Accounting Standards

2016–17

Extant at 30 April 2016

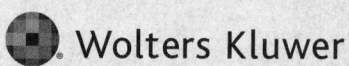

Wolters Kluwer

Wolters Kluwer (UK) Limited
145 London Road
Kingston upon Thames
KT2 6SR
Tel: 0844 561 8166
Fax: 0208 547 2638
Email: cch@wolterskluwer.com
website: www.cch.co.uk

ISBN 978-1-78540-252-4

British Library Cataloguing-in-Publication Data.
A catalogue record for this book is available from the British Library.

Typeset by Innodata Inc., India.

Printed in Spain by Rotabook, S.L.

Contents

Part Five ICAEW Technical Releases

Preface

This book presents, in one convenient bound volume, all UK accounting standards extant at 30 April 2016 and related guidance. These have been updated for amendments made since the documents were originally issued.

The main change since the last volume has been the further amendments made to the new body of UK accounting standards. Probably the most significant changes relate to small and micro entities, so as well as the August 2014 version of FRS 102 (effective for periods from 1 January 2015) we have added the September 2015 version of FRS 102 that includes the new section 1A setting out the small entities regime effective from 1 January 2016 (with early adoption from 1 January 2015 permitted or required as set out in paragraph 45 of the advice to issue the amendments). The new micros standard, FRS 105, along with the May 2016 amendments to bring limited liability partnerships and qualifying partnerships within the scope of the micro-entities regime, is also included. These amendments to FRS 105 are applicable for accounting periods beginning on or after 1 January 2016, with early application permitted from 1 January 2015 in conjunction with the changes in legislation. Other less radical amendments include the March 2016 updates to FRS 102 in respect of fair value disclosures for financial institutions and retirement benefit schemes, and minor amendments from July 2015 to FRSs 100 and 101.

Old UK GAAP standards have now been withdrawn, and hence are not included; the only exception is the FRSSE, which is included here (albeit in its 2015 incarnation) since it is available for the last time for 2015 year ends. Added this year, though, are the FRC's Staff Education Notes, which are not formally part of FRS 102 but provide valuable help in its interpretation. We have also included the FRC's 2014 version of 'True and Fair' and the 2016 FRC Policy on Developing Statements of Recommended Practice (SORPs); the new UK GAAP SORPs themselves are available on CCH online.

As in previous years, footnotes and editorial notes have been added to refer to any major changes to legal or other references included in standards. However, these are not intended to provide a comprehensive summary. No attempt has been made to update any references to legislation in the Republic of Ireland.

If you have a comment on the editorial content of Accounting Standards 2016–17, please email your views to us at uk-contentqueries@wolterskluwer.com.

Julia Bowyer ACA

Content Manager, Audit and Accounting

Wolters Kluwer UK

Preface

Part One

Overview and Statement of Principles

Overview of the financial reporting framework

(July 2015)

Contents

The FRC is responsible for promoting high quality corporate governance and reporting to foster investment. We set the UK Corporate Governance and Stewardship Codes as well as UK standards for accounting, auditing and actuarial work. We represent UK interests in international standard-setting. We also monitor and take action to promote the quality of corporate reporting and auditing. We operate independent disciplinary arrangements for accountants and actuaries, and oversee the regulatory activities of the accountancy and actuarial professional bodies.

The FRC does not accept any liability to any party for any loss, damage or costs howsoever arising, whether directly or indirectly, whether in contract, tort or otherwise from any action or decision taken (or not taken) as a result of any person relying on or otherwise using this document or arising from any omission from it.

The Financial Reporting Council Limited is a company limited by guarantee.

Registered in England number 2486368. Registered Office: 8th Floor, 125 London Wall, London EC2Y 5AS

1 INTRODUCTION

As a consequence of the changes to company law arising from the implementation of the   **1.1**
EU Accounting Directive, it has been necessary to make amendments to UK and Republic
of Ireland (RoI) accounting standards to ensure continued consistency between the revised
legal frameworks and the financial reporting framework. This has also given the FRC the
opportunity to reconsider the most appropriate way that accounting standards can support
the new micro-entities regime.

The changes to company law predominantly affect the small companies regime, however   **1.2**
other more minor amendments affect other aspects of UK and Republic of Ireland
accounting standards.

This overview describes the financial reporting framework that will be applicable for   **1.3**
accounting periods beginning on or after 1 January 2016 (early application is permitted
subject to the provisions in each standard).

2 THE FINANCIAL REPORTING FRAMEWORK

Company law recognises two financial reporting frameworks – IFRS and UK and Ireland   **2.1**
GAAP (generally accepted accounting practice).

Publicly listed companies are required to apply IFRS in the preparation of their group   **2.2**
accounts but may choose between IFRS and UK and Ireland GAAP for the preparation
of their individual parent accounts. Other entities have a free choice between the two
frameworks.

FRS 100 *Application of Financial Reporting Requirements* sets out the overall framework,   **2.3**
which can be illustrated as follows:

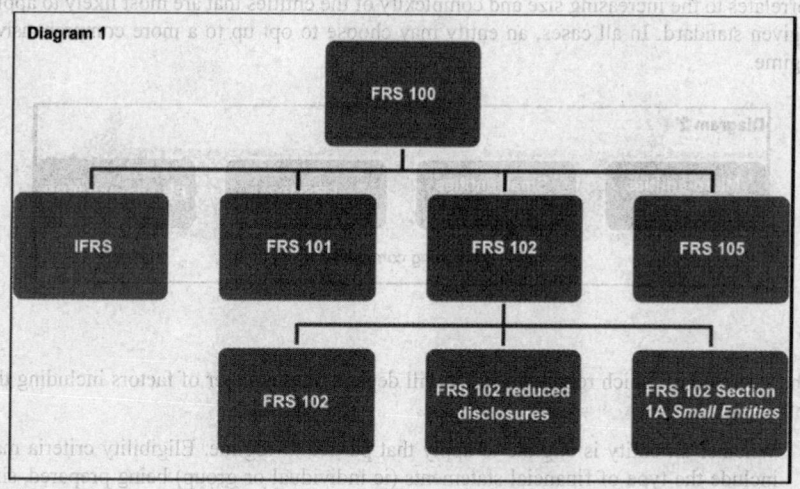

Diagram 1

UK and Ireland GAAP

The UK and Ireland GAAP reporting framework is made up of five regimes, three   **2.4**
of which are available within FRS 102 *The Financial Reporting Standard applicable
in the UK and Republic of Ireland*. The other two are FRS 101 *Reduced Disclosure*

Framework and FRS 105 *The Financial Reporting Standard applicable to the Micro-entities Regime.*

Table 1: UK and Ireland GAAP					
Framework	**Micro-entities regime**	**Small entities regime**	**FRS 102**	**Reduced disclosure framework (FRS 101)**	**Reduced disclosures for subsidiaries and ultimate parents (FRS 102)**
Related accounting standard(s)	FRS 105	Section 1A *Small Entities* of FRS 102	FRS 102	FRS 101	Paragraphs 1.8 to 1.13 of FRS 102

2.5   Smaller entities have a choice between three core UK GAAP regimes subject to meeting relevant criteria:

- the micro-entities regime (FRS 105);
- the small entities regime (Section 1A *Small Entities* of FRS 102); and
- FRS 102.

2.6   Entities that are part of a group may apply either of the reduced disclosure regimes. These additional options are discussed in more detail in Section 4 *Additional options for entities that are part of a group.*

The core UK GAAP and Ireland regimes

2.7   The financial reporting requirements of each standard get progressively more complex and comprehensive the further up the suite of standards you go. The increase in complexity correlates to the increasing size and complexity of the entities that are most likely to apply a given standard. In all cases, an entity may choose to opt up to a more comprehensive regime.

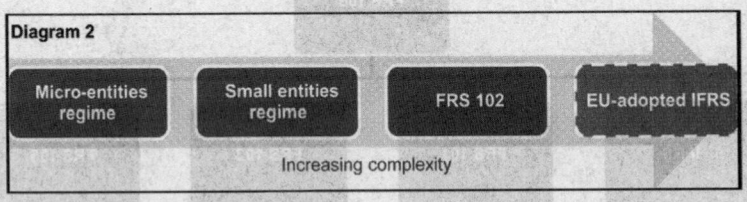

Diagram 2

Micro-entities regime → Small entities regime → FRS 102 → EU-adopted IFRS

Increasing complexity

2.8   The selection of which regime to apply will depend on a number of factors including the following:

- Whether an entity is eligible to apply that particular regime. Eligibility criteria may include the type of financial statements (ie individual or group) being prepared, size thresholds and entity type.
- Where a choice of regime exists, entities should consider which of the regimes is the most appropriate to the individual circumstances of the entity. Factors to consider will differ from entity to entity and may relate to certain characteristics or restrictions of a particular regime, the resources available and the information needs of users of the accounts, amongst many others.

The following table outlines the key eligibility criteria for the micro-entities and small entities regimes. Entities should refer to the detailed eligibility criteria in the relevant legislation in order to determine if they are eligible or not. **2.9**

Table 2: UK Eligibility criteria		
Regime	Micro-entities regime[1]	Small entities regime[2]
Source of eligibility criteria	Sections 384A to 384B of the Companies Act 2006.	Sections 382 to 384 of the Companies Act 2006.
Eligible entities	• Companies only (Note: Whilst the legislation and consequently FRS 105 uses the term micro-entities regime, it is only currently available in law to companies.)	• Companies • Limited liability partnerships[3] • Any other type of entity that would have met the criteria of the small companies regime had it been a company incorporated under company law (for example charities)
Size thresholds	A company qualifies if it does not exceed two or more of the following criteria: • Turnover £632,000 • Balance sheet total £312,000 • No. of employees 10	A company[3] qualifies if it does not exceed two or more of the following criteria: • Turnover £10.2m • Balance sheet total £5.1m • No. of employees 50

[1] *For Irish entities, if legislation is enacted, the equivalent thresholds are: Turnover €700,000, Balance sheet total €350,000 and Number of employees 10.*

[2] *For Irish entities, qualification as a small company is set out in section 350 of The Companies Act 2014. The current equivalent size criteria are: Turnover not exceeding €8.8m, Balance Sheet total not exceeding €4.4m, and number of employees not exceeding 50. The equivalent thresholds after implementation of the EU Accounting Directive have not yet been set, however the limits in the Directive are: Turnover at or above €8m and not exceeding €12m; Balance sheet total at or above €4m and not exceeding €6m.*

[3] *As set out in the The Limited Liability Partnerships (Accounts and Audit) (Application of Companies Act 2006) Regulations 2008 (SI 2008/1911). The thresholds differ from those applicable to companies.*

Table 2: UK Eligibility criteria		
Regime	**Micro-entities regime[1]**	**Small entities regime[2]**
Ineligible entities	<ul><li>Any companies excluded from the small companies regime</li><li>Financial institutions including credit and insurance institutions</li><li>Charities</li><li>Small parent companies that choose to prepare group accounts</li><li>Companies that are not parent companies but their accounts are included in group accounts</li></ul>	<ul><li>Public companies</li><li>Financial institutions including insurance companies and banking companies</li></ul>

2.10 The following decision tree will help an entity identify the options that may be open to it in selecting its reporting regime:

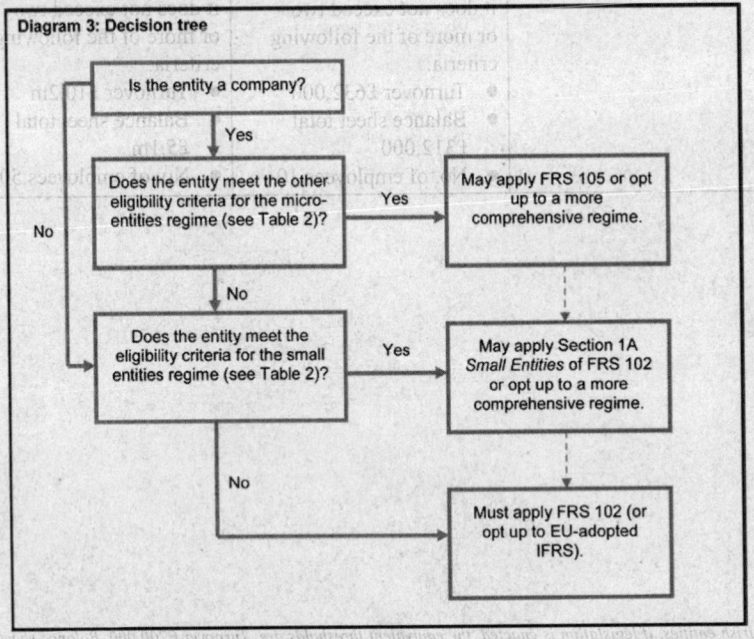

3 KEY FEATURES OF THE CORE UK AND IRELAND GAAP REGIMES

FRS 102

3.1 FRS 102 was first issued in March 2013 and is effective for accounting periods beginning on or after 1 January 2015. Subsequent amendments have revised it responding to both issues raised by stakeholders and changes in company law, with the most recent revision being in July 2015. For convenience, a revised edition of FRS 102 will be published periodically to incorporate any recent amendments, usually after any significant amendments have been issued.

FRS 102 replaced over 70 accounting standards and UITF Abstracts spanning more than   **3.2**
2,400 pages, with one succinct standard of a little over 300 pages. It reflects developments in the way businesses operate and uses up-to-date accounting treatment and language. One of the key improvements in financial reporting is that FRS 102 requires the recognition of financial instruments and disclosure of the risks associated with those instruments. It also improves intellectual mobility and reduces the costs of education and training.

The micro-entities regime (FRS 105)

Micro-entities are the smallest of entities (with turnover of up to £632,000) and a subset   **3.3**
of small entities. The accounting standard for micro-entities, FRS 105, has been developed around the legal framework and simplified the requirements of FRS 102 for this group of entities.

Although FRS 105 is the least complex standard, every entity that is eligible to apply it   **3.4**
should consider whether the regime meets its individual needs. It is important to remember that the micro-entities regime is optional even if an entity meets the eligibility criteria.

The micro-entities regime requires limited disclosures and constrains the accounting   **3.5**
policies that can be applied:

- The only primary statements required are a balance sheet and profit and loss account. There is no requirement to prepare a statement of cash flows, a statement of comprehensive income or a statement of changes in equity. Further, the information presented in the balance sheet and profit and loss account is condensed (for example 'fixed assets' is not disaggregated into tangible fixed assets, intangible assets, investment properties etc).
- No assets can be measured at fair value or a revalued amount. This means that land and buildings and investment properties can only be measured at cost and previous revaluations gains would need to be removed on transition.
- Micro-entities' accounts are **only** required to disclose the following:
  - the total amount of any financial commitments, guarantees or contingencies that are not included in the balance sheet;
  - an indication of the nature and form of any valuable security which has been provided;
  - the amounts of advances and credits granted to its directors with indications of interest rates, main conditions and any amounts repaid or written off or waived; and
  - any commitments entered into on their behalf by way of guarantees of any kind, with an indication of the total for each category.

- However, micro-entities may voluntarily choose to disclose more information.
- Micro-entities' accounts that comply with the minimal legal requirements are presumed to give a true and fair view. There is no requirement for directors to consider what additional information may be needed in order for the accounts to give a true and fair view.

In addition to these legal constraints, FRS 105 is simplified further, for example: **3.6**

- deferred tax and equity-settled share-based payments shall not be recognised; and
- all accounting policy choices have been removed, including the options to capitalise development costs and borrowing costs.

More detailed discussion of the additional simplifications can be found in FRS 105.

Comparison to the FRSSE

3.7   For entities previously applying the FRSSE, Appendix 1 to this document sets out the key differences between that standard and FRS 105. In the majority of instances, the accounting treatment of FRS 105 is either simpler or the same as that of the FRSSE.

The small entities regime (Section 1A Small Entities of FRS 102)

3.8   The thresholds for the small entities regime have increased resulting in more entities qualifying as small.

3.9   Similarly to FRS 105, Section 1A *Small Entities* of FRS 102 has been developed around the legal framework from the requirements of FRS 102.

3.10   The requirements of the small entities regime are more comprehensive than the micro-entities regime and the recognition and measurement requirements of Section 1A are the same as those set out in the rest of FRS 102. In relation to recognition and measurement, key differences between the small entities regime and the micro-entities regime include the use of fair value and revaluation accounting and the additional accounting requirements in respect of derivatives, deferred tax and equity-settled share-based payments.

3.11   The law only mandates a limited number of specified disclosures. However, unlike the micro-entities regime, directors of small entities are legally obligated to prepare accounts that give a true and fair view whereas micro-entity accounts are automatically presumed to give a true and fair view if the legal minimum is adhered to. In practical terms this will require more judgement of directors of small entities in considering what additional information (if any) is needed to ensure the accounts give a true and fair view. Section 1A of FRS 102 provides additional guidance to assist directors.

Comparison to the FRSSE

3.12   For entities previously applying the FRSSE, Appendix 2 to this document sets out the key differences between that standard and Section 1A of FRS 102. In the main, the requirements of Section 1A and the FRSSE are the same. However, there are a handful of key differences in accounting treatment between the two standards worth noting, including the recognition of additional financial instruments such as derivatives like interest rate swaps and foreign exchange contracts.

4 ADDITIONAL OPTIONS FOR ENTITIES THAT ARE PART OF A GROUP

4.1   For entities that are part of a group and included in the consolidated financial statements (known as qualifying entities), UK and Ireland GAAP provides an additional two further reporting regimes. Both regimes aim to make group reporting more efficient and cost-effective by permitting consistent accounting policies to be applied across a group, but with reduced disclosures.

Table 3: Eligibility criteria		
Regime	Reduced disclosure framework (FRS 101)	Reduced disclosures for subsidiaries and ultimate parents (FRS 102)
Source of eligibility criteria	Definition of a qualifying entity as set out in the glossary to FRS 101.	Definition of a qualifying entity as set out in the glossary to FRS 102.
Eligible entities	A member of a group: • where the parent prepares publicly available consolidated financial statements which are intended to give a true and fair view; and • that is included in the consolidation	A member of a group: • where the parent prepares publicly available consolidated financial statements which are intended to give a true and fair view; and • that is included in the consolidation
Size thresholds	None	None
Ineligible entities	Charities	None

Each regime is based on a different underlying reporting framework: **4.2**

• FRS 101 *Reduced Disclosure Framework* is based on EU-adopted IFRS; whereas
• the reduced disclosures for subsidiaries and ultimate parents in FRS 102 are based on FRS 102.

In essence, entities applying either reduced disclosure regime are required to otherwise   **4.3**
apply the underlying requirements of the related standard (ie EU-adopted IFRS or FRS 102)
but are permitted to take advantage of certain disclosure exemptions.

Both reduced disclosure regimes are optional.   **4.4**

Appendix I
Key differences between FRS 105 and the FRSSE

Table 4: Key differences between FRS 105 and the FRSSE	
Key features of FRS 105:	
Presumed true and fair view	Financial statements prepared in accordance with the legal requirements of the micro-entities regime are presumed to give a true and fair view, therefore directors are not required to consider what additional information is required for the financial statements of the entity to give a true and fair view. This is in contrast to the FRSSE where directors were legally obligated to ensure the financial statements provided a true and fair view.
Preparation of only two primary statements required	Micro-entities are only required to prepare a balance sheet and profit and loss account and not a statement of recognised gains and losses (STRGL) or a cash flow statement.
Significantly condensed formats of statements	The statutory formats for the balance sheet and profit and loss accounts are significantly condensed, for example 'current assets' is not disaggregated into stocks, debtors, investments and cash.
Significantly reduced number of disclosures	Micro-entities are only legally required to provide two disclosures, and are not required to provide any more. However, micro-entities can voluntarily provide more disclosures. This is in contrast to the FRSSE which mandates significantly more disclosures.
Simplified accounting treatment	FRS 105 has simplified the accounting treatment for some transactions. For example, micro-entities shall not account for deferred tax.
Fair value and revaluation accounting not permitted	Micro-entities are not permitted to fair value or revalue any assets or liabilities, therefore all assets and liabilities (such as land and buildings and investment properties) must be held at cost. This is in contrast to the FRSSE which permitted or required certain assets to be revalued.
No accounting policy choices	All accounting policy options have been removed. In general, the mandatory treatments result in earlier recognition of income / expenses in the profit and loss account rather than deferring on the balance sheet.
More helpful guidance included	In many instances, the requirements of FRS 105 do not differ from those of the FRSSE, but more guidance is provided in FRS 105 to help preparers apply and interpret the treatment required.
Not all company law requirements are reproduced	FRS 105 does not reproduce all the reporting requirements from company law applicable to micro-entities unlike the FRSSE, but does incorporate those relating to the financial statements. Micro-entities will need to satisfy themselves that they have met all their legal requirements.
Terminology used consistent with FRS 102	FRS 105 uses terminology consistent with FRS 102 such as 'statement of financial position' rather than 'balance sheet'. A table of equivalence is included in Appendix II to FRS 105 for convenience.

Appendix II
Key differences between Section 1A
Small Entities of FRS 102 and the FRSSE

Table 5: Key differences between Section 1A of FRS 102 and the FRSSE	
Key features of Section 1A of FRS 102:	
Preparation of only two primary statements required	Small entities are only required to prepare a balance sheet and profit and loss account and not a statement of recognised gains and losses (STRGL) or a cash flow statement.
Reduced number of mandatory disclosures	Small entities are only legally required to provide a limited number of specified disclosures. However, directors of small entities are still required to ensure the financial statements provide a true and fair view and therefore must consider what additional information may be needed to achieve this and provide that information.
More helpful guidance included	In many instances, the requirements of Section 1A of FRS 102 do not differ from those of the FRSSE, however more guidance is provided in FRS 102 to help preparers apply and interpret the treatment required.
Improved reporting for financial instruments	FRS 102 will require recognition of some financial instruments that the FRSSE did not. In particular, small entities will need to recognise derivatives such as options, swaps and forward contracts at fair value.
Removal of contract rate accounting for foreign currency transactions	FRS 102 does not permit the use of contract rate accounting in relation to foreign currency transactions and a small entity must apply the hedge accounting requirements of FRS 102 instead if they wish to achieve similar accounting results.
Deferred tax arising on revaluations	FRS 102 requires small entities to recognise deferred tax arising on revaluations of fixed assets.
Addition of the performance method of accounting for government grants	FRS 102 permits an accounting policy choice between the accruals method (the method mandated in the FRSSE) and the performance method in relation to government grants. The performance method is simpler to apply and may lead to earlier recognition of income in the profit and loss account in some circumstances.
Gains / losses on investment properties recognised in profit or loss	FRS 102 requires that gains and losses on investment properties must be recognised in profit or loss, rather than in reserves as previously required by the FRSSE.
Not all company law requirements are reproduced	Section 1A of FRS 102 does not reproduce all the reporting requirements from company law applicable to small entities unlike the FRSSE, but does include those relating to the financial statements. Small entities will need to satisfy themselves that they have met all their legal requirements.
Terminology used consistent with FRS 102	Section 1A of FRS 102 uses terminology consistent with the rest of FRS 102 such as 'statement of financial position' rather than 'balance sheet'. A table of equivalence is included in Appendix III to FRS 102 for convenience.

Statement of principles for financial reporting

The Statement of Principles for Financial Reporting was agreed on by the Accounting Standards Board in October 1999. At that time, the Board comprised:

Sir David Tweedie   (Chairman)

Allan Cook CBE   (Technical Director)

David Allvey

Ian Brindle

Dr John Buchanan

John Coombe

Raymond Hinton

Huw Jones

Professor Geoffrey Whittington

Ken Wild

Contents

Detailed list of contents

Chapter 5: Recognition in Financial Statements

Principles

Explanation

Chapter 6: Measurement in Financial Statements

Principles

Explanation

Chapter 7: Presentation of financial information

Principles

Explanation

Chapter 8: Accounting for interests in other entities

Principles

Explanation

Statement of principles for financial reporting

Introduction

PURPOSE

This Statement of Principles for Financial Reporting sets out the principles that the **1**
Accounting Standards Board believes should underlie the preparation and presentation of
general purpose financial statements.[1]

The primary purpose of articulating such principles is to provide a coherent frame of **2**
reference to be used by the Board in the development and review of accounting standards
and by others who interact with the Board during the standard-setting process.

Such a frame of reference should clarify the conceptual underpinnings of proposed **3**
accounting standards and should enable standards to be developed on a consistent basis
by reducing the need to debate fundamental issues each time a standard is developed
or revised. As such, it will play an important role in the development of accounting
standards. It is expected that it will play a similar role in the development of Statements of
Recommended Practice.

The Statement is being published because knowledge of the principles should assist **4**
preparers and users of financial statements, as well as auditors and others, to understand
the Board's approach to formulating accounting standards and the nature and function of
information reported in general purpose financial statements. The principles will also help
preparers and auditors faced with new or emerging issues to carry out an initial analysis of
the issues involved in the absence of applicable accounting standards.

STATUS

The Statement of Principles is not an accounting standard, nor does it have a status that is **5**
equivalent to an accounting standard. It therefore does not contain requirements on how
financial statements should be prepared or presented.

SCOPE

Types of financial report

Financial information takes many different forms. For the purposes of the Statement, it has **6**
been categorised:

(a) *special purpose financial reports*—Financial information prepared by the entity
    itself at the behest of, and in the form specified by, persons who have the authority
    to obtain the information they require to meet their needs. Regulatory returns, tax
    returns and financial reports prepared for bankers are examples of such reports.

(b) *general purpose financial reports*—Financial information that, although prepared by
    the entity itself, is not in the form of a special purpose financial report. Such reports
    comprise:

    (i) *general purpose financial statements*—for example, annual financial
        statements and the financial statements contained in interim reports, preliminary

[1] *The meaning of the term 'general purpose financial statements' is explained in paragraph 6(b)(i).*

announcements and summary financial statements. General purpose financial statements are generally referred to in the Statement hereafter simply as 'financial statements'.

(ii)   *other types of general purpose financial report*—for example, directors' reports, statements by the chairman, operating and financial reviews, historical summaries and trend information (such as five-year summaries), letters to shareholders and similar items.

(c)   *other financial information*—Financial information that has not been prepared by the reporting entity itself, such as news articles and analysts' reports.

A diagram summarising and providing examples of the various categories of financial information is on page 12.

7   The primary focus of the Statement of Principles is on those financial statements that are required to give a true and fair view of the reporting entity's financial performance and financial position. For most entities, those statements will be their full annual financial statements. The Statement's principles will also be applicable to financial statements that are intended to be consistent with financial statements required to give a true and fair view (such as financial statements contained in interim reports, preliminary announcements and summary financial statements), although additional considerations are relevant in the context of such statements.

8   Whilst the Statement does not address to any significant extent other types of general purpose financial report, it will be relevant to such reports insofar as they provide financial information that is intended to be consistent with the financial statements.

Types of entity

9   The principles in the Statement are intended to be relevant to the financial statements of profit-oriented reporting entities, regardless of their size and whether they are private or public sector entities.[2] The Statement is, broadly speaking, also relevant to the financial statements of not-for-profit entities, although some of the principles need to be re-expressed and others need changes of emphasis before they can be applied to that sector.

---

[2] *The application of accounting standards to the public sector is discussed more fully in the Foreword to Accounting Standards.*

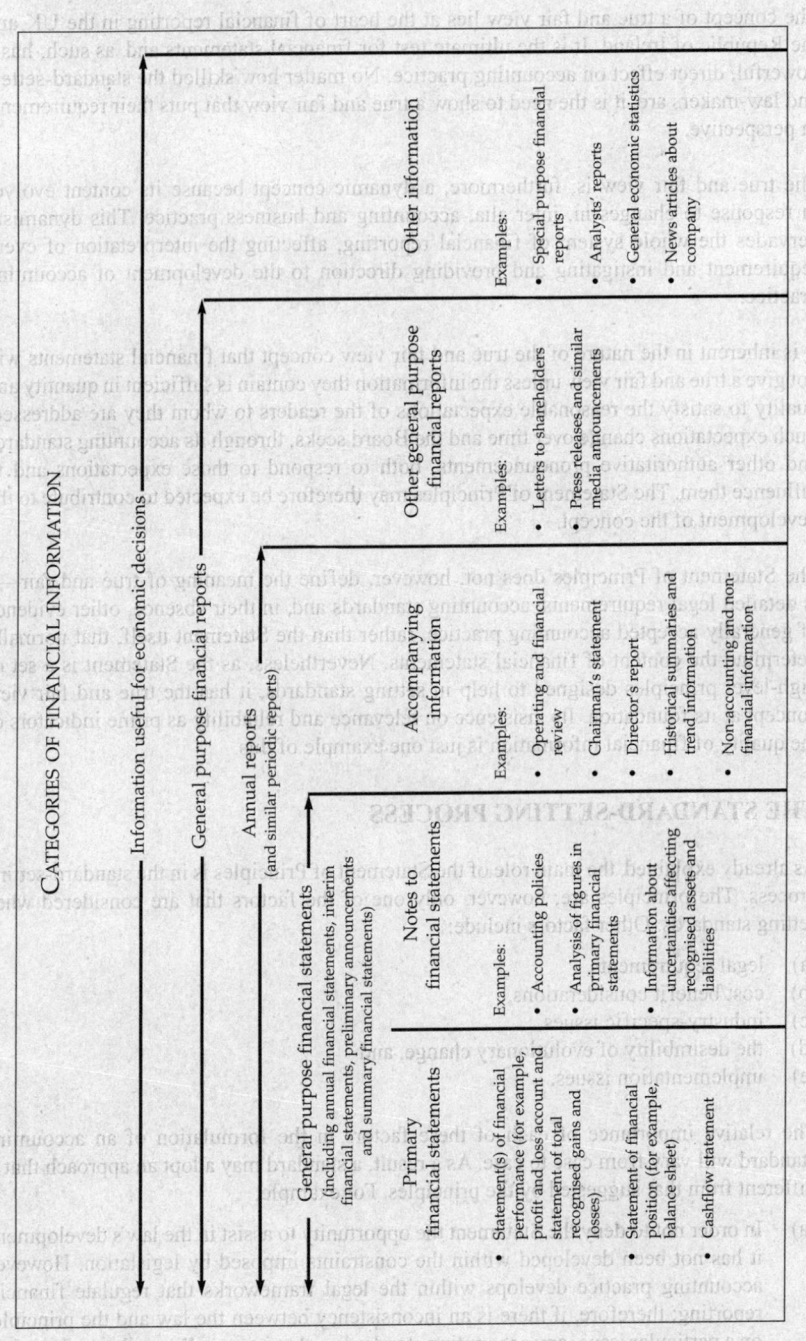

CATEGORIES OF FINANCIAL INFORMATION

Information useful for economic decisions

General purpose financial reports

Annual reports
(and similar periodic reports)

Other information

Examples:
- Special purpose financial reports
- Analysts' reports
- General economic statistics
- News articles about company

Other general purpose financial reports

Examples:
- Letters to shareholders
- Press releases and similar media announcements

Accompanying information

Examples:
- Operating and financial review
- Chairman's statement
- Director's report
- Historical summaries and trend information
- Non-accounting and non-financial information

General purpose financial statements
(including annual financial statements, interim financial statements, preliminary announcements and summary financial statements)

Notes to financial statements

Examples:
- Accounting policies
- Analysis of figures in primary financial statements
- Information about uncertainties affecting recognised assets and liabilities

Primary financial statements

Examples:
- Statement(s) of financial performance (for example, profit and loss account and statement of total recognised gains and losses)
- Statement of financial position (for example, balance sheet)
- Cashflow statement

TRUE AND FAIR

10   The concept of a true and fair view lies at the heart of financial reporting in the UK and the Republic of Ireland. It is the ultimate test for financial statements and, as such, has a powerful, direct effect on accounting practice. No matter how skilled the standard-setters and law-makers are, it is the need to show a true and fair view that puts their requirements in perspective.

11   The true and fair view is, furthermore, a dynamic concept because its content evolves in response to changes in, inter alia, accounting and business practice. This dynamism pervades the whole system of financial reporting, affecting the interpretation of every requirement and instigating and providing direction to the development of accounting practice.

12   It is inherent in the nature of the true and fair view concept that financial statements will not give a true and fair view unless the information they contain is sufficient in quantity and quality to satisfy the reasonable expectations of the readers to whom they are addressed. Such expectations change over time and the Board seeks, through its accounting standards and other authoritative pronouncements, both to respond to those expectations and to influence them. The Statement of Principles may therefore be expected to contribute to the development of the concept.

13   The Statement of Principles does not, however, define the meaning of true and fair—it is detailed legal requirements, accounting standards and, in their absence, other evidence of generally accepted accounting practice, rather than the Statement itself, that normally determine the content of financial statements. Nevertheless, as the Statement is a set of high-level principles designed to help in setting standards, it has the true and fair view concept at its foundation. Its insistence on relevance and reliability as prime indicators of the quality of financial information is just one example of this.

THE STANDARD-SETTING PROCESS

14   As already explained, the main role of the Statement of Principles is in the standard-setting process. The principles are, however, only one of the factors that are considered when setting standards. Other factors include:

(a)   legal requirements,
(b)   cost/benefit considerations,
(c)   industry-specific issues,
(d)   the desirability of evolutionary change, and
(e)   implementation issues.

15   The relative importance of each of these factors in the formulation of an accounting standard will vary from case to case. As a result, a standard may adopt an approach that is different from that suggested by the principles. For example:

(a)   In order not to deny the Statement the opportunity to assist in the law's development, it has not been developed within the constraints imposed by legislation. However, accounting practice develops within the legal frameworks that regulate financial reporting; therefore, if there is an inconsistency between the law and the principles on a particular issue, any accounting standard on that issue will usually need to adopt an approach that is different from that suggested by the principles.[3]

---

[3] *The relationship between the accounting requirements imposed by legislation and the Statement of Principles and the inconsistencies between the two are explained in Appendix I.*

(b)   In setting standards the Board weighs the costs and benefits of its proposals to ensure that they are justified on cost/benefit grounds, and this may also result in an accounting standard adopting an approach that is different from that suggested by the principles. The benefits of new accounting practices will come from improvements in economic decision-making by users. The costs will include the costs of preparation and might also include, for example, the possible loss or diminution of competitive position.

As legal requirements, accounting techniques and markets evolve, the Board believes that it will be possible to reduce the number of conflicts between the Statement and accounting standards and that fewer new conflicts will emerge.   **16**

It will be made clear in each accounting standard how the standard relates to the Statement of Principles.   **17**

REVISIONS TO THE STATEMENT

The Statement may be revised from time to time in the light of the Board's experience of working with it and in response to developments in accounting thought.   **18**

Chapter 1: The objective of Financial Statements

Put simply, the objective of financial statements is to provide information that is useful to those for whom they are prepared. However, the objective needs to be expressed more precisely if it is to be of any use in determining the form and content of financial statements. This chapter does that by considering the persons for whom financial statements are prepared, the information needs of such persons and the role that financial statements play in meeting those needs.

PRINCIPLES

- The objective of financial statements is to provide information about the reporting entity's financial performance and financial position that is useful to a wide range of users for assessing the stewardship of the entity's management and for making economic decisions.
- That objective can usually be met by focusing exclusively on the information needs of present and potential investors, the defining class of user.
- Present and potential investors need information about the reporting entity's financial performance and financial position that is useful to them in evaluating the entity's ability to generate cash (including the timing and certainty of its generation) and in assessing the entity's financial adaptability.

EXPLANATION

The objective of financial statements

Useful to a wide range of users

1.1   Financial information about the activities and resources of an entity is typically of interest to many people. Although some of these people are able to command the preparation of special purpose financial reports in order to obtain the information they need, the rest— usually the vast majority—rely on general purpose financial reports, such as financial statements and other financial information. Many people are therefore potentially interested in an entity's financial statements.

1.2   It does not follow that financial statements are prepared specifically for all those interested persons. However, although there continues to be debate about for whom precisely they are prepared, there is no doubt that they are prepared for a range of persons that extends far beyond existing investors. These persons are referred to in the Statement as the 'users'.

Useful for making economic decisions

1.3   The persons potentially interested in an entity's financial statements need information on that entity for a variety of purposes.

(a)   *Present and potential investors (hereafter generally referred to simply as* 'investors'*).* In its stewardship role, management is accountable for the safekeeping of the entity's resources and for their proper, efficient and profitable use. Providers of risk capital are interested in information that helps them to assess how effectively management has fulfilled this role. They are also interested in information that is useful in taking decisions about their investment or potential investment in the entity. They are, as a result, concerned with the risk inherent in, and return provided by, their investments, and need information on the entity's financial performance and financial position that helps them to assess its cash-generation abilities and its financial adaptability.

(b)   *Lenders.* Lenders are interested in information that helps them to assess whether their loans will be repaid, and related interest will be paid, when due. Similarly, potential lenders are interested in information that helps them to decide whether to lend to the entity and on what terms.

(c)   *Suppliers and other trade creditors.* Suppliers and other trade creditors are interested in information that helps them to decide whether to sell to the entity and to assess the likelihood that amounts owing to them will be paid when due.

(d)   *Employees.* Employees are interested in information on their employer's stability and profitability, with particular reference to that part (for example, the subsidiary or branch) of the entity in which they work. They are also interested in information that enables them to assess their employer's ability to provide remuneration, employment opportunities and retirement and other benefits.

(e)   *Customers.* Customers are interested in information about the entity's continued existence. That is especially so when they have a long-term involvement with, or are dependent on, the entity, as will generally be the case if product warranties are involved or if specialised replacement parts may be needed.

(f)   *Governments and their agencies.* Governments and their agencies are interested in the allocation of resources and, therefore, the activities of entities. They also require information that assists them in regulating the activities of entities, assessing taxation and providing a basis for national statistics. Although much of this information is obtained through special purpose financial reports, its consistency with published general purpose financial reports such as financial statements often needs to be demonstrated.

(g)   *The public.* Entities affect members of the public in a variety of ways. For example, they may make a substantial contribution to a local economy by providing employment and using local suppliers. The public, including the local community, may therefore be interested in information that is useful in assessing the trends and recent developments in the entity's prosperity and the range of its activities.

This analysis illustrates that, although those potentially interested in an entity's financial statements need that information for a variety of purposes, all the purposes involve taking informed economic decisions. Even present investors assessing the stewardship of the entity's management do so in order to decide whether, amongst other things, to hold or sell their investment in the entity and to reappoint or replace the management.   **1.4**

Information on financial performance and financial position

The economic decisions for which users need financial statements will not all be the same. Although different decisions usually require different information, there is, as can be seen from paragraph 1.3, some overlap in the information required: all potential users are interested, to varying degrees, in the financial performance and financial position of the entity as a whole.   **1.5**

General purpose financial reports focus on this common interest of users. Their objective is therefore to provide information about the financial performance and financial position of an entity that is useful to a wide range of users for assessing the stewardship of management and for making economic decisions (including those based on assessments of the stewardship of management).   **1.6**

As financial statements are the principal means of communicating accounting information on an entity to interested parties and are a central feature of general purpose financial reporting, they carry much of the burden that is placed on general purpose financial reporting to meet this objective.   **1.7**

The limitations of financial statements

1.8   Financial statements do not seek to meet all the information needs of users: users will usually have to supplement the information they obtain from financial statements with information from other sources. Furthermore, financial statements have various inherent limitations that make them an imperfect vehicle for reflecting the full effects of transactions and other events on a reporting entity's financial performance and financial position. For example:

   (a)   they are a conventionalised representation of transactions and other events that involves a substantial degree of classification and aggregation and the allocation of the effects of continuous operations to discrete reporting periods.

   (b)   they focus on the financial effects of transactions and other events and do not focus to any significant extent on their non-financial effects or on non-financial information in general.

   (c)   they provide information that is largely historical and therefore do not reflect future events or transactions that may enhance or impair the entity's operations, nor do they anticipate the impact of potential changes in the economic environment.

1.9   These inherent limitations mean that some information on the financial performance and financial position of the reporting entity can be provided only by general purpose financial reports other than financial statements—or in some cases is better provided by such reports. For example, although a description of the business environment and markets in which a reporting entity operates and the strategies it has adopted is usually needed to put into context the numerical information provided by the financial statements, it is generally better to provide such information in the material accompanying the financial statements than in the financial statements themselves.[4]

Investors as the defining class of user

1.10   As explained in paragraph 1.3, the perspective from which investors view financial performance and financial position is one that focuses on the entity's cash-generation ability and financial adaptability. This perspective is also of fundamental importance to other users, because an entity's ability to generate cash and to respond to unexpected needs and opportunities ultimately determines its capacity over the medium to long term to repay loans, meet interest payments, pay employees and suppliers, and undertake investment. For example, although in origin the perspective of lenders and other creditors differs from that of investors, they require similar information to investors when their interests are long-term or the risk of loss is significant. That is because they will want to use that information as a frame of reference against which to evaluate the more specific information they obtain.

1.11   Therefore, in preparing financial statements, the rebuttable assumption is made that financial statements that focus on the interest that investors have in the reporting entity's financial performance and financial position will, in effect, also be focusing on the common interest that all users have in that entity's financial performance and financial position.

1.12   It follows that, in determining which information to include in the financial statements and how to present that information, it can usually be presumed that:

   (a)   information that is needed by investors will be given in either the financial statements or some other general purpose financial report; and

   (b)   information that is not needed by investors need not be given in the financial statements.

---

[4] *Accompanying information is discussed in Chapter 7.*

The information required by investors

Financial performance

The financial performance of an entity comprises the return it obtains on the resources it controls, the components of that return and the characteristics of those components. **1.13**

Investors require information on financial performance because such information: **1.14**

(a) provides an account of the stewardship of management and is useful in assessing the past and anticipated performance of the entity;

(b) is useful in assessing the entity's capacity to generate cash flows from its existing resource base and in forming judgements about the effectiveness with which the entity has employed its resources and might employ additional resources; and

(c) provides feedback on previous assessments of financial performance and can therefore assist users in modifying their assessments for, or in developing expectations about, future periods.

Financial position

An entity's financial position encompasses the economic resources it controls, its financial structure, its liquidity and solvency, its risk profile and risk management approach, and its capacity to adapt to changes in the environment in which it operates. **1.15**

Investors require information on financial position because: **1.16**

(a) information about the economic resources controlled and the use made of them in the past helps in assessing the stewardship of management and the entity's ability to generate cash in the future;

(b) information about financial structure is useful in assessing how future cash flows will be distributed among those with an interest in or claims on the entity. It is also useful in assessing how successful the entity has been in managing its resources, its requirements for future finance and its ability to raise that finance;

(c) information about liquidity and solvency helps in assessing the ability of the entity to meet its financial commitments as they fall due;

(d) information on an entity's risk profile and risk management approach is useful in evaluating its current performance and financial adaptability, and in assessing its ability to generate cash in the future; and

(e) information on an entity's capacity to adapt to changing circumstances (in other words, its financial adaptability) is useful in assessing the extent to which the entity is at risk, or able to benefit, from unexpected changes.

Generation and use of cash

Information about the ways in which an entity generates and uses cash in its operations, its investment activities and its financing activities provides an additional perspective on its financial performance—one that is largely free from allocation and valuation issues. **1.17**

Investors need such information because it is useful in assessing and reviewing previous assessments of: **1.18**

(a) liquidity and solvency;

(b) the relationship between profits and cash flows;

(c) the implications that financial performance has for future cash flows; and

(d) other aspects of financial adaptability.

Financial adaptability

1.19   An entity's financial adaptability is its ability to take effective action to alter the amount and timing of its cash flows so that it can respond to unexpected needs or opportunities.

1.20   Financial adaptability is desirable for an entity because it helps it to mitigate the risks associated with operations, which in turn helps it to survive during a time of low (or possibly negative) cash flows from operations. It may also enable an entity to take advantage of unexpected investment opportunities. On the other hand, it also generally involves making sacrifices. For example, although holding assets that are readily marketable provides some financial adaptability, the rate of return involved may be lower than could be earned from holding less liquid assets.

1.21   The extent to which—and the ways in which—it is desirable for an entity to be financially adaptable will depend on the risks the entity faces and on the appetite for risk of its investors.

1.22   Financial adaptability comes from several sources, including the ability to:

(a)   raise new capital, perhaps by issuing debt securities, at short notice;
(b)   repay capital or debt at short notice;
(c)   obtain cash by selling assets without disrupting continuing operations; and
(d)   achieve a rapid improvement in the net cash inflows generated by operations.

Chapter 2: The Reporting Entity

It is important that entities that ought to prepare and publish financial statements do, in fact, do so and that those financial statements report on all relevant activities and resources. This chapter focuses on these issues—in other words, on identifying and circumscribing the reporting entity.

PRINCIPLES

- An entity should prepare and publish financial statements if there is a legitimate demand for the information that its financial statements would provide and it is a cohesive economic unit.
- The boundary of the reporting entity is determined by the scope of its control. For this purpose, first direct control and, secondly, direct plus indirect control are taken into account.

EXPLANATION

Entities that should prepare and publish financial statements

It is essential that entities that ought to prepare and publish financial statements do, in fact, do so. For similar reasons, if there is no justification for an entity to prepare and publish financial statements, it should not be required to do so.   **2.1**

For the preparation of financial statements to be justified in any particular case, there needs to be a legitimate demand for the information that the financial statements would provide. This means, inter alia, that the information provided by the financial statements will need to be useful and that the benefits to be derived by providing the financial statements will need to exceed the costs of doing so.   **2.2**

The financial statements of an entity will report on the entity's transactions and on other events that affect its financial performance and financial position. However, if the information provided by the financial statements is to be useful, the entity that is the subject of the financial statements (the reporting entity) needs to be a cohesive economic unit. This ensures accountability—the reporting entity is held to account for all the things it can control—and it gives the reporting entity a determinable boundary—because activities and resources are either within its control or outside its control.   **2.3**

The boundary of a reporting entity

The control an entity exerts can be direct or indirect.   **2.4**

(a)   An entity has direct control of an asset if it has the ability in its own right to obtain the future economic benefits embodied in that asset and to restrict others' access to those benefits. An entity has direct control of its own activities and resources but does not have direct control of any other activities and resources.

(b)   An entity indirectly controls an asset if it has control of an entity that has direct control of the asset.[5] A parent company therefore has indirect control of the activities and resources of its subsidiary.

---

[5] *For simplicity, the discussion in this chapter assumes that one entity (the parent) directly controls the other (the subsidiary). However, the discussion applies equally if the parent controls the subsidiary by controlling one or more other entities that themselves control the subsidiary. It also applies when a parent's control of its subsidiary is achieved through the combined influence of itself and other entities that it controls.*

2.5   If the boundary of the reporting entity is determined by reference to direct control only, when one entity controls another, there will be two reporting entities: the controlling entity and its activities and resources; and the controlled entity and its activities and resources. On the other hand, if the boundary is determined by reference to direct plus indirect control, there will in the same circumstances be a reporting entity that comprises the controlling entity, the controlled entity and all their activities and resources. This reporting entity is often referred to as 'the group'.

2.6   Both these approaches result in useful information being provided, and both are therefore used in the model described in the Statement.

   (a)   Direct control is used to determine the boundary of the reporting entity that prepares single entity financial statements. Those financial statements will therefore deal with the gains, losses, assets and liabilities directly controlled or borne by the entity but no other gains, losses, assets or liabilities.

   (b)   Direct plus indirect control is used to determine the boundary of the reporting entity that prepares consolidated financial statements. Those financial statements will deal with the gains, losses, assets and liabilities directly controlled or borne by the entity as well as those that are indirectly controlled or borne by that entity through its control of other entities.

2.7   It may be that, although an entity can influence another entity, it does not control it. Such entities do not comprise a single reporting entity.[6]

What is control?

2.8   Control has two aspects: the ability to deploy the economic resources involved and the ability to benefit (or to suffer) from their deployment. To have control, an entity must have both these abilities.

2.9   This can be contrasted with the position in a trusteeship or agency arrangement, where the abilities are held by different parties. For example, in a trusteeship, the trustee—unless required to act in a predetermined way—has the power to deploy the trust's resources whilst the beneficiaries benefit from their deployment.

2.10 Control in the context of assets and liabilities is considered in more detail in Chapter 4; indirect control—through control over other entities—is considered in the paragraphs below.

Controlling an entity

When does one entity control another?

2.11 An entity will have control of a second entity if it has the ability to direct that entity's operating and financial policies with a view to gaining economic benefit from its activities.

2.12 Control may be evidenced in a variety of ways depending on its basis (for example ownership or other rights) and the way in which it is exercised (interventionist or not). Although control of another entity has traditionally involved share ownership and voting rights, that need not be the case. Indeed, some forms of control do not involve an investment of any kind.[7]

---

[6] *The accounting treatment of such relationships is addressed in Chapter 8.*

[7] *Although control need not involve an investment, for simplicity this chapter uses the term* **'investor'** *to mean 'entity with the interest in the other entity' and* **'investee'** *to mean 'entity in which the investor has an interest'.*

There is no single piece of evidence that is proof of an investor's control in all circumstances, although evidence that will help to determine whether control exists can be obtained by considering:

2.13

(a)   the respective rights held;

(b)   the inflows and outflows of benefit; and

(c)   exposure to risk—how and to what extent the investor suffers or gains from variability in outcome.

These sources of evidence are interrelated because the rights an investor holds in the investee usually determine its entitlement to benefits generated by the investee and therefore usually its exposure to risk from variations in the benefits that the investee generates.

2.14

When determining whether the investor controls the investee, it is the relationship between the entities in practice, rather than the theoretical level of influence, that is important. The paragraphs below explain some of the factors that may need to be taken into account in determining whether control exists.

2.15

Powers of veto and reserve powers

Control implies the ability to restrict others from directing the financial and operating policies of the controlled entity. Powers of veto and reserve powers may therefore form part of the rights by which an investor exercises control. However, such powers are unlikely to form the sole basis of control because they do not provide a basis for deploying the resources of the investee nor do they ensure the corresponding flows of benefit.

2.16

Predetermined operating and financial policies

An investee whose operating and financial policies are predetermined will be controlled by the investor if the investor gains the benefits arising from the investee's net assets and is exposed to the risks inherent in them (ie the variability of outcome).

2.17

Latent control

If an investor has the ability to control an investee, it is usually presumed to be exercising control, even if such control is not apparent. Generally speaking, the only evidence that could rebut this presumption is evidence that a third entity is actually deploying the investee's resources on its own behalf and benefiting from them. It is, for example, not enough to show that the investee appears to be independent—it may be implementing the operating and financial policies desired by its investor without being given explicit instructions to do so.

2.18

Management but not control

Control needs to be distinguished from management. If an entity manages a second entity on its own behalf (ie it expects to benefit from the net assets of the second entity other than merely receiving a management fee) then it controls the second entity because it has the two abilities referred to in paragraph 2.8. A fee structure that in substance amounts to an interest in the net assets of an entity is treated as an ability to benefit (or to suffer) from the deployment of those net assets (sometimes referred to as an equity interest), whatever it is called.

2.19

2.20   On the other hand, if an entity manages the second entity on behalf of another party, it is not exposed to the benefits arising from, or risks inherent in, the activities of the second entity because the manager's interest in the managed entity is normally limited to its fee. As such, it does not have the second ability referred to in paragraph 2.8 and therefore does not have control of the second entity.

Chapter 3: The Qualitative Characteristics of Financial Information

In deciding which information to include in financial statements, when to include it and how to present it, the aim is to ensure that financial statements yield information that is useful. This chapter considers the qualities of financial information that make it useful.

PRINCIPLES

- Information provided by financial statements needs to be relevant and reliable and, if a choice exists between relevant and rel?able approaches that are mutually exclusive, the approach chosen needs to be the one that results in the relevance of the information provided being maximised.
- Information is relevant if it has the ability to influence the economic decisions of users and is provided in time to influence those decisions.
- Information is reliable if:

  (a)   it can be depended upon by users to represent faithfully what it either purports to represent or could reasonably be expected to represent, and therefore reflects the substance of the transactions and other events that have taken place;

  (b)   it is free from deliberate or systematic bias and material error and is complete; and

  (c)   in its preparation under conditions of uncertainty, a degree of caution has been applied in exercising the necessary judgements.

- Information in financial statements needs to be comparable.
- As an aid to comparability, information in financial statements needs to be prepared and presented in a way that enables users to discern and evaluate similarities in, and differences between, the nature and effects of transactions and other events over time and across different reporting entities.
- Information provided by financial statements needs to be understandable, although information should not be excluded from the financial statements simply because it would not be understood by some users.
- Information is understandable if its significance can be perceived by users that have a reasonable knowledge of business and economic activities and accounting and a willingness to study with reasonable diligence the information provided.
- Information that is material needs to be given in the financial statements and information that is not material need not be given.
- Information is material to the financial statements if its misstatement or omission might reasonably be expected to influence the economic decisions of users.

The relationship between these characteristics is portrayed in the diagram on the following page.

EXPLANATION

Relevance

Relevance is a general quality that is used as a selection criterion at all stages of the financial reporting process. Information provided by financial statements needs to be relevant. Furthermore, where choices have to be made between options that are relevant and reliable but mutually exclusive, the option selected should be the one that results in the relevance of the information package as a whole being maximised—in other words, the one that is reliable and would be of most use in taking economic decisions.   **3.1**

Information is relevant if it has the ability to influence the economic decisions of users and is provided in time to influence those decisions.   **3.2**

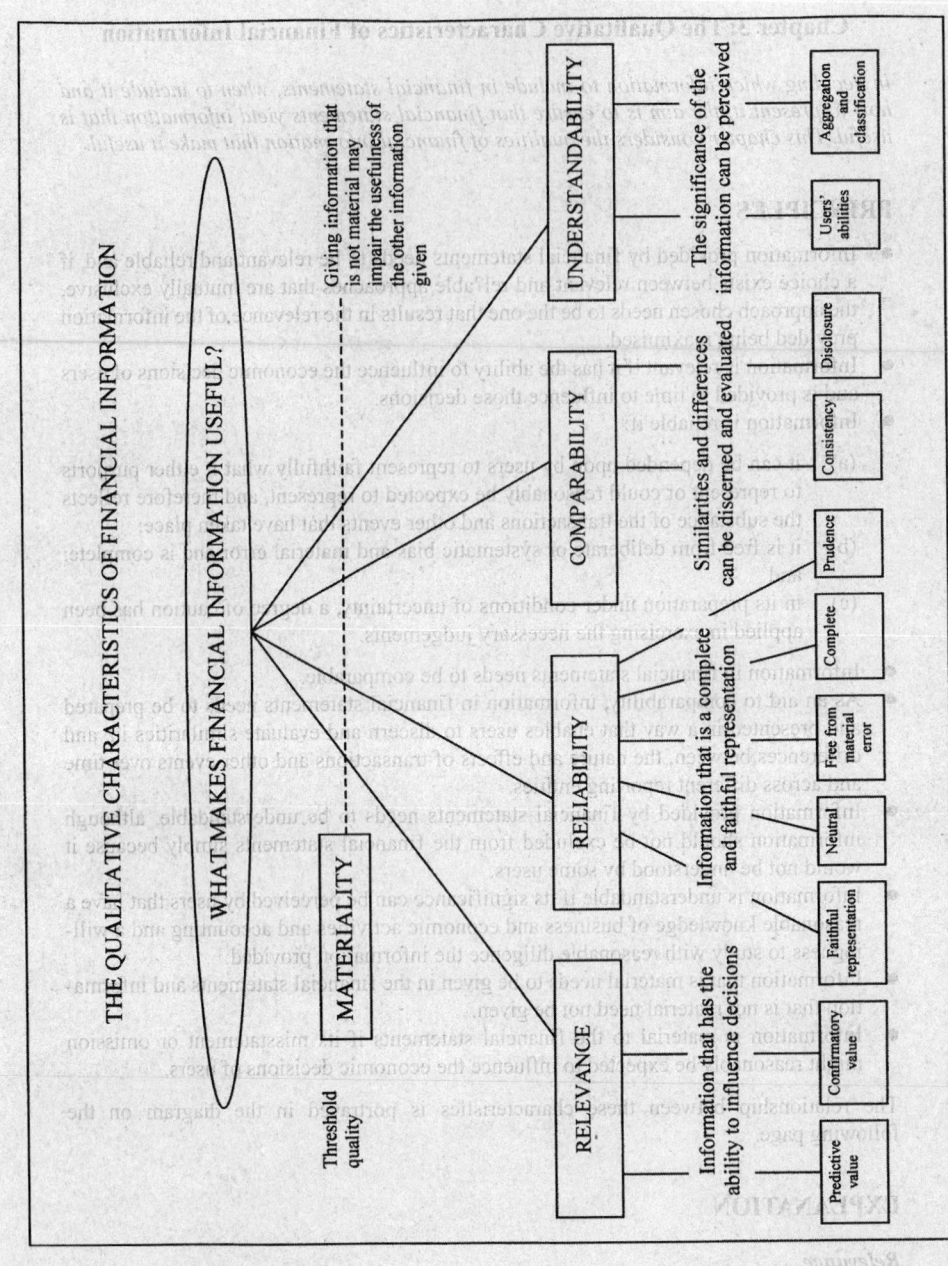

THE QUALITATIVE CHARACTERISTICS OF FINANCIAL INFORMATION

WHAT MAKES FINANCIAL INFORMATION USEFUL?

MATERIALITY

Threshold quality

Giving information that is not material may impair the usefulness of the other information given

RELEVANCE

Information that has the ability to influence decisions

Predictive value

Confirmatory value

RELIABILITY

Information that is a complete and faithful representation

Faithful representation

Neutral

Free from material error

Complete

Prudence

COMPARABILITY

Similarities and differences can be discerned and evaluated

Consistency

Disclosure

UNDERSTANDABILITY

The significance of the information can be perceived

Users' abilities

Aggregation and classification

Relevant information has predictive value or confirmatory value. It has predictive value if **3.3**
it helps users to evaluate or assess past, present or future events, and it does not need to be in
the form of an explicit forecast to have predictive value. Information has confirmatory value
if it helps users to confirm or correct their past evaluations and assessments. Information
may have both predictive value and confirmatory value. For example, information about
the current level and structure of asset holdings helps users to assess the entity's ability
to exploit opportunities and react to adverse situations. The same information helps to
confirm past assessments about the structure of the entity and the outcome of operations.

The ability to use information in financial statements to make assessments is enhanced by **3.4**
the way in which it is presented. For example, the predictive value of information provided
by the financial performance statement is enhanced if unusual or infrequent items of gains
or losses are disclosed and if information is provided that helps users to assess the likely
incidence of similarly unusual or infrequent gains or losses in the future. In the same
way, presentations that help users to understand the recurring/non-recurring nature of the
various gains and losses also improve the predictive value of the performance statement.

Maximising the relevance of financial information involves maximising its predictive and **3.5**
confirmatory value.

There are a number of different perspectives from which an entity's financial performance **3.6**
and financial position could be viewed and the perspective adopted could have a significant
effect on the assets and liabilities recognised and on their carrying amounts. In view of the
objective of financial statements, the perspective that is usually most relevant is based on
the assumption that the entity is to continue in operational existence for the foreseeable
future. This perspective is commonly referred to as the going concern assumption.

Reliability

Information provided by financial statements needs to be reliable. **3.7**

Information is reliable if: **3.8**

(a)   it can be depended upon by users to represent faithfully what it either purports to
      represent or could reasonably be expected to represent;
(b)   it is free from deliberate or systematic bias (ie it is neutral);
(c)   it is free from material error;
(d)   it is complete within the bounds of materiality; and
(e)   in its preparation under conditions of uncertainty, a degree of caution (ie prudence)
      has been applied in exercising judgement and making the necessary estimates.

Faithful representation

The portrayal of a transaction or other event in the financial statements depends, inter alia, **3.9**
on:

(a)   the rights and obligations arising and the weight attached to each;
(b)   how the rights and obligations to which most weight has been attached are
      characterised;
(c)   which measurement basis (or bases) and presentation techniques are used to depict
      the rights and obligations; and
(d)   the way in which the elements arising from the transaction or other event are
      presented in the financial statements.

3.10   A transaction or other event is faithfully represented in the financial statements if the way in which it is recognised, measured and presented in those statements corresponds closely to the effect of that transaction or event.

3.11   It needs to be borne in mind that most financial information is subject to some risk of being less than a faithful representation of what it purports to portray. This is partly due to inherent difficulties in identifying the transactions and other events to be dealt with and in identifying the consequences of such transactions and events that need to be measured. It reflects the difficulties in devising and applying measurement and presentation techniques that can convey messages that reflect those transactions and events. Furthermore, references to faithful representation need to be understood in the context of the Statement as a whole, which limits the kind of information that may properly be included in financial statements.

3.12   Faithful representation involves identifying *all* the rights and obligations arising from the transaction or event, giving greater weight to those that are likely to have a commercial effect in practice, then accounting for and presenting the transaction or other event in a way that reflects that commercial effect—in other words, in a way that reflects its substance.

3.13   The substance of a transaction or other event is not always consistent with that suggested by its legal form: although the effects of the legal characteristics of a transaction or other event are themselves a part of its substance and commercial effect, they have to be construed in the context of the transaction as a whole, including any related transactions. For example, an entity may pass legal ownership of an item of property to another party, yet, when the circumstances are looked at as a whole, it may be found that arrangements exist that ensure that the entity continues to have access to the future economic benefits embodied in that item of property. In such circumstances, the accounting needs to reflect this continuing interest.

3.14   A group or series of transactions that achieves an overall commercial effect will often need to be viewed as a whole in order to be accounted for in accordance with its substance.

Neutrality

3.15   The information provided by financial statements needs to be neutral—in other words, free from deliberate or systematic bias. Financial information is not neutral if it has been selected or presented in such a way as to influence the making of a decision or judgement in order to achieve a predetermined result or outcome.

Complete and free from material error

3.16   In requiring information provided by financial statements to represent faithfully what it purports to represent and to be neutral, there is an implication that the information is complete and free from error—at least within the bounds of materiality. Information that contains a material error or has been omitted for reasons other than materiality can cause the financial statements to be false or misleading and thus unreliable and deficient in terms of their relevance.

3.17   This reference to being complete within the bounds of materiality is important because completeness is relative: financial statements are a highly aggregated portrayal of an entity's financial performance and financial position and therefore cannot show everything.

Prudence

Uncertainty surrounds many of the events and circumstances that are reported on in the financial statements and it is dealt with in those statements by disclosing the nature and extent of the uncertainty involved and by exercising prudence.   **3.18**

Prudence is the inclusion of a degree of caution in the exercise of the judgements needed in making the estimates required under conditions of uncertainty, such that gains and assets are not overstated and losses and liabilities are not understated. In particular, under such conditions it requires more confirmatory evidence about the existence of, and a greater reliability of measurement for, assets and gains than is required for liabilities and losses.   **3.19**

However, it is not necessary to exercise prudence where there is no uncertainty. Nor is it appropriate to use prudence as a reason for, for example, creating hidden reserves or excessive provisions, deliberately understating assets or gains, or deliberately overstating liabilities or losses, because that would mean that the financial statements are not neutral and, therefore, are not reliable.   **3.20**

Comparability

Information in an entity's financial statements gains greatly in usefulness if it can be compared with similar information about the entity for some other period or point in time in order to identify trends in financial performance and financial position. Information about an entity is also much more useful if it can be compared with similar information about other entities in order to evaluate their relative financial performance and financial position.   **3.21**

Information in financial statements therefore needs to be comparable—at least as far as is possible. Furthermore, to help users to make comparisons, such information needs to be prepared and presented in a way that enables users to discern and evaluate similarities in, and differences between, the nature and effects of transactions and other events taking place over time and across different reporting entities. This can usually be achieved through a combination of consistency and disclosure of accounting policies.   **3.22**

Consistency

Comparability generally implies consistency throughout the reporting entity within each accounting period and from one period to the next. However, consistency is not an end in itself nor should it be allowed to become an impediment to the introduction of improved accounting practices. Consistency can also be useful in enhancing comparability between entities, although it should not be confused with a need for absolute uniformity.   **3.23**

Disclosure of accounting policies

In order to determine whether consistency exists or to assist in the making of comparisons despite inconsistencies, users need to be able to identify any differences between: **3.24**

(a)   the accounting policies adopted by an entity to account for like transactions and other events;
(b)   the accounting policies adopted from period to period by an entity; and
(c)   the accounting policies adopted by different entities.

Disclosure of the accounting policies employed in the preparation of the financial statements, of any changes in those policies and of the effects of such changes therefore enhances the usefulness of financial statements.   **3.25**

Understandability

3.26   Information provided by financial statements needs to be understandable—in other words, users need to be able to perceive its significance.

3.27   Whether financial information is understandable will depend on:

(a)   the way in which the effects of transactions and other events are characterised, aggregated and classified. For example, information that does not properly reflect and communicate the substance of transactions and other events will not help users to understand the entity's financial performance or financial position.

(b)   the way in which the information is presented. (This is considered further in Chapter 7.)

(c)   the capabilities of users. Those preparing financial statements are entitled to assume that users have a reasonable knowledge of business and economic activities and accounting and a willingness to study with reasonable diligence the information provided.

Materiality

3.28   Materiality is the final test of what information should be given in a particular set of financial statements. While the paragraphs above describe the characteristics that, if present, will mean that the usefulness of the financial information has been maximised, the materiality test asks whether the resulting information content is of such significance as to require its inclusion in the financial statements.

3.29   Materiality is therefore a threshold quality that is demanded of all information given in the financial statements. Furthermore, when immaterial information is given in the financial statements, the resulting clutter can impair the understandability of the other information provided. In such circumstances, the immaterial information will need to be excluded.

3.30   An item of information is material to the financial statements if its misstatement or omission might reasonably be expected to influence the economic decisions of users of those financial statements, including their assessments of management's stewardship.

3.31   Whether information is material will depend on the size and nature of the item in question judged in the particular circumstances of the case. The principal factors to be taken into account are set out below. It will usually be a combination of these factors, rather than any one in particular, that will determine materiality.

(a)   The item's size is judged in the context both of the financial statements as a whole and of the other information available to users that would affect their evaluation of the financial statements. This includes, for example, considering how the item affects the evaluation of trends and similar considerations.

(b)   Consideration is given to the item's nature in relation to:

(i)   the transactions or other events giving rise to it;

(ii)   the legality, sensitivity, normality and potential consequences of the event or transaction;

(iii)   the identity of the parties involved; and

(iv)   the particular headings and disclosures that are affected.

3.32   If there are two or more similar items, the materiality of the items in aggregate as well as of the items individually needs to be considered.

Constraints on the qualitative characteristics

On occasion, a conflict will arise between the characteristics of relevance, reliability, comparability and understandability. In such circumstances, a trade-off needs to be found that still enables the objective of financial statements to be met. **3.33**

Relevance and reliability

Sometimes the information that is the most relevant is not the most reliable and vice versa. Choosing the amount at which to measure an asset or liability will sometimes involve just such a conflict. In such circumstances, it will usually be appropriate to use the information that is the most relevant of whichever information is reliable.8 **3.34**

Conflict between relevance and reliability can also arise over the timeliness of information. That is because a delay in providing information can make it out-of-date, which will affect its relevance, yet reporting on transactions and other events before all the uncertainties involved are resolved may affect the information's reliability. On the other hand, leaving information out of the financial statements because of reliability concerns may affect the completeness, and therefore reliability, of the information that is provided. Although financial information should generally be made available as soon as it is reliable and entities should do all that they reasonably can to speed up the process necessary to make information reliable, financial information should not be provided until it is reliable. **3.35**

Neutrality and prudence

There can also be tension between two aspects of reliability—neutrality and prudence— because, whilst neutrality involves freedom from deliberate or systematic bias, prudence is a potentially biased concept that seeks to ensure that, under conditions of uncertainty, gains and assets are not overstated and losses and liabilities are not understated. This tension exists only where there is uncertainty, because it is only then that prudence needs to be exercised. When there is uncertainty, the competing demands of neutrality and prudence are reconciled by finding a balance that ensures that the deliberate and systematic understatement of gains and assets and overstatement of losses and liabilities do not occur. **3.36**

Understandability

It may not always be possible to present a piece of relevant, reliable and comparable information in a way that can be understood by all the users with the capabilities described in paragraph 3.27(c). However, information that is relevant and reliable should not be excluded from the financial statements simply because it is too difficult for some users to understand. **3.37**

---

8 *Choosing between alternative measurement bases is considered in Chapter 6*

Chapter 4: The elements of Financial Statements

UITF Abstract 34: Pre-contract costs;UITF Information Sheet No 59; UITF Information Sheet No 60; UITF Information Sheet No 62; UITF Abstract 37: Purchases and sales of own shares; UITF Abstract 38: Accounting for ESOP Trusts

Elements of financial statements are the building blocks with which financial statements are constructed—the classes of items that financial statements comprise. This chapter identifies those elements and explains their attributes.

PRINCIPLES

- The elements of the financial statements are:

   (a)   assets
   (b)   liabilities
   (c)   ownership interest[9]
   (d)   gains[10]
   (e)   losses[11]
   (f)   contributions from owners
   (g)   distributions to owners.

- Assets are rights or other access to future economic benefits controlled by an entity as a result of past transactions or events.
- Liabilities are obligations of an entity to transfer economic benefits as a result of past transactions or events.
- Ownership interest is the residual amount found by deducting all of the entity's liabilities from all of the entity's assets.
- Gains are increases in ownership interest not resulting from contributions from owners.
- Losses are decreases in ownership interest not resulting from distributions to owners.
- Contributions from owners are increases in ownership interest resulting from transfers from owners in their capacity as owners.
- Distributions to owners are decreases in ownership interest resulting from transfers to owners in their capacity as owners.

EXPLANATION

The elements of financial statements

Depicting the effects of transactions and other events

4.1   Financial statements need to reflect, in an appropriate manner and as far as is practicable, the effects of transactions and other events on the reporting entity's financial performance and financial position. This involves a high degree of classification and aggregation. Order is imposed on this process by specifying and defining the classes of items—the elements of financial statements—that encapsulate the key aspects of the effects of those transactions and other events.

---

[9] *This element is given various descriptions in financial statements including, for example, equity, owners' equity, shareholders' equity, equity capital, capital, capital and reserves, partners' capital, shareholders' funds, proprietorship and ownership.*

[10] *This term incorporates all forms of income and revenue as well as all recognised gains (realised and unrealised) on non-revenue items.*

[11] *This term incorporates all forms of expenses, sometimes referred to as revenue expenditure, and all recognised losses (realised and unrealised) on non-revenue items.*

The elements of financial statements are: **4.2**

(a)   in the case of the balance sheet (or statement of financial position)—assets, liabilities and ownership interest;

(b)   in the case of the profit and loss account and any other statement of financial performance—gains and losses;

(c)   contributions from owners; and

(d)   distributions to owners.

Contributions from owners and distributions to owners are not the same as, and need to   **4.3** be distinguished from, other increases or decreases in ownership interest (in other words, gains and losses), which is why they are elements even though they are not identified with any particular primary financial statement.

Elements have been specified and defined to analyse comprehensively the way in which the   **4.4** financial effects of transactions and other events are represented in financial statements. However, as the cash flow statement represents only one type of financial effect—cash flows—analysis into elements is not relevant to that statement.

Recognition

Simply because a transaction or other event results, say, in a new asset being created, it   **4.5** does not follow that that new asset will be recognised. The criteria that need to be met before the effects of a transaction or other event on the elements will be recognised are considered in Chapter 5.

Assets

Definition

Assets are defined as follows: **4.6**

> Assets are rights or other access to future economic benefits controlled by an entity as a result of past transactions or events.

UITF Abstract 32: Employee benefit trusts and other intermediate payment arrangements

Although assets commonly have other features that help identify them—for example, they   **4.7** may be acquired at a cost and they may be tangible, exchangeable or legally enforceable— those features are not essential characteristics of an asset and their absence is not sufficient in itself to preclude an item from qualifying as an asset.

Rights or other access

An asset is not the item of property itself, but rather the rights or other access to some or   **4.8** all of the future economic benefits derived from the item of property.[12]

These rights or other access can be obtained in various ways. Often they are obtained   **4.9** by legal ownership of the underlying item of property. Such ownership usually gives the owner access to a number of future economic benefits, including the ability to use the

---

[12] *The term 'item of property' has been used in this chapter to differentiate between the control of rights or other access to future economic benefits (the asset) and the thing from which those future economic benefits are derived (the item of property). It is recognised however that, in other contexts, the term may have a different meaning and could, for example, refer to the subdivided property rights.*

item of property, to sell or exchange it or to exploit its value by, for example, pledging it as security for borrowing.

4.10   However, legal rights to future economic benefits derived from an item of property can be obtained without having legal ownership of the property itself, as is the case, for example, where property is leased.

4.11   Other legal rights that give rise to assets include the right to require other parties to make payments or render services and the right to use a patent or trade mark.

4.12   Access to future economic benefits—and therefore an asset—can also exist in the absence of legal rights. An example might be an unpatented invention.

Future economic benefits

4.13   Capacity to obtain future economic benefits is the essence of an asset and is common to all assets irrespective of their form. Therefore, to be an asset, the right or other access must be capable, singly or in combination with other assets, of yielding economic benefits.

4.14   This future economic benefit need not, however, be certain. Indeed, there is always some uncertainty whether expected future economic benefits will be obtained either to the extent expected or at all. In some cases, that uncertainty is so great that the asset is not recognised.[13]

4.15   Future economic benefits eventually result in net cash inflows to the entity. Assets are not, however, always direct representations of cash flows: they are rights and other access to the future economic benefits that can generate or be used to generate future cash flows. In particular:

   (a)   cash (including bank deposits) can be exchanged for virtually any goods or service that is available or it can be saved and exchanged for them in the future. The command that cash gives over resources is the basis of its future economic benefits.
   (b)   debtors, investments and similar assets represent future economic benefits because they are direct claims to cash inflows that are expected to occur when customers pay their accounts, when investees pay interest or dividends, or when an investment is repaid or sold.
   (c)   payments made to external parties for services to be received from them in the future (such as prepayments) result in access to future economic benefits because they represent rights to receive services or to return of the payment.
   (d)   other assets provide access to future economic benefits through their ability to be:

        (i)   exchanged for cash, claims to cash or other goods and services;
        (ii)   used to provide goods or services; or
        (iii) used to settle liabilities.

4.16   As there does not need to be certainty that the economic benefits will arise, items that represent the right to exchange property on terms that will or may be favourable are also assets. For example, an option to acquire an asset will, subject to the other criteria being met, be an asset even if the price payable under the option is currently more than the market price of the asset.

Controlled by the entity

4.17   The definition of an asset requires that the rights or other access to future economic benefits are controlled by the reporting entity. An entity will control the rights or other

---

[13] *The recognition process is discussed in Chapter 5.*

access if it has the ability both to obtain for itself any economic benefits that will arise and to prevent or limit the access of others to those benefits.

This control does not need to be legally enforceable, which means that weight can be given to economic and social sanctions when these are effective in inducing entities to fulfil promises or to comply with widely accepted business practices or customs. **4.18**

The requirement that the rights or other access should be controlled by the entity treating them as its asset means that a particular right or other access to future economic benefits will appear in only one set of single entity financial statements, because such rights or access can be directly controlled by only one entity. (As indirect control is important in determining the boundaries of reporting entities, a right that is directly controlled by one entity and indirectly controlled by a second—through its control of the first entity—will be an asset both of the first entity and of the reporting entity that comprises both entities, ie the group.[14]) **4.19**

On the other hand, a single item of property may give rise to assets of more than one entity. If two entities control the rights to different future economic benefits from the same item of property, both entities will have an asset (subject to the other aspects of the definition being met). However, although the item of property underlying the asset will be the same, the assets will be different because the future economic benefits are different. For example, if an entity leases an item of property to another entity, both entities will recognise an asset based on rights relating to the leased item of property although, as the lessor's rights will not be identical to the lessee's, the assets will not be the same. **4.20**

An item of property will be an asset of an entity even though that entity cannot dispose of it without fundamentally changing the nature of its business, as would be the case if, for example, a hotel company with one hotel sold its hotel or a television franchise company sold its franchise. In such cases, although the rights to future economic benefits derived from the hotel or television franchise are the essence of the entity's business, it controls those rights and is therefore still in a position to choose if and when to realise the economic benefits involved. On the other hand, it is generally not possible for an entity to choose if and when to realise the economic benefits derivable from factors such as its market share, superior management or good labour relations because the rights or other access to such benefits cannot be controlled independently of the business as a whole. The entity therefore does not have the control of these benefits envisaged by the Statement, which means that such factors are not assets of the entity. **4.21**

Past transactions or events

If the reporting entity's control of the rights or other access to the future economic benefits involved is to represent an asset, it needs to be the result of past transactions or events. A reporting entity that has access to future economic benefits but did not, until after the balance sheet date, have the ability to restrict the access of others to those benefits, did not have an asset at the balance sheet date. **4.22**

Liabilities

Definition

Liabilities are defined as follows: **4.23**

> Liabilities are obligations of an entity to transfer economic benefits as a result of past transactions or events.

---

[14] *Determining the boundaries of reporting entities is considered in Chapter 2.*

Obligations

4.24   For there to be a liability there must be an obligation that might result in the transfer of economic benefits.

4.25   The notion of an obligation implies that the entity is not free to avoid the outflow of resources. If an obligation exists, although an entity may offer inducements to its creditors to cancel or postpone settlement, it will not be able to insist that they accept such an offer.

4.26   Although many liabilities are based on legal obligations, a legal obligation is not a necessary condition: a liability can exist in the absence of legal obligations if commercial considerations create a constructive obligation.

4.27   A decision to transfer economic benefits does not, in itself, create a constructive obligation because the transfer can be avoided by changing the decision. On the other hand, a constructive obligation would be created if such a decision was coupled with an event that both created a valid expectation that the entity involved would implement that decision and meant that the entity could not realistically withdraw from it. For example, a constructive obligation may be created by communicating a decision to follow a particular course of action to another party. Such an obligation may also be created by an established pattern of past practice.

4.28   When preparing financial statements, it is usually most relevant to assume that the reporting entity is to continue in operational existence for the foreseeable future. It does not follow from this assumption, however, that, in preparing financial statements, the entity should be treated as being obliged to adopt a course of action that will enable it to continue in operational existence. Even if an obligation needs to be incurred to enable the entity to continue existing operations, until the entity ceases to be able to avoid the outflow of resources involved, there will be no obligation and, therefore, no liability.

Transfer of economic benefits

4.29   Certainty that the obligation will result in a transfer of future economic benefits is not necessary. Obligations that are not likely to result in a transfer of economic benefits—such as the guarantee of another entity's debt where that entity is expected to remain solvent— are liabilities, even though they may not be recognised in financial statements (or may be recognised with a carrying amount of nil).

4.30   Similarly, although many liabilities involve transfers of known amounts of cash, that need not be the case: a liability could involve an obligation to transfer an uncertain amount, and it could involve an obligation to transfer economic benefits other than cash—for example, by providing services or by undertaking to repair goods that are the subject of warranties. The recognition criteria described in Chapter 5 will filter out those liabilities that involve too much uncertainty to be recognised in the primary financial statements.

Past transactions or events

4.31   For a liability to exist at the balance sheet date, the obligation to transfer economic benefits must have resulted from a past transaction or event. For example, in the circumstances described in paragraph 4.27—where the event that gave rise to the obligation was the communication of the decision to transfer economic benefits—the liability will have existed at the balance sheet date only if the communication took place on or before that date.

Sometimes a series of events must take place before the entity will have an obligation to transfer economic benefits. In such circumstances, whether the obligation exists depends on whether any of the events that have still to take place are under the entity's control. If they are, the entity retains discretion to avoid the transfer, so no obligation exists. For example, as long as it is possible to avoid a penalty clause in a contract by performing, a liability in respect of the penalty will not arise. In contrast, an obligation to repair goods subject to warranty cannot be avoided once the goods have been sold on terms that include the warranty, so the sale marks the inception of the liability. **4.32**

Offsetting rights and obligations

When a transaction or other event gives rise to a number of rights and obligations, it is necessary to consider whether some or all of those rights and obligations need to be offset either with each other or with rights and obligations that arise from other transactions or events. This raises issues of: **4.33**

(a)   definition—when do rights and obligations represent separate assets and liabilities and when should some or all of them be aggregated or offset? This issue is considered in paragraphs 4.34-4.36.
(b)   recognition—when should rights that represent an asset and obligations that represent a liability be combined and recognised as a single asset or liability? This Statement envisages no circumstances in which assets and liabilities will be treated in this way.
(c)   presentation—when is it appropriate to present assets offset against liabilities (or vice versa) in the balance sheet? This issue is considered in Chapter 7.

If a right to receive future economic benefits and an obligation to transfer future economic benefits exist and the reporting entity has the ability—which is assured—to insist on net settlement of the balances, the right and obligation together form a single asset or liability regardless of how the parties intend to settle the balances. **4.34**

When an entity enters into an agreement with another, it usually obtains certain rights and, in exchange, accepts certain obligations. Before any act of performance under the agreement has taken place, the entity does not have control of the future economic benefits arising from performance, nor does it have an obligation to transfer economic benefits that arise on performance. What it does have, however, is a contract that represents a net position comprising a combined right and obligation either to participate in the exchange or alternatively to be compensated (or to compensate) for the consequences of the exchange not taking place. Initially, the rights and obligations are likely to be exactly offsetting, although that will often not remain the case. The rights and obligations arising under such unperformed executory contracts together represent a single asset or liability. **4.35**

It may be that the contract has been performed partially but is equally proportionately unperformed—in other words, that both parties to the contract have still to perform to an equal degree the actions promised by and required of them under the contract. In such a case, although the rights and obligations relating to the performed part of the contract may represent separate assets and liabilities, the rights and obligations relating to the unperformed part will together represent a single asset or liability. **4.36**

Ownership interest

Ownership interest is defined as follows:

Ownership interest is the residual amount found by deducting all of the entity's liabilities from all of the entity's assets. **4.37**

4.38   Since ownership interest is defined as a residual interest, the distinction between liabilities and ownership interest is highly significant. Owners invest in an entity in the hope of a return, at least part of which will usually be provided by the transfer to them from the entity of economic benefits (for example the payment of dividends). However, owners, unlike creditors, do not have the ability to insist that a transfer is made to them regardless of the circumstances: theirs is a residual interest in the assets of the entity after all the liabilities have been deducted.

Gains and losses

Definitions

4.39   Financial statements draw a distinction between changes in ownership interest arising from transactions with owners in their capacity as owners and other changes. These latter changes are gains and losses and are defined as follows:

> Gains are increases in ownership interest not resulting from contributions from owners.

> Losses are decreases in ownership interest not resulting from distributions to owners.

UITF Abstract 32: Employee benefit trusts and other intermediate payment arrangements

4.40   The terms 'gains' and 'losses' therefore include items that are often referred to as 'revenue' and 'expenses', as well as gains and losses arising from, for example, the disposal of fixed assets and the remeasurement of assets and liabilities.

Offsetting gains and losses

4.41   Some transactions give rise to a gain (or a loss) that is the net of two amounts: the revenue or income arising from the transaction and the expenses or costs incurred in generating that revenue. For example, the profit that arises on selling an item of stock is the difference between the sale proceeds and the cost of the item sold. For the purpose of the Statement, the sale proceeds and cost of the item sold are separate items—the former being a gain and the latter a loss. Whether such gains and losses are shown separately in the financial statements is a presentation issue and is considered in Chapter 7.

Contributions from owners and distributions to owners

Definitions

4.42   The remaining elements of financial statements relate to transactions with the owners in their capacity as owners and are defined as follows:

> Contributions from owners are increases in ownership interest resulting from transfers from owners in their capacity as owners.

> Distributions to owners are decreases in ownership interest resulting from transfers to owners in their capacity as owners.

In their capacity as owners

4.43   Contributions from, and distributions to, owners include only those transactions to which owners are a party in their capacity as owners. Increases or decreases in ownership interest that result from transactions entered into with owners in other capacities (for example, as customers or suppliers) are gains or losses. In some cases a single transaction combines a transaction with owners in their capacity as owners and a transaction with them in some other capacity.

Contributions from owners

Contributions from owners involve the owners making a contribution to the entity by transferring assets, performing services, or accepting ownership interest in satisfaction of liabilities. Rights in the ownership interest are usually granted in return for a contribution from owners. **4.44**

Distributions to owners

Distributions to owners include the payment of dividends and the return of capital. A purchase by a company of its own shares is an example of a return of capital and is therefore reflected in financial statements by reducing the amount of ownership interest. **4.45**

Chapter 5: Recognition in Financial Statements

See also UITF Abstract 36 *Contracts for sales of capacity*; UITF Abstract 34: Pre-contract costs; UITF Abstract 26: Barter transactions for advertising

When the reporting entity undertakes a transaction or when some other relevant event occurs, the effect of that transaction or event on the elements of financial statements will need to be recognised in the financial statements if certain criteria are met. This chapter considers that recognition process.

PRINCIPLES

- If a transaction or other event has created a new asset or liability or added to an existing asset or liability, that effect will be recognised[15] if:

  (a) sufficient evidence exists that the new asset or liability has been created or that there has been an addition to an existing asset or liability; and

  (b) the new asset or liability or the addition to the existing asset or liability can be measured at a monetary amount with sufficient reliability.

- In a transaction involving the provision of services or goods for a net gain, the recognition criteria described above will be met on the occurrence of the critical event in the operating cycle involved.

- An asset or liability will be wholly or partly derecognised[16] if:

  (a) sufficient evidence exists that a transaction or other past event has eliminated[17] all or part of a previously recognised asset or liability; or

  (b) although the item continues to be an asset or a liability, the criteria for recognition are no longer met.

EXPLANATION

The recognition process

The stages of the recognition process

5.1   The objective of financial statements is achieved to a large extent through the recognition of elements in the primary financial statements—in other words, the depiction of elements both in words and by monetary amounts and the inclusion of those amounts in the primary financial statement totals. This recognition process has the following stages:

  (a) initial recognition, which is where an item is depicted in the primary financial statements for the first time;

  (b) subsequent remeasurement, which involves changing the amount at which an already recognised asset or liability is stated in the primary financial statements; and

  (c) derecognition, which is where an item that was until then recognised ceases to be recognised.

---

[15] *The term '**recognised**' is used in the Statement to mean depicting an item both in words and by a monetary amount and including that amount in the primary financial statement totals.*

[16] *The term '**derecognised**' is used in the Statement to mean that an item ceases to be recognised.*

[17] *To simplify the text, the word '**eliminated**' is used in this chapter in place of the phrase 'consumed, transferred, disposed of, expired, settled or extinguished'.*

Transactions and events other than transactions

The recognition process requires that all events that may have an effect on elements of the financial statements are, as far as is possible, identified and reflected in an appropriate manner in the financial statements.   **5.2**

Transactions are the most common form of such events and are therefore the most common reason for recognising and derecognising items. Events other than transactions may nevertheless also result in the recognition or derecognition of items. For example: **5.3**

(a)   events such as discovery, growth, extraction, processing or innovation may result in the creation of new assets that may meet the recognition criteria. Similarly, the imposition of a penalty by a court may create a new liability that meets the recognition criteria.

(b)   events (such as a fire) that cause damage to an asset and events (such as the elapse of time) that result in an obligation expiring may result in a need to derecognise the asset or liability involved.

The effect of transactions and other events

No matter what element or change in element is being considered, the starting point for the recognition process is the effect that the transaction or other event involved has had on the reporting entity's assets and liabilities, because it is the assets and liabilities that demonstrate the lasting effect of changes in other elements. The interrelationship between the elements means that the recognition of one item as an element (or the recognition of a change in an element, including its derecognition) will inevitably result in the recognition of, or change in, another element. Thus, if a new asset is recognised, there will also be recognised a decrease in another asset, a new or increased liability, a gain, or a contribution from owners (or a combination of these).   **5.4**

A transaction or other event could have one of several effects on a reporting entity's assets and liabilities.   **5.5**

(a)   It might create a new asset or liability or add to an existing asset or liability. When this is the case, it will be necessary to determine whether the new asset or liability (or the addition thereto) should be recognised, because not all assets and liabilities are recognised. Paragraphs 5.12-5.21 consider initial recognition in detail.

(b)   It might provide additional evidence about an existing but unrecognised asset or liability and, as a result, enable that item to be recognised. This is also considered in paragraphs 5.12-5.21.

(c)   It might change some aspect of an already recognised asset or liability. This change may involve:

(i)   the nature of the item. For example, an item of raw material may be converted through the production process into finished goods. Similarly, convertible debt may be converted into equity shares. A change in the nature of an item will usually require a change in description, possibly by reclassification from one balance sheet caption to another or by renaming within a balance sheet caption. The amount at which the item is stated in the financial statements may also need to be changed.

(ii)   a change to the flow of benefits associated with an already recognised asset or liability. For example, the market value of a property may change as a result of changes in its development or income potential. Doubts about the creditworthiness of a debtor may alter perceptions of the collectability of the amount due from that debtor. Similarly, new information may cause the reporting entity to alter its estimate of the amount to be paid out to settle a liability of uncertain amount. A change in the flow of benefits associated with an item may require a change in the amount at which the item is stated. Changes in the amount at which an item is stated (in other words, subsequent remeasurements) are considered in Chapter 6.

(d)   It might involve transferring, using up or consuming an asset or settling, extinguishing or transferring a liability. On the other hand, it might leave intact certain of the rights to future economic benefits inherent in an asset whilst transferring, using up or consuming others, or it might leave intact certain obligations inherent in a liability whilst settling, extinguishing or transferring others. In all such circumstances it will be necessary to consider whether the existing asset or liability that has been affected should be derecognised in whole or in part. Paragraphs 5.22-5.25 consider derecognition further.

5.6   The references in the definitions of assets and liabilities to past transactions or events ensure that the non-cash effects of transactions and other events will, as far as is possible, be reflected in the financial statements in the accounting period in which they occur and not, for example, in the period in which any cash involved is received or paid. This is commonly referred to as the 'accruals concept'.

5.7   Whether the reporting entity is a going concern can play a significant role in the recognition process. For example, some contracts stipulate that the rights they give one party to the contract will lapse if that party discontinues its operations. Similarly, the reliability of measures—an important factor in the recognition process—may be affected if the reporting entity is not able to continue its operations. As explained in Chapter 3, the qualitative characteristic of relevance usually requires the going concern assumption to be applied.

Uncertainty and the recognition process

5.8   Ideally, all assets, liabilities, gains, losses and other elements would be recognised immediately they arise. Similarly, in an ideal world an asset or liability would be derecognised as soon as it had ceased to exist or would be remeasured as soon as the need for remeasurement arose. In practice, however, entities operate in an uncertain environment and this uncertainty may sometimes make it necessary to delay the recognition process.

5.9   If uncertainty exists, totally reliable information will become available only when the uncertainty has resolved itself. However, to defer a stage of the recognition process until the uncertainty has resolved itself will often reduce the relevance of the financial statements. It may also reduce their reliability because they will not represent faithfully the transactions and other events of the reporting period. Financial statements achieve a balance between these competing demands by seeking to provide information that has no more than an acceptable degree of uncertainty but not seeking to provide information that is totally free from uncertainty.

5.10   In the business environment, uncertainty usually exists in a continuum, so the recognition process involves selecting the point on the continuum at which uncertainty becomes acceptable. The exact location of this point on the continuum will vary, depending on circumstances. For example, if additional information about the possible outcomes of an obligation is disclosed, it will usually be possible to recognise a liability despite this uncertainty. Furthermore, if a number of similar uncertain items are involved, it may be practicable to determine a sufficiently reliable measure for the items taken as a whole despite the impracticality of determining a sufficiently reliable measure for each item individually.

5.11   There will nevertheless be circumstances in which it is not possible to reduce the uncertainty to an acceptable level. If that is the case, the recognition process will be deferred until such time as the uncertainty has been reduced to an acceptable level (and the effect of the transaction or other event will instead usually be reported in the notes to the financial statements).

Initial recognition

Categories of uncertainty

In the initial recognition process, there are two broad categories of uncertainty that could arise:

5.12

(a) element uncertainty, which involves uncertainty whether an item exists and meets the definitions of the elements of financial statements; and

(b) measurement uncertainty, which concerns the appropriate monetary amount at which to recognise the item.

Element uncertainty

Whether the rights or other access that underlie a potential asset exist, whether they are controlled by the reporting entity and whether they may yield future economic benefits may all be subject to uncertainty. Similarly, in the case of a potential liability there could be uncertainty whether the obligation exists and whether that obligation might require the reporting entity to transfer economic benefits.

5.13

Uncertainty of this kind (element uncertainty) is countered by evidence—the more evidence there is about an item and the better the quality of that evidence, the less uncertainty there will be over the item's existence and nature. To recognise an item it is necessary to have sufficient evidence, both in amount and quality, that the item exists and is an asset or liability of the reporting entity. This is reflected in the first of the two criteria for initial recognition, which requires that sufficient evidence must exist that a new asset or liability has been created or that there has been an addition to an existing asset or liability.

5.14

What constitutes sufficient evidence is a matter of judgement in the particular circumstances of each case although, while the evidence needs to be adequate, it need not be (and often cannot be) conclusive. The main source of evidence will be past or present experience with the item itself or with similar items, including:

5.15

(a) evidence provided by the event that has given rise to the possible asset or liability;

(b) past experience with similar items (for example, successful research and development in the past);

(c) current information directly relating to the possible asset or liability; and

(d) evidence provided by transactions of other entities in similar assets and liabilities.

Measurement uncertainty

To recognise an item, it is necessary to attribute a monetary amount to it. This involves two steps: selecting a suitable measurement basis (ie historical cost or current value) for the item and determining an appropriate monetary amount for the basis chosen.[18]

5.16

Uncertainty about the appropriate monetary amount at which to recognise the item (in other words, measurement uncertainty) is reflected in the second of the criteria for initial recognition, which requires that the new asset or liability or addition to an existing asset or liability can be measured at a monetary amount with sufficient reliability.

5.17

---

[18] *The measurement process is described in Chapter 6.*

Prudence

5.18   As explained earlier, in order to recognise a loss (or gain), it is necessary to consider whether there is sufficient evidence that a decrease (or increase) in ownership interest has occurred and whether the amount of the loss (or gain) can be measured with sufficient reliability. As explained in Chapter 3, if there is uncertainty prudence requires:

(a)   more confirmatory evidence about the existence of an asset or gain than about the existence of a liability or loss; and

(b)   a greater reliability of measurement for assets and gains than for liabilities and losses.

5.19   However, the exercise of prudence does not justify the omission of assets or gains when there is sufficient evidence of occurrence and reliability of measurement or the inclusion of liabilities or losses when there is not. Nor does it justify any other deliberate and systematic overstatement of liabilities or losses or deliberate and systematic understatement of assets or gains.

Unperformed contracts

5.20   As explained in Chapter 4, when an entity enters into an agreement with another party, it obtains certain rights and, in exchange, accepts certain obligations. Before any act of performance under the agreement has taken place, the entity will have only a net position comprising a combined right and obligation either to participate in the exchange or alternatively to be compensated (or to compensate) for the consequences of the exchange not taking place. Although this right and the obligation will usually be in balance initially, changing circumstances may cause an imbalance to arise, in which case the net position will be either an asset or a liability.

5.21   This asset or liability will be recognised if the recognition criteria described in paragraphs 5.14 and 5.17 are met (and if the amount at which the asset or liability is to be measured is not nil). In particular:

(a)   the criterion that sufficient evidence must exist that the new asset or liability has been created will generally be met if it can be shown that the agreement is enforceable and, as a result, that a party to the agreement cannot cancel it (or otherwise fail to perform in accordance with it) without being obliged to compensate for such non-performance.

(b)   the criterion that the new asset or liability must be capable of being measured at a monetary amount with sufficient reliability is dealt with in Chapter 6.

(c)   if the historical cost basis of measurement is being used, the carrying amount will be the cost of entering into the agreement, which is usually nil. In effect, therefore, the contract is recognised at nil. An unperformed non-derivative contract with no initial cost will nevertheless be recognised if it has become an onerous contract.

Derecognition

Derecognition because the asset or liability has been eliminated

5.22   Assets tend, in due course, to be consumed, transferred or otherwise disposed of, or they expire. For example, cash may be spent, debtors may be collected, raw materials may be consumed or processed, finished goods may be sold and the service potential of a machine may be fully used up. Similarly, liabilities tend to be settled, extinguished, transferred, or they expire. For example, creditors may be paid, a warranty attaching to goods sold may expire, long-term debt may be exchanged for other debt and obligations to perform in accordance with agreed contractual terms may be met. In all such circumstances, it may be necessary to derecognise some or all of the asset or liability involved.

It is usually relatively simple to determine whether and when a previously recognised asset or liability needs to be derecognised. For example, using the examples given in the previous paragraph, the cash will be derecognised when it is paid out, the raw materials as they are being used and so on (in other words, when the asset is eliminated). However, some transactions leave intact certain of the rights to future benefits inherent in an asset (or obligations inherent in a liability) while eliminating others. In such circumstances, analysis is required to ascertain whether the effect of the transaction should be reflected by derecognising some or all of the assets and liabilities involved. For example, if the reporting entity no longer has control of some of the rights that previously constituted an asset while retaining control of some of the other rights, the asset may need to be partially derecognised (or the existing asset completely derecognised and a new asset recognised instead).   **5.23**

Ideally, an asset or liability would be derecognised as soon as it has been eliminated. However, there will sometimes be uncertainty about an item's continued existence. In such circumstances, derecognition will not take place until sufficient evidence exists that the transaction or other event has resulted in the elimination of the item. When there is uncertainty, prudence usually requires more confirmatory evidence about the existence of, and a greater reliability of measurement for, assets than is required for liabilities. This tends to mean that, if there is any significant uncertainty about an asset's continued existence, it will be derecognised. However, in the case of a liability, more evidence of its elimination will be needed before it will be derecognised.   **5.24**

Derecognition because the criteria for recognition are no longer met

After initial recognition, an asset or liability will usually continue to be recognised until it has been eliminated, at which point it will be derecognised. It is possible, however, that although there has been no significant change in the inherent nature of an already recognised asset or liability—in other words, although the asset or liability has not been eliminated—the criteria for recognition described in paragraphs 5.14 and 5.17 are no longer met. For example, an event may have occurred since initial recognition that has resulted in there no longer being sufficient evidence that the asset or liability concerned exists. Similarly, an event may have created additional uncertainty and, as a result, a previously recognised asset or liability can no longer be measured with sufficient reliability. On the rare occasions when this is the case, that asset or liability will be derecognised even though it has not been eliminated.   **5.25**

Revenue recognition

It was explained earlier in the chapter that, because of the interrelationship between the elements, the starting point for the recognition process is always the effect that the transaction or other event involved has had on the reporting entity's assets and liabilities. For example, assuming that no contribution from owners or transfer to owners is involved: **5.26**

(a) if the effect of the transaction or other event is to increase the entity's recognised net assets, a gain will be recognised.

(b) a loss will be recognised if, and to the extent that, previously recognised assets have been reduced or eliminated or cease to qualify for recognition as assets without a commensurate increase in other assets or reduction in liabilities. Similarly, a loss will be recognised when, and to the extent, that a liability is incurred or increased without a commensurate increase in recognised assets or a reduction in other liabilities.

5.27   However, although the starting point for the recognition process may be the effect on assets and liabilities, the notions of matching and the critical event in the operating cycle will often help in identifying these effects.

Matching

5.28   Matching has two forms.

(a)   Time matching involves the recognition of receipts (and payments) directly associated with the passage of time as gains (and losses) on a systematic basis over the course of the period involved. For example, rent paid at the beginning of a rental period is recognised as a loss over the course of the rental period, with amounts paid in advance of such recognition being recognised as an asset.

(b)   Revenue/expenditure matching involves the recognition of expenditure directly associated with the generation of specific gains as a loss in the same period as the gains are recognised, rather than in the period in which the expenditure is incurred. For example, the cost incurred in obtaining or producing an item of stock is recognised in the performance statement as a loss in the same reporting period as the gain on selling that item, and in the meantime is recognised as an asset.

5.29   Almost all expenditure is undertaken with a view to acquiring some form of benefit in exchange. Consequently, if matching were used in an unrestricted way, it would be possible to delay the recognition in the performance statement of most items of expenditure insofar as the hoped-for benefits still lay in the future. The Statement imposes a degree of discipline on this process because only items that meet the definitions of, and relevant recognition criteria for, assets, liabilities or ownership interest are recognised in the balance sheet.

5.30   This means that the Statement does not use the notion of matching as the main driver of the recognition process. Nevertheless, the Statement envisages that:

(a)   if the future economic benefits embodied in the asset are eliminated at a single point in time, it is at that point that the asset will be derecognised and a loss recognised; and

(b)   if the future economic benefits are eliminated over several accounting periods—typically because they are being consumed over a period of time—the cost of the asset that comprises the future economic benefits will be recognised as a loss in the performance statement over those accounting periods.

5.31   When expenditure is being allocated to more than one accounting period, the amount allocated to each accounting period will depend on the circumstances involved, although the aim is always to recognise the expenditure as a loss on a systematic basis over the periods in which the asset delivers up its benefits. For example, if the association of the expenditure with the generation of specific gains can be only broadly or indirectly determined, it will often be necessary to assume that the asset declines in a systematic manner over its expected life.

5.32   Two implications of adopting the approach in the Statement, rather than using matching as a main driver of recognition, are that:

(a)   expenditure or some other form of loss that cannot justifiably be shown to be associated with control of rights or other access to future economic benefits will be recognised in the performance statement as a loss in the period in which it is incurred; and

(b)   expenditure incurred with a view to future economic benefits but whose relationship to such benefits is too uncertain to warrant recognition of an asset will be recognised immediately as a loss.

Critical event in the operating cycle

Sometimes it is easier to identify the appropriate point at which to recognise gains[19] arising from the provision of services or goods—and therefore changes to the entity's assets and liabilities—by focusing on the operating cycle of the reporting entity and, in particular, on the critical event in that cycle.   **5.33**

The critical event is the point in an operating cycle at which there will usually be sufficient evidence that the gain exists and it will usually be possible to measure that gain with sufficient reliability. In other words, it is the point at which the recognition criteria described earlier in the chapter will be met and the gain and related change to assets and liabilities will be recognised.   **5.34**

For many types of transaction, the critical event in the operating cycle is synonymous with full performance. In such cases a gain will be recognised when the entity providing the service or goods has fully performed. That need not, however, be the case: the critical event could occur at other times in the cycle and there could be more than one critical event in the cycle.   **5.35**

The identity of the critical event or events of an operating cycle will depend on the particular circumstances involved. For example: **5.36**

(a)   if the reporting entity has carried out all its obligations under an agreement except for a few minor acts of performance, the critical event will have occurred.

(b)   if a sale is contingent upon acceptance by the buyer, the critical event will usually ~~~~~~ acceptance unless the act of acceptance creates substantial uncertainty whether the contractual ~~~~~~~~~~~~ will be met. The critical event will not usually have occurred if the likelihood of the goods or services not being accepted is significant.

(c)   the operating cycle might involve a contract that is performed in stages, for each of which there is a critical event. (Contracts to build large buildings are usually an example of such an operating cycle.) In such circumstances, the gain that is expected to be earned on the contract as a whole will need to be allocated among the critical events.

---

[19] *In order to keep the explanation simple, it has been assumed in paragraphs 5.33-5.36 that the transaction being discussed is expected to generate a net profit and that the issue is therefore when to recognise that profit when using the historical cost basis of measurement. If the contract is expected to generate a loss the historical cost carrying amount will be adjusted immediately to reflect that expected loss.*

Chapter 6: Measurement in Financial Statements

Measuring an asset or liability entails deciding on the measurement basis to be used and determining the monetary amount that is appropriate for that basis. It may also involve revising the monetary amount when certain events occur. This chapter describes the measurement process and explains how a choice is made between the measurement bases available.

PRINCIPLES

- In drawing up financial statements, a measurement basis—either historical cost or current value[20]—needs to be selected for each category of assets or liabilities. The basis selected will be the one that best meets the objective of financial statements and the demands of the qualitative characteristics of financial information, bearing in mind the nature of the assets or liabilities concerned and the circumstances involved.
- An asset or liability being measured using the historical cost basis is recognised initially at transaction cost. An asset or liability being measured using the current value basis is recognised initially at its current value at the time it was acquired or assumed.
- Subsequent remeasurement will occur if it is necessary to ensure that:

   (a)   assets measured at historical cost are carried at the lower of cost and recoverable amount;

   (b)   monetary items denominated in foreign currency are carried at amounts based on up-to-date exchange rates; and

   (c)   assets and liabilities measured on the current value basis are carried at up-to-date current values.

- Such remeasurements, however, will be recognised only if:

   (a)   there is sufficient evidence that the monetary amount of the asset or liability has changed; and

   (b)   the new amount of the asset or liability can be measured with sufficient reliability.

EXPLANATION

Alternative bases of measurement

6.1   Assets and liabilities have several different monetary attributes that could be represented in financial statements. Assets could, for example, be stated at historical cost, replacement cost or net realisable value and liabilities could, for example, be stated at historical cost, the cost of discharging the liability by the most economical means available or (in some cases) the amount that the entity could currently raise by issuing a similar debt security. The single most important characteristic that distinguishes these monetary attributes (which are known as measurement bases) is whether they are based on historical cost or current value. This chapter concentrates on that distinction.

6.2   These measurement bases could be used in financial statements in one of several ways. In particular:

   (a)   a single measurement basis could be used for all assets and liabilities. For example, all assets and liabilities could be measured using historical cost. This is known as the

---

[20] *The term* **historical cost** *is, unless stated otherwise, used in the Statement to refer to the particular version of the historical cost basis described in paragraph 6.18. Similarly, the term* **current value** *is used to refer to the value determined in accordance with paragraphs 6.7-6.9.*

historical cost system. Alternatively, all assets and liabilities could be measured at current value. This is known as the current value system.

(b) some categories of assets or liabilities could be measured on a historical cost basis and some on a current value basis. This is known as the mixed measurement system. In reality there is not one mixed measurement system but many, each involving a different mix of historical cost and current value.

The mixed measurement system permits the measurement basis to be selected separately for each category of assets or liabilities. It also permits the use of historical cost (or current value) for all assets and liabilities if historical cost (or current value) is the most appropriate measure for each of those categories. Thus it can be adapted to fit the particular circumstances involved.   **6.3**

The Statement therefore envisages that the mixed measurement system will be used and it focuses on the mix of historical cost and current value to be adopted. In doing so, it describes a framework that would guide the choice of basis for each category of assets or liabilities.   **6.4**

One approach that is not appropriate is to remeasure a category of assets or liabilities at current value, then retain those assets or liabilities at that same amount indefinitely or for a long period of time. Such measures will usually soon cease to be up-to-date current values and will then be neither a historical cost nor a current value. As such, they disturb the comparability and consistency of accounting measurement and are not consistent with the principles contained in the Statement.   **6.5**

Alternative measures of current value

The current value of an asset could be determined by reference to entry value (replacement cost), exit value (net realisable value) or value in use (discounted present value of the cash flows expected from continuing use and ultimate sale by the present owner). For some assets (for example investments in actively traded securities), these three alternative measures of current value produce very similar amounts, with only small differences due to transaction costs. However, for other assets (for example fixed assets specific to the business), differences between the alternative measures can be material.   **6.6**

It is therefore necessary to select from these alternative measures of current value the measure that maximises the relevance of the current value basis. Current value is at its most relevant when it reflects the loss that the entity would suffer if it were deprived of the asset involved. That measure, which is often referred to as the 'deprival value' or the 'value to the business', will depend on the circumstances involved.   **6.7**

(a) In most cases, as the entity will be putting the asset to profitable use, the asset's value in its most profitable use (in other words, its recoverable amount) will exceed its replacement cost. In such circumstances, the entity will, if deprived of the asset, replace it, and the current value of the asset will be its current replacement cost.

(b) An asset will not be replaced if the cost of replacing it exceeds its recoverable amount. In such circumstances, the asset's current value is that recoverable amount.

   (i) When the most profitable use of an asset is to sell it, the asset's recoverable amount will be the amount that can be obtained by selling it, net of selling expenses; in other words, its net realisable value.

   (ii) When the most profitable use of an asset is to consume it—for example by continuing to operate it—its recoverable amount will be the present value of the future cash flows obtainable and cash flows obviated as a result of the asset's continued use and ultimate disposal, net of any expenses that would need to be incurred; in other words, its value in use.

6.8   This can be portrayed diagrammatically as follows:

Click here to see a diagram showing the value to the business rule

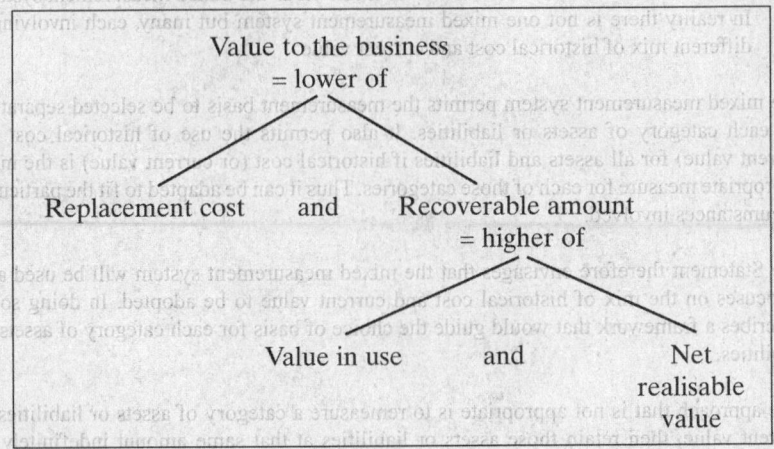

Value to the business
= lower of

Replacement cost   and   Recoverable amount
= higher of

Value in use   and   Net realisable value

6.9   It is possible to select a current value for a liability in a similar manner (using the concept of 'relief value'). The relief value of a liability is the lowest amount at which the entity could divest itself of the obligation involved—in other words, the lowest amount at which the liability could, hypothetically, be settled.

The measurement process

6.10   It is not the function of financial statements to represent directly the total value that the reporting entity would fetch in an exchange transaction. Instead, the financial statements provide information designed to assist users to make judgements about the entity's financial performance and financial position and it is these judgements, in combination with other information, that enable, inter alia, a value for the entity to be assessed. The purpose of the measurement process is therefore to measure the effects of the transactions and events of the period on the financial performance and financial position of the entity.

Initial recognition

6.11   An asset or liability that is being measured using the historical cost basis will be recognised initially at transaction cost or, if an event other than a transaction is involved, at its fair value at the time it was acquired or assumed. The transaction cost of an asset acquired or liability assumed is the fair value of the consideration given or received in exchange for that asset or liability.

6.12   An asset or liability that is being measured using the current value basis will be recognised initially at its current value at the time it was acquired or assumed.

6.13   This means that, regardless of the measurement basis used, assets and liabilities that arise from transactions carried out at fair value—which is the vast majority of assets and liabilities—will be measured on initial recognition at their transaction cost. That is because, in the case of such a transaction, the fair value of the consideration paid or received (ie the transaction cost) is equal to the current value of the asset or liability at the time of acquisition.

It can generally be assumed that, in the absence of evidence to the contrary, a transaction has been carried out at fair value. In such circumstances, the transaction cost involved can be determined by reference to the fair value of either the asset (or liability) acquired or the consideration paid (or received); whichever fair value is easiest to measure will usually be used. For example (and assuming in both cases that there is no evidence suggesting that the transaction was not carried out at fair value):

6.14

(a)   if the reporting entity purchases mining rights in exchange for an immediate cash payment, those rights would usually be measured on initial recognition at the cash amount because that amount is easier to measure than the fair value of the rights.

(b)   if the entity purchases an asset from an employee for an immediate cash payment, it may not be clear whether it also involves a payment for services provided by the employee. Where such uncertainty exists, it may be easier to measure the fair value of the asset purchased than the fair value of the services provided. If the former amount is, for example, less than the amount of the payment, the difference will be remuneration.

If an asset or liability arises from a transaction that was not carried out at fair value, it will often be more appropriate to measure the asset or liability at current value rather than historical cost. Choosing a measurement basis is considered in paragraphs 6.23-6.29.

6.15

The initial recognition criteria described in Chapter 5 stipulate that, to be recognised, the asset or liability involved needs to be capable of being measured at a monetary amount with sufficient reliability. Whether a measure is sufficiently reliable for inclusion in primary financial statements depends on the quantity and quality of the evidence available to confirm that the measure has the attributes of reliability described in Chapter 3. A measure derived from a generally accepted valuation methodology and supported by a reasonable amount of confirmatory evidence will usually be a sufficiently reliable measure.

6.16

Subsequent remeasurement

If a *pure* historical cost measurement basis is being used, the carrying amount of an asset or liability will always be the amount at which it was initially recognised; in other words, there is no subsequent remeasurement stage. The carrying amount of an asset or liability measured at historical cost may nevertheless need to be changed so that the item remains at cost. For example, as work is carried out on work-in-progress, so the carrying amount is changed to reflect the additional costs incurred. Similarly, in the case of assets that are consumed over more than one accounting period (such as fixed assets), the amount at which the asset was recognised initially will be reduced over the expected life of the asset so as to allocate the asset's cost over its expected life. Adjustments may also need to be made to the carrying amount of other assets and liabilities to reflect cost and income allocations. These adjustments are not remeasurements; they are adjustments to maintain the carrying amount at an amount based on historical cost.

6.17

In practice, however, this 'pure historical cost basis' is rarely used. Instead, to make historical cost more relevant to the needs of users, a variation is used that involves a limited amount of remeasurement. The purpose of this remeasurement is to ensure that:

6.18

(a)   assets are not reported at amounts greater than their recoverable amount; and

(b)   monetary assets and liabilities denominated in currencies other than the reporting currency are stated at an amount that is based on up-to-date exchange rates.

All references in the Statement to the historical cost basis are, unless stated otherwise, references to this version of the historical cost basis.

6.19 When the current value basis of measurement is being used, remeasurement takes place to ensure that the assets or liabilities involved are measured at an up-to-date current value. Such remeasurements will, however, be recognised in the financial statements only if:

(a) there is sufficient evidence that the amount of the asset or liability has changed. For example, if consideration is being given to writing down the carrying amount of an asset to its recoverable amount, there will need to be sufficient evidence that the asset's recoverable amount is lower than its carrying amount; and

(b) the new amount of the asset or liability is capable of being measured with sufficient reliability.

6.20 What constitutes sufficient evidence is a matter of judgement in the particular circumstances of each case although, whilst the evidence will need to be adequate, it need not (and often cannot) be conclusive. Relevant considerations as to whether the evidence is sufficient will include its persuasiveness and whether the change implies that a gain or a loss has occurred.[21]

6.21 Although the nature of the evidence will vary from item to item, its primary source will be past or present experience with the item itself or with similar items. This will include evidence provided by:

(a) current information directly relating to the item (eg the current physical condition of items of stock, their current selling price, and current levels of orders for them).

(b) other entities' transactions in similar assets and liabilities. If such transactions are frequent and the items traded are very similar to the item held by the reporting entity (ie there is an efficient market in homogeneous items), such evidence will often be sufficient. However, as the frequency of transactions decreases or differences between the items traded and the item held by the reporting entity increase, the evidence will become less persuasive and is less likely to be sufficient on its own.

(c) past experience with a group of similar items (eg the levels of losses arising in the past on stock of different ages).

6.22 The issues to be considered in deciding whether the new amount of the asset or liability is capable of being measured with sufficient reliability are identical to the reliability of measurement issues considered in the context of initial recognition (see paragraph 6.16).

Choosing a measurement basis and deciding whether to change it

6.23 In choosing the measurement basis to be used for a particular category of assets or liabilities, the aim is to select the basis that is most appropriate bearing in mind:

(a) the objective of financial statements and the qualitative characteristics of financial information, in particular relevance and reliability;

(b) the nature of the assets or liabilities concerned; and

(c) the particular circumstances involved.

6.24 Although these factors may not change, the measurement basis that best meets them may. For example, to the extent that markets develop, measurement bases that were once thought unreliable may become reliable. Similarly, to the extent that access to markets develops, so a measurement basis that was once thought insufficiently relevant may become the most relevant measure available.

---

[21] *These factors, and the sources of evidence referred to in paragraph 6.21, are broadly similar to those that need to be taken into account when considering, in the initial recognition stage, whether there is sufficient evidence that an asset or liability itself has been changed (see paragraph 5.15).*

Although it is often difficult to make general statements about the appropriate measurement basis for any particular category of assets or liabilities, the observations set out in paragraphs 6.26-6.29 can be made. **6.25**

The need for financial information to be relevant means that, in selecting a measurement basis, the focus will be on providing information about financial performance and financial position that is useful in evaluating the reporting entity's cash-generation abilities and in assessing its financial adaptability. **6.26**

The carrying amounts of assets and liabilities need to be sufficiently reliable.[22] If only one of the measures available is reliable, it will be the one used provided that it is also relevant. On the other hand, if both the historical cost measure and the current value measure are reliable, the better measure to use will be the one that is the most relevant. **6.27**

Current value measures are sometimes characterised as less reliable than historical cost measures. Such a characterisation tends to assume, however, that all historical cost measures are transaction-based and involve little estimation, which is not the case. For example, adjustments made to the historical cost carrying value of debtors to make allowance for bad and doubtful debts involve a degree of estimation that is not dissimilar to that involved in estimating current values not derived from an active market—and the results are often of broadly similar reliability. There is a similar level of estimation involved in determining the cost of self-generated assets and by-products, and generally in all circumstances involving allocations of substantial amounts of indirect costs. The hurdle that a measure must clear to be deemed reliable is set at the same height for current value measures as for historical cost measures. **6.28**

Assessments of relevance and reliability need to take into account what the asset or liability represents. For example, if an entity 'stores' its spare cash by making an investment, that investment's relevance to the entity will be derived from the specific future cash flows that it represents rights to. The measure that will most faithfully represent those rights will generally be current value. Similarly, if an entity has a liability of uncertain amount, that liability's relevance to the entity will be derived from the most up-to-date information about those uncertainties. The measure that most faithfully represents those uncertainties will again generally be current value. **6.29**

Measurement issues

Going concern

Financial statements are usually prepared—and measures are usually arrived at—on the basis that the reporting entity is a going concern because measures based on break-up values tend not to be relevant to users seeking to assess the entity's cash-generation ability and financial adaptability. **6.30**

Discounting

Most transactions take place at fair value. Rational buyers and sellers will ensure that this fair value reflects the time value of money and the risk associated with the future expected cash flows, which means that market prices generally will reflect such factors. **6.31**

This chapter has explained that assets will, depending on the circumstances, be carried in the financial statements at historical cost, replacement cost, net realisable value or value in use and that liabilities will, again depending on the circumstances, be carried at **6.32**

---

[22] *What the characteristic of reliability entails is considered in detail in Chapter 3 and is also dealt with in paragraphs 6.16 and 6.35-6.38.*

historical cost or the lowest amount at which the liability could be settled. Historical cost and replacement cost are both market prices and will therefore, for the reason set out in paragraph 6.31, take into account the time value of money and the risk associated with the future expected cash flows.

6.33   To be consistent, these factors need also to be reflected in the other measures that can be used to determine the carrying amount of assets (in other words, value in use and net realisable value) and the carrying amount of any liabilities measured by reference to expected future cash flows. It follows that, when basing carrying amounts on future cash flows, those cash flows will need to be discounted.

6.34   The discount rate used will reflect the risks associated with the future expected cash flows involved (unless those future expected cash flows are already risk-adjusted) and the time value of money. As such, it will reflect the risks specific to the item being measured but not the more general risks of the entity as a whole.[23]

Arriving at a measure in the face of uncertainty

6.35   It is quite common for there to be uncertainty about the appropriate monetary amount at which to measure an asset or liability. The existence of this uncertainty (measurement uncertainty) is acknowledged in the initial recognition and subsequent remeasurement criteria, both of which insist that the monetary amount at which an asset or liability is to be recognised is capable of being measured with sufficient reliability.

6.36   If uncertainty exists, the only way to determine an appropriate monetary amount for the asset or liability is through the use of estimates. As long as a generally accepted estimation method is used and the measure is supported by a reasonable amount of confirmatory evidence—prudence requires a greater reliability of measurement for assets (and gains) than for liabilities (and losses)—the use of estimates is acceptable and will not prevent the measure from being sufficiently reliable to be used in the financial statements.

6.37   Estimating an appropriate carrying amount will often involve adopting one of the following approaches.

    (a)   If there is a reasonably efficient market for the item or for very similar items, a market-based measure such as a market price could be used as the carrying amount because the market consensus over the amount of the benefits inherent in the item is likely to mean that the measure will be reliable.

    (b)   If the entity has a group of homogeneous but not identical items, the expected value of the entire group could be used, provided the group is of a sufficient size and there is sufficient evidence of the various possible outcomes and their probabilities to permit an explicit calculation of expected value.[24]

---

[23] *Discounting is discussed in greater detail in a Working Paper 'Discounting in Financial Reporting' published by the Board in April 1997.*

[24] *Expected value is a weighted average of all possible outcomes, calculated using the probability of occurrence of an outcome as its weight. For a group of similar items, individual items will have different outcomes, and the number of items having a particular outcome will be related to the probability of that outcome. Hence, the expected value will represent a reasonable estimate of the monetary amount of the benefits associated with the entire group. For instance, in considering a large portfolio of non-interest bearing debts, it may be unlikely that any individual debt will prove to be bad, but some degree of non-payment is normally expected; hence a loss representing this expected reduction in economic benefits is recognised. If each debt were to be considered individually and measured at its most likely outcome, each debtor might be judged more likely than not to pay, and hence no bad debt provision would be made. However, this would not represent a reasonable measure of future economic benefits for the entire group.*

(c)   If neither of these approaches is practicable, a best estimate will need to be used. If there is a minimum amount that is reasonably assured, the item will be stated at no less than that minimum amount, and a higher amount will be used if that is a better estimate.

If the monetary amount at which an asset or liability is recognised is subject to significant uncertainty, the degree of uncertainty surrounding the estimate will usually be disclosed in order to avoid the impression that the outcome is certain. Such a disclosure might provide details of the significant assumptions and measurement basis used, the range of possible outcomes, and the principal factors that affect the outcome.   **6.38**

Capital maintenance adjustments and changing prices

Put simply, accounting profit is the return the reporting entity has earned on its capital. Therefore, in order to account properly for accounting profit, it is necessary to differentiate between return on capital and return of capital. This involves defining and measuring the capital of the entity.   **6.39**

Under the accounting model described by the Statement and adopted by almost all profit-making entities, the capital of the entity is defined as the monetary amount of ownership interest (the financial capital maintenance concept) and is measured in nominal amounts.   **6.40**

With this approach, the capital of the entity will be maintained if the amount of gains during a period is at least equal to the amount of losses in that period. This means that any surplus of gains over losses during a period represents a return on capital for that period.   **6.41**

Whilst this approach is satisfactory under conditions of stable prices, it is open to criticism when general or specific price changes are significant.   **6.42**

(a)   General price changes can affect the significance of reported profits and of ownership interest. If this problem is acute, an approach will need to be adopted that involves recognising profit only after adjustments have been made to maintain the purchasing power of the entity's financial capital.
(b)   Specific price changes can affect the significance of reported profits and financial position. If the problem is acute, it will be necessary to adopt a system of accounting that informs the user of the significance of specific price changes for the entity's financial performance and financial position.

Chapter 7: Presentation of financial information

Good presentation ensures that the essential messages of the financial statements are communicated clearly and effectively and in as simple and straightforward a manner as possible. This chapter explains what good presentation entails. It also considers the information that often accompanies financial statements and explains some of the roles fulfilled by such information.

PRINCIPLES

- Financial statements comprise primary financial statements and supporting notes that amplify and explain the primary financial statements. The primary financial statements themselves comprise the statement of financial performance,[25] the statement of financial position or balance sheet, and the cash flow statement.
- The presentation of information on financial performance focuses on the components of that performance and on the characteristics of those components.
- The presentation of information on financial position focuses on the types and functions of assets and liabilities held and on the relationships between them.
- The presentation of cash flow information will show the extent to which the entity's various activities generate and use cash, and will distinguish in particular between those cash flows that result from operations and those that result from other activities.
- Disclosure of information in the notes to the financial statements is not a substitute for recognition and does not correct or justify any misrepresentation or omission in the primary financial statements.

EXPLANATION

Presentation of information in financial statements

Clear, effective and simple communication

7.1   As financial statements are a means of communication, the objective of the presentation adopted is to communicate clearly and effectively and in as simple and straightforward a manner as is possible without loss of relevance or reliability and without unnecessarily increasing the length of the financial statements.

Highly structured and aggregated

7.2   Even if it were practicable it would not be appropriate for financial statements to report every single aspect of every relevant transaction and event: the mass of detail would obscure the message. The presentation of information in financial statements therefore involves a high degree of interpretation, simplification, abstraction and aggregation—in other words, a loss of detailed information. Nevertheless, if this process is carried out in an orderly manner, greater knowledge will result because such a presentation will:

(a)   convey information that would otherwise have been obscured;
(b)   highlight those items, and relationships between items, that are generally of most significance;
(c)   facilitate comparability between different entities' financial statements; and
(d)   be more understandable to users.

---

[25] *Although many entities in the UK and the Republic of Ireland at present prepare two statements of financial performance, the number of statements prepared is a matter of convention and legal requirement; no significant financial reporting principle is involved. For simplicity, however, the Statement generally refers to 'the statement of financial performance'.*

The primary focus of financial statements is on the entity's cash generation and financial adaptability. This focus is met through a set of interrelated reports (known as the primary financial statements) on: **7.3**

(a)   financial performance (the profit and loss account and the statement of total recognised gains and losses are examples of financial performance statements);
(b)   financial position (the balance sheet); and
(c)   cash inflows and outflows (the cash flow statement),

and a series of supporting disclosures (the notes to the financial statements).

The notes and primary financial statements form an integrated whole, with the notes amplifying and explaining the statements by, for example, providing: **7.4**

(a)   more detailed information on items recognised in the primary financial statements. Good presentation strikes a balance between the detail provided on the face of the primary financial statements and that provided in the notes, thus avoiding cluttering up the former and obscuring their message.
(b)   context for, or an alternative view of, items recognised in the primary financial statements. For instance, if a balance sheet includes a liability that is in dispute, the related note might disclose the range of possible outcomes. Similarly, the notes usually provide segmental information to supplement the primary financial statements, which focus on the reporting entity in aggregate.
(c)   relevant information that it is not practicable to incorporate in the primary financial statements, for example because of pervasive uncertainty.

The notes to the financial statements therefore represent a very important part of the overall information package. Nevertheless, disclosure of information in the notes is not a substitute for recognition and does not correct or justify any misrepresentation in or omission from the primary financial statements.   **7.5**

Classification

In order to facilitate the analysis of the information provided, items that are similar are presented together in the financial statements and distinguished from dissimilar items.   **7.6**

The classifications used to achieve this also have regard to the additional insights that can be obtained by considering the relationships between different classes of items, for example the relative sizes of profits and capital employed or debtors and sales.   **7.7**

Classifications that are similar or related are presented in financial statements in a manner that highlights that similarity or relationship. For example, different kinds of current assets are shown adjacent to each other, and current liabilities are usually shown in a manner that highlights their relationship to current assets.   **7.8**

Good presentation

Statement of financial performance

The financial performance of a reporting entity is made up of components that exhibit differing characteristics in terms of, for example, nature, cause, function, relative continuity or recurrence, stability, risk, predictability and reliability. All these components are relevant to an assessment of financial performance and therefore need to be reported on in the statement of financial performance, although their individual characteristics   **7.9** mean that some will carry more weight in some assessments of financial performance than others.

7.10   Information on financial performance needs to be presented in a way that focuses attention on these components and on their key characteristics. Therefore, although it is not of fundamental importance whether one or more than one performance statement is provided, the presentation—including the headings used and the items that appear under each heading—is important. Good presentation of financial performance information typically involves:

(a)   recognising only gains and losses in the statement of financial performance.

(b)   classifying components by reference to a combination of function (such as production, selling and administrative) and of the nature of the item (such as employment costs, interest payable and amounts written off investments).

(c)   distinguishing amounts that are affected in different ways by changes in economic conditions or business activity (for example, by providing segmental information or by presenting income from continuing and discontinued operations as separate components).

(d)   identifying separately:

(i)   items that are unusual in amount or incidence judged by the experience of previous periods or expectations of the future.

(ii)   items that have special characteristics, such as financing costs and taxation.

(iii)   items that are related primarily to the profits of future, rather than current, accounting periods, such as some research and development expenditure.

7.11   Gains and losses are generally not offset in presenting information on financial performance. For example, as explained in Chapter 4, if a transaction involves both a receipt and a cost (as is the case, for example, when an item of stock is sold), the transaction will usually be best presented by showing the gain (the receipt) separately from the loss (the cost). However, gains and losses will be offset if:

(a)   they relate to the same event or circumstance; and

(b)   disclosing the gross components is not likely to be useful for an assessment of either future results or the effects of past transactions and events.

For example, if a profit is made on the disposal of a fixed asset, that profit is usually best presented by showing it as a gain rather than by showing the sales proceeds as a gain separately from the depreciated cost of the asset.

Balance sheet

7.12   In assessing the financial position of an entity, users are most interested in the types and amounts of assets and liabilities held and the relationship between them, and in the function of the various assets. Information on the reporting entity's financial position therefore needs to be presented in a way that focuses attention on these aspects. Good presentation typically involves:

(a)   recognising only assets, liabilities and ownership interest in the balance sheet;

(b)   delineating the entity's resource structure (major classes and amounts of assets) and its financial structure (major classes and amounts of liabilities and ownership interest). The main basis for deciding the number of classes and the content of each is that the result will help users to assess the nature, amounts and liquidity of available resources and the nature, amounts and timing of obligations that require or may require liquid resources for settlement.

(c)   distinguishing assets by function. For example, assets held for sale will be reported separately from assets held on a continuing basis for use in the entity's activities.

In presenting information on the reporting entity's financial position, assets will not be offset against liabilities.[26]

7.13

Cash flow statement

Cash flow information will be of most use if it shows the extent to which the entity's activities generate and use cash, distinguishing in particular cash flows that are the result of operations from cash flows that result from other activities. This might include, for example, showing separately cash received from trading activities, cash used to repay debt, cash used to distribute dividends and cash reinvested.

7.14

Accompanying information

Financial statements are often accompanied and complemented by information that does not form part of the financial statements. Examples of such information include five-year trend information, operating and financial reviews, directors' reports and statements by the chairman. The Statement refers to such information as accompanying information.[27]

7.15

Although accompanying information generally has the same objective as financial statements, it usually comprises a different kind of information. For example, it often includes:

7.16

(a) narrative disclosures describing and explaining the entity's activities;
(b) historical summaries and trend information;
(c) non-accounting, and non-financial, information; and
(d) evolutionary or experimental disclosures that are not considered suitable for inclusion in the financial statements.

Some of the accompanying information therefore deals with matters that are not in the financial statements and some deals with matters that are in the financial statements, but from a different perspective. However, none of the accompanying information will be inconsistent with the information in the financial statements.

7.17

The more complex entities and their transactions become, the more users need an objective and comprehensive analysis and explanation of the main features underlying their financial performance and financial position. Such disclosures, which are typically included in the reporting entity's operating and financial review, are best presented in the context of a discussion of the entity's business as a whole and will be most useful if they discuss:

7.18

(a) the main factors underlying the entity's financial performance, including the principal risks, uncertainties and trends involved in each of the main business areas and how the entity is responding to them;
(b) the dynamics of the entity's financial position, including the strategies being adopted on capital structure and treasury policy; and
(c) the activities and expenditure of the period that can be regarded as a form of investment in the future.

---

[26] *The offsetting of rights and obligations to produce a single asset or liability is considered in paragraphs 4.33-4.36.*

[27] *Such information is sometimes referred to as 'supplementary information'. However, the Statement avoids that term because it is also sometimes used to refer to certain information that is included within the financial statements.*

Highlights and summary indicators

7.19   Financial statements and accompanying information sometimes include amounts, ratios, and other computations that attempt to distil key information about the reporting entity's financial performance and financial position. Such highlights and summary indicators cannot, on their own, provide a basis for meaningful analysis or prudent decision-making. It is therefore essential that they are not presented in a way that exaggerates their importance.

7.20   That having been said, well-presented highlights and summary indicators are useful to users who:

(a)   require only very basic information, such as the amount of sales or dividends; or

(b)   will proceed to a detailed appraisal of all the financial information, since highlights and summary indicators may suggest particular aspects of the information that need to be analysed further.

7.21   As already mentioned, financial statements are a means of communication. Therefore, notwithstanding the limited usefulness of highlights and summary indicators, if such information is provided it needs to be presented in a manner and context that enable its meaning to be communicated to users. This will often entail explaining the reasons for changes in the relative or absolute size of the figures from one period to the next.

Chapter 8: Accounting for interests in other entities

Financial statements need to reflect the effect on the reporting entity's financial performance and financial position of its interests in other entities. This involves various measurement and presentation issues. Rather than being dealt with in the relevant chapters and therefore in isolation from each other, they are dealt with together in this chapter. For similar reasons, various consolidation issues are dealt with in this chapter.

PRINCIPLES

- Single entity financial statements and consolidated financial statements present the interests the reporting entity may have in other entities from different perspectives.
- In single entity financial statements, interests in other entities are dealt with by focusing on the income and (depending on the measurement basis adopted) capital growth arising from those interests.
- In consolidated financial statements, the way in which interests in other entities are dealt with depends on the degree of influence involved.
  - (a) An interest that involves control of another entity's operating and financial policies is dealt with by incorporating the controlled entity as part of the reporting entity.
  - (b) An interest that involves joint control of, or significant influence over, another entity's operating and financial policies is dealt with by recognising the reporting entity's share of that other entity's results and resources in a way that does not involve showing those results and resources in the performance statement and balance sheet as if they were controlled by the reporting entity.
  - (c) Other interests are dealt with in the same way as any other asset.
- Although consolidated financial statements are the financial statements of the group as a whole, they are prepared from the perspective of the parent's shareholders and, as a result, ultimately focus on the parent's ownership interest in its subsidiaries. The effect on benefit flows of any outside equity interest in the subsidiaries will therefore be separately identified.
- Consolidated financial statements reflect the whole of the parent's investment in its subsidiaries, including purchased goodwill.
- A transaction involving the amalgamation of two or more reporting entities is reflected in the consolidated financial statements in accordance with its character. Therefore, a transaction that is of the character of:
  - (a) an acquisition is reflected in the consolidated financial statements as if the acquirer purchased the acquiree's assets and liabilities as a bundle of assets and liabilities on the open market.
  - (b) a merger is reflected in the consolidated financial statements as if the new reporting entity, comprising all the parties to the transaction, had always existed.

EXPLANATION

Degree of influence

Although an entity's interest in a second entity may take many different forms, the key factor in determining its effect on the first entity's financial performance and financial position is the degree of influence it exerts over the operating and financial policies of the second entity involved. **8.1**

The degree of influence exerted will depend on the facts of each particular case. Ownership of shares is usually the main basis of influence because owning voting rights confers influence. However, while the level of ownership of shares and voting rights is indicative **8.2** of an entity's relationship with its investee,[28] it is not by itself sufficient to define the relationship because of the possible effect of other agreements, arrangements or working practices. Indeed, any mixture of share ownership, voting rights or agreements, formal or informal, can provide a means of influencing or controlling another entity.

8.3   The highest degree of influence that an entity can have over an investee is control. As Chapter 2 explains, control comprises the ability to deploy the economic resources involved and to benefit (or to suffer) by their deployment. Other degrees of influence have these same aspects; in effect, the ability to influence the activities of the investee with a view to gaining economic benefits from that influence.

8.4   Although it is possible to classify the degree of influence that an entity has over its investee in an almost infinite number of ways, it is sufficient for the purposes of the Statement to classify it as follows:

(a)   *Control*—where the entity controls the investee.

(b)   *Joint control*—where the entity does not itself control the investee, but shares control through some form of arrangement jointly with others.

(c)   *Significant influence*—where the entity has neither control nor joint control, but exerts a degree of influence over the investee's operating and financial policies that is at the least a significant influence and at the most just short of control.

(d)   *Lesser or no influence*—where any influence that the entity has over the investee's operating and financial policies is less than a significant influence.

Reflecting the effects of interests in other entities

Consolidated financial statements and single entity financial statements

8.5   The effect on the entity's financial performance and financial position of an interest in an investee is reflected in the first entity's financial statements in different ways depending on the type of financial statements being prepared.

(a)   Financial statements of a reporting entity whose boundary has been drawn by reference to the scope of its direct control—in other words, single entity financial statements—take a narrow view of the reporting entity's interests in other entities and, as a result, reflect only the income and (depending on the measurement basis adopted) capital growth arising from those interests.

(b)   Financial statements of a reporting entity whose boundary has been drawn by reference to the scope of the entity's control (both direct and indirect)—in other words, consolidated financial statements—present an expanded view of the reporting entity's interests in other entities that reflects the reporting entity's influence over, and its accountability for, the activities and resources of its investees.

8.6   Because of the narrow view taken in single entity financial statements, interests in other entities are treated like any other asset in those financial statements. On the other hand, the treatment of such interests in the consolidated financial statements will depend on the degree of influence involved, as explained more fully in paragraphs 8.7-8.10.

---

[28] *Although it is not necessary for an interest in another entity to involve an investment, that is the most common form. For simplicity, therefore, this chapter uses the term 'investee' to mean 'entity in which the first entity has an interest'.*

Interests involving control

As already explained in Chapter 2, if an entity controls[29] one or more other entities, the controlling entity (the parent) and the controlled entities (the subsidiaries) will be a reporting entity (the group). The group's financial statements (consolidated financial statements) are prepared by aggregating the gains, losses, assets, liabilities and cash flows of the parent and its subsidiaries. This ensures that the effects on the parent's financial performance and financial position of its interests in its subsidiaries are fully reflected in the financial statements.   **8.7**

Paragraphs 8.11-8.13 consider various issues relating to the preparation of consolidated financial statements.   **8.8**

Interests involving joint control or significant influence

If the reporting entity shares joint control of, or exercises significant influence over, another entity, it will be directly involved in and affected by that other entity's activities. Its interest in its investee is therefore reflected in the consolidated financial statements in a way that: **8.9**

(a)   recognises the reporting entity's share of the results and net assets of the investee; and

(b)   does not misrepresent the extent of its influence over the investee—in other words, it does not treat activities and resources that are not controlled by the reporting entity as if they are controlled by the reporting entity. At present, the only commonly recognised method of accounting for investments that achieves this end is the equity method of accounting. This is where the reporting entity's share of the results and net assets of the investee are brought into its financial statements on a single line in the performance statement and balance sheet respectively. There are different types of equity method, usually involving the presentation of a greater or lesser degree of information than that just described, but in each case the reporting entity's share of the net results and of the position of the investee are not combined in the primary financial statements on a line-by-line basis with the reporting entity's own activities and resources.

Interests involving lesser or no influence

If the reporting entity's influence over its investee does not involve control, joint control or significant influence, the reporting entity will not be accountable for the investee's activities. In such circumstances, the only amounts recognised in the consolidated financial statements will be the investment (if any) and any income derived therefrom.   **8.10**

Consolidated financial statements

The gains, losses, assets, liabilities and cash flows of all subsidiaries are reflected in full in the consolidated financial statements, even if a subsidiary is not wholly-owned. This reflects the parent's ability, through its control, to deploy both its own economic resources and those of its subsidiaries even where it does not wholly own the subsidiaries.   **8.11**

However, the extent of outside ownership interests is an important factor in considering the parent's access and exposure to the results of its subsidiaries. Therefore, although   **8.12**

[29] *For simplicity, the discussion in the chapter assumes that the ultimate parent has 'direct' control of all its subsidiaries. However, it applies equally to situations in which the parent controls its subsidiary through its control of that subsidiary's parent. It also applies when the parent's control of its subsidiary is achieved through the combined influence of itself and other entities that it controls.*

consolidated financial statements are the financial statements of the group as a whole, they ultimately focus on the parent's ownership interest in the entities within its control. The effect of any outside equity interest (the minority interest) on benefit flows will therefore be separately identified in the financial statements.

8.13   Purchased goodwill (sometimes referred to as goodwill arising on acquisition) is the part of a parent's investment in its subsidiary that has not been attributed to the separately identified assets and liabilities of the subsidiary. Although it is not an asset in itself, it is part of a larger asset (the investment). Furthermore, it does not represent a decrease in that larger asset's value and therefore a loss: it represents part of the asset's value. Therefore, if the parent's investment is to be fully reflected in the group's financial statements and the parent is to be held accountable for its investment in full, purchased goodwill needs to be recognised as if it were an asset.

Accounting for business combinations

8.14   An amalgamation of two or more reporting entities—sometimes referred to as a business combination—can take a number of different forms. All these forms can be characterised as either:

(a)   a purchase—such transactions are commonly referred to as acquisitions; or

(b)   a uniting of interests—such transactions are commonly referred to as mergers.

8.15   An acquisition is a business combination that is in the nature of an acquisition by one entity of another entity. The transaction therefore results in an existing reporting entity being enlarged and is reflected in the consolidated financial statements by treating the assets and liabilities of the entity acquired and the purchased goodwill as if the transaction was the purchase of a bundle of assets and liabilities on the open market.

8.16   On the other hand, a merger is in the nature of a coming together of two entities to form a new reporting entity. This is reflected in the financial statements of the new reporting entity comprising all the parties to the transaction as if that entity had always existed. As a result, the assets and liabilities of each party to the transaction are treated as if they were acquired by the new reporting entity at the time that they were acquired by the party concerned: none of the assets or liabilities is treated as being purchased at the time of the business combination as part of a bundle of assets and liabilities on the open market.

Contents of Appendices

Appendix I
The Statement and the legal requirements concerning the Form and content of Financial Statements

INTRODUCTION

The Statement was not developed within the constraints imposed by the law. As a result, there was a risk that inconsistencies could arise between the Statement and the law that would invalidate the Statement as a frame of reference for standard-setting. The purpose of this appendix is to: **1**

(a) explain why the approach was nevertheless adopted;
(b) describe the main respects in which legislation is inconsistent with the Statement; and
(c) explain why these inconsistencies do not prevent the Statement from being an acceptable framework to be used by standard-setters.

WHY THE STATEMENT WAS NOT DEVELOPED WITHIN LEGAL CONSTRAINTS

There are two main reasons why the Statement was developed without taking into account the legal frameworks that regulate financial reporting. First, on a practical level, the Statement is intended to be relevant to the financial statements of all profit-oriented organisations, and it would have been difficult to develop a set of principles that was both consistent in all respects with all the legal requirements relating to such financial statements and also sufficiently detailed for the Board's purposes. Secondly, there was a concern that, if the Statement of Principles was developed within the constraints imposed by the law, it would be denied the opportunity to assist in the development of that law. This would have been a pity because it is framework documents such as the Statement that provide direction to the development of such legal frameworks and help to ensure that such development takes place in a coherent way. **2**

It is nevertheless recognised that the approach would not have been appropriate, despite these reasons, if there had been many significant differences between the Statement and the various legal frameworks involved. Paragraphs 4-13 describe briefly the main inconsistencies that exist at present between the principles in the Statement and the legal requirements that apply in Great Britain to the form and content of individual and group accounts prepared by companies that are not banks or insurance companies. Paragraph 14 concludes that these inconsistencies do not invalidate the Statement as a frame of reference to be used in the development of accounting standards for such entities. Although the paragraphs below deal with one type of entity only, the inconsistencies identified are believed to be typical of those that exist in the case of other entities. As a result, it is believed that the conclusion reached in paragraph 14 can be applied to all entities. **3**

MAIN INCONSISTENCIES BETWEEN THE STATEMENT AND THE LAW

The reporting entity

Section 258 of the Companies Act 1985 identifies subsidiary undertakings by a list of tests. Although these tests are founded mainly on the concept of control, they may in some cases either fail to identify as a subsidiary undertaking an entity that is controlled by another or they may identify as a subsidiary undertaking an entity that is not controlled. Hence those companies that are identified as subsidiary undertakings by applying the Companies Act tests may not always correspond to those the Statement would identify as subsidiaries. **4**

5   In practice, this difference tends not to be a problem because of other factors. For example, the Act's requirements concerning the treatment of subsidiaries that involve severe long-term restrictions on the rights of the parent reduce the practical effect of this difference in approach, as do the treatments of quasi-subsidiaries and jointly controlled entities required by FRS 5 'Reporting the Substance of Transactions' and FRS 9 'Associates and Joint Ventures'.

The elements of financial statements

6   One implication of the Act is that proposed dividends are required to be recognised as liabilities, although they would not usually fall within the Statement's definition of a liability.

Recognition

7   The Act states that only profits realised at the balance sheet date can be included in the profit and loss account (Schedule 4, paragraph 12). The Act defines realised profits, but does so in a way that allows the precise meaning of the term to be capable of development. The Statement adopts a different approach in which, rather than restrict the recognition of gains in the statement or statements of financial performance to those that are realised, it restricts their recognition to those that can be measured with sufficient reliability and for which sufficient evidence exists that they have actually arisen.

8   Although the Statement and the Act clearly adopt different approaches, the way in which the Act defines a realised profit means that the exact effect of this difference is not clear. The potential inconsistency described in paragraph 12—concerning the number and format of the statement or statements of financial performance—makes the effect of the difference in approach even less clear.

Measurement

9   The Statement envisages that, if the current value basis of measurement is regarded as the most appropriate measurement basis for a particular category of assets, all assets within that category will be recognised at their current value. That current value will, furthermore, be determined by reference to the value to the business rule. However, although the Act (Schedule 4, paragraph 31) permits:

(a)   intangible fixed assets other than goodwill to be included at current cost;

(b)   tangible fixed assets to be included at market value or current cost;

(c)   fixed asset investments to be included at market value or directors' valuation; and

(d)   current asset investments and stocks to be included at current cost,

current assets other than investments and stocks are required to be included in the balance sheet at the lower of cost and net realisable value (Schedule 4, paragraphs 22 and 23). Thus, for some assets the Act requires the use of measurement bases that may differ from those suggested by the Statement. It also means that the Act does not permit the use of the range of current value measures that are envisaged by the Statement's value to the business rule.[30] [31]

---

[30] *Legislative proposals are being prepared by the European Commission to permit a wider use of current values in the measurement of financial instruments. This demonstrates both that the constraints of law are not immutable and that desirable change can be motivated by accounting developments guided by the framework described in the Statement.*

[31] *These proposals have now been adopted.*

The Statement also envisages that some categories of liabilities could be measured at current value, whereas the Act does not specifically refer to this possibility.   **10**

Presentation

The balance sheet and profit and loss account of a company must be prepared in accordance with one of the statutory formats (although these formats may, subject to certain constraints, be adapted to suit the particular circumstances). Some specific items are also required to be shown in every profit and loss account (Schedule 4, paragraphs 1-3). These requirements may necessitate a presentation that differs in certain respects from what would be suggested by following the presentation principles set out in the Statement. These inconsistencies can, however, generally be overcome by providing additional disclosures.   **11**

The Act requires in most cases the preparation of, inter alia, a profit and loss account in one of the statutory formats and it makes no reference to any other performance statement. The Statement, on the other hand, is less specific about the format of any profit and loss account provided, and it acknowledges that entities may prepare more than one performance statement or may alternatively prepare a single statement that is more comprehensive than the profit and loss account the Act requires. As such, although the preparation of a profit and loss account in one of the statutory formats would meet the requirements of the Act *and* (subject to the point made in the preceding paragraph) be consistent with the Statement, other presentations possible under the Statement may not comply with the Act's requirements.   **12**

The Act requires the profit and loss account to show separately the aggregate amount of any dividends paid and proposed (Schedule 4, paragraph 3(7)). The Statement envisages that, as dividends are a distribution to owners and not a gain or loss, they will not be reported in a performance statement but will instead be reported in the reconciliation of movements in shareholders' funds.   **13**

THE STATEMENT AS A SATISFACTORY FRAME OF REFERENCE FOR STANDARD-SETTERS

Of the inconsistencies identified above, probably the most significant is the one relating to the recognition of gains: the Act requires that only profits realised at the balance sheet date are to be recognised in the profit and loss account, whilst the Statement adopts an approach that is not based on the notion of realisation. Although, as already mentioned, the precise effect of this difference in approach is not clear, the Board does not believe that this difference in approach invalidates the statement as a satisfactory frame of reference for standard-setting. It notes, for example, that realised profits are defined in the Act in a way that is intended to enable its meaning to develop. It also notes that EU legislative proposals are being prepared which, if implemented, would permit the recognition in the profit and loss account of certain gains that might not be regarded by some as realised profits. This suggests that the legal requirements in this area are capable of evolving in response to the reasonable demands of accounting practice. In such circumstances, it seems appropriate that the Statement of Principles should try to give direction to, rather than merely follow, such changes.   **14**

As the Statement is expected to provide direction to the development of the legal requirements concerning the form and content of financial statements, the Board's expectation is that inconsistencies between the Statement and legal requirements will tend to be temporary and that the law will not be a permanent impediment to the adoption of approaches consistent with the Statement.   **15**

NORTHERN IRELAND AND THE REPUBLIC OF IRELAND

16   The following table gives the references to legislation in Northern Ireland and in the Republic of Ireland corresponding to the legislation in Great Britain referred to in this appendix.

Paragraph	Great Britain	Northern Ireland	Republic of Ireland*
	Companies Act 1985	Companies (Northern Ireland) Order 1986	
4	Section 258	Article 266	GAR 1992, Regulation 4
7	Schedule 4, paragraph 12	Schedule 4, paragraph 12	CAA 1986, section 5
9	Schedule 4, paragraphs 22 and 23	Schedule 4, paragraphs 22 and 23	CAA 1986, Schedule, paragraphs 10 and 11
9	Schedule 4, paragraph 31	Schedule 4, paragraph 31	CAA 1986, Schedule, paragraph 19
11	Schedule 4, paragraphs 1-3	Schedule 4, paragraphs 1-3	CAA 1986, section 4
13	Schedule 4, paragraph 3(7)	Schedule 4, paragraph 3(7)	CAA 1986, section 4(15)

* CAA 1986 = Companies (Amendment) Act 1986;
  GAR 1992 = European Communities (Companies: Group Accounts) Regulations 1992

Appendix II
The Statement and IASC's 'framework for the preparation and presentation of Financial Statements'

It is the Board's view that a common set of principles is necessary to achieve further harmonisation in international accounting practice. For that reason, the Statement of Principles is based on the International Accounting Standards Committee's 'Framework for the Preparation and Presentation of Financial Statements' (the IASC Framework), which was itself derived from the Statements of Financial Accounting Concepts issued in the USA by the Financial Accounting Standards Board.[32]   **1**

This appendix compares the Statement with the IASC Framework and highlights and explains the main differences. The appendix does not deal in detail with any other conceptual documents, although the principles and explanations in the Statement are similar to those set out in the conceptual statements issued by other leading accounting standard-setters, including those in Australia, Canada, New Zealand and the USA.   **2**

The Statement is much more detailed than the IASC Framework, which means that it deals with many issues on which the IASC Framework is silent. These differences in detail have not been treated as differences for the purposes of this appendix.   **3**

The commentary below follows the structure and order of the Statement and it uses the headings of that document.   **4**

INTRODUCTION

There are no significant differences between the two documents.   **5**

CHAPTER 1: THE OBJECTIVE OF FINANCIAL STATEMENTS

The objective of financial statements set out in the Statement is almost identical to that set out in the IASC Framework, although there are two minor differences.   **6**

(a) The Statement's description of the objective refers specifically to information that is useful for 'assessing the stewardship of management', while the IASC Framework's description does not. However, as both documents refer to providing information that is useful for making economic decisions and agree that the reason why the stewardship of management is assessed is to take economic decisions, this difference is of no practical effect.

(b) Although the objective in the IASC Framework refers to providing information about changes in financial position while the Statement's objective does not, it is clear from both documents that it is expected that such information will be provided.

Only the Statement refers to the notion of a defining class of user (the investor). This notion is used in the Statement to give a focus that would otherwise be lacking for the selection and presentation of financial information.   **7**

CHAPTER 2: THE REPORTING ENTITY

This chapter deals with two separate reporting entity issues: identifying a reporting entity and determining the boundary of a reporting entity. The two documents adopt a similar   **8**

[32] *The IASC framework was adopted by the International Accounting Standards Board (IASB) in April 2001.*

approach to the first issue, although neither deals with it in any detail. Only the Statement deals with the second issue. It was thought that the Statement would not be complete if it did not explain which activities and resources should be reported on in financial statements.

CHAPTER 3: THE QUALITATIVE CHARACTERISTICS OF FINANCIAL INFORMATION

9　In most respects the two documents adopt the same approach to the desirable characteristics of financial information. For example, they both identify relevance, reliability, understandability and comparability as qualitative characteristics, and they describe those characteristics in very similar terms. There are however some differences:

(a)　Materiality is not treated in the same way in that, while the IASC Framework treats it as a subcategory of relevance and describes it as a quantitative characteristic, the Statement treats it as a separate characteristic and describes it as relating to both the nature and size of the item. However, the overall effect of the two documents will be the same because they agree that information should be included in the financial statements if it might reasonably be expected to influence the economic decisions of users and it can be excluded if it is not expected to have that effect.

(b)　The IASC Framework describes the accruals basis and the going concern assumption as underlying assumptions. Although the Statement does not give them such a title, their role and the way in which they are described are, to all intents and purposes, the same.

These differences are minor and will have little effect in practice.

CHAPTER 4: THE ELEMENTS OF FINANCIAL STATEMENTS

10　The two documents adopt the same approach to this subject, although:

(a)　the elements that the Statement refers to as ownership interest, gains and losses are referred to by the IASC Framework as equity, income and expenses;

(b)　the Statement defines as elements contributions by owners and distributions to owners while, in the IASC Framework, these are merely movements within owners' equity.

These differences are essentially concerned with nomenclature rather than principle.

CHAPTER 5: RECOGNITION IN FINANCIAL STATEMENTS

11　Both the IASC Framework and the Statement approach the initial recognition process by asking whether a new asset or liability has been created (or an existing one has been added to), then applying recognition criteria to that new (or increased) asset or liability to determine whether it should be recognised. Both documents also adopt similar recognition criteria, although they are described in slightly different terms in that, while the Statement's criteria require, inter alia, that sufficient evidence should exist that the new asset or liability has been created or that there has been an addition to an existing asset or liability, the IASC Framework refers to it needing to be probable that any future economic benefit associated with the item will flow to or from the enterprise. The Board believes that this difference reflects a development in accounting thought since the publication of the IASC Framework.

12　The Statement deals with derecognition, a topic not covered in the IASC Framework. The Board believes that this reflects the fact that, as transactions and the instruments transacted have become more complex since the IASC Framework was published, greater emphasis than hitherto needs to be placed on the principles that underlie the derecognition process.

CHAPTER 6: MEASUREMENT IN FINANCIAL STATEMENTS

The Statement and the IASC Framework adopt different approaches to the subject of measurement. For example, while the IASC Framework briefly describes the measurement bases that might be used, the Statement goes on to develop a framework to guide the choice of measurement basis. It also discusses the measurement bases much more extensively than the IASC Framework and it uses the value to the business model to decide between alternative measures of current value. This material has been included in the Statement in order to help introduce a degree of consistency into the measurement process. For similar reasons, the Statement, unlike the IASC Framework, discusses subsequent remeasurement in detail.   **13**

CHAPTER 7: PRESENTATION OF FINANCIAL INFORMATION

The IASC Framework contains very little on this subject. The Statement nevertheless deals with it because the Board believes that good presentation is an essential element in effective financial reporting.   **14**

CHAPTER 8: ACCOUNTING FOR INTERESTS IN OTHER ENTITIES

Although the IASC Framework contains no material on this subject, the Statement deals with it because the Board believes it is an important issue.   **15**

Appendix III
Background to issues dealt with in the statement

BACKGROUND TO THE STATEMENT OF PRINCIPLES

1   When the Board was formed in 1990, it recognised that, if it was to develop accounting standards that were consistent with each other, it needed to develop a coherent frame of reference to guide it in its work. Indeed, one of the recommendations of the committee that recommended that the Accounting Standards Board should be established was that further work on a conceptual framework should be undertaken.[33]

2   The frame of reference that the Board subsequently developed became the basis for a series of discussion drafts of individual chapters that were published in the early 1990s. Those drafts were revised and reissued together, in 1995, as an exposure draft of the complete Statement of Principles for Financial Reporting. A second exposure draft was published in March 1999.

3   The Board started to develop its frame of reference by looking to the accounting principles that, at that time, underpinned accounting practice in the UK. However, those principles were found wanting because:

(a)   they were developed piecemeal at different times in response to particular problems and were not consistent with one another.

(b)   some of them had not kept up with modern developments. For example, many had their origins in accounting solutions devised for manufacturing companies with an emphasis on accounting for stocks and fixed assets. Some of those principles are not as effective in coping with the more complex financial reporting issues of today, such as those arising from intangibles and complex contractual arrangements.

(c)   some of them were out of line with developments internationally.

The Board therefore concluded that, although many of those principles continued to be relevant and appropriate, some would have to be modified and some additional principles were needed to produce a framework that was consistent, up-to-date and reasonably complete.

4   The main principles in this Statement are derived from that informal frame of reference. Many of them have been examined closely over the last nine years during the development of new accounting standards (and the revision of existing ones) and have benefited from that examination, with some of the principles being refined and some developed further as a result. Furthermore, a number of the principles now play significant roles in accounting standards and have found general acceptance. For example:

(a)   FRS 2 *Accounting for Subsidiary Undertakings* uses the reporting entity concept described in Chapter 2 of the Statement;

(b)   FRS 4 *Capital Instruments*, FRS 5 *Reporting the Substance of Transactions*, FRS 7 *Fair Values in Acquisition Accounting* and FRS 12 *Provisions, Contingent Liabilities and Contingent Assets* are based on the definitions of assets and liabilities set out in Chapter 4; and

(c)   FRS 11 *Impairment of Fixed Assets and Goodwill* uses the recoverable amount notion described in Chapter 6.

Therefore, although in places the Statement may sound unfamiliar, it actually bears a close resemblance to much of existing practice.

---

[33] *See 'The Making of Accounting Standards': Report of the Review Committee under the Chairmanship of Sir Ron Dearing CB (1988).*

The Board has in its work programme a number of projects that are exploring further some   5
of the issues covered in the Statement. Although it is possible that this work may result in
changes needing to be made to what is said in the Statement, that does not create a difficulty
because the Board does not regard the Statement as its final word on the principles that
underlie financial reporting. Accounting thought is continually evolving and it is only to be
expected that the Statement will need to be revised from time to time.

Editor's note: The most obvious subsequent product of the Statement is FRS 18 'Accounting Policies'
which is based on a number of the principles covered in the Statement.

The remainder of this appendix discusses, and sets out the rationale behind, aspects of the   6
Statement that would benefit from a fuller explanation. The discussion is organised by
reference to the sections in the Statement (ie Introduction, Chapter 1 etc) to which they
relate.

INTRODUCTION

General purpose financial statements

The Statement classifies financial information into special purpose financial reports,   7
general purpose financial reports and other financial information, and explains that annual
financial statements prepared to comply with companies legislation are examples of a
general purpose financial report. Describing annual financial statements in this way is not
intended to imply that such statements are all-purpose financial statements, because they
are not. The term 'general purpose financial reports' has been used because it highlights
the difference between special purpose financial reports and other financial reports.

Smaller entities and not-for-profit entities

Although the principles set out in the Statement are intended to be relevant to the financial   8
statements of all profit-oriented entities, it has been prepared with large entities uppermost
in mind: accounting issues are generally at their most complex where large entities are
involved and it is only right that the Board should seek to prepare a Statement that will
help it to address these issues. That does not mean, however, that the Statement would
have been fundamentally different had it been prepared with smaller entities in mind. The
principles in Chapters 2-8, for example, would have remained unchanged. As the financial
statements of small entities probably have a narrower range of users and tend to be used
for a narrower range of purposes, the objective of those financial statements might have
needed to be expressed differently. This difference would, however, be one of application
rather than principle.

The Statement explains that, although it is relevant to the financial statements of not-for-   9
profit entities, some of the principles need to be re-expressed and others need changes
of emphasis before they can be applied to that sector. The Board has requested its Public
Sector and Not-for-profit Committee to study the issue and make recommendations in due
course.

CHAPTER 1: THE OBJECTIVE OF FINANCIAL STATEMENTS

A wide range of users

Although it is sometimes suggested that the legal position is that a company's annual   10
financial statements are prepared for its shareholders only, neither companies legislation
nor, so far as the Board is aware, case law suggests that the courts should or would take

such a view. Indeed, since companies legislation requires companies to put a copy of their annual financial statements on the public record, it is clear that the law envisages that those financial statements will be used by the public at large—a much wider range of people than existing shareholders. This position is reflected in the Statement.

11   It is not reasonable to expect financial statements to meet the information needs of everyone who chooses to use them. They focus on the common interest that users have in the financial performance and financial position of the reporting entity as a whole. That means that they do not address the special interests that many users will have and they do not satisfy all users equally well. Users will therefore usually need to supplement the information they obtain from financial statements with information from other sources.

Investors as the defining class of user

12   The Statement explains that investors are to be treated as the defining class of user. Investors are interested in financial information on the reporting entity as a whole. Other users require exactly the same information as a frame of reference against which to judge the more specialised information they obtain from other sources. For example, although potential lenders will gather specialised information from a range of sources to help them decide whether, and at what price, to lend to the reporting entity, they will also use information derived from the financial statements of the entity as a whole.

Economic decisions and stewardship

13   The Statement explains that the financial statements provide information that is useful in assessing stewardship and for making economic decisions. At first sight these objectives— assessing stewardship and making economic decisions—seem mutually exclusive because stewardship reports are often thought to be limited to the use of historical cost whereas decision-useful reports are thought to require the comprehensive use of current values. The Board does not, however, believe that they are mutually exclusive.

(a)   Stewardship reports are limited to using historical cost only if a very narrow view is taken of what a stewardship report entails. However, the Statement takes a broad view in that it regards stewardship as being not merely about the safekeeping and proper use of an entity's resources but also about their efficient and profitable use.

(b)   The need for financial statements to provide information that is relevant for making economic decisions seems to suggest that more assets and liabilities than hitherto should be measured at current value. However, it does not necessarily follow that there needs to be comprehensive use of current values: experience shows that much historical cost information can also have predictive value.

CHAPTER 2: THE REPORTING ENTITY

Identifying a reporting entity

14   Although those who are entrusted with resources by others are accountable to them for those resources and should therefore probably provide them with a set of accounts, when the Statement considers which entities should prepare financial statements it is considering a much wider issue: which entities should prepare financial statements and make them available to a wide range of users? This is a complex issue and, as it has been the practice in the UK and the Republic of Ireland for legislators to determine which profit-oriented entities should prepare financial statements, is an issue that the Statement discusses in general terms only.

The boundary of the reporting entity

There are two main approaches that can be used to determine the boundary of a reporting   **15**
entity: one approach concentrates wholly on ownership (the proprietary view) and the
other concentrates on the group as an entity, unified and encompassed by the parent's
control (the entity view).

(a)   The proprietary view regards ownership and the resulting access to benefits as
      of paramount interest to users. As a result, ownership is used to provide the basis
      of consolidated financial statements. On a strict proprietary view, the investor's
      ability to influence or even control its investee is irrelevant: consolidated financial
      statements will aggregate the parent's direct and indirect ownership interests in a
      proportional consolidation (the line-by-line consolidation of the investor's share of
      each item) as this shows the parent's access to benefit from all of its investments.

(b)   On the entity view, the parent's ability to control its subsidiaries is all-important,
      regardless of the size of its ownership interest in the activities of the entity that
      it directs. The consolidated financial statements therefore consolidate in full the
      assets and liabilities of any entity that the parent controls—even if the entity is not
      a wholly-owned subsidiary—and the parent's ownership interest and any outside
      equity interest in a subsidiary are treated merely as part of an overall ownership
      interest.

The appropriate perspective to use depends on the relative usefulness of the information   **16**
each provides. The Statement regards the entity view as providing the most useful
information, and therefore uses control to determine the boundary of a reporting entity.

Single entity financial statements of parent companies

The Statement explains that, once a reporting entity has been identified, two boundaries   **17**
will be drawn—one based on direct control and one based on direct plus indirect control.
This means that, where a company is controlled by another company, both companies will
be reporting entities as will the group of companies that they constitute.

Some commentators suggest that, because the activities and resources of a parent and its   **18**
subsidiary are difficult to separate economically, it is inappropriate for an entity to report
on the activities it carries out and the resources it holds in isolation from the activities and
resources of its subsidiaries. This view suggests that companies preparing consolidated
financial statements should not also be expected to prepare single entity financial
statements. Some might argue that the present legal position—in which parent companies
are not required to prepare profit and loss accounts—could be used to support this view.
However, if it is inappropriate for a parent to report on the activities it carries out and the
resources it holds in isolation from the activities and resources of its subsidiaries, it would
seem to follow that it is also inappropriate for those subsidiaries to report in isolation from
their parent; in other words, subsidiaries whose activities and resources are reported on in
consolidated financial statements should not be required to prepare single entity financial
statements. That is not the present legal position.

The Board's view is that, although the usefulness of single entity financial statements has   **19**
decreased as the structure of business organisations has become more complex, single
entity financial statements—whether for parent companies or subsidiaries—still have a
role to play, albeit a much narrower role than that of the financial statements of the group
as a whole. Drawing a boundary by reference to direct control reflects this view.

CHAPTER 3: THE QUALITATIVE CHARACTERISTICS OF FINANCIAL INFORMATION

Materiality and relevance

20   Although the Statement of Principles expects the financial information given in financial statements to be both material and relevant, it describes these two characteristics in similar ways. In particular, the tests of whether information is material and whether it is relevant are both based on influencing the economic decisions of users—although relevance involves *the ability* to influence decisions while materiality involves the reasonable expectation that decisions *will* be influenced. Similarly, both characteristics involve a consideration of the size and nature of the items or information involved. There are, however, important differences between the characteristics.

   (a)   Materiality is a threshold characteristic—a discrete test—used to decide whether to include information in the financial statements. If an item of information is material, it will need to be included and if it is not, it need not be included. Relevance, on the other hand, is a 'continuous' quality; one item of information will be more relevant than another and the information given will (subject to other constraints) be that which is the most relevant.

   (b)   Put simply, characteristics such as relevance, reliability, comparability and understandability provide direction to the financial reporting selection process, thus enabling the usefulness of the information to be maximised. The materiality test, which recognises that some information has to be left out of financial statements, then asks whether the information is useful enough to be given.

Prudence

21   Accounting practice has evolved significantly over the last thirty years and, as a result, has become much more sophisticated in the way that it seeks to reflect the nuances of business activity. This is acknowledged in the Statement through its emphasis on specific principles rather than general notions and assumptions. In the case of prudence, for example, the smoothing of reported profits has become as great a concern as their overstatement and, as a result, the deliberate understatement of assets and gains and the deliberate overstatement of liabilities and losses are no longer seen as a virtue. Indeed, it is now widely accepted that the use of prudence in this way can seriously affect the quality of the information provided.

22   This has been reflected in international practice for some time now. For example, the framework documents published by the International Accounting Standards Committee (IASC) and the accounting standard-setters in Canada and the USA describe prudence (sometimes referred to as conservatism) as involving a degree of caution in the exercise of the judgements needed in making the estimates required under conditions of uncertainty. The standard-setters in Australia and New Zealand have adopted a similar approach, although they have subsumed prudence within the notion of reliability.

23   The Statement's approach to prudence is consistent with the way in which accounting practice has evolved and with the approaches adopted internationally. It:

   (a)   treats prudence as one of the attributes that need to be present if financial information prepared under conditions of uncertainty is to be reliable;

   (b)   describes prudence as the inclusion of a degree of caution in the exercise of the judgements needed in making the estimates required under conditions of uncertainty; and

   (c)   makes it clear that prudence is a potentially biased concept and that care should therefore be taken to ensure that it does not result in the deliberate and systematic understatement of assets and gains and the overstatement of liabilities and losses.

Understandability

In an ideal world, financial statements would be prepared in a way that makes them intelligible to all users, regardless of their level of expertise or experience. However, as entities are increasingly complex and many of them enter into increasingly complex transactions, it can be difficult to represent their financial performance and financial position both faithfully and in a way that can be understood by all users. The Statement recognises this by explaining that the basis on which financial statements are to be prepared is that users have a reasonable knowledge of business and economic activities and accounting.

24

This means that financial statements will not always be capable of being understood by all users. Although this sounds an unsatisfactory state of affairs, it is, in fact, the present position. Users who do not have a reasonable knowledge of business and economic activities and accounting use the services of those who have that knowledge to help them derive information from the financial statements.

25

Relevance versus reliability

Although it is sometimes argued that the characteristics of relevance and reliability are often in conflict, such conflicts are exaggerated. As the Statement makes clear, reliability is a hurdle to be cleared (ie is the information sufficiently reliable?), not a competition that has to be won (ie is this information the most reliable?). This means that the approach to be adopted in preparing the financial statements will be the one that is the most relevant of those that are reliable. A conflict will therefore arise between the characteristics only in the rare circumstances in which the reliable approaches are not relevant and the relevant approaches are not reliable.

26

CHAPTER 4: THE ELEMENTS OF FINANCIAL STATEMENTS

Identifying the elements

In essence, the preparation of financial statements involves finding the best way to categorise financial information about the transactions and other events that affect a reporting entity's financial performance and financial position. It is generally accepted that the best way to report this information is to focus on what has happened to the entity over the reporting period (for example, revenues and expenses, gains and losses, cash flows, and capital transactions) and what is its position as a result (assets and liabilities). These effects will inevitably have to be reflected in the financial statements in a highly aggregated form, and the Statement envisages that order will be imposed on this process by specifying and defining the classes of items (elements) that encapsulate the key aspects of those effects.

27

Should the definitions of the elements be interrelated and, if so, which definitions should be based on which?

The performance statement elements and the balance sheet elements could, in theory, be defined independently of each other. However, such an approach risks leaving gaps or creating areas of overlap. It would also have been inconsistent with the notion that primary financial statements should articulate, a fundamental and long-accepted characteristic of such statements. The Statement therefore uses definitions that are interrelated.

28

It follows that either the balance sheet elements should be based on the definitions of the performance statement elements or vice versa. As the accounting process is essentially about allocating the effects of transactions and other events to reporting periods, it might

29

seem more logical to define the performance statement elements and then base the balance sheet elements on those definitions. This approach requires the use of robust definitions of the performance statement elements in order to provide the unity, order and discipline needed for an effective framework. Those definitions need therefore to be precise and comprehensive, and they need to avoid placing reliance on management intent or referring to generally accepted accounting principles. However, accounting standard-setters around the world have carried out an exhaustive search for robust definitions of performance statement elements and have concluded that such definitions do not exist. On the other hand, robust definitions of balance sheet elements do exist. The Statement, like all the conceptual documents developed by all the leading accounting standard-setters around the world, therefore defines the balance sheet elements and bases the definitions of the performance statement elements on those definitions.

How many elements should there be and how should they be defined?

30   It is obviously both important and necessary to distinguish cash flows and capital transactions from other things that happen to an entity. It is, however, not immediately clear whether it is important or realistic to treat, say, all the credits in the performance statement as a single type of element and expect them to meet a single definition (and all the debits as a separate single element and expect them to meet a single definition). A similar question arises concerning the debits and credits in the balance sheet.

31   Reporting on the financial performance and financial position of an entity involves providing an account of the reporting entity's use of, and command over, economic resources. The Statement therefore bases its definitions on flows and prospective flows of future economic benefits embodied in economic resources. Thus, assets are defined as 'rights or other access to future economic benefits controlled by an entity as a result of past transactions or events', liabilities as 'obligations of an entity to transfer economic benefits as a result of past transactions or events', and, apart from ownership interest, no other balance sheet elements are identified.

32   As the items in the profit and loss account are typically referred to as revenue, expenses, gains and losses, it would seem natural to use similar terminology in the Statement. Indeed, that is the approach adopted in the USA by the Financial Accounting Standards Board. However, as it has been decided that the definitions of the performance statement elements should be based on the definitions of the balance sheet elements, it is possible to define the credits in the performance statement in terms of increases in net assets not resulting from capital contributions and the debits in the performance statement as decreases in net assets not resulting from capital distributions. The issue the Board therefore had to consider was whether more comprehensive definitions should be used in order to differentiate between types of performance statement debits and credits.

33   At the moment, the Board is carrying out a review of FRS 3 *Reporting Financial Performance*. As part of this work, it is considering possible ways of restructuring the performance statements that are provided at present. It may be that, as a result of this work, it will conclude that gains and revenue should be differentiated from each other. Similarly, it may be concluded that losses and expenses should be differentiated from each other. However, until then, there does not appear to be sufficient reason for the Statement of Principles to distinguish revenue from gains and expenses from losses. It therefore identifies one credit performance statement element (gains) and one debit performance statement element (losses). IASC's 'Framework for the Preparation and Presentation of Financial Statements' adopts the same approach, except that it calls the two elements 'income' and 'expenses'.

It is recognised that, by not differentiating gains from revenue (and losses from expenses), items that are commonly referred to as 'revenue' (and 'expenses') have had to be referred to in the Statement as 'gains' (and 'losses') or vice versa. That is not ideal but is not regarded as sufficient reason to justify differentiation.   **34**

Implications of the approach adopted to specifying and defining the elements

Under the approach adopted in the Statement, if costs are to be carried forward (ie deferred) to a subsequent period to match income being earned in that period, they will need to meet the definition of an asset (and meet the relevant recognition criteria). This will mean, inter alia, asking whether the costs to be deferred constitute future economic benefits. It is recognised that the application of this approach in practice will result in some of the costs that are at present deferred and shown as assets being recognised as losses because they do not represent future economic benefits. Similarly, some of the credit items that are deferred at present in the balance sheet might, under the principles, need instead to be recognised as income because they do not qualify as liabilities. Nevertheless, the Board believes that the approach provides what is needed for an effective framework.   **35**

It is worth noting that the Statement's approach is almost identical to the approach adopted in the conceptual documents of IASC and the other leading accounting standard-setters around the world, including the standard-setters in Australia, Canada, New Zealand and the USA. It is also worth noting that the definitions of assets and liabilities set out in the Statement already provide the foundation for several UK accounting standards, including FRS 5*Reporting the Substance of Transactions*. Indeed, through the Board's own work, the work of UK bodies preparing Statements of Recommended Practice, and the work of the aforementioned standard-setters, the elements and their definitions have for many years now been playing an important role in the standard-setting process throughout the world.   **36**

It has nevertheless been suggested by some that the approach means that the balance sheet will become the main accounting statement and the performance statement will be relegated to a statement of residual amounts. It means nothing of the kind. First, the Board accepts that the primary focus of users is on the performance statement and that this is likely to remain the case for the foreseeable future. Secondly, using definitions of assets and liabilities to define gains and losses is merely a means to an end—that end being to improve the quality of financial statements in general and, through the discipline that the definitions will impose on the recognition of gains and losses, performance statements in particular.   **37**

It has also been suggested in the past that the approach means that the profit or loss for the period will be the difference between the opening and closing balance sheets, adjusted for capital contributions and distributions. Although it is correct to say that the amount of the difference is equal to the total of all the components of financial performance, it is an oversimplification to suggest that this means that the difference is regarded as the profit or loss for the period. The Board has spent much time and energy since its inception on improving the way in which financial performance is reported, and the focus of this work has been the need to move away from placing so much significance on any one line of the performance statement. FRS 3—which was issued in 1992—makes it clear that the focus of performance reporting should be on the components of financial performance and on the characteristics of those components. This is also the approach adopted in the Statement.   **38**

Finally, some commentators have suggested that, by defining the performance statement elements by reference to movements in assets and liabilities, the Statement will shift the focus of accounting away from transactions. The Board does not agree with this suggestion. Accounting is a process that is primarily concerned with allocating the effects   **39** of transactions to reporting periods, and the approach set out in the Statement will achieve exactly that.

CHAPTER 5: RECOGNITION IN FINANCIAL STATEMENTS

The role of realisation in the Statement

40   The Statement envisages that all gains and losses will be recognised in a performance statement. Furthermore, as the Statement does not specify different recognition criteria for different performance statements (or for different parts of the same, single performance statement), realised profits may conceivably be shown alongside unrealised profits.

41   An alternative approach might have been to base recognition on the notions of realisation and realised profit. For example, the Statement could have assumed that only realised gains would be recognised in the performance statements. It could, alternatively, have assumed that realised gains would be recognised in one performance statement (or in one part of a single performance statement) while unrealised gains would be recognised in a second performance statement (such as the statement of total recognised gains and losses) or in a separate part of the single performance statement. The main reasons that are usually put forward in support of this approach, and the counter-arguments, are set out below.

Companies legislation

42   Companies legislation specifies that companies should include only profits realised at the balance sheet date in their profit and loss account. It could be argued that, for this reason alone, realisation should be acknowledged as a recognition criterion.

43   However, the development of the Statement has not been constrained by legal requirements because the Board believes that accounting practice evolves best if regard is had in documents such as the Statement of Principles to what is deemed to be right rather than what is required by law. The implications of this for the Statement of Principles are considered in Appendix I.

Distributable profits

44   Companies making distributions of income to their shareholders must make them from distributable profits. It is therefore sometimes argued that, if users are to have a proper understanding of the level of sustainable dividends and of the prospects of dividend growth, it is important that the level of distributable profits is reported and that dividends paid and payable are reported in the context of those distributable profits.

45   However, in practice—and particularly for a group—the potential for distributions, whether from profits or return of capital, is dependent on many factors, including companies legislation in the countries in which the operations are carried out, corporate structure, currency and dividend controls, and the entity's financial adaptability. In these circumstances it is unrealistic to suppose that distributability per se can serve as a primary focus of the presentation of financial performance.

Realisation as a criterion for determining what should be recognised

46   Regardless of the legal requirements, it is a desirable attribute of items included in the profit and loss account, particularly gains, that their existence should be reasonably

certain. The realisation notion is one means of determining whether the existence of a gain is reasonably certain. However, in the Board's view, it is not necessarily the best way.

The realisation notion originally came into use in order to protect creditors from the   **47** uncertainties that arise in accruals accounting, and its purpose was to try to ensure that profits were not overstated and that there was sufficient cash available to distribute those profits without the company becoming insolvent. In this guise the notion was understood to involve the conversion into cash of non-cash resources and rights to cash.

As business practice developed, so the purpose of the notion changed and it came to be used   **48** to ensure that only gains that were reasonably certain and unlikely to reverse were included in the profit and loss account. Similarly, its meaning evolved to include conversion into claims to cash.

Developments since then have, however, made even this version of the notion irrelevant   **49** in some areas. For example, it is now often possible to be reasonably certain that a gain exists and to measure that gain reliably even if no disposal has occurred. Furthermore, the introduction of cash flow statements means that cash-based profit and loss accounts have largely been outgrown. A number of attempts have been made to update the notion to take account of these developments. For example, it has been suggested that changes in the market value of securities for which an active market exists are also realised, even though no claim to cash is involved. Similarly, some have suggested that the test should be extended to include gains that are realisable, in other words capable of being converted into cash or claims for cash.

However, in general it is not a good idea to bend a term so that it has a meaning other   **50** than its natural meaning. A better approach in this case would seem to be to focus on the underlying objective and then encapsulate that objective in the recognition criteria. It is the Board's view that the objective is to recognise a gain only if there is reasonable certainty that it exists and if it can be measured reliably. The initial recognition and subsequent remeasurement criteria set out in the Statement are designed to achieve that end.

CHAPTER 6: MEASUREMENT IN FINANCIAL STATEMENTS

The mixed measurement system

For many years entities carried all their assets and liabilities in their balance sheet at   **51** historical cost. However, the relevance of such measures in periods when prices have moved markedly has often been questioned and, to counteract this perceived fading relevance, the majority of larger UK listed companies now measure some of their assets at current values and some at cost. (According to Company Reporting No 80 (February 1997), more than 65 per cent of the companies in that journal's database had adopted this approach.)

Although this approach is commonly referred to as the modified historical cost basis,   **52** that term is something of a misnomer because it is a mixed measurement system. The Statement therefore uses this latter term.

The Statement explains that assets and liabilities have a number of different monetary   **53** attributes that could be represented in financial statements. It also explains that the single most important characteristic that distinguishes these monetary attributes is whether they are based on historical cost or current value. The remainder of its discussion is expressed in terms of this distinction.

54   In theory, the Statement could have adopted one of three broad approaches to measurement.

(a)   It could have assumed strict adherence to historical cost in all circumstances. In view of existing practice, this would have been a revolutionary step. For example, when respondents to the Accounting Standards Committee's ED 51 'Accounting for fixed assets and revaluations' (1990) were asked whether it would be practicable to prohibit the carrying of selected fixed assets at revalued amounts, 96 per cent of those who answered the question believed it was not practicable.

(b)   It could have assumed the adoption of a comprehensive current value system under which all assets and all liabilities, or at least the great majority of them, would be carried at current values. This too would have been a revolutionary step and it is not an approach that the Board has considered in the past nor is it one that it expects to consider in the foreseeable future.

(c)   It could have assumed the continuance of the present, mixed measurement system. Previous consultations have shown that the majority of respondents favour this approach. For example, just over 70 per cent of those who responded to the Board's Discussion Paper 'The Role of Valuation in Financial Reporting' (1993) favoured continued use of the mixed measurement system.

55   In preparing the Statement, the Board has assumed the continued use of the mixed measurement system. This system has the advantage of requiring reporting entities to match the measurement basis used for a particular category of assets or liabilities to the circumstances relating to that category and, in so doing, acknowledges the different trade-offs between relevance and reliability in the measurement of different types of balance sheet item. The system is also flexible in that the mix of historical cost and current value can be changed as accounting thought develops and markets evolve.

Choosing a measurement basis

56   The main focus of the Statement's chapter on measurement is the measurement debate that is of most relevance today—what mix of historical cost and current value should be used. The Statement provides a framework to guide the choice of an appropriate measurement basis for each balance sheet category and thereby helps to apply some discipline and logic to the selection process. This should result in an improvement in the relevance and comparability of the information being provided.

57   The characteristic of relevance plays a major role in the framework described in the Statement. Current value information can be relevant in two rather different ways.

(a)   For assets that generate cash flows indirectly through use—such as property, plant and equipment—a current value gives an up-to-date measure of the total resources invested and provides a basis for calculating the current cost of using the asset within the period.

(b)   For assets and liabilities that represent rights to specific future cash flows—financial assets and financial liabilities—the market price gives the value of those cash flows at that time.

58   Whereas for the first type of balance sheet item some degree of choice may be appropriate for each entity in determining whether market values should be used as the basis of measure, the same flexibility may be less appropriate if extended to the second type because of their more direct relationship to future cash flows.

59   As the Statement explains, although the factors that should be used to determine the most appropriate measurement basis are unlikely to change, the measurement basis that best meets those factors may. Indeed, the Board expects that, if markets develop, greater use will probably be made of current value because measures that were once thought not relevant or unreliable may become both the most relevant measure and reliable. That having been said, it is unlikely that the framework set out in the Statement will suggest the use of current values other than for certain types of investments, commodity stocks and financial instruments. Under the framework, the practice of measuring some fixed assets at current value is also likely to continue.

CHAPTER 7: PRESENTATION OF FINANCIAL INFORMATION

Presentation of gains and losses

The way in which information on financial performance is presented is of fundamental importance to the quality of financial reporting. The Statement does not, however, deal with this matter in any detail, primarily because it is an issue that is being actively considered in the Board's review of FRS 3. If that review identifies principles about the presentation of gains and losses that could usefully be incorporated in the Statement, the Statement will be amended.   **60**

Dividends paid and payable

The Statement makes it clear that, regardless of the number of performance statements prepared, they will deal with gains and losses only and no items that are not gains and losses will be recognised in them. As dividends paid and payable are not gains and losses, the Statement envisages that they will not be included in the profit and loss account or other performance statement. Although that seems logical—dividends are not a component of financial performance—it is not consistent with how such dividends are dealt with at present. This issue is being considered as part of the review of FRS 3.[34]   **61**

Recycling

The Statement explains that items that are not gains or losses are not included in the performance statement, which means that the notion of recycling[35] is not consistent with the principles. This is another matter that is being considered in the review of FRS 3.   **62**

CHAPTER 8: ACCOUNTING FOR INTERESTS IN OTHER ENTITIES

Accounting for minority interests

As explained in paragraph 15, there are, in theory, two opposing perspectives from which minority interests could be viewed when preparing consolidated financial statements: one perspective concentrates wholly on ownership (the proprietary view) and the other on the group as an entity, unified and encompassed by the parent's control (the entity view). The Statement considers that the entity view provides the most useful information and therefore uses control to determine the boundary of a reporting entity.   **63**

One implication of adopting the entity view is that all subsidiaries, even those that are not wholly-owned, will be fully consolidated. However, it is useful to show the extent of outside ownership interests since this is an important factor in determining the interest of investors in the reporting entity as a whole. This important feature—ownership—would be   **64**

---

[34] See FRED 22 'Revision of FRS 3 'Reporting Financial Performance'.'

[35] By 'recycling' the Statement means recognising a gain or loss in the performance statement in one period then, in a later period, recognising some or all of that gain or loss under a different heading in either the same or a different performance statement because the nature of the item is deemed to have changed in some way.

ignored if the focus was exclusively on the entity view. The Statement therefore envisages that any outside equity interests in entities within the parent's control will be identified in the primary financial statements. In this way the financial statements will reflect the parent's ownership interests in the entities within its control.

Part Two

Accounting Standards

Foreword to Accounting Standards

(March 2015)

Contents

Editor's note: This revised foreword supersedes Foreword to Accounting Standards (2012).

The FRC is responsible for promoting high quality corporate governance and reporting to foster investment. We set the UK Corporate Governance and Stewardship Codes as well as UK standards for accounting, auditing and actuarial work. We represent UK interests in international standard-setting. We also monitor and take action to promote the quality of corporate reporting and auditing. We operate independent disciplinary arrangements for accountants and actuaries, and oversee the regulatory activities of the accountancy and actuarial professional bodies.

The FRC does not accept any liability to any party for any loss, damage or costs howsoever arising, whether directly or indirectly, whether in contract, tort or otherwise from any action or decision taken (or not taken) as a result of any person relying on or otherwise using this document or arising from any omission from it.

FOREWORD TO ACCOUNTING STANDARDS

Introduction

This foreword explains the scope, authority and identification of accounting standards, **1**
issued by the Financial Reporting Council (FRC), for the purposes of the *Companies Act 2006* (the Act) and Regulations made thereunder.

This foreword relates to financial statements prepared in accordance with UK and Republic **2**
of Ireland legislation and accounting standards (for companies these are referred to in the Act as 'Companies Act accounts'). It does not apply to financial statements prepared in accordance with EU-adopted IFRS (for companies these are referred to in the Act as 'IAS accounts').

Scope of accounting standards

Directors of companies incorporated under the Act are required by the Act to prepare **3**
financial statements that give a true and fair view of:

(a) the assets, liabilities and financial position of the company and, where relevant, the group at the end of the reporting period; and

(b) the profit or loss of the company and, where relevant, the group for the reporting period.

In the case of a micro-entity, financial statements drawn up in accordance with the micro-entity provisions of company law are presumed to give a true and fair view.

Accounting standards are applicable to the financial statements of a reporting entity[1] that **4**
are required to give a true and fair view of its financial position at the reporting date[2] and of its profit or loss (or income and expenditure) for the reporting period.

The whole essence of accounting standards is to provide for recognition, measurement, **5**
presentation and disclosure for specific aspects of financial reporting in a way that reflects economic reality and hence provides a true and fair view.

More information about the 'true and fair' concept can be found on the FRC's website **6**
at http://frc.org.uk/Our-Work/Codes-Standards/Accounting-and-Reporting-Policy/True-and-Fair.aspx.

Authority for issuing accounting standards

The FRC, in accordance with the *Statutory Auditors (Amendment of Companies Act 2006* **7**
and Delegation of Functions etc) Order 2012 (SI 2012/1741), is a prescribed body for issuing accounting standards in the UK. In the Republic of Ireland the accounting standards issued by the FRC are promulgated by the Institute of Chartered Accountants in Ireland (ICAI). The objective of the FRC and ICAI is a regime of accounting standards common to both the United Kingdom and the Republic of Ireland.

---

[1] *This includes entities incorporated under the Act and preparing Companies Act accounts, and also entities that are not constituted as companies, but are otherwise required to prepare financial statements that give a true and fair view.*

[2] *For companies this is the accounting reference date.*

8   In relation to the setting of accounting standards the FRC has identified that its objective is to enable users of accounts to receive high-quality, understandable financial reporting proportionate to the size and complexity of the entity and users' information needs.

Identification of accounting standards

9   Accounting standards developed by the FRC will be designated Financial Reporting Standards (FRSs)[3].

10   The FRC may issue FRSs that relate to other aspects of financial reporting, but which are not accounting standards.

11   Each FRS will indicate its status, ie that it is an accounting standard or, if not, the circumstances in which it may be applied. For the avoidance of doubt, those FRSs issued prior to the issue of this edition of the *Foreword to Accounting Standards* are accounting standards.

12   The FRC may issue other material with, or alongside, an FRS. This material is only part of an accounting standard where it is identified as an integral part of an FRS that is an accounting standard.

Early adoption of Financial Reporting Exposure Drafts

13   An exposure draft is issued for comment and is subject to revision. Until it is finalised as an accounting standard the requirements of any existing accounting standards that would be affected by proposals in the exposure draft remain in force.

14   Some reporting entities may wish to provide additional information reflecting proposals in an exposure draft. In the FRC's view there are two ways that this can be achieved:

(a)   Insofar as the information does not conflict with existing accounting standards, it could be incorporated into the financial statements. It should be remembered, however, that the proposals may change before forming part of an accounting standard and the consequences of a change to the proposals should be considered.

(b)   The information could be provided in supplementary form.

15   Similar considerations apply to consultation documents or discussion documents issued by the FRC, and to proposals to amend FRSs that are not accounting standards.

Withdrawal of Foreword to Accounting Standards (issued November 2012)

16   The *Foreword to Accounting Standards* issued by the FRC in November 2012 is superseded by this Foreword and is accordingly withdrawn.

---

[3] *For accounting periods beginning on or after 1 January 2015, as set out in FRS 100 Application of Financial Reporting Requirements, a number of accounting standards were withdrawn. Some of these accounting standards did not have the designation FRS, but were nevertheless accounting standards and continue to be applicable to accounting periods beginning prior to 1 January 2015.*

FRS 100
Application of Financial Reporting Requirements

(September 2015)

Contents

Appendices

FRS 100 Application of Financial Reporting Requirements

(September 2015)

Editor's note: This revised version (issued in September 2015) incorporates recently published amendments; most notably the incorporation of amendments issued in July 2015. The amended version of FRS 100 updates the version issued in November 2012 for the following: a) the withdrawal of FRS 27 *Life Assurance* (as set out in FRS 103 *Insurance Contracts* issued in March 2014); b) consequential amendments to FRS 102 included in FRS 104 *Interim Financial Reporting* issued in March 2015; c) Amendments to FRS 100 issued in July 2015; d) an editorial amendment to paragraph A2.19 to include a reference to the Strategic Report; and e) some minor typographical or presentational corrections. This revised standard is effective for accounting periods beginning on or after 1 January 2016.

SUMMARY

(i)   With effect from 1 January 2015 the Financial Reporting Council (FRC) revised financial reporting standards for the United Kingdom and Republic of Ireland. The revision fundamentally reformed financial reporting, replacing the extant standards with five Financial Reporting Standards:

    (a)   FRS 100 *Application of Financial Reporting Requirements*;

    (b)   FRS 101 *Reduced Disclosure Framework*;

    (c)   FRS 102 *The Financial Reporting Standard applicable in the UK and Republic of Ireland*;

    (d)   FRS 103 *Insurance Contracts*; and

    (e)   FRS 104 *Interim Financial Reporting*.

The FRC has also issued FRS 105 The *Financial Reporting Standard applicable to the Micro-entities Regime* to support the implementation of the new micro-entities regime.

(ii)   The FRC's overriding objective in setting accounting standards is to enable users of accounts to receive high-quality understandable financial reporting proportionate to the size and complexity of the entity and users' information needs.

(iii) In meeting this objective, the FRC aims to provide succinct financial reporting standards that:

    (a)   have consistency with international accounting standards through the application of an IFRS-based solution unless an alternative clearly better meets the overriding objective;

    (b)   reflect up-to-date thinking and developments in the way entities operate and the transactions they undertake;

    (c)   balance consistent principles for accounting by all UK and Republic of Ireland entities with practical solutions, based on size, complexity, public interest and users' information needs;

    (d)   promote efficiency within groups; and

    (e)   are cost-effective to apply.

(iv)   The requirements in this Financial Reporting Standard (FRS) take into consideration the findings from all relevant consultations.

(v)   This FRS sets out the financial reporting requirements for UK and Republic of Ireland entities. Financial statements (whether consolidated financial statements or individual financial statements) that are within the scope of this FRS must be prepared in accordance with the following requirements:

    (a)   If the financial statements are those of an entity that is eligible to apply FRS 105, they may be prepared in accordance with that standard.

    (b)   If the financial statements are those of an entity that is not eligible to apply FRS 105, or of an entity that is eligible to apply FRS 105 but chooses not to do so, they must be prepared in accordance with FRS 102, EU-adopted IFRS or, if the financial statements are the individual financial statements of a qualifying entity, FRS 101[1].

(vi)   FRS 101 sets out a reduced disclosure framework which addresses the financial reporting requirements and disclosure exemptions for the individual financial statements of subsidiaries and ultimate parents that otherwise apply the recognition, measurement and disclosure requirements of EU-adopted IFRS.

---

[1] *Under company law in the Republic of Ireland, certain entities are permitted to prepare 'Companies Act accounts' using a financial reporting framework based on accounting standards other than those issued by the FRC.*

FRS 102 is a single financial reporting standard that applies to the financial statements of **(vii)**
entities that are not applying EU-adopted IFRS, FRS 101 or the FRSSE.

FRS 105 sets out the financial reporting requirements for micro-entities, as defined by **(viii)**
company law, choosing to apply the micro-entities regime.

This edition of FRS 100 issued in September 2015 updates the edition of FRS 100 issued **(ix)**
in November 2012 for the following:

(a)   the withdrawal of FRS 27 *Life Assurance* (as set out in FRS 103 *Insurance Contracts*
       issued in March 2014);
(b)   consequential amendments to FRS 102 included in FRS 104 *Interim Financial
       Reporting* issued in March 2015;
(c)   *Amendments to FRS 100* issued in July 2015;
(d)   an editorial amendment to paragraph A2.19 to include a reference to the Strategic
       Report; and
(e)   some minor typographical or presentational corrections.

FRS 100 APPLICATION OF FINANCIAL REPORTING REQUIREMENTS

Objective

1   The objective of this Financial Reporting Standard (FRS) is to set out the applicable financial reporting framework for entities preparing financial statements in accordance with legislation, regulations or accounting standards applicable in the United Kingdom and Republic of Ireland.

Scope

2   This FRS applies to financial statements that are intended to give a true and fair view of the assets, liabilities, financial position and profit or loss for a period.

Abbreviations and definitions

3   The terms **Accounting Directive, Act, date of transition, EU-adopted IFRS, financial institution, FRS 100, FRS 101, FRS 102, FRS 105, IAS Regulation, IFRS, individual financial statements, public benefit entity, qualifying entity, small entity** and **SORP** are defined in the glossary included as Appendix I to this FRS.

Basis of preparation of financial statements

4   Financial statements (whether consolidated financial statements or individual financial statements) that are within the scope of this FRS, and that are not required by the IAS Regulation or other legislation or regulation to be prepared in accordance with EU-adopted IFRS, must be prepared in accordance with the following requirements:

   (a)   If the financial statements are those of an entity that is eligible to apply FRS 105[2], they may be prepared in accordance with that standard;

   (b)   If the financial statements are those of an entity that is not eligible to apply FRS 105, or of an entity that is eligible to apply FRS 105 but chooses not to do so, they must[3] be prepared in accordance with FRS 102, EU-adopted IFRS[4] or, if the financial statements are the individual financial statements of a qualifying entity, FRS 101.[5]

Application of statements of recommended practice (SORPs)

5   If an entity's financial statements are prepared in accordance with FRS 102 SORPs will apply in the circumstances set out in that FRS.

---

[2] *The eligibility criteria for applying FRS 105 are set out in legislation and FRS 105. In establishing whether the eligibility criteria have been met turnover and balance sheet total shall be measured in accordance with FRS 105; the measurement of turnover and balance sheet total in accordance with FRS 101 or FRS 102 need not be considered.*

[3] *Under company law in the Republic of Ireland, certain entities are permitted to prepare 'Companies Act accounts' using a financial reporting framework based on accounting standards other than those issued by the FRC.*

[4] *Some entities are prohibited from applying EU-adopted IFRS, for example section 395(2) of the Act states that 'the individual accounts of a company that is a charity must be Companies Act individual accounts', and section 403(3) of the Act mirrors this for the group accounts of a parent company that is a charity.*

[5] *Individual accounts that are prepared by a company in accordance with FRS 101, FRS 102 or FRS 105 are Companies Act individual accounts (section 395(1)(a) of the Act), whereas individual accounts that are prepared by a company in accordance with EU-adopted IFRS are IAS individual accounts (section 395(1)(b) of the Act).*

When a SORP applies, an entity, other than a small entity applying the small entities **6**
regime in FRS 102, shall state in its financial statements the title of the SORP and whether
its financial statements have been prepared in accordance with the SORP's provisions that
are currently in effect[6]. In the event of a departure from those provisions, the entity shall
give a brief description of how the financial statements depart from the recommended
practice set out in the SORP, which shall include:

(a) for any treatment that is not in accordance with the SORP, the reasons why the
     treatment adopted is judged more appropriate to the entity's particular circumstances;
     and

(b) brief details of any disclosures recommended by the SORP that have not been
     provided, and the reasons why they have not been provided.

A small entity applying the small entities regime in FRS 102 is encouraged to provide
these disclosures.

SORPs recommend particular accounting treatments and disclosures with the aim of **7**
narrowing areas of difference and variety between comparable entities. Compliance
with a SORP that has been generally accepted by an industry or sector leads to enhanced
comparability between the financial statements of entities in that industry or sector.
Comparability is further enhanced if users are made aware of the extent to which an entity
complies with a SORP, and the reasons for any departures. The effect of a departure from
a SORP need not be quantified, except in those rare cases where such quantification is
necessary for the entity's financial statements to give a true and fair view.

Entities whose financial statements do not fall within the scope of a SORP may, if the **8**
SORP is otherwise relevant to them, nevertheless choose to comply with the SORP's
recommendations when preparing financial statements, provided that the SORP does not
conflict with the requirements of the framework adopted. Where this is the case, entities
are encouraged to disclose that fact.

Statement of compliance

Where an entity prepares its financial statements in accordance with FRS 101 or FRS 102, **9**
it shall include a statement of compliance in the notes to the financial statements in
accordance with the requirements set out in the relevant standard unless it is a small entity
applying the small entities regime in FRS 102, in which case it is encouraged to include a
statement of compliance in the notes to the financial statements.

Date from which effective and transitional arrangements

An entity shall apply this FRS for accounting periods beginning on or after 1 January 2016. **10**
Early application of this FRS is permitted, providing an entity also applies the edition of
FRS 101, FRS 102 and FRS 105 effective for accounting periods beginning on or after
1 January 2016 and is subject to the early application provisions set out in those standards.
An entity choosing not to apply these amendments to accounting periods beginning before
1 January 2016 shall not adopt the associated amendments made to FRS 101, FRS 102 nor
FRS 105 to accounting periods beginning before 1 January 2016. If an entity applies this
FRS before 1 January 2016 it shall disclose that fact, unless the entity is a micro-entity or
a small entity. A small entity is encouraged to provide this disclosure.

On first-time application of this FRS, or when an entity changes the basis of preparation of **11**
its financial statements within the requirements of this FRS, it shall apply the transitional
arrangements relevant to its circumstances as follows:

---

[6] *The provisions of a SORP will cease to have effect, for example, to the extent that they conflict with a more recent
financial reporting standard.*

(a)   An entity transitioning to EU-adopted IFRS shall apply the transitional arrangements set out in IFRS 1 *First-time Adoption of International Financial Reporting Standards* as adopted by the EU.

(b)   A qualifying entity transitioning to FRS 101 shall, unless it is applying EU-adopted IFRS prior to the date of transition (see paragraph 12), apply the requirements of paragraphs 6 to 33 of IFRS 1 as adopted by the EU including the relevant appendices except for the requirement of paragraphs 6 and 21 to present an opening statement of financial position at the date of transition; references to IFRSs in IFRS 1 are interpreted to mean EU-adopted IFRS as amended in accordance with paragraph 5(b) of FRS 101.

(c)   An entity transitioning to FRS 102 shall apply the transitional arrangements set out in that standard.

(d)   An entity transitioning to FRS 105 shall apply the transitional arrangements set out in FRS 105.

12   A qualifying entity applying EU-adopted IFRS prior to the date of transition to FRS 101 will then be preparing Companies Act individual accounts in accordance with section 395(1)(a) of the Act and thus will no longer be preparing IAS individual accounts in accordance with section 395(1)(b) of the Act.[7] It shall consider whether amendments are required to comply with paragraph 5(b) of FRS 101, but it does not reapply the provisions of IFRS 1. Where amendments to the recognition, measurement and disclosure requirements of EU-adopted IFRS in accordance with paragraph 5(b) of FRS 101 are required, the entity shall determine whether the amendments have a material effect on the first financial statements presented. Where there is:

(a)   no material effect, the qualifying entity shall disclose that it has undergone transition to FRS 101 and a brief narrative of the disclosure exemptions adopted, for all periods presented; or

(b)   a material effect, the qualifying entity's first financial statements shall include:

(i)   a description of the nature of each material change in accounting policy;

(ii)   reconciliations of its equity determined in accordance with EU-adopted IFRS to its equity determined in accordance with FRS 101 for both the date of transition to FRS 101 and for the end of the latest period presented in the entity's most recent annual financial statements prepared in accordance with EU-adopted IFRS; and

(iii)   a reconciliation of the profit or loss determined in accordance with EU-adopted IFRS to its profit or loss determined in accordance with FRS 101 for the latest period presented in the entity's most recent annual financial statements prepared in accordance with EU-adopted IFRS.

13   Where paragraph 12(b) applies but it is impracticable to apply the amendments retrospectively, a qualifying entity shall apply the amendments to the earliest period for which it is practicable to do so, and it shall identify the data presented for prior periods that are not comparable with data for the period in which it prepares its first financial statements that conform with the reduced disclosure framework set out in FRS 101.

Withdrawal of current accounting standards

14   The following SSAPs, FRSs and UITF Abstracts are superseded on the early application of this FRS. These SSAPs, FRSs and UITF Abstracts will be withdrawn for accounting periods beginning on or after 1 January 2015.

---

[7] *Further relevant information can be found at paragraph A2.14 of Appendix II.*

SSAP 4	*Accounting for government grants;*
SSAP 5	*Accounting for value added tax;*
SSAP 9	*Stocks and long-term contracts;*
SSAP 13	*Accounting for research and development;*
SSAP 19	*Accounting for investment properties;*
SSAP 20	*Foreign currency translation;*
SSAP 21	*Accounting for leases and hire purchase contracts; including the Guidance Notes on SSAP 21;*
SSAP 25	*Segmental reporting;*
FRS 1	*Cash flow statements (revised 1996);*
FRS 2	*Accounting for subsidiary undertakings;*
FRS 3	*Reporting financial performance;*
FRS 4	*Capital instruments;*
FRS 5	*Reporting the substance of transactions;*
FRS 6	*Acquisitions and mergers;*
FRS 7	*Fair values in acquisition accounting;*
FRS 8	*Related party disclosures;*
FRS 9	*Associates and joint ventures;*
FRS 10	*Goodwill and intangible assets;*
FRS 11	*Impairment of fixed assets and goodwill;*
FRS 12	*Provisions, contingent liabilities and contingent assets;*
FRS 13	*Derivatives and other financial instruments: disclosures;*
FRS 15	*Tangible fixed assets;*
FRS 16	*Current tax;*
FRS 17	*Retirement benefits;*
FRS 18	*Accounting policies;*
FRS 19	*Deferred tax;*
FRS 20 (IFRS 2)	*Share-based payment;*
FRS 21 (IAS 10)	*Events after the balance sheet date;*
FRS 22 (IAS 33)	*Earnings per share;*
FRS 23 (IAS 21)	*The effects of changes in foreign exchange rates;*
FRS 24 (IAS 29)	*Financial reporting in hyperinflationary economies;*
FRS 25 (IAS 32)	*Financial instruments: Presentation;*
FRS 26 (IAS 39)	*Financial instruments: Recognition and Measurement;*
FRS 27	*Life Assurance;*
FRS 28	*Corresponding amounts;*
FRS 29 (IFRS 7)	*Financial instruments: Disclosures;*
FRS 30	*Heritage assets;*
UITF Abstract 4:	*Presentation of long-term debtors in current assets;*
UITF Abstract 5:	*Transfers from current assets to fixed assets;*
UITF Abstract 9:	*Accounting for operations in hyper-inflationary economies;*
UITF Abstract 11:	*Capital instruments: Issuer call options;*
UITF Abstract 15:	*Disclosure of substantial acquisitions (Revised 1999);*
UITF Abstract 19:	*Tax on gains and losses on foreign currency borrowings that hedge an investment in a foreign enterprise;*
UITF Abstract 21:	*Accounting issues arising from the proposed introduction of the euro;*
UITF Abstract 22:	*The acquisition of a Lloyd's business;*
UITF Abstract 23:	*Application of the transitional rules in FRS 15;*
UITF Abstract 24:	*Accounting for start-up costs;*
UITF Abstract 25:	*National Insurance contributions on share option gains;*
UITF Abstract 26:	*Barter transactions for advertising;*
UITF Abstract 27:	*Revision to estimates of the useful economic life of goodwill and intangible assets;*
UITF Abstract 28:	*Operating lease incentives;*

UITF Abstract 29:	*Website development costs;*
UITF Abstract 31:	*Exchanges of businesses or other non-monetary assets for an interest in a subsidiary, joint venture or associate;*
UITF Abstract 32:	*Employee benefit trusts and other intermediate payment arrangements;*
UITF Abstract 34:	*Pre-contract costs;*
UITF Abstract 35:	*Death-in-service and incapacity benefits;*
UITF Abstract 36:	*Contracts for sales of capacity;*
UITF Abstract 38:	*Accounting for ESOP trusts;*
UITF Abstract 39:	*(IFRIC Interpretation 2) Members' shares in co-operative entities and similar instruments;*
UITF Abstract 40:	*Revenue recognition and service contracts;*
UITF Abstract 41:	*(IFRIC Interpretation 8) Scope of FRS 20 (IFRS 2);*
UITF Abstract 42:	*(IFRIC Interpretation 9) Reassessment of embedded derivatives;*
UITF Abstract 43:	*The interpretation of equivalence for the purposes of section 228A of the Companies Act 1985;*
UITF Abstract 44:	*(IFRIC Interpretation 11) FRS 20 (IFRS 2) Group and Treasury Share Transactions;*
UITF Abstract 45:	*(IFRIC Interpretation 6) Liabilities arising from participating in a specific market – Waste electrical and electronic equipment;*
UITF Abstract 46:	*(IFRIC Interpretation 16) Hedges of a net investment in a foreign operation;*
UITF Abstract 47:	*(IFRIC Interpretation 19) Extinguishing financial liabilities with equity instruments;* and
UITF Abstract 48:	*Accounting implications of the replacement of the retail prices index with the consumer prices index for retirement benefits.*

15   The following statements are also withdrawn:

Statement of Principles for Financial Reporting;
Statement of Principles for Financial Reporting – Interpretation for public benefit entities;
Reporting Statement: Retirement Benefits – Disclosures;
Reporting Statement: Preliminary announcements; and
Reporting Statement: Half-yearly financial reports.

15A   The *Financial Reporting Standard for Smaller Entities* (effective January 2015) (FRSSE) is superseded on the early application of the amendments set out in *Amendments to FRS 100* (and the related amendments to other accounting standards, particularly FRS 102 and FRS 105) issued in July 2015 and the early application of *The Companies, Partnerships and Groups (Accounts and Reports) Regulations 2015* (SI 2015/980) and is withdrawn for accounting periods beginning on or after 1 January 2016.

APPLICATION GUIDANCE: THE INTERPRETATION OF EQUIVALENCE

This application guidance forms an integral part of FRS 100

Introduction

Section 401 of the Act exempts, subject to certain conditions, an intermediate parent from the requirement to prepare consolidated financial statements where its parent is not established under the law of an EEA state. The exemption is conditional on the company and all of its subsidiaries being included in consolidated financial statements for a larger group drawn up to the same date, or an earlier date in the same financial year, and those financial statements must be drawn up: **AG1**

(a) in accordance with, or in a manner that is equivalent to, the Accounting Directive (Section 401(2)(b)(i) and (ii));

(b) in accordance with EU-adopted IFRS (Section 401(2)(b)(iii)); or

(c) in accordance with accounting standards which are equivalent to EU-adopted IFRS, as determined in accordance with the EU mechanism (see paragraph AG7) (Section 401(2)(b)(iv)).

FRS 101 and FRS 102 permit certain exemptions from disclosures, but those exemptions are in some cases subject to **equivalent** disclosures being included in the consolidated financial statements of the group in which the entity is consolidated.   **AG2**

This Application Guidance provides guidance on interpreting the meaning of equivalence in the two circumstances set out above.   **AG3**

Section 401 of the Companies Act 2006

Use of the exemption in section 401(2)(b)(ii) requires an analysis of a particular set of consolidated financial statements to determine whether they are drawn up in a manner equivalent to consolidated financial statements that are drawn up in accordance with the Accounting Directive. This Application Guidance aims to assist entities in adopting a consistent approach to this issue. In the absence of this guidance, companies and their auditors might feel obliged to take an overly cautious approach in response to uncertainty about whether the exemptions can be used.   **AG4**

It is generally accepted that the reference to equivalence in section 401(2)(b)(ii) of the Act does not mean compliance with every detail of the Accounting Directive. When assessing whether consolidated financial statements of a higher non-EEA parent are drawn up in a manner equivalent to consolidated financial statements drawn up in accordance with the Accounting Directive, it is necessary to consider whether they meet the basic requirements of the Accounting Directive; in particular the requirement to give a true and fair view, without implying strict conformity with each and every provision. A qualitative approach is more in keeping with the deregulatory nature of the exemption than a requirement to consider the detailed requirements on a checklist basis.   **AG5**

The consequences of the exemptions in section 401(2)(b) and adopting the principle in paragraph AG5 in relation to section 401(2)(b)(ii) are that consolidated financial statements of the higher parent will meet the exemption or the test of equivalence in the Accounting Directive if they are intended to give a true and fair view and: **AG6**

(a) are prepared in accordance with FRS 102;

(b) are prepared in accordance with EU-adopted IFRS;

(c)   are prepared in accordance with IFRS, subject to the consideration of the reasons for any failure by the European Commission to adopt a standard or interpretation; or

(d)   are prepared using other GAAPs which are closely related to IFRS, subject to consideration of the effect of any differences from EU-adopted IFRS.

Consolidated financial statements of the higher parent prepared using other GAAPs or the IFRS for SMEs should be assessed for equivalence with the Accounting Directive based on the particular facts, including the similarities to and differences from the Accounting Directive.

AG7   A mechanism to determine the equivalence of the Generally Accepted Accounting Principles (GAAP) from third countries was established in 2007. Subsequently, the European Commission has identified as equivalent to IFRS the following:

GAAP	Applicable from
GAAP of Japan	1 January 2009
GAAP of the United States of America	1 January 2009
GAAP of the People's Republic of China	1 January 2012
GAAP of Canada	1 January 2012
GAAP of the Republic of Korea	1 January 2012

Further, third country issuers shall be permitted to prepare their annual consolidated financial statements and half-yearly consolidated financial statements in accordance with the Generally Accepted Accounting Principles of the Republic of India for financial years starting before 1 January 2015. For reporting periods beginning on or after 1 January 2015, in relation to GAAP of the Republic of India, equivalence should be assessed on the basis of the particular facts.

Equivalent disclosures are included in the consolidated financial statements of the group

AG8   In deciding whether the consolidated financial statements of the parent provide disclosures which are equivalent to the requirements of EU-adopted IFRS or FRS 102, from which relief is provided in paragraphs 8 to 9 of FRS 101 and paragraphs 1.12 to 1.13 of FRS 102 respectively, it is necessary to consider whether the consolidated financial statements of the parent provide disclosures that meet the basic disclosure requirements of the relevant standard or interpretation issued (or adopted) by the relevant standard setter, without requiring strict conformity with each and every disclosure. This assessment should be based on the particular facts, including the similarities to and differences from the requirements of the relevant standard from which relief is provided.

AG9   The concept of 'equivalence' described in paragraph AG8 is intended to be aligned to that described for section 401 of the Act.

AG10   Disclosure exemptions for subsidiaries are permitted where the relevant disclosure requirements are met in the consolidated financial statements, even where the disclosures are made in aggregate or in an abbreviated form, or in relation to intra-group balances, those intra-group balances have been eliminated on consolidation. If, however, no disclosure is made in the consolidated financial statements on the grounds of materiality, the relevant disclosures should be made at the subsidiary level if material in those financial statements.

APPROVAL BY THE FRC

Financial Reporting Standard 100 *Application of Financial Reporting Requirements* was approved for issue by the Board of the Financial Reporting Council on 1 November 2012, following its consideration of the Accounting Council's advice for this FRS.

Amendments to FRS 100 Application of Financial Reporting Requirements was approved for issue by the Board of the Financial Reporting Council on 1 July 2015, following its consideration of the Accounting Council's Advice.

THE ACCOUNTING COUNCIL'S ADVICE TO THE FRC TO ISSUE FRS 100

Introduction

1   This report provides an overview of the main issues which have been considered by the Accounting Council in advising the Financial Reporting Council (FRC) to issue FRS 100 *Application of Financial Reporting Requirements*. The FRC, in accordance with the *Statutory Instrument Statutory Auditors (Amendment of Companies Act 2006 and Delegation of Functions etc) Order 2012* (SI 2012/1741), is the prescribed body for issuing accounting standards in the UK. *The Foreword to Accounting Standards* sets out the application of accounting standards in the Republic of Ireland.

2   In accordance with *FRC Codes and Standards: procedures*, any proposal to issue, amend or withdraw a code or standard is put to the FRC with the full advice of the relevant Councils and/or the Codes & Standards Committee. Ordinarily, the FRC will only reject the advice put to it where:

● it is apparent that a significant group of stakeholders has not been adequately consulted;
● the necessary assessment of the impact of the proposal has not been completed, including an analysis of costs and benefits;
● insufficient consideration has been given to the timing or cost of implementation; or
● the cumulative impact of a number of proposals would make the adoption of an otherwise satisfactory proposal inappropriate.

3   The FRC has established the Accounting Council as the relevant Council to assist it in the setting of accounting standards.

Advice

4   The Accounting Council is advising the FRC to issue:

FRS 100 *Application of Financial Reporting Requirements*; and
FRS 101 *Reduced Disclosure Framework*.

5   FRS 102 *The Financial Reporting Standard Applicable in the UK and Republic of Ireland* completes the new suite of financial reporting standards. The Accounting Council will provide its advice to the FRC on FRS 102 in that standard.

Background

6   Accounting standards were formerly developed by the Accounting Standards Board (ASB). The ASB commenced its project to update accounting standards in 2002; Appendix III provides a history of the previous consultations and a summary of how the overall proposals have developed.[8]

7   The ASB (and subsequently the Accounting Council) gave careful consideration to the project's objective and intended effects during its consultations on updating accounting standards. In developing the requirements in this FRS, FRS 101 and FRS 102, the overriding objective is:

To enable users of accounts to receive high-quality understandable financial reporting proportionate to the size and complexity of the entity and users' information needs.

---

[8] *References in this section and Appendix III are made to the FRC, ASB or Accounting Council, as appropriate in terms of the time period and context of the reference.*

In achieving this objective, the ASB decided (and the Accounting Council subsequently   **8**
agreed) that it should provide succinct financial reporting standards that:

- have consistency with global accounting standards through the application of an IFRS-
  based solution unless an alternative clearly better meets the overriding objective;
- reflect up-to-date thinking and developments in the way businesses operate and the
  transactions they undertake;
- balance consistent principles for accounting by all UK and Republic of Ireland
  entities with practical solutions, based on size, complexity, public interest and users'
  information needs;
- promote efficiency within groups; and
- are cost-effective to apply.

The requirements in this FRS were principally consulted on in two exposure drafts; FRED 43   **9**
Application of Financial Reporting Requirements issued in October 2010, and FRED 46
Application of Financial Reporting Requirements (revised) issued in January 2012.

A differential financial reporting system and the elimination of 'public accountability'

In the early stages of developing this FRS, the ASB consulted on whether to introduce   **10**
a differential financial reporting system. A differential system requires an entity
to apply specified accounting standards as prescribed based on the size, nature or
other differentiating feature of the entity. FRED 43 set out proposals for a differential
financial reporting system based on three tiers of entities using public accountability and
size as differentiators. The proposals in FRED 43 would have extended the application
of EU-adopted IFRS to those entities with public accountability[9]. Whilst there was some
support for a differential financial reporting system, entities that would be required to
apply EU-adopted IFRS did not support the proposal, principally on the basis of costs and
benefits.

The ASB gave careful consideration to the concerns raised and concluded that public   **11**
accountability (and therefore the differential financial reporting system) could be
eliminated if it were to extend the proposals by including additional requirements
in FRED 44 *Financial Reporting Standard for Medium-sized Entities* for entities with
publicly traded debt or equity, and for financial institutions, so that the proposals in that
FRED applied to a broader group of entities. FRED 44 proposed to replace the majority
of extant financial reporting standards with a single standard based on the International
Financial Reporting Standard for Small and Medium-sized Entities (IFRS for SMEs). As
a consequence, FRED 44 was revised and FRED 48 issued, which addressed a broader
group of entities including those previously considered to have public accountability,
single entities listed on a regulated market, entities listed on a non-regulated market and
additional disclosure requirements for financial instruments held by financial institutions.

Respondents to FRED 46 supported the removal of the public accountability criteria   **12**
and the Accounting Council agreed to advise the FRC not to extend the application of
EU-adopted IFRS beyond that already required by company law or other legislation or
regulation.

---

[9] *FRED 43 defined an entity as having public accountability if:*
(a) as at the reporting date, its debt or equity instruments are traded in a public market or it is in the process of issuing such instruments for trading in a public market (a domestic or foreign stock exchange or an over-the-counter market, including local and regional markets); or
(b) as one of its primary businesses, it holds assets in a fiduciary capacity for a broad group of outsiders and/or it is a deposit taking entity for a broad group of outsiders. This is typically the case for banks, credit unions, insurance companies, securities brokers/dealers, mutual funds or investment banks.

13   Once this FRS becomes effective, there will be five FRSs applicable in the UK and
     Republic of Ireland:

     ● FRS 100 *Application of Financial Reporting Requirements;*
     ● FRS 101 *Reduced Disclosure Framework;*
     ● FRS 102 *The Financial Reporting Standard applicable in the UK and Republic of
       Ireland;*
     ● *Financial Reporting Standard for Smaller Entities* (effective January 2015) (the
       FRSSE); and
     ● FRS 27 *Life assurance.*[10]

FRS 101 Reduced disclosure framework

14   FRS 101 was developed in response to concerns that arose from earlier consultations
     (see Appendix III). Respondents to those consultations (and particularly the 2009 Policy
     Proposal) noted that a move to the IFRS for SMEs for subsidiaries of entities that apply
     EU-adopted IFRS would require recognition and measurement differences to be monitored
     and maintained at group level, and yet the alternative of a move to EU-adopted IFRS would
     increase disclosure in comparison to current accounting standards. The ASB therefore
     developed a reduced disclosure framework to address these concerns.

15   Further details regarding the development of FRS 101 are located in the Accounting
     Council's Advice to the FRC accompanying that FRS.

FRS 102 The Financial Reporting Standard applicable in the UK and Republic of Ireland

16   FRS 102 will replace the majority of current accounting standards applicable in the UK
     and Republic of Ireland with a single FRS based on the IFRS for SMEs. Details of the
     development of FRS 102 will be set out in the Accounting Council's Advice to the FRC
     accompanying that FRS. One member of the Accounting Council considers that the level
     of input from users does not constitute adequate consultation, despite extensive efforts at
     outreach, and holds an alternative view on aspects of the Accounting Council's expected
     advice on FRS 102.

The Financial Reporting Standard for Smaller Entities (FRSSE)

17   The Accounting Council advises the FRC (consistent with FREDs 43 and 46) to retain the
     FRSSE for a period following the application of FRS 102, with a view to consulting again
     on the FRSSE's future in the short to medium term.

18   The eligibility criteria for applying the FRSSE are set out in paragraph 8 of the FRSSE.
     One of the criteria is that the entity must be 'small' as defined in company law. Turnover
     and balance sheet total should be measured in accordance with the FRSSE for the purposes
     of establishing whether the entity is 'small'; the measurement of turnover and balance
     sheet total in accordance with FRS 101 or FRS 102 need not be considered.

19   The Accounting Council also advises the FRC to undertake further consultation to address
     the implications for the FRSSE of:

     (a)   the European Commission proposals arising from its review of the EU Accounting
           Directives (an initial proposed Directive was issued in October 2011); and
     (b)   the Directive on annual accounts of micro-entities that was approved by the European
           Council in February 2012.

---

[10] *At the time of approving this advice consideration is being given to updating FRS 27.*

The amendments to the FRSSE set out in this FRS arise as a consequence of withdrawing **20** current accounting standards.

Statements of Recommended Practice (SORPs)

In its 2009 Policy Proposal, the ASB's recommendation was to remove almost all of the **21** SORPs. Respondents to the Policy Proposal questioned this and many noted that SORPs contribute to improving the quality of financial reporting in the UK. Instead FRED 43 proposed to streamline the number of SORPs in existence. Respondents to FRED 43 were supportive of this revised proposal. The decision, however, to eliminate the definition of public accountability and thereby broaden the scope of entities eligible to apply FRS 102 had a consequential impact on the SORPs (for example, pension funds would no longer be required to apply EU-adopted IFRS), so the ASB amended its proposals again in FRED 48.

The proposals in FRED 48 received support and the Accounting Council is now advising **22** the FRC that they be taken forward, as follows:

SORP	Accounting Council Advice
Accounting for insurance business	A separate consultation will be undertaken on accounting for insurance
Accounting for oil & gas	The SORP-making body has indicated that they do not believe that it would make sense to update the 2001 SORP
Authorised funds	Update to be based on FRS 102
Banking segments	Withdraw
Charities	Update to be based on FRS 102
Financial reports of pension funds	Update for consistency with FRS 102 to supplement Section 34 of FRS 102
Further and higher education	Update to be based on FRS 102
Investment companies	Update to be based on FRS 102
Leasing	Withdraw
Limited liability partnerships	Update to be based on FRS 102
Registered social housing providers	Update to be based on FRS 102

In response to a request for clarification as to the role of the SORPs, the Accounting **23** Council is advising the FRC that a reference to the application of SORPs be included in this FRS and in Section 10 *Accounting policies, estimates and errors* of FRS 102, to note that they are a source of guidance on accounting policies.

Clarification of equivalence

FRS 101 and FRS 102 permit certain exemptions from disclosures, which are in some cases **24** subject to equivalent disclosures being included in the consolidated financial statements of the group in which the entity is consolidated. Clarification on interpreting the meaning of the term equivalence is included in Application Guidance I of this FRS.

Withdrawn publications

25   Paragraph 14 of this FRS sets out the withdrawal of current accounting standards. For the avoidance of doubt, the Accounting Council (and FRC) will also not proceed with developing the following superseded Financial Reporting Exposure Drafts (FREDs):

> Leases: Implementation of a new approach
> IASB Exposure draft of a proposed IFRS for small and medium-sized entities (Issued April 2007)
> FRED 22 *Revision of FRS 3 Reporting financial performance*
> FRED 28 *Inventories: Construction and service contracts*
> FRED 29 *Property, plant and equipment: Borrowing costs*
> FRED 32 *Disposal of non-current assets and presentation of discontinued operations*
> FRED 36 *Business combinations*
> FRED 37 *Intangible assets (IAS 38) and FRED 38 Impairment of assets (IAS 36)*
> FRED 39 *Amendments to FRS 12 Provisions, contingent liabilities and contingent assets and FRS 17 Retirement benefits*
> FRED 43 *Application of Financial Reporting Requirements*
> FRED 44 *The Financial Reporting Standards for Medium-sized Entities*
> FRED 45 *The Financial Reporting Standard for Public Benefit Entities*

Effective date and early application

26   In reassessing the effective date as proposed in FREDs 46 to 48, the Accounting Council supports the previous view of the ASB that application should be deferred to January 2015 for the following reasons:

(a)   although the revisions to the ASB's original proposals should ease the transition, an 18 month period between the publication of the final standard and effective date should be retained as there are significant changes to the accounting requirements for financial instruments; and

(b)   the effective date should take into consideration the process of updating the SORPs.

27   This decision was reassessed by the Accounting Council when it considered the responses to FREDs 46 to 48. It decided that it was not necessary to have the same early application provisions for FRS 101, FRS 102 and the FRSSE (effective January 2015) and that specific requirements relating to early application should be set out separately in each standard.

Approval of this advice

28   This advice to the FRC was approved by the nine members of the Accounting Council on 25 October 2012. The Accounting Council is comprised of the following members:

Roger Marshall   (Chair of the Accounting Council)
Nick Anderson
Dr Richard Barker
Edward Beale
Peter Elwin
Ken Lever
Robert Overend
Andy Simmonds
Pauline Wallace

THE ACCOUNTING COUNCIL'S ADVICE TO THE FRC TO ISSUE AMENDMENTS TO FRS 100

Introduction

This report provides an overview of the main issues that have been considered by the **1** Accounting Council in advising the Financial Reporting Council (FRC) to issue *Amendments to FRS 100 Application of Financial Reporting Requirements* incorporating the Council's advice following the Consultation Document *Accounting standards for small entities – Implementation of the EU Accounting Directive* and FRED 60 *Draft amendments to FRS 100 and FRS 101*.

The FRC, in accordance with the *Statutory Auditors (Amendment of Companies Act 2006* **2** *and Delegation of Functions etc) Order 2012* (SI 2012/1741), is a prescribed body for issuing accounting standards in the UK. The *Foreword to Accounting Standards* sets out the application of accounting standards in the Republic of Ireland.

In accordance with the *FRC Codes and Standards: procedures*, any proposal to issue, **3** amend or withdraw a code or standard is put to the FRC Board with the full advice of the relevant Councils and/or the Codes & Standards Committee. Ordinarily, the FRC Board will only reject the advice put to it where:

(a) it is apparent that a significant group of stakeholders has not been adequately consulted;
(b) the necessary assessment of the impact of the proposal has not been completed, including an analysis of costs and benefits;
(c) insufficient consideration has been given to the timing or cost of implementation; or
(d) the cumulative impact of a number of proposals would make the adoption of an otherwise satisfactory proposal inappropriate.

The FRC has established the Accounting Council as the relevant Council to assist it in the **4** setting of accounting standards.

Advice

The Accounting Council is advising the FRC to issue *Amendments to FRS 100 Application* **5** *of Financial Reporting Requirements*.

The Accounting Council advises that these proposals will update the framework of **6** accounting standards and maintain consistency of accounting standards with company law.

The Accounting Council's Advice to the FRC to issue FRS 100 *Application of Financial* **7** *Reporting Requirements* was set out in the standard. The Accounting Council's Advice to the FRC in respect of these amendments will be included in the revised FRS 100.

Background

The new EU Accounting Directive (Directive 2013/34/EU of the European Parliament and **8** of the Council of 26 June 2013) is being implemented in the UK and Republic of Ireland. In doing so there are changes to company law to reflect new requirements and, where considered appropriate, to take advantage of new options that are available. Accounting standards are developed within the context of company law and amendments are also required to accounting standards.

9   In September 2014, the FRC issued a Consultation Document *Accounting standards for small entities – Implementation of the EU Accounting Directive*[11] (the Consultation Document), outlining its proposal that the *Financial Reporting Standard for Smaller Entities* (FRSSE) would be withdrawn. A small number of amendments to FRS 100 would also be necessary to maintain consistency with company law. The Accounting Council considered the responses to the Consultation Document in developing FRED 60 *Draft amendments to FRS 100 and FRS 101*. It has also considered the responses to FRED 60, which was issued in February 2015, in developing its advice on these amendments.

Objective

10   In developing its advice to the FRC, the Accounting Council was guided by the overriding objective to enable users of accounts to receive high-quality understandable financial reporting proportionate to the size and complexity of the entity and users' information needs.

11   In meeting this objective, the FRC aims to provide succinct financial reporting standards that:

(a)   have consistency with international accounting standards through the application of an IFRS-based solution unless an alternative clearly better meets the overriding objective;

(b)   reflect up-to-date thinking and developments in the way entities operate and the transactions they undertake;

(c)   balance consistent principles for accounting by all UK and Republic of Ireland entities with practical solutions, based on size, complexity, public interest and users' information needs;

(d)   promote efficiency within groups; and

(e)   are cost-effective to apply.

Small entities regime

12   In the Consultation Document and FRED 60 the FRC proposed that the FRSSE should be withdrawn and that it should be replaced with:

(a)   a new standard for micro-entities, FRS 105 *The Financial Reporting Standard applicable to the Micro-entities Regime*; and

(b)   for small entities ineligible for or choosing not to apply the micro-entities regime, it should be replaced with a new Section 1A *Small Entities* within FRS 102.

This proposal was supported by respondents and the Accounting Council advises that the FRSSE is withdrawn, with consequential amendments made to FRS 100 *Application of Financial Reporting Requirements* to set out the revised framework.

Other minor amendments

13   The Accounting Council advises that other minor amendments are made to FRS 100 for compliance with company law. This principally relates to the *Application Guidance: The Interpretation of Equivalence*.

14   One respondent to FRED 60 requested clarification relating to the meaning of equivalent disclosures included in the consolidated financial statements in relation to intra-group balances eliminated on consolidation. The Accounting Council agreed that this could

[11] *Available on the FRC website (www.frc.org.uk).*

usefully be clarified whilst amendments were being made to the *Application Guidance: The Interpretation of Equivalence* and advises that it is made clear that, provided relevant disclosures have been made in the consolidated financial statements, the exemption is permitted when intra-group balances have been eliminated on consolidation. This is, of course, subject to any disclosures that are required by law.

Effective date

The Accounting Council advises that the amendments to FRS 100 arising from the implementation of the new Accounting Directive are effective for accounting periods beginning on or after 1 January 2016, with early application available providing an entity also applies the edition of FRS 101, FRS 102 or FRS 105 effective for accounting periods beginning on or after 1 January 2016 and subject to the early application provisions set out in those standards.

15

Approval of this Advice

This advice to the FRC was approved by the Accounting Council on 4 June 2015.

16

Appendix I
Glossary

Accounting Directive	Directive 2013/34/EU of the European Parliament and of the Council of 26 June 2013
Act	The Companies Act 2006
date of transition	The beginning of the earliest period for which an entity presents full comparative information under a given standard in its first financial statements that comply with that standard.
EU-adopted IFRS	IFRS that have been adopted in the European Union in accordance with EU Regulation 1606/2002.
financial institution	Any of the following: (a) a bank which is: 　(i) a firm with a Part IV permission[12] which includes accepting deposits and: 　　(a) which is a credit institution; or 　　(b) whose Part IV permission includes a requirement that it complies with the rules in the General Prudential sourcebook and the Prudential sourcebook for Banks, Building Societies and Investment Firms relating to banks, but which is not a building society, a friendly society or a credit union; 　(ii) an EEA bank which is a full credit institution; (b) a building society which is defined in section 119(1) of the Building Societies Act 1986 as a building society incorporated (or deemed to be incorporated) under that act; (c) a credit union, being a body corporate registered under the Industrial and Provident Societies Act 1965 as a credit union in accordance with the Credit Unions Act 1979, which is an authorised person; (d) custodian bank, broker-dealer or stockbroker; (e) an entity that undertakes the business of effecting or carrying out insurance contracts, including general and life assurance entities; (f) an incorporated friendly society incorporated under the Friendly Societies Act 1992 or a registered friendly society registered under section 7(1)(a) of the Friendly Societies Act 1974 or any enactment which it replaced, including any registered branches; (g) an investment trust, Irish investment company, venture capital trust, mutual fund, exchange traded fund, unit trust, open-ended investment company (OEIC); (h) a retirement benefit plan; or 　(i) any other entity whose principal activity is to generate wealth or manage risk through financial instruments. This is intended to cover entities that have business activities similar to those listed above but are not specifically included in the list above. A parent entity whose sole activity is to hold investments in other group entities is not a financial institution.

---

[12] *As defined in section 40(4) of the Financial Services and Markets Act 2000 or references to equivalent provisions of any successor legislation.*

FRS 100	FRS 100 *Application of Financial Reporting Requirements*
FRS 101	FRS 101 *Reduced Disclosure Framework*
FRS 102	FRS 102 *The Financial Reporting Standard applicable in the UK and Republic of Ireland*
FRS 105	FRS 105 *The Financial Reporting Standard applicable to the Micro-entities Regime*
IAS Regulation	EU Regulation 1606/2002
IFRS	Standards and interpretations issued (or adopted) by the International Accounting Standards Board (IASB). They comprise: (a) International Financial Reporting Standards; (b) International Accounting Standards; and (c) Interpretations developed by the IFRS Interpretations Committee (the Interpretations Committee) or the former Standing Interpretations Committee (SIC).
individual financial statements	The accounts that are required to be prepared by an entity in accordance with the **Act** or relevant legislation, for example: (a) 'individual accounts', as set out in section 394 of the Act; (b) 'statement of accounts', as set out in section 132 of the Charities Act 2011; or (c) 'individual accounts', as set out in section 72A of the Building Societies Act 1986. Separate financial statements are included in the meaning of this term.
public benefit entity	An entity whose primary objective is to provide goods or services for the general public, community or social benefit and where any equity is provided with a view to supporting the entity's primary objectives rather than with a view to providing a financial return to equity providers, shareholders or members.
qualifying entity (for the purposes of FRS 100 and FRS 101)	A member of a group where the parent of that group prepares publicly available consolidated financial statements which are intended to give a true and fair view (of the assets, liabilities, financial position and profit or loss) and that member is included in the consolidation[13]. A charity may not be a qualifying entity.
small entity	(a) A company meeting the definition of a small company as set out in section 382 or 383 of the **Act** and not excluded from the small companies regime by section 384; (b) an LLP qualifying as small and not excluded from the small LLPs regime, as set out in LLP Regulations; or (c) any other entity that would have met the criteria in (a) had it been a company incorporated under company law.
Statement of Recommended Practice (SORP)	An extant Statement of Recommended Practice developed in accordance with *SORPs: Policy and Code of Practice*. SORPs recommend accounting practices for specialised industries or sectors. They supplement accounting standards and other legal and regulatory requirements in the light of the special factors prevailing or transactions undertaken in a particular industry or sector.

[13] *As set out in section 474(1) of the Act.*

Appendix II
Note on legal requirements

INTRODUCTION

A2.1   This appendix provides an overview of how the requirements in FRS 100 address United Kingdom company law requirements. It is therefore written from the perspective of a company to which the Companies Act 2006 applies[14]. Appendix IV discusses the Republic of Ireland legal references.

A2.2   Many entities that are not constituted as companies apply accounting standards promulgated by the FRC for the purposes of preparing financial statements that present a true and fair view. A brief consideration of the legal framework for some other entities can be found at A2.20 and A2.21. For those entities that are within the scope of a SORP, the relevant SORP may provide more details on the legal framework.

A2.3   References to the Act in this appendix are to the *Companies Act 2006*. References to the Regulations are to *The Large and Medium-sized Companies and Groups (Accounts and Reports) Regulations 2008* (SI 2008/410).

APPLICABLE ACCOUNTING FRAMEWORK

A2.4   Group accounts of certain parent entities (those with securities admitted for trading on a regulated market in an EU Member State) are required by Article 4 of EU Regulation 1606/2002 (IAS Regulation) to be prepared in accordance with EU-adopted IFRS.

A2.5   All other entities, except those that are eligible and choose to apply FRS 105 *The Financial Reporting Standard applicable to the Micro-entities Regime*, must apply either FRS 102 *The Financial Reporting Standard applicable in the UK and Republic of Ireland*, EU-adopted IFRS or, for financial statements that are the individual financial statements of a qualifying entity, FRS 101 *Reduced Disclosure Framework*[15].

A2.6   Section 395(1) of the Act states:

> A company's individual accounts may be prepared–
> (a)   in accordance with section 396 ('Companies Act individual accounts'), or
> (b)   in accordance with international accounting standards ('IAS individual accounts').

Section 403(2) of the Act states:

> The group accounts of other companies may be prepared–
> (a)   in accordance with section 404 ('Companies Act group accounts'), or
> (b)   in accordance with international accounting standards ('IAS group accounts').

A2.7   Accounts prepared in accordance with EU-adopted IFRS are therefore within the scope of the IAS Regulation. All other accounts are classified as either 'Companies Act individual accounts', including those of qualifying entities applying FRS 101, or 'Companies Act group accounts' and are therefore required to comply with the applicable provisions of Parts 15 and 16 of the Act and with the Regulations.

---

[14] *Some charities are also companies, and are therefore required to apply the requirements of both the Companies Act 2006 and the Charities Act 2011.*

[15] *Under company law in the Republic of Ireland, certain companies are permitted to prepare Companies Act accounts using a financial reporting framework based on accounting standards other than those issued by the FRC.*

Financial reporting by small entities

The Small Companies and Groups (Accounts and Directors' Report) Regulations 2008   **A2.8**
(SI 2008/409) set out the legal framework for both the micro-entities regime and the
small companies regime, with the eligibility criteria for both set out in Part 15 of the Act.
FRS 105 and FRS 102 contain notes on legal requirements applicable to these regimes.

[Deleted]   **A2.9**

[Deleted]   **A2.10**

[Deleted]   **A2.11**

[Deleted]   **A2.12**

Financial reporting by charitable companies

Section 395(2) of the Act states that 'the individual accounts of a company that is a charity   **A2.13**
must be Companies Act individual accounts', and section 403(3) of the Act mirrors this for
a parent company that is a charity.

Moving between IAS accounts and Companies Act accounts

Sections 395 and 403 of the Act restrict an entity's ability to move from preparing IAS   **A2.14**
individual accounts to preparing Companies Act individual accounts and from preparing
IAS group accounts to preparing Companies Act group accounts respectively. A company
or group is permitted to switch from IAS accounts to Companies Act accounts preparation:

(a)   if there is a 'relevant change in circumstance' (as defined in the Act); or
(b)   for financial years ending on or after 1 October 2012, for a reason other than a
      relevant change of circumstance, once in a five year period.[16]

For example, provided the condition in section 395(4A) is met, a subsidiary company   **A2.15**
which previously prepared IAS individual accounts is permitted to move to preparing
Companies Act individual accounts in applying FRS 101 or FRS 102, providing it is also
complying with other requirements of the Act, such as those relating to consistency of
financial reporting within groups

Consistency of financial reporting within groups

Section 407 of the Act requires that the directors of the parent company secure that   **A2.16**
individual accounts of a parent company and each of its subsidiaries[17] are prepared using
the same financial reporting framework, except to the extent that in the directors' opinion
there are good reasons for not doing so.

In addition, consistency is not required in the following situations:

(a)   when the parent company does not prepare consolidated accounts; or
(b)   when some subsidiaries are charities (consistency is not needed between the
      framework used for these and for other subsidiaries).

---

[16] *The Companies and Limited Liability Partnership (Accounts and Audit Exemptions and Change of Accounting Framework) Regulations 2012 (SI 2012/2301).*

[17] *This only applies to accounts of subsidiaries that are required to be prepared under Part 15 of the Act.*

Where the directors of a parent company prepare IAS group accounts and IAS individual accounts, there only has to be consistency across the individual financial statements of the subsidiaries.

A2.17   All companies, other than those which elect or are required to prepare IAS individual accounts in accordance with law, prepare Companies Act individual accounts.

APPLICABILITY OF UK COMPANY LAW TO ENTITIES PREPARING IAS ACCOUNTS

A2.18   Entities that prepare IAS accounts, either voluntarily or because they are required to do so by law, only need apply certain sections of the Act as it relates to financial reporting. They are not required to comply with Schedules 1 and 6 to the Regulations (for companies and groups), nor with Schedules 2 or 3 (for banks and insurance companies). Schedules 4, 5, 7 and 8 to the Regulations are, however, still applicable.

A2.19   The sections of parts 15 and 16 of the Act that contain financial reporting requirements applying to IAS accounts, as well as to Companies Act accounts, are as follows (in some cases the requirements only apply to companies meeting certain criteria):

Section 410A	*Off-balance sheet arrangements*;
Section 411	*Employee numbers and costs*;
Section 412	*Directors' benefits: Remuneration*;
Section 413	*Directors' benefits: Advances, credit and guarantees*;
Sections 414A to 414D	*Strategic Report*;
Sections 415 to 419	*Directors' Report*;
Sections 420 to 421	*Directors' Remuneration Report*; and
Section 494	*Services provided by auditor and associates and related remuneration.*

ENTITIES NOT SUBJECT TO COMPANY LAW

A2.20   Many entities that may apply FRS 102 are not companies, but are nevertheless required by their governing legislation or other regulation or requirement, to prepare financial statements that present a true and fair view of the financial performance and financial position of the reporting entity. However, the FRC sets accounting standards within the framework of the Act and therefore it is the company law requirements that the FRC primarily considered when developing FRS 102. Entities preparing financial statements within other legal frameworks will need to satisfy themselves that FRS 102 does not conflict with any relevant legal obligations.

A2.21   However, the FRC notes the following:

Legislation	Overview of requirements
Building Societies Act 1986	The annual accounts of a building society shall give a true and fair view of the income and expenditure for the year and the balance sheet shall give a true and fair view of the state of affairs of the society at the end of the financial year.
	Regulations make further requirements about the form and content of building society accounts, which do not appear inconsistent with the requirement of FRS 102.

Legislation	Overview of requirements
Charity law in England and Wales: Charities Act 2011 and regulations made thereunder	All charities are required to prepare accounts. The regulations require financial statements (other than cash-based receipts and payments accounts prepared by smaller charities) to present a true and fair view of the incoming resources, application of resources and the balance sheet, and to be prepared in accordance with the SORP. However company charities prepare their accounts in accordance with UK company law to give a 'true and fair view'. The Charities SORP (FRS 102) is compatible with the legal requirements, clarifying how they apply to accounting by charities applying FRS 102. UK Company law prohibits charities from preparing IAS accounts.
Charity law in Scotland: Charities and Trustee Investments Act (Scotland) 2005 and regulations made thereunder	All charities are required to prepare accounts. The regulations require financial statements (other than cash-based receipts and payments accounts prepared by smaller charities) to present a true and fair view of the incoming resources, application of resources and the balance sheet, and to be prepared in accordance with the SORP. These regulations apply equally to company charities.
Charity law in Northern Ireland: Charities Act (Northern Ireland) 2008	The Charities Act 2008 has yet to come fully into effect. The Act provides for all charities to prepare accounts. The Act provides for regulations concerning the financial statements. The financial statements other than cash-based receipts and payments accounts prepared by smaller charities are to present a true and fair view of the incoming resources, application of resources and the balance sheet. However company charities prepare their accounts in accordance with UK company law to give a 'true and fair view'.
Friendly and Industrial and Provident Societies Act 1968	Every Society shall prepare a revenue account and a balance sheet giving a true and fair view of the income and expenditure and state of affairs of the Society. FRS 102 does not appear to give rise to any legal conflicts for Societies. However, Societies often carry out activities that are regulated and may be required to comply with additional regulations on top of the legal requirements and accounting standards. Some Societies fall within the scope of SORPs, which reflect the requirements of FRS 102.
Friendly Societies Act 1992	Every society shall prepare a balance sheet and an income and expenditure account for each financial year giving a true and fair view of the affairs of the society and its income and expenditure for the year. The Regulations[18] make further requirements about the form and content of friendly society accounts, which do not appear inconsistent with the requirements of FRS 102.

[18] *The Friendly Societies (Accounts and Related Provisions) Regulations 1994 (as amended).*

Legislation	Overview of requirements
The Occupational Pension Schemes (Requirement to obtain Audited Accounts and a Statement from the Auditor) Regulations 1996	The accounts of pension funds within the scope of the regulations should show a true and fair view of the transactions during the year, assets held at the end of the year and liabilities of the scheme, other than those to pay pensions and benefits. FRS 102 includes retirement benefit plans as a specialised activity.

Appendix III
Previous consultations

HISTORY OF PREVIOUS CONSULTATIONS

The requirements in FRSs 100 to 102 are the outcome of a lengthy and extensive consultation. The FRC (and formerly the ASB) together with the Department for Business, Innovation and Skills have consulted on the future of accounting standards in the UK and Republic of Ireland (RoI) over a ten-year period.   **A3.1**

Table 1 – Consultations conducted

Year	Consultation
2002	DTI[19] consults on adoption of IAS Regulation
2004	Discussion Paper – Strategy for Convergence with IFRS
2005	Exposure Draft – Policy Statement: The Role of the ASB
2006	Public Meeting and Proposals for Comment
2006	Press Notice seeking views
2007	Consultation Paper – Proposed IFRS for SMEs
2009	Consultation Paper – Policy Proposal: The future of UK GAAP
2010	Request for Responses – Development of the Impact Assessment
2010	Financial Reporting Exposure Drafts 43 and 44
2011	Financial Reporting Exposure Draft 45
2012	Financial Reporting Exposure Drafts 46, 47 and 48

2004

In 2004 the Discussion Paper contained two key elements underpinning the proposals: firstly that UK and Republic of Ireland (RoI) accounting standards should be based on IFRS and secondly that a phased approach to the introduction of the standards should be adopted.   **A3.2**

The ASB embarked on the phased approach and issued a number of standards based on IFRS. The majority of respondents agreed with a framework based on IFRS, and although supportive overall, the response to the phased approach was mixed.   **A3.3**

2005

In its 2005 Exposure Draft (2005 ED) of a Policy Statement *Accounting standard-setting in a changing environment: The role of the Accounting Standards Board*, amongst other aspects of its role, the ASB identified its intention to converge with IFRS by implementing new IFRS in the UK as soon as possible. It also proposed to continue the phased approach to adopting UK accounting standards based on older IFRSs, but recognised there was little case for being more prescriptive than IFRS.   **A3.4**

---

[19] *The Department of Trade and Industry (DTI) was a United Kingdom government department which was replaced with the announcement of the creation of the Department for Business, Enterprise and Regulatory Reform and the Department for Innovation, Universities and Skills on 28 June 2007, which were themselves merged into the Department for Business, Innovation and Skills (BIS) on 6 June 2009.*

A3.5   Although the ASB had, in the 2005 ED, wanted to move the debate on to how it would seek to influence the IASB's agenda, respondents' main concern remained about convergence. In 2005, the ASB issued an exposure draft proposing the IASB's standard on Business Combinations be adopted in the UK and RoI. This exposure draft highlighted the complexity of a mixed set of UK accounting standards, with some based on IFRSs and others developed independently by the ASB. The majority of respondents continued to agree with the aim of basing UK accounting standards on IFRS, but a broader set of views on how to achieve this was emerging.

A3.6   As time progressed the ASB formed the view that convergence by adopting certain IFRSs was not meeting the needs of its constituents, which no longer included quoted groups. The ASB was concerned about the complexity of certain IFRSs, and it noted that introducing them piecemeal created complications and anomalies within the body of current FRSs. This arose because IFRS-based standards were not an exact replacement for current FRSs and many consequential amendments were required to 'fit' each replacement IFRS-based standard into the existing body of UK FRS. The ASB agreed to continue with its convergence programme, but decided to re-examine how to achieve this.

2006

A3.7   The ASB published revised proposals to be discussed at the 2006 public meeting. By this time the IASB had started its IFRS for SMEs project, and the ASB decided this might have a role as one of the tiers in the UK financial reporting framework. The ASB proposed a 'big bang' with new IFRS-based UK accounting standards mandatory from a single date, 1 January 2009. The ASB's proposal was for a three-tier system, with Tier 1 being EU-adopted IFRS, and the other two tiers being developed as the IASB progressed with its project on the IFRS for SMEs.

A3.8   Those attending the public meeting supported the aim of basing UK and RoI accounting standards on IFRS and adapting them to ensure they were appropriate for the entities applying them.

A3.9   Taking this feedback into account, later in 2006 the ASB issued a Press Notice (PN 289) seeking views on its current thinking:
    (a)   All quoted and publicly accountable companies should apply EU-adopted IFRS.
    (b)   The FRSSE should be retained and extended to include medium-sized entities.
    (c)   UK subsidiaries of groups applying full IFRS should apply EU-adopted IFRS, but with reduced disclosure requirements.
    (d)   No firm decision on the remainder (Tier 2), but options included extending the FRSSE, extending full IFRS, maintaining separate UK accounting standards or some combination of these.

A3.10   The responses were mixed, but there was agreement that whatever the solution, it should be based on IFRS and there should be different reporting tiers to ensure proportionality.

2007

A3.11   The IASB published an exposure draft of its IFRS for SMEs in early 2007; shortly afterwards the ASB published its own consultation paper. This sought views on how the IFRS for SMEs might fit into the future UK financial reporting framework, for example whether it might be appropriate for Tier 2, with the FRSSE continuing for those eligible for the small companies' regime.

Feedback on the IFRS for SMEs was largely positive: it would be suitable for Tier 2, it was **A3.12**
international, it was compatible with IFRS, and it represented a significant simplification.
Overall, it was seen as a workable alternative to IFRS. In addition, respondents wanted
to retain the FRSSE (because it reduces the regulatory burden on smaller entities) and to
give subsidiaries the option of applying the IFRS for SMEs as well as a reduced disclosure
regime if applying full IFRS.

2009

The IFRS for SMEs was published in 2009, allowing the ASB to further develop its proposals **A3.13**
in the Consultation Paper *Policy Proposal: The future of UK GAAP*. The proposals were
largely consistent with the cumulative results of the preceding consultations and included:

(a) a move to an IFRS-based framework;
(b) a three-tier approach;
(c) publicly accountable entities would be Tier 1 and would apply EU-adopted IFRS;
(d) small companies would be Tier 3 and continue to apply the FRSSE; and
(e) other entities would be Tier 2 and should apply a UK and RoI accounting standard
based on the IFRS for SMEs.

The only significant proposal that was inconsistent with respondents' previous comments **A3.14**
was that subsidiaries should simply apply the requirement of the tier they individually
met – respondents had wanted subsidiaries to be able to take advantage of disclosure
exemptions, and at that time the ASB had yet to be convinced that significant cost savings
were available from a reduced disclosure framework. Taking into account the feedback
received, this proposal was subsequently reversed and the reduced disclosure framework
was incorporated into FREDs 43 and then 46, and it is now set out in FRS 101.

In addition to the many useful and detailed points made, some common themes included **A3.15**
general agreement that change was needed to UK accounting standards and that there was
support for many of the changes proposed in the consultation paper.

2010 onwards

The request for responses to aid development of the Impact Assessment focused on **A3.16**
obtaining feedback on the expected costs, benefits and impact of the proposals subsequently
set out in FREDs 43 and 44, rather than on the accounting principles. As the focus was
on costs and benefits no specific question was asked about the principle of the proposed
introduction of an IFRS-based framework, but nevertheless respondents commented on
this: of the 32 responses received only 12.5% did not agree with the introduction of an
IFRSbased framework.

FRED 43 and 44 issued in October 2010 set out the draft suggested text for two new **A3.17**
accounting standards that would replace the majority of extant Financial Reporting
Standards (current FRS) in the UK and RoI. The ASB issued a supplementary FRED
addressing specific needs of public benefit entities (FRED 45) in March 2011. The ASB
then updated FREDs 43, 44 and 45, replacing them with the revised FREDs 46, 47 and 48
in January 2012, by eliminating the concept of public accountability and by introducing
a number of accounting treatment options that are available in EU-adopted IFRS. The
Accounting Council's advice to the FRC to issue FRSs 100 to 102 includes more discussion
of the feedback received on FREDs 43 to 48 and how the proposals have been refined and
developed into the standards.

HOW HAVE THE PROPOSALS BEEN DEVELOPED?

A3.18   As set out above, the FRC, the Accounting Council (and previously the ASB) have consulted regularly on the future of financial reporting in the UK and RoI. Over the consultations the ASB's (and the Accounting Council's) thinking has evolved based on careful consideration of the feedback at each stage. Whilst responses were sometimes mixed, there has been agreement that:

(a)   current FRS, which are a mixture of Statements of Standard Accounting Practice (SSAPs) issued by the Consultative Committee of Accounting Bodies, FRSs developed and issued by the ASB and IFRS-based standards issued by the ASB to converge with international standards, are an uncomfortable mismatch that lack strong underlying principles or cohesion; and

(b)   whatever the solution, it should be based on IFRS and there should be different reporting tiers to ensure proportionality.

A3.19   During the consultation process to date, the Accounting Council and formerly the ASB have been guided by the following principles:

(a)   The framework must be fit for purpose, so that each entity required to produce true and fair financial statements under UK and RoI law will deliver financial statements that are suited to the needs of its primary users. The Accounting Council has kept in close contact with constituent users on this point, including investors, creditor institutions and the tax authorities.

(b)   The framework must be proportionate, so that preparing entities are not unduly burdened by costs that outweigh the benefit to them and to the primary users of information in their financial statements. The FRC believes that the proposals will produce a lower cost regime, while enhancing user benefits. It has carried out a consultation stage impact assessment with input from interested parties, and will continue to assess cost-benefit issues.

(c)   The framework must be in line with UK company law. This determines which entities must produce true and fair financial statements. Exemptions within the law have generally been retained. The detailed requirements of the Companies Act 2006 are driven to a great extent by the European Accounting Directives, which are being revised[20].

(d)   The framework must be future-proofed, where possible. The FRC will continue to monitor the situation and has sovereignty over UK accounting standards (subject to the law). Changes to the Accounting Directives may lead to further developments, for example the European Council and European Parliament decision to permit Member States an option to treat micro-entities as a separate category of Company and exempt them from certain accounting requirements.

SUMMARY OF OUTREACH

A3.20   During the development and throughout the consultation period of FREDs 43 to 48, the ASB undertook an extensive programme of outreach aimed at raising awareness of the proposals and to address the view (held by some) that previous consultations had not gathered sufficient evidence to support and test the assumptions made.

A3.21   As part of the outreach programme to obtain both formal and informal feedback, a series of meetings and events took place with users, including with lenders to small and medium-sized entities. Lenders noted that financial statements are an important part of their decision-making process when considering whether to provide finance and, whilst a

---

[20] *The EU's consultation process on review of the Accounting Directives is summarised at http://ec.europa.eu/ internal_market/accounting/sme_accounting/review_directives_en.htm*

decision to provide finance is not based on financial statements alone, they provide useful information and verification to the lender.

Although the ASB and the Accounting Council employed their best efforts to obtain feedback from users (a constituent group historically difficult to engage with formally) it is disappointing that limited formal responses were received and the Accounting Council has not been more successful in obtaining input from users.   **A3.22**

In addition, a review was made of academic research that addressed the users of the financial statements of small and medium-sized entities. The conclusion drawn from the research was that many entities requested financial statements from Companies House when considering whether to trade with another entity. The European Federation of Accountants and Auditors (EFAA) issued, in May 2011, a statement that identified the users of financial statements, noting who the users of SMEs' financial statements are and that information on the public record assists all users of financial statements of SMEs by providing, in an efficient manner, basic information that protects their rights.   **A3.23**

The ASB considered that the outreach programme had gleaned information from people who would not normally submit formal responses to a consultation and provided very useful information that could be used in developing the next stage of the project. The ASB noted that whilst this information was not part of the public record, as are formal consultation responses, it could use the information to assist in developing the revised FREDs 46 to 48, supplementing information contained in responses, and would seek further comment in the next stage of its deliberations.   **A3.24**

The Accounting Council continued the work of the ASB in finalising FRSs 100 to 102. The responses to FREDs 46 to 48 were analysed and discussed, and engagements were conducted to take into account the views and suggestions of all relevant associations and contacts. Respondents and outreach contacts were satisfied with FREDs 46 to 48, and many of the response letters were forthcoming in their overall praise for the proposals. A significant number of constituents anticipated cost savings arising from the application of FRS 101. Many respondents considered that FRS 102 would improve UK accounting standards, in particular by introducing requirements for accounting for financial instruments. Further they considered that the improvements will be achieved in a way that will be proportionate to the needs of users, and that once the transition phase has been overcome, it will have the effect of reducing the reporting burden on those UK companies that adopt it.   **A3.25**

Appendix IV
Republic of Ireland (RoI) legal references

A4.1   Appendix IV: *Republic of Ireland (RoI) legal references* will be updated as appropriate for both the Companies Act 2014 and the Irish legislation implementing the EU Accounting Directive once the latter has been made. This will be made available on the FRC website and included in the next edition of FRS 100.

FRS 101
Reduced Disclosure Framework – Disclosure exemptions from EU-adopted IFRS for qualifying entities

(September 2015)

Contents

The Accounting Council's Advice to the FRC to issue Amendments to FRS 101 – 2014/15 Cycle and Other Minor Amendments

Appendices

Prospective amendments: FRED 63 (December 2015) proposes amendments to this Standard (see Part Five).

Editor's note: This revised version incorporates various amendments, most notably amendments issued in July 2015. The amended version of FRS 101 *Reduced Disclosure Framework* updates the version issued in August 2014 for the following: a) *Amendments to FRS 101 Reduced Disclosure Framework – 2014/15 cycle* and other minor amendments issued in July 2015; and b) some minor typographical or presentational corrections. This revised standard is effective for accounting periods beginning on or after 1 January 2016 except for the amendments arising from FRED 57 (i.e. paragraphs 5, 7A, 8j and AG1(d)) which are effective for annual periods beginning on or after 1 January 2015.

SUMMARY

(i) With effect from 1 January 2015 the Financial Reporting Council (FRC) revised financial reporting standards in the United Kingdom and Republic of Ireland. The revisions fundamentally reformed financial reporting, replacing the extant standards with five Financial Reporting Standards:

    (a)   FRS 100 *Application of Financial Reporting Requirements*;

    (b)   FRS 101 *Reduced Disclosure Framework*;

    (c)   FRS 102 *The Financial Reporting Standard applicable in the UK and Republic of Ireland*;

    (d)   FRS 103 *Insurance Contracts*; and

    (e)   FRS 104 *Interim Financial Reporting*.

The FRC has also issued FRS 105 *The Financial Reporting Standard applicable to the Micro-entities Regime* to support the implementation of the new micro-entities regime.

(ii) The FRC's overriding objective in setting accounting standards is to enable users of accounts to receive high-quality understandable financial reporting proportionate to the size and complexity of the entity and users' information needs.

(iii) In meeting this objective, the FRC aims to provide succinct financial reporting standards that:

    (a)   have consistency with international accounting standards through the application of an IFRS-based solution unless an alternative clearly better meets the overriding objective;

    (b)   reflect up-to-date thinking and developments in the way entities operate and the transactions they undertake;

    (c)   balance consistent principles for accounting by all UK and Republic of Ireland entities with practical solutions, based on size, complexity, public interest and users' information needs;

    (d)   promote efficiency within groups; and

    (e)   are cost-effective to apply.

(iv) The requirements in this Financial Reporting Standard (FRS) take into consideration the findings from all relevant consultations.

(v) This FRS sets out a reduced disclosure framework which addresses the financial reporting requirements and disclosure exemptions for the individual financial statements of subsidiaries and ultimate parents that otherwise apply the recognition, measurement and disclosure requirements of EU-adopted IFRS. It is envisaged that the provision of these disclosure exemptions could result in cost savings in the preparation of financial statements of subsidiaries and ultimate parents, without reducing the quality of financial reporting.

(vi) Disclosure exemptions are available to a qualifying entity, as defined in the glossary to this FRS, in its individual financial statements (but not in consolidated financial statements which it is required or voluntarily chooses to prepare). However, a qualifying entity which is a financial institution is not exempt from the disclosure requirements of IFRS 7 *Financial Instruments: Disclosures*, IFRS 13 *Fair Value Measurement* to the extent that they apply to financial instruments, and paragraphs 134 to 136 of IAS 1 *Presentation of Financial Statements*.

(vii) A qualifying entity may apply the reduced disclosure framework regardless of whether the financial reporting framework applied in the consolidated financial statements of the group is based on standards and interpretations issued (or adopted) by the International Accounting Standards Board.

Financial statements prepared by a qualifying entity in accordance with this FRS are not **(viii)**
accounts prepared in accordance with EU-adopted IFRS. A qualifying entity must ensure
it complies with any relevant legal requirements applicable to it. For example, individual
financial statements prepared by companies in accordance with this FRS are Companies
Act accounts and not IAS accounts as set out in section 395(1) of the Act, and therefore
such accounts must comply with the requirements of the Act and any relevant regulations
such as the *Large and Medium-Sized Companies and Groups (Accounts and Reports)
Regulations 2008* (SI 2008/410).

Disclosure exemptions are also available to qualifying entities applying the recognition **(ix)**
and measurement principles of FRS 102; the relevant financial reporting requirements and
disclosure exemptions are set out in that FRS.

This edition of FRS 101 issued in September 2015 updates the edition of FRS 101 issued **(x)**
in August 2014 for the following amendments:

(a)   *Amendments to FRS 101 Reduced Disclosure Framework – 2014/15 cycle and
      other minor amendments* issued in July 2015; and
(b)   some minor typographical or presentational corrections.

FRS 101 REDUCED DISCLOSURE FRAMEWORK

Disclosure exemptions from EU-adopted IFRS for qualifying entities

Objective

1   The objective of this Financial Reporting Standard (FRS) is to set out the disclosure exemptions (a reduced disclosure framework) for the individual financial statements of subsidiaries, including intermediate parents, and ultimate parents that otherwise apply the recognition, measurement and disclosure requirements of EU-adopted IFRS.

Scope

2   This FRS may be applied to the individual financial statements of a qualifying entity, as defined in the glossary, that are intended to give a true and fair view of the assets, liabilities, financial position and profit or loss for a period.

3   A qualifying entity which is required to prepare consolidated financial statements (for example, if the entity is required by section 399 of the Act to prepare group accounts, and is not entitled to any of the exemptions in sections 400 to 402 of the Act), or which voluntarily chooses to do so, may not apply this FRS in its consolidated financial statements.

Abbreviations and definitions

4   The terms **Act**, **date of transition**, **EU-adopted IFRS**, **financial institution**, **FRS 100**, **FRS 101**, **FRS 102**, **IAS Regulation**, **IFRS**, **individual financial statements**, **public benefit entity**, **qualifying entity** and **Regulations** are defined in the glossary included as Appendix I to this FRS.

4A   Financial statements prepared by qualifying entities in accordance with this FRS are not accounts prepared in accordance with EU-adopted IFRS. A qualifying entity must ensure it complies with any relevant legal requirements applicable to it. For example, individual financial statements prepared by companies in accordance with this FRS are Companies Act accounts and not IAS accounts as set out in section 395(1) of the Act, and therefore such accounts must comply with the requirements of the Act and any relevant regulations such as the *Large and Medium-Sized Companies and Groups (Accounts and Reports) Regulations 2008* (SI 2008/410).

Reduced disclosures for subsidiaries and ultimate parents

5   A qualifying entity applying this FRS to its individual financial statements may take advantage of the disclosure exemptions in paragraphs 7A to 9, subject to paragraph 7, provided that:

(a)   Its shareholders have been notified in writing about, and do not object to, the use of the disclosure exemptions. Objections to the use of the disclosure exemptions may be served on the qualifying entity, in accordance with reasonable specified timeframes and format requirements, by a shareholder that is the immediate parent of the entity, or by a shareholder or shareholders holding in aggregate 5% or more of the total allotted shares in the entity or more than half of the allotted shares in the entity that are not held by the immediate parent.

(b)   It otherwise applies as its financial reporting framework the recognition, measurement and disclosure requirements of EU-adopted IFRS, but makes amendments to EU-adopted IFRS requirements where necessary in order to comply with the Act and the Regulations. This is to ensure that the financial statements prepared by companies in accordance with this FRS, comply with the requirements of the Act and Regulations. The Application Guidance to this FRS sets out the amendments necessary to remove conflicts between EU-adopted IFRS and the Act and Regulations. For the avoidance of doubt, the Application Guidance is an integral part of this FRS and is applicable to any qualifying entity applying this FRS, including those that are not companies.

(c)   It discloses in the notes to its financial statements:

    (i)   a brief narrative summary of the disclosure exemptions adopted; and

    (ii)   the name of the parent[1] of the group in whose consolidated financial statements its financial statements are consolidated, and from where those financial statements may be obtained.

[Deleted]   **6**

A qualifying entity which is a financial institution may take advantage in its individual   **7** financial statements of the disclosure exemptions set out in paragraphs 8 to 9 of this FRS, except for:

(a)   the disclosure exemptions from IFRS 7 *Financial Instruments: Disclosures* (see paragraph 8(d));

(b)   the disclosure exemptions from IFRS 13 *Fair Value Measurement* (see paragraph 8(e)) to the extent that they apply to financial instruments[2]; and

(c)   the disclosure exemptions from paragraphs 134 to 136 of IAS 1 *Presentation of Financial Statements* (see paragraph 8(g)).

On first-time adoption of this standard, a qualifying entity shall apply the requirements   **7A** of paragraphs 6 to 33 of IFRS 1 *First-time adoption of International Financial Reporting Standards* except for the requirement of paragraphs 6 and 21 to present an opening statement of financial position at the date of transition. References to IFRS in IFRS 1 shall be interpreted as references to EU-adopted IFRS as amended in accordance with paragraph 5(b) of this FRS.

A qualifying entity may take advantage of the following disclosure exemptions, from when   **8** the relevant standard is applied[3]:

(a)   The requirements of paragraphs 45(b) and 46 to 52 of IFRS 2 *Share-based Payment*, provided that for a qualifying entity that is:

    (i)   a subsidiary, the share-based payment arrangement concerns equity instruments of another group entity;

    (ii)   an ultimate parent, the share-based payment arrangement concerns its own equity instruments and its separate financial statements are presented alongside the consolidated financial statements of the group;

    and, in both cases, provided that equivalent disclosures are included in the consolidated financial statements of the group in which the entity is consolidated.

(b)   The requirements of paragraphs 62, B64(d), B64(e), B64(g), B64(h), B64(j) to B64(m), B64(n)(ii), B64(o)(ii), B64(p), B64(q)(ii), B66 and B67 of IFRS 3 *Business*

---

[1] *The parent identified in the definition of the term 'qualifying entity' (see the glossary included as Appendix I to this FRS).*

[2] *A qualifying entity that is a financial institution may take advantage in its individual financial statements of the disclosure exemptions from IFRS 13 (see paragraph 8(e)) to the extent that they apply to assets and liabilities other than financial instruments.*

[3] *Where a paragraph within a given standard cross-refers to an exempted paragraph listed above, the qualifying entity is permitted to still take the exemption.*

Combinations provided that equivalent disclosures are included in the consolidated financial statements of the group in which the entity is consolidated.

(c) The requirements of paragraph 33(c) of IFRS 5 *Non-current Assets Held for Sale and Discontinued Operations* provided that equivalent disclosures are included in the consolidated financial statements of the group in which the entity is consolidated.

(d) The requirements of IFRS 7 *Financial Instruments: Disclosures*, provided that equivalent disclosures are included in the consolidated financial statements of the group in which the entity is consolidated[4].

(e) The requirements of paragraphs 91 to 99 of IFRS 13 *Fair Value Measurement*, provided that equivalent disclosures are included in the consolidated financial statements of the group in which the entity is consolidated[4].

(f) The requirement in paragraph 38 of IAS 1 *Presentation of Financial Statements* to present comparative information in respect of:

    (i) paragraph 79(a)(iv) of IAS 1;

    (ii) paragraph 73(e) of IAS 16 *Property, Plant and Equipment*;

    (iii) paragraph 118(e) of IAS 38 *Intangible Assets*;

    (iv) paragraphs 76 and 79(d) of IAS 40 *Investment Property*; and

    (v) paragraph 50 of IAS 41 *Agriculture*.

(g) The requirements of paragraphs 10(d), 10(f), 16, 38A, 38B, 38C, 38D, 40A, 40B, 40C, 40D, 111 and 134 to 136 of IAS 1 *Presentation of Financial Statements*.
For accounting periods beginning before 1 January 2013, paragraphs 38A, 38B, 38C, 38D, 40A, 40B, 40C and 40D of IAS 1 (effective 1 January 2013) should be replaced with paragraphs 39 and 40 of IAS 1 (effective 1 January 2009).

(h) The requirements of IAS 7 *Statement of Cash Flows*.

(i) The requirements of paragraphs 30 and 31 of IAS 8 *Accounting Policies, Changes in Accounting Estimates and Errors*.

(j) The requirements of paragraphs 17 and 18A of IAS 24 *Related Party Disclosures*.

(k) The requirements in IAS 24 *Related Party Disclosures* to disclose related party transactions entered into between two or more members of a group, provided that any subsidiary which is a party to the transaction is wholly owned by such a member.

(l) The requirements of paragraphs 130(f)(ii), 130(f)(iii), 134(d) to 134(f) and 135(c) to 135(e) of IAS 36 *Impairment of Assets*, provided that equivalent disclosures are included in the consolidated financial statements of the group in which the entity is consolidated.

Prospective amendments: FRED 63 (December 2015) proposes amendments to this paragraph with effect for annual periods beginning on or after [date].

9   Reference should be made to the Application Guidance to FRS 100 in deciding whether the consolidated financial statements of the group provide disclosures which are equivalent to the requirements of EU-adopted IFRS, from which relief is provided in paragraph 8 of this FRS.

Statement of compliance

10   Where a qualifying entity prepares its financial statements in accordance with FRS 101, it shall state in the notes to the financial statements: '*These financial statements were prepared in accordance with Financial Reporting Standard 101 Reduced Disclosure Framework.*'. The financial statements of such an entity do not comply with all of the requirements of EU-adopted IFRS and shall not therefore contain the unreserved statement of compliance referred to in paragraph 3 of IFRS 1 and otherwise required by paragraph 16 of IAS 1 *Presentation of Financial Statements*.

---

[4] *It should be noted that companies which are subject to the requirements of the Act and Regulations are legally required to provide disclosures related to financial instruments, including those measured at fair value. Further guidance in relation to financial instruments measured at fair value is provided in Appendix II Note on legal requirements.*

Date from which effective and transitional arrangements

A qualifying entity may apply this FRS for accounting periods beginning on or after   **11**
1 January 2015. Early application of this FRS is permitted. If an entity applies this
FRS before 1 January 2015 it shall disclose that fact.

In July 2015 amendments were made to this FRS as a consequence of changes made   **12**
to EU-adopted IFRS and to maintain consistency with company law. In relation to
the amendments set out in *Amendments to FRS 101 – 2014/15 cycle and other minor
amendments* a qualifying entity shall apply:

(a)   the amendments to paragraphs 5, 7A and 8(j) arising from the 2014/15 cycle for
      accounting periods beginning on or after 1 January 2015 (subject also to the effective
      date of the relevant EU-adopted IFRS). Early application is permitted; and

(b)   the amendments arising for consistency with company law for accounting periods
      beginning on or after 1 January 2016. Early application is:

      (i)   permitted for accounting periods beginning on or after 1 January 2015 provided
             that *The Companies, Partnerships, and Groups (Accounts and Reports)
             Regulations 2015* (SI 2015/980) are applied from the same date;

      (ii)   required if a qualifying entity applies *The Companies, Partnerships, and
             Groups (Accounts and Reports) Regulations 2015* (SI 2015/980) to a reporting
             period beginning before 1 January 2016.

If an entity applies these amendments early it shall disclose that fact.

APPLICATION GUIDANCE: AMENDMENTS TO INTERNATIONAL FINANCIAL REPORTING STANDARDS AS ADOPTED IN THE EUROPEAN UNION FOR COMPLIANCE WITH THE ACT AND THE REGULATIONS

This application guidance forms an integral part of FRS 101

AG1 In accordance with the Act, an entity may prepare Companies Act accounts or IAS accounts. A qualifying entity which applies FRS 101 prepares Companies Act accounts. This Application Guidance to FRS 101 sets out amendments to EUadopted IFRS that are necessary to achieve compliance with the Act and related Regulations (deleted text is struck through and inserted text is underlined):

   (a) Paragraph D16 of IFRS 1 *First-time Adoption of International Financial Reporting Standards* is amended as follows:

   If a subsidiary becomes a first-time adopter later than its parent, the subsidiary shall, in its financial statements, measure its assets and liabilities at either:

      (a) the carrying amounts that would be included in the parent's consolidated financial statements, based on the parent's date of transition to IFRSs, if no adjustments were made for consolidation procedures and for the effects of the business combination in which the parent acquired the subsidiary; or

      (b) the carrying amounts required by the rest of this IFRS, based on the subsidiary's date of transition to IFRSs. These carrying amounts could differ from those described in (a):

        (i) when the exemptions in this IFRS result in measurements that depend on the date of transition to IFRSs;

        (ii) when the accounting policies used in the subsidiary's financial statements differ from those in the consolidated financial statements. For example, the subsidiary may use as its accounting policy the cost model in IAS 16 *Property, Plant and Equipment*, whereas the group may use the revaluation model.

   A similar election is available to an associate or joint venture that becomes a first-time adopter later than an entity that has significant influence or joint control over it.

   A qualifying entity that applies this provision must ensure that its assets and liabilities are measured in compliance with FRS 101.

   (b) Paragraph D17 of IFRS 1 *First-time Adoption of International Financial Reporting Standards* is amended as follows:

   However, if an entity becomes a first-time adopter later than its subsidiary (or associate or joint venture) the entity shall, in its consolidated financial statements, measure the assets and liabilities of the subsidiary (or associate or joint venture) at the same carrying amounts as in the financial statements of the subsidiary (or associate or joint venture), after adjusting for consolidation and equity accounting adjustments and for the effects of the business combination in which the entity acquired the subsidiary. Similarly, if a parent becomes a first-time adopter for its separate financial statements earlier or later than for its consolidated financial statements, it shall measure its assets and liabilities at the same amounts in both financial statements, except for consolidation adjustments.

   A qualifying entity that applies this provision must ensure that its assets and liabilities are measured in compliance with FRS 101.

   (c) Paragraph 34 of IFRS 3 *Business Combinations* is amended as follows:

   Occasionally, an acquirer will make a bargain purchase, which is a business combination in which the amount in paragraph 32(b) exceeds the aggregate of the amounts specified in paragraph 32(a). If that excess remains after applying the requirements in paragraph 36, the acquirer shall recognise ~~and separately disclose~~ the resulting ~~gain in profit or loss~~ excess on the face of the statement of financial position on the acquisition date, immediately below goodwill, and followed by a subtotal of the net amount of goodwill and the excess. The ~~gain~~ excess shall be attributed to the acquirer. Subsequently, the excess up to the fair value of the non-monetary assets acquired shall be recognised in profit or loss in the periods in which the non-monetary assets are recovered. Any excess exceeding the fair value of non-monetary assets acquired shall be recognised in profit or loss in the periods expected to be benefited.

(d) Contingent consideration balances arising from business combinations whose acquisition dates preceded the date when an entity first applied the amendments to company law set out in *The Companies, Partnerships and Groups (Accounts and Reports) Regulations 2015* (SI 2015/980) shall not be adjusted as a result of the change in company law (ie generally the start of accounting periods beginning on or after 1 January 2016). Instead the entity's previous accounting policies for contingent consideration shall continue to apply. Contingent consideration balances arising from business combinations whose acquisition dates are on or after the date an entity first applied the amendments to company law set out in *The Companies, Partnerships and Groups (Accounts and Reports) Regulations 2015* (SI 2015/980) shall be accounted for in accordance with IFRS 3 *Business Combinations* (Revised 2008).

(e) [Deleted]

(f) Without amending paragraph B63(a) of IFRS 3 *Business Combinations*, its requirement shall be read in conjunction with paragraph A2.8 of this standard.

(fA) Paragraph 14(a) of IFRS 4 *Insurance Contracts* is amended as follows:

(a) unless otherwise required by the regulatory framework that applies to the entity, shall not recognise as a liability any provisions for possible future claims, if those claims arise under insurance contracts that are not in existence at the end of the reporting period (such as catastrophe provisions and equalisation provisions). The presentation of any such liabilities shall follow the requirements of the Regulations (or other legal framework that applies to that entity).

(g) Paragraph 33 of IFRS 5 *Non-current Assets Held for Sale and Discontinued Operations* is amended as follows:

An entity shall disclose:

(a) a single amount in the statement of comprehensive income comprising the total of:

(i) the post-tax profit or loss of discontinued operations and

(ii) the post-tax gain or loss recognised on the measurement to fair value less costs to sell or on the disposal of the assets or disposal group(s) constituting the discontinued operation.

(b) an analysis of the single amount in (a) into:

(i) the revenue, expenses and pre-tax profit or loss of discontinued operations;

(ii) the related income tax expense as required by paragraph 81(h) of IAS 12;

(iii) the gain or loss recognised on the measurement to fair value less costs to sell or on the disposal of the assets or disposal group(s) constituting the discontinued operation; and

(iv) the related income tax expense as required by paragraph 81(h) of IAS 12.

The analysis ~~may be~~ shall be presented in ~~the notes or in the statement of comprehensive income. If it is presented In~~ the statement of comprehensive income ~~it shall be presented~~ in a ~~section~~ column identified as relating to discontinued operations, ie separately from continuing operations; a total column shall also be presented. The analysis is not required for disposal groups that are newly acquired subsidiaries that meet the criteria to be classified as held for sale on acquisition (see paragraph 11).

(c)   the net cash flows attributable to the operating, investing and financing activities of discontinued operations. These disclosures may be presented either in the notes or in the financial statements. These disclosures are not required for disposal groups that are newly acquired subsidiaries that meet the criteria to be classified as held for sale on acquisition (see paragraph 11).

(d)   the amount of income from continuing operations and from discontinued operations attributable to owners of the parent. These disclosures ~~may be~~ are presented ~~either in the notes or~~ in the statement of comprehensive income.

(h)   Paragraph 53A and corresponding footnote are inserted into IAS 1 *Presentation of Financial Statements* as follows:

Statement of financial position

Information to be presented in the statement of financial position

53A A qualifying entity choosing to apply paragraph 1A(1) of Schedule 1 to the Regulations and adapt one of the balance sheet formats shall apply the relevant presentation requirements of IAS 1 *Presentation of Financial Statements*. A qualifying entity not permitted or not choosing to apply paragraph 1A(1) of Schedule 1 to the Regulations shall comply with the balance sheet format requirements of the Act* instead of paragraphs 54 to 76 of IAS 1.

[Footnote text]

* An entity shall apply, as required by company law, either Part 1 *General Rules and Formats* of Schedule 1 to the Regulations; Part 1 *General Rules and Formats* of Schedule 2 to the Regulations; Part 1 *General Rules and Formats* of Schedule 3 to the Regulations; or Part 1 *General Rules and Formats* of Schedule 1 to the LLP Regulations.

(i)   Paragraph 81C and corresponding footnote are inserted into IAS 1 *Presentation of Financial Statements* as follows:

Information to be presented in profit or loss

81C A qualifying entity choosing to apply paragraph 1A(2) of Schedule 1 to the Regulations and adapt one of the profit and loss account formats shall apply the relevant presentation requirements of IAS 1 *Presentation of Financial Statements*, and in addition shall disclose 'profit or loss before taxation'. A qualifying entity not permitted or not choosing to apply paragraph 1A(2) of Schedule 1 to the Regulations shall present the components of profit or loss in the statement of comprehensive income (in either the single statement or two statement approach) in accordance with the profit and loss account format requirements of the Act* instead of paragraphs 82 and 85 to 86 of IAS 1.

[Footnote text]

* An entity shall apply, as required by company law, either Part 1 *General Rules and Formats* of Schedule 1 to the Regulations; Part 1 *General Rules and Formats* of Schedule 2 to the Regulations; Part 1 *General Rules and Formats* of Schedule 3 to the Regulations; or Part 1 *General Rules and Formats* of Schedule 1 to the LLP Regulations.

(j)   Paragraph 87 of IAS 1 *Presentation of Financial Statements* is amended and paragraphs 87A and 87B are inserted into IAS 1 as follows:

87 ~~An~~ qualifying entity applying Schedule 1 to the Regulations shall not present or describe any items of income and expense as 'extraordinary items' in the statement of comprehensive income (or in the income statement, if presented) or in the notes.

A qualifying entity applying Schedule 2 or Schedule 3 to the Regulations or Schedule 1 to the LLP Regulations shall apply paragraphs 87A and 87B.

87A Ordinary activities are any activities which are undertaken by a reporting entity as part of its business and such related activities in which the reporting entity engages in furtherance of, incidental to, or arising from, these activities. Ordinary activities include any effects on the reporting entity of any event in the various environments in which it operates, including the political, regulatory, economic and geographical environments, irrespective of the frequency or unusual nature of the events.

87B Extraordinary items are material items possessing a high degree of abnormality which arise from events or transactions that fall outside the ordinary activities of the reporting entity and which are not expected to recur. They do not include items occurring within the entity's ordinary activities that are required to be disclosed by IAS 1.97, nor do they include prior period items merely because they relate to a prior period.

(k)   Paragraph 88 of IAS 1 *Presentation of Financial Statements* is amended as follows:

An entity shall recognise all items of income and expense arising in a period in profit or loss unless an IFRS requires or permits otherwise, or unless prohibited by the Act.

(l)   Paragraph 28 of IAS 16 *Property, Plant and Equipment* is deleted.

(m)   Paragraph 24 of IAS 20 *Accounting for Government Grants and Disclosure of Government Assistance* is amended as follows:

Government grants related to assets, including non-monetary grants at fair value, shall be presented in the statement of financial position ~~either~~ by setting up the grant as deferred income ~~or by deducting the grant in arriving at the carrying amount of the asset~~.

(n)   Paragraph 25 of IAS 20 *Accounting for Government Grants and Disclosure of Government Assistance* is deleted.

(o)   Paragraph 26 of IAS 20 *Accounting for Government Grants and Disclosure of Government Assistance* is amended as follows:

~~One method recognises the~~ The grant is recognised as deferred income that is recognised in profit or loss on a systematic basis over the useful life of the asset.

(p)   Paragraph 27 of IAS 20 *Accounting for Government Grants and Disclosure of Government Assistance* is deleted.

(q)   Paragraph 28 of IAS 20 *Accounting for Government Grants and Disclosure of Government Assistance* is amended as follows:

The purchase of assets and the receipt of related grants can cause major movements in the cash flow of an entity. For this reason and in order to show the gross investment in assets, such movements are ~~often~~ disclosed as separate items in the statement of cash flows ~~regardless of whether or not the grant is deducted from the related asset for presentation purposes in the statement of financial position~~.

(r)   Paragraph 29 of IAS 20 *Accounting for Government Grants and Disclosure of Government Assistance* is amended as follows:

Grants related to income are presented as part of profit or loss, either separately or under a general heading such as 'Other income'; ~~alternatively,~~ they are not deducted in reporting the related expense.

(s)   Paragraph 92 of IAS 37 *Provisions, Contingent Liabilities and Contingent Assets* is amended as follows:

92 In extremely rare cases, disclosure of some or all of the information required by paragraphs 84–89 can be expected to prejudice seriously the position of the entity in a dispute with other parties on the subject matter of the provision, contingent liability or contingent asset. In such cases, an entity need not disclose all of the information required by those paragraphs insofar as it relates to the dispute, but shall disclose at least the following ~~general nature of the dispute, together with the fact that, and reason why, the information has not been disclosed~~.

In relation to provisions, the following information shall be given:

(a) a table showing the reconciliation required by paragraph 84 in aggregate, including the source and application of any amounts transferred to or from provisions during the reporting period;

(b) particulars of each provision in any case where the amount of the provision is material; and

(c) the fact that, and reason why, the information required by paragraphs 84 and 85 has not been disclosed.

In relation to contingent liabilities, the following information shall be given:

(a) particulars and the total amount of any contingent liabilities (excluding those which arise out of insurance contracts) that are not included in the statement of financial position;

(b) the total amount of contingent liabilities which are undertaken on behalf of or for the benefit of:

(i) any parent or fellow subsidiary of the entity;

(ii) any subsidiary of the entity; or

(iii) any entity in which the reporting entity has a participating interest, shall each be stated separately; and

(c) the fact that, and reason why, the information required by paragraph 86 has not been disclosed.

In relation to contingent assets, the entity shall disclose the general nature of the dispute, together with the fact that, and reason why, the information required by paragraph 89 has not been disclosed.

APPROVAL BY THE FRC

Financial Reporting Standard 101 *Reduced Disclosure Framework* was approved for issue by the Board of the Financial Reporting Council on 1 November 2012, following its consideration of the Accounting Council's Advice for this FRS.

Amendments to FRS 101 Reduced Disclosure Framework (2013/14 Cycle) was approved for issue by the Board of the Financial Reporting Council on 2 July 2014, following its consideration of the Accounting Council's Advice.

Amendments to FRS 101 Reduced Disclosure Framework – 2014/15 cycle and other minor amendments was approved for issue by the Board of the Financial Reporting Council on 1 July 2015, following its consideration of the Accounting Council's Advice.

THE ACCOUNTING COUNCIL'S ADVICE TO THE FRC TO ISSUE FRS 101

Introduction

1   This report provides an overview of the main issues which have been considered by the Accounting Council in advising the Financial Reporting Council (FRC) to issue FRS 101 *Reduced Disclosure Framework*. The FRC, in accordance with the Statutory Instrument *Statutory Auditors (Amendment of Companies Act 2006 and Delegation of Functions etc) Order 2012* (SI 2012/1741), is the prescribed body for issuing accounting standards in the UK. *The Foreword to Accounting Standards* sets out the application of accounting standards in the Republic of Ireland.

2   In accordance with FRC *Codes and Standards: procedures*, any proposal to issue, amend or withdraw a code or standard is put to the FRC with the full advice of the relevant Councils and/or the Codes & Standards Committee. Ordinarily, the FRC will only reject the advice put to it where:

- it is apparent that a significant group of stakeholders has not been adequately consulted;
- the necessary assessment of the impact of the proposal has not been completed, including an analysis of costs and benefits;
- insufficient consideration has been given to the timing or cost of implementation; or
- the cumulative impact of a number of proposals would make the adoption of an otherwise satisfactory proposal inappropriate.

3   The FRC has established the Accounting Council as the relevant Council to assist it in the setting of accounting standards.

Advice

4   The Accounting Council is advising the FRC to issue:

FRS 100 *Application of Financial Reporting Requirements*; and
FRS 101 *Reduced Disclosure Framework*.

5   FRS 102 *The Financial Reporting Standard Applicable in the UK and Republic of Ireland* completes the new suite of financial reporting standards. The Accounting Council will provide its advice to the FRC on FRS 102 in that standard.

Background

6   Accounting standards were formerly developed by the Accounting Standards Board (ASB). The ASB commenced its project to update accounting standards in 2002; Appendix III provides a history of the previous consultations and a summary of how the overall proposals have developed[5].

7   FRS 101 was developed in response to concerns that arose from earlier consultations (see Appendix III). Respondents to those consultations (and particularly the 2009 Policy Proposal) noted that a move to the IFRS for SMEs for subsidiaries of entities that apply EU-adopted IFRS would require recognition and measurement differences to be monitored and maintained at group level, and yet the alternative of a move to EU-adopted IFRS would increase disclosure in comparison to current accounting standards. The ASB therefore developed a reduced disclosure framework to address these concerns.

---

[5] *References in this section and Appendix III are made to the FRC, ASB or Accounting Council, as appropriate in terms of the time period and context of the reference.*

The reduced disclosure framework principles

In developing the reduced disclosure framework, the ASB set principles for determining **8** which of the disclosure requirements in EU-adopted IFRS should be applied by qualifying entities. Setting principles provides a structure for future amendments to the reduced disclosure framework as new and revised IFRSs are adopted in the EU. The principles are specific to qualifying entities, so the impact on preparers and users of qualifying entity individual financial statements is a common theme to be considered in applying the principles. The agreed principles, which were first introduced when FRED 47 *Reduced Disclosure Framework* was issued, are as follows:

(a) Relevance:
    Does the disclosure requirement provide information that is capable of making a difference to the decisions made by the users of the financial statements of a qualifying entity?
(b) Cost constraint on useful financial reporting:
    Does the disclosure requirement impose costs on the preparers of the financial statements of a qualifying entity that are not justified by the benefits to the users of those financial statements?
(c) Avoid gold plating:
    Does the disclosure requirement override an existing exemption provided by company law in the UK?

The Accounting Council is advising the FRC to adopt these principles. **9**

The scope of the reduced disclosure framework

The reduced disclosure framework was first proposed in FRED 43 *Application of* **10** *Financial Reporting Requirements*, and revised proposals were issued in FRED 47. FRED 43 proposed that qualifying subsidiaries could apply the reduced disclosure framework. The scope of the framework was extended beyond subsidiaries in FRED 47, so that the ultimate parent of a group may take advantage of the disclosure framework in its individual financial statements. Intermediate parents are subsidiaries and so were already included within the scope of the reduced disclosure framework.

The ASB decided, in clarifying the scope of the reduced disclosure framework in FRED 47, **11** that a qualifying entity which is required to prepare consolidated financial statements (for example, if the entity is required by section 399 of the Act to prepare group accounts, and is not entitled to any of the exemptions in sections 400 to 402 of the Act), or a qualifying entity which voluntarily chooses to prepare consolidated financial statements, should not be permitted to apply the reduced disclosure framework in its consolidated financial statements. The ASB recognised that entities which are required or voluntarily choose to prepare consolidated financial statements generally have users with greater information requirements than the users of entities which only prepare individual financial statements. The ASB's decision not to extend the reduced disclosure framework to consolidated financial statements was questioned by a few respondents to FRED 47. The Accounting Council noted that the concerns raised were industry-specific and held the view previously identified that users of these financial statements had greater information requirements. The Accounting Council is therefore advising the FRC that the scope of the FRS remains unchanged from that proposed in FRED 47.

Application of the reduced disclosure framework to financial institutions

FRED 43 proposed that a subsidiary with public accountability should not be permitted **12** to apply the reduced disclosure framework (see the Accounting Council's Advice to the

FRC for FRS 100). With the elimination of 'public accountability' as a differentiator for a financial reporting system in FRED 46 (which replaced FRED 43), the ASB reconsidered which entities should be eligible to apply the reduced disclosure framework.

13   FRED 47 proposed consistent disclosure requirements for financial institutions, between those financial institutions that would be required to provide additional disclosures in accordance with FRED 48 and those financial institutions that are a qualifying entity taking advantage of the reduced disclosure framework. The ASB sought views on whether qualifying entities which are financial institutions should:

(a)   provide disclosures required by IFRS 7 *Financial Instrument: Disclosures* and the disclosure requirements of IFRS 13 *Fair Value Measurement*; or

(b)   provide disclosures required by IFRS 7 except for paragraphs 6, 7, 9(b), 16, 27A, 31, 33, 36, 37, 38, 39, 40 and 41 (this would provide consistency with disclosures required by FRED 48), and from paragraphs 92 to 99 of IFRS 13 (all disclosure requirements except the disclosure objectives).

14   Respondents had mixed views. Some held the view that a qualifying entity that is a financial institution should be permitted some exemptions from financial instrument disclosures in line with those in FRED 48, but others constituents disagreed on the basis that financial instruments are a significant part of the business for financial institutions and that those entities should provide an appropriate level of disclosure. The Accounting Council is advising the FRC that there should be no exemptions from IFRS 7 for financial institutions. This is also simple to apply and ensures financial institutions provide appropriate disclosure about their financial instruments.

15   Some respondents noted that there was an inconsistency in the application of the disclosure requirements in IFRS 13 between financial institutions and other entities. The inconsistency arose because financial institutions were required to provide disclosures for assets and liabilities held at fair value that are not financial instruments whereas other entities were exempt. The Accounting Council therefore considers that FRS 101 should clarify that a qualifying entity which is a financial institution is restricted from taking advantage of the disclosure exemptions from IFRS 13 only to the extent that they apply to financial instruments.

16   The Accounting Council is also advising the FRC that financial institutions should not be permitted to take advantage of the exemption from applying the capital disclosure requirements in IAS 1 *Presentation of Financial Statements*. Responses to FRED 47 had noted that capital disclosures provide relevant information for financial institutions.

Related party exemption for the reduced disclosure framework

17   In issuing FRED 47 the ASB decided to include an exemption in the reduced disclosure framework from disclosing a related party transaction in accordance with IAS 24 *Related Party Disclosures* where the related party transaction was entered into between two or more members of a group, provided that any subsidiary which is a party to a transaction is wholly owned by such a member. This exemption is consistent with company law and was well-received by constituents; the Accounting Council advises the FRC to carry the exemption forward into FRS 101. The exemption set out in paragraph 8(k) of FRS 101 should only be applied where all subsidiaries which are a party to the transaction are wholly owned by a member of the group. The provision of this exemption is in line with principle 3 in paragraph 8 of this report.

***Extension of the reduced disclosure framework to recently issued International
Financial Reporting Standards and amendments***

The reduced disclosure framework principles (see paragraph 7) were applied in FRED 47   **18**
to those IFRSs issued or amended in 2011, including:

(a)   IFRS 9 *Financial Instruments* (as revised in 2011);
(b)   IFRS 10 *Consolidated Financial Statements*;
(c)   IFRS 11 *Joint Arrangements*;
(d)   IFRS 12 *Disclosure of Interests in Other Entities;*
(e)   IFRS 13 *Fair Value Measurement*;
(f)   IAS 1 *Presentation of Financial Statements* (as revised in 2011);
(g)   IAS 19 *Employee Benefits* (as revised in 2011);
(h)   IAS 27 *Separate Financial Statements* (as revised in 2011); and
(i)   IAS 28 *Investments in Associates and Joint Ventures* (as revised in 2011).

The Accounting Council subsequently considered the application of the reduced disclosure   **19**
framework principles to *Annual Improvements to IFRSs 2009–2011 Cycle* which was
issued by the IASB in May 2012. The application of the reduced disclosure framework
principles leads the Accounting Council to advise the FRC (paragraph 8(g) of FRS 101)
to provide disclosure exemptions from paragraphs 38A, 38B, 38C, 38D, 40A, 40B, 40C
and 40D of IAS 1 *Presentation of Financial Statements*. Paragraphs 38A, 38B, 38C and
38D are concerned with comparative information in respect of the preceding period, and
paragraphs 40A, 40B, 40C and 40D are concerned with a statement of financial position
as at the beginning of the preceding period.

The Accounting Council advises the FRC to update FRS 101 at regular intervals, to ensure   **20**
that the disclosure framework maintains consistency with EU-adopted IFRS.

The precedence of the Companies Act

The presentation requirements applicable to the statement of financial position and the   **21**
statement of comprehensive income in IAS 1 have been amended in the Application
Guidance of FRS 101 to clarify that a qualifying entity must comply with the company law
format requirements. The Accounting Council advises the FRC to reconsider the format
requirements of FRS 101 should the Government decide to amend company law at a future
date.

Approval of this advice

This advice to the FRC was approved by the nine members of the Accounting Council on   **22**
25 October 2012. The Accounting Council is comprised of the following members:

Roger Marshall   (Chair of the Accounting Council)
Nick Anderson
Dr Richard Barker
Edward Beale
Peter Elwin
Ken Lever
Robert Overend
Andy Simmonds
Pauline Wallace

THE ACCOUNTING COUNCIL'S ADVICE TO THE FRC TO ISSUE AMENDMENTS TO FRS 101 REDUCED DISCLOSURE FRAMEWORK (2013/14 CYCLE)

Introduction

1   This section provides an overview of the main issues that have been considered by the Accounting Council in advising the Financial Reporting Council (FRC) to issue *Amendments to FRS 101 Reduced Disclosure Framework (2013/14 Cycle)*.

2   The FRC, in accordance with the *Statutory Auditors (Amendment of Companies Act 2006 and Delegation of Functions etc) Order 2012* (SI 2012/1741), is a prescribed body for issuing accounting standards in the UK. The *Foreword to Accounting Standards* sets out the application of accounting standards in the Republic of Ireland.

3   In accordance with the *FRC Codes and Standards: procedures*, any proposal to issue, amend or withdraw a code or standard is put to the FRC Board with the full advice of the relevant Councils and/or the Codes & Standards Committee. Ordinarily, the FRC Board will only reject the advice put to it where:

   (a)   it is apparent that a significant group of stakeholders has not been adequately consulted;
   (b)   the necessary assessment of the impact of the proposal has not been completed, including an analysis of costs and benefits;
   (c)   insufficient consideration has been given to the timing or cost of implementation; or
   (d)   the cumulative impact of a number of proposals would make the adoption of an otherwise satisfactory proposal inappropriate.

4   The FRC has established the Accounting Council as the relevant Council to assist it in the setting of accounting standards.

Advice

5   The Accounting Council is advising the FRC to issue *Amendments to FRS 101 Reduced Disclosure Framework (2013/14 Cycle)* to ensure that FRS 101 continues to maintain consistency with EU-adopted IFRS and continues to promote efficiencies in reporting for groups.

6   The Accounting Council's Advice to the FRC to issue FRS 101 *Reduced Disclosure Framework* was set out in that standard. When these amendments are finalised, the Accounting Council's Advice to the FRC on these amendments will be included in the revised FRS 101.

Background

7   The Accounting Council advised the FRC to update FRS 101 at regular intervals to ensure that the disclosure framework maintains consistency with EU-adopted IFRS[6] so that it remains effective as EU-adopted IFRS develops.

8   The Accounting Council also advised the FRC that the following principles should be applied when determining which of the disclosure requirements in EU-adopted IFRS should be applied by qualifying entities:

---

[6] *Paragraph 20 of the Accounting Council's Advice to the FRC to issue FRS 101.*

1   Relevance:
     Does the disclosure requirement provide information that is capable of making
     a difference to the decisions made by the users of the financial statements of a
     qualifying entity?
2   Cost constraint on useful financial reporting:
     Does the disclosure requirement impose costs on the preparers of the financial
     statements of a qualifying entity that are not justified by the benefits to the users of
     those financial statements?
3   Avoid gold plating:
     Does the disclosure requirement override an existing exemption provided by
     company law in the UK?

The Accounting Council considered the responses to the consultation *Financial Reporting*   9
Exposure Draft 53: Amendments to FRS 101 Reduced Disclosure Framework (2013/14)
(FRED 53) which was issued in December 2013, in developing its advice.

IASB projects completed since those considered in the development of FRS 101

The IASB has completed six projects since those considered in the development of   10
FRS 101:

IFRS		Date issued by IASB	Endorsed by EU
1	IAS 32 *Financial Instruments: Presentation* – Offsetting Financial Assets And Financial Liabilities (amendment)	Dec 2011	Dec 2012
2	Disclosures – Offsetting Financial Assets and Financial Liabilities (Amendments to IFRS 7)	Dec 2011	Dec 2012
3	Government loans (amendments to IFRS 1)	Mar 2012	Mar 2013
4	Consolidated Financial Statements, Joint Arrangements and Disclosure of Interests in Other Entities: Transition Guidance (Amendments to IFRS 10, IFRS 11 and IFRS 12)	Jun 2012	Apr 2013
5	Investment Entities (Amendments to IFRS 10, IFRS 12 and IAS 27)	Oct 2012	Nov 2013
6	Recoverable Amount Disclosures for Non-Financial Assets (Amendment to IAS 36)	May 2013	Dec 2013

The amendments[7] resulting from these projects were reviewed in the context of the reduced   11
disclosure framework for any amendments that:

(a)   alter disclosure requirements, as consideration will need to be given as to whether
       changes should be made to the disclosure exemptions permitted in FRS 101; and/or
(b)   are inconsistent with current UK legal requirements, as consideration will need to be
       given to whether changes should be made to the Application Guidance: *Amendments*
       to International Financial Reporting Standards as Adopted in the European Union
       for Compliance with the Act and the Regulations to FRS 101.

---

[7] *The full IASB documents setting out the amendments for each project are available on the IASB website*
(www.ifrs.org).

Investment Entities (Amendments to IFRS 10, IFRS 12 and IAS 27)

12   The amendments resulting from this IASB project introduced into IFRS 10 *Consolidated Financial Statements* an exception from consolidation of subsidiaries for parents that are investment entities. These amendments require an investment entity to measure those subsidiaries at fair value through profit or loss in accordance with IFRS 9 *Financial Instruments* in its consolidated and separate financial statements. The amendments also introduce new disclosure requirements for investment entities into IFRS 12 *Disclosure of Interests in Other Entities* and IAS 27 *Separate Financial Statements*.

Compliance with UK company law

13   Several respondents questioned whether the proposed amendment to the Application Guidance of FRS 101 in relation to IFRS 10 was necessary given that IFRS 10 is only applicable to the preparation of consolidated financial statements, and FRS 101 is only applicable to the preparation of the individual financial statements of a qualifying entity.

14   Although FRS 101 is not applicable to the preparation of consolidated financial statements, the amendments to IFRS 10 in respect of investment entities will have a knock-on effect on the preparation of individual financial statements as paragraph 11A of IAS 27 states that 'if a parent is required, in accordance with paragraph 31 of IFRS 10, to measure its investment in a subsidiary at fair value through profit or loss in accordance with IFRS 9, it shall also account for those investments in the same way in its separate financial statements'[8].

15   However, the Accounting Council noted the respondents' concerns and advises that the proposed amendment to the Application Guidance set out in FRED 53 is not made but additional guidance is inserted into Appendix II *Note on legal requirements*, in particular to clarify that a qualifying entity that meets the definition of an investment entity under IFRS 10 must measure its investments in subsidiaries at fair value through profit or loss in its individual financial statements.

Disclosure exemptions

16   The Accounting Council considers that the new disclosure requirements in IFRS 12 and IAS 27 in respect of qualifying entities that are investment entities are relevant to a user's understanding of the qualifying entity's financial statements, particularly as no consolidated financial statements would have been prepared in respect of the exempt subsidiaries. Further, the qualifying entity would also be a financial institution and these disclosures relate to its financial instruments. The Accounting Council advises that no exemption should be given for these new disclosure requirements.

17   A respondent to the consultation questioned whether the Accounting Council had considered paragraphs 24 to 31 of IFRS 12 in relation to unconsolidated structured entities as paragraph 6(b) of IFRS 12 states that 'this IFRS does not apply to ... an entity's separate financial statements to which IAS 27 Separate Financial Statements applies. However, if an entity has interests in unconsolidated structured entities and prepares separate financial statements as its only financial statements, it shall apply the requirements in paragraph 24–31 when preparing those financial statements.'

18   The Accounting Council had not specifically considered paragraph 6(b) of IFRS 12 in developing the proposals in FRED 53, but on further consideration advises that the disclosures required by that paragraph provide relevant information and no exemption

---

[8] *As set out in the Appendix I Glossary, separate financial statements are included in the meaning of individual financial statements.*

should be given in FRS 101. For the avoidance of doubt, the other requirements of IFRS 12 do not apply to the preparation of individual financial statements and therefore are not relevant to financial statements prepared by qualifying entities applying FRS 101.

Recoverable Amount Disclosures for Non-Financial Assets (Amendment to IAS 36)

The Accounting Council noted that FRS 101 already allows disclosure exemptions for qualifying entities against paragraphs 134(d) to 134(f) and 135(c) to 135(e) of IAS 36. These disclosures relate to cash-generating units that, either individually or in combination, have a significant amount of goodwill or intangible assets with indefinite useful lives allocated to them. These exemptions are only permitted if equivalent disclosures are included in the consolidated financial statements of the group. **19**

The IASB has made amendments to the disclosure requirements of paragraph 130(f) of IAS 36 in relation to fair value, where fair value less costs of disposal is the recoverable amount of an individual asset or cash-generating unit. **20**

The Accounting Council considered that, on balance, the additional detailed disclosure requirements of paragraph 130(f) of IAS 36 are unlikely to provide relevant information to users of the financial statements of qualifying entities, given that general information on impairments will be disclosed through the requirements of paragraphs 130(a) to (e). **21**

In addition, this detailed information would be available in the consolidated financial statements, and if no disclosure is made in the consolidated financial statements on the grounds of materiality, the relevant disclosures would need to be made at subsidiary level[9]. **22**

The Accounting Council noted, however, that should an exemption be permitted for paragraph 130(f) in its entirety, basic information about the basis of measurement of the fair value would be lost, and an imbalance between the disclosure requirements relating to fair value less costs of disposal and value in use would exist. Therefore the Accounting Council advises that: **23**

(a) an exemption should not be permitted against the requirements of paragraph 130(f) (i) and entities should provide disclosure of the level of the fair value hierarchy used in measuring fair value; and

(b) an exemption should be permitted against subparagraphs 130(f)(ii) and 130(f) (iii), provided that equivalent disclosures are included the consolidated financial statements of the group.

This proposed disclosure exemption was supported by all respondents and the Accounting Council advises that paragraph 8(l) of FRS 101 is amended to include this exemption. **24**

Editorial amendment to paragraph 6 of FRS 101

It has been brought to the attention of the Accounting Council that the drafting of paragraph 6 of FRS 101 does not accurately reflect the requirements of paragraph 36(4) of Schedule 1 to the *Large and Medium-sized Companies and Groups (Accounts and Reports) Regulations 2008* (SI 2008/410) (the Regulations) and is potentially confusing. **25**

The Accounting Council proposed in FRED 53 that paragraph 6 should be amended and paragraph 4A be inserted to remind entities that financial statements prepared under **26**

---

[9] *As required by paragraph AG10 of the Application Guidance to FRS 100 Application of Financial Reporting Requirements.*

FRS 101 are not IAS Accounts but Companies Act Accounts, and therefore qualifying entities must comply with the Act and the Regulations.

27   In general, respondents welcomed the insertion of paragraph 4A and the proposed simplification of paragraph 6. However, some noted that entities which are not companies can apply FRS 101 and therefore the drafting of paragraphs 4A and 6 needed to be revisited. The Accounting Council acknowledged this point and advises that the drafting of paragraph 4A is further improved to reflect this fact, and consequential amendments to the paragraphs (ix) of the Summary and A2.3 of Appendix II are made for consistency.

28   In light of the proposed insertion of paragraph 4A, some respondents commented that further consideration of the drafting of paragraph 5(b) is needed to clarify whether the Application Guidance to FRS 101 is applicable to all qualifying entities or to companies only. The Accounting Council noted that its intention was that all entities applying FRS 101 (regardless of whether they are a company or otherwise) should use the same recognition and measurement bases, in line with the principle adopted in developing FRS 102. Although direct comparability across entities applying FRS 101 is not critical, given that the standard only applies to the individual financial statements of group entities where the most common user is likely to be the parent entity, the Accounting Council nonetheless noted that in general, users will have an expectation that all financial statements prepared in accordance with FRS 101 will be applying a consistent recognition and measurement framework.

29   The Accounting Council acknowledged that the standard as originally drafted was not clear on this point and therefore it advises that paragraph 5(b) is amended to clarify for any avoidance of doubt that the Application Guidance (which amends EU-adopted IFRS to remove conflicts with company law) is an integral part of the FRS and is applicable to all entities, not just companies, applying FRS 101.

30   In reconsidering paragraph 6 of FRS 101, the Accounting Council considered whether the same underlying principle should be applied to disclosure requirements, and it drew a distinction between the recognition and measurement framework and the availability of reduced disclosures. It noted that the key objective of FRS 101 is to promote more efficient group reporting by permitting qualifying entities exemptions from certain disclosure requirements set out in EU-adopted IFRS. However, in some circumstances, the level of exemptions that can be taken by a qualifying entity may be restricted by legal requirements applicable to the entity.

31   This is the case for companies (and limited liability partnerships (LLPs)) that measure financial instruments at fair value subject to the requirements of paragraph 36(4) of Schedule 1 to the relevant regulations. FRS 101 provides an exemption against the disclosure requirements of IFRS 7 *Financial Instruments: Disclosures* and IFRS 13 *Fair Value Measurement*; however companies (and LLPs) with financial instruments of this nature are required by law to provide certain disclosures.

32   In relation to paragraph 6 of FRS 101 (which was intended to help companies to identify the disclosure requirements necessary to comply with paragraph 36(4) of Schedule 1 to the Regulations), the Accounting Council concluded that this paragraph should not be mandatory for all qualifying entities (despite footnote 2 of FRS 101 which states otherwise) given that entities that are not subject to the Regulations would otherwise have been permitted to take advantage of the exemptions from the disclosure requirements of IFRS 7 and IFRS 13.

33   The Accounting Council noted that the equivalent requirement in FRS 102 does not specifically state that it is applicable to all qualifying entities but rather it is only applicable

to qualifying entities that have *'financial instruments held at fair value subject to the requirements of paragraph 36(4) of Schedule 1 to the Regulations'*[10]; this infers that it is only applicable to companies, indicating that there is inconsistency between the two standards.

In light of this, the Accounting Council concluded that paragraph 6 of FRS 101 should not be applicable to all qualifying entities and is simply an interpretation of a company law disclosure requirement which restricts the level of exemptions that a company can take. It therefore advises that paragraph 6 of FRS 101 is deleted and further explanatory guidance is inserted into Appendix II *Note on legal requirements*. 34

In inserting further guidance into Appendix II, the Accounting Council noted that a company will comply with the requirements of paragraph 36(4) of Schedule 1 to the Regulations if it provides the disclosures required by IAS 32 or IFRS 7 as at 5 September 2006. However, the most practical solution would be for a qualifying entity to provide the disclosures required by IFRS 7 as entities may find it difficult to obtain a copy of IAS 32 as at that date. IFRS 7 has been amended since September 2006 but the Accounting Council advises that if an entity applies the current version of IFRS 7 (extant at the date of this Advice), it will still be complying with the requirements of the Regulations. 35

Date from which effective and transitional arrangements

The effective date of FRS 101 is for accounting periods beginning on or after 1 January 2015 with early application permitted. 36

The amendments resulting from both the *Investment Entities (Amendments to IFRS 10, IFRS 12 and IAS 27)* project and the *Recoverable Amount Disclosures for Non-Financial Assets (Amendments to IAS 36)* project have an effective date for accounting periods beginning on or after 1 January 2014 with early application permitted as set out in IFRS 10 and IAS 36. 37

The Accounting Council advises that the amendments to FRS 101 have the same effective date as currently stated in FRS 101 and early adoption is permitted to the extent that a qualifying entity can apply the amendments of the underlying IFRSs (ie IFRS 10 and IAS 36). 38

Approval of this Advice

This advice to the FRC was approved by the Accounting Council on 19 June 2014. 39

---

[10] *See paragraph 1.8 of FRS 102.*

THE ACCOUNTING COUNCIL'S ADVICE TO THE FRC TO ISSUE AMENDMENTS TO FRS 101 – 2014/15 CYCLE AND OTHER MINOR AMENDMENTS

Introduction

1   This section provides an overview of the main issues that have been considered by the Accounting Council in advising the Financial Reporting Council (FRC) to issue *Amendments to FRS 101 Reduced Disclosure Framework – 2014/15 cycle and other minor amendments*.

2   The FRC, in accordance with the *Statutory Auditors (Amendment of Companies Act 2006 and Delegation of Functions etc) Order 2012* (SI 2012/1741), is a prescribed body for issuing accounting standards in the UK. The *Foreword to Accounting Standards* sets out the application of accounting standards in the Republic of Ireland.

3   In accordance with the *FRC Codes and Standards: procedures*, any proposal to issue, amend or withdraw a code or standard is put to the FRC Board with the full advice of the relevant Councils and/or the Codes & Standards Committee. Ordinarily, the FRC Board will only reject the advice put to it where:

   (a)   it is apparent that a significant group of stakeholders has not been adequately consulted;
   (b)   the necessary assessment of the impact of the proposal has not been completed, including an analysis of costs and benefits;
   (c)   insufficient consideration has been given to the timing or cost of implementation; or
   (d)   the cumulative impact of a number of proposals would make the adoption of an otherwise satisfactory proposal inappropriate.

4   The FRC has established the Accounting Council as the relevant Council to assist it in the setting of accounting standards.

Advice

5   The Accounting Council is advising the FRC to issue *Amendments to FRS 101 Reduced Disclosure Framework – 2014/15 cycle and other minor amendments* to ensure FRS 101 maintains consistency with IFRS and company law and continues to be effective.

6   The Accounting Council's Advice to the FRC to issue FRS 101 *Reduced Disclosure Framework* was set out in the standard. The Accounting Council's Advice to the FRC in respect of these amendments will be included in the revised FRS 101.

Background

7   The Accounting Council advised the FRC to update FRS 101 at regular intervals to ensure that the reduced disclosure framework maintains consistency with EUadopted IFRS.

8   The Accounting Council also advised the FRC that the following principles should be applied when determining which of the disclosure requirements in EU-adopted IFRS should be applied by qualifying entities:

   (1)   Relevance:
         Does the disclosure requirement provide information that is capable of making a difference to the decisions made by the users of the financial statements of a qualifying entity?

(2) Cost constraint on useful financial reporting:
   Does the disclosure requirement impose costs on the preparers of the financial statements of a qualifying entity that are not justified by the benefits to the users of those financial statements?
(3) Avoid gold plating:
   Does the disclosure requirement override an existing exemption provided by company law in the UK?

FRS 101 also requires limited other amendments for compliance with company law **9** following the implementation of the new Accounting Directive.

The Accounting Council considered the responses to: **10**

(a) FRED 57 *Draft amendments to FRS 101 Reduced Disclosure Framework (2014/15 Cycle)*, which was issued in December 2014; and
(b) FRED 60 *Draft amendments to FRS 100 Application of Financial Reporting Requirements and FRS 101 Reduced Disclosure Framework*, which was issued in February 2015,

in developing its advice.

IASB projects completed since the 2013/14 cycle

The IASB has completed 13 projects since those considered in the review for the 2013/14 **11** cycle performed in August 2013:

	IFRS	IFRS Date issued by IASB	Effective date	Endorsed by EU
1	IFRIC 21 *Levies*	May 2013	1 Jan 2014	Jun 2014
2	Novation of Derivatives and Continuation of Hedge Accounting – Amendments to IAS 39	Jun 2013	1 Jan 2014	Dec 2013
3	IFRS 9 *Financial Instruments* – Hedge Accounting and amendments to IFRS 9, IFRS 7 and IAS 39	Nov 2013	1 Jan 2018	Expected H2 2015
4	Defined Benefit Plans: Employee Contributions – Amendments to IAS 19	Nov 2013	1 Jul 2014	Dec 2014
5	Annual Improvements to IFRSs 2010–2012 Cycle	Dec 2013	1 Jul 2014	Dec 2014
6	Annual Improvements to IFRSs 2011–2013 Cycle	Dec 2013	1 Jul 2014	Dec 2014
7	IFRS 14 *Regulatory Deferral Accounts*	Jan 2014	1 Jan 2016	Not endorsed
8	IFRS 15 *Revenue from Contracts with Customers*	May 2014	1 Jan 2017	To be decided
9	Accounting for Acquisitions of Interests in Joint Operations	May 2014	1 Jan 2016	Expected Q4 2015
10	Clarification of Acceptable Methods of Depreciation and Amortisation	May 2014	1 Jan 2016	Expected Q4 2015
11	Agriculture: Bearer Plants – Amendments to IAS 16 and IAS 41	Jun 2014	1 Jan 2016	Expected Q4 2015
12	IFRS 9 Financial Instruments – Classification and Measurement, Impairments	Jun 2014	1 Jan 2018	Expected H2 2015
13	Equity Method in Separate Financial Statements (Amendments to IAS 27)	Aug 2014	1 Jan 2016	Expected Q4 2015

12   The Accounting Council advises that consideration of the final project listed above (*Equity Method in Separate Financial Statements (Amendments to IAS 27)*) should be deferred until the 2015/16 cycle as its application in the UK was not permitted at the time of the review, but changes to company law made as part of the implementation of the EU Accounting Directive mean that it will be permitted for accounting periods beginning on or after 1 January 2015 (if an entity adopts the changes to company law early).

13   The amendments[11] resulting from the remaining 12 projects were reviewed in the context of the reduced disclosure framework for any amendments that:

[11] *The full IASB documents setting out the amendments for each project are available on the IASB website (www.ifrs.org).*

(a) alter disclosure requirements, as consideration will need to be given to whether changes should be made to the disclosure exemptions permitted in FRS 101; and/or

(b) are inconsistent with current UK legal requirements, as consideration will need to be given to whether changes should be made to the Application Guidance: *Amendments to International Financial Reporting Standards as Adopted in the European Union for Compliance with the Act and the Regulations* to FRS 101.

The most significant amendments / standards are considered below.   14

IAS 24 Related Party Disclosures – Key management services from management entities

The *Annual Improvements to IFRSs (2010–2012 Cycle)* introduces three main changes to   15
IAS 24 *Related Party Disclosures*:

(a) Insertion of paragraph 9(b)(viii) changing the definition of a related party to clarify that a management entity that provides key management personnel services to the reporting entity is a related party.

(b) Insertion of paragraph 17A which states that where an entity obtains key management personnel services from a management entity, it is not required to apply paragraph 17 which requires disclosure of key management personnel compensation.

(c) Insertion of paragraph 18A which requires an entity that obtains key management personnel services from a management entity to disclose amounts incurred for the provision of those services.

The Council noted that FRS 101 currently allows an exemption against paragraph 17   16
of IAS 24 (which requires disclosure of key management personnel compensation) on the basis that company law requires disclosure of directors' emoluments and further information about key management personnel compensation is unlikely to be relevant to the users of a qualifying entity's financial statements.

The majority of the respondents to FRED 57 supported this proposal.   17

The Council advises that on the basis that FRS 101 already allows an exemption   18
against paragraph 17 it considers that FRS 101 should also allow an exemption against paragraph 18A.

IFRS 15 Revenue from Contracts with Customers

The disclosure requirements of IFRS 15 *Revenue from Contracts with Customers*   19
are significantly more detailed than those currently required by IAS 18 *Revenue* and IAS 11 *Construction Contracts*, and the Council notes that the majority of the additional requirements are qualitative in nature, around judgements exercised in the recognition and measurement of revenue.

The Council also notes that paragraph 111 of IFRS 15 calls for entities to consider the level   20
of detail necessary to satisfy the disclosure objective to provide sufficient information to enable users of financial statements to understand the nature, amount, timing and uncertainty of revenue and cash flows arising from contracts with customers, and how much emphasis to place on each of the various requirements, requiring that entities aggregate/disaggregate as appropriate. So although the disclosure requirements are extensive, there is scope for entities to apply judgement in their preparation.

IFRS 15 is effective for accounting periods beginning on or after 1 January 2017 (albeit   21
early adoption is permitted), although the IASB is currently consulting on deferring the effective date by one year to 1 January 2018. At this stage, with the effective date some

way off and the European Union endorsement process not yet complete, the Council advises that no exemptions from the disclosure requirements of IFRS 15 should be added to FRS 101. The majority of respondents to FRED 57 supported this proposal.

22   IFRS 15 will be applicable from the same date for both entities applying IFRS and those qualifying entities applying FRS 101. The Council advises that IFRS 15 should be revisited as part of the 2015/16 cycle in order to consider whether any disclosure exemptions are appropriate in FRS 101; two respondents to FRED 57 commented that in their view exemptions would be appropriate.

IFRS 9 Financial Instruments

23   IFRS 9 *Financial Instruments* issued in July 2014 combines the outputs from the classification and measurement, hedge accounting and impairment projects to date, and amends the requirements of IFRS 7 *Financial Instruments: Disclosures*. EFRAG indicates that endorsement may be expected in H2 2015.

24   The Accounting Council advises that the existing position of FRS 101 (ie that financial institutions are not permitted any exemptions against the disclosure requirements of IFRS 7 or the financial instruments disclosures in IFRS 13 *Fair Value Measurement* and that non-financial institutions are permitted exemptions) should remain even after IFRS 9 is endorsed.

2013/14 cycle: IFRS 1 First-time Adoption of International Financial Reporting Standards – Presentation of an opening statement of financial position on transition

25   The Council noted its earlier advice to revisit a query raised by a respondent to the 2013/14 cycle highlighting that although FRS 101 provides an explicit exemption from paragraph 10(f) of IAS 1 *Presentation of Financial Statements* there is no explicit exemption from a similar requirement set out in paragraph 21 (and paragraph 6) of IFRS 1 *First-time Adoption of International Financial Reporting Standards* to present a third statement of financial position:

   (a)   Paragraph 10(f) of IAS 1 requires the presentation of a statement of financial position as at the beginning of the preceding period when an entity applies an accounting policy retrospectively or makes a retrospective restatement of its financial statements.

   (b)   Paragraph 6 of IFRS 1 requires an entity to prepare and present an opening statement of financial position at the date of transition, and paragraph 21 of IFRS 1 requires that an entity's first IFRS financial statements should include at least three statements of financial position.

26   The Council advises in addition to the apparent inconsistency within FRS 101 as noted above, paragraph 35.7 of the IFRS for SMEs was amended in developing FRS 102 *The Financial Reporting Standard applicable in the UK and Republic of Ireland* to require the preparation of, but not the presentation of, an opening statement of financial position in the first set of financial statements prepared under FRS 102. Therefore the Council advises that an exemption from the requirement in IFRS 1 to present an opening statement of financial position on transition to FRS 101 should be permitted.

27   All the respondents to FRED 57 agreed with this proposal, and some respondents noted that a consequential amendment would be necessary to paragraph 11(b) of FRS 100 *Application of Financial Reporting Requirements*. The Accounting Council agrees with this comment and advises that paragraph 11(b) of FRS 100 is amended for consistency.

This amendment is set out in *Amendments to FRS 100 Application of Financial Reporting Requirements* issued in July 2015.

Editorial amendments to the Application Guidance to FRS 101

IFRS 3 Business Combinations – Contingent consideration

The *Annual Improvements to IFRSs (2010–2012 Cycle)* amended the requirements in 28 relation to contingent consideration set out in paragraphs 40 and 58 of IFRS 3 *Business Combinations*.

The Application Guidance to FRS 101 already amends paragraphs 39 and 40, and deletes 29 paragraph 58 of IFRS 3 for compliance with company law which prior to the implementation of the new Accounting Directive did not permit contingent consideration to be measured at fair value. Therefore, FRED 57 proposed an amendment to the Application Guidance to ensure the underlying text from IFRS 3 is correct. However, as these requirements of IFRS 3 are no longer inconsistent with company law, FRED 60 proposed deleting this paragraph. As a result, the Council advises paragraph AG1(d) is deleted and replaced with a new paragraph AG1(d) that sets out transitional provisions arising from the change in company law.

IFRS 5 Discontinued Operations and Assets Held for Sale

The IASB issued a set of editorial amendments in July 2012 which included the deletion 30 of paragraph 33(b)(iv) of IFRS 5 *Discontinued Operations and Assets Held for Sale*. Therefore FRED 57 proposed that the underlying text included in paragraph AG1(g) of the Application Guidance to FRS 101 was amended to reflect this editorial amendment. However, in September 2014 (after the cut-off period for this review cycle) the IASB retracted this editorial amendment and therefore the proposed amendment of paragraph AG1(g) of the Application Guidance to FRS 101 is no longer necessary and has not been made.

Implementation of the new Accounting Directive

The new EU Accounting Directive (Directive 2013/34/EU of the European Parliament and 31 of the Council of 26 June 2013) is being implemented in the UK and Republic of Ireland. In doing so there are changes to company law to reflect new requirements and, where considered appropriate, to take advantage of new options that are available. Accounting standards are developed within the context of company law and amendments will also be required to accounting standards.

In September 2014, the FRC issued a Consultation Document *Accounting standards* 32 *for small entities – Implementation of the EU Accounting Directive*[12] (the Consultation Document), outlining its proposal that a small number of amendments to FRS 101 *Reduced Disclosure Framework* would be necessary to maintain consistency with company law. The Accounting Council considered the responses to the Consultation Document in developing FRED 60 *Draft amendments to FRS 100 and FRS 101*. It has also considered the responses to FRED 60, which was issued in February 2015, in developing its advice on these amendments.

---

[12] *Available on the FRC website (www.frc.org.uk).*

Amendments to FRS 101

33   A small number of amendments, principally to the Application Guidance to FRS 101, are necessary to maintain consistency between FRS 101 and company law.

34   The amendments proposed include:

(a)   Greater flexibility in relation to the format of the profit and loss account and balance sheet, which will allow entities choosing this option to adopt a presentation that is closer to that applied by entities preparing 'IAS accounts'.

(b)   Revisions to certain requirements relating to financial instruments that are, or may be, measured at fair value. The new Accounting Directive permits measurement of certain financial instruments at fair value where it is in accordance with EU-adopted IFRS; previously this was restricted to IFRS endorsed by 5 September 2006. The consequences of this change have been considered. As a result, there is no longer a prohibition on measuring contingent consideration at fair value[13] and the Accounting Council advises that the relevant amendment to IFRS can be deleted.

(c)   Prohibiting the reversal of impairment losses for goodwill.

35   The Accounting Council noted that, following amendments proposed to the 'seriously prejudicial' disclosure exemption in FRS 102 *The Financial Reporting Standard applicable in the UK and Republic of Ireland* some respondents to FRED 60 suggested that FRS 101 should include an amendment to paragraph 92 of IAS 37 *Provisions, Contingent Liabilities and Contingent Assets* to note that the exemption does not apply to disclosures that are required by company law (for example by paragraphs 59 and 63 of the Regulations). Although this was already covered by paragraph 4A of FRS 101, which notes that the requirements of the Regulations must be complied with, the Accounting Council advises that this constraint on the exemption in IAS 37 should be specifically highlighted in FRS 101 and it is set out in new paragraph AG1(s) of the Application Guidance to FRS 101.

Future amendments to FRS 101

36   The Accounting Council notes that IFRS 9 *Financial Instruments* has not yet been endorsed for use in the EU, and therefore is not yet applicable to an entity applying FRS 101. However, the Accounting Council notes that one aspect of its recognition and measurement requirements is inconsistent with company law. This relates to where changes in fair value shall be presented. Once IFRS 9 has been endorsed the Accounting Council intends to advise that, for entities applying FRS 101, recording fair value gains and losses attributable to changes in credit risk in other comprehensive income in accordance with IFRS 9 will usually be a departure from the requirement of paragraph 40 of Schedule 1 to the Regulations, for the overriding purpose of giving a true and fair view.

37   The Accounting Council notes that company law will permit the use of the equity method in an entity's individual financial statements for accounting periods beginning on or after 1 January 2016 (or with early application from 1 January 2015) and therefore when it considers the recent amendment to IAS 27 *Separate Financial Statements* as part of the next annual review of FRS 101, it expects to advise that amendments are not necessary to FRS 101 for compliance with company law.

---

[13] *Although paragraph 36(3) of the Regulations will continue to prohibit the measurement of contingent consideration at fair value through profit or loss (as required by IFRS 3 **Business Combinations**), this measurement will now be permitted through paragraph 36(4) of the Regulations.*

Date from which effective and transitional arrangements

The effective date of FRS 101 is for accounting periods beginning on or after 1 January 2015   **38**
with early application permitted. A qualifying entity is permitted to apply EU-adopted
IFRS extant at the time of preparing its financial statements.

The Accounting Council advises that the amendments to FRS 101 arising from FRED 57   **39**
have the same effective date as currently stated in FRS 101 and early adoption is permitted
to the extent that a qualifying entity can apply the amendments of the underlying IFRSs.

The Accounting Council advises that the amendments to FRS 101 arising from the   **40**
implementation of the new Accounting Directive are effective for accounting periods
beginning on or after 1 January 2016, with early application:

(a)   permitted for accounting periods beginning on or after 1 January 2015 provided that
      The Companies, Partnerships and Groups (Accounts and Reports) Regulations 2015
      (SI 2015/980) are applied from the same date; and
(b)   required if an entity applies *The Companies, Partnerships and Groups (Accounts
      and Reports) Regulations 2015* (SI 2015/980) to a reporting period beginning before
      1 January 2016.

Approval of this Advice

This advice to the FRC was approved by the Accounting Council on 4 June 2015.   **41**

Appendix I
Glossary

Act	The Companies Act 2006
date of transition	The beginning of the earliest period for which an entity presents full comparative information under a given standard in its first financial statements that comply with that standard.
EU-adopted IFRS	IFRS that have been adopted in the European Union in accordance with EU Regulation 1606/2002

financial institution	Any of the following:
	(a) a bank which is:
	 (i) a firm with a Part IV permission[14] which includes accepting deposits and:
	   (a) which is a credit institution; or
	   (b) whose Part IV permission includes a requirement that it complies with the rules in the General Prudential sourcebook and the Prudential sourcebook for Banks, Building Societies and Investment Firms relating to banks, but which is not a building society, a friendly society or a credit union;
	 (ii) an EEA bank which is a full credit institution;
	(b) a building society which is defined in section 119(1) of the Building Societies Act 1986 as a building society incorporated (or deemed to be incorporated) under that act;
	(c) a credit union, being a body corporate registered under the Industrial and Provident Societies Act 1965 as a credit union in accordance with the Credit Unions Act 1979, which is an authorised person;
	(d) custodian bank, broker-dealer or stockbroker;
	(e) an entity that undertakes the business of effecting or carrying out insurance contracts, including general and life assurance entities;
	(f) an incorporated friendly society incorporated under the Friendly Societies Act 1992 or a registered friendly society registered under section 7(1)(a) of the Friendly Societies Act 1974 or any enactment which it replaced, including any registered branches;
	(g) an investment trust, Irish investment company, venture capital trust, mutual fund, exchange traded fund, unit trust, open-ended investment company (OEIC);
	(h) a retirement benefit plan; or
	(i) any other entity whose principal activity is to generate wealth or manage risk through financial instruments. This is intended to cover entities that have business activities similar to those listed above but are not specifically included in the list above.
	A parent entity whose sole activity is to hold investments in other group entities is not a financial institution.

[14] *As defined in section 40(4) of the Financial Services and Markets Act 2000 or references to equivalent provisions of any successor legislation.*

FRS 100	FRS 100 *Application of Financial Reporting Requirements*
FRS 101	FRS 101 *Reduced Disclosure Framework*
FRS 102	FRS 102 *The Financial Reporting Standard applicable in the UK and Republic of Ireland*
IAS Regulation	EU Regulation 1606/2002
IFRS	Standards and interpretations issued (or adopted) by the International Accounting Standards Board (IASB). They comprise: (a) International Financial Reporting Standards; (b) International Accounting Standards; and (c) Interpretations developed by the IFRS Interpretations Committee (the Interpretations Committee) or the former Standing Interpretations Committee (SIC).
individual financial statements	The accounts that are required to be prepared by an entity in accordance with the Act or relevant legislation, for example: (a) 'individual accounts', as set out in section 394 of the Act;' (b) 'statement of accounts', as set out in section 132 of the Charities Act 2011; or (c) 'individual accounts', as set out in section 72A of the Building Societies Act 1986. Separate financial statements are included in the meaning of this term.
public benefit entity	An entity whose primary objective is to provide goods or services for the general public, community or social benefit and where any equity is provided with a view to supporting the entity's primary objectives rather than with a view to providing a financial return to equity providers, shareholders or members.
qualifying entity	A member of a group where the parent of that group prepares publicly available consolidated financial statements which are intended to give a true and fair view (of the assets, liabilities, financial position and profit or loss) and that member is included in the consolidation[15]. A charity may not be a qualifying entity.
Regulations	The Large and Medium-sized Companies and Groups (Accounts and Reports) Regulations 2008 (SI 2008/410)

---

[15]*As set out in section 474(1) of the Act.*

Appendix II
Note on legal requirements

INTRODUCTION

A2.1   This appendix provides an overview of how the requirements in FRS 101 address United Kingdom company law requirements. It is therefore written from the perspective of a company to which the Companies Act 2006 applies. Limited liability partnerships (LLPs) are subject to similar legal requirements and therefore may find this appendix useful (see paragraph A2.21). Appendix IV discusses Republic of Ireland legal references.

A2.2   References to the Act in this appendix are to the *Companies Act 2006*. References to the Regulations are to *The Large and Medium-sized Companies and Groups (Accounts and Reports) Regulations 2008* (SI 2008/410) as amended by *The Companies, Partnerships and Groups (Accounts and Reports) Regulations 2015* (SI 2015/980). References to specific provisions are to Schedule 1 to the Regulations; entities applying Schedules 2 or 3 should read them as referring to the equivalent paragraph in those schedules.

COMPANIES ACT ACCOUNTS

A2.3   For companies, accounts prepared in accordance with EU-adopted IFRS are 'IAS accounts', and are within the scope of EU Regulation 1606/2002 (IAS Regulation). As stated in paragraph 4A of FRS 101, where a company prepares accounts in accordance with FRS 101, those accounts are Companies Act accounts and not IAS accounts as set out in section 395 of the Act. Therefore those accounts must comply with the applicable provisions of Parts 15 and 16 of the Act and with the Regulations.

APPLICABLE ACCOUNTING FRAMEWORK

Consistency of financial reporting within groups

A2.4   Section 407 of the Act requires that the directors of the parent company secure that individual accounts of a parent company and each of its subsidiaries are prepared using the same financial reporting framework, except to the extent that in the directors' opinion there are good reasons for not doing so.

In addition, consistency is not required in the following situations:

(a)   when the parent company does not prepare consolidated accounts; or

(b)   when some subsidiaries are charities (consistency is not needed between the framework used for these and for other subsidiaries).

Where the directors of a parent company prepare IAS group accounts and IAS individual accounts, there only has to be consistency across the individual financial statements of the subsidiaries.

A2.5   All companies, other than those which elect or are required to prepare IAS individual accounts in accordance with the Act, prepare Companies Act individual accounts.

Financial instruments measured at fair value

A2.5A   Paragraph 8 of FRS 101 permits qualifying entities that are not financial institutions to take advantage of exemptions from the disclosure requirements of IFRS 7 *Financial Instruments: Disclosures* and IFRS 13 *Fair Value Measurement*. However, as noted in paragraph 4A of FRS 101 a qualifying entity must comply with any relevant legal requirements that are applicable to it.

Paragraph 36 of Schedule 1 to the Regulations states that: **A2.6**

(1)   *Subject to sub-paragraphs (2) to (5), financial instruments (including derivatives) may be included at fair value.*
(2)   *Sub-paragraph (1) does not apply to financial instruments that constitute liabilities unless—*
       (a)   *they are held as part of a trading portfolio,*
       (b)   *they are derivatives, or*
       (c)   *they are financial instruments falling within sub-paragraph (4).*
(3)   *Unless they are financial instruments falling within sub-paragraph (4), sub-paragraph (1) does not apply to—*
       (a)   *financial instruments (other than derivatives) held to maturity,*
       (b)   *loans and receivables originated by the company and not held for trading purposes,*
       (c)   *interests in subsidiary undertakings, associated undertakings and joint ventures,*
       (d)   *equity instruments issued by the company,*
       (e)   *contracts for contingent consideration in a business combination, or*
       (f)   *other financial instruments with such special characteristics that the instruments, according to generally accepted accounting principles or practice, should be accounted for differently from other financial instruments.*
(4)   *Financial instruments which under international accounting standards may be included in accounts at fair value, may be so included, provided that the disclosures required by such accounting standards are made.*
       [...]

A qualifying entity that has financial instruments measured at fair value in accordance with   **A2.7**
the requirements of paragraph 36(4) of Schedule 1 to the Regulations (or equivalent[16]), is legally required to provide the relevant disclosures set out in international accounting standards adopted by the European Commission. Such disclosures should be based on extant standards.

[Not used]   **A2.7A**

[Not used]   **A2.7B**

[Not used]   **A2.7C**

In addition, qualifying entities that are preparing Companies Act accounts must provide   **A2.7D**
the disclosures required by paragraph 55 of Schedule 1 to the Regulations which sets out requirements relating to financial instruments measured at fair value.

Non-amortisation of goodwill

A qualifying entity preparing accounts in accordance with FRS 101 may have recognised   **A2.8**
goodwill which, in accordance with IFRS 3 *Business Combinations*, is not amortised. The non-amortisation of goodwill conflicts with paragraph 22 of Schedule 1 to the Regulations, which requires acquired goodwill to be written off over its useful economic life. As such,

---

[16] *The* Small Companies and Groups (Accounts and Directors' Report) Regulations 2008 *(SI 2008/409) contain an identical provision for companies subject to the small companies regime,* The Large and Medium-sized Limited Liability Partnerships (Accounts) Regulations 2008 *(SI 2008/1913) and* The Small Limited Liability Partnerships (Accounts) Regulations 2008 *(SI 2008/1912) contain similar requirements for limited liability partnerships (see paragraph A2.21).*

the non-amortisation of goodwill will usually be a departure, for the overriding purpose of giving a true and fair view, from the requirement of paragraph 22 of Schedule 1 to the Regulations. In this circumstance there will need to be given in the notes to the accounts 'particulars of the departure, the reasons for it and its effect' (paragraph 10(2) of Schedule 1 to the Regulations). This is not a new instance of the use of the 'true and fair override' as paragraph 18 of FRS 10 *Goodwill and intangible* assets noted that it would have been required by companies applying paragraph 17 of FRS 10 which states 'Where goodwill and intangible assets are regarded as having indefinite useful economic lives, they should not be amortised.'

A2.8A   In addition, similar considerations may apply to intangible assets that are not amortised because they have an indefinite life and intangible assets that have a residual value that is not zero.

Presentation and formats

A2.9   A qualifying entity preparing accounts in accordance with FRS 101 must comply with the company law format requirements applicable to the statement of financial position and the statement of comprehensive income.

A2.9A   A qualifying entity choosing to apply paragraphs 1A(1) and 1A(2) of Schedule 1 to the Regulations, which permit a company to adapt the formats providing that the information given is at least equivalent to that which would have been required by the formats set out in the Regulations, shall apply the relevant presentation requirements of IAS 1, subject to:

(a)   the disclosure of profit or loss before taxation and the amendment to IFRS 5 *Non-current Assets Held for Sale and Discontinued Operations* set out in paragraph AG1(g) of this FRS; and

(b)   any further disaggregation of the statement of financial position, for example in relation to trade and other receivables and trade and other payables, (which may be provided in the notes to the financial statements) that is necessary to meet the requirement to give equivalent information.

This option is not available to a qualifying entity applying Schedule 2 or Schedule 3 to the Regulations or Schedule 1 to the LLP Regulations.

A2.9B   For a qualifying entity not permitted or not choosing to apply paragraphs 1A(1) and 1A(2) of Schedule 1 to the Regulations the format and presentation requirements of IAS 1 *Presentation of Financial Statements* may conflict with those in company law because of the following:

(a)   Differences in the definition of 'fixed assets'[17] (the term used in the Regulations) and 'non-current assets' (the term used in EU-adopted IFRS).

(b)   Differences in the definition of 'current assets' as the term is used in the Regulations and EU-adopted IFRS.

(c)   Differences in the definition of 'creditors falling due within or after one year' (the terms used in the Regulations) and 'current and non-current liabilities' (the term used in EU-adopted IFRS). Under the Act a loan is treated as due for repayment on the earliest date on which a lender could require repayment, whilst under EU-adopted IFRS the due date is based on when the entity expects to settle the liability or has no unconditional right to defer payment.

(d)   The Act requires presentation of debtors falling due after more than one year within current assets. Under EU-adopted IFRS those items would be presented in non-current assets. UITF Abstract 4 *Presentation of long-term debtors in current assets* (the UITF's consensus is reproduced below in paragraph A2.10) addressed the inclusion of debtors due after more than one year within 'current assets'.

---

[17] *Assets of an entity which are intended for use on a continuing basis in the entity's activities.*

In relation to paragraph A2.9(d), in most cases it will be satisfactory to disclose the size of debtors due after more than one year in the notes to the accounts. There will be some instances, however, where the amount is so material in the context of the total net current assets that in the absence of disclosure of the debtors due after more than one year on the face of the balance sheet readers may misinterpret the accounts. In such circumstances, the amount should be disclosed on the face of the balance sheet within current assets.   **A2.10**

Schedule 2 and Schedule 3 to the Regulations and the LLP Regulations require the separate disclosure of extraordinary items in the profit and loss account. A qualifying entity preparing financial statements in accordance with FRS 101 must therefore disclose items that are deemed to be extraordinary items separately in the statement of comprehensive income. Entities should note that extraordinary items are extremely rare as they relate to highly abnormal events or transactions.   **A2.11**

Prospective amendments: FRED 63 (December 2015) proposes insertion of paragraph A2.11A and the sub-heading preceding it with effect for annual periods beginning on or after [date].

Realised profits

Paragraph 13(a) of Schedule 1 to the Regulations requires that only profits realised at the balance sheet date are included in the profit and loss account, a requirement modified from that in Article 3.1(c)(aa) of the Fourth Directive[18] which refers to profits 'made' at the balance sheet date.   **A2.12**

Paragraph 39 of Schedule 1 to the Regulations allows stocks, investment property and living animals and plants to be held at fair value in Companies Act accounts.   **A2.13**

Paragraph 40(2) of Schedule 1 to the Regulations then requires that, in general, movements in the value of financial instruments, stocks, investment properties or living animals or plants are recognised in the profit and loss account, notwithstanding the usual restrictions allowing only realised profits and losses to be included in the profit and loss account. Paragraph 40 of Schedule 1 to the Regulations thereby overrides the requirements of Paragraph 13(a) of Schedule 1.   **A2.14**

Entities measuring investment properties, living animals or plants, or financial instruments at fair value should note that they may transfer such amounts to a separate non-distributable reserve instead of carrying them forward in retained earnings but are not required to do so. Presenting fair value movements that are not distributable profits in a separate reserve may assist with the identification of profits available for that purpose.   **A2.15**

Entities should also continue to note that whether profits are available for distribution must be determined in accordance with applicable law. Entities may also refer to the Technical Release 02/10 *Guidance on Realised and Distributable Profits under the Companies Act 2006* issued by the Institute of Chartered Accountants in England and Wales and the Institute of Chartered Accountants of Scotland or any successor document, to determine profits available for distribution.   **A2.16**

Accounting for investment entities

FRS 101 is not applicable to the preparation of consolidated financial statements as it is only applicable to the individual financial statements of a qualifying entity. However, the requirement set out in paragraph 11A of IAS 27 *Separate Financial Statements* which states: **A2.17**

---

[18] *European Commission, Council Directive 78/660/EEC.*

"If a parent is required, in accordance with paragraph 31 of IFRS 10 to measure its investment in a subsidiary at fair value through profit or loss in accordance with IFRS 9, it shall also account for its investment in a subsidiary in the same way in its separate financial statements."

will be applicable to the treatment of investments in subsidiaries in the individual financial statements of a qualifying entity applying FRS 101, if the entity meets the definition of an investment entity in IFRS 10 *Consolidated Financial Statements*. In other words, a qualifying entity that meets the definition of an investment entity under IFRS 10 must measure its investment in subsidiaries at fair value through profit or loss in its individual financial statements.

A2.18   The Regulations permit investments in subsidiaries to be measured on three different bases as follows:

(a)   at historical cost using the historical cost accounting rules;

(b)   at fair value with fair value movements recognised in reserves using the alternative accounting rules; or

(c)   at fair value with fair value movements recognised in profit or loss using the fair value accounting rules.

A2.19   The requirement to measure investments in subsidiaries at fair value through profit or loss under paragraph 11A of IAS 27 does not conflict with these requirements but merely restricts the measurement bases that an investment entity may apply to such investments.

A2.20   Paragraph 36(4) of Schedule 1 to the Regulations permits investments in subsidiaries to be measured at fair value provided that international accounting standards adopted in the EU allow such measurement, and that an entity makes the disclosures required by such standards. IAS 39 *Financial Instruments: Recognition and Measurement* which was endorsed by the EU in November 2004 and was applicable to accounting periods beginning on or after 1 January 2005, permits the designation of financial instruments at fair value through profit or loss on initial recognition. As noted in paragraph A2.7 such disclosures should be based on extant standards.

LLPS

A2.21   Limited liability partnerships (LLPs) applying FRS 101 will be doing so in conjunction with the LLP Regulations. In many cases these Regulations are similar to the Regulations, limiting the situations in which legal matters relevant to the financial statements of LLPs are not addressed in this Appendix. However, amendments made to the Regulations by *The Companies, Partnerships and Groups (Accounts and Reports) Regulations 2015* (SI 2015/980) have not been reflected in the LLP Regulations. This gives rise to some differences for LLPs. Areas where this may have an impact include:

(a)   the flexibility available in relation to the format of the balance sheet and of the profit and loss account;

(b)   the scope of financial instruments that can be measured at fair value through profit or loss;

(c)   the reversal of impairment losses in relation to goodwill; and

(d)   the application of merger accounting.

If following the requirements of FRS 101 would lead to a conflict with applicable legislation, an LLP shall instead apply its own legal requirements and consider whether disclosure of a departure from FRS 101 is required.

Table I Areas for consideration by a qualifying entity preparing accounts in accordance with FRS 101 *Reduced Disclosure Framework*, in order to ensure compliance with the Act

IFRS	Explanation/potential issues	Amendment to EU-adopted IFRS
IFRS 1	*Assets and liabilities of a parent or subsidiaries*	Restricted the application of the first-time adoption options in IFRS 1 D16 and D17 to situations where the measurement of assets and liabilities in the subsidiary's or parent's individual financial statements based on the consolidated financial statements would comply with FRS 101.
	IFRS 1 provides an option for a subsidiary which becomes a first-time adopter later than its parent, which allows the subsidiary to measure its assets and liabilities at the carrying amounts that would be included in the parent's consolidated financial statements, based on the parent's date of transition to IFRS (D16).	
	Under IFRS 1, if a parent becomes a first-time adopter later than in its consolidated financial statements, it shall measure its assets and liabilities at the same carrying amounts as in the consolidated financial statements (D17).	
	Entities preparing their financial statements in accordance with FRS 101 must comply with the measurement requirements of the Act, which may be inconsistent with those of EU-adopted IFRS applied in the consolidated financial statements.	
IFRS 3	*Negative goodwill*	Amended IFRS 3.34 to align with FRS 102, Section 19 *Business Combinations and Goodwill*, paragraph 19.24.
	IFRS 3 requires that negative goodwill is recognised as a gain in profit or loss at the acquisition date (IFRS 3.34). The Act does not contain accounting requirements for a negative consolidation difference subsequent to recognition. Nevertheless, the Seventh Directive[19] sets out conditions under which a negative consolidation difference may be transferred to the profit and loss account. The conditions under the Seventh Accounting Directive may be inconsistent with the recognition requirements for negative goodwill under EU-adopted IFRS.	

[19] *European Commission, Council Directive 83/349/EEC*

IFRS	Explanation/potential issues	Amendment to EU-adopted IFRS
IFRS 5	*Analysis of results of discontinued operation* IFRS 5 allows the analysis of post-tax results of discontinued operations to be presented on the face of the statement of comprehensive income or in the notes (IFRS 5.33). The Regulations require an entity to show totals for turnover, profit or loss before taxation and tax arising from ordinary activities on the face of the profit and loss account.	Removed the option in IFRS 5.33 to present the analysis in the notes to the accounts. The information must be presented on the face of the statement of comprehensive income in a columnar format.
IAS 1	*Formats* The format requirements applicable under IAS 1 and those under the Regulations may be incompatible.	IAS 1.53A and IAS 1.81C are inserted to disapply IAS 1.54 to IAS 1.76, IAS 1.82 and IAS 1.84 to IAS 1.86, unless certain options in Schedule 1 to the Regulations are chosen.
	Extraordinary items IAS 1 does not permit the presentation of extraordinary items (IAS 1.87) however, for some companies and LLPs the Regulations (and LLP Regulations) require it.	Amended IAS 1.87 and inserted IAS 1.87A and IAS 1.87B to include the definition of extraordinary items consistent with that in FRS 102, Section 5 *Statement of comprehensive income and income statement*, paragraphs 5.10A and 5.10B.
	Realised profits IAS 1 requires the recognition of all income and expenses in profit or loss, unless otherwise required or permitted by an IFRS (IAS 1.88). The Regulations require that only profits realised at the balance sheet date are included in the profit and loss account (see paragraphs A2.12 to A2.15 above).	Amended IAS 1.88 to clarify the precedence of the Act.

IFRS	Explanation/potential issues	Amendment to EU-adopted IFRS
IAS 16	*Government grants* IAS 16.28 permits the carrying amount of property, plant and equipment to be reduced by government grants in accordance with IAS 20. Off-setting of items that represent assets against items that represent liabilities is prohibited under the Regulations, unless specifically permitted or required. This option in EU-adopted IFRS is not compliant with the Regulations.	Deleted IAS 16.28.
IAS 20	*Balance sheet off-setting* IAS 20.24 contains an option which permits government grants related to assets to be deducted in arriving at the carrying amount of the asset. Off-setting of items that represent assets against items that represent liabilities is prohibited under the Regulations, unless specifically permitted or required. This option in EU-adopted IFRS is not compliant with the Regulations. *Profit and loss account off-setting* IAS 20.29 contains an option which permits grants related to income to be deducted in reporting the related expense. Off-setting of items that represent income against items that represent expenditure is prohibited under the Regulations, unless specifically permitted or required. This option in EU-adopted IFRS is not compliant with the Regulations.	Amended IAS 20.24, IAS 20.26, IAS 20.28 and deleted IAS 20.25 and IAS 20.27 to remove the off-set option. Amended IAS 20.29 to remove the off-set option.

Appendix III
Previous consultations

HISTORY OF PREVIOUS CONSULTATIONS

A3.1   The requirements in FRSs 100 to 102 are the outcome of a lengthy and extensive consultation. The FRC (and formerly the ASB) together with the Department for Business, Innovation and Skills have consulted on the future of accounting standards in the UK and Republic of Ireland (RoI) over a ten year period.

Table 1 – Consultations conducted

Year	Consultation
2002	DTI[20] consults on adoption of IAS Regulation
2004	Discussion Paper – Strategy for Convergence with IFRS
2005	Exposure Draft – Policy Statement: The Role of the ASB
2006	Public Meeting and Proposals for Comment
2006	Press Notice seeking views
2007	Consultation Paper – Proposed IFRS for SMEs
2009	Consultation Paper – Policy Proposal: The future of UK GAAP
2010	Request for Responses – Development of the Impact Assessment
2010	Financial Reporting Exposure Drafts 43 and 44
2011	Financial Reporting Exposure Draft 45
2012	Financial Reporting Exposure Drafts 46, 47 and 48

2004

A3.2   In 2004 the Discussion Paper contained two key elements underpinning the proposals: firstly that UK and Republic of Ireland (RoI) accounting standards should be based on IFRS and secondly that a phased approach to the introduction of the standards should be adopted.

A3.3   The ASB embarked on the phased approach and issued a number of standards based on IFRS. The majority of respondents agreed with a framework based on IFRS, and although supportive overall, the response to the phased approach was mixed.

2005

A3.4   In its 2005 Exposure Draft (2005 ED) of a Policy Statement *Accounting standard-setting in a changing environment: The role of the Accounting Standards Board*, amongst other aspects of its role, the ASB identified its intention to converge with IFRS by implementing new IFRS in the UK as soon as possible. It also proposed to continue the phased approach to

---

[20] *The Department of Trade and Industry (DTI) was a United Kingdom government department which was replaced with the announcement of the creation of the Department for Business, Enterprise and Regulatory Reform and the Department for Innovation, Universities and Skills on 28 June 2007, which were themselves merged into the Department for Business, Innovation and Skills (BIS) on 6 June 2009.*

adopting UK accounting standards based on older IFRSs, but recognised there was little case for being more prescriptive than IFRS.

Although the ASB had, in the 2005 ED, wanted to move the debate on to how it would seek to influence the IASB's agenda, respondents' main concern remained about convergence. In 2005, the ASB issued an exposure draft proposing the IASB's standard on Business Combinations be adopted in the UK and RoI. This exposure draft highlighted the complexity of a mixed set of UK accounting standards, with some based on IFRSs and others developed independently by the ASB. The majority of respondents continued to agree with the aim of basing UK accounting standards on IFRS, but a broader set of views on how to achieve this was emerging. **A3.5**

As time progressed the ASB formed the view that convergence by adopting certain IFRSs was not meeting the needs of its constituents, which no longer included quoted groups. The ASB was concerned about the complexity of certain IFRSs, and it noted that introducing them piecemeal created complications and anomalies within the body of current FRSs. This arose because IFRS-based standards were not an exact replacement for current FRSs and many consequential amendments were required to 'fit' each replacement IFRS-based standard into the existing body of UK FRS. The ASB agreed to continue with its convergence programme, but decided to re-examine how to achieve this. **A3.6**

2006

The ASB published revised proposals to be discussed at the 2006 public meeting. By this time the IASB had started its IFRS for SMEs project, and the ASB decided this might have a role as one of the tiers in the UK financial reporting framework. The ASB proposed a 'big bang' with new IFRS-based UK accounting standards mandatory from a single date, 1 January 2009. The ASB's proposal was for a three-tier system, with Tier 1 being EU-adopted IFRS, and the other two tiers being developed as the IASB progressed with its project on the IFRS for SMEs. **A3.7**

Those attending the public meeting supported the aim of basing UK and RoI accounting standards on IFRS and adapting them to ensure they were appropriate for the entities applying them. **A3.8**

Taking this feedback into account, later in 2006 the ASB issued a Press Notice (PN 289) seeking views on its current thinking: **A3.9**

(a) All quoted and publicly accountable companies should apply EU-adopted IFRS.
(b) The FRSSE should be retained and extended to include medium-sized entities.
(c) UK subsidiaries of groups applying full IFRS should apply EU-adopted IFRS, but with reduced disclosure requirements.
(d) No firm decision on the remainder (Tier 2), but options included extending the FRSSE, extending full IFRS, maintaining separate UK accounting standards or some combination of these.

The responses were mixed, but there was agreement that whatever the solution, it should be based on IFRS and there should be different reporting tiers to ensure proportionality. **A3.10**

2007

The IASB published an exposure draft of its IFRS for SMEs in early 2007; shortly afterwards the ASB published its own consultation paper. This sought views on how the IFRS for SMEs might fit into the future UK financial reporting framework, for example **A3.11** whether it might be appropriate for Tier 2, with the FRSSE continuing for those eligible for the small companies' regime.

A3.12   Feedback on the IFRS for SMEs was largely positive: it would be suitable for Tier 2, it was international, it was compatible with IFRSs, and it represented a significant simplification. Overall, it was seen as a workable alternative to IFRS. In addition, respondents wanted to retain the FRSSE (because it reduces the regulatory burden on smaller entities) and to give subsidiaries the option of applying the IFRS for SMEs as well as a reduced disclosure regime if applying full IFRS.

2009

A3.13   The IFRS for SMEs was published in 2009, allowing the ASB to further develop its proposals in the Consultation Paper *Policy Proposal: The future of UK GAAP*. The proposals were largely consistent with the cumulative results of the preceding consultations and included:

(a)   a move to an IFRS-based framework;
(b)   a three-tier approach;
(c)   publicly accountable entities would be Tier 1 and would apply EU-adopted IFRS;
(d)   small companies would be Tier 3 and continue to apply the FRSSE; and
(e)   other entities would be Tier 2 and should apply a UK and RoI accounting standard based on the IFRS for SMEs.

A3.14   The only significant proposal that was inconsistent with respondents' previous comments was that subsidiaries should simply apply the requirement of the tier they individually met – respondents had wanted subsidiaries to be able to take advantage of disclosure exemptions, and at that time the ASB had yet to be convinced that significant cost savings were available from a reduced disclosure framework. Taking into account the feedback received, this proposal was subsequently reversed and the reduced disclosure framework was incorporated into FREDs 43 and then 46, and it is now set out in FRS 101.

A3.15   In addition to the many useful and detailed points made, some common themes included general agreement that change was needed to UK accounting standards and that there was support for many of the changes proposed in the consultation paper.

2010 onwards

A3.16   The request for responses to aid development of the Impact Assessment focused on obtaining feedback on the expected costs, benefits and impact of the proposals subsequently set out in FREDs 43 and 44, rather than on the accounting principles. As the focus was on costs and benefits no specific question was asked about the principle of the proposed introduction of an IFRS-based framework, but nevertheless respondents commented on this: of the 32 responses received only 12.5% did not agree with the introduction of an IFRS-based framework.

A3.17   FREDs 43 and 44 issued in October 2010 set out the draft suggested text for two new accounting standards that would replace the majority of extant Financial Reporting Standards (current FRS) in the UK and RoI. The ASB issued a supplementary FRED addressing specific needs of public benefit entities (FRED 45) in March 2011. The ASB then updated FREDs 43, 44 and 45, replacing them with the revised FREDs 46, 47 and 48 in January 2012, by eliminating the concept of public accountability and by introducing a number of accounting treatment options that are available in EU-adopted IFRS. The Accounting Council's advice to the FRC to issue FRSs 100 to 102 includes more discussion of the feedback received on FREDs 43 to 48 and how the proposals have been refined and developed into the standards.

HOW HAVE THE PROPOSALS BEEN DEVELOPED?

As set out above, the FRC, the Accounting Council (and previously the ASB) have consulted   **A3.18**
regularly on the future of financial reporting in the UK and RoI. Over the consultations the
ASB's (and the Accounting Council's) thinking has evolved based on careful consideration
of the feedback at each stage. Whilst responses were sometimes mixed, there has been
agreement that:

(a)   current FRS, which are a mixture of Statements of Standard Accounting Practice
       (SSAPs) issued by the Consultative Committee of Accounting Bodies, FRSs
       developed and issued by the ASB and IFRS-based standards issued by the ASB to
       converge with international standards, are an uncomfortable mismatch that lack
       strong underlying principles or cohesion; and
(b)   whatever the solution, it should be based on IFRS and there should be different
       reporting tiers to ensure proportionality.

During the consultation process to date, the Accounting Council and formerly the ASB   **A3.19**
have been guided by the following principles:

(a)   The framework must be fit for purpose, so that each entity required to produce true
       and fair financial statements under UK and RoI law will deliver financial statements
       that are suited to the needs of its primary users. The Accounting Council has kept
       in close contact with constituent users on this point, including investors, creditor
       institutions and the tax authorities.
(b)   The framework must be proportionate, so that preparing entities are not unduly
       burdened by costs that outweigh the benefit to them and to the primary users of
       information in their financial statements. The FRC believes that the proposals will
       produce a lower cost regime, while enhancing user benefits. It has carried out a
       consultation stage impact assessment with input from interested parties, and will
       continue to assess cost-benefit issues.
(c)   The framework must be in line with UK company law. This determines which
       entities must produce true and fair financial statements. Exemptions within the law
       have generally been retained. The detailed requirements of the Companies Act 2006
       are driven to a great extent by the European Accounting Directives, which are being
       revised[21].
(d)   The framework must be future-proofed, where possible. The FRC will continue to
       monitor the situation and has sovereignty over UK accounting standards (subject to
       the law). Changes to the Accounting Directives may lead to further developments,
       for example the European Council and European Parliament decision to permit
       Member States an option to treat micro-entities as a separate category of Company
       and exempt them from certain accounting requirements.

SUMMARY OF OUTREACH

During the development and throughout the consultation period of FREDs 43 to 48, the   **A3.20**
ASB undertook an extensive programme of outreach aimed at raising awareness of the
proposals and to address the view (held by some) that previous consultations had not
gathered sufficient evidence to support and test the assumptions made.

As part of the outreach programme to obtain both formal and informal feedback, a   **A3.21**
series of meetings and events took place with users, including with lenders to small and
medium-sized entities. Lenders noted that financial statements are an important part of
their decision-making process when considering whether to provide finance and, whilst a

---

[21] *The EU's consultation process on review of the Accounting Directives is summarised at http://ec.europa.eu/
internal_market/accounting/sme_accounting/review_directives_en.htm*

decision to provide finance is not based on financial statements alone, they provide useful information and verification to the lender.

A3.22   Although the ASB and the Accounting Council employed their best efforts to obtain feedback from users (a constituent group historically difficult to engage with formally) it is disappointing that limited formal responses were received and the Accounting Council has not been more successful in obtaining input from users.

A3.23   In addition, a review was made of academic research that addressed the users of the financial statements of small and medium-sized entities. The conclusion drawn from the research was that many entities requested financial statements from Companies House when considering whether to trade with another entity. The European Federation of Accountants and Auditors (EFAA) issued, in May 2011, a statement that identified the users of financial statements, noting who the users of SMEs' financial statements are and that information on the public record assists all users of financial statements of SMEs' by providing, in an efficient manner, basic information that protects their rights.

A3.24   The ASB considered that the outreach programme had gleaned information from people who would not normally submit formal responses to a consultation and provided very useful information that could be used in developing the next stage of the project. The ASB noted that whilst this information was not part of the public record, as are formal consultation responses, it could use the information to assist in developing the revised FREDs 46 to 48, supplementing information contained in responses, and would seek further comment in the next stage of its deliberations.

A3.25   The Accounting Council continued the work of the ASB in finalising FRSs 100 to 102. The responses to FREDs 46 to 48 were analysed and discussed, and engagements were conducted to take into account the views and suggestions of all relevant associations and contacts. Respondents and outreach contacts were satisfied with FREDs 46 to 48, and many of the response letters were forthcoming in their overall praise for the proposals. A significant number of constituents anticipated cost savings arising from the application of FRS 101. Many respondents considered that FRS 102 would improve UK accounting standards, in particular by introducing requirements for accounting for financial instruments. Further they considered that the improvements will be achieved in a way that will be proportionate to the needs of users, and that once the transition phase has been overcome, it will have the effect of reducing the reporting burden on those UK companies that adopt it.

Appendix IV
Republic of Ireland (RoI) legal references

Appendix IV: *Republic of Ireland (RoI) legal references* will be updated as appropriate for both the Companies Act 2014 and the Irish legislation implementing the EU Accounting Directive once the latter has been made. This will be made available on the FRC website and included in the next edition of FRS 101.

A4.1

FRS 102
The Financial Reporting Standard
applicable in the UK and Republic of Ireland (2014)

(August 2014)

Contents

Paragraphs

Summary

FRS 102 The Financial Reporting Standard applicable in the UK and Republic of Ireland

Approval by the FRC

The Accounting Council's Advice to the FRC to issue FRS 102

Appendices

Prospective amendments: Amendments to FRS 102 *The Financial Reporting Standard applicable in the UK and Republic of Ireland* – Small entities and other minor amendments (July 2015) amends FRS 102 with effect for annual periods beginning on or after 1 January 2016.

Editor's note: The FRC has issued this revised edition of FRS 102 which incorporates a) editorial amendments, issued on 19 March 2014, to Section 11 *Basic Financial Instruments*, Section 12 *Other Financial Instruments Issues* and Section 35 *Transition to this FRS*; b) *Amendments to FRS 102 – Basic financial instruments and Hedge accounting* issued in July 2014; and c) the correction of some minor typographical errors. This Standard will be effective for accounting periods beginning on or after 1 January 2015.

Amendments to FRS 102 *The Financial Reporting Standard applicable in the UK and Republic of Ireland* – Pension obligations (February 2015) amended this Standard with effect for annual periods beginning on or after 1 January 2015.

This standard was amended by FRS 104 (March 2015) with effect for interim periods commencing on or after 1 January 2015 with early application permitted.

This standard was amended by FRS 102 – Editorial amendments and clarification statements (last updated 16 April 2015).

SUMMARY

(i)   In 2012, 2013 and 2014 the Financial Reporting Council (FRC) revised financial reporting standards in the United Kingdom and Republic of Ireland. The revisions fundamentally reformed financial reporting, replacing the extant standards with four Financial Reporting Standards:

   (a)   FRS 100 *Application of Financial Reporting Requirements*;

   (b)   FRS 101 *Reduced Disclosure Framework*;

   (c)   FRS 102 *The Financial Reporting Standard applicable in the UK and Republic of Ireland*; and

   (d)   FRS 103 *Insurance Contracts*.

(ii)   The revisions made by the FRC followed a sustained and detailed period of consultation. The FRC made these fundamental changes recognising that the introduction of International Financial Reporting Standards for listed groups in 2002 (with application from 2005) called into question the need for two sets of financial reporting standards. Evidence from consultation supported a move towards an international-based framework for financial reporting, but one that was proportionate to the needs of preparers and users.

(iii)   The FRC's overriding objective in setting accounting standards is to enable users of accounts to receive high-quality understandable financial reporting proportionate to the size and complexity of the entity and users' information needs.

(iv)   In meeting this objective, the FRC aims to provide succinct financial reporting standards that:

   (a)   have consistency with international accounting standards through the application of an IFRS-based solution unless an alternative clearly better meets the overriding objective;

   (b)   reflect up-to-date thinking and developments in the way entities operate and the transactions they undertake;

   (c)   balance consistent principles for accounting by all UK and Republic of Ireland entities with practical solutions, based on size, complexity, public interest and users' information needs;

   (d)   promote efficiency within groups; and

   (e)   are cost-effective to apply.

(v)   The requirements in this Financial Reporting Standard (FRS) take into consideration the findings from the previous consultations on the future of financial reporting in the UK and Republic of Ireland that took place between 2002 and 2014.

(vi)   This FRS is a single financial reporting standard that applies to the financial statements of entities that are not applying EU-adopted IFRS, FRS 101 or the FRSSE[1].

The Financial Reporting Standard applicable in the UK and Republic of Ireland and the IFRS for SMEs

(vii)   This FRS aims to provide entities with succinct financial reporting requirements. The requirements in this FRS are based on the International Accounting Standards Board's (IASB) International Financial Reporting Standard for Small and Medium-sized Entities (IFRS for SMEs) issued in 2009. The IFRS for SMEs is intended to apply to the general purpose financial statements of, and other financial reporting by, entities that in many countries are referred to by a variety of terms including 'small and medium-sized', 'private' and 'non-publicly accountable'.

---

[1] *This FRS does not, however apply to the preparation of 'Companies Act accounts' of certain companies under company law in the Republic of Ireland. Please refer to Appendix VI for further details.*

(viii) The Accounting Standards Board (ASB)[2] first consulted on the use of the IFRS for SMEs to replace extant Financial Reporting Standards in the United Kingdom and Republic of Ireland in 2006. In 2010 the ASB issued a financial reporting exposure draft (FRED 44 *Financial Reporting Standard for Medium-sized Entities*) proposing the application of the IFRS for SMEs to entities that did not have public accountability and were not eligible to apply the FRSSE. Entities with public accountability would have been required to apply EU-adopted IFRS; respondents to the proposals were not supportive of the extension of the application of EU-adopted IFRS. Based on this feedback, the ASB decided to amend the IFRS for SMEs so that it is relevant to a broader group of preparers and users.

(ix) The IFRS for SMEs is a simplification of the principles in IFRS for recognising and measuring assets, liabilities, income and expenses; in most cases it includes only the simpler accounting treatment where IFRS permit accounting options, it contains fewer disclosures and it is drafted more succinctly than IFRS. Whilst respondents to FRED 44 welcomed simplification, many did not support the removal of accounting options where those options were permitted in extant FRS. As a consequence, the ASB amended the IFRS for SMEs to include accounting options in current FRS and permitted by IFRS, but not included in the IFRS for SMEs.

(x) The ASB also issued FRED 45 *Financial Reporting Standard for Public Benefit Entities* in 2011 that addressed the accounting for some transactions and circumstances that are common to public benefit entities. Respondents to FRED 45 noted that it was difficult to identify when the requirements in the FRED should be applied. The ASB consequently decided to combine the requirements of FREDs 44 and 45 into one FRS.

(xi) The FRC has thus modified the IFRS for SMEs substantially, both in terms of the scope of entities eligible to apply it and in terms of the accounting treatments provided. To reflect this wider scope the proposed name of the standard was revised to FRS 102 *Financial Reporting Standard applicable in the UK and Republic of Ireland*.

(xii) FRS 102 is designed to apply to the general purpose financial statements and financial reporting of entities including those that are not constituted as companies and those that are not profit-oriented. General purpose financial statements are intended to focus on the common information needs of a wide range of users; shareholders, lenders, other creditors, employees and members of the public, for example.

Organisation of FRS 102

(xiii) FRS 102 is organised by topic with each topic presented in a separate numbered section. Cross-references to paragraphs are identified by section followed by paragraph number. Paragraph numbers are in the form of xx.yy, where xx is the section number and yy is the sequential paragraph number within that section. Those paragraphs that apply solely to public benefit entities are identified by the prefix 'PBE'[3]. In order to maintain consistency with the paragraph numbering of the IFRS for SMEs, when a paragraph from the IFRS for SMEs has been deleted and not replaced with an alternative paragraph, the phrase [not used] is given. In examples that include monetary amounts, the measuring unit is Currency Unit (abbreviated as CU).

(xiv) All the paragraphs of FRS 102 have equal authority. Some sections include appendices of implementation guidance or examples. Some of these are an integral part of the

---

[2] *The Financial Reporting Council (FRC) became the prescribed body for issuing accounting standards on 2 July 2012; the prescribed body was previously the Accounting Standards Board (ASB). References in this section and Appendix V are made to the FRC, ASB or Accounting Council, as appropriate in terms of the time period and context of the reference.*

[3] *In some cases 'PBE' prefixed paragraphs also apply to other entities in a public benefit entity group.*

FRS while others provide guidance concerning its application; each specifies its status.

(xv) This FRS is set out in Sections 1 to 35 and the Glossary (Appendix I). Terms defined in the Glossary are in **bold type** the first time they appear in each section and subsection within Section 34.

(xvi) This edition of FRS 102 issued in August 2014 updates the edition of FRS 102 issued in March 2013 for the following:

(a) an editorial amendment to Section 11 *Basic Financial Instruments* and Section 12 *Other Financial Instruments Issues* in relation to the presentation requirements for financial instruments issued on 19 March 2014;

(b) an editorial amendment to Section 35 *Transition to this FRS* in relation to the transitional exemptions for service concession arrangements issued on 19 March 2014;

(c) *Amendments to FRS 102 – Basic financial instruments and Hedge accounting* issued in July 2014; and

(d) the correction of some minor typographical errors.

FRS 102 THE FINANCIAL REPORTING STANDARD APPLICABLE IN THE UK AND REPUBLIC OF IRELAND

Section 1 Scope

Scope of this Financial Reporting Standard

1.1   This FRS applies to **financial statements** that are intended to give a true and fair view of a reporting entity's **financial position** and **profit or loss** (or **income and expenditure**) for a period.

1.2   The requirements of this FRS are applicable to **public benefit entities** and other entities, not just to companies. However, those paragraph numbers prefixed with 'PBE' shall only be applied by public benefit entities, and shall not be applied directly, or by analogy, by entities that are not public benefit entities, other than, where specifically directed, entities within a **public benefit entity group**.

Prospective amendments: Amendments to FRS 102 *The Financial Reporting Standard applicable in the UK and Republic of Ireland* – Small entities and other minor amendments (July 2015) inserts paragraph 1.2A with effect for annual periods beginning on or after 1 January 2016.

Basis of preparation of financial statements

1.3   As stated in **FRS 100**, an entity that is required by the **IAS Regulation** (or other legislation or regulation) to prepare **consolidated financial statements** in accordance with **EU-adopted IFRS** must do so. The **individual financial statements** of such an entity, or the individual financial statements or consolidated financial statements of any other entity within the scope of FRS 100, must be prepared in accordance with the following requirements:

(a)   If the financial statements are those of an entity that is eligible to apply the **FRSSE**[4], they may be prepared in accordance with that standard.

(b)   If the financial statements are those of an entity that is not eligible to apply the FRSSE, or of an entity that is eligible to apply the FRSSE but chooses not to do so, they must[5] be prepared in accordance with this FRS, EU-adopted IFRS or **FRS 101**[6].

Prospective amendments: Amendments to FRS 102 *The Financial Reporting Standard applicable in the UK and Republic of Ireland* – Small entities and other minor amendments (July 2015) amends paragraph 1.3 and footnote 4 with effect for annual periods beginning on or after 1 January 2016.

---

[4] *The eligibility criteria for applying the FRSSE are set out in paragraph 8 of the FRSSE. One of the criteria is that the entity must be 'small' as defined in company law. Turnover and balance sheet total should be measured in accordance with the FRSSE for the purposes of establishing whether the entity is 'small'; the measurement of turnover and balance sheet total in accordance with FRS 101 or FRS 102 need not be considered.*

[5] *Under company law in the Republic of Ireland, certain companies are permitted to prepare 'Companies Act accounts' using accounting standards other than those issued by the FRC. Please refer to Appendix VI for further details.*

[6] *Individual financial statements that are prepared by a company in accordance with FRS 101 or FRS 102 are Companies Act individual accounts (section 395(1)(a) of the Act), whereas those prepared in accordance with EU-adopted IFRS are IAS individual accounts (section 395(1)(b) of the Act).*

An entity whose **ordinary shares** or **potential ordinary shares** are **publicly traded**, or that files, or is in the process of filing, its financial statements with a securities commission or other regulatory organisation for the purpose of issuing ordinary shares in a public market, or an entity that chooses to disclose earnings per share, shall apply IAS 33 *Earnings per Share* (as adopted in the EU).   **1.4**

An entity whose debt or equity instruments are publicly traded, or that files, or is in the process of filing, its financial statements with a securities commission or other regulatory organisation for the purpose of issuing any class of instruments in a public market, or an entity that chooses to provide information described as segment information, shall apply IFRS 8 *Operating Segments* (as adopted in the EU). If an entity discloses disaggregated information, but the information does not comply with the requirements of IFRS 8, it shall not describe the information as segment information.   **1.5**

An entity shall apply FRS 103 *Insurance Contracts* to: **1.6**

(a)   **insurance contracts** (including **reinsurance contracts**) that it issues and reinsurance contracts that it holds; and

(b)   **financial instruments** with a **discretionary participation feature** that it issues.

When applying IAS 33, IFRS 8 and IFRS 6 *Exploration for and Evaluation of Mineral Resources* (see paragraph 34.11), references made to other IFRSs within those standards shall be taken to be references to the relevant section or paragraph in this FRS.   **1.7**

Reduced disclosures for subsidiaries (and ultimate parents)

A **qualifying entity** (for the purposes of this FRS) which is not a **financial institution** may take advantage in its individual financial statements of the disclosure exemptions set out in paragraph 1.12. In relation to paragraph 1.12(c) for **financial liabilities** that are held at **fair value** that are either part of a trading portfolio or are **derivatives**, the qualifying entity can take advantage of those exemptions. Where the qualifying entity has financial instruments held at fair value subject to the requirements of paragraph 36(4) of Schedule 1 to the **Regulations**, it must apply the disclosure requirements of Section 11 *Basic Financial Instruments* to those financial instruments held at fair value.   **1.8**

A qualifying entity (for the purposes of this FRS) which is a financial institution may take advantage in its individual financial statements of the disclosure exemptions set out in paragraph 1.12, except for the disclosure exemptions from Section 11 and Section 12 *Other Financial Instruments Issues*.   **1.9**

A qualifying entity (for the purposes of this FRS) which is required to prepare consolidated financial statements (for example, if the entity is required by section 399 of the **Act** to prepare consolidated financial statements, and is not entitled to any of the exemptions in sections 400 to 402 of the Act), or which voluntarily chooses to do so, may not take advantage of the disclosure exemptions set out in paragraph 1.12 in its consolidated financial statements.   **1.10**

A qualifying entity (for the purposes of this FRS) may take advantage of the disclosure exemptions in paragraph 1.12, in accordance with paragraphs 1.8 to 1.10, provided that: **1.11**

(a)   Its shareholders have been notified in writing about, and do not object to, the use of the disclosure exemptions. Objections to the use of the disclosure exemptions may be served on the qualifying entity, in accordance with reasonable specified timeframes and format requirements, by a shareholder that is the immediate **parent** of the entity, or by a shareholder or shareholders holding in aggregate 5% or more of the total allotted shares in the entity or more than half of the allotted shares in the entity that are not held by the immediate parent.

(b)   It otherwise applies the **recognition**, **measurement** and disclosure requirements of this FRS.

(c)   It discloses in the **notes** to its financial statements:

    (i)   a brief narrative summary of the disclosure exemptions adopted; and

    (ii)   the name of the parent[7] of the **group** in whose consolidated financial statements its financial statements are consolidated, and from where those financial statements may be obtained.

1.12   A qualifying entity (for the purposes of this FRS) may take advantage of the following disclosure exemptions:

(a)   The requirements of Section 4 *Statement of Financial Position* paragraph 4.12(a)(iv).

(b)   The requirements of Section 7 *Statement of Cash Flows* and Section 3 *Financial Statement Presentation* paragraph 3.17(d).

(c)   The requirements of Section 11 paragraphs 11.39 to 11.48A and Section 12 paragraphs 12.26 to 12.29A providing the equivalent disclosures required by this FRS are included in the consolidated financial statements of the group in which the entity is consolidated.

(d)   The requirements of Section 26 *Share-based Payment* paragraphs 26.18(b), 26.19 to 26.21 and 26.23, provided that for a qualifying entity that is:

    (i)   a **subsidiary**, the share-based payment arrangement concerns equity instruments of another group entity;

    (ii)   an ultimate parent, the share-based payment arrangement concerns its own equity instruments and its **separate financial statements** are presented alongside the consolidated financial statements of the group;

    and, in both cases, provided that the equivalent disclosures required by this FRS are included in the consolidated financial statements of the group in which the entity is consolidated.

(e)   The requirement of Section 33 *Related Party Disclosures* paragraph 33.7.

Prospective amendments: Amendments to FRS 102 *The Financial Reporting Standard applicable in the UK and Republic of Ireland* – Small entities and other minor amendments (July 2015) amends paragraph 1.12 with effect for annual periods beginning on or after 1 January 2016.

1.13   Reference shall be made to the Application Guidance to FRS 100 in deciding whether the consolidated financial statements of the parent provide disclosures which are equivalent to the requirements of this FRS (ie the full requirements of this FRS when not applying the disclosure exemptions) from which relief is provided in paragraph 1.12.

Date from which effective and transitional arrangements

1.14   An entity shall apply this FRS for accounting periods beginning on or after 1 January 2015. Early application is permitted for accounting periods ending on or after 31 December 2012. For entities that are within the scope of a SORP, early application is permitted for accounting periods ending on or after 31 December 2012 providing it does not conflict with the requirements of a current SORP or legal requirements for the preparation of financial statements. If an entity applies this FRS before 1 January 2015 it shall disclose that fact.

---

[7] *The parent identified in the definition of the term 'qualifying entity'.*

This FRS permits a financial instrument (provided it meets certain criteria) to be designated on initial recognition as a **financial asset** or financial liability at fair value through profit or loss. Entities that have applied this FRS in financial statements authorised for issue prior to 1 August 2014 are permitted in their first financial statements authorised for issue on or after 1 August 2014 to designate, as at the date of transition to this FRS, any financial asset or financial liability at fair value through profit or loss provided the asset or liability meets the criteria in paragraph 11.14(b) at that date. Entities that have applied this FRS in financial statements authorised for issue prior to 1 August 2014 are permitted in their first financial statements authorised for issue on or after 1 August 2014 to de-designate any financial asset or financial liability previously designated at fair value through profit or loss and classify and measure the financial instrument in accordance with Section 11.

1.14A

This FRS permits entities to apply hedge accounting, provided certain qualifying conditions are met. Entities that have applied this FRS in financial statements authorised for issue prior to 1 August 2014 are permitted to apply hedge accounting to a hedging relationship existing on or before 31 July 2014 as set out in Section 12 of this FRS from a date no earlier than the conditions of paragraphs 12.18(a) to (c) are met, provided the conditions of paragraphs 12.18(d) and (e) are met no later than the date the first financial statements issued on or after 1 August 2014 are authorised for issue. This choice applies to each hedging relationship existing on or before 31 July 2014. This choice only applies in respect of the first financial statements that comply with this FRS that are authorised for issue on or after 1 August 2014.

1.14B

In a fair value hedge the cumulative **hedging gain or loss** on the hedged item from the date hedge accounting commenced, shall be recorded in retained earnings (or if appropriate, another category of **equity**). In a cash flow hedge and net investment hedge, the lower of the following (in absolute amounts) shall be recorded in equity (in respect of cash flow hedges in the cash flow hedge reserve):

(a)   the cumulative gain or loss on the hedging instrument from the date hedge accounting commenced to the reporting date of the last financial statements authorised for issue prior to 1 August 2014; and

(b)   the cumulative change in fair value (ie the present value of the cumulative change of expected future cash flows) on the hedged item from the date hedge accounting commenced to the reporting date of the last financial statements authorised for issue prior to 1 August 2014.

Prospective amendments: Amendments to FRS 102 *The Financial Reporting Standard applicable in the UK and Republic of Ireland* – Small entities and other minor amendments (July 2015) inserts paragraph 1.15 with effect for annual periods beginning on or after 1 January 2016.

Section 1A *Small Entities*

Prospective amendments: Amendments to FRS 102 *The Financial Reporting Standard applicable in the UK and Republic of Ireland* – Small entities and other minor amendments (July 2015) inserts a new Section 1A and its appendices with effect for annual periods beginning on or after 1 January 2016.

Section 2 Concepts and Pervasive Principles

Scope of this section

This section describes the **objective of financial statements** of entities within the scope of this FRS and the qualities that make the information in the **financial statements** of entities

2.1

within the scope of this FRS useful. It also sets out the concepts and basic principles underlying the financial statements of entities within the scope of this FRS.

2.1A   Although this section sets out the concepts and pervasive principles underlying financial statements, in some circumstances there may be inconsistencies between the concepts and principles in this section of the FRS and the specific requirements of another section. In these circumstances the specific requirements of the other section within the FRS take precedence over this section.

Objective of financial statements

2.2   The objective of financial statements is to provide information about the **financial position**, **performance** and **cash flows** of an entity that is useful for economic decision-making by a broad range of users who are not in a position to demand reports tailored to meet their particular information needs.

2.3   Financial statements also show the results of the stewardship of management – the accountability of management for the resources entrusted to it.

Qualitative characteristics of information in financial statements

Understandability

2.4   The information provided in financial statements should be presented in a way that makes it comprehensible by users who have a reasonable knowledge of **business** and economic activities and accounting and a willingness to study the information with reasonable diligence. However, the need for **understandability** does not allow relevant information to be omitted on the grounds that it may be too difficult for some users to understand.

Relevance

2.5   The information provided in financial statements must be relevant to the decision-making needs of users. Information has the quality of **relevance** when it is capable of influencing the economic decisions of users by helping them evaluate past, present or future events or confirming, or correcting, their past evaluations.

Materiality

2.6   Information is **material** – and therefore has relevance – if its omission or misstatement, individually or collectively, could influence the economic decisions of users taken on the basis of the financial statements. Materiality depends on the size and nature of the omission or misstatement judged in the surrounding circumstances. The size or nature of the item, or a combination of both, could be the determining factor. However, it is inappropriate to make, or leave uncorrected, immaterial departures from this FRS to achieve a particular presentation of an entity's financial position, financial performance or cash flows.

Reliability

2.7   The information provided in financial statements must be reliable. Information is reliable when it is free from material **error** and bias and represents faithfully that which it either purports to represent or could reasonably be expected to represent. Financial statements are not free from bias (ie not neutral) if, by the selection or presentation of information, they are intended to influence the making of a decision or judgement in order to achieve a predetermined result or outcome.

Substance over form

Transactions and other events and conditions should be accounted for and presented   **2.8**
in accordance with their substance and not merely their legal form. This enhances the
reliability of financial statements.

Prudence

The uncertainties that inevitably surround many events and circumstances are   **2.9**
acknowledged by the disclosure of their nature and extent and by the exercise of **prudence**
in the preparation of the financial statements. Prudence is the inclusion of a degree of
caution in the exercise of the judgements needed in making the estimates required under
conditions of uncertainty, such that **assets** or **income** are not overstated and **liabilities**
or **expenses** are not understated. However, the exercise of prudence does not allow the
deliberate understatement of assets or income, or the deliberate overstatement of liabilities
or expenses. In short, prudence does not permit bias.

Completeness

To be reliable, the information in financial statements must be complete within the bounds   **2.10**
of materiality and cost. An omission can cause information to be false or misleading and
thus unreliable and deficient in terms of its relevance.

Comparability

Users must be able to compare the financial statements of an entity through time to identify   **2.11**
trends in its financial position and performance. Users must also be able to compare
the financial statements of different entities to evaluate their relative financial position,
performance and cash flows. Hence, the **measurement** and display of the financial effects
of like transactions and other events and conditions must be carried out in a consistent way
throughout an entity and over time for that entity, and in a consistent way across entities. In
addition, users must be informed of the **accounting policies** employed in the preparation
of the financial statements, and of any changes in those policies and the effects of such
changes.

Timeliness

To be relevant, financial information must be able to influence the economic decisions of   **2.12**
users. **Timeliness** involves providing the information within the decision time frame. If
there is undue delay in the reporting of information it may lose its relevance. Management
may need to balance the relative merits of timely reporting and the provision of reliable
information. In achieving a balance between relevance and reliability, the overriding
consideration is how best to satisfy the needs of users in making economic decisions.

Balance between benefit and cost

The benefits derived from information should exceed the cost of providing it. The evaluation   **2.13**
of benefits and costs is substantially a judgemental process. Furthermore, the costs are not
necessarily borne by those users who enjoy the benefits, and often the benefits of the
information are enjoyed by a broad range of external users.

Financial reporting information helps capital providers make better decisions, which   **2.14**
results in more efficient functioning of capital markets and a lower cost of capital for the

economy as a whole. Individual entities also enjoy benefits, including improved access to capital markets, favourable effect on public relations, and perhaps lower costs of capital. The benefits may also include better management decisions because financial information used internally is often based at least partly on information prepared for general purpose financial reporting purposes.

Financial position

2.15   The financial position of an entity is the relationship of its assets, liabilities and **equity** as of a specific date as presented in the **statement of financial position**. These are defined as follows:

(a)   An asset is a resource controlled by the entity as a result of past events and from which future economic benefits are expected to flow to the entity.

(b)   A liability is a present obligation of the entity arising from past events, the settlement of which is expected to result in an outflow from the entity of resources embodying economic benefits.

(c)   Equity is the residual interest in the assets of the entity after deducting all its liabilities.

2.16   Some items that meet the definition of an asset or a liability may not be recognised as assets or liabilities in the statement of financial position because they do not satisfy the criteria for **recognition** in paragraphs 2.27 to 2.32. In particular, the expectation that future economic benefits will flow to or from an entity must be sufficiently certain to meet the probability criterion before an asset or liability is recognised.

Assets

2.17   The future economic benefit of an asset is its potential to contribute, directly or indirectly, to the flow of **cash** and **cash equivalents** to the entity. Those cash flows may come from using the asset or from disposing of it.

2.18   Many assets, for example **property, plant and equipment**, have a physical form. However, physical form is not essential to the existence of an asset. Some assets are intangible.

2.19   In determining the existence of an asset, the right of ownership is not essential. Thus, for example, property held on a **lease** is an asset if the entity controls the benefits that are expected to flow from the property.

Liabilities

2.20   An essential characteristic of a liability is that the entity has a present obligation to act or perform in a particular way. The obligation may be either a legal obligation or a **constructive obligation**. A legal obligation is legally enforceable as a consequence of a binding contract or statutory requirement. A constructive obligation is an obligation that derives from an entity's actions when:

(a)   by an established pattern of past practice, published policies or a sufficiently specific current statement, the entity has indicated to other parties that it will accept certain responsibilities; and

(b)   as a result, the entity has created a valid expectation on the part of those other parties that it will discharge those responsibilities.

2.21   The settlement of a present obligation usually involves the payment of cash, transfer of other assets, provision of services, the replacement of that obligation with another obligation, or conversion of the obligation to equity. An obligation may also be extinguished by other means, such as a creditor waiving or forfeiting its rights.

Equity

Equity is the residual interest in the assets of the entity after deducting all its liabilities. It may be sub-classified in the statement of financial position. For example, in a corporate entity, sub-classifications may include funds contributed by shareholders, retained earnings and **gains** or losses recognised in **other comprehensive income**. **2.22**

Performance

Performance is the relationship of the income and expenses of an entity during a **reporting period**. This FRS permits entities to present performance in a single financial statement (a **statement of comprehensive income**) or in two financial statements (an **income statement** and a statement of comprehensive income). **Total comprehensive income** and **profit or loss** are frequently used as measures of performance or as the basis for other measures, such as return on investment or earnings per share. Income and expenses are defined as follows: **2.23**

(a) Income is increases in economic benefits during the reporting period in the form of inflows or enhancements of assets or decreases of liabilities that result in increases in equity, other than those relating to contributions from equity investors.

(b) Expenses are decreases in economic benefits during the reporting period in the form of outflows or depletions of assets or incurrences of liabilities that result in decreases in equity, other than those relating to distributions to equity investors.

The recognition of income and expenses results directly from the recognition and measurement of assets and liabilities. Criteria for the recognition of income and expenses are discussed in paragraphs 2.27 to 2.32. **2.24**

Income

The definition of income encompasses both **revenue** and gains. **2.25**

(a) Revenue is income that arises in the course of the ordinary activities of an entity and is referred to by a variety of names including sales, fees, interest, dividends, royalties and rent.

(b) Gains are other items that meet the definition of income but are not revenue. When gains are recognised in the statement of comprehensive income, they are usually displayed separately because knowledge of them is useful for making economic decisions.

Expenses

The definition of expenses encompasses losses as well as those expenses that arise in the course of the ordinary activities of the entity. **2.26**

(a) Expenses that arise in the course of the ordinary activities of the entity include, for example, cost of sales, wages and **depreciation**. They usually take the form of an outflow or depletion of assets such as cash and cash equivalents, **inventory**, or property, plant and equipment.

(b) Losses are other items that meet the definition of expenses and may arise in the course of the ordinary activities of the entity. When losses are recognised in the statement of comprehensive income, they are usually presented separately because knowledge of them is useful for making economic decisions.

Recognition of assets, liabilities, income and expenses

2.27   Recognition is the process of incorporating in the statement of financial position or statement of comprehensive income an item that meets the definition of an asset, liability, equity, income or expense and satisfies the following criteria:

(a)   it is **probable** that any future economic benefit associated with the item will flow to or from the entity; and

(b)   the item has a cost or value that can be measured reliably.

2.28   The failure to recognise an item that satisfies those criteria is not rectified by disclosure of the accounting policies used or by **notes** or explanatory material.

The probability of future economic benefit

2.29   The concept of probability is used in the first recognition criterion to refer to the degree of uncertainty that the future economic benefits associated with the item will flow to or from the entity. Assessments of the degree of uncertainty attaching to the flow of future economic benefits are made on the basis of the evidence relating to conditions at the end of the reporting period available when the financial statements are prepared. Those assessments are made individually for individually significant items, and for a group for a large population of individually insignificant items.

Reliability of measurement

2.30   The second criterion for the recognition of an item is that it possesses a cost or value that can be measured with reliability. In many cases, the cost or value of an item is known. In other cases it must be estimated. The use of reasonable estimates is an essential part of the preparation of financial statements and does not undermine their reliability. When a reasonable estimate cannot be made, the item is not recognised in the financial statements.

2.31   An item that fails to meet the recognition criteria may qualify for recognition at a later date as a result of subsequent circumstances or events.

2.32   An item that fails to meet the criteria for recognition may nonetheless warrant disclosure in the notes or explanatory material or in supplementary schedules. This is appropriate when knowledge of the item is relevant to the evaluation of the financial position, performance and changes in financial position of an entity by the users of financial statements.

Measurement of assets, liabilities, income and expenses

2.33   Measurement is the process of determining the monetary amounts at which an entity measures assets, liabilities, income and expenses in its financial statements. Measurement involves the selection of a basis of measurement. This FRS specifies which measurement basis an entity shall use for many types of assets, liabilities, income and expenses.

2.34   Two common measurement bases are historical cost and **fair value**:

(a)   For assets, historical cost is the amount of cash or cash equivalents paid or the fair value of the consideration given to acquire the asset at the time of its acquisition. For liabilities, historical cost is the amount of proceeds of cash or cash equivalents received or the fair value of non-cash assets received in exchange for the obligation at the time the obligation is incurred, or in some circumstances (for example, **income tax**) the amounts of cash or cash equivalents expected to be paid to settle the liability in the normal course of business. Amortised historical cost is the historical cost of an asset or liability plus or minus that portion of its historical cost previously recognised as an expense or income.

(b)   Fair value is the amount for which an asset could be exchanged, a liability settled, or an equity instrument granted could be exchanged, between knowledgeable, willing parties in an arm's length transaction. In the absence of any specific guidance provided in the relevant section of this FRS, where fair value measurement is permitted or required the guidance in paragraphs 11.27 to 11.32 shall be applied.

Pervasive recognition and measurement principles

The requirements for recognising and measuring assets, liabilities, income and expenses in this FRS are based on pervasive principles that are derived from the IASB *Framework for the Preparation and Presentation of Financial Statements*[8] and from **EU-adopted IFRS**. In the absence of a requirement in this FRS that applies specifically to a transaction or other event or condition, paragraph 10.4 provides guidance for making a judgement and paragraph 10.5 establishes a hierarchy for an entity to follow in deciding on the appropriate accounting policy in the circumstances. The second level of that hierarchy requires an entity to look to the definitions, recognition criteria and measurement concepts for assets, liabilities, income and expenses and the pervasive principles set out in this section.   **2.35**

Accrual basis

An entity shall prepare its financial statements, except for cash flow information, using the **accrual basis** of accounting. On the accrual basis, items are recognised as assets, liabilities, equity, income or expenses when they satisfy the definitions and recognition criteria for those items.   **2.36**

Recognition in financial statements

Assets

An entity shall recognise an asset in the statement of financial position when it is probable that the future economic benefits will flow to the entity and the asset has a cost or value that can be measured reliably. An asset is not recognised in the statement of financial position when expenditure has been incurred for which it is considered not probable that economic benefits will flow to the entity beyond the current reporting period. Instead such a transaction results in the recognition of an expense in the statement of comprehensive income (or in the income statement, if presented).   **2.37**

An entity shall not recognise a **contingent asset** as an asset. However, when the flow of future economic benefits to the entity is virtually certain, then the related asset is not a contingent asset, and its recognition is appropriate.   **2.38**

Liabilities

An entity shall recognise a liability in the statement of financial position when: **2.39**

---

[8] *In 2010 the IASB issued the Conceptual Framework for Financial Reporting, which superseded the Framework for the Preparation and Presentation of Financial Statements.*

(a)   the entity has an obligation at the end of the reporting period as a result of a past event;

(b)   it is probable that the entity will be required to transfer resources embodying economic benefits in settlement; and

(c)   the settlement amount can be measured reliably.

2.40   A **contingent liability** is either a possible but uncertain obligation or a present obligation that is not recognised because it fails to meet one or both of the conditions (b) and (c) in paragraph 2.39. An entity shall not recognise a contingent liability as a liability, except for contingent liabilities of an acquiree in a **business combination** (see Section 19 *Business Combinations and Goodwill*).

Income

2.41   The recognition of income results directly from the recognition and measurement of assets and liabilities. An entity shall recognise income in the statement of comprehensive income (or in the income statement, if presented) when an increase in future economic benefits related to an increase in an asset or a decrease of a liability has arisen that can be measured reliably.

Expenses

2.42   The recognition of expenses results directly from the recognition and measurement of assets and liabilities. An entity shall recognise expenses in the statement of comprehensive income (or in the income statement, if presented) when a decrease in future economic benefits related to a decrease in an asset or an increase of a liability has arisen that can be measured reliably.

Total comprehensive income and profit or loss

2.43   Total comprehensive income is the arithmetical difference between income and expenses. It is not a separate element of financial statements, and a separate recognition principle is not needed for it.

2.44   Profit or loss is the arithmetical difference between income and expenses other than those items of income and expense that this FRS classifies as items of other comprehensive income. It is not a separate element of financial statements, and a separate recognition principle is not needed for it.

2.45   Generally this FRS does not allow the recognition of items in the statement of financial position that do not meet the definition of assets or of liabilities regardless of whether they result from applying the notion commonly referred to as the 'matching concept' for measuring profit or loss.

Measurement at initial recognition

2.46   At initial recognition, an entity shall measure assets and liabilities at historical cost unless this FRS requires initial measurement on another basis such as fair value.

Subsequent measurement

Financial assets and financial liabilities

An entity measures basic **financial assets** and basic **financial liabilities** at **amortised cost**   **2.47**
less impairment except for:

(a) investments in non-convertible preference shares and non-puttable ordinary and
     preference shares that are **publicly traded** or whose fair value can otherwise be
     measured reliably, which are measured at fair value with changes in fair value
     recognised in profit or loss; and
(b) any financial instruments that upon their initial recognition were designated by the
     entity as at fair value through profit or loss.

An entity generally measures all other financial assets and financial liabilities at fair value,   **2.48**
with changes in fair value recognised in profit or loss, unless this FRS requires or permits
measurement on another basis such as cost or amortised cost.

Non-financial assets

Most non-financial assets that an entity initially recognised at historical cost are   **2.49**
subsequently measured on other measurement bases. For example:

(a) An entity measures property, plant and equipment using either the cost model or the
     revaluation model.
(b) An entity measures inventories at the lower of cost and selling price less costs to
     complete and sell.

Measurement of assets at amounts lower than initial historical cost is intended to ensure
that an asset is not measured at an amount greater than the entity expects to recover from
the sale or use of that asset.

For certain types of non-financial assets, this FRS permits or requires measurement at fair   **2.50**
value. For example:

(a) Investments in **associates** and **joint ventures** that an entity measures at fair value
     (see paragraphs 14.4(b) and 14.4B, and 15.9(b) and 15.9B respectively).
(b) **Investment property** that an entity measures at fair value (see paragraph 16.7).
(c) **Biological assets** that an entity measures at fair value less estimated costs to sell in
     accordance with the fair value model (see paragraph 34.3A(a)) and **agricultural
     produce** that an entity measures, at the point of harvest, at fair value less estimated
     costs to sell in accordance with either the fair value model (see paragraph 34.3A(a))
     or cost model (see paragraph 34.9).
(d) Property, plant and equipment that an entity measures in accordance with the
     revaluation model (see paragraph 17.15B).
(e) **Intangible assets** that an entity measures in accordance with the revaluation model
     (see paragraph 18.18B).

Liabilities other than financial liabilities

Most liabilities other than financial liabilities are measured at the best estimate of the   **2.51**
amount that would be required to settle the obligation at the **reporting date**.

Offsetting

2.52   An entity shall not offset assets and liabilities, or income and expenses, unless required or permitted by an FRS.

(a)   Measuring assets net of valuation allowances (for example, allowances for inventory obsolescence and allowances for uncollectible receivables) is not offsetting.

(b)   If an entity's normal **operating activities** do not include buying and selling **fixed assets**, including investments and operating assets, then the entity reports gains and losses on disposal of such assets by deducting from the proceeds on disposal the **carrying amount** of the asset and related selling expenses.

Section 3 Financial Statement Presentation

Scope of this section

3.1   This section explains **fair presentation** of **financial statements**, what compliance with this FRS requires, and what is a complete set of financial statements.

Prospective amendments: Amendments to FRS 102 *The Financial Reporting Standard applicable in the UK and Republic of Ireland* – Small entities and other minor amendments (July 2015) amends paragraph 3.1 with effect for annual periods beginning on or after 1 January 2016.

Prospective amendments: Amendments to FRS 102 *The Financial Reporting Standard applicable in the UK and Republic of Ireland* – Small entities and other minor amendments (July 2015) inserts paragraph 3.1A with effect for annual periods beginning on or after 1 January 2016.

Fair presentation

3.2   Financial statements shall present fairly the **financial position**, financial **performance** and **cash flows** of an entity. Fair presentation requires the faithful representation of the effects of transactions, other events and conditions in accordance with the definitions and **recognition** criteria for **assets**, **liabilities**, **income** and **expenses** set out in Section 2 *Concepts and Pervasive Principles*.

(a)   The application of this FRS, with additional disclosure when necessary, is presumed to result in financial statements that achieve a fair presentation of the financial position, financial performance and cash flows of entities within the scope of this FRS.

(b)   [Not used]

The additional disclosures referred to in (a) are necessary when compliance with the specific requirements in this FRS is insufficient to enable users to understand the effect of particular transactions, other events and conditions on the entity's financial position and financial performance.

Prospective amendments: Amendments to FRS 102 *The Financial Reporting Standard applicable in the UK and Republic of Ireland* – Small entities and other minor amendments (July 2015) amends paragraph 3.2 and the heading before paragraph 3.2 with effect for annual periods beginning on or after 1 January 2016.

Compliance with this FRS

An entity whose financial statements comply with this FRS shall make an explicit and unreserved statement of such compliance in the **notes**. Financial statements shall not be described as complying with this FRS unless they comply with all the requirements of this FRS.

3.3

A **public benefit entity** that applies the 'PBE' prefixed paragraphs shall make an explicit and unreserved statement that it is a public benefit entity.

PBE3.3A

In the extremely rare circumstances when management concludes that compliance with this FRS would be so misleading that it would conflict with the **objective of financial statements** of entities within the scope of this FRS set out in Section 2, the entity shall depart from that requirement in the manner set out in paragraph 3.5.

3.4

Prospective amendments: Amendments to FRS 102 *The Financial Reporting Standard applicable in the UK and Republic of Ireland* – Small entities and other minor amendments (July 2015) amends paragraph 3.4 with effect for annual periods beginning on or after 1 January 2016.

When an entity departs from a requirement of this FRS in accordance with paragraph 3.4, or from a requirement of applicable legislation, it shall disclose the following:

3.5

(a)   that management has concluded that the financial statements present fairly the entity's financial position, financial performance and cash flows;

(b)   that it has complied with this FRS or applicable legislation, except that it has departed from a particular requirement of this FRS or applicable legislation to achieve a fair presentation; and

(c)   the nature of the departure, including the treatment that this FRS or applicable legislation would require, the reason why that treatment would be so misleading in the circumstances that it would conflict with the objective of financial statements set out in Section 2, and the treatment adopted[9].

Prospective amendments: Amendments to FRS 102 *The Financial Reporting Standard applicable in the UK and Republic of Ireland* – Small entities and other minor amendments (July 2015) amends paragraph 3.5 (footnote 9 is deleted and subsequent footnotes are renumbered sequentially) with effect for annual periods beginning on or after 1 January 2016.

When an entity has departed from a requirement of this FRS or applicable legislation in a prior period, and that departure affects the amounts recognised in the financial statements for the current period, it shall make the disclosures set out in paragraph 3.5(c).

3.6

[Not used]

3.7

Going concern

When preparing financial statements, the management of an entity using this FRS shall make an assessment of the entity's ability to continue as a **going concern**. An entity is a going concern unless management either intends to liquidate the entity or to cease

3.8

[9] *For companies sections 396(5) and 404(5) of the Companies Act 2006 require that 'If in special circumstances compliance with any of [the Regulations and any other provisions made by or under the Act] is inconsistent with the requirement to give a true and fair view, the directors must depart from that provision to the extent necessary to give a true and fair view. Particulars of any such departure, the reasons for it and its effect must be given in a note to the accounts.'*

trading, or has no realistic alternative but to do so. In assessing whether the going concern assumption is appropriate, management takes into account all available information about the future, which is at least, but is not limited to, twelve months from the date when the financial statements are authorised for issue.

3.9   When management is aware, in making its assessment, of **material** uncertainties related to events or conditions that cast significant doubt upon the entity's ability to continue as a going concern, the entity shall disclose those uncertainties. When an entity does not prepare financial statements on a going concern basis, it shall disclose that fact, together with the basis on which it prepared the financial statements and the reason why the entity is not regarded as a going concern.

Frequency of reporting

3.10   An entity shall present a complete set of financial statements (including comparative information as set out in paragraph 3.14) at least annually. When the end of an entity's **reporting period** changes and the annual financial statements are presented for a period longer or shorter than one year, the entity shall disclose the following:

(a)   that fact;

(b)   the reason for using a longer or shorter period; and

(c)   the fact that comparative amounts presented in the financial statements (including the related notes) are not entirely comparable.

Consistency of presentation

3.11   An entity shall retain the presentation and classification of items in the financial statements from one period to the next unless:

(a)   it is apparent, following a significant change in the nature of the entity's operations or a review of its financial statements, that another presentation or classification would be more appropriate having regard to the criteria for the selection and application of **accounting policies** in Section 10 *Accounting Policies, Estimates and Errors*; or

(b)   this FRS, or another applicable FRS or FRC Abstract, requires a change in presentation.

3.12   When the presentation or classification of items in the financial statements is changed, an entity shall reclassify comparative amounts unless the reclassification is **impracticable**. When comparative amounts are reclassified, an entity shall disclose the following:

(a)   the nature of the reclassification;

(b)   the amount of each item or class of items that is reclassified; and

(c)   the reason for the reclassification.

3.13   If it is impracticable to reclassify comparative amounts, an entity shall disclose why reclassification was not practicable.

Comparative information

3.14   Except when this FRS permits or requires otherwise, an entity shall present comparative information in respect of the preceding period for all amounts presented in the current period's financial statements. An entity shall include comparative information for narrative and descriptive information when it is relevant to an understanding of the current period's financial statements.

Materiality and aggregation

An entity shall present separately each material class of similar items. An entity shall **3.15** present separately items of a dissimilar nature or function unless they are immaterial.

Financial statements result from processing large numbers of transactions or other events **3.16** that are aggregated into classes according to their nature or function. The final stage in the process of aggregation and classification is the presentation of condensed and classified data, which form line items in the financial statements. If a line item is not individually material, it is aggregated with other items either in those statements or in the notes. An item that may not warrant separate presentation in those statements may warrant separate presentation in the notes.

An entity need not provide a specific disclosure required by this FRS if the information is **3.16A** not material.

Complete set of financial statements

A complete set of financial statements of an entity shall include all of the following: **3.17**

(a)   a **statement of financial position** as at the **reporting date**;
(b)   either:

> (i)   a single **statement of comprehensive income** for the reporting period displaying all items of income and expense recognised during the period including those items recognised in determining **profit or loss** (which is a subtotal in the statement of comprehensive income) and items of **other comprehensive income**; or
>
> (ii)   a separate **income statement** and a separate statement of comprehensive income. If an entity chooses to present both an income statement and a statement of comprehensive income, the statement of comprehensive income begins with profit or loss and then displays the items of other comprehensive income;

(c)   a **statement of changes in equity** for the reporting period;
(d)   a **statement of cash flows** for the reporting period; and
(e)   notes, comprising a summary of significant accounting policies and other explanatory information.

If the only changes to **equity** during the periods for which financial statements are **3.18** presented arise from profit or loss, payment of dividends, corrections of prior period **errors**, and changes in accounting policy, the entity may present a single **statement of income and retained earnings** in place of the statement of comprehensive income and statement of changes in equity (see paragraph 6.4).

If an entity has no items of other comprehensive income in any of the periods for which **3.19** financial statements are presented, it may present only an income statement, or it may present a statement of comprehensive income in which the 'bottom line' is labelled 'profit or loss'.

Because paragraph 3.14 requires comparative amounts in respect of the previous period for **3.20** all amounts presented in the financial statements, a complete set of financial statements means that an entity shall present, as a minimum, two of each of the required financial statements and related notes.

In a complete set of financial statements, an entity shall present each financial statement **3.21** with equal prominence.

3.22   An entity may use titles for the financial statements other than those used in this FRS as long as they are not misleading.

Identification of the financial statements

3.23   An entity shall clearly identify each of the financial statements and the notes and distinguish them from other information in the same document. In addition, an entity shall display the following information prominently, and repeat it when necessary for an understanding of the information presented:

(a)   the name of the reporting entity and any change in its name since the end of the preceding reporting period;

(b)   whether the financial statements cover the individual entity or a group of entities;

(c)   the date of the end of the reporting period and the period covered by the financial statements;

(d)   the **presentation currency**, as defined in Section 30 *Foreign Currency Translation*; and

(e)   the level of rounding, if any, used in presenting amounts in the financial statements.

3.24   An entity shall disclose the following in the notes:

(a)   the legal form of the entity, its country of incorporation and the address of its registered office (or principal place of business, if different from the registered office); and

(b)   a description of the nature of the entity's operations and its principal activities, unless this is disclosed in the business review (or similar statement) accompanying the financial statements.

Presentation of information not required by this FRS

3.25   This FRS does not address presentation of **interim financial reports**. An entity that prepares such reports shall describe the basis for preparing and presenting the information. **FRS 104** sets out a basis for the preparation and presentation of interim financial reports that an entity may apply.

Editor's note: FRS 104 (March 2015) amended this paragraph 3.25 with effect for interim periods commencing on or after 1 January 2015 with early application permitted.

Section 4 Statement of Financial Position

Scope of this section

4.1   This section sets out the information that is to be presented in a **statement of financial position** and how to present it. The statement of financial position (which is referred to as the balance sheet in the **Act**) presents an entity's **assets, liabilities** and **equity** as of a specific date – the end of the **reporting period**. This section applies to all entities, whether or not they report under the Act. Entities that do not report under the Act should comply with the requirements of this section, and with the **Regulations** (or, where applicable, the **LLP Regulations**) where referred to in this section, except to the extent that these requirements are not permitted by any statutory framework under which such entities report.

Prospective amendments: Amendments to FRS 102 *The Financial Reporting Standard applicable in the UK and Republic of Ireland* – Small entities and other minor amendments

(July 2015) inserts paragraph 4.1A with effect for annual periods beginning on or after 1 January 2016.

Information to be presented in the statement of financial position

An entity shall present a statement of financial position in accordance with one of the following requirements for a balance sheet: **4.2**

(a)   Part 1 *General Rules and Formats* of Schedule 1 to the Regulations.
(b)   Part 1 *General Rules and Formats* of Schedule 2 to the Regulations.
(c)   Part 1 *General Rules and Formats* of Schedule 3 to the Regulations.
(d)   Part 1 *General Rules and Formats* of Schedule 1 to the LLP Regulations.

The consolidated statement of financial position of a **group** shall be presented in accordance with the requirements for a consolidated balance sheet in Schedule 6 to the Regulations or Schedule 3 to the LLP Regulations.

Prospective amendments: Amendments to FRS 102 *The Financial Reporting Standard applicable in the UK and Republic of Ireland* – Small entities and other minor amendments (July 2015) inserts paragraph 4.2A with effect for annual periods beginning on or after 1 January 2016.

Prospective amendments: Amendments to FRS 102 *The Financial Reporting Standard applicable in the UK and Republic of Ireland* – Small entities and other minor amendments (July 2015) inserts paragraph 4.2B with effect for annual periods beginning on or after 1 January 2016.

Prospective amendments: Amendments to FRS 102 *The Financial Reporting Standard applicable in the UK and Republic of Ireland* – Small entities and other minor amendments (July 2015) inserts paragraph 4.2C with effect for annual periods beginning on or after 1 January 2016.

Prospective amendments: Amendments to FRS 102 *The Financial Reporting Standard applicable in the UK and Republic of Ireland* – Small entities and other minor amendments (July 2015) inserts paragraph 4.2D with effect for annual periods beginning on or after 1 January 2016.

An entity shall present additional line items, headings and subtotals in the statement of financial position when such presentation is relevant to an understanding of the entity's **financial position**. **4.3**

Debtors due after more than one year

[Not used] **4.4**

In instances where the amount of debtors due after more than one year is so **material** in the context of the total net current assets that in the absence of disclosure of the debtors due after more than one year on the face of the statement of financial position readers may misinterpret the **financial statements**, the amount should be disclosed on the face of the statement of financial position within **current assets**. In most cases it will be satisfactory to disclose the amount due after more than one year in the **notes** to the financial statements. **4.4A**

Prospective amendments: Amendments to FRS 102 *The Financial Reporting Standard applicable in the UK and Republic of Ireland* – Small entities and other minor amendments

(July 2015) amends paragraph 4.4A with effect for annual periods beginning on or after 1 January 2016.

4.5 [Not used]

4.6 [Not used]

Creditors: amounts falling due within one year

4.7 An entity shall classify a creditor as due within one year when the entity does not have an unconditional right, at the end of the reporting period, to defer settlement of the creditor for at least twelve months after the **reporting date**.

Prospective amendments: Amendments to FRS 102 *The Financial Reporting Standard applicable in the UK and Republic of Ireland* – Small entities and other minor amendments (July 2015) amends paragraph 4.7 with effect for annual periods beginning on or after 1 January 2016.

4.8 [Not used]

Information to be presented either in the statement of financial position or in the notes

4.9 [Not used]

4.10 [Not used]

4.11 [Not used]

4.12 An entity with share capital shall disclose the following, either in the statement of financial position or in the notes:

(a)   For each class of share capital:

(i)   [Not used]

(ii)   The number of shares issued and fully paid, and issued but not fully paid.

(iii) Par value per share, or that the shares have no par value.

(iv)   A reconciliation of the number of shares outstanding at the beginning and at the end of the period. This reconciliation need not be presented for prior periods.

(v)   The rights, preferences and restrictions attaching to that class including restrictions on the distribution of dividends and the repayment of capital.

(vi)   Shares in the entity held by the entity or by its **subsidiaries**, **associates**, or **joint ventures**.

(vii) Shares reserved for issue under options and contracts for the sale of shares, including the terms and amounts.

(b)   A description of each reserve within equity.

4.13 An entity without share capital, such as a partnership or trust, shall disclose information equivalent to that required by paragraph 4.12(a), showing changes during the period in each category of equity, and the rights, preferences and restrictions attaching to each category of equity.

Information to be presented in the notes

If, at the reporting date, an entity has a binding sale agreement for a major disposal of   **4.14**
assets, or a **disposal group**, the entity shall disclose the following information:

(a)   a description of the asset(s) or the disposal group;
(b)   a description of the facts and circumstances of the sale; and
(c)   the **carrying amount** of the assets or, for a disposal group, the carrying amounts of
       the underlying assets and liabilities.

Section 5 Statement of Comprehensive Income and Income Statement

Scope of this section

This section requires an entity to present its **total comprehensive income** for a period – ie its   **5.1**
financial **performance** for the period – in one or two statements. It sets out the information
that is to be presented in those statements and how to present it. This section applies to all
entities, whether or not they report under the **Act**. Entities that do not report under the Act
should comply with the requirements of this section, and with the **Regulations** (or, where
applicable, the **LLP Regulations**) where referred to in this section, except to the extent
that these requirements are not permitted by any statutory framework under which such
entities report. If an entity meets specified conditions and chooses to do so, it may present
a **statement of income and retained earnings** as set out in Section 6 *Statement of Change
in Equity and Statement of Income and Retained Earnings*.

Prospective amendments: Amendments to FRS 102 *The Financial Reporting Standard
applicable in the UK and Republic of Ireland* – Small entities and other minor amendments
(July 2015) inserts paragraph 5.1A with effect for annual periods beginning on or after
1 January 2016.

Presentation of total comprehensive income

An entity shall present its total comprehensive income for a period either: **5.2**

(a)   in a single **statement of comprehensive income**, in which case the statement of
       comprehensive income presents all items of **income** and **expense** recognised in the
       period; or
(b)   in two statements – an **income statement** (which is referred to as the profit and loss
       account in the Act) and a statement of comprehensive income – in which case the
       income statement presents all items of income and expense recognised in the period
       except those that are recognised in total comprehensive income outside of **profit or
       loss** as permitted or required by this FRS.

A change from the single-statement approach to the two-statement approach, or vice versa,   **5.3**
is a change in **accounting policy** to which Section 10 *Accounting Policies, Estimates and
Errors* applies.

Single-statement approach

[Not used]   **5.4**

An entity shall present, in the statement of comprehensive income, the items to be included   **5.5**
in a profit and loss account in accordance with one of the following requirements:

(a)   Part 1 *General Rules and Formats* of Schedule 1 to the Regulations;
(b)   Part 1 *General Rules and Formats* of Schedule 2 to the Regulations;
(c)   Part 1 *General Rules and Formats* of Schedule 3 to the Regulations; or
(d)   Part 1 *General Rules and Formats* of Schedule 1 to the LLP Regulations.

The consolidated statement of comprehensive income of a **group** shall be presented in accordance with the requirements for a consolidated profit and loss account of Schedule 6 to the Regulations or Schedule 3 to the LLP Regulations.

5.5A   In addition an entity shall include, in the statement of comprehensive income, line items that present the following amounts for the period:

(a)   Classified by nature (excluding amounts in (b)), the components of **other comprehensive income** recognised as part of total comprehensive income outside profit or loss as permitted or required by this FRS. An entity may present the components of other comprehensive income either:

(i)   net of related tax effects; or
(ii)   before the related tax effects with one amount shown for the aggregate amount of **income tax** relating to those components.

(b)   Its share of the other comprehensive income of **associates** and **jointly controlled entities** accounted for by the equity method.
(c)   Total comprehensive income.

Prospective amendments: Amendments to FRS 102 *The Financial Reporting Standard applicable in the UK and Republic of Ireland* – Small entities and other minor amendments (July 2015) inserts paragraph 5.5B with effect for annual periods beginning on or after 1 January 2016.

Prospective amendments: Amendments to FRS 102 *The Financial Reporting Standard applicable in the UK and Republic of Ireland* – Small entities and other minor amendments (July 2015) inserts paragraph 5.5C with effect for annual periods beginning on or after 1 January 2016.

5.6   An entity shall present the following items as allocations of profit or loss and other comprehensive income in the statement of comprehensive income for the period:

(a)   Profit or loss for the period attributable to:

(i)   **non-controlling interest**; and
(ii)   **owners** of the **parent**.

(b)   Total comprehensive income for the period attributable to:

(i)   non-controlling interest; and
(ii)   owners of the parent.

Two-statement approach

5.7   Under the two-statement approach, an entity shall present in an income statement, the items to be included in a profit and loss account in accordance with one of the following requirements:

(a)   Part 1 *General Rules and Formats* of Schedule 1 to the Regulations;
(b)   Part 1 *General Rules and Formats* of Schedule 2 to the Regulations;
(c)   Part 1 *General Rules and Formats* of Schedule 3 to the Regulations; or
(d)   Part 1 *General Rules and Formats* of Schedule 1 to the LLP Regulations.

The consolidated income statement of a group shall be presented in accordance with the requirements for a consolidated profit and loss account of Schedule 6 to the Regulations or Schedule 3 to the LLP Regulations.

Prospective amendments: Amendments to FRS 102 *The Financial Reporting Standard applicable in the UK and Republic of Ireland* – Small entities and other minor amendments (July 2015) inserts new paragraph 5.7A with effect for annual periods beginning on or after 1 January 2016.

If an entity presents profit or loss in an income statement, it shall present the information required in paragraph 5.6(a) in that statement.   **5.7A**

Prospective amendments: Amendments to FRS 102 *The Financial Reporting Standard applicable in the UK and Republic of Ireland* – Small entities and other minor amendments (July 2015) renumber of paragraph 5.7A into 5.7B with effect for annual periods beginning on or after 1 January 2016.

The statement of comprehensive income shall begin with profit or loss as its first line and shall display, as a minimum, line items that present the amounts in paragraphs 5.5A and 5.6(b) for the period.   **5.7B**

Prospective amendments: Amendments to FRS 102 *The Financial Reporting Standard applicable in the UK and Republic of Ireland* – Small entities and other minor amendments (July 2015) renumber of paragraph 5.7B into 5.7C with effect for annual periods beginning on or after 1 January 2016.

Requirements applicable to both approaches

In addition to the requirements of paragraphs 5.5 or 5.7, as a minimum, **turnover** must be presented on the face of the income statement (or statement of comprehensive income if presented).   **5.7C**

Prospective amendments: Amendments to FRS 102 *The Financial Reporting Standard applicable in the UK and Republic of Ireland* – Small entities and other minor amendments (July 2015) renumber of paragraph 5.7C into 5.7D with effect for annual periods beginning on or after 1 January 2016.

An entity shall also disclose on the face of the income statement (or statement of comprehensive income if presented) an amount comprising the total of: **5.7D**

(a)   the post-tax profit or loss of **discontinued operations**; and
(b)   the post-tax gain or loss attributable to the impairment or on the disposal of the **assets** or **disposal group(s)** constituting discontinued operations.

A line-by-line analysis shall be presented in the income statement (or statement of comprehensive income if presented), in a column identified as relating to discontinued operations, ie separately from continuing operations; a total column shall also be presented.

Prospective amendments: Amendments to FRS 102 *The Financial Reporting Standard applicable in the UK and Republic of Ireland* – Small entities and other minor amendments (July 2015) renumber of paragraph 5.7D into 5.7E and in renumbered paragraph 5.7E the terms 'discontinued operation', 'assets' and 'disposal group(s)' are no longer shown in bold type with effect for annual periods beginning on or after 1 January 2016.

5.7E   An entity shall re-present the disclosures in paragraph 5.7D for prior periods presented in the **financial statements** so that the disclosures relate to all operations that have been discontinued by the end of the **reporting period** for the latest period presented.

Prospective amendments: Amendments to FRS 102 *The Financial Reporting Standard applicable in the UK and Republic of Ireland* – Small entities and other minor amendments (July 2015) renumber of paragraph 5.7E into 5.7F with effect for annual periods beginning on or after 1 January 2016.

5.8   Under this FRS, the effects of corrections of **material errors** and changes in accounting policies are presented as retrospective adjustments of prior periods rather than as part of profit or loss in the period in which they arise (see Section 10).

5.9   An entity shall present additional line items, headings and subtotals in the statement of comprehensive income (and in the income statement, if presented), when such presentation is relevant to an understanding of the entity's financial performance.

5.9A   When items included in total comprehensive income are material, an entity shall disclose their nature and amount separately, in the statement of comprehensive income (and in the income statement, if presented) or in the **notes**.

5.9B   This FRS does not require disclosure of 'operating profit'. However, if an entity elects to disclose the results of **operating activities** the entity should ensure that the amount disclosed is representative of activities that would normally be regarded as 'operating'. For example, it would be inappropriate to exclude items clearly related to operations (such as inventory write-downs and restructuring and relocation expenses) because they occur irregularly or infrequently or are unusual in amount. Similarly, it would be inappropriate to exclude items on the grounds that they do not involve **cash flows**, such as **depreciation** and **amortisation** expenses.

Ordinary activities and extraordinary items

Prospective amendments: Amendments to FRS 102 *The Financial Reporting Standard applicable in the UK and Republic of Ireland* – Small entities and other minor amendments (July 2015) inserts new paragraph 5.10 with effect for annual periods beginning on or after 1 January 2016.

5.10   Ordinary activities are any activities which are undertaken by a reporting entity as part of its business and such related activities in which the reporting entity engages in furtherance of, incidental to, or arising from, these activities. Ordinary activities include any effects on the reporting entity of any event in the various environments in which it operates, including the political, regulatory, economic and geographical environments, irrespective of the frequency or unusual nature of the events.

Prospective amendments: Amendments to FRS 102 *The Financial Reporting Standard applicable in the UK and Republic of Ireland* – Small entities and other minor amendments (July 2015) renumbers paragraph 5.10 into 5.10A with effect for annual periods beginning on or after 1 January 2016.

5.10A   Extraordinary items are material items possessing a high degree of abnormality which arise from events or transactions that fall outside the ordinary activities of the reporting entity and which are not expected to recur. The additional line items required to be presented by paragraph 5.9 and material items required to be disclosed by paragraph 5.9A, are not extraordinary items when they arise from the ordinary activities of the entity. Extraordinary items do not include prior period items merely because they relate to a prior period.

Prospective amendments: Amendments to FRS 102 *The Financial Reporting Standard applicable in the UK and Republic of Ireland* – Small entities and other minor amendments (July 2015) renumbers paragraph 5.10A into 5.10B with effect for annual periods beginning on or after 1 January 2016.

Analysis of expenses

Unless otherwise required under the Regulations, an entity shall present an analysis of expenses using a classification based on either the nature of expenses or the function of expenses within the entity, whichever provides information that is reliable and more relevant.   **5.11**

Analysis by nature of expense

(a)   Under this method of classification, expenses are aggregated in the statement of comprehensive income (or in the income statement, under the two-statement approach) according to their nature (eg depreciation, raw materials and consumables and staff costs), and are not reallocated among various functions within the entity.

Analysis by function of expense

(b)   Under this method of classification, expenses are aggregated according to their function as part of cost of sales or, for example, the costs of distribution or administrative activities.

Appendix to Section 5

Example showing presentation of discontinued operations

This appendix accompanies, but is not part of, Section 5. It provides guidance on applying the requirements of Section 5 paragraph 5.7D for presenting discontinued operations. The example illustrates the presentation of comprehensive income in a single statement and the classification of expenses within profit by function. A columnar format is used in order to present a single line item as required by paragraph 5.7D, while still complying with the requirements of the Act to show totals for ordinary activities of items such as turnover, profit or loss before taxation and tax.

Statement of comprehensive income

for the year ended 31 December 20X1

	Continuing operations	20X1 Discontinued operations	Total	Continuing operations (as restated)	20X0 Discontinued operations (as restated)	Total
	CU	CU	CU	CU	CU	CU
Turnover	4,200	1,232	5,432	3,201	1,500	4,701
Cost of Sales	(2,591)	(1,104)	(3,695)	(2,281)	(1,430)	(3,711)
Gross profit	1,609	128	1,737	920	70	990
Administrative expenses	(452)	(110)	(562)	(418)	(120)	(538)
Other operating income	212	–	212	198	–	198
Profit on disposal of operations	–	301	301	–	–	–
Operating profit	1,369	319	1,688	700	(50)	650
Interest receivable and similar income	14	–	14	16	–	16
Interest payable and similar charges	(208)	–	(208)	(208)	–	(208)
Profit on ordinary activities before tax	1,175	319	1,494	508	(50)	458
Taxation	(390)	(4)	(394)	(261)	3	(258)
Profit on ordinary activities after taxation and profit for the financial year	785	315	1,100	247	(47)	200
Other comprehensive income						
Actuarial losses on defined benefit pension plans			(108)			(68)
Deferred tax movement relating to actuarial losses			28			18
Total comprehensive income for the year			1,020			150

Section 6 Statement of Changes in Equity and Statement of Income and Retained Earnings

Scope of this section

6.1 This section sets out requirements for presenting the changes in an entity's **equity** for a period, either in a statement of changes in equity or, if specified conditions are met and an entity chooses, in a **statement of income and retained earnings**.

Prospective amendments: Amendments to FRS 102 *The Financial Reporting Standard applicable in the UK and Republic of Ireland* – Small entities and other minor amendments (July 2015) inserts paragraph 6.1A with effect for annual periods beginning on or after 1 January 2016.

Statement of changes in equity

Purpose

The statement of changes in equity presents an entity's **profit or loss** for a **reporting period**, **other comprehensive income** for the period, the effects of changes in **accounting policies** and corrections of **material errors** recognised in the period, and the amounts of investments by, and dividends and other distributions to, equity investors during the period.

6.2

Information to be presented in the statement of changes in equity

An entity shall present a statement of changes in equity showing in the statement:

6.3

(a)   **total comprehensive income** for the period, showing separately the total amounts attributable to **owners** of the **parent** and to **non-controlling interests**;

(b)   for each component of equity, the effects of **retrospective application** or retrospective restatement recognised in accordance with Section 10 *Accounting Policies, Estimates and Errors*; and

(c)   for each component of equity, a reconciliation between the **carrying amount** at the beginning and the end of the period, separately disclosing changes resulting from:

   (i)   profit or loss;

   (ii)   other comprehensive income; and

   (iii) the amounts of investments by, and dividends and other distributions to, owners, showing separately issues of shares, purchase of own share transactions, dividends and other distributions to owners, and changes in ownership interests in **subsidiaries** that do not result in a loss of **control**.

Information to be presented in the statement of changes in equity or in the notes

For each component of equity, an entity shall present, either in the statement of changes in equity or in the **notes**, an analysis of other comprehensive income by item (see paragraph 6.3(c)(ii)).

6.3A

Statement of income and retained earnings

Purpose

The statement of income and retained earnings presents an entity's profit or loss and changes in retained earnings for a reporting period. Paragraph 3.18 permits an entity to present a statement of income and retained earnings in place of a **statement of comprehensive income** and a statement of changes in equity if the only changes to its equity during the periods for which **financial statements** are presented arise from profit or loss, payment of dividends, corrections of prior period material errors, and changes in accounting policy.

6.4

Information to be presented in the statement of income and retained earnings

An entity shall present, in the statement of income and retained earnings, the following items in addition to the information required by Section 5 *Statement of Comprehensive Income and Income Statement*:

6.5

(a)   retained earnings at the beginning of the reporting period;

(b)   dividends declared and paid or payable during the period;

(c)   restatements of retained earnings for corrections of prior period material errors;

(d)   restatements of retained earnings for changes in accounting policy; and

(e)   retained earnings at the end of the reporting period.

Section 7 Statement of Cash Flows

Scope of this section

7.1   This section sets out the information that is to be presented in a **statement of cash flows** and how to present it. The statement of cash flows provides information about the changes in **cash** and **cash equivalents** of an entity for a **reporting period**, showing separately changes from **operating activities, investing activities** and **financing activities**.

7.1A   This section and paragraph 3.17(d) do not apply to:

(a)   mutual life assurance companies;

(b)   **retirement benefit plans**; or

(c)   investment funds that meet all the following conditions:

(i)   substantially all of the entity's investments are highly liquid;

(ii)   substantially all of the entity's investments are carried at market value; and

(iii)   the entity provides a statement of changes in net assets.

Prospective amendments: Amendments to FRS 102 *The Financial Reporting Standard applicable in the UK and Republic of Ireland* – Small entities and other minor amendments (July 2015) inserts paragraph 7.1B with effect for annual periods beginning on or after 1 January 2016.

Cash equivalents

7.2   Cash equivalents are short-term, highly liquid investments that are readily convertible to known amounts of cash and that are subject to an insignificant risk of changes in value. Therefore, an investment normally qualifies as a cash equivalent only when it has a short maturity of, say, three months or less from the date of acquisition. Bank overdrafts are normally considered financing activities similar to borrowings. However, if they are repayable on demand and form an integral part of an entity's cash management, bank overdrafts are a component of cash and cash equivalents.

Information to be presented in the statement of cash flows

7.3   An entity shall present a statement of cash flows that presents **cash flows** for a reporting period classified by operating activities, investing activities and financing activities.

Operating activities

7.4   Operating activities are the principal revenue-producing activities of the entity. Therefore, cash flows from operating activities generally result from the transactions and other events and conditions that enter into the determination of **profit or loss**. Examples of cash flows from operating activities are:

(a)   cash receipts from the sale of goods and the rendering of services;

(b)   cash receipts from royalties, fees, commissions and other revenue;

(c)   cash payments to suppliers for goods and services;

(d)   cash payments to and on behalf of employees;

(e)   cash payments or refunds of **income tax**, unless they can be specifically identified with financing and investing activities;
(f)   cash receipts and payments from investments, loans and other contracts held for dealing or trading purposes, which are similar to **inventory** acquired specifically for resale; and
(g)   cash advances and loans made to other parties by **financial institutions**.

Some transactions, such as the sale of an item of plant by a manufacturing entity, may give rise to a **gain** or loss that is included in profit or loss. However, the cash flows relating to such transactions are cash flows from investing activities.

Investing activities

Investing activities are the acquisition and disposal of long-term assets and other investments not included in cash equivalents. Examples of cash flows arising from investing activities are: **7.5**

(a)   cash payments to acquire **property, plant and equipment** (including self-constructed property, plant and equipment), **intangible assets** and other long-term assets. These payments include those relating to capitalised development costs and self-constructed property, plant and equipment;
(b)   cash receipts from sales of property, plant and equipment, intangibles and other long-term assets;
(c)   cash payments to acquire **equity** or debt instruments of other entities and interests in **joint ventures** (other than payments for those instruments classified as cash equivalents or held for dealing or trading);
(d)   cash receipts from sales of equity or debt instruments of other entities and interests in joint ventures (other than receipts for those instruments classified as cash equivalents or held for dealing or trading);
(e)   cash advances and loans made to other parties (except those made by financial institutions – see paragraph 7.4(g));
(f)   cash receipts from the repayment of advances and loans made to other parties;
(g)   cash payments for futures contracts, forward contracts, option contracts and swap contracts, except when the contracts are held for dealing or trading, or the payments are classified as financing activities; and
(h)   cash receipts from futures contracts, forward contracts, option contracts and swap contracts, except when the contracts are held for dealing or trading, or the receipts are classified as financing activities.

When a contract is accounted for as a hedge (see Section 12 *Other Financial Instruments Issues*), an entity shall classify the cash flows of the contract in the same manner as the cash flows of the item being hedged.

Financing activities

Financing activities are activities that result in changes in the size and composition of the contributed equity and borrowings of an entity. Examples of cash flows arising from financing activities are: **7.6**

(a)   cash proceeds from issuing shares or other equity instruments;
(b)   cash payments to **owners** to acquire or redeem the entity's shares;
(c)   cash proceeds from issuing debentures, loans, notes, bonds, mortgages and other short-term or long-term borrowings;
(d)   cash repayments of amounts borrowed; and
(e)   cash payments by a lessee for the reduction of the outstanding **liability** relating to a **finance lease**.

Reporting cash flows from operating activities

7.7   An entity shall present cash flows from operating activities using either:

(a)   the indirect method, whereby profit or loss is adjusted for the effects of non-cash transactions, any deferrals or accruals of past or future operating cash receipts or payments, and items of **income** or **expense** associated with investing or financing cash flows; or

(b)   the direct method, whereby major classes of gross cash receipts and gross cash payments are disclosed.

Indirect method

7.8   Under the indirect method, the net cash flow from operating activities is determined by adjusting profit or loss for the effects of:

(a)   changes during the period in inventories and operating receivables and payables;

(b)   non-cash items such as **depreciation**, **provisions**, **deferred tax**, accrued income (expenses) not yet received (paid) in cash, unrealised foreign currency gains and losses, undistributed profits of **associates**, and **non-controlling interests**; and

(c)   all other items for which the cash effects relate to investing or financing.

Direct method

7.9   Under the direct method, net cash flow from operating activities is presented by disclosing information about major classes of gross cash receipts and gross cash payments. Such information may be obtained either:

(a)   from the accounting records of the entity; or

(b)   by adjusting sales, cost of sales and other items in the **statement of comprehensive income** (or the **income statement**, if presented) for:

(i)   changes during the period in inventories and operating receivables and payables;

(ii)   other non-cash items; and

(iii)   other items for which the cash effects are investing or financing cash flows.

Reporting cash flows from investing and financing activities

7.10   An entity shall present separately major classes of gross cash receipts and gross cash payments arising from investing and financing activities, except to the extent that net presentation is permitted by paragraphs 7.10A to 7.10E. The aggregate cash flows arising from acquisitions and from disposals of **subsidiaries** or other business units shall be presented separately and classified as investing activities.

Reporting cash flows on a net basis

7.10A   Cash flows arising from the following operating, investing or financing activities may be reported on a net basis:

(a)   cash receipts and payments on behalf of customers when the cash flows reflect the activities of the customer rather than those of the entity; and

(b)   cash receipts and payments for items in which the turnover is quick, the amounts are large, and the maturities are short.

Examples of cash receipts and payments referred to in paragraph 7.10A(a) are: **7.10B**

(a)   the acceptance and repayment of demand deposits of a bank;
(b)   funds held for customers by an investment entity; and
(c)   rents collected on behalf of, and paid over to, the owners of properties.

Examples of cash receipts and payments referred to in paragraph 7.10A(b) are advances **7.10C**
made for, and the repayment of:

(a)   principal amounts relating to credit card customers;
(b)   the purchase and sale of investments; and
(c)   other short-term borrowings, for example, those which have a maturity period of
      three months or less.

Financial institutions may report cash flows described in paragraph 34.33 on a net basis.   **7.10D**

A financial institution that undertakes the business of effecting or carrying out **insurance** **7.10E**
contracts, other than mutual life assurance companies scoped out of this section in
paragraph 7.1A(a), should include the cash flows of their long-term business only to the
extent of cash transferred and available to meet the obligations of the company or group
as a whole.

Foreign currency cash flows

An entity shall record cash flows arising from transactions in a foreign currency in the **7.11**
entity's **functional currency** by applying to the foreign currency amount the exchange rate
between the functional currency and the foreign currency at the date of the cash flow or an
exchange rate that approximates the actual rate (for example, a weighted average exchange
rate for the period).

An entity shall translate cash flows of a foreign subsidiary at the exchange rate between the **7.12**
entity's functional currency and the foreign currency at the date of the cash flow or at an
exchange rate that approximates the actual rate (for example, a weighted average exchange
rate for the period).

Unrealised gains and losses arising from changes in foreign currency exchange rates are **7.13**
not cash flows. However, to reconcile cash and cash equivalents at the beginning and the
end of the period, the effect of exchange rate changes on cash and cash equivalents held
or due in a foreign currency must be presented in the statement of cash flows. Therefore,
the entity shall remeasure cash and cash equivalents held during the reporting period (such
as amounts of foreign currency held and foreign currency bank accounts) at period-end
exchange rates. The entity shall present the resulting unrealised gain or loss separately
from cash flows from operating, investing and financing activities.

Interest and dividends

An entity shall present separately cash flows from interest and dividends received and paid. **7.14**
The entity shall classify these cash flows consistently from period to period as operating,
investing or financing activities.

An entity may classify interest paid and interest and dividends received as operating cash **7.15**
flows because they are included in profit or loss. Alternatively, the entity may classify
interest paid and interest and dividends received as financing cash flows and investing
cash flows respectively, because they are costs of obtaining financial resources or returns
on investments.

7.16   An entity may classify dividends paid as a financing cash flow because they are a cost of obtaining financial resources. Alternatively, the entity may classify dividends paid as a component of cash flows from operating activities because they are paid out of operating cash flows.

Income tax

7.17   An entity shall present separately cash flows arising from income tax and shall classify them as cash flows from operating activities unless they can be specifically identified with financing and investing activities. When tax cash flows are allocated over more than one class of activity, the entity shall disclose the total amount of taxes paid.

Non-cash transactions

7.18   An entity shall exclude from the statement of cash flows investing and financing transactions that do not require the use of cash or cash equivalents. An entity shall disclose such transactions elsewhere in the **financial statements** in a way that provides all the relevant information about those investing and financing activities.

7.19   Many investing and financing activities do not have a direct impact on current cash flows even though they affect the capital and asset structure of an entity. The exclusion of non-cash transactions from the statement of cash flows is consistent with the objective of a statement of cash flows because these items do not involve cash flows in the current period. Examples of non-cash transactions are:

(a)   the acquisition of assets either by assuming directly related liabilities or by means of a finance lease;

(b)   the acquisition of an entity by means of an equity issue; and

(c)   the conversion of debt to equity.

Components of cash and cash equivalents

7.20   An entity shall present the components of cash and cash equivalents and shall present a reconciliation of the amounts presented in the statement of cash flows to the equivalent items presented in the **statement of financial position**. However, an entity is not required to present this reconciliation if the amount of cash and cash equivalents presented in the statement of cash flows is identical to the amount similarly described in the statement of financial position.

7.20A   Entities applying Part 1 *General Rules and Formats* of Schedule 2 to the **Regulations** should include as cash, only cash and balances at central banks and loans and advances to banks repayable on demand.

Other disclosures

7.21   An entity shall disclose, together with a commentary by management, the amount of significant cash and cash equivalent balances held by the entity that are not available for use by the entity. Cash and cash equivalents held by an entity may not be available for use by the entity because of, among other reasons, foreign exchange controls or legal restrictions.

Section 8 Notes to the Financial Statements

Scope of this section

This section sets out the principles underlying information that is to be presented in the **notes**   **8.1**
to the **financial statements** and how to present it. Notes contain information in addition
to that presented in the **statement of financial position**, **statement of comprehensive
income** (if presented), **income statement** (if presented), combined **statement of income
and retained earnings** (if presented), **statement of changes in equity** (if presented),
and **statement of cash flows**. Notes provide narrative descriptions or disaggregations of
items presented in those statements and information about items that do not qualify for
recognition in those statements. In addition to the requirements of this section, nearly
every other section of this FRS requires disclosures that are normally presented in the
notes.

Structure of the notes

The notes shall: **8.2**

(a)   present information about the basis of preparation of the financial statements and the
specific **accounting policies** used, in accordance with paragraphs 8.5 to 8.7;
(b)   disclose the information required by this FRS that is not presented elsewhere in the
financial statements; and
(c)   provide information that is not presented elsewhere in the financial statements but is
relevant to an understanding of any of them.

An entity shall, as far as practicable, present the notes in a systematic manner. An entity   **8.3**
shall cross-reference each item in the financial statements to any related information in
the notes.

An entity normally presents the notes in the following order: **8.4**

(a)   a statement that the financial statements have been prepared in compliance with this
FRS (see paragraph 3.3);
(b)   a summary of significant accounting policies applied (see paragraph 8.5);
(c)   supporting information for items presented in the financial statements, in the
sequence in which each statement and each line item is presented; and
(d)   any other disclosures.

Prospective amendments: Amendments to FRS 102 *The Financial Reporting Standard
applicable in the UK and Republic of Ireland* – Small entities and other minor amendments
(July 2015) inserts a new footnote (to be sequentially numbered) is inserted after the word
'normally' in paragraph 8.4 (subsequent footnotes are renumbered sequentially), with
effect for annual periods beginning on or after 1 January 2016.

Disclosure of accounting policies

An entity shall disclose the following in the summary of significant accounting policies: **8.5**

(a)   the measurement basis (or bases) used in preparing the financial statements; and
(b)   the other accounting policies used that are relevant to an understanding of the
financial statements.

Information about judgements

8.6   An entity shall disclose, in the summary of significant accounting policies or other notes, the judgements, apart from those involving estimations (see paragraph 8.7), that management has made in the process of applying the entity's accounting policies and that have the most significant effect on the amounts recognised in the financial statements.

Information about key sources of estimation uncertainty

8.7   An entity shall disclose in the notes information about the key assumptions concerning the future, and other key sources of estimation uncertainty at the reporting date, that have a significant risk of causing a **material** adjustment to the **carrying amounts** of **assets** and **liabilities** within the next financial year. In respect of those assets and liabilities, the notes shall include details of:

(a)   their nature; and

(b)   their carrying amount as at the end of the **reporting period**.

Section 9 Consolidated and Separate Financial Statements

Scope of this section

9.1   This section applies to all **parents** that present **consolidated financial statements** (which are referred to as group accounts in the **Act**) intended to give a true and fair view of the **financial position** and **profit or loss** (or **income and expenditure**) of their **group**, whether or not they report under the Act. Parents that do not report under the Act should comply with the requirements of this section, and of the Act where referred to in this section, except to the extent that these requirements are not permitted by any statutory framework under which such entities report. This section also includes guidance on **individual financial statements** and **separate financial statements**.

Requirement to present consolidated financial statements

9.2   Except as permitted or required by paragraph 9.3, a parent entity shall present consolidated financial statements in which it consolidates all its investments in **subsidiaries** in accordance with this FRS. A parent entity need only prepare consolidated accounts under the Act if it is a parent at the year end.

9.3   A parent is exempt from the requirement to prepare consolidated financial statements on any one of the following grounds:

(a)   The parent is a wholly-owned subsidiary and its immediate parent is established under the law of an EEA State. Exemption is conditional on compliance with certain further conditions set out in section 400(2) of the Act.

(b)   The parent is a majority-owned subsidiary and meets all the conditions for exemption as a wholly-owned subsidiary set out in section 400(2) of the Act as well as the additional conditions set out in section 400(1)(b) of the Act.

(c)   The parent is a wholly-owned subsidiary of another entity and that parent is not established under the law of an EEA State. Exemption is conditional on compliance with certain further conditions set out in section 401(2) of the Act.

(d)   The parent is a majority-owned subsidiary and meets all of the conditions for exemption as a wholly-owned subsidiary set out in section 401(2) of the Act as well as the additional conditions set out in section 401(1)(b) of the Act.

(e)   The parent, and group headed by it, qualify as small as set out in section 383 of the Act and the group is not ineligible as set out in section 384 of the Act.

(f) All of the parent's subsidiaries are required to be excluded from consolidation by paragraph 9.9.

(g) For parents not reporting under the Act, if its statutory framework does not require the preparation of consolidated financial statements.

In sub-paragraphs (a) to (d), the parent is not exempt if any of its securities are admitted to trading on a regulated market of any EEA State within the meaning of Directive 2004/39/EC.

Prospective amendments: Amendments to FRS 102 *The Financial Reporting Standard applicable in the UK and Republic of Ireland* – Small entities and other minor amendments (July 2015) amends of paragraph 9.3 with effect for annual periods beginning on or after 1 January 2016.

A subsidiary is an entity that is controlled by the parent. **Control** is the power to govern the financial and operating policies of an entity so as to obtain benefits from its activities.   **9.4**

Control is presumed to exist when the parent owns, directly or indirectly through subsidiaries, more than half of the voting power of an entity. That presumption may be overcome in exceptional circumstances if it can be clearly demonstrated that such ownership does not constitute control. Control also exists when the parent owns half or less of the voting power of an entity but it has: **9.5**

(a) power over more than half of the voting rights by virtue of an agreement with other investors;

(b) power to govern the financial and operating policies of the entity under a statute or an agreement;

(c) power to appoint or remove the majority of the members of the board of directors or equivalent governing body and control of the entity is by that board or body; or

(d) power to cast the majority of votes at meetings of the board of directors or equivalent governing body and control of the entity is by that board or body.

Control can also be achieved by having options or convertible instruments that are currently exercisable or by having an agent with the ability to direct the activities for the benefit of the controlling entity.   **9.6**

Control can also exist when the parent has the power to exercise, or actually exercises, dominant influence or control over the undertaking or it and the undertaking are managed on a unified basis.   **9.6A**

[Not used]   **9.7**

A subsidiary is not excluded from consolidation because its business activities are dissimilar to those of the other entities within the consolidation. Relevant information is provided by consolidating such subsidiaries and disclosing additional information in the consolidated financial statements about the different business activities of subsidiaries.   **9.8**

A subsidiary is not excluded from consolidation because the information necessary for the preparation of consolidated financial statements cannot be obtained without disproportionate **expense** or undue delay, unless its inclusion is not **material** (individually or collectively for more than one subsidiary) for the purposes of giving a true and fair view in the context of the group.   **9.8A**

A subsidiary shall be excluded from consolidation where: **9.9**

(a) severe long-term restrictions substantially hinder the exercise of the rights of the parent over the **assets** or management of the subsidiary; or

(b)   the interest in the subsidiary is **held exclusively with a view to subsequent resale**; and the subsidiary has not previously been consolidated in the consolidated financial statements prepared in accordance with this FRS.

9.9A   A subsidiary excluded from consolidation on the grounds set out in paragraph 9.9(a) shall be measured using an accounting policy selected by the parent in accordance with paragraph 9.26, except where the parent still exercises a significant influence over the subsidiary. If this is the case, the parent should treat the subsidiary as an associate using the equity method set out in paragraph 14.8.

9.9B   A subsidiary excluded from consolidation on the grounds set out in paragraph 9.9(b) which is:

(a)   **held as part of an investment portfolio** shall be measured at **fair value** with changes in fair value recognised in profit or loss;[10] or

(b)   not held as part of an investment portfolio shall be measured using an **accounting policy** selected by the parent in accordance with paragraph 9.26.

Special purpose entities

9.10   An entity may be created to accomplish a narrow objective (eg to effect a **lease**, undertake **research** and **development** activities, securitise **financial assets** or facilitate employee shareholdings under remuneration schemes, such as Employee Share Ownership Plans (ESOPs)). Such a special purpose entity (SPE) may take the form of a corporation, trust, partnership or unincorporated entity. Often, SPEs are created with legal arrangements that impose strict requirements over the operations of the SPE.

9.11   Except as permitted or required by paragraph 9.3, a parent entity shall prepare consolidated financial statements that include the entity and any SPEs that are controlled by that entity. In addition to the circumstances described in paragraph 9.5, the following circumstances may indicate that an entity controls a SPE (this is not an exhaustive list):

(a)   the activities of the SPE are being conducted on behalf of the entity according to its specific business needs;

(b)   the entity has the ultimate decision-making powers over the activities of the SPE even if the day-to-day decisions have been delegated;

(c)   the entity has rights to obtain the majority of the benefits of the SPE and therefore may be exposed to risks incidental to the activities of the SPE; and

(d)   the entity retains the majority of the residual or ownership risks related to the SPE or its assets.

9.12   Paragraphs 9.10 and 9.11 do not apply to **post-employment benefit plans** or other long-term employee benefit plans to which Section 28 *Employee Benefits* applies. A special purpose entity that is an intermediate payment arrangement shall be accounted for in accordance with paragraphs 9.33 to 9.38.

Consolidation procedures

9.13   The consolidated financial statements present financial information about the group as a single economic entity. In preparing consolidated financial statements, an entity shall:

(a)   combine the **financial statements** of the parent and its subsidiaries line by line by adding together like items of assets, **liabilities**, **equity**, **income** and expenses;

---

[10] *Additional disclosures may need to be provided in accordance with company law (see Appendix IV, paragraph A4.17).*

(b) eliminate the **carrying amount** of the parent's investment in each subsidiary and the parent's portion of equity of each subsidiary;

(c) measure and present **non-controlling interest** in the profit or loss of consolidated subsidiaries for the **reporting period** separately from the interest of the **owners** of the parent; and

(d) measure and present non-controlling interest in the net assets of consolidated subsidiaries separately from the parent shareholders' equity in them. Non-controlling interest in the net assets consists of:

    (i) the amount of the non-controlling interest's share in the net amount of the identifiable assets, liabilities and contingent liabilities recognised and measured in accordance with Section 19 *Business Combinations and Goodwill* at the date of the original combination; and

    (ii) the non-controlling interest's share of changes in equity since the date of the combination.

The proportions of profit or loss and changes in equity allocated to the owners of the parent and to the non-controlling interest are determined on the basis of existing ownership interests and do not reflect the possible exercise or conversion of options or convertible instruments. **9.14**

Intragroup balances and transactions

Intragroup balances and transactions, including income, expenses and dividends, are eliminated in full. Profits and losses resulting from intragroup transactions that are recognised in assets, such as **inventory** and **property, plant and equipment**, are eliminated in full. Intragroup losses may indicate an impairment that requires **recognition** in the consolidated financial statements (see Section 27 *Impairment of Assets*). Section 29 *Income Tax* applies to **timing differences** that arise from the elimination of profits and losses resulting from intragroup transactions. **9.15**

Uniform reporting date and reporting period

The financial statements of the parent and its subsidiaries used in the preparation of the consolidated financial statements shall be prepared as of the same **reporting date**, and for the same reporting period, unless it is **impracticable** to do so. Where the reporting date and reporting period of a subsidiary are not the same as the parent's reporting date and reporting period, the consolidated financial statements must be made up: **9.16**

(a) from the financial statements of the subsidiary as of its last reporting date before the parent's reporting date, adjusted for the effects of significant transactions or events that occur between the date of those financial statements and the date of the consolidated financial statements, provided that reporting date is no more than three months before that of the parent; or

(b) from interim financial statements prepared by the subsidiary as at the parent's reporting date.

Uniform accounting policies

Consolidated financial statements shall be prepared using uniform accounting policies for like transactions and other events and conditions in similar circumstances. If a member of the group uses accounting policies other than those adopted in the consolidated financial statements for like transactions and events in similar circumstances, appropriate adjustments are made to its financial statements in preparing the consolidated financial statements. **9.17**

Acquisition and disposal of subsidiaries

9.18   The income and expenses of a subsidiary are included in the consolidated financial statements from the **acquisition date**, except when a **business combination** is accounted for by using the merger accounting method under Section 19 or, for certain public benefit entity combinations, Section 34 *Specialised Activities*. The income and expenses of a subsidiary are included in the consolidated financial statements until the date on which the parent ceases to control the subsidiary. A parent may cease to control a subsidiary with or without a change in absolute or relative ownership levels. This could occur, for example, when a subsidiary becomes subject to the control of a government, court, administrator or regulator.

Disposal – where control is lost

9.18A   Where a parent ceases to control a subsidiary, a **gain** or loss is recognised in the consolidated statement of comprehensive income (or in the **income statement**, if presented) calculated as the difference between:

(a)   the proceeds from the disposal (or the event that resulted in the loss of control); and

(b)   the proportion of the carrying amount of the subsidiary's net assets, including any related **goodwill**, disposed of (or lost) as at the date of disposal (or date control is lost).

The cumulative amount of any exchange differences that relate to a foreign subsidiary recognised in equity in accordance with Section 30 *Foreign Currency Translation* is not recognised in profit or loss as part of the gain or loss on disposal of the subsidiary and shall be transferred directly to retained earnings.

9.18B   The gain or loss arising on the disposal shall also include those amounts that have been recognised in **other comprehensive income** in relation to that subsidiary, where those amounts are required to be reclassified to profit or loss upon disposal in accordance with other sections of this FRS. Amounts that are not required to be reclassified to profit or loss upon disposal of the related assets or liabilities in accordance with other sections of this FRS shall be transferred directly to retained earnings.

9.19   If an entity ceases to be a subsidiary but the investor (former parent) continues to hold:

(a)   an investment that is not an **associate** (see paragraph 9.19(b)) or a **jointly controlled entity** (see paragraph 9.19(c)), that investment shall be accounted for as a financial asset in accordance with Section 11 *Basic Financial Instruments* or Section 12 *Other Financial Instruments Issues* from the date the entity ceases to be a subsidiary;

(b)   an associate, that associate shall be accounted for in accordance with Section 14 *Investments in Associates*; or

(c)   a jointly controlled entity, that jointly controlled entity shall be accounted for in accordance with Section 15 *Investments in Joint Ventures*.

The carrying amount of the net assets (and goodwill) attributable to the investment at the date that the entity ceases to be a subsidiary shall be regarded as the cost on initial **measurement** of the financial asset, investment in associate or jointly controlled entity, as appropriate. In applying the equity method to investments in associate or jointly controlled entities as required in sub-paragraphs (b) and (c) above, paragraph 14.8(c) shall not be applied.

Disposal – where control is retained

Where a parent reduces its holding in a subsidiary and control is retained, it shall be accounted for as a transaction between equity holders and the resulting change in non-controlling interest shall be accounted for in accordance with paragraph 22.19. No gain or loss shall be recognised at the date of disposal.

9.19A

Acquisition – Control achieved in stages

Where a parent acquires control of a subsidiary in stages, the transaction shall be accounted for in accordance with paragraphs 19.11A and 19.14 applied at the date control is achieved.

9.19B

Acquisition – Increasing a controlling interest in a subsidiary

Where a parent increases its controlling interest in a subsidiary, the identifiable assets and liabilities and a **provision** for **contingent liabilities** of the subsidiary shall not be revalued to fair value and no additional goodwill shall be recognised at the date the controlling interest is increased.

9.19C

The transaction shall be accounted for as a transaction between equity holders and the resulting change in non-controlling interest shall be accounted for in accordance with paragraph 22.19.

9.19D

Non-controlling interest in subsidiaries

An entity shall present non-controlling interest in the consolidated statement of financial position within equity, separately from the equity of the owners of the parent.

9.20

An entity shall disclose non-controlling interest in the profit or loss of the group separately in the **statement of comprehensive income** (or income statement, if presented).

9.21

Profit or loss and each component of other comprehensive income shall be attributed to the owners of the parent and to non-controlling interest. **Total comprehensive income** shall be attributed to the owners of the parent and to non-controlling interest even if this results in non-controlling interest having a deficit balance.

9.22

Disclosures in consolidated financial statements

The following disclosures shall be made in consolidated financial statements:

9.23

(a)   the fact that the statements are consolidated financial statements;
(b)   the basis for concluding that control exists when the parent does not own, directly or indirectly through subsidiaries, more than half of the voting power;
(c)   any difference in the reporting date of the financial statements of the parent and its subsidiaries used in the preparation of the consolidated financial statements;
(d)   the nature and extent of any significant restrictions (eg resulting from borrowing arrangements or regulatory requirements) on the ability of subsidiaries to transfer funds to the parent in the form of cash dividends or to repay loans; and
(e)   the name of any subsidiary excluded from consolidation and the reason for exclusion.

Individual and separate financial statements

Preparation of individual and separate financial statements

9.23A   The requirements for the preparation of individual financial statements are set out in the Act or other statutory framework.

9.24   Separate financial statements are those prepared by a parent in which the investments in subsidiaries, associates or jointly controlled entities are accounted for either at cost or fair value rather than on the basis of the reported results and net assets of the investees. Separate financial statements are included within the meaning of individual financial statements.

9.25   An entity that is not a parent shall account for any investments in associates and any interests in jointly controlled entities in accordance with paragraph 14.4 or 15.9, as appropriate in its individual financial statements.

Accounting policy election in separate financial statements

9.26   When an entity that is a parent prepares separate financial statements and describes them as conforming to this FRS, those financial statements shall comply with all of the requirements of this FRS. The parent shall select and adopt a policy of accounting for its investments in subsidiaries, associates and jointly controlled entities either:

(a)   at cost less impairment;
(b)   at fair value with changes in fair value recognised in other comprehensive income in accordance with paragraphs 17.15E and 17.15F; or
(c)   at fair value with changes in fair value recognised in profit or loss (paragraphs 11.27 to 11.32 provide guidance on fair value).

The entity shall apply the same accounting policy for all investments in a single class (subsidiaries, associates or jointly controlled entities), but it can elect different policies for different classes.

9.26A   A parent that is exempt in accordance with paragraph 9.3 from the requirement to present consolidated financial statements, and presents separate financial statements as its only financial statements, shall account for its investments in subsidiaries, associates and jointly controlled entities in accordance with paragraph 9.26.

Disclosures in separate financial statements

9.27   When a parent prepares separate financial statements, those separate financial statements shall disclose:

(a)   that the statements are separate financial statements; and
(b)   a description of the methods used to account for the investments in subsidiaries, jointly controlled entities and associates.

9.27A   A parent that uses one of the exemptions from presenting consolidated financial statements (described in paragraph 9.3) shall disclose the grounds on which the parent is exempt.

9.27B   When a parent adopts a policy of accounting for its investments in subsidiaries, associates or jointly controlled entities at fair value with changes in fair value recognised in profit or loss, it must comply with the requirements of paragraph 36(4) of Schedule 1 to the **Regulations** by applying the disclosure requirements of Section 11 *Basic Financial Instruments* to those investments.

[Not used] 9.28

[Not used] 9.29

[Not used] 9.30

Exchanges of businesses or other non-monetary assets for an interest in a subsidiary, jointly controlled entity or associate

Where a reporting entity exchanges a **business**, or other non-monetary assets, for an 9.31
interest in another entity, and that other entity thereby becomes a subsidiary, **jointly controlled entity** or associate of the reporting entity, the following accounting treatment shall apply in the consolidated financial statements of the reporting entity:

(a) To the extent that the reporting entity retains an ownership interest in the business, or other non-monetary assets, exchanged, even if that interest is then held through the other entity, that retained interest, including any related goodwill, is treated as having been owned by the reporting entity throughout the transaction and should be included at its pre-transaction carrying amount.

(b) Goodwill should be recognised as the difference between:

(i) the fair value of the consideration given; and

(ii) the fair value of the reporting entity's share of the pre-transaction identifiable net assets of the other entity.

The consideration given for the interest acquired in the other entity will include that part of the business, or other non-monetary assets, exchanged and no longer owned by the reporting entity. The consideration may also include **cash** or monetary assets to achieve equalisation of values. Where it is difficult to value the consideration given, the best estimate of its value may be given by valuing what is acquired.

(c) To the extent that the fair value of the consideration received by the reporting entity exceeds the carrying value of the part of the business, or other non-monetary assets exchanged and no longer owned by the reporting entity, and any related goodwill together with any cash given up, the reporting entity should recognise a gain. Any unrealised gain arising on the exchange shall be recognised in other comprehensive income.

(d) To the extent that the fair value of the consideration received by the reporting entity is less than the carrying value of the part of the business, or other non-monetary assets no longer owned by the reporting entity, and any related goodwill, together with any cash given up, the reporting entity should recognise a loss. This loss should be recognised either as an impairment in accordance with Section 27 *Impairment of Assets* or, for any loss remaining after an impairment review of the relevant assets, in profit or loss.

No gain or loss should be recognised in those rare cases where the artificiality or lack 9.32
of substance of the transaction is such that a gain or loss on the exchange could not be justified. Where a gain or loss on the exchange is not taken into account because the transaction is artificial or has no substance, the circumstances should be explained.

Intermediate payment arrangements

Intermediate payment arrangements may take a variety of forms: 9.33

(a) The intermediary is usually established by a sponsoring entity and constituted as a trust, although other arrangements are possible.

(b) The relationship between the sponsoring entity and the intermediary may take different forms. For example, when the intermediary is constituted as a trust, the sponsoring entity will not have a right to direct the intermediary's activities. However, in these and other cases the sponsoring entity may give advice to the intermediary or may be relied on by the intermediary to provide the information it needs to carry out its activities. Sometimes, the way the intermediary has been set up gives it little discretion in the broad nature of its activities.

(c)   The arrangements are most commonly used to pay employees, although they are sometimes used to compensate suppliers of goods and services other than employee services. Sometimes the sponsoring entity's employees and other suppliers are not the only beneficiaries of the arrangement. Other beneficiaries may include past employees and their dependants, and the intermediary may be entitled to make charitable donations.

(d)   The precise identity of the persons or entities that will receive payments from the intermediary, and the amounts that they will receive, are not usually agreed at the outset.

(e)   The sponsoring entity often has the right to appoint or veto the appointment of the intermediary's trustees (or its directors or the equivalent).

(f)   The payments made to the intermediary and the payments made by the intermediary are often cash payments but may involve other transfers of value.

Examples of intermediate payment arrangements are employee share ownership plans (ESOPs) and employee benefit trusts that are used to facilitate employee shareholdings under remuneration schemes. In a typical employee benefit trust arrangement for share-based payments, an entity makes payments to a trust or guarantees borrowing by the trust, and the trust uses its funds to accumulate assets to pay the entity's employees for services the employees have rendered to the entity.

Although the trustees of an intermediary must act at all times in accordance with the interests of the beneficiaries of the intermediary, most intermediaries (particularly those established as a means of remunerating employees) are specifically designed so as to serve the purposes of the sponsoring entity, and to ensure that there will be minimal risk of any conflict arising between the duties of the trustees of the intermediary and the interest of the sponsoring entity, such that there is nothing to encumber implementation of the wishes of the sponsoring entity in practice. Where this is the case, the sponsoring entity has de facto control.

Accounting for intermediate payment arrangements

9.34   When a sponsoring entity makes payments (or transfers assets) to an intermediary, there is a rebuttable presumption that the entity has exchanged one asset for another and that the payment itself does not represent an immediate expense. To rebut this presumption at the time the payment is made to the intermediary, the entity must demonstrate:

(a)   it will not obtain future economic benefit from the amounts transferred; or

(b)   it does not have control of the right or other access to the future economic benefit it is expected to receive.

9.35   Where a payment to an intermediary is an exchange by the sponsoring entity of one asset for another, any assets that the intermediary acquires in a subsequent exchange transaction will also be under the control of the entity. Accordingly, assets and liabilities of the intermediary shall be accounted for by the sponsoring entity as an extension of its own business and recognised in its own individual financial statements. An asset will cease to be recognised as an asset of the sponsoring entity when, for example, the asset of the intermediary vests unconditionally with identified beneficiaries.

9.36   A sponsoring entity may distribute its own equity instruments, or other equity instruments, to an intermediary in order to facilitate employee shareholdings under a remuneration scheme. Where this is the case and the sponsoring entity has control, or de facto control, of the assets and liabilities of the intermediary, the commercial effect is that the sponsoring entity is, for all practical purposes, in the same position as if it had purchased the shares directly.

Where an intermediary holds the sponsoring entity's equity instruments, the sponsoring entity shall account for the equity instruments as if it had purchased them directly. The sponsoring entity shall account for the assets and liabilities of the intermediary in its individual financial statements as follows: **9.37**

(a) The consideration paid for the equity instruments of the sponsoring entity shall be deducted from equity until such time that the equity instruments **vest** unconditionally with employees.

(b) Consideration paid or received for the purchase or sale of the sponsoring entity's own equity instruments shall be shown as separate amounts in the **statement of changes in equity**.

(c) Other assets and liabilities of the intermediary shall be recognised as assets and liabilities of the sponsoring entity.

(d) No gain or loss shall be recognised in profit or loss or other comprehensive income on the purchase, sale, issue or cancellation of the entity's own equity instruments.

(e) Finance costs and any administration expenses shall be recognised on an accruals basis rather than as funding payments are made to the intermediary.

(f) Any dividend income arising on the sponsoring entity's own equity instruments shall be excluded from profit or loss and deducted from the aggregate of dividends paid.

Disclosures in individual and separate financial statements

When a sponsoring entity recognises the assets and liabilities held by an intermediary, it should disclose sufficient information in the **notes** to its financial statements to enable users to understand the significance of the intermediary and the arrangement in the context of the sponsoring entity's financial statements. This should include: **9.38**

(a) a description of the main features of the intermediary including the arrangements for making payments and for distributing equity instruments;

(b) any restrictions relating to the assets and liabilities of the intermediary;

(c) the amount and nature of the assets and liabilities held by the intermediary, which have not yet vested unconditionally with the beneficiaries of the arrangement;

(d) the amount that has been deducted from equity and the number of equity instruments held by the intermediary, which have not yet vested unconditionally with the beneficiaries of the arrangement;

(e) for entities that have their equity instruments listed or **publicly traded** on a stock exchange or market, the market value of the equity instruments held by the intermediary which have not yet vested unconditionally with employees;

(f) the extent to which the equity instruments are under option to employees, or have been conditionally gifted to them; and

(g) the amount that has been deducted from the aggregate dividends paid by the sponsoring entity.

Section 10 Accounting Policies, Estimates and Errors

Scope of this section

This section provides guidance for selecting and applying the **accounting policies** used in preparing **financial statements**. It also covers **changes in accounting estimates** and corrections of **errors** in prior period financial statements. **10.1**

Selection and application of accounting policies

10.2   Accounting policies are the specific principles, bases, conventions, rules and practices applied by an entity in preparing and presenting financial statements.

10.3   If an FRS or FRC Abstract specifically addresses a transaction, other event or condition, an entity shall apply that FRS or FRC Abstract. However, the entity need not follow a requirement in an FRS or FRC Abstract if the effect of doing so would not be **material**.

10.4   If an FRS or FRC Abstract does not specifically address a transaction, other event or condition, an entity's management shall use its judgement in developing and applying an accounting policy that results in information that is:

(a)   relevant to the economic decision-making needs of users; and
(b)   reliable, in that the financial statements:

    (i)   represent faithfully the **financial position**, financial **performance** and **cash flows** of the entity;
    (ii)   reflect the economic substance of transactions, other events and conditions, and not merely the legal form;
    (iii)   are neutral, ie free from bias;
    (iv)   are prudent; and
    (v)   are complete in all material respects.

10.5   In making the judgement described in paragraph 10.4, management shall refer to and consider the applicability of the following sources in descending order:

(a)   the requirements and guidance in an FRS or FRC Abstract dealing with similar and related issues;
(b)   where an entity's financial statements are within the scope of a **Statement of Recommended Practice (SORP)** the requirements and guidance in that SORP dealing with similar and related issues; and
(c)   the definitions, **recognition** criteria and measurement concepts for **assets**, **liabilities**, **income** and **expenses** and the pervasive principles in Section 2 *Concepts and Pervasive Principles*.

10.6   In making the judgement described in paragraph 10.4, management may also consider the requirements and guidance in **EU-adopted IFRS** dealing with similar and related issues. Paragraphs 1.4 to 1.7 require certain entities to apply IAS 33 *Earnings per Share* (as adopted in the EU) , IFRS 8 *Operating Segments* (as adopted in the EU) or IFRS 6 *Exploration for and Evaluation of Mineral Resources*.

Consistency of accounting policies

10.7   An entity shall select and apply its accounting policies consistently for similar transactions, other events and conditions, unless an FRS or FRC Abstract specifically requires or permits categorisation of items for which different policies may be appropriate. If an FRS or FRC Abstract requires or permits such categorisation, an appropriate accounting policy shall be selected and applied consistently to each category.

Changes in accounting policies

10.8   An entity shall change an accounting policy only if the change:

(a)   is required by an FRS or FRC Abstract; or

(b)   results in the financial statements providing reliable and more relevant information about the effects of transactions, other events or conditions on the entity's financial position, financial performance or cash flows.

The following are not changes in accounting policies: **10.9**

(a)   the application of an accounting policy for transactions, other events or conditions that differ in substance from those previously occurring;

(b)   the application of a new accounting policy for transactions, other events or conditions that did not occur previously or were not material; and

(c)   a change to the cost model when a reliable measure of **fair value** is no longer available (or vice versa) for an asset that an FRS or FRC Abstract would otherwise require or permit to be measured at fair value.

If an FRS or FRC Abstract allows a choice of accounting treatment (including the   **10.10** measurement basis) for a specified transaction or other event or condition and an entity changes its previous choice, that is a change in accounting policy.

The initial application of a policy to revalue assets in accordance with Section 17 *Property,*   **10.10A** *Plant and Equipment* or Section 18 *Intangible Assets other than Goodwill* is a change in accounting policy to be dealt with as a revaluation in accordance with those sections, rather than in accordance with paragraphs 10.11 and 10.12.

Applying changes in accounting policies

An entity shall account for changes in accounting policy as follows: **10.11**

(a)   an entity shall account for a change in accounting policy resulting from a change in the requirements of an FRS or FRC Abstract in accordance with the transitional provisions, if any, specified in that amendment;

(b)   when an entity has elected to follow IAS 39 *Financial Instruments: Recognition and Measurement* and/or IFRS 9 *Financial Instruments* instead of following Section 11 *Basic Financial Instruments* and Section 12 *Other Financial Instruments Issues* as permitted by paragraph 11.2, and the requirements of IAS 39 and/or IFRS 9 change, the entity shall account for that change in accounting policy in accordance with the transitional provisions, if any, specified in the revised IAS 39 and/or IFRS 9; and

(c)   when an entity is required or has elected to follow IAS 33 *Earnings per Share*, IFRS 8 *Operating Segments* or IFRS 6 *Exploration for and Evaluation of Mineral Resources* and the requirements of those standards change, the entity shall account for that change in accounting policy in accordance with the transitional provisions, if any, specified in those standards as amended; and

(d)   an entity shall account for all other changes in accounting policy retrospectively (see paragraph 10.12).

Retrospective application

When a change in accounting policy is applied retrospectively in accordance with   **10.12** paragraph 10.11, the entity shall apply the new accounting policy to comparative information for prior periods to the earliest date for which it is practicable, as if the new accounting policy had always been applied. When it is **impracticable** to determine the individual-period effects of a change in accounting policy on comparative information for one or more prior periods presented, the entity shall apply the new accounting policy to the **carrying amounts** of assets and liabilities as at the beginning of the earliest period for which **retrospective application** is practicable, which may be the current period, and shall make a corresponding adjustment to the opening balance of each affected component of **equity** for that period.

Disclosure of a change in accounting policy

10.13   When an amendment to an FRS or FRC Abstract has an effect on the current period or any prior period, or might have an effect on future periods, an entity shall disclose the following:

(a)   the nature of the change in accounting policy;

(b)   for the current period and each prior period presented, to the extent practicable, the amount of the adjustment for each financial statement line item affected;

(c)   the amount of the adjustment relating to periods before those presented, to the extent practicable; and

(d)   an explanation if it is impracticable to determine the amounts to be disclosed in (b) or (c) above.

Financial statements of subsequent periods need not repeat these disclosures.

10.14   When a voluntary change in accounting policy has an effect on the current period or any prior period, an entity shall disclose the following:

(a)   the nature of the change in accounting policy;

(b)   the reasons why applying the new accounting policy provides reliable and more relevant information;

(c)   to the extent practicable, the amount of the adjustment for each financial statement line item affected, shown separately:

(i)   for the current period;

(ii)   for each prior period presented; and

(iii) in the aggregate for periods before those presented; and

(d)   an explanation if it is impracticable to determine the amounts to be disclosed in (c) above.

Financial statements of subsequent periods need not repeat these disclosures.

Changes in accounting estimates

10.15   A **change in accounting estimate** is an adjustment of the carrying amount of an asset or a liability, or the amount of the periodic consumption of an asset, that results from the assessment of the present status of, and expected future benefits and obligations associated with, assets and liabilities. Changes in accounting estimates result from new information or new developments and, accordingly, are not corrections of errors. When it is difficult to distinguish a change in an accounting policy from a change in an accounting estimate, the change is treated as a change in an accounting estimate.

10.16   An entity shall recognise the effect of a change in an accounting estimate, other than a change to which paragraph 10.17 applies, **prospectively** by including it in **profit or loss** in:

(a)   the period of the change, if the change affects that period only; or

(b)   the period of the change and future periods, if the change affects both.

10.17   To the extent that a change in an accounting estimate gives rise to changes in assets and liabilities, or relates to an item of equity, the entity shall recognise it by adjusting the carrying amount of the related asset, liability or equity item in the period of the change.

Disclosure of a change in estimate

An entity shall disclose the nature of any change in an accounting estimate and the effect   **10.18**
of the change on assets, liabilities, income and expense for the current period. If it is
practicable for the entity to estimate the effect of the change in one or more future periods,
the entity shall disclose those estimates.

Corrections of prior period errors

Prior period errors are omissions from, and misstatements in, an entity's financial   **10.19**
statements for one or more prior periods arising from a failure to use, or misuse of, reliable
information that:

(a)   was available when financial statements for those periods were authorised for issue;
      and
(b)   could reasonably be expected to have been obtained and taken into account in the
      preparation and presentation of those financial statements.

Such errors include the effects of mathematical mistakes, mistakes in applying accounting   **10.20**
policies, oversights or misinterpretations of facts, and fraud.

To the extent practicable, an entity shall correct a material prior period error retrospectively   **10.21**
in the first financial statements authorised for issue after its discovery by:

(a)   restating the comparative amounts for the prior period(s) presented in which the
      error occurred; or
(b)   if the error occurred before the earliest prior period presented, restating the opening
      balances of assets, liabilities and equity for the earliest prior period presented.

When it is impracticable to determine the period-specific effects of a material error on   **10.22**
comparative information for one or more prior periods presented, the entity shall restate
the opening balances of assets, liabilities and equity for the earliest period for which
retrospective restatement is practicable (which may be the current period).

Disclosure of prior period errors

An entity shall disclose the following about material prior period errors: **10.23**

(a)   the nature of the prior period error;
(b)   for each prior period presented, to the extent practicable, the amount of the correction
      for each financial statement line item affected;
(c)   to the extent practicable, the amount of the correction at the beginning of the earliest
      prior period presented; and
(d)   an explanation if it is not practicable to determine the amounts to be disclosed in (b)
      or (c) above.

Financial statements of subsequent periods need not repeat these disclosures.

Section 11 Basic Financial Instruments

Scope of Sections 11 and 12

Section 11 *Basic Financial Instruments* and Section 12 *Other Financial Instruments*   **11.1**
Issues together deal with recognising, derecognising, measuring and disclosing **financial**
instruments (financial assets and **financial liabilities**). Section 11 applies to basic

financial instruments and is relevant to all entities. Section 12 applies to other, more complex financial instruments and transactions. If an entity enters into only basic financial instrument transactions then Section 12 is not applicable. However, even entities with only basic financial instruments shall consider the scope of Section 12 to ensure they are exempt.

PBE11.1A **Public benefit entities** and other members of a **public benefit entity group** that make or receive **public benefit entity concessionary loans** shall refer to the relevant paragraphs of Section 34 *Specialised Activities* for the accounting requirements for such loans.

Accounting policy choice

11.2 An entity shall choose to apply either:

(a) the provisions of both Section 11 and Section 12 in full; or

(b) the **recognition** and **measurement** provisions of IAS 39 *Financial Instruments: Recognition and Measurement* (as adopted for use in the EU), the disclosure requirements of Sections 11 and 12 and the presentation requirements of paragraphs 11.38A or 12.25B; or

(c) the recognition and measurement provisions of IFRS 9 *Financial Instruments* and/ or IAS 39 (as amended following the publication of IFRS 9), the disclosure requirements of Sections 11 and 12 and the presentation requirements of paragraphs 11.38A or 12.25B;

to account for all of its financial instruments. Where an entity chooses (b) or (c) it applies the scope of the relevant standard to its financial instruments. An entity's choice of (a), (b) or (c) is an **accounting policy** choice. Paragraphs 10.8 to 10.14 contain requirements for determining when a change in accounting policy is appropriate, how such a change should be accounted for and what information should be disclosed about the change.

Prospective amendments: Amendments to FRS 102 *The Financial Reporting Standard applicable in the UK and Republic of Ireland* – Small entities and other minor amendments (July 2015) amends paragraph 11.2 with effect for annual periods beginning on or after 1 January 2016.

Prospective amendments: Amendments to FRS 102 *The Financial Reporting Standard applicable in the UK and Republic of Ireland* – Small entities and other minor amendments (July 2015) inserts paragraph 11.2A with effect for annual periods beginning on or after 1 January 2016.

Introduction to Section 11

11.3 A financial instrument is a contract that gives rise to a financial asset of one entity and a financial liability or equity instrument of another entity.

11.4 [Not used]

11.5 Basic financial instruments within the scope of Section 11 are those that satisfy the conditions in paragraph 11.8. Examples of financial instruments that normally satisfy those conditions include:

(a) **cash**;

(b) demand and fixed-term deposits when the entity is the depositor, eg bank accounts;

(c) commercial paper and commercial bills held;

(d) accounts, notes and loans receivable and payable;

(e) bonds and similar debt instruments;

(f)   investments in non-convertible preference shares and non-puttable ordinary and preference shares; and

(g)   commitments to receive a loan and commitments to make a loan to another entity that meet the conditions of paragraph 11.8(c).

Examples of financial instruments that do not normally satisfy the conditions in paragraph 11.8, and are therefore within the scope of Section 12, include: **11.6**

(a)   asset-backed securities, such as collateralised mortgage obligations, repurchase agreements and securitised packages of receivables;

(b)   options, rights, warrants, futures contracts, forward contracts and interest rate swaps that can be settled in cash or by exchanging another financial instrument;

(c)   financial instruments that qualify and are designated as hedging instruments in accordance with the requirements in Section 12; and

(d)   commitments to make a loan to another entity and commitments to receive a loan, if the commitment can be settled net in cash.

(e)   [not used]

Scope of Section 11

Section 11 applies to all financial instruments meeting the conditions of paragraph 11.8 except for the following: **11.7**

(a)   Investments in **subsidiaries, associates** and **joint ventures** that are accounted for in accordance with Section 9 *Consolidated and Separate Financial Statements*, Section 14 *Investments in Associates* or Section 15 *Investments in Joint Ventures*.

(b)   Financial instruments that meet the definition of an entity's own equity and the equity component of **compound financial instruments** issued by the reporting entity that contain both a **liability** and an equity component (see Section 22 *Liabilities and Equity*).

(c)   **Leases**, to which Section 20 *Leases* applies. However, the **derecognition** requirements in paragraphs 11.33 to 11.35 and impairment accounting requirements in paragraphs 11.21 to 11.26 apply to derecognition and impairment of receivables recognised by a lessor and the derecognition requirements in paragraphs 11.36 to 11.38 apply to payables recognised by a lessee arising under a **finance lease**. Section 12 applies to leases with characteristics specified in paragraph 12.3(f).

(d)   Employers' rights and obligations under employee benefit plans, to which Section 28 *Employee Benefits* applies, although paragraphs 11.27 to 11.32 do apply in determining the **fair value** of **plan assets**.

(e)   Financial instruments, contracts and obligations to which Section 26 *Share-based Payment* applies, and contracts within the scope of paragraph 12.5.

(f)   **Insurance contracts** (including **reinsurance contracts**) that the entity issues and reinsurance contracts that the entity holds (see FRS 103 *Insurance Contracts*).

(g)   Financial instruments issued by an entity with a **discretionary participation feature** (see FRS 103 *Insurance Contracts*).

(h)   Reimbursement assets accounted for in accordance with Section 21 *Provisions and Contingencies*.

(i)   **Financial guarantee contracts** (see Section 21).

A reporting entity that issues the financial instruments set out in (f) or (g) or holds the financial instruments in (f) is required by paragraph 1.6 of this FRS to apply FRS 103 to those financial instruments.

Prospective amendments: Amendments to FRS 102 *The Financial Reporting Standard applicable in the UK and Republic of Ireland* – Small entities and other minor amendments

(July 2015) amends paragraph 11.7(d) the term 'fair value' is no longer shown in bold type with effect for annual periods beginning on or after 1 January 2016.

Basic financial instruments

11.8   An entity shall account for the following financial instruments as basic financial instruments in accordance with Section 11:

(a)   cash;

(b)   a debt instrument (such as an account, note, or loan receivable or payable) that meets the conditions in paragraph 11.9 and is not a financial instrument described in paragraph 11.6(b);

(c)   commitments to receive or make a loan to another entity that:

(i)   cannot be settled net in cash; and

(ii)   when the commitment is executed, are expected to meet the conditions in paragraph 11.9; and

(d)   an investment in non-convertible preference shares and non-puttable **ordinary shares** or preference shares.

11.9   The conditions a debt instrument shall satisfy in accordance with paragraph 11.8(b) are:

(a)   The contractual return to the holder (the lender), assessed in the currency in which the debt instrument is denominated, is:

(i)   a fixed amount;

(ii)   a positive fixed rate or a positive variable rate[11]; or

(iii)   [not used]

(iv)   a combination of a positive or a negative fixed rate and a positive variable rate (eg LIBOR plus 200 basis points or LIBOR less 50 basis points, but not 500 basis points less LIBOR).

(aA)   The contract may provide for repayments of the principal or the return to the holder (but not both) to be linked to a single relevant observable index of general price inflation of the currency in which the debt instrument is denominated, provided such links are not leveraged.

(aB)   The contract may provide for a determinable variation of the return to the holder during the life of the instrument, provided that:

(i)   the new rate satisfies condition (a) and the variation is not contingent on future events other than:

(1)   a change of a contractual variable rate;

(2)   to protect the holder against credit deterioration of the issuer;

(3)   changes in levies applied by a central bank or arising from changes in relevant taxation or law; or

(ii)   the new rate is a market rate of interest and satisfies condition (a).

Contractual terms that give the lender the unilateral option to change the terms of the contract are not determinable for this purpose.

(b)   There is no contractual provision that could, by its terms, result in the holder losing the principal amount or any interest attributable to the current period or prior periods. The fact that a debt instrument is subordinated to other debt instruments is not an example of such a contractual provision.

---

[11] *A variable rate for this purpose is a rate which varies over time and is linked to a single observable interest rate or to a single relevant observable index of general price inflation of the currency in which the instrument is denominated, provided such links are not leveraged.*

(c) Contractual provisions that permit the issuer (the borrower) to prepay a debt instrument or permit the holder (the lender) to put it back to the issuer before maturity are not contingent on future events other than to protect:

    (i) the holder against the credit deterioration of the issuer (eg defaults, credit downgrades or loan covenant violations), or a change in control of the issuer; or

    (ii) the holder or issuer against changes in levies applied by a central bank or arising from changes in relevant taxation or law.

The inclusion of contractual terms that, as a result of the early termination, require the issuer to compensate the holder for the early termination does not, in itself, constitute a breach of this condition.

(d) [not used]

(e) Contractual provisions may permit the extension of the term of the debt instrument, provided that the return to the holder and any other contractual provisions applicable during the extended term satisfy the conditions of paragraphs (a) to (c).

Examples – Debt instruments

1 A zero-coupon loan

For a zero-coupon loan, the holder's return is the difference between the nominal value of the loan and the issue price. The holder (lender) receives a fixed amount when the loan matures and the issuer (borrower) repays the loan. The return to the holder meets the condition of paragraph 11.9(a)(i).

2 A fixed interest rate loan with an initial tie-in period which reverts to the bank's standard variable interest rate after the tie-in period

The initial fixed rate is a return permitted by paragraph 11.9(a)(ii). A bank's standard variable interest rate is an observable interest rate and, in accordance with the definition of a variable rate, is a permissible link. In accordance with paragraph 11.9(a)(ii) the variable rate should be a positive rate.

The variation of the interest rate after the tie-in period is non-contingent and since the new rate (ie the bank's standard variable rate) meets the condition of paragraph 11.9(a), paragraph 11.9(aB)(i) is met.

3 A loan with interest payable at the bank's standard variable rate plus 1% throughout the life of the loan

As discussed under Example 2 above, a bank's standard variable rate is a permitted variable rate in accordance with the definition of variable rate. The combination of a positive fixed rate (ie plus 1%) and a positive variable rate is a permitted return under paragraph 11.9(a)(iv). The combination of a bank's standard variable rate plus a fixed interest rate of 1% therefore meets the condition in paragraph 11.9(a)(iv).

4 A loan with interest payable at the bank's standard variable rate less 1% throughout the life of the loan, with the condition that the interest rate can never fall below 2%

Paragraph 11.9(aB)(i)(a) permits variation of a return to a holder (lender) that is contingent on a change of a contractual variable rate. In this example the contractual variable rate is the bank's standard variable rate. The variation of

---

Examples – Debt instruments

the return to the holder is between the bank's standard variable rate less 1 and 2%, depending on the bank's standard variable rate. For example, if the bank's standard variable rate is less than 3%, the return to the holder is fixed at 2%; if the bank's standard variable rate is higher than 3%, the return to the holder is the bank's standard variable rate less 1%. The contractual variation meets the condition of paragraph 11.9(aB)(i)(1).

The holder is protected against the risk of losing the principal amount of the loan via the interest rate floor of 2%. The requirement of paragraph 11.9(b) is therefore also met.

5 Interest on a loan is referenced to 2 times the bank's standard variable rate

In accordance with the definition of a variable rate, the contractual interest rate payable can be linked to a single observable interest rate. A bank's standard variable rate is an observable rate and meets the definition of a variable rate, but the rate in this example is 2 times the bank's standard variable rate and the link to the observable interest rate is leveraged. Therefore, the rate in this example is not a variable rate as described in paragraph 11.9(a). The instrument is measured at fair value in accordance with Section 12.

6 Interest on a loan is charged at 10% less 6-month LIBOR over the life of the loan

The effect of combining a negative variable rate with a positive fixed rate is that the interest on the loan increases as and when the variable rate decreases and vice versa (so called inverse floating interest).

Under paragraph 11.9(a)(iv) the combination of positive or negative fixed rate and positive variable rate is a permitted return. The variable rate (6-month LIBOR) meets the definition of a variable rate, as the rate is a quoted interest rate. However, since the variable rate is negative (minus 6-month LIBOR), the rate is in breach of paragraph 11.9(a)(iv). The instrument is measured at fair value in accordance with Section 12.

7 Interest on a GBP denominated mortgage is linked to the UK Land Registry House Price Index (HPI) plus 3%

In accordance with paragraph 11.9(aA) the holder's return may be linked to an index of general price inflation of the currency of the debt instrument. The mortgage is denominated in GBP and a permitted inflation index would be an index that measures general price inflation of goods and services denominated in GBP.

The HPI measures inflation for residential properties in the UK and is not a measure of general price inflation. The return to the holder therefore fails to meet the condition in paragraph 11.9(aA). The instrument is measured at fair value in accordance with Section 12.

11.10 Examples of financial instruments that would normally satisfy the conditions in paragraph 11.9 are:

(a) trade accounts and notes receivable and payable, and loans from banks or other third parties;

(b) accounts payable in a foreign currency. However, any change in the account payable because of a change in the exchange rate is recognised in **profit or loss** as required by paragraph 30.10;

(c)   loans to or from subsidiaries or associates that are due on demand; and

(d)   a debt instrument that would become immediately receivable if the issuer defaults on an interest or principal payment (such a provision does not violate the conditions in paragraph 11.9).

Prospective amendments: Amendments to FRS 102 *The Financial Reporting Standard applicable in the UK and Republic of Ireland* – Small entities and other minor amendments (July 2015) amends paragraph 11.10(b) the term 'profit or loss' is no longer shown in bold type with effect for annual periods beginning on or after 1 January 2016.

Examples of financial instruments that do not satisfy the conditions in paragraph 11.9 (and are therefore within the scope of Section 12) include: **11.11**

(a)   an investment in another entity's equity instruments other than non-convertible preference shares and non-puttable ordinary and preference shares (see paragraph 11.8(d)); and

(b)   [not used]

(c)   [not used]

(d)   investments in convertible debt, because the return to the holder can vary with the price of the issuer's equity shares rather than just with market interest rates.

(e)   [not used]

Initial recognition of financial assets and liabilities

An entity shall recognise a financial asset or a financial liability only when the entity becomes a party to the contractual provisions of the instrument. **11.12**

Initial measurement

When a financial asset or financial liability is recognised initially, an entity shall measure it at the transaction price (including **transaction costs** except in the initial measurement of financial assets and liabilities that are measured at fair value through profit or loss) unless the arrangement constitutes, in effect, a financing transaction. A financing transaction may take place in connection with the sale of goods or services, for example, if payment is deferred beyond normal business terms or is financed at a rate of interest that is not a market rate. If the arrangement constitutes a financing transaction, the entity shall measure the financial asset or financial liability at the **present value** of the future payments discounted at a market rate of interest for a similar debt instrument. **11.13**

Examples – financial assets
1   For a long-term loan made to another entity, a receivable is recognised at the present value of cash receivable (including interest payments and repayment of principal) from that entity.
2   For goods sold to a customer on short-term credit, a receivable is recognised at the undiscounted amount of cash receivable from that entity, which is normally the invoice price.
3   For an item sold to a customer on two-years interest-free credit, a receivable is recognised at the current cash sale price for that item (in financing transactions conducted on an arm's length basis the cash sales price would normally approximate to the present value). If the current cash sale price is not known, it may be estimated as the present value of the cash receivable discounted using the **prevailing market rate(s)** of interest for a similar receivable.
4   For a cash purchase of another entity's ordinary shares, the investment is recognised at the amount of cash paid to acquire the shares.

Prospective amendments: Amendments to FRS 102 *The Financial Reporting Standard applicable in the UK and Republic of Ireland* – Small entities and other minor amendments (July 2015) amends this example with effect for annual periods beginning on or after 1 January 2016.

Examples – financial liabilities
1   For a loan received from a bank, a payable is recognised initially at the present value of cash payable to the bank (eg including interest payments and repayment of principal).
2   For goods purchased from a supplier on short-term credit, a payable is recognised at the undiscounted amount owed to the supplier, which is normally the invoice price.

Prospective amendments: Amendments to FRS 102 *The Financial Reporting Standard applicable in the UK and Republic of Ireland* – Small entities and other minor amendments (July 2015) amends this example with effect for annual periods beginning on or after 1 January 2016.

Subsequent measurement

11.14   At the end of each **reporting period**, an entity shall measure financial instruments as follows, without any deduction for transaction costs the entity may incur on sale or other disposal:

(a)   Debt instruments that meet the conditions in paragraph 11.8(b) shall be measured at **amortised cost** using the **effective interest method**. Paragraphs 11.15 to 11.20 provide guidance on determining amortised cost using the effective interest method. Debt instruments that are payable or receivable within one year shall be measured at the undiscounted amount of the cash or other consideration expected to be paid or received (ie net of impairment – see paragraphs 11.21 to 11.26) unless the arrangement constitutes, in effect, a financing transaction (see paragraph 11.13). If the arrangement constitutes a financing transaction, the entity shall measure the debt instrument at the present value of the future payments discounted at a market rate of interest for a similar debt instrument.

(b)   Debt instruments that meet the conditions in paragraph 11.8(b) and commitments to receive a loan and to make a loan to another entity that meet the conditions in paragraph 11.8(c) may upon their initial recognition be designated by the entity as at fair value through profit or loss (paragraphs 11.27 to 11.32 provide guidance on fair value) provided doing so results in more relevant information, because either:

(i)   it eliminates or significantly reduces a measurement or recognition inconsistency (sometimes referred to as 'an accounting mismatch') that would otherwise arise from measuring assets or debt instruments or recognising the **gains** and losses on them on different bases; or

(ii)   a group of debt instruments or financial assets and debt instruments is managed and its performance is evaluated on a fair value basis, in accordance with a documented risk management or investment strategy, and information about the group is provided internally on that basis to the entity's **key management personnel** (as defined in Section 33 *Related Party Disclosures*, paragraph 33.6), for example members of the entity's board of directors and its chief executive officer.

(c)   Commitments to receive a loan and to make a loan to another entity that meet the conditions in paragraph 11.8(c) shall be measured at cost (which sometimes is nil) less impairment.

(d)   Investments in non-convertible preference shares and non-puttable ordinary shares or preference shares shall be measured as follows (paragraphs 11.27 to 11.32 provide guidance on fair value):

  (i)   if the shares are **publicly traded** or their fair value can otherwise be measured reliably, the investment shall be measured at fair value with changes in fair value recognised in profit or loss; and

  (ii)   all other such investments shall be measured at cost less impairment.

Impairment or uncollectability must be assessed for financial assets in (a), (c) and (d)(ii) above. Paragraphs 11.21 to 11.26 provide guidance.

Prospective amendments: Amendments to FRS 102 *The Financial Reporting Standard applicable in the UK and Republic of Ireland* – Small entities and other minor amendments (July 2015) amends this paragraph 11.14(a) the term 'amortised cost' is no longer shown in bold type with effect for annual periods beginning on or after 1 January 2016.

Amortised cost and effective interest method

The amortised cost of a financial asset or financial liability at each **reporting date** is the net of the following amounts: **11.15**

(a)   the amount at which the financial asset or financial liability is measured at initial recognition;

(b)   minus any repayments of the principal;

(c)   plus or minus the cumulative amortisation using the effective interest method of any difference between the amount at initial recognition and the maturity amount;

(d)   minus, in the case of a financial asset, any reduction (directly or through the use of an allowance account) for impairment or uncollectability.

Financial assets and financial liabilities that have no stated interest rate (and do not constitute a financing transaction) and are classified as payable or receivable within one year are initially measured at an undiscounted amount in accordance with paragraph 11.14(a). Therefore, (c) above does not apply to them.

The effective interest method is a method of calculating the amortised cost of a financial asset or a financial liability (or a group of financial assets or financial liabilities) and of allocating the interest income or interest expense over the relevant period. The **effective interest rate** is the rate that exactly discounts estimated future cash payments or receipts through the expected life of the financial instrument or, when appropriate, a shorter period, to the **carrying amount** of the financial asset or financial liability. The effective interest rate is determined on the basis of the carrying amount of the financial asset or liability at initial recognition. Under the effective interest method: **11.16**

(a)   the amortised cost of a financial asset (liability) is the present value of future cash receipts (payments) discounted at the effective interest rate; and

(b)   the interest expense (income) in a period equals the carrying amount of the financial liability (asset) at the beginning of a period multiplied by the effective interest rate for the period.

When calculating the effective interest rate, an entity shall estimate cash flows considering all contractual terms of the financial instrument (eg prepayment, call and similar options) and known credit losses that have been incurred, but it shall not consider possible future credit losses not yet incurred.   **11.17**

When calculating the effective interest rate, an entity shall amortise any related fees, finance charges paid or received (such as 'points'), transaction costs and other premiums   **11.18** or discounts over the expected life of the instrument, except as follows. The entity shall use a shorter period if that is the period to which the fees, finance charges paid or received, transaction costs, premiums or discounts relate. This will be the case when the variable to which the fees, finance charges paid or received, transaction costs, premiums or discounts relate is repriced to market rates before the expected maturity of the instrument. In such a case, the appropriate amortisation period is the period to the next such repricing date.

11.19   For variable rate financial assets and variable rate financial liabilities, periodic re-estimation of cash flows to reflect changes in market rates of interest alters the effective interest rate. If a variable rate financial asset or variable rate financial liability is recognised initially at an amount equal to the principal receivable or payable at maturity, re-estimating the future interest payments normally has no significant effect on the carrying amount of the asset or liability.

11.20   If an entity revises its estimates of payments or receipts, the entity shall adjust the carrying amount of the financial asset or financial liability (or group of financial instruments) to reflect actual and revised estimated cash flows. The entity shall recalculate the carrying amount by computing the present value of estimated future cash flows at the financial instrument's original effective interest rate. The entity shall recognise the adjustment as **income** or **expense** in profit or loss at the date of the revision.

Example of determining amortised cost for a five-year loan using the effective interest method

On 1 January 20X0, an entity acquires a bond for Currency Units (CU)900, incurring transaction costs of CU50. Interest of CU40 is receivable annually, in arrears, over the next five years (31 December 20X0 to 31 December 20X4). The bond has a mandatory redemption of CU1100 on 31 December 20X4.

Year	Carrying amount at beginning of period	Interest income at 6.9583%*	Cash inflow	Carrying amount at end of period
	CU	CU	CU	CU
20X0	950.00	66.11	(40.00)	976.11
20X1	976.11	67.92	(40.00)	1,004.03
20X2	1,004.03	69.86	(40.00)	1,033.89
20X3	1,033.89	71.94	(40.00)	1,065.83
20X4	1,065.83	74.16	(40.00)	1,100.00
			(1,100.00)	0

* The effective interest rate of 6.9583% is the rate that discounts the expected cash flows on the bond to the initial carrying amount:

$40/(1.069583)^1 + 40/(1.069583)^2 + 40/(1.069583)^3 + 40/(1.069583)^4 + 1,140/(1.069583)^5 = 950$

Impairment of financial instruments measured at cost or amortised cost

Recognition

11.21   At the end of each reporting period, an entity shall assess whether there is objective evidence of impairment of any financial assets that are measured at cost or amortised cost. If there is objective evidence of impairment, the entity shall recognise an **impairment loss** in profit or loss immediately.

Objective evidence that a financial asset or group of assets is impaired includes observable data that come to the attention of the holder of the asset about the following loss events: **11.22**

(a)   significant financial difficulty of the issuer or obligor;

(b)   a breach of contract, such as a default or delinquency in interest or principal payments;

(c)   the creditor, for economic or legal reasons relating to the debtor's financial difficulty, granting to the debtor a concession that the creditor would not otherwise consider;

(d)   it has become **probable** that the debtor will enter bankruptcy or other financial reorganisation; and

(e)   observable data indicating that there has been a measurable decrease in the estimated future cash flows from a group of financial assets since the initial recognition of those assets, even though the decrease cannot yet be identified with the individual financial assets in the group, such as adverse national or local economic conditions or adverse changes in industry conditions.

Other factors may also be evidence of impairment, including significant changes with an adverse effect that have taken place in the technological, market, economic or legal environment in which the issuer operates.   **11.23**

An entity shall assess the following financial assets individually for impairment: **11.24**

(a)   all equity instruments regardless of significance; and

(b)   other financial assets that are individually significant.

An entity shall assess other financial assets for impairment either individually or grouped on the basis of similar **credit risk** characteristics.

Measurement

An entity shall measure an impairment loss on the following instruments measured at cost or amortised cost as follows: **11.25**

(a)   For an instrument measured at amortised cost in accordance with paragraph 11.14(a), the impairment loss is the difference between the asset's carrying amount and the present value of estimated cash flows discounted at the asset's original effective interest rate. If such a financial instrument has a variable interest rate, the discount rate for measuring any impairment loss is the current effective interest rate determined under the contract.

(b)   For an instrument measured at cost less impairment in accordance with paragraph 11.14(c) and (d)(ii) the impairment loss is the difference between the asset's carrying amount and the best estimate (which will necessarily be an approximation) of the amount (which might be zero) that the entity would receive for the asset if it were to be sold at the reporting date.

Reversal

If, in a subsequent period, the amount of an impairment loss decreases and the decrease can be related objectively to an event occurring after the impairment was recognised (such as an improvement in the debtor's credit rating), the entity shall reverse the previously recognised impairment loss either directly or by adjusting an allowance account. The reversal shall not result in a carrying amount of the financial asset (net of any allowance account) that exceeds what the carrying amount would have been had the impairment not previously been recognised. The entity shall recognise the amount of the reversal in profit or loss immediately.   **11.26**

Fair value

11.27   Paragraph 11.14(b) and other sections of this FRS make reference to the fair value guidance in paragraphs 11.27 to 11.32, including Section 9 *Consolidated and Separate Financial Statements*, Section 12 *Other Financial Instruments Issues*, Section 13 *Inventories*, Section 14 *Investments in Associates*, Section 15 *Investments in Joint Ventures*, Section 16 *Investment Property*, Section 17 *Property, Plant and Equipment*, Section 18 *Intangible Assets other than Goodwill*, Section 27 *Impairment of Assets*, Section 28 *Employee Benefits* (in relation to plan assets) and Section 34 *Specialised Activities*. In applying the fair value guidance to assets or liabilities accounted for in accordance with those sections, the reference to ordinary shares or preference shares in these paragraphs should be read to include the types of assets and liabilities addressed in those sections.

Paragraph 11.14(d)(i) requires an investment in non-convertible preference shares and non-puttable ordinary shares or preference shares to be measured at fair value if the shares are publicly traded or if their fair value can otherwise be measured reliably. An entity shall use the following hierarchy to estimate the fair value of the shares:

(a)   The best evidence of fair value is a quoted price for an identical asset in an **active market**. Quoted in an active market in this context means quoted prices are readily and regularly available and those prices represent actual and regularly occurring market transactions on an arm's length basis. The quoted price is usually the current bid price.

(b)   When quoted prices are unavailable, the price of a recent transaction for an identical asset provides evidence of fair value as long as there has not been a significant change in economic circumstances or a significant lapse of time since the transaction took place. If the entity can demonstrate that the last transaction price is not a good estimate of fair value (eg because it reflects the amount that an entity would receive or pay in a forced transaction, involuntary liquidation or distress sale), that price is adjusted.

(c)   If the market for the asset is not active and recent transactions of an identical asset on their own are not a good estimate of fair value, an entity estimates the fair value by using a valuation technique. The objective of using a valuation technique is to estimate what the transaction price would have been on the measurement date in an arm's length exchange motivated by normal business considerations.

Valuation technique

11.28   Valuation techniques include using recent arm's length market transactions for an identical asset between knowledgeable, willing parties, if available, reference to the current fair value of another asset that is substantially the same as the asset being measured, discounted cash flow analysis and option pricing models. If there is a valuation technique commonly used by market participants to price the asset and that technique has been demonstrated to provide reliable estimates of prices obtained in actual market transactions, the entity uses that technique.

11.29   The objective of using a valuation technique is to establish what the transaction price would have been on the measurement date in an arm's length exchange motivated by normal business considerations. Fair value is estimated on the basis of the results of a valuation technique that makes maximum use of market inputs, and relies as little as possible on entity-determined inputs. A valuation technique would be expected to arrive at a reliable estimate of the fair value if:

(a)   it reasonably reflects how the market could be expected to price the asset; and

(b)   the inputs to the valuation technique reasonably represent market expectations and measures of the risk return factors inherent in the asset.

No active market

The fair value of ordinary shares or preference shares that do not have a quoted market price in an active market is reliably measurable if: **11.30**

(a)   the variability in the range of reasonable fair value estimates is not significant for that asset; or
(b)   the probabilities of the various estimates within the range can be reasonably assessed and used in estimating fair value.

There are many situations in which the variability in the range of reasonable fair value   **11.31**
estimates of assets that do not have a quoted market price is likely not to be significant. Normally it is possible to estimate the fair value of ordinary shares or preference shares that an entity has acquired from an outside party. However, if the range of reasonable fair value estimates is significant and the probabilities of the various estimates cannot be reasonably assessed, an entity is precluded from measuring the ordinary shares or preference shares at fair value.

If a reliable measure of fair value is no longer available for an asset measured at fair value   **11.32**
(eg ordinary shares or preference shares measured at fair value through profit or loss), its carrying amount at the last date the asset was reliably measurable becomes its new cost. The entity shall measure the ordinary shares or preference shares at this cost amount less impairment until a reliable measure of fair value becomes available.

Derecognition of a financial asset

An entity shall derecognise a financial asset only when: **11.33**

(a)   the contractual rights to the cash flows from the financial asset expire or are settled; or
(b)   the entity transfers to another party substantially all of the risks and rewards of ownership of the financial asset; or
(c)   the entity, despite having retained some significant risks and rewards of ownership, has transferred control of the asset to another party and the other party has the practical ability to sell the asset in its entirety to an unrelated third party and is able to exercise that ability unilaterally and without needing to impose additional restrictions on the transfer. In this case, the entity shall:

   (i)   derecognise the asset; and
   (ii)   recognise separately any rights and obligations retained or created in the transfer.

The carrying amount of the transferred asset shall be allocated between the rights or obligations retained and those transferred on the basis of their relative fair values at the transfer date. Newly created rights and obligations shall be measured at their fair values at that date. Any difference between the consideration received and the amounts recognised and derecognised in accordance with this paragraph shall be recognised in profit or loss in the period of the transfer.

If a transfer does not result in derecognition because the entity has retained significant risks   **11.34**
and rewards of ownership of the transferred asset, the entity shall continue to recognise the transferred asset in its entirety and shall recognise a financial liability for the consideration received. The asset and liability shall not be offset. In subsequent periods, the entity shall recognise any income on the transferred asset and any expense incurred on the financial liability.

11.35   If a transferor provides non-cash collateral (such as debt or equity instruments) to the transferee, the accounting for the collateral by the transferor and the transferee depends on whether the transferee has the right to sell or repledge the collateral and on whether the transferor has defaulted. The transferor and transferee shall account for the collateral as follows:

(a)   If the transferee has the right by contract or custom to sell or repledge the collateral, the transferor shall reclassify that asset in its **statement of financial position** (eg as a loaned asset, pledged equity instruments or repurchase receivable) separately from other assets.

(b)   If the transferee sells collateral pledged to it, it shall recognise the proceeds from the sale and a liability measured at fair value for its obligation to return the collateral.

(c)   If the transferor defaults under the terms of the contract and is no longer entitled to redeem the collateral, it shall derecognise the collateral, and the transferee shall recognise the collateral as its asset initially measured at fair value or, if it has already sold the collateral, derecognise its obligation to return the collateral.

(d)   Except as provided in (c), the transferor shall continue to carry the collateral as its asset, and the transferee shall not recognise the collateral as an asset.

Example: Transfer that qualifies for derecognition

An entity sells a group of its accounts receivable to a bank at less than their face amount. The entity continues to handle collections from the debtors on behalf of the bank, including sending monthly statements, and the bank pays the entity a market-rate fee for servicing the receivables. The entity is obliged to remit promptly to the bank any and all amounts collected, but it has no obligation to the bank for slow payment or non-payment by the debtors. In this case, the entity has transferred to the bank substantially all of the risks and rewards of ownership of the receivables. Accordingly, it removes the receivables from its statement of financial position (ie derecognises them), and it shows no liability in respect of the proceeds received from the bank. The entity recognises a loss calculated as the difference between the carrying amount of the receivables at the time of sale and the proceeds received from the bank. The entity recognises a liability to the extent that it has collected funds from the debtors but has not yet remitted them to the bank.

Example: Transfer that does not qualify for derecognition

The facts are the same as the preceding example except that the entity has agreed to buy back from the bank any receivables for which the debtor is in arrears as to principal or interest for more than 120 days.

In this case, the entity has retained the risk of slow payment or non-payment by the debtors – a significant risk with respect to receivables. Accordingly, the entity does not treat the receivables as having been sold to the bank, and it does not derecognise them. Instead, it treats the proceeds from the bank as a loan secured by the receivables. The entity continues to recognise the receivables as an asset until they are collected or written off as uncollectible.

Derecognition of a financial liability

An entity shall derecognise a financial liability (or a part of a financial liability) only when it is extinguished – ie when the obligation specified in the contract is discharged, is cancelled or expires.   **11.36**

If an existing borrower and lender exchange financial instruments with substantially different terms, the entities shall account for the transaction as an extinguishment of the original financial liability and the recognition of a new financial liability. Similarly, an entity shall account for a substantial modification of the terms of an existing financial liability or a part of it (whether or not attributable to the financial difficulty of the debtor) as an extinguishment of the original financial liability and the recognition of a new financial liability.   **11.37**

The entity shall recognise in profit or loss any difference between the carrying amount of the financial liability (or part of a financial liability) extinguished or transferred to another party and the consideration paid, including any non-cash assets transferred or liabilities assumed.   **11.38**

Presentation

A financial asset and a financial liability shall be offset and the net amount presented in the statement of financial position when, and only when, an entity: **11.38A**

(a)   currently has a legally enforceable right to set off the recognised amounts; and

(b)   intends either to settle on a net basis, or to realise the asset and settle the liability simultaneously.

Disclosures

The disclosures below make reference to disclosures for financial liabilities measured at fair value through profit or loss. Entities that have only basic financial instruments (and therefore do not apply Section 12), and have not chosen to designate financial instruments as at fair value through profit or loss (in accordance with paragraph 11.14(b)) will not have any financial liabilities measured at fair value through profit or loss and hence will not need to provide such disclosures.   **11.39**

Prospective amendments: Amendments to FRS 102 *The Financial Reporting Standard applicable in the UK and Republic of Ireland* – Small entities and other minor amendments (July 2015) amends this paragraph 11.39 with effect for annual periods beginning on or after 1 January 2016.

Disclosure of accounting policies for financial instruments

In accordance with paragraph 8.5, an entity shall disclose, in the summary of significant accounting policies, the measurement basis (or bases) used for financial instruments and the other accounting policies used for financial instruments that are relevant to an understanding of the **financial statements**.   **11.40**

Statement of financial position – categories of financial assets and financial liabilities

11.41   An entity shall disclose the carrying amounts of each of the following categories of financial assets and financial liabilities at the reporting date, in total, either in the statement of financial position or in the **notes**:

(a)   financial assets measured at fair value through profit or loss (paragraphs 11.14(b), 11.14(d)(i), 12.8 and 12.9);

(b)   financial assets that are debt instruments measured at amortised cost (paragraph 11.14(a));

(c)   financial assets that are equity instruments measured at cost less impairment (paragraphs 11.14(d)(ii), 12.8 and 12.9);

(d)   financial liabilities measured at fair value through profit or loss (paragraphs 11.14(b), 12.8 and 12.9). Financial liabilities that are not held as part of a trading portfolio and are not **derivatives** shall be shown separately;

(e)   financial liabilities measured at amortised cost (paragraph 11.14(a)); and

(f)   loan commitments measured at cost less impairment (paragraph 11.14(c)).

11.42   An entity shall disclose information that enables users of its financial statements to evaluate the significance of financial instruments for its **financial position** and **performance**. For example, for long-term debt such information would normally include the terms and conditions of the debt instrument (such as interest rate, maturity, repayment schedule, and restrictions that the debt instrument imposes on the entity).

11.43   For all financial assets and financial liabilities measured at fair value, the entity shall disclose the basis for determining fair value, eg quoted market price in an active market or a valuation technique. When a valuation technique is used, the entity shall disclose the assumptions applied in determining fair value for each class of financial assets or financial liabilities. For example, if applicable, an entity discloses information about the assumptions relating to prepayment rates, rates of estimated credit losses, and interest rates or discount rates.

11.44   If a reliable measure of fair value is no longer available for ordinary or preference shares measured at fair value through profit or loss, the entity shall disclose that fact.

Derecognition

11.45   If an entity has transferred financial assets to another party in a transaction that does not qualify for derecognition (see paragraphs 11.33 to 11.35), the entity shall disclose the following for each class of such financial assets:

(a)   the nature of the assets;

(b)   the nature of the risks and rewards of ownership to which the entity remains exposed; and

(c)   the carrying amounts of the assets and of any associated liabilities that the entity continues to recognise.

Collateral

11.46   When an entity has pledged financial assets as collateral for liabilities or **contingent liabilities**, it shall disclose the following:

(a)   the carrying amount of the financial assets pledged as collateral; and

(b)   the terms and conditions relating to its pledge.

Defaults and breaches on loans payable

For **loans payable** recognised at the reporting date for which there is a breach of terms or default of principal, interest, sinking fund, or redemption terms that has not been remedied by the reporting date, an entity shall disclose the following:

11.47

(a)   details of that breach or default;

(b)   the carrying amount of the related loans payable at the reporting date; and

(c)   whether the breach or default was remedied, or the terms of the loans payable were renegotiated, before the financial statements were authorised for issue.

Items of income, expense, gains or losses

An entity shall disclose the following items of income, expense, gains or losses:

11.48

(a)   income, expense, net gains or net losses, including changes in fair value, recognised on:

    (i)   financial assets measured at fair value through profit or loss;

    (ii)   financial liabilities measured at fair value through profit or loss (with separate disclosure of movements on those which are not held as part of a trading portfolio and are not derivatives);

    (iii)   financial assets measured at amortised cost; and

    (iv)   financial liabilities measured at amortised cost;

(b)   total interest income and total interest expense (calculated using the effective interest method) for financial assets or financial liabilities that are not measured at fair value through profit or loss; and

(c)   the amount of any impairment loss for each class of financial asset. A class of financial asset is a grouping that is appropriate to the nature of the information disclosed and that takes into account the characteristics of the financial assets.

Financial instruments at fair value through profit or loss

The following disclosures are required only for financial instruments at fair value through profit or loss that are not held as part of a trading portfolio and are not derivatives:

11.48A

(a)   The amount of change, during the period and cumulatively, in the fair value of the financial instrument that is attributable to changes in the credit risk of that instrument, determined either:

    (i)   as the amount of change in its fair value that is not attributable to changes in market conditions that give rise to **market risk**; or

    (ii)   using an alternative method the entity believes more faithfully represents the amount of change in its fair value that is attributable to changes in the credit risk of the instrument.

(b)   The method used to establish the amount of change attributable to changes in own credit risk, or, if the change cannot be measured reliably or is not **material**, that fact.

(c)   The difference between the financial liability's carrying amount and the amount the entity would be contractually required to pay at maturity to the holder of the obligation.

(d)   If an instrument contains both a liability and an equity feature, and the instrument has multiple features that substantially modify the cash flows and the values of those features are interdependent (such as a callable convertible debt instrument), the existence of those features.

(e)   Any difference between the fair value at initial recognition and the amount that would be determined at that date using a valuation technique, and the amount recognised in profit or loss.

(f)   Information that enables users of the entity's financial statements to evaluate the nature and extent of relevant risks arising from financial instruments to which the entity is exposed at the end of the reporting period. These risks typically include, but are not limited to, credit risk, **liquidity risk** and market risk. The disclosure should include both the entity's exposure to each type of risk and how it manages those risks.

Prospective amendments: Amendments to FRS 102 *The Financial Reporting Standard applicable in the UK and Republic of Ireland* – Small entities and other minor amendments (July 2015) amends this paragraph 11.48A and inserts a new footnote (to be sequentially numbered) is inserted (subsequent footnotes are renumbered sequentially) with effect for annual periods beginning on or after 1 January 2016.

Financial institutions

11.48B   A **financial institution** (other than a **retirement benefit plan**) shall, in addition, apply the requirements of paragraph 34.17.

11.48C   A retirement benefit plan shall, in addition, apply the requirements of paragraphs 34.39 to 34.48.

Section 12 Other Financial Instruments Issues

Scope of Sections 11 and 12

12.1   Section 11 *Basic Financial Instruments* and Section 12 *Other Financial Instruments Issues* together deal with recognising, derecognising, measuring, and disclosing **financial instruments** (**financial assets** and **financial liabilities**). Section 11 applies to basic financial instruments and is relevant to all entities. Section 12 applies to other, more complex financial instruments and transactions. If an entity enters into only basic financial instrument transactions then Section 12 is not applicable. However, even entities with only basic financial instruments shall consider the scope of Section 12 to ensure they are exempt.

PBE12.1A   **Public benefit entities** or other members of a **public benefit entity group** that make or receive **public benefit entity concessionary loans** shall refer to the relevant paragraphs of Section 34 *Specialised Activities* for the accounting requirements for such loans.

Accounting policy choice

12.2   An entity shall choose to apply either:

(a)   the provisions of both Section 11 and Section 12 in full; or

(b)   the **recognition** and **measurement** provisions of IAS 39 *Financial Instruments: Recognition and Measurement* (as adopted for use in the EU), the disclosure requirements of Sections 11 and 12 and the presentation requirements of paragraphs 11.38A or 12.25B; or

(c)   the recognition and measurement provisions of IFRS 9 *Financial Instruments* and/ or IAS 39 (as amended following the publication of IFRS 9), the disclosure requirements of Sections 11 and 12 and the presentation requirements of paragraph 11.38A or 12.25B;

to account for all of its financial instruments. Where an entity chooses (b) or (c) it applies the scope of the relevant standard to its financial instruments. An entity's choice of (a), (b) or (c) is an **accounting policy** choice. Paragraphs 10.8 to 10.14 contain requirements for determining when a change in accounting policy is appropriate, how such a change should be accounted for and what information should be disclosed about the change in accounting policy.

Prospective amendments: Amendments to FRS 102 *The Financial Reporting Standard applicable in the UK and Republic of Ireland* – Small entities and other minor amendments (July 2015) amends this paragraph 12.2 with effect for annual periods beginning on or after 1 January 2016.

Prospective amendments: Amendments to FRS 102 *The Financial Reporting Standard applicable in the UK and Republic of Ireland* – Small entities and other minor amendments (July 2015) inserts paragraph 12.2A with effect for annual periods beginning on or after 1 January 2016.

Scope of Section 12

Section 12 applies to all financial instruments except the following: **12.3**

(a)   Those covered by Section 11.

(b)   Investments in **subsidiaries** (see Section 9 *Consolidated and Separate Financial Statements*), **associates** (see Section 14 *Investments in Associates*) and **joint ventures** (see Section 15 *Investments in Joint Ventures*).

(c)   Employers' rights and obligations under employee benefit plans (see Section 28 *Employee Benefits*).

(d)   **Insurance contracts** (including **reinsurance contracts**) that the entity issues and reinsurance contracts that the entity holds (see FRS 103 *Insurance Contracts*).

(e)   Financial instruments that meet the definition of an entity's own **equity** and the equity component of **compound financial instruments** issued by the reporting entity that contain both a **liability** and an equity component (see Section 22 *Liabilities and Equity*).

(f)   **Leases** (see Section 20 *Leases*) unless the lease could, as a result of non-typical contractual terms, result in a loss to the lessor or the lessee.

(g)   Contracts for contingent consideration in a **business combination** (see Section 19 *Business Combinations and Goodwill*). This exemption applies only to the acquirer.

(h)   Any forward contract between an acquirer and a selling shareholder to buy or sell an acquiree that will result in a business combination at a future **acquisition date**. The term of the forward contract should not exceed a reasonable period normally necessary to obtain any required approvals and to complete the transaction.

(i)   Financial instruments, contracts and obligations to which Section 26 *Share-based Payment* applies, except for contracts within the scope of paragraph 12.5.

(j)   Financial instruments issued by an entity with a **discretionary participation feature** (see FRS 103).

(k)   Reimbursement assets accounted for in accordance with Section 21 *Provisions and Contingencies*.

(l)   **Financial guarantee contracts** (see Section 21).

A reporting entity that issues the financial instruments set out in (d) or (j) or holds the financial instruments set out in (d) is required by paragraph 1.6 to apply FRS 103 to those financial instruments.

12.4   Most contracts to buy or sell a non-financial item such as a commodity, **inventory**, or **property, plant and equipment** are excluded from this section because they are not financial instruments. However, this section applies to all contracts that impose risks on the buyer or seller that are not typical of contracts to buy or sell non-financial items. For example, this section applies to contracts that, as a result of its contractual terms, could result in a loss to the buyer or seller that is unrelated to changes in the price of the non-financial item, changes in foreign exchange rates, or a default by one of the counterparties.

12.5   In addition to the contracts described in paragraph 12.4, this section applies to contracts to buy or sell non-financial items if the contract can be settled net in **cash** or another financial instrument, or by exchanging financial instruments as if the contracts were financial instruments, with the following exception: contracts that were entered into and continue to be held for the purpose of the receipt or delivery of a non-financial item in accordance with the entity's expected purchase, sale or usage requirements are not financial instruments for the purposes of this section.

Initial recognition of financial assets and liabilities

12.6   An entity shall recognise a financial asset or a financial liability only when the entity becomes a party to the contractual provisions of the instrument.

Initial measurement

12.7   When a financial asset or financial liability is recognised initially, an entity shall measure it at its **fair value**, which is normally the transaction price (including **transaction costs** except in the initial measurement of financial assets and liabilities that are measured at fair value through profit or loss). If payment for an asset is deferred beyond normal business terms or is financed at a rate of interest that is not a market rate, the entity shall initially measure the asset at the **present value** of the future payments discounted at a market rate of interest for a similar debt instrument.

Prospective amendments: Amendments to FRS 102 *The Financial Reporting Standard applicable in the UK and Republic of Ireland* – Small entities and other minor amendments (July 2015) amends of this paragraph 12.7 the term 'fair value' is no longer shown in bold type with effect for annual periods beginning on or after 1 January 2016.

Subsequent measurement

12.8   At the end of each **reporting period**, an entity shall measure all financial instruments within the scope of Section 12 at fair value and recognise changes in fair value in **profit or loss**, except as follows:

(a)   investments in equity instruments that are not **publicly traded** and whose fair value cannot otherwise be measured reliably and contracts linked to such instruments that, if exercised, will result in delivery of such instruments, shall be measured at cost less impairment;

(b)   hedging instruments in a designated hedging relationship accounted for in accordance with paragraph 12.23; and

(c)   financial instruments that are not permitted by the **Regulations** or the **LLP Regulations** to be measured at fair value through profit or loss shall be measured at **amortised cost** in accordance with paragraphs 11.15 to 11.20.

Prospective amendments: Amendments to FRS 102 *The Financial Reporting Standard applicable in the UK and Republic of Ireland* – Small entities and other minor amendments (July 2015) amends of this paragraph 12.8 and 12.8(c) the terms 'profit or loss', 'Regulations', 'LLP Regulations' and 'amortised cost' are no longer shown in bold type with effect for annual periods beginning on or after 1 January 2016.

If a reliable measure of fair value is no longer available for an equity instrument (or a contract linked to such an instrument) that is not publicly traded but is measured at fair value through profit or loss, its fair value at the last date the instrument was reliably measurable is treated as the cost of the instrument. The entity shall measure the instrument at this cost amount less impairment until a reliable measure of fair value becomes available. | **12.9**

Fair value

An entity shall apply the guidance on fair value in paragraphs 11.27 to 11.32 to fair value measurements in accordance with this section as well as for fair value measurements in accordance with Section 11. | **12.10**

The fair value of a financial liability that is due on demand is not less than the amount payable on demand, discounted from the first date that the amount could be required to be paid. | **12.11**

An entity shall not include transaction costs in the initial measurement of financial assets and liabilities that will be measured subsequently at fair value through profit or loss. | **12.12**

Impairment of financial instruments measured at cost or amortised cost

An entity shall apply the guidance on impairment of a financial instrument measured at cost in paragraphs 11.21 to 11.26 to financial instruments measured at cost less impairment in accordance with this section. | **12.13**

Derecognition of a financial asset or financial liability

An entity shall apply the **derecognition** requirements in paragraphs 11.33 to 11.38 to financial assets and financial liabilities to which this section applies. | **12.14**

Hedge accounting

A hedging relationship consists of a hedging instrument and a hedged item. Provided the qualifying conditions in paragraph 12.18 are met, an entity may apply hedge accounting. | **12.15**

Hedged items

A hedged item can be a recognised **asset** or liability, an unrecognised **firm commitment**, a **highly probable forecast transaction** or a **net investment in a foreign operation**, or a component of any such item, provided the item is reliably measurable. | **12.16**

For hedge accounting purposes, only assets, liabilities, firm commitments or a highly probable forecast transaction with a party external to the reporting entity can be a hedged item. Hedge accounting can be applied to transactions between entities in the same **group** only in the **individual financial statements** of those entities, except for: | **12.16A**

(a) transactions with subsidiaries, where the subsidiaries are not consolidated in the **consolidated financial statements**;

(b)   the foreign currency risk of intragroup **monetary items** that result in an exposure to foreign exchange **gains** or losses that are not fully eliminated on consolidation in accordance with Section 30 *Foreign Currency Translation*; and

(c)   the foreign currency risk of highly probable forecast intragroup transactions, provided the transactions are denominated in a currency other than the **functional currency** of the entity entering into the transactions and the foreign currency risk affects consolidated profit or loss.

12.16B   A group of items, including components of items, can be an eligible hedged item provided that all of the following conditions are met:

(a)   it consists of items that are individually eligible hedged items;

(b)   the items in the group share the same risk;

(c)   the items in the group are managed together on a group basis for risk management purposes; and

(d)   it does not include items with offsetting risk positions.

12.16C   A component of an item comprises less than the entire fair value change or **cash flow** variability of an item. The following components of an item (including combinations thereof) may be a hedged item:

(a)   changes in the cash flows or fair value attributable to a separately identifiable and reliably measureable specific risk or risks, including cash flow and fair value changes above or below a specified price or other variable;

(b)   one or more selected contractual cash flows; or

(c)   a specified part of the nominal amount of an item.

Hedging instruments

12.17   An instrument may be a hedging instrument provided all of the following conditions are met:

(a)   it is a financial instrument measured at fair value through profit or loss;

(b)   it is a contract with a party external to the reporting entity (ie external to the group or individual entity that is being reported on); and

(c)   it is not a written option, except as described in paragraph 12.17C.

12.17A   An instrument (or a combination of such instruments) meeting the conditions of paragraph 12.17, may only be a hedging instrument:

(a)   in its entirety; or

(b)   a proportion of such an instrument or a proportion of a combination of such instruments, eg 50% of the nominal amount of the instrument.

12.17B   For a hedge of foreign currency risk, the foreign currency risk component of a financial instrument, provided that it is not a financial instrument as described in paragraph 11.6(b), may be a hedging instrument.

12.17C   A written option is not a hedging instrument unless the written option is an offset to or is combined with a purchased option and the effect of the offset or combination is not a net written option. An example of a combination of a written and a purchased option that is not a net written option is a zero cost interest rate collar.

Conditions for hedge accounting

12.18   An entity may apply hedge accounting to a hedging relationship from the date all of the following conditions are met:

(a)   the hedging relationship consists only of a hedging instrument and a hedged item as described in paragraphs 12.16 to 12.17C;

(b)   the hedging relationship is consistent with the entity's risk management objectives for undertaking hedges;

(c)   there is an economic relationship between the hedged item and the hedging instrument;

(d)   the entity has documented the hedging relationship so that the risk being hedged, the hedged item and the hedging instrument are clearly identified; and

(e)   the entity has determined and documented causes of hedge ineffectiveness.

An economic relationship between a hedged item and hedging instrument exists when the entity expects that the values of the hedged item and hedging instrument will typically move in opposite directions in response to movements in the same risk, which is the hedged risk.   **12.18A**

Accounting for qualifying hedging relationships

There are three types of hedging relationships: **12.19**

(a)   fair value hedge: a hedge of the exposure to changes in fair value of a recognised asset or liability or an unrecognised firm commitment, or a component of any such item, that are attributable to a particular risk and could affect profit or loss;

(b)   cash flow hedge: a hedge of the exposure to variability in cash flows that is attributable to a particular risk associated with all, or a component of, a recognised asset or liability (such as all or some future interest payments on variable rate debt) or a highly probable forecast transaction, and could affect profit or loss; and

(c)   hedge of a net investment in a foreign operation.

Issued 16 April 2015

Net investment hedges in foreign operations that are branches

During 2013 it had been brought to the FRC's attention that, in relation to net investment hedges of foreign operations, there appeared to be an inconsistency between FRS 102 *The Financial Reporting Standard applicable in the UK and Republic of Ireland* and the Accounting Council's Advice to the FRC, and that this could potentially lead to confusion.

The FRC subsequently revised the hedge accounting requirements in July 2014. The Accounting Council did not revisit its original Advice, which was issued in March 2013, when the hedge accounting requirements were amended, but issued Advice on the new hedge accounting requirements. This new Advice is also included in FRS 102 and does not contain references to hedges of a net investment in a foreign operation.

A hedge of a net investment in a foreign operation remains a permitted type of hedging relationship (see paragraph 12.19(c) of FRS 102) and FRS 102 therefore continues to permit hedge accounting for net investments in foreign branches in the separate financial statements of a parent, provided the conditions in paragraph 12.18 of FRS 102 are met.

A hedge of the foreign currency risk of an unrecognised firm commitment may be accounted for as a fair value hedge or as a cash flow hedge.   **12.19A**

Fair value hedges

12.20   A fair value hedge shall be accounted for as follows from the date the conditions in paragraph 12.18 are met:

(a)   the gain or loss on the hedging instrument shall be recognised in profit or loss; and

(b)   the **hedging gain or loss** on the hedged item shall adjust the carrying amount of the hedged item (if applicable) and be recognised in profit or loss. When a hedged item is an unrecognised firm commitment, the cumulative hedging gain or loss on the hedged item is recognised as an asset or liability with a corresponding gain or loss recognised in profit or loss.

12.21   When an unrecognised firm commitment to acquire an asset or assume a liability is the hedged item, the initial carrying amount of the asset or liability that results from the entity meeting the firm commitment is adjusted to include the cumulative hedging gain or loss of the hedged item that was recognised in the statement of financial position.

12.22   Any adjustment arising from paragraph 12.20(b) shall be amortised to profit or loss if the hedged item is a financial instrument measured at amortised cost. Amortisation may begin as soon as an adjustment exists and shall begin no later than when the hedged item ceases to be adjusted for hedging gains and losses. The amortisation is based on a recalculated effective interest rate at the date amortisation begins.

Cash flow hedges

12.23   A cash flow hedge shall be accounted for as follows from the date the conditions in paragraph 12.18 are met:

(a)   the separate component of equity associated with the hedged item (cash flow hedge reserve) is adjusted to the lower of the following (in absolute amounts):

(i)   the cumulative gain or loss on the hedging instrument from the date the conditions of paragraph 12.18 are met; and

(ii)   the cumulative change in fair value on the hedged item (ie the **present value** of the cumulative change of expected future cash flows) from the date the conditions of paragraph 12.18 are met;

(b)   the portion of the gain or loss on the hedging instrument that is determined to be an effective hedge (ie the portion that is offset by the change in the cash flow hedge reserve calculated in accordance with (a)) shall be recognised in **other comprehensive income**;

(c)   any remaining gain or loss on the hedging instrument (or any gain or loss required to balance the change in the cash flow hedge reserve calculated in accordance with (a)), is hedge ineffectiveness that shall be recognised in profit or loss; and

(d)   the amount that has been accumulated in the cash flow hedge reserve in accordance with (a) shall be accounted for as follows:

(i)   if a hedged forecast transaction subsequently results in the recognition of a non-financial asset or non-financial liability, or a hedged forecast transaction for a non-financial asset or non-financial liability becomes a firm commitment for which fair value hedge accounting is applied, the entity shall remove that amount from the cash flow hedge reserve and include it directly in the initial cost or other carrying amount of the asset or liability;

(ii)   for cash flow hedges other than those covered by (i), that amount shall be reclassified from the cash flow hedge reserve to profit or loss in the same period or periods during which the hedged expected future cash flows affect profit or loss (for example, in the periods that interest income or interest expense is recognised or when a forecast sale occurs); and

(iii)   if the amount is a loss, and all or part of that loss is not expected to be recovered, the amount of the loss not expected to be recovered shall be reclassified to profit or loss immediately.

Hedges of a net investment in a foreign operation

Hedges of a net investment in a foreign operation, including a hedge of a monetary item that is accounted for as part of the net investment (see Section 30), shall be accounted for similarly to cash flow hedges from the date the conditions of paragraph 12.18 are met: **12.24**

(a)   the portion of the gain or loss on the hedging instrument that is determined to be an effective hedge shall be recognised in other comprehensive income (see paragraphs 12.23(a) and (b)); and
(b)   the ineffective portion shall be recognised in profit or loss.

The cumulative gain or loss on the hedging instrument relating to the effective portion of the hedge that has been accumulated in equity shall not be reclassified from equity to profit or loss on disposal or partial disposal of the foreign operation.

Discontinuing hedge accounting

The entity may discontinue hedge accounting provided the entity has documented its election.   **12.25**

The entity shall discontinue hedge accounting when:

(a)   the hedging instrument has expired, is sold, terminated or exercised; or
(b)   the conditions for hedge accounting in paragraph 12.18 are no longer met.

In all cases, hedge accounting shall be discontinued prospectively.

In a fair value hedge, any adjustment arising from paragraph 12.20(b) is dealt with in accordance with paragraph 12.22.   **12.25A**

In a cash flow hedge, if the hedged future cash flows are no longer expected to occur, the amount that has been accumulated in the cash flow hedge reserve in accordance with paragraph 12.23(a) shall be reclassified from the cash flow hedge reserve to profit or loss immediately. If the hedged future cash flows are still expected to occur (for example a future cash flow that is no longer highly probable may still be expected to occur), the cumulative gain or loss in the cash flow hedge reserve is dealt with in accordance with paragraph 12.23(d).

In a net investment hedge, in accordance with paragraph 12.24, the amount that has been accumulated in equity is not reclassified to profit or loss.

Presentation

A financial asset and a financial liability shall be offset and the net amount presented in the **statement of financial position** when, and only when, an entity: **12.25B**

(a)   currently has a legally enforceable right to set off the recognised amounts; and
(b)   intends either to settle on a net basis, or to realise the asset and settle the liability simultaneously.

Disclosures

12.26   An entity applying this section shall make all of the disclosures required in Section 11 incorporating in those disclosures, financial instruments that are within the scope of this section as well as those within the scope of Section 11. For financial instruments in the scope of this section that are not held as part of a trading portfolio and are not **derivative** instruments, an entity shall provide additional disclosures as set out in paragraph 11.48A. In addition, if the entity uses hedge accounting, it shall make the additional disclosures in paragraphs 12.27 to 12.29A.

12.27   An entity shall disclose the following separately for each type of hedging relationship described in paragraph 12.19:

(a)   a description of the hedge;

(b)   a description of the financial instruments designated as hedging instruments and their fair values at the **reporting date**; and

(c)   the nature of the risks being hedged, including a description of the hedged item.

12.28   If an entity uses hedge accounting for a fair value hedge it shall disclose the following:

(a)   the amount of the change in fair value of the hedging instrument recognised in profit or loss for the period; and

(b)   the amount of the change in fair value of the hedged item recognised in profit or loss for the period.

12.29   If an entity uses hedge accounting for a cash flow hedge it shall disclose the following:

(a)   the periods when the cash flows are expected to occur and when they are expected to affect profit or loss;

(b)   a description of any forecast transaction for which hedge accounting had previously been used, but which is no longer expected to occur;

(c)   the amount of the change in fair value of the hedging instrument that was recognised in other comprehensive income during the period;

(d)   the amount, if any, that was reclassified from equity to profit or loss for the period; and

(e)   the amount, if any, of any excess of the fair value of the hedging instrument over the change in the fair value of the expected cash flows that was recognised in profit or loss for the period.

12.29A   If an entity uses hedge accounting for a net investment in a foreign operation it shall disclose separately the amounts recognised in other comprehensive income in accordance with paragraph 12.24(a) and the amounts recognised in profit or loss in accordance with paragraph 12.24(b).

Appendix to Section 12

Examples of hedge accounting

This appendix accompanies, but is not part of, Section 12. It provides guidance for applying the requirements of paragraphs 12.15 to 12.25A.

Example 1

Fair value hedge accounting – Hedge of forward foreign currency risk of an unrecognised firm commitment

In accordance with paragraph 12.19A, a hedge of the foreign currency risk of an unrecognised firm commitment may be accounted for as a cash flow or fair value hedge. This example illustrates fair value hedge accounting.

On 9 June 20X5 an entity enters into a purchase agreement with a third party over a non-financial asset in a foreign currency (FC) for FC515,000. On the same day, the entity enters into a forward currency contract to buy FC500,000 for CU1,000,000. Under the purchase agreement, the non-financial asset will be delivered and paid for on 30 March 20X6, the same day the forward currency contract is required to be settled.   **12A.1**

In this example the hedged item is the total of the commitment of FC515,000 and the hedging instrument is the forward contract to buy FC500,000. Since the nominal amounts of the two contracts do not match, hedge ineffectiveness arises. It should be noted that in practice an entity could avoid ineffectiveness arising for this reason by identifying an amount of FC500,000 of the total commitment as the hedged item in accordance with paragraph 12.16C.

For simplification, this example disregards other sources of ineffectiveness, eg counter party credit risk associated with the forward currency contract.

The entity's financial year ends on 31 December.

This example assumes that the qualifying conditions for hedge accounting in paragraph 12.18 are met from 9 June 20X5.

The table below sets out the applicable forward exchange rates, the fair value of the forward currency contract (the hedging instrument) and the hedging gains/losses on the purchase commitment (the hedged item) on the relevant dates. This example ignores the effects of discounting.

	9 Jun 20X5	31 Dec 20X5	30 Mar 20X6
Forward exchange rate (CU:FC)	2:1	2.2:1	2.16:1
Forward currency contract (hedging instrument)			
Fair value	nil	FC500,000 × CU0.2:FC = CU100,000	FC500,000 × CU0.16:FC = CU80,000†
Fair value change	nil	CU100,000 − 0 = CU100,000	CU80,000 − CU100,000 = (CU20,000)
Purchase commitment (hedged item)			
Cumulative hedging (loss)‡	nil	(FC515,000) × CU0.2:FC = (CU103,000)	(FC515,000) × CU0.16:FC = (CU82,400)
Hedging (loss)/gain	nil	(CU103,000) − 0 = (CU103,000)	(CU82,400) − (CU103,000) = CU20,600

Key to table:
† This is the fair value of the contract prior to settlement.
‡ In accordance with paragraph 12.20(b), the commitment is fair valued only for the hedged risk, which in this example is the forward exchange rate risk.

12A.2   Hedge accounting:

Note that there are no hedge accounting entries on 9 June 20X5.

31 December 20X5

(1)   In accordance with paragraph 12.20(a) the fair value gain of CU100,000 on the forward currency contract is recognised in profit or loss.
(2)   In accordance with paragraph 12.20(b) the cumulative hedging loss of CU103,000 on the commitment is recorded as a liability with a corresponding loss recognised in profit or loss.

Accounting entries:

Ref		Debit	Credit
(1)	Forward currency contract	CU100,000	
	Profit or loss		CU100,000
(2)	Profit or loss	CU103,000	
	Hedged item (commitment)		CU103,000

30 March 20X6

(1)   In accordance with paragraph 12.20(a) the fair value loss of CU20,000 on the forward currency contract is recognised in profit or loss.
(2)   In accordance with paragraph 12.20(b) the hedging gain on the commitment of CU20,600 is recognised in profit or loss with a corresponding adjustment to the recognised liability from CU103,000 to CU82,400.
(3)   In accordance with paragraph 12.21 the non-financial asset's carrying amount is adjusted to include the cumulative hedging loss on the hedged item of CU82,400.

Note A: For illustrative purposes the accounting entry in respect of the settlement of the forward currency contract in cash for CU80,000 is shown below.
Note B: For illustrative purposes the accounting entry for the purchase of the non-financial asset at the applicable spot rate of FC2.16:CU for CU1,112,400 (settled in cash) is shown below.

Accounting entries:

Ref		Debit	Credit
(1)	Profit or loss	CU20,000	
	Forward currency contract		CU20,000
(2)	Hedged item (commitment)	CU20,600	
	Profit or loss		CU20,600
(3)	Hedged item (commitment)	CU82,400	
	Property, plant and equipment (PP&E)		CU82,400
(A)	Cash	CU80,000	
	Forward currency contract		CU80,000
(B)	Property, plant and equipment (PP&E)	CU1,112,400	
	Cash		CU1,112,400

Editor's note: This paragraph of Example 1 was amended by FRS 102 – Editorial amendments and clarification statements (last updated 16 April 2015) – Editorial amendment regarding Examples of hedge accounting: Example 1 (issued 17 September 2014).

Example 2

Cash flow hedge accounting – Hedge of variability in cash flows in a floating rate loan due to interest rate risk

This example illustrates the accounting for a cash flow hedge of interest rate risk associated with a floating rate loan. The entity borrows money at a floating rate and enters into an interest rate swap with the effect of paying a fixed rate overall.

On 1 January 20X5, an entity borrows CU10,000,000 from a bank at a floating rate of 3-month LIBOR plus 2.5%. The interest is payable annually in arrears on 31 December. The loan is repayable on 31 December 20X7.

12A.3

On 1 January 20X5 the entity also enters into an interest rate swap with a third party, under which it receives 6-month LIBOR and pays a fixed rate of interest of 4.5%. The notional amount of the swap is CU10,000,000. The swap is settled annually in arrears on 31 December and expires on 31 December 20X7.

The LIBOR rates on the loan and the interest rate swap are reset and fixed annually in advance on 31 December based on the expected LIBOR rates applicable at that time. Note that in practice the loan and swap interest rates would be reset more frequently than assumed for the purpose of simplification in this example.

The entity hedges the variability of the interest rate payments on the bank loan based on 3-month LIBOR. It should be noted that because the entity receives interest based on 6-month LIBOR under the interest rate swap, ineffectiveness will arise because the expected cash flows of the hedged item and the hedging instrument differ. The fair value of the interest rate swap may be affected by other factors that cause ineffectiveness, for example counter party credit risk, but these have been disregarded in this example.

There are no transaction costs.

The entity's financial year ends on 31 December.

This example assumes that the qualifying conditions for hedge accounting in paragraph 12.18 are met from 1 January 20X5.

The table in paragraph 12A.5 summarises the impact of hedge accounting on the interest rate swap, profit or loss and other comprehensive income.

The table below sets out the applicable LIBOR rates, interest payments and swap settlements. The fair values of the interest rate swap and the hedged item shown in the table are shown for illustrative purposes only.

Note that in practice, when forecasted variable interest rate payments are the hedged item, the fair value of a hypothetical swap, that would be expected to perfectly offset the hedged cash flows, is used as a proxy of the fair value of the hedged item. The hypothetical derivative in this scenario is a fixed to floating interest rate swap with terms that match those of the loan and a fixed rate of 4.3%, which for the purpose of this example, is the interest rate where the fair value of the hypothetical swap is nil at the inception of the hedging relationship.

	1 Jan 20X5	31 Dec 20X5	31 Dec 20X6	31 Dec 20X7
Actual 3-month LIBOR	4.3%	5%	3%	n/a
Actual 6-month LIBOR	4.5%	4.9%	3.2%	n/a
Interest payments based on 3-month LIBOR	n/a	CU10m × (4.3% + 2.5%) = CU680,000	CU10m × (5% + 2.5%) = CU750,000	CU10m × (3% + 2.5%) = CU550,000
Interest rate swap (hedging instrument)				
Fair value	nil	CU78,000	(CU89,000)†	(CU130,000)‡
Fair value change	nil	CU78,000 − 0 = CU78,000	(CU89,000) − CU78,000 = (CU167,000)	(CU130,000) − (CU40,000)§ − (CU89,000) = (CU1,000)
Swap settlement receipts/(payments) based on 6-month LIBOR	n/a	CU10m × (4.5% − 4.5%) = nil	CU10m × (4.9% − 4.5%) = CU40,000	CU10m * (3.2% − 4.5%) = (CU130,000)
Hedged item				
Fair value	nil	(CU137,000)	CU59,000	CU130,000

Key to table:
†*This valuation is determined before the receipt of the cash settlement of CU40,000 due on 31 December 20X6.*
‡*This valuation is determined before the payment of the cash settlement of CU130,000 due on 31 December 20X7.*
§*CU40,000 is the settlement of the interest rate swap as at 31 December 20X6 which affects the fair value of the swap, but is not included in the fair value of the swap at 31 December 20X6 of CU89,000.*

12A.4   Hedge accounting:

31 December 20X5

(1)   In accordance with paragraph 12.23(a), the cash flow hedge reserve is adjusted to the lower of (in absolute amounts) the cumulative gain on the hedging instrument (ie the interest rate swap), which equals its fair value, of CU78,000 and the cumulative change in fair value of the hedged item, which equals its fair value of (CU137,000). In accordance with paragraph 12.23(b), the gain of CU78,000 on the interest rate swap is recognised in other comprehensive income.

(2)   The fixed interest element on the hypothetical swap is CU430,000, the same amount as the variable rate component. The variability of the 3-month LIBOR did therefore not affect profit or loss during the period. The reclassification adjustment in accordance with paragraph 12.23(d)(ii) is nil. (Note that no accounting entry is shown below.)

Note A: For illustrative purposes the accounting entry for interest payments is shown below. Note that in practice the accrual and payment of interest may be recorded in separate accounting entries.

Accounting entries:

Note that the accounting entries shown are only those relevant to demonstrate the effects of hedge accounting. In practice other accounting entries would be required, eg an entry to recognise the loan liability.

Ref		Debit	Credit
(1)	Interest rate swap	CU78,000	
	Other comprehensive income		CU78,000
(A)	Profit or loss	CU680,000	
	Cash		CU680,000

31 December 20X6

(1) In accordance with paragraph 12.23(a), the cash flow hedge reserve is adjusted to the lower of (in absolute amounts) the cumulative loss on the hedging instrument (ie the interest rate swap) which equals its fair value of (CU89,000) and the cumulative change in fair value of the hedged item, which equals its fair value of CU59,000. The cash flow hedge reserve moves from CU78,000 to (CU59,000), a change of (CU137,000).

   In accordance with paragraph 12.23(b), a loss of CU137,000 on the interest rate swap is recognised in other comprehensive income, as this part of the loss is fully off-set by the change in the cash flow hedge reserve. The remainder of the loss on the interest rate swap of CU30,000 is recognised in profit or loss, as required by paragraph 12.23(c).

(2) The fixed interest element on the hypothetical swap is CU430,000, whilst the variable rate component is CU500,000. The variability of the 3-month LIBOR affects profit or loss during the period by CU70,000. Accordingly, the reclassification adjustment in accordance with paragraph 12.23(d)(ii) is CU70,000.

Note A: For illustrative purposes the accounting entry for interest payments is shown below. Note that in practice the accrual and payment of interest may be recorded in separate accounting entries.

Note B: For illustrative purposes the accounting entry for the settlement of the swap is shown below.

Accounting entries:

Ref		Debit	Credit
(1)	Other comprehensive income	CU137,000	
	Profit or loss	CU30,000	
	Interest rate swap		CU167,000
(2)	Other comprehensive income	CU70,000	
	Profit or loss		CU70,000
(A)	Profit or loss	CU750,000	
	Cash		CU750,000
(B)	Cash	CU40,000	
	Interest rate swap		CU40,000

31 December 20X7

(1) In accordance with paragraph 12.23(a), the cash flow hedge reserve is adjusted to the lower of (in absolute amounts) the cumulative loss on the hedging instrument (ie the interest rate swap) which equals the fair value of (CU130,000) and the cumulative change in fair value of the hedged item, which equals its fair value of CU130,000. The cash flow hedge reserve moves from (CU129,000) to (CU130,000), a change of (CU1,000). In accordance with paragraph 12.23(b), the loss of CU1,000 on the interest rate swap is recognised in other comprehensive income.

(2) The fixed interest element on the hypothetical swap is CU430,000, whilst the variable rate component is CU300,000. The variability of the 3-month LIBOR affects profit or loss during the period by (CU130,000). Accordingly, the reclassification adjustment in accordance with paragraph 12.23(d)(ii) is (CU130,000).

Note A: For illustrative purposes the accounting entry for interest payments is shown below. Note that in practice the accrual and payment of interest may be recorded in separate accounting entries.

Note B: For illustrative purposes the accounting entry for the settlement of the swap is shown below.

Accounting entries:

Ref		Debit	Credit
(1)	Other comprehensive income	CU1,000	
	Interest rate swap		CU1,000
(2)	Profit or loss	CU130,000	
	Other comprehensive income		CU130,000
(A)	Profit or loss	CU550,000	
	Cash		CU550,000
(B)	Interest rate swap	CU130,000	
	Cash		CU130,000

12A.5 The table below summarises the effects of the accounting entries shown in paragraph 12A.4 on the interest rate swap, profit or loss and other comprehensive income.

Description	Interest rate swap	Other comprehensive income	Profit or loss
31 December 20X5			
Opening balance	nil	nil†	–
Interest on the loan			CU680,000
Interest rate swap fair value movement	CU78,000	(CU78,000)	–
Closing balance	**CU78,000**	**(CU78,000)**‡	**–**

Description	Interest rate swap	Other comprehensive income	Profit or loss
31 December 20X6			
Opening balance	**CU78,000**	**(CU78,000)†**	–
Interest on the loan			CU750,000
Interest rate swap fair value movement	(CU167,000)	CU137,000	CU30,000
Settlement receipt interest rate swap	(40,000)	–	–
Reclassification from cash flow hedge reserve	–	CU70,000	(CU70,000)
Closing balance	**(CU129,000)**	**CU129,000†**	–
31 December 20X7			
Opening balance	**(CU129,000)**	**CU129,000†**	–
Interest on the loan			CU550,000
Interest rate swap movement	(1,000)	1,000	–
Settlement payment interest rate swap	CU130,000	–	–
Reclassification from cash flow hedge reserve	–	(CU130,000)	CU130,000
Closing balance	**nil**	**nil†**	–

Key to table:
† This is the balance of the cash flow hedge reserve.

Example 3

Hedge accounting: Net investment in a foreign operation

This example illustrates the accounting for a net investment hedge in the consolidated financial statements. The entity has a foreign operation and hedges its exposure to foreign currency risk in the foreign operation by the use of a foreign currency loan.

On 1 April 20X5 an entity with functional currency CU acquires an investment in an overseas subsidiary (with functional currency FC) at a cost of FC1,200,000. On the same day the entity takes out a loan with a third party of FC1,200,000 to finance the investment. This example disregards the effects of interest or other transaction costs associated with the loan.   **12A.6**

This example assumes that the carrying amount of the investment denominated in FC is impaired below FC1,200,000 as presented in the table below, which causes ineffectiveness.

The entity's financial year ends on 31 December.

This example assumes that the qualifying conditions for hedge accounting in paragraph 12.18 are met from 1 April 20X5.

The table below sets out the applicable exchange rates, the carrying amount of the loan and the foreign exchange gains and losses on the loan as determined in accordance with Section 30, as well as the retranslation differences on the foreign investment recognised in other comprehensive income in accordance with Section 30.

	1 Apr 20X5	31 Dec 20X5	31 Dec 20X6
Spot exchange rate CU:FC	0.35:1	0.3:1	0.45:1
Loan (hedging instrument)			
Carrying amount under Section 30	(FC1,200,000) × CU0.35:FC = (CU420,000)	(FC1,200,000) × CU0.35:FC = (CU420,000)	(FC1,200,000) × CU0.45:FC = (CU540,000)
Cumulative gain/(loss)	nil	(CU360,000) − (CU420,000) = CU60,000	(CU540,000) − (CU420,000) = (CU120,000)
Gain/(loss)	nil	(CU360,000) − (CU420,000) = CU60,000	(CU540,000) − (CU360,000) = (CU180,000)
Investment in foreign operation (hedged item)			
Retranslation difference in accordance with Section 30	nil	(CU55,000)†	CU157,500‡
Cumulative retranslation differences	nil	(CU55,000) − 0 = (CU55,000)	CU157,500 + (CU55,000) = CU102,500

Key to table:

†*This is the exchange difference referred to in paragraph 30.20 which is recognised in other comprehensive income. The amount under paragraph 30.20(a) is CU5,000 and under paragraph 30.20(b) (CU60,000). The calculation is based on the translation of the FC200,000 loss at the average rate of 0.325CU:FC.*

‡*This is the exchange difference referred to in paragraph 30.20 which is recognised in other comprehensive income. The amount under paragraph 30.20(a) is CU7,500 and under paragraph 30.20(b) CU150,000. The calculation is based on the translation of the FC100,000 profit at the average rate of 0.375CU:FC.*

12A.7   Hedge accounting:

31 December 20X5

A component of equity is adjusted to the lower of (in absolute amounts) the cumulative exchange gain on the loan of CU60,000 and the cumulative retranslation difference on the net investment of (CU55,000).

In accordance with paragraph 12.24(a), a gain of CU55,000 on the loan is recognised in other comprehensive income. The remainder of the gain of CU5,000 is recognised in profit or loss, as required by paragraph 12.24(b).

Accounting entry:

Note that only the accounting entry in relation to hedge accounting as described in paragraph 12.24 is shown. Other accounting entries in relation to the loan and the investment in the foreign operation would be required in practice.

	Debit	Credit
Loan	CU60,000	
Other comprehensive income		CU55,000
Profit or loss		CU5,000

31 December 20X6

A component of equity is adjusted to the lower of (in absolute amounts) the cumulative exchange loss on the loan of CU120,000 and the cumulative exchange difference on the net investment of CU102,500.

The amount recorded in equity changes from CU55,000 to (CU102,500), a change of (CU157,500). In accordance with paragraph 12.24(a) a loss of CU157,500 on the loan is recognised in other comprehensive income. The remainder of the loss of CU22,500 is recorded in profit or loss, as required by paragraph 12.24(b).

Accounting entry:

	Debit	Credit
Other comprehensive income	CU157,500	
Profit or loss	CU22,500	
Loan		CU180,000

Section 13 Inventories

Scope of this section

This section sets out the principles for recognising and measuring **inventories**. Inventories are **assets**:   **13.1**

(a)   held for sale in the ordinary course of business;

(b)   in the process of production for such sale; or

(c)   in the form of materials or supplies to be consumed in the production process or in the rendering of services.

This section applies to all inventories, except: **13.2**

(a)   work in progress arising under **construction contracts**, including directly related service contracts (see Section 23 *Revenue*);

(b)   **financial instruments** (see Section 11 *Basic Financial Instruments* and Section 12 *Other Financial Instruments Issues*); and

(c)   **biological assets** related to **agricultural activity** and **agricultural produce** at the point of harvest (see Section 34 *Specialised Activities*).

This section does not apply to the **measurement** of inventories measured at **fair value less**   **13.3** **costs to sell** through **profit or loss** at each reporting date.

Prospective amendments: Amendments to FRS 102 *The Financial Reporting Standard applicable in the UK and Republic of Ireland –* Small entities and other minor amendments (July 2015) amends this paragraph 13.3 with effect for annual periods beginning on or after 1 January 2016.

Measurement of inventories

An entity shall measure inventories at the lower of **cost** and estimated selling price less   **13.4** costs to complete and sell.

Inventories held for distribution at no or nominal consideration shall be measured at   **13.4A** cost adjusted, when applicable, for any loss of **service potential**.

Prospective amendments: Amendments to FRS 102 *The Financial Reporting Standard applicable in the UK and Republic of Ireland* – Small entities and other minor amendments (July 2015) amends this paragraph 13.4A with effect for annual periods beginning on or after 1 January 2016.

Cost of inventories

13.5   An entity shall include in the cost of inventories all costs of purchase, costs of conversion and other costs incurred in bringing the inventories to their present location and condition.

13.5A Where inventories are acquired through a **non-exchange transaction**, their cost shall be measured at their **fair value** as at the date of acquisition. For **public benefit entities** and entities within a **public benefit entity group**, this requirement only applies to inventories that are recognised as a result of the requirements for incoming resources from non-exchange transactions as prescribed in Section 34 *Specialised Activities*.

Costs of purchase

13.6   The costs of purchase of inventories comprise the purchase price, import duties and other taxes (other than those subsequently recoverable by the entity from the taxing authorities), and transport, handling and other costs directly attributable to the acquisition of finished goods, materials and services. Trade discounts, rebates and other similar items are deducted in determining the costs of purchase.

13.7   An entity may purchase inventories on deferred settlement terms. In some cases, the arrangement effectively contains an unstated financing element, for example, a difference between the purchase price for normal credit terms and the deferred settlement amount. In these cases, the difference is recognised as interest expense over the period of the financing and is not added to the cost of the inventories unless the inventory is a **qualifying asset** (see Section 25 *Borrowing Costs*) and the entity adopts a policy of capitalisation of borrowing costs.

Costs of conversion

13.8   The costs of conversion of inventories include costs directly related to the units of production, such as direct labour. They also include a systematic allocation of fixed and variable production overheads that are incurred in converting materials into finished goods. Fixed production overheads are those indirect costs of production that remain relatively constant regardless of the volume of production, such as **depreciation** and maintenance of factory buildings and equipment, and the cost of factory management and administration. Variable production overheads are those indirect costs of production that vary directly, or nearly directly, with the volume of production, such as indirect materials and indirect labour.

13.8A Production overheads include the costs for obligations (recognised and measured in accordance with Section 21 *Provisions and Contingencies*) for dismantling, removing and restoring a site on which an item of **property, plant and equipment** is located that are incurred during the **reporting period** as a consequence of having used that item of property, plant and equipment to produce inventory during that period.

Allocation of production overheads

13.9   An entity shall allocate fixed production overheads to the costs of conversion on the basis of the normal capacity of the production facilities. Normal capacity is the production expected to be achieved on average over a number of periods or seasons under normal circumstances, taking into account the loss of capacity resulting from planned maintenance. The actual level of production may be used if it approximates normal capacity. The amount of fixed overhead allocated to each unit of production is not increased as a consequence of low production or idle plant. Unallocated overheads are recognised as an **expense** in the period in which they are incurred. In periods of abnormally high production, the amount of fixed overhead allocated to each unit of production is decreased so that inventories are not measured above cost. Variable production overheads are allocated to each unit of production on the basis of the actual use of the production facilities.

Joint products and by-products

A production process may result in more than one product being produced simultaneously. **13.10**
This is the case, for example, when joint products are produced or when there is a main product and a by-product. When the costs of raw materials or conversion of each product are not separately identifiable, an entity shall allocate them between the products on a rational and consistent basis. The allocation may be based, for example, on the relative sales value of each product either at the stage in the production process when the products become separately identifiable, or at the completion of production. Most by-products, by their nature, are immaterial. When this is the case, the entity shall measure them at selling price less costs to complete and sell and deduct this amount from the cost of the main product. As a result, the **carrying amount** of the main product is not materially different from its cost.

Other costs included in inventories

An entity shall include other costs in the cost of inventories only to the extent that they are **13.11**
incurred in bringing the inventories to their present location and condition.

[Not used] **13.12**

Costs excluded from inventories

Examples of costs excluded from the cost of inventories and recognised as expenses in the **13.13**
period in which they are incurred are:

(a) abnormal amounts of wasted materials, labour or other production costs;
(b) storage costs, unless those costs are necessary during the production process before a further production stage;
(c) administrative overheads that do not contribute to bringing inventories to their present location and condition; and
(d) selling costs.

Cost of inventories of a service provider

To the extent that service providers have inventories, they measure them at the costs of **13.14**
their production. These costs consist primarily of the labour and other costs of personnel directly engaged in providing the service, including supervisory personnel, and attributable overheads. Labour and other costs relating to sales and general administrative personnel are not included but are recognised as expenses in the period in which they are incurred. The cost of inventories of a service provider does not include profit margins or non-attributable overheads that are often factored into prices charged by service providers.

Cost of agricultural produce harvested from biological assets

13.15   Section 34 requires that inventories comprising agricultural produce that an entity has harvested from its biological assets should be measured on initial **recognition**, at the point of harvest, at either their fair value less estimated costs to sell or the lower of cost and estimated selling price less costs to complete and sell. This becomes the cost of the inventories at that date for application of this section.

Techniques for measuring cost, such as standard costing, retail method and most recent purchase price

13.16   An entity may use techniques such as the standard cost method, the retail method or most recent purchase price for measuring the cost of inventories if the result approximates cost. Standard costs take into account normal levels of materials and supplies, labour, efficiency and capacity utilisation. They are regularly reviewed and, if necessary, revised in the light of current conditions. The retail method measures cost by reducing the sales value of the inventory by the appropriate percentage gross margin.

Cost formulas

13.17   An entity shall measure the cost of inventories of items that are not ordinarily interchangeable and goods or services produced and segregated for specific projects by using specific identification of their individual costs.

13.18   An entity shall measure the cost of inventories, other than those dealt with in paragraph 13.17, by using the first-in, first-out (FIFO) or weighted average cost formula. An entity shall use the same cost formula for all inventories having a similar nature and use to the entity. For inventories with a different nature or use, different cost formulas may be justified. The last-in, first-out method (LIFO) is not permitted by this FRS.

Impairment of inventories

13.19   Paragraphs 27.2 to 27.4 require an entity to assess at the end of each reporting period whether any inventories are impaired, ie the carrying amount is not fully recoverable (eg because of damage, obsolescence or declining selling prices). If an item (or group of items) of inventory is impaired, those paragraphs require the entity to measure the inventory at its selling price less costs to complete and sell, and to recognise an **impairment loss**. Those paragraphs also require a reversal of a prior impairment in some circumstances.

Recognition as an expense

13.20   When inventories are sold, the entity shall recognise the carrying amount of those inventories as an expense in the period in which the related **revenue** is recognised.

13.20A   When inventories held for distribution at no or nominal consideration are distributed, the carrying amount of those inventories shall be recognised as an expense.

13.21   Some inventories may be allocated to other asset accounts, for example, inventory used as a component of self-constructed property, plant or equipment. Inventories allocated to another asset in this way are accounted for subsequently in accordance with the section of this FRS relevant to that type of asset.

Disclosures

An entity shall disclose the following: **13.22**

(a) the **accounting policies** adopted in measuring inventories, including the cost formula used;

(b) the total carrying amount of inventories and the carrying amount in classifications appropriate to the entity;

(c) the amount of inventories recognised as an expense during the period;

(d) impairment losses recognised or reversed in profit or loss in accordance with Section 27; and

(e) the total carrying amount of inventories pledged as security for **liabilities**.

Section 14 Investments in Associates

Scope of this section

This section applies to accounting for **associates** in **consolidated financial statements**. **14.1** This section also applies to accounting for investments in associates in the **individual financial statements** of an investor that is not a **parent**. An entity that is a parent shall account for its investments in associates in its **separate financial statements** in accordance with paragraphs 9.26 and 9.26A, as appropriate.

Associates defined

An associate is an entity, including an unincorporated entity such as a partnership, over **14.2** which the investor has **significant influence** and that is neither a **subsidiary** nor an interest in a **joint venture**.

Significant influence is the power to participate in the financial and operating policy **14.3** decisions of the associate but is not **control** or **joint control** over those policies.

(a) If an investor holds, directly or indirectly (eg through subsidiaries), 20% or more of the voting power of the associate, it is presumed that the investor has significant influence, unless it can be clearly demonstrated that this is not the case.

(b) Conversely, if the investor holds, directly or indirectly (eg through subsidiaries), less than 20% of the voting power of the associate, it is presumed that the investor does not have significant influence, unless such influence can be clearly demonstrated.

(c) A substantial or majority ownership by another investor does not preclude an investor from having significant influence.

Measurement – accounting policy election

An investor that is not a parent but that has an investment in one or more associates shall, **14.4** in its individual financial statements, account for all of its investments in associates using either:

(a) the cost model in accordance with paragraphs 14.5 to 14.6;

(b) [not used]

(c) the fair value model in accordance with paragraphs 14.9 to 14.10A; or

(d) at fair value with changes in fair value recognised in profit or loss (paragraphs 11.27 to 11.32 provide guidance on fair value).

14.4A An investor that is a parent shall, in its consolidated financial statements, account for all of its investments in associates using the equity method in accordance with paragraph 14.8, except as required by paragraph 14.4B.

14.4B Where an investor is a parent and has an associate that is **held as part of an investment portfolio**, the associate shall be measured at **fair value** with changes in fair value recognised in **profit or loss** in the consolidated financial statements.

Cost model

14.5 An investor that is not a parent, that chooses to adopt the cost model, shall measure its investments in associates at cost less any accumulated **impairment losses** recognised in accordance with Section 27 *Impairment of Assets*.

14.6 The investor shall recognise dividends and other distributions received from the investment as **income** without regard to whether the distributions are from accumulated profits of the associate arising before or after the date of acquisition.

14.7 [Not used]

Equity method

14.8 Under the equity method of accounting, an equity investment is initially recognised at the transaction price (including **transaction costs**) and is subsequently adjusted to reflect the investor's share of the profit or loss, **other comprehensive income** and **equity** of the associate.

   (a) *Distributions and other adjustments to carrying amount.* Distributions received from the associate reduce the **carrying amount** of the investment. Adjustments to the carrying amount may also be required as a consequence of changes in the associate's equity arising from items of other comprehensive income.

   (b) *Potential voting rights.* Although potential voting rights are considered in deciding whether significant influence exists, an investor shall measure its share of profit or loss and other comprehensive income of the associate and its share of changes in the associate's equity on the basis of present ownership interests. Those measurements shall not reflect the possible exercise or conversion of potential voting rights.

   (c) *Implicit goodwill and fair value adjustments.* On acquisition of the investment in an associate, an investor shall account for any difference (whether positive or negative) between the cost of acquisition and the investor's share of the fair values of the net identifiable assets of the associate in accordance with paragraphs 19.22 to 19.24. An investor shall adjust its share of the associate's profits or losses after acquisition to account for additional **depreciation** or **amortisation** of the associate's depreciable or amortisable assets (including **goodwill**) on the basis of the excess of their fair values over their carrying amounts at the time the investment was acquired.

   (d) *Impairment.* If there is an indication that an investment in an associate may be impaired, an investor shall test the entire carrying amount of the investment for impairment in accordance with Section 27 as a single **asset**. Any goodwill included as part of the carrying amount of the investment in the associate is not tested separately for impairment but, rather, as part of the test for impairment of the investment as a whole.

   (e) *Investor's transactions with associates.* The investor shall eliminate unrealised profits and losses resulting from upstream (associate to investor) and downstream (investor to associate) transactions to the extent of the investor's interest in the associate. Unrealised losses on such transactions may provide evidence of an impairment of the asset transferred.

(f)   *Date of associate's financial statements.* In applying the equity method, the investor shall use the **financial statements** of the associate as of the same date as the financial statements of the investor unless it is **impracticable** to do so. If it is impracticable, the investor shall use the most recent available financial statements of the associate, with adjustments made for the effects of any significant transactions or events occurring between the accounting period ends.

(g)   *Associate's accounting policies.* If the associate uses **accounting policies** that differ from those of the investor, the investor shall adjust the associate's financial statements to reflect the investor's accounting policies for the purpose of applying the equity method unless it is impracticable to do so.

(h)   *Losses in excess of investment.* If an investor's share of losses of an associate equals or exceeds the carrying amount of its investment in the associate, the investor shall discontinue recognising its share of further losses. After the investor's interest is reduced to zero, the investor shall recognise additional losses by a **provision** (see Section 21 *Provisions and Contingencies*) only to the extent that the investor has incurred legal or **constructive obligations** or has made payments on behalf of the associate. If the associate subsequently reports profits, the investor shall resume recognising its share of those profits only after its share of the profits equals the share of losses not recognised.

(i)   *Discontinuing the equity method.* An investor shall cease using the equity method from the date that significant influence ceases and, provided the associate does not become a subsidiary in accordance with *Section 19 Business Combinations and Goodwill* or a joint venture in accordance with Section 15 *Investments in Joint Ventures*, shall account for the investment as follows:

(i)   If the investor loses significant influence over an associate as a result of a full or partial disposal, it shall derecognise that associate and recognise in profit or loss the difference between the proceeds from the disposal and the carrying amount of the investment in the associate relating to the proportion disposed of or lost at the date significant influence is lost. The investor shall account for any retained interest using Section 11 *Basic Financial Instruments* or Section 12 *Other Financial Instruments Issues*, as appropriate. The carrying amount of the investment at the date that it ceases to be an associate shall be regarded as its cost on initial **measurement** as a **financial asset**; and

(ii)   If an investor loses significant influence for reasons other than a partial disposal of its investment, the investor shall regard the carrying amount of the investment at that date as a new cost basis and shall account for the investment using Sections 11 or 12, as appropriate.

The gain or loss arising on the disposal shall also include those amounts that have been recognised in **other comprehensive income** in relation to that associate, where those amounts are required to be reclassified to profit or loss upon disposal in accordance with other sections of this FRS. Amounts that are not required to be reclassified to profit or loss upon disposal of the related assets or liabilities in accordance with other sections of this FRS shall be transferred directly to retained earnings.

Fair value model

When an investment in an associate is recognised initially, an investor that is not a parent, that chooses to adopt the fair value model, shall measure it at the transaction price.   **14.9**

At each reporting date, an investor that is not a parent, that chooses to adopt the fair value model, shall measure its investments in associates at fair value, with changes in fair value recognised in other comprehensive income in accordance with paragraphs 17.15E and 17.15F, using the fair value guidance in paragraphs 11.27 to 11.32. An investor using the   **14.10** fair value model shall use the cost model for any investment in an associate for which it is impracticable to measure fair value reliably without undue cost or effort.

14.10A   The investor shall recognise dividends and other distributions received from the investment as income without regard to whether the distributions are from accumulated profits of the associate arising before or after the date of acquisition.

Presentation in individual and consolidated financial statements

14.11   Unless otherwise required under the Regulations, an investor shall classify investments in associates as **fixed assets**.

Disclosures in individual and consolidated financial statements

14.12   The financial statements shall disclose:

(a)   the accounting policy for investments in associates;

(b)   the carrying amount of investments in associates; and

(c)   the fair value of investments in associates accounted for using the equity method for which there are published price quotations.

14.13   For investments in associates accounted for in accordance with the cost model, an investor shall disclose the amount of dividends and other distributions recognised as income.

14.14   For investments in associates accounted for in accordance with the equity method, an investor shall disclose separately its share of the profit or loss of such associates and its share of any **discontinued operations** of such associates.

14.15   For investments in associates accounted for in accordance with the fair value model, an investor shall make the disclosures required by paragraphs 11.43 and 11.44.

14.15A   The individual financial statements of an investor that is not a parent shall disclose summarised financial information about the investments in the associates, along with the effect of including those investments as if they had been accounted for using the equity method. Investing entities that are exempt from preparing consolidated financial statements, or would be exempt if they had subsidiaries, are exempt from this requirement.

Section 15 Investments in Joint Ventures

Scope of this section

15.1   This section applies to accounting for **joint ventures** in **consolidated financial statements**, for investments in joint ventures in the **individual financial statements** of a **venturer** that is not a **parent**, and for investment in **jointly controlled operations** and **jointly controlled assets** in the **separate financial statements** of a venturer that is a parent. A venturer that is a parent shall account for interests in **jointly controlled entities** in its **separate financial statements** in accordance with paragraphs 9.26 and 9.26A, as appropriate.

Joint ventures defined

15.2   **Joint control** is the contractually agreed sharing of **control** over an economic activity, and exists only when the strategic financial and operating decisions relating to the activity require the unanimous consent of the parties sharing control (the venturers).

A joint venture is a contractual arrangement whereby two or more parties undertake an economic activity that is subject to joint control. Joint ventures can take the form of jointly controlled operations, jointly controlled assets, or jointly controlled entities.   **15.3**

Jointly controlled operations

The operation of some joint ventures involves the use of the **assets** and other resources of the venturers rather than the establishment of a corporation, partnership or other entity, or a financial structure that is separate from the venturers themselves. Each venturer uses its own **property, plant and equipment** and carries its own **inventories**. It also incurs its own **expenses** and **liabilities** and raises its own finance, which represent its own obligations. The joint venture activities may be carried out by the venturer's employees alongside the venturer's similar activities. The joint venture agreement usually provides a means by which the **revenue** from the sale of the joint product and any expenses incurred in common are shared among the venturers.   **15.4**

In respect of its interests in jointly controlled operations, a venturer shall recognise in its **financial statements**:   **15.5**

(a)   the assets that it controls and the liabilities that it incurs; and

(b)   the expenses that it incurs and its share of the **income** that it earns from the sale of goods or services by the joint venture.

Jointly controlled assets

Some joint ventures involve the joint control, and often the joint ownership, by the venturers of one or more assets contributed to, or acquired for the purpose of, the joint venture and dedicated to the purposes of the joint venture.   **15.6**

In respect of its interest in a jointly controlled asset, a venturer shall recognise in its financial statements: **15.7**

(a)   its share of the jointly controlled assets, classified according to the nature of the assets;

(b)   any liabilities that it has incurred;

(c)   its share of any liabilities incurred jointly with the other venturers in relation to the joint venture;

(d)   any income from the sale or use of its share of the output of the joint venture, together with its share of any expenses incurred by the joint venture; and

(e)   any expenses that it has incurred in respect of its interest in the joint venture.

Jointly controlled entities

A jointly controlled entity is a joint venture that involves the establishment of a corporation, partnership or other entity in which each venturer has an interest. The entity operates in the same way as other entities, except that a contractual arrangement between the venturers establishes joint control over the economic activity of the entity.   **15.8**

Measurement – accounting policy election

A venturer that is not a parent but has one or more interests in jointly controlled entities shall, in its individual financial statements, account for all of its interests in jointly controlled entities using either: **15.9**

(a)   the cost model in accordance with paragraphs 15.10 to 15.11;

(b)   [not used]

(c)   the fair value model in accordance with paragraphs 15.14 to 15.15A; or

(d)   at fair value with changes in fair value recognised in profit or loss (paragraphs 11.27 to 11.32 provide guidance on fair value).

15.9A   A venturer that is a parent shall, in its consolidated financial statements, account for all of its investments in jointly controlled entities using the equity method in accordance with paragraph 15.13, except as required by paragraph 15.9B.

15.9B   A venture that is a parent, shall measure its investments in jointly controlled entities **held as part of an investment portfolio** at **fair value** with changes in fair value recognised in **profit or loss** in the consolidated financial statements.

Cost model

15.10   A venturer that is not a parent, that chooses to adopt the cost model, shall measure its investments in jointly controlled entities, at cost less any accumulated **impairment losses** recognised in accordance with Section 27 *Impairment of Assets*.

15.11   The venturer shall recognise distributions received from the investment as income without regard to whether the distributions are from accumulated profits of the jointly controlled entity arising before or after the date of acquisition.

15.12   [Not used]

Equity method

15.13   A venturer shall measure its investments in jointly controlled entities by the equity method using the procedures in accordance with paragraph 14.8 (substituting 'joint control' where that paragraph refers to 'significant influence', and 'jointly controlled entity' where that paragraph refers to 'associate').

Fair value model

15.14   When an investment in a jointly controlled entity is recognised initially, a venturer that is not a parent, that chooses to adopt the fair value model, shall measure it at the transaction price.

15.15   At each reporting date, a venturer that is not a parent, that chooses to adopt the fair value model, shall measure its investments in jointly controlled entities at fair value using the fair value guidance in paragraphs 11.27 to 11.32. Changes in fair value shall be recognised in accordance with paragraphs 17.15E and 17.15F. A venturer using the fair value model shall use the cost model for any investment in a jointly controlled entity for which it is **impracticable** to measure fair value reliably without undue cost or effort.

15.15A   The venturer shall recognise dividends and other distributions received from the investment as income without regard to whether the distributions are from accumulated profits of the jointly controlled entity arising before or after the date of acquisition.

Transactions between a venturer and a joint venture

15.16   When a venturer contributes or sells assets to a joint venture, **recognition** of any portion of a **gain** or loss from the transaction shall reflect the substance of the transaction. While the assets are retained by the joint venture, and provided the venturer has transferred the significant risks and rewards of ownership, the venturer shall recognise only that portion of the gain or loss that is attributable to the interests of the other venturers. The venturer shall recognise the full amount of any loss when the contribution or sale provides evidence of an impairment loss.

When a venturer purchases assets from a joint venture, the venturer shall not recognise its **15.17** share of the profits of the joint venture from the transaction until it resells the assets to an independent party. A venturer shall recognise its share of the losses resulting from these transactions in the same way as profits except that losses shall be recognised immediately when they represent an impairment loss.

If investor does not have joint control

An investor in a joint venture that does not have joint control shall account for that **15.18** investment in accordance with Section 11 *Basic Financial Instruments* or Section 12 *Other Financial Instruments Issues* or, if it has **significant influence** in the joint venture, in accordance with Section 14 *Investments in Associates*.

Disclosures in individual and consolidated financial statements

The financial statements shall disclose the following: **15.19**

(a)   the **accounting policy** for recognising investments in jointly controlled entities;
(b)   the **carrying amount** of investments in jointly controlled entities;
(c)   the fair value of investments in jointly controlled entities accounted for using the equity method for which there are published price quotations; and
(d)   the aggregate amount of its commitments relating to joint ventures, including its share in the capital commitments that have been incurred jointly with other venturers, as well as its share of the capital commitments of the joint ventures themselves.

For jointly controlled entities accounted for in accordance with the equity method, the **15.20** venturer shall disclose separately its share of the profit or loss of such investments and its share of any **discontinued operations** of such jointly controlled entities.

For jointly controlled entities accounted for in accordance with the fair value model, the **15.21** venturer shall make the disclosures required by paragraphs 11.43 and 11.44.

The individual financial statements of a venturer that is not a parent shall disclose **15.21A** summarised financial information about the investments in the jointly controlled entities, along with the effect of including those investments as if they had been accounted for using the equity method. Investing entities that are exempt from preparing consolidated financial statements, or would be exempt if they had subsidiaries, are exempt from this requirement.

Section 16 Investment Property

Scope of this section

This section applies to accounting for investments in land or buildings that meet the **16.1** definition of **investment property** in paragraph 16.2 and some property interests held by a lessee under an **operating lease** (see paragraph 16.3) that are treated like investment property. Only investment property whose **fair value** can be measured reliably without undue cost or effort on an on-going basis is accounted for in accordance with this section at fair value through **profit or loss**. All other investment property is accounted for as **property, plant and equipment** using the cost model in Section 17 *Property, Plant and*

Equipment and remains within the scope of Section 17 unless a reliable measure of fair value becomes available and it is expected that fair value will be reliably measurable on an on-going basis.

Definition and initial recognition of investment property

16.2   Investment property is property (land or a building, or part of a building, or both) held by the owner or by the lessee under a **finance lease** to earn rentals or for capital appreciation or both, rather than for:

(a)   use in the production or supply of goods or services or for administrative purposes; or

(b)   sale in the ordinary course of business.

16.3   A property interest that is held by a lessee under an operating lease may be classified and accounted for as investment property using this section if, and only if, the property would otherwise meet the definition of an investment property and the lessee can measure the fair value of the property interest without undue cost or effort on an on-going basis. This classification alternative is available on a property-by-property basis.

16.3A   Property held primarily for the provision of social benefits, eg social housing held by a **public benefit entity**, shall not be classified as investment property and shall be accounted for as property, plant and equipment in accordance with Section 17.

16.4   Mixed use property shall be separated between investment property and property, plant and equipment. However, if the fair value of the investment property component cannot be measured reliably without undue cost or effort, the entire property shall be accounted for as property, plant and equipment in accordance with Section 17.

Measurement at initial recognition

16.5   An entity shall measure investment property at its cost at initial **recognition**. The cost of a purchased investment property comprises its purchase price and any directly attributable expenditure such as legal and brokerage fees, property transfer taxes and other transaction costs. If payment is deferred beyond normal credit terms, the cost is the **present value** of all future payments. An entity shall determine the cost of a self-constructed investment property in accordance with paragraphs 17.10 to 17.14.

16.6   The initial cost of a property interest held under a **lease** and classified as an investment property shall be as prescribed for a finance lease by paragraphs 20.9 and 20.10, even if the lease would otherwise be classified as an operating lease if it was in the scope of Section 20 *Leases*. In other words, the **asset** is recognised at the lower of the fair value of the property and the present value of the **minimum lease payments**. An equivalent amount is recognised as a **liability** in accordance with paragraphs 20.9 and 20.10. Any premium paid for a lease is treated as part of the minimum lease payments for this purpose, and is therefore included in the cost of the asset, but is excluded from the liability.

Measurement after recognition

16.7   Investment property whose fair value can be measured reliably without undue cost or effort shall be measured at fair value at each **reporting date** with changes in fair value recognised in profit or loss. If a property interest held under a lease is classified as investment property, the item accounted for at fair value is that interest and not the underlying property. Paragraphs 11.27 to 11.32 provide guidance on determining fair value. An entity shall account for all other investment property as property, plant and equipment using the cost model in Section 17.

Transfers

If a reliable measure of fair value is no longer available without undue cost or effort for an item of investment property measured using the fair value model, the entity shall thereafter account for that item as property, plant and equipment in accordance with Section 17 until a reliable measure of fair value becomes available. The **carrying amount** of the investment property on that date becomes its cost under Section 17. Paragraph 16.10(e) (iii) requires disclosure of this change. It is a change of circumstances and not a change in **accounting policy**.   **16.8**

Other than as required by paragraph 16.8, an entity shall transfer a property to, or from, investment property only when the property first meets, or ceases to meet, the definition of investment property.   **16.9**

Disclosures

An entity shall disclose the following for all investment property accounted for at fair value through profit or loss (paragraph 16.7):   **16.10**

(a)   the methods and significant assumptions applied in determining the fair value of investment property;

(b)   the extent to which the fair value of investment property (as measured or disclosed in the **financial statements**) is based on a valuation by an independent valuer who holds a recognised and relevant professional qualification and has recent experience in the location and class of the investment property being valued. If there has been no such valuation, that fact shall be disclosed;

(c)   the existence and amounts of restrictions on the realisability of investment property or the remittance of **income** and proceeds of disposal;

(d)   contractual obligations to purchase, construct or develop investment property or for repairs, maintenance or enhancements; and

(e)   a reconciliation between the carrying amounts of investment property at the beginning and end of the period, showing separately:

(i)   additions, disclosing separately those additions resulting from acquisitions through **business combinations**;

(ii)   net gains or losses from fair value adjustments;

(iii)   transfers to property, plant and equipment when a reliable measure of fair value is no longer available without undue cost or effort (see paragraph 16.8);

(iv)   transfers to and from **inventories** and owner-occupied property; and

(v)   other changes.

This reconciliation need not be presented for prior periods.

In accordance with Section 20 *Leases*, an entity shall provide all relevant disclosures required in that section about leases into which it has entered.   **16.11**

Section 17 Property, Plant and Equipment

Scope

This section applies to the accounting for **property, plant and equipment** and to **investment property** whose **fair value** cannot be measured reliably without undue cost or   **17.1** effort. Section 16 *Investment Property* applies to investment property whose fair value can be measured reliably without undue cost or effort.

17.2   Property, plant and equipment are tangible assets that:

(a)   are held for use in the production or supply of goods or services, for rental to others, or for administrative purposes; and

(b)   are expected to be used during more than one period;

17.3   Property, plant and equipment does not include:

(a)   **biological assets** related to **agricultural activity** (see Section 34 *Specialised Activities*) or **heritage assets** (see Section 34); or

(b)   mineral rights and mineral reserves, such as oil, natural gas and similar non-regenerative resources (see Section 34).

Recognition

17.4   An entity shall apply the **recognition** criteria in paragraph 2.27 in determining whether to recognise an item of property, plant or equipment. Therefore, the entity shall recognise the cost of an item of property, plant and equipment as an **asset** if, and only if:

(a)   it is **probable** that future economic benefits associated with the item will flow to the entity; and

(b)   the cost of the item can be measured reliably.

17.5   Spare parts and servicing equipment are usually carried as **inventory** and recognised in **profit or loss** as consumed. However, major spare parts and stand-by equipment are property, plant and equipment when an entity expects to use them during more than one period. Similarly, if the spare parts and servicing equipment can be used only in connection with an item of property, plant and equipment, they are considered property, plant and equipment.

17.6   Parts of some items of property, plant and equipment may require replacement at regular intervals (eg the roof of a building). An entity shall add to the **carrying amount** of an item of property, plant and equipment the cost of replacing part of such an item when that cost is incurred if the replacement part is expected to provide incremental future benefits to the entity. The carrying amount of those parts that are replaced is derecognised in accordance with paragraphs 17.27 to 17.30. Paragraph 17.16 provides that if the major components of an item of property, plant and equipment have significantly different patterns of consumption of economic benefits, an entity shall allocate the initial cost of the asset to its major components and depreciate each such component separately over its **useful life**.

17.7   A condition of continuing to operate an item of property, plant and equipment (eg a bus) may be performing regular major inspections for faults regardless of whether parts of the item are replaced. When each major inspection is performed, its cost is recognised in the carrying amount of the item of property, plant and equipment as a replacement if the recognition criteria are satisfied. Any remaining carrying amount of the cost of the previous major inspection (as distinct from physical parts) is derecognised. This is done regardless of whether the cost of the previous major inspection was identified in the transaction in which the item was acquired or constructed. If necessary, the estimated cost of a future similar inspection may be used as an indication of what the cost of the existing inspection component was when the item was acquired or constructed.

17.8   Land and buildings are separable assets, and an entity shall account for them separately, even when they are acquired together.

Measurement at initial recognition

An entity shall measure an item of property, plant and equipment at initial recognition at its cost. **17.9**

Elements of cost

The cost of an item of property, plant and equipment comprises all of the following: **17.10**

(a) Its purchase price, including legal and brokerage fees, import duties and non-refundable purchase taxes, after deducting trade discounts and rebates.

(b) Any costs directly attributable to bringing the asset to the location and condition necessary for it to be capable of operating in the manner intended by management. These can include the costs of site preparation, initial delivery and handling, installation and assembly, and testing of functionality.

(c) The initial estimate of the costs, recognised and measured in accordance with Section 21 *Provisions and Contingencies*, of dismantling and removing the item and restoring the site on which it is located, the obligation for which an entity incurs either when the item is acquired or as a consequence of having used the item during a particular period for purposes other than to produce inventories during that period.

(d) Any **borrowing costs** capitalised in accordance with paragraph 25.2.

The following costs are not costs of an item of property, plant and equipment, and an entity shall recognise them as an **expense** when they are incurred: **17.11**

(a) costs of opening a new facility;

(b) costs of introducing a new product or service (including costs of advertising and promotional activities);

(c) costs of conducting business in a new location or with a new class of customer (including costs of staff training); and

(d) administration and other general overhead costs.

The **income** and related expenses of incidental operations during construction or development of an item of property, plant and equipment are recognised in profit or loss if those operations are not necessary to bring the item to its intended location and operating condition. **17.12**

Measurement of cost

The cost of an item of property, plant and equipment is the cash price equivalent at the recognition date. If payment is deferred beyond normal credit terms, the cost is the **present value** of all future payments. **17.13**

Exchanges of assets

An item of property, plant or equipment may be acquired in exchange for a non-monetary asset or assets, or a combination of monetary and non-monetary assets. An entity shall measure the cost of the acquired asset at fair value unless: **17.14**

(a) the exchange transaction lacks commercial substance; or

(b) the fair value of neither the asset received nor the asset given up is reliably measurable. In that case, the asset's cost is measured at the carrying amount of the asset given up.

Measurement after initial recognition

17.15   An entity shall measure all items of property, plant and equipment after initial recognition using the cost model (in accordance with paragraph 17.15A) or the revaluation model (in accordance with paragraphs 17.15B to 17.15F). Where the revaluation model is selected, this shall be applied to all items of property, plant and equipment in the same class (ie having a similar nature, function or use in the business). An entity shall recognise the costs of day-to-day servicing of an item of property, plant and equipment in profit or loss in the period in which the costs are incurred.

Cost model

17.15A   Under the cost model, an entity shall measure an item of property, plant and equipment at cost less any accumulated **depreciation** and any accumulated **impairment losses**.

Revaluation model

17.15B   Under the revaluation model, an item of property, plant and equipment whose fair value can be measured reliably shall be carried at a revalued amount, being its fair value at the date of revaluation less any subsequent accumulated depreciation and subsequent accumulated impairment losses. Revaluations shall be made with sufficient regularity to ensure that the carrying amount does not differ materially from that which would be determined using fair value at the end of the **reporting period**.

17.15C   The fair value of land and buildings is usually determined from market-based evidence by appraisal that is normally undertaken by professionally qualified valuers. The fair value of items of plant and equipment is usually their market value determined by appraisal. Paragraphs 11.27 to 11.32 provide further guidance on determining fair value.

17.15D   If there is no market-based evidence of fair value because of the specialised nature of the item of property, plant and equipment and the item is rarely sold, except as part of a continuing business, an entity may need to estimate fair value using an income or a **depreciated replacement cost** approach.

Reporting gains and losses on revaluations

17.15E   If an asset's carrying amount is increased as a result of a revaluation, the increase shall be recognised in **other comprehensive income** and accumulated in **equity**. However, the increase shall be recognised in profit or loss to the extent that it reverses a revaluation decrease of the same asset previously recognised in profit or loss.

17.15F   The decrease of an asset's carrying amount as a result of a revaluation shall be recognised in other comprehensive income to the extent of any previously recognised revaluation increase accumulated in equity, in respect of that asset. If a revaluation decrease exceeds the accumulated revaluation gains accumulated in equity in respect of that asset, the excess shall be recognised in **profit or loss**.

Depreciation

17.16   If the major components of an item of property, plant and equipment have significantly different patterns of consumption of economic benefits, an entity shall allocate the initial cost of the asset to its major components and depreciate each such component separately over its useful life. Other assets shall be depreciated over their useful lives as a single asset.

There are some exceptions, such as land which generally has an unlimited useful life and therefore is not usually depreciated.

The depreciation charge for each period shall be recognised in profit or loss unless another section of this FRS requires the cost to be recognised as part of the cost of an asset. For example, the depreciation of manufacturing property, plant and equipment is included in the costs of inventories (see Section 13 *Inventories*).   **17.17**

Depreciable amount and depreciation period

An entity shall allocate the **depreciable amount** of an asset on a systematic basis over its useful life.   **17.18**

Factors such as a change in how an asset is used, significant unexpected wear and tear, technological advancement, and changes in market prices may indicate that the **residual value** or useful life of an asset has changed since the most recent annual **reporting date**. If such indicators are present, an entity shall review its previous estimates and, if current expectations differ, amend the residual value, depreciation method or useful life. The entity shall account for the change in residual value, depreciation method or useful life as a change in an accounting estimate in accordance with paragraphs 10.15 to 10.18.   **17.19**

Depreciation of an asset begins when it is available for use, ie when it is in the location and condition necessary for it to be capable of operating in the manner intended by management. Depreciation of an asset ceases when the asset is derecognised. Depreciation does not cease when the asset becomes idle or is retired from active use unless the asset is fully depreciated. However, under usage methods of depreciation the depreciation charge can be zero while there is no production.   **17.20**

An entity shall consider all the following factors in determining the useful life of an asset: **17.21**

(a)   The expected usage of the asset. Usage is assessed by reference to the asset's expected capacity or physical output.

(b)   Expected physical wear and tear, which depends on operational factors such as the number of shifts for which the asset is to be used and the repair and maintenance programme, and the care and maintenance of the asset while idle.

(c)   Technical or commercial obsolescence arising from changes or improvements in production, or from a change in the market demand for the product or service output of the asset.

(d)   Legal or similar limits on the use of the asset, such as the expiry dates of related **leases**.

Depreciation method

An entity shall select a depreciation method that reflects the pattern in which it expects to consume the asset's future economic benefits. The possible depreciation methods include the straight-line method, the diminishing balance method and a method based on usage such as the units of production method.   **17.22**

If there is an indication that there has been a significant change since the last annual reporting date in the pattern by which an entity expects to consume an asset's future economic benefits, the entity shall review its present depreciation method and, if current expectations differ, change the depreciation method to reflect the new pattern. The entity shall account for the change as a change in an accounting estimate in accordance with paragraphs 10.15 to 10.18.   **17.23**

Impairment

Recognition and measurement of impairment

17.24   At each reporting date, an entity shall apply Section 27 *Impairment of Assets* to determine whether an item or group of items of property, plant and equipment is impaired and, if so, how to recognise and measure the impairment loss. That section explains when and how an entity reviews the carrying amount of its assets, how it determines the **recoverable amount** of an asset, and when it recognises or reverses an impairment loss.

Compensation for impairment

17.25   An entity shall include in profit or loss, compensation from third parties for items of property, plant and equipment that were impaired, lost or given up only when the compensation is virtually certain.

Property, plant and equipment held for sale

17.26   Paragraph 27.9(f) states that a plan to dispose of an asset before the previously expected date is an indicator of impairment that triggers the calculation of the asset's recoverable amount for the purpose of determining whether the asset is impaired.

Derecognition

17.27   An entity shall derecognise an item of property, plant and equipment:

(a)   on disposal; or

(b)   when no future economic benefits are expected from its use or disposal.

17.28   An entity shall recognise the **gain** or loss on the **derecognition** of an item of property, plant and equipment in profit or loss when the item is derecognised (unless Section 20 *Leases* requires otherwise on a sale and leaseback). The entity shall not classify such gains as **revenue**.

17.29   In determining the date of disposal of an item, an entity shall apply the criteria in Section 23 *Revenue* for recognising revenue from the sale of goods. Section 20 applies to disposal by a sale and leaseback.

17.30   An entity shall determine the gain or loss arising from the derecognition of an item of property, plant and equipment as the difference between the net disposal proceeds, if any, and the carrying amount of the item.

Disclosures

17.31   An entity shall disclose the following for each class of property, plant and equipment:

(a)   the measurement bases used for determining the gross carrying amount;

(b)   the depreciation methods used;

(c)   the useful lives or the depreciation rates used;

(d)   the gross carrying amount and the accumulated depreciation (aggregated with accumulated impairment losses) at the beginning and end of the reporting period;

(e)   a reconciliation of the carrying amount at the beginning and end of the reporting period showing separately:

(i) additions;

(ii) disposals;

(iii) acquisitions through **business combinations**;

(iv) revaluations;

(v) transfers to or from investment property if a reliable measure of fair value becomes available or unavailable (see paragraph 16.8);

(vi) impairment losses recognised or reversed in profit or loss in accordance with Section 27 *Impairment of Assets*;

(vii) depreciation; and

(viii) other changes.

This reconciliation need not be presented for prior periods.

The entity shall also disclose the following: 17.32

(a) the existence and carrying amounts of property, plant and equipment to which the entity has restricted title or that is pledged as security for **liabilities**; and

(b) the amount of contractual commitments for the acquisition of property, plant and equipment.

If items of property, plant and equipment are stated at revalued amounts, the following   17.32A
shall be disclosed:

(a) the effective date of the revaluation;

(b) whether an independent valuer was involved;

(c) the methods and significant assumptions applied in estimating the items' fair values; and

(d) for each revalued class of property, plant and equipment, the carrying amount that would have been recognised had the assets been carried under the cost model.

Section 18 Intangible Assets other than Goodwill

Scope of this section

This section applies to accounting for all **intangible assets** other than **goodwill**   18.1
(see Section 19 *Business Combinations and Goodwill*) and intangible assets held by an entity for sale in the ordinary course of business (see Section 13 *Inventories* and Section 23 *Revenue*).

This section does not apply to the accounting for **deferred acquisition costs** and intangible   18.1A
assets arising from contracts in the scope of FRS 103 *Insurance Contracts*, except for the disclosure requirements in this section which apply to intangible assets arising from contracts in the scope of FRS 103.

An intangible asset is an identifiable non-monetary asset without physical substance. Such   18.2
an **asset** is identifiable when:

(a) it is separable, ie capable of being separated or divided from the entity and sold, transferred, licensed, rented or exchanged, either individually or together with a related contract, asset or **liability**; or

(b) it arises from contractual or other legal rights, regardless of whether those rights are transferable or separable from the entity or from other rights and obligations.

This section does not apply to the following: 18.3

(a) **financial assets** (see Section 11 *Basic Financial Instruments* and Section 12 *Other Financial Instruments Issues*);

(b)   **heritage assets** (see Section 34 *Specialised Activities*); or

(c)   mineral rights and mineral reserves, such as oil, natural gas and similar non-regenerative resources (see Section 34).

Recognition

General principle for recognising intangible assets

18.4   An entity shall apply the **recognition** criteria in paragraph 2.27 in determining whether to recognise an intangible asset. Therefore, the entity shall recognise an intangible asset as an asset if, and only if:

(a)   it is **probable** that the expected future economic benefits that are attributable to the asset will flow to the entity; and

(b)   the cost or value of the asset can be measured reliably.

18.5   An entity shall assess the probability of expected future economic benefits using reasonable and supportable assumptions that represent management's best estimate of the economic conditions that will exist over the **useful life** of the asset.

18.6   An entity uses judgement to assess the degree of certainty attached to the flow of future economic benefits that are attributable to the use of the asset on the basis of the evidence available at the time of initial recognition, giving greater weight to external evidence.

18.7   The probability recognition criterion in paragraph 18.4(a) is always considered satisfied for intangible assets that are separately acquired.

Acquisition as part of a business combination

18.8   An intangible asset acquired in a **business combination** is normally recognised as an asset because its **fair value** can be measured with sufficient **reliability**. However, an intangible asset acquired in a business combination is not recognised when it arises from legal or other contractual rights and there is no history or evidence of exchange transactions for the same or similar assets, and otherwise estimating fair value would be dependent on immeasurable variables.

Internally generated intangible assets

18.8A   To assess whether an internally generated intangible asset meets the criteria for recognition, an entity classifies the generation of the asset into:

(a)   a **research** phase; and

(b)   a **development** phase.

18.8B   If an entity cannot distinguish the research phase from the development phase of an internal project to create an intangible asset, the entity treats the expenditure on that project as if it were incurred in the research phase only.

18.8C[12]   An entity shall recognise expenditure on the following items as an **expense** and shall not recognise such expenditure as intangible assets:

(a)   Internally generated brands, logos, publishing titles, customer lists and items similar in substance.

[12] *Is paragraph 18.15 in the IFRS for SMEs.*

(b) Start-up activities (ie start-up costs), which include establishment costs such as legal and secretarial costs incurred in establishing a legal entity, expenditure to open a new facility or business (ie pre-opening costs) and expenditure for starting new operations or launching new products or processes (ie pre-operating costs).

(c) Training activities.

(d) Advertising and promotional activities (unless it meets the definition of **inventories held for distribution at no or nominal consideration** (see paragraph 13.4A)).

(e) Relocating or reorganising part or all of an entity.

(f) Internally generated goodwill.

Paragraph 18.8C does not preclude recognising a prepayment as an asset when payment for goods or services has been made in advance of the delivery of the goods or the rendering of the services.   **18.8D**[13]

Research phase

No intangible asset arising from research (or from the research phase of an internal project) shall be recognised. Expenditure on research (or on the research phase of an internal project) shall be recognised as an expense when it is incurred.   **18.8E**

In the research phase of an internal project, an entity cannot demonstrate that an intangible asset exists that will generate probable future economic benefits.   **18.8F**

Examples of research activities are: **18.8G**

(a) Activities aimed at obtaining new knowledge.

(b) The search for, evaluation and final selection of, applications of research findings and other knowledge.

(c) The search for alternatives for materials, devices, products, processes, systems or services.

(d) The formulation, design, evaluation and final selection of possible alternatives for new or improved material, devices, projects, processes, systems or services.

Development phase

An entity may recognise an intangible asset arising from development (or from the development phase of an internal project) if, and only if, an entity can demonstrate all of the following: **18.8H**

(a) The technical feasibility of completing the intangible asset so that it will be available for use or sale.

(b) Its intention to complete the intangible asset and use or sell it.

(c) Its ability to use or sell the intangible asset.

(d) How the intangible asset will generate probable future economic benefits. Among other things, the entity can demonstrate the existence of a market for the output of the intangible asset or the intangible asset itself or, if it is to be used internally, the usefulness of the intangible asset.

(e) The availability of adequate technical, financial and other resources to complete the development and to use or sell the intangible asset.

(f) Its ability to measure reliably the expenditure attributable to the intangible asset during its development.

---

[13] *Is paragraph 18.16 in the IFRS for SMEs.*

18.8I   In the development phase of an internal project, an entity can, in some instances, identify an intangible asset and demonstrate that the asset will generate probable future economic benefits. This is because the development phase of a project is further advanced than the research phase.

18.8J   Examples of development activities are:

(a)   The design, construction and testing of pre-production or pre-use prototypes and models.

(b)   The design of tools, jigs, moulds and dies involving new technology.

(c)   The design, construction and operation of a pilot plant that is not of a scale economically feasible for commercial production.

(d)   The design, construction and testing of a chosen alternative for new or improved materials, devices, products, processes, systems or services.

18.8K   Where an entity adopts a policy of capitalising expenditure in the development phase that meets the conditions of paragraph 18.8H, that policy shall be applied consistently to all expenditure that meets the requirements of paragraph 18.8H. Expenditure that does not meet the conditions of paragraph 18.8H is expensed as incurred.

Initial measurement

18.9   An entity shall measure an intangible asset initially at cost.

Separate acquisition

18.10   The cost of a separately acquired intangible asset comprises:

(a)   its purchase price, including import duties and non-refundable purchase taxes, after deducting trade discounts and rebates; and

(b)   any directly attributable cost of preparing the asset for its intended use.

Internally generated intangible assets

18.10A   The cost of an internally generated intangible asset for the purpose of paragraph 18.9 is the sum of expenditure incurred from the date when the intangible asset first meets the recognition criteria in paragraphs 18.4 and 18.8H.

18.10B   The cost of an internally generated intangible asset comprises all directly attributable costs necessary to create, produce and prepare the asset to be capable of operating in the manner intended by management. Examples of directly attributable costs are:

(a)   costs of materials and services used or consumed in generating the intangible asset;

(b)   costs of **employee benefits** (as defined in Section 28 *Employee Benefits*) arising from the generation of the intangible asset;

(c)   fees to register a legal right; and

(d)   **amortisation** of patents and licences that are used to generate the intangible asset.

Section 25 *Borrowing Costs* specifies criteria for the recognition of interest as an element of the cost of an internally generated intangible asset.

Acquisition as part of a business combination

18.11   If an intangible asset is acquired in a business combination, the cost of that intangible asset is its fair value at the **acquisition date**.

Acquisition by way of a grant

If an intangible asset is acquired by way of a grant, the cost of that intangible asset is its fair value at the date the grant is received or receivable in accordance with Section 24 *Government Grants*. 18.12

Exchanges of assets

An intangible asset may be acquired in exchange for a non-monetary asset or assets, or a combination of monetary and non-monetary assets. An entity shall measure the cost of such an intangible asset at fair value unless: 18.13

(a) the exchange transaction lacks commercial substance; or
(b) the fair value of neither the asset received nor the asset given up is reliably measurable. In that case, the asset's cost is measured at the **carrying amount** of the asset given up.

[Replaced by paragraph 18.8A] 18.14

[Moved to paragraph 18.8C] 18.15

[Moved to paragraph 18.8D] 18.16

Past expenses not to be recognised as an asset

Expenditure on an intangible item that was initially recognised as an expense shall not be recognised at a later date as part of the cost of an asset. 18.17

Measurement after initial recognition

An entity shall measure intangible assets after initial recognition using the cost model (in accordance with paragraph 18.18A) or the revaluation model (in accordance with paragraphs 18.18B to 18.18H). Where the revaluation model is selected, this shall be applied to all intangible assets in the same class. If an intangible asset in a class of revalued intangible assets cannot be revalued because there is no **active market** for this asset, the asset shall be carried at its cost less any accumulated amortisation and impairment losses. 18.18

Cost model

Under the cost model, an entity shall measure its assets at cost less any accumulated amortisation and any accumulated **impairment losses**. The requirements for amortisation are set out in paragraphs 18.19 to 18.24. 18.18A

Revaluation model

Under the revaluation model, an intangible asset shall be carried at a revalued amount, being its fair value at the date of revaluation less any subsequent accumulated amortisation and subsequent accumulated impairment losses, provided that the fair value can be determined by reference to an active market. The requirements for amortisation are set out in paragraphs 18.19 to 18.24. 18.18B

The revaluation model does not allow: 18.18C

(a)   the revaluation of intangible assets that have not previously been recognised as assets; or

(b)   the initial recognition of intangible assets at amounts other than cost.

18.18D   Revaluations shall be made with sufficient regularity to ensure that the carrying amount does not differ materially from that which would be determined using fair value at the end of the **reporting period**.

18.18E   If the fair value of a revalued intangible asset can no longer be determined by reference to an active market in accordance with the requirements of paragraph 18.18B, the carrying amount of the asset shall be its revalued amount at the date of the last revaluation by reference to the active market, less any subsequent accumulated amortisation and any subsequent accumulated impairment losses.

18.18F   The revaluation model is applied after an asset has been initially recognised at cost. However, if only part of the cost of an intangible asset is recognised as an asset because the asset did not meet the criteria for recognition until part of the way through the process (see paragraph 18.10A), the revaluation model may be applied to the whole of that asset.

Reporting gains and losses on revaluations

18.18G   If an asset's carrying amount is increased as a result of a revaluation, the increase shall be recognised in **other comprehensive income** and accumulated in **equity**. However, the increase shall be recognised in **profit or loss** to the extent that it reverses a revaluation decrease of the same asset previously recognised in profit or loss.

18.18H   The decrease of an asset's carrying amount as a result of a revaluation shall be recognised in other comprehensive income to the extent of any previously recognised revaluation increase accumulated in equity, in respect of that asset. If a revaluation decrease exceeds the accumulated revaluation gains recognised in equity in respect of that asset, the excess shall be recognised in profit or loss.

Amortisation over useful life

18.19   For the purpose of this FRS, all intangible assets shall be considered to have a finite useful life. The useful life of an intangible asset that arises from contractual or other legal rights shall not exceed the period of the contractual or other legal rights, but may be shorter depending on the period over which the entity expects to use the asset. If the contractual or other legal rights are conveyed for a limited term that can be renewed, the useful life of the intangible asset shall include the renewal period(s) only if there is evidence to support renewal by the entity without significant cost.

18.20   If an entity is unable to make a reliable estimate of the useful life of an intangible asset, the life shall not exceed five years.

Prospective amendments: Amendments to FRS 102 *The Financial Reporting Standard applicable in the UK and Republic of Ireland* – Small entities and other minor amendments (July 2015) amends this paragraph 18.20 with effect for annual periods beginning on or after 1 January 2016.

Amortisation period and amortisation method

18.21   An entity shall allocate the **depreciable amount** of an intangible asset on a systematic basis over its useful life. The amortisation charge for each period shall be recognised in profit or loss, unless another section of this FRS requires the cost to be recognised as part of the cost of an asset. For example, the amortisation of an intangible asset may be included in the costs of **inventories** or **property, plant and equipment**.

Amortisation begins when the intangible asset is available for use, ie when it is in the location and condition necessary for it to be usable in the manner intended by management. Amortisation ceases when the asset is derecognised. The entity shall choose an amortisation method that reflects the pattern in which it expects to consume the asset's future economic benefits. If the entity cannot determine that pattern reliably, it shall use the straight-line method.   **18.22**

Residual value

An entity shall assume that the **residual value** of an intangible asset is zero unless: **18.23**

(a)   there is a commitment by a third party to purchase the asset at the end of its useful life; or

(b)   there is an active market for the asset and:

   (i)   residual value can be determined by reference to that market; and

   (ii)   it is probable that such a market will exist at the end of the asset's useful life.

Review of amortisation period and amortisation method

Factors such as a change in how an intangible asset is used, technological advancement, and changes in market prices may indicate that the residual value or useful life of an intangible asset has changed since the most recent annual **reporting date**. If such indicators are present, an entity shall review its previous estimates and, if current expectations differ, amend the residual value, amortisation method or useful life. The entity shall account for the change in residual value, amortisation method or useful life as a change in an accounting estimate in accordance with paragraphs 10.15 to 10.18.   **18.24**

Recoverability of the carrying amount – impairment losses

To determine whether an intangible asset is impaired, an entity shall apply Section 27 *Impairment of Assets*. That section explains when and how an entity reviews the carrying amount of its assets, how it determines the **recoverable amount** of an asset, and when it recognises or reverses an impairment loss.   **18.25**

Retirements and disposals

An entity shall derecognise an intangible asset, and shall recognise a **gain** or loss in profit or loss: **18.26**

(a)   on disposal; or

(b)   when no future economic benefits are expected from its use or disposal.

Disclosures

An entity shall disclose the following for each class of intangible assets: **18.27**

(a)   the useful lives or the amortisation rates used and the reasons for choosing those periods;

(b)   the amortisation methods used;

(c) the gross carrying amount and any accumulated amortisation (aggregated with accumulated impairment losses) at the beginning and end of the reporting period;

(d) the line item(s) in the **statement of comprehensive income** (or in the **income statement**, if presented) in which any amortisation of intangible assets is included; and

(e) a reconciliation of the carrying amount at the beginning and end of the reporting period showing separately:

(i) additions, indicating separately those from internal development and those acquired separately;

(ii) disposals;

(iii) acquisitions through business combinations;

(iv) revaluations;

(v) amortisation;

(vi) impairment losses; and

(vii) other changes.

This reconciliation need not be presented for prior periods.

18.28 An entity shall also disclose:

(a) a description, the carrying amount and remaining amortisation period of any individual intangible asset that is **material** to the entity's **financial statements**;

(b) for intangible assets acquired by way of a grant and initially recognised at fair value (see paragraph 18.12):

(i) the fair value initially recognised for these assets; and

(ii) their carrying amounts.

(c) the existence and carrying amounts of intangible assets to which the entity has restricted title or that are pledged as security for liabilities; and

(d) the amount of contractual commitments for the acquisition of intangible assets.

18.29 An entity shall disclose the aggregate amount of research and development expenditure recognised as an expense during the period (ie the amount of expenditure incurred internally on research and development that has not been capitalised as an intangible asset or as part of the cost of another asset that meets the recognition criteria in this FRS).

18.29A If intangible assets are accounted for at revalued amounts, an entity shall disclose the following:

(a) the effective date of the revaluation;

(b) whether an independent valuer was involved;

(c) the methods and significant assumptions applied in estimating the assets' fair values; and

(d) for each revalued class of intangible assets, the carrying amount that would have been recognised had the assets been carried under the cost model.

Section 19 Business Combinations and Goodwill

Scope of this section

19.1 This section applies to accounting for **business combinations**. It provides guidance on identifying the acquirer, measuring the cost of the business combination, and allocating that cost to the **assets** acquired and **liabilities** and **provisions** for **contingent liabilities** assumed. It also addresses accounting for **goodwill** both at the time of a business combination and subsequently.

This section specifies the accounting for all business combinations except: **19.2**

(a)   the formation of a **joint venture**; and

(b)   acquisition of a group of assets that does not constitute a **business**.

In addition, **public benefit entities** shall consider the requirements of Section 34   **PBE19.2A**
Specialised Activities in accounting for **public benefit entity combinations**.

Business combinations defined

A business combination is the bringing together of separate entities or businesses into   **19.3**
one reporting entity. The result of nearly all business combinations is that one entity, the
acquirer, obtains **control** of one or more other businesses, the acquiree. The **acquisition
date** is the date on which the acquirer obtains control of the acquiree.

A business combination may be structured in a variety of ways for legal, taxation or   **19.4**
other reasons. It may involve the purchase by an entity of the **equity** of another entity,
the purchase of all the net assets of another entity, the assumption of the liabilities of
another entity, or the purchase of some of the net assets of another entity that together form
one or more businesses.

A business combination may be effected by the issue of equity instruments, the transfer   **19.5**
of **cash**, **cash equivalents** or other assets, or a mixture of these. The transaction may
be between the shareholders of the combining entities or between one entity and the
shareholders of another entity. It may involve the establishment of a new entity to control
the combining entities or net assets transferred, or the restructuring of one or more of the
combining entities.

Purchase method

All business combinations shall be accounted for by applying the purchase method,   **19.6**
except for:

(a)   **group reconstructions** which may be accounted for by using the merger accounting
method (see paragraphs 19.27 to 19.33); and

(b)   public benefit entity **combinations that are in substance a gift** or that are a **merger**
which shall be accounted for in accordance with Section 34 *Specialised Activities*.

Applying the purchase method involves the following steps: **19.7**

(a)   identifying an acquirer;

(b)   measuring the cost of the business combination; and

(c)   allocating, at the acquisition date, the cost of the business combination to the assets
acquired and liabilities and provisions for contingent liabilities assumed.

Identifying the acquirer

An acquirer shall be identified for all business combinations accounted for by applying   **19.8**
the purchase method. The acquirer is the combining entity that obtains control of the
other combining entities or businesses.

Control is the power to govern the financial and operating policies of an entity or business   **19.9**
so as to obtain benefits from its activities. Control of one entity by another is described in
Section 9 *Consolidated and Separate Financial Statements*.

19.10   Although it may sometimes be difficult to identify an acquirer, there are usually indications that one exists. For example:

(a)   If the **fair value** of one of the combining entities is significantly greater than that of the other combining entity, the entity with the greater fair value is likely to be the acquirer.

(b)   If the business combination is effected through an exchange of voting ordinary equity instruments for cash or other assets, the entity giving up cash or other assets is likely to be the acquirer.

(c)   If the business combination results in the management of one of the combining entities being able to dominate the selection of the management team of the resulting combined entity, the entity whose management is able so to dominate is likely to be the acquirer.

Cost of a business combination

19.11   The acquirer shall measure the cost of a business combination as the aggregate of:

(a)   the fair values, at the acquisition date, of assets given, liabilities incurred or assumed, and equity instruments issued by the acquirer, in exchange for control of the acquiree; plus

(b)   any costs directly attributable to the business combination.

19.11A   Where control is achieved following a series of transactions, the cost of the business combination is the aggregate of the fair values of the assets given, liabilities assumed and equity instruments issued by the acquirer at the date of each transaction in the series.

Adjustments to the cost of a business combination contingent on future events

19.12   When a business combination agreement provides for an adjustment to the cost of the combination contingent on future events, the acquirer shall include the estimated amount of that adjustment in the cost of the combination at the acquisition date if the adjustment is **probable** and can be measured reliably.

19.13   However, if the potential adjustment is not recognised at the acquisition date but subsequently becomes probable and can be measured reliably, the additional consideration shall be treated as an adjustment to the cost of the combination.

Allocating the cost of a business combination to the assets acquired and liabilities and contingent liabilities assumed

19.14   The acquirer shall, at the acquisition date, allocate the cost of a business combination by recognising the acquiree's identifiable assets and liabilities and a provision for those contingent liabilities (that satisfy the **recognition** criteria in paragraph 19.20) at their fair values at that date, except for the items specified in paragraphs 19.15A to 19.15C. Any difference between the cost of the business combination and the acquirer's interest in the net amount of the identifiable assets, liabilities and provisions for contingent liabilities so recognised shall be accounted for in accordance with paragraphs 19.22 to 19.24.

19.15   Except for the items specified in paragraphs 19.15A to 19.15C, the acquirer shall recognise separately the acquiree's identifiable assets, liabilities and contingent liabilities at the acquisition date only if they satisfy the following criteria at that date:

(a)   In the case of an asset other than an **intangible asset**, it is probable that any associated future economic benefits will flow to the acquirer, and its fair value can be measured reliably.

(b) In the case of a liability other than a contingent liability, it is probable that an outflow of resources will be required to settle the obligation, and its fair value can be measured reliably.

(c) In the case of an intangible asset or a contingent liability, its fair value can be measured reliably.

The acquirer shall recognise and measure a **deferred tax asset** or **liability** arising from the assets acquired and liabilities assumed in accordance with Section 29 *Income Tax*.   **19.15A**

The acquirer shall recognise and measure a liability (or asset, if any) related to the acquiree's employee benefit arrangements in accordance with Section 28 *Employee Benefits*.   **19.15B**

The acquirer shall recognise and measure a share-based payment in accordance with Section 26 *Share-based Payment*.   **19.15C**

The acquirer's **statement of comprehensive income** shall incorporate the acquiree's profits or losses after the acquisition date by including the acquiree's **income** and **expenses** based on the cost of the business combination to the acquirer. For example, depreciation expense included after the acquisition date in the acquirer's statement of comprehensive income that relates to the acquiree's depreciable assets shall be based on the fair values of those depreciable assets at the acquisition date, ie their cost to the acquirer.   **19.16**

Application of the purchase method starts from the acquisition date, which is the date on which the acquirer obtains control of the acquiree. Because control is the power to govern the financial and operating policies of an entity or business so as to obtain benefits from its activities, it is not necessary for a transaction to be closed or finalised at law before the acquirer obtains control. All pertinent facts and circumstances surrounding a business combination shall be considered in assessing when the acquirer has obtained control.   **19.17**

In accordance with paragraph 19.14, the acquirer recognises separately only the identifiable assets, liabilities and contingent liabilities of the acquiree that existed at the acquisition date and satisfy the recognition criteria in paragraph 19.15 (except for the items specified in paragraphs 19.15A to 19.15C). Therefore: **19.18**

(a) the acquirer shall recognise liabilities for terminating or reducing the activities of the acquiree as part of allocating the cost of the combination only to the extent that the acquiree has, at the acquisition date, an existing liability for restructuring recognised in accordance with Section 21 *Provisions and Contingencies*; and

(b) the acquirer, when allocating the cost of the combination, shall not recognise liabilities for future losses or other costs expected to be incurred as a result of the business combination.

If the initial accounting for a business combination is incomplete by the end of the **reporting period** in which the combination occurs, the acquirer shall recognise in its **financial statements** provisional amounts for the items for which the accounting is incomplete. Within twelve months after the acquisition date, the acquirer shall retrospectively adjust the provisional amounts recognised as assets and liabilities at the acquisition date (ie account for them as if they were made at the acquisition date) to reflect new information obtained. Beyond twelve months after the acquisition date, adjustments to the initial accounting for a business combination shall be recognised only to correct a **material error** in accordance with Section 10 *Accounting Policies, Estimates and Errors*.   **19.19**

Contingent liabilities

19.20   Paragraph 19.15(c) specifies that the acquirer recognises separately a provision for a contingent liability of the acquiree only if its fair value can be measured reliably. If its fair value cannot be measured reliably:

(a)   there is a resulting effect on the amount recognised as goodwill or the amount accounted for in accordance with paragraph 19.24; and

(b)   the acquirer shall disclose the information about that contingent liability as required by Section 21.

19.21   After their initial recognition, the acquirer shall measure contingent liabilities that are recognised separately in accordance with paragraph 19.15(c) at the higher of:

(a)   the amount that would be recognised in accordance with Section 21; and

(b)   the amount initially recognised less amounts previously recognised as **revenue** in accordance with Section 23 *Revenue*.

Goodwill

19.22   The acquirer shall, at the acquisition date:

(a)   recognise goodwill acquired in a business combination as an asset; and

(b)   initially measure that goodwill at its cost, being the excess of the cost of the business combination over the acquirer's interest in the net amount of the identifiable assets, liabilities and contingent liabilities recognised and measured in accordance with paragraphs 19.15, 19.15A to 19.15C.

19.23   After initial recognition, the acquirer shall measure goodwill acquired in a business combination at cost less accumulated **amortisation** and accumulated **impairment losses**:

(a)   An entity shall follow the principles in paragraphs 18.19 to 18.24 for amortisation of goodwill. Goodwill shall be considered to have a finite **useful life**, and shall be amortised on a systematic basis over its life. If an entity is unable to make a reliable estimate of the useful life of goodwill, the life shall not exceed five years.

(b)   An entity shall follow Section 27 *Impairment of Assets* for recognising and measuring the impairment of goodwill.

Prospective amendments: Amendments to FRS 102 *The Financial Reporting Standard applicable in the UK and Republic of Ireland* – Small entities and other minor amendments (July 2015) amends this paragraph 19.23(a) with effect for annual periods beginning on or after 1 January 2016.

Excess over cost of acquirer's interest in the net fair value of acquiree's identifiable assets, liabilities and contingent liabilities

19.24   If the acquirer's interest in the net amount of the identifiable assets, liabilities and provisions for contingent liabilities recognised in accordance with paragraph 19.14 exceeds the cost of the business combination (also referred to as 'negative goodwill'), the acquirer shall:

(a)   Reassess the identification and **measurement** of the acquiree's assets, liabilities and provisions for contingent liabilities and the measurement of the cost of the combination.

(b)   Recognise and separately disclose the resulting excess on the face of the **statement of financial position** on the acquisition date, immediately below goodwill, and followed by a subtotal of the net amount of goodwill and the excess.

(c)   Recognise subsequently the excess up to the fair value of non-monetary assets acquired in profit or loss in the periods in which the non-monetary assets are recovered. Any excess exceeding the fair value of non-monetary assets acquired shall be recognised in profit or loss in the periods expected to be benefited.

Disclosures

For business combinations effected during the reporting period

For each business combination, excluding any group reconstructions, that was effected during the period, the acquirer shall disclose the following: **19.25**

(a)   the names and descriptions of the combining entities or businesses;
(b)   the acquisition date;
(c)   the percentage of voting equity instruments acquired;
(d)   the cost of the combination and a description of the components of that cost (such as cash, equity instruments and debt instruments);
(e)   the amounts recognised at the acquisition date for each class of the acquiree's assets, liabilities and contingent liabilities, including goodwill;
(f)   [not used]
(g)   the useful life of goodwill, and if this exceeds five years, supporting reasons for this; and
(h)   the periods in which the excess recognised in accordance with paragraph 19.24 will be recognised in profit or loss.

Prospective amendments: Amendments to FRS 102 *The Financial Reporting Standard applicable in the UK and Republic of Ireland* – Small entities and other minor amendments (July 2015) amends this paragraph 19.25(g) with effect for annual periods beginning on or after 1 January 2016.

The acquirer shall disclose, separately for each material business combination that occurred during the reporting period, the amounts of revenue and profit or loss of the acquiree since the acquisition date included in the consolidated statement of comprehensive income for the reporting period. The disclosure may be provided in aggregate for business combinations that occurred during the reporting period which, individually, are not material.   **19.25A**

For all business combinations

An acquirer shall disclose a reconciliation of the **carrying amount** of goodwill at the beginning and end of the reporting period, showing separately: **19.26**

(a)   changes arising from new business combinations;
(b)   amortisation;
(c)   impairment losses;
(d)   disposals of previously acquired businesses; and
(e)   other changes.

This reconciliation need not be presented for prior periods.

An acquirer shall disclose a reconciliation of the carrying amount of the excess recognised in accordance with paragraph 19.24 at the beginning and end of the reporting period, showing separately: **19.26A**

(a)   changes arising from new business combinations;
(b)   amounts recognised in profit or loss in accordance with paragraph 19.24(c);
(c)   disposals of previously acquired businesses; and

(d)   other changes.

This reconciliation need not be presented for prior periods.

Group reconstructions

19.27   Group reconstructions may be accounted for by using the merger accounting method provided:

(a)   the use of the merger accounting method is not prohibited by company law or other relevant legislation;

(b)   the ultimate equity holders remain the same, and the rights of each equity holder, relative to the others, are unchanged; and

(c)   no **non-controlling interest** in the net assets of the **group** is altered by the transfer.

Applicability to various structures of business combinations

19.28   The provisions of paragraphs 19.29 to 19.33, which are explained by reference to an acquirer or issuing entity that issues shares as consideration for the transfer to it of shares in the other parties to the combination, should also be read so as to apply to other arrangements that achieve similar results.

Merger accounting method

19.29   With the merger accounting method the carrying values of the assets and liabilities of the parties to the combination are not required to be adjusted to fair value, although appropriate adjustments shall be made to achieve uniformity of **accounting policies** in the combining entities.

19.30   The results and cash flows of all the combining entities shall be brought into the financial statements of the combined entity from the beginning of the financial year in which the combination occurred, adjusted so as to achieve uniformity of accounting policies. The comparative information shall be restated by including the **total comprehensive income** for all the combining entities for the previous reporting period and their statement of financial position for the previous **reporting date**, adjusted as necessary to achieve uniformity of accounting policies.

19.31   The difference, if any, between the nominal value of the shares issued plus the fair value of any other consideration given, and the nominal value of the shares received in exchange shall be shown as a movement on other reserves in the **consolidated financial statements**. Any existing balances on the share premium account or capital redemption reserve of the new subsidiary shall be brought in by being shown as a movement on other reserves. These movements shall be shown in the **statement of changes in equity**.

19.32   Merger expenses are not to be included as part of this adjustment, but shall be charged to the statement of comprehensive income as part of profit or loss of the combined entity at the effective date of the group reconstruction.

Disclosures

19.33   For each group reconstruction, that was effected during the period, the combined entity shall disclose the following:

(a)   the names of the combining entities (other than the reporting entity);

(b)   whether the combination has been accounted for as an acquisition or a merger; and

(c)   the date of the combination.

Section 20 Leases

Scope of this section

This section covers accounting for all **leases** other than: 20.1

(a)   leases to explore for or use minerals, oil, natural gas and similar non-regenerative resources (see Section 34 *Specialised Activities*);

(b)   licensing agreements for such items as motion picture films, video recordings, plays, manuscripts, patents and copyrights (see Section 18 *Intangible Assets other than Goodwill*);

(c)   **measurement** of property held by lessees that is accounted for as **investment property** and measurement of investment property provided by lessors under **operating leases** (see Section 16 *Investment Property*);

(d)   measurement of **biological assets** held by lessees under **finance leases** and biological assets provided by lessors under operating leases (see Section 34); and

(e)   leases that could lead to a loss to the lessor or the lessee as a result of non-typical contractual terms (see paragraph 12.3(f)).

(f)   [not used]

This section applies to agreements that transfer the right to use **assets** even though   20.2
substantial services by the lessor may be called for in connection with the operation or maintenance of such assets. This section does not apply to agreements that are contracts for services that do not transfer the right to use assets from one contracting party to the other.

Some arrangements do not take the legal form of a lease but convey rights to use assets   20.3
in return for payments. Examples of arrangements in which one entity (the supplier) may convey a right to use an asset to another entity (the purchaser), often together with related services, may include outsourcing arrangements, telecommunication contracts that provide rights to capacity and take-or-pay contracts.

Determining whether an arrangement is, or contains, a lease shall be based on the substance   20.3A
of the arrangement and requires an assessment of whether:

(a)   fulfilment of the arrangement is dependent on the use of a specific asset or assets. Although a specific asset may be explicitly identified in an arrangement, it is not the subject of a lease if fulfilment of the arrangement is not dependent on the use of the specified asset. An asset is implicitly specified if, for example, the supplier owns or leases only one asset with which to fulfil the obligation and it is not economically feasible or practicable for the supplier to perform its obligation through the use of alternative assets; and

(b)   the arrangement conveys a right to use the asset. This will be the case where the arrangement conveys to the purchaser the right to control the use of the underlying asset.

Classification of leases

A lease is classified as a finance lease if it transfers substantially all the risks and rewards   20.4
incidental to ownership. A lease is classified as an operating lease if it does not transfer substantially all the risks and rewards incidental to ownership.

Whether a lease is a finance lease or an operating lease depends on the substance of the   20.5
transaction rather than the form of the contract. Examples of situations that individually or in combination would normally lead to a lease being classified as a finance lease are:

(a) the lease transfers ownership of the asset to the lessee by the end of the **lease term**;

(b) the lessee has the option to purchase the asset at a price that is expected to be sufficiently lower than the **fair value** at the date the option becomes exercisable for it to be reasonably certain, at the **inception of the lease**, that the option will be exercised;

(c) the lease term is for the major part of the economic life of the asset even if title is not transferred;

(d) at the inception of the lease the **present value** of the **minimum lease payments** amounts to at least substantially all of the fair value of the leased asset; and

(e) the leased assets are of such a specialised nature that only the lessee can use them without major modifications.

20.6 Indicators of situations that individually or in combination could also lead to a lease being classified as a finance lease are:

(a) if the lessee can cancel the lease, the lessor's losses associated with the cancellation are borne by the lessee;

(b) **gains** or losses from the fluctuation in the **residual value** of the leased asset accrue to the lessee (eg in the form of a rent rebate equalling most of the sales proceeds at the end of the lease); and

(c) the lessee has the ability to continue the lease for a secondary period at a rent that is substantially lower than market rent.

20.7 The examples and indicators in paragraphs 20.5 and 20.6 are not always conclusive. If it is clear from other features that the lease does not transfer substantially all risks and rewards incidental to ownership, the lease is classified as an operating lease. For example, this may be the case if ownership of the asset is transferred to the lessee at the end of the lease for a variable payment equal to the asset's then fair value, or if there are **contingent rents**, as a result of which the lessee does not have substantially all risks and rewards incidental to ownership.

20.8 Lease classification is made at the inception of the lease and is not changed during the term of the lease unless the lessee and the lessor agree to change the provisions of the lease (other than simply by renewing the lease), in which case the lease classification shall be re-evaluated.

Financial statements of lessees: finance leases

Initial recognition

20.9 At the **commencement of the lease term**, a lessee shall recognise its rights of use and obligations under finance leases as assets and **liabilities** in its **statement of financial position** at amounts equal to the fair value of the leased asset or, if lower, the present value of the minimum lease payments, determined at the inception of the lease. Any initial direct costs of the lessee (incremental costs that are directly attributable to negotiating and arranging a lease) are added to the amount recognised as an asset.

20.10 The present value of the minimum lease payments shall be calculated using the **interest rate implicit in the lease**. If this cannot be determined, the **lessee's incremental borrowing rate** shall be used.

Subsequent measurement

20.11 A lessee shall apportion minimum lease payments between the finance charge and the reduction of the outstanding liability using the **effective interest method**

(see paragraphs 11.15 to 11.20). The lessee shall allocate the finance charge to each period during the lease term so as to produce a constant periodic rate of interest on the remaining balance of the liability. A lessee shall charge contingent rents as **expenses** in the periods in which they are incurred.

A lessee shall depreciate an asset leased under a finance lease in accordance with Section 17 **20.12** *Property, Plant and Equipment*. If there is no reasonable certainty that the lessee will obtain ownership by the end of the lease term, the asset shall be fully depreciated over the shorter of the lease term and its **useful life**. A lessee shall also assess at each **reporting date** whether an asset leased under a finance lease is impaired (see Section 27 *Impairment of Assets*).

Disclosures

A lessee shall make the following disclosures for finance leases: **20.13**

(a) for each **class of asset**, the net **carrying amount** at the end of the **reporting period**;
(b) the total of future minimum lease payments at the end of the reporting period, for each of the following periods:

    (i)   not later than one year;
    (ii) later than one year and not later than five years; and
    (iii) later than five years; and

(c) a general description of the lessee's significant leasing arrangements including, for example, information about contingent rent, renewal or purchase options and escalation clauses, subleases, and restrictions imposed by lease arrangements.

In addition, the requirements for disclosure about assets in accordance with Sections 17 **20.14** and 27 apply to lessees for assets leased under finance leases.

Financial statements of lessees: operating leases

Recognition and measurement

A lessee shall recognise lease payments under operating leases (excluding costs for services **20.15** such as insurance and maintenance) as an expense over the lease term on a straight-line basis unless either:

(a) another systematic basis is representative of the time pattern of the user's benefit, even if the payments are not on that basis; or
(b) the payments to the lessor are structured to increase in line with expected general inflation (based on published indexes or statistics) to compensate for the lessor's expected inflationary cost increases. If payments to the lessor vary because of factors other than general inflation, then this condition (b) is not met.

Example of applying paragraph 20.15(b):
X operates in a jurisdiction in which the consensus forecast by local banks is that the general price level index, as published by the government, will increase by an average of 10% annually over the next five years. X leases some office space from Y for five years under an operating lease. The lease payments are structured to reflect the expected 10% annual general inflation over the five-year term of the lease as follows:

Year 1	CU100,000
Year 2	CU110,000

Example of applying paragraph 20.15(b):	
Year 3	CU121,000
Year 4	CU133,000
Year 5	CU146,000

X recognises annual rent expense equal to the amounts owed to the lessor as shown above. If the escalating payments are not clearly structured to compensate the lessor for expected inflationary cost increases based on published indexes or statistics, then X recognises annual rent expense on a straight-line basis: CU122,000 each year (sum of the amounts payable under the lease divided by five years).

20.15A   A lessee shall recognise the aggregate benefit of **lease incentives** as a reduction to the expense recognised in accordance with paragraph 20.15 over the lease term, on a straight-line basis unless another systematic basis is representative of the time pattern of the lessee's benefit from the use of the leased asset. Any costs incurred by the lessee (for example costs for termination of a pre-existing lease, relocation or leasehold improvements) shall be accounted for in accordance with the applicable section of this FRS.

20.15B   Where an operating lease becomes an **onerous contract** an entity shall also apply Section 21 *Provisions and Contingencies*.

Disclosures

20.16   A lessee shall make the following disclosures for operating leases:

(a)   the total of future minimum lease payments under non-cancellable operating leases for each of the following periods:

    (i)   not later than one year;
    (ii)   later than one year and not later than five years; and
    (iii)   later than five years; and

(b)   lease payments recognised as an expense.
(c)   [not used]

Financial statements of lessors: finance leases

Initial recognition and measurement

20.17   A lessor shall recognise assets held under a finance lease in its statement of financial position and present them as a receivable at an amount equal to the net investment in the lease. The **net investment in a lease** is the lessor's **gross investment in the lease** discounted at the interest rate implicit in the lease. The gross investment in the lease is the aggregate of:

(a)   the minimum lease payments receivable by the lessor under a finance lease; and
(b)   any unguaranteed residual value accruing to the lessor.

20.18   For finance leases other than those involving manufacturer or dealer lessors, initial direct costs (costs that are incremental and directly attributable to negotiating and arranging a lease) are included in the initial measurement of the finance lease receivable and reduce the amount of **income** recognised over the lease term.

Subsequent measurement

The **recognition** of finance income shall be based on a pattern reflecting a constant 20.19
periodic rate of return on the lessor's net investment in the finance lease. Lease payments
relating to the period, excluding costs for services, are applied against the gross investment
in the lease to reduce both the principal and the unearned finance income. If there is an
indication that the estimated unguaranteed residual value used in computing the lessor's
gross investment in the lease has changed significantly, the income allocation over the
lease term is revised, and any reduction in respect of amounts accrued is recognised
immediately in **profit or loss**.

Manufacturer or dealer lessors

Manufacturers or dealers often offer to customers the choice of either buying or leasing 20.20
an asset. A finance lease of an asset by a manufacturer or dealer lessor gives rise to two
types of income:

(a) profit or loss equivalent to the profit or loss resulting from an outright sale of the
asset being leased, at normal selling prices, reflecting any applicable volume or trade
discounts; and

(b) finance income over the lease term.

The sales **revenue** recognised at the commencement of the lease term by a manufacturer 20.21
or dealer lessor is the fair value of the asset or, if lower, the present value of the minimum
lease payments accruing to the lessor, computed at a market rate of interest. The cost of
sale recognised at the commencement of the lease term is the cost, or carrying amount
if different, of the leased asset less the present value of the unguaranteed residual value.
The difference between the sales revenue and the cost of sale is the selling profit, which is
recognised in accordance with the entity's policy for outright sales.

If artificially low rates of interest are quoted, selling profit shall be restricted to that which 20.22
would apply if a market rate of interest were charged. Costs incurred by manufacturer or
dealer lessors in connection with negotiating and arranging a lease shall be recognised as
an expense when the selling profit is recognised.

Disclosures

A lessor shall make the following disclosures for finance leases: 20.23

(a) a reconciliation between the gross investment in the lease at the end of the reporting
period, and the present value of minimum lease payments receivable at the end of
the reporting period. In addition, a lessor shall disclose the gross investment in the
lease and the present value of minimum lease payments receivable at the end of the
reporting period, for each of the following periods:

   (i) not later than one year;
   (ii) later than one year and not later than five years; and
   (iii) later than five years;

(b) unearned finance income;

(c) the unguaranteed residual values accruing to the benefit of the lessor;

(d) the accumulated allowance for uncollectible minimum lease payments receivable;

(e) contingent rents recognised as income in the period; and

(f) a general description of the lessor's significant leasing arrangements, including,
for example, information about contingent rent, renewal or purchase options and
escalation clauses, subleases, and restrictions imposed by lease arrangements.

Financial statements of lessors: operating leases

Recognition and measurement

20.24 A lessor shall present assets subject to operating leases in its statement of financial position according to the nature of the asset.

20.25 A lessor shall recognise lease income from operating leases (excluding amounts for services such as insurance and maintenance) in profit or loss on a straight-line basis over the lease term, unless either:

(a) another systematic basis is representative of the time pattern of the lessee's benefit from the leased asset, even if the receipt of payments is not on that basis; or

(b) the payments to the lessor are structured to increase in line with expected general inflation (based on published indexes or statistics) to compensate for the lessor's expected inflationary cost increases. If payments to the lessor vary according to factors other than inflation, then condition (b) is not met.

20.25A A lessor shall recognise the aggregate cost of lease incentives as a reduction to the income recognised in accordance with paragraph 20.25 over the lease term on a straight-line basis, unless another systematic basis is representative of the time pattern over which the lessor's benefit from the leased asset is diminished.

20.26 A lessor shall recognise as an expense, costs, including **depreciation**, incurred in earning the lease income. The depreciation policy for depreciable leased assets shall be consistent with the lessor's normal depreciation policy for similar assets.

20.27 A lessor shall add to the carrying amount of the leased asset any initial direct costs it incurs in negotiating and arranging an operating lease and shall recognise such costs as an expense over the lease term on the same basis as the lease income.

20.28 To determine whether a leased asset has become impaired, a lessor shall apply Section 27.

20.29 A manufacturer or dealer lessor does not recognise any selling profit on entering into an operating lease because it is not the equivalent of a sale.

Disclosures

20.30 A lessor shall disclose the following for operating leases:

(a) the future minimum lease payments under non-cancellable operating leases for each of the following periods:

(i) not later than one year;
(ii) later than one year and not later than five years; and
(iii) later than five years;

(b) total contingent rents recognised as income; and

(c) a general description of the lessor's significant leasing arrangements, including, for example, information about contingent rent, renewal or purchase options and escalation clauses, and restrictions imposed by lease arrangements.

20.31 In addition, the requirements for disclosure about assets in accordance with Sections 17 and 27 apply to lessors for assets provided under operating leases.

Sale and leaseback transactions

A sale and leaseback transaction involves the sale of an asset and the leasing back of the same asset. The lease payment and the sale price are usually interdependent because they are negotiated as a package. The accounting treatment of a sale and leaseback transaction depends on the type of lease.

20.32

Sale and leaseback transaction results in a finance lease

If a sale and leaseback transaction results in a finance lease, the seller-lessee shall not recognise immediately, as income, any excess of sales proceeds over the carrying amount. Instead, the seller-lessee shall defer such excess and amortise it over the lease term.

20.33

Sale and leaseback transaction results in an operating lease

If a sale and leaseback transaction results in an operating lease, and it is clear that the transaction is established at fair value, the seller-lessee shall recognise any profit or loss immediately. If the sale price is below fair value, the seller-lessee shall recognise any profit or loss immediately unless the loss is compensated for by future lease payments at below market price. In that case the seller-lessee shall defer and amortise such loss in proportion to the lease payments over the period for which the asset is expected to be used. If the sale price is above fair value, the seller-lessee shall defer the excess over fair value and amortise it over the period for which the asset is expected to be used.

20.34

Disclosures

Disclosure requirements for lessees and lessors apply equally to sale and leaseback transactions. The required description of significant leasing arrangements includes description of unique or unusual provisions of the agreement or terms of the sale and leaseback transactions.

20.35

Section 21 Provisions and Contingencies

Scope of this section

This section applies to all **provisions** (ie **liabilities** of uncertain timing or amount), **contingent liabilities** and **contingent assets** except those provisions covered by other sections of this FRS. Where those other sections contain no specific requirements to deal with contracts that have become onerous, this section applies to those contracts.

21.1

This section applies to **financial guarantee contracts** unless:

21.1A

(a) an entity has chosen to apply IAS 39 *Financial Instruments: Recognition and Measurement* and/or IFRS 9 *Financial Instruments* to its **financial instruments** (see paragraphs 11.2 and 12.2); or

(b) an entity has elected under FRS 103 *Insurance Contracts* to continue the application of insurance contract accounting.

This section does not apply to financial instruments (including loan commitments) that are within the scope of Section 11 *Basic Financial Instruments* and 12 *Other Financial Instruments Issues*. This section does not apply to **insurance contracts** (including **reinsurance contracts**) that an entity issues and reinsurance contracts that the entity holds, or financial instruments issued by an entity with a **discretionary participation feature** that are within the scope of FRS 103 *Insurance Contracts*.

21.1B

21.2   The requirements in this section do not apply to executory contracts unless they are **onerous contracts**. Executory contracts are contracts under which neither party has performed any of its obligations or both parties have partially performed their obligations to an equal extent.

21.3   The word 'provision' is sometimes used in the context of such items as **depreciation**, impairment of **assets**, and uncollectible receivables. Those are adjustments of the **carrying amounts** of assets, rather than **recognition** of liabilities, and therefore are not covered by this section.

Initial recognition

21.4   An entity shall recognise a provision only when:

    (a)   the entity has an obligation at the **reporting date** as a result of a past event;

    (b)   it is **probable** (ie more likely than not) that the entity will be required to transfer economic benefits in settlement; and

    (c)   the amount of the obligation can be estimated reliably.

21.5   The entity shall recognise the provision as a liability in the **statement of financial position** and shall recognise the amount of the provision as an **expense**, unless another section of this FRS requires the cost to be recognised as part of the cost of an asset such as **inventories** or **property, plant and equipment**.

21.6   The condition in paragraph 21.4(a) means that the entity has no realistic alternative to settling the obligation. This can happen when the entity has a legal obligation that can be enforced by law or when the entity has a **constructive obligation** because the past event (which may be an action of the entity) has created valid expectations in other parties that the entity will discharge the obligation. Obligations that will arise from the entity's future actions (ie the future conduct of its business) do not satisfy the condition in paragraph 21.4(a), no matter how likely they are to occur and even if they are contractual. To illustrate, because of commercial pressures or legal requirements, an entity may intend or need to carry out expenditure to operate in a particular way in the future (for example, by fitting smoke filters in a particular type of factory). Because the entity can avoid the future expenditure by its future actions, for example by changing its method of operation or selling the factory, it has no present obligation for that future expenditure and no provision is recognised.

Initial measurement

21.7   An entity shall measure a provision at the best estimate of the amount required to settle the obligation at the reporting date. The best estimate is the amount an entity would rationally pay to settle the obligation at the end of the **reporting period** or to transfer it to a third party at that time.

    (a)   When the provision involves a large population of items, the estimate of the amount reflects the weighting of all possible outcomes by their associated probabilities. The provision will therefore be different depending on whether the probability of a loss of a given amount is, for example, 60% or 90%. Where there is a continuous range of possible outcomes, and each point in that range is as likely as any other, the mid-point of the range is used.

    (b)   When the provision arises from a single obligation, the individual most likely outcome may be the best estimate of the amount required to settle the obligation. However, even in such a case, the entity considers other possible outcomes. When other possible outcomes are either mostly higher or mostly lower than the most likely outcome, the best estimate will be a higher or lower amount.

When the effect of the time value of money is **material**, the amount of a provision shall be the **present value** of the amount expected to be required to settle the obligation. The discount rate (or rates) shall be a pre-tax rate (or rates) that reflect(s) current market assessments of the time value of money and risks specific to the liability. The risks specific to the liability shall be reflected either in the discount rate or in the estimation of the amounts required to settle the obligation, but not both.

An entity shall exclude **gains** from the expected disposal of assets from the **measurement** of a provision.   **21.8**

When some or all of the amount required to settle a provision may be reimbursed **21.9** by another party (eg through an insurance claim), the entity shall recognise the reimbursement as a separate asset only when it is virtually certain that the entity will receive the reimbursement on settlement of the obligation. The amount recognised for the reimbursement shall not exceed the amount of the provision. The reimbursement receivable shall be presented in the statement of financial position as an asset and shall not be offset against the provision. In the **statement of comprehensive income** (or in the **income statement**, if presented) the expense relating to a provision may be presented net of the amount recognised for a reimbursement.

Subsequent measurement

An entity shall charge against a provision only those expenditures for which the provision **21.10** was originally recognised.

An entity shall review provisions at each reporting date and adjust them to reflect the **21.11** current best estimate of the amount that would be required to settle the obligation at that reporting date. Any adjustments to the amounts previously recognised shall be recognised in **profit or loss** unless the provision was originally recognised as part of the cost of an asset (see paragraph 21.5). When a provision is measured at the present value of the amount expected to be required to settle the obligation, the unwinding of the discount shall be recognised as a finance cost in profit or loss in the period it arises.

Onerous contracts

If an entity has an **onerous contract**, the present obligation under the contract shall be **21.11A** recognised and measured as a provision (see Example 2 of the Appendix to this section).

Future operating losses

Provisions shall not be recognised for future operating losses (see Example 1 of the **21.11B** Appendix to this section).

Restructuring

A **restructuring** gives rise to a constructive obligation only when an entity: **21.11C**

(a)   has a detailed formal plan for the restructuring identifying at least:

    (i)   the business or part of a business concerned;
    (ii)   the principal locations affected;
    (iii) the location, function, and approximate number of employees who will be compensated for terminating their services;
    (iv) the expenditures that will be undertaken; and
    (v)   when the plan will be implemented; and

(b)　has raised a valid expectation in those affected that it will carry out the restructuring by starting to implement that plan or announcing its main features to those affected by it.

21.11D　An entity recognises a provision for restructuring costs only when it has a legal or constructive obligation at the reporting date to carry out the restructuring.

Contingent liabilities

21.12　A contingent liability is either a possible but uncertain obligation or a present obligation that is not recognised because it fails to meet one or both of the conditions (b) and (c) in paragraph 21.4. An entity shall not recognise a contingent liability as a liability, except for provisions for contingent liabilities of an acquiree in a **business combination** (see paragraphs 19.20 and 19.21). Disclosure of a contingent liability is required by paragraph 21.15 unless the possibility of an outflow of resources is remote. When an entity is jointly and severally liable for an obligation, the part of the obligation that is expected to be met by other parties is treated as a contingent liability.

Contingent assets

21.13　An entity shall not recognise a contingent asset as an asset. Disclosure of a contingent asset is required by paragraph 21.16 when an inflow of economic benefits is probable. However, when the flow of future economic benefits to the entity is virtually certain, then the related asset is not a contingent asset, and its recognition is appropriate.

Disclosures

Disclosures about provisions

21.14　For each class of provision, an entity shall disclose the following:

(a)　a reconciliation showing:

    (i)　the carrying amount at the beginning and end of the period;

    (ii)　additions during the period, including adjustments that result from changes in measuring the discounted amount;

    (iii)　amounts charged against the provision during the period; and

    (iv)　unused amounts reversed during the period;

(b)　a brief description of the nature of the obligation and the expected amount and timing of any resulting payments;

(c)　an indication of the uncertainties about the amount or timing of those outflows; and

(d)　the amount of any expected reimbursement, stating the amount of any asset that has been recognised for that expected reimbursement.

Comparative information for prior periods is not required.

Disclosures about contingent liabilities

21.15　Unless the possibility of any outflow of resources in settlement is remote, an entity shall disclose, for each class of contingent liability at the reporting date, a brief description of the nature of the contingent liability and, when practicable:

(a)　an estimate of its financial effect, measured in accordance with paragraphs 21.7 to 21.11;

(b)   an indication of the uncertainties relating to the amount or timing of any outflow; and

(c)   the possibility of any reimbursement.

If it is **impracticable** to make one or more of these disclosures, that fact shall be stated.

Disclosures about contingent assets

If an inflow of economic benefits is probable (more likely than not) but not virtually   **21.16**
certain, an entity shall disclose a description of the nature of the contingent assets at the
end of the reporting period, and, when practicable, an estimate of their financial effect,
measured using the principles set out in paragraphs 21.7 to 21.11. If it is impracticable to
make this disclosure, that fact shall be stated.

Prejudicial disclosures

In extremely rare cases, disclosure of some or all of the information required by   **21.17**
paragraphs 21.14 to 21.16 can be expected to prejudice seriously the position of the entity
in a dispute with other parties on the subject matter of the provision, contingent liability
or contingent asset. In such cases, an entity need not disclose the information, but shall
disclose the general nature of the dispute, together with the fact that, and reason why, the
information has not been disclosed.

Prospective amendments: Amendments to FRS 102 *The Financial Reporting Standard*
applicable in the UK and Republic of Ireland – Small entities and other minor amendments
(July 2015) amends this paragraph 21.17 with effect for annual periods beginning on or
after 1 January 2016.

Disclosure about financial guarantee contracts

An entity shall disclose the nature and business purpose of the financial guarantee   **21.17A**
contracts it has issued. If applicable, an entity shall also provide the disclosures required
by paragraphs 21.14 and 21.15.

Appendix to Section 21

Examples of recognising and measuring provisions

This appendix accompanies, but is not part of, Section 21. It provides guidance for applying
the requirements of Section 21 in recognising and measuring provisions.

All of the entities in the examples in this appendix have 31 December as their reporting
date. In all cases, it is assumed that a reliable estimate can be made of any outflows
expected. In some examples the circumstances described may have resulted in impairment
of the assets; this aspect is not dealt with in the examples. References to 'best estimate'
are to the present value amount, when the effect of the time value of money is material.

Example 1 Future operating losses

An entity determines that it is probable that a segment of its operations will incur future   **21A.1**
operating losses for several years.

Present obligation as a result of a past obligating event: There is no past event that obliges
the entity to pay out resources.

Conclusion: The entity does not recognise a provision for future operating losses. Expected future losses do not meet the definition of a liability. The expectation of future operating losses may be an indicator that one or more assets are impaired (see Section 27 *Impairment of Assets*).

Example 2 Onerous contracts

21A.2   An onerous contract is one in which the unavoidable costs of meeting the obligations under the contract exceed the economic benefits expected to be received under it. The unavoidable costs under a contract reflect the least net cost of exiting from the contract, which is the lower of the cost of fulfilling it and any compensation or penalties arising from failure to fulfil it. For example, an entity may be contractually required under an operating lease to make payments to lease an asset for which it no longer has any use.

Present obligation as a result of a past obligating event: The entity is contractually required to pay out resources for which it will not receive commensurate benefits.

Conclusion: If an entity has a contract that is onerous, the entity recognises and measures the present obligation under the contract as a provision.

Example 3 Restructurings

21A.3   [Moved to paragraph 21.11C]

Example 4 Warranties

21A.4   A manufacturer gives warranties at the time of sale to purchasers of its product. Under the terms of the contract for sale, the manufacturer undertakes to make good, by repair or replacement, manufacturing defects that become apparent within three years from the date of sale. On the basis of experience, it is probable (ie more likely than not) that there will be some claims under the warranties.

Present obligation as a result of a past obligating event: The obligating event is the sale of the product with a warranty, which gives rise to a legal obligation.

An outflow of resources embodying economic benefits in settlement: Probable for the warranties as a whole.

Conclusion: The entity recognises a provision for the best estimate of the costs of making good under the warranty products sold before the reporting date.

Illustration of calculations:

In 20X0, goods are sold for CU1,000,000. Experience indicates that 90% of products sold require no warranty repairs; 6% of products sold require minor repairs costing 30% of the sale price; and 4% of products sold require major repairs or replacement costing 70% of sale price. Therefore estimated warranty costs are:

CU1,000,000 × 90% × 0 =	CU0
CU1,000,000 × 6% × 30% =	CU18,000
CU1,000,000 × 4% × 70% =	CU28,000
Total	CU46,000

The expenditures for warranty repairs and replacements for products sold in 20X0 are expected to be made 60% in 20X1, 30% in 20X2, and 10% in 20X3, in each case at the end of the period. Because the estimated cash flows already reflect the probabilities of the cash outflows, and assuming there are no other risks or uncertainties that must be reflected, to determine the present value of those cash flows the entity uses a 'risk-free' discount rate based on government bonds with the same term as the expected cash outflows (6% for one-year bonds and 7% for two-year and three-year bonds). Calculation of the present value, at the end of 20X0, of the estimated cash flows related to the warranties for products sold in 20X0 is as follows:

Year		Expected cash payments (CU)	Discount rate	Discount factor	Present value (CU)
1	60% × CU46,000	27,600	6%	0.9434 (at 6% for 1 year)	26,038
2	30% × CU46,000	13,800	7%	0.8734 (at 7% for 2 years)	12,053
3	10% × CU46,000	4,600	7%	0.8163 (at 7% for 3 years)	3,755
Total					41,846

The entity will recognise a warranty obligation of CU41,846 at the end of 20X0 for products sold in 20X0.

Example 5 Refunds policy

21A.5

A retail store has a policy of refunding purchases by dissatisfied customers, even though it is under no legal obligation to do so. Its policy of making refunds is generally known.

Present obligation as a result of a past obligating event: The obligating event is the sale of the product, which gives rise to a constructive obligation because the conduct of the store has created a valid expectation on the part of its customers that the store will refund purchases.

An outflow of resources embodying economic benefits in settlement: Probable that a proportion of goods will be returned for refund.

Conclusion: The entity recognises a provision for the best estimate of the amount required to settle the refunds.

Example 6 Closure of a division: no implementation before end of reporting period

21A.6

On 12 December 20X0 the board of an entity decided to close down a division. Before the end of the reporting period (31 December 20X0) the decision was not communicated to any of those affected and no other steps were taken to implement the decision.

Present obligation as a result of a past obligating event: There has been no obligating event, and so there is no obligation.

Conclusion: The entity does not recognise a provision.

Example 7 Closure of a division: communication and implementation before end of reporting period

21A.7   On 12 December 20X0 the board of an entity decided to close a division making a particular product. On 20 December 20X0 a detailed plan for closing the division was agreed by the board, letters were sent to customers warning them to seek an alternative source of supply, and redundancy notices were sent to the staff of the division.

Present obligation as a result of a past obligating event: The obligating event is the communication of the decision to the customers and employees, which gives rise to a constructive obligation from that date, because it creates a valid expectation that the division will be closed.

An outflow of resources embodying economic benefits in settlement: Probable.

Conclusion: The entity recognises a provision at 31 December 20X0 for the best estimate of the costs that would be incurred to close the division at the reporting date.

Example 8 Staff retraining as a result of changes in the income tax system

21A.8   The government introduces changes to the income tax system. As a result of those changes, an entity in the financial services sector will need to retrain a large proportion of its administrative and sales workforce in order to ensure continued compliance with tax regulations. At the end of the reporting period, no retraining of staff has taken place.

Present obligation as a result of a past obligating event: The tax law change does not impose an obligation on an entity to do any retraining. An obligating event for recognising a provision (the retraining itself) has not taken place.

Conclusion: The entity does not recognise a provision.

Example 9 A court case

21A.9   A customer has sued Entity X, seeking damages for injury the customer allegedly sustained from using a product sold by Entity X. Entity X disputes liability on grounds that the customer did not follow directions in using the product. Up to the date the board authorised the financial statements for the year to 31 December 20X1 for issue, the entity's lawyers advise that it is probable that the entity will not be found liable. However, when the entity prepares the financial statements for the year to 31 December 20X2, its lawyers advise that, owing to developments in the case, it is now probable that the entity will be found liable.

(a)   At 31 December 20X1

Present obligation as a result of a past obligating event: On the basis of the evidence available when the financial statements were approved, there is no obligation as a result of past events.

Conclusion: No provision is recognised. The matter is disclosed as a contingent liability unless the probability of any outflow is regarded as remote.

(b)   At 31 December 20X2

Present obligation as a result of a past obligating event: On the basis of the evidence available, there is a present obligation. The obligating event is the sale of the product to the customer.

An outflow of resources embodying economic benefits in settlement: Probable.

Conclusion: A provision is recognised at the best estimate of the amount to settle the obligation at 31 December 20X2, and the expense is recognised in profit or loss. It is not a correction of an error in 20X1 because, on the basis of the evidence available when the 20X1 financial statements were approved, a provision should not have been recognised at that time.

Section 22 Liabilities and Equity

Scope of this section

This section establishes principles for classifying **financial instruments** as either **liabilities**   **22.1** or **equity** and deals with the accounting for **compound financial instruments**. It also addresses the issue of equity instruments and distributions to individuals or other parties acting in their capacity as investors in equity instruments (ie in their capacity as **owners**) and the accounting for purchases of own equity. This section also deals with the accounting for **non-controlling interests** in **consolidated financial statements**. Section 26 *Share-based Payment* addresses accounting for a transaction in which the entity receives goods or services (including employee services) as consideration for its equity instruments (including shares or **share options**) from employees and other vendors acting in their capacity as vendors of goods and services.

This section shall be applied to all types of financial instruments except: **22.2**

(a) Investments in **subsidiaries**, **associates** and **joint ventures** that are accounted for in accordance with Section 9 *Consolidated and Separate Financial Statements*, Section 14 *Investments in Associates* or Section 15 *Investments in Joint Ventures*.

(b) Employers' rights and obligations under employee benefit plans, to which Section 28 *Employee Benefits* applies.

(c) Contracts for contingent consideration in a **business combination** (see Section 19 *Business Combinations and Goodwill*). This exemption applies only to the acquirer.

(d) Financial instruments, contracts and obligations under **share-based payment transactions** to which Section 26 applies, except that paragraphs 22.3 to 22.6 shall be applied to **treasury shares** issued, purchased, sold, transferred or cancelled in connection with employee share option plans, employee share purchase plans, and all other share-based payment arrangements.

(e) **Insurance contracts** (including **reinsurance contracts**) that an entity issues and reinsurance contracts that it holds (see FRS 103 *Insurance Contracts*).

(f) Financial instruments with a **discretionary participation feature** that an entity issues (see FRS 103).

(g) **Financial guarantee contracts** (see Section 21 *Provisions and Contingencies*).

A reporting entity that issues the financial instruments set out in (e) and (f) or holds the financial instruments set out (e) is required by paragraph 1.6 to apply FRS 103 to those financial instruments.

Classification of an instrument as liability or equity

Equity is the residual interest in the **assets** of an entity after deducting all its liabilities.   **22.3** Equity includes investments by the owners of the entity, plus additions to those investments earned through profitable operations and retained for use in the entity's operations, minus reductions to owners' investments as a result of unprofitable operations and distributions to owners.

A **financial liability** is any liability that is:

(a)   a contractual obligation:

    (i)   to deliver **cash** or another **financial asset** to another entity; or

    (ii)   to exchange financial assets or financial liabilities with another entity under conditions that are potentially unfavourable to the entity; or

(b)   a contract that will or may be settled in the entity's own equity instruments and:

    (i)   under which the entity is or may be obliged to deliver a variable number of the entity's own equity instruments; or

    (ii)   which will or may be settled other than by the exchange of a fixed amount of cash or another financial asset for a fixed number of the entity's own equity instruments. For this purpose the entity's own equity instruments do not include instruments that are themselves contracts for the future receipt or delivery of the entity's own equity instruments.

22.3A   A financial instrument, where the issuer does not have the unconditional right to avoid settling in cash or by delivery of another financial asset (or otherwise to settle it in such a way that it would be a financial liability) and where settlement is dependent on the occurrence or non-occurrence of uncertain future events beyond the control of the issuer and the holder, is a financial liability of the issuer unless:

(a)   the part of the contingent settlement provision that could require settlement in cash or another financial asset (or otherwise in such a way that it would be a financial liability) is not genuine;

(b)   the issuer can be required to settle the obligation in cash or another financial asset (or otherwise to settle it in such a way that it would be a financial liability) only in the event of liquidation of the issuer; or

(c)   the instrument has all the features and meets the conditions in paragraph 22.4.

22.4   Some financial instruments that meet the definition of a liability are classified as equity because they represent the residual interest in the net assets of the entity:

(a)   A puttable instrument is a financial instrument that gives the holder the right to sell that instrument back to the issuer for cash or another financial asset or is automatically redeemed or repurchased by the issuer on the occurrence of an uncertain future event or the death or retirement of the instrument holder. A puttable instrument that has all of the following features is classified as an equity instrument:

    (i)   It entitles the holder to a pro rata share of the entity's net assets in the event of the entity's liquidation. The entity's net assets are those assets that remain after deducting all other claims on its assets.

    (ii)   The instrument is in the class of instruments that is subordinate to all other classes of instruments.

    (iii)   All financial instruments in the class of instruments that is subordinate to all other classes of instruments have identical features.

    (iv)   Apart from the contractual obligation for the issuer to repurchase or redeem the instrument for cash or another financial asset, the instrument does not include any contractual obligation to deliver cash or another financial asset to another entity, or to exchange financial assets or financial liabilities with another entity under conditions that are potentially unfavourable to the entity, and it is not a contract that will or may be settled in the entity's own equity instruments as set out in paragraph 22.3(b) of the definition of a financial liability.

    (v)   The total expected **cash flows** attributable to the instrument over the life of the instrument are based substantially on the **profit or loss**, the change in the recognised net assets or the change in the **fair value** of the recognised and unrecognised net assets of the entity over the life of the instrument (excluding any effects of the instrument).

(b)   Instruments, or components of instruments, that are subordinate to all other classes of instruments are classified as equity if they impose on the entity an obligation to deliver to another party a pro rata share of the net assets of the entity only on liquidation.

The following are examples of instruments that are either classified as liabilities or equity: **22.5**

(a)   An instrument of the type described in paragraph 22.4(b) is classified as a liability if the distribution of net assets on liquidation is subject to a maximum amount (a ceiling). For example, if on liquidation the holders of the instrument receive a pro rata share of the net assets, but this amount is limited to a ceiling and the excess net assets are distributed to a charity organisation or the government, the instrument is not classified as equity.

(b)   A puttable instrument is classified as equity if, when the put option is exercised, the holder receives a pro rata share of the net assets of the entity determined by:

  (i)   dividing the entity's net assets on liquidation into units of equal amounts; and

  (ii)   multiplying that amount by the number of the units held by the financial instrument holder.

However, if the holder is entitled to an amount measured on some other basis the instrument is classified as a liability.

(c)   An instrument is classified as a liability if it obliges the entity to make payments to the holder before liquidation, such as a mandatory dividend.

(d)   A puttable instrument that is classified as equity in a subsidiary's **financial statements** is classified as a liability in the consolidated financial statements.

(e)   A preference share that provides for mandatory redemption by the issuer for a fixed or determinable amount at a fixed or determinable future date, or gives the holder the right to require the issuer to redeem the instrument at or after a particular date for a fixed or determinable amount, is a financial liability.

Members' shares in co-operative entities and similar instruments are equity if: **22.6**

(a)   the entity has an unconditional right to refuse redemption of the members' shares; or

(b)   redemption is unconditionally prohibited by local law, regulation or the entity's governing charter.

Original issue of shares or other equity instruments

An entity shall recognise the issue of shares or other equity instruments as equity when it   **22.7**
issues those instruments and another party is obliged to provide cash or other resources to the entity in exchange for the instruments.

(a)   [Not used]

(b)   If the entity receives the cash or other resources before the equity instruments are issued, and the entity cannot be required to repay the cash or other resources received, the entity shall recognise the corresponding increase in equity to the extent of consideration received.

(c)   To the extent that the equity instruments have been subscribed for but not issued (or called up), and the entity has not yet received the cash or other resources, the entity shall not recognise an increase in equity.

An entity shall measure the equity instruments at the fair value of the cash or other resources   **22.8**
received or receivable, net of direct costs of issuing the equity instruments. If payment is deferred and the time value of money is **material**, the initial **measurement** shall be on a **present value** basis.

22.9 An entity shall account for the **transaction costs** of an equity transaction as a deduction from equity, net of any related income tax benefit.

22.10 How the increase in equity arising on the issue of shares or other equity instruments is presented in the **statement of financial position** is determined by applicable laws. For example, the par value (or other nominal value) of shares and the amount paid in excess of par value may be presented separately.

Exercise of options, rights and warrants

22.11 An entity shall apply the principles in paragraphs 22.7 to 22.10 to equity issued by means of exercise of options, rights, warrants and similar equity instruments.

Capitalisation or bonus issues of shares and share splits

22.12 A capitalisation or bonus issue (sometimes referred to as a stock dividend) is the issue of new shares to shareholders in proportion to their existing holdings. For example, an entity may give its shareholders one dividend or bonus share for every five shares held. A share split (sometimes referred to as a stock split) is the dividing of an entity's existing shares into multiple shares. For example, in a share split, each shareholder may receive one additional share for each share held. In some cases, the previously outstanding shares are cancelled and replaced by new shares. Capitalisation and bonus issues and share splits do not change total equity. An entity shall reclassify amounts within equity as required by applicable laws.

Convertible debt or similar compound financial instruments

22.13 On issuing convertible debt or similar compound financial instruments that contain both a liability and an equity component, an entity shall allocate the proceeds between the liability component and the equity component. To make the allocation, the entity shall first determine the amount of the liability component as the fair value of a similar liability that does not have a conversion feature or similar associated equity component. The entity shall allocate the residual amount as the equity component. Transaction costs shall be allocated between the debt component and the equity component on the basis of their relative fair values.

22.14 The entity shall not revise the allocation in a subsequent period.

22.15 In periods after the instruments were issued, the entity shall account for the liability component as a financial instrument in accordance with Section 11 *Basic Financial Instruments* or Section 12 *Other Financial Instruments Issues* as appropriate. The appendix to this section illustrates the issuer's accounting for convertible debt where the liability component is a basic financial instrument.

Treasury shares

22.16 Treasury shares are the equity instruments of an entity that have been issued and subsequently reacquired by the entity. An entity shall deduct from equity the fair value of the consideration given for the treasury shares. The entity shall not recognise a **gain** or loss in profit or loss on the purchase, sale, transfer or cancellation of treasury shares.

Distributions to owners

An entity shall reduce equity for the amount of distributions to its owners (holders of its **22.17** equity instruments).

An entity shall disclose the fair value of any non-cash assets that have been distributed to **22.18** its owners during the **reporting period**, except when the non-cash assets are ultimately controlled by the same parties both before and after the distribution.

Non-controlling interest and transactions in shares of a consolidated subsidiary

In the consolidated financial statements, a non-controlling interest in the net assets of **22.19** a subsidiary is included in equity. An entity shall treat changes in a parent's controlling interest in a subsidiary that do not result in a loss of **control** as transactions with equity holders in their capacity as equity holders. Accordingly, the **carrying amount** of the non-controlling interest shall be adjusted to reflect the change in the parent's interest in the subsidiary's net assets. Any difference between the amount by which the non-controlling interest is so adjusted and the fair value of the consideration paid or received, if any, shall be recognised directly in equity and attributed to equity holders of the parent. An entity shall not recognise a gain or loss on these changes. Also, an entity shall not recognise any change in the carrying amounts of assets (including goodwill) or liabilities as a result of such transactions.

Appendix to Section 22

Example of the issuer's accounting for convertible debt

The appendix accompanies, but is not part of, Section 22. It provides guidance for applying the requirements of paragraphs 22.13 to 22.15.

On 1 January 20X5 an entity issues 500 convertible bonds. The bonds are issued at par with a face value of CU100 per bond and are for a five-year term, with no transaction costs. The total proceeds from the issue are CU50,000. Interest is payable annually in arrears at an annual interest rate of 4%. Each bond is convertible, at the holder's discretion, into 25 ordinary shares at any time up to maturity. At the time the bonds are issued, the market interest rate for similar debt that does not have the conversion option is 6%.

When the instrument is issued, the liability component must be valued first, and the difference between the total proceeds on issue (which is the fair value of the instrument in its entirety) and the fair value of the liability component is assigned to the equity component. The fair value of the liability component is calculated by determining its present value using the discount rate of 6%. The calculations and journal entries are illustrated below:

	CU
Proceeds from the bond issue (A)	50,000
Present value of principal at the end of five years (see calculations below)	37,363
Present value of interest payable annually in arrears for five years	8,425
Present value of liability, which is the fair value of liability component (B)	45,788
Residual, which is the fair value of the equity component (A) – (B)	4,212

The issuer of the bonds makes the following journal entry at issue on 1 January 20X5:

Dr	Cash	CU50,000	
Cr	Financial Liability – Convertible bond		CU45,788
Cr	Equity		CU4,212

The CU4,212 represents a discount on issue of the bonds, so the entry could also be shown 'gross':

Dr	Cash	CU50,000	
Dr	Financial Liability – Convertible bond discount	CU4,212	
Cr	Financial Liability – Convertible bond		CU50,000
Cr	Equity		CU4,212

After issue, the issuer will amortise the bond discount according to the following table:

	(a) Interest payment	(b) Total interest expense = 6% × (e)	(c) Amortisation of bond discount = (b) – (a)	(d) Bond discount = (d) – (c)	(e) Net liability = 50,000 – (d)
	CU	CU	CU	CU	CU
1/1/20X5				4,212	45,788
31/12/20X5	2,000	2,747	747	3,465	46,535
31/12/20X6	2,000	2,792	792	2,673	47,327
31/12/20X7	2,000	2,840	840	1,833	48,167
31/12/20X8	2,000	2,890	890	943	49,057
31/12/20X9	2,000	2,943	943	0	50,000
Totals	10,000	14,212	4,212		

At the end of 20X5, the issuer would make the following journal entry:

Dr	Interest expense	CU2,747	
Cr	Bond discount		CU747
Cr	Cash		CU2,000

Calculations

Present value of principal of CU50,000 at 6%

$CU50,000/(1.06)^5 = 37,363$

Present value of the interest annuity of CU2,000 (= CU50,000 × 4%) payable at the end of each of five years

The CU2,000 annual interest payments are an annuity: a cash flow stream with a limited number (n) of periodic payments (C), receivable at dates 1 to n. To calculate the present value of this annuity, future payments are discounted by the periodic rate of interest (i) using the following formula:

$$PV = C/i \times [1 - 1/(1 + i)^n]$$

Therefore, the present value of the CU2,000 interest payments is $(2,000/.06) \times [1 - [(1/1.06)^5] = 8,425$

This is equivalent to the sum of the present values of the five individual CU2,000 payments, as follows:

	CU
Present value of interest payment at 31 December 20X5 = 2,000/1.06	1,887
Present value of interest payment at 31 December 20X6 = $2,000/1.06^2$	1,780
Present value of interest payment at 31 December 20X7 = $2,000/1.06^3$	1,679
Present value of interest payment at 31 December 20X8 = $2,000/1.06^4$	1,584
Present value of interest payment at 31 December 20X9 = $2,000/1.06^5$	1,495
Total	8,425

Yet another way to calculate this is to use a table of present value of an ordinary annuity in arrears, five periods, interest rate of 6% per period. (Such tables are easily found on the Internet.) The present value factor is 4.2124. Multiplying this by the annuity payment of CU2,000 determines the present value of CU8,425.

Section 23 Revenue

Scope of this section

This section shall be applied in accounting for **revenue** arising from the following transactions and events: **23.1**

(a) the sale of goods (whether produced by the entity for the purpose of sale or purchased for resale);
(b) the rendering of services;
(c) **construction contracts** in which the entity is the contractor; and
(d) the use by others of entity assets yielding interest, royalties or dividends.

Revenue or other income arising from some transactions and events is dealt with in other sections of this FRS: **23.2**

(a) lease agreements (see Section 20 *Leases*);
(b) dividends and other income arising from investments that are accounted for using the equity method (see Section 14 *Investments in Associates* and Section 15 *Investments in Joint Ventures*);
(c) changes in the **fair value** of **financial assets** and **financial liabilities** or their disposal (see Section 11 *Basic Financial Instruments* and Section 12 *Other Financial Instruments Issues*);
(d) changes in the fair value of **investment property** (see Section 16 *Investment Property*);
(e) initial **recognition** and changes in the fair value of **biological assets** related to **agricultural activity** (see Section 34 *Specialised Activities*); and
(f) initial recognition of **agricultural produce** (see Section 34).

This section excludes revenue or other income arising from transactions and events dealt with in FRS 103 *Insurance Contracts*.   **23.2A**

Measurement of revenue

23.3 An entity shall measure revenue at the fair value of the consideration received or receivable. The fair value of the consideration received or receivable takes into account the amount of any trade discounts, prompt settlement discounts and volume rebates allowed by the entity.

23.4 An entity shall include in revenue only the gross inflows of economic benefits received and receivable by the entity on its own account. An entity shall exclude from revenue all amounts collected on behalf of third parties such as sales taxes, goods and services taxes and value added taxes. In an agency relationship, an entity (the **agent**) shall include in revenue only the amount of its commission. The amounts collected on behalf of the principal are not revenue of the entity.

Deferred payment

23.5 When the inflow of **cash** or **cash equivalents** is deferred, and the arrangement constitutes in effect a financing transaction, the fair value of the consideration is the **present value** of all future receipts determined using an **imputed rate of interest**. A financing transaction arises when, for example, an entity provides interest-free credit to the buyer or accepts a note receivable bearing a below-market interest rate from the buyer as consideration for the sale of goods. The imputed rate of interest is the more clearly determinable of either:

(a) the prevailing rate for a similar instrument of an issuer with a similar credit rating; or

(b) a rate of interest that discounts the nominal amount of the instrument to the current cash sales price of the goods or services.

An entity shall recognise the difference between the present value of all future receipts and the nominal amount of the consideration as interest revenue in accordance with paragraphs 23.28 and 23.29 and Section 11.

Exchanges of goods or services

23.6 An entity shall not recognise revenue:

(a) when goods or services are exchanged for goods or services that are of a similar nature and value; or

(b) when goods or services are exchanged for dissimilar goods or services but the transaction lacks commercial substance.

23.7 An entity shall recognise revenue when goods are sold or services are exchanged for dissimilar goods or services in a transaction that has commercial substance. In that case, the entity shall measure the transaction:

(a) at the fair value of the goods or services received adjusted by the amount of any cash or cash equivalents transferred;

(b) if the amount under (a) cannot be measured reliably, then at the fair value of the goods or services given up adjusted by the amount of any cash or cash equivalents transferred; or

(c) if the fair value of neither the goods or services received nor the goods or services given up can be measured reliably, then at the **carrying amount** of the goods or services given up adjusted by the amount of any cash or cash equivalents transferred.

Identification of the revenue transaction

23.8 An entity usually applies the revenue recognition criteria in this section separately to each transaction. However, an entity applies the recognition criteria to the separately identifiable components of a single transaction when necessary to reflect the substance of the transaction. For example, an entity applies the recognition criteria to the separately identifiable components of a single transaction when the selling price of a product includes an identifiable amount for subsequent servicing. Conversely, an entity applies the recognition criteria to two or more transactions together when they are linked in such a way that the commercial effect cannot be understood without reference to the series of transactions as a whole. For example, an entity applies the recognition criteria to two or more transactions together when it sells goods and, at the same time, enters into a separate agreement to repurchase the goods at a later date, thus negating the substantive effect of the transaction.

Sometimes, as part of a sales transaction, an entity grants its customer a loyalty award that the customer may redeem in the future for free or discounted goods or services. In this case, in accordance with paragraph 23.8, the entity shall account for the award credits as a separately identifiable component of the initial sales transaction. The entity shall allocate the fair value of the consideration received or receivable in respect of the initial sale between the award credits and the other components of the sale. The consideration allocated to the award credits shall be measured by reference to their fair value, ie the amount for which the award credits could be sold separately. **23.9**

Sale of goods

An entity shall recognise revenue from the sale of goods when all the following conditions are satisfied: **23.10**

(a) the entity has transferred to the buyer the significant risks and rewards of ownership of the goods;

(b) the entity retains neither continuing managerial involvement to the degree usually associated with ownership nor effective control over the goods sold;

(c) the amount of revenue can be measured reliably;

(d) it is **probable** that the economic benefits associated with the transaction will flow to the entity; and

(e) the costs incurred or to be incurred in respect of the transaction can be measured reliably.

The assessment of when an entity has transferred the significant risks and rewards of ownership to the buyer requires an examination of the circumstances of the transaction. In most cases, the transfer of the risks and rewards of ownership coincides with the transfer of the legal title or the passing of possession to the buyer. This is the case for most retail sales. In other cases, the transfer of risks and rewards of ownership occurs at a time different from the transfer of legal title or the passing of possession. **23.11**

An entity does not recognise revenue if it retains significant risks and rewards of ownership. Examples of situations in which the entity may retain the significant risks and rewards of ownership are: **23.12**

(a) when the entity retains an obligation for unsatisfactory performance not covered by normal warranties;

(b) when the receipt of the revenue from a particular sale is contingent on the buyer selling the goods;

(c) when the goods are shipped subject to installation and the installation is a significant part of the contract that has not yet been completed; and

(d) when the buyer has the right to rescind the purchase for a reason specified in the sales contract, or at the buyer's sole discretion without any reason, and the entity is uncertain about the probability of return.

23.13   If an entity retains only an insignificant risk of ownership, the transaction is a sale and the entity recognises the revenue. For example, a seller recognises revenue when it retains the legal title to the goods solely to protect the collectability of the amount due. Similarly an entity recognises revenue when it offers a refund if the customer finds the goods faulty or is not satisfied for other reasons, and the entity can estimate the returns reliably. In such cases, the entity recognises a **provision** for returns in accordance with Section 21 *Provisions and Contingencies.*

Rendering of services

23.14   When the outcome of a transaction involving the rendering of services can be estimated reliably, an entity shall recognise revenue associated with the transaction by reference to the stage of completion of the transaction at the end of the **reporting period** (sometimes referred to as the percentage of completion method). The outcome of a transaction can be estimated reliably when all the following conditions are satisfied:

(a)   the amount of revenue can be measured reliably;

(b)   it is probable that the economic benefits associated with the transaction will flow to the entity;

(c)   the stage of completion of the transaction at the end of the reporting period can be measured reliably; and

(d)   the costs incurred for the transaction and the costs to complete the transaction can be measured reliably.

Paragraphs 23.21 to 23.27 provide guidance for applying the percentage of completion method.

23.15   When services are performed by an indeterminate number of acts over a specified period of time, an entity recognises revenue on a straight-line basis over the specified period unless there is evidence that some other method better represents the stage of completion. When a specific act is much more significant than any other act, the entity postpones recognition of revenue until the significant act is executed.

23.16   When the outcome of the transaction involving the rendering of services cannot be estimated reliably, an entity shall recognise revenue only to the extent of the **expenses** recognised that are recoverable.

Construction contracts

23.17   When the outcome of a construction contract can be estimated reliably, an entity shall recognise contract revenue and contract costs associated with the construction contract as revenue and expenses respectively by reference to the stage of completion of the contract activity at the end of the reporting period (often referred to as the percentage of completion method). Reliable estimation of the outcome requires reliable estimates of the stage of completion, future costs and collectability of billings. Paragraphs 23.21 to 23.27 provide guidance for applying the percentage of completion method.

23.18   When a contract covers a number of **assets**, the construction of each asset shall be treated as a separate construction contract when:

(a)   separate proposals have been submitted for each asset;

(b)   each asset has been subject to separate negotiation, and the contractor and customer are able to accept or reject that part of the contract relating to each asset; and

(c)   the costs and revenues of each asset can be identified.

A group of contracts, whether with a single customer or with several customers, shall be treated as a single construction contract when: **23.20**

(a)   the group of contracts is negotiated as a single package;

(b)   the contracts are so closely interrelated that they are, in effect, part of a single project with an overall profit margin; and

(c)   the contracts are performed concurrently or in a continuous sequence.

Percentage of completion method

This method is used to recognise revenue from rendering services (see paragraphs 23.14 to 23.16) and from construction contracts (see paragraphs 23.17 to 23.20). An entity shall review and, when necessary, revise the estimates of revenue and costs as the service transaction or construction contract progresses.   **23.21**

An entity shall determine the stage of completion of a transaction or contract using the method that measures most reliably the work performed. Possible methods include: **23.22**

(a)   the proportion that costs incurred for work performed to date bear to the estimated total costs. Costs incurred for work performed to date do not include costs relating to future activity, such as for materials or prepayments;

(b)   surveys of work performed; and

(c)   completion of a physical proportion of the contract work or the completion of a proportion of the service contract.

Progress payments and advances received from customers often do not reflect the work performed.

An entity shall recognise costs that relate to future activity on the transaction or contract, such as for materials or prepayments, as an asset if it is probable that the costs will be recovered.   **23.23**

An entity shall recognise as an expense immediately any costs whose recovery is not probable.   **23.24**

When the outcome of a construction contract cannot be estimated reliably: **23.25**

(a)   an entity shall recognise revenue only to the extent of contract costs incurred that it is probable will be recoverable; and

(b)   the entity shall recognise contract costs as an expense in the period in which they are incurred.

When it is probable that total contract costs will exceed total contract revenue on a construction contract, the expected loss shall be recognised as an expense immediately, with a corresponding provision for an **onerous contract** (see Section 21).   **23.26**

If the collectability of an amount already recognised as contract revenue is no longer probable, the entity shall recognise the uncollectible amount as an expense rather than as an adjustment of the amount of contract revenue.   **23.27**

Interest, royalties and dividends

23.28 An entity shall recognise revenue arising from the use by others of entity assets yielding interest, royalties and dividends on the bases set out in paragraph 23.29 when:

(a)   it is probable that the economic benefits associated with the transaction will flow to the entity; and

(b)   the amount of the revenue can be measured reliably.

23.29 An entity shall recognise revenue on the following bases:

(a)   Interest shall be recognised using the **effective interest method** as described in paragraphs 11.15 to 11.20. When calculating the **effective interest rate**, an entity shall include any related fees, finance charges paid or received (such as 'points'), **transaction costs** and other premiums or discounts.

(b)   Royalties shall be recognised on an **accrual basis** in accordance with the substance of the relevant agreement.

(c)   Dividends shall be recognised when the shareholder's right to receive payment is established.

Disclosures

General disclosures about revenue

23.30 An entity shall disclose:

(a)   the **accounting policies** adopted for the recognition of revenue, including the methods adopted to determine the stage of completion of transactions involving the rendering of services; and

(b)   the amount of each category of revenue recognised during the period, showing separately, at a minimum, revenue arising from:

(i)   the sale of goods;
(ii)   the rendering of services;
(iii) interest;
(iv)   royalties;
(v)   dividends;
(vi)   commissions;
(vii) grants; and
(viii) any other significant types of revenue.

Disclosures relating to revenue from construction contracts

23.31 An entity shall disclose the following:

(a)   the amount of contract revenue recognised as revenue in the period;
(b)   the methods used to determine the contract revenue recognised in the period; and
(c)   the methods used to determine the stage of completion of contracts in progress.

23.32 An entity shall present:

(a)   the gross amount due from customers for contract work, as an asset; and
(b)   the gross amount due to customers for contract work, as a **liability**.

Appendix to Section 23

Examples of revenue recognition under the principles in Section 23

This appendix accompanies, but is not part of, Section 23. It provides guidance for applying the requirements of Section 23 in recognising revenue.

The following examples focus on particular aspects of a transaction and are not a comprehensive discussion of all the relevant factors that might influence the recognition of revenue. The examples generally assume that the amount of revenue can be measured reliably, it is probable that the economic benefits will flow to the entity and the costs incurred or to be incurred can be measured reliably.   **23A.1**

Sale of goods

The law in different countries may cause the recognition criteria in Section 23 to be met at different times. In particular, the law may determine the point in time at which the entity transfers the significant risks and rewards of ownership. Therefore, the examples in this appendix need to be read in the context of the laws relating to the sale of goods in the country in which the transaction takes place.   **23A.2**

Example 1 'Bill and hold' sales, in which delivery is delayed at the buyer's request but the buyer takes title and accepts billing

The seller recognises revenue when the buyer takes title, provided: **23A.3**

(a)   it is probable that delivery will be made;
(b)   the item is on hand, identified and ready for delivery to the buyer at the time the sale is recognised;
(c)   the buyer specifically acknowledges the deferred delivery instructions; and
(d)   the usual payment terms apply.

Revenue is not recognised when there is simply an intention to acquire or manufacture the goods in time for delivery.

Example 2 Goods shipped subject to conditions: installation and inspection

The seller normally recognises revenue when the buyer accepts delivery, and installation and inspection are complete. However, revenue is recognised immediately upon the buyer's acceptance of delivery when: **23A.4**

(a)   the installation process is simple, for example the installation of a factory-tested television receiver that requires only unpacking and connection of power and antennae; or
(b)   the inspection is performed only for the purposes of final determination of contract prices, for example, shipments of iron ore, sugar or soya beans.

Example 3 Goods shipped subject to conditions: on approval when the buyer has negotiated a limited right of return

If there is uncertainty about the possibility of return, the seller recognises revenue when the shipment has been formally accepted by the buyer or the goods have been delivered and the time period for rejection has elapsed.   **23A.5**

Example 4 Goods shipped subject to conditions: consignment sales under which the recipient (buyer) undertakes to sell the goods on behalf of the shipper (seller)

23A.6   The shipper recognises revenue when the goods are sold by the recipient to a third party.

Example 5 Goods shipped subject to conditions: cash on delivery sales

23A.7   The seller recognises revenue when delivery is made and cash is received by the seller or its agent.

Example 6 Layaway sales under which the goods are delivered only when the buyer makes the final payment in a series of instalments

23A.8   The seller recognises revenue from such sales when the goods are delivered. However, when experience indicates that most such sales are consummated, revenue may be recognised when a significant deposit is received, provided the goods are on hand, identified and ready for delivery to the buyer.

Example 7 Orders when payment (or partial payment) is received in advance of delivery for goods not currently held in inventory, for example, the goods are still to be manufactured or will be delivered direct to the buyer from a third party

23A.9   The seller recognises revenue when the goods are delivered to the buyer.

Example 8 Sale and repurchase agreements (other than swap transactions) under which the seller concurrently agrees to repurchase the same goods at a later date, or when the seller has a call option to repurchase, or the buyer has a put option to require the repurchase, by the seller, of the goods

23A.10   For a sale and repurchase agreement on an asset other than a financial asset, the seller must analyse the terms of the agreement to ascertain whether, in substance, the risks and rewards of ownership have been transferred to the buyer. If they have been transferred, the seller recognises revenue. When the seller has retained the risks and rewards of ownership, even though legal title has been transferred, the transaction is a financing arrangement and does not give rise to revenue. For a sale and repurchase agreement on a financial asset, the derecognition provisions of Section 11 apply.

Example 9 Sales to intermediate parties, such as distributors, dealers or others for resale

23A.11   The seller generally recognises revenue from such sales when the risks and rewards of ownership have been transferred. However, when the buyer is acting, in substance, as an agent, the sale is treated as a consignment sale.

Example 10 Subscriptions to publications and similar items

23A.12   When the items involved are of similar value in each time period, the seller recognises revenue on a straight-line basis over the period in which the items are dispatched. When the items vary in value from period to period, the seller recognises revenue on the basis of the sales value of the item dispatched in relation to the total estimated sales value of all items covered by the subscription.

Example 11 Instalment sales, under which the consideration is receivable in instalments

The seller recognises revenue attributable to the sales price, exclusive of interest, at the date of sale. The sale price is the present value of the consideration, determined by discounting the instalments receivable at the imputed rate of interest. The seller recognises the interest element as revenue using the effective interest method.   **23A.13**

Example 12 Agreements for the construction of real estate

An entity that undertakes the construction of real estate, directly or through subcontractors, and enters into an agreement with one or more buyers before construction is complete, shall account for the agreement using the percentage of completion method, only if: **23A.14**

(a) the buyer is able to specify the major structural elements of the design of the real estate before construction begins and/or specify major structural changes once construction is in progress (whether it exercises that ability or not); or

(b) the buyer acquires and supplies construction materials and the entity provides only construction services.

If the entity is required to provide services together with construction materials in order to perform its contractual obligation to deliver real estate to the buyer, the agreement shall be accounted for as the sale of goods. In this case, the buyer does not obtain control or the significant risks and rewards of ownership of the work in progress in its current state as construction progresses. Rather, the transfer occurs only on delivery of the completed real estate to the buyer.   **23A.15**

Example 13 Sale with customer loyalty award

An entity sells product A for CU100. Purchasers of product A get an award credit enabling them to buy product B for CU10. The normal selling price of product B is CU18. The entity estimates that 40% of the purchasers of product A will use their award to buy product B at CU10. The normal selling price of product A, after taking into account discounts that are usually offered but that are not available during this promotion, is CU95.   **23A.16**

The fair value of the award credit is 40% × [CU18 − CU10] = CU3.20. The entity allocates the total revenue of CU100 between product A and the award credit by reference to their relative fair values of CU95 and CU3.20 respectively. Therefore: **23A.17**

(a) Revenue for product A is CU100 × [CU95 / (CU95 + CU3.20)] = CU96.74

(b) Revenue for product B is CU100 × [CU3.20 / (CU95 + CU3.20)] = CU3.26

Rendering of services

Example 14 Installation fees

The seller recognises installation fees as revenue by reference to the stage of completion of the installation, unless they are incidental to the sale of a product, in which case they are recognised when the goods are sold.   **23A.18**

Example 15 Servicing fees included in the price of the product

When the selling price of a product includes an identifiable amount for subsequent servicing (eg after sales support and product enhancement on the sale of software), the seller defers that amount and recognises it as revenue over the period during which the service is performed. The amount deferred is that which will cover the expected costs of the services under the agreement, together with a reasonable profit on those services.   **23A.19**

Example 16 Advertising commissions

23A.20   Media commissions are recognised when the related advertisement or commercial appears before the public. Production commissions are recognised by reference to the stage of completion of the project.

Example 17 Insurance agency commissions

23A.21   Insurance agency commissions received or receivable that do not require the agent to render further service are recognised as revenue by the agent on the effective commencement or renewal dates of the related policies. However, when it is probable that the agent will be required to render further services during the life of the policy, the agent defers the commission, or part of it, and recognises it as revenue over the period during which the policy is in force.

Example 17A Financial services fees

23A.21A   The recognition of revenue for financial service fees depends on the purposes for which the fees are assessed and the basis of accounting for any associated financial instrument. The description of fees for financial services may not be indicative of the nature and substance of the services provided. Therefore it is necessary to distinguish between fees that are an integral part of the effective interest rate of a financial instrument, fees that are earned as services are provided, and fees that are earned on the execution of a significant act.

Example 18 Admission fees

23A.22   The seller recognises revenue from artistic performances, banquets and other special events when the event takes place. When a subscription to a number of events is sold, the seller allocates the fee to each event on a basis that reflects the extent to which services are performed at each event.

Example 19 Tuition fees

23A.23   The seller recognises revenue over the period of instruction.

Example 20 Initiation, entrance and membership fees

23A.24   Revenue recognition depends on the nature of the services provided. If the fee permits only membership, and all other services or products are paid for separately, or if there is a separate annual subscription, the fee is recognised as revenue when no significant uncertainty about its collectability exists. If the fee entitles the member to services or publications to be provided during the membership period, or to purchase goods or services at prices lower than those charged to non-members, it is recognised on a basis that reflects the timing, nature and value of the benefits provided.

Franchise fees

23A.25   Franchise fees may cover the supply of initial and subsequent services, equipment and other tangible assets, and know-how. Accordingly, franchise fees are recognised as revenue on a basis that reflects the purpose for which the fees were charged. The following methods of franchise fee recognition are appropriate.

Example 21 Franchise fees: Supplies of equipment and other tangible assets

23A.26   The franchisor recognises the fair value of the assets sold as revenue when the items are delivered or title passes.

Example 22 Franchise fees: Supplies of initial and subsequent services

The franchisor recognises fees for the provision of continuing services, whether part of the initial fee or a separate fee, as revenue as the services are rendered. When the separate fee does not cover the cost of continuing services together with a reasonable profit, part of the initial fee, sufficient to cover the costs of continuing services and to provide a reasonable profit on those services, is deferred and recognised as revenue as the services are rendered.   23A.27

The franchise agreement may provide for the franchisor to supply equipment, inventories, or other tangible assets at a price lower than that charged to others or a price that does not provide a reasonable profit on those sales. In these circumstances, part of the initial fee, sufficient to cover estimated costs in excess of that price and to provide a reasonable profit on those sales, is deferred and recognised over the period the goods are likely to be sold to the franchisee. The balance of an initial fee is recognised as revenue when performance of all the initial services and other obligations required of the franchisor (such as assistance with site selection, staff training, financing and advertising) has been substantially accomplished.   23A.28

The initial services and other obligations under an area franchise agreement may depend on the number of individual outlets established in the area. In this case, the fees attributable to the initial services are recognised as revenue in proportion to the number of outlets for which the initial services have been substantially completed.   23A.29

If the initial fee is collectible over an extended period and there is a significant uncertainty that it will be collected in full, the fee is recognised as cash instalments are received.   23A.30

Example 23 Franchise fees: Continuing franchise fees

Fees charged for the use of continuing rights granted by the agreement, or for other services provided during the period of the agreement, are recognised as revenue as the services are provided or the rights used.   23A.31

Example 24 Franchise fees: Agency transactions

Transactions may take place between the franchisor and the franchisee that, in substance, involve the franchisor acting as agent for the franchisee. For example, the franchisor may order supplies and arrange for their delivery to the franchisee at no profit. Such transactions do not give rise to revenue.   23A.32

Example 25 Fees from the development of customised software

The software developer recognises fees from the development of customised software as revenue by reference to the stage of completion of the development, including completion of services provided for post-delivery service support.   23A.33

Interest, royalties and dividends

Example 26 Licence fees and royalties

The licensor recognises fees and royalties paid for the use of an entity's assets (such as trademarks, patents, software, music copyright, record masters and motion picture films) in accordance with the substance of the agreement. As a practical matter, this may be on a straight-line basis over the life of the agreement, for example, when a licensee has the right to use specified technology for a specified period of time.   23A.34

23A.35 An assignment of rights for a fixed fee or non-refundable guarantee under a non-cancellable contract that permits the licensee to exploit those rights freely and the licensor has no remaining obligations to perform is, in substance, a sale. An example is a licensing agreement for the use of software when the licensor has no obligations after delivery. Another example is the granting of rights to exhibit a motion picture film in markets in which the licensor has no control over the distributor and expects to receive no further revenues from the box office receipts. In such cases, revenue is recognised at the time of sale.

23A.36 In some cases, whether or not a licence fee or royalty will be received is contingent on the occurrence of a future event. In such cases, revenue is recognised only when it is probable that the fee or royalty will be received, which is normally when the event has occurred.

Section 24 Government Grants

Scope of this section

24.1 This section specifies the accounting for all **government grants**. A government grant is assistance by government in the form of a transfer of resources to an entity in return for past or future compliance with specified conditions relating to the **operating activities** of the entity.

24.2 Government grants exclude those forms of government assistance that cannot reasonably have a value placed upon them and transactions with government that cannot be distinguished from the normal trading transactions of the entity.

24.3 This section does not cover government assistance that is provided for an entity in the form of benefits that are available in determining **taxable profit (tax loss)**, or are determined or limited on the basis of income tax liability. Examples of such benefits are income tax holidays, investment tax credits, accelerated depreciation allowances and reduced income tax rates. Section 29 *Income Tax* covers accounting for taxes based on **income**.

Recognition and measurement

24.3A Government grants, including non-monetary grants shall not be recognised until there is reasonable assurance that:

    (a)   the entity will comply with the conditions attaching to them; and

    (b)   the grants will be received.

24.4 An entity shall recognise grants either based on the performance model or the accrual model. This policy choice shall be applied on a class-by-class basis.

24.5 An entity shall measure grants at the **fair value** of the **asset** received or receivable.

24.5A Where a grant becomes repayable it shall be recognised as a **liability** when the repayment meets the definition of a liability.

Performance model

24.5B An entity applying the performance model shall recognise grants as follows:

    (a)   A grant that does not impose specified future **performance-related conditions** on the recipient is recognised in income when the grant proceeds are received or receivable.

(b)   A grant that imposes specified future performance-related conditions on the recipient is recognised in income only when the performance-related conditions are met.

(c)   Grants received before the **revenue recognition** criteria are satisfied are recognised as a liability.

Accrual model

An entity applying the accrual model shall classify grants either as a grant relating to revenue or a grant relating to assets.

24.5C

Grants relating to revenue shall be recognised in income on a systematic basis over the periods in which the entity recognises the related costs for which the grant is intended to compensate.

24.5D

A grant that becomes receivable as compensation for **expenses** or losses already incurred or for the purpose of giving immediate financial support to the entity with no future related costs shall be recognised in income in the period in which it becomes receivable.

24.5E

Grants relating to assets shall be recognised in income on a systematic basis over the expected **useful life** of the asset.

24.5F

Where part of a grant relating to an asset is deferred it shall be recognised as deferred income and not deducted from the **carrying amount** of the asset.

24.5G

Disclosures

An entity shall disclose the following:

24.6

(a)   the **accounting policy** adopted for grants in accordance with paragraph 24.4;
(b)   the nature and amounts of grants recognised in the **financial statements**;
(c)   unfulfilled conditions and other contingencies attaching to grants that have been recognised in income; and
(d)   an indication of other forms of government assistance from which the entity has directly benefited.

For the purpose of the disclosure required by paragraph 24.6(d), government assistance is action by government designed to provide an economic benefit specific to an entity or range of entities qualifying under specified criteria. Examples include free technical or marketing advice, the provision of guarantees, and loans at nil or low interest rates.

24.7

Section 25 Borrowing Costs

Scope of this section

This section specifies the accounting for **borrowing costs**. Borrowing costs are interest and other costs that an entity incurs in connection with the borrowing of funds. Borrowing costs include:

25.1

(a)   interest expense calculated using the **effective interest method** as described in Section 11 *Basic Financial Instruments*;
(b)   finance charges in respect of **finance leases** recognised in accordance with Section 20 *Leases*; and
(c)   exchange differences arising from foreign currency borrowings to the extent that they are regarded as an adjustment to interest costs.

Recognition

25.2 An entity may adopt a policy of capitalising borrowing costs that are directly attributable to the acquisition, construction or production of a **qualifying asset** as part of the cost of that **asset**. Where an entity adopts a policy of capitalisation of borrowing costs, it shall be applied consistently to a class of qualifying assets. Where an entity does not adopt a policy of capitalising borrowing costs, all borrowing costs shall be recognised as an **expense** in **profit or loss** in the period in which they are incurred.

25.2A The borrowing costs that are directly attributable to the acquisition, construction or production of a qualifying asset are those borrowing costs that would have been avoided if the expenditure on the qualifying asset had not been made.

25.2B To the extent that an entity borrows funds specifically for the purpose of obtaining a qualifying asset, the entity shall determine the amount of borrowing costs eligible for capitalisation as the actual borrowing costs incurred on that borrowing during the period less any investment income on the temporary investment of those borrowings.

25.2C To the extent that funds applied to obtain a qualifying asset form part of the entity's general borrowings, the amount of borrowing costs eligible for capitalisation are determined by applying a capitalisation rate to the expenditure on that asset. For this purpose the expenditure on the asset is the average **carrying amount** of the asset during the period, including borrowing costs previously capitalised. The capitalisation rate used in an accounting period shall be the weighted average of rates applicable to the entity's general borrowings that are outstanding during the period. This excludes borrowings by the entity that are specifically for the purpose of obtaining other qualifying assets. The amount of borrowing costs that an entity capitalises during a period shall not exceed the amount of borrowing costs it incurred during that period.

25.2D An entity shall:

    (a)   capitalise borrowing costs as part of the cost of a qualifying asset from the point when it first incurs both expenditure on the asset and borrowing costs, and undertakes activities necessary to prepare the asset for its intended use or sale;

    (b)   suspend capitalisation during extended periods where active development of the asset has paused; and

    (c)   cease capitalisation when substantially all the activities necessary to prepare the qualifying asset for its intended use or sale are complete.

Disclosures

25.3 Paragraph 5.5 sets out the presentation requirements for items of profit or loss, including interest payable. Paragraph 11.48(b) requires disclosure of total interest expense (using the effective interest method) for **financial liabilities** that are not at fair value through profit or loss. When a policy of capitalising borrowing costs is not adopted, this section does not require any additional disclosure.

25.3A Where a policy of capitalisation is adopted, an entity shall disclose:

    (a)   the amount of borrowing costs capitalised in the period; and

    (b)   the capitalisation rate used.

Section 26 Share-based Payment

Scope of this section

This section specifies the accounting for all **share-based payment transactions** including: **26.1**

(a)   **equity-settled share-based payment transactions**, in which the entity:

    (i)   receives goods or services as consideration for its own equity instruments (including shares or **share options**); or

    (ii) receives goods or services but has no obligation to settle the transaction with supplier;

(b)   **cash-settled share-based payment transactions**, in which the entity acquires goods or services by incurring a **liability** to transfer **cash** or other assets to the supplier of those goods or services for amounts that are based on the price (or value) of the entity's shares or other equity instruments of the entity or another group entity; and

(c)   transactions in which the entity receives or acquires goods or services and the terms of the arrangement provide either the entity or the supplier of those goods or services with a choice of whether the entity settles the transaction in cash (or other assets) or by issuing equity instruments.

A share-based payment transaction may be settled by another group entity (or a shareholder   **26.1A** of any group entity) on behalf of the entity receiving or acquiring the goods or services. Paragraph 26.1 also applies to an entity that:

(a)   receives goods or services when another entity in the same group (or shareholder of any group entity) has the obligation to settle the share-based payment transaction; or

(b)   has an obligation to settle a share-based payment transaction when another entity in the same group receives the goods or services

unless the transaction is clearly for a purpose other than payment for goods or services supplied to the entity receiving them.

Cash-settled share-based payment transactions include share appreciation rights. For   **26.2** example, an entity might grant share appreciation rights to employees as part of their remuneration package, whereby the employees will become entitled to a future cash payment (rather than an equity instrument), based on the increase in the entity's share price from a specified level over a specified period of time. Or an entity might grant to its employees a right to receive a future cash payment by granting to them a right to shares (including shares to be issued upon the exercise of share options) that are redeemable, either mandatorily (eg upon cessation of employment) or at the employee's option.

Recognition

An entity shall recognise the goods or services received or acquired in a share-based   **26.3** payment transaction when it obtains the goods or as the services are received. The entity shall recognise a corresponding increase in **equity** if the goods or services were received in an equity-settled share-based payment transaction, or a liability if the goods or services were acquired in a cash-settled share-based payment transaction.

When the goods or services received or acquired in a share-based payment transaction do   **26.4** not qualify for **recognition** as assets, the entity shall recognise them as **expenses**.

Recognition when there are vesting conditions

26.5   If the share-based payments granted to employees **vest** immediately, the employee is not required to complete a specified period of service before becoming unconditionally entitled to those share-based payments. In the absence of evidence to the contrary, the entity shall presume that services rendered by the employee as consideration for the share-based payments have been received. In this case, on **grant date** the entity shall recognise the services received in full, with a corresponding increase in equity or liabilities.

26.6   If the share-based payments do not vest until the employee completes a specified period of service, the entity shall presume that the services to be rendered by the counterparty as consideration for those share-based payments will be received in the future, during the vesting period. The entity shall account for those services as they are rendered by the employee during the vesting period, with a corresponding increase in equity or liabilities.

Measurement of equity-settled share-based payment transactions

Measurement principle

26.7   For equity-settled share-based payment transactions, an entity shall measure the goods or services received, and the corresponding increase in equity, at the **fair value** of the goods or services received, unless that fair value cannot be estimated reliably. If the entity cannot estimate reliably the fair value of the goods or services received, the entity shall measure their value, and the corresponding increase in equity, by reference to the fair value of the equity instruments granted measured in accordance with paragraphs 26.10 and 26.11. To apply this requirement to transactions with employees and others providing similar services, the entity shall measure the fair value of the services received by reference to the fair value of the equity instruments granted, because typically it is not possible to estimate reliably the fair value of the services received.

26.8   For transactions with employees (including others providing similar services), the fair value of the equity instruments shall be measured at grant date. For transactions with parties other than employees, the measurement date is the date when the entity obtains the goods or the counterparty renders service.

26.9   A grant of equity instruments might be conditional on employees satisfying specified **vesting conditions** related to service or performance. An example of a vesting condition relating to service is where a grant of shares or share options is conditional on the employee remaining in the entity's employ for a specified period of time. Examples of vesting conditions relating to performance are where a grant of shares or share options is conditional on the entity achieving a specified growth in profit (an example of a non-market condition) or a specified increase in the entity's share price (an example of a **market condition**). All vesting conditions related solely to employee service or to a non-market performance condition shall be taken into account when estimating the number of equity instruments expected to vest. Subsequently, the entity shall revise that estimate, if necessary, if new information indicates that the number of equity instruments expected to vest differs from previous estimates. On the vesting date, the entity shall revise the estimate to equal the number of equity instruments that ultimately vested. All market conditions and non-vesting conditions shall be taken into account when estimating the fair value of the shares or share options at the measurement date, with no subsequent adjustment irrespective of the outcome of the market or non-vesting condition, provided that all other vesting conditions are satisfied.

Shares

An entity shall measure the fair value of shares (and the related goods or services received) using the following three-tier measurement hierarchy: **26.10**

(a) If an observable market price is available for the equity instruments granted, use that price.
(b) If an observable market price is not available, measure the fair value of equity instruments granted using entity-specific observable market data such as:

    (i) a recent transaction in the entity's shares; or
    (ii) a recent independent fair valuation of the entity or its principal assets.

(c) If an observable market price is not available and obtaining a reliable **measurement** of fair value under (b) is **impracticable**, indirectly measure the fair value of the shares using a valuation method that uses market data to the greatest extent practicable to estimate what the price of those equity instruments would be on the grant date in an arm's length transaction between knowledgeable, willing parties. The entity's directors shall use their judgement to apply a generally accepted valuation methodology for valuing equity instruments that is appropriate to the circumstances of the entity.

Share options and equity-settled share appreciation rights

An entity shall measure the fair value of share options and equity-settled share appreciation rights (and the related goods or services received) using the following three-tier measurement hierarchy: **26.11**

(a) If an observable market price is available for the equity instruments granted, use that price.
(b) If an observable market price is not available, measure the fair value of share options and share appreciation rights granted using entity-specific observable market data such as for a recent transaction in the share options.
(c) If an observable market price is not available and obtaining a reliable measurement of fair value under (b) is impracticable, indirectly measure the fair value of share options or share appreciation rights using an alternative valuation methodology such as an option pricing model. The inputs for an option pricing model (such as the weighted average share price, exercise price, expected volatility, option life, expected dividends and the risk-free interest rate) shall use market data to the greatest extent possible. Paragraph 26.10 provides guidance on determining the fair value of the shares used in determining the weighted average share price. The entity shall derive an estimate of expected volatility consistent with the valuation methodology used to determine the fair value of the shares.

Modifications to the terms and conditions on which equity instruments were granted

If an entity modifies the vesting conditions in a manner that is beneficial to the employee, for example, by reducing the exercise price of an option or reducing the vesting period or by modifying or eliminating a performance condition, the entity shall take the modified vesting conditions into account in accounting for the share-based payment transaction, as follows: **26.12**

(a) If the modification increases the fair value of the equity instruments granted (or increases the number of equity instruments granted) measured immediately before and after the modification, the entity shall include the incremental fair value granted in the measurement of the amount recognised for services received as consideration for the equity instruments granted. The incremental fair value granted is the difference between the fair value of the modified equity instrument and that of the original equity instrument, both estimated as at the date of the modification. If the modification occurs during the vesting period, the incremental fair value granted is included in the measurement of the amount recognised for services received over the period from the modification date until the date when the modified equity instruments vest, in addition to the amount based on the grant date fair value of the original equity instruments, which is recognised over the remainder of the original vesting period.

(b) If the modification reduces the total fair value of the share-based payment arrangement, or apparently is not otherwise beneficial to the employee, the entity shall nevertheless continue to account for the services received as consideration for the equity instruments granted as if that modification had not occurred.

Cancellations and settlements

26.13   An entity shall account for a cancellation or settlement of an equity-settled share-based payment award as an acceleration of vesting, and therefore shall recognise immediately the amount that otherwise would have been recognised for services received over the remainder of the vesting period.

Cash-settled share-based payment transactions

26.14   For cash-settled share-based payment transactions, an entity shall measure the goods or services acquired and the liability incurred at the fair value of the liability. Until the liability is settled, the entity shall remeasure the fair value of the liability at each **reporting date** and at the date of settlement, with any changes in fair value recognised in **profit or loss** for the period.

Share-based payment transactions with cash alternatives

26.15   Some share-based payment transactions give either the entity or the counterparty a choice of settling the transaction in cash (or other assets) or by transfer of equity instruments. In such a case, the entity shall account for the transaction as a cash-settled share-based payment transaction unless either:

(a) the entity has a past practice of settling by issuing equity instruments; or

(b) the option has no commercial substance because the cash settlement amount bears no relationship to, and is likely to be lower in value than, the fair value of the equity instrument.

In circumstances (a) and (b), the entity shall account for the transaction as an equity-settled share-based payment transaction in accordance with paragraphs 26.7 to 26.13.

Prospective amendments: Amendments to FRS 102 *The Financial Reporting Standard applicable in the UK and Republic of Ireland* – Small entities and other minor amendments (July 2015) deletes this paragraph 26.15 and replaced with new paragraphs 26.15 to 26.15B with effect for annual periods beginning on or after 1 January 2016.

Group plans

26.16   If a share-based payment award is granted by an entity to the employees of one or more members in the **group**, the members are permitted, as an alternative to the treatment set out in paragraphs 26.3 to 26.15, to recognise and measure the share-based payment expense on the basis of a reasonable allocation of the expense for the group.

Government-mandated plans

Some jurisdictions have programmes established under law by which equity investors   **26.17**
(such as employees) are able to acquire equity without providing goods or services that
can be specifically identified (or by providing goods or services that are clearly less than
the fair value of the equity instruments granted). This indicates that other consideration
has been or will be received (such as past or future employee services). These are equity-
settled share-based payment transactions within the scope of this section. The entity shall
measure the unidentifiable goods or services received (or to be received) as the difference
between the fair value of the share-based payment and the fair value of any identifiable
goods or services received (or to be received) measured at the grant date.

Disclosures

An entity shall disclose the following information about the nature and extent of share-   **26.18**
based payment arrangements that existed during the period:

(a)   A description of each type of share-based payment arrangement that existed at
      any time during the period, including the general terms and conditions of each
      arrangement, such as vesting requirements, the maximum term of options granted,
      and the method of settlement (eg whether in cash or equity). An entity with
      substantially similar types of share-based payment arrangements may aggregate this
      information.
(b)   The number and weighted average exercise prices of share options for each of the
      following groups of options:

      (i)   outstanding at the beginning of the period;
      (ii)   granted during the period;
      (iii)   forfeited during the period;
      (iv)   exercised during the period;
      (v)   expired during the period;
      (vi)   outstanding at the end of the period; and
      (vii)   exercisable at the end of the period.

For equity-settled share-based payment arrangements, an entity shall disclose information   **26.19**
about how it measured the fair value of goods or services received or the value of the
equity instruments granted. If a valuation methodology was used, the entity shall disclose
the method and its reason for choosing it.

For cash-settled share-based payment arrangements, an entity shall disclose information   **26.20**
about how the liability was measured.

For share-based payment arrangements that were modified during the period, an entity   **26.21**
shall disclose an explanation of those modifications.

If the entity is part of a group share-based payment plan, and it recognises and measures   **26.22**
its share-based payment expense on the basis of a reasonable allocation of the expense
recognised for the group, it shall disclose that fact and the basis for the allocation
(see paragraph 26.16).

An entity shall disclose the following information about the effect of share-based payment   **26.23**
transactions on the entity's profit or loss for the period and on its **financial position**:

(a)   the total expense recognised in profit or loss for the period; and
(b)   the total **carrying amount** at the end of the period for liabilities arising from share-
      based payment transactions.

Section 27 Impairment of Assets

Objective and scope

27.1   An **impairment loss** occurs when the **carrying amount** of an **asset** exceeds its **recoverable amount**. This section shall be applied in accounting for the impairment of all assets other than the following, for which other sections of this FRS establish impairment requirements:

(a)   assets arising from **construction contracts** (see Section 23 *Revenue*);

(b)   **deferred tax assets** (see Section 29 *Income Tax*);

(c)   assets arising from **employee benefits** (see Section 28 *Employee Benefits*);

(d)   **financial assets** within the scope of Section 11 *Basic Financial Instruments* or Section 12 *Other Financial Instruments Issues*;

(e)   **investment property** measured at **fair value** (see Section 16 *Investment Property*); and

(f)   **biological assets** related to **agricultural activity** measured at fair value less estimated costs to sell (see Section 34 *Specialised Activities*).

27.1A   This section shall not apply in accounting for the impairment of **deferred acquisition costs** and **intangible assets** arising from contracts within the scope of FRS 103 *Insurance Contracts*.

Impairment of inventories

Selling price less costs to complete and sell

27.2   An entity shall assess at each **reporting date** whether any **inventories** are impaired. The entity shall make the assessment by comparing the carrying amount of each item of inventory (or group of similar items – see paragraph 27.3) with its selling price less costs to complete and sell. If an item of inventory (or group of similar items) is impaired, the entity shall reduce the carrying amount of the inventory (or the group) to its selling price less costs to complete and sell. That reduction is an impairment loss and it is recognised immediately in **profit or loss**.

27.3   If it is **impracticable** to determine the selling price less costs to complete and sell for inventories item by item, the entity may group items of inventory relating to the same product line that have similar purposes or end uses and are produced and marketed in the same geographical area for the purpose of assessing impairment.

Reversal of impairment

27.4   An entity shall make a new assessment of selling price less costs to complete and sell at each subsequent reporting date. When the circumstances that previously caused inventories to be impaired no longer exist or when there is clear evidence of an increase in selling price less costs to complete and sell because of changed economic circumstances, the entity shall reverse the amount of the impairment (ie the reversal is limited to the amount of the original impairment loss) so that the new carrying amount is the lower of the cost and the revised selling price less costs to complete and sell.

Impairment of assets other than inventories

General principles

If, and only if, the recoverable amount of an asset is less than its carrying amount, the entity shall reduce the carrying amount of the asset to its recoverable amount. That reduction is an impairment loss. Paragraphs 27.11 to 27.20A provide guidance on measuring recoverable amount.   **27.5**

An entity shall recognise an impairment loss immediately in profit or loss, unless the asset is carried at a revalued amount in accordance with another section of this FRS (for example, in accordance with the revaluation model in Section 17 *Property, Plant and Equipment*). Any impairment loss of a revalued asset shall be treated as a revaluation decrease in accordance with that other section.   **27.6**

Indicators of impairment

An entity shall assess at each reporting date whether there is any indication that an asset may be impaired. If any such indication exists, the entity shall estimate the recoverable amount of the asset. If there is no indication of impairment, it is not necessary to estimate the recoverable amount.   **27.7**

If it is not possible to estimate the recoverable amount of the individual asset, an entity shall estimate the recoverable amount of the **cash-generating unit** to which the asset belongs. This may be the case because measuring recoverable amount requires forecasting **cash flows**, and sometimes individual assets do not generate cash flows by themselves. An asset's cash-generating unit is the smallest identifiable group of assets that includes the asset and generates cash inflows that are largely independent of the cash inflows from other assets or groups of assets.   **27.8**

In assessing whether there is any indication that an asset may be impaired, an entity shall consider, as a minimum, the following indications: **27.9**

External sources of information

(a)   During the period, an asset's market value has declined significantly more than would be expected as a result of the passage of time or normal use.

(b)   Significant changes with an adverse effect on the entity have taken place during the period, or will take place in the near future, in the technological, market, economic or legal environment in which the entity operates or in the market to which an asset is dedicated.

(c)   Market interest rates or other market rates of return on investments have increased during the period, and those increases are likely to affect materially the discount rate used in calculating an asset's **value in use** and decrease the asset's **fair value less costs to sell**.

(d)   The carrying amount of the net assets of the entity is more than the estimated fair value of the entity as a whole (such an estimate may have been made, for example, in relation to the potential sale of part or all of the entity).

Internal sources of information

(e)   Evidence is available of obsolescence or physical damage of an asset.

(f)   Significant changes with an adverse effect on the entity have taken place during the period, or are expected to take place in the near future, in the extent to which, or manner in which, an asset is used or is expected to be used. These changes include the asset becoming idle, plans to discontinue or restructure the operation to which an asset belongs, plans to dispose of an asset before the previously expected date, and reassessing the **useful life** of an asset as finite rather than indefinite.

(g)   Evidence is available from internal reporting that indicates that the economic performance of an asset is, or will be, worse than expected. In this context economic performance includes operating results and cash flows.

27.10   If there is an indication that an asset may be impaired, this may indicate that the entity should review the remaining useful life, the **depreciation (amortisation)** method or the **residual value** for the asset and adjust it in accordance with the section of this FRS applicable to the asset (eg Section 17 *Property, Plant and Equipment* and Section 18 *Intangible Assets other than Goodwill*), even if no impairment loss is recognised for the asset.

Measuring recoverable amount

27.11   The recoverable amount of an asset or a cash-generating unit is the higher of its fair value less costs to sell and its value in use. If it is not possible to estimate the recoverable amount of an individual asset, references to an asset in paragraphs 27.12 to 27.20A should be read as references also to an asset's cash-generating unit.

27.12   It is not always necessary to determine both an asset's fair value less costs to sell and its value in use. If either of these amounts exceeds the asset's carrying amount, the asset is not impaired and it is not necessary to estimate the other amount.

27.13   If there is no reason to believe that an asset's value in use materially exceeds its fair value less costs to sell, the asset's fair value less costs to sell may be used as its recoverable amount. This will often be the case for an asset that is held for disposal.

Fair value less costs to sell

27.14   Fair value less costs to sell is the amount obtainable from the sale of an asset in an arm's length transaction between knowledgeable, willing parties, less the costs of disposal. The best evidence of the fair value less costs to sell of an asset is a price in a binding sale agreement in an arm's length transaction or a market price in an **active market**. If there is no binding sale agreement or active market for an asset, fair value less costs to sell is based on the best information available to reflect the amount that an entity could obtain, at the reporting date, from the disposal of the asset in an arm's length transaction between knowledgeable, willing parties, after deducting the costs of disposal. In determining this amount, an entity considers the outcome of recent transactions for similar assets within the same industry.

27.14A   When determining an asset's fair value less costs to sell, consideration shall be given to any restrictions imposed on that asset. Costs to sell shall also include the cost of obtaining relaxation of a restriction where necessary in order to enable the asset to be sold. If a restriction would also apply to any potential purchaser of an asset, the fair value of the asset may be lower than that of an asset whose use is not restricted.

Value in use

27.15   Value in use is the **present value** of the future cash flows expected to be derived from an asset. This present value calculation involves the following steps:

(a)   estimating the future cash inflows and outflows to be derived from continuing use of the asset and from its ultimate disposal; and

(b)   applying the appropriate discount rate to those future cash flows.

The following elements shall be reflected in the calculation of an asset's value in use: **27.16**

(a)   an estimate of the future cash flows the entity expects to derive from the asset;
(b)   expectations about possible variations in the amount or timing of those future cash flows;
(c)   the time value of money, represented by the current market risk-free rate of interest;
(d)   the price for bearing the uncertainty inherent in the asset; and
(e)   other factors, such as illiquidity, that market participants would reflect in pricing the future cash flows the entity expects to derive from the asset.

In measuring value in use, estimates of future cash flows shall include: **27.17**

(a)   projections of cash inflows from the continuing use of the asset;
(b)   projections of cash outflows that are necessarily incurred to generate the cash inflows from continuing use of the asset (including cash outflows to prepare the asset for use) and can be directly attributed, or allocated on a reasonable and consistent basis, to the asset; and
(c)   net cash flows, if any, expected to be received (or paid) for the disposal of the asset at the end of its useful life in an arm's length transaction between knowledgeable, willing parties.

The entity may wish to use any recent financial budgets or forecasts to estimate the cash flows, if available. To estimate cash flow projections beyond the period covered by the most recent budgets or forecasts an entity may wish to extrapolate the projections based on the budgets or forecasts using a steady or declining growth rate for subsequent years, unless an increasing rate can be justified.

Estimates of future cash flows shall not include: **27.18**

(a)   cash inflows or outflows from **financing activities**; or
(b)   income tax receipts or payments.

Future cash flows shall be estimated for the asset in its current condition. Estimates of   **27.19**
future cash flows shall not include estimated future cash inflows or outflows that are expected to arise from:

(a)   a future restructuring to which an entity is not yet committed; or
(b)   improving or enhancing the asset's performance.

The discount rate (rates) used in the present value calculation shall be a pre-tax rate (rates)   **27.20**
that reflect(s) current market assessments of:

(a)   the time value of money; and
(b)   the risks specific to the asset for which the future cash flow estimates have not been adjusted.

The discount rate (rates) used to measure an asset's value in use shall not reflect risks for which the future cash flow estimates have been adjusted, to avoid double-counting.

For assets held for their **service potential**, a cash flow driven valuation (such as value in   **27.20A**
use) may not be appropriate. In these circumstances **value in use (in respect of assets held for their service potential)** is determined by the present value of the asset's remaining service potential plus the net amount the entity will receive from its disposal. In some cases this may be taken to be costs avoided by possession of the asset. Therefore, **depreciated replacement cost**, may be a suitable measurement model but other approaches may be used where more appropriate.

Recognising and measuring an impairment loss for a cash-generating unit

27.21   An impairment loss shall be recognised for a cash-generating unit if, and only if, the recoverable amount of the unit is less than the carrying amount of the unit. The impairment loss shall be allocated to reduce the carrying amount of the assets of the unit in the following order:

(a)   first, to reduce the carrying amount of any **goodwill** allocated to the cash-generating unit; and

(b)   then, to the other assets of the unit pro rata on the basis of the carrying amount of each asset in the cash-generating unit.

27.22   However, an entity shall not reduce the carrying amount of any asset in the cash-generating unit below the highest of:

(a)   its fair value less costs to sell (if determinable);

(b)   its value in use (if determinable); and

(c)   zero.

27.23   Any excess amount of the impairment loss that cannot be allocated to an asset because of the restriction in paragraph 27.22 shall be allocated to the other assets of the unit pro rata on the basis of the carrying amount of those other assets.

Additional requirements for impairment of goodwill

27.24   Goodwill, by itself, cannot be sold. Nor does it generate cash flows to an entity that are independent of the cash flows of other assets. As a consequence, the fair value of goodwill cannot be measured directly. Therefore, the fair value of goodwill must be derived from **measurement** of the fair value of the cash-generating unit(s) of which the goodwill is a part.

27.25   For the purpose of impairment testing, goodwill acquired in a **business combination** shall, from the **acquisition date**, be allocated to each of the acquirer's cash-generating units that are expected to benefit from the synergies of the combination, irrespective of whether other assets or **liabilities** of the acquiree are assigned to those units.

27.26   Part of the recoverable amount of a cash-generating unit is attributable to the **non-controlling interest** in goodwill. For the purpose of impairment testing of a non-wholly-owned cash-generating unit with goodwill, the carrying amount of that unit is notionally adjusted, before being compared with its recoverable amount, by grossing up the carrying amount of goodwill allocated to the unit to include the goodwill attributable to the non-controlling interest. This notionally adjusted carrying amount is then compared with the recoverable amount of the unit to determine whether the cash-generating unit is impaired.

27.27   If goodwill cannot be allocated to individual cash-generating units (or groups of cash-generating units) on a non-arbitrary basis, then for the purposes of testing goodwill the entity shall test the impairment of goodwill by determining the recoverable amount of either:

(a)   the acquired entity in its entirety, if the goodwill relates to an acquired entity that has not been integrated. Integrated means the acquired **business** has been restructured or dissolved into the reporting entity or other **subsidiaries**; or

(b)   the entire group of entities, excluding any entities that have not been integrated, if the goodwill relates to an entity that has been integrated.

In applying this paragraph, an entity will need to separate goodwill into goodwill relating to entities that have been integrated and goodwill relating to entities that have not been integrated. Also the entity shall follow the requirements for cash-generating units in this section when calculating the recoverable amount of, and allocating impairment losses and reversals to assets belonging to, the acquired entity or group of entities.

Reversal of an impairment loss

An impairment loss recognised for all assets, including goodwill, shall be reversed in a subsequent period if and only if the reasons for the impairment loss have ceased to apply.   **27.28**

Prospective amendments: Amendments to FRS 102 *The Financial Reporting Standard applicable in the UK and Republic of Ireland* – Small entities and other minor amendments (July 2015) amends this paragraph 27.28 with effect for annual periods beginning on or after 1 January 2016.

An entity shall assess at each reporting date whether there is any indication that an impairment loss recognised in prior periods may no longer exist or may have decreased. Indications that an impairment loss may have decreased or may no longer exist are generally the opposite of those set out in paragraph 27.9. If any such indication exists, the entity shall determine whether all or part of the prior impairment loss should be reversed. The procedure for making that determination will depend on whether the prior impairment loss on the asset was based on: **27.29**

(a)   the recoverable amount of that individual asset (see paragraph 27.30); or

(b)   the recoverable amount of the cash-generating unit to which the asset belongs (see paragraph 27.31).

Prospective amendments: Amendments to FRS 102 *The Financial Reporting Standard applicable in the UK and Republic of Ireland* – Small entities and other minor amendments (July 2015) amends this paragraph 27.29 with effect for annual periods beginning on or after 1 January 2016.

Reversal where recoverable amount was estimated for an individual impaired asset

When the prior impairment loss was based on the recoverable amount of the individual impaired asset, the following requirements apply: **27.30**

(a)   The entity shall estimate the recoverable amount of the asset at the current reporting date.

(b)   If the estimated recoverable amount of the asset exceeds its carrying amount, the entity shall increase the carrying amount to recoverable amount, subject to the limitation described in (c) below. That increase is a reversal of an impairment loss. The entity shall recognise the reversal immediately in profit or loss unless the asset is carried at revalued amount in accordance with another section of this FRS (for example, the revaluation model in Section 17 *Property, plant and equipment*). Any reversal of an impairment loss of a revalued asset shall be treated as a revaluation increase in accordance with the relevant section of this FRS.

(c)   The reversal of an impairment loss shall not increase the carrying amount of the asset above the carrying amount that would have been determined (net of amortisation or depreciation) had no impairment loss been recognised for the asset in prior years.

(d)   After a reversal of an impairment loss is recognised, the entity shall adjust the depreciation (amortisation) charge for the asset in future periods to allocate the asset's revised carrying amount, less its residual value (if any), on a systematic basis over its remaining useful life.

Reversal when recoverable amount was estimated for a cash-generating unit

27.31 When the original impairment loss was based on the recoverable amount of the cash-generating unit to which the asset, including goodwill belongs, the following requirements apply:

(a) The entity shall estimate the recoverable amount of that cash-generating unit at the current reporting date.

(b) If the estimated recoverable amount of the cash-generating unit exceeds its carrying amount, that excess is a reversal of an impairment loss. The entity shall allocate the amount of that reversal to the assets of the unit, pro rata with the carrying amounts of those assets and goodwill in the order set out below, subject to the limitation described in (c) below. Those increases in carrying amounts shall be treated as reversals of impairment losses and recognised immediately in profit or loss unless an asset is carried at revalued amount in accordance with another section of this FRS (for example, the revaluation model in Section 17 *Property, plant and equipment*). Any reversal of an impairment loss of a revalued asset shall be treated as a revaluation increase in accordance with the relevant section of this FRS.

(i) First the assets (other than goodwill) of the unit pro rata on the basis of the carrying amount of each asset in the cash-generating unit; and

(ii) then to any goodwill allocated to the cash-generating unit.

(c) In allocating a reversal of an impairment loss for a cash-generating unit, the reversal shall not increase the carrying amount of any asset above the lower of:

(i) its recoverable amount; and

(ii) the carrying amount that would have been determined (net of amortisation or depreciation) had no impairment loss been recognised for the asset in prior periods.

(d) Any excess amount of the reversal of the impairment loss that cannot be allocated to an asset because of the restriction in (c) above shall be allocated pro rata to the other assets of the cash-generating unit.

(e) After a reversal of an impairment loss is recognised, if applicable, the entity shall adjust the depreciation (amortisation) charge for each asset in the cash-generating unit in future periods to allocate the asset's revised carrying amount, less its residual value (if any), on a systematic basis over its remaining useful life.

Prospective amendments: Amendments to FRS 102 *The Financial Reporting Standard applicable in the UK and Republic of Ireland* – Small entities and other minor amendments (July 2015) amends this paragraph 27.31 with effect for annual periods beginning on or after 1 January 2016.

Disclosures

27.32 An entity shall disclose the following for each **class of assets** indicated in paragraph 27.33:

(a) the amount of impairment losses recognised in profit or loss during the period and the line item(s) in the **statement of comprehensive income** (or in the **income statement**, if presented) in which those impairment losses are included; and

(b) the amount of reversals of impairment losses recognised in profit or loss during the period and the line item(s) in the statement of comprehensive income (or in the income statement, if presented) in which those impairment losses are reversed.

An entity shall disclose the information required by paragraph 27.32 for each of the following classes of asset:

27.33

(a)   inventories;
(b)   **property, plant and equipment** (including investment property accounted for by the cost method);
(c)   goodwill;
(d)   **intangible assets** other than goodwill;
(e)   investments in **associates**; and
(f)   investments in **joint ventures**.

An entity shall disclose a description of the events and circumstances that led to the **recognition** or reversal of the impairment loss.

27.33A

Section 28 Employee Benefits

Scope of this section

Employee benefits are all forms of consideration given by an entity in exchange for service rendered by employees, including directors and management. This section applies to all employee benefits, except for **share-based payment transactions**, which are covered by Section 26 *Share-based Payment*. Employee benefits covered by this section will be one of the following four types:

28.1

(a)   short-term employee benefits, which are employee benefits (other than **termination benefits**) that are expected to be settled wholly before twelve months after the end of the **reporting period** in which the employees render the related service;
(b)   **post-employment benefits**, which are employee benefits (other than termination benefits and short-term employee benefits) that are payable after the completion of employment;
(c)   other long-term employee benefits, which are all employee benefits, other than short-term employee benefits, post-employment benefits and termination benefits; or
(d)   termination benefits, which are employee benefits provided in exchange for the termination of an employee's employment as a result of either:

   (i)   an entity's decision to terminate an employee's employment before the normal retirement date; or
   (ii)   an employee's decision to accept voluntary redundancy in exchange for those benefits.

[Not used]

28.2

General recognition principle for all employee benefits

An entity shall recognise the cost of all employee benefits to which its employees have become entitled as a result of service rendered to the entity during the reporting period:

28.3

(a)   As a **liability**, after deducting amounts that have been paid either directly to the employees or as a contribution to an employee benefit fund[14]. If the amount paid exceeds the obligation arising from service before the **reporting date**, an entity shall

---

[14] *Contributions to an employee benefit fund that is an intermediate payment arrangement shall be accounted for in accordance with paragraphs 9.33 to 9.38, and as a result if the employer is a sponsoring entity the assets and liabilities of the intermediary will be accounted for by the sponsoring entity as an extension of its own business. In which case the payment to the employee benefit fund does not extinguish the liability of the employer.*

recognise that excess as an asset to the extent that the prepayment will lead to a reduction in future payments or a cash refund.

(b)   As an **expense**, unless another section of this FRS requires the cost to be recognised as part of the cost of an asset such as **inventories** (for example in accordance with paragraph 13.8) or **property, plant and equipment** (in accordance with paragraph 17.10).

Short-term employee benefits

Examples

28.4   Short-term employee benefits include items such as the following, if expected to be settled wholly before 12 months after the end of the annual reporting period in which the employees render the related service:

(a)   wages, salaries and social security contributions;

(b)   paid annual leave and paid sick leave;

(c)   profit-sharing and bonuses; and

(d)   non-monetary benefits (such as medical care, housing, cars and free or subsidised goods or services) for current employees.

Measurement of short-term benefits generally

28.5   When an employee has rendered service to an entity during the reporting period, the entity shall measure the amounts recognised in accordance with paragraph 28.3 at the undiscounted amount of short-term employee benefits expected to be paid in exchange for that service.

Recognition and measurement: Short-term compensated absences

28.6   An entity may compensate employees for absence for various reasons including annual leave and sick leave. Some short-term compensated absences accumulate – they can be carried forward and used in future periods if the employee does not use the current period's entitlement in full. Examples include annual leave and sick leave. An entity shall recognise the expected cost of **accumulating compensated absences** when the employees render service that increases their entitlement to future compensated absences. The entity shall measure the expected cost of accumulating compensated absences at the undiscounted additional amount that the entity expects to pay as a result of the unused entitlement that has accumulated at the end of the reporting period. The entity shall present this amount as falling due within one year at the reporting date.

28.7   An entity shall recognise the cost of other (non-accumulating) compensated absences when the absences occur. The entity shall measure the cost of non-accumulating compensated absences at the undiscounted amount of salaries and wages paid or payable for the period of absence.

Recognition: Profit-sharing and bonus plans

28.8   An entity shall recognise the expected cost of profit-sharing and bonus payments only when:

(a)   the entity has a present legal or **constructive obligation** to make such payments as a result of past events (this means that the entity has no realistic alternative but to make the payments); and

(b)   a reliable estimate of the obligation can be made.

Post-employment benefits: Distinction between defined contribution plans and defined benefit plans

Post-employment benefits include, for example: **28.9**

(a)   retirement benefits, such as pensions; and
(b)   other post-employment benefits, such as post-employment life insurance and post-employment medical care.

Arrangements whereby an entity provides post-employment benefits are **post-employment benefit plans**. An entity shall apply this section to all such arrangements whether or not they involve the establishment of a separate entity to receive contributions and to pay benefits. In some cases, these arrangements are imposed by law rather than by action of the entity. In some cases, these arrangements arise from actions of the entity even in the absence of a formal, documented plan.

Post-employment benefit plans are classified as either **defined contribution plans** or   **28.10**
defined benefit plans, depending on their principal terms and conditions:

(a)   Defined contribution plans are post-employment benefit plans under which an entity pays fixed contributions into a separate entity (a fund) and has no legal or constructive obligation to pay further contributions or to make direct benefit payments to employees if the fund does not hold sufficient assets to pay all employee benefits relating to employee service in the current and prior periods. Thus, the amount of the post-employment benefits received by the employee is determined by the amount of contributions paid by an entity (and perhaps also the employee) to a post-employment benefit plan or to an insurer, together with investment returns arising from the contributions.
(b)   Defined benefit plans are post-employment benefit plans other than defined contribution plans. Under defined benefit plans, the entity's obligation is to provide the agreed benefits to current and former employees, and actuarial risk (that benefits will cost more or less than expected) and investment risk (that returns on assets set aside to fund the benefits will differ from expectations) are borne, in substance, by the entity. If actuarial or investment experience is worse than expected, the entity's obligation may be increased, and vice versa if actuarial or investment experience is better than expected.

Multi-employer plans and state plans

Multi-employer plans and **state plans** are classified as defined contribution plans or   **28.11**
defined benefit plans on the basis of the terms of the plan, including any constructive obligation that goes beyond the formal terms. However, if sufficient information is not available to use defined benefit accounting for a multi-employer plan that is a defined benefit plan, an entity shall account for the plan in accordance with paragraphs 28.13 and 28.13A as if it was a defined contribution plan and make the disclosures required by paragraphs 28.40 and 28.40A. An entity shall account for a state plan in the same way as for a multi-employer plan.

Where an entity participates in a defined benefit plan, which is a multi-employer plan   **28.11A**
that in accordance with paragraph 28.11 is accounted for as if the plan were a defined contribution plan, and the entity has entered into an agreement with the multi-employer plan that determines how the entity will fund a deficit, the entity shall recognise a liability for the contributions payable that arise from the agreement (to the extent that they relate to the deficit) and the resulting expense in **profit or loss** in accordance with paragraphs 28.13 and 28.13A.

Insured benefits

28.12   An entity may pay insurance premiums to fund a post-employment benefit plan. The entity shall treat such a plan as a defined contribution plan unless the entity has a legal or constructive obligation either:

(a)   to pay the employee benefits directly when they become due; or

(b)   to pay further amounts if the insurer does not pay all future employee benefits relating to employee service in the current and prior periods.

A constructive obligation could arise indirectly through the plan, through the mechanism for setting future premiums, or through a **related party** relationship with the insurer. If the entity retains such a legal or constructive obligation, the entity shall treat the plan as a defined benefit plan.

Post-employment benefits: Defined contribution plans

Recognition and measurement

28.13   An entity shall recognise the contribution payable for a period:

(a)   As a liability, after deducting any amount already paid. If contribution payments exceed the contribution due for service before the reporting date, an entity shall recognise that excess as an asset to the extent that the prepayment will lead to a reduction in future payments or a cash refund.

(b)   As an expense, unless another section of this FRS requires the cost to be recognised as part of the cost of an asset such as inventories or property, plant and equipment.

28.13A   When contributions to a defined contribution plan (or a defined benefit plan which, in accordance with paragraph 28.11, is accounted for as a defined contribution plan) are not expected to be settled wholly within 12 months after the end of the reporting period in which the employees render the related service, the liability shall be measured at the **present value** of the contributions payable using the methodology for selecting a discount rate specified in paragraph 28.17. The unwinding of the discount shall be recognised as a finance cost in profit or loss in the period in which it arises.

Post-employment benefits: Defined benefit plans

Recognition

28.14   In applying the general **recognition** principle in paragraph 28.3 to defined benefit plans, an entity shall recognise:

(a)   a liability for its obligations under defined benefit plans net of **plan assets** – its '**net defined benefit liability**' (see paragraphs 28.15 to 28.22); and

(b)   the net change in that liability during the period as the cost of its defined benefit plans during the period (see paragraphs 28.23 to 28.27).

Measurement of the net defined benefit liability

28.15   An entity shall measure the net defined benefit liability for its obligations under defined benefit plans at the net total of the following amounts:

(a) the present value of its obligations under defined benefit plans (its **defined benefit obligation**) at the reporting date (paragraphs 28.16 to 28.21A provide guidance for measuring this obligation); minus

(b) the **fair value** at the reporting date of plan assets (if any) out of which the obligations are to be settled. Paragraphs 11.27 to 11.32 establish requirements for determining the fair values of those plan assets, except that, if the asset is an insurance policy that exactly matches the amount and timing of some or all of the benefits payable under the plan, the fair value of the asset is deemed to be the present value of the related obligation.

Where an entity has measured its defined benefit obligation using the **projected unit credit method** (including the use of appropriate **actuarial assumptions**), as set out in paragraph 28.18, it shall not recognise any additional liabilities to reflect differences between these assumptions and those used for the most recent actuarial valuation of the plan for funding purposes. For the avoidance of doubt, no additional liabilities shall be recognised in respect of an agreement with the defined benefit plan to fund a deficit (such as a schedule of contributions). **28.15A**

Editor's note: Amendments to FRS 102 The Financial Reporting Standard applicable in the UK and Republic of Ireland – Pension obligations (February 2015) added paragraph 28.15A with effect for annual periods beginning on or after 1 January 2015.

Inclusion of both vested and unvested benefits

The present value of an entity's obligations under defined benefit plans at the reporting date shall reflect the estimated amount of benefit that employees have earned in return for their service in the current and prior periods, including benefits that are not yet **vested** (see paragraph 28.26) and including the effects of benefit formulas that give employees greater benefits for later years of service. This requires the entity to determine how much benefit is attributable to the current and prior periods on the basis of the plan's benefit formula and to make estimates (actuarial assumptions) about demographic variables (such as employee turnover and mortality) and financial variables (such as future increases in salaries and medical costs) that influence the cost of the benefit. The actuarial assumptions shall be unbiased (neither imprudent nor excessively conservative), mutually compatible, and selected to lead to the best estimate of the future **cash flows** that will arise under the plan. **28.16**

Editor's note: Amendments to FRS 102 The Financial Reporting Standard applicable in the UK and Republic of Ireland – Pension obligations (February 2015) amended paragraph 28.16 with effect for annual periods beginning on or after 1 January 2015.

Discounting

An entity shall measure its defined benefit obligation on a discounted present value basis. The entity shall determine the rate used to discount the future payments by reference to market yields at the reporting date on high quality corporate bonds. In countries with no deep market in such bonds, the entity shall use the market yields (at the reporting date) on government bonds. The currency and term of the corporate bonds or government bonds shall be consistent with the currency and estimated period of the future payments. **28.17**

Actuarial valuation method

An entity shall use the projected unit credit method to measure its defined benefit obligation and the related expense. If defined benefits are based on future salaries, the projected unit **28.18** credit method requires an entity to measure its defined benefit obligations on a basis that reflects estimated future salary increases. Additionally, the projected unit credit method requires an entity to make various actuarial assumptions in measuring the defined benefit obligation, including discount rates, employee turnover, mortality, and (for defined benefit medical plans) medical cost trend rates.

Editor's note: Amendments to FRS 102 The Financial Reporting Standard applicable in the UK and Republic of Ireland – Pension obligations (February 2015) amended paragraph 28.18 with effect for annual periods beginning on or after 1 January 2015.

28.19   [Not used]

28.20   This FRS does not require an entity to engage an independent actuary to perform the comprehensive actuarial valuation needed to calculate its defined benefit obligation. Nor does it require that a comprehensive actuarial valuation must be done annually. In the periods between comprehensive actuarial valuations, if the principal actuarial assumptions have not changed significantly the defined benefit obligation can be measured by adjusting the prior period measurement for changes in employee demographics such as number of employees and salary levels.

Plan introductions, changes, curtailments and settlements

28.21   If a defined benefit plan has been introduced or the benefits have changed in the current period, the entity shall increase or decrease its net defined benefit liability to reflect the change, and shall recognise the increase (decrease) as an expense (**income**) in measuring **profit or loss** in the current reporting period.

28.21A   If a defined benefit plan has been curtailed (ie benefits or group of covered employees are reduced) or settled (the relevant part of the employer's obligation is completely discharged) in the current period, the defined benefit obligation shall be decreased or eliminated, and the entity shall recognise the resulting **gain** or loss in profit or loss in the current period.

Defined benefit plan asset

28.22   If the present value of the defined benefit obligation at the reporting date is less than the fair value of plan assets at that date, the plan has a surplus. An entity shall recognise a plan surplus as a defined benefit plan asset only to the extent that it is able to recover the surplus either through reduced contributions in the future or through refunds from the plan.

Cost of a defined benefit plan

28.23   An entity shall recognise the cost of a defined benefit plan, except to the extent that another section of this FRS requires part or all of the cost to be recognised as part of the cost of an asset, as follows:

(a)   the change in the net defined benefit liability arising from employee service rendered during the reporting period in profit or loss;

(b)   net interest on the net defined benefit liability during the reporting period in profit or loss;

(c)   the cost of plan introductions, benefit changes, curtailments and settlements in profit or loss (see paragraphs 28.21 and 28.21A); and

(d)   remeasurement of the net defined benefit liability in **other comprehensive income**.

Some defined benefit plans require employees or third parties to contribute to the cost of the plan. Contributions by employees reduce the cost of the benefits to the entity.

The net interest on the net defined benefit liability shall be determined by multiplying the net defined benefit liability by the discount rate in paragraph 28.17, both as determined at the start of the annual reporting period, taking account of any changes in the net defined benefit liability during the period as a result of contribution and benefit payments.   **28.24**

The net interest on the net defined benefit liability can be viewed as comprising interest cost on the defined benefit obligation and interest income on plan assets excluding the effect of any surplus that is not recoverable in accordance with paragraph 28.22.   **28.24A**

Interest income on plan assets, excluding the effect of any surplus that is not recoverable in accordance with paragraph 28.22, is a component of the return on plan assets, and is determined by multiplying the fair value of the plan assets by the discount rate specified in paragraph 28.17 both as determined at the start of the annual reporting period, taking account of any changes in the plan assets held during the period as a result of contribution and benefit payments. The difference between the interest income on plan assets and the return on plan assets is included in the remeasurement of the net defined benefit liability.   **28.24B**

Remeasurement of the net defined benefit liability comprises: **28.25**

(a)   **actuarial gains and losses**;
(b)   the return on plan assets, excluding amounts included in net interest on the net defined benefit liability; and
(c)   any change in the amount of a defined benefit plan surplus that is not recoverable (see paragraph 28.22), excluding amounts included in net interest on the net defined benefit liability.

Editor's note: Amendments to FRS 102 The Financial Reporting Standard applicable in the UK and Republic of Ireland – Pension obligations (February 2015) amended paragraph 28.25 with effect for annual periods beginning on or after 1 January 2015.

Remeasurement of the net defined benefit liability recognised in other comprehensive income shall not be reclassified to profit or loss in a subsequent period.   **28.25A**

Employee service gives rise to an obligation under a defined benefit plan even if the benefits are conditional on future employment (in other words, they are not yet vested). Employee service before the vesting date gives rise to a constructive obligation because, at each successive reporting date, the amount of future service that an employee will have to render before becoming entitled to the benefit is reduced. In measuring its defined benefit obligation, an entity considers the probability that some employees may not satisfy vesting requirements. Similarly, although some post-employment benefits (such as post-employment medical benefits) become payable only if a specified event occurs when an employee is no longer employed (such as an illness), an obligation is created when the employee renders service that will provide entitlement to the benefit if the specified event occurs. The probability that the specified event will occur affects the **measurement** of the obligation, but does not determine whether the obligation exists.   **28.26**

If defined benefits are reduced for amounts that will be paid to employees under government-sponsored plans, an entity shall measure its defined benefit obligations on a basis that reflects the benefits payable under the government plans, but only if: **28.27**

(a)   those plans were enacted before the reporting date; or

(b)   past history, or other reliable evidence, indicates that those state benefits will change in some predictable manner, for example, in line with future changes in general price levels or general salary levels.

Reimbursements

28.28   If an entity is virtually certain that another party will reimburse some or all of the expenditure required to settle a defined benefit obligation, the entity shall recognise its right to reimbursement as a separate asset. An entity shall treat that asset in the same way as plan assets.

Other long-term employee benefits

28.29   Other long-term employee benefits include items such as the following, if not expected to be settled wholly before 12 months after the end of the annual reporting period in which the employees render the related service:

(a)   long-term paid absences such as long-service or sabbatical leave;

(b)   other long-service benefits;

(c)   long-term disability benefits;

(d)   profit-sharing and bonuses; and

(e)   deferred remuneration.

28.30   An entity shall recognise a liability for other long-term employee benefits measured at the net total of the following amounts:

(a)   the present value of the benefit obligation at the reporting date (calculated using the methodology for selecting a discount rate in paragraph 28.17); minus

(b)   the fair value at the reporting date of plan assets (if any) out of which the obligations are to be settled directly.

An entity shall recognise the change in the liability in profit or loss, except to the extent that this FRS requires or permits their inclusion in the cost of an asset.

Termination benefits

28.31   An entity may be committed, by legislation, by contractual or other agreements with employees or their representatives or by a constructive obligation based on business practice, custom or a desire to act equitably, to make payments (or provide other benefits) to employees when it terminates their employment. Such payments are termination benefits.

Recognition

28.32   Because termination benefits do not provide an entity with future economic benefits, an entity shall recognise them as an expense in profit or loss immediately.

28.33   When an entity recognises termination benefits, the entity may also have to account for a curtailment of retirement benefits or other employee benefits.

28.34   An entity shall recognise termination benefits as a liability and an expense only when the entity is demonstrably committed either:

(a)   to terminate the employment of an employee or group of employees before the normal retirement date; or

(b)   to provide termination benefits as a result of an offer made in order to encourage voluntary redundancy.

An entity is demonstrably committed to a termination only when the entity has a detailed formal plan for the termination[15] and is without realistic possibility of withdrawal from the plan.   **28.35**

Measurement

An entity shall measure termination benefits at the best estimate of the expenditure that would be required to settle the obligation at the reporting date. In the case of an offer made to encourage voluntary redundancy, the measurement of termination benefits shall be based on the number of employees expected to accept the offer.   **28.36**

When termination benefits are due more than 12 months after the end of the reporting period, they shall be measured at their discounted present value using the methodology for selecting a discount rate specified in paragraph 28.17.   **28.37**

Group plans

Where an entity participates in a defined benefit plan that shares risks between entities under common control it shall obtain information about the plan as a whole measured in accordance with this FRS on the basis of assumptions that apply to the plan as a whole. If there is a contractual agreement or stated policy for charging the net defined benefit cost of a defined benefit plan as a whole measured in accordance with this FRS to individual group entities, the entity shall, in its **individual financial statements**, recognise the net defined benefit cost of a defined benefit plan so charged. If there is no such agreement or policy, the net defined benefit cost of a defined benefit plan shall be recognised in the individual financial statements of the group entity which is legally responsible for the plan. The other group entities shall, in their individual financial statements, recognise a cost equal to their contribution payable for the period.   **28.38**

Disclosures

Disclosures about short-term employee benefits

This section does not require specific disclosures about short-term employee benefits.   **28.39**

Disclosures about defined contribution plans

An entity shall disclose the amount recognised in profit or loss as an expense for defined contribution plans.   **28.40**

If an entity treats a defined benefit multi-employer plan as a defined contribution plan because sufficient information is not available to use defined benefit accounting (see paragraph 28.11) it shall: **28.40A**

(a)   disclose the fact that it is a defined benefit plan and the reason why it is being accounted for as a defined contribution plan, along with any available information about the plan's surplus or deficit and the implications, if any, for the entity;

---

[15] *An example of the features of a detailed formal plan for restructuring, which may include termination benefits, is given in paragraph 21.11C.*

(b)   include a description of the extent to which the entity can be liable to the plan for other entities' obligations under the terms and conditions of the multi-employer plan; and

(c)   disclose how any liability recognised in accordance with paragraph 28.11A has been determined.

Disclosures about defined benefit plans

28.41   An entity shall disclose the following information about defined benefit plans (except for any defined multi-employer benefit plans that are accounted for as a defined contribution plan in accordance with paragraphs 28.11 and 28.11A, for which the disclosures in paragraphs 28.40 and 28.40A apply instead). If an entity has more than one defined benefit plan, these disclosures may be made in aggregate, separately for each plan, or in such groupings as are considered to be the most useful:

(a)   A general description of the type of plan, including **funding** policy. This includes the amount and timing of the future payments to be made by the entity under any agreement with the defined benefit plan to fund a deficit (such as a schedule of contributions).

(b)   [Not used]

(c)   [Not used]

(d)   The date of the most recent comprehensive actuarial valuation and, if it was not as of the reporting date, a description of the adjustments that were made to measure the defined benefit obligation at the reporting date.

(e)   A reconciliation of opening and closing balances for each of the following:

(i)   the defined benefit obligation;

(ii)   the fair value of plan assets; and

(iii) any reimbursement right recognised as an asset.

(f)   Each of the reconciliations in paragraph 28.41(e) shall show each of the following, if applicable:

(i)   the change in the defined benefit liability arising from employee service rendered during the reporting period in profit or loss;

(ii)   interest income or expense;

(iii) remeasurement of the defined benefit liability, showing separately actuarial gains and losses and the return on plan assets less amounts included in (ii) above; and

(iv)   plan introductions, changes, curtailments and settlements.

(g)   The total cost relating to defined benefit plans for the period, disclosing separately the amounts:

(i)   recognised in profit or loss as an expense; and

(ii)   included in the cost of an asset.

(h)   For each major class of plan assets, which shall include, but is not limited to, equity instruments, debt instruments, property, and all other assets, the percentage or amount that each major class constitutes of the fair value of the total plan assets at the reporting date.

(i)   The amounts included in the fair value of plan assets for:

(i)   each class of the entity's own **financial instruments**; and

(ii)   any property occupied by, or other assets used by, the entity.

(j)   The return on plan assets.

(k)   The principal actuarial assumptions used, including, when applicable:

(i)   the discount rates;

(ii)   [not used]

(iii)   the expected rates of salary increases;

(iv)   medical cost trend rates; and

(v)   any other **material** actuarial assumptions used.

The reconciliations in (e) and (f) above need not be presented for prior periods.

Editor's note: Amendments to FRS 102 The Financial Reporting Standard applicable in the UK and Republic of Ireland – Pension obligations (February 2015) amended paragraph 28.41(a) with effect for annual periods beginning on or after 1 January 2015.

If an entity participates in a defined benefit plan that shares risks between entities under common control (see paragraph 28.38) it shall disclose the following information: **28.41A**

(a)   The contractual agreement or stated policy for charging the cost of a defined benefit plan or the fact that there is no policy.

(b)   The policy for determining the contribution to be paid by the entity.

(c)   If the entity accounts for an allocation of the net defined benefit cost, all the information required in paragraph 28.41.

(d)   If the entity accounts for the contributions payable for the period, the information about the plan as a whole required by paragraph 28.41(a), (d), (h) and (i).

This information can be disclosed by cross-reference to disclosures in another group entity's **financial statements** if:

(i)   that group entity's financial statements separately identify and disclose the information required about the plan; and

(ii)   that group entity's financial statements are available to users of the financial statements on the same terms as the financial statements of the entity and at the same time as, or earlier than, the financial statements of the entity.

Disclosures about other long-term benefits

For each category of other long-term benefits that an entity provides to its employees, the entity shall disclose the nature of the benefit, the amount of its obligation and the extent of funding at the reporting date.   **28.42**

Disclosures about termination benefits

For each category of termination benefits that an entity provides to its employees, the entity shall disclose the nature of the benefit, its **accounting policy**, and the amount of its obligation and the extent of funding at the reporting date.   **28.43**

When there is uncertainty about the number of employees who will accept an offer of termination benefits, a **contingent liability** exists. Section 21 *Provisions and Contingencies* requires an entity to disclose information about its contingent liabilities unless the possibility of an outflow in settlement is remote.   **28.44**

Section 29 Income Tax

Scope of this section

For the purpose of this FRS, **income tax** includes all domestic and foreign taxes that are based on **taxable profit**. Income tax also includes taxes, such as withholding taxes, that are payable by a **subsidiary**, **associate** or **joint venture** on distributions to the reporting entity.   **29.1**

29.2 This section covers accounting for income tax. It requires an entity to recognise the current and future tax consequences of transactions and other events that have been recognised in the **financial statements**. These recognised tax amounts comprise **current tax** and **deferred tax**. Current tax is tax payable (refundable) in respect of the taxable profit (tax loss) for the current period or past **reporting periods**. Deferred tax represents the future tax consequences of transactions and events recognised in the financial statements of the current and previous periods. This section also requires that deferred tax is recognised in respect of **assets** (other than **goodwill**) and **liabilities** recognised as a result of a **business combination**.

29.2A This section also covers accounting for value added tax (VAT) and other similar sales taxes, which are not income taxes.

Recognition and measurement of current tax

29.3 An entity shall recognise a current tax liability for tax payable on taxable profit for the current and past periods. If the amount of tax paid for the current and past periods exceeds the amount of tax payable for those periods, the entity shall recognise the excess as a current tax asset.

29.4 An entity shall recognise a current tax asset for the benefit of a tax loss that can be carried back to recover tax paid in a previous period.

29.5 An entity shall measure a current tax liability (asset) at the amount of tax it expects to pay (recover) using the tax rates and laws that have been enacted or **substantively enacted** by the **reporting date**.

Recognition of deferred tax

Timing differences

29.6 Deferred tax shall be recognised in respect of all **timing differences** at the reporting date, except as otherwise required by paragraphs 29.7 to 29.9 and 29.11 below. Timing differences are differences between taxable profits and **total comprehensive income** as stated in the financial statements that arise from the inclusion of **income** and **expenses** in tax assessments in periods different from those in which they are recognised in financial statements.

29.7 Unrelieved tax losses and other **deferred tax assets** shall be recognised only to the extent that it is **probable** that they will be recovered against the reversal of **deferred tax liabilities** or other future taxable profits (the very existence of unrelieved tax losses is strong evidence that there may not be other future taxable profits against which the losses will be relieved).

29.8 Deferred tax shall be recognised when the tax allowances for the cost of a **fixed asset** are received before or after the **depreciation** of the fixed asset is recognised in **profit or loss**. If and when all conditions for retaining the tax allowances have been met, the deferred tax shall be reversed.

29.9 Deferred tax shall be recognised when income or expenses from a subsidiary, associate, branch, or interest in joint venture have been recognised in the financial statements, and will be assessed to or allowed for tax in a future period, except where:

(a)   the reporting entity is able to control the reversal of the timing difference; and
(b)   it is probable that the timing difference will not reverse in the foreseeable future.

Such timing differences may arise, for example, where there are undistributed profits in a subsidiary, associate, branch or interest in a joint venture.

Permanent differences

Permanent differences arise because certain types of **income** and expenses are non-taxable or disallowable, or because certain tax charges or allowances are greater or smaller than the corresponding income or expense in the financial statements. Deferred tax shall not be recognised on permanent differences except for circumstances set out in paragraph 29.11.

29.10

Business combinations

When the amount that can be deducted for tax for an asset (other than goodwill) that is recognised in a business combination is less (more) than the value at which it is recognised, a deferred tax liability (asset) shall be recognised for the additional tax that will be paid (avoided) in respect of that difference. Similarly, a deferred tax asset (liability) shall be recognised for the additional tax that will be avoided (paid) because of a difference between the value at which a liability is recognised and the amount that will be assessed for tax. The amount attributed to goodwill shall be adjusted by the amount of deferred tax recognised.

29.11

Issued 12 November 2013

Clarification statement in relation to deferred tax arising on a business combination

Paragraph 29.11 of FRS 102 requires an entity to recognise a deferred tax asset or liability for the difference between the amount that can be deducted for tax for an asset (other than goodwill) that is acquired in a business combination and the value at which it is recognised.

The phrase 'the amount that can be deducted for tax' is not a defined term in FRS 102 and it has been brought to the FRC's attention that the meaning of this phrase would benefit from clarification.

In applying this paragraph an entity should consider the manner in which it expects, at the end of the reporting period, to recover or settle the carrying amount of its assets and liabilities. This assessment should include consideration of all taxes, including operating taxes and taxes arising from the sale of the item, if appropriate.

Measurement of deferred tax

An entity shall measure a deferred tax liability (asset) using the tax rates and laws that have been enacted or substantively enacted by the reporting date that are expected to apply to the reversal of the timing difference except for the cases dealt with in paragraphs 29.15 and 29.16 below.

29.12

When different tax rates apply to different levels of taxable profit, an entity shall measure deferred tax expense (income) and related deferred tax liabilities (assets) using the average enacted or substantively enacted rates that it expects to be applicable to the taxable profit (tax loss) of the periods in which it expects the deferred tax asset to be realised or the deferred tax liability to be settled.

29.13

29.14   In some jurisdictions, income taxes are payable at a higher or lower rate if part or all of the profit or retained earnings is paid out as a dividend to shareholders of the entity. In other jurisdictions, income taxes may be refundable or payable if part or all of the profit or retained earnings is paid out as a dividend to shareholders of the entity. In both of those circumstances, an entity shall measure current and deferred taxes at the tax rate applicable to undistributed profits until the entity recognises a liability to pay a dividend. When the entity recognises a liability to pay a dividend, it shall recognise the resulting current or deferred tax liability (asset), and the related **tax expense** (income).

29.15   Deferred tax relating to a non-depreciable asset that is measured using the revaluation model in Section 17 *Property, Plant and Equipment* shall be measured using the tax rates and allowances that apply to the sale of the asset.

29.16   Deferred tax relating to **investment property** that is measured at **fair value** in accordance with Section 16 *Investment Property* shall be measured using the tax rates and allowances that apply to sale of the asset, except for investment property that has a limited **useful life** and is held within a business model whose objective is to consume substantially all of the economic benefits embodied in the property over time.

Measurement of both current and deferred tax

29.17   An entity shall not discount current or deferred tax assets and liabilities.

Withholding tax on dividends

29.18   When an entity pays dividends to its shareholders, it may be required to pay a portion of the dividends to taxation authorities on behalf of shareholders. Outgoing dividends and similar amounts payable shall be recognised at an amount that includes any withholding tax but excludes other taxes, such as attributable tax credits.

29.19   Incoming dividends and similar income receivable shall be recognised at an amount that includes any withholding tax but excludes other taxes, such as attributable tax credits. Any withholding tax suffered shall be shown as part of the tax charge.

Value Added Tax ('VAT') and other similar sales taxes

29.20   **Turnover** shown in profit or loss shall exclude VAT and other similar sales taxes on taxable outputs and VAT imputed under the flat rate VAT scheme. Expenses shall exclude recoverable VAT and other similar recoverable sales taxes. Irrecoverable VAT allocable to fixed assets and to other items disclosed separately in the financial statements shall be included in their cost where practicable and **material**.

Presentation

Allocation in comprehensive income and equity

29.21   An entity shall present changes in a current tax liability (asset) and changes in a deferred tax liability (asset) as tax expense (income) with the exception of those changes arising on the initial **recognition** of a business combination which shall be dealt with in accordance with paragraph 29.11.

29.22   An entity shall present tax expense (income) in the same component of **total comprehensive income** (ie continuing or **discontinued operations**, and profit or loss or

other comprehensive income) or **equity** as the transaction or other event that resulted in the tax expense (income).

Presentation in the statement of financial position

An entity shall present deferred tax liabilities within provisions for liabilities and deferred tax assets within debtors. **29.23**

Offsetting

An entity shall offset current tax assets and current tax liabilities, if and only if, it has a legally enforceable right to set off the amounts and it intends either to settle on a net basis or to realise the asset and settle the liability simultaneously. **29.24**

An entity shall offset deferred tax assets and deferred tax liabilities if, and only if: **29.24A**

(a) the entity has a legally enforceable right to set off current tax assets against current tax liabilities; and

(b) the deferred tax assets and deferred tax liabilities relate to income taxes levied by the same taxation authority on either the same taxable entity or different taxable entities which intend either to settle current tax liabilities and assets on a net basis, or to realise the assets and settle the liabilities simultaneously, in each future period in which significant amounts of deferred tax liabilities or assets are expected to be settled or recovered.

Disclosures

An entity shall disclose information that enables users of its financial statements to evaluate the nature and financial effect of the current and deferred tax consequences of recognised transactions and other events. **29.25**

An entity shall disclose separately the major components of tax expense (income). Such components of tax expense (income) may include: **29.26**

(a) current tax expense (income);

(b) any adjustments recognised in the period for current tax of prior periods;

(c) the amount of deferred tax expense (income) relating to the origination and reversal of timing differences;

(d) the amount of deferred tax expense (income) relating to changes in tax rates or the imposition of new taxes;

(e) adjustments to deferred tax expense (income) arising from a change in the tax status of the entity or its shareholders; and

(f) the amount of tax expense (income) relating to changes in **accounting policies** and **material errors** (see Section 10 *Accounting Policies, Estimates and Errors*).

An entity shall disclose the following separately: **29.27**

(a) the aggregate current and deferred tax relating to items that are recognised as items of other comprehensive income or equity;

(b) a reconciliation between:

(i) the tax expense (income) included in profit or loss; and

(ii) the profit or loss on ordinary activities before tax multiplied by the applicable tax rate;

(c)   the amount of the net reversal of deferred tax assets and deferred tax liabilities expected to occur during the year beginning after the **reporting period** together with a brief explanation for the expected reversal;

(d)   an explanation of changes in the applicable tax rate(s) compared with the previous reporting period;

(e)   the amount of deferred tax liabilities and deferred tax assets at the end of the reporting period for each type of timing difference and the amount of unused tax losses and tax credits;

(f)   the expiry date, if any, of timing differences, unused tax losses and unused tax credits; and

(g)   in the circumstances described in paragraph 29.14, an explanation of the nature of the potential income tax consequences that would result from the payment of dividends to its shareholders.

Section 30 Foreign Currency Translation

Scope of this section

30.1   An entity can conduct foreign activities in two ways. It may have transactions in foreign currencies or it may have **foreign operations**. In addition, an entity may present its **financial statements** in a foreign currency. This section prescribes how to include foreign currency transactions and foreign operations in the financial statements of an entity and how to translate financial statements into a **presentation currency**. Hedge accounting of foreign currency items is dealt with in Section 12 *Other Financial Instruments Issues*.

Functional currency

30.2   Each entity shall identify its **functional currency**. An entity's functional currency is the currency of the primary economic environment in which the entity operates.

30.3   The primary economic environment in which an entity operates is normally the one in which it primarily generates and expends **cash**. Therefore, the following are the most important factors an entity considers in determining its functional currency:

(a)   the currency:

  (i)   that mainly influences sales prices for goods and services (this will often be the currency in which sales prices for its goods and services are denominated and settled); and

  (ii)   of the country whose competitive forces and regulations mainly determine the sales prices of its goods and services; and

(b)   the currency that mainly influences labour, material and other costs of providing goods or services (this will often be the currency in which such costs are denominated and settled).

30.4   The following factors may also provide evidence of an entity's functional currency:

(a)   the currency in which funds from **financing activities** (issuing debt and equity instruments) are generated; and

(b)   the currency in which receipts from **operating activities** are usually retained.

30.5   The following additional factors are considered in determining the functional currency of a foreign operation, and whether its functional currency is the same as that of the reporting entity (the reporting entity, in this context, being the entity that has the foreign operation as its **subsidiary**, branch, **associate** or **joint venture**):

(a)   Whether the activities of the foreign operation are carried out as an extension of the reporting entity, rather than being carried out with a significant degree of autonomy. An example of the former is when the foreign operation only sells goods imported from the reporting entity and remits the proceeds to it. An example of the latter is when the operation accumulates cash and other **monetary items**, incurs **expenses**, generates **income** and arranges borrowings, all substantially in its local currency.

(b)   Whether transactions with the reporting entity are a high or a low proportion of the foreign operation's activities.

(c)   Whether **cash flows** from the activities of the foreign operation directly affect the cash flows of the reporting entity and are readily available for remittance to it.

(d)   Whether cash flows from the activities of the foreign operation are sufficient to service existing and normally expected debt obligations without funds being made available by the reporting entity.

Reporting foreign currency transactions in the functional currency

Initial recognition

A foreign currency transaction is a transaction that is denominated or requires settlement   **30.6** in a foreign currency, including transactions arising when an entity:

(a)   buys or sells goods or services whose price is denominated in a foreign currency;

(b)   borrows or lends funds when the amounts payable or receivable are denominated in a foreign currency; or

(c)   otherwise acquires or disposes of **assets**, or incurs or settles **liabilities**, denominated in a foreign currency.

An entity shall record a foreign currency transaction, on initial **recognition** in the functional   **30.7** currency, by applying to the foreign currency amount the spot exchange rate between the functional currency and the foreign currency at the date of the transaction.

The date of a transaction is the date on which the transaction first qualifies for recognition   **30.8** in accordance with this FRS. For practical reasons, a rate that approximates the actual rate at the date of the transaction is often used, for example, an average rate for a week or a month might be used for all transactions in each foreign currency occurring during that period. However, if exchange rates fluctuate significantly, the use of the average rate for a period is inappropriate.

Reporting at the end of the subsequent reporting periods

At the end of each **reporting period**, an entity shall: **30.9**

(a)   translate foreign currency monetary items using the **closing rate**;

(b)   translate non-monetary items that are measured in terms of historical cost in a foreign currency using the exchange rate at the date of the transaction; and

(c)   translate non-monetary items that are measured at **fair value** in a foreign currency using the exchange rates at the date when the fair value was determined.

An entity shall recognise, in **profit or loss** in the period in which they arise, exchange   **30.10** differences arising on the settlement of monetary items or on translating monetary items at rates different from those at which they were translated on initial recognition during the period or in previous periods, except as described in paragraph 30.13.

When another section of this FRS requires a **gain** or loss on a non-monetary item to be   **30.11** recognised in **other comprehensive income**, an entity shall recognise any exchange component of that gain or loss in other comprehensive income. Conversely, when a gain or loss on a non-monetary item is recognised in profit or loss, an entity shall recognise any exchange component of that gain or loss in profit or loss.

Net investment in a foreign operation

30.12   An entity may have a monetary item that is receivable from or payable to a foreign operation. An item for which settlement is neither planned nor likely to occur in the foreseeable future is, in substance, a part of the entity's net investment in that foreign operation, and is accounted for in accordance with paragraph 30.13. Such monetary items may include long-term receivables or loans. They do not include trade receivables or trade payables.

30.13   Exchange differences arising on a monetary item that forms part of a reporting entity's **net investment in a foreign operation** shall be recognised in profit or loss in the **separate financial statements** of the reporting entity or the **individual financial statements** of the foreign operation, as appropriate. In the financial statements that include the foreign operation and the reporting entity (eg **consolidated financial statements** when the foreign operation is a subsidiary), such exchange differences shall be recognised in other comprehensive income and accumulated in **equity**. They shall not be recognised in profit or loss on disposal of the net investment.

Change in functional currency

30.14   When there is a change in an entity's functional currency, the entity shall apply the translation procedures applicable to the new functional currency prospectively from the date of the change.

30.15   As noted in paragraphs 30.2 to 30.5, the functional currency of an entity reflects the underlying transactions, events and conditions that are relevant to the entity. Accordingly, once the functional currency is determined, it can be changed only if there is a change to those underlying transactions, events and conditions. For example, a change in the currency that mainly influences the sales prices of goods and services may lead to a change in an entity's functional currency.

30.16   The effect of a change in functional currency is accounted for prospectively. In other words, an entity translates all items into the new functional currency using the exchange rate at the date of the change. The resulting translated amounts for non-monetary items are treated as their historical cost.

Use of a presentation currency other than the functional currency

Translation to the presentation currency

30.17   An entity may present its financial statements in any currency (or currencies). If the presentation currency differs from the entity's functional currency, the entity shall translate its items of income and expense and **financial position** into the presentation currency. For example, when a **group** contains individual entities with different functional currencies, the items of income and expense and financial position of each entity are expressed in a common currency so that consolidated financial statements may be presented.

30.18   An entity whose functional currency is not the currency of a hyperinflationary economy shall translate its results and financial position into a different presentation currency using the following procedures:

(a) assets and liabilities for each **statement of financial position** presented (ie including comparatives) shall be translated at the closing rate at the date of that statement of financial position;

(b) income and expenses for each **statement of comprehensive income** (ie including comparatives) shall be translated at exchange rates at the dates of the transactions; and

(c) all resulting exchange differences shall be recognised in other comprehensive income.

For practical reasons, an entity may use a rate that approximates the exchange rates at the **30.19** dates of the transactions, for example an average rate for the period to translate income and expense items. However, if exchange rates fluctuate significantly, the use of the average rate for a period is inappropriate.

The exchange differences referred to in paragraph 30.18(c) result from: **30.20**

(a) translating income and expenses at the exchange rates at the dates of the transactions and assets and liabilities at the closing rate; and

(b) translating the opening net assets at a closing rate that differs from the previous closing rate.

When the exchange differences relate to a foreign operation that is consolidated but not wholly-owned, accumulated exchange differences arising from translation and attributable to the **non-controlling interest** are allocated to, and recognised as part of, non-controlling interest in the consolidated statement of financial position.

An entity whose functional currency is the currency of a hyperinflationary economy **30.21** shall adjust its results and financial position using the procedures specified in Section 31 *Hyperinflation* before applying the requirements of this section.

Translation of a foreign operation into the investor's presentation currency

In incorporating the assets, liabilities, income and expenses of a foreign operation with **30.22** those of the reporting entity, the entity shall follow normal consolidation procedures, such as the elimination of intragroup balances and intragroup transactions of a subsidiary (see Section 9 *Consolidated and Separate Financial Statements*) and the translation procedures set out in paragraphs 30.17 to 30.21. An intragroup monetary asset (or liability), whether short-term or long-term, cannot be eliminated against the corresponding intragroup liability (or asset) without showing the results of currency fluctuations in the consolidated financial statements. This is because the monetary item represents a commitment to convert one currency into another and exposes the reporting entity to a gain or loss through currency fluctuations. Accordingly, in the consolidated financial statements, a reporting entity continues to recognise such an exchange difference in profit or loss or, if it arises from the circumstances described in paragraph 30.13, the entity shall recognise it in other comprehensive income.

Any **goodwill** arising on the acquisition of a foreign operation and any fair value adjustments **30.23** to the **carrying amounts** of assets and liabilities arising on the acquisition of that foreign operation shall be treated as assets and liabilities of the foreign operation. Thus, they shall be expressed in the functional currency of the foreign operation and shall be translated at the closing rate in accordance with paragraph 30.18.

Disclosures

30.24   In paragraphs 30.26 and 30.27, references to functional currency apply, in the case of a group, to the functional currency of the **parent**.

30.25   An entity shall disclose the following:

(a)   the amount of exchange differences recognised in profit or loss during the period, except for those arising on **financial instruments** measured at fair value through profit or loss in accordance with Sections 11 *Basic Financial Instruments* and Section 12.

(b)   the amount of exchange differences arising during the period and classified in equity at the end of the period.

30.26   An entity shall disclose the currency in which the financial statements are presented. When the presentation currency is different from the functional currency, an entity shall state that fact and shall disclose the functional currency and the reason for using a different presentation currency.

30.27   When there is a change in the functional currency of either the reporting entity or a significant foreign operation, the entity shall disclose that fact and the reason for the change in functional currency.

Section 31 Hyperinflation

Scope of this section

31.1   This section applies to an entity whose **functional currency** is the currency of a hyperinflationary economy. It requires such an entity to prepare **financial statements** that have been adjusted for the effects of hyperinflation.

Hyperinflationary economy

31.2   This section does not establish an absolute rate at which an economy is deemed hyperinflationary. An entity shall make that judgement by considering all available information including, but not limited to, the following possible indicators of hyperinflation:

(a)   The general population prefers to keep its wealth in non-monetary assets or in a relatively stable foreign currency. Amounts of local currency held are immediately invested to maintain purchasing power.

(b)   The general population regards monetary amounts not in terms of the local currency but in terms of a relatively stable foreign currency. Prices may be quoted in that currency.

(c)   Sales and purchases on credit take place at prices that compensate for the expected loss of purchasing power during the credit period, even if the period is short.

(d)   Interest rates, wages and prices are linked to a price index.

(e)   The cumulative inflation rate over three years is approaching, or exceeds, 100%.

Measuring unit in the financial statements

31.3   All amounts in the financial statements of an entity whose functional currency is the currency of a hyperinflationary economy shall be stated in terms of the measuring unit current at the end of the **reporting period**. The comparative information for the previous period required by paragraph 3.14, and any information presented in respect of earlier periods, shall also be stated in terms of the measuring unit current at the **reporting date**.

The restatement of financial statements in accordance with this section requires the use of a general price index that reflects changes in general purchasing power. In most economies there is a recognised general price index, normally produced by the government, that entities will follow.   **31.4**

Procedures for restating historical cost financial statements

Statement of financial position

Statement of financial position amounts not expressed in terms of the measuring unit current at the end of the reporting period are restated by applying a general price index.   **31.5**

Monetary items are not restated because they are expressed in terms of the measuring unit current at the end of the reporting period. Monetary items are money held and items to be received or paid in money.   **31.6**

Assets and **liabilities** linked by agreement to changes in prices, such as index-linked bonds and loans, are adjusted in accordance with the agreement and presented at this adjusted amount in the restated statement of financial position.   **31.7**

All other assets and liabilities are non-monetary: **31.8**

(a)   Some non-monetary items are carried at amounts current at the end of the reporting period, such as net realisable value and **fair value**, so they are not restated. All other non-monetary assets and liabilities are restated.

(b)   Most non-monetary items are carried at cost or cost less **depreciation**; hence they are expressed at amounts current at their date of acquisition. The restated cost, or cost less depreciation, of each item is determined by applying to its historical cost and accumulated depreciation the change in a general price index from the date of acquisition to the end of the reporting period.

(c)   The restated amount of a non-monetary item is reduced, in accordance with Section 27 *Impairment of Assets*, when it exceeds its **recoverable amount**.

At the beginning of the first period of application of this section, the components of **equity**, except retained earnings, are restated by applying a general price index from the dates the components were contributed or otherwise arose. Restated retained earnings are derived from all the other amounts in the restated statement of financial position.   **31.9**

At the end of the first period and in subsequent periods, all components of owners' equity are restated by applying a general price index from the beginning of the period or the date of contribution, if later. The changes for the period in owners' equity are disclosed in accordance with Section 6 *Statement of Changes in Equity and Statement of Income and Retained Earnings*.   **31.10**

Statement of comprehensive income and income statement

All items in the **statement of comprehensive income** (and in the **income statement**, if presented) shall be expressed in terms of the measuring unit current at the end of the reporting period. Therefore, all amounts need to be restated by applying the change in the general price index from the dates when the items of **income** and **expenses** were initially recognised in the financial statements. If general inflation is approximately even throughout the period, and the items of income and expense arose approximately evenly throughout the period, an average rate of inflation may be appropriate.   **31.11**

Statement of cash flows

31.12   An entity shall express all items in the **statement of cash flows** in terms of the measuring unit current at the end of the reporting period.

Gain or loss on net monetary position

31.13   In a period of inflation, an entity holding an excess of monetary assets over monetary liabilities loses purchasing power, and an entity with an excess of monetary liabilities over monetary assets gains purchasing power, to the extent the assets and liabilities are not linked to a price level. An entity shall include in **profit or loss** the **gain** or loss on the net monetary position. An entity shall offset the adjustment to those assets and liabilities linked by agreement to changes in prices made in accordance with paragraph 31.7 against the gain or loss on net monetary position.

Economies ceasing to be hyperinflationary

31.14   When an economy ceases to be hyperinflationary and an entity discontinues the preparation and presentation of financial statements prepared in accordance with this section, it shall treat the amounts expressed in the **presentation currency** at the end of the previous reporting period as the basis for the **carrying amounts** in its subsequent financial statements.

Disclosures

31.15   An entity to which this section applies shall disclose the following:

(a)   the fact that financial statements and other prior period data have been restated for changes in the general purchasing power of the functional currency;

(b)   the identity and level of the price index at the reporting date and changes during the current reporting period and the previous reporting period; and

(c)   amount of gain or loss on monetary items.

Section 32 Events after the End of the Reporting Period

Scope of this section

32.1   This section defines events after the end of the **reporting period** and sets out principles for recognising, measuring and disclosing those events.

Events after the end of the reporting period defined

32.2   Events after the end of the reporting period are those events, favourable and unfavourable, that occur between the end of the reporting period and the date when the **financial statements** are authorised for issue. There are two types of events:

(a)   those that provide evidence of conditions that existed at the end of the reporting period (adjusting events after the end of the reporting period); and

(b)   those that are indicative of conditions that arose after the end of the reporting period (non-adjusting events after the end of the reporting period).

32.3   Events after the end of the reporting period include all events up to the date when the financial statements are authorised for issue, even if those events occur after the public announcement of **profit or loss** or other selected financial information.

Recognition and measurement

Adjusting events after the end of the reporting period

An entity shall adjust the amounts recognised in its financial statements, including related **32.4**
disclosures, to reflect adjusting events after the end of the reporting period.

The following are examples of adjusting events after the end of the reporting period **32.5**
that require an entity to adjust the amounts recognised in its financial statements, or to
recognise items that were not previously recognised:

(a)   The settlement after the end of the reporting period of a court case that confirms
      that the entity had a present obligation at the end of the reporting period. The entity
      adjusts any previously recognised **provision** related to this court case in accordance
      with Section 21 *Provisions and Contingencies* or recognises a new provision. The
      entity does not merely disclose a **contingent liability**. Rather, the settlement provides
      additional evidence to be considered in determining the provision that should be
      recognised at the end of the reporting period in accordance with Section 21.

(b)   The receipt of information after the end of the reporting period indicating that an **asset**
      was impaired at the end of the reporting period, or that the amount of a previously
      recognised **impairment loss** for that asset needs to be adjusted. For example:

      (i)   the bankruptcy of a customer that occurs after the end of the reporting period
             usually confirms that a loss existed at the end of the reporting period on a trade
             receivable and that the entity needs to adjust the **carrying amount** of the trade
             receivable; and

      (ii)   the sale of **inventories** after the end of the reporting period may give evidence
             about their selling price at the end of the reporting period for the purpose of
             assessing impairment at that date.

(c)   The determination after the end of the reporting period of the cost of assets purchased,
      or the proceeds from assets sold, before the end of the reporting period.

(d)   The determination after the end of the reporting period of the amount of profit-
      sharing or bonus payments, if the entity had a legal or **constructive obligation** at the
      end of the reporting period to make such payments as a result of events before that
      date (see Section 28 *Employee Benefits*).

(e)   The discovery of fraud or **errors** that show that the financial statements are incorrect.

Non-adjusting events after the end of the reporting period

An entity shall not adjust the amounts recognised in its financial statements to reflect non- **32.6**
adjusting events after the end of the reporting period.

Examples of non-adjusting events after the end of the reporting period include: **32.7**

(a)   A decline in market value of investments between the end of the reporting period and
      the date when the financial statements are authorised for issue. The decline in market
      value does not normally relate to the condition of the investments at the end of the
      reporting period, but reflects circumstances that have arisen subsequently. Therefore,
      an entity does not adjust the amounts recognised in its financial statements for
      the investments. Similarly, the entity does not update the amounts disclosed for
      the investments as at the end of the reporting period, although it may need to give
      additional disclosure in accordance with paragraph 32.10.

(b)   An amount that becomes receivable as a result of a favourable judgement or
      settlement of a court case after the **reporting date** but before the financial statements
      are authorised for issued. This would be a **contingent asset** at the reporting date
      (see paragraph 21.13), and disclosure may be required by paragraph 21.16. However,

agreement on the amount of damages for a judgement that was reached before the reporting date, but was not previously recognised because the amount could not be measured reliably, may constitute an adjusting event.

Further examples of non-adjusting events are set out in paragraph 32.11.

Going concern

32.7A   An entity shall not prepare its financial statements on a **going concern** basis if management determines after the reporting period either that it intends to liquidate the entity or to cease trading, or that it has no realistic alternative but to do so.

32.7B   Deterioration in operating results and **financial position** after the reporting period may indicate a need to consider whether the going concern assumption is still appropriate. If the going concern assumption is no longer appropriate, the effect is so pervasive that this section requires a fundamental change in the basis of accounting, rather than an adjustment to the amounts recognised within the original basis of accounting and therefore the disclosure requirements of paragraph 3.9 apply.

Dividends

32.8   If an entity declares dividends to holders of its equity instruments after the end of the reporting period, the entity shall not recognise those dividends as a **liability** at the end of the reporting period because no obligation exists at that time. The amount of the dividend may be presented as a segregated component of retained earnings at the end of the reporting period.

Disclosure

Date of authorisation for issue

32.9   An entity shall disclose the date when the financial statements were authorised for issue and who gave that authorisation. If the entity's **owners** or others have the power to amend the financial statements after issue, the entity shall disclose that fact.

Non-adjusting events after the end of the reporting period

32.10   An entity shall disclose the following for each category of non-adjusting event after the end of the reporting period:

(a)   the nature of the event; and

(b)   an estimate of its financial effect or a statement that such an estimate cannot be made.

32.11   The following are examples of non-adjusting events after the end of the reporting period that would generally result in disclosure. The disclosures will reflect information that becomes known after the end of the reporting period but before the financial statements are authorised for issue:

(a)   a major **business combination** or disposal of a major **subsidiary**;

(b)   announcement of a plan to discontinue an operation;

(c)   major purchases of assets, disposals or plans to dispose of assets, or expropriation of major assets by government;

(d)   the destruction of a major production plant by a fire;

(e)   announcement, or commencement of the implementation, of a major restructuring;

(f)   issues or repurchases of an entity's debt or equity instruments;

(g)   abnormally large changes in asset prices or foreign exchange rates;

(h)   changes in tax rates or tax laws enacted or announced that have a significant effect on current and **deferred tax assets and liabilities**;

(i)   entering into significant commitments or contingent liabilities, for example, by issuing significant guarantees; and

(j)   commencement of major litigation arising solely out of events that occurred after the end of the reporting period.

Section 33 Related Party Disclosures

Scope of this section

This section requires an entity to include in its **financial statements** the disclosures necessary to draw attention to the possibility that its **financial position** and **profit or loss** have been affected by the existence of **related parties** and by transactions and outstanding balances with such parties.

33.1

Disclosures need not be given of transactions entered into between two or more members of a **group**, provided that any **subsidiary** which is a party to the transaction is wholly owned by such a member.

33.1A

Related party defined

A related party is a person or entity that is related to the entity that is preparing its financial statements (the reporting entity).

33.2

(a)   A person or a **close member of that person's family** is related to a reporting entity if that person:

   (i)   has **control** or **joint control** over the reporting entity;

   (ii)   has **significant influence** over the reporting entity; or

   (iii) is a member of the **key management personnel** of the reporting entity or of a **parent** of the reporting entity.

(b)   An entity is related to a reporting entity if any of the following conditions apply:

   (i)   the entity and the reporting entity are members of the same group (which means that each parent, subsidiary and fellow subsidiary is related to the others).

   (ii)   one entity is an **associate** or **joint venture** of the other entity (or an associate or joint venture of a member of a group of which the other entity is a member).

   (iii) both entities are joint ventures of the same third party.

   (iv)   one entity is a joint venture of a third party and the other entity is an associate of the third entity.

   (v)   the entity is a **post-employment benefit plan** for the benefit of employees of either the reporting entity or an entity related to the reporting entity. If the reporting entity is itself such a plan, the sponsoring employers are also related to the reporting entity.

   (vi)   the entity is controlled or jointly controlled by a person identified in (a).

   (vii) a person identified in (a)(i) has significant influence over the entity or is a member of the key management personnel of the entity (or of a parent of the entity).

Prospective amendments: Amendments to FRS 102 *The Financial Reporting Standard applicable in the UK and Republic of Ireland – Small entities and other minor amendments*

(July 2015) amends this paragraph 33.2 with effect for annual periods beginning on or after 1 January 2016.

33.3   In considering each possible related party relationship, an entity shall assess the substance of the relationship and not merely the legal form.

33.4   In the context of this FRS, the following are not related parties:

(a)   Two entities simply because they have a director or other member of key management personnel in common or because a member of key management personnel of one entity has significant influence over the other entity.

(b)   Two **venturers** simply because they share joint control over a joint venture.

(c)   Any of the following simply by virtue of their normal dealings with an entity (even though they may affect the freedom of action of an entity or participate in its decision-making process):

(i)   providers of finance;

(ii)   trade unions;

(iii)   public utilities; and

(iv)   government departments and agencies.

(d)   A customer, supplier, franchisor, distributor or general agent with whom an entity transacts a significant volume of business, merely by virtue of the resulting economic dependence.

33.4A   In the definition of a related party, an associate includes subsidiaries of the associate and a joint venture includes subsidiaries of the joint venture. Therefore, for example, an associate's subsidiary and the investor that has significant influence over the associate are related to each other.

Disclosures

Disclosure of parent-subsidiary relationships

33.5   Relationships between a parent and its subsidiaries shall be disclosed irrespective of whether there have been **related party transactions**. An entity shall disclose the name of its parent and, if different, the ultimate controlling party. If neither the entity's parent nor the ultimate controlling party produces financial statements available for public use, the name of the next most senior parent that does so (if any) shall also be disclosed.

Disclosure of key management personnel compensation

33.6   Key management personnel are those persons having authority and responsibility for planning, directing and controlling the activities of the entity, directly or indirectly, including any director (whether executive or otherwise) of that entity. Compensation includes all **employee benefits** (as defined in Section 28 *Employee Benefits*) including those in the form of share-based payments (see Section 26 *Share-based Payment*). Employee benefits include all forms of consideration paid, payable or provided by the entity, or on behalf of the entity (eg by its parent or by a shareholder), in exchange for services rendered to the entity. It also includes such consideration paid on behalf of a parent of the entity in respect of goods or services provided to the entity.

33.7   An entity shall disclose key management personnel compensation in total.

Disclosure of related party transactions

33.8 A related party transaction is a transfer of resources, services or obligations between a reporting entity and a related party, regardless of whether a price is charged. Examples of related party transactions that are common to entities within the scope of this FRS include, but are not limited to:

(a) transactions between an entity and its principal **owner(s)**;

(b) transactions between an entity and another entity when both entities are under the common control of a single entity or person; and

(c) transactions in which an entity or person that controls the reporting entity incurs **expenses** directly that otherwise would have been borne by the reporting entity.

33.9 If an entity has related party transactions, it shall disclose the nature of the related party relationship as well as information about the transactions, outstanding balances and commitments necessary for an understanding of the potential effect of the relationship on the financial statements. Those disclosure requirements are in addition to the requirements in paragraph 33.7 to disclose key management personnel compensation. At a minimum, disclosures shall include:

(a) The amount of the transactions.

(b) The amount of outstanding balances and:

    (i) their terms and conditions, including whether they are secured, and the nature of the consideration to be provided in settlement; and

    (ii) details of any guarantees given or received.

(c) Provisions for uncollectible receivables related to the amount of outstanding balances.

(d) The expense recognised during the period in respect of bad or doubtful debts due from related parties.

Such transactions could include purchases, sales, or transfers of goods or services, **leases**, guarantees and settlements by the entity on behalf of the related party or vice versa.

33.10 An entity shall make the disclosures required by paragraph 33.9 separately for each of the following categories:

(a) entities with control, joint control or significant influence over the entity;

(b) entities over which the entity has control, joint control or significant influence;

(c) key management personnel of the entity or its parent (in the aggregate); and

(d) other related parties.

Prospective amendments: Amendments to FRS 102 *The Financial Reporting Standard applicable in the UK and Republic of Ireland* – Small entities and other minor amendments (July 2015) amends this paragraph 33.10 with effect for annual periods beginning on or after 1 January 2016.

33.11 An entity is exempt from the disclosure requirements of paragraph 33.9 in relation to:

(a) a **state** (a national, regional or local government) that has control, joint control or significant influence over the reporting entity; and

(b) another entity that is a related party because the same state has control, joint control or significant influence over both the reporting entity and the other entity.

However, the entity must still disclose a parent-subsidiary relationship as required by paragraph 33.5.

33.12 The following are examples of transactions that shall be disclosed if they are with a related party:

(a)   purchases or sales of goods (finished or unfinished);

(b)   purchases or sales of property and other **assets**;

(c)   rendering or receiving of services;

(d)   leases;

(e)   transfers of **research** and **development**;

(f)   transfers under licence agreements;

(g)   transfers under finance arrangements (including loans and equity contributions in **cash** or in kind);

(h)   provision of guarantees or collateral;

(i)   settlement of **liabilities** on behalf of the entity or by the entity on behalf of another party; and

(j)   participation by a parent or subsidiary in a **defined benefit plan** that shares risks between group entities.

33.13 An entity shall not state that related party transactions were made on terms equivalent to those that prevail in arm's length transactions unless such terms can be substantiated.

33.14 An entity may disclose items of a similar nature in the aggregate except when separate disclosure is necessary for an understanding of the effects of related party transactions on the financial statements of the entity.

Section 34 Specialised Activities

Scope of this section

34.1 This section sets out the financial reporting requirements for entities applying this FRS involved in the following types of specialised activities:

(a)   Agriculture (see paragraphs 34.2 to 34.10A);

(b)   Extractive Activities (see paragraphs 34.11 to 34.11C);

(c)   Service Concession Arrangements (see paragraphs 34.12 to 34.16A);

(d)   Financial Institutions (see paragraphs 34.17 to 34.33);

(e)   Retirement Benefit Plans: Financial Statements (see paragraphs 34.34 to 34.48);

(f)   Heritage Assets (see paragraphs 34.49 to 34.56);

(g)   Funding Commitments (see paragraphs 34.57 to 34.63);

(h)   Incoming Resources from Non-Exchange Transactions (see paragraphs 34.64 to 34.74);

(i)   Public Benefit Entity Combinations (see paragraphs 34.75 to 34.86); and

(j)   Public Benefit Entity Concessionary Loans (see paragraphs 34.87 to 34.97).

Agriculture

34.2 An entity using this FRS that is engaged in **agricultural activity** shall determine an **accounting policy** for each class of **biological asset** and its related **agricultural produce**.

Recognition

34.3 An entity shall recognise a biological asset or an item of agricultural produce when, and only when:

(a)   the entity controls the **asset** as a result of past events;
(b)   it is **probable** that future economic benefits associated with the asset will flow to the entity; and
(c)   the **fair value** or cost of the asset can be measured reliably.

Measurement

For each class of biological asset and its related agricultural produce an entity shall choose as its accounting policy either: **34.3A**

(a)   the fair value model set out in paragraphs 34.4 to 34.7A; or
(b)   the cost model set out in paragraphs 34.8 to 34.10A.

If an entity has chosen the fair value model for a class of biological asset and its related agricultural produce, it shall not subsequently change its accounting policy to the cost model.   **34.3B**

Measurement – fair value model

An entity applying the fair value model shall measure a biological asset on initial **recognition** and at each **reporting date** at its **fair value less costs to sell**. Changes in fair value less costs to sell shall be recognised in **profit or loss**.   **34.4**

Agricultural produce harvested from an entity's biological assets shall be measured at the point of harvest at its fair value less costs to sell. Such **measurement** is the cost at that date when applying Section 13 *Inventories* or another applicable section of this FRS.   **34.5**

In determining fair value, an entity shall consider the following: **34.6**

(a)   If an **active market** exists for a biological asset or agricultural produce in its present location and condition, the quoted price in that market is the appropriate basis for determining the fair value of that asset. If an entity has access to different active markets, the entity shall use the price existing in the market that it expects to use.
(b)   If an active market does not exist, an entity uses one or more of the following, when available, in determining fair value:

   (i)   the most recent market transaction price, provided that there has not been a significant change in economic circumstances between the date of that transaction and the end of the **reporting period**;
   (ii)   market prices for similar assets with adjustment to reflect differences; and
   (iii)   sector benchmarks such as the value of an orchard expressed per export tray, bushel, or hectare, and the value of cattle expressed per kilogram of meat.

(c)   In some cases, the information sources listed in (b) may suggest different conclusions as to the fair value of a biological asset or an item of agricultural produce. An entity considers the reasons for those differences, to arrive at the most reliable estimate of fair value within a relatively narrow range of reasonable estimates.
(d)   In some circumstances, fair value may be readily determinable even though market determined prices or values are not available for a biological asset in its present condition. An entity shall consider whether the **present value** of expected net cash flows from the asset discounted at a current market determined rate results in a reliable measure of fair value.

If the fair value of a biological asset cannot be measured reliably, the entity shall apply the cost model to that biological asset in accordance with paragraphs 34.8 and 34.10A until such time that the fair value can be reliably measured.   **34.6A**

Disclosures – fair value model

34.7   An entity shall disclose the following for each class of biological asset measured using the fair value model:

(a)   A description of each class of biological asset.

(b)   The methods and significant assumptions applied in determining the fair value of each class of biological asset.

(c)   A reconciliation of changes in the **carrying amount** of each class of biological asset between the beginning and the end of the current period. The reconciliation shall include:

    (i)   the **gain** or loss arising from changes in fair value less costs to sell;

    (ii)   increases resulting from purchases;

    (iii)   decreases attributable to sales;

    (iv)   decreases resulting from harvest;

    (v)   increases resulting from **business combinations**; and

    (vi)   other changes.

This reconciliation need not be presented for prior periods.

34.7A   If an entity measures any individual biological assets at cost in accordance with paragraph 34.6A, it shall explain why fair value cannot be reliably measured. If the fair value of such a biological asset becomes reliably measurable during the current period an entity shall explain why fair value has become reliably measurable and the effect of the change.

34.7B   An entity shall disclose the methods and significant assumptions applied in determining the fair value at the point of harvest of each class of agricultural produce.

Measurement – cost model

34.8   An entity applying the cost model shall measure biological assets at cost less any accumulated **depreciation** and any accumulated **impairment losses**.

34.9   In applying the cost model, agricultural produce harvested from an entity's biological assets shall be measured at the point of harvest at either:

(a)   the lower of cost and estimated selling price less costs to complete and sell; or

(b)   its fair value less costs to sell. Any gain or loss arising on initial recognition of agricultural produce at fair value less costs to sell shall be included in profit or loss for the period in which it arises.

Such measurement is the cost at that date when applying Section 13 or another applicable section of this FRS.

Disclosures – cost model

34.10   An entity shall disclose the following for each class of biological asset measured using the cost model:

(a)   a description of each class of biological asset;

(b)   [not used]

(c)   the depreciation method used;

(d)   the useful lives or the depreciation rates used; and

(e)   a reconciliation of changes in the carrying amount of each class of biological asset between the beginning and the end of the current period. The reconciliation shall include:

    (i)   increases resulting from purchases;

    (ii)   decreases attributable to sales;

    (iii) decreases resulting from harvest;

    (iv) increases resulting from business combinations;

    (v)   impairment losses recognised or reversed in profit or loss in accordance with Section 27 *Impairment of Assets*; and

    (vi) other changes.

This reconciliation need not be presented for prior periods.

An entity shall disclose, for any agricultural produce measured at fair value less costs to sell, the methods and significant assumptions applied in determining the fair value at the point of harvest of each class of agricultural produce.   **34.10A**

Extractive Activities

An entity using this FRS that is engaged in the exploration for and/or evaluation of mineral resources (extractive activities) shall apply the requirements of IFRS 6 *Exploration for and Evaluation of Mineral Resources*.   **34.11**

When applying the requirements of IFRS 6, references made to other IFRSs within that standard shall be taken to be references to the relevant section or paragraph within this FRS.   **34.11A**

Notwithstanding the requirements of paragraph 34.11A, when applying paragraph 21 of IFRS 6, a **cash-generating unit** or group of cash-generating units shall be no larger than an **operating segment** and the reference to IFRS 8 *Operating Segments* shall be ignored.   **34.11B**

On first-time adoption of this FRS if it is not practical to apply a particular requirement of paragraph 18 of IFRS 6 to previous comparative amounts, an entity shall disclose that fact.   **34.11C**

Service Concession Arrangements

A **service concession arrangement** is an arrangement whereby a public sector body, or a **public benefit entity** (the grantor) contracts with a private sector entity (the operator) to construct (or upgrade), operate and maintain **infrastructure assets** for a specified period of time (concession period). The operator is paid for its services over the period of the arrangement. A common feature of a service concession arrangement is the public service nature of the obligation undertaken by the operator, whereby the arrangement contractually obliges the operator to provide services to, or on behalf of, the grantor for the benefit of the public.   **34.12**

Specifically an arrangement is a service concession arrangement when the following conditions apply: **34.12A**

(a)   the grantor controls or regulates what services the operator must provide using the infrastructure assets, to whom, and at what price; and

(b)   the grantor controls, through ownership, beneficial entitlement or otherwise, any significant **residual interest** in the assets at the end of the term of the arrangement.

Where the infrastructure assets have no significant **residual value** at the end of the term of the arrangement (ie the arrangement is for its entire useful life), then the arrangement shall be accounted for as a service concession if the conditions in (a) are met.

For the purpose of condition (b), the grantor's control over any significant residual interest should both restrict the operator's practical ability to sell or pledge the infrastructure assets and give the grantor a continuing right of use throughout the concession period.

34.12B   A service concession arrangement shall be accounted for in accordance with the requirements of paragraphs 34.12E to 34.16A.

34.12C   A service concession arrangement may contain a group of contracts and sub-arrangements as elements of the service concession arrangement as a whole. Such an arrangement shall be treated as a whole when the group of contracts and sub-arrangements are linked in such a way that the commercial effect cannot be understood without reference to them as a whole. Accordingly, the contractual terms of certain contracts or arrangements may meet both the scope requirements of paragraphs 34.12 and 34.12A, and Section 20 *Leases*. Where this is the case, the requirements of this section shall prevail.

34.12D   Where an arrangement does not meet the requirements of paragraphs 34.12 and 34.12A, it shall be accounted for in accordance with Section 17 *Property, Plant and Equipment*, Section 18 *Intangible Assets other than Goodwill*, Section 20 or Section 23 *Revenue*, based on the nature of the arrangement.

Accounting by grantors – Finance lease liability model

34.12E   The infrastructure assets shall be recognised as **assets** of the grantor together with a **liability** for its obligations under the service concession arrangement.

34.12F   The grantor shall initially recognise the infrastructure assets and associated liability in accordance with paragraphs 20.9 and 20.10. If as a result of applying paragraphs 20.9 and 20.10 the grantor has not recognised a liability to make payments to the operator, it shall not recognise the infrastructure assets.

34.12G   The liability shall be recognised as a finance lease liability and subsequently accounted for in accordance with paragraph 20.11.

34.12H   The infrastructure assets shall be recognised as **property, plant and equipment** or as **intangible assets**, as appropriate, and subsequently accounted for in accordance with Section 17 or Section 18.

Accounting by operators

Treatment of the operator's rights over the infrastructure

34.12I   Infrastructure assets shall not be recognised as property, plant and equipment by the operator because the contractual service arrangement does not convey the right to control the use of the public service assets to the operator. The operator has access to operate the infrastructure to provide the public service on behalf of the grantor in accordance with the terms specified in the arrangement.

Recognition and measurement of consideration

There are two principal categories of service concession arrangements: **34.13**

(a) In one, the operator receives a **financial asset** – an unconditional contractual right to receive a specified or determinable amount of **cash** or another financial asset from, or at the direction of, the grantor in return for constructing (or upgrading) the infrastructure assets, and then operating and maintaining the asset for a specified period of time. This category includes guarantees by the grantor to pay for any shortfall between amounts received from users of the public service and specified or determinable amounts.

(b) In the other, the operator receives an **intangible asset** - a right to charge for use of the infrastructure assets that it constructs (or upgrades) and then operates and maintains for a specified period of time. A right to charge users is not an unconditional right to receive cash because the amounts are contingent on the extent to which the public uses the service.

Sometimes, a single arrangement may contain both types: to the extent that the grantor has given an unconditional guarantee of payment for the construction (or upgrade) of the infrastructure assets, the operator has a financial asset; to the extent that the operator receives a right to charge the public for using the service the operator has an intangible asset.

Accounting – financial asset model

The operator shall recognise a financial asset to the extent that it has an unconditional   **34.14** contractual right to receive cash or another financial asset from, or at the direction of, the grantor for the construction (or upgrade) services. The operator shall initially recognise the financial asset at fair value for the consideration received or receivable, based on the fair value of the construction (or upgrade) services provided. Thereafter, it shall account for the financial asset in accordance with Section 11 *Basic Financial Instruments* and Section 12 *Other Financial Instruments Issues*.

Accounting – intangible asset model

The operator shall recognise an intangible asset to the extent that it receives a right (a   **34.15** licence) to charge users of the public service. The operator shall initially recognise the intangible asset at fair value for the consideration received or receivable, based on the fair value of the construction (or upgrade) services provided. Thereafter, it shall account for the intangible asset in accordance with Section 18.

Operating services

The operator shall account for **revenue** in accordance with Section 23 for the operating   **34.16** services it performs.

Borrowing costs

Borrowing costs attributable to the arrangement shall be recognised as an **expense**, in   **34.16A** accordance with Section 25 *Borrowing Costs*, in the period in which they are incurred unless the operator has an intangible asset. In this case borrowing costs attributable to the arrangement may be capitalised in accordance with Section 25 where a policy of capitalisation has been adopted in accordance with that section.

Financial Institutions

34.17   A **financial institution** (other than a **retirement benefit plan**) applying this FRS shall, in addition to the disclosure requirements in Section 11 *Basic Financial Instruments* and Section 12 *Other Financial Instruments Issues*, provide the disclosures in paragraphs 34.19 to 34.33. The disclosures in paragraphs 34.19 to 34.33 are required to be provided in:

(a)   the **individual financial statements** of a financial institution (other than a retirement benefit plan); and

(b)   the **consolidated financial statements** of a **group** containing a financial institution (other than a retirement benefit plan) when the **financial instruments** held by the financial institution are **material** to the group. Where this is the case, the disclosures apply regardless of whether the principal activity of the group is being a financial institution or not. The disclosures in paragraphs 34.19 to 34.33 only need to be given in respect of financial instruments held by entities within the group that are financial institutions (other than retirement benefit plans).

34.18   A retirement benefit plan shall provide the disclosures in paragraphs 34.35 to 34.48 of this FRS.

Disclosures

Significance of financial instruments for financial position and performance

34.19   A financial institution shall disclose information that enables users of its **financial statements** to evaluate the significance of financial instruments for its **financial position** and **performance**.

34.20   A financial institution shall disclose a disaggregation of the **statement of financial position** line item by class of financial instrument. A class is a grouping of financial instruments that is appropriate to the nature of the information disclosed and that takes into account the characteristics of those financial instruments.

Impairment

34.21   Where a financial institution uses a separate allowance account to record impairments, it shall disclose a reconciliation of changes in that account during the period for each class of **financial asset**.

Fair value

34.22   For financial instruments held at **fair value** in the statement of financial position, a financial institution shall disclose for each class of financial instrument, an analysis of the level in the fair value hierarchy (as set out in paragraph 11.27) into which the fair value measurements are categorised.

Nature and extent of risks arising from financial instruments

34.23   A financial institution shall disclose information that enables users of its financial statements to evaluate the nature and extent of **credit risk**, **liquidity risk** and **market risk** arising from financial instruments to which the financial institution is exposed at the end of the **reporting period**.

For each type of risk arising from financial instruments, a financial institution shall disclose: **34.24**

(a)   the exposures to risk and how they arise;

(b)   its objectives, policies and processes for managing the risk and the methods used to measure the risk; and

(c)   any changes in (a) or (b) from the previous period.

Credit risk

A financial institution shall disclose by class of financial instrument: **34.25**

(a)   The amount that best represents its maximum exposure to credit risk at the end of the reporting period. This disclosure is not required for financial instruments whose **carrying amount** best represents the maximum exposure to credit risk.

(b)   A description of collateral held as security and of other credit enhancements, and the extent to which these mitigate credit risk.

(c)   The amount by which any related credit **derivatives** or similar instruments mitigate that maximum exposure to credit risk.

(d)   Information about the credit quality of **financial assets** that are neither past due nor impaired.

A financial institution shall provide, by class of financial asset, an analysis of: **34.26**

(a)   the age of financial assets that are past due as at the end of the reporting period but not impaired; and

(b)   the financial assets that are individually determined to be impaired as at the end of the reporting period, including the factors the financial institution considered in determining that they are impaired.

When a financial institution obtains financial or non-financial assets during the period by taking possession of collateral it holds as security or calling on other credit enhancements (eg guarantees), and such **assets** meet the **recognition** criteria in other sections, a financial institution shall disclose: **34.27**

(a)   the nature and carrying amount of the assets obtained; and

(b)   when the assets are not readily convertible into **cash**, its policies for disposing of such assets or for using them in its operations.

Liquidity risk

A financial institution shall provide a maturity analysis for **financial liabilities** that shows the remaining contractual maturities at undiscounted amounts separated between derivative and non-derivative financial liabilities.   **34.28**

Market risk

A financial institution shall provide a sensitivity analysis for each type of market risk (eg interest rate risk, currency risk, other price risk) it is exposed to, showing the impact on **profit or loss** and **equity**. Details of the methods and assumptions used should be provided.   **34.29**

If a financial institution prepares a sensitivity analysis, such as value-at-risk, that reflects interdependencies between risk variables (eg interest rates and exchange rates) and uses it to manage **financial risks**, it may use that sensitivity analysis instead.   **34.30**

Capital

34.31   A financial institution shall disclose information that enables users of its financial statements to evaluate the entity's objectives, policies and processes for managing capital. A financial institution shall disclose the following:

(a)   Qualitative information about its objectives, policies and processes for managing capital, including:

(i)   a description of what it manages as capital;

(ii)   when an entity is subject to externally imposed capital requirements, the nature of those requirements and how those requirements are incorporated into the management of capital; and

(iii)   how it is meeting its objectives for managing capital.

(b)   Summary quantitative data about what it manages as capital. Some entities regard some financial liabilities (eg some forms of subordinated debt) as part of capital. Other entities regard capital as excluding some components of equity (eg components arising from cash flow hedges).

(c)   Any changes in (a) and (b) from the previous period.

(d)   Whether during the period it complied with any externally imposed capital requirements to which it is subject.

(e)   When the entity has not complied with such externally imposed capital requirements, the consequences of such non-compliance.

A financial institution bases these disclosures on the information provided internally to **key management personnel**.

34.32   A financial institution may manage capital in a number of ways and be subject to a number of different capital requirements. For example, a conglomerate may include entities that undertake insurance activities and banking activities and those entities may operate in several jurisdictions. When an aggregate disclosure of capital requirements and how capital is managed would not provide useful information or would distort a financial statement user's understanding of the financial institution's capital resources, the financial institution shall disclose separate information for each capital requirement to which the entity is subject.

Reporting cash flows on a net basis

34.33   A financial institution that presents a statement of cash flow in accordance with Section 7 *Statement of Cash Flows* may report cash flows arising from each of the following activities on a net basis:

(a)   cash receipts and payments for the acceptance and repayment of deposits with a fixed maturity date;

(b)   the placement of deposits with and withdrawal of deposits from other financial institutions; and

(c)   cash advances and loans made to customers and the repayment of those advances and loans.

This paragraph does not impose a requirement to produce a cash flow statement.

Retirement Benefit Plans: Financial Statements

34.34   An entity applying this FRS that is a **retirement benefit plan** shall also apply the requirements of paragraphs 34.35 to 34.48. A retirement benefit plan may be a **defined benefit plan**, a **defined contribution plan**, or have both defined benefit and defined contribution elements. The **financial statements** shall distinguish between defined benefit and defined contribution elements, where **material**.

Requirements applicable to both defined benefit plans and defined contribution plans

A retirement benefit plan need not comply with the requirements of paragraph 3.17. The financial statements of a retirement benefit plan shall contain as part of the financial statements: **34.35**

(a)   a statement of changes in **net assets available for benefits** (which can also be called a Fund Account) (see paragraph 34.37);
(b)   a statement of net assets available for benefits (see paragraph 34.38); and
(c)   **notes**, comprising a summary of significant **accounting policies** and other explanatory information.

At each **reporting date**, the net assets available for benefits shall be measured in accordance with paragraph 28.15(b). Changes in fair value shall be recognised in the statements of changes in net assets available for benefits.   **34.36**

Statement of changes in net assets available for benefits (Fund Account)

The financial statements of a retirement benefit plan, whether defined contribution or defined benefit, shall present the following in the statement of changes in net assets available for benefits: **34.37**

(a)   employer contributions;
(b)   employee contributions;
(c)   investment income such as interest and dividends;
(d)   other income;
(e)   benefits paid or payable (analysed, for example, as retirement, death and disability benefits, and lump sum payments);
(f)   administrative expenses;
(g)   other expenses;
(h)   taxes on income;
(i)   profits and losses on disposal of investments and changes in value of investments; and
(j)   transfers from and to other plans.

Statement of net assets available for benefits

The financial statements of a retirement benefit plan, whether defined contribution or defined benefit, shall present the following in the statement of net assets available for benefits: **34.38**

(a)   **assets** at the end of the period suitably classified; and
(b)   **liabilities** other than the actuarial **present value** of promised retirement benefits.

The basis of valuation of assets shall be presented in the notes to the financial statements.

Disclosures

Assets other than financial instruments held at fair value

Where a retirement benefit plan holds assets other than financial instruments at fair value in accordance with paragraph 34.36, it shall apply the disclosure requirements of the relevant section of this FRS, for example in relation to **investment property** it shall provide the disclosures required by paragraph 16.10.   **34.39**

Significance of financial instruments for financial position and performance

34.40 A retirement benefit plan shall disclose information that enables users of its financial statements to evaluate the significance of financial instruments for its **financial position** and **performance**.

34.41 A retirement benefit plan shall disclose a disaggregation of the statement of net assets available for benefits by class of financial instrument. A class is a grouping of financial instruments that is appropriate to the nature of the information disclosed and that takes into account the characteristics of those financial instruments.

Fair value

34.42 For financial instruments held at fair value in the statement of net assets available for benefits, a retirement benefit plan shall disclose for each class of financial instrument, an analysis of the level in the fair value hierarchy (as set out in paragraph 11.27) into which the fair value measurements are categorised.

Nature and extent of risks arising from financial instruments

34.43 A retirement benefit plan shall disclose information that enables users of its financial statements to evaluate the nature and extent of **credit risk** and **market risk** arising from financial instruments to which the retirement benefit plan is exposed at the end of the **reporting period**.

34.44 For each type of credit and market risk arising from financial instruments, a retirement benefit plan shall disclose:

(a) the exposures to risk and how they arise;

(b) its objectives, policies and processes for managing the risk and the methods used to measure the risk; and

(c) any changes in (a) or (b) from the previous period.

In relation to credit risk, a retirement benefit plan shall, in addition, provide the disclosures set out in paragraphs 34.45 and 34.46.

Credit risk

34.45 A retirement benefit plan shall disclose by class of financial instrument:

(a) The amount that best represents its maximum exposure to credit risk at the end of the reporting period. This disclosure is not required for financial instruments whose **carrying amount** best represents the maximum exposure to credit risk.

(b) A description of collateral held as security and of other credit enhancements, and the extent to which these mitigate credit risk.

(c) The amount by which any related credit **derivatives** or similar instruments mitigate that maximum exposure to credit risk.

(d) Information about the credit quality of financial assets that are neither past due nor impaired.

34.46 When a retirement benefit plan obtains financial or non-financial assets during the period by taking possession of collateral it holds as security or calling on other credit enhancements (eg guarantees), and such assets meet the **recognition** criteria in other sections, a retirement benefit plan shall disclose:

(a)   the nature and carrying amount of the assets obtained; and

(b)   when the assets are not readily convertible into **cash**, its policies for disposing of such assets or for retaining them.

Defined benefit plans – actuarial liabilities

A defined benefit plan is not required to recognise a liability in relation to the promised retirement benefits.   **34.47**

A defined benefit plan shall disclose, in a report alongside the financial statements, information regarding the actuarial present value of promised retirement benefits including: **34.48**

(a)   a statement of the actuarial present value of promised retirement benefits, based on the most recent valuation of the scheme;

(b)   the date of the most recent valuation of the scheme; and

(c)   the significant actuarial assumptions made and the method used to calculate the actuarial present value of promised retirement benefits.

Heritage Assets

All **heritage assets** shall be accounted for in accordance with the requirements of paragraphs 34.50 to 34.56. These paragraphs do not apply to **investment property**, **property, plant and equipment** or **intangible assets** which fall within the scope of Section 16 *Investment Properties*, Section 17 *Property, Plant and Equipment* and Section 18 *Intangible Assets other than Goodwill*.   **34.49**

Works of art and similar objects are sometimes held by commercial entities but are not heritage assets because they are not maintained principally for their contribution to knowledge and culture. These assets shall therefore be accounted for in accordance with Section 17. Heritage assets used by the entity itself, for example historic buildings used for teaching by education establishments, shall also be accounted for in accordance with Section 17. This is based on the view that an operational perspective is likely to be most relevant for most users of **financial statements**. However, entities that use historic buildings and similar assets may wish to consider whether it is appropriate to apply the disclosures required by paragraphs 34.55 and 34.56.   **34.50**

Recognition and measurement

An entity shall recognise and measure heritage assets in accordance with Section 17 (ie using the cost model or revaluation model), subject to the requirements set out in paragraphs 34.52 to 34.53 below.   **34.51**

Heritage assets shall be recognised in the **statement of financial position** separately from other assets.   **34.52**

Where heritage assets have previously been capitalised or are recently purchased, information on the cost or value of the asset will be available. Where this information is not available, and cannot be obtained at a cost which is commensurate with the benefits to users of the financial statements, the assets shall not be recognised in the statement of financial position, but must be disclosed in accordance with the requirements below.   **34.53**

At each **reporting date**, an entity shall apply Section 27 *Impairment of Assets* to determine whether a heritage asset is impaired and, if so, how to recognise and measure the **impairment loss**. A heritage asset may be impaired, for example where it has suffered physical deterioration, breakage or doubts arise as to its authenticity.   **34.54**

Disclosure

34.55   An entity shall disclose the following for all heritage assets it holds:

(a)   An indication of the nature and scale of heritage assets held by the entity.

(b)   The policy for the acquisition, preservation, management and disposal of heritage assets (including a description of the records maintained by the entity of its collection of heritage assets and information on the extent to which access to the assets is permitted).

(c)   The **accounting policies** adopted for heritage assets, including details of the measurement bases used.

(d)   For heritage assets that have not been recognised in the statement of financial position, the **notes** to the financial statements shall:

(i)   explain the reasons why;

(ii)   describe the significance and nature of those assets; and

(iii)   disclose information that is helpful in assessing the value of those heritage assets.

(e)   Where heritage assets are recognised in the statement of financial position the following disclosure is required:

(i)   the **carrying amount** of heritage assets at the beginning of the **reporting period** and the reporting date, including an analysis between classes or groups of heritage assets recognised at cost and those recognised at valuation; and

(ii)   where assets are recognised at valuation, sufficient information to assist in understanding the valuation being recognised (date of valuation, method used, whether carried out by external valuer and if so their qualification and any significant limitations on the valuation).

(f)   A summary of transactions relating to heritage assets for the reporting period and each of the previous four reporting periods disclosing:

(i)   the cost of acquisitions of heritage assets;

(ii)   the value of heritage assets acquired by donations;

(iii)   the carrying amount of heritage assets disposed of in the period and proceeds received; and

(iv)   any impairment recognised in the period.

The summary shall show separately those transactions included in the statement of financial position and those that are not.

(g)   In exceptional circumstances where it is **impracticable** to obtain a valuation of heritage assets acquired by donation the reason shall be stated.

Disclosures can be aggregated for groups or classes of heritage assets, provided this does not obscure significant information.

34.56   Where it is impracticable to do so, the disclosures required by paragraph 34.55(f) need not be given for any accounting period earlier than the previous comparable period, and a statement to the effect that it is impracticable shall be made.

Funding Commitments

34.57   An entity that commits to provide resources to other entities shall apply the requirements of paragraphs 34.58 to 34.63 and the accompanying guidance at Appendix A to this section, except for commitments to make a loan to which entities shall apply Section 11 *Basic Financial Instruments* or Section 12 *Other Financial Instruments Issues*, as applicable.

When applying these paragraphs, the requirements of Section 2 *Concepts and Pervasive Principles* and Section 21 *Provisions and Contingencies* shall also be taken into consideration.

34.58

Recognition

An entity shall recognise a **liability** and, usually, a corresponding **expense**, when it has made a commitment that it will provide resources to another party, if, and only if:

34.59

(a) the definition and **recognition** criteria for a liability have been satisfied;

(b) the obligation (which may be a **constructive obligation**) is such that the entity cannot realistically withdraw from it; and

(c) the entitlement of the other party to the resources does not depend on the satisfaction of **performance-related conditions**.

Commitments that are performance-related will be recognised when those performance-related conditions are met.

34.60

Measurement

An entity shall measure any recognised liability at the **present value** of the resources committed.

34.61

Disclosure

An entity that has made a commitment shall disclose the following:

34.62

(a) the commitment made;

(b) the time-frame of that commitment;

(c) any performance-related conditions attached to that commitment; and

(d) details of how that commitment will be funded.

The above disclosures may be made in aggregate, providing that such aggregation does not obscure significant information. However, separate disclosure shall be made for recognised and unrecognised commitments.

34.63

Incoming Resources from Non-Exchange Transactions

The accounting for **government grants** is addressed in Section 24 *Government Grants*.

PBE34.64

Paragraphs PBE34.67 to PBE34.74 and the accompanying guidance at Appendix B to this section apply to other resources received from non-**exchange transactions** by **public benefit entities** or entities within a **public benefit entity group**. A non-exchange transaction is a transaction whereby an entity receives value from another entity without directly giving approximately equal value in exchange or gives value to another entity without directly receiving approximately equal value in exchange.

PBE34.65

Non-exchange transactions include, but are not limited to, donations (of **cash**, goods, and services) and legacies.

PBE34.66

Recognition and measurement

An entity shall recognise receipts of resources from non-exchange transactions as follows:

PBE34.67

(a)   Transactions that do not impose specified future performance-related conditions on the recipient are recognised in **income** when the resources are received or receivable.

(b)   Transactions that do impose specified future performance-related conditions on the recipient are recognised in income only when the performance-related conditions are met.

(c)   Where resources are received before the **revenue recognition** criteria are satisfied, a **liability** is recognised.

PBE34.68   The existence of a **restriction** does not prohibit a resource from being recognised in income when receivable.

PBE34.69   When applying the requirements of paragraph PBE34.67, an entity must take into consideration whether the resource can be measured reliably and whether the benefits of recognising the resource outweigh the costs.

PBE34.70   Therefore, where it is not practicable to estimate the value of the resource with sufficient **reliability**, the income shall be included in the financial period when the resource is sold.

PBE34.71   An entity shall recognise a liability for any resource that has previously been received and recognised in income when, as a result of a subsequent failure to meet restrictions or performance-related conditions attached to it, repayment becomes **probable**.

PBE34.72   Donations of services that can be reasonably quantified will usually result in the recognition of income and an **expense**. An **asset** will be recognised only when those services are used for the production of an asset and the services received will be capitalised as part of the cost of that asset.

PBE34.73   An entity shall measure incoming resources from non-exchange transactions as follows:

(a)   Donated services and facilities, that would otherwise have been purchased, shall be measured at the value to the entity.

(b)   All other incoming resources from non-exchange transactions shall be measured at the **fair value** of the resources received or receivable.

Disclosure

PBE34.74   An entity shall disclose the following:

(a)   the nature and amounts of resources receivable from non-exchange transactions recognised in the **financial statements**;

(b)   any unfulfilled conditions or other contingencies attaching to resources from non-exchange transactions that have not been recognised in income; and

(c)   an indication of other forms of resources from non-exchange transactions from which the entity has benefited.

Public Benefit Entity Combinations

PBE34.75   Paragraphs PBE34.76 to PBE34.86 apply only to **public benefit entities** for the following categories of **entity combinations** which involve a whole entity or parts of an entity combining with another entity:

(a)   combinations at nil or nominal consideration which are in substance a gift; and

(b)   combinations which meet the definition and criteria of a **merger**.

PBE34.76   Combinations which are determined to be acquisitions shall be accounted for in accordance with Section 19 *Business Combinations and Goodwill*.

Combinations that are in substance a gift

Accounting treatment and disclosure

A **combination that is in substance a gift** shall be accounted for in accordance with Section 19 except for the matters addressed in paragraphs PBE34.78 and PBE34.79 below.   **PBE34.77**

Any excess of the **fair value** of the **assets** received over the fair value of the **liabilities** assumed is recognised as a **gain** in **income and expenditure**. This gain represents the gift of the value of one entity to another and shall be recognised as income.   **PBE34.78**

Any excess of the fair value of the liabilities assumed over the fair value of the assets received is recognised as a loss in income and expenditure. This loss represents the net obligations assumed, for which the receiving entity has not received a financial reward and shall be recognised as an **expense**.   **PBE34.79**

Combinations that are a merger

An entity combination that is a merger shall apply merger accounting as prescribed below.   **PBE34.80**

Prospective amendments: Amendments to FRS 102 *The Financial Reporting Standard applicable in the UK and Republic of Ireland* – Small entities and other minor amendments (July 2015) amends this paragraph PBE34.80 with effect for annual periods beginning on or after 1 January 2016.

Any entity combination which is neither a combination that is in substance a gift nor a merger shall be accounted for as an acquisition in accordance with Section 19.   **PBE34.81**

Prospective amendments: Amendments to FRS 102 *The Financial Reporting Standard applicable in the UK and Republic of Ireland* – Small entities and other minor amendments (July 2015) amends this paragraph PBE34.81 with effect for annual periods beginning on or after 1 January 2016.

Accounting treatment

Under merger accounting the carrying value of the assets and liabilities of the parties to the combination are not adjusted to fair value, although adjustments shall be made to achieve uniformity of **accounting policies** across the combining entities.   **PBE34.82**

The results and **cash flows** of all the combining entities shall be brought into the **financial statements** of the newly formed entity from the beginning of the financial period in which the merger occurs.   **PBE34.83**

The comparative amounts shall be restated by including the results for all the combining entities for the previous accounting period and their **statement of financial positions** for the previous **reporting date**. The comparative figures shall be marked as 'combined' figures.   **PBE34.84**

All costs associated with the merger shall be charged as an expense in the period incurred.   **PBE34.85**

Disclosure

For each entity combination accounted for as a merger in the **reporting period** the following shall be disclosed in the newly formed entity's financial statements: **PBE34.86**

(a)   the names and descriptions of the combining entities or businesses;

(b)   the date of the merger;

(c)   an analysis of the principal components of the current year's **total comprehensive income** to indicate:

    (i)   the amounts relating to the newly formed merged entity for the period after the date of the merger; and

    (ii)   the amounts relating to each party to the merger up to the date of the merger.

(d)   an analysis of the previous year's total comprehensive income between each party to the merger;

(e)   the aggregate carrying value of the net assets of each party to the merger at the date of the merger; and

(f)   the nature and amount of any significant adjustments required to align accounting policies and an explanation of any further adjustments made to net assets as a result of the merger.

Public Benefit Entity Concessionary Loans

PBE34.87   Paragraphs PBE34.89 to PBE34.97 address the **recognition**, **measurement** and disclosure of **public benefit entity concessionary loan** arrangements within the **financial statements of public benefit entities** or entities within a **public benefit entity group** making or receiving public benefit entity concessionary loans. These paragraphs apply to public benefit entity concessionary loan arrangements only and are not applicable to loans which are at a market rate or to other commercial arrangements.

PBE34.88   Public benefit entity concessionary loans are loans made or received between a public benefit entity or an entity within the public benefit entity group, and another party at below the **prevailing market rate** of interest that are not repayable on demand and are for the purposes of furthering the objectives of the public benefit entity or public benefit entity **parent**.

Accounting treatment

PBE34.89   Entities making or receiving public benefit entity concessionary loans shall use either:

(a)   the recognition, measurement and disclosure requirements in Section 11 *Basic Financial Instruments* or Section 12 *Other Financial Instruments Issues* (for example, Section 11 requires initial measurement at **fair value** and subsequent measurement at **amortised cost** using the **effective interest method**); or

(b)   the accounting treatment set out in paragraphs PBE34.90 to PBE34.97 below.

A public benefit entity or an entity within a public benefit entity group shall apply the same **accounting policy** to concessionary loans both made and received.

Initial measurement

PBE34.90   A public benefit entity or an entity within a public benefit entity group making or receiving concessionary loans shall initially measure these arrangements at the amount received or paid and recognise them in the **statement of financial position**.

Subsequent measurement

PBE34.91   In subsequent years, the **carrying amount** of concessionary loans in the financial statements shall be adjusted to reflect any accrued interest payable or receivable.

To the extent that a loan that has been made is irrecoverable, an **impairment loss** shall be recognised in **income and expenditure**.

PBE34.92

Presentation and disclosure

The entity shall present concessionary loans made and concessionary loans received either as a separate line items on the face of the statement of financial position or in the **notes** to the financial statements.

PBE34.93

Concessionary loans shall be presented separately between amounts repayable or receivable within one year and amounts repayable or receivable after more than one year.

PBE34.94

The entity shall disclose in the summary of significant accounting policies the measurement basis used for concessionary loans and any other accounting policies which are relevant to the understanding of these transactions within the financial statements.

PBE34.95

The entity shall disclose the following:

PBE34.96

(a) the terms and conditions of concessionary loan arrangements, for example the interest rate, any security provided and the terms of the repayment; and

(b) the value of concessionary loans which have been committed but not taken up at the year end.

Concessionary loans made or received shall be disclosed separately. However multiple loans made or received may be disclosed in aggregate, providing that such aggregation does not obscure significant information.

PBE34.97

Appendix A to Section 34

Guidance on funding commitments (paragraphs 34.57 to 34.63)

This guidance is an integral part of the Standard.

Entities often make commitments to provide cash or other resources to other entities. In such a case, it is necessary to determine whether the commitment should be recognised as a liability. The definition of a liability requires that there be a present obligation, and not merely an expectation of a future outflow.

34A.1

A general statement that the entity intends to provide resources to certain classes of potential beneficiaries in accordance with its objectives does not in itself give rise to a liability, as the entity may amend or withdraw its policy, and potential beneficiaries do not have the ability to insist on their fulfilment. Similarly, a promise to provide cash conditional on the receipt of future income in itself may not give rise to a liability where the entity cannot be required to fulfil it if the future income is not received and it is probable that the economic benefits will not be transferred.

34A.2

A liability is recognised only for a commitment that gives the recipient a valid expectation that payment will be made and from which the grantor cannot realistically withdraw. One of the implications of this is that a liability only exists where the commitment has been communicated to the recipient.

34A.3

Commitments are not recognised if they are subject to performance-related conditions. In such a case, the entity is required to fulfil its commitment only when the performance-related conditions are met and no liability exists until that time.

34A.4

34A.5   A commitment may contain conditions that are not performance-related conditions. For example, a requirement to provide an annual financial report to the grantor may serve mainly as an administrative tool because failure to comply would not release the grantor from its commitment. This may be distinguished from a requirement to submit a detailed report for review and consideration by the grantor of how funds will be utilised in order to secure payment. A mere restriction on the specific purpose for which funds are to be used does not in itself constitute a performance-related condition.

34A.6   For funding commitments that are not recognised, it is important that full and informative disclosures are made of their existence and of the sources of funding for these unrecognised commitments.

Appendix B to Section 34

Guidance on incoming resources from non-exchange transactions (paragraphs 34.64 to 34.74)

This guidance is an integral part of the Standard.

Recognition

PBE34B.1   The receipt of resources will usually result in an entity recognising an asset and corresponding income for the fair value of resources when those resources become received or receivable. Instances when this may differ include where:

(a)   an entity received those resources in the form of services (see paragraphs PBE34B.8 to PBE34B.12); or

(b)   there are performance-related conditions attached to the resources, which have yet to be fulfilled (see paragraphs PBE34B.13 to PBE34B.14).

PBE34B.2   Resources shall only be recognised when the fair value of the incoming resources can be measured reliably.

PBE34B.3   The concepts of materiality (see paragraph 2.6), and balance between benefit and cost (see paragraph 2.13) should be considered when deciding which resources received shall be recognised in the financial statements.

PBE34B.4   When it is impracticable to recognise resources from non-exchange transactions, the income is recognised in the period in which the resources are sold or distributed. The most common example is that of high volume, low value second-hand goods donated for resale.

Legacies

PBE34B.5   Donations in the form of legacies are recognised when it is probable that the legacy will be received and its value can be measured reliably. These criteria will normally be met following probate once the executor(s) of the estate has established that there are sufficient assets in the estate, after settling liabilities, to pay the legacy.

PBE34B.6   Evidence that the executor(s) has determined that a payment can be made, may arise on the agreement of the estate's accounts or notification that payment will be made. Where notification is received after the year-end but it is clear that the executor(s) has agreed prior to the year-end that the legacy can be paid, the legacy is accrued in the financial statements. The certainty and measurability of the receipt may be affected by subsequent events such as valuations and disputes.

Entities that are in receipt of numerous immaterial legacies for which individual identification would be burdensome may take a portfolio approach.   **PBE34B.7**

Services

Donated services that can be reasonably quantified shall be recognised in the financial statements when they are received.   **PBE34B.8**

Donated services that are consumed immediately are usually recognised as an expense. However, there may be circumstances when a service is used in the production of an asset, for example erecting a building. In these cases, the associated donated service (eg plumbing and electrical services) would be recognised as a part of the cost of that asset.   **PBE34B.9**

Donated services that can be reasonably quantified include donated facilities, such as office accommodation, services that would otherwise have been purchased and services usually provided by an individual or an entity as part of their trade or profession for a fee.   **PBE34B.10**

It is expected that contributions made by volunteers cannot be reasonably quantified and therefore these services shall not be recognised.   **PBE34B.11**

Paragraph PBE34.74(c) requires an entity to disclose other forms of resources from non-exchange transactions from which the entity has benefited. This will include the disclosure of unrecognised volunteer services.   **PBE34B.12**

Performance-related conditions

Some resources are given with performance-related conditions attached which require the recipient to use the resources to provide a specified level of service in order to be entitled to retain the resources. An entity will not recognise income from those resources until these performance-related conditions have been met.   **PBE34B.13**

However, some requirements are stated so broadly that they do not actually impose a performance-related condition on the recipient. In these cases the recipient will recognise income on receipt of the transfer of resources.   **PBE34B.14**

Measurement

Paragraph PBE34.73(a) requires donated services and facilities to be measured at the value to the entity. This requirement only applies to those services and facilities that would otherwise have been purchased by the entity. The value placed on these services and facilities should be the estimated value to the entity of the service or facility received, this will be the price the entity estimates it would pay in the open market for a service or facility of equivalent utility to the entity.   **PBE34B.15**

Paragraph PBE34.73(b) requires resources received or receivable, that are not services or facilities, to be measured at their fair value. These fair values are usually the price that the entity would have to pay on the open market for an equivalent resource.   **PBE34B.16**

When there is no direct evidence of an open market value for an equivalent item a value may be derived from sources such as: **PBE34B.17**

(a)   the cost of the item to the donor; or

(b)   in the case of goods that are expected to be sold, the estimated resale value (which may reflect the amount actually realised) after deducting the cost to sell the goods.

PBE34B.18   Donated services are recognised as income and an equivalent amount shall be recognised as an expense in income and expenditure, unless the expense can be capitalised as part of the cost of an asset.

Section 35 Transition to this FRS

Scope of this section

35.1   This section applies to a **first-time adopter of this FRS**, regardless of whether its previous accounting framework was **EU-adopted IFRS** or another set of generally accepted accounting principles (GAAP) such as its national accounting standards, or another framework such as the local income tax basis.

35.2   Notwithstanding the requirements in paragraphs 35.3 and 35.4, an entity that has applied **FRS 102** in a previous **reporting period**, but whose most recent previous annual **financial statements** did not contain an explicit and unreserved statement of compliance with this FRS, must either apply this section or else apply FRS 102 retrospectively in accordance with Section 10 *Accounting Policies, Changes in Estimates and Errors* as if the entity had never stopped applying this FRS.

First-time adoption

35.3   A first-time adopter of this FRS shall apply this section in its first financial statements that conform to this FRS.

35.4   An entity's first financial statements that conform to this FRS are the first financial statements[16] in which the entity makes an explicit and unreserved statement in those financial statements of compliance with this FRS. Financial statements prepared in accordance with this FRS are an entity's first such financial statements if, for example, the entity:

    (a)   did not present financial statements for previous periods;

    (b)   presented its most recent previous financial statements under previous UK and Republic of Ireland requirements that are therefore not consistent with this FRS in all respects; or

    (c)   presented its most recent previous financial statements in conformity with EU-adopted IFRS.

35.5   Paragraph 3.17 defines a complete set of financial statements.

35.6   Paragraph 3.14 requires an entity to disclose, in a complete set of financial statements, comparative information in respect of the preceding period for all amounts presented in the financial statements, as well as specified comparative narrative and descriptive information. An entity may present comparative information in respect of more than one preceding period. Therefore, an entity's **date of transition** to this FRS is the beginning of the earliest period for which the entity presents full comparative information in accordance with this FRS in its first financial statements that comply with this FRS.

Procedures for preparing financial statements at the date of transition

35.7   Except as provided in paragraphs 35.9 to 35.11B, an entity shall, in its opening **statement of financial position** as of its date of transition to this FRS (ie the beginning of the earliest period presented):

---

[16] *This excludes interim financial statements.*

(a) recognise all **assets** and **liabilities** whose **recognition** is required by this FRS;
(b) not recognise items as assets or liabilities if this FRS does not permit such recognition;
(c) reclassify items that it recognised under its previous financial reporting framework as one type of asset, liability or component of **equity**, but are a different type of asset, liability or component of equity under this FRS; and
(d) apply this FRS in measuring all recognised assets and liabilities.

This section does not require the opening statement of financial position to be presented.

The **accounting policies** that an entity uses in its opening statement of financial position under this FRS may differ from those that it used for the same date using its previous financial reporting framework. The resulting adjustments arise from transactions, other events or conditions before the date of transition to this FRS. Therefore, an entity shall recognise those adjustments directly in retained earnings (or, if appropriate, another category of equity) at the date of transition to this FRS.   **35.8**

On first-time adoption of this FRS, an entity shall not retrospectively change the accounting that it followed under its previous financial reporting framework for any of the following transactions: **35.9**

(a) *Derecognition of financial assets and financial liabilities;*
    Financial assets and liabilities derecognised under an entity's previous accounting framework before the date of transition shall not be recognised upon adoption of this FRS. Conversely, for financial assets and liabilities that would have been derecognised under this FRS in a transaction that took place before the date of transition, but that were not derecognised under an entity's previous accounting framework, an entity may choose:
    (i) to derecognise them on adoption of this FRS; or
    (ii) to continue to recognise them until disposed of or settled.
(b) [Not used]
(c) *Accounting estimates.*
(d) *Discontinued operations.*
(e) *Measuring non-controlling interests:*

The requirements:

    (i) to allocate **profit or loss** and **total comprehensive income** between non-controlling interest and **owners** of the **parent**;
    (ii) for accounting for changes in the parent's ownership interest in a subsidiary that do not result in a loss of control; and
    (iii) for accounting for a loss of control over a subsidiary

shall be applied prospectively from the date of transition to this FRS (or from such earlier date as this FRS is applied to restate **business combination**s – see paragraph 35.10(a)).

An entity may use one or more of the following exemptions in preparing its first financial statements that conform to this FRS: **35.10**

(a) *Business combinations, including group reconstructions*
    A first-time adopter may elect not to apply Section 19 *Business Combinations and Goodwill* to business combinations that were effected before the date of transition to this FRS. However, if a first-time adopter restates any business combination to comply with Section 19, it shall restate all later business combinations. If a first-time adopter does not apply Section 19 retrospectively, the first-time adopter shall recognise and measure all its assets and liabilities acquired or assumed in a past business combination at the date of transition to this FRS in accordance with paragraphs 35.7 to 35.9 or if applicable, with paragraphs 35.10(b) to (r) except for:

(i)   **intangible assets** other than **goodwill** – intangible assets subsumed within goodwill shall not be separately recognised; and

(ii)   goodwill – no adjustment shall be made to the carrying value of goodwill.

(b)   *Share-based payment transactions*

A first-time adopter is not required to apply Section 26 *Share-based Payment* to equity instruments that were granted before the date of transition to this FRS, or to liabilities arising from share-based payment transactions that were settled before the date of transition to this FRS. Except that a first-time adopter previously applying FRS 20 *(IFRS 2) Share-based Payment* or IFRS 2 *Share-based Payment* shall, in relation to equity instruments that were granted before the date of transition to this FRS, apply either FRS 20 / IFRS 2 (as applicable) or Section 26 of this FRS at the date of transition.

(c)   *Fair value as deemed cost*

A first-time adopter may elect to measure an:

(i)   item of **property, plant and equipment**;

(ii)   **investment property**; or

(iii)   intangible asset which meets the recognition criteria and the criteria for revaluation in Section 18 *Intangible Assets other than Goodwill*

on the date of transition to this FRS at its **fair value** and use that fair value as its **deemed cost** at that date.

(d)   *Revaluation as deemed cost*

A first-time adopter may elect to use a previous GAAP revaluation of an:

(i)   item of property, plant and equipment;

(ii)   investment property; or

(iii)   intangible asset which meets the recognition criteria and the criteria for revaluation in Section 18

at, or before, the date of transition to this FRS as its deemed cost at the revaluation date.

(e)   [Not used]

(f)   *Individual and separate financial statements*

When an entity prepares individual or **separate financial statements**, paragraphs 9.26, 14.4 and 15.9 require the entity to account for its investments in **subsidiaries**, **associates**, and **jointly controlled entities** either at cost less impairment or at fair value.

If a first-time adopter measures such an investment at cost, it shall measure that investment at one of the following amounts in its individual or separate opening statement of financial position, as appropriate, prepared in accordance with this FRS:

(i)   cost determined in accordance with Section 9 *Consolidated and Separate Financial Statements*, Section 14 *Investments in Associates* or Section 15 *Investments in Joint Ventures*; or

(ii)   deemed cost, which shall be the **carrying amount** at the date of transition as determined under the entity's previous GAAP.

(g)   *Compound financial instruments*

Paragraph 22.13 requires an entity to split a **compound financial instrument** into its liability and equity components at the date of issue. A first-time adopter need not separate those two components if the liability component is not outstanding at the date of transition to this FRS.

(h)   [Not used]

(i)   *Service concession arrangements – Accounting by operators*

A first-time adopter is not required to apply paragraphs 34.12I to 34.16A to service concession arrangements that were entered into before the date of transition to this FRS. Such **service concession arrangements** shall continue to be accounted for using the same accounting policies being applied at the date of transition to this FRS.

(j)   ***Extractive activities***

A first-time adopter that under a previous GAAP accounted for exploration and development costs for oil and gas properties in the development or production phases, in cost centres that included all properties in a large geographical area may elect to measure oil and gas assets at the date of transition to this FRS on the following basis:

(i)   Exploration and evaluation assets at the amount determined under the entity's previous GAAP.

(ii)   Assets in the development or production phases at the amount determined for the cost centre under the entity's previous GAAP. The entity shall allocate this amount to the cost centre's underlying assets pro rata using reserve volumes or reserve values as of that date.

The entity shall test exploration and evaluation assets and assets in the development and production phases for impairment at the date of transition to this FRS in accordance with Section 34 *Specialised Activities* or Section 27 *Impairment of Assets* of this FRS respectively, and if necessary, reduce the amount determined in accordance with (i) or (ii) above. For the purposes of this paragraph, oil and gas assets comprise only those assets used in the exploration, evaluation, development or production of oil and gas.

(k)   ***Arrangements containing a lease***

A first-time adopter may elect to determine whether an arrangement existing at the date of transition to this FRS contains a **lease** (see paragraph 20.3A) on the basis of facts and circumstances existing at that date, rather than when the arrangement was entered into.

(l)   ***Decommissioning liabilities included in the cost of property, plant and equipment***

Paragraph 17.10(c) states that the cost of an item of property, plant and equipment includes the initial estimate of the costs of dismantling and removing the item and restoring the site on which it is located, the obligation for which an entity incurs either when the item is acquired or as a consequence of having used the item during a particular period for purposes other than to produce **inventories** during that period. A first-time adopter may elect to measure this component of the cost of an item of property, plant and equipment at the date of transition to this FRS, rather than on the date(s) when the obligation initially arose.

(m)   ***Dormant companies***[17]

A company within the Companies Act definition of a dormant company may elect to retain its accounting policies for reported assets, liabilities and equity at the date of transition to this FRS until there is any change to those balances or the company undertakes any new transactions.

(n)   ***Deferred development costs as a deemed cost***

A first-time adopter may elect to measure the carrying amount at the date of transition to this FRS for development costs deferred in accordance with SSAP 13 *Accounting for research and development* as its deemed cost at that date.

(o)   ***Borrowing costs***

An entity electing to adopt an accounting policy of capitalising **borrowing costs** as part of the cost of a **qualifying asset** may elect to treat the date of transition to this FRS as the date on which capitalisation commences.

(p)   ***Lease incentives***

A first-time adopter is not required to apply paragraphs 20.15A and 20.25A to **lease incentives** provided the term of the lease commenced before the date of transition to this FRS. The first-time adopter shall continue to recognise any residual benefit or cost associated with these lease incentives on the same basis as that applied at the date of transition to this FRS.

(q)   ***Public benefit entity combinations***

A first-time adopter may elect not to apply paragraphs PBE34.75 to PBE34.86 relating to **public benefit entity combinations** to combinations that were effected

---

[17] *Irish company law does not contain an equivalent definition.*

before the date of transition to this FRS. However, if on first-time adoption a **public benefit entity** restates any entity combination to comply with this section, it shall restate all later entity combinations.

(r) *Assets and liabilities of subsidiaries, associates and joint ventures*

If a subsidiary becomes a first-time adopter later than its parent, the subsidiary shall in its financial statements measure its assets and liabilities at either:

  (i) the carrying amounts that would be included in the parent's **consolidated financial statements**, based on the parent's date of transition to this FRS, if no adjustments were made for consolidation procedures and for the effects of the business combination in which the parent acquired the subsidiary; or

  (ii) the carrying amounts required by the rest of this FRS, based on the subsidiary's date of transition to this FRS. These carrying amounts could differ from those described in (i) when:

      (a) the exemptions in this FRS result in measurements that depend on the date of transition to this FRS; or

      (b) the accounting policies used in the subsidiary's financial statements differ from those in the consolidated financial statements. For example, the subsidiary may use as its accounting policy the cost model in Section 17 *Property, Plant and Equipment*, whereas the **group** may use the revaluation model.

A similar election is available to an associate or **joint venture** that becomes a first-time adopter later than an entity that has **significant influence** or **joint control** over it.

However, if an entity becomes a first-time adopter later than its subsidiary (or associate or joint venture) the entity shall, in its consolidated financial statements, measure the assets and liabilities of the subsidiary (or associate or joint venture) at the same carrying amounts as in the financial statements of the subsidiary (or associate or joint venture), after adjusting for consolidation (and equity accounting) adjustments and for the effects of the business combination in which the entity acquired the subsidiary (or transaction in which it acquired the associate or joint venture). Similarly, if a parent becomes a first-time adopter for its separate financial statements earlier or later than for its consolidated financial statements, it shall measure its assets and liabilities at the same amounts in both financial statements, except for consolidation adjustments.

(s) *Designation of previously recognised financial instruments*

This FRS permits a financial instrument (provided it meets certain criteria) to be designated on initial recognition as a financial asset or financial liability at fair value through profit or loss. Despite this an entity is permitted to designate, as at the date of transition to this FRS, any financial asset or financial liability at fair value through profit or loss provided the asset or liability meets the criteria in paragraph 11.14(b) at that date.

(t) *Hedge accounting*

  (i) *A hedging relationship existing on the date of transition*

      A first-time adopter may choose to apply hedge accounting to a hedging relationship of a type described in paragraph 12.19 which exists on the date of transition between a **hedging instrument** and a **hedged item**, provided the conditions of paragraphs 12.18(a) to (c) are met on the date of transition to this FRS and the conditions of paragraphs 12.18(d) and (e) are met no later than the date the first financial statements that comply with this FRS are authorised for issue. This choice applies to each hedging relationship existing on the date of transition.

      Hedge accounting as set out in Section 12 *Other Financial Instruments Issues* of this FRS may commence from a date no earlier than the conditions of paragraphs 12.18(a) to (c) are met. In a fair value hedge the cumulative **hedging**

gain or loss on the hedged item from the date hedge accounting commenced to the date of transition, shall be recorded in retained earnings (or if appropriate, another category of equity). In a cash flow hedge and net investment hedge, the lower of the following (in absolute amounts) shall be recorded in equity (in respect of cash flow hedges in the cash flow hedge reserve):

  (a) the cumulative gain or loss on the hedging instrument from the date hedge accounting commenced to the date of transition; and

  (b) the cumulative change in fair value (ie the present value of the cumulative change of expected future cash flows) on the hedged item from the date hedge accounting commenced to the date of transition.

 (ii) *A hedging relationship that ceased to exist before the date of transition because the hedging instrument has expired, was sold, terminated or exercised prior to the date of transition*

A first-time adopter may elect not to adjust the carrying amount of an asset or liability for previous GAAP accounting effects of a hedging relationship that has ceased to exist.

A first-time adopter may elect to account for amounts deferred in equity in a cash flow hedge under a previous GAAP, as described in paragraph 12.23(d) from the date of transition. Any amounts deferred in equity in relation to a hedge of a **net investment in a foreign operation** under a previous GAAP shall not be reclassified to profit or loss on disposal or partial disposal of the foreign operation.

(iii) *A hedging relationship that commenced after the date of transition*

A first-time adopter may elect to apply hedge accounting to a hedging relationship of a type described in paragraph 12.19 that commenced after the date of transition between a hedging instrument and a hedged item, starting from the date the conditions of paragraphs 12.18(a) to (c) are met, provided that the conditions of paragraphs 12.18(d) and (e) are met no later than the date the first financial statements that comply with this FRS are authorised for issue.

The choice applies to each hedging relationship that commenced after the date of transition.

(iv) *Entities taking the accounting policy choice under paragraphs 11.2(b) or (c) or paragraphs 12.2(b) or (c) to apply IAS 39 Financial Instruments: Recognition and Measurement or IFRS 9 Financial Instruments*

A first-time adopter adopting an accounting policy set out in paragraphs 11.2(b) or (c) or paragraphs 12.2(b) or (c) shall not apply the transitional provisions of paragraphs (i) to (iii) above. Such a first-time adopter shall apply the transitional requirements applicable to hedge accounting in IFRS 1 *First–time adoption of International Financial Reporting Standards*, paragraphs B4 to B6, except that the designation and documentation of a hedging relationship may be completed after the date of transition, and no later than the date the first financial statements that comply with this FRS are authorised for issue, if the hedging relationship is to qualify for hedge accounting from the date of transition.

A first-time adopter adopting an accounting policy set out in paragraphs 11.2(b) or (c) or paragraphs 12.2(b) or (c) that has entered into a hedging relationship as described in IAS 39 or IFRS 9 in the period between the date of transition and the **reporting date** for the first financial statements that comply with this FRS may elect to apply hedge accounting prospectively from the date all qualifying conditions for hedge accounting in IAS 39 or IFRS 9 are met, except that an entity shall complete the formal designation and documentation of a hedging relationship no later than the date the first financial statements that comply with this FRS are authorised for issue.

Prospective amendments: Amendments to FRS 102 *The Financial Reporting Standard applicable in the UK and Republic of Ireland* – Small entities and other minor amendments (July 2015) amends this paragraph 35.10 with effect for annual periods beginning on or after 1 January 2016.

35.11   If it is **impracticable** for an entity to restate the opening statement of financial position at the date of transition for one or more of the adjustments required by paragraph 35.7, the entity shall apply paragraphs 35.7 to 35.10 for such adjustments in the earliest period for which it is practicable to do so, and shall identify the data presented for prior periods that are not comparable with data for the period in which it prepares its first financial statements that conform to this FRS. If it is impracticable for an entity to provide any disclosures required by this FRS for any period before the period in which it prepares its first financial statements that conform to this FRS, the omission shall be disclosed.

35.11A   Where applicable to the transactions, events or arrangements affected by applying these exemptions, an entity may continue to use the exemptions that are applied at the date of transition to this FRS when preparing subsequent financial statements, until such time when the assets and liabilities associated with those transactions, events or arrangements are derecognised.

35.11B   Where there is subsequently a significant change in the circumstances or conditions associated with transactions, events or arrangements that existed at the date of transition, to which an exemption has been applied, an entity shall reassess the appropriateness of applying that exemption in preparing subsequent financial statements in order to maintain **fair presentation** in accordance with Section 3 *Financial Statement Presentation*.

Disclosures

Explanation of transition to this FRS

35.12   An entity shall explain how the transition from its previous financial reporting framework to this FRS affected its reported **financial position** and financial **performance**.

Reconciliations

35.13   To comply with paragraph 35.12, an entity's first financial statements prepared using this FRS shall include:

(a)   A description of the nature of each change in accounting policy.

(b)   Reconciliations of its equity determined in accordance with its previous financial reporting framework to its equity determined in accordance with this FRS for both of the following dates:

(i)   the date of transition to this FRS; and

(ii)   the end of the latest period presented in the entity's most recent annual financial statements determined in accordance with its previous financial reporting framework.

(c)   A reconciliation of the profit or loss determined in accordance with its previous financial reporting framework for the latest period in the entity's most recent annual financial statements to its profit or loss determined in accordance with this FRS for the same period.

If an entity becomes aware of **errors** made under its previous financial reporting framework, the reconciliations required by paragraphs 35.13(b) and (c) shall, to the extent practicable, distinguish the correction of those errors from changes in accounting policies. **35.14**

If an entity did not present financial statements for previous periods, it shall disclose that fact in its first financial statements that conform to this FRS. **35.15**

APPROVAL BY THE FRC

Financial Reporting Standard 102 *The Financial Reporting Standard applicable in the UK and Republic of Ireland* was approved for issue by the Financial Reporting Council on 5 March 2013, following its consideration of the Accounting Council's Advice for this FRS.

Amendments to FRS 102 The Financial Reporting Standard applicable in the UK and Republic of Ireland – Basic financial instruments and Hedge accounting was approved for issue by the Financial Reporting Council on 2 July 2014, following its consideration of the Accounting Council's Advice.

THE ACCOUNTING COUNCIL'S ADVICE TO THE FRC TO ISSUE FRS 102

Introduction

1   This report provides an overview of the main issues that have been considered by the Accounting Council in advising the Financial Reporting Council (FRC) to issue FRS 102 *The Financial Reporting Standard applicable in the UK and Republic of Ireland*. The FRC, in accordance with the Statutory Auditors (Amendment of Companies Act 2006 and Delegation of Functions etc) Order 2012 (SI 2012/1741), is the prescribed body for issuing accounting standards in the UK. The Foreword to Accounting Standards sets out the application of accounting standards in the Republic of Ireland.

2   In accordance with the *FRC Codes and Standards: procedures*, any proposal to issue, amend or withdraw a code or standard is put to the FRC Board with the full advice of the relevant Councils and/or the Codes & Standards Committee. Ordinarily, the FRC Board will only reject the advice put to it where:

- it is apparent that a significant group of stakeholders has not been adequately consulted;
- the necessary assessment of the impact of the proposal has not been completed, including an analysis of costs and benefits;
- insufficient consideration has been given to the timing or cost of implementation; or
- the cumulative impact of a number of proposals would make the adoption of an otherwise satisfactory proposal inappropriate.

3   The FRC has established the Accounting Council as the relevant Council to assist it in the setting of accounting standards.

Advice

4   All but one member of the Accounting Council is advising the FRC to issue FRS 102 *The Financial Reporting Standard Applicable in the UK and Republic of Ireland*.

5   One member of the Accounting Council, Edward Beale, does not agree with some aspects of the Accounting Council's advice and his dissenting view is set out in the appendix to the Accounting Council's Advice.

6   FRS 100 *Application of Financial Reporting Requirements* and FRS 101 *Reduced Disclosure Framework* which are also part of this suite of financial reporting standards were issued by the FRC in November 2012. The Accounting Council's advice to the FRC on those standards is contained in those standards.

Background

7   Accounting standards were formerly developed by the Accounting Standards Board (ASB). The ASB commenced its project to update accounting standards in 2002; Appendix V provides a history of the previous consultations and a summary of how the overall proposals have developed.[18]

8   FRS 102 was developed from the IASB's IFRS for SMEs to replace the majority of UK accounting standards in a single volume.

---

[18] *References in this section and Appendix V are made to the FRC, ASB or Accounting Council, as appropriate in terms of the time period and context of the reference.*

Objective

During its consultations on updating accounting standards, the ASB (and subsequently the   **9**
FRC) gave careful consideration to its objective and the intended effects. In developing the
requirements in this FRS, FRS 100 and FRS 101, the overriding objective is:

To enable users of accounts to receive high-quality understandable financial reporting
proportionate to the size and complexity of the entity and users' information needs.

In achieving this objective, the Accounting Council decided (and the FRC subsequently   **10**
adopted this decision) that it should provide succinct financial reporting standards that:

- have consistency with global accounting standards through the application of an IFRS-
  based solution unless an alternative clearly better meets the overriding objective;
- reflect up-to-date thinking and developments in the way businesses operate and the
  transactions they undertake;
- balance consistent principles for accounting by all UK and Republic of Ireland
  entities with practical solutions, based on size, complexity, public interest and users'
  information needs;
- promote efficiency within groups; and
- are cost-effective to apply.

The requirements in this FRS were principally consulted on in four exposure drafts: **11**

- FRED 44 Financial Reporting Standard for Medium-sized Entities issued in
  October 2010;
- FRED 45 Financial Reporting Standard for Public Benefit Entities issued in
  March 2011;
- FRED 48 Financial Reporting Standard applicable in the UK and Republic of Ireland
  issued in January 2012; and
- Amendment to FRED 48 issued in October 2012.

Consultation with stakeholders

The Accounting Council has obtained feedback from stakeholders throughout the project   **12**
in a variety of ways. Appendix V sets out a history of the consultation on this project. In
addition to formal consultation through exposure drafts, and previous consultation papers,
feedback has been obtained through an extensive programme of outreach aimed at raising
awareness of the proposals and to address the view (held by some) that earlier consultations
had not gathered sufficient evidence to support and test its assumptions.

The Accounting Council recognised that sometimes stakeholders who will be affected by   **13**
the outcome of a proposal can be difficult to engage in formal, written consultation. As a
result, and in accordance with the principles of Better Regulation it developed an outreach
programme that would reach beyond those stakeholders that typically respond to Exposure
Drafts.

As part of the outreach programme a series of meetings and events took place with   **14**
lenders to small and medium-sized entities. Lenders noted that financial statements are
an important part of their decision-making process when considering providing finance
and whilst a decision to provide finance is not based on financial statements alone, they
provide useful information and verification to the lender.

In addition, a review was made of academic research that addressed the users of small   **15**
and medium-sized entities' financial statements. The conclusion drawn from the research
was that many entities requested financial statements from Companies House when

considering whether to trade with another entity. The European Federation of Accountants and Auditors (EFAA) issued in May 2011 a statement that identified the users of financial statements noting who the users of SMEs financial statements are and that information on the public record assists all users of financial statements of SMEs by providing, in an efficient manner, basic information that protects their rights.

16   The Accounting Council considers that the outreach programme, across the project as a whole, has gleaned information from stakeholders who would not normally submit formal responses to a consultation and provided very useful information. The Accounting Council noted that whilst this information was not part of the public record, as formal consultation responses are, it could use the information to assist in finalising the standards, which supplemented the information contained in formal responses.

Consultation with stakeholders carried out by others

17   In addition to the consultation and outreach work carried out by the Accounting Council itself, the Accounting Council notes that some respondents, notably the accountancy institutes, conducted their own outreach amongst their members in determining their responses to the exposure drafts.

Classification of respondents

18   When analysing responses to consultations it has been the Accounting Council's practice to classify respondents into a number of standard categories in order to determine whether similar views are consistently held by a particular category of respondents. This classification is set out in the Feedback Statement that accompanies this FRS.

19   The classification of respondents only allows respondents to be classified to a single category and is based on the main perspective articulated in the response. However, the Accounting Council notes that many people that are interested in financial reporting and respond to consultations have a number of different perspectives, for example those that prepare financial statements often also use the financial statements of customers, suppliers and competitors in making decisions about running their business.

20   Therefore, there is an inherent limitation in the classification of respondents, which tends to underestimate the number of users of financial statements that have responded.

Using the IFRS for SMEs as a basis

21   Set out in Appendix V is a history of previous consultations. The ASB first started to consider the future of UK and Republic of Ireland accounting standards following the EU decision to require consolidated accounts of listed companies to comply with IFRS. The long held view is that there can be no justification for two different sets of accounting standards in the UK. Consequently, throughout the various consultations it has been proposed that the new accounting standards should have consistency with global accounting standards; this has continually been supported by the majority of respondents. Therefore the Accounting Council has proceeded with the project on this basis. The Impact Assessment accompanying this standard sets out alternative strategic options that the Accounting Council considered in framing the project (including UK accounting standards not based on IFRS), but taking into account consultation responses these were rejected. Therefore the Accounting Council developed the standard within the strategic context of an IFRS-based solution.

The Accounting Council noted that the IFRS for SMEs: **22**

- is a way of achieving a consistent accounting framework, as it is a simplification of IFRS;
- was developed by the IASB and published in 2009, reflecting more up-to-date thinking and developments than current FRS, especially for financial instruments;
- is a single book setting out clear accounting requirements; and
- is a cost effective way of updating current FRS.

The Accounting Council noted that one of the most significant changes being introduced   **23**
in this standard is the changes to the recognition, measurement and disclosures related
to financial instruments. Current FRSs contain limited requirements on accounting
for financial instruments for unlisted entities or those that do not apply the fair value
accounting rules. Entities use derivatives to manage risk and it is important that financial
statements recognise and provide disclosures about the effect of those instruments on the
entity's performance and position. The Accounting Council believes that the approach
under current FRSs, where derivatives are not recognised, does not adequately reflect
the risks arising from financial instruments. FRS 102 will lead to an improvement in
accounting for financial instruments.

The Accounting Council adopted guidelines for developing this standard from the IFRS for   **24**
SMEs, and noted that some pragmatism was required in determining when it would be
appropriate to diverge from the IFRS for SMEs. The objective is high-quality understandable
financial reporting, and the standard needs to work within the legal framework in the UK
and Republic of Ireland, including enabling the provisions of company law to be adhered
to. The guidelines also balance high-quality understandable financial reporting and cost
effective application. The high degree of support from respondents for the strategic thrust
of the approach to developing the new standards suggested that respondents were prepared
to balance high-quality financial reporting and costs/benefits. The Accounting Council
therefore concluded that its objective and guidelines for making changes to the IFRS for
SMEs should be:

In amending the IFRS for SMEs for application in the UK and Republic of Ireland
(RoI) the FRC maintains its commitment to:

(a)   ensuring high-quality financial reporting by UK and RoI entities applying
      FRS 102;
(b)   operate under an international accounting framework; and
(c)   acknowledge that users' preference for consistent financial reporting must be
      balanced with costs to preparers.

The guidelines when considering amendments to the IFRS for SMEs are:

(a)   changes should be made to permit accounting treatments that exist in FRSs at the
      transition date that align with EU-adopted IFRS;
(b)   changes should be consistent with EU-adopted IFRS unless a non-IFRS-
      based solution clearly better meets the objective of providing high-quality
      understandable financial reporting proportionate to the size and complexity of
      the entity and the users' information needs. In these cases elements of an IFRS-
      based solution may nevertheless be retained;
(c)   use should be made, where possible, of existing exemptions in company law to
      avoid gold-plating; and
(d)   changes should be made to provide clarification, by reference to EU-adopted
      IFRS, that will avoid unnecessary diversity in practice.

25   The Accounting Council noted that by providing clarifications within FRS 102 when compared with the IFRS for SMEs it could avoid unnecessary diversity in practice. Similarly, whilst maintaining its commitment to high-quality financial reporting and a global framework, the Accounting Council determined that it should amend the IFRS for SMEs by reference to EU-adopted IFRS.

Amendments made to the IFRS for SMEs in developing FRS 102

26   In developing FRS 102 from the IFRS for SMEs, the Accounting Council advises that a number of amendments should be made to the IFRS for SMEs. The following table identifies the more significant amendments and which of the guidelines were applied in making those amendments. Where an amendment is marked ✓✓ it indicates that the amendment is as a consequence of the decision that the scope of FRS 102 is different from that of the IFRS for SMEs.

Amendment	Guideline				Law
	a)	b)	c)	d)	
Scope					
Elimination of public accountability		✓			
Cross-references to IFRS 8 and IAS 33 for listed entities.				✓✓	
Definition of a financial institution				✓	
Inclusion of public benefit entities		✓			
Presentation					
True and fair override					✓
Statement of financial position					✓
Statement of comprehensive income, including discontinued operations					✓
Statement of changes in equity	✓				
Consolidated financial statements					
Consistency with the Act					✓
ESOPs		✓			
Subsidiaries held exclusively for resale, including in an investment portfolio	✓				
Changes in stake and gains or losses on disposals	✓			✓	✓
Exchanges of businesses for interests in another business (was UITF Abstract 31)				✓	
Accounting policies					
Clarification of when to refer to a SORP in developing accounting policies		✓			
Financial instruments					
Disclosures required by financial institutions (might be considered an expansion of paragraph 11.42 for those entities)				✓✓	

Amendment	Guideline				Law
	a)	b)	c)	d)	
Treatment of loan covenants for determining whether an instrument is basic	✓				
Disclosures for certain financial instruments required by law					✓
Hedge accounting is permitted for a net investment in a foreign operation and in respect of foreign exchange risks in a debt instrument measured at amortised cost	✓	✓			
Borrowing costs may be capitalised in certain circumstances	✓				
Public benefit entities can account for concessionary loans at transaction amount		✓	✓		
Fair value option	✓				
Option to apply IAS 39 or IFRS 9 recognition and measurement requirements	✓				
Financial guarantee contracts scoped out of financial instrument accounting		✓			
Property, plant and equipment					
Revaluation	✓				
Intangible assets					
Capitalisation of development costs	✓				
Revaluation after initial recognition	✓				
Where unable to make a reliable estimate of useful life, it should not exceed 5 years.					✓
Business combinations and goodwill					
Permit merger accounting for group reconstructions			✓		
Permit merger accounting by public benefit entities		✓	✓		
Where unable to make a reliable estimate of useful life of goodwill, it should not exceed 5 years.					✓
Leases					
Clarification of definitions				✓	
Clarification of scope for 'arrangements that contain a lease'				✓	
Liabilities and equity					
Clarification of whether an instrument is a financial liability or equity in certain circumstances				✓	
Only disclosure required for non-cash distributions to owners				✓	

Amendment	Guideline				Law
	a)	b)	c)	d)	
Grants					
Introduction of accrual method as an option for accounting for government grants	✓				
Share-based payment					
Clarification that option pricing models are not required particularly for unquoted shares				✓	
Share-based payments granted by another group entity				✓	
Employee benefits					
Presentation of the cost of a defined benefit pension is consistent with IAS 19's 2011 amendments.		✓			
Recognition of liability by entities in multi-employer schemes with a schedule of funding for a deficit				✓	
Income tax					
Timing differences plus approach		✓			
Revised disclosure requirements		✓			
Guidance on accounting for VAT				✓	
Related party disclosures					
Disclosure exemption for wholly-owned entities			✓		
Specialised activities					
Agriculture – permit historical cost model for biological assets.		✓			
Extractive industries – refer to IFRS 6	✓				
Service concession arrangements – grantors				✓ ✓	
Service concession arrangements – operators				✓	
Retirement benefit plans		✓			
Heritage assets		✓			
Funding commitments				✓ ✓	
PBE – incoming resources from non-exchange transactions (including performance-related conditions and restrictions)		✓ ✓			

Scope of FRS 102

27　In an earlier consultation the Accounting Council proposed a differential financial reporting system based on three tiers of entities using public accountability as a differentiator, which would have required some entities to apply EU-adopted IFRS that would not otherwise have been required to do so. Several concerns were noted about this; the more significant include:

(a)   the costs for those entities that would be required to apply EU-adopted IFRS could not be justified in relation to the benefit to users of those entities financial statements;

(b)   inconsistencies in the recognition and measurement requirements between EU-adopted IFRS and the proposals at the time for FRS 102 would reduce comparability between entities; and

(c)   the application guidance addressing the definition of public accountability remained unclear despite the guidance being developed further from the Policy Proposal.

The Accounting Council wanted to address the concerns from respondents that the costs for those entities that would be required to apply EU-adopted IFRS could not be justified in relation to the benefit to users of those entities' financial statements. As a result it proposed eliminating public accountability as a differentiator and determined that FRS 102 should be applied by entities that were not required to apply EU-adopted IFRS, nor were eligible and chose to apply the FRSSE. Respondents agreed with this approach.   **28**

As a consequence various entities that are outside the scope of the IFRS for SMEs are within the scope of FRS 102, typically these are financial institutions.   **29**

The Accounting Council noted that a significant number of public benefit entities apply UK accounting standards, and would be within the scope of FRS 102.   **30**

Consequences of the scope of FRS 102

As the scope of FRS 102 is wider than the scope of the IFRS for SMEs, there are areas not addressed in the IFRS for SMEs that might be relevant to the broader group of entities applying FRS 102.   **31**

In considering these areas the Accounting Council reflected on users' needs for additional information relevant to entities that are listed but not on a regulated market, ie those entities that were in part (a) of the definition of public accountability but were not required by EU Regulation to apply EU-adopted IFRS. This identified that earnings per share, operating segments and accounting for insurance contracts were not addressed in the IFRS for SMEs and accounting requirements would need to be set in these areas.   **32**

The Accounting Council, however, noted that in addressing the needs of this broader group of entities it should not lose sight of its objective to provide succinct financial reporting standards. Consequently, consideration was given to whether entities listed on a non-regulated market could apply EU-adopted IFRS for the areas identified by including cross references to EU-adopted IFRS in FRS 102 rather than setting out the requirements in the FRS itself.   **33**

The Accounting Council broadly termed as financial institutions those entities that, in accordance with FRED 43 were within the scope of part (b) of the definition of public accountability, (ie entities that hold assets in a fiduciary capacity or take deposits, including credit unions, building societies and investment entities). In considering the users' needs for financial information on financial institutions the Accounting Council noted that FRS 102 set out improvements, from current FRS, for the recognition and measurement of financial instruments, however, it had limited specific disclosure requirements for financial instruments. The Accounting Council decided that if it were to eliminate the definition of public accountability it would need to address the disclosure requirements for financial institutions, noting that financial instruments are central to the business model of these entities and how such entities generate wealth and manage risk.   **34**

Having identified that it would need to improve the disclosure requirements for financial institutions if it were to remove the definition of public accountability, the Accounting   **35**

Council sought to find a clear definition of a financial institution. Various options were considered including whether to retain part (b) of the definition of publicly accountable, however this approach was rejected because it did not address the application difficulties raised by respondents to FRED 43.

36   The second option considered was to use the definition in section 467(1) of the Companies Act 2006; one advantage was that this was in part basing the definition on whether the entity was regulated or not.

37   The third option was simply to list the types of entity which should provide additional disclosures for financial instruments. In this regard the Accounting Council gave consideration to its previous accounting standard FRS 13 *Derivatives and Financial Instrument: Disclosures*, which applied a differential disclosure regime depending on the category of entity. On balance the Accounting Council decided that a list of entities provided the clearest approach to determine which entities should be defined as financial institutions. However, the Accounting Council also agreed with some respondents to FRED 48 that a principle behind entities selected for inclusion on the list should be articulated. As a result the Accounting Council added a final item to the list, intended to capture any entities similar to those listed above, which would also add an element of future-proofing to the definition. The Accounting Council advises that a parent entity whose sole activity is to hold investments in other group entities is not a financial institution, but notes that a subsidiary entity engaged solely in treasury activities for the group as a whole is likely to meet the definition of a financial institution.

38   Having undertaken the analysis above, it was concluded that public accountability could be eliminated and FRS 102 could apply to a broader group of entities than the IFRS for SMEs. To address the users' information needs for entities listed on a non-regulated market, FRS 102 includes cross-referencing to EU-adopted IFRS and additional disclosure requirements have been inserted for financial instruments held by financial institutions.

39   The Accounting Council observed that if it were to require a financial institution applying FRS 102 to disclose additional information regarding its financial instruments, it also needed to consider its proposals for reduced disclosures. It decided that financial institutions applying reduced disclosures would not be permitted exemptions from the additional disclosures for financial institutions.

40   The Accounting Council considered whether broadening the scope of FRS 102 would increase the pressure to update the standard (in line with changes being made to full IFRS) more frequently than on a three-year cycle. The Accounting Council agreed that there may be circumstances where FRS 102 would require updating in an interim period between the three-year cycles, but where this occurred the amendments proposed should be limited.

Presentation

41   The Accounting Council considered feedback to FRED 44 and to the draft case studies prepared by its staff that were posted on its website that addressed the interaction between FRED 44 and the presentation formats required by company law. The Accounting Council noted that there were specific conflicts between the IFRS for SMEs and the formats, specifically the definition of current assets differed between the two sets of requirements.

42   The Accounting Council considered whether to replicate the requirements set out in company law for the information to be presented in the statement of financial position and the income statement, but was concerned that this would add clutter to FRS 102 which was not consistent with its objectives. However, it needed to work within company law and whilst it had encouraged changes to simplify the Accounting Directives it was unlikely

such change would take place in the near future. The Accounting Council decided that it should promote only formats already determined in company law. This would have the consequence of all entities being required to comply with the company law formats, promoting consistency amongst all those preparing financial statements intended to give a true and fair view.

In amending the IFRS for SMEs to include the Companies Act formats, it was noted that   **43** the ASB had had a long-standing policy that company law formats on their own were not sufficient and should be supplemented to highlight a range of important components of financial performance to aid users' understanding of the performance of the entity. Therefore some requirements from FRS 3 *Reporting Financial Performance*, notably covering acquisitions, exceptional items and discontinued operations need to be factored in. The IFRS for SMEs was amended so that FRS 102 includes:

(a)   the disclosure of post-acquisition revenue and profit or loss of an acquiree in a business combination in the notes to the financial statements;

(b)   no mandatory requirement to disclose an operating profit line but guidance, based on IAS 1 *Presentation of Financial Statements*, on matters to consider where entities choose to present operating profit; and

(c)   the inclusion of an explicit requirement to disclose material items.

The existing FRS 3 requirement to show separately on the face of the profit and loss   **44** account: profits or losses on sale or termination of an operation; costs of a fundamental reorganisation materially affecting the operation and profits; and losses on disposal of fixed assets (all of which would still have to be disclosed where material) has not been included.

The Accounting Council advises that, in view of the company law requirement that turnover   **45** includes the turnover from discontinued operations, a practical way of presenting this and the post-tax profit or loss on discontinued operations would be for the information about discontinued operations to be presented via a columnar approach. An example illustrating this is set out in FRS 102.

Consolidated financial statements

Definitions of control, parent and subsidiary

The Accounting Council notes that the definitions of control, parent and subsidiary   **46** included in FRS 102 are consistent with the IFRS for SMEs (and based on EU-adopted IFRS prior to the issuing of IFRS 10 *Consolidated Financial Statements*), but differ from those used in current FRS. Some respondents queried whether the definitions should be based on company law. The Accounting Council rejected this suggestion, but noted that by using the IFRS for SMEs definitions (consistently with its objective and guidelines), it was widening the application of control to include certain special purpose entities within the definition of a group. However, as noted below, the Accounting Council advises that this should not include employee benefit trusts and ESOPs (which should continue to be accounted for as if they are assets and liabilities of the sponsoring entity).

Employee benefit trusts, ESOPs and similar arrangements

In clarifying the requirements for consolidation, including considering consistency with   **47** company law requirements, the Accounting Council noted that the accounting treatment for employee benefit trusts, ESOPs or similar arrangements would give rise to a change in accounting from current FRS. The removal of UITF Abstract 38 *Accounting for ESOP trusts* would mean that such arrangements would no longer be included in individual financial statements but only in consolidated financial statements. Further, for an entity with such an arrangement, which is not a parent entity, a change in accounting requirements would lead to the preparation of 'group' financial statements where they would otherwise not have been required. Therefore the Accounting Council decided to retain the accounting treatment from UITF Abstract 32 *Employee benefit trusts and other intermediate payment arrangements* which are included in Section 9 *Consolidated and Separate Financial Statements* of FRS 102.

Investment entities exemption from consolidation

48   In September 2011 the IASB issued an exposure draft proposing to exempt qualifying investment entities from consolidating their investments. The accounting requirements were finalised and published as an amendment to IFRS 10 *Consolidated Financial Statements*, IFRS 12 *Disclosure of Interests in Other Entities* and IAS 27 *Separate Financial Statements* in October 2012. The Accounting Council noted that without a similar exemption in FRS 102, investment entities eligible to apply FRS 102, would need to elect to prepare EU-adopted IFRS in order to take advantage of the exemption. The Accounting Council did not consider this to be a logical or meaningful outcome and therefore sought to find a solution.

49   Section 405(3) of the Companies Act sets out the circumstances in which a subsidiary may be excluded from consolidation and the Accounting Council must work within these requirements. Section 405(3) permits a subsidiary to be excluded from consolidation on the following grounds:

(a)   severe long-term restrictions substantially hinder the exercise of the rights of the parent company over the assets or management of that subsidiary;

(b)   the information necessary for the preparation of group accounts cannot be obtained without disproportion expense or undue delay; or

(c)   the interest of the parent company is held exclusively with a view to subsequent resale.

50   Taking into account the IASB's publication of *Investment Entities* (Amendments to IFRS 10, IFRS 12 and IAS 27) in October 2012, the Accounting Council advises that the definition of an interest held exclusively with a view to subsequent resale should include interests held as part of an investment portfolio.

51   FRS 102 permits that subsidiaries excluded from consolidation may be measured at fair value through profit or loss. This is a departure from the requirements of the Companies Act for the overriding purpose of giving a true and fair view in the consolidated financial statements.

Changes in stake and gains or losses on disposals

52   The Accounting Council noted that the requirements of the IFRS for SMEs in relation to changes in stake and gains and losses on disposals were not entirely coherent being based partly on IFRS 3 *Business combinations* (issued 2004) and partly on IFRS 3 *Business combinations* (revised 2008), and further some of the requirements are not consistent with company law provisions on the recognition of unrealised gains.

53   The Accounting Council considered that a coherent model for increases and decreases in stakes held in another entity was required, and that it must be consistent with company law. As a result the requirements of Section 9 *Consolidated and Separate Financial Statements* and Section 19 *Business Combinations and Goodwill* are now based on IFRS 3 (issued 2004), providing an IFRS-based solution that is consistent with company law.

Distribution of non-cash assets to owners

The Accounting Council had also been asked to clarify that the distribution of non-cash assets to owners did not apply to distributions within groups. In considering this requirement, the Accounting Council noted a distinction between the disposal of an asset at fair value followed by a distribution to shareholders of the profit, and making a distribution of the asset to shareholders. In its view, a distribution to shareholders does not generate a profit, whereas a disposal does generate a profit that may then be distributed to shareholders. The Accounting Council decided, given it did not support the accounting requirement, to remove the requirement in the IFRS for SMEs to recognise a liability to pay a dividend for a non-cash asset at fair value and to require disclosure of the fair value of the assets distributed to shareholders.   **54**

Financial instruments

In FREDs 43 and 44 the ASB noted that current FRSs were in need of updating and that they permitted certain transactions not to be recorded. Sections 11 *Basic Financial Instruments* and 12 *Other Financial Instruments Issues* of FRED 44 proposed to address these weaknesses in current FRS. The Accounting Council noted that the IFRS for SMEs has simplified the accounting for financial instruments when compared with IAS 39 *Financial Instruments: Recognition and Measurement*, whilst generally achieving similar accounting. However, there will be areas where those familiar with IAS 39 will need to take care to ensure compliance with FRS 102, for example the hierarchy to be used in determining the fair value of an asset set out in paragraph 11.27 is not the same as the 'fair value hierarchy' set out in IAS 39.   **55**

The Accounting Council carefully considered the views of respondents to FRED 44 concerning the proposed accounting for financial instruments set out in the FRED.   **56**

The Accounting Council noted the concern, primarily from the social housing sector, that recognition of derivatives used for hedging purposes at fair value may result in volatility in profit or loss. It considered carefully the requirement to recognise derivatives at fair value but noted that any changes to the financial instrument proposals should be consistent with the guidelines for amending the IFRS for SMEs. The Accounting Council concluded that it would not be consistent with the objective of providing high-quality information, or the guidelines for amending the IFRS for SMEs, to change the recognition requirements for derivatives. Recognition of derivatives, and associated disclosure, will provide relevant information to users about the risks an entity has in relation to its financial instruments.   **57**

Impact of the IASB hedge accounting and impairment projects

The requirements for hedge accounting and impairment of financial assets in FRS 102 are based on the requirements of IAS 39. The IASB is currently reviewing hedge accounting and impairment requirements (including developing an 'expected loss' model for the recognition of impairments of financial assets) and the Accounting Council is reluctant to propose new accounting requirements in respect of these areas before the IASB's projects are finalised in IFRS 9 *Financial Instruments*. The Accounting Council is concerned that doing so would risk financial instruments requirements in FRS 102 being out of line with both IFRS 9 and IAS 39. Simultaneously, the Accounting Council believes that the next scheduled amendment date for FRS 102 is too far in the future and consequential amendments to FRS 102 may therefore be untimely for entities that would like to apply the new IFRS 9 accounting requirements without undue delay. For that reason the Accounting Council agreed that a proposed amendment to FRS 102 would be issued for public consultation once the IASB has completed the hedge accounting and impairment projects and IFRS 9 has been updated; it is likely that there will be two separate exposure   **58** drafts, one addressing each topic. The Accounting Council intends to make amendments to FRS 102 (should the consultation determine this is appropriate) prior its effective date, although the exact timetable of any possible amendment is dependent upon when the IASB completes the impairment and hedge accounting requirements in IFRS 9.

Financial instruments accounting policy choices

59   In order to allow entities applying FRS 102 maximum flexibility, entities have a choice of either:

(a)   applying the requirements of Sections 11 and 12 of FRS 102;

(b)   applying the recognition and measurement requirements in IAS 39 (as adopted for use in the EU) as the standard applies prior to the application of IFRS 9; or

(c)   applying IFRS 9 (as far as it has replaced the requirements in IAS 39) and IAS 39 (as far it remains applicable if IFRS 9 is applied).

By providing these accounting policy choices entities have the flexibility to apply the accounting requirements of IFRS 9 without delay should they wish to do so[19]. Entities that elect to account for financial instruments by applying the requirements of Sections 11 and 12, especially those entities that choose to apply FRS 102 before its effective date, may be required to change their accounting for financial instruments should some of the requirements in Sections 11 and 12 be amended for consistency with the principles of IFRS 9 in respect of hedge and impairment accounting, once those have been determined.

Disclosures by financial institutions

60   Having defined financial institutions, the Accounting Council advises that additional disclosures should be provided for the financial instruments held by these entities. It developed a proportionate set of disclosures for financial institutions, using IFRS 7 *Financial Instruments: Disclosures* as the basis.

Fair value option

61   A number of respondents to FRED 48 noted that bonds within the scope of Section 11 must be measured at amortised cost, even if they are managed on a fair value basis or their measurement at amortised cost introduces measurement differences, and suggested that an option to measure such items at fair value should be permitted in FRS 102. The Accounting Council agreed that, consistently with EU-adopted IFRS, an option should be available to designate financial assets and liabilities to be measured at fair value through profit or loss.

Hedge accounting

62   In light of the comments received in response to FREDs 44 and 48, and in order to reduce inconsistencies with EU-adopted IFRS, the Accounting Council advises that hedge accounting of a net investment in a foreign operation in consolidated financial statements be permitted and that entities are permitted to hedge foreign exchange risk arising in a debt instrument measured at amortised cost. Consistently with EU-adopted IFRS the Accounting Council also advises that hedge accounting of a net investment in a foreign operation should not be permitted in the separate financial statements of a parent.

---

[19] *As FRS 102 is a UK and Republic of Ireland accounting standard, IFRS 9 can be applied through FRS 102 in advance of EU endorsement.*

Financial guarantee contracts

Respondents to FRED 48 asked for clarification of the accounting requirements for   **63**
financial guarantee contracts. The accounting for financial guarantee contracts is within
the scope of Section 21 *Provisions and Contingencies* unless an entity has chosen to
apply IAS 39 and/or IFRS 9, or has an existing accounting policy of insurance contract
accounting for financial guarantee contracts and chooses to continue to apply that policy
under FRS 103 *Insurance Contracts*.

Group reconstructions

The Accounting Council advises that FRS 102 should retain the current accounting   **64**
permitted by FRS 6 *Acquisitions and mergers* for group reconstructions. The Accounting
Council noted that whilst EU-adopted IFRS does not provide accounting requirements for
the accounting for business combinations under common control the accounting provided
by FRS 6 is well understood and provides useful requirements. It therefore decided to carry
forward these requirements into FRS 102. In practice, the Accounting Council does not
expect the introduction of FRS 102 to change the accounting for group reconstructions.
For example, where a combination is effected by using a newly formed parent company to
hold the shares of each of the parties to a combination, the accounting treatment depends
on the substance of the business combination being effected.

Leases

Leases are accounted for in accordance with the requirements of Section 20 *Leases*, except   **65**
for those leases falling within the scope of Section 12, which are those that could result in
a loss to the lessor or the lessee as a result of non-typical contractual terms, for example
those that are unrelated to:

(a)   changes in the price of the leased asset;
(b)   changes in foreign exchange rates; or
(c)   a default by one of the counterparties.

The Accounting Council notes that the reference to 'changes in the price of the leased   **66**
asset' is framed widely and in practice it does not expect many leases to fall within the
scope of Section 12.

Grants

A number of respondents, particularly from the public benefit entity sector, raised   **67**
concerns about the proposed changes to the recognition requirements for grants received
from government and other bodies. The proposals in FRED 44 based the recognition of
income from grants on when an entity fulfilled the performance criteria stipulated in the
grant. This would have been a change from both current FRS and EU-adopted IFRS which
attempt to match grant income with the related expenditure. The Accounting Council
observed that the IFRS for SMEs used an approach not in current EU-adopted IFRSs.

The Accounting Council reviewed the concerns of entities noting that it could amend the   **68**
performance criterion approach to provide application guidance on performance outcome.
This approach would require a research project to be undertaken and cause delay to the
finalisation of FRS 102. An alternative was to amend the requirements in the IFRS for
SMEs so that they were consistent with EU-adopted IFRS and defer a research project
on the accounting for grants until after the publication of FRS 102. However, respondents
also noted that some entities, mainly in the public benefit entity sector, currently
recognised income from grants on the basis of performance criteria and that reverting to

the requirements of EU-adopted IFRS (which is similar to current FRS) would introduce a change for these entities. The Accounting Council did not wish to implement a change for entities that might be reversed when it subsequently undertook a research project on grant accounting. It therefore concluded it should allow entities a choice between the accounting requirements of the IFRS for SMEs and those in EU-adopted IFRS.

69   The Accounting Council recognises that the respondents to FRED 44 highlighted an inconsistency in current practice and that the solution in FRS 102 is therefore, an interim solution until completion on a research project is undertaken.

70   Respondents have further commented that as Section 24 *Government Grants* is restricted to government grants, grants received by public benefit entities from other sources will be accounted for in accordance with Section 34 *Specialised Activities: Incoming Resources from Non-Exchange Transactions*, and there is now the possibility that the accounting for grants depends on the source of the grant, rather than whether or not the underlying terms and conditions of the grants differ. Whilst this is not ideal, the Accounting Council advises permitting the accrual model for government grants in accordance with its guidelines for amending the IFRS for SMEs as an interim solution to avoid changes in accounting that might be reversed in the future.

71   For those entities that apply the performance model to capital grants, either as an accounting policy choice for government grants, or through applying Section 34 to grants from other sources, the Accounting Council notes that there may be a change from current accounting practice, which may lead to greater volatility in the income statement. The effect of this volatility can be explained in the notes to the financial statements.

Share-based payment

72   The Accounting Council noted that at present entities in the UK and Republic of Ireland[20] that enter into share-based payment transactions are required to apply FRS 20 (IFRS 2) *Share-based Payment*. However, for unlisted entities it can be difficult to apply option pricing models and therefore the benefits outweigh the costs. As a result the Accounting Council advises that directors apply judgement by using models that are appropriate to the entity's circumstance. The Accounting Council considers that this provides a cost effective way of recognising the cost of share-based payments.

Employee benefits

73   The Accounting Council noted that the requirements of FRS 17 *Retirement benefits* are broadly consistent with the equivalent requirements of IAS 19 *Employee Benefits*, which form the basis of the IFRS for SMEs in this area, including the principles for the measurement of the net defined benefit liability and the recognition of plan deficits and surpluses. The disclosure requirements of FRS 102 for defined benefit pension plans are reduced when compared with those in FRS 17.

Cost of a defined benefit plan

74   Respondents noted that the presentation requirements for post-employment benefit plans were not clear in FRED 44. Specifically a request was made to clarify where the difference between the actual return on plan assets and expected return on plan assets should be presented. The Accounting Council, in considering this request, noted that the presentation requirements in IAS 19 had been amended in 2011. The amendments to IAS 19 were

---

[20] *Other than those applying the FRSSE.*

consistent with the ASB's recommendations in its report following the consultation document *The Financial Reporting of Pensions*. In view of this, the Accounting Council decided to update FRS 102 to be consistent with the revised IAS 19, which requires an entity to recognise the net change in the defined benefit liability as follows:

(a)   the change in the defined benefit liability arising from employee service rendered during the reporting period in profit or loss;

(b)   net interest on the net defined benefit liability in profit or loss; and

(c)   remeasurement of the net defined benefit liability in other comprehensive income.

In advising this amendment, the Accounting Council also noted that the accounting   **75**
requirements in the IFRS for SMEs for group pension plan arrangements were more stringent than those set out in IAS 19 (revised 2011). The Accounting Council therefore decided to update these requirements to be consistent with the IAS 19 (revised 2011).

Group defined benefit pension plans

Consistently with IAS 19 (revised 2011), paragraph 28.38 of FRS 102 requires entities   **76**
participating in a group defined benefit pension plan to recognise the net defined benefit cost in their individual financial statements where a relevant agreement or policy exists. Otherwise the entity that is legally responsible for the group pension plan will recognise the entire net defined benefit cost in its individual financial statements. The Accounting Council noted that although this paragraph only refers explicitly to the cost of the pension plan, the net defined benefit cost is calculated by reference to both the defined benefit obligation and the fair value of plan assets. Therefore paragraph 28.38 does require the recognition of the relevant net defined benefit liability in the individual financial statements of any group entities recognising a net defined benefit cost.

Multi-employer defined benefit plans

In October 2012 the FRC issued an exposure draft of proposed amendments to FRED   **77**
48, including amendments to Section 28 *Employee Benefits*. These amendments related to multi-employer defined benefit plans that are accounted for as defined contribution plans. The Accounting Council is aware that diversity in accounting practice had arisen in relation to entities who participate in a defined benefit multi-employer plan, who account for that plan as a defined contribution plan and who have entered into a funding agreement for future payments relating to past service liabilities, to recognise a liability in relation to the deficit in the plan in their financial statements.

Consistently with the guidelines for amending the IFRS for SMEs, the Accounting Council   **78**
advises incorporating the relevant requirement from IAS 19 and notes that the IASB's basis for conclusions said that 'In relation to the funding of a deficit, […] this principle [is] consistent with the recognition of a provision in accordance with IAS 37.'

The Accounting Council also advises clarifying the measurement requirements for such   **79**
a liability. In the circumstances that the entity has entered into a funding agreement for future payments relating to past service it shall recognise those future payments as a liability, discounted using the methodology for selecting a discount rate for post-employment benefit liabilities. The Accounting Council debated whether the discount rate should alternatively be based on the entity's cost of capital, but decided to advise the use of a rate consistent with the methodology used for accounting for other pension liabilities.

The Accounting Council noted that some respondents to the exposure draft disagreed   **80**
with the proposed amendment or requested a delay in implementation, but the Accounting Council believes that where participants in a multi-employer defined benefit pension plan

have entered into an agreement to fund a deficit, and have applied defined contribution accounting, a liability exists and its recognition provides useful information to users.

81   Some respondents suggested that FRS 102 should also address situations where a multi-employer pension plan was in surplus, and entered into an agreement to distribute that surplus to the participating employers. Although the Accounting Council noted that this is addressed in IAS 19, it expected that the situation would arise rarely in practice, and considered that entities would be able to determine the appropriate accounting using the principles set out in FRS 102. Therefore it does not advise making an amendment for this.

Income tax

82   In FRED 44 the ASB proposed using the text of IAS 12 *Income Taxes* in place of the IFRS for SMEs section on income tax. The ASB had amended the tax section of the IFRS for SMEs because it had been based on proposals subsequently abandoned by the IASB and therefore the IFRS for SMEs was not consistent with full IFRS. Respondents to the Policy Proposal had not supported retaining the IFRS for SMEs requirements in this area. Respondents to FRED 44 had accepted that the IFRS for SMEs treatment could not be used, but did not support the ASB's proposal to replace the tax section with IAS 12.

83   In developing FRED 48 the ASB considered what would be the most suitable alternative, and took into account the findings of its research work with EFRAG in developing the Discussion Paper *Improving the Financial Reporting of Income Tax* (issued in December 2011), as well as its commitment to an IFRS-based solution and the requirements of FRS 19 *Deferred Tax* from which entities would be transitioning. It set out an alternative approach that based the recognition requirements on timing differences, with additional recognition requirements for certain temporary differences that are not timing differences, which was referred to as a 'timing differences plus' approach. The advantages of this approach seemed to be that it would:

(a)   provide useful information to users of financial statements; and

(b)   provide the simple solution preparers were looking for that was close to current FRS and that would give the same answers as IFRSs in most cases.

84   Most respondents supported the 'timing differences plus' approach, which has therefore been retained in FRS 102.

85   The most significant change to the requirements in current FRS is that the proposed approach requires the recognition of the deferred tax implications of the revaluation of assets. Gains and losses recognised on a revaluation are timing differences and the tax effects should be recognised. Such a requirement is consistent with IAS 12 and the IFRS for SMEs.

86   Another significant change from current FRS is that discounting of current and deferred tax is not allowed which is consistent with the IFRS for SMEs.

87   Under IAS 12 deferred tax is not generally recognised on the initial recognition of an asset, except that of assets and liabilities arising from a business combination. No specific exception for this is necessary under the 'timing differences plus' approach as no timing difference arises. The proposed treatment is therefore consistent in this respect with IAS 12.

88   A pure timing difference approach does not provide complete consistency with the requirements of IAS 12. In particular, IAS 12 requires that deferred tax is recognised in respect of the difference between the amount recognised on a business combination for assets and liabilities (other than goodwill) and the amount that will be allowed for or assessed to tax in respect of such assets and liabilities. These differences are not timing

differences. In order to maintain consistency with IFRS on this major issue, the Accounting Council agreed to supplement the timing difference approach with a requirement to recognise deferred tax on business combinations.

However, the 'timing differences plus' approach adopted in FRS 102 does not ensure   **89** complete consistency with the requirements of IAS 12. For example FRS 102 does not permit the recognition of deferred tax:

(a)   where the tax deduction (or estimated future deduction) for share-based payment exceeds the cumulative amount of the related remuneration expense; and

(b)   in some cases, where the tax basis of an asset is changed, for example where legislation changes the amount of future tax relief relating to the asset.

The Accounting Council considered, however, that the differences from IAS 12 were likely   **90** to be relatively rare and that in such cases the relevance of the information produced in accordance with IAS 12 was unclear.

The proposed disclosure requirements have been reviewed in the light of comments on   **91** FRED 48. In particular the requirement to disclose differences between the current tax charge and a standard rate of tax for the next three years has been replaced by a requirement to disclose expected net reversals of timing differences for the next year. The requirement to disclose is on a net basis, which takes account of both the reversal of existing timing differences and the origination of new ones. The net basis provides information that is relevant to the entity's future cash flows, and hence is more relevant than disclosure on a gross basis. The Accounting Council considers that the additional benefit of disclosure on a net basis outweighed the cost to preparers of forecasting future new timing differences.

Related party disclosures

In response to feedback from respondents, the Accounting Council advises that the   **92** company law exemption from disclosing intra-group related party transactions should be included in FRS 102.

Some respondents raised the issue of a possible exemption from the disclosure of   **93** outstanding balances as well as transactions. However, the Accounting Council noted that there is a separate legal requirement, in relation to the format of the balance sheet which requires disclosure of outstanding balances in aggregate for group undertakings and, separately, for undertakings in which the company has a participating interest. As Section 33 *Related Party Disclosures* requires disclosure in aggregate for a category of related parties, one of which is 'entities over which the entity has control, joint control or significant influence' this should be met by compliance with the requirements of Section 4 *Statement of Financial Position*. As a result it is not possible to provide an effective exemption from the disclosure of outstanding balances with group undertakings.

Specialised activities

Agriculture

The IFRS for SMEs includes guidance for specialised activities including agriculture. The   **94** proposed requirements for agriculture are a predominately fair value model and are based on IAS 41 *Agriculture*. Respondents questioned the proposed requirements noting that current FRSs do not set out accounting requirements and although the proposals included an exemption from applying fair value where there is undue cost or effort, the fair value information is inconsistent with the way most agricultural businesses are managed and would not benefit the users of financial statements.

95   The Accounting Council evaluated the comments raised and advises that entities engaged in agricultural activities should be permitted an accounting policy choice for their biological assets, between the cost model and fair value model set out in the IFRS for SMEs.

96   The Accounting Council noted that both the cost model and the fair value model, as set out in the IFRS for SMEs, require agricultural produce to be measured at the point of harvest at fair value less costs to sell. However, it considered that respondents in favour of the cost model would have expected the cost model to mean that both biological assets and agricultural produce would be measured at cost.

97   The Accounting Council noted that agricultural produce should be capable of measurement at fair value without undue cost or effort, and should provide more relevant information to users. However, it noted that respondents argued that agricultural businesses often manage their business on the basis of cost information and advises that agricultural produce should be permitted to be measured at cost. The Accounting Council advises limiting the use of the cost model for agricultural produce to those entities that have chosen the cost model for biological assets; however these entities should also have the option of using the fair value model for agricultural produce.

Extractive activities

98   Respondents noted that the requirements of the IFRS for SMEs in relation to extractive activities were not consistent with IFRS 6 *Exploration for and Evaluation of Mineral Resources*, and the application of the IFRS for SMEs requirements, in conjunction with other elements of FRS 102 would significantly change accounting practices for entities engaged in extractive activities. It would be likely that no assets could be recognised from the costs of exploration activities, yet entities applying EU-adopted IFRS would be permitted to recognise such assets.

99   The Accounting Council agreed that entities applying FRS 102 should not be prohibited from applying accounting policies that are available to those entities applying EU-adopted IFRS, and advises that the requirements of IFRS 6 are incorporated into FRS 102 by cross reference.

Service concession arrangements

100   Respondents raised two main issues relating to the accounting for service concession arrangements. The first was that the requirements of the IFRS for SMEs in relation to the accounting by operators had been over-simplified when compared with IFRIC 12 *Service Concession Arrangements*. The Accounting Council agreed and FRS 102 includes additional clarification of the principles of accounting by operators for service concession arrangements, which were developed from IFRIC 12.

101   The second issue related to grantors, with some respondents noting that grantors might be within the scope of FRS 102. This was addressed in the October 2012 exposure draft of proposed amendments to FRED 48 issued by the FRC.

102   EU-adopted IFRS does not address accounting by grantors of service concession arrangements; grantors are expected to be outside the scope of EU-adopted IFRS. As a result, and consistently with the guidelines for amending the IFRS for SMEs, the Accounting Council sought to develop accounting for grantors that is consistent with the principles underpinning the accounting by operators of service concession arrangements, which is set out in IFRIC 12. The scope of IFRIC 12 is such that the grantor controls the residual interest in the infrastructure asset, and therefore for service concession arrangements meeting the definition in FRS 102, the Accounting Council advises that

the grantor recognises its interest in the infrastructure asset usually as property, plant and equipment, with a corresponding liability measured using a finance lease model.

The Accounting Council noted that the International Public Sector Accounting Standards Board (IPSASB) has issued a standard IPSAS 32 *Service Concession Arrangements: Grantor*, which includes two models for accounting by the grantor, depending on the terms of the arrangement with the operator. In addition to the finance lease model advised by the Accounting Council, IPSAS 32 includes a 'grant of right to the operator model' which applies to 'user-pays' arrangements. The Accounting Council does not advise the application of this model because it appears to result in the recognition as liabilities of amounts that may not meet the definition of a liability. However, some respondents to the exposure draft suggested that this model should be permitted. The Accounting Council advises that further research should be carried out on the most appropriate accounting for user-pays service concession arrangements, but that this should not delay the issue of FRS 102.   **103**

The Accounting Council considered whether transitional provisions should be available for grantors. It noted that for some grantors, the proposals would result in recognising assets and liabilities for the infrastructure assets that are not presently recognised. It considered that this provides more relevant information to users, and therefore advises the FRC that transitional provisions should not be available. As a result grantors will not be permitted to apply the transitional exemptions that are available to operators, as set out in FRS 102 paragraph 35.10(i), by analogy.   **104**

Retirement benefit plans

FRED 43 proposed that retirement benefit plans were publicly accountable and therefore should apply EU-adopted IFRS, but having decided to eliminate the definition of publicly accountable, retirement benefit plans are now within the scope of FRS 102, yet the IFRS for SMEs contains no specific provisions for retirement benefit plans.   **105**

The Accounting Council considered whether to direct retirement benefit plans to IAS 26 *Accounting and Reporting by Retirement Benefit Plans* and request that the Statement of Recommended Practice (SORP) *Financial Reports of Pension Schemes* be updated to be consistent with IAS 26. This option was, however, rejected based on feedback which suggested that the application of IAS 26 would be difficult for two reasons: **106**

(a)   legal accounting and reporting requirements in the UK are different to those in IAS 26; and

(b)   IAS 26 itself makes references to other IFRSs and the interaction between these references and FRS 102 would be complicated.

A further complication would arise as the SORP would also provide application guidance for retirement benefit plans.

Following this feedback the Accounting Council decided to develop, as part of the specialised activities section, accounting requirements for retirement benefit pla financial statements that could be supplemented by the SORP.

In developing the proposals, the Accounting Council considered the issue of whether the financial statements of retirement benefit plans need to provide disc' pension liabilities and the related funding of the plan. Following fee the Accounting Council decided that such information should not financial statements, but provided alongside it, as is currently the case

109   The Accounting Council advises that because of the way in which retirement benefit plans use financial instruments they should be considered to be financial institutions. However, not all of the disclosure requirements for financial institutions are relevant to retirement benefit plans and it will be more user-friendly to have all requirements in one place. Therefore Section 34 sets out all the requirements for retirement benefit plans in one sub-section.

Insurance contracts

110   FRED 48 proposed that entities with insurance contracts should apply IFRS 4 *Insurance Contracts* to those contracts. In addition, insurance-related contracts not meeting the definition of an insurance contract shall usually be accounted for as financial instruments in accordance with Sections 11 and 12.

111   The FRC also has FRS 27 *Life Assurance* in issue. The Accounting Council debated the various options for setting out the requirements for entities engaged in insurance business, and decided that it should advise the FRC to issue a separate accounting standard on insurance contracts, FRS 103 *Insurance Contracts*. An exposure draft of this standard will be available after FRS 102 has been issued, but FRS 102 cross-refers to it. The Accounting Council's Advice to the FRC to issue FRS 103 will be set out in that standard.

Other options available in EU-adopted IFRS

112   Respondents to FRED 44, in general, supported the use of the IFRS for SMEs as a base for a future financial reporting standard in the UK and Republic of Ireland. There were, however, concerns raised that would require careful consideration, most notably the removal of certain accounting treatments (options) that are available in current FRSs and EU-adopted IFRS but were not proposed in FRED 44.

113   Responses from the housing associations particularly focused on how the removal of options might have behavioural implications that the Accounting Council should take into consideration. The housing associations noted that:

(a)   the removal of the options would reduce comparability between entities that apply EU-adopted IFRS and those applying FRED 44 for entities operating in the same market, for example entities applying FRED 44 would not be permitted to revalue property, plant and equipment whereas entities applying EU-adopted IFRS could; and

(b)   the inability to include borrowing costs as part of the costs of property, plant and equipment may cause some housing associations to breach terms and conditions of current financing arrangements; this gave potential for banks and other lenders to renegotiate existing financing arrangements but at a higher cost of capital.

114   Other respondents noted that removal of the accounting options was potentially an over-simplification for the UK and Republic of Ireland. These respondents noted the IFRS for SMEs had been developed by the IASB for countries that had a less developed financial reporting framework than the UK and Republic of Ireland. They considered that as options existed in current FRSs the simplification had not been justified by the Accounting Council.

5   A further view put forward by respondents was that retaining the options that existed in current FRS would reduce transition costs and ease transition between the different standards and also with EU-adopted IFRS.

Application of the guidelines permitted the introduction of accounting options that exist   **116**
in current FRS and EU-adopted IFRS that respondents had highlighted as reducing
comparability. FRS 102 therefore includes accounting options for:

(a)   capitalisation of borrowing costs;
(b)   revaluation of property, plant and equipment and intangible assets; and
(c)   capitalisation of development costs, in certain circumstances.

Providing clarifications in FRS 102

Having agreed guidelines that include making amendments to the IFRS for SMEs to provide   **117**
clarifications, the Accounting Council considered relevant requests from respondents.
Some clarifications were made by reference to EU-adopted IFRS (see column (d) of the
table at paragraph 26 of the Accounting Council's Advice), others were made by reference
to current FRS, for example whether there is an interaction with company law. As a result
a number of clarifications have been made, examples include:

(a)   disclosure requirements for discontinued operations;
(b)   treatment of loan covenants, so that the treatment is consistent with IFRS 9 *Financial
      Instruments*;
(c)   financial instruments that would be equity under IAS 32 *Financial Instruments:
      Presentation* are not liabilities, when an entity is required to prepare consolidated
      financial statements;
(d)   when an investor that is not a parent but has an investment in one or more associates
      and/or jointly controlled entities shall account for its investments and/or jointly
      controlled entities using either cost or fair value;
(e)   the presumed life for goodwill, in particular when an entity is otherwise unable to
      make a reliable estimate shall not be in excess of five years and thereby consistent
      with company law. The same also applies to intangible assets;
(f)   accounting treatment for group share-based payments where the award is granted by
      the parent or another group entity; and
(g)   that option pricing models are not required for the value of shared-based payments,
      particularly for unquoted shares or share options.

Other matters

The Accounting Council considered whether to provide guidance for the term 'undue cost   **118**
or effort' where respondents had sought clarification. The Accounting Council noted that
Section 2 *Concepts and Pervasive Principles* discussed the balance between benefit and
cost and that no further clarification was required.

The retention of Urgent Issue Task Force (UITF) Abstracts

FREDs 43 and 44 proposed to withdraw all UITF Abstracts except UITF Abstract 43   **119**
The Interpretation of equivalence for the purposes of section 228A of the Companies Act.
Respondents to the FRED proposed that in addition to UITF Abstract 43, other UITF
Abstracts should be retained. The Accounting Council gave consideration to this request
and noted that rather than retain UITF Abstracts, consistent with its objective to provide
succinct financial reporting standards, it should incorporate any guidance into FRS 102.

Based on feedback the Accounting Council advises that the following accounting   **120**
requirements of UITF Abstracts are retained by incorporation, as follows:

	UITF Abstract	Action
4	*Presentation of long-term debtors in current assets*	Incorporated into the legal appendix.
31	*Exchange of businesses or other non-monetary assets for an interest in a subsidiary, joint venture or associate*	Additional paragraphs 9.31 and 9.32 are inserted.
32	*Employee benefit trusts and other intermediate payment arrangements*	Additional paragraphs are inserted into Section 9.
43	*The interpretation of equivalence for the purposes of section 228A of the Companies Act 1985*	The guidance has been updated and included as Application Guidance to FRS 100.

121 The Accounting Council decided to advise the withdrawal of UITF Abstract 48 *Accounting implications of the replacement of the retail prices index with the consumer prices index for retirement benefits* as the circumstance it addressed were related to a one time period which has now expired.

Interaction with company law

122 The Accounting Council gave careful consideration to the comments received to its draft legal appendix set out in FREDs 44 and 48. The Accounting Council agreed with respondents' views that the appendix should address entities that are not companies.

123 The Accounting Council also considered whether it should retain, as proposed in FRED 44, accounting options that had been removed because the option conflicted with company law, where an entity that is not a company would not be restricted in the same way as a company. For example, SSAP 4 *Accounting for government grants* contained an option that was not permitted by the company law.

124 The Accounting Council confirmed the position it had taken in developing FRED 44 that options that existed in the IFRS for SMEs, but not permitted by company law, should be removed. This would promote consistency between reporting entities regardless of the legal framework under which they operate.

Public benefit entities (PBEs)

125 The Consultation Paper *Policy Proposal: The Future of UK GAAP* (issued in 2009) set out 10 issues that could be included in a Public Benefit Entities (PBEs) specific standard. However, these 10 issues were refined to six which were deemed to be those most significant and relevant to the PBE sectors that were not satisfactorily addressed by the IFRS for SMEs. These six issues were:

(a)   Concessionary loans;
(b)   Property held for the provision of social benefits;
(c)   Entity combinations;
(d)   Impairment of assets: public benefit considerations;
(e)   Funding commitments; and
(f)   Incoming resources from non-exchange transactions.

Concessionary loans

Paragraphs have been inserted into Section 34 *Specialised Activities* to address the accounting requirements for PBEs making and receiving concessionary loans.   **126**

There are two main accounting treatments to consider when determining the basis for the measurement of concessionary loans; the amount paid or received, and fair value. This has been the subject of significant discussion and debate by the Accounting Council, taking into account the information that users of PBE accounts may consider useful and the difficulties that may arise for smaller organisations in measuring concessionary loans at fair value.   **127**

Accounting for concessionary loans at the amount paid or received rather than fair value is not consistent with the accounting requirements set out in either Section 11 of FRS 102, EU-adopted IFRS or IPSAS 29 *Financial Instruments: Recognition and Measurement* (which require that such arrangements are measured and recognised in the financial statements at their fair value).   **128**

Nevertheless the Accounting Council advises that due to the difficulties that smaller PBEs may face with using fair value, PBEs that make or receive concessionary loans may have the option of measuring such loans at either the amount paid or received or at fair value. However, PBEs that make and receive concessionary loans must apply the same measurement method to both. Further the Accounting Council proposes that the same accounting may be applied by other wholly-owned entities in a public benefit entity group, to eliminate the need to restate concessionary loans made or received for the purposes of furthering the PBEs objectives on consolidation.   **129**

Presentation and disclosure of concessionary loan arrangements are an important part of the proposals for concessionary loans and the Accounting Council concluded that the disclosure requirements in FRS 102 will provide sufficient information to understand and interpret the impact of this type of transaction on the financial statements.   **130**

Property held for the provision of social benefits

Subsequent to FRED 45, the Accounting Council decided that the requirements for property held for the provision of social benefits should apply to all entities applying FRS 102 and should not be restricted to PBEs.   **131**

Consideration was given as to whether properties that are held for the provision of social benefits meet the definition of an investment property. The definition of investment property in paragraph 16.2 of FRS 102, excludes properties held for use in the production or supply of goods and services or for administrative purposes. A property held to earn rentals and/or for capital appreciation, but not used in the production or supply of goods or services, meets this definition. The Accounting Council noted that although many PBEs that engage in the provision of social housing receive rental income, their primary purpose is to provide social benefits.   **132**

Provision of social housing is akin to supplying a service and therefore, property held for the primary purpose of providing social benefits should be excluded from the scope of investment property and be accounted for as property, plant and equipment.   **133**

The Accounting Council acknowledges that PBEs may hold 'investment properties' which are not held primarily to provide social benefits and will return market value rentals and/or are held for their capital appreciation. FRS 102 requires those properties to be accounted for as investment properties.   **134**

Public benefit entity combinations

135   In considering the issue of entity combinations involving two or more public benefit entities, the Accounting Council noted that there is some debate over whether the use of acquisition accounting for all combinations would be appropriate. In particular whether acquisition accounting reflects the substance of a transaction if there is a gift of one entity to another in a combination at nil or nominal consideration, or where two or more organisations genuinely merge to form a new entity.

136   Where there is a combination of entities at nil or nominal consideration which is in substance a gift, it is appropriate to follow the same accounting principles as donations of assets (as set out in Section 34 *Specialised Activities: Incoming Resources from Non-Exchange Transactions*) by recognising the fair value of the assets received and liabilities assumed as a gain or loss in income and expenditure.

137   Accounting for combinations that meet the definition of a merger requires a different methodology to acquisition accounting in order to reflect the true substance of the transaction. Whilst it is not anticipated that all combinations involving two or more public benefit entities are mergers or that merger accounting will generally be applicable to such combinations it is considered appropriate to retain merger accounting in certain circumstances. In considering this matter it was noted that the accounting requirements for PBEs in some jurisdictions, for example, the US and Australia have recently been reviewed and noted that merger accounting has been retained for the public and not-for-profit sectors.

138   In retaining merger accounting, the Accounting Council considered the criteria to be met for a merger. The criteria set out in FRS 6 *Acquisitions and Mergers* provided a starting point, but are framed in the context of the commercial sector and therefore the criteria have been adapted to make them more appropriate for public benefit entities. In particular, a criterion has been added to include consideration of the impact of the combination on beneficiaries and the benefits to which they are entitled.

139   One specific concern highlighted in relation to the requirements of FRS 6, is the need to restate comparatives by adding together the previous periods' reported figures of each of the combining entities. This does not reflect the substance of the transaction as the historical parties which formed the entity did not exist in the previous accounting period and therefore FRS 102 requires that comparatives are marked as 'combined' to make it clear that they are a combination of previously reported figures for the combining entities.

Impairment of assets

140   FRS 102 requires impaired assets to be measured at the lower of their fair value less costs to sell and their value in use. In a for-profit context, value in use is determined by measuring the present value of the cash flows derived from the asset. However, often PBE assets are held for their service potential rather than their ability to generate cash flows. In such a case it is sometimes impossible to determine value in use by reference to cash flows and it is more appropriate to regard value in use as the present value of future service potential rather than cash flows.

141   International Public Sector Accounting Standard (IPSAS) 21 *Impairment of Non-Cash Generating Assets* permits value in use to be determined by any of three approaches:

(a)   depreciated replacement cost (DRC);
(b)   restoration cost; and
(c)   the service units approach.

Restoration cost and the service units approach are applications of DRC as DRC is used as the starting point. DRC reflects the cash outflows that are saved through ownership of an asset and is likely to be widely applicable and appropriate for PBEs. Therefore FRS 102 permits a service potential driven valuation to be used for assets held for their service potential.

The use of DRC is not mandated; other methods that value service potential rather   **142** than cash flows may be used if those methods are more appropriate in those particular circumstances.

FRED 45 only allowed this alternative valuation method for PBEs, however subsequent   **143** to that consultation, the Accounting Council advises that any entity that holds an asset for service potential can use a service potential valuation method. It is not expected that, for example, headquarters buildings that do not generate cash flows independently of other assets or groups of assets but nevertheless contribute to the cash-generating activities of the entity, will usually be measured on the basis of their service potential.

The Accounting Council also discussed whether a restriction on the use of an asset would   **144** affect its fair value. As an asset's fair value is based on the amount that an entity could obtain, restrictions might impact on the fair value where they prevent a purchaser from using the asset for another purpose that would be more valuable than that required by the restriction. In addition, the costs to sell should include the costs of breaking the restriction.

Another issue for discussion was indicators of impairment. Although the indicators   **145** provided in FRS 102 are mainly linked to the expected cash flow of an asset and as such may not necessarily be relevant to some PBE assets, the Accounting Council considered that they must, as a minimum, be considered by PBEs as possible indicators of impairment.

In addition, the Accounting Council noted that other accounting literature (eg IPSAS 21   **146** and SORPs) identified other indicators of impairment including:

(a)   cessation, or near cessation of the demand or need for services provided by the asset;
(b)   social, demographic or environmental changes resulting in a reduction of beneficiaries; and
(c)   a major loss of key employees associated with particular activities.

The Accounting Council concluded that it would not be appropriate to include these   **147** indicators in FRS 102, as they are not exclusively relevant to PBEs and because the indicators given in FRS 102 will continue to apply to PBEs. Therefore, their inclusion would make such entities subject to a confusing list of overlapping indicators. The indicators given in FRS 102 are merely minimum requirements, and recognition of an impairment loss is required irrespective of whether any of the given indicators are met.

The Accounting Council also considered whether to specify that an indicator of impairment   **148** was present where an asset's service potential was not fully utilised and noted that an entity may require standby or surplus capacity to ensure that it has adequate capacity to provide services at all times. For example, a building that provides accommodation for the homeless may not be used to full capacity during the summer months but is utilised fully during winter. In this circumstance, the surplus capacity is part of the required service potential of the asset and the asset is not impaired. For this reason, it was concluded that it would be inappropriate to specify that the unutilised capacity should be treated as an indicator of impairment.

Funding commitments

149   The Accounting Council also discussed when to recognise a commitment to provide funding in a non-exchange transaction. The *Statement of Principles: Interpretation for Public Benefit Entities* previously addressed this issue, and it was considered necessary to incorporate these details into FRS 102 to be used in conjunction with Sections 2 *Concepts and Pervasive Principles* and 21 *Provisions and Contingencies*.

150   The issue was identified as being particularly important because many PBEs provide funding on an on-going basis and there is little guidance on how such multi-year commitments should be recognised.

151   The Accounting Council considered when a liability for such a commitment should be recognised and determined that an entity would only recognise a liability if the commitment to provide funding was made unconditionally, and the grantor could not realistically withdraw from the commitment. In this situation, an entity would recognise a liability for the present value of the total funding promised.

152   As this is an application of the principles in Sections 2 and 21, the Accounting Council advises that the requirements for funding commitments should apply to all entities and not just PBEs.

Incoming resources from non-exchange transactions

153   The receipt of resources from non-exchange transactions is an inflow of resources that is highly significant for many PBEs: the receipt of donations, grants and legacies from non-exchange transactions are a major source of their funding and this issue is not addressed in the IFRS for SMEs apart from in Section 24 *Government Grants*.

154   The Accounting Council considered that for PBE financial statements to be complete, they should reflect the benefit that the inflow of these resources had to the entity. FRS 102 requires, in principle, PBEs to value the resources they receive from non-exchange transactions at their fair value. The Accounting Council discussed whether using fair value would overstate the value of a donation where the entity is unable to exploit fully an asset, and the equivalent service potential could be derived from a lower value asset. Being able to achieve the same service potential from a lower value asset might suggest that the value of the donated asset should be at the lower value. However, FRS 102 requires donated assets to be valued at their fair value. This reflects that the circumstances described above would rarely occur. In many cases, an entity would be able to sell the donated asset and if appropriate, purchase a cheaper asset with the equivalent service potential.

155   Incorporating an exception for donated assets which may not be fully exploited would make the application of FRS 102 more onerous, as it would require all entities in receipt of donated assets (except those intended for resale) to consider whether they would be able to exploit the asset fully. This would be subjective and may incur the risk of understatement of the value of donated assets.

156   The Accounting Council noted that where goods are donated for subsequent sale (for example donations to charity shops), it could be argued that the donated goods should be valued only when they are sold. This is not consistent with the accruals concept which requires the financial statements to recognise goods when they are received. However, the Accounting Council advises, on pragmatic grounds, that donated goods should only be recognised as income on receipt when the item is material, can be measured reliably and if the benefits of recognising the item outweigh the costs. Further the Accounting Council proposes that the same accounting may be applied by other wholly-owned entities in a public benefit entity group, to eliminate the need to restate goods donated for subsequent sale on consolidation (for example where a charity operates it shops through a subsidiary that is a non-charitable company).

FRS 102 requires donated services that would otherwise have been purchased to **157** be accounted for at their estimated value to the recipient. This is a pragmatic solution recognising that there are potential issues in determining a value for volunteer services and their contribution to the organisation and notes that quantifying this type of service may not be practicable. There is an argument to suggest that valuing volunteer services could be measured by reference to a metric such as the minimum wage, however this measure does not take into consideration an organisation's requirements for volunteers. In addition, this would be attributing an arbitrary value onto a volunteer's time which may not be reflective of their skills, experience or role and to determine a different method of valuation would be very subjective.

However, when a service is provided voluntarily for which the entity would otherwise **158** have to pay (eg legal or financial advice) the value of that service should be recognised in the financial statements where, as will usually be the case, its value can be reasonably quantified.

Other PBE issues

The Accounting Council discussed the issue of reporting entity control and the indicators **159** of control that may be specific to the PBE sectors. The indicators of control set out in Section 9 *Consolidated and Separate Financial Statements* of FRS 102 focus on benefits, and in the PBE sectors benefit can be in the form of indirect benefit through a PBE's beneficiaries or benefit which furthers a PBE's activities. Following discussion of these issues the Accounting Council advises that FRS 102 can be interpreted and applied to PBEs and therefore no separate guidance for PBEs is considered necessary.

A number of additional topics were identified through the development of FRS 102, which **160** may be considered in the future and as possible updates to FRS 102. The following table summarises these subjects:

Narrative Reporting	To consider narrative reporting requirements for public benefit entities and any specific matters.
Fresh Start Accounting	To consider the concept of fresh start accounting as an alternative accounting treatment for entity combinations where the effect of a combination is to create a new entity that cannot be reasonably portrayed as the enlargement of a pre-existing party.
Social Benefit Obligations	To consider if and how social benefit obligations should be recognised and measured in the financial statements. The International Public Sector Accounting Standards Board currently have a project addressing this issue and it is likely to be most productive to await the outcome of that work.
Fund Accounting	To consider how fund accounting would be applied in accordance with the requirements of FRS 102 for segmental reporting.

Transition to FRS 102

161   The Accounting Council noted that FRS 102 does not permit goodwill to have an indefinite useful life, unlike current FRS. On transition to FRS 102 entities that previously determined that goodwill had an indefinite useful life will need to reassess goodwill to determine its remaining useful life, and subsequently amortise the goodwill over that period.

Effective date

162   FREDs 43 and 44 proposed an effective date for accounting periods beginning on or after 1 July 2013, with early application being permitted. Respondents' views regarding the proposals were very mixed with some calling for earlier adoption and others for deferral of the proposals.

163   The Accounting Council took into consideration its decision that FRS 102 would apply to a broader scope of entities and its revised guidelines for amending the IFRS for SMEs in relation to the effective date. The Accounting Council noted that:

(a)   Although the revisions to its original proposals should ease the transition, an 18 month period between the publication of the final standard and effective date should be retained as there are significant changes to the accounting requirements for financial instruments.

(b)   The IASB's decision to revise the effective date of IFRS 9 *Financial Instruments* to 2015. The ASB noted that entities that apply current FRS without FRS 26, who wished to move to the proposed reduced disclosure framework would not be able to apply IFRS 9 until it was adopted by the EU. Consequently such entities would need to apply IAS 39 *Financial Instruments: Recognition and Measurement* for an interim period. The costs associated with these changes were not justifiable.

(c)   The effective date needed to take into consideration the updating of the SORPs that is required.

164   The Accounting Council advises that the effective date of FRS 102 should be accounting periods beginning on or after 1 January 2015.

165   The Accounting Council also considered whether to permit early application of FRS 102. It noted that as FRS 102 represents an improvement in financial reporting it would not be appropriate to prevent early application of its requirements. However, the Accounting Council advises that early application of FRS 102 should not be permitted for accounting periods before those ending on or after 31 December 2012, which is consistent with the first date at which it is likely to be practical for entities applying FRS 101 to apply that standard.

166   The Accounting Council also considered the early application of FRS 102 by entities that are within the scope of a SORP. It noted that most of the SORPs require updating for consistency with FRS 102, and for charities there are legal requirements relating to the application of the SORP. The Accounting Council therefore advises that early application should be permitted for entities applying a SORP provided that FRS 102 does not conflict with the requirements of a current SORP or legal requirements for the preparation of financial statements.

Approval of this advice

This advice to the FRC was approved by eight of the nine members of the Accounting   **167**
Council on 17 January 2013. Mr Beale dissented from the approval of the advice and
his dissenting view is set out in the Appendix to the Accounting Council's advice. The
Accounting Council is comprised of the following members:

Roger Marshall   (Chair of the Accounting Council)
Nick Anderson
Dr Richard Barker
Edward Beale
Peter Elwin
Ken Lever
Robert Overend
Andy Simmonds
Pauline Wallace

APPENDIX TO THE ACCOUNTING COUNCIL'S ADVICE TO THE FRC TO ISSUE FRS 102

Dissenting view of Mr Beale

1   Mr Beale agrees that it is fundamental that financial statements should provide useful information to users, who are defined as being: investors not involved in management, customers and suppliers, including suppliers of capital and of non-equity finance. He agrees with the Accounting Council that it is disappointing that despite extensive outreach activities, the Accounting Council has not received more feedback from users, both formal and informal, on whether or not financial statements prepared in accordance with FRS 102 will meet their information needs.

2   Mr Beale does not believe that the consultation responses from industry representative bodies[21], and from organisations which are both preparers and users, can be considered to be input from users since these responses are from a preparer perspective.

3   The informal input received by the FRC staff supports FRS 102 as drafted, and is generally consistent with the input from preparers and industry representative bodies. However, this informal input is inconsistent with the five[22] formal consultation responses received from users and the informal input received personally by Mr Beale. This inconsistency in the content of informal input may be due to the informal input received by FRC staff being from providers of non-equity finance whereas the informal input received by Mr Beale has been from directors (who are both users and preparers) and investors.

4   This informal input received by FRC staff in relation to FRS 102 differs from comments that FRC staff have recently received on other projects:

  (a)   from credit analysts and bond fund managers in relation to the financial statements of listed entities[23] (that there is not sufficient forward looking information on cash flows and challenging the usefulness of fair value); and

  (b)   as part of the Financial Reporting Laboratory's work on a single figure for remuneration[24] (regarding valuation of equity incentives and pension costs).

5   In Mr Beale's experience users are concerned with issues identified by the FRC in *Louder than Words*[25], which they believe have not been adequately addressed in FRS 102. In his analysis, the common thread behind these user concerns is a desire for clearer, more understandable, information, from which they can derive better predictions about future cash flows on a going concern basis, even at the expense of further divergence from IFRS. Understandability is crucial to confidence in the integrity of financial reporting, and thus maximising the benefits from accounts. Despite the importance of maintaining consistency with IFRS, Mr Beale believes that the FRC should not be issuing new accounting standards perpetuating problems identified in existing standards.

---

[21] *Some of which have been classified in the Feedback Statements as 'user representative bodies'.*

[22] *Four of these formal consultation responses are from users connected to Mr Beale and include three responses to FREDs 43 and 44, of which two were formally classified as being from preparers and one from an academic.*

[23] *http://www.frc.org.uk/getattachment/b0eff085-b542-4eaf-bc36-d52e26eb3833/How-credit-analysts-view-and-use-the-financial-statements.aspx*

[24] *http://frc.org.uk/getattachment/5310093d-c092-45e1-8106-278ae7ac1a4b/A-single-figure-for-remuneration.aspx*

[25] *http://www.frc.org.uk/getattachment/7d952925-74ea-4deb-b659-e9242b09f2fa/Louder-than-words.aspx*

In particular Mr Beale believes that there are significant further opportunities to improve   **6**
the balance between costs and benefits in the sections of FRS 102 dealing with: Financial
Instruments, Deferred Tax, Defined Benefit Pension Schemes, and Equity Settled Share-
based Payments. This is discussed further below. In his view FRS 102 could have achieved
clearer reporting in the above areas by departing further from the IFRS for SMEs,
thus better meeting users' needs for high-quality financial information in line with the
overriding objective.

The FRC needs to consider whether the extensive outreach activities undertaken constitute   **7**
'adequate consultation'. In Mr Beale's opinion the determination of 'adequate consultation'
should be based on the outcome from the consultation process and, regrettably, there has
been virtually no formal input from the people who will be using accounts prepared under
FRS 102. Based on the consultation responses from users and the informal input from
users that he has received, Mr Beale is advising that the FRC defer approval of FRS 102
until it has a better understanding of the degree of support from users, and in the meantime
to work on improving the balance between costs and benefits in the areas outlined above.

In Mr Beale's experience, users do not consider UK GAAP to be in need of urgent   **8**
replacement, and will not be concerned about any delays to FRS 102 necessary to
determine the degree of user support and resolve any outstanding issues.

Further opportunities to improve the balance between costs and benefits

There are two issues of principle underpinning the areas of FRS 102 that, in Mr Beale's   **9**
opinion, can be significantly improved:

(a) Since the purpose of accounts is to supply useful information to users, the most
     important concepts underpinning accounting standards should be 'relevance'
     (include information that is useful to users) and its converse, 'materiality' (exclude
     information that is not useful). All other accounting concepts should clearly be
     subsidiary to these. Such an emphasis on the priority attributable to 'relevance'
     and 'materiality' will promote measurement of assets and liabilities in a manner
     that conveys useful information to users, and will normally exclude mark to model
     valuations, and limit application of fair value elsewhere.

(b) At present some assets and liabilities are revalued, and some unrealised profits
     are taken to earnings. To ensure a principled base for accounting standards the
     FRC needs to determine general principles covering (i) when it is appropriate
     for assets and liabilities to be revalued, and (ii) whether unrealised profits arising
     from revaluations should be recognised in earnings or as a movement in reserves.
     A consistent approach to revaluation of items such as fixed assets and financial
     instruments, and a consistent approach to profit recognition, cannot be achieved
     without such principles. In his opinion, for the purposes of FRS 102: assets should
     be revalued when there is a sufficiently liquid market for their market value to be
     determined reliably, or when an impairment provision is necessary; liabilities should
     only be revalued when there are changes to the amount required to settle them when
     they fall due; and unrealised profits should not be included within earnings, except
     for profits on liquid investments.

In Mr Beale's opinion, opportunities to significantly improve the balance of costs
and benefits within FRS 102 exist in four areas, two of general application: financial
instruments, and deferred tax; and two of more limited application: equity settled share
based payments and defined benefit pension schemes. These are summarised below.

Financial instruments

10   Current FRSs have been criticised in that they allow certain financial instruments not to be recorded. Such criticism is incorrect in that the existence of, and details about, these financial instruments should (where 'material') be recorded in the notes to the accounts. This criticism has been used by some to justify moving to an IFRS based approach to accounting for financial instruments, which has been widely criticised, and which is not the most cost effective approach to providing users of accounts with the information that they desire.

11   Many different assets and liabilities fall within the definition of financial instruments and attempting to deal with all of these in the same manner introduces unnecessary complexity. The two sections on financial instruments include three to four pages of rules on which section should be applied, and are written in a language which is in places very difficult for people not accustomed to IFRS to understand. These sections have also been drafted to cater for financial institutions as well as ordinary businesses, and this exacerbates the difficulty that non-experts will have in applying them. Preparers of accounts will generally only refer to accounting standards once a year in the lead up to preparation of their annual accounts. FRS 102 needs to be readily understandable for such preparers, and there is a risk that if accounting standards are not sufficiently accessible they will be applied in a manner that generates unnecessary complexity and clutter.

12   The two sections on financial instruments should be redrafted in language that is understandable to the normal businessperson and is not the preserve of experts. Redrafting of these sections should focus on the information that users need relating to ordinary businesses, with additional requirements for financial institutions dealt with in the section for specialised activities, by expanding the part relating to financial institutions, and which can in turn refer to IAS 39 *Financial Instruments: Recognition and Measurement*, IFRS 7 *Financial Instruments: Disclosure* and IFRS 9 *Financial Instruments* where appropriate.

13   Users need different 'information sets' on financial instruments that are: fixed assets, current assets and liabilities; and FRS 102 should consider financial instruments in these three categories, rather than trying to cover all three categories with one set of rules. Prudence should be incorporated where necessary so that the treatment of assets is not necessarily the mirror of the treatment of liabilities.

Financial assets

14   For normal businesses, financial assets should be carried at fair value when the principles for revaluation set out above are met, and failing that at cost less any necessary impairment provision. Income should be recognised in a prudent manner: as it is earned (eg interest on a daily basis), or when it can be reliably measured (eg dividends).

15   Circumstances may arise which cause the valuation basis of financial assets to change, but such situations are unlikely to occur frequently outside financial institutions. Where they do occur, the consequences of reclassifications can be made obvious to users of accounts through note disclosures. Strict anti-abuse rules are not necessary. A clear analysis in the notes can highlight where reclassification is potentially being abused to manage earnings, so that users can discuss their concerns with management, auditors or regulators as appropriate. Any additional requirements considered necessary for financial institutions can be dealt with in the section for specialised activities.

Financial liabilities

When a financial liability is included in the balance sheet at a value which is different **16** from the amount required to settle the liability when it falls due, disclosure of amount of principal repayable is necessary, so that users can understand the underlying cash flow. The notes then show two different values for the same liability. This duplication of valuation bases creates extra cost to both preparers and users of accounts and risks causing confusion. Confusion can be minimised by using the settlement value in the statement of financial position, rather than fair values or amortised cost, recognising deferred financing costs where necessary, and providing information in the notes about financing costs and settlement dates. Interested users will then have the information necessary to perform their own comparisons with other businesses, as well as clearer information on the business's funding requirements.

The above approach to liabilities could lead to extensive disclosures for financial institutions **17** and others where there are a large number of different types of financial liability. The section on specialised activities should set out an approach for the aggregation of necessary disclosures and allow an opt into IFRS 9/IAS 39.

Impairment of financial assets

Impairment provisions are only allowed in FRS 102 where there is 'objective evidence' **18** of impairment. Businesses are not allowed to make provision for expected losses, even where there is past experience supporting the likelihood of such losses. Expected loss provisions should be allowed now, before IFRS 9 has been updated, to avoid assets being overvalued. A clear analysis in the notes will highlight where impairment provisions are potentially being abused to manage earnings, so that users can discuss their concerns with management, auditors or regulators as appropriate. Additional requirements may be imposed on financial institutions through the section on specialised activities.

Hedging

Hedge accounting is only permitted in FRS 102 if 'specified criteria' are met. In the past **19** similar restrictions have led to businesses not hedge accounting for financial instruments acquired, or entered into, for hedging purposes. The purpose of accounting standards is not to promote good management but good reporting. Accounting standards are not the appropriate way to attempt to stop the miss-selling, or miss-buying, of derivatives. There needs to be transparency over hedges entered into so that the effect of hedges in managing risk can be understood by users of accounts. This can be achieved by linked accounting for hedges and items being hedged, so that accounting faithfully represents the underlying commercial activity.

Concerns over earnings management can be alleviated by disclosure of the impact on **20** earnings of hedges closed out in a different period to the risk that they purported to hedge. Businesses other than financial institutions should be able to allay concerns over the effectiveness of hedges by explaining how their limited number of material risks are being hedged. Financial institutions may have too many hedges to be able to provide this information in a meaningful manner and an alternative approach for such businesses should be set out in the section on specialised activities.

Deferred tax

As the recent ASB/EFRAG discussion paper on tax identified, users want to know how **21** future tax payments will differ from the amount calculated by applying the standard tax rate to future profits. This difference will be in part due to future actions and in part due to past actions.

22   The section of FRS 102 on deferred tax is not predicated on a going concern basis, and in effect identifies the impact on future tax payments if the business ceases trading. As such, except for the disclosure of amounts expected to reverse in the next period, the approach in FRS 102 is of little relevance to most users and will create disclosures which will generally be ignored by users.

23   The disclosure required by FRS 102 of the amount of the deferred tax provision which will be released in the next period is of limited usefulness. This is only part of the difference between expected tax cost and standard tax rate. Prediction of the element due to future actions is not currently required.

24   The information that users need can best be provided by way of disclosure of the expected future tax rate and any other material information that may influence future tax payments, eg losses carried forward. A deferred tax provision should not be made because this does not provide useful information in a cost effective manner. The exception to this is that the logic behind revaluing certain items dictates that, for consistency, the tax impact of such revaluations needs to be recognised too.

Equity settled share-based payments

25   As identified by the recent financial reporting laboratory work on valuation of remuneration, users do not understand the complex models used to value equity settled share based payments. The cost of creating these values is therefore wasted.

26   These valuation models also generate a substantial amount of clutter when trying to explain how the valuation is arrived at.

27   It should also be noted that the standard valuation models assume liquid markets and negligible spreads. These assumptions are not appropriate for the types of businesses that will be applying FRS 102. Given the lack of guidance in FRS 102, and the complexity of the valuation models, in Mr Beale's opinion it is highly likely that preparers will use inappropriate valuation models, or use valuation models in inappropriate ways, and that users will not have enough knowledge to identify this.

28   Unless there is a liquid market to provide a relevant value for equity settled share based payments, their existence should be disclosed in the notes to the accounts, and there should be no notional cost in the income statement.

Defined benefit pension schemes

29   The information relating to defined benefit pension schemes that users need is: the current cost of providing the benefit, the expected additional payments required to make good any funding deficit (or payment holiday because of funding surpluses) and an explanation of the contingent liability in respect of potential future funding shortfalls.

30   At present there is a requirement to prepare a fund valuation solely for accounting purposes and then to consolidate the net assets or, more usually, liabilities of the fund. Changes in the net assets/liabilities are then split into three parts and recognised in operating costs, financing costs and other comprehensive income. This is supplemented by extensive disclosures. However, the disclosures do not require information about the uncertainties or

sensitivities attached to the valuation inputs eg the time periods over which payments out of the fund will be made, discount and inflation rates, and other risks inherent in the fund.

Most users do not understand pension scheme valuations. They see fund valuations which are massively volatile, and perceive most current requirements as adding to clutter and generating additional preparation costs for no benefit.   **31**

Clutter could be reduced by not consolidating the pension fund, but instead disclosing the level of normal contributions being made and providing for contributions required to make good any funding shortfall. Changes in this liability to make good any funding shortfall should be expensed and explained. In addition disclosures should be made describing the contingent liability to fund any future increases in fund deficits. Those users who do understand pension scheme valuations can obtain the more detailed information that they are likely to want about pension scheme funding from the fund valuation prepared for that purpose, which should be made available on demand or on a web site. Such an approach would save the costs associated with preparing a valuation solely for accounting purposes as well as reducing clutter in the accounts.   **32**

Training costs

Maintaining limited UK GAAP differences from IFRS will marginally increase the cost of training accountants, but should improve their employability, and will increase the challenge on the IASB to further improve IFRS, thereby improving the balance between benefits and costs overall.   **33**

THE ACCOUNTING COUNCIL'S ADVICE TO THE FRC TO ISSUE AMENDMENTS TO FRS 102 – BASIC FINANCIAL INSTRUMENTS AND HEDGE ACCOUNTING

Introduction

1   This report provides an overview of the main issues that have been considered by the Accounting Council in advising the Financial Reporting Council (FRC) to issue *Amendments to FRS 102 The Financial Reporting Standard applicable in the UK and Republic of Ireland – Basic financial instruments and Hedge accounting*.

2   The FRC, in accordance with the *Statutory Auditors (Amendment of Companies Act 2006 and Delegation of Functions etc) Order 2012* (SI 2012/1741), is a prescribed body for issuing accounting standards in the UK. The *Foreword to Accounting Standards* sets out the application of accounting standards in the Republic of Ireland.

3   In accordance with the *FRC Codes and Standards: procedures*, any proposal to issue, amend or withdraw a code or standard is put to the FRC Board with the full advice of the relevant Councils and/or the Codes & Standards Committee. Ordinarily, the FRC Board will only reject the advice put to it where:

   (a)   it is apparent that a significant group of stakeholders has not been adequately consulted;

   (b)   the necessary assessment of the impact of the proposal has not been completed, including an analysis of costs and benefits;

   (c)   insufficient consideration has been given to the timing or cost of implementation; or

   (d)   the cumulative impact of a number of proposals would make the adoption of an otherwise satisfactory proposal inappropriate.

4   The FRC has established the Accounting Council as the relevant Council to assist it in the setting of accounting standards.

Advice

5   The Accounting Council is advising the FRC to issue *Amendments to FRS 102 The Financial Reporting Standard applicable in the UK and Republic of Ireland – Basic financial instruments and Hedge accounting* to:

   (a)   remove the unintended accounting consequences arising for the classification of certain financial instruments. It believes these changes will result in a reduction in the cost of compliance for entities within the scope of the standard; and

   (b)   to make the application of the hedge accounting requirements easier and more cost effective to apply for entities that choose to take advantage of this option.

6   The Accounting Council's Advice to the FRC in FRS 102 *The Financial Reporting Standard applicable in the UK and Republic of Ireland* is supplemented by the inclusion of its advice on these amendments.

Background

7   The FRC issued FRS 102 in March 2013, which is effective for accounting periods beginning on or after 1 January 2015.

8   After the publication of FRS 102, feedback from constituents indicated that the implementation of the accounting requirements of FRS 102 for loans with common

contractual features could have unintended consequences for many entities. The amendments to Section 11 *Basic Financial Instruments* address the issues identified and take into account responses to FRED 54 *Draft Amendments to FRS 102 Financial Reporting Standard applicable in the UK and Ireland – Basic financial instruments.*

At the time of issue of FRS 102, the Accounting Council and the FRC were of the view that the standard should reflect up-to-date thinking on hedge accounting, but the IASB had not yet finalised the hedge accounting requirements in IFRS 9 *Financial Instruments.* The Accounting Council advised the FRC at that time that amending the hedge accounting requirements in FRS 102 prior to the IASB finalising the hedge accounting requirements in IFRS 9, would risk implementing hedge accounting requirements in FRS 102 that were inconsistent with IFRS. **9**

The hedge accounting amendments to FRS 102 were developed based on the hedge accounting requirements in IFRS 9 and take into account the responses to FRED 51 Draft Amendments to FRS 102 Financial Reporting Standard applicable in the UK and Ireland – Hedge Accounting. **10**

Objective

The FRC gives careful consideration to its objective and the intended effects when developing new accounting standards or requirements for the UK and Republic of Ireland. In developing accounting standards, including FRS 102, the overriding objective of the FRC is: **11**

> To enable users of accounts to receive high-quality understandable financial reporting proportionate to the size and complexity of the entity and users' information needs.

In meeting this objective, the FRC aims to provide succinct financial reporting standards that: **12**

(a) have consistency with global accounting standards through the application of an IFRS-based solution unless an alternative clearly better meets the overriding objective;
(b) reflect up-to-date thinking and developments in the way businesses operate and the transactions they undertake;
(c) balance consistent principles for accounting by all UK and Republic of Ireland entities with practical solutions, based on size, complexity, public interest and users' information needs;
(d) promote efficiency within groups; and
(e) are cost-effective to apply.

Basic financial instruments

Rules vs principles-based solution

The classification of financial instruments as 'basic' or 'other' in FRS 102 is dependent on a list of prescriptive conditions. The Accounting Council considered whether a principles-based solution to relaxing the conditions, based on the principle articulated in IFRS 9 in respect of the classification of financial assets, would be more effective, but advises retaining the rules-based conditions of FRS 102 instead, for the following reasons: **13**

(a)   the IFRS 9 principle is yet untested in practice and, at the time of giving the advice, the IASB is currently debating possible amendments to IFRS 9; and

(b)   the IFRS 9 principle in relation to the classification of financial instruments only applies to financial assets. The classification conditions in FRS 102, however, apply equally to debt instruments that are assets or liabilities.

Interaction with Regulations or LLP Regulations on measurement of certain financial instruments

14   Subsequent to receiving the responses to FRED 54, the Accounting Council was made aware of an additional issue in relation to a conflict between the Regulations and LLP Regulations and the requirements in FRS 102, as originally issued, on measurement of some financial liabilities. The original text of FRS 102 could have resulted in the standard requiring certain financial liabilities to be measured at fair value where such measurement may be prohibited by the Regulations. The Regulations prohibit the measurement of financial liabilities at fair value, except for those held as part of a trading portfolio, that are derivatives or where permitted by EU-adopted IFRS.

15   For example, the original text of FRS 102 would have required certain financial liabilities, where the cash outflows are linked to non-financial variables specific to one party to the contract, to be classified as non-basic and measured at fair value. Fair value measurement is not permitted for such liabilities under EU-adopted IFRS and so would be prohibited by the Regulations.

16   Such liabilities commonly arise in insurance contracts where the amount an insurer is liable to pay depends on the occurrence of insured events specific to the insured party and its activities.

17   The Accounting Council is aware that there are divergent views on what constitutes a 'non-financial variable' in other cases. For example, there is no clear consensus as to whether measures of performance such as turnover, profits or EBITDA are 'non-financial variables…specific to a party to the contract'. The Accounting Council is unable to resolve this divergence as to do so would involve interpreting EU-adopted IFRS on an issue that the IFRS Interpretations Committee has so far not reached a definitive conclusion.

18   Similarly, FRS 102 would have required that financial assets which are similarly linked to non-financial variables specific to one party to the contract, be classified as non-basic and measured at fair value through profit or loss. Although Regulations permit financial assets to be classified at fair value, this classification is only available as permitted by EU-adopted IFRS, which in some cases is restricted to fair value through other comprehensive income.

19   The Accounting Council also notes that there may be other non-basic financial assets and liabilities that EU-adopted IFRS, and hence the Regulations, would not permit to be measured at fair value through profit or loss although it expected that such instruments would be rare in practice.

20   As a result, the Accounting Council advises the inclusion of an exception in Section 12 in respect of non-basic financial instruments where the Regulations would not permit the use of fair value through profit or loss, instead requiring them to be measured at amortised cost. In advising this, the Accounting Council is conscious that this exception would be applicable to a small number of entities under a narrow set of circumstances.

Loans in the social housing sector

In response to FRED 54, a number of respondents from the social housing sector raised   **21**
concerns about the classification of certain lending arrangements common within that
sector. It was noted that a number of these arrangements were structured in different
ways but often to achieve the same economic outcome. After detailed consideration
the Accounting Council advises that a loan cannot be classified as basic if it includes
contractual terms giving the lender the unilateral option to change the terms of that loan,
for example from a pre-determined fixed rate to a variable rate or to a different fixed rate
chosen by the lender, even if the holder can avoid it by repaying the loan.

Structured financial instruments

In response to FRED 54, a number of respondents raised questions about the classification   **22**
of certain financial instruments that were structured in a complex way and requested
that the final amendment clarify their classification in accordance with FRS 102. The
Accounting Council noted that such structured financial instruments are not based on
contracts that are standardised across an industry. As a result, the repayment of principal
and interest on such loans can be impacted in a complex way by a number of different
variables defined in the contractual terms. The Accounting Council noted that it was not
possible to conclude on the classification of such financial instruments without a close
reading of the individual contracts and an understanding of the detailed clauses. Therefore,
the Accounting Council advises that the reporting entity's directors should apply their
judgement to determine whether the contractual terms enable a financial instrument to be
classified as basic in accordance with the requirements in FRS 102.

Classification subsequent to initial recognition

The Accounting Council noted that the initial classification assessment of a financial   **23**
instrument should take into account the relevant clauses dealing with the returns and any
subsequent contractual variations relating to returns, prepayments and extensions of terms
etc. Once the classification of a financial instrument is determined at initial recognition, no
re-assessment is required at subsequent dates unless there is a modification of contractual
terms.

Hedge accounting

The previous hedge accounting requirements in FRS 102 narrowly defined the types of   **24**
permitted arrangements that may qualify for hedge accounting, which was not necessarily
representative of an entity's risk management objectives and hedging practices.

The Accounting Council's aim was to develop new hedge accounting requirements that   **25**
allow for a reflection of an entity's hedging activities in the financial statements that is
consistent with the entity's risk management objectives and are, as far as appropriate for
constituents of FRS 102, consistent with IFRS.

These amendments to FRS 102 have been developed on the basis of IFRS, and substantively   **26**
adopt the terminology and hedge accounting requirements in IFRS 9, with notable
exceptions described in more detail below. The Accounting Council has been mindful that
the requirements in IFRS 9 deal with hedging transactions that can be far more complex
than those typically entered into by entities applying FRS 102. The departures from
the requirements in IFRS 9 are therefore intended to simplify the application of hedge
accounting.

Eligible hedged items

27   The Accounting Council was requested to reconsider the exclusion of explicit macro-hedging provisions in FRS 102, similar to those in IAS 39 *Financial Instruments: Recognition and Measurement*. After consideration of the specific concerns of entities that raised this as an issue, the Accounting Council concluded that in the interest of developing straight-forward hedge accounting requirements that are relevant for a majority of entities, it retains its previous advice stated in FRED 51. Entities wishing to apply the IFRS macro-hedging provisions are able to apply the accounting policy choice in FRS 102 to apply IAS 39 and/or IFRS 9 instead.

Qualifying hedge accounting conditions

28   The qualifying hedge accounting conditions in FRS 102 have been simplified compared to the criteria set out in IFRS 9, with the aim of making hedge accounting easier to apply.

29   Under the amended hedge accounting requirements it is not necessary to achieve a prescribed level of effectiveness in a hedging relationship in order to qualify for hedge accounting, but an economic relationship between the hedged item and the hedging instrument has to exist. In response to feedback on FRED 51, an explanation has been added of when an economic relationship between a hedged item and a hedging instrument exists, which is in line with IFRS 9.

30   The Accounting Council notes that although a quantitative assessment of hedge effectiveness is not required, it is nevertheless important for entities to identify the different factors that affect the valuation of the hedging instrument and hedged item, including factors that may be a source of hedge ineffectiveness. Entities are therefore required to identify and document causes of hedge ineffectiveness before they commence hedge accounting, to ensure that ineffectiveness is properly captured in profit or loss.

31   Entities are required to document a hedging relationship, to avoid hedge accounting being misused. The hedge documentation requirements are, however, relatively informal and undemanding and should not be an administrative burden for entities in practice.

Discontinuing hedge accounting

32   These amendments permit entities to discontinue hedge accounting voluntarily. This is a departure from IFRS 9. The Accounting Council considered that the restrictions in IFRS 9 on discontinuance are unnecessarily onerous, and instead has retained the existing option of voluntary discontinuation. An entity must document the election to discontinue hedge accounting, which is consistent with the requirement for documentation at the start of hedge accounting.

Disclosure

33   These amendments retain substantially the disclosure requirements of FRS 102. The disclosure requirements in relation to the hedge accounting requirements in IFRS 9, contained in IFRS 7 *Financial Instruments: Disclosure* focus on risks and risk mitigation through hedging. The Accounting Council notes that risk disclosures are not generally required in FRS 102, except for financial institutions.

Transitional provisions for first-time adopters of FRS 102

The Accounting Council's aim was to develop transitional provisions that are consistent   **34**
with the permissive hedge accounting regime of FRS 102 and give entities a choice over
whether to commence, continue or end hedge accounting on transition to FRS 102. Some
respondents to FRED 51 were concerned that this flexibility may be abused, as it allows
entities to apply a degree of hindsight. The Accounting Council is mindful of this possible
exploitation of the transitional provisions. Nevertheless, on balance it believes that in
the interests of the majority of entities, especially entities that have not applied hedge
accounting before, flexibility should take precedence over restrictions aimed at preventing
abuse.

The Accounting Council is conscious that entities may have applied diverse hedge   **35**
accounting practices before the adoption of FRS 102. Entities may have applied the hedge
accounting requirements in accordance with FRS 26 (IAS 39) *Financial Instruments:
Recognition and Measurement* or may have applied synthetic accounting practices
permitted under SSAP 20 *Foreign currency translation.* Accommodating these different
accounting practices introduces complexity that the transitional provisions need to
address. Under the transitional provisions, regardless of what accounting practices were
applied previously, entities have the choice to continue hedge accounting in accordance
with FRS 102, provided the conditions for hedge accounting are met. Entities that elect not
to apply the FRS 102 hedge accounting requirements, have to comply with the applicable
measurement requirements for assets and liabilities set out elsewhere in FRS 102 from the
date of transition.

The amendments are issued after the date of transition to FRS 102 for many entities. The   **36**
transitional provisions take this into account by providing an extended deadline for hedge
documentation on first-time adoption.

Alternative reporting of economic hedges

The Accounting Council advises modifying the provision in Section 11 to allow the   **37**
designation of loan commitments at fair value through profit or loss (in addition to the
designation of debt instruments at fair value through profit or loss). This will have the
effect of allowing economic hedge accounting where an entity balances the risks from a
first instrument by taking out a second which is measured at fair value: it will be able to
choose to measure the first at fair value too, thus matching the movements in profit and
reflecting, in financial reporting, the combined economic effect of the instruments.

Impairment provisions

Originally it was planned to amend FRS 102 prior to its effective date in respect of the   **38**
requirements relating to hedge accounting and the impairment of financial assets. The
IASB's project on the new IFRS impairment model is delayed and the FRC's consultation on
introducing equivalent requirements in FRS 102 has therefore been deferred. Respondents
to FRED 51 requested the exemption of certain entities from the requirement to adopt the
impairment accounting requirements in FRS 102 until the new impairment requirements
in FRS 102 are finalised.

The Accounting Council deliberated on the likely impact of the adoption of the impairment   **39**
accounting requirements in FRS 102. It concluded that the incurred loss impairment
model in FRS 102 is consistent with UK GAAP, as applicable prior to the introduction of
FRS 102. The Accounting Council considers that it is therefore unnecessary to provide a
temporary relief from the impairment accounting requirements in FRS 102.

Effective date

40   The Accounting Council advises that the amendments should be effective from the effective date of FRS 102 (ie accounting periods beginning on or after 1 January 2015), and therefore no amendment to the effective date is required.

Approval of this advice

41   This advice to the FRC was approved by the Accounting Council on 19 June 2014.

Appendix I
Glossary

This glossary is an integral part of the Standard.

accounting policies	The specific principles, bases, conventions, rules and practices applied by an entity in preparing and presenting **financial statements**.
accrual basis (of accounting)	The effects of transactions and other events are recognised when they occur (and not as **cash** or its equivalent is received or paid) and they are recorded in the accounting records and reported in the **financial statements** of the periods to which they relate.
accumulating compensated absences	Compensated absences that are carried forward and can be used in future periods if the current period's entitlement is not used in full.
acquisition date	The date on which the acquirer obtains **control** of the acquiree.
Act	The Companies Act 2006
active market	A market in which all the following conditions exist: (a) the items traded in the market are homogeneous; (b) willing buyers and sellers can normally be found at any time; and (c) prices are available to the public.
actuarial assumptions	An entity's unbiased and mutually compatible best estimates of the demographic and financial variables that will determine the ultimate cost of providing post-employment benefits.
actuarial gains and losses	Changes in the **present value** of the **defined benefit obligation** resulting from: (a) experience adjustments (the effects of differences between the previous **actuarial assumptions** and what has actually occurred); and (b) the effects of changes in actuarial assumptions.
agent	An entity is acting as an agent when it does not have exposure to the significant risks and rewards associated with the sale of goods or the rendering of services. One feature indicating that an entity is acting as an agent is that the amount the entity earns is predetermined, being either a fixed fee per transaction or a stated percentage of the amount billed to the customer.
agricultural activity	The management by an entity of the biological transformation of **biological assets** for sale, into agricultural produce or into additional biological assets.
agricultural produce	The harvested product of the entity's **biological assets**.
amortisation	The systematic allocation of the **depreciable amount** of an **asset** over its **useful life**.

amortised cost (of a financial asset or financial liability)	The amount at which the **financial asset** or **financial liability** is measured at initial **recognition** minus principal repayments, plus or minus the cumulative **amortisation** using the **effective interest method** of any difference between that initial amount and the maturity amount, and minus any reduction (directly or through the use of an allowance account) for impairment or uncollectability.
asset	A resource controlled by the entity as a result of past events and from which future economic benefits are expected to flow to the entity.

asset held by a long-term employee benefit fund	An **asset** (other than non-transferable financial instruments issued by the reporting entity) that:
	(a) is held by an entity (a fund) that is legally separate from the reporting entity and exists solely to pay or fund **employee benefits**; and
	(b) is available to be used only to pay or fund employee benefits, is not available to the reporting entity's own creditors (even in bankruptcy), and cannot be returned to the reporting entity, unless either:
	   (i) the remaining assets of the fund are sufficient to meet all the related employee benefit obligations of the plan or the reporting entity; or
	   (ii) the assets are returned to the reporting entity to reimburse it for employee benefits already paid.

associate	An entity, including an unincorporated entity such as a partnership, over which the investor has **significant influence** and that is neither a **subsidiary** nor an interest in a **joint venture**.
biological asset	A living animal or plant.
borrowing costs	Interest and other costs incurred by an entity in connection with the borrowing of funds.
business	An integrated set of activities and **assets** conducted and managed for the purpose of providing: (a) a return to investors; or (b) lower costs or other economic benefits directly and proportionately to policyholders or participants. A business generally consists of inputs, processes applied to those inputs, and resulting outputs that are, or will be, used to generate **revenues**. If **goodwill** is present in a transferred set of activities and assets, the transferred set shall be presumed to be a business.
business combination	The bringing together of separate entities or **businesses** into one reporting entity.
carrying amount	The amount at which an **asset** or **liability** is recognised in the **statement of financial position**.
cash	Cash on hand and demand deposits.
cash equivalents	Short-term, highly liquid investments that are readily convertible to known amounts of **cash** and that are subject to an insignificant risk of changes in value.
cash flows	Inflows and outflows of **cash** and **cash equivalents**.

cash-generating unit	The smallest identifiable group of **assets** that generates cash inflows that are largely independent of the cash inflows from other assets or groups of assets.
cash-settled share-based payment transaction	A **share-based payment transaction** in which the entity acquires goods or services by incurring a **liability** to transfer **cash** or other **assets** to the supplier of those goods or services for amounts that are based on the price (or value) of the entity's shares or other equity instruments of the entity or another group entity.
change in accounting estimate	An adjustment of the **carrying amount** of an **asset** or a **liability**, or the amount of the periodic consumption of an asset, that results from the assessment of the present status of, and expected future benefits and obligations associated with, assets and liabilities. Changes in accounting estimates result from new information or new developments and, accordingly, are not corrections of **errors**.
class of assets	A grouping of **assets** of a similar nature and use in an entity's operations.
close members of the family of a person	Those family members who may be expected to influence, or be influenced by, that person in their dealings with the entity including: (a) that person's children and spouse or domestic partner; (b) children of that person's spouse or domestic partner; and (c) dependants of that person or that person's spouse or domestic partner.
closing rate	The spot exchange rate at the end of the **reporting period**.
combination that is in substance is a gift	A combination carried out at nil or nominal consideration that is not a fair value exchange but in substance the gift of one entity to another.
commencement of lease term	The date from which the lessee is entitled to exercise its right to use the leased asset. It is the date of initial **recognition** of the **lease** (ie the recognition of the **assets**, **liabilities**, **income** or **expenses** resulting from the lease, as appropriate).
component of an entity	Operations and **cash flows** that can be clearly distinguished, operationally and for financial reporting purposes, from the rest of the entity.
compound financial instrument	A financial instrument that, from the issuer's perspective, contains both a **liability** and an **equity** element.
consolidated financial statements	The financial statements of a **parent** and its **subsidiaries** presented as those of a single economic entity.
construction contract	A contract specifically negotiated for the construction of an asset or a combination of assets that are closely interrelated or interdependent in terms of their design, technology and function or their ultimate purpose or use.

constructive obligation	An obligation that derives from an entity's actions where: (a) by an established pattern of past practice, published policies or a sufficiently specific current statement, the entity has indicated to other parties that it will accept certain responsibilities; and (b) as a result, the entity has created a valid expectation on the part of those other parties that it will discharge those responsibilities.
contingent asset	A possible **asset** that arises from past events and whose existence will be confirmed only by the occurrence or non-occurrence of one or more uncertain future events not wholly within the control of the entity.

contingent liability	(a) a possible obligation that arises from past events and whose existence will be confirmed only by the occurrence or non-occurrence of one or more uncertain future events not wholly within the control of the entity; or
	 (b) a present obligation that arises from past events but is not recognised because:
	    (i) it is not **probable** that an outflow of resources embodying economic benefits will be required to settle the obligation; or
	    (ii) the amount of the obligation cannot be measured with sufficient **reliability**.

contingent rent	That portion of the lease payments that is not fixed in amount but is based on the future amount of a factor that changes other than with the passage of time (eg percentage of future sales, amount of future use, future price indices, and future market rates of interest).
control (of an entity)	The power to govern the financial and operating policies of an entity so as to obtain benefits from its activities.
credit risk	The risk that one party to a financial instrument will cause a financial loss for the other party by failing to discharge an obligation.
current assets	**Assets** of an entity which are not intended for use on a continuing basis in the entity's activities.
current tax	The amount of income tax payable (refundable) in respect of the taxable profit (tax loss) for the current period or past **reporting periods**.
date of transition	The beginning of the earliest period for which an entity presents full comparative information in a given standard in its first **financial statements** that comply with that standard.
deemed cost	An amount used as a surrogate for cost or depreciated cost at a given date. Subsequent **depreciation** or **amortisation** assumes that the entity had initially recognised the **asset** or **liability** at the given date and that its cost was equal to the deemed cost.
deferred acquisition costs	Costs arising from the conclusion of **insurance contracts** that are incurred during a **reporting period** but which relate to a subsequent reporting period.

deferred tax	Income tax payable (recoverable) in respect of the **taxable profit (tax loss)** for future **reporting periods** as a result of past transactions or events.
deferred tax assets	Income tax recoverable in future **reporting periods** in respect of: (a) future tax consequences of transactions and events recognised in the **financial statements** of the current and previous periods; (b) the carry forward of unused tax losses; and (c) the carry forward of unused tax credits.
deferred tax liabilities	Income tax payable in future **reporting periods** in respect of future tax consequences of transactions and events recognised in the **financial statements** of the current and previous periods.
defined benefit obligation (present value of)	The **present value**, without deducting any **plan assets**, of expected future payments required to settle the obligation resulting from employee service in the current and prior periods.
defined benefit plans	**Post-employment benefit plans** other than **defined contribution plans**.
defined contribution plans	**Post-employment benefit plans** under which an entity pays fixed contributions into a separate entity (a fund) and has no legal or **constructive obligation** to pay further contributions or to make direct benefit payments to employees if the fund does not hold sufficient **assets** to pay all **employee benefits** relating to employee service in the current and prior periods.
depreciable amount	The cost of an **asset**, or other amount substituted for cost (in the **financial statements**), less its residual value.
depreciated replacement cost	The most economic cost required for the entity to replace the **service potential** of an **asset** (including the amount that the entity will receive from its disposal at the end of its **useful life**) at the **reporting date**.
depreciation	The systematic allocation of the **depreciable amount** of an **asset** over its **useful life**.
derecognition	The removal of a previously recognised **asset** or **liability** from an entity's **statement of financial position**.

derivative	A financial instrument or other contract with all three of the following characteristics: (a) its value changes in response to the change in a specified interest rate, financial instrument price, commodity price, foreign exchange rate, index of prices or rates, credit rating or credit index, or other variable (sometimes called the 'underlying'), provided in the case of a non-financial variable that the variable is not specific to a party to the contract; (b) it requires no initial net investment or an initial net investment that is smaller than would be required for other types of contracts that would be expected to have a similar response to changes in market factors; and (c) it is settled at a future date.
development	The application of **research** findings or other knowledge to a plan or design for the production of new or substantially improved materials, devices, products, processes, systems or services before the start of commercial production or use.
discontinued operation	A **component of an entity** that has been disposed of and: (a) represented a separate major line of business or geographical area of operations; (b) was part of a single co-ordinated plan to dispose of a separate major line of business or geographical area of operations; or (c) was a subsidiary acquired exclusively with a view to resale.

discretionary participation feature	A contractual right to receive, as a supplement to guaranteed benefits, additional benefits:
	(a) that are likely to be a significant portion of the total contractual benefits;
	(b) whose amount or timing is contractually at the discretion of the issuer; and
	(c) that are contractually based on:
	    (i) the performance of a specified pool of contracts or a specified type of contract;
	    (ii) realised and/or unrealised investment returns on a specified pool of **assets** held by the issuer; or
	    (iii) the **profit or loss** of the company, fund or other entity that issues the contract.

disposal group	A group of **assets** to be disposed of, by sale or otherwise, together as a group in a single transaction, and **liabilities** directly associated with those assets that will be transferred in the transaction. The group includes **goodwill** acquired in a **business combination** if the group is a **cash-generating unit** to which goodwill has been allocated in accordance with the requirements of paragraphs 27.24 to 27.27 of this FRS.
effective interest method	A method of calculating the **amortised cost** of a **financial asset** or a **financial liability** (or a group of financial assets or financial liabilities) and of allocating the interest income or interest expense over the relevant period.

effective interest rate	The rate that exactly discounts estimated future cash payments or receipts through the expected life of the financial instrument or, when appropriate, a shorter period to the **carrying amount** of the **financial asset** or **financial liability**.
employee benefits	All forms of consideration given by an entity in exchange for service rendered by employees.
entity combination	See **business combination**.
equity	The residual interest in the **assets** of the entity after deducting all its **liabilities**.
equity-settled share-based payment transaction	A **share-based payment transaction** in which the entity: (a) receives goods or services as consideration for its own equity instruments (including shares or **share options**); or (b) receives goods or services but has no obligation to settle the transaction with the supplier.
errors	Omissions from, and misstatements in, the entity's financial statements for one or more prior periods arising from a failure to use, or misuse of, reliable information that: (a) was available when financial statements for those periods were authorised for issue; and (b) could reasonably be expected to have been obtained and taken into account in the preparation and presentation of those financial statements.
expenses	Decreases in economic benefits during the **reporting period** in the form of outflows or depletions of **assets** or incurrences of **liabilities** that result in decreases in **equity**, other than those relating to distributions to equity investors.
EU-adopted IFRS	IFRS that have been adopted in the European Union in accordance with EU Regulation 1606/2002.
fair presentation	Faithful representation of the effects of transactions, other events and conditions in accordance with the definitions and **recognition** criteria for **assets**, **liabilities**, **income** and **expenses** unless the override stated in paragraph 3.4 applies.
fair value	The amount for which an **asset** could be exchanged, a **liability** settled, or an equity instrument granted could be exchanged, between knowledgeable, willing parties in an arm's length transaction. In the absence of any specific guidance provided in the relevant section of this FRS, the guidance in paragraphs 11.27 to 11.32 shall be used in determining fair value.

fair value less costs to sell	The amount obtainable from the sale of an **asset** or **cash-generating unit** in an arm's length transaction between knowledgeable, willing parties, less the costs of disposal.
finance lease	A **lease** that transfers substantially all the risks and rewards incidental to ownership of an **asset**. Title may or may not eventually be transferred. A lease that is not a finance lease is an operating lease.

financial asset	Any **asset** that is:
	(a) **cash**;
	(b) an equity instrument of another entity;
	(c) a contractual right:
	    (i) to receive cash or another financial asset from another entity, or
	    (ii) to exchange financial assets or **financial liabilities** with another entity under conditions that are potentially favourable to the entity; or
	(d) a contract that will or may be settled in the entity's own equity instruments and:
	    (i) under which the entity is or may be obliged to receive a variable number of the entity's own equity instruments; or
	    (ii) that will or may be settled other than by the exchange of a fixed amount of cash or another financial asset for a fixed number of the entity's own equity instruments. For this purpose the entity's own equity instruments do not include instruments that are themselves contracts for the future receipt or delivery of the entity's own equity instruments.

financial guarantee contract	A contract that requires the issuer to make specified payments to reimburse the holder for a loss it incurs because a specified debtor fails to make payments when due in accordance with the original or modified terms of a debt instrument.

| financial institution | Any of the following:
(a) a bank which is:
  (i) a firm with a Part IV permission[26] which includes accepting deposits and:
    (a) which is a credit institution; or
    (b) whose Part IV permission includes a requirement that it complies with the rules in the General Prudential sourcebook and the Prudential sourcebook for Banks, Building Societies and Investment Firms relating to banks, but which is not a building society, a friendly society or a credit union;
  (ii) an EEA bank which is a full credit institution;
(b) a building society which is defined in section 119(1) of the Building Societies Act 1986 as a building society incorporated (or deemed to be incorporated) under that act;
(c) a credit union, being a body corporate registered under the Industrial and Provident Societies Act 1965 as a credit union in accordance with the Credit Unions Act 1979, which is an authorised person;
(d) custodian bank, broker-dealer or stockbroker;
(e) an entity that undertakes the business of effecting or carrying out **insurance contracts**, including general and life assurance entities;
(f) an incorporated friendly society incorporated under the Friendly Societies Act 1992 or a registered friendly society registered under section 7(1)(a) of the Friendly Societies Act 1974 or any enactment which it replaced, including any registered branches;
(g) an investment trust, Irish Investment Company[27], venture capital trust, mutual fund, exchange traded fund, unit trust, open-ended investment company (OEIC);
(h) a **retirement benefit plan**; or
(i) any other entity whose principal activity is to generate wealth or manage risk through financial instruments. This is intended to cover entities that have business activities similar to those listed above but are not specifically included in the list above.
A **parent** entity whose sole activity is to hold investments in other group entities is not a financial institution. |
| **financial instrument** | A contract that gives rise to a **financial asset** of one entity and a **financial liability** or equity instrument of another entity. |

[26] *As defined in section 40(4) of the Financial Services and Markets Act 2000 or references to equivalent provisions of any successor legislation.*

[27] *An Irish Investment Company is a corporate vehicle as defined by section 47(3) of the Companies (Amendment) Act 1983 and paragraph 58 of the Schedule to the Companies (Amendment) Act 1986, and regulated by the Central Bank of Ireland.*

financial liability	Any **liability** that is:
	(a) a contractual obligation:
	(i) to deliver **cash** or another **financial asset** to another entity; or
	(ii) to exchange financial assets or financial liabilities with another entity under conditions that are potentially unfavourable to the entity, or
	(b) a contract that will or may be settled in the entity's own equity instruments and:
	(i) under which the entity is or may be obliged to deliver a variable number of the entity's own equity instruments; or
	(ii) will or may be settled other than by the exchange of a fixed amount of cash or another financial asset for a fixed number of the entity's own equity instruments. For this purpose the entity's own equity instruments do not include instruments that are themselves contracts for the future receipt or delivery of the entity's own equity instruments.
financial position	The relationship of the **assets**, **liabilities** and **equity** of an entity as reported in the **statement of financial position**.
financial statements	Structured representation of the **financial position**, financial **performance** and **cash flows** of an entity.
financial risk	The risk of a possible future change in one or more of a specified interest rate, financial instrument price, commodity price, foreign exchange rate, index of prices or rates, credit rating or credit index or other variable, provided in the case of a non-financial variable that the variable is not specific to a party to the contract.
financing activities	Activities that result in changes in the size and composition of the contributed **equity** and borrowings of the entity.
firm commitment	A binding agreement for the exchange of a specified quantity of resources at a specified price on a specified future date or dates.
first-time adopter of this FRS	An entity that presents its first annual **financial statements** that conform to this FRS, regardless of whether its previous accounting framework was **EU-adopted IFRS** or another set of accounting standards.
fixed assets	**Assets** of an entity which are intended for use on a continuing basis in the entity's activities.
forecast transaction	An uncommitted but anticipated future transaction.
foreign operation	An entity that is a **subsidiary**, **associate**, **joint venture** or branch of a reporting entity, the activities of which are based or conducted in a country or currency other than those of the reporting entity.
FRS 100	FRS 100 *Application of Financial Reporting Requirements*.
FRS 101	FRS 101 *Reduced Disclosure Framework*
FRS 102	FRS 102 *The Financial Reporting Standard applicable in the UK and Republic of Ireland*
FRS 103	FRS 103 *Insurance Contracts*

FRS 104	FRS 104 *Interim Financial Reporting*
FRSSE	The extant version[28] of the *Financial Reporting Standard for Smaller Entities*.
functional currency	The currency of the primary economic environment in which the entity operates.
funding (of post-employment benefits)	Contributions by an entity, and sometimes its employees, into an entity, or fund, that is legally separate from the reporting entity and from which the **employee benefits** are paid.
gains	Increases in economic benefits that meet the definition of **income** but are not **revenue**.
general purpose financial statements (generally referred to simply as financial statements)	**Financial statements** directed to the general financial information needs of a wide range of users who are not in a position to demand reports tailored to meet their particular information needs.
going concern	An entity is a going concern unless management either intends to liquidate the entity or to cease trading, or has no realistic alternative but to do so.
goodwill	Future economic benefits arising from **assets** that are not capable of being individually identified and separately recognised.
government grant	Assistance by government in the form of a transfer of resources to an entity in return for past or future compliance with specified conditions relating to the **operating activities** of the entity. Government refers to government, government agencies and similar bodies whether local, national or international.
grant date	The date at which the entity and another party (including an employee) agree to a share-based payment arrangement, being when the entity and the counterparty have a shared understanding of the terms and conditions of the arrangement. At grant date the entity confers on the counterparty the right to **cash**, other **assets**, or equity instruments of the entity, provided the specified vesting conditions, if any, are met. If that agreement is subject to an approval process (for example, by shareholders), grant date is the date when that approval is obtained.
gross investment in a lease	The aggregate of: (a) the **minimum lease payments** receivable by the lessor under a **finance lease**; and (b) any unguaranteed **residual value** accruing to the lessor.
group	A **parent** and all its **subsidiaries**.

[28] *At the date of issue of this FRS, the extant version of the FRSSE is the Financial Reporting Standard for Smaller Entities (effective April 2008). The Financial Reporting Standard for Smaller Entities (effective January 2015) will replace it as the extant standard from 1 January 2015.*

group reconstruction	Any one of the following arrangements: (a) the transfer of an equity holding in a **subsidiary** from one group entity to another; (b) the addition of a new **parent** entity to a **group**; (c) the transfer of equity holdings in one or more subsidiaries of a group to a new entity that is not a group entity but whose equity holders are the same as those of the group's parent; or (d) the combination into a group of two or more entities that before the combination had the same equity holders.
hedging gain or loss	The change in fair value of a hedged item that is attributable to the hedged risk.
held exclusively with a view to subsequent resale	An interest: (a) for which a purchaser has been identified or is being sought, and which is reasonably expected to be disposed of within approximately one year of its date of acquisition; or (b) that was acquired as a result of the enforcement of a security, unless the interest has become part of the continuing activities of the **group** or the holder acts as if it intends the interest to become so; or (c) which is **held as part of an investment portfolio**.
held as part of an investment portfolio	An interest is held as part of an investment portfolio if its value to the investor is through **fair value** as part of a directly or indirectly held basket of investments rather than as media through which the investor carries out **business**. A basket of investments is indirectly held if an investment fund holds a single investment in a second investment fund which, in turn, holds a basket of investments.
heritage assets	Tangible and **intangible assets** with historic, artistic, scientific, technological, geophysical, or environmental qualities that are held and maintained principally for their contribution to knowledge and culture.
highly probable	Significantly more likely than **probable**.
IAS Regulation	EU Regulation 1606/2002.
IFRS (International Financial Reporting Standards)	Standards and interpretations issued (or adopted) by the International Accounting Standards Board (IASB). They comprise: (a) International Financial Reporting Standards; (b) International Accounting Standards; and (c) Interpretations developed by the IFRS Interpretations Committee (IFRIC) or the former Standing Interpretations Committee (SIC).

impairment loss	The amount by which the **carrying amount** of an **asset** exceeds: (a) in the case of **inventories**, its selling price less costs to complete and sell; or (b) in the case of other assets, its **recoverable amount**.
impracticable	Applying a requirement is impracticable when the entity cannot apply it after making every reasonable effort to do so.
imputed rate of interest	The more clearly determinable of either: (a) the prevailing rate for a similar instrument of an issuer with a similar credit rating; or (b) a rate of interest that discounts the nominal amount of the instrument to the current cash sales price of the goods or services.
inception of the lease	The earlier of the date of the lease agreement and the date of commitment by the parties to the principal provisions of the **lease**.
income	Increases in economic benefits during the **reporting period** in the form of inflows or enhancements of **assets** or decreases of **liabilities** that result in increases in **equity**, other than those relating to contributions from equity investors.
income and expenditure	The total of **income** less **expenses**, excluding the components of **other comprehensive income**. In the for-profit sector this is known as **profit or loss**.
income statement	**Financial statement** that presents all items of **income** and **expense** recognised in a **reporting period**, excluding the items of **other comprehensive income** (referred to as the profit and loss account in the **Act**).
income tax	All domestic and foreign taxes that are based on **taxable profits**. Income tax also includes taxes, such as withholding taxes, that are payable by a **subsidiary**, **associate** or **joint venture** on distributions to the reporting entity.
individual financial statements	The accounts that are required to be prepared by an entity in accordance with the Act or relevant legislation, for example: (a) 'individual accounts', as set out in section 394 of the Act; (b) 'statement of accounts', as set out in section 132 of the Charities Act 2011; or (c) 'individual accounts', as set out in section 72A of the Building Societies Act 1986. **Separate financial statements** are included in the meaning of this term.
infrastructure assets	Infrastructure for public services, such as roads, bridges, tunnels, prisons, hospitals, airports, water distribution facilities, energy supply and telecommunications networks.
insurance contract	A contract under which one party (the insurer) accepts significant insurance risk from another party (the policyholder) by agreeing to compensate the policyholder if a specified uncertain future event (the insured event) adversely affects the policyholder.

intangible asset	An identifiable non-monetary asset without physical substance. Such an **asset** is identifiable when: (a) it is separable, ie capable of being separated or divided from the entity and sold, transferred, licensed, rented or exchanged, either individually or together with a related contract, asset or **liability**; or (b) it arises from contractual or other legal rights, regardless of whether those rights are transferable or separable from the entity or from other rights and obligations.

interest rate implicit in the lease	The discount rate that, at the **inception of the lease**, causes the aggregate **present value** of:
	(a) the **minimum lease payments**; and
	(b) the unguaranteed **residual value** to be equal to the sum of:
	    (i) the **fair value** of the leased asset; and
	    (ii) any initial direct costs of the lessor.

interim financial report	A financial report containing either a complete set of **financial statements** or a set of condensed financial statements for an **interim period**.
interim period	A financial **reporting period** shorter than a full financial year.
intrinsic value	The difference between the fair value of the shares to which the counterparty has the (conditional or unconditional) right to subscribe or which it has the right to receive, and the price (if any) the counterparty is (or will be) required to pay for those shares. For example, a share option with an exercise price of CU15, on a share with a fair value of CU20, has an intrinsic value of CU5.
inventories	Assets: (a) held for sale in the ordinary course of business; (b) in the process of production for such sale; or (c) in the form of materials or supplies to be consumed in the production process or in the rendering of services.
inventories held for distribution at no or nominal consideration	Assets that are: (a) held for distribution at no or nominal consideration in the ordinary course of operations; (b) in the process of production for distribution at no or nominal consideration in the ordinary course of operations; or (c) in the form of material or supplies to be consumed in the production process or in the rendering of services at no or nominal consideration.
investing activities	The acquisition and disposal of long-term assets and other investments not included in **cash equivalents**.
investment property	Property (land or a building, or part of a building, or both) held by the owner or by the lessee under a **finance lease** to earn rentals or for capital appreciation or both, rather than for: (a) use in the production or supply of goods or services or for administrative purposes, or (b) sale in the ordinary course of **business**.

joint control	The contractually agreed sharing of **control** over an economic activity. It exists only when the strategic financial and operating decisions relating to the activity require the unanimous consent of the parties sharing control (the **venturers**).
joint venture	A contractual arrangement whereby two or more parties undertake an economic activity that is subject to **joint control**. Joint ventures can take the form of jointly controlled operations, jointly controlled assets, or **jointly controlled entities**.
jointly controlled entity	A **joint venture** that involves the establishment of a corporation, partnership or other entity in which each **venturer** has an interest. The entity operates in the same way as other entities, except that a contractual arrangement between the venturers establishes **joint control** over the economic activity of the entity.
key management personnel	Those persons having authority and responsibility for planning, directing and controlling the activities of the entity, directly or indirectly, including any director (whether executive or otherwise) of that entity.
lease	An agreement whereby the lessor conveys to the lessee in return for a payment or series of payments the right to use an **asset** for an agreed period of time.
lease incentives	Incentives provided by the lessor to the lessee to enter into a new or renew an operating lease. Examples of such incentives include up-front cash payments to the lessee, the reimbursement or assumption by the lessor of costs of the lessee (such as relocation costs, leasehold improvements and costs associated with pre-existing lease commitments of the lessee), or initial periods of the **lease** provided by the lessor rent-free or at a reduced rent.
lease term	The non-cancellable period for which the lessee has contracted to **lease** the **asset** together with any further terms for which the lessee has the option to continue to lease the asset, with or without further payment, when at the **inception of the lease** it is reasonably certain that the lessee will exercise the option.
lessee's incremental borrowing rate (of interest)	The rate of interest the lessee would have to pay on a similar **lease** or, if that is not determinable, the rate that, at the **inception of the lease,** the lessee would incur to borrow over a similar term, and with a similar security, the funds necessary to purchase the **asset**.
liability	A present obligation of the entity arising from past events, the settlement of which is expected to result in an outflow from the entity of resources embodying economic benefits.
liquidity risk	The risk that an entity will encounter difficulty in meeting obligations associated with **financial liabilities** that are settled by delivering **cash** or another **financial asset**.

LLP Regulations	The Large and Medium-sized Limited Liability Partnerships (Accounts) Regulations 2008 (SI 2008/1913).
loans payable	**Financial liabilities** other than short-term trade payables on normal credit terms.
market condition	A condition upon which the exercise price, vesting or exercisability of an equity instrument depends that is related to the market price of the entity's equity instruments, such as attaining a specified share price or a specified amount of **intrinsic value** of a **share option**, or achieving a specified target that is based on the market price of the entity's equity instruments relative to an index of market prices of equity instruments of other entities.
market risk	The risk that the **fair value** or future **cash flows** of a financial instrument will fluctuate because of changes in market prices. Market risk comprises three types of risk: currency risk, interest rate risk and other price risk. Interest rate risk – the risk that the fair value or future cash flows of a financial instrument will fluctuate because of changes in market interest rates. Currency risk – the risk that the fair value or future cash flows of a financial instrument will fluctuate because of changes in foreign exchange rates. Other price risk – the risk that the fair value or future cash flows of a financial instrument will fluctuate because of changes in market prices (other than those arising from interest rate risk or currency risk), whether those changes are caused by factors specific to the financial instrument or its issuer, or factors affecting all similar financial instruments traded in the market.
material	Omissions or misstatements of items are material if they could, individually or collectively, influence the economic decisions of users taken on the basis of the **financial statements**. Materiality depends on the size and nature of the omission or misstatement judged in the surrounding circumstances. The size or nature of the item, or a combination of both, could be the determining factor.
measurement	The process of determining the monetary amounts at which the elements of the **financial statements** are to be recognised and carried in the **statement of financial position** and **statement of comprehensive income**.

merger	An **entity combination** that results in the creation of a new reporting entity formed from the combining parties, in which the controlling parties of the combining entities come together in a partnership for the mutual sharing of risks and benefits of the newly formed entity and in which no party to the combination in substance obtains **control** over any other, or is otherwise seen to be dominant.
	All of the following criteria must be met for an entity combination to meet the definition of a merger:
	(a) no party to the combination is portrayed as either acquirer or acquiree, either by its own board or management or by that of another party to the combination;
	(b) there is no significant change to the classes of beneficiaries of the combining entities or the purpose of the benefits provided as a result of the combination; and
	(c) all parties to the combination, as represented by the members of the board, participate in establishing the management structure of the combined entity and in selecting the management personnel, and such decisions are made on the basis of a consensus between the parties to the combination rather than purely by exercise of voting rights.
minimum lease payments	The payments over the **lease term** that the lessee is or can be required to make, excluding **contingent rent**, costs for services and taxes to be paid by and reimbursed to the lessor, together with:
	(a) for a lessee, any amounts guaranteed by the lessee or by a party related to the lessee; or
	(b) for a lessor, any **residual value** guaranteed to the lessor by:
	(i) the lessee;
	(ii) a party related to the lessee; or
	(iii) a third party unrelated to the lessor that is financially capable of discharging the obligations under the guarantee.
	However, if the lessee has an option to purchase the **asset** at a price that is expected to be sufficiently lower than **fair value** at the date the option becomes exercisable for it to be reasonably certain, at the **inception of the lease**, that the option will be exercised, the minimum lease payments comprise the minimum payments payable over the lease term to the expected date of exercise of this purchase option and the payment required to exercise it.
monetary items	Units of currency held and **assets** and **liabilities** to be received or paid in a fixed or determinable number of units of currency.

multi-employer (benefit) plans	**Defined contribution plans** (other than **state plans**) or **defined benefit plans** (other than state plans) that: (a) pool the **assets** contributed by various entities that are not under common control, and (b) use those assets to provide benefits to employees of more than one entity, on the basis that contribution and benefit levels are determined without regard to the identity of the entity that employs the employees concerned.
net assets available for benefits	The **assets** of a plan less **liabilities** other than the actuarial **present value** of promised retirement benefits
net defined benefit liability	The **present value** of the **defined benefit obligation** at the **reporting date** minus the **fair value** at the reporting date of **plan assets** (if any) out of which the obligations are to be settled.
net investment in a foreign operation	The amount of the reporting entity's interest in the net assets of that operation.
net investment in a lease	The **gross investment in a lease** discounted at the **interest rate implicit in the lease**.
non-controlling interest	The **equity** in a **subsidiary** not attributable, directly or indirectly, to a **parent**.
non-exchange transaction	A transaction whereby an entity receives value from another entity without directly giving approximately equal value in exchange, or gives value to another entity without directly receiving approximately equal value in exchange.
notes (to financial statements)	Notes contain information in addition to that presented in the **statement of financial position**, **statement of comprehensive income**, **income statement** (if presented), combined **statement of income and retained earnings** (if presented), **statement of changes in equity** and **statement of cash flows**. Notes provide narrative descriptions or disaggregations of items presented in those statements and information about items that do not qualify for **recognition** in those statements.
notional amount	The quantity of currency units, shares, bushels, pounds or other units specified in a financial instrument contract.
objective of financial statements	To provide information about the **financial position**, **performance** and **cash flows** of an entity that is useful for economic decision-making by a broad range of users who are not in a position to demand reports tailored to meet their particular information needs.
onerous contract	A contract in which the unavoidable costs of meeting the obligations under the contract exceed the economic benefits expected to be received under it.
operating activities	The principal revenue-producing activities of the entity and other activities that are not investing or **financing activities**.
operating lease	A **lease** that does not transfer substantially all the risks and rewards incidental to ownership. A lease that is not an operating lease is a **finance lease**.

operating segment	An operating segment is a **component of an entity**: (a) that engages in business activities from which it may earn **revenues** and incur **expenses** (including revenues and expenses relating to transactions with other components of the same entity); (b) whose operating results are regularly reviewed by the entity's chief operating decision maker to make decisions about resources to be allocated to the segment and assess its **performance**; and (c) for which discrete financial information is available.
ordinary share	An equity instrument that is subordinate to all other classes of equity instrument.
other comprehensive income	Items of **income** and **expense** (including reclassification adjustments) that are not recognised in **profit or loss** as required or permitted by this FRS.
owners	Holders of instruments classified as **equity**.
parent	An entity that has one or more **subsidiaries**.
performance	The relationship of the **income** and **expenses** of an entity, as reported in the **statement of comprehensive income**.
performance-related condition	A condition that requires the performance of a particular level of service or units of output to be delivered, with payment of, or entitlement to, the resources conditional on that performance.
permanent differences	Differences between an entity's **taxable profits** and its **total comprehensive income** as stated in the **financial statements**, other than **timing differences**.
plan assets (of an employee benefit plan)	(a) **assets held by a long-term employee benefit fund**; and (b) **qualifying insurance policies**.
post-employment benefits	**Employee benefits** (other than **termination benefits** and short-term employee benefits) that are payable after the completion of employment.
post-employment benefit plans	Formal or informal arrangements under which an entity provides **post-employment benefits** for one or more employees.
potential ordinary share	A financial instrument or other contract that may entitle its holder to **ordinary shares**.
present value	A current estimate of the present discounted value of the future net **cash flows** in the normal course of **business**.
presentation currency	The currency in which the **financial statements** are presented.
prevailing market rate	The rate of interest that would apply to the entity in an open market for a similar financial instrument.

principal	An entity is acting as a principal when it has exposure to the significant risks and rewards associated with the sale of goods or the rendering of services. Features that indicate that an entity is acting as a principal include: (a) the entity has the primary responsibility for providing the goods or services to the customer or for fulfilling the order, for example by being responsible for the acceptability of the products or services ordered or purchased by the customer; (b) the entity has inventory risk before or after the customer order, during shipping or on return; (c) the entity has latitude in establishing prices, either directly or indirectly, for example by providing additional goods or services; and (d) the entity bears the customer's credit risk for the amount receivable from the customer.
probable	More likely than not.
profit or loss	The total of **income** less **expenses**, excluding the components of **other comprehensive income**.
projected unit credit method	An actuarial valuation method that sees each period of service as giving rise to an additional unit of benefit entitlement and measures each unit separately to build up the final obligation (sometimes known as the accrued benefit method pro-rated on service or as the benefit/years of service method).
property, plant and equipment	Tangible assets that: (a) are held for use in the production or supply of goods or services, for rental to others, or for administrative purposes, and (b) are expected to be used during more than one period.
prospectively (applying a change in accounting policy)	Applying the new **accounting policy** to transactions, other events and conditions occurring after the date as at which the policy is changed.
provision	A **liability** of uncertain timing or amount.
prudence	The inclusion of a degree of caution in the exercise of the judgements needed in making the estimates required under conditions of uncertainty, such that **assets** or **income** are not overstated and **liabilities** or **expenses** are not understated.

public benefit entity	An entity whose primary objective is to provide goods or services for the general public, community or social benefit and where any **equity** is provided with a view to supporting the entity's primary objectives rather than with a view to providing a financial return to equity providers, shareholders or members.[29]
public benefit entity concessionary loan	A loan made or received between a **public benefit entity** or an entity within a **public benefit entity group** and another party: (a) at below the **prevailing market rate** of interest; (b) that is not repayable on demand; and (c) is for the purposes of furthering the objectives of the public benefit entity or public benefit entity **parent**.
public benefit entity group	A **public benefit entity parent** and all of its wholly-owned **subsidiaries**.
publicly traded (debt or equity instruments)	Traded, or in process of being issued for trading, in a public market (a domestic or foreign stock exchange or an over-the-counter market, including local and regional markets).
qualifying asset	An **asset** that necessarily takes a substantial period of time to get ready for its intended use or sale. Depending on the circumstances any of the following may be qualifying assets: (a) **inventories**; (b) manufacturing plants; (c) power generation facilities; (d) **intangible assets**; and (e) **investment properties**. **Financial assets**, and inventories that are produced over a short period of time, are not qualifying assets. Assets that are ready for their intended use or sale when acquired are not qualifying assets.
qualifying entity (for the purposes of this FRS)	A member of a **group** where the **parent** of that group prepares publicly available **consolidated financial statements** which are intended to give a true and fair view (of the **assets**, **liabilities**, **financial position** and **profit or loss**) and that member is included in the consolidation[30].

[29] *The term public benefit entity does not necessarily imply that the purpose of the entity is for the benefit of the public as a whole. For example, many PBEs exist for the direct benefit of a particular group of people, although it is possible that society as a whole also benefits indirectly. The important factor is what the primary purpose of such an entity is, and that it does not exist primarily to provide economic benefit to its investors. Organisations such as mutual insurance companies, other mutual co-operative entities and clubs that provide dividends or other economic benefits directly and proportionately to their owners, members or participants are not PBEs.*

Some PBEs undertake certain activities that are intended to make a surplus in order to fund their primary activities. Consideration should be given to the primary purpose of an entity's (or group's) activities in assessing whether it meets the definition of a PBE.

PBEs may have received contributions in the form of equity, even though the entity does not have a primary profit motive. However, because of the fundamental nature of public benefit entities, any such contributions are made by the equity holders of the entity primarily to enable the provision of goods or services to beneficiaries rather than with a view to a financial return for themselves. This is different from the position of lenders; loans do not fall into the category of equity.

[30] *As set out in section 474(1) of the Act.*

qualifying insurance policies	An insurance policy[31] issued by an insurer that is not a **related party** of the reporting entity, if the proceeds of the policy:
	(a) can be used only to pay or fund **employee benefits** under a **defined benefit plan**; and
	(b) are not available to the reporting entity's own creditors (even in bankruptcy) and cannot be paid to the reporting entity, unless either:
	  (i) the proceeds represent surplus **assets** that are not needed for the policy to meet all the related employee benefit obligations; or
	  (ii) the proceeds are returned to the reporting entity to reimburse it for employee benefits already paid.

recognition	The process of incorporating in the **statement of financial position** or **statement of comprehensive income** an item that meets the definition of an asset, liability, equity, income or expense and satisfies the following criteria: (a) it is **probable** that any future economic benefit associated with the item will flow to or from the entity; and (b) the item has a cost or value that can be measured with **reliability**.
recoverable amount	The higher of an **asset's** (or **cash-generating unit's**) **fair value less costs to sell** and its value in use.
Regulations	The Large and Medium-sized Companies and Groups (Accounts and Reports) Regulations 2008 (SI 2008/410).
reinsurance contract	An **insurance contract** issued by one insurer (the reinsurer) to compensate another insurer (the cedant) for losses on one or more contracts issued by the cedant.

related party	A related party is a person or entity that is related to the entity that is preparing its **financial statements** (the reporting entity).
	(a) A person or a close member of that person's family is related to a reporting entity if that person:
	  (i) has **control** or **joint control** over the reporting entity;
	  (ii) has **significant influence** over the reporting entity; or
	  (iii) is a member of the **key management personnel** of the reporting entity or of a **parent** of the reporting entity.
	(b) An entity is related to a reporting entity if any of the following conditions apply:
	  (i) the entity and the reporting entity are members of the same **group** (which means that each parent, **subsidiary** and fellow subsidiary is related to the others).
	  (ii) one entity is an **associate** or **joint venture** of the other entity (or of a member of a group of which the other entity is a member).

[31] *A qualifying insurance policy is not necessarily an insurance contract.*

	(iii) both entities are joint ventures of the same third entity.
	(iv) one entity is a joint venture of a third entity and the other entity is an associate of the third entity.
	(v) the entity is a **post-employment benefit plan** for the benefit of employees of either the reporting entity or an entity related to the reporting entity. If the reporting entity is itself such a plan, the sponsoring employers are also related to the reporting entity.
	(vi) the entity is controlled or jointly controlled by a person identified in (a).
	(vii) a person identified in (a)(i) has significant influence over the entity or is a member of the key management personnel of the entity (or of a parent of the entity).
related party transaction	A transfer of resources, services or obligations between a reporting entity and a **related party**, regardless of whether a price is charged.
relevance	The quality of information that allows it to influence the economic decisions of users by helping them evaluate past, present or future events or confirming, or correcting, their past evaluations.
reliability	The quality of information that makes it free from **material error** and bias and represents faithfully that which it either purports to represent or could reasonably be expected to represent.
reporting date	The end of the latest period covered by **financial statements** or by an interim financial report.
reporting period	The period covered by **financial statements** or by an **interim financial report**.
research	Original and planned investigation undertaken with the prospect of gaining new scientific or technical knowledge and understanding.
residual value (of an asset)	The estimated amount that an entity would currently obtain from disposal of an **asset**, after deducting the estimated costs of disposal, if the asset were already of the age and in the condition expected at the end of its **useful life**.
restriction	A requirement that limits or directs the purposes for which a resource may be used that does not meet the definition of a **performance-related condition**.
restructuring	A restructuring is a programme that is planned and controlled by management and materially changes either: (a) the scope of a business undertaken by an entity; or (b) the manner in which that business is conducted.

retirement benefit plan	Arrangements whereby an entity provides benefits for employees on or after termination of service (either in the form of an annual **income** or as a lump sum) when such benefits, or the contributions towards them, can be determined or estimated in advance of retirement from the provisions of a document or from the entity's practice.
retrospective application (of an accounting policy)	Applying a new **accounting policy** to transactions, other events and conditions as if that policy had always been applied.
revenue	The gross inflow of economic benefits during the period arising in the course of the ordinary activities of an entity when those inflows result in increases in **equity**, other than increases relating to contributions from equity participants.
separate financial statements	Those presented by a **parent** in which the investments in **subsidiaries**, **associates** or **jointly controlled entities** are accounted for either at cost or **fair value** rather than on the basis of the reported results and net assets of the investees. Separate financial statements are included within the meaning of **individual financial statements**.
service concession arrangement	An arrangement whereby a public sector body or a **public benefit entity** (the grantor) contracts with a private sector entity (the operator) to construct (or upgrade), operate and maintain **infrastructure assets** for a specified period of time (the concession period).
service potential	The economic utility of an **asset**, based on the total benefit expected to be derived by the entity from use (and/or through sale) of the asset.
share-based payment transaction	A transaction in which the entity: (a) receives goods or services (including employee services) as consideration for its own equity instruments (including shares or **share options**); or (b) receives goods or services but has no obligation to settle the transaction with supplier; or (c) acquires goods or services by incurring **liabilities** to the supplier of those goods or services for amounts that are based on the price (or value) of the entity's shares or other equity instruments of the entity or another group entity.
share option	A contract that gives the holder the right, but not the obligation, to subscribe to the entity's shares at a fixed or determinable price for a specific period of time.
significant influence	Significant influence is the power to participate in the financial and operating policy decisions of the **associate** but is not **control** or **joint control** over those policies.
Statement of Recommended Practice (SORP)	An extant Statement of Recommended Practice developed in accordance with *SORPs: Policy and Code of Practice*. SORPs recommend accounting practices for specialised industries or sectors. They supplement accounting standards and other legal and regulatory requirements in the light of the special factors prevailing or transactions undertaken in a particular industry or sector.

state	A national, regional, or local government.
state (employee benefit) plan	Employee benefit plans established by legislation to cover all entities (or all entities in a particular category, for example a specific industry) and operated by national or local government or by another body (for example an autonomous agency created specifically for this purpose) which is not subject to control or influence by the reporting entity.
statement of cash flows	**Financial statement** that provides information about the changes in **cash** and **cash equivalents** of an entity for a period, showing separately changes during the period from operating, investing and **financing activities**.
statement of comprehensive income	**Financial statement** that presents all items of **income** and **expense** recognised in a period, including those items recognised in determining **profit or loss** (which is a subtotal in the statement of comprehensive income) and items of **other comprehensive income**. If an entity chooses to present both an **income statement** and a statement of comprehensive income, the statement of comprehensive income begins with profit or loss and then displays the items of other comprehensive income.
statement of financial position	**Financial statement** that presents the relationship of an entity's **assets**, **liabilities** and **equity** as of a specific date (referred to as the balance sheet in the **Act**).
statement of income and retained earnings	**Financial statement** that presents the **profit or loss** and changes in retained earnings for a **reporting period**.
subsidiary	An entity, including an unincorporated entity such as a partnership, that is **controlled** by another entity (known as the **parent**).
substantively enacted	Tax rates shall be regarded as substantively enacted when the remaining stages of the enactment process historically have not affected the outcome and are unlikely to do so. A UK tax rate shall be regarded as having been substantively enacted if it is included in either: (a) a Bill that has been passed by the House of Commons and is awaiting only passage through the House of Lords and Royal Assent; or (b) a resolution having statutory effect that has been passed under the Provisional Collection of Taxes Act 1968. (Such a resolution could be used to collect taxes at a new rate before that rate has been enacted. In practice, corporation tax rates are now set a year ahead to avoid having to invoke the Provisional Collection of Taxes Act for the quarterly payment system.) A Republic of Ireland tax rate can be regarded as having been substantively enacted if it is included in a Bill that has been passed by the Dail.
tax expense	The aggregate amount included in **total comprehensive income** or **equity** for the **reporting period** in respect of **current tax** and **deferred tax**.

taxable profit (tax loss)	The profit (loss) for a **reporting period** upon which income taxes are payable or recoverable, determined in accordance with the rules established by the taxation authorities. Taxable profit equals taxable income less amounts deductible from taxable income.
termination benefits	**Employee benefits** provided in exchange for the termination of an employee's employment as a result of either: (a) an entity's decision to terminate an employee's employment before the normal retirement date; or (b) an employee's decision to accept voluntary redundancy in exchange for those benefits.
timing differences	Differences between **taxable profits** and **total comprehensive income** as stated in the **financial statements** that arise from the inclusion of **income** and **expenses** in tax assessments in periods different from those in which they are recognised in financial statements.
timeliness	Providing the information in **financial statements** within the decision time frame.
total comprehensive income	The change in **equity** during a period resulting from transactions and other events, other than those changes resulting from transactions from equity participants (equal to the sum of **profit or loss** and **other comprehensive income**).
transaction costs (financial instruments)	Incremental costs that are directly attributable to the acquisition, issue or disposal of a **financial asset** or **financial liability**, or the issue or reacquisition of an entity's **own equity instrument**. An incremental cost is one that would not have been incurred if the entity had not acquired, issued or disposed of the financial asset or financial liability, or had not issued or reacquired its own equity instrument.
treasury shares	An entity's own equity instruments, held by that entity or other members of the consolidated group.
turnover	The amounts derived from the provision of goods and services falling within the entity's ordinary activities, after deduction of: (a) trade discounts; (b) value added tax; and (c) any other taxes based on the amounts so derived.
understandability	The presentation of information in a way that makes it comprehensible by users who have a reasonable knowledge of **business** and economic activities and accounting and a willingness to study the information with reasonable diligence.
useful life	The period over which an **asset** is expected to be available for use by an entity or the number of production or similar units expected to be obtained from the asset by an entity.
value in use	The **present value** of the future **cash flows** expected to be derived from an **asset** or **cash-generating unit**.

value in use (in respect of assets held for their service potential)	When the future economic benefits of an **asset** are not primarily dependent on the asset's ability to generate net cash inflows, **value in use** (in respect of assets held for their **service potential**) is the **present value** to the entity of the asset's remaining service potential if it continues to be used, plus the net amount that the entity will receive from its disposal at the end of its **useful life**.
venturer	A party to a **joint venture** that has **joint control** over that joint venture.
vest	Become an entitlement. Under a share-based payment arrangement, a counterparty's right to receive **cash**, other **assets** or equity instruments of the entity vests when the counterparty's entitlement is no longer conditional on the satisfaction of any vesting conditions.
vested benefits	Benefits, the rights to which, under the conditions of a **retirement benefit plan**, are not conditional on continued employment.

Editor's note: FRS 104 (March 2015) amended this appendix with effect for interim periods commencing on or after 1 January 2015 with early application permitted.

Prospective amendments: Amendments to FRS 102 *The Financial Reporting Standard applicable in the UK and Republic of Ireland* – Small entities and other minor amendments (July 2015) amends Appendix I and inserted new glossary terms and footnotes will be renumbered sequentially with effect for annual periods beginning on or after 1 January 2016.

Appendix II
Significant differences between FRS 102 and the IFRS for SMEs

Section		Changes to the IFRS for SMEs
1	Scope of this FRS	This section of the IFRS for SMEs has been replaced. The IFRS for SMEs applies to small and medium sized entities that do not have public accountability and publish general purpose financial statements. FRS 100 *Application of Financial Reporting Requirements* sets out the scope of entities applying this FRS.
		Paragraphs 1.14A and 1.14B are added to provide transitional provisions in respect of the designation of financial instruments at fair value and hedge accounting which are available to entities that have authorised for issue financial statements compliant with this FRS prior to 1 August 2014.
2	Concepts and Pervasive Principles	No significant changes.
3	Financial Statement Presentation	The requirements in paragraph 3.7 are deleted and requirements set out in the Act are referred to for the use of the true and fair override.
		Paragraph 3.16 is amended to clarify the role of materiality in the preparation of financial statements. Paragraph 3.16A is inserted to specify that disclosures are not required if the information is not material.
4	Statement of Financial Position	The requirements of this section have predominantly been removed and replaced by the requirements set out in the Act. Entities that do not report under the Act comply with the requirements of this section, and of the Regulations, except to the extent that these requirements are not permitted by any statutory framework under which such entities report.
5	Statement of Comprehensive Income and Income Statement	The requirements of this section have predominantly been removed and replaced by the requirements set out in the Act. Entities that do not report under the Act comply with the requirements of this section and of the Regulations except to the extent that these requirements are not permitted by any statutory framework under which such entities report.
		Paragraph 5.10 has been amended and paragraph 5.10A is inserted to comply with the Act and includes the definition of an extraordinary item.

Section		Changes to the IFRS for SMEs
6	Statement of Changes in Equity and Statement of Income and Retained Earnings	Paragraph 6.3A is inserted to require presentation for each component of equity an analysis of other comprehensive income by item, either in the notes, or in the statement of changes in equity.
7	Statement of Cash Flows	The scope of this section is amended to exclude mutual life assurance companies, pension funds and certain investment funds.
		Paragraphs 7.10A to 7.10E are inserted to require the reporting of cash flows on a net basis in some circumstances.
		Paragraphs 7.11 and 7.12 are amended to provide some relaxation of the exchange rates permitted to be used.
8	Notes to the Financial Statements	No significant changes.
9	Consolidated and Separate Financial Statements	The scope of this section is amended to clarify that it applies to all parent entities that present consolidated financial statements intended to give a true and fair view.
		The requirements to present consolidated financial statements are amended to comply with the Act.
		Paragraph 9.9 requires a subsidiary that is held exclusively with a view to subsequent resale because it is held as part of an investment portfolio, to be excluded from consolidation. Such subsidiaries are required to be measured at fair value with changes recognised in profit or loss. This exemption is required irrespective of whether the subsidiary was previously consolidated under previous GAAP, prior to transition to FRS 102. In addition paragraphs 14.4B and 15.9B are inserted to require an investor that has investments in associates or jointly controlled entities that are held as part of an investment portfolio to measure those investments at fair value with the changes recognised in profit or loss in their consolidated financial statements.
		Clarification is added to paragraph 9.10 that Employee Share Ownership Plans and similar arrangements are Special Purpose Entities.

Section		Changes to the IFRS for SMEs
		Paragraph 9.16 is amended to comply with paragraph 2(2) of Schedule 6 to the Regulations in order to require a subsidiary's financial statements, which are included in the consolidated financial statements, to be for the same reporting period (financial year) and as at the same reporting date (year-end). Where it is not practicable to align the subsidiary's reporting date (year-end) with the parent's, paragraph 9.16 has been amended to specify which financial statements of the subsidiary are permitted to be used in the consolidation.
		Paragraphs 9.18A and 9.18B are inserted to clarify the treatment of a disposal where control is lost.
		Paragraph 9.19A is inserted to clarify the treatment of the disposal where control is retained.
		Paragraph 9.19B is inserted to clarify the treatment of an acquisition made in stages.
		Paragraphs 9.19C and 9.19D are inserted to clarify the treatment of non-controlling interest when a parent changes its holding in a subsidiary but control is retained.
		Paragraphs 9.23A to 9.25 are amended to clarify the distinction between the individual financial statements and separate financial statements and that the Act specifies when individual financial statements are required to be prepared.
		Paragraphs 9.28 to 9.30 relating to combined financial statements are deleted.
		Paragraphs 9.31 and 9.32 provide guidance on exchanges of businesses or other non-monetary assets for an interest in a subsidiary, joint venture or associate. This guidance was previously contained in UITF Abstract 31 *Exchanges of businesses or other non-monetary assets for an interest in a subsidiary, joint venture or associate.*
		Paragraphs 9.33 to 9.38 are inserted to provide guidance on the accounting treatment for intermediate payment arrangements. These were previously contained in UITF Abstract 32 *Employee benefit trusts and other intermediate payment arrangements.*

Section		Changes to the IFRS for SMEs
10	Accounting Policies, Estimates and Errors	Paragraph 10.5 clarifies when an entity is required to refer to SORPs in developing an accounting policy.
		Paragraph 10.10A is inserted to bring the accounting treatment for changes in accounting policy relating to property, plant and equipment (Section 17) and intangible assets (Section 18) in line with IAS 10 *Accounting Policies, Estimate and Errors*.
11	Basic Financial Instruments	The scope of Section 11 is amended to clarify that certain financial instruments are not within its scope.
		Paragraph 11.8(b) is amended to clarify that instruments as described in paragraph 11.6(b) are not debt instruments accounted for under Section 11.
		Paragraph 11.9(a) is amended to clarify the permissible contractual returns to the lender.
		Paragraph 11.9(aA) is added to include some contractual provisions that provide for a linkage of repayments and/or returns to the lender based on inflation.
		Paragraph 11.9(aB) is added to permit certain variations of the return to the holder during the life of the instrument.
		Paragraph 11.9(c) is amended to clarify that contractual prepayment provisions which are contingent future events exclude those which protect the holder from credit deterioration, changes in central bank levies or tax changes and to clarify when compensation payments do not breach the condition.
		The text of paragraph 11.9(d) is deleted as it is no longer needed.
		Paragraph 11.9(e) is added to permit certain contractual extension options.
		Examples are inserted after paragraph 11.9 to illustrate the application of paragraph 11.9.
		Paragraphs 11.11(b) and (c) are deleted as the instruments shown as examples are excluded from debt instruments within the scope of Section 11 under paragraph 11.8(b).
		Paragraph 11.14(b) is inserted to clarify that entities may choose to designate debt instruments and loan commitments as fair value through profit or loss under certain circumstances.

Section		Changes to the IFRS for SMEs
		Paragraph 11.38A is inserted to allow offsetting of certain financial assets and financial liabilities in the statement of financial position.
		Paragraph 11.48A is inserted to provide disclosures required in accordance with the Regulations for financial instruments that are not held as part of a trading portfolio and are not derivatives.
		Paragraphs 11.48B and 11.48C require additional disclosures for financial institutions.
12	Other Financial Instruments Issues	The scope of Section 12 is amended to exclude financial instruments issued by an entity with a discretionary participation feature, reimbursement assets and financial guarantee contracts.
		Paragraph 12.8(c) is added to clarify when financial instruments within the scope of Section 12 should not be measured at amortised cost.
		Paragraphs 12.15 to 12.29 are deleted and replaced with paragraphs 12.15 to 12.29A to include revised hedge accounting requirements which have the following effect:
		(a) the scope of permissible hedged items and hedging instruments is expanded;
		(b) the hedge accounting conditions are revised and simplified;
		(c) it determines three hedge accounting models, ie cash flow, fair value and net investment hedges;
		(d) it clarifies that the cumulative amount of foreign exchange differences relating to a hedge of a net investment in a foreign operation is not reclassified to profit or loss on disposal or partial disposal; and
		(e) it introduces a documentation requirement in cases of voluntary hedge accounting discontinuation.
		Paragraph 12.25B is inserted to allow offsetting of certain financial assets and financial liabilities in the statement of financial position.
		Paragraph 12.26 is amended to comply with requirements set out in the Act.
		The Appendix to Section 12 is inserted to illustrate by way of example the application of the hedge accounting requirements.

Section		Changes to the IFRS for SMEs
13	Inventories	Paragraphs 13.4A and 13.20A are inserted to provide guidance on inventories held for distribution at no or nominal consideration.
		Paragraph 13.5A is inserted to provide guidance on inventory acquired through non-exchange transactions.
		Paragraph 13.8A is inserted to clarify the treatment for provisions made against dismantling and restoration costs (of PPE) in the cost of inventory.
		Paragraph 13.12 is deleted because of the revisions to the hedge accounting requirements.
		Paragraph 13.15 is amended to allow for the inclusion of a cost model for agricultural produce in Section 34 *Specialised Activities*.
14	Investments in Associates	The scope of this section is amended to clarify its application to consolidated financial statements and to the financial statements of an entity that is not a parent but which holds investments in associates.
		Paragraph 14.4(b) of the IFRS for SMEs is deleted as the equity method of accounting for investments in associates in individual financial statements is not compliant with company law. Paragraph 14.4(d) is inserted to allow non-parent investors to account for investments in associates at fair value with changes recognised in profit or loss.
		Paragraphs 14.4B is inserted to require an investor that is a parent which has investments in associates that are held as part of an investment portfolio to measure those investments at fair value with the changes recognised in profit or loss in their consolidated financial statements.
		Paragraph 14.9 is amended to require transaction costs to be included as part of the transaction price on initial recognition.
		Paragraph 14.10 is amended to require changes in fair value to be recognised through other comprehensive income, in accordance with paragraphs 17.15E and 17.15F, when the fair value model is applied, rather than through profit or loss.
		Paragraph 14.15A is inserted to provide information about associates held by entities that are not parents.

Section		Changes to the IFRS for SMEs
15	Investments in Joint Ventures	The scope of this section is amended to clarify its application to consolidated financial statements and to the financial statements of a venture that is not a parent.
		Paragraph 15.9(b) of the IFRS for SMEs is deleted as the equity method of accounting for interests in jointly controlled entities in individual financial statements is not compliant with company law. Paragraph 15.9(d) is inserted to allow non-parent investors to account for investments in jointly controlled entities at fair value with the changes recognised in profit or loss.
		Paragraph 15.9B is inserted to require an investor that is a parent which has investments in jointly controlled entities that are held as part of an investment portfolio to measure those investments at fair value with the changes recognised in profit or loss in their consolidated financial statements.
		Paragraph 15.14 is amended to require transaction costs to be included as part of the transaction price on initial recognition.
		Paragraph 15.15 is amended to require changes in fair value to be recognised through other comprehensive income, in accordance with paragraphs 17.15E and 17.15F, when the fair value model is applied, rather than through profit or loss.
		Paragraph 15.21A is inserted to provide information about associates held by entities that are not parents.
16	Investment Property	No significant changes.
17	Property, Plant and Equipment	Section 17 is amended to provide, after initial recognition, that an entity may use the cost model or revaluation model.
18	Intangible Assets other than Goodwill	Section 18 is amended to permit entities to recognise intangible assets that result from expenditure incurred on the internal development of an intangible item (subject to certain criteria). The section provides guidance on what comprises the cost of an internally generated intangible asset and the criteria for initial recognition.
		The section is also amended to provide, after initial recognition, that an entity may use the cost model or revaluation model.

Section		Changes to the IFRS for SMEs
19	Business Combinations and Goodwill	Section 19 is amended to permit the use of merger accounting method for group reconstructions. The merger method is set out in paragraphs 19.29 to 19.33.
		Paragraphs 19.15A to 19.15C are inserted to provide guidance on the treatment of deferred tax assets or liabilities, employee benefit arrangements and share-based payments of a subsidiary on acquisition.
		Paragraph 19.23(a) is amended to comply with company law such that, where an entity is unable to make a reliable estimate of the useful life of goodwill, the life shall be presumed not to exceed five years rather than 10 years as set out in the IFRS for SMEs.
		Paragraph 19.24 is amended and paragraph 19.26A is inserted to comply with the requirements of the Act for bargain purchases (negative goodwill).
20	Leases	The scope of Section 20 is amended to include operating leases that are onerous within its scope.
		Paragraphs 20.15A and 20.25A are inserted to clarify the treatment of operating lease incentives for lessees and lessors respectively.
		Paragraph 20.15B is inserted to provide guidance on the treatment of onerous operating lease contracts.
21	Provisions and Contingencies	The scope of Section 21 is amended to include financial guarantee contracts. Paragraph 21.17A is inserted to provide guidance on the accounting treatment of financial guarantee contracts.
22	Liabilities and Equity	Paragraph 22.3A is inserted to clarify that a financial instrument where the issuer does not have the unconditional right to avoid settling in cash or by delivery of another financial asset (or otherwise to settle it in such a way that it would be a financial liability); and where settlement is dependent on the occurrence or non-occurrence of uncertain future events beyond the control of the issuer and the holder, is a financial liability of the issuer unless specific circumstances apply.
		The requirement for an entity to recognise a liability at fair value when non-cash assets are distributed to owners is removed and only disclosure is required in paragraph 22.18.
23	Revenue	No significant changes.

Section		Changes to the IFRS for SMEs
24	Government Grants	Paragraphs 24.5C to 24.5G are inserted to allow an additional model of accounting for grants (the accrual model). The model permits entities to recognise grant income on a systematic basis over the period in which the entity recognises the related costs for which the grant is intended to compensate.
25	Borrowing Costs	Section 25 is amended to allow an option that permits entities to capitalise borrowing costs that are directly attributable to the acquisition, construction or production of a qualifying asset.
26	Share-based Payment	The definition of equity-settled share based payments has been amended to align with the revised IFRS 2 definition. It is clarified that option pricing models do not have to be applied in all circumstances.
27	Impairment of Assets	Paragraph 27.20A is inserted to provide guidance on the treatment of impairments on assets held for their service potential.
		Paragraph 27.31 is amended to allow the reversal of impairment losses against goodwill.
		Paragraph 27.33A is inserted to include a descriptive disclosure requirement of the events and circumstances that led to the recognition or reversal of the impairment loss.
28	Employee Benefits	The presentation of the cost of a defined benefit plan and the accounting for group plans have been amended to be consistent with the requirements of IAS 19 *Employee Benefits* as amended in 2011.
		Paragraph 28.11A is inserted to require the recognition of a liability on a defined benefit multi-employer plan, which is accounted as defined contribution scheme, where funding of a deficit has been agreed.
		Paragraph 28.19 is deleted to remove the option to use a simplified valuation method in measuring the liability.
29	Income Tax	Section 29 of the IFRS for SMEs has been entirely replaced with revised requirements.
30	Foreign Currency Translation	No significant changes.
31	Hyperinflation	No significant changes.
32	Events after the End of the Reporting Period	Paragraphs 32.7A and 32.7B are inserted to provide guidance on the impact of changes in an entity's going concern status.

Section		Changes to the IFRS for SMEs
33	Related Party Disclosures	Paragraph 33.1A is inserted to include the exemption from disclosure of related party transactions for wholly-owned entities available in the Act.
34	Specialised Activities	Agriculture – this sub-section is amended to allow the option to hold biological assets and agricultural produce at cost.
		Extractives – this sub-section has been amended to require application of IFRS 6.
		Service concession arrangements – this sub-section is amended to clarify the accounting by operators and provide guidance to grantors.
		The following additional sub-sections are inserted:
		• Financial Institutions;
		• Retirement Benefit Plans: Financial Statements;
		• Heritage Assets;
		• Funding Commitments;
		• Incoming Resources from Non-Exchange Transactions;
		• Public Benefit Entity Combinations; and
		• Public Benefit Entity Concessionary Loans.
35	Transition to this FRS	Amendments to this section reflect the changes in preceding sections.

Prospective amendments: Amendments to FRS 102 *The Financial Reporting Standard applicable in the UK and Republic of Ireland* – Small entities and other minor amendments (July 2015) amends Appendix II with effect for annual periods beginning on or after 1 January 2016.

Appendix III
Table of equivalence for UK Companies Act terminology

The following table compares company law terminology with broadly equivalent terminology used in FRS 102. In some cases there are minor differences between the broadly equivalent definitions, which are also summarised below.

Company law terminology	FRS 102 terminology
Accounting reference date	Reporting date
Accounts	Financial statements
Associated undertaking	Associate
Balance sheet	Statement of financial position
Capital and reserves	Equity
Cash at bank and in hand	Cash[32]
Debtors	Trade receivables
Diminution in value [of assets]	Impairment
Financial year	Reporting period
Group [accounts]	Consolidated [financial statements]
IAS	EU-adopted IFRS
Individual [accounts]	Individual [financial statements]
Interest payable and similar charges	Finance costs
Interest receivable and similar income	Finance income/Investment income
Minority interests	Non-controlling interest
Net realisable value [of any current asset]	Estimated selling price less costs to complete and sell
Parent undertaking	Parent
Profit and loss account	Income statement (under the two-statement approach)
	Part of the statement of comprehensive income (under the single- statement approach)
Related undertakings[33]	Subsidiaries, associates and joint ventures
Stocks	Inventories
Subsidiary undertaking	Subsidiary
Tangible assets	Includes: Property, plant equipment; Investment property
Trade creditors	Trade payables

[32] *FRS 102 requires the cash flow statement to reconcile the movement in cash and cash equivalents. Disclosure is required of reconciliation between amounts presented in the statement of financial position (ie cash) and cash and cash equivalents.*

[33] *This would also include entities in which a company has at least a 20% holding, but which are not a subsidiary, joint venture or an associate. A shareholding of 20% is presumed to give significant influence to the holder, such that the investment would be classified as an associate, therefore in practice there are unlikely to be many related undertakings that are not subsidiaries, joint ventures or associates.*

Appendix IV
Note on legal requirements

INTRODUCTION

This appendix provides an overview of how the requirements in FRS 102 address United **A4.1**
Kingdom company law requirements. It is therefore written from the perspective of a
company to which the Companies Act 2006 applies[34]. Appendix VI contains the Republic
of Ireland legal references.

Many entities that are not constituted as companies apply accounting standards promulgated **A4.2**
by the FRC for the purposes of preparing financial statements that present a true and
fair view[35]. A brief consideration of the legal framework for some other entities can be
found at A4.41 and A4.42. For those entities that are within the scope of a Statement of
Recommended Practice (SORP), the relevant SORP will provide more details on the legal
framework.

References to the Act in this appendix are to the *Companies Act 2006*. References to **A4.3**
the Regulations are to *The Large and Medium-sized Companies and Groups (Accounts
and Reports) Regulations 2008* (SI 2008/410). References to specific provisions are to
Schedule 1 to the Regulations; entities applying Schedules 2, 3 or 6 should read them as
referring to the equivalent paragraph in those schedules.

Prospective amendments: Amendments to FRS 102 *The Financial Reporting Standard
applicable in the UK and Republic of Ireland* – Small entities and other minor amendments
(July 2015) amends this paragraph A4.3 with effect for annual periods beginning on or
after 1 January 2016.

APPLICABLE ACCOUNTING FRAMEWORK

Group accounts of certain parent entities (those with securities admitted to trading **A4.4**
on a regulated market in an EU Member State) are required by Article 4 of EU
Regulation 1606/2002 (IAS Regulation) to be prepared in accordance with EU-adopted
IFRS.

All other entities, except those that are eligible to apply the *Financial Reporting Standard* **A4.5**
for Smaller Entities (effective January 2015) (FRSSE), must apply[36] either FRS 102 *The
Financial Reporting Standard applicable in the UK and Republic of Ireland*, EU-adopted
IFRS or FRS 101 (if the financial statements are the individual financial statements of a
qualifying entity eligible to apply FRS 101 *Reduced Disclosure Framework*).

Prospective amendments: Amendments to FRS 102 *The Financial Reporting Standard
applicable in the UK and Republic of Ireland* – Small entities and other minor amendments
(July 2015) amends this paragraph A4.5 with effect for annual periods beginning on or
after 1 January 2016.

[34] *Some charities are also companies, and are therefore required to apply the requirements of both the
Companies Act 2006 and the Charities Act 2011.*
[35] *More information about the 'true and fair' concept can be found on the FRC's website at http://www.frc.org.
uk/Our-Work/Codes-Standards/Accounting-and-Reporting-Policy/True-and-Fair.aspx.*
[36] *Under company law in the Republic of Ireland, certain entities are permitted to prepare Companies Act
accounts using accounting standards other than those issued by the FRC. Please refer to Appendix VI for
further details.*

A4.6   Section 395(1) of the Act states:

"A company's individual accounts may be prepared –

    (a)   in accordance with section 396 ('Companies Act individual accounts'), or

    (b)   in accordance with international accounting standards ('IAS individual accounts')."

Section 403(2) of the Act states:

"The group accounts of other companies may be prepared –

    (a)   in accordance with section 404 ('Companies Act group accounts'), or

    (b)   in accordance with international accounting standards ('IAS group accounts')."

A4.7   Accounts prepared in accordance with FRS 102 are classified as either 'Companies Act individual accounts', including those of qualifying entities applying FRS 102, or 'Companies Act group accounts' and are therefore required to comply with the applicable provisions of Parts 15 and 16 of the Act and with the Regulations.

Consistency of financial reporting within groups

A4.8   Section 407 of the Act requires that the directors of the parent company secure that individual accounts of a parent company and each of its subsidiaries are prepared using the same financial reporting framework, except to the extent that in the directors' opinion there are good reasons for not doing so.

In addition, consistency is not required in the following situations:

    (a)   when the parent company does not prepare consolidated financial statements; or

    (b)   when some subsidiaries are charities (consistency is not needed between the framework used for these and for other subsidiaries).

Where the directors of a parent company prepare IAS group accounts and IAS individual accounts, there only has to be consistency across the individual financial statements of the subsidiaries.

A4.9   All companies, other than those which elect or are required to prepare IAS individual accounts in accordance with the Act, prepare Companies Act individual accounts.

APPLICATION OF FRS 102

Compliance with company law

A4.10   The FRS has been developed for application in the UK and Republic of Ireland, using the IFRS for SMEs as a basis. Part of that development process included making amendments to the IFRS for SMEs to ensure compliance with the Act and the Regulations. For example, changes were made to eliminate options that are not permitted by company law. However, FRS 102 is not intended to be a one-stop-shop for all accounting and legal requirements, and although the FRC believes FRS 102 is not inconsistent with company law, compliance with FRS 102 alone will often be insufficient to ensure compliance with all the disclosure requirements set out in the Act and the Regulations. As a result preparers will continue to be required to have regard to the requirements of company law in addition to accounting standards.

This appendix does not list every legal requirement, but instead focuses on those areas where greater judgement might be required in determining compliance with the law. **A4.11**

Prospective amendments: Amendments to FRS 102 *The Financial Reporting Standard applicable in the UK and Republic of Ireland* – Small entities and other minor amendments (July 2015) inserts a sub-heading after paragraph A4.11 and paragraphs A4.11A to A4.11E with effect for annual periods beginning on or after 1 January 2016.

Financial instruments measured at fair value

All preparers of Companies Act accounts must comply with the requirements of paragraph 36 of Schedule 1 to the Regulations, which provides that: **A4.12**

"(1) Subject to sub-paragraphs (2) to (5), financial instruments (including derivatives) may be included at fair value.

(2) Sub-paragraph (1) does not apply to financial instruments that constitute liabilities unless –

   (a)   they are held as part of a trading portfolio,

   (b)   they are derivatives, or

   (c)   they are financial instruments falling within sub-paragraph (4).

(3) Unless they are financial instruments falling within sub-paragraph (4), subparagraph (1) does not apply to –

   (a)   financial instruments (other than derivatives) held to maturity,

   (b)   loans and receivables originated by the company and not held for trading purposes,

   (c)   interests in subsidiary undertakings, associated undertakings and joint ventures,

   (d)   equity instruments issued by the company,

   (e)   contracts for contingent consideration in a business combination, or

   (f)   other financial instruments with such special characteristics that the instruments, according to generally accepted accounting principles or practice, should be accounted for differently from other financial instruments.

(4) Financial instruments that, under international accounting standards adopted by the European Commission on or before 5th September 2006 in accordance with the IAS Regulation, may be included in accounts at fair value, may be so included, provided that the disclosures required by such accounting standards are made.

(5) [...]"

Prospective amendments: Amendments to FRS 102 *The Financial Reporting Standard applicable in the UK and Republic of Ireland* – Small entities and other minor amendments (July 2015) amends this paragraph A4.12 with effect for annual periods beginning on or after 1 January 2016.

In limited circumstances, an entity applying this FRS to its financial instruments that are classified as non-basic in accordance with Section 11 *Basic Financial Instruments* may be prohibited, by paragraph 36 of Schedule 1 to the Regulations, to measure those financial instruments at fair value through profit or loss in accordance with the requirements of this FRS. The Regulations prohibit the measurement of certain financial instruments at fair value through profit or loss, unless the instruments could be designated for such measurement under EU-adopted IFRS. EU-adopted IFRS permits designation at fair value through profit or loss upon initial recognition for financial instruments where: doing so eliminates or reduces a measurement or recognition inconsistency; or a group of financial instruments is managed and their performance evaluated on a fair value basis; or for a **A4.12A** hybrid financial instruments which contains a component that, if recognised separately, would meet the definition of a derivative. Paragraph 12.8(c) of this FRS is applicable to the measurement of financial instruments prohibited under the Regulations to be measured at fair value through profit or loss and requires them to be measured at amortised cost.

Prospective amendments: Amendments to FRS 102 *The Financial Reporting Standard applicable in the UK and Republic of Ireland* – Small entities and other minor amendments (July 2015) insert paragraphs A4.12B, A4.12C and A4.12D with effect for annual periods beginning on or after 1 January 2016.

A4.13   An entity applying this FRS and holding financial instruments measured at fair value either in accordance with Sections 11 or 12 *Other Financial Instruments Issues* may be required to provide the disclosures required by paragraph 36(4) of Schedule 1 to the Regulations. The disclosures as required by paragraph 36(4) have been incorporated into Section 11. Some of the Section 11 disclosure requirements apply to all financial instruments measured at fair value, whilst others (see paragraph 11.48A of FRS 102) apply only to financial instruments that are not held as part of a trading portfolio and are not derivatives. The disclosure requirements of paragraph 11.48A will predominantly apply to certain financial liabilities, however, there may be instances where paragraph 36(3) of Schedule 1 to the Regulations requires that the disclosures must also be provided in relation to financial assets, for example investments in subsidiaries, associates or jointly controlled entities measured at fair value (see paragraph 9.27B of FRS 102).

Prospective amendments: Amendments to FRS 102 *The Financial Reporting Standard applicable in the UK and Republic of Ireland* – Small entities and other minor amendments (July 2015) amends this paragraph A4.13 with effect for annual periods beginning on or after 1 January 2016.

Requirement to present financial statements

A4.14   FRS 102 does not prescribe which entities prepare financial statements and preparers should apply the requirements of the Act in determining whether financial statements (either individual or consolidated) are required. FRS 102 sets out the requirements for a complete set of financial statements that present fairly the financial position, financial performance and cash flows of an entity, where these are required by law, or other regulation or requirement.

Prospective amendments: Amendments to FRS 102 *The Financial Reporting Standard applicable in the UK and Republic of Ireland* – Small entities and other minor amendments (July 2015) amends this paragraph A4.14 with effect for annual periods beginning on or after 1 January 2016.

A4.15   A parent company preparing consolidated financial statements under section 434(2) of the Act must publish its company financial statements together with the consolidated financial statements, although section 408 of the Act provides an exemption from including the company's individual profit and loss account.

Subsidiaries excluded from consolidation

A4.16   Paragraph 9.9(b) of Section 9 *Consolidated and Separate Financial Statements* requires a group to exclude subsidiaries from consolidation on the grounds that they are held exclusively with a view to subsequent resale. By defining 'held exclusively with a view to subsequent resale' in FRS 102 to include those interests that are held as part of an investment portfolio, subsidiaries held as part of such an investment portfolio are excluded from consolidation in accordance with section 405(3) of the Act and an entity will not need to apply the true and fair override in this circumstance.

Paragraph 9.9B(a) requires a group to measure subsidiaries excluded from consolidation by virtue of paragraph 9.9(b) and held as part of an investment portfolio, at fair value through profit or loss. The measurement at fair value through profit and loss is a departure from the requirements of paragraph 36 of Schedule 1 to the Regulations, for the overriding purpose of giving a true and fair view in the consolidated financial statements. In this circumstance, entities must provide in the notes to the financial statements the 'particulars of the departure, the reasons for it and its effect' (paragraph 10(2) of Schedule 1 to the Regulations).   **A4.17**

Prospective amendments: Amendments to FRS 102 *The Financial Reporting Standard applicable in the UK and Republic of Ireland* – Small entities and other minor amendments (July 2015) amends this paragraph A4.17 with effect for annual periods beginning on or after 1 January 2016.

Calculation of goodwill where a business combination is achieved in stages

Paragraph 9 of Schedule 6 to the Regulations sets out the requirements for the acquisition method of accounting, which results in goodwill (or negative goodwill) being calculated as the difference between: **A4.18**

(a) the fair value of the group's share of identifiable assets and liabilities of the subsidiary at the date control is achieved; and

(b) the total acquisition cost of the interests held by the group in that subsidiary.

This applies even where part of the acquisition cost arises from purchases at earlier dates.

In most cases, this method provides a practical means of applying acquisition accounting because it does not require retrospective assessments of the fair value of the identifiable assets and liabilities of the subsidiary. In certain circumstances, however, not using fair values at the dates of earlier purchases while using acquisition costs which in part relate to earlier purchases may result in accounting that is inconsistent with the way the investment has been treated previously and, for that reason, may fail to give a true and fair view.   **A4.19**

For example, an undertaking that has been treated as an associate may then be acquired by that group as a subsidiary. Using the method required by the Regulations and paragraph 9.19B of FRS 102 to calculate goodwill on such an acquisition has the effect that the group's share of profits or losses and reserve movements of its associate becomes reclassified as goodwill (usually negative goodwill). A similar problem may arise where the group has substantially restated its investment in an undertaking that subsequently becomes its subsidiary. For example, where such an investment has been written down because it is impaired, the effect of applying the Regulations' method of acquisition accounting would be to increase reserves and create an asset (goodwill).   **A4.20**

In the rare cases where the method for calculating goodwill set out in the Regulations and in paragraph 9.19B of FRS 102 would be misleading, the goodwill should be calculated as the sum of goodwill arising from each purchase of an interest in the relevant undertaking adjusted as necessary for any subsequent impairment. Goodwill arising on each purchase should be calculated as the difference between the cost of that purchase and the fair value at the date of that purchase of the identifiable assets and liabilities attributable to the interest purchased. The difference between the goodwill calculated using this method and that calculated using the method provided by the Regulations and FRS 102 is shown in reserves. Section 404(5) of the Act sets out the disclosures required in cases where the statutory requirement is not applied. Paragraph 3.5 of FRS 102 sets out the disclosures   **A4.21** when an entity departs from a requirement of FRS 102 or from a requirement of applicable legislation.

Netting

A4.22   FRS 102 permits an expense relating to a provision to be presented net of the amount recognised for a reimbursement (which may only be recognised if it is virtually certain it will be received) (see paragraph 21.9 of FRS 102). Paragraph 8 of Schedule 1 to the Regulations requires that 'Amounts in respect of items representing assets or income may not be set off against amounts in respect of items representing liabilities or expenditure (as the case may be), or vice versa.' The reimbursement asset is recognised separately from the underlying obligation to reflect the fact that the entity often will continue to be liable if the third party from which the reimbursement is due fails to pay. On the other hand, the net presentation in the income statement reflects the cost to the entity and net presentation therefore does not conflict with the Regulation.

A4.23   FRS 102 requires that a financial asset and financial liability are offset and the net amount presented in the statement of financial position, if certain criteria are met (see paragraph 11.38A of FRS 102). The net presentation does not conflict with paragraph 8 of Schedule 1 to the Regulations, because provided the criteria for the net presentation are met, the presentation reflects the expected net cash flows from settling two or more separate financial instruments.

Recording investments at cost

A4.24   Paragraph 9.26 of FRS 102 requires that in an investor's separate financial statements its investments in subsidiaries are accounted for at cost less impairment, or at fair value. Where the cost model is applied, sections 611 to 615 of the Act set out the treatment where 'merger relief' or 'group reconstruction relief' are available. These reliefs reduce the amount required to be included in share premium; they also (in section 615) allow the initial carrying amount to be adjusted downwards so it is equal to either the previous carrying amount of the investment in the transferor's books or the nominal value of the shares issued, depending on which relief applies. If the fair value model in paragraph 9.26 is used, then the relief in section 615 is not available, so the investment's carrying value may not be reduced, although the provisions in sections 611 and 612 remain relevant in respect of amounts required to be recorded in share premium.

Realised profits

A4.25   Paragraph 13(a) of Schedule 1 to the Regulations requires that only profits realised at the reporting date are included in profit or loss, a requirement modified from that in Article 31.1(c)(aa) of the Fourth Directive which refers to profits 'made' at the balance sheet date.

A4.26   Paragraph 36(4) and paragraph 39 of Schedule 1 to the Regulations allow that financial instruments, investment property, and living animals and plants that may under international accounting standards be held at fair value, may also be held at fair value in Companies Act accounts.

Prospective amendments: Amendments to FRS 102 *The Financial Reporting Standard applicable in the UK and Republic of Ireland* – Small entities and other minor amendments (July 2015) amends this paragraph A4.26 with effect for annual periods beginning on or after 1 January 2016.

Paragraph 40(2) of Schedule 1 to the Regulations then requires that movements in the value of financial instruments, investment properties and living animals and plants are recognised in the profit and loss account, notwithstanding the usual restrictions allowing only realised profits and losses to be included in the profit and loss account. Paragraph 40 of Schedule 1 to the Regulations thereby overrides the requirements of paragraph 13(a) of Schedule 1. **A4.27**

Entities measuring financial instruments, investment properties, and living animals and plants at fair value should note that they may transfer such amounts to a separate non-distributable reserve, instead of a transfer to retained earnings, but are not required to do so. Presenting fair value movements, that are not distributable profits, in the separate reserve may assist with the identification of profits available for that purpose. **A4.28**

The determination of profits available for distribution is a complex area where accounting and company law interface. In determining profits available for distribution an entity may refer to Technical Release 02/10 *Guidance on realised and distributable profits under the Companies Act 2006* issued by the Institute of Chartered Accountants in England and Wales and the Institute of Chartered Accountants of Scotland, or any successor document, to determine profits available for distribution.. **A4.29**

Merger accounting

Paragraph 10 of Schedule 6 to the Regulations permits the use of merger accounting in certain circumstances. FRS 102 requires the application of the purchase method of accounting for all business combinations within the scope of Section 19 *Business Combinations and Goodwill*, other than group reconstructions. Paragraph 19.27 permits merger accounting for group reconstructions. Section 34 *Specialised Activities* requires that combinations by public benefit entities meeting certain criteria are accounted for as a merger. FRS 102 therefore restricts the circumstances in which merger accounting may be applied. **A4.30**

Prospective amendments: Amendments to FRS 102 *The Financial Reporting Standard applicable in the UK and Republic of Ireland* – Small entities and other minor amendments (July 2015) amends this paragraph A4.30, with the second part of the paragraph now shown as a separate paragraph A4.30A with effect for annual periods beginning on or after 1 January 2016.

Treasury shares

Paragraph 22.16 of FRS 102 sets out the accounting requirements when an entity purchases its own equity instruments (ie treasury shares). **A4.31**

Companies subject to the Act, need to comply with the accounting requirements of paragraph 22.16 as well as with the requirements of the Act when they purchase their own equity and hold it in treasury (Sections 690 to 708 and 724 to 732, respectively). **A4.32**

Measurement of investments in associates and jointly controlled entities for an investor, which is not a parent

Paragraph 36 of Schedule 1 to the Regulations sets out the fair value accounting rules and permits investments in associates and joint ventures to be measured at fair value through profit or loss only where they are permitted to be treated as financial instruments in accordance with IAS Regulation. EU-adopted IFRS does allow investments in subsidiaries, associates and jointly controlled entities to be measured in accordance with **A4.33**

IAS 39 *Financial Instruments Recognition and Measurement* within separate financial statements (as set out in IAS 27 *Consolidated and Separate Financial Statements*).

A4.34   Therefore, where the fair value model is applied by an investor, changes in fair value may be recognised through profit or loss, or other comprehensive income. Under the alternative accounting rules set out in Section C of Schedule 1 to the Regulations, the initial recognition of the investment must include any expenses that are incidental to the acquisition of the investment.

Measurement of inventories held for distribution at no or nominal value

A4.35   Paragraph 24(1) of Schedule 1 to the Regulations requires that if the net realisable value of any current asset is lower than its purchase price or production cost, the amount to be included in respect of that asset must be the net realisable value. However, paragraph 32(5) permits stocks to be included at their current cost, when applying the alternative accounting rules.

Prospective amendments: Amendments to FRS 102 *The Financial Reporting Standard applicable in the UK and Republic of Ireland* – Small entities and other minor amendments (July 2015) amends this paragraph A4.35 with effect for annual periods beginning on or after 1 January 2016.

A4.36   Inventories held for distribution at no or nominal value include items that might be distributed to beneficiaries by public benefit entities and items such as advertising and promotional material. As the items will be distributed at no or nominal cost, the net realisable value will usually be lower than the purchase price.

A4.37   However, paragraph 13.4A of FRS 102 requires inventories held for distribution at no or nominal cost to be measured at cost. Although the alternative accounting rules require measurement at current cost, for inventories held for distribution at no or nominal value, there is unlikely to be a significant difference between cost and current cost.

Prospective amendments: Amendments to FRS 102 *The Financial Reporting Standard applicable in the UK and Republic of Ireland* – Small entities and other minor amendments (July 2015) amends this paragraph A4.37 and paragraph A4.37A and the sub-heading preceding it are to be inserted with effect for annual periods beginning on or after 1 January 2016.

Accounts formats

A4.38   Sections 4 and 5 of FRS 102 require entities to apply one of the profit and loss account and balance sheet formats set out in the Regulations and LLP Regulations, when preparing their statement of comprehensive income (single-statement approach) or income statement (two-statement approach) and statement of financial position, respectively.

Prospective amendments: Amendments to FRS 102 *The Financial Reporting Standard applicable in the UK and Republic of Ireland* – Small entities and other minor amendments (July 2015) amends this paragraph A4.38 with effect for annual periods beginning on or after 1 January 2016.

Discontinued operations

A4.39   FRS 102 requires an entity with discontinued operations, to provide an analysis between continuing operations and discontinued operations of each of the line items on the face of the statement of comprehensive income, or income statement, up to and including post-tax profit or loss for the period and illustrates this presentation in a columnar format. This is in order to present the post-tax results of those operations, combined with the profit or loss on their disposal, as a single line item while still complying with the requirement of company law to show totals for ordinary activities of items such as turnover, profit or loss before taxation and tax.

Long-term debtors

UITF Abstract 4 *Presentation of long-term debtors in current assets* addressed the inclusion of debtors due after more than one year within 'current assets'; that UITF consensus has been withdrawn, but its conclusions remain valid and have been included in paragraph 4.4A of FRS 102. **A4.40**

Entities not subject to company law

Many entities that apply FRS 102 are not companies, but are nevertheless required by their governing legislation, or other regulation or requirement to prepare financial statements that present a true and fair view of the financial performance and financial position of the reporting entity. However, the FRC sets accounting standards within the framework of the Act and therefore it is the company law requirements that the FRC primarily considered when developing FRS 102. Entities preparing financial statements within other legal frameworks will need to satisfy themselves that FRS 102 does not conflict with any relevant legal obligations. **A4.41**

However, the FRC notes the following: **A4.42**

Legislation	Overview of requirements
Building Societies Act 1986	The annual accounts of a building society shall give a true and fair of the income and expenditure for the year and the balance sheet shall give a true and fair view of the state of affairs of the society at the end of the financial year.
	Regulations make further requirements about the form and content of building society accounts, which do not appear inconsistent with the requirement of FRS 102.
Charity law in England and Wales: Charities Act 2011 and regulations made thereunder	All charities are required to prepare accounts. The regulations require financial statements (other than cash-based receipts and payments accounts prepared by smaller charities) to present a true and fair view of the incoming resources, application of resources and the balance sheet, and to be prepared in accordance with the SORP. However company charities prepare their accounts in accordance with UK company law to give a 'true and fair view'.
	The Charities SORP 2005 requires the application of accounting standards and is compatible with the legal requirements, clarifying how they apply to accounting by charities. The SORP will be updated to reflect the requirements of FRS 102.
	UK company law prohibits charities from preparing IAS accounts.

Legislation	Overview of requirements
Charity law in Scotland: Charities and Trustee Investments Act (Scotland) 2005 and regulations made thereunder	All charities are required to prepare accounts. The regulations require financial statements (other than cash-based receipts and payments accounts prepared by smaller charities) to present a true and fair view of the incoming resources, application of resources and the balance sheet, and to be prepared in accordance with the SORP. These regulations apply equally to company charities.
Charity law in Northern Ireland: Charities Act (Northern Ireland) 2008	The Charities Act 2008 has yet to come fully into effect. The Act provides for all charities to prepare accounts. The Act provides for regulations concerning the financial statements. The financial statements other than cash-based receipts and payments accounts prepared by smaller charities are to present a true and fair view of the incoming resources, application of resources and the balance sheet. However company charities prepare their accounts in accordance with UK company law to give a 'true and fair view'.
Friendly and Industrial and Provident Societies Act 1968	Every Society shall prepare a revenue account and a balance sheet giving a true and fair view of the income and expenditure and state of affairs of the Society. FRS 102 does not appear to give rise to any legal conflicts for Societies. However, Societies often carry out activities that are regulated and may be required to comply with additional regulations on top of the legal requirements and accounting standards. Some Societies fall within the scope of SORPs, which may be updated to reflect the requirements of FRS 102.
Friendly Societies Act 1992	Every society shall prepare a balance sheet and an income and expenditure account for each financial year giving a true and fair view of the affairs of the society and its income and expenditure for the year. The Regulations[37] make further requirements about the form and content of friendly society accounts, which do not appear inconsistent with the requirements of FRS 102.
The Occupational Pension Schemes (Requirement to obtain Audited Accounts and a Statement from the Auditor) Regulations 1996	The accounts of pension funds within the scope of the regulations should show a true and fair view of the transactions during the year, assets held at the end of the year and liabilities of the scheme, other than those to pay pensions and benefits. FRS 102 includes retirement benefit plans as a specialised activity.

Prospective amendments: Amendments to FRS 102 *The Financial Reporting Standard applicable in the UK and Republic of Ireland* – Small entities and other minor amendments (July 2015) insert paragraphs A4.43 to A4.47 and the related sub-headings with effect for annual periods beginning on or after 1 January 2016.

---

[37] *The Friendly Societies (Accounts and Related Provisions) Regulations 1994 (as amended).*

Appendix V
Previous consultations

The requirements in FRSs 100 to 102 are the outcome of a lengthy and extensive consultation. The FRC (and formerly the ASB) together with the Department for Business, Innovation and Skills have consulted on the future of accounting standards in the UK and Republic of Ireland (RoI) over a ten-year period.   **A5.1**

Table 1 – Consultations conducted

Year	Consultation
2002	DTI[38] consults on adoption of IAS Regulation
2004	Discussion Paper – Strategy for Convergence with IFRS
2005	Exposure Draft – Policy Statement: The Role of the ASB
2006	Public Meeting and Proposals for Comment
2006	Press Notice seeking views
2007	Consultation Paper – Proposed IFRS for SMEs
2009	Consultation Paper – Policy Proposal: The future of UK GAAP
2010	Request for Responses – Development of the Impact Assessment
2010	Financial Reporting Exposure Drafts 43 and 44
2011	Financial Reporting Exposure Draft 45
2012	Financial Reporting Exposure Drafts 46, 47 and 48
2012	Financial Reporting Exposure Draft: Amendment to FRED 48

2004

In 2004 the Discussion Paper contained two key elements underpinning the proposals: firstly that UK and Republic of Ireland (RoI) accounting standards should be based on IFRS and secondly that a phased approach to the introduction of the standards should be adopted.   **A5.2**

The ASB embarked on the phased approach and issued a number of standards based on IFRS. The majority of respondents agreed with a framework based on IFRS, and although supportive overall, the response to the phased approach was mixed.   **A5.3**

2005

In its 2005 Exposure Draft (2005 ED) of a Policy Statement *Accounting standard-setting in a changing environment: The role of the Accounting Standards Board*, amongst other aspects of its role, the ASB identified its intention to converge with IFRS by implementing new IFRS in the UK as soon as possible. It also proposed to continue the phased approach to   **A5.4**

---

[38] *The Department of Trade and Industry (DTI) was a United Kingdom government department which was replaced with the announcement of the creation of the Department for Business, Enterprise and Regulatory Reform and the Department for Innovation, Universities and Skills on 28 June 2007, which were themselves merged into the Department for Business, Innovation and Skills (BIS) on 6 June 2009.*

adopting UK accounting standards based on older IFRSs, but recognised there was little case for being more prescriptive than IFRS.

A5.5   Although the ASB had, in the 2005 ED, wanted to move the debate on to how it would seek to influence the IASB's agenda, respondents' main concern remained about convergence. In 2005, the ASB issued an exposure draft proposing the IASB's standard on Business Combinations be adopted in the UK and RoI. This exposure draft highlighted the complexity of a mixed set of UK accounting standards, with some based on IFRSs and others developed independently by the ASB. The majority of respondents continued to agree with the aim of basing UK accounting standards on IFRS, but a broader set of views on how to achieve this was emerging.

A5.6   As time progressed the ASB formed the view that convergence by adopting certain IFRSs was not meeting the needs of its constituents, which no longer included quoted groups. The ASB was concerned about the complexity of certain IFRSs, and it noted that introducing them piecemeal created complications and anomalies within the body of current FRSs. This arose because IFRS-based standards were not an exact replacement for current FRSs and many consequential amendments were required to 'fit' each replacement IFRS-based standard into the existing body of UK FRS. The ASB agreed to continue with its convergence programme, but decided to re-examine how to achieve this.

2006

A5.7   The ASB published revised proposals to be discussed at the 2006 public meeting. By this time the IASB had started its IFRS for SMEs project, and the ASB decided this might have a role as one of the tiers in the UK financial reporting framework. The ASB proposed a 'big bang' with new IFRS-based UK accounting standards mandatory from a single date, 1 January 2009. The ASB's proposal was for a three-tier system, with Tier 1 being EU-adopted IFRS, and the other two tiers being developed as the IASB progressed with its project on the IFRS for SMEs.

A5.8   Those attending the public meeting supported the aim of basing UK and RoI accounting standards on IFRS and adapting them to ensure they were appropriate for the entities applying them.

A5.9   Taking this feedback into account, later in 2006 the ASB issued a Press Notice (PN 289) seeking views on its current thinking:

(a)   All quoted and publicly accountable companies should apply EU-adopted IFRS.

(b)   The FRSSE should be retained and extended to include medium-sized entities.

(c)   UK subsidiaries of groups applying full IFRS should apply EU-adopted IFRS, but with reduced disclosure requirements.

(d)   No firm decision on the remainder (Tier 2), but options included extending the FRSSE, extending full IFRS, maintaining separate UK accounting standards or some combination of these.

A5.10   The responses were mixed, but there was agreement that whatever the solution, it should be based on IFRS and there should be different reporting tiers to ensure proportionality.

2007

A5.11   The IASB published an exposure draft of its IFRS for SMEs in early 2007; shortly afterwards the ASB published its own consultation paper. This sought views on how the IFRS for SMEs might fit into the future UK financial reporting framework, for example whether it might be appropriate for Tier 2, with the FRSSE continuing for those eligible for the small companies' regime.

Feedback on the IFRS for SMEs was largely positive: it would be suitable for Tier 2, it was international, it was compatible with IFRS, and it represented a significant simplification. Overall, it was seen as a workable alternative to IFRS. In addition, respondents wanted to retain the FRSSE (because it reduces the regulatory burden on smaller entities) and to give subsidiaries the option of applying the IFRS for SMEs as well as a reduced disclosure regime if applying full IFRS.   **A5.12**

2009

The IFRS for SMEs was published in 2009, allowing the ASB to further develop its proposals in the Consultation Paper *Policy Proposal: The future of UK GAAP*. The proposals were largely consistent with the cumulative results of the preceding consultations and included: **A5.13**

(a)   a move to an IFRS-based framework;
(b)   a three-tier approach;
(c)   publicly accountable entities would be Tier 1 and would apply EU-adopted IFRS;
(d)   small companies would be Tier 3 and continue to apply the FRSSE; and
(e)   other entities would be Tier 2 and should apply a UK and RoI accounting standard based on the IFRS for SMEs.

The only significant proposal that was inconsistent with respondents' previous comments was that subsidiaries should simply apply the requirement of the tier they individually met – respondents had wanted subsidiaries to be able to take advantage of disclosure exemptions, and at that time the ASB had yet to be convinced that significant cost savings were available from a reduced disclosure framework. Taking into account the feedback received, this proposal was subsequently reversed and the reduced disclosure framework was incorporated into FREDs 43 and then 46, and it is now set out in FRS 101.   **A5.14**

In addition to the many useful and detailed points made, some common themes included general agreement that change was needed to UK accounting standards and that there was support for many of the changes proposed in the consultation paper.   **A5.15**

2010 ONWARDS

The request for responses to aid development of the Impact Assessment focused on obtaining feedback on the expected costs, benefits and impact of the proposals subsequently set out in FREDs 43 and 44, rather than on the accounting principles. As the focus was on costs and benefits no specific question was asked about the principle of the proposed introduction of an IFRS-based framework, but nevertheless respondents commented on this: of the 32 responses received only 12.5% did not agree with the introduction of an IFRS-based framework.   **A5.16**

FRED 43 and 44 issued in October 2010 set out the draft suggested text for two new accounting standards that would replace the majority of extant Financial Reporting Standards (current FRS) in the UK and RoI. The ASB issued a supplementary FRED addressing specific needs of public benefit entities (FRED 45) in March 2011. The ASB then updated FREDs 43, 44 and 45, replacing them with the revised FREDs 46, 47 and 48 in January 2012, by eliminating the concept of public accountability and by introducing a number of accounting treatment options that are available in EU-adopted IFRS. The Accounting Council's advice to the FRC to issue FRSs 100 to 102 includes more discussion of the feedback received on FREDs 43 to 48 and how the proposals have been refined and developed into the standards.   **A5.17**

HOW HAVE THE PROPOSALS BEEN DEVELOPED?

A5.18   As set out above, the FRC, the Accounting Council (and previously the ASB) have consulted regularly on the future of financial reporting in the UK and RoI. Over the consultations the ASB's (and the Accounting Council's) thinking has evolved based on careful consideration of the feedback at each stage. Whilst responses were sometimes mixed, there has been agreement that:

(a)   current FRS, which are a mixture of Statements of Standard Accounting Practice (SSAPs) issued by the Consultative Committee of Accounting Bodies, FRSs developed and issued by the ASB and IFRS-based standards issued by the ASB to converge with international standards, are an uncomfortable mismatch that lack strong underlying principles or cohesion; and

(b)   whatever the solution, it should be based on IFRS and there should be different reporting tiers to ensure proportionality.

A5.19   During the consultation process to date, the Accounting Council and formerly the ASB have been guided by the following principles:

(a)   The framework must be fit for purpose, so that each entity required to produce true and fair financial statements under UK and RoI law will deliver financial statements that are suited to the needs of its primary users. The Accounting Council has kept in close contact with constituent users on this point, including investors, creditor institutions and the tax authorities.

(b)   The framework must be proportionate, so that preparing entities are not unduly burdened by costs that outweigh the benefit to them and to the primary users of information in their financial statements. The FRC believes that the proposals will produce a lower cost regime, while enhancing user benefits. It has carried out a consultation stage impact assessment with input from interested parties, and will continue to assess cost-benefit issues.

(c)   The framework must be in line with UK company law. This determines which entities must produce true and fair financial statements. Exemptions within the law have generally been retained. The detailed requirements of the Companies Act 2006 are driven to a great extent by the European Accounting Directives, which are being revised[39].

(d)   The framework must be future-proofed, where possible. The FRC will continue to monitor the situation and has sovereignty over UK accounting standards (subject to the law). Changes to the Accounting Directives may lead to further developments, for example the European Council and European Parliament decision to permit Member States an option to treat micro-entities as a separate category of Company and exempt them from certain accounting requirements.

SUMMARY OF OUTREACH

A5.20   During the development and throughout the consultation period of FREDs 43 to 48, the ASB undertook an extensive programme of outreach aimed at raising awareness of the proposals and to address the view (held by some) that previous consultations had not gathered sufficient evidence to support and test the assumptions made.

A5.21   As part of the outreach programme to obtain both formal and informal feedback, a series of meetings and events took place with users, including with lenders to small and medium-sized entities. Lenders noted that financial statements are an important part of their decision-making process when considering whether to provide finance and, whilst a

---

[39] *The EU's consultation process on review of the Accounting Directives is summarised at http://ec.europa.eu/ internal_market/accounting/sme_accounting/review_directives_en.htm*

decision to provide finance is not based on financial statements alone, they provide useful information and verification to the lender.

Although the ASB and the Accounting Council employed their best efforts to obtain feedback from users (a constituent group historically difficult to engage with formally) it is disappointing that limited formal responses were received and the Accounting Council has not been more successful in obtaining input from users.   **A5.22**

In addition, a review was made of academic research that addressed the users of the financial statements of small and medium-sized entities. The conclusion drawn from the research was that many entities requested financial statements from Companies House when considering whether to trade with another entity. The European Federation of Accountants and Auditors (EFAA) issued, in May 2011, a statement that identified the users of financial statements, noting who the users of SMEs' financial statements are and that information on the public record assists all users of financial statements of SMEs by providing, in an efficient manner, basic information that protects their rights.   **A5.23**

The ASB considered that the outreach programme had gleaned information from people who would not normally submit formal responses to a consultation and provided very useful information that could be used in developing the next stage of the project. The ASB noted that whilst this information was not part of the public record, as are formal consultation responses, it could use the information to assist in developing the revised FREDs 46 to 48, supplementing information contained in responses, and would seek further comment in the next stage of its deliberations.   **A5.24**

The Accounting Council continued the work of the ASB in finalising FRSs 100 to 102. The responses to FREDs 46 to 48 were analysed and discussed, and engagements were conducted to take into account the views and suggestions of all relevant associations and contacts. Respondents and outreach contacts were satisfied with FREDs 46 to 48, and many of the response letters were forthcoming in their overall praise for the proposals. A significant number of constituents anticipated cost savings arising from the application of FRS 101. Many respondents considered that FRS 102 would improve UK accounting standards, in particular by introducing requirements for accounting for financial instruments. Further they considered that the improvements will be achieved in a way that will be proportionate to the needs of users, and that once the transition phase has been overcome, it will have the effect of reducing the reporting burden on those UK companies that adopt it.   **A5.25**

Appendix VI
Republic of Ireland (RoI) legal references

Prospective amendments: Amendments to FRS 102 *The Financial Reporting Standard applicable in the UK and Republic of Ireland* – Small entities and other minor amendments (July 2015) deletes Appendix VI and will be updated as appropriate for both the Companies Act 2014 and the Irish legislation implementing the EU Accounting Directive once the latter has been made. This will be included in the next edition of FRS 102 with effect for annual periods beginning on or after 1 January 2016.

INTRODUCTION

A6.1   The table below outlines the provisions in the Companies Acts 1963 to 2012 and related Regulations which implement EC Accounting Directives (Irish company law), corresponding to the provisions of the UK *Companies Act 2006* (the 2006 Act) and the UK *Large and Medium-sized Companies and Groups (Accounts and Reports) Regulations 2008* (the 2008 Regulations) (SI 2008/410) referred to in this FRS.

A6.2   The principal Irish companies' legislation referred to in the table below is:

- The Companies Act 1963 (1963 Act);
- The Companies (Amendment) Act 1983 (1983 Act);
- The Companies (Amendment) Act 1986 (1986 Act);
- The Companies Act 1990 (1990 Act);
- The Companies (Amendment) (No 2) Act 1999;
- The European Communities (Companies: Group Accounts) Regulations 1992 – S.I. No. 201 of 1992 (Group Accounts Regulations 1992 or GAR 1992);
- The European Communities (Credit Institutions: Accounts) Regulations 1992 – S.I. No. 294 of 1992 (Credit Institutions Regulations 1992 or CIR 1992);
- The European Communities (Insurance Undertakings: Accounts) Regulations 1996 – S.I. No. 23 of 1996 (Insurance Undertakings Regulations 1996 or IUR 1996).

A6.3   General references are made in this FRS to UK legislation such as the '2006 Act', 'Companies Act 2006 ('and the Regulations')', 'the Companies Act', 'the Act', 'the Large and Medium-sized Companies and Groups (Accounts and Reports) Regulations, 2008', 'the 2008 Regulations' and 'the Regulations'. In an Irish context reference should be made to the relevant sections and paragraphs of Irish companies' legislation. Such general references are not dealt with in the table below. References in the text to 'IAS accounts' are equivalent to 'IFRS accounts' in Irish company law.

A6.4   The following Irish legislation is also referenced in the table below:

- The Building Societies Act 1989;
- The Credit Union Acts 1997 to 2012;
- The Central Bank Act 1971;
- The Charities Act 2009;
- The Friendly Societies Acts 1896 to 1977;
- The Friendly Societies (Amendment) Act 1977;
- The Friendly Societies Regulations 1988 – S.I. No. 74 of 1988;
- The Industrial and Provident Societies (Amendment) Act 1978;
- The Pensions Act 1990; and
- The Occupational Pension Schemes (Disclosure of Information) Regulations 2006 – S.I. No. 301 of 2006.

COMPANIES ACT ACCOUNTS UNDER IRISH COMPANY LAW

Certain companies are permitted under Irish company law to prepare their Companies Act accounts using accounting standards other than those issued by the Financial Reporting Council (FRC) and promulgated by the Institute of Chartered Accountants in Ireland in respect of their application in the Republic of Ireland. Specifically: A6.5

- Pursuant to the Companies (Miscellaneous Provisions) Act 2009, as amended by the Companies (Amendment) Act 2012, relevant parent undertakings are permitted to prepare 'Companies Act individual accounts' and/or 'Companies Act group accounts' in accordance with US GAAP, as modified to ensure consistency with Irish company law.
- Investment companies subject to Part XIII of the Companies Act 1990 or the European Communities (Undertakings for Collective Investment in Transferable Securities) Regulations 2011 may adopt an alternative body of accounting standards, being standards which apply in the United States of America, Canada or Japan in preparing 'Companies Act individual accounts'.

Such companies, therefore, may adopt standards other than those issued by the FRC in preparing Companies Act accounts under Irish company law.   A6.6

SMALL COMPANIES UNDER IRISH COMPANY LAW

There is no equivalent to the UK *small companies regime* (see Sections 381 to 384 of the 2006 Act) in Irish company law. Section 8 of the Companies (Amendment) Act 1986 (as amended by the European Union (Accounts) Regulations 2012 (S.I. No. 304 of 2012)) defines small companies for the purposes of Irish company law. However, whilst Sections 10 and 12 provide certain exemptions for such companies in relation to their financial statements that are filed with the Registrar of Companies, there are no exemptions for individual or group accounts prepared for members. Under Section 8 (as amended) the qualifying conditions for a company to be treated as a small company in respect of any financial year are as follows: A6.7

- The amount of turnover for that year does not exceed €8,800,000;
- The balance sheet total for that year does not exceed €4,400,000; and
- Average number of employees does not exceed 50.

Except for companies in their first financial year, Section 8(1)(a) provides that companies qualify to be treated as small if, in respect of that year and the financial year immediately preceding that year, the company satisfies at least two of the above criteria. Section 9 provides that where a company has qualified as small, it continues to be so qualified until it does not meet two of the above three criteria for two consecutive years. Similarly, where a company no longer qualifies as small, two consecutive years of meeting two of the three criteria are required to qualify again as small.   A6.8

The following do not qualify as small under Irish company law: A6.9

- Companies subject to the European Communities (Credit Institutions: Accounts) Regulations 1992;
- Companies subject to the European Communities (Insurance Undertakings: Accounts) Regulations 1996;
- Private companies whose securities are admitted to trading on a regulated market.

SIZE EXEMPTIONS FROM THE PREPARATION OF GROUP ACCOUNTS UNDER IRISH COMPANY LAW

A6.10   An Irish parent company within the scope of the European Communities (Companies: Group Accounts) Regulations 1992 is exempt from the requirement to prepare group accounts if it, together with its subsidiaries, meets the size and other criteria set out in Regulation 7 of those Regulations. The size criteria in summary require that the parent and subsidiaries together meet two of the following three conditions:

- The amount of turnover for that year does not exceed €15,236,858;
- The balance sheet total for that year does not exceed €7,618,428; and
- Average number of employees does not exceed 250.

A6.11   Except for the year in which a company becomes a parent undertaking, the exemption can only be availed of if two of the three conditions are met in respect of the financial year and the immediately preceding financial year.

A6.12   Exemptions from preparing group accounts on the basis of size, in accordance with Regulation 7 of the European Communities (Companies: Group Accounts) Regulations 1992, are only available to parent companies that are private companies and are not available to parent companies subject to the European Communities (Credit Institutions: Accounts) Regulations 1992 or the European Communities (Insurance Undertakings: Accounts) Regulations 1996.

A6.13   As there is currently no legislative equivalent to merger relief in the Republic of Ireland, no relief from the requirement of Section 62(1) to establish a share premium account is available. Section 149(5) provides that pre-acquisition profits of an acquired subsidiary may not, for any purpose, be treated in the holding company's accounts as revenue profits. Section 149(5) contains a provision that, where the directors and auditors are satisfied and so certify that it would be fair and reasonable and would not prejudice the rights and interests of any person, the profits or losses attributable to any shares in a subsidiary may be treated in a manner otherwise than in accordance with this subsection.

A6.14   Accordingly, in considering whether merger accounting may be applied, directors and auditors should consider the consequences of providing such certification.

OTHER NOTES

A6.15   As noted in paragraph A4.3 of Appendix IV of this FRS, while the UK company law references are made to Schedule 1 to the 2008 Regulations, UK entities applying Schedules 2 (banking companies), 3 (insurance companies) or 6 (Companies Act group accounts) to those Regulations should read them as referring to the equivalent paragraphs in those Schedules. In the table below, the corresponding or similar provisions in Irish company law are specifically set out.

A6.16   The table below is intended as a reference guide to the corresponding or similar provisions in Irish company law and does not purport to be complete. It should be noted that not all Irish legal provisions are equivalent to the corresponding UK legal provisions and reference should be made to the Irish legislation for an understanding of relevant requirements. In some cases reference may need to be made to other parts of Irish company law.

Section 1: Scope

Paragraph	UK references	RoI references						
	2006 Act and the 2008 Regulations (unless otherwise stated)	1963 Act	1983 Act	1986 Act	1990 Act	GAR 1992	CIR 1992	IUR 1996
1.3(b) (Footnote 6)	Section 395(1)(a)	Section 148(2)(a)					Regulation 5(1)	Regulation 5(1)
1.3(b) (Footnote 6)	Section 395(1)(b)	Section 148(2)(b)					Regulation 5(1)	Regulation 5(1)
1.8	Paragraph 36(4) of Schedule 1			Paragraph 22AA of Part IIIA of the Schedule		Regulation 15 (applying the Schedule to the 1986 Act)	Paragraphs 46A(4A) and 46A(4B) of Part I and paragraph 1 of Part II of the Schedule	
1.10	Section 399	Section 150(1)				Regulations 5 and 7	Regulation 7(3)	Regulation 10(3)
1.10	Sections 400 to 401					Regulations 8, 9 and 9A	Regulations 8 and 8A	Regulations 12 and 12A
1.10	Section 402	Section 150(1A)*					Paragraph 2 of Part II of the Schedule	Regulation 10(1A)*

*Section 150(1A) of the 1963 Act and Regulation 10(1A) of the IUR 1996 contain an exemption from preparing group accounts which is similar but not identical to Section 402.

Section 3: Financial Statements Presentation

Paragraph	UK references: 2006 Act and the 2008 Regulations (unless otherwise stated)	RoI references: 1963 Act	1983 Act	1986 Act	1990 Act	GAR 1992	CIR 1992	IUR 1996
3.5 (Footnote 9)	Section 396(5)			Section 3(1)(d) and (e)		Regulation 14(3) and (4)	Regulation 5(1A) (d) and (e) and Regulation 7(7)(d) and (e)	Regulation 5(1A) (d) and (e) and Regulation 10(7)(d) and (e)

Section 4: Statement of Financial Position and Section 5: Statement of Comprehensive Income and Income Statement

Paragraph	UK references: 2006 Act and the 2008 Regulations (unless otherwise stated)	RoI references: 1963 Act	1983 Act	1986 Act	1990 Act	GAR 1992	CIR 1992	IUR 1996
4.2, 5.5 and 5.7	Part 1 *General Rules and Formats of* Schedule 1 to the Regulations			Part 1 of the Schedule				
4.2, 5.5 and 5.7	Part 1 *General Rules and Formats of* Schedule 2 to the Regulations						Chapter 1 of Part I of the Schedule	

Paragraph	UK references 2006 Act and the 2008 Regulations (unless otherwise stated)	RoI references 1963 Act	1983 Act	1986 Act	1990 Act	GAR 1992	CIR 1992	IUR 1996
4.2, 5.5 and 5.7	Part 1 *General Rules and Formats* of Schedule 3 to the Regulations							Part I of the Schedule
4.2, 5.5 and 5.7	Schedule 6 to the Regulations					Regulation 15 (applying the Schedule to the 1986 Act)	Paragraph 1 of Part II of the Schedule (applying Part I of the Schedule)	Paragraph 1 of Part IV of the Schedule (applying Part I of the Schedule)
4.2, 5.5 and 5.7	Schedule 1 and Schedule 3 to the LLP Regulations	There is no equivalent Irish LLP legislation.						

Section 7: Statement of Cash Flows

Paragraph	UK references 2006 Act and the 2008 Regulations (unless otherwise stated)	RoI references 1963 Act	1983 Act	1986 Act	1990 Act	GAR 1992	CIR 1992	IUR 1996
7.20A	Part 1 *General Rules and Formats* of Schedule 2 to the Regulations						Chapter 1 of Part I of the Schedule	

Section 9: Consolidated and Separate Financial Statements

Paragraph	UK references 2006 Act and the 2008 Regulations (unless otherwise stated)	RoI references 1963 Act	1983 Act	1986 Act	1990 Act	GAR 1992	CIR 1992	IUR 1996
9.3(a) and (b)	Section 400(2)					Regulations 8(3) and 9	Regulation 8(3)	Regulation 12(3)
9.3(b)	Section 400(1)(b)					Regulations 8(1) and 9	Regulations 8(1), (2) and (6)	Regulations 12(1), (2) and (6)
9.3(c) and (d)	Section 401(2)					Regulation 9A(3)	Regulation 8A(3)	Regulation 12A(3)
9.3(d)	Section 401(1)(b)					Regulation 9A(1)(b)	Regulation 8A(1)(b)	Regulation 12A(1)(b)
9.3(e)	Section 383	Please refer to the note above in the introduction to this table – Size exemptions from the preparation of group accounts under Irish company law.						
9.3(e)	Section 384	Please refer to the note above in the introduction to this table – Size exemptions from the preparation of group accounts under Irish company law.						
9.27B	Paragraph 36(4) of Schedule 1 to the Regulations			Paragraph 22AA of Part IIIA of the Schedule		Regulation 15 (applying the Schedule to the 1986 Act)	Paragraphs 46A(4A) and 46A(4B) of Part I and paragraph 1 of Part II of the Schedule	

Section 35: Transition to this FRS

	UK references	RoI references							
Paragraph	**2006 Act and the 2008 Regulations (unless otherwise stated)**	**1963 Act**	**1983 Act**	**1986 Act**	**1990 Act**	**GAR 1992**	**CIR 1992**	**IUR 1996**
35.10(m)	Companies Act definition of a dormant company	There is no equivalent definition in Irish company law.						

The Accounting Council's Advice to the FRC to issue FRS 102

Paragraph	UK references	RoI references						
	2006 Act and the 2008 Regulations (unless otherwise stated)	1963 Act	1983 Act	1986 Act	1990 Act	GAR 1992	CIR 1992	IUR 1996
36	Section 467(1)			Sections 2 and 8				
49	Section 405(3)					Regulation 11	Paragraph 2(3) of Part II of the Schedule	Paragraph 2(3) of Part IV of the Schedule

APPENDIX I: GLOSSARY

Paragraph	UK references 2006 Act and the 2008 Regulations (unless otherwise stated)	RoI references						
		1963 Act	1983 Act	1986 Act	1990 Act	GAR 1992	CIR 1992	IUR 1996
'financial institution' and footnote 26	Part IV permission; Section 40(4) of the Financial Services and Markets Act 2000	There is no equivalent legislation in Ireland to the Financial Services and Markets Act 2000. Banks in Ireland are licensed under Section 9 of the Central Bank Act 1971.						
'financial institution'	Section 119(1) of the Building Societies Act 1986	Section 2(1) of the Building Societies Act 1989						
'financial institution'	Industrial and Provident Societies Act 1965 and Credit Unions Act 1979	Credit Union Acts 1997 to 2012						
'financial institution'	Friendly Societies Act 1992; section 7(1)(a) of the Friendly Societies Act 1974	Friendly Societies Acts 1896 to 1977						
'individual financial statements'	Section 394	Section 148						
'individual financial statements'	Section 132 of the Charities Act 2011	Section 48 of the Charities Act 2009 provides that all charities are to prepare an annual statement of accounts, the form and content of which can be prescribed by Regulations of the Minister. Section 48 is, at the date of publication of this FRS, not commenced and no Regulations regarding the form and content of charities' annual statements of accounts have been published. Charity companies are required to prepare financial statements which give a true and fair view in accordance with the Companies Acts. Sections 148(3) and 150(4) of the 1963 Act require that companies 'not trading for the acquisition of gain by the members' must prepare Companies Act accounts (ie not IFRS accounts), and this definition may apply to many Irish charity companies.						

Paragraph	UK references	RoI references						
	2006 Act and the 2008 Regulations (unless otherwise stated)	**1963 Act**	**1983 Act**	**1986 Act**	**1990 Act**	**GAR 1992**	**CIR 1992**	**IUR 1996**
'individual financial statements'	Section 72A of the Building Societies Act 1986	Section 77 of the Building Societies Act 1989 requires the preparation of (a) an income and expenditure account giving a true and fair view of its income and expenditure for that year, (b) a balance sheet giving a true and fair view of the state of its affairs as at the end of that year, and (c) a statement of the source and application of funds giving a true and fair view of the manner in which its business has been financed and in which its financial resources have been used during that year.						
'LLP Regulations'	The Large and Medium-sized Limited Liability Partnerships (Accounts) Regulations 2008 (SI 2008/1913)	There is no equivalent Irish LLP legislation						
'qualifying entity' (footnote 30)	Section 474(1)					Regulation 3(1)	Paragraph 1 of Part IV of the Schedule	

APPENDIX II: SIGNIFICANT DIFFERENCES BETWEEN FRS 102 AND THE IFRS FOR SMES

Paragraph	UK references	RoI references						
	2006 Act and the 2008 Regulations (unless otherwise stated)	1963 Act	1983 Act	1986 Act	1990 Act	GAR 1992	CIR 1992	IUR 1996
Section 9	Paragraph 2(2) of Schedule 6 to the Regulations					Regulation 26(2)	Paragraph 3(3) of Part II of the Schedule	Paragraph 3(3) of Part IV of the Schedule
Section 9	Paragraph 13(a) of Schedule 1 to the Regulations			Section 5(c)(i)		Regulation 28 (applying Section 5 of the 1986 Act)	Paragraph 19(a) of Part I and paragraph 1 of Part II of the Schedule	Regulation 7(c)(i) and paragraph 13 of Part IV of the Schedule
Sections 14 and 15	Paragraph 27 of Schedule 1 to the Regulations			Paragraph 14 of Part II of the Schedule		Regulation 15 (applying the Schedule to the 1986 Act)	Paragraph 36 of Part I of the Schedule and paragraph 1 of Part II of the Schedule	Paragraphs 7 to 8 of Part II of the Schedule and paragraph 13 of Part IV of the Schedule
Sections 14 and 15	Section C of Schedule 1 to the Regulations			Part III of the Schedule		Regulation 15 (applying the Schedule to the 1986 Act)	Paragraphs 39 to 44 of Part I of the Schedule and paragraph 1 of Part II of the Schedule	Chapter 2 of Part II of the Schedule and paragraph 13 of Part IV of the Schedule
Sections 14 and 15	Paragraph 36 of Schedule 1 to the Regulations			Paragraphs 22A and 22AA of Part IIIA of the Schedule		Regulation 15 (applying the Schedule to the 1986 Act)	Paragraph 46A of Part I and paragraph 1 of Part II of the Schedule	

APPENDIX IV: NOTE ON LEGAL REQUIREMENTS

Paragraph	UK references: 2006 Act and the 2008 Regulations (unless otherwise stated)	RoI references: 1963 Act	1983 Act	1986 Act	1990 Act	GAR 1992	CIR 1992	IUR 1996
A4.1 (Footnote 34)	Charities Act 2011	Section 48 of the Charities Act 2009 provides that all charities are to prepare an annual statement of accounts, the form and content of which can be prescribed by Regulations of the Minister. Section 48 is, at the date of publication of this FRS, not commenced and no Regulations regarding the form and content of charities' annual statements of accounts have been published. Charity companies are required to prepare financial statements which give a true and fair view in accordance with the Companies Acts. Sections 148(3) and 150(4) of the 1963 Act require that companies 'not trading for the acquisition of gain by the members' must prepare Companies Act accounts (i.e. not IFRS accounts), and this definition may apply to many Irish charity companies.						
A4.3	Schedule 1 to the Regulations			Sections 4, 5 and 6 and the Schedule				
A4.3	Schedule 2 to the Regulations						Part I of the Schedule	
A4.3	Schedule 3 to the Regulations							Regulations 6, 7 and 8 and Parts I, II and III of the Schedule
A4.3	Schedule 6 to the Regulations					Regulations 15 to 35 & the Schedule	Part II of the Schedule	Regulations 6, 7, 8 and 10 and Parts I, II and III, as modified by Part IV of the Schedule
A4.6	Section 395(1)	Section 148(2)					Regulation 5	Regulation 5
A4.6	Section 396	Section 149		Section 3			Regulation 5	Regulation 5
A4.6	Section 403(2)	Section 150(3)						
A4.6	Section 404	Section 150A and 151				Regulation 14	Regulation 7	Regulation 10

Paragraph	UK references 2006 Act and the 2008 Regulations (unless otherwise stated)	RoI references 1963 Act	1983 Act	1986 Act	1990 Act	GAR 1992	CIR 1992	IUR 1996
A4.7	'Accounts prepared in accordance with FRS 102 are ... required to comply with the applicable provisions of Parts 15 and 16 of the Act and with the Regulations'	Sections 148, 149, 150, 150A, 150C, 151, 152, 153, 156, 161D and 191		Sections 3 to 6, 16, 16A and 17 and the Schedule	Sections 41 to 43 and Section 63	Regulations 2 to 35 and the Schedule	Regulations 2, 5, 7, 8, 8A, 9 and 10 and the Schedule	Regulations 2, 5, 6, 7, 8, 10, 11, 12, 12A and 13 and the Schedule
	See also Section 33(4) of the Companies (Amendment) (No.2) Act 1999							
A4.8	Section 407	Section 150C						
A4.12 and A4.12A	Paragraph 36 of Schedule 1 to the Regulations			Paragraphs 22A and 22AA of Part IIIA of the Schedule		Regulation 15 (applying the Schedule to the 1986 Act)	Paragraph 46A of Part I of the Schedule and paragraph 1 of Part II of the Schedule	
A4.13	Paragraph 36(4) of Schedule 1 to the Regulations			Paragraph 22AA of Part IIIA of the Schedule		Regulation 15 (applying the Schedule to the 1986 Act)	Paragraphs 46A(4A) and 46A(4B) of Part I and paragraph 1 of Part II of the Schedule	
A4.13	Paragraph 36(3) of Schedule 1 to the Regulations			Paragraph 22A(3) of Part IIIA of the Schedule		Regulation 15 (applying the Schedule to the 1986 Act)	Paragraph 46A(4) of Part I and paragraph 1 of Part II of the Schedule	
A4.15	Section 434(2)			Section 19(3A)			Regulation 6(4)	
A4.15	Section 408	Sections 148(8) and (9)		Sections 7(1A) and (1B)				Regulation 9(4)

| | UK references | RoI references | | | | | | |
Paragraph	2006 Act and the 2008 Regulations (unless otherwise stated)	1963 Act	1983 Act	1986 Act	1990 Act	GAR 1992	CIR 1992	IUR 1996
A4.16	Section 405(3)					Regulation 11	Paragraph 2(3) of Part II of the Schedule	Paragraph 2(3) of Part IV of the Schedule
A4.17	Paragraph 36 of Schedule 1 to the Regulations			Paragraphs 22A and 22AA of Part IIIA of the Schedule		Regulation 15 (applying the Schedule to the 1986 Act)	Paragraph 46A of Part I and paragraph 1 of Part II of the Schedule	
A4.17	Paragraph 10(2) of Schedule 1 to the Regulations			Section 6		Regulation 28 (applying Section 6 of the 1986 Act)	Paragraph 22 of Part I and paragraph 1 of Part II of the Schedule	Regulation 8
A4.18	Paragraph 9 of Schedule 6 to the Regulations					Regulation 19	Paragraph 10 of Part II of the Schedule	Paragraph 9 of Part IV of the Schedule
A4.21	Section 404(5)					Regulation 14(3) and (4)	Regulation 7(7)(d) and (e)	Regulation 10(7)(d) and (e)
A4.22 and A4.23	Paragraph 8 of Schedule 1 to the Regulations			Section 4(11)		Regulation 15 (applying Section 4 of the 1986 Act)	Paragraph 5 of Part I and paragraph 1 of Part II of the Schedule	Regulation 6(9) and paragraph 3(1) of Part IV of the Schedule
A4.24	Sections 611–615	There are no corresponding Irish provisions to Sections 611–615 (group reconstruction and merger relief)						
A4.25 and A4.27	Paragraph 13(a) of Schedule 1 to the Regulations			Section 5(c)(i)		Regulation 28 (applying Section 5 of the 1986 Act)	Paragraph 19(a) of Part I and paragraph 1 of Part II of the Schedule	Regulation 7(c)(i) and paragraph 13 of Part IV of the Schedule

Paragraph	UK references	RoI references						
	2006 Act and the 2008 Regulations (unless otherwise stated)	1963 Act	1983 Act	1986 Act	1990 Act	GAR 1992	CIR 1992	IUR 1996
A4.26	Paragraph 36(4) of Schedule 1 to the Regulations			Paragraph 22AA of Part IIIA of the Schedule		Regulation 15 (applyingtheSchedule to the 1986 Act)	Paragraphs 46A(4A) and 46A(4B) of Part I and paragraph 1 of Part II of the Schedule	
A4.26	Paragraph 39 of Schedule 1 to the Regulations			Paragraph 22CA of Part IIIA of the Schedule		Regulation 15 (applyingtheSchedule to the 1986 Act)	Paragraph 46BA of Part I and paragraph 1 of Part II of the Schedule	
A4.27	Paragraphs 40 and 40(2) of Schedule 1 to the Regulations			Sections 22D and 22D(2) of Part IIIA of the Schedule		Regulation 15 (applyingtheSchedule to the 1986 Act)	Paragraphs 46C and 46C(1) of Part I and paragraph 1 of Part II of the Schedule	
A4.30	Paragraph 10 of Schedule 6 to the Regulations	Sections 62 and 149(5)*				Regulation 21	Paragraph 11 of Part II of the Schedule	Paragraph 10 of Part IV of the Schedule
		* Please refer to the note above in the introduction to this table – merger accounting.						
A4.32	Sections 690 to 708	Section 72			Part XI			
A4.32	Sections 724 to 732		Section 43A		Section 209			

| Paragraph | UK references | RoI references | | | | | | |
	2006 Act and the 2008 Regulations (unless otherwise stated)	1963 Act	1983 Act	1986 Act	1990 Act	GAR 1992	CIR 1992	IUR 1996
A4.33	Paragraph 36 of Schedule 1 to the Regulations			Paragraphs 22A and 22AA of Part IIIA of the Schedule		Regulation 15 (applying the Schedule to the 1986 Act)	Paragraph 46A of Part I and paragraph 1 of Part II of the Schedule	
A4.34	Section C of Schedule 1 to the Regulations			Part III of the Schedule		Regulation 15 (applying the Schedule to the 1986 Act)	Section B of Chapter II of Part I of the Schedule and paragraph 1 of Part II of the Schedule	Chapter 2 of Part II of the Schedule
A4.35	Paragraph 24(1) of Schedule 1 to the Regulations			Paragraph 11(1) of the Schedule		Regulation 15 (applying the Schedule to the 1986 Act)	Paragraph 33(1) of Part I of the Schedule and paragraph 1 of Part II of the Schedule	Paragraph 5(2) of Part II of the Schedule and paragraph 13 of Part IV of the Schedule
A4.35	Paragraph 32(5) of Schedule 1 to the Regulations			Paragraph 19(5) of the Schedule		Regulation 15 (applying the Schedule to the 1986 Act)	Paragraph 41(4) of Part I of the Schedule and paragraph 1 of Part II of the Schedule	Paragraph 15(2) of Part II of the Schedule and paragraph 13 of Part IV of the Schedule
A4.38	LLP Regulations	There is no equivalent Irish legislation.						
A4.42	Building Societies Act 1986	Building Societies Act 1989, Part VII, Section 77(1)						
A4.42	Charities Act 2011 and regulations made thereunder	Section 48 of the Charities Act 2009 provides that all charities are to prepare an annual statement of accounts, the form and content of which can be prescribed by Regulations of the Minister. Section 48 is, at the date of publication of this FRS, not commenced and no Regulations regarding the form and content of charities' annual statements of accounts have been published. Charity companies are required to prepare financial statements which give a true and fair view in accordance with the Companies Acts. Sections 148(3) and 150(4) of the 1963 Act require that companies 'not trading for the acquisition of gain by the members' must prepare Companies Act accounts (i.e. not IFRS accounts), and this definition may apply to many Irish charity companies.						

Paragraph	UK references 2006 Act and the 2008 Regulations (unless otherwise stated)	RoI references 1963 Act	1983 Act	1986 Act	1990 Act	GAR 1992	CIR 1992	IUR 1996
A4.42	Friendly and Industrial and Provident Societies Act 1968	Section 30 of Part IV of the Industrial and Provident Societies (Amendment) Act, 1978; Regulation 4 of the Friendly Societies Regulations 1988, pursuant to Section 3 of the Friendly Societies (Amendment) Act 1977						
A4.42 and Footnote 37	Friendly Societies Act 1992 and Friendly Societies (Accounts and Related Provisions) Regulations 1994 (as amended)	Regulation 4 of the Friendly Societies Regulations 1988, pursuant to Section 3 to the Friendly Societies (Amendment) Act 1977						
A4.42	The Occupational Pension Schemes (Requirement to obtain Audited Accounts and a Statement from the Auditor) Regulations 1996	Section 56 of the Pensions Act 1990; Regulation 5 and paragraphs 1 and 2(a)(ii) of Schedule A to the Occupational Pension Schemes (Disclosure of Information) Regulations 2006.						

APPENDIX V: PREVIOUS CONSULTATIONS

Paragraph	UK references		RoI references						
	2006 Act and the 2008 Regulations (unless otherwise stated)	'small companies' regime'	1963 Act	1983 Act	1986 Act	1990 Act	GAR 1992	CIR 1992	IUR 1996
A5.11			There are no equivalent provisions in Irish company law to the UK small companies regime or to the Small Companies and Groups (Accounts and Directors' Report) Regulations 2008. Small companies are defined in Section 8 of the 1986 Act. Please refer to the note above in the introduction to this table.						

FRS 102
The Financial Reporting Standard applicable in the UK and Republic of Ireland (2015)

(September 2015)

Contents

Approval by the FRC

The Accounting Council's Advice to the FRC to issue FRS 102

Appendices

Prospective amendments: Amendments to FRS 102 The Financial Reporting Standard applicable in the UK and Republic of Ireland – Fair value hierarchy disclosures (March 2016) amends this Standard with effect for annual periods beginning on or after 1 January 2017.

Editor's note: This revised version issued by the FRC incorporates recently published amendments, most notably the incorporation of amendments issued in July 2015. The amended version of FRS 102 *The Financial Reporting Standard applicable in the UK and Republic of Ireland* updates the version issued in August 2014 for the following: a) an editorial amendment to Section 12 *Other Financial Instruments Issues* in relation to the examples of hedge accounting issued on 17 September 2014; b) Amendments to FRS 102 – Pension obligations issued in February 2015; c) consequential amendments to FRS 102 included in FRS 104 *Interim Financial Reporting* issued in March 2015; d) Amendments to FRS 102 – Small entities and other minor amendments issued in July 2015; and e) some minor typographical or presentational corrections. This revised standard is effective for accounting periods beginning on or after 1 January 2016.

SUMMARY

(i)   With effect from 1 January 2015 the Financial Reporting Council (FRC) revised financial reporting standards in the United Kingdom and Republic of Ireland. The revisions fundamentally reformed financial reporting, replacing the extant standards with five Financial Reporting Standards:

    (a)   FRS 100 *Application of Financial Reporting Requirements*;

    (b)   FRS 101 *Reduced Disclosure Framework*;

    (c)   FRS 102 *The Financial Reporting Standard applicable in the UK and Republic of Ireland*;

    (d)   FRS 103 *Insurance Contracts*; and

    (e)   FRS 104 *Interim Financial Reporting*.

The FRC has also issued FRS 105 *The Financial Reporting Standard applicable to the Micro-entities Regime* to support the implementation of the new micro-entities regime.

(ii)   The FRC's overriding objective in setting accounting standards is to enable users of accounts to receive high-quality understandable financial reporting proportionate to the size and complexity of the entity and users' information needs.

(iii)   In meeting this objective, the FRC aims to provide succinct financial reporting standards that:

    (a)   have consistency with international accounting standards through the application of an IFRS-based solution unless an alternative clearly better meets the overriding objective;

    (b)   reflect up-to-date thinking and developments in the way entities operate and the transactions they undertake;

    (c)   balance consistent principles for accounting by all UK and Republic of Ireland entities with practical solutions, based on size, complexity, public interest and users' information needs;

    (d)   promote efficiency within groups; and

    (e)   are cost-effective to apply.

(iv)   The requirements in this Financial Reporting Standard (FRS) take into consideration the findings from all relevant consultations.

(v)   This FRS is a single financial reporting standard that applies to the financial statements of entities that are not applying EU-adopted IFRS, FRS 101 or FRS 105[1].

The Financial Reporting Standard applicable in the UK and Republic of Ireland and the IFRS for SMEs

(vi)   This FRS aims to provide entities with succinct financial reporting requirements. The requirements in this FRS are based on the International Accounting Standards Board's (IASB) International Financial Reporting Standard for Small and Medium-sized Entities (IFRS for SMEs) issued in 2009. The IFRS for SMEs is intended to apply to the general purpose financial statements of, and other financial reporting by, entities that in many countries are referred to by a variety of terms including 'small and medium-sized', 'private' and 'non-publicly accountable'.

---

[1] *This FRS does not, however apply to the preparation of 'Companies Act accounts' of certain companies under company law in the Republic of Ireland.*

The FRC has modified the IFRS for SMEs substantially, both in terms of the scope of **(vii)** entities eligible to apply it and in terms of the accounting treatments provided. To reflect this wider scope the proposed name of the standard was revised to FRS 102 *Financial Reporting Standard applicable in the UK and Republic of Ireland*.

FRS 102 is designed to apply to the general purpose financial statements and financial **(viii)** reporting of entities including those that are not constituted as companies and those that are not profit-oriented. General purpose financial statements are intended to focus on the common information needs of a wide range of users; shareholders, lenders, other creditors, employees and members of the public, for example.

Organisation of FRS 102

FRS 102 is organised by topic with each topic presented in a separate numbered section. **(ix)** Cross-references to paragraphs are identified by section followed by paragraph number. Paragraph numbers are in the form of xx.yy, where xx is the section number and yy is the sequential paragraph number within that section. Those paragraphs that apply solely to public benefit entities are identified by the prefix 'PBE'[2]. In order to maintain consistency with the paragraph numbering of the IFRS for SMEs, when a paragraph from the IFRS for SMEs has been deleted and not replaced with an alternative paragraph, the phrase [not used] is given. In examples that include monetary amounts, the measuring unit is Currency Unit (abbreviated as CU).

All the paragraphs of FRS 102 have equal authority. Some sections include appendices of **(x)** implementation guidance or examples. Some of these are an integral part of the FRS while others provide guidance concerning its application; each specifies its status.

This FRS is set out in Sections 1 to 35 and the Glossary (Appendix I). Terms defined in **(xi)** the Glossary are in **bold type** the first time they appear in each section and sub-section within Section 34.

This edition of FRS 102 issued in September 2015 updates the edition of FRS 102 issued **(xii)** in August 2014 for the following:

(a)   an editorial amendment to Section 12 *Other Financial Instruments Issues* in relation to the examples of hedge accounting issued on 17 September 2014;
(b)   *Amendments to FRS 102 – Pension obligations* issued in February 2015;
(c)   consequential amendments to FRS 102 included in FRS 104 *Interim Financial Reporting* issued in March 2015;
(d)   *Amendments to FRS 102 – Small entities and other minor amendments* issued in July 2015; and
(e)   some minor typographical or presentational corrections.

---

[2] *In some cases 'PBE' prefixed paragraphs also apply to other entities in a public benefit entity group.*

FRS 102 THE FINANCIAL REPORTING STANDARD APPLICABLE IN THE UK AND REPUBLIC OF IRELAND

Section 1 Scope

Scope of this Financial Reporting Standard

1.1   This FRS applies to **financial statements** that are intended to give a true and fair view of a reporting entity's **financial position** and **profit or loss** (or **income and expenditure**) for a period.

1.2   The requirements of this FRS are applicable to **public benefit entities** and other entities, not just to companies. However, those paragraph numbers prefixed with 'PBE' shall only be applied by public benefit entities, and shall not be applied directly, or by analogy, by entities that are not public benefit entities, other than, where specifically directed, entities within a **public benefit entity group**.

1.2A   An entity applying this FRS must ensure it complies with any relevant legal requirements applicable to it. This FRS does not necessarily contain all legal disclosure requirements. In relation to small companies (see Section 1A *Small Entities*) most legal disclosure requirements are included, but, for example, those only relevant when the financial statements have been audited are not included.

Basis of preparation of financial statements

1.3   As stated in **FRS 100**, an entity that is required by the **IAS Regulation** (or other legislation or regulation) to prepare **consolidated financial statements** in accordance with **EU-adopted IFRS** must do so. The **individual financial statements** of such an entity, or the individual financial statements or consolidated financial statements of any other entity within the scope of FRS 100, must be prepared in accordance with the following requirements:

(a)   If the financial statements are the individual financial statements of an entity that is eligible to apply **FRS 105**[3], they may be prepared in accordance with that standard.

(b)   If the financial statements are those of an entity that is not eligible to apply FRS 105, or of an entity that is eligible to apply FRS 105 but chooses not to do so, they must[4] be prepared in accordance with this FRS, EU-adopted IFRS or **FRS 101**[5].

1.4   An entity whose **ordinary shares** or **potential ordinary shares** are **publicly traded,** or that files, or is in the process of filing, its financial statements with a securities commission or other regulatory organisation for the purpose of issuing ordinary shares in a public market, or an entity that chooses to disclose earnings per share, shall apply IAS 33 *Earnings per Share* (as adopted in the EU).

1.5   An entity whose debt or equity instruments are publicly traded, or that files, or is in the process of filing, its financial statements with a securities commission or other regulatory organisation for the purpose of issuing any class of instruments in a public market, or an

---

[3] *The eligibility criteria for applying FRS 105 are set out in legislation and FRS 105. In establishing whether the eligibility criteria have been met turnover and balance sheet total shall be measured in accordance with FRS 105; the measurement of turnover and balance sheet total in accordance with FRS 101 or FRS 102 need not be considered.*

[4] *Under company law in the Republic of Ireland, certain companies are permitted to prepare 'Companies Act accounts' using accounting standards other than those issued by the FRC.*

[5] *Individual financial statements that are prepared by a company in accordance with FRS 101 or FRS 102 are Companies Act individual accounts (section 395(1)(a) of the Act), whereas those prepared in accordance with EU-adopted IFRS are IAS individual accounts (section 395(1)(b) of the Act).*

entity that chooses to provide information described as segment information, shall apply IFRS 8 *Operating Segments* (as adopted in the EU). If an entity discloses disaggregated information, but the information does not comply with the requirements of IFRS 8, it shall not describe the information as segment information.

An entity shall apply FRS 103 *Insurance Contracts* to: **1.6**

(a)   **insurance contracts** (including **reinsurance contracts**) that it issues and reinsurance contracts that it holds; and

(b)   **financial instruments** with a **discretionary participation feature** that it issues.

When applying IAS 33, IFRS 8 and IFRS 6 *Exploration for and Evaluation of Mineral* **1.7** *Resources* (see paragraph 34.11), references made to other IFRSs within those standards shall be taken to be references to the relevant section or paragraph in this FRS.

Reduced disclosures for subsidiaries (and ultimate parents)

A **qualifying entity** (for the purposes of this FRS) which is not a **financial institution** **1.8** may take advantage in its individual financial statements of the disclosure exemptions set out in paragraph 1.12. In relation to paragraph 1.12(c) for **financial liabilities** that are held at **fair value** that are either part of a trading portfolio or are **derivatives**, the qualifying entity can take advantage of those exemptions. Where the qualifying entity has financial instruments held at fair value subject to the requirements of paragraph 36(4) of Schedule 1 to the **Regulations**, it must apply the disclosure requirements of Section 11 *Basic Financial Instruments* to those financial instruments held at fair value.

A qualifying entity (for the purposes of this FRS) which is a financial institution may **1.9** take advantage in its individual financial statements of the disclosure exemptions set out in paragraph 1.12, except for the disclosure exemptions from Section 11 and Section 12 *Other Financial Instruments Issues*.

A qualifying entity (for the purposes of this FRS) which is required to prepare consolidated **1.10** financial statements (for example, if the entity is required by section 399 of the **Act** to prepare consolidated financial statements, and is not entitled to any of the exemptions in sections 400 to 402 of the Act), or which voluntarily chooses to do so, may not take advantage of the disclosure exemptions set out in paragraph 1.12 in its consolidated financial statements.

A qualifying entity (for the purposes of this FRS) may take advantage of the disclosure **1.11** exemptions in paragraph 1.12, in accordance with paragraphs 1.8 to 1.10, provided that:

(a)   Its shareholders have been notified in writing about, and do not object to, the use of the disclosure exemptions. Objections to the use of the disclosure exemptions may be served on the qualifying entity, in accordance with reasonable specified timeframes and format requirements, by a shareholder that is the immediate **parent** of the entity, or by a shareholder or shareholders holding in aggregate 5 per cent or more of the total allotted shares in the entity or more than half of the allotted shares in the entity that are not held by the immediate parent.

(b)   It otherwise applies the **recognition**, **measurement** and disclosure requirements of this FRS.

(c)   It discloses in the **notes** to its financial statements:

  (i)   a brief narrative summary of the disclosure exemptions adopted; and

  (ii)   the name of the parent[6] of the **group** in whose consolidated financial statements its financial statements are consolidated, and from where those financial statements may be obtained.

---

[6] *The parent identified in the definition of the term 'qualifying entity'.*

1.12   A qualifying entity (for the purposes of this FRS) may take advantage of the following disclosure exemptions:

(a)   The requirements of Section 4 *Statement of Financial Position* paragraph 4.12(a)(iv).

(b)   The requirements of Section 7 *Statement of Cash Flows* and Section 3 *Financial Statement Presentation* paragraph 3.17(d).

(c)   The requirements of Section 11 paragraphs 11.41(b), 11.41(c), 11.41(e), 11.41(f), 11.42, 11.44, 11.45, 11.47, 11.48(a)(iii), 11.48(a)(iv), 11.48(b) and 11.48(c) and Section 12 paragraphs 12.26 (in relation to those cross-referenced paragraphs from which a disclosure exemption is available), 12.27, 12.29(a), 12.29(b), and 12.29A providing disclosures equivalent to those required by this FRS are included in the consolidated financial statements of the group in which the entity is consolidated.

(d)   The requirements of Section 26 *Share-based Payment* paragraphs 26.18(b), 26.19 to 26.21 and 26.23, provided that for a qualifying entity that is:

(i)   a **subsidiary**, the share-based payment arrangement concerns equity instruments of another group entity;

(ii)   an ultimate parent, the share-based payment arrangement concerns its own equity instruments and its **separate financial statements** are presented alongside the consolidated financial statements of the group;

and, in both cases, provided that the equivalent disclosures required by this FRS are included in the consolidated financial statements of the group in which the entity is consolidated.

(e)   The requirement of Section 33 *Related Party Disclosures* paragraph 33.7.

1.13   Reference shall be made to the Application Guidance to FRS 100 in deciding whether the consolidated financial statements of the parent provide disclosures which are equivalent to the requirements of this FRS (ie the full requirements of this FRS when not applying the disclosure exemptions) from which relief is provided in paragraph 1.12.

Date from which effective and transitional arrangements

1.14   An entity shall apply this FRS for accounting periods beginning on or after 1 January 2015. Early application is permitted for accounting periods ending on or after 31 December 2012. For entities that are within the scope of a SORP, early application is permitted for accounting periods ending on or after 31 December 2012 providing it does not conflict with the requirements of a current SORP or legal requirements for the preparation of financial statements. If an entity applies this FRS before 1 January 2015 it shall disclose that fact.

1.14A   This FRS permits a financial instrument (provided it meets certain criteria) to be designated on initial recognition as a **financial asset** or financial liability at fair value through profit or loss. Entities that have applied this FRS in financial statements authorised for issue prior to 1 August 2014 are permitted in their first financial statements authorised for issue on or after 1 August 2014 to designate, as at the date of transition to this FRS, any financial asset or financial liability at fair value through profit or loss provided the asset or liability meets the criteria in paragraph 11.14(b) at that date. Entities that have applied this FRS in financial statements authorised for issue prior to 1 August 2014 are permitted in their first financial statements authorised for issue on or after 1 August 2014 to de-designate any financial asset or financial liability previously designated at fair value through profit or loss and classify and measure the financial instrument in accordance with Section 11.

1.14B   This FRS permits entities to apply hedge accounting, provided certain qualifying conditions are met. Entities that have applied this FRS in financial statements authorised for issue prior to 1 August 2014 are permitted to apply hedge accounting to a hedging relationship existing on or before 31 July 2014 as set out in Section 12 of this FRS from a date no earlier than the conditions of paragraphs 12.18(a) to (c) are met, provided the conditions of paragraphs 12.18(d) and (e) are met no later than the date the first financial statements issued on or after 1 August 2014 are authorised for issue. This choice applies to each hedging relationship existing on or before 31 July 2014. This choice only applies in respect of the first financial statements that comply with this FRS that are authorised for issue on or after 1 August 2014.

In a fair value hedge the cumulative **hedging gain or loss** on the hedged item from the date hedge accounting commenced, shall be recorded in retained earnings (or if appropriate, another category of **equity**). In a cash flow hedge and net investment hedge, the lower of the following (in absolute amounts) shall be recorded in equity (in respect of cash flow hedges in the cash flow hedge reserve):

(a)   the cumulative gain or loss on the hedging instrument from the date hedge accounting commenced to the reporting date of the last financial statements authorised for issue prior to 1 August 2014; and

(b)   the cumulative change in fair value (ie the present value of the cumulative change of expected future cash flows) on the hedged item from the date hedge accounting commenced to the reporting date of the last financial statements authorised for issue prior to 1 August 2014.

In July 2015 amendments were made to this FRS to incorporate the new small entities regime and make other amendments necessary to maintain consistency with company law. An entity shall apply the amendments set out in *Amendments to FRS 102 – Small entities and other minor amendments* (the July 2015 amendments) other than the replacement of paragraph 26.15 with new paragraphs 26.15 to 26.15B for accounting periods beginning on or after 1 January 2016. Early application is: **1.15**

(a)   permitted for accounting periods beginning on or after 1 January 2015 provided that *The Companies, Partnerships and Groups (Accounts and Reports) Regulations 2015* (SI 2015/980) are applied from the same date; and

(b)   required if an entity applies *The Companies, Partnerships and Groups (Accounts and Reports) Regulations 2015* (SI 2015/980) to a reporting period beginning before 1 January 2016.

For entities not subject to company law, early application is permitted from 1 January 2015.

If an entity applies the July 2015 amendments before 1 January 2016 it shall disclose that fact, unless it is a **small entity**, in which case it is encouraged to disclose that fact.

Prospective amendments: Amendments to FRS 102 The Financial Reporting Standard applicable in the UK and Republic of Ireland – Fair value hierarchy disclosures (March 2016) inserts paragraph 1.16 with effect for annual periods beginning on or after 1 January 2017.

Section 1A Small Entities

Scope of this section

This section sets out the information that shall be presented and disclosed in the **financial statements** of a **small entity** that chooses to apply the small entities regime. Unless excluded below, all of the requirements of this FRS apply to a small entity, including the **recognition** and **measurement** requirements. **1A.1**

Unless a small entity chooses to apply EU-adopted IFRS, or if eligible, FRS 101, a small entity that chooses not to apply the small entities regime shall apply FRS 102 excluding Section 1A. **1A.2**

1A.3   References to a small entity in paragraphs 1A.4 to 1A.22 and the Appendices to Section 1A are to a small entity that chooses to apply the small entities regime.

1A.4   This section applies to all small entities applying the small entities regime, whether or not they report under the **Act**. Small entities that do not report under the Act shall comply with the requirements of this section, and with the **Small Companies Regulations** (or, where applicable, the **Small LLP Regulations**) where referred to in this section, except to the extent that these requirements are not permitted by any statutory framework under which such entities report.

True and fair view

1A.5   The financial statements of a small entity shall give a true and fair view of the **assets**, **liabilities**, **financial position** and **profit or loss** of the small entity for the **reporting period** (Section 393 of the Act).

1A.6   A small entity may need to provide disclosures in addition to those set out in this section in order to comply with the requirement of paragraph 1A.5 (see also paragraphs 1A.16 and 1A.17).

Complete set of financial statements of a small entity

1A.7   A small entity is not required to comply with the requirements of paragraphs 3.3, PBE3.3A, 3.9, 3.17,.3.18, 3.19 and 3.24(b) which relate to presentation and disclosure requirements that are not required of small companies in company law, Section 4 *Statement of Financial Position*, Section 5 *Statement of Comprehensive Income and Income Statement*, Section 6 *Statement of Changes in Equity and Statement of Income and Retained Earnings* and Section 7 *Statement of Cash Flows*.

1A.8   Instead a complete set of financial statements of a small entity shall include all of the following:

   (a)   a **statement of financial position** as at the **reporting date** in accordance with paragraph 1A.12;
   (b)   an **income statement** for the reporting period in accordance with paragraph 1A.14; and
   (c)   **notes** in accordance with paragraphs 1A.16 to 1A.20.

1A.9   In addition to the statements required by company law and set out in paragraph 1A.8:

   (a)   when a small entity recognises **gains** or losses in **other comprehensive income** it is encouraged to present a statement of total comprehensive income (see Section 5); and
   (b)   when a small entity has transactions with equity holders it is encouraged to present a statement of changes in equity, or a **statement of income and retained earnings**, (see Section 6),

in order to meet the requirements of paragraph 1A.5.

1A.10   In accordance with paragraph 3.14 a small entity shall present comparative information in respect of the preceding period for all amounts presented in the current period's financial statements, except when this FRS permits or requires otherwise.

1A.11   In accordance with paragraph 3.22 a small entity may use titles for the financial statements other than those used in this FRS as long as they are not misleading.

Information to be presented in the statement of financial position

A small entity shall present a statement of financial position in accordance with the requirements for a balance sheet set out in either Part 1 *General Rules and Formats* of Schedule 1 to the Small Companies Regulations or Part 1 *General Rules and Formats* of Schedule 1 to the Small LLP Regulations.   **1A.12**

Guidance on applying these requirements is set out in Appendix A to this section, which shall be applied by a small entity.   **1A.13**

Information to be presented in the income statement

A small entity shall present its profit or loss for a period in an income statement in accordance with the requirements for a profit and loss account set out in either Part 1 *General Rules and Formats* of Schedule 1 to the Small Companies Regulations or Part 1 *General Rules and Formats* of Schedule 1 to the Small LLP Regulations.   **1A.14**

Guidance on applying these requirements is set out in in Appendix B to this section, which shall be applied by a small entity.   **1A.15**

Information to be presented in the notes to the financial statements

A small entity shall present sufficient information in the notes to the financial statements to meet the requirement for the financial statements to give a true and fair view of the assets, liabilities, financial position and profit or loss of the small entity for the reporting period.   **1A.16**

A small entity is not required to comply with the disclosure requirements of Section 3 (to the extent set out in paragraph 1A.7) and Sections 8 to 35 of this FRS. However, because those disclosures are usually considered relevant to giving a true and fair view, a small entity is encouraged to consider and provide any of those disclosures that are relevant to **material** transactions, other events or conditions of the small entity in order to meet the requirement set out in paragraphs 1A.5 and 1A.16. In accordance with paragraph 3.16A a small entity need not provide a specific disclosure (including those set out in paragraph 1A.18 and Appendix C to this section) if the information is not material.   **1A.17**

As a minimum, where relevant to its transactions, other events and conditions, a small entity shall provide the disclosures set out in Appendix C to this section.   **1A.18**

The paragraphs of this FRS that are cross-referenced in Appendix C are also highlighted in those sections by including an * in the left-hand margin.   **1A.19**

In addition, a small entity is encouraged to make the disclosures set out in Appendix D to this section, which may nevertheless be necessary to give a true and fair view.   **1A.20**

Voluntary preparation of consolidated financial statements

A small entity that is a **parent** entity is not required to prepare **consolidated financial statements**.   **1A.21**

If a small entity that is a parent voluntarily chooses to prepare consolidated financial statements it: **1A.22**

(a)   shall apply the consolidation procedures set out in Section 9 *Consolidated and Separate Financial Statements*;

(b)   is encouraged to provide the disclosures set out in paragraph 9.23;

(c)   shall comply so far as practicable with the requirements of Section 1A as if it were a single entity (Schedule 6 of the Small Companies Regulations, paragraph 1(1)), subject to any restrictions or exemptions set out in legislation; and

(d)   shall provide any disclosures required by Schedule 6 of the Small Companies Regulations.

Appendix A to Section 1A

Guidance on adapting the balance sheet formats

This appendix is an integral part of the Standard.

1AA.1   As set out in paragraph 1A.12 a small entity shall present a statement of financial position in accordance with the requirements for a balance sheet set out in either Part 1 *General Rules and Formats* of Schedule 1 to the Small Companies Regulations or Part 1 *General Rules and Formats* of Schedule 1 to the Small LLP Regulations. This results in three alternatives:

(a)   apply the required balance sheet formats as set out in legislation (subject to any permitted flexibility);

(b)   draw up an abridged balance sheet (see paragraph 1AA.2); or

(c)   adapt one of the balance sheet formats (see paragraphs 1AA.3 to 1AA.6).

Abridged balance sheet

1AA.2   A small entity choosing to apply paragraph 1A(1) of Schedule 1 to the Small Companies Regulations and draw up an abridged balance sheet must still meet the requirement for the financial statements to give a true and fair view. A small entity shall therefore also consider the requirements of paragraph 1A.16, and provide any additional disclosure that is necessary in the notes to the financial statements, for example in relation to disaggregating the information in the balance sheet.

Adapted balance sheet

1AA.3   A small entity choosing to apply paragraph 1B(1) of Schedule 1 to the Small Companies Regulations and adapt one of the balance sheet formats shall, as a minimum, include in its statement of financial position line items that present the following, distinguishing between those items that are **current** and those that are **non-current**:

(a)   **property, plant and equipment**;

(b)   **investment property** carried at **fair value** through profit or loss;

(c)   **intangible assets**;

(d)   **financial assets** (excluding amounts shown under (e), (f), (j) and (k));

(e)   investments in **associates**;

(f)   investments in **jointly controlled entities**;

(g)   **biological assets** carried at cost less accumulated **depreciation** and impairment;

(h)   biological assets carried at fair value through profit or loss;

(i)   **inventories**;

(j)   trade and other receivables;

(k)   **cash** and **cash equivalents**;

(l)   trade and other payables;

(m)   **provisions**;

(n)   financial liabilities (excluding amounts shown under (l) and (m));

(o)   liabilities and assets for **current tax**;

(p)   **deferred tax liabilities** and **deferred tax assets** (classified as non-current);
(q)   **non-controlling interest**, presented within equity separately from the equity attributable to the owners of the parent; and
(r)   equity attributable to the owners of the parent.

A small entity choosing to apply paragraph 1B(1) of Schedule 1 to the Small Companies Regulations and adapt one of the balance sheet formats shall also disclose, either in the statement of financial position or in the notes, the following sub-classifications of the line items presented: **1AA.4**

(a)   property, plant and equipment in classifications appropriate to the small entity;
(b)   **goodwill** and other intangible assets;
(c)   investments, showing separately shares and loans;
(d)   trade and other receivables, showing separately amounts due from **related parties** and amounts due from other parties;
(e)   trade and other payables, showing separately amounts payable to trade suppliers and amounts payable to related parties; and
(f)   classes of equity, such as called up share capital, share premium, retained earnings, revaluation reserve, fair value reserve and other reserves.

The descriptions used in paragraphs 1AA.3 and 1AA.4, and the ordering of items or aggregation of similar items, may be amended according to the nature of the small entity and its transactions, to provide information that is relevant to an understanding of the small entity's financial position, providing the information given is at least equivalent to that required by the balance sheet format had it not been adapted.   **1AA.5**

In order to comply with the requirement to distinguish between those items that are current and those that are non-current a small entity shall present current and non-current assets, and current and non-current liabilities, as separate classifications in its statement of financial position.   **1AA.6**

Appendix B to Section 1A

Guidance on adapting the profit and loss account formats

This appendix is an integral part of the Standard.

As set out in paragraph 1A.14 a small entity shall present its profit or loss for a period in an income statement in accordance with the requirements for a profit and loss account set out in either Part 1 *General Rules and Formats* of Schedule 1 to the Small Companies Regulations or Part 1 *General Rules and Formats* of Schedule 1 to the Small LLP Regulations. This results in three alternatives: **1AB.1**

(a)   apply the required profit and loss account formats as set out in legislation (subject to any permitted flexibility);
(b)   draw up an abridged profit and loss account (see paragraph 1AB.2); or
(c)   adapt one of the profit and loss account formats (see paragraphs 1AB.3 and 1AB.4).

Abridged profit and loss account

A small entity choosing to apply paragraph 1A(2) of Schedule 1 to the Small Companies Regulations and draw up an abridged profit and loss account must still meet the requirement for the financial statements to give a true and fair view. A small entity shall therefore also consider the requirements of paragraph 1A.16 and provide any additional disclosure that is necessary in the notes to the financial statements, for example in relation to disaggregating gross profit or loss and disclosing turnover.   **1AB.2**

Adapted profit and loss account

1AB.3   A small entity choosing to apply paragraph 1B(2) of Schedule 1 to the Small Companies Regulations and adapt one of the profit and loss account formats shall, as a minimum, include in its income statement line items that present the following amounts for the period:

(a)   **revenue**;

(b)   finance costs;

(c)   share of the profit or loss of investments in associates (see Section 14 *Investments in Associates*) and jointly controlled entities (see Section 15 *Investments in Joint Ventures*) accounted for using the equity method;

(d)   profit or loss before taxation;

(e)   **tax expense** excluding tax allocated to other comprehensive income or equity; and

(f)   profit or loss.

1AB.4   A small entity may include additional line items in the income statement and it amends the descriptions used in paragraph 1AB.3, and the ordering of items, when this is necessary to explain the elements of financial performance, providing the information given is at least equivalent to that required by the profit and loss account format had it not been adapted.

Appendix C to Section 1A

Disclosure requirements for small entities

This appendix is an integral part of the Standard.

This appendix sets out the disclosure requirements for small entities based on the requirements of company law. These are shown in italic font in the paragraphs below. Other than substituting company law terminology with the equivalent terminology used in FRS 102 (see Appendix III) the drafting is as close as possible to that set out in company law. References to Schedule 1 are to Schedule 1 of the Small Companies Regulations.

Where there is a similar disclosure requirement in FRS 102 this has been indicated and those paragraphs of FRS 102 that have been cross-referenced are also highlighted by including an * in the left-hand margin. In many cases compliance with the similar requirement of FRS 102 will result in compliance with the requirements below.

1AC.1   As a minimum, where relevant to its transactions, other events and conditions, a small entity shall provide the disclosures set out in this Appendix.

1AC.2   *The notes must be presented in the order in which, where relevant, the items to which they relate are presented in the statement of financial position and in the income statement. (Schedule 1, paragraph 42(2))*

Paragraphs 8.3 and 8.4 address similar requirements.

Accounting policies

1AC.3   *The accounting policies adopted by the small entity in determining the amounts to be included in respect of items shown in the statement of financial position and in determining the profit or loss of the small entity must be stated (including such policies with respect to the depreciation and impairment of assets). (Schedule 1, paragraph 44)*

Paragraph 8.5 addresses similar requirements. Including information about the judgements made in applying the small entity's accounting policies, as set out in paragraph 8.6, may be useful to users of the small entity's financial statements.

If any amount is included in a small entity's statement of financial position in respect of development costs, the note on accounting policies must include the following information: **1AC.4**

(a)   *the period over which the amount of those costs originally capitalised is being or is to be written off; and*

(b)   *the reasons for capitalising the development costs in question. (Schedule 1, paragraph 21(2))*

Paragraph 18.27(a) addresses similar requirements to paragraph 1AC.4(a).

Where development costs are shown or included as an asset in the small entity's financial statements and the amount is not treated as a realised loss because there are special circumstances justifying this, a note to the financial statements must state the reasons for showing development costs as an asset and that it is not a realised loss. (Section 844 of the Act)   **1AC.5**

Where in exceptional cases the useful life of intangible assets cannot be reliably estimated, there must be disclosed in a note to the financial statements the period over which those intangible assets are being written off and the reasons for choosing that period. (Schedule 1, paragraph 22(4))   **1AC.6**

Intangible assets include goodwill. Paragraphs 18.27(a) and 19.25(g) address similar requirements.

Changes in presentation and accounting policies and corrections of prior period errors

Where there is a change in the presentation of a small entity's statement of financial position or income statement, particulars of any such change must be given in a note to the financial statements in which the new presentation is first used, and the reasons for the change must be explained. (Schedule 1, paragraph 2(2))   **1AC.7**

Paragraphs 3.12 and 3.13 address similar requirements.

Where the corresponding amount for the immediately preceding financial year is not comparable with the amount to be shown for the item in question in respect of the reporting period, and the corresponding amount is adjusted, the particulars of the non-comparability and of any adjustment must be disclosed in a note to the financial statements. (Schedule 1, paragraph 7(2))   **1AC.8**

This is likely to be relevant where there has either been a change in accounting policy or the correction of a material prior period error. Paragraphs 10.13, 10.14 and 10.23 address similar requirements.

Where any amount relating to a preceding reporting period is included in any item in the income statement, the effect must be stated. (Schedule 1, paragraph 61(1))   **1AC.9**

True and fair override

If it appears to the small entity that there are special reasons for departing from any of the principles set out in company law in preparing the small entity's financial statements in respect of any reporting period, it may do so, in which case particulars of the departure, the reasons for it, and its effects must be given in the notes to the financial statements. (Schedule 1, paragraph 10(2))   **1AC.10**

This is only expected to occur in special circumstances. Paragraphs 3.4 and 3.5 address similar requirements.

Notes supporting the statement of financial position

1AC.11   *Where an asset or liability relates to more than one item in the statement of financial position, the relationship of such asset or liability to the relevant items must be disclosed either under those items or in the notes to the financial statements. (Schedule 1, paragraph 9A)*

Fixed assets

1AC.12   *In respect of each item which is shown under the general item 'fixed assets' in the small entity's statement of financial position the following information must be given:*

(a)   *the aggregate amounts (on the basis of cost or revaluation) in respect of that item as at the date of the beginning of the reporting period and as at the reporting date respectively;*

(b)   *the effect on any amount shown in the statement of financial position in respect of that item of:*

   (i)   *any revision of the amount in respect of any assets included under that item made during the reporting period as a result of revaluation;*

   (ii)   *acquisitions during the reporting period of any assets;*

   (iii)   *disposals during the reporting period of any assets; and*

   (iv)   *any transfers of assets of the small entity to and from that item during the reporting period. (Schedule 1, paragraphs 48(1) and 48(2))*

1AC.13   *In respect of each item within paragraph 1AC.12 there must also be stated:*

(a)   *the cumulative amount of provisions for depreciation and impairment of assets included under that item as at the date of the beginning of the reporting period and as at the reporting date respectively;*

(b)   *the amount of any such provisions made in respect of the reporting period;*

(c)   *the amount of any adjustments made in respect of any such provisions during the reporting period in consequence of the disposal of any assets; and*

(d)   *the amount of any other adjustments made in respect of any such provisions during the reporting period. (Schedule 1, paragraph 48(3))*

These two paragraphs apply to all fixed assets, including investment property, property, plant and equipment, intangible assets (including goodwill), fixed asset investments, biological assets and heritage assets recognised in the statement of financial position.

Each item refers to a class of fixed assets shown separately either in the statement of financial position, or in the notes to the financial statements.

These reconciliations need not be presented for prior periods.

Paragraph 16.10(e) addresses similar requirements for investment property. Paragraphs 17.31(d) and (e) address similar requirements for property, plant and equipment. Paragraphs 18.27(c) and (e) address similar requirements for intangible assets other than goodwill. Paragraph 19.26 addresses similar requirements for goodwill. Paragraphs 34.7(c) and 34.10(e) address similar requirements for biological assets. Paragraphs 34.55(e) and (f) address similar requirements for heritage assets recognised in the statement of financial position.

Fixed assets measured at revalued amounts

When fixed assets are measured at revalued amounts the items affected and the basis   **1AC.14**
of valuation adopted in determining the amounts of the assets in question in the case
of each such item must be disclosed in the note on accounting policies. (Schedule 1,
paragraph 34(2))

These requirements apply when:

● investments in subsidiaries, associates and joint ventures are measured at fair value with
changes in fair value recognised in other comprehensive income. Paragraph 9.27(b)
addresses a similar disclosure requirement;
● property, plant and equipment are revalued using the revaluation model set out
in paragraphs 17.15B to 17.15F. Paragraph 17.31(a) addresses a similar disclosure
requirement; and
● intangible assets other than goodwill are revalued using the revaluation model set out
in paragraphs 18.18B to 18.18H.

These requirements do not apply to investment property and biological assets measured at
fair value through profit or loss.

Where any fixed assets of the small entity (other than listed investments) are included   **1AC.15**
under any item shown in the small entity's statement of financial position at a revalued
amount, the following information must be given:

(a) *the years (so far as they are known to the directors) in which the assets were severally*
valued and the several values;
(b) *in the case of assets that have been valued during the reporting period, the names of*
the persons who valued them or particulars of their qualifications for doing so and
(whichever is stated) the bases of valuation used by them. (Schedule 1, paragraph 49)

Paragraphs 17.32A(a) and (c), 18.29A(a) and (c) and 34.55(e)(ii) address similar
requirements. These paragraphs do not require the names or qualifications of the persons
who valued the fixed assets to be disclosed; paragraphs 17.32A(b) and 18.29A(b) address
only whether or not the valuer was independent.

These requirements apply in the same circumstances as those set out in paragraph 1AC.14.

In the case of each item in the statement of financial position measured at a revalued   **1AC.16**
amount, the comparable amounts determined according to the historical cost accounting
rules must be shown in a note to the financial statements. (Schedule 1, paragraph 34(3))

The comparable amounts refers to the aggregate amount of cost and the aggregate of
accumulated depreciation and accumulated impairment losses that would have been
required according to the historical cost accounting rules (Schedule 1, paragraph 34(4)).

Paragraphs 17.32A(d) and 18.29A(d) address similar requirements.

These requirements apply in the same circumstances as those set out in paragraph 1AC.14.

Where fixed assets are measured at revalued amounts the following information must be   **1AC.17**
given in tabular form:

(a) *movements in the revaluation reserve in the reporting period, with an explanation of*
the tax treatment of items therein; and
(b) *the carrying amount in the statement of financial position that would have been*
recognised had the fixed assets not been revalued. (Schedule 1, paragraph 54(2))

Paragraphs 6.3A, 17.32A(d), 18.29A(d) and 29.27(a) address similar requirements.

These requirements apply in the same circumstances as those set out in paragraph 1AC.14.

1AC.18   *The treatment for taxation purposes of amounts credited or debited to the revaluation reserve must be disclosed in a note to the financial statements. (Schedule 1, paragraph 35(6))*

Paragraph 29.27(a) addresses similar requirements.

These requirements apply in the same circumstances as those set out in paragraph 1AC.14.

Capitalisation of borrowing costs

1AC.19   *When a small entity adopts a policy of capitalising borrowing costs, the inclusion of interest in determining the cost of the asset and the amount of the interest so included is disclosed in a note to the financial statements. (Schedule 1, paragraph 27(3))*

Paragraph 25.3A(a) addresses a similar requirement to the second part of this.

Impairment of assets

1AC.20   *Provisions for impairment of fixed assets (including fixed asset investments) must be disclosed separately in a note to the financial statements if not shown separately in the income statement. (Schedule 1, paragraph 19(3))*

Paragraph 27.32(a) addresses similar requirements.

1AC.21   *Any provisions for impairment of fixed assets that are reversed because the reasons for which they were made have ceased to apply must be disclosed (either separately or in aggregate) in a note to the financial statements if not shown separately in the income statement. (Schedule 1, paragraph 20(2))*

Paragraph 27.32(b) addresses similar requirements.

Fair value measurement

1AC.22   *Where financial instruments or other assets have been measured at fair value through profit or loss there must be stated:*

(a)   *the significant assumptions underlying the valuation models and techniques used to determine the fair values;*

(b)   *for each category of financial instrument or other asset, the fair value of the assets in that category and the change in value:*

  (i)   *included directly in the income statement; or*

  (ii)   *credited to or (as the case may be) debited from the fair value reserve,*

in respect of those assets. (Schedule 1, paragraphs 51(2)(a) and (b))

This does not apply where financial instruments or other assets are measured at fair value only on initial recognition.

This applies where financial instruments, certain inventories, investment property and biological assets are subsequently measured at fair value through profit or loss, which is permitted or required by paragraphs 9.26(c), 11.14(b), 11.14(d)(i), 12.8, 13.4A, 14.4(d), 15.9(d), 16.7 and 34.4.

Paragraphs 11.41(a), 11.41(d), 11.43, 11.48(a)(i), 11.48(a)(ii), 12.28, 12.29(c), and 12.29(e) address similar disclosure requirements for financial instruments. Paragraphs 16.10(a) and 16.10(e)(ii) address similar disclosure requirements for investment property. Paragraphs 34.7(b) and 34.7(c)(i) address similar disclosure requirements for biological assets.

Where financial instruments or other assets have been measured at fair value through **1AC.23**
profit or loss there must be stated for each class of derivatives, the extent and nature of the instruments, including significant terms and conditions that may affect the amount, timing and certainty of future cash flows. (Schedule 1, paragraph 51(2)(c))

Where any amount is transferred to or from the fair value reserve during the reporting **1AC.24**
period, there must be stated in tabular form:

(a) *the amount of the reserve as at the beginning of the reporting period and as at the reporting date respectively; and*
(b) *the amount transferred to or from the reserve during that year. (Schedule 1, paragraph 51(3))*

Paragraphs 6.3A, 12.29(c) and 12.29(d) address similar requirements.

The treatment for taxation purposes of amounts credited or debited to the fair value reserve **1AC.25**
must be disclosed in a note to the financial statements. (Schedule 1, paragraph 41(2))

Paragraph 29.27(a) addresses similar requirements.

Financial instruments measured at fair value

Financial instruments which under international accounting standards may be included in **1AC.26**
accounts at fair value, may be so included, provided that the disclosures required by such accounting standards are made. (Schedule 1, paragraph 36(4))

This only applies in certain circumstances; for example, it does not apply to derivatives. It applies where investments in subsidiaries, associates and joint ventures are measured at fair value through profit or loss. When it applies, the disclosures required by Section 11 that relate to financial assets and financial liabilities measured at fair value, including paragraph 11.48A, shall be given.

Indebtedness, guarantees and financial commitments

For the aggregate of all items shown under 'creditors' in the small entity's statement of **1AC.27**
financial position there must be stated the aggregate of the following amounts:

(a) *the amount of any debts included under 'creditors' which are payable or repayable otherwise than by instalments and fall due for payment or repayment after the end of the period of five years beginning with the day next following the reporting date; and*
(b) *in the case of any debts so included which are payable or repayable by instalments, the amount of any instalments which fall due for payment after the end of that period. (Schedule 1, paragraph 55(1))*

In respect of each item shown under 'creditors' in the small entity's statement of financial **1AC.28**
position there must be stated the aggregate amount of any debts included under that item in respect of which any security has been given by the small entity with an indication of the nature and form of any such security. (Schedule 1, paragraph 55(2))

Paragraphs 11.46, 13.22(e), 16.10(c), 17.32(a) and 18.28(c) address similar requirements.

1AC.29   *The total amount of any financial commitments, guarantees and contingencies that are not included in the balance sheet must be stated. (Schedule 1, paragraph 57(1))*

The total amount of any commitments concerning pensions must be separately disclosed. (Schedule 1, paragraph 57(3))

The total amount of any commitments which are undertaken on behalf of or for the benefit of:

(a)   *any parent, fellow subsidiary or any subsidiary of the small entity; or*

(b)   *any undertaking in which the small entity has a participating interest,*

must be separately stated and those within (a) must also be stated separately from those within (b). (Schedule 1, paragraph 57(4))

Such commitments can arise in a variety of situations, including in relation to group entities, investments, property, plant and equipment, leases and pension obligations. Paragraphs 15.19(d), 16.10(d), 17.32(b), 18.28(d), 20.16, 21.15, 28.40A(a), 28.40A(b), 28.41A(d), 33.9(b)(ii) and 34.62 address similar requirements.

1AC.30   *An indication of the nature and form of any valuable security given by the small entity in respect of commitments, guarantees and contingencies within paragraph 1AC.29 must be given. (Schedule 1, paragraph 57(2))*

Paragraphs 11.46, 13.22(e), 16.10(c), 17.32(a) and 18.28(c) address similar requirements.

1AC.31   *If in any reporting period a small entity is or has been party to arrangements that are not reflected in its statement of financial position and at the reporting date the risks or benefits arising from those arrangements are material the nature and business purpose of the arrangements must be given in the notes to the financial statements to the extent necessary for enabling the financial position of the small entity to be assessed. (Section 410A of the Act)*

Examples of off-balance sheet arrangements include risk and benefit-sharing arrangements or obligations arising from a contract such as debt factoring, combined sale and repurchase arrangements, consignment stock arrangements, take or pay arrangements, securitisation arranged through separate entities, pledged assets, operating lease arrangements, outsourcing and the like. In many cases the disclosures about financial commitments and contingencies required by paragraphs 1AC.29 and 1AC.30 will also address such arrangements.

Notes supporting the income statement

1AC.32   *The amount and nature of any individual items of income or expenses of exceptional size or incidence must be stated. (Schedule 1, paragraph 61(2))*

Paragraph 5.9A addresses a similar requirement in relation to material items.

1AC.33   *The notes to a small entity's financial statements must disclose the average number of persons employed by the small entity in the reporting period. (Section 411 of the Act)*

Related party disclosures

1AC.34   *Where the small entity is a subsidiary, the following information must be given in respect of the parent of the smallest group for which consolidated financial statements are drawn up of which the small entity is a member:*

(a)   *the name of the parent which draws up the consolidated financial statements;*
(b)   *the address of the parent's registered office (whether in or outside the UK); or*
(c)   *if it is unincorporated, the address of its principal place of business. (Schedule 1, paragraph 65)*

Paragraph 33.5 addresses a similar requirement to paragraph (a).

Particulars must be given of material transactions the small entity has entered into that have not been concluded under normal market conditions with: **1AC.35**

(a)   *owners holding a participating interest in the small entity;*
(b)   *companies in which the small entity itself has a participating interest; and*
(c)   *the small entity's directors [or members of its governing body].*

Particulars must include:

(a)   *the amount of such transactions;*
(b)   *the nature of the related party relationship; and*
(c)   *other information about the transactions necessary for an understanding of the financial position of the small entity.*

Information about individual transactions may be aggregated according to their nature, except where separate information is necessary for an understanding of the effects of the related party transactions on the financial position of the small entity.

Particulars need not be given of transactions entered into between two or more members of a group, provided that any subsidiary which is a party to the transaction is wholly-owned by such a member. (Schedule 1, paragraph 66)

Although disclosure is only required of material transactions with the specified related parties that have not been concluded under normal market conditions, small entities disclosing all transactions with such related parties would still be compliant with company law.

Transactions with directors, or members of an entity's governing body, include directors' remuneration and dividends paid to directors.

Paragraphs 33.9 and 33.14 address similar requirements for all related parties.

Details of advances and credits granted by the small entity to its directors and guarantees of any kind entered into by the small entity on behalf of its directors must be shown in the notes to the financial statements.   **1AC.36**

The details required of an advance or credit are:

(a)   *its amount;*
(b)   *an indication of the interest rate;*
(c)   *its main conditions;*
(d)   *any amounts repaid;*
(e)   *any amounts written off; and*
(f)   *any amounts waived.*

There must also be stated in the notes to the financial statements the totals of amounts stated under (a), (d), (e) and (f).

The details required of a guarantee are:

(a)   *its main terms;*

(b)   *the amount of the maximum liability that may be incurred by the small entity; and*

(c)   *any amount paid and any liability incurred by the small entity for the purpose of fulfilling the guarantee (including any loss incurred by reason of enforcement of the guarantee).*

There must also be stated in the notes to the financial statements the totals of amounts stated under (b) and (c). (Section 413 of the Act)

Paragraph 33.9 addresses similar requirements for all related parties.

A small entity that is not a company shall provide this disclosure in relation to members of its governing body.

Other

1AC.37   *The financial statements must state:*

(a)   *the part of the UK in which the small entity is registered;*

(b)   *the small entity's registered number;*

(c)   *whether the small entity is a public or a private company and whether the small entity is limited by shares or by guarantee;*

(d)   *the address of the small entity's registered office; and*

(e)   *where appropriate, the fact that the entity is being wound up. (Section 396 of the Act)*

Paragraph 3.24(a) addresses similar requirements.

1AC.38   *Where items to which Arabic numbers are given in any of the formats have been combined, unless they are not material, the individual amounts of any items which have been combined must be disclosed in a note to the financial statements. (Schedule 1, paragraph 4(3))*

1AC.39   *The nature and financial effect of material events arising after the reporting date which are not reflected in the income statement or statement of financial position must be stated. (Schedule 1, paragraph 64)*

Paragraphs 32.10 and 32.11 address similar requirements.

Appendix D to Section 1A

Additional disclosures encouraged for small entities

This appendix is an integral part of the Standard.

1AD.1   Where relevant to its transactions, other events and conditions, a small entity is encouraged to provide the following disclosures:

(a)   a statement of compliance with this FRS as set out in paragraph 3.3, adapted to refer to Section 1A;

(b)   a statement that it is a public benefit entity as set out in paragraph PBE3.3A;

(c)   the disclosures relating to going concern set out in paragraph 3.9;

(d)   dividends declared and paid or payable during the period (for example, as set out in paragraph 6.5(b)); and

(e)   on first-time adoption of this FRS an explanation of how the transition has affected its financial position and financial performance as set out in paragraph 35.13.

Section 2 Concepts and Pervasive Principles

Scope of this section

This section describes the **objective of financial statements** of entities within the scope of   2.1
this FRS and the qualities that make the information in the **financial statements** of entities
within the scope of this FRS useful. It also sets out the concepts and basic principles
underlying the financial statements of entities within the scope of this FRS.

Although this section sets out the concepts and pervasive principles underlying financial   2.1A
statements, in some circumstances there may be inconsistencies between the concepts and
principles in this section of the FRS and the specific requirements of another section. In
these circumstances the specific requirements of the other section within the FRS take
precedence over this section.

Objective of financial statements

The objective of financial statements is to provide information about the **financial**   2.2
position, **performance** and **cash flows** of an entity that is useful for economic decision-
making by a broad range of users who are not in a position to demand reports tailored to
meet their particular information needs.

Financial statements also show the results of the stewardship of management—the   2.3
accountability of management for the resources entrusted to it.

Qualitative characteristics of information in financial statements

Understandability

The information provided in financial statements should be presented in a way that makes   2.4
it comprehensible by users who have a reasonable knowledge of **business** and economic
activities and accounting and a willingness to study the information with reasonable
diligence. However, the need for **understandability** does not allow relevant information
to be omitted on the grounds that it may be too difficult for some users to understand.

Relevance

The information provided in financial statements must be relevant to the decision-making   2.5
needs of users. Information has the quality of **relevance** when it is capable of influencing
the economic decisions of users by helping them evaluate past, present or future events or
confirming, or correcting, their past evaluations.

Materiality

Information is **material**—and therefore has relevance—if its omission or misstatement,   2.6
individually or collectively, could influence the economic decisions of users taken on the
basis of the financial statements. Materiality depends on the size and nature of the omission
or misstatement judged in the surrounding circumstances. The size or nature of the item,
or a combination of both, could be the determining factor. However, it is inappropriate to
make, or leave uncorrected, immaterial departures from this FRS to achieve a particular
presentation of an entity's financial position, financial performance or cash flows.

Reliability

The information provided in financial statements must be reliable. Information is reliable   2.7
when it is free from material **error** and bias and represents faithfully that which it either

purports to represent or could reasonably be expected to represent. Financial statements are not free from bias (ie not neutral) if, by the selection or presentation of information, they are intended to influence the making of a decision or judgement in order to achieve a predetermined result or outcome.

Substance over form

2.8   Transactions and other events and conditions should be accounted for and presented in accordance with their substance and not merely their legal form. This enhances the **reliability** of financial statements.

Prudence

2.9   The uncertainties that inevitably surround many events and circumstances are acknowledged by the disclosure of their nature and extent and by the exercise of **prudence** in the preparation of the financial statements. Prudence is the inclusion of a degree of caution in the exercise of the judgements needed in making the estimates required under conditions of uncertainty, such that **assets** or **income** are not overstated and **liabilities** or **expenses** are not understated. However, the exercise of prudence does not allow the deliberate understatement of assets or income, or the deliberate overstatement of liabilities or expenses. In short, prudence does not permit bias.

Completeness

2.10   To be reliable, the information in financial statements must be complete within the bounds of materiality and cost. An omission can cause information to be false or misleading and thus unreliable and deficient in terms of its relevance.

Comparability

2.11   Users must be able to compare the financial statements of an entity through time to identify trends in its financial position and performance. Users must also be able to compare the financial statements of different entities to evaluate their relative financial position, performance and cash flows. Hence, the **measurement** and display of the financial effects of like transactions and other events and conditions must be carried out in a consistent way throughout an entity and over time for that entity, and in a consistent way across entities. In addition, users must be informed of the **accounting policies** employed in the preparation of the financial statements, and of any changes in those policies and the effects of such changes.

Timeliness

2.12   To be relevant, financial information must be able to influence the economic decisions of users. **Timeliness** involves providing the information within the decision time frame. If there is undue delay in the reporting of information it may lose its relevance. Management may need to balance the relative merits of timely reporting and the provision of reliable information. In achieving a balance between relevance and reliability, the overriding consideration is how best to satisfy the needs of users in making economic decisions.

Balance between benefit and cost

2.13   The benefits derived from information should exceed the cost of providing it. The evaluation of benefits and costs is substantially a judgemental process. Furthermore, the costs are not necessarily borne by those users who enjoy the benefits, and often the benefits of the information are enjoyed by a broad range of external users.

Financial reporting information helps capital providers make better decisions, which results in more efficient functioning of capital markets and a lower cost of capital for the economy as a whole. Individual entities also enjoy benefits, including improved access to capital markets, favourable effect on public relations, and perhaps lower costs of capital. The benefits may also include better management decisions because financial information used internally is often based at least partly on information prepared for general purpose financial reporting purposes.   **2.14**

Financial position

The financial position of an entity is the relationship of its assets, liabilities and **equity** as of a specific date as presented in the **statement of financial position**. These are defined as follows: **2.15**

(a)   An asset is a resource controlled by the entity as a result of past events and from which future economic benefits are expected to flow to the entity.

(b)   A liability is a present obligation of the entity arising from past events, the settlement of which is expected to result in an outflow from the entity of resources embodying economic benefits.

(c)   Equity is the residual interest in the assets of the entity after deducting all its liabilities.

Some items that meet the definition of an asset or a liability may not be recognised as assets or liabilities in the statement of financial position because they do not satisfy the criteria for **recognition** in paragraphs 2.27 to 2.32. In particular, the expectation that future economic benefits will flow to or from an entity must be sufficiently certain to meet the probability criterion before an asset or liability is recognised.   **2.16**

Assets

The future economic benefit of an asset is its potential to contribute, directly or indirectly, to the flow of **cash** and **cash equivalents** to the entity. Those cash flows may come from using the asset or from disposing of it.   **2.17**

Many assets, for example **property, plant and equipment**, have a physical form. However, physical form is not essential to the existence of an asset. Some assets are intangible.   **2.18**

In determining the existence of an asset, the right of ownership is not essential. Thus, for example, property held on a **lease** is an asset if the entity controls the benefits that are expected to flow from the property.   **2.19**

Liabilities

An essential characteristic of a liability is that the entity has a present obligation to act or perform in a particular way. The obligation may be either a legal obligation or a **constructive obligation**. A legal obligation is legally enforceable as a consequence of a binding contract or statutory requirement. A constructive obligation is an obligation that derives from an entity's actions when: **2.20**

(a)   by an established pattern of past practice, published policies or a sufficiently specific current statement, the entity has indicated to other parties that it will accept certain responsibilities; and

(b)   as a result, the entity has created a valid expectation on the part of those other parties that it will discharge those responsibilities.

2.21   The settlement of a present obligation usually involves the payment of cash, transfer of other assets, provision of services, the replacement of that obligation with another obligation, or conversion of the obligation to equity. An obligation may also be extinguished by other means, such as a creditor waiving or forfeiting its rights.

Equity

2.22   Equity is the residual interest in the assets of the entity after deducting all its liabilities. It may be sub-classified in the statement of financial position. For example, in a corporate entity, sub-classifications may include funds contributed by shareholders, retained earnings and **gains** or losses recognised in **other comprehensive income**.

Performance

2.23   Performance is the relationship of the income and expenses of an entity during a **reporting period**. This FRS permits entities to present performance in a single financial statement (a **statement of comprehensive income**) or in two financial statements (an **income statement** and a statement of comprehensive income). **Total comprehensive income** and **profit or loss** are frequently used as measures of performance or as the basis for other measures, such as return on investment or earnings per share. Income and expenses are defined as follows:

(a)   Income is increases in economic benefits during the reporting period in the form of inflows or enhancements of assets or decreases of liabilities that result in increases in equity, other than those relating to contributions from equity investors.

(b)   Expenses are decreases in economic benefits during the reporting period in the form of outflows or depletions of assets or incurrences of liabilities that result in decreases in equity, other than those relating to distributions to equity investors.

2.24   The recognition of income and expenses results directly from the recognition and measurement of assets and liabilities. Criteria for the recognition of income and expenses are discussed in paragraphs 2.27 to 2.32.

Income

2.25   The definition of income encompasses both **revenue** and gains.

(a)   Revenue is income that arises in the course of the ordinary activities of an entity and is referred to by a variety of names including sales, fees, interest, dividends, royalties and rent.

(b)   Gains are other items that meet the definition of income but are not revenue. When gains are recognised in the statement of comprehensive income, they are usually displayed separately because knowledge of them is useful for making economic decisions.

Expenses

2.26   The definition of expenses encompasses losses as well as those expenses that arise in the course of the ordinary activities of the entity.

(a)   Expenses that arise in the course of the ordinary activities of the entity include, for example, cost of sales, wages and **depreciation**. They usually take the form of an outflow or depletion of assets such as cash and cash equivalents, **inventory**, or property, plant and equipment.

(b)   Losses are other items that meet the definition of expenses and may arise in the course of the ordinary activities of the entity. When losses are recognised in the statement of comprehensive income, they are usually presented separately because knowledge of them is useful for making economic decisions.

Recognition of assets, liabilities, income and expenses

Recognition is the process of incorporating in the statement of financial position or statement of comprehensive income an item that meets the definition of an asset, liability, equity, income or expense and satisfies the following criteria: **2.27**

(a)   it is **probable** that any future economic benefit associated with the item will flow to or from the entity; and

(b)   the item has a cost or value that can be measured reliably.

The failure to recognise an item that satisfies those criteria is not rectified by disclosure of the accounting policies used or by **notes** or explanatory material. **2.28**

The probability of future economic benefit

The concept of probability is used in the first recognition criterion to refer to the degree of uncertainty that the future economic benefits associated with the item will flow to or from the entity. Assessments of the degree of uncertainty attaching to the flow of future economic benefits are made on the basis of the evidence relating to conditions at the end of the reporting period available when the financial statements are prepared. Those assessments are made individually for individually significant items, and for a group for a large population of individually insignificant items. **2.29**

Reliability of measurement

The second criterion for the recognition of an item is that it possesses a cost or value that can be measured with reliability. In many cases, the cost or value of an item is known. In other cases it must be estimated. The use of reasonable estimates is an essential part of the preparation of financial statements and does not undermine their reliability. When a reasonable estimate cannot be made, the item is not recognised in the financial statements. **2.30**

An item that fails to meet the recognition criteria may qualify for recognition at a later date as a result of subsequent circumstances or events. **2.31**

An item that fails to meet the criteria for recognition may nonetheless warrant disclosure in the notes or explanatory material or in supplementary schedules. This is appropriate when knowledge of the item is relevant to the evaluation of the financial position, performance and changes in financial position of an entity by the users of financial statements. **2.32**

Measurement of assets, liabilities, income and expenses

Measurement is the process of determining the monetary amounts at which an entity measures assets, liabilities, income and expenses in its financial statements. Measurement involves the selection of a basis of measurement. This FRS specifies which measurement basis an entity shall use for many types of assets, liabilities, income and expenses. **2.33**

Two common measurement bases are historical cost and **fair value**: **2.34**

(a)   For assets, historical cost is the amount of cash or cash equivalents paid or the fair value of the consideration given to acquire the asset at the time of its acquisition. For liabilities, historical cost is the amount of proceeds of cash or cash equivalents received or the fair value of non-cash assets received in exchange for the obligation at the time the obligation is incurred, or in some circumstances (for example,

income tax) the amounts of cash or cash equivalents expected to be paid to settle the liability in the normal course of business. Amortised historical cost is the historical cost of an asset or liability plus or minus that portion of its historical cost previously recognised as an expense or income.

(b)　Fair value is the amount for which an asset could be exchanged, a liability settled, or an equity instrument granted could be exchanged, between knowledgeable, willing parties in an arm's length transaction. In the absence of any specific guidance provided in the relevant section of this FRS, where fair value measurement is permitted or required the guidance in paragraphs 11.27 to 11.32 shall be applied.

Pervasive recognition and measurement principles

2.35　The requirements for recognising and measuring assets, liabilities, income and expenses in this FRS are based on pervasive principles that are derived from the IASB *Framework for the Preparation and Presentation of Financial Statements*[7] and from **EU-adopted IFRS**. In the absence of a requirement in this FRS that applies specifically to a transaction or other event or condition, paragraph 10.4 provides guidance for making a judgement and paragraph 10.5 establishes a hierarchy for an entity to follow in deciding on the appropriate accounting policy in the circumstances. The second level of that hierarchy requires an entity to look to the definitions, recognition criteria and measurement concepts for assets, liabilities, income and expenses and the pervasive principles set out in this section.

Accrual basis

2.36　An entity shall prepare its financial statements, except for cash flow information, using the **accrual basis** of accounting. On the accrual basis, items are recognised as assets, liabilities, equity, income or expenses when they satisfy the definitions and recognition criteria for those items.

Recognition in financial statements

Assets

2.37　An entity shall recognise an asset in the statement of financial position when it is probable that the future economic benefits will flow to the entity and the asset has a cost or value that can be measured reliably. An asset is not recognised in the statement of financial position when expenditure has been incurred for which it is considered not probable that economic benefits will flow to the entity beyond the current reporting period. Instead such a transaction results in the recognition of an expense in the statement of comprehensive income (or in the income statement, if presented).

2.38　An entity shall not recognise a **contingent asset** as an asset. However, when the flow of future economic benefits to the entity is virtually certain, then the related asset is not a contingent asset, and its recognition is appropriate.

Liabilities

2.39　An entity shall recognise a liability in the statement of financial position when:

(a)　the entity has an obligation at the end of the reporting period as a result of a past event;

---

[7] *In 2010 the IASB issued the Conceptual Framework for Financial Reporting, which superseded the Framework for the Preparation and Presentation of Financial Statements.*

(b)   it is probable that the entity will be required to transfer resources embodying economic benefits in settlement; and

(c)   the settlement amount can be measured reliably.

A **contingent liability** is either a possible but uncertain obligation or a present obligation   2.40
that is not recognised because it fails to meet one or both of the conditions (b) and (c) in
paragraph 2.39. An entity shall not recognise a contingent liability as a liability, except for
contingent liabilities of an acquiree in a **business combination** (see Section 19 *Business
Combinations and Goodwill*).

Income

The recognition of income results directly from the recognition and measurement of assets   2.41
and liabilities. An entity shall recognise income in the statement of comprehensive income
(or in the income statement, if presented) when an increase in future economic benefits
related to an increase in an asset or a decrease of a liability has arisen that can be measured
reliably.

Expenses

The recognition of expenses results directly from the recognition and measurement of   2.42
assets and liabilities. An entity shall recognise expenses in the statement of comprehensive
income (or in the income statement, if presented) when a decrease in future economic
benefits related to a decrease in an asset or an increase of a liability has arisen that can be
measured reliably.

Total comprehensive income and profit or loss

Total comprehensive income is the arithmetical difference between income and expenses.   2.43
It is not a separate element of financial statements, and a separate recognition principle is
not needed for it.

Profit or loss is the arithmetical difference between income and expenses other than those   2.44
items of income and expense that this FRS classifies as items of other comprehensive
income. It is not a separate element of financial statements, and a separate recognition
principle is not needed for it.

Generally this FRS does not allow the recognition of items in the statement of financial   2.45
position that do not meet the definition of assets or of liabilities regardless of whether
they result from applying the notion commonly referred to as the 'matching concept' for
measuring profit or loss.

Measurement at initial recognition

At initial recognition, an entity shall measure assets and liabilities at historical cost unless   2.46
this FRS requires initial measurement on another basis such as fair value.

Subsequent measurement

Financial assets and financial liabilities

An entity measures basic **financial assets** and basic **financial liabilities** at amortised cost   2.47
less impairment except for:

(a)   investments in non-convertible preference shares and non-puttable ordinary and preference shares that are **publicly traded** or whose fair value can otherwise be measured reliably, which are measured at fair value with changes in fair value recognised in profit or loss; and

(b)   any financial instruments that upon their initial recognition were designated by the entity as at fair value through profit or loss.

2.48   An entity generally measures all other financial assets and financial liabilities at fair value, with changes in fair value recognised in profit or loss, unless this FRS requires or permits measurement on another basis such as cost or amortised cost.

Non-financial assets

2.49   Most non-financial assets that an entity initially recognised at historical cost are subsequently measured on other measurement bases. For example:

(a)   An entity measures property, plant and equipment using either the cost model or the revaluation model.

(b)   An entity measures inventories at the lower of cost and selling price less costs to complete and sell.

Measurement of assets at amounts lower than initial historical cost is intended to ensure that an asset is not measured at an amount greater than the entity expects to recover from the sale or use of that asset.

2.50   For certain types of non-financial assets, this FRS permits or requires measurement at fair value. For example:

(a)   Investments in **associates** and **joint ventures** that an entity measures at fair value (see paragraphs 14.4(b) and 14.4B, and 15.9(b) and 15.9B respectively).

(b)   **Investment property** that an entity measures at fair value (see paragraph 16.7).

(c)   **Biological assets** that an entity measures at fair value less estimated costs to sell in accordance with the fair value model (see paragraph 34.3A(a)) and **agricultural produce** that an entity measures, at the point of harvest, at fair value less estimated costs to sell in accordance with either the fair value model (see paragraph 34.3A(a)) or cost model (see paragraph 34.9).

(d)   Property, plant and equipment that an entity measures in accordance with the revaluation model (see paragraph 17.15B).

(e)   **Intangible assets** that an entity measures in accordance with the revaluation model (see paragraph 18.18B).

Liabilities other than financial liabilities

2.51   Most liabilities other than financial liabilities are measured at the best estimate of the amount that would be required to settle the obligation at the **reporting date**.

Offsetting

2.52   An entity shall not offset assets and liabilities, or income and expenses, unless required or permitted by an FRS.

(a)   Measuring assets net of valuation allowances (for example, allowances for inventory obsolescence and allowances for uncollectible receivables) is not offsetting.

(b)   If an entity's normal **operating activities** do not include buying and selling **fixed assets**, including investments and operating assets, then the entity reports gains and losses on disposal of such assets by deducting from the proceeds on disposal the **carrying amount** of the asset and related selling expenses.

Section 3 Financial Statement Presentation

Scope of this section

This section explains that the **financial statements** of an entity shall give a true and fair view, what compliance with this FRS requires, and what is a complete set of financial statements.   **3.1**

A **small entity** applying Section 1A *Small Entities* is not required to comply with paragraphs 3.3, PBE3.3A, 3.9, 3.17, 3.18, 3.19 and 3.24(b).   **3.1A**

True and fair view

The financial statements shall give a true and fair view of the **assets**, **liabilities**, **financial position**, financial **performance** and, when required to be presented, **cash flows** of an entity.   **3.2**

(a)   The application of this FRS, with additional disclosure when necessary, is presumed to result in financial statements that give a true and fair view of the financial position, financial performance and, when required to be presented, cash flows of entities within the scope of this FRS.

(b)   [Not used]

The additional disclosures referred to in (a) are necessary when compliance with the specific requirements in this FRS is insufficient to enable users to understand the effect of particular transactions, other events and conditions on the entity's financial position and financial performance.

Compliance with this FRS

An entity whose financial statements comply with this FRS shall make an explicit and unreserved statement of such compliance in the **notes**. Financial statements shall not be described as complying with this FRS unless they comply with all the requirements of this FRS.   **3.3**

A **public benefit entity** that applies the 'PBE' prefixed paragraphs shall make an explicit and unreserved statement that it is a public benefit entity.   **PBE3.3A**

In special circumstances when management concludes that compliance with any requirement of this FRS or applicable legislation (only when it allows for a true and fair override) is inconsistent with the requirement to give a true and fair view, the entity shall depart from that requirement in the manner set out in paragraph 3.5.   *** 3.4**

When an entity departs from a requirement of this FRS in accordance with paragraph 3.4, or from a requirement of applicable legislation, it shall disclose the following: *** 3.5**

(a)   that management has concluded that the financial statements give a true and fair view of the entity's financial position, financial performance and, when required to be presented, cash flows;

(b)   that it has complied with this FRS or applicable legislation, except that it has departed from a particular requirement of this FRS or applicable legislation to the extent necessary to give a true and fair view; and

(c)   the nature and effect of the departure, including the treatment that this FRS or applicable legislation would require, the reason why that treatment would be so misleading in the circumstances that it would conflict with the objective of financial statements set out in Section 2, and the treatment adopted.

3.6   When an entity has departed from a requirement of this FRS or applicable legislation in a prior period, and that departure affects the amounts recognised in the financial statements for the current period, it shall make the disclosures set out in paragraph 3.5(c).

3.7   [Not used]

Going concern

3.8   When preparing financial statements, the management of an entity using this FRS shall make an assessment of the entity's ability to continue as a **going concern**. An entity is a going concern unless management either intends to liquidate the entity or to cease trading, or has no realistic alternative but to do so. In assessing whether the going concern assumption is appropriate, management takes into account all available information about the future, which is at least, but is not limited to, twelve months from the date when the financial statements are authorised for issue.

3.9   When management is aware, in making its assessment, of **material** uncertainties related to events or conditions that cast significant doubt upon the entity's ability to continue as a going concern, the entity shall disclose those uncertainties. When an entity does not prepare financial statements on a going concern basis, it shall disclose that fact, together with the basis on which it prepared the financial statements and the reason why the entity is not regarded as a going concern.

Frequency of reporting

3.10   An entity shall present a complete set of financial statements (including comparative information as set out in paragraph 3.14) at least annually. When the end of an entity's **reporting period** changes and the annual financial statements are presented for a period longer or shorter than one year, the entity shall disclose the following:

   (a)   that fact;
   (b)   the reason for using a longer or shorter period; and
   (c)   the fact that comparative amounts presented in the financial statements (including the related notes) are not entirely comparable.

Consistency of presentation

3.11   An entity shall retain the presentation and classification of items in the financial statements from one period to the next unless:

   (a)   it is apparent, following a significant change in the nature of the entity's operations or a review of its financial statements, that another presentation or classification would be more appropriate having regard to the criteria for the selection and application of **accounting policies** in Section 10 *Accounting Policies, Estimates and Errors*; or
   (b)   this FRS, or another applicable FRS or FRC Abstract, requires a change in presentation.

* 3.12   When the presentation or classification of items in the financial statements is changed, an entity shall reclassify comparative amounts unless the reclassification is **impracticable**. When comparative amounts are reclassified, an entity shall disclose the following:

   (a)   the nature of the reclassification;
   (b)   the amount of each item or class of items that is reclassified; and
   (c)   the reason for the reclassification.

If it is impracticable to reclassify comparative amounts, an entity shall disclose why reclassification was not practicable.   *** 3.13**

Comparative information

Except when this FRS permits or requires otherwise, an entity shall present comparative information in respect of the preceding period for all amounts presented in the current period's financial statements. An entity shall include comparative information for narrative and descriptive information when it is relevant to an understanding of the current period's financial statements.   **3.14**

Materiality and aggregation

An entity shall present separately each material class of similar items. An entity shall present separately items of a dissimilar nature or function unless they are immaterial.   **3.15**

Financial statements result from processing large numbers of transactions or other events that are aggregated into classes according to their nature or function. The final stage in the process of aggregation and classification is the presentation of condensed and classified data, which form line items in the financial statements. If a line item is not individually material, it is aggregated with other items either in those statements or in the notes. An item that may not warrant separate presentation in those statements may warrant separate presentation in the notes.   **3.16**

An entity need not provide a specific disclosure required by this FRS if the information is not material.   **3.16A**

Complete set of financial statements

A complete set of financial statements of an entity shall include all of the following: **3.17**

(a)   a **statement of financial position** as at the **reporting date**;
(b)   either:
     (i)   a single **statement of comprehensive income** for the reporting period displaying all items of income and expense recognised during the period including those items recognised in determining **profit or loss** (which is a subtotal in the statement of comprehensive income) and items of **other comprehensive income**; or
     (ii)   a separate **income statement** and a separate statement of comprehensive income. If an entity chooses to present both an income statement and a statement of comprehensive income, the statement of comprehensive income begins with profit or loss and then displays the items of other comprehensive income;
(c)   a **statement of changes in equity** for the reporting period;
(d)   a **statement of cash flows** for the reporting period; and
(e)   notes, comprising a summary of significant accounting policies and other explanatory information.

If the only changes to **equity** during the periods for which financial statements are presented arise from profit or loss, payment of dividends, corrections of prior period **errors**, and changes in accounting policy, the entity may present a single **statement of income and retained earnings** in place of the statement of comprehensive income and statement of changes in equity (see paragraph 6.4).   **3.18**

3.19   If an entity has no items of other comprehensive income in any of the periods for which financial statements are presented, it may present only an income statement, or it may present a statement of comprehensive income in which the 'bottom line' is labelled 'profit or loss'.

3.20   Because paragraph 3.14 requires comparative amounts in respect of the previous period for all amounts presented in the financial statements, a complete set of financial statements means that an entity shall present, as a minimum, two of each of the required financial statements and related notes.

3.21   In a complete set of financial statements, an entity shall present each financial statement with equal prominence.

3.22   An entity may use titles for the financial statements other than those used in this FRS as long as they are not misleading.

Identification of the financial statements

3.23   An entity shall clearly identify each of the financial statements and the notes and distinguish them from other information in the same document. In addition, an entity shall display the following information prominently, and repeat it when necessary for an understanding of the information presented:

(a)   the name of the reporting entity and any change in its name since the end of the preceding reporting period;

(b)   whether the financial statements cover the individual entity or a group of entities;

(c)   the date of the end of the reporting period and the period covered by the financial statements;

(d)   the **presentation currency**, as defined in Section 30 *Foreign Currency Translation*; and

(e)   the level of rounding, if any, used in presenting amounts in the financial statements.

3.24   An entity shall disclose the following in the notes:

* (a)   the legal form of the entity, its country of incorporation and the address of its registered office (or principal place of business, if different from the registered office); and

(b)   a description of the nature of the entity's operations and its principal activities, unless this is disclosed in the business review (or similar statement) accompanying the financial statements.

Presentation of information not required by this FRS

3.25   This FRS does not address presentation of **interim financial reports**. An entity that prepares such reports shall describe the basis for preparing and presenting the information. **FRS 104** sets out a basis for the preparation and presentation of interim financial reports that an entity may apply.

Section 4 Statement of Financial Position

Scope of this section

4.1   This section sets out the information that is to be presented in a **statement of financial position** and how to present it. The statement of financial position (which is referred to as the balance sheet in the **Act**) presents an entity's **assets, liabilities** and **equity** as of a specific date—the end of the **reporting period**. This section applies to all entities, whether or not they report under the Act. Entities that do not report under the Act should comply with the requirements of this section, and with the **Regulations** (or, where applicable, the **LLP Regulations**) where referred to in this section, except to the extent that these requirements are not permitted by any statutory framework under which such entities report.

A **small entity** applying Section 1A *Small Entities* is not required to comply with this section.   **4.1A**

Information to be presented in the statement of financial position

An entity shall present a statement of financial position in accordance with one of the following requirements for a balance sheet: **4.2**

(a)   Part 1 *General Rules and Formats* of Schedule 1 to the Regulations.
(b)   Part 1 *General Rules and Formats* of Schedule 2 to the Regulations.
(c)   Part 1 *General Rules and Formats* of Schedule 3 to the Regulations.
(d)   Part 1 *General Rules and Formats* of Schedule 1 to the LLP Regulations.

The consolidated statement of financial position of a **group** shall be presented in accordance with the requirements for a consolidated balance sheet in Schedule 6 to the Regulations or Schedule 3 to the LLP Regulations.

An entity choosing to apply paragraph 1A(1) of Schedule 1 to the Regulations and adapt one of the balance sheet formats shall, as a minimum, include in its statement of financial position line items that present the following, distinguishing between those items that are **current** and those that are **non-current**:   **4.2A**

(a)   **property, plant and equipment**;
(b)   **investment property** carried at **fair value** through profit or loss;
(c)   **intangible assets**;
(d)   **financial assets** (excluding amounts shown under (e), (f), (j) and (k));
(e)   investments in **associates**;
(f)   investments in **jointly controlled entities**;
(g)   **biological assets** carried at cost less accumulated **depreciation** and impairment;
(h)   biological assets carried at fair value through profit or loss;
(i)   **inventories**;
(j)   trade and other receivables;
(k)   **cash** and **cash equivalents**;
(l)   trade and other payables;
(m)   **provisions**;
(n)   financial liabilities (excluding amounts shown under (l) and (m));
(o)   liabilities and assets for **current tax**;
(p)   **deferred tax liabilities** and **deferred tax assets** (classified as non-current);
(q)   **non-controlling interest**, presented within equity separately from the equity attributable to the owners of the **parent**; and
(r)   equity attributable to the owners of the parent.

An entity choosing to apply paragraph 1A(1) of Schedule 1 to the Regulations shall also disclose, either in the statement of financial position or in the **notes**, the following sub-classifications of the line items presented: **4.2B**

(a)   property, plant and equipment in classifications appropriate to the entity;
(b)   intangible assets and **goodwill** in classifications appropriate to the entity;
(c)   investments, showing separately shares and loans;

(d)   trade and other receivables showing separately amounts due from **related parties**, amounts due from other parties, prepayments and receivables arising from accrued income not yet billed;

(e)   inventories, showing separately amounts of inventories:

    (i)   held for sale in the ordinary course of business;

    (ii)   in the process of production for such sale; and

    (iii)   in the form of materials or supplies to be consumed in the production process or in the rendering of services.

(f)   trade and other payables, showing separately amounts payable to trade suppliers, payable to related parties, deferred income and accruals; and

(g)   classes of equity, such as share capital, share premium, retained earnings, revaluation reserve, fair value reserve and other reserves.

4.2C   The descriptions used in paragraphs 4.2A and 4.2B, and the ordering of items or aggregation of similar items, may be amended according to the nature of the entity and its transactions, to provide information that is relevant to an understanding of the entity's financial position, providing the information given is at least equivalent to that required by the balance sheet format had it not been adapted.

4.2D   In order to comply with the requirement to distinguish between those items that are current and those that are non-current an entity shall present current and non-current assets, and current and non-current liabilities, as separate classifications in its statement of financial position.

4.3   An entity shall present additional line items, headings and subtotals in the statement of financial position when such presentation is relevant to an understanding of the entity's **financial position**.

Debtors due after more than one year

4.4   [Not used]

4.4A   Unless an entity chooses to apply paragraph 1A(1) of Schedule 1 to the Regulations, in instances where the amount of debtors due after more than one year is so **material** in the context of the total net current assets that in the absence of disclosure of the debtors due after more than one year on the face of the statement of financial position readers may misinterpret the **financial statements**, the amount should be disclosed on the face of the statement of financial position within **current assets**. In most cases it will be satisfactory to disclose the amount due after more than one year in the **notes** to the financial statements.

4.5   [Not used]

4.6   [Not used]

Creditors: amounts falling due within one year

4.7   Unless an entity chooses to apply paragraph 1A(1) of Schedule 1 to the Regulations, an entity shall classify a creditor as due within one year when the entity does not have an unconditional right, at the end of the reporting period, to defer settlement of the creditor for at least 12 months after the **reporting date**. For example, this would be the case if the earliest date on which the lender, exercising all available options and rights, could require repayment or (as the case may be) payment was within 12 months after the reporting date.

[Not used]   **4.8**

Information to be presented either in the statement of financial position or in the notes

[Not used]   **4.9**

[Not used]   **4.10**

[Not used]   **4.11**

An entity with share capital shall disclose the following, either in the statement of financial   **4.12**
position or in the notes:

(a)   For each class of share capital:

    (i)   [Not used]

    (ii)   The number of shares issued and fully paid, and issued but not fully paid.

    (iii)   Par value per share, or that the shares have no par value.

    (iv)   A reconciliation of the number of shares outstanding at the beginning and
    at the end of the period. This reconciliation need not be presented for prior
    periods.

    (v)   The rights, preferences and restrictions attaching to that class including
    restrictions on the distribution of dividends and the repayment of capital.

    (vi)   Shares in the entity held by the entity or by its **subsidiaries**, **associates**, or
    joint ventures.

    (vii)   Shares reserved for issue under options and contracts for the sale of shares,
    including the terms and amounts.

(b)   A description of each reserve within equity.

An entity without share capital, such as a partnership or trust, shall disclose information   **4.13**
equivalent to that required by paragraph 4.12(a), showing changes during the period in
each category of equity, and the rights, preferences and restrictions attaching to each
category of equity.

Information to be presented in the notes

If, at the reporting date, an entity has a binding sale agreement for a major disposal of   **4.14**
assets, or a **disposal group**, the entity shall disclose the following information:

(a)   a description of the asset(s) or the disposal group;

(b)   a description of the facts and circumstances of the sale; and

(c)   the **carrying amount** of the assets or, for a disposal group, the carrying amounts of
    the underlying assets and liabilities.

Section 5 Statement of Comprehensive Income and Income Statement

Scope of this section

This section requires an entity to present its **total comprehensive income** for a period—   **5.1**
ie its financial **performance** for the period—in one or two statements. It sets out the
information that is to be presented in those statements and how to present it. This section
applies to all entities, whether or not they report under the **Act**. Entities that do not
report under the Act should comply with the requirements of this section, and with the
Regulations (or, where applicable, the **LLP Regulations**) where referred to in this section,
except to the extent that these requirements are not permitted by any statutory framework

under which such entities report. If an entity meets specified conditions and chooses to do so, it may present a **statement of income and retained earnings** as set out in Section 6 *Statement of Change in Equity and Statement of Income and Retained Earnings.*

5.1A   A **small entity** applying Section 1A *Small Entities* is not required to comply with this section.

Presentation of total comprehensive income

5.2   An entity shall present its total comprehensive income for a period either:

(a)   in a single **statement of comprehensive income**, in which case the statement of comprehensive income presents all items of **income** and **expense** recognised in the period; or

(b)   in two statements—an **income statement** (which is referred to as the profit and loss account in the Act) and a statement of comprehensive income—in which case the income statement presents all items of income and expense recognised in the period except those that are recognised in total comprehensive income outside of **profit or loss** as permitted or required by this FRS.

5.3   A change from the single-statement approach to the two-statement approach, or vice versa, is a change in **accounting policy** to which Section 10 *Accounting Policies, Estimates and Errors* applies.

Single-statement approach

5.4   [Not used]

5.5   An entity shall present, in the statement of comprehensive income, the items to be included in a profit and loss account in accordance with one of the following requirements:

(a)   Part 1 *General Rules and Formats* of Schedule 1 to the Regulations;
(b)   Part 1 *General Rules and Formats* of Schedule 2 to the Regulations;
(c)   Part 1 *General Rules and Formats* of Schedule 3 to the Regulations; or
(d)   Part 1 *General Rules and Formats* of Schedule 1 to the LLP Regulations.

The consolidated statement of comprehensive income of a **group** shall be presented in accordance with the requirements for a consolidated profit and loss account of Schedule 6 to the Regulations or Schedule 3 to the LLP Regulations.

5.5A   In addition an entity shall include, in the statement of comprehensive income, line items that present the following amounts for the period:

(a)   Classified by nature (excluding amounts in (b)), the components of **other comprehensive income** recognised as part of total comprehensive income outside profit or loss as permitted or required by this FRS. An entity may present the components of other comprehensive income either:

(i)   net of related tax effects; or
(ii)   before the related tax effects with one amount shown for the aggregate amount of **income tax** relating to those components.

(b)   Its share of the other comprehensive income of **associates** and **jointly controlled entities** accounted for by the equity method.
(c)   Total comprehensive income.

An entity choosing to apply paragraph 1A(2) of Schedule 1 to the Regulations and adapt one of the profit and loss account formats shall, as a minimum, include in its statement of comprehensive income line items that present the following amounts for the period: **5.5B**

(a) **revenue**;
(b) finance costs;
(c) share of the profit or loss of investments in **associates** (see Section 14 *Investments in Associates*) and **jointly controlled entities** (see Section 15 *Investments in Joint Ventures*) accounted for using the equity method;
(d) profit or loss before taxation;
(e) **tax expense** excluding tax allocated to items (h) and (i) below or to **equity** (see paragraph 29.27);
(f) as set out in paragraph 5.7E (including a column identified as **discontinued operations**) a single amount comprising the total of:

    (i) the post-tax profit or loss of a discontinued operation, and
    (ii) the post-tax gain or loss recognised on the remeasurement of the impairment or on the disposal of the **assets** or **disposal group(s)** constituting discontinued operations.

(g) profit or loss;
(h) each item of other comprehensive income classified by nature (excluding amounts in (i));
(i) share of other comprehensive income of associates and jointly controlled entities accounted for by the equity method; and
(j) total comprehensive income.

An entity may include additional line items in the income statement and amend the descriptions used in paragraph 5.5B, and the ordering of items, when this is necessary to explain the elements of financial performance, providing the information given is at least equivalent to that required by the profit and loss account format had it not been adapted. **5.5C**

An entity shall present the following items as allocations of profit or loss and other comprehensive income in the statement of comprehensive income for the period: **5.6**

(a) Profit or loss for the period attributable to:

    (i) **non-controlling interest**; and
    (ii) **owners** of the **parent**.

(b) Total comprehensive income for the period attributable to:

    (i) non-controlling interest; and
    (ii) owners of the parent.

Two-statement approach

Under the two-statement approach, an entity shall present in an income statement, the items to be included in a profit and loss account in accordance with one of the following requirements: **5.7**

(a) Part 1 *General Rules and Formats* of Schedule 1 to the Regulations;
(b) Part 1 *General Rules and Formats* of Schedule 2 to the Regulations;
(c) Part 1 *General Rules and Formats* of Schedule 3 to the Regulations; or
(d) Part 1 *General Rules and Formats* of Schedule 1 to the LLP Regulations.

The consolidated income statement of a group shall be presented in accordance with the requirements for a consolidated profit and loss account of Schedule 6 to the Regulations or Schedule 3 to the LLP Regulations.

5.7A An entity choosing to apply paragraph 1A(2) of Schedule 1 to the Regulations and adapt one of the profit and loss account formats shall, as a minimum, include in its income statement line items that present the amounts in paragraphs 5.5B(a) to 5.5B(g), with profit or loss as the last line. The statement of comprehensive income shall begin with profit or loss as its first line and shall display, as a minimum, line items that present the amounts in paragraphs 5.5B(h) to 5.5B(j) and paragraph 5.6(b) for the period, with total comprehensive income as the last line.

5.7B If an entity presents profit or loss in an income statement, it shall present the information required in paragraph 5.6(a) in that statement.

5.7C The statement of comprehensive income shall begin with profit or loss as its first line and shall display, as a minimum, line items that present the amounts in paragraphs 5.5A and 5.6(b) for the period.

Requirements applicable to both approaches

5.7D In addition to the requirements of paragraphs 5.5 or 5.7, as a minimum, **turnover** must be presented on the face of the income statement (or statement of comprehensive income if presented).

5.7E An entity shall also disclose on the face of the income statement (or statement of comprehensive income if presented) an amount comprising the total of:

(a) the post-tax profit or loss of discontinued operations; and
(b) the post-tax gain or loss attributable to the impairment or on the disposal of the assets or disposal group(s) constituting discontinued operations.

A line-by-line analysis shall be presented in the income statement (or statement of comprehensive income if presented), in a column identified as relating to discontinued operations, ie separately from continuing operations; a total column shall also be presented.

5.7F An entity shall re-present the disclosures in paragraph 5.7D for prior periods presented in the **financial statements** so that the disclosures relate to all operations that have been discontinued by the end of the **reporting period** for the latest period presented.

5.8 Under this FRS, the effects of corrections of **material errors** and changes in accounting policies are presented as retrospective adjustments of prior periods rather than as part of profit or loss in the period in which they arise (see Section 10).

5.9 An entity shall present additional line items, headings and subtotals in the statement of comprehensive income (and in the income statement, if presented), when such presentation is relevant to an understanding of the entity's financial performance.

* 5.9A When items included in total comprehensive income are material, an entity shall disclose their nature and amount separately, in the statement of comprehensive income (and in the income statement, if presented) or in the **notes**.

5.9B This FRS does not require disclosure of 'operating profit'. However, if an entity elects to disclose the results of **operating activities** the entity should ensure that the amount disclosed is representative of activities that would normally be regarded as 'operating'. For example, it would be inappropriate to exclude items clearly related to operations (such as inventory write-downs and restructuring and relocation expenses) because they occur irregularly or infrequently or are unusual in amount. Similarly, it would be inappropriate to exclude items on the grounds that they do not involve **cash flows**, such as **depreciation** and **amortisation** expenses.

Ordinary activities and extraordinary items

An entity applying paragraph 5.5(a) or 5.7(a) shall not present or describe any items of income or expense as 'extraordinary items' in the statement of comprehensive income (or in the income statement, if presented) or in the notes.   **5.10**

Paragraphs 5.10A and 5.10B apply to entities applying paragraphs 5.5(b), 5.5(c), 5.5(d), 5.7(b), 5.7(c) or 5.7(d).

Ordinary activities are any activities which are undertaken by a reporting entity as part of its business and such related activities in which the reporting entity engages in furtherance of, incidental to, or arising from, these activities. Ordinary activities include any effects on the reporting entity of any event in the various environments in which it operates, including the political, regulatory, economic and geographical environments, irrespective of the frequency or unusual nature of the events.   **5.10A**

Extraordinary items are material items possessing a high degree of abnormality which arise from events or transactions that fall outside the ordinary activities of the reporting entity and which are not expected to recur. The additional line items required to be presented by paragraph 5.9 and material items required to be disclosed by paragraph 5.9A, are not extraordinary items when they arise from the ordinary activities of the entity. Extraordinary items do not include prior period items merely because they relate to a prior period.   **5.10B**

Analysis of expenses

Unless otherwise required under the Regulations, an entity shall present an analysis of expenses using a classification based on either the nature of expenses or the function of expenses within the entity, whichever provides information that is reliable and more relevant.   **5.11**

Analysis by nature of expense

(a) Under this method of classification, expenses are aggregated in the statement of comprehensive income (or in the income statement, under the two-statement approach) according to their nature (eg depreciation, raw materials and consumables and staff costs), and are not reallocated among various functions within the entity.

Analysis by function of expense

(b) Under this method of classification, expenses are aggregated according to their function as part of cost of sales or, for example, the costs of distribution or administrative activities.

Appendix to Section 5

Example showing presentation of discontinued operations

This appendix accompanies, but is not part of, Section 5. It provides guidance on applying the requirements of Section 5 paragraph 5.7E for presenting discontinued operations. The example illustrates the presentation of comprehensive income in a single statement and the classification of expenses within profit by function. A columnar format is used in order to present a single line item as required by paragraph 5.7E, while still complying with the requirements of the Act to show totals for ordinary activities of items such as turnover, profit or loss before taxation and tax.

Statement of comprehensive income

for the year ended 31 December 20X1

	20X1			20X0		
	Continuing operations	Discontinued operations	Total	Continuing operations (as restated)	Discontinued operations (as restated)	Total
	CU	CU	CU	CU	CU	CU
Turnover	4,200	1,232	5,432	3,201	1,500	4,701
Cost of Sales	(2,591)	(1,104)	(3,695)	(2,281)	(1,430)	(3,711)
Gross profit	1,609	128	1,737	920	70	990
Administrative expenses	(452)	(110)	(562)	(418)	(120)	(538)
Other operating income	212	—	212	198	—	198
Profit on disposal of operations		301	301			
Operating profit	1,369	319	1,688	700	(50)	650
Interest receivable and similar income	14	—	14	16	—	16
Interest payable and similar charges	(208)	—	(208)	(208)	—	(208)
Profit on ordinary activities before tax	1,175	319	1,494	508	(50)	458
Taxation	(390)	(4)	(394)	(261)	3	(258)
Profit on ordinary activities after taxation and profit for the financial year	785	315	1,100	247	(47)	200
Other comprehensive income						
Actuarial losses on defined benefit pension plans			(108)			(68)
Deferred tax movement relating to actuarial losses			28			18
Total comprehensive income for the year			1,020			150

Section 6 Statement of Changes in Equity and Statement of Income and Retained Earnings

Scope of this section

6.1 This section sets out requirements for presenting the changes in an entity's **equity** for a period, either in a statement of changes in equity or, if specified conditions are met and an entity chooses, in a **statement of income and retained earnings**.

6.1A A **small entity** applying Section 1A *Small Entities* is not required to comply with this section. However, paragraph 1A.9 encourages a small entity to present a statement of changes in equity or a statement of income and retained earnings.

Statement of changes in equity

Purpose

The statement of changes in equity presents an entity's **profit or loss** for a **reporting period**, **other comprehensive income** for the period, the effects of changes in **accounting policies** and corrections of **material errors** recognised in the period, and the amounts of investments by, and dividends and other distributions to, equity investors during the period.   6.2

Information to be presented in the statement of changes in equity

An entity shall present a statement of changes in equity showing in the statement: 6.3

(a)   **total comprehensive income** for the period, showing separately the total amounts attributable to **owners** of the **parent** and to **non-controlling interests**;

(b)   for each component of equity, the effects of **retrospective application** or retrospective restatement recognised in accordance with Section 10 *Accounting Policies, Estimates and Errors*; and

(c)   for each component of equity, a reconciliation between the **carrying amount** at the beginning and the end of the period, separately disclosing changes resulting from:

   (i)   profit or loss;

   (ii) other comprehensive income; and

   (iii) the amounts of investments by, and dividends and other distributions to, owners, showing separately issues of shares, purchase of own share transactions, dividends and other distributions to owners, and changes in ownership interests in **subsidiaries** that do not result in a loss of **control**.

Information to be presented in the statement of changes in equity or in the notes

For each component of equity, an entity shall present, either in the statement of changes in equity or in the **notes**, an analysis of other comprehensive income by item (see paragraph 6.3(c)(ii)).   * 6.3A

Statement of income and retained earnings

Purpose

The statement of income and retained earnings presents an entity's profit or loss and changes in retained earnings for a reporting period. Paragraph 3.18 permits an entity to present a statement of income and retained earnings in place of a **statement of comprehensive income** and a statement of changes in equity if the only changes to its equity during the periods for which **financial statements** are presented arise from profit or loss, payment of dividends, corrections of prior period material errors, and changes in accounting policy.   6.4

Information to be presented in the statement of income and retained earnings

An entity shall present, in the statement of income and retained earnings, the following items in addition to the information required by Section 5 *Statement of Comprehensive Income and Income Statement*:   6.5

(a)   retained earnings at the beginning of the reporting period;

(b)   dividends declared and paid or payable during the period;

(c)   restatements of retained earnings for corrections of prior period material errors;

(d)   restatements of retained earnings for changes in accounting policy; and

(e)   retained earnings at the end of the reporting period.

Section 7 Statement of Cash Flows

Scope of this section

7.1   This section sets out the information that is to be presented in a **statement of cash flows** and how to present it. The statement of cash flows provides information about the changes in **cash** and **cash equivalents** of an entity for a **reporting period**, showing separately changes from **operating activities**, **investing activities** and **financing activities**.

7.1A   This section and paragraph 3.17(d) do not apply to:

(a)   mutual life assurance companies;

(b)   **retirement benefit plans**; or

(c)   investment funds that meet all the following conditions:

(i)   substantially all of the entity's investments are highly liquid;

(ii)   substantially all of the entity's investments are carried at market value; and

(iii)   the entity provides a statement of changes in net assets.

7.1B   A **small entity** is not required to comply with this section.

Cash equivalents

7.2   Cash equivalents are short-term, highly liquid investments that are readily convertible to known amounts of cash and that are subject to an insignificant risk of changes in value. Therefore, an investment normally qualifies as a cash equivalent only when it has a short maturity of, say, three months or less from the date of acquisition. Bank overdrafts are normally considered financing activities similar to borrowings. However, if they are repayable on demand and form an integral part of an entity's cash management, bank overdrafts are a component of cash and cash equivalents.

Information to be presented in the statement of cash flows

7.3   An entity shall present a statement of **cash flows** that presents cash flows for a reporting period classified by operating activities, investing activities and financing activities.

Operating activities

7.4   Operating activities are the principal revenue-producing activities of the entity. Therefore, cash flows from operating activities generally result from the transactions and other events and conditions that enter into the determination of **profit or loss**. Examples of cash flows from operating activities are:

(a)   cash receipts from the sale of goods and the rendering of services;

(b)   cash receipts from royalties, fees, commissions and other revenue;

(c)   cash payments to suppliers for goods and services;

(d)   cash payments to and on behalf of employees;

(e)   cash payments or refunds of **income tax**, unless they can be specifically identified with financing and investing activities;

(f)   cash receipts and payments from investments, loans and other contracts held for dealing or trading purposes, which are similar to **inventory** acquired specifically for resale; and

(g)   cash advances and loans made to other parties by **financial institutions**.

Some transactions, such as the sale of an item of plant by a manufacturing entity, may give rise to a **gain** or loss that is included in profit or loss. However, the cash flows relating to such transactions are cash flows from investing activities.

Investing activities

Investing activities are the acquisition and disposal of long-term assets and other   **7.5**
investments not included in cash equivalents. Examples of cash flows arising from
investing activities are:

(a)   cash payments to acquire **property, plant and equipment** (including self-
      constructed property, plant and equipment), **intangible assets** and other long-term
      assets. These payments include those relating to capitalised development costs and
      self-constructed property, plant and equipment;

(b)   cash receipts from sales of property, plant and equipment, intangibles and other long-
      term assets;

(c)   cash payments to acquire **equity** or debt instruments of other entities and interests
      in **joint ventures** (other than payments for those instruments classified as cash
      equivalents or held for dealing or trading);

(d)   cash receipts from sales of equity or debt instruments of other entities and interests in
      joint ventures (other than receipts for those instruments classified as cash equivalents
      or held for dealing or trading);

(e)   cash advances and loans made to other parties (except those made by financial
      institutions – see paragraph 7.4(g));

(f)   cash receipts from the repayment of advances and loans made to other parties;

(g)   cash payments for futures contracts, forward contracts, option contracts and swap
      contracts, except when the contracts are held for dealing or trading, or the payments
      are classified as financing activities; and

(h)   cash receipts from futures contracts, forward contracts, option contracts and swap
      contracts, except when the contracts are held for dealing or trading, or the receipts
      are classified as financing activities.

When a contract is accounted for as a hedge (see Section 12 *Other Financial Instruments
Issues*), an entity shall classify the cash flows of the contract in the same manner as the
cash flows of the item being hedged.

Financing activities

Financing activities are activities that result in changes in the size and composition of   **7.6**
the contributed equity and borrowings of an entity. Examples of cash flows arising from
financing activities are:

(a)   cash proceeds from issuing shares or other equity instruments;

(b)   cash payments to **owners** to acquire or redeem the entity's shares;

(c)   cash proceeds from issuing debentures, loans, notes, bonds, mortgages and other
      short-term or long-term borrowings;

(d)   cash repayments of amounts borrowed; and

(e)   cash payments by a lessee for the reduction of the outstanding **liability** relating to a
      finance lease.

Reporting cash flows from operating activities

An entity shall present cash flows from operating activities using either: **7.7**

(a)   the indirect method, whereby profit or loss is adjusted for the effects of non-cash
      transactions, any deferrals or accruals of past or future operating cash receipts or
      payments, and items of **income** or **expense** associated with investing or financing
      cash flows; or

(b)   the direct method, whereby major classes of gross cash receipts and gross cash
      payments are disclosed.

Indirect method

7.8   Under the indirect method, the net cash flow from operating activities is determined by adjusting profit or loss for the effects of:

(a)   changes during the period in inventories and operating receivables and payables;

(b)   non-cash items such as **depreciation**, **provisions**, **deferred tax**, accrued income (expenses) not yet received (paid) in cash, unrealised foreign currency gains and losses, undistributed profits of **associates**, and **non-controlling interests**; and

(c)   all other items for which the cash effects relate to investing or financing.

Direct method

7.9   Under the direct method, net cash flow from operating activities is presented by disclosing information about major classes of gross cash receipts and gross cash payments. Such information may be obtained either:

(a)   from the accounting records of the entity; or

(b)   by adjusting sales, cost of sales and other items in the **statement of comprehensive income** (or the **income statement**, if presented) for:

(i)   changes during the period in inventories and operating receivables and payables;

(ii)   other non-cash items; and

(iii)   other items for which the cash effects are investing or financing cash flows.

Reporting cash flows from investing and financing activities

7.10   An entity shall present separately major classes of gross cash receipts and gross cash payments arising from investing and financing activities, except to the extent that net presentation is permitted by paragraphs 7.10A to 7.10E. The aggregate cash flows arising from acquisitions and from disposals of **subsidiaries** or other business units shall be presented separately and classified as investing activities.

Reporting cash flows on a net basis

7.10A   Cash flows arising from the following operating, investing or financing activities may be reported on a net basis:

(a)   cash receipts and payments on behalf of customers when the cash flows reflect the activities of the customer rather than those of the entity; and

(b)   cash receipts and payments for items in which the turnover is quick, the amounts are large, and the maturities are short.

7.10B   Examples of cash receipts and payments referred to in paragraph 7.10A(a) are:

(a)   the acceptance and repayment of demand deposits of a bank;

(b)   funds held for customers by an investment entity; and

(c)   rents collected on behalf of, and paid over to, the owners of properties.

7.10C   Examples of cash receipts and payments referred to in paragraph 7.10A(b) are advances made for, and the repayment of:

(a)   principal amounts relating to credit card customers;

(b)   the purchase and sale of investments; and

(c)   other short-term borrowings, for example, those which have a maturity period of three months or less.

Financial institutions may report cash flows described in paragraph 34.33 on a net basis.	**7.10D**

A financial institution that undertakes the business of effecting or carrying out **insurance contracts**, other than mutual life assurance companies scoped out of this section in paragraph 7.1A(a), should include the cash flows of their long-term business only to the extent of cash transferred and available to meet the obligations of the company or group as a whole. **7.10E**

Foreign currency cash flows

An entity shall record cash flows arising from transactions in a foreign currency in the entity's **functional currency** by applying to the foreign currency amount the exchange rate between the functional currency and the foreign currency at the date of the cash flow or an exchange rate that approximates the actual rate (for example, a weighted average exchange rate for the period). **7.11**

An entity shall translate cash flows of a foreign subsidiary at the exchange rate between the entity's functional currency and the foreign currency at the date of the cash flow or at an exchange rate that approximates the actual rate (for example, a weighted average exchange rate for the period). **7.12**

Unrealised gains and losses arising from changes in foreign currency exchange rates are not cash flows. However, to reconcile cash and cash equivalents at the beginning and the end of the period, the effect of exchange rate changes on cash and cash equivalents held or due in a foreign currency must be presented in the statement of cash flows. Therefore, the entity shall remeasure cash and cash equivalents held during the reporting period (such as amounts of foreign currency held and foreign currency bank accounts) at period-end exchange rates. The entity shall present the resulting unrealised gain or loss separately from cash flows from operating, investing and financing activities. **7.13**

Interest and dividends

An entity shall present separately cash flows from interest and dividends received and paid. The entity shall classify these cash flows consistently from period to period as operating, investing or financing activities. **7.14**

An entity may classify interest paid and interest and dividends received as operating cash flows because they are included in profit or loss. Alternatively, the entity may classify interest paid and interest and dividends received as financing cash flows and investing cash flows respectively, because they are costs of obtaining financial resources or returns on investments. **7.15**

An entity may classify dividends paid as a financing cash flow because they are a cost of obtaining financial resources. Alternatively, the entity may classify dividends paid as a component of cash flows from operating activities because they are paid out of operating cash flows. **7.16**

Income tax

An entity shall present separately cash flows arising from income tax and shall classify them as cash flows from operating activities unless they can be specifically identified with financing and investing activities. When tax cash flows are allocated over more than one class of activity, the entity shall disclose the total amount of taxes paid. **7.17**

Non-cash transactions

7.18 An entity shall exclude from the statement of cash flows investing and financing transactions that do not require the use of cash or cash equivalents. An entity shall disclose such transactions elsewhere in the **financial statements** in a way that provides all the relevant information about those investing and financing activities.

7.19 Many investing and financing activities do not have a direct impact on current cash flows even though they affect the capital and asset structure of an entity. The exclusion of non-cash transactions from the statement of cash flows is consistent with the objective of a statement of cash flows because these items do not involve cash flows in the current period. Examples of non-cash transactions are:

    (a)   the acquisition of assets either by assuming directly related liabilities or by means of a finance lease;

    (b)   the acquisition of an entity by means of an equity issue; and

    (c)   the conversion of debt to equity.

Components of cash and cash equivalents

7.20 An entity shall present the components of cash and cash equivalents and shall present a reconciliation of the amounts presented in the statement of cash flows to the equivalent items presented in the **statement of financial position**. However, an entity is not required to present this reconciliation if the amount of cash and cash equivalents presented in the statement of cash flows is identical to the amount similarly described in the statement of financial position.

7.20A Entities applying Part 1 *General Rules and Formats* of Schedule 2 to the **Regulations** should include as cash, only cash and balances at central banks and loans and advances to banks repayable on demand.

Other disclosures

7.21 An entity shall disclose, together with a commentary by management, the amount of significant cash and cash equivalent balances held by the entity that are not available for use by the entity. Cash and cash equivalents held by an entity may not be available for use by the entity because of, among other reasons, foreign exchange controls or legal restrictions.

Section 8 Notes to the Financial Statements

Scope of this section

8.1 This section sets out the principles underlying information that is to be presented in the **notes** to the **financial statements** and how to present it. Notes contain information in addition to that presented in the **statement of financial position**, **statement of comprehensive income** (if presented), **income statement** (if presented), combined **statement of income and retained earnings** (if presented), **statement of changes in equity** (if presented), and **statement of cash flows**. Notes provide narrative descriptions or disaggregations of items presented in those statements and information about items that do not qualify for **recognition** in those statements. In addition to the requirements of this section, nearly every other section of this FRS requires disclosures that are normally presented in the notes.

Structure of the notes

The notes shall: **8.2**

(a)   present information about the basis of preparation of the financial statements and the
      specific **accounting policies** used, in accordance with paragraphs 8.5 to 8.7;
(b)   disclose the information required by this FRS that is not presented elsewhere in the
      financial statements; and
(c)   provide information that is not presented elsewhere in the financial statements but is
      relevant to an understanding of any of them.

An entity shall, as far as practicable, present the notes in a systematic manner. An entity   *** 8.3**
shall cross-reference each item in the financial statements to any related information in
the notes.

An entity normally[8] presents the notes in the following order: *** 8.4**

(a)   a statement that the financial statements have been prepared in compliance with this
      FRS (see paragraph 3.3);
(b)   a summary of significant accounting policies applied (see paragraph 8.5);
(c)   supporting information for items presented in the financial statements, in the
      sequence in which each statement and each line item is presented; and
(d)   any other disclosures.

Disclosure of accounting policies

An entity shall disclose the following in the summary of significant accounting policies: *** 8.5**

(a)   the measurement basis (or bases) used in preparing the financial statements; and
(b)   the other accounting policies used that are relevant to an understanding of the
      financial statements.

Information about judgements

An entity shall disclose, in the summary of significant accounting policies or other   *** 8.6**
notes, the judgements, apart from those involving estimations (see paragraph 8.7), that
management has made in the process of applying the entity's accounting policies and that
have the most significant effect on the amounts recognised in the financial statements.

Information about key sources of estimation uncertainty

An entity shall disclose in the notes information about the key assumptions concerning the   **8.7**
future, and other key sources of estimation uncertainty at the reporting date, that have a
significant risk of causing a **material** adjustment to the **carrying amounts** of **assets** and
liabilities within the next financial year. In respect of those assets and liabilities, the notes
shall include details of:

(a)   their nature; and
(b)   their carrying amount as at the end of the **reporting period**.

---

[8] *Company law requires the notes to be presented in the order in which, where relevant, the items to which they relate
are presented in the statement of financial position and in the income statement.*

Section 9 Consolidated and Separate Financial Statements

Scope of this section

9.1   This section applies to all **parents** that present **consolidated financial statements** (which are referred to as group accounts in the **Act**) intended to give a true and fair view of the **financial position** and **profit or loss** (or **income and expenditure**) of their **group**, whether or not they report under the Act. Parents that do not report under the Act should comply with the requirements of this section, and of the Act where referred to in this section, except to the extent that these requirements are not permitted by any statutory framework under which such entities report. This section also includes guidance on **individual financial statements** and **separate financial statements**.

Requirement to present consolidated financial statements

9.2   Except as permitted or required by paragraph 9.3, a parent entity shall present consolidated financial statements in which it consolidates all its investments in **subsidiaries** in accordance with this FRS. A parent entity need only prepare consolidated accounts under the Act if it is a parent at the year end.

9.3   A parent is exempt from the requirement to prepare consolidated financial statements on any one of the following grounds:

When its immediate parent is established under the law of an EEA State (Section 400 of the Act):

(a)   The parent is a wholly-owned subsidiary. Exemption is conditional on compliance with certain further conditions set out in section 400(2) of the Act.

(b)   The immediate parent holds 90% or more of the allotted shares in the entity and the remaining shareholders have approved the exemption. Exemption is conditional on compliance with certain further conditions set out in section 400(2) of the Act.

(bA) The immediate parent holds more than 50% (but less than 90%) of the allotted shares in the entity, and notice requesting the preparation of consolidated financial statements has not been served on the entity by shareholders holding in aggregate at least 5% of the allotted shares in the entity. Exemption is conditional on compliance with certain further conditions set out in section 400(2) of the Act.

When its parent is not established under the law of an EEA State (Section 401 of the Act):

(c)   The parent is a wholly-owned subsidiary. Exemption is conditional on compliance with certain further conditions set out in section 401(2) of the Act.

(d)   The parent holds 90% or more of the allotted shares in the entity and the remaining shareholders have approved the exemption. Exemption is conditional on compliance with certain further conditions set out in section 401(2) of the Act.

(dA) The parent holds more than 50% (but less than 90%) of the allotted shares in the entity, and notice requesting the preparation of consolidated financial statements has not been served on the entity by shareholders holding in aggregate at least 5% of the allotted shares in the entity. Exemption is conditional on compliance with certain further conditions set out in section 401(2) of the Act.

Other situations

(e)   The parent, and the group headed by it, qualify as small as set out in section 383 of the Act and the parent and the group are considered eligible for the exemption as determined by reference to sections 384 and 399(2A) of the Act.

(f)   All of the parent's subsidiaries are required to be excluded from consolidation by paragraph 9.9 (Section 402 of the Act).

(g)   For a parent not reporting under the Act, if its statutory framework does not require the preparation of consolidated financial statements.

In sub-paragraphs (a) to (dA), the parent is not exempt if any of its transferable securities are admitted to trading on a regulated market of any EEA State within the meaning of Directive 2004/39/EC.

A subsidiary is an entity that is controlled by the parent. **Control** is the power to govern the financial and operating policies of an entity so as to obtain benefits from its activities.   **9.4**

Control is presumed to exist when the parent owns, directly or indirectly through subsidiaries, more than half of the voting power of an entity. That presumption may be overcome in exceptional circumstances if it can be clearly demonstrated that such ownership does not constitute control. Control also exists when the parent owns half or less of the voting power of an entity but it has: **9.5**

(a)   power over more than half of the voting rights by virtue of an agreement with other investors;

(b)   power to govern the financial and operating policies of the entity under a statute or an agreement;

(c)   power to appoint or remove the majority of the members of the board of directors or equivalent governing body and control of the entity is by that board or body; or

(d)   power to cast the majority of votes at meetings of the board of directors or equivalent governing body and control of the entity is by that board or body.

Control can also be achieved by having options or convertible instruments that are currently exercisable or by having an agent with the ability to direct the activities for the benefit of the controlling entity.   **9.6**

Control can also exist when the parent has the power to exercise, or actually exercises, dominant influence or control over the undertaking or it and the undertaking are managed on a unified basis.   **9.6A**

[Not used]   **9.7**

A subsidiary is not excluded from consolidation because its business activities are dissimilar to those of the other entities within the consolidation. Relevant information is provided by consolidating such subsidiaries and disclosing additional information in the consolidated financial statements about the different business activities of subsidiaries.   **9.8**

A subsidiary is not excluded from consolidation because the information necessary for the preparation of consolidated financial statements cannot be obtained without disproportionate **expense** or undue delay, unless its inclusion is not **material** (individually or collectively for more than one subsidiary) for the purposes of giving a true and fair view in the context of the group.   **9.8A**

A subsidiary shall be excluded from consolidation where: **9.9**

(a)   severe long-term restrictions substantially hinder the exercise of the rights of the parent over the **assets** or management of the subsidiary; or

(b)   the interest in the subsidiary is **held exclusively with a view to subsequent resale**; and the subsidiary has not previously been consolidated in the consolidated financial statements prepared in accordance with this FRS.

A subsidiary excluded from consolidation on the grounds set out in paragraph 9.9(a) shall be measured using an accounting policy selected by the parent in accordance with paragraph 9.26, except where the parent still exercises a significant influence over the   **9.9A** subsidiary. If this is the case, the parent should treat the subsidiary as an associate using the equity method set out in paragraph 14.8.

9.9B   A subsidiary excluded from consolidation on the grounds set out in paragraph 9.9(b) which is:

(a)   **held as part of an investment portfolio** shall be measured at **fair value** with changes in fair value recognised in profit or loss;[9] or

(b)   not held as part of an investment portfolio shall be measured using an **accounting policy** selected by the parent in accordance with paragraph 9.26.

Special purpose entities

9.10   An entity may be created to accomplish a narrow objective (eg to effect a **lease**, undertake **research** and **development** activities, securitise **financial assets** or facilitate employee shareholdings under remuneration schemes, such as Employee Share Ownership Plans (ESOPs)). Such a special purpose entity (SPE) may take the form of a corporation, trust, partnership or unincorporated entity. Often, SPEs are created with legal arrangements that impose strict requirements over the operations of the SPE.

9.11   Except as permitted or required by paragraph 9.3, a parent entity shall prepare consolidated financial statements that include the entity and any SPEs that are controlled by that entity. In addition to the circumstances described in paragraph 9.5, the following circumstances may indicate that an entity controls a SPE (this is not an exhaustive list):

(a)   the activities of the SPE are being conducted on behalf of the entity according to its specific business needs;

(b)   the entity has the ultimate decision-making powers over the activities of the SPE even if the day-to-day decisions have been delegated;

(c)   the entity has rights to obtain the majority of the benefits of the SPE and therefore may be exposed to risks incidental to the activities of the SPE; and

(d)   the entity retains the majority of the residual or ownership risks related to the SPE or its assets.

9.12   Paragraphs 9.10 and 9.11 do not apply to **post-employment benefit plans** or other long-term employee benefit plans to which Section 28 *Employee Benefits* applies. A special purpose entity that is an intermediate payment arrangement shall be accounted for in accordance with paragraphs 9.33 to 9.38.

Consolidation procedures

9.13   The consolidated financial statements present financial information about the group as a single economic entity. In preparing consolidated financial statements, an entity shall:

(a)   combine the **financial statements** of the parent and its subsidiaries line by line by adding together like items of assets, **liabilities**, **equity**, **income** and expenses;

(b)   eliminate the **carrying amount** of the parent's investment in each subsidiary and the parent's portion of equity of each subsidiary;

(c)   measure and present **non-controlling interest** in the profit or loss of consolidated subsidiaries for the **reporting period** separately from the interest of the **owners** of the parent; and

---

[9] *Additional disclosures may need to be provided in accordance with company law (see Appendix IV, paragraph A4.17).*

(d)   measure and present non-controlling interest in the net assets of consolidated subsidiaries separately from the parent shareholders' equity in them. Non-controlling interest in the net assets consists of:

    (i)   the amount of the non-controlling interest's share in the net amount of the identifiable assets, liabilities and contingent liabilities recognised and measured in accordance with Section 19 *Business Combinations and Goodwill* at the date of the original combination; and

    (ii)   the non-controlling interest's share of changes in equity since the date of the combination.

The proportions of profit or loss and changes in equity allocated to the owners of the parent and to the non-controlling interest are determined on the basis of existing ownership interests and do not reflect the possible exercise or conversion of options or convertible instruments.   **9.14**

Intragroup balances and transactions

Intragroup balances and transactions, including income, expenses and dividends, are eliminated in full. Profits and losses resulting from intragroup transactions that are recognised in assets, such as **inventory** and **property, plant and equipment**, are eliminated in full. Intragroup losses may indicate an impairment that requires **recognition** in the consolidated financial statements (see Section 27 *Impairment of Assets*). Section 29 *Income Tax* applies to **timing differences** that arise from the elimination of profits and losses resulting from intragroup transactions.   **9.15**

Uniform reporting date and reporting period

The financial statements of the parent and its subsidiaries used in the preparation of the consolidated financial statements shall be prepared as of the same **reporting date**, and for the same reporting period, unless it is **impracticable** to do so. Where the reporting date and reporting period of a subsidiary are not the same as the parent's reporting date and reporting period, the consolidated financial statements must be made up: **9.16**

(a)   from the financial statements of the subsidiary as of its last reporting date before the parent's reporting date, adjusted for the effects of significant transactions or events that occur between the date of those financial statements and the date of the consolidated financial statements, provided that reporting date is no more than three months before that of the parent; or

(b)   from interim financial statements prepared by the subsidiary as at the parent's reporting date.

Uniform accounting policies

Consolidated financial statements shall be prepared using uniform accounting policies for like transactions and other events and conditions in similar circumstances. If a member of the group uses accounting policies other than those adopted in the consolidated financial statements for like transactions and events in similar circumstances, appropriate adjustments are made to its financial statements in preparing the consolidated financial statements.   **9.17**

Acquisition and disposal of subsidiaries

The income and expenses of a subsidiary are included in the consolidated financial statements from the **acquisition date**, except when a **business combination** is accounted   **9.18** for by using the merger accounting method under Section 19 or, for certain public benefit entity combinations, Section 34 *Specialised Activities*. The income and expenses of a subsidiary are included in the consolidated financial statements until the date on which the parent ceases to control the subsidiary. A parent may cease to control a subsidiary with or without a change in absolute or relative ownership levels. This could occur, for example, when a subsidiary becomes subject to the control of a government, court, administrator or regulator.

Disposal – where control is lost

9.18A   Where a parent ceases to control a subsidiary, a **gain** or loss is recognised in the consolidated statement of comprehensive income (or in the **income statement**, if presented) calculated as the difference between:

(a)   the proceeds from the disposal (or the event that resulted in the loss of control); and

(b)   the proportion of the carrying amount of the subsidiary's net assets, including any related **goodwill**, disposed of (or lost) as at the date of disposal (or date control is lost).

The cumulative amount of any exchange differences that relate to a foreign subsidiary recognised in equity in accordance with Section 30 *Foreign Currency Translation* is not recognised in profit or loss as part of the gain or loss on disposal of the subsidiary and shall be transferred directly to retained earnings.

9.18B   The gain or loss arising on the disposal shall also include those amounts that have been recognised in **other comprehensive income** in relation to that subsidiary, where those amounts are required to be reclassified to profit or loss upon disposal in accordance with other sections of this FRS. Amounts that are not required to be reclassified to profit or loss upon disposal of the related assets or liabilities in accordance with other sections of this FRS shall be transferred directly to retained earnings.

9.19   If an entity ceases to be a subsidiary but the investor (former parent) continues to hold:

(a)   an investment that is not an **associate** (see paragraph 9.19(b)) or a **jointly controlled entity** (see paragraph 9.19(c)), that investment shall be accounted for as a financial asset in accordance with Section 11 *Basic Financial Instruments* or Section 12 *Other Financial Instruments Issues* from the date the entity ceases to be a subsidiary;

(b)   an associate, that associate shall be accounted for in accordance with Section 14 *Investments in Associates*; or

(c)   a jointly controlled entity, that jointly controlled entity shall be accounted for in accordance with Section 15 *Investments in Joint Ventures*.

The carrying amount of the net assets (and goodwill) attributable to the investment at the date that the entity ceases to be a subsidiary shall be regarded as the cost on initial **measurement** of the financial asset, investment in associate or jointly controlled entity, as appropriate. In applying the equity method to investments in associate or jointly controlled entities as required in sub-paragraphs (b) and (c) above, paragraph 14.8(c) shall not be applied.

Disposal – where control is retained

9.19A   Where a parent reduces its holding in a subsidiary and control is retained, it shall be accounted for as a transaction between equity holders and the resulting change in non-controlling interest shall be accounted for in accordance with paragraph 22.19. No gain or loss shall be recognised at the date of disposal.

Acquisition – Control achieved in stages

Where a parent acquires control of a subsidiary in stages, the transaction shall be accounted   **9.19B**
for in accordance with paragraphs 19.11A and 19.14 applied at the date control is achieved.

Acquisition – Increasing a controlling interest in a subsidiary

Where a parent increases its controlling interest in a subsidiary, the identifiable assets and   **9.19C**
liabilities and a **provision** for **contingent liabilities** of the subsidiary shall not be revalued
to fair value and no additional goodwill shall be recognised at the date the controlling
interest is increased.

The transaction shall be accounted for as a transaction between equity holders and the   **9.19D**
resulting change in non-controlling interest shall be accounted for in accordance with
paragraph 22.19.

Non-controlling interest in subsidiaries

An entity shall present non-controlling interest in the consolidated statement of financial   **9.20**
position within equity, separately from the equity of the owners of the parent.

An entity shall disclose non-controlling interest in the profit or loss of the group separately   **9.21**
in the **statement of comprehensive income** (or income statement, if presented).

Profit or loss and each component of other comprehensive income shall be attributed to the   **9.22**
owners of the parent and to non-controlling interest. **Total comprehensive income** shall
be attributed to the owners of the parent and to non-controlling interest even if this results
in non-controlling interest having a deficit balance.

Disclosures in consolidated financial statements

The following disclosures shall be made in consolidated financial statements: **9.23**

(a)   the fact that the statements are consolidated financial statements;
(b)   the basis for concluding that control exists when the parent does not own, directly or
      indirectly through subsidiaries, more than half of the voting power;
(c)   any difference in the reporting date of the financial statements of the parent and its
      subsidiaries used in the preparation of the consolidated financial statements;
(d)   the nature and extent of any significant restrictions (eg resulting from borrowing
      arrangements or regulatory requirements) on the ability of subsidiaries to transfer
      funds to the parent in the form of cash dividends or to repay loans; and
(e)   the name of any subsidiary excluded from consolidation and the reason for exclusion.

Individual and separate financial statements

Preparation of individual and separate financial statements

The requirements for the preparation of individual financial statements are set out in the   **9.23A**
Act or other statutory framework.

Separate financial statements are those prepared by a parent in which the investments in   **9.24**
subsidiaries, associates or jointly controlled entities are accounted for either at cost or fair
value rather than on the basis of the reported results and net assets of the investees. Separate
financial statements are included within the meaning of individual financial statements.

9.25   An entity that is not a parent shall account for any investments in associates and any interests in jointly controlled entities in accordance with paragraph 14.4 or 15.9, as appropriate in its individual financial statements.

Accounting policy election in separate financial statements

9.26   When an entity that is a parent prepares separate financial statements and describes them as conforming to this FRS, those financial statements shall comply with all of the requirements of this FRS. The parent shall select and adopt a policy of accounting for its investments in subsidiaries, associates and jointly controlled entities either:

(a)   at cost less impairment;

(b)   at fair value with changes in fair value recognised in other comprehensive income in accordance with paragraphs 17.15E and 17.15F; or

(c)   at fair value with changes in fair value recognised in profit or loss (paragraphs 11.27 to 11.32 provide guidance on fair value).

The entity shall apply the same accounting policy for all investments in a single class (subsidiaries, associates or jointly controlled entities), but it can elect different policies for different classes.

9.26A   A parent that is exempt in accordance with paragraph 9.3 from the requirement to present consolidated financial statements, and presents separate financial statements as its only financial statements, shall account for its investments in subsidiaries, associates and jointly controlled entities in accordance with paragraph 9.26.

Disclosures in separate financial statements

9.27   When a parent prepares separate financial statements, those separate financial statements shall disclose:

(a)   that the statements are separate financial statements; and

* (b)   a description of the methods used to account for the investments in subsidiaries, jointly controlled entities and associates.

9.27A   A parent that uses one of the exemptions from presenting consolidated financial statements (described in paragraph 9.3) shall disclose the grounds on which the parent is exempt.

9.27B   When a parent adopts a policy of accounting for its investments in subsidiaries, associates or jointly controlled entities at fair value with changes in fair value recognised in profit or loss, it must comply with the requirements of paragraph 36(4) of Schedule 1 to the **Regulations** by applying the disclosure requirements of Section 11 *Basic Financial Instruments* to those investments.

9.28   [Not used]

9.29   [Not used]

9.30   [Not used]

Exchanges of businesses or other non-monetary assets for an interest in a subsidiary, jointly controlled entity or associate

9.31   Where a reporting entity exchanges a **business**, or other non-monetary assets, for an interest in another entity, and that other entity thereby becomes a subsidiary, jointly controlled entity or associate of the reporting entity, the following accounting treatment shall apply in the consolidated financial statements of the reporting entity:

(a) To the extent that the reporting entity retains an ownership interest in the business, or other non-monetary assets, exchanged, even if that interest is then held through the other entity, that retained interest, including any related goodwill, is treated as having been owned by the reporting entity throughout the transaction and should be included at its pre-transaction carrying amount.

(b) Goodwill should be recognised as the difference between:

   (i) the fair value of the consideration given; and

   (ii) the fair value of the reporting entity's share of the pre-transaction identifiable net assets of the other entity.

   The consideration given for the interest acquired in the other entity will include that part of the business, or other non-monetary assets, exchanged and no longer owned by the reporting entity. The consideration may also include **cash** or monetary assets to achieve equalisation of values. Where it is difficult to value the consideration given, the best estimate of its value may be given by valuing what is acquired.

(c) To the extent that the fair value of the consideration received by the reporting entity exceeds the carrying value of the part of the business, or other non-monetary assets exchanged and no longer owned by the reporting entity, and any related goodwill together with any cash given up, the reporting entity should recognise a gain. Any unrealised gain arising on the exchange shall be recognised in other comprehensive income.

(d) To the extent that the fair value of the consideration received by the reporting entity is less than the carrying value of the part of the business, or other non-monetary assets no longer owned by the reporting entity, and any related goodwill, together with any cash given up, the reporting entity should recognise a loss. This loss should be recognised either as an impairment in accordance with Section 27 *Impairment of Assets* or, for any loss remaining after an impairment review of the relevant assets, in profit or loss.

9.32   No gain or loss should be recognised in those rare cases where the artificiality or lack of substance of the transaction is such that a gain or loss on the exchange could not be justified. Where a gain or loss on the exchange is not taken into account because the transaction is artificial or has no substance, the circumstances should be explained.

Intermediate payment arrangements

9.33   Intermediate payment arrangements may take a variety of forms:

(a) The intermediary is usually established by a sponsoring entity and constituted as a trust, although other arrangements are possible.

(b) The relationship between the sponsoring entity and the intermediary may take different forms. For example, when the intermediary is constituted as a trust, the sponsoring entity will not have a right to direct the intermediary's activities. However, in these and other cases the sponsoring entity may give advice to the intermediary or may be relied on by the intermediary to provide the information it needs to carry out its activities. Sometimes, the way the intermediary has been set up gives it little discretion in the broad nature of its activities.

(c) The arrangements are most commonly used to pay employees, although they are sometimes used to compensate suppliers of goods and services other than employee services. Sometimes the sponsoring entity's employees and other suppliers are not the only beneficiaries of the arrangement. Other beneficiaries may include past employees and their dependants, and the intermediary may be entitled to make charitable donations.

(d)   The precise identity of the persons or entities that will receive payments from the intermediary, and the amounts that they will receive, are not usually agreed at the outset.

(e)   The sponsoring entity often has the right to appoint or veto the appointment of the intermediary's trustees (or its directors or the equivalent).

(f)   The payments made to the intermediary and the payments made by the intermediary are often cash payments but may involve other transfers of value.

Examples of intermediate payment arrangements are employee share ownership plans (ESOPs) and employee benefit trusts that are used to facilitate employee shareholdings under remuneration schemes. In a typical employee benefit trust arrangement for share-based payments, an entity makes payments to a trust or guarantees borrowing by the trust, and the trust uses its funds to accumulate assets to pay the entity's employees for services the employees have rendered to the entity.

Although the trustees of an intermediary must act at all times in accordance with the interests of the beneficiaries of the intermediary, most intermediaries (particularly those established as a means of remunerating employees) are specifically designed so as to serve the purposes of the sponsoring entity, and to ensure that there will be minimal risk of any conflict arising between the duties of the trustees of the intermediary and the interest of the sponsoring entity, such that there is nothing to encumber implementation of the wishes of the sponsoring entity in practice. Where this is the case, the sponsoring entity has de facto control.

Accounting for intermediate payment arrangements

9.34   When a sponsoring entity makes payments (or transfers assets) to an intermediary, there is a rebuttable presumption that the entity has exchanged one asset for another and that the payment itself does not represent an immediate expense. To rebut this presumption at the time the payment is made to the intermediary, the entity must demonstrate:

(a)   it will not obtain future economic benefit from the amounts transferred; or

(b)   it does not have control of the right or other access to the future economic benefit it is expected to receive.

9.35   Where a payment to an intermediary is an exchange by the sponsoring entity of one asset for another, any assets that the intermediary acquires in a subsequent exchange transaction will also be under the control of the entity. Accordingly, assets and liabilities of the intermediary shall be accounted for by the sponsoring entity as an extension of its own business and recognised in its own individual financial statements. An asset will cease to be recognised as an asset of the sponsoring entity when, for example, the asset of the intermediary vests unconditionally with identified beneficiaries.

9.36   A sponsoring entity may distribute its own equity instruments, or other equity instruments, to an intermediary in order to facilitate employee shareholdings under a remuneration scheme. Where this is the case and the sponsoring entity has control, or de facto control, of the assets and liabilities of the intermediary, the commercial effect is that the sponsoring entity is, for all practical purposes, in the same position as if it had purchased the shares directly.

9.37   Where an intermediary holds the sponsoring entity's equity instruments, the sponsoring entity shall account for the equity instruments as if it had purchased them directly. The sponsoring entity shall account for the assets and liabilities of the intermediary in its individual financial statements as follows:

(a)   The consideration paid for the equity instruments of the sponsoring entity shall be deducted from equity until such time that the equity instruments **vest** unconditionally with employees.

(b)   Consideration paid or received for the purchase or sale of the sponsoring entity's own equity instruments shall be shown as separate amounts in the **statement of changes in equity**.

(c)   Other assets and liabilities of the intermediary shall be recognised as assets and liabilities of the sponsoring entity.

(d)   No gain or loss shall be recognised in profit or loss or other comprehensive income on the purchase, sale, issue or cancellation of the entity's own equity instruments.

(e)   Finance costs and any administration expenses shall be recognised on an accruals basis rather than as funding payments are made to the intermediary.

(f)   Any dividend income arising on the sponsoring entity's own equity instruments shall be excluded from profit or loss and deducted from the aggregate of dividends paid.

Disclosures in individual and separate financial statements

When a sponsoring entity recognises the assets and liabilities held by an intermediary, it should disclose sufficient information in the **notes** to its financial statements to enable users to understand the significance of the intermediary and the arrangement in the context of the sponsoring entity's financial statements. This should include: **9.38**

(a)   a description of the main features of the intermediary including the arrangements for making payments and for distributing equity instruments;

(b)   any restrictions relating to the assets and liabilities of the intermediary;

(c)   the amount and nature of the assets and liabilities held by the intermediary, which have not yet vested unconditionally with the beneficiaries of the arrangement;

(d)   the amount that has been deducted from equity and the number of equity instruments held by the intermediary, which have not yet vested unconditionally with the beneficiaries of the arrangement;

(e)   for entities that have their equity instruments listed or **publicly traded** on a stock exchange or market, the market value of the equity instruments held by the intermediary which have not yet vested unconditionally with employees;

(f)   the extent to which the equity instruments are under option to employees, or have been conditionally gifted to them; and

(g)   the amount that has been deducted from the aggregate dividends paid by the sponsoring entity.

Section 10 Accounting Policies, Estimates and Errors

Scope of this section

This section provides guidance for selecting and applying the **accounting policies** used in preparing **financial statements**. It also covers **changes in accounting estimates** and corrections of **errors** in prior period financial statements.   **10.1**

Selection and application of accounting policies

Accounting policies are the specific principles, bases, conventions, rules and practices applied by an entity in preparing and presenting financial statements.   **10.2**

If an FRS or FRC Abstract specifically addresses a transaction, other event or condition, an entity shall apply that FRS or FRC Abstract. However, the entity need not follow a requirement in an FRS or FRC Abstract if the effect of doing so would not be **material**.   **10.3**

10.4   If an FRS or FRC Abstract does not specifically address a transaction, other event or condition, an entity's management shall use its judgement in developing and applying an accounting policy that results in information that is:

(a)   relevant to the economic decision-making needs of users; and

(b)   reliable, in that the financial statements:

   (i)   represent faithfully the **financial position**, financial **performance** and **cash flows** of the entity;

   (ii)   reflect the economic substance of transactions, other events and conditions, and not merely the legal form;

   (iii)   are neutral, ie free from bias;

   (iv)   are prudent; and

   (v)   are complete in all material respects.

10.5   In making the judgement described in paragraph 10.4, management shall refer to and consider the applicability of the following sources in descending order:

(a)   the requirements and guidance in an FRS or FRC Abstract dealing with similar and related issues;

(b)   where an entity's financial statements are within the scope of a **Statement of Recommended Practice (SORP)** the requirements and guidance in that SORP dealing with similar and related issues; and

(c)   the definitions, **recognition** criteria and measurement concepts for **assets**, **liabilities**, **income** and **expenses** and the pervasive principles in Section 2 *Concepts and Pervasive Principles*.

10.6   In making the judgement described in paragraph 10.4, management may also consider the requirements and guidance in **EU-adopted IFRS** dealing with similar and related issues. Paragraphs 1.4 to 1.7 require certain entities to apply IAS 33 *Earnings per Share* (as adopted in the EU) , IFRS 8 *Operating Segments* (as adopted in the EU) or IFRS 6 *Exploration for and Evaluation of Mineral Resources*.

Consistency of accounting policies

10.7   An entity shall select and apply its accounting policies consistently for similar transactions, other events and conditions, unless an FRS or FRC Abstract specifically requires or permits categorisation of items for which different policies may be appropriate. If an FRS or FRC Abstract requires or permits such categorisation, an appropriate accounting policy shall be selected and applied consistently to each category.

Changes in accounting policies

10.8   An entity shall change an accounting policy only if the change:

(a)   is required by an FRS or FRC Abstract; or

(b)   results in the financial statements providing reliable and more relevant information about the effects of transactions, other events or conditions on the entity's financial position, financial performance or cash flows.

10.9   The following are not changes in accounting policies:

(a)   the application of an accounting policy for transactions, other events or conditions that differ in substance from those previously occurring;

(b)   the application of a new accounting policy for transactions, other events or conditions that did not occur previously or were not material; and

(c) a change to the cost model when a reliable measure of **fair value** is no longer available (or vice versa) for an asset that an FRS or FRC Abstract would otherwise require or permit to be measured at fair value.

If an FRS or FRC Abstract allows a choice of accounting treatment (including the measurement basis) for a specified transaction or other event or condition and an entity changes its previous choice, that is a change in accounting policy.   **10.10**

The initial application of a policy to revalue assets in accordance with Section 17 *Property, Plant and Equipment* or Section 18 *Intangible Assets other than Goodwill* is a change in accounting policy to be dealt with as a revaluation in accordance with those sections, rather than in accordance with paragraphs 10.11 and 10.12.   **10.10A**

Applying changes in accounting policies

An entity shall account for changes in accounting policy as follows: **10.11**

(a) an entity shall account for a change in accounting policy resulting from a change in the requirements of an FRS or FRC Abstract in accordance with the transitional provisions, if any, specified in that amendment;

(b) when an entity has elected to follow IAS 39 *Financial Instruments: Recognition and Measurement* and/or IFRS 9 *Financial Instruments* instead of following Section 11 *Basic Financial Instruments* and Section 12 *Other Financial Instruments Issues* as permitted by paragraph 11.2, and the requirements of IAS 39 and/or IFRS 9 change, the entity shall account for that change in accounting policy in accordance with the transitional provisions, if any, specified in the revised IAS 39 and/or IFRS 9; and

(c) when an entity is required or has elected to follow IAS 33, IFRS 8 or IFRS 6 and the requirements of those standards change, the entity shall account for that change in accounting policy in accordance with the transitional provisions, if any, specified in those standards as amended; and

(d) an entity shall account for all other changes in accounting policy retrospectively (see paragraph 10.12).

Retrospective application

When a change in accounting policy is applied retrospectively in accordance with paragraph 10.11, the entity shall apply the new accounting policy to comparative information for prior periods to the earliest date for which it is practicable, as if the new accounting policy had always been applied. When it is **impracticable** to determine the individual-period effects of a change in accounting policy on comparative information for one or more prior periods presented, the entity shall apply the new accounting policy to the **carrying amounts** of assets and liabilities as at the beginning of the earliest period for which **retrospective application** is practicable, which may be the current period, and shall make a corresponding adjustment to the opening balance of each affected component of **equity** for that period.   **10.12**

Disclosure of a change in accounting policy

When an amendment to an FRS or FRC Abstract has an effect on the current period or any prior period, or might have an effect on future periods, an entity shall disclose the following: *** 10.13**

(a) the nature of the change in accounting policy;

(b) for the current period and each prior period presented, to the extent practicable, the amount of the adjustment for each financial statement line item affected;

(c)   the amount of the adjustment relating to periods before those presented, to the extent practicable; and

(d)   an explanation if it is impracticable to determine the amounts to be disclosed in (b) or (c) above.

Financial statements of subsequent periods need not repeat these disclosures.

* **10.14**   When a voluntary change in accounting policy has an effect on the current period or any prior period, an entity shall disclose the following:

(a)   the nature of the change in accounting policy;

(b)   the reasons why applying the new accounting policy provides reliable and more relevant information;

(c)   to the extent practicable, the amount of the adjustment for each financial statement line item affected, shown separately:

(i)   for the current period;

(ii)   for each prior period presented; and

(iii) in the aggregate for periods before those presented; and

(d)   an explanation if it is impracticable to determine the amounts to be disclosed in (c) above.

Financial statements of subsequent periods need not repeat these disclosures.

Changes in accounting estimates

10.15   A **change in accounting estimate** is an adjustment of the carrying amount of an asset or a liability, or the amount of the periodic consumption of an asset, that results from the assessment of the present status of, and expected future benefits and obligations associated with, assets and liabilities. Changes in accounting estimates result from new information or new developments and, accordingly, are not corrections of errors. When it is difficult to distinguish a change in an accounting policy from a change in an accounting estimate, the change is treated as a change in an accounting estimate.

10.16   An entity shall recognise the effect of a change in an accounting estimate, other than a change to which paragraph 10.17 applies, **prospectively** by including it in **profit or loss** in:

(a)   the period of the change, if the change affects that period only; or

(b)   the period of the change and future periods, if the change affects both.

10.17   To the extent that a change in an accounting estimate gives rise to changes in assets and liabilities, or relates to an item of equity, the entity shall recognise it by adjusting the carrying amount of the related asset, liability or equity item in the period of the change.

Disclosure of a change in estimate

10.18   An entity shall disclose the nature of any change in an accounting estimate and the effect of the change on assets, liabilities, income and expense for the current period. If it is practicable for the entity to estimate the effect of the change in one or more future periods, the entity shall disclose those estimates.

Corrections of prior period errors

Prior period errors are omissions from, and misstatements in, an entity's financial statements for one or more prior periods arising from a failure to use, or misuse of, reliable information that: **10.19**

(a)   was available when financial statements for those periods were authorised for issue; and

(b)   could reasonably be expected to have been obtained and taken into account in the preparation and presentation of those financial statements.

Such errors include the effects of mathematical mistakes, mistakes in applying accounting policies, oversights or misinterpretations of facts, and fraud.   **10.20**

To the extent practicable, an entity shall correct a material prior period error retrospectively in the first financial statements authorised for issue after its discovery by: **10.21**

(a)   restating the comparative amounts for the prior period(s) presented in which the error occurred; or

(b)   if the error occurred before the earliest prior period presented, restating the opening balances of assets, liabilities and equity for the earliest prior period presented.

When it is impracticable to determine the period-specific effects of a material error on comparative information for one or more prior periods presented, the entity shall restate the opening balances of assets, liabilities and equity for the earliest period for which retrospective restatement is practicable (which may be the current period).   **10.22**

Disclosure of prior period errors

An entity shall disclose the following about material prior period errors: *** 10.23**

(a)   the nature of the prior period error;

(b)   for each prior period presented, to the extent practicable, the amount of the correction for each financial statement line item affected;

(c)   to the extent practicable, the amount of the correction at the beginning of the earliest prior period presented; and

(d)   an explanation if it is not practicable to determine the amounts to be disclosed in (b) or (c) above.

Financial statements of subsequent periods need not repeat these disclosures.

Section 11 Basic Financial Instruments

Scope of Sections 11 and 12

Section 11 *Basic Financial Instruments* and Section 12 *Other Financial Instruments Issues* together deal with recognising, derecognising, measuring and disclosing **financial instruments** (**financial assets** and **financial liabilities**). Section 11 applies to basic financial instruments and is relevant to all entities. Section 12 applies to other, more complex financial instruments and transactions. If an entity enters into only basic financial instrument transactions then Section 12 is not applicable. However, even entities with only basic financial instruments shall consider the scope of Section 12 to ensure they are exempt.   **11.1**

Public benefit entities and other members of a **public benefit entity group** that make or receive **public benefit entity concessionary loans** shall refer to the relevant paragraphs of Section 34 *Specialised Activities* for the accounting requirements for such loans.   **PBE11.1A**

Accounting policy choice

11.2   An entity shall choose to apply either:

   (a)   the provisions of both Section 11 and Section 12 in full; or

   (b)   the **recognition** and **measurement** provisions of IAS 39 *Financial Instruments: Recognition and Measurement* (as adopted for use in the EU), the disclosure requirements of Sections 11 and 12 and the presentation requirements of paragraphs 11.38A or 12.25B; or

   (c)   the recognition and measurement provisions of IFRS 9 *Financial Instruments* and/or IAS 39 (as amended following the publication of IFRS 9) subject to the restriction in paragraph 11.2A, the disclosure requirements of Sections 11 and 12 and the presentation requirements of paragraphs 11.38A or 12.25B;

   to account for all of its financial instruments. Where an entity chooses (b) or (c) it applies the scope of the relevant standard to its financial instruments. An entity's choice of (a), (b) or (c) is an **accounting policy** choice. Paragraphs 10.8 to 10.14 contain requirements for determining when a change in accounting policy is appropriate, how such a change should be accounted for and what information should be disclosed about the change.

11.2A   An entity, including an entity that is not a company, that has made the accounting policy choice in paragraph 11.2(c) to apply the recognition and measurement provisions of IFRS 9 shall depart from the provisions of IFRS 9 as follows:

   A financial asset that is not permitted by the **Small Companies Regulations**, the **Regulations, the Small LLP Regulations** or the **LLP Regulations** to be measured at **fair value** through **profit or loss** shall be measured at **amortised cost** in accordance with paragraphs 5.4.1 to 5.4.4 of IFRS 9.

Introduction to Section 11

11.3   A financial instrument is a contract that gives rise to a financial asset of one entity and a financial liability or equity instrument of another entity.

11.4   [Not used]

11.5   Basic financial instruments within the scope of Section 11 are those that satisfy the conditions in paragraph 11.8. Examples of financial instruments that normally satisfy those conditions include:

   (a)   **cash**;

   (b)   demand and fixed-term deposits when the entity is the depositor, eg bank accounts;

   (c)   commercial paper and commercial bills held;

   (d)   accounts, notes and loans receivable and payable;

   (e)   bonds and similar debt instruments;

   (f)   investments in non-convertible preference shares and non-puttable ordinary and preference shares; and

   (g)   commitments to receive a loan and commitments to make a loan to another entity that meet the conditions of paragraph 11.8(c).

11.6   Examples of financial instruments that do not normally satisfy the conditions in paragraph 11.8, and are therefore within the scope of Section 12, include:

   (a)   asset-backed securities, such as collateralised mortgage obligations, repurchase agreements and securitised packages of receivables;

   (b)   options, rights, warrants, futures contracts, forward contracts and interest rate swaps that can be settled in cash or by exchanging another financial instrument;

(c)   financial instruments that qualify and are designated as hedging instruments in accordance with the requirements in Section 12; and

(d)   commitments to make a loan to another entity and commitments to receive a loan, if the commitment can be settled net in cash.

(e)   [not used]

Scope of Section 11

Section 11 applies to all financial instruments meeting the conditions of paragraph 11.8 except for the following: **11.7**

(a)   Investments in **subsidiaries, associates** and **joint ventures** that are accounted for in accordance with Section 9 *Consolidated and Separate Financial Statements*, Section 14 *Investments in Associates* or Section 15 *Investments in Joint Ventures*.

(b)   Financial instruments that meet the definition of an entity's own equity and the equity component of **compound financial instruments** issued by the reporting entity that contain both a **liability** and an equity component (see Section 22 *Liabilities and Equity*).

(c)   **Leases**, to which Section 20 *Leases* applies. However, the **derecognition** requirements in paragraphs 11.33 to 11.35 and impairment accounting requirements in paragraphs 11.21 to 11.26 apply to derecognition and impairment of receivables recognised by a lessor and the derecognition requirements in paragraphs 11.36 to 11.38 apply to payables recognised by a lessee arising under a **finance lease**. Section 12 applies to leases with characteristics specified in paragraph 12.3(f).

(d)   Employers' rights and obligations under employee benefit plans, to which Section 28 *Employee Benefits* applies, although paragraphs 11.27 to 11.32 do apply in determining the fair value of **plan assets**.

(e)   Financial instruments, contracts and obligations to which Section 26 *Share-based Payment* applies, and contracts within the scope of paragraph 12.5.

(f)   **Insurance contracts** (including **reinsurance contracts**) that the entity issues and reinsurance contracts that the entity holds (see FRS 103 *Insurance Contracts*).

(g)   Financial instruments issued by an entity with a **discretionary participation feature** (see FRS 103 *Insurance Contracts*).

(h)   Reimbursement assets accounted for in accordance with Section 21 *Provisions and Contingencies*.

(i)   **Financial guarantee contracts** (see Section 21).

A reporting entity that issues the financial instruments set out in (f) or (g) or holds the financial instruments in (f) is required by paragraph 1.6 of this FRS to apply FRS 103 to those financial instruments.

Basic financial instruments

An entity shall account for the following financial instruments as basic financial instruments in accordance with Section 11:   **11.8**

(a)   cash;

(b)   a debt instrument (such as an account, note, or loan receivable or payable) that meets the conditions in paragraph 11.9 and is not a financial instrument described in paragraph 11.6(b);

(c)   commitments to receive or make a loan to another entity that:

(i)   cannot be settled net in cash; and

(ii)   when the commitment is executed, are expected to meet the conditions in paragraph 11.9; and

(d) an investment in non-convertible preference shares and non-puttable **ordinary shares** or preference shares.

11.9 The conditions a debt instrument shall satisfy in accordance with paragraph 11.8(b) are:

(a) The contractual return to the holder (the lender), assessed in the currency in which the debt instrument is denominated, is:

    (i) a fixed amount;

    (ii) a positive fixed rate or a positive variable rate[10]; or

    (iii) [not used]

    (iv) a combination of a positive or a negative fixed rate and a positive variable rate (eg LIBOR plus 200 basis points or LIBOR less 50 basis points, but not 500 basis points less LIBOR).

(aA) The contract may provide for repayments of the principal or the return to the holder (but not both) to be linked to a single relevant observable index of general price inflation of the currency in which the debt instrument is denominated, provided such links are not leveraged.

(aB) The contract may provide for a determinable variation of the return to the holder during the life of the instrument, provided that:

    (i) the new rate satisfies condition (a) and the variation is not contingent on future events other than:

        (1) a change of a contractual variable rate;

        (2) to protect the holder against credit deterioration of the issuer;

        (3) changes in levies applied by a central bank or arising from changes in relevant taxation or law; or

    (ii) the new rate is a market rate of interest and satisfies condition (a).

Contractual terms that give the lender the unilateral option to change the terms of the contract are not determinable for this purpose.

(b) There is no contractual provision that could, by its terms, result in the holder losing the principal amount or any interest attributable to the current period or prior periods. The fact that a debt instrument is subordinated to other debt instruments is not an example of such a contractual provision.

(c) Contractual provisions that permit the issuer (the borrower) to prepay a debt instrument or permit the holder (the lender) to put it back to the issuer before maturity are not contingent on future events other than to protect:

    (i) the holder against the credit deterioration of the issuer (eg defaults, credit downgrades or loan covenant violations), or a change in control of the issuer; or

    (ii) the holder or issuer against changes in levies applied by a central bank or arising from changes in relevant taxation or law.

The inclusion of contractual terms that, as a result of the early termination, require the issuer to compensate the holder for the early termination does not, in itself, constitute a breach of this condition.

(d) [Not used]

(e) Contractual provisions may permit the extension of the term of the debt instrument, provided that the return to the holder and any other contractual provisions applicable during the extended term satisfy the conditions of paragraphs (a) to (c).

---

[10] *A variable rate for this purpose is a rate which varies over time and is linked to a single observable interest rate or to a single relevant observable index of general price inflation of the currency in which the instrument is denominated, provided such links are not leveraged.*

Examples – Debt instruments

1   A zero-coupon loan

For a zero-coupon loan, the holder's return is the difference between the nominal value of the loan and the issue price. The holder (lender) receives a fixed amount when the loan matures and the issuer (borrower) repays the loan. The return to the holder meets the condition of paragraph 11.9(a)(i).

2   A fixed interest rate loan with an initial tie-in period which reverts to the bank's standard variable interest rate after the tie-in period

The initial fixed rate is a return permitted by paragraph 11.9(a)(ii). A bank's standard variable interest rate is an observable interest rate and, in accordance with the definition of a variable rate, is a permissible link. In accordance with paragraph 11.9(a)(ii) the variable rate should be a positive rate.

The variation of the interest rate after the tie-in period is non-contingent and since the new rate (ie the bank's standard variable rate) meets the condition of paragraph 11.9(a), paragraph 11.9(aB)(i) is met.

3   A loan with interest payable at the bank's standard variable rate plus 1 per cent throughout the life of the loan

As discussed under Example 2 above, a bank's standard variable rate is a permitted variable rate in accordance with the definition of variable rate. The combination of a positive fixed rate (ie plus 1 per cent) and a positive variable rate is a permitted return under paragraph 11.9(a)(iv). The combination of a bank's standard variable rate plus a fixed interest rate of 1 per cent therefore meets the condition in paragraph 11.9(a)(iv).

4   A loan with interest payable at the bank's standard variable rate less 1 per cent throughout the life of the loan, with the condition that the interest rate can never fall below 2 per cent

Paragraph 11.9(aB)(i)(1) permits variation of a return to a holder (lender) that is contingent on a change of a contractual variable rate. In this example the contractual variable rate is the bank's standard variable rate. The variation of the return to the holder is between the bank's standard variable rate less 1 and 2 per cent, depending on the bank's standard variable rate. For example, if the bank's standard variable rate is less than 3 per cent, the return to the holder is fixed at 2 per cent; if the bank's standard variable rate is higher than 3 per cent, the return to the holder is the bank's standard variable rate less 1 per cent. The contractual variation meets the condition of paragraph 11.9(aB)(i)(1).

The holder is protected against the risk of losing the principal amount of the loan via the interest rate floor of 2 per cent. The requirement of paragraph 11.9(b) is therefore also met.

5   Interest on a loan is referenced to 2 times the bank's standard variable rate

In accordance with the definition of a variable rate, the contractual interest rate payable can be linked to a single observable interest rate. A bank's standard variable rate is an observable rate and meets the definition of a variable rate, but the rate in this example is 2 times the bank's standard variable rate and the link to the observable interest rate is leveraged. Therefore, the rate in this example is not a variable rate as described in paragraph 11.9(a). The instrument is measured at fair value in accordance with Section 12.

Examples – Debt instruments

6 **Interest on a loan is charged at 10 per cent less 6-month LIBOR over the life of the loan**

The effect of combining a negative variable rate with a positive fixed rate is that the interest on the loan increases as and when the variable rate decreases and vice versa (so called inverse floating interest).

Under paragraph 11.9(a)(iv) the combination of positive or negative fixed rate and positive variable rate is a permitted return. The variable rate (6-month LIBOR) meets the definition of a variable rate, as the rate is a quoted interest rate. However, since the variable rate is negative (minus 6-month LIBOR), the rate is in breach of paragraph 11.9(a)(iv). The instrument is measured at fair value in accordance with Section 12.

7 **Interest on a GBP denominated mortgage is linked to the UK Land Registry House Price Index (HPI) plus 3 per cent**

In accordance with paragraph 11.9(aA) the holder's return may be linked to an index of general price inflation of the currency of the debt instrument. The mortgage is denominated in GBP and a permitted inflation index would be an index that measures general price inflation of goods and services denominated in GBP.

The HPI measures inflation for residential properties in the UK and is not a measure of general price inflation. The return to the holder therefore fails to meet the condition in paragraph 11.9(aA). The instrument is measured at fair value in accordance with Section 12.

11.10   Examples of financial instruments that would normally satisfy the conditions in paragraph 11.9 are:

(a)   trade accounts and notes receivable and payable, and loans from banks or other third parties;

(b)   accounts payable in a foreign currency. However, any change in the account payable because of a change in the exchange rate is recognised in profit or loss as required by paragraph 30.10;

(c)   loans to or from subsidiaries or associates that are due on demand; and

(d)   a debt instrument that would become immediately receivable if the issuer defaults on an interest or principal payment (such a provision does not violate the conditions in paragraph 11.9).

11.11   Examples of financial instruments that do not satisfy the conditions in paragraph 11.9 (and are therefore within the scope of Section 12) include:

(a)   an investment in another entity's equity instruments other than non-convertible preference shares and non-puttable ordinary and preference shares (see paragraph 11.8(d)); and

(b)   [not used]

(c)   [not used]

(d)   investments in convertible debt, because the return to the holder can vary with the price of the issuer's equity shares rather than just with market interest rates.

(e)   [not used]

Initial recognition of financial assets and liabilities

11.12   An entity shall recognise a financial asset or a financial liability only when the entity becomes a party to the contractual provisions of the instrument.

Initial measurement

When a financial asset or financial liability is recognised initially, an entity shall measure **11.13**
it at the transaction price (including **transaction costs** except in the initial measurement of
financial assets and liabilities that are measured at fair value through profit or loss) unless
the arrangement constitutes, in effect, a financing transaction. A financing transaction may
take place in connection with the sale of goods or services, for example, if payment is
deferred beyond normal business terms or is financed at a rate of interest that is not a
market rate. If the arrangement constitutes a financing transaction, the entity shall measure
the financial asset or financial liability at the **present value** of the future payments
discounted at a market rate of interest for a similar debt instrument.

Examples – financial assets

1   For a long-term loan at a market rate of interest made to another entity, a receivable
    is recognised at the amount of the cash advanced to that entity plus transaction costs
    incurred by the entity (see the example following paragraph 11.20).

2   For goods sold to a customer on short-term credit, a receivable is recognised at the
    undiscounted amount of cash receivable from that entity, which is normally the
    invoice price.

3   For an item sold to a customer on two-years interest-free credit, a receivable is
    recognised at the current cash sale price for that item (in financing transactions
    conducted on an arm's length basis the cash sales price would normally approximate
    to the present value). If the current cash sale price is not known, it may be estimated
    as the present value of the cash receivable discounted using the **prevailing market
    rate(s)** of interest for a similar receivable.

4   For a cash purchase of another entity's ordinary shares, the investment is recognised
    at the amount of cash paid to acquire the shares.

Examples – financial liabilities

1   For a loan received from a bank at a market rate of interest, a payable is recognised
    initially at the amount of the cash received from the bank less separately incurred
    transaction costs.

2   For goods purchased from a supplier on short-term credit, a payable is recognised at
    the undiscounted amount owed to the supplier, which is normally the invoice price.

Subsequent measurement

At the end of each **reporting period**, an entity shall measure financial instruments as **11.14**
follows, without any deduction for transaction costs the entity may incur on sale or other
disposal:

(a)   Debt instruments that meet the conditions in paragraph 11.8(b) shall be measured
      at amortised cost using the **effective interest method**. Paragraphs 11.15 to 11.20
      provide guidance on determining amortised cost using the effective interest method.
      Debt instruments that are payable or receivable within one year shall be measured
      at the undiscounted amount of the cash or other consideration expected to be paid
      or received (ie net of impairment—see paragraphs 11.21 to 11.26) unless the
      arrangement constitutes, in effect, a financing transaction (see paragraph 11.13). If
      the arrangement constitutes a financing transaction, the entity shall measure the debt
      instrument at the present value of the future payments discounted at a market rate of
      interest for a similar debt instrument.

(b)   Debt instruments that meet the conditions in paragraph 11.8(b) and commitments to receive a loan and to make a loan to another entity that meet the conditions in paragraph 11.8(c) may upon their initial recognition be designated by the entity as at fair value through profit or loss (paragraphs 11.27 to 11.32 provide guidance on fair value) provided doing so results in more relevant information, because either:

   (i)   it eliminates or significantly reduces a measurement or recognition inconsistency (sometimes referred to as 'an accounting mismatch') that would otherwise arise from measuring assets or debt instruments or recognising the **gains** and losses on them on different bases; or

   (ii)   a group of debt instruments or financial assets and debt instruments is managed and its performance is evaluated on a fair value basis, in accordance with a documented risk management or investment strategy, and information about the group is provided internally on that basis to the entity's **key management personnel** (as defined in Section 33 *Related Party Disclosures*, paragraph 33.6), for example members of the entity's board of directors and its chief executive officer.

(c)   Commitments to receive a loan and to make a loan to another entity that meet the conditions in paragraph 11.8(c) shall be measured at cost (which sometimes is nil) less impairment.

(d)   Investments in non-convertible preference shares and non-puttable ordinary shares or preference shares shall be measured as follows (paragraphs 11.27 to 11.32 provide guidance on fair value):

   (i)   if the shares are **publicly traded** or their fair value can otherwise be measured reliably, the investment shall be measured at fair value with changes in fair value recognised in profit or loss; and

   (ii)   all other such investments shall be measured at cost less impairment.

Impairment or uncollectability must be assessed for financial assets in (a), (c) and (d)(ii) above. Paragraphs 11.21 to 11.26 provide guidance.

Amortised cost and effective interest method

11.15   The amortised cost of a financial asset or financial liability at each **reporting date** is the net of the following amounts:

(a)   the amount at which the financial asset or financial liability is measured at initial recognition;

(b)   minus any repayments of the principal;

(c)   plus or minus the cumulative amortisation using the effective interest method of any difference between the amount at initial recognition and the maturity amount;

(d)   minus, in the case of a financial asset, any reduction (directly or through the use of an allowance account) for impairment or uncollectability.

Financial assets and financial liabilities that have no stated interest rate (and do not constitute a financing transaction) and are classified as payable or receivable within one year are initially measured at an undiscounted amount in accordance with paragraph 11.14(a). Therefore, (c) above does not apply to them.

11.16   The effective interest method is a method of calculating the amortised cost of a financial asset or a financial liability (or a group of financial assets or financial liabilities) and of allocating the interest income or interest expense over the relevant period. The **effective interest rate** is the rate that exactly discounts estimated future cash payments or receipts through the expected life of the financial instrument or, when appropriate, a shorter period, to the **carrying amount** of the financial asset or financial liability. The effective interest rate is determined on the basis of the carrying amount of the financial asset or liability at initial recognition. Under the effective interest method:

(a)   the amortised cost of a financial asset (liability) is the present value of future cash receipts (payments) discounted at the effective interest rate; and

(b)   the interest expense (income) in a period equals the carrying amount of the financial liability (asset) at the beginning of a period multiplied by the effective interest rate for the period.

When calculating the effective interest rate, an entity shall estimate cash flows considering all contractual terms of the financial instrument (eg prepayment, call and similar options) and known credit losses that have been incurred, but it shall not consider possible future credit losses not yet incurred.   **11.17**

When calculating the effective interest rate, an entity shall amortise any related fees, finance charges paid or received (such as 'points'), transaction costs and other premiums or discounts over the expected life of the instrument, except as follows. The entity shall use a shorter period if that is the period to which the fees, finance charges paid or received, transaction costs, premiums or discounts relate. This will be the case when the variable to which the fees, finance charges paid or received, transaction costs, premiums or discounts relate is repriced to market rates before the expected maturity of the instrument. In such a case, the appropriate amortisation period is the period to the next such repricing date.   **11.18**

For variable rate financial assets and variable rate financial liabilities, periodic re-estimation of cash flows to reflect changes in market rates of interest alters the effective interest rate. If a variable rate financial asset or variable rate financial liability is recognised initially at an amount equal to the principal receivable or payable at maturity, re-estimating the future interest payments normally has no significant effect on the carrying amount of the asset or liability.   **11.19**

If an entity revises its estimates of payments or receipts, the entity shall adjust the carrying amount of the financial asset or financial liability (or group of financial instruments) to reflect actual and revised estimated cash flows. The entity shall recalculate the carrying amount by computing the present value of estimated future cash flows at the financial instrument's original effective interest rate. The entity shall recognise the adjustment as **income** or **expense** in profit or loss at the date of the revision.   **11.20**

Example of determining amortised cost for a five-year loan using the effective interest method

On 1 January 20X0, an entity acquires a bond for Currency Units (CU)900, incurring transaction costs of CU50. Interest of CU40 is receivable annually, in arrears, over the next five years (31 December 20X0 to 31 December 20X4). The bond has a mandatory redemption of CU1100 on 31 December 20X4.

Year	Carrying amount at beginning of period	Interest income at 6.9583%*	Cash inflow	Carrying amount at end of period
	CU	CU	CU	CU
20X0	950.00	66.11	(40.00)	976.11
20X1	976.11	67.92	(40.00)	1,004.03
20X2	1,004.03	69.86	(40.00)	1,033.89
20X3	1,033.89	71.94	(40.00)	1,065.83
20X4	1,065.83	74.16	(40.00)	1,100.00
			(1,100.00)	0

* The effective interest rate of 6.9583 per cent is the rate that discounts the expected cash flows on the bond to the initial carrying amount:
$$40/(1.069583)^1 + 40/(1.069583)^2 + 40/(1.069583)^3 + 40/(1.069583)^4 + 1,140/(1.069583)^5 = 950$$

Impairment of financial instruments measured at cost or amortised cost

Recognition

11.21   At the end of each reporting period, an entity shall assess whether there is objective evidence of impairment of any financial assets that are measured at cost or amortised cost. If there is objective evidence of impairment, the entity shall recognise an **impairment loss** in profit or loss immediately.

11.22   Objective evidence that a financial asset or group of assets is impaired includes observable data that come to the attention of the holder of the asset about the following loss events:

(a)   significant financial difficulty of the issuer or obligor;

(b)   a breach of contract, such as a default or delinquency in interest or principal payments;

(c)   the creditor, for economic or legal reasons relating to the debtor's financial difficulty, granting to the debtor a concession that the creditor would not otherwise consider;

(d)   it has become **probable** that the debtor will enter bankruptcy or other financial reorganisation; and

(e)   observable data indicating that there has been a measurable decrease in the estimated future cash flows from a group of financial assets since the initial recognition of those assets, even though the decrease cannot yet be identified with the individual financial assets in the group, such as adverse national or local economic conditions or adverse changes in industry conditions.

11.23   Other factors may also be evidence of impairment, including significant changes with an adverse effect that have taken place in the technological, market, economic or legal environment in which the issuer operates.

11.24   An entity shall assess the following financial assets individually for impairment:

(a)   all equity instruments regardless of significance; and

(b)   other financial assets that are individually significant.

An entity shall assess other financial assets for impairment either individually or grouped on the basis of similar **credit risk** characteristics.

Measurement

11.25   An entity shall measure an impairment loss on the following instruments measured at cost or amortised cost as follows:

(a)   For an instrument measured at amortised cost in accordance with paragraph 11.14(a), the impairment loss is the difference between the asset's carrying amount and the present value of estimated cash flows discounted at the asset's original effective interest rate. If such a financial instrument has a variable interest rate, the discount rate for measuring any impairment loss is the current effective interest rate determined under the contract.

(b)   For an instrument measured at cost less impairment in accordance with paragraph 11.14(c) and (d)(ii) the impairment loss is the difference between the asset's carrying amount and the best estimate (which will necessarily be an approximation) of the amount (which might be zero) that the entity would receive for the asset if it were to be sold at the reporting date.

Reversal

11.26   If, in a subsequent period, the amount of an impairment loss decreases and the decrease can be related objectively to an event occurring after the impairment was recognised (such as an improvement in the debtor's credit rating), the entity shall reverse the previously recognised impairment loss either directly or by adjusting an allowance account. The reversal shall not result in a carrying amount of the financial asset (net of any allowance account) that exceeds what the carrying amount would have been had the impairment not previously been recognised. The entity shall recognise the amount of the reversal in profit or loss immediately.

Fair value

Paragraph 11.14(b) and other sections of this FRS make reference to the fair value guidance in paragraphs 11.27 to 11.32, including Section 9 *Consolidated and Separate Financial Statements*, Section 12 *Other Financial Instruments Issues*, Section 13 *Inventories*, Section 14 *Investments in Associates*, Section 15 *Investments in Joint Ventures*, Section 16 *Investment Property*, Section 17 *Property, Plant and Equipment*, Section 18 *Intangible Assets other than Goodwill*, Section 27 *Impairment of Assets*, Section 28 *Employee Benefits* (in relation to plan assets) and Section 34 *Specialised Activities*. In applying the fair value guidance to assets or liabilities accounted for in accordance with those sections, the reference to ordinary shares or preference shares in these paragraphs should be read to include the types of assets and liabilities addressed in those sections.

11.27

Paragraph 11.14(d)(i) requires an investment in non-convertible preference shares and non-puttable ordinary shares or preference shares to be measured at fair value if the shares are publicly traded or if their fair value can otherwise be measured reliably. An entity shall use the following hierarchy to estimate the fair value of the shares:

(a)   The best evidence of fair value is a quoted price for an identical asset in an **active market**. Quoted in an active market in this context means quoted prices are readily and regularly available and those prices represent actual and regularly occurring market transactions on an arm's length basis. The quoted price is usually the current bid price.

(b)   When quoted prices are unavailable, the price of a recent transaction for an identical asset provides evidence of fair value as long as there has not been a significant change in economic circumstances or a significant lapse of time since the transaction took place. If the entity can demonstrate that the last transaction price is not a good estimate of fair value (eg because it reflects the amount that an entity would receive or pay in a forced transaction, involuntary liquidation or distress sale), that price is adjusted.

(c)   If the market for the asset is not active and recent transactions of an identical asset on their own are not a good estimate of fair value, an entity estimates the fair value by using a valuation technique. The objective of using a valuation technique is to estimate what the transaction price would have been on the measurement date in an arm's length exchange motivated by normal business considerations.

Valuation technique

Valuation techniques include using recent arm's length market transactions for an identical asset between knowledgeable, willing parties, if available, reference to the current fair value of another asset that is substantially the same as the asset being measured, discounted cash flow analysis and option pricing models. If there is a valuation technique commonly used by market participants to price the asset and that technique has been demonstrated to provide reliable estimates of prices obtained in actual market transactions, the entity uses that technique.

11.28

The objective of using a valuation technique is to establish what the transaction price would have been on the measurement date in an arm's length exchange motivated by normal business considerations. Fair value is estimated on the basis of the results of a

11.29

valuation technique that makes maximum use of market inputs, and relies as little as possible on entity-determined inputs. A valuation technique would be expected to arrive at a reliable estimate of the fair value if:

(a)   it reasonably reflects how the market could be expected to price the asset; and

(b)   the inputs to the valuation technique reasonably represent market expectations and measures of the risk return factors inherent in the asset.

No active market

11.30   The fair value of ordinary shares or preference shares that do not have a quoted market price in an active market is reliably measurable if:

(a)   the variability in the range of reasonable fair value estimates is not significant for that asset; or

(b)   the probabilities of the various estimates within the range can be reasonably assessed and used in estimating fair value.

11.31   There are many situations in which the variability in the range of reasonable fair value estimates of assets that do not have a quoted market price is likely not to be significant. Normally it is possible to estimate the fair value of ordinary shares or preference shares that an entity has acquired from an outside party. However, if the range of reasonable fair value estimates is significant and the probabilities of the various estimates cannot be reasonably assessed, an entity is precluded from measuring the ordinary shares or preference shares at fair value.

11.32   If a reliable measure of fair value is no longer available for an asset measured at fair value (eg ordinary shares or preference shares measured at fair value through profit or loss), its carrying amount at the last date the asset was reliably measurable becomes its new cost. The entity shall measure the ordinary shares or preference shares at this cost amount less impairment until a reliable measure of fair value becomes available.

Derecognition of a financial asset

11.33   An entity shall derecognise a financial asset only when:

(a)   the contractual rights to the cash flows from the financial asset expire or are settled; or

(b)   the entity transfers to another party substantially all of the risks and rewards of ownership of the financial asset; or

(c)   the entity, despite having retained some significant risks and rewards of ownership, has transferred control of the asset to another party and the other party has the practical ability to sell the asset in its entirety to an unrelated third party and is able to exercise that ability unilaterally and without needing to impose additional restrictions on the transfer. In this case, the entity shall:

(i)   derecognise the asset; and

(ii)   recognise separately any rights and obligations retained or created in the transfer.

The carrying amount of the transferred asset shall be allocated between the rights or obligations retained and those transferred on the basis of their relative fair values at the transfer date. Newly created rights and obligations shall be measured at their fair values at that date. Any difference between the consideration received and the amounts recognised and derecognised in accordance with this paragraph shall be recognised in profit or loss in the period of the transfer.

If a transfer does not result in derecognition because the entity has retained significant risks **11.34**
and rewards of ownership of the transferred asset, the entity shall continue to recognise the
transferred asset in its entirety and shall recognise a financial liability for the consideration
received. The asset and liability shall not be offset. In subsequent periods, the entity shall
recognise any income on the transferred asset and any expense incurred on the financial liability.

If a transferor provides non-cash collateral (such as debt or equity instruments) to the **11.35**
transferee, the accounting for the collateral by the transferor and the transferee depends
on whether the transferee has the right to sell or repledge the collateral and on whether the
transferor has defaulted. The transferor and transferee shall account for the collateral as
follows:

(a) If the transferee has the right by contract or custom to sell or repledge the collateral,
the transferor shall reclassify that asset in its **statement of financial position** (eg as
a loaned asset, pledged equity instruments or repurchase receivable) separately from
other assets.
(b) If the transferee sells collateral pledged to it, it shall recognise the proceeds from the
sale and a liability measured at fair value for its obligation to return the collateral.
(c) If the transferor defaults under the terms of the contract and is no longer entitled
to redeem the collateral, it shall derecognise the collateral, and the transferee shall
recognise the collateral as its asset initially measured at fair value or, if it has already
sold the collateral, derecognise its obligation to return the collateral.
(d) Except as provided in (c), the transferor shall continue to carry the collateral as its
asset, and the transferee shall not recognise the collateral as an asset.

Example: Transfer that qualifies for derecognition

An entity sells a group of its accounts receivable to a bank at less than their face
amount. The entity continues to handle collections from the debtors on behalf of the
bank, including sending monthly statements, and the bank pays the entity a market-rate
fee for servicing the receivables. The entity is obliged to remit promptly to the bank any
and all amounts collected, but it has no obligation to the bank for slow payment or non-
payment by the debtors. In this case, the entity has transferred to the bank substantially
all of the risks and rewards of ownership of the receivables. Accordingly, it removes the
receivables from its statement of financial position (ie derecognises them), and it shows
no liability in respect of the proceeds received from the bank. The entity recognises a
loss calculated as the difference between the carrying amount of the receivables at the
time of sale and the proceeds received from the bank. The entity recognises a liability
to the extent that it has collected funds from the debtors but has not yet remitted them
to the bank.

Example: Transfer that does not qualify for derecognition

The facts are the same as the preceding example except that the entity has agreed to buy
back from the bank any receivables for which the debtor is in arrears as to principal or
interest for more than 120 days.

In this case, the entity has retained the risk of slow payment or non-payment by the
debtors—a significant risk with respect to receivables. Accordingly, the entity does
not treat the receivables as having been sold to the bank, and it does not derecognise
them. Instead, it treats the proceeds from the bank as a loan secured by the receivables.
The entity continues to recognise the receivables as an asset until they are collected or
written off as uncollectible.

Derecognition of a financial liability

11.36   An entity shall derecognise a financial liability (or a part of a financial liability) only when it is extinguished—ie when the obligation specified in the contract is discharged, is cancelled or expires.

11.37   If an existing borrower and lender exchange financial instruments with substantially different terms, the entities shall account for the transaction as an extinguishment of the original financial liability and the recognition of a new financial liability. Similarly, an entity shall account for a substantial modification of the terms of an existing financial liability or a part of it (whether or not attributable to the financial difficulty of the debtor) as an extinguishment of the original financial liability and the recognition of a new financial liability.

11.38   The entity shall recognise in profit or loss any difference between the carrying amount of the financial liability (or part of a financial liability) extinguished or transferred to another party and the consideration paid, including any non-cash assets transferred or liabilities assumed.

Presentation

11.38A   A financial asset and a financial liability shall be offset and the net amount presented in the statement of financial position when, and only when, an entity:

(a)   currently has a legally enforceable right to set off the recognised amounts; and

(b)   intends either to settle on a net basis, or to realise the asset and settle the liability simultaneously.

Disclosures

11.39   The disclosures below make reference to disclosures for certain financial instruments measured at fair value through profit or loss. Entities that have only basic financial instruments (and therefore do not apply Section 12), and have not chosen to designate financial instruments as at fair value through profit or loss (in accordance with paragraph 11.14(b)) will not have any financial instruments measured at fair value through profit or loss and hence will not need to provide such disclosures.

Disclosure of accounting policies for financial instruments

11.40   In accordance with paragraph 8.5, an entity shall disclose, in the summary of significant accounting policies, the measurement basis (or bases) used for financial instruments and the other accounting policies used for financial instruments that are relevant to an understanding of the **financial statements**.

Statement of financial position – categories of financial assets and financial liabilities

11.41   An entity shall disclose the carrying amounts of each of the following categories of financial assets and financial liabilities at the reporting date, in total, either in the statement of financial position or in the **notes**:

*(a)   financial assets measured at fair value through profit or loss (paragraphs 11.14(b), 11.14(d)(i), 12.8 and 12.9);

(b)   financial assets that are debt instruments measured at amortised cost (paragraph 11.14(a));

(c)   financial assets that are equity instruments measured at cost less impairment (paragraphs 11.14(d)(ii), 12.8 and 12.9);

*(d)   financial liabilities measured at fair value through profit or loss (paragraphs 11.14(b), 12.8 and 12.9). Financial liabilities that are not held as part of a trading portfolio and are not **derivatives** shall be shown separately;

(e)   financial liabilities measured at amortised cost (paragraph 11.14(a)); and

(f)   loan commitments measured at cost less impairment (paragraph 11.14(c)).

An entity shall disclose information that enables users of its financial statements to evaluate **11.42** the significance of financial instruments for its **financial position** and **performance**. For example, for long-term debt such information would normally include the terms and conditions of the debt instrument (such as interest rate, maturity, repayment schedule, and restrictions that the debt instrument imposes on the entity).

For all financial assets and financial liabilities measured at fair value, the entity shall *** 11.43** disclose the basis for determining fair value, eg quoted market price in an active market or a valuation technique. When a valuation technique is used, the entity shall disclose the assumptions applied in determining fair value for each class of financial assets or financial liabilities. For example, if applicable, an entity discloses information about the assumptions relating to prepayment rates, rates of estimated credit losses, and interest rates or discount rates.

If a reliable measure of fair value is no longer available for ordinary or preference shares **11.44** measured at fair value through profit or loss, the entity shall disclose that fact.

Derecognition

If an entity has transferred financial assets to another party in a transaction that does not **11.45** qualify for derecognition (see paragraphs 11.33 to 11.35), the entity shall disclose the following for each class of such financial assets:

(a)   the nature of the assets;

(b)   the nature of the risks and rewards of ownership to which the entity remains exposed; and

(c)   the carrying amounts of the assets and of any associated liabilities that the entity continues to recognise.

Collateral

When an entity has pledged financial assets as collateral for liabilities or **contingent** *** 11.46** **liabilities**, it shall disclose the following:

(a)   the carrying amount of the financial assets pledged as collateral; and

(b)   the terms and conditions relating to its pledge.

Defaults and breaches on loans payable

For **loans payable** recognised at the reporting date for which there is a breach of terms or **11.47** default of principal, interest, sinking fund, or redemption terms that has not been remedied by the reporting date, an entity shall disclose the following:

(a)   details of that breach or default;

(b)   the carrying amount of the related loans payable at the reporting date; and

(c)   whether the breach or default was remedied, or the terms of the loans payable were renegotiated, before the financial statements were authorised for issue.

Items of income, expense, gains or losses

11.48   An entity shall disclose the following items of income, expense, gains or losses:

(a)   income, expense, net gains or net losses, including changes in fair value, recognised on:

*(i)   financial assets measured at fair value through profit or loss;

*(ii)   financial liabilities measured at fair value through profit or loss (with separate disclosure of movements on those which are not held as part of a trading portfolio and are not derivatives);

(iii)   financial assets measured at amortised cost; and

(iv)   financial liabilities measured at amortised cost;

(b)   total interest income and total interest expense (calculated using the effective interest method) for financial assets or financial liabilities that are not measured at fair value through profit or loss; and

(c)   the amount of any impairment loss for each class of financial asset. A class of financial asset is a grouping that is appropriate to the nature of the information disclosed and that takes into account the characteristics of the financial assets.

Financial instruments at fair value through profit or loss

* 11.48A   An entity, including an entity that is not a company, shall provide the following disclosures only for financial instruments measured at fair value through profit or loss in accordance with paragraph 36(4) of Schedule 1 to the Regulations[11]. This does not include financial liabilities held as part of a trading portfolio nor derivatives. The required disclosures are:

(a)   The amount of change, during the period and cumulatively, in the fair value of the financial instrument that is attributable to changes in the credit risk of that instrument, determined either:

(i)   as the amount of change in its fair value that is not attributable to changes in market conditions that give rise to **market risk**; or

(ii)   using an alternative method the entity believes more faithfully represents the amount of change in its fair value that is attributable to changes in the credit risk of the instrument.

(b)   The method used to establish the amount of change attributable to changes in own credit risk, or, if the change cannot be measured reliably or is not **material**, that fact.

(c)   For a financial liability, the difference between the financial liability's carrying amount and the amount the entity would be contractually required to pay at maturity to the holder of the obligation.

(d)   If an instrument contains both a liability and an equity feature, and the instrument has multiple features that substantially modify the cash flows and the values of those features are interdependent (such as a callable convertible debt instrument), the existence of those features.

(e)   If there is a difference between the fair value of a financial instrument at initial recognition and the amount determined at that date using a valuation technique, the aggregate difference yet to be recognised in profit or loss at the beginning and end of the period and a reconciliation of the changes in the balance of this difference.

(f)   Information that enables users of the entity's financial statements to evaluate the nature and extent of relevant risks arising from financial instruments to which the entity is exposed at the end of the reporting period. These risks typically include, but are not limited to, credit risk, **liquidity risk** and market risk. The disclosure should include both the entity's exposure to each type of risk and how it manages those risks.

---

[11] *And the equivalent requirements of the Small Companies Regulations, the Small LLP Regulations and the LLP Regulations.*

Financial institutions

A **financial institution** (other than a **retirement benefit plan**) shall, in addition, apply the requirements of paragraph 34.17.   **11.48B**

A retirement benefit plan shall, in addition, apply the requirements of paragraphs 34.39 to 34.48.   **11.48C**

Section 12 Other Financial Instruments Issues

Scope of Sections 11 and 12

Section 11 *Basic Financial Instruments* and Section 12 *Other Financial Instruments Issues* together deal with recognising, derecognising, measuring, and disclosing **financial instruments** (**financial assets** and **financial liabilities**). Section 11 applies to basic financial instruments and is relevant to all entities. Section 12 applies to other, more complex financial instruments and transactions. If an entity enters into only basic financial instrument transactions then Section 12 is not applicable. However, even entities with only basic financial instruments shall consider the scope of Section 12 to ensure they are exempt.   **12.1**

Public benefit entities or other members of a **public benefit entity group** that make or receive **public benefit entity concessionary loans** shall refer to the relevant paragraphs of Section 34 *Specialised Activities* for the accounting requirements for such loans.   **PBE12.1A**

Accounting policy choice

An entity shall choose to apply either: **12.2**

(a)   the provisions of both Section 11 and Section 12 in full; or

(b)   the **recognition** and **measurement** provisions of IAS 39 *Financial Instruments: Recognition and Measurement* (as adopted for use in the EU), the disclosure requirements of Sections 11 and 12 and the presentation requirements of paragraphs 11.38A or 12.25B; or

(c)   the recognition and measurement provisions of IFRS 9 *Financial Instruments* and/or IAS 39 (as amended following the publication of IFRS 9) subject to the restriction in paragraph 12.2A, the disclosure requirements of Sections 11 and 12 and the presentation requirements of paragraph 11.38A or 12.25B;

to account for all of its financial instruments. Where an entity chooses (b) or (c) it applies the scope of the relevant standard to its financial instruments. An entity's choice of (a), (b) or (c) is an **accounting policy** choice. Paragraphs 10.8 to 10.14 contain requirements for determining when a change in accounting policy is appropriate, how such a change should be accounted for and what information should be disclosed about the change in accounting policy.

An entity, including an entity that is not a company, that has made the accounting policy choice in paragraph 12.2(c) to apply the recognition and measurement provisions of IFRS 9 shall depart from those provisions of IFRS 9 as follows: **12.2A**

A financial asset that is not permitted by the **Small Companies Regulations**, the **Regulations, the Small LLP Regulations** or the **LLP Regulations** to be measured at **fair value** through **profit or loss** shall be measured at **amortised cost** in accordance with paragraphs 5.4.1 to 5.4.4 of IFRS 9.

Scope of Section 12

12.3   Section 12 applies to all financial instruments except the following:

(a)   Those covered by Section 11.

(b)   Investments in **subsidiaries** (see Section 9 *Consolidated and Separate Financial Statements*), **associates** (see Section 14 *Investments in Associates*) and **joint ventures** (see Section 15 *Investments in Joint Ventures*).

(c)   Employers' rights and obligations under employee benefit plans (see Section 28 *Employee Benefits*).

(d)   **Insurance contracts** (including **reinsurance contracts**) that the entity issues and reinsurance contracts that the entity holds (see FRS 103 *Insurance Contracts*).

(e)   Financial instruments that meet the definition of an entity's own **equity** and the equity component of **compound financial instruments** issued by the reporting entity that contain both a **liability** and an equity component (see Section 22 *Liabilities and Equity*).

(f)   **Leases** (see Section 20 *Leases*) unless the lease could, as a result of non-typical contractual terms, result in a loss to the lessor or the lessee.

(g)   Contracts for contingent consideration in a **business combination** (see Section 19 *Business Combinations and Goodwill*). This exemption applies only to the acquirer.

(h)   Any forward contract between an acquirer and a selling shareholder to buy or sell an acquiree that will result in a business combination at a future **acquisition date**. The term of the forward contract should not exceed a reasonable period normally necessary to obtain any required approvals and to complete the transaction.

(i)   Financial instruments, contracts and obligations to which Section 26 *Share-based Payment* applies, except for contracts within the scope of paragraph 12.5.

(j)   Financial instruments issued by an entity with a **discretionary participation feature** (see FRS 103).

(k)   Reimbursement assets accounted for in accordance with Section 21 *Provisions and Contingencies*.

(l)   **Financial guarantee contracts** (see Section 21).

A reporting entity that issues the financial instruments set out in (d) or (j) or holds the financial instruments set out in (d) is required by paragraph 1.6 to apply FRS 103 to those financial instruments.

12.4   Most contracts to buy or sell a non-financial item such as a commodity, **inventory**, or **property, plant and equipment** are excluded from this section because they are not financial instruments. However, this section applies to all contracts that impose risks on the buyer or seller that are not typical of contracts to buy or sell non-financial items. For example, this section applies to contracts that, as a result of its contractual terms, could result in a loss to the buyer or seller that is unrelated to changes in the price of the non-financial item, changes in foreign exchange rates, or a default by one of the counterparties.

12.5   In addition to the contracts described in paragraph 12.4, this section applies to contracts to buy or sell non-financial items if the contract can be settled net in **cash** or another financial instrument, or by exchanging financial instruments as if the contracts were financial instruments, with the following exception: contracts that were entered into and continue to be held for the purpose of the receipt or delivery of a non-financial item in accordance with the entity's expected purchase, sale or usage requirements are not financial instruments for the purposes of this section.

Initial recognition of financial assets and liabilities

12.6   An entity shall recognise a financial asset or a financial liability only when the entity becomes a party to the contractual provisions of the instrument.

Initial measurement

When a financial asset or financial liability is recognised initially, an entity shall measure
it at its fair value, which is normally the transaction price (including **transaction costs**
except in the initial measurement of financial assets and liabilities that are measured at fair
value through profit or loss). If payment for an asset is deferred beyond normal business
terms or is financed at a rate of interest that is not a market rate, the entity shall initially
measure the asset at the **present value** of the future payments discounted at a market rate
of interest for a similar debt instrument.

12.7

Subsequent measurement

At the end of each **reporting period**, an entity shall measure all financial instruments
within the scope of Section 12 at fair value and recognise changes in fair value in profit or
loss, except as follows:

12.8

(a)   investments in equity instruments that are not **publicly traded** and whose fair value
      cannot otherwise be measured reliably and contracts linked to such instruments that,
      if exercised, will result in delivery of such instruments, shall be measured at cost less
      impairment;
(b)   hedging instruments in a designated hedging relationship accounted for in accordance
      with paragraph 12.23; and
(c)   financial instruments that are not permitted by the Small Company Regulations, the
      Regulations, the Small LLP Regulations or the LLP Regulations to be measured at
      fair value through profit or loss shall be measured at amortised cost in accordance
      with paragraphs 11.15 to 11.20.

If a reliable measure of fair value is no longer available for an equity instrument (or a contract
linked to such an instrument) that is not publicly traded but is measured at fair value through
profit or loss, its fair value at the last date the instrument was reliably measurable is treated
as the cost of the instrument. The entity shall measure the instrument at this cost amount less
impairment until a reliable measure of fair value becomes available.

12.9

Fair value

An entity shall apply the guidance on fair value in paragraphs 11.27 to 11.32 to fair value
measurements in accordance with this section as well as for fair value measurements in
accordance with Section 11.

12.10

The fair value of a financial liability that is due on demand is not less than the amount payable
on demand, discounted from the first date that the amount could be required to be paid.

12.11

An entity shall not include transaction costs in the initial measurement of financial assets
and liabilities that will be measured subsequently at fair value through profit or loss.

12.12

Impairment of financial instruments measured at cost or amortised cost

An entity shall apply the guidance on impairment of a financial instrument measured at
cost in paragraphs 11.21 to 11.26 to financial instruments measured at cost less impairment
in accordance with this section.

12.13

Derecognition of a financial asset or financial liability

An entity shall apply the **derecognition** requirements in paragraphs 11.33 to 11.38 to
financial assets and financial liabilities to which this section applies.

12.14

Hedge accounting

12.15   A hedging relationship consists of a hedging instrument and a hedged item. Provided the qualifying conditions in paragraph 12.18 are met, an entity may apply hedge accounting.

Hedged items

12.16   A hedged item can be a recognised **asset** or liability, an unrecognised **firm commitment**, a **highly probable forecast transaction** or a **net investment in a foreign operation**, or a component of any such item, provided the item is reliably measurable.

12.16A   For hedge accounting purposes, only assets, liabilities, firm commitments or a highly probable forecast transaction with a party external to the reporting entity can be a hedged item. Hedge accounting can be applied to transactions between entities in the same **group** only in the **individual financial statements** of those entities, except for:

(a)   transactions with subsidiaries, where the subsidiaries are not consolidated in the **consolidated financial statements**;

(b)   the foreign currency risk of intragroup **monetary items** that result in an exposure to foreign exchange **gains** or losses that are not fully eliminated on consolidation in accordance with Section 30 *Foreign Currency Translation*; and

(c)   the foreign currency risk of highly probable forecast intragroup transactions, provided the transactions are denominated in a currency other than the **functional currency** of the entity entering into the transactions and the foreign currency risk affects consolidated profit or loss.

12.16B   A group of items, including components of items, can be an eligible hedged item provided that all of the following conditions are met:

(a)   it consists of items that are individually eligible hedged items;

(b)   the items in the group share the same risk;

(c)   the items in the group are managed together on a group basis for risk management purposes; and

(d)   it does not include items with offsetting risk positions.

12.16C   A component of an item comprises less than the entire fair value change or **cash flow** variability of an item. The following components of an item (including combinations thereof) may be a hedged item:

(a)   changes in the cash flows or fair value attributable to a separately identifiable and reliably measureable specific risk or risks, including cash flow and fair value changes above or below a specified price or other variable;

(b)   one or more selected contractual cash flows; or

(c)   a specified part of the nominal amount of an item.

Hedging instruments

12.17   An instrument may be a hedging instrument provided all of the following conditions are met:

(a)   it is a financial instrument measured at fair value through profit or loss;

(b)   it is a contract with a party external to the reporting entity (ie external to the group or individual entity that is being reported on); and

(c)   it is not a written option, except as described in paragraph 12.17C.

12.17A   An instrument (or a combination of such instruments) meeting the conditions of paragraph 12.17, may only be a hedging instrument:

(a)   in its entirety; or
(b)   a proportion of such an instrument or a proportion of a combination of such instruments, eg 50 per cent of the nominal amount of the instrument.

For a hedge of foreign currency risk, the foreign currency risk component of a financial instrument, provided that it is not a financial instrument as described in paragraph 11.6(b), may be a hedging instrument.   **12.17B**

A written option is not a hedging instrument unless the written option is an offset to or is combined with a purchased option and the effect of the offset or combination is not a net written option. An example of a combination of a written and a purchased option that is not a net written option is a zero cost interest rate collar.   **12.17C**

Conditions for hedge accounting

An entity may apply hedge accounting to a hedging relationship from the date all of the following conditions are met: **12.18**

(a)   the hedging relationship consists only of a hedging instrument and a hedged item as described in paragraphs 12.16 to 12.17C;
(b)   the hedging relationship is consistent with the entity's risk management objectives for undertaking hedges;
(c)   there is an economic relationship between the hedged item and the hedging instrument;
(d)   the entity has documented the hedging relationship so that the risk being hedged, the hedged item and the hedging instrument are clearly identified; and
(e)   the entity has determined and documented causes of hedge ineffectiveness.

An economic relationship between a hedged item and hedging instrument exists when the entity expects that the values of the hedged item and hedging instrument will typically move in opposite directions in response to movements in the same risk, which is the hedged risk.   **12.18A**

Accounting for qualifying hedging relationships

There are three types of hedging relationships: **12.19**

(a)   fair value hedge: a hedge of the exposure to changes in fair value of a recognised asset or liability or an unrecognised firm commitment, or a component of any such item, that are attributable to a particular risk and could affect profit or loss;
(b)   cash flow hedge: a hedge of the exposure to variability in cash flows that is attributable to a particular risk associated with all, or a component of, a recognised asset or liability (such as all or some future interest payments on variable rate debt) or a highly probable forecast transaction, and could affect profit or loss; and
(c)   hedge of a net investment in a foreign operation.

A hedge of the foreign currency risk of an unrecognised firm commitment may be accounted for as a fair value hedge or as a cash flow hedge.   **12.19A**

Fair value hedges

A fair value hedge shall be accounted for as follows from the date the conditions in paragraph 12.18 are met: **12.20**

(a)   the gain or loss on the hedging instrument shall be recognised in profit or loss; and
(b)   the **hedging gain or loss** on the hedged item shall adjust the carrying amount of the hedged item (if applicable) and be recognised in profit or loss. When a hedged item is an unrecognised firm commitment, the cumulative hedging gain or loss on the

hedged item is recognised as an asset or liability with a corresponding gain or loss recognised in profit or loss.

12.21 When an unrecognised firm commitment to acquire an asset or assume a liability is the hedged item, the initial carrying amount of the asset or liability that results from the entity meeting the firm commitment is adjusted to include the cumulative hedging gain or loss of the hedged item that was recognised in the statement of financial position.

12.22 Any adjustment arising from paragraph 12.20(b) shall be amortised to profit or loss if the hedged item is a financial instrument measured at amortised cost. Amortisation may begin as soon as an adjustment exists and shall begin no later than when the hedged item ceases to be adjusted for hedging gains and losses. The amortisation is based on a recalculated effective interest rate at the date amortisation begins.

Cash flow hedges

12.23 A cash flow hedge shall be accounted for as follows from the date the conditions in paragraph 12.18 are met:

(a) the separate component of equity associated with the hedged item (cash flow hedge reserve) is adjusted to the lower of the following (in absolute amounts):

    (i) the cumulative gain or loss on the hedging instrument from the date the conditions of paragraph 12.18 are met; and

    (ii) the cumulative change in fair value on the hedged item (ie the present value of the cumulative change of expected future cash flows) from the date the conditions of paragraph 12.18 are met;

(b) the portion of the gain or loss on the hedging instrument that is determined to be an effective hedge (ie the portion that is offset by the change in the cash flow hedge reserve calculated in accordance with (a)) shall be recognised in **other comprehensive income**;

(c) any remaining gain or loss on the hedging instrument (or any gain or loss required to balance the change in the cash flow hedge reserve calculated in accordance with (a)), is hedge ineffectiveness that shall be recognised in profit or loss; and

(d) the amount that has been accumulated in the cash flow hedge reserve in accordance with (a) shall be accounted for as follows:

    (i) if a hedged forecast transaction subsequently results in the recognition of a non-financial asset or non-financial liability, or a hedged forecast transaction for a non-financial asset or non-financial liability becomes a firm commitment for which fair value hedge accounting is applied, the entity shall remove that amount from the cash flow hedge reserve and include it directly in the initial cost or other carrying amount of the asset or liability;

    (ii) for cash flow hedges other than those covered by (i), that amount shall be reclassified from the cash flow hedge reserve to profit or loss in the same period or periods during which the hedged expected future cash flows affect profit or loss (for example, in the periods that interest income or interest expense is recognised or when a forecast sale occurs); and

    (iii) if the amount is a loss, and all or part of that loss is not expected to be recovered, the amount of the loss not expected to be recovered shall be reclassified to profit or loss immediately.

Hedges of a net investment in a foreign operation

12.24 Hedges of a net investment in a foreign operation, including a hedge of a monetary item that is accounted for as part of the net investment (see Section 30), shall be accounted for similarly to cash flow hedges from the date the conditions of paragraph 12.18 are met:

(a)   the portion of the gain or loss on the hedging instrument that is determined to be an effective hedge shall be recognised in other comprehensive income (see paragraphs 12.23(a) and (b)); and

(b)   the ineffective portion shall be recognised in profit or loss.

The cumulative gain or loss on the hedging instrument relating to the effective portion of the hedge that has been accumulated in equity shall not be reclassified from equity to profit or loss on disposal or partial disposal of the foreign operation.

Discontinuing hedge accounting

The entity may discontinue hedge accounting provided the entity has documented its election.   **12.25**

The entity shall discontinue hedge accounting when:

(a)   the hedging instrument has expired, is sold, terminated or exercised; or

(b)   the conditions for hedge accounting in paragraph 12.18 are no longer met.

In all cases, hedge accounting shall be discontinued prospectively.

In a fair value hedge, any adjustment arising from paragraph 12.20(b) is dealt with in accordance with paragraph 12.22.   **12.25A**

In a cash flow hedge, if the hedged future cash flows are no longer expected to occur, the amount that has been accumulated in the cash flow hedge reserve in accordance with paragraph 12.23(a) shall be reclassified from the cash flow hedge reserve to profit or loss immediately. If the hedged future cash flows are still expected to occur (for example a future cash flow that is no longer highly probable may still be expected to occur), the cumulative gain or loss in the cash flow hedge reserve is dealt with in accordance with paragraph 12.23(d).

In a net investment hedge, in accordance with paragraph 12.24, the amount that has been accumulated in equity is not reclassified to profit or loss.

Presentation

A financial asset and a financial liability shall be offset and the net amount presented in the **statement of financial position** when, and only when, an entity: **12.25B**

(a)   currently has a legally enforceable right to set off the recognised amounts; and

(b)   intends either to settle on a net basis, or to realise the asset and settle the liability simultaneously.

Disclosures

An entity applying this section shall make all of the disclosures required in Section 11 incorporating in those disclosures, financial instruments that are within the scope of this section as well as those within the scope of Section 11. For financial instruments in the scope of this section that are not held as part of a trading portfolio and are not **derivative** instruments, an entity shall provide additional disclosures as set out in paragraph 11.48A. In addition, if the entity uses hedge accounting, it shall make the additional disclosures in paragraphs 12.27 to 12.29A.   **12.26**

An entity shall disclose the following separately for each type of hedging relationship described in paragraph 12.19:   **12.27**

(a)   a description of the hedge;

(b)   a description of the financial instruments designated as hedging instruments and their fair values at the **reporting date**; and

(c)   the nature of the risks being hedged, including a description of the hedged item.

* **12.28**   If an entity uses hedge accounting for a fair value hedge it shall disclose the following:

(a)   the amount of the change in fair value of the hedging instrument recognised in profit or loss for the period; and

(b)   the amount of the change in fair value of the hedged item recognised in profit or loss for the period.

12.29   If an entity uses hedge accounting for a cash flow hedge it shall disclose the following:

(a)   the periods when the cash flows are expected to occur and when they are expected to affect profit or loss;

(b)   a description of any forecast transaction for which hedge accounting had previously been used, but which is no longer expected to occur;

*(c)   the amount of the change in fair value of the hedging instrument that was recognised in other comprehensive income during the period;

*(d)   the amount, if any, that was reclassified from equity to profit or loss for the period; and

*(e)   the amount, if any, of any excess of the fair value of the hedging instrument over the change in the fair value of the expected cash flows that was recognised in profit or loss for the period.

12.29A   If an entity uses hedge accounting for a net investment in a foreign operation it shall disclose separately the amounts recognised in other comprehensive income in accordance with paragraph 12.24(a) and the amounts recognised in profit or loss in accordance with paragraph 12.24(b).

Appendix to Section 12

Examples of hedge accounting

This appendix accompanies, but is not part of, Section 12. It provides guidance for applying the requirements of paragraphs 12.15 to 12.25A.

Example 1

Fair value hedge accounting – Hedge of forward foreign currency risk of an unrecognised firm commitment

In accordance with paragraph 12.19A, a hedge of the foreign currency risk of an unrecognised firm commitment may be accounted for as a cash flow or fair value hedge. This example illustrates fair value hedge accounting.

12A.1   On 9 June 20X5 an entity enters into a purchase agreement with a third party over a non-financial asset in a foreign currency (FC) for FC515,000. On the same day, the entity enters into a forward currency contract to buy FC500,000 for CU1,000,000. Under the purchase agreement, the non-financial asset will be delivered and paid for on 30 March 20X6, the same day the forward currency contract is required to be settled.

In this example the hedged item is the total of the commitment of FC515,000 and the hedging instrument is the forward contract to buy FC500,000. Since the nominal amounts of the two contracts do not match, hedge ineffectiveness arises. It should be noted that in practice an entity could avoid ineffectiveness arising for this reason by identifying an amount of FC500,000 of the total commitment as the hedged item in accordance with paragraph 12.16C.

For simplification, this example disregards other sources of ineffectiveness, eg counter party credit risk associated with the forward currency contract.

The entity's financial year ends on 31 December.

This example assumes that the qualifying conditions for hedge accounting in paragraph 12.18 are met from 9 June 20X5.

The table below sets out the applicable forward exchange rates, the fair value of the forward currency contract (the hedging instrument) and the hedging gains/losses on the purchase commitment (the hedged item) on the relevant dates. This example ignores the effects of discounting.

	9 Jun 20X5	31 Dec 20X5	30 Mar 20X6
Forward exchange rate (CU:FC)	2:1	2.2:1	2.16:1
Forward currency contract (hedging instrument)			
Fair value	nil	FC500,000 × CU0.2:FC = CU100,000	FC500,000 × CU0.16:FC = CU80,000†
Fair value change	nil	CU100,000 − 0 = CU100,000	CU80,000 − CU100,000 = (CU20,000)
Purchase commitment (hedged item)			
Cumulative hedging (loss)‡	nil	(FC515,000) × CU0.2:FC = (CU103,000)	(FC515,000) × CU0.16:FC = (CU82,400)
Hedging (loss)/ gain	nil	(CU103,000) − 0 = (CU103,000)	(CU82,400) − (CU103,000) = CU20,600

Key to table:
† *This is the fair value of the contract prior to settlement.*
‡ *In accordance with paragraph 12.20(b), the commitment is fair valued only for the hedged risk, which in this example is the forward exchange rate risk.*

Hedge accounting: **12A.2**

Note that there are no hedge accounting entries on 9 June 20X5.

31 December 20X5
(1)   In accordance with paragraph 12.20(a) the fair value gain of CU100,000 on the forward currency contract is recognised in profit or loss.
(2)   In accordance with paragraph 12.20(b) the cumulative hedging loss of CU103,000 on the commitment is recorded as a liability with a corresponding loss recognised in profit or loss.

Accounting entries:

Ref		Debit	Credit
(1)	Forward currency contract	CU100,000	
	Profit or loss		CU100,000
(2)	Profit or loss	CU103,000	
	Hedged item (commitment)		CU103,000

30 March 20X6

(1) In accordance with paragraph 12.20(a) the fair value loss of CU20,000 on the forward currency contract is recognised in profit or loss.

(2) In accordance with paragraph 12.20(b) the hedging gain on the commitment of CU20,600 is recognised in profit or loss with a corresponding adjustment to the recognised liability from CU103,000 to CU82,400.

(3) In accordance with paragraph 12.21 the non-financial asset's carrying amount is adjusted to include the cumulative hedging loss on the hedged item of CU82,400.

Note A: For illustrative purposes the accounting entry in respect of the settlement of the forward currency contract in cash for CU80,000 is shown below.

Note B: For illustrative purposes the accounting entry for the purchase of the non-financial asset at the applicable spot rate of FC2.16:CU for CU1,112,400 (settled in cash) is shown below.

Accounting entries:

Ref		Debit	Credit
(1)	Profit or loss	CU20,000	
	Forward currency contract		CU20,000
(2)	Hedged item (commitment)	CU20,600	
	Profit or loss		CU20,600
(3)	Hedged item (commitment)	CU82,400	
	Property, plant and equipment (PP&E)		CU82,400
(A)	Cash	CU80,000	
	Forward currency contract		CU80,000
(B)	Property, plant and equipment (PP&E)	CU1,112,400	
	Cash		CU1,112,400

Example 2

Cash flow hedge accounting – Hedge of variability in cash flows in a floating rate loan due to interest rate risk

This example illustrates the accounting for a cash flow hedge of interest rate risk associated with a floating rate loan. The entity borrows money at a floating rate and enters into an interest rate swap with the effect of paying a fixed rate overall.

12A.3   On 1 January 20X5, an entity borrows CU10,000,000 from a bank at a floating rate of 3-month LIBOR plus 2.5 per cent. The interest is payable annually in arrears on 31 December. The loan is repayable on 31 December 20X7.

On 1 January 20X5 the entity also enters into an interest rate swap with a third party, under which it receives 6-month LIBOR and pays a fixed rate of interest of 4.5 per cent. The notional amount of the swap is CU10,000,000. The swap is settled annually in arrears on 31 December and expires on 31 December 20X7.

The LIBOR rates on the loan and the interest rate swap are reset and fixed annually in advance on 31 December based on the expected LIBOR rates applicable at that time. Note that in practice the loan and swap interest rates would be reset more frequently than assumed for the purpose of simplification in this example.

The entity hedges the variability of the interest rate payments on the bank loan based on 3-month LIBOR. It should be noted that because the entity receives interest based on 6-month LIBOR under the interest rate swap, ineffectiveness will arise because the expected cash flows of the hedged item and the hedging instrument differ. The fair value of the interest rate swap may be affected by other factors that cause ineffectiveness, for example counter party credit risk, but these have been disregarded in this example.

There are no transaction costs.

The entity's financial year ends on 31 December.

This example assumes that the qualifying conditions for hedge accounting in paragraph 12.18 are met from 1 January 20X5.

The table in paragraph 12A.5 summarises the impact of hedge accounting on the interest rate swap, profit or loss and other comprehensive income.

The table below sets out the applicable LIBOR rates, interest payments and swap settlements. The fair values of the interest rate swap and the hedged item shown in the table are shown for illustrative purposes only.

Note that in practice, when forecasted variable interest rate payments are the hedged item, the fair value of a hypothetical swap, that would be expected to perfectly offset the hedged cash flows, is used as a proxy of the fair value of the hedged item. The hypothetical derivative in this scenario is a fixed to floating interest rate swap with terms that match those of the loan and a fixed rate of 4.3 per cent, which for the purpose of this example, is the interest rate where the fair value of the hypothetical swap is nil at the inception of the hedging relationship.

	1 Jan 20X5	31 Dec 20X5	31 Dec 20X6	31 Dec 20X7
Actual 3-month LIBOR	4.3%	5%	3%	n/a
Actual 6-month LIBOR	4.5%	4.9%	3.2%	n/a
Interest payments based on 3-month LIBOR	n/a	CU10m × (4.3% + 2.5%) = CU680,000	CU10m × (5% + 2.5%) = CU750,000	CU10m × (3% + 2.5%) = CU550,000
Interest rate swap (hedging instrument)				
Fair value	nil	CU78,000	(CU89,000)†	(CU130,000)‡
Fair value change	nil	CU78,000 – 0 = CU78,000	(CU89,000) – CU78,000 = (CU167,000)	(CU130,000) – (CU40,000)§ – (CU89,000) = (CU1,000)

	1 Jan 20X5	31 Dec 20X5	31 Dec 20X6	31 Dec 20X7
Swap settlement receipts/(payments) based on 6-month LIBOR	n/a	CU10m × (4.5% – 4.5%) = nil	CU10m × (4.9% – 4.5%) = CU40,000	CU10m * (3.2% – 4.5%) = (CU130,000)
Hedged item				
Fair value	nil	(CU137,000)	CU59,000	CU130,000

Key to table:
† This valuation is determined before the receipt of the cash settlement of CU40,000 due on 31 December 20X6.
‡ This valuation is determined before the payment of the cash settlement of CU130,000 due on 31 December 20X7.
§ CU40,000 is the settlement of the interest rate swap as at 31 December 20X6 which affects the fair value of the swap, but is not included in the fair value of the swap at 31 December 20X6 of CU89,000.

12A.4   Hedge accounting:

31 December 20X5

(1)   In accordance with paragraph 12.23(a), the cash flow hedge reserve is adjusted to the lower of (in absolute amounts) the cumulative gain on the hedging instrument (ie the interest rate swap), which equals its fair value, of CU78,000 and the cumulative change in fair value of the hedged item, which equals its fair value of (CU137,000).

In accordance with paragraph 12.23(b), the gain of CU78,000 on the interest rate swap is recognised in other comprehensive income.

(2)   The fixed interest element on the hypothetical swap is CU430,000, the same amount as the variable rate component. The variability of the 3-month LIBOR did therefore not affect profit or loss during the period. The reclassification adjustment in accordance with paragraph 12.23(d)(ii) is nil. (Note that no accounting entry is shown below.)

Note A: For illustrative purposes the accounting entry for interest payments is shown below. Note that in practice the accrual and payment of interest may be recorded in separate accounting entries.

Accounting entries:

Note that the accounting entries shown are only those relevant to demonstrate the effects of hedge accounting. In practice other accounting entries would be required, eg an entry to recognise the loan liability.

Ref		Debit	Credit
(1)	Interest rate swap	CU78,000	
	Other comprehensive income		CU78,000
(A)	Profit or loss	CU680,000	
	Cash		CU680,000

31 December 20X6

(1)   In accordance with paragraph 12.23(a), the cash flow hedge reserve is adjusted to the lower of (in absolute amounts) the cumulative loss on the hedging instrument (ie the interest rate swap) which equals its fair value of (CU89,000) and the cumulative change in fair value of the hedged item, which equals its fair value of CU59,000. The cash flow hedge reserve moves from CU78,000 to (CU59,000), a change of (CU137,000).

In accordance with paragraph 12.23(b), a loss of CU137,000 on the interest rate swap is recognised in other comprehensive income, as this part of the loss is fully off-set by the change in the cash flow hedge reserve. The remainder of the loss on the interest rate swap of CU30,000 is recognised in profit or loss, as required by paragraph 12.23(c).

(2)   The fixed interest element on the hypothetical swap is CU430,000, whilst the variable rate component is CU500,000. The variability of the 3-month LIBOR affects profit or loss during the period by CU70,000. Accordingly, the reclassification adjustment in accordance with paragraph 12.23(d)(ii) is CU70,000.

Note A: For illustrative purposes the accounting entry for interest payments is shown below. Note that in practice the accrual and payment of interest may be recorded in separate accounting entries.

Note B: For illustrative purposes the accounting entry for the settlement of the swap is shown below.

Accounting entries:

Ref	Description	Debit	Credit
(1)	Other comprehensive income	CU137,000	
	Profit or loss	CU30,000	
	Interest rate swap		CU167,000
(2)	Other comprehensive income	CU70,000	
	Profit or loss		CU70,000
(A)	Profit or loss	CU750,000	
	Cash		CU750,000
(B)	Cash	CU40,000	
	Interest rate swap		CU40,000

31 December 20X7

(1)   In accordance with paragraph 12.23(a), the cash flow hedge reserve is adjusted to the lower of (in absolute amounts) the cumulative loss on the hedging instrument (ie the interest rate swap) which equals the fair value of (CU130,000) and the cumulative change in fair value of the hedged item, which equals its fair value of CU130,000.

The cash flow hedge reserve moves from (CU129,000) to (CU130,000), a change of (CU1,000). In accordance with paragraph 12.23(b), the loss of CU1,000 on the interest rate swap is recognised in other comprehensive income.

(2)   The fixed interest element on the hypothetical swap is CU430,000, whilst the variable rate component is CU300,000. The variability of the 3-month LIBOR affects profit or loss during the period by (CU130,000). Accordingly, the reclassification adjustment in accordance with paragraph 12.23(d)(ii) is (CU130,000).

Note A: For illustrative purposes the accounting entry for interest payments is shown below. Note that in practice the accrual and payment of interest may be recorded in separate accounting entries.

Note B: For illustrative purposes the accounting entry for the settlement of the swap is shown below.

Accounting entries:

Ref		Debit	Credit
(1)	Other comprehensive income	CU1,000	
	Interest rate swap		CU1,000
(2)	Profit or loss	CU130,000	
	Other comprehensive income		CU130,000
(A)	Profit or loss	CU550,000	
	Cash		CU550,000
(B)	Interest rate swap	CU130,000	
	Cash		CU130,000

12A.5 The table below summarises the effects of the accounting entries shown in paragraph 12A.4 on the interest rate swap, profit or loss and other comprehensive income.

Description	Interest rate swap	Other comprehensive income	Profit or loss
31 December 20X5			
Opening balance	**nil**	**nil†**	**–**
Interest on the loan			CU680,000
Interest rate swap fair value movement	CU78,000	(CU78,000)	–
Closing balance	**CU78,000**	**(CU78,000)†**	**–**
31 December 20X6			
Opening balance	**CU78,000**	**(CU78,000)†**	**–**
Interest on the loan			CU750,000
Interest rate swap fair value movement	(CU167,000)	CU137,000	CU30,000
Settlement receipt interest rate swap	(40,000)	–	–
Reclassification from cash flow hedge reserve		CU70,000	(CU70,000)
Closing balance	**(CU129,000)**	**CU129,000†**	**–**
31 December 20X7			
Opening balance	**(CU129,000)**	**CU129,000†**	**–**
Interest on the loan			CU550,000
Interest rate swap movement	(1,000)	1,000	–
Settlement payment interest rate swap	CU130,000	–	–
Reclassification from cash flow hedge reserve	–	(CU130,000)	CU130,000
Closing balance	**nil**	**nil†**	**–**

Key to table:
†: *This is the balance of the cash flow hedge reserve.*

Example 3

Hedge accounting: Net investment in a foreign operation

This example illustrates the accounting for a net investment hedge in the consolidated financial statements. The entity has a foreign operation and hedges its exposure to foreign currency risk in the foreign operation by the use of a foreign currency loan.

On 1 April 20X5 an entity with functional currency CU acquires an investment in an overseas subsidiary (with functional currency FC) at a cost of FC1,200,000. On the same day the entity takes out a loan with a third party of FC1,200,000 to finance the investment. This example disregards the effects of interest or other transaction costs associated with the loan.   **12A.6**

This example assumes that the carrying amount of the investment denominated in FC is impaired below FC1,200,000 as presented in the table below, which causes ineffectiveness.

The entity's financial year ends on 31 December.

This example assumes that the qualifying conditions for hedge accounting in paragraph 12.18 are met from 1 April 20X5.

The table below sets out the applicable exchange rates, the carrying amount of the loan and the foreign exchange gains and losses on the loan as determined in accordance with Section 30, as well as the retranslation differences on the foreign investment recognised in other comprehensive income in accordance with Section 30.

	1 Apr 20X5	31 Dec 20X5	31 Dec 20X6
Spot exchange rate CU:FC	0.35:1	0.3:1	0.45:1
Loan (hedging instrument)			
Carrying amount under Section 30	(FC1,200,000) × CU0.35:FC = (CU420,000)	(FC1,200,000) × CU0.3:FC = (CU360,000)	(FC1,200,000) × CU0.45:FC = (CU540,000)
Cumulative gain/(loss)	nil	(CU360,000) – (CU420,000) = CU60,000	(CU540,000) – (CU420,000) = (CU120,000)
Gain/(loss)	nil	(CU360,000) – (CU420,000) = CU60,000	(CU540,000) – (CU360,000) = (CU180,000)
Investment in foreign operation (hedged item)			
Retranslation difference in accordance with Section 30	nil	(CU55,000)†	CU157,500‡
Cumulative retranslation differences	nil	(CU55,000) – 0 = (CU55,000)	CU157,500 + (CU55,000) = CU102,500

Key to table:
† *This is the exchange difference referred to in paragraph 30.20 which is recognised in other comprehensive income. The amount under paragraph 30.20(a) is CU5,000 and under paragraph 30.20(b) (CU60,000). The calculation is based on the translation of the FC200,000 loss at the average rate of 0.325CU:FC.*
‡ *This is the exchange difference referred to in paragraph 30.20 which is recognised in other comprehensive income. The amount under paragraph 30.20(a) is CU7,500 and under paragraph 30.20(b) CU150,000. The calculation is based on the translation of the FC100,000 profit at the average rate of 0.375CU:FC.*

12A.7   Hedge accounting:

31 December 20X5

A component of equity is adjusted to the lower of (in absolute amounts) the cumulative exchange gain on the loan of CU60,000 and the cumulative retranslation difference on the net investment of (CU55,000).

In accordance with paragraph 12.24(a), a gain of CU55,000 on the loan is recognised in other comprehensive income. The remainder of the gain of CU5,000 is recognised in profit or loss, as required by paragraph 12.24(b).

Accounting entry:

Note that only the accounting entry in relation to hedge accounting as described in paragraph 12.24 is shown. Other accounting entries in relation to the loan and the investment in the foreign operation would be required in practice.

	Debit	Credit
Loan	CU60,000	
Other comprehensive income		CU55,000
Profit or loss		CU5,000

31 December 20X6

A component of equity is adjusted to the lower of (in absolute amounts) the cumulative exchange loss on the loan of CU120,000 and the cumulative exchange difference on the net investment of CU102,500.

The amount recorded in equity changes from CU55,000 to (CU102,500), a change of (CU157,500). In accordance with paragraph 12.24(a) a loss of CU157,500 on the loan is recognised in other comprehensive income. The remainder of the loss of CU22,500 is recorded in profit or loss, as required by paragraph 12.24(b).

Accounting entry:

	Debit	Credit
Other comprehensive income	CU157,500	
Profit or loss	CU22,500	
Loan		CU180,000

Section 13 Inventories

Scope of this section

13.1   This section sets out the principles for recognising and measuring **inventories**. Inventories are **assets**:

(a)   held for sale in the ordinary course of business;

(b)   in the process of production for such sale; or

(c)   in the form of materials or supplies to be consumed in the production process or in the rendering of services.

This section applies to all inventories, except: **13.2**

(a)   work in progress arising under **construction contracts**, including directly related service contracts (see Section 23 *Revenue*);

(b)   **financial instruments** (see Section 11 *Basic Financial Instruments* and Section 12 *Other Financial Instruments Issues*); and

(c)   **biological assets** related to **agricultural activity** and **agricultural produce** at the point of harvest (see Section 34 *Specialised Activities*).

Other than the disclosure requirements in paragraph 13.22, this section does not apply to   **13.3** the **measurement** of inventories at **fair value less costs to sell** through **profit or loss** at each **reporting date**. Inventories shall not be measured at fair value less costs to sell unless it is a more relevant measure of the entity's **performance** because the entity operates in an **active market** where sale can be achieved at published prices, and inventory is a store of readily realisable value.

Measurement of inventories

An entity shall measure inventories at the lower of **cost** and estimated selling price less   **13.4** costs to complete and sell.

Inventories held for distribution at no or nominal consideration shall be measured   **13.4A** at the lower of cost adjusted, when applicable, for any loss of **service potential** and replacement cost.

Cost of inventories

An entity shall include in the cost of inventories all costs of purchase, costs of conversion   **13.5** and other costs incurred in bringing the inventories to their present location and condition.

Where inventories are acquired through a **non-exchange transaction**, their cost shall be   **13.5A** measured at their **fair value** as at the date of acquisition. For **public benefit entities** and entities within a **public benefit entity group**, this requirement only applies to inventories that are recognised as a result of the requirements for incoming resources from non-exchange transactions as prescribed in Section 34 *Specialised Activities*.

Costs of purchase

The costs of purchase of inventories comprise the purchase price, import duties and other   **13.6** taxes (other than those subsequently recoverable by the entity from the taxing authorities), and transport, handling and other costs directly attributable to the acquisition of finished goods, materials and services. Trade discounts, rebates and other similar items are deducted in determining the costs of purchase.

An entity may purchase inventories on deferred settlement terms. In some cases, the   **13.7** arrangement effectively contains an unstated financing element, for example, a difference between the purchase price for normal credit terms and the deferred settlement amount. In these cases, the difference is recognised as interest expense over the period of the financing and is not added to the cost of the inventories unless the inventory is a **qualifying asset** (see Section 25 *Borrowing Costs*) and the entity adopts a policy of capitalisation of borrowing costs.

Costs of conversion

13.8   The costs of conversion of inventories include costs directly related to the units of production, such as direct labour. They also include a systematic allocation of fixed and variable production overheads that are incurred in converting materials into finished goods. Fixed production overheads are those indirect costs of production that remain relatively constant regardless of the volume of production, such as **depreciation** and maintenance of factory buildings and equipment, and the cost of factory management and administration. Variable production overheads are those indirect costs of production that vary directly, or nearly directly, with the volume of production, such as indirect materials and indirect labour.

13.8A   Production overheads include the costs for obligations (recognised and measured in accordance with Section 21 *Provisions and Contingencies*) for dismantling, removing and restoring a site on which an item of **property, plant and equipment** is located that are incurred during the **reporting period** as a consequence of having used that item of property, plant and equipment to produce inventory during that period.

Allocation of production overheads

13.9   An entity shall allocate fixed production overheads to the costs of conversion on the basis of the normal capacity of the production facilities. Normal capacity is the production expected to be achieved on average over a number of periods or seasons under normal circumstances, taking into account the loss of capacity resulting from planned maintenance. The actual level of production may be used if it approximates normal capacity. The amount of fixed overhead allocated to each unit of production is not increased as a consequence of low production or idle plant. Unallocated overheads are recognised as an **expense** in the period in which they are incurred. In periods of abnormally high production, the amount of fixed overhead allocated to each unit of production is decreased so that inventories are not measured above cost. Variable production overheads are allocated to each unit of production on the basis of the actual use of the production facilities.

Joint products and by-products

13.10   A production process may result in more than one product being produced simultaneously. This is the case, for example, when joint products are produced or when there is a main product and a by-product. When the costs of raw materials or conversion of each product are not separately identifiable, an entity shall allocate them between the products on a rational and consistent basis. The allocation may be based, for example, on the relative sales value of each product either at the stage in the production process when the products become separately identifiable, or at the completion of production. Most by-products, by their nature, are immaterial. When this is the case, the entity shall measure them at selling price less costs to complete and sell and deduct this amount from the cost of the main product. As a result, the **carrying amount** of the main product is not materially different from its cost.

Other costs included in inventories

13.11   An entity shall include other costs in the cost of inventories only to the extent that they are incurred in bringing the inventories to their present location and condition.

13.12   [Not used]

Costs excluded from inventories

Examples of costs excluded from the cost of inventories and recognised as expenses in the period in which they are incurred are: **13.13**

(a)   abnormal amounts of wasted materials, labour or other production costs;
(b)   storage costs, unless those costs are necessary during the production process before a further production stage;
(c)   administrative overheads that do not contribute to bringing inventories to their present location and condition; and
(d)   selling costs.

Cost of inventories of a service provider

To the extent that service providers have inventories, they measure them at the costs of their production. These costs consist primarily of the labour and other costs of personnel directly engaged in providing the service, including supervisory personnel, and attributable overheads. Labour and other costs relating to sales and general administrative personnel are not included but are recognised as expenses in the period in which they are incurred. The cost of inventories of a service provider does not include profit margins or non-attributable overheads that are often factored into prices charged by service providers.   **13.14**

Cost of agricultural produce harvested from biological assets

Section 34 requires that inventories comprising agricultural produce that an entity has harvested from its biological assets should be measured on initial **recognition**, at the point of harvest, at either their fair value less estimated costs to sell or the lower of cost and estimated selling price less costs to complete and sell. This becomes the cost of the inventories at that date for application of this section.   **13.15**

Techniques for measuring cost, such as standard costing, retail method and most recent purchase price

An entity may use techniques such as the standard cost method, the retail method or most recent purchase price for measuring the cost of inventories if the result approximates cost. Standard costs take into account normal levels of materials and supplies, labour, efficiency and capacity utilisation. They are regularly reviewed and, if necessary, revised in the light of current conditions. The retail method measures cost by reducing the sales value of the inventory by the appropriate percentage gross margin.   **13.16**

Cost formulas

An entity shall measure the cost of inventories of items that are not ordinarily interchangeable and goods or services produced and segregated for specific projects by using specific identification of their individual costs.   **13.17**

An entity shall measure the cost of inventories, other than those dealt with in paragraph 13.17, by using the first-in, first-out (FIFO) or weighted average cost formula. An entity shall use the same cost formula for all inventories having a similar nature and use to the entity. For inventories with a different nature or use, different cost formulas may be justified. The last-in, first-out method (LIFO) is not permitted by this FRS.   **13.18**

Impairment of inventories

13.19　Paragraphs 27.2 to 27.4 require an entity to assess at the end of each reporting period whether any inventories are impaired, ie the carrying amount is not fully recoverable (eg because of damage, obsolescence or declining selling prices). If an item (or group of items) of inventory is impaired, those paragraphs require the entity to measure the inventory at its selling price less costs to complete and sell, and to recognise an **impairment loss**. Those paragraphs also require a reversal of a prior impairment in some circumstances.

Recognition as an expense

13.20　When inventories are sold, the entity shall recognise the carrying amount of those inventories as an expense in the period in which the related **revenue** is recognised.

13.20A　When inventories held for distribution at no or nominal consideration are distributed, the carrying amount of those inventories shall be recognised as an expense.

13.21　Some inventories may be allocated to other asset accounts, for example, inventory used as a component of self-constructed property, plant or equipment. Inventories allocated to another asset in this way are accounted for subsequently in accordance with the section of this FRS relevant to that type of asset.

Disclosures

13.22　An entity shall disclose the following:

(a)　the **accounting policies** adopted in measuring inventories, including the cost formula used;

(b)　the total carrying amount of inventories and the carrying amount in classifications appropriate to the entity;

(c)　the amount of inventories recognised as an expense during the period;

(d)　impairment losses recognised or reversed in profit or loss in accordance with Section 27; and

*(e)　the total carrying amount of inventories pledged as security for **liabilities**.

Section 14 Investments in Associates

Scope of this section

14.1　This section applies to accounting for **associates** in **consolidated financial statements**. This section also applies to accounting for investments in associates in the **individual financial statements** of an investor that is not a **parent**. An entity that is a parent shall account for its investments in associates in its **separate financial statements** in accordance with paragraphs 9.26 and 9.26A, as appropriate.

Associates defined

14.2　An associate is an entity, including an unincorporated entity such as a partnership, over which the investor has **significant influence** and that is neither a **subsidiary** nor an interest in a **joint venture**.

14.3　Significant influence is the power to participate in the financial and operating policy decisions of the associate but is not **control** or **joint control** over those policies.

(a)   If an investor holds, directly or indirectly (eg through subsidiaries), 20 per cent or more of the voting power of the associate, it is presumed that the investor has significant influence, unless it can be clearly demonstrated that this is not the case.

(b)   Conversely, if the investor holds, directly or indirectly (eg through subsidiaries), less than 20 per cent of the voting power of the associate, it is presumed that the investor does not have significant influence, unless such influence can be clearly demonstrated.

(c)   A substantial or majority ownership by another investor does not preclude an investor from having significant influence.

Measurement—accounting policy election

An investor that is not a parent but that has an investment in one or more associates shall, in its individual financial statements, account for all of its investments in associates using either: **14.4**

(a)   the cost model in accordance with paragraphs 14.5 to 14.6;

(b)   [not used]

(c)   the fair value model in accordance with paragraphs 14.9 to 14.10A; or

(d)   at fair value with changes in fair value recognised in profit or loss (paragraphs 11.27 to 11.32 provide guidance on fair value).

An investor that is a parent shall, in its consolidated financial statements, account for all of its investments in associates using the equity method in accordance with paragraph 14.8, except as required by paragraph 14.4B.   **14.4A**

Where an investor is a parent and has an associate that is **held as part of an investment portfolio**, the associate shall be measured at **fair value** with changes in fair value recognised in **profit or loss** in the consolidated financial statements.   **14.4B**

Cost model

An investor that is not a parent, that chooses to adopt the cost model, shall measure its investments in associates at cost less any accumulated **impairment losses** recognised in accordance with Section 27 *Impairment of Assets*.   **14.5**

The investor shall recognise dividends and other distributions received from the investment as **income** without regard to whether the distributions are from accumulated profits of the associate arising before or after the date of acquisition.   **14.6**

[Not used]   **14.7**

Equity method

Under the equity method of accounting, an equity investment is initially recognised at the transaction price (including **transaction costs**) and is subsequently adjusted to reflect the investor's share of the profit or loss, **other comprehensive income** and **equity** of the associate.   **14.8**

(a)   *Distributions and other adjustments to carrying amount.* Distributions received from the associate reduce the **carrying amount** of the investment. Adjustments to the carrying amount may also be required as a consequence of changes in the associate's equity arising from items of other comprehensive income.

(b)   *Potential voting rights.* Although potential voting rights are considered in deciding whether significant influence exists, an investor shall measure its share of profit or loss and other comprehensive income of the associate and its share of changes in the associate's equity on the basis of present ownership interests. Those measurements shall not reflect the possible exercise or conversion of potential voting rights.

(c) *Implicit goodwill and fair value adjustments.* On acquisition of the investment in an associate, an investor shall account for any difference (whether positive or negative) between the cost of acquisition and the investor's share of the fair values of the net identifiable assets of the associate in accordance with paragraphs 19.22 to 19.24. An investor shall adjust its share of the associate's profits or losses after acquisition to account for additional **depreciation** or **amortisation** of the associate's depreciable or amortisable assets (including **goodwill**) on the basis of the excess of their fair values over their carrying amounts at the time the investment was acquired.

(d) *Impairment.* If there is an indication that an investment in an associate may be impaired, an investor shall test the entire carrying amount of the investment for impairment in accordance with Section 27 as a single **asset**. Any goodwill included as part of the carrying amount of the investment in the associate is not tested separately for impairment but, rather, as part of the test for impairment of the investment as a whole.

(e) *Investor's transactions with associates.* The investor shall eliminate unrealised profits and losses resulting from upstream (associate to investor) and downstream (investor to associate) transactions to the extent of the investor's interest in the associate. Unrealised losses on such transactions may provide evidence of an impairment of the asset transferred.

(f) *Date of associate's financial statements.* In applying the equity method, the investor shall use the **financial statements** of the associate as of the same date as the financial statements of the investor unless it is **impracticable** to do so. If it is impracticable, the investor shall use the most recent available financial statements of the associate, with adjustments made for the effects of any significant transactions or events occurring between the accounting period ends.

(g) *Associate's accounting policies.* If the associate uses **accounting policies** that differ from those of the investor, the investor shall adjust the associate's financial statements to reflect the investor's accounting policies for the purpose of applying the equity method unless it is impracticable to do so.

(h) *Losses in excess of investment.* If an investor's share of losses of an associate equals or exceeds the carrying amount of its investment in the associate, the investor shall discontinue recognising its share of further losses. After the investor's interest is reduced to zero, the investor shall recognise additional losses by a **provision** (see Section 21 *Provisions and Contingencies*) only to the extent that the investor has incurred legal or **constructive obligations** or has made payments on behalf of the associate. If the associate subsequently reports profits, the investor shall resume recognising its share of those profits only after its share of the profits equals the share of losses not recognised.

(i) *Discontinuing the equity method.* An investor shall cease using the equity method from the date that significant influence ceases and, provided the associate does not become a subsidiary in accordance with *Section 19 Business Combinations and Goodwill* or a joint venture in accordance with Section 15 *Investments in Joint Ventures*, shall account for the investment as follows:

  (i) If the investor loses significant influence over an associate as a result of a full or partial disposal, it shall derecognise that associate and recognise in profit or loss the difference between the proceeds from the disposal and the carrying amount of the investment in the associate relating to the proportion disposed of or lost at the date significant influence is lost. The investor shall account for any retained interest using Section 11 *Basic Financial Instruments* or Section 12 *Other Financial Instruments Issues*, as appropriate. The carrying amount of the investment at the date that it ceases to be an associate shall be regarded as its cost on initial **measurement** as a **financial asset**; and

(ii)   If an investor loses significant influence for reasons other than a partial disposal of its investment, the investor shall regard the carrying amount of the investment at that date as a new cost basis and shall account for the investment using Sections 11 or 12, as appropriate.

The gain or loss arising on the disposal shall also include those amounts that have been recognised in **other comprehensive income** in relation to that associate, where those amounts are required to be reclassified to profit or loss upon disposal in accordance with other sections of this FRS. Amounts that are not required to be reclassified to profit or loss upon disposal of the related assets or liabilities in accordance with other sections of this FRS shall be transferred directly to retained earnings.

Fair value model

When an investment in an associate is recognised initially, an investor that is not a parent, that chooses to adopt the fair value model, shall measure it at the transaction price.   14.9

At each reporting date, an investor that is not a parent, that chooses to adopt the fair value   14.10
model, shall measure its investments in associates at fair value, with changes in fair value recognised in other comprehensive income in accordance with paragraphs 17.15E and 17.15F, using the fair value guidance in paragraphs 11.27 to 11.32. An investor using the fair value model shall use the cost model for any investment in an associate for which it is impracticable to measure fair value reliably without undue cost or effort.

The investor shall recognise dividends and other distributions received from the investment   14.10A
as income without regard to whether the distributions are from accumulated profits of the associate arising before or after the date of acquisition.

Presentation in individual and consolidated financial statements

Unless otherwise required under the Regulations, an investor shall classify investments in   14.11
associates as **fixed assets**.

Disclosures in individual and consolidated financial statements

The financial statements shall disclose: 14.12

(a)   the accounting policy for investments in associates;
(b)   the carrying amount of investments in associates; and
(c)   the fair value of investments in associates accounted for using the equity method for which there are published price quotations.

For investments in associates accounted for in accordance with the cost model, an investor   14.13
shall disclose the amount of dividends and other distributions recognised as income.

For investments in associates accounted for in accordance with the equity method, an   14.14
investor shall disclose separately its share of the profit or loss of such associates and its share of any **discontinued operations** of such associates.

For investments in associates accounted for in accordance with the fair value model, an   14.15
investor shall make the disclosures required by paragraphs 11.43 and 11.44.

The individual financial statements of an investor that is not a parent shall disclose   14.15A
summarised financial information about the investments in the associates, along with the effect of including those investments as if they had been accounted for using the

equity method. Investing entities that are exempt from preparing consolidated financial statements, or would be exempt if they had subsidiaries, are exempt from this requirement.

Section 15 Investments in Joint Ventures

Scope of this section

15.1   This section applies to accounting for **joint ventures** in **consolidated financial statements**, for investments in joint ventures in the **individual financial statements** of a **venturer** that is not a **parent**, and for investment in **jointly controlled operations** and **jointly controlled assets** in the **separate financial statements** of a venturer that is a parent. A venturer that is a parent shall account for interests in **jointly controlled entities** in its **separate financial statements** in accordance with paragraphs 9.26 and 9.26A, as appropriate.

Joint ventures defined

15.2   **Joint control** is the contractually agreed sharing of **control** over an economic activity, and exists only when the strategic financial and operating decisions relating to the activity require the unanimous consent of the parties sharing control (the venturers).

15.3   A joint venture is a contractual arrangement whereby two or more parties undertake an economic activity that is subject to joint control. Joint ventures can take the form of jointly controlled operations, jointly controlled assets, or jointly controlled entities.

Jointly controlled operations

15.4   The operation of some joint ventures involves the use of the **assets** and other resources of the venturers rather than the establishment of a corporation, partnership or other entity, or a financial structure that is separate from the venturers themselves. Each venturer uses its own **property, plant and equipment** and carries its own **inventories**. It also incurs its own **expenses** and **liabilities** and raises its own finance, which represent its own obligations. The joint venture activities may be carried out by the venturer's employees alongside the venturer's similar activities. The joint venture agreement usually provides a means by which the **revenue** from the sale of the joint product and any expenses incurred in common are shared among the venturers.

15.5   In respect of its interests in jointly controlled operations, a venturer shall recognise in its **financial statements**:

(a)   the assets that it controls and the liabilities that it incurs; and

(b)   the expenses that it incurs and its share of the **income** that it earns from the sale of goods or services by the joint venture.

Jointly controlled assets

15.6   Some joint ventures involve the joint control, and often the joint ownership, by the venturers of one or more assets contributed to, or acquired for the purpose of, the joint venture and dedicated to the purposes of the joint venture.

15.7   In respect of its interest in a jointly controlled asset, a venturer shall recognise in its financial statements:

(a)   its share of the jointly controlled assets, classified according to the nature of the assets;

(b)   any liabilities that it has incurred;

(c)   its share of any liabilities incurred jointly with the other venturers in relation to the joint venture;

(d)   any income from the sale or use of its share of the output of the joint venture, together with its share of any expenses incurred by the joint venture; and

(e)   any expenses that it has incurred in respect of its interest in the joint venture.

Jointly controlled entities

A jointly controlled entity is a joint venture that involves the establishment of a corporation, partnership or other entity in which each venturer has an interest. The entity operates in the same way as other entities, except that a contractual arrangement between the venturers establishes joint control over the economic activity of the entity.   **15.8**

Measurement—accounting policy election

A venturer that is not a parent but has one or more interests in jointly controlled entities shall, in its individual financial statements, account for all of its interests in jointly controlled entities using either: **15.9**

(a)   the cost model in accordance with paragraphs 15.10 to 15.11;

(b)   [not used]

(c)   the fair value model in accordance with paragraphs 15.14 to 15.15A; or

(d)   at fair value with changes in fair value recognised in profit or loss (paragraphs 11.27 to 11.32 provide guidance on fair value).

A venturer that is a parent shall, in its consolidated financial statements, account for all of its investments in jointly controlled entities using the equity method in accordance with paragraph 15.13, except as required by paragraph 15.9B.   **15.9A**

A venture that is a parent, shall measure its investments in jointly controlled entities **held as part of an investment portfolio** at **fair value** with changes in fair value recognised in **profit or loss** in the consolidated financial statements.   **15.9B**

Cost model

A venturer that is not a parent, that chooses to adopt the cost model, shall measure its investments in jointly controlled entities, at cost less any accumulated **impairment losses** recognised in accordance with Section 27 *Impairment of Assets.*   **15.10**

The venturer shall recognise distributions received from the investment as income without regard to whether the distributions are from accumulated profits of the jointly controlled entity arising before or after the date of acquisition.   **15.11**

[Not used]   **15.12**

Equity method

A venturer shall measure its investments in jointly controlled entities by the equity method using the procedures in accordance with paragraph 14.8 (substituting 'joint control' where that paragraph refers to 'significant influence', and 'jointly controlled entity' where that paragraph refers to 'associate').   **15.13**

Fair value model

When an investment in a jointly controlled entity is recognised initially, a venturer that is not a parent, that chooses to adopt the fair value model, shall measure it at the transaction price.   **15.14**

15.15 At each reporting date, a venturer that is not a parent, that chooses to adopt the fair value model, shall measure its investments in jointly controlled entities at fair value using the fair value guidance in paragraphs 11.27 to 11.32. Changes in fair value shall be recognised in accordance with paragraphs 17.15E and 17.15F. A venturer using the fair value model shall use the cost model for any investment in a jointly controlled entity for which it is **impracticable** to measure fair value reliably without undue cost or effort.

15.15A The venturer shall recognise dividends and other distributions received from the investment as income without regard to whether the distributions are from accumulated profits of the jointly controlled entity arising before or after the date of acquisition.

Transactions between a venturer and a joint venture

15.16 When a venturer contributes or sells assets to a joint venture, **recognition** of any portion of a **gain** or loss from the transaction shall reflect the substance of the transaction. While the assets are retained by the joint venture, and provided the venturer has transferred the significant risks and rewards of ownership, the venturer shall recognise only that portion of the gain or loss that is attributable to the interests of the other venturers. The venturer shall recognise the full amount of any loss when the contribution or sale provides evidence of an impairment loss.

15.17 When a venturer purchases assets from a joint venture, the venturer shall not recognise its share of the profits of the joint venture from the transaction until it resells the assets to an independent party. A venturer shall recognise its share of the losses resulting from these transactions in the same way as profits except that losses shall be recognised immediately when they represent an impairment loss.

If investor does not have joint control

15.18 An investor in a joint venture that does not have joint control shall account for that investment in accordance with Section 11 *Basic Financial Instruments* or Section 12 *Other Financial Instruments Issues* or, if it has **significant influence** in the joint venture, in accordance with Section 14 *Investments in Associates*.

Disclosures in individual and consolidated financial statements

15.19 The financial statements shall disclose the following:

(a)   the **accounting policy** for recognising investments in jointly controlled entities;
(b)   the **carrying amount** of investments in jointly controlled entities;
(c)   the fair value of investments in jointly controlled entities accounted for using the equity method for which there are published price quotations; and
*(d)   the aggregate amount of its commitments relating to joint ventures, including its share in the capital commitments that have been incurred jointly with other venturers, as well as its share of the capital commitments of the joint ventures themselves.

15.20 For jointly controlled entities accounted for in accordance with the equity method, the venturer shall disclose separately its share of the profit or loss of such investments and its share of any **discontinued operations** of such jointly controlled entities.

15.21 For jointly controlled entities accounted for in accordance with the fair value model, the venturer shall make the disclosures required by paragraphs 11.43 and 11.44.

15.21A The individual financial statements of a venturer that is not a parent shall disclose summarised financial information about the investments in the jointly controlled entities, along with the effect of including those investments as if they had been accounted for using the equity method. Investing entities that are exempt from preparing consolidated financial statements, or would be exempt if they had subsidiaries, are exempt from this requirement.

Section 16 Investment Property

Scope of this section

This section applies to accounting for investments in land or buildings that meet the definition of **investment property** in paragraph 16.2 and some property interests held by a lessee under an **operating lease** (see paragraph 16.3) that are treated like investment property. Only investment property whose **fair value** can be measured reliably without undue cost or effort on an on-going basis is accounted for in accordance with this section at fair value through **profit or loss**. All other investment property is accounted for as **property, plant and equipment** using the cost model in Section 17 *Property, Plant and Equipment* and remains within the scope of Section 17 unless a reliable measure of fair value becomes available and it is expected that fair value will be reliably measurable on an on-going basis.   **16.1**

Definition and initial recognition of investment property

Investment property is property (land or a building, or part of a building, or both) held by the owner or by the lessee under a **finance lease** to earn rentals or for capital appreciation or both, rather than for: **16.2**

(a)   use in the production or supply of goods or services or for administrative purposes; or

(b)   sale in the ordinary course of business.

A property interest that is held by a lessee under an operating lease may be classified and accounted for as investment property using this section if, and only if, the property would otherwise meet the definition of an investment property and the lessee can measure the fair value of the property interest without undue cost or effort on an on-going basis. This classification alternative is available on a property-by-property basis.   **16.3**

Property held primarily for the provision of social benefits, eg social housing held by a **public benefit entity**, shall not be classified as investment property and shall be accounted for as property, plant and equipment in accordance with Section 17.   **16.3A**

Mixed use property shall be separated between investment property and property, plant and equipment. However, if the fair value of the investment property component cannot be measured reliably without undue cost or effort, the entire property shall be accounted for as property, plant and equipment in accordance with Section 17.   **16.4**

Measurement at initial recognition

An entity shall measure investment property at its cost at initial **recognition**. The cost of a purchased investment property comprises its purchase price and any directly attributable expenditure such as legal and brokerage fees, property transfer taxes and other transaction costs. If payment is deferred beyond normal credit terms, the cost is the **present value** of all future payments. An entity shall determine the cost of a self-constructed investment property in accordance with paragraphs 17.10 to 17.14.   **16.5**

16.6   The initial cost of a property interest held under a **lease** and classified as an investment property shall be as prescribed for a finance lease by paragraphs 20.9 and 20.10, even if the lease would otherwise be classified as an operating lease if it was in the scope of Section 20 *Leases*. In other words, the **asset** is recognised at the lower of the fair value of the property and the present value of the **minimum lease payments**. An equivalent amount is recognised as a **liability** in accordance with paragraphs 20.9 and 20.10. Any premium paid for a lease is treated as part of the minimum lease payments for this purpose, and is therefore included in the cost of the asset, but is excluded from the liability.

Measurement after recognition

16.7   Investment property whose fair value can be measured reliably without undue cost or effort shall be measured at fair value at each **reporting date** with changes in fair value recognised in profit or loss. If a property interest held under a lease is classified as investment property, the item accounted for at fair value is that interest and not the underlying property. Paragraphs 11.27 to 11.32 provide guidance on determining fair value. An entity shall account for all other investment property as property, plant and equipment using the cost model in Section 17.

Transfers

16.8   If a reliable measure of fair value is no longer available without undue cost or effort for an item of investment property measured using the fair value model, the entity shall thereafter account for that item as property, plant and equipment in accordance with Section 17 until a reliable measure of fair value becomes available. The **carrying amount** of the investment property on that date becomes its cost under Section 17. Paragraph 16.10(e) (iii) requires disclosure of this change. It is a change of circumstances and not a change in **accounting policy**.

16.9   Other than as required by paragraph 16.8, an entity shall transfer a property to, or from, investment property only when the property first meets, or ceases to meet, the definition of investment property.

Disclosures

16.10   An entity shall disclose the following for all investment property accounted for at fair value through profit or loss (paragraph 16.7):

*(a)   the methods and significant assumptions applied in determining the fair value of investment property;

(b)   the extent to which the fair value of investment property (as measured or disclosed in the **financial statements**) is based on a valuation by an independent valuer who holds a recognised and relevant professional qualification and has recent experience in the location and class of the investment property being valued. If there has been no such valuation, that fact shall be disclosed;

*(c)   the existence and amounts of restrictions on the realisability of investment property or the remittance of **income** and proceeds of disposal;

*(d)   contractual obligations to purchase, construct or develop investment property or for repairs, maintenance or enhancements; and

*(e)   a reconciliation between the carrying amounts of investment property at the beginning and end of the period, showing separately:

(i)   additions, disclosing separately those additions resulting from acquisitions through **business combinations**;

*(ii)   net gains or losses from fair value adjustments;
(iii)   transfers to property, plant and equipment when a reliable measure of fair value is no longer available without undue cost or effort (see paragraph 16.8);
(iv)   transfers to and from **inventories** and owner-occupied property; and
(v)   other changes.

This reconciliation need not be presented for prior periods.

In accordance with Section 20 *Leases*, an entity shall provide all relevant disclosures required in that section about leases into which it has entered.   **16.11**

Section 17 Property, Plant and Equipment

Scope

This section applies to the accounting for **property, plant and equipment** and to **investment property** whose **fair value** cannot be measured reliably without undue cost or effort. Section 16 *Investment Property* applies to investment property whose fair value can be measured reliably without undue cost or effort.   **17.1**

Property, plant and equipment are tangible assets that: **17.2**

(a)   are held for use in the production or supply of goods or services, for rental to others, or for administrative purposes; and
(b)   are expected to be used during more than one period;

Property, plant and equipment does not include: **17.3**

(a)   **biological assets** related to **agricultural activity** (see Section 34 *Specialised Activities*) or **heritage assets** (see Section 34); or
(b)   mineral rights and mineral reserves, such as oil, natural gas and similar non-regenerative resources (see Section 34).

Recognition

An entity shall apply the **recognition** criteria in paragraph 2.27 in determining whether to recognise an item of property, plant or equipment. Therefore, the entity shall recognise the cost of an item of property, plant and equipment as an **asset** if, and only if: **17.4**

(a)   it is **probable** that future economic benefits associated with the item will flow to the entity; and
(b)   the cost of the item can be measured reliably.

Spare parts and servicing equipment are usually carried as **inventory** and recognised in **profit or loss** as consumed. However, major spare parts and stand-by equipment are property, plant and equipment when an entity expects to use them during more than one period. Similarly, if the spare parts and servicing equipment can be used only in connection with an item of property, plant and equipment, they are considered property, plant and equipment.   **17.5**

Parts of some items of property, plant and equipment may require replacement at regular intervals (eg the roof of a building). An entity shall add to the **carrying amount** of an item of property, plant and equipment the cost of replacing part of such an item when that cost is incurred if the replacement part is expected to provide incremental future benefits to the entity. The carrying amount of those parts that are replaced is derecognised in accordance with paragraphs 17.27 to 17.30. Paragraph 17.16   **17.6** provides that if the major components of an item of property, plant and equipment have significantly different patterns of consumption of economic benefits, an entity shall allocate the initial cost of the asset to its major components and depreciate each such component separately over its **useful life**.

17.7   A condition of continuing to operate an item of property, plant and equipment (eg a bus) may be performing regular major inspections for faults regardless of whether parts of the item are replaced. When each major inspection is performed, its cost is recognised in the carrying amount of the item of property, plant and equipment as a replacement if the recognition criteria are satisfied. Any remaining carrying amount of the cost of the previous major inspection (as distinct from physical parts) is derecognised. This is done regardless of whether the cost of the previous major inspection was identified in the transaction in which the item was acquired or constructed. If necessary, the estimated cost of a future similar inspection may be used as an indication of what the cost of the existing inspection component was when the item was acquired or constructed.

17.8   Land and buildings are separable assets, and an entity shall account for them separately, even when they are acquired together.

Measurement at initial recognition

17.9   An entity shall measure an item of property, plant and equipment at initial recognition at its cost.

Elements of cost

17.10   The cost of an item of property, plant and equipment comprises all of the following:

(a)   Its purchase price, including legal and brokerage fees, import duties and non-refundable purchase taxes, after deducting trade discounts and rebates.

(b)   Any costs directly attributable to bringing the asset to the location and condition necessary for it to be capable of operating in the manner intended by management. These can include the costs of site preparation, initial delivery and handling, installation and assembly, and testing of functionality.

(c)   The initial estimate of the costs, recognised and measured in accordance with Section 21 *Provisions and Contingencies*, of dismantling and removing the item and restoring the site on which it is located, the obligation for which an entity incurs either when the item is acquired or as a consequence of having used the item during a particular period for purposes other than to produce inventories during that period.

(d)   Any **borrowing costs** capitalised in accordance with paragraph 25.2.

17.11   The following costs are not costs of an item of property, plant and equipment, and an entity shall recognise them as an **expense** when they are incurred:

(a)   costs of opening a new facility;

(b)   costs of introducing a new product or service (including costs of advertising and promotional activities);

(c)   costs of conducting business in a new location or with a new class of customer (including costs of staff training); and

(d)   administration and other general overhead costs.

17.12   The **income** and related expenses of incidental operations during construction or development of an item of property, plant and equipment are recognised in profit or loss if those operations are not necessary to bring the item to its intended location and operating condition.

Measurement of cost

The cost of an item of property, plant and equipment is the cash price equivalent at the recognition date. If payment is deferred beyond normal credit terms, the cost is the **present value** of all future payments.   **17.13**

Exchanges of assets

An item of property, plant or equipment may be acquired in exchange for a non-monetary asset or assets, or a combination of monetary and non-monetary assets. An entity shall measure the cost of the acquired asset at fair value unless: **17.14**

(a) the exchange transaction lacks commercial substance; or

(b) the fair value of neither the asset received nor the asset given up is reliably measurable. In that case, the asset's cost is measured at the carrying amount of the asset given up.

Measurement after initial recognition

An entity shall measure all items of property, plant and equipment after initial recognition using the cost model (in accordance with paragraph 17.15A) or the revaluation model (in accordance with paragraphs 17.15B to 17.15F). Where the revaluation model is selected, this shall be applied to all items of property, plant and equipment in the same class (ie having a similar nature, function or use in the business). An entity shall recognise the costs of day-to-day servicing of an item of property, plant and equipment in profit or loss in the period in which the costs are incurred.   **17.15**

Cost model

Under the cost model, an entity shall measure an item of property, plant and equipment at cost less any accumulated **depreciation** and any accumulated **impairment losses**.   **17.15A**

Revaluation model

Under the revaluation model, an item of property, plant and equipment whose fair value can be measured reliably shall be carried at a revalued amount, being its fair value at the date of revaluation less any subsequent accumulated depreciation and subsequent accumulated impairment losses. Revaluations shall be made with sufficient regularity to ensure that the carrying amount does not differ materially from that which would be determined using fair value at the end of the **reporting period**.   **17.15B**

The fair value of land and buildings is usually determined from market-based evidence by appraisal that is normally undertaken by professionally qualified valuers. The fair value of items of plant and equipment is usually their market value determined by appraisal. Paragraphs 11.27 to 11.32 provide further guidance on determining fair value.   **17.15C**

If there is no market-based evidence of fair value because of the specialised nature of the item of property, plant and equipment and the item is rarely sold, except as part of a continuing business, an entity may need to estimate fair value using an income or a **depreciated replacement cost** approach.   **17.15D**

Reporting gains and losses on revaluations

If an asset's carrying amount is increased as a result of a revaluation, the increase shall be recognised in **other comprehensive income** and accumulated in **equity**. However, the increase shall be recognised in profit or loss to the extent that it reverses a revaluation decrease of the same asset previously recognised in profit or loss.   **17.15E**

17.15F   The decrease of an asset's carrying amount as a result of a revaluation shall be recognised in other comprehensive income to the extent of any previously recognised revaluation increase accumulated in equity, in respect of that asset. If a revaluation decrease exceeds the accumulated revaluation gains accumulated in equity in respect of that asset, the excess shall be recognised in **profit or loss**.

Depreciation

17.16   If the major components of an item of property, plant and equipment have significantly different patterns of consumption of economic benefits, an entity shall allocate the initial cost of the asset to its major components and depreciate each such component separately over its useful life. Other assets shall be depreciated over their useful lives as a single asset. There are some exceptions, such as land which generally has an unlimited useful life and therefore is not usually depreciated.

17.17   The depreciation charge for each period shall be recognised in profit or loss unless another section of this FRS requires the cost to be recognised as part of the cost of an asset. For example, the depreciation of manufacturing property, plant and equipment is included in the costs of inventories (see Section 13 *Inventories*).

Depreciable amount and depreciation period

17.18   An entity shall allocate the **depreciable amount** of an asset on a systematic basis over its useful life.

17.19   Factors such as a change in how an asset is used, significant unexpected wear and tear, technological advancement, and changes in market prices may indicate that the **residual value** or useful life of an asset has changed since the most recent annual **reporting date**. If such indicators are present, an entity shall review its previous estimates and, if current expectations differ, amend the residual value, depreciation method or useful life. The entity shall account for the change in residual value, depreciation method or useful life as a change in an accounting estimate in accordance with paragraphs 10.15 to 10.18.

17.20   Depreciation of an asset begins when it is available for use, ie when it is in the location and condition necessary for it to be capable of operating in the manner intended by management. Depreciation of an asset ceases when the asset is derecognised. Depreciation does not cease when the asset becomes idle or is retired from active use unless the asset is fully depreciated. However, under usage methods of depreciation the depreciation charge can be zero while there is no production.

17.21   An entity shall consider all the following factors in determining the useful life of an asset:

   (a)   The expected usage of the asset. Usage is assessed by reference to the asset's expected capacity or physical output.

   (b)   Expected physical wear and tear, which depends on operational factors such as the number of shifts for which the asset is to be used and the repair and maintenance programme, and the care and maintenance of the asset while idle.

   (c)   Technical or commercial obsolescence arising from changes or improvements in production, or from a change in the market demand for the product or service output of the asset.

   (d)   Legal or similar limits on the use of the asset, such as the expiry dates of related **leases**.

Depreciation method

An entity shall select a depreciation method that reflects the pattern in which it expects to consume the asset's future economic benefits. The possible depreciation methods include the straight-line method, the diminishing balance method and a method based on usage such as the units of production method.   **17.22**

If there is an indication that there has been a significant change since the last annual reporting date in the pattern by which an entity expects to consume an asset's future economic benefits, the entity shall review its present depreciation method and, if current expectations differ, change the depreciation method to reflect the new pattern. The entity shall account for the change as a change in an accounting estimate in accordance with paragraphs 10.15 to 10.18.   **17.23**

Impairment

Recognition and measurement of impairment

At each reporting date, an entity shall apply Section 27 *Impairment of Assets* to determine whether an item or group of items of property, plant and equipment is impaired and, if so, how to recognise and measure the impairment loss. That section explains when and how an entity reviews the carrying amount of its assets, how it determines the **recoverable amount** of an asset, and when it recognises or reverses an impairment loss.   **17.24**

Compensation for impairment

An entity shall include in profit or loss, compensation from third parties for items of property, plant and equipment that were impaired, lost or given up only when the compensation is virtually certain.   **17.25**

Property, plant and equipment held for sale

Paragraph 27.9(f) states that a plan to dispose of an asset before the previously expected date is an indicator of impairment that triggers the calculation of the asset's recoverable amount for the purpose of determining whether the asset is impaired.   **17.26**

Derecognition

An entity shall derecognise an item of property, plant and equipment: **17.27**

(a)   on disposal; or
(b)   when no future economic benefits are expected from its use or disposal.

An entity shall recognise the **gain** or loss on the **derecognition** of an item of property, plant and equipment in profit or loss when the item is derecognised (unless Section 20 *Leases* requires otherwise on a sale and leaseback). The entity shall not classify such gains as **revenue**.   **17.28**

In determining the date of disposal of an item, an entity shall apply the criteria in Section 23 *Revenue* for recognising revenue from the sale of goods. Section 20 applies to disposal by a sale and leaseback.   **17.29**

An entity shall determine the gain or loss arising from the derecognition of an item of property, plant and equipment as the difference between the net disposal proceeds, if any, and the carrying amount of the item.   **17.30**

Disclosures

17.31   An entity shall disclose the following for each class of property, plant and equipment:

*(a)   the measurement bases used for determining the gross carrying amount;

(b)   the depreciation methods used;

(c)   the useful lives or the depreciation rates used;

*(d)   the gross carrying amount and the accumulated depreciation (aggregated with accumulated impairment losses) at the beginning and end of the reporting period;

*(e)   a reconciliation of the carrying amount at the beginning and end of the reporting period showing separately:

(i)   additions;

(ii)   disposals;

(iii)   acquisitions through **business combinations**;

(iv)   revaluations;

(v)   transfers to or from investment property if a reliable measure of fair value becomes available or unavailable (see paragraph 16.8);

(vi)   impairment losses recognised or reversed in profit or loss in accordance with Section 27 *Impairment of Assets*;

(vii)   depreciation; and

(viii)   other changes.

This reconciliation need not be presented for prior periods.

17.32   The entity shall also disclose the following:

*(a)   the existence and carrying amounts of property, plant and equipment to which the entity has restricted title or that is pledged as security for **liabilities**; and

*(b)   the amount of contractual commitments for the acquisition of property, plant and equipment.

17.32A   If items of property, plant and equipment are stated at revalued amounts, the following shall be disclosed:

*(a)   the effective date of the revaluation;

(b)   whether an independent valuer was involved;

*(c)   the methods and significant assumptions applied in estimating the items' fair values; and

*(d)   for each revalued class of property, plant and equipment, the carrying amount that would have been recognised had the assets been carried under the cost model.

Section 18 Intangible Assets other than Goodwill

Scope of this section

18.1   This section applies to accounting for all **intangible assets** other than **goodwill** (see Section 19 *Business Combinations and Goodwill*) and intangible assets held by an entity for sale in the ordinary course of business (see Section 13 *Inventories* and Section 23 *Revenue*).

18.1A   This section does not apply to the accounting for **deferred acquisition costs** and intangible assets arising from contracts in the scope of FRS 103 *Insurance Contracts*, except for the disclosure requirements in this section which apply to intangible assets arising from contracts in the scope of FRS 103.

18.2   An intangible asset is an identifiable non-monetary asset without physical substance. Such an **asset** is identifiable when:

(a)   it is separable, ie capable of being separated or divided from the entity and sold, transferred, licensed, rented or exchanged, either individually or together with a related contract, asset or **liability**; or

(b)   it arises from contractual or other legal rights, regardless of whether those rights are transferable or separable from the entity or from other rights and obligations.

This section does not apply to the following: **18.3**

(a)   **financial assets** (see Section 11 *Basic Financial Instruments* and Section 12 *Other Financial Instruments Issues*);

(b)   **heritage assets** (see Section 34 *Specialised Activities*); or

(c)   mineral rights and mineral reserves, such as oil, natural gas and similar non-regenerative resources (see Section 34).

Recognition

General principle for recognising intangible assets

An entity shall apply the **recognition** criteria in paragraph 2.27 in determining whether to   **18.4** recognise an intangible asset. Therefore, the entity shall recognise an intangible asset as an asset if, and only if:

(a)   it is **probable** that the expected future economic benefits that are attributable to the asset will flow to the entity; and

(b)   the cost or value of the asset can be measured reliably.

An entity shall assess the probability of expected future economic benefits using reasonable   **18.5** and supportable assumptions that represent management's best estimate of the economic conditions that will exist over the **useful life** of the asset.

An entity uses judgement to assess the degree of certainty attached to the flow of future   **18.6** economic benefits that are attributable to the use of the asset on the basis of the evidence available at the time of initial recognition, giving greater weight to external evidence.

The probability recognition criterion in paragraph 18.4(a) is always considered satisfied   **18.7** for intangible assets that are separately acquired.

Acquisition as part of a business combination

An intangible asset acquired in a **business combination** is normally recognised as an asset   **18.8** because its **fair value** can be measured with sufficient **reliability**. However, an intangible asset acquired in a business combination is not recognised when it arises from legal or other contractual rights and there is no history or evidence of exchange transactions for the same or similar assets, and otherwise estimating fair value would be dependent on immeasurable variables.

Internally generated intangible assets

To assess whether an internally generated intangible asset meets the criteria for recognition,   **18.8A** an entity classifies the generation of the asset into:

(a)   a **research** phase; and

(b)   a **development** phase.

If an entity cannot distinguish the research phase from the development phase of an internal   **18.8B** project to create an intangible asset, the entity treats the expenditure on that project as if it were incurred in the research phase only.

18.8C   An entity shall recognise expenditure on the following items as an **expense** and shall not recognise such expenditure as intangible assets:

(a)   Internally generated brands, logos, publishing titles, customer lists and items similar in substance.

(b)   Start-up activities (ie start-up costs), which include establishment costs such as legal and secretarial costs incurred in establishing a legal entity, expenditure to open a new facility or business (ie pre-opening costs) and expenditure for starting new operations or launching new products or processes (ie pre-operating costs).

(c)   Training activities.

(d)   Advertising and promotional activities (unless it meets the definition of **inventories held for distribution at no or nominal consideration** (see paragraph 13.4A)).

(e)   Relocating or reorganising part or all of an entity.

(f)   Internally generated goodwill.

18.8D   Paragraph 18.8C does not preclude recognising a prepayment as an asset when payment for goods or services has been made in advance of the delivery of the goods or the rendering of the services.

Research phase

18.8E   No intangible asset arising from research (or from the research phase of an internal project) shall be recognised. Expenditure on research (or on the research phase of an internal project) shall be recognised as an expense when it is incurred.

18.8F   In the research phase of an internal project, an entity cannot demonstrate that an intangible asset exists that will generate probable future economic benefits.

18.8G   Examples of research activities are:

(a)   Activities aimed at obtaining new knowledge.

(b)   The search for, evaluation and final selection of, applications of research findings and other knowledge.

(c)   The search for alternatives for materials, devices, products, processes, systems or services.

(d)   The formulation, design, evaluation and final selection of possible alternatives for new or improved material, devices, projects, processes, systems or services.

Development phase

18.8H   An entity may recognise an intangible asset arising from development (or from the development phase of an internal project) if, and only if, an entity can demonstrate all of the following:

(a)   The technical feasibility of completing the intangible asset so that it will be available for use or sale.

(b)   Its intention to complete the intangible asset and use or sell it.

(c)   Its ability to use or sell the intangible asset.

(d)   How the intangible asset will generate probable future economic benefits. Among other things, the entity can demonstrate the existence of a market for the output of the intangible asset or the intangible asset itself or, if it is to be used internally, the usefulness of the intangible asset.

(e)   The availability of adequate technical, financial and other resources to complete the development and to use or sell the intangible asset.

(f)   Its ability to measure reliably the expenditure attributable to the intangible asset during its development.

In the development phase of an internal project, an entity can, in some instances, identify an intangible asset and demonstrate that the asset will generate probable future economic benefits. This is because the development phase of a project is further advanced than the research phase.   **18.8I**

Examples of development activities are: **18.8J**

(a)   The design, construction and testing of pre-production or pre-use prototypes and models.

(b)   The design of tools, jigs, moulds and dies involving new technology.

(c)   The design, construction and operation of a pilot plant that is not of a scale economically feasible for commercial production.

(d)   The design, construction and testing of a chosen alternative for new or improved materials, devices, products, processes, systems or services.

Where an entity adopts a policy of capitalising expenditure in the development phase that meets the conditions of paragraph 18.8H, that policy shall be applied consistently to all expenditure that meets the requirements of paragraph 18.8H. Expenditure that does not meet the conditions of paragraph 18.8H is expensed as incurred.   **18.8K**

Initial measurement

An entity shall measure an intangible asset initially at cost.   **18.9**

Separate acquisition

The cost of a separately acquired intangible asset comprises: **18.10**

(a)   its purchase price, including import duties and non-refundable purchase taxes, after deducting trade discounts and rebates; and

(b)   any directly attributable cost of preparing the asset for its intended use.

Internally generated intangible assets

The cost of an internally generated intangible asset for the purpose of paragraph 18.9 is the sum of expenditure incurred from the date when the intangible asset first meets the recognition criteria in paragraphs 18.4 and 18.8H.   **18.10A**

The cost of an internally generated intangible asset comprises all directly attributable costs necessary to create, produce and prepare the asset to be capable of operating in the manner intended by management. Examples of directly attributable costs are: **18.10B**

(a)   costs of materials and services used or consumed in generating the intangible asset;

(b)   costs of **employee benefits** (as defined in Section 28 *Employee Benefits*) arising from the generation of the intangible asset;

(c)   fees to register a legal right; and

(d)   **amortisation** of patents and licences that are used to generate the intangible asset.

Section 25 *Borrowing Costs* specifies criteria for the recognition of interest as an element of the cost of an internally generated intangible asset.

Acquisition as part of a business combination

If an intangible asset is acquired in a business combination, the cost of that intangible asset is its fair value at the **acquisition date**.   **18.11**

Acquisition by way of a grant

18.12   If an intangible asset is acquired by way of a grant, the cost of that intangible asset is its fair value at the date the grant is received or receivable in accordance with Section 24 *Government Grants*.

Exchanges of assets

18.13   An intangible asset may be acquired in exchange for a non-monetary asset or assets, or a combination of monetary and non-monetary assets. An entity shall measure the cost of such an intangible asset at fair value unless:

(a)   the exchange transaction lacks commercial substance; or

(b)   the fair value of neither the asset received nor the asset given up is reliably measurable. In that case, the asset's cost is measured at the **carrying amount** of the asset given up.

18.14   [Replaced by paragraph 18.8A]

18.15   [Moved to paragraph 18.8C]

18.16   [Moved to paragraph 18.8D]

Past expenses not to be recognised as an asset

18.17   Expenditure on an intangible item that was initially recognised as an expense shall not be recognised at a later date as part of the cost of an asset.

Measurement after initial recognition

18.18   An entity shall measure intangible assets after initial recognition using the cost model (in accordance with paragraph 18.18A) or the revaluation model (in accordance with paragraphs 18.18B to 18.18H). Where the revaluation model is selected, this shall be applied to all intangible assets in the same class. If an intangible asset in a class of revalued intangible assets cannot be revalued because there is no **active market** for this asset, the asset shall be carried at its cost less any accumulated amortisation and impairment losses.

Cost model

18.18A   Under the cost model, an entity shall measure its assets at cost less any accumulated amortisation and any accumulated **impairment losses**. The requirements for amortisation are set out in paragraphs 18.19 to 18.24.

Revaluation model

18.18B   Under the revaluation model, an intangible asset shall be carried at a revalued amount, being its fair value at the date of revaluation less any subsequent accumulated amortisation and subsequent accumulated impairment losses, provided that the fair value can be determined by reference to an active market. The requirements for amortisation are set out in paragraphs 18.19 to 18.24.

18.18C   The revaluation model does not allow:

(a)   the revaluation of intangible assets that have not previously been recognised as assets; or

(b)   the initial recognition of intangible assets at amounts other than cost.

Revaluations shall be made with sufficient regularity to ensure that the carrying amount does not differ materially from that which would be determined using fair value at the end of the **reporting period**. **18.18D**

If the fair value of a revalued intangible asset can no longer be determined by reference to an active market in accordance with the requirements of paragraph 18.18B, the carrying amount of the asset shall be its revalued amount at the date of the last revaluation by reference to the active market, less any subsequent accumulated amortisation and any subsequent accumulated impairment losses. **18.18E**

The revaluation model is applied after an asset has been initially recognised at cost. However, if only part of the cost of an intangible asset is recognised as an asset because the asset did not meet the criteria for recognition until part of the way through the process (see paragraph 18.10A), the revaluation model may be applied to the whole of that asset. **18.18F**

Reporting gains and losses on revaluations

If an asset's carrying amount is increased as a result of a revaluation, the increase shall be recognised in **other comprehensive income** and accumulated in **equity**. However, the increase shall be recognised in **profit or loss** to the extent that it reverses a revaluation decrease of the same asset previously recognised in profit or loss. **18.18G**

The decrease of an asset's carrying amount as a result of a revaluation shall be recognised in other comprehensive income to the extent of any previously recognised revaluation increase accumulated in equity, in respect of that asset. If a revaluation decrease exceeds the accumulated revaluation gains recognised in equity in respect of that asset, the excess shall be recognised in profit or loss. **18.18H**

Amortisation over useful life

For the purpose of this FRS, all intangible assets shall be considered to have a finite useful life. The useful life of an intangible asset that arises from contractual or other legal rights shall not exceed the period of the contractual or other legal rights, but may be shorter depending on the period over which the entity expects to use the asset. If the contractual or other legal rights are conveyed for a limited term that can be renewed, the useful life of the intangible asset shall include the renewal period(s) only if there is evidence to support renewal by the entity without significant cost. **18.19**

If, in exceptional cases, an entity is unable to make a reliable estimate of the useful life of an intangible asset, the life shall not exceed 10 years. **18.20**

Amortisation period and amortisation method

An entity shall allocate the **depreciable amount** of an intangible asset on a systematic basis over its useful life. The amortisation charge for each period shall be recognised in profit or loss, unless another section of this FRS requires the cost to be recognised as part of the cost of an asset. For example, the amortisation of an intangible asset may be included in the costs of **inventories** or **property, plant and equipment**. **18.21**

Amortisation begins when the intangible asset is available for use, ie when it is in the location and condition necessary for it to be usable in the manner intended by management. Amortisation ceases when the asset is derecognised. The entity shall choose an amortisation method that reflects the pattern in which it expects to consume the asset's future economic benefits. If the entity cannot determine that pattern reliably, it shall use the straight-line method. **18.22**

Residual value

18.23   An entity shall assume that the **residual value** of an intangible asset is zero unless:

  (a)   there is a commitment by a third party to purchase the asset at the end of its useful life; or

  (b)   there is an active market for the asset and:

    (i)   residual value can be determined by reference to that market; and

    (ii)   it is probable that such a market will exist at the end of the asset's useful life.

Review of amortisation period and amortisation method

18.24   Factors such as a change in how an intangible asset is used, technological advancement, and changes in market prices may indicate that the residual value or useful life of an intangible asset has changed since the most recent annual **reporting date**. If such indicators are present, an entity shall review its previous estimates and, if current expectations differ, amend the residual value, amortisation method or useful life. The entity shall account for the change in residual value, amortisation method or useful life as a change in an accounting estimate in accordance with paragraphs 10.15 to 10.18.

Recoverability of the carrying amount—impairment losses

18.25   To determine whether an intangible asset is impaired, an entity shall apply Section 27 *Impairment of Assets*. That section explains when and how an entity reviews the carrying amount of its assets, how it determines the **recoverable amount** of an asset, and when it recognises or reverses an impairment loss.

Retirements and disposals

18.26   An entity shall derecognise an intangible asset, and shall recognise a **gain** or loss in profit or loss:

  (a)   on disposal; or

  (b)   when no future economic benefits are expected from its use or disposal.

Disclosures

18.27   An entity shall disclose the following for each class of intangible assets:

  *(a)   the useful lives or the amortisation rates used and the reasons for choosing those periods;

  (b)   the amortisation methods used;

  *(c)   the gross carrying amount and any accumulated amortisation (aggregated with accumulated impairment losses) at the beginning and end of the reporting period;

  (d)   the line item(s) in the **statement of comprehensive income** (or in the **income statement**, if presented) in which any amortisation of intangible assets is included; and

  *(e)   a reconciliation of the carrying amount at the beginning and end of the reporting period showing separately:

    (i)   additions, indicating separately those from internal development and those acquired separately;

    (ii)   disposals;

    (iii)   acquisitions through business combinations;

    (iv)   revaluations;

(v) amortisation;

(vi) impairment losses; and

(vii) other changes.

This reconciliation need not be presented for prior periods.

An entity shall also disclose: **18.28**

(a) a description, the carrying amount and remaining amortisation period of any individual intangible asset that is **material** to the entity's **financial statements**;

(b) for intangible assets acquired by way of a grant and initially recognised at fair value (see paragraph 18.12):

  (i) the fair value initially recognised for these assets; and

  (ii) their carrying amounts.

*(c) the existence and carrying amounts of intangible assets to which the entity has restricted title or that are pledged as security for liabilities; and

*(d) the amount of contractual commitments for the acquisition of intangible assets.

An entity shall disclose the aggregate amount of research and development expenditure recognised as an expense during the period (ie the amount of expenditure incurred internally on research and development that has not been capitalised as an intangible asset or as part of the cost of another asset that meets the recognition criteria in this FRS). **18.29**

If intangible assets are accounted for at revalued amounts, an entity shall disclose the following: **18.29A**

*(a) the effective date of the revaluation;

(b) whether an independent valuer was involved;

*(c) the methods and significant assumptions applied in estimating the assets' fair values; and

*(d) for each revalued class of intangible assets, the carrying amount that would have been recognised had the assets been carried under the cost model.

Section 19 Business Combinations and Goodwill

Scope of this section

This section applies to accounting for **business combinations**. It provides guidance on identifying the acquirer, measuring the cost of the business combination, and allocating that cost to the **assets** acquired and **liabilities** and **provisions** for **contingent liabilities** assumed. It also addresses accounting for **goodwill** both at the time of a business combination and subsequently. **19.1**

This section specifies the accounting for all business combinations except: **19.2**

(a) the formation of a **joint venture**; and

(b) acquisition of a group of assets that does not constitute a **business**.

In addition, **public benefit entities** shall consider the requirements of Section 34 *Specialised Activities* in accounting for **public benefit entity combinations**. **PBE19.2A**

Business combinations defined

A business combination is the bringing together of separate entities or businesses into one reporting entity. The result of nearly all business combinations is that one entity, the **19.3** acquirer, obtains **control** of one or more other businesses, the acquiree. The **acquisition date** is the date on which the acquirer obtains control of the acquiree.

19.4　A business combination may be structured in a variety of ways for legal, taxation or other reasons. It may involve the purchase by an entity of the **equity** of another entity, the purchase of all the net assets of another entity, the assumption of the liabilities of another entity, or the purchase of some of the net assets of another entity that together form one or more businesses.

19.5　A business combination may be effected by the issue of equity instruments, the transfer of **cash**, **cash equivalents** or other assets, or a mixture of these. The transaction may be between the shareholders of the combining entities or between one entity and the shareholders of another entity. It may involve the establishment of a new entity to control the combining entities or net assets transferred, or the restructuring of one or more of the combining entities.

Purchase method

19.6　All business combinations shall be accounted for by applying the purchase method, except for:

(a)　**group reconstructions** which may be accounted for by using the merger accounting method (see paragraphs 19.27 to 19.33); and

(b)　public benefit entity **combinations that are in substance a gift** or that are a **merger** which shall be accounted for in accordance with Section 34 *Specialised Activities*.

19.7　Applying the purchase method involves the following steps:

(a)　identifying an acquirer;

(b)　measuring the cost of the business combination; and

(c)　allocating, at the acquisition date, the cost of the business combination to the assets acquired and liabilities and provisions for contingent liabilities assumed.

Identifying the acquirer

19.8　An acquirer shall be identified for all business combinations accounted for by applying the purchase method. The acquirer is the combining entity that obtains control of the other combining entities or businesses.

19.9　Control is the power to govern the financial and operating policies of an entity or business so as to obtain benefits from its activities. Control of one entity by another is described in Section 9 *Consolidated and Separate Financial Statements*.

19.10　Although it may sometimes be difficult to identify an acquirer, there are usually indications that one exists. For example:

(a)　If the **fair value** of one of the combining entities is significantly greater than that of the other combining entity, the entity with the greater fair value is likely to be the acquirer.

(b)　If the business combination is effected through an exchange of voting ordinary equity instruments for cash or other assets, the entity giving up cash or other assets is likely to be the acquirer.

(c)　If the business combination results in the management of one of the combining entities being able to dominate the selection of the management team of the resulting combined entity, the entity whose management is able so to dominate is likely to be the acquirer.

Cost of a business combination

The acquirer shall measure the cost of a business combination as the aggregate of: **19.11**

(a)   the fair values, at the acquisition date, of assets given, liabilities incurred or assumed, and equity instruments issued by the acquirer, in exchange for control of the acquiree; plus

(b)   any costs directly attributable to the business combination.

Where control is achieved following a series of transactions, the cost of the business   **19.11A**
combination is the aggregate of the fair values of the assets given, liabilities assumed and
equity instruments issued by the acquirer at the date of each transaction in the series.

Adjustments to the cost of a business combination contingent on future events

When a business combination agreement provides for an adjustment to the cost of the   **19.12**
combination contingent on future events, the acquirer shall include the estimated amount
of that adjustment in the cost of the combination at the acquisition date if the adjustment is
probable and can be measured reliably.

However, if the potential adjustment is not recognised at the acquisition date but   **19.13**
subsequently becomes probable and can be measured reliably, the additional consideration
shall be treated as an adjustment to the cost of the combination.

**Allocating the cost of a business combination to the assets acquired and liabilities and
contingent liabilities assumed**

The acquirer shall, at the acquisition date, allocate the cost of a business combination   **19.14**
by recognising the acquiree's identifiable assets and liabilities and a provision for those
contingent liabilities (that satisfy the **recognition** criteria in paragraph 19.20) at their fair
values at that date, except for the items specified in paragraphs 19.15A to 19.15C. Any
difference between the cost of the business combination and the acquirer's interest in the
net amount of the identifiable assets, liabilities and provisions for contingent liabilities so
recognised shall be accounted for in accordance with paragraphs 19.22 to 19.24.

Except for the items specified in paragraphs 19.15A to 19.15C, the acquirer shall recognise   **19.15**
separately the acquiree's identifiable assets, liabilities and contingent liabilities at the
acquisition date only if they satisfy the following criteria at that date:

(a)   In the case of an asset other than an **intangible asset**, it is probable that any associated
future economic benefits will flow to the acquirer, and its fair value can be measured
reliably.

(b)   In the case of a liability other than a contingent liability, it is probable that an
outflow of resources will be required to settle the obligation, and its fair value can be
measured reliably.

(c)   In the case of an intangible asset or a contingent liability, its fair value can be
measured reliably.

The acquirer shall recognise and measure a **deferred tax asset** or **liability** arising from the   **19.15A**
assets acquired and liabilities assumed in accordance with Section 29 *Income Tax*.

The acquirer shall recognise and measure a liability (or asset, if any) related to the acquiree's   **19.15B**
employee benefit arrangements in accordance with Section 28 *Employee Benefits*.

The acquirer shall recognise and measure a share-based payment in accordance with   **19.15C**
Section 26 *Share-based Payment*.

19.16   The acquirer's **statement of comprehensive income** shall incorporate the acquiree's profits or losses after the acquisition date by including the acquiree's **income** and **expenses** based on the cost of the business combination to the acquirer. For example, depreciation expense included after the acquisition date in the acquirer's statement of comprehensive income that relates to the acquiree's depreciable assets shall be based on the fair values of those depreciable assets at the acquisition date, ie their cost to the acquirer.

19.17   Application of the purchase method starts from the acquisition date, which is the date on which the acquirer obtains control of the acquiree. Because control is the power to govern the financial and operating policies of an entity or business so as to obtain benefits from its activities, it is not necessary for a transaction to be closed or finalised at law before the acquirer obtains control. All pertinent facts and circumstances surrounding a business combination shall be considered in assessing when the acquirer has obtained control.

19.18   In accordance with paragraph 19.14, the acquirer recognises separately only the identifiable assets, liabilities and contingent liabilities of the acquiree that existed at the acquisition date and satisfy the recognition criteria in paragraph 19.15 (except for the items specified in paragraphs 19.15A to 19.15C). Therefore:

  (a)   the acquirer shall recognise liabilities for terminating or reducing the activities of the acquiree as part of allocating the cost of the combination only to the extent that the acquiree has, at the acquisition date, an existing liability for restructuring recognised in accordance with Section 21 *Provisions and Contingencies*; and

  (b)   the acquirer, when allocating the cost of the combination, shall not recognise liabilities for future losses or other costs expected to be incurred as a result of the business combination.

19.19   If the initial accounting for a business combination is incomplete by the end of the **reporting period** in which the combination occurs, the acquirer shall recognise in its **financial statements** provisional amounts for the items for which the accounting is incomplete. Within twelve months after the acquisition date, the acquirer shall retrospectively adjust the provisional amounts recognised as assets and liabilities at the acquisition date (ie account for them as if they were made at the acquisition date) to reflect new information obtained. Beyond twelve months after the acquisition date, adjustments to the initial accounting for a business combination shall be recognised only to correct a **material error** in accordance with Section 10 *Accounting Policies, Estimates and Errors*.

Contingent liabilities

19.20   Paragraph 19.15(c) specifies that the acquirer recognises separately a provision for a contingent liability of the acquiree only if its fair value can be measured reliably. If its fair value cannot be measured reliably:

  (a)   there is a resulting effect on the amount recognised as goodwill or the amount accounted for in accordance with paragraph 19.24; and

  (b)   the acquirer shall disclose the information about that contingent liability as required by Section 21.

19.21   After their initial recognition, the acquirer shall measure contingent liabilities that are recognised separately in accordance with paragraph 19.15(c) at the higher of:

  (a)   the amount that would be recognised in accordance with Section 21; and

  (b)   the amount initially recognised less amounts previously recognised as **revenue** in accordance with Section 23 *Revenue*.

Goodwill

The acquirer shall, at the acquisition date: **19.22**

(a)   recognise goodwill acquired in a business combination as an asset; and

(b)   initially measure that goodwill at its cost, being the excess of the cost of the business
        combination over the acquirer's interest in the net amount of the identifiable assets,
        liabilities and contingent liabilities recognised and measured in accordance with
        paragraphs 19.15, 19.15A to 19.15C.

After initial recognition, the acquirer shall measure goodwill acquired in a business   **19.23**
combination at cost less accumulated **amortisation** and accumulated **impairment losses**:

(a)   An entity shall follow the principles in paragraphs 18.19 to 18.24 for amortisation
        of goodwill. Goodwill shall be considered to have a finite **useful life**, and shall be
        amortised on a systematic basis over its life. If, in exceptional cases, an entity is
        unable to make a reliable estimate of the useful life of goodwill, the life shall not
        exceed 10 years.

(b)   An entity shall follow Section 27 *Impairment of Assets* for recognising and measuring
        the impairment of goodwill.

**Excess over cost of acquirer's interest in the net fair value of acquiree's identifiable
assets, liabilities and contingent liabilities**

If the acquirer's interest in the net amount of the identifiable assets, liabilities and provisions   **19.24**
for contingent liabilities recognised in accordance with paragraph 19.14 exceeds the cost
of the business combination (also referred to as 'negative goodwill'), the acquirer shall:

(a)   Reassess the identification and **measurement** of the acquiree's assets, liabilities
        and provisions for contingent liabilities and the measurement of the cost of the
        combination.

(b)   Recognise and separately disclose the resulting excess on the face of the **statement
        of financial position** on the acquisition date, immediately below goodwill, and
        followed by a subtotal of the net amount of goodwill and the excess.

(c)   Recognise subsequently the excess up to the fair value of non-monetary assets
        acquired in profit or loss in the periods in which the non-monetary assets are
        recovered. Any excess exceeding the fair value of non-monetary assets acquired
        shall be recognised in profit or loss in the periods expected to be benefited.

Disclosures

For business combinations effected during the reporting period

For each business combination, excluding any group reconstructions, that was effected   **19.25**
during the period, the acquirer shall disclose the following:

(a)   the names and descriptions of the combining entities or businesses;

(b)   the acquisition date;

(c)   the percentage of voting equity instruments acquired;

(d)   the cost of the combination and a description of the components of that cost (such as
        cash, equity instruments and debt instruments);

(e)   the amounts recognised at the acquisition date for each class of the acquiree's assets,
        liabilities and contingent liabilities, including goodwill;

(f)   [not used]

*(g)   the useful life of goodwill, and if this cannot be reliably estimated, supporting
        reasons for the period chosen; and

(h)   the periods in which the excess recognised in accordance with paragraph 19.24 will be recognised in profit or loss.

19.25A   The acquirer shall disclose, separately for each material business combination that occurred during the reporting period, the amounts of revenue and profit or loss of the acquiree since the acquisition date included in the consolidated statement of comprehensive income for the reporting period. The disclosure may be provided in aggregate for business combinations that occurred during the reporting period which, individually, are not material.

For all business combinations

* 19.26   An acquirer shall disclose a reconciliation of the **carrying amount** of goodwill at the beginning and end of the reporting period, showing separately:

(a)   changes arising from new business combinations;
(b)   amortisation;
(c)   impairment losses;
(d)   disposals of previously acquired businesses; and
(e)   other changes.

This reconciliation need not be presented for prior periods.

19.26A   An acquirer shall disclose a reconciliation of the carrying amount of the excess recognised in accordance with paragraph 19.24 at the beginning and end of the reporting period, showing separately:

(a)   changes arising from new business combinations;
(b)   amounts recognised in profit or loss in accordance with paragraph 19.24(c);
(c)   disposals of previously acquired businesses; and
(d)   other changes.

This reconciliation need not be presented for prior periods.

Group reconstructions

19.27   Group reconstructions may be accounted for by using the merger accounting method provided:

(a)   the use of the merger accounting method is not prohibited by company law or other relevant legislation;
(b)   the ultimate equity holders remain the same, and the rights of each equity holder, relative to the others, are unchanged; and
(c)   no **non-controlling interest** in the net assets of the **group** is altered by the transfer.

Applicability to various structures of business combinations

19.28   The provisions of paragraphs 19.29 to 19.33, which are explained by reference to an acquirer or issuing entity that issues shares as consideration for the transfer to it of shares in the other parties to the combination, should also be read so as to apply to other arrangements that achieve similar results.

Merger accounting method

19.29   With the merger accounting method the carrying values of the assets and liabilities of the parties to the combination are not required to be adjusted to fair value, although appropriate adjustments shall be made to achieve uniformity of **accounting policies** in the combining entities.

The results and cash flows of all the combining entities shall be brought into the financial statements of the combined entity from the beginning of the financial year in which the combination occurred, adjusted so as to achieve uniformity of accounting policies. The comparative information shall be restated by including the **total comprehensive income** for all the combining entities for the previous reporting period and their statement of financial position for the previous **reporting date**, adjusted as necessary to achieve uniformity of accounting policies. **19.30**

The difference, if any, between the nominal value of the shares issued plus the fair value of any other consideration given, and the nominal value of the shares received in exchange shall be shown as a movement on other reserves in the **consolidated financial statements**. Any existing balances on the share premium account or capital redemption reserve of the new subsidiary shall be brought in by being shown as a movement on other reserves. These movements shall be shown in the **statement of changes in equity**. **19.31**

Merger expenses are not to be included as part of this adjustment, but shall be charged to the statement of comprehensive income as part of profit or loss of the combined entity at the effective date of the group reconstruction. **19.32**

Disclosures

For each group reconstruction, that was effected during the period, the combined entity shall disclose the following: **19.33**

(a)   the names of the combining entities (other than the reporting entity);
(b)   whether the combination has been accounted for as an acquisition or a merger; and
(c)   the date of the combination.

Section 20 Leases

Scope of this section

This section covers accounting for all **leases** other than: **20.1**

(a)   leases to explore for or use minerals, oil, natural gas and similar non-regenerative resources (see Section 34 *Specialised Activities*);
(b)   licensing agreements for such items as motion picture films, video recordings, plays, manuscripts, patents and copyrights (see Section 18 *Intangible Assets other than Goodwill*);
(c)   **measurement** of property held by lessees that is accounted for as **investment property** and measurement of investment property provided by lessors under **operating leases** (see Section 16 *Investment Property*);
(d)   measurement of **biological assets** held by lessees under **finance leases** and biological assets provided by lessors under operating leases (see Section 34); and
(e)   leases that could lead to a loss to the lessor or the lessee as a result of non-typical contractual terms (see paragraph 12.3(f)).
(f)   [not used]

This section applies to agreements that transfer the right to use **assets** even though substantial services by the lessor may be called for in connection with the operation or maintenance of such assets. This section does not apply to agreements that are contracts for services that do not transfer the right to use assets from one contracting party to the other. **20.2**

Some arrangements do not take the legal form of a lease but convey rights to use assets in return for payments. Examples of arrangements in which one entity (the supplier) may **20.3** convey a right to use an asset to another entity (the purchaser), often together with related services, may include outsourcing arrangements, telecommunication contracts that provide rights to capacity and take-or-pay contracts.

20.3A   Determining whether an arrangement is, or contains, a lease shall be based on the substance of the arrangement and requires an assessment of whether:

(a)   fulfilment of the arrangement is dependent on the use of a specific asset or assets. Although a specific asset may be explicitly identified in an arrangement, it is not the subject of a lease if fulfilment of the arrangement is not dependent on the use of the specified asset. An asset is implicitly specified if, for example, the supplier owns or leases only one asset with which to fulfil the obligation and it is not economically feasible or practicable for the supplier to perform its obligation through the use of alternative assets; and

(b)   the arrangement conveys a right to use the asset. This will be the case where the arrangement conveys to the purchaser the right to control the use of the underlying asset.

Classification of leases

20.4   A lease is classified as a finance lease if it transfers substantially all the risks and rewards incidental to ownership. A lease is classified as an operating lease if it does not transfer substantially all the risks and rewards incidental to ownership.

20.5   Whether a lease is a finance lease or an operating lease depends on the substance of the transaction rather than the form of the contract. Examples of situations that individually or in combination would normally lead to a lease being classified as a finance lease are:

(a)   the lease transfers ownership of the asset to the lessee by the end of the **lease term**;

(b)   the lessee has the option to purchase the asset at a price that is expected to be sufficiently lower than the **fair value** at the date the option becomes exercisable for it to be reasonably certain, at the **inception of the lease**, that the option will be exercised;

(c)   the lease term is for the major part of the economic life of the asset even if title is not transferred;

(d)   at the inception of the lease the **present value** of the **minimum lease payments** amounts to at least substantially all of the fair value of the leased asset; and

(e)   the leased assets are of such a specialised nature that only the lessee can use them without major modifications.

20.6   Indicators of situations that individually or in combination could also lead to a lease being classified as a finance lease are:

(a)   if the lessee can cancel the lease, the lessor's losses associated with the cancellation are borne by the lessee;

(b)   **gains** or losses from the fluctuation in the **residual value** of the leased asset accrue to the lessee (eg in the form of a rent rebate equalling most of the sales proceeds at the end of the lease); and

(c)   the lessee has the ability to continue the lease for a secondary period at a rent that is substantially lower than market rent.

20.7   The examples and indicators in paragraphs 20.5 and 20.6 are not always conclusive. If it is clear from other features that the lease does not transfer substantially all risks and rewards incidental to ownership, the lease is classified as an operating lease. For example, this may be the case if ownership of the asset is transferred to the lessee at the end of the lease for a variable payment equal to the asset's then fair value, or if there are **contingent rents**, as a result of which the lessee does not have substantially all risks and rewards incidental to ownership.

Lease classification is made at the inception of the lease and is not changed during the term of the lease unless the lessee and the lessor agree to change the provisions of the lease (other than simply by renewing the lease), in which case the lease classification shall be re-evaluated. **20.8**

Financial statements of lessees: finance leases

Initial recognition

At the **commencement of the lease term**, a lessee shall recognise its rights of use and obligations under finance leases as assets and **liabilities** in its **statement of financial position** at amounts equal to the fair value of the leased asset or, if lower, the present value of the minimum lease payments, determined at the inception of the lease. Any initial direct costs of the lessee (incremental costs that are directly attributable to negotiating and arranging a lease) are added to the amount recognised as an asset. **20.9**

The present value of the minimum lease payments shall be calculated using the **interest rate implicit in the lease**. If this cannot be determined, the **lessee's incremental borrowing rate** shall be used. **20.10**

Subsequent measurement

A lessee shall apportion minimum lease payments between the finance charge and the reduction of the outstanding liability using the **effective interest method** (see paragraphs 11.15 to 11.20). The lessee shall allocate the finance charge to each period during the lease term so as to produce a constant periodic rate of interest on the remaining balance of the liability. A lessee shall charge contingent rents as **expenses** in the periods in which they are incurred. **20.11**

A lessee shall depreciate an asset leased under a finance lease in accordance with Section 17 *Property, Plant and Equipment*. If there is no reasonable certainty that the lessee will obtain ownership by the end of the lease term, the asset shall be fully depreciated over the shorter of the lease term and its **useful life**. A lessee shall also assess at each **reporting date** whether an asset leased under a finance lease is impaired (see Section 27 *Impairment of Assets*). **20.12**

Disclosures

A lessee shall make the following disclosures for finance leases: **20.13**

(a) for each **class of asset**, the net **carrying amount** at the end of the **reporting period**;

(b) the total of future minimum lease payments at the end of the reporting period, for each of the following periods:

    (i) not later than one year;

    (ii) later than one year and not later than five years; and

    (iii) later than five years; and

(c) a general description of the lessee's significant leasing arrangements including, for example, information about contingent rent, renewal or purchase options and escalation clauses, subleases, and restrictions imposed by lease arrangements.

In addition, the requirements for disclosure about assets in accordance with Sections 17 and 27 apply to lessees for assets leased under finance leases. **20.14**

Financial statements of lessees: operating leases

Recognition and measurement

20.15　A lessee shall recognise lease payments under operating leases (excluding costs for services such as insurance and maintenance) as an expense over the lease term on a straight-line basis unless either:

(a)　another systematic basis is representative of the time pattern of the user's benefit, even if the payments are not on that basis; or

(b)　the payments to the lessor are structured to increase in line with expected general inflation (based on published indexes or statistics) to compensate for the lessor's expected inflationary cost increases. If payments to the lessor vary because of factors other than general inflation, then this condition (b) is not met.

Example of applying paragraph 20.15(b):	
X operates in a jurisdiction in which the consensus forecast by local banks is that the general price level index, as published by the government, will increase by an average of 10 per cent annually over the next five years. X leases some office space from Y for five years under an operating lease. The lease payments are structured to reflect the expected 10 per cent annual general inflation over the five-year term of the lease as follows:	
Year 1	CU100,000
Year 2	CU110,000
Year 3	CU121,000
Year 4	CU133,000
Year 5	CU146,000
X recognises annual rent expense equal to the amounts owed to the lessor as shown above. If the escalating payments are not clearly structured to compensate the lessor for expected inflationary cost increases based on published indexes or statistics, then X recognises annual rent expense on a straight-line basis: CU122,000 each year (sum of the amounts payable under the lease divided by five years).	

20.15A　A lessee shall recognise the aggregate benefit of **lease incentives** as a reduction to the expense recognised in accordance with paragraph 20.15 over the lease term, on a straight-line basis unless another systematic basis is representative of the time pattern of the lessee's benefit from the use of the leased asset. Any costs incurred by the lessee (for example costs for termination of a pre-existing lease, relocation or leasehold improvements) shall be accounted for in accordance with the applicable section of this FRS.

20.15B　Where an operating lease becomes an **onerous contract** an entity shall also apply Section 21 *Provisions and Contingencies*.

Disclosures

* 20.16　A lessee shall make the following disclosures for operating leases:

(a)　the total of future minimum lease payments under non-cancellable operating leases for each of the following periods:

(i)　not later than one year;

(ii)　later than one year and not later than five years; and

(iii)　later than five years; and

(b)   lease payments recognised as an expense.

(c)   [not used]

Financial statements of lessors: finance leases

Initial recognition and measurement

A lessor shall recognise assets held under a finance lease in its statement of financial position and present them as a receivable at an amount equal to the net investment in the lease. The **net investment in a lease** is the lessor's **gross investment in the lease** discounted at the interest rate implicit in the lease. The gross investment in the lease is the aggregate of:

20.17

(a)   the minimum lease payments receivable by the lessor under a finance lease; and

(b)   any unguaranteed residual value accruing to the lessor.

For finance leases other than those involving manufacturer or dealer lessors, initial direct costs (costs that are incremental and directly attributable to negotiating and arranging a lease) are included in the initial measurement of the finance lease receivable and reduce the amount of **income** recognised over the lease term.

20.18

Subsequent measurement

The **recognition** of finance income shall be based on a pattern reflecting a constant periodic rate of return on the lessor's net investment in the finance lease. Lease payments relating to the period, excluding costs for services, are applied against the gross investment in the lease to reduce both the principal and the unearned finance income. If there is an indication that the estimated unguaranteed residual value used in computing the lessor's gross investment in the lease has changed significantly, the income allocation over the lease term is revised, and any reduction in respect of amounts accrued is recognised immediately in **profit or loss**.

20.19

Manufacturer or dealer lessors

Manufacturers or dealers often offer to customers the choice of either buying or leasing an asset. A finance lease of an asset by a manufacturer or dealer lessor gives rise to two types of income:

20.20

(a)   profit or loss equivalent to the profit or loss resulting from an outright sale of the asset being leased, at normal selling prices, reflecting any applicable volume or trade discounts; and

(b)   finance income over the lease term.

The sales **revenue** recognised at the commencement of the lease term by a manufacturer or dealer lessor is the fair value of the asset or, if lower, the present value of the minimum lease payments accruing to the lessor, computed at a market rate of interest. The cost of sale recognised at the commencement of the lease term is the cost, or carrying amount if different, of the leased asset less the present value of the unguaranteed residual value. The difference between the sales revenue and the cost of sale is the selling profit, which is recognised in accordance with the entity's policy for outright sales.

20.21

If artificially low rates of interest are quoted, selling profit shall be restricted to that which would apply if a market rate of interest were charged. Costs incurred by manufacturer or dealer lessors in connection with negotiating and arranging a lease shall be recognised as an expense when the selling profit is recognised.

20.22

Disclosures

20.23   A lessor shall make the following disclosures for finance leases:

(a)   a reconciliation between the gross investment in the lease at the end of the reporting period, and the present value of minimum lease payments receivable at the end of the reporting period. In addition, a lessor shall disclose the gross investment in the lease and the present value of minimum lease payments receivable at the end of the reporting period, for each of the following periods:

(i)   not later than one year;

(ii)   later than one year and not later than five years; and

(iii)   later than five years;

(b)   unearned finance income;

(c)   the unguaranteed residual values accruing to the benefit of the lessor;

(d)   the accumulated allowance for uncollectible minimum lease payments receivable;

(e)   contingent rents recognised as income in the period; and

(f)   a general description of the lessor's significant leasing arrangements, including, for example, information about contingent rent, renewal or purchase options and escalation clauses, subleases, and restrictions imposed by lease arrangements.

Financial statements of lessors: operating leases

Recognition and measurement

20.24   A lessor shall present assets subject to operating leases in its statement of financial position according to the nature of the asset.

20.25   A lessor shall recognise lease income from operating leases (excluding amounts for services such as insurance and maintenance) in profit or loss on a straight-line basis over the lease term, unless either:

(a)   another systematic basis is representative of the time pattern of the lessee's benefit from the leased asset, even if the receipt of payments is not on that basis; or

(b)   the payments to the lessor are structured to increase in line with expected general inflation (based on published indexes or statistics) to compensate for the lessor's expected inflationary cost increases. If payments to the lessor vary according to factors other than inflation, then condition (b) is not met.

20.25A   A lessor shall recognise the aggregate cost of lease incentives as a reduction to the income recognised in accordance with paragraph 20.25 over the lease term on a straight-line basis, unless another systematic basis is representative of the time pattern over which the lessor's benefit from the leased asset is diminished.

20.26   A lessor shall recognise as an expense, costs, including **depreciation**, incurred in earning the lease income. The depreciation policy for depreciable leased assets shall be consistent with the lessor's normal depreciation policy for similar assets.

20.27   A lessor shall add to the carrying amount of the leased asset any initial direct costs it incurs in negotiating and arranging an operating lease and shall recognise such costs as an expense over the lease term on the same basis as the lease income.

20.28   To determine whether a leased asset has become impaired, a lessor shall apply Section 27.

20.29   A manufacturer or dealer lessor does not recognise any selling profit on entering into an operating lease because it is not the equivalent of a sale.

Disclosures

A lessor shall disclose the following for operating leases: **20.30**

(a)   the future minimum lease payments under non-cancellable operating leases for each of the following periods:

      (i)   not later than one year;

      (ii)   later than one year and not later than five years; and

      (iii) later than five years;

(b)   total contingent rents recognised as income; and

(c)   a general description of the lessor's significant leasing arrangements, including, for example, information about contingent rent, renewal or purchase options and escalation clauses, and restrictions imposed by lease arrangements.

In addition, the requirements for disclosure about assets in accordance with Sections 17   **20.31**
and 27 apply to lessors for assets provided under operating leases.

Sale and leaseback transactions

A sale and leaseback transaction involves the sale of an asset and the leasing back of the   **20.32**
same asset. The lease payment and the sale price are usually interdependent because they
are negotiated as a package. The accounting treatment of a sale and leaseback transaction
depends on the type of lease.

Sale and leaseback transaction results in a finance lease

If a sale and leaseback transaction results in a finance lease, the seller-lessee shall not   **20.33**
recognise immediately, as income, any excess of sales proceeds over the carrying amount.
Instead, the seller-lessee shall defer such excess and amortise it over the lease term.

Sale and leaseback transaction results in an operating lease

If a sale and leaseback transaction results in an operating lease, and it is clear that the   **20.34**
transaction is established at fair value, the seller-lessee shall recognise any profit or loss
immediately. If the sale price is below fair value, the seller-lessee shall recognise any
profit or loss immediately unless the loss is compensated for by future lease payments
at below market price. In that case the seller-lessee shall defer and amortise such loss in
proportion to the lease payments over the period for which the asset is expected to be used.
If the sale price is above fair value, the seller-lessee shall defer the excess over fair value
and amortise it over the period for which the asset is expected to be used.

Disclosures

Disclosure requirements for lessees and lessors apply equally to sale and leaseback   **20.35**
transactions. The required description of significant leasing arrangements includes
description of unique or unusual provisions of the agreement or terms of the sale and
leaseback transactions.

Section 21 Provisions and Contingencies

Scope of this section

This section applies to all **provisions** (ie **liabilities** of uncertain timing or amount),   **21.1**
contingent liabilities and **contingent assets** except those provisions covered by other

sections of this FRS. Where those other sections contain no specific requirements to deal with contracts that have become onerous, this section applies to those contracts.

21.1A   This section applies to **financial guarantee contracts** unless:

(a)   an entity has chosen to apply IAS 39 *Financial Instruments: Recognition and Measurement* and/or IFRS 9 *Financial Instruments* to its **financial instruments** (see paragraphs 11.2 and 12.2); or

(b)   an entity has elected under FRS 103 *Insurance Contracts* to continue the application of insurance contract accounting.

21.1B   This section does not apply to financial instruments (including loan commitments) that are within the scope of Section 11 *Basic Financial Instruments* and 12 *Other Financial Instruments Issues*. This section does not apply to **insurance contracts** (including **reinsurance contracts**) that an entity issues and reinsurance contracts that the entity holds, or financial instruments issued by an entity with a **discretionary participation feature** that are within the scope of FRS 103 *Insurance Contracts*.

21.2   The requirements in this section do not apply to executory contracts unless they are **onerous contracts**. Executory contracts are contracts under which neither party has performed any of its obligations or both parties have partially performed their obligations to an equal extent.

21.3   The word 'provision' is sometimes used in the context of such items as **depreciation**, impairment of **assets**, and uncollectible receivables. Those are adjustments of the **carrying amounts** of assets, rather than **recognition** of liabilities, and therefore are not covered by this section.

Initial recognition

21.4   An entity shall recognise a provision only when:

(a)   the entity has an obligation at the **reporting date** as a result of a past event;

(b)   it is **probable** (ie more likely than not) that the entity will be required to transfer economic benefits in settlement; and

(c)   the amount of the obligation can be estimated reliably.

21.5   The entity shall recognise the provision as a liability in the **statement of financial position** and shall recognise the amount of the provision as an **expense**, unless another section of this FRS requires the cost to be recognised as part of the cost of an asset such as **inventories** or **property, plant and equipment**.

21.6   The condition in paragraph 21.4(a) means that the entity has no realistic alternative to settling the obligation. This can happen when the entity has a legal obligation that can be enforced by law or when the entity has a **constructive obligation** because the past event (which may be an action of the entity) has created valid expectations in other parties that the entity will discharge the obligation. Obligations that will arise from the entity's future actions (ie the future conduct of its business) do not satisfy the condition in paragraph 21.4(a), no matter how likely they are to occur and even if they are contractual. To illustrate, because of commercial pressures or legal requirements, an entity may intend or need to carry out expenditure to operate in a particular way in the future (for example, by fitting smoke filters in a particular type of factory). Because the entity can avoid the future expenditure by its future actions, for example by changing its method of operation or selling the factory, it has no present obligation for that future expenditure and no provision is recognised.

Initial measurement

An entity shall measure a provision at the best estimate of the amount required to settle the **21.7** obligation at the reporting date. The best estimate is the amount an entity would rationally pay to settle the obligation at the end of the **reporting period** or to transfer it to a third party at that time.

(a)   When the provision involves a large population of items, the estimate of the amount reflects the weighting of all possible outcomes by their associated probabilities. The provision will therefore be different depending on whether the probability of a loss of a given amount is, for example, 60 per cent or 90 per cent. Where there is a continuous range of possible outcomes, and each point in that range is as likely as any other, the mid-point of the range is used.

(b)   When the provision arises from a single obligation, the individual most likely outcome may be the best estimate of the amount required to settle the obligation. However, even in such a case, the entity considers other possible outcomes. When other possible outcomes are either mostly higher or mostly lower than the most likely outcome, the best estimate will be a higher or lower amount.

When the effect of the time value of money is **material**, the amount of a provision shall be the **present value** of the amount expected to be required to settle the obligation. The discount rate (or rates) shall be a pre-tax rate (or rates) that reflect(s) current market assessments of the time value of money and risks specific to the liability. The risks specific to the liability shall be reflected either in the discount rate or in the estimation of the amounts required to settle the obligation, but not both.

An entity shall exclude **gains** from the expected disposal of assets from the **measurement** **21.8** of a provision.

When some or all of the amount required to settle a provision may be reimbursed by another **21.9** party (eg through an insurance claim), the entity shall recognise the reimbursement as a separate asset only when it is virtually certain that the entity will receive the reimbursement on settlement of the obligation. The amount recognised for the reimbursement shall not exceed the amount of the provision. The reimbursement receivable shall be presented in the statement of financial position as an asset and shall not be offset against the provision. In the **statement of comprehensive income** (or in the **income statement**, if presented) the expense relating to a provision may be presented net of the amount recognised for a reimbursement.

Subsequent measurement

An entity shall charge against a provision only those expenditures for which the provision **21.10** was originally recognised.

An entity shall review provisions at each reporting date and adjust them to reflect the **21.11** current best estimate of the amount that would be required to settle the obligation at that reporting date. Any adjustments to the amounts previously recognised shall be recognised in **profit or loss** unless the provision was originally recognised as part of the cost of an asset (see paragraph 21.5). When a provision is measured at the present value of the amount expected to be required to settle the obligation, the unwinding of the discount shall be recognised as a finance cost in profit or loss in the period it arises.

Onerous contracts

21.11A   If an entity has an **onerous contract**, the present obligation under the contract shall be recognised and measured as a provision (see Example 2 of the Appendix to this section).

Future operating losses

21.11B   Provisions shall not be recognised for future operating losses (see Example 1 of the Appendix to this section).

Restructuring

21.11C   A **restructuring** gives rise to a constructive obligation only when an entity:

(a)   has a detailed formal plan for the restructuring identifying at least:

(i)   the business or part of a business concerned;

(ii)   the principal locations affected;

(iii)   the location, function, and approximate number of employees who will be compensated for terminating their services;

(iv)   the expenditures that will be undertaken; and

(v)   when the plan will be implemented; and

(b)   has raised a valid expectation in those affected that it will carry out the restructuring by starting to implement that plan or announcing its main features to those affected by it.

21.11D   An entity recognises a provision for restructuring costs only when it has a legal or constructive obligation at the reporting date to carry out the restructuring.

Contingent liabilities

21.12   A contingent liability is either a possible but uncertain obligation or a present obligation that is not recognised because it fails to meet one or both of the conditions (b) and (c) in paragraph 21.4. An entity shall not recognise a contingent liability as a liability, except for provisions for contingent liabilities of an acquiree in a **business combination** (see paragraphs 19.20 and 19.21). Disclosure of a contingent liability is required by paragraph 21.15 unless the possibility of an outflow of resources is remote. When an entity is jointly and severally liable for an obligation, the part of the obligation that is expected to be met by other parties is treated as a contingent liability.

Contingent assets

21.13   An entity shall not recognise a contingent asset as an asset. Disclosure of a contingent asset is required by paragraph 21.16 when an inflow of economic benefits is probable. However, when the flow of future economic benefits to the entity is virtually certain, then the related asset is not a contingent asset, and its recognition is appropriate.

Disclosures

Disclosures about provisions

21.14   For each class of provision, an entity shall disclose the following:

(a)   a reconciliation showing:

(i)   the carrying amount at the beginning and end of the period;

(ii)   additions during the period, including adjustments that result from changes in measuring the discounted amount;

(iii) amounts charged against the provision during the period; and

(iv)   unused amounts reversed during the period;

(b)   a brief description of the nature of the obligation and the expected amount and timing of any resulting payments;

(c)   an indication of the uncertainties about the amount or timing of those outflows; and

(d)   the amount of any expected reimbursement, stating the amount of any asset that has been recognised for that expected reimbursement.

Comparative information for prior periods is not required.

Disclosures about contingent liabilities

Unless the possibility of any outflow of resources in settlement is remote, an entity shall disclose, for each class of contingent liability at the reporting date, a brief description of the nature of the contingent liability and, when practicable: *** 21.15**

(a)   an estimate of its financial effect, measured in accordance with paragraphs 21.7 to 21.11;

(b)   an indication of the uncertainties relating to the amount or timing of any outflow; and

(c)   the possibility of any reimbursement.

If it is **impracticable** to make one or more of these disclosures, that fact shall be stated.

Disclosures about contingent assets

If an inflow of economic benefits is probable (more likely than not) but not virtually certain, an entity shall disclose a description of the nature of the contingent assets at the end of the reporting period, and, when practicable, an estimate of their financial effect, measured using the principles set out in paragraphs 21.7 to 21.11. If it is impracticable to make this disclosure, that fact shall be stated.   **21.16**

Prejudicial disclosures

In extremely rare cases, disclosure of some or all of the information required by paragraphs 21.14 to 21.16 can be expected to prejudice seriously the position of the entity in a dispute with other parties on the subject matter of the provision, contingent liability or contingent asset. In such cases, an entity need not disclose all of the information required by those paragraphs insofar as it relates to the dispute, but shall disclose at least the following.   **21.17**

In relation to provisions, the following information shall be given:

(a)   a table showing the reconciliation required by paragraph 21.14(a) in aggregate, including the source and application of any amounts transferred to or from provisions during the reporting period;

(b)   particulars of each provision in any case where the amount of the provision is material; and

(c)   the fact that, and reason why, the information required by paragraph 21.14 has not been disclosed.

In relation to contingent liabilities, the following information shall be given:

(a)   particulars and the total amount of any contingent liabilities (excluding those which arise out of insurance contracts) that are not included in the statement of financial position;

(b)   the total amount of contingent liabilities which are undertaken on behalf of or for the benefit of:

    (i)   any **parent** or fellow **subsidiary** of the entity;

    (ii)   any subsidiary of the entity; or

    (iii)   any entity in which the reporting entity has a participating interest,

    shall each be stated separately; and

(c)   the fact that, and reason why, the information required by paragraph 21.15 has not been disclosed.

In relation to contingent assets, the entity shall disclose the general nature of the dispute, together with the fact that, and reason why, the information required by paragraph 21.16 has not been disclosed.

Disclosure about financial guarantee contracts

21.17A   An entity shall disclose the nature and business purpose of the financial guarantee contracts it has issued. If applicable, an entity shall also provide the disclosures required by paragraphs 21.14 and 21.15.

Appendix to Section 21

Examples of recognising and measuring provisions

This appendix accompanies, but is not part of, Section 21. It provides guidance for applying the requirements of Section 21 in recognising and measuring provisions.

All of the entities in the examples in this appendix have 31 December as their reporting date. In all cases, it is assumed that a reliable estimate can be made of any outflows expected. In some examples the circumstances described may have resulted in impairment of the assets; this aspect is not dealt with in the examples. References to 'best estimate' are to the present value amount, when the effect of the time value of money is material.

Example 1 Future operating losses

21A.1   An entity determines that it is probable that a segment of its operations will incur future operating losses for several years.

Present obligation as a result of a past obligating event: There is no past event that obliges the entity to pay out resources.

Conclusion: The entity does not recognise a provision for future operating losses. Expected future losses do not meet the definition of a liability. The expectation of future operating losses may be an indicator that one or more assets are impaired (see Section 27 *Impairment of Assets*).

Example 2 Onerous contracts

21A.2   An onerous contract is one in which the unavoidable costs of meeting the obligations under the contract exceed the economic benefits expected to be received under it. The unavoidable costs under a contract reflect the least net cost of exiting from the contract, which is the lower of the cost of fulfilling it and any compensation or penalties arising from failure to fulfil it. For example, an entity may be contractually required under an operating lease to make payments to lease an asset for which it no longer has any use.

Present obligation as a result of a past obligating event: The entity is contractually required to pay out resources for which it will not receive commensurate benefits.

Conclusion: If an entity has a contract that is onerous, the entity recognises and measures the present obligation under the contract as a provision.

Example 3 Restructurings

[Moved to paragraph 21.11C]   21A.3

Example 4 Warranties

A manufacturer gives warranties at the time of sale to purchasers of its product. Under   21A.4
the terms of the contract for sale, the manufacturer undertakes to make good, by repair or
replacement, manufacturing defects that become apparent within three years from the date
of sale. On the basis of experience, it is probable (ie more likely than not) that there will be
some claims under the warranties.

Present obligation as a result of a past obligating event: The obligating event is the sale of
the product with a warranty, which gives rise to a legal obligation.

An outflow of resources embodying economic benefits in settlement: Probable for the
warranties as a whole.

Conclusion: The entity recognises a provision for the best estimate of the costs of making
good under the warranty products sold before the reporting date.

Illustration of calculations:

In 20X0, goods are sold for CU1,000,000. Experience indicates that 90 per cent of
products sold require no warranty repairs; 6 per cent of products sold require minor
repairs costing 30 per cent of the sale price; and 4 per cent of products sold require major
repairs or replacement costing 70 per cent of sale price. Therefore estimated warranty
costs are:

CU1,000,000 × 90% × 0 =	CU0
CU1,000,000 × 6% × 30% =	CU18,000
CU1,000,000 × 4% × 70% =	CU28,000
Total	CU46,000

The expenditures for warranty repairs and replacements for products sold in 20X0
are expected to be made 60 per cent in 20X1, 30 per cent in 20X2, and 10 per cent in
20X3, in each case at the end of the period. Because the estimated cash flows already
reflect the probabilities of the cash outflows, and assuming there are no other risks or
uncertainties that must be reflected, to determine the present value of those cash flows
the entity uses a 'risk-free' discount rate based on government bonds with the same
term as the expected cash outflows (6 per cent for one-year bonds and 7 per cent for
two-year and three-year bonds). Calculation of the present value, at the end of 20X0,
of the estimated cash flows related to the warranties for products sold in 20X0 is as
follows:

Year	Expected cash payments (CU)	Discount rate	Discount factor	Present value (CU)
1	60% × CU46,000	27,600	6%	0.9434 (at 6% for 1 year)	26,038
2	30% × CU46,000	13,800	7%	0.8734 (at 7% for 2 years)	12,053
3	10% × CU46,000	4,600	7%	0.8163 (at 7% for 3 years)	3,755
Total				41,846

The entity will recognise a warranty obligation of CU41,846 at the end of 20X0 for products sold in 20X0.

Example 5 Refunds policy

21A.5   A retail store has a policy of refunding purchases by dissatisfied customers, even though it is under no legal obligation to do so. Its policy of making refunds is generally known.

Present obligation as a result of a past obligating event: The obligating event is the sale of the product, which gives rise to a constructive obligation because the conduct of the store has created a valid expectation on the part of its customers that the store will refund purchases.

An outflow of resources embodying economic benefits in settlement: Probable that a proportion of goods will be returned for refund.

Conclusion: The entity recognises a provision for the best estimate of the amount required to settle the refunds.

Example 6 Closure of a division: no implementation before end of reporting period

21A.6   On 12 December 20X0 the board of an entity decided to close down a division. Before the end of the reporting period (31 December 20X0) the decision was not communicated to any of those affected and no other steps were taken to implement the decision.

Present obligation as a result of a past obligating event: There has been no obligating event, and so there is no obligation.

Conclusion: The entity does not recognise a provision.

Example 7 Closure of a division: communication and implementation before end of reporting period

21A.7   On 12 December 20X0 the board of an entity decided to close a division making a particular product. On 20 December 20X0 a detailed plan for closing the division was agreed by the board, letters were sent to customers warning them to seek an alternative source of supply, and redundancy notices were sent to the staff of the division.

Present obligation as a result of a past obligating event: The obligating event is the communication of the decision to the customers and employees, which gives rise to a constructive obligation from that date, because it creates a valid expectation that the division will be closed.

An outflow of resources embodying economic benefits in settlement: Probable.

Conclusion: The entity recognises a provision at 31 December 20X0 for the best estimate of the costs that would be incurred to close the division at the reporting date.

Example 8 Staff retraining as a result of changes in the income tax system

The government introduces changes to the income tax system. As a result of those changes, an entity in the financial services sector will need to retrain a large proportion of its administrative and sales workforce in order to ensure continued compliance with tax regulations. At the end of the reporting period, no retraining of staff has taken place.

21A.8

Present obligation as a result of a past obligating event: The tax law change does not impose an obligation on an entity to do any retraining. An obligating event for recognising a provision (the retraining itself) has not taken place.

Conclusion: The entity does not recognise a provision.

Example 9 A court case

A customer has sued Entity X, seeking damages for injury the customer allegedly sustained from using a product sold by Entity X. Entity X disputes liability on grounds that the customer did not follow directions in using the product. Up to the date the board authorised the financial statements for the year to 31 December 20X1 for issue, the entity's lawyers advise that it is probable that the entity will not be found liable. However, when the entity prepares the financial statements for the year to 31 December 20X2, its lawyers advise that, owing to developments in the case, it is now probable that the entity will be found liable.

21A.9

(a)   At 31 December 20X1
      Present obligation as a result of a past obligating event: On the basis of the evidence available when the financial statements were approved, there is no obligation as a result of past events.
      Conclusion: No provision is recognised. The matter is disclosed as a contingent liability unless the probability of any outflow is regarded as remote.
(b)   At 31 December 20X2

Present obligation as a result of a past obligating event: On the basis of the evidence available, there is a present obligation. The obligating event is the sale of the product to the customer.

An outflow of resources embodying economic benefits in settlement: Probable.

Conclusion: A provision is recognised at the best estimate of the amount to settle the obligation at 31 December 20X2, and the expense is recognised in profit or loss. It is not a correction of an error in 20X1 because, on the basis of the evidence available when the 20X1 financial statements were approved, a provision should not have been recognised at that time.

Section 22 Liabilities and Equity

Scope of this section

22.1   This section establishes principles for classifying **financial instruments** as either **liabilities** or **equity** and deals with the accounting for **compound financial instruments**. It also addresses the issue of equity instruments and distributions to individuals or other parties acting in their capacity as investors in equity instruments (ie in their capacity as **owners**) and the accounting for purchases of own equity. This section also deals with the accounting for **non-controlling interests** in **consolidated financial statements**. Section 26 *Share-based Payment* addresses accounting for a transaction in which the entity receives goods or services (including employee services) as consideration for its equity instruments (including shares or **share options**) from employees and other vendors acting in their capacity as vendors of goods and services.

22.2   This section shall be applied to all types of financial instruments except:

   (a)   Investments in **subsidiaries**, **associates** and **joint ventures** that are accounted for in accordance with Section 9 *Consolidated and Separate Financial Statements*, Section 14 *Investments in Associates* or Section 15 *Investments in Joint Ventures*.

   (b)   Employers' rights and obligations under employee benefit plans, to which Section 28 *Employee Benefits* applies.

   (c)   Contracts for contingent consideration in a **business combination** (see Section 19 *Business Combinations and Goodwill*). This exemption applies only to the acquirer.

   (d)   Financial instruments, contracts and obligations under **share-based payment transactions** to which Section 26 applies, except that paragraphs 22.3 to 22.6 shall be applied to **treasury shares** issued, purchased, sold, transferred or cancelled in connection with employee share option plans, employee share purchase plans, and all other share-based payment arrangements.

   (e)   **Insurance contracts** (including **reinsurance contracts**) that an entity issues and reinsurance contracts that it holds (see FRS 103 *Insurance Contracts*).

   (f)   Financial instruments with a **discretionary participation feature** that an entity issues (see FRS 103).

   (g)   **Financial guarantee contracts** (see Section 21 *Provisions and Contingencies*).

   A reporting entity that issues the financial instruments set out in (e) and (f) or holds the financial instruments set out (e) is required by paragraph 1.6 to apply FRS 103 to those financial instruments.

Classification of an instrument as liability or equity

22.3   Equity is the residual interest in the **assets** of an entity after deducting all its liabilities. Equity includes investments by the owners of the entity, plus additions to those investments earned through profitable operations and retained for use in the entity's operations, minus reductions to owners' investments as a result of unprofitable operations and distributions to owners.

   A **financial liability** is any liability that is:

   (a)   a contractual obligation:

      (i)   to deliver **cash** or another **financial asset** to another entity; or

      (ii)   to exchange financial assets or financial liabilities with another entity under conditions that are potentially unfavourable to the entity; or

(b)   a contract that will or may be settled in the entity's own equity instruments and:

  (i)   under which the entity is or may be obliged to deliver a variable number of the entity's own equity instruments; or

  (ii)   which will or may be settled other than by the exchange of a fixed amount of cash or another financial asset for a fixed number of the entity's own equity instruments. For this purpose the entity's own equity instruments do not include instruments that are themselves contracts for the future receipt or delivery of the entity's own equity instruments.

A financial instrument, where the issuer does not have the unconditional right to avoid settling in cash or by delivery of another financial asset (or otherwise to settle it in such a way that it would be a financial liability) and where settlement is dependent on the occurrence or non-occurrence of uncertain future events beyond the control of the issuer and the holder, is a financial liability of the issuer unless: **22.3A**

(a)   the part of the contingent settlement provision that could require settlement in cash or another financial asset (or otherwise in such a way that it would be a financial liability) is not genuine;

(b)   the issuer can be required to settle the obligation in cash or another financial asset (or otherwise to settle it in such a way that it would be a financial liability) only in the event of liquidation of the issuer; or

(c)   the instrument has all the features and meets the conditions in paragraph 22.4.

Some financial instruments that meet the definition of a liability are classified as equity because they represent the residual interest in the net assets of the entity: **22.4**

(a)   A puttable instrument is a financial instrument that gives the holder the right to sell that instrument back to the issuer for cash or another financial asset or is automatically redeemed or repurchased by the issuer on the occurrence of an uncertain future event or the death or retirement of the instrument holder. A puttable instrument that has all of the following features is classified as an equity instrument:

  (i)   It entitles the holder to a pro rata share of the entity's net assets in the event of the entity's liquidation. The entity's net assets are those assets that remain after deducting all other claims on its assets.

  (ii)   The instrument is in the class of instruments that is subordinate to all other classes of instruments.

  (iii)   All financial instruments in the class of instruments that is subordinate to all other classes of instruments have identical features.

  (iv)   Apart from the contractual obligation for the issuer to repurchase or redeem the instrument for cash or another financial asset, the instrument does not include any contractual obligation to deliver cash or another financial asset to another entity, or to exchange financial assets or financial liabilities with another entity under conditions that are potentially unfavourable to the entity, and it is not a contract that will or may be settled in the entity's own equity instruments as set out in paragraph 22.3(b) of the definition of a financial liability.

  (v)   The total expected **cash flows** attributable to the instrument over the life of the instrument are based substantially on the **profit or loss**, the change in the recognised net assets or the change in the **fair value** of the recognised and unrecognised net assets of the entity over the life of the instrument (excluding any effects of the instrument).

(b)   Instruments, or components of instruments, that are subordinate to all other classes of instruments are classified as equity if they impose on the entity an obligation to deliver to another party a pro rata share of the net assets of the entity only on liquidation.

22.5   The following are examples of instruments that are either classified as liabilities or equity:

(a)   An instrument of the type described in paragraph 22.4(b) is classified as a liability if the distribution of net assets on liquidation is subject to a maximum amount (a ceiling). For example, if on liquidation the holders of the instrument receive a pro rata share of the net assets, but this amount is limited to a ceiling and the excess net assets are distributed to a charity organisation or the government, the instrument is not classified as equity.

(b)   A puttable instrument is classified as equity if, when the put option is exercised, the holder receives a pro rata share of the net assets of the entity determined by:

(i)   dividing the entity's net assets on liquidation into units of equal amounts; and

(ii)   multiplying that amount by the number of the units held by the financial instrument holder.

However, if the holder is entitled to an amount measured on some other basis the instrument is classified as a liability.

(c)   An instrument is classified as a liability if it obliges the entity to make payments to the holder before liquidation, such as a mandatory dividend.

(d)   A puttable instrument that is classified as equity in a subsidiary's **financial statements** is classified as a liability in the consolidated financial statements.

(e)   A preference share that provides for mandatory redemption by the issuer for a fixed or determinable amount at a fixed or determinable future date, or gives the holder the right to require the issuer to redeem the instrument at or after a particular date for a fixed or determinable amount, is a financial liability.

22.6   Members' shares in co-operative entities and similar instruments are equity if:

(a)   the entity has an unconditional right to refuse redemption of the members' shares; or

(b)   redemption is unconditionally prohibited by local law, regulation or the entity's governing charter.

Original issue of shares or other equity instruments

22.7   An entity shall recognise the issue of shares or other equity instruments as equity when it issues those instruments and another party is obliged to provide cash or other resources to the entity in exchange for the instruments.

(a)   [Not used]

(b)   If the entity receives the cash or other resources before the equity instruments are issued, and the entity cannot be required to repay the cash or other resources received, the entity shall recognise the corresponding increase in equity to the extent of consideration received.

(c)   To the extent that the equity instruments have been subscribed for but not issued (or called up), and the entity has not yet received the cash or other resources, the entity shall not recognise an increase in equity.

22.8   An entity shall measure the equity instruments at the fair value of the cash or other resources received or receivable, net of direct costs of issuing the equity instruments. If payment is deferred and the time value of money is **material**, the initial **measurement** shall be on a **present value** basis.

22.9   An entity shall account for the **transaction costs** of an equity transaction as a deduction from equity, net of any related income tax benefit.

22.10   How the increase in equity arising on the issue of shares or other equity instruments is presented in the **statement of financial position** is determined by applicable laws. For example, the par value (or other nominal value) of shares and the amount paid in excess of par value may be presented separately.

Exercise of options, rights and warrants

An entity shall apply the principles in paragraphs 22.7 to 22.10 to equity issued by means   **22.11**
of exercise of options, rights, warrants and similar equity instruments.

Capitalisation or bonus issues of shares and share splits

A capitalisation or bonus issue (sometimes referred to as a stock dividend) is the issue of   **22.12**
new shares to shareholders in proportion to their existing holdings. For example, an entity
may give its shareholders one dividend or bonus share for every five shares held. A share
split (sometimes referred to as a stock split) is the dividing of an entity's existing shares into
multiple shares. For example, in a share split, each shareholder may receive one additional
share for each share held. In some cases, the previously outstanding shares are cancelled and
replaced by new shares. Capitalisation and bonus issues and share splits do not change total
equity. An entity shall reclassify amounts within equity as required by applicable laws.

Convertible debt or similar compound financial instruments

On issuing convertible debt or similar compound financial instruments that contain both a   **22.13**
liability and an equity component, an entity shall allocate the proceeds between the liability
component and the equity component. To make the allocation, the entity shall first determine
the amount of the liability component as the fair value of a similar liability that does not have
a conversion feature or similar associated equity component. The entity shall allocate the
residual amount as the equity component. Transaction costs shall be allocated between the
debt component and the equity component on the basis of their relative fair values.

The entity shall not revise the allocation in a subsequent period.   **22.14**

In periods after the instruments were issued, the entity shall account for the liability   **22.15**
component as a financial instrument in accordance with Section 11 *Basic Financial
Instruments* or Section 12 *Other Financial Instruments Issues* as appropriate. The appendix
to this section illustrates the issuer's accounting for convertible debt where the liability
component is a basic financial instrument.

Treasury shares

Treasury shares are the equity instruments of an entity that have been issued and   **22.16**
subsequently reacquired by the entity. An entity shall deduct from equity the fair value of
the consideration given for the treasury shares. The entity shall not recognise a **gain** or loss
in profit or loss on the purchase, sale, transfer or cancellation of treasury shares.

Distributions to owners

An entity shall reduce equity for the amount of distributions to its owners (holders of its   **22.17**
equity instruments).

An entity shall disclose the fair value of any non-cash assets that have been distributed to   **22.18**
its owners during the **reporting period**, except when the non-cash assets are ultimately
controlled by the same parties both before and after the distribution.

Non-controlling interest and transactions in shares of a consolidated subsidiary

In the consolidated financial statements, a non-controlling interest in the net assets of a   **22.19**
subsidiary is included in equity. An entity shall treat changes in a parent's controlling

interest in a subsidiary that do not result in a loss of **control** as transactions with equity holders in their capacity as equity holders. Accordingly, the **carrying amount** of the non-controlling interest shall be adjusted to reflect the change in the parent's interest in the subsidiary's net assets. Any difference between the amount by which the non-controlling interest is so adjusted and the fair value of the consideration paid or received, if any, shall be recognised directly in equity and attributed to equity holders of the parent. An entity shall not recognise a gain or loss on these changes. Also, an entity shall not recognise any change in the carrying amounts of assets (including goodwill) or liabilities as a result of such transactions.

Appendix to Section 22

Example of the issuer's accounting for convertible debt

The appendix accompanies, but is not part of, Section 22. It provides guidance for applying the requirements of paragraphs 22.13 to 22.15.

On 1 January 20X5 an entity issues 500 convertible bonds. The bonds are issued at par with a face value of CU100 per bond and are for a five-year term, with no transaction costs. The total proceeds from the issue are CU50,000. Interest is payable annually in arrears at an annual interest rate of 4 per cent. Each bond is convertible, at the holder's discretion, into 25 ordinary shares at any time up to maturity. At the time the bonds are issued, the market interest rate for similar debt that does not have the conversion option is 6 per cent.

When the instrument is issued, the liability component must be valued first, and the difference between the total proceeds on issue (which is the fair value of the instrument in its entirety) and the fair value of the liability component is assigned to the equity component. The fair value of the liability component is calculated by determining its present value using the discount rate of 6 per cent. The calculations and journal entries are illustrated below:

	CU
Proceeds from the bond issue (A)	50,000
Present value of principal at the end of five years (see calculations below)	37,363
Present value of interest payable annually in arrears for five years	8,425
Present value of liability, which is the fair value of liability component (B)	45,788
Residual, which is the fair value of the equity component (A) – (B)	4,212

The issuer of the bonds makes the following journal entry at issue on 1 January 20X5:

Dr Cash	CU50,000	
Cr Financial Liability – Convertible bond		CU45,788
Cr Equity		CU4,212

The CU4,212 represents a discount on issue of the bonds, so the entry could also be shown 'gross':

Dr Cash	CU50,000	
Dr Financial Liability – Convertible bond discount	CU4,212	
Cr Financial Liability – Convertible bond		CU50,000
Cr Equity		CU4,212

After issue, the issuer will amortise the bond discount according to the following table:

	(a) Interest payment	(b) Total interest expense = 6% × (e)	(c) Amortisation of bond discount = (b) – (a)	(d) Bond discount = (d) – (c)	(e) Net liability = 50,000 – (d)
	CU	CU	CU	CU	CU
1/1/20X5				4,212	45,788
31/12/20X5	2,000	2,747	747	3,465	46,535
31/12/20X6	2,000	2,792	792	2,673	47,327
31/12/20X7	2,000	2,840	840	1,833	48,167
31/12/20X8	2,000	2,890	890	943	49,057
31/12/20X9	2,000	2,943	943	0	50,000
Totals	10,000	14,212	4,212		

At the end of 20X5, the issuer would make the following journal entry:

Dr Interest expense	CU2,747	
Cr Bond discount		CU747
Cr Cash		CU2,000

Calculations

Present value of principal of CU50,000 at 6 per cent

$CU50,000/(1.06)^5 = 37,363$

Present value of the interest annuity of CU2,000 (= CU50,000 × 4 per cent) payable at the end of each of five years

The CU2,000 annual interest payments are an annuity: a cash flow stream with a limited number (n) of periodic payments (C), receivable at dates 1 to n. To calculate the present value of this annuity, future payments are discounted by the periodic rate of interest (i) using the following formula:

$PV = C/i × [1 – 1/(1 + i)^n]$

Therefore, the present value of the CU2,000 interest payments is $(2,000/.06) × [1 – [(1/1.06)^5] = 8,425$

This is equivalent to the sum of the present values of the five individual CU2,000 payments, as follows:

	CU
Present value of interest payment at 31 December 20X5 = 2,000/1.06	1,887
Present value of interest payment at 31 December 20X6 = 2,000/1.06²	1,780
Present value of interest payment at 31 December 20X7 = 2,000/1.06³	1,679
Present value of interest payment at 31 December 20X8 = 2,000/1.06⁴	1,584
Present value of interest payment at 31 December 20X9 = 2,000/1.06⁵	1,495
Total	8,425

Yet another way to calculate this is to use a table of present value of an ordinary annuity in arrears, five periods, interest rate of 6 per cent per period. (Such tables are easily found on the Internet.) The present value factor is 4.2124. Multiplying this by the annuity payment of CU2,000 determines the present value of CU8,425.

Section 23 Revenue

Scope of this section

23.1   This section shall be applied in accounting for **revenue** arising from the following transactions and events:

(a)   the sale of goods (whether produced by the entity for the purpose of sale or purchased for resale);

(b)   the rendering of services;

(c)   **construction contracts** in which the entity is the contractor; and

(d)   the use by others of entity assets yielding interest, royalties or dividends.

23.2   Revenue or other income arising from some transactions and events is dealt with in other sections of this FRS:

(a)   lease agreements (see Section 20 *Leases*);

(b)   dividends and other income arising from investments that are accounted for using the equity method (see Section 14 *Investments in Associates* and Section 15 *Investments in Joint Ventures*);

(c)   changes in the **fair value** of **financial assets** and **financial liabilities** or their disposal (see Section 11 *Basic Financial Instruments* and Section 12 *Other Financial Instruments Issues*);

(d)   changes in the fair value of **investment property** (see Section 16 *Investment Property*);

(e)   initial **recognition** and changes in the fair value of **biological assets** related to **agricultural activity** (see Section 34 *Specialised Activities*); and

(f)   initial recognition of **agricultural produce** (see Section 34).

23.2A   This section excludes revenue or other income arising from transactions and events dealt with in FRS 103 *Insurance Contracts*.

Measurement of revenue

23.3   An entity shall measure revenue at the fair value of the consideration received or receivable. The fair value of the consideration received or receivable takes into account the amount of any trade discounts, prompt settlement discounts and volume rebates allowed by the entity.

23.4   An entity shall include in revenue only the gross inflows of economic benefits received and receivable by the entity on its own account. An entity shall exclude from revenue all amounts collected on behalf of third parties such as sales taxes, goods and services taxes and value added taxes. In an agency relationship, an entity (the **agent**) shall include in revenue only the amount of its commission. The amounts collected on behalf of the **principal** are not revenue of the entity.

Deferred payment

23.5   When the inflow of **cash** or **cash equivalents** is deferred, and the arrangement constitutes in effect a financing transaction, the fair value of the consideration is the **present value** of all future receipts determined using an **imputed rate of interest**. A financing transaction arises when, for example, an entity provides interest-free credit to the buyer or accepts a note receivable bearing a below-market interest rate from the buyer as consideration for the sale of goods. The imputed rate of interest is the more clearly determinable of either:

(a)   the prevailing rate for a similar instrument of an issuer with a similar credit rating; or

(b)   a rate of interest that discounts the nominal amount of the instrument to the current cash sales price of the goods or services.

An entity shall recognise the difference between the present value of all future receipts and the nominal amount of the consideration as interest revenue in accordance with paragraphs 23.28 and 23.29 and Section 11.

Exchanges of goods or services

An entity shall not recognise revenue: 23.6

(a)   when goods or services are exchanged for goods or services that are of a similar nature and value; or

(b)   when goods or services are exchanged for dissimilar goods or services but the transaction lacks commercial substance.

An entity shall recognise revenue when goods are sold or services are exchanged for   23.7
dissimilar goods or services in a transaction that has commercial substance. In that case, the entity shall measure the transaction:

(a)   at the fair value of the goods or services received adjusted by the amount of any cash or cash equivalents transferred;

(b)   if the amount under (a) cannot be measured reliably, then at the fair value of the goods or services given up adjusted by the amount of any cash or cash equivalents transferred; or

(c)   if the fair value of neither the goods or services received nor the goods or services given up can be measured reliably, then at the **carrying amount** of the goods or services given up adjusted by the amount of any cash or cash equivalents transferred.

Identification of the revenue transaction

An entity usually applies the revenue recognition criteria in this section separately to each   23.8
transaction. However, an entity applies the recognition criteria to the separately identifiable components of a single transaction when necessary to reflect the substance of the transaction. For example, an entity applies the recognition criteria to the separately identifiable components of a single transaction when the selling price of a product includes an identifiable amount for subsequent servicing. Conversely, an entity applies the recognition criteria to two or more transactions together when they are linked in such a way that the commercial effect cannot be understood without reference to the series of transactions as a whole. For example, an entity applies the recognition criteria to two or more transactions together when it sells goods and, at the same time, enters into a separate agreement to repurchase the goods at a later date, thus negating the substantive effect of the transaction.

Sometimes, as part of a sales transaction, an entity grants its customer a loyalty award   23.9
that the customer may redeem in the future for free or discounted goods or services. In this case, in accordance with paragraph 23.8, the entity shall account for the award credits as a separately identifiable component of the initial sales transaction. The entity shall allocate the fair value of the consideration received or receivable in respect of the initial sale between the award credits and the other components of the sale. The consideration allocated to the award credits shall be measured by reference to their fair value, ie the amount for which the award credits could be sold separately.

Sale of goods

An entity shall recognise revenue from the sale of goods when all the following conditions   23.10
are satisfied:

(a)   the entity has transferred to the buyer the significant risks and rewards of ownership of the goods;

(b)   the entity retains neither continuing managerial involvement to the degree usually associated with ownership nor effective control over the goods sold;

(c)   the amount of revenue can be measured reliably;

(d)   it is **probable** that the economic benefits associated with the transaction will flow to the entity; and

(e)   the costs incurred or to be incurred in respect of the transaction can be measured reliably.

23.11   The assessment of when an entity has transferred the significant risks and rewards of ownership to the buyer requires an examination of the circumstances of the transaction. In most cases, the transfer of the risks and rewards of ownership coincides with the transfer of the legal title or the passing of possession to the buyer. This is the case for most retail sales. In other cases, the transfer of risks and rewards of ownership occurs at a time different from the transfer of legal title or the passing of possession.

23.12   An entity does not recognise revenue if it retains significant risks and rewards of ownership. Examples of situations in which the entity may retain the significant risks and rewards of ownership are:

(a)   when the entity retains an obligation for unsatisfactory performance not covered by normal warranties;

(b)   when the receipt of the revenue from a particular sale is contingent on the buyer selling the goods;

(c)   when the goods are shipped subject to installation and the installation is a significant part of the contract that has not yet been completed; and

(d)   when the buyer has the right to rescind the purchase for a reason specified in the sales contract, or at the buyer's sole discretion without any reason, and the entity is uncertain about the probability of return.

23.13   If an entity retains only an insignificant risk of ownership, the transaction is a sale and the entity recognises the revenue. For example, a seller recognises revenue when it retains the legal title to the goods solely to protect the collectability of the amount due. Similarly an entity recognises revenue when it offers a refund if the customer finds the goods faulty or is not satisfied for other reasons, and the entity can estimate the returns reliably. In such cases, the entity recognises a **provision** for returns in accordance with Section 21 *Provisions and Contingencies*.

Rendering of services

23.14   When the outcome of a transaction involving the rendering of services can be estimated reliably, an entity shall recognise revenue associated with the transaction by reference to the stage of completion of the transaction at the end of the **reporting period** (sometimes referred to as the percentage of completion method). The outcome of a transaction can be estimated reliably when all the following conditions are satisfied:

(a)   the amount of revenue can be measured reliably;

(b)   it is probable that the economic benefits associated with the transaction will flow to the entity;

(c)   the stage of completion of the transaction at the end of the reporting period can be measured reliably; and

(d)   the costs incurred for the transaction and the costs to complete the transaction can be measured reliably.

Paragraphs 23.21 to 23.27 provide guidance for applying the percentage of completion method.

When services are performed by an indeterminate number of acts over a specified period of time, an entity recognises revenue on a straight-line basis over the specified period unless there is evidence that some other method better represents the stage of completion. When a specific act is much more significant than any other act, the entity postpones recognition of revenue until the significant act is executed.   **23.15**

When the outcome of the transaction involving the rendering of services cannot be estimated reliably, an entity shall recognise revenue only to the extent of the **expenses** recognised that are recoverable.   **23.16**

Construction contracts

When the outcome of a construction contract can be estimated reliably, an entity shall recognise contract revenue and contract costs associated with the construction contract as revenue and expenses respectively by reference to the stage of completion of the contract activity at the end of the reporting period (often referred to as the percentage of completion method). Reliable estimation of the outcome requires reliable estimates of the stage of completion, future costs and collectability of billings. Paragraphs 23.21 to 23.27 provide guidance for applying the percentage of completion method.   **23.17**

The requirements of this section are usually applied separately to each construction contract. However, in some circumstances, it is necessary to apply this section to the separately identifiable components of a single contract or to a group of contracts together in order to reflect the substance of a contract or a group of contracts.   **23.18**

When a contract covers a number of **assets**, the construction of each asset shall be treated as a separate construction contract when: **23.19**

(a)   separate proposals have been submitted for each asset;
(b)   each asset has been subject to separate negotiation, and the contractor and customer are able to accept or reject that part of the contract relating to each asset; and
(c)   the costs and revenues of each asset can be identified.

A group of contracts, whether with a single customer or with several customers, shall be treated as a single construction contract when: **23.20**

(a)   the group of contracts is negotiated as a single package;
(b)   the contracts are so closely interrelated that they are, in effect, part of a single project with an overall profit margin; and
(c)   the contracts are performed concurrently or in a continuous sequence.

Percentage of completion method

This method is used to recognise revenue from rendering services (see paragraphs 23.14 to 23.16) and from construction contracts (see paragraphs 23.17 to 23.20). An entity shall review and, when necessary, revise the estimates of revenue and costs as the service transaction or construction contract progresses.   **23.21**

An entity shall determine the stage of completion of a transaction or contract using the method that measures most reliably the work performed. Possible methods include: **23.22**

(a)   the proportion that costs incurred for work performed to date bear to the estimated total costs. Costs incurred for work performed to date do not include costs relating to future activity, such as for materials or prepayments;
(b)   surveys of work performed; and

(c)   completion of a physical proportion of the contract work or the completion of a proportion of the service contract.

Progress payments and advances received from customers often do not reflect the work performed.

23.23   An entity shall recognise costs that relate to future activity on the transaction or contract, such as for materials or prepayments, as an asset if it is probable that the costs will be recovered.

23.24   An entity shall recognise as an expense immediately any costs whose recovery is not probable.

23.25   When the outcome of a construction contract cannot be estimated reliably:

(a)   an entity shall recognise revenue only to the extent of contract costs incurred that it is probable will be recoverable; and

(b)   the entity shall recognise contract costs as an expense in the period in which they are incurred.

23.26   When it is probable that total contract costs will exceed total contract revenue on a construction contract, the expected loss shall be recognised as an expense immediately, with a corresponding provision for an **onerous contract** (see Section 21).

23.27   If the collectability of an amount already recognised as contract revenue is no longer probable, the entity shall recognise the uncollectible amount as an expense rather than as an adjustment of the amount of contract revenue.

Interest, royalties and dividends

23.28   An entity shall recognise revenue arising from the use by others of entity assets yielding interest, royalties and dividends on the bases set out in paragraph 23.29 when:

(a)   it is probable that the economic benefits associated with the transaction will flow to the entity; and

(b)   the amount of the revenue can be measured reliably.

23.29   An entity shall recognise revenue on the following bases:

(a)   Interest shall be recognised using the **effective interest method** as described in paragraphs 11.15 to 11.20. When calculating the **effective interest rate**, an entity shall include any related fees, finance charges paid or received (such as 'points'), **transaction costs** and other premiums or discounts.

(b)   Royalties shall be recognised on an **accrual basis** in accordance with the substance of the relevant agreement.

(c)   Dividends shall be recognised when the shareholder's right to receive payment is established.

Disclosures

General disclosures about revenue

23.30   An entity shall disclose:

(a)   the **accounting policies** adopted for the recognition of revenue, including the methods adopted to determine the stage of completion of transactions involving the rendering of services; and

(b)   the amount of each category of revenue recognised during the period, showing separately, at a minimum, revenue arising from:

(i)   the sale of goods;
(ii)   the rendering of services;
(iii)   interest;
(iv)   royalties;
(v)   dividends;
(vi)   commissions;
(vii) grants; and
(viii) any other significant types of revenue.

Disclosures relating to revenue from construction contracts

An entity shall disclose the following: **23.31**

(a)   the amount of contract revenue recognised as revenue in the period;
(b)   the methods used to determine the contract revenue recognised in the period; and
(c)   the methods used to determine the stage of completion of contracts in progress.

An entity shall present: **23.32**

(a)   the gross amount due from customers for contract work, as an asset; and
(b)   the gross amount due to customers for contract work, as a **liability**.

Appendix to Section 23

Examples of revenue recognition under the principles in Section 23

This appendix accompanies, but is not part of, Section 23. It provides guidance for applying the requirements of Section 23 in recognising revenue.

The following examples focus on particular aspects of a transaction and are not a   **23A.1**
comprehensive discussion of all the relevant factors that might influence the recognition of revenue. The examples generally assume that the amount of revenue can be measured reliably, it is probable that the economic benefits will flow to the entity and the costs incurred or to be incurred can be measured reliably.

Sale of goods

The law in different countries may cause the recognition criteria in Section 23 to be met at   **23A.2**
different times. In particular, the law may determine the point in time at which the entity transfers the significant risks and rewards of ownership. Therefore, the examples in this appendix need to be read in the context of the laws relating to the sale of goods in the country in which the transaction takes place.

Example 1 'Bill and hold' sales, in which delivery is delayed at the buyer's request but the buyer takes title and accepts billing

The seller recognises revenue when the buyer takes title, provided: **23A.3**

(a)   it is probable that delivery will be made;
(b)   the item is on hand, identified and ready for delivery to the buyer at the time the sale is recognised;
(c)   the buyer specifically acknowledges the deferred delivery instructions; and
(d)   the usual payment terms apply.

Revenue is not recognised when there is simply an intention to acquire or manufacture the goods in time for delivery.

Example 2 Goods shipped subject to conditions: installation and inspection

23A.4   The seller normally recognises revenue when the buyer accepts delivery, and installation and inspection are complete. However, revenue is recognised immediately upon the buyer's acceptance of delivery when:

(a)   the installation process is simple, for example the installation of a factory-tested television receiver that requires only unpacking and connection of power and antennae; or

(b)   the inspection is performed only for the purposes of final determination of contract prices, for example, shipments of iron ore, sugar or soya beans.

Example 3 Goods shipped subject to conditions: on approval when the buyer has negotiated a limited right of return

23A.5   If there is uncertainty about the possibility of return, the seller recognises revenue when the shipment has been formally accepted by the buyer or the goods have been delivered and the time period for rejection has elapsed.

Example 4 Goods shipped subject to conditions: consignment sales under which the recipient (buyer) undertakes to sell the goods on behalf of the shipper (seller)

23A.6   The shipper recognises revenue when the goods are sold by the recipient to a third party.

Example 5 Goods shipped subject to conditions: cash on delivery sales

23A.7   The seller recognises revenue when delivery is made and cash is received by the seller or its agent.

Example 6 Layaway sales under which the goods are delivered only when the buyer makes the final payment in a series of instalments

23A.8   The seller recognises revenue from such sales when the goods are delivered. However, when experience indicates that most such sales are consummated, revenue may be recognised when a significant deposit is received, provided the goods are on hand, identified and ready for delivery to the buyer.

Example 7 Orders when payment (or partial payment) is received in advance of delivery for goods not currently held in inventory, for example, the goods are still to be manufactured or will be delivered direct to the buyer from a third party

23A.9   The seller recognises revenue when the goods are delivered to the buyer.

Example 8 Sale and repurchase agreements (other than swap transactions) under which the seller concurrently agrees to repurchase the same goods at a later date, or when the seller has a call option to repurchase, or the buyer has a put option to require the repurchase, by the seller, of the goods

23A.10   For a sale and repurchase agreement on an asset other than a financial asset, the seller must analyse the terms of the agreement to ascertain whether, in substance, the risks and rewards of ownership have been transferred to the buyer. If they have been transferred, the seller recognises revenue. When the seller has retained the risks and rewards of ownership, even though legal title has been transferred, the transaction is a financing arrangement and does not give rise to revenue. For a sale and repurchase agreement on a financial asset, the derecognition provisions of Section 11 apply.

Example 9 Sales to intermediate parties, such as distributors, dealers or others for resale

The seller generally recognises revenue from such sales when the risks and rewards of ownership have been transferred. However, when the buyer is acting, in substance, as an agent, the sale is treated as a consignment sale.

23A.11

Example 10 Subscriptions to publications and similar items

When the items involved are of similar value in each time period, the seller recognises revenue on a straight-line basis over the period in which the items are dispatched. When the items vary in value from period to period, the seller recognises revenue on the basis of the sales value of the item dispatched in relation to the total estimated sales value of all items covered by the subscription.

23A.12

Example 11 Instalment sales, under which the consideration is receivable in instalments

The seller recognises revenue attributable to the sales price, exclusive of interest, at the date of sale. The sale price is the present value of the consideration, determined by discounting the instalments receivable at the imputed rate of interest. The seller recognises the interest element as revenue using the effective interest method.

23A.13

Example 12 Agreements for the construction of real estate

An entity that undertakes the construction of real estate, directly or through subcontractors, and enters into an agreement with one or more buyers before construction is complete, shall account for the agreement using the percentage of completion method, only if:

23A.14

(a)   the buyer is able to specify the major structural elements of the design of the real estate before construction begins and/or specify major structural changes once construction is in progress (whether it exercises that ability or not); or

(b)   the buyer acquires and supplies construction materials and the entity provides only construction services.

If the entity is required to provide services together with construction materials in order to perform its contractual obligation to deliver real estate to the buyer, the agreement shall be accounted for as the sale of goods. In this case, the buyer does not obtain control or the significant risks and rewards of ownership of the work in progress in its current state as construction progresses. Rather, the transfer occurs only on delivery of the completed real estate to the buyer.

23A.15

Example 13 Sale with customer loyalty award

An entity sells product A for CU100. Purchasers of product A get an award credit enabling them to buy product B for CU10. The normal selling price of product B is CU18. The entity estimates that 40 per cent of the purchasers of product A will use their award to buy product B at CU10. The normal selling price of product A, after taking into account discounts that are usually offered but that are not available during this promotion, is CU95.

23A.16

The fair value of the award credit is 40 per cent × [CU18 – CU10] = CU3.20. The entity allocates the total revenue of CU100 between product A and the award credit by reference to their relative fair values of CU95 and CU3.20 respectively. Therefore:

23A.17

    (a)   Revenue for product A is CU100 × [CU95 / (CU95 + CU3.20)] = CU96.74

    (b)   Revenue for product B is CU100 × [CU3.20 / (CU95 + CU3.20)] = CU3.26

Rendering of services

Example 14 Installation fees

23A.18   The seller recognises installation fees as revenue by reference to the stage of completion of the installation, unless they are incidental to the sale of a product, in which case they are recognised when the goods are sold.

Example 15 Servicing fees included in the price of the product

23A.19   When the selling price of a product includes an identifiable amount for subsequent servicing (eg after sales support and product enhancement on the sale of software), the seller defers that amount and recognises it as revenue over the period during which the service is performed. The amount deferred is that which will cover the expected costs of the services under the agreement, together with a reasonable profit on those services.

Example 16 Advertising commissions

23A.20   Media commissions are recognised when the related advertisement or commercial appears before the public. Production commissions are recognised by reference to the stage of completion of the project.

Example 17 Insurance agency commissions

23A.21   Insurance agency commissions received or receivable that do not require the agent to render further service are recognised as revenue by the agent on the effective commencement or renewal dates of the related policies. However, when it is probable that the agent will be required to render further services during the life of the policy, the agent defers the commission, or part of it, and recognises it as revenue over the period during which the policy is in force.

Example 17A Financial services fees

23A.21A   The recognition of revenue for financial service fees depends on the purposes for which the fees are assessed and the basis of accounting for any associated financial instrument. The description of fees for financial services may not be indicative of the nature and substance of the services provided. Therefore it is necessary to distinguish between fees that are an integral part of the effective interest rate of a financial instrument, fees that are earned as services are provided, and fees that are earned on the execution of a significant act.

Example 18 Admission fees

23A.22   The seller recognises revenue from artistic performances, banquets and other special events when the event takes place. When a subscription to a number of events is sold, the seller allocates the fee to each event on a basis that reflects the extent to which services are performed at each event.

Example 19 Tuition fees

23A.23   The seller recognises revenue over the period of instruction.

Example 20 Initiation, entrance and membership fees

Revenue recognition depends on the nature of the services provided. If the fee permits only membership, and all other services or products are paid for separately, or if there is a separate annual subscription, the fee is recognised as revenue when no significant uncertainty about its collectability exists. If the fee entitles the member to services or publications to be provided during the membership period, or to purchase goods or services at prices lower than those charged to non-members, it is recognised on a basis that reflects the timing, nature and value of the benefits provided.

23A.24

Franchise fees

Franchise fees may cover the supply of initial and subsequent services, equipment and other tangible assets, and know-how. Accordingly, franchise fees are recognised as revenue on a basis that reflects the purpose for which the fees were charged. The following methods of franchise fee recognition are appropriate.

23A.25

Example 21 Franchise fees: Supplies of equipment and other tangible assets

The franchisor recognises the fair value of the assets sold as revenue when the items are delivered or title passes.

23A.26

Example 22 Franchise fees: Supplies of initial and subsequent services

The franchisor recognises fees for the provision of continuing services, whether part of the initial fee or a separate fee, as revenue as the services are rendered. When the separate fee does not cover the cost of continuing services together with a reasonable profit, part of the initial fee, sufficient to cover the costs of continuing services and to provide a reasonable profit on those services, is deferred and recognised as revenue as the services are rendered.

23A.27

The franchise agreement may provide for the franchisor to supply equipment, inventories, or other tangible assets at a price lower than that charged to others or a price that does not provide a reasonable profit on those sales. In these circumstances, part of the initial fee, sufficient to cover estimated costs in excess of that price and to provide a reasonable profit on those sales, is deferred and recognised over the period the goods are likely to be sold to the franchisee. The balance of an initial fee is recognised as revenue when performance of all the initial services and other obligations required of the franchisor (such as assistance with site selection, staff training, financing and advertising) has been substantially accomplished.

23A.28

The initial services and other obligations under an area franchise agreement may depend on the number of individual outlets established in the area. In this case, the fees attributable to the initial services are recognised as revenue in proportion to the number of outlets for which the initial services have been substantially completed.

23A.29

If the initial fee is collectible over an extended period and there is a significant uncertainty that it will be collected in full, the fee is recognised as cash instalments are received.

23A.30

Example 23 Franchise fees: Continuing franchise fees

Fees charged for the use of continuing rights granted by the agreement, or for other services provided during the period of the agreement, are recognised as revenue as the services are provided or the rights used.

23A.31

Example 24 Franchise fees: Agency transactions

23A.32   Transactions may take place between the franchisor and the franchisee that, in substance, involve the franchisor acting as agent for the franchisee. For example, the franchisor may order supplies and arrange for their delivery to the franchisee at no profit. Such transactions do not give rise to revenue.

Example 25 Fees from the development of customised software

23A.33   The software developer recognises fees from the development of customised software as revenue by reference to the stage of completion of the development, including completion of services provided for post-delivery service support.

Interest, royalties and dividends

Example 26 Licence fees and royalties

23A.34   The licensor recognises fees and royalties paid for the use of an entity's assets (such as trademarks, patents, software, music copyright, record masters and motion picture films) in accordance with the substance of the agreement. As a practical matter, this may be on a straight-line basis over the life of the agreement, for example, when a licensee has the right to use specified technology for a specified period of time.

23A.35   An assignment of rights for a fixed fee or non-refundable guarantee under a non-cancellable contract that permits the licensee to exploit those rights freely and the licensor has no remaining obligations to perform is, in substance, a sale. An example is a licensing agreement for the use of software when the licensor has no obligations after delivery. Another example is the granting of rights to exhibit a motion picture film in markets in which the licensor has no control over the distributor and expects to receive no further revenues from the box office receipts. In such cases, revenue is recognised at the time of sale.

23A.36   In some cases, whether or not a licence fee or royalty will be received is contingent on the occurrence of a future event. In such cases, revenue is recognised only when it is probable that the fee or royalty will be received, which is normally when the event has occurred.

Section 24 Government Grants

Scope of this section

24.1   This section specifies the accounting for all **government grants**. A government grant is assistance by government in the form of a transfer of resources to an entity in return for past or future compliance with specified conditions relating to the **operating activities** of the entity.

24.2   Government grants exclude those forms of government assistance that cannot reasonably have a value placed upon them and transactions with government that cannot be distinguished from the normal trading transactions of the entity.

24.3   This section does not cover government assistance that is provided for an entity in the form of benefits that are available in determining **taxable profit (tax loss)**, or are determined or limited on the basis of income tax liability. Examples of such benefits are income tax holidays, investment tax credits, accelerated depreciation allowances and reduced income tax rates. Section 29 *Income Tax* covers accounting for taxes based on **income**.

Recognition and measurement

Government grants, including non-monetary grants shall not be recognised until there is reasonable assurance that:	24.3A

(a)   the entity will comply with the conditions attaching to them; and
(b)   the grants will be received.

An entity shall recognise grants either based on the performance model or the accrual model. This policy choice shall be applied on a class-by-class basis.	24.4

An entity shall measure grants at the **fair value** of the **asset** received or receivable.	24.5

Where a grant becomes repayable it shall be recognised as a **liability** when the repayment meets the definition of a liability.	24.5A

Performance model

An entity applying the performance model shall recognise grants as follows:	24.5B

(a)   A grant that does not impose specified future **performance-related conditions** on the recipient is recognised in income when the grant proceeds are received or receivable.
(b)   A grant that imposes specified future performance-related conditions on the recipient is recognised in income only when the performance-related conditions are met.
(c)   Grants received before the **revenue recognition** criteria are satisfied are recognised as a liability.

Accrual model

An entity applying the accrual model shall classify grants either as a grant relating to revenue or a grant relating to assets.	24.5C

Grants relating to revenue shall be recognised in income on a systematic basis over the periods in which the entity recognises the related costs for which the grant is intended to compensate.	24.5D

A grant that becomes receivable as compensation for **expenses** or losses already incurred or for the purpose of giving immediate financial support to the entity with no future related costs shall be recognised in income in the period in which it becomes receivable.	24.5E

Grants relating to assets shall be recognised in income on a systematic basis over the expected **useful life** of the asset.	24.5F

Where part of a grant relating to an asset is deferred it shall be recognised as deferred income and not deducted from the **carrying amount** of the asset.	24.5G

Disclosures

An entity shall disclose the following:	24.6

(a)   the **accounting policy** adopted for grants in accordance with paragraph 24.4;
(b)   the nature and amounts of grants recognised in the **financial statements**;
(c)   unfulfilled conditions and other contingencies attaching to grants that have been recognised in income; and
(d)   an indication of other forms of government assistance from which the entity has directly benefited.

24.7   For the purpose of the disclosure required by paragraph 24.6(d), government assistance is action by government designed to provide an economic benefit specific to an entity or range of entities qualifying under specified criteria. Examples include free technical or marketing advice, the provision of guarantees, and loans at nil or low interest rates.

Section 25 Borrowing Costs

Scope of this section

25.1   This section specifies the accounting for **borrowing costs**. Borrowing costs are interest and other costs that an entity incurs in connection with the borrowing of funds. Borrowing costs include:

(a)   interest expense calculated using the **effective interest method** as described in Section 11 *Basic Financial Instruments*;

(b)   finance charges in respect of **finance leases** recognised in accordance with Section 20 *Leases*; and

(c)   exchange differences arising from foreign currency borrowings to the extent that they are regarded as an adjustment to interest costs.

Recognition

25.2   An entity may adopt a policy of capitalising borrowing costs that are directly attributable to the acquisition, construction or production of a **qualifying asset** as part of the cost of that **asset**. Where an entity adopts a policy of capitalisation of borrowing costs, it shall be applied consistently to a class of qualifying assets. Where an entity does not adopt a policy of capitalising borrowing costs, all borrowing costs shall be recognised as an **expense** in **profit or loss** in the period in which they are incurred.

25.2A   The borrowing costs that are directly attributable to the acquisition, construction or production of a qualifying asset are those borrowing costs that would have been avoided if the expenditure on the qualifying asset had not been made.

25.2B   To the extent that an entity borrows funds specifically for the purpose of obtaining a qualifying asset, the entity shall determine the amount of borrowing costs eligible for capitalisation as the actual borrowing costs incurred on that borrowing during the period less any investment income on the temporary investment of those borrowings.

25.2C   To the extent that funds applied to obtain a qualifying asset form part of the entity's general borrowings, the amount of borrowing costs eligible for capitalisation are determined by applying a capitalisation rate to the expenditure on that asset. For this purpose the expenditure on the asset is the average **carrying amount** of the asset during the period, including borrowing costs previously capitalised. The capitalisation rate used in an accounting period shall be the weighted average of rates applicable to the entity's general borrowings that are outstanding during the period. This excludes borrowings by the entity that are specifically for the purpose of obtaining other qualifying assets. The amount of borrowing costs that an entity capitalises during a period shall not exceed the amount of borrowing costs it incurred during that period.

25.2D   An entity shall:

(a)   capitalise borrowing costs as part of the cost of a qualifying asset from the point when it first incurs both expenditure on the asset and borrowing costs, and undertakes activities necessary to prepare the asset for its intended use or sale;

(b)   suspend capitalisation during extended periods where active development of the asset has paused; and

(c)   cease capitalisation when substantially all the activities necessary to prepare the qualifying asset for its intended use or sale are complete.

Disclosures

Paragraph 5.5 sets out the presentation requirements for items of profit or loss, including interest payable. Paragraph 11.48(b) requires disclosure of total interest expense (using the effective interest method) for **financial liabilities** that are not at fair value through profit or loss. When a policy of capitalising borrowing costs is not adopted, this section does not require any additional disclosure.   **25.3**

Where a policy of capitalisation is adopted, an entity shall disclose: **25.3A**

*(a)   the amount of borrowing costs capitalised in the period; and
(b)   the capitalisation rate used.

Section 26 Share-based Payment

Scope of this section

This section specifies the accounting for all **share-based payment transactions** including: **26.1**

(a)   **equity-settled share-based payment transactions**, in which the entity:
   (i)   receives goods or services as consideration for its own equity instruments (including shares or **share options**); or
   (ii)   receives goods or services but has no obligation to settle the transaction with supplier;
(b)   **cash-settled share-based payment transactions**, in which the entity acquires goods or services by incurring a **liability** to transfer **cash** or other assets to the supplier of those goods or services for amounts that are based on the price (or value) of the entity's shares or other equity instruments of the entity or another group entity; and
(c)   transactions in which the entity receives or acquires goods or services and the terms of the arrangement provide either the entity or the supplier of those goods or services with a choice of whether the entity settles the transaction in cash (or other assets) or by issuing equity instruments.

A share-based payment transaction may be settled by another group entity (or a shareholder of any group entity) on behalf of the entity receiving or acquiring the goods or services. Paragraph 26.1 also applies to an entity that: **26.1A**

(a)   receives goods or services when another entity in the same group (or shareholder of any group entity) has the obligation to settle the share-based payment transaction; or
(b)   has an obligation to settle a share-based payment transaction when another entity in the same group receives the goods or services

unless the transaction is clearly for a purpose other than payment for goods or services supplied to the entity receiving them.

Cash-settled share-based payment transactions include share appreciation rights. For example, an entity might grant share appreciation rights to employees as part of their remuneration package, whereby the employees will become entitled to a future cash payment (rather than an equity instrument), based on the increase in the entity's share price from a specified level over a specified period of time. Or an entity might grant to its employees a right to receive a future cash payment by granting to them a right to shares (including shares to be issued upon the exercise of share options) that are redeemable, either mandatorily (eg upon cessation of employment) or at the employee's option.   **26.2**

Recognition

26.3   An entity shall recognise the goods or services received or acquired in a share-based payment transaction when it obtains the goods or as the services are received. The entity shall recognise a corresponding increase in **equity** if the goods or services were received in an equity-settled share-based payment transaction, or a liability if the goods or services were acquired in a cash-settled share-based payment transaction.

26.4   When the goods or services received or acquired in a share-based payment transaction do not qualify for **recognition** as assets, the entity shall recognise them as **expenses**.

Recognition when there are vesting conditions

26.5   If the share-based payments granted to employees **vest** immediately, the employee is not required to complete a specified period of service before becoming unconditionally entitled to those share-based payments. In the absence of evidence to the contrary, the entity shall presume that services rendered by the employee as consideration for the share-based payments have been received. In this case, on **grant date** the entity shall recognise the services received in full, with a corresponding increase in equity or liabilities.

26.6   If the share-based payments do not vest until the employee completes a specified period of service, the entity shall presume that the services to be rendered by the counterparty as consideration for those share-based payments will be received in the future, during the vesting period. The entity shall account for those services as they are rendered by the employee during the vesting period, with a corresponding increase in equity or liabilities.

Measurement of equity-settled share-based payment transactions

Measurement principle

26.7   For equity-settled share-based payment transactions, an entity shall measure the goods or services received, and the corresponding increase in equity, at the **fair value** of the goods or services received, unless that fair value cannot be estimated reliably. If the entity cannot estimate reliably the fair value of the goods or services received, the entity shall measure their value, and the corresponding increase in equity, by reference to the fair value of the equity instruments granted measured in accordance with paragraphs 26.10 and 26.11. To apply this requirement to transactions with employees and others providing similar services, the entity shall measure the fair value of the services received by reference to the fair value of the equity instruments granted, because typically it is not possible to estimate reliably the fair value of the services received.

26.8   For transactions with employees (including others providing similar services), the fair value of the equity instruments shall be measured at grant date. For transactions with parties other than employees, the measurement date is the date when the entity obtains the goods or the counterparty renders service.

26.9   A grant of equity instruments might be conditional on employees satisfying specified vesting conditions related to service or performance. An example of a vesting condition relating to service is where a grant of shares or share options is conditional on the employee remaining in the entity's employ for a specified period of time. Examples of vesting conditions relating to performance are where a grant of shares or share options is conditional on the entity achieving a specified growth in profit (an example of a non-market condition) or a specified increase in the entity's share price (an example of a **market condition**). All vesting conditions related solely to employee service or to a non-market performance condition shall be taken into account when estimating the number of equity instruments expected to vest. Subsequently, the entity shall revise that estimate, if necessary, if new information indicates that the number of equity instruments expected to vest differs from previous estimates. On the vesting date, the entity shall revise the estimate to equal the number of equity instruments that ultimately vested. All market conditions and non-vesting conditions shall be taken into account when estimating the fair value of the shares or share options at the measurement date, with no subsequent adjustment irrespective of the outcome of the market or non-vesting condition, provided that all other vesting conditions are satisfied.

Shares

An entity shall measure the fair value of shares (and the related goods or services received) using the following three-tier measurement hierarchy: **26.10**

(a) If an observable market price is available for the equity instruments granted, use that price.

(b) If an observable market price is not available, measure the fair value of equity instruments granted using entity-specific observable market data such as:

  (i)   a recent transaction in the entity's shares; or
  (ii) a recent independent fair valuation of the entity or its principal assets.

(c) If an observable market price is not available and obtaining a reliable **measurement** of fair value under (b) is **impracticable**, indirectly measure the fair value of the shares using a valuation method that uses market data to the greatest extent practicable to estimate what the price of those equity instruments would be on the grant date in an arm's length transaction between knowledgeable, willing parties. The entity's directors shall use their judgement to apply a generally accepted valuation methodology for valuing equity instruments that is appropriate to the circumstances of the entity.

Share options and equity-settled share appreciation rights

An entity shall measure the fair value of share options and equity-settled share appreciation rights (and the related goods or services received) using the following three-tier measurement hierarchy: **26.11**

(a) If an observable market price is available for the equity instruments granted, use that price.

(b) If an observable market price is not available, measure the fair value of share options and share appreciation rights granted using entity-specific observable market data such as for a recent transaction in the share options.

(c) If an observable market price is not available and obtaining a reliable measurement of fair value under (b) is impracticable, indirectly measure the fair value of share options or share appreciation rights using an alternative valuation methodology such as an option pricing model. The inputs for an option pricing model (such as the weighted average share price, exercise price, expected volatility, option life, expected dividends and the risk-free interest rate) shall use market data to the greatest extent possible. Paragraph 26.10 provides guidance on determining the fair value of the shares used in determining the weighted average share price. The entity shall derive an estimate of expected volatility consistent with the valuation methodology used to determine the fair value of the shares.

Modifications to the terms and conditions on which equity instruments were granted

If an entity modifies the vesting conditions in a manner that is beneficial to the employee, for example, by reducing the exercise price of an option or reducing the vesting period or by modifying or eliminating a performance condition, the entity shall take the modified   **26.12** vesting conditions into account in accounting for the share-based payment transaction, as follows:

(a) If the modification increases the fair value of the equity instruments granted (or increases the number of equity instruments granted) measured immediately before and after the modification, the entity shall include the incremental fair value granted in the measurement of the amount recognised for services received as consideration for the equity instruments granted. The incremental fair value granted is the difference between the fair value of the modified equity instrument and that of the original equity instrument, both estimated as at the date of the modification. If the modification occurs during the vesting period, the incremental fair value granted is included in the measurement of the amount recognised for services received over the period from the modification date until the date when the modified equity instruments vest, in addition to the amount based on the grant date fair value of the original equity instruments, which is recognised over the remainder of the original vesting period.

(b) If the modification reduces the total fair value of the share-based payment arrangement, or apparently is not otherwise beneficial to the employee, the entity shall nevertheless continue to account for the services received as consideration for the equity instruments granted as if that modification had not occurred.

Cancellations and settlements

26.13 An entity shall account for a cancellation or settlement of an equity-settled share-based payment award as an acceleration of vesting, and therefore shall recognise immediately the amount that otherwise would have been recognised for services received over the remainder of the vesting period.

Cash-settled share-based payment transactions

26.14 For cash-settled share-based payment transactions, an entity shall measure the goods or services acquired and the liability incurred at the fair value of the liability. Until the liability is settled, the entity shall remeasure the fair value of the liability at each **reporting date** and at the date of settlement, with any changes in fair value recognised in **profit or loss** for the period.

Share-based payment transactions with cash alternatives

26.15 Some share-based payment transactions give either the entity or the counterparty a choice of settling the transaction in cash (or other assets) or by the transfer of equity instruments.

26.15A When the entity has a choice of settlement of the transaction in cash (or other assets) or by the transfer of equity instruments, the entity shall account for the transaction as a wholly equity-settled share-based payment transaction in accordance with paragraphs 26.7 to 26.13 unless:

(a) the choice of settlement in equity instruments has no commercial substance (eg because the entity is legally prohibited from issuing shares); or

(b) the entity has a past practice or a stated policy of settling in cash, or generally settles in cash whenever the counterparty asks for cash settlement.

In circumstances (a) and (b) the entity shall account for the transaction as a wholly cash-settled transaction in accordance with paragraph 26.14.

26.15B When the counterparty has a choice of settlement of the transaction in cash (or other assets) or by the transfer of equity instruments, the entity shall account for the transaction as a wholly cash-settled share-based payment transaction in accordance with paragraph 26.14 unless:

(a)   the choice of settlement in cash (or other assets) has no commercial substance because the cash settlement amount (or value of the other assets) bears no relationship to, and is likely to be lower in value than, the fair value of the equity instruments.

In circumstance (a) the entity shall account for the transaction as a wholly equity-settled transaction in accordance with paragraphs 26.7 to 26.13.

Group plans

If a share-based payment award is granted by an entity to the employees of one or more   **26.16**
members in the **group**, the members are permitted, as an alternative to the treatment set out
in paragraphs 26.3 to 26.15, to recognise and measure the sharebased payment expense on
the basis of a reasonable allocation of the expense for the group.

Government-mandated plans

Some jurisdictions have programmes established under law by which equity investors   **26.17**
(such as employees) are able to acquire equity without providing goods or services that
can be specifically identified (or by providing goods or services that are clearly less than
the fair value of the equity instruments granted). This indicates that other consideration
has been or will be received (such as past or future employee services). These are equity-
settled share-based payment transactions within the scope of this section. The entity shall
measure the unidentifiable goods or services received (or to be received) as the difference
between the fair value of the share-based payment and the fair value of any identifiable
goods or services received (or to be received) measured at the grant date.

Disclosures

An entity shall disclose the following information about the nature and extent of share-   **26.18**
based payment arrangements that existed during the period:

(a)   A description of each type of share-based payment arrangement that existed at
      any time during the period, including the general terms and conditions of each
      arrangement, such as vesting requirements, the maximum term of options granted,
      and the method of settlement (eg whether in cash or equity). An entity with
      substantially similar types of share-based payment arrangements may aggregate this
      information.
(b)   The number and weighted average exercise prices of share options for each of the
      following groups of options:

      (i)   outstanding at the beginning of the period;
      (ii)   granted during the period;
      (iii)   forfeited during the period;
      (iv)   exercised during the period;
      (v)   expired during the period;
      (vi)   outstanding at the end of the period; and
      (vii)   exercisable at the end of the period.

For equity-settled share-based payment arrangements, an entity shall disclose information   **26.19**
about how it measured the fair value of goods or services received or the value of the
equity instruments granted. If a valuation methodology was used, the entity shall disclose
the method and its reason for choosing it.

26.20   For cash-settled share-based payment arrangements, an entity shall disclose information about how the liability was measured.

26.21   For share-based payment arrangements that were modified during the period, an entity shall disclose an explanation of those modifications.

26.22   If the entity is part of a group share-based payment plan, and it recognises and measures its share-based payment expense on the basis of a reasonable allocation of the expense recognised for the group, it shall disclose that fact and the basis for the allocation (see paragraph 26.16).

26.23   An entity shall disclose the following information about the effect of share-based payment transactions on the entity's profit or loss for the period and on its **financial position**:

   (a)   the total expense recognised in profit or loss for the period; and

   (b)   the total **carrying amount** at the end of the period for liabilities arising from share-based payment transactions.

Section 27 Impairment of Assets

Objective and scope

27.1   An **impairment loss** occurs when the **carrying amount** of an **asset** exceeds its **recoverable amount**. This section shall be applied in accounting for the impairment of all assets other than the following, for which other sections of this FRS establish impairment requirements:

   (a)   assets arising from **construction contracts** (see Section 23 *Revenue*);

   (b)   **deferred tax assets** (see Section 29 *Income Tax*);

   (c)   assets arising from **employee benefits** (see Section 28 *Employee Benefits*);

   (d)   **financial assets** within the scope of Section 11 *Basic Financial Instruments* or Section 12 *Other Financial Instruments Issues*;

   (e)   **investment property** measured at **fair value** (see Section 16 *Investment Property*); and

   (f)   **biological assets** related to **agricultural activity** measured at fair value less estimated costs to sell (see Section 34 *Specialised Activities*).

27.1A   This section shall not apply in accounting for the impairment of **deferred acquisition costs** and **intangible assets** arising from contracts within the scope of FRS 103 *Insurance Contracts*.

Impairment of inventories

Selling price less costs to complete and sell

27.2   An entity shall assess at each **reporting date** whether any **inventories** are impaired. The entity shall make the assessment by comparing the carrying amount of each item of inventory (or group of similar items – see paragraph 27.3) with its selling price less costs to complete and sell. If an item of inventory (or group of similar items) is impaired, the entity shall reduce the carrying amount of the inventory (or the group) to its selling price less costs to complete and sell. That reduction is an impairment loss and it is recognised immediately in **profit or loss**.

27.3   If it is **impracticable** to determine the selling price less costs to complete and sell for inventories item by item, the entity may group items of inventory relating to the same product line that have similar purposes or end uses and are produced and marketed in the same geographical area for the purpose of assessing impairment.

Reversal of impairment

An entity shall make a new assessment of selling price less costs to complete and sell at   **27.4**
each subsequent reporting date. When the circumstances that previously caused inventories
to be impaired no longer exist or when there is clear evidence of an increase in selling price
less costs to complete and sell because of changed economic circumstances, the entity
shall reverse the amount of the impairment (ie the reversal is limited to the amount of the
original impairment loss) so that the new carrying amount is the lower of the cost and the
revised selling price less costs to complete and sell.

Impairment of assets other than inventories

General principles

If, and only if, the recoverable amount of an asset is less than its carrying amount, the entity   **27.5**
shall reduce the carrying amount of the asset to its recoverable amount. That reduction is an
impairment loss. Paragraphs 27.11 to 27.20A provide guidance on measuring recoverable
amount.

An entity shall recognise an impairment loss immediately in profit or loss, unless the   **27.6**
asset is carried at a revalued amount in accordance with another section of this FRS (for
example, in accordance with the revaluation model in Section 17 *Property, Plant and
Equipment*). Any impairment loss of a revalued asset shall be treated as a revaluation
decrease in accordance with that other section.

Indicators of impairment

An entity shall assess at each reporting date whether there is any indication that an asset   **27.7**
may be impaired. If any such indication exists, the entity shall estimate the recoverable
amount of the asset. If there is no indication of impairment, it is not necessary to estimate
the recoverable amount.

If it is not possible to estimate the recoverable amount of the individual asset, an entity   **27.8**
shall estimate the recoverable amount of the **cash-generating unit** to which the asset
belongs. This may be the case because measuring recoverable amount requires forecasting
cash flows, and sometimes individual assets do not generate cash flows by themselves.
An asset's cash-generating unit is the smallest identifiable group of assets that includes
the asset and generates cash inflows that are largely independent of the cash inflows from
other assets or groups of assets.

In assessing whether there is any indication that an asset may be impaired, an entity shall   **27.9**
consider, as a minimum, the following indications:

External sources of information
(a)   During the period, an asset's market value has declined significantly more than
      would be expected as a result of the passage of time or normal use.
(b)   Significant changes with an adverse effect on the entity have taken place during the
      period, or will take place in the near future, in the technological, market, economic
      or legal environment in which the entity operates or in the market to which an asset
      is dedicated.
(c)   Market interest rates or other market rates of return on investments have increased
      during the period, and those increases are likely to affect materially the discount rate
      used in calculating an asset's **value in use** and decrease the asset's **fair value less
      costs to sell**.

(d)   The carrying amount of the net assets of the entity is more than the estimated fair value of the entity as a whole (such an estimate may have been made, for example, in relation to the potential sale of part or all of the entity).

Internal sources of information

(e)   Evidence is available of obsolescence or physical damage of an asset.

(f)   Significant changes with an adverse effect on the entity have taken place during the period, or are expected to take place in the near future, in the extent to which, or manner in which, an asset is used or is expected to be used. These changes include the asset becoming idle, plans to discontinue or restructure the operation to which an asset belongs, plans to dispose of an asset before the previously expected date, and reassessing the **useful life** of an asset as finite rather than indefinite.

(g)   Evidence is available from internal reporting that indicates that the economic performance of an asset is, or will be, worse than expected. In this context economic performance includes operating results and cash flows.

27.10   If there is an indication that an asset may be impaired, this may indicate that the entity should review the remaining useful life, the **depreciation (amortisation)** method or the **residual value** for the asset and adjust it in accordance with the section of this FRS applicable to the asset (eg Section 17 *Property, Plant and Equipment* and Section 18 *Intangible Assets other than Goodwill*), even if no impairment loss is recognised for the asset.

Measuring recoverable amount

27.11   The recoverable amount of an asset or a cash-generating unit is the higher of its fair value less costs to sell and its value in use. If it is not possible to estimate the recoverable amount of an individual asset, references to an asset in paragraphs 27.12 to 27.20A should be read as references also to an asset's cash-generating unit.

27.12   It is not always necessary to determine both an asset's fair value less costs to sell and its value in use. If either of these amounts exceeds the asset's carrying amount, the asset is not impaired and it is not necessary to estimate the other amount.

27.13   If there is no reason to believe that an asset's value in use materially exceeds its fair value less costs to sell, the asset's fair value less costs to sell may be used as its recoverable amount. This will often be the case for an asset that is held for disposal.

Fair value less costs to sell

27.14   Fair value less costs to sell is the amount obtainable from the sale of an asset in an arm's length transaction between knowledgeable, willing parties, less the costs of disposal. The best evidence of the fair value less costs to sell of an asset is a price in a binding sale agreement in an arm's length transaction or a market price in an **active market**. If there is no binding sale agreement or active market for an asset, fair value less costs to sell is based on the best information available to reflect the amount that an entity could obtain, at the reporting date, from the disposal of the asset in an arm's length transaction between knowledgeable, willing parties, after deducting the costs of disposal. In determining this amount, an entity considers the outcome of recent transactions for similar assets within the same industry.

27.14A   When determining an asset's fair value less costs to sell, consideration shall be given to any restrictions imposed on that asset. Costs to sell shall also include the cost of obtaining relaxation of a restriction where necessary in order to enable the asset to be sold. If a restriction would also apply to any potential purchaser of an asset, the fair value of the asset may be lower than that of an asset whose use is not restricted.

Value in use

Value in use is the **present value** of the future cash flows expected to be derived from an asset. This present value calculation involves the following steps:

27.15

(a)   estimating the future cash inflows and outflows to be derived from continuing use of the asset and from its ultimate disposal; and

(b)   applying the appropriate discount rate to those future cash flows.

The following elements shall be reflected in the calculation of an asset's value in use:

27.16

(a)   an estimate of the future cash flows the entity expects to derive from the asset;

(b)   expectations about possible variations in the amount or timing of those future cash flows;

(c)   the time value of money, represented by the current market risk-free rate of interest;

(d)   the price for bearing the uncertainty inherent in the asset; and

(e)   other factors, such as illiquidity, that market participants would reflect in pricing the future cash flows the entity expects to derive from the asset.

In measuring value in use, estimates of future cash flows shall include:

27.17

(a)   projections of cash inflows from the continuing use of the asset;

(b)   projections of cash outflows that are necessarily incurred to generate the cash inflows from continuing use of the asset (including cash outflows to prepare the asset for use) and can be directly attributed, or allocated on a reasonable and consistent basis, to the asset; and

(c)   net cash flows, if any, expected to be received (or paid) for the disposal of the asset at the end of its useful life in an arm's length transaction between knowledgeable, willing parties.

The entity may wish to use any recent financial budgets or forecasts to estimate the cash flows, if available. To estimate cash flow projections beyond the period covered by the most recent budgets or forecasts an entity may wish to extrapolate the projections based on the budgets or forecasts using a steady or declining growth rate for subsequent years, unless an increasing rate can be justified.

Estimates of future cash flows shall not include:

27.18

(a)   cash inflows or outflows from **financing activities**; or

(b)   income tax receipts or payments.

Future cash flows shall be estimated for the asset in its current condition. Estimates of future cash flows shall not include estimated future cash inflows or outflows that are expected to arise from:

27.19

(a)   a future restructuring to which an entity is not yet committed; or

(b)   improving or enhancing the asset's performance.

The discount rate (rates) used in the present value calculation shall be a pre-tax rate (rates) that reflect(s) current market assessments of:

27.20

(a)   the time value of money; and

(b)   the risks specific to the asset for which the future cash flow estimates have not been adjusted.

The discount rate (rates) used to measure an asset's value in use shall not reflect risks for which the future cash flow estimates have been adjusted, to avoid double-counting.

27.20A   For assets held for their **service potential**, a cash flow driven valuation (such as value in use) may not be appropriate. In these circumstances **value in use (in respect of assets held for their service potential)** is determined by the present value of the asset's remaining service potential plus the net amount the entity will receive from its disposal. In some cases this may be taken to be costs avoided by possession of the asset. Therefore, **depreciated replacement cost**, may be a suitable measurement model but other approaches may be used where more appropriate.

Recognising and measuring an impairment loss for a cash-generating unit

27.21   An impairment loss shall be recognised for a cash-generating unit if, and only if, the recoverable amount of the unit is less than the carrying amount of the unit. The impairment loss shall be allocated to reduce the carrying amount of the assets of the unit in the following order:

(a)   first, to reduce the carrying amount of any **goodwill** allocated to the cash-generating unit; and

(b)   then, to the other assets of the unit pro rata on the basis of the carrying amount of each asset in the cash-generating unit.

27.22   However, an entity shall not reduce the carrying amount of any asset in the cash-generating unit below the highest of:

(a)   its fair value less costs to sell (if determinable);

(b)   its value in use (if determinable); and

(c)   zero.

27.23   Any excess amount of the impairment loss that cannot be allocated to an asset because of the restriction in paragraph 27.22 shall be allocated to the other assets of the unit pro rata on the basis of the carrying amount of those other assets.

Additional requirements for impairment of goodwill

27.24   Goodwill, by itself, cannot be sold. Nor does it generate cash flows to an entity that are independent of the cash flows of other assets. As a consequence, the fair value of goodwill cannot be measured directly. Therefore, the fair value of goodwill must be derived from **measurement** of the fair value of the cash-generating unit(s) of which the goodwill is a part.

27.25   For the purpose of impairment testing, goodwill acquired in a **business combination** shall, from the **acquisition date**, be allocated to each of the acquirer's cash-generating units that are expected to benefit from the synergies of the combination, irrespective of whether other assets or **liabilities** of the acquiree are assigned to those units.

27.26   Part of the recoverable amount of a cash-generating unit is attributable to the **non-controlling interest** in goodwill. For the purpose of impairment testing of a non-wholly-owned cash-generating unit with goodwill, the carrying amount of that unit is notionally adjusted, before being compared with its recoverable amount, by grossing up the carrying amount of goodwill allocated to the unit to include the goodwill attributable to the non-controlling interest. This notionally adjusted carrying amount is then compared with the recoverable amount of the unit to determine whether the cash-generating unit is impaired.

27.27   If goodwill cannot be allocated to individual cash-generating units (or groups of cash-generating units) on a non-arbitrary basis, then for the purposes of testing goodwill the entity shall test the impairment of goodwill by determining the recoverable amount of either:

(a)　the acquired entity in its entirety, if the goodwill relates to an acquired entity that has not been integrated. Integrated means the acquired **business** has been restructured or dissolved into the reporting entity or other **subsidiaries**; or

(b)　the entire group of entities, excluding any entities that have not been integrated, if the goodwill relates to an entity that has been integrated.

In applying this paragraph, an entity will need to separate goodwill into goodwill relating to entities that have been integrated and goodwill relating to entities that have not been integrated. Also the entity shall follow the requirements for cash-generating units in this section when calculating the recoverable amount of, and allocating impairment losses and reversals to assets belonging to, the acquired entity or group of entities.

Reversal of an impairment loss

An impairment loss recognised for goodwill shall not be reversed in a subsequent period.　**27.28**

For all assets other than goodwill, if and only if the reasons for the impairment loss have ceased　**27.29**
to apply, an impairment loss shall be reversed in a subsequent period. An entity shall assess at each reporting date whether there is any indication that an impairment loss recognised in prior periods may no longer exist or may have decreased. Indications that an impairment loss may have decreased or may no longer exist are generally the opposite of those set out in paragraph 27.9. If any such indication exists, the entity shall determine whether all or part of the prior impairment loss should be reversed. The procedure for making that determination will depend on whether the prior impairment loss on the asset was based on:

(a)　the recoverable amount of that individual asset (see paragraph 27.30); or

(b)　the recoverable amount of the cash-generating unit to which the asset belongs (see paragraph 27.31).

Reversal where recoverable amount was estimated for an individual impaired asset

When the prior impairment loss was based on the recoverable amount of the individual　**27.30**
impaired asset, the following requirements apply:

(a)　The entity shall estimate the recoverable amount of the asset at the current reporting date.

(b)　If the estimated recoverable amount of the asset exceeds its carrying amount, the entity shall increase the carrying amount to recoverable amount, subject to the limitation described in (c) below. That increase is a reversal of an impairment loss. The entity shall recognise the reversal immediately in profit or loss unless the asset is carried at revalued amount in accordance with another section of this FRS (for example, the revaluation model in Section 17 *Property, plant and equipment*). Any reversal of an impairment loss of a revalued asset shall be treated as a revaluation increase in accordance with the relevant section of this FRS.

(c)　The reversal of an impairment loss shall not increase the carrying amount of the asset above the carrying amount that would have been determined (net of amortisation or depreciation) had no impairment loss been recognised for the asset in prior years.

(d)　After a reversal of an impairment loss is recognised, the entity shall adjust the depreciation (amortisation) charge for the asset in future periods to allocate the asset's revised carrying amount, less its residual value (if any), on a systematic basis over its remaining useful life.

Reversal when recoverable amount was estimated for a cash-generating unit

When the original impairment loss was based on the recoverable amount of the cash-　**27.31**
generating unit to which the asset, including goodwill belongs, the following requirements apply:

(a)   The entity shall estimate the recoverable amount of that cash-generating unit at the current reporting date.

(b)   If the estimated recoverable amount of the cash-generating unit exceeds its carrying amount, that excess is a reversal of an impairment loss. The entity shall allocate the amount of that reversal to the assets of the unit, except for goodwill, pro rata with the carrying amounts of those assets, subject to the limitation described in (c) below. Those increases in carrying amounts shall be treated as reversals of impairment losses and recognised immediately in profit or loss unless an asset is carried at revalued amount in accordance with another section of this FRS (for example, the revaluation model in Section 17 *Property, plant and equipment*). Any reversal of an impairment loss of a revalued asset shall be treated as a revaluation increase in accordance with the relevant section of this FRS.

(c)   In allocating a reversal of an impairment loss for a cash-generating unit, the reversal shall not increase the carrying amount of any asset above the lower of:

    (i)   its recoverable amount; and
    (ii)   the carrying amount that would have been determined (net of amortisation or depreciation) had no impairment loss been recognised for the asset in prior periods.

(d)   Any excess amount of the reversal of the impairment loss that cannot be allocated to an asset because of the restriction in (c) above shall be allocated pro rata to the other assets of the cash-generating unit, except for goodwill.

(e)   After a reversal of an impairment loss is recognised, if applicable, the entity shall adjust the depreciation (amortisation) charge for each asset in the cash-generating unit in future periods to allocate the asset's revised carrying amount, less its residual value (if any), on a systematic basis over its remaining useful life.

Disclosures

27.32   An entity shall disclose the following for each **class of assets** indicated in paragraph 27.33:

*(a)   the amount of impairment losses recognised in profit or loss during the period and the line item(s) in the **statement of comprehensive income** (or in the **income statement**, if presented) in which those impairment losses are included; and

*(b)   the amount of reversals of impairment losses recognised in profit or loss during the period and the line item(s) in the statement of comprehensive income (or in the income statement, if presented) in which those impairment losses are reversed.

27.33   An entity shall disclose the information required by paragraph 27.32 for each of the following classes of asset:

(a)   inventories;
(b)   **property, plant and equipment** (including investment property accounted for by the cost method);
(c)   goodwill;
(d)   **intangible assets** other than goodwill;
(e)   investments in **associates**; and
(f)   investments in **joint ventures**.

27.33A   An entity shall disclose a description of the events and circumstances that led to the **recognition** or reversal of the impairment loss.

Section 28 Employee Benefits

Scope of this section

Employee benefits are all forms of consideration given by an entity in exchange for service   **28.1**
rendered by employees, including directors and management. This section applies to all
employee benefits, except for **share-based payment transactions**, which are covered by
Section 26 *Share-based Payment*. Employee benefits covered by this section will be one
of the following four types:

(a)   short-term employee benefits, which are employee benefits (other than **termination
      benefits**) that are expected to be settled wholly before twelve months after the end of
      the **reporting period** in which the employees render the related service;
(b)   **post-employment benefits**, which are employee benefits (other than termination
      benefits and short-term employee benefits) that are payable after the completion of
      employment;
(c)   other long-term employee benefits, which are all employee benefits, other than
      short-term employee benefits, post-employment benefits and termination benefits;
      or
(d)   termination benefits, which are employee benefits provided in exchange for the
      termination of an employee's employment as a result of either:

      (i)   an entity's decision to terminate an employee's employment before the normal
            retirement date; or
      (ii) an employee's decision to accept voluntary redundancy in exchange for those
            benefits.

[Not used]   **28.2**

General recognition principle for all employee benefits

An entity shall recognise the cost of all employee benefits to which its employees have   **28.3**
become entitled as a result of service rendered to the entity during the reporting period:

(a)   As a **liability**, after deducting amounts that have been paid either directly to the
      employees or as a contribution to an employee benefit fund[12]. If the amount paid
      exceeds the obligation arising from service before the **reporting date**, an entity shall
      recognise that excess as an asset to the extent that the prepayment will lead to a
      reduction in future payments or a cash refund.
(b)   As an **expense**, unless another section of this FRS requires the cost to be recognised
      as part of the cost of an asset such as **inventories** (for example in accordance with
      paragraph 13.8) or **property, plant and equipment** (in accordance with paragraph
      17.10).

Short-term employee benefits

Examples

Short-term employee benefits include items such as the following, if expected to be   **28.4**
settled wholly before 12 months after the end of the annual reporting period in which the
employees render the related service:

---

[12] *Contributions to an employee benefit fund that is an intermediate payment arrangement shall be accounted for
in accordance with paragraphs 9.33 to 9.38, and as a result if the employer is a sponsoring entity the assets and
liabilities of the intermediary will be accounted for by the sponsoring entity as an extension of its own business. In
which case the payment to the employee benefit fund does not extinguish the liability of the employer.*

(a)   wages, salaries and social security contributions;

(b)   paid annual leave and paid sick leave;

(c)   profit-sharing and bonuses; and

(d)   non-monetary benefits (such as medical care, housing, cars and free or subsidised goods or services) for current employees.

Measurement of short-term benefits generally

28.5   When an employee has rendered service to an entity during the reporting period, the entity shall measure the amounts recognised in accordance with paragraph 28.3 at the undiscounted amount of short-term employee benefits expected to be paid in exchange for that service.

Recognition and measurement: Short-term compensated absences

28.6   An entity may compensate employees for absence for various reasons including annual leave and sick leave. Some short-term compensated absences accumulate—they can be carried forward and used in future periods if the employee does not use the current period's entitlement in full. Examples include annual leave and sick leave. An entity shall recognise the expected cost of **accumulating compensated absences** when the employees render service that increases their entitlement to future compensated absences. The entity shall measure the expected cost of accumulating compensated absences at the undiscounted additional amount that the entity expects to pay as a result of the unused entitlement that has accumulated at the end of the reporting period. The entity shall present this amount as falling due within one year at the reporting date.

28.7   An entity shall recognise the cost of other (non-accumulating) compensated absences when the absences occur. The entity shall measure the cost of non-accumulating compensated absences at the undiscounted amount of salaries and wages paid or payable for the period of absence.

Recognition: Profit-sharing and bonus plans

28.8   An entity shall recognise the expected cost of profit-sharing and bonus payments only when:

(a)   the entity has a present legal or **constructive obligation** to make such payments as a result of past events (this means that the entity has no realistic alternative but to make the payments); and

(b)   a reliable estimate of the obligation can be made.

Post-employment benefits: Distinction between defined contribution plans and defined benefit plans

28.9   Post-employment benefits include, for example:

(a)   retirement benefits, such as pensions; and

(b)   other post-employment benefits, such as post-employment life insurance and post-employment medical care.

Arrangements whereby an entity provides post-employment benefits are **post-employment benefit plans**. An entity shall apply this section to all such arrangements whether or not they involve the establishment of a separate entity to receive contributions and to pay benefits. In some cases, these arrangements are imposed by law rather than by action of the entity. In some cases, these arrangements arise from actions of the entity even in the absence of a formal, documented plan.

Post-employment benefit plans are classified as either **defined contribution plans** or **defined benefit plans**, depending on their principal terms and conditions:

    28.10

(a)   Defined contribution plans are post-employment benefit plans under which an entity pays fixed contributions into a separate entity (a fund) and has no legal or constructive obligation to pay further contributions or to make direct benefit payments to employees if the fund does not hold sufficient assets to pay all employee benefits relating to employee service in the current and prior periods. Thus, the amount of the post-employment benefits received by the employee is determined by the amount of contributions paid by an entity (and perhaps also the employee) to a post-employment benefit plan or to an insurer, together with investment returns arising from the contributions.

(b)   Defined benefit plans are post-employment benefit plans other than defined contribution plans. Under defined benefit plans, the entity's obligation is to provide the agreed benefits to current and former employees, and actuarial risk (that benefits will cost more or less than expected) and investment risk (that returns on assets set aside to fund the benefits will differ from expectations) are borne, in substance, by the entity. If actuarial or investment experience is worse than expected, the entity's obligation may be increased, and vice versa if actuarial or investment experience is better than expected.

Multi-employer plans and state plans

Multi-employer plans and **state plans** are classified as defined contribution plans or defined benefit plans on the basis of the terms of the plan, including any constructive obligation that goes beyond the formal terms. However, if sufficient information is not available to use defined benefit accounting for a multi-employer plan that is a defined benefit plan, an entity shall account for the plan in accordance with paragraphs 28.13 and 28.13A as if it was a defined contribution plan and make the disclosures required by paragraphs 28.40 and 28.40A. An entity shall account for a state plan in the same way as for a multi-employer plan.

    28.11

Where an entity participates in a defined benefit plan, which is a multi-employer plan that in accordance with paragraph 28.11 is accounted for as if the plan were a defined contribution plan, and the entity has entered into an agreement with the multi-employer plan that determines how the entity will fund a deficit, the entity shall recognise a liability for the contributions payable that arise from the agreement (to the extent that they relate to the deficit) and the resulting expense in **profit or loss** in accordance with paragraphs 28.13 and 28.13A.

    28.11A

Insured benefits

An entity may pay insurance premiums to fund a post-employment benefit plan. The entity shall treat such a plan as a defined contribution plan unless the entity has a legal or constructive obligation either:

    28.12

(a)   to pay the employee benefits directly when they become due; or

(b)   to pay further amounts if the insurer does not pay all future employee benefits relating to employee service in the current and prior periods.

A constructive obligation could arise indirectly through the plan, through the mechanism for setting future premiums, or through a **related party** relationship with the insurer. If the entity retains such a legal or constructive obligation, the entity shall treat the plan as a defined benefit plan.

Post-employment benefits: Defined contribution plans

Recognition and measurement

28.13   An entity shall recognise the contribution payable for a period:

(a)   As a liability, after deducting any amount already paid. If contribution payments exceed the contribution due for service before the reporting date, an entity shall recognise that excess as an asset to the extent that the prepayment will lead to a reduction in future payments or a cash refund.

(b)   As an expense, unless another section of this FRS requires the cost to be recognised as part of the cost of an asset such as inventories or property, plant and equipment.

28.13A   When contributions to a defined contribution plan (or a defined benefit plan which, in accordance with paragraph 28.11, is accounted for as a defined contribution plan) are not expected to be settled wholly within 12 months after the end of the reporting period in which the employees render the related service, the liability shall be measured at the **present value** of the contributions payable using the methodology for selecting a discount rate specified in paragraph 28.17. The unwinding of the discount shall be recognised as a finance cost in profit or loss in the period in which it arises.

Post-employment benefits: Defined benefit plans

Recognition

28.14   In applying the general **recognition** principle in paragraph 28.3 to defined benefit plans, an entity shall recognise:

(a)   a liability for its obligations under defined benefit plans net of **plan assets**—its '**net defined benefit liability**' (see paragraphs 28.15 to 28.22); and

(b)   the net change in that liability during the period as the cost of its defined benefit plans during the period (see paragraphs 28.23 to 28.27).

Measurement of the net defined benefit liability

28.15   An entity shall measure the net defined benefit liability for its obligations under defined benefit plans at the net total of the following amounts:

(a)   the present value of its obligations under defined benefit plans (its **defined benefit obligation**) at the reporting date (paragraphs 28.16 to 28.21A provide guidance for measuring this obligation); minus

(b)   the **fair value** at the reporting date of plan assets (if any) out of which the obligations are to be settled. Paragraphs 11.27 to 11.32 establish requirements for determining the fair values of those plan assets, except that, if the asset is an insurance policy that exactly matches the amount and timing of some or all of the benefits payable under the plan, the fair value of the asset is deemed to be the present value of the related obligation.

28.15A   Where an entity has measured its defined benefit obligation using the **projected unit credit method** (including the use of appropriate **actuarial assumptions**), as set out in paragraph 28.18, it shall not recognise any additional liabilities to reflect differences between these assumptions and those used for the most recent actuarial valuation of the plan for funding purposes. For the avoidance of doubt, no additional liabilities shall be recognised in respect of an agreement with the defined benefit plan to fund a deficit (such as a schedule of contributions).

Inclusion of both vested and unvested benefits

The present value of an entity's obligations under defined benefit plans at the reporting **28.16**
date shall reflect the estimated amount of benefit that employees have earned in return
for their service in the current and prior periods, including benefits that are not yet
vested (see paragraph 28.26) and including the effects of benefit formulas that give
employees greater benefits for later years of service. This requires the entity to
determine how much benefit is attributable to the current and prior periods on the
basis of the plan's benefit formula and to make estimates (actuarial assumptions) about
demographic variables (such as employee turnover and mortality) and financial variables
(such as future increases in salaries and medical costs) that influence the cost of the
benefit. The actuarial assumptions shall be unbiased (neither imprudent nor excessively
conservative), mutually compatible, and selected to lead to the best estimate of the future
cash flows that will arise under the plan.

Discounting

An entity shall measure its defined benefit obligation on a discounted present value basis. **28.17**
The entity shall determine the rate used to discount the future payments by reference to
market yields at the reporting date on high quality corporate bonds. In countries with no
deep market in such bonds, the entity shall use the market yields (at the reporting date) on
government bonds. The currency and term of the corporate bonds or government bonds
shall be consistent with the currency and estimated period of the future payments.

Actuarial valuation method

An entity shall use the projected unit credit method to measure its defined benefit obligation **28.18**
and the related expense. If defined benefits are based on future salaries, the projected unit
credit method requires an entity to measure its defined benefit obligations on a basis that
reflects estimated future salary increases. Additionally, the projected unit credit method
requires an entity to make various actuarial assumptions in measuring the defined benefit
obligation, including discount rates, employee turnover, mortality, and (for defined benefit
medical plans) medical cost trend rates.

[Not used] **28.19**

This FRS does not require an entity to engage an independent actuary to perform the **28.20**
comprehensive actuarial valuation needed to calculate its defined benefit obligation. Nor
does it require that a comprehensive actuarial valuation must be done annually. In the
periods between comprehensive actuarial valuations, if the principal actuarial assumptions
have not changed significantly the defined benefit obligation can be measured by adjusting
the prior period measurement for changes in employee demographics such as number of
employees and salary levels.

Plan introductions, changes, curtailments and settlements

If a defined benefit plan has been introduced or the benefits have changed in the current **28.21**
period, the entity shall increase or decrease its net defined benefit liability to reflect the
change, and shall recognise the increase (decrease) as an expense (**income**) in measuring
profit or loss in the current reporting period.

If a defined benefit plan has been curtailed (ie benefits or group of covered employees **28.21A**
are reduced) or settled (the relevant part of the employer's obligation is completely
discharged) in the current period, the defined benefit obligation shall be decreased or
eliminated, and the entity shall recognise the resulting **gain** or loss in profit or loss in the
current period.

Defined benefit plan asset

28.22   If the present value of the defined benefit obligation at the reporting date is less than the fair value of plan assets at that date, the plan has a surplus. An entity shall recognise a plan surplus as a defined benefit plan asset only to the extent that it is able to recover the surplus either through reduced contributions in the future or through refunds from the plan.

Cost of a defined benefit plan

28.23   An entity shall recognise the cost of a defined benefit plan, except to the extent that another section of this FRS requires part or all of the cost to be recognised as part of the cost of an asset, as follows:

  (a)   the change in the net defined benefit liability arising from employee service rendered during the reporting period in profit or loss;

  (b)   net interest on the net defined benefit liability during the reporting period in profit or loss;

  (c)   the cost of plan introductions, benefit changes, curtailments and settlements in profit or loss (see paragraphs 28.21 and 28.21A); and

  (d)   remeasurement of the net defined benefit liability in **other comprehensive income**.

Some defined benefit plans require employees or third parties to contribute to the cost of the plan. Contributions by employees reduce the cost of the benefits to the entity.

28.24   The net interest on the net defined benefit liability shall be determined by multiplying the net defined benefit liability by the discount rate in paragraph 28.17, both as determined at the start of the annual reporting period, taking account of any changes in the net defined benefit liability during the period as a result of contribution and benefit payments.

28.24A   The net interest on the net defined benefit liability can be viewed as comprising interest cost on the defined benefit obligation and interest income on plan assets excluding the effect of any surplus that is not recoverable in accordance with paragraph 28.22.

28.24B   Interest income on plan assets, excluding the effect of any surplus that is not recoverable in accordance with paragraph 28.22, is a component of the return on plan assets, and is determined by multiplying the fair value of the plan assets by the discount rate specified in paragraph 28.17 both as determined at the start of the annual reporting period, taking account of any changes in the plan assets held during the period as a result of contribution and benefit payments. The difference between the interest income on plan assets and the return on plan assets is included in the remeasurement of the net defined benefit liability.

28.25   Remeasurement of the net defined benefit liability comprises:

  (a)   **actuarial gains and losses**;

  (b)   the return on plan assets, excluding amounts included in net interest on the net defined benefit liability; and

  (c)   any change in the amount of a defined benefit plan surplus that is not recoverable (see paragraph 28.22), excluding amounts included in net interest on the net defined benefit liability.

28.25A   Remeasurement of the net defined benefit liability recognised in other comprehensive income shall not be reclassified to profit or loss in a subsequent period.

28.26   Employee service gives rise to an obligation under a defined benefit plan even if the benefits are conditional on future employment (in other words, they are not yet vested). Employee service before the vesting date gives rise to a constructive obligation because, at each successive reporting date, the amount of future service that an employee will have to render before becoming entitled to the benefit is reduced. In measuring its defined benefit obligation, an entity considers the probability that some employees may not satisfy vesting requirements. Similarly, although some post-employment benefits (such as post-employment medical benefits) become payable only if a specified event occurs when an employee is no longer employed (such as an illness), an obligation is created when the employee renders service that will provide entitlement to the benefit if the specified event occurs. The probability that the specified event will occur affects the **measurement** of the obligation, but does not determine whether the obligation exists.

If defined benefits are reduced for amounts that will be paid to employees under government-sponsored plans, an entity shall measure its defined benefit obligations on a basis that reflects the benefits payable under the government plans, but only if: **28.27**

(a) those plans were enacted before the reporting date; or
(b) past history, or other reliable evidence, indicates that those state benefits will change in some predictable manner, for example, in line with future changes in general price levels or general salary levels.

Reimbursements

If an entity is virtually certain that another party will reimburse some or all of the expenditure required to settle a defined benefit obligation, the entity shall recognise its right to reimbursement as a separate asset. An entity shall treat that asset in the same way as plan assets. **28.28**

Other long-term employee benefits

Other long-term employee benefits include items such as the following, if not expected to be settled wholly before 12 months after the end of the annual reporting period in which the employees render the related service: **28.29**

(a) long-term paid absences such as long-service or sabbatical leave;
(b) other long-service benefits;
(c) long-term disability benefits;
(d) profit-sharing and bonuses; and
(e) deferred remuneration.

An entity shall recognise a liability for other long-term employee benefits measured at the net total of the following amounts: **28.30**

(a) the present value of the benefit obligation at the reporting date (calculated using the methodology for selecting a discount rate in paragraph 28.17); minus
(b) the fair value at the reporting date of plan assets (if any) out of which the obligations are to be settled directly.

An entity shall recognise the change in the liability in profit or loss, except to the extent that this FRS requires or permits their inclusion in the cost of an asset.

Termination benefits

An entity may be committed, by legislation, by contractual or other agreements with employees or their representatives or by a constructive obligation based on business practice, custom or a desire to act equitably, to make payments (or provide other benefits) to employees when it terminates their employment. Such payments are termination benefits. **28.31**

Recognition

28.32   Because termination benefits do not provide an entity with future economic benefits, an entity shall recognise them as an expense in profit or loss immediately.

28.33   When an entity recognises termination benefits, the entity may also have to account for a curtailment of retirement benefits or other employee benefits.

28.34   An entity shall recognise termination benefits as a liability and an expense only when the entity is demonstrably committed either:

    (a)   to terminate the employment of an employee or group of employees before the normal retirement date; or

    (b)   to provide termination benefits as a result of an offer made in order to encourage voluntary redundancy.

28.35   An entity is demonstrably committed to a termination only when the entity has a detailed formal plan for the termination[13] and is without realistic possibility of withdrawal from the plan.

Measurement

28.36   An entity shall measure termination benefits at the best estimate of the expenditure that would be required to settle the obligation at the reporting date. In the case of an offer made to encourage voluntary redundancy, the measurement of termination benefits shall be based on the number of employees expected to accept the offer.

28.37   When termination benefits are due more than 12 months after the end of the reporting period, they shall be measured at their discounted present value using the methodology for selecting a discount rate specified in paragraph 28.17.

Group plans

28.38   Where an entity participates in a defined benefit plan that shares risks between entities under common control it shall obtain information about the plan as a whole measured in accordance with this FRS on the basis of assumptions that apply to the plan as a whole. If there is a contractual agreement or stated policy for charging the net defined benefit cost of a defined benefit plan as a whole measured in accordance with this FRS to individual group entities, the entity shall, in its individual financial statements, recognise the net defined benefit cost of a defined benefit plan so charged. If there is no such agreement or policy, the net defined benefit cost of a defined benefit plan shall be recognised in the individual financial statements of the group entity which is legally responsible for the plan. The other group entities shall, in their **individual financial statements**, recognise a cost equal to their contribution payable for the period.

Disclosures

Disclosures about short-term employee benefits

28.39   This section does not require specific disclosures about short-term employee benefits.

---

[13] *An example of the features of a detailed formal plan for restructuring, which may include termination benefits, is given in paragraph 21.11C.*

Disclosures about defined contribution plans

An entity shall disclose the amount recognised in profit or loss as an expense for defined contribution plans.   **28.40**

If an entity treats a defined benefit multi-employer plan as a defined contribution plan because sufficient information is not available to use defined benefit accounting (see paragraph 28.11) it shall: **28.40A**

*(a)   disclose the fact that it is a defined benefit plan and the reason why it is being accounted for as a defined contribution plan, along with any available information about the plan's surplus or deficit and the implications, if any, for the entity;

*(b)   include a description of the extent to which the entity can be liable to the plan for other entities' obligations under the terms and conditions of the multi-employer plan; and

(c)   disclose how any liability recognised in accordance with paragraph 28.11A has been determined.

Disclosures about defined benefit plans

An entity shall disclose the following information about defined benefit plans (except for any defined multi-employer benefit plans that are accounted for as a defined contribution plan in accordance with paragraphs 28.11 and 28.11A, for which the disclosures in paragraphs 28.40 and 28.40A apply instead). If an entity has more than one defined benefit plan, these disclosures may be made in aggregate, separately for each plan, or in such groupings as are considered to be the most useful: **28.41**

(a)   A general description of the type of plan, including **funding** policy. This includes the amount and timing of the future payments to be made by the entity under any agreement with the defined benefit plan to fund a deficit (such as a schedule of contributions).

(b)   [Not used]

(c)   [Not used]

(d)   The date of the most recent comprehensive actuarial valuation and, if it was not as of the reporting date, a description of the adjustments that were made to measure the defined benefit obligation at the reporting date.

(e)   A reconciliation of opening and closing balances for each of the following:

(i)   the defined benefit obligation;

(ii)   the fair value of plan assets; and

(iii) any reimbursement right recognised as an asset.

(f)   Each of the reconciliations in paragraph 28.41(e) shall show each of the following, if applicable:

(i)   the change in the defined benefit liability arising from employee service rendered during the reporting period in profit or loss;

(ii)   interest income or expense;

(iii) remeasurement of the defined benefit liability, showing separately actuarial gains and losses and the return on plan assets less amounts included in (ii) above; and

(iv)   plan introductions, changes, curtailments and settlements.

(g)   The total cost relating to defined benefit plans for the period, disclosing separately the amounts:

(i)   recognised in profit or loss as an expense; and

(ii)   included in the cost of an asset.

(h)　For each major class of plan assets, which shall include, but is not limited to, equity instruments, debt instruments, property, and all other assets, the percentage or amount that each major class constitutes of the fair value of the total plan assets at the reporting date.

(i)　The amounts included in the fair value of plan assets for:

(i)　each class of the entity's own **financial instruments**; and

(ii)　any property occupied by, or other assets used by, the entity.

(j)　The return on plan assets.

(k)　The principal actuarial assumptions used, including, when applicable:

(i)　the discount rates;

(ii)　[not used]

(iii)　the expected rates of salary increases;

(iv)　medical cost trend rates; and

(v)　any other **material** actuarial assumptions used.

The reconciliations in (e) and (f) above need not be presented for prior periods.

28.41A　If an entity participates in a defined benefit plan that shares risks between entities under common control (see paragraph 28.38) it shall disclose the following information:

(a)　The contractual agreement or stated policy for charging the cost of a defined benefit plan or the fact that there is no policy.

(b)　The policy for determining the contribution to be paid by the entity.

(c)　If the entity accounts for an allocation of the net defined benefit cost, all the information required in paragraph 28.41.

*(d)　If the entity accounts for the contributions payable for the period, the information about the plan as a whole required by paragraph 28.41(a), (d), (h) and (i).

This information can be disclosed by cross-reference to disclosures in another group entity's **financial statements** if:

(i)　that group entity's financial statements separately identify and disclose the information required about the plan; and

(ii)　that group entity's financial statements are available to users of the financial statements on the same terms as the financial statements of the entity and at the same time as, or earlier than, the financial statements of the entity.

Disclosures about other long-term benefits

28.42　For each category of other long-term benefits that an entity provides to its employees, the entity shall disclose the nature of the benefit, the amount of its obligation and the extent of funding at the reporting date.

Disclosures about termination benefits

28.43　For each category of termination benefits that an entity provides to its employees, the entity shall disclose the nature of the benefit, its **accounting policy**, and the amount of its obligation and the extent of funding at the reporting date.

28.44　When there is uncertainty about the number of employees who will accept an offer of termination benefits, a **contingent liability** exists. Section 21 *Provisions and Contingencies* requires an entity to disclose information about its contingent liabilities unless the possibility of an outflow in settlement is remote.

Section 29 Income Tax

Scope of this section

For the purpose of this FRS, **income tax** includes all domestic and foreign taxes that are based on **taxable profit**. Income tax also includes taxes, such as withholding taxes, that are payable by a **subsidiary**, **associate** or **joint venture** on distributions to the reporting entity.   29.1

This section covers accounting for income tax. It requires an entity to recognise the current and future tax consequences of transactions and other events that have been recognised in the **financial statements**. These recognised tax amounts comprise **current tax** and **deferred tax**. Current tax is tax payable (refundable) in respect of the taxable profit (tax loss) for the current period or past **reporting periods**. Deferred tax represents the future tax consequences of transactions and events recognised in the financial statements of the current and previous periods. This section also requires that deferred tax is recognised in respect of **assets** (other than **goodwill**) and **liabilities** recognised as a result of a **business combination**.   29.2

This section also covers accounting for value added tax (VAT) and other similar sales taxes, which are not income taxes.   29.2A

Recognition and measurement of current tax

An entity shall recognise a current tax liability for tax payable on taxable profit for the current and past periods. If the amount of tax paid for the current and past periods exceeds the amount of tax payable for those periods, the entity shall recognise the excess as a current tax asset.   29.3

An entity shall recognise a current tax asset for the benefit of a tax loss that can be carried back to recover tax paid in a previous period.   29.4

An entity shall measure a current tax liability (asset) at the amount of tax it expects to pay (recover) using the tax rates and laws that have been enacted or **substantively enacted** by the **reporting date**.   29.5

Recognition of deferred tax

Timing differences

Deferred tax shall be recognised in respect of all **timing differences** at the reporting date, except as otherwise required by paragraphs 29.7 to 29.9 and 29.11 below. Timing differences are differences between taxable profits and **total comprehensive income** as stated in the financial statements that arise from the inclusion of **income** and **expenses** in tax assessments in periods different from those in which they are recognised in financial statements.   29.6

Unrelieved tax losses and other **deferred tax assets** shall be recognised only to the extent that it is **probable** that they will be recovered against the reversal of **deferred tax liabilities** or other future taxable profits (the very existence of unrelieved tax losses is strong evidence that there may not be other future taxable profits against which the losses will be relieved).   29.7

Deferred tax shall be recognised when the tax allowances for the cost of a **fixed asset** are received before or after the **depreciation** of the fixed asset is recognised in **profit or loss**. If and when all conditions for retaining the tax allowances have been met, the deferred tax shall be reversed.   29.8

29.9   Deferred tax shall be recognised when income or expenses from a subsidiary, associate, branch, or interest in joint venture have been recognised in the financial statements, and will be assessed to or allowed for tax in a future period, except where:

(a)   the reporting entity is able to control the reversal of the timing difference; and

(b)   it is probable that the timing difference will not reverse in the foreseeable future.

Such timing differences may arise, for example, where there are undistributed profits in a subsidiary, associate, branch or interest in a joint venture.

Permanent differences

29.10   **Permanent differences** arise because certain types of **income** and expenses are non-taxable or disallowable, or because certain tax charges or allowances are greater or smaller than the corresponding income or expense in the financial statements. Deferred tax shall not be recognised on permanent differences except for circumstances set out in paragraph 29.11.

Business combinations

29.11   When the amount that can be deducted for tax for an asset (other than goodwill) that is recognised in a business combination is less (more) than the value at which it is recognised, a deferred tax liability (asset) shall be recognised for the additional tax that will be paid (avoided) in respect of that difference. Similarly, a deferred tax asset (liability) shall be recognised for the additional tax that will be avoided (paid) because of a difference between the value at which a liability is recognised and the amount that will be assessed for tax. The amount attributed to goodwill shall be adjusted by the amount of deferred tax recognised.

Measurement of deferred tax

29.12   An entity shall measure a deferred tax liability (asset) using the tax rates and laws that have been enacted or substantively enacted by the reporting date that are expected to apply to the reversal of the timing difference except for the cases dealt with in paragraphs 29.15 and 29.16 below.

29.13   When different tax rates apply to different levels of taxable profit, an entity shall measure deferred tax expense (income) and related deferred tax liabilities (assets) using the average enacted or substantively enacted rates that it expects to be applicable to the taxable profit (tax loss) of the periods in which it expects the deferred tax asset to be realised or the deferred tax liability to be settled.

29.14   In some jurisdictions, income taxes are payable at a higher or lower rate if part or all of the profit or retained earnings is paid out as a dividend to shareholders of the entity. In other jurisdictions, income taxes may be refundable or payable if part or all of the profit or retained earnings is paid out as a dividend to shareholders of the entity. In both of those circumstances, an entity shall measure current and deferred taxes at the tax rate applicable to undistributed profits until the entity recognises a liability to pay a dividend. When the entity recognises a liability to pay a dividend, it shall recognise the resulting current or deferred tax liability (asset), and the related **tax expense** (income).

29.15   Deferred tax relating to a non-depreciable asset that is measured using the revaluation model in Section 17 *Property, Plant and Equipment* shall be measured using the tax rates and allowances that apply to the sale of the asset.

Deferred tax relating to **investment property** that is measured at **fair value** in accordance with Section 16 *Investment Property* shall be measured using the tax rates and allowances that apply to sale of the asset, except for investment property that has a limited **useful life** and is held within a business model whose objective is to consume substantially all of the economic benefits embodied in the property over time.   **29.16**

Measurement of both current and deferred tax

An entity shall not discount current or deferred tax assets and liabilities.   **29.17**

Withholding tax on dividends

When an entity pays dividends to its shareholders, it may be required to pay a portion of the dividends to taxation authorities on behalf of shareholders. Outgoing dividends and similar amounts payable shall be recognised at an amount that includes any withholding tax but excludes other taxes, such as attributable tax credits.   **29.18**

Incoming dividends and similar income receivable shall be recognised at an amount that includes any withholding tax but excludes other taxes, such as attributable tax credits. Any withholding tax suffered shall be shown as part of the tax charge.   **29.19**

Value Added Tax ('VAT') and other similar sales taxes

Turnover shown in profit or loss shall exclude VAT and other similar sales taxes on taxable outputs and VAT imputed under the flat rate VAT scheme. Expenses shall exclude recoverable VAT and other similar recoverable sales taxes. Irrecoverable VAT allocable to fixed assets and to other items disclosed separately in the financial statements shall be included in their cost where practicable and **material**.   **29.20**

Presentation

Allocation in comprehensive income and equity

An entity shall present changes in a current tax liability (asset) and changes in a deferred tax liability (asset) as tax expense (income) with the exception of those changes arising on the initial **recognition** of a business combination which shall be dealt with in accordance with paragraph 29.11.   **29.21**

An entity shall present tax expense (income) in the same component of **total comprehensive income** (ie continuing or **discontinued operations**, and profit or loss or **other comprehensive income**) or **equity** as the transaction or other event that resulted in the tax expense (income).   **29.22**

Presentation in the statement of financial position

An entity shall present deferred tax liabilities within provisions for liabilities and deferred tax assets within debtors.   **29.23**

Offsetting

An entity shall offset current tax assets and current tax liabilities, if and only if, it has a legally enforceable right to set off the amounts and it intends either to settle on a net basis or to realise the asset and settle the liability simultaneously.   **29.24**

29.24A   An entity shall offset deferred tax assets and deferred tax liabilities if, and only if:

(a)   the entity has a legally enforceable right to set off current tax assets against current tax liabilities; and

(b)   the deferred tax assets and deferred tax liabilities relate to income taxes levied by the same taxation authority on either the same taxable entity or different taxable entities which intend either to settle current tax liabilities and assets on a net basis, or to realise the assets and settle the liabilities simultaneously, in each future period in which significant amounts of deferred tax liabilities or assets are expected to be settled or recovered.

Disclosures

29.25   An entity shall disclose information that enables users of its financial statements to evaluate the nature and financial effect of the current and deferred tax consequences of recognised transactions and other events.

29.26   An entity shall disclose separately the major components of tax expense (income). Such components of tax expense (income) may include:

(a)   current tax expense (income);

(b)   any adjustments recognised in the period for current tax of prior periods;

(c)   the amount of deferred tax expense (income) relating to the origination and reversal of timing differences;

(d)   the amount of deferred tax expense (income) relating to changes in tax rates or the imposition of new taxes;

(e)   adjustments to deferred tax expense (income) arising from a change in the tax status of the entity or its shareholders; and

(f)   the amount of tax expense (income) relating to changes in **accounting policies** and **material errors** (see Section 10 *Accounting Policies, Estimates and Errors*).

29.27   An entity shall disclose the following separately:

*(a)   the aggregate current and deferred tax relating to items that are recognised as items of other comprehensive income or equity;

(b)   a reconciliation between:

(i)   the tax expense (income) included in profit or loss; and

(ii)   the profit or loss on ordinary activities before tax multiplied by the applicable tax rate;

(c)   the amount of the net reversal of deferred tax assets and deferred tax liabilities expected to occur during the year beginning after the **reporting period** together with a brief explanation for the expected reversal;

(d)   an explanation of changes in the applicable tax rate(s) compared with the previous reporting period;

(e)   the amount of deferred tax liabilities and deferred tax assets at the end of the reporting period for each type of timing difference and the amount of unused tax losses and tax credits;

(f)   the expiry date, if any, of timing differences, unused tax losses and unused tax credits; and

(g)   in the circumstances described in paragraph 29.14, an explanation of the nature of the potential income tax consequences that would result from the payment of dividends to its shareholders.

Section 30 Foreign Currency Translation

Scope of this section

An entity can conduct foreign activities in two ways. It may have transactions in foreign currencies or it may have **foreign operations**. In addition, an entity may present its **financial statements** in a foreign currency. This section prescribes how to include foreign currency transactions and foreign operations in the financial statements of an entity and how to translate financial statements into a **presentation currency**. Hedge accounting of foreign currency items is dealt with in Section 12 *Other Financial Instruments Issues*.

30.1

Functional currency

Each entity shall identify its **functional currency**. An entity's functional currency is the currency of the primary economic environment in which the entity operates.

30.2

The primary economic environment in which an entity operates is normally the one in which it primarily generates and expends **cash**. Therefore, the following are the most important factors an entity considers in determining its functional currency:

30.3

(a)   the currency:

   (i)   that mainly influences sales prices for goods and services (this will often be the currency in which sales prices for its goods and services are denominated and settled); and

   (ii)   of the country whose competitive forces and regulations mainly determine the sales prices of its goods and services; and

(b)   the currency that mainly influences labour, material and other costs of providing goods or services (this will often be the currency in which such costs are denominated and settled).

The following factors may also provide evidence of an entity's functional currency:

30.4

(a)   the currency in which funds from **financing activities** (issuing debt and equity instruments) are generated; and

(b)   the currency in which receipts from **operating activities** are usually retained.

The following additional factors are considered in determining the functional currency of a foreign operation, and whether its functional currency is the same as that of the reporting entity (the reporting entity, in this context, being the entity that has the foreign operation as its **subsidiary**, branch, **associate** or **joint venture**):

30.5

(a)   Whether the activities of the foreign operation are carried out as an extension of the reporting entity, rather than being carried out with a significant degree of autonomy. An example of the former is when the foreign operation only sells goods imported from the reporting entity and remits the proceeds to it. An example of the latter is when the operation accumulates cash and other **monetary items**, incurs **expenses**, generates **income** and arranges borrowings, all substantially in its local currency.

(b)   Whether transactions with the reporting entity are a high or a low proportion of the foreign operation's activities.

(c)   Whether **cash flows** from the activities of the foreign operation directly affect the cash flows of the reporting entity and are readily available for remittance to it.

(d)   Whether cash flows from the activities of the foreign operation are sufficient to service existing and normally expected debt obligations without funds being made available by the reporting entity.

Reporting foreign currency transactions in the functional currency

Initial recognition

30.6 A foreign currency transaction is a transaction that is denominated or requires settlement in a foreign currency, including transactions arising when an entity:

(a) buys or sells goods or services whose price is denominated in a foreign currency;

(b) borrows or lends funds when the amounts payable or receivable are denominated in a foreign currency; or

(c) otherwise acquires or disposes of **assets**, or incurs or settles **liabilities**, denominated in a foreign currency.

30.7 An entity shall record a foreign currency transaction, on initial **recognition** in the functional currency, by applying to the foreign currency amount the spot exchange rate between the functional currency and the foreign currency at the date of the transaction.

30.8 The date of a transaction is the date on which the transaction first qualifies for recognition in accordance with this FRS. For practical reasons, a rate that approximates the actual rate at the date of the transaction is often used, for example, an average rate for a week or a month might be used for all transactions in each foreign currency occurring during that period. However, if exchange rates fluctuate significantly, the use of the average rate for a period is inappropriate.

Reporting at the end of the subsequent reporting periods

30.9 At the end of each **reporting period**, an entity shall:

(a) translate foreign currency monetary items using the **closing rate**;

(b) translate non-monetary items that are measured in terms of historical cost in a foreign currency using the exchange rate at the date of the transaction; and

(c) translate non-monetary items that are measured at **fair value** in a foreign currency using the exchange rates at the date when the fair value was determined.

30.10 An entity shall recognise, in **profit or loss** in the period in which they arise, exchange differences arising on the settlement of monetary items or on translating monetary items at rates different from those at which they were translated on initial recognition during the period or in previous periods, except as described in paragraph 30.13.

30.11 When another section of this FRS requires a **gain** or loss on a non-monetary item to be recognised in **other comprehensive income**, an entity shall recognise any exchange component of that gain or loss in other comprehensive income. Conversely, when a gain or loss on a non-monetary item is recognised in profit or loss, an entity shall recognise any exchange component of that gain or loss in profit or loss.

Net investment in a foreign operation

30.12 An entity may have a monetary item that is receivable from or payable to a foreign operation. An item for which settlement is neither planned nor likely to occur in the foreseeable future is, in substance, a part of the entity's net investment in that foreign operation, and is accounted for in accordance with paragraph 30.13. Such monetary items may include long-term receivables or loans. They do not include trade receivables or trade payables.

30.13 Exchange differences arising on a monetary item that forms part of a reporting entity's **net investment in a foreign operation** shall be recognised in profit or loss in the **separate**

financial statements of the reporting entity or the **individual financial statements** of the foreign operation, as appropriate. In the financial statements that include the foreign operation and the reporting entity (eg **consolidated financial statements** when the foreign operation is a subsidiary), such exchange differences shall be recognised in other comprehensive income and accumulated in **equity**. They shall not be recognised in profit or loss on disposal of the net investment.

Change in functional currency

When there is a change in an entity's functional currency, the entity shall apply the translation procedures applicable to the new functional currency prospectively from the date of the change.   **30.14**

As noted in paragraphs 30.2 to 30.5, the functional currency of an entity reflects the underlying transactions, events and conditions that are relevant to the entity. Accordingly, once the functional currency is determined, it can be changed only if there is a change to those underlying transactions, events and conditions. For example, a change in the currency that mainly influences the sales prices of goods and services may lead to a change in an entity's functional currency.   **30.15**

The effect of a change in functional currency is accounted for prospectively. In other words, an entity translates all items into the new functional currency using the exchange rate at the date of the change. The resulting translated amounts for non-monetary items are treated as their historical cost.   **30.16**

Use of a presentation currency other than the functional currency

Translation to the presentation currency

An entity may present its financial statements in any currency (or currencies). If the presentation currency differs from the entity's functional currency, the entity shall translate its items of income and expense and **financial position** into the presentation currency. For example, when a **group** contains individual entities with different functional currencies, the items of income and expense and financial position of each entity are expressed in a common currency so that consolidated financial statements may be presented.   **30.17**

An entity whose functional currency is not the currency of a hyperinflationary economy shall translate its results and financial position into a different presentation currency using the following procedures: **30.18**

(a) assets and liabilities for each **statement of financial position** presented (ie including comparatives) shall be translated at the closing rate at the date of that statement of financial position;

(b) income and expenses for each **statement of comprehensive income** (ie including comparatives) shall be translated at exchange rates at the dates of the transactions; and

(c) all resulting exchange differences shall be recognised in other comprehensive income.

For practical reasons, an entity may use a rate that approximates the exchange rates at the dates of the transactions, for example an average rate for the period to translate income and expense items. However, if exchange rates fluctuate significantly, the use of the average rate for a period is inappropriate.   **30.19**

30.20   The exchange differences referred to in paragraph 30.18(c) result from:

(a)   translating income and expenses at the exchange rates at the dates of the transactions and assets and liabilities at the closing rate; and

(b)   translating the opening net assets at a closing rate that differs from the previous closing rate.

When the exchange differences relate to a foreign operation that is consolidated but not wholly-owned, accumulated exchange differences arising from translation and attributable to the **non-controlling interest** are allocated to, and recognised as part of, non-controlling interest in the consolidated statement of financial position.

30.21   An entity whose functional currency is the currency of a hyperinflationary economy shall adjust its results and financial position using the procedures specified in Section 31 *Hyperinflation* before applying the requirements of this section.

Translation of a foreign operation into the investor's presentation currency

30.22   In incorporating the assets, liabilities, income and expenses of a foreign operation with those of the reporting entity, the entity shall follow normal consolidation procedures, such as the elimination of intragroup balances and intragroup transactions of a subsidiary (see Section 9 *Consolidated and Separate Financial Statements*) and the translation procedures set out in paragraphs 30.17 to 30.21. An intragroup monetary asset (or liability), whether short-term or long-term, cannot be eliminated against the corresponding intragroup liability (or asset) without showing the results of currency fluctuations in the consolidated financial statements. This is because the monetary item represents a commitment to convert one currency into another and exposes the reporting entity to a gain or loss through currency fluctuations. Accordingly, in the consolidated financial statements, a reporting entity continues to recognise such an exchange difference in profit or loss or, if it arises from the circumstances described in paragraph 30.13, the entity shall recognise it in other comprehensive income.

30.23   Any **goodwill** arising on the acquisition of a foreign operation and any fair value adjustments to the **carrying amounts** of assets and liabilities arising on the acquisition of that foreign operation shall be treated as assets and liabilities of the foreign operation. Thus, they shall be expressed in the functional currency of the foreign operation and shall be translated at the closing rate in accordance with paragraph 30.18.

Disclosures

30.24   In paragraphs 30.26 and 30.27, references to functional currency apply, in the case of a group, to the functional currency of the **parent**.

30.25   An entity shall disclose the following:

(a)   the amount of exchange differences recognised in profit or loss during the period, except for those arising on **financial instruments** measured at fair value through profit or loss in accordance with Sections 11 *Basic Financial Instruments* and Section 12.

(b)   the amount of exchange differences arising during the period and classified in equity at the end of the period.

30.26   An entity shall disclose the currency in which the financial statements are presented. When the presentation currency is different from the functional currency, an entity shall state that fact and shall disclose the functional currency and the reason for using a different presentation currency.

When there is a change in the functional currency of either the reporting entity or a significant foreign operation, the entity shall disclose that fact and the reason for the change in functional currency.

30.27

Section 31 Hyperinflation

Scope of this section

This section applies to an entity whose **functional currency** is the currency of a hyperinflationary economy. It requires such an entity to prepare **financial statements** that have been adjusted for the effects of hyperinflation.

31.1

Hyperinflationary economy

This section does not establish an absolute rate at which an economy is deemed hyperinflationary. An entity shall make that judgement by considering all available information including, but not limited to, the following possible indicators of hyperinflation:

31.2

(a)   The general population prefers to keep its wealth in non-monetary assets or in a relatively stable foreign currency. Amounts of local currency held are immediately invested to maintain purchasing power.

(b)   The general population regards monetary amounts not in terms of the local currency but in terms of a relatively stable foreign currency. Prices may be quoted in that currency.

(c)   Sales and purchases on credit take place at prices that compensate for the expected loss of purchasing power during the credit period, even if the period is short.

(d)   Interest rates, wages and prices are linked to a price index.

(e)   The cumulative inflation rate over three years is approaching, or exceeds, 100 per cent.

Measuring unit in the financial statements

All amounts in the financial statements of an entity whose functional currency is the currency of a hyperinflationary economy shall be stated in terms of the measuring unit current at the end of the **reporting period**. The comparative information for the previous period required by paragraph 3.14, and any information presented in respect of earlier periods, shall also be stated in terms of the measuring unit current at the **reporting date**.

31.3

The restatement of financial statements in accordance with this section requires the use of a general price index that reflects changes in general purchasing power. In most economies there is a recognised general price index, normally produced by the government, that entities will follow.

31.4

Procedures for restating historical cost financial statements

Statement of financial position

Statement of financial position amounts not expressed in terms of the measuring unit current at the end of the reporting period are restated by applying a general price index.

31.5

Monetary items are not restated because they are expressed in terms of the measuring unit current at the end of the reporting period. Monetary items are money held and items to be received or paid in money.

31.6

Assets and **liabilities** linked by agreement to changes in prices, such as index-linked bonds and loans, are adjusted in accordance with the agreement and presented at this adjusted amount in the restated statement of financial position.

31.7

31.8   All other assets and liabilities are non-monetary:

(a)   Some non-monetary items are carried at amounts current at the end of the reporting period, such as net realisable value and **fair value**, so they are not restated. All other non-monetary assets and liabilities are restated.

(b)   Most non-monetary items are carried at cost or cost less **depreciation**; hence they are expressed at amounts current at their date of acquisition. The restated cost, or cost less depreciation, of each item is determined by applying to its historical cost and accumulated depreciation the change in a general price index from the date of acquisition to the end of the reporting period.

(c)   The restated amount of a non-monetary item is reduced, in accordance with Section 27 *Impairment of Assets*, when it exceeds its **recoverable amount**.

31.9   At the beginning of the first period of application of this section, the components of **equity**, except retained earnings, are restated by applying a general price index from the dates the components were contributed or otherwise arose. Restated retained earnings are derived from all the other amounts in the restated statement of financial position.

31.10   At the end of the first period and in subsequent periods, all components of owners' equity are restated by applying a general price index from the beginning of the period or the date of contribution, if later. The changes for the period in owners' equity are disclosed in accordance with Section 6 *Statement of Changes in Equity and Statement of Income and Retained Earnings*.

Statement of comprehensive income and income statement

31.11   All items in the **statement of comprehensive income** (and in the **income statement**, if presented) shall be expressed in terms of the measuring unit current at the end of the reporting period. Therefore, all amounts need to be restated by applying the change in the general price index from the dates when the items of **income** and **expenses** were initially recognised in the financial statements. If general inflation is approximately even throughout the period, and the items of income and expense arose approximately evenly throughout the period, an average rate of inflation may be appropriate.

Statement of cash flows

31.12   An entity shall express all items in the **statement of cash flows** in terms of the measuring unit current at the end of the reporting period.

Gain or loss on net monetary position

31.13   In a period of inflation, an entity holding an excess of monetary assets over monetary liabilities loses purchasing power, and an entity with an excess of monetary liabilities over monetary assets gains purchasing power, to the extent the assets and liabilities are not linked to a price level. An entity shall include in **profit or loss** the **gain** or loss on the net monetary position. An entity shall offset the adjustment to those assets and liabilities linked by agreement to changes in prices made in accordance with paragraph 31.7 against the gain or loss on net monetary position.

Economies ceasing to be hyperinflationary

31.14   When an economy ceases to be hyperinflationary and an entity discontinues the preparation and presentation of financial statements prepared in accordance with this section, it shall treat the amounts expressed in the **presentation currency** at the end of the previous reporting period as the basis for the **carrying amounts** in its subsequent financial statements.

Disclosures

An entity to which this section applies shall disclose the following: **31.15**

(a)   the fact that financial statements and other prior period data have been restated for changes in the general purchasing power of the functional currency;

(b)   the identity and level of the price index at the reporting date and changes during the current reporting period and the previous reporting period; and

(c)   amount of gain or loss on monetary items.

Section 32 Events after the End of the Reporting Period

Scope of this section

This section defines events after the end of the **reporting period** and sets out principles for recognising, measuring and disclosing those events.   **32.1**

Events after the end of the reporting period defined

Events after the end of the reporting period are those events, favourable and unfavourable, that occur between the end of the reporting period and the date when the **financial statements** are authorised for issue. There are two types of events: **32.2**

(a)   those that provide evidence of conditions that existed at the end of the reporting period (adjusting events after the end of the reporting period); and

(b)   those that are indicative of conditions that arose after the end of the reporting period (non-adjusting events after the end of the reporting period).

Events after the end of the reporting period include all events up to the date when the financial statements are authorised for issue, even if those events occur after the public announcement of **profit or loss** or other selected financial information.   **32.3**

Recognition and measurement

Adjusting events after the end of the reporting period

An entity shall adjust the amounts recognised in its financial statements, including related disclosures, to reflect adjusting events after the end of the reporting period.   **32.4**

The following are examples of adjusting events after the end of the reporting period that require an entity to adjust the amounts recognised in its financial statements, or to recognise items that were not previously recognised: **32.5**

(a)   The settlement after the end of the reporting period of a court case that confirms that the entity had a present obligation at the end of the reporting period. The entity adjusts any previously recognised **provision** related to this court case in accordance with Section 21 *Provisions and Contingencies* or recognises a new provision. The entity does not merely disclose a **contingent liability**. Rather, the settlement provides additional evidence to be considered in determining the provision that should be recognised at the end of the reporting period in accordance with Section 21.

(b)   The receipt of information after the end of the reporting period indicating that an **asset** was impaired at the end of the reporting period, or that the amount of a previously recognised **impairment loss** for that asset needs to be adjusted. For example:

(i)   the bankruptcy of a customer that occurs after the end of the reporting period usually confirms that a loss existed at the end of the reporting period on a trade receivable and that the entity needs to adjust the **carrying amount** of the trade receivable; and

(ii) the sale of **inventories** after the end of the reporting period may give evidence about their selling price at the end of the reporting period for the purpose of assessing impairment at that date.

(c) The determination after the end of the reporting period of the cost of assets purchased, or the proceeds from assets sold, before the end of the reporting period.

(d) The determination after the end of the reporting period of the amount of profit-sharing or bonus payments, if the entity had a legal or **constructive obligation** at the end of the reporting period to make such payments as a result of events before that date (see Section 28 *Employee Benefits*).

(e) The discovery of fraud or **errors** that show that the financial statements are incorrect.

Non-adjusting events after the end of the reporting period

32.6   An entity shall not adjust the amounts recognised in its financial statements to reflect non-adjusting events after the end of the reporting period.

32.7   Examples of non-adjusting events after the end of the reporting period include:

(a) A decline in market value of investments between the end of the reporting period and the date when the financial statements are authorised for issue. The decline in market value does not normally relate to the condition of the investments at the end of the reporting period, but reflects circumstances that have arisen subsequently. Therefore, an entity does not adjust the amounts recognised in its financial statements for the investments. Similarly, the entity does not update the amounts disclosed for the investments as at the end of the reporting period, although it may need to give additional disclosure in accordance with paragraph 32.10.

(b) An amount that becomes receivable as a result of a favourable judgement or settlement of a court case after the **reporting date** but before the financial statements are authorised for issued. This would be a **contingent asset** at the reporting date (see paragraph 21.13), and disclosure may be required by paragraph 21.16. However, agreement on the amount of damages for a judgement that was reached before the reporting date, but was not previously recognised because the amount could not be measured reliably, may constitute an adjusting event.

Further examples of non-adjusting events are set out in paragraph 32.11.

Going concern

32.7A   An entity shall not prepare its financial statements on a **going concern** basis if management determines after the reporting period either that it intends to liquidate the entity or to cease trading, or that it has no realistic alternative but to do so.

32.7B   Deterioration in operating results and **financial position** after the reporting period may indicate a need to consider whether the going concern assumption is still appropriate. If the going concern assumption is no longer appropriate, the effect is so pervasive that this section requires a fundamental change in the basis of accounting, rather than an adjustment to the amounts recognised within the original basis of accounting and therefore the disclosure requirements of paragraph 3.9 apply.

Dividends

32.8   If an entity declares dividends to holders of its equity instruments after the end of the reporting period, the entity shall not recognise those dividends as a **liability** at the end of the reporting period because no obligation exists at that time. The amount of the dividend may be presented as a segregated component of retained earnings at the end of the reporting period.

Disclosure

Date of authorisation for issue

An entity shall disclose the date when the financial statements were authorised for issue and who gave that authorisation. If the entity's **owners** or others have the power to amend the financial statements after issue, the entity shall disclose that fact.   32.9

Non-adjusting events after the end of the reporting period

An entity shall disclose the following for each category of non-adjusting event after the end of the reporting period: * 32.10

(a)   the nature of the event; and
(b)   an estimate of its financial effect or a statement that such an estimate cannot be made.

The following are examples of non-adjusting events after the end of the reporting period that would generally result in disclosure. The disclosures will reflect information that becomes known after the end of the reporting period but before the financial statements are authorised for issue: * 32.11

(a)   a major **business combination** or disposal of a major **subsidiary**;
(b)   announcement of a plan to discontinue an operation;
(c)   major purchases of assets, disposals or plans to dispose of assets, or expropriation of major assets by government;
(d)   the destruction of a major production plant by a fire;
(e)   announcement, or commencement of the implementation, of a major restructuring;
(f)   issues or repurchases of an entity's debt or equity instruments;
(g)   abnormally large changes in asset prices or foreign exchange rates;
(h)   changes in tax rates or tax laws enacted or announced that have a significant effect on current and **deferred tax assets and liabilities**;
(i)   entering into significant commitments or contingent liabilities, for example, by issuing significant guarantees; and
(j)   commencement of major litigation arising solely out of events that occurred after the end of the reporting period.

Section 33 Related Party Disclosures

Scope of this section

This section requires an entity to include in its **financial statements** the disclosures necessary to draw attention to the possibility that its **financial position** and **profit or loss** have been affected by the existence of **related parties** and by transactions and outstanding balances with such parties.   33.1

Disclosures need not be given of transactions entered into between two or more members of a **group**, provided that any **subsidiary** which is a party to the transaction is wholly owned by such a member.   33.1A

Related party defined

33.2   A related party is a person or entity that is related to the entity that is preparing its financial statements (the reporting entity).

(a)   A person or a **close member of that person's family** is related to a reporting entity if that person:

(i)   has **control** or **joint control** over the reporting entity;

(ii)   has **significant influence** over the reporting entity; or

(iii)   is a member of the **key management personnel** of the reporting entity or of a **parent** of the reporting entity.

(b)   An entity is related to a reporting entity if any of the following conditions apply:

(i)   the entity and the reporting entity are members of the same group (which means that each parent, subsidiary and fellow subsidiary is related to the others).

(ii)   one entity is an **associate** or **joint venture** of the other entity (or an associate or joint venture of a member of a group of which the other entity is a member).

(iii)   both entities are joint ventures of the same third party.

(iv)   one entity is a joint venture of a third entity and the other entity is an associate of the third entity.

(v)   the entity is a **post-employment benefit plan** for the benefit of employees of either the reporting entity or an entity related to the reporting entity. If the reporting entity is itself such a plan, the sponsoring employers are also related to the reporting entity.

(vi)   the entity is controlled or jointly controlled by a person identified in (a).

(vii)   a person identified in (a)(i) has significant influence over the entity or is a member of the key management personnel of the entity (or of a parent of the entity).

(viii)   the entity, or any member of a group of which it is a part, provides key management personnel services to the reporting entity or to the parent of the reporting entity.

33.3   In considering each possible related party relationship, an entity shall assess the substance of the relationship and not merely the legal form.

33.4   In the context of this FRS, the following are not related parties:

(a)   Two entities simply because they have a director or other member of key management personnel in common or because a member of key management personnel of one entity has significant influence over the other entity.

(b)   Two **venturers** simply because they share joint control over a joint venture.

(c)   Any of the following simply by virtue of their normal dealings with an entity (even though they may affect the freedom of action of an entity or participate in its decision-making process):

(i)   providers of finance;

(ii)   trade unions;

(iii)   public utilities; and

(iv)   government departments and agencies.

(d)   A customer, supplier, franchisor, distributor or general agent with whom an entity transacts a significant volume of business, merely by virtue of the resulting economic dependence.

33.4A   In the definition of a related party, an associate includes subsidiaries of the associate and a joint venture includes subsidiaries of the joint venture. Therefore, for example, an associate's subsidiary and the investor that has significant influence over the associate are related to each other.

Disclosures

Disclosure of parent-subsidiary relationships

Relationships between a parent and its subsidiaries shall be disclosed irrespective of whether there have been **related party transactions**. An entity shall disclose the name of its parent and, if different, the ultimate controlling party. If neither the entity's parent nor the ultimate controlling party produces financial statements available for public use, the name of the next most senior parent that does so (if any) shall also be disclosed.   *** 33.5**

Disclosure of key management personnel compensation

Key management personnel are those persons having authority and responsibility for planning, directing and controlling the activities of the entity, directly or indirectly, including any director (whether executive or otherwise) of that entity. Compensation includes all **employee benefits** (as defined in Section 28 *Employee Benefits*) including those in the form of share-based payments (see Section 26 *Share-based Payment*). Employee benefits include all forms of consideration paid, payable or provided by the entity, or on behalf of the entity (eg by its parent or by a shareholder), in exchange for services rendered to the entity. It also includes such consideration paid on behalf of a parent of the entity in respect of goods or services provided to the entity.   **33.6**

An entity shall disclose key management personnel compensation in total.   **33.7**

Disclosure of related party transactions

A related party transaction is a transfer of resources, services or obligations between a reporting entity and a related party, regardless of whether a price is charged. Examples of related party transactions that are common to entities within the scope of this FRS include, but are not limited to: **33.8**

(a)   transactions between an entity and its principal **owner(s)**;
(b)   transactions between an entity and another entity when both entities are under the common control of a single entity or person; and
(c)   transactions in which an entity or person that controls the reporting entity incurs **expenses** directly that otherwise would have been borne by the reporting entity.

If an entity has related party transactions, it shall disclose the nature of the related party relationship as well as information about the transactions, outstanding balances and commitments necessary for an understanding of the potential effect of the relationship on the financial statements. Those disclosure requirements are in addition to the requirements in paragraph 33.7 to disclose key management personnel compensation. At a minimum, disclosures shall include: *** 33.9**

(a)   The amount of the transactions.
(b)   The amount of outstanding balances and:

    (i)   their terms and conditions, including whether they are secured, and the nature of the consideration to be provided in settlement; and
  *(ii)   details of any guarantees given or received.

(c)   Provisions for uncollectible receivables related to the amount of outstanding balances.
(d)   The expense recognised during the period in respect of bad or doubtful debts due from related parties.

Such transactions could include purchases, sales, or transfers of goods or services, **leases**, guarantees and settlements by the entity on behalf of the related party or vice versa.

33.10 An entity shall make the disclosures required by paragraph 33.9 separately for each of the following categories:

(a) entities with control, joint control or significant influence over the entity;
(b) entities over which the entity has control, joint control or significant influence;
(c) key management personnel of the entity or its parent (in the aggregate);
(d) entities that provide key management personnel services to the entity; and
(e) other related parties.

33.11 An entity is exempt from the disclosure requirements of paragraph 33.9 in relation to:

(a) a **state** (a national, regional or local government) that has control, joint control or significant influence over the reporting entity; and
(b) another entity that is a related party because the same state has control, joint control or significant influence over both the reporting entity and the other entity.

However, the entity must still disclose a parent-subsidiary relationship as required by paragraph 33.5.

33.12 The following are examples of transactions that shall be disclosed if they are with a related party:

(a) purchases or sales of goods (finished or unfinished);
(b) purchases or sales of property and other **assets**;
(c) rendering or receiving of services;
(d) leases;
(e) transfers of **research** and **development**;
(f) transfers under licence agreements;
(g) transfers under finance arrangements (including loans and equity contributions in **cash** or in kind);
(h) provision of guarantees or collateral;
(i) settlement of **liabilities** on behalf of the entity or by the entity on behalf of another party; and
(j) participation by a parent or subsidiary in a **defined benefit plan** that shares risks between group entities.

33.13 An entity shall not state that related party transactions were made on terms equivalent to those that prevail in arm's length transactions unless such terms can be substantiated.

*33.14 An entity may disclose items of a similar nature in the aggregate except when separate disclosure is necessary for an understanding of the effects of related party transactions on the financial statements of the entity.

Section 34 Specialised Activities

Scope of this section

34.1 This section sets out the financial reporting requirements for entities applying this FRS involved in the following types of specialised activities:

(a) Agriculture (see paragraphs 34.2 to 34.10A);
(b) Extractive Activities (see paragraphs 34.11 to 34.11C);
(c) Service Concession Arrangements (see paragraphs 34.12 to 34.16A);
(d) Financial Institutions (see paragraphs 34.17 to 34.33);

(e)   Retirement Benefit Plans: Financial Statements (see paragraphs 34.34 to 34.48);
(f)   Heritage Assets (see paragraphs 34.49 to 34.56);
(g)   Funding Commitments (see paragraphs 34.57 to 34.63);
(h)   Incoming Resources from Non-Exchange Transactions (see paragraphs 34.64 to 34.74);
(i)   Public Benefit Entity Combinations (see paragraphs 34.75 to 34.86); and
(j)   Public Benefit Entity Concessionary Loans (see paragraphs 34.87 to 34.97).

Agriculture

An entity using this FRS that is engaged in **agricultural activity** shall determine an **accounting policy** for each class of **biological asset** and its related **agricultural produce**.   **34.2**

Recognition

An entity shall recognise a biological asset or an item of agricultural produce when, and only when: **34.3**

(a)   the entity controls the **asset** as a result of past events;
(b)   it is **probable** that future economic benefits associated with the asset will flow to the entity; and
(c)   the **fair value** or cost of the asset can be measured reliably.

Measurement

For each class of biological asset and its related agricultural produce an entity shall choose as its accounting policy either: **34.3A**

(a)   the fair value model set out in paragraphs 34.4 to 34.7A; or
(b)   the cost model set out in paragraphs 34.8 to 34.10A.

If an entity has chosen the fair value model for a class of biological asset and its related agricultural produce, it shall not subsequently change its accounting policy to the cost model.   **34.3B**

Measurement – fair value model

An entity applying the fair value model shall measure a biological asset on initial **recognition** and at each **reporting date** at its **fair value less costs to sell**. Changes in fair value less costs to sell shall be recognised in **profit or loss**.   **34.4**

Agricultural produce harvested from an entity's biological assets shall be measured at the point of harvest at its fair value less costs to sell. Such **measurement** is the cost at that date when applying Section 13 *Inventories* or another applicable section of this FRS.   **34.5**

In determining fair value, an entity shall consider the following: **34.6**

(a)   If an **active market** exists for a biological asset or agricultural produce in its present location and condition, the quoted price in that market is the appropriate basis for determining the fair value of that asset. If an entity has access to different active markets, the entity shall use the price existing in the market that it expects to use.
(b)   If an active market does not exist, an entity uses one or more of the following, when available, in determining fair value:

(i)   the most recent market transaction price, provided that there has not been a significant change in economic circumstances between the date of that transaction and the end of the **reporting period**;

(ii)   market prices for similar assets with adjustment to reflect differences; and

(iii)   sector benchmarks such as the value of an orchard expressed per export tray, bushel, or hectare, and the value of cattle expressed per kilogram of meat.

(c)   In some cases, the information sources listed in (b) may suggest different conclusions as to the fair value of a biological asset or an item of agricultural produce. An entity considers the reasons for those differences, to arrive at the most reliable estimate of fair value within a relatively narrow range of reasonable estimates.

(d)   In some circumstances, fair value may be readily determinable even though market determined prices or values are not available for a biological asset in its present condition. An entity shall consider whether the present value of expected net cash flows from the asset discounted at a current market determined rate results in a reliable measure of fair value.

34.6A   If the fair value of a biological asset cannot be measured reliably, the entity shall apply the cost model to that biological asset in accordance with paragraphs 34.8 and 34.10A until such time that the fair value can be reliably measured.

Disclosures – fair value model

34.7   An entity shall disclose the following for each class of biological asset measured using the fair value model:

(a)   A description of each class of biological asset.

*(b)   The methods and significant assumptions applied in determining the fair value of each class of biological asset.

*(c)   A reconciliation of changes in the **carrying amount** of each class of biological asset between the beginning and the end of the current period. The reconciliation shall include:

　　*(i)   the **gain** or loss arising from changes in fair value less costs to sell;

　　(ii)   increases resulting from purchases;

　　(iii)   decreases attributable to sales;

　　(iv)   decreases resulting from harvest;

　　(v)   increases resulting from **business combinations**; and

　　(vi)   other changes.

This reconciliation need not be presented for prior periods.

34.7A   If an entity measures any individual biological assets at cost in accordance with paragraph 34.6A, it shall explain why fair value cannot be reliably measured. If the fair value of such a biological asset becomes reliably measurable during the current period an entity shall explain why fair value has become reliably measurable and the effect of the change.

34.7B   An entity shall disclose the methods and significant assumptions applied in determining the fair value at the point of harvest of each class of agricultural produce.

Measurement – cost model

34.8   An entity applying the cost model shall measure biological assets at cost less any accumulated **depreciation** and any accumulated **impairment losses**.

34.9   In applying the cost model, agricultural produce harvested from an entity's biological assets shall be measured at the point of harvest at either:

(a)   the lower of cost and estimated selling price less costs to complete and sell; or

(b)   its fair value less costs to sell. Any gain or loss arising on initial recognition of agricultural produce at fair value less costs to sell shall be included in profit or loss for the period in which it arises.

Such measurement is the cost at that date when applying Section 13 or another applicable section of this FRS.

Disclosures – cost model

An entity shall disclose the following for each class of biological asset measured using the cost model: 34.10

(a) a description of each class of biological asset;
(b) [not used]
(c) the depreciation method used;
(d) the useful lives or the depreciation rates used; and
*(e) a reconciliation of changes in the carrying amount of each class of biological asset between the beginning and the end of the current period. The reconciliation shall include:

(i) increases resulting from purchases;
(ii) decreases attributable to sales;
(iii) decreases resulting from harvest;
(iv) increases resulting from business combinations;
(v) impairment losses recognised or reversed in profit or loss in accordance with Section 27 *Impairment of Assets*; and
(vi) other changes.

This reconciliation need not be presented for prior periods.

An entity shall disclose, for any agricultural produce measured at fair value less costs to sell, the methods and significant assumptions applied in determining the fair value at the point of harvest of each class of agricultural produce. 34.10A

Extractive Activities

An entity using this FRS that is engaged in the exploration for and/or evaluation of mineral resources (extractive activities) shall apply the requirements of IFRS 6 *Exploration for and Evaluation of Mineral Resources*. 34.11

When applying the requirements of IFRS 6, references made to other IFRSs within that standard shall be taken to be references to the relevant section or paragraph within this FRS. 34.11A

Notwithstanding the requirements of paragraph 34.11A, when applying paragraph 21 of IFRS 6, a **cash-generating unit** or group of cash-generating units shall be no larger than an **operating segment** and the reference to IFRS 8 *Operating Segments* shall be ignored. 34.11B

On first-time adoption of this FRS if it is not practical to apply a particular requirement of paragraph 18 of IFRS 6 to previous comparative amounts, an entity shall disclose that fact. 34.11C

Service Concession Arrangements

A **service concession arrangement** is an arrangement whereby a public sector body, or a **public benefit entity** (the grantor) contracts with a private sector entity (the operator) to construct (or upgrade), operate and maintain **infrastructure assets** for a specified period of time (concession period). The operator is paid for its services over the period of the arrangement. A common feature of a service concession arrangement is the public service nature of the obligation undertaken by the operator, whereby the arrangement contractually obliges the operator to provide services to, or on behalf of, the grantor for the benefit of the public. 34.12

34.12A   Specifically an arrangement is a service concession arrangement when the following conditions apply:

(a)   the grantor controls or regulates what services the operator must provide using the infrastructure assets, to whom, and at what price; and

(b)   the grantor controls, through ownership, beneficial entitlement or otherwise, any significant **residual interest** in the assets at the end of the term of the arrangement.

Where the infrastructure assets have no significant **residual value** at the end of the term of the arrangement (ie the arrangement is for its entire useful life), then the arrangement shall be accounted for as a service concession if the conditions in (a) are met.

For the purpose of condition (b), the grantor's control over any significant residual interest should both restrict the operator's practical ability to sell or pledge the infrastructure assets and give the grantor a continuing right of use throughout the concession period.

34.12B   A service concession arrangement shall be accounted for in accordance with the requirements of paragraphs 34.12E to 34.16A.

34.12C   A service concession arrangement may contain a group of contracts and sub-arrangements as elements of the service concession arrangement as a whole. Such an arrangement shall be treated as a whole when the group of contracts and sub-arrangements are linked in such a way that the commercial effect cannot be understood without reference to them as a whole. Accordingly, the contractual terms of certain contracts or arrangements may meet both the scope requirements of paragraphs 34.12 and 34.12A, and Section 20 *Leases*. Where this is the case, the requirements of this section shall prevail.

34.12D   Where an arrangement does not meet the requirements of paragraphs 34.12 and 34.12A, it shall be accounted for in accordance with Section 17 *Property, Plant and Equipment*, Section 18 *Intangible Assets other than Goodwill*, Section 20 or Section 23 *Revenue*, based on the nature of the arrangement.

Accounting by grantors – Finance lease liability model

34.12E   The infrastructure assets shall be recognised as **assets** of the grantor together with a **liability** for its obligations under the service concession arrangement.

34.12F   The grantor shall initially recognise the infrastructure assets and associated liability in accordance with paragraphs 20.9 and 20.10. If as a result of applying paragraphs 20.9 and 20.10 the grantor has not recognised a liability to make payments to the operator, it shall not recognise the infrastructure assets.

34.12G   The liability shall be recognised as a finance lease liability and subsequently accounted for in accordance with paragraph 20.11.

34.12H   The infrastructure assets shall be recognised as **property, plant and equipment** or as **intangible assets**, as appropriate, and subsequently accounted for in accordance with Section 17 or Section 18.

Accounting by operators

Treatment of the operator's rights over the infrastructure

34.12I   Infrastructure assets shall not be recognised as property, plant and equipment by the operator because the contractual service arrangement does not convey the right to control the use of the public service assets to the operator. The operator has access to operate the infrastructure to provide the public service on behalf of the grantor in accordance with the terms specified in the arrangement.

Recognition and measurement of consideration

There are two principal categories of service concession arrangements: **34.13**

(a)   In one, the operator receives a **financial asset** – an unconditional contractual right to receive a specified or determinable amount of **cash** or another financial asset from, or at the direction of, the grantor in return for constructing (or upgrading) the infrastructure assets, and then operating and maintaining the asset for a specified period of time. This category includes guarantees by the grantor to pay for any shortfall between amounts received from users of the public service and specified or determinable amounts.

(b)   In the other, the operator receives an **intangible asset** – a right to charge for use of the infrastructure assets that it constructs (or upgrades) and then operates and maintains for a specified period of time. A right to charge users is not an unconditional right to receive cash because the amounts are contingent on the extent to which the public uses the service.

Sometimes, a single arrangement may contain both types: to the extent that the grantor has given an unconditional guarantee of payment for the construction (or upgrade) of the infrastructure assets, the operator has a financial asset; to the extent that the operator receives a right to charge the public for using the service the operator has an intangible asset.

Accounting – financial asset model

The operator shall recognise a financial asset to the extent that it has an unconditional   **34.14** contractual right to receive cash or another financial asset from, or at the direction of, the grantor for the construction (or upgrade) services. The operator shall initially recognise the financial asset at fair value for the consideration received or receivable, based on the fair value of the construction (or upgrade) services provided. Thereafter, it shall account for the financial asset in accordance with Section 11 *Basic Financial Instruments* and Section 12 *Other Financial Instruments Issues*.

Accounting – intangible asset model

The operator shall recognise an intangible asset to the extent that it receives a right (a   **34.15** licence) to charge users of the public service. The operator shall initially recognise the intangible asset at fair value for the consideration received or receivable, based on the fair value of the construction (or upgrade) services provided. Thereafter, it shall account for the intangible asset in accordance with Section 18.

Operating services

The operator shall account for **revenue** in accordance with Section 23 for the operating   **34.16** services it performs.

Borrowing costs

Borrowing costs attributable to the arrangement shall be recognised as an **expense**, in   **34.16A** accordance with Section 25 *Borrowing Costs*, in the period in which they are incurred unless the operator has an intangible asset. In this case borrowing costs attributable to the arrangement may be capitalised in accordance with Section 25 where a policy of capitalisation has been adopted in accordance with that section.

Financial Institutions

34.17   A **financial institution** (other than a **retirement benefit plan**) applying this FRS shall, in addition to the disclosure requirements in Section 11 *Basic Financial Instruments* and Section 12 *Other Financial Instruments Issues*, provide the disclosures in paragraphs 34.19 to 34.33. The disclosures in paragraphs 34.19 to 34.33 are required to be provided in:

(a)   the **individual financial statements** of a financial institution (other than a retirement benefit plan); and

(b)   the **consolidated financial statements** of a **group** containing a financial institution (other than a retirement benefit plan) when the **financial instruments** held by the financial institution are **material** to the group. Where this is the case, the disclosures apply regardless of whether the principal activity of the group is being a financial institution or not. The disclosures in paragraphs 34.19 to 34.33 only need to be given in respect of financial instruments held by entities within the group that are financial institutions (other than retirement benefit plans).

34.18   A retirement benefit plan shall provide the disclosures in paragraphs 34.35 to 34.48 of this FRS.

Disclosures

Significance of financial instruments for financial position and performance

34.19   A financial institution shall disclose information that enables users of its **financial statements** to evaluate the significance of financial instruments for its **financial position** and **performance**.

34.20   A financial institution shall disclose a disaggregation of the **statement of financial position** line item by class of financial instrument. A class is a grouping of financial instruments that is appropriate to the nature of the information disclosed and that takes into account the characteristics of those financial instruments.

Impairment

34.21   Where a financial institution uses a separate allowance account to record impairments, it shall disclose a reconciliation of changes in that account during the period for each class of **financial asset**.

Fair value

34.22   For financial instruments held at **fair value** in the statement of financial position, a financial institution shall disclose for each class of financial instrument, an analysis of the level in the fair value hierarchy (as set out in paragraph 11.27) into which the fair value measurements are categorised.

Prospective amendments: Amendments to FRS 102 The Financial Reporting Standard applicable in the UK and Republic of Ireland – Fair value hierarchy disclosures (March 2016) amends paragraph 34.22 with effect for annual periods beginning on or after 1 January 2017.

Nature and extent of risks arising from financial instruments

34.23   A financial institution shall disclose information that enables users of its financial statements to evaluate the nature and extent of **credit risk**, **liquidity risk** and **market risk**

arising from financial instruments to which the financial institution is exposed at the end of the **reporting period**.

For each type of risk arising from financial instruments, a financial institution shall disclose:

34.24

(a)   the exposures to risk and how they arise;

(b)   its objectives, policies and processes for managing the risk and the methods used to measure the risk; and

(c)   any changes in (a) or (b) from the previous period.

Credit risk

A financial institution shall disclose by class of financial instrument:

34.25

(a)   The amount that best represents its maximum exposure to credit risk at the end of the reporting period. This disclosure is not required for financial instruments whose **carrying amount** best represents the maximum exposure to credit risk.

(b)   A description of collateral held as security and of other credit enhancements, and the extent to which these mitigate credit risk.

(c)   The amount by which any related credit **derivatives** or similar instruments mitigate that maximum exposure to credit risk.

(d)   Information about the credit quality of **financial assets** that are neither past due nor impaired.

A financial institution shall provide, by class of financial asset, an analysis of:

34.26

(a)   the age of financial assets that are past due as at the end of the reporting period but not impaired; and

(b)   the financial assets that are individually determined to be impaired as at the end of the reporting period, including the factors the financial institution considered in determining that they are impaired.

When a financial institution obtains financial or non-financial assets during the period by taking possession of collateral it holds as security or calling on other credit enhancements (eg guarantees), and such **assets** meet the **recognition** criteria in other sections, a financial institution shall disclose:

34.27

(a)   the nature and carrying amount of the assets obtained; and

(b)   when the assets are not readily convertible into **cash**, its policies for disposing of such assets or for using them in its operations.

Prospective amendments: Amendments to FRS 102 The Financial Reporting Standard applicable in the UK and Republic of Ireland – Fair value hierarchy disclosures (March 2016) amends paragraph 34.27 with effect for annual periods beginning on or after 1 January 2017.

Liquidity risk

A financial institution shall provide a maturity analysis for **financial liabilities** that shows the remaining contractual maturities at undiscounted amounts separated between derivative and non-derivative financial liabilities.

34.28

Market risk

A financial institution shall provide a sensitivity analysis for each type of market risk (eg interest rate risk, currency risk, other price risk) it is exposed to, showing the impact

34.29

on **profit or loss** and **equity**. Details of the methods and assumptions used should be provided.

34.30   If a financial institution prepares a sensitivity analysis, such as value-at-risk, that reflects interdependencies between risk variables (eg interest rates and exchange rates) and uses it to manage **financial risks**, it may use that sensitivity analysis instead.

Capital

34.31   A financial institution shall disclose information that enables users of its financial statements to evaluate the entity's objectives, policies and processes for managing capital. A financial institution shall disclose the following:

(a)   Qualitative information about its objectives, policies and processes for managing capital, including:

(i)   a description of what it manages as capital;

(ii)   when an entity is subject to externally imposed capital requirements, the nature of those requirements and how those requirements are incorporated into the management of capital; and

(iii)   how it is meeting its objectives for managing capital.

(b)   Summary quantitative data about what it manages as capital. Some entities regard some financial liabilities (eg some forms of subordinated debt) as part of capital. Other entities regard capital as excluding some components of equity (eg components arising from cash flow hedges).

(c)   Any changes in (a) and (b) from the previous period.

(d)   Whether during the period it complied with any externally imposed capital requirements to which it is subject.

(e)   When the entity has not complied with such externally imposed capital requirements, the consequences of such non-compliance.

A financial institution bases these disclosures on the information provided internally to **key management personnel**.

34.32   A financial institution may manage capital in a number of ways and be subject to a number of different capital requirements. For example, a conglomerate may include entities that undertake insurance activities and banking activities and those entities may operate in several jurisdictions. When an aggregate disclosure of capital requirements and how capital is managed would not provide useful information or would distort a financial statement user's understanding of the financial institution's capital resources, the financial institution shall disclose separate information for each capital requirement to which the entity is subject.

Reporting cash flows on a net basis

34.33   A financial institution that presents a statement of cash flow in accordance with Section 7 *Statement of Cash Flows* may report cash flows arising from each of the following activities on a net basis:

(a)   cash receipts and payments for the acceptance and repayment of deposits with a fixed maturity date;

(b)   the placement of deposits with and withdrawal of deposits from other financial institutions; and

(c)   cash advances and loans made to customers and the repayment of those advances and loans.

This paragraph does not impose a requirement to produce a cash flow statement.

Retirement Benefit Plans: Financial Statements

An entity applying this FRS that is a **retirement benefit plan** shall also apply the requirements of paragraphs 34.35 to 34.48. A retirement benefit plan may be a **defined benefit plan**, a **defined contribution plan**, or have both defined benefit and defined contribution elements. The **financial statements** shall distinguish between defined benefit and defined contribution elements, where **material**. **34.34**

Requirements applicable to both defined benefit plans and defined contribution plans

A retirement benefit plan need not comply with the requirements of paragraph 3.17. The financial statements of a retirement benefit plan shall contain as part of the financial statements: **34.35**

(a) a statement of changes in **net assets available for benefits** (which can also be called a Fund Account) (see paragraph 34.37);
(b) a statement of net assets available for benefits (see paragraph 34.38); and
(c) **notes**, comprising a summary of significant **accounting policies** and other explanatory information.

At each **reporting date**, the net assets available for benefits shall be measured in accordance with paragraph 28.15(b). Changes in fair value shall be recognised in the statements of changes in net assets available for benefits. **34.36**

Statement of changes in net assets available for benefits (Fund Account)

The financial statements of a retirement benefit plan, whether defined contribution or defined benefit, shall present the following in the statement of changes in net assets available for benefits: **34.37**

(a) employer contributions;
(b) employee contributions;
(c) investment income such as interest and dividends;
(d) other income;
(e) benefits paid or payable (analysed, for example, as retirement, death and disability benefits, and lump sum payments);
(f) administrative expenses;
(g) other expenses;
(h) taxes on income;
(i) profits and losses on disposal of investments and changes in value of investments; and
(j) transfers from and to other plans.

Statement of net assets available for benefits

The financial statements of a retirement benefit plan, whether defined contribution or defined benefit, shall present the following in the statement of net assets available for benefits: **34.38**

(a) **assets** at the end of the period suitably classified; and
(b) **liabilities** other than the actuarial **present value** of promised retirement benefits.

The basis of valuation of assets shall be presented in the notes to the financial statements.

Disclosures

Assets other than financial instruments held at fair value

34.39 Where a retirement benefit plan holds assets other than financial instruments at fair value in accordance with paragraph 34.36, it shall apply the disclosure requirements of the relevant section of this FRS, for example in relation to **investment property** it shall provide the disclosures required by paragraph 16.10.

Significance of financial instruments for financial position and performance

34.40 A retirement benefit plan shall disclose information that enables users of its financial statements to evaluate the significance of financial instruments for its **financial position** and **performance**.

34.41 A retirement benefit plan shall disclose a disaggregation of the statement of net assets available for benefits by class of financial instrument. A class is a grouping of financial instruments that is appropriate to the nature of the information disclosed and that takes into account the characteristics of those financial instruments.

Fair value

34.42 For financial instruments held at fair value in the statement of net assets available for benefits, a retirement benefit plan shall disclose for each class of financial instrument, an analysis of the level in the fair value hierarchy (as set out in paragraph 11.27) into which the fair value measurements are categorised.

Prospective amendments: Amendments to FRS 102 The Financial Reporting Standard applicable in the UK and Republic of Ireland – Fair value hierarchy disclosures (March 2016) amends paragraph 34.42 with effect for annual periods beginning on or after 1 January 2017.

Nature and extent of risks arising from financial instruments

34.43 A retirement benefit plan shall disclose information that enables users of its financial statements to evaluate the nature and extent of **credit risk** and **market risk** arising from financial instruments to which the retirement benefit plan is exposed at the end of the **reporting period**.

34.44 For each type of credit and market risk arising from financial instruments, a retirement benefit plan shall disclose:

(a)   the exposures to risk and how they arise;

(b)   its objectives, policies and processes for managing the risk and the methods used to measure the risk; and

(c)   any changes in (a) or (b) from the previous period.

In relation to credit risk, a retirement benefit plan shall, in addition, provide the disclosures set out in paragraphs 34.45 and 34.46.

Credit risk

34.45 A retirement benefit plan shall disclose by class of financial instrument:

(a)   The amount that best represents its maximum exposure to credit risk at the end of the reporting period. This disclosure is not required for financial instruments whose **carrying amount** best represents the maximum exposure to credit risk.

(b) A description of collateral held as security and of other credit enhancements, and the extent to which these mitigate credit risk.

(c) The amount by which any related credit **derivatives** or similar instruments mitigate that maximum exposure to credit risk.

(d) Information about the credit quality of financial assets that are neither past due nor impaired.

When a retirement benefit plan obtains financial or non-financial assets during the period by taking possession of collateral it holds as security or calling on other credit enhancements (eg guarantees), and such assets meet the **recognition** criteria in other sections, a retirement benefit plan shall disclose: **34.46**

(a) the nature and carrying amount of the assets obtained; and

(b) when the assets are not readily convertible into **cash**, its policies for disposing of such assets or for retaining them.

Defined benefit plans – actuarial liabilities

A defined benefit plan is not required to recognise a liability in relation to the promised retirement benefits. **34.47**

A defined benefit plan shall disclose, in a report alongside the financial statements, information regarding the actuarial present value of promised retirement benefits including: **34.48**

(a) a statement of the actuarial present value of promised retirement benefits, based on the most recent valuation of the scheme;

(b) the date of the most recent valuation of the scheme; and

(c) the significant actuarial assumptions made and the method used to calculate the actuarial present value of promised retirement benefits.

Heritage Assets

All **heritage assets** shall be accounted for in accordance with the requirements of paragraphs 34.50 to 34.56. These paragraphs do not apply to **investment property, property, plant and equipment** or **intangible assets** which fall within the scope of Section 16 *Investment Properties*, Section 17 *Property, Plant and Equipment* and Section 18 *Intangible Assets other than Goodwill*. **34.49**

Works of art and similar objects are sometimes held by commercial entities but are not heritage assets because they are not maintained principally for their contribution to knowledge and culture. These assets shall therefore be accounted for in accordance with Section 17. Heritage assets used by the entity itself, for example historic buildings used for teaching by education establishments, shall also be accounted for in accordance with Section 17. This is based on the view that an operational perspective is likely to be most relevant for most users of **financial statements**. However, entities that use historic buildings and similar assets may wish to consider whether it is appropriate to apply the disclosures required by paragraphs 34.55 and 34.56. **34.50**

Recognition and measurement

An entity shall recognise and measure heritage assets in accordance with Section 17 (ie using the cost model or revaluation model), subject to the requirements set out in paragraphs 34.52 to 34.53 below. **34.51**

Heritage assets shall be recognised in the **statement of financial position** separately from other assets. **34.52**

34.53   Where heritage assets have previously been capitalised or are recently purchased, information on the cost or value of the asset will be available. Where this information is not available, and cannot be obtained at a cost which is commensurate with the benefits to users of the financial statements, the assets shall not be recognised in the statement of financial position, but must be disclosed in accordance with the requirements below.

34.54   At each **reporting date**, an entity shall apply Section 27 *Impairment of Assets* to determine whether a heritage asset is impaired and, if so, how to recognise and measure the **impairment loss**. A heritage asset may be impaired, for example where it has suffered physical deterioration, breakage or doubts arise as to its authenticity.

Disclosure

34.55   An entity shall disclose the following for all heritage assets it holds:

(a)   An indication of the nature and scale of heritage assets held by the entity.

(b)   The policy for the acquisition, preservation, management and disposal of heritage assets (including a description of the records maintained by the entity of its collection of heritage assets and information on the extent to which access to the assets is permitted).

(c)   The **accounting policies** adopted for heritage assets, including details of the measurement bases used.

(d)   For heritage assets that have not been recognised in the statement of financial position, the **notes** to the financial statements shall:

    (i)   explain the reasons why;

    (ii)   describe the significance and nature of those assets; and

    (iii)   disclose information that is helpful in assessing the value of those heritage assets.

*(e)   Where heritage assets are recognised in the statement of financial position the following disclosure is required:

    (i)   the **carrying amount** of heritage assets at the beginning of the **reporting period** and the reporting date, including an analysis between classes or groups of heritage assets recognised at cost and those recognised at valuation; and

    *(ii)   where assets are recognised at valuation, sufficient information to assist in understanding the valuation being recognised (date of valuation, method used, whether carried out by external valuer and if so their qualification and any significant limitations on the valuation).

*(f)   A summary of transactions relating to heritage assets for the reporting period and each of the previous four reporting periods disclosing:

    (i)   the cost of acquisitions of heritage assets;

    (ii)   the value of heritage assets acquired by donations;

    (iii)   the carrying amount of heritage assets disposed of in the period and proceeds received; and

    (iv)   any impairment recognised in the period.

The summary shall show separately those transactions included in the statement of financial position and those that are not.

(g)   In exceptional circumstances where it is **impracticable** to obtain a valuation of heritage assets acquired by donation the reason shall be stated.

Disclosures can be aggregated for groups or classes of heritage assets, provided this does not obscure significant information.

Where it is impracticable to do so, the disclosures required by paragraph 34.55(f) need not be given for any accounting period earlier than the previous comparable period, and a statement to the effect that it is impracticable shall be made.   **34.56**

Funding Commitments

An entity that commits to provide resources to other entities shall apply the requirements of paragraphs 34.58 to 34.63 and the accompanying guidance at Appendix A to this section, except for commitments to make a loan to which entities shall apply Section 11 *Basic Financial Instruments* or Section 12 *Other Financial Instruments Issues*, as applicable.   **34.57**

When applying these paragraphs, the requirements of Section 2 *Concepts and Pervasive Principles* and Section 21 *Provisions and Contingencies* shall also be taken into consideration.   **34.58**

Recognition

An entity shall recognise a **liability** and, usually, a corresponding **expense**, when it has made a commitment that it will provide resources to another party, if, and only if: **34.59**

(a) the definition and **recognition** criteria for a liability have been satisfied;

(b) the obligation (which may be a **constructive obligation**) is such that the entity cannot realistically withdraw from it; and

(c) the entitlement of the other party to the resources does not depend on the satisfaction of **performance-related conditions**.

Commitments that are performance-related will be recognised when those performance-related conditions are met.   **34.60**

Measurement

An entity shall measure any recognised liability at the **present value** of the resources committed.   **34.61**

Disclosure

An entity that has made a commitment shall disclose the following: *** 34.62**

(a) the commitment made;

(b) the time-frame of that commitment;

(c) any performance-related conditions attached to that commitment; and

(d) details of how that commitment will be funded.

The above disclosures may be made in aggregate, providing that such aggregation does not obscure significant information. However, separate disclosure shall be made for recognised and unrecognised commitments.   **34.63**

Incoming Resources from Non-Exchange Transactions

The accounting for **government grants** is addressed in Section 24 *Government Grants*.   **PBE34.64**

Paragraphs PBE34.67 to PBE34.74 and the accompanying guidance at Appendix B to this section apply to other resources received from **non-exchange transactions** by **public benefit entities** or entities within a **public benefit entity group**. A non-exchange transaction is a transaction whereby an entity receives value from another entity without   **PBE34.65** directly giving approximately equal value in exchange or gives value to another entity without directly receiving approximately equal value in exchange.

PBE34.66   Non-exchange transactions include, but are not limited to, donations (of **cash**, goods, and services) and legacies.

Recognition and measurement

PBE34.67   An entity shall recognise receipts of resources from non-exchange transactions as follows:

   (a)   Transactions that do not impose specified future performance-related conditions on the recipient are recognised in **income** when the resources are received or receivable.

   (b)   Transactions that do impose specified future performance-related conditions on the recipient are recognised in income only when the performance-related conditions are met.

   (c)   Where resources are received before the **revenue recognition** criteria are satisfied, a **liability** is recognised.

PBE34.68   The existence of a **restriction** does not prohibit a resource from being recognised in income when receivable.

PBE34.69   When applying the requirements of paragraph PBE34.67, an entity must take into consideration whether the resource can be measured reliably and whether the benefits of recognising the resource outweigh the costs.

PBE34.70   Therefore, where it is not practicable to estimate the value of the resource with sufficient **reliability**, the income shall be included in the financial period when the resource is sold.

PBE34.71   An entity shall recognise a liability for any resource that has previously been received and recognised in income when, as a result of a subsequent failure to meet restrictions or performance-related conditions attached to it, repayment becomes **probable**.

PBE34.72   Donations of services that can be reasonably quantified will usually result in the recognition of income and an **expense**. An **asset** will be recognised only when those services are used for the production of an asset and the services received will be capitalised as part of the cost of that asset.

PBE34.73   An entity shall measure incoming resources from non-exchange transactions as follows:

   (a)   Donated services and facilities, that would otherwise have been purchased, shall be measured at the value to the entity.

   (b)   All other incoming resources from non-exchange transactions shall be measured at the **fair value** of the resources received or receivable.

Disclosure

PBE34.74   An entity shall disclose the following:

   (a)   the nature and amounts of resources receivable from non-exchange transactions recognised in the **financial statements**;

   (b)   any unfulfilled conditions or other contingencies attaching to resources from non-exchange transactions that have not been recognised in income; and

   (c)   an indication of other forms of resources from non-exchange transactions from which the entity has benefited.

Public Benefit Entity Combinations

Paragraphs PBE34.76 to PBE34.86 apply only to **public benefit entities** for the following categories of **entity combinations** which involve a whole entity or parts of an entity combining with another entity:	**PBE34.75**

(a)   combinations at nil or nominal consideration which are in substance a gift; and

(b)   combinations which meet the definition and criteria of a **merger**.

Combinations which are determined to be acquisitions shall be accounted for in accordance with Section 19 *Business Combinations and Goodwill*.	**PBE34.76**

Combinations that are in substance a gift

Accounting treatment and disclosure

A **combination that is in substance a gift** shall be accounted for in accordance with Section 19 except for the matters addressed in paragraphs PBE34.78 and PBE34.79 below.	**PBE34.77**

Any excess of the **fair value** of the **assets** received over the fair value of the **liabilities** assumed is recognised as a **gain** in **income and expenditure**. This gain represents the gift of the value of one entity to another and shall be recognised as income.	**PBE34.78**

Any excess of the fair value of the liabilities assumed over the fair value of the assets received is recognised as a loss in income and expenditure. This loss represents the net obligations assumed, for which the receiving entity has not received a financial reward and shall be recognised as an **expense**.	**PBE34.79**

Combinations that are a merger

Unless it is not permitted by the statutory framework under which a public benefit entity reports, an entity combination that is a merger shall apply merger accounting as prescribed below. If merger accounting is not permitted, an entity combination shall be accounted for as an acquisition in accordance with Section 19.	**PBE34.80**

Any entity combination:	**PBE34.81**

(a)   which is neither a combination that is in substance a gift nor a merger; or

(b)   for which merger accounting is not permitted by the statutory framework under which the public benefit entity reports

shall be accounted for as an acquisition in accordance with Section 19.

Accounting treatment

Under merger accounting the carrying value of the assets and liabilities of the parties to the combination are not adjusted to fair value, although adjustments shall be made to achieve uniformity of **accounting policies** across the combining entities.	**PBE34.82**

The results and **cash flows** of all the combining entities shall be brought into the **financial statements** of the newly formed entity from the beginning of the financial period in which the merger occurs.	**PBE34.83**

The comparative amounts shall be restated by including the results for all the combining entities for the previous accounting period and their **statement of financial positions** for the previous **reporting date**. The comparative figures shall be marked as 'combined' figures.	**PBE34.84**

PBE34.85 All costs associated with the merger shall be charged as an expense in the period incurred.

Disclosure

PBE34.86 For each entity combination accounted for as a merger in the **reporting period** the following shall be disclosed in the newly formed entity's financial statements:

(a) the names and descriptions of the combining entities or businesses;

(b) the date of the merger;

(c) an analysis of the principal components of the current year's **total comprehensive income** to indicate:

    (i) the amounts relating to the newly formed merged entity for the period after the date of the merger; and

    (ii) the amounts relating to each party to the merger up to the date of the merger.

(d) an analysis of the previous year's total comprehensive income between each party to the merger;

(e) the aggregate carrying value of the net assets of each party to the merger at the date of the merger; and

(f) the nature and amount of any significant adjustments required to align accounting policies and an explanation of any further adjustments made to net assets as a result of the merger.

Public Benefit Entity Concessionary Loans

PBE34.87 Paragraphs PBE34.89 to PBE34.97 address the **recognition**, **measurement** and disclosure of **public benefit entity concessionary loan** arrangements within the **financial statements** of **public benefit entities** or entities within a **public benefit entity group** making or receiving public benefit entity concessionary loans. These paragraphs apply to public benefit entity concessionary loan arrangements only and are not applicable to loans which are at a market rate or to other commercial arrangements.

PBE34.88 Public benefit entity concessionary loans are loans made or received between a public benefit entity or an entity within the public benefit entity group, and another party at below the **prevailing market rate** of interest that are not repayable on demand and are for the purposes of furthering the objectives of the public benefit entity or public benefit entity **parent**.

Accounting treatment

PBE34.89 Entities making or receiving public benefit entity concessionary loans shall use either:

(a) the recognition, measurement and disclosure requirements in Section 11 *Basic Financial Instruments* or Section 12 *Other Financial Instruments Issues* (for example, Section 11 requires initial measurement at **fair value** and subsequent measurement at **amortised cost** using the **effective interest method**); or

(b) the accounting treatment set out in paragraphs PBE34.90 to PBE34.97 below.

A public benefit entity or an entity within a public benefit entity group shall apply the same **accounting policy** to concessionary loans both made and received.

Initial measurement

PBE34.90 A public benefit entity or an entity within a public benefit entity group making or receiving concessionary loans shall initially measure these arrangements at the amount received or paid and recognise them in the **statement of financial position**.

Subsequent measurement

In subsequent years, the **carrying amount** of concessionary loans in the financial statements shall be adjusted to reflect any accrued interest payable or receivable.

PBE34.91

To the extent that a loan that has been made is irrecoverable, an **impairment loss** shall be recognised in **income and expenditure**.

PBE34.92

Presentation and disclosure

The entity shall present concessionary loans made and concessionary loans received either as a separate line items on the face of the statement of financial position or in the **notes** to the financial statements.

PBE34.93

Concessionary loans shall be presented separately between amounts repayable or receivable within one year and amounts repayable or receivable after more than one year.

PBE34.94

The entity shall disclose in the summary of significant accounting policies the measurement basis used for concessionary loans and any other accounting policies which are relevant to the understanding of these transactions within the financial statements.

PBE34.95

The entity shall disclose the following:

PBE34.96

(a) the terms and conditions of concessionary loan arrangements, for example the interest rate, any security provided and the terms of the repayment; and

(b) the value of concessionary loans which have been committed but not taken up at the year end.

Concessionary loans made or received shall be disclosed separately. However multiple loans made or received may be disclosed in aggregate, providing that such aggregation does not obscure significant information.

PBE34.97

Appendix A to Section 34

Guidance on funding commitments (paragraphs 34.57 to 34.63)

This guidance is an integral part of the Standard.

Entities often make commitments to provide cash or other resources to other entities. In such a case, it is necessary to determine whether the commitment should be recognised as a liability. The definition of a liability requires that there be a present obligation, and not merely an expectation of a future outflow.

34A.1

A general statement that the entity intends to provide resources to certain classes of potential beneficiaries in accordance with its objectives does not in itself give rise to a liability, as the entity may amend or withdraw its policy, and potential beneficiaries do not have the ability to insist on their fulfilment. Similarly, a promise to provide cash conditional on the receipt of future income in itself may not give rise to a liability where the entity cannot be required to fulfil it if the future income is not received and it is probable that the economic benefits will not be transferred.

34A.2

A liability is recognised only for a commitment that gives the recipient a valid expectation that payment will be made and from which the grantor cannot realistically withdraw. One of the implications of this is that a liability only exists where the commitment has been communicated to the recipient.

34A.3

34A.4   Commitments are not recognised if they are subject to performance-related conditions. In such a case, the entity is required to fulfil its commitment only when the performance-related conditions are met and no liability exists until that time.

34A.5   A commitment may contain conditions that are not performance-related conditions. For example, a requirement to provide an annual financial report to the grantor may serve mainly as an administrative tool because failure to comply would not release the grantor from its commitment. This may be distinguished from a requirement to submit a detailed report for review and consideration by the grantor of how funds will be utilised in order to secure payment. A mere restriction on the specific purpose for which funds are to be used does not in itself constitute a performance-related condition.

34A.6   For funding commitments that are not recognised, it is important that full and informative disclosures are made of their existence and of the sources of funding for these unrecognised commitments.

Appendix B to Section 34

Guidance on incoming resources from non-exchange transactions (paragraphs 34.64 to 34.74)

This guidance is an integral part of the Standard.

Recognition

PBE34B.1   The receipt of resources will usually result in an entity recognising an asset and corresponding income for the fair value of resources when those resources become received or receivable. Instances when this may differ include where:

(a)   an entity received those resources in the form of services (see paragraphs PBE34B.8 to PBE34B.12); or

(b)   there are performance-related conditions attached to the resources, which have yet to be fulfilled (see paragraphs PBE34B.13 to PBE34B.14).

PBE34B.2   Resources shall only be recognised when the fair value of the incoming resources can be measured reliably.

PBE34B.3   The concepts of materiality (see paragraph 2.6), and balance between benefit and cost (see paragraph 2.13) should be considered when deciding which resources received shall be recognised in the financial statements.

PBE34B.4   When it is impracticable to recognise resources from non-exchange transactions, the income is recognised in the period in which the resources are sold or distributed. The most common example is that of high volume, low value second-hand goods donated for resale.

Legacies

PBE34B.5   Donations in the form of legacies are recognised when it is probable that the legacy will be received and its value can be measured reliably. These criteria will normally be met following probate once the executor(s) of the estate has established that there are sufficient assets in the estate, after settling liabilities, to pay the legacy.

PBE34B.6   Evidence that the executor(s) has determined that a payment can be made, may arise on the agreement of the estate's accounts or notification that payment will be made. Where notification is received after the year-end but it is clear that the executor(s) has agreed prior to the year-end that the legacy can be paid, the legacy is accrued in the financial statements. The certainty and measurability of the receipt may be affected by subsequent events such as valuations and disputes.

Entities that are in receipt of numerous immaterial legacies for which individual identification would be burdensome may take a portfolio approach.   **PBE34B.7**

Services

Donated services that can be reasonably quantified shall be recognised in the financial statements when they are received.   **PBE34B.8**

Donated services that are consumed immediately are usually recognised as an expense. However, there may be circumstances when a service is used in the production of an asset, for example erecting a building. In these cases, the associated donated service (eg plumbing and electrical services) would be recognised as a part of the cost of that asset.   **PBE34B.9**

Donated services that can be reasonably quantified include donated facilities, such as office accommodation, services that would otherwise have been purchased and services usually provided by an individual or an entity as part of their trade or profession for a fee.   **PBE34B.10**

It is expected that contributions made by volunteers cannot be reasonably quantified and therefore these services shall not be recognised.   **PBE34B.11**

Paragraph PBE34.74(c) requires an entity to disclose other forms of resources from non-exchange transactions from which the entity has benefited. This will include the disclosure of unrecognised volunteer services.   **PBE34B.12**

Performance-related conditions

Some resources are given with performance-related conditions attached which require the recipient to use the resources to provide a specified level of service in order to be entitled to retain the resources. An entity will not recognise income from those resources until these performance-related conditions have been met.   **PBE34B.13**

However, some requirements are stated so broadly that they do not actually impose a performance-related condition on the recipient. In these cases the recipient will recognise income on receipt of the transfer of resources.   **PBE34B.14**

Measurement

Paragraph PBE34.73(a) requires donated services and facilities to be measured at the value to the entity. This requirement only applies to those services and facilities that would otherwise have been purchased by the entity. The value placed on these services and facilities should be the estimated value to the entity of the service or facility received, this will be the price the entity estimates it would pay in the open market for a service or facility of equivalent utility to the entity.   **PBE34B.15**

Paragraph PBE34.73(b) requires resources received or receivable, that are not services or facilities, to be measured at their fair value. These fair values are usually the price that the entity would have to pay on the open market for an equivalent resource.   **PBE34B.16**

When there is no direct evidence of an open market value for an equivalent item a value may be derived from sources such as: **PBE34B.17**

(a)   the cost of the item to the donor; or

(b)   in the case of goods that are expected to be sold, the estimated resale value (which may reflect the amount actually realised) after deducting the cost to sell the goods.

PBE34B.18   Donated services are recognised as income and an equivalent amount shall be recognised as an expense in income and expenditure, unless the expense can be capitalised as part of the cost of an asset.

Section 35 Transition to this FRS

Scope of this section

35.1   This section applies to a **first-time adopter of this FRS**, regardless of whether its previous accounting framework was **EU-adopted IFRS** or another set of generally accepted accounting principles (GAAP) such as its national accounting standards, or another framework such as the local income tax basis.

35.2   Notwithstanding the requirements in paragraphs 35.3 and 35.4, an entity that has applied **FRS 102** in a previous **reporting period**, but whose most recent previous annual **financial statements** did not contain an explicit and unreserved statement of compliance with this FRS, must either apply this section or else apply FRS 102 retrospectively in accordance with Section 10 *Accounting Policies, Changes in Estimates and Errors* as if the entity had never stopped applying this FRS.

First-time adoption

35.3   A first-time adopter of this FRS shall apply this section in its first financial statements that conform to this FRS.

35.4   An entity's first financial statements that conform to this FRS are the first financial statements[14] in which the entity makes an explicit and unreserved statement in those financial statements of compliance with this FRS. Financial statements prepared in accordance with this FRS are an entity's first such financial statements if, for example, the entity:

(a)   did not present financial statements for previous periods;

(b)   presented its most recent previous financial statements under previous UK and Republic of Ireland requirements that are therefore not consistent with this FRS in all respects; or

(c)   presented its most recent previous financial statements in conformity with EU-adopted IFRS.

35.5   Paragraph 3.17 defines a complete set of financial statements.

35.6   Paragraph 3.14 requires an entity to disclose, in a complete set of financial statements, comparative information in respect of the preceding period for all amounts presented in the financial statements, as well as specified comparative narrative and descriptive information. An entity may present comparative information in respect of more than one preceding period. Therefore, an entity's **date of transition** to this FRS is the beginning of the earliest period for which the entity presents full comparative information in accordance with this FRS in its first financial statements that comply with this FRS.

---

[14] *This excludes interim financial statements.*

Procedures for preparing financial statements at the date of transition

Except as provided in paragraphs 35.9 to 35.11B, an entity shall, in its opening **statement**   **35.7**
of financial position as of its date of transition to this FRS (ie the beginning of the earliest
period presented):

(a)   recognise all **assets** and **liabilities** whose **recognition** is required by this FRS;
(b)   not recognise items as assets or liabilities if this FRS does not permit such recognition;
(c)   reclassify items that it recognised under its previous financial reporting framework
       as one type of asset, liability or component of equity, but are a different type of asset,
       liability or component of equity under this FRS; and
(d)   apply this FRS in measuring all recognised assets and liabilities.

This section does not require the opening statement of financial position to be presented.

The **accounting policies** that an entity uses in its opening statement of financial position   **35.8**
under this FRS may differ from those that it used for the same date using its previous
financial reporting framework. The resulting adjustments arise from transactions, other
events or conditions before the date of transition to this FRS. Therefore, an entity shall
recognise those adjustments directly in retained earnings (or, if appropriate, another
category of equity) at the date of transition to this FRS.

On first-time adoption of this FRS, an entity shall not retrospectively change the accounting   **35.9**
that it followed under its previous financial reporting framework for any of the following
transactions:

(a)   ***Derecognition of financial assets and financial liabilities:***
       Financial assets and liabilities derecognised under an entity's previous accounting
       framework before the date of transition shall not be recognised upon adoption
       of this FRS. Conversely, for financial assets and liabilities that would have been
       derecognised under this FRS in a transaction that took place before the date of
       transition, but that were not derecognised under an entity's previous accounting
       framework, an entity may choose:

       (i)   to derecognise them on adoption of this FRS; or
       (ii)   to continue to recognise them until disposed of or settled.

(b)   [Not used]
(c)   *Accounting estimates.*
(d)   ***Discontinued operations.***
(e)   *Measuring **non-controlling interests***:

       The requirements:

       (i)   to allocate **profit or loss** and **total comprehensive income** between non-
              controlling interest and **owners** of the **parent**;
       (ii)   for accounting for changes in the parent's ownership interest in a subsidiary
              that do not result in a loss of control; and
       (iii) for accounting for a loss of control over a subsidiary

       shall be applied prospectively from the date of transition to this FRS (or from such
       earlier date as this FRS is applied to restate **business combinations**—see paragraph
       35.10(a)).

An entity may use one or more of the following exemptions in preparing its first financial   **35.10**
statements that conform to this FRS:

(a)   ***Business combinations, including group reconstructions***
       A first-time adopter may elect not to apply Section 19 *Business Combinations and*
       Goodwill to business combinations that were effected before the date of transition

to this FRS. However, if a first-time adopter restates any business combination to comply with Section 19, it shall restate all later business combinations. If a first-time adopter does not apply Section 19 retrospectively, the first-time adopter shall recognise and measure all its assets and liabilities acquired or assumed in a past business combination at the date of transition to this FRS in accordance with paragraphs 35.7 to 35.9 or if applicable, with paragraphs 35.10(b) to (r) except for:

(i) **intangible assets** other than **goodwill** – intangible assets subsumed within goodwill shall not be separately recognised; and

(ii) goodwill – no adjustment shall be made to the carrying value of goodwill.

(b) *Share-based payment transactions*

A first-time adopter is not required to apply Section 26 *Share-based Payment* to equity instruments (including the equity component of share-based payment transactions previously treated as compound instruments) that were granted before the date of transition to this FRS, or to liabilities arising from share-based payment transactions that were settled before the date of transition to this FRS. Except that a first-time adopter previously applying FRS 20 *(IFRS 2) Share-based Payment* or IFRS 2 *Share-based Payment* shall, in relation to equity instruments (including the equity component of share-based payment transactions previously treated as compound instruments) that were granted before the date of transition to this FRS, apply either FRS 20/IFRS 2 (as applicable) or Section 26 of this FRS at the date of transition.

In addition, for a small entity that first adopts this FRS for an accounting period that commences before 1 January 2017, this exemption is extended to equity instruments that were granted before the start of the first reporting period that complies with this FRS, provided that the small entity did not previously apply FRS 20 or IFRS 2. A small entity that chooses to apply this exemption shall provide disclosures in accordance with paragraph 1AC.31.

(c) *Fair value as deemed cost*

A first-time adopter may elect to measure an:

(i) item of **property, plant and equipment**;

(ii) **investment property**; or

(iii) intangible asset which meets the recognition criteria and the criteria for revaluation in Section 18 *Intangible Assets other than Goodwill*

on the date of transition to this FRS at its fair value and use that **fair value** as its **deemed cost** at that date.

(d) *Revaluation as deemed cost*

A first-time adopter may elect to use a previous GAAP revaluation of an:

(i) item of property, plant and equipment;

(ii) investment property; or

(iii) intangible asset which meets the recognition criteria and the criteria for revaluation in Section 18

at, or before, the date of transition to this FRS as its deemed cost at the revaluation date.

(e) [Not used]

(f) *Individual and separate financial statements*

When an entity prepares individual or **separate financial statements**, paragraphs 9.26, 14.4 and 15.9 require the entity to account for its investments in **subsidiaries**, **associates**, and **jointly controlled entities** either at cost less impairment or at fair value.

If a first-time adopter measures such an investment at cost, it shall measure that investment at one of the following amounts in its individual or separate opening statement of financial position, as appropriate, prepared in accordance with this FRS:

(i)   cost determined in accordance with Section 9 *Consolidated and Separate Financial Statements*, Section 14 *Investments in Associates* or Section 15 *Investments in Joint Ventures*; or

(ii) deemed cost, which shall be the **carrying amount** at the date of transition as determined under the entity's previous GAAP.

(g) ***Compound financial instruments***
Paragraph 22.13 requires an entity to split a **compound financial instrument** into its liability and equity components at the date of issue. A first-time adopter need not separate those two components if the liability component is not outstanding at the date of transition to this FRS.

(h) [Not used]

(i) ***Service concession arrangements – Accounting by operators***
A first-time adopter is not required to apply paragraphs 34.12I to 34.16A to **service concession arrangements** that were entered into before the date of transition to this FRS. Such service concession arrangements shall continue to be accounted for using the same accounting policies being applied at the date of transition to this FRS.

(j) ***Extractive activities***
A first-time adopter that under a previous GAAP accounted for exploration and development costs for oil and gas properties in the development or production phases, in cost centres that included all properties in a large geographical area may elect to measure oil and gas assets at the date of transition to this FRS on the following basis:

(i)   Exploration and evaluation assets at the amount determined under the entity's previous GAAP.

(ii) Assets in the development or production phases at the amount determined for the cost centre under the entity's previous GAAP. The entity shall allocate this amount to the cost centre's underlying assets pro rata using reserve volumes or reserve values as of that date.

The entity shall test exploration and evaluation assets and assets in the development and production phases for impairment at the date of transition to this FRS in accordance with Section 34 *Specialised Activities* or Section 27 *Impairment of Assets* of this FRS respectively, and if necessary, reduce the amount determined in accordance with (i) or (ii) above. For the purposes of this paragraph, oil and gas assets comprise only those assets used in the exploration, evaluation, development or production of oil and gas.

(k) ***Arrangements containing a lease***
A first-time adopter may elect to determine whether an arrangement existing at the date of transition to this FRS contains a **lease** (see paragraph 20.3A) on the basis of facts and circumstances existing at that date, rather than when the arrangement was entered into.

(l) ***Decommissioning liabilities included in the cost of property, plant and equipment***
Paragraph 17.10(c) states that the cost of an item of property, plant and equipment includes the initial estimate of the costs of dismantling and removing the item and restoring the site on which it is located, the obligation for which an entity incurs either when the item is acquired or as a consequence of having used the item during a particular period for purposes other than to produce **inventories** during that period. A first-time adopter may elect to measure this component of the cost of an item of property, plant and equipment at the date of transition to this FRS, rather than on the date(s) when the obligation initially arose.

(m) ***Dormant companies***
A company within the Companies Act definition of a dormant company may elect to retain its accounting policies for reported assets, liabilities and equity at the date of transition to this FRS until there is any change to those balances or the company undertakes any new transactions.

(n)   **Deferred development costs as a deemed cost**
A first-time adopter may elect to measure the carrying amount at the date of transition to this FRS for development costs deferred in accordance with SSAP 13 *Accounting for research and development* as its deemed cost at that date.

(o)   **Borrowing costs**
An entity electing to adopt an accounting policy of capitalising **borrowing costs** as part of the cost of a **qualifying asset** may elect to treat the date of transition to this FRS as the date on which capitalisation commences.

(p)   **Lease incentives**
A first-time adopter is not required to apply paragraphs 20.15A and 20.25A to **lease incentives** provided the term of the lease commenced before the date of transition to this FRS. The first-time adopter shall continue to recognise any residual benefit or cost associated with these lease incentives on the same basis as that applied at the date of transition to this FRS.

(q)   **Public benefit entity combinations**
A first-time adopter may elect not to apply paragraphs PBE34.75 to PBE34.86 relating to **public benefit entity combinations** to combinations that were effected before the date of transition to this FRS. However, if on first-time adoption a **public benefit entity** restates any entity combination to comply with this section, it shall restate all later entity combinations.

(r)   **Assets and liabilities of subsidiaries, associates and joint ventures**
If a subsidiary becomes a first-time adopter later than its parent, the subsidiary shall in its financial statements measure its assets and liabilities at either:

   (i)   the carrying amounts that would be included in the parent's **consolidated financial statements**, based on the parent's date of transition to this FRS, if no adjustments were made for consolidation procedures and for the effects of the business combination in which the parent acquired the subsidiary; or

   (ii)   the carrying amounts required by the rest of this FRS, based on the subsidiary's date of transition to this FRS. These carrying amounts could differ from those described in (i) when:

      (a)   the exemptions in this FRS result in measurements that depend on the date of transition to this FRS; or

      (b)   the accounting policies used in the subsidiary's financial statements differ from those in the consolidated financial statements. For example, the subsidiary may use as its accounting policy the cost model in Section 17 *Property, Plant and Equipment*, whereas the **group** may use the revaluation model.

A similar election is available to an associate or **joint venture** that becomes a first-time adopter later than an entity that has **significant influence** or **joint control** over it.

However, if an entity becomes a first-time adopter later than its subsidiary (or associate or joint venture) the entity shall, in its consolidated financial statements, measure the assets and liabilities of the subsidiary (or associate or joint venture) at the same carrying amounts as in the financial statements of the subsidiary (or associate or joint venture), after adjusting for consolidation (and equity accounting) adjustments and for the effects of the business combination in which the entity acquired the subsidiary (or transaction in which it acquired the associate or joint venture). Similarly, if a parent becomes a first-time adopter for its separate financial statements earlier or later than for its consolidated financial statements, it shall measure its assets and liabilities at the same amounts in both financial statements, except for consolidation adjustments.

(s)   **Designation of previously recognised financial instruments**
This FRS permits a financial instrument (provided it meets certain criteria) to be designated on initial recognition as a financial asset or financial liability at fair value through profit or loss. Despite this an entity is permitted to designate, as at the date

of transition to this FRS, any financial asset or financial liability at fair value through profit or loss provided the asset or liability meets the criteria in paragraph 11.14(b) at that date.

(t)   **Hedge accounting**

(i)   *A hedging relationship existing on the date of transition*

A first-time adopter may choose to apply hedge accounting to a hedging relationship of a type described in paragraph 12.19 which exists on the date of transition between a **hedging instrument** and a **hedged item**, provided the conditions of paragraphs 12.18(a) to (c) are met on the date of transition to this FRS and the conditions of paragraphs 12.18(d) and (e) are met no later than the date the first financial statements that comply with this FRS are authorised for issue. This choice applies to each hedging relationship existing on the date of transition.

Hedge accounting as set out in Section 12 *Other Financial Instruments Issues* of this FRS may commence from a date no earlier than the conditions of paragraphs 12.18(a) to (c) are met. In a fair value hedge the cumulative **hedging gain or loss** on the hedged item from the date hedge accounting commenced to the date of transition, shall be recorded in retained earnings (or if appropriate, another category of equity). In a cash flow hedge and net investment hedge, the lower of the following (in absolute amounts) shall be recorded in equity (in respect of cash flow hedges in the cash flow hedge reserve):

(a)   the cumulative gain or loss on the hedging instrument from the date hedge accounting commenced to the date of transition; and

(b)   the cumulative change in fair value (ie the present value of the cumulative change of expected future cash flows) on the hedged item from the date hedge accounting commenced to the date of transition.

(ii)   *A hedging relationship that ceased to exist before the date of transition because the hedging instrument has expired, was sold, terminated or exercised prior to the date of transition*

A first-time adopter may elect not to adjust the carrying amount of an asset or liability for previous GAAP accounting effects of a hedging relationship that has ceased to exist.

A first-time adopter may elect to account for amounts deferred in equity in a cash flow hedge under a previous GAAP, as described in paragraph 12.23(d) from the date of transition. Any amounts deferred in equity in relation to a hedge of a **net investment in a foreign operation** under a previous GAAP shall not be reclassified to profit or loss on disposal or partial disposal of the foreign operation.

(iii)   *A hedging relationship that commenced after the date of transition*

A first-time adopter may elect to apply hedge accounting to a hedging relationship of a type described in paragraph 12.19 that commenced after the date of transition between a hedging instrument and a hedged item, starting from the date the conditions of paragraphs 12.18(a) to (c) are met, provided that the conditions of paragraphs 12.18(d) and (e) are met no later than the date the first financial statements that comply with this FRS are authorised for issue.

The choice applies to each hedging relationship that commenced after the date of transition.

(iv)   *Entities taking the accounting policy choice under paragraphs 11.2(b) or (c) or paragraphs 12.2(b) or (c) to apply IAS 39 Financial Instruments: Recognition and Measurement or IFRS 9 Financial Instruments*

A first-time adopter adopting an accounting policy set out in paragraphs 11.2(b) or (c) or paragraphs 12.2(b) or (c) shall not apply the transitional provisions of paragraphs (i) to (iii) above. Such a first-time adopter shall apply the transitional requirements applicable to hedge accounting in IFRS 1

First–time adoption of International Financial Reporting Standards, paragraphs B4 to B6, except that the designation and documentation of a hedging relationship may be completed after the date of transition, and no later than the date the first financial statements that comply with this FRS are authorised for issue, if the hedging relationship is to qualify for hedge accounting from the date of transition.

A first-time adopter adopting an accounting policy set out in paragraphs 11.2(b) or (c) or paragraphs 12.2(b) or (c) that has entered into a hedging relationship as described in IAS 39 or IFRS 9 in the period between the date of transition and the **reporting date** for the first financial statements that comply with this FRS may elect to apply hedge accounting prospectively from the date all qualifying conditions for hedge accounting in IAS 39 or IFRS 9 are met, except that an entity shall complete the formal designation and documentation of a hedging relationship no later than the date the first financial statements that comply with this FRS are authorised for issue.

(u)   *Small entities – fair value measurement of financial instruments*

A small entity that first adopts this FRS for an accounting period that commences before 1 January 2017 need not restate comparative information to comply with the fair value measurement requirements of Section 11 *Basic Financial Instruments* or Section 12, unless those financial instruments were measured at fair value in accordance with the small entity's previous accounting framework.

A small entity that chooses to present comparative information that does not comply with the fair value measurement requirements of Sections 11 and 12 in its first year of adoption:

(a)   shall apply its existing accounting policies to the relevant financial instruments in the comparative information and is encouraged to disclose this fact;

(b)   shall disclose the accounting policies applied (in accordance with paragraph 1AC.3); and

(c)   shall treat any adjustment between the statement of financial position at the comparative period's reporting date and the statement of financial position at the start of the first reporting period that complies with Sections 11 and 12 as an adjustment, in the current reporting period, to opening equity.

(v)   *Small entities – financing transactions involving related parties*

A small entity that first adopts this FRS for an accounting period that commences before 1 January 2017 need not restate comparative information to comply with the requirements of paragraph 11.13 only insofar as they related to financing transactions involving **related parties**.

A small entity that chooses to present comparative information that does not comply with the financing transaction requirements of Section 11 in its first year of adoption:

(a)   shall apply its existing accounting policies to the relevant financial instruments in the comparative information and is encouraged to disclose this fact;

(b)   shall disclose the accounting policies applied (in accordance with paragraph 1AC.3); and

(c)   shall treat any adjustment between the statement of financial position at the comparative period's reporting date and the statement of financial position at the start of the first reporting period that complies with paragraph 11.13 as an adjustment, in the current reporting period, to opening equity. The **present value** of the financial asset or financial liability at the start of the first reporting period that complies with this FRS may be determined on the basis of the facts and circumstances existing at that date, rather than when the arrangement was entered into.

If it is **impracticable** for an entity to restate the opening statement of financial position at the date of transition for one or more of the adjustments required by paragraph 35.7, the entity shall apply paragraphs 35.7 to 35.10 for such adjustments in the earliest period for which it is practicable to do so, and shall identify the data presented for prior periods that are not comparable with data for the period in which it prepares its first financial statements that conform to this FRS. If it is impracticable for an entity to provide any disclosures required by this FRS for any period before the period in which it prepares its first financial statements that conform to this FRS, the omission shall be disclosed.   **35.11**

Where applicable to the transactions, events or arrangements affected by applying these exemptions, an entity may continue to use the exemptions that are applied at the date of transition to this FRS when preparing subsequent financial statements, until such time when the assets and liabilities associated with those transactions, events or arrangements are derecognised.   **35.11A**

Where there is subsequently a significant change in the circumstances or conditions associated with transactions, events or arrangements that existed at the date of transition, to which an exemption has been applied, an entity shall reassess the appropriateness of applying that exemption in preparing subsequent financial statements in order to maintain **fair presentation** in accordance with Section 3 *Financial Statement Presentation*.   **35.11B**

Disclosures

Explanation of transition to this FRS

An entity shall explain how the transition from its previous financial reporting framework to this FRS affected its reported **financial position** and financial **performance**.   **35.12**

Reconciliations

To comply with paragraph 35.12, an entity's first financial statements prepared using this FRS shall include: **35.13**

(a) A description of the nature of each change in accounting policy.
(b) Reconciliations of its equity determined in accordance with its previous financial reporting framework to its equity determined in accordance with this FRS for both of the following dates:

   (i) the date of transition to this FRS; and
   (ii) the end of the latest period presented in the entity's most recent annual financial statements determined in accordance with its previous financial reporting framework.

(c) A reconciliation of the profit or loss determined in accordance with its previous financial reporting framework for the latest period in the entity's most recent annual financial statements to its profit or loss determined in accordance with this FRS for the same period.

If an entity becomes aware of **errors** made under its previous financial reporting framework, the reconciliations required by paragraphs 35.13(b) and (c) shall, to the extent practicable, distinguish the correction of those errors from changes in accounting policies.   **35.14**

If an entity did not present financial statements for previous periods, it shall disclose that fact in its first financial statements that conform to this FRS.   **35.15**

APPROVAL BY THE FRC

Financial Reporting Standard 102 *The Financial Reporting Standard applicable in the UK and Republic of Ireland* was approved for issue by the Financial Reporting Council on 5 March 2013, following its consideration of the Accounting Council's Advice for this FRS.

Amendments to FRS 102 The Financial Reporting Standard applicable in the UK and Republic of Ireland – Basic financial instruments and Hedge accounting was approved for issue by the Financial Reporting Council on 2 July 2014, following its consideration of the Accounting Council's Advice.

Amendments to FRS 102 The Financial Reporting Standard applicable in the UK and Republic of Ireland – Pension obligations was approved for issue by the Board of the Financial Reporting Council on 25 February 2015, following its consideration of the Accounting Council's Advice.

Amendments to FRS 102 The Financial Reporting Standard applicable in the UK and Republic of Ireland – Small entities and other minor amendments was approved for issue by the Board of the Financial Reporting Council on 1 July 2015, following its consideration of the Accounting Council's Advice.

THE ACCOUNTING COUNCIL'S ADVICE TO THE FRC TO ISSUE FRS 102

Introduction

This report provides an overview of the main issues that have been considered by the   1
Accounting Council in advising the Financial Reporting Council (FRC) to issue FRS 102
The Financial Reporting Standard applicable in the UK and Republic of Ireland. The
FRC, in accordance with the Statutory Auditors (Amendment of Companies Act 2006
and Delegation of Functions etc) Order 2012 (SI 2012/1741), is the prescribed body for
issuing accounting standards in the UK. The Foreword to Accounting Standards sets out
the application of accounting standards in the Republic of Ireland.

In accordance with the *FRC Codes and Standards: procedures*, any proposal to issue,   2
amend or withdraw a code or standard is put to the FRC Board with the full advice of the
relevant Councils and/or the Codes & Standards Committee. Ordinarily, the FRC Board
will only reject the advice put to it where:

- it is apparent that a significant group of stakeholders has not been adequately consulted;
- the necessary assessment of the impact of the proposal has not been completed, including an analysis of costs and benefits;
- insufficient consideration has been given to the timing or cost of implementation; or
- the cumulative impact of a number of proposals would make the adoption of an otherwise satisfactory proposal inappropriate.

The FRC has established the Accounting Council as the relevant Council to assist it in the   3
setting of accounting standards.

Advice

All but one member of the Accounting Council is advising the FRC to issue FRS 102 *The*   4
Financial Reporting Standard Applicable in the UK and Republic of Ireland.

One member of the Accounting Council, Edward Beale, does not agree with some aspects   5
of the Accounting Council's advice and his dissenting view is set out in the appendix to
the Accounting Council's Advice.

FRS 100 *Application of Financial Reporting Requirements* and FRS 101 *Reduced*   6
Disclosure Framework which are also part of this suite of financial reporting standards
were issued by the FRC in November 2012. The Accounting Council's advice to the FRC
on those standards is contained in those standards.

Background

Accounting standards were formerly developed by the Accounting Standards Board   7
(ASB). The ASB commenced its project to update accounting standards in 2002; Appendix
V provides a history of the previous consultations and a summary of how the overall
proposals have developed.[15]

FRS 102 was developed from the IASB's IFRS for SMEs to replace the majority of UK   8
accounting standards in a single volume.

---

[15] *References in this section and Appendix V are made to the FRC, ASB or Accounting Council, as appropriate in
terms of the time period and context of the reference.*

Objective

9   During its consultations on updating accounting standards, the ASB (and subsequently the FRC) gave careful consideration to its objective and the intended effects. In developing the requirements in this FRS, FRS 100 and FRS 101, the overriding objective is:

> To enable users of accounts to receive high-quality understandable financial reporting proportionate to the size and complexity of the entity and users' information needs.

10   In achieving this objective, the Accounting Council decided (and the FRC subsequently adopted this decision) that it should provide succinct financial reporting standards that:

- have consistency with global accounting standards through the application of an IFRS-based solution unless an alternative clearly better meets the overriding objective;
- reflect up-to-date thinking and developments in the way businesses operate and the transactions they undertake;
- balance consistent principles for accounting by all UK and Republic of Ireland entities with practical solutions, based on size, complexity, public interest and users' information needs;
- promote efficiency within groups; and
- are cost-effective to apply.

11   The requirements in this FRS were principally consulted on in four exposure drafts:

- FRED 44 *Financial Reporting Standard for Medium-sized Entitles* issued in October 2010;
- FRED 45 *Financial Reporting Standard for Public Benefit Entities* issued in March 2011;
- FRED 48 *Financial Reporting Standard applicable in the UK and Republic of Ireland* issued in January 2012; and
- Amendment to FRED 48 issued in October 2012.

Consultation with stakeholders

12   The Accounting Council has obtained feedback from stakeholders throughout the project in a variety of ways. Appendix V sets out a history of the consultation on this project. In addition to formal consultation through exposure drafts, and previous consultation papers, feedback has been obtained through an extensive programme of outreach aimed at raising awareness of the proposals and to address the view (held by some) that earlier consultations had not gathered sufficient evidence to support and test its assumptions.

13   The Accounting Council recognised that sometimes stakeholders who will be affected by the outcome of a proposal can be difficult to engage in formal, written consultation. As a result, and in accordance with the principles of Better Regulation it developed an outreach programme that would reach beyond those stakeholders that typically respond to Exposure Drafts.

14   As part of the outreach programme a series of meetings and events took place with lenders to small and medium-sized entities. Lenders noted that financial statements are an important part of their decision-making process when considering providing finance and whilst a decision to provide finance is not based on financial statements alone, they provide useful information and verification to the lender.

15   In addition, a review was made of academic research that addressed the users of small and medium-sized entities' financial statements. The conclusion drawn from the research

was that many entities requested financial statements from Companies House when considering whether to trade with another entity. The European Federation of Accountants and Auditors (EFAA) issued in May 2011 a statement that identified the users of financial statements noting who the users of SMEs financial statements are and that information on the public record assists all users of financial statements of SMEs by providing, in an efficient manner, basic information that protects their rights.

The Accounting Council considers that the outreach programme, across the project as a whole, has gleaned information from stakeholders who would not normally submit formal responses to a consultation and provided very useful information. The Accounting Council noted that whilst this information was not part of the public record, as formal consultation responses are, it could use the information to assist in finalising the standards, which supplemented the information contained in formal responses.   **16**

Consultation with stakeholders carried out by others

In addition to the consultation and outreach work carried out by the Accounting Council itself, the Accounting Council notes that some respondents, notably the accountancy institutes, conducted their own outreach amongst their members in determining their responses to the exposure drafts.   **17**

Classification of respondents

When analysing responses to consultations it has been the Accounting Council's practice to classify respondents into a number of standard categories in order to determine whether similar views are consistently held by a particular category of respondents. This classification is set out in the Feedback Statement that accompanies this FRS.   **18**

The classification of respondents only allows respondents to be classified to a single category and is based on the main perspective articulated in the response. However, the Accounting Council notes that many people that are interested in financial reporting and respond to consultations have a number of different perspectives, for example those that prepare financial statements often also use the financial statements of customers, suppliers and competitors in making decisions about running their business.   **19**

Therefore, there is an inherent limitation in the classification of respondents, which tends to underestimate the number of users of financial statements that have responded.   **20**

Using the IFRS for SMEs as a basis

Set out in Appendix V is a history of previous consultations. The ASB first started to consider the future of UK and Republic of Ireland accounting standards following the EU decision to require consolidated accounts of listed companies to comply with IFRS. The long held view is that there can be no justification for two different sets of accounting standards in the UK. Consequently, throughout the various consultations it has been proposed that the new accounting standards should have consistency with global accounting standards; this has continually been supported by the majority of respondents. Therefore the Accounting Council has proceeded with the project on this basis. The Impact Assessment accompanying this standard sets out alternative strategic options that the Accounting Council considered in framing the project (including UK accounting standards not based on IFRS), but taking into account consultation responses these were rejected. Therefore the Accounting Council developed the standard within the strategic context of an IFRS-based solution.   **21**

22   The Accounting Council noted that the IFRS for SMEs:

- is a way of achieving a consistent accounting framework, as it is a simplification of IFRS;
- was developed by the IASB and published in 2009, reflecting more up-to-date thinking and developments than current FRS, especially for financial instruments;
- is a single book setting out clear accounting requirements; and
- is a cost effective way of updating current FRS.

23   The Accounting Council noted that one of the most significant changes being introduced in this standard is the changes to the recognition, measurement and disclosures related to financial instruments. Current FRSs contain limited requirements on accounting for financial instruments for unlisted entities or those that do not apply the fair value accounting rules. Entities use derivatives to manage risk and it is important that financial statements recognise and provide disclosures about the effect of those instruments on the entity's performance and position. The Accounting Council believes that the approach under current FRSs, where derivatives are not recognised, does not adequately reflect the risks arising from financial instruments. FRS 102 will lead to an improvement in accounting for financial instruments.

24   The Accounting Council adopted guidelines for developing this standard from the IFRS for SMEs, and noted that some pragmatism was required in determining when it would be appropriate to diverge from the IFRS for SMEs. The objective is high-quality understandable financial reporting, and the standard needs to work within the legal framework in the UK and Republic of Ireland, including enabling the provisions of company law to be adhered to. The guidelines also balance high-quality understandable financial reporting and cost effective application. The high degree of support from respondents for the strategic thrust of the approach to developing the new standards suggested that respondents were prepared to balance high-quality financial reporting and costs/benefits. The Accounting Council therefore concluded that its objective and guidelines for making changes to the IFRS for SMEs should be:

In amending the IFRS for SMEs for application in the UK and Republic of Ireland (RoI) the FRC maintains its commitment to:

(a)   ensuring high-quality financial reporting by UK and RoI entities applying FRS 102;

(b)   operate under an international accounting framework; and

(c)   acknowledge that users' preference for consistent financial reporting must be balanced with costs to preparers.

The guidelines when considering amendments to the IFRS for SMEs are:

(a)   changes should be made to permit accounting treatments that exist in FRSs at the transition date that align with EU-adopted IFRS;

(b)   changes should be consistent with EU-adopted IFRS unless a non-IFRS-based solution clearly better meets the objective of providing high-quality understandable financial reporting proportionate to the size and complexity of the entity and the users' information needs. In these cases elements of an IFRS-based solution may nevertheless be retained;

(c)   use should be made, where possible, of existing exemptions in company law to avoid gold-plating; and

(d)   changes should be made to provide clarification, by reference to EU-adopted IFRS, that will avoid unnecessary diversity in practice.

The Accounting Council noted that by providing clarifications within FRS 102 when compared with the IFRS for SMEs it could avoid unnecessary diversity in practice. Similarly, whilst maintaining its commitment to high-quality financial reporting and a global framework, the Accounting Council determined that it should amend the IFRS for SMEs by reference to EU-adopted IFRS.

25

Amendments made to the IFRS for SMEs in developing FRS 102

In developing FRS 102 from the IFRS for SMEs, the Accounting Council advises that a number of amendments should be made to the IFRS for SMEs. The following table identifies the more significant amendments and which of the guidelines were applied in making those amendments. Where an amendment is marked ✓✓ it indicates that the amendment is as a consequence of the decision that the scope of FRS 102 is different from that of the IFRS for SMEs.

26

Amendment	Guideline				Law
	a)	b)	c)	d)	
Scope					
Elimination of public accountability		✓			
Cross-references to IFRS 8 and IAS 33 for listed entities.				✓✓	
Definition of a financial institution				✓	
Inclusion of public benefit entities		✓			
Presentation					
True and fair override					✓
Statement of financial position					✓
Statement of comprehensive income, including discontinued operations					✓
Statement of changes in equity	✓				
Consolidated financial statements					
Consistency with the Act					✓
ESOPs		✓			
Subsidiaries held exclusively for resale, including in an investment portfolio	✓				
Changes in stake and gains or losses on disposals	✓		✓✓	✓	
Exchanges of businesses for interests in another business (was UITF Abstract 31)				✓	
Accounting policies					
Clarification of when to refer to a SORP in developing accounting policies		✓			
Financial instruments					
Disclosures required by financial institutions (might be considered an expansion of paragraph 11.42 for those entities)			✓✓		
Treatment of loan covenants for determining whether an instrument is basic	✓				

Amendment	Guideline	Law
Disclosures for certain financial instruments required by law		✓
Hedge accounting is permitted for a net investment in a foreign operation and in respect of foreign exchange risks in a debt instrument measured at amortised cost	✓ ✓	
Borrowing costs may be capitalised in certain circumstances		
Public benefit entities can account for concessionary loans at transaction amount	✓✓	
Fair value option	✓	
Option to apply IAS 39 or IFRS 9 recognition and measurement requirements	✓	
Financial guarantee contracts scoped out of financial instrument accounting	✓	
Property, plant and equipment		
Revaluation	✓	
Intangible assets		
Capitalisation of development costs	✓	
Revaluation after initial recognition	✓	
Where unable to make a reliable estimate of useful life, it should not exceed 5 years.		
Business combinations and goodwill		
Permit merger accounting for group reconstructions	✓	
Permit merger accounting by public benefit entities	✓✓	
Where unable to make a reliable estimate of useful life of goodwill, it should not exceed 5 years.		✓
Leases		
Clarification of definitions		✓
Clarification of scope for 'arrangements that contain a lease'		✓
Liabilities and equity		
Clarification of whether an instrument is a financial liability or equity in certain circumstances		✓
Only disclosure required for non-cash distributions to owners	✓	
Grants		
Introduction of accrual method as an option for accounting for government grants	✓	

Amendment	Guideline		Law
Share-based payment			
Clarification that option pricing models are not required particularly for unquoted shares		✓	
Share-based payments granted by another group entity		✓	
Employee benefits			
Presentation of the cost of a defined benefit pension is consistent with IAS 19's 2011 amendments.	✓		
Recognition of liability by entities in multi-employer schemes with a schedule of funding for a deficit		✓	
Income tax			
Timing differences plus approach	✓		
Revised disclosure requirements	✓		
Guidance on accounting for VAT		✓	
Related party disclosures			
Disclosure exemption for wholly-owned entities	✓		
Specialised activities			
Agriculture – permit historical cost model for biological assets.	✓		
Extractive industries – refer to IFRS 6	✓		
Service concession arrangements – grantors		✓✓	
Service concession arrangements – operators		✓✓	
Retirement benefit plans	✓		
Heritage assets	✓		
Funding commitments		✓✓	
PBE – incoming resources from non-exchange transactions (including performance-related conditions and restrictions)	✓✓		

Scope of FRS 102

In an earlier consultation the Accounting Council proposed a differential financial reporting system based on three tiers of entities using public accountability as a differentiator, which would have required some entities to apply EU-adopted IFRS that would not otherwise have been required to do so. Several concerns were noted about this; the more significant include:

(a)   the costs for those entities that would be required to apply EU-adopted IFRS could not be justified in relation to the benefit to users of those entities financial statements;

(b)   inconsistencies in the recognition and measurement requirements between EU-adopted IFRS and the proposals at the time for FRS 102 would reduce comparability between entities; and

(c)   the application guidance addressing the definition of public accountability remained unclear despite the guidance being developed further from the Policy Proposal.

28   The Accounting Council wanted to address the concerns from respondents that the costs for those entities that would be required to apply EU-adopted IFRS could not be justified in relation to the benefit to users of those entities' financial statements. As a result it proposed eliminating public accountability as a differentiator and determined that FRS 102 should be applied by entities that were not required to apply EU-adopted IFRS, nor were eligible and chose to apply the FRSSE. Respondents agreed with this approach.

29   As a consequence various entities that are outside the scope of the IFRS for SMEs are within the scope of FRS 102, typically these are financial institutions.

30   The Accounting Council noted that a significant number of public benefit entities apply UK accounting standards, and would be within the scope of FRS 102.

Consequences of the scope of FRS 102

31   As the scope of FRS 102 is wider than the scope of the IFRS for SMEs, there are areas not addressed in the IFRS for SMEs that might be relevant to the broader group of entities applying FRS 102.

32   In considering these areas the Accounting Council reflected on users' needs for additional information relevant to entities that are listed but not on a regulated market, ie those entities that were in part (a) of the definition of public accountability but were not required by EU Regulation to apply EU-adopted IFRS. This identified that earnings per share, operating segments and accounting for insurance contracts were not addressed in the IFRS for SMEs and accounting requirements would need to be set in these areas.

33   The Accounting Council, however, noted that in addressing the needs of this broader group of entities it should not lose sight of its objective to provide succinct financial reporting standards. Consequently, consideration was given to whether entities listed on a non-regulated market could apply EU-adopted IFRS for the areas identified by including cross references to EU-adopted IFRS in FRS 102 rather than setting out the requirements in the FRS itself.

34   The Accounting Council broadly termed as financial institutions those entities that, in accordance with FRED 43 were within the scope of part (b) of the definition of public accountability, (ie entities that hold assets in a fiduciary capacity or take deposits, including credit unions, building societies and investment entities). In considering the users' needs for financial information on financial institutions the Accounting Council noted that FRS 102 set out improvements, from current FRS, for the recognition and measurement of financial instruments, however, it had limited specific disclosure requirements for financial instruments. The Accounting Council decided that if it were to eliminate the definition of public accountability it would need to address the disclosure requirements for financial institutions, noting that financial instruments are central to the business model of these entities and how such entities generate wealth and manage risk.

35   Having identified that it would need to improve the disclosure requirements for financial institutions if it were to remove the definition of public accountability, the Accounting Council sought to find a clear definition of a financial institution. Various options were considered including whether to retain part (b) of the definition of publicly accountable, however this approach was rejected because it did not address the application difficulties raised by respondents to FRED 43.

The second option considered was to use the definition in section 467(1) of the Companies   **36**
Act 2006; one advantage was that this was in part basing the definition on whether the
entity was regulated or not.

The third option was simply to list the types of entity which should provide additional   **37**
disclosures for financial instruments. In this regard the Accounting Council gave
consideration to its previous accounting standard FRS 13 *Derivatives and Financial
Instrument: Disclosures*, which applied a differential disclosure regime depending on
the category of entity. On balance the Accounting Council decided that a list of entities
provided the clearest approach to determine which entities should be defined as financial
institutions. However, the Accounting Council also agreed with some respondents to FRED
48 that a principle behind entities selected for inclusion on the list should be articulated.
As a result the Accounting Council added a final item to the list, intended to capture any
entities similar to those listed above, which would also add an element of future-proofing
to the definition. The Accounting Council advises that a parent entity whose sole activity
is to hold investments in other group entities is not a financial institution, but notes that a
subsidiary entity engaged solely in treasury activities for the group as a whole is likely to
meet the definition of a financial institution.

Having undertaken the analysis above, it was concluded that public accountability could   **38**
be eliminated and FRS 102 could apply to a broader group of entities than the IFRS for
SMEs. To address the users' information needs for entities listed on a non-regulated
market, FRS 102 includes cross-referencing to EU-adopted IFRS and additional disclosure
requirements have been inserted for financial instruments held by financial institutions.

The Accounting Council observed that if it were to require a financial institution   **39**
applying FRS 102 to disclose additional information regarding its financial instruments,
it also needed to consider its proposals for reduced disclosures. It decided that financial
institutions applying reduced disclosures would not be permitted exemptions from the
additional disclosures for financial institutions.

The Accounting Council considered whether broadening the scope of FRS 102 would   **40**
increase the pressure to update the standard (in line with changes being made to full IFRS)
more frequently than on a three-year cycle. The Accounting Council agreed that there may
be circumstances where FRS 102 would require updating in an interim period between the
three-year cycles, but where this occurred the amendments proposed should be limited.

Presentation

The Accounting Council considered feedback to FRED 44 and to the draft case studies   **41**
prepared by its staff that were posted on its website that addressed the interaction between
FRED 44 and the presentation formats required by company law. The Accounting Council
noted that there were specific conflicts between the IFRS for SMEs and the formats,
specifically the definition of current assets differed between the two sets of requirements.

The Accounting Council considered whether to replicate the requirements set out in   **42**
company law for the information to be presented in the statement of financial position and
the income statement, but was concerned that this would add clutter to FRS 102 which was
not consistent with its objectives. However, it needed to work within company law and
whilst it had encouraged changes to simplify the Accounting Directives it was unlikely
such change would take place in the near future. The Accounting Council decided that
it should promote only formats already determined in company law. This would have
the consequence of all entities being required to comply with the company law formats,
promoting consistency amongst all those preparing financial statements intended to give
a true and fair view.

43   In amending the IFRS for SMEs to include the Companies Act formats, it was noted that the ASB had had a long-standing policy that company law formats on their own were not sufficient and should be supplemented to highlight a range of important components of financial performance to aid users' understanding of the performance of the entity. Therefore some requirements from FRS 3 *Reporting Financial Performance*, notably covering acquisitions, exceptional items and discontinued operations need to be factored in. The IFRS for SMEs was amended so that FRS 102 includes:

(a)   the disclosure of post-acquisition revenue and profit or loss of an acquiree in a business combination in the notes to the financial statements;

(b)   no mandatory requirement to disclose an operating profit line but guidance, based on IAS 1 *Presentation of Financial Statements*, on matters to consider where entities choose to present operating profit; and

(c)   the inclusion of an explicit requirement to disclose material items.

44   The existing FRS 3 requirement to show separately on the face of the profit and loss account: profits or losses on sale or termination of an operation; costs of a fundamental reorganisation materially affecting the operation and profits; and losses on disposal of fixed assets (all of which would still have to be disclosed where material) has not been included.

45   The Accounting Council advises that, in view of the company law requirement that turnover includes the turnover from discontinued operations, a practical way of presenting this and the post-tax profit or loss on discontinued operations would be for the information about discontinued operations to be presented via a columnar approach. An example illustrating this is set out in FRS 102.

Consolidated financial statements

Definitions of control, parent and subsidiary

46   The Accounting Council notes that the definitions of control, parent and subsidiary included in FRS 102 are consistent with the IFRS for SMEs (and based on EUadopted IFRS prior to the issuing of IFRS 10 *Consolidated Financial Statements*), but differ from those used in current FRS. Some respondents queried whether the definitions should be based on company law. The Accounting Council rejected this suggestion, but noted that by using the IFRS for SMEs definitions (consistently with its objective and guidelines), it was widening the application of control to include certain special purpose entities within the definition of a group. However, as noted below, the Accounting Council advises that this should not include employee benefit trusts and ESOPs (which should continue to be accounted for as if they are assets and liabilities of the sponsoring entity).

Employee benefit trusts, ESOPs and similar arrangements

47   In clarifying the requirements for consolidation, including considering consistency with company law requirements, the Accounting Council noted that the accounting treatment for employee benefit trusts, ESOPs or similar arrangements would give rise to a change in accounting from current FRS. The removal of UITF Abstract 38 *Accounting for ESOP trusts* would mean that such arrangements would no longer be included in individual financial statements but only in consolidated financial statements. Further, for an entity with such an arrangement, which is not a parent entity, a change in accounting requirements would lead to the preparation of 'group' financial statements where they would otherwise not have been required. Therefore the Accounting Council decided to retain the accounting treatment from UITF Abstract 32 *Employee benefit trusts and other intermediate payment arrangements* which are included in Section 9 *Consolidated and Separate Financial Statements* of FRS 102.

Investment entities exemption from consolidation

In September 2011 the IASB issued an exposure draft proposing to exempt qualifying investment entities from consolidating their investments. The accounting requirements were finalised and published as an amendment to IFRS 10 *Consolidated Financial Statements*, IFRS 12 *Disclosure of Interests in Other Entities* and IAS 27 *Separate Financial Statements* in October 2012. The Accounting Council noted that without a similar exemption in FRS 102, investment entities eligible to apply FRS 102, would need to elect to prepare EU-adopted IFRS in order to take advantage of the exemption. The Accounting Council did not consider this to be a logical or meaningful outcome and therefore sought to find a solution.

48

Section 405(3) of the Companies Act sets out the circumstances in which a subsidiary may be excluded from consolidation and the Accounting Council must work within these requirements. Section 405(3) permits a subsidiary to be excluded from consolidation on the following grounds:

49

(a) severe long-term restrictions substantially hinder the exercise of the rights of the parent company over the assets or management of that subsidiary;
(b) the information necessary for the preparation of group accounts cannot be obtained without disproportion expense or undue delay; or
(c) the interest of the parent company is held exclusively with a view to subsequent resale.

Taking into account the IASB's publication of *Investment Entities* (Amendments to IFRS 10, IFRS 12 and IAS 27) in October 2012, the Accounting Council advises that the definition of an interest held exclusively with a view to subsequent resale should include interests held as part of an investment portfolio.

50

FRS 102 permits that subsidiaries excluded from consolidation may be measured at fair value through profit or loss. This is a departure from the requirements of the Companies Act for the overriding purpose of giving a true and fair view in the consolidated financial statements.

51

Changes in stake and gains or losses on disposals

The Accounting Council noted that the requirements of the IFRS for SMEs in relation to changes in stake and gains and losses on disposals were not entirely coherent being based partly on IFRS 3 *Business combinations* (issued 2004) and partly on IFRS 3 *Business combinations* (revised 2008), and further some of the requirements are not consistent with company law provisions on the recognition of unrealised gains.

52

The Accounting Council considered that a coherent model for increases and decreases in stakes held in another entity was required, and that it must be consistent with company law. As a result the requirements of Section 9 *Consolidated and Separate Financial Statements* and Section 19 *Business Combinations and Goodwill* are now based on IFRS 3 (issued 2004), providing an IFRS-based solution that is consistent with company law.

53

Distribution of non-cash assets to owners

The Accounting Council had also been asked to clarify that the distribution of non-cash assets to owners did not apply to distributions within groups. In considering this requirement, the Accounting Council noted a distinction between the disposal of an asset at fair value followed by a distribution to shareholders of the profit, and making a distribution of the asset to shareholders. In its view, a distribution to shareholders does not

54

generate a profit, whereas a disposal does generate a profit that may then be distributed to shareholders. The Accounting Council decided, given it did not support the accounting requirement, to remove the requirement in the IFRS for SMEs to recognise a liability to pay a dividend for a non-cash asset at fair value and to require disclosure of the fair value of the assets distributed to shareholders.

Financial instruments

55   In FREDs 43 and 44 the ASB noted that current FRSs were in need of updating and that they permitted certain transactions not to be recorded. Sections 11 *Basic Financial Instruments* and 12 *Other Financial Instruments Issues* of FRED 44 proposed to address these weaknesses in current FRS. The Accounting Council noted that the IFRS for SMEs has simplified the accounting for financial instruments when compared with IAS 39 *Financial Instruments: Recognition and Measurement*, whilst generally achieving similar accounting. However, there will be areas where those familiar with IAS 39 will need to take care to ensure compliance with FRS 102, for example the hierarchy to be used in determining the fair value of an asset set out in paragraph 11.27 is not the same as the 'fair value hierarchy' set out in IAS 39.

56   The Accounting Council carefully considered the views of respondents to FRED 44 concerning the proposed accounting for financial instruments set out in the FRED.

57   The Accounting Council noted the concern, primarily from the social housing sector, that recognition of derivatives used for hedging purposes at fair value may result in volatility in profit or loss. It considered carefully the requirement to recognise derivatives at fair value but noted that any changes to the financial instrument proposals should be consistent with the guidelines for amending the IFRS for SMEs. The Accounting Council concluded that it would not be consistent with the objective of providing high-quality information, or the guidelines for amending the IFRS for SMEs, to change the recognition requirements for derivatives. Recognition of derivatives, and associated disclosure, will provide relevant information to users about the risks an entity has in relation to its financial instruments.

Impact of the IASB hedge accounting and impairment projects

58   The requirements for hedge accounting and impairment of financial assets in FRS 102 are based on the requirements of IAS 39. The IASB is currently reviewing hedge accounting and impairment requirements (including developing an 'expected loss' model for the recognition of impairments of financial assets) and the Accounting Council is reluctant to propose new accounting requirements in respect of these areas before the IASB's projects are finalised in IFRS 9 *Financial Instruments*. The Accounting Council is concerned that doing so would risk financial instruments requirements in FRS 102 being out of line with both IFRS 9 and IAS 39. Simultaneously, the Accounting Council believes that the next scheduled amendment date for FRS 102 is too far in the future and consequential amendments to FRS 102 may therefore be untimely for entities that would like to apply the new IFRS 9 accounting requirements without undue delay. For that reason the Accounting Council agreed that a proposed amendment to FRS 102 would be issued for public consultation once the IASB has completed the hedge accounting and impairment projects and IFRS 9 has been updated; it is likely that there will be two separate exposure drafts, one addressing each topic. The Accounting Council intends to make amendments to FRS 102 (should the consultation determine this is appropriate) prior its effective date, although the exact timetable of any possible amendment is dependent upon when the IASB completes the impairment and hedge accounting requirements in IFRS 9.

Financial instruments accounting policy choices

In order to allow entities applying FRS 102 maximum flexibility, entities have a choice   **59**
of either:

(a)   applying the requirements of Sections 11 and 12 of FRS 102;

(b)   applying the recognition and measurement requirements in IAS 39 (as adopted for use in the EU) as the standard applies prior to the application of IFRS 9; or

(c)   applying IFRS 9 (as far as it has replaced the requirements in IAS 39) and IAS 39 (as far it remains applicable if IFRS 9 is applied).

By providing these accounting policy choices entities have the flexibility to apply the accounting requirements of IFRS 9 without delay should they wish to do so[16]. Entities that elect to account for financial instruments by applying the requirements of Sections 11 and 12, especially those entities that choose to apply FRS 102 before its effective date, may be required to change their accounting for financial instruments should some of the requirements in Sections 11 and 12 be amended for consistency with the principles of IFRS 9 in respect of hedge and impairment accounting, once those have been determined.

Disclosures by financial institutions

Having defined financial institutions, the Accounting Council advises that additional   **60**
disclosures should be provided for the financial instruments held by these entities. It developed a proportionate set of disclosures for financial institutions, using IFRS 7 *Financial Instruments: Disclosures* as the basis.

Fair value option

A number of respondents to FRED 48 noted that bonds within the scope of Section 11   **61**
must be measured at amortised cost, even if they are managed on a fair value basis or their measurement at amortised cost introduces measurement differences, and suggested that an option to measure such items at fair value should be permitted in FRS 102. The Accounting Council agreed that, consistently with EU-adopted IFRS, an option should be available to designate financial assets and liabilities to be measured at fair value through profit or loss.

Hedge accounting

In light of the comments received in response to FREDs 44 and 48, and in order to reduce   **62**
inconsistencies with EU-adopted IFRS, the Accounting Council advises that hedge accounting of a net investment in a foreign operation in consolidated financial statements be permitted and that entities are permitted to hedge foreign exchange risk arising in a debt instrument measured at amortised cost. Consistently with EU-adopted IFRS the Accounting Council also advises that hedge accounting of a net investment in a foreign operation should not be permitted in the separate financial statements of a parent.

Financial guarantee contracts

Respondents to FRED 48 asked for clarification of the accounting requirements for   **63**
financial guarantee contracts. The accounting for financial guarantee contracts is within the scope of Section 21 *Provisions and Contingencies* unless an entity has chosen to

[16] *As FRS 102 is a UK and Republic of Ireland accounting standard, IFRS 9 can be applied through FRS 102 in advance of EU endorsement.*

apply IAS 39 and/or IFRS 9, or has an existing accounting policy of insurance contract accounting for financial guarantee contracts and chooses to continue to apply that policy under FRS 103 *Insurance Contracts*.

Group reconstructions

64   The Accounting Council advises that FRS 102 should retain the current accounting permitted by FRS 6 *Acquisitions and mergers* for group reconstructions. The Accounting Council noted that whilst EU-adopted IFRS does not provide accounting requirements for the accounting for business combinations under common control the accounting provided by FRS 6 is well understood and provides useful requirements. It therefore decided to carry forward these requirements into FRS 102. In practice, the Accounting Council does not expect the introduction of FRS 102 to change the accounting for group reconstructions. For example, where a combination is effected by using a newly formed parent company to hold the shares of each of the parties to a combination, the accounting treatment depends on the substance of the business combination being effected.

Leases

65   Leases are accounted for in accordance with the requirements of Section 20 *Leases*, except for those leases falling within the scope of Section 12, which are those that could result in a loss to the lessor or the lessee as a result of non-typical contractual terms, for example those that are unrelated to:

(a)   changes in the price of the leased asset;

(b)   changes in foreign exchange rates; or

(c)   a default by one of the counterparties.

66   The Accounting Council notes that the reference to 'changes in the price of the leased asset' is framed widely and in practice it does not expect many leases to fall within the scope of Section 12.

Grants

67   A number of respondents, particularly from the public benefit entity sector, raised concerns about the proposed changes to the recognition requirements for grants received from government and other bodies. The proposals in FRED 44 based the recognition of income from grants on when an entity fulfilled the performance criteria stipulated in the grant. This would have been a change from both current FRS and EU-adopted IFRS which attempt to match grant income with the related expenditure. The Accounting Council observed that the IFRS for SMEs used an approach not in current EU-adopted IFRSs.

68   The Accounting Council reviewed the concerns of entities noting that it could amend the performance criterion approach to provide application guidance on performance outcome. This approach would require a research project to be undertaken and cause delay to the finalisation of FRS 102. An alternative was to amend the requirements in the IFRS for SMEs so that they were consistent with EU-adopted IFRS and defer a research project on the accounting for grants until after the publication of FRS 102. However, respondents also noted that some entities, mainly in the public benefit entity sector, currently recognised income from grants on the basis of performance criteria and that reverting to the requirements of EU-adopted IFRS (which is similar to current FRS) would introduce a change for these entities. The Accounting Council did not wish to implement a change for entities that might be reversed when it subsequently undertook a research project on grant accounting. It therefore concluded it should allow entities a choice between the accounting requirements of the IFRS for SMEs and those in EU-adopted IFRS.

The Accounting Council recognises that the respondents to FRED 44 highlighted an   69
inconsistency in current practice and that the solution in FRS 102 is therefore, an interim
solution until completion on a research project is undertaken.

Respondents have further commented that as Section 24 *Government Grants* is restricted   70
to government grants, grants received by public benefit entities from other sources will be
accounted for in accordance with Section 34 *Specialised Activities: Incoming Resources
from Non-Exchange Transactions*, and there is now the possibility that the accounting for
grants depends on the source of the grant, rather than whether or not the underlying terms
and conditions of the grants differ. Whilst this is not ideal, the Accounting Council advises
permitting the accrual model for government grants in accordance with its guidelines for
amending the IFRS for SMEs as an interim solution to avoid changes in accounting that
might be reversed in the future.

For those entities that apply the performance model to capital grants, either as an accounting   71
policy choice for government grants, or through applying Section 34 to grants from other
sources, the Accounting Council notes that there may be a change from current accounting
practice, which may lead to greater volatility in the income statement. The effect of this
volatility can be explained in the notes to the financial statements.

Share-based payment

The Accounting Council noted that at present entities in the UK and Republic of Ireland[17]   72
that enter into share-based payment transactions are required to apply FRS 20 *(IFRS 2)
Share-based Payment*. However, for unlisted entities it can be difficult to apply option
pricing models and therefore the benefits outweigh the costs. As a result the Accounting
Council advises that directors apply judgement by using models that are appropriate to the
entity's circumstance. The Accounting Council considers that this provides a cost effective
way of recognising the cost of share-based payments.

Employee benefits

The Accounting Council noted that the requirements of FRS 17 *Retirement benefits*   73
are broadly consistent with the equivalent requirements of IAS 19 *Employee Benefits*,
which form the basis of the IFRS for SMEs in this area, including the principles for the
measurement of the net defined benefit liability and the recognition of plan deficits and
surpluses. The disclosure requirements of FRS 102 for defined benefit pension plans are
reduced when compared with those in FRS 17.

Cost of a defined benefit plan

Respondents noted that the presentation requirements for post-employment benefit plans   74
were not clear in FRED 44. Specifically a request was made to clarify where the difference
between the actual return on plan assets and expected return on plan assets should be
presented. The Accounting Council, in considering this request, noted that the presentation
requirements in IAS 19 had been amended in 2011. The amendments to IAS 19 were
consistent with the ASB's recommendations in its report following the consultation
document *The Financial Reporting of Pensions*. In view of this, the Accounting Council
decided to update FRS 102 to be consistent with the revised IAS 19, which requires an
entity to recognise the net change in the defined benefit liability as follows:

---

[17] *Other than those applying the FRSSE.*

(a)   the change in the defined benefit liability arising from employee service rendered during the reporting period in profit or loss;

(b)   net interest on the net defined benefit liability in profit or loss; and

(c)   remeasurement of the net defined benefit liability in other comprehensive income.

75   In advising this amendment, the Accounting Council also noted that the accounting requirements in the IFRS for SMEs for group pension plan arrangements were more stringent than those set out in IAS 19 (revised 2011). The Accounting Council therefore decided to update these requirements to be consistent with the IAS 19 (revised 2011).

Group defined benefit pension plans

76   Consistently with IAS 19 (revised 2011), paragraph 28.38 of FRS 102 requires entities participating in a group defined benefit pension plan to recognise the net defined benefit cost in their individual financial statements where a relevant agreement or policy exists. Otherwise the entity that is legally responsible for the group pension plan will recognise the entire net defined benefit cost in its individual financial statements. The Accounting Council noted that although this paragraph only refers explicitly to the cost of the pension plan, the net defined benefit cost is calculated by reference to both the defined benefit obligation and the fair value of plan assets. Therefore paragraph 28.38 does require the recognition of the relevant net defined benefit liability in the individual financial statements of any group entities recognising a net defined benefit cost.

Multi-employer defined benefit plans

77   In October 2012 the FRC issued an exposure draft of proposed amendments to FRED 48, including amendments to Section 28 *Employee Benefits*. These amendments related to multi-employer defined benefit plans that are accounted for as defined contribution plans. The Accounting Council is aware that diversity in accounting practice had arisen in relation to entities who participate in a defined benefit multi-employer plan, who account for that plan as a defined contribution plan and who have entered into a funding agreement for future payments relating to past service liabilities, to recognise a liability in relation to the deficit in the plan in their financial statements.

78   Consistently with the guidelines for amending the IFRS for SMEs, the Accounting Council advises incorporating the relevant requirement from IAS 19 and notes that the IASB's basis for conclusions said that 'In relation to the funding of a deficit, [...] this principle [is] consistent with the recognition of a provision in accordance with IAS 37.'

79   The Accounting Council also advises clarifying the measurement requirements for such a liability. In the circumstances that the entity has entered into a funding agreement for future payments relating to past service it shall recognise those future payments as a liability, discounted using the methodology for selecting a discount rate for post-employment benefit liabilities. The Accounting Council debated whether the discount rate should alternatively be based on the entity's cost of capital, but decided to advise the use of a rate consistent with the methodology used for accounting for other pension liabilities.

80   The Accounting Council noted that some respondents to the exposure draft disagreed with the proposed amendment or requested a delay in implementation, but the Accounting Council believes that where participants in a multi-employer defined benefit pension plan have entered into an agreement to fund a deficit, and have applied defined contribution accounting, a liability exists and its recognition provides useful information to users.

Some respondents suggested that FRS 102 should also address situations where a multi-employer pension plan was in surplus, and entered into an agreement to distribute that surplus to the participating employers. Although the Accounting Council noted that this is addressed in IAS 19, it expected that the situation would arise rarely in practice, and considered that entities would be able to determine the appropriate accounting using the principles set out in FRS 102. Therefore it does not advise making an amendment for this.   **81**

Income tax

In FRED 44 the ASB proposed using the text of IAS 12 *Income Taxes* in place of the IFRS for SMEs section on income tax. The ASB had amended the tax section of the IFRS for SMEs because it had been based on proposals subsequently abandoned by the IASB and therefore the IFRS for SMEs was not consistent with full IFRS. Respondents to the Policy Proposal had not supported retaining the IFRS for SMEs requirements in this area. Respondents to FRED 44 had accepted that the IFRS for SMEs treatment could not be used, but did not support the ASB's proposal to replace the tax section with IAS 12.   **82**

In developing FRED 48 the ASB considered what would be the most suitable alternative, and took into account the findings of its research work with EFRAG in developing the Discussion Paper *Improving the Financial Reporting of Income Tax* (issued in December 2011), as well as its commitment to an IFRS-based solution and the requirements of FRS 19 *Deferred Tax* from which entities would be transitioning. It set out an alternative approach that based the recognition requirements on timing differences, with additional recognition requirements for certain temporary differences that are not timing differences, which was referred to as a 'timing differences plus' approach. The advantages of this approach seemed to be that it would: **83**

(a)   provide useful information to users of financial statements; and
(b)   provide the simple solution preparers were looking for that was close to current FRS and that would give the same answers as IFRSs in most cases.

Most respondents supported the 'timing differences plus' approach, which has therefore been retained in FRS 102.   **84**

The most significant change to the requirements in current FRS is that the proposed approach requires the recognition of the deferred tax implications of the revaluation of assets. Gains and losses recognised on a revaluation are timing differences and the tax effects should be recognised. Such a requirement is consistent with IAS 12 and the IFRS for SMEs.   **85**

Another significant change from current FRS is that discounting of current and deferred tax is not allowed which is consistent with the IFRS for SMEs.   **86**

Under IAS 12 deferred tax is not generally recognised on the initial recognition of an asset, except that of assets and liabilities arising from a business combination. No specific exception for this is necessary under the 'timing differences plus' approach as no timing difference arises. The proposed treatment is therefore consistent in this respect with IAS 12.   **87**

A pure timing difference approach does not provide complete consistency with the requirements of IAS 12. In particular, IAS 12 requires that deferred tax is recognised in respect of the difference between the amount recognised on a business combination for assets and liabilities (other than goodwill) and the amount that will be allowed for or assessed to tax in respect of such assets and liabilities. These differences are not timing differences. In order to maintain consistency with IFRS on this major issue, the Accounting   **88**

Council agreed to supplement the timing difference approach with a requirement to recognise deferred tax on business combinations.

89   However, the 'timing differences plus' approach adopted in FRS 102 does not ensure complete consistency with the requirements of IAS 12. For example FRS 102 does not permit the recognition of deferred tax:

    (a)   where the tax deduction (or estimated future deduction) for share-based payment exceeds the cumulative amount of the related remuneration expense; and

    (b)   in some cases, where the tax basis of an asset is changed, for example where legislation changes the amount of future tax relief relating to the asset.

90   The Accounting Council considered, however, that the differences from IAS 12 were likely to be relatively rare and that in such cases the relevance of the information produced in accordance with IAS 12 was unclear.

91   The proposed disclosure requirements have been reviewed in the light of comments on FRED 48. In particular the requirement to disclose differences between the current tax charge and a standard rate of tax for the next three years has been replaced by a requirement to disclose expected net reversals of timing differences for the next year. The requirement to disclose is on a net basis, which takes account of both the reversal of existing timing differences and the origination of new ones. The net basis provides information that is relevant to the entity's future cash flows, and hence is more relevant than disclosure on a gross basis. The Accounting Council considers that the additional benefit of disclosure on a net basis outweighed the cost to preparers of forecasting future new timing differences.

Related party disclosures

92   In response to feedback from respondents, the Accounting Council advises that the company law exemption from disclosing intra-group related party transactions should be included in FRS 102.

93   Some respondents raised the issue of a possible exemption from the disclosure of outstanding balances as well as transactions. However, the Accounting Council noted that there is a separate legal requirement, in relation to the format of the balance sheet which requires disclosure of outstanding balances in aggregate for group undertakings and, separately, for undertakings in which the company has a participating interest. As Section 33 *Related Party Disclosures* requires disclosure in aggregate for a category of related parties, one of which is 'entities over which the entity has control, joint control or significant influence' this should be met by compliance with the requirements of Section 4 *Statement of Financial Position*. As a result it is not possible to provide an effective exemption from the disclosure of outstanding balances with group undertakings.

Specialised activities

Agriculture

94   The IFRS for SMEs includes guidance for specialised activities including agriculture. The proposed requirements for agriculture are a predominately fair value model and are based on IAS 41 *Agriculture*. Respondents questioned the proposed requirements noting that current FRSs do not set out accounting requirements and although the proposals included an exemption from applying fair value where there is undue cost or effort, the fair value information is inconsistent with the way most agricultural businesses are managed and would not benefit the users of financial statements.

The Accounting Council evaluated the comments raised and advises that entities engaged in   **95**
agricultural activities should be permitted an accounting policy choice for their biological
assets, between the cost model and fair value model set out in the IFRS for SMEs.

The Accounting Council noted that both the cost model and the fair value model, as set out   **96**
in the IFRS for SMEs, require agricultural produce to be measured at the point of harvest
at fair value less costs to sell. However, it considered that respondents in favour of the
cost model would have expected the cost model to mean that both biological assets and
agricultural produce would be measured at cost.

The Accounting Council noted that agricultural produce should be capable of measurement   **97**
at fair value without undue cost or effort, and should provide more relevant information to
users. However, it noted that respondents argued that agricultural businesses often manage
their business on the basis of cost information and advises that agricultural produce should
be permitted to be measured at cost. The Accounting Council advises limiting the use of
the cost model for agricultural produce to those entities that have chosen the cost model
for biological assets; however these entities should also have the option of using the fair
value model for agricultural produce.

Extractive activities

Respondents noted that the requirements of the IFRS for SMEs in relation to extractive   **98**
activities were not consistent with IFRS 6 *Exploration for and Evaluation of Mineral
Resources*, and the application of the IFRS for SMEs requirements, in conjunction with
other elements of FRS 102 would significantly change accounting practices for entities
engaged in extractive activities. It would be likely that no assets could be recognised
from the costs of exploration activities, yet entities applying EUadopted IFRS would be
permitted to recognise such assets.

The Accounting Council agreed that entities applying FRS 102 should not be prohibited   **99**
from applying accounting policies that are available to those entities applying EU-adopted
IFRS, and advises that the requirements of IFRS 6 are incorporated into FRS 102 by cross
reference.

Service concession arrangements

Respondents raised two main issues relating to the accounting for service concession   **100**
arrangements. The first was that the requirements of the IFRS for SMEs in relation to
the accounting by operators had been over-simplified when compared with IFRIC 12
Service Concession Arrangements. The Accounting Council agreed and FRS 102 includes
additional clarification of the principles of accounting by operators for service concession
arrangements, which were developed from IFRIC 12.

The second issue related to grantors, with some respondents noting that grantors might be   **101**
within the scope of FRS 102. This was addressed in the October 2012 exposure draft of
proposed amendments to FRED 48 issued by the FRC.

EU-adopted IFRS does not address accounting by grantors of service concession   **102**
arrangements; grantors are expected to be outside the scope of EU-adopted IFRS. As
a result, and consistently with the guidelines for amending the IFRS for SMEs, the
Accounting Council sought to develop accounting for grantors that is consistent with the
principles underpinning the accounting by operators of service concession arrangements,
which is set out in IFRIC 12. The scope of IFRIC 12 is such that the grantor controls
the residual interest in the infrastructure asset, and therefore for service concession

arrangements meeting the definition in FRS 102, the Accounting Council advises that the grantor recognises its interest in the infrastructure asset usually as property, plant and equipment, with a corresponding liability measured using a finance lease model.

103   The Accounting Council noted that the International Public Sector Accounting Standards Board (IPSASB) has issued a standard IPSAS 32 *Service Concession Arrangements: Grantor*, which includes two models for accounting by the grantor, depending on the terms of the arrangement with the operator. In addition to the finance lease model advised by the Accounting Council, IPSAS 32 includes a 'grant of right to the operator model' which applies to 'user-pays' arrangements. The Accounting Council does not advise the application of this model because it appears to result in the recognition as liabilities of amounts that may not meet the definition of a liability. However, some respondents to the exposure draft suggested that this model should be permitted. The Accounting Council advises that further research should be carried out on the most appropriate accounting for user-pays service concession arrangements, but that this should not delay the issue of FRS 102.

104   The Accounting Council considered whether transitional provisions should be available for grantors. It noted that for some grantors, the proposals would result in recognising assets and liabilities for the infrastructure assets that are not presently recognised. It considered that this provides more relevant information to users, and therefore advises the FRC that transitional provisions should not be available. As a result grantors will not be permitted to apply the transitional exemptions that are available to operators, as set out in FRS 102 paragraph 35.10(i), by analogy.

Retirement benefit plans

105   FRED 43 proposed that retirement benefit plans were publicly accountable and therefore should apply EU-adopted IFRS, but having decided to eliminate the definition of publicly accountable, retirement benefit plans are now within the scope of FRS 102, yet the IFRS for SMEs contains no specific provisions for retirement benefit plans.

106   The Accounting Council considered whether to direct retirement benefit plans to IAS 26 *Accounting and Reporting by Retirement Benefit Plans* and request that the Statement of Recommended Practice (SORP) *Financial Reports of Pension Schemes* be updated to be consistent with IAS 26. This option was, however, rejected based on feedback which suggested that the application of IAS 26 would be difficult for two reasons:

(a)   legal accounting and reporting requirements in the UK are different to those in IAS 26; and

(b)   IAS 26 itself makes references to other IFRSs and the interaction between these references and FRS 102 would be complicated.

A further complication would arise as the SORP would also provide application guidance for retirement benefit plans.

107   Following this feedback the Accounting Council decided to develop, as part of the specialised activities section, accounting requirements for retirement benefit plans financial statements that could be supplemented by the SORP.

108   In developing the proposals, the Accounting Council considered the issue of whether the financial statements of retirement benefit plans need to provide disclosure regarding the pension liabilities and the related funding of the plan. Following feedback from respondents, the Accounting Council decided that such information should not be recognised in the financial statements, but provided alongside it, as is currently the case.

The Accounting Council advises that because of the way in which retirement benefit   **109**
plans use financial instruments they should be considered to be financial institutions.
However, not all of the disclosure requirements for financial institutions are relevant to
retirement benefit plans and it will be more user-friendly to have all requirements in one
place. Therefore Section 34 sets out all the requirements for retirement benefit plans in
one sub-section.

Insurance contracts

FRED 48 proposed that entities with insurance contracts should apply IFRS 4 *Insurance*   **110**
Contracts to those contracts. In addition, insurance-related contracts not meeting the
definition of an insurance contract shall usually be accounted for as financial instruments
in accordance with Sections 11 and 12.

The FRC also has FRS 27 *Life Assurance* in issue. The Accounting Council debated the   **111**
various options for setting out the requirements for entities engaged in insurance business,
and decided that it should advise the FRC to issue a separate accounting standard on
insurance contracts, FRS 103 *Insurance Contracts*. An exposure draft of this standard will
be available after FRS 102 has been issued, but FRS 102 cross-refers to it. The Accounting
Council's Advice to the FRC to issue FRS 103 will be set out in that standard.

Other options available in EU-adopted IFRS

Respondents to FRED 44, in general, supported the use of the IFRS for SMEs as a base   **112**
for a future financial reporting standard in the UK and Republic of Ireland. There were,
however, concerns raised that would require careful consideration, most notably the
removal of certain accounting treatments (options) that are available in current FRSs and
EU-adopted IFRS but were not proposed in FRED 44.

Responses from the housing associations particularly focused on how the removal of   **113**
options might have behavioural implications that the Accounting Council should take into
consideration. The housing associations noted that:

(a)   the removal of the options would reduce comparability between entities that apply
      EU-adopted IFRS and those applying FRED 44 for entities operating in the same
      market, for example entities applying FRED 44 would not be permitted to revalue
      property, plant and equipment whereas entities applying EU-adopted IFRS could;
      and
(b)   the inability to include borrowing costs as part of the costs of property, plant and
      equipment may cause some housing associations to breach terms and conditions of
      current financing arrangements; this gave potential for banks and other lenders to
      renegotiate existing financing arrangements but at a higher cost of capital.

Other respondents noted that removal of the accounting options was potentially an   **114**
oversimplification for the UK and Republic of Ireland. These respondents noted the
IFRS for SMEs had been developed by the IASB for countries that had a less developed
financial reporting framework than the UK and Republic of Ireland. They considered
that as options existed in current FRSs the simplification had not been justified by the
Accounting Council.

A further view put forward by respondents was that retaining the options that existed   **115**
in current FRS would reduce transition costs and ease transition between the different
standards and also with EU-adopted IFRS.

116   Application of the guidelines permitted the introduction of accounting options that exist in current FRS and EU-adopted IFRS that respondents had highlighted as reducing comparability. FRS 102 therefore includes accounting options for:

(a)   capitalisation of borrowing costs;

(b)   revaluation of property, plant and equipment and intangible assets; and

(c)   capitalisation of development costs, in certain circumstances.

Providing clarifications in FRS 102

117   Having agreed guidelines that include making amendments to the IFRS for SMEs to provide clarifications, the Accounting Council considered relevant requests from respondents. Some clarifications were made by reference to EU-adopted IFRS (see column (d) of the table at paragraph 26 of the Accounting Council's Advice), others were made by reference to current FRS, for example whether there is an interaction with company law. As a result a number of clarifications have been made, examples include:

(a)   disclosure requirements for discontinued operations;

(b)   treatment of loan covenants, so that the treatment is consistent with IFRS 9 *Financial Instruments*;

(c)   financial instruments that would be equity under IAS 32 *Financial Instruments: Presentation* are not liabilities, when an entity is required to prepare consolidated financial statements;

(d)   when an investor that is not a parent but has an investment in one or more associates and/or jointly controlled entities shall account for its investments and/or jointly controlled entities using either cost or fair value;

(e)   the presumed life for goodwill, in particular when an entity is otherwise unable to make a reliable estimate shall not be in excess of five years and thereby consistent with company law. The same also applies to intangible assets;

(f)   accounting treatment for group share-based payments where the award is granted by the parent or another group entity; and

(g)   that option pricing models are not required for the value of shared-based payments, particularly for unquoted shares or share options.

Other matters

118   The Accounting Council considered whether to provide guidance for the term 'undue cost or effort' where respondents had sought clarification. The Accounting Council noted that Section 2 *Concepts and Pervasive Principles* discussed the balance between benefit and cost and that no further clarification was required.

The retention of Urgent Issue Task Force (UITF) Abstracts

119   FREDs 43 and 44 proposed to withdraw all UITF Abstracts except UITF Abstract 43 *The Interpretation of equivalence for the purposes of section 228A of the Companies Act*. Respondents to the FRED proposed that in addition to UITF Abstract 43, other UITF Abstracts should be retained. The Accounting Council gave consideration to this request and noted that rather than retain UITF Abstracts, consistent with its objective to provide succinct financial reporting standards, it should incorporate any guidance into FRS 102.

120   Based on feedback the Accounting Council advises that the following accounting requirements of UITF Abstracts are retained by incorporation, as follows:

UITF Abstract		Action
4	*Presentation of long-term debtors in current assets*	Incorporated into the legal appendix.
31	*Exchange of businesses or other non-monetary assets for an interest in a subsidiary, joint venture or associate*	Additional paragraphs 9.31 and 9.32 are inserted.
32	*Employee benefit trusts and other intermediate payment arrangements*	Additional paragraphs are inserted into Section 9.
43	*The interpretation of equivalence for the purposes of section 228A of the Companies Act 1985*	The guidance has been updated and included as Application Guidance to FRS 100.

The Accounting Council decided to advise the withdrawal of UITF Abstract 48 *Accounting*   **121**
implications of the replacement of the retail prices index with the consumer prices index
for retirement benefits as the circumstance it addressed were related to a one time period
which has now expired.

Interaction with company law

The Accounting Council gave careful consideration to the comments received to its   **122**
draft legal appendix set out in FREDs 44 and 48. The Accounting Council agreed with
respondents' views that the appendix should address entities that are not companies.

The Accounting Council also considered whether it should retain, as proposed in FRED   **123**
44, accounting options that had been removed because the option conflicted with company
law, where an entity that is not a company would not be restricted in the same way as a
company. For example, SSAP 4 *Accounting for government grants* contained an option
that was not permitted by the company law.

The Accounting Council confirmed the position it had taken in developing FRED 44 that   **124**
options that existed in the IFRS for SMEs, but not permitted by company law, should be
removed. This would promote consistency between reporting entities regardless of the
legal framework under which they operate.

Public benefit entities (PBEs)

The Consultation Paper *Policy Proposal: The Future of UK GAAP* (issued in 2009) set   **125**
out 10 issues that could be included in a Public Benefit Entities (PBEs) specific standard.
However, these 10 issues were refined to six which were deemed to be those most
significant and relevant to the PBE sectors that were not satisfactorily addressed by the
IFRS for SMEs. These six issues were:

(a)   Concessionary loans;
(b)   Property held for the provision of social benefits;
(c)   Entity combinations;
(d)   Impairment of assets: public benefit considerations;
(e)   Funding commitments; and
(f)   Incoming resources from non-exchange transactions.

Concessionary loans

Paragraphs have been inserted into Section 34 *Specialised Activities* to address the   **126**
accounting requirements for PBEs making and receiving concessionary loans.

127   There are two main accounting treatments to consider when determining the basis for the measurement of concessionary loans; the amount paid or received, and fair value. This has been the subject of significant discussion and debate by the Accounting Council, taking into account the information that users of PBE accounts may consider useful and the difficulties that may arise for smaller organisations in measuring concessionary loans at fair value.

128   Accounting for concessionary loans at the amount paid or received rather than fair value is not consistent with the accounting requirements set out in either Section 11 of FRS 102, EU-adopted IFRS or IPSAS 29 *Financial Instruments: Recognition and Measurement* (which require that such arrangements are measured and recognised in the financial statements at their fair value).

129   Nevertheless the Accounting Council advises that due to the difficulties that smaller PBEs may face with using fair value, PBEs that make or receive concessionary loans may have the option of measuring such loans at either the amount paid or received or at fair value. However, PBEs that make and receive concessionary loans must apply the same measurement method to both. Further the Accounting Council proposes that the same accounting may be applied by other wholly-owned entities in a public benefit entity group, to eliminate the need to restate concessionary loans made or received for the purposes of furthering the PBEs objectives on consolidation.

130   Presentation and disclosure of concessionary loan arrangements are an important part of the proposals for concessionary loans and the Accounting Council concluded that the disclosure requirements in FRS 102 will provide sufficient information to understand and interpret the impact of this type of transaction on the financial statements.

Property held for the provision of social benefits

131   Subsequent to FRED 45, the Accounting Council decided that the requirements for property held for the provision of social benefits should apply to all entities applying FRS 102 and should not be restricted to PBEs.

132   Consideration was given as to whether properties that are held for the provision of social benefits meet the definition of an investment property. The definition of investment property in paragraph 16.2 of FRS 102, excludes properties held for use in the production or supply of goods and services or for administrative purposes. A property held to earn rentals and/or for capital appreciation, but not used in the production or supply of goods or services, meets this definition. The Accounting Council noted that although many PBEs that engage in the provision of social housing receive rental income, their primary purpose is to provide social benefits.

133   Provision of social housing is akin to supplying a service and therefore, property held for the primary purpose of providing social benefits should be excluded from the scope of investment property and be accounted for as property, plant and equipment.

134   The Accounting Council acknowledges that PBEs may hold 'investment properties' which are not held primarily to provide social benefits and will return market value rentals and/or are held for their capital appreciation. FRS 102 requires those properties to be accounted for as investment properties.

Public benefit entity combinations

In considering the issue of entity combinations involving two or more public benefit entities, the Accounting Council noted that there is some debate over whether the use of acquisition accounting for all combinations would be appropriate. In particular whether acquisition accounting reflects the substance of a transaction if there is a gift of one entity to another in a combination at nil or nominal consideration, or where two or more organisations genuinely merge to form a new entity. **135**

Where there is a combination of entities at nil or nominal consideration which is in substance a gift, it is appropriate to follow the same accounting principles as donations of assets (as set out in Section 34 *Specialised Activities: Incoming Resources from Non-Exchange Transactions*) by recognising the fair value of the assets received and liabilities assumed as a gain or loss in income and expenditure. **136**

Accounting for combinations that meet the definition of a merger requires a different methodology to acquisition accounting in order to reflect the true substance of the transaction. Whilst it is not anticipated that all combinations involving two or more public benefit entities are mergers or that merger accounting will generally be applicable to such combinations it is considered appropriate to retain merger accounting in certain circumstances. In considering this matter it was noted that the accounting requirements for PBEs in some jurisdictions, for example, the US and Australia have recently been reviewed and noted that merger accounting has been retained for the public and not-for-profit sectors. **137**

In retaining merger accounting, the Accounting Council considered the criteria to be met for a merger. The criteria set out in FRS 6 *Acquisitions and Mergers* provided a starting point, but are framed in the context of the commercial sector and therefore the criteria have been adapted to make them more appropriate for public benefit entities. In particular, a criterion has been added to include consideration of the impact of the combination on beneficiaries and the benefits to which they are entitled. **138**

One specific concern highlighted in relation to the requirements of FRS 6, is the need to restate comparatives by adding together the previous periods' reported figures of each of the combining entities. This does not reflect the substance of the transaction as the historical parties which formed the entity did not exist in the previous accounting period and therefore FRS 102 requires that comparatives are marked as 'combined' to make it clear that they are a combination of previously reported figures for the combining entities. **139**

Impairment of assets

FRS 102 requires impaired assets to be measured at the lower of their fair value less costs to sell and their value in use. In a for-profit context, value in use is determined by measuring the present value of the cash flows derived from the asset. However, often PBE assets are held for their service potential rather than their ability to generate cash flows. In such a case it is sometimes impossible to determine value in use by reference to cash flows and it is more appropriate to regard value in use as the present value of future service potential rather than cash flows. **140**

International Public Sector Accounting Standard (IPSAS) 21 *Impairment of Non-Cash Generating Assets* permits value in use to be determined by any of three approaches: **141**

(a) depreciated replacement cost (DRC);
(b) restoration cost; and
(c) the service units approach.

Restoration cost and the service units approach are applications of DRC as DRC is used as the starting point. DRC reflects the cash outflows that are saved through ownership of an asset and is likely to be widely applicable and appropriate for PBEs. Therefore FRS 102 permits a service potential driven valuation to be used for assets held for their service potential.

142   The use of DRC is not mandated; other methods that value service potential rather than cash flows may be used if those methods are more appropriate in those particular circumstances.

143   FRED 45 only allowed this alternative valuation method for PBEs, however subsequent to that consultation, the Accounting Council advises that any entity that holds an asset for service potential can use a service potential valuation method. It is not expected that, for example, headquarters buildings that do not generate cash flows independently of other assets or groups of assets but nevertheless contribute to the cash-generating activities of the entity, will usually be measured on the basis of their service potential.

144   The Accounting Council also discussed whether a restriction on the use of an asset would affect its fair value. As an asset's fair value is based on the amount that an entity could obtain, restrictions might impact on the fair value where they prevent a purchaser from using the asset for another purpose that would be more valuable than that required by the restriction. In addition, the costs to sell should include the costs of breaking the restriction.

145   Another issue for discussion was indicators of impairment. Although the indicators provided in FRS 102 are mainly linked to the expected cash flow of an asset and as such may not necessarily be relevant to some PBE assets, the Accounting Council considered that they must, as a minimum, be considered by PBEs as possible indicators of impairment.

146   In addition, the Accounting Council noted that other accounting literature (eg IPSAS 21 and SORPs) identified other indicators of impairment including:

   (a)   cessation, or near cessation of the demand or need for services provided by the asset;
   (b)   social, demographic or environmental changes resulting in a reduction of beneficiaries; and
   (c)   a major loss of key employees associated with particular activities.

147   The Accounting Council concluded that it would not be appropriate to include these indicators in FRS 102, as they are not exclusively relevant to PBEs and because the indicators given in FRS 102 will continue to apply to PBEs. Therefore, their inclusion would make such entities subject to a confusing list of overlapping indicators. The indicators given in FRS 102 are merely minimum requirements, and recognition of an impairment loss is required irrespective of whether any of the given indicators are met.

148   The Accounting Council also considered whether to specify that an indicator of impairment was present where an asset's service potential was not fully utilised and noted that an entity may require standby or surplus capacity to ensure that it has adequate capacity to provide services at all times. For example, a building that provides accommodation for the homeless may not be used to full capacity during the summer months but is utilised fully during winter. In this circumstance, the surplus capacity is part of the required service potential of the asset and the asset is not impaired. For this reason, it was concluded that it would be inappropriate to specify that the unutilised capacity should be treated as an indicator of impairment.

Funding commitments

The Accounting Council also discussed when to recognise a commitment to provide   **149**
funding in a non-exchange transaction. The *Statement of Principles: Interpretation for
Public Benefit Entities* previously addressed this issue, and it was considered necessary to
incorporate these details into FRS 102 to be used in conjunction with Sections 2 *Concepts
and Pervasive Principles* and 21 *Provisions and Contingencies*.

The issue was identified as being particularly important because many PBEs provide   **150**
funding on an on-going basis and there is little guidance on how such multi-year
commitments should be recognised.

The Accounting Council considered when a liability for such a commitment should be   **151**
recognised and determined that an entity would only recognise a liability if the commitment
to provide funding was made unconditionally, and the grantor could not realistically
withdraw from the commitment. In this situation, an entity would recognise a liability for
the present value of the total funding promised.

As this is an application of the principles in Sections 2 and 21, the Accounting Council   **152**
advises that the requirements for funding commitments should apply to all entities and not
just PBEs.

Incoming resources from non-exchange transactions

The receipt of resources from non-exchange transactions is an inflow of resources that is   **153**
highly significant for many PBEs: the receipt of donations, grants and legacies from non-
exchange transactions are a major source of their funding and this issue is not addressed in
the IFRS for SMEs apart from in Section 24 *Government Grants*.

The Accounting Council considered that for PBE financial statements to be complete,   **154**
they should reflect the benefit that the inflow of these resources had to the entity.
FRS 102 requires, in principle, PBEs to value the resources they receive from non-exchange
transactions at their fair value. The Accounting Council discussed whether using fair value
would overstate the value of a donation where the entity is unable to exploit fully an asset,
and the equivalent service potential could be derived from a lower value asset. Being able
to achieve the same service potential from a lower value asset might suggest that the value
of the donated asset should be at the lower value. However, FRS 102 requires donated
assets to be valued at their fair value. This reflects that the circumstances described above
would rarely occur. In many cases, an entity would be able to sell the donated asset and if
appropriate, purchase a cheaper asset with the equivalent service potential.

Incorporating an exception for donated assets which may not be fully exploited would   **155**
make the application of FRS 102 more onerous, as it would require all entities in receipt of
donated assets (except those intended for resale) to consider whether they would be able to
exploit the asset fully. This would be subjective and may incur the risk of understatement
of the value of donated assets.

The Accounting Council noted that where goods are donated for subsequent sale (for   **156**
example donations to charity shops), it could be argued that the donated goods should be
valued only when they are sold. This is not consistent with the accruals concept which
requires the financial statements to recognise goods when they are received. However, the
Accounting Council advises, on pragmatic grounds, that donated goods should only be
recognised as income on receipt when the item is material, can be measured reliably and
if the benefits of recognising the item outweigh the costs. Further the Accounting Council
proposes that the same accounting may be applied by other wholly-owned entities in a

public benefit entity group, to eliminate the need to restate goods donated for subsequent sale on consolidation (for example where a charity operates it shops through a subsidiary that is a non-charitable company).

157   FRS 102 requires donated services that would otherwise have been purchased to be accounted for at their estimated value to the recipient. This is a pragmatic solution recognising that there are potential issues in determining a value for volunteer services and their contribution to the organisation and notes that quantifying this type of service may not be practicable. There is an argument to suggest that valuing volunteer services could be measured by reference to a metric such as the minimum wage, however this measure does not take into consideration an organisation's requirements for volunteers. In addition, this would be attributing an arbitrary value onto a volunteer's time which may not be reflective of their skills, experience or role and to determine a different method of valuation would be very subjective.

158   However, when a service is provided voluntarily for which the entity would otherwise have to pay (eg legal or financial advice) the value of that service should be recognised in the financial statements where, as will usually be the case, its value can be reasonably quantified.

Other PBE issues

159   The Accounting Council discussed the issue of reporting entity control and the indicators of control that may be specific to the PBE sectors. The indicators of control set out in Section 9 *Consolidated and Separate Financial Statements* of FRS 102 focus on benefits, and in the PBE sectors benefit can be in the form of indirect benefit through a PBE's beneficiaries or benefit which furthers a PBE's activities. Following discussion of these issues the Accounting Council advises that FRS 102 can be interpreted and applied to PBEs and therefore no separate guidance for PBEs is considered necessary.

160   A number of additional topics were identified through the development of FRS 102, which may be considered in the future and as possible updates to FRS 102. The following table summarises these subjects:

Narrative Reporting	To consider narrative reporting requirements for public benefit entities and any specific matters.
Fresh Start Accounting	To consider the concept of fresh start accounting as an alternative accounting treatment for entity combinations where the effect of a combination is to create a new entity that cannot be reasonably portrayed as the enlargement of a pre-existing party.
Social Benefit Obligations	To consider if and how social benefit obligations should be recognised and measured in the financial statements. The International Public Sector Accounting Standards Board currently have a project addressing this issue and it is likely to be most productive to await the outcome of that work.
Fund Accounting	To consider how fund accounting would be applied in accordance with the requirements of FRS 102 for segmental reporting.

Transition to FRS 102

161   The Accounting Council noted that FRS 102 does not permit goodwill to have an indefinite useful life, unlike current FRS. On transition to FRS 102 entities that previously determined that goodwill had an indefinite useful life will need to reassess goodwill to determine its remaining useful life, and subsequently amortise the goodwill over that period.

Effective date

FREDs 43 and 44 proposed an effective date for accounting periods beginning on or after 1 July 2013, with early application being permitted. Respondents' views regarding the proposals were very mixed with some calling for earlier adoption and others for deferral of the proposals.   **162**

The Accounting Council took into consideration its decision that FRS 102 would apply to a broader scope of entities and its revised guidelines for amending the IFRS for SMEs in relation to the effective date. The Accounting Council noted that: **163**

(a) Although the revisions to its original proposals should ease the transition, an 18 month period between the publication of the final standard and effective date should be retained as there are significant changes to the accounting requirements for financial instruments.

(b) The IASB's decision to revise the effective date of IFRS 9 *Financial Instruments* to 2015. The ASB noted that entities that apply current FRS without FRS 26, who wished to move to the proposed reduced disclosure framework would not be able to apply IFRS 9 until it was adopted by the EU. Consequently such entities would need to apply IAS 39 *Financial Instruments: Recognition and Measurement* for an interim period. The costs associated with these changes were not justifiable.

(c) The effective date needed to take into consideration the updating of the SORPs that is required.

The Accounting Council advises that the effective date of FRS 102 should be accounting periods beginning on or after 1 January 2015.   **164**

The Accounting Council also considered whether to permit early application of FRS 102. It noted that as FRS 102 represents an improvement in financial reporting it would not be appropriate to prevent early application of its requirements. However, the Accounting Council advises that early application of FRS 102 should not be permitted for accounting periods before those ending on or after 31 December 2012, which is consistent with the first date at which it is likely to be practical for entities applying FRS 101 to apply that standard.   **165**

The Accounting Council also considered the early application of FRS 102 by entities that are within the scope of a SORP. It noted that most of the SORPs require updating for consistency with FRS 102, and for charities there are legal requirements relating to the application of the SORP. The Accounting Council therefore advises that early application should be permitted for entities applying a SORP provided that FRS 102 does not conflict with the requirements of a current SORP or legal requirements for the preparation of financial statements.   **166**

Approval of this advice

This advice to the FRC was approved by eight of the nine members of the Accounting Council on 17 January 2013. Mr Beale dissented from the approval of the advice and his dissenting view is set out in the Appendix to the Accounting Council's advice. The Accounting Council is comprised of the following members: **167**

Roger Marshall   (Chair of the Accounting Council)
Nick Anderson
Dr Richard Barker
Edward Beale
Peter Elwin
Ken Lever
Robert Overend
Andy Simmonds
Pauline Wallace

APPENDIX TO THE ACCOUNTING COUNCIL'S ADVICE TO THE FRC TO ISSUE FRS 102

Dissenting view of Mr Beale

1   Mr Beale agrees that it is fundamental that financial statements should provide useful information to users, who are defined as being: investors not involved in management, customers and suppliers, including suppliers of capital and of non-equity finance. He agrees with the Accounting Council that it is disappointing that despite extensive outreach activities, the Accounting Council has not received more feedback from users, both formal and informal, on whether or not financial statements prepared in accordance with FRS 102 will meet their information needs.

2   Mr Beale does not believe that the consultation responses from industry representative bodies[18], and from organisations which are both preparers and users, can be considered to be input from users since these responses are from a preparer perspective.

3   The informal input received by the FRC staff supports FRS 102 as drafted, and is generally consistent with the input from preparers and industry representative bodies. However, this informal input is inconsistent with the five[19] formal consultation responses received from users and the informal input received personally by Mr Beale. This inconsistency in the content of informal input may be due to the informal input received by FRC staff being from providers of non-equity finance whereas the informal input received by Mr Beale has been from directors (who are both users and preparers) and investors.

4   This informal input received by FRC staff in relation to FRS 102 differs from comments that FRC staff have recently received on other projects:

(a)   from credit analysts and bond fund managers in relation to the financial statements of listed entities[20] (that there is not sufficient forward looking information on cash flows and challenging the usefulness of fair value); and

(b)   as part of the Financial Reporting Laboratory's work on a single figure for remuneration[21] (regarding valuation of equity incentives and pension costs).

5   In Mr Beale's experience users are concerned with issues identified by the FRC in *Louder than Words*[22], which they believe have not been adequately addressed in FRS 102. In his analysis, the common thread behind these user concerns is a desire for clearer, more understandable, information, from which they can derive better predictions about future cash flows on a going concern basis, even at the expense of further divergence from IFRS. Understandability is crucial to confidence in the integrity of financial reporting, and thus maximising the benefits from accounts. Despite the importance of maintaining consistency with IFRS, Mr Beale believes that the FRC should not be issuing new accounting standards perpetuating problems identified in existing standards.

---

[18] *Some of which have been classified in the Feedback Statements as 'user representative bodies'.*

[19] *Four of these formal consultation responses are from users connected to Mr Beale and include three responses to FREDs 43 and 44, of which two were formally classified as being from preparers and one from an academic.*

[20] *http://www.frc.org.uk/getattachment/b0eff085-b542-4eaf-bc36-d52e26eb3833/How-credit-analysts-view-and-use-the-financial-statements.aspx*

[21] *http://frc.org.uk/getattachment/5310093d-c092-45e1-8106-278ae7ac1a4b/A-single-figure-for-remuneration.aspx*

[22] *http://www.frc.org.uk/getattachment/7d952925-74ea-4deb-b659-e9242b09f2fa/Louder-than-words.aspx*

In particular Mr Beale believes that there are significant further opportunities to improve   **6**
the balance between costs and benefits in the sections of FRS 102 dealing with: Financial
Instruments, Deferred Tax, Defined Benefit Pension Schemes, and Equity Settled Share-
based Payments. This is discussed further below. In his view FRS 102 could have achieved
clearer reporting in the above areas by departing further from the IFRS for SMEs,
thus better meeting users' needs for high-quality financial information in line with the
overriding objective.

The FRC needs to consider whether the extensive outreach activities undertaken   **7**
constitute 'adequate consultation'. In Mr Beale's opinion the determination of 'adequate
consultation' should be based on the outcome from the consultation process and,
regrettably, there has been virtually no formal input from the people who will be using
accounts prepared under FRS 102. Based on the consultation responses from users and
the informal input from users that he has received, Mr Beale is advising that the FRC
defer approval of FRS 102 until it has a better understanding of the degree of support
from users, and in the meantime to work on improving the balance between costs and
benefits in the areas outlined above.

In Mr Beale's experience, users do not consider UK GAAP to be in need of urgent   **8**
replacement, and will not be concerned about any delays to FRS 102 necessary to
determine the degree of user support and resolve any outstanding issues.

Further opportunities to improve the balance between costs and benefits

There are two issues of principle underpinning the areas of FRS 102 that, in Mr Beale's   **9**
opinion, can be significantly improved:

(a)   Since the purpose of accounts is to supply useful information to users, the most
      important concepts underpinning accounting standards should be 'relevance'
      (include information that is useful to users) and its converse, 'materiality' (exclude
      information that is not useful). All other accounting concepts should clearly be
      subsidiary to these. Such an emphasis on the priority attributable to 'relevance'
      and 'materiality' will promote measurement of assets and liabilities in a manner
      that conveys useful information to users, and will normally exclude mark to model
      valuations, and limit application of fair value elsewhere.

(b)   At present some assets and liabilities are revalued, and some unrealised profits
      are taken to earnings. To ensure a principled base for accounting standards the
      FRC needs to determine general principles covering (i) when it is appropriate
      for assets and liabilities to be revalued, and (ii) whether unrealised profits arising
      from revaluations should be recognised in earnings or as a movement in reserves.
      A consistent approach to revaluation of items such as fixed assets and financial
      instruments, and a consistent approach to profit recognition, cannot be achieved
      without such principles. In his opinion, for the purposes of FRS 102: assets should
      be revalued when there is a sufficiently liquid market for their market value to be
      determined reliably, or when an impairment provision is necessary; liabilities should
      only be revalued when there are changes to the amount required to settle them when
      they fall due; and unrealised profits should not be included within earnings, except
      for profits on liquid investments.

In Mr Beale's opinion, opportunities to significantly improve the balance of costs
and benefits within FRS 102 exist in four areas, two of general application: financial
instruments, and deferred tax; and two of more limited application: equity settled
share based payments and defined benefit pension schemes. These are summarised
below.

Financial instruments

10   Current FRSs have been criticised in that they allow certain financial instruments not to be recorded. Such criticism is incorrect in that the existence of, and details about, these financial instruments should (where 'material') be recorded in the notes to the accounts. This criticism has been used by some to justify moving to an IFRS based approach to accounting for financial instruments, which has been widely criticised, and which is not the most cost effective approach to providing users of accounts with the information that they desire.

11   Many different assets and liabilities fall within the definition of financial instruments and attempting to deal with all of these in the same manner introduces unnecessary complexity. The two sections on financial instruments include three to four pages of rules on which section should be applied, and are written in a language which is in places very difficult for people not accustomed to IFRS to understand. These sections have also been drafted to cater for financial institutions as well as ordinary businesses, and this exacerbates the difficulty that non-experts will have in applying them. Preparers of accounts will generally only refer to accounting standards once a year in the lead up to preparation of their annual accounts. FRS 102 needs to be readily understandable for such preparers, and there is a risk that if accounting standards are not sufficiently accessible they will be applied in a manner that generates unnecessary complexity and clutter.

12   The two sections on financial instruments should be redrafted in language that is understandable to the normal businessperson and is not the preserve of experts. Redrafting of these sections should focus on the information that users need relating to ordinary businesses, with additional requirements for financial institutions dealt with in the section for specialised activities, by expanding the part relating to financial institutions, and which can in turn refer to IAS 39 *Financial Instruments: Recognition and Measurement*, IFRS 7 *Financial Instruments: Disclosure* and IFRS 9 *Financial Instruments* where appropriate.

13   Users need different 'information sets' on financial instruments that are: fixed assets, current assets and liabilities; and FRS 102 should consider financial instruments in these three categories, rather than trying to cover all three categories with one set of rules. Prudence should be incorporated where necessary so that the treatment of assets is not necessarily the mirror of the treatment of liabilities.

Financial assets

14   For normal businesses, financial assets should be carried at fair value when the principles for revaluation set out above are met, and failing that at cost less any necessary impairment provision. Income should be recognised in a prudent manner: as it is earned (eg interest on a daily basis), or when it can be reliably measured (eg dividends).

15   Circumstances may arise which cause the valuation basis of financial assets to change, but such situations are unlikely to occur frequently outside financial institutions. Where they do occur, the consequences of reclassifications can be made obvious to users of accounts through note disclosures. Strict anti-abuse rules are not necessary. A clear analysis in the notes can highlight where reclassification is potentially being abused to manage earnings, so that users can discuss their concerns with management, auditors or regulators as appropriate. Any additional requirements considered necessary for financial institutions can be dealt with in the section for specialised activities.

Financial liabilities

When a financial liability is included in the balance sheet at a value which is different   **16**
from the amount required to settle the liability when it falls due, disclosure of amount
of principal repayable is necessary, so that users can understand the underlying cash
flow. The notes then show two different values for the same liability. This duplication of
valuation bases creates extra cost to both preparers and users of accounts and risks causing
confusion. Confusion can be minimised by using the settlement value in the statement of
financial position, rather than fair values or amortised cost, recognising deferred financing
costs where necessary, and providing information in the notes about financing costs and
settlement dates. Interested users will then have the information necessary to perform their
own comparisons with other businesses, as well as clearer information on the business's
funding requirements.

The above approach to liabilities could lead to extensive disclosures for financial institutions   **17**
and others where there are a large number of different types of financial liability. The
section on specialised activities should set out an approach for the aggregation of necessary
disclosures and allow an opt into IFRS 9/IAS 39.

Impairment of financial assets

Impairment provisions are only allowed in FRS 102 where there is 'objective evidence'   **18**
of impairment. Businesses are not allowed to make provision for expected losses, even
where there is past experience supporting the likelihood of such losses. Expected loss
provisions should be allowed now, before IFRS 9 has been updated, to avoid assets being
overvalued. A clear analysis in the notes will highlight where impairment provisions are
potentially being abused to manage earnings, so that users can discuss their concerns
with management, auditors or regulators as appropriate. Additional requirements may be
imposed on financial institutions through the section on specialised activities.

Hedging

Hedge accounting is only permitted in FRS 102 if 'specified criteria' are met. In the past   **19**
similar restrictions have led to businesses not hedge accounting for financial instruments
acquired, or entered into, for hedging purposes. The purpose of accounting standards is
not to promote good management but good reporting. Accounting standards are not the
appropriate way to attempt to stop the miss-selling, or miss-buying, of derivatives. There
needs to be transparency over hedges entered into so that the effect of hedges in managing
risk can be understood by users of accounts. This can be achieved by linked accounting
for hedges and items being hedged, so that accounting faithfully represents the underlying
commercial activity.

Concerns over earnings management can be alleviated by disclosure of the impact on   **20**
earnings of hedges closed out in a different period to the risk that they purported to
hedge. Businesses other than financial institutions should be able to allay concerns over
the effectiveness of hedges by explaining how their limited number of material risks are
being hedged. Financial institutions may have too many hedges to be able to provide
this information in a meaningful manner and an alternative approach for such businesses
should be set out in the section on specialised activities.

Deferred tax

As the recent ASB/EFRAG discussion paper on tax identified, users want to know how   **21**
future tax payments will differ from the amount calculated by applying the standard tax

rate to future profits. This difference will be in part due to future actions and in part due to past actions.

22   The section of FRS 102 on deferred tax is not predicated on a going concern basis, and in effect identifies the impact on future tax payments if the business ceases trading. As such, except for the disclosure of amounts expected to reverse in the next period, the approach in FRS 102 is of little relevance to most users and will create disclosures which will generally be ignored by users.

23   The disclosure required by FRS 102 of the amount of the deferred tax provision which will be released in the next period is of limited usefulness. This is only part of the difference between expected tax cost and standard tax rate. Prediction of the element due to future actions is not currently required.

24   The information that users need can best be provided by way of disclosure of the expected future tax rate and any other material information that may influence future tax payments, eg losses carried forward. A deferred tax provision should not be made because this does not provide useful information in a cost effective manner. The exception to this is that the logic behind revaluing certain items dictates that, for consistency, the tax impact of such revaluations needs to be recognised too.

Equity settled share-based payments

25   As identified by the recent financial reporting laboratory work on valuation of remuneration, users do not understand the complex models used to value equity settled share based payments. The cost of creating these values is therefore wasted.

26   These valuation models also generate a substantial amount of clutter when trying to explain how the valuation is arrived at.

27   It should also be noted that the standard valuation models assume liquid markets and negligible spreads. These assumptions are not appropriate for the types of businesses that will be applying FRS 102. Given the lack of guidance in FRS 102, and the complexity of the valuation models, in Mr Beale's opinion it is highly likely that preparers will use inappropriate valuation models, or use valuation models in inappropriate ways, and that users will not have enough knowledge to identify this.

28   Unless there is a liquid market to provide a relevant value for equity settled share based payments, their existence should be disclosed in the notes to the accounts, and there should be no notional cost in the income statement.

Defined benefit pension schemes

29   The information relating to defined benefit pension schemes that users need is: the current cost of providing the benefit, the expected additional payments required to make good any funding deficit (or payment holiday because of funding surpluses) and an explanation of the contingent liability in respect of potential future funding shortfalls.

30   At present there is a requirement to prepare a fund valuation solely for accounting purposes and then to consolidate the net assets or, more usually, liabilities of the fund. Changes in the net assets/liabilities are then split into three parts and recognised in operating costs, financing costs and other comprehensive income. This is supplemented by extensive disclosures. However, the disclosures do not require information about the uncertainties or sensitivities attached to the valuation inputs eg the time periods over

which payments out of the fund will be made, discount and inflation rates, and other risks inherent in the fund.

Most users do not understand pension scheme valuations. They see fund valuations which are massively volatile, and perceive most current requirements as adding to clutter and generating additional preparation costs for no benefit. **31**

Clutter could be reduced by not consolidating the pension fund, but instead disclosing the level of normal contributions being made and providing for contributions required to make good any funding shortfall. Changes in this liability to make good any funding shortfall should be expensed and explained. In addition disclosures should be made describing the contingent liability to fund any future increases in fund deficits. Those users who do understand pension scheme valuations can obtain the more detailed information that they are likely to want about pension scheme funding from the fund valuation prepared for that purpose, which should be made available on demand or on a web site. Such an approach would save the costs associated with preparing a valuation solely for accounting purposes as well as reducing clutter in the accounts. **32**

Training costs

Maintaining limited UK GAAP differences from IFRS will marginally increase the cost of training accountants, but should improve their employability, and will increase the challenge on the IASB to further improve IFRS, thereby improving the balance between benefits and costs overall. **33**

THE ACCOUNTING COUNCIL'S ADVICE TO THE FRC TO ISSUE AMENDMENTS TO FRS 102 – BASIC FINANCIAL INSTRUMENTS AND HEDGE ACCOUNTING

Introduction

1   This report provides an overview of the main issues that have been considered by the Accounting Council in advising the Financial Reporting Council (FRC) to issue *Amendments to FRS 102 The Financial Reporting Standard applicable in the UK and Republic of Ireland – Basic financial instruments and Hedge accounting.*

2   The FRC, in accordance with the *Statutory Auditors (Amendment of Companies Act 2006 and Delegation of Functions etc) Order 2012* (SI 2012/1741), is a prescribed body for issuing accounting standards in the UK. The *Foreword to Accounting Standards* sets out the application of accounting standards in the Republic of Ireland.

3   In accordance with the *FRC Codes and Standards: procedures*, any proposal to issue, amend or withdraw a code or standard is put to the FRC Board with the full advice of the relevant Councils and/or the Codes & Standards Committee. Ordinarily, the FRC Board will only reject the advice put to it where:

(a)   it is apparent that a significant group of stakeholders has not been adequately consulted;

(b)   the necessary assessment of the impact of the proposal has not been completed, including an analysis of costs and benefits;

(c)   insufficient consideration has been given to the timing or cost of implementation; or

(d)   the cumulative impact of a number of proposals would make the adoption of an otherwise satisfactory proposal inappropriate.

4   The FRC has established the Accounting Council as the relevant Council to assist it in the setting of accounting standards.

Advice

5   The Accounting Council is advising the FRC to issue *Amendments to FRS 102 The Financial Reporting Standard applicable in the UK and Republic of Ireland – Basic financial instruments and Hedge accounting* to:

(a)   remove the unintended accounting consequences arising for the classification of certain financial instruments. It believes these changes will result in a reduction in the cost of compliance for entities within the scope of the standard; and

(b)   to make the application of the hedge accounting requirements easier and more cost effective to apply for entities that choose to take advantage of this option.

6   The Accounting Council's Advice to the FRC in FRS 102 *The Financial Reporting Standard applicable in the UK and Republic of Ireland* is supplemented by the inclusion of its advice on these amendments.

Background

7   The FRC issued FRS 102 in March 2013, which is effective for accounting periods beginning on or after 1 January 2015.

8   After the publication of FRS 102, feedback from constituents indicated that the implementation of the accounting requirements of FRS 102 for loans with common contractual features could have unintended consequences for many entities. The

amendments to Section 11 *Basic Financial Instruments* address the issues identified and take into account responses to FRED 54 *Draft Amendments to FRS 102 Financial Reporting Standard applicable in the UK and Ireland – Basic financial instruments.*

At the time of issue of FRS 102, the Accounting Council and the FRC were of the view that the standard should reflect up-to-date thinking on hedge accounting, but the IASB had not yet finalised the hedge accounting requirements in IFRS 9 *Financial Instruments.* The Accounting Council advised the FRC at that time that amending the hedge accounting requirements in FRS 102 prior to the IASB finalising the hedge accounting requirements in IFRS 9, would risk implementing hedge accounting requirements in FRS 102 that were inconsistent with IFRS. 9

The hedge accounting amendments to FRS 102 were developed based on the hedge accounting requirements in IFRS 9 and take into account the responses to FRED 51 *Draft Amendments to FRS 102 Financial Reporting Standard applicable in the UK and Ireland – Hedge Accounting.* 10

Objective

The FRC gives careful consideration to its objective and the intended effects when developing new accounting standards or requirements for the UK and Republic of Ireland. In developing accounting standards, including FRS 102, the overriding objective of the FRC is: 11

> To enable users of accounts to receive high-quality understandable financial reporting proportionate to the size and complexity of the entity and users' information needs.

In meeting this objective, the FRC aims to provide succinct financial reporting standards that: 12

(a) have consistency with global accounting standards through the application of an IFRS-based solution unless an alternative clearly better meets the overriding objective;

(b) reflect up-to-date thinking and developments in the way businesses operate and the transactions they undertake;

(c) balance consistent principles for accounting by all UK and Republic of Ireland entities with practical solutions, based on size, complexity, public interest and users' information needs;

(d) promote efficiency within groups; and

(e) are cost-effective to apply.

Basic financial instruments

Rules vs principles-based solution

The classification of financial instruments as 'basic' or 'other' in FRS 102 is dependent on a list of prescriptive conditions. The Accounting Council considered whether a principles-based solution to relaxing the conditions, based on the principle articulated in IFRS 9 in respect of the classification of financial assets, would be more effective, but advises retaining the rules-based conditions of FRS 102 instead, for the following reasons: 13

(a) the IFRS 9 principle is yet untested in practice and, at the time of giving the advice, the IASB is currently debating possible amendments to IFRS 9; and

(b)   the IFRS 9 principle in relation to the classification of financial instruments only applies to financial assets. The classification conditions in FRS 102, however, apply equally to debt instruments that are assets or liabilities.

Interaction with Regulations or LLP Regulations on measurement of certain financial instruments

14   Subsequent to receiving the responses to FRED 54, the Accounting Council was made aware of an additional issue in relation to a conflict between the Regulations and LLP Regulations and the requirements in FRS 102, as originally issued, on measurement of some financial liabilities. The original text of FRS 102 could have resulted in the standard requiring certain financial liabilities to be measured at fair value where such measurement may be prohibited by the Regulations. The Regulations prohibit the measurement of financial liabilities at fair value, except for those held as part of a trading portfolio, that are derivatives or where permitted by EU-adopted IFRS.

15   For example, the original text of FRS 102 would have required certain financial liabilities, where the cash outflows are linked to non-financial variables specific to one party to the contract, to be classified as non-basic and measured at fair value. Fair value measurement is not permitted for such liabilities under EU-adopted IFRS and so would be prohibited by the Regulations.

16   Such liabilities commonly arise in insurance contracts where the amount an insurer is liable to pay depends on the occurrence of insured events specific to the insured party and its activities.

17   The Accounting Council is aware that there are divergent views on what constitutes a 'non-financial variable' in other cases. For example, there is no clear consensus as to whether measures of performance such as turnover, profits or EBITDA are 'non-financial variables ... specific to a party to the contract'. The Accounting Council is unable to resolve this divergence as to do so would involve interpreting EU-adopted IFRS on an issue that the IFRS Interpretations Committee has so far not reached a definitive conclusion.

18   Similarly, FRS 102 would have required that financial assets which are similarly linked to non-financial variables specific to one party to the contract, be classified as non-basic and measured at fair value through profit or loss. Although Regulations permit financial assets to be classified at fair value, this classification is only available as permitted by EU-adopted IFRS, which in some cases is restricted to fair value through other comprehensive income.

19   The Accounting Council also notes that there may be other non-basic financial assets and liabilities that EU-adopted IFRS, and hence the Regulations, would not permit to be measured at fair value through profit or loss although it expected that such instruments would be rare in practice.

20   As a result, the Accounting Council advises the inclusion of an exception in Section 12 in respect of non-basic financial instruments where the Regulations would not permit the use of fair value through profit or loss, instead requiring them to be measured at amortised cost. In advising this, the Accounting Council is conscious that this exception would be applicable to a small number of entities under a narrow set of circumstances.

Loans in the social housing sector

21   In response to FRED 54, a number of respondents from the social housing sector raised concerns about the classification of certain lending arrangements common within that sector. It was noted that a number of these arrangements were structured in different

ways but often to achieve the same economic outcome. After detailed consideration the Accounting Council advises that a loan cannot be classified as basic if it includes contractual terms giving the lender the unilateral option to change the terms of that loan, for example from a pre-determined fixed rate to a variable rate or to a different fixed rate chosen by the lender, even if the holder can avoid it by repaying the loan.

Structured financial instruments

In response to FRED 54, a number of respondents raised questions about the classification   **22**
of certain financial instruments that were structured in a complex way and requested that the final amendment clarify their classification in accordance with FRS 102. The Accounting Council noted that such structured financial instruments are not based on contracts that are standardised across an industry. As a result, the repayment of principal and interest on such loans can be impacted in a complex way by a number of different variables defined in the contractual terms. The Accounting Council noted that it was not possible to conclude on the classification of such financial instruments without a close reading of the individual contracts and an understanding of the detailed clauses. Therefore, the Accounting Council advises that the reporting entity's directors should apply their judgement to determine whether the contractual terms enable a financial instrument to be classified as basic in accordance with the requirements in FRS 102.

Classification subsequent to initial recognition

The Accounting Council noted that the initial classification assessment of a financial   **23**
instrument should take into account the relevant clauses dealing with the returns and any subsequent contractual variations relating to returns, prepayments and extensions of terms etc. Once the classification of a financial instrument is determined at initial recognition, no re-assessment is required at subsequent dates unless there is a modification of contractual terms.

Hedge accounting

The previous hedge accounting requirements in FRS 102 narrowly defined the types of   **24**
permitted arrangements that may qualify for hedge accounting, which was not necessarily representative of an entity's risk management objectives and hedging practices.

The Accounting Council's aim was to develop new hedge accounting requirements that   **25**
allow for a reflection of an entity's hedging activities in the financial statements that is consistent with the entity's risk management objectives and are, as far as appropriate for constituents of FRS 102, consistent with IFRS.

These amendments to FRS 102 have been developed on the basis of IFRS, and substantively   **26**
adopt the terminology and hedge accounting requirements in IFRS 9, with notable exceptions described in more detail below. The Accounting Council has been mindful that the requirements in IFRS 9 deal with hedging transactions that can be far more complex than those typically entered into by entities applying FRS 102. The departures from the requirements in IFRS 9 are therefore intended to simplify the application of hedge accounting.

Eligible hedged items

The Accounting Council was requested to reconsider the exclusion of explicit macrohedging   **27**
provisions in FRS 102, similar to those in IAS 39 *Financial Instruments: Recognition and Measurement*. After consideration of the specific concerns of entities that raised this as an

issue, the Accounting Council concluded that in the interest of developing straight-forward hedge accounting requirements that are relevant for a majority of entities, it retains its previous advice stated in FRED 51. Entities wishing to apply the IFRS macrohedging provisions are able to apply the accounting policy choice in FRS 102 to apply IAS 39 and/or IFRS 9 instead.

Qualifying hedge accounting conditions

28   The qualifying hedge accounting conditions in FRS 102 have been simplified compared to the criteria set out in IFRS 9, with the aim of making hedge accounting easier to apply.

29   Under the amended hedge accounting requirements it is not necessary to achieve a prescribed level of effectiveness in a hedging relationship in order to qualify for hedge accounting, but an economic relationship between the hedged item and the hedging instrument has to exist. In response to feedback on FRED 51, an explanation has been added of when an economic relationship between a hedged item and a hedging instrument exists, which is in line with IFRS 9.

30   The Accounting Council notes that although a quantitative assessment of hedge effectiveness is not required, it is nevertheless important for entities to identify the different factors that affect the valuation of the hedging instrument and hedged item, including factors that may be a source of hedge ineffectiveness. Entities are therefore required to identify and document causes of hedge ineffectiveness before they commence hedge accounting, to ensure that ineffectiveness is properly captured in profit or loss.

31   Entities are required to document a hedging relationship, to avoid hedge accounting being misused. The hedge documentation requirements are, however, relatively informal and undemanding and should not be an administrative burden for entities in practice.

Discontinuing hedge accounting

32   These amendments permit entities to discontinue hedge accounting voluntarily. This is a departure from IFRS 9. The Accounting Council considered that the restrictions in IFRS 9 on discontinuance are unnecessarily onerous, and instead has retained the existing option of voluntary discontinuation. An entity must document the election to discontinue hedge accounting, which is consistent with the requirement for documentation at the start of hedge accounting.

Disclosure

33   These amendments retain substantially the disclosure requirements of FRS 102. The disclosure requirements in relation to the hedge accounting requirements in IFRS 9, contained in IFRS 7 *Financial Instruments: Disclosure* focus on risks and risk mitigation through hedging. The Accounting Council notes that risk disclosures are not generally required in FRS 102, except for financial institutions.

Transitional provisions for first-time adopters of FRS 102

34   The Accounting Council's aim was to develop transitional provisions that are consistent with the permissive hedge accounting regime of FRS 102 and give entities a choice over whether to commence, continue or end hedge accounting on transition to FRS 102. Some respondents to FRED 51 were concerned that this flexibility may be abused, as it allows entities to apply a degree of hindsight. The Accounting Council is mindful of this possible exploitation of the transitional provisions. Nevertheless, on balance it believes that in the

interests of the majority of entities, especially entities that have not applied hedge accounting before, flexibility should take precedence over restrictions aimed at preventing abuse.

The Accounting Council is conscious that entities may have applied diverse hedge accounting   **35** practices before the adoption of FRS 102. Entities may have applied the hedge accounting requirements in accordance with FRS 26 (IAS 39) *Financial Instruments: Recognition and Measurement* or may have applied synthetic accounting practices permitted under SSAP 20 *Foreign currency translation*. Accommodating these different accounting practices introduces complexity that the transitional provisions need to address. Under the transitional provisions, regardless of what accounting practices were applied previously, entities have the choice to continue hedge accounting in accordance with FRS 102, provided the conditions for hedge accounting are met. Entities that elect not to apply the FRS 102 hedge accounting requirements, have to comply with the applicable measurement requirements for assets and liabilities set out elsewhere in FRS 102 from the date of transition.

The amendments are issued after the date of transition to FRS 102 for many entities. The   **36** transitional provisions take this into account by providing an extended deadline for hedge documentation on first-time adoption.

Alternative reporting of economic hedges

The Accounting Council advises modifying the provision in Section 11 to allow the   **37** designation of loan commitments at fair value through profit or loss (in addition to the designation of debt instruments at fair value through profit or loss). This will have the effect of allowing economic hedge accounting where an entity balances the risks from a first instrument by taking out a second which is measured at fair value: it will be able to choose to measure the first at fair value too, thus matching the movements in profit and reflecting, in financial reporting, the combined economic effect of the instruments.

Impairment provisions

Originally it was planned to amend FRS 102 prior to its effective date in respect of the   **38** requirements relating to hedge accounting and the impairment of financial assets. The IASB's project on the new IFRS impairment model is delayed and the FRC's consultation on introducing equivalent requirements in FRS 102 has therefore been deferred. Respondents to FRED 51 requested the exemption of certain entities from the requirement to adopt the impairment accounting requirements in FRS 102 until the new impairment requirements in FRS 102 are finalised.

The Accounting Council deliberated on the likely impact of the adoption of the impairment   **39** accounting requirements in FRS 102. It concluded that the incurred loss impairment model in FRS 102 is consistent with UK GAAP, as applicable prior to the introduction of FRS 102. The Accounting Council considers that it is therefore unnecessary to provide a temporary relief from the impairment accounting requirements in FRS 102.

Effective date

The Accounting Council advises that the amendments should be effective from the   **40** effective date of FRS 102 (ie accounting periods beginning on or after 1 January 2015), and therefore no amendment to the effective date is required.

Approval of this advice

This advice to the FRC was approved by the Accounting Council on 19 June 2014.   **41**

THE ACCOUNTING COUNCIL'S ADVICE TO THE FRC TO ISSUE AMENDMENTS TO FRS 102 – PENSION OBLIGATIONS

Introduction

1　This report provides an overview of the main issues that have been considered by the Accounting Council in advising the Financial Reporting Council (FRC) to issue *Amendments to FRS 102 The Financial Reporting Standard applicable in the UK and Republic of Ireland – Pension obligations*.

2　The FRC, in accordance with the *Statutory Auditors (Amendment of Companies Act 2006 and Delegation of Functions etc) Order 2012* (SI 2012/1741), is a prescribed body for issuing accounting standards in the UK. The *Foreword to Accounting Standards* sets out the application of accounting standards in the Republic of Ireland.

3　In accordance with the *FRC Codes and Standards: procedures*, any proposal to issue, amend or withdraw a code or standard is put to the FRC Board with the full advice of the relevant Councils and/or the Codes & Standards Committee. Ordinarily, the FRC Board will only reject the advice put to it where:

(a)　it is apparent that a significant group of stakeholders has not been adequately consulted;

(b)　the necessary assessment of the impact of the proposal has not been completed, including an analysis of costs and benefits;

(c)　insufficient consideration has been given to the timing or cost of implementation; or

(d)　the cumulative impact of a number of proposals would make the adoption of an otherwise satisfactory proposal inappropriate.

4　The FRC has established the Accounting Council as the relevant Council to assist it in the setting of accounting standards.

Advice

5　The Accounting Council is advising the FRC to issue *Amendments to FRS 102 The Financial Reporting Standard applicable in the UK and Republic of Ireland – Pension obligations*.

6　The amendments will resolve an issue of uncertainty over the requirements of FRS 102 in relation to a commitment to make payments under a 'schedule of contributions' to a defined benefit pension plan which the entity accounts for on a defined benefit basis, and therefore reduce potential diversity in practice and the cost of compliance with FRS 102.

7　The Accounting Council's Advice to the FRC to issue FRS 102 *The Financial Reporting Standard applicable in the UK and Republic of Ireland* was set out in that standard. The Accounting Council's Advice to the FRC on these amendments will be included in the revised FRS 102.

Background

8　After the publication of FRS 102 in March 2013 the FRC issued, in October 2013, a Press Notice[23] addressing the accounting in accordance with EU-adopted IFRS for a 'schedule of contributions' payable by an entity to a defined benefit pension plan. Subsequently

---

[23] *FRC PN 089 Findings of the FRC in respect of the accounts of WH Smith Plc for the year ended 31 August 2012.*

the FRC received enquiries about the accounting for similar circumstances by entities applying FRS 102.

The issue concerns whether or not an entity applying FRS 102 should have regard to the **9** principles of IFRIC 14 *IAS 19 – The Limit on a Defined Benefit Asset, Minimum Funding Requirements and their Interaction* where it might be relevant to its circumstances. There appeared to be a diversity of views on the matter, and because the potential implications for an entity's financial statements could be significant the FRC decided to address the matter outside the intended three-yearly review cycle for FRS 102.

The Accounting Council considered the responses to the consultation FRED 55 *Draft* **10** *Amendments to FRS 102 – Pension obligations*, which was issued in August 2014, in developing its advice.

Objective

In developing its advice to the FRC, the Accounting Council was guided by the overriding **11** objective to enable users of accounts to receive high-quality understandable financial reporting proportionate to the size and complexity of the entity and users' information needs.

In meeting this objective, the FRC aims to provide succinct financial reporting standards **12** that:

(a) have consistency with international accounting standards through the application of an IFRS-based solution unless an alternative clearly better meets the overriding objective;

(b) reflect up-to-date thinking and developments in the way entities operate and the transactions they undertake;

(c) balance consistent principles for accounting by all UK and Republic of Ireland entities with practical solutions, based on size, complexity, public interest and users' information needs;

(d) promote efficiency within groups; and

(e) are cost-effective to apply.

Proportionate measurement of the net defined benefit liability for a defined benefit plan

The Accounting Council considered whether FRS 102 required an entity with a defined **13** benefit plan to consider the principles of IFRIC 14 in interpreting its requirements to measure the net defined benefit liability. The Accounting Council noted that there appeared to be uncertainty over this issue and that there was the possibility of significant diversity arising in accounting practice, particularly because the amounts that might be recognised (or not) could be very significant.

The Accounting Council considers that for entities applying FRS 102, the recognition **14** of the net defined benefit liability or asset (which may be limited by paragraph 28.22) for a defined benefit pension plan as the net total of the present value of the obligations under the plan and the fair value of the plan assets is a proportionate way to measure the present obligation to employees as a result of service rendered. It noted that in some circumstances IFRIC 14 would result in an additional liability being recognised in relation to a schedule of contributions that had been agreed with the defined benefit plan in order to address a deficit that had arisen on the basis of the funding assumptions. It further noted that the measurement of the present value of the obligations under the plan for funding purposes differs from the measurement for accounting purposes, but they are different measurements of the same obligation, not separate obligations.

15   Therefore the Accounting Council advises that, as a practical and proportionate solution, in measuring its defined benefit obligation an entity need not include the present value of contributions payable that arise from an agreement with the defined benefit plan to fund a deficit. The Accounting Council also advises that Section 28 *Employee Benefits* explicitly states that, in applying FRS 102, no additional liabilities shall be recognised in respect of an agreement with the defined benefit plan to fund a deficit (such as a schedule of contributions). This should ensure there are no divergent interpretations of the scope of Section 21 *Provisions and Contingencies* in relation to a schedule of contributions, because they are clearly within the scope of Section 28, and therefore outside the scope of Section 21.

16   The Accounting Council considered another potential solution to determining whether or not an additional obligation should be recognised in certain circumstances. It noted the interaction with the recognition of a defined benefit plan asset, and considered whether removing the restriction on recognising a defined benefit plan asset in some circumstances might be an alternative solution. However, the Accounting Council rejected this because it could have the unintended consequence of permitting an asset to be recognised where other factors would indicate the reporting entity was not able to recover the surplus.

17   These amendments to FRS 102 do not affect the accounting for a schedule of contributions or other funding agreement between a reporting entity and a multi-employer plan, which is set out in paragraph 28.11A of FRS 102. Where an entity participates in a defined benefit plan that is a multi-employer plan accounted for as if it were a defined contribution plan, it shall recognise a liability for the contributions payable that arise from the agreement (to the extent that they relate to a deficit) because this is the most cost-effective way of recognising the entity's obligation to employees as a result of service rendered. This contrasts with the approach for defined benefit plans because the obligation has already been recognised as the net defined benefit liability.

18   The majority of respondents to FRED 55 supported the proposal.

Effect of a restriction on the recoverability of a plan surplus

19   The Accounting Council also noted that FRS 102 does not specify where an entity shall recognise the effects of a restriction on the recoverability of a plan surplus, and therefore FRS 102 would require it to be recognised in profit or loss. A plan surplus may be irrecoverable because the entity is not able to recover the surplus through reduced contributions in the future or through refunds from the plan (see paragraph 28.22 of FRS 102). The Accounting Council considers that, except for any amount included in net interest on the net defined benefit liability, the effect of any such restriction should be recognised in other comprehensive income and advises that paragraph 28.25 is amended so that any such amounts are part of remeasurements, and therefore recognised in other comprehensive income. This is consistent with IAS 19 *Employee Benefits*.

Disclosure

20   Four respondents to FRED 55 commented on the benefits of an entity disclosing the amounts it had committed to pay under a schedule of contributions, and some requested clarification that the requirement in paragraph 28.41(a) of FRS 102 to disclose the funding policy was intended to include such disclosure.

The Accounting Council agreed that the disclosure of information about the amount and timing of payments intended to fund a deficit in a defined benefit plan would be useful information for users of financial statements. Although this should already be covered by the requirement to describe the funding policy, the Accounting Council advises that paragraph 28.41(a) is amended to clarify this.

21

Effective date

The Accounting Council advises that these amendments should be effective from the effective date of FRS 102 (ie accounting periods beginning on or after 1 January 2015), and therefore no amendment to the effective date of FRS 102 is required.

22

Approval of this Advice

This advice to the FRC was approved by the Accounting Council on 15 January 2015.

23

THE ACCOUNTING COUNCIL'S ADVICE TO THE FRC TO ISSUE AMENDMENTS TO FRS 102 – SMALL ENTITIES AND OTHER MINOR AMENDMENTS

Introduction

1   This report provides an overview of the main issues that have been considered by the Accounting Council in advising the Financial Reporting Council (FRC) to issue *Amendments to FRS 102 The Financial Reporting Standard applicable in the UK and Republic of Ireland – Small entities and other minor amendments* incorporating the Council's advice following the Consultation Document *Accounting standards for small entities – Implementation of the EU Accounting Directive*, FRED 59 *Draft Amendments to FRS 102 The Financial Reporting Standard applicable in the UK and Republic of Ireland – Small entities and other minor amendments* and FRED 61 *Draft amendments to FRS 102 – Share-based payment arrangements with cash alternatives*.

2   The FRC, in accordance with the *Statutory Auditors (Amendment of Companies Act 2006 and Delegation of Functions etc) Order 2012* (SI 2012/1741), is a prescribed body for issuing accounting standards in the UK. The *Foreword to Accounting Standards* sets out the application of accounting standards in the Republic of Ireland.

3   In accordance with the *FRC Codes and Standards: procedures*, any proposal to issue, amend or withdraw a code or standard is put to the FRC Board with the full advice of the relevant Councils and/or the Codes & Standards Committee. Ordinarily, the FRC Board will only reject the advice put to it where:

   (a)   it is apparent that a significant group of stakeholders has not been adequately consulted;
   (b)   the necessary assessment of the impact of the proposal has not been completed, including an analysis of costs and benefits;
   (c)   insufficient consideration has been given to the timing or cost of implementation; or
   (d)   the cumulative impact of a number of proposals would make the adoption of an otherwise satisfactory proposal inappropriate.

4   The FRC has established the Accounting Council as the relevant Council to assist it in the setting of accounting standards.

Advice

5   The Accounting Council is advising the FRC to issue *Amendments to FRS 102 The Financial Reporting Standard applicable in the UK and Republic of Ireland – Small entities and other minor amendments*.

6   The Accounting Council advises that these proposals will maintain consistency of accounting standards with company law and will improve the financial reporting by small entities by, for example, requiring the recognition of various financial instruments that the *Financial Reporting Standard for Smaller Entities (effective January 2015)* (FRSSE) does not currently require.

7   The Accounting Council's Advice to the FRC to issue FRS 102 *The Financial Reporting Standard applicable in the UK and Republic of Ireland* was set out in the standard. The Accounting Council's Advice to the FRC in respect of these amendments will be included in the revised FRS 102.

Background

The new EU Accounting Directive (Directive 2013/34/EU of the European Parliament and   8
of the Council of 26 June 2013) is being implemented in the UK and Republic of Ireland.
In doing so there are changes to company law to reflect new requirements and, where
considered appropriate, to take advantage of new options that are available. Accounting
standards are developed within the context set by company law; when company law
changes, amendments may also be required to accounting standards.

In September 2014, the FRC issued a Consultation Document *Accounting standards*   9
for small entities – Implementation of the EU Accounting Directive[24] (the Consultation
Document), outlining its proposal that small entities will apply FRS 102 *The Financial*
Reporting Standard applicable in the UK and Republic of Ireland. It was proposed that
a new section would be inserted into FRS 102 setting out the presentation and disclosure
requirements applicable to small entities, which would be based on the new legal
provisions, and as a consequence the FRSSE would be withdrawn. A small number of other
amendments to FRS 102 would also be necessary to maintain consistency with company
law. The Accounting Council considered the responses to the Consultation Document in
developing FRED 59. It has also considered the responses to FRED 59, which was issued
in February 2015, in developing its advice on these amendments.

In addition, in April 2015 the FRC issued FRED 61 to address an implementation issue in   10
relation to FRS 102. The responses to FRED 61 have also been considered in developing
this advice.

Objective

In developing its advice to the FRC, the Accounting Council was guided by the overriding   11
objective to enable users of accounts to receive high-quality understandable financial
reporting proportionate to the size and complexity of the entity and users' information
needs.

In meeting this objective, the FRC aims to provide succinct financial reporting standards   12
that:

(a) have consistency with international accounting standards through the application
     of an IFRS-based solution unless an alternative clearly better meets the overriding
     objective;
(b) reflect up-to-date thinking and developments in the way entities operate and the
     transactions they undertake;
(c) balance consistent principles for accounting by all UK and Republic of Ireland
     entities with practical solutions, based on size, complexity, public interest and users'
     information needs;
(d) promote efficiency within groups; and
(e) are cost-effective to apply.

Small entities regime

In the Consultation Document, the FRC proposed that the FRSSE should be withdrawn and   13
that, for small entities ineligible for the micro-entities regime, it should be replaced with
a new Section 1A *Small Entities* within FRS 102. It was proposed that Section 1A would
set out the presentation and disclosure requirements applicable to small entities, whilst
the recognition and measurement requirements of the remainder of FRS 102 would apply.

[24] *Available on the FRC website (www.frc.org.uk).*

This proposal was supported by the majority of respondents. In particular, respondents supported the proposals that:

(a)   the FRSSE should be withdrawn (see FRED 60 *Draft amendments to FRS 100 and FRS 101*);

(b)   Section 1A should apply to all entities (that are required to prepare financial statements that present a true and fair view) meeting the relevant criteria and not just companies; and

(c)   small entities should apply the same recognition and measurement criteria as other entities applying FRS 102.

14   FRED 59 set out these proposals in more detail.

15   The Accounting Council notes that, whilst the financial statements of a small company must give a true and fair view, the new legal framework for small companies restricts the specific disclosures that may be required of small companies. As these restrictions do not apply to entities that are not companies, the Accounting Council considered whether to have two small entities regimes, one applying to companies and one to other entities. As set out in the Consultation Document and FRED 59, the Accounting Council advises that it may be confusing to have two different sets of presentation and disclosure requirements for small entities, depending on legal form, particularly when the overall objective of the financial statements is the same (that they give a true and fair view), and therefore Section 1A should apply to all entities meeting the relevant criteria.

16   Eligibility for the small companies regime is set out in company law. The Accounting Council advises that Section 1A should apply to companies eligible for the small companies regime, LLPs eligible for the small LLPs regime and any other entity that would have met the criteria for the small companies regime had they been companies. This is broadly the same as the scope of the FRSSE. At the time of giving this advice the Accounting Council notes that different thresholds apply to the small companies regime and the small LLPs regime and entities will need to take care to ensure they are eligible to apply Section 1A.

Presentation and disclosure

17   A key feature of the new small companies regime set out in the new Accounting Directive is that it specifies the maximum mandatory disclosures to be included in a small company's financial statements, which may not be added to. However, the financial statements of a small company must still give a true and fair view of the financial performance and financial position of the entity; this has been emphasised in Section 1A. The directors of a company will need to consider whether additional disclosures are necessary to give a true and fair view and, if so, provide those additional disclosures.

18   The Accounting Council advises that, as the disclosures required by FRS 102 of larger entities are those that are usually considered necessary (but not necessarily sufficient) to give a true and fair view, a small entity should be encouraged to consider all of these disclosures in order to determine the additional disclosures necessary in its own circumstances.

19   In addition, the Accounting Council considers that it will be helpful to small entities applying FRS 102 for the disclosures required by law to be included and cross-referenced to the same or similar disclosures elsewhere in FRS 102. This has been set out in Appendix C to Section 1A, where the drafting of the disclosures is as close as possible to the company law requirements, with a note of the source of the legal requirement, and an indication of which paragraphs of FRS 102 address similar requirements.

There are a small number of specific disclosures that the Accounting Council considers   **20**
will be particularly useful to users of the financial statements of a small entity, including
a statement of compliance with FRS 102 and a note of dividends declared and paid or
payable. The Accounting Council advises specifically encouraging small entities to
provide these disclosures.

Another feature of the small companies regime is that additional 'statements' may not   **21**
be required of small companies. This includes a statement of comprehensive income, a
statement of changes in equity and the cash flow statement. Section 1A makes it clear that
such statements are not required of small entities, but the Accounting Council considers that
a statement of comprehensive income and a statement of changes in equity (or statement of
income and retained earnings) will be useful to users of the financial statements of a small
entity in explaining the financial performance for the reporting period and the effect that
this has had on financial position. Therefore the Accounting Council advises that a small
entity is encouraged to provide these statements.

The Accounting Council notes that, although the FRSSE encouraged the presentation of a   **22**
cash flow statement by small entities, FRS 1 (Revised 1996) *Cash flow statements* simply
exempted small entities from presenting a cash flow statement on the basis that it was not
required by company law for a small company. The Accounting Council advises retaining
the exemption from FRS 1. As a result, a small entity choosing to apply 'full' FRS 102 is
not required to present a cash flow statement.

Recognition and measurement

The Accounting Council advises that small entities should follow the recognition and   **23**
measurement requirements of FRS 102. This will improve financial reporting by small
entities by, for example, requiring the recognition of various financial instruments that
the FRSSE does not currently require, such as derivatives like interest rate swaps and
forward foreign currency contracts. Almost all respondents to FRED 59 agreed with this;
those that did not generally suggested that changes should be made to FRS 102 that would
apply to all entities. These suggestions will be considered as part of the triennial review
of FRS 102.

In FRS 105 *The Financial Reporting Standard applicable to the Micro-entities Regime*   **24**
the Accounting Council has considered and applied a set of principles for simplifying
the recognition and measurement requirements for micro-entities. For the larger small
entities within the scope of FRS 102 the Accounting Council advises that the principle it
has applied is that there should not be recognition and measurement differences from the
requirements applicable to larger entities. This reinstates the principle of consistency in
accounting policies between those entities that are smaller and those that are larger that
applied when the FRSSE was originally developed.

A small number of additional transitional provisions have been provided for small entities   **25**
applying FRS 102 for the first time for an accounting period that commences before
1 January 2017 (see paragraphs 42 to 44).

Other matters relating to the small entities regime

Some respondents to FRED 59 noted that Section 1A did not address situations where   **26**
a small entity voluntarily chooses to prepare consolidated financial statements. The
Accounting Council advises that this is addressed in Section 1A.

27   Company law and the new Accounting Directive restrict the disclosures that can be required of small companies in relation to related party transactions. In particular, disclosure can only be required of transactions not conducted under normal market conditions. Respondents noted that it could be burdensome for a small entity to identify those related party transactions that were not conducted under normal market conditions, because a significant degree of judgement would be involved. Instead, disclosure of all transactions with the specified related parties would meet the legal disclosure requirement. The Accounting Council notes that the Accounting Regulatory Committee reached a conclusion in 2007 that disclosing all related party transactions would comply with the requirement to disclose those not conducted under normal market conditions (as previously set out in paragraph 36 of Appendix IV to FRS 8 *Related Party Disclosures*). Therefore it advises including guidance in Appendix C to Section 1A that notes that although disclosure is only required of material transactions with the specified related parties that have not been concluded under normal market conditions, small entities disclosing all transactions with such related parties would still be compliant with company law.

True and fair view

28   In Section 1A the drafting of various requirements is as close as possible to the company law requirements, reflecting the need for the financial statements of a small entity to give a true and fair view. The Accounting Council noted that Section 3 *Financial Statement Presentation* expressed some of the same requirements in a different way, and advises that Section 3 is amended to more closely reflect the requirements of company law. These changes are not considered to have any substantive effect as 'true and fair' and 'presents fairly' are synonymous, being different articulations of the same concept, as confirmed by legal opinion.

Other minor amendments

29   A small number of other amendments were also necessary to maintain consistency between FRS 102 and company law. This was not a comprehensive review of the requirements of FRS 102.

30   The amendments include:

(a)   Greater flexibility in relation to the format of the profit and loss account and balance sheet, which will allow entities choosing this option to adopt a presentation that is closer to that applied by entities preparing 'IAS accounts'. The Accounting Council advises that these new options available in company law should be available to entities applying FRS 102, but that a framework should be provided in FRS 102 to assist entities applying it.

(b)   Revisions to certain requirements relating to financial instruments that are, or may be, measured at fair value. The new Accounting Directive permits measurement of certain financial instruments at fair value where it is in accordance with EU-adopted IFRS; previously this was restricted to IFRS endorsed by 5 September 2006. The consequences of this change, as well as any interaction with IFRS 9 *Financial Instruments* that was issued in July 2014 and which an entity may make an accounting policy choice to apply under paragraphs 11.2(c) and 12.2(c), have been considered. As a result, the Accounting Council advises that some amendments are made for compliance with company law, although these are only likely to affect a minority of entities applying FRS 102. In addition, Appendix IV: *Note on legal requirements* advises that entities applying IFRS 9 will need to consider an override of the Regulations for the purposes of giving a true and fair view, in order to recognise certain fair value gains or losses in other comprehensive income.

(c)   Revising the 'seriously prejudicial' exemption that applies, in extremely rare circumstances, to disclosure of provisions and contingencies. The Accounting Council notes that company law requires certain disclosures in relation to provisions and contingencies, and that it advises consistency of disclosure by entities that are companies and those that are not. Therefore the 'seriously prejudicial' exemption has been redrafted to remind companies of the legal disclosure requirements and ensure that equivalent disclosures are provided by all entities.

(d)   Revising the maximum period over which goodwill and other intangible assets may be amortised to 10 years, in those exceptional cases where an entity is unable to make a reliable estimate of the asset's useful economic life. The Accounting Council advises that, as this only applies in exceptional cases, the change in the maximum period so soon after it was introduced in the first edition of FRS 102 should have a limited impact in practice.

(e)   Prohibiting the reversal of impairment losses for goodwill.

(f)   Clarifying that a public benefit entity may apply merger accounting to an entity combination that is a merger provided that it is permitted by the statutory framework under which it reports. The new Accounting Directive only permits companies to apply merger accounting for group reconstructions and the Accounting Council advises that this amendment is made to ensure merger accounting is not applied by public benefit entities that are companies where not permitted in law. Some respondents to FRED 59 suggested that FRS 102 should continue to require the use of merger accounting by all public benefit entity combinations meeting the definition and criteria of a merger, through requiring the use of the true and fair override. The Accounting Council noted that 'true mergers' (other than those that might be considered group reconstructions) are not likely to be common. However, Appendix IV: *Note on legal requirements* notes that an individual public benefit entity may apply the true and fair override if it considers it appropriate to its circumstances, and provides the corresponding disclosures.

(g)   Amending the definitions of a 'related party' and 'turnover' in accordance with changes in company law.

(h)   Clarifying in paragraph 1.12(c) that, because company law requires certain disclosures relating to financial instruments, a qualifying entity choosing to provide reduced disclosures will not be exempt from all the disclosure requirements of Sections 11 and 12. This was previously addressed in paragraph A4.10, which notes that preparers need to have regard to the requirements of company law in addition to accounting standards.

The Accounting Council noted that in relation to small entities, Section 1A of FRS 102   **31** will include all the disclosure requirements set out in company law, but that FRS 102 does not presently include all the equivalent disclosures for larger entities. The majority of respondents to the Consultation Document agreed that the current approach for larger entities should not be amended because this would increase the length of FRS 102 and make it potentially less user-friendly, especially as a significant number of larger entities applying FRS 102 are not companies and the additional disclosure requirements would not be applicable to them. Some respondents suggested including any additional disclosures as an appendix, but noted that this could be considered as part of the triennial review of FRS 102. The Accounting Council advises not amending FRS 102 for additional disclosures for larger entities at present, but notes that the suggestion of an appendix could be reconsidered at a later date.

The Accounting Council noted that in some areas the amendments made to the Regulations   **32** and the Small Companies Regulations make new accounting options available alongside existing requirements. In these areas it is not necessary to amend FRS 102, as it already complies with the existing requirements. The Accounting Council considered the following two areas:

(a)   Equity method in individual accounts – paragraph 29A of the Regulations and the Small Companies Regulations permits participating interests to be accounted for in the financial statements of an investor using the equity method. FRS 102 already includes a number of options for accounting for such investments (see paragraph 9.26) and the Accounting Council does not advise introducing this option at present.

(b)   Contingent consideration in a business combination – an amendment to paragraph 36 of the Regulations and the Small Companies Regulations would permit contingent consideration in a business combination to be measured and remeasured at fair value, which would be consistent with EU-adopted IFRS (IFRS 3 *Business Combinations* (revised 2008)). The Accounting Council notes that the requirements of FRS 102 are based on IFRS 3 (issued 2004) and does not advise amending the accounting for contingent consideration outside the context of a wider review of the accounting for business combinations. Therefore an amendment to accounting for contingent consideration in a business combination is not proposed at present.

33   In addition, the following amendments are advised:

(a)   Two of the examples following paragraph 11.13 are being amended for clarity.

(b)   The reduced disclosures for subsidiaries, set out in paragraphs 1.8 to 1.13, have been amended in relation to financial instruments measured at fair value through profit or loss to ensure they are consistent with company law disclosure requirements.

Residents' Management Companies

34   In considering the feedback received from the FRC's previous consultations, the Accounting Council noted that no clear consensus existed amongst respondents on the appropriate basis of accounting in the statutory financial statements of residents' management companies[25] where service charge monies are held on trust in accordance with section 42 of the Landlord and Tenant Act 1987. However, there was general agreement that no change should be made to FRS 102, or any other relevant financial reporting standard (including FRS 105), to address such a narrow and sector-specific issue.

35   The Accounting Council considered this issue carefully. It assessed the case for further intervention by reference to the FRC's published *Principles for the development of Codes, Standards and Guidance*[26] and, in particular, the extent to which the anticipated benefits from any changes to current practices would outweigh the costs incurred by the entities involved. It agreed with respondents that this matter does not merit a change in accounting standards, and therefore advises that no changes are made to FRS 102 (or FRS 105) that are specific to residents' management companies.

Share-based payment arrangements with cash alternatives

36   After the introduction of FRS 102, it was brought to the FRC's attention that the accounting it required for share-based payment transactions that give the reporting entity an option to settle in cash or equity could result in the recognition of a liability even though the conditions for the recognition of a liability under the standard were not clearly met. The Accounting Council notes that the requirement to account for such transactions as cash-settled is more onerous than the requirements under EU-adopted IFRS, under which they

---

[25] *An organisation which may be referred to in the lease, which is responsible for the provision of services, and manages and arranges maintenance of the property, but which does not necessarily have any legal interest in the property.*

[26] *This can be found on the FRC's website at www.frc.org.uk/FRC-Documents/FRC/About-the-FRC/Principles-for-the-development-of-Codes.pdf.*

would generally be treated as equity-settled, since it requires the measurement of the obligation at fair value at each reporting date.

The Accounting Council therefore advises that FRS 102 should be amended with the result that such transactions are accounted for as equity-settled share-based payment arrangements unless the option to settle in equity has no commercial substance or the entity has created a valid expectation that it would settle in cash. 37

In some schemes the recipient may have an option to request settlement in cash or equity instruments. If an entity cannot avoid settling in cash should the recipient request it, FRS 102 requires the entity to account for the transaction as cash-settled by measuring the goods or services acquired at the fair value of the liability unless the cash settlement option has no commercial substance. The Accounting Council notes that this requirement is different to EU-adopted IFRS which requires the separate recognition of debt and equity components. The Accounting Council continues to believe that the simpler requirements of FRS 102 provide a practical and proportionate solution for those applying the standard and notes that this is generally consistent with the requirements in the IFRS for SMEs. In FRED 61 the exemption from cash-settlement accounting when the option to settle in cash has no commercial substance was omitted and the Accounting Council advises that this be retained in FRS 102. 38

The FRC had consulted on additional amendments that would have resulted in cash-settlement treatment for all share-based payment arrangements with terms that could result in the transfer of cash on the occurrence of an event outside the control of either party to the transaction. Some respondents commented that this could result in the recognition of a liability in situations when the probability of settlement in cash is remote. They also noted that the accounting for such transactions is under consideration by the IASB and its Interpretation Committee who have so far been unable to reach a conclusion. For the reasons noted by these respondents, the Accounting Council advises that FRS 102 should not be amended in this regard, but the need for further amendment be re-considered as part of the next review of the standard. 39

The FRC did not propose any additional transitional exemptions for entities that had chosen to early adopt FRS 102 and had granted awards under share-based payment arrangements that would be affected by the changes in FRED 61. The majority of respondents agreed that there was no need for additional transitional exemptions as such instances would be very rare and early adopters would have had the benefit of the transitional exemption for awards granted before the date of transition. 40

However, some respondents did identify an issue with the transitional exemption where greater clarity is needed. The transitional exemption in paragraph 35.10(b) of FRS 102 refers only to equity instruments granted before the date of transition. Some respondents noted that it was not clear if this reference also applies to the equity components of instruments that had been treated as compound instruments under FRS 20 or IFRS 2. The Accounting Council notes that the transitional exemption was intended to alleviate the costs of transition in respect of equity-settled share-based payment arrangements for companies that had previously applied the FRSSE, where such arrangements were not recognised, and for companies that had previously applied FRS 20 / IFRS 2 should FRS 102 require different accounting. As FRS 20 / IFRS 2 can result in compound instruments being partly accounted for as equity-settled and partly as cash-settled, the Accounting Council agrees it should be clarified that the reference to equity instruments includes the equity component of compound instruments accounted for in accordance with FRS 20 / IFRS 2. The Accounting Council also notes that there is no need for transitional exemptions to be added for liabilities not settled at the transition date, including those arising from arrangements previously treated as compound instruments, because the 41 liability will not continue to be measured in the same way under FRS 102, being the fair value of the liability.

Transitional provisions for small entities

42   The Accounting Council considered whether transitional provisions should be provided for small entities applying FRS 102 for the first time. The Accounting Council noted that FRS 102 already includes Section 35 *Transition to this FRS*, which applies to any first-time adopter of FRS 102, which has a significant number of optional exemptions from full retrospective application of FRS 102 that are designed to reduce the burden of first-time adoption. This is particularly where it may be difficult to restate historical transactions on the basis otherwise required by FRS 102 because the relevant data would not have been obtained at the time the transaction occurred.

43   The Accounting Council advised in FRED 59 that no further transitional provisions were necessary for small entities that are not already provided for. Although the majority of respondents to FRED 59 agreed with this assessment, a small number of respondents suggested that additional transitional provisions should be made available. These suggestions related to areas where additional burdens may be incurred in applying FRS 102 for the first time because an entity's transition date to FRS 102 occurred before these amendments were finalised.

44   The Accounting Council considered these suggestions carefully and agreed to provide additional transitional exemptions for all small entities applying FRS 102 for the first time for an accounting period that commences before 1 January 2017. These relate to equity-settled share-based payment arrangements, financial instruments measured at fair value and financing transactions with related parties. On first-time application they provide relief from the full application of FRS 102 in the comparative period.

Effective date

45   The Accounting Council advises that, other than the replacement of paragraph 26.15 with new paragraphs 26.15 to 26.15B, these amendments should be effective for accounting periods beginning on or after 1 January 2016, with early application:

    (a)   permitted for accounting periods beginning on or after 1 January 2015 provided that *The Companies, Partnerships and Groups (Accounts and Reports) Regulations 2015* (SI 2015/980) are applied from the same date; and

    (b)   required if an entity applies *The Companies, Partnerships and Groups (Accounts and Reports) Regulations 2015* (SI 2015/980) to a reporting period beginning before 1 January 2016.

46   The Accounting Council advises that the replacement of paragraph 26.15 with new paragraphs 26.15 to 26.15B shall be effective for accounting periods beginning on or after 1 January 2015, with early application permitted in line with FRS 102 generally.

Approval of this Advice

47   This advice to the FRC was approved by the Accounting Council on 16 June 2015.

Appendix I
Glossary

This glossary is an integral part of the Standard.

accounting policies	The specific principles, bases, conventions, rules and practices applied by an entity in preparing and presenting **financial statements**.
accrual basis (of accounting)	The effects of transactions and other events are recognised when they occur (and not as **cash** or its equivalent is received or paid) and they are recorded in the accounting records and reported in the **financial statements** of the periods to which they relate.
accumulating compensated absences	Compensated absences that are carried forward and can be used in future periods if the current period's entitlement is not used in full.
acquisition date	The date on which the acquirer obtains **control** of the acquiree.
Act	The Companies Act 2006
active market	A market in which all the following conditions exist: (a) the items traded in the market are homogeneous; (b) willing buyers and sellers can normally be found at any time; and (c) prices are available to the public.
actuarial assumptions	An entity's unbiased and mutually compatible best estimates of the demographic and financial variables that will determine the ultimate cost of providing post-employment benefits.
actuarial gains and losses	Changes in the **present value** of the **defined benefit obligation** resulting from: (a) experience adjustments (the effects of differences between the previous **actuarial assumptions** and what has actually occurred); and (b) the effects of changes in actuarial assumptions.
agent	An entity is acting as an agent when it does not have exposure to the significant risks and rewards associated with the sale of goods or the rendering of services. One feature indicating that an entity is acting as an agent is that the amount the entity earns is predetermined, being either a fixed fee per transaction or a stated percentage of the amount billed to the customer.
agricultural activity	The management by an entity of the biological transformation of **biological assets** for sale, into agricultural produce or into additional biological assets.
agricultural produce	The harvested product of the entity's **biological assets**.
amortisation	The systematic allocation of the **depreciable amount** of an **asset** over its **useful life**.

amortised cost (of a financial asset or financial liability)	The amount at which the **financial asset** or **financial liability** is measured at initial **recognition** minus principal repayments, plus or minus the cumulative **amortisation** using the **effective interest method** of any difference between that initial amount and the maturity amount, and minus any reduction (directly or through the use of an allowance account) for impairment or uncollectability.
asset	A resource controlled by the entity as a result of past events and from which future economic benefits are expected to flow to the entity.
asset held by a long-term employee benefit fund	An **asset** (other than non-transferable financial instruments issued by the reporting entity) that: (a) is held by an entity (a fund) that is legally separate from the reporting entity and exists solely to pay or fund **employee benefits**; and (b) is available to be used only to pay or fund employee benefits, is not available to the reporting entity's own creditors (even in bankruptcy), and cannot be returned to the reporting entity, unless either: (i) the remaining assets of the fund are sufficient to meet all the related employee benefit obligations of the plan or the reporting entity; or (ii) the assets are returned to the reporting entity to reimburse it for employee benefits already paid.
associate	An entity, including an unincorporated entity such as a partnership, over which the investor has **significant influence** and that is neither a **subsidiary** nor an interest in a **joint venture**.
biological asset	A living animal or plant.
borrowing costs	Interest and other costs incurred by an entity in connection with the borrowing of funds.
business	An integrated set of activities and **assets** conducted and managed for the purpose of providing: (a) a return to investors; or (b) lower costs or other economic benefits directly and proportionately to policyholders or participants. A business generally consists of inputs, processes applied to those inputs, and resulting outputs that are, or will be, used to generate **revenues**. If **goodwill** is present in a transferred set of activities and assets, the transferred set shall be presumed to be a business.
business combination	The bringing together of separate entities or **businesses** into one reporting entity.
carrying amount	The amount at which an **asset** or **liability** is recognised in the **statement of financial position**.
cash	Cash on hand and demand deposits.
cash equivalents	Short-term, highly liquid investments that are readily convertible to known amounts of **cash** and that are subject to an insignificant risk of changes in value.
cash flows	Inflows and outflows of **cash** and **cash equivalents**.

cash-generating unit	The smallest identifiable group of **assets** that generates cash inflows that are largely independent of the cash inflows from other assets or groups of assets.
cash-settled share-based payment transaction	A **share-based payment transaction** in which the entity acquires goods or services by incurring a **liability** to transfer **cash** or other **assets** to the supplier of those goods or services for amounts that are based on the price (or value) of the entity's shares or other equity instruments of the entity or another group entity.
change in accounting estimate	An adjustment of the **carrying amount** of an **asset** or a **liability**, or the amount of the periodic consumption of an asset, that results from the assessment of the present status of, and expected future benefits and obligations associated with, assets and liabilities. Changes in accounting estimates result from new information or new developments and, accordingly, are not corrections of **errors**.
class of assets	A grouping of **assets** of a similar nature and use in an entity's operations.
close members of the family of a person	Those family members who may be expected to influence, or be influenced by, that person in their dealings with the entity including: (a) that person's children and spouse or domestic partner; (b) children of that person's spouse or domestic partner; and (c) dependants of that person or that person's spouse or domestic partner.
closing rate	The spot exchange rate at the end of the **reporting period**
combination that is in substance is a gift	A combination carried out at nil or nominal consideration that is not a fair value exchange but in substance the gift of one entity to another.
commencement of lease term	The date from which the lessee is entitled to exercise its right to use the leased asset. It is the date of initial **recognition** of the **lease** (ie the recognition of the **assets**, **liabilities**, **income** or **expenses** resulting from the lease, as appropriate).
component of an entity	Operations and **cash flows** that can be clearly distinguished, operationally and for financial reporting purposes, from the rest of the entity.
compound financial instrument	A financial instrument that, from the issuer's perspective, contains both a **liability** and an **equity** element.
consolidated financial statements	The financial statements of a **parent** and its **subsidiaries** presented as those of a single economic entity.
construction contract	A contract specifically negotiated for the construction of an **asset** or a combination of assets that are closely interrelated or interdependent in terms of their design, technology and function or their ultimate purpose or use.

constructive obligation	An obligation that derives from an entity's actions where: (a) by an established pattern of past practice, published policies or a sufficiently specific current statement, the entity has indicated to other parties that it will accept certain responsibilities; and (b) as a result, the entity has created a valid expectation on the part of those other parties that it will discharge those responsibilities.
contingent asset	A possible **asset** that arises from past events and whose existence will be confirmed only by the occurrence or non-occurrence of one or more uncertain future events not wholly within the control of the entity.
contingent liability	(a) a possible obligation that arises from past events and whose existence will be confirmed only by the occurrence or non-occurrence of one or more uncertain future events not wholly within the control of the entity; or (b) a present obligation that arises from past events but is not recognised because: (i) it is not **probable** that an outflow of resources embodying economic benefits will be required to settle the obligation; or (ii) the amount of the obligation cannot be measured with sufficient **reliability**.
contingent rent	That portion of the lease payments that is not fixed in amount but is based on the future amount of a factor that changes other than with the passage of time (eg percentage of future sales, amount of future use, future price indices, and future market rates of interest).
control (of an entity)	The power to govern the financial and operating policies of an entity so as to obtain benefits from its activities.
credit risk	The risk that one party to a financial instrument will cause a financial loss for the other party by failing to discharge an obligation.
current assets	**Assets** of an entity which: (a) for an entity choosing to apply paragraph 1A(1) of Schedule 1 to the Regulations, are not **non-current assets**; or (b) for all other entities, are not fixed assets.
current liabilities **(for the purposes of an entity applying paragraph 1A(1) of Schedule 1 to the Regulations)**	**Liabilities** of the entity which: (a) it expects to settle in its normal operating cycle; (b) it holds primarily for the purpose of trading; (c) are due to be settled within 12 months after the **reporting period**; or (d) it does not have an unconditional right to defer settlement for at least 12 months after the reporting period.
current tax	The amount of income tax payable (refundable) in respect of the taxable profit (tax loss) for the current period or past **reporting periods**.

date of transition	The beginning of the earliest period for which an entity presents full comparative information in a given standard in its first **financial statements** that comply with that standard.
deemed cost	An amount used as a surrogate for cost or depreciated cost at a given date. Subsequent **depreciation** or **amortisation** assumes that the entity had initially recognised the **asset** or **liability** at the given date and that its cost was equal to the deemed cost.
deferred acquisition costs	Costs arising from the conclusion of **insurance contracts** that are incurred during a **reporting period** but which relate to a subsequent reporting period.
deferred tax	Income tax payable (recoverable) in respect of the **taxable profit (tax loss)** for future **reporting periods** as a result of past transactions or events.
deferred tax assets	Income tax recoverable in future **reporting periods** in respect of: (a) future tax consequences of transactions and events recognised in the **financial statements** of the current and previous periods; (b) the carry forward of unused tax losses; and (c) the carry forward of unused tax credits.
deferred tax liabilities	Income tax payable in future **reporting periods** in respect of future tax consequences of transactions and events recognised in the **financial statements** of the current and previous periods.
defined benefit obligation (present value of)	The **present value**, without deducting any **plan assets**, of expected future payments required to settle the obligation resulting from employee service in the current and prior periods.
defined benefit plans	**Post-employment benefit plans** other than **defined contribution plans.**
defined contribution plans	**Post-employment benefit plans** under which an entity pays fixed contributions into a separate entity (a fund) and has no legal or **constructive obligation** to pay further contributions or to make direct benefit payments to employees if the fund does not hold sufficient **assets** to pay all **employee benefits** relating to employee service in the current and prior periods.
depreciable amount	The cost of an **asset**, or other amount substituted for cost (in the **financial statements**), less its residual value.
depreciated replacement cost	The most economic cost required for the entity to replace the **service potential** of an **asset** (including the amount that the entity will receive from its disposal at the end of its **useful life**) at the **reporting date**.
depreciation	The systematic allocation of the **depreciable amount** of an **asset** over its **useful life**.
derecognition	The removal of a previously recognised **asset** or **liability** from an entity's **statement of financial position**.

derivative	A financial instrument or other contract with all three of the following characteristics: (a) its value changes in response to the change in a specified interest rate, financial instrument price, commodity price, foreign exchange rate, index of prices or rates, credit rating or credit index, or other variable (sometimes called the 'underlying'), provided in the case of a non-financial variable that the variable is not specific to a party to the contract; (b) it requires no initial net investment or an initial net investment that is smaller than would be required for other types of contracts that would be expected to have a similar response to changes in market factors; and (c) it is settled at a future date.
development	The application of **research** findings or other knowledge to a plan or design for the production of new or substantially improved materials, devices, products, processes, systems or services before the start of commercial production or use.
discontinued operation	A **component of an entity** that has been disposed of and: (a) represented a separate major line of **business** or geographical area of operations; (b) was part of a single co-ordinated plan to dispose of a separate major line of business or geographical area of operations; or (c) was a **subsidiary** acquired exclusively with a view to resale.

discretionary participation feature	A contractual right to receive, as a supplement to guaranteed benefits, additional benefits:
	(a) that are likely to be a significant portion of the total contractual benefits;
	(b) whose amount or timing is contractually at the discretion of the issuer; and
	(c) that are contractually based on:
	   (i) the performance of a specified pool of contracts or a specified type of contract;
	   (ii) realised and/or unrealised investment returns on a specified pool of **assets** held by the issuer; or
	   (iii) the **profit or loss** of the company, fund or other entity that issues the contract.

disposal group	A group of **assets** to be disposed of, by sale or otherwise, together as a group in a single transaction, and **liabilities** directly associated with those assets that will be transferred in the transaction. The group includes **goodwill** acquired in a **business combination** if the group is a **cash-generating unit** to which goodwill has been allocated in accordance with the requirements of paragraphs 27.24 to 27.27 of this FRS.
effective interest method	A method of calculating the **amortised cost** of a **financial asset** or a **financial liability** (or a group of financial assets or financial liabilities) and of allocating the interest income or interest expense over the relevant period.

effective interest rate	The rate that exactly discounts estimated future cash payments or receipts through the expected life of the financial instrument or, when appropriate, a shorter period to the **carrying amount** of the **financial asset** or **financial liability**.
employee benefits	All forms of consideration given by an entity in exchange for service rendered by employees.
entity combination	See **business combination**.
equity	The residual interest in the **assets** of the entity after deducting all its **liabilities**.
equity-settled share-based payment transaction	A **share-based payment transaction** in which the entity: (a) receives goods or services as consideration for its own equity instruments (including shares or **share options**); or (b) receives goods or services but has no obligation to settle the transaction with the supplier.
errors	Omissions from, and misstatements in, the entity's **financial statements** for one or more prior periods arising from a failure to use, or misuse of, reliable information that: (a) was available when financial statements for those periods were authorised for issue; and (b) could reasonably be expected to have been obtained and taken into account in the preparation and presentation of those financial statements.
expenses	Decreases in economic benefits during the **reporting period** in the form of outflows or depletions of **assets** or incurrences of **liabilities** that result in decreases in **equity**, other than those relating to distributions to equity investors.
EU-adopted IFRS	IFRS that have been adopted in the European Union in accordance with EU Regulation 1606/2002.
fair value	The amount for which an **asset** could be exchanged, a **liability** settled, or an equity instrument granted could be exchanged, between knowledgeable, willing parties in an arm's length transaction. In the absence of any specific guidance provided in the relevant section of this FRS, the guidance in paragraphs 11.27 to 11.32 shall be used in determining fair value.
fair value less costs to sell	The amount obtainable from the sale of an **asset** or **cash-generating unit** in an arm's length transaction between knowledgeable, willing parties, less the costs of disposal.
finance lease	A **lease** that transfers substantially all the risks and rewards incidental to ownership of an **asset**. Title may or may not eventually be transferred. A lease that is not a finance lease is an operating lease.

financial asset	Any **asset** that is:
	(a) **cash**;
	(b) an equity instrument of another entity;
	(c) a contractual right:
	   (i) to receive cash or another financial asset from another entity, or
	   (ii) to exchange financial assets or **financial liabilities** with another entity under conditions that are potentially favourable to the entity; or
	(d) a contract that will or may be settled in the entity's own equity instruments and:
	   (i) under which the entity is or may be obliged to receive a variable number of the entity's own equity instruments; or
	   (ii) that will or may be settled other than by the exchange of a fixed amount of cash or another financial asset for a fixed number of the entity's own equity instruments. For this purpose the entity's own equity instruments do not include instruments that are themselves contracts for the future receipt or delivery of the entity's own equity instruments.

financial guarantee contract	A contract that requires the issuer to make specified payments to reimburse the holder for a loss it incurs because a specified debtor fails to make payments when due in accordance with the original or modified terms of a debt instrument.

financial institution	Any of the following:
	(a) a bank which is:
	   (i) a firm with a Part IV permission[27] which includes accepting deposits and:
	     (a) which is a credit institution; or
	     (b) whose Part IV permission includes a requirement that it complies with the rules in the General Prudential sourcebook and the Prudential sourcebook for Banks, Building Societies and Investment Firms relating to banks, but which is not a building society, a friendly society or a credit union;
	   (ii) an EEA bank which is a full credit institution;
	(b) a building society which is defined in section 119(1) of the Building Societies Act 1986 as a building society incorporated (or deemed to be incorporated) under that act;
	(c) a credit union, being a body corporate registered under the Industrial and Provident Societies Act 1965 as a credit union in accordance with the Credit Unions Act 1979, which is an authorised person;
	(d) custodian bank, broker-dealer or stockbroker;

[27] *As defined in section 40(4) of the Financial Services and Markets Act 2000 or references to equivalent provisions of any successor legislation.*

	(e) an entity that undertakes the business of effecting or carrying out **insurance contracts**, including general and life assurance entities; (f) an incorporated friendly society incorporated under the Friendly Societies Act 1992 or a registered friendly society registered under section 7(1)(a) of the Friendly Societies Act 1974 or any enactment which it replaced, including any registered branches; (g) an investment trust, Irish investment company, venture capital trust, mutual fund, exchange traded fund, unit trust, open-ended investment company (OEIC); (h) a **retirement benefit plan**; or (i) any other entity whose principal activity is to generate wealth or manage risk through financial instruments. This is intended to cover entities that have business activities similar to those listed above but are not specifically included in the list above. A **parent** entity whose sole activity is to hold investments in other group entities is not a financial institution.
financial instrument	A contract that gives rise to a **financial asset** of one entity and a **financial liability** or equity instrument of another entity.

financial liability	Any **liability** that is:
	
	(a) a contractual obligation:
	    (i) to deliver **cash** or another **financial asset** to another entity; or
	    (ii) to exchange financial assets or financial liabilities with another entity under conditions that are potentially unfavourable to the entity, or
	
	(b) a contract that will or may be settled in the entity's own equity instruments and:
	    (i) under which the entity is or may be obliged to deliver a variable number of the entity's own equity instruments; or
	    (ii) will or may be settled other than by the exchange of a fixed amount of cash or another financial asset for a fixed number of the entity's own equity instruments. For this purpose the entity's own equity instruments do not include instruments that are themselves contracts for the future receipt or delivery of the entity's own equity instruments.

financial position	The relationship of the **assets**, **liabilities** and **equity** of an entity as reported in the **statement of financial position**.
financial statements	Structured representation of the **financial position**, financial **performance** and **cash flows** of an entity.
financial risk	The risk of a possible future change in one or more of a specified interest rate, financial instrument price, commodity price, foreign exchange rate, index of prices or rates, credit rating or credit index or other variable, provided in the case of a non-financial variable that the variable is not specific to a party to the contract.

financing activities	Activities that result in changes in the size and composition of the contributed **equity** and borrowings of the entity.
firm commitment	A binding agreement for the exchange of a specified quantity of resources at a specified price on a specified future date or dates.
first-time adopter of this FRS	An entity that presents its first annual **financial statements** that conform to this FRS, regardless of whether its previous accounting framework was **EU-adopted IFRS** or another set of accounting standards.
fixed assets	**Assets** of an entity which are intended for use on a continuing basis in the entity's activities.
forecast transaction	An uncommitted but anticipated future transaction.
foreign operation	An entity that is a **subsidiary**, **associate**, **joint venture** or branch of a reporting entity, the activities of which are based or conducted in a country or currency other than those of the reporting entity.
FRS 100	FRS 100 *Application of Financial Reporting Requirements*
FRS 101	FRS 101 *Reduced Disclosure Framework*
FRS 102	FRS 102 *The Financial Reporting Standard applicable in the UK and Republic of Ireland*
FRS 103	FRS 103 *Insurance Contracts*
FRS 104	FRS 104 *Interim Financial Reporting*
FRS 105	FRS 105 *The Financial Reporting Standard applicable to the Micro-entities Regime*
functional currency	The currency of the primary economic environment in which the entity operates.
funding (of post-employment benefits)	Contributions by an entity, and sometimes its employees, into an entity, or fund, that is legally separate from the reporting entity and from which the **employee benefits** are paid.
gains	Increases in economic benefits that meet the definition of **income** but are not **revenue**.
general purpose financial statements (generally referred to simply as financial statements)	**Financial statements** directed to the general financial information needs of a wide range of users who are not in a position to demand reports tailored to meet their particular information needs.
going concern	An entity is a going concern unless management either intends to liquidate the entity or to cease trading, or has no realistic alternative but to do so.
goodwill	Future economic benefits arising from **assets** that are not capable of being individually identified and separately recognised.

government grant	Assistance by government in the form of a transfer of resources to an entity in return for past or future compliance with specified conditions relating to the **operating activities** of the entity. Government refers to government, government agencies and similar bodies whether local, national or international.
grant date	The date at which the entity and another party (including an employee) agree to a share-based payment arrangement, being when the entity and the counterparty have a shared understanding of the terms and conditions of the arrangement. At grant date the entity confers on the counterparty the right to **cash**, other **assets**, or equity instruments of the entity, provided the specified vesting conditions, if any, are met. If that agreement is subject to an approval process (for example, by shareholders), grant date is the date when that approval is obtained.
gross investment in a lease	The aggregate of: (a) the **minimum lease payments** receivable by the lessor under a **finance lease**; and (b) any unguaranteed **residual value** accruing to the lessor.
group	A **parent** and all its **subsidiaries**.
group reconstruction	Any one of the following arrangements: (a) the transfer of an equity holding in a **subsidiary** from one group entity to another; (b) the addition of a new **parent** entity to a **group**; (c) the transfer of equity holdings in one or more subsidiaries of a group to a new entity that is not a group entity but whose equity holders are the same as those of the group's parent; or (d) the combination into a group of two or more entities that before the combination had the same equity holders.
hedging gain or loss	The change in fair value of a hedged item that is attributable to the hedged risk.
held exclusively with a view to subsequent resale	An interest: (a) for which a purchaser has been identified or is being sought, and which is reasonably expected to be disposed of within approximately one year of its date of acquisition; or (b) that was acquired as a result of the enforcement of a security, unless the interest has become part of the continuing activities of the **group** or the holder acts as if it intends the interest to become so; or (c) which is **held as part of an investment portfolio**.

held as part of an investment portfolio	An interest is held as part of an investment portfolio if its value to the investor is through **fair value** as part of a directly or indirectly held basket of investments rather than as media through which the investor carries out **business**. A basket of investments is indirectly held if an investment fund holds a single investment in a second investment fund which, in turn, holds a basket of investments.
heritage assets	Tangible and **intangible assets** with historic, artistic, scientific, technological, geophysical, or environmental qualities that are held and maintained principally for their contribution to knowledge and culture.
highly probable	Significantly more likely than **probable**.
IAS Regulation	EU Regulation 1606/2002
IFRS (International Financial Reporting Standards)	Standards and interpretations issued (or adopted) by the International Accounting Standards Board (IASB). They comprise: (a) International Financial Reporting Standards; (b) International Accounting Standards; and (c) Interpretations developed by the IFRS Interpretations Committee (IFRIC) or the former Standing Interpretations Committee (SIC).
impairment loss	The amount by which the **carrying amount** of an **asset** exceeds: (a) in the case of **inventories**, its selling price less costs to complete and sell; or (b) in the case of other assets, its **recoverable amount**.
impracticable	Applying a requirement is impracticable when the entity cannot apply it after making every reasonable effort to do so.
imputed rate of interest	The more clearly determinable of either: (a) the prevailing rate for a similar instrument of an issuer with a similar credit rating; or (b) a rate of interest that discounts the nominal amount of the instrument to the current cash sales price of the goods or services.
inception of the lease	The earlier of the date of the lease agreement and the date of commitment by the parties to the principal provisions of the **lease**.
income	Increases in economic benefits during the **reporting period** in the form of inflows or enhancements of **assets** or decreases of **liabilities** that result in increases in **equity**, other than those relating to contributions from equity investors.
income and expenditure	The total of **income** less **expenses**, excluding the components of **other comprehensive income**. In the for-profit sector this is known as **profit or loss**.
income statement	**Financial statement** that presents all items of **income** and **expense** recognised in a **reporting period**, excluding the items of **other comprehensive income** (referred to as the profit and loss account in the **Act**).

income tax	All domestic and foreign taxes that are based on **taxable profits**. Income tax also includes taxes, such as withholding taxes, that are payable by a **subsidiary**, **associate** or **joint venture** on distributions to the reporting entity.
individual financial statements	The accounts that are required to be prepared by an entity in accordance with the Act or relevant legislation, for example: (a) 'individual accounts', as set out in section 394 of the Act; (b) 'statement of accounts', as set out in section 132 of the Charities Act 2011; or (c) 'individual accounts', as set out in section 72A of the Building Societies Act 1986. **Separate financial statements** are included in the meaning of this term.
infrastructure assets	Infrastructure for public services, such as roads, bridges, tunnels, prisons, hospitals, airports, water distribution facilities, energy supply and telecommunications networks.
insurance contract	A contract under which one party (the insurer) accepts significant insurance risk from another party (the policyholder) by agreeing to compensate the policyholder if a specified uncertain future event (the insured event) adversely affects the policyholder.
intangible asset	An identifiable non-monetary asset without physical substance. Such an **asset** is identifiable when: (a) it is separable, ie capable of being separated or divided from the entity and sold, transferred, licensed, rented or exchanged, either individually or together with a related contract, asset or **liability**; or (b) it arises from contractual or other legal rights, regardless of whether those rights are transferable or separable from the entity or from other rights and obligations.

interest rate implicit in the lease	The discount rate that, at the **inception of the lease**, causes the aggregate **present value** of:
	(a) the **minimum lease payments**; and
	(b) the unguaranteed **residual value** to be equal to the sum of:
	  (i) the **fair value** of the leased asset; and
	  (ii) any initial direct costs of the lessor.

interim financial report	A financial report containing either a complete set of **financial statements** or a set of condensed financial statements for an **interim period**.
interim period	A financial **reporting period** shorter than a full financial year.
intrinsic value	The difference between the fair value of the shares to which the counterparty has the (conditional or unconditional) right to subscribe or which it has the right to receive, and the price (if any) the counterparty is (or will be) required to pay for those shares. For example, a share option with an exercise price of CU15, on a share with a fair value of CU20, has an intrinsic value of CU5.

inventories	**Assets**: (a) held for sale in the ordinary course of business; (b) in the process of production for such sale; or (c) in the form of materials or supplies to be consumed in the production process or in the rendering of services.
inventories held for distribution at no or nominal consideration	**Assets** that are: (a) held for distribution at no or nominal consideration in the ordinary course of operations; (b) in the process of production for distribution at no or nominal consideration in the ordinary course of operations; or (c) in the form of material or supplies to be consumed in the production process or in the rendering of services at no or nominal consideration.
investing activities	The acquisition and disposal of long-term assets and other investments not included in **cash equivalents**.
investment property	Property (land or a building, or part of a building, or both) held by the owner or by the lessee under a **finance lease** to earn rentals or for capital appreciation or both, rather than for: (a) use in the production or supply of goods or services or for administrative purposes, or (b) sale in the ordinary course of **business**.
joint control	The contractually agreed sharing of **control** over an economic activity. It exists only when the strategic financial and operating decisions relating to the activity require the unanimous consent of the parties sharing control (the **venturers**).
joint venture	A contractual arrangement whereby two or more parties undertake an economic activity that is subject to **joint control**. Joint ventures can take the form of jointly controlled operations, jointly controlled assets, or **jointly controlled entities**.
jointly controlled entity	A **joint venture** that involves the establishment of a corporation, partnership or other entity in which each **venturer** has an interest. The entity operates in the same way as other entities, except that a contractual arrangement between the venturers establishes **joint control** over the economic activity of the entity.
key management personnel	Those persons having authority and responsibility for planning, directing and controlling the activities of the entity, directly or indirectly, including any director (whether executive or otherwise) of that entity.
lease	An agreement whereby the lessor conveys to the lessee in return for a payment or series of payments the right to use an **asset** for an agreed period of time.
lease incentives	Incentives provided by the lessor to the lessee to enter into a new or renew an operating lease. Examples of such incentives include up-front cash payments to the lessee, the reimbursement or assumption by the lessor of costs of the lessee (such as relocation costs, leasehold improvements and costs associated with pre-existing lease commitments of the lessee), or initial periods of the **lease** provided by the lessor rent-free or at a reduced rent.

lease term	The non-cancellable period for which the lessee has contracted to **lease** the **asset** together with any further terms for which the lessee has the option to continue to lease the asset, with or without further payment, when at the **inception of the lease** it is reasonably certain that the lessee will exercise the option.
lessee's incremental borrowing rate (of interest)	The rate of interest the lessee would have to pay on a similar **lease** or, if that is not determinable, the rate that, at the **inception of the lease**, the lessee would incur to borrow over a similar term, and with a similar security, the funds necessary to purchase the **asset**.
liability	A present obligation of the entity arising from past events, the settlement of which is expected to result in an outflow from the entity of resources embodying economic benefits.
liquidity risk	The risk that an entity will encounter difficulty in meeting obligations associated with **financial liabilities** that are settled by delivering **cash** or another **financial asset**.
LLP Regulations	The Large and Medium-sized Limited Liability Partnerships (Accounts) Regulations 2008 (SI 2008/1913)
loans payable	**Financial liabilities** other than short-term trade payables on normal credit terms.
market condition	A condition upon which the exercise price, vesting or exercisability of an equity instrument depends that is related to the market price of the entity's equity instruments, such as attaining a specified share price or a specified amount of **intrinsic value** of a **share option**, or achieving a specified target that is based on the market price of the entity's equity instruments relative to an index of market prices of equity instruments of other entities.
market risk	The risk that the **fair value** or future **cash flows** of a financial instrument will fluctuate because of changes in market prices. Market risk comprises three types of risk: currency risk, interest rate risk and other price risk.
	Interest rate risk – the risk that the fair value or future cash flows of a financial instrument will fluctuate because of changes in market interest rates.
	Currency risk – the risk that the fair value or future cash flows of a financial instrument will fluctuate because of changes in foreign exchange rates.
	Other price risk – the risk that the fair value or future cash flows of a financial instrument will fluctuate because of changes in market prices (other than those arising from interest rate risk or currency risk), whether those changes are caused by factors specific to the financial instrument or its issuer, or factors affecting all similar financial instruments traded in the market.
material	Omissions or misstatements of items are material if they could, individually or collectively, influence the economic decisions of users taken on the basis of the **financial statements**. Materiality depends on the size and nature of the omission or misstatement judged in the surrounding circumstances. The size or nature of the item, or a combination of both, could be the determining factor.

measurement	The process of determining the monetary amounts at which the elements of the **financial statements** are to be recognised and carried in the **statement of financial position** and **statement of comprehensive income**.
merger	An **entity combination** that results in the creation of a new reporting entity formed from the combining parties, in which the controlling parties of the combining entities come together in a partnership for the mutual sharing of risks and benefits of the newly formed entity and in which no party to the combination in substance obtains **control** over any other, or is otherwise seen to be dominant. All of the following criteria must be met for an entity combination to meet the definition of a merger: (a) no party to the combination is portrayed as either acquirer or acquiree, either by its own board or management or by that of another party to the combination; (b) there is no significant change to the classes of beneficiaries of the combining entities or the purpose of the benefits provided as a result of the combination; and (c) all parties to the combination, as represented by the members of the board, participate in establishing the management structure of the combined entity and in selecting the management personnel, and such decisions are made on the basis of a consensus between the parties to the combination rather than purely by exercise of voting rights.
minimum lease payments	The payments over the **lease term** that the lessee is or can be required to make, excluding **contingent rent**, costs for services and taxes to be paid by and reimbursed to the lessor, together with: (a) for a lessee, any amounts guaranteed by the lessee or by a party related to the lessee; or (b) for a lessor, any **residual value** guaranteed to the lessor by: (i) the lessee; (ii) a party related to the lessee; or (iii) a third party unrelated to the lessor that is financially capable of discharging the obligations under the guarantee. However, if the lessee has an option to purchase the **asset** at a price that is expected to be sufficiently lower than **fair value** at the date the option becomes exercisable for it to be reasonably certain, at the **inception of the lease**, that the option will be exercised, the minimum lease payments comprise the minimum payments payable over the lease term to the expected date of exercise of this purchase option and the payment required to exercise it.
monetary items	Units of currency held and **assets** and **liabilities** to be received or paid in a fixed or determinable number of units of currency.

multi-employer (benefit) plans	**Defined contribution plans** (other than **state plans**) or **defined benefit plans** (other than state plans) that: (a) pool the **assets** contributed by various entities that are not under common control, and (b) use those assets to provide benefits to employees of more than one entity, on the basis that contribution and benefit levels are determined without regard to the identity of the entity that employs the employees concerned.
net assets available for benefits	The **assets** of a plan less **liabilities** other than the actuarial **present value** of promised retirement benefits
net defined benefit liability	The **present value** of the **defined benefit obligation** at the **reporting date** minus the **fair value** at the reporting date of **plan assets** (if any) out of which the obligations are to be settled.
net investment in a foreign operation	The amount of the reporting entity's interest in the net assets of that operation.
net investment in a lease	The **gross investment in a lease** discounted at the **interest rate implicit in the lease**.
non-controlling interest	The **equity** in a **subsidiary** not attributable, directly or indirectly, to a **parent**.
non-current assets	**Assets** of the entity which: (a) it does not expect to realise, or intend to sell or consume, in its normal operating cycle; (b) it does not hold primarily for the purpose of trading; (c) it does not expect to realise within 12 months after the **reporting period**; or (d) are **cash** or **cash equivalents** restricted from being exchanged or used to settle a **liability** for at least 12 months after the reporting period.
non-current liabilities	**Liabilities** of the entity which are not **current liabilities**.
non-exchange transaction	A transaction whereby an entity receives value from another entity without directly giving approximately equal value in exchange, or gives value to another entity without directly receiving approximately equal value in exchange.
notes (to financial statements)	Notes contain information in addition to that presented in the **statement of financial position, statement of comprehensive income, income statement** (if presented), combined **statement of income and retained earnings** (if presented), **statement of changes in equity** and **statement of cash flows**. Notes provide narrative descriptions or disaggregations of items presented in those statements and information about items that do not qualify for **recognition** in those statements.
notional amount	The quantity of currency units, shares, bushels, pounds or other units specified in a financial instrument contract.

objective of financial statements	To provide information about the **financial position**, **performance** and, when required to be presented, **cash flows** of an entity that is useful for economic decision-making by a broad range of users who are not in a position to demand reports tailored to meet their particular information needs.
onerous contract	A contract in which the unavoidable costs of meeting the obligations under the contract exceed the economic benefits expected to be received under it.
operating activities	The principal revenue-producing activities of the entity and other activities that are not investing or **financing activities**.
operating lease	A **lease** that does not transfer substantially all the risks and rewards incidental to ownership. A lease that is not an operating lease is a **finance lease**.
operating segment	An operating segment is a **component of an entity**: (a) that engages in business activities from which it may earn **revenues** and incur **expenses** (including revenues and expenses relating to transactions with other components of the same entity); (b) whose operating results are regularly reviewed by the entity's chief operating decision maker to make decisions about resources to be allocated to the segment and assess its **performance**; and (c) for which discrete financial information is available.
ordinary share	An equity instrument that is subordinate to all other classes of equity instrument.
other comprehensive income	Items of **income** and **expense** (including reclassification adjustments) that are not recognised in **profit or loss** as required or permitted by this FRS.
owners	Holders of instruments classified as **equity**.
parent	An entity that has one or more **subsidiaries**.
performance	The relationship of the **income** and **expenses** of an entity, as reported in the **statement of comprehensive income**.
performance-related condition	A condition that requires the performance of a particular level of service or units of output to be delivered, with payment of, or entitlement to, the resources conditional on that performance.
permanent differences	Differences between an entity's **taxable profits** and its **total comprehensive income** as stated in the **financial statements**, other than **timing differences**.
plan assets (of an employee benefit plan)	(a) **assets held by a long-term employee benefit fund**; and (b) **qualifying insurance policies**.
post-employment benefits	**Employee benefits** (other than **termination benefits** and short-term employee benefits) that are payable after the completion of employment.

post-employment benefit plans	Formal or informal arrangements under which an entity provides **post-employment benefits** for one or more employees.
potential ordinary share	A financial instrument or other contract that may entitle its holder to **ordinary shares**.
present value	A current estimate of the present discounted value of the future net **cash flows** in the normal course of **business**.
presentation currency	The currency in which the **financial statements** are presented.
prevailing market rate	The rate of interest that would apply to the entity in an open market for a similar financial instrument.
principal	An entity is acting as a principal when it has exposure to the significant risks and rewards associated with the sale of goods or the rendering of services. Features that indicate that an entity is acting as a principal include: (a) the entity has the primary responsibility for providing the goods or services to the customer or for fulfilling the order, for example by being responsible for the acceptability of the products or services ordered or purchased by the customer; (b) the entity has inventory risk before or after the customer order, during shipping or on return; (c) the entity has latitude in establishing prices, either directly or indirectly, for example by providing additional goods or services; and (d) the entity bears the customer's credit risk for the amount receivable from the customer.
probable	More likely than not.
profit or loss	The total of **income** less **expenses**, excluding the components of **other comprehensive income**.
projected unit credit method	An actuarial valuation method that sees each period of service as giving rise to an additional unit of benefit entitlement and measures each unit separately to build up the final obligation (sometimes known as the accrued benefit method pro-rated on service or as the benefit/years of service method).
property, plant and equipment	Tangible assets that: (a) are held for use in the production or supply of goods or services, for rental to others, or for administrative purposes, and (b) are expected to be used during more than one period.
prospectively (applying a change in accounting policy)	Applying the new **accounting policy** to transactions, other events and conditions occurring after the date as at which the policy is changed.
provision	A **liability** of uncertain timing or amount.

prudence	The inclusion of a degree of caution in the exercise of the judgements needed in making the estimates required under conditions of uncertainty, such that **assets** or **income** are not overstated and **liabilities** or **expenses** are not understated.
public benefit entity	An entity whose primary objective is to provide goods or services for the general public, community or social benefit and where any **equity** is provided with a view to supporting the entity's primary objectives rather than with a view to providing a financial return to equity providers, shareholders or members.[28]
public benefit entity concessionary loan	A loan made or received between a **public benefit entity** or an entity within a **public benefit entity group** and another party: (a) at below the **prevailing market rate** of interest; (b) that is not repayable on demand; and (c) is for the purposes of furthering the objectives of the public benefit entity or public benefit entity **parent**.
public benefit entity group	A **public benefit entity parent** and all of its wholly-owned **subsidiaries**.
publicly traded (debt or equity instruments)	Traded, or in process of being issued for trading, in a public market (a domestic or foreign stock exchange or an over-the-counter market, including local and regional markets).
qualifying asset	An **asset** that necessarily takes a substantial period of time to get ready for its intended use or sale. Depending on the circumstances any of the following may be qualifying assets: (a) **inventories**; (b) manufacturing plants; (c) power generation facilities; (d) **intangible assets**; and (e) **investment properties**. **Financial assets**, and inventories that are produced over a short period of time, are not qualifying assets. Assets that are ready for their intended use or sale when acquired are not qualifying assets.

[28] *The term public benefit entity does not necessarily imply that the purpose of the entity is for the benefit of the public as a whole. For example, many PBEs exist for the direct benefit of a particular group of people, although it is possible that society as a whole also benefits indirectly. The important factor is what the primary purpose of such an entity is, and that it does not exist primarily to provide economic benefit to its investors. Organisations such as mutual insurance companies, other mutual co-operative entities and clubs that provide dividends or other economic benefits directly and proportionately to their owners, members or participants are not PBEs.*

Some PBEs undertake certain activities that are intended to make a surplus in order to fund their primary activities. Consideration should be given to the primary purpose of an entity's (or group's) activities in assessing whether it meets the definition of a PBE.

PBEs may have received contributions in the form of equity, even though the entity does not have a primary profit motive. However, because of the fundamental nature of public benefit entities, any such contributions are made by the equity holders of the entity primarily to enable the provision of goods or services to beneficiaries rather than with a view to a financial return for themselves. This is different from the position of lenders; loans do not fall into the category of equity.

qualifying entity (for the purposes of this FRS)	A member of a **group** where the **parent** of that group prepares publicly available **consolidated financial statements** which are intended to give a true and fair view (of the **assets**, **liabilities**, **financial position** and **profit or loss**) and that member is included in the consolidation[29].

qualifying insurance policies	An insurance policy[30] issued by an insurer that is not a **related party** of the reporting entity, if the proceeds of the policy:
	(a) can be used only to pay or fund **employee benefits** under a **defined benefit plan**; and
	(b) are not available to the reporting entity's own creditors (even in bankruptcy) and cannot be paid to the reporting entity, unless either:
	    (i) the proceeds represent surplus **assets** that are not needed for the policy to meet all the related employee benefit obligations; or
	    (ii) the proceeds are returned to the reporting entity to reimburse it for employee benefits already paid.

recognition	The process of incorporating in the **statement of financial position** or **statement of comprehensive income** an item that meets the definition of an asset, liability, equity, income or expense and satisfies the following criteria: (a) it is **probable** that any future economic benefit associated with the item will flow to or from the entity; and (b) the item has a cost or value that can be measured with **reliability**.
recoverable amount	The higher of an **asset's** (or **cash-generating unit's**) **fair value less costs to sell** and its value in use.
Regulations	The Large and Medium-sized Companies and Groups (Accounts and Reports) Regulations 2008 (SI 2008/410)
reinsurance contract	An **insurance contract** issued by one insurer (the reinsurer) to compensate another insurer (the cedant) for losses on one or more contracts issued by the cedant.

related party	A related party is a person or entity that is related to the entity that is preparing its **financial statements** (the reporting entity).
	(a) A person or a close member of that person's family is related to a reporting entity if that person:
	    (i) has **control** or **joint control** over the reporting entity;
	    (ii) has **significant influence** over the reporting entity; or
	    (iii) is a member of the **key management personnel** of the reporting entity or of a **parent** of the reporting entity.
	(b) An entity is related to a reporting entity if any of the following conditions apply:

---

[29] *As set out in section 474(1) of the Act.*

[30] *A qualifying insurance policy is not necessarily an insurance contract.*

	(i) the entity and the reporting entity are members of the same **group** (which means that each parent, **subsidiary** and fellow subsidiary is related to the others).
	(ii) one entity is an **associate** or **joint venture** of the other entity (or of a member of a group of which the other entity is a member).
	(iii) both entities are joint ventures of the same third entity.
	(iv) one entity is a joint venture of a third entity and the other entity is an associate of the third entity.
	(v) the entity is a **post-employment benefit plan** for the benefit of employees of either the reporting entity or an entity related to the reporting entity. If the reporting entity is itself such a plan, the sponsoring employers are also related to the reporting entity.
	(vi) the entity is controlled or jointly controlled by a person identified in (a).
	(vii) a person identified in (a)(i) has significant influence over the entity or is a member of the key management personnel of the entity (or of a parent of the entity).
	(viii) the entity, or any member of a group of which it is a part, provides key management personnel services to the reporting entity or to the parent of the reporting entity.
related party transaction	A transfer of resources, services or obligations between a reporting entity and a **related party**, regardless of whether a price is charged.
relevance	The quality of information that allows it to influence the economic decisions of users by helping them evaluate past, present or future events or confirming, or correcting, their past evaluations.
reliability	The quality of information that makes it free from **material error** and bias and represents faithfully that which it either purports to represent or could reasonably be expected to represent.
reporting date	The end of the latest period covered by **financial statements** or by an **interim financial report**.
reporting period	The period covered by **financial statements** or by an **interim financial report**.
research	Original and planned investigation undertaken with the prospect of gaining new scientific or technical knowledge and understanding.
residual value (of an asset)	The estimated amount that an entity would currently obtain from disposal of an **asset**, after deducting the estimated costs of disposal, if the asset were already of the age and in the condition expected at the end of its **useful life**.

restriction	A requirement that limits or directs the purposes for which a resource may be used that does not meet the definition of a **performance-related condition**.
restructuring	A restructuring is a programme that is planned and controlled by management and materially changes either: (a) the scope of a business undertaken by an entity; or (b) the manner in which that business is conducted.
retirement benefit plan	Arrangements whereby an entity provides benefits for employees on or after termination of service (either in the form of an annual **income** or as a lump sum) when such benefits, or the contributions towards them, can be determined or estimated in advance of retirement from the provisions of a document or from the entity's practice.
retrospective application (of an accounting policy)	Applying a new **accounting policy** to transactions, other events and conditions as if that policy had always been applied.
revenue	The gross inflow of economic benefits during the period arising in the course of the ordinary activities of an entity when those inflows result in increases in **equity**, other than increases relating to contributions from equity participants.
separate financial statements	Those presented by a **parent** in which the investments in **subsidiaries**, **associates** or **jointly controlled entities** are accounted for either at cost or **fair value** rather than on the basis of the reported results and net assets of the investees. Separate financial statements are included within the meaning of **individual financial statements**.
service concession arrangement	An arrangement whereby a public sector body or a **public benefit entity** (the grantor) contracts with a private sector entity (the operator) to construct (or upgrade), operate and maintain **infrastructure assets** for a specified period of time (the concession period).
service potential	The economic utility of an **asset**, based on the total benefit expected to be derived by the entity from use (and/or through sale) of the asset.
share-based payment transaction	A transaction in which the entity: (a) receives goods or services (including employee services) as consideration for its own equity instruments (including shares or **share options**); or (b) receives goods or services but has no obligation to settle the transaction with supplier; or (c) acquires goods or services by incurring **liabilities** to the supplier of those goods or services for amounts that are based on the price (or value) of the entity's shares or other equity instruments of the entity or another group entity.
share option	A contract that gives the holder the right, but not the obligation, to subscribe to the entity's shares at a fixed or determinable price for a specific period of time.

significant influence	Significant influence is the power to participate in the financial and operating policy decisions of the **associate** but is not **control** or **joint control** over those policies.
Small Companies Regulations	The Small Companies and Groups (Accounts and Directors' Report) Regulations 2008 (SI 2008/409)
small entity	(a) A company meeting the definition of a small company as set out in section 382 or 383 of the **Act** and not excluded from the small companies regime by section 384; (b) an LLP qualifying as small and not excluded from the small LLPs regime, as set out in LLP Regulations; or (c) any other entity that would have met the criteria in (a) had it been a company incorporated under company law.
Small LLP Regulations	The Small Limited Liability Partnership (Accounts) Regulations 2008 (SI 2008/1912)
Statement of Recommended Practice (SORP)	An extant Statement of Recommended Practice developed in accordance with *SORPs: Policy and Code of Practice.* SORPs recommend accounting practices for specialised industries or sectors. They supplement accounting standards and other legal and regulatory requirements in the light of the special factors prevailing or transactions undertaken in a particular industry or sector.
state	A national, regional, or local government.
state (employee benefit) plan	Employee benefit plans established by legislation to cover all entities (or all entities in a particular category, for example a specific industry) and operated by national or local government or by another body (for example an autonomous agency created specifically for this purpose) which is not subject to control or influence by the reporting entity.
statement of cash flows	**Financial statement** that provides information about the changes in **cash** and **cash equivalents** of an entity for a period, showing separately changes during the period from operating, investing and **financing activities**.
statement of comprehensive income	**Financial statement** that presents all items of **income** and **expense** recognised in a period, including those items recognised in determining **profit or loss** (which is a subtotal in the statement of comprehensive income) and items of **other comprehensive income**. If an entity chooses to present both an **income statement** and a statement of comprehensive income, the statement of comprehensive income begins with profit or loss and then displays the items of other comprehensive income.
statement of financial position	**Financial statement** that presents the relationship of an entity's **assets**, **liabilities** and **equity** as of a specific date (referred to as the balance sheet in the **Act**).
statement of income and retained earnings	**Financial statement** that presents the **profit or loss** and changes in retained earnings for a **reporting period**.

subsidiary	An entity, including an unincorporated entity such as a partnership, that is **controlled** by another entity (known as the **parent**).
substantively enacted	Tax rates shall be regarded as substantively enacted when the remaining stages of the enactment process historically have not affected the outcome and are unlikely to do so. A UK tax rate shall be regarded as having been substantively enacted if it is included in either: (a) a Bill that has been passed by the House of Commons and is awaiting only passage through the House of Lords and Royal Assent; or (b) a resolution having statutory effect that has been passed under the Provisional Collection of Taxes Act 1968. (Such a resolution could be used to collect taxes at a new rate before that rate has been enacted. In practice, corporation tax rates are now set a year ahead to avoid having to invoke the Provisional Collection of Taxes Act for the quarterly payment system.) A Republic of Ireland tax rate can be regarded as having been substantively enacted if it is included in a Bill that has been passed by the Dail.
tax expense	The aggregate amount included in **total comprehensive income** or **equity** for the **reporting period** in respect of **current tax** and **deferred tax**.
taxable profit (tax loss)	The profit (loss) for a **reporting period** upon which income taxes are payable or recoverable, determined in accordance with the rules established by the taxation authorities. Taxable profit equals taxable income less amounts deductible from taxable income.
termination benefits	**Employee benefits** provided in exchange for the termination of an employee's employment as a result of either: (a) an entity's decision to terminate an employee's employment before the normal retirement date; or (b) an employee's decision to accept voluntary redundancy in exchange for those benefits.
timing differences	Differences between **taxable profits** and **total comprehensive income** as stated in the **financial statements** that arise from the inclusion of **income** and **expenses** in tax assessments in periods different from those in which they are recognised in financial statements.
timeliness	Providing the information in **financial statements** within the decision time frame.
total comprehensive income	The change in **equity** during a period resulting from transactions and other events, other than those changes resulting from transactions from equity participants (equal to the sum of **profit or loss** and **other comprehensive income**).

transaction costs (financial instruments)	Incremental costs that are directly attributable to the acquisition, issue or disposal of a **financial asset** or **financial liability**, or the issue or reacquisition of an entity's **own equity instrument**. An incremental cost is one that would not have been incurred if the entity had not acquired, issued or disposed of the financial asset or financial liability, or had not issued or reacquired its own equity instrument.
treasury shares	An entity's own equity instruments, held by that entity or other members of the consolidated group.
turnover	The amounts derived from the provision of goods and services after deduction of: (a) trade discounts; (b) value added tax; and (c) any other taxes based on the amounts so derived.
understandability	The presentation of information in a way that makes it comprehensible by users who have a reasonable knowledge of business and economic activities and accounting and a willingness to study the information with reasonable diligence.
useful life	The period over which an **asset** is expected to be available for use by an entity or the number of production or similar units expected to be obtained from the asset by an entity.
value in use	The **present value** of the future **cash flows** expected to be derived from an **asset** or **cash-generating unit**.
value in use (in respect of assets held for their service potential)	When the future economic benefits of an **asset** are not primarily dependent on the asset's ability to generate net cash inflows, **value in use** (in respect of assets held for their **service potential**) is the **present value** to the entity of the asset's remaining service potential if it continues to be used, plus the net amount that the entity will receive from its disposal at the end of its **useful life**.
venturer	A party to a **joint venture** that has **joint control** over that joint venture.
vest	Become an entitlement. Under a share-based payment arrangement, a counterparty's right to receive **cash**, other **assets** or equity instruments of the entity vests when the counterparty's entitlement is no longer conditional on the satisfaction of any vesting conditions.
vested benefits	Benefits, the rights to which, under the conditions of a **retirement benefit plan**, are not conditional on continued employment.

Appendix II
Significant differences between FRS 102 and the IFRS for SMEs

Section		Changes to the IFRS for SMEs (July 2009)
1	Scope of this FRS	This section of the IFRS for SMEs has been replaced. The IFRS for SMEs applies to small and medium sized entities that do not have public accountability and publish general purpose financial statements. FRS 100 *Application of Financial Reporting Requirements* sets out the scope of entities applying this FRS.
		Paragraphs 1.14A and 1.14B are added to provide transitional provisions in respect of the designation of financial instruments at fair value and hedge accounting which are available to entities that have authorised for issue financial statements compliant with this FRS prior to 1 August 2014.
1A	Small Entities	This section has been inserted to set out the information that is to be presented and disclosed in the financial statements of a small entity, based on the legal framework for small companies.
2	Concepts and Pervasive Principles	No significant changes.
3	Financial Statement Presentation	The drafting of the requirements has been more closely aligned with the drafting of company law.
		The requirements in paragraph 3.7 are deleted.
		Paragraph 3.16 is amended to clarify the role of materiality in the preparation of financial statements. Paragraph 3.16A is inserted to specify that disclosures are not required if the information is not material.
4	Statement of Financial Position	The requirements of this section have predominantly been removed and replaced by the requirements set out in the Act. Entities that do not report under the Act comply with the requirements of this section, and of the Regulations, except to the extent that these requirements are not permitted by any statutory framework under which such entities report.
5	Statement of Comprehensive Income and Income Statement	The requirements of this section have predominantly been removed and replaced by the requirements set out in the Act. Entities that do not report under the Act comply with the requirements of this section and of the Regulations except to the extent that these requirements are not permitted by any statutory framework under which such entities report.
		Paragraph 5.10 has been amended and paragraphs 5.10A and 5.10B are inserted to comply with the Regulations and include the definition of an extraordinary item.

Section		Changes to the IFRS for SMEs (July 2009)
6	Statement of Changes in Equity and Statement of Income and Retained Earnings	Paragraph 6.3A is inserted to require presentation for each component of equity an analysis of other comprehensive income by item, either in the notes, or in the statement of changes in equity.
7	Statement of Cash Flows	The scope of this section is amended to exclude mutual life assurance companies, pension funds and certain investment funds.
		Paragraphs 7.10A to 7.10E are inserted to require the reporting of cash flows on a net basis in some circumstances.
		Paragraphs 7.11 and 7.12 are amended to provide some relaxation of the exchange rates permitted to be used.
8	Notes to the Financial Statements	No significant changes.
9	Consolidated and Separate Financial Statements	The scope of this section is amended to clarify that it applies to all parent entities that present consolidated financial statements intended to give a true and fair view.
		The requirements to present consolidated financial statements are amended to comply with the Act.
		Paragraph 9.9 requires a subsidiary that is held exclusively with a view to subsequent resale because it is held as part of an investment portfolio, to be excluded from consolidation. Such subsidiaries are required to be measured at fair value with changes recognised in profit or loss. This exemption is required irrespective of whether the subsidiary was previously consolidated under previous GAAP, prior to transition to FRS 102. In addition paragraphs 14.4B and 15.9B are inserted to require an investor that has investments in associates or jointly controlled entities that are held as part of an investment portfolio to measure those investments at fair value with the changes recognised in profit or loss in their consolidated financial statements.
		Clarification is added to paragraph 9.10 that Employee Share Ownership Plans and similar arrangements are Special Purpose Entities.
		Paragraph 9.16 is amended to comply with paragraph 2(2) of Schedule 6 to the Regulations in order to require a subsidiary's financial statements, which are included in the consolidated financial statements, to be for the same reporting period (financial year) and as at the same reporting date (year-end). Where it is not practicable to align the subsidiary's reporting date (year-end) with the parent's, paragraph 9.16 has been amended to specify which financial statements of the subsidiary are permitted to be used in the consolidation.

Section		Changes to the IFRS for SMEs (July 2009)
		Paragraphs 9.18A and 9.18B are inserted to clarify the treatment of a disposal where control is lost.
		Paragraph 9.19A is inserted to clarify the treatment of the disposal where control is retained.
		Paragraph 9.19B is inserted to clarify the treatment of an acquisition made in stages.
		Paragraphs 9.19C and 9.19D are inserted to clarify the treatment of non-controlling interest when a parent changes its holding in a subsidiary but control is retained.
		Paragraphs 9.23A to 9.25 are amended to clarify the distinction between the individual financial statements and separate financial statements and that the Act specifies when individual financial statements are required to be prepared.
		Paragraphs 9.28 to 9.30 relating to combined financial statements are deleted.
		Paragraphs 9.31 and 9.32 provide guidance on exchanges of businesses or other non-monetary assets for an interest in a subsidiary, joint venture or associate. This guidance was previously contained in UITF Abstract 31 *Exchanges of businesses or other non-monetary assets for an interest in a subsidiary, joint venture or associate*.
		Paragraphs 9.33 to 9.38 are inserted to provide guidance on the accounting treatment for intermediate payment arrangements. These were previously contained in UITF Abstract 32 *Employee benefit trusts and other intermediate payment arrangements*.
10	Accounting Policies, Estimates and Errors	Paragraph 10.5 clarifies when an entity is required to refer to SORPs in developing an accounting policy.
		Paragraph 10.10A is inserted to bring the accounting treatment for changes in accounting policy relating to property, plant and equipment (Section 17) and intangible assets (Section 18) in line with IAS 10 *Accounting Policies, Estimate and Errors*.
11	Basic Financial Instruments	The scope of Section 11 is amended to clarify that certain financial instruments are not within its scope.
		Paragraph 11.2A is inserted to ensure that an entity choosing to apply the recognition and measurement requirements of IFRS 9 complies with the Regulations.
		Paragraph 11.8(b) is amended to clarify that instruments as described in paragraph 11.6(b) are not debt instruments accounted for under Section 11.

Section	Changes to the IFRS for SMEs (July 2009)
	Paragraph 11.9(a) is amended to clarify the permissible contractual returns to the lender.
	Paragraph 11.9(aA) is added to include some contractual provisions that provide for a linkage of repayments and/or returns to the lender based on inflation.
	Paragraph 11.9(aB) is added to permit certain variations of the return to the holder during the life of the instrument.
	Paragraph 11.9(c) is amended to clarify that contractual prepayment provisions which are contingent future events exclude those which protect the holder from credit deterioration, changes in central bank levies or tax changes and to clarify when compensation payments do not breach the condition.
	The text of paragraph 11.9(d) is deleted as it is no longer needed.
	Paragraph 11.9(e) is added to permit certain contractual extension options.
	Examples are inserted after paragraph 11.9 to illustrate the application of paragraph 11.9.
	Paragraphs 11.11(b) and (c) are deleted as the instruments shown as examples are excluded from debt instruments within the scope of Section 11 under paragraph 11.8(b).
	Paragraph 11.14(b) is inserted to clarify that entities may choose to designate debt instruments and loan commitments as fair value through profit or loss under certain circumstances.
	Paragraph 11.38A is inserted to allow offsetting of certain financial assets and financial liabilities in the statement of financial position.
	Paragraph 11.48A is inserted to provide disclosures required in accordance with the Regulations for certain financial instruments held at fair value.
	Paragraphs 11.48B and 11.48C require additional disclosures for financial institutions.
12 Other Financial Instruments Issues	The scope of Section 12 is amended to exclude financial instruments issued by an entity with a discretionary participation feature, reimbursement assets and financial guarantee contracts.
	Paragraph 12.2A is inserted to ensure that an entity choosing to apply the recognition and measurement requirements of IFRS 9 complies with the Regulations.
	Paragraph 12.8(c) is added to clarify when financial instruments within the scope of Section 12 should be measured at amortised cost.

Section	Changes to the IFRS for SMEs (July 2009)
	Paragraphs 12.15 to 12.29 are deleted and replaced with paragraphs 12.15 to 12.29A to include revised hedge accounting requirements which have the following effect:
	(a) the scope of permissible hedged items and hedging instruments is expanded;
	(b) the hedge accounting conditions are revised and simplified;
	(c) it determines three hedge accounting models, ie cash flow, fair value and net investment hedges;
	(d) it clarifies that the cumulative amount of foreign exchange differences relating to a hedge of a net investment in a foreign operation is not reclassified to profit or loss on disposal or partial disposal; and
	(e) it introduces a documentation requirement in cases of voluntary hedge accounting discontinuation.
	Paragraph 12.25B is inserted to allow offsetting of certain financial assets and financial liabilities in the statement of financial position.
	Paragraph 12.26 is amended to comply with requirements set out in the Act.
	The Appendix to Section 12 is inserted to illustrate by way of example the application of the hedge accounting requirements.
13 Inventories	Paragraph 13.3 is amended to permit inventory to be measured at fair value less costs to sell through profit or loss in certain circumstances.
	Paragraphs 13.4A and 13.20A are inserted to provide guidance on inventories held for distribution at no or nominal consideration.
	Paragraph 13.5A is inserted to provide guidance on inventory acquired through non-exchange transactions.
	Paragraph 13.8A is inserted to clarify the treatment for provisions made against dismantling and restoration costs (of PPE) in the cost of inventory.
	Paragraph 13.12 is deleted because of the revisions to the hedge accounting requirements.
	Paragraph 13.15 is amended to allow for the inclusion of a cost model for agricultural produce in Section 34 *Specialised Activities*.

Section		Changes to the IFRS for SMEs (July 2009)
14	Investments in Associates	The scope of this section is amended to clarify its application to consolidated financial statements and to the financial statements of an entity that is not a parent but which holds investments in associates.
		Paragraph 14.4(b) of the IFRS for SMEs is deleted as the equity method of accounting for investments in associates in individual financial statements is not compliant with company law. Paragraph 14.4(d) is inserted to allow non-parent investors to account for investments in associates at fair value with changes recognised in profit or loss.
		Paragraphs 14.4B is inserted to require an investor that is a parent which has investments in associates that are held as part of an investment portfolio to measure those investments at fair value with the changes recognised in profit or loss in their consolidated financial statements.
		Paragraph 14.9 is amended to require transaction costs to be included as part of the transaction price on initial recognition.
		Paragraph 14.10 is amended to require changes in fair value to be recognised through other comprehensive income, in accordance with paragraphs 17.15E and 17.15F, when the fair value model is applied, rather than through profit or loss.
		Paragraph 14.15A is inserted to provide information about associates held by entities that are not parents.
15	Investments in Joint Ventures	The scope of this section is amended to clarify its application to consolidated financial statements and to the financial statements of a venture that is not a parent.
		Paragraph 15.9(b) of the IFRS for SMEs is deleted as the equity method of accounting for interests in jointly controlled entities in individual financial statements is not compliant with company law. Paragraph 15.9(d) is inserted to allow non-parent investors to account for investments in jointly controlled entities at fair value with the changes recognised in profit or loss.
		Paragraph 15.9B is inserted to require an investor that is a parent which has investments in jointly controlled entities that are held as part of an investment portfolio to measure those investments at fair value with the changes recognised in profit or loss in their consolidated financial statements.
		Paragraph 15.14 is amended to require transaction costs to be included as part of the transaction price on initial recognition.

Section		Changes to the IFRS for SMEs (July 2009)
		Paragraph 15.15 is amended to require changes in fair value to be recognised through other comprehensive income, in accordance with paragraphs 17.15E and 17.15F, when the fair value model is applied, rather than through profit or loss.
		Paragraph 15.21A is inserted to provide information about associates held by entities that are not parents.
16	Investment Property	No significant changes.
17	Property, Plant and Equipment	Section 17 is amended to provide, after initial recognition, that an entity may use the cost model or revaluation model.
18	Intangible Assets other than Goodwill	Section 18 is amended to permit entities to recognise intangible assets that result from expenditure incurred on the internal development of an intangible item (subject to certain criteria). The section provides guidance on what comprises the cost of an internally generated intangible asset and the criteria for initial recognition.
		The section is also amended to provide, after initial recognition, that an entity may use the cost model or revaluation model.
19	Business Combinations and Goodwill	Section 19 is amended to permit the use of the merger accounting method for group reconstructions. The merger method is set out in paragraphs 19.29 to 19.33.
		Paragraphs 19.15A to 19.15C are inserted to provide guidance on the treatment of deferred tax assets or liabilities, employee benefit arrangements and share-based payments of a subsidiary on acquisition.
		Paragraph 19.24 is amended and paragraph 19.26A is inserted to comply with the requirements of the Act for bargain purchases (negative goodwill).
20	Leases	The scope of Section 20 is amended to include operating leases that are onerous within its scope.
		Paragraphs 20.15A and 20.25A are inserted to clarify the treatment of operating lease incentives for lessees and lessors respectively.
		Paragraph 20.15B is inserted to provide guidance on the treatment of onerous operating lease contracts.
21	Provisions and Contingencies	The scope of Section 21 is amended to include financial guarantee contracts. Paragraph 21.17A is inserted to provide guidance on the accounting treatment of financial guarantee contracts.
		Paragraph 21.17 is amended to comply with disclosure requirements set out in the Regulations.

Section		Changes to the IFRS for SMEs (July 2009)
22	Liabilities and Equity	Paragraph 22.3A is inserted to clarify that a financial instrument where the issuer does not have the unconditional right to avoid settling in cash or by delivery of another financial asset (or otherwise to settle it in such a way that it would be a financial liability); and where settlement is dependent on the occurrence or non-occurrence of uncertain future events beyond the control of the issuer and the holder, is a financial liability of the issuer unless specific circumstances apply.
		The requirement for an entity to recognise a liability at fair value when non-cash assets are distributed to owners is removed and only disclosure is required in paragraph 22.18.
23	Revenue	No significant changes.
24	Government Grants	Paragraphs 24.5C to 24.5G are inserted to allow an additional model of accounting for grants (the accrual model). The model permits entities to recognise grant income on a systematic basis over the period in which the entity recognises the related costs for which the grant is intended to compensate.
25	Borrowing Costs	Section 25 is amended to allow an option that permits entities to capitalise borrowing costs that are directly attributable to the acquisition, construction or production of a qualifying asset.
26	Share-based Payment	The definition of equity-settled share based payments has been amended to align with the revised IFRS 2 definition. It is clarified that option pricing models do not have to be applied in all circumstances.
		Paragraph 26.15 has been replaced with new paragraphs 26.15 to 26.15B to bring the accounting for share-based payment arrangements with cash alternatives closer to that required by IFRS 2 when the entity has the settlement choice.
27	Impairment of Assets	Paragraph 27.20A is inserted to provide guidance on the treatment of impairments on assets held for their service potential.
		Paragraph 27.33A is inserted to include a descriptive disclosure requirement of the events and circumstances that led to the recognition or reversal of the impairment loss.
28	Employee Benefits	The presentation of the cost of a defined benefit plan and the accounting for group plans have been amended to be consistent with the requirements of IAS 19 *Employee Benefits* as amended in 2011.

Section		Changes to the IFRS for SMEs (July 2009)
		Paragraph 28.11A is inserted to require the recognition of a liability on a defined benefit multi-employer plan, which is accounted as defined contribution scheme, where funding of a deficit has been agreed.
		Paragraph 28.19 is deleted to remove the option to use a simplified valuation method in measuring the liability.
29	Income Tax	Section 29 of the IFRS for SMEs has been entirely replaced with revised requirements.
30	Foreign Currency Translation	No significant changes.
31	Hyperinflation	No significant changes.
32	Events after the End of the Reporting Period	Paragraphs 32.7A and 32.7B are inserted to provide guidance on the impact of changes in an entity's going concern status.
33	Related Party Disclosures	Paragraph 33.1A is inserted to include the exemption from disclosure of related party transactions for wholly-owned entities available in the Act.
		The definition of a related party in paragraph 33.2 is amended for consistency with company law.
34	Specialised Activities	Agriculture – this sub-section is amended to allow the option to hold biological assets and agricultural produce at cost.
		Extractives – this sub-section has been amended to require application of IFRS 6.
		Service concession arrangements – this sub-section is amended to clarify the accounting by operators and provide guidance to grantors.
		The following additional sub-sections are inserted: • Financial Institutions; • Retirement Benefit Plans: Financial Statements; • Heritage Assets; • Funding Commitments; • Incoming Resources from Non-Exchange Transactions; • Public Benefit Entity Combinations; and • Public Benefit Entity Concessionary Loans.
35	Transition to this FRS	Amendments to this section reflect the changes in preceding sections and the different effective date for small entities.

Appendix III
Table of equivalence for
UK Companies Act terminology

The following table compares company law terminology with broadly equivalent terminology used in FRS 102. In some cases there are minor differences between the broadly equivalent definitions, which are also summarised below.

Company law terminology	FRS 102 terminology
Accounting reference date	Reporting date
Accounts	Financial statements
Associated undertaking	Associate
Balance sheet	Statement of financial position
Capital and reserves	Equity
Cash at bank and in hand	Cash[31]
Debtors	Trade receivables
Diminution in value [of assets]	Impairment
Financial year	Reporting period
Group [accounts]	Consolidated [financial statements]
IAS	EU-adopted IFRS
Individual [accounts]	Individual [financial statements]
Interest payable and similar charges	Finance costs
Interest receivable and similar income	Finance income/Investment income
Minority interests	Non-controlling interest
Net realisable value [of any current asset]	Estimated selling price less costs to complete and sell
Parent undertaking	Parent
Profit and loss account	Income statement (under the two-statement approach) Part of the statement of comprehensive income (under the single-statement approach)
Related undertakings[32]	Subsidiaries, associates and joint ventures
Stocks	Inventories
Subsidiary undertaking	Subsidiary
Tangible assets	Includes: Property, plant equipment; Investment property
Trade creditors	Trade payables

[31] *FRS 102 requires the cash flow statement to reconcile the movement in cash and cash equivalents. Disclosure is required of reconciliation between amounts presented in the statement of financial position (ie cash) and cash and cash equivalents.*

[32] *This would also include entities in which a company has at least a 20 per cent holding, but which are not a subsidiary, joint venture or an associate. A shareholding of 20 per cent is presumed to give significant influence to the holder, such that the investment would be classified as an associate, therefore in practice there are unlikely to be many related undertakings that are not subsidiaries, joint ventures or associates.*

Appendix IV
Note on legal requirements

INTRODUCTION

This appendix provides an overview of how the requirements in FRS 102 address United Kingdom company law requirements. It is therefore written from the perspective of a company to which the Companies Act 2006 applies[33]. Appendix VI discusses the Republic of Ireland legal references. **A4.1**

Many entities that are not constituted as companies apply accounting standards promulgated by the FRC for the purposes of preparing financial statements that present a true and fair view[34]. A brief consideration of the legal framework for some other entities can be found at A4.41 and A4.42. For those entities that are within the scope of a Statement of Recommended Practice (SORP), the relevant SORP will provide more details on the legal framework. **A4.2**

References to the Act in this appendix are to the *Companies Act 2006*. References to the Regulations are to *The Large and Medium-sized Companies and Groups (Accounts and Reports) Regulations 2008* (SI 2008/410) as amended by *The Companies, Partnerships and Groups (Accounts and Reports) Regulations 2015* (SI 2015/980) following the implementation of the EU Accounting Directive. References to specific provisions are to Schedule 1 to the Regulations; entities applying Schedules 2, 3 or 6 should read them as referring to the equivalent paragraph in those schedules; and small entities applying the Small Companies Regulations should read them as referring to the equivalent paragraph in Schedule 1 to the Small Companies Regulations. Similar provisions generally also apply to limited liability partnerships applying the Small LLP Regulations or the LLP Regulations although some differences do exist (see paragraphs A4.43 to A4.47). **A4.3**

---

[33] *Some charities are also companies, and are therefore required to apply the requirements of both the* Companies Act 2006 *and the* Charities Act 2011.

[34] *More information about the 'true and fair' concept can be found on the FRC's website at http://www.frc.org.uk/ Our-Work/Codes-Standards/Accounting-and-Reporting-Policy/True-and-Fair.aspx.*

APPLICABLE ACCOUNTING FRAMEWORK

A4.4   Group accounts of certain parent entities (those with securities admitted to trading on a regulated market in an EU Member State) are required by Article 4 of EU Regulation 1606/2002 (IAS Regulation) to be prepared in accordance with EU-adopted IFRS.

A4.5   All other entities, except those that are eligible to apply FRS 105 *The Financial Reporting Standard applicable to the Micro-entities Regime*, must apply[35] either FRS 102 *The Financial Reporting Standard applicable in the UK and Republic of Ireland*, EU-adopted IFRS or FRS 101 *Reduced Disclosure Framework* (if the financial statements are the individual financial statements of a qualifying entity eligible to apply FRS 101).

A4.6   Section 395(1) of the Act states:

'A company's individual accounts may be prepared—

(a)   in accordance with section 396 ('Companies Act individual accounts'), or

(b)   in accordance with international accounting standards ('IAS individual accounts').'

Section 403(2) of the Act states:

'The group accounts of other companies may be prepared—

(a)   in accordance with section 404 ('Companies Act group accounts'), or

(b)   in accordance with international accounting standards ('IAS group accounts').'

A4.7   Accounts prepared in accordance with FRS 102 are classified as either 'Companies Act individual accounts', including those of qualifying entities applying FRS 102, or 'Companies Act group accounts' and are therefore required to comply with the applicable provisions of Parts 15 and 16 of the Act and with the Regulations.

Consistency of financial reporting within groups

A4.8   Section 407 of the Act requires that the directors of the parent company secure that individual accounts of a parent company and each of its subsidiaries are prepared using the same financial reporting framework, except to the extent that in the directors' opinion there are good reasons for not doing so.

In addition, consistency is not required in the following situations:

(a)   when the parent company does not prepare consolidated financial statements; or

(b)   when some subsidiaries are charities (consistency is not needed between the framework used for these and for other subsidiaries).

Where the directors of a parent company prepare IAS group accounts and IAS individual accounts, there only has to be consistency across the individual financial statements of the subsidiaries.

A4.9   All companies, other than those which elect or are required to prepare IAS individual accounts in accordance with the Act, prepare Companies Act individual accounts.

---

[35] *Under company law in the Republic of Ireland, certain entities are permitted to prepare Companies Act accounts using accounting standards other than those issued by the FRC.*

APPLICATION OF FRS 102

Compliance with company law

The FRS has been developed for application in the UK and Republic of Ireland, using the IFRS for SMEs as a basis. Part of that development process included making amendments to the IFRS for SMEs to ensure compliance with the Act and the Regulations. For example, changes were made to eliminate options that are not permitted by company law. However, FRS 102 is not intended to be a one-stop-shop for all accounting and legal requirements, and although the FRC believes FRS 102 is not inconsistent with company law, compliance with FRS 102 alone will often be insufficient to ensure compliance with all the disclosure requirements set out in the Act and the Regulations. As a result preparers will continue to be required to have regard to the requirements of company law in addition to accounting standards.

A4.10

This appendix does not list every legal requirement, but instead focuses on those areas where greater judgement might be required in determining compliance with the law.

A4.11

Small companies

The definition of a small company is contained in sections 382 and 383 of the Act; certain companies are excluded from the small companies regime by section 384. Subject to certain conditions and exclusions, the qualifying conditions are met by a company in a year in which it does not exceed two or more of the following criteria:

A4.11A

(a)	Turnover	£10.2 million
(b)	Balance sheet total	£5.1 million
(c)	Average number of employees	50

A parent company qualifies as a small company in relation to a financial year only if the group that it heads qualifies as small (as set out in section 383 of the Act).

A4.11B

The Small Companies Regulations set out the small companies regime. Although FRS 102 was developed on the basis of the Regulations (which apply to large and medium-sized companies) the recognition and measurement requirements of FRS 102 should also be consistent with the Small Companies Regulations.

A4.11C

In accordance with section 393 of the Act the directors of any company, including a small company, must not approve accounts unless they are satisfied that they give a true and fair view of the assets, liabilities, financial position and profit or loss of the company. In order to achieve this, a company, including a small company, may need to provide disclosures additional to those required by company law. In relation to small companies, paragraph 1A.16 of FRS 102 reflects this requirement and paragraph 1A.17 encourages a small company to consider all other disclosures in FRS 102 to determine any additional disclosures to provide.

A4.11D

The Small Companies Regulations include options for small companies to prepare an abridged balance sheet and an abridged profit and loss account. In order to take this option small companies must comply with the additional legal requirement that all members of the company have consented to the drawing up of abridged financial statements (which may only be given in respect of the preceding financial year). In accordance with paragraph 1A(4) of Schedule 1 to the Small Companies Regulations this option is not available to small entities that are charities. When a small entity that is not a company chooses to prepare abridged financial statements it should ensure that:

A4.11E

(a)   similar consent is obtained from the members of its governing body, taking into account its legal form; and

(b)   abridged financial statements would not be prohibited by relevant laws or regulation.

Financial instruments measured at fair value

A4.12   All preparers of Companies Act accounts must comply with the requirements of paragraph 36 of Schedule 1 to the Regulations, which provides that:

'(1)   Subject to sub-paragraphs (2) to (5), financial instruments (including derivatives) may be included at fair value.

(2)   Sub-paragraph (1) does not apply to financial instruments that constitute liabilities unless—

    (a)   they are held as part of a trading portfolio,

    (b)   they are derivatives, or

    (c)   they are financial instruments falling within sub-paragraph (4).

(3)   Unless they are financial instruments falling within sub-paragraph (4), sub-paragraph (1) does not apply to –

    (a)   financial instruments (other than derivatives) held to maturity,

    (b)   loans and receivables originated by the company and not held for trading purposes,

    (c)   interests in subsidiary undertakings, associated undertakings and joint ventures,

    (d)   equity instruments issued by the company,

    (e)   contracts for contingent consideration in a business combination, or

    (f)   other financial instruments with such special characteristics that the instruments, according to generally accepted accounting principles or practice, should be accounted for differently from other financial instruments.

(4)   Financial instruments which under international accounting standards may be included in accounts at fair value, may be so included, provided that the disclosures required by such accounting standards are made.

(5)   […]'

A4.12A   In limited circumstances, an entity applying this FRS to its financial instruments that are classified as non-basic in accordance with Section 11 *Basic Financial Instruments* may be prohibited, by paragraph 36 of Schedule 1 to the Regulations, to measure those financial instruments at fair value through profit or loss in accordance with the requirements of this FRS. The Regulations prohibit the measurement of certain financial instruments at fair value through profit or loss, unless the instruments could be designated for such measurement under EU-adopted IFRS. EU-adopted IFRS permits designation at fair value through profit or loss upon initial recognition for financial instruments where: doing so eliminates or reduces a measurement or recognition inconsistency; or a group of financial instruments is managed and their performance evaluated on a fair value basis; or for a hybrid financial instruments which contains a component that, if recognised separately, would meet the definition of a derivative. Paragraph 12.8(c) of this FRS is applicable to the measurement of financial instruments prohibited under the Regulations to be measured at fair value through profit or loss and requires them to be measured at amortised cost.

A4.12B   Further, an entity that has made the accounting policy choice in paragraph 11.2(c) or paragraph 12.2(c) to apply the recognition and measurement provisions of IFRS 9 *Financial Instruments* shall depart from those provisions of IFRS 9 where the measurement of financial assets at fair value through profit or loss is not permitted by paragraph 36 of Schedule 1 to the Regulations. This can occur in relation to financial assets because the classification and measurement requirements of IFRS 9 are not identical to the equivalent requirements of IAS 39 *Financial Instruments: Recognition and Measurement*, which is the standard presently adopted by the EU and is therefore the reference point for paragraph 36(4) of Schedule 1 to the Regulations.

Paragraph 40 of Schedule 1 to the Regulations requires companies to include fair value gains and losses on financial instruments measured at fair value in the profit and loss account, except when the financial instrument is a hedging instrument or an available for sale security. Therefore, for those companies making the accounting policy choice, in accordance with paragraph 11.2(c) and 12.2(c) of FRS 102, to apply the recognition and measurement requirements of IFRS 9 *Financial Instruments*, recording fair value gains and losses attributable to changes in credit risk in other comprehensive income in accordance with IFRS 9 will usually be a departure from the requirement of paragraph 40 of Schedule 1 to the Regulations, for the overriding purpose of giving a true and fair view.   **A4.12C**

Entities that are preparing Companies Act accounts must provide the disclosures required by paragraph 55 of Schedule 1 to the Regulations, which sets out requirements relating to financial instruments measured at fair value through profit or loss. Most of these disclosures will be satisfied by equivalent requirements of FRS 102, but entities will need to take care to ensure appropriate disclosure of derivatives is provided.   **A4.12D**

An entity applying this FRS and holding financial instruments measured at fair value may be required to provide the disclosures required by paragraph 36(4) of Schedule 1 to the Regulations. The disclosures required by paragraph 36(4) have been incorporated into Section 11. Some of the Section 11 disclosure requirements apply to all financial instruments measured at fair value, whilst others (see paragraph 11.48A of FRS 102) apply only to certain financial instruments (this does not include financial liabilities held as part of a trading portfolio nor derivatives). The disclosure requirements of paragraph 11.48A will predominantly apply to certain financial liabilities, however, there may be instances where paragraph 36(3) of Schedule 1 to the Regulations requires that the disclosures must also be provided in relation to financial assets, for example investments in subsidiaries, associates or jointly controlled entities measured at fair value (see paragraph 9.27B of FRS 102).   **A4.13**

Requirement to present financial statements

FRS 102 does not prescribe which entities prepare financial statements and preparers should apply the requirements of the Act in determining whether financial statements (either individual or consolidated) are required. FRS 102 sets out the requirements for a complete set of financial statements that give a true and fair view of the financial position, financial performance and, where required to be presented, cash flows of an entity, where these are required by law, or other regulation or requirement.   **A4.14**

A parent company preparing consolidated financial statements under section 434(2) of the Act must publish its company financial statements together with the consolidated financial statements, although section 408 of the Act provides an exemption from including the company's individual profit and loss account.   **A4.15**

Subsidiaries excluded from consolidation

Paragraph 9.9(b) of Section 9 *Consolidated and Separate Financial Statements* requires a group to exclude subsidiaries from consolidation on the grounds that they are held exclusively with a view to subsequent resale. By defining 'held exclusively with a view to subsequent resale' in FRS 102 to include those interests that are held as part of an investment portfolio, subsidiaries held as part of such an investment portfolio are excluded from consolidation in accordance with section 405(3) of the Act and an entity will not need to apply the true and fair override in this circumstance.   **A4.16**

A4.17　Paragraph 9.9B(a) requires a group to measure subsidiaries excluded from consolidation by virtue of paragraph 9.9(b) and held as part of an investment portfolio, at fair value through profit or loss. The measurement at fair value through profit and loss, in circumstances where it would not be required by IFRS 10 *Consolidated Financial Statements*, is a departure from the requirements of paragraph 36 of Schedule 1 to the Regulations, for the overriding purpose of giving a true and fair view in the consolidated financial statements. In this circumstance entities must provide, in the notes to the financial statements, the 'particulars of the departure, the reasons for it and its effect' (paragraph 10(2) of Schedule 1 to the Regulations).

Calculation of goodwill where a business combination is achieved in stages

A4.18　Paragraph 9 of Schedule 6 to the Regulations sets out the requirements for the acquisition method of accounting, which results in goodwill (or negative goodwill) being calculated as the difference between:

(a)　the fair value of the group's share of identifiable assets and liabilities of the subsidiary at the date control is achieved; and

(b)　the total acquisition cost of the interests held by the group in that subsidiary.

This applies even where part of the acquisition cost arises from purchases at earlier dates.

A4.19　In most cases, this method provides a practical means of applying acquisition accounting because it does not require retrospective assessments of the fair value of the identifiable assets and liabilities of the subsidiary. In certain circumstances, however, not using fair values at the dates of earlier purchases while using acquisition costs which in part relate to earlier purchases may result in accounting that is inconsistent with the way the investment has been treated previously and, for that reason, may fail to give a true and fair view.

A4.20　For example, an undertaking that has been treated as an associate may then be acquired by that group as a subsidiary. Using the method required by the Regulations and paragraph 9.19B of FRS 102 to calculate goodwill on such an acquisition has the effect that the group's share of profits or losses and reserve movements of its associate becomes reclassified as goodwill (usually negative goodwill). A similar problem may arise where the group has substantially restated its investment in an undertaking that subsequently becomes its subsidiary. For example, where such an investment has been written down because it is impaired, the effect of applying the Regulations' method of acquisition accounting would be to increase reserves and create an asset (goodwill).

A4.21　In the rare cases where the method for calculating goodwill set out in the Regulations and in paragraph 9.19B of FRS 102 would be misleading, the goodwill should be calculated as the sum of goodwill arising from each purchase of an interest in the relevant undertaking adjusted as necessary for any subsequent impairment. Goodwill arising on each purchase should be calculated as the difference between the cost of that purchase and the fair value at the date of that purchase of the identifiable assets and liabilities attributable to the interest purchased. The difference between the goodwill calculated using this method and that calculated using the method provided by the Regulations and FRS 102 is shown in reserves. Section 404(5) of the Act sets out the disclosures required in cases where the statutory requirement is not applied. Paragraph 3.5 of FRS 102 sets out the disclosures when an entity departs from a requirement of FRS 102 or from a requirement of applicable legislation.

Netting

FRS 102 permits an expense relating to a provision to be presented net of the amount recognised for a reimbursement (which may only be recognised if it is virtually certain it will be received) (see paragraph 21.9 of FRS 102). Paragraph 8 of Schedule 1 to the Regulations requires that 'Amounts in respect of items representing assets or income may not be set off against amounts in respect of items representing liabilities or expenditure (as the case may be), or vice versa.' The reimbursement asset is recognised separately from the underlying obligation to reflect the fact that the entity often will continue to be liable if the third party from which the reimbursement is due fails to pay. On the other hand, the net presentation in the income statement reflects the cost to the entity and net presentation therefore does not conflict with the Regulations.

A4.22

FRS 102 requires that a financial asset and financial liability are offset and the net amount presented in the statement of financial position, if certain criteria are met (see paragraph 11.38A of FRS 102). The net presentation does not conflict with paragraph 8 of Schedule 1 to the Regulations, because provided the criteria for the net presentation are met, the presentation reflects the expected net cash flows from settling two or more separate financial instruments.

A4.23

Recording investments at cost

Paragraph 9.26 of FRS 102 requires that in an investor's separate financial statements its investments in subsidiaries are accounted for at cost less impairment, or at fair value. Where the cost model is applied, sections 611 to 615 of the Act set out the treatment where 'merger relief' or 'group reconstruction relief' are available. These reliefs reduce the amount required to be included in share premium; they also (in section 615) allow the initial carrying amount to be adjusted downwards so it is equal to either the previous carrying of the investment in the transferor's books or the nominal value of the shares issued, depending on which relief applies. If the fair value model in paragraph 9.26 is used, then the relief in section 615 is not available, so the investment's carrying value may not be reduced, although the provisions in sections 611 and 612 remain relevant in respect of amounts required to be recorded in share premium.

A4.24

Realised profits

Paragraph 13(a) of Schedule 1 to the Regulations requires that only profits realised at the reporting date are included in profit or loss, a requirement modified from that in Article 31.1(c)(aa) of the Fourth Directive which refers to profits 'made' at the balance sheet date.

A4.25

Paragraph 36 and paragraph 39 of Schedule 1 to the Regulations allow financial instruments, stocks, investment property, and living animals and plants to be held at fair value in Companies Act accounts.

A4.26

Paragraph 40(2) of Schedule 1 to the Regulations then requires that movements in the value of financial instruments, investment properties and living animals and plants are recognised in the profit and loss account, notwithstanding the usual restrictions allowing only realised profits and losses to be included in the profit and loss account. Paragraph 40 of Schedule 1 to the Regulations thereby overrides the requirements of paragraph 13(a) of Schedule 1.

A4.27

Entities measuring financial instruments, investment properties, and living animals and plants at fair value should note that they may transfer such amounts to a separate non-distributable reserve, instead of a transfer to retained earnings, but are not required to

A4.28

do so. Presenting fair value movements, that are not distributable profits, in the separate reserve may assist with the identification of profits available for that purpose.

A4.29   The determination of profits available for distribution is a complex area where accounting and company law interface. In determining profits available for distribution an entity may refer to Technical Release 02/10 *Guidance on realised and distributable profits under the Companies Act 2006* issued by the Institute of Chartered Accountants in England and Wales and the Institute of Chartered Accountants of Scotland, or any successor document, to determine profits available for distribution.

Merger accounting

A4.30   Paragraph 10 of Schedule 6 to the Regulations states:
'The conditions for accounting for an acquisition as a merger are—

(a)   that the undertaking whose shares are acquired is ultimately controlled by the same party both before and after the acquisition,

(b)   that the control referred to in paragraph (a) is not transitory, and

(c)   that adoption of the merger method accords with generally accepted accounting principles or practice.'

Therefore, paragraph 10 of Schedule 6 to the Regulations permits the use of merger accounting in certain limited circumstances, which is generally consistent with paragraph 19.27 of FRS 102 (group reconstructions). If an entity considers that, for the overriding purpose of giving a true and fair view, merger accounting should be applied in circumstances other than those set out in paragraph 10 of Schedule 6 to the Regulations, it may do so providing the relevant disclosures are made in the notes to the financial statements.

A4.30A   Section 34 *Specialised Activities* requires that combinations by public benefit entities meeting certain criteria are accounted for as a merger, unless this is not permitted by the relevant statutory framework. FRS 102 therefore does not extend the use of merger accounting beyond its applicability in company law, or other relevant statutory framework. If a public benefit entity that is a company considers that, for the overriding purpose of giving a true and fair view, merger accounting should be applied in circumstances other than those set out in paragraph 10 of Schedule 6 to the Regulations, it may do so providing the relevant disclosures are made in the notes to the financial statements.

Treasury shares

A4.31   Paragraph 22.16 of FRS 102 sets out the accounting requirements when an entity purchases its own equity instruments (ie treasury shares).

A4.32   Companies subject to the Act, need to comply with the accounting requirements of paragraph 22.16 as well as with the requirements of the Act when they purchase their own equity and hold it in treasury (Sections 690 to 708 and 724 to 732, respectively).

Measurement of investments in associates and jointly controlled entities for an investor, which is not a parent

A4.33   Paragraph 36 of Schedule 1 to the Regulations sets out the fair value accounting rules and permits investments in associates and joint ventures to be measured at fair value through profit or loss only where they are permitted to be treated as financial instruments in accordance with IAS Regulation. EU-adopted IFRS does allow investments in subsidiaries, associates and jointly controlled entities to be measured in accordance with

IAS 39 *Financial Instruments Recognition and Measurement* within separate financial statements (as set out in IAS 27 *Consolidated and Separate Financial Statements*).

Therefore, where the fair value model is applied by an investor, changes in fair value may be recognised through profit or loss, or other comprehensive income. Under the alternative accounting rules set out in Section C of Schedule 1 to the Regulations, the initial recognition of the investment must include any expenses that are incidental to the acquisition of the investment.   **A4.34**

Measurement of inventories held for distribution at no or nominal value

Paragraph 24(1) of Schedule 1 to the Regulations requires that if the net realisable value of any current asset is lower than its purchase price or production cost, the amount to be included in respect of that asset must be the net realisable value. However, paragraph 39 permits stocks to be included at their fair value, when applying fair value accounting.   **A4.35**

Inventories held for distribution at no or nominal value include items that might be distributed to beneficiaries by public benefit entities and items such as advertising and promotional material. As the items will be distributed at no or nominal cost, the net realisable value will usually be lower than the purchase price.   **A4.36**

Paragraph 13.4A of FRS 102 requires inventories held for distribution at no or nominal cost to be measured at the lower of cost (adjusted for any loss in service potential) and replacement cost. This is an application of fair value accounting. For inventories, including those held for distribution at no or nominal value (particularly items distributed to beneficiaries by public benefit entities), there is unlikely to be a significant difference between replacement cost and fair value.   **A4.37**

Amortisation of intangible assets

Paragraph 22 of Schedule 1 to the Regulations requires intangible assets to be written off over their useful economic lives. This is broadly consistent with paragraph 18.21 of FRS 102, except that FRS 102 allows for the possibility that an intangible asset will have a residual value, in which case it is the depreciable amount that shall be amortised, not the cost (or revalued amount) of the intangible asset. In practice it will be uncommon for an intangible asset to have a residual value (paragraph 18.23 requires an entity to assume that the residual value is zero other than in specific circumstances). In those cases where an intangible asset has a residual value that is not zero, the amortisation of the depreciable amount of an intangible asset over its useful economic life is a departure from the requirements of paragraph 22 of Schedule 1 to the Regulations for the overriding purpose of giving a true and fair view. In these circumstances entities must provide, in the notes to the financial statements, the 'particulars of the departure, the reasons for it and its effect' (paragraph 10(2) of Schedule 1 to the Regulations).   **A4.37A**

Accounts formats

Sections 1A, 4 and 5 of FRS 102 require entities to apply one of the profit and loss account and balance sheet formats set out in the Small Companies Regulations, the Regulations, the Small LLP Regulations and the LLP Regulations, when preparing their statement of comprehensive income (single-statement approach) or income statement (two-statement approach) and statement of financial position, respectively. The *General Rules* preceding *The Required Formats for Accounts* include certain flexibilities for companies (but not LLPs at present), this includes permitting adaptation of the formats, providing the adapted presentation is equivalent to that set out in the formats and that it is consistent with generally   **A4.38** accepted accounting practice. For entities within its scope FRS 102 sets out a framework for the information to be presented by those entities choosing to adapt the formats.

Discontinued operations

A4.39   FRS 102 requires an entity with discontinued operations, to provide an analysis between continuing operations and discontinued operations of each of the line items on the face of the statement of comprehensive income, or income statement, up to and including post-tax profit or loss for the period and illustrates this presentation in a columnar format. This is in order to present the post-tax results of those operations, combined with the profit or loss on their disposal, as a single line item while still complying with the requirement of company law to show totals for ordinary activities of items such as turnover, profit or loss before taxation and tax.

Long-term debtors

A4.40   UITF Abstract 4 *Presentation of long-term debtors in current assets* addressed the inclusion of debtors due after more than one year within 'current assets'; that UITF consensus has been withdrawn, but its conclusions remain valid and have been included in paragraph 4.4A of FRS 102.

Entities not subject to company law

A4.41   Many entities that apply FRS 102 are not companies, but are nevertheless required by their governing legislation, or other regulation or requirement to prepare financial statements that present a true and fair view of the financial performance and financial position of the reporting entity. However, the FRC sets accounting standards within the framework of the Act and therefore it is the company law requirements that the FRC primarily considered when developing FRS 102. Entities preparing financial statements within other legal frameworks will need to satisfy themselves that FRS 102 does not conflict with any relevant legal obligations.

A4.42   However, the FRC notes the following:

Legislation	Overview of requirements
Building Societies Act 1986	The annual accounts of a building society shall give a true and fair view of the income and expenditure for the year and the balance sheet shall give a true and fair view of the state of affairs of the society at the end of the financial year. Regulations make further requirements about the form and content of building society accounts, which do not appear inconsistent with the requirement of FRS 102.
Charity law in England and Wales: Charities Act 2011 and regulations made thereunder	All charities are required to prepare accounts. The regulations require financial statements (other than cash-based receipts and payments accounts prepared by smaller charities) to present a true and fair view of the incoming resources, application of resources and the balance sheet, and to be prepared in accordance with the SORP. However company charities prepare their accounts in accordance with UK company law to give a 'true and fair view'.

Legislation	Overview of requirements
	The Charities SORP (FRS 102) is compatible with the legal requirements, clarifying how they apply to accounting by charities applying FRS 102.
	UK company law prohibits charities from preparing IAS accounts.
Charity law in Scotland: Charities and Trustee Investments Act (Scotland) 2005 and regulations made thereunder	All charities are required to prepare accounts. The regulations require financial statements (other than cash-based receipts and payments accounts prepared by smaller charities) to present a true and fair view of the incoming resources, application of resources and the balance sheet, and to be prepared in accordance with the SORP. These regulations apply equally to company charities.
Charity law in Northern Ireland: Charities Act (Northern Ireland) 2008	The Charities Act 2008 has yet to come fully into effect. The Act provides for all charities to prepare accounts. The Act provides for regulations concerning the financial statements. The financial statements other than cash-based receipts and payments accounts prepared by smaller charities are to present a true and fair view of the incoming resources, application of resources and the balance sheet.
	However company charities prepare their accounts in accordance with UK company law to give a 'true and fair view'.
Friendly and Industrial and Provident Societies Act 1968	Every Society shall prepare a revenue account and a balance sheet giving a true and fair view of the income and expenditure and state of affairs of the Society.
	FRS 102 does not appear to give rise to any legal conflicts for Societies. However, Societies often carry out activities that are regulated and may be required to comply with additional regulations on top of the legal requirements and accounting standards. Some Societies fall within the scope of SORPs, which reflect the requirements of FRS 102.
Friendly Societies Act 1992	Every society shall prepare a balance sheet and an income and expenditure account for each financial year giving a true and fair view of the affairs of the society and its income and expenditure for the year.
	The Regulations[36] make further requirements about the form and content of friendly society accounts, which do not appear inconsistent with the requirements of FRS 102.
The Occupational Pension Schemes (Requirement to obtain Audited Accounts and a Statement from the Auditor) Regulations 1996	The accounts of pension funds within the scope of the regulations should show a true and fair view of the transactions during the year, assets held at the end of the year and liabilities of the scheme, other than those to pay pensions and benefits.
	FRS 102 includes retirement benefit plans as a specialised activity.

[36] *The Friendly Societies (Accounts and Related Provisions) Regulations 1994 (as amended).*

A4.43   Limited liability partnerships (LLPs) will be applying FRS 102 in conjunction with the LLP Regulations or the Small LLP Regulations. In many cases these regulations are similar to the Regulations or the Small Companies Regulations, which reduces the situations in which legal matters relevant to the financial statements of LLPs are not addressed in this Appendix. However, the amendments made to the Regulations and the Small Companies Regulations by *The Companies, Partnerships and Groups (Accounts and Reports) Regulations 2015* (SI 2015/980) have not been reflected in the LLP Regulations or the Small LLP Regulations. This gives rise to some differences for LLPs.

SMALL LLPS

A4.44   The thresholds that are part of the qualifying conditions of a small company and a small LLP have diverged, with the thresholds for a small LLP being lower than those for a small company. Of LLPs, only those qualifying as small (and not otherwise excluded) in accordance with the LLP Regulations, will be able to apply Section 1A *Small Entities*.

A4.45   A small LLP choosing to apply Section 1A shall provide the following disclosures:

(a)   those set out in Appendix C to Section 1A;
(b)   those required by the Small LLP Regulations that are additional to those set out in Appendix C to Section 1A; and
(c)   any additional disclosures necessary to meet the requirement to give a true and fair view, as set out in paragraph 1A.17.

In accordance with paragraph 1A.20 a small LLP is also encouraged to provide the disclosures set out in Appendix D to Section 1A.

ALL LLPS

A4.46   In a relatively small number of areas *The Companies, Partnerships and Groups (Accounts and Reports) Regulations 2015* (SI 2015/980) made changes to the recognition and measurement requirements applicable to companies. These changes have not been made to the LLP Regulations or the Small LLP Regulations and therefore, in a small number of cases, the requirements of FRS 102 will be inconsistent with the LLP Regulations and the Small LLP Regulations. Areas where this may have an impact include:

(a)   the flexibility available in relation to the format of the balance sheet and of the profit and loss account;
(b)   the scope of financial instruments that can be measured at fair value through profit or loss;
(c)   the reversal of impairment losses in relation to goodwill; and
(d)   the application of merger accounting.

If following the requirements of FRS 102 would lead to a conflict with applicable legislation, an LLP shall instead apply its own legal requirements and consider whether disclosure of a departure from FRS 102 is required.

LLP CONSOLIDATED FINANCIAL STATEMENTS

A4.47   When LLPs prepare consolidated financial statements, whether mandatorily or voluntarily, there will also be differences between company law and the similar requirements applicable to LLPs. If following the requirements of FRS 102 would lead to a conflict with applicable legislation, an LLP shall instead apply its own legal requirements and consider whether disclosure of a departure from FRS 102 is required.

Appendix V
Previous consultations

The requirements in FRSs 100 to 102 are the outcome of a lengthy and extensive consultation. The FRC (and formerly the ASB) together with the Department for Business, Innovation and Skills have consulted on the future of accounting standards in the UK and Republic of Ireland (RoI) over a ten-year period.

A5.1

Year	Consultation
2002	DTI[37] consults on adoption of IAS Regulation
2004	Discussion Paper – Strategy for Convergence with IFRS
2005	Exposure Draft – Policy Statement: The Role of the ASB
2006	Public Meeting and Proposals for Comment
2006	Press Notice seeking views
2007	Consultation Paper – Proposed IFRS for SMEs
2009	Consultation Paper – Policy Proposal: The future of UK GAAP
2010	Request for Responses – Development of the Impact Assessment
2010	Financial Reporting Exposure Drafts 43 and 44
2011	Financial Reporting Exposure Draft 45
2012	Financial Reporting Exposure Drafts 46, 47 and 48
2012	Financial Reporting Exposure Draft: Amendment to FRED 48

---

[37] *The Department of Trade and Industry (DTI) was a United Kingdom government department which was replaced with the announcement of the creation of the Department for Business, Enterprise and Regulatory Reform and the Department for Innovation, Universities and Skills on 28 June 2007, which were themselves merged into the Department for Business, Innovation and Skills (BIS) on 6 June 2009.*

2004

A5.2   In 2004 the Discussion Paper contained two key elements underpinning the proposals: firstly that UK and Republic of Ireland (RoI) accounting standards should be based on IFRS and secondly that a phased approach to the introduction of the standards should be adopted.

A5.3   The ASB embarked on the phased approach and issued a number of standards based on IFRS. The majority of respondents agreed with a framework based on IFRS, and although supportive overall, the response to the phased approach was mixed.

2005

A5.4   In its 2005 Exposure Draft (2005 ED) of a Policy Statement *Accounting standard-setting in a changing environment: The role of the Accounting Standards Board*, amongst other aspects of its role, the ASB identified its intention to converge with IFRS by implementing new IFRS in the UK as soon as possible. It also proposed to continue the phased approach to adopting UK accounting standards based on older IFRSs, but recognised there was little case for being more prescriptive than IFRS.

A5.5   Although the ASB had, in the 2005 ED, wanted to move the debate on to how it would seek to influence the IASB's agenda, respondents' main concern remained about convergence. In 2005, the ASB issued an exposure draft proposing the IASB's standard on Business Combinations be adopted in the UK and RoI. This exposure draft highlighted the complexity of a mixed set of UK accounting standards, with some based on IFRSs and others developed independently by the ASB. The majority of respondents continued to agree with the aim of basing UK accounting standards on IFRS, but a broader set of views on how to achieve this was emerging.

A5.6   As time progressed the ASB formed the view that convergence by adopting certain IFRSs was not meeting the needs of its constituents, which no longer included quoted groups. The ASB was concerned about the complexity of certain IFRSs, and it noted that introducing them piecemeal created complications and anomalies within the body of current FRSs. This arose because IFRS-based standards were not an exact replacement for current FRSs and many consequential amendments were required to 'fit' each replacement IFRS-based standard into the existing body of UK FRS. The ASB agreed to continue with its convergence programme, but decided to re-examine how to achieve this.

2006

A5.7   The ASB published revised proposals to be discussed at the 2006 public meeting. By this time the IASB had started its IFRS for SMEs project, and the ASB decided this might have a role as one of the tiers in the UK financial reporting framework. The ASB proposed a 'big bang' with new IFRS-based UK accounting standards mandatory from a single date, 1 January 2009. The ASB's proposal was for a three-tier system, with Tier 1 being EU-adopted IFRS, and the other two tiers being developed as the IASB progressed with its project on the IFRS for SMEs.

A5.8   Those attending the public meeting supported the aim of basing UK and RoI accounting standards on IFRS and adapting them to ensure they were appropriate for the entities applying them.

A5.9   Taking this feedback into account, later in 2006 the ASB issued a Press Notice (PN 289) seeking views on its current thinking:

(a)   All quoted and publicly accountable companies should apply EU-adopted IFRS.
(b)   The FRSSE should be retained and extended to include medium-sized entities.
(c)   UK subsidiaries of groups applying full IFRS should apply EU-adopted IFRS, but with reduced disclosure requirements.
(d)   No firm decision on the remainder (Tier 2), but options included extending the FRSSE, extending full IFRS, maintaining separate UK accounting standards or some combination of these.

The responses were mixed, but there was agreement that whatever the solution, it should be based on IFRS and there should be different reporting tiers to ensure proportionality.   **A5.10**

2007

The IASB published an exposure draft of its IFRS for SMEs in early 2007; shortly afterwards the ASB published its own consultation paper. This sought views on how the IFRS for SMEs might fit into the future UK financial reporting framework, for example whether it might be appropriate for Tier 2, with the FRSSE continuing for those eligible for the small companies' regime.   **A5.11**

Feedback on the IFRS for SMEs was largely positive: it would be suitable for Tier 2, it was international, it was compatible with IFRS, and it represented a significant simplification. Overall, it was seen as a workable alternative to IFRS. In addition, respondents wanted to retain the FRSSE (because it reduces the regulatory burden on smaller entities) and to give subsidiaries the option of applying the IFRS for SMEs as well as a reduced disclosure regime if applying full IFRS.   **A5.12**

2009

The IFRS for SMEs was published in 2009, allowing the ASB to further develop its proposals in the Consultation Paper *Policy Proposal: The future of UK GAAP*. The proposals were largely consistent with the cumulative results of the preceding consultations and included: **A5.13**

(a)   a move to an IFRS-based framework;
(b)   a three-tier approach;
(c)   publicly accountable entities would be Tier 1 and would apply EU-adopted IFRS;
(d)   small companies would be Tier 3 and continue to apply the FRSSE; and
(e)   other entities would be Tier 2 and should apply a UK and RoI accounting standard based on the IFRS for SMEs.

The only significant proposal that was inconsistent with respondents' previous comments was that subsidiaries should simply apply the requirement of the tier they individually met – respondents had wanted subsidiaries to be able to take advantage of disclosure exemptions, and at that time the ASB had yet to be convinced that significant cost savings were available from a reduced disclosure framework. Taking into account the feedback received, this proposal was subsequently reversed and the reduced disclosure framework was incorporated into FREDs 43 and then 46, and it is now set out in FRS 101.   **A5.14**

In addition to the many useful and detailed points made, some common themes included general agreement that change was needed to UK accounting standards and that there was support for many of the changes proposed in the consultation paper.   **A5.15**

2010 ONWARDS

The request for responses to aid development of the Impact Assessment focused on obtaining feedback on the expected costs, benefits and impact of the proposals subsequently   **A5.16** set out in FREDs 43 and 44, rather than on the accounting principles. As the focus was on costs and benefits no specific question was asked about the principle of the proposed introduction of an IFRS-based framework, but nevertheless respondents commented on this: of the 32 responses received only 12.5 per cent did not agree with the introduction of an IFRS-based framework.

A5.17   FRED 43 and 44 issued in October 2010 set out the draft suggested text for two new accounting standards that would replace the majority of extant Financial Reporting Standards (current FRS) in the UK and RoI. The ASB issued a supplementary FRED addressing specific needs of public benefit entities (FRED 45) in March 2011. The ASB then updated FREDs 43, 44 and 45, replacing them with the revised FREDs 46, 47 and 48 in January 2012, by eliminating the concept of public accountability and by introducing a number of accounting treatment options that are available in EU-adopted IFRS. The Accounting Council's advice to the FRC to issue FRSs 100 to 102 includes more discussion of the feedback received on FREDs 43 to 48 and how the proposals have been refined and developed into the standards.

HOW HAVE THE PROPOSALS BEEN DEVELOPED?

A5.18   As set out above, the FRC, the Accounting Council (and previously the ASB) have consulted regularly on the future of financial reporting in the UK and RoI. Over the consultations the ASB's (and the Accounting Council's) thinking has evolved based on careful consideration of the feedback at each stage. Whilst responses were sometimes mixed, there has been agreement that:

(a)   current FRS, which are a mixture of Statements of Standard Accounting Practice (SSAPs) issued by the Consultative Committee of Accounting Bodies, FRSs developed and issued by the ASB and IFRS-based standards issued by the ASB to converge with international standards, are an uncomfortable mismatch that lack strong underlying principles or cohesion; and

(b)   whatever the solution, it should be based on IFRS and there should be different reporting tiers to ensure proportionality.

A5.19   During the consultation process to date, the Accounting Council and formerly the ASB have been guided by the following principles:

(a)   The framework must be fit for purpose, so that each entity required to produce true and fair financial statements under UK and RoI law will deliver financial statements that are suited to the needs of its primary users. The Accounting Council has kept in close contact with constituent users on this point, including investors, creditor institutions and the tax authorities.

(b)   The framework must be proportionate, so that preparing entities are not unduly burdened by costs that outweigh the benefit to them and to the primary users of information in their financial statements. The FRC believes that the proposals will produce a lower cost regime, while enhancing user benefits. It has carried out a consultation stage impact assessment with input from interested parties, and will continue to assess cost-benefit issues.

(c)   The framework must be in line with UK company law. This determines which entities must produce true and fair financial statements. Exemptions within the law have generally been retained. The detailed requirements of the Companies Act 2006 are driven to a great extent by the European Accounting Directives, which are being revised[38].

---

[38] *The EU's consultation process on review of the Accounting Directives is summarised at http://ec.europa.eu/ internal_market/ accounting/sme_accounting/review_directives_en.htm*

(d)   The framework must be future-proofed, where possible. The FRC will continue to monitor the situation and has sovereignty over UK accounting standards (subject to the law). Changes to the Accounting Directives may lead to further developments, for example the European Council and European Parliament decision to permit Member States an option to treat micro-entities as a separate category of Company and exempt them from certain accounting requirements.

SUMMARY OF OUTREACH

During the development and throughout the consultation period of FREDs 43 to 48, the ASB undertook an extensive programme of outreach aimed at raising awareness of the proposals and to address the view (held by some) that previous consultations had not gathered sufficient evidence to support and test the assumptions made.   **A5.20**

As part of the outreach programme to obtain both formal and informal feedback, a series of meetings and events took place with users, including with lenders to small and medium-sized entities. Lenders noted that financial statements are an important part of their decision-making process when considering whether to provide finance and, whilst a decision to provide finance is not based on financial statements alone, they provide useful information and verification to the lender.   **A5.21**

Although the ASB and the Accounting Council employed their best efforts to obtain feedback from users (a constituent group historically difficult to engage with formally) it is disappointing that limited formal responses were received and the Accounting Council has not been more successful in obtaining input from users.   **A5.22**

In addition, a review was made of academic research that addressed the users of the financial statements of small and medium-sized entities. The conclusion drawn from the research was that many entities requested financial statements from Companies House when considering whether to trade with another entity. The European Federation of Accountants and Auditors (EFAA) issued, in May 2011, a statement that identified the users of financial statements, noting who the users of SMEs' financial statements are and that information on the public record assists all users of financial statements of SMEs by providing, in an efficient manner, basic information that protects their rights.   **A5.23**

The ASB considered that the outreach programme had gleaned information from people who would not normally submit formal responses to a consultation and provided very useful information that could be used in developing the next stage of the project. The ASB noted that whilst this information was not part of the public record, as are formal consultation responses, it could use the information to assist in developing the revised FREDs 46 to 48, supplementing information contained in responses, and would seek further comment in the next stage of its deliberations.   **A5.24**

The Accounting Council continued the work of the ASB in finalising FRSs 100 to 102. The responses to FREDs 46 to 48 were analysed and discussed, and engagements were conducted to take into account the views and suggestions of all relevant associations and contacts. Respondents and outreach contacts were satisfied with FREDs 46 to 48, and many of the response letters were forthcoming in their overall praise for the proposals. A significant number of constituents anticipated cost savings arising from the application of FRS 101. Many respondents considered that FRS 102 would improve UK accounting standards, in particular by introducing requirements for accounting for financial instruments. Further they considered that the improvements will be achieved in a way that will be proportionate to the needs of users, and that once the transition phase has been overcome, it will have the effect of reducing the reporting burden on those UK companies that adopt it.   **A5.25**

Appendix VI
Republic of Ireland (RoI) legal references

A6.1   Appendix VI: *Republic of Ireland (RoI) legal references* will be updated as appropriate for both the Companies Act 2014 and the Irish legislation implementing the EU Accounting Directive once the latter has been made. This will be made available on the FRC website and included in the next edition of FRS 102.

Amendments to FRS 102
The Financial Reporting Standard applicable
in the UK and Republic of Ireland – Fair value
hierarchy disclosures

(March 2016)

Contents

Editor's note: The FRC has published these amendments that are relevant only to financial institutions and retirement benefit plans as defined in FRS 102. These amendments apply for accounting periods beginning on or after 1 January 2017. Early application is permitted with immediate effect. If an entity applies these amendments to an accounting period beginning before 1 January 2017 it shall disclose that fact.

SUMMARY

With effect from 1 January 2015 the Financial Reporting Council (FRC) revised financial **(i)**
reporting standards in the United Kingdom and Republic of Ireland. The revisions
fundamentally reformed financial reporting, replacing the extant standards with five
Financial Reporting Standards:

(a) FRS 100 *Application of Financial Reporting Requirements*;
(b) FRS 101 *Reduced Disclosure Framework*;
(c) FRS 102 *The Financial Reporting Standard applicable in the UK and Republic of Ireland*;
(d) FRS 103 *Insurance Contracts*; and
(e) FRS 104 *Interim Financial Reporting*.

The FRC has also issued FRS 105 *The Financial Reporting Standard applicable to the Micro-entities Regime* to support the implementation of the new micro-entities regime.

These limited amendments to FRS 102 simplify the preparation of disclosures about
financial instruments for financial institutions and retirement benefit plans.

The FRC's overriding objective in setting accounting standards is to enable users of **(ii)**
accounts to receive high-quality understandable financial reporting proportionate to the
size and complexity of the entity and users' information needs.

In meeting this objective, the FRC aims to provide succinct financial reporting standards **(iii)**
that:

(a) have consistency with international accounting standards through the application
     of an IFRS-based solution unless an alternative clearly better meets the overriding
     objective;
(b) reflect up-to-date thinking and developments in the way entities operate and the
     transactions they undertake;
(c) balance consistent principles for accounting by all UK and Republic of Ireland
     entities with practical solutions, based on size, complexity, public interest and users'
     information needs;
(d) promote efficiency within groups; and
(e) are cost-effective to apply.

Amendments to FRS 102 – Fair value hierarchy disclosures

These amendments to FRS 102, which are relevant only to financial institutions and **(iv)**
retirement benefit plans, were consulted on in FRED 62 *Draft amendments to FRS 102 – Fair value hierarchy disclosures*. They relate to the disclosure of financial instruments in
an analysis based on the fair value hierarchy. Taking into account the feedback to FRED 62
these amendments simplify the preparation of disclosures about financial instruments
for the entities affected, whilst increasing the consistency with disclosures required by
EU-adopted IFRS that users of the financial statements will often be familiar with.

AMENDMENTS TO FRS 102 *THE FINANCIAL REPORTING STANDARD APPLICABLE IN THE UK AND REPUBLIC OF IRELAND*

Amendments to Section 1 Scope

1   The following paragraph sets out the amendments to Section 1 *Scope* (inserted text is underlined).

2   Paragraph 1.16 is inserted as follows:

> 1.16 In March 2016 amendments were made to paragraphs 34.22 and 34.42 of this FRS, revising the disclosure requirements for financial institutions and retirement benefit plans. An entity shall apply these amendments for accounting periods beginning on or after 1 January 2017. Early application is permitted. If an entity applies these amendments to an accounting period beginning before 1 January 2017 it shall disclose that fact.

Amendments to Section 34 Specialised Activities

3   The following paragraphs set out the amendments to Section 34 *Specialised Activities* (deleted text is struck through, inserted text is underlined).

4   Paragraph 34.22 is amended as follows:

> 34.22 For financial instruments held at **fair value** in the statement of financial position, a financial institution shall disclose for each class of financial instrument, an analysis of the level in the following fair value hierarchy (as set out in paragraph 11.27) into which the fair value measurements are categorised. A fair value measurement is categorised in its entirety on the basis of the lowest level input that is significant to the fair value measurement in its entirety.
>
> - Level 1: The unadjusted quoted price in an **active market** for identical **assets** or **liabilities** that the entity can access at the measurement date.
> - Level 2: Inputs other than quoted prices included within Level 1 that are observable (ie developed using market data) for the asset or liability, either directly or indirectly.
> - Level 3: Inputs are unobservable (ie for which market data is unavailable) for the asset or liability.

5   In paragraph 34.27 'assets' will no longer be shown in bold type.

6   Paragraph 34.42 is amended as follows:

> 34.42 For financial instruments held at fair value in the statement of net assets available for benefits, a retirement benefit plan shall disclose for each class of financial instrument, an analysis of the level in the following fair value hierarchy (as set out in paragraph 11.27) into which the fair value measurements are categorised. A fair value measurement is categorised in its entirety on the basis of the lowest level input that is significant to the fair value measurement in its entirety.
>
> - Level 1: The unadjusted quoted price in an **active market** for identical assets or liabilities that the entity can access at the measurement date.
> - Level 2: Inputs other than quoted prices included within Level 1 that are observable (ie developed using market data) for the asset or liability, either directly or indirectly.
> - Level 3: Inputs are unobservable (ie for which market data is unavailable) for the asset or liability.

APPROVAL BY THE FRC

Amendments to FRS 102 The Financial Reporting Standard applicable in the UK and Republic of Ireland – Fair value hierarchy disclosures was approved for issue by the Board of the Financial Reporting Council on 3 March 2016, following its consideration of the Accounting Council's Advice.

THE ACCOUNTING COUNCIL'S ADVICE TO THE FRC TO ISSUE *AMENDMENTS TO FRS 102 – FAIR VALUE HIERARCHY DISCLOSURES*

Introduction

1   This report provides an overview of the main issues that have been considered by the Accounting Council in advising the Financial Reporting Council (FRC) to issue *Amendments to FRS 102 The Financial Reporting Standard applicable in the UK and Republic of Ireland – Fair value hierarchy disclosures*.

2   The FRC, in accordance with the *Statutory Auditors (Amendment of Companies Act 2006 and Delegation of Functions etc) Order 2012* (SI 2012/1741), is a prescribed body for issuing accounting standards in the UK. The *Foreword to Accounting Standards* sets out the application of accounting standards in the Republic of Ireland.

3   In accordance with the *FRC Codes and Standards: procedures*, any proposal to issue, amend or withdraw a code or standard is put to the FRC Board with the full advice of the relevant Councils and/or the Codes & Standards Committee. Ordinarily, the FRC Board will only reject the advice put to it where:

   (a)   it is apparent that a significant group of stakeholders has not been adequately consulted;

   (b)   the necessary assessment of the impact of the proposal has not been completed, including an analysis of costs and benefits;

   (c)   insufficient consideration has been given to the timing or cost of implementation; or

   (d)   the cumulative impact of a number of proposals would make the adoption of an otherwise satisfactory proposal inappropriate.

4   The FRC has established the Accounting Council as the relevant Council to assist it in the setting of accounting standards.

Advice

5   The Accounting Council is advising the FRC to issue *Amendments to FRS 102 The Financial Reporting Standard applicable in the UK and Republic of Ireland – Fair value hierarchy disclosures*.

6   The Accounting Council advises that these amendments will reduce the costs of complying with FRS 102 *The Financial Reporting Standard applicable in the UK and Republic of Ireland* for financial institutions and retirement benefit plans, whilst increasing the consistency with disclosures required by EU-adopted IFRS that users of the financial statements will often be familiar with.

7   The Accounting Council's Advice to the FRC to issue FRS 102 was set out in the standard. The Accounting Council's Advice to the FRC in respect of these amendments will be included in the revised FRS 102.

Background

8   The FRC had received feedback that amending the fair value disclosure requirements applicable to financial institutions and retirement benefit plans would reduce the costs of complying with FRS 102, and allow these entities to provide information to users that is more consistent with EU-adopted IFRS. This should also make it easier for users to make comparisons between the financial statements of these entities and those applying EU-adopted IFRS.

The FRC consulted on proposals to address this in FRED 62 *Draft amendments to FRS 102 – Fair value hierarchy disclosures.* The responses to FRED 62 confirmed the earlier feedback.   **9**

Amendments to FRS 102

In developing its advice to the FRC, the Accounting Council was guided by the overriding   **10** objective to enable users of accounts to receive high-quality understandable financial reporting proportionate to the size and complexity of the entity and users' information needs.

In meeting this objective, the FRC aims to provide succinct financial reporting standards   **11** that:

(a)   have consistency with international accounting standards through the application of an IFRS-based solution unless an alternative clearly better meets the overriding objective;

(b)   reflect up-to-date thinking and developments in the way entities operate and the transactions they undertake;

(c)   balance consistent principles for accounting by all UK and Republic of Ireland entities with practical solutions, based on size, complexity, public interest and users' information needs;

(d)   promote efficiency within groups; and

(e)   are cost-effective to apply.

After FRS 102 was issued the FRC received feedback, for example in response to FRED 54   **12** *Draft amendments to FRS 102 – Basic financial instruments,* from the representative bodies of some financial institutions and retirement benefit plans suggesting that the disclosure requirements for these entities, relating to financial instruments held at fair value, could be made more cost-effective, whilst increasing their usefulness to users of the financial statements. For those users familiar with the IFRS disclosures, the consistency of disclosure with IFRS may also reduce costs or effort of comparison and the possibility of confusion. No amendments were made at the time of finalising the amendments resulting from FRED 54, because this issue was outside the scope of that consultation. However, the FRC agreed to consult on this issue as part of the triennial review of FRS 102.

Following the postponement of the triennial review of FRS 102 by one year, the FRC   **13** consulted on proposals to amend the disclosure requirements for financial institutions and retirement benefit plans in FRED 62 issued in November 2015. The amendments do not affect any other entities applying FRS 102, and do not otherwise disrupt the three-year stable platform for small entities.

In advising that an amendment be made to FRS 102, the Accounting Council carefully   **14** considered how to balance the desire for stability in FRS 102 with requests for improvements that are expected to lead to greater efficiency. The Accounting Council concluded that as the amendment affected only a small number of entities (and that stability would be retained for the remainder) and related to streamlining disclosures it was appropriate to advise a change in FRS 102 outside the triennial review. This was supported by the respondents to FRED 62, a number of whom encouraged the amendments to be finalised as soon as possible.

The Accounting Council noted that paragraphs 34.22 and 34.42 of FRS 102 required   **15** financial institutions and retirement benefit plans, respectively, to provide disclosures about financial instruments held at fair value analysed by the level of the fair value hierarchy in paragraph 11.27 of FRS 102. This hierarchy is not the same as the hierarchy set out in

IFRS 13 *Fair Value Measurement*, and therefore the disclosures provided by a financial institution or retirement benefit plan applying FRS 102 would not be directly comparable to those provided by an entity applying EU-adopted IFRS. The SORPs for Authorised Funds, Investment Trust Companies and Pension Schemes require, or permit, additional disclosure from entities within their scope in order to improve this comparability. The Accounting Council also noted that some financial institutions previously applied FRS 29 *Financial instruments: Disclosures*, which required disclosure according to a fair value hierarchy that is consistent with IFRS 13, and therefore for these entities FRS 102 had introduced a departure from IFRS.

16   In order to make FRS 102 more cost-effective, the Accounting Council advises that financial institutions and retirement benefit plans should categorise fair value measurements into levels consistent with the fair value hierarchy set out in IFRS 13. This is consistent with the aims for developing and maintaining FRS 102.

Impact on other entities applying FRS 102

17   Other than financial institutions and retirement benefit plans, entities applying FRS 102 are not required to provide disclosures in accordance with the fair value hierarchy as paragraph 11.43 requires information about the basis for determining fair value, but does not require this to be categorised according to the fair value hierarchy in paragraph 11.27. Therefore the amendments do not impact on any other entities applying FRS 102.

18   The Accounting Council notes, however, that this leads to an inconsistency within FRS 102, whereby the hierarchy described in paragraph 11.27 for the purposes of determining a process for estimating fair values will no longer be consistent with the hierarchy used for disclosure purposes in Section 34 *Specialised Activities*. Therefore the Accounting Council advises that, as part of the first triennial review of FRS 102, consideration should be given to revising paragraph 11.27. Respondents to FRED 62 agreed with this conclusion.

Effective date

19   The Accounting Council advises that these amendments to FRS 102 should be effective for accounting periods beginning on or after 1 January 2017, with early adoption permitted.

20   However, as the amendments relate to disclosure only, and early application is permitted, an entity may be able to apply the amendments to financial statements for periods ending on 31 December 2015 if those financial statements are approved after these amendments are issued.

21   The Accounting Council also notes that amendments to the relevant SORPs will not be necessary before any changes to FRS 102 can take effect because a change in accounting standards after a SORP has been issued means that any inconsistent provisions of a SORP cease to have effect. The relevant SORPs will, however, require amendment in due course.

Approval of this Advice

22   This advice to the FRC was approved by the Accounting Council on 25 February 2016.

FRS 103
Insurance Contracts – Consolidated accounting and reporting requirements for entities in the UK and Republic of Ireland issuing insurance contracts

(March 2014)

Contents

Paragraphs

Prospective amendments: FRED 64 (December 2015) proposes amendments to this Standard.

Editor's note: This accounting standard issued by the FRC is relevant to entities applying FRS 102 that have insurance contracts. This standard replaces the withdrawn FRS 27 *Life Assurance* and ABI Statement Of Recommended Practice on Accounting For Insurance Business (SORP) (December 2005) with effect for accounting periods beginning on or after 1 January 2015.

SUMMARY

(i)   In 2012 and 2013 the Financial Reporting Council (FRC) revised financial reporting standards in the United Kingdom and Republic of Ireland. The revisions fundamentally reformed financial reporting, replacing almost all extant standards with three Financial Reporting Standards:

> FRS 100   *Application of Financial Reporting Requirements;*
> FRS 101   *Reduced Disclosure Framework;* and
> FRS 102   *The Financial Reporting Standard applicable in the UK and Republic of Ireland.*
> FRS 103   *Insurance Contracts* is a fourth standard added to the suite of accounting standards, which is relevant to entities applying FRS 102 that have insurance contracts.

(ii)   The FRC's overriding objective in setting accounting standards is to enable users of accounts to receive high-quality understandable financial reporting proportionate to the size and complexity of the entity and users' information needs.

(iii) In meeting this objective, the FRC aims to provide succinct financial reporting standards that:

(a)   have consistency with international accounting standards through the application of an IFRS-based solution unless an alternative clearly better meets the overriding objective;

(b)   reflect up-to-date thinking and developments in the way entities operate and the transactions they undertake;

(c)   balance consistent principles for accounting by all UK and Republic of Ireland entities with practical solutions, based on size, complexity, public interest and users' information needs;

(d)   promote efficiency within groups; and

(e)   are cost-effective to apply.

(iv)   The requirements in this Financial Reporting Standard (FRS) take into consideration:

(a)   the findings from the previous consultations on the future of financial reporting in the UK and Republic of Ireland that took place between 2002 and 2012, which includes responses to the Discussion Paper *Insurance Accounting – Mind the UK GAAP* issued in 2012; and

(b)   the responses to FRED 49: Draft FRS 103 *Insurance Contracts* issued in July 2013.

(v)   Entities that are applying FRS 102, whether or not they are 'insurance companies', shall also apply this FRS to insurance contracts (including reinsurance contracts) that the entity issues and reinsurance contracts that the entity holds, and to other financial instruments that the entity issues with a discretionary participation feature.

FRS 103 *Insurance Contracts*

(vi)   This FRS (and the accompanying non-mandatory Implementation Guidance) consolidates existing financial reporting requirements and guidance for insurance contracts. The requirements in this FRS (and the guidance in the accompanying non-mandatory Implementation Guidance) are based on the International Accounting Standards Board's (IASB) IFRS 4 *Insurance Contracts* extant in 2013 (except to the extent that it was amended by IFRS 13 *Fair Value Measurement*), the requirements of FRS 27 *Life Assurance* (prior to it being withdrawn by this standard) and elements of the Association of British Insurers' *Statement of Recommended Practice on Accounting for Insurance Business* (the ABI SORP) (published in December 2005 and amended in December 2006).

In particular, this FRS:

(a)   allows entities, generally, to continue with their existing accounting policies for insurance contracts including the appropriate measurement of long-term insurance business, whilst permitting limited improvements to accounting by insurers; and

(b)   requires disclosure that:

(i)   identifies and explains the amounts in an insurer's financial statements arising from the insurance contracts (including reinsurance contracts) it issues and reinsurance contracts that it holds;

(ii)   relate to the financial strength of entities carrying on long-term insurance business; and

(iii) helps users of those financial statements understand the amount, timing and uncertainty of future cash flows from those insurance contracts.

(vii) This FRS allows entities, generally, to continue with their current accounting practices for insurance contracts, but permits entities the same flexibility to make improvements (subject to legal and regulatory requirements) as entities in the UK and Republic of Ireland applying IFRS 4 have, because the FRC does not want the standard to be more onerous to apply than IFRS 4. Nevertheless, this FRS is part of a suite of new accounting standards, including FRS 102, that improve financial reporting for financial instruments (other than insurance contracts); some of the requirements of FRS 102 and of this FRS in relation to financial instruments will lead to changes for insurers.

(viii) One of the reasons that this FRS permits entities to, generally, continue with their current accounting practice is that the FRC expects this FRS to have a limited life. The FRC expects to review this standard once the IASB has issued its updated standard on insurance contracts. The most appropriate timing for this review cannot be determined at the present time. The FRC may make interim amendments to FRS 103 once changes in the regulatory regime for insurers have been finalised.

Entities that are not legally constituted as insurance providers

(ix) Some entities that are not legally constituted as insurance providers may be issuing contracts meeting the definition of an insurance contract in this FRS. Examples include appliance servicing agreements and some product warranty arrangements (when issued by another party for the manufacturer, dealer or retailer). Although such contracts are within the scope of this FRS an entity should generally be able to continue to apply its previous accounting policies to such contracts, as noted above, although additional considerations may be relevant, for example the liability adequacy test and additional disclosures to those provided in the past.

Organisation of FRS 103

(x)   All the paragraphs of FRS 103 have equal authority. Some appendices are an integral part of the FRS while others provide guidance concerning its application; each specifies its status. FRS 103 is accompanied by non-mandatory Implementation Guidance providing guidance on applying:

(a)   the requirements of FRS 103;

(b)   the requirements and principles of FRS 102 by entities with general insurance business or long-term insurance business; and

(c)   the requirements of Schedule 3 to the Regulations.

(xi)   The elements of the ABI SORP that have been included are largely set out in Section 2 *Guidance for entities with general insurance business or long-term insurance business* of the Implementation Guidance.

(xii)   This FRS is set out in Sections 1 to 6, the Glossary (Appendix I) and the Definition of an Insurance Contract (Appendix II). Terms defined in the Glossary are in **bold type** the first time they appear in each section in the FRS.

FRS 103 INSURANCE CONTRACTS – CONSOLIDATED ACCOUNTING AND REPORTING REQUIREMENTS FOR ENTITIES IN THE UK AND REPUBLIC OF IRELAND ISSUING INSURANCE CONTRACTS

Section 1 Scope

Scope of this Financial Reporting Standard

1.1   This FRS applies to **financial statements** prepared by an entity that applies **FRS 102** and that are intended to give a true and fair view of a reporting entity's **financial position** and **profit or loss** (or income and expenditure) for a period.

1.2   An entity that applies FRS 102 shall apply this FRS to:

(a)   **insurance contracts** (including **reinsurance contracts**) that it issues and reinsurance contracts that it holds; and

(b)   **financial instruments** (other than insurance contracts) that it issues with a **discretionary participation feature** (see paragraph 2.30).

1.3   This FRS applies to entities with insurance contracts and financial instruments with discretionary participation features within the scope of paragraph 1.2 as follows:

(a)   Section 1 Scope, Section 2 *Accounting Policies, Recognition and Measurement*, Section 4 *Disclosure* and Section 6 *Transition to this FRS* apply to all entities applying this FRS.

(b)   Section 3 *Recognition and Measurement: Requirements for entities with long-term insurance business* and Section 5 *Disclosure: Additional requirements for with-profits business* only apply to entities with **long-term insurance business**.

(c)   Appendix II: *Definition of an insurance contract* applies to all entities.

The **Regulations** (or other legal framework that applies to the entity) may set out requirements in addition to those within this FRS.

1.4   The Implementation Guidance accompanying this FRS provides additional guidance for applying:

(a)   the requirements of this FRS;

(b)   the requirements or principles of FRS 102 by entities with **general insurance business** or long-term insurance business; and

(c)   the requirements of Schedule 3 to the Regulations.

In particular the Implementation Guidance may be relevant as follows:

(a)   Section 1: *Guidance for entities with long-term business* provides guidance on applying Section 3 of FRS 103.

(b)   Section 2: *Guidance for entities with general insurance business or long-term business* provides guidance for all entities applying FRS 103.

(c)   Section 3: *Guidance on capital disclosures for entities with long-term insurance business* applies to entities with long-term insurance business.

Paragraph 2.3 permits entities to change their **accounting policies**, either on adoption   **1.5**
of this FRS or subsequently, providing the new accounting policies meet certain
criteria. Entities that are setting accounting policies in relation to insurance contracts, or
other financial instruments with discretionary participation features, for the first time,
shall first consider the requirements of Section 3, the Regulations and any relevant parts
of FRS 102, as a means of establishing current practice as a benchmark before assessing
whether to set accounting policies that differ from those benchmark policies in accordance
with paragraph 2.3. The Implementation Guidance accompanying this FRS also provides
guidance.

This FRS does not address other aspects of accounting by **insurers**, such as accounting   **1.6**
for **financial assets** held by insurers and **financial liabilities** issued by insurers
(see Sections 11 *Basic Financial Instruments*, 12 *Other Financial Instruments Issues*
and 34 *Specialised Activities* of FRS 102), except in paragraph 1.8 and in the transitional
provisions in paragraph 6.4.

An entity shall not apply this FRS to: **1.7**

(a)   product warranties issued directly by a manufacturer, dealer or retailer (see Sections 21
      Provisions and Contingencies and 23 *Revenue* of FRS 102);
(b)   employers' assets and **liabilities** under employee benefit plans (see Sections 26
      Share-based Payment and 28 *Employee Benefits* of FRS 102) and retirement benefit
      obligations reported by defined benefit retirement plans (see Section 34 of FRS 102);
(c)   contractual rights or contractual obligations that are contingent on the future use
      of, or right to use, a non-financial item (for example, some licence fees, royalties,
      contingent lease payments and similar items), as well as a lessee's residual value
      guarantee embedded in a finance lease (see Sections 18 *Intangible Assets other than
      Goodwill*, 20 *Leases* and 23 of FRS 102);
(d)   **financial guarantee contracts** unless the issuer has previously asserted explicitly
      that it regards such contracts as insurance contracts and has used accounting
      applicable to insurance contracts, in which case the issuer may elect to apply either
      Section 21 of FRS 102 or this FRS to such financial guarantee contracts. The issuer
      may make that election contract by contract, but the election for each contract is
      irrevocable;
(e)   contingent consideration payable or receivable in a **business combination**
      (see Section 19 *Business Combinations and Goodwill* of FRS 102); or
(f)   **direct insurance contracts** that the entity holds (ie direct insurance contracts in
      which the entity is the **policyholder**) (for which an accounting policy shall be
      selected in accordance with the principles of FRS 102). However, a **cedant** shall
      apply this FRS to reinsurance contracts that it holds.

Some contracts that have the legal form of an insurance contract do not meet the definition   **1.8**
of an insurance contract in this FRS. Paragraph A2.19 provides examples of items that are
not insurance contracts, and paragraphs A2.20 to A2.24 provide further information on
accounting for contracts that are not insurance contracts.

For ease of reference, this FRS describes any entity that issues an insurance contract as   **1.9**
an insurer, whether or not the issuer is regarded as an insurer for legal or supervisory
purposes.

A reinsurance contract is a type of insurance contract. Accordingly, all references in this   **1.10**
FRS to insurance contracts also apply to reinsurance contracts.

Date from which effective and transitional arrangements

1.11   An entity shall apply this FRS for accounting periods beginning on or after 1 January 2015. Early application is permitted provided that if an entity applies this FRS before 1 January 2015 it shall:

(a)   also apply FRS 102 from the same date and is not subject to the transitional arrangements in paragraph 1.14 of FRS 102 relating to entities within the scope of a SORP; and

(b)   disclose the fact that it has applied FRS 103 before 1 January 2015.

Prospective amendments: FRED 64 (December 2015) proposes insertion paragraph 1.11A with effect for annual periods beginning on or after [date].

Compliance with this FRS

1.12   An entity whose financial statements comply with this FRS shall, in addition to its statement of compliance with FRS 102 (made in accordance with paragraphs 3.3 to 3.6 of FRS 102), make an explicit and unreserved statement of compliance with this FRS in the **notes to the financial statements**.

Withdrawal of FRS 27

1.13   FRS 27 *Life Assurance* is superseded on the early application of this FRS. FRS 27 will be withdrawn for accounting periods beginning on or after 1 January 2015.

Consequential amendment to FRS 101 *Reduced Disclosure Framework*

1.14   The following consequential amendment is made to **FRS 101** (inserted text is underlined):

Paragraph (fA) of the Application Guidance: *Amendments to International Financial Reporting Standards as Adopted in the European Union for Compliance with the Act and Regulations* is inserted as follows:

(fA)   Paragraph 14(a) of IFRS 4 *Insurance Contracts* is amended as follows:

(a)   unless otherwise required by the regulatory framework that applies to the entity, shall not recognise as a liability any provisions for possible future claims, if those claims arise under insurance contracts that are not in existence at the end of the reporting period (such as catastrophe provisions and equalisation provisions). The presentation of any such liabilities shall follow the requirements of the Regulations (or other legal framework that applies to the entity).

Section 2 Accounting Policies, Recognition and Measurement

Scope of this section

2.1   This section provides guidance for selecting and applying the **accounting policies** used in the **recognition** and measurement of **insurance contracts** when preparing **financial statements**. Entities with **long-term insurance business** shall also apply the requirements of Section 3 *Recognition and Measurement: Requirements for entities with long-term insurance business* in selecting accounting policies for long-term insurance business.

Changes in accounting policy

2.2   Paragraphs 2.3 to 2.11 apply both to changes made by an **insurer** that already applies this FRS and to changes made by an insurer adopting this FRS for the first time.

As an exception to paragraph 10.8 of **FRS 102** an insurer may change its accounting   **2.3**
policies for insurance contracts if, and only if, the change makes the financial statements
more relevant to the economic decision-making needs of users and no less reliable, or
more reliable and no less relevant to those needs. An insurer shall judge relevance and
reliability by the criteria in paragraph 10.4 of FRS 102 and the qualitative characteristics of
information in financial statements set out in Section 2 *Concepts and Pervasive Principles*
of FRS 102.

To justify changing its accounting policies for insurance contracts, an insurer shall show that   **2.4**
the change brings its financial statements closer to meeting the criteria in paragraph 10.4
of FRS 102, but the change need not achieve full compliance with those criteria. The
following specific issues are discussed below:

(a)   current interest rates (paragraph 2.5);
(b)   continuation of existing practices (paragraph 2.6);
(c)   prudence (paragraph 2.7);
(d)   future investment margins (paragraphs 2.8 to 2.10); and
(e)   shadow accounting (paragraph 2.11).

Current market interest rates

An insurer is permitted, but not required, to change its accounting policies so that it   **2.5**
remeasures designated **insurance liabilities**[1] to reflect current market interest rates and
recognises changes in those **liabilities** in **profit or loss**. At that time, it may also introduce
accounting policies that require other current estimates and assumptions for the designated
liabilities. The election in this paragraph permits an insurer to change its accounting
policies for designated liabilities, without applying those policies consistently to all similar
liabilities as Section 10 *Accounting Policies, Estimates and Errors* of FRS 102 would
otherwise require. If an insurer designates liabilities for this election, it shall continue
to apply current market interest rates (and, if applicable, the other current estimates and
assumptions) consistently in all periods to all these liabilities until they are extinguished.

Continuation of existing practices

An insurer may continue the following practices, but the introduction of any of them does   **2.6**
not satisfy paragraph 10.8(b) of FRS 102:

(a)   unless otherwise required by the **Regulations** (or other legal framework that applies
to the entity), measuring insurance liabilities on an undiscounted basis.
(b)   measuring contractual rights to future investment management fees at an amount
that exceeds their **fair value** as implied by a comparison with current fees charged
by other market participants for similar services. It is likely that the fair value at
inception of those contractual rights equals the origination costs paid, unless
future investment management fees and related costs are out of line with market
comparables.
(c)   as an exception to paragraph 9.17 of FRS 102, using non-uniform accounting policies
for the insurance contracts (and related **deferred acquisition costs** and related
intangible assets, if any) of subsidiaries, except as permitted by paragraph 2.5.
If those accounting policies are not uniform, an insurer may change them if the
change does not make the accounting policies more diverse and also satisfies the
other requirements in this FRS.

---

[1] *In this paragraph, insurance liabilities include related deferred acquisition costs and related intangible assets, such
as those discussed in paragraphs 2.27 and 2.28.*

Prudence

2.7   An insurer need not change its accounting policies for insurance contracts to eliminate excessive prudence. However, if an insurer already measures its insurance contracts with sufficient prudence, it shall not introduce additional prudence.

Future investment margins

2.8   An insurer need not change its accounting policies for insurance contracts to eliminate future investment margins. However, there is a rebuttable presumption that an insurer's financial statements will become less relevant and reliable if it introduces an accounting policy that reflects future investment margins in the measurement of insurance contracts, unless those margins affect the contractual payments. Two examples of accounting policies that reflect those margins are:

(a)   using a discount rate that reflects the estimated return on the insurer's assets; or

(b)   projecting the returns on those assets at an estimated rate of return, **discounting** those projected returns at a different rate and including the result in the measurement of the liability.

2.9   Provided it is permitted by the Regulations an insurer may overcome the rebuttable presumption described in paragraph 2.8 if, and only if, the other components of a change in accounting policies increase the relevance and reliability of its financial statements sufficiently to outweigh the decrease in relevance and reliability caused by the inclusion of future investment margins. For example, suppose that an insurer's **existing accounting policies** for insurance contracts involve excessively prudent assumptions set at inception and a discount rate prescribed by a regulator without direct reference to market conditions, and ignore some embedded **options and guarantees**. The insurer might make its financial statements more relevant and no less reliable by switching to a comprehensive investor-oriented basis of accounting that is widely used and involves:

(a)   current estimates and assumptions;

(b)   a reasonable (but not excessively prudent) adjustment to reflect risk and uncertainty;

(c)   measurements that reflect both the intrinsic value and time value of embedded options and guarantees; and

(d)   a current market discount rate, even if that discount rate reflects the estimated return on the insurer's assets.

2.10   In some measurement approaches, the discount rate is used to determine the **present value** of a future profit margin. That profit margin is then attributed to different periods using a formula. In those approaches, the discount rate affects the measurement of the liability only indirectly. In particular, the use of a less appropriate discount rate has a limited or no effect on the measurement of the liability at inception. However, in other approaches, the discount rate determines the measurement of the liability directly. In the latter case, because the introduction of an asset-based discount rate has a more significant effect, it is highly unlikely that an insurer could overcome the rebuttable presumption described in paragraph 2.8.

Shadow accounting

2.11   In some accounting models, realised gains or losses on an insurer's assets have a direct effect on the measurement of some or all of (a) its insurance liabilities, (b) related deferred acquisition costs and (c) related intangible assets, such as those described in paragraphs 2.27

and 2.28. An insurer is permitted, but not required, to change its accounting policies so that a recognised but unrealised gain or loss on an asset affects those measurements in the same way that a realised gain or loss does. The related adjustment to the insurance liability (or deferred acquisition costs or intangible assets) shall be recognised in other comprehensive income if, and only if, the unrealised gains or losses are recognised in other comprehensive income. This practice is sometimes described as 'shadow accounting'.

Exemption from some requirements of FRS 102

Paragraphs 10.4 to 10.6 of FRS 102 set out how an entity's management shall use its judgement in developing and applying an accounting policy if no FRS or FRC Abstract applies specifically to a transaction, other event or condition. However, this FRS exempts an insurer from the considerations in paragraphs 10.4 to 10.6 of FRS 102 in relation to its accounting policies for: **2.12**

(a)   insurance contracts that it issues (including related **acquisition costs** and related intangible assets, such as those described in paragraphs 2.27 and 2.28, and paragraphs 3.16 to 3.18); and
(b)   **reinsurance contracts** that it holds.

Nevertheless, this FRS does not exempt an insurer from some implications of the considerations in paragraphs 10.4 to 10.6 of FRS 102. Specifically, an insurer: **2.13**

(a)   unless otherwise required by the regulatory framework that applies to the entity, shall not recognise as a liability any provisions for possible future **claims**, if those claims arise under insurance contracts that are not in existence at the end of the **reporting period** (such as **catastrophe provisions** and **equalisation provisions**). The presentation of any such liabilities shall follow the requirements of the Regulations (or other legal framework that applies to the entity);
(b)   shall carry out the **liability adequacy test** described in paragraphs 2.14 to 2.18;
(c)   shall remove an insurance liability (or a part of an insurance liability) from its **statement of financial position** when, and only when, it is extinguished—ie when the obligation specified in the contract is discharged or cancelled or expires;
(d)   shall not offset:
   (i)   **reinsurance assets** against the related insurance liabilities; or
   (ii)   income or expense from reinsurance contracts against the expense or income from the related insurance contracts; and
(e)   shall consider whether its reinsurance assets are impaired (see paragraph 2.19).

Liability adequacy test

An insurer shall assess at the end of each reporting period whether its recognised insurance liabilities are adequate, using current estimates of future cash flows under its insurance contracts. If that assessment shows that the carrying amount of its insurance liabilities (less related deferred acquisition costs and related intangible assets, such as those discussed in paragraphs 2.27 and 2.28) is inadequate in the light of the estimated future cash flows, the entire deficiency shall be recognised in profit or loss. **2.14**

2.15   If an insurer applies a liability adequacy test that meets specified minimum requirements, this FRS imposes no further requirements. The minimum requirements are the following:

(a)   The test considers current estimates of all contractual cash flows, and of related cash flows such as claims handling costs, as well as cash flows resulting from embedded options and guarantees.

(b)   If the test shows that the liability is inadequate, the entire deficiency is recognised in profit or loss.

2.16   If an insurer's accounting policies do not require a liability adequacy test that meets the minimum requirements of paragraph 2.15, the insurer shall:

(a)   determine the carrying amount of the relevant insurance liabilities[2] less the carrying amount of:

(i)   any related deferred acquisition costs; and

(ii)   any related intangible assets, such as those acquired in a **business combination** or **portfolio transfer** (see paragraphs 2.27 and 2.28). However, related reinsurance assets are not considered because an insurer accounts for them separately (see paragraph 2.19); and

(b)   determine whether the amount described in (a) is less than the carrying amount that would be required if the relevant insurance liabilities were within the scope of Section 21 *Provisions and Contingencies* of FRS 102. If it is less, the insurer shall recognise the entire difference in profit or loss and decrease the carrying amount of the related deferred acquisition costs or related intangible assets or increase the carrying amount of the relevant insurance liabilities.

2.17   If an insurer's liability adequacy test meets the minimum requirements of paragraph 2.15, the test is applied at the level of aggregation specified in that test. If its liability adequacy test does not meet those minimum requirements, the comparison described in paragraph 2.16 shall be made at the level of a portfolio of contracts that are subject to broadly similar risks and managed together as a single portfolio.

2.18   The amount described in paragraph 2.16(b) (ie the result of applying Section 21 of FRS 102) shall reflect future investment margins (see paragraphs 2.8 to 2.10) if, and only if, the amount described in paragraph 2.16(a) also reflects those margins.

Impairment of reinsurance assets

2.19   If a **cedant**'s reinsurance asset is impaired, the cedant shall reduce its carrying amount accordingly and recognise that impairment loss in profit or loss. A reinsurance asset is impaired if, and only if:

(a)   there is objective evidence, as a result of an event that occurred after initial recognition of the reinsurance asset, that the cedant may not receive all amounts due to it under the terms of the contract; and

(b)   that event has a reliably measurable impact on the amounts that the cedant will receive from the **reinsurer**.

Embedded derivatives

2.20   An entity applying this FRS shall determine whether it has any **separable embedded derivatives**. Subject to paragraphs 2.21 and 2.22, if the separable embedded derivative

---

[2] *The relevant insurance liabilities are those insurance liabilities (and related deferred acquisition costs and related intangible assets) for which the insurer's accounting policies do not require a liability adequacy test that meets the minimum requirements of paragraph 2.15.*

is not itself an insurance contract, the entity shall separate the **embedded derivative** from the host contract and account for it in accordance with Sections 11 *Basic Financial Instruments* and 12 *Other Financial Instruments Issues* of FRS 102 (or, if the entity has made the accounting policy choice under paragraphs 11.2(b) or (c), or paragraphs 12.2(b) or (c) of FRS 102 to apply the recognition and measurement provisions of either IAS 39 *Financial Instruments: Recognition and Measurement* or IFRS 9 *Financial Instruments*, the disclosure requirements of Section 11 of FRS 102 and the recognition and measurement requirements of IAS 39 or IFRS 9, as applicable) as if it is a **financial instrument**. For an entity that is a **financial institution** the disclosure requirements of paragraphs 34.17 to 34.33 of FRS 102 also apply to any separable embedded derivatives.

As an exception to the requirements in paragraph 2.20, an insurer need not separate, and 2.21
measure at fair value, a **policyholder's** option to **surrender** an insurance contract for a fixed amount (or for an amount based on a fixed amount and an interest rate), even if the exercise price differs from the carrying amount of the host insurance liability. However, the requirements in paragraph 2.20 do apply to a put option or cash **surrender option** embedded in an insurance contract if the surrender value varies in response to the change in a financial variable (such as an **equity** or commodity price or index), or a non-financial variable that is not specific to a party to the contract. Furthermore, those requirements also apply if the holder's ability to exercise a put option or cash surrender option is triggered by a change in such a variable (for example, a put option that can be exercised if a stock market index reaches a specified level).

Paragraph 2.21 applies equally to options to surrender a financial instrument containing a 2.22
discretionary participation feature.

Unbundling of deposit components

Some insurance contracts contain both an insurance component and a **deposit component**. 2.23
In some cases, an insurer is required or permitted to **unbundle** those components:

(a)   Unbundling is required if both the following conditions are met:

  (i)   the insurer can measure the deposit component (including any embedded surrender options) separately (ie without considering the insurance component); and

  (ii)   the insurer's accounting policies do not otherwise require it to recognise all obligations and rights arising from the deposit component.

(b)   Unbundling is permitted, but not required, if the insurer can measure the deposit component separately as in (a)(i) but its accounting policies require it to recognise all obligations and rights arising from the deposit component, regardless of the basis used to measure those rights and obligations.

(c)   Unbundling is prohibited if an insurer cannot measure the deposit component separately as in (a)(i).

The following is an example of a case when an insurer's accounting policies do not 2.24
require it to recognise all obligations arising from a deposit component. A cedant receives compensation for losses from a reinsurer, but the contract obliges the cedant to repay the compensation in future years. That obligation arises from a deposit component. If the cedant's accounting policies would otherwise permit it to recognise the compensation as income without recognising the resulting obligation, unbundling is required.

To unbundle a contract, an insurer shall: 2.25

(a)   apply this FRS to the insurance component; and
(b)   apply Section 11 or 12 of FRS 102 (or, if the entity has made the accounting policy choice under paragraphs 11.2(b) or (c), or paragraphs 12.2(b) or (c) of FRS 102 to apply the recognition and measurement provisions of either IAS 39 or

IFRS 9, the disclosure requirements of Section 11 of FRS 102 and the recognition and measurement requirements of IAS 39 or IFRS 9, as applicable) to the deposit component.

Reporting foreign currency transactions in the functional currency

2.26   Paragraph 30.9 of FRS 102 requires an entity, at the end of each reporting period, to translate foreign currency monetary items using the closing rate and non-monetary items using the exchange rate at the date of the transaction or the date when fair value was determined (for non-monetary items measured at fair value). For the purposes of applying the requirements of Section 30 *Foreign Currency Translation* of FRS 102 an entity shall treat all assets and liabilities arising from an insurance contract as monetary items.

Insurance contracts acquired in a business combination or portfolio transfer

2.27   To comply with Section 19 *Business Combinations and Goodwill* of FRS 102, an insurer shall, at the acquisition date, measure at fair value the insurance liabilities assumed and **insurance assets** acquired in a business combination. However, an insurer is permitted, but not required, to use an expanded presentation that splits the fair value of acquired insurance contracts into two components:

(a)   a liability measured in accordance with the insurer's accounting policies for insurance contracts that it issues; and

(b)   an intangible asset, representing the difference between (i) the fair value of the contractual insurance rights acquired and insurance obligations assumed and (ii) the amount described in (a). As an exception to Section 18 *Intangible Assets other than Goodwill* of FRS 102, the subsequent measurement of this asset shall be consistent with the measurement of the related insurance liability.

2.28   An insurer acquiring a portfolio of insurance contracts may use the expanded presentation described in paragraph 2.27.

2.29   The intangible assets described in paragraphs 2.27 and 2.28 are excluded from the scope of Sections 18 and 27 *Impairment of Assets* of FRS 102. However, Sections 18 and 27 of FRS 102 apply to customer lists and customer relationships reflecting the expectation of future contracts that are not part of the contractual insurance rights and contractual insurance obligations that existed at the date of a business combination or portfolio transfer.

Discretionary participation features

Discretionary participation features in insurance contracts

2.30   Some insurance contracts contain a discretionary participation feature as well as a **guaranteed element**. The issuer of such a contract:

(a)   may, but need not, recognise the guaranteed element separately from the discretionary participation feature. If the issuer does not recognise them separately, it shall classify the whole contract as a liability. If the issuer classifies them separately, it shall classify the guaranteed element as a liability;

(b)   shall, if it recognises the discretionary participation feature separately from the guaranteed element, classify that feature as either a liability or a separate component of equity (where this is permitted by the Regulations). The issuer may split that feature into liability and equity components and shall use a consistent accounting policy for that split. The issuer shall not classify that feature as an intermediate category that is neither liability nor equity;

(c) may recognise all premiums received as revenue without separating any portion that relates to the equity component. The resulting changes in the guaranteed element and in the portion of the discretionary participation feature classified as a liability shall be recognised in profit or loss. If part or all of the discretionary participation feature is classified in equity, a portion of profit or loss may be attributable to that feature (in the same way that a portion may be attributable to **non-controlling interests**). Where legislation permits the discretionary participation feature to be classified as a component of equity, the issuer shall recognise the portion of profit or loss attributable to any equity component as an allocation of profit or loss, not as expense or income (see Section 5 *Statement of Comprehensive Income and Income Statement* of FRS 102);

(d) shall, if it has made an accounting policy choice in accordance with paragraphs 11.2(b) or (c), or paragraphs 12.2(b) or (c) of FRS 102 to apply the recognition and measurement provisions of either IAS 39 or IFRS 9, and the contract contains an embedded derivative within the scope of IAS 39 or IFRS 9, apply IAS 39 or IFRS 9 to that embedded derivative; and

(e) shall, in all respects not described in paragraphs 2.13 to 2.19 and 2.30(a) to (d), continue its existing accounting policies for such contracts, unless it changes those accounting policies in a way that complies with paragraphs 2.2 to 2.11.

Discretionary participation features in financial instruments other than insurance contracts

The requirements in paragraph 2.30 also apply to a financial instrument other than an insurance contract that contains a discretionary participation feature. In addition: **2.31**

(a) If the issuer classifies the entire discretionary participation feature as a liability, it shall apply the liability adequacy test in paragraphs 2.14 to 2.18 to the whole contract (ie both the guaranteed element and the discretionary participation feature). The issuer need not determine the amount that would result from applying IAS 39, IFRS 9 or Sections 11 and 12 of FRS 102 (depending on the entity's accounting policy choice) to the guaranteed element.

(b) If the issuer classifies part or all of that feature as a separate component of equity, the liability recognised for the whole contract shall not be less than the amount that would result from applying IAS 39, IFRS 9 or Sections 11 and 12 of FRS 102 (depending on the entity's accounting policy choice) to the guaranteed element. That amount shall include the intrinsic value of an option to surrender the contract, but need not include its time value if paragraph 2.22 exempts that option from measurement at fair value. The issuer need not disclose the amount that would result from applying IAS 39, IFRS 9 or Sections 11 and 12 of FRS 102 (depending on the entity's accounting policy choice) to the guaranteed element, nor need it present that amount separately. Furthermore, the issuer need not determine that amount if the total liability recognised is clearly higher.

(c) Although these contracts are financial instruments, the issuer may continue to recognise the premiums for those contracts as revenue and recognise as an expense the resulting increase in the carrying amount of the liability.

(d) Although these contracts are financial instruments, an issuer shall disclose the total interest expense recognised in profit or loss, but need not calculate such interest expense using the **effective interest method**.

Recognition in the Income Statement for entities required to maintain a non-technical account

Exchange gains and losses

2.32   Where Section 30 of FRS 102 requires entities to include exchange differences within profit or loss, these differences shall be dealt with through the **non-technical account** except for long-term insurance business where exchange differences shall be recognised in the **technical account** for long-term business. In respect of paragraph 30.18(c) of FRS 102 in the case of the long-term insurance business, where appropriate, entities may recognise the resulting exchange differences in the **fund for future appropriations (FFA)**.

Employee benefits

2.33   In applying paragraph 28.23(b) of FRS 102 the net interest on the net defined benefit liability during the reporting period shall be recognised, as appropriate, in the technical account for long-term insurance business or the non-technical account.

2.34   As an exception to paragraph 28.23(d) of FRS 102 the remeasurement of the net defined benefit liability which is not attributable to **owners** shall be treated as an amount, the allocation of which, either to policyholders or to owners, has not been determined by the **reporting date**. It shall be included as a separate line in the technical account for long-term insurance business immediately above the line for transfer to or from the fund for future appropriations, and reflected in that transfer. The impact shall be disclosed separately in the **notes to the financial statements**.

Section 3 Recognition and Measurement: Requirements for entities with long-term insurance business

Scope of this section

3.1   This section sets out requirements for entities applying this FRS that are carrying out **long-term insurance business**:

(a)   Paragraphs 3.3 to 3.10 and 3.16 to 3.18 apply to all long-term insurance business.

(b)   Paragraphs 3.11 to 3.15 apply to **with-profits business** and with-profits funds, to which the **Prudential Regulatory Authority (PRA) realistic capital regime** is being applied, either voluntarily or compulsorily.

Prospective amendments: FRED 64 (December 2015) proposes amendments to this paragraph with effect for annual periods beginning on or after [date].

3.2   Where an entity has changed its **accounting policies** in accordance with paragraph 2.3, and its new accounting policies are no longer consistent with this section, the requirements of this section that are no longer consistent with the entity's accounting policies need not be applied.

Gross premiums written

3.3   Premiums, including those for inwards reinsurance business, shall be recognised when due for payment. Where the amount due is not known, for example with certain pensions business, estimates should be used. For **linked business** the due date for payment may be taken as the date when the **liability** is established.

3.4   Reinsurance outwards premiums shall be recognised when paid or payable.

Claims recognition

Claims payable on maturity shall be recognised when the claims become due for payment   **3.5**
and claims payable on death shall be recognised on notification. Where a claim is payable
and the policy or contract remains in force, the relevant instalments shall be recognised
when due for payment. There should be consistent treatment between the **recognition** of
the claim in the **technical account** for long-term business and the calculation of the long-
term business provision and/or the provision for linked liabilities as appropriate.

Surrenders shall be included within **claims incurred** and recognised either when paid   **3.6**
or at the earlier date on which, following notification, the policy ceases to be included
within the calculation of the long-term business provision and/or the provision for linked
liabilities.

Deferred acquisition costs

Acquisition costs shall not be deferred for with-profits funds to which the PRA realistic   **3.7**
capital regime is being applied, either voluntarily or compulsorily.

Prospective amendments: FRED 64 (December 2015) proposes amendments to this
paragraph with effect for annual periods beginning on or after [date].

Except as required by paragraph 3.7, acquisition costs shall be deferred except to the   **3.8**
extent that:

(a)   the costs in question have already been recovered (for example where the design of
      the policy provides for the recovery of costs as incurred);
(b)   the net present value of margins within the **insurance contracts** is not expected
      to be sufficient to cover **deferred acquisition costs** after providing for contractual
      liabilities to **policyholders** and expenses; and
(c)   the receipt of future premiums or the achievement of future margins is insufficiently
      certain based on estimates of future expected discontinuance rates or other experience.

Advertising costs shall not be deferred unless they are directly attributable to the acquisition   **3.9**
of new business.

Deferred acquisition costs that are carried forward shall be amortised over a period no   **3.10**
longer than one in which, net of any related **deferred tax** provision, they are expected to
be recoverable out of margins on related insurance contracts in force at the **reporting date**,
and in a similar profile to those margins.

Measurement of with-profits liabilities and related assets

The established accounting treatment for long-term insurance business is to measure   **3.11**
liabilities for policyholder benefits under the **modified statutory solvency basis (MSSB)**.
This FRS requires those with-profits funds within the scope of the PRA realistic capital
regime to use the **realistic value of liabilities** as the basis for the estimated value of the
liabilities to be included in the **financial statements**.

Prospective amendments: FRED 64 (December 2015) proposes amendments to this
paragraph with effect for annual periods beginning on or after [date].

For with-profits funds to which the PRA realistic capital regime is being applied, either   **3.12**
voluntarily or compulsorily:

(a)   liabilities to policyholders arising from with-profits business shall be stated at the amount of the realistic value of liabilities adjusted to exclude the shareholders' share of projected future **bonuses**;

(b)   **reinsurance recoveries** that are recognised shall be measured on a basis that is consistent with the value of the policyholder liabilities to which the reinsurance applies;

(c)   an amount may be recognised for the present value of future profits on **non-participating business** written in a with-profits fund if:

   (i)   the non-participating business is measured on a realistic basis for the purposes of the regulatory returns made under the PRA realistic capital regime;

   (ii)   the value is determined in accordance with the PRA regulations; and

   (iii)   the determination of the realistic value of liabilities in that with-profits fund takes account, directly or indirectly, of this value;

(d)   where a with-profits life fund has an interest in a subsidiary or associate and the determination of the realistic value of liabilities to with-profits policyholders takes account of a value of that interest at an amount in excess of the net amounts included in the entity's consolidated accounts, an amount may be recognised representing this excess; and

(e)   adjustments to reflect the consequential tax effects of (a) to (d) above shall be made.

Adjustments from the MSSB necessary to meet the above requirements, including the recognition of an amount in accordance with paragraph 3.12(c) or 3.12(d), shall be included in **profit or loss**. An amount equal and opposite to the net amount of these adjustments shall be transferred to or from the **fund for future appropriations (FFA)** and also included in profit or loss.

Prospective amendments: FRED 64 (December 2015) proposes amendments to this paragraph with effect for annual periods beginning on or after [date].

3.13   In the case of a **mutual**, an FFA or retained surplus account is maintained that represents amounts that have not yet been allocated to specific policyholders. For such entities, the adjustments required by paragraph 3.12 will be offset within profit or loss by a transfer directly to or from this FFA or retained surplus account, with the result that overall profit or loss for the year will be unchanged.

3.14   The realistic value of liabilities shall exclude the amount which represents the shareholders' share of future bonuses. Similar adjustments shall be made if other amounts due to shareholders would otherwise be included in the realistic value of liabilities.

3.15   An entity is permitted to recognise the excess of the market value of a subsidiary over the net amounts included in the consolidated financial statements as a deduction from the sub-total of the FFA and liabilities to policyholders in the same way as the **value of in-force insurance business (VIF)** described in paragraph IG1.3 of the Implementation Guidance.

Value of in-force life assurance business

3.16   Banking and other non-insurance entities with insurance subsidiaries sometimes account for the insurance business in their consolidated financial statements on an **embedded value** or similar basis under which, in addition to the value of the retained surplus in the insurance subsidiary, an asset is recognised for the VIF. This FRS permits the continuation of such a practice only if the valuation policy is amended, if necessary, to exclude from the measurement of the value of the future profit to shareholders any value attributable to future investment margins.

No value shall be attributed to in-force long-term insurance business other than: **3.17**

(a)　in accordance with paragraphs 3.12(c), 3.12(d) or 3.16 above; or
(b)　amounts recognised as an **intangible asset** as part of the allocation of **fair values** under acquisition accounting in accordance with paragraph 2.27.

Where the value attributable to a VIF asset recognised under paragraph 3.16 or paragraph 3.17(b) includes an amount in relation to non-participating business for which the entity also recognises an amount under paragraph 3.12(c) or 3.12(d), the amount recognised under paragraph 3.12(c) or 3.12(d) shall be reduced to exclude the amount that is included in relation to that business under paragraph 3.16 or paragraph 3.17(b). **3.18**

Section 4 Disclosure

Scope of this section

This section describes the disclosures to be provided by **insurers** in addition to the disclosure requirements of **FRS 102**. **4.1**

In accordance with paragraph 8.5 of FRS 102, an entity shall disclose, in the summary of significant **accounting policies**, in relation to both **insurance contracts** and financial instruments that it issues with a **discretionary participation feature**: **4.2**

(a)　the measurement basis (or bases) used; and
(b)　the other accounting policies used that are relevant to an understanding of the **financial statements**.

Insurers that have **liabilities** arising from **with-profits business** shall also apply Section 5 *Disclosure: Additional requirements for with-profits business* of this FRS. **4.3**

Explanation of recognised amounts from insurance contracts

An insurer shall disclose information that identifies and explains the amounts in its financial statements arising from insurance contracts. **4.4**

To comply with paragraph 4.4 an insurer shall disclose: **4.5**

(a)　the recognised assets, liabilities, income and expense (and, if it presents its statement of cash flows using the direct method, cash flows) arising from insurance contracts. Furthermore, if the insurer is a **cedant**, it shall disclose:
　　(i)　gains and losses recognised in **profit or loss** on buying reinsurance; and
　　(ii)　if the cedant defers and amortises gains and losses arising on buying reinsurance, the amortisation for the period and the amounts remaining unamortised at the beginning and end of the period;
(b)　the process used to determine the assumptions that have the greatest effect on the measurement of the recognised amounts described in (b). When practicable, an insurer shall also give quantified disclosure of those assumptions;
(c)　the effect of changes in assumptions used to measure **insurance assets** and **insurance liabilities**, showing separately the effect of each change that has a material effect on the financial statements; and
(d)　reconciliations of changes in insurance liabilities, **reinsurance assets** and, if any, related **deferred acquisition costs**.

4.6   Schedule 3 to the **Regulations** requires disclosure of the total amount of commissions for direct business including acquisition, renewal, collection and portfolio management. For this purpose, commission shall exclude payments made to employees of the undertaking.

Nature and extent of risks arising from insurance contracts

4.7   An insurer shall disclose information that enables users of its financial statements to evaluate the nature and extent of risks arising from insurance contracts.

4.8   To comply with paragraph 4.7, an insurer shall disclose:

(a)   its objectives, policies and processes for managing risks arising from insurance contracts and the methods used to manage those risks;

(b)   information about **insurance risk** (both before and after risk mitigation by reinsurance), including information about:

(i)   sensitivity to insurance risk (see paragraph 4.9);

(ii)   concentrations of insurance risk, including a description of how management determines concentrations and a description of the shared characteristic that identifies each concentration (eg type of **insured event**, geographical area, or currency); and

(iii)   actual **claims** compared with previous estimates (ie claims development). The disclosure about claims development shall go back to the period when the earliest material claim arose for which there is still uncertainty about the amount and timing of the claims payments, but need not go back more than ten years. An insurer need not disclose this information for claims for which uncertainty about the amount and timing of claims payments is typically resolved within one year;

(c)   information about **credit risk**, **liquidity risk** and **market risk** that, as a **financial institution**, Section 34 *Specialised Activities* of FRS 102 would require if the insurance contracts were within the scope of Sections 11 *Basic Financial Instruments* and 12 *Other Financial Instruments Issues* of FRS 102. However:

(i)   an insurer need not provide the maturity analyses required by paragraph 34.28 of FRS 102 if it discloses information about the estimated timing of the net cash outflows resulting from recognised insurance liabilities instead. This may take the form of an analysis, by estimated timing, of the amounts recognised in the **statement of financial position**;

(ii)   if an insurer uses an alternative method to manage sensitivity to market conditions, such as an **embedded value** analysis, it may use that sensitivity analysis to meet the requirement in paragraph 34.29 of FRS 102. Such an insurer shall also provide the disclosures required by paragraph 34.30 of FRS 102; and

(d)   information about exposures to market risk arising from **embedded derivatives** contained in a host insurance contract if the insurer is not required to, and does not, measure the embedded derivatives at **fair value**.

4.9   To comply with paragraph 4.8(b)(i), an insurer shall disclose either (a) or (b) as follows:

(a)   A sensitivity analysis that shows how profit or loss and **equity** would have been affected if changes in the relevant risk variable that were reasonably possible at the end of the **reporting period** had occurred; the methods and assumptions used in preparing the sensitivity analysis; and any changes from the previous period in the methods and assumptions used. However, if an insurer uses an alternative method to manage sensitivity to market conditions, such as an embedded value analysis, it may meet this requirement by disclosing that alternative sensitivity analysis and the disclosures required by paragraph 34.30 of FRS 102.

(b)   Qualitative information about sensitivity, and information about those terms and conditions of insurance contracts that have a material effect on the amount, timing and uncertainty of the insurer's future cash flows.

Financial instruments, other than insurance contracts, containing discretionary participation features

An insurer that has financial instruments, other than insurance contracts, that it issues with a discretionary participation feature shall, in relation to those financial instruments, disclose: **4.10**

(a)   the carrying amount of those financial instruments at the **reporting date**, in total, either in the statement of financial position or in the **notes to the financial statements**; and

(b)   the information required by paragraphs 11.42 and 11.48 of FRS 102.

Section 5 Disclosure: Additional requirements for with-profits business

Scope of this section

This section describes the disclosures to be provided by **insurers** that have liabilities arising from **with-profits business**, in addition to the disclosure requirements of **FRS 102** and Section 4 *Disclosure* of this FRS.   **5.1**

Where an entity has changed its **accounting policies** in accordance with paragraph 2.3, and its new accounting policies are no longer consistent with policies on which the disclosure requirements of this section are based, the requirements of this section that are no longer consistent with the entity's accounting policies need not be applied.   **5.2**

Disclosure and presentation relating to with-profits business

Amounts recognised under paragraph 3.12(c) or 3.12(d) shall be presented in one of the following ways: **5.3**

(a)   Where it is possible to apportion the amount recognised between an amount relating to liabilities to **policyholders** and an amount relating to the **fund for future appropriation (FFA)**, these portions shall be presented in the **statement of financial position** as a deduction in arriving at the amount of liabilities to policyholders and the FFA respectively.

(b)   Where it is not possible to make a reasonably approximate apportionment of the amount recognised, the amount shall be presented in the statement of financial position as a separate item deducted from a sub-total of liabilities to policyholders and the FFA.

(c)   Where the presentation under paragraph 5.3(a) or 5.3(b) does not comply with statutory requirements for balance sheet presentation applying to the entity, the amount recognised under paragraph 3.12(c) or 3.12(d) shall be recognised as an asset.

The **FFA** shall be disclosed separately in the statement of financial position, and not combined with technical provisions or other liabilities. Entities that consolidate interests in an entity carrying on **long-term insurance business** on a basis that combines the FFA and   **5.4** technical provisions into a single amount of liabilities to policyholders are required to show these elements separately.

5.5   Where the balance on the FFA of a with-profits life fund is negative, as a result of the transfer made in accordance with paragraph 3.12 or otherwise, the entity shall include in the **notes to the financial statements** an explanation of the nature of the negative balance and the circumstances in which it arose, and why no action to eliminate it has been considered necessary.

Section 6 Transition to this FRS

Scope of this section

6.1   The transitional provisions in paragraphs 6.3 and 6.4 apply to both an entity that is already applying **FRS 102** when it first applies this FRS and an entity that applies both FRS 102 and this FRS together for the first time.

6.2   Section 35 *Transition to this FRS* of FRS 102 also applies to a first-time adopter of FRS 102.

Disclosure

6.3   In applying paragraph 4.8(b)(iii), an entity need not disclose information about **claims** development that occurred earlier than five years before the end of the first financial year in which it applies this FRS. Furthermore, if it is impracticable, when an entity first applies this FRS, to prepare information about claims development that occurred before the beginning of the earliest period for which an entity presents full comparative information that complies with this FRS, the entity shall disclose that fact.

Re-designation of financial assets

6.4   If an **insurer** changes its **accounting policies** for **insurance liabilities**, it is permitted, but not required, to reclassify some or all of its **financial assets** as a financial asset at **fair value** through **profit or loss** provided those assets meet the criteria in paragraph 11.14(b) of FRS 102 (or if the entity has made the accounting policy choice under paragraphs 11.2(b) or (c), or paragraphs 12.2(b) or (c) of FRS 102 to apply the **recognition** and measurement provisions of either IAS 39 *Financial Instruments: Recognition and Measurement* or IFRS 9 Financial Instruments, the relevant requirements of IAS 39 or IFRS 9, as applicable) at that date. This reclassification is permitted if an insurer changes accounting policies when it first applies this FRS and if it makes a subsequent policy change permitted by paragraph 2.3. The reclassification is a change in accounting policy and Section 10 *Accounting Policies, Estimates and Errors* of FRS 102 applies.

APPROVAL BY THE FRC

Financial Reporting Standard 103 *Insurance Contracts* was approved for issue by the Financial Reporting Council on 5 March 2014, following its consideration of the Accounting Council's Advice for this FRS.

THE ACCOUNTING COUNCIL'S ADVICE TO THE FRC TO ISSUE FRS 103

Introduction

This report provides an overview of the main issues that have been considered by the **1**
Accounting Council in advising the Financial Reporting Council (FRC) to issue FRS 103
Insurance Contracts. The FRC, in accordance with the *Statutory Auditors (Amendment of
Companies Act 2006 and Delegation of Functions etc) Order 2012* (SI 2012/1741), is the
prescribed body for issuing accounting standards in the UK. The Foreword to Accounting
Standards sets out the application of accounting standards in the Republic of Ireland.

In accordance with the *FRC Codes and Standards: procedures*, any proposal to issue, **2**
amend or withdraw a code or standard is put to the FRC Board with the full advice of the
relevant Councils and/or the Codes & Standards Committee. Ordinarily, the FRC Board
will only reject the advice put to it where:

- it is apparent that a significant group of stakeholders has not been adequately consulted;
- the necessary assessment of the impact of the proposal has not been completed,
  including an analysis of costs and benefits;
- insufficient consideration has been given to the timing or cost of implementation; or
- the cumulative impact of a number of proposals would make the adoption of an
  otherwise satisfactory proposal inappropriate.

The FRC has established the Accounting Council as the relevant Council to assist it in the **3**
setting of accounting standards.

Advice

When FRS 102 *The Financial Reporting Standard applicable in the UK and Republic of* **4**
Ireland was issued in March 2013 it referred to the accounting for insurance contracts
being addressed by FRS 103 *Insurance Contracts*, which was yet to be completed. A
standard on insurance contracts was required to fill a gap in current accounting standards.
Respondents agreed with the proposal to develop FRS 103 from IFRS 4 *Insurance
Contracts*, in accordance with the FRC's overall objective for the future of UK GAAP.

FRS 103 largely permits insurers to continue with their existing accounting policies for **5**
insurance contracts and as a result the incremental costs of implementation, in addition
to those that will be incurred in implementing FRS 102, are not significant. Overall the
introduction of FRS 103 will have a positive impact on financial reporting.

Therefore, the Accounting Council is advising the FRC to issue FRS 103 *Insurance* **6**
Contracts.

FRS 100 *Application of Financial Reporting Requirements* and FRS 101 *Reduced* **7**
Disclosure Framework which were both issued in November 2012 and FRS 102 which
was issued in March 2013, are also part of this suite of financial reporting standards. The
Accounting Council's advice to the FRC on those standards is contained in those standards.

Background

8   Accounting standards were formerly developed by the Accounting Standards Board (ASB)[3] . The ASB commenced its project to update accounting standards in 2002; the FRC issued FRS 100 and FRS 101 in November 2012 and FRS 102 in March 2013. FRS 103 supplements FRS 102 for entities with insurance contracts.

9   FRS 103 was developed from IFRS 4 *Insurance Contracts*. It also contains much of the requirements of FRS 27 *Life Assurance* (prior to it being withdrawn by this standard) and elements of the Association of British Insurers' *Statement of Recommended Practice on Accounting for Insurance Business* (the ABI SORP) (published in December 2005 and amended in December 2006).

10   The requirements in this FRS take into consideration:

   (a)   the findings from the previous consultations on the future of financial reporting in the UK and Republic of Ireland that took place between 2002 and 2012, which includes responses to the Discussion Paper *Insurance Accounting – Mind the UK GAAP* issued in 2012; and

   (b)   the responses to FRED 49: Draft FRS 103 *Insurance Contracts* issued in July 2013.

Objective

11   During its consultations on updating accounting standards, the ASB (and subsequently the FRC) gave careful consideration to its objective and the intended effects. In developing the requirements for the future of UK GAAP, including this FRS, the overriding objective is:

> To enable users of accounts to receive high-quality understandable financial reporting proportionate to the size and complexity of the entity and users' information needs.

12   In achieving this objective, the Accounting Council decided (and the FRC subsequently adopted this decision) that it should provide succinct financial reporting standards that:

   ● have consistency with global accounting standards through the application of an IFRS-based solution unless an alternative clearly better meets the overriding objective;

   ● reflect up-to-date thinking and developments in the way businesses operate and the transactions they undertake;

   ● balance consistent principles for accounting by all UK and Republic of Ireland entities with practical solutions, based on size, complexity, public interest and users' information needs;

   ● promote efficiency within groups; and

   ● are cost-effective to apply.

Using IFRS 4 Insurance Contracts as a basis for FRS 103

13   The recently issued accounting standards have consistency with global accounting standards, where appropriate, with FRS 102 being based upon the IFRS for SMEs. FRS 103 has been developed in accordance with the same overall objective and principles and is applicable to those entities applying FRS 102 that have insurance contracts. It is based upon IFRS 4 and it must be consistent with FRS 102 where relevant. One of the options

---

[3] *References in this section are made to the FRC, ASB or Accounting Council, as appropriate in terms of the time period and context of the reference.*

the Accounting Council previously explored, but rejected, was including a requirement in FRS 102 for entities with insurance contracts to apply IFRS 4.

In developing FRS 103 the Accounting Council aimed to provide a financial reporting **14** framework for entities with insurance contracts that allows them to generally continue with their existing accounting policies, whilst consolidating and modernising the relevant accounting requirements. FRS 103 is also deregulatory in some areas, for example, by permitting entities to improve their accounting policies and by including best practice guidance that will allow entities some flexibility in how they comply with the disclosure principles.

In using IFRS 4 as a basis for FRS 103, however, the Accounting Council noted that **15** IFRS 4 does not set specific requirements for the underlying recognition and measurement of insurance contracts, reflecting the fact that it was an interim standard issued by the IASB to facilitate harmonisation between jurisdictions pending completion of the second phase of its insurance contracts project. Therefore the Accounting Council advises that in developing FRS 103 the text of IFRS 4 should be supplemented by some of the existing requirements and practice in accounting for insurance contracts in the UK and Republic of Ireland.

As a result, much of FRS 27, which was issued by the ASB after Lord Penrose's *Report of* **16** *the Equitable Life Inquiry* and is still relevant to entities with long-term insurance business, has been incorporated into FRS 103 or the accompanying Implementation Guidance, along with elements of the ABI SORP providing guidance on applying the requirements of FRS 27 and company law applicable to insurance companies. The Accounting Council advises that when FRS 103 becomes effective, FRS 27 should be withdrawn.

FRS 103 and the accompanying Implementation Guidance consolidate all relevant, **17** existing accounting requirements and guidance applicable to entities with insurance contracts, other than company law and the requirements of the PRA Handbook. This is consistent with the FRC's general approach to setting accounting standards and eliminates unnecessary duplication. The ABI has confirmed that it will withdraw the ABI SORP once FRS 103 is effective.

The Accounting Council notes the prospective commencement of Solvency II, which at the **18** time of giving this advice is currently expected for 1 January 2016, in the light of which it will review whether or not consequential changes to FRS 103 will be required in due course.

The Accounting Council also notes that the IASB has a long-running active project to **19** revise IFRS 4; the aims of this project are 'to provide a single principle-based Standard to account for all types of insurance contracts, including reinsurance contracts that an insurer holds'. Once the IASB has issued its new standard[4], the Accounting Council advises that the FRC should review the requirements of FRS 103. The most appropriate timing for this review cannot be determined at the present time.

The Accounting Council has been mindful of not imposing multiple changes in accounting **20** and reporting on insurers, in quick succession, where this can be avoided. It is also cognisant that, given the complexity and conceptual nature of the issues being addressed by the IASB's insurance contracts project, the development, at this time, of a UK-specific accounting basis for insurers was unlikely to be supported.

---

[4] *An Exposure Draft ED/2013/7 Insurance Contracts was issued in June 2013.*

21   The respondents to FRED 49 supported the introduction of a standard based on that exposure draft, and agreed that the resulting standard should be expected to be an interim standard that will be reviewed following further industry developments.

22   Therefore, following analysis of the options and consideration of the feedback from respondents, the Accounting Council advises the FRC that FRS 103 should be issued, and its requirements should be kept under review in the light of regulatory and accounting changes affecting the insurance industry that are discussed above.

Supplementing IFRS 4 from FRS 27 and the ABI SORP

23   In developing FRS 103 from IFRS 4 the Accounting Council was mindful that UK accounting standards should not be more restrictive than EU-adopted IFRS, unless this was necessary for compliance with company law.

24   In order to supplement IFRS 4, FRS 27 and the ABI SORP were reviewed, with material incorporated as follows:

    (a)   requirements that should be a core part of the standard;

    (b)   material that provided important guidance for applying the requirements of FRS 103 or FRS 102 and should be included as Implementation Guidance; or

    (c)   material that was guidance in nature, but was either repeating other requirements (including the PRA Handbook and Schedule 3 to the Regulations), or concerned matters where diversity in practice was unlikely to arise, which has not been incorporated into FRS 103.

25   Paragraphs that have been sourced from the ABI SORP, and to a lesser extent those from FRS 27, have been revised where they needed updating, for example, to reflect new legislative requirements or for consistency with FRS 102; changes in language for consistency with FRS 102 are not intended to result in a change in meaning. In relation to taxation in entities with long-term insurance business, where a new taxation regime was introduced on 1 January 2013, new guidance has been drafted and incorporated into Section 2 *Guidance for entities with general insurance business or long-term insurance business* of the Implementation Guidance.

Definition of an insurance contract

26   FRS 102 includes a definition of an insurance contract, which will be new to entities applying FRS 102 (and FRS 103) that have not previously applied FRS 26 (IAS 39) *Financial Instruments: Recognition and Measurement*. The definition requires entities to assess whether their contracts meet the definition of insurance (and therefore fall within the scope of FRS 103) or do not meet the definition and therefore fall within Section 11 *Basic Financial Instruments* or Section 12 *Other Financial Instruments Issues* of FRS 102.

27   The definition in FRS 102 is expanded upon in Appendix II: *Definition of an Insurance Contract* of FRS 103. It includes examples of contracts that are, and are not, insurance contracts.

Continuation of existing accounting policies

28   Notwithstanding the need for insurers to make a distinction between insurance and investment contracts, FRS 103 largely permits insurers to continue with their existing accounting policies for insurance contracts. The Accounting Council advises a period of stability in financial reporting for insurance contracts in advance of the expected regulatory

changes from Solvency II and the future new accounting standard from the IASB. There are a small number of exceptions to this principle.

Improvement of existing accounting policies

IFRS 4 permits entities to improve their accounting policies for insurance contracts in **29** certain circumstances, providing they continue to comply with any other relevant legal or regulatory requirements. Although the majority of respondents to FRED 49 agreed with this proposal and the rationale for it (ie that FRS 103 should not be more restrictive than EU-adopted IFRS or FRS 101), some did not. Those disagreeing raised concerns about the potential to reduce consistency of reporting between entities in the insurance industry and that it would be easier to change accounting policies for insurance contracts than FRS 102 would permit for other transactions. The Accounting Council considered these concerns and noted that some of the respondents acknowledged that their concerns may not have a significant effect in practice because there is limited evidence of UK entities applying IFRS 4 taking advantage of this option, and therefore it is not clear that it will be widely used by entities applying FRS 103.

Therefore the Accounting Council advises that this option is included in FRS 103 to ensure **30** that entities applying FRS 103 will have the same flexibility as those entities in the UK and Republic of Ireland that are applying EU-adopted IFRS and FRS 101. In addition, Section 3 *Recognition and Measurement: Requirements for entities with long-term insurance business* and Section 5 *Disclosure: Additional requirements for with-profits business* note that entities that have improved their accounting policies will no longer have to comply with the requirements of those sections (which are based on the requirements of FRS 27 and the ABI SORP) where these are no longer consistent with their accounting policies.

New entrants

The Accounting Council noted that any new entrants to the insurance market would **31** not have existing accounting policies for insurance contracts. Therefore to provide new entrants with the same benchmark accounting policies and the same flexibility to make improvements, the Accounting Council advises that new entrants shall first consider the sections of FRS 103 based on the requirements of FRS 27 and the ABI SORP, as a means to establishing current practice before considering whether to 'improve' those benchmark accounting policies.

Entities that are not legally constituted as insurance providers

Some entities that are not legally constituted as insurance providers may be issuing **32** contracts meeting the definition of an insurance contract in FRS 103. Examples include appliance servicing agreements, and some product warranty arrangements. Although such contracts are within the scope of FRS 103 an entity previously applying an accounting policy based on FRS 12 *Provisions, contingent liabilities and contingent assets* or some other method will be able to continue to apply a similar policy based on Section 21 *Provisions and Contingencies* of FRS 102. However, an entity may, alternatively, choose to apply the recognition and measurement requirements of FRS 103.

Although an entity with such contracts should generally be able to continue to apply its **33** previous accounting policies to such contracts on first-time application of FRS 103, it will need to consider other requirements of FRS 103, for example the liability adequacy test and may need to provide additional disclosures to those provided in the past.

Excessive prudence

34   The Accounting Council notes that paragraph 95 of the ABI SORP explained that claims provisions should be set such that there is no adverse run-off deviation. This may lead to provisions containing excessive prudence – an issue acknowledged by paragraph 2.7, which allows the practice to continue, but prevents it being introduced or extended. Excessive prudence is contrary to Section 2 *Concepts and Pervasive Principles* and Section 21 of FRS 102, and as such the Accounting Council recommends that paragraph IG2.10 of the Implementation Guidance prevents excessive prudence being applied where a new accounting policy is being introduced (ie there is no change for existing accounting policies).

Embedded derivatives

35   Entities that are applying FRS 103 will also be applying FRS 102. FRS 102 does not require entities to identify separable embedded derivatives, but instead, as a simplification from full IFRS, a contract with certain non-typical features shall be measured at fair value. The Accounting Council considered whether a similar approach should be applied to insurance contracts, but advises that for insurance contracts more relevant information will be provided to users if separable embedded derivatives are recognised and measured separately from the host contract (unless the embedded derivative is itself an insurance contract).

Insurance contracts denominated in foreign currencies

36   Some respondents to FRED 49 identified a further area where compliance with FRS 102, for entities that had not previously applied FRS 26, would lead to a change from existing accounting policies. This relates to insurance contracts held in a foreign currency, which are not held by an overseas subsidiary. Some of the assets and liabilities recognised in relation to an insurance contract would be monetary items and some would be non-monetary items, and as a result applying the requirements of FRS 102 would lead to some being retranslated at the reporting date, whilst others would not, resulting in accounting mismatches in the income statement.

37   As a result the Accounting Council advises that all assets and liabilities arising from an insurance contract shall be treated as monetary items for the purposes of reporting foreign currency transactions in the functional currency.

Compliance with company law

38   There are a small number of areas where IFRS 4 conflicts with the requirements of Schedule 3 to the Regulations, and therefore in developing FRS 103 amendments have been made to the text from IFRS 4 to ensure compliance with company law. The three principal examples are:

   (a)   Equalisation provisions – provisions for future claims arising under insurance contracts that are not in existence at the end of the reporting period are prohibited under IFRS 4, but may be a requirement under a regulatory framework that applies to the entity (for example INSPRU 1.4), with separate presentation required by the Regulations. An amendment has been made in paragraph 2.13(a) to reflect these legal and regulatory requirements. In addition, a consequential amendment to FRS 101 is made to ensure consistent accounting by insurers applying either FRS 101 or FRS 103.

   (b)   Equity treatment for discretionary participation features – IFRS 4 gives entities options for the presentation of the discretionary participation feature of a contract, if it is separated. However, the Regulations specifically prevent presentation as part of equity and paragraph 2.30(c) reflects this.

(c) Discounting – IFRS 4 permits an entity to continue measuring insurance liabilities on an undiscounted basis but does not allow an entity to choose a new policy without discounting. However, the Regulations state when discounting is permitted or prohibited. An amendment has been made in paragraph 2.6 to reflect this legal requirement and would not restrict a new entrant's ability to apply discounting where it is required by the Regulations.

Applicability to insurance contracts and to insurance companies

The Accounting Council acknowledges that there are challenges in bringing the texts of IFRS 4, FRS 27 and the ABI SORP together into FRS 103 and the accompanying Implementation Guidance, as a result of each being written at different times (and therefore potentially using different language) for different purposes: **39**

(a) IFRS 4 applies to insurance contracts, as defined in the standard;
(b) FRS 27 applies to all entities that have a life assurance business; and
(c) the ABI SORP applies to insurance companies and groups that are subject to the requirements of Schedule 3 to the Regulations.

FRS 103 applies to insurance contracts, but where requirements from FRS 27 or the ABI SORP have been incorporated their application has been restricted in the scope of each section, where necessary, to avoid extending those requirements to all entities with insurance contracts unnecessarily.   **40**

Disclosure

The disclosure principles set out in FRS 103 require entities to disclose the amounts recognised in the financial statements, and the related risks and uncertainties with those balances. These provisions are complementary to the disclosure requirements of Section 11 and the *Financial Institutions* sub-section of Section 34 *Specialised Activities* of FRS 102.   **41**

The Accounting Council noted that, for financial instruments, other than insurance contracts with discretionary participation features, IFRS 4 does not contain disclosure requirements, because they are within the scope of IFRS 7 *Financial Instruments: Disclosures*. Therefore, it advises that for such contracts, FRS 103 requires entities to provide the relevant disclosures from Section 11 of FRS 102. This will maintain consistency with the requirements of EU-adopted IFRS for these instruments, but implemented in a proportionate manner.   **42**

FRS 103, consistently with IFRS 4, includes a requirement that entities present claims development information. Disclosure of this information is also required by the Regulations, but FRS 103 goes further than the Regulations in requiring information over a 10-year period. The Accounting Council advises that, as this does not contradict the Regulations and respondents confirmed that the information should generally be available to management, for consistency with global accounting standards the requirement is included in FRS 103.   **43**

Captive insurers

Some respondents to FRED 49 noted that there were no disclosure exemptions proposed for captive insurers and considered that it might be appropriate to provide some, given that there would often be limited interest outside the relevant group in the financial statements of a captive insurer. A captive insurer is one that provides insurance cover for other entities   **44** in the group to which it belongs, and only a small part, if any, of its risk exposure relates to entities outside the group.

45   The Accounting Council considered this issue. It noted that an insurer is a financial institution (as defined in FRS 102) and that in developing FRS 102 (and FRS 101) it had advised that entities that are financial institutions should not be permitted to provide reduced disclosures in relation to financial instruments, because they are a significant part of their business, including in relation to treasury subsidiaries. The Accounting Council considers that this reasoning also holds for captive insurers, especially because it notes that equivalent disclosures will not always be given in the consolidated financial statements; at group level the relevant risks will not be reported as insurance risks. Therefore it is important that the insurance risk taken on by the captive insurer is appropriately disclosed in its individual financial statements. Therefore the Accounting Council advises that no disclosure exemptions should be permitted for captive insurers in relation to insurance contracts (or other financial instruments).

Disclosure: Capital

46   Prior to the application of FRS 102 there were no specific capital disclosure requirements for entities with general insurance business unless they applied FRS 26, in which case some general requirements were contained in FRS 29 (IFRS 7) *Financial Instruments: Disclosure*. For entities with long-term insurance business, there were capital and liability disclosure requirements in FRS 27.

47   FRS 102 requires all financial institutions (including insurance companies) to make the disclosures regarding capital set out in paragraphs 34.31 and 34.32 of FRS 102. In addition, the Implementation Guidance accompanying FRS 103 includes best practice guidance in Section 3: *Guidance on capital disclosures for entities with long-term insurance business* for entities with long-term insurance business on meeting this requirement in relation to life assurance capital and liability. These disclosures were previously required by FRS 27. This may provide entities with some flexibility over how they meet the requirements, but the Accounting Council does not anticipate a reduction in the usefulness of the information disclosed.

48   The Accounting Council considered whether to expand the applicability of the long-term insurance business capital disclosures to all insurers, but this was rejected as being unduly onerous on entities with general insurance business, in the context of an accounting standard that consolidates existing practice, pending future developments relating to the accounting and regulatory environment for insurers. FRED 49 asked for respondents' views on whether the guidance in Section 3 of the Implementation Guidance should be considered best practice for other financial institutions as well. The feedback received was generally that this should be considered in the context of a review of FRS 102, not the development of FRS 103, and that some modification would be necessary in order for this to be applicable to other financial institutions. The Accounting Council notes these views and advises that the first three-yearly review of FRS 102 should consider the effectiveness of its disclosure requirements for financial institutions and whether or not any amendment is required.

49   The Accounting Council advises the following changes are made to the requirements of FRS 27 when incorporated into FRS 103:

(a)   90% subsidiary exemptions
      To maintain the consistency with FRS 101 and FRS 102, the disclosure exemptions
      for 90% subsidiaries in paragraph 31 of FRS 27 have not been brought into FRS 103,

because FRS 102 does not permit qualifying entities that are financial institutions exemptions from disclosures relating to financial instruments. Whilst this will change the level of disclosures needed by subsidiaries, the Accounting Council considers that these disclosures are useful, and that the information will be readily available as a result of the associated regulatory reporting to the PRA.

(b)   Disclosures on requirements and targets

Paragraph 45(a) of FRS 27 gives an option for entities to disclose information on the capital requirements or capital targets set by management. In developing the Implementation Guidance the Accounting Council advises changing 'or' to 'and' so that disclosure of both the requirement and management's targets are best practice. The Accounting Council considers that this is effectively required by paragraph 45(d) of FRS 27, and so is a clarification of an existing requirement.

Implementation Guidance accompanying draft FRS 103

The Implementation Guidance accompanying FRS 103 is not mandatory. **50** Section 2 of the Implementation Guidance contains material originally in the ABI SORP which the Accounting Council considers provides useful guidance on the application of the requirements of FRS 102, FRS 103 and company law.

The Accounting Council also notes that the Technical Actuarial Standards issued by the **51** FRC[5] apply to a wide range of actuarial work and may be relevant when implementing aspects of FRS 103.

Memorandum of Understanding concerning FRS 27 *Life Assurance*

In December 2004 a Memorandum of Understanding concerning FRS 27 *Life Assurance* **52** was entered into by the Accounting Standards Board, the Association of British Insurers and certain entities with life assurance activities concerning the application of the requirements of FRS 27 in financial statements prepared in accordance with EU-adopted IFRS.

As this was relevant only at a particular point in time and FRS 27 is now being withdrawn, **53** the FRC will also withdraw the Memorandum of Understanding once FRS 103 is effective.

Approval of this advice

This advice to the FRC was approved by the nine members of the Accounting Council on **54** 13 February 2014.

[5] *In RoI, the guidance issued by the Society of Actuaries in Ireland in ASPLA1 and ASPLA3 may be relevant.*

Appendix I
Glossary

This appendix is an integral part of the FRS.

accounting policies	The specific principles, bases, conventions, rules and practices applied by an entity in preparing and presenting **financial statements**.
acquisition costs	Costs arising from the conclusion of **insurance contracts** including direct costs and indirect costs connected with the processing of proposals and the issuing of policies. Further details are set out in note 6 to the Notes on the Profit and loss Account format in Schedule 3 to the **Regulations**.
Act	The Companies Act 2006
amortised cost (of a financial asset or financial liability)	The amount at which the **financial asset** or **financial liability** is measured at initial **recognition** minus principal repayments, plus or minus the cumulative **amortisation** using the **effective interest method** of any difference between that initial amount and the maturity amount, and minus any reduction (directly or through the use of an allowance account) for impairment or uncollectability.
bonuses	Amounts allocated to **policyholders** under **with-profits** contracts whose existence but not size is specified in the contract. Bonuses may be regular, occasional or terminal.
business combination	The bringing together of separate entities or businesses into one reporting entity.
catastrophe provision	Amount recognised over **reporting periods** between catastrophe events to provide contingency against future catastrophe **claims**.
category of business	Groupings of **general insurance business** with similar characteristics (such as patterns of risk, **claims** incurrence and settlement patterns, and setting of premiums).
cedant	The **policyholder** under a **reinsurance contract**.
claim	The amount payable under an **insurance contract** arising from the occurrence of an **insured event**.
claims incurred	A **claim** is incurred when the event giving rise to the claim occurs. Claims incurred include paid claims and movements in outstanding claims.

claims outstanding	In relation to **general insurance business**: The amounts provided to cover the estimated ultimate cost of settling **claims** arising out of events which have occurred by the **reporting date**, including incurred but not reported (IBNR) claims and claims handling expenses, less amounts already paid in respect of those claims. In relation to **long-term insurance business**: The amounts provided to cover the estimated ultimate cost of settling claims arising out of events, which have been notified by the reporting date being the sums due to beneficiaries together with claims handling expenses, less amounts already paid in respect of those claims.
credit risk	The risk that one party to a **financial instrument** will cause a financial loss for the other party by failing to discharge an obligation.
deferred acquisition costs	Costs arising from the conclusion of **insurance contracts** that are incurred during a **reporting period** but which relate to a subsequent reporting period and are carried forward to subsequent reporting periods. In relation to **general insurance business**: Costs relating to the unexpired period of risk of contracts in force at the **reporting date**. In relation to **long-term insurance business**: Costs relating to contracts in-force at the reporting date in the expectation that they will be recoverable out of future margins within **insurance contracts** after providing for contractual liabilities.
deferred tax	Income tax payable (recoverable) in respect of the taxable profit (tax loss) for future **reporting periods** as a result of past transactions or events.
delegated authority	Agreement for another entity (eg a broker) to underwrite business in the entity's own name.
deposit component	A contractual component that is not accounted for as a **derivative** under Sections 11 and 12 of **FRS 102** and would be within the scope of FRS 102 if it were a separate instrument.
derivative	A **financial instrument** or other contract with all three of the following characteristics: (a) its value changes in response to the change in a specified interest rate, financial instrument price, commodity price, foreign exchange rate, index of prices or rates, credit rating or credit index, or other variable (sometimes called the 'underlying'), provided in the case of a non-financial variable that the variable is not specific to a party to the contract; (b) it requires no initial net investment or an initial net investment that is smaller than would be required for other types of contracts that would be expected to have a similar response to changes in market factors; and (c) it is settled at a future date.

deterministic approach	A method which calculates the value of a policy under a defined scenario and a single set of assumptions.
direct insurance contract	An **insurance contract** that is not a **reinsurance contract**.
discontinued operation	A component of an entity that has been disposed of and: (a) represented a separate major line of business or geographical area of operations; (b) was part of a single co-ordinated plan to dispose of a separate major line of business or geographical area of operations; or (c) was a subsidiary acquired exclusively with a view to resale.
discounting	The reduction to **present value** at a given date of future cash flows at an assumed date by the application of an appropriate discount factor reflecting the time value of money.

discretionary participation feature	A contractual right to receive, as a supplement to **guaranteed benefits**, additional benefits:
	(a) that are likely to be a significant portion of the total contractual benefits;
	(b) whose amount or timing is contractually at the discretion of the issuer; and
	(c) that are contractually based on:
	  (i) the performance of a specified pool of contracts or a specified type of contract;
	  (ii) realised and/or unrealised **investment returns** on a specified pool of assets held by the issuer; or
	  (iii) the **profit or loss** of the company, fund or other entity that issues the contract.

earned premium	For **general insurance business**, earned premium is the proportion of **written premiums** (including where relevant those of previous **reporting periods**) attributable to the risks borne by the **insurer** during the **reporting period**.
effective interest method	A method of calculating the **amortised cost** of a **financial asset** or a **financial liability** (or a group of **financial assets** or **financial liabilities**) and of allocating the interest income or interest expense over the relevant period.
embedded derivative	A component of a hybrid (combined) instrument that also includes a non-derivative host contract—with the effect that some of the cash flows of the combined instrument vary in a way similar to a stand-alone **derivative**. A **derivative** that is attached to a **financial instrument** but is contractually transferable independently of that instrument, or has a different counterparty from that instrument, is not an embedded derivative, but a separate **financial instrument**.
embedded value	A measure of the consolidated value of shareholder's interests in the business, calculated as free surplus plus required capital plus the **value of in-force life assurance business (VIF)**. Different approaches are adopted in terms of methodology and valuation basis, with most entities tending to adopt either the CFO Forum's EEV or MCEV principles.

equalisation provisions	As defined in the relevant regulatory framework (eg **INSPRU**).
equity	The residual interest in the assets of the entity after deducting all its **liabilities**.
EU-adopted IFRS	**IFRS** that have been adopted in the European Union in accordance with EU Regulation 1606/2002
existing accounting policies	The **accounting policies** adopted by a reporting entity in its last annual **financial statements** before adoption of this FRS.
fair value	The amount for which an asset could be exchanged, or a **liability** settled, between knowledgeable, willing parties in an arm's length transaction. In the absence of any specific guidance provided in the relevant section of this FRS, the guidance in paragraphs 11.27 to 11.32 of **FRS 102** shall be used in determining fair value.
financial asset	Any asset that is: (a) cash; (b) an equity instrument of another entity; (c) a contractual right: (i) to receive cash or another financial asset from another entity; or (ii) to exchange financial assets or **financial liabilities** with another entity under conditions that are potentially favourable to the entity; or (d) a contract that will or may be settled in the entity's own equity instruments and: (i) under which the entity is or may be obliged to receive a variable number of the entity's own equity instruments; or (ii) that will or may be settled other than by the exchange of a fixed amount of cash or another financial asset for a fixed number of the entity's own equity instruments. For this purpose the entity's own equity instruments do not include instruments that are themselves contracts for the future receipt or delivery of the entity's own equity instruments.
financial guarantee contract	A contract that requires the issuer to make specified payments to reimburse the holder for a loss it incurs because a specified debtor fails to make payment when due in accordance with the original or modified terms of a debt instrument.

financial institution	Any of the following:
	(a) a bank which is:
	    (i) a firm with a Part 4A permission[6] which includes accepting deposits and:
	        (a) which is a credit institution; or
	        (b) whose Part 4A permission includes a requirement that it complies with the rules in the General Prudential sourcebook and the Prudential sourcebook for Banks, Building Societies and Investment Firms relating to banks, but which is not a building society, a friendly society or a credit union;
	    (ii) an EEA bank which is a full credit institution;
	(b) a building society which is defined in section 119(1) of the Building Societies Act 1986 as a building society incorporated (or deemed to be incorporated) under that Act;
	(c) a credit union, being a body corporate registered under the Industrial and Provident Societies Act 1965 as a credit union in accordance with the Credit Unions Act 1979, which is an authorised person;
	(d) custodian bank, broker-dealer or stockbroker;
	(e) an entity that undertakes the business of effecting or carrying out **insurance contracts**, including general and life assurance entities;
	(f) an incorporated friendly society incorporated under the Friendly Societies Act 1992 or a registered friendly society registered under section 7(1)(a) of the Friendly Societies Act 1974 or any enactment which it replaced, including any registered branches;
	(g) an investment trust, Irish Investment Company[7], venture capital trust, mutual fund, exchange traded fund, unit trust, open-ended investment company (OEIC);
	(h) a retirement benefit plan; or
	(i) any other entity whose principal activity is to generate wealth or manage risk through **financial instruments**. This is intended to cover entities that have business activities similar to those listed above but are not specifically included in the list above.
	A parent entity whose sole activity is to hold investments in other group entities is not a financial institution.

financial instrument	A contract that gives rise to a **financial asset** of one entity and a **financial liability** or equity instrument of another entity.

---

[6] *As defined in section 55A of the Financial Services and Markets Act 2000 or references to equivalent provisions of any successor legislation.*

[7] *An Irish Investment Company is a corporate vehicle as defined by section 47(3) of the Companies (Amendment) Act 1983 and paragraph 58 of the Schedule to the Companies (Amendment) Act 1986, and regulated by the Central Bank of Ireland.*

financial liability	Any **liability** that is:
	(a) a contractual obligation:
	    (i) to deliver cash or another **financial asset** to another entity; or
	    (ii) to exchange financial assets or financial liabilities with another entity under conditions that are potentially unfavourable to the entity; or
	(b) a contract that will or may be settled in the entity's own equity instruments and:
	    (i) under which the entity is or may be obliged to deliver a variable number of the entity's own equity instruments; or
	    (ii) will or may be settled other than by the exchange of a fixed amount of cash or another financial asset for a fixed number of the entity's own equity instruments. For this purpose the entity's own equity instruments do not include instruments that are themselves contracts for the future receipt or delivery of the entity's own equity instruments.

financial position	The relationship of the assets, **liabilities** and **equity** of an entity as reported in the **statement of financial position**.
financial reinsurance	Where a **reinsurance contract** is intended, either in whole or in part, to mitigate the requirement to establish prudent provisions, and/or to provide an element of financing, the identifiable elements of the contract which do not transfer **significant insurance risk** are considered to be financial reinsurance.
financial risk	The risk of a possible future change in one or more of a specified interest rate, **financial instrument** price, commodity price, foreign exchange rate, index of prices or rates, credit rating or credit index or other variable, provided in the case of a non-financial variable that the variable is not specific to a party to the contract.
financial statements	Structured representation of the **financial position**, financial performance and cash flows of an entity.
FRS 101	FRS 101 *Reduced Disclosure Framework*
FRS 102	FRS 102 *The Financial Reporting Standard applicable in the UK and Republic of Ireland*
FRS 103	FRS 103 *Insurance Contracts*
fund for future appropriations (FFA)	The balance sheet item required by Schedule 3 to the **Regulations** to comprise all funds the allocation of which, either to **policyholders** or to shareholders, has not been determined by the end of the **reporting period**.

general insurance business	**Insurance contracts** (including reinsurance) falling within one of the classes of insurance specified in Part I of Schedule 1 to the Financial Services and Markets Act 2000 (Regulated Activities) Order 2001 (SI 2001/544).
gross premium method	A form of actuarial valuation of **liabilities** arising under long-term insurance contracts where the premiums brought into account are the full amounts receivable under the contract. The method includes explicit estimates of cash flows for: (a) premiums, adjusted for renewals and lapses; (b) expected claims and for **with-profits business** future regular but not occasional or terminal **bonuses**; (c) costs of maintaining contracts; and (d) future renewal expenses. Cash flows are discounted at the valuation interest rate. The methodology may be set out in the relevant regulatory framework. For UK companies this is included in the **PRA** Handbook. The discount rate is based on the expected return on the assets deemed to back the **liabilities** as prescribed by the PRA Handbook. This may be further constrained by a maximum rate set by the PRA. This will be adjusted to reflect any further risks although, under this method, most of the key risks will be reflected in the modelling of the cash flows. For **linked business**, allowance may be made for the purchase of future units required by the contract terms and credit is taken for future charges permitted under those terms.
guaranteed benefits	Payments or other benefits to which a particular **policyholder** or investor has an unconditional right that is not subject to the contractual discretion of the issuer.
guaranteed element	An obligation to pay **guaranteed benefits**, included in a contract that contains a **discretionary participation feature**.
IFRS (International Financial Reporting Standards)	Standards and interpretations issued (or adopted) by the International Accounting Standards Board (IASB). They comprise: (a) International Financial Reporting Standards; (b) International Accounting Standards; and (c) Interpretations developed by the IFRS Interpretations Committee (IFRIC) or the former Standing Interpretations Committee (SIC).
income statement	**Financial statement** that presents all items of income and expense recognised in a **reporting period**, excluding the items of other comprehensive income (referred to as the profit and loss account in the **Act**).
INSPRU	See **Prudential sourcebook for insurers (INSPRU)**.
insurance asset	An **insurer's** net contractual rights under an **insurance contract**.

insurance contract	A contract under which one party (the **insurer**) accepts **significant insurance risk** from another party (the **policyholder**) by agreeing to compensate the policyholder if a specified uncertain future event (the **insured event**) adversely affects the policyholder. (See Appendix II for guidance on this definition.)
insurance liability	An **insurer's** net contractual obligations under an **insurance contract**.
insurance risk	Risk, other than **financial risk**, transferred from the holder of a contract to the issuer.
insured event	An uncertain future event that is covered by an **insurance contract** and creates **insurance risk**.
insurer	The party that has an obligation under an **insurance contract** to compensate a **policyholder** if an **insured event** occurs.
intangible asset	An identifiable non-monetary asset without physical substance. Such an asset is identifiable when: (a) it is separable, ie capable of being separated or divided from the entity and sold, transferred, licensed, rented or exchanged, either individually or together with a related contract, asset or **liability**; or (b) it arises from contractual or other legal rights, regardless of whether those rights are transferable or separable from the entity or from other rights and obligations.
investment contract	Contract that has the legal form of an **insurance contract** but does not expose the **insurer** to **significant insurance risk**, for example life insurance contracts in which the insurer bears no significant mortality risk.
investment return	Comprises all investment income, **realised investment gains and losses** and movements in **unrealised investment gains and losses**. It also includes investment expenses and charges and, if appropriate, interest payable.
liability	A present obligation of the entity arising from past events, the settlement of which is expected to result in an outflow from the entity of resources embodying economic benefits.
liability adequacy test	An assessment of whether the carrying amount of an **insurance liability** needs to be increased (or the carrying amount of related **deferred acquisition costs** or related **intangible assets** decreased), based on a review of future cash flows.
linked business	**Long-term insurance business** where the benefits payable to **policyholders** are wholly or partly to be determined by reference to the value of, or the income from, property of any description or by reference to fluctuations in, or in an index of, the value of property of any description.
liquidity risk	The risk that an entity will encounter difficulty in meeting obligations associated with **financial liabilities** that are settled by delivering cash or another **financial asset**.

longer term rate of investment return	An estimate of the long-term trend **investment return** for the relevant category of investments having regard to past performance, current trends and future expectations.
long-term fund	The fund or funds maintained by an undertaking in respect of its **long-term insurance business** in accordance with the **PRA** rules.
long-term insurance business	**Insurance contracts** (including reinsurance) falling within one of the classes of insurance specified in Part II of Schedule 1 to the Financial Services and Markets Act 2000 (Regulated Activities) Order 2001 (SI 2001/544).
market risk	The risk that the **fair value** or future cash flows of a **financial instrument** will fluctuate because of changes in market prices. Market risk comprises three types of risk: currency risk, interest rate risk and other price risk. Interest rate risk – the risk that the fair value or future cash flows of a financial instrument will fluctuate because of changes in market interest rates. Currency risk – the risk that the fair value or future cash flows of a financial instrument will fluctuate because of changes in foreign exchange rates. Other price risk – the risk that the fair value or future cash flows of a financial instrument will fluctuate because of changes in market prices (other than those arising from interest rate risk or currency risk), whether those changes are caused by factors specific to the financial instrument or its issuer, or factors affecting all similar financial instruments traded in the market.
modified statutory solvency basis (MSSB)	The basis for determining **insurance liabilities** which is the **statutory solvency basis** adjusted for the following items: (a) to defer new business **acquisition costs** incurred where the benefit of such costs will be obtained in subsequent **reporting periods**; and (b) to treat investment, resilience and similar reserves, or reserves held in respect of general contingencies or the specific contingency that the fund will be closed to new business, where such items are held within the **long-term fund**, as reserves rather than provisions. These are included, as appropriate, within shareholders' capital and reserves or the **fund for future appropriations (FFA)**.
mutual	As defined in the **PRA** Handbook.
net premium method	An actuarial valuation of **liabilities** arising under **long-term insurance contracts** where the premium brought into account at any valuation date is that which, on the valuation assumptions regarding interest, mortality and disability, will exactly provide for the benefits guaranteed. A variation of the net premium method involves **zillmerisation**. The detailed methodology for UK companies is included in regulations contained in the **PRA** Handbook.
non-controlling interest	The **equity** in a **subsidiary** not attributable, directly or indirectly, to a **parent**.

non-participating business	**Long-term insurance business** where **policyholders** are not entitled to share in the surplus of the relevant **long-term fund**.
non-technical account	The section of the **income statement** (referred to as the profit and loss account in the **Act**) prescribed by Part 1 of Schedule 3 to the **Regulations** in addition to the **technical accounts** for **general** and **long-term insurance business**.
notes (to financial statements)	Notes contain information in addition to that presented in the **statement of financial position**, statement of comprehensive income, **income statement** (if presented), combined statement of income and retained earnings (if presented), statement of changes in equity and statement of cash flows. Notes provide narrative descriptions or disaggregations of items presented in those statements and information about items that do not qualify for **recognition** in those statements.
options and guarantees	Features of life assurance contracts that: (a) confer potentially valuable guarantees underlying the level or nature of **policyholder** benefits; or (b) are options to change these benefits exercisable at the discretion of the **policyholder**. For the purposes of this FRS, the term is used to refer only to those options and guarantees whose potential value is affected by the behaviour of financial variables.
owners	Holders of instruments classified as **equity**.
pipeline premiums	Premiums written but not reported to the undertaking by the **reporting date**.
policyholder	A party that has a right to compensation under an **insurance contract** if an **insured event** occurs.
portfolio claims	Amounts payable by one **insurer** to another in consideration for a contract whereby the latter agrees to assume responsibility for the unpaid **claims incurred** by the former prior to a date specified in the contract.
portfolio premiums	Amounts payable by one **insurer** to another in consideration for a contract whereby the latter agrees to assume responsibility for the **claims** arising on a portfolio of in-force business written by the former from a future date until the expiry of the policies.
portfolio transfer	The bulk transfer of contracts or risks to another entity.
present value	A current estimate of the present discounted value of the future net cash flows in the normal course of business.
principles and practices of financial management (PPFM)	The statement that the **PRA** requires each **with-profits** life fund to make available to its **policyholders** containing, inter alia, a description of the fund's investment management and bonus distribution policies.
profit or loss	The total of income less expenses, excluding the components of other comprehensive income.

Prudential Regulatory Authority (PRA)	The division of the Bank of England responsible for the prudential regulation and supervision of banks, building societies, credit unions, **insurers** and major investment firms in the UK.
Prudential sourcebook for insurers (INSPRU)	The section of the **PRA** Handbook detailing the prudential rules for **insurers**, including capital requirements, credit, market and **liquidity risk**.
realised investment gains and losses	(a) For investments included in the **financial statements** at **fair value**, the difference between the net proceeds on disposal and their purchase price. (b) For investments included at **amortised cost**, the difference between the net proceeds on disposal and the latest carrying value (or if acquired after the last **reporting date**, the purchase price).
realistic capital regime	As set out in section 1.3 of **INSPRU**[8].
realistic value of liabilities	That element of the amount defined by rule 1.3.40 in **INSPRU**, excluding current **liabilities** falling within the definition in rule 1.3.190 that are recognised separately in the **statement of financial position**.
recognition	The process of incorporating in the **statement of financial position** or statement of comprehensive income an item that meets the definition of an asset, **liability**, **equity**, income or expense and satisfies the following criteria: (a) it is probable that any future economic benefit associated with the item will flow to or from the entity; and (b) the item has a cost or value that can be measured with reliability.
Regulations	The Large and Medium-sized Companies and Groups (Accounts and Reports) Regulations 2008 (SI 2008/410)
regulatory capital resources	An entity's capital resources as calculated in accordance with the capital resources table in **INSPRU**.
reinsurance assets	A **cedant**'s net contractual rights under a **reinsurance contract**.
reinsurance contract	An **insurance contract** issued by one **insurer** (the **reinsurer**) to compensate another **insurer** (the **cedant**) for losses on one or more contracts issued by the **cedant**. Retrocession is the reinsurance outwards of risks previously accepted by an **insurer** as reinsurance inwards. The recipient is known as the retrocessionaire.
reinsurance recovery	The amount recoverable or recovered from a **reinsurer** (or retrocessionaire) under a **reinsurance contract**.
reinsurer	The party that has an obligation under a **reinsurance contract** to compensate a **cedant** if an **insured event** occurs.
reporting date	The end of the latest period covered by **financial statements** or by an interim financial report.

[8] *References to the PRA's Prudential sourcebook for insurers, and to individual rules therein, are to the rules made on 1 April 2013 by the FCA and PRA Handbook Designation (General Modifications) Instrument 2013.*

reporting period	The period covered by **financial statements** or by an interim financial report.
restructuring	A restructuring is a programme that is planned and controlled by management and materially changes either: (a) the scope of a business undertaken by an entity; or (b) the manner in which that business is conducted.
run-off deviation	For **general insurance business**, the difference (before any reduction in respect of **discounting**) between: (a) the provisions made at the beginning of the **reporting period** for outstanding **claims incurred** in previous reporting periods; and (b) the payments made during the reporting period on account of claims incurred in previous reporting periods and the claims provision at the end of the reporting period for such outstanding claims.
separable embedded derivative	An **embedded derivative** where: (a) the economic characteristics and risks of the **embedded derivative** are not closely related to the economic characteristics and risks of the host contract; (b) a separate instrument with the same terms as the **embedded derivative** would meet the definition of a **derivative**; and (c) the hybrid (combined) instrument is not measured at **fair value** with changes in **fair value** recognised in **profit or loss**. The guidance in IAS 39 and IFRS 4 shall be used in determining whether an **embedded derivative** is separable.
significant insurance risk	An **insured event** or risk which could cause an **insurer** to pay significant additional benefits in any scenario, excluding scenarios that lack commercial substance.
statement of financial position	**Financial statement** that presents the relationship of an entity's assets, **liabilities** and **equity** as of a specific date (referred to as the balance sheet in the **Act**).
statutory solvency basis	The basis of determination of **insurance liabilities** in accordance with rule 1 of **INSPRU**.
structured settlement	An arrangement by consent between the parties concerned or under a Court Order whereby damages in the form of a lump sum are replaced by a smaller lump sum and a series of periodic payments. These are also referred to as Periodic Payment Orders or PPOs.
surrender	To cease paying premiums such that the **insurance contract** ceases to have effect.
surrender option	The option to **surrender** an **insurance contract** in return for some form of reduced **claim**.

technical account	In relation to **general insurance business**: The section of the **income statement** (referred to as the profit and loss account in the **Act**) for recording insurance business within the classes specified in Part I of Schedule 1 to the Regulated Activities Order which must be prepared in accordance with the format prescribed in Part I of Schedule 3 to the **Regulations**. In relation to **long-term insurance business**: The section of the income statement (referred to as the profit and loss account in the Act) for recording insurance business within the classes specified in Part II of Schedule 1 to the Regulated Activities Order, which must be prepared in accordance with the format prescribed in Part I of Schedule 3 to the Regulations.
unbundle	To account for the components of a contract as if they were separate contracts.
unearned premiums provision	For **general insurance business**, the proportion of **written premiums** relating to periods of risk after the **reporting date**, which are deferred to subsequent **reporting periods**.
unexpired risks provision	The excess of the estimated value of **claims** and expenses likely to arise after the end of the **reporting period** from contracts concluded before that date, insofar as their estimated value exceeds the provision for unearned premiums (after deduction of any **acquisition costs** deferred), and any premiums receivable under those contracts.
unrealised investment gains and losses	The difference between the **fair value** at the **reporting date** of investments held on that date and their purchase price. Movements in unrealised investment gains and losses comprise: (a) the increase/decrease in the **reporting period** in the value of investments held at the reporting date; and (b) the reversal of unrealised investment gains and losses recognised in earlier reporting periods in respect of investment disposals of the current period.
value of in-force life assurance business (VIF)	The net **present value** of the shareholders' interest in the expected after tax cash flows from **long-term insurance business,** on the assumption that all assets backing the business will be distributed over time to in-force **policyholders** and/or shareholders. The calculation of VIF should allow for uncertainties associated with the assessment of future cash flows, as well as for the time value of money. VIF includes both the shareholders' interest which is expected to arise in the form of cash flows over the lifetime of current in-force contracts and the interest in the surplus assets which, in practice, is not expected to be distributed over this period.

with-profits business	**Long-term insurance business** where **policyholders** are contractually entitled to share in the surplus of the relevant **long-term fund**. A with-profits contract is an example of a contract with a **discretionary participation feature**.
written premiums	In relation to **general insurance business**: Premiums, which an **insurer** is contractually entitled to receive from the insured in relation to contracts of insurance. These are premiums on contracts entered into during the **reporting period** and adjustments arising in the reporting period to premiums receivable in respect of contracts entered into in previous **reporting periods**. In relation to **long-term insurance business**: Premiums to which the insurer is contractually entitled becoming due for payment in the reporting period.
zillmerisation	A variation of the **net premium method** which increases the future premiums valued to take account of **acquisition costs** incurred.

Prospective amendments: FRED 64 (December 2015) proposes amendments to the glossary terms and definitions above with effect for annual periods beginning on or after [date].

Appendix II
Definition of an insurance contract

This appendix is an integral part of the FRS.

A2.1   This appendix gives guidance on the definition of an **insurance contract** in Appendix I. It addresses the following issues:

(a)   the term 'uncertain future event' (paragraphs A2.2 to A2.4);

(b)   payments in kind (paragraphs A2.5 to A2.7);

(c)   **insurance risk** and other risks (paragraphs A2.8 to A2.17);

(d)   examples of insurance contracts (paragraphs A2.18 to A2.24);

(e)   **significant insurance risk** (paragraphs A2.25 to A2.31); and

(f)   changes in the level of insurance risk (paragraphs A2.32 and A2.33).

UNCERTAIN FUTURE EVENT

A2.2   Uncertainty (or risk) is the essence of an insurance contract. Accordingly, at least one of the following is uncertain at the inception of an insurance contract:

(a)   whether an **insured event** will occur;

(b)   when it will occur; or

(c)   how much the **insurer** will need to pay if it occurs.

A2.3   In some insurance contracts, the insured event is the discovery of a loss during the term of the contract, even if the loss arises from an event that occurred before the inception of the contract. In other insurance contracts, the insured event is an event that occurs during the term of the contract, even if the resulting loss is discovered after the end of the contract term.

A2.4   Some insurance contracts cover events that have already occurred, but whose financial effect is still uncertain. An example is a **reinsurance contract** that covers the direct insurer against adverse development of **claims** already reported by **policyholders**. In such contracts, the insured event is the discovery of the ultimate cost of those claims.

PAYMENTS IN KIND

A2.5   Some insurance contracts require or permit payments to be made in kind. An example is when the insurer replaces a stolen article directly, instead of reimbursing the policyholder. Another example is when an insurer uses its own hospitals and medical staff to provide medical services covered by the contracts.

A2.6   Some fixed-fee service contracts in which the level of service depends on an uncertain event meet the definition of an insurance contract in this FRS but are not regulated as insurance contracts. One example is a maintenance contract in which the service provider agrees to repair specified equipment after a malfunction. The fixed service fee is based on the expected number of malfunctions, but it is uncertain whether a particular machine will break down. The malfunction of the equipment adversely affects its owner and the contract compensates the owner (in kind, rather than cash). Another example is a contract for car breakdown services in which the provider agrees, for a fixed annual fee, to provide roadside assistance or tow the car to a nearby garage. The latter contract could meet the definition of an insurance contract even if the provider does not agree to carry out repairs or replace parts.

Applying the FRS to the contracts described in paragraph A2.6 is likely to be no more burdensome than applying FRS 102 if such contracts were outside the scope of this FRS: **A2.7**

(a) There are unlikely to be material liabilities for malfunctions and breakdowns that have already occurred.

(b) If Section 23 *Revenue* of FRS 102 applied, the service provider would recognise revenue by reference to the stage of completion (and subject to other specified criteria). That approach is also acceptable under this FRS, which permits the service provider to continue its **existing accounting policies** for these contracts unless they involve practices prohibited by paragraph 2.13.

(c) If this FRS did not apply to these contracts, the service provider would apply Section 21 *Provisions and Contingencies* of FRS 102 to determine whether the contracts are onerous.

DISTINCTION BETWEEN INSURANCE RISK AND OTHER RISKS

The definition of an insurance contract refers to insurance risk, which this FRS defines as risk, other than **financial risk**, transferred from the holder of a contract to the issuer. A contract that exposes the issuer to financial risk without significant insurance risk is not an insurance contract. **A2.8**

The definition of financial risk in Appendix I: *Glossary* includes a list of financial and non-financial variables. That list includes non-financial variables that are not specific to a party to the contract, such as an index of earthquake losses in a particular region or an index of temperatures in a particular city. It excludes non-financial variables that are specific to a party to the contract, such as the occurrence or non-occurrence of a fire that damages or destroys an asset of that party. Furthermore, the risk of changes in the **fair value** of a non-financial asset is not a financial risk if the fair value reflects not only changes in market prices for such assets (a financial variable) but also the condition of a specific non-financial asset held by a party to a contract (a non-financial variable). For example, if a guarantee of the residual value of a specific car exposes the guarantor to the risk of changes in the car's physical condition, that risk is insurance risk, not financial risk. **A2.9**

Some contracts expose the issuer to financial risk, in addition to significant insurance risk. For example, many life insurance contracts both guarantee a minimum rate of return to policyholders (creating financial risk) and promise death benefits that at some times significantly exceed the policyholder's account balance (creating insurance risk in the form of mortality risk). Such contracts are insurance contracts. **A2.10**

Under some contracts, an insured event triggers the payment of an amount linked to a price index. Such contracts are insurance contracts, provided the payment that is contingent on the insured event can be significant. For example, a life-contingent annuity linked to a cost-of-living index transfers insurance risk because payment is triggered by an uncertain event—the survival of the annuitant. The link to the price index is an **embedded derivative**, but it also transfers insurance risk. If the resulting transfer of insurance risk is significant, the embedded derivative meets the definition of an insurance contract (which need not be separated and measured at fair value). **A2.11**

The definition of insurance risk refers to risk that the insurer accepts from the policyholder. In other words, insurance risk is a pre-existing risk transferred from the policyholder to the insurer. Thus, a new risk created by the contract is not insurance risk. **A2.12**

The definition of an insurance contract refers to an adverse effect on the policyholder. The definition does not limit the payment by the insurer to an amount equal to the financial impact of the adverse event. For example, the definition does not exclude 'new-for-old' **A2.13** coverage that pays the policyholder sufficient to permit replacement of a damaged old asset by a new asset. Similarly, the definition does not limit payment under a term life insurance contract to the financial loss suffered by the deceased's dependants, nor does it preclude the payment of predetermined amounts to quantify the loss caused by death or an accident.

A2.14 Some contracts require a payment if a specified uncertain event occurs, but do not require an adverse effect on the policyholder as a precondition for payment. Such a contract is not an insurance contract even if the holder uses the contract to mitigate an underlying risk exposure. For example, if the holder uses a **derivative** to hedge an underlying non-financial variable that is correlated with cash flows from an asset of the entity, the derivative is not an insurance contract because payment is not conditional on whether the holder is adversely affected by a reduction in the cash flows from the asset. Conversely, the definition of an insurance contract refers to an uncertain event for which an adverse effect on the policyholder is a contractual precondition for payment. This contractual precondition does not require the insurer to investigate whether the event actually caused an adverse effect, but permits the insurer to deny payment if it is not satisfied that the event caused an adverse effect.

A2.15 Lapse or persistency risk (ie the risk that the counterparty will cancel the contract earlier or later than the issuer had expected in pricing the contract) is not insurance risk because the payment to the counterparty is not contingent on an uncertain future event that adversely affects the counterparty. Similarly, expense risk (ie the risk of unexpected increases in the administrative costs associated with the servicing of a contract, rather than in costs associated with insured events) is not insurance risk because an unexpected increase in expenses does not adversely affect the counterparty.

A2.16 Therefore, a contract that exposes the issuer to lapse risk, persistency risk or expense risk is not an insurance contract unless it also exposes the issuer to insurance risk. However, if the issuer of that contract mitigates that risk by using a second contract to transfer part of that risk to another party, the second contract exposes that other party to insurance risk.

A2.17 An insurer can accept significant insurance risk from the policyholder only if the insurer is an entity separate from the policyholder. In the case of a **mutual** insurer, the mutual accepts risk from each policyholder and pools that risk. Although policyholders bear that pooled risk collectively in their capacity as **owners**, the mutual has still accepted the risk that is the essence of an insurance contract.

EXAMPLES OF INSURANCE CONTRACTS

A2.18 The following are examples of contracts that are insurance contracts, if the transfer of insurance risk is significant:

   (a) insurance against theft or damage to property.

   (b) insurance against product liability, professional liability, civil liability or legal expenses.

   (c) life insurance and prepaid funeral plans (although death is certain, it is uncertain when death will occur or, for some types of life insurance, whether death will occur within the period covered by the insurance).

   (d) life-contingent annuities and pensions (ie contracts that provide compensation for the uncertain future event—the survival of the annuitant or pensioner—to assist the annuitant or pensioner in maintaining a given standard of living, which would otherwise be adversely affected by his or her survival).

   (e) disability and medical cover.

(f)   surety bonds, fidelity bonds, performance bonds and bid bonds (ie contracts that provide compensation if another party fails to perform a contractual obligation, for example an obligation to construct a building).

(g)   credit insurance that provides for specified payments to be made to reimburse the holder for a loss it incurs because a specified debtor fails to make payment when due under the original or modified terms of a debt instrument. These contracts could have various legal forms, such as that of a guarantee, some types of letter of credit, a credit derivative default contract or an insurance contract. However, although these contracts meet the definition of an insurance contract, they also meet the definition of a **financial guarantee contract** in FRS 102 and are within the scope of Section 21 of FRS 102, not this FRS (see paragraph 1.7(d)). Nevertheless, if an issuer of financial guarantee contracts has previously asserted explicitly that it regards such contracts as insurance contracts and has used accounting applicable to insurance contracts, the issuer may elect to apply either Section 21 of FRS 102 or this FRS to such financial guarantee contracts.

(h)   product warranties. Product warranties issued by another party for goods sold by a manufacturer, dealer or retailer are within the scope of this FRS. However, product warranties issued directly by a manufacturer, dealer or retailer are outside its scope, because they are within the scope of Sections 21 and 23 of FRS 102.

(i)   title insurance (ie insurance against the discovery of defects in title to land that were not apparent when the insurance contract was written). In this case, the insured event is the discovery of a defect in the title, not the defect itself.

(j)   travel assistance (ie compensation in cash or in kind to policyholders for losses suffered while they are travelling). Paragraphs A2.6 and A2.7 discuss some contracts of this kind.

(k)   catastrophe bonds that provide for reduced payments of principal, interest or both if a specified event adversely affects the issuer of the bond (unless the specified event does not create significant insurance risk, for example if the event is a change in an interest rate or foreign exchange rate).

(l)   insurance swaps and other contracts that require a payment based on changes in climatic, geological or other physical variables that are specific to a party to the contract.

(m)   reinsurance contracts.

The following are examples of items that are not insurance contracts: **A2.19**

(a)   **investment contracts** that have the legal form of an insurance contract but do not expose the insurer to significant insurance risk, for example life insurance contracts in which the insurer bears no significant mortality risk (such contracts are non-insurance **financial instruments** or service contracts, see paragraphs A2.20 and A2.21).

(b)   contracts that have the legal form of insurance, but pass all significant insurance risk back to the policyholder through non-cancellable and enforceable mechanisms that adjust future payments by the policyholder as a direct result of insured losses, for example some **financial reinsurance** contracts or some group contracts (such contracts are normally non-insurance financial instruments or service contracts, see paragraphs A2.20 and A2.21).

(c)   self-insurance, in other words retaining a risk that could have been covered by insurance (there is no insurance contract because there is no agreement with another party).

(d)   contracts (such as gambling contracts) that require a payment if a specified uncertain future event occurs, but do not require, as a contractual precondition for payment, that the event adversely affects the policyholder. However, this does not preclude the specification of a predetermined payout to quantify the loss caused by a specified event such as death or an accident (see also paragraph A2.13).

(e) derivatives that expose one party to financial risk but not insurance risk, because they require that party to make payment based solely on changes in one or more of a specified interest rate, financial instrument price, commodity price, foreign exchange rate, index of prices or rates, credit rating or credit index or other variable, provided in the case of a non-financial variable that the variable is not specific to a party to the contract (see FRS 102).

(f) a credit-related guarantee (or letter of credit, credit derivative default contract or credit insurance contract) that requires payments even if the holder has not incurred a loss on the failure of the debtor to make payments when due.

(g) contracts that require a payment based on a climatic, geological or other physical variable that is not specific to a party to the contract (commonly described as weather derivatives).

(h) catastrophe bonds that provide for reduced payments of principal, interest or both, based on a climatic, geological or other physical variable that is not specific to a party to the contract.

A2.20 If the contracts described in paragraph A2.19 create **financial assets** or **financial liabilities**, they are within the scope of Sections 11 *Basic Financial Instruments* and 12 *Other Financial Instruments Issues* of FRS 102. Among other things, this means that the parties to the contract use what is sometimes called deposit accounting, which involves the following:

(a) one party recognises the consideration received as a financial liability, rather than as revenue; and

(b) the other party recognises the consideration paid as a financial asset, rather than as an expense.

A2.21 If the contracts described in paragraph A2.19 do not create financial assets or financial liabilities, Section 23 of FRS 102 applies. Under Section 23 of FRS 102, revenue associated with a transaction involving the rendering of services is recognised by reference to the stage of completion of the transaction if the outcome of the transaction can be estimated reliably.

Examples of revenue recognition under the principles in Section 23 of FRS 102

A2.22 Examples 15, 17 and 17A in the appendix to Section 23 of FRS 102 are relevant to the **recognition** of revenue for the types of contract described in paragraph A2.19.

A2.23 Where the consideration for a contract meeting the definition of an investment contract comprises both a fee for the origination and an ongoing charge for the provision of (eg investment management) services, the insurance undertaking shall record the origination fee as revenue on the date on which it becomes entitled to it where it can be demonstrated that the undertaking has no further obligations in respect of the fee.

A2.24 Incremental costs that are directly attributable to securing an investment management contract are recognised as an asset if they can be identified separately and measured reliably and if it is probable that they will be recovered. The asset represents the entity's contractual right to benefit from providing investment management services and is amortised as the entity recognises the related revenue. If the entity has a portfolio of investment management contracts, it may assess their recoverability on a portfolio basis.

SIGNIFICANT INSURANCE RISK

A contract is an insurance contract only if it transfers significant insurance risk. Paragraphs A2.8 to A2.21 discuss insurance risk. The following paragraphs discuss the assessment of whether insurance risk is significant. **A2.25**

Insurance risk is significant if, and only if, an insured event could cause an insurer to pay significant additional benefits in any scenario, excluding scenarios that lack commercial substance (ie have no discernible effect on the economics of the transaction). If significant additional benefits would be payable in scenarios that have commercial substance, the condition in the previous sentence may be met even if the insured event is extremely unlikely or even if the expected (ie probability-weighted) **present value** of contingent cash flows is a small proportion of the expected present value of all the remaining contractual cash flows. **A2.26**

The additional benefits described in paragraph A2.26 refer to amounts that exceed those that would be payable if no insured event occurred (excluding scenarios that lack commercial substance). Those additional amounts include claims handling and claims assessment costs, but exclude: **A2.27**

(a) the loss of the ability to charge the policyholder for future services. For example, in an investment-linked life insurance contract, the death of the policyholder means that the insurer can no longer perform investment management services and collect a fee for doing so. However, this economic loss for the insurer does not reflect insurance risk, just as a mutual fund manager does not take on insurance risk in relation to the possible death of the client. Therefore, the potential loss of future investment management fees is not relevant in assessing how much insurance risk is transferred by a contract;

(b) waiver on death of charges that would be made on cancellation or **surrender**. Because the contract brought those charges into existence, the waiver of these charges does not compensate the policyholder for a pre-existing risk. Hence, they are not relevant in assessing how much insurance risk is transferred by a contract;

(c) a payment conditional on an event that does not cause a significant loss to the holder of the contract. For example, consider a contract that requires the issuer to pay one million currency units if an asset suffers physical damage causing an insignificant economic loss of one currency unit to the holder. In this contract, the holder transfers to the insurer the insignificant risk of losing one currency unit. At the same time, the contract creates non-insurance risk that the issuer will need to pay 999,999 currency units if the specified event occurs. Because the issuer does not accept significant insurance risk from the holder, this contract is not an insurance contract;

(d) possible **reinsurance recoveries**. The insurer accounts for these separately.

An insurer shall assess the significance of insurance risk contract by contract, rather than by reference to materiality to the **financial statements**[9]. Thus, insurance risk may be significant even if there is a minimal probability of material losses for a whole book of contracts. This contract-by-contract assessment makes it easier to classify a contract as an insurance contract. However, if a relatively homogeneous book of small contracts is known to consist of contracts that all transfer insurance risk, an insurer need not examine each contract within that book to identify a few non-derivative contracts that transfer insignificant insurance risk. **A2.28**

---

[9] *For this purpose, contracts entered into simultaneously with a single counterparty (or contracts that are otherwise interdependent) form a single contract.*

A2.29 It follows from paragraphs A2.26 to A2.28 that if a contract pays a death benefit exceeding the amount payable on survival, the contract is an insurance contract unless the additional death benefit is insignificant (judged by reference to the contract rather than to an entire book of contracts). As noted in paragraph A2.27(b), the waiver on death of cancellation or surrender charges is not included in this assessment if this waiver does not compensate the policyholder for a pre-existing risk. Similarly, an annuity contract that pays out regular sums for the rest of a policyholder's life is an insurance contract, unless the aggregate life-contingent payments are insignificant.

A2.30 Paragraph A2.26 refers to additional benefits. These additional benefits could include a requirement to pay benefits earlier if the insured event occurs earlier and the payment is not adjusted for the time value of money. An example is whole life insurance for a fixed amount (in other words, insurance that provides a fixed death benefit whenever the policyholder dies, with no expiry date for the cover). It is certain that the policyholder will die, but the date of death is uncertain. The insurer will suffer a loss on those individual contracts for which policyholders die early, even if there is no overall loss on the whole book of contracts.

A2.31 If an insurance contract is **unbundled** into a **deposit component** and an insurance component, the significance of insurance risk transfer is assessed by reference to the insurance component. The significance of insurance risk transferred by an embedded derivative is assessed by reference to the embedded derivative.

CHANGES IN THE LEVEL OF INSURANCE RISK

A2.32 Some contracts do not transfer any insurance risk to the issuer at inception, although they do transfer insurance risk at a later time. For example, consider a contract that provides a specified **investment return** and includes an option for the policyholder to use the proceeds of the investment on maturity to buy a life-contingent annuity at the current annuity rates charged by the insurer to other new annuitants when the policyholder exercises the option. The contract transfers no insurance risk to the issuer until the option is exercised, because the insurer remains free to price the annuity on a basis that reflects the insurance risk transferred to the insurer at that time. However, if the contract specifies the annuity rates (or a basis for setting the annuity rates), the contract transfers insurance risk to the issuer at inception.

A2.33 A contract that qualifies as an insurance contract remains an insurance contract until all rights and obligations are extinguished or expire.

Appendix III
Tables of concordance between FRS 103, FRS 27 and the ABI SORP

This appendix maps the source material in FRS 27 and the ABI SORP into the FRS.

FRS 27

Source paragraph	Location in FRS 103/ IG	Notes
1	Summary (vi)	
2	Appendix I	Integrated into Appendix I: Glossary
3	Not used	Not applicable under FRS 103
4	3.7 and 3.12	
5	5.3	
6	3.11	
7	IG1.1	
8	Not used	
9	Not used	
10	3.14	
11	Not used	
12	Not used	
13	IG1.3	Significant deletions/amendments to the text
14	IG1.5	Significant deletions/amendments to the text
15	IG1.6	
16	3.15	Significant deletions/amendments to the text
17	IG1.10	
18	3.13	
19	IG1.11	
20	IG1.12	
21	IG1.13	Significant deletions/amendments to the text
22	Not used	Covered by the Regulations
23	5.5	
24	5.4	
25	Not used	
26	Not used	
27	3.16	Significant deletions/amendments to the text
28	3.17	
29	3.18	
30	Not used	Covered by paragraph 8.5 of FRS 102
31	Not used	Subsidiary exemption from disclosure no longer applicable

Source paragraph	Location in FRS 103/ IG	Notes
32	IG3.1	
33	IG3.2	
34	IG3.3	
35	IG3.4	
36	Not used	
37	IG3.5	
38	IG3.6	
39	IG3.7	
40	IG3.8	
41	IG3.9	Provides guidance on best practice
42	IG3.10	
43	IG3.11	
44	IG3.12	Significant deletions/amendments to the text
45	IG3.13	
46	Not used	
47	Not used	
48	IG3.14	
49	IG3.16	Significant deletions/amendments to the text
50	IG3.17	
51	IG3.18	Provides guidance on best practice
52	IG3.19	
53	IG3.20	
54	Not used	
55	IG3.21	
56	IG3.22	Provides guidance on best practice
57	Not used	
58	IG3.23	
59	IG3.15	Paragraph moved to before FRS 27.49
60	Not used	

ABI SORP

Source section / paragraph	Paragraphs used	Location in FRS 103/IG
Definitions	Various	Integrated into Appendix I: Glossary
Gross written premiums	83, 84, 85, 87, 88, 89, 90, 91	IG2.1 – IG2.8
Claims	94, 95, 99, 100, 101	IG2.9 – IG2.13
Discounting	105, 106, 107, 108, 110, 112, 113	IG2.14 – IG2.20
Unexpired risks provision	117, 118, 119, 120, 121, 122, 123	IG2.21 – IG2.27
Equalisation reserves	125	IG2.28
Portfolio premiums and claims	127, 128, 129, 130	IG2.29 – IG2.32
Structured settlements	131	IG2.33
Deferred acquisition costs	132, 133, 135	IG2.34 – IG2.36
Measurement of with-profits liabilities and related assets	149, 151, 152, 153, 154	IG1.2, IG1.4 and IG1.7 – IG1.9
Examples of revenue recognition	159, 161	A2.23 – A2.24
Premiums	163, 164	3.3 – 3.4
Claims	166, 167	3.5 – 3.6
Deferred acquisition costs	171, 174, 175*	3.8 – 3.10 * 175 is placed before 171
Technical provisions	178, 180, 182, 183, 184, 185, 186, 187, 188*, 189**, 190, 191	IG2.38 – IG2.49 * 188 is placed after 184 ** 189 is placed after 191
Fund for future appropriations	194, 195	IG2.50 – IG2.51
Reserves relating to long term business	196, 197	IG2.52 – IG2.53
Present value of acquired in-force business	200, 201	IG2.54 – IG2.55
Disaggregated information about single and regular premiums	213*, 214, 216*, 217	IG2.56 – IG2.58 * 213 and 216 are combined, and placed after 214
Commission	218	4.6
Exchange gains and losses	219	2.32
Income Statement	225, 226	IG2.59 – IG2.60
Retirement benefits	230, 232*, 234*	2.33 – 2.34 * 232 and 234 are combined

Source section / paragraph	Paragraphs used	Location in FRS 103/IG
Valuation of reinsurance asset	259, 260	IG2.61 Combined with FRS 27.12
Reinsurance balance	264	IG2.62
Allocation of investment return	290, 291, 292, 293, 295, 296, 297, 298, 305	IG2.63 – IG2.71
The longer term rate of investment return	299, 300, 301, 302, 303, 304	IG2.72 – IG2.77
Investments in unit trusts/OEICs	311	IG2.78

Appendix IV
Note on Legal Requirements

INTRODUCTION

This appendix provides an overview of how the requirements in FRS 103 address United Kingdom company law requirements. It is therefore written from the perspective of a company to which the Companies Act 2006 applies. Appendix V contains the Republic of Ireland legal references.　**A4.1**

Many entities that are not constituted as companies apply accounting standards promulgated by the FRC for the purposes of preparing financial statements that present a true and fair view[10]. A brief consideration of the legal framework for some other entities can be found at A4.3.　**A4.2**

Entities not subject to company law

Many entities that apply FRS 103 are not companies, but are nevertheless required by their governing legislation, or other regulation or requirement to prepare financial statements that present a true and fair view of the financial performance and financial position of the reporting entity. However, the FRC sets accounting standards within the framework of the Act and therefore it is the company law requirements that the FRC primarily considered when developing FRS 103. Entities preparing financial statements within other legal frameworks will need to satisfy themselves that FRS 103 does not conflict with any relevant legal obligations.　**A4.3**

The FRC notes the following:

Legislation	Overview of requirements
Friendly Societies Act 1992	Every society shall prepare a balance sheet and an income and expenditure account for each financial year giving a true and fair view of the affairs of the society and its income and expenditure for the year. The Friendly Societies (Accounts and Related Provisions) Regulations 1994 (as amended) make further requirements about the form and content of friendly society accounts, which do not generally appear inconsistent with the requirements of FRS 102 and FRS 103. However, for a non-directive society (as defined in the regulations) the regulations set out a different required format.
Industrial and Provident Societies Act 1965	The Insurance Accounts Directive (Miscellaneous Insurance Undertakings) Regulations 2008 require every society that is an insurance undertaking to prepare its financial statements substantially as though it were a company registered under the Companies Act 2006.

---

[10] *More information about the 'true and fair' concept can be found on the FRC's website at http://www.frc.org.uk/ Our-Work/Codes-Standards/Accounting-and-Reporting-Policy/True-and-Fair.aspx.*

Legislation	Overview of requirements
Insurance Accounts Directive (Lloyd's Syndicate and Aggregate Accounts) Regulations 2008	In respect of each syndicate managing agents shall prepare accounts on an underwriting year basis that give a true and fair view of the results of that underwriting year.

Prospective amendments: FRED 64 (December 2015) proposes amendments to the table in paragraph A4.3 with effect for annual periods beginning on or after [date].

Appendix V
Republic of Ireland (RoI) Legal References

INTRODUCTION

The table below outlines the provisions of the Companies Acts 1963 to 2013 and related   **A5.1**
Regulations which implement EC Accounting Directives in Ireland (Irish company law)
which correspond to the provisions of UK company law referred to in the FRS.

In an Irish context, the principal legislation of relevance is the European Communities   **A5.2**
(Insurance Undertakings: Accounts) Regulations 1996 (SI No. 23 of 1996) (Insurance
Undertakings Regulations 1996 or IUR 1996).

The following Irish legislation is also referenced in the table below: **A5.3**

- European Communities (Non-life Insurance) Framework Regulations 1994 – SI 359
  of 1994;
- European Communities (Life Assurance) Framework Regulations 1994 – SI 360 of
  1994;
- The Building Societies Act 1989;
- The Credit Union Acts 1997 and 2012;
- The Central Bank Act 1971;
- The Charities Act 2009; and
- The Friendly Societies Acts 1896 to 1977.

Throughout the FRS, general references are made to 'the Regulations', which are defined   **A5.4**
in the Glossary as the UK Large and Medium-sized Companies and Groups (Accounts and
Reports) Regulations 2008 (SI 2008/410). Schedule 3 and Schedule 6 of those Regulations
apply to UK insurance companies preparing Companies Act individual accounts and
Companies Act group accounts respectively. General references are also made in this
FRS to 'the Act', which is defined in the Glossary as the (UK) 'Companies Act 2006'.
Such general references to 'the Regulations' and 'the Act' in the FRS are not included in
the table below. In an Irish context, reference should be made to the relevant provisions of
the Irish legislation outlined above.

OTHER NOTES

The table below is intended to serve as a general reference guide to the corresponding or   **A5.5**
similar provisions in Irish law and does not purport to be complete. It should be noted that
not all of the Irish legal provisions in the table below are equivalent to the corresponding UK
legal provisions and reference should be made to the Irish legislation for an understanding
of relevant requirements. In some cases reference may need to be made to other parts of
Irish legislation.

Furthermore, the table below does not address the regulatory aspects of accounting for   **A5.6**
insurance contracts. Where this FRS makes reference to the handbook, regulations, rules
or guidance of the UK Prudential Regulatory Authority (PRA), reference should be made
in an Irish context to the regulatory requirements and guidance of the Central Bank of
Ireland as well as legislation applicable to insurance undertakings. Of particular relevance
in this regard are SI 359 of 1994 and SI 360 of 1994, as noted above. It should also be
noted that there are some differences between the UK and Irish regulatory requirements,
for example the 'PRA Realistic Capital Regime' for with-profits insurance business is not
relevant in Ireland.

SECTION 1: SCOPE

Paragraph	UK Reference	RoI Reference
1.4	Schedule 3 to the Regulations	Insurance Undertakings Regulations 1996

SECTION 4: DISCLOSURE

Paragraph	UK Reference	RoI Reference
4.6	Schedule 3 to the Regulations	Insurance Undertakings Regulations 1996

ACCOUNTING COUNCIL'S ADVICE TO THE FRC TO ISSUE FRS 103 INSURANCE CONTRACTS

Paragraph	UK Reference	RoI Reference
24, 38, 39	Schedule 3 to the Regulations	Insurance Undertakings Regulations 1996

APPENDIX I: GLOSSARY

Paragraph	UK Reference	RoI Reference
'Acquisition costs'	Note 6 to the Notes on the Profit and Loss Account format in Schedule 3 to the Regulations	Note 6 to the Notes on the profit and loss account format in Section B of Chapter 2 of Part I of the Schedule to the Insurance Undertakings Regulations 1996
'Financial institution' and Footnote 6	Part 4A permission; Section 55A of the Financial Services and Markets Act 2000	There is no equivalent legislation in Ireland to the Financial Services and Markets Act 2000. Banks in Ireland are licensed under Section 9 of the Central Bank Act 1971
'Financial institution'	Section 119(1) of the Building Societies Act 1986	Section 2(1) of the Building Societies Act 1989
'Financial institution'	Industrial and Provident Societies Act 1965 and Credit Unions Act 1979	Credit Union Acts 1997 to 2012
'Financial institution'	Friendly Societies Act 1992; section 7(1)(a) of the Friendly Societies Act 1974	Friendly Societies Acts 1896 to 1977
'Fund for future appropriations (FFA)'	Schedule 3 to the Regulations	Insurance Undertakings Regulations 1996
'General insurance business'	Part I of Schedule 1 to the Financial Services and Markets Act 2000 (Regulated Activities) Order 2001 (SI 2001/544)	Annex 1 of SI 359 of 1994
'Long term insurance business'	Part II of Schedule 1 to the Financial Services and Markets Act 2000 (Regulated Activities) Order 2001 (SI 2001/544)	Annex 1 of SI 360 of 1994

Paragraph	UK Reference	RoI Reference
'Non-technical account'	Part 1 of Schedule 3 to the Regulations	Section B of Chapter 2 of Part 1 of the Schedule to the Insurance Undertakings Regulations 1996
'Technical account'	Part I of Schedule 1 to the Regulated Activities Order	Annex 1 of SI 359 of 1994
'Technical account'	Part II of Schedule 1 to the Regulated Activities Order	Annex 1 of SI 360 of 1994
'Technical account'	Part I of Schedule 3 to the Regulations	Section B of Chapter 2 of Part 1 of the Schedule to the Insurance Undertakings Regulations 1996

APPENDIX IV: NOTE ON LEGAL REQUIREMENTS

Paragraph	UK Reference	RoI Reference
A4.3	Friendly Societies Act 1992	Friendly Societies Acts 1896 to 1977
A4.3	Industrial and Provident Societies Acts 1965	The Industrial and Provident Societies (Amendment) Act 1978
A4.3	Insurance Accounts Directive (Lloyd's Syndicate and Aggregate Accounts) Regulations 2008	There is no equivalent legislation in Ireland.

Amendments to FRS 103:
Insurance Contracts – Solvency II

(May 2016)

Contents

Editor's note: These amendments are effective for accounting periods beginning on or after 1 January 2016. Early adoption is not permitted, consistent with the effective date of the new regulatory framework.

SUMMARY

(i)   With effect from 1 January 2015, the Financial Reporting Council (FRC) revised financial reporting standards in the United Kingdom and Republic of Ireland. The revisions fundamentally reformed financial reporting, replacing the extant standards with five Financial Reporting Standards:

    (a)   FRS 100 *Application of Financial Reporting Requirements*;

    (b)   FRS 101 *Reduced Disclosure Framework*;

    (c)   FRS 102 *The Financial Reporting Standard applicable in the UK and Republic of Ireland*;

    (d)   FRS 103 *Insurance Contracts*; and

    (e)   FRS 104 *Interim Financial Reporting*.

The FRC has also issued FRS 105 *The Financial Reporting Standard applicable to the Micro-entities Regime* to support the implementation of the new micro-entities regime. It is effective from 1 January 2016 with early application permitted.

These limited amendments to FRS 103 update it to reflect the implementation, from 1 January 2016, of the Solvency II Directive.

(ii)   The FRC's overriding objective in setting accounting standards is to enable users of accounts to receive high-quality understandable financial reporting proportionate to the size and complexity of the entity and users' information needs.

(iii)   In meeting this objective, the FRC aims to provide succinct financial reporting standards that:

    (a)   have consistency with international accounting standards through the application of an IFRS-based solution unless an alternative clearly better meets the overriding objective;

    (b)   reflect up-to-date thinking and developments in the way entities operate and the transactions they undertake;

    (c)   balance consistent principles for accounting by all UK and Republic of Ireland entities with practical solutions, based on size, complexity, public interest and users' information needs;

    (d)   promote efficiency within groups; and

    (e)   are cost-effective to apply.

AMENDMENTS TO FRS 103 – SOLVENCY II

(iv)   These amendments to FRS 103 update the terminology and definitions used for changes in the regulatory framework, following the implementation of the Solvency II Directive. Established accounting policies can continue to be applied if an entity so chooses.

AMENDMENTS TO FRS 103 *INSURANCE CONTRACTS*

Amendments to Section 1 Scope

The following paragraphs set out the amendments to Section 1 *Scope* (deleted text is struck through, inserted text is underlined).   **1**

Paragraph 1.5 is amended as follows: **2**

> 1.5 Paragraph 2.3 permits entities to change their **accounting policies**, either on adoption of this FRS or subsequently, providing their new accounting policies meet certain criteria. Entities that are setting accounting policies in relation to insurance contracts, or other financial instruments with discretionary participation features, for the first time, shall <u>for long-term insurance business either:</u>
>
> <u>(a)</u> first consider the requirements of Section 3, the Regulations and any relevant parts of FRS 102, ~~as a means of establishing current practice~~ as a benchmark before assessing whether to set accounting policies that differ from those benchmark policies in accordance with paragraph 2.3<u>; or</u>
>
> <u>(b) establish accounting policies that are based on the rules under the</u> **Solvency II Directive** <u>for the recognition and measurement of technical provisions, and any relevant requirements of this FRS, the Regulations and FRS 102. In doing so an entity shall make appropriate adjustments to the Solvency II rules to ensure that the accounting policies result in information that is relevant and reliable.</u>
>
> The Implementation Guidance accompanying this FRS also provides guidance.

Paragraph 1.11A is inserted as follows: **3**

> <u>1.11A In May 2016 amendments were made to this FRS, to update it for changes in the regulatory framework. An entity shall apply these amendments for accounting periods ending on or after 1 January 2016.</u>

Amendments to Section 2 Accounting Policies, Recognition and Measurement

The following paragraph sets out the amendments to Section 2 *Accounting Policies, Recognition and Measurement* (inserted text is underlined).   **4**

Paragraph 2.3A is inserted as follows: **5**

> 2.3A <u>One basis for changing accounting policies might be to enable them to be more consistent with the rules under the</u> **Solvency II Directive** <u>for the recognition and measurement of technical provisions. In doing so an entity shall make appropriate adjustments to the Solvency II rules to meet the requirements of paragraph 2.3.</u>

Amendments to Section 3 Recognition and Measurement: Requirements for entities with long-term insurance business

The following paragraphs set out the amendments to Section 3 *Recognition and Measurement: Requirements for entities with long-term insurance business* (deleted text is struck through, inserted text is underlined).   **6**

7   Paragraph 3.1 is amended as follows (and 'realistic capital regime' is no longer shown in bold type):

    3.1 This section sets out requirements for entities applying this FRS that are carrying out **long-term insurance business**:

    (a)   Paragraphs 3.3 to 3.9~~10~~ and 3.16 to 3.18 apply to all long-term insurance business.

    (b)   Paragraphs 3.10~~1~~ to 3.15 apply to **with-profits business** and with-profits funds, to which the **Prudential Regulatory Authority (PRA)** realistic capital regime (as set out in section 1.3 of **INSPRU** as at 31 December 2015) ~~i~~was being applied, either voluntarily or compulsorily, prior to 1 January 2016.

8   Paragraph 3.1A is inserted as follows:

    3.1A This section sets out the benchmark for setting **accounting policies** for long-term insurance business as at 1 January 2015. Entities are permitted to change their accounting policies in accordance with paragraph 2.3. Entities that are setting accounting policies for the first time may apply this benchmark in accordance with paragraph 1.5(a) or are permitted to set alternative policies in accordance with paragraph 1.5(b).

9   Paragraph 3.2 is amended as follows:

    3.2 Where an entity has changed its **accounting policies** in accordance with paragraph 2.3 or adopted accounting policies in accordance with paragraph 1.5(b), and its ~~new~~ accounting policies are ~~no longer~~not consistent with this section, the requirements of this section that are ~~no longer~~not consistent with the entity's accounting policies need not be applied.

10   Paragraph 3.7 is amended as follows, and renumbered as paragraph 3.10:

    3.7~~10~~ **Acquisition costs** shall not be deferred for with-profits funds ~~to which the PRA realistic capital regime is being applied, either voluntarily or compulsorily~~.

11   Paragraphs 3.8 is amended as follows, and renumbered as paragraph 3.7:

    3.8~~7~~ Except as required by paragraph 3.~~10~~7, acquisition costs shall be deferred except to the extent that:

    (a)   …

12   Paragraphs 3.9 and 3.10 are renumbered as paragraphs 3.8 and 3.9.

13   Paragraph 3.11 is amended as follows:

    3.11 The established accounting treatment for long-term insurance business is to measure liabilities for policyholder benefits under the **modified statutory solvency basis (MSSB)**. This FRS requires ~~those~~ with-profits funds ~~within the scope of the PRA realistic capital regime~~ to use the **realistic value of liabilities** as the basis for the estimated value of the liabilities to be included in the **financial statements**.

Paragraph 3.12 is amended as follows: **14**

3.12 For with-profits funds ~~to which the PRA realistic capital regime is being applied, either voluntarily or compulsorily~~:

(a) liabilities to policyholders arising from with-profits business shall be stated at the amount of the realistic value of liabilities adjusted to exclude the shareholders' share of projected future **bonuses**;

(b) **reinsurance recoveries** that are recognised shall be measured on a basis that is consistent with the value of the policyholder liabilities to which the reinsurance applies;

(c) an amount may be recognised for the **present value** of future profits on **non-participating business** written in a with-profits fund if:

(i) ~~the non-participating business is measured on a realistic basis for the purposes of the regulatory returns made under the PRA realistic capital regime;~~

(ii) ~~the value is determined in accordance with the PRA regulations; and~~

(iii) the determination of the realistic value of liabilities in that with-profits fund takes account, directly or indirectly, of this value;

(d) where a with-profits life fund has an interest in a subsidiary or associate and the determination of the realistic value of liabilities to with-profits policyholders takes account of a value of that interest at an amount in excess of the net amounts included in the entity's consolidated accounts, an amount may be recognised representing this excess; and

(e) adjustments to reflect the consequential tax effects of (a) to (d) above shall be made.

Adjustments from the MSSB necessary to meet the above requirements, including the recognition of an amount in accordance with paragraph 3.12(c) or 3.12(d), shall be included in **profit or loss**. An amount equal and opposite to the net amount of these adjustments shall be transferred to or from the **fund for future appropriations (FFA)** and also included in profit or loss.

Amendments to Section 4 Disclosure

The following paragraph sets out the amendments to Section 4 *Disclosure* (deleted text is struck through, inserted text is underlined). **15**

Paragraph 4.5 is amended as follows: **16**

4.5 To comply with paragraph 4.4 an insurer shall disclose:

(a) ...

(b) the process used to determine the assumptions that have the greatest effect on the measurement of the recognised amounts described in (ab). When practicable, an insurer shall also give quantified disclosure of those assumptions;

(c) ...

Amendments to Appendix I: Glossary

17   The following glossary terms and definitions, and footnote 8 (subsequent footnotes will be renumbered sequentially), are deleted:

~~long-term fund~~	~~The fund or funds maintained by an undertaking in respect of its **long-term insurance business** in accordance with the PRA rules.~~
~~realistic capital regime~~	~~As set out in section 1.3 of INSPRU[8].~~

~~[8] References to the PRA's Prudential sourcebook for insurers, and to individual rules therein, are to the rules made on 1 April 2013 by the FCA and PRA Handbook Designation (General Modifications) Instrument 2013.~~

18   The following glossary term and definition is inserted in alphabetical order:

Solvency II Directive	<u>Directive 2009/138/EC of the European Parliament and of the Council of 25 November 2009 on the taking-up and pursuit of the business of Insurance and Reinsurance (Solvency II), as amended by Directive 2013/58/EU, and as implemented in the United Kingdom and Republic of Ireland.</u>

19   The following glossary terms and definitions are amended as follows (deleted text is struck through, inserted text is underlined):

equalisation provisions	As defined in the relevant regulatory framework ~~(eg INSPRU)~~.
gross premium method	A form of actuarial valuation of **liabilities** arising under long-term insurance contracts where the premiums brought into account are the full amounts receivable under the contract. The method includes explicit estimates of cash flows for: (a) premiums, adjusted for renewals and lapses; (b) expected claims and for **with-profits business** future regular but not occasional or terminal **bonuses**; (c) costs of maintaining contracts; and (d) future renewal expenses. Cash flows are discounted at the valuation interest rate. The methodology may be set out in the relevant regulatory framework. ~~For UK companies this is included in the PRA Handbook.~~ The discount rate is based on the expected return on the assets deemed to back the **liabilities** ~~as prescribed by the PRA Handbook. This may be further constrained by a maximum rate set by the PRA~~. This will be adjusted to reflect any further risks although, under this method, most of the key risks will be reflected in the modelling of the cash flows. For **linked business**, allowance may be made for the purchase of future units required by the contract terms and credit is taken for future charges permitted under those terms.
modified statutory solvency (MSSB)	The basis for determining **insurance liabilities** which is the **statutory solvency basis** adjusted for the following items:

	(a) to defer new business **acquisition costs** incurred where the benefit of such costs will be obtained in subsequent **reporting periods**; and
	(b) to treat investment, resilience and similar reserves, or reserves held in respect of general contingencies or the specific contingency that the fund will be closed to new business, where such items are held in respect of **long-term insurance business** ~~within the long-term fund~~, as reserves rather than provisions. These are included, as appropriate, within shareholders' capital and reserves or the **fund for future appropriations (FFA)**.
mutual	As defined in the **PRA** ~~Handbook~~Rulebook.
net premium method	An actuarial valuation of **liabilities** arising under long-term **insurance contracts** where the premium brought into account at any valuation date is that which, on the valuation assumptions regarding interest, mortality and disability, will exactly provide for the benefits guaranteed. A variation of the net premium method involves **zillmerisation**. The detailed methodology for UK companies is included in regulations contained in the **PRA** ~~Handbook~~Rulebook as at 31 December 2015.
non-participating business	**Long-term insurance business** where **policyholders** are not entitled to share in the surplus of the relevant ~~long-term fund~~ long-term business.
principles and practices of financial management (PPFM)	The statement that the **PRA** Financial Conduct Authority requires each **with-profits** life fund to make available to its **policyholders** containing, inter alia, a description of the fund's investment management and bonus distribution policies.
Prudential sourcebook for insurers (INSPRU)	The section of the **PRA**~~Handbook~~Rulebook detailing the prudential rules for **insurers**, including capital requirements, credit, market and **liquidity risk** for periods ending before 1 January 2016.
realistic value of liabilities	That element of the amount defined by rule 1.3.40 ~~in~~of **INSPRU** as at 31 December 2015, excluding current **liabilities** falling within the definition set out in rule 1.3.190 of INSPRU as at 31 December 2015 that are recognised separately in the **statement of financial position**.
regulatory capital resources	An entity's capital resources as calculated in accordance with ~~the capital resources table in INSPRU~~regulatory framework.
statutory solvency basis	The basis of determination of **insurance liabilities** in accordance with rule 1 of **INSPRU** as at 31 December 2015.
with-profits business	**Long-term insurance business** ~~where policyholders are contractually entitled to share in the surplus of the relevant long-term fund~~which provides benefits through eligibility to participate in discretionary distributions based on profits arising from the **insurer**'s business or from a particular part of the insurer's business. A with-profits contract is an example of a contract with a **discretionary participation feature**.

Amendments to Appendix IV: Note on legal requirements

20   The following paragraph sets out the amendments to Appendix IV: *Note on legal requirements* (deleted text is struck through, inserted text is underlined).

21   The table in paragraph A4.3 is amended as follows (only the line that is amended is shown here):

Legislation	Overview of requirements
~~Industrial and Provident Societies Act 1965~~ Co-operative and Community Benefit Societies Act 2014	The Insurance Accounts Directive (Miscellaneous Insurance Undertakings) Regulations 2008 require every society that is an insurance undertaking to prepare its financial statements substantially as though it were a company registered under the Companies Act 2006.

AMENDMENTS TO IMPLEMENTATION GUIDANCE TO ACCOMPANY FRS 103 *INSURANCE CONTRACTS*

Amendments to Implementation Guidance – Section 1 Guidance for entities with long-term insurance business

22   The following paragraphs set out the amendments to Implementation Guidance – Section 1 *Guidance for entities with long-term insurance business* (deleted text is struck through, inserted text is underlined).

23   Paragraph IG1.1 is amended as follows (footnote 1 is not amended and is not repeated here):

IG1.1 An entity may, but is not required to, adopt the requirements of paragraph 3.12 of **FRS 103** *Insurance Contracts* for UK[1] **with-profits business** that does not fall within the scope of ~~the **PRA realistic capital regime** or for which the PRA has granted a full waiver from compliance with this regime~~paragraph 3.1(b) of FRS 103. If an entity changes its **accounting policy** for such with-profits business it shall only do so in accordance with paragraph 2.3 of FRS 103.

24   Paragraph IG1.2 is amended as follows:

IG1.2 The shareholders' share of projected future **bonuses** deducted in accordance with paragraph 3.12(a) of FRS 103 should be calculated as the value of future transfers to shareholders calculated using market consistent financial assumptions, and assuming that transfers take place at a level consistent with those assumptions used to calculate the **realistic value of liabilities**~~within the PRA realistic balance sheet~~. Where an explicit assumption is not required in order to calculate the **liabilities** ~~under the PRA's approach~~ then continuation of the current profit sharing arrangements should be assumed unless the firm has plans to change this approach. Non-economic projection assumptions should be consistent with those used in determining the realistic value of liabilities~~elsewhere in the realistic balance sheet~~. The amount deducted in accordance with this paragraph should be taken to the **fund for future appropriations (FFA)**. If shareholders transfers have been included as part of the ~~PRA~~ realistic value of liabilit~~ies~~y (or otherwise included in liabilities) then the amount of such transfers should be taken out of liabilities and included in the FFA, together with any related tax liability. If shareholders transfers have not been set up as part of the ~~PRA~~ realistic value of liabilit~~ies~~y or elsewhere, no adjustment is required.

Paragraph IG1.3 is amended as follows and 'realistic value of liabilities' is no longer shown in bold type: **25**

IG1.3 ~~Under the PRA realistic capital regime~~In determining the realistic value of liabilities, a with-profits life fund may take account of~~includes within assets~~ the value of future profits expected to arise from any **non-participating business** that forms part of the with-profits fund—sometimes referred to as the **value of in-force life assurance business (VIF)**. Excluding the VIF from the **statement of financial position** whilst recognising the realistic value of liabilities in full, and valuing the non-participating liabilities in the with-profits fund on a statutory basis, would give rise to an inconsistency in the fund's net assets. An entity is therefore permitted to recognise the VIF if that business has been taken into account in measuring the liability, in the circumstances of paragraph 3.12(c) of FRS 103, even though there is not a direct link between the value of the asset and the amount of the liabilities. Where there is not a direct link between the value of the business and the amount of realistic liabilities, but the value is taken into account in determining those liabilities, it is appropriate to recognise the total value of the business. Although not separately identifiable, any excess value over that included in realistic liabilities will be taken to the FFA.

Paragraph IG1.4 is amended as follows: **26**

IG1.4 Paragraph 3.12(c) of FRS 103 permits an amount to be recognised for VIF on non-participating business written in a with-profits fund when~~: (i) the non-participating business is measured on this basis for the purposes of the regulatory returns made under the PRA realistic capital regime; (ii) the VIF is calculated on the basis used in the PRA realistic capital regime; and (iii)~~ the determination of the realistic value of liabilities takes account of this value either directly or indirectly. Where with-profits **policyholders** are entitled to a share of the profits on non-participating business it would generally be expected that the determination of the realistic liabilities would take account, directly or indirectly, of the value of future profits on this business.

Paragraph IG1.6 is amended as follows: **27**

IG1.6 The VIF recognised within assets ~~for regulatory purposes~~as described in paragraph IG1.3~~2~~ is determined as the discounted value of future profits expected to arise from the policies, taking into account liabilities relating to the policies measured on th~~e~~a **statutory solvency basis**. ~~When~~This includes adjustments ~~are~~ made onto a **modified statutory solvency basis (MSSB)** for the purposes of the **financial statements** (for example, to adjust liabilities to exclude certain additional reserves included in the liabilities ~~for regulatory purposes~~when measured on the statutory solvency basis, or where future income included in the VIF covers **deferred acquisition costs** included in the ~~MSSB~~statement of financial position)~~.~~ ~~A~~a corresponding adjustment to the value of in-force policies will need to be made in order to ensure a consistent valuation.

Paragraph IG1.7 is amended as follows: **28**

IG1.7 Paragraph 3.12 of FRS 103 ~~requires~~permits ~~that~~ the recognition of a VIF asset ~~recognised~~when the ~~should be~~ determine~~d~~ation ~~in accordance with~~ of the realistic value of liabilities takes account of this value~~capital regime requirements~~. Paragraph IG1.4 explains that the value calculated ~~under the realistic capital regime requirements~~ must be adjusted to ensure consistency where adjustments have been made onto the MSSB measurement basis in relation to non-participating contracts. The measurement of the VIF asset ~~recognised in accordance with the realistic capital regime~~ may take into account the release of capital requirements for non-participating business. It would not be appropriate to recognise this release of capital requirements within the VIF asset presented in the accounts because the MSSB liabilities do not include an allowance for capital. Therefore the amount of the VIF asset ~~determined for the purposes of the PRA realistic capital regime~~ should be adjusted accordingly.

29   Paragraph IG1.8 is amended as follows:

IG1.8 The profit recognition profile for non-participating contracts which do not satisfy FRS 103's definition of an insurance contract or contain a **discretionary participation feature** will be determined by the requirements of Sections 11, 12 and 23 of **FRS 102**. Where these contracts are written in a with-profits fund, paragraph IG1.4 will apply but the VIF recognised for such contracts ~~for the purposes of the PRA's realistic capital regime~~ should be adjusted to reflect the difference in the profit recognition bases between the basis used to determine the VIF ~~used in~~taken into account in determining the realistic value of liabilities~~capital regime~~ and the profit recognition profile determined by FRS 102.

30   Paragraph IG1.9 is amended as follows:

IG1.9 Paragraph 3.12(d) of FRS 103 permits that when~~re~~ a with-profits fund has an interest in a subsidiary or associate and the determination of~~that is valued for PRA regulatory purposes~~ the realistic value of liabilities takes account of a value for that interest at an amount in excess of the net amounts that would be included in the entity's consolidated accounts, an amount may be recognised representing this excess ~~if the determination of the realistic value of liabilities to with-profits policyholders takes account of this value~~. As explained in paragraph 3.15 of FRS 103 this situation could arise where the subsidiary or associate writes non-participating business and the value of the subsidiary or associate ~~recognised for PRA reporting purposes~~ incorporates the VIF of non-participating business written in the subsidiary or associate. The value of the subsidiary or associate ~~recognised for PRA reporting purposes~~ is reduced by the subsidiary's or associate's capital requirement as noted in rule 1.3.33(3) of **INSPRU** as at 31 December 2015. When preparing both consolidated and non-consolidated accounts, the excess value that may be recognised should therefore be taken as the excess before deduction of the subsidiary's or associate's capital requirement.

31   Paragraph IG1.10 is amended as follows:

IG1.10 Where the amounts on a 'realistic' basis determined in accordance with paragraph 3.12 of FRS 103 are different from the amounts on th~~e~~a MSSB, a corresponding amount is transferred to or from the FFA, so that there is no effect on **equity**. The potential shareholders' share corresponding to additional bonuses to policyholders that have been included in the policyholders' liability should be accounted for in the FFA. As a result, there will generally be no change in the profit for the **reporting period** except where the adjustments result in a negative balance on the FFA and the entity determines that this negative balance should result in a deduction from equity through **profit or loss**.

32   Paragraph IG1.11 is amended as follows:

IG1.11 Entities with with-profits business within the scope of paragraph 3.1(b) of FRS 103~~the PRA realistic capital regime~~ are required to measure the liability of that business in respect of **options and guarantees** relating to policyholders either at **fair value** or at an amount estimated using a **market-consistent stochastic model** ~~in accordance with PRA regulations~~.

Paragraph IG1.12 is amended as follows (footnote 2 is not amended and is not repeated here): **33**

> IG1.12 For all entities with **long-term insurance business**, the best basis for measuring policyholders' options and guarantees is one that includes their time value[2]. Any **deterministic approach** to valuation of a policy with a guarantee or optionality feature will generally fail to deal appropriately with the time value of the option. Therefore stochastic modelling techniques to evaluate the range of potential outcomes should be used unless a market value for the option is available. The ~~PRA realistic capital regime~~regulatory framework includes a requirement to value options and guarantees on this basis. For the liabilities of businesses not falling within the scope of the ~~PRA realistic capital regime~~paragraph 3.1(b) of FRS 103, entities are encouraged, but not required, to adopt these valuation techniques. Where options are not valued on this basis, additional disclosures are required; these are set out in paragraph IG3.14(c).

Paragraph IG1.13 is amended as follows: **34**

> IG1.13 In determining the value of guarantees and options under the ~~PRA realistic capital regime~~regulatory framework, the entity will take into account under each scenario in the market-consistent stochastic modelling management actions it anticipates would be taken in response to variations in market variables (such as changing the balance of the investment portfolio between debt instruments and equity, varying the amount charged to policyholders, or varying its bonus policy) that will affect the amount payable under the guarantee or option. Such actions must be realistically capable of being implemented within the timescale assumed in the scenario analysis, and be consistent with the entity's published **principles and practices of financial managements (PPFM)**.

Amendments to Implementation Guidance – Section 2 Guidance for entities with general insurance business or long-term insurance business

The following paragraphs set out the amendments to Implementation Guidance – Section 2 **35** *Guidance for entities with general insurance business or long-term insurance business* (deleted text is struck through, inserted text is underlined).

Paragraph IG2.28 is amended as follows: **36**

> IG2.28 Disclosure should be made where an equalisation reserve has been established in accordance with the **PRA** ~~Handbook~~Rulebook. Where equalisation reserves are established, an entity should disclose the following in the notes to the financial statements:
>
> (a) that the amounts provided are not liabilities because they are in addition to the provisions required to meet the anticipated ultimate cost of settlement of outstanding claims at the reporting date;
>
> (b) notwithstanding this, they are required by Schedule 3 to the Regulations to be included within technical provisions; and
>
> (c) the impact of the equalisation reserves on **equity** and the effect of movements in the reserves on the profit or loss for the reporting period.

Paragraph IG2.42 is amended as follows: **37**

> IG2.42 The long-term business provision may be calculated on the basis used for regulatory reporting ~~under PRA rules~~subject to appropriate adjustments including:

(a) reassessment of the provisions and reserves included in the statutory liabilities for solvency purposes to consider the extent to which they should be included in the long-term business provision. This will require the exclusion of the appropriate proportion of reserves (such as investment reserves, reserves to cover general contingencies and reserves to cover the specific contingency of the fund being closed to new business). Any amount in excess of the necessary provision should be disclosed in the financial statements as a reserve or in the **fund for future appropriations (FFA)** as appropriate; and

(b) (b) the reversal of any reduction in policyholder liabilities in the regulatory returns where these liabilities already implicitly take account of a pension fund surplus through future expense assumptions which reflect lower expected contributions.

38   Paragraph IG2.48 is amended as follows:

> IG2.48 The net assets held to cover linked liabilities at the reporting date may differ from the technical provisions for linked liabilities. The reasons for any significant mismatching should be disclosed. In practice this should apply only to overseas companies included in consolidated financial statements because of the requirements of rule 3.1.57 of **INSPRU**.

39   In paragraph IG2.50 the first occurrence of 'FFA' is replaced by 'fund for future appropriations (FFA)' in bold type.

40   Paragraph IG2.53 is amended as follows:

> IG2.53 The investment return (which includes movements in realised and **unrealised investment gains and losses**) and related tax charges on assets representing reserves which are held for within the relevant **long-term insurance business** long-term fund for solvency purposes under the PRA rules should be credited to the technical account for long-term business. Allocations may then be made as appropriate to the **non-technical account** in accordance with paragraphs IG2.65 and IG2.66 or to the FFA. When the regulatory framework does not require the entity to set up a long-term fund for its long-term insurance business, the entity shall make the allocations as appropriate between the technical and non-technical account and disclose the basis of its allocation in the notes to the financial statements.

41   The rubric before paragraph IG2.56 is amended as follows:

> *Paragraphs IG2.56 to IG2.58* provide guidance for applying the requirements of paragraphs 2 and 3 of the instructions for completing Form 47 in the PRA rules. They *are only relevant to long-term insurance business.*

42   Paragraph IG2.60 is amended as follows:

> IG2.60 On consolidation, the profit or loss of any non-insurance entity belonging to the long-term fund (as defined in **INSRPU** as at 31 December 2015) may be included directly in the technical account for long-term business. Where material, more detailed disclosure should be provided in the notes to the financial statements. Where an entity carrying on general insurance business is owned by an asset of the long-term fund insurance business, the profit or loss of this business should be transferred from the non-technical account to the technical account for long-term business using new lines for this purpose.

APPROVAL BY THE FRC

Amendments to FRS 103 Insurance Contracts – Solvency II was approved for issue by the Board of the Financial Reporting Council on 19 May 2016, following its consideration of the Corporate Reporting Council's Advice.

THE CORPORATE REPORTING COUNCIL'S ADVICE TO THE FRC TO ISSUE *AMENDMENTS TO FRS 103 – SOLVENCY II*

Introduction

1   This report provides an overview of the main issues that have been considered by the Corporate Reporting Council in advising the Financial Reporting Council (FRC) to issue *Amendments to FRS 103 Insurance Contracts – Solvency II*.

2   The FRC, in accordance with the *Statutory Auditors (Amendment of Companies Act 2006 and Delegation of Functions etc) Order 2012* (SI 2012/1741), is a prescribed body for issuing accounting standards in the UK. The *Foreword to Accounting Standards* sets out the application of accounting standards in the Republic of Ireland.

3   In accordance with the *FRC Codes and Standards: procedures*, any proposal to issue, amend or withdraw a code or standard is put to the FRC Board with the full advice of the relevant Councils and/or the Codes & Standards Committee. Ordinarily, the FRC Board will only reject the advice put to it where:

(a)   it is apparent that a significant group of stakeholders has not been adequately consulted;

(b)   the necessary assessment of the impact of the proposal has not been completed, including an analysis of costs and benefits;

(c)   insufficient consideration has been given to the timing or cost of implementation; or

(d)   the cumulative impact of a number of proposals would make the adoption of an otherwise satisfactory proposal inappropriate.

4   The FRC has established the Corporate Reporting Council as the relevant Council to assist it in the setting of accounting standards.

Advice

5   The Corporate Reporting Council is advising the FRC to issue *Amendments to FRS 103 Insurance Contracts – Solvency II*.

6   The Corporate Reporting Council advises that these proposals will update FRS 103 *Insurance Contracts* for changes in the regulatory framework and ensure that established accounting policies can continue to be applied if an entity so chooses.

7   The Accounting Council's Advice[1] to the FRC to issue FRS 103 was set out in that standard. The Corporate Reporting Council's Advice to the FRC in respect of these amendments will be included in the revised FRS 103.

Background

8   When FRS 103 was issued in March 2014 the Accounting Council advised the FRC to review, in due course, whether or not consequential changes to FRS 103 would be required for the commencement of Solvency II.

9   As Solvency II is effective from 1 January 2016 this review has now been carried out and the Corporate Reporting Council advises that limited amendments are made to FRS 103 to reflect the changes in the regulatory regime. The Corporate Reporting Council does not advise making any other changes to FRS 103 at this time.

---

[1] *From 1 April 2016 the Accounting Council was renamed as the Corporate Reporting Council.*

The FRC consulted on the proposals for amendments to FRS 103 in FRED 64 *Draft* **10** *amendments to FRS 103 – Solvency II*. The responses to FRED 64 have been considered in developing this advice.

Amendments to FRS 103

FRS 103 makes a number of references to the PRA realistic capital regime, which was **11** replaced by Solvency II from 1 January 2016. In addition, it refers to the Prudential sourcebook for insurers (INSPRU), which was replaced from the same date. As these references are out of date, amendments are required to FRS 103.

In considering the amendments that are required, the Corporate Reporting Council advises **12** that entities should be permitted to continue to apply established accounting practices in their financial statements, if they choose to do so. It notes that FRS 103 already includes the ability for an insurer to change its accounting policies for insurance contracts if it judges certain criteria are met, and therefore there is no need to introduce specific new accounting policies relating to Solvency II.

In response to suggestions from respondents to FRED 64, the Corporate Reporting **13** Council advises making it clearer in FRS 103 that one basis for changing accounting policies might be in order to achieve greater alignment with Solvency II. This is reflected in paragraph 2.3A.

Scope of Section 3 Recognition and Measurement: Requirements for entities with long-term insurance business of FRS 103

The Corporate Reporting Council notes that paragraph 3.1(b) of FRS 103 describes the **14** circumstances in which the requirements for with-profits liabilities and related assets apply, which was based on those to which the PRA realistic capital regime applied. The Corporate Reporting Council considered the following two options for revising the description of the scope of these requirements:

(a)   describe more fully the current scope; or
(b)   describe the scope by reference to Solvency II.

The Corporate Reporting Council noted that describing the scope by reference to Solvency **15** II may extend the application of the relevant requirements of FRS 103 to entities not previously within their scope. As the Corporate Reporting Council's aim was to limit the amount of change in accounting policies that would be required, the Corporate Reporting Council advises effectively retaining the existing definition, but qualifying it to note that entities are within the scope of the requirements if they applied the realistic capital regime prior to 1 January 2016.

Revised definitions

Some of the key definitions within FRS 103 were based, either directly or indirectly, on the **16** rules of INSPRU. As a result of INSPRU being replaced by Solvency II for many insurers, these definitions needed revising. In FRED 64 the FRC proposed a revised description for the 'established method of accounting for long-term insurance business' (to replace the modified statutory solvency basis) and that both that definition and the definition of the 'realistic value of liabilities' should be principles-based, and consistent with accounting policies applied in periods ending before 1 January 2016.

Respondents noted that the definitions described features that could be attributed to many **17** bases and included the term 'appropriate' without further guidance. Some respondents suggested that retaining the current definitions, but clarifying that the references to INSPRU were to INSPRU as at 31 December 2015, would be a preferable solution. The Corporate Reporting Council noted that, as it did not intend the changes to FRS 103 to result in changes in accounting practice, however the phrases were defined, in practical terms entities would need to refer to INSPRU as at 31 December 2015 in order to continue with their existing accounting policies. Therefore the Corporate Reporting Council advises retaining the existing definitions of the 'modified statutory solvency basis' and the 'realistic value of liabilities', and amending them to refer to INSPRU as at 31 December 2015. The Corporate Reporting Council noted that the PRA Rulebook can be accessed 'as at' a certain date, and therefore this is a practical solution.

New entrants

18   Some of the respondents to FRED 64 noted that paragraph 1.5 of FRS 103 required new entrants establishing accounting policies for insurance contracts for the first time to consider the requirements of Section 3 of FRS 103 as a means of establishing current practice as a benchmark before assessing whether to 'improve' those policies. They noted that this might be unduly burdensome as new entrants would be required to assess their accounting policies against a benchmark which they would not need to consider for regulatory reporting purposes.

19   The Corporate Reporting Council considered the framework that should apply to new entrants, which might include both entirely new entities and new entities established within an existing group or business, as a result of a business reorganisation. Section 3 of FRS 103 was developed from previous UK accounting practice, and does not have an equivalent in IFRS. As a result, some respondents suggested that Section 3 of FRS 103 could be deleted, which would be consistent with IFRS and have little, or no, practical effect on existing entities.

20   The Corporate Reporting Council advises that a benchmark should be retained, in order to maintain a consistent starting point for insurers selecting their accounting policies for insurance contracts for the first time. The Corporate Reporting Council also notes that, although existing entities are not required to change their accounting policies, the change in regulatory regime may be a trigger for some entities to 'improve' their accounting policies, in order to make them more consistent with the new regulatory framework. As a result, 'current practice' may be evolving. Therefore, in light of the fact that the current benchmark is based on the previous regulatory regime, and the possible changes in current practice, the Corporate Reporting Council advises permitting two alternative starting points for new entrants. One is the requirements of Section 3 of FRS 102, and the other is to establish policies that are consistent with the relevant requirements of the Solvency II Directive, subject to any appropriate adjustments.

Accounting policies based on the requirements of Solvency II

21   The Corporate Reporting Council considered whether aspects of the rules under the Solvency II Directive might need amendment for use in measuring liabilities for financial reporting purposes. The Corporate Reporting Council advises that appropriate adjustments may be necessary in order to ensure that the financial statements meet the qualitative characteristics of information in financial statements (as set out in Section 2 *Concepts and Pervasive Principles* of FRS 102). This is reflected in paragraphs 1.5(b) and 2.3A of FRS 103.

22   The Corporate Reporting Council notes that items to consider, when determining whether and to what extent appropriate adjustments are required, might include the following:

(a)   transitional adjustments that may be made for regulatory purposes;

(b)   the volatility adjustment to the discount rate that is made for regulatory purposes;

(c)   the risk margin that is applied for regulatory purposes; and

(d)   'surplus funds' when these reflect contractual obligations of cash flows to policyholders.

Regulatory framework

Not all entities applying FRS 103 will be subject to the same regulatory framework.   **23**
In some instances the regulatory framework will set requirements relating to amounts to be recognised in the financial statements. When FRS 103 refers to a requirement of the regulatory framework, the Corporate Reporting Council advises that an entity shall apply the requirements of the regulatory framework that applies to it. This may result in differences in accounting between some entities. For example, most entities will not be required by the regulatory framework to recognise an equalisation provision from 1 January 2016.

Effective date

The Corporate Reporting Council advises that these amendments should be effective   **24**
for accounting periods ending on or after 1 January 2016. Early adoption should not be permitted because this is consistent with the effective date of the new regulatory framework.

Future development of FRS 103

When FRS 103 was issued, the Accounting Council advised that, in addition to reviewing   **25**
FRS 103 when Solvency II was implemented, once the IASB had issued its new insurance standard the requirements of FRS 103 should be reviewed. This project has not yet been completed by the IASB, and consequently it is still not possible to determine the appropriate timing for this further review of FRS 103.

Approval of this advice

This advice to the FRC was approved by the Corporate Reporting Council on 10 May 2016.   **26**

FRS 104
Interim Financial Reporting

(March 2015)

Contents

Appendices

Editor's note: This standard published by the FRC on interim reporting is for entities that apply FRS 102 in their annual financial statements. It is effective for interim periods commencing on or after 1 January 2015, with early application permitted.

FRS 104 is based on IAS 34 Interim Financial Reporting, the international standard on interim reporting with certain adaptations and replaces the existing Accounting Standards Board (ASB) Statement Half-yearly financial reports, issued in 2007.

The standard does not impose an obligation on entities to produce interim financial reports. However, entities that make a statement of compliance with it are required to apply all of its provisions. For example, the standard applies to those listed investment trusts which report under UK GAAP. The FRC has also withdrawn the ASB Statement Preliminary announcements.

SUMMARY

(i)   In 2012, 2013 and 2014 the Financial Reporting Council (FRC) revised accounting standards in the United Kingdom (UK) and Republic of Ireland (RoI). The revisions fundamentally reformed financial reporting, replacing the extant standards with four Financial Reporting Standards:

    (a)   FRS 100 *Application of Financial Reporting Requirements*;

    (b)   FRS 101 *Reduced Disclosure Framework*;

    (c)   FRS 102 *The Financial Reporting Standard applicable in the UK and Republic of Ireland*; and

    (d)   FRS 103 *Insurance Contracts*.

(ii)   The FRC's overriding objective in setting financial reporting standards is to enable users of accounts to receive high-quality understandable financial reporting proportionate to the size and complexity of the entity and users' information needs.

(iii)   In meeting this objective, the FRC aims to provide succinct financial reporting standards that:

    (a)   have consistency with international accounting standards through the application of an IFRS-based solution unless an alternative clearly better meets the overriding objective;

    (b)   reflect up-to-date thinking and developments in the way entities operate and the transactions they undertake;

    (c)   balance consistent principles for accounting by all UK and RoI entities with practical solutions, based on size, complexity, public interest and users' information needs;

    (d)   promote efficiency within groups; and

    (e)   are cost-effective to apply.

(iv)   Financial Reporting Standard 104 *Interim Financial Reporting* replaces the Statement *Half-yearly financial reports* issued by the Accounting Standards Board (ASB) in 2007 (ASB Statement Half-yearly reports). The change from a Statement to a Financial Reporting Standard has no effect on the scope of entities required to prepare an interim financial report nor on the extent to which entities that prepare an interim financial report are required to comply with this standard. The scope of FRS 104 and the extent to which its application is mandatory is explained further below. FRS 104 is not an accounting standard[1].

(v)   The FRC also withdraws the Statement *Preliminary announcements* issued by the ASB in 1998 (ASB Statement Preliminary announcements).

---

[1] *Refer to the* Foreword to Accounting Standards *issued in March 2015 for more detail on accounting standards.*

Reasons for replacing the ASB Statement Half-yearly reports

When FRS 102 was issued, the FRC decided that FRS 102 should not contain interim reporting requirements, but that instead the existing reporting guidance contained in the ASB Statement Half-yearly reports should be reviewed.   **(vi)**

The ASB updated the ASB Statement Half-yearly reports in July 2007 for the implementation of the EU Transparency Directive (Directive 2004/109/EC) in the UK and the RoI which resulted in the introduction of the Disclosure and Transparency Rules (DTRs) and the Transparency (Directive 2004/109/EC) Regulations 2007 respectively. Issuers continue to have the same reporting obligations under the DTRs[2] in relation to half-yearly financial reports, but a replacement of the ASB Statement Half-yearly reports is necessary because of the revisions to the annual financial reporting requirements referred to in paragraph (i) above.   **(vii)**

With the publication of FRS 104 the ASB Statement Half-yearly reports is withdrawn.   **(viii)**

Reasons for withdrawing the ASB Statement Preliminary announcements

The ASB Statement Preliminary announcements was published in 1998 and has not subsequently been updated to reflect regulatory changes and market practice developments. The guidance contained therein is therefore out of date and the ASB Statement Preliminary announcements is withdrawn with immediate effect. However, the FRC will, as part of a future project, evaluate whether reporting guidance on certain aspects of preliminary announcements would be useful.   **(ix)**

FRS 104 Interim Financial Reporting

FRS 104 is based on the interim financial reporting requirements promulgated by the International Accounting Standards Board in IAS 34 *Interim Financial Reporting*. We conducted a two-month consultation on these interim reporting requirements in FRED 56 Draft *FRS 104 Interim Financial Reporting*, which closed in January 2015.   **(x)**

FRS 104 does not require any entity to prepare an interim report, nor does it change the extent to which laws or regulations may require the preparation of such a report. Entities should consider whether any such laws or regulations apply to them. For example, paragraph 4.2.2R of the DTRs requires listed entities within the scope of that rule to prepare a half-yearly financial report that must include a condensed set of financial statements, such as the interim financial report described in FRS 104. Similarly, AIM companies are required under the AIM Rules for Companies issued by the London Stock Exchange to prepare a half-yearly report.   **(xi)**

Where an entity does prepare an interim financial report, FRS 104 does not, in itself, require such reports to be prepared in accordance with FRS 104. However, laws or regulations may contain such a requirement. Paragraph 4.2.10R of the DTRs set out that UK issuers within the scope of that rule which do not apply EU-adopted IFRS in their annual financial statements can prepare their condensed interim financial statements in accordance with IAS 34 or pronouncements on interim reporting issued by the FRC. FRS 104 replaces the ASB Statement Half-yearly reports as the FRC's pronouncement on interim reporting, described in paragraph 4.2.10(4)R of the DTRs.   **(xii)**

---

[2] *References to the UK DTRs should also be read as references to the Irish Transparency (Directive 2004/109/EC) Regulations 2007, including any subsequent amendments thereto.*

(xiii)   FRS 104 is intended for use in the preparation of interim reports by entities that apply FRS 102 when preparing their annual financial statements. Entities applying FRS 101 to prepare the annual financial statements may also use FRS 104 as a basis for their interim financial reports.

(xiv)   As explained above, FRS 104 does not impose an obligation on entities to produce interim financial reports nor does it mandate its application by any entity. However, entities that make a statement of compliance with this standard are required to apply all of the provisions of FRS 104.

(xv)   FRS 104 is effective for interim periods commencing on or after 1 January 2015, with early application being permitted.

Organisation of FRS 104

(xvi)   In order to maintain consistency with the paragraph numbering of IAS 34, when a paragraph in IAS 34 has been deleted and has not been replaced with an alternative paragraph in FRS 104, the phrase [not used] is stated. Some paragraphs have been deleted in IAS 34 and are marked as [deleted]. These paragraphs are also identified as [deleted] in FRS 104.

(xvii)   Terms defined in the Glossary (Appendix I) are in **bold type** the first time they appear in FRS 104.

FRS 104 INTERIM FINANCIAL REPORTING

Objective

Timely and **reliable** interim financial reporting can improve the ability of investors, creditors or others to understand an entity's capacity to generate earnings and **cash flows** and its **financial position** and liquidity.

1

This FRS sets out content, **recognition** and **measurement** principles for **interim financial reports**.

1A

Scope

This FRS, in itself, does not require an entity to prepare interim financial reports. Where an entity is required by laws or regulations or voluntarily chooses to prepare interim financial reports it may voluntarily choose to apply this FRS. This FRS does not mandate how frequently or how soon after the end of an **interim period** interim financial reports should be issued.

2

This FRS is intended for use by entities that prepare annual **financial statements** in accordance with **FRS 102**. If entities that prepare the annual financial statements in accordance with **FRS 101** apply this FRS, references made in this FRS to FRS 102 shall be read as references to the equivalent requirements in **EU-adopted IFRS** as amended by paragraph AG1 of FRS 101.

2A

An entity that makes a statement of compliance with this FRS shall comply with all of the provisions of this FRS. This FRS does need not be applied to immaterial items.

3

UK issuers not using EU-adopted IFRS that, as provided for in DTR 4.2.10(4)R[3], include a statement in their half-yearly financial report that the condensed set of financial statements has been prepared in accordance with pronouncements on interim reporting issued by the FRC, shall apply this FRS.

3A

[Not used]

4

Content of an interim financial report

[Not used]

5

In the interest of timeliness and cost and to avoid repetition of information previously reported, an entity may be required to or may elect to provide less information at interim dates as compared with its annual financial statements. This FRS defines the minimum components of an interim financial report as including condensed interim financial statements and selected explanatory notes (see paragraph 8). The interim financial report is intended to provide an update on the most recent complete set of annual financial statements. Accordingly, it focuses on new activities, events, and circumstances and does not duplicate information previously reported.

6

Nothing in this FRS is intended to prohibit or discourage an entity from publishing a complete set of financial statements as described in Section 3 Financial Statement Presentation of FRS 102, instead of the condensed interim financial statements and selected

7

---

[3] *Irish issuers should read references to the UK DTRs as references to the Irish Transparency (Directive 2004/109/EC) Regulations 2007, including any subsequent amendments thereto.*

explanatory notes described in paragraph 8. A complete set of financial statements shall include all of the disclosures required by this FRS as well as the disclosures required by FRS 102. The recognition and measurement requirements set out in this FRS also apply to a complete set of financial statements.

Minimum components of an interim financial report

8   An interim financial report shall include, at a minimum, the following components:

(a)   a condensed **statement of financial position**;
(b)   a single condensed **statement of comprehensive income** or a separate condensed **income statement** and a separate condensed statement of comprehensive income;
(c)   a condensed statement of changes in equity;
(d)   a condensed **statement of cash flows**; and
(e)   selected explanatory notes.

8A   An entity shall present a single condensed statement of comprehensive income or a separate condensed income statement and a separate condensed statement of comprehensive income (see paragraph 8(b)), consistent with the basis of presentation applied in its most recent annual financial statements.

8B   An entity that has presented a single **statement of income and retained earnings** in place of the statement of comprehensive income and statement of changes in equity in accordance with paragraph 3.18 of FRS 102 in its most recent annual financial statements, is permitted to present a single condensed statement of income and retained earnings if, during any of the periods for which the interim financial statements are required to be presented in accordance with paragraph 20A, the only changes to **equity** arise from **profit or loss**, payment of dividends, corrections of prior period **errors** or changes in **accounting policies**.

8C   An entity that has presented only an income statement, or a statement of comprehensive income in which the 'bottom line' is labelled 'profit or loss' in accordance with paragraph 3.19 of FRS 102 in its most recent annual financial statements, is permitted to use the same basis of presentation if there are no items of **other comprehensive income** in any of the periods for which the interim financial statements are required to be presented in accordance with paragraph 20B.

8D   When the presentation of the components of the interim financial statements will be changed in its next annual financial statements an entity is permitted to present the components of the interim financial statements on that new basis, instead of the basis applied in its most recent annual financial statements as required by paragraphs 8A to 8C.

8E   An entity may use titles for the statements other than those used in this FRS as long as they are not misleading.

8F   Paragraph 8(d) does not apply to entities that will not present a statement of cash flows in its next annual financial statements.

Form and content of interim financial statements

9   If an entity publishes a complete set of financial statements in its interim financial report, the form and content of those statements shall conform to the requirements of Section 3 of FRS 102 for a complete set of financial statements. An entity that will not present a statement of cash flows in its next annual financial statements is not required to include that statement in its interim financial report.

The condensed interim financial statements shall include, at a minimum, each of the **10** headings and subtotals that were included in the entity's most recent annual financial statements and the selected explanatory notes as required by this FRS. Additional line items or notes shall be included if their omission would make the condensed interim financial statements misleading.

An entity shall present basic and diluted earnings per share for an interim period when the **11** entity has presented earnings per share information in accordance with IAS 33 *Earnings per Share* (as adopted in the EU) in its most recent annual financial statements.

If an entity presents basic and diluted earnings per share, it shall do so in the statement that **11A** presents the components of profit or loss (see paragraph 8(b)).

[Not used] **12**

[Deleted] **13**

[Not used] **14**

Significant events and transactions

An entity shall include in its interim financial report an explanation of events and **15** transactions that are significant to an understanding of the changes in financial position and **performance** of the entity since the end of the last annual **reporting period**. Information disclosed in relation to those events and transactions shall update the relevant information presented in the most recent annual financial report.

A user of an entity's interim financial report will have access to the most recent annual **15A** financial report of that entity. Therefore, it is unnecessary for the interim financial report to provide relatively insignificant updates to the information that was reported in the most recent annual financial report.

The following is a list of events and transactions for which disclosures would be required, **15B** if they are significant, either in the notes to the interim financial statements or, if disclosed elsewhere in the interim financial report, cross-referred to the disclosure in the notes to the interim financial statements. Disclosure of this information is required in an entity's interim financial report only if the entity would be required to make the disclosure in its annual financial statements. This list is not exhaustive:

(a) the write-down of **inventories** to net realisable value and the reversal of such a write-down;
(b) recognition of a loss from the impairment of **financial assets**, **property, plant and equipment**, **intangible assets**, or other **assets**, and the reversal of such an **impairment loss**;
(c) the reversal of any **provisions** for the costs of **restructuring**;
(d) acquisitions and disposals of items of property, plant and equipment;
(e) commitments for the purchase of property, plant and equipment;
(f) litigation settlements;
(g) corrections of prior period errors;
(h) changes in the business or economic circumstances that affect the **fair value** of the entity's financial assets and **financial liabilities**, where those assets or liabilities are measured at fair value;
(i) any loan default or breach of a loan agreement that has not been remedied on or before the end of the reporting period;

(j)   **related party transactions**, unless the transaction was entered into between two or more members of a **group**, provided that any **subsidiary** which is party to the transaction is wholly owned by such a member; and

(k)   [not used]

(l)   [not used]

(m)   changes in **contingent liabilities** or **contingent assets**.

15C   Individual sections of FRS 102 provide guidance regarding disclosure requirements for many of the items listed in paragraph 15B. When an event or transaction is significant to an understanding of the changes in an entity's financial position or performance since the last annual reporting period, its interim financial report should provide an explanation of and an update to the relevant information included in the financial statements of the last annual reporting period.

16-18   [Deleted]

Other disclosures

16A   In addition to disclosing significant events and transactions in accordance with paragraphs 15–15C, an entity shall include the following information, either in the notes to its interim financial statements or, if disclosed elsewhere in the interim financial report, cross-referred to the information in the notes to the interim financial statements (the information shall normally be reported on a financial year-to-date basis):

(a)   A statement that the same accounting policies and methods of computation are followed in the interim financial statements as compared with the most recent annual financial statements or, if those policies or methods have been changed, a description of the nature and effect of the change.[4]

(b)   Explanatory comments about the seasonality or cyclicality of interim operations.

(c)   The nature and amount of items affecting assets, **liabilities**, equity, profit or loss or cash flows that are unusual because of their nature, size or incidence.

(d)   The nature and amount of changes in estimates of amounts reported in prior interim periods of the current financial year or changes in estimates of amounts reported in prior financial years.

(e)   Issues, repurchases and repayments of debt and equity securities.

(f)   Dividends paid (aggregate or per share) separately for **ordinary shares** and other shares.

(g)   The following segment information (disclosure of segment information is required in an entity's interim financial report only if the entity has presented segment information in accordance with IFRS 8 *Operating Segments* (as adopted in the EU) in its most recent annual financial statements):

(i)   **Revenues** from external customers, if included in the measure of segment profit or loss reviewed by the chief operating decision maker or otherwise regularly provided to the chief operating decision maker.

(ii)   Intersegment revenues, if included in the measure of segment profit or loss reviewed by the chief operating decision maker or otherwise regularly provided to the chief operating decision maker.

(iii)   A measure of segment profit or loss.

(iv)   A measure of total assets and liabilities for a particular reportable segment if such amounts are regularly provided to the chief operating decision maker and

---

[4] *Where a company is subject to the UK Corporate Governance Code, provision C.1.3 requires its directors to state, in the annual and half-yearly financial statements, whether they consider it appropriate to adopt the going concern basis of accounting and to identify any material uncertainties to the company's ability to do so for a period of at least twelve months from the date of approval of the financial statements.*

if there has been a **material** change from the amount disclosed in the most recent annual financial statements for that reportable segment.

(v) A description of differences from the most recent annual financial statements in the basis of segmentation or in the basis of measurement of segment profit or loss.

(vi) A reconciliation of the total of the reportable segments' measures of profit or loss to the entity's profit or loss before **tax expense** (tax income) and **discontinued operations**. However, if an entity allocates to reportable segments items such as tax expense (tax income), the entity may reconcile the total of the segments' measures of profit or loss to profit or loss after those items. Material reconciling items shall be separately identified and described in that reconciliation.

(h) Events after the interim period that have not been reflected in the financial statements for the interim period.

(i) The effect of changes in the composition of the entity during the interim period, including **business combinations**, obtaining or losing control of subsidiaries and long-term investments, restructurings, and discontinued operations. In the case of business combinations, the entity shall disclose the information required by paragraphs 19.25 and 19.25A of FRS 102 (disclosure of this information is required in an entity's interim financial report only if the entity would be required to make the disclosure in the annual financial statements).

(j) For **financial instruments** disclosures that help users of interim financial reports to evaluate the significance of financial instruments measured at fair value; the entity shall disclose the information required by paragraphs 11.43, 11.48A(e) and 34.22 of FRS 102 (disclosure of this information is required in an entity's interim financial report only if the entity would be required to make the disclosure in its annual financial statements).

(k) [Not used]

An interim financial report that covers part of an annual financial reporting period during which an entity transitions from one financial reporting framework to another shall, in order to comply with the disclosure requirements in paragraph 16A(a), disclose the following information: **16B**

(a) a description of the nature of each change in accounting policy;

(b) a reconciliation of its equity determined in accordance with its previous financial reporting framework to its equity determined in accordance with the new financial reporting framework for the following dates:

(i) the **date of transition** to the new financial reporting framework; and

(ii) at the end of the comparable year-to-date period of the immediately preceding financial year; and

(c) a reconciliation of profit or loss determined in accordance with its previous financial reporting framework for the comparable interim period (current and if different year-to-date) of the immediately preceding financial year.

The requirements of paragraph 35.14 of FRS 102 apply in respect of the reconciliations presented.

Disclosure of compliance with this FRS

If an entity's interim financial report is in compliance with this FRS, that fact shall be disclosed. **19**

Periods for which interim financial statements are required to be presented

20   Interim financial reports shall include interim financial statements (condensed or complete) for periods as follows:

(a)   A statement of financial position as of the end of the current interim period and a comparative statement of financial position as of the end of the immediately preceding financial year.

(b)   A single statement of comprehensive income or separate statements of income and of comprehensive income for the current interim period and, if different, cumulatively for the current financial year to date, with a comparative single statement of comprehensive income or separate statements of income and of comprehensive income for the comparable interim period (current and, if different, year-to-date) of the immediately preceding financial year. Paragraph 8A sets out when an entity shall present a single statement of comprehensive income or separate statements of income and of comprehensive income.

(c)   A statement of changes in equity cumulatively for the current financial year to date, with a comparative statement for the comparable year-to-date period of the immediately preceding financial year.

(d)   A statement of cash flows cumulatively for the current financial year-to-date, with a comparative statement for the comparable year-to-date period of the immediately preceding financial year. This requirement does not apply to entities that do not present a statement of cash flows in accordance with paragraphs 8F or 9.

20A   An entity that presents a single condensed statement of income and retained earnings in place of the statement of comprehensive income and statement of changes in equity in accordance with paragraph 8B, shall present a single condensed statement of income and retained earnings for the periods set out in paragraph 20(b).

20B   An entity that presents an income statement, or a statement of comprehensive income in which the 'bottom line' is labelled 'profit or loss' in accordance with paragraph 8C, shall present an income statement, or a statement of comprehensive income on that basis for the periods set out in paragraph 20(b).

21   For an entity whose business is highly seasonal, financial information for the 12 months up to the end of the interim period and comparative information for the prior 12-month period may be useful. Accordingly, entities whose business is highly seasonal are encouraged to consider reporting such information in addition to the information called for in paragraps 20 to 20B.

22   See paragraphs A2.1 and A2.2 of Appendix II *Illustrations and Examples* to this FRS for illustrative examples of the periods that shall be presented by an entity that reports half-yearly and an entity that reports quarterly.

Materiality

23   In deciding how to recognise, measure, classify, or disclose an item for interim financial reporting purposes, materiality shall be assessed in relation to the interim period financial data. In making assessments of materiality, it shall be recognised that interim measurements may rely on estimates to a greater extent than measurements of annual financial data.

24   As described in paragraph 2.6 of FRS 102, an item is material if its omission or misstatement could influence the economic decisions of users of the financial statements.

25   While judgement is always required in assessing materiality, this FRS bases the recognition and disclosure decision on data for the interim period by itself for reasons

of understandability of the interim figures. Thus, for example, unusual items, changes in accounting policies or estimates, and errors are recognised and disclosed on the basis of materiality in relation to interim period data to avoid misleading inferences that might result from non-disclosure. The overriding goal is to ensure that an interim financial report includes all information that is **relevant** to understanding an entity's financial position and performance during the interim period.

[Not used]   26-27

Recognition and measurement

Same accounting policies as annual

An entity shall apply the same accounting policies in its interim financial statements as   28
are applied in its most recent annual financial statements, except for accounting policy changes made after the date of the most recent annual financial statements that are to be reflected in the next annual financial statements.

The frequency of an entity's reporting (annual, half-yearly or quarterly) shall not affect   28A
the measurement of its annual results, with the exception described in paragraph 30(a). To achieve that objective, measurements for interim reporting purposes shall be made on a year-to-date basis.

Year-to-date measurements may involve changes in estimates of amounts reported in prior   29
interim periods of the current financial year, but the principles for recognising assets, liabilities, **income**, and **expenses** for interim periods are the same as in annual financial statements.

To illustrate: 30

(a)   The principles for recognising and measuring losses from inventory write-downs, restructurings, or impairments in an interim period are the same as those that an entity would follow if it prepared only annual financial statements. However, if such items are recognised and measured in one interim period and the estimate changes in a subsequent interim period of that financial year, the original estimate is changed in the subsequent interim period either by accrual of an additional amount of loss or by reversal of the previously recognised amount, unless the reversal of a previously recognised impairment is prohibited by FRS 102.
(b)   A cost that does not meet the definition of an asset at the end of an interim period is not deferred in the statement of financial position either to await future information as to whether it has met the definition of an asset or to smooth earnings over interim periods within a financial year.
(c)   **Income tax** expense is recognised in each interim period based on the best estimate of the weighted average annual income tax rate expected for the full financial year, using the tax rates and laws that have been enacted or **substantively enacted** at the end of an interim reporting period. Amounts accrued for income tax expense in one interim period may have to be adjusted in a subsequent interim period of that financial year if the estimate of the annual income tax rate changes.

Under Section 2 *Concepts and Pervasive Principles* of FRS 102, recognition is the '...   31
process of incorporating in the statement of financial position or statement of comprehensive income an item that meets the definition of an asset, liability, equity, income or expense and satisfies the ... criteria [for recognition]'. The definitions of assets, liabilities, equity, income, and expenses are fundamental to recognition, at the end of both annual and interim financial reporting periods.

32   For assets, the same tests of future economic benefits apply at interim dates and at the end of an entity's financial year. Costs that, by their nature, would not qualify as assets at financial year-end would not qualify at interim dates either. Similarly, a liability at the end of an interim reporting period must represent an existing obligation at that date, just as it must at the end of an annual reporting period.

33   An essential characteristic of income (revenue) and expenses is that the related inflows and outflows of assets and liabilities have already taken place. If those inflows or outflows have taken place, the related revenue and expense are recognised; otherwise they are not recognised. Section 2 of FRS 102 states that 'an entity shall recognise expenses in the statement of comprehensive income (or in the income statement, if presented) when a decrease in future economic benefits related to a decrease in an asset or an increase of a liability has arisen that can be measured reliably'. Section 2 of FRS 102 does not allow the recognition of items in the statement of financial position which do not meet the definition of assets or liabilities.

34   In measuring the assets, liabilities, equity, income, expenses, and cash flows reported in its financial statements, an entity that reports only annually is able to take into account information that becomes available throughout the financial year. Its measurements are, in effect, on a year-to-date basis.

35   An entity uses information available when the interim financial report is being prepared. Amounts of income and expenses reported in the current interim period will reflect any changes in estimates of amounts reported in the last published financial statements. The amounts reported in the last published financial statements, whether at the end of a prior interim period or at the end of the prior financial year, are not retrospectively adjusted for a **change in accounting estimate**. Paragraph 16A(d) requires that the nature and amount of any significant changes in estimates are disclosed.

36   [Not used]

Revenues received seasonally, cyclically, or occasionally

37   Revenues that are received seasonally, cyclically, or occasionally within a financial year shall not be anticipated or deferred as of an interim date if anticipation or deferral would not be appropriate at the end of the entity's financial year.

38   Examples include dividend revenue, royalties, and government grants. Additionally, some entities consistently earn more revenues in certain interim periods of a financial year than in other interim periods, for example, seasonal revenues of retailers. Such revenues are recognised when they occur.

Costs incurred unevenly during the financial year

39   Costs that are incurred unevenly during an entity's financial year shall be anticipated or deferred for interim reporting purposes if, and only if, it is also appropriate to anticipate or defer that type of cost at the end of the financial year.

40   See paragraphs A2.3 to A2.38 of Appendix II to this FRS for illustrative examples of applying the requirements set out in paragraphs 28 to 39.

Use of estimates

The measurement procedures to be followed in an interim financial report shall be   **41**
designed to ensure that the resulting information is reliable and that all material financial
information that is relevant to an understanding of the financial position or performance
of the entity is appropriately disclosed. While measurements in both annual and interim
financial reports are often based on reasonable estimates, the preparation of interim
financial reports generally will require a greater use of estimation methods than annual
financial reports.

See paragraphs A2.39 to A2.47 of Appendix II to this FRS for illustrative examples of the   **42**
use of estimates in interim periods.

Restatement of previously reported interim periods

A change in accounting policy, other than one for which the transition is specified in   **43**
FRS 102, shall be reflected by:

(a)   restating the financial statements of prior interim periods of the current financial
      year and the comparable interim periods of any prior financial years that will be
      restated in the annual financial statements in accordance with Section 10 *Accounting
      Policies, Estimates and Errors* of FRS 102; or
(b)   when it is **impracticable** to determine the cumulative effect at the beginning of the
      financial year of applying a new accounting policy to all prior periods, adjusting
      the financial statements of prior interim periods of the current financial year, and
      comparable interim periods of prior financial years to apply the new accounting
      policy **prospectively** from the earliest date practicable.

One objective of the preceding principle is to ensure that a single accounting policy is   **44**
applied to a particular class of transactions throughout an entire financial year. Under
Section 10 of FRS 102, a change in accounting policy is reflected by **retrospective
application**, with restatement of prior period financial data as far back as is practicable.
However, if the cumulative amount of the adjustment relating to prior financial years is
impracticable to determine, then under Section 10 of FRS 102 the new policy is applied
prospectively from the earliest date practicable. The effect of the principle in paragraph 43
is to require that within the current financial year any change in accounting policy is
applied either retrospectively or, if that is not practicable, prospectively, from no later than
the beginning of the financial year.

To allow accounting changes to be reflected as of an interim date within the financial   **45**
year would allow two differing accounting policies to be applied to a particular class
of transactions within a single financial year. The result would be interim allocation
difficulties, obscured operating results, and complicated analysis and understandability of
interim period information.

Effective date

This FRS is effective for interim periods beginning on or after 1 January 2015. Early   **46**
application is permitted if an entity also applies FRS 101 or FRS 102 for an accounting
period beginning before 1 January 2015.

[Not used]   **47-56**

Consequential amendments to FRS 100 Application of Financial Reporting Requirements

57   Paragraph 15 is amended as follows (deleted text is struck through, inserted text is underlined):

> 15 The following statements are also withdrawn:
>
> Statement of Principles for Financial Reporting
> Statement of Principles for Financial Reporting – Interpretation for public benefit entities
> Reporting Statement: Retirement Benefits – Disclosures~~:~~
> <u>Reporting Statement: Preliminary announcements (withdrawn in March 2015)</u>
> <u>Reporting Statement: Half-yearly financial reports (withdrawn in March 2015).</u>

Consequential amendments to FRS 102 The Financial Reporting Standard applicable in the UK and Republic of Ireland

58   Paragraph 3.25 and the Glossary are amended as set out below (inserted text is underlined). The new glossary term is inserted in alphabetical order:

> 3.25 This FRS does not address presentation of **interim financial reports**. An entity that prepares such reports shall describe the basis for preparing and presenting the information. <u>FRS 104 sets out a basis for the preparation and presentation of interim financial reports that an entity may apply.</u>

Appendix I: Glossary

FRS 104	FRS 104 *Interim Financial Reporting*

APPROVAL BY THE FRC

Financial Reporting Standard FRS 104 *Interim Financial Reporting* was approved for issue by the Financial Reporting Council on 4 March 2015, following its consideration of the Accounting Council's Advice for this FRS.

THE ACCOUNTING COUNCIL'S ADVICE TO THE FRC TO ISSUE FRS 104

Introduction

This report provides an overview of the main issues that have been considered by the Accounting Council in advising the Financial Reporting Council (FRC) to issue FRS 104 *Interim Financial Reporting*.   **1**

In accordance with the *FRC Codes and Standards: procedures*, any proposal to issue, amend or withdraw a code or standard is put to the FRC Board with the full advice of the relevant Councils and/or the Codes & Standards Committee. Ordinarily, the FRC Board will only reject the advice put to it where: **2**

(a) it is apparent that a significant group of stakeholders has not been adequately consulted;

(b) the necessary assessment of the impact of the proposal has not been completed, including an analysis of costs and benefits;

(c) insufficient consideration has been given to the timing or cost of implementation; or

(d) the cumulative impact of a number of proposals would make the adoption of an otherwise satisfactory proposal inappropriate.

The FRC has established the Accounting Council as the relevant Council to assist it in the setting of financial reporting standards.   **3**

Advice

The Accounting Council is advising the FRC to issue FRS 104 *Interim Financial Reporting* to: **4**

(a) Replace the existing interim financial reporting guidance in the Reporting Statement *Half-yearly financial reporting* issued by the Accounting Standards Board (ASB) in 2007 (ASB Statement Half-yearly reports). FRS 104 is based on IFRS to ensure that the FRC's revised interim and annual reporting requirements are based on a consistent framework.

(b) Withdraw the Reporting Statement *Preliminary announcements* issued by the ASB in 1998 (ASB Statement Preliminary announcements) because its content is out of date.

Background

The ASB issued the ASB Statement Half-yearly reports in July 2007 in response to the introduction of the Disclosure and Transparency Rules (DTRs)[5] and the more comprehensive half-yearly financial reporting requirements contained therein. When FRS 102 *The Financial Reporting Standard applicable in the UK and Republic of Ireland* was issued, the FRC decided that FRS 102 should not contain interim reporting requirements, but that instead the existing reporting guidance contained in the ASB Statement Half-yearly reports should be reviewed.   **5**

Since the ASB Statement Preliminary announcements was published in 1998 it has not been updated to reflect regulatory changes and market practice developments.   **6**

---

[5] *References to the Disclosure and Transparency Rules applicable in the UK should be read to include references to the Transparency (Directive 2004/109/EC) Regulations 2007, including any subsequent amendments thereto, applicable in the Republic of Ireland.*

7   The FRC consulted on the proposals to replace the ASB Statement Half-yearly reports and withdraw the ASB Statement Preliminary announcements in FRED 56 *Draft FRS 104 Interim Financial Reporting*. The Accounting Council's advice takes into account the responses to FRED 56.

Objective

8   The FRC gives careful consideration to its objective and the intended effects when developing new financial reporting standards or requirements for the UK and Republic of Ireland. In developing financial reporting standards, including FRS 104, the overriding objective of the FRC is to enable users of accounts to receive high-quality understandable financial reporting proportionate to the size and complexity of the entity and users' information needs.

9   In meeting this objective, the FRC aims to provide succinct financial reporting standards that:

   (a)   have consistency with global accounting standards through the application of an IFRS-based solution unless an alternative clearly better meets the overriding objective;

   (b)   reflect up-to-date thinking and developments in the way businesses operate and the transactions they undertake;

   (c)   balance consistent principles for accounting by all UK and Republic of Ireland entities with practical solutions, based on size, complexity, public interest and users' information needs;

   (d)   promote efficiency within groups; and

   (e)   are cost-effective to apply.

10   The objectives of FRS 104 are to introduce UK and Irish interim reporting requirements that, consistent with the annual reporting requirements, are based on an IFRS-framework and to promote the publication of useful financial information at an interim date.

FRS 104 Interim Financial Reporting

Basis and scope of FRS 104

11   The FRC consulted on the introduction of interim financial reporting requirements in FRS 102 in FRED 48 *The Financial Reporting Standard applicable in the UK and Republic of Ireland* during 2012. The FRC proposed that entities preparing interim financial reports should apply IAS 34 *Interim Financial Reporting*. Respondents agreed with this proposal.

12   In line with the proposal in FRED 48, FRED 56 proposed interim reporting requirements based on IAS 34, although with certain adaptations to tailor the reporting requirements for entities that prepare their annual financial statements in accordance with FRS 102. Respondents to FRED 56 agreed with this proposal.

13   FRS 104 has been developed primarily for entities preparing the annual financial statements in accordance with FRS 102. We are mindful, however, that a small number of entities may prepare the annual financial statements in accordance with FRS 101 *Reduced Disclosure Framework*. These entities may be required to produce half-yearly financial reports in accordance with the DTRs because, although being a member of a larger group, they have issued their own listed debt securities.

14   Considering that only a small minority of entities that use FRS 101 will also produce interim financial reports, it is in the Accounting Council's view not an effective solution

to develop a separate set of interim reporting requirements solely for entities that apply FRS 101. Instead, as set out in FRS 104, these entities should apply the same requirements applicable to entities that use FRS 102, except that any reference to a specific requirement in FRS 102 is read as a reference to the equivalent requirement in EU-adopted IFRS, as amended by paragraph AG1 of FRS 101. A majority of respondents to FRED 56 supported this approach.

Key changes to IAS 34

The reporting requirements of IAS 34 have been adapted for application by entities that **15** prepare their annual financial statements in accordance with FRS 102. The key changes made to IAS 34 for the purpose of developing FRS 104 include (please refer to Appendix III *Significant differences between FRS 104 and IAS 34* of FRS 104 for more detail):

(a)   Disclosures that are not required by FRS 102 have been deleted. For example certain fair value disclosure requirements that apply under IAS 34 have not been repeated in FRS 104.

(b)   Some disclosure requirements, for example those in relation to fair value measurements and business combinations, apply only if the entity would be required to make the same disclosures in the annual financial statements. This exempts entities that are not financial institutions and entities that report in accordance with FRS 101 from disclosing information in the interim financial report that they are not required to disclose in the annual financial statements.

(c)   Related party disclosures may be omitted for transactions between wholly owned members of a group since FRS 102 exempts such transactions from disclosure in the annual financial statements.

(d)   Disclosure requirements that apply when an entity adopts a new financial reporting framework for the first time have been inserted. Similar disclosures are required under IFRS, although they are not part of IAS 34.

(e)   The annual financial statements disclosure requirements in paragraph 26 of IAS 34 concerning significant changes of estimates reported in an interim period have been deleted because FRS 104 addresses only reporting requirements in interim financial reports.

(f)   FRS 102 permits the presentation of simplified primary financial statements under certain circumstances. These presentation requirements have been included in FRS 104 to ensure consistency of presentation in the annual and interim financial statements.

(g)   Entities that are not required to present a cash flow statement in the annual financial statements are also exempt from this requirement in the interim financial report.

(h)   The principle that the frequency of reporting should not affect the measurement of the annual results has been qualified where FRS 102 would prohibit a reversal of an impairment charge[6]. This is consistent with the requirements in IFRIC 10 *Interim Financial Reporting and Impairment*.

(i)   The preparation requirements in paragraph 14 of IAS 34 pertaining to consolidated interim financial reports have been deleted, because entities that apply FRS 104 will generally prepare entity-only annual financial statements and interim financial reports.

Respondents to FRED 56 largely supported these adaptations of IAS 34. In particular **16** they agreed that FRS 104 should not impose disclosure requirements that exceed those applicable to the annual financial statements of an entity.

---

[6] *FRS 102 as issued in August 2014 does not prohibit the reversal of impairments. However, as set out in FRED 59 Draft amendments to FRS 102 The Financial Reporting Standard applicable in the UK and Republic of Ireland - Small entities and other minor amendments issued in February 2015, the FRC proposes to amend FRS 102 in respect of the reversal of goodwill impairment charges.*

17   A number of respondents recommended that the Appendices to IAS 34 should be repeated in FRS 104 as they provide useful guidance for preparers. The Accounting Council agrees with this feedback and advises that the appendices should be included as non-mandatory guidance in FRS 104 adapted for use by entities that prepare their annual financial statements in accordance with FRS 102.

Other information included in the interim financial report

18   FRS 104 sets out the minimum components of an interim financial report and, consistent with IAS 34, requires only the inclusion of a set of interim financial statements and explanatory notes. Laws and regulations may, however, set out additional narrative reporting requirements. For example, the DTRs require entities to prepare an interim management report.

19   A minority of respondents to FRED 56 suggested that the FRC should issue separate guidance on narrative reporting in interim financial reports. The Accounting Council advises that FRS 104 should not include additional narrative reporting requirements because entities applying FRS 104 would then be subject to reporting requirements that exceed those of entities that apply IFRS and prepare their interim financial reports in accordance with IAS 34.

Comparative information

20   FRS 104 requires entities to present comparative period information and the comparatives have to be presented on the same basis as the current period information. Entities which adopt FRS 102 for accounting periods beginning on or after 1 January 2015 are therefore required to restate the comparative period information in accordance with FRS 102. Additionally, as set out in paragraph 16B of FRS 104, entities should provide explanations of the effect of the accounting policy changes and reconciliations of equity and profit or loss. The Accounting Council advises that these disclosures are necessary for users of interim financial reports to understand the impact of the adoption of FRS 102. Respondents to FRED 56 supported the Accounting Council's position.

Preliminary announcements

21   The ASB Statement Preliminary announcements issued in 1998 is out of date. A majority of respondents to FRED 56 therefore supported the proposed withdrawal. A small number of respondents, however, suggested that the FRC should issue new guidance in this area. The Accounting Council retains its advice that the ASB Statement Preliminary announcements should be withdrawn as soon as possible. The FRC should consider whether new guidance in this area is useful, as part of a future project.

Effective date

22   The interim financial reporting requirements replacing the ASB Statement Half-yearly reports are effective from the same date as FRS 102 and apply to interim periods beginning on or after 1 January 2015. Some respondents to FRED 56 suggested that FRS 104 should be available for application sooner. The Accounting Council advises that early application should be permitted, provided that an entity applies FRS 101 or FRS 102 to an accounting period beginning before 1 January 2015.

Approval of this advice

23   This advice to the FRC was approved by the Accounting Council on 12 February 2015.

Appendix I
Glossary

This glossary is an integral part of FRS 104.

accounting policies	The specific principles, bases, conventions, rules and practices applied by an entity in preparing and presenting **financial statements**.
asset	A resource controlled by the entity as a result of past events and from which future economic benefits are expected to flow to the entity.
associate	An entity, including an unincorporated entity such as a partnership, over which the investor has **significant influence** and that is neither a **subsidiary** nor an interest in a **joint venture**.
business	An integrated set of activities and **assets** conducted and managed for the purpose of providing: (a) a return to investors; or (b) lower costs or other economic benefits directly and proportionately to policyholders or participants. A business generally consists of inputs, processes applied to those inputs, and resulting outputs that are, or will be, used to generate **revenues**. If **goodwill** is present in a transferred set of activities and assets, the transferred set shall be presumed to be a business.
business combination	The bringing together of separate entities or **businesses** into one reporting entity.
carrying amount	The amount at which an **asset** or **liability** is recognised in the **statement of financial position**.
cash	Cash on hand and demand deposits.
cash equivalents	Short-term, highly liquid investments that are readily convertible to known amounts of **cash** and that are subject to an insignificant risk of changes in value.
cash flows	Inflows and outflows of **cash** and **cash equivalents**.
cash-generating unit	The smallest identifiable group of **assets** that generates cash inflows that are largely independent of the cash inflows from other assets or groups of assets.
change in accounting estimate	An adjustment of the **carrying amount** of an **asset** or a **liability**, or the amount of the periodic consumption of an asset, that results from the assessment of the present status of, and expected future benefits and obligations associated with, assets and liabilities. Changes in accounting estimates result from new information or new developments and, accordingly, are not corrections of **errors**.
component of an entity	Operations and **cash flows** that can be clearly distinguished, operationally and for financial reporting purposes, from the rest of the entity.

contingent asset	A possible **asset** that arises from past events and whose existence will be confirmed only by the occurrence or non-occurrence of one or more uncertain future events not wholly within the control of the entity.

contingent liability	(a) a possible obligation that arises from past events and whose existence will be confirmed only by the occurrence or non-occurrence of one or more uncertain future events not wholly within the control of the entity; or
	
	(b) a present obligation that arises from past events but is not recognised because:
	
	    (i) it is not probable that an outflow of resources embodying economic benefits will be required to settle the obligation; or
	
	    (ii) the amount of the obligation cannot be measured with sufficient reliability.

control (of an entity)	The power to govern the financial and operating policies of an entity so as to obtain benefits from its activities.
current tax	The amount of income tax payable (refundable) in respect of the taxable profit (tax loss) for the current period or past **reporting periods**.
date of transition	The beginning of the earliest period for which an entity presents full comparative information in a given standard in its first **financial statements** that comply with that standard.
deferred tax	Income tax payable (recoverable) in respect of the **taxable profit (tax loss)** for future **reporting periods** as a result of past transactions or events.
discontinued operation	A **component of an entity** that has been disposed of and: (a) represented a separate major line of **business** or geographical area of operations; (b) was part of a single co-ordinated plan to dispose of a separate major line of business or geographical area of operations; or (c) was a **subsidiary** acquired exclusively with a view to resale.
DTRs	Disclosure and Transparency Rules issued by the Financial Conduct Authority.
employee benefits	All forms of consideration given by an entity in exchange for service rendered by employees.
equity	The residual interest in the **assets** of the entity after deducting all its **liabilities**.
errors	Omissions from, and misstatements in, the entity's **financial statements** for one or more prior periods arising from a failure to use, or misuse of, reliable information that: (a) was available when financial statements for those periods were authorised for issue; and (b) could reasonably be expected to have been obtained and taken into account in the preparation and presentation of those financial statements.

EU-adopted IFRS	**IFRS** that have been adopted in the European Union in accordance with EU Regulation 1606/2002.
expenses	Decreases in economic benefits during the **reporting period** in the form of outflows or depletions of **assets** or incurrences of **liabilities** that result in decreases in **equity**, other than those relating to distributions to equity investors.
fair value	The amount for which an **asset** could be exchanged, a **liability** settled, or an equity instrument granted could be exchanged, between knowledgeable, willing parties in an arm's length transaction. The guidance in paragraphs 11.27 to 11.32 of **FRS 102** shall be used in determining fair value.
fair value less costs to sell	The amount obtainable from the sale of an **asset** or **cash-generating unit** in an arm's length transaction between knowledgeable, willing parties, less the costs of disposal.

financial asset	Any **asset** that is:
	
	(a) **cash**;
	
	(b) an equity instrument of another entity;
	
	(c) a contractual right:
	
	    (i) to receive cash or another financial asset from another entity; or
	
	    (ii) to exchange financial assets or **financial liabilities** with another entity under conditions that are potentially favourable to the entity; or
	
	(d) a contract that will or may be settled in the entity's own equity instruments and:
	
	    (i) under which the entity is or may be obliged to receive a variable number of the entity's own equity instruments; or
	
	    (ii) that will or may be settled other than by the exchange of a fixed amount of cash or another financial asset for a fixed number of the entity's own equity instruments. For this purpose the entity's own equity instruments do not include instruments that are themselves contracts for the future receipt or delivery of the entity's own equity instruments.

financial instrument	A contract that gives rise to a **financial asset** of one entity and a **financial liability** or equity instrument of another entity.

financial liability	Any **liability** that is:
	
	(a) a contractual obligation:
	
	    (i) to deliver **cash** or another **financial asset** to another entity; or
	
	    (ii) to exchange financial assets or financial liabilities with another entity under conditions that are potentially unfavourable to the entity; or
	
	(b) a contract that will or may be settled in the entity's own equity instruments and:
	
	    (i) under which the entity is or may be obliged to deliver a variable number of the entity's own equity instruments; or
	
	    (ii) will or may be settled other than by the exchange of a fixed amount of cash or another financial asset for a fixed number of the entity's own equity instruments. For this purpose the entity's own equity instruments do not include instruments that are themselves contracts for the future receipt or delivery of the entity's own equity instruments.

financial position	The relationship of the **assets**, **liabilities** and **equity** of an entity as reported in the **statement of financial position**.
financial statements	Structured representation of the **financial position**, financial **performance** and **cash flows** of an entity.
financing activities	Activities that result in changes in the size and composition of the contributed **equity** and borrowings of the entity.
FRS 101	FRS 101 *Reduced Disclosure Framework*
FRS 102	FRS 102 *The Financial Reporting Standard applicable in the UK and Republic of Ireland*
goodwill	Future economic benefits arising from **assets** that are not capable of being individually identified and separately recognised.
group	A **parent** and all its **subsidiaries**.
IFRS (International Financial Reporting Standards)	Standards and interpretations issued (or adopted) by the International Accounting Standards Board (IASB). They comprise: (a) International Financial Reporting Standards; (b) International Accounting Standards; and (c) Interpretations developed by the IFRS Interpretations Committee (IFRIC) or the former Standing Interpretations Committee (SIC).
impairment loss	The amount by which the **carrying amount** of an **asset** exceeds: (a) in the case of **inventories**, its selling price less costs to complete and sell; or (b) in the case of other assets, its **recoverable amount**.
impracticable	Applying a requirement is impracticable when the entity cannot apply it after making every reasonable effort to do so.

income	Increases in economic benefits during the **reporting period** in the form of inflows or enhancements of **assets** or decreases of **liabilities** that result in increases in **equity**, other than those relating to contributions from equity investors.
income statement	**Financial statement** that presents all items of **income** and **expense** recognised in a **reporting period**, excluding the items of **other comprehensive income**.
income tax	All domestic and foreign taxes that are based on **taxable profits**. Income tax also includes taxes, such as withholding taxes, that are payable by a **subsidiary**, **associate** or **joint venture** on distributions to the reporting entity.
intangible asset	An identifiable non-monetary asset without physical substance. Such an **asset** is identifiable when: (a) it is separable, ie capable of being separated or divided from the entity and sold, transferred, licensed, rented or exchanged, either individually or together with a related contract, asset or **liability**; or (b) it arises from contractual or other legal rights, regardless of whether those rights are transferable or separable from the entity or from other rights and obligations.
interim financial report	A financial report containing either a complete set of **financial statements** or a set of condensed financial statements for an **interim period**.
interim period	A financial **reporting period** shorter than a full financial year.
inventories	**Assets**: (a) held for sale in the ordinary course of business; (b) in the process of production for such sale; or (c) in the form of materials or supplies to be consumed in the production process or in the rendering of services.
joint control	The contractually agreed sharing of **control** over an economic activity. It exists only when the strategic financial and operating decisions relating to the activity require the unanimous consent of the parties sharing control (the **venturers**).
joint venture	A contractual arrangement whereby two or more parties undertake an economic activity that is subject to **joint control**. Joint ventures can take the form of jointly controlled operations, jointly controlled assets, or **jointly controlled entities**.
jointly controlled entity	A **joint venture** that involves the establishment of a corporation, partnership or other entity in which each **venturer** has an interest. The entity operates in the same way as other entities, except that a contractual arrangement between the venturers establishes **joint control** over the economic activity of the entity.

key management personnel	Those persons having authority and responsibility for planning, directing and controlling the activities of the entity, directly or indirectly, including any director (whether executive or otherwise) of that entity.
liability	A present obligation of the entity arising from past events, the settlement of which is expected to result in an outflow from the entity of resources embodying economic benefits.
material	Omissions or misstatements of items are material if they could, individually or collectively, influence the economic decisions of users taken on the basis of the **financial statements**. Materiality depends on the size and nature of the omission or misstatement judged in the surrounding circumstances. The size or nature of the item, or a combination of both, could be the determining factor.
measurement	The process of determining the monetary amounts at which the elements of the **financial statements** are to be recognised and carried in the **statement of financial position** and **statement of comprehensive income**.
ordinary share	An equity instrument that is subordinate to all other classes of equity instrument.
other comprehensive income	Items of **income** and **expense** (including reclassification adjustments) that are not recognised in **profit or loss** as required or permitted by **FRS 102**.
parent	An entity that has one or more **subsidiaries**.
performance	The relationship of the **income** and **expenses** of an entity, as reported in the **statement of comprehensive income**.
post-employment benefits	**Employee benefits** (other than **termination benefits** and short-term employee benefits) that are payable after the completion of employment.
post-employment benefit plans	Formal or informal arrangements under which an entity provides **post-employment benefits** for one or more employees.
present value	A current estimate of the present discounted value of the future net **cash flows** in the normal course of **business**.
probable	More likely than not.
profit or loss	The total of **income** less **expenses**, excluding the components of **other comprehensive income**.
property, plant and equipment	Tangible **assets** that: (a) are held for use in the production or supply of goods or services, for rental to others, or for administrative purposes; and (b) are expected to be used during more than one period.
prospectively (applying a change in accounting policy)	Applying the new **accounting policy** to transactions, other events and conditions occurring after the date as at which the policy is changed.
provision	A **liability** of uncertain timing or amount.

recognition	The process of incorporating in the **statement of financial position** or **statement of comprehensive income** an item that meets the definition of an **asset, liability, equity, income** or **expense** and satisfies the following criteria: (a) it is **probable** that any future economic benefit associated with the item will flow to or from the entity; and (b) the item has a cost or value that can be measured with **reliability**.
recoverable amount	The higher of an **asset's** (or **cash-generating unit's**) **fair value less costs to sell** and its **value in use**.

related party	A related party is a person or entity that is related to the entity that is preparing its **financial statements** (the reporting entity).
	
	(a) A person or a close member of that person's family is related to a reporting entity if that person:
	    (i) has **control** or **joint control** over the reporting entity;
	    (ii) has **significant influence** over the reporting entity; or
	    (iii) is a member of the **key management personnel** of the reporting entity or of a **parent** of the reporting entity.
	
	(b) An entity is related to a reporting entity if any of the following conditions apply:
	    (i) the entity and the reporting entity are members of the same **group** (which means that each parent, **subsidiary** and fellow subsidiary is related to the others).
	    (ii) one entity is an **associate** or **joint venture** of the other entity (or of a member of a group of which the other entity is a member).
	    (iii) both entities are joint ventures of the same third entity.
	    (iv) one entity is a joint venture of a third entity and the other entity is an associate of the third entity.
	    (v) the entity is a **post-employment benefit plan** for the benefit of employees of either the reporting entity or an entity related to the reporting entity. If the reporting entity is itself such a plan, the sponsoring employers are also related to the reporting entity.
	    (vi) the entity is controlled or jointly controlled by a person identified in (a).
	    (vii) a person identified in (a)(i) has **significant influence** over the entity or is a member of the key management personnel of the entity (or of a parent of the entity).
	    (viii) the entity, or any member of a group of which it is a part, provides key management personnel services to the reporting entity or to the parent of the reporting entity.

related party transaction	A transfer of resources, services or obligations between a reporting entity and a **related party**, regardless of whether a price is charged.
relevant or relevance	The quality of information that allows it to influence the economic decisions of users by helping them evaluate past, present or future events or confirming, or correcting, their past evaluations.
reliable or reliability	The quality of information that makes it free from **material error** and bias and represents faithfully that which it either purports to represent or could reasonably be expected to represent.
reporting period	The period covered by **financial statements** or by an **interim financial report**.
restructuring	A restructuring is a programme that is planned and controlled by management and materially changes either: (a) the scope of a business undertaken by an entity; or (b) the manner in which that business is conducted.
retrospective application (of an accounting policy)	Applying a new **accounting policy** to transactions, other events and conditions as if that policy had always been applied.
revenue	The gross inflow of economic benefits during the period arising in the course of the ordinary activities of an entity when those inflows result in increases in **equity**, other than increases relating to contributions from equity participants.
significant influence	Significant influence is the power to participate in the financial and operating policy decisions of the **associate** but is not **control** or **joint control** over those policies.
statement of cash flows	**Financial statement** that provides information about the changes in **cash** and **cash equivalents** of an entity for a period, showing separately changes during the period from operating, investing and **financing activities**.
statement of comprehensive income	**Financial statement** that presents all items of **income** and **expense** recognised in a period, including those items recognised in determining **profit or loss** (which is a subtotal in the statement of comprehensive income) and items of **other comprehensive income**. If an entity chooses to present both an **income statement** and a statement of comprehensive income, the statement of comprehensive income begins with profit or loss and then displays the items of other comprehensive income.
statement of financial position	**Financial statement** that presents the relationship of an entity's **assets**, **liabilities** and **equity** as of a specific date.
statement of income and retained earnings	**Financial statement** that presents the **profit or loss** and changes in retained earnings for a **reporting period**.
subsidiary	An entity, including an unincorporated entity such as a partnership, that is **controlled** by another entity (known as the **parent**).

substantively enacted	Tax rates shall be regarded as substantively enacted when the remaining stages of the enactment process historically have not affected the outcome and are unlikely to do so. A UK tax rate shall be regarded as having been substantively enacted if it is included in either: (a) a Bill that has been passed by the House of Commons and is awaiting only passage through the House of Lords and Royal Assent; or (b) a resolution having statutory effect that has been passed under the Provisional Collection of Taxes Act 1968. (Such a resolution could be used to collect taxes at a new rate before that rate has been enacted. In practice, corporation tax rates are now set a year ahead to avoid having to invoke the Provisional Collection of Taxes Act for the quarterly payment system.) A Republic of Ireland tax rate can be regarded as having been substantively enacted if it is included in a Bill that has been passed by the Dáil.
tax expense	The aggregate amount included in **total comprehensive income** or **equity** for the **reporting period** in respect of **current tax** and **deferred tax**.
taxable profit (tax loss)	The profit (loss) for a **reporting period** upon which income taxes are payable or recoverable, determined in accordance with the rules established by the taxation authorities. Taxable profit equals taxable income less amounts deductible from taxable income.
termination benefits	**Employee benefits** provided in exchange for the termination of an employee's employment as a result of either: (a) an entity's decision to terminate an employee's employment before the normal retirement date; or (b) an employee's decision to accept voluntary redundancy in exchange for those benefits.
timely or timeliness	Providing the information in **financial statements** within the decision time frame.
total comprehensive income	The change in **equity** during a period resulting from transactions and other events, other than those changes resulting from transactions from equity participants (equal to the sum of **profit or loss** and **other comprehensive income**).
value in use	The **present value** of the future **cash flows** expected to be derived from an **asset** or **cash-generating unit**.
venturer	A party to a **joint venture** that has **joint control** over that joint venture.

Appendix II
Illustrations and examples

This appendix accompanies, but is not part of FRS 104. It provides guidance for applying some of the requirements in FRS 104.

ILLUSTRATION OF PERIODS REQUIRED TO BE PRESENTED

The following examples illustrate the application of the principle in paragraph 20 of FRS 104.

Entity publishes interim financial reports half-yearly

A2.1   The entity's financial year ends on 31 December (calendar year). The entity will present the following financial statements (condensed or complete) as identified by a tickmark ✓ in its half-yearly interim financial report for the six-month period ending on 30 June 20X1:

	30 Jun 20X0	31 Dec 20X0	30 Jun 20X1
Statement of financial position as at	✗	✓	✓
Single statement of comprehensive income or separate statements of income and comprehensive income for the six-month period ending on	✓	✗	✓
Statement of changes in equity for the six-month period ending on	✓	✗	✓
Statement of cash flows for the six-month period ending on	✓	✗	✓

Entity publishes interim financial reports quarterly

A2.2   The entity's financial year ends on 31 December (calendar year). The entity will present the financial statements (condensed or complete) as shown in paragraph A2.1 and the financial statements (condensed or complete) shown below as identified by a tickmark ✓ in its quarterly interim financial report for the six-month period ending on 30 June 20X1:

	30 Jun 20X0	31 Dec 20X0	30 Jun 20X1
Single statement of comprehensive income or separate statements of income and comprehensive income for the three-month period ending on	✓	✗	✓

EXAMPLES OF APPLYING THE RECOGNITION AND MEASUREMENT PRINCIPLES

The following are examples of applying the general recognition and measurement principles set out in paragraphs 28–39 of FRS 104.

Employer payroll taxes and insurance contributions

If employer payroll taxes or contributions to government-sponsored insurance funds are assessed on an annual basis, the employer's related expense is recognised in interim periods using an estimated average annual effective payroll tax or contribution rate, even though a large portion of the payments may be made early in the financial year. A common example is an employer payroll tax or insurance contribution that is imposed up to a certain maximum level of earnings per employee. For higher income employees, the maximum income is reached before the end of the financial year, and the employer makes no further payments through the end of the year.

A2.3

Major planned periodic maintenance or overhaul

The cost of a planned major periodic maintenance or overhaul or other seasonal expenditure that is expected to occur late in the year is not anticipated for interim reporting purposes unless an event has caused the entity to have a legal or constructive obligation. The mere intention or necessity to incur expenditure related to the future is not sufficient to give rise to an obligation.

A2.4

Provisions

A provision is recognised when an entity has no realistic alternative but to make a transfer of economic benefits as a result of an event that has created a legal or constructive obligation. The amount of the obligation is adjusted upward or downward, with a corresponding loss or gain recognised in profit or loss, if the entity's best estimate of the amount of the obligation changes.

A2.5

FRS 104 requires that an entity applies the same criteria for recognising and measuring a provision at an interim date as it would at the end of its financial year. The existence or non-existence of an obligation to transfer benefits is not a function of the length of the reporting period. It is a question of fact.

A2.6

Year-end bonuses

The nature of year-end bonuses varies widely. Some are earned simply by continued employment during a time period. Some bonuses are earned based on a monthly, quarterly, or annual measure of operating result. They may be purely discretionary, contractual, or based on years of historical precedent.

A2.7

A bonus is anticipated for interim reporting purposes if, and only if:

A2.8

(a) the bonus is a legal obligation or past practice would make the bonus a constructive obligation for which the entity has no realistic alternative but to make the payments; and

(b) a reliable estimate of the obligation can be made.

Section 28 *Employee Benefits* of FRS 102 provides guidance.

Contingent lease payments

Contingent lease payments can be an example of a legal or constructive obligation that is recognised as a liability. If a lease provides for contingent payments based on the lessee achieving a certain level of annual sales, an obligation can arise in the interim periods of the financial year before the required annual level of sales has been achieved,

A2.9

if that required level of sales is expected to be achieved and the entity, therefore, has no realistic alternative but to make the future lease payment.

Intangible assets

A2.10   An entity will apply the definition and recognition criteria for an intangible asset in the same way in an interim period as in an annual period. Costs incurred before the recognition criteria for an intangible asset are met are recognised as an expense. Costs incurred after the specific point in time at which the criteria are met are recognised as part of the cost of an intangible asset. 'Deferring' costs as assets in an interim statement of financial position in the hope that the recognition criteria will be met later in the financial year is not justified.

Pensions

A2.11   The cost of a defined benefit plan for an interim period is calculated on a year-to-date basis. For the measurement of the defined benefit obligation at an interim reporting date refer to paragraph A2.42.

Vacations, holidays, and other short-term compensated absences

A2.12   Accumulating paid absences are those that are carried forward and can be used in future periods if the current period's entitlement is not used in full. Section 28 of FRS 102 requires that an entity measure the expected cost of an obligation for accumulating paid absences at the amount the entity expects to pay as a result of the unused entitlement that has accumulated at the end of the reporting period. That principle is also applied at the end of interim financial reporting periods. Conversely, an entity recognises no expense or liability for non-accumulating paid absences at the end of an interim reporting period, just as it recognises none at the end of an annual reporting period.

Other planned but irregularly occurring costs

A2.13   An entity's budget may include certain costs expected to be incurred irregularly during the financial year, such as charitable contributions and employee training costs. Those costs generally are discretionary even though they are planned and tend to recur from year to year. Recognising an obligation at the end of an interim financial reporting period for such costs that have not yet been incurred generally is not consistent with the definition of a liability.

Measuring interim income tax expense

A2.14   Interim period income tax expense is accrued using the tax rate that would be applicable to expected total annual earnings; that is, the estimated average annual effective income tax rate applied to the pre-tax income of the interim period.

A2.15   This is consistent with the basic concept set out in paragraph 28 of FRS 104 that the same accounting recognition and measurement principles shall be applied in an interim financial report as are applied in annual financial statements. Income taxes are assessed on an annual basis. Interim period income tax expense is calculated by applying to an interim period's pre-tax income the tax rate that would be applicable to expected total annual earnings; that is, the estimated average annual effective income tax rate. That estimated average annual rate would reflect a blend of the progressive tax rate structure expected to be applicable to the full year's earnings including enacted or substantively enacted changes in the income tax rates scheduled to take effect later in the financial year. The estimated average annual income tax rate would be re-estimated on a year-to-date basis, consistent with paragraph 28 of FRS 104. Paragraph 16A of FRS 104 requires disclosure of a significant change in estimate.

To the extent practicable, a separate estimated average annual effective income tax rate   **A2.16** is determined for each taxing jurisdiction and applied individually to the interim period pre-tax income of each jurisdiction. Similarly, if different income tax rates apply to different categories of income (such as capital gains or income earned in particular industries), to the extent practicable a separate rate is applied to each individual category of interim period pre-tax income. While that degree of precision is desirable, it may not be achievable in all cases, and a weighted average of rates across jurisdictions or across categories of income is used if it is a reasonable approximation of the effect of using more specific rates.

To illustrate the application of the foregoing principle, an entity reporting quarterly expects   **A2.17** to earn Currency Units (CU)10,000 pre-tax each quarter and operates in a jurisdiction with a tax rate of 20 per cent on the first CU20,000 of annual earnings and 30 per cent on all additional earnings. Actual earnings match expectations. The following table shows the amount of income tax expense that is reported in each quarter:

	1st Quarter	2nd Quarter	3rd Quarter	4th Quarter	Annual
Tax expense	CU2,500	CU2,500	CU2,500	CU2,500	CU10,000

CU10,000 of tax is expected to be payable for the full year on CU40,000 of pre-tax income.

As another illustration, an entity reports quarterly, earns CU15,000 pre-tax profit in the   **A2.18** first quarter but expects to incur losses of CU5,000 in each of the three remaining quarters (thus having zero income for the year), and operates in a jurisdiction in which its estimated average annual income tax rate is expected to be 20 per cent. The following table shows the amount of income tax expense that is reported in each quarter:

	1st Quarter	2nd Quarter	3rd Quarter	4th Quarter	Annual
Tax expense	CU3,000	CU(1,000)	CU(1,000)	CU(1,000)	nil

Difference in financial reporting year and tax year

If the financial reporting year and the income tax year differ, income tax expense for   **A2.19** the interim periods of that financial reporting year is measured using separate weighted average estimated effective tax rates for each of the income tax years applied to the portion of pre-tax income earned in each of those income tax years.

To illustrate, an entity's financial reporting year ends on 30 June and it reports quarterly. Its   **A2.20** taxable year ends on 31 December. For the financial year that begins 1 July, Year 1 and ends 30 June, Year 2, the entity earns CU10,000 pre-tax each quarter. The estimated average annual income tax rate is 30 per cent in Year 1 and 40 per cent in Year 2.

	Quarter ending 30 Sep Year 1	Quarter ending 31 Dec Year 1	Quarter ending 31 Mar Year 2	Quarter ending 30 Jun Year 2	Year ending 30 Jun Year 2
Tax expense	CU3,000	CU3,000	CU4,000	CU4,000	CU14,000

Tax credits

A2.21   Some tax jurisdictions give taxpayers credits against the tax payable based on amounts of capital expenditures, exports, research and development expenditures, or other bases. Anticipated tax benefits of this type for the full year are generally reflected in computing the estimated annual effective income tax rate, because those credits are granted and calculated on an annual basis under most tax laws and regulations. On the other hand, tax benefits that relate to a one-off event are recognised in computing income tax expense in that interim period, in the same way that special tax rates applicable to particular categories of income are not blended into a single effective annual tax rate.

Tax loss and tax credit carrybacks and carryforwards

A2.22   The benefits of a tax loss carryback are reflected in the interim period in which the related tax loss occurs. Section 29 *Income Tax* of FRS 102 provides that 'an entity shall recognise a current tax asset for the benefit of a tax loss that can be carried back to recover tax paid in a previous period'. A corresponding reduction of tax expense or increase of tax income is also recognised.

A2.23   Section 29 of FRS 102 provides that unrelieved tax losses shall only be recognised to the extent that it is probable that they will be recovered against the reversal of deferred tax liabilities or other future taxable profits.

A2.24   To illustrate, an entity that reports quarterly has an operating loss carryforward of CU10,000 for income tax purposes at the start of the current financial year for which a deferred tax asset has not been recognised. The entity earns CU10,000 in the first quarter of the current year and expects to earn CU10,000 in each of the three remaining quarters. Excluding the carryforward, the estimated average annual income tax rate is expected to be 40 per cent. Tax expense is as follows:

	1st Quarter	2nd Quarter	3rd Quarter	4th Quarter	Annual
Tax expense	CU3,000	CU3,000	CU3,000	CU3,000	CU12,000

Contractual or anticipated purchase price changes

A2.25   Volume rebates or discounts and other contractual changes in the prices of raw materials, labour, or other purchased goods and services are anticipated in interim periods, by both the payer and the recipient, if it is probable that they have been earned or will take effect. Thus, contractual rebates and discounts are anticipated but discretionary rebates and discounts are not anticipated because the resulting asset or liability would not satisfy the conditions set out in FRS 102 that an asset must be a resource controlled by the entity as a result of a past event and that a liability must be a present obligation whose settlement is expected to result in an outflow of resources.

Depreciation and amortisation

A2.26   Depreciation and amortisation for an interim period is based only on assets owned during that interim period. It does not take into account asset acquisitions or dispositions planned for later in the financial year.

Inventories

Inventories are measured for interim financial reporting by the same principles as at financial year-end. Section 13 *Inventories* of FRS 102 establishes standards for recognising and measuring inventories. Inventories pose particular problems at the end of any financial reporting period because of the need to determine inventory quantities, costs, and net realisable values. Nonetheless, the same measurement principles are applied for inventories at an interim date. To save cost and time, entities often use estimates to measure inventories at interim dates to a greater extent than at the end of annual reporting periods. Following are examples of how to apply the net realisable value test at an interim date and how to treat manufacturing variances at interim dates.

A2.27

Net realisable value of inventories

The net realisable value of inventories is determined by reference to selling prices and related costs to complete and dispose at interim dates. An entity will reverse a write-down to net realisable value in a subsequent interim period only if it would be appropriate to do so at the end of the financial year.

A2.28

[Deleted]

A2.29

Interim period manufacturing cost variances

Price, efficiency, spending, and volume variances of a manufacturing entity are recognised in income at interim reporting dates to the same extent that those variances are recognised in income at financial year-end. Deferral of variances that are expected to be absorbed by year-end is not appropriate because it could result in reporting inventory at the interim date at more or less than its portion of the actual cost of manufacture.

A2.30

Foreign currency translation gains and losses

Foreign currency translation gains and losses are measured for interim financial reporting by the same principles as at financial year-end.

A2.31

Section 30 *Foreign Currency Translation* of FRS 102 specifies how to translate the financial statements for foreign operations into the presentation currency, including guidelines for using average or closing foreign exchange rates and guidelines for recognising the resulting adjustments in profit or loss, or in other comprehensive income. Consistently with Section 30 of FRS 102, the actual average and closing rates for the interim period are used. Entities do not anticipate future changes in foreign exchange rates in the remainder of the current financial year in translating foreign operations at an interim date.

A2.32

If Section 30 of FRS 102 requires translation adjustments to be recognised as income or expense in the period in which they arise, that principle is applied during each interim period. Entities do not defer some foreign currency translation adjustments at an interim date if the adjustment is expected to reverse before the end of the financial year.

A2.33

Interim financial reporting in hyperinflationary economies

Interim financial reports in hyperinflationary economies are prepared by the same principles as at financial year-end.

A2.34

Section 31 *Hyperinflation* of FRS 102 requires that the financial statements of an entity that reports in the currency of a hyperinflationary economy shall be stated in terms of the

A2.35

measuring unit current at the end of the reporting period, and the gain or loss on the net monetary position is included in profit or loss. Also, comparative financial data reported for prior periods are restated to the current measuring unit.

A2.36 Entities follow those same principles at interim dates, thereby presenting all interim data in the measuring unit as of the end of the interim period, with the resulting gain or loss on the net monetary position included in the interim period's profit or loss. Entities do not annualise the recognition of the gain or loss. Nor do they use an estimated annual inflation rate in preparing an interim financial report in a hyperinflationary economy.

Impairment of assets

A2.37 Section 27 *Impairment of Assets* of FRS 102 requires that an impairment loss be recognised if the recoverable amount has declined below carrying amount.

A2.38 FRS 104 requires that an entity shall apply the same impairment testing, recognition, and reversal criteria at an interim date as it would at the end of its financial year. That does not mean, however, that an entity must necessarily make a detailed impairment calculation at the end of each interim period. Rather, an entity will review for indications of significant impairment since the end of the most recent financial year to determine whether such a calculation is needed.

EXAMPLES OF THE USE OF ESTIMATES

The following examples illustrate the application of the principle in paragraph 41 of FRS 104.

Inventories

A2.39 Full stock-taking and valuation procedures may not be required for inventories at interim dates, although it may be done at financial year-end. It may be sufficient to make estimates at interim dates based on sales margins.

Classifications of assets and liabilities

A2.40 Entities may do a more thorough investigation for classifying assets as current or fixed assets and liabilities as due within one year or after more than one year (or an equivalent classification between current and non-current assets and liabilities) at annual reporting dates than at interim dates.

Provisions

A2.41 Determination of the appropriate amount of a provision (such as a provision for warranties, environmental costs, and site restoration costs) may be complex and often costly and time-consuming. Entities sometimes engage outside experts to assist in the annual calculations. Making similar estimates at interim dates often entails updating of the prior annual provision rather than the engaging of outside experts to do a new calculation.

Pensions

A2.42 Section 28 of FRS 102 requires an entity to determine the present value of defined benefit obligations and the fair value of plan assets at the end of each reporting period. FRS 102 does not require an entity to involve a professionally qualified actuary in the measurement of the obligations nor does FRS 102 require an annual comprehensive actuarial valuation. For interim reporting purposes, the defined benefit obligation can often be reliably measured by extrapolation of the latest actuarial valuation adjusted for changes in employee demographics such as number of employees and salary levels.

Income taxes

Entities may calculate income tax expense and deferred income tax liability at annual dates by applying the tax rate for each individual jurisdiction to measures of income for each jurisdiction. Paragraph A2.16 acknowledges that while that degree of precision is desirable at interim reporting dates as well, it may not be achievable in all cases, and a weighted average of rates across jurisdictions or across categories of income is used if it is a reasonable approximation of the effect of using more specific rates.

A2.43

Contingencies

The measurement of contingencies may involve the opinions of legal experts or other advisers. Formal reports from independent experts are sometimes obtained with respect to contingencies. Such opinions about litigation, claims, assessments, and other contingencies and uncertainties may or may not also be needed at interim dates.

A2.44

Revaluations and fair value accounting

Section 17 *Property, Plant and Equipment* of FRS 102 allows an entity to choose as its accounting policy the revaluation model whereby items of property, plant and equipment are revalued to fair value. Similarly, Section 16 *Investment Property* of FRS 102 requires an entity to measure the fair value of investment property. For those measurements, an entity that relies on professionally qualified valuers at annual reporting dates is not required to rely on them at interim reporting dates.

A2.45

[Not used]

A2.46

Specialised industries

Because of complexity, costliness, and time, interim period measurements in specialised industries might be less precise than at financial year-end. An example would be calculation of insurance reserves by insurance companies.

A2.47

Appendix III
Significant differences between FRS 104 and IAS 34

Paragraphs in FRS 104	Changes made to IAS 34
2 to 3A	The scope of FRS 104 has been amended to reflect that FRS 104 is intended for use by entities that prepare annual financial statements in accordance with FRS 102.
	It sets out when entities preparing half-yearly financial reports in accordance with the DTRs shall apply FRS 104.
	FRS 104 does not contain recommendations or requirements as to whether, when or how frequently an entity should prepare interim financial reports.
4 to 5	These paragraphs have been deleted.
	Definitions of terms are included in the Glossary to FRS 104.
	Entities that elect to prepare a complete set of financial statements refer to FRS 102 for the content requirements; these are not repeated in FRS 104.
8A	This paragraph clarifies when an entity presents a single statement of comprehensive income or separate statements of income and comprehensive income in the interim financial report.
8B to 8D	An entity is permitted to apply the exemptions in paragraphs 3.18 and 3.19 of FRS 102 in the interim financial statements under certain conditions.
8E	This new paragraph repeats requirements contained in paragraph 5 of IAS 34.
8F	This paragraph grants entities a conditional exemption from the preparation of a statement of cash flows.
9	A conditional exemption from the preparation of a statement of cash flows is provided to entities consistent with paragraph 8F of FRS 104.
12	This paragraph has been deleted.
14	This paragraph has been deleted.
	The requirements are not relevant for entities that apply FRS 102.
	Entities that prepare interim financial reports in accordance with FRS 104 will generally prepare them on an entity-only basis.
15B	It has been clarified that entities are permitted to include cross-references in the notes from disclosures made elsewhere in the interim financial report.
	Disclosure of the information is only required if the information would be disclosable in the annual financial statements.
	Paragraphs 15B(j), (k) and (l) have been amended or deleted because disclosures required by these paragraphs in IAS 34 are not required in the annual financial statements under FRS 102.

Paragraphs in FRS 104	Changes made to IAS 34
16A	It has been clarified that entities are permitted to include cross-references in the notes from disclosures made elsewhere in the interim financial report.
	Paragraphs 16A(i) and (j) have been amended to limit the disclosure requirements to those required by FRS 102 in annual financial statements. An entity that is not required to make the disclosures in the annual financial statements is exempt from providing the disclosures in the interim financial report.
	Paragraph 16A(k) has been deleted because similar disclosures are not required by FRS 102 in annual financial statements.
19	References to compliance with IFRSs have been deleted as not applicable for entities applying FRS 104.
20A to 20B	The requirements have been clarified in respect of entities that apply any of the presentational options provided for in paragraphs 8B to 8C of FRS 104.
26 to 27	These paragraphs have been deleted.
	FRS 104 does not set out disclosure requirements pertaining to annual financial statements.
35 to 36	The requirements of these paragraphs have been consolidated in paragraph 35 of FRS 104.
	Paragraph 36 has been deleted.
46 to 56	The effective date requirements have been amended in FRS 104.
	Paragraphs 47 to 56 have been deleted as they are not needed in FRS 104.

Appendix IV
Table of comparison between terminology used in the DTRs and FRS 104

The following table compares broadly equivalent terminology used in the Disclosure and Transparency Rules (DTRs) with terminology used in FRS 104.

Terminology used in the DTRs	Terminology used in FRS 104
Balance sheet	Statement of financial position
Condensed set of financial statements	Condensed interim financial statements and selected explanatory notes
Half-yearly financial report	Interim financial report
Profit and loss account	Income statement (under the two-statement approach)
	Part of the statement of comprehensive income (under the single-statement approach)

Appendix V
Note on UK regulatory requirements

This Appendix provides an overview of how the requirements in FRS 104 complement the legal reporting requirements set out in the Disclosure and Transparency Rules (DTRs) of the United Kingdom (UK) Financial Conduct Authority (FCA). **A5.1**

SCOPE

FRS 104 does not specify whether, how frequently or how soon after the end of an interim period an entity should present interim financial reports. The DTRs set out requirements in this regard. **A5.2**

Issuers that are required to publish half-yearly financial reports in accordance with the DTRs must include a responsibility statement in the report. In accordance with paragraph 4.2.10R of the DTRs, a person making the responsibility statement will satisfy the requirement to confirm that the condensed set of financial statements gives a true and fair view of the assets, liabilities, financial position and profit or loss of the issuer (or the undertakings included in the consolidation as a whole) by including a statement that the condensed set of financial statements has been prepared in accordance with IAS 34 *Interim Financial Reporting* or, for UK issuers not using EU-adopted IFRS, pronouncements on interim reporting issued by the Financial Reporting Council[7]. **A5.3**

FRS 104 constitutes the pronouncement on interim reporting for UK issuers not using EU-adopted IFRS as described in the preceding paragraph. The application of FRS 104 is conditional upon the person making the responsibility statement having reasonable grounds to be satisfied that the condensed set of financial statements prepared in accordance with FRS 104 is not misleading. **A5.4**

CONTENT AND BASIS OF PREPARATION OF THE INTERIM FINANCIAL STATEMENTS

In accordance with the DTRs, an issuer that is required to prepare consolidated accounts must prepare the condensed set of financial statements in accordance with IAS 34 and the requirements set out in FRS 104 do not apply to these issuers. **A5.5**

An issuer that is not required to prepare consolidated accounts must, as a minimum, apply the content and preparation requirements set out in paragraph 4.2.5R of the DTRs. The content and preparation requirements of FRS 104 are consistent with those set out in the DTRs, although they are more prescriptive and detailed. **A5.6**

As required by the DTRs and FRS 104, the accounting policies and presentation applied to the interim financial statements should be consistent with those of the most recent annual financial statements, unless changes are made in the next annual financial statements. In that case the new accounting policies and presentation must be reflected in the interim financial statements. An interim financial report prepared in the year of adoption of FRS 102 *The Financial Reporting Standard applicable in the UK and Republic of Ireland* must therefore be prepared in accordance with the new FRS 102 compliant accounting policies and presentation requirements. FRS 104 also requires certain transitional **A5.7**

---

[7] *At the time of the publication of FRS 104 the DTRs refer to pronouncements on interim reporting issued by the Accounting Standard Board. Following the publication of FRS 104 the FCA will seek a change to the DTRs so that the DTRs refer to pronouncements on interim reporting issued by the FRC.*

disclosures in the first set of interim financial statements that is prepared in accordance with the new FRS 102 compliant accounting policies.

CROSS-REFERENCING TO THE INTERIM MANAGEMENT REPORT

A5.8 Paragraphs 4.2.7R and 4.2.8R of the DTRs require issuers to publish an interim management report and specify certain minimum disclosures. Where FRS 104 requires disclosure of the same information in the interim financial statements, an issuer is permitted to include a cross-reference to the information disclosed in the interim management report, instead of duplicating the same information in the notes.

Appendix VI
Republic of Ireland legal references

In the Republic of Ireland (RoI) the Investment Funds Companies and Miscellaneous Provisions Act 2006 provides for, inter alia, the implementation of certain aspects of the EU Transparency Directive (Directive 2004/109/EC). Where entities fall within the scope of the EU Transparency Directive, the half-yearly reporting requirements are set out in Regulation 6(2) of the Transparency (Directive 2004/109/EC) Regulations 2007.

A6.1

FRS 104 includes various references to the requirements of the Disclosure and Transparency Rules (DTRs) of the Financial Conduct Authority as they apply to issuers whose home state is the United Kingdom. The tables below outline the corresponding provisions in the Transparency (Directive 2004/109/EC) Regulations 2007, including subsequent amendments thereto (Transparency Regulations), as they apply to Irish issuers.

A6.2

FRS 104 constitutes the pronouncement on interim reporting for Irish issuers not using EU-adopted IFRS, as provided for in Regulation 8(5)(d)(ii) of the Transparency Regulations.

A6.3

SUMMARY

Paragraph	DTRs reference	Transparency Regulations reference
xi	Paragraph 4.2.2R	Regulation 6(2)
xii	Paragraphs 4.2.10R and 4.2.10(4)R	Regulations 6(3)(c) and 8(5) (a) to (d)

FRS 104

Paragraph	DTRs reference	Transparency Regulations reference
3A	Paragraph 4.2.10(4)R	Regulations 8(5) (a) to (d)

APPENDIX I: GLOSSARY

'DTRs'	Equivalent aspects of the EU Transparency Directive are implemented in the Republic of Ireland through the Transparency (Directive 2004/109/EC) Regulations 2007, including subsequent amendments thereto.

APPENDIX V: NOTE ON UK REGULATORY REQUIREMENTS

Paragraph	DTRs reference	Transparency Regulations reference
A5.3	Paragraph 4.2.10R	Regulations 6(3)(c) and 8(5)
A5.6	Paragraph 4.2.5R	Regulation 7
A5.9	Paragraphs 4.2.7R and 4.2.8R	Regulations 8(2) and 8(3)

FRS 105
The Financial Reporting Standard applicable to the Micro-entities Regime

(July 2015)

Contents

This standard was amended by Amendments to FRS 105: The Financial Reporting Standard applicable to the micro-entities regime - Limited Liability Partnerships and Qualifying Partnerships (May 2016) to bring limited liability partnerships and qualifying partnerships within the scope of the micro-entities regime. These amendments are applicable for accounting periods beginning on or after 1 January 2016, with early application permitted from 1 January 2015 if the new legislation The Limited Liability Partnerships, Partnerships and Groups (Accounts and Audit) Regulations 2016 are also applied from that date.

Editor's note: This new accounting standard published by the FRC is based on FRS 102 but its accounting requirements are adapted to satisfy the legal requirements applicable to micro-entities and to reflect the simpler nature and smaller size of micro-entities. FRS 105 is effective for periods beginning on or after 1 January 2016, with early adoption permitted.

SUMMARY

With effect from 1 January 2015 the Financial Reporting Council (FRC) revised financial   **(i)**
reporting standards in the United Kingdom and Republic of Ireland. The revisions
fundamentally reformed financial reporting, replacing the extant standards with five
Financial Reporting Standards:

(a)   FRS 100 *Application of Financial Reporting Requirements*;
(b)   FRS 101 *Reduced Disclosure Framework*;
(c)   FRS 102 *The Financial Reporting Standard applicable in the UK and Republic of
      Ireland*;
(d)   FRS 103 *Insurance Contracts*; and
(e)   FRS 104 *Interim Financial Reporting*.

The revisions made by the FRC followed a sustained and detailed period of consultation.   **(ii)**
The FRC made these fundamental changes recognising that the introduction of International
Financial Reporting Standards for listed groups in 2002 (with application from 2005)
called into question the need for two sets of financial reporting standards. Evidence from
consultation supported a move towards an international-based framework for financial
reporting, but one that was proportionate to the needs of preparers and users.

The FRC's overriding objective in setting accounting standards is to enable users of   **(iii)**
accounts to receive high-quality understandable financial reporting proportionate to the
size and complexity of the entity and users' information needs.

In meeting this objective, the FRC aims to provide succinct financial reporting standards   **(iv)**
that:

(a)   have consistency with international accounting standards through the application
      of an IFRS-based solution unless an alternative clearly better meets the overriding
      objective;
(b)   reflect up-to-date thinking and developments in the way entities operate and the
      transactions they undertake;
(c)   balance consistent principles for accounting by all UK and Republic of Ireland
      entities with practical solutions, based on size, complexity, public interest and users'
      information needs;
(d)   promote efficiency within groups; and
(e)   are cost-effective to apply.

FRS 105 *The Financial Reporting Standard applicable to the Micro-entities Regime* is   **(v)**
an accounting standard intended for financial statements of companies which qualify for
the micro-entities regime. FRS 105 is effective for accounting periods beginning on or
after 1 January 2016. Early application is permitted. The FRC withdraws the Financial
Reporting Standard for Smaller Entities from the effective date of this FRS.

Development of FRS 105

In November 2013, *The Small Companies (Micro-entities' Accounts) Regulations 2013*   **(vi)**
(SI 2013/3008) were made which amended *The Small Companies and Groups (Accounts
and Directors' Report) Regulations 2008* (SI 2008/409). The amendment introduced a
new optional reporting framework for companies that meet the qualifying criteria of a
micro-entity. In response to this change of UK company law and the revision of financial
reporting standards in the United Kingdom and Republic of Ireland set out in paragraph (i),
the FRC developed FRS 105.

(vii)   In February 2015 the FRC issued Financial Reporting Exposure Draft (FRED) 58 *Draft FRS 105 The Financial Reporting Standard applicable to the Micro-entities Regime* to consult on the new accounting standard for micro-entities. Respondents were generally supportive of the proposed requirements and comments made during the consultation were taken into account when FRS 105 was finalised.

(viii)   FRS 105 is based on FRS 102, but its accounting requirements are adapted to satisfy the legal requirements applicable to micro-entities and to reflect the simpler nature and smaller size of micro-entities.

(ix)   The application of the micro-entities regime is optional, however, a micro-entity that chooses to prepare its financial statements in accordance with the micro-entities regime is required to apply FRS 105. A company that qualifies for this regime, but chooses not to apply it, is required to apply another accounting standard. The possible options are set out in FRS 100 *Application of Financial Reporting Requirements*.

(x)   At the same time as the FRC issues FRS 105, the FRC also makes amendments to FRS 102 to incorporate consequential changes resulting from the *The Companies, Partnerships and Groups (Accounts and Reports) Regulations 2015* (SI 2015/980). FRS 105 takes into account any relevant changes made to FRS 102 in this regard.

Organisation of FRS 105

(xi)   FRS 105 is organised by topic with each topic presented in a separate numbered section. Cross-references to paragraphs are identified by section followed by paragraph number. Paragraph numbers are in the form of xx.yy, where xx is the section number and yy is the sequential paragraph number within that section.

(xii)   In examples that include monetary amounts, the measuring unit is Currency Unit (abbreviated as CU)

(xiii)   All the paragraphs of FRS 105 have equal authority. Some sections include appendices of implementation guidance or examples. Some of these are an integral part of this FRS while others provide guidance concerning its application; each specifies its status.

(xiv)   FRS 105 is set out in Sections 1 to 28 and the Glossary (Appendix I). Terms defined in the glossary are in **bold type** the first time they appear in each section.

(xv)   Where references to other sections or paragraphs are made, these are in reference to FRS 105 unless otherwise stated.

FRS 105 THE FINANCIAL REPORTING STANDARD APPLICABLE TO THE MICRO-ENTITIES REGIME

Section 1 Scope

Scope of this Financial Reporting Standard

1.1   This FRS applies to the **financial statements** of a **micro-entity**. The financial statements of a micro-entity prepared in accordance with this FRS that include the **micro-entity minimum accounting items** are presumed in law to show a true and fair view of the micro-entity's **financial position** and **profit or loss** in accordance with the **micro-entities regime**.

References to a micro-entity in this FRS are to a micro-entity that chooses to apply the micro-entities regime.   **1.2**

This FRS permits, but does not require, a micro-entity to include information additional to the micro-entity minimum accounting items in its financial statements. If a micro-entity includes additional information it shall have regard to any requirement of Section 1A *Small Entities* of **FRS 102** that relates to that information.   **1.3**

Date from which effective

A micro-entity applying the micro-entities regime shall apply this FRS for accounting periods beginning on or after 1 January 2016. Early application is permitted.   **1.4**

Section 2 Concepts and Pervasive Principles

Scope of this section

This section sets out the concepts and basic principles that generally underlie the **recognition** and **measurement** of transactions of **micro-entities** within the scope of this FRS.   **2.1**

Financial position

The **financial position** of a micro-entity is the relationship of its **assets**, **liabilities** and **equity** as of a specific date as presented in the **statement of financial position**. These are defined as follows: **2.2**

(a) An asset is a resource controlled by the micro-entity as a result of past events and from which future economic benefits are expected to flow to the micro-entity.
(b) A liability is a present obligation of the micro-entity arising from past events, the settlement of which is expected to result in an outflow from the micro-entity of resources embodying economic benefits.
(c) Equity is the residual interest in the assets of the micro-entity after deducting all its liabilities.

Some items that meet the definition of an asset or a liability may not be recognised as assets or liabilities in the statement of financial position because they do not satisfy the criteria for recognition in paragraphs 2.22 and 2.24. In particular, the expectation that future economic benefits will flow to or from a micro-entity must be sufficiently certain to meet the probability criterion before an asset or liability is recognised.   **2.3**

Assets

The future economic benefit of an asset is its potential to contribute, directly or indirectly, to the flow of cash to the micro-entity. Those cash flows may come from using the asset or from disposing of it.   **2.4**

Many assets, for example **property, plant and equipment**, have a physical form. However, physical form is not essential to the existence of an asset. Some assets are intangible.   **2.5**

In determining the existence of an asset, the right of ownership is not essential. Thus, for example, property held on a **lease** is an asset if the micro-entity controls the benefits that are expected to flow from the property.   **2.6**

Liabilities

2.7   An essential characteristic of a liability is that the micro-entity has a present obligation to act or perform in a particular way. The obligation may be either a legal obligation or a **constructive obligation**. A legal obligation is legally enforceable as a consequence of a binding contract or statutory requirement. A constructive obligation is an obligation that derives from a micro-entity's actions when:

(a)   by an established pattern of past practice, published policies or a sufficiently specific current statement, the micro-entity has indicated to other parties that it will accept certain responsibilities; and

(b)   as a result, the micro-entity has created a valid expectation on the part of those other parties that it will discharge those responsibilities.

2.8   The settlement of a present obligation usually involves the payment of cash, transfer of other assets, provision of services, the replacement of that obligation with another obligation, or conversion of the obligation to equity. An obligation may also be extinguished by other means, such as a creditor waiving or forfeiting its rights.

Equity

2.9   Equity is the residual interest in the assets of the micro-entity after deducting all its liabilities.

Performance

2.10   **Performance** is the relationship of the **income** and **expenses** of a micro-entity during a **reporting period**. Income and expenses are defined as follows:

(a)   Income is increases in economic benefits during the reporting period in the form of inflows or enhancements of assets or decreases of liabilities that result in increases in equity, other than those relating to contributions from equity investors.

(b)   Expenses are decreases in economic benefits during the reporting period in the form of outflows or depletions of assets or incurrences of liabilities that result in decreases in equity, other than those relating to distributions to equity investors.

2.11   The recognition of income and expenses results directly from the recognition and measurement of assets and liabilities. Criteria for the recognition of income and expenses are discussed in paragraphs 2.26 and 2.27.

Income

2.12   The definition of income encompasses both **revenue** and **gains**.

(a)   Revenue is income that arises in the course of the ordinary activities of a micro-entity and is referred to by a variety of names including sales, fees, interest, dividends, royalties and rent.

(b)   Gains are other items that meet the definition of income but are not revenue.

Expenses

2.13   The definition of expenses encompasses losses as well as those expenses that arise in the course of the ordinary activities of the micro-entity.

(a)   Expenses that arise in the course of the ordinary activities of the micro-entity include, for example, cost of sales, wages and **depreciation**. They usually take the form of an outflow or depletion of assets such as cash, **inventory**, or property, plant and equipment.

(b)   Losses are other items that meet the definition of expenses and may arise in the course of the ordinary activities of the micro-entity.

Recognition of assets, liabilities, income and expenses

Recognition is the process of incorporating in the statement of financial position or **income statement** an item that meets the definition of an asset, liability, equity, income or expense and satisfies the following criteria: **2.14**

(a)   it is **probable** that any future economic benefit associated with the item will flow to or from the micro-entity; and

(b)   the item has a cost or value that can be measured reliably.

The uncertainties that inevitably surround many events and circumstances are acknowledged by the exercise of **prudence** in the preparation of the financial statements. Prudence is the inclusion of a degree of caution in the exercise of the judgements needed in making the estimates required under conditions of uncertainty, such that assets or income are not overstated and liabilities or expenses are not understated. However, the exercise of prudence does not allow the deliberate understatement of assets or income, or the deliberate overstatement of liabilities or expenses. In short, prudence does not permit bias.   **2.15**

The probability of future economic benefit

The concept of probability is used in the first recognition criterion to refer to the degree of uncertainty that the future economic benefits associated with the item will flow to or from the micro-entity. Assessments of the degree of uncertainty attaching to the flow of future economic benefits are made on the basis of the evidence relating to conditions at the end of the reporting period available when the financial statements are prepared. Those assessments are made individually for individually significant items, and for a group for a large population of individually insignificant items.   **2.16**

Reliability of measurement

The second criterion for the recognition of an item is that it possesses a cost or value that can be measured with reliability. In many cases, the cost or value of an item is known. In other cases it must be estimated. The use of reasonable estimates is an essential part of the preparation of financial statements and does not undermine their reliability. When a reasonable estimate cannot be made, the item is not recognised in the financial statements.   **2.17**

An item that fails to meet the recognition criteria may qualify for recognition at a later date as a result of subsequent circumstances or events.   **2.18**

Measurement of assets, liabilities, income and expenses

Measurement is the process of determining the monetary amounts at which a micro-entity measures assets, liabilities, income and expenses in its financial statements. Measurement involves the selection of a basis of measurement. This FRS specifies which measurement basis a micro-entity shall use for many types of assets, liabilities, income and expenses.   **2.19**

Pervasive recognition and measurement principles

2.20   In the absence of a requirement in this FRS that applies specifically to a transaction or other event or condition, paragraph 8.4 provides guidance for making a judgement and paragraph 8.5 requires a micro-entity to look to the definitions, recognition criteria and measurement concepts for assets, liabilities, income and expenses and the pervasive principles set out in this section.

Accrual basis

2.21   A micro-entity shall prepare its financial statements using the **accrual basis** of accounting. On the accrual basis, items are recognised as assets, liabilities, equity, income or expenses when they satisfy the definitions and recognition criteria for those items.

Recognition in financial statements

Assets

2.22   A micro-entity shall recognise an asset in the statement of financial position when it is probable that the future economic benefits will flow to the micro-entity and the asset has a cost or value that can be measured reliably. An asset is not recognised in the statement of financial position when expenditure has been incurred for which it is considered not probable that economic benefits will flow to the micro-entity beyond the current reporting period. Instead such a transaction results in the recognition of an expense in the income statement.

2.23   A micro-entity shall not recognise a **contingent asset** as an asset. When the flow of future economic benefits to the micro-entity is virtually certain, then the related asset is not a contingent asset, and its recognition is appropriate.

Liabilities

2.24   A micro-entity shall recognise a liability in the statement of financial position when:

    (a)   the micro-entity has an obligation at the end of the reporting period as a result of a past event;

    (b)   it is probable that the micro-entity will be required to transfer resources embodying economic benefits in settlement; and

    (c)   the settlement amount can be measured reliably.

2.25   A **contingent liability** is either a possible but uncertain obligation or a present obligation that is not recognised because it fails to meet one or both of the conditions (b) and (c) in paragraph 2.24.

Income

2.26   The recognition of income results directly from the recognition and measurement of assets and liabilities. A micro-entity shall recognise income in the income statement when an increase in future economic benefits related to an increase in an asset or a decrease of a liability has arisen that can be measured reliably.

Expenses

The recognition of expenses results directly from the recognition and measurement of assets and liabilities. A micro-entity shall recognise expenses in the income statement when a decrease in future economic benefits related to a decrease in an asset or an increase of a liability has arisen that can be measured reliably.   **2.27**

Profit or loss

Profit or loss is the arithmetical difference between income and expenses. It is not a separate element of financial statements, and a separate recognition principle is not needed for it.   **2.28**

Generally this FRS does not allow the recognition of items in the statement of financial position that do not meet the definition of assets or of liabilities regardless of whether they result from applying the notion commonly referred to as the 'matching concept' for measuring profit or loss.   **2.29**

Measurement at initial recognition

At initial recognition, a micro-entity shall measure assets and liabilities at cost.   **2.30**

Under limited circumstances this FRS requires a micro-entity to estimate the cost of an asset or liability based on its **fair value**. Where this FRS requires a micro-entity to determine the fair value of an asset or liability, it shall use the following hierarchy to estimate the fair value: **2.31**

(a) The best evidence of fair value is the open market price for an identical asset or liability in an **active market**.

(b) When an open market price is not available, the price of a recent transaction for an identical asset or liability provides evidence of fair value as long as there has not been significant change in economic circumstances or a significant lapse of time since the transaction took place.

(c) If neither (a) nor (b) above are available, the fair value shall be estimated using a valuation technique. The objective of using a valuation technique is to estimate what the price of a recent transaction for an identical asset or liability would have been on the measurement date in an arm's length exchange motivated by normal business considerations.

Subsequent measurement

Financial assets and financial liabilities

A micro-entity measures **financial assets** and **financial liabilities** as follows: **2.32**

(a) Investments in preference shares or **ordinary shares** and investments in **subsidiaries** and **associates** and interests in **jointly controlled entities** shall be measured at cost less impairment.

(b) **Derivatives** are measured at cost adjusted for amounts recognised in profit or loss over the term of the instruments and any impairment loss.

(c) **Financial instruments** other than financial instruments covered by paragraphs (a) and (b) are measured at cost adjusted for the allocation of interest, the amortisation of any **transaction costs** included in the cost of the instruments and any impairment loss.

Non-financial assets

2.33   **Property, plant and equipment, investment property** and **biological assets** are measured at cost less accumulated depreciation and accumulated **impairment losses**.

2.34   **Inventories** are measured at the lower of cost and selling price less costs to complete and sell.

2.35   Measurement of assets at amounts lower than their initial historical cost is intended to ensure that an asset is not measured at an amount greater than the micro-entity expects to recover from the sale or use of that asset.

Liabilities other than financial liabilities

2.36   Most liabilities other than financial liabilities are measured at the best estimate of the amount that would be required to settle the obligation at the **reporting date**.

Offsetting

2.37   A micro-entity shall not offset assets and liabilities, or income and expenses, unless required or permitted by this FRS.

(a)   Measuring assets net of valuation allowances (for example, allowances for inventory obsolescence and allowances for uncollectible receivables) is not offsetting.

(b)   If a micro-entity's normal **operating activities** do not include buying and selling **fixed assets**, including investments and operating assets, then the micro-entity reports gains and losses on disposal of such assets by deducting from the proceeds on disposal the **carrying amount** of the asset and related selling expenses.

Section 3 Financial Statement Presentation

Scope of this section

3.1   This section explains what compliance with this FRS requires and what makes up a complete set of **financial statements** for a **micro-entity**.

Presumed true and fair view

3.2   The financial statements of a micro-entity that comply with this FRS are presumed in law to give a true and fair view of the **financial position** and **profit or loss** of the micro-entity in accordance with the **micro-entities regime**.

Going concern

3.3   When preparing financial statements using this FRS, the management of a micro-entity shall make an assessment of whether the going concern basis of accounting is appropriate. The going concern basis of accounting is appropriate unless management either intends to liquidate the micro-entity or to cease trading, or has no realistic alternative but to do so. In assessing whether the going concern basis of accounting is appropriate, management takes into account all available information about the future, which is at least, but is not limited to, 12 months from the date when the financial statements are authorised for issue.

Frequency of reporting

A micro-entity shall present a complete set of financial statements (including comparative information as set out in paragraph 3.7) at the end of each **reporting period**. **3.4**

Consistency of presentation

A micro-entity shall retain the presentation and classification of items in the financial statements from one period to the next unless: **3.5**

(a) it is apparent, following a significant change in the nature of the micro-entity's operations or a review of its financial statements, that another presentation or classification would be more appropriate having regard to the criteria for the selection and application of **accounting policies** in Section 8 *Accounting Policies, Estimates and Errors*; or

(b) this FRS requires a change in presentation.

When the presentation or classification of items in the financial statements is changed, a micro-entity shall reclassify comparative amounts unless the reclassification is **impracticable**. **3.6**

Comparative information

Except when this FRS permits or requires otherwise, a micro-entity shall present comparative information in respect of the preceding period for all amounts presented in the current period's financial statements. **3.7**

Materiality

A micro-entity need not provide a specific disclosure required by this FRS if the information is not **material**. This exemption does not apply to the disclosures required by paragraph 6.2(a). **3.8**

Complete set of financial statements

A complete set of financial statements of a micro-entity shall include the following: **3.9**

(a) a **statement of financial position** as at the **reporting date** with **notes** included at the foot of the statement; and

(b) an **income statement** for the reporting period.

Because paragraph 3.7 requires comparative amounts in respect of the previous period for all amounts presented in the financial statements, a complete set of financial statements means that a micro-entity shall present, as a minimum, two of each of the required financial statements and related notes. **3.10**

In a complete set of financial statements, a micro-entity shall present each financial statement with equal prominence. **3.11**

A micro-entity may use titles for the financial statements other than those used in this FRS as long as they are not misleading. **3.12**

Identification of the financial statements

3.13   A micro-entity shall clearly identify each of the financial statements and the notes. In addition, a micro-entity shall display the following information prominently, and repeat it when necessary for an understanding of the information presented:

(a)   the name of the reporting entity and any change in its name since the end of the preceding reporting period;

(b)   the date of the end of the reporting period and the period covered by the financial statements;

(c)   the presentation currency; and

(d)   the level of rounding, if any, used in presenting amounts in the financial statements.

Statement of compliance with the micro-entity provisions

3.14   In accordance with section 414(3) of the **Act**, financial statements prepared in accordance with the **micro-entity provisions** shall on the **statement of financial position**, in a prominent position above the signature, contain a statement that the financial statements are prepared in accordance with the micro-entity provisions.

Section 4 Statement of Financial Position

Scope of this section

4.1   This section sets out the information that is to be presented in a **statement of financial position** and how to present it. The statement of financial position (which is referred to as the balance sheet in the **Act**) presents a **micro-entity's assets, liabilities** and **equity** as of a specific date – the end of the **reporting period**.

4.2   A micro-entity is permitted, but not required, to present information additional to that required by this section. Paragraph 1.3 applies to any additional information presented.

Information to be presented in the statement of financial position

4.3   A micro-entity shall present a statement of financial position in accordance with one of the formats set out in Section C of Part 1 of Schedule 1 to the **Small Companies Regulations**, as follows:

Format 1	**CU**	**CU**
Called up share capital not paid		X
Fixed assets		X
Current assets	X	
Prepayments and accrued income	X	
Creditors: amounts falling due within one year	(X)	
Net current assets / (liabilities)		X/(X)
Total assets less current liabilities		X
Creditors: amounts falling due after more than one year		(X)
Provisions for liabilities		(X)

Format 1	CU	CU
Accruals and deferred income		(X)
		X
Capital and reserves		X

Format 2	CU	CU
Assets		
Called up share capital not paid		X
Fixed assets		X
Current assets		X
Prepayments and accrued income		X
		X
Capital, Reserves and Liabilities		
Capital and reserves		X
Provisions for liabilities		X
Creditors		
Amounts falling due within one year	X	
Amounts falling due after one year	X	
		X
Accruals and deferred income		X
		X

Creditors: amounts falling due within one year

A micro-entity shall classify a creditor as due within one year when the micro-entity does not have an unconditional right, at the end of the reporting period, to defer settlement of the creditor for at least 12 months after the **reporting date**.   **4.4**

Section 5 Income Statement

Scope of this section

This section requires a **micro-entity** to present its **profit or loss** for a period, ie its financial **performance** for the period. It sets out the information that is to be presented in the **income statement** (which is referred to as the profit and loss account in the **Act**) and how to present it.   **5.1**

A micro-entity is permitted, but not required, to present information additional to that required by this section. Paragraph 1.3 applies to any additional information presented.   **5.2**

Presentation of profit or loss

A micro-entity shall present its profit or loss for a period in an income statement in accordance with Section C of Part 1 of Schedule 1 to the **Small Companies Regulations**, as follows: **5.3**

	CU
Turnover	X
Other income	X
Cost of raw materials and consumables	(X)
Staff costs	(X)
Depreciation and other amounts written off assets	(X)
Other charges	(X)
Tax	(X)
Profit or loss	X / (X)

5.4   Under this FRS, the effects of corrections of **material errors** and changes in **accounting policies** are presented as retrospective adjustments of prior periods rather than as part of profit or loss in the period in which they arise (see Section 8 *Accounting Policies, Estimates and Errors*).

Section 6 Notes to the Financial Statements

Scope of this section

6.1   This section sets out the information that shall be disclosed in the **notes** to the **financial statements** and where. A **micro-entity** is permitted, but not required, to disclose information additional to that required by this section. Paragraph 1.3 applies to any additional information disclosed.

Structure and content of the notes

6.2   In accordance with section 472(1A) of the **Act**, the notes to the financial statements of a micro-entity shall be presented at the foot of the **statement of financial position** and shall include the following information:

(a)   advances, credit and guarantees granted to directors as required by section 413 of the Act (see paragraph 6A.1 in the Appendix to this Section); and

(b)   financial commitments, guarantees and contingencies as required by regulation 5A of, and paragraph 57 of Part 3 of Schedule 1 to, the **Small Companies Regulations** (see paragraphs 6A.2 and 6A.3 in the Appendix to this Section).

Appendix to Section 6

Company law disclosure requirements

This appendix is an integral part of this FRS.

This appendix sets out the company law disclosure requirements referred to in paragraph 6.2. Other than substituting company law terminology with the equivalent terminology used in this FRS (see Appendix II Table of equivalence for UK Companies Act terminology), the text is as close as possible to that set out in company law.

Where this FRS contains a disclosure requirement related to a company law requirement this has been indicated.

Details of advances and credits granted by a micro-entity to its directors and guarantees   **6A.1**
of any kind entered into by a micro-entity on behalf of its directors must be shown in the
notes to the financial statements.

The details required of an advance or credit are:

(a)   *its amount;*
(b)   *an indication of the interest rate;*
(c)   *its main conditions;*
(d)   *any amounts repaid;*
(e)   *any amounts written off; and*
(f)   *any amounts waived.*

*There must also be stated in the notes to the financial statements the totals of amounts
stated under (a), (d), (e) and (f).*

The details required of a guarantee are:

(a)   *its main terms;*
(b)   *the amount of the maximum liability that may be incurred by a micro-entity;*
(c)   *any amount paid and any liability incurred by a micro-entity for the purpose of
fulfilling the guarantee (including any loss incurred by reason of enforcement of the
guarantee).*

*There must also be stated in the notes to the financial statements the totals of amounts
stated under (b) and (c). (Section 413 of the Act)*

The total amount of any financial commitments, guarantees and contingencies that are not   **6A.2**
included in the statement of financial position must be stated. (Schedule 1, paragraph 57(1))

*The total amount of any commitments concerning pensions must be separately disclosed.
(Schedule 1, paragraph 57(3))*

The total amount of any commitments which are undertaken on behalf of or for the benefit of:

(a)   *any parent, fellow subsidiary or any subsidiary of a micro-entity; or*
(b)   *any undertaking in which a micro-entity has a participating interest,*

*must be separately stated and those within (a) must also be stated separately from those
within (b). (Schedule 1, paragraph 57(4))*

The following paragraphs in this FRS address these disclosure requirements within the
context of specific transactions:

(a)   Section 9 *Financial Instruments*: paragraph 9.28
(b)   Section 11 *Investments in Joint Ventures*: paragraph 11.9
(c)   Section 12 *Property, Plant and Equipment and Investment Property*: paragraph 12.28
(d)   Section 13 *Intangible Assets other than Goodwill*: paragraph 13.17
(e)   Section 14 *Business Combinations and Goodwill*: paragraph 14.3
(f)   Section 15 *Leases*: paragraphs 15.17 and 15.33.
(g)   Section 16 *Provisions and Contingencies*: paragraph 16.19
(h)   Section 23 *Employee Benefits*: paragraph 23.22.
(i)   Section 27 *Specialised Activities*: paragraph 27.5.

6A.3   *An indication of the nature and form of any valuable security given by the micro-entity in respect of commitments, guarantees and contingencies within paragraph 6A.2. must be given. (Schedule 1, paragraph 57(2))*

The following paragraphs in this FRS address these disclosure requirements within the context of specific transactions:

(a)   Section 9 *Financial Instruments*: paragraph 9.29.
(b)   Section 10 *Inventories*: paragraph 10.22.
(c)   Section 12 *Property, Plant and Equipment and Investment Property*: paragraph 12.29.
(d)   Section 13 *Intangible Assets other than Goodwill*: paragraph 13.18.
(e)   Section 27 *Specialised Activities*: paragraph 27.6.

Section 7 Subsidiaries, Associates, Jointly Controlled Entities and Intermediate Payment Arrangements

Scope of this section

7.1   This section sets out how a **micro-entity** shall account for investments in **subsidiaries** and **associates**, interests in **jointly controlled entities** and intermediate payment arrangements.

Investments in subsidiaries, associates and interests in jointly controlled entities

7.2   A micro-entity shall account for any investments in subsidiaries and associates and any interests in jointly controlled entities in accordance with Section 9 *Financial Instruments*.

Consolidated financial statements

7.3   An entity that is required or chooses to present **consolidated financial statements** is excluded from the **micro-entities regime** (sections 384A(8) and 384B(2) of the **Act**) and shall not apply this FRS.

Intermediate payment arrangements (eg ESOPs)

7.4   Intermediate payment arrangements may take a variety of forms:

(a)   The intermediary is usually established by the micro-entity and constituted as a trust, although other arrangements are possible.
(b)   The relationship between the micro-entity and the intermediary may take different forms. For example, when the intermediary is constituted as a trust, the micro-entity will not have a right to direct the intermediary's activities. However, in these and other cases the micro-entity may give advice to the intermediary or may be relied on by the intermediary to provide the information it needs to carry out its activities. Sometimes, the way the intermediary has been set up gives it little discretion in the broad nature of its activities.
(c)   The arrangements are most commonly used to pay employees, although they are sometimes used to compensate suppliers of goods and services other than employee services. Sometimes the micro-entity's employees and other suppliers are not the only beneficiaries of the arrangement. Other beneficiaries may include past employees and their dependants, and the intermediary may be entitled to make charitable donations.
(d)   The precise identity of the persons or entities that will receive payments from the intermediary, and the amounts that they will receive, are not usually agreed at the outset.

(e)   The micro-entity often has the right to appoint or veto the appointment of the intermediary's trustees (or its directors or the equivalent).
(f)   The payments made to the intermediary and the payments made by the intermediary are often cash payments but may involve other transfers of value.

Examples of intermediate payment arrangements are employee share ownership plans (ESOPs) and employee benefit trusts that are used to facilitate employee shareholdings under remuneration schemes. In a typical employee benefit trust arrangement for **share-based payment transactions**, a micro-entity makes payments to a trust or guarantees borrowing by the trust, and the trust uses its funds to accumulate assets to pay the micro-entity's employees for services the employees have rendered to the micro-entity.

Although the trustees of an intermediary must act at all times in accordance with the interests of the beneficiaries of the intermediary, most intermediaries (particularly those established as a means of remunerating employees) are specifically designed so as to serve the purposes of the micro-entity, and to ensure that there will be minimal risk of any conflict arising between the duties of the trustees of the intermediary and the interest of the micro-entity, such that there is nothing to encumber implementation of the wishes of the micro-entity in practice. Where this is the case, the micro-entity has de facto **control**.

Accounting for intermediate payment arrangements

When a micro-entity makes payments (or transfers **assets**) to an intermediary, there is a rebuttable presumption that the entity has exchanged one asset for another and that the payment itself does not represent an immediate **expense**. To rebut this presumption at the time the payment is made to the intermediary, the micro-entity must demonstrate: **7.5**

(a)   it will not obtain future economic benefit from the amounts transferred; or
(b)   it does not have control of the right or other access to the future economic benefit it is expected to receive.

Where a payment to an intermediary is an exchange by the micro-entity of one asset for another, any assets that the intermediary acquires in a subsequent exchange transaction will also be under the control of the micro-entity. Accordingly, assets and **liabilities** of the intermediary shall be accounted for by the micro-entity as an extension of its own business and recognised in its **financial statements**. An asset will cease to be recognised as an asset of the micro-entity when, for example, the asset of the intermediary **vests** unconditionally with identified beneficiaries.   **7.6**

A micro-entity may distribute its own equity instruments, or other equity instruments, to an intermediary in order to facilitate employee shareholdings under a remuneration scheme. Where this is the case and the micro-entity has control, or de facto control, of the assets and liabilities of the intermediary, the commercial effect is that the micro-entity is, for all practical purposes, in the same position as if it had purchased the shares directly.   **7.7**

Where an intermediary holds the micro-entity's equity instruments, the micro-entity shall account for the equity instruments as if it had purchased them directly. The micro-entity shall account for the assets and liabilities of the intermediary in its financial statements as follows: **7.8**

(a)   The consideration paid for the equity instruments of the sponsoring entity shall be deducted from equity until such time that the equity instruments vest unconditionally with employees.
(b)   Other assets and liabilities of the intermediary shall be recognised as assets and liabilities of the micro-entity.

(c)   No **gain** or loss shall be recognised in **profit or loss** on the purchase, sale, issue or cancellation of the micro-entity's own equity instruments.

(d)   Finance costs and any administration expenses shall be recognised on an **accruals basis** rather than as funding payments are made to the intermediary.

(e)   Any dividend income arising on the micro-entity's own equity instruments shall be excluded from profit or loss and deducted from the aggregate of dividends paid.

Section 8 Accounting Policies, Estimates and Errors

Scope of this section

8.1   This section provides guidance for selecting and applying the **accounting policies** used in preparing **financial statements**. It also covers **changes in accounting estimates** and corrections of **errors** in prior period financial statements.

Selection and application of accounting policies

8.2   Accounting policies are the specific principles, bases, conventions, rules and practices applied by a **micro-entity** in preparing and presenting financial statements.

8.3   If this FRS specifically addresses a transaction, other event or condition, a micro-entity shall apply this FRS. However, the micro-entity need not follow a requirement in this FRS if the effect of doing so would not be **material**. This exemption does not apply to the disclosures required by paragraph 6.2(a).

8.4   If this FRS does not specifically address a transaction, other event or condition, a micro-entity's management shall use its judgement in developing and applying an accounting policy that results in information that:

(a)   represents faithfully the transactions, other events or conditions;

(b)   reflects the economic substance of the transactions, other events and conditions, and not merely the legal form;

(c)   is neutral, ie free from bias; and

(d)   is **prudent**.

8.5   In making the judgement described in paragraph 8.4, management shall refer to and consider the definitions, **recognition** criteria and **measurement** concepts for **assets**, **liabilities**, **income** and **expenses** and the pervasive principles in Section 2 *Concepts and Pervasive Principles*. A micro-entity is not required to provide any disclosures other than those required by Section 6 *Notes to the Financial Statements* in respect of these transactions or events.

Consistency of accounting policies

8.6   A micro-entity shall select and apply its accounting policies consistently for similar transactions, other events and conditions.

Changes in accounting policies

8.7   A micro-entity shall change an accounting policy only if the change:

(a)   is required by this FRS; or

(b)   results in the financial statements providing reliable and more relevant information about the effects of transactions, other events or conditions on the micro-entity's **financial position** and financial **performance**.

The following are not changes in accounting policies: **8.8**

(a)   the application of an accounting policy for transactions, other events or conditions that differ in substance from those previously occurring; and
(b)   the application of a new accounting policy for transactions, other events or conditions that did not occur previously or were not material.

Applying changes in accounting policies

A micro-entity shall account for changes in accounting policy as follows: **8.9**

(a)   a micro-entity shall account for a change in accounting policy resulting from a change in the requirements of this FRS in accordance with the transitional provisions, if any, specified in that amendment; and
(b)   a micro-entity shall account for all other changes in accounting policy retrospectively (see paragraph 8.10).

Retrospective application

When a change in accounting policy is applied retrospectively in accordance with   **8.10** paragraph 8.9, the micro-entity shall apply the new accounting policy to comparative information for prior periods to the earliest date for which it is practicable, as if the new accounting policy had always been applied. When it is **impracticable** to determine the individual-period effects of a change in accounting policy on comparative information for one or more prior periods presented, the micro-entity shall apply the new accounting policy to the **carrying amounts** of assets and liabilities as at the beginning of the earliest period for which **retrospective application** is practicable, which may be the current period, and shall make a corresponding adjustment to the opening balance of each affected component of **equity** for that period.

Changes in accounting estimates

A **change in accounting estimate** is an adjustment of the carrying amount of an asset   **8.11** or a liability, or the amount of the periodic consumption of an asset, that results from the assessment of the present status of, and expected future benefits and obligations associated with, assets and liabilities. Changes in accounting estimates result from new information or new developments and, accordingly, are not corrections of errors. When it is difficult to distinguish a change in an accounting policy from a change in an accounting estimate, the change is treated as a change in an accounting estimate.

A micro-entity shall recognise the effect of a change in an accounting estimate, other than a   **8.12** change to which paragraph 8.13 applies, **prospectively** by including it in **profit or loss** in:

(a)   the period of the change, if the change affects that period only; or
(b)   the period of the change and future periods, if the change affects both.

To the extent that a change in an accounting estimate gives rise to changes in assets and   **8.13** liabilities, or relates to an item of equity, the micro-entity shall recognise it by adjusting the carrying amount of the related asset, liability or equity item in the period of the change.

Corrections of prior period errors

8.14   Prior period errors are omissions from, and misstatements in, a micro-entity's financial statements for one or more prior periods arising from a failure to use, or misuse of, reliable information that:

(a)   was available when financial statements for those periods were authorised for issue; and

(b)   could reasonably be expected to have been obtained and taken into account in the preparation and presentation of those financial statements.

8.15   Such errors include the effects of mathematical mistakes, mistakes in applying accounting policies, oversights or misinterpretations of facts, and fraud.

8.16   To the extent practicable, a micro-entity shall correct a material prior period error retrospectively in the first financial statements authorised for issue after its discovery by:

(a)   restating the comparative amounts for the prior period(s) presented in which the error occurred; or

(b)   if the error occurred before the earliest prior period presented, restating the opening balances of assets, liabilities and equity for the earliest prior period presented.

8.17   When it is impracticable to determine the period-specific effects of a material error on comparative information for one or more prior periods presented, the micro-entity shall restate the opening balances of assets, liabilities and equity for the earliest period for which retrospective restatement is practicable (which may be the current period).

Section 9 Financial Instruments

Scope of this section

9.1   This section deals with the **recognition**, **derecognition**, **measurement** and disclosure of **financial instruments** (**financial assets** and **financial liabilities**).

9.2   All financial instruments are accounted for in accordance with this section, unless they are excluded by paragraph 9.3. Examples of financial instruments in the scope of this section include:

(a)   cash;

(b)   accounts receivable and payable (trade debtors and creditors);

(c)   commercial paper and commercial bills held;

(d)   demand and fixed-term deposits with banks or similar institutions;

(e)   bonds, loans and similar instruments;

(f)   investments;

(g)   options, warrants, futures contracts, forward contracts and interest rate swaps.

9.3   This section does not apply to the following financial instruments:

(a)   Financial instruments that meet the definition of a **micro-entity's** own **equity**, and the equity component of **compound financial instruments** issued by the reporting micro-entity that contain both a liability and an equity component (see Section 17 *Liabilities and Equity*).

(b)   **Leases**, to which Section 15 *Leases* applies. However, the derecognition requirements in paragraphs 9.21 to 9.23 and impairment accounting requirements in paragraphs 9.16 to 9.19 apply to derecognition and impairment of receivables recognised by a lessor and the derecognition requirements in paragraphs 9.25 and 9.26 apply to payables recognised by a lessee arising under a **finance lease**.

(c) Employers' rights and obligations under employee benefit plans, to which Section 23 *Employee Benefits* applies.

(d) Financial instruments, contracts and obligations to which Section 21 *Share-based Payment* applies.

(e) Reimbursement assets and **financial guarantee contracts** accounted for in accordance with Section 16 *Provisions and Contingencies*.

(f) Contracts for contingent consideration in a **business combination** (see Section 14 *Business Combinations and Goodwill*). This exemption applies only to the acquirer.

Initial recognition of financial assets and liabilities

A micro-entity shall recognise a financial asset or a financial liability only when the micro-entity becomes a party to the contractual provisions of the instrument.   **9.4**

Initial measurement

A financial asset or financial liability is recognised initially at its cost. The cost is measured at the transaction price.   **9.5**

Examples – Transaction price of a financial asset or liability

1 For a loan the transaction price is the amount borrowed or loaned.

2 For trade receivables or payables (trade debtors or trade creditors) the transaction price equals the invoice price unless payment is deferred beyond normal credit terms (see paragraph 9.6).

3 For an investment the transaction price is the consideration given (eg cash paid to acquire the investment).

4 For an option the transaction price is the premium paid to purchase the option.

When a micro-entity purchases **inventory, property, plant and equipment, investment property** or sells goods or services with settlement deferred beyond normal credit terms, the transaction price is the cash price available on the date of the transaction (see Sections 10 *Inventories*, 12 *Property, Plant and Equipment* and *Investment Property* and 18 *Revenue* respectively).   **9.6**

Example – Transaction price when payment is deferred

A micro-entity sells goods to a customer for CU100. Customers are usually required to pay within 14 days of the invoice date, but the micro-entity agrees with the customer that payment will be deferred for one year. The micro-entity sells the same item for CU90, if payment is received within the usual credit terms.

The cash price for the goods and thereby the transaction price is CU90.

Transaction costs shall be added to the cost of a financial asset or shall be deducted from the cost of a financial liability, unless they are not **material** in which case they are recognised immediately as an **expense** in **profit or loss**.   **9.7**

> **Examples – Transaction costs**
>
> 1 A micro-entity receives a bank loan of CU500. The bank charges CU5 in arrangement fees. The micro-entity determines that the transaction costs are immaterial and recognises them immediately in profit or loss as an expense. The cost of the loan is CU500.
>
> 2 A micro-entity is making an investment and buys shares in another entity for CU1,000. The micro-entity incurs legal fees and other transaction costs totalling CU100. The micro-entity determines that the transaction costs are material and includes them in the cost of the investment. The total cost of the investment is CU1,100.
>
> 3 A micro-entity takes out a forward foreign currency exchange contract and is charged a fee of CU30. The micro-entity determines that the transaction costs are material. The total cost of the forward foreign currency exchange contract is CU30.

Subsequent measurement

9.8 At the end of each **reporting period**, a micro-entity shall measure financial instruments as follows, without any deduction for transaction costs the micro-entity may incur on sale or other disposal:

(a) Investments in preference shares or **ordinary shares** and investments in **subsidiaries** and **associates** and interests in **jointly controlled entities** shall be measured at cost less impairment.

(b) **Derivatives** shall be measured as set out in paragraph 9.10.

(c) Financial instruments other than those covered by paragraphs (a) and (b) shall be measured as set out in paragraphs 9.12 to 9.15.

All financial assets must be assessed for impairment or uncollectability. See paragraphs 9.16 to 9.19.

Derivatives

9.9 Derivatives include forward foreign currency exchange contracts and interest rate swaps. More examples are given in paragraph 9.2(g).

9.10 The transaction price of a financial instrument that is a derivative plus any transaction costs not immediately recognised in profit or loss (see paragraph 9.7) less any **impairment losses** recognised to date, is allocated to profit or loss over the term of the contract on a straight-line basis, unless another systematic basis of allocation is more appropriate.

Contractual payments

9.11 Under a derivative contract a micro-entity may be required to make or may be entitled to receive payments. A micro-entity shall recognise amounts payable or receivable as they accrue.

Financial instruments measured in accordance with paragraph 9.8(c)

9.12 Financial instruments other than those covered in paragraphs 9.8(a) and 9.8(b) are measured as follows:

(a)   the transaction price (see paragraph 9.5);

(b)   plus, in the case of a financial asset, or minus in the case of a financial liability, transaction costs not yet recognised in profit or loss (see paragraph 9.15);

(c)   plus the cumulative interest income or expense recognised in profit or loss to date (see paragraphs 9.13 and 9.14);

(d)   minus all repayments of principal and all interest payments or receipts to date;

(e)   minus, in the case of a financial asset, any reduction (directly or through the use of an allowance account) for impairment or uncollectability (see paragraphs 9.16 to 9.19).

Allocation of interest income or expense

Total interest income or expense is the difference between the initial transaction price and the total amount of the subsequent contractual receipts or payments, excluding transaction costs.   **9.13**

A micro-entity shall allocate total interest income or expense over the term of the contract as follows: **9.14**

(a)   For transactions where settlement is deferred beyond normal credit terms (see paragraph 9.6), total interest income or expense shall be allocated on a straight-line basis over the term of the contract.

(b)   In all other cases, interest income or expense is allocated at a constant rate on the financial asset's or financial liability's **carrying amount** excluding transaction costs not yet recognised in profit or loss (see paragraph 9.12(b)). The applicable rate will normally be the contractual rate of interest and may be a variable or a fixed rate.

Transaction costs

Transaction costs not immediately recognised in profit or loss in accordance with paragraph 9.7, are recognised in profit or loss on a straight-line basis over the term of the contract.   **9.15**

Example 1: Measurement of a loan liability

A micro-entity receives a loan of CU1,000 on 1 January 20X0. The micro-entity pays loan arrangement fees of CU50. The contractual interest rate is five per cent payable annually in arrears on 31 December. The loan is repayable after two years. The micro-entity's annual reporting period ends on 31 December.

The micro-entity determines that the loan arrangement fees (transaction costs) are material and on 1 January 20X0 recognises the loan at its transaction price of CU1,000 less the transaction costs of CU50. The transactions costs of CU50 are recognised in the profit and loss account on a straight-line basis over two years, ie CU25 each year.

The carrying value of the loan is as follows:

Year	Carrying amount at 1 Jan	Interest at 5%	Transaction costs in profit or loss	Cash payments	Carrying amount at 31 Dec
	CU	CU	CU	CU	CU
20X0	(950)	(50)	(25)	50	(975)
20X1	(975)	(50)	(25)	1,050	0

Example 2: Measurement of a loan asset

A micro-entity makes an interest-free loan of CU900 on 1 January 20X0. The loan is repayable after two years. In 20X1 the micro-entity agrees that the borrower only needs to repay CU450 which is paid on 31 December 20X1. The micro-entity's annual reporting period ends on 31 December.

The loan is recognised at its transaction price of CU900 on 1 January 20X0. In 20X1 an impairment loss for the uncollectability of CU450 is recognised. The carrying amount of the loan is as follows:

Year	Carrying amount at 1 Jan	Impairment	Cash receipts	Carrying amount at 31 Dec
	CU	CU	CU	CU
20X0	900	-	-	900
20X1	900	(450)	(450)	0

Impairment of financial assets

Recognition and measurement

9.16   At the end of each reporting period, a micro-entity shall assess whether there is evidence of impairment of any financial asset.

9.17   Evidence that a financial asset could be impaired includes the following events:

(a)   significant financial difficulty of the debtor;

(b)   a breach of contract, such as a default or delinquency in interest or principal payments;

(c)   the creditor, for economic or legal reasons relating to the debtor's financial difficulty, granting to the debtor a concession that the creditor would not otherwise consider;

(d)   it has become **probable** that the debtor will enter bankruptcy or other financial reorganisation;

(e)   declining market values of the asset or similar assets;

(f)   significant changes with an adverse effect on the asset that have taken place in the technological, market, economic or legal environment; and

(g)   the contract has become an **onerous contract**.

9.18   A micro-entity shall measure an impairment loss for financial assets as set out below. An impairment loss is immediately recognised in profit or loss.

(a)   An investment in preference shares or ordinary shares and an investment in subsidiaries and associates and an interest in jointly controlled entities is impaired and an impairment loss shall be recognised if the asset's carrying amount exceeds the best estimate of the asset's selling price as at the **reporting date**.

(b)   An asset that is a derivative is impaired and an impairment loss shall be recognised if the asset's carrying value exceeds the asset's **fair value less costs to sell**.

(c)   An asset measured in accordance with paragraph 9.8(c), is impaired and an impairment loss shall be recognised, if the asset's carrying amount exceeds the total of estimated net cash flows that can be generated from the asset. When the effect of the time value of money is material, the amount of the net cash flows shall be the present value of the estimated net cash flows. The discount rate shall be the asset's current contractual interest rate.

Reversal

A micro-entity shall reverse a previously recognised impairment loss if in a subsequent period the amount of an impairment loss decreases and the decrease can be related to an event occurring after the impairment was recognised (eg an improvement in the debtor's credit rating). The micro-entity shall recognise the amount of the reversal in profit or loss immediately.   **9.19**

Onerous contracts

At each reporting date a micro-entity shall assess whether a derivative constitutes an onerous contract. A derivative is an onerous contract when the expected unavoidable payments exceed the economic benefits expected to be received from the derivative. A derivative which does not mitigate a specific risk or risks of a micro-entity is an onerous contract when the expected payments exceed the expected cash receipts under the contract. The present obligation arising from an onerous contract shall be measured in accordance with Section 16.   **9.20**

Example: Assessment of whether a derivative is onerous

A micro-entity takes out a loan with a variable rate of interest. In order to mitigate the risk of fluctuating interest payments, the micro-entity enters into an interest rate swap. Through the interest rate swap the micro-entity pays a fixed rate of interest and receives a variable rate of interest equal to the interest on the loan.

Scenario 1:

Interest rates are going down and as a result the payments made by the micro-entity under the interest rate swap are higher than the receipts. The interest rate swap is not an onerous contract because the micro-entity continues to benefit from the interest rate swap by effectively paying a fixed rate of interest on the loan.

Scenario 2:

The micro-entity repays the loan early, but the interest rate swap cannot be terminated. The micro-entity expects that the payments due under the interest rate swap exceed the receipts. The interest rate swap is an onerous contract because the micro-entity no longer derives a benefit from it.

Derecognition of a financial asset

A micro-entity shall derecognise a financial asset only when: **9.21**

(a)   the contractual rights to the cash flows from the financial asset expire or are settled;
(b)   the micro-entity transfers to another party substantially all of the risks (eg slow or non-payment risk) and rewards of ownership (eg future cash flows from a debtor); or
(c)   when no future economic benefits are expected from holding it or its disposal.

A micro-entity shall recognise any **gain** or loss on the derecognition of a financial asset in profit or loss when the item is derecognised.   **9.22**

If a micro-entity received any proceeds from the transfer of a financial asset, but the conditions in paragraph 9.21 are not met, a micro-entity shall continue to recognise the asset in its entirety and shall recognise a financial liability for the consideration received. The asset and liability shall not be offset. In subsequent periods, the micro-entity shall recognise any **income** on the transferred asset and any expense incurred on the financial liability.   **9.23**

Example 1: Debt factoring arrangement that qualifies for derecognition

A micro-entity sells a group of its accounts receivable to a bank at less than their carrying amount. The micro-entity is obliged to remit promptly to the bank all amounts collected, but it has no obligation to the bank for slow payment or non-payment by the debtors.

In this case, the micro-entity has transferred to the bank substantially all of the risks and rewards of ownership of the receivables. Accordingly, it removes the receivables from its statement of financial position (ie derecognises them), and it shows no liability in respect of the proceeds received from the bank. The micro-entity recognises a loss calculated as the difference between the carrying amount of the receivables at the time of sale and the proceeds received from the bank. The micro-entity recognises a liability to the extent that it has collected funds from the debtors but has not yet remitted them to the bank.

Example 2: Debt factoring arrangement that does not qualify for derecognition

The facts are the same as in the preceding example except that the micro-entity has agreed to buy back from the bank any receivables for which the debtor is in arrears as to principal or interest for more than 120 days.

In this case, the micro-entity has retained the risk of slow payment or non-payment by the debtors – a significant risk with respect to receivables. Accordingly, the micro-entity does not treat the receivables as having been sold to the bank, and it does not derecognise them. Instead, it treats the proceeds from the bank as a loan. The micro-entity continues to recognise the receivables as an asset until they are collected or written off as uncollectible.

Transfers of non-cash collateral

9.24   When a micro-entity participates in arrangements where it provides or receives financial assets other than cash as collateral (eg a micro-entity pledges commercial papers as security against a loan), the micro-entity shall apply the requirements of paragraphs 11.35(b) to 11.35(d) of **FRS 102**.

Derecognition of a financial liability

9.25   A micro-entity shall derecognise a financial liability (or a part of a financial liability) only when it is extinguished – ie when the obligation specified in the contract is discharged, is cancelled or expires.

9.26   A micro-entity shall recognise any gain or loss on the derecognition of a financial liability (or a part of a financial liability) in profit or loss when the item is derecognised.

Presentation

9.27   A financial asset and a financial liability shall be offset and the net amount presented in the **statement of financial position** when, and only when, a micro-entity:

(a)   currently has a legally enforceable right to set off the recognised amounts; and

(b)   intends either to settle on a net basis, or to realise the asset and settle the liability simultaneously.

Disclosures in the notes

A micro-entity shall determine the amount of any financial commitments, guarantees and **9.28** contingencies not recognised in the statement of financial position arising from its financial instruments and disclose that amount within the total amount of financial commitments, guarantees and contingencies (see paragraph 6A.2).

A micro-entity shall disclose an indication of the nature and form of any financial **9.29** asset given as security in respect of its commitments, guarantees and contingencies (see paragraph 6A.3).

Section 10 Inventories

Scope of this section

This section sets out the principles for recognising and measuring **inventories**. **10.1**

This section applies to all inventories, except: **10.2**

(a) work in progress arising under **construction contracts**, including directly related service contracts (see Section 18 *Revenue*); and

(b) **biological assets** related to **agricultural activity** and **agricultural produce** at the point of harvest (see Section 27 *Specialised Activities*).

Measurement of inventories

A **micro-entity** shall measure inventories at the lower of cost and estimated selling price **10.3** less costs to complete and sell.

Cost of inventories

A micro-entity shall include in the cost of inventories all costs of purchase, costs of **10.4** conversion and other costs incurred in bringing the inventories to their present location and condition.

Where inventories are acquired through a **non-exchange transaction**, their cost shall be **10.5** measured at their **fair value** at the date of acquisition.

Costs of purchase

The costs of purchase of inventories comprise the purchase price, import duties and **10.6** other taxes (other than those subsequently recoverable by the micro-entity from the taxing authorities), and transport, handling and other costs directly attributable to the acquisition of finished goods, materials and services. Trade discounts, rebates and other similar items are deducted in determining the costs of purchase.

If payment is deferred beyond normal credit terms, the purchase price is the cash price **10.7** available at the date of purchase. Any excess of the deferred payment amount over the cash price available at the date of purchase is recognised as interest and accounted for in accordance with paragraph 9.14(a).

Costs of conversion

10.8 The costs of conversion of inventories include costs directly related to the units of production, such as direct labour. They also include a systematic allocation of fixed and variable production overheads that are incurred in converting materials into finished goods. Fixed production overheads are those indirect costs of production that remain relatively constant regardless of the volume of production, such as **depreciation** and maintenance of factory buildings and equipment, and the cost of factory management and administration. Variable production overheads are those indirect costs of production that vary directly, or nearly directly, with the volume of production, such as indirect materials and indirect labour.

10.9 Production overheads include the costs for obligations (recognised and measured in accordance with Section 16 *Provisions and Contingencies*) for dismantling, removing and restoring a site on which an item of **property, plant and equipment** is located that are incurred during the **reporting period** as a consequence of having used that item of property, plant and equipment to produce inventory during that period.

Allocation of production overheads

10.10 A micro-entity shall allocate fixed production overheads to the costs of conversion on the basis of the normal capacity of the production facilities. Normal capacity is the production expected to be achieved on average over a number of periods or seasons under normal circumstances, taking into account the loss of capacity resulting from planned maintenance. The actual level of production may be used if it approximates normal capacity. The amount of fixed overhead allocated to each unit of production is not increased as a consequence of low production or idle plant. Unallocated overheads are recognised as an **expense** in the period in which they are incurred. In periods of abnormally high production, the amount of fixed overhead allocated to each unit of production is decreased so that inventories are not measured above cost. Variable production overheads are allocated to each unit of production on the basis of the actual use of the production facilities.

Other costs included in inventories

10.11 A micro-entity shall include other costs in the cost of inventories only to the extent that they are incurred in bringing the inventories to their present location and condition.

Costs excluded from inventories

10.12 Examples of costs excluded from the cost of inventories and recognised as expenses in the period in which they are incurred are:

(a) abnormal amounts of wasted materials, labour or other production costs;
(b) storage costs, unless those costs are necessary during the production process before a further production stage;
(c) administrative overheads that do not contribute to bringing inventories to their present location and condition; and
(d) selling costs.

Cost of inventories of a service provider

10.13 To the extent that service providers have inventories, they measure them at the costs of their production. These costs consist primarily of the labour and other costs of personnel directly engaged in providing the service, including supervisory personnel, and attributable overheads. Labour and other costs relating to sales and general administrative personnel are not included but are recognised as expenses in the period in which they are incurred. The cost of inventories of a service provider does not include profit margins or non-attributable overheads that are often factored into prices charged by service providers.

Cost of agricultural produce harvested from biological assets

Section 27 requires that inventories comprising agricultural produce that a micro-entity has harvested from its biological assets should be measured on initial **recognition**, at the point of harvest, at the lower of cost and estimated selling price less costs to complete and sell. This becomes the cost of the inventories at that date for application of this section.   **10.14**

Techniques for measuring cost, such as standard costing, retail method and most recent purchase price

A micro-entity may use techniques such as the standard cost method, the retail method or most recent purchase price for measuring the cost of inventories if the result approximates cost. Standard costs take into account normal levels of materials and supplies, labour, efficiency and capacity utilisation. They are regularly reviewed and, if necessary, revised in the light of current conditions. The retail method measures cost by reducing the sales value of the inventory by the appropriate percentage gross margin.   **10.15**

Cost formulas

A micro-entity shall measure the cost of inventories of items that are not ordinarily interchangeable and goods or services produced and segregated for specific projects by using specific identification of their individual costs.   **10.16**

A micro-entity shall measure the cost of inventories, other than those dealt with in paragraph 10.16, by using the first-in, first-out (FIFO) or weighted average cost formula. A micro-entity shall use the same cost formula for all inventories having a similar nature and use to the micro-entity. For inventories with a different nature or use, different cost formulas may be justified. The last-in, first-out method (LIFO) is not permitted by this FRS.   **10.17**

Impairment of inventories

Implicit in the requirement for a micro-entity to measure inventories at the lower of cost and estimated selling price less costs to complete, is a requirement that a micro-entity shall assess at the end of each reporting period whether any inventories are impaired, ie the **carrying amount** is not fully recoverable (eg because of damage, obsolescence or declining selling prices). If an item (or group of items) of inventory is impaired, the micro-entity shall recognise an **impairment loss**.   **10.18**

When the circumstances that previously caused inventories to be impaired no longer exist or when there is clear evidence of an increase in selling price less costs to complete and sell because of changed economic circumstances, the micro-entity shall reverse the amount of the impairment (ie the reversal is limited to the amount of the original impairment loss).   **10.19**

Recognition as an expense

When inventories are sold, the micro-entity shall recognise the carrying amount of those inventories as an expense in the period in which the related **revenue** is recognised.   **10.20**

10.21   Some inventories may be allocated to other asset accounts, for example, inventory used as a component of self-constructed property, plant or equipment. Inventories allocated to another **asset** in this way are accounted for subsequently in accordance with the section of this FRS relevant to that type of asset.

Disclosure in the notes

10.22   A micro-entity shall disclose an indication of the nature and form of any items of inventory given as security in respect of its commitments, guarantees and contingencies (see paragraph 6A.3).

Section 11 Investments in Joint Ventures

Scope of this section

11.1   This section applies to the accounting for investments in **joint ventures** that are **jointly controlled** operations and jointly controlled **assets**.

11.2   A **micro-entity** shall refer to Section 7 *Subsidiaries, Associates, Jointly Controlled Entities and Intermediate Payment Arrangements* which sets out the requirements for investments in joint ventures that are **jointly controlled entities**.

Joint ventures defined

11.3   Joint control is the contractually agreed sharing of **control** over an economic activity, and exists only when the strategic financial and operating decisions relating to the activity require the unanimous consent of the parties sharing control (the **venturers**).

11.4   A joint venture is a contractual arrangement whereby two or more parties undertake an economic activity that is subject to joint control. Joint ventures can take the form of jointly controlled operations, jointly controlled assets, or jointly controlled entities.

Jointly controlled operations

11.5   The operation of some joint ventures involves the use of the assets and other resources of the venturers rather than the establishment of a corporation, partnership or other entity, or a financial structure that is separate from the venturers themselves. Each venturer uses its own **property, plant and equipment** and carries its own **inventories**. It also incurs its own **expenses** and **liabilities** and raises its own finance, which represent its own obligations. The joint venture activities may be carried out by the venturer's employees alongside the venturer's similar activities. The joint venture agreement usually provides a means by which the **revenue** from the sale of the joint product and any expenses incurred in common are shared among the venturers.

11.6   In respect of its interests in jointly controlled operations, a venturer shall recognise in its **financial statements**:

    (a)   the assets that it controls and the liabilities that it incurs; and

    (b)   the expenses that it incurs and its share of the **income** that it earns from the sale of goods or services by the joint venture.

Jointly controlled assets

Some joint ventures involve the joint control, and often the joint ownership, by the venturers of one or more assets contributed to, or acquired for the purpose of, the joint venture and dedicated to the purposes of the joint venture.   **11.7**

In respect of its interest in a jointly controlled asset, a venturer shall recognise in its financial statements: **11.8**

(a)   its share of the jointly controlled assets, classified in accordance with the format adopted set out in Section 4 *Statement of Financial Position*;
(b)   any liabilities that it has incurred;
(c)   its share of any liabilities incurred jointly with the other venturers in relation to the joint venture;
(d)   any income from the sale or use of its share of the output of the joint venture, together with its share of any expenses incurred by the joint venture; and
(e)   any expenses that it has incurred in respect of its interest in the joint venture.

Disclosure in the notes

A micro-entity shall determine the amount of any financial commitments, guarantees and contingencies not recognised in the **statement of financial position** arising from its jointly controlled operations and jointly controlled assets and disclose that amount within the total amount of financial commitments, guarantees and contingencies (see paragraph 6A.2).   **11.9**

Section 12 Property, Plant and Equipment and Investment Property

Scope of this section

This section applies to the accounting for **property, plant and equipment** and **investment property**.   **12.1**

Property, plant and equipment does not include **biological assets** related to **agricultural activity** (see Section 27 *Specialised Activities*).   **12.2**

Recognition

A **micro-entity** shall recognise the cost of an item of property, plant and equipment or investment property as an **asset** if, and only if: **12.3**

(a)   it is **probable** that future economic benefits associated with the item will flow to the micro-entity; and
(b)   the cost of the item can be measured reliably.

Spare parts and servicing equipment are usually carried as **inventory** and recognised in **profit or loss** as consumed. However, major spare parts and stand-by equipment are property, plant and equipment when a micro-entity expects to use them during more than one period. Similarly, if the spare parts and servicing equipment can be used only in connection with an item of property, plant and equipment, they are considered property, plant and equipment.   **12.4**

Parts of some items of property, plant and equipment or investment property may require replacement at regular intervals (eg the roof of a building). A micro-entity shall add to the **carrying amount** of an item of property, plant and equipment or investment property the cost of replacing part of such an item when that cost is incurred if the replacement part is   **12.5** expected to provide incremental future benefits to the micro-entity. The carrying amount of those parts that are replaced is derecognised in accordance with paragraphs 12.26 and 12.27.

12.6 A condition of continuing to operate an item of property, plant and equipment (eg a bus) or investment property may be performing regular major inspections for faults regardless of whether parts of the item are replaced. When each major inspection is performed, its cost is recognised in the carrying amount of the item of property, plant and equipment or investment property as a replacement if the **recognition** criteria are satisfied. Any remaining carrying amount of the cost of the previous major inspection (as distinct from physical parts) is derecognised. This is done regardless of whether the cost of the previous major inspection was identified in the transaction in which the item was acquired or constructed. If necessary, the estimated cost of a future similar inspection may be used as an indication of what the cost of the existing inspection component was when the item was acquired or constructed.

12.7 Land and buildings are separable assets, and a micro-entity shall account for them separately, even when they are acquired together.

Measurement at initial recognition

12.8 A micro-entity shall measure an item of property, plant and equipment or investment property at initial recognition at its cost.

Elements of cost

12.9 The cost of an item of property, plant and equipment or investment property comprises all of the following:

(a)   Its purchase price, including legal and brokerage fees, import duties and non-refundable purchase taxes, after deducting trade discounts and rebates.

(b)   Any costs directly attributable to bringing the asset to the location and condition necessary for it to be capable of operating in the manner intended by management. These can include the costs of site preparation, initial delivery and handling, installation and assembly, and testing of functionality.

(c)   The initial estimate of the costs, recognised and measured in accordance with Section 16 *Provisions and Contingencies*, of dismantling and removing the item and restoring the site on which it is located, the obligation for which a micro-entity incurs either when the item is acquired or as a consequence of having used the item during a particular period for purposes other than to produce inventories during that period.

12.10 The following costs are not costs of an item of property, plant and equipment or investment property, and a micro-entity shall recognise them as an **expense** when they are incurred:

(a)   costs of opening a new facility;

(b)   costs of introducing a new product or service (including costs of advertising and promotional activities);

(c)   costs of conducting business in a new location or with a new class of customer (including costs of staff training); and

(d)   administration and other general overhead costs.

12.11 The **income** and related **expenses** of incidental operations during construction or development of an item of property, plant and equipment or investment property are recognised in **profit or loss** if those operations are not necessary to bring the item to its intended location and operating condition.

Measurement of cost

The cost of an item of property, plant and equipment or investment property is the cash   **12.12**
price equivalent at the recognition date. If payment is deferred beyond normal credit terms,
the cost is the cash price available at the recognition date. Any excess of the deferred
payment amount over the cash price available at the recognition date is recognised as
interest and accounted for in accordance with paragraph 9.14(a).

Exchanges of assets

An item of property, plant or equipment or investment property may be acquired in exchange   **12.13**
for a non-monetary asset or assets, or a combination of monetary and non-monetary assets.
A micro-entity shall measure the cost of the acquired asset at **fair value** unless:

(a)   the exchange transaction lacks commercial substance; or
(b)   the fair value of neither the asset received nor the asset given up is reliably
      measurable. In that case, the asset's cost is measured at the carrying amount of the
      asset given up.

Measurement after initial recognition

A micro-entity shall measure all items of property, plant and equipment and investment   **12.14**
property after initial recognition at cost less any accumulated **depreciation** and any
accumulated **impairment losses**. A micro-entity shall recognise the costs of day-to-day
servicing of an item of property, plant and equipment or investment property in profit or
loss in the period in which the costs are incurred.

Depreciation

If the major components of an item of property, plant and equipment or investment property   **12.15**
have significantly different patterns of consumption of economic benefits, a micro-entity
shall allocate the initial cost of the asset to its major components and depreciate each
such component separately over its **useful life**. Other assets shall be depreciated over their
useful lives as a single asset. There are some exceptions, such as land which generally has
an unlimited useful life and therefore is not usually depreciated.

The depreciation charge for each period shall be recognised in profit or loss unless   **12.16**
another section of this FRS requires the cost to be recognised as part of the cost of an asset.
For example, the depreciation of manufacturing property, plant and equipment is included
in the costs of inventories (see Section 10 *Inventories*).

Depreciable amount and depreciation period

A micro-entity shall allocate the **depreciable amount** of an asset on a systematic basis   **12.17**
over its useful life.

Factors may indicate that the **residual value** or useful life of an asset has changed since   **12.18**
the most recent annual **reporting date**. If such indicators are present, a micro-entity
shall review its previous estimates and, if current expectations differ, amend the residual
value, depreciation method or useful life. The micro-entity shall account for the change in
residual value, depreciation method or useful life as a change in an accounting estimate in
accordance with paragraphs 8.11 to 8.13.

12.19   Depreciation of an asset begins when it is available for use, ie when it is in the location and condition necessary for it to be capable of operating in the manner intended by management. Depreciation of an asset ceases when the asset is derecognised. Depreciation does not cease when the asset becomes idle or is retired from active use unless the asset is fully depreciated. However, under usage methods of depreciation the depreciation charge can be zero while there is no production.

12.20   A micro-entity shall consider all the following factors in determining the useful life of an asset:

(a)   The expected usage of the asset. Usage is assessed by reference to the asset's expected capacity or physical output.

(b)   Expected physical wear and tear, which depends on operational factors such as the number of shifts for which the asset is to be used and the repair and maintenance programme, and the care and maintenance of the asset while idle.

(c)   Technical or commercial obsolescence arising from changes or improvements in production, or from a change in the market demand for the product or service output of the asset.

(d)   Legal or similar limits on the use of the asset, such as the expiry dates of related **leases**.

Depreciation method

12.21   A micro-entity shall select a depreciation method that reflects the pattern in which it expects to consume the asset's future economic benefits. The possible depreciation methods include the straight-line method, the diminishing balance method and a method based on usage such as the units of production method.

12.22   If there is an indication that there has been a significant change since the last annual reporting date in the pattern by which a micro-entity expects to consume an asset's future economic benefits, the micro-entity shall review its present depreciation method and, if current expectations differ, change the depreciation method to reflect the new pattern. The micro-entity shall account for the change as a change in an accounting estimate in accordance with paragraphs 8.11 to 8.13.

Impairment

Recognition and measurement of impairment

12.23   At each reporting date, a micro-entity shall apply Section 22 *Impairment of Assets* to determine whether an item or group of items of property, plant and equipment or investment property is impaired and, if so, how to recognise and measure the impairment loss. That section explains when and how a micro-entity reviews the carrying amount of its assets, how it determines the **recoverable amount** of an asset, and when it recognises or reverses an impairment loss.

Compensation for impairment

12.24   An entity shall include in profit or loss, compensation from third parties for items of property, plant and equipment or investment property that were impaired, lost or given up only when the compensation is virtually certain.

Property, plant and equipment or investment property held for sale

Paragraph 22.7(f) states that a plan to dispose of an asset before the previously expected   **12.25**
date is an indicator of impairment that triggers the calculation of the asset's recoverable
amount for the purpose of determining whether the asset is impaired.

Derecognition

A micro-entity shall **derecognise** an item of property, plant and equipment or investment   **12.26**
property:

(a)   on disposal; or
(b)   when no future economic benefits are expected from its use or disposal.

A micro-entity shall recognise the **gain** or loss on the derecognition of an item of property,   **12.27**
plant and equipment or investment property in profit or loss when the item is derecognised
(unless Section 15 *Leases* requires otherwise on a sale and leaseback). The micro-entity
shall not classify such gains as **turnover** in the **income statement**.

Disclosure in the notes

A micro-entity shall determine the amount of any financial commitments not recognised   **12.28**
in the **statement of financial position** for the acquisition of property, plant and equipment
or investment property and disclose that amount within the total amount of financial
commitments, guarantees and contingencies (see paragraph 6A.2).

A micro-entity shall disclose an indication of the nature and form of any items of property,   **12.29**
plant and equipment or investment property given as security in respect of its commitments,
guarantees and contingencies (see paragraph 6A.3).

Section 13 Intangible Assets other than Goodwill

Scope of this section

This section applies to the accounting for all separately acquired **intangible assets** and   **13.1**
internally generated intangible assets, other than intangible assets held by a **micro-entity**
for sale in the ordinary course of business (see Section 10 *Inventories* and Section 18
Revenue).

For the accounting of intangible assets acquired as part of a **business combination**   **13.2**
including **goodwill** see Section 14 *Business Combinations and Goodwill*.

Recognition

A micro-entity shall recognise all separately acquired intangible assets.   **13.3**

An internally generated intangible shall not be recognised as an **asset**. All expenditure   **13.4**
incurred shall be recognised as an **expense** immediately in **profit or loss**.

A micro-entity shall recognise the expenditure on the following items as an expense and   **13.5**
shall not recognise such expenditure as intangible assets (the list is not exhaustive):

(a)   Expenditure on **research** and **development** activities.
(b)   Internally generated brands, logos, publishing titles, customer lists and items similar
      in substance.

(c)   Start-up activities (ie start-up costs), which include establishment costs such as legal and secretarial costs incurred in establishing a legal entity, expenditure to open a new facility or business (ie pre-opening costs) and expenditure for starting new operations or launching new products or processes (ie pre-operating costs).

(d)   Training activities.

(e)   Advertising and promotional activities.

(f)   Relocating or reorganising part or all of a micro-entity.

(g)   Internally generated goodwill.

Initial measurement

13.6   A micro-entity shall measure a separately acquired intangible asset initially at cost which comprises:

(a)   its purchase price, including import duties and non-refundable purchase taxes, after deducting trade discounts and rebates; and

(b)   any directly attributable cost of preparing the asset for its intended use.

Exchanges of assets

13.7   An intangible asset may be acquired in exchange for a non-monetary asset or assets, or a combination of monetary and non-monetary assets. A micro-entity shall measure the cost of such an intangible asset at **fair value** unless:

(a)   the exchange transaction lacks commercial substance; or

(b)   the fair value of neither the asset received nor the asset given up is reliably measurable. In that case, the asset's cost is measured at the **carrying amount** of the asset given up.

Measurement after initial recognition

13.8   A micro-entity shall measure a separately acquired intangible asset after initial recognition at cost less any accumulated **amortisation** and any accumulated **impairment losses**. The requirements for amortisation are set out in paragraphs 13.9 to 13.14.

Amortisation over useful life

13.9   Intangible assets shall be considered to have a finite **useful life**. The useful life of an intangible asset that arises from contractual or other legal rights shall not exceed the period of the contractual or other legal rights, but may be shorter depending on the period over which the micro-entity expects to use the asset. If the contractual or other legal rights are conveyed for a limited term that can be renewed, the useful life of the intangible asset shall include the renewal period(s) only if there is evidence to support renewal by the micro-entity without significant cost.

13.10   If, in exceptional cases, a micro-entity is unable to make a reliable estimate of the useful life of an intangible asset, the life shall not exceed ten years.

Amortisation period and amortisation method

13.11   A micro-entity shall allocate the **depreciable amount** of an intangible asset on a systematic basis over its useful life. The amortisation charge for each period shall be recognised in profit or loss, unless another section of this FRS requires the cost to be recognised as part of the cost of an asset. For example, the amortisation of an intangible asset may be included in the costs of **inventories** or **property, plant and equipment**.

Amortisation begins when the intangible asset is available for use, ie when it is in the location and condition necessary for it to be usable in the manner intended by management. Amortisation ceases when the asset is derecognised. The micro-entity shall choose an amortisation method that reflects the pattern in which it expects to consume the asset's future economic benefits. If the micro-entity cannot determine that pattern reliably, it shall use the straight-line method.   **13.12**

Residual value

A micro-entity shall assume that the **residual value** of an intangible asset is zero unless: **13.13**

(a) there is a commitment by a third party to purchase the asset at the end of its useful life; or

(b) there is an **active market** for the asset and:

    (i)   residual value can be determined by reference to that market; and

    (ii) it is **probable** that such a market will exist at the end of the asset's useful life.

Review of amortisation period and amortisation method

Factors may indicate that the residual value or useful life of an intangible asset has changed since the most recent annual **reporting date**. If such indicators are present, a micro-entity shall review its previous estimates and, if current expectations differ, amend the residual value, amortisation method or useful life. The micro-entity shall account for the change in residual value, amortisation method or useful life as a change in an accounting estimate in accordance with paragraphs 8.11 to 8.13.   **13.14**

Recoverability of the carrying amount—impairment losses

To determine whether a separately acquired intangible asset is impaired, a micro-entity shall apply Section 22 *Impairment of Assets*. That section explains when and how a micro-entity reviews the carrying amount of its assets, how it determines the **recoverable amount** of an asset, and when it recognises or reverses an **impairment loss**.   **13.15**

Retirements and disposals

A micro-entity shall derecognise a separately acquired intangible asset, and shall recognise a **gain** or loss in profit or loss: **13.16**

(a) on disposal; or

(b) when no future economic benefits are expected from its use or disposal.

Disclosure in the notes

A micro-entity shall determine the amount of any financial commitments, guarantees and contingencies not recognised in the **statement of financial position** for the acquisition of separately acquired intangible assets and disclose that amount within the total amount of financial commitments, guarantees and contingencies (see paragraph 6A.2).   **13.17**

13.18   A micro-entity shall disclose an indication of the nature and form of any intangible assets given as security in respect of its commitments, guarantees and contingencies (see paragraph 6A.3).

Section 14 Business Combinations and Goodwill

Accounting for a trade and asset acquisition

14.1   Where a **micro-entity** effects a **business combination** by acquiring the trade and **assets** of another **business,** it shall apply Section 19 *Business Combinations and Goodwill* of **FRS 102**, except for the following:

(a)   a micro-entity shall not separately identify and recognise **intangible assets**;

(b)   a micro-entity shall not recognise a **deferred tax asset** or **liability**;

(c)   a micro-entity shall not apply paragraph 19.23 of FRS 102, but instead apply paragraph 14.2 of this FRS;

(d)   a micro-entity shall not recognise and measure a **share-based payment transaction** in accordance with Section 28 *Employee Benefit* of FRS 102, but instead apply Section 23 *Employee Benefits* of this FRS; and

(e)   a micro-entity is not required to provide any of the disclosures.

Goodwill arising on a trade and asset acquisition

14.2   Where a micro-entity has recognised **goodwill** acquired in a trade and asset acquisition (in accordance with paragraph 19.22 of FRS 102), the micro-entity shall measure that goodwill at cost less accumulated **amortisation** and accumulated **impairment losses**:

(a)   A micro-entity shall follow the principles in paragraphs 13.9 to 13.14 of this FRS for amortisation of goodwill. Goodwill shall be considered to have a finite **useful life**, and shall be amortised on a systematic basis over its life. If, in exceptional cases, a micro-entity is unable to make a reliable estimate of the useful life of goodwill, the life shall not exceed ten years.

(b)   A micro-entity shall follow Section 22 *Impairment of Assets* of this FRS for recognising and measuring the impairment of goodwill.

Disclosure in the notes

14.3   A micro-entity shall determine the amount of any financial commitments, guarantees and contingencies not recognised in the **statement of financial position** for trade and asset acquisitions and disclose that amount within the total amount of financial commitments, guarantees and contingencies (see paragraph 6A.2).

Section 15 Leases

Scope of this section

15.1   This section covers accounting for all **leases** other than licensing agreements for such items as motion picture films, video recordings, plays, manuscripts, patents and copyrights (see Section 13 *Intangible Assets other than Goodwill*).

15.2   This section applies to agreements that transfer the right to use **assets** even though substantial services by the lessor may be called for in connection with the operation or maintenance of such assets. This section does not apply to agreements that are contracts for services that do not transfer the right to use assets from one contracting party to the other.

Some arrangements do not take the legal form of a lease but convey rights to use assets in return for payments. Examples of such arrangements may include outsourcing arrangements, telecommunication contracts that provide rights to capacity and take-or-pay contracts. **15.3**

Determining whether an arrangement is, or contains, a lease shall be based on the substance of the arrangement. **15.4**

Classification of leases

A lease is classified as a **finance lease** if it transfers substantially all the risks and rewards incidental to ownership. A lease is classified as an **operating lease** if it does not transfer substantially all the risks and rewards incidental to ownership. **15.5**

Whether a lease is a finance lease or an operating lease depends on the substance of the transaction rather than the form of the contract. Examples of situations that individually or in combination would normally lead to a lease being classified as a finance lease are: **15.6**

(a) the lease transfers ownership of the asset to the lessee by the end of the **lease term**;
(b) the lessee has the option to purchase the asset at a price that is expected to be sufficiently lower than the **fair value** at the date the option becomes exercisable for it to be reasonably certain, at the **inception of the lease**, that the option will be exercised;
(c) the lease term is for the major part of the economic life of the asset even if title is not transferred;
(d) at the inception of the lease the **present value** of the **minimum lease payments** amounts to at least substantially all of the fair value of the leased asset; and
(e) the leased assets are of such a specialised nature that only the lessee can use them without major modifications.

Indicators of situations that individually or in combination could also lead to a lease being classified as a finance lease are: **15.7**

(a) if the lessee can cancel the lease, the lessor's losses associated with the cancellation are borne by the lessee;
(b) **gains** or losses from the fluctuation in the **residual value** of the leased asset accrue to the lessee (eg in the form of a rent rebate equalling most of the sales proceeds at the end of the lease); and
(c) the lessee has the ability to continue the lease for a secondary period at a rent that is substantially lower than market rent.

The examples and indicators in paragraphs 15.6 and 15.7 are not always conclusive. If it is clear from other features that the lease does not transfer substantially all risks and rewards incidental to ownership, the lease is classified as an operating lease. For example, this may be the case if ownership of the asset is transferred to the lessee at the end of the lease for a variable payment equal to the asset's then fair value, or if there are **contingent rents**, as a result of which the lessee does not have substantially all risks and rewards incidental to ownership. **15.8**

Lease classification is made at the inception of the lease and is not changed during the term of the lease unless the lessee and the lessor agree to change the provisions of the lease (other than simply by renewing the lease), in which case the lease classification shall be re-evaluated. **15.9**

Financial statements of lessees: finance leases

Initial recognition

15.10   At the **commencement of the lease term**, a lessee shall recognise its rights of use and obligations under finance leases as assets and **liabilities** in its **statement of financial position** at amounts equal to the fair value of the leased asset or, if lower, the present value of the minimum lease payments, determined at the inception of the lease. Any initial direct costs of the lessee (incremental costs that are directly attributable to negotiating and arranging a lease) are added to the amount recognised as an asset.

15.11   The present value of the minimum lease payments shall be calculated using the **interest rate implicit in the lease**. If this cannot be determined, the **lessee's incremental borrowing rate** shall be used.

Subsequent measurement

15.12   A lessee shall apportion minimum lease payments between the finance charge and the reduction of the outstanding liability. The lessee shall allocate the finance charge to each period during the lease term so as to produce a constant periodic rate of interest on the remaining balance of the liability. A lessee shall charge **contingent rents** as **expenses** in the periods in which they are incurred.

15.13   A lessee shall depreciate an asset leased under a finance lease in accordance with Section 12 *Property, Plant and Equipment and Investment Property*. If there is no reasonable certainty that the lessee will obtain ownership by the end of the lease term, the asset shall be fully depreciated over the shorter of the lease term and its **useful life**. A lessee shall also assess at each **reporting date** whether an asset leased under a finance lease is impaired (see Section 22 *Impairment of Assets*).

Financial statements of lessees: operating leases

Recognition and measurement

15.14   A lessee shall recognise lease payments under operating leases (excluding costs for services such as insurance and maintenance) as an expense over the lease term on a straight-line basis unless another systematic basis is representative of the time pattern of the user's benefit, even if the payments are not on that basis.

15.15   A lessee shall recognise the aggregate benefit of **lease incentives** as a reduction to the expense recognised in accordance with paragraph 15.14 over the lease term, on a straight-line basis unless another systematic basis is representative of the time pattern of the lessee's benefit from the use of the leased asset. Any costs incurred by the lessee (for example costs for termination of a pre-existing lease, relocation or leasehold improvements) shall be accounted for in accordance with the applicable section.

15.16   Where an operating lease becomes an **onerous contract** a **micro-entity** shall also apply Section 16 *Provisions and Contingencies*.

Disclosure in the notes

A micro-entity shall determine the amount of any financial commitments, guarantees and contingencies not recognised in the statement of financial position arising from operating leases and disclose that amount within the total amount of financial commitments, guarantees and contingencies (see paragraph 6A.2). | **15.17**

Financial statements of lessors: finance leases

Initial recognition and measurement

A lessor shall recognise assets held under a finance lease in its statement of financial position and present them as a receivable at an amount equal to the **net investment in the lease**. The net investment in a lease is the lessor's **gross investment in the lease** discounted at the interest rate implicit in the lease. The gross investment in the lease is the aggregate of: | **15.18**

(a) the minimum lease payments receivable by the lessor under a finance lease; and
(b) any unguaranteed residual value accruing to the lessor.

For finance leases other than those involving manufacturer or dealer lessors, initial direct costs (costs that are incremental and directly attributable to negotiating and arranging a lease) are included in the initial measurement of the finance lease receivable and reduce the amount of **income** recognised over the lease term. | **15.19**

Subsequent measurement

The **recognition** of finance income shall be based on a pattern reflecting a constant periodic rate of return on the lessor's net investment in the finance lease. Lease payments relating to the period, excluding costs for services, are applied against the gross investment in the lease to reduce both the principal and the unearned finance income. If there is an indication that the estimated unguaranteed residual value used in computing the lessor's gross investment in the lease has changed significantly, the income allocation over the lease term is revised, and any reduction in respect of amounts accrued is recognised immediately in **profit or loss**. | **15.20**

Manufacturer or dealer lessors

Manufacturers or dealers often offer to customers the choice of either buying or leasing an asset. A finance lease of an asset by a manufacturer or dealer lessor gives rise to two types of income: | **15.21**

(a) profit or loss equivalent to the profit or loss resulting from an outright sale of the asset being leased, at normal selling prices, reflecting any applicable volume or trade discounts; and
(b) finance income over the lease term.

The sales **revenue** recognised at the commencement of the lease term by a manufacturer or dealer lessor is the fair value of the asset or, if lower, the present value of the minimum lease payments accruing to the lessor, computed at a market rate of interest. The cost of sale recognised at the commencement of the lease term is the cost, or **carrying amount** if different, of the leased asset less the present value of the unguaranteed residual value. The difference between the sales revenue and the cost of sale is the selling profit, which is recognised in accordance with the micro-entity's policy for outright sales. | **15.22**

15.23   If artificially low rates of interest are quoted, selling profit shall be restricted to that which would apply if a market rate of interest were charged. Costs incurred by manufacturer or dealer lessors in connection with negotiating and arranging a lease shall be recognised as an expense when the selling profit is recognised.

Financial statements of lessors: operating leases

Recognition and measurement

15.24   A lessor shall recognise lease income from operating leases (excluding amounts for services such as insurance and maintenance) in profit or loss on a straight-line basis over the lease term unless another systematic basis is representative of the time pattern of the lessee's benefit from the leased asset, even if the receipt of payments is not on that basis.

15.25   A lessor shall recognise the aggregate cost of lease incentives as a reduction to the income recognised in accordance with paragraph 15.24 over the lease term on a straight-line basis, unless another systematic basis is representative of the time pattern over which the lessor's benefit from the leased asset is diminished.

15.26   A lessor shall recognise as an expense, costs, including **depreciation**, incurred in earning the lease income. The depreciation policy for depreciable leased assets shall be consistent with the lessor's normal depreciation policy for similar assets.

15.27   A lessor shall add to the carrying amount of the leased asset any initial direct costs it incurs in negotiating and arranging an operating lease and shall recognise such costs as an expense over the lease term on the same basis as the lease income.

15.28   To determine whether a leased asset has become impaired, a lessor shall apply Section 22.

15.29   A manufacturer or dealer lessor does not recognise any selling profit on entering into an operating lease because it is not the equivalent of a sale.

Sale and leaseback transactions

15.30   A sale and leaseback transaction involves the sale of an asset and the leasing back of the same asset. The lease payment and the sale price are usually interdependent because they are negotiated as a package. The accounting treatment of a sale and leaseback transaction depends on the type of lease.

Sale and leaseback transaction results in a finance lease

15.31   If a sale and leaseback transaction results in a finance lease, the seller-lessee shall not recognise immediately, as income, any excess of sales proceeds over the carrying amount. Instead, the seller-lessee shall defer such excess and amortise it over the lease term.

Sale and leaseback transaction results in an operating lease

15.32   If a sale and leaseback transaction results in an operating lease, and it is clear that the transaction is established at fair value, the seller-lessee shall recognise any profit or loss immediately. If the sale price is below fair value, the seller-lessee shall recognise any profit or loss immediately unless the loss is compensated for by future lease payments at below market price. In that case the seller-lessee shall defer and amortise such loss in proportion to the lease payments over the period for which the asset is expected to be used. If the sale price is above fair value, the seller-lessee shall defer the excess over fair value and amortise it over the period for which the asset is expected to be used.

Disclosure in the notes

A micro-entity shall determine the amount of any financial commitments, guarantees and contingencies not recognised in the statement of financial position arising from a sale and lease back transaction and disclose that amount within the total amount of financial commitments, guarantees and contingencies (see paragraph 6A.2).   **15.33**

Section 16 Provisions and Contingencies

Scope of this section

This section applies to all **provisions**, **contingent liabilities** and **contingent assets** except those provisions covered by other sections of this FRS. Where those other sections contain no specific requirements to deal with contracts that have become onerous, this section applies to those contracts.   **16.1**

This section does not apply to **financial instruments** that are within the scope of Section 9 *Financial Instruments* unless the contracts are **onerous contracts** or **financial guarantee contracts**.   **16.2**

The requirements in this section do not apply to executory contracts unless they are onerous contracts. Executory contracts are contracts under which neither party has performed any of its obligations or both parties have partially performed their obligations to an equal extent.   **16.3**

The word 'provision' is sometimes used in the context of such items as **depreciation**, impairment of **assets**, and uncollectible receivables. Those are adjustments of the **carrying amounts** of assets, rather than **recognition** of **liabilities**, and therefore are not covered by this section.   **16.4**

Initial recognition

A **micro-entity** shall recognise a provision only when: **16.5**

(a)   the micro-entity has an obligation at the **reporting date** as a result of a past event;

(b)   it is **probable** (ie more likely than not) that the micro-entity will be required to transfer economic benefits in settlement; and

(c)   the amount of the obligation can be estimated reliably.

The micro-entity shall recognise the provision as a liability in the **statement of financial position** and shall recognise the amount of the provision as an **expense**, unless another section of this FRS requires the cost to be recognised as part of the cost of an asset such as **inventories** or **property, plant and equipment**.   **16.6**

The condition in paragraph 16.5(a) means that the micro-entity has no realistic alternative to settling the obligation. This can happen when the micro-entity has a legal obligation that can be enforced by law or when the micro-entity has a **constructive obligation** because the past event (which may be an action of the micro-entity) has created valid expectations in other parties that the micro-entity will discharge the obligation. Obligations that will arise from the micro-entity's future actions (ie the future conduct of its business) do not satisfy the condition in paragraph 16.5(a), no matter how likely they are to occur and even if they are contractual. To illustrate, because of commercial pressures or legal requirements, a   **16.7** micro-entity may intend or need to carry out expenditure to operate in a particular way in the future (for example, by fitting smoke filters in a particular type of factory). Because the micro-entity can avoid the future expenditure by its future actions, for example by changing its method of operation or selling the factory, it has no present obligation for that future expenditure and no provision is recognised.

Initial measurement

16.8   A micro-entity shall measure a provision at the best estimate of the amount required to settle the obligation at the reporting date. The best estimate is the amount a micro-entity would rationally pay to settle the obligation at the end of the **reporting period** or to transfer it to a third party at that time.

(a)   When the provision involves a large population of items, the estimate of the amount reflects the weighting of all possible outcomes by their associated probabilities. The provision will therefore be different depending on whether the probability of a loss of a given amount is, for example, 60 per cent or 90 per cent. Where there is a continuous range of possible outcomes, and each point in that range is as likely as any other, the mid-point of the range is used.

(b)   When the provision arises from a single obligation, the individual most likely outcome may be the best estimate of the amount required to settle the obligation. However, even in such a case, the micro-entity considers other possible outcomes. When other possible outcomes are either mostly higher or mostly lower than the most likely outcome, the best estimate will be a higher or lower amount.

When the effect of the time value of money is **material**, the amount of a provision shall be the **present value** of the amount expected to be required to settle the obligation. The discount rate (or rates) shall be a pre-tax rate (or rates) that reflect(s) current market assessments of the time value of money and risks specific to the liability. The risks specific to the liability shall be reflected either in the discount rate or in the estimation of the amounts required to settle the obligation, but not both.

16.9   A micro-entity shall exclude **gains** from the expected disposal of assets from the **measurement** of a provision.

16.10   When some or all of the amount required to settle a provision may be reimbursed by another party (eg through an insurance claim), the micro-entity shall recognise the reimbursement as a separate asset only when it is virtually certain that the micro-entity will receive the reimbursement on settlement of the obligation. The amount recognised for the reimbursement shall not exceed the amount of the provision. The reimbursement receivable shall be presented in the statement of financial position as an asset and shall not be offset against the provision. In the **income statement** the expense relating to a provision may be presented net of the amount recognised for a reimbursement.

Subsequent measurement

16.11   A micro-entity shall charge against a provision only those expenditures for which the provision was originally recognised.

16.12   A micro-entity shall review provisions at each reporting date and adjust them to reflect the current best estimate of the amount that would be required to settle the obligation at that reporting date. Any adjustments to the amounts previously recognised shall be recognised in **profit or loss** unless the provision was originally recognised as part of the cost of an asset (see paragraph 16.6). When a provision is measured at the present value of the amount expected to be required to settle the obligation, the unwinding of the discount shall be recognised as interest expense in profit or loss in the period it arises.

Onerous contracts

If a micro-entity has an onerous contract, the present obligation under the contract shall be recognised and measured as a provision (see Example 2 of the Appendix to this section). **16.13**

Future operating losses

Provisions shall not be recognised for future operating losses (see Example 1 of the Appendix to this section). **16.14**

Restructuring

A **restructuring** gives rise to a constructive obligation only when a micro-entity: **16.15**

(a) has a detailed formal plan for the restructuring identifying at least:

   (i) the business or part of a business concerned;
   (ii) the principal locations affected;
   (iii) the location, function, and approximate number of employees who will be compensated for terminating their services;
   (iv) the expenditures that will be undertaken; and
   (v) when the plan will be implemented; and

(b) has raised a valid expectation in those affected that it will carry out the restructuring by starting to implement that plan or announcing its main features to those affected by it.

A micro-entity recognises a provision for restructuring costs only when it has a legal or constructive obligation at the reporting date to carry out the restructuring. **16.16**

Contingent liabilities

A contingent liability is either a possible but uncertain obligation or a present obligation that is not recognised because it fails to meet one or both of the conditions (b) and (c) in paragraph 16.5. A micro-entity shall not recognise a contingent liability as a liability, except for provisions for contingent liabilities of an acquiree in a trade and asset acquisition (see Section 14 *Business Combinations and Goodwill*). Paragraph 16.19 sets out the disclosure requirements for a contingent liability. When a micro-entity is jointly and severally liable for an obligation, the part of the obligation that is expected to be met by other parties is treated as a contingent liability. **16.17**

Contingent assets

A micro-entity shall not recognise a contingent asset as an asset. However, when the flow of future economic benefits to the micro-entity is virtually certain, then the related asset is not a contingent asset, and its recognition is appropriate. **16.18**

Disclosures in the notes

A micro-entity shall determine the amount of any financial commitments, guarantees and contingencies not recognised in the statement of financial position and disclose that **16.19** amount within the total amount of financial commitments, guarantees and contingencies (see paragraph 6A.2). A micro-entity is not required to disclose the amount of a contingent liability where the possibility of an outflow of resources is remote.

Appendix to Section 16

Examples of recognising and measuring provisions

This appendix accompanies, but is not part of, Section 16. It provides guidance for applying the requirements of Section 16 in recognising and measuring provisions.

All of the micro-entities in the examples in this appendix have 31 December as their reporting date. In all cases, it is assumed that a reliable estimate can be made of any outflows expected. In some examples the circumstances described may have resulted in impairment of the assets; this aspect is not dealt with in the examples. References to 'best estimate' are to the present value amount, when the effect of the time value of money is material.

Example 1 Future operating losses

16A.1   A micro-entity determines that it is probable that it will incur future operating losses for several years.

Present obligation as a result of a past obligating event: There is no past event that obliges the micro-entity to pay out resources.

Conclusion: The micro-entity does not recognise a provision for future operating losses. Expected future losses do not meet the definition of a liability. The expectation of future operating losses may be an indicator that one or more assets are impaired (see Section 22 *Impairment of Assets* of this FRS).

Example 2 Onerous contracts

16A.2   An onerous contract is one in which the unavoidable costs of meeting the obligations under the contract exceed the economic benefits expected to be received under it. The unavoidable costs under a contract reflect the least net cost of exiting from the contract, which is the lower of the cost of fulfilling it and any compensation or penalties arising from failure to fulfil it. For example, a micro-entity may be contractually required under an operating lease to make payments to lease an asset for which it no longer has any use.

Present obligation as a result of a past obligating event: The micro-entity is contractually required to pay out resources for which it will not receive commensurate benefits.

Conclusion: If a micro-entity has a contract that is onerous, the micro-entity recognises and measures the present obligation under the contract as a provision.

Example 3 Warranties

16A.3   A manufacturer gives warranties at the time of sale to purchasers of its product. Under the terms of the contract for sale, the manufacturer undertakes to make good, by repair or replacement, manufacturing defects that become apparent within three years from the date of sale. On the basis of experience, it is probable (ie more likely than not) that there will be some claims under the warranties.

Present obligation as a result of a past obligating event: The obligating event is the sale of the product with a warranty, which gives rise to a legal obligation.

An outflow of resources embodying economic benefits in settlement: Probable for the warranties as a whole.

Conclusion: The micro-entity recognises a provision for the best estimate of the costs of making good under the warranty products sold before the reporting date.

Illustration of calculations:

In 20X0, goods are sold for CU100,000. Experience indicates that 90 per cent of products sold require no warranty repairs; six per cent of products sold require minor repairs costing 30 per cent of the sale price; and four per cent of products sold require major repairs or replacement costing 70 per cent of sale price. Therefore estimated warranty costs are:

CU100,000 × 90% × 0 =	CU0
CU100,000 × 6% × 30% =	CU1,800
CU100,000 × 4% × 70% =	CU2,800
Total	CU4,600

The expenditures for warranty repairs and replacements for products sold in 20X0 are expected to be made 60 per cent in 20X1, 30 per cent in 20X2, and ten per cent in 20X3, in each case at the end of the period. Because the estimated cash flows already reflect the probabilities of the cash outflows, and assuming there are no other risks or uncertainties that must be reflected, to determine the present value of those cash flows the micro-entity uses a 'risk-free' discount rate based on government bonds with the same term as the expected cash outflows (six per cent for one-year bonds and seven per cent for two-year and three-year bonds). Calculation of the present value, at the end of 20X0, of the estimated cash flows related to the warranties for products sold in 20X0 is as follows:

Year	Expected cash payments (CU)		Discount rate	Discount factor	Present value (CU)
1	60% × CU4,600	2,760	6%	0.9434 (at 6% for 1 year)	2,604
2	30% × CU4,600	1,380	7%	0.8734 (at 7% for 2 years)	1,205
3	10% × CU4,600	460	7%	0.8163 (at 7% for 3 years)	375
Total					4,184

The micro-entity will recognise a warranty obligation of CU4,184 at the end of 20X0 for products sold in 20X0.

Example 4 Refunds policy

16A.4   A retail store has a policy of refunding purchases by dissatisfied customers, even though it is under no legal obligation to do so. Its policy of making refunds is generally known.

Present obligation as a result of a past obligating event: The obligating event is the sale of the product, which gives rise to a constructive obligation because the conduct of the store has created a valid expectation on the part of its customers that the store will refund purchases.

An outflow of resources embodying economic benefits in settlement: Probable that a proportion of goods will be returned for refund.

Conclusion: The micro-entity recognises a provision for the best estimate of the amount required to settle the refunds.

Example 5 Closure of a division: no implementation before end of reporting period

16A.5   On 12 December 20X0 the board of a micro-entity decided to close down a division. Before the end of the reporting period (31 December 20X0) the decision was not communicated to any of those affected and no other steps were taken to implement the decision.

Present obligation as a result of a past obligating event: There has been no obligating event, and so there is no obligation.

Conclusion: The micro-entity does not recognise a provision.

Example 6 Closure of a division: communication and implementation before end of reporting period

16A.6   On 12 December 20X0 the board of a micro-entity decided to close a division making a particular product. On 20 December 20X0 a detailed plan for closing the division was agreed by the board, letters were sent to customers warning them to seek an alternative source of supply, and redundancy notices were sent to the staff of the division.

Present obligation as a result of a past obligating event: The obligating event is the communication of the decision to the customers and employees, which gives rise to a constructive obligation from that date, because it creates a valid expectation that the division will be closed.

An outflow of resources embodying economic benefits in settlement: Probable.

Conclusion: The micro-entity recognises a provision at 31 December 20X0 for the best estimate of the costs that would be incurred to close the division at the reporting date.

Example 7 Staff retraining as a result of changes in the income tax system

16A.7   The government introduces changes to the income tax system. As a result of those changes, a micro-entity will need to retrain a large proportion of its administrative and sales workforce in order to ensure continued compliance with tax regulations. At the end of the reporting period, no retraining of staff has taken place.

Present obligation as a result of a past obligating event: The tax law change does not impose an obligation on a micro-entity to do any retraining. An obligating event for recognising a provision (the retraining itself) has not taken place.

Conclusion: The micro-entity does not recognise a provision.

Example 8 A court case

A customer has sued Micro-entity X, seeking damages for injury the customer allegedly sustained from using a product sold by Micro-entity X. Micro-entity X disputes liability on grounds that the customer did not follow directions in using the product. Up to the date the financial statements for the year to 31 December 20X1 were authorised for issue, the micro-entity's lawyers advise that it is probable that the micro-entity will not be found liable. However, when the micro-entity prepares the financial statements for the year to 31 December 20X2, its lawyers advise that, owing to developments in the case, it is now probable that the micro-entity will be found liable.

16A.8

(a)   At 31 December 20X1

Present obligation as a result of a past obligating event: On the basis of the evidence available when the financial statements were approved, there is no obligation as a result of past events.

Conclusion: No provision is recognised, but the micro-entity shall make the disclosures required by paragraph 16.19.

(b)   At 31 December 20X2

Present obligation as a result of a past obligating event: On the basis of the evidence available, there is a present obligation. The obligating event is the sale of the product to the customer.

An outflow of resources embodying economic benefits in settlement: Probable.

Conclusion: A provision is recognised at the best estimate of the amount to settle the obligation at 31 December 20X2, and the expense is recognised in profit or loss. It is not a correction of an error in 20X1 because, on the basis of the evidence available when the 20X1 financial statements were approved, a provision should not have been recognised at that time.

Section 17 Liabilities and Equity

Scope of this section

This section establishes principles for classifying **financial instruments** as either **liabilities** or **equity** and deals with the accounting for **compound financial instruments**, such as convertible debt. It also addresses the issue of equity instruments, distributions to individuals or other parties acting in their capacity as investors in equity instruments (ie in their capacity as **owners**) and the accounting for purchases of own equity.

17.1

This section shall be applied to all types of financial instruments except:

17.2

(a)   Investments in **subsidiaries** and **associates** and interests in **jointly controlled entities** that are accounted for in accordance with Section 9 *Financial Instruments*.

(b)   Employers' rights and obligations under employee benefit plans to which Section 23 *Employee Benefits* applies.

(c)   Financial instruments, contracts and obligations under **share-based payment transactions** to which Section 21 *Share-based Payment* applies, except that paragraph 17.14 shall be applied to **treasury shares** issued, purchased, sold, transferred or cancelled in connection with employee share option plans, employee share purchase plans, and all other share-based payment arrangements.

(d)   **Financial guarantee contracts** (see Section 16 *Provisions and Contingencies*).

Classification of an instrument as liability or equity

17.3   Equity is the residual interest in the **assets** of a **micro-entity** after deducting all its liabilities. Equity includes investments by the owners of the micro-entity, plus additions to those investments earned through profitable operations and retained for use in the micro-entity's operations, minus reductions to owners' investments as a result of unprofitable operations and distributions to owners.

17.4   A financial instrument is classified as equity where the issuer can be required to settle an obligation in cash or by delivery of another **financial asset** (or otherwise to settle it in such a way that it would be a **financial liability**) only in the event of the liquidation of the issuer.

17.5   A financial instrument is a financial liability of the issuer where the issuer does not have an unconditional right to avoid settling an obligation in cash or by delivery of another financial asset (or otherwise to settle it in such a way that it would be a financial liability), other than for the reason described in paragraph 17.4.

17.6   Examples of instruments and their classification as equity or liabilities are set out below:

   (a)   An instrument is classified as equity if the only payment holders of the instruments are entitled to receive is a pro rata share of the net assets of the micro-entity on liquidation.

   (b)   An instrument is classified as a liability if it obliges the micro-entity to make payments to the holder before liquidation, such as a mandatory dividend.

   (c)   A preference share that provides for mandatory redemption by the issuer for a fixed or determinable amount at a fixed or determinable future date, or gives the holder the right to require the issuer to redeem the instrument at or after a particular date for a fixed or determinable amount, is a financial liability.

Original issue of shares or other equity instruments

17.7   A micro-entity shall recognise the issue of shares or other equity instruments as equity when it issues those instruments and another party is obliged to provide cash or other resources to the micro-entity in exchange for the instruments.

   (a)   If the micro-entity receives the cash or other resources before the equity instruments are issued, and the micro-entity cannot be required to repay the cash or other resources received, the micro-entity shall recognise the corresponding increase in equity to the extent of consideration received.

   (b)   To the extent that the equity instruments have been subscribed for but not issued (or called up), and the micro-entity has not yet received the cash or other resources, the micro-entity shall not recognise an increase in equity.

17.8   A micro-entity shall measure the equity instruments at the **fair value** of the cash or other resources received or receivable, net of direct costs of issuing the equity instruments.

17.9   A micro-entity shall account for the **transaction costs** of an equity transaction as a deduction from equity, net of any related **income tax** benefit.

Exercise of options, rights and warrants

17.10   A micro-entity shall apply the principles in paragraphs 17.7 to 17.9 to equity issued by means of exercise of options, rights, warrants and similar equity instruments.

Convertible debt and similar compound financial instruments

On issuing convertible debt, or a similar compound financial instrument, a micro-entity **17.11** shall allocate the proceeds between the liability component and the equity component of the instrument. To make the allocation, the micro-entity shall first determine the amount of the liability component as the fair value of a similar liability that does not have a conversion feature or similar associated equity component. The micro-entity shall allocate the residual amount as the equity component. Transaction costs shall be allocated between the debt component and the equity component on the basis of their relative fair values.

The micro-entity shall not revise the allocation in a subsequent period. **17.12**

In periods after the instruments were issued, the micro-entity shall account for the liability **17.13** component as a financial instrument in accordance with Section 9. The example shown in the Appendix to Section 22 *Liabilities and Equity* of **FRS 102** illustrates the accounting for convertible debt by an issuer.

Treasury shares

Treasury shares are the equity instruments of a micro-entity that have been issued and **17.14** subsequently reacquired by the micro-entity. A micro-entity shall deduct from equity the fair value of the consideration given for the treasury shares. The micro-entity shall not recognise a **gain** or loss in **profit or loss** on the purchase, sale, transfer or cancellation of treasury shares.

Distributions to owners

A micro-entity shall reduce its equity reserves for the amount of distributions to its owners **17.15** (holders of its equity instruments).

Section 18 Revenue

Scope of this section

This section shall be applied in accounting for **revenue** arising from the following **18.1** transactions and events:

(a) the sale of goods (whether produced by the **micro-entity** for the purpose of sale or purchased for resale);
(b) the rendering of services;
(c) **construction contracts** in which the micro-entity is the contractor; and
(d) the use by others of micro-entity **assets** yielding interest, royalties or dividends.

Revenue or other **income** arising from **lease** agreements is dealt with in Section 15 *Leases*. **18.2**

Measurement of revenue

A micro-entity shall measure revenue at the amount receivable, taking into account any trade **18.3** discounts, prompt settlement discounts and volume rebates allowed by the micro-entity.

A micro-entity shall include in revenue only the gross inflows of economic benefits received **18.4** and receivable by the micro-entity on its own account. A micro-entity shall exclude from revenue all amounts collected on behalf of third parties such as sales taxes, goods and services taxes and value added taxes. In an agency relationship, a micro-entity (the **agent**) shall include in revenue only the amount of its commission. The amounts collected on behalf of the **principal** are not revenue of the micro-entity.

Deferred payment

18.5   If payment is deferred beyond normal credit terms, the amount of revenue recognised is equal to the cash price available on the transaction date. Any excess of the deferred payment amount over the cash price available on the transaction date is recognised as interest and accounted for in accordance with paragraph 9.14(a).

Exchanges of goods or services

18.6   A micro-entity shall not recognise revenue:

(a)   when goods or services are exchanged for goods or services that are of a similar nature and value; or

(b)   when goods or services are exchanged for dissimilar goods or services but the transaction lacks commercial substance.

18.7   A micro-entity shall recognise revenue when goods are sold or services are exchanged for dissimilar goods or services in a transaction that has commercial substance. In that case, the micro-entity shall measure the transaction:

(a)   at the **fair value** of the goods or services received, adjusted by the amount of any cash transferred;

(b)   if the amount under (a) cannot be measured reliably, then at the fair value of the goods or services given up adjusted by the amount of any cash transferred; or

(c)   if the fair value of neither the goods or services received nor the goods or services given up can be measured reliably, then at the **carrying amount** of the goods or services given up adjusted by the amount of any cash transferred.

Identification of the revenue transaction

18.8   A micro-entity shall apply the **recognition** criteria to the separately identifiable components of a single transaction when necessary to reflect the substance of the transaction. For example, a micro-entity applies the recognition criteria to the separately identifiable components of a single transaction when the selling price of a product includes an identifiable amount for subsequent servicing. Conversely, a micro-entity applies the recognition criteria to two or more transactions together when they are linked in such a way that the commercial effect cannot be understood without reference to the series of transactions as a whole.

Sale of goods

18.9   A micro-entity shall recognise revenue from the sale of goods when all the following conditions are satisfied:

(a)   the micro-entity has transferred to the buyer the significant risks and rewards of ownership of the goods;

(b)   the micro-entity retains neither continuing managerial involvement to the degree usually associated with ownership nor effective control over the goods sold;

(c)   the amount of revenue can be measured reliably;

(d)   it is **probable** that the economic benefits associated with the transaction will flow to the micro-entity; and

(e) the costs incurred or to be incurred in respect of the transaction can be measured reliably.

The assessment of when a micro-entity has transferred the significant risks and rewards of ownership to the buyer requires an examination of the circumstances of the transaction. In most cases, the transfer of the risks and rewards of ownership coincides with the transfer of the legal title or the passing of possession to the buyer. This is the case for most retail sales. In other cases, the transfer of risks and rewards of ownership occurs at a time different from the transfer of legal title or the passing of possession. **18.10**

A micro-entity does not recognise revenue if it retains significant risks and rewards of ownership. Examples of situations in which the micro-entity may retain the significant risks and rewards of ownership are: **18.11**

(a) when the micro-entity retains an obligation for unsatisfactory performance not covered by normal warranties;
(b) when the receipt of the revenue from a particular sale is contingent on the buyer selling the goods;
(c) when the goods are shipped subject to installation and the installation is a significant part of the contract that has not yet been completed; and
(d) when the buyer has the right to rescind the purchase for a reason specified in the sales contract, or at the buyer's sole discretion without any reason, and the micro-entity is uncertain about the probability of return.

If an entity retains only an insignificant risk of ownership, the transaction is a sale and the entity recognises the revenue. For example, a seller recognises revenue when it retains the legal title to the goods solely to protect the collectability of the amount due. Similarly, an entity recognises revenue when it offers a refund if the customer finds the goods faulty or is not satisfied for other reasons, and the entity can estimate the returns reliably. In such cases, the entity recognises a **provision** for returns in accordance with Section 16 *Provisions and Contingencies*. **18.12**

Rendering of services

When the outcome of a transaction involving the rendering of services can be estimated reliably, a micro-entity shall recognise revenue associated with the transaction by reference to the stage of completion of the transaction at the end of the **reporting period** (sometimes referred to as the percentage of completion method). The outcome of a transaction can be estimated reliably when all the following conditions are satisfied: **18.13**

(a) the amount of revenue can be measured reliably;
(b) it is probable that the economic benefits associated with the transaction will flow to the micro-entity;
(c) the stage of completion of the transaction at the end of the reporting period can be measured reliably; and
(d) the costs incurred for the transaction and the costs to complete the transaction can be measured reliably.

Paragraphs 18.18 to 18.24 provide guidance for applying the percentage of completion method.

When services are performed by an indeterminate number of acts over a specified period of time, a micro-entity recognises revenue on a straight-line basis over the specified period unless there is evidence that some other method better represents the stage of completion. When a specific act is much more significant than any other act, the micro-entity postpones recognition of revenue until the significant act is executed. **18.14**

18.15   When the outcome of the transaction involving the rendering of services cannot be estimated reliably, a micro-entity shall recognise revenue only to the extent of the **expenses** recognised that are recoverable.

Construction contracts

18.16   When the outcome of a construction contract can be estimated reliably, a micro-entity shall recognise contract revenue and contract costs associated with the construction contract as revenue and expenses respectively by reference to the stage of completion of the contract activity at the end of the reporting period (often referred to as the percentage of completion method). Reliable estimation of the outcome requires reliable estimates of the stage of completion, future costs and collectability of billings. Paragraphs 18.18 to 18.24 provide guidance for applying the percentage of completion method.

18.17   The requirements of this section are usually applied separately to each construction contract. However, in some circumstances, it is necessary to apply this section to the separately identifiable components of a single contract or to a group of contracts together in order to reflect the substance of a contract or a group of contracts.

Percentage of completion method

18.18   This method is used to recognise revenue from rendering services (see paragraphs 18.13 to 18.15) and from construction contracts (see paragraphs 18.16 and 18.17). A micro-entity shall review and, when necessary, revise the estimates of revenue and costs as the service transaction or construction contract progresses.

18.19   A micro-entity shall determine the stage of completion of a transaction or contract using the method that measures most reliably the work performed. Possible methods include:

(a)   the proportion that costs incurred for work performed to date bear to the estimated total costs. Costs incurred for work performed to date do not include costs relating to future activity, such as for materials or prepayments;

(b)   surveys of work performed; and

(c)   completion of a physical proportion of the contract work or the completion of a proportion of the service contract.

Progress payments and advances received from customers often do not reflect the work performed.

18.20   A micro-entity shall recognise costs that relate to future activity on the transaction or contract, such as for materials or prepayments, as an asset if it is probable that the costs will be recovered.

18.21   A micro-entity shall recognise as an expense immediately any costs whose recovery is not probable.

18.22   When the outcome of a construction contract cannot be estimated reliably:

(a)   a micro-entity shall recognise revenue only to the extent of contract costs incurred that it is probable will be recoverable; and

(b)   the micro-entity shall recognise contract costs as an expense in the period in which they are incurred.

18.23   When it is probable that total contract costs will exceed total contract revenue on a construction contract, the expected loss shall be recognised as an expense immediately, with a corresponding provision for an **onerous contract** (see Section 16 *Provisions and Contingencies*).

If the collectability of an amount already recognised as contract revenue is no longer probable, the micro-entity shall recognise the uncollectible amount as an expense rather than as an adjustment of the amount of contract revenue.   **18.24**

Interest, royalties and dividends

A micro-entity shall recognise revenue arising from the use by others of micro-entity assets   **18.25**
yielding interest, royalties and dividends on the bases set out in paragraph 18.26 when:

(a)   it is probable that the economic benefits associated with the transaction will flow to the micro-entity; and
(b)   the amount of the revenue can be measured reliably.

A micro-entity shall recognise revenue on the following bases: **18.26**

(a)   Interest income shall be recognised in accordance with Section 9 *Financial Instruments*.
(b)   Royalties shall be recognised on an **accrual basis** in accordance with the substance of the relevant agreement.
(c)   Dividends shall be recognised when the shareholder's right to receive payment is established.

Appendix to Section 18

Examples of revenue recognition under the principles in Section 18

This appendix accompanies, but is not part of, Section 18. It provides guidance for applying the requirements of Section 18 in recognising revenue.

The following examples focus on particular aspects of a transaction and are not a   **18A.1**
comprehensive discussion of all the relevant factors that might influence the recognition of revenue. The examples generally assume that the amount of revenue can be measured reliably, it is probable that the economic benefits will flow to the micro-entity and the costs incurred or to be incurred can be measured reliably.

Sale of goods

The law in different countries may cause the recognition criteria in Section 18 to be   **18A.2**
met at different times. In particular, the law may determine the point in time at which the micro-entity transfers the significant risks and rewards of ownership. Therefore, the examples in this appendix need to be read in the context of the laws relating to the sale of goods in the country in which the transaction takes place.

Example 1 'Bill and hold' sales, in which delivery is delayed at the buyer's request but the buyer takes title and accepts billing

The seller recognises revenue when the buyer takes title, provided: **18A.3**

(a)   it is probable that delivery will be made;
(b)   the item is on hand, identified and ready for delivery to the buyer at the time the sale is recognised;
(c)   the buyer specifically acknowledges the deferred delivery instructions; and

(d)   the usual payment terms apply.

Revenue is not recognised when there is simply an intention to acquire or manufacture the goods in time for delivery.

Example 2 Goods shipped subject to conditions: installation and inspection

18A.4   The seller normally recognises revenue when the buyer accepts delivery, and installation and inspection are complete. However, revenue is recognised immediately upon the buyer's acceptance of delivery when:

(a)   the installation process is simple, for example the installation of a factory-tested television receiver that requires only unpacking and connection of power and antennae; or

(b)   the inspection is performed only for the purposes of final determination of contract prices, for example, shipments of iron ore, sugar or soya beans.

Example 3 Goods shipped subject to conditions: on approval when the buyer has negotiated a limited right of return

18A.5   If there is uncertainty about the possibility of return, the seller recognises revenue when the shipment has been formally accepted by the buyer or the goods have been delivered and the time period for rejection has elapsed.

Example 4 Goods shipped subject to conditions: consignment sales under which the recipient (buyer) undertakes to sell the goods on behalf of the shipper (seller)

18A.6   The shipper recognises revenue when the goods are sold by the recipient to a third party.

Example 5 Goods shipped subject to conditions: cash on delivery sales

18A.7   The seller recognises revenue when delivery is made and cash is received by the seller or its agent.

Example 6 Layaway sales under which the goods are delivered only when the buyer makes the final payment in a series of instalments

18A.8   The seller recognises revenue from such sales when the goods are delivered. However, when experience indicates that most such sales are consummated, revenue may be recognised when a significant deposit is received, provided the goods are on hand, identified and ready for delivery to the buyer.

Example 7 Orders when payment (or partial payment) is received in advance of delivery for goods not currently held in inventory, for example, the goods are still to be manufactured or will be delivered direct to the buyer from a third party

18A.9   The seller recognises revenue when the goods are delivered to the buyer.

Example 8 Sale and repurchase agreements (other than swap transactions) under which the seller concurrently agrees to repurchase the same goods at a later date, or when the seller has a call option to repurchase, or the buyer has a put option to require the repurchase, by the seller, of the goods

For a sale and repurchase agreement on an asset other than a financial asset, the seller must analyse the terms of the agreement to ascertain whether, in substance, the risks and rewards of ownership have been transferred to the buyer. If they have been transferred, the seller recognises revenue. When the seller has retained the risks and rewards of ownership, even though legal title has been transferred, the transaction is a financing arrangement and does not give rise to revenue. For a sale and repurchase agreement on a financial asset, the derecognition provisions of Section 9 apply.   **18A.10**

Example 9 Sales to intermediate parties, such as distributors, dealers or others for resale

The seller generally recognises revenue from such sales when the risks and rewards of ownership have been transferred. However, when the buyer is acting, in substance, as an agent, the sale is treated as a consignment sale.   **18A.11**

Example 10 Subscriptions to publications and similar items

When the items involved are of similar value in each time period, the seller recognises revenue on a straight-line basis over the period in which the items are dispatched. When the items vary in value from period to period, the seller recognises revenue on the basis of the sales value of the item dispatched in relation to the total estimated sales value of all items covered by the subscription.   **18A.12**

Example 11 Instalment sales, under which the consideration is receivable in instalments

The seller recognises revenue based on the cash price a customer would pay at the date of sale. If the total amount paid through instalments is greater than the cash price payable at the date of sale, any excess is recognised as interest and accounted for in accordance with paragraph 9.14(a).   **18A.13**

Example 12 Agreements for the construction of real estate

A micro-entity that undertakes the construction of real estate, directly or through subcontractors, and enters into an agreement with one or more buyers before construction is complete, shall account for the agreement using the percentage of completion method, only if: **18A.14**

(a)   the buyer is able to specify the major structural elements of the design of the real estate before construction begins and/or specify major structural changes once construction is in progress (whether it exercises that ability or not); or

(b)   the buyer acquires and supplies construction materials and the micro-entity provides only construction services.

If the micro-entity is required to provide services together with construction materials in order to perform its contractual obligation to deliver real estate to the buyer, the agreement shall be accounted for as the sale of goods. In this case, the buyer does not obtain control or the significant risks and rewards of ownership of the work in progress in its current state as construction progresses. Rather, the transfer occurs only on delivery of the completed real estate to the buyer.   **18A.15**

Example 13 Sale with customer loyalty award

18A.16　A micro-entity sells product A for CU100. Purchasers of product A get an award credit enabling them to buy product B for CU10. The normal selling price of product B is CU18. The micro-entity estimates that 40 per cent of the purchasers of product A will use their award to buy product B at CU10. The normal selling price of product A, after taking into account discounts that are usually offered but that are not available during this promotion, is CU95.

18A.17　The fair value of the award credit is 40 per cent × [CU18 − CU10] = CU3.20. The micro-entity allocates the total revenue of CU100 between product A and the award credit by reference to their relative fair values of CU95 and CU3.20 respectively. Therefore:

　　(a)　Revenue for product A is CU100 × [CU95 / (CU95 + CU3.20)] = CU96.74

　　(b)　Revenue for product B is CU100 × [CU3.20 / (CU95 + CU3.20)] = CU3.26

Rendering of services

Example 14 Installation fees

18A.18　The seller recognises installation fees as revenue by reference to the stage of completion of the installation, unless they are incidental to the sale of a product, in which case they are recognised when the goods are sold.

Example 15 Servicing fees included in the price of the product

18A.19　When the selling price of a product includes an identifiable amount for subsequent servicing (eg after sales support and product enhancement on the sale of software), the seller defers that amount and recognises it as revenue over the period during which the service is performed. The amount deferred is that which will cover the expected costs of the services under the agreement, together with a reasonable profit on those services.

Example 16 Advertising commissions

18A.20　Media commissions are recognised when the related advertisement or commercial appears before the public. Production commissions are recognised by reference to the stage of completion of the project.

Example 17 Admission fees

18A.21　The seller recognises revenue from artistic performances, banquets and other special events when the event takes place. When a subscription to a number of events is sold, the seller allocates the fee to each event on a basis that reflects the extent to which services are performed at each event.

Example 18 Tuition fees

18A.22　The seller recognises revenue over the period of instruction.

Example 19 Initiation, entrance and membership fees

18A.23　Revenue recognition depends on the nature of the services provided. If the fee permits only membership, and all other services or products are paid for separately, or if there is a separate annual subscription, the fee is recognised as revenue when no significant uncertainty about its collectability exists. If the fee entitles the member to services or publications to be provided during the membership period, or to purchase goods or services at prices lower than those charged to non-members, it is recognised on a basis that reflects the timing, nature and value of the benefits provided.

Franchise fees

Franchise fees may cover the supply of initial and subsequent services, equipment and other tangible assets, and know-how. Accordingly, franchise fees are recognised as revenue on a basis that reflects the purpose for which the fees were charged. The following methods of franchise fee recognition are appropriate.   **18A.24**

Example 20 Franchise fees: Supplies of equipment and other tangible assets

The franchisor recognises the fair value of the assets sold as revenue when the items are delivered or title passes.   **18A.25**

Example 21 Franchise fees: Supplies of initial and subsequent services

The franchisor recognises fees for the provision of continuing services, whether part of the initial fee or a separate fee, as revenue as the services are rendered. When the separate fee does not cover the cost of continuing services together with a reasonable profit, part of the initial fee, sufficient to cover the costs of continuing services and to provide a reasonable profit on those services, is deferred and recognised as revenue as the services are rendered.   **18A.26**

The franchise agreement may provide for the franchisor to supply equipment, inventories, or other tangible assets at a price lower than that charged to others or a price that does not provide a reasonable profit on those sales. In these circumstances, part of the initial fee, sufficient to cover estimated costs in excess of that price and to provide a reasonable profit on those sales, is deferred and recognised over the period the goods are likely to be sold to the franchisee. The balance of an initial fee is recognised as revenue when performance of all the initial services and other obligations required of the franchisor (such as assistance with site selection, staff training, financing and advertising) has been substantially accomplished.   **18A.27**

The initial services and other obligations under an area franchise agreement may depend on the number of individual outlets established in the area. In this case, the fees attributable to the initial services are recognised as revenue in proportion to the number of outlets for which the initial services have been substantially completed.   **18A.28**

If the initial fee is collectible over an extended period and there is a significant uncertainty that it will be collected in full, the fee is recognised as cash instalments are received.   **18A.29**

Example 22 Franchise fees: Continuing franchise fees

Fees charged for the use of continuing rights granted by the agreement, or for other services provided during the period of the agreement, are recognised as revenue as the services are provided or the rights used.   **18A.30**

Example 23 Franchise fees: Agency transactions

18A.31   Transactions may take place between the franchisor and the franchisee that, in substance, involve the franchisor acting as agent for the franchisee. For example, the franchisor may order supplies and arrange for their delivery to the franchisee at no profit. Such transactions do not give rise to revenue.

Example 24 Fees from the development of customised software

18A.32   The software developer recognises fees from the development of customised software as revenue by reference to the stage of completion of the development, including completion of services provided for post-delivery service support.

Interest, royalties and dividends

Example 25 Licence fees and royalties

18A.33   The licensor recognises fees and royalties paid for the use of its assets (such as trademarks, patents, software, music copyright, record masters and motion picture films) in accordance with the substance of the agreement. As a practical matter, this may be on a straight-line basis over the life of the agreement, for example, when a licensee has the right to use specified technology for a specified period of time.

18A.34   An assignment of rights for a fixed fee or non-refundable guarantee under a non-cancellable contract that permits the licensee to exploit those rights freely and the licensor has no remaining obligations to perform is, in substance, a sale. An example is a licensing agreement for the use of software when the licensor has no obligations after delivery. Another example is the granting of rights to exhibit a motion picture film in markets in which the licensor has no control over the distributor and expects to receive no further revenues from the box office receipts. In such cases, revenue is recognised at the time of sale.

18A.35   In some cases, whether or not a licence fee or royalty will be received is contingent on the occurrence of a future event. In such cases, revenue is recognised only when it is probable that the fee or royalty will be received, which is normally when the event has occurred.

Section 19 Government Grants

Scope of this section

19.1   This section specifies the accounting for all **government grants**.

19.2   Government grants exclude those forms of government assistance that cannot reasonably have a value placed upon them and transactions with government that cannot be distinguished from the normal trading transactions of the **micro-entity**.

Recognition and measurement

19.3   Government grants, including non-monetary grants, shall not be recognised until there is reasonable assurance that:

(a)   the micro-entity will comply with the conditions attaching to them; and
(b)   the grants will be received.

A micro-entity shall measure grants at the **fair value** of the **asset** received or receivable.   **19.4**

Where a grant becomes repayable it shall be recognised as a **liability** when the repayment meets the definition of a liability.   **19.5**

A micro-entity shall classify government grants either as a grant relating to revenue or a grant relating to assets.   **19.6**

Government grants relating to revenue shall be recognised in income on a systematic basis over the periods in which the micro-entity recognises the related costs for which the grant is intended to compensate.   **19.7**

A government grant that becomes receivable as compensation for **expenses** or losses already incurred or for the purpose of giving immediate financial support to the entity with no future related costs shall be recognised as **income** in **profit or loss** in the period in which it becomes receivable.   **19.8**

Government grants relating to assets shall be recognised in income on a systematic basis over the expected **useful life** of the asset.   **19.9**

Where part of a government grant relating to an asset is deferred it shall be recognised as deferred income and not deducted from the **carrying amount** of the asset.   **19.10**

Section 20 Borrowing Costs

Scope of this section

This section specifies the accounting for **borrowing costs**. Borrowing costs include: **20.1**

(a)   interest expense recognised in accordance with Section 9 *Financial Instruments*;
(b)   finance charges in respect of **finance leases** recognised in accordance with Section 15 *Leases*; and
(c)   exchange differences arising from foreign currency borrowings to the extent that they are regarded as an adjustment to interest costs.

Recognition

A **micro-entity** shall recognise all borrowing costs as an **expense** in **profit or loss** in the period in which they are incurred.   **20.2**

Section 21 Share-based Payment

Scope of this section

This section specifies the accounting for all **share-based payment transactions** including: **21.1**

(a)   **equity-settled share-based payment transactions**;
(b)   **cash-settled share-based payment transactions**; and
(c)   transactions in which the **micro-entity** receives or acquires goods or services and the terms of the arrangement provide either the micro-entity or the supplier of those goods or services with a choice of whether the micro-entity settles the transaction in cash (or other **assets**) or by issuing equity instruments.

Equity-settled share-based payment transactions

21.2   A micro-entity shall not account for equity-settled share-based payments transactions until shares are issued, at which point the micro-entity shall apply the requirements of Section 17 *Liabilities and Equity*.

Cash-settled share-based payment transactions

21.3   A micro-entity shall recognise the goods or services received or acquired in a cash-settled share-based payment transaction when it obtains the goods or as the services are received and recognise a corresponding **liability**.

21.4   If the cash-settled share-based payments granted to employees **vest** immediately, the employee is not required to complete a specified period of service before becoming unconditionally entitled to those cash-settled share-based payments. In the absence of evidence to the contrary, the micro-entity shall presume that services rendered by the employee as consideration for the share-based payments have been received. In this case, on **grant date** the micro-entity shall recognise the services received in full, with a corresponding liability.

21.5   If the cash-settled share-based payments do not vest until the employee completes a specified period of service, the micro-entity shall presume that the services to be rendered by the employee as consideration for those cash-settled share-based payments will be received in the future, during the vesting period. The micro-entity shall account for those services as they are rendered by the employee during the vesting period, with a corresponding increase in the liability.

21.6   When the goods or services received or acquired in a cash-settled share-based payment transaction do not qualify for **recognition** as assets, the micro-entity shall recognise them as **expenses**.

21.7   A micro-entity shall measure the goods and services acquired and the liability incurred in accordance with the measurement requirements for a provision in Section 16 *Provisions and Contingencies*.

Share-based payment transactions with cash alternatives

21.8   Some share-based payment transactions give either the micro-entity or the counterparty a choice of settling the transaction in cash (or other assets) or by the transfer of equity instruments.

21.9   When the micro-entity has a choice of settlement of the transaction in cash (or other assets) or by the transfer of equity instruments, the micro-entity shall account for the whole transaction as set out in paragraph 21.2 unless:

   (a)   the choice of settlement in equity instruments has no commercial substance (eg because the micro-entity is legally prohibited from issuing shares); or

   (b)   the micro-entity has a past practice or a stated policy of settling in cash, or generally settles in cash whenever the counterparty asks for cash settlement.

   In circumstances (a) and (b) the micro-entity shall account for the transaction as a wholly cash-settled transaction in accordance with paragraphs 21.3 to 21.7.

21.10   When the counterparty has a choice of settlement of the transaction in cash (or other assets) or by the transfer of equity instruments, the micro-entity shall account for the transaction as a wholly cash-settled share-based payment transaction in accordance with paragraphs 21.3 to 21.7 unless:

(a)   the choice of settlement in cash (or other assets) has no commercial substance because the cash settlement amount (or value of the other assets) bears no relationship to, and is likely to be lower in value than, the **fair value** of the equity instruments.

In circumstance (a) the entity shall account for the whole transaction as set out in paragraph 21.2.

Section 22 Impairment of Assets

Objective and scope

An **impairment loss** occurs when the **carrying amount** of an **asset** exceeds its **recoverable amount**. This section shall be applied in accounting for the impairment of all assets (including **goodwill**), other than the following, for which other sections of this FRS establish impairment requirements: **22.1**

(a)   assets arising from **construction contracts** (see Section 18 *Revenue*);
(b)   **financial assets** within the scope of Section 9 *Financial Instruments*; and
(c)   **inventories** (see Section 10 *Inventories*).

Impairment of assets

General principles

If, and only if, the recoverable amount of an asset is less than its carrying amount, the **micro-entity** shall reduce the carrying amount of the asset to its recoverable amount.   **22.2**

If it is not possible to estimate the recoverable amount of the individual asset, a micro-entity shall estimate the recoverable amount of the **cash-generating unit** to which the asset belongs. This may be the case because measuring the recoverable amount requires forecasting cash flows, and sometimes individual assets do not generate cash flows by themselves. An impairment loss for a cash-generating unit shall be recognised and measured in accordance with the relevant requirements of Section 27 *Impairment of Assets* of **FRS 102**.   **22.3**

A micro-entity that has goodwill acquired in a **business combination** shall apply the additional impairment requirements applicable to goodwill in paragraphs 27.24 to 27.27 of FRS 102.   **22.4**

A micro-entity shall recognise an impairment loss immediately in **profit or loss**.   **22.5**

Indicators of impairment

A micro-entity shall assess at each **reporting date** whether there is any indication that an asset may be impaired. If any such indication exists, the micro-entity shall estimate the recoverable amount of the asset. If there is no indication of impairment, it is not necessary to estimate the recoverable amount.   **22.6**

In assessing whether there is any indication that an asset may be impaired, a micro-entity shall consider, as a minimum, the following indications: **22.7**

External sources of information

(a) During the period, an asset's market value has declined significantly more than would be expected as a result of the passage of time or normal use.

(b) Significant changes with an adverse effect on the micro-entity have taken place during the period, or will take place in the near future, in the technological, market, economic or legal environment in which the micro-entity operates or in the market to which an asset is dedicated.

(c) Market interest rates or other market rates of return on investments have increased during the period, and those increases are likely to affect materially the discount rate used in calculating an asset's **value in use** and decrease the asset's **fair value less costs to sell**.

(d) The carrying amount of the net assets of the micro-entity is more than the estimated **fair value** of the micro-entity as a whole (such an estimate may have been made, for example, in relation to the potential sale of part or all of the micro-entity).

Internal sources of information

(e) Evidence is available of obsolescence or physical damage of an asset.

(f) Significant changes with an adverse effect on the micro-entity have taken place during the period, or are expected to take place in the near future, in the extent to which, or manner in which, an asset is used or is expected to be used. These changes include the asset becoming idle, plans to discontinue or restructure the operation to which an asset belongs, plans to dispose of an asset before the previously expected date, and reassessing the **useful life** of an asset as finite rather than indefinite.

(g) Evidence is available from internal reporting that indicates that the economic performance of an asset is, or will be, worse than expected. In this context economic performance includes operating results and cash flows.

22.8 If there is an indication that an asset may be impaired, this may indicate that the micro-entity should review the remaining useful life, the **depreciation (amortisation)** method or the **residual value** for the asset and adjust it in accordance with the section of this FRS applicable to the asset (eg Section 12 *Property, Plant and Equipment and Investment Property* and Section 13 *Intangible Assets other than Goodwill*), even if no impairment loss is recognised for the asset.

Measuring recoverable amount

22.9 The recoverable amount of an asset is the higher of its fair value less costs to sell and its value in use.

22.10 It is not always necessary to determine both an asset's fair value less costs to sell and its value in use. If either of these amounts exceeds the asset's carrying amount, the asset is not impaired and it is not necessary to estimate the other amount.

22.11 If there is no reason to believe that an asset's value in use materially exceeds its fair value less costs to sell, the asset's fair value less costs to sell may be used as its recoverable amount. This will often be the case for an asset that is held for disposal.

Fair value less costs to sell

22.12 Fair value less costs to sell is the amount obtainable from the sale of an asset in an arm's length transaction between knowledgeable, willing parties, less the costs of disposal. The best evidence of the fair value less costs to sell of an asset is a price in a binding sale agreement in an arm's length transaction or a market price in an **active market**. If there is no binding sale agreement or active market for an asset, fair value less costs to sell is based on the best information available to reflect the amount that a micro-entity could obtain, at the reporting date, from the disposal of the asset in an arm's length transaction between knowledgeable, willing parties, after deducting the costs of disposal. In determining this amount, a micro-entity considers the outcome of recent transactions for similar assets within the same industry.

When determining an asset's fair value less costs to sell, consideration shall be given to any restrictions imposed on that asset. Costs to sell shall also include the cost of obtaining relaxation of a restriction where necessary in order to enable the asset to be sold. If a restriction would also apply to any potential purchaser of an asset, the fair value of the asset may be lower than that of an asset whose use is not restricted.   **22.13**

Value in use

Value in use is the **present value** of the future cash flows expected to be derived from an asset. This present value calculation involves the following steps: **22.14**

(a)   estimating the future cash inflows and outflows to be derived from the continuing use of the asset and from its ultimate disposal; and

(b)   applying the appropriate discount rate to those future cash flows.

In measuring value in use, estimates of future cash flows shall include: **22.15**

(a)   projections of cash inflows from the continuing use of the asset;

(b)   projections of cash outflows that are necessarily incurred to generate the cash inflows from continuing use of the asset (including cash outflows to prepare the asset for use) and can be directly attributed, or allocated on a reasonable and consistent basis, to the asset; and

(c)   net cash flows, if any, expected to be received (or paid) for the disposal of the asset at the end of its useful life in an arm's length transaction between knowledgeable, willing parties.

The micro-entity may wish to use any recent financial budgets or forecasts to estimate the cash flows, if available, and extrapolate the projections using a steady or declining growth rate for subsequent years, unless an increasing rate can be justified.

Estimates of future cash flows shall not include: **22.16**

(a)   cash inflows or outflows from **financing activities**; or

(b)   income tax receipts or payments.

Future cash flows shall be estimated for the asset in its current condition. Estimates of future cash flows shall not include estimated future cash inflows or outflows that are expected to arise from: **22.17**

(a)   a future **restructuring** to which a micro-entity is not yet committed; or

(b)   improving or enhancing the asset's performance.

The discount rate(s) used in the present value calculation shall be a pre-tax rate(s) that reflect(s) current market assessments of: **22.18**

(a)   the time value of money; and

(b)   the risks specific to the asset for which the future cash flow estimates have not been adjusted.

The discount rate(s) used to measure an asset's value in use shall not reflect risks for which the future cash flow estimates have been adjusted, to avoid double-counting.

Reversal of an impairment loss

22.19   An impairment loss recognised for **goodwill** shall not be reversed in a subsequent period[1].

22.20   For all assets other than goodwill, if and only if the reasons for the impairment loss have ceased to apply, an impairment loss shall be reversed in a subsequent period. A micro-entity shall assess at each reporting date whether there is any indication that an impairment loss recognised in prior periods may no longer exist or may have decreased. Indications that an impairment loss may have decreased or may no longer exist are generally the opposite of those set out in paragraph 22.7. If any such indication exists, the micro-entity shall determine whether all or part of the prior impairment loss should be reversed.

Reversal where recoverable amount was estimated for an individual impaired asset

22.21   When the prior impairment loss was based on the recoverable amount of the individual impaired asset, the following requirements apply:

(a)   The micro-entity shall estimate the recoverable amount of the asset at the current reporting date.

(b)   If the estimated recoverable amount of the asset exceeds its carrying amount, the micro-entity shall increase the carrying amount to recoverable amount, subject to the limitation described in paragraph (c) below. That increase is a reversal of an impairment loss. The micro-entity shall recognise the reversal immediately in profit or loss.

(c)   The reversal of an impairment loss shall not increase the carrying amount of the asset above the carrying amount that would have been determined (net of amortisation or depreciation) had no impairment loss been recognised for the asset in prior years.

(d)   After a reversal of an impairment loss is recognised, the micro-entity shall adjust the depreciation (amortisation) charge for the asset in future periods to allocate the asset's revised carrying amount, less its residual value (if any), on a systematic basis over its remaining useful life.

Section 23 Employee Benefits

Scope of this section

23.1   **Employee benefits** are all forms of consideration given by a **micro-entity** in exchange for service rendered by employees, including directors and management. This section applies to all employee benefits, except for **share-based payment transactions**, which are covered by Section 21 *Share-based Payment*. Employee benefits covered by this section will be one of the following four types:

(a)   short-term employee benefits, which are employee benefits (other than **termination benefits**) that are expected to be settled wholly before 12 months after the end of the **reporting period** in which the employees render the related service;

---

[1] *The prohibition of the reversal of goodwill impairment losses is subject to the introduction of the same requirement in company law. Prior to that change being made this FRS requires the reversal of goodwill if the conditions set out in paragraph 22.20 are met.*

(b) **post-employment benefits**, which are employee benefits (other than termination benefits and short-term employee benefits) that are payable after the completion of employment;

(c) other long-term employee benefits, which are all employee benefits, other than short-term employee benefits, post-employment benefits and termination benefits; or

(d) termination benefits, which are employee benefits provided in exchange for the termination of an employee's employment as a result of either:

  (i) a micro-entity's decision to terminate an employee's employment before the normal retirement date; or

  (ii) an employee's decision to accept voluntary redundancy in exchange for those benefits.

General recognition principle for all employee benefits

A micro-entity shall recognise the cost of all employee benefits to which its employees have become entitled as a result of service rendered to the micro-entity during the reporting period:

23.2

(a) As a **liability**, after deducting amounts that have been paid directly to the employees or as a contribution to an employee benefit fund[2]. If the amount paid exceeds the obligation arising from service before the **reporting date**, a micro-entity shall recognise that excess as an **asset** to the extent that the prepayment will lead to a reduction in future payments or a cash refund.

(b) As an **expense**, unless another section of this FRS requires the cost to be recognised as part of the cost of an asset such as **inventories** (for example in accordance with paragraph 10.8) or **property, plant and equipment** (in accordance with paragraph 12.9).

Short-term employee benefits

Examples

Short-term employee benefits include items such as the following, if expected to be settled wholly before 12 months after the end of the annual reporting period in which the employees render the related service:

23.3

(a) wages, salaries and social security contributions;

(b) paid annual leave and paid sick leave;

(c) profit-sharing and bonuses; and

(d) non-monetary benefits (such as medical care, housing, cars and free or subsidised goods or services) for current employees.

Measurement of short-term benefits generally

When an employee has rendered service to a micro-entity during the reporting period, the micro-entity shall measure the amounts recognised in accordance with paragraph 23.2 at

23.4

---

[2] *Contributions to an employee benefit fund that is an intermediate payment arrangement shall be accounted for in accordance with Section 7 Subsidiaries, Associates, Jointly Controlled Entities and Intermediate Payment Arrangements, and as a result if the employer is a sponsoring micro-entity the assets and liabilities of the intermediary will be accounted for by the sponsoring micro-entity as an extension of its own business. In which case the payment to the employee benefit fund does not extinguish the liability of the employer.*

the undiscounted amount of short-term employee benefits expected to be paid in exchange for that service.

Recognition and measurement: Short-term compensated absences

23.5   A micro-entity may compensate employees for absence for various reasons including annual leave and sick leave. Some short-term compensated absences accumulatethey can be carried forward and used in future periods if the employee does not use the current period's entitlement in full. Examples include annual leave and sick leave. A micro-entity shall recognise the expected cost of **accumulating compensated absences** when the employees render service that increases their entitlement to future compensated absences. The micro-entity shall measure the expected cost of accumulating compensated absences at the undiscounted additional amount that the micro-entity expects to pay as a result of the unused entitlement that has accumulated at the end of the reporting period. The micro-entity shall present this amount as falling due within one year at the reporting date.

23.6   A micro-entity shall recognise the cost of other (non-accumulating) compensated absences when the absences occur. The micro-entity shall measure the cost of non-accumulating compensated absences at the undiscounted amount of salaries and wages paid or payable for the period of absence.

Recognition: Profit-sharing and bonus plans

23.7   A micro-entity shall recognise the expected cost of profit-sharing and bonus payments only when:

   (a)   the micro-entity has a present legal or **constructive obligation** to make such payments as a result of past events (this means that the micro-entity has no realistic alternative but to make the payments); and

   (b)   a reliable estimate of the obligation can be made.

Post-employment benefits: Distinction between defined contribution plans and defined benefit plans

23.8   Post-employment benefits include, for example:

   (a)   retirement benefits, such as pensions; and

   (b)   other post-employment benefits, such as post-employment life insurance and post-employment medical care.

Arrangements whereby a micro-entity provides post-employment benefits are **post-employment benefit plans**. A micro-entity shall apply this section to all such arrangements whether or not they involve the establishment of a separate entity to receive contributions and to pay benefits. In some cases, these arrangements are imposed by law rather than by action of the micro-entity. In some cases, these arrangements arise from actions of the micro-entity even in the absence of a formal, documented plan.

23.9   Post-employment benefit plans are classified as either **defined contribution plans** or **defined benefit plans**, depending on their principal terms and conditions:

   (a)   Defined contribution plans are post-employment benefit plans under which a micro-entity pays fixed contributions into a separate entity (a fund) and has no legal or constructive obligation to pay further contributions or to make direct benefit payments to employees if the fund does not hold sufficient assets to pay all employee benefits relating to employee service in the current and prior periods. The amount of the post-employment benefits received by the employee is determined by the amount of contributions paid by a micro-entity (and perhaps also the employee) to a post-employment benefit plan or to an insurer, together with investment returns arising from the contributions.

(b) Defined benefit plans are post-employment benefit plans other than defined contribution plans. Under defined benefit plans, the micro-entity's obligation is to provide the agreed benefits to current and former employees, and actuarial risk (that benefits will cost more or less than expected) and investment risk (that returns on assets set aside to fund the benefits will differ from expectations) are borne, in substance, by the micro-entity. If actuarial or investment experience is worse than expected, the micro-entity's obligation may be increased, and vice versa if actuarial or investment experience is better than expected.

Post-employment benefit plans

Recognition and measurement – requirements applicable to all plans

When contributions to a defined contribution or defined benefit plan are not expected to be settled wholly within 12 months after the end of the reporting period in which the employees render the related service, the liability recognised in accordance with paragraph 23.2(a) shall be measured at the **present value** of the contributions payable using the methodology for selecting a discount rate specified in paragraph 23.11. The unwinding of the discount shall be recognised as interest expense in **profit or loss** in the period in which it arises. **23.10**

A micro-entity shall determine the rate used to discount the future payments by reference to market yields at the reporting date on high quality corporate bonds. In countries with no deep market in such bonds, the micro-entity shall use the market yields (at the reporting date) on government bonds. The currency and term of the corporate bonds or government bonds shall be consistent with the currency and estimated period of the future payments. **23.11**

Recognition and measurement – requirements applicable to defined benefit plans

When a micro-entity participates in a defined benefit plan (which may include a **multi-employer plan** or **state plan**) and has entered into an agreement with the plan that determines how the micro-entity will fund a deficit (such as a schedule of contributions), the micro-entity shall recognise a liability for the contributions payable that arise from the agreement (to the extent that they relate to the deficit) and the resulting expense in profit or loss in accordance with paragraphs 23.2 and 23.10. **23.12**

Where a micro-entity participates in a defined benefit plan that shares risks between entities under common control it shall recognise a cost equal to its contribution payable for the period. If a micro-entity is legally responsible for the plan and has entered into an agreement with the plan that determines how a deficit will be funded, the micro-entity shall recognise a liability for the contributions payable that arise from the agreement (to the extent that they relate to the deficit) and the resulting expense in profit or loss in accordance with paragraphs 23.2 and 23.10. **23.13**

Other long-term employee benefits

Other long-term employee benefits include items such as the following, if not expected to be settled wholly before 12 months after the end of the annual reporting period in which the employees render the related service: **23.14**

(a) long-term paid absences such as long-service or sabbatical leave;
(b) other long-service benefits;

(c)   long-term disability benefits;

(d)   profit-sharing and bonuses; and

(e)   deferred remuneration.

23.15   A micro-entity shall recognise a liability for other long-term employee benefits measured at the present value of the benefit obligation at the reporting date calculated using the methodology for selecting a discount rate in paragraph 23.11. The unwinding of the discount shall be recognised as interest expense in profit or loss in the period in which it arises.

Termination benefits

23.16   A micro-entity may be committed, by legislation, by contractual or other agreements with employees or their representatives or by a constructive obligation based on business practice, custom or a desire to act equitably, to make payments (or provide other benefits) to employees when it terminates their employment. Such payments are termination benefits.

Recognition

23.17   Because termination benefits do not provide a micro-entity with future economic benefits, a micro-entity shall recognise them as an expense in profit or loss immediately.

23.18   A micro-entity shall recognise termination benefits as a liability and an expense only when the micro-entity is demonstrably committed either:

(a)   to terminate the employment of an employee or group of employees before the normal retirement date; or

(b)   to provide termination benefits as a result of an offer made in order to encourage voluntary redundancy.

23.19   A micro-entity is demonstrably committed to a termination only when the micro-entity has a detailed formal plan for the termination[3] and is without realistic possibility of withdrawal from the plan.

Measurement

23.20   A micro-entity shall measure termination benefits at the best estimate of the expenditure that would be required to settle the obligation at the reporting date. In the case of an offer made to encourage voluntary redundancy, the measurement of termination benefits shall be based on the number of employees expected to accept the offer.

23.21   When termination benefits are due more than 12 months after the end of the reporting period, they shall be measured at their discounted present value using the methodology for selecting a discount rate specified in paragraph 23.11.

---

[3] *An example of the features of a detailed formal plan for restructuring, which may include termination benefits, is given in paragraph 16.15.*

Disclosures in the notes

A micro entity shall disclose any commitment not recognised in the statement of financial position concerning pensions separately from other financial commitments, guarantees and contingencies (see paragraph 6A.2).   **23.22**

Section 24 Income Tax

Scope of this section

For the purpose of this FRS, **income tax** includes all domestic and foreign taxes that are based on **taxable profit**.   **24.1**

This section covers accounting for income tax. It requires a **micro-entity** to recognise the **current tax** consequences of transactions and other events that have been recognised in the **financial statements**. Current tax is tax payable (refundable) in respect of the taxable profit (tax loss) for the current period or past **reporting periods**. This section prohibits the recognition of **deferred tax** which represents the future tax consequences of transactions and events recognised in the financial statements of the current and previous periods.   **24.2**

This section also covers accounting for value added tax (VAT) and other similar sales taxes, which are not income taxes.   **24.3**

Current tax

A micro-entity shall recognise a current tax **liability** for tax payable on taxable profit for the current and past periods. If the amount of tax paid for the current and past periods exceeds the amount of tax payable for those periods, the micro-entity shall recognise the excess as a current tax **asset**.   **24.4**

A micro-entity shall recognise a current tax asset for the benefit of a tax loss that can be carried back to recover tax paid in a previous period.   **24.5**

A micro-entity shall measure a current tax liability (asset) at the amount of tax it expects to pay (recover) using the tax rates and laws that have been enacted or **substantively enacted** by the **reporting date**.   **24.6**

Deferred tax

A micro-entity shall not recognise deferred tax.   **24.7**

Measurement of current tax

A micro-entity shall not discount current tax assets and liabilities.   **24.8**

Withholding tax on dividends

When a micro-entity pays dividends to its shareholders, it may be required to pay a portion of the dividends to taxation authorities on behalf of shareholders. Outgoing dividends and similar amounts payable shall be recognised at an amount that includes any withholding tax but excludes other taxes, such as attributable tax credits.   **24.9**

24.10   Incoming dividends and similar income receivable shall be recognised at an amount that includes any withholding tax but excludes other taxes, such as attributable tax credits. Any withholding tax suffered shall be shown as part of the tax charge.

Value Added Tax and other similar sales taxes

24.11   **Turnover** included in **profit or loss** shall exclude VAT and other similar sales taxes on taxable outputs and VAT imputed under the flat rate VAT scheme. **Expenses** shall exclude recoverable VAT and other similar recoverable sales taxes. Irrecoverable VAT allocable to **fixed assets** and to other items separately recognised shall be included in their cost where practicable and **material**.

Presentation

Allocation in profit or loss

24.12   A micro-entity shall present changes in a current tax liability (asset) as **tax expense (income)**.

Offsetting

24.13   A micro-entity shall offset current tax assets and current tax liabilities, if and only if, it has a legally enforceable right to set off the amounts and it intends either to settle on a net basis or to realise the asset and settle the liability simultaneously.

Section 25 Foreign Currency Translation

Scope of this section

25.1   A **micro-entity** may have transactions in foreign currencies. This section prescribes how to include foreign currency transactions in the financial statements of a micro-entity. Where a micro-entity has a foreign branch, the micro-entity should refer to the requirements of Section 30 *Foreign Currency Translation* of **FRS 102** to determine if the foreign branch has a different functional currency, and if so, should apply the requirements of Section 30 of FRS 102 to those transactions undertaken by the foreign branch.

Reporting foreign currency transactions

Initial recognition

25.2   A foreign currency transaction is a transaction that is denominated or requires settlement in a foreign currency, including transactions arising when a micro-entity:

(a)   buys or sells goods or services whose price is denominated in a foreign currency;

(b)   borrows or lends funds when the amounts payable or receivable are denominated in a foreign currency; or

(c)   otherwise acquires or disposes of **assets**, or incurs or settles **liabilities**, denominated in a foreign currency.

25.3   A micro-entity shall record a foreign currency transaction by applying to the foreign currency amount the spot exchange rate at the date of the transaction unless:

(a)   the transaction is to be settled at a contracted rate, in which case that rate shall be used; or

(b) where a trading transaction is covered by a related or matching forward contract, in which case the rate of exchange specified in that contract shall be used.

The date of a transaction is the date on which the transaction first qualifies for **recognition** 25.4
in accordance with this FRS. For practical reasons, a rate that approximates the actual rate at the date of the transaction is often used, for example, an average rate for a week or a month might be used for all transactions in each foreign currency occurring during that period. However, if exchange rates fluctuate significantly, the use of the average rate for a period is inappropriate.

Reporting at the end of the subsequent reporting periods

At the end of each **reporting period**, unless it is applying a contracted rate in accordance 25.5
with paragraph 25.3 a micro-entity shall:

(a) translate foreign currency **monetary items** using the **closing rate**; and
(b) translate non-monetary items that are measured in terms of historical cost in a foreign currency using the exchange rate at the date of the transaction.

A micro-entity shall recognise, in **profit or loss** in the period in which they arise, exchange 25.6
differences arising on the settlement of monetary items or on translating monetary items at rates different from those at which they were translated on initial recognition during the period or in previous periods.

Section 26 Events after the End of the Reporting Period

Scope of this section

This section defines events after the end of the **reporting period** and sets out principles for 26.1
recognising and measuring those events.

Events after the end of the reporting period defined

Events after the end of the reporting period are those events, favourable and unfavourable, 26.2
that occur between the end of the reporting period and the date when the financial statements are authorised for issue. There are two types of events:

(a) those that provide evidence of conditions that existed at the end of the reporting period (adjusting events after the end of the reporting period); and
(b) those that are indicative of conditions that arose after the end of the reporting period (non-adjusting events after the end of the reporting period).

Events after the end of the reporting period include all events up to the date when the 26.3
financial statements are authorised for issue, even if those events occur after the public announcement of **profit or loss** or other selected financial information.

Recognition and measurement

Adjusting events after the end of the reporting period

A **micro-entity** shall adjust the amounts recognised in its **financial statements** to reflect 26.4
adjusting events after the end of the reporting period.

26.5   The following are examples of adjusting events after the end of the reporting period that require a micro-entity to adjust the amounts recognised in its financial statements, or to recognise items that were not previously recognised:

(a)   The settlement after the end of the reporting period of a court case that confirms that the micro-entity had a present obligation at the end of the reporting period. The micro-entity adjusts any previously recognised **provision** related to this court case in accordance with Section 16 *Provisions and Contingencies* or recognises a new provision. The micro-entity does not merely disclose a **contingent liability**. Rather, the settlement provides additional evidence to be considered in determining the provision that should be recognised at the end of the reporting period in accordance with Section 16.

(b)   The receipt of information after the end of the reporting period indicating that an **asset** was impaired at the end of the reporting period, or that the amount of a previously recognised **impairment loss** for that asset needs to be adjusted. For example:

(i)   the bankruptcy of a customer that occurs after the end of the reporting period usually confirms that a loss existed at the end of the reporting period on a trade receivable and that the micro-entity needs to adjust the **carrying amount** of the trade receivable; and

(ii)   the sale of **inventories** after the end of the reporting period may give evidence about their selling price at the end of the reporting period for the purpose of assessing impairment at that date.

(c)   The determination after the end of the reporting period of the cost of assets purchased, or the proceeds from assets sold, before the end of the reporting period.

(d)   The determination after the end of the reporting period of the amount of profit-sharing or bonus payments, if the micro-entity had a legal or **constructive obligation** at the end of the reporting period to make such payments as a result of events before that date (see Section 23 *Employee Benefits*).

(e)   The discovery of fraud or **errors** that show that the financial statements are incorrect.

Non-adjusting events after the end of the reporting period

26.6   A micro-entity shall not adjust the amounts recognised in its financial statements to reflect non-adjusting events after the end of the reporting period.

26.7   Examples of non-adjusting events after the end of the reporting period include:

(a)   A decline in market value of investments between the end of the reporting period and the date when the financial statements are authorised for issue. The decline in market value does not normally relate to the condition of the investments at the end of the reporting period, but reflects circumstances that have arisen subsequently. Therefore, a micro-entity does not adjust the amounts recognised in its financial statements for the investments.

(b)   An amount that becomes receivable as a result of a favourable judgement or settlement of a court case after the **reporting date** but before the financial statements are authorised for issue. This would be a **contingent asset** at the reporting date (see paragraph 16.18). However, agreement on the amount of damages for a judgement that was reached before the reporting date, but was not previously recognised because the amount could not be measured reliably, may constitute an adjusting event.

Going concern

26.8   A micro-entity shall not prepare its financial statements on a going concern basis if management determines after the end of the reporting period that it either intends to liquidate the micro-entity or to cease trading, or that it has no realistic alternative but to do so.

Deterioration in operating results and **financial position** after the reporting period may lead management to determine that they intend to liquidate the micro-entity or to cease trading or that they have no realistic alternative but to do so. If the going concern basis of accounting is no longer appropriate, the effect is so pervasive that this section requires a fundamental change in the basis of accounting.   **26.9**

Dividends

If a micro-entity declares dividends to holders of its equity instruments after the end of the reporting period, the micro-entity shall not recognise those dividends as a **liability** at the end of the reporting period because no obligation exists at that time.   **26.10**

Section 27 Specialised Activities

Scope of this section

This section sets out the financial reporting requirements for **micro-entities** involved in agriculture.   **27.1**

Agriculture

Recognition

A micro-entity that is engaged in **agricultural activity** shall recognise a **biological asset** or an item of **agricultural produce** when, and only when: **27.2**

(a)   the micro-entity controls the **asset** as a result of past events;
(b)   it is **probable** that future economic benefits associated with the asset will flow to the micro-entity; and
(c)   the cost of the **asset** can be measured reliably.

Measurement

A micro-entity shall measure biological assets at cost less any accumulated **depreciation** and any accumulated **impairment losses**.   **27.3**

Agricultural produce harvested from a micro-entity's biological assets shall be measured at the point of harvest at the lower of cost and estimated selling price less costs to complete and sell.   **27.4**

Such measurement is the cost at that date when applying Section 10 *Inventories* or another applicable section of this FRS.

Disclosure in the notes

A micro-entity shall determine the amount of any financial commitments, guarantees and contingencies not recognised in the **statement of financial position** for the acquisition of a biological asset and disclose that amount within the total amount of financial commitments, guarantees and contingencies (see paragraph 6A.2).   **27.5**

27.6   A micro-entity shall disclose an indication of the nature and form of any biological asset or item of agricultural produce given as security in respect of its commitments, guarantees and contingencies (see paragraph 6A.3).

Section 28 Transition to this FRS

Scope of this section

28.1   This section applies to a **first-time adopter of this FRS**, regardless of its previous accounting framework.

28.2   Notwithstanding the requirements in paragraphs 28.3 and 28.4, a **micro-entity** that has applied this FRS in a previous **reporting period**, but whose most recent previous annual **financial statements** were prepared in accordance with a different accounting framework, must either apply this section or else apply this FRS retrospectively in accordance with Section 8 *Accounting Policies, Changes in Estimates and Errors* as if the micro-entity had never stopped applying this FRS.

First-time adoption

28.3   A first-time adopter of this FRS shall apply this section in its first financial statements that conform to this FRS.

28.4   A micro-entity's first financial statements that conform to this FRS are the first financial statements prepared in accordance with this FRS if, for example, the micro-entity:

(a)   did not present financial statements for previous periods; or

(b)   presented its most recent previous financial statements under previous UK and Republic of Ireland requirements or **FRS 102** and that are therefore not consistent with this FRS in all respects.

28.5   Paragraph 3.9 defines a complete set of financial statements for a micro-entity.

28.6   Paragraph 3.10 requires a micro-entity to disclose, in a complete set of financial statements, comparative information in respect of the preceding period for all amounts presented in the financial statements. Therefore, a micro-entity's **date of transition** to this FRS is the beginning of the earliest period for which the micro-entity presents full comparative information in accordance with this FRS in its first financial statements that comply with this FRS.

Procedures for preparing financial statements at the date of transition

28.7   Except as provided in paragraphs 28.9 to 28.11, a micro-entity shall, in its opening **statement of financial position** as of its date of transition to this FRS (ie the beginning of the earliest period presented):

(a)   recognise all **assets** and **liabilities** whose **recognition** is required by this FRS;

(b)   not recognise items as assets or liabilities if this FRS does not permit such recognition;

(c)   reclassify items that it recognised under its previous financial reporting framework as one type of asset, liability or component of **equity**, but are a different type of asset, liability or component of equity under this FRS; and

(d)   apply this FRS in **measuring** all recognised assets and liabilities.

This section does not require the opening statement of financial position to be presented.

The **accounting policies** that a micro-entity uses in its opening statement of financial **28.8**
position under this FRS may differ from those that it used for the same date using its
previous financial reporting framework. The resulting adjustments arise from transactions,
other events or conditions before the date of transition to this FRS. Therefore, a micro-entity
shall recognise those adjustments directly in equity reserves at the date of transition to this
FRS.

On first-time adoption of this FRS, a micro-entity shall not retrospectively change the **28.9**
accounting that it followed under its previous financial reporting framework for any of the
following transactions:

(a) *Derecognition of financial assets and financial liabilities*
    Financial assets and **financial liabilities** derecognised under a micro-entity's
    previous accounting framework before the date of transition shall not be recognised
    upon adoption of this FRS. Conversely, for financial assets and liabilities that would
    have been derecognised under this FRS in a transaction that took place before the
    date of transition, but that were not derecognised under a micro-entity's previous
    accounting framework, a micro-entity may choose:

    (i)   to derecognise them on adoption of this FRS; or
    (ii) to continue to recognise them until disposed of or settled.

(b) *Accounting estimates*.

A micro-entity may use one or more of the following exemptions in preparing its first **28.10**
financial statements that conform to this FRS:

(a) *Business combinations and goodwill*
    A first-time adopter is not required to apply Section 14 *Business Combinations and
    Goodwill* to **business combinations** that were effected before the date of transition
    to this FRS. However, if a first-time adopter restates any business combination to
    comply with Section 14, it shall restate all later business combinations. If a first-
    time adopter does not apply Section 14 retrospectively, the first-time adopter
    shall recognise and measure all its assets and liabilities acquired or assumed in a
    past business combination at the date of transition to this FRS in accordance with
    paragraphs 28.7 to 28.9 or, if applicable, with paragraphs 28.10(b) to (h) except that
    no adjustment shall be made to the **carrying amount** of **goodwill**.

(b) *Share-based payment transactions*
    A first-time adopter is not required to apply Section 21 *Share-based Payment* to
    obligations arising from **share-based payment transactions** that were settled before
    the date of transition to this FRS.

(c) *Investment properties*
    A first-time adopter is not required to retrospectively apply paragraph 12.15 to
    determine the depreciated cost of each of the major components of an **investment
    property** at the date of transition to this FRS. If this exemption is applied, a first-
    time adopter shall:

    (i)   Determine the total cost of the investment property including all of its
          components. Where no **depreciation** had been charged under the micro-entity's
          previous financial reporting framework, this can be calculated by reversing
          any revaluation **gains** or losses previously recorded in equity reserves.
    (ii) The cost of land, if any, shall be separated from buildings.
    (iii) Estimate the total depreciated cost of the investment property (excluding land)
          at the date of transition to this FRS, by recognising accumulated depreciation
          since the date of initial acquisition calculated on the basis of the **useful life**
          of the most significant component of the item of investment property (eg the
          main structural elements of the building).

(iv)   A portion of the estimated total depreciated cost calculated in paragraph (iii) shall then be allocated to each of the other major components (ie excluding the most significant component identified above) to determine their depreciated cost. The allocation should be made on a reasonable and consistent basis. For example, a possible basis of allocation is to multiply the current cost to replace the component by the ratio of its remaining useful life to the expected useful life of a replacement component.

(v)   Any amount of the total depreciated cost not allocated under paragraph (iv) shall be allocated to the most significant component of the investment property.

(d)   *Compound financial instruments*

Paragraph 17.11 requires a micro-entity to split a **compound financial instrument** into its liability and equity components at the date of issue. A first-time adopter need not separate those two components if the liability component is not outstanding at the date of transition to this FRS.

(e)   *Arrangements containing a lease*

A first-time adopter may elect to determine whether an arrangement existing at the date of transition to this FRS contains a **lease** (see paragraph 15.4) on the basis of facts and circumstances existing at that date, rather than when the arrangement was entered into.

(f)   *Decommissioning liabilities included in the cost of property, plant and equipment or investment property*

Paragraph 12.9(c) states that the cost of an item of **property, plant and equipment** or **investment property** includes the initial estimate of the costs of dismantling and removing the item and restoring the site on which it is located, the obligation for which a micro-entity incurs either when the item is acquired or as a consequence of having used the item during a particular period for purposes other than to produce **inventories** during that period. A first-time adopter may elect to measure this component of the cost of an item of property, plant and equipment or investment property at the date of transition to this FRS, rather than on the date(s) when the obligation initially arose.

(g)   *Dormant companies*

A company within the **Act's** definition of a dormant company may elect to retain its accounting policies for reported assets, liabilities and equity at the date of transition to this FRS until there is any change to those balances or the company undertakes any new transactions.

(h)   *Lease incentives*

A first-time adopter is not required to apply paragraphs 15.15 and 15.25 to **lease incentives** provided the term of the lease commenced before the date of transition to this FRS. The first-time adopter shall continue to recognise any residual benefit or cost associated with these lease incentives on the same basis as that applied at the date of transition to this FRS.

28.11   If it is **impracticable** for a micro-entity to restate the opening statement of financial position at the date of transition for one or more of the adjustments required by paragraph 28.7, the micro-entity shall apply paragraphs 28.7 to 28.10 for such adjustments in the earliest period for which it is practicable to do so.

28.12   Where applicable to the transactions, events or arrangements affected by applying these exemptions, a micro-entity may continue to use the exemptions that are applied at the date of transition to this FRS when preparing subsequent financial statements, until such time when the assets and liabilities associated with those transactions, events or arrangements are derecognised.

APPROVAL BY THE FRC

Financial Reporting Standard 105 *The Financial Reporting Standard applicable to the Micro-entities Regime* was approved for issue by the Financial Reporting Council on 1 July 2015, following its consideration of the Accounting Council's Advice for this FRS.

THE ACCOUNTING COUNCIL'S ADVICE TO THE FRC TO ISSUE FRS 105

Introduction

1   This report provides an overview of the main issues that have been considered by the Accounting Council in advising the Financial Reporting Council (FRC) to issue FRS 105 *The Financial Reporting Standard applicable to the Micro-entities Regime*, incorporating the Council's advice following the publication of Financial Reporting Exposure Draft (FRED) 58 *Draft FRS 105 The Financial Reporting Standard applicable to the Micro-entities Regime* and FRED 50 *Draft FRC Abstract 1 Residential Management Companies' Financial Statements and Consequential Amendments to the FRSSE.*

2   The FRC, in accordance with the *Statutory Auditors (Amendment of Companies Act 2006 and Delegation of Functions etc) Order 2012* (SI 2012/1741), is a prescribed body for issuing accounting standards in the UK. The *Foreword to Accounting Standards* sets out the application of accounting standards in the Republic of Ireland.

3   In accordance with the *FRC Codes and Standards: procedures*, any proposal to issue, amend or withdraw a code or standard is put to the FRC Board with the full advice of the relevant Councils and/or the Codes & Standards Committee. Ordinarily, the FRC Board will only reject the advice put to it where:

    (a)   it is apparent that a significant group of stakeholders has not been adequately consulted;

    (b)   the necessary assessment of the impact of the proposal has not been completed, including an analysis of costs and benefits;

    (c)   insufficient consideration has been given to the timing or cost of implementation; or

    (d)   the cumulative impact of a number of proposals would make the adoption of an otherwise satisfactory proposal inappropriate.

4   The FRC has established the Accounting Council as the relevant Council to assist it in the setting of accounting standards.

Advice

5   The Accounting Council is advising the FRC to issue FRS 105 *The Financial Reporting Standard applicable to the Micro-entities Regime* to facilitate the effective adoption of the micro-entities regime introduced by company law. FRS 105 has been developed from the recognition and measurement requirements of FRS 102 *The Financial Reporting Standard applicable in the UK and Republic of Ireland*, adapted for compliance with the specific company law requirements applicable to the micro-entities regime and other appropriate simplifications.

6   The Accounting Council's Advice on FRS 102 is contained in that standard.

Background

7   The micro-entities regime was introduced in UK company law in 2013 with significantly reduced financial statements presentation and disclosure requirements. In order to reflect the legal requirements of the new micro-entities regime, the FRC amended the *Financial Reporting Standard for Smaller Entities* (FRSSE) in April 2014, but this was intended to be a temporary solution until the FRC developed a new standard for entities that prepare financial statements under the micro-entities regime.

In February 2015, the FRC published FRED 58 to consult on a new accounting standard for micro-entities.   **8**

In August 2013, the FRC issued FRED 50, a consultation on residential management companies' financial statements which is relevant in the context of the reporting by micro-entities.   **9**

The Accounting Council has considered the responses to FREDs 50 and 58 and took them into account when issuing its advice.   **10**

Objective

The FRC gives careful consideration to its objective and the intended effects when developing new accounting standards or requirements for the UK and Republic of Ireland. In developing accounting standards, including FRS 105, the overriding objective of the FRC is to enable users of accounts to receive high-quality understandable financial reporting proportionate to the size and complexity of the entity and users' information needs.   **11**

In meeting this objective, the FRC aims to provide succinct financial reporting standards that: **12**

(a)   have consistency with global accounting standards through the application of an IFRS-based solution unless an alternative clearly better meets the overriding objective;

(b)   reflect up-to-date thinking and developments in the way businesses operate and the transactions they undertake;

(c)   balance consistent principles for accounting by all UK and Republic of Ireland entities with practical solutions, based on size, complexity, public interest and users' information needs;

(d)   promote efficiency within groups; and

(e)   are cost-effective to apply.

Consistent recognition and measurement requirements with FRS 102

The Accounting Council is of the view that the reporting requirements for all small entities (including micro-entities) should be based on FRS 102 because it improves consistency across the financial reporting framework in the UK and Republic of Ireland.   **13**

To that end, FRED 58 proposed that FRS 105 applies the recognition and measurement requirements of FRS 102, adapted where necessary to reflect the legal requirements of the micro-entities regime and simplified further to reflect the size and nature of micro-entities.   **14**

Respondents to the consultation supported that FRS 105 should be developed from FRS 102 and the standard has been finalised on that basis.   **15**

The Accounting Council notes that it would not otherwise have recommended some of the simplifications made in FRS 105, including the omission of some of the disclosures required by FRS 102, if they had not been necessary to ensure legal compliance with the micro-entities regime. For example, the Accounting Council continues to believe that investment property should always, where practicable, be measured at fair value as this provides more relevant information to users of the financial statements on an investment property company's financial position and performance. However, company law prohibits the revaluation of any asset by micro-entities and instead requires that fixed assets are measured at cost less depreciation and impairment.   **16**

Amendments to FRS 102 to align FRS 105 with the legal requirements

Scope

17   FRS 105 is an accounting standard applicable to the preparation of the financial statements of a micro-entity which are presumed in law to give a true and fair view in accordance with the micro-entities regime.

18   During its deliberations, the Accounting Council was requested to consider whether FRS 105 could be applied to financial statements prepared for the purpose of submission to the tax authorities by unincorporated businesses and individuals that, if they were companies, would be eligible to apply the micro-entities regime.

19   The Accounting Council notes that the form and content of financial statements prepared for tax purposes is a matter for the relevant tax authorities to determine and believes it is therefore not possible for the FRC to explicitly permit or prohibit the application of FRS 105 for such purpose. The Accounting Council notes that compliance with FRS 105 by businesses incorporated as companies that meet the conditions to apply the micros-entities regime will result in financial statements that in law are presumed to give a true and fair view.

20   The availability of the micro-entities regime is restricted to the smallest of companies and some types of entities are excluded. For example, charities and financial institutions are ineligible to report under this regime. For that reason, in contrast to FRS 102, FRS 105 does not contain any specific requirements that only apply to these entities.

21   The micro-entities regime is not available to entities that are required or choose to prepare consolidated financial statements. FRS 105 therefore does not contain accounting requirements that are relevant for the preparation of consolidated financial statements.

Presentation and disclosure

22   The micro-entities regime specifies certain minimum presentation and disclosure requirements. Financial statements which include the prescribed minimum accounting items are presumed in law to give a true and fair view and no further disclosures need to be made. FRS 105 has been adapted to reflect the legal minimum presentation and disclosure requirements.

Recognition and measurement

23   The micro-entities regime prohibits the use of the Alternative Accounting Rules or the Fair Value Rules set out in company law and therefore micro-entities are not permitted to revalue or subsequently measure assets or liabilities at fair value. To take account of the legal restrictions on fair value measurement, FRS 105 does not allow the subsequent measurement of any asset or liability at fair value. This affects in particular financial instruments and investment properties which a micro-entity has to measure at depreciated cost.

Further simplifications over and above the legal requirements

24   The micro-entities regime is intended to be deregulatory and the Accounting Council believes it is appropriate to simplify some of the accounting requirements applicable under FRS 102. The Accounting Council considers that simplifications would be appropriate if:

(a) the benefits of applying the accounting treatment in FRS 102 do not outweigh the burden for micro-entities and an alternative, more straightforward, treatment could be identified;

(b) the lack of detail in the formats of the financial statements and/or supporting disclosures would limit the understanding of the financial information presented; and/or

(c) transactions occur infrequently amongst micro-entities.

The Accounting Council notes that permitting accounting policy choices in FRS 105 would add complexity for preparers of a micro-entity's financial statements and could cause confusion to users due to the lack of detail in the formats of the financial statements and lack of supporting disclosures to explain the policy choice taken. As a result, the Accounting Council advises that FRS 105 should not contain accounting policy options, except on first-time adoption of FRS 105.   **25**

The Accounting Council advises that first-time adopters of FRS 105 should be given a choice on whether they apply the requirements of FRS 105 fully retrospectively or whether they apply one or more of the transitional exemptions. Although this introduces a degree of complexity for preparers and users, the Accounting Council believes transitional exemptions are important for a smooth transition and not allowing a choice would disadvantage micro-entities unnecessarily over entities that transition to FRS 102.   **26**

In all other cases where accounting policy options are provided in FRS 102 they should be removed in FRS 105. The Accounting Council advises that FRS 105 should mandate the most straightforward and easy to apply option.   **27**

The key areas where simplifications have been made are: **28**

(a) Prohibition of accounting for deferred taxation on the basis that this is a complex area of accounting and the lack of disclosure in a micro-entity's financial statements make it impossible to distinguish between current and deferred tax.

(b) Prohibition of accounting for equity-settled share-based payments prior to the issue of the shares, because of the prohibition to use fair value measurements and lack of supporting disclosure in the financial statements.

(c) A requirement that the contributions payable to any post-employment benefit plans are accounted for as an expense, subject to a requirement for defined benefit plans to recognise a liability for a schedule of contributions to the extent that it relates to the deficit. The simplification was made on the basis that very few micro-entities will have defined benefit pension schemes.

(d) The distinction between functional and presentation currency is removed as it will be very rare for micro-entities to have a different functional and presentational currency.

(e) Requirement to use contracted rates to translate foreign currency denominated assets and liabilities rather than spot rates. This will simplify the accounting when micro-entities enter into foreign currency forward contracts.

(f) All borrowing and development costs must be expensed, because this is considered the simplest option of accounting for these costs.

(g) Mandating the application of the accrual model to account for government grants because this is considered the simplest method of accounting for these transactions.

(h) Simplifications in relation to the accounting for financial instruments as far as the allocation of interest and transaction costs is concerned. The effective interest rate method is considered too onerous to apply by micro-entities.

(i) Removal of the requirement to impute a market-rate of interest in lending arrangements conducted at non-market rates because considering the nature and size of micro-entities the costs of mandating this requirement would exceed the benefits.

(j) Simplified requirements for classifying financial instruments as equity or debt because most micro-entities will issue simple equity instruments.

(k)   Prohibition of the recognition of separately identifiable intangible assets in a trade and asset acquisition because these are not required items in the financial statements formats.

(l)   Removal of the requirements concerning accounting for hyperinflation because this is unlikely to be an issue for micro-entities.

(m) Removal of accounting requirements relating to specialised activities including extractive activities, service concessions, heritage assets and funding commitments because micro-entities will not typically enter into these transactions.

Feedback on the proposed simplification from respondents to FRED 58

29   Most respondents supported the proposed simplifications and the principles applied by the Accounting Council to assess whether a simplification is appropriate. It was noted that some stakeholders are of the view that the recognition of deferred tax should be permitted or required in FRS 105. However, after having considered these comments the Accounting Council retains its view that without additional disclosure the benefits of requiring micro-entities to account for deferred tax do not exceed the costs.

30   FRED 58 proposed that government grants should be accounted for using the performance model. The views of respondents on whether FRS 105 should require the performance or accrual model were divided. The evidence provided by respondents suggests that the accrual model may in practice be easier to apply than the performance model and the Accounting Council therefore advises that FRS 105 should mandate the accrual model.

Determining accounting policies where FRS 105 does not contain requirements

31   A micro-entity that enters into a transaction that is not specifically covered in FRS 105 is required to refer to the concepts and pervasive principles set out in Section 2 *Concepts and Pervasive Principles* of FRS 105 in determining its accounting policies. The Accounting Council notes that micro-entities are not required to refer to other accounting standards or authoritative guidance because these requirements may be inconsistent with the legal requirements of the micro-entities regime.

Transitional provisions – fair value / revaluation as deemed cost

32   The micro-entities regime requires micro-entities to apply the historical cost accounting rules, which require fixed assets to be included at purchase price or production cost. Therefore the Accounting Council advises that it would be inconsistent with the legal framework for micro-entities to provide in FRS 105 a transitional exemption to allow micro-entities to carry forward previous revaluations of property, plant and equipment or the fair value of investment properties or investments in shares as deemed cost.

33   FRS 105 provides a transitional exemption in respect of the determination of the depreciated historical cost of investment properties. Under the transitional exemption a micro-entity is permitted, for the purpose of estimating accumulated depreciation at the date of transition, to treat an investment property as if it were a single asset with a useful economic life equal to that of its most significant component, which is likely to be comprised of its main structural elements such as foundations, walls etc. This exempts a micro-entity from having to determine the historical cost of each component that has been replaced in the past and the depreciation that would have been charged since their initial recognition.

The Accounting Council notes that the micro-entities regime is optional and that if a micro-entity wishes to retain revalued amounts in its financial statement it could continue to apply the small company regime, rather than moving to the micro-entities regime.   **34**

Structure and language of FRS 105

FRS 105 should be as easily accessible and understandable as possible. A number of respondents to FRED 58 suggested that the accessibility of FRS 105 could be enhanced by departing from the section and paragraph numbering of FRS 102. The Accounting Council agrees and advises that FRS 105 should where possible maintain consistency with the language and terminology used in FRS 102, but use its own structure (ie section and paragraph numbering).   **35**

Residents' management companies

In considering the feedback received from the FRC's previous consultations, the Accounting Council noted that no clear consensus existed amongst respondents on the appropriate basis of accounting in the statutory financial statements of residents' management companies[4] where service charge monies are held on trust in accordance with section 42 of the Landlord and Tenant Act 1987. However, there was general agreement that no change should be made to FRS 105, or any other relevant financial reporting standard (including FRS 102), to address such a narrow and sector-specific issue.   **36**

The Accounting Council considered this issue carefully. It assessed the case for further intervention by reference to the FRC's published *Principles for the development of Codes, Standards and Guidance*[5] and, in particular, the extent to which the anticipated benefits from any changes to current practices would outweigh the costs incurred by the entities involved. It agreed with respondents that this matter does not merit a change in accounting standards, and therefore advises that no changes are made to FRS 105 (or FRS 102) that are specific to residents' management companies.   **37**

Effective date

FRS 105 is effective for accounting periods commencing on or after 1 January 2016, in line with the mandatory effective date of the consequential amendments to FRS 102 resulting from the UK's new small companies regime. Early application of FRS 105 is permitted.   **38**

See Appendix IV *Republic of Ireland (RoI) legal references* of FRS 105 for information on the applicability of the micro-entities regime in the Republic of Ireland.   **39**

Approval of this advice

This advice to the FRC was approved by the Accounting Council on 16 June 2015.   **40**

---

[4] *An organisation which may be referred to in the lease, which is responsible for the provision of services, and manages and arranges maintenance of the property, but which does not necessarily have any legal interest in the property.*

[5] *This can be found on the FRC's website at www.frc.org.uk/FRC-Documents/FRC/About-the-FRC/Principles-for-the-development-of-Codes.pdf.*

Appendix I
Glossary

This glossary is an integral part of this FRS.

accounting policies	The specific principles, bases, conventions, rules and practices applied by an entity in preparing and presenting **financial statements**.
accrual basis (of accounting)	The effects of transactions and other events are recognised when they occur (and not as cash or its equivalent is received or paid) and they are recorded in the accounting records and reported in the **financial statements** of the periods to which they relate.
accumulating compensated absences	Compensated absences that are carried forward and can be used in future periods if the current period's entitlement is not used in full.
Act	The Companies Act 2006
active market	A market in which all the following conditions exist: (a) the items traded in the market are homogeneous; (b) willing buyers and sellers can normally be found at any time; and (c) prices are available to the public.
agent	An entity is acting as an agent when it does not have exposure to the significant risks and rewards associated with the sale of goods or the rendering of services. One feature indicating that an entity is acting as an agent is that the amount the entity earns is predetermined, being either a fixed fee per transaction or a stated percentage of the amount billed to the customer.
agricultural activity	The management by an entity of the biological transformation of **biological assets** for sale, into **agricultural produce** or into additional biological assets.
agricultural produce	The harvested product of the entity's **biological assets**.
amortisation	The systematic allocation of the **depreciable amount** of an **asset** over its **useful life**.

asset	A resource controlled by the entity as a result of past events and from which future economic benefits are expected to flow to the entity.
associate	An entity, including an unincorporated entity such as a partnership, over which the investor has **significant influence** and that is neither a **subsidiary** nor an interest in a **joint venture**.
biological asset	A living animal or plant.
borrowing costs	Interest and other costs incurred by an entity in connection with the borrowing of funds.
business	An integrated set of activities and **assets** conducted and managed for the purpose of providing: (a) a return to investors; or (b) lower costs or other economic benefits directly and proportionately to policyholders or participants. A business generally consists of inputs, processes applied to those inputs, and resulting outputs that are, or will be, used to generate **revenues**. If **goodwill** is present in a transferred set of activities and assets, the transferred set shall be presumed to be a business.
business combination	The bringing together of separate entities or **businesses** into one reporting entity.
carrying amount	The amount at which an **asset** or **liability** is recognised in the **statement of financial position**.
cash-generating unit	The smallest identifiable group of **assets** that generates cash inflows that are largely independent of the cash inflows from other assets or groups of assets.
cash-settled share-based payment transaction	A **share-based payment transaction** in which the entity acquires goods or services by incurring a **liability** to transfer cash or other **assets** to the supplier of those goods or services for amounts that are based on the price (or value) of the entity's shares or other equity instruments of the entity or another group entity.

change in accounting estimate	An adjustment of the **carrying amount** of an **asset** or a **liability**, or the amount of the periodic consumption of an asset, that results from the assessment of the present status of, and expected future benefits and obligations associated with, assets and liabilities. Changes in accounting estimates result from new information or new developments and, accordingly, are not corrections of **errors**.
closing rate	The spot exchange rate at the end of the **reporting period**.
commencement of lease term	The date from which the lessee is entitled to exercise its right to use the leased asset. It is the date of initial **recognition** of the **lease** (ie the recognition of the **assets**, **liabilities**, **income** or **expenses** resulting from the lease, as appropriate).
compound financial instrument	A **financial instrument** that, from the issuer's perspective, contains both a **liability** and an **equity** element.
consolidated financial statements	The **financial statements** of a **parent** and its **subsidiaries** presented as those of a single economic entity.
construction contract	A contract specifically negotiated for the construction of an **asset** or a combination of assets that are closely interrelated or interdependent in terms of their design, technology and function or their ultimate purpose or use.
constructive obligation	An obligation that derives from an entity's actions where: (a) by an established pattern of past practice, published policies or a sufficiently specific current statement, the entity has indicated to other parties that it will accept certain responsibilities; and (b) as a result, the entity has created a valid expectation on the part of those other parties that it will discharge those responsibilities
contingent asset	A possible **asset** that arises from past events and whose existence will be confirmed only by the occurrence or non-occurrence of one or more uncertain future events not wholly within the control of the entity.

contingent liability	(a) a possible obligation that arises from past events and whose existence will be confirmed only by the occurrence or non-occurrence of one or more uncertain future events not wholly within the control of the entity; or
	
	(b) a present obligation that arises from past events but is not recognised because:
	
	   (i) it is not **probable** that an outflow of resources embodying economic benefits will be required to settle the obligation; or
	
	   (ii) the amount of the obligation cannot be measured with sufficient reliability.

contingent rent	That portion of the lease payments that is not fixed in amount but is based on the future amount of a factor that changes other than with the passage of time (eg percentage of future sales, amount of future use, future price indices, and future market rates of interest).
control (of an entity)	The power to govern the financial and operating policies of an entity so as to obtain benefits from its activities.
current tax	The amount of **income tax** payable (refundable) in respect of the **taxable profit (tax loss)** for the current period or past **reporting periods**.
date of transition	The beginning of the earliest period for which an entity presents full comparative information in a given standard in its first financial statements that comply with that standard.
deferred tax	Income tax payable (recoverable) in respect of the **taxable profit (tax loss)** for future **reporting periods** as a result of past transactions or events.
defined benefit plans	**Post-employment benefit plans** other than **defined contribution plans**.
defined contribution plans	**Post-employment benefit plans** under which an entity pays fixed contributions into a separate entity (a fund) and has no legal or **constructive obligation** to pay further contributions or to make direct benefit payments to employees if the fund does not hold sufficient **assets** to pay all **employee benefits** relating to employee service in the current and prior periods.

depreciable amount	The cost of an **asset**, or other amount substituted for cost (in the **financial statements**), less its **residual value**.
depreciation	The systematic allocation of the **depreciable amount** of an **asset** over its **useful life**.
derecognition	The removal of a previously recognised **asset** or **liability** from an entity's **statement of financial position**.
derivative	Is a **financial instrument** with the following three characteristics: (a) its value changes in response to the change in a specified interest rate, financial instrument price, commodity price, foreign exchange rate, index of prices or rates, credit rating or credit index, or other variable (sometimes called the 'underlying'), provided in the case of a non-financial variable that the variable is not specific to a party to the contract; (b) it requires no initial net investment or an initial net investment that is smaller than would be required for other types of contracts that would be expected to have a similar response to changes in market factors; and (c) it is settled at a future date.
development	The application of **research** findings or other knowledge to a plan or design for the production of new or substantially improved materials, devices, products, processes, systems or services before the start of commercial production or use.
employee benefits	All forms of consideration given by an entity in exchange for service rendered by employees.
equity	The residual interest in the **assets** of the entity after deducting all its **liabilities**.
equity-settled share-based payment transaction	A **share-based payment transaction** in which the entity: (a) receives goods or services as consideration for its own equity instruments (including shares or **share options**); or (b) receives goods or services but has no obligation to settle the transaction with the supplier.

errors	Omissions from, and misstatements in, the entity's **financial statements** for one or more prior periods arising from a failure to use, or misuse of, reliable information that:
	(a) was available when financial statements for those periods were authorised for issue; and
	(b) could reasonably be expected to have been obtained and taken into account in the preparation and presentation of those financial statements.
expenses	Decreases in economic benefits during the **reporting period** in the form of outflows or depletions of **assets** or incurrences of **liabilities** that result in decreases in **equity**, other than those relating to distributions to equity investors.
fair value	The amount for which an **asset** could be exchanged, a **liability** settled, or an equity instrument granted could be exchanged, between knowledgeable, willing parties in an arm's length transaction. In the absence of any specific guidance provided in the relevant section of this FRS, the guidance in paragraph 2.31 shall be used in determining fair value.
fair value less costs to sell	The amount obtainable from the sale of an **asset** in an arm's length transaction between knowledgeable, willing parties, less the costs of disposal.
finance lease	A **lease** that transfers substantially all the risks and rewards incidental to ownership of an **asset**. Title may or may not eventually be transferred. A lease that is not a finance lease is an **operating lease**.
financial asset	Any **asset** that is:
	(a) cash;
	(b) an equity instrument of another entity;
	(c) a contractual right:
	(i) to receive cash or another financial asset from another entity; or
	(ii) to exchange financial assets or **financial liabilities** with another entity under conditions that are potentially favourable to the entity; or

	(d) a contract that will or may be settled in the entity's own equity instruments and: (i) under which the entity is or may be obliged to receive a variable number of the entity's own equity instruments; or (ii) that will or may be settled other than by the exchange of a fixed amount of cash or another financial asset for a fixed number of the entity's own equity instruments. For this purpose the entity's own equity instruments do not include instruments that are themselves contracts for the future receipt or delivery of the entity's own equity instruments.
financial guarantee contract	A contract that requires the issuer to make specified payments to reimburse the holder for a loss it incurs because a specified debtor fails to make payments when due in accordance with the original or modified terms of a debt instrument.
financial instrument	A contract that gives rise to a **financial asset** of one entity and a **financial liability** or equity instrument of another entity.

financial liability	Any **liability** that is:
	
	(a) a contractual obligation:
	
	   (i) to deliver cash or another **financial asset** to another entity; or
	
	   (ii) to exchange financial assets or financial liabilities with another entity under conditions that are potentially unfavourable to the entity, or
	
	(b) a contract that will or may be settled in the entity's own equity instruments and:
	
	   (i) under which the entity is or may be obliged to deliver a variable number of the entity's own equity instruments; or
	
	   (ii) will or may be settled other than by the exchange of a fixed amount of cash or another financial asset for a fixed number of the entity's own equity instruments. For this purpose the entity's own equity instruments do not include instruments that are themselves contracts for the future receipt or delivery of the entity's own equity instruments.

financial position	The relationship of the **assets**, **liabilities** and **equity** of an entity as reported in the **statement of financial position**.
financial statements	A structured presentation of the **financial position** and financial **performance** of an entity.
financing activities	Activities that result in changes in the size and composition of the contributed **equity** and borrowings of the entity.
first-time adopter of this FRS	An entity that presents its first annual **financial statements** that conform to this FRS, regardless of its previous accounting framework.
fixed assets	**Assets** of an entity which are intended for use on a continuing basis in the entity's activities.
FRS 102	FRS 102 *The Financial Reporting Standard applicable in the UK and Republic of Ireland*
gains	Increases in economic benefits that meet the definition of **income** but are not **revenue**.

goodwill	Future economic benefits arising from **assets** that are not capable of being individually identified and separately recognised.
government grant	Assistance by government in the form of a transfer of resources to an entity in return for past or future compliance with specified conditions relating to the **operating activities** of the entity. Government refers to government, government agencies and similar bodies whether local, national or international.
grant date	The date at which the entity and another party (including an employee) agree to a share-based payment arrangement, being when the entity and the counterparty have a shared understanding of the terms and conditions of the arrangement. At grant date the entity confers on the counterparty the right to cash, other **assets**, or equity instruments of the entity, provided the specified vesting conditions, if any, are met. If that agreement is subject to an approval process (for example, by shareholders), grant date is the date when that approval is obtained.
gross investment in a lease	The aggregate of: (a) the **minimum lease payments** receivable by the lessor under a **finance lease**; and (b) any unguaranteed **residual value** accruing to the lessor.
impairment loss	The amount by which the **carrying amount** of an asset exceeds: (a) in the case of **inventories**, its selling price less costs to complete and sell; (b) in the case of **financial assets** the amounts as set out in paragraph 9.18; or (c) in the case of any other asset, its **recoverable amount**.
impracticable	Applying a requirement is impracticable when the entity cannot apply it after making every reasonable effort to do so.
inception of the lease	The earlier of the date of the lease agreement and the date of commitment by the parties to the principal provisions of the **lease**.

income	Increases in economic benefits during the **reporting period** in the form of inflows or enhancements of **assets** or decreases of **liabilities** that result in increases in **equity**, other than those relating to contributions from equity investors.
income statement	**Financial statement** that presents all items of **income** and **expense** recognised in a **reporting period** (referred to as the profit and loss account in the **Act**).
income tax	All domestic and foreign taxes that are based on **taxable profits**. Income tax also includes taxes, such as withholding taxes, that are payable by a **subsidiary**, **associate** or **joint venture** on distributions to the reporting entity.
intangible asset	An identifiable non-monetary asset without physical substance. Such an **asset** is identifiable when: (a) it is separable, ie capable of being separated or divided from the entity and sold, transferred, licensed, rented or exchanged, either individually or together with a related contract, asset or **liability**; or (b) it arises from contractual or other legal rights, regardless of whether those rights are transferable or separable from the entity or from other rights and obligations.
interest rate implicit in the lease	The discount rate that, at the **inception of the lease**, causes the aggregate **present value** of: (a) the **minimum lease payments**; and (b) the unguaranteed **residual value** to be equal to the sum of: (i) the **fair value** of the leased **asset**; and (ii) any initial direct costs of the lessor.
inventories	Assets: (a) held for sale in the ordinary course of business; (b) in the process of production for such sale; or (c) in the form of materials or supplies to be consumed in the production process or in the rendering of services.

investment property	Property (land or a building, or part of a building, or both) held by the owner or by the lessee under a **finance lease** to earn rentals or for capital appreciation or both, rather than for:
	(a) use in the production or supply of goods or services or for administrative purposes; or
	(b) sale in the ordinary course of business.
joint control	The contractually agreed sharing of **control** over an economic activity. It exists only when the strategic financial and operating decisions relating to the activity require the unanimous consent of the parties sharing control (the **venturers**).
joint venture	A contractual arrangement whereby two or more parties undertake an economic activity that is subject to **joint control**. Joint ventures can take the form of jointly controlled operations, jointly controlled **assets**, or **jointly controlled entities**.
jointly controlled entity	A **joint venture** that involves the establishment of a corporation, partnership or other entity in which each **venturer** has an interest. The entity operates in the same way as other entities, except that a contractual arrangement between the venturers establishes **joint control** over the economic activity of the entity.
lease	An agreement whereby the lessor conveys to the lessee in return for a payment or series of payments the right to use an **asset** for an agreed period of time.
lease incentives	Incentives provided by the lessor to the lessee to enter into a new or renew an **operating lease**. Examples of such incentives include up-front cash payments to the lessee, the reimbursement or assumption by the lessor of costs of the lessee (such as relocation costs, leasehold improvements and costs associated with pre-existing lease commitments of the lessee), or initial periods of the **lease** provided by the lessor rent-free or at a reduced rent.

lease term	The non-cancellable period for which the lessee has contracted to **lease** the **asset** together with any further terms for which the lessee has the option to continue to lease the asset, with or without further payment, when at the **inception of the lease** it is reasonably certain that the lessee will exercise the option.
lessee's incremental borrowing rate (of interest)	The rate of interest the lessee would have to pay on a similar **lease** or, if that is not determinable, the rate that, at the **inception of the lease**, the lessee would incur to borrow over a similar term, and with a similar security, the funds necessary to purchase the **asset**.
liability	A present obligation of the entity arising from past events, the settlement of which is expected to result in an outflow from the entity of resources embodying economic benefits.
material	Omissions or misstatements of items are material if they could, individually or collectively, influence the economic decisions of users taken on the basis of the **financial statements**. Materiality depends on the size and nature of the omission or misstatement judged in the surrounding circumstances. The size or nature of the item, or a combination of both, could be the determining factor.
measurement	The process of determining the monetary amounts at which the elements of the **financial statements** are to be recognised and carried in the **statement of financial position** and **income statement**.
micro-entity	Is an entity that meets all of the following conditions: (a) it is a company established under company law; (b) it qualifies as a micro-entity in accordance with section 384A of the **Act**; and (c) it is not excluded from being treated as a micro-entity under section 384B of the Act. Micro-entities are a subset of small companies as defined in the Act.

micro-entity minimum accounting items	The item of information required under the **micro-entities regime** to be contained in the **financial statements** of a **micro-entity**. These are set out in Sections 4 *Statement of Financial Position*, 5 *Income Statement* and 6 *Notes to the Financial Statements* of this FRS.
micro-entity provisions	Means any provisions of Part 15, Part 16 or regulations under Part 15 of the **Act** relating specifically to the individual accounts of an entity which qualifies as a **micro-entity**.
micro-entities regime	The legal requirements and exemptions relating to the preparation of the **financial statements** of **micro-entities** as set out in the **Act** and **Small Companies Regulations**.
minimum lease payments	The payments over the **lease term** that the lessee is or can be required to make, excluding **contingent rent**, costs for services and taxes to be paid by and reimbursed to the lessor, together with:
	(a) for a lessee, any amounts guaranteed by the lessee or by a party related to the lessee; or
	(b) for a lessor, any **residual value** guaranteed to the lessor by:
	(i) the lessee;
	(ii) a party related to the lessee; or
	(iii) a third party unrelated to the lessor that is financially capable of discharging the obligations under the guarantee.
	However, if the lessee has an option to purchase the **asset** at a price that is expected to be sufficiently lower than **fair value** at the date the option becomes exercisable for it to be reasonably certain, at the **inception of the lease**, that the option will be exercised, the minimum lease payments comprise the minimum payments payable over the lease term to the expected date of exercise of this purchase option and the payment required to exercise it.
monetary items	Units of currency held and **assets** and **liabilities** to be received or paid in a fixed or determinable number of units of currency.

multi-employer (benefit) plans	**Defined contribution plans** (other than **state plans**) or **defined benefit plans** (other than state plans) that: (a) pool the **assets** contributed by various entities that are not under common control; and (b) use those assets to provide benefits to employees of more than one entity, on the basis that contribution and benefit levels are determined without regard to the identity of the entity that employs the employees concerned.
net investment in a lease	The **gross investment in a lease** discounted at the **interest rate implicit in the lease**.
non-exchange transaction	A transaction whereby an entity receives value from another entity without directly giving approximately equal value in exchange, or gives value to another entity without directly receiving approximately equal value in exchange.
notes (to the financial statements prepared under this FRS)	Notes contain information in addition to that presented in the **statement of financial position** and **income statement**. Notes are required to be presented at the foot of the statement of financial position.
onerous contract	A contract in which the unavoidable costs of meeting the obligations under the contract exceed the economic benefits expected to be received under it.
operating activities	The principal revenue-producing activities of the entity and other activities that are not investing or **financing activities**.
operating lease	A **lease** that does not transfer substantially all the risks and rewards incidental to ownership. A lease that is not an operating lease is a **finance lease**.
ordinary share	An equity instrument that is subordinate to all other classes of equity instrument.
owners	Holders of instruments classified as **equity**.
parent	An entity that has one or more **subsidiaries**.
performance	The relationship of the **income** and **expenses** of a **micro-entity**, as reported in the **income statement**.

post-employment benefits	**Employee benefits** (other than **termination benefits** and short-term employee benefits) that are payable after the completion of employment.
post-employment benefit plans	Formal or informal arrangements under which an entity provides **post-employment benefits** for one or more employees.
present value	A current estimate of the present discounted value of the future net **cash flows** in the normal course of business.
principal	An entity is acting as a principal when it has exposure to the significant risks and rewards associated with the sale of goods or the rendering of services. Features that indicate that an entity is acting as a principal include:
	(a) the entity has the primary responsibility for providing the goods or services to the customer or for fulfilling the order, for example by being responsible for the acceptability of the products or services ordered or purchased by the customer;
	(b) the entity has **inventory** risk before or after the customer order, during shipping or on return;
	(c) the entity has latitude in establishing prices, either directly or indirectly, for example by providing additional goods or services; and
	(d) the entity bears the customer's credit risk for the amount receivable from the customer.
probable	More likely than not.
profit or loss	The total of **income** less **expenses**.
property, plant and equipment	Tangible assets that:
	are held for use in the production or supply of goods or services, for rental to others, or for administrative purposes; and
	are expected to be used during more than one period.
prospectively (applying a change in accounting policy)	Applying the new **accounting policy** to transactions, other events and conditions occurring after the date as at which the policy is changed.
provision	A **liability** of uncertain timing or amount.

prudence	The inclusion of a degree of caution in the exercise of the judgements needed in making the estimates required under conditions of uncertainty, such that **assets** or **income** are not overstated and **liabilities** or **expenses** are not understated.
recognition	The process of incorporating in the **statement of financial position** or **income statement** an item that meets the definition of an **asset**, **liability**, **equity**, **income** or **expense** and satisfies the following criteria: (a) it is **probable** that any future economic benefit associated with the item will flow to or from the **entity**; and (b) the item has a cost or value that can be measured with reliability.
recoverable amount	The higher of an **asset's** (or **cash-generating unit's**) **fair value less costs to sell** and its **value in use**.
reporting date	The end of the latest period covered by **financial statements**.
reporting period	The period covered by **financial statements**.
research	Original and planned investigation undertaken with the prospect of gaining new scientific or technical knowledge and understanding.
residual value (of an asset)	The estimated amount that an entity would currently obtain from disposal of an **asset**, after deducting the estimated costs of disposal, if the asset were already of the age and in the condition expected at the end of its **useful life**.
restructuring	A restructuring is a programme that is planned and controlled by management and materially changes either: (a) the scope of a business undertaken by an entity; or (b) the manner in which that business is conducted.
retrospective application (of an accounting policy)	Applying a new **accounting policy** to transactions, other events and conditions as if that policy had always been applied.

revenue	The gross inflow of economic benefits during the period arising in the course of the ordinary activities of an entity when those inflows result in increases in **equity**, other than increases relating to contributions from equity participants.
share-based payment transaction	A transaction in which the entity: (a) receives goods or services (including employee services) as consideration for its own equity instruments (including shares or **share options**); or (b) receives goods or services but has no obligation to settle the transaction with supplier; or (c) acquires goods or services by incurring **liabilities** to the supplier of those goods or services for amounts that are based on the price (or value) of the entity's shares or other equity instruments of the entity or another group entity.
share option	A contract that gives the holder the right, but not the obligation, to subscribe to the entity's shares at a fixed or determinable price for a specific period of time.
significant influence	Is the power to participate in the financial and operating policy decisions of the **associate** but is not **control** or **joint control** over those policies.
Small Companies Regulations	The Small Companies and Groups (Accounts and Directors' Report) Regulations 2008 (SI 2008/409)
state (employee benefit) plan	Employee benefit plans established by legislation to cover all entities (or all entities in a particular category, for example a specific industry) and operated by national or local government or by another body (for example an autonomous agency created specifically for this purpose) which is not subject to control or influence by the reporting entity.
statement of financial position	**Financial statement** that presents the relationship of an entity's **assets**, **liabilities** and **equity** as of a specific date (referred to as the balance sheet in the **Act**).
subsidiary	An entity, including an unincorporated entity such as a partnership, that is **controlled** by another entity (known as the **parent**).

substantively enacted	Tax rates shall be regarded as substantively enacted when the remaining stages of the enactment process historically have not affected the outcome and are unlikely to do so. A UK tax rate shall be regarded as having been substantively enacted if it is included in either: (a) a Bill that has been passed by the House of Commons and is awaiting only passage through the House of Lords and Royal Assent; or (b) a resolution having statutory effect that has been passed under the Provisional Collection of Taxes Act 1968. (Such a resolution could be used to collect taxes at a new rate before that rate has been enacted. In practice, corporation tax rates are now set a year ahead to avoid having to invoke the Provisional Collection of Taxes Act for the quarterly payment system.) A Republic of Ireland tax rate can be regarded as having been substantively enacted if it is included in a Bill that has been passed by the Dail.
tax expense	The aggregate amount included in **profit or loss** or **equity** for the **reporting period** in respect of **current tax**.
taxable profit (tax loss)	The profit (loss) for a **reporting period** upon which **income taxes** are payable or recoverable, determined in accordance with the rules established by the taxation authorities. Taxable profit equals taxable income less amounts deductible from taxable **income**.
termination benefits	**Employee benefits** provided in exchange for the termination of an employee's employment as a result of either: (a) an entity's decision to terminate an employee's employment before the normal retirement date; or (b) an employee's decision to accept voluntary redundancy in exchange for those benefits.

transaction costs (financial instruments)	Incremental costs that are directly attributable to the acquisition, issue or disposal of a **financial asset** or **financial liability**, or the issue or reacquisition of an entity's own equity instrument. An incremental cost is one that would not have been incurred if the entity had not acquired, issued or disposed of the financial asset or financial liability, or had not issued or reacquired its own equity instrument.
treasury shares	An entity's own equity instruments that are held by the entity.
turnover	The amounts derived from the provision of goods and services after deduction of: (a) trade discounts; (b) value added tax; and (c) any other taxes based on the amounts so derived.
useful life	The period over which an **asset** is expected to be available for use by an entity or the number of production or similar units expected to be obtained from the asset by an entity.
value in use	The **present value** of the future cash flows expected to be derived from an **asset** or **cash-generating unit**.
venturer	A party to a **joint venture** that has **joint control** over that joint venture.
vest	Become an entitlement. Under a share-based payment arrangement, a counterparty's right to receive cash, other **assets** or equity instruments of the entity vests when the counterparty's entitlement is no longer conditional on the satisfaction of any vesting conditions.

Appendix II
Table of equivalence for UK Companies Act terminology

The following table compares company law terminology with broadly equivalent terminology used in this FRS. In some cases there are minor differences between the broadly equivalent definitions, which are also summarised below.

Company law terminology	FRS 105 terminology
Accounting reference date	Reporting date
Accounts	Financial statements
Balance sheet	Statement of financial position
Capital and reserves	Equity
Cash at bank and in hand	Cash
Debtors	Trade receivables
Diminution in value [of assets]	Impairment
Financial year	Reporting period
Net realisable value [of any current asset]	Estimated selling price less costs to complete and sell
Profit and loss account	Income statement
Stocks	Inventories
Tangible assets	Includes: property, plant and equipment and investment property
Trade creditors	Trade payables

Appendix III
Note on legal requirements

INTRODUCTION

A3.1　This appendix provides an overview of how the requirements of FRS 105 address UK company law requirements. It is therefore written from the perspective of a company to which *The Small Companies and Groups (Accounts and Directors' Report) Regulations 2008* (SI 2008/409) amended by *The Small Companies (Micro-Entities' Accounts) Regulations 2013* (SI 2013/3008) and *The Companies, Partnerships and Groups (Accounts and Reports) Regulations 2015* (SI 2015/980) apply.

A3.2　*The Small Companies (Micro-Entities' Accounts) Regulations 2013* were made in November 2013 and apply to the financial statements of micro-entities for accounting periods ending on or after 30 September 2013 for companies filing their accounts on or after 1 December 2013.

A3.3　The definition of a micro-entity is contained in sections 384A and 384B of the Companies Act 2006 (Act). The qualifying conditions are met by a company in a year in which it does not exceed two or more of the following criteria:

(a) Turnover	£632,000
(b) Balance sheet total	£316,000
(c) Number of employees	10

A3.4　For any company, other than a newly incorporated company, to qualify as a micro-entity, the qualifying conditions must be met for two consecutive years. A company will cease to qualify as a micro-entity if it fails to meet the qualifying conditions for two consecutive years. However, if a company which qualified as a micro-entity in one period no longer meets the criteria for a micro-entity in the next period, the company may continue to claim the exemptions available in the next period. If that company then reverts back to being a micro-entity by meeting the criteria, the exemptions will continue uninterrupted.

A3.5　Certain companies are excluded by section 384B of the Act from being treated as micro-entities, including those excluded from the small companies regime for reasons of public interest (as set out in section 384), certain financial institutions, charities, those voluntarily preparing group accounts and those included in group accounts. The Act should be referred to for a full list of excluded companies.

A3.6　Entities that are not companies, such as limited liability partnerships (LLPs), do not meet the definition of a micro-entity.

APPLICABLE ACCOUNTING FRAMEWORK

A3.7　Accounts prepared in accordance with FRS 105 are classified as 'Companies Act individual accounts' for the purposes of section 395 of the Act and are therefore required to comply with the applicable provisions of Parts 15 and 16 of the Act and with the Regulations referred to in paragraph A3.1.

FAIR VALUE AT INITIAL RECOGNITION

The Small Companies (Micro-Entities'Accounts) Regulations 2013 state that micro-entities are not permitted to apply the Alternative Accounting Rules or the Fair Value Rules as set out in company law. Therefore micro-entities are only permitted to apply the Historical Cost Accounting Rules. **A3.8**

FRS 105 states that certain types of assets and liabilities must be measured at fair value at initial recognition, for example inventories acquired through a non-exchange transaction. This does not breach the prohibition against fair value accounting as the use of a fair value is a method of estimating cost at initial recognition. **A3.9**

TRUE AND FAIR VIEW

FRS 105 is an accounting standard and all accounting standards issued by the Financial Reporting Council are applicable to the preparation of financial statements that are intended to give a true and fair view. Financial statements of a micro-entity that include the minimum accounting items specified by *The Small Companies (Micro-Entities'Accounts) Regulations 2013* are presumed in law to give a true and fair view. **A3.10**

DISTRIBUTABLE PROFITS

The determination of profits available for distribution is a complex area where accounting and company law interface. In determining profits available for distribution any entity may refer to Technical Release 02/10 *Guidance on realised and distributable profits under the Companies Act 2006* issued by the Institute of Chartered Accountants in England and Wales and the Institute of Chartered Accountants of Scotland, or any successor document, to determine profits available for distribution. **A3.11**

Appendix IV
Republic of Ireland (RoI) legal references

A4.1 At the time of issuing FRS 105, the micro-entities legislation is not available for application in the Republic of Ireland. However, the Irish Department of Jobs, Enterprise and Innovation has consulted on the possible enactment of this legislation in its *Consultation on the transposition of the EU Accounting Directive 2013/34/EU.*

A4.2 If legislation giving effect to the micro-entities option is enacted in Ireland, FRS 105 will be available for application in line with the effective date of the relevant legislation and will be updated to include Republic of Ireland legal references.

Amendments to FRS 105: The Financial Reporting Standard applicable to the Micro-entities Regime – Limited Liability Partnerships and Qualifying Partnerships

May 2016

Contents

Editor's note: The FRC issued amendments to FRS 105 to bring limited liability partnerships and qualifying partnerships within the scope of the micro-entities regime. These amendments are applicable for accounting periods beginning on or after 1 January 2016, with early application permitted from 1 January 2015 if the new legislation *The Limited Liability Partnerships, Partnerships and Groups (Accounts and Audit) Regulations* 2016 are also applied from that date.

SUMMARY

With effect from 1 January 2015 the Financial Reporting Council (FRC) revised financial   (i)
reporting standards in the United Kingdom and Republic of Ireland. The revisions
fundamentally reformed financial reporting, replacing the extant standards with five
Financial Reporting Standards:

(a)   FRS 100 *Application of Financial Reporting Requirements*;
(b)   FRS 101 *Reduced Disclosure Framework*;
(c)   FRS 102 *The Financial Reporting Standard applicable in the UK and Republic of Ireland*;
(d)   FRS 103 *Insurance Contracts*; and
(e)   FRS 104 *Interim Financial Reporting*.

The FRC has also issued FRS 105 *The Financial Reporting Standard applicable to the Micro-entities Regime* to support the implementation of the new micro-entities regime. It
is effective from 1 January 2016 with early application permitted.

These limited amendments to FRS 105 extend its scope to include eligible limited liability
partnerships (LLPs) and qualifying partnerships, following a change in legislation. For
LLPs and qualifying partnerships early application is permitted only for accounting
periods beginning on or after 1 January 2015.

The FRC's overriding objective in setting accounting standards is to enable users of   (ii)
accounts to receive high-quality understandable financial reporting proportionate to the
size and complexity of the entity and users' information needs.

In meeting this objective, the FRC aims to provide succinct financial reporting standards   (iii)
that:

(a)   have consistency with international accounting standards through the application
      of an IFRS-based solution unless an alternative clearly better meets the overriding
      objective;
(b)   reflect up-to-date thinking and developments in the way entities operate and the
      transactions they undertake;
(c)   balance consistent principles for accounting by all UK and Republic of Ireland
      entities with practical solutions, based on size, complexity, public interest and users'
      information needs;
(d)   promote efficiency within groups; and
(e)   are cost-effective to apply.

Amendments to FRS 105 – Limited Liability Partnerships and Qualifying Partnerships

In November 2013 the Government introduced an optional new reporting framework   (iv)
for companies that meet the qualifying criteria of a micro-entity. In response the FRC
developed FRS 105 which may be used by eligible companies.

These amendments to FRS 105 extend its scope to include eligible LLPs and qualifying   (v)
partnerships following a change in legislation. The use of the micro-entities regime
remains optional.

These amendments are applicable to accounting periods beginning on or after   (vi)
1 January 2016. Early application is permitted for accounting periods beginning on or
after 1 January 2015.

AMENDMENTS TO FRS 105 *THE FINANCIAL REPORTING STANDARD APPLICABLE TO THE MICRO-ENTITIES REGIME*

Amendments to Section 1 Scope

1　The following paragraph sets out the amendments to Section 1 *Scope* (inserted text is underlined).

2　Paragraph 1.5 is inserted as follows:

1.5 In May 2016 amendments were made to this FRS to extend its scope to include **limited liability partnerships (LLPs)** and **qualifying partnerships** following a change in legislation. An LLP or a qualifying partnership which qualifies as a micro-entity and is applying the micro-entities regime shall apply this FRS for accounting periods beginning on or after 1 January 2016. Early application by a micro-entity that is an LLP or a qualifying partnership is:

(a)　permitted for accounting periods beginning on or after 1 January 2015 provided that *The Limited Liability Partnerships, Partnerships and Groups (Accounts and Audit) Regulations 2016* (SI 2016/575) are applied from the same date; and

(b)　required if the LLP or qualifying partnership applies *The Limited Liability Partnerships, Partnerships and Groups (Accounts and Audit) Regulations 2016* (SI 2016/575) to a reporting period beginning before 1 January 2016.

Amendments to Section 3 Financial Statement Presentation

3　The following paragraph sets out the amendments to Section 3 *Financial Statement Presentation* (inserted text is underlined).

4　A new footnote (to be sequentially numbered) is inserted after the word 'Act' in paragraph 3.14 (subsequent footnotes are renumbered sequentially) as follows:

footnote Or, when relevant, Regulation 12 of the *Limited Liability Partnerships (Accounts and Audit) (Application of Companies Act 2006) Regulations 2008* (SI 2008/1911).

Amendments to Section 4 Statement of Financial Position

5　The following paragraph sets out the amendments to Section 4 *Statement of Financial Position* (deleted text is struck through, inserted text is underlined).

6　Paragraph 4.3 is amended and a new footnote (to be sequentially numbered) is inserted (subsequent footnotes are renumbered sequentially) as follows:

4.3 A micro-entity shall present a statement of financial position in accordance with one of the formats set out in Section C of Part 1 of Schedule 1 to the **Small Companies Regulations** or Section C of Part 1 of Schedule 1 to the **Small LLP Regulations**footnote, as followsillustrated below:

Format 1	**CU**	**CU**
Called up share capital not paid		X
Fixed assets		X
Current assets	X	
Prepayments and accrued income	X	
Creditors: amounts falling due within one year	(X)	
Net current assets / (liabilities)		X/(X)
Total assets less current liabilities		X

Format 1   CU   CU
Creditors: amounts falling due after more than one year   (X)
Provisions for liabilities   (X)
Accruals and deferred income   (X)
                                                                               ‾X‾

Capital and reserves   X

Format 2   CU   CU
Assets
Called up share capital not paid   X
Fixed assets   X
Current assets   X
Prepayments and accrued income   X
                                                                               ‾X‾

Capital, Reserves and Liabilities
Capital and reserves   X
Provisions for liabilities   X
Creditors
Amounts falling due within one year   X
Amounts falling due after one year   X
                                                                               X
Accruals and deferred income   X
                                                                               ‾X‾

footnote LLPs shall describe the items as set out in the Small LLP Regulations. In particular, 'Called up share capital not paid' shall not be used and 'Loans and other debts due to members' and 'Members' other interests' shall be used instead of 'Capital and reserves'.

Amendments to Section 5 Income Statement

The following paragraph sets out the amendments to Section 5 *Income Statement* (deleted   **7**
text is struck through, inserted text is underlined).

Paragraph 5.3 is amended and a new footnote (to be sequentially numbered) is inserted   **8**
(subsequent footnotes are renumbered sequentially) as follows:

5.3 A micro-entity shall present its profit or loss for a period in an income statement in accordance with Section C of Part 1 of Schedule 1 to the **Small Companies Regulations** or Section C of Part 1 of Schedule 1 to the **Small LLP Regulations**, as ~~follows~~illustrated below:

                                                                               CU
Turnover   X
Other income   X
Cost of raw materials and consumables   (X)
Staff costs   (X)
Depreciation and other amounts written off assets   (X)
Other charges   (X)
Tax   (X)
Profit or loss footnote   X / (X)

footnote LLPs shall describe this item as 'Profit or loss for the financial year before members' remuneration and profit shares'.

Amendments to Section 6 Notes to the Financial Statements

9   The following paragraphs set out the amendments to Section 6 *Notes to the Financial Statements* (deleted text is struck through, inserted text is underlined).

10   Paragraph 6.3 is inserted as follows:

6.3 In accordance with Regulation 30 of the *Limited Liability Partnerships (Accounts and Audit) (Application of Companies Act 2006) Regulations 2008* (SI 2008/1911), the notes to the financial statements of an **LLP** which qualifies as a micro-entity shall be presented at the foot of the statement of financial position and shall include financial commitments, guarantees and contingencies as required by paragraph 55 of Part 3 of Schedule 1 to the **Small LLPs Regulations** (see paragraphs 6A.2 and 6A.3 in the Appendix to this Section).

11   Paragraphs 6A.2 and 6A.3 are amended as follows:

6A.2 *The total amount of any financial commitments, guarantees and contingencies that are not included in the statement of financial position must be stated. (Schedule 1, paragraph 57(1) of Schedule 1 to the Small Companies Regulations or paragraph 55(1) of Schedule 1 to the Small LLPs Regulations)*

The total amount of any commitments concerning pensions must be separately disclosed. (Schedule 1, paragraph 57(3) of Schedule 1 to the Small Companies Regulations or paragraph 55(3) of Schedule 1 to the Small LLPs Regulations)

The total amount of any commitments which are undertaken on behalf of or for the benefit of:

(a)   *any parent, fellow subsidiary or any subsidiary of a micro-entity; or*

(b)   *any undertaking in which a micro-entity has a participating interest,*

must be separately stated and those within (a) must also be stated separately from those within (b). (Schedule 1, paragraph 57(4) of Schedule 1 to the Small Companies Regulations or paragraph 55(4) of Schedule 1 to the Small LLPs Regulations)

The following paragraphs …

6A.3 *An indication of the nature and form of any valuable security given by the micro-entity in respect of commitments, guarantees and contingencies within paragraph 6A.2 must be given. (Schedule 1, paragraph 57(2) of Schedule 1 to the Small Companies Regulations or paragraph 55(2) of Schedule 1 to the Small LLPs Regulations)*

The following paragraphs …

Amendments to Section 7 Subsidiaries, Associates, Jointly Controlled Entities and Intermediate Payment Arrangements

12   The following paragraph sets out the amendment to Section 7 *Subsidiaries, Associates, Jointly Controlled Entities and Intermediate Payment Arrangements* (inserted text is underlined).

13   A new footnote (to be sequentially numbered) is inserted after the word 'Act' in paragraph 7.3 (subsequent footnotes are renumbered sequentially) as follows:

footnote Or, when relevant, Regulation 5A of the *Limited Liability Partnerships (Accounts and Audit) (Application of Companies Act 2006) Regulations 2008* (SI 2008/1911).

Amendments to Section 22 Impairment of Assets

The following paragraph sets out the amendments to Section 22 *Impairment of Assets*.   14

Footnote 1 in paragraph 22.19 is deleted (subsequent footnotes are renumbered   15
sequentially).

Amendments to Appendix I: Glossary

The following paragraphs set out the amendments to Appendix I: *Glossary* (deleted text is   16
struck through, inserted text is underlined).

The following glossary terms and definitions are inserted in alphabetical order: 17

limited liability partnership (LLP)	A limited liability partnership formed under the Limited Liability Partnerships Act 2000 or the Limited Liability Partnerships Act (Northern Ireland) 2002.
qualifying partnership	A partnership meeting the definition of a qualifying partnership as set out in the Partnerships (Accounts) Regulations 2008 (SI 2008/569).
Small LLP Regulations	The Small Limited Liability Partnership (Accounts) Regulations 2008 (SI 2008/1912)

The following glossary terms and definitions are amended as follows: 18

micro-entity	~~Is an entity that meets all of the following conditions:~~
	~~(a) it is a company established under company law;~~
	~~(b) it qualifies as a micro-entity in accordance with section 384A of the Act; and~~
	~~(c) it is not excluded from being treated as a micro-entity under section 384B of the Act.~~
	~~Micro-entities are a subset of small companies as defined in the Act.~~
	(a) A company meeting the definition of a micro-entity as set out in section 384A of the **Act**, and not prevented from applying the micro-entity provisions by section 384B of the Act;
	(b) an **LLP** which qualifies as a micro-entity and is not prevented from applying the micro-entity provisions in accordance with Regulation 5A of the *Limited Liability Partnerships (Accounts and Audit) (Application of Companies Act 2006) Regulations 2008* (SI 2008/1911); or
	(c) a **qualifying partnership** that would meet the definition of a micro-entity as set out in section 384A of the Act, and not be prevented from applying the micro-entity provisions by section 384B of the Act, if the partnership were a company.

micro-entity provisions	~~Means a~~(a) Any provisions of Part 15, Part 16 or regulations <u>made</u> under Part 15 of the **Act**<u>; or</u> <u>(b) any provisions of the **Small LLP Regulations**,</u> relating specifically to the individual accounts of an entity which qualifies as a **micro-entity**.
micro-entities regime	The legal requirements and exemptions relating to the preparation of the **financial statements** of **micro-entities** as set out in the **Act**<u>, the</u> ~~and~~ **Small Companies Regulations** <u>and the **Small LLP Regulations**</u>.

Amendments to Appendix III: Note on legal requirements

19   The following paragraphs set out the amendments to Appendix III: *Note on legal requirements* (deleted text is struck through, inserted text is underlined).

20   Paragraph A3.1 is amended as follows:

A3.1 This appendix provides an overview of how the requirements of FRS 105 address UK company law requirements. It is therefore written from the perspective of a company to which *The Small Companies and Groups (Accounts and Directors' Report) Regulations 2008* (SI 2008/409) amended by *The Small Companies (Micro-Entities' Accounts) Regulations 2013* (SI 2013/3008) and *The Companies, Partnerships and Groups (Accounts and Reports) Regulations 2015* (SI 2015/980) apply. <u>The same provisions generally apply to limited liability partnerships (LLPs) and qualifying partnerships following amendments to legislation made in *The Limited Liability Partnerships, Partnerships and Groups (Accounts and Audit) Regulations 2016* (SI 2016/575) (see paragraph A3.6).</u>

21   Paragraph A3.6 is amended as follows:

A3.6 <u>*The Limited Liability Partnerships, Partnerships and Groups (Accounts and Audit) Regulations 2016* (SI 2016/575) were made in May 2016 and extend the micro-entities regime to LLPs and qualifying partnerships for accounting periods beginning on or after 1 January 2016 with early application permitted for accounting periods beginning on or after 1 January 2015. LLPs and qualifying partnerships are eligible to apply the micro-entities regime, provided they meet the relevant conditions, which mirror the requirements of sections 384A and 384B of the Act for companies.</u> Entities that are not companies, ~~such as limited liability partnerships (LLPs)~~, <u>or qualifying partnerships</u> do not meet the definition of a micro-entity.

APPROVAL BY THE FRC

Amendments to *FRS 105 The Financial Reporting Standard applicable to the Micro-entities Regime – Limited Liability Partnerships and Qualifying Partnerships* was approved by the Board of the Financial Reporting Council for issue on 17 May 2016, following its consideration of the Corporate Reporting Council's Advice.

THE CORPORATE REPORTING COUNCIL'S ADVICE TO THE FRC TO ISSUE *AMENDMENTS TO FRS 105 – LIMITED LIABILITY PARTNERSHIPS AND QUALIFYING PARTNERSHIPS*

Introduction

1   This report provides an overview of the main issues that have been considered by the Corporate Reporting Council in advising the Financial Reporting Council (FRC) to issue *Amendments to FRS 105 The Financial Reporting Standard applicable to the Micro-entities Regime – Limited Liability Partnerships and Qualifying Partnerships*.

2   The FRC, in accordance with the *Statutory Auditors (Amendment of Companies Act 2006 and Delegation of Functions etc) Order 2012* (SI 2012/1741), is a prescribed body for issuing accounting standards in the UK. The *Foreword to Accounting Standards* sets out the application of accounting standards in the Republic of Ireland.

3   In accordance with the *FRC Codes and Standards: procedures*, any proposal to issue, amend or withdraw a code or standard is put to the FRC Board with the full advice of the relevant Councils and/or the Codes & Standards Committee. Ordinarily, the FRC Board will only reject the advice put to it where:

(a)   it is apparent that a significant group of stakeholders has not been adequately consulted;

(b)   the necessary assessment of the impact of the proposal has not been completed, including an analysis of costs and benefits;

(c)   insufficient consideration has been given to the timing or cost of implementation; or

(d)   the cumulative impact of a number of proposals would make the adoption of an otherwise satisfactory proposal inappropriate.

4   The FRC has established the Corporate Reporting Council as the relevant Council to assist it in the setting of accounting standards.

Advice

5   The Corporate Reporting Council is advising the FRC to issue *Amendments to FRS 105 The Financial Reporting Standard applicable to the Micro-entities Regime – Limited Liability Partnerships and Qualifying Partnerships*.

6   The amendments update FRS 105 *The Financial Reporting Standard applicable to the Micro-entities Regime* in line with changes in UK legislation which have extended the micro-entities regime to limited liability partnerships (LLPs) and qualifying partnerships.

7   The Accounting Council's Advice[1] to the FRC to issue FRS 105 *The Financial Reporting Standard applicable to the Micro-entities Regime* was set out in that standard. The Corporate Reporting Council's Advice to the FRC in respect of these amendments will be included in the revised FRS 105.

Background

8   When FRS 105 was issued, UK company law restricted the availability of the new micro-entities regime to eligible companies. FRS 105 reflected this legal restriction. In May 2016 Regulations were made which extended the micro-entities regime to LLPs and qualifying partnerships.

---

[1] *From 1 April 2016 the Accounting Council was renamed as the Corporate Reporting Council.*

In accordance with the FRC's *Framework for developing Standards, Statements of*   **9**
Practice, Codes and Guidance, these amendments have been assessed as not requiring a
formal consultation. FRS 105 was developed to support the existing micro-entities regime
for companies, which as a result of a change in legislation has been extended to LLPs and
qualifying partnerships, and these amendments simply extend the scope of FRS 105 (with
some consequential amendments) consistently with the change in legislation.

Amendments to FRS 105

In developing its advice to the FRC, the Corporate Reporting Council was guided by the   **10**
overriding objective to enable users of accounts to receive high-quality understandable
financial reporting proportionate to the size and complexity of the entity and users'
information needs.

In meeting this objective, the FRC aims to provide succinct financial reporting standards   **11**
that:

(a)   have consistency with international accounting standards through the application
      of an IFRS-based solution unless an alternative clearly better meets the overriding
      objective;
(b)   reflect up-to-date thinking and developments in the way entities operate and the
      transactions they undertake;
(c)   balance consistent principles for accounting by all UK and Republic of Ireland
      entities with practical solutions, based on size, complexity, public interest and users'
      information needs;
(d)   promote efficiency within groups; and
(e)   are cost-effective to apply.

The Corporate Reporting Council advises that, as the micro-entities regime is now available   **12**
to LLPs and qualifying partnerships, FRS 105 should be updated to reflect the extent to
which the micro-entities regime is available in law. In order to achieve this the definition
of a micro-entity and other related glossary terms have been updated.

The presentation and disclosure requirements applicable to the financial statements of   **13**
LLPs and qualifying partnerships that adopt the micro-entities regime are almost identical
to those applicable to the financial statements of companies that are micro-entities. Where
there are differences these have been reflected in the amendments to FRS 105.

The Corporate Reporting Council advises that the current recognition and measurement   **14**
requirements of FRS 105 are also suitable for LLPs and qualifying partnerships applying
the micro-entities regime and therefore no amendments have been made to the recognition
and measurement requirements of FRS 105.

Effective date

The Corporate Reporting Council advises that in line with the effective date of the changes   **15**
in legislation, the amendments to FRS 105 should be effective for accounting periods
beginning on or after 1 January 2016 with early adoption permitted for accounting periods
beginning on or after 1 January 2015.

Approval of this Advice

This advice to the FRC was approved by the Corporate Reporting Council on 14 April 2016.   **16**

Financial Reporting Standard for Smaller Entities (effective January 2015)

(July 2013)

Contents

Editor's note: Amendments to the FRSSE – Micro-entities (April 2014) has amended this document.

Editor's note: This FRSSE (effective January 2015) superseded FRSSE (effective April 2008) with effect for reporting periods beginning on or after 1 January 2015, although early adoption is permitted. This FRSSE is however withdrawn for periods beginning on or after 1 January 2016.

STATUS OF THE FRSSE

General

1   The Financial Reporting Standard for Smaller Entities (effective January 2015) (the FRSSE) prescribes the basis, for those entities within its scope that have chosen to adopt it, for preparing and presenting their financial statements. The definitions and accounting treatments are consistent with the requirements of companies legislation.

2   Reporting entities that apply the FRSSE, together with FRS 100 *Application of Financial Reporting Requirements*, are exempt from complying with other Financial Reporting Standards (FRSs).

3   For the convenience of companies using the FRSSE, the requirements of company law in the United Kingdom on full financial statements have been reflected in this standard. THESE ARE SHOWN IN SMALL CAPITALS TO DISTINGUISH THEM FROM THE REQUIREMENTS OF THE FRSSE[1]. The legal requirements set out in the FRSSE are intended to reflect company law, including the Companies Act 2006 and amendments and Regulations issued thereunder which are effective from 6 April 2008. This does not affect directors' responsibilities regarding compliance with company law and in all matters regarding interpretation of the legal requirements reference should be to the relevant legislation.

4   The significant differences between this version of the FRSSE (effective January 2015) and the FRSSE (effective April 2008) are in respect of the revised reporting framework introduced into the UK effective January 2015. As part of the revised reporting framework, the FRC has withdrawn extant Financial Reporting Standards and Urgent Issues Task Force (UITF) Abstracts. It has made consequential amendments to the FRSSE where it previously referred to standards or Abstracts that are now withdrawn.

5   Financial statements will generally be prepared using accepted practice and, accordingly, for transactions or events not dealt with in the FRSSE, smaller entities should first have regard to their own existing accounting policies. Where an entity applying the FRSSE undertakes a new transaction not dealt with in the FRSSE for which it has no existing policy, in developing a new policy it should have regard to FRS 102 *The Financial Reporting Standard applicable in the UK and Republic of Ireland*, not as a mandatory document, but as a means of establishing current practice.

5A   Public benefit entities (PBEs), only, shall have regard to the requirements in FRS 102 that are specific to PBEs not as mandatory requirements, but as a means of establishing current practice.

---

[1] *The detail of the requirements in company law in the Republic of Ireland in many cases differs from the UK requirements reflected in the FRSSE. Tables showing the source of legislative requirements in British law and the equivalent sources in Northern Ireland and the Republic of Ireland are available on the FRC website (frc.org. uk/Our-Work/Codes-Standards/Accounting-and-Reporting-Policy/FRSSE.aspx). In addition, there are a number of Republic of Ireland legal requirements that are not reflected in the FRSSE. There is no equivalent to SI 2008/409 The Small Companies and Groups (Accounts and Directors' Report) Regulations 2008 providing certain exemptions for small companies when preparing annual accounts for shareholders. Exemptions from company law requirements for small companies in the Republic of Ireland are therefore limited and relate primarily to information that must be filed with the Companies Registration Office. This does not affect directors' responsibilities regarding compliance with company law and in all matters regarding interpretation of the legal requirements in the Republic of Ireland reference should be to the relevant legislation.*

Criteria

When considering the application of accounting standards, including FRS 102 *The* **6**
Financial Reporting Standard applicable in the UK and Republic of Ireland, to smaller
entities, the FRC has had, and will continue to have, regard to the following criteria:[2]

(a)   The standard or requirement is likely to be regarded as having general application
      and as an essential element of generally accepted accounting practice for all entities.
(b)   The standard or requirement is likely to lead to a transaction being treated in a way
      that would be readily recognised by the proprietor or manager of the business as
      corresponding to his or her understanding of the transaction.
(c)   The standard or requirement is likely to meet the information needs and legitimate
      expectations of a user of a small entity's accounts.
(d)   The standard or requirement results in disclosures that are likely to be meaningful
      and comprehensive to such a user. Where disclosures are aimed at a particular group
      of users, that group would be likely to receive the information, given that they may
      have access only to abbreviated accounts.
(e)   The requirements of the standard significantly augment the treatment prescribed by
      legislation.
(f)   The treatment prescribed by the standard or requirement is compatible with that
      already used, or expected to be used, by the Inland Revenue in computing taxable
      profits.
(g)   The standard or requirement provides the least cumbersome method of achieving the
      desired accounting treatment and/or disclosure for an entity that is not complex.
(h)   The standard provides guidance that is expected to be widely relevant to the
      transactions of small entities and is written in terms that can be understood by such
      businesses.
(i)   The measurement methods prescribed in the standard are likely to be reasonably
      practical for small entities.

The satisfaction of a majority of the above criteria would suggest that the standard or **7**
requirement under consideration may also be appropriate for application to smaller entities,
whereas failure to satisfy a majority of the above criteria would suggest that exemption, or
differing treatment, from the standard, or a specific requirement within that standard, may
be more appropriate.

Scope

The FRSSE may be applied to all financial statements intended to give a true and fair view **8**
of the financial position and profit or loss (or income and expenditure) of all entities[3] that
are:

(a)   small companies or small groups as defined in companies legislation[4] preparing
      Companies Act individual or group accounts; or
(b)   entities that would also qualify under (a) if they had been incorporated under
      companies legislation, with the exception of building societies.

---

[2] *Legal advice has been obtained that in accounting standards smaller entities may properly be allowed exemptions
or differing treatments provided that there are rational grounds for doing so: see Appendix I.*

[3] *Some older accounting standards are drafted in terms of application to companies. References to companies and
associated terms, such as board of directors and shareholders, in the FRSSE should therefore be taken to apply also
to unincorporated entities.*

[4] *The legal definitions of small companies and small groups in the UK are set out in Appendix I. In the Republic of
Ireland the FRSSE can be applied to those companies meeting the criteria as set out in companies legislation that
allow them to be treated as 'small' for the purposes of filing information with the Companies Registration Office.*

9   Accordingly, the FRSSE does not apply to:

(a)   large or medium-sized companies, groups and other entities;

(b)   public companies;

(c)   companies preparing individual or group accounts in accordance with international accounting standards;

(d)   companies preparing individual or group accounts in accordance with the fair value accounting rules for certain assets and liabilities set out in Section D of Schedule 1 of Regulation 2008/409 to the Companies Act 2006[5];

(e)   a company that is an authorised insurance company, a banking company, an emoney issuer, an MifId investment firm[6] or a UCITS management company or a company that carries on insurance market activity;

(f)   a person (other than a small company) who has permission under Part 4 of the Financial Services and Markets Act 2000 (in the UK) to carry on a regulated activity or, notwithstanding the definition of a small company in the legislation, companies authorised under the Investment Intermediaries Act 1995 (in the Republic of Ireland); or

(g)   members of an ineligible group. A group is ineligible if any of its members is:

(i)   A public company;

(ii)   A body corporate (other than a company) whose shares are admitted to trading on a regulated market in an EEA State;

(iii)   A person (other than a small company) who has permission under Part 4 of the Financial Services and Markets Act 2000 to carry on a regulated activity;

(iv)   A small company that is an authorised insurance company, a banking company, an e-money issuer, a MifId investment firm or a UCITS management company; or

(v)   A person who carries on insurance market activity.

10   Reporting entities that are entitled to adopt the FRSSE, but choose not to do so, are required to apply EU-adopted IFRS, FRS 101 *Reduced Disclosure Framework* (in the individual financial statements of qualifying entities) or FRS 102 *The Financial Reporting Standard applicable in the UK and Republic of* Ireland, in accordance with the requirements of FRS 100 *Application of Financial Reporting Requirements,* when preparing financial statements intended to give a true and fair view of the assets, liabilities, financial position and profit or loss of the entity[7].

Statements of Recommended Practice

11   Statements of Recommended Practice (SORPs) and other equivalent guidance may specify the circumstances, if any, in which entities in the industry or sector addressed in the SORP or equivalent guidance may adopt the current version of the FRSSE.

12   Where SORPs are drafted on the basis of the requirements of FRS 102 *The Financial Reporting Standard applicable in the UK and Republic of Ireland,* financial statements cannot be said to comply with those SORPs if they are prepared in accordance with the FRSSE.

---

[5] *Companies accounting for fixed assets and investments at valuation are not precluded from using the FRSSE.*

[6] *The Markets in Financial Instruments Directive (Consequential Amendments) Regulations 2007 (SI 2007/2932) substituted the term 'MifId investment firm' for 'ISD investment firm'.*

[7] *Under company law in the Republic of Ireland, certain companies are permitted to prepare Companies Act accounts using a financial reporting framework based on accounting standards other than those issued by the FRC.*

FINANCIAL REPORTING STANDARD FOR SMALLER ENTITIES (EFFECTIVE JANUARY 2015)

A OBJECTIVE

The objective of the FRSSE is to ensure that reporting entities falling within its scope **1** provide in their financial statements information about the financial position, performance and financial adaptability of the entity that is useful to users in assessing the stewardship of management and for making economic decisions, recognising that the balance between users' needs in respect of stewardship and economic decision-making for smaller entities is different from that for other reporting entities.

B STATEMENT OF STANDARD ACCOUNTING PRACTICE

1 Scope

The FRSSE may be applied to all financial statements intended to give a true and fair view **1.1** of the financial position and profit or loss (or income and expenditure) of all entities that are:

(a) companies incorporated under **companies legislation**[8] and entitled to the exemptions available in the legislation for small companies when filing accounts with the Registrar of Companies;[9] or

(b) entities that would have come into category (a) above had they been companies incorporated under **companies legislation,** excluding building societies. While not bound by the requirements of **companies legislation** reflected in the FRSSE (set out in SMALL CAPITALS), such entities shall have regard to the **accounting principles,** presentation and disclosure requirements in **companies legislation** (or other equivalent legislation) that, taking into account the FRSSE, are necessary to present a true and fair view.

A **micro-entity** preparing its financial statements in accordance with section 393(1A) of **1.2** the **Act**:

(a) shall disregard all presentation and disclosure requirements of the FRSSE (including those relating to the formats for the balance sheet and profit and loss account), except those set out in paragraphs 2.40 to 2.42, which are only applicable to **micro-entities**. However, where a **micro-entity** chooses to provide AN ITEM OF INFORMATION ADDITIONAL TO THE **MICRO-ENTITY MINIMUM ACCOUNTING ITEMS,** IT SHALL HAVE REGARD TO the requirements of the FRSSE RELATING TO THAT ITEM;

(b) shall not choose to adopt an accounting policy of revaluation in respect of **tangible fixed assets**, which would otherwise be permitted by paragraph 6.23;

(c) shall not choose to measure fixed asset investments at a market value, which would otherwise be permitted by paragraph 6.30;

(d) shall account for any **investment properties** in accordance with paragraphs 6.19 to 6.22 rather than paragraphs 6.50 to 6.53;

(e) shall not choose to measure current asset investments at current cost in accordance with paragraph 8.13.

---

[8] *Terms appearing in* **bold** *in the text are explained in the Definitions set out in Part C.*

[9] *The legal definitions of small companies and small groups in the UK are set out in Appendix I. In the Republic of Ireland the FRSSE can be applied to those companies meeting the criteria as set out in companies legislation that allow them to be treated as 'small' for the purposes of filing information with the Companies Registration Office.*

If this results in a change in **accounting policy**, for example because fixed assets that were previously revalued are now accounted for at cost less **depreciation** and impairment, that change shall be accounted for in accordance with paragraph 2.10 by restating the amounts for the current and corresponding periods on the basis of the new policy.

Editor's note: Amendments to the FRSSE – Micro-entities (April 2014) has added this paragraph 1.2.

2   General

Requirement to prepare financial statements

2.1   THE **DIRECTORS** MUST PREPARE FOR EACH **FINANCIAL YEAR** OF THE COMPANY[10] –

(A)   A BALANCE SHEET AS AT THE LAST DAY OF THE **FINANCIAL YEAR**; AND

(B)   A PROFIT AND LOSS ACCOUNT.

True and fair view

2.2   THE BALANCE SHEET MUST GIVE A TRUE AND FAIR VIEW OF THE STATE OF AFFAIRS OF THE COMPANY AS AT THE END OF THE **FINANCIAL YEAR**; AND THE PROFIT AND LOSS ACCOUNT MUST GIVE A TRUE AND FAIR VIEW OF THE PROFIT OR LOSS OF THE COMPANY FOR THE **FINANCIAL YEAR**. THE DIRECTORS OF A COMPANY MUST, IN DETERMINING HOW AMOUNTS ARE PRESENTED WITHIN ITEMS IN THE PROFIT AND LOSS ACCOUNT AND BALANCE SHEET, HAVE REGARD TO THE SUBSTANCE OF THE REPORTED TRANSACTION OR ARRANGEMENT, IN ACCORDANCE WITH GENERALLY ACCEPTED ACCOUNTING PRINCIPLES OR PRACTICE. To determine the substance of a transaction it is necessary to identify whether the transaction has given rise to new **assets** or **liabilities** for the reporting entity and whether it has changed the entity's existing **assets** or **liabilities**.

2.2A   For a **micro-entity** preparing its financial statements in accordance with section 393(1A) of the **Act** that COMPRISE ONLY **MICRO-ENTITY MINIMUM ACCOUNTING ITEMS**:

(A)   THE **MICRO-ENTITY MINIMUM ACCOUNTING ITEMS** ARE PRESUMED TO GIVE A TRUE AND FAIR VIEW; AND

(b)   paragraphs 2.3 to 2.5 and 2.18 do not apply.

Editor's note: Amendments to the FRSSE – Micro-entities (April 2014) has added this paragraph 2.2A.

2.3   IF IN SPECIAL CIRCUMSTANCES COMPLIANCE WITH ANY OF THE PROVISIONS OF THE FRSSE OR COMPANIES ACT IS INCONSISTENT WITH THE REQUIREMENT TO GIVE A TRUE AND FAIR VIEW, THE **DIRECTORS** MUST DEPART FROM THAT PROVISION TO THE EXTENT NECESSARY TO GIVE A TRUE AND FAIR VIEW. PARTICULARS OF THE DEPARTURE, THE REASONS FOR IT AND ITS EFFECT MUST BE GIVEN IN A NOTE TO THE ACCOUNTS as follows:

(a)   a statement that there has been a departure from the requirements of the FRSSE or Companies Act and that the departure is necessary to give a true and fair view;

(b)   a statement of the treatment that the FRSSE or Companies Act would normally require and a description of the treatment adopted;

(c)   a statement of the reasons why the treatment prescribed would not give a true and fair view; and

(d)   a description of how the position shown in the financial statements is different as a result of the departure, normally with quantification, except where:

(i)   quantification is already evident in the financial statements themselves; or

(ii)   the effect cannot be reasonably quantified, in which case the **directors** shall explain the circumstances.

---

[10] Text appearing in SMALL CAPITALS refers to UK company legislation requirements.

Where a departure continues in subsequent financial statements, the disclosures shall be made in all subsequent statements and shall include comparative amounts for the previous period. Where a departure affects only the comparative amounts, the disclosures shall be given for those comparative amounts. **2.4**

Where there is doubt whether applying provisions of the FRSSE would be sufficient to give a true and fair view, adequate explanation shall be given in the notes to the accounts of the transaction or arrangement concerned and the treatment adopted. **2.5**

Accounting principles and policies

The financial statements shall state that they have been prepared in accordance with the Financial Reporting Standard for Smaller Entities (effective January 2015)[11]. **2.6**

Financial statements shall include: **2.7**

(a)   a description of each material **accounting policy** followed;
(b)   details of any changes to the **accounting policies** followed in the preceding period including, in addition to the disclosures necessary for **prior period adjustments**, a brief explanation of why each new **accounting policy** is thought more appropriate and, where practicable, an indication of the effect of the change on the results for the current period; and
(c)   where the effect of a change to an **estimation technique** is material, a description of the change and, where practicable, the effect on the results for the current period.

THE **ACCOUNTING POLICIES** ADOPTED BY THE COMPANY IN DETERMINING THE AMOUNTS TO BE INCLUDED IN RESPECT OF ITEMS SHOWN IN THE BALANCE SHEET AND IN DETERMINING THE PROFIT OR LOSS OF THE COMPANY MUST BE STATED (INCLUDING SUCH POLICIES WITH RESPECT TO THE **DEPRECIATION** AND DIMINUTION IN VALUE OF ASSETS). **2.8**

Accounting policies and **estimation techniques** shall be consistent with the requirements of the FRSSE and of **companies legislation** (or other equivalent legislation). Where this permits a choice, an entity shall select the policies and techniques most appropriate to its particular circumstances for the purpose of giving a true and fair view, taking account of the objectives of relevance, **reliability**, comparability and understandability. **2.9**

Accounting policies MUST BE APPLIED CONSISTENTLY WITHIN THE SAME ACCOUNTS AND FROM ONE **FINANCIAL YEAR** TO THE NEXT. They shall be reviewed regularly to ensure that they remain the most appropriate to the entity's particular circumstances for the purpose of giving a true and fair view. However, in judging whether a new policy is more appropriate than the existing policy, due weight shall be given to the impact on consistency and comparability. Following a change in **accounting policy**, the amounts for the current and corresponding periods shall be restated on the basis of the new policies. **2.10**

IN DETERMINING THE AGGREGATE AMOUNT OF ANY ITEM, THE AMOUNT OF EACH INDIVIDUAL ASSET OR LIABILITY THAT FALLS TO BE TAKEN INTO ACCOUNT MUST BE DETERMINED SEPARATELY. AMOUNTS IN RESPECT OF ASSETS OR INCOME MAY NOT BE SET OFF AGAINST AMOUNTS IN RESPECT OF LIABILITIES OR EXPENDITURE (AS THE CASE MAY BE), OR VICE VERSA. **2.11**

[11] *This statement may be included with the note of accounting policies or, for those entities taking advantage of the exemptions for small companies in companies legislation, in the statement required by companies legislation to be given on the balance sheet. For example, in Great Britain the combined statement could read as follows 'These accounts have been prepared in accordance with the provisions applicable to small companies within Part 15 of the Companies Act 2006 and with the Financial Reporting Standard for Smaller Entities (effective January 2015).' If abbreviated accounts are also to be prepared, the statement referring to the Financial Reporting Standard for Smaller Entities (effective January 2015) shall be included with the note of accounting policies so that it is reproduced in the abbreviated accounts.*

Going concern

2.12   THE COMPANY IS PRESUMED TO BE CARRYING ON BUSINESS AS A GOING CONCERN. When preparing financial statements, **directors** shall assess whether there are significant doubts about the entity's ability to continue as a going concern. Any material uncertainties, of which the **directors** are aware in making their assessment, shall be disclosed. Where the period considered by the **directors** in making this assessment has been limited to a period of less than one year from the date of approval of the financial statements, that fact shall be stated. The financial statements shall not be prepared on a going concern basis if the **directors** determine after the balance sheet date either that they intend to liquidate the entity or to cease trading, or that they have no realistic alternative but to do so.

Prudence

2.13   THE AMOUNT OF ANY ITEM MUST BE DETERMINED ON A PRUDENT BASIS. Prudence is the inclusion of a degree of caution in the exercise of the judgements needed in making the estimates required under conditions of uncertainty, such that gains and assets are not overstated and liabilities are not understated. However it is not necessary to exercise prudence where there is no uncertainty. Nor is it appropriate to use prudence as a reason to understate deliberately assets or gains or overstate liabilities or losses.

Accruals

2.14   The financial statements, with the exception of cash flow information, shall be prepared on the accruals basis of accounting. HENCE, ALL INCOME AND CHARGES RELATING TO THE **FINANCIAL YEAR** TO WHICH THE ACCOUNTS RELATE MUST BE TAKEN INTO ACCOUNT, WITHOUT REGARD TO THE DATE OF PAYMENT OR RECEIPT.

Prior period adjustments

2.15   **Prior period adjustments** shall be accounted for by restating the comparative figures for the preceding period in the primary statements and notes and adjusting the opening balance of reserves for the cumulative effect. The cumulative effect of the adjustments shall also be noted at the foot of the statement of **total recognised gains and losses** of the current period. The effect of **prior period adjustments** on the results for the preceding period shall be disclosed where practicable.

Formats – general rules

2.16   THE FORMATS FOR THE BALANCE SHEET AND PROFIT AND LOSS ACCOUNT ARE SET OUT BELOW. A COMPANY'S INDIVIDUAL ACCOUNTS MUST COMPLY WITH THE PROVISIONS SET OUT BELOW AS TO THE FORM AND CONTENT OF THE BALANCE SHEET AND PROFIT AND LOSS ACCOUNT AND ADDITIONAL INFORMATION TO BE PROVIDED BY WAY OF NOTES TO THE ACCOUNTS.

2.17   THE **DIRECTORS** OF THE COMPANY MUST ADOPT THE SAME FORMAT IN PREPARING THE ACCOUNTS FOR SUBSEQUENT **FINANCIAL YEARS** OF THE COMPANY UNLESS, IN THEIR OPINION, THERE ARE SPECIAL REASONS FOR A CHANGE. PARTICULARS OF ANY CHANGE IN THE FORMAT ADOPTED IN A COMPANY'S PROFIT AND LOSS ACCOUNT OR BALANCE SHEET MUST BE DISCLOSED, AND THE REASONS FOR THE CHANGE MUST BE EXPLAINED IN A NOTE TO THE ACCOUNTS IN WHICH THE NEW FORMAT IS FIRST ADOPTED.

2.18   WHERE COMPLIANCE WITH THE PROVISIONS OF COMPANIES LEGISLATION AS TO THE MATTERS TO BE INCLUDED IN A COMPANY'S INDIVIDUAL ACCOUNTS OR IN NOTES TO THOSE ACCOUNTS WOULD NOT BE SUFFICIENT TO GIVE A TRUE AND FAIR VIEW, THE NECESSARY ADDITIONAL INFORMATION MUST BE GIVEN IN THE ACCOUNTS OR IN A NOTE TO THEM.

ANY ITEM REQUIRED TO BE SHOWN IN THE ACCOUNTS MAY BE SHOWN IN GREATER DETAIL THAN **2.19**
REQUIRED BY THE FORMAT ADOPTED. THE ACCOUNTS MAY INCLUDE AN ITEM REPRESENTING OR
COVERING THE AMOUNT OF ANY ASSET OR LIABILITY, INCOME OR EXPENDITURE NOT OTHERWISE
COVERED BY ANY OF THE ITEMS LISTED IN THE FORMAT ADOPTED[12].

ITEMS LISTED IN THE FORMATS MUST NOT BE INCLUDED IF THERE IS NO AMOUNT TO BE SHOWN FOR **2.20**
THAT ITEM IN RESPECT OF THE **FINANCIAL YEAR** TO WHICH THE ACCOUNTS RELATE AND FOR THE
IMMEDIATELY PRECEDING **FINANCIAL YEAR**.

IN PREPARING THE BALANCE SHEET OR PROFIT AND LOSS ACCOUNT, THE **DIRECTORS** MUST ADAPT **2.21**
THE ARRANGEMENT, HEADINGS AND SUBHEADINGS OF ITEMS TO WHICH AN ARABIC NUMBER IS
ASSIGNED IN THE FORMATS, WHERE THE SPECIAL NATURE OF THE COMPANY'S BUSINESS REQUIRES
SUCH ADAPTATION.

ITEMS TO WHICH ARABIC NUMBERS ARE ASSIGNED IN ANY OF THE FORMATS MAY BE COMBINED FOR **2.22**
ANY **FINANCIAL YEAR** IF:

(A) THEIR INDIVIDUAL AMOUNTS ARE NOT MATERIAL TO ASSESSING THE STATE OF AFFAIRS OR
     PROFIT AND LOSS OF THE COMPANY FOR THAT YEAR; OR
(B) THEIR COMBINATION FACILITATES THAT ASSESSMENT OF THE BALANCE SHEET OR PROFIT AND
     LOSS ACCOUNT. WHERE THIS APPLIES, THE INDIVIDUAL AMOUNTS OF ANY ITEMS WHICH HAVE
     BEEN COMBINED MUST BE DISCLOSED IN A NOTE TO THE ACCOUNTS.

Corresponding amounts for the previous accounting period shall be shown for every item **2.23**
disclosed in the balance sheet, profit and loss account and notes to the financial statements.
Where there is no amount to be shown for an item in the balance sheet or profit and
loss account for the current accounting period but a corresponding amount can be shown
for the previous accounting period, the corresponding amount shall be shown. Where a
corresponding amount is not comparable with that for the current accounting period, it
shall be adjusted and particulars of the adjustment and the reasons for it shall be disclosed
in a note to the financial statements. Corresponding amounts are not required in relation
to any amounts stated in the notes to the financial statements for the items listed below:

(a) details of additions, disposals, revaluations, transfers and cumulative depreciation of
     fixed assets;
(b) transfers to or from reserves and provisions and the source and application of any
     transfers;
(c) details of a company's shareholdings in subsidiary undertakings; and
(d) details of a company's significant holdings in undertakings other than subsidiary
     undertakings.

IF NOT GIVEN IN THE COMPANY'S ACCOUNTS, THERE MUST BE STATED BY WAY OF A NOTE TO THOSE **2.24**
ACCOUNTS ANY AMOUNT SET ASIDE OR PROPOSED TO BE SET ASIDE, OR WITHDRAWN OR PROPOSED TO
BE WITHDRAWN FROM RESERVES. FOR EACH RESERVE DISCLOSED SEPARATELY IN THE ACCOUNTS, THE
FOLLOWING INFORMATION MUST BE PROVIDED:

(A) THE AMOUNT OF THE RESERVE AT THE BEGINNING AND THE END OF THE **FINANCIAL YEAR**;
(B) ANY AMOUNTS TRANSFERRED TO OR FROM THE RESERVES DURING THE YEAR; AND
(C) THE SOURCE AND APPLICATION OF THE AMOUNTS TRANSFERRED.

FOR THE AGGREGATE OF ALL ITEMS SHOWN AS CREDITORS IN THE BALANCE SHEET, THE AGGREGATE **2.25**
OF THE AMOUNTS WHICH FALL DUE FOR PAYMENT MORE THAN FIVE YEARS AFTER THE END OF THE
CURRENT PERIOD MUST BE DISCLOSED. AMOUNTS PAYABLE OR REPAYABLE BY INSTALMENTS AND
THOSE PAYABLE OR REPAYABLE OTHERWISE THAN BY INSTALMENTS SHALL BE SEPARATELY DISCLOSED.

---

[12] *PRELIMINARY EXPENSES, EXPENSES OF AND COMMISSION ON ANY ISSUE OF SHARES OR DEBENTURES AND COSTS OF RESEARCH SHALL
NOT BE TREATED AS ASSETS.*

2.26   FOR EACH ITEM SHOWN UNDER CREDITORS, THE AGGREGATE AMOUNT OF ANY DEBTS INCLUDED WHERE ANY SECURITY HAS BEEN GIVEN BY THE COMPANY MUST BE DISCLOSED.

Balance sheet format[13]

2.27   THE BALANCE SHEET MUST SHOW THE ITEMS LISTED IN THE ORDER, AND UNDER THE HEADINGS AND SUB-HEADINGS, SHOWN IN THE FORMAT BELOW[14].

BALANCE SHEET FORMAT[15]

A.   CALLED UP SHARE CAPITAL NOT PAID

B.   FIXED ASSETS

    I.   INTANGIBLE ASSETS

        1.   GOODWILL

        2.   OTHER INTANGIBLE ASSETS

    II.   TANGIBLE ASSETS

        1.   LAND AND BUILDINGS

        2.   PLANT AND MACHINERY ETC

    III.   INVESTMENTS

        1.   SHARES IN GROUP UNDERTAKINGS AND PARTICIPATING INTERESTS

        2.   LOANS TO GROUP UNDERTAKINGS AND UNDERTAKINGS IN WHICH THE COMPANY HAS A PARTICIPATING INTEREST

        3.   OTHER INVESTMENTS OTHER THAN LOANS

        4.   OTHER INVESTMENTS

C.   CURRENT ASSETS

    I.   STOCKS

        1.   STOCKS

        2.   PAYMENTS ON ACCOUNT

    II.   DEBTORS[16]

        1.   TRADE DEBTORS

        2.   AMOUNTS OWED BY GROUP UNDERTAKINGS AND UNDERTAKINGS IN WHICH THE COMPANY HAS A PARTICIPATING INTEREST

        3.   OTHER DEBTORS

    III.   INVESTMENTS

        1.   SHARES IN GROUP UNDERTAKINGS

        2.   OTHER INVESTMENTS

    IV.   CASH AT BANK AND IN HAND

D.   PREPAYMENTS AND ACCRUED INCOME[17]

E.   CREDITORS: AMOUNTS FALLING DUE WITHIN ONE YEAR

        1.   BANK LOANS AND OVERDRAFTS

        2.   TRADE CREDITORS

        3.   AMOUNTS OWED TO GROUP UNDERTAKINGS AND UNDERTAKINGS IN WHICH THE COMPANY HAS A PARTICIPATING INTEREST

---

[13] *An alternative format is available under companies legislation and may be adopted.*

[14] *Note: this does not mean that the items, headings and sub-headings need be identified by the letters and numbers assigned to them in the format.*

[15] *There are certain differences in the format requirements for the balance sheet under companies legislation in the Republic of Ireland. The format requirements are contained in* Part 1 of the Schedule to the Companies (Amendment) Act 1986 *with references available in the derivation tables on the FRC website.*

[16] *THE AMOUNT FALLING DUE AFTER MORE THAN ONE YEAR SHALL BE SHOWN SEPARATELY FOR EACH ITEM INCLUDED UNDER DEBTORS UNLESS THE AGGREGATE AMOUNT OF DEBTORS FALLING DUE AFTER MORE THAN ONE YEAR IS DISCLOSED IN THE NOTES TO THE ACCOUNTS.*

[17] *THIS ITEM MAY ALTERNATIVELY BE INCLUDED UNDER ITEM C.II.3.*

> 4. OTHER CREDITORS[18]
>
> F. NET CURRENT ASSETS/LIABILITIES[19]
> G. TOTAL ASSETS LESS CURRENT LIABILITIES
> H. CREDITORS: AMOUNTS FALLING DUE AFTER MORE THAN ONE YEAR
>> 1. BANK LOANS AND OVERDRAFTS
>> 2. TRADE CREDITORS
>> 3. AMOUNTS OWED TO GROUP UNDERTAKINGS AND UNDERTAKINGS IN WHICH THE COMPANY HAS A PARTICIPATING INTEREST
>> 4. OTHER CREDITORS
> I. PROVISIONS FOR LIABILITIES
> J. ACCRUALS AND DEFERRED INCOME[20]
> K. CAPITAL AND RESERVES
>> I. CALLED UP SHARE CAPITAL
>> II. SHARE PREMIUM ACCOUNT
>> III. REVALUATION RESERVE
>> IV. OTHER RESERVES
>> V. PROFIT AND LOSS ACCOUNT

Profit and loss account formats[21]

THE FORMAT OF THE PROFIT AND LOSS ACCOUNT MUST COMPLY WITH ONE OF THE FORMATS SET OUT BELOW. **2.28**

THE ACCOUNT MUST SHOW THE ITEMS LISTED IN THE ORDER, AND UNDER THE HEADINGS AND SUB-HEADINGS, SHOWN IN THE FORMATS SET OUT BELOW[22]. **2.29**

> ## PROFIT AND LOSS ACCOUNT FORMAT 1[23]
> 1. TURNOVER
> 2. COST OF SALES[24]
> 3. GROSS PROFIT OR LOSS
> 4. DISTRIBUTION COSTS
> 5. ADMINISTRATIVE EXPENSES
> 6. OTHER OPERATING INCOME
> 7. INCOME FROM SHARES IN GROUP UNDERTAKINGS
> 8. INCOME FROM PARTICIPATING INTERESTS
> 9. INCOME FROM OTHER FIXED ASSET INVESTMENTS
> 10. OTHER INTEREST RECEIVABLE AND SIMILAR INCOME
> 11. AMOUNTS WRITTEN OFF INVESTMENTS

---

[18] *ITEMS E4, H4 AND J: THERE SHALL BE SHOWN SEPARATELY THE AMOUNT OF ANY CONVERTIBLE LOANS AND THE AMOUNT OF CREDITORS IN RESPECT OF TAXATION AND SOCIAL SECURITY.*

[19] *IN DETERMINING THE AMOUNT TO BE SHOWN UNDER THIS ITEM ANY PREPAYMENTS AND ACCRUED INCOME MUST BE TAKEN INTO ACCOUNT.*

[20] *THIS ITEM MAY ALTERNATIVELY BE INCLUDED UNDER ITEM E4 OR H4 OR BOTH (AS THE CASE MAY REQUIRE).*

[21] *Alternative formats are available under companies legislation and may be adopted.*

[22] *Note, this does not mean that the items, headings and sub-headings need be identified by the letters and numbers assigned to them in the formats.*

[23] *There are certain differences in the format requirements for the profit and loss account under companies legislation in the Republic of Ireland. The format requirements are contained in Part 1 of the Schedule to the Companies (Amendment) Act 1986. References are available in the derivation tables on the FRC website.*

[24] *COST OF SALES, DISTRIBUTION COSTS AND ADMINISTRATIVE EXPENSES SHALL INCLUDE THE PROVISIONS FOR DEPRECIATION AND DIMINUTIONS IN VALUE OF ASSETS. THESE AMOUNTS SHALL ALSO BE SEPARATELY DISCLOSED IN A NOTE TO THE ACCOUNTS.*

12.   INTEREST PAYABLE AND SIMILAR CHARGES
12A. PROFIT OR LOSS ON ORDINARY ACTIVITIES BEFORE TAXATION
13.   TAX ON PROFIT OR LOSS ON ORDINARY ACTIVITIES
14.   PROFIT OR LOSS ON ORDINARY ACTIVITIES AFTER TAXATION[25]
19.   OTHER TAXES NOT SHOWN UNDER THE ABOVE ITEMS
20.   Profit or loss for the financial year

PROFIT AND LOSS ACCOUNT FORMAT 2

1.   TURNOVER
2.   CHANGE IN STOCKS OF FINISHED GOODS AND IN WORK IN PROGRESS
3.   OWN WORK CAPITALISED
4.   OTHER OPERATING INCOME
5.   A. RAW MATERIALS AND CONSUMABLES
     B. OTHER EXTERNAL CHARGES
6.   STAFF COSTS:
     A. WAGES AND SALARIES
     B. SOCIAL SECURITY COSTS
     C. OTHER PENSION COSTS
7.   A. DEPRECIATION AND OTHER AMOUNTS WRITTEN OFF TANGIBLE AND INTANGIBLE FIXED
         ASSETS
     B. EXCEPTIONAL AMOUNTS WRITTEN OFF CURRENT ASSETS
8.   OTHER OPERATING CHARGES
9.   INCOME FROM SHARES IN GROUP UNDERTAKINGS
10. INCOME FROM PARTICIPATING INTERESTS
11. INCOME FROM OTHER FIXED ASSET INVESTMENTS
12. OTHER INTEREST RECEIVABLE AND SIMILAR INCOME
13. AMOUNTS WRITTEN OFF INVESTMENTS
14. INTEREST PAYABLE AND SIMILAR CHARGES
14A. PROFIT OR LOSS ON ORDINARY ACTIVITIES BEFORE TAXATION
15. TAX ON PROFIT OR LOSS ON ORDINARY ACTIVITIES
16. PROFIT OR LOSS ON ORDINARY ACTIVITIES AFTER TAXATION[26]
21. OTHER TAXES NOT SHOWN UNDER THE ABOVE ITEMS
22. PROFIT OR LOSS FOR THE FINANCIAL YEAR

Approval and signing of accounts

2.30   A COMPANY'S ANNUAL ACCOUNTS MUST BE APPROVED BY THE BOARD OF **DIRECTORS** AND SIGNED ON BEHALF OF THE BOARD BY A DIRECTOR OF THE COMPANY. THE SIGNATURE MUST BE ON THE COMPANY'S BALANCE SHEET. The date on which the financial statements are approved by the board of **directors** shall be disclosed in the financial statements. THE BALANCE SHEET MUST CONTAIN, IN A PROMINENT POSITION ABOVE THE SIGNATURE, A STATEMENT THAT THE ACCOUNTS HAVE BEEN PREPARED IN ACCORDANCE WITH THE PROVISIONS APPLICABLE TO SMALL COMPANIES WITHIN PART 15 OF THE COMPANIES ACT 2006.

2.31   EVERY COPY OF THE BALANCE SHEET WHICH IS PUBLISHED BY OR ON BEHALF OF THE BOARD MUST STATE THE NAME OF THE PERSON WHO SIGNED THE BALANCE SHEET ON BEHALF OF THE BOARD.

2.32   THE COPY OF THE COMPANY'S BALANCE SHEET WHICH IS DELIVERED TO THE REGISTRAR MUST STATE THE NAME OF THE PERSON WHO SIGNED IT ON BEHALF OF THE BOARD.

---

[25] *Extraordinary items, which are extremely rare, shall be shown separately after the profit or loss on ordinary activities after taxation.*

[26] *Extraordinary items, which are extremely rare, shall be shown separately after the profit or loss on ordinary activities after taxation.*

IF ANNUAL ACCOUNTS ARE APPROVED WHICH DO NOT COMPLY WITH THE REQUIREMENTS OF THE COMPANIES ACT, EVERY DIRECTOR OF THE COMPANY WHO KNOWS THAT THEY DO NOT COMPLY OR IS RECKLESS AS TO WHETHER THEY COMPLY COMMITS AN OFFENCE AND IS LIABLE TO A FINE. FOR THIS PURPOSE, EVERY DIRECTOR OF THE COMPANY AT THE TIME THE ACCOUNTS ARE APPROVED SHALL BE TAKEN TO BE A PARTY TO THEIR APPROVAL UNLESS HE SHOWS THAT HE TOOK ALL REASONABLE STEPS TO SECURE COMPLIANCE WITH THOSE REQUIREMENTS OR, AS THE CASE MAY BE, PREVENT THEIR BEING APPROVED.
2.33

IF A COPY OF THE BALANCE SHEET —
2.34

(A) IS LAID BEFORE THE COMPANY, OR OTHERWISE CIRCULATED, PUBLISHED OR ISSUED, WITHOUT THE BALANCE SHEET HAVING BEEN SIGNED OR WITHOUT THE REQUIRED STATEMENT OF THE SIGNATORY'S NAME BEING INCLUDED; OR

(B) IS DELIVERED TO THE REGISTRAR WITHOUT BEING SIGNED;

EVERY PERSON WHO WAS A DIRECTOR OF THE COMPANY COMMITS AN OFFENCE AND IS LIABLE TO A FINE.

Delivery to the registrar

THE COPY OF THE FINANCIAL STATEMENTS DELIVERED TO THE REGISTRAR MUST STATE IN A PROMINENT POSITION THE REGISTERED NUMBER OF THE COMPANY, BE SIGNED BY, AND STATE THE NAME OF, THE **DIRECTORS** WHO SIGNED ON BEHALF OF THE BOARD AND REGISTERED AUDITORS AS APPROPRIATE.
2.35

THE FINANCIAL STATEMENTS MUST ALSO CONTAIN A STATEMENT IN A PROMINENT POSITION ON THE BALANCE SHEET THAT THEY HAVE BEEN PREPARED IN ACCORDANCE WITH THE SPECIAL PROVISIONS IN PART 15 OF THE COMPANIES ACT 2006 RELATING TO SMALL COMPANIES.
2.36

Exemptions from audit

WHERE A COMPANY MEETS THE CONDITIONS FOR EXEMPTION FROM AUDIT, AND HAS TAKEN ADVANTAGE OF THAT EXEMPTION, THE BALANCE SHEET MUST CONTAIN A STATEMENT BY THE **DIRECTORS** THAT:
2.37

(A) FOR THE YEAR IN QUESTION, THE COMPANY WAS ENTITLED TO EXEMPTION (UNDER SECTIONS 475 AND 477 OF THE COMPANIES ACT 2006);

(B) NO MEMBER OR MEMBERS ELIGIBLE TO DO SO HAVE DEPOSITED A NOTICE REQUESTING AN AUDIT WITHIN THE SPECIFIED TIME PERIOD; AND

(C) THE **DIRECTORS** ACKNOWLEDGE THEIR RESPONSIBILITIES FOR COMPLYING WITH THE REQUIREMENTS OF THE COMPANIES ACT 2006 WITH RESPECT TO ACCOUNTING RECORDS AND FOR PREPARING ACCOUNTS WHICH GIVE A TRUE AND FAIR VIEW OF THE STATE OF AFFAIRS OF THE COMPANY AS AT THE END OF THE **FINANCIAL YEAR** AND OF ITS PROFIT OR LOSS FOR THE **FINANCIAL YEAR** IN ACCORDANCE WITH THE REQUIREMENTS OF SECTIONS 394 AND 395 (DUTY TO PREPARE INDIVIDUAL COMPANY ACCOUNTS AND APPLICABLE ACCOUNTING FRAMEWORK), AND WHICH OTHERWISE COMPLY WITH THE REQUIREMENTS OF THE COMPANIES ACT 2006 RELATING TO ACCOUNTS, SO FAR AS APPLICABLE TO THE COMPANY.

WHERE THE **DIRECTORS** HAVE TAKEN ADVANTAGE OF THE EXEMPTION FROM AUDIT DUE TO THE FACT THAT THE COMPANY IS DORMANT, AND THE COMPANY HAS DURING THE **FINANCIAL YEAR** IN QUESTION ACTED AS AN AGENT FOR ANY PERSON, THE FACT THAT IT HAS SO ACTED MUST BE STATED.
2.38

Liability Limitation Agreement

WHERE EXEMPTION FROM AUDIT IS NOT AVAILABLE, OR THE DIRECTORS HAVE NOT TAKEN ADVANTAGE OF THE EXEMPTION FROM AUDIT AND THE COMPANY HAS ENTERED INTO A LIABILITY LIMITATION AGREEMENT WITH ITS AUDITORS, THE NOTES TO THE ACCOUNTS MUST DISCLOSE THE PRINCIPAL TERMS OF THE AGREEMENT AND EITHER THE DATE OF THE RESOLUTION APPROVING THE AGREEMENT OR THE AGREEMENT'S PRINCIPAL TERMS OR THE DATE OF THE RESOLUTION WAIVING THE NEED FOR SUCH APPROVAL.
2.39

Financial statements of a micro-entity

2.40   A **micro-entity** preparing its financial statements in accordance with section 393(1A) of the **Act** shall prepare a balance sheet in which only those items listed in the following formats must be shown, where applicable:

BALANCE SHEET FORMAT 1

A.   CALLED UP SHARE CAPITAL NOT PAID
B.   FIXED ASSETS
C.   CURRENT ASSETS
D.   PREPAYMENTS AND ACCRUED INCOME
E.   CREDITORS: AMOUNTS FALLING DUE WITHIN ONE YEAR
F.   NET CURRENT ASSETS (LIABILITIES)
G.   TOTAL ASSETS LESS CURRENT LIABILITIES
H.   CREDITORS: AMOUNTS FALLING DUE AFTER MORE THAN ONE YEAR
I.   PROVISIONS FOR LIABILITIES
J.   ACCRUALS AND DEFERRED INCOME
K.   CAPITAL AND RESERVES

BALANCE SHEET FORMAT 2

ASSETS

A.   CALLED UP SHARE CAPITAL NOT PAID
B.   FIXED ASSETS
C.   CURRENT ASSETS
D.   PREPAYMENTS AND ACCRUED INCOME

LIABILITIES

A.   CAPITAL AND RESERVES
B.   PROVISIONS FOR LIABILITIES
C.   CREDITORS

THE BALANCE SHEET MUST CONTAIN, IN A PROMINENT POSITION ABOVE THE SIGNATURE, A STATEMENT THAT THE ACCOUNTS ARE PREPARED IN ACCORDANCE WITH THE MICRO-ENTITY PROVISIONS in Part 15 of the Companies Act 2006.

Editor's note: Amendments to the FRSSE – Micro-entities (April 2014) has added this paragraph 2.40 and the sub-heading above.

2.41   A **micro-entity** preparing its financial statements in accordance with section 393(1A) of the **Act** shall prepare a profit and loss account in which only the following items must be shown, where applicable:

A.   TURNOVER
B.   OTHER INCOME
C.   COST OF RAW MATERIALS AND CONSUMABLES
D.   STAFF COSTS
E.   DEPRECIATION AND OTHER AMOUNTS WRITTEN OFF ASSETS
F.   OTHER CHARGES
G.   TAX
H.   PROFIT OR LOSS

Editor's note: Amendments to the FRSSE – Micro-entities (April 2014) has added this paragraph 2.41.

A **micro-entity** preparing its financial statements in accordance with section 393(1A) of the **Act** shall prepare notes to the financial statements, to be disclosed at the foot of the balance sheet, providing disclosure of: **2.42**

(a)   guarantees and other financial commitments, as follows:

    (I)   PARTICULARS MUST BE GIVEN OF ANY CHARGE ON THE ASSETS OF THE COMPANY TO SECURE THE LIABILITIES OF ANY OTHER PERSON, INCLUDING, WHERE PRACTICABLE, THE AMOUNT SECURED.

    (II)   THE FOLLOWING INFORMATION MUST BE GIVEN WITH RESPECT TO ANY OTHER CONTINGENT LIABILITY NOT PROVIDED FOR:

        (A)   THE AMOUNT OR ESTIMATED AMOUNT OF THAT LIABILITY;

        (B)   ITS LEGAL NATURE; AND

        (C)   WHETHER ANY VALUABLE SECURITY HAS BEEN PROVIDED BY THE COMPANY IN CONNECTION WITH THAT LIABILITY AND IF SO, WHAT.

    (III)   THERE MUST BE STATED, WHERE PRACTICABLE, THE AGGREGATE AMOUNT OR ESTIMATED AMOUNT OF CONTRACTS FOR CAPITAL EXPENDITURE, SO FAR AS NOT PROVIDED FOR.

    (IV)   PARTICULARS MUST BE GIVEN OF:

        (A)   ANY PENSIONS COMMITMENTS INCLUDED UNDER ANY PROVISION SHOWN IN THE COMPANY' BALANCE SHEET; AND

        (B)   ANY SUCH COMMITMENTS FOR WHICH NO PROVISION HAS BEEN MADE.

AND WHERE ANY SUCH COMMITMENT RELATES WHOLLY OR PARTLY TO PENSIONS PAYABLE TO PAST DIRECTORS OF THE COMPANY SEPARATE PARTICULARS MUST BE GIVEN OF THAT COMMITMENT AS FAR AS IT RELATES TO SUCH PENSIONS.

    (V)   PARTICULARS MUST ALSO BE GIVEN OF ANY OTHER FINANCIAL COMMITMENTS THAT:

        (A)   HAVE NOT BEEN PROVIDED FOR; AND

        (B)   ARE RELEVANT TO ASSESSING THE COMPANY' STATE OF AFFAIRS.

    (VI)   COMMITMENTS WITHIN ANY OF SUB-PARAGRAPHS (I) TO (V) WHICH ARE UNDERTAKEN ON BEHALF OF OR FOR THE BENEFIT OF (A) ANY PARENT UNDERTAKING OR FELLOW SUBSIDIARY UNDERTAKING, OR (B) ANY SUBSIDIARY UNDERTAKING OF THE COMPANY, MUST BE STATED SEPARATELY FROM THE OTHER COMMITMENTS. COMMITMENTS WITHIN PARAGRAPH (A) MUST ALSO BE STATED SEPARATELY FROM THOSE WITHIN PARAGRAPH (B).

(b)   directors' benefits: advances, credit and guarantees as follows:

    (I)   DETAILS OF:

        (A)   ADVANCES AND CREDITS GRANTED BY THE COMPANY TO ITS DIRECTORS; AND

        (B)   GUARANTEES OF ANY KIND ENTERED INTO BY THE COMPANY ON BEHALF OF ITS DIRECTORS.

    (II)   THE DETAILS REQUIRED OF AN ADVANCE OR CREDIT ARE:

        (A)   ITS AMOUNT;

        (B)   AN INDICATION OF THE INTEREST RATE;

        (C)   ITS MAIN CONDITIONS; AND

        (D)   ANY AMOUNTS REPAID.

    (III)   THE DETAILS REQUIRED OF A GUARANTEE ARE:

        (A)   ITS MAIN TERMS;

        (B)   THE AMOUNT OF THE MAXIMUM LIABILITY THAT MAY BE INCURRED BY THE COMPANY; AND

(C) ANY AMOUNT PAID AND ANY LIABILITY INCURRED BY THE COMPANY FOR THE PURPOSE OF FULFILLING THE GUARANTEE (INCLUDING ANY LOSS INCURRED BY REASON OF ENFORCEMENT OF THE GUARANTEE).

(IV) THERE MUST ALSO BE STATED THE TOTALS:

(A) OF AMOUNTS STATED UNDER PARAGRAPH (II)(A);

(B) OF AMOUNTS STATED UNDER PARAGRAPH (II)(D);

(C) OF AMOUNTS STATED UNDER PARAGRAPH (III)(B); AND

(D) OF AMOUNTS STATED UNDER PARAGRAPH (III)(C).

(V) REFERENCES IN THIS PARAGRAPH TO THE DIRECTORS OF A COMPANY ARE TO THE PERSONS WHO WERE A DIRECTOR AT ANY TIME IN THE FINANCIAL YEAR TO WHICH THE FINANCIAL STATEMENTS RELATE.

(VI) THE REQUIREMENTS OF THIS PARAGRAPH APPLY IN RELATION TO EVERY ADVANCE, CREDIT OR GUARANTEE SUBSISTING AT ANY TIME IN THE FINANCIAL YEAR TO WHICH THE FINANCIAL STATEMENTS RELATE:

(A) WHENEVER IT WAS ENTERED INTO; AND

(B) WHETHER OR NOT THE PERSON CONCERNED WAS A DIRECTOR OF THE COMPANY IN QUESTION AT THE TIME IT WAS ENTERED INTO.

Editor's note: Amendments to the FRSSE – Micro-entities (April 2014) has added this paragraph 2.42.

3   *Profit and loss account*

General

3.1   All gains and losses **recognised** in the financial statements for the period shall be included in the profit and loss account or the statement of **total recognised gains and losses**. ONLY PROFITS THAT ARE REALISED AT THE BALANCE SHEET DATE MUST BE INCLUDED IN THE PROFIT AND LOSS ACCOUNT. ALL LIABILITIES WHICH HAVE ARISEN IN RESPECT OF THE PERIOD OR IN RESPECT OF A PREVIOUS FINANCIAL YEAR MUST BE TAKEN INTO ACCOUNT, INCLUDING THOSE WHICH ONLY BECOME APPARENT BETWEEN THE BALANCE SHEET DATE AND THE DATE ON WHICH IT IS SIGNED.

3.2   Gains and losses may be excluded from the profit and loss account only if they are specifically permitted or required to be taken direct to reserves by this standard or by **companies legislation** or equivalent legislation.

3.3   WHERE AN AMOUNT RELATING TO ANY PRECEDING **FINANCIAL YEAR** IS INCLUDED IN THE PROFIT AND LOSS ACCOUNT, THE EFFECT OF ITS INCLUSION MUST BE STATED.

3.4   IF THE COMPANY HAS SUPPLIED GEOGRAPHICAL MARKETS OUTSIDE THE UNITED KINGDOM DURING THE **FINANCIAL YEAR**, THE PERCENTAGE OF TURNOVER THAT IS ATTRIBUTABLE TO THOSE MARKETS MUST BE SEPARATELY DISCLOSED. IN ANALYSING THE SOURCE OF TURNOVER, REGARD MUST BE PAID TO THE MANNER IN WHICH THE COMPANY'S ACTIVITIES ARE ORGANISED.

Exceptional items

3.5   All **exceptional items**, other than those included in the items listed in the next paragraph, shall be credited or charged in arriving at the profit or loss on **ordinary activities** by inclusion under the statutory format headings to which they relate. The amount of each **exceptional item**, either individually or as an aggregate of items of a similar type, shall be disclosed separately by way of a note, or on the face of the profit and loss account if that degree of prominence is necessary in order to give a true and fair view. An adequate description of each **exceptional item** shall be given to enable its nature to be understood.

The effect must be stated of any transactions that are exceptional by virtue of size or incidence though they fall within the ordinary activities of the company.

The following items, including provisions in respect of such items, shall be shown separately **3.6** on the face of the profit and loss account after operating profit (which is normally profit before income from shares in group undertakings) and before interest:

(a)   profits or losses on the sale or termination of an operation;

(b)   costs of a fundamental reorganisation or restructuring having a material effect on the nature and focus of the reporting entity's operations; and

(c)   profits or losses on the disposal of fixed assets.

Profit or loss on disposal

The profit or loss on the disposal of an asset shall be accounted for in the profit and **3.7** loss account of the period in which the disposal occurs as the difference between the net sale proceeds and the net carrying amount, whether carried at historical cost (less any provisions made) or at a valuation. Profit or loss on disposal of a previously acquired business shall include the attributable amount of **purchased goodwill** that has previously been eliminated against reserves as a matter of **accounting policy** and has not previously been charged in the profit and loss account.

Disclosure of auditor remuneration

Where a small company chooses not to take advantage of the exemption in the Companies **3.8** Act 2006 relating to the audit of accounts, the remuneration of the company's auditor, including sums paid in respect of expenses, must be disclosed in a note to the accounts, including the nature and estimated monetary value of any benefits in kind. Where more than one person has been appointed as a company's auditor in respect of the period to which the accounts relate, separate disclosure is required in respect of the remuneration of each such person.

4   Revenue recognition

Basic principles[27]

A seller recognises revenue under an **exchange transaction** with a customer when, and to **4.1** the extent that, it obtains the **right to consideration** in exchange for its **performance**. At the same time, it typically recognises a new asset, usually a debtor.

When a seller receives payment from a customer in advance of **performance**, it recognises **4.2** a liability equal to the amount received, representing its **obligation** under the contract. When the seller obtains the **right to consideration** through its **performance**, that liability is reduced and the amount of the reduction in the liability is simultaneously reported as revenue.

A seller may obtain a **right to consideration** when some, but not all, of its contractual **4.3** **obligations** have been fulfilled. Where a seller has partially performed its contractual **obligations**, it recognises revenue to the extent that it has obtained the **right to consideration** through its **performance**.

Revenue shall be measured at the **fair value** of the **right to consideration**. Subject to **4.4** paragraphs 4.5-4.6 or other evidence to the contrary, this will normally be the price

---

[27] *Guidance on the practical considerations for recognising revenue in respect of service contracts, bill and hold arrangements, presentation of turnover as principal or as agent and sales with rights of return is given in Appendix III.*

specified in the contractual arrangement, net of discounts, value added tax and similar sales taxes.

4.5 Where the effect of the time value of money is material to reported revenue, the amount of revenue **recognised** shall be the present value of the cash inflows expected to be received from the customer in settlement. The unwinding of the discount shall be credited to finance income as this represents a gain from a financing transaction.

4.6 Where at the time revenue is **recognised** on a transaction there is a significant risk that there will be default on the amount of consideration due and the effect is material to reported revenue, an adjustment to the price specified in the contractual arrangement will be necessary to arrive at the amount of revenue to be **recognised**.

4.7 Subsequent adjustments to a debtor as a result of changes in the time value of money and credit risk shall not be included within revenue.

Turnover

4.8 Turnover (which may be described as 'sales' in a seller's financial statements) is the revenue resulting from **exchange transactions** under which a seller supplies to customers the goods or services that it is in business to provide.[28]

4.9 A seller may enter into other **exchange transactions** such as the sale of fixed assets. Such transactions do not normally give rise to turnover, as they do not normally fall within the class of transactions set out in paragraph 4.8.

Contracts for services

4.10 Where there are distinguishable phases of a single contract it may be appropriate to account for the contract as two or more separate transactions, provided the value of each phase can be reliably estimated.

4.11 Contracts for services should not be accounted for as long-term contracts unless they involve the provision of a single service, or a number of services that constitute a single project.

4.12 A contract for services should be accounted for as a long-term contract where contract activity falls into different accounting periods and it is concluded that the effect is material. In determining whether contracts should be accounted for as long-term contracts, the aggregate effect of all such contracts on the financial statements as a whole should be considered.

4.13 Where the substance of a contract is that the seller's contractual obligations are performed gradually over time, revenue should be recognised as contract activity progresses to reflect the seller's partial performance of its contractual obligations. The amount of revenue should reflect the accrual of the right to consideration as contract activity progresses by reference to value of the work performed.

4.14 Where the substance of a contract is that a right to consideration does not arise until the occurrence of a critical event, revenue is not recognised until that event occurs. This only applies where the right to consideration is conditional or contingent on a specified future event or outcome, the occurrence of which is outside the control of the seller.

---

[28] *These transactions are often referred to as being part of the seller's operating activities.*

The amount of revenue recognised on any contract for services should reflect any **4.15** uncertainties as to the amount that the customer will accept and pay.

5 Statement of total recognised gains and losses

A primary statement shall be presented, with the same prominence as the profit and loss **5.1** account, showing the **total of recognised gains and losses** and its components. The components shall be the gains and losses that are **recognised** in the period insofar as they are attributable to shareholders, excluding transactions with shareholders.[29] Where the only **recognised** gains and losses are the results included in the profit and loss account no separate statement to this effect need be made.

6 Fixed assets and goodwill

Disclosure

THE FOLLOWING INFORMATION MUST BE PROVIDED FOR ALL FIXED ASSETS AND GOODWILL: **6.1**

(A)   THE COST OR VALUATION AT THE BEGINNING AND THE END OF THE YEAR; AND
(B)   THE EFFECT OF ANY:

    (I)   REVALUATION MADE DURING THE YEAR;
    (II)   ACQUISITIONS DURING THE YEAR;
    (III)   DISPOSALS DURING THE YEAR; AND
    (IV)   TRANSFERS DURING THE YEAR.

THE FOLLOWING INFORMATION MUST BE PROVIDED IN RESPECT OF PROVISIONS FOR DEPRECIATION OR **6.2** DIMINUTION IN VALUE:

(A)   THE CUMULATIVE AMOUNT OF SUCH PROVISIONS AS AT THE BEGINNING AND END OF THE YEAR;
(B)   THE AMOUNT OF ANY SUCH PROVISIONS MADE DURING THE YEAR;
(C)   THE AMOUNT OF ANY ADJUSTMENTS MADE ON DISPOSAL DURING THE YEAR; AND
(D)   THE AMOUNT OF ANY OTHER ADJUSTMENTS MADE DURING THE YEAR.

Research and development

The cost of fixed assets acquired or constructed in order to provide facilities for **research** **6.3** **and development** activities over a number of accounting periods shall be capitalised and written off over their useful lives through the profit and loss account.

Expenditure on **pure** and **applied research** shall be written off in the period of expenditure **6.4** through the profit and loss account.

Development expenditure shall be written off in the period of expenditure except in the **6.5** following circumstances when it may be deferred to future periods:

(a)   there is a clearly defined project; and
(b)   the related expenditure is separately identifiable; and
(c)   the outcome of such a project has been assessed with reasonable certainty as to:

    (i)   its technical feasibility; and
    (ii)   its ultimate commercial viability considered in the light of factors such as likely market conditions (including competing products), public opinion, consumer and environmental legislation; and

---

[29] *An illustration of a statement of total recognised gains and losses is given in Appendix III.*

(d)   the aggregate of the deferred **development** costs, any further **development** costs, and related production, selling and administration costs is reasonably expected to be exceeded by related future sales or other revenues; and

(e)   adequate resources exist, or are reasonably expected to be available, to enable the project to be completed and to provide any consequential increases in working capital.

6.6   In the foregoing circumstances **development** expenditure may be deferred to the extent that its recovery can be reasonably regarded as assured.

6.7   If an **accounting policy** of deferral of **development** expenditure is adopted, it shall be applied to all **development** projects that meet the criteria in paragraph 6.5.

6.8   If **development** costs are deferred to future periods, they shall be amortised. The amortisation shall commence with the commercial production or application of the product, service, process or system and shall be allocated on a systematic basis to each accounting period, by reference to either the sale or use of the product, service, process or system or the period over which these are expected to be sold or used.

6.9   Deferred **development** expenditure for each product shall be reviewed at the end of each accounting period and where the circumstances that justified the deferral of expenditure no longer apply, or are considered doubtful, the expenditure, to the extent to which it is considered to be irrecoverable, shall be written off immediately project by project.

6.10   The amount of deferred **development** expenditure carried forward at the beginning and end of the period shall be disclosed under **intangible assets** in the balance sheet or in the notes to the balance sheet. THE REASON FOR CAPITALISING THESE COSTS AND THE PERIOD OVER WHICH THEY ARE BEING DEPRECIATED MUST BE DISCLOSED IN A NOTE TO THE ACCOUNTS. IF **DEVELOPMENT** COSTS ARE NOT TREATED AS A REALISED LOSS, THIS MUST BE STATED TOGETHER WITH AN EXPLANATION OF THE CIRCUMSTANCES RELIED UPON BY THE **DIRECTORS** TO JUSTIFY THEIR DECISION.

Other intangible assets and goodwill

6.11   **Positive purchased goodwill** and purchased **intangible assets** shall be capitalised. Internally generated goodwill and intangible assets shall not be capitalised.

6.12   An **intangible asset** purchased with a business shall be **recognised** separately from the **purchased goodwill** if its value can be measured reliably.

6.13   Capitalised goodwill and **intangible assets** shall be considered to have a finite useful life, and shall be **depreciated** on a straight-line (or more appropriate) basis over their **useful economic lives.** If an entity is unable to make a reliable estimate of the useful life of goodwill or intangible assets, the life shall be presumed not to exceed five years. THE PERIOD CHOSEN FOR DEPRECIATING GOODWILL AND THE REASONS FOR CHOOSING THAT PERIOD MUST BE DISCLOSED IN A NOTE TO THE ACCOUNTS.

6.14   The **residual value** assigned to goodwill shall be zero. A higher **residual value** may be assigned to an **intangible asset** only when this value can be established reliably, for example when it has been agreed contractually.

6.15   **Useful economic lives** shall be reviewed at the end of each reporting period and revised if necessary, subject to the constraint that the revised life shall not exceed 20 years from the date of acquisition. The carrying amount at the date of revision shall be **depreciated** over the revised estimate of remaining **useful economic life**.

Goodwill and **intangible assets** shall not be revalued. **6.16**

If an acquisition appears to give rise to negative goodwill, **fair values** shall be checked to ensure that those of the acquired **assets** have not been overstated and those of the acquired **liabilities** have not been understated. Once this has been done, remaining negative goodwill up to the **fair values** of the non-monetary **assets** acquired shall be released in the profit and loss account over the lives of those assets. Any additional negative goodwill shall be **recognised** in the profit and loss account over the period expected to benefit from it. The amount of negative goodwill on the balance sheet and the period(s) in which it is being written back shall be disclosed. **6.17**

Tangible fixed assets

Except as set out in paragraph 1.2, paragraphs 6.19-6.26 apply to all **tangible fixed assets** other than **investment properties**. **6.18**

Editor's note: Amendments to the FRSSE – Micro-entities (April 2014) has amended the words in this paragraph.

A **tangible fixed asset** shall initially be measured at its cost, then written down to its **recoverable amount** if necessary. The initial carrying amount of a **tangible fixed asset** received as a gift or donation by a charity shall be its current value, i.e. the lower of replacement cost and **recoverable amount**, at the date it is received.[30] WHERE THERE IS NO RECORD OF THE PURCHASE PRICE OR PRODUCTION COST OF AN ASSET, OR ANY SUCH RECORD CANNOT BE OBTAINED WITHOUT UNREASONABLE EXPENSE OR DELAY, THE VALUE ASCRIBED MUST BE THE EARLIEST AVAILABLE RECORD OF ITS VALUE. PARTICULARS MUST BE GIVEN OF ANY CASE WHERE THE PURCHASE PRICE OR PRODUCTION COST OF ANY ASSET IS FOR THE FIRST TIME DETERMINED IN THIS WAY. **6.19**

Costs that are directly attributable to bringing the **tangible fixed asset** into working condition for its intended use shall be included in its measurement. Other costs shall not be included. An entity may adopt an **accounting policy** of capitalising **finance costs** (such as interest). Where such a policy is adopted, **finance costs** that are directly attributable to the construction of **tangible fixed assets** shall be capitalised as part of the cost of those assets. The total amount of **finance costs** capitalised during a period shall not exceed the total amount of **finance costs** incurred during that period. WHERE APPLICABLE, THE NOTES TO THE ACCOUNTS MUST DISCLOSE THAT FINANCE COSTS ARE INCLUDED IN DETERMINING THE COST OF THE ASSET AND THE AMOUNT OF FINANCE COSTS SO INCLUDED. **6.20**

Capitalisation of directly attributable costs, including **finance costs**, shall be suspended during extended periods in which active **development** is interrupted. Capitalisation shall cease when substantially all the activities that are necessary to get the **tangible fixed asset** ready for use are complete, even if the asset has not yet been brought into use. **6.21**

Subsequent expenditure shall be capitalised only if: **6.22**

(a) it enhances the economic benefits of a **tangible fixed asset** in excess of the previously assessed standard of performance (i.e. if it is an 'improvement'); or

(b) it replaces or restores a component that has been separately depreciated over its **useful economic life**.

Otherwise it shall be **recognised** in the profit and loss account as it is incurred.

---

[30] *Generally, where issues of practicality or of cost-benefit arise, these will be addressed in the relevant sector-specific guidance and Statements of Recommended Practice (SORPs).*

6.23   Where an entity adopts an **accounting policy** of revaluation in respect of a **tangible fixed asset**, its carrying amount shall be its market value (or the best estimate thereof) as at the balance sheet date. Where the **directors** believe that market value is not an appropriate basis, current value (i.e. the lower of replacement cost and **recoverable amount**) may be used instead. Where a **tangible fixed asset** is revalued, all **tangible fixed assets** of the same class (i.e. having a similar nature, function or use in the business) shall be revalued, but a policy of revaluation need not be applied to all classes of **tangible fixed assets**.

6.24   It may be possible to establish with reasonable **reliability** the values of certain **tangible fixed assets**, other than properties, by reference to active second-hand markets or appropriate publicly available indices. For other **tangible fixed assets**, including properties, a valuation shall be performed by an experienced valuer (i.e. one who has recognised and relevant recent professional experience, and sufficient knowledge of the state of the market, in the location and category of the **tangible fixed asset** being valued) at least every five years. It shall be updated by an experienced valuer in the intervening years where it is likely that there has been a material change in value.[31]

6.25   Revaluation losses caused only by changing market prices shall be **recognised** in the statement of **total recognised gains and losses** until the carrying amount of the asset reaches its depreciated historical cost. Other revaluation losses shall be **recognised** in the profit and loss account.

6.26   Revaluation gains shall be **recognised** in the statement of **total recognised gains and losses**, except to the extent (after adjusting for subsequent **depreciation**) that they reverse revaluation losses on the same asset that were previously **recognised** in the profit and loss account. To that extent they shall be **recognised** in the profit and loss account. The adjustment for subsequent **depreciation** is to achieve the same overall effect that would have been reached had the original downward revaluation reflected in the profit and loss account not occurred.

6.27   WHERE TANGIBLE FIXED ASSETS HAVE BEEN REVALUED EITHER — THE COMPARABLE AMOUNTS DETERMINED UNDER THE HISTORICAL COST ACCOUNTING RULES (i.e. the aggregate historical cost amount that would have been included had the **assets** not been revalued, reflecting any write-downs to **recoverable amount** that would have been necessary); OR THE DIFFERENCES BETWEEN THOSE AMOUNTS AND THE CORRESPONDING AMOUNTS ACTUALLY SHOWN IN THE BALANCE SHEET MUST BE SHOWN SEPARATELY IN THE BALANCE SHEET OR IN A NOTE TO THE ACCOUNTS.

6.28   WHERE TANGIBLE FIXED ASSETS ARE CONSTANTLY BEING REPLACED AND THEIR VALUE IS NOT MATERIAL TO ASSESSING THE COMPANY'S STATE OF AFFAIRS AND THEIR QUANTITY, VALUE AND COMPOSITION ARE NOT SUBJECT TO MATERIAL VARIATION, THEY MAY BE INCLUDED AT A FIXED QUANTITY AND VALUE.

6.29   WHERE TANGIBLE FIXED ASSETS HAVE BEEN REVALUED, THE YEAR IN WHICH THEY WERE VALUED MUST BE DISCLOSED. IN THE CASE OF ASSETS THAT HAVE BEEN REVALUED DURING THE CURRENT FINANCIAL YEAR, THE NAMES OF THE PERSONS WHO VALUED THEM OR PARTICULARS OF THEIR QUALIFICATIONS FOR DOING SO AND THE BASES OF THE VALUATION MUST BE DISCLOSED.

Investments

6.30   FIXED ASSET INVESTMENTS MUST INITIALLY BE MEASURED AT COST. ALTERNATIVELY, THEY MAY BE MEASURED AT A MARKET VALUE DETERMINED AS AT THE DATE OF THEIR LAST VALUATION OR ON ANY OTHER VALUE DETERMINED ON A BASIS WHICH APPEARS TO THE **DIRECTORS** TO BE APPROPRIATE IN THE CIRCUMSTANCES OF THE COMPANY (IN THE LATTER CASE, THE METHOD OF VALUATION ADOPTED AND

---

[31] *Where, for cost/benefit reasons, alternative approaches are set out in relevant sector-specific guidance and SORPs, these may be adopted instead of the approach in paragraph 6.24.*

OF THE REASONS FOR ADOPTING IT MUST BE DISCLOSED IN A NOTE TO THE ACCOUNTS). Gains and losses shall be **recognised** (in the profit and loss account or statement of **total recognised gains and losses**) using the same basis applied to **tangible fixed assets** in paragraphs 6.25 and 6.26 above.

WHERE FIXED ASSET INVESTMENTS HAVE BEEN REVALUED EITHER — THE COMPARABLE AMOUNTS DETERMINED UNDER THE HISTORICAL COST ACCOUNTING RULES (i.e. the aggregate historical cost amount that would have been included had the **assets** not been revalued, reflecting any write-downs to **recoverable amount** that would have been necessary); OR THE DIFFERENCES BETWEEN THOSE AMOUNTS AND THE CORRESPONDING AMOUNTS ACTUALLY SHOWN IN THE BALANCE SHEET MUST BE SHOWN SEPARATELY IN THE BALANCE SHEET OR IN A NOTE TO THE ACCOUNTS. **6.31**

THE AGGREGATE AMOUNT OF LISTED INVESTMENTS INCLUDED UNDER EACH ITEM OF INVESTMENTS SHOWN IN THE BALANCE SHEET MUST BE DISCLOSED. FOR EACH ITEM WHICH INCLUDES LISTED INVESTMENTS, THE FOLLOWING MUST BE DISCLOSED: **6.32**

(A) THE AGGREGATE MARKET VALUE OF THE LISTED INVESTMENTS WHERE IT DIFFERS FROM THEIR BALANCE SHEET AMOUNT; AND

(B) BOTH THE MARKET VALUE AND THE STOCK EXCHANGE VALUE OF ANY INVESTMENTS, OF WHICH THE MARKET VALUE IS TAKEN AS BEING HIGHER THAN THE STOCK EXCHANGE VALUE.

WHERE THE COMPANY HAS, AT THE END OF THE **FINANCIAL YEAR**, A SIGNIFICANT HOLDING IN AN UNDERTAKING (WHICH IS NOT A SUBSIDIARY UNDERTAKING OF THE COMPANY) WHICH REPRESENTS 20 PER CENT OR MORE OF THE NOMINAL VALUE OF ANY CLASS OF SHARES IN THE UNDERTAKING, OR MORE THAN 20 PER CENT OF THE BOOK VALUE OF THE INVESTING COMPANY'S TOTAL ASSETS, THE FOLLOWING MUST BE STATED IN RELATION TO THAT UNDERTAKING:[32,33,34] **6.33**

(A) THE NAME OF THE UNDERTAKING;

(B) IF THE UNDERTAKING IS INCORPORATED OUTSIDE THE UNITED KINGDOM, THE COUNTRY IN WHICH IT IS INCORPORATED;

(C) IF IT IS UNINCORPORATED, THE ADDRESS OF ITS PRINCIPAL PLACE OF BUSINESS;

(D) THE IDENTITY AND PROPORTION OF THE NOMINAL VALUE OF EACH CLASS OF SHARES HELD;

(E) THE AGGREGATE AMOUNT OF THE CAPITAL AND RESERVES OF THE UNDERTAKING AS AT THE END OF THE MOST RECENT **FINANCIAL YEAR** ENDING WITH OR BEFORE THAT OF THE INVESTING COMPANY; AND

(F) ITS PROFIT OR LOSS FOR THAT YEAR.

Revaluation reserve

GAINS AND LOSSES ARISING ON THE REVALUATION OF **ASSETS** THAT HAVE BEEN **RECOGNISED** IN THE STATEMENT OF **TOTAL RECOGNISED GAINS AND LOSSES** MUST BE CREDITED, OR DEBITED, TO A SEPARATE REVALUATION RESERVE. **6.34**

---

[32] *If the directors of the company are of opinion the number of undertakings in respect of which the company is required to disclose information is such that compliance would result in information of excessive length being given, the information need only be given in respect of the undertakings principally affecting the figures shown in the company's annual accounts. Where the disclosures are limited in this way, the notes shall include a statement that the information is given only with respect to such undertakings and full details must be annexed to the company's next annual return.*

[33] INFORMATION NEED NOT BE DISCLOSED WITH RESPECT TO AN UNDERTAKING WHICH IS ESTABLISHED UNDER THE LAW OF A COUNTRY OUTSIDE THE UNITED KINGDOM OR CARRIES ON BUSINESS OUTSIDE THE UNITED KINGDOM, IF IN THE OPINION OF THE DIRECTORS OF THE COMPANY THE DISCLOSURE WOULD BE SERIOUSLY PREJUDICIAL TO THE BUSINESS OF THAT UNDERTAKING, OR TO THE BUSINESS OF THE COMPANY OR ANY OF ITS SUBSIDIARY UNDERTAKINGS, AND THE SECRETARY OF STATE AGREES THAT THE INFORMATION NEED NOT BE DISCLOSED. WHERE ADVANTAGE IS TAKEN OF THIS, THAT FACT SHALL BE STATED IN A NOTE TO THE COMPANY'S ANNUAL ACCOUNTS. THIS STATUTORY EXEMPTION IS NOT AVAILABLE IN THE REPUBLIC OF IRELAND.

[34] *Disclosure requirements for holdings in subsidiary undertakings are set out in paragraphs 15.17.*

6.35   AMOUNTS MAY BE TRANSFERRED FROM THE REVALUATION RESERVE TO THE PROFIT AND LOSS ACCOUNT WHEN THEY ARE REALISED. FOR **TANGIBLE FIXED ASSETS**, THIS WILL NORMALLY RESULT IN AN ANNUAL TRANSFER FROM THE REVALUATION RESERVE TO THE PROFIT AND LOSS ACCOUNT OVER THE **USEFUL ECONOMIC LIFE** OF THE **ASSET** (I.E. IN LINE WITH THE **DEPRECIATION** CHARGE). REALISATION MAY ALSO OCCUR ON THE EVENTUAL DISPOSAL OF THE **ASSET**.

6.36   THE TREATMENT FOR TAXATION PURPOSES OF AMOUNTS CREDITED OR DEBITED TO THE REVALUATION RESERVE MUST BE DISCLOSED IN A NOTE TO THE ACCOUNTS.

Depreciation

6.37   Paragraphs 6.38-6.43 apply to all **tangible fixed assets** other than **investment properties**.

6.38   The cost (or revalued amount) less estimated **residual value** of a **tangible fixed asset** shall be depreciated on a systematic basis over its **useful economic life**. The **depreciation** method used shall reflect as fairly as possible the pattern in which the asset's economic benefits are consumed by the entity. The **depreciation** charge for each period shall be **recognised** as an expense in the profit and loss account unless it is permitted to be included in the carrying amount of another **asset**.

6.39   Where a **tangible fixed asset** comprises two or more major components with substantially different **useful economic lives**, each component shall be accounted for separately for **depreciation** purposes and depreciated over its individual **useful economic life**. With certain exceptions, such as sites used for extractive purposes or landfill, land has an unlimited life and therefore is not depreciated.

6.40   The **useful economic lives** and **residual values** of **tangible fixed assets** shall be reviewed regularly and, when necessary, revised. On revision, the carrying amount of the **tangible fixed asset** at the date of revision less the revised **residual value** shall be depreciated over the revised remaining **useful economic life**.

6.41   A change from one method of providing **depreciation** to another is permissible only on the grounds that the new method will give a fairer presentation of the results and of the financial position. Such a change does not, however, constitute a change of **accounting policy**; the carrying amount of the **tangible fixed asset** is depreciated using the revised method over the remaining **useful economic life**, beginning in the period in which the change is made.

6.42   The following shall be disclosed in the financial statements for (1) land and buildings and (2) other **tangible fixed assets** in aggregate:

   (a)   the **depreciation** methods used;
   (b)   the useful economic lives or the depreciation rates used; and
   (c)   where material, the financial effect of a change during the period in either the estimate of **useful economic lives** or the estimate of **residual values**.

6.43   Where there has been a change in the **depreciation** method used, the effect, if material, shall be disclosed in the period of change. The reason for the change shall also be disclosed.

Write-downs to recoverable amount

6.44   Paragraphs 6.45-6.48 apply to capitalised goodwill and all fixed assets (i.e. **tangible fixed assets**, **intangible assets** and **investments**) except **investment properties** and financial instruments (other than investments in subsidiaries, associates and joint ventures).

6.45   Fixed assets and goodwill shall be carried in the balance sheet at no more than **recoverable amount**. If the net book amount of a fixed asset or goodwill is considered not to be recoverable in full at the balance sheet date, the net book amount shall be written down to the estimated **recoverable amount**, which shall then be written off over the remaining **useful economic life** of the asset.

At each reporting date an assessment shall be carried out of whether there is any indication that an asset should be written down (ie whether its carrying amount is more than its recoverable amount). If any such indication exists, the recoverable amount of the asset shall be estimated. If there is no indication that an asset should be written down, it is not necessary to estimate the recoverable amount.   **6.45A**

In assessing whether there is any indication that an asset should be written down, the following might be considered: **6.45B**

(a)   During the period, an asset's market value has declined significantly more than would be expected as a result of the passage of time or normal use.

(b)   Significant changes with an adverse effect on an asset, or the entity, have taken place during the period, or will take place in the near future, (for example external factors such as technological, market, economic or legal changes or internal factors such as the asset becoming idle, or plans to dispose of an asset before the previously expected date).

(c)   Market interest rates have increased during the period, and those increases are likely to affect materially the asset's recoverable amount.

(d)   Evidence is available of obsolescence or physical damage of an asset.

(e)   Evidence is available from internal reporting that indicates that operating results or cash flows from the use of the asset are, or will be, worse than expected.

If there is an indication that an asset should be written down, this may indicate that the entity should review the remaining useful economic life, the depreciation method or the residual value of the asset and adjust it in accordance with paragraph 6.40 even if no loss is recognised for writing down the asset.   **6.45C**

If the **recoverable amount** of a **tangible fixed asset** or investment subsequently increases as a result of a change in economic conditions or in the expected use of the asset, the net book amount shall be written back to the lower of **recoverable amount** and the amount at which the asset would have been recorded had the original writedown not been made.   **6.46**

If the **recoverable amount** of an **intangible asset** or capitalised goodwill subsequently increases, the net book amount shall be written back only if an external event caused the original write-down and subsequent external events clearly and demonstrably reverse the effects of that event in a way that was not foreseen when the original writedown was calculated.   **6.47**

Write-downs (and any reversals) to **recoverable amount** shall be charged (or credited) in the profit and loss account for the period. However, write-downs of revalued **tangible fixed assets** that reverse previous revaluation gains simply as a result of changing market prices shall instead be **recognised** in the statement of **total recognised gains and losses**, to the extent that the carrying amount of the asset is greater than its depreciated historical cost. ANY AMOUNTS WHICH ARE NOT SHOWN IN THE PROFIT AND LOSS ACCOUNT MUST BE DISCLOSED (EITHER SEPARATELY OR IN AGGREGATE) IN A NOTE TO THE ACCOUNTS.   **6.48**

WHERE FIXED ASSETS ARE NOT ACTUALLY REVALUED IN THE BALANCE SHEET BUT THEIR VALUE IS CONSIDERED BY THE **DIRECTORS**, A NOTE TO THE ACCOUNTS MUST STATE THE FOLLOWING: **6.49**

(A)   THAT THE **DIRECTORS** HAVE CONSIDERED THE VALUE OF SOME OR ALL OF THE FIXED ASSETS OF THE COMPANY, WITHOUT ACTUALLY REVALUING THOSE ASSETS;

(B)   THAT THE **DIRECTORS** ARE SATISFIED THAT THE AGGREGATE VALUE OF THOSE ASSETS AT THE TIME IN QUESTION IS OR WAS NOT LESS THAN THE AGGREGATE AMOUNT AT WHICH THEY WERE THEN STATED IN THE COMPANY'S ACCOUNTS; AND

(C)   THE ASSETS AFFECTED ARE ACCORDINGLY STATED IN THE ACCOUNTS ON THE BASIS THAT A REVALUATION OF THE COMPANY'S FIXED ASSETS TOOK PLACE AT THAT TIME.

Investment properties

6.50   **Investment properties** shall not be subject to periodic charges for **depreciation** except for properties held on lease, which shall be **depreciated** at least over the period when the unexpired term is 20 years or less.

6.51   **Investment properties** shall be included in the balance sheet at their market value and the carrying value shall be displayed prominently either on the face of the balance sheet or in the notes.

6.52   The names of the persons making the valuation, or particulars of their qualifications, shall be disclosed together with the bases of valuation used by them. If a person making a valuation is an employee or officer of the company or group that owns the property this fact shall be disclosed.

6.53   Changes in the market value of **investment properties** shall not be taken to the profit and loss account but shall be taken to the statement of **total recognised gains and losses** (being a movement on an investment revaluation reserve), unless a deficit (or its reversal) on an individual **investment property** is expected to be permanent, in which case it shall be charged (or credited) in the profit and loss account of the period.

Government grants[35]

6.54   Subject to paragraph 6.55, **government grants** shall be **recognised** in the profit and loss account so as to match them with the expenditure towards which they are intended to contribute. To the extent that the grant is made as a contribution towards expenditure on a fixed asset, in principle it may be deducted from the purchase price or production cost of that asset. However, the option to deduct **government grants** from the purchase price or production costs of fixed assets is not available to companies governed by the accounting and reporting requirements of UK **companies legislation.** In such cases, the amount so deferred shall be treated as deferred income.

6.55   A **government grant** shall not be **recognised** in the profit and loss account until the conditions for its receipt have been complied with and there is reasonable assurance that the grant will be received.

6.56   Potential liabilities to repay grants either in whole or in part in specified circumstances shall be provided for only to the extent that repayment is probable. The repayment of a **government grant** shall be accounted for by setting off the repayment against any unamortised deferred income relating to the grant. Any excess shall be charged immediately to the profit and loss account.

6.57   The following information shall be disclosed in the financial statements:

(a)   the effects of **government grants** on the results for the period and/or the financial position of the entity; and

(b)   where the results of the period are affected materially by the receipt of forms of **government** assistance other than grants, the nature of that assistance and, to the extent that the effects on the financial statements can be measured, an estimate of those effects.

---

[35] *Additional specific legal requirements relating to government grants in the Republic of Ireland are included in the derivation tables on the FRC website.*

7 Leases

Hire purchase and leasing

Those **hire purchase contracts** which are of a financing nature shall be accounted for on a basis similar to that set out below for **finance leases**. Conversely, other **hire purchase contracts** shall be accounted for on a basis similar to that set out below for **operating leases**.   **7.1**

Accounting by lessees

A **finance lease** shall be recorded in the balance sheet of a lessee as an asset and as an **obligation** to pay future rentals. At the **inception** of the lease, the sum to be recorded both as an asset and as a liability shall normally be the **fair value** of the asset.   **7.2**

In those cases where the **fair value** of the asset does not give a realistic estimate of the cost to the lessee of the asset and of the **obligation** entered into, a better estimate shall be used. In principle this shall approximate to the present value of the **minimum lease payments**, derived by discounting them at the interest rate implicit in the lease. An example of where this might be used would be where the lessee has benefited from grants and capital allowances that enable the **minimum lease payments** under a **finance lease** to be adjusted to a total that is less than the **fair value** of the asset. A negative **finance charge** shall not be shown.   **7.3**

The total **finance charge** under a **finance lease** shall be allocated to accounting periods during the **lease term** so as to produce a constant periodic rate of charge on the remaining balance of the **obligation** for each accounting period, or a reasonable approximation thereto. The straight-line method may provide such a reasonable approximation.   **7.4**

The rental under an **operating lease** shall be charged on a straight-line basis over the **lease term** even if the payments are not made on such a basis, unless another systematic and rational basis is more appropriate.   **7.5**

Incentives to sign a lease, in whatever form they may take, shall be spread by the lessee on a straight-line basis over the **lease term** or, if shorter than the full **lease term**, over the period to the review date on which the rent is first expected to be adjusted to the prevailing market rate.   **7.6**

An **asset** leased under a **finance lease** shall be depreciated over the shorter of the **lease term** or its useful life. However, in the case of a **hire purchase contract** that has the characteristics of a **finance lease**, the asset shall be depreciated over its useful life.   **7.7**

Accounting by lessors

The amount due from the lessee under a **finance lease** shall be recorded in the balance sheet of a lessor as a debtor at the amount of the **net investment** in the lease after making provisions for items such as bad and doubtful rentals receivable.   **7.8**

The total **gross earnings** under **finance leases** shall be **recognised** on a systematic and rational basis. This will normally be a constant periodic rate of return on the lessor's **net investment**.   **7.9**

Rental income from an **operating lease** shall be **recognised** on a straight-line basis over the period of the lease, even if the payments are not made on such a basis, unless another systematic and rational basis is more representative of the time pattern in which the benefit from the **leased** asset is receivable.   **7.10**

7.11 An asset held for use in **operating leases** by a lessor shall be recorded as a fixed **asset** and **depreciated** over its useful life.

Manufacturer/dealer lessor

7.12 A manufacturer or dealer lessor shall not **recognise** a selling profit under an **operating lease**. The selling profit under a **finance lease** shall be restricted to the excess of the **fair value** of the **asset** over the manufacturer's or dealer's cost less any grants receivable by the manufacturer or dealer towards the purchase, construction or use of the **asset**.

Sale and leaseback transactions – accounting by the seller/lessee

7.13 In a sale and leaseback transaction that results in a **finance lease**, any apparent profit or loss (i.e. the difference between the sale price and the previous carrying value) shall be deferred and amortised in the financial statements of the seller/lessee over the shorter of the **lease term** and the useful life of the **asset**.

7.14 If the leaseback is an **operating lease**:

(a)   any profit or loss shall be **recognised** immediately, provided it is clear that the transaction is established at **fair value**;

(b)   if the sale price is below **fair value** any profit or loss shall be **recognised** immediately, except that if the apparent loss is compensated for by future rentals at below market price it shall to that extent be deferred and amortised over the remainder of the **lease term** (or, if shorter, the period during which the reduced rentals are chargeable); or

(c)   if the sale price is above **fair value**, the excess over **fair value** shall be deferred and amortised over the shorter of the remainder of the **lease term** and the period to the next rent review (if any).

Sale and leaseback transactions – accounting by the buyer/lessor

7.15 A buyer/lessor shall account for a sale and leaseback in the same way as other leases are accounted for, i.e. using the methods set out in paragraphs 7.8-7.12.

Disclosure by lessees

7.16 Disclosure shall be made of:

(a)   either:

(i)   the gross amounts of **assets** that are held under **finance leases** together with the related accumulated **depreciation** for (1) land and buildings and (2) other fixed **assets** in aggregate; or

(ii)   alternatively to being shown separately from that in respect of owned fixed **assets**, the information in (i) above may be integrated with it, such that the totals of gross amount, accumulated **depreciation**, net amount and **depreciation** allocated for the period for (1) land and buildings and (2) other fixed assets in aggregate for **assets** held under **finance leases** are included with similar amounts for owned fixed **assets**. Where this alternative treatment is adopted, the net amount of **assets** held under **finance leases** and the amount of **depreciation** allocated for the period in respect of **assets** under **finance leases** included in the overall total shall be disclosed separately.

(b)   the amounts of **obligations** related to **finance leases** (net of **finance charges** allocated to future periods). These shall be disclosed separately from other **obligations** and liabilities, either on the face of the balance sheet or in the notes to the accounts.

(c)   the amount of any commitments existing at the balance sheet date in respect of **finance leases** that have been entered into but whose **inception** occurs after the year end.

In respect of **operating leases**, the lessee shall disclose the payments that it is committed to make during the next year, analysed into those in which the commitment expires within that year, those expiring in the second to fifth years inclusive, and those expiring over five years from the balance sheet date.   7.17

Disclosure by lessors

Disclosure shall be made of: 7.18

(a)   the gross amounts of **assets** held for use in **operating leases** and the related accumulated **depreciation** charges;

(b)   the cost of assets acquired, whether by purchase or **finance lease**, for the purpose of letting under **finance leases**; and

(c)   the **net investment** in (i) **finance leases** and (ii) **hire purchase contracts** at each balance sheet date.

8   Current assets

Stocks and long-term contracts[36]

The amount at which stocks are stated in the financial statements shall be the total of the lower of cost and **net realisable value** of the separate items of stock or of groups of similar items.   8.1

WHERE THERE IS NO RECORD OF THE PURCHASE PRICE OR PRODUCTION COST OF STOCK THE VALUE ASCRIBED MUST BE THE EARLIEST AVAILABLE RECORD OF ITS VALUE. PARTICULARS MUST BE GIVEN OF ANY CASE WHERE THE PURCHASE PRICE OR PRODUCTION COST OF ANY ASSET IS FOR THE FIRST TIME DETERMINED IN THIS WAY.   8.2

FINANCE COSTS (SUCH AS INTEREST) THAT ARE DIRECTLY ATTRIBUTABLE TO THE ACQUISITION, CONSTRUCTION OR PRODUCTION OF STOCK MAY BE INCLUDED AS PART OF THE COST. IN SUCH CIRCUMSTANCES, THE NOTES TO THE ACCOUNTS MUST DISCLOSE THAT FINANCE COSTS ARE INCLUDED IN DETERMINING THE COST OF THE **ASSET** AND THE AMOUNT OF FINANCE COSTS SO INCLUDED.   8.3

WHERE STOCKS ARE CONSTANTLY BEING REPLACED AND THEIR VALUE IS NOT MATERIAL TO ASSESSING THE COMPANY'S STATE OF AFFAIRS AND THEIR QUANTITY, VALUE AND COMPOSITION ARE NOT SUBJECT TO MATERIAL VARIATION, THEY MAY BE INCLUDED AT A FIXED QUANTITY AND VALUE.   8.4

DISTRIBUTION COSTS MAY NOT BE INCLUDED IN THE PRODUCTION COSTS OF STOCKS.   8.5

Long-term contracts shall be assessed on a contract-by-contract basis and reflected in the profit and loss account by recording turnover and related costs as contract activity progresses. Turnover is ascertained in a manner appropriate to the stage of completion of the contract, the business and the industry in which it operates.   8.6

Where it is considered that the outcome of a **long-term contract** can be assessed with reasonable certainty before its conclusion, the prudently calculated **attributable profit** shall be **recognised** in the profit and loss account as the difference between the reported turnover and related costs for that contract.   8.7

---

[36] *Guidance on the practical considerations of arriving at amounts at which stocks and long-term contracts are stated in financial statements is given in Appendix III.*

8.8   **Long-term contracts** shall be disclosed in the balance sheet as follows:

(a)   The amount by which recorded turnover is in excess of payments on account shall be classified as 'amounts recoverable on contracts' and separately disclosed within debtors.

(b)   The balance of payments on account (in excess of the amounts (i) matched with turnover and (ii) offset against **long-term contract** balances) shall be classified as payments on account and separately disclosed within creditors.

(c)   The amount of **long-term contracts**, at costs incurred, net of amounts transferred to cost of sales, after deducting **foreseeable losses** and payments on account not matched with turnover, shall be classified as 'long-term contract balances' and separately disclosed within the balance sheet heading 'stocks'. The balance sheet note shall disclose separately the balances of:

(i)   net cost less **foreseeable losses**; and

(ii)   applicable payments on account.

(d)   The amount by which the provision or accrual for **foreseeable losses** exceeds the costs incurred (after transfers to cost of sales) shall be included within either 'provisions for liabilities' or 'creditors' as appropriate.

Consignment stock[37]

8.9   Where **consignment stock** is in substance an **asset** of the dealer, the stock shall be **recognised** as such on the dealer's balance sheet, together with a corresponding liability to the manufacturer. Any deposit shall be deducted from the **liability** and the excess classified as a trade creditor. Where stock is not in substance an **asset** of the dealer, the stock shall not be included on the dealer's balance sheet until the transfer of title has crystallised. Any deposit shall be included under 'other debtors'.

Debt factoring[38]

8.10   Where the entity has transferred to the factor all significant benefits (i.e. the future cash flows from payment by the debtors) and all significant risks (i.e. slow payment risk and the risk of bad debts) relating to the debts, and has no **obligation** to repay the factor, the debts shall be removed from the entity's balance sheet and no **liability** shall be shown in respect of the proceeds received from the factor. A profit or loss shall be **recognised,** calculated as the difference between the carrying amount of the debts and the proceeds received.

8.11   Where the entity has retained significant benefits and risks relating to factored debts, and all the following conditions are met:

(a)   there is absolutely no doubt that the entity's exposure to loss is limited to a fixed monetary amount (e.g. because there is no recourse or such recourse has a fixed monetary ceiling);

(b)   amounts received from the factor are secured only on the debts factored;

(c)   the debts factored are capable of separate identification;

(d)   the debt factor has no recourse to other debts or assets;

(e)   the entity has no right to reacquire the debts in the future; and

(f)   the factor has no right to return the debts even in the event of the cessation of the factoring agreement,

---

[37] *A table illustrating the considerations affecting the treatment of consignment stock is given in Appendix III.*

[38] *Similar arrangements, such as invoice discounting, shall be accounted for in the same way as debt factoring. A table illustrating the considerations affecting the treatment of debt factoring is given in Appendix III.*

then the factored debts shall be shown gross (after providing for bad debts, credit protection charges and any accrued interest) separately on the face of the balance sheet. Any amounts received from the factor in respect of those debts, to the extent that they are not returnable, shall be shown as deductions therefrom on the face of the balance sheet (a 'linked presentation'). The financial statements shall include a note stating that the entity is not required to support bad debts in respect of factored debts and that the factors have stated in writing that they will not seek recourse other than out of factored debts. The interest element of the factor's charges shall be **recognised** as it accrues and included in the profit and loss account with other interest charges.

In all other cases a separate presentation shall be adopted. A gross **asset** (equivalent in amount to the gross amount of the debts) shall be shown on the balance sheet of the entity within **assets** and a corresponding **liability** in respect of the proceeds received from the factor shall be shown within **liabilities**. The interest element of the factor's charges and other factoring costs shall be **recognised** as they accrue and included in the profit and loss account with other interest charges. **8.12**

Current asset investments

CURRENT **ASSET** INVESTMENTS MUST INITIALLY BE STATED IN THE FINANCIAL STATEMENTS AT THE LOWER OF COST AND **NET REALISABLE VALUE**. ALTERNATIVELY, THEY MAY BE MEASURED AT THEIR CURRENT COST. Gains and losses shall be **recognised** (in the profit and loss account or statement of **total recognised gains and losses**) using the same basis applied to **tangible fixed assets** in paragraphs 6.25 and 6.26 above. **8.13**

WHERE LISTED SHARES ARE HELD AS A CURRENT **ASSET** INVESTMENT, THE FOLLOWING INFORMATION MUST BE DISCLOSED: **8.14**

(A)   THE AGGREGATE MARKET VALUE OF THOSE INVESTMENTS WHERE IT DIFFERS FROM THEIR BALANCE SHEET AMOUNT; AND

(B)   BOTH THE MARKET VALUE AND THE STOCK EXCHANGE VALUE OF ANY INVESTMENTS, OF WHICH THE MARKET VALUE IS TAKEN AS BEING HIGHER THAN THE STOCK EXCHANGE VALUE.

Start-up costs and pre-contract costs

Start-up costs shall be accounted for on a basis consistent with the accounting treatment of similar costs incurred as part of the entity's on-going activities. In cases where there are no such similar costs, **start-up** costs that do not meet the criteria for **recognition** as **assets** under another specific requirement of the FRSSE shall be **recognised** as an expense when they are incurred. They shall not be carried forward as an **asset**. **8.15**

Pre-contract costs shall be expensed as incurred, except that **directly attributable costs** shall be **recognised** as an **asset** when it is virtually certain that a contract will be obtained and the contract is expected to result in future net cash inflows with a present value no less than all amounts **recognised** as an **asset**. Costs incurred before the **asset recognition** criteria are met shall not be **recognised** as an **asset**. **8.16**

9   Taxation

General

Tax (current and **deferred**) shall be **recognised** in the profit and loss account, except to the extent that it is attributable to a gain or loss that is or has been **recognised** directly in the statement of **total recognised gains and losses** (in which case the tax shall also be **recognised** directly in that statement). **9.1**

9.2   The material components of the (current and **deferred**) **tax** charge (or credit) for the period shall be disclosed separately.

9.3   Any special circumstances that affect the overall tax charge or credit for the period, or may affect those of future periods, shall be disclosed by way of a note to the profit and loss account and their individual effects quantified. The effects of a fundamental change in the basis of taxation shall be included in the tax charge or credit for the period and separately disclosed on the face of the profit and loss account.

Deferred tax

9.4   **Deferred tax** shall be **recognised** in respect of all **timing differences** that have originated but not reversed by the balance sheet date; however, **deferred tax** shall not be **recognised** on:

   (a)   revaluation gains and losses unless, by the balance sheet date, the entity has entered into a binding agreement to sell the **asset** and has revalued the **asset** to the selling price; or

   (b)   taxable gains arising on revaluations or sales if it is more likely than not that the gain will be rolled over into a replacement **asset**.

9.5   Unrelieved tax losses and other **deferred tax assets** shall be **recognised** only to the extent that it is more likely than not that they will be recovered against the reversal of **deferred tax liabilities** or other future taxable profits (the very existence of unrelieved tax losses is strong evidence that there may not be 'other future taxable profits' against which the losses will be relieved).

9.6   **Deferred tax** shall be **recognised** when the tax allowances for the cost of a fixed **asset** are received before or after the **depreciation** of the fixed **asset** is **recognised** in the profit and loss account. However, if and when all conditions for retaining the tax allowances have been met, the **deferred tax** shall be reversed.

9.7   Deferred tax shall not be recognised on permanent differences.

9.8   **Deferred tax** shall be measured at the average tax rates that would apply when the **timing differences** are expected to reverse, based on tax rates and laws that have been enacted by the balance sheet date.

9.9   The discounting of **deferred tax assets** and **liabilities** is not required. However, if an entity does adopt a policy of discounting, all **deferred tax** balances that have been measured by reference to undiscounted cash flows and for which the impact of discounting is material shall be discounted. Where discounting is used, the unwinding of the discount shall be shown as a component of the tax charge and disclosed separately.

9.10   The **deferred tax** balance and its material components shall be disclosed.

9.11   The movement between the opening and closing net **deferred tax** balances, and the material components of this movement, shall be disclosed.

9.12   If **assets** have been revalued, or if their market values have been disclosed in a note, the amount of tax that would be payable or recoverable if the **assets** were sold at the values shown shall be disclosed.

Tax on dividends

Outgoing dividends and similar amounts payable shall be **recognised** at an amount that includes any **withholding tax** but excludes other taxes, such as attributable **tax credits**. **9.13**

Incoming dividends and similar income receivable shall be **recognised** at an amount that includes any **withholding tax** but excludes other taxes, such as attributable **tax credits**. Any **withholding tax** suffered shall be shown as part of the tax charge. **9.14**

Value added tax (VAT)

Turnover shown in the profit and loss account shall exclude either VAT on taxable outputs or VAT imputed under the flat rate VAT scheme. Irrecoverable VAT allocable to fixed **assets** and to other items disclosed separately in the financial statements shall be included in their cost where practicable and material. **9.15**

10   Pensions

The cost of a **defined contribution scheme** is equal to the contributions payable to the scheme for the accounting period. The cost shall be **recognised** within operating profit in the profit and loss account. **10.1**

PARTICULARS MUST BE GIVEN OF ANY PENSION COMMITMENTS INCLUDED UNDER ANY PROVISION SHOWN IN THE COMPANY'S BALANCE SHEET AND ANY SUCH COMMITMENTS FOR WHICH NO PROVISION HAS BEEN MADE. WHERE ANY SUCH COMMITMENT RELATES WHOLLY OR PARTLY TO PENSIONS PAYABLE TO PAST **DIRECTORS** OF THE COMPANY, SEPARATE PARTICULARS MUST BE GIVEN OF THAT COMMITMENT, SO FAR AS IT RELATES TO SUCH PENSIONS. **10.2**

The following disclosures shall be made in respect of a **defined contribution scheme**: **10.3**

(a)   the nature of the scheme (i.e. defined contribution);
(b)   the cost for the period; and
(c)   any outstanding or prepaid contributions at the balance sheet date.

An employer participating in a **defined benefit scheme** shall refer to Appendix II 'Accounting for retirement benefits: defined benefit schemes'. **10.4**

11 Provisions, contingent liabilities and contingent assets

The requirements in paragraphs 11.2 to 11.8 do not apply to pensions, **deferred tax** and leases, which are covered by more specific requirements of the FRSSE. **11.1**

Provisions

A **provision** shall be **recognised** when, and only when, it is probable (i.e. more likely than not) that a present **obligation** exists, as a result of a past event, and that it will require a transfer of economic benefits in settlement that can be estimated reliably. The amount **recognised** as a **provision** shall be the best estimate of the expenditure required to settle the **obligation** at the balance sheet date. Where the effect of the time value of money is material, the amount of a **provision** shall be the present value of the expenditures expected **11.2** to be required to settle the **obligation**. Where discounting is used, the unwinding of the discount shall be shown as other finance costs adjacent to interest.[39]

11.3   Where some or all of the expenditure required to settle a **provision** may be reimbursed by another party (e.g. through an insurance claim), the reimbursement shall be **recognised**, as a separate **asset**, only when it is virtually certain to be received if the entity settles the **obligation**. In the profit and loss account, the expense relating to the **provision** may be presented net of the recovery. Gains from the expected disposal of **assets** shall be excluded from the measurement of a provision.

11.4   **Provisions** shall be reviewed at each balance sheet date and adjusted to reflect the current best estimate.

11.5   A **provision** shall be used only for expenditures for which the **provision** was originally **recognised**.

11.6   FOR EACH CLASS OF **PROVISION** THE FOLLOWING INFORMATION MUST BE PROVIDED:

(A)   THE AMOUNT OF THE **PROVISION** AT THE BEGINNING AND THE END OF THE **FINANCIAL YEAR**;
(B)   ANY AMOUNTS TRANSFERRED TO OR FROM THE **PROVISION** DURING THE YEAR;
(C)   THE SOURCE AND APPLICATION OF THE AMOUNTS TRANSFERRED; AND
(D)   PARTICULARS OF EACH MATERIAL **PROVISION** INCLUDED UNDER 'OTHER PROVISIONS' IN THE COMPANY'S BALANCE SHEET IN ANY CASE WHERE THE AMOUNT OF THAT **PROVISION** IS MATERIAL.

THE DISCLOSURES SET OUT ABOVE ARE NOT REQUIRED WHERE THE MOVEMENT CONSISTS OF THE APPLICATION OF A **PROVISION** FOR THE PURPOSE FOR WHICH IT WAS ESTABLISHED.

Contingent liabilities and contingent assets

11.7   Contingent liabilities and **contingent assets** shall not be **recognised.**

11.8   The following shall be disclosed for **contingent liabilities**, except where their existence is remote, and for probable **contingent assets**:

(a)   a brief description of the nature of the contingent item; and
(b)   where practicable, an estimate of its financial effect; and
(c)   ITS LEGAL NATURE.

11.9   DETAILS MUST BE PROVIDED WHERE ANY VALUABLE SECURITY HAS BEEN PROVIDED BY THE COMPANY IN CONNECTION WITH A **CONTINGENT LIABILITY** AND IF SO, WHAT.

11.10   WHERE PRACTICABLE, THE AGGREGATE AMOUNT, OR ESTIMATED AMOUNT, OF CONTRACTS FOR CAPITAL EXPENDITURE NOT PROVIDED FOR MUST BE DISCLOSED. DETAILS OF ANY OTHER FINANCIAL COMMITMENTS NOT PROVIDED FOR WHICH ARE RELEVANT TO ASSESSING THE COMPANY'S STATE OF AFFAIRS MUST ALSO BE DISCLOSED.

11.11   PARTICULARS MUST BE GIVEN OF ANY CHARGE ON THE ASSETS OF THE COMPANY TO SECURE THE LIABILITIES OF ANY OTHER PERSON, INCLUDING WHERE PRACTICABLE, THE AMOUNT SECURED.

---

[39] *There are a number of acceptable methods of discounting, and the appropriate discount rate depends on the method adopted. However, if cash flows are expressed in future prices and have been adjusted for risk, it will be appropriate to discount them at a risk-free rate such as a market rate on relevant government bonds. An illustrative example of a provision calculated using discounting is given in Appendix III.*

12 Financial instruments, share capital and share-based payments

General

A **financial instrument**, or its component parts, shall be classified as a **financial** **12.1** **liability**, a **financial asset** or an **equity instrument** in accordance with the substance of the contractual arrangement rather than its legal form. Some **financial instruments** take the legal form of equity but are **liabilities** in substance and others may combine features associated with **equity instruments** and features associated with **financial liabilities**. For example a preference share that provides for mandatory redemption by the issuer for a fixed or determinable amount at a fixed or determinable future date, or gives the holder the right to require the issuer to redeem the instrument at or after a particular date for a fixed or determinable amount, is a **financial liability**.

The **finance costs** of **borrowings** shall be allocated to periods over the **term** of the **12.2** **borrowings** at a constant rate on the carrying amount. All **finance costs** shall be charged in the profit and loss account.

Borrowings shall be initially stated in the balance sheet at the **fair value** of consideration **12.3** received. The carrying amount of **borrowings** shall be increased by the **finance cost** in respect of the reporting period and reduced by payments made in respect of the **borrowings** in that period.

Where an **arrangement fee** is such as to represent a significant additional cost of finance **12.4** when compared with the interest payable over the life of the instrument, the treatment set out in paragraph 12.2 shall be followed. Where this is not the case it shall be charged in the profit and loss account immediately it is incurred.

THE AMOUNT OF ANY CONVERTIBLE DEBT ISSUED MUST BE SEPARATELY DISCLOSED FROM OTHER **12.5** LIABILITIES.

Dividends relating to a **financial instrument** or a component that is a **financial liability** **12.6** shall be recognised as expense in profit or loss. Distributions to holders of an **equity instrument** shall be debited by the entity directly to equity, net of any related income tax benefit. If an entity declares dividends after the balance sheet date, the dividends shall not be **recognised** as a **liability** at the balance sheet date.

THE NOTES TO THE ACCOUNTS MUST STATE: **12.7**

(A)   THE AGGREGATE AMOUNT OF DIVIDENDS PAID IN THE FINANCIAL YEAR (OTHER THAN THOSE FOR WHICH A LIABILITY EXISTED AT THE IMMEDIATELY PRECEDING BALANCE SHEET DATE);

(B)   THE AGGREGATE AMOUNT OF DIVIDENDS THAT THE COMPANY IS LIABLE TO PAY AT THE BALANCE SHEET DATE; AND

(C)   THE AGGREGATE AMOUNT OF DIVIDENDS THAT ARE PROPOSED BEFORE THE DATE OF APPROVAL OF THE ACCOUNTS, AND NOT OTHERWISE DISCLOSED UNDER PARAGRAPH (A) OR (B) ABOVE.

IF ANY FIXED CUMULATIVE DIVIDENDS ON THE COMPANY'S SHARES ARE IN ARREARS, THE AMOUNT **12.8** OF THE ARREARS AND THE PERIOD FOR WHICH EACH CLASS OF DIVIDENDS IS IN ARREARS MUST BE DISCLOSED.

The company's share capital

12.9   THE FOLLOWING INFORMATION MUST BE DISCLOSED WITH RESPECT TO THE COMPANY'S SHARE CAPITAL:

(A)   WHERE SHARES OF MORE THAN ONE CLASS HAVE BEEN ALLOTTED, THE NUMBER AND AGGREGATE NOMINAL VALUE OF SHARES OF EACH CLASS ALLOTTED;

(B)   FOR ANY PART OF THE ALLOTTED SHARE CAPITAL THAT CONSISTS OF REDEEMABLE SHARES:

(I)   THE EARLIEST AND LATEST DATES ON WHICH THE COMPANY HAS THE POWER TO REDEEM THOSE SHARES;

(II)   WHETHER THOSE SHARES MUST BE REDEEMED IN ANY EVENT OR ARE LIABLE TO BE REDEEMED AT THE OPTION OF THE COMPANY OR OF THE SHAREHOLDER; AND

(III)   WHETHER ANY (AND, IF SO, WHAT) PREMIUM IS PAYABLE ON REDEMPTION.

12.10   IF THE COMPANY HAS ALLOTTED ANY SHARES DURING THE PERIOD, THE FOLLOWING INFORMATION MUST BE DISCLOSED:

(A)   THE CLASSES OF SHARES ALLOTTED; AND

(B)   FOR EACH CLASS, THE NUMBER ALLOTTED, THEIR AGGREGATE NOMINAL VALUE, AND THE CONSIDERATION RECEIVED BY THE COMPANY FOR THE ALLOTMENT.

12.11   THE AMOUNT OF ALLOTTED SHARE CAPITAL AND THE AMOUNT OF CALLED UP SHARE CAPITAL WHICH HAS BEEN PAID UP MUST BE SEPARATELY DISCLOSED.

12.12   THE NUMBER, DESCRIPTION AND AMOUNT OF SHARES IN THE COMPANY HELD BY OR ON BEHALF OF ITS **SUBSIDIARY UNDERTAKINGS** MUST BE DISCLOSED UNLESS THE SUBSIDIARY UNDERTAKING IS CONCERNED AS A PERSONAL REPRESENTATIVE OR A TRUSTEE.

Share-based payments

12.13   An entity which undertakes **share-based payment arrangements**, including transactions with **employees or others providing similar services** shall account for them as follows.

Cash-settled share-based payment transactions

(a)   An entity shall recognise the goods or services received or acquired when it obtains the goods or as the services are received. If the goods or services received or acquired do not qualify for recognition as **assets**, they shall be **recognised** as expenses. The entity shall **recognise** a corresponding **liability.**

(b)   **The amount of the goods or services and the corresponding liability recognised** shall be the best estimate of the expenditure required to settle the **liability** at the balance sheet date. The **liability** shall be remeasured at each balance sheet date and at the date of settlement.

(c)   Information shall be disclosed in a note to describe the principal terms and conditions of cash settled share-based payment transactions that exist during the period, including their current and potential financial effect.

Equity-settled share-based payment arrangements

(d)   Information shall be disclosed in a note to describe the principal terms and conditions of any equity settled share-based payment arrangements that exist during the period including, the number of shares and the number of employees and others potentially involved, the grant date, any performance conditions and over what periods these apply and, where applicable, any option exercise prices.

Where the terms of the arrangement provide the counterparty with the choice of whether the entity settles the transaction in cash (or other assets) or by issuing **equity instruments**, the transaction, shall be accounted for as a cash-settled transaction in accordance with paragraph 12.13 (a) to (c) above. The liability shall be measured at the best estimate of the amount required to settle it at the balance sheet date if the counterparty were to opt for cash settlement. If the obligation is eventually settled by the issue of equity instruments, the liability previously recognised should be treated as the proceeds of issue of those instruments. **12.14**

Where the entity and not the counterparty has the choice of settlement method, the arrangement shall be treated as either an equity-settled transaction in accordance with paragraph 12.13(d) or a cash-settled transaction in accordance with paragraph 12.13 (a) to (c), as appropriate in the entity's circumstances. **12.15**

13   Foreign currency translation

Transactions in foreign currencies

WHERE SUMS ORIGINALLY DENOMINATED IN FOREIGN CURRENCIES HAVE BEEN BROUGHT INTO ACCOUNT UNDER ANY ITEMS SHOWN IN THE BALANCE SHEET OR PROFIT AND LOSS ACCOUNT, THE BASIS ON WHICH THOSE SUMS HAVE BEEN TRANSLATED INTO **LOCAL CURRENCY** MUST BE DISCLOSED. **13.1**

Subject to the provisions of paragraphs 13.4 and 13.6, each **asset**, **liability**, revenue or cost arising from a transaction denominated in a foreign currency shall be translated into the **local currency** at the **exchange rate** in operation on the date on which the transaction occurred; if the rates do not fluctuate significantly, an average rate for a period may be used as an approximation. Where the transaction is to be settled at a contracted rate, that rate shall be used. Where a trading transaction is covered by a related or matching **forward contract**, the rate of exchange specified in that contract may be used. **13.2**

Subject to the special provisions of paragraph 13.6, which relate to the treatment of foreign equity investments financed by foreign currency **borrowings**, no subsequent **translations** shall normally be made once non-monetary **assets** have been translated and recorded. **13.3**

At each balance sheet date, monetary **assets** and **liabilities** denominated in a foreign currency shall be translated by using the **closing rate** or, where appropriate, the rates of exchange fixed under the terms of the relevant transactions. Where there are related or matching **forward contracts** in respect of trading transactions, the rates of exchange specified in those contracts may be used. **13.4**

All exchange gains or losses on settled transactions and unsettled **monetary items** shall be reported as part of the profit or loss for the period from **ordinary activities**. **13.5**

Where a company has used foreign currency **borrowings** to finance, or to provide a hedge against, its foreign equity investments and the conditions set out in this paragraph apply, the equity investments may be denominated in the appropriate foreign currencies and the carrying amounts translated at the end of each accounting period at **closing rates** for inclusion in the investing company's financial statements. Where investments are treated in this way, any exchange differences arising shall be taken to reserves and the exchange gains or losses on the foreign currency **borrowings** shall then be offset, as a reserve movement, against these exchange differences. The conditions that must apply are as follows: **13.6**

(a)   in any accounting period, exchange gains or losses arising on the **borrowings** may be offset only to the extent of exchange differences arising on the equity investments;

(b)   the foreign currency **borrowings**, whose exchange gains or losses are used in the offset process, shall not exceed, in the aggregate, the total amount of cash that the investments are expected to be able to generate, whether from profits or otherwise; and

(c)   the accounting treatment adopted shall be applied consistently from period to period.

Incorporating accounts of foreign entities

13.7   When preparing accounts for a company and its **foreign entities** (which includes the incorporation of the results of associated companies or foreign branches into those of an investing company) the **closing rate/net investment** method of translating the **local currency** financial statements shall normally be used.

13.8   Exchange differences arising from the retranslation of the opening **net investment** in a **foreign entity** at the **closing rate** shall be recorded as a movement on reserves.

13.9   The profit and loss account of a **foreign entity** accounted for under the **closing rate/net investment** method shall be translated at the **closing rate** or at an average rate for the period. Where an average rate is used, the difference between the profit and loss account translated at an average rate and at the **closing rate** shall be recorded as a movement on reserves. The average rate used shall be calculated by the method considered most appropriate for the circumstances of the **foreign entity**.

13.10   In those circumstances where the trade of the **foreign entity** is more dependent on the economic environment of the investing company's currency than that of its own reporting currency, the transactions of the foreign operation shall be reported as though all of its transactions had been entered into by the investing company itself in its own currency, as stated in paragraphs 13.2-13.5.

13.11   The method used for translating the financial statements of each **foreign entity** shall be applied consistently from period to period unless its financial and other operational relationships with the investing company change.

13.12   Where foreign currency **borrowings** have been used to finance, or provide a hedge against, group equity investments in **foreign entities**, exchange gains or losses on the **borrowings**, which would otherwise have been taken to the profit and loss account, may be offset as reserve movements against exchange differences arising on the retranslation of the **net investments** provided that:

(a)   the relationships between the investing company and the **foreign entities** concerned justify the use of the **closing rate** method for consolidation purposes;

(b)   in any accounting period, the exchange gains and losses arising on foreign currency **borrowings** are offset only to the extent of the exchange differences arising on the **net investments** in **foreign entities**;

(c)   the foreign currency **borrowings**, whose exchange gains or losses are used in the offset process, shall not exceed, in the aggregate, the total amount of cash that the **net investments** are expected to be able to generate, whether from profits or otherwise; and

(d)   the accounting treatment is applied consistently from period to period.

Where the provisions of paragraph 13.6 have been applied in the investing company's financial statements to a foreign equity investment that is neither a subsidiary nor an associated company, the same offset procedure may be applied in the **consolidated financial statements**.

14 Post balance sheet events

An entity shall adjust the amounts **recognised** in its financial statements to reflect adjusting **events after the balance sheet date**. **14.1**

An entity shall not adjust the amounts **recognised** in its financial statements to reflect non-adjusting **events after the balance sheet date**. **14.2**

If non-adjusting **events after the balance sheet date** are material, non-disclosure could influence the economic decisions of users taken on the basis of the financial statements. Accordingly, an entity shall disclose the following for each material category of non-adjusting event after the balance sheet date: **14.3**

(a)   the nature of the event; and
(b)   an estimate of its financial effect, or a statement that such an estimate cannot be made.

The date on which the financial statements are approved for issue and who gave that approval shall be disclosed in the financial statements. **14.4**

15 Related party disclosures

Where the reporting entity: **15.1**

(a)   purchases, sells or transfers goods and other **assets** or **liabilities**; or
(b)   renders or receives services; or
(c)   provides or receives finance or financial support; (irrespective of whether a price is charged) to, from or on behalf of a **related party**, then such material[40] transactions shall be disclosed, including:

(i)   the names of the transacting **related parties**;
(ii)   a description of the relationship between the parties;
(iii)   a description of the transactions;
(iv)   the amounts involved;
(v)   any other elements of the transactions necessary for an understanding of the financial statements;
(vi)   the amounts due to or from **related parties** at the balance sheet date and provisions for doubtful debts due from such parties at that date; and
(vii)   amounts written off in the period in respect of debts due to or from **related parties**.

Personal guarantees given by **directors** in respect of **borrowings** by the reporting entity shall be disclosed in the notes to the financial statements. **15.2**

AMOUNTS INCLUDED IN THE PROFIT AND LOSS ACCOUNT UNDER 'INVESTMENT INCOME' AND 'OTHER INTEREST RECEIVABLE AND SIMILAR INCOME' THAT WERE RECEIVED, OR ARE RECEIVABLE FROM GROUP UNDERTAKINGS, MUST BE SHOWN SEPARATELY. **15.3**

AMOUNTS INCLUDED IN THE PROFIT AND LOSS ACCOUNT UNDER 'INTEREST PAYABLE AND SIMILAR CHARGES' PAID, OR PAYABLE, TO GROUP UNDERTAKINGS, MUST BE SHOWN SEPARATELY. **15.4**

COMMITMENTS WHICH ARE UNDERTAKEN ON BEHALF OF OR FOR THE BENEFIT OF (A) ANY PARENT UNDERTAKING OR FELLOW **SUBSIDIARY UNDERTAKING**, OR (B) ANY **SUBSIDIARY UNDERTAKING** OF THE COMPANY, MUST BE DISCLOSED SEPARATELY FROM THOSE COMMITMENTS DISCLOSED UNDER **15.5**

---

[40] *The materiality of a related party transaction shall be judged in terms of its significance to the reporting entity.*

PARAGRAPHS 10.2 AND 11.8 TO 11.11, AND COMMITMENTS UNDERTAKEN UNDER (A) MUST BE DISCLOSED SEPARATELY FROM THOSE UNDERTAKEN UNDER (B).

15.6   Other transactions with **related parties** may be disclosed on an aggregated basis (aggregation of similar transactions by type of **related party**) unless disclosure of an individual transaction, or connected transactions, is necessary for an understanding of the impact of the transactions on the financial statements of the reporting entity or is required by law.

15.7   Disclosure, as a **related party** transaction, is not required of:

(a)   pension contributions paid to a pension fund;

(b)   emoluments in respect of services as an employee of the reporting entity;

(c)   transactions with the parties listed below simply as a result of their role as:

(i)   providers of finance in the course of their business in that regard;

(ii)   utility companies;

(iii)   **government** departments and their sponsored bodies; or

(iv)   a customer, supplier, franchiser, distributor or general agent; or

(d)   related party transactions entered into between two or more members of a group, provided that any subsidiary which is a party to the transaction is wholly owned by such a member.

15.8   When the reporting entity is controlled by another party, there shall be disclosure of the **related party** relationship and the name of that party and, if different, that of the ultimate controlling party. If the controlling party or ultimate controlling party of the reporting entity is not known, that fact shall be disclosed. This information shall be disclosed irrespective of whether any transactions have taken place between the controlling parties and the reporting entity.

15.9   WHERE THE COMPANY IS A **SUBSIDIARY UNDERTAKING,** THE FOLLOWING INFORMATION MUST BE GIVEN WITH RESPECT TO THE COMPANY (IF ANY) REGARDED BY THE DIRECTORS AS BEING THE COMPANY'S ULTIMATE PARENT COMPANY:

(A)   THE NAME OF THAT COMPANY; AND

(B)   ITS COUNTRY OF INCORPORATION IF OUTSIDE THE UNITED KINGDOM AND IF KNOWN TO THE DIRECTORS.

Parent undertaking drawing up accounts for larger group[41]

15.10   WHERE THE COMPANY IS A **SUBSIDIARY UNDERTAKING,** THE FOLLOWING INFORMATION MUST BE GIVEN WITH RESPECT TO THE PARENT UNDERTAKING OF:

(A)   THE LARGEST GROUP OF WHICH IT IS A MEMBER FOR WHICH GROUP ACCOUNTS ARE DRAWN UP; AND

(B)   THE SMALLEST SUCH GROUP OF UNDERTAKINGS:

(I)   THE NAME OF THE PARENT UNDERTAKING;

(II)   THE COUNTRY OF INCORPORATION, IF OUTSIDE THE UNITED KINGDOM;

(III)   IF UNINCORPORATED, THE ADDRESS OF ITS PRINCIPAL PLACE OF BUSINESS; AND

---

[41] *INFORMATION NEED NOT BE DISCLOSED WITH RESPECT TO AN UNDERTAKING WHICH IS ESTABLISHED UNDER THE LAW OF A COUNTRY OUTSIDE THE UNITED KINGDOM OR CARRIES ON BUSINESS OUTSIDE THE UNITED KINGDOM, IF IN THE OPINION OF THE DIRECTORS OF THE COMPANY THE DISCLOSURE WOULD BE SERIOUSLY PREJUDICIAL TO THE BUSINESS OF THAT UNDERTAKING, OR TO THE BUSINESS OF THE COMPANY OR ANY OF ITS SUBSIDIARY UNDERTAKINGS, AND THE SECRETARY OF STATE AGREES THAT THE INFORMATION NEED NOT BE DISCLOSED. WHERE ADVANTAGE IS TAKEN OF THIS EXEMPTION, THAT FACT SHALL BE STATED IN A NOTE TO THE COMPANY'S ANNUAL ACCOUNTS. This statutory exemption is not available in the Republic of Ireland.*

(IV)   IF COPIES OF EITHER OF THE GROUP ACCOUNTS REFERRED TO IN (A) OR (B) ABOVE ARE AVAILABLE TO THE PUBLIC, THE ADDRESS FROM WHICH THEY MAY BE OBTAINED.

Directors' benefits: advances, credit and guarantees

15.11 INFORMATION ABOUT THE FOLLOWING DIRECTORS' BENEFITS MUST BE PROVIDED IN THE NOTES TO THE ACCOUNTS. FOR THE PURPOSES OF THIS SECTION, THE DIRECTORS OF A COMPANY ARE THE PERSONS WHO WERE A DIRECTOR AT ANY TIME IN THE FINANCIAL YEAR TO WHICH THE ACCOUNTS RELATE:

(A)   ADVANCES AND CREDITS GRANTED BY THE COMPANY TO ITS DIRECTORS; AND
(B)   GUARANTEES OF ANY KIND ENTERED INTO BY THE COMPANY ON BEHALF OF ITS DIRECTORS.

15.12 THE INFORMATION REQUIRED FOR AN ADVANCE OR CREDIT IS AS FOLLOWS:

(A)   ITS AMOUNT;
(B)   AN INDICATION OF THE INTEREST RATE;
(C)   ITS MAIN CONDITIONS; AND
(D)   ANY AMOUNTS REPAID.

15.13 THE INFORMATION REQUIRED FOR A GUARANTEE IS AS FOLLOWS:

(A)   ITS MAIN TERMS;
(B)   THE AMOUNT OF THE MAXIMUM LIABILITY THAT MAY BE INCURRED BY THE COMPANY (OR ITS SUBSIDIARY); AND
(C)   ANY AMOUNT PAID AND ANY LIABILITY INCURRED BY THE COMPANY (OR ITS SUBSIDIARY) FOR THE PURPOSE OF FULFILLING THE GUARANTEE (INCLUDING ANY LOSS INCURRED BY REASON OF ENFORCEMENT OF THE GUARANTEE).

15.14 THERE MUST ALSO BE DISCLOSED IN THE NOTES TO THE ACCOUNTS THE TOTALS OF AMOUNTS STATED UNDER PARAGRAPHS 15.12(A); 15.12(D); 15.13(B) AND 15.13(C) ABOVE.

15.15 THE REQUIREMENTS OF THIS SECTION APPLY IN RELATION TO EVERY ADVANCE, CREDIT OR GUARANTEE SUBSISTING AT ANY TIME IN THE FINANCIAL YEAR TO WHICH THE ACCOUNTS RELATE:

(A)   WHENEVER IT WAS ENTERED INTO;
(B)   WHETHER OR NOT THE PERSON WAS A DIRECTOR OF THE COMPANY IN QUESTION AT THE TIME IT WAS ENTERED INTO; AND
(C)   IN THE CASE OF AN ADVANCE, CREDIT OR GUARANTEE INVOLVING A SUBSIDIARY UNDERTAKING OF THAT COMPANY, WHETHER OR NOT THAT UNDERTAKING WAS SUCH A SUBSIDIARY UNDERTAKING AT THE TIME IT WAS ENTERED INTO.

Subsidiary undertakings

15.16 THE FOLLOWING INFORMATION MUST BE GIVEN WHERE AT THE END OF THE **FINANCIAL YEAR** THE COMPANY HAS **SUBSIDIARY UNDERTAKINGS**:

(A)   THE NAME OF EACH **SUBSIDIARY UNDERTAKING** MUST BE STATED; AND
(B)   WITH RESPECT TO EACH **SUBSIDIARY UNDERTAKING** IF IT IS INCORPORATED OUTSIDE THE UNITED KINGDOM, THE COUNTRY IN WHICH IT IS INCORPORATED; IF IT IS UNINCORPORATED, THE ADDRESS OF ITS PRINCIPAL PLACE OF BUSINESS.

Holdings in subsidiary undertakings[42]

15.17 THERE MUST BE STATED IN RELATION TO SHARES OF EACH CLASS HELD BY THE COMPANY IN A **SUBSIDIARY UNDERTAKING** —

---

[42] *Disclosure requirements for holdings in undertakings other than subsidiary undertakings are set out in paragraph 6.33.*

(A)   THE IDENTITY OF THE CLASS; AND

(B)   THE PROPORTION OF THE NOMINAL VALUE OF THE SHARES OF THAT CLASS REPRESENTED BY THOSE SHARES.

THE SHARES HELD BY THE COMPANY ITSELF MUST BE DISTINGUISHED FROM THOSE ATTRIBUTED TO THE COMPANY WHICH ARE HELD BY OR ON BEHALF OF A SUBSIDIARY UNDERTAKING.

Financial information about subsidiary undertakings

15.18   THERE MUST BE DISCLOSED WITH RESPECT TO EACH **SUBSIDIARY UNDERTAKING** –

(A)   THE AGGREGATE AMOUNT OF ITS CAPITAL AND RESERVES AS AT THE END OF ITS RELEVANT **FINANCIAL YEAR**; AND

(B)   ITS PROFIT OR LOSS FOR THAT YEAR.

15.19   THAT INFORMATION NEED NOT BE GIVEN IF:

(A)   THE COMPANY IS EXEMPT BY VIRTUE OF SECTION 400 AND 401 OF THE COMPANIES ACT 2006 FROM THE REQUIREMENT TO PREPARE GROUP ACCOUNTS;

(B)   THE COMPANY'S INVESTMENT IN THE **SUBSIDIARY UNDERTAKING** IS INCLUDED IN THE COMPANY'S ACCOUNTS BY WAY OF THE EQUITY METHOD OF VALUATION;

(C)   THE **SUBSIDIARY UNDERTAKING** IS NOT REQUIRED BY ANY PROVISION OF THE COMPANIES ACT 2006 TO DELIVER A COPY OF ITS BALANCE SHEET FOR ITS RELEVANT **FINANCIAL YEAR** AND DOES NOT OTHERWISE PUBLISH THAT BALANCE SHEET IN THE UNITED KINGDOM OR ELSEWHERE, AND THE COMPANY'S HOLDING IS LESS THAN 50 PER CENT OF THE NOMINAL VALUE OF THE SHARES IN THE UNDERTAKING; OR

(D)   IT IS NOT MATERIAL.

15.20   THE 'RELEVANT **FINANCIAL YEAR**' OF A **SUBSIDIARY UNDERTAKING** IS –

(A)   IF ITS **FINANCIAL YEAR** ENDS WITH THAT OF THE COMPANY, THAT YEAR; AND

(B)   IF NOT, ITS **FINANCIAL YEAR** ENDING LAST BEFORE THE END OF THE COMPANY'S **FINANCIAL YEAR**.

Membership of certain undertakings

15.21   THE FOLLOWING INFORMATION MUST BE GIVEN WHERE, AT THE END OF THE **FINANCIAL YEAR**, THE COMPANY IS A MEMBER OF A **QUALIFYING UNDERTAKING**:

(A)   THE NAME AND LEGAL FORM OF THE UNDERTAKING; AND

(B)   THE ADDRESS OF THE UNDERTAKING'S REGISTERED OFFICE (WHETHER IN OR OUTSIDE THE UNITED KINGDOM) OR, IF IT DOES NOT HAVE SUCH AN OFFICE, ITS HEAD OFFICE (WHETHER IN OR OUTSIDE THE UNITED KINGDOM).

15.22   WHERE THE UNDERTAKING IS A QUALIFYING PARTNERSHIP THERE MUST ALSO BE STATED EITHER –

(A)   THAT A COPY OF THE LATEST ACCOUNTS OF THE UNDERTAKING HAS BEEN OR IS TO BE APPENDED TO THE COPY OF THE COMPANY'S ACCOUNTS SENT TO THE REGISTRAR UNDER SECTION 444 OF THE COMPANIES ACT 2006; OR

(B)   THE NAME OF AT LEAST ONE BODY CORPORATE (WHICH MAY BE THE COMPANY) IN WHOSE GROUP ACCOUNTS THE UNDERTAKING HAS BEEN OR IS TO BE DEALT WITH ON A CONSOLIDATED BASIS.

INFORMATION OTHERWISE REQUIRED BY PARAGRAPH 15.21 ABOVE NEED NOT BE GIVEN IF IT IS NOT MATERIAL. **15.23**

INFORMATION OTHERWISE REQUIRED BY PARAGRAPH 15.22 (B) ABOVE NEED NOT BE GIVEN IF THE NOTES TO THE COMPANY'S ACCOUNTS DISCLOSE THAT THE COMPANY IS EXEMPT BECAUSE THE PARTNERSHIP IS DEALT WITH ON A CONSOLIDATED BASIS IN GROUP ACCOUNTS PREPARED BY (I) A MEMBER OF THE PARTNERSHIP ESTABLISHED UNDER LAW, OR (II) A PARENT UNDERTAKING OF SUCH A MEMBER. **15.24**

16 Consolidated financial statements

IF, AT THE END OF A FINANCIAL YEAR, A COMPANY SUBJECT TO THE SMALL COMPANIES REGIME IS A PARENT COMPANY, THE DIRECTORS, AS WELL AS PREPARING INDIVIDUAL ACCOUNTS FOR THE YEAR, MAY PREPARE GROUP ACCOUNTS FOR THE YEAR. **16.1**

Where the reporting entity is preparing **consolidated financial statements**, it should have regard to paragraph 5 of the Status of the FRSSE as a means of developing its policies and practices for the preparation of its consolidated financial statements. **16.2**

Form and content of small group accounts[43]

WHERE A SMALL COMPANY HAS PREPARED INDIVIDUAL ACCOUNTS IN ACCORDANCE WITH THE LEGAL REQUIREMENTS REFLECTED IN THE FRSSE AND IS PREPARING GROUP ACCOUNTS IN RESPECT OF THE SAME YEAR PARAGRAPHS 16.4 TO 16.8 APPLY. **16.3**

IN PREPARING GROUP ACCOUNTS, A COMPANY SHALL HAVE REGARD TO THE LEGAL REQUIREMENTS REFLECTED IN THE FRSSE AND THE PROVISIONS OF SCHEDULE 6 OF THE SMALL COMPANIES AND GROUPS (ACCOUNTS AND DIRECTORS' REPORT) REGULATION (SI 2008/409). ANY REFERENCES IN THAT SCHEDULE TO COMPLIANCE WITH THE PROVISIONS OF 'SCHEDULE 6' SHALL BE CONSTRUED AS REFERENCES TO THE LEGAL REQUIREMENTS REFLECTED IN THE FRSSE. **16.4**

IN PREPARING GROUP ACCOUNTS, DETAILS MUST BE SHOWN IN THE NOTES TO THE GROUP ACCOUNTS OF: **16.5**

(A) ADVANCES AND CREDITS GRANTED TO THE DIRECTORS OF THE PARENT COMPANY, BY THAT COMPANY, OR BY ANY OF ITS SUBSIDIARY UNDERTAKINGS; AND

(B) GUARANTEES OF ANY KIND ENTERED INTO ON BEHALF OF THE DIRECTORS OF THE PARENT COMPANY, BY THAT COMPANY OR BY ANY OF ITS SUBSIDIARY UNDERTAKINGS.

THE BALANCE SHEET FORMAT SET OUT IN PARAGRAPH 2.27 SHALL BE MODIFIED AS FOLLOWS. FOR ITEM B.III 'INVESTMENTS' SUBSTITUTE: **16.6**

"B.III INVESTMENTS

1. SHARES IN GROUP UNDERTAKINGS

2. INTERESTS IN ASSOCIATED UNDERTAKINGS

3. OTHER PARTICIPATING INTERESTS

4. LOANS TO GROUP UNDERTAKINGS AND UNDERTAKINGS IN WHICH A PARTICIPATING INTEREST IS HELD

5. OTHER INVESTMENTS OTHER THAN LOANS

6. OTHERS."

---

[43] *There are no special provisions in Republic of Ireland company law that relate to the preparation of group accounts by small companies. See Appendix I.*

16.7 THE PROFIT AND LOSS ACCOUNT FORMAT SET OUT IN PARAGRAPH 2.29 SHALL BE MODIFIED BY REPLACING THE ITEM HEADED 'INCOME FROM PARTICIPATING INTERESTS'[44] BY TWO ITEMS: 'INCOME FROM INTERESTS IN ASSOCIATED UNDERTAKINGS' AND 'INCOME FROM OTHER PARTICIPATING INTERESTS'.

16.8 WHERE GROUP ACCOUNTS ARE PREPARED THE BALANCE SHEET MUST CONTAIN IN A PROMINENT POSITION ON THE BALANCE SHEET, ABOVE THE SIGNATURE REQUIRED BY PARAGRAPH 2.30, THAT THEY ARE PREPARED IN ACCORDANCE WITH THE SPECIAL PROVISIONS IN PART 15 OF THE COMPANIES ACT 2006 RELATING TO SMALL COMPANIES.

17 *Directors' remuneration*

17.1 THE OVERALL TOTAL OF THE FOLLOWING ITEMS MUST BE DISCLOSED IN RESPECT OF DIRECTORS' REMUNERATION:

(A)   THE OVERALL AMOUNT OF REMUNERATION PAID TO OR RECEIVABLE BY **DIRECTORS** IN RESPECT OF **QUALIFYING SERVICES**;

(B)   THE OVERALL AMOUNT OF MONEY PAID TO OR RECEIVABLE BY **DIRECTORS** AND THE NET VALUE OF ASSETS (OTHER THAN MONEY, SHARE OPTIONS OR SHARES) RECEIVED OR RECEIVABLE BY DIRECTORS, UNDER LONG TERM INCENTIVE SCHEMES IN RESPECT OF QUALIFYING SERVICES; AND

(C)   THE OVERALL VALUE OF ANY COMPANY CONTRIBUTIONS PAID, OR TREATED AS PAID, TO A **PENSION SCHEME** IN RESPECT OF **DIRECTORS' QUALIFYING SERVICES** AND BY REFERENCE TO WHICH THE RATE OR AMOUNT OF ANY MONEY PURCHASE BENEFITS THAT MAY BECOME PAYABLE WILL BE CALCULATED.

IN THE CASE OF **MONEY PURCHASE SCHEMES** AND **DEFINED BENEFIT SCHEMES**, DISCLOSE THE NUMBER OF **DIRECTORS** (IF ANY) TO WHOM **RETIREMENT BENEFITS** ARE ACCRUING IN RESPECT OF **QUALIFYING SERVICES**.

17.2 DISCLOSURE MUST BE PROVIDED OF THE AGGREGATE AMOUNTS OF ANY COMPENSATION TO

DIRECTORS OR PAST **DIRECTORS** IN RESPECT OF LOSS OF OFFICE, INCLUDING BENEFITS OTHER THAN IN CASH, AND THE ESTIMATED MONEY VALUE OF SUCH BENEFITS AND THEIR NATURE.

17.3 DISCLOSURE MUST BE PROVIDED OF THE AGGREGATE AMOUNT OF ANY CONSIDERATION PAID TO, OR RECEIVABLE BY, THIRD PARTIES[45] FOR MAKING AVAILABLE THE SERVICES OF ANY PERSON:

(A)   AS A **DIRECTOR** OF THE COMPANY; OR

(B)   WHILE **DIRECTOR** OF THE COMPANY, AS **DIRECTOR** OF ANY SUBSIDIARY UNDERTAKING, OR OTHERWISE IN CONNECTION WITH THE MANAGEMENT OF THE AFFAIRS OF THE COMPANY OR ANY OF ITS **SUBSIDIARY UNDERTAKINGS**.

THE REFERENCE TO CONSIDERATION INCLUDES BENEFITS OTHER THAN IN CASH AND THE ESTIMATED MONEY VALUE OF SUCH BENEFITS AND THEIR NATURE MUST BE DISCLOSED.

---

[44] *That is item 8 in format 1 and item 10 in format 2.*

[45] *THIRD PARTIES ARE PERSONS OTHER THAN (1) THE DIRECTOR HIMSELF OR A PERSON CONNECTED WITH HIM OR BODY CORPORATE CONTROLLED BY HIM, AND (2) THE COMPANY OR ANY OF ITS SUBSIDIARY UNDERTAKINGS. Sections 252 and 253 of the Companies Act 2006 define what is meant by 'Persons connected with a director' and 'Member of the **director's family**'. Amounts paid to or receivable by a person connected with a director, or a body corporate controlled by a director, shall be included instead within the disclosures set out in paragraph 17.1.*

18   The directors' report

Introduction

THE DIRECTORS OF A COMPANY MUST PREPARE A DIRECTORS' REPORT FOR EACH INDIVIDUAL FINANCIAL **18.1**
YEAR OF THE COMPANY. THE FOLLOWING DISCLOSURES MUST BE PROVIDED IN THE DIRECTORS' REPORT:

(A)   THE PRINCIPAL ACTIVITIES OF THE COMPANY;
(B)   DETAILS OF THE COMPANY'S **DIRECTORS**;
(C)   POLITICAL DONATIONS AND EXPENDITURE;
(D)   CHARITABLE DONATIONS;
(E)   ACQUISITION OF OWN SHARES; AND
(F)   EMPLOYMENT, ETC OF DISABLED PERSONS.

A DIRECTOR OF A COMPANY IS LIABLE TO COMPENSATE THE COMPANY FOR ANY UNTRUE OR MISLEADING **18.2**
STATEMENT IN THE DIRECTORS' REPORT OR ANY OMISSION FROM IT IF HE KNEW THE STATEMENT TO BE
UNTRUE OR MISLEADING OR HE KNEW THE OMISSION TO BE DISHONEST CONCEALMENT OF A MATERIAL
FACT.

WHERE THE COMPANY IS A PARENT AND CHOOSES TO PREPARE GROUP ACCOUNTS, THE DIRECTORS' **18.3**
REPORT MUST BE A GROUP REPORT RELATING TO THE UNDERTAKINGS INCLUDED IN THE CONSOLIDATION.

The principal activities of the company

THE REPORT MUST STATE THE PRINCIPAL ACTIVITIES OF THE COMPANY AND ITS SUBSIDIARIES DURING **18.4**
THE YEAR. These activities will be the various classes of business in which the company
operates.

Details of the company's directors

THE REPORT MUST STATE THE NAMES OF THE PERSONS WHO, AT ANY TIME DURING THE **FINANCIAL** **18.5**
YEAR, WERE **DIRECTORS** OF THE COMPANY.

Disclosure of qualifying third party indemnity provisions

IF, WHEN A DIRECTORS' REPORT IS APPROVED, ANY QUALIFYING THIRD PARTY INDEMNITY PROVISION **18.6**
(WHETHER MADE BY THE COMPANY OR OTHERWISE) IS IN FORCE OR WAS IN FORCE DURING THE
FINANCIAL YEAR FOR THE BENEFIT OF ONE OR MORE DIRECTORS OF THE COMPANY (OR OF AN
ASSOCIATED COMPANY), THE REPORT MUST STATE THAT ANY SUCH PROVISION IS OR WAS IN FORCE.

Political donations and expenditure and charitable donations

IF THE COMPANY OR THE COMPANY AND ITS SUBSIDIARIES, HAS IN THE **FINANCIAL YEAR** MADE **18.7**
ANY POLITICAL DONATION TO ANY POLITICAL PARTY OR OTHER POLITICAL ORGANISATION, OR MADE
ANY POLITICAL DONATION TO ANY INDEPENDENT ELECTION CANDIDATE, OR INCURRED ANY POLITICAL
EXPENDITURE, AND THE AMOUNT OF THE DONATION OR EXPENDITURE OR (AS THE CASE MAY BE) THE
AGGREGATE AMOUNT OF ALL DONATIONS AND EXPENDITURE EXCEEDED £2,000, THEN THE DIRECTORS'
REPORT MUST DISCLOSE THE FOLLOWING PARTICULARS:

(A)   FOR POLITICAL DONATIONS — THE NAME OF EACH POLITICAL PARTY, OTHER POLITICAL
      ORGANISATION OR INDEPENDENT ELECTION CANDIDATE TO WHOM SUCH A DONATION HAS BEEN
      MADE AND THE TOTAL AMOUNT GIVEN TO THAT PARTY, ORGANISATION OR CANDIDATE BY WAY
      OF SUCH DONATIONS IN THE FINANCIAL YEAR; AND
(B)   FOR POLITICAL EXPENDITURE — THE TOTAL AMOUNT INCURRED BY WAY OF SUCH EXPENDITURE
      IN THE FINANCIAL YEAR.

18.8   IF THE COMPANY, OR THE COMPANY AND ITS SUBSIDIARIES MADE ANY CONTRIBUTION TO A NONEU POLITICAL PARTY, THE DIRECTORS' REPORT MUST CONTAIN A STATEMENT OF THE AMOUNT OF THE CONTRIBUTION OR, IF IT HAS MADE TWO OR MORE SUCH CONTRIBUTIONS IN THE YEAR, A STATEMENT OF THE TOTAL AMOUNT OF THE CONTRIBUTIONS.

18.9   IF THE COMPANY, OR THE COMPANY AND ITS SUBSIDIARIES, HAS IN THE FINANCIAL YEAR GIVEN MONEY FOR CHARITABLE PURPOSES AND THE MONEY GIVEN EXCEEDS £2,000 THE AMOUNT GIVEN FOR EACH OF THE PURPOSES FOR WHICH MONEY HAS BEEN GIVEN MUST BE DISCLOSED.

Acquisition of own shares[46]

18.10   WHERE THE COMPANY ACQUIRES ITS OWN SHARES, EITHER BY PURCHASE OR ACQUISITION BY FORFEITURE, THE DIRECTORS' REPORT MUST STATE:

(A)   THE NUMBER AND NOMINAL VALUE OF SHARES PURCHASED, THE AGGREGATE CONSIDERATION PAID FOR THE SHARES AND THE REASONS FOR THE PURCHASE;

(B)   THE NUMBER AND NOMINAL VALUE OF SHARES ACQUIRED;

(C)   THE MAXIMUM NUMBER AND NOMINAL VALUE OF SHARES ACQUIRED OR CHARGED DURING THE YEAR; AND

(D)   THE NUMBER AND NOMINAL VALUE OF SUCH SHARES ACQUIRED WHICH WERE DISPOSED OF IN THE YEAR. THE AMOUNT OF MONEY RECEIVED SHALL BE DISCLOSED WHERE THE SHARES WERE DISPOSED OF FOR MONEY.

IN EACH OF THE ABOVE CASES, THE PERCENTAGE OF THE CALLED-UP SHARE CAPITAL WHICH THEY REPRESENT AND, IN EACH CASE WHERE SHARES HAVE BEEN CHARGED, THE AMOUNT OF THE CHARGE MUST BE STATED.

Employment, etc of disabled persons

18.11   WHERE THE AVERAGE NUMBER OF EMPLOYEES EXCEEDS 250, THE DIRECTORS' REPORT MUST INCLUDE A STATEMENT DESCRIBING THE POLICY WHICH THE COMPANY HAS ADOPTED FOR:

(A)   GIVING FULL AND FAIR CONSIDERATION TO APPLICATIONS FOR EMPLOYMENT BY DISABLED PERSONS, HAVING REGARD TO THEIR PARTICULAR APTITUDES AND ABILITIES;

(B)   CONTINUING EMPLOYMENT AND APPROPRIATE TRAINING FOR EMPLOYEES OF THE COMPANY WHO BECAME DISABLED DURING THE PERIOD WHEN THEY WERE EMPLOYED BY THE COMPANY; AND

(C)   OTHERWISE FOR THE TRAINING, CAREER DEVELOPMENT AND PROMOTION OF DISABLED PERSONS EMPLOYED BY THE COMPANY.

Statement as to disclosure of information to auditors

18.12   WHERE A SMALL COMPANY CHOOSES NOT TO TAKE ADVANTAGE OF THE EXEMPTION IN THE COMPANIES ACT 2006 RELATING TO THE AUDIT OF ACCOUNTS, THE DIRECTORS' REPORT MUST CONTAIN A STATEMENT THAT, SO FAR AS EACH OF THE DIRECTORS AT THE TIME THE REPORT IS APPROVED ARE AWARE:

(A)   THERE IS NO RELEVANT AUDIT INFORMATION OF WHICH THE COMPANY'S AUDITORS ARE UNAWARE; AND

(B)   THE DIRECTORS HAVE TAKEN ALL STEPS THAT THEY OUGHT TO HAVE TAKEN TO MAKE THEMSELVES AWARE OF ANY RELEVANT AUDIT INFORMATION AND TO ESTABLISH THAT THE AUDITORS ARE AWARE OF THAT INFORMATION.

---

[46] *THESE DISCLOSURE REQUIREMENTS APPLY WHERE OWN SHARES ARE: (I) PURCHASED BY THE COMPANY OR ACQUIRED BY THE COMPANY BY FORFEITURE OR SURRENDER IN LIEU OF FORFEITURE; (II) ACQUIRED BY THE COMPANY OTHERWISE THAN FOR VALUABLE CONSIDERATION; (III) ACQUIRED BY A NOMINEE OF THE COMPANY WITHOUT FINANCIAL ASSISTANCE FROM THE COMPANY, OR BY ANY PERSON WITH FINANCIAL ASSISTANCE FROM THE COMPANY, AND, IN EITHER CASE, THE COMPANY HAS A BENEFICIAL INTEREST IN THE SHARES; OR (IV) MADE SUBJECT TO A LIEN OR CHARGE UNDER s150 OR s6(3) OF THE CONSEQUENTIAL PROVISIONS ACT 1985.*

Approval and signing of the directors' report

THE DIRECTORS' REPORT MUST BE APPROVED BY THE BOARD OF **DIRECTORS** AND SIGNED ON BEHALF OF THE BOARD BY A **DIRECTOR** OR THE SECRETARY OF THE COMPANY. EVERY COPY OF THE DIRECTORS' REPORT WHICH IS PUBLISHED BY OR ON BEHALF OF THE BOARD MUST STATE THE NAME OF THE PERSON WHO SIGNED IT ON BEHALF OF THE BOARD. **18.13**

THE COPY OF THE DIRECTORS' REPORT WHICH IS DELIVERED TO THE REGISTRAR MUST STATE THE NAME OF THE PERSON WHO SIGNED IT ON BEHALF OF THE BOARD. **18.14**

IF THE DIRECTORS' REPORT IS PREPARED IN ACCORDANCE WITH THE SMALL COMPANIES REGIME, IT MUST CONTAIN A STATEMENT TO THAT EFFECT IN A PROMINENT POSITION ABOVE THE SIGNATURE. **18.15**

IF A DIRECTORS' REPORT IS APPROVED THAT DOES NOT COMPLY WITH THE REQUIREMENTS OF THE COMPANIES ACT 2006, THEN EVERY DIRECTOR OF THE COMPANY WHO KNEW THAT IT DID NOT COMPLY OR WAS RECKLESS AS TO WHETHER IT COMPLIED AND FAILED TO TAKE REASONABLE STEPS TO SECURE COMPLIANCE WITH THOSE REQUIREMENTS OR, AS THE CASE MAY BE, TO PREVENT THE REPORT FROM BEING APPROVED, COMMITS AN OFFENCE AND IS LIABLE TO A FINE. **18.16**

19 Date from which effective and transitional arrangements

Except as set out in paragraph 19.1A, the accounting practices set out in this Financial Reporting Standard for Smaller Entities (effective January 2015) shall be regarded as standard in respect of financial statements relating to accounting periods beginning on or after 1 January 2015. Earlier application is permitted. **19.1**

Editor's note: Amendments to the FRSSE – Micro-entities (April 2014) has amended the words in this paragraph.

In the FRSSE (effective January 2015): 'The accounting practices for **micro-entities** set out in paragraphs 1.2, 2.2A and 2.40 to 2.42 of this Financial Reporting Standard for Smaller Entities (effective January 2015) shall be regarded as standard in respect of the financial statements of **micro-entities** relating to accounting periods ending on or after 30 September 2013 for companies filing their accounts on or after 1 December 2013. Earlier application is not permitted.' **19.1A**

Editor's note: Amendments to the FRSSE – Micro-entities (April 2014) has added this paragraph 19.1A.

Transitional arrangements – goodwill

All goodwill that was eliminated against reserves in accordance with an **accounting policy** permitted until 23 March 1999 may remain eliminated against reserves thereafter.[47] Alternatively, in its first accounting period beginning on or after 23 March 1999, an entity may reinstate by prior period adjustment all goodwill previously eliminated against reserves. **19.2**

Transitional arrangements – tangible fixed assets

Where, for its first accounting period ending on or after 23 March 2000, an entity does not adopt an **accounting policy** of revaluation, but the carrying amount of its **tangible fixed assets** reflects previous revaluations, it may: **19.3**

---

[47] *The treatment of such amounts on disposal of a business is set out in paragraph 3.7.*

(a) retain the book amounts. In these circumstances the entity shall disclose the fact that the transitional provisions of the FRSSE are being followed and that the valuation has not been updated and give the date of the last revaluation; or

(b) restate the carrying amount of the **tangible fixed assets** to historical cost (less restated accumulated **depreciation**), as a change in **accounting policy**.

19.4   Where, for its first accounting period ending on or after 23 March 2000, an entity separates **tangible fixed assets** into different components with significantly different useful economic lives for **depreciation** purposes, the changes shall be dealt with as a prior period adjustment, as a change in **accounting policy**. Other revisions to the useful economic lives and **residual values** of **tangible fixed assets** are not the result of a change in **accounting policy** and shall be treated in accordance with paragraph 6.40 and not as **prior period adjustments**.

20   *Withdrawal of the FRSSE (effective April 2008)*

20.1   The Financial Reporting Standard for Smaller Entities (effective January 2015) supersedes the FRSSE (effective April 2008).

C DEFINITIONS

The following definitions shall apply in the FRSSE and in particular in the Statement of Standard Accounting Practice set out in sections 1-20 of Part B.

accounting policies	Those principles, bases, conventions, rules and practices applied by an entity that specify how the effects of transactions and other events are to be reflected in its financial statements through: (i) recognising; (ii) selecting measurement bases for; and (iii) presenting **assets, liabilities**, gains, losses and changes to shareholders' funds. Accounting policies do not include **estimation techniques**. Accounting policies define the process whereby transactions and other events are reflected in financial statements. For example, an accounting policy for a particular type of expenditure may specify whether an **asset** or a loss is to be **recognised**; the basis on which it is to be measured; and where in the profit and loss account or balance sheet it is to be presented.
act	The Companies Act 2006
actuarial gains and losses	Changes in actuarial deficits or surpluses that arise because events have not coincided with the actuarial assumptions made for the last valuation or because the actuarial assumptions have changed.
applied research	Original or critical investigation undertaken in order to gain new scientific or technical knowledge and directed towards a specific practical aim or objective.
arrangement fees	The costs that are incurred directly in connection with the issue of a **capital instrument** (i.e. those costs that would not have been incurred if the specific instrument in question had not been issued).
assets	Rights or other access to future economic benefits controlled by an entity as a result of past transactions or events.
attributable profit (on long-term contracts)	That part of the total profit currently estimated to arise over the duration of the contract, after allowing for estimated remedial and maintenance costs and increases in costs so far as not recoverable under the terms of the contract, that fairly reflects the profit attributable to that part of the work performed at the accounting date. (There can be no attributable profit until the profitable outcome of the contract can be assessed with reasonable certainty.)
borrowings	Capital instruments that are classified as liabilities.

capital instruments	All instruments that are issued (or arrangements entered into) by reporting entities as a means of raising finance, including shares, debentures, loans and debt instruments, options and warrants that give the holder the right to subscribe for or obtain capital instruments. In the case of **consolidated financial statements** the term includes capital instruments issued by subsidiaries except those that are held by another member of the group that is included in the consolidation.
cash-settled share-based payment transaction	A **share-based payment transaction** in which the entity acquires goods or services by incurring a **liability** to transfer cash or other **assets** to the supplier of those goods or services for amounts that are based on the price (or value) of the entity's shares or other **equity instruments** of the entity.
close members of the family of a person	Close members of the family of a person are those family members, who may be expected to influence, or be influenced by, that person in their dealings with the entity and include: (a) that person's children and spouse or domestic partner; (b) children of that person's spouse or domestic partner; and (c) dependents of that person or that person's spouse or domestic partner.
closing rate	The closing rate is the **exchange rate** for spot transactions ruling at the balance sheet date and is the mean of the buying and selling rates at the close of business on the day for which the rate is to be ascertained.
companies legislation	(a) In the United Kingdom, the Companies Act 2006; and (b) In the Republic of Ireland, the Companies Acts 1963-2003 and all other Regulations to be read as one with the Companies Acts.
consignment stock	Consignment stock is stock held by one party (the 'dealer') but legally owned by another (the 'manufacturer'), on terms that give the dealer the right to sell the stock in the normal course of its business or, at its option, to return it unsold to the legal owner.
consolidated financial statements	The financial statements of a group prepared by consolidation. A group is a parent undertaking and its subsidiary undertakings. Consolidation is the process of adjusting and combining financial information from the individual financial statements of a parent undertaking and its subsidiary undertakings to prepare consolidated financial statements that present financial information for the group as a single economic entity.

contingent asset	A possible **asset** that arises from past events and whose existence will be confirmed only by the occurrence of one or more uncertain future events not wholly within the entity's control.

contingent liability	(a) A possible **obligation** that arises from past events and whose existence will be confirmed only by the occurrence of one or more uncertain future events not wholly within the entity's control; or
	
	(b) an **obligation** at the balance sheet date that arises from past events but is not **recognised** as a **provision** because:
	
	    (i) it is not probable that a transfer of economic benefits will be required to settle the **obligation**; or
	
	    (ii) the amount of the **obligation** cannot be measured with sufficient **reliability**.

cost (of stock)	Cost is defined as being that expenditure which has been incurred in the normal course of business in bringing the product or service to its present location and condition. This expenditure should include, in addition to cost of purchase, such costs of conversion (including, for example, attributable overheads) as are appropriate to that location and condition. BORROWING COSTS THAT ARE DIRECTLY ATTRIBUTABLE TO THE ACQUISITION, CONSTRUCTION OR PRODUCTION OF STOCK MAY BE INCLUDED AS PART OF THE COST.
current service cost	The increase in the present value of the **scheme liabilities** expected to arise from employee service in the current period.
current tax	The amount of tax estimated to be payable or recoverable in respect of the taxable profit or loss for a period, along with adjustments to estimates in respect of previous periods.
curtailment	An event that reduces the expected years of future service of present employees or reduces for a number of employees the accrual of defined benefits for some or all of their future service.
deferred tax	Estimated future tax consequences of transactions and events **recognised** in the financial statements of the current and previous periods.
defined benefit scheme	A pension or other **retirement benefit** scheme other than a **defined contribution scheme**. Normally, the scheme rules define the benefits independently of the contributions payable, and the benefits are not directly related to the investments of the scheme.
defined contribution scheme	A pension or other **retirement benefit** scheme into which an employer pays regular contributions fixed as an amount or as a percentage of pay. The employer will have no legal or constructive **obligation** to pay further contributions if the scheme does not have sufficient **assets** to pay all employee benefits relating to employee service in the current and prior periods.

depreciation	The measure of the cost or revalued amount of the economic benefits of a fixed **asset** that have been consumed during the period. Consumption includes the wearing out, using up or other reduction in the **useful economic life** of a fixed **asset** whether arising from use, effluxion of time or obsolescence through either changes in technology or demand for the goods and services produced by the **asset**.
development	Use of scientific or technical knowledge in order to produce new or substantially improved materials, devices, products or services, to install new processes or systems before the commencement of commercial production or commercial applications, or to improve substantially those already produced or installed.
directly attributable costs	The costs that relate directly to securing the specific contract after the asset recognition criteria for **pre-contract costs** are met, if they can be separately identified and measured reliably.
directors	The directors of a company or other body, the partners, proprietors, committee of management or trustees of other forms of entity, or equivalent persons responsible for directing the entity's affairs and preparing its financial statements.
DIRECTOR'S FAMILY	THE MEMBERS OF A DIRECTOR'S FAMILY ARE; (A)　THE DIRECTOR'S SPOUSE OR CIVIL PARTNER; (B)　ANY OTHER PERSON (WHETHER OF A DIFFERENT SEX OR THE SAME SEX) WITH WHOM THE DIRECTOR LIVES AS PARTNER IN AN ENDURING FAMILY RELATIONSHIP; (C)　THE DIRECTOR'S CHILDREN OR STEP-CHILDREN; (D)　ANY CHILDREN OR STEP-CHILDREN OF A PERSON WITHIN PARAGRAPH (B) (AND WHO ARE NOT CHILDREN OR STEPCHILDREN OF THE DIRECTOR) WHO LIVE WITH THE DIRECTOR AND HAVE NOT ATTAINED THE AGE OF 18; AND (E)　THE DIRECTOR'S PARENTS. IT EXCLUDES A PERSON WHO IS A DIRECTOR OF THE COMPANY.
employees and others providing similar services	Individuals who render personal services to the entity and either (a) the individuals are regarded as employees for legal or tax purposes, (b) the individuals work for the entity under its direction in the same way as individuals who are regarded as employees for legal or tax purposes, or (c) the services rendered are similar to those rendered by employees. For example, the term encompasses all management personnel, i.e. those persons having authority and responsibility for planning, directing and controlling the activities of the entity, including non-executive directors.
equity instrument	Any contract that evidences a residual interest in the assets of an entity after deducting all of its liabilities.

equity instrument granted	The right (conditional or unconditional) to an equity instrument of the entity conferred by the entity on another party, under a share-based payment arrangement.
equity-settled share-based payment transaction	A **share-based payment transaction** in which the entity receives goods or services as consideration for **equity instruments** of the entity (including shares or share options).
estimation techniques	The methods adopted by an entity to arrive at estimated monetary amounts, corresponding to the measurement bases selected, for **assets**, **liabilities**, gains, losses and changes to shareholders' funds.
	Estimation techniques implement the measurement aspects of **accounting policies**. An **accounting policy** will specify the basis on which an item is to be measured; where there is uncertainty over the monetary amount corresponding to that basis, the amount will be arrived at by using an estimation technique.
	Estimation techniques include, for example:
	(a) methods of **depreciation**, such as straight-line and reducing balance, applied in the context of a particular measurement basis, used to estimate the proportion of the economic benefits of a tangible fixed asset consumed in a period; and
	(b) different methods used to estimate the proportion of trade debts that will not be recovered, particularly where such methods consider a population as a whole rather than individual balances.
events after the balance sheet date	Those events, both favourable and unfavourable, that occur between the balance sheet date and the date when financial statements are authorised for issue. Two types of events can be identified:
	Adjusting events
	(a) those that provide evidence of conditions that existed at the balance sheet date; and
	Non-adjusting events
	(b) those that are indicative of conditions that arose after the balance sheet date.
exceptional items	Material items that derive from events or transactions that fall within the **ordinary activities** of the reporting entity and individually or, if of a similar type, in aggregate need to be disclosed by virtue of their size or incidence if the financial statements are to give a true and fair view.
exchange rate	An exchange rate is a rate at which two currencies may be exchanged for each other at a particular point in time; different rates apply for spot and forward transactions.
exchange transaction	A transaction in which one party supplies goods or services to another party in exchange for a consideration, usually monetary.

fair value	Fair value is the amount at which an **asset** or **liability** could be exchanged in an arm's length transaction between informed and willing parties, other than in a forced or liquidation sale, less, where applicable, any grants receivable towards the purchase or use of an **asset**.
finance charge (on a lease)	The finance charge is the amount borne by the lessee over the **lease term**, representing the difference between the total of the **minimum lease payments** (including any residual amounts guaranteed by the lessee) and the amount at which the lessee records the leased asset at the **inception** of the lease.
finance costs (of a capital instrument)	The difference between the net proceeds of a **capital instrument** and the total amount of the payments (or other transfer of economic benefits) that the issuer may be required to make in respect of the instrument other than **arrangement fees**.
finance lease	A finance lease is a lease that transfers substantially all the risks and rewards of ownership of an asset to the lessee. It should be presumed that such a transfer of risks and rewards occurs if at the **inception** of a lease the present value of the **minimum lease payments**, including any initial payment, amounts to substantially all (normally 90 per cent or more) of the **fair value** of the leased asset. The present value should be calculated by using the interest rate implicit in the lease. If the **fair value** of the asset is not determinable an estimate thereof should be used.
financial asset	Any asset that is: (a) cash; (b) an equity instrument of another entity; (c) a contractual right: (i) to receive cash or another financial asset from another entity; or (ii) to exchange financial assets or financial liabilities with another entity under conditions that are potentially favourable to the entity; or (d) a contract that will or may be settled in the entity's own equity instruments and is: (i) a non-derivative for which the entity is or may be obliged to receive a variable number of the entity's own equity instruments; or (ii) a derivative that will or may be settled other than by the exchange of a fixed amount of cash or another financial asset for a fixed number of the entity's own equity instruments. For this purpose the entity's own equity instruments do not include instruments that are themselves contracts for the future receipt or delivery of the entity's own equity instruments.

financial instrument	Any contract that gives rise to a **financial asset** of one entity and a **financial liability** or equity instrument of another entity.

financial liability	Any liability that is:
	
	(a) a contractual obligation:
	
	   (i) to deliver cash or another financial asset to another entity; or
	
	   (ii) to exchange financial assets or financial liabilities with another entity under conditions that are potentially unfavourable to the entity; or
	
	(b) a contract that will or may be settled in the entity's own equity instruments and is:
	
	   (i) a non-derivative for which the entity is or may be obliged to deliver a variable number of the entity's own equity instruments; or
	
	   (ii) a derivative that will or may be settled other than by the exchange of a fixed amount of cash or another financial asset for a fixed number of the entity's own equity instruments. For this purpose the entity's own equity instruments do not include instruments that are themselves contracts for the future receipt or delivery of the entity's own equity instruments.

FINANCIAL YEAR	A COMPANY'S **FINANCIAL YEAR** BEGINS WITH THE FIRST DAY OF ITS ACCOUNTING REFERENCE PERIOD AND ENDS WITH THE LAST DAY OF THAT PERIOD OR SUCH OTHER DATE, NOT MORE THAN SEVEN DAYS BEFORE OR AFTER THE END OF THAT PERIOD, AS THE **DIRECTORS** MAY DETERMINE.
foreign entity	A foreign entity is a subsidiary, associated company or branch whose operations are based in a country other than that of the investing company or whose **assets** and **liabilities** are denominated mainly in a foreign currency.
foreseeable losses (on a long-term contract)	Losses that are currently estimated to arise over the duration of the contract (after allowing for estimated remedial and maintenance costs and increases in costs so far as not recoverable under the terms of the contract). This estimate is required irrespective of: (a) whether work has yet commenced on such contracts; (b) the proportion of work carried out at the accounting date; or (c) the amount of profits expected to arise on other contracts.
forward contract	A forward contract is an agreement to exchange different currencies at a specified future date and at a specified rate. The difference between the specified rate and the spot rate ruling on the date the contract was entered into is the discount or premium on the forward contract.

government	Government includes government and inter-governmental agencies and similar bodies whether local, national or international.
government grants	Government grants are assistance by **government** in the form of cash or transfers of assets to an entity in return for past or future compliance with certain conditions relating to the operating activities of the entity.
grant date for share-based payment arrangements	The date at which the entity and another party (including an employee) agree to a share-based payment arrangement, being when the entity and the counterparty have a shared understanding of the terms and conditions of the arrangement. At grant date the entity confers on the counterparty the right to cash, other **assets**, or **equity instruments** of the entity, provided the specified vesting conditions, if any, are met. If that agreement is subject to an approval process (for example, by shareholders), grant date is the date when that approval is obtained.
gross earnings (from a lease)	Gross earnings comprise the lessor's gross finance income over the **lease term**, representing the difference between its gross investment in the lease and the cost of the leased **asset** less any grants receivable towards the purchase or use of the **asset**.
hire purchase contract	A hire purchase contract is a contract for the hire of an **asset** that contains a **provision** giving the hirer an option to acquire legal title to the **asset** upon the fulfilment of certain conditions stated in the contract.
identifiable assets and liabilities	Identifiable assets and liabilities are the **assets** and **liabilities** of an entity that are capable of being disposed of or settled separately, without disposing of a business of the entity.
inception (of a lease)	The inception of a lease is the earlier of the time the asset is brought into use and the date from which rentals first accrue.
intangible assets	Intangible assets are non-financial fixed **assets** that do not have physical substance but are **identifiable** and are controlled by the entity through custody or legal rights.
interest cost	The expected increase during the period in the present value of the **scheme liabilities** because the benefits are one period closer to **settlement**.

investment property	An investment property is an interest in land and/or buildings: (a) in respect of which construction work and development have been completed; and (b) which is held for its investment potential, any rental income being negotiated at arm's length, but excluding: (i) a property that is owned and occupied by a company for its own purposes; and (ii) a property let to and occupied by another group company.
key management personnel	Key management personnel are those persons having authority and responsibility for planning, directing and controlling the activities of the entity, directly or indirectly, including any director (whether executive or otherwise) of that entity.
lease term	The lease term is the period for which the lessee has contracted to lease the **asset** and any further terms for which the lessee has the option to continue to lease the **asset** with or without further payment, which option it is reasonably certain at the **inception** of the lease that the lessee will exercise.
liabilities	An entity's **obligations** to transfer economic benefits as a result of past transactions or events.
local currency	An entity's local currency is the currency of the primary economic environment in which it operates and generates net cash flows.
long-term contract	A contract entered into for the design, manufacture or construction of a single substantial **asset** or the provision of a service (or of a combination of **assets** or services that together constitute a single project) where the time taken substantially to complete the contract is such that the contract activity falls into different accounting periods. A contract that is required to be accounted for as long-term by the FRSSE will usually extend for a period exceeding one year. However, a duration exceeding one year is not an essential feature of a long-term contract. Some contracts with a shorter duration than one year should be accounted for as long-term contracts if they are sufficiently material to the activity of the period that not to record turnover and **attributable profit** would lead to distortion of the period's turnover and results such that the financial statements would not give a true and fair view, provided that the policy is applied consistently within the reporting entity and from year to year.
micro-entity	As defined in sections 384A and 384B of the **Act**, which are summarised in Appendix I *Note on legal requirements for companies*.

micro-entity minimum accounting items	The items of information required by the **Act** or regulations to be contained in the individual accounts of a company which qualifies as a **micro-entity**. These are set out in paragraphs 2.40 to 2.42.
minimum lease payments	The minimum lease payments are the minimum payments over the remaining part of the **lease term** (excluding charges for services and taxes to be paid by the lessor) and: (a) in the case of the lessee any residual amounts guaranteed by it or by a party related to it; or (b) in the case of the lessor any residual amounts guaranteed by the lessee or by an independent third party.
monetary items	Monetary items are money held and amounts to be received or paid in money and should be categorised as either short-term or long-term. Short-term monetary items are those that fall due within one year of the balance sheet date.
MONEY PURCHASE SCHEME	A DEFINED CONTRIBUTION SCHEME UNDER WHICH ALL OF THE BENEFITS THAT MAY BECOME PAYABLE ARE CALCULATED BY REFERENCE TO THE PAYMENTS MADE OR TREATED AS MADE BY THE SCHEME MEMBER AND WHICH ARE NOT AVERAGE SALARY BENEFITS.
net investment (in a foreign entity)	The net investment that a company has in a **foreign entity** is its effective equity stake and comprises its proportion of such **foreign entity's** net assets; in appropriate circumstances, intragroup loans and other deferred balances may be regarded as part of the effective equity stake.
net investment (in a lease)	The net investment in a lease at a point in time comprises: (a) the gross investment in a lease (i.e. the total of the **minimum lease payments** and that portion of the **residual value** of the **leased asset**, the realisation of which by the lessor is not assured or is guaranteed solely by a party related to the lessor); less (b) **gross earnings** allocated to future periods.
net realisable value (of fixed assets)	Net realisable value of a fixed asset is the amount at which the asset could be disposed of, less any direct selling costs.
net realisable value (of stocks and long-term contracts)	The actual or estimated selling price (net of trade but before settlement discounts) less: (a) all further costs to completion; and (b) all costs to be incurred in marketing, selling and distributing.

obligation	An obligation may be either a legal obligation (derived, for example, from a contract or legislation) or a constructive obligation, where the entity has indicated to other parties that it will accept certain responsibilities and has created valid expectations in those other parties that it will discharge those responsibilities.
operating lease	An operating lease is a lease other than a **finance lease**.
ordinary activities	Any activities that are undertaken by a reporting entity as part of its business and such related activities in which the reporting entity engages in furtherance of, incidental to, or arising from, these activities. Ordinary activities include the effects on the reporting entity of any event in the various environments in which it operates, including the political, regulatory, economic and geographical environments, irrespective of the frequency or unusual nature of the events.
past service cost	The increase in the present value of the **scheme liabilities** related to employee service in prior periods arising in the current period as a result of the introduction of, or improvement to, **retirement benefits**.
pension schemes	A pension scheme is an arrangement (other than accident insurance) to provide pension and/or other benefits for members on leaving service or retiring and, after a member's death, for his/ her dependants.
performance	The fulfilment of the seller's contractual **obligations** to a customer through the supply of goods and services.
permanent differences	Differences between an entity's taxable profits and its results as stated in the financial statements that arise because certain types of income and expenditure are non-taxable or disallowable, or because certain tax charges or allowances have no corresponding amount in the financial statements.
pre-contract costs	The costs of tendering for and securing contracts to supply products or services.
prior period adjustments	Material adjustments applicable to prior periods arising from changes in **accounting policies** or from the correction of fundamental errors. They do not include normal recurring adjustments or corrections of accounting estimates made in prior periods.

projected unit method	An accrued benefits valuation method in which the **scheme liabilities** make allowance for projected earnings. An accrued benefits valuation method is a valuation method in which the **scheme liabilities** at the valuation date relate to: (a) the benefits for pensioners and deferred pensioners (i.e. individuals who have ceased to be active members but are entitled to benefits payable at a later date) and their dependants, allowing where appropriate for future increases; and (b) the accrued benefits for members in service on the valuation date. The accrued benefits are the benefits for service up to a given point in time, whether vested rights or not. Guidance on the projected unit method is given in the Guidance Note GN26 issued by the Faculty and Institute of Actuaries.
provision	A **liability** of uncertain timing or amount.
public benefit entities	An entity whose primary objective is to provide goods or services for the general public, community or social benefit and where any equity is provided with a view to supporting the entity's primary objectives rather than with a view to providing a financial return to equity providers, shareholders or members.
purchased goodwill	Purchased goodwill is goodwill that is established as a result of the purchase of a business accounted for as an acquisition. It represents the difference between the cost of the acquired business and the aggregate of the **fair values** recorded for the **identifiable assets and liabilities** acquired. Positive goodwill arises when the acquisition cost exceeds the aggregate **fair values** of the **identifiable assets and liabilities**. Negative goodwill arises when the aggregate **fair values** of the **identifiable assets and liabilities** of the entity exceed the acquisition cost.
pure (or basic) research	Experimental or theoretical work undertaken primarily to acquire new scientific or technological knowledge for its own sake rather than directed towards any specific aim or application.
QUALIFYING SERVICES	SERVICES AS A DIRECTOR OF THE COMPANY OR SERVICES WHILE DIRECTOR OF THE COMPANY AND AS DIRECTOR OF ANY OF ITS SUBSIDIARY UNDERTAKINGS OR OTHERWISE IN CONNECTION WITH THE MANAGEMENT OF THE AFFAIRS OF THE COMPANY OR ANY OF ITS SUBSIDIARIES.

QUALIFYING THIRD PARTY INDEMNITY PROVISION	A PROVISION BY WHICH A COMPANY DIRECTLY OR INDIRECTLY PROVIDES AN INDEMNITY FOR A DIRECTOR OF THE COMPANY OR AN ASSOCIATED COMPANY WHICH SATISFIES THE FOLLOWING THREE CONDITIONS: (A) THE PROVISION DOES NOT PROVIDE ANY INDEMNITY AGAINST ANY LIABILITY INCURRED BY THE DIRECTOR TO THE COMPANY OR ANY ASSOCIATED COMPANY; (B) THE PROVISION DOES NOT PROVIDE ANY INDEMNITY AGAINST ANY LIABILITY INCURRED BY THE DIRECTOR TO PAY A FINE IMPOSED BY CRIMINAL PROCEEDINGS OR PAY A PENALTY TO A REGULATORY AUTHORITY IN RESPECT OF NON-COMPLIANCE; (C) THE PROVISION DOES NOT PROVIDE ANY INDEMNITY AGAINST ANY LIABILITY INCURRED BY THE DIRECTOR (I) IN DEFENDING ANY CRIMINAL PROCEEDINGS IN WHICH HE IS CONVICTED OR (II) IN DEFENDING ANY CIVIL PROCEEDINGS BROUGHT BY THE COMPANY OR AN ASSOCIATED COMPANY IN WHICH JUDGEMENT IS GIVEN AGAINST HIM, OR (III) IN WHICH THE COURT REFUSES TO GRANT RELIEF IN CONNECTION WITH ANY APPLICATION UNDER THE FOLLOWING PROVISIONS: ACQUISITION OF SHARES BY INNOCENT NOMINEE, OR GENERAL POWER TO GRANT RELIEF IN CASE OF HONEST AND REASONABLE CONDUCT.
QUALIFYING UNDERTAKING	A QUALIFYING PARTNERSHIP OR AN UNLIMITED COMPANY EACH OF WHOSE MEMBERS IS (I) A LIMITED COMPANY, OR (II) ANOTHER UNLIMITED COMPANY EACH OF WHOSE MEMBERS IS A LIMITED COMPANY, OR (III) A SCOTTISH PARTNERSHIP EACH OF WHOSE MEMBERS IS A LIMITED COMPANY. THIS INCLUDES ANY COMPARABLE UNDERTAKING INCORPORATED IN OR FORMED UNDER THE LAW OF ANY COUNTRY OR TERRITORY OUTSIDE UNITED KINGDOM.
recognised	Recognition is the process of incorporating an item into the primary financial statements under the appropriate heading. It involves depiction of the item in words and by a monetary amount and inclusion of that amount in the statement totals.
recoverable amount	Recoverable amount of an **asset** is the higher of the amounts that can be obtained from selling the **asset** (i.e. **net realizable value**) or continuing to use the **asset** in the business (i.e. value in use). Value in use is calculated as the present value of the future cash flows[48] obtainable as a result of the **asset's** continued use (including those resulting from its ultimate disposal), or a reasonable estimate thereof.
regular (pension) cost	The consistent ongoing cost **recognised** under the actuarial method used.

[48] *This calculation may not be relevant for fixed assets held by charities and other not-for-profit entities, where they are not held for the purpose of generating cash flows.*

related parties	A related party is a person or entity that is related to the entity that is preparing its financial statements (in this Standard referred to as the 'reporting entity').
	(a) A person or a close member of that person's family is related to a reporting entity if that person:
	(i) has control or joint control over the reporting entity;
	(ii) has significant influence over the reporting entity; or
	(b) is a member of the **key management personnel** of the reporting entity or of a parent of the reporting entity. An entity is related to a reporting entity if any of the following conditions applies:
	(i) The entity and the reporting entity are members of the same group (which means that each parent, subsidiary and fellow subsidiary is related to the others).
	(ii) One entity is an associate or joint venture of the other entity (or an associate or joint venture of a member of a group of which the other entity is a member).
	(iii) Both entities are joint ventures of the same third party.
	(iv) One entity is a joint venture of a third entity and the other entity is an associate of the third entity.
	(v) The entity is a retirement benefit scheme for the benefit of employees of either the reporting entity or an entity related to the reporting entity. If the reporting entity is itself such a scheme, the sponsoring employers are also related to the reporting entity.
	(vi) The entity is controlled or jointly controlled by a person identified in (a).
	(vii) A person identified in (a)(i) has significant influence over the entity or is a member of the key management personnel of the entity (or of a parent of the entity).

reliability	Financial information is reliable if:
	(a) it can be depended upon by users to represent faithfully what it either purports to represent or could reasonably be expected to represent, and therefore reflects the substance of the transactions and other events that have taken place;
	(b) it is free from deliberate or systematic bias (i.e. it is neutral);
	(c) it is free from material error;
	(d) it is complete within the bounds of materiality; and
	(e) under conditions of uncertainty, it has been prudently prepared (i.e. a degree of caution has been applied in exercising judgement and making the necessary estimates).
research and development expenditure	Research and development expenditure means expenditure falling into one or more of the broad categories of **pure (or basic) research**, **applied research** and **development** (except to the extent that it relates to locating or exploiting oil, gas or mineral deposits or is reimbursable by third parties either directly or under the terms of a firm contract to develop and manufacture at an agreed price calculated to reimburse both elements of expenditure).
residual value	Residual value is the realisable value of an **asset** at the end of its **useful economic life**, based on prices prevailing at the date of acquisition or revaluation, where this has taken place. Residual values do not take account of future price changes Realisation costs should be deducted in arriving at the residual value.
retirement benefits	All forms of consideration given by an employer in exchange for services rendered by employees that are payable after the completion of employment. Retirement benefits do not include termination benefits payable as a result of either (i) an employer's decision to terminate an employee's employment before the normal retirement date or (ii) an employee's decision to accept voluntary redundancy in exchange for those benefits, because these are not given in exchange for services rendered by employees.
right to consideration	A seller's right to the amount received or receivable in exchange for its **performance**. This right does not necessarily correspond to amounts falling due in accordance with a schedule of stage payments which may be specified in a contractual arrangement. Whilst stage payments will often be timed to coincide with **performance**, they may not correspond exactly. Stage payments reflect only the agreed timing of payment, whereas a right to consideration arises through the seller's **performance**.

scheme liabilities	The **liabilities** of a defined benefit scheme for outgoings due after the valuation date. Scheme liabilities measured using the **projected unit method** reflect the benefits that the employer is committed to provide for service up to the valuation date.
settlement	An irrevocable action that relieves the employer (or the **defined benefit scheme**) of the primary responsibility for a pension **obligation** and eliminates significant risks relating to the **obligation** and the **assets** used to effect the settlement.
share-based payment transaction	A transaction in which the entity receives goods or services as consideration for **equity instruments** of the entity (including shares or share options), or acquires goods or services by incurring **liabilities** to the supplier of those goods or services for amounts that are based on the price of the entity's shares or other **equity instruments** of the entity.
SOCIAL SECURITY COSTS	ANY CONTRIBUTIONS BY THE ENTITY TO ANY STATE SOCIAL SECURITY OR PENSION SCHEME, FUND OR ARRANGEMENT.
start-up costs	Costs arising from those one-time activities related to opening a new facility, introducing a new product or service, conducting business in a new territory, conducting business with a new class of customer, initiating a new process in an existing facility, starting some new operation and similar items. They include costs of relocating or reorganising part or all of an entity, costs related to organising a new entity, and expenses and losses incurred both before and after opening.
SUBSIDIARY UNDERTAKINGS[49]	AN UNDERTAKING IS A SUBSIDIARY OF A PARENT UNDERTAKING WHERE THE PARENT: (A) HOLDS A MAJORITY OF THE VOTING RIGHTS IN THE UNDERTAKING; OR (B) IS A MEMBER OF THE UNDERTAKING AND HAS THE RIGHT TO APPOINT OR REMOVE A MAJORITY OF ITS BOARD OF DIRECTORS; OR (C) HAS THE RIGHT TO EXERCISE A DOMINANT INFLUENCE OVER THE UNDERTAKING BY VIRTUE OF PROVISIONS CONTAINED IN ITS MEMORANDUM OR ARTICLES OR BY VIRTUE OF A CONTROL CONTRACT; OR (D) IS A MEMBER OF THE UNDERTAKING AND CONTROLS ALONE, PURSUANT TO AN AGREEMENT WITH OTHER SHAREHOLDERS OR MEMBERS, A MAJORITY OF THE VOTING RIGHTS IN THE UNDERTAKING; OR (E) HAS THE POWER TO EXERCISE, OR ACTUALLY EXERCISES, DOMINANT INFLUENCE OR CONTROL OVER THE UNDERTAKING; OR (F) THE PARENT AND THE SUBSIDIARY UNDERTAKING ARE MANAGED ON A UNIFIED BASIS.

[49] *In case of doubt, reference should be made to the full definition in section 1162 of the Companies Act 2006.*

tangible fixed assets	**Assets** that have physical substance and are held for use in the production or supply of goods or services, for rental to others, or for administrative purposes on a continuing basis in the reporting entity's activities.
tax credit	The tax credit given under UK legislation to the recipient of a dividend from a UK company.
term (of a capital instrument)	The period from the date of issue of the **capital instrument** to the date at which it will expire, be redeemed, or be cancelled. If either party has the option to require the instrument to be redeemed or cancelled and, under the terms of the instrument, it is uncertain whether such an option will be exercised, the term should be taken to end on the earliest date at which the instrument would be redeemed or cancelled on exercise of such an option. If either party has the right to extend the period of an instrument, the term should not include the period of the extension if there is a genuine commercial possibility that the period will not be extended.
timing differences	Differences between taxable profits and the results as stated in the financial statements that arise from the inclusion of gains and losses in tax assessments in periods different from those in which they are **recognised** in financial statements. For example, a timing difference would arise when tax allowances for the cost of a fixed asset are accelerated or decelerated, i.e. received before or after the **depreciation** of the fixed asset is **recognized** in the profit and loss account.
total recognised gains and losses	The total of all gains and losses of the reporting entity that are **recognised** in a period and are attributable to the shareholders.
translation	Translation is the process whereby financial data denominated in one currency are expressed in terms of another currency. It includes both the expression of individual transactions in terms of another currency and the expression of a complete set of financial statements prepared in one currency in terms of another currency.
useful economic life	The useful economic life of a tangible fixed asset is the period over which the entity expects to derive economic benefit from that asset.
withholding tax	Tax on dividends or other income that is deducted by the payer of the income and paid to the tax authorities wholly on behalf of the recipient.

Editor's note: Amendments to the FRSSE – Micro-entities (April 2014) have inserted the definitions of 'act', 'micro-entity' and 'micro-entity minimum accounting items'.

D   VOLUNTARY DISCLOSURES

The disclosures below are not mandatory and do not form part of the Statement of Standard Accounting Practice. The Board, however, encourages reporting entities voluntarily to include the following disclosures in their financial statements.

Cash flow information[50]

1   Reporting entities are encouraged, but not required, to provide a cash flow statement using the indirect method as explained below.[51]

2   The indirect method starts with operating profit (which is normally profit before income from shares in group undertakings) and adjusts it for non-cash charges and credits to reconcile it with cash generated from operations. Other sources and applications of cash are shown to arrive at total cash generated (or utilised) in the period.

3   Cash is taken as 'cash at bank and in hand' less overdrafts repayable on demand, which should be reconciled to the balance sheet.

4   Cash flows are shown net of any attributable value added tax or other sales tax unless the tax is irrecoverable by the reporting entity.

5   It is recommended that material transactions not resulting in movements of cash of the reporting entity are disclosed by way of note, if disclosure is necessary for an understanding of the underlying transactions.

E   APPROVAL BY THE FRC

FRS 100 *Application of Financial Reporting Requirements* was approved for issue by the Board of the Financial Reporting Council on 1 November 2012, following its consideration of the Accounting Council's advice for that standard. The consequential amendments to the FRSSE were set out in paragraphs 16(a) to (x) of FRS 100.

---

[50] *The Board's reasoning for including a voluntary recommendation for cash flow information is set out in Appendix IV.*

[51] *An illustrative example of a cash flow statement using the indirect method is given in Appendix III.*

Appendix I
Note on Legal Requirements for Companies

THE UNITED KINGDOM

Companies Act 2006, sections 382 to 384

The definition of a small company is contained in sections 382 and 383 of the Companies **1**
Act 2006. The qualifying conditions are met by a company in a year in which it does not
exceed two or more of the following criteria:

(a)   Turnover of £6,500,000
(b)   Balance sheet total of £3,260,000
(c)   Average number of employees is 50

For any company, other than a newly incorporated company, to qualify as small, the
qualifying conditions must be met for two consecutive years. A company will cease to
qualify as small if it fails to meet the qualifying conditions for two consecutive years.
However, if a company which qualified as small in one period no longer meets the criteria
for small in the next period, the company may continue to claim the exemption available in
the next period. If that company then reverts back to being small by meeting the criteria,
the exemption will continue uninterrupted.

Certain companies are excluded by section 384 from the 'small company' criteria for **2**
reasons of public interest. These are any entity that is, or is in a group that includes:

(a)   a public company;
(b)   a small company that is an authorised insurance company, a banking company, an
      emoney issuer, a MifId investment firm or a UCITS management company or a
      company that carries on insurance market activity;
(c)   a body corporate (other than a company) whose shares are admitted to trading on a
      regulated market in an EEA State; or
(d)   a person (other than a small company) who has permission under Part 4 of the
      Financial Services and Markets Act 2000 to carry on a regulated activity.

A parent company shall not be treated as qualifying as a small company in relation to a **3**
financial year unless the group headed by it qualifies as a small group.

The definition of a small group is contained in section 383. The qualifying conditions are **4**
met by a group in a year in which it does not exceed two or more of the following criteria:

(1)   Aggregate turnover of £6,500,000 net (or £7,800,000 gross).
(2)   Aggregate balance sheet total of £3,260,000 net (or £3,900,000 gross).
(3)   Aggregate number of employees is 50.

'Net' means after the set-offs and other adjustments required by Schedule 6 of the Small
Companies and Groups (Accounts and Directors' Report) Regulations 2008 in the case
of group accounts, and 'gross' means without those set-offs and adjustments. A company
may satisfy the relevant requirements on the basis of either the net or the gross figure[52].

---

[52] *Reference should also be made to Schedule 6 of the Large and Medium-sized Companies and Groups (Accounts and Reports) Regulations 2008 because it is possible that after the set-offs and other adjustments required by that Schedule, a group which started off large or medium-sized could become small.*

REPUBLIC OF IRELAND

5   The following table shows the references in companies legislation in the Republic of Ireland that correspond to the references in paragraphs 1-4 above.

United Kingdom	Republic of Ireland
Sections 382 and 383	Companies (Amendment) Act 1986, sections 2, 8 and 9
Sections 384	No equivalent
The Small Companies and Groups (Accounts and Directors' Report) Regulations 2008	No equivalent

The qualifying conditions for the definition of a small company may be met by a company in a year in which it does not exceed two or more of the following criteria:

(1)   Turnover of €3.81 million.
(2)   Balance sheet total of €1.9 million.
(3)   Average number of employees is 50.

The FRSSE can be applied to those companies meeting the criteria as set out in the Republic of Ireland Companies Acts that allow them to be treated as 'small' for the purposes of filing information with the Companies Registration Office. Small groups are not defined in Republic of Ireland legislation. However, in the Republic of Ireland, for the purposes of the FRSSE, small groups should meet, on a consolidated basis, the same legal conditions as are required for small companies. If a group does not qualify as small, then the parent undertaking of that group, even if it qualifies as a small company under Republic of Ireland legislation, is not entitled to adopt the FRSSE.

DERIVATION TABLES FOR LEGAL REQUIREMENTS REFERRED TO IN THE FRSSE

6   Derivation tables for all the legal requirements referred to in the FRSSE are available from the FRC website at frc.org.uk/Our-Work/Codes-Standards/Accounting-and-Reporting-Policy/FRSSE.aspx in the derivation tables which indicates the source of company law in the United Kingdom and the Republic of Ireland.

7   Republic of Ireland users of the FRSSE should note that the requirements of company law as shown in SMALL CAPITALS in the text of the FRSSE relate to UK company law as applicable to small companies. The corresponding reference to Republic of Ireland companies legislation is shown in Table 1 of the derivation tables However, Republic of Ireland users should note that the detail of the Republic of Ireland legal requirements in many cases differs from UK company law.

8   In addition, there are a number of Republic of Ireland legal requirements that are not reflected in the FRSSE. There is no equivalent to the Small Companies and Groups (Accounts and Directors' Report) Regulations 2008 providing certain exemptions for small companies when preparing annual accounts for shareholders. Exemptions from company law requirements for small companies in the Republic of Ireland are limited and relate primarily to information that must be filed with the Companies Registration Office. These additional requirements are referenced in Table 2 of the derivation tables.

9   There are no special provisions in Republic of Ireland company law that relate to the preparation of group accounts by small entities. The general requirement for the preparation of group accounts is contained in section 150 of the Companies Act 1963.

Regulation 7 of the EC (Companies: Group Accounts) Regulations 1992, SI 201/1992, contains an exemption from the requirement to prepare group accounts for certain undertakings to whom the above Regulation applies. The legal references are given in Table 2 of the derivation tables.

Republic of Ireland users should refer to the underlying legislation when using the FRSSE. **10** The Republic of Ireland legal requirements set out in the derivation tables are intended to reflect company law as applicable to accounting periods beginning on or after 6 April 2008.

STATUS OF THE FRSSE

Legal advice has been obtained that in accounting standards smaller entities may properly **11** be allowed exemptions or different treatment provided that such differences are justified on rational grounds. The Board will have regard to the criteria given in the 'Status of the FRSSE' section in determining whether such rational grounds exist.

The summary of advice regarding the status of the FRSSE given by Richard Sykes QC in **12** December 1995 is reproduced below:

"I do not see any conflict with the law or likely weakening of the authority of ASB or FRRP[53] as respects the upholding of Standards provided that

(i) the treatment required by the FRSSE is the same as that required by existing Standards or is a simplified version of that treatment; or

(ii) in a case where a future Standard calls for a new treatment for Big GAAP[54] Companies only and which is also likely to be significant to small companies, ASB is able to justify on rational grounds any lack of a change in treatment for smaller entities when the FRSSE is in due course revised;

(iii) in a case where in the future the FRSSE requires a treatment which is materially different from then existing Standards on a significant matter ASB is able to justify on rational grounds such different treatment in the case of smaller entities.

(iv) it is recognised that the starting point for deciding how a smaller entity will account for something not covered by the FRSSE will be existing practice and that the smaller entity must be able to justify its departure from such practice on rational grounds related to its size. Where the matter is covered by a Big GAAP Standard, that Standard would provide the obvious source in determining existing practice.

Rational grounds for justifying different treatments might include:

(i) the different nature of entities;

(ii) particularly if the different treatment is in the area of disclosure, the different users of their financial statements; and

(iii) established practices existing at the time of issue of a Standard or FRSSE revision."

MICRO-ENTITIES

The *Small Companies (Micro-Entities' Accounts) Regulations 2013* (the Micro- Entities' **13** Accounts Regulations) were made in November 2013 and apply to the financial statements

---

[53] *Financial Reporting Review Panel.*

[54] *Generally accepted accounting practice.*

of micro-entities for accounting periods ending on or after 30 September 2013 for companies filing their accounts on or after 1 December 2013.

Editor's note: Amendments to the FRSSE – Micro-entities (April 2014) has added this paragraph 13 and the sub-heading above.

14   The definition of a micro-entity is contained in sections 384A and 384B of the Companies Act 2006. The qualifying conditions are met by a company in a year in which it does not exceed two or more of the following criteria:

Turnover	£632,000
Balance sheet total	£316,000
Number of employees	10

For any company, other than a newly incorporated company, to qualify as a micro-entity, the qualifying conditions must be met for two consecutive years. A company will cease to qualify as a micro-entity if it fails to meet the qualifying conditions for two consecutive years. However, if a company which qualified as a micro-entity in one period no longer meets the criteria for a micro-entity in the next period, the company may continue to claim the exemptions available in the next period. If that company then reverts back to being a micro-entity by meeting the criteria, the exemptions will continue uninterrupted.

Editor's note: Amendments to the FRSSE – Micro-entities (April 2014) has added this paragraph 14.

15   Certain companies are excluded by section 384B from being treated as micro-entities, including those excluded from the small companies regime for reasons of public interest (as set out in section 384), certain financial institutions, charities, those voluntarily preparing group accounts and those included in group accounts. The **Act** should be referred to for a full list of excluded companies.

Editor's note: Amendments to the FRSSE – Micro-entities (April 2014) has added this paragraph 15.

16   Entities that are not companies, such as limited liability partnerships (LLPs), cannot meet the definition of a micro-entity.

Editor's note: Amendments to the FRSSE – Micro-entities (April 2014) has added this paragraph 16.

17   Micro-entities preparing financial statements comprising only the micro-entity minimum accounting items shall apply the specific paragraphs of the FRSSE applicable to micro-entities. This will allow micro-entities to take advantage of the reduced presentation and disclosure requirements whilst complying with the generally accepted recognition and measurement requirements of the FRSSE, except that the Micro-Entities' Accounts Regulations simplify the measurement bases available for fixed assets and certain current assets. The effect of this is that micro-entities may not revalue any fixed assets, including investment property or measure any current asset investments at current cost.

Editor's note: Amendments to the FRSSE – Micro-entities (April 2014) has added this paragraph 17.

18   Similar legislation is not currently applicable in the Republic of Ireland.

Editor's note: Amendments to the FRSSE – Micro-entities (April 2014) has added this paragraph 18.

Appendix II
Accounting for Retirement Benefits:
Defined Benefit Schemes

The following requirements should be regarded as standard:

(a) **Assets** in a **defined benefit scheme** should be measured at their **fair value** at the balance sheet date.

(b) **Defined benefit scheme liabilities** should be measured on an actuarial basis using the **projected unit method**. The **scheme liabilities** comprise both any benefits promised under the formal terms of the scheme and any constructive **obligations** for further benefits.

(c) The assumptions underlying the valuation should be mutually compatible and lead to the best estimate of the future cash flows that will arise under the **scheme liabilities**. The assumptions are ultimately the responsibility of the **directors** (or equivalent) but should be set upon advice given by an actuary. Any assumptions that are affected by economic conditions (financial assumptions) should reflect market expectations at the balance sheet date.

(d) **Defined benefit scheme liabilities** should be discounted at the current rate of return on a high quality corporate bond of equivalent currency and term.

(e) Full actuarial valuations by a professionally qualified actuary should be obtained for a **defined benefit scheme** at intervals not exceeding three years. The actuary should review the most recent actuarial valuation at the balance sheet date and update it to reflect current conditions.

(f) The surplus/deficit in a **defined benefit scheme** is the excess/shortfall of the value of the **assets** in the scheme over/below the present value of the **scheme liabilities**. The employer should **recognise** an **asset** to the extent that it is able to recover a surplus either through reduced contributions in the future or through refunds from the scheme. The employer should **recognise** a **liability** to the extent that it reflects its legal or constructive **obligation**.

(g) Any unpaid contributions to the scheme should be presented in the balance sheet as a creditor due within one year. The defined benefit **asset** or **liability** should be presented separately on the face of the balance sheet:

    (i) in balance sheets of the type prescribed for small companies in the United Kingdom by the Small Companies and Groups (Accounts and Directors' Report) Regulations 2008[55], format 1 after item J Accruals and deferred income but before item K Capital and reserves; and

    (ii) in balance sheets of the type prescribed for small companies in the United Kingdom by the Small Companies and Groups (Accounts and Directors' Report) Regulations 2008, format 2: any **asset** after ASSETS item D Prepayments and accrued income and any **liability** after LIABILITIES item D Accruals and deferred income.

(h) The **deferred tax** relating to the defined benefit **asset** or **liability** should be offset against the defined benefit **asset** or **liability** and not included with other **deferred tax assets** or **liabilities**:

(i) The components of the change in the defined benefit **asset** or **liability** (other than those arising from contributions to the scheme) should be presented separately in the performance statements as follows:

---

[55] *There is no equivalent to Statutory Instrument 2008/409* The Small Companies and Groups (Accounts and Directors Report) Regulations 2008 *in companies legislation in the Republic of Ireland. See the derivation table on the FRC website for Republic of Ireland legal requirements.*

(i) the **current service cost** should be included within operating profit in the profit and loss account;

(ii) the net of the **interest cost** and the expected return on assets should be included as other finance costs (or income) adjacent to interest;

(iii) actuarial gains and losses should be recognised in the statement of total recognised gains and losses;

(iv) **past service costs** should be **recognised** in the profit and loss account in the period in which the increases in benefit vest; and

(v) losses arising on a **settlement** or **curtailment** should be **recognised** in the profit and loss account when the employer becomes demonstrably committed to the transaction (gains should only be **recognised** once all parties whose consent is required are irrevocably committed).

(j) The following disclosures should be made in respect of a **defined benefit scheme**:

(i) the nature of the scheme (i.e. **defined benefit**);

(ii) the date of the most recent full actuarial valuation on which the amounts in the financial statements are based. If the actuary is an employee or officer of the reporting entity, or of the group of which it is a member, this fact should be disclosed;

(iii) the contribution made in respect of the accounting period and any agreed contribution rates for future years; and

(iv) for closed schemes and those in which the age profile of the active membership is rising significantly, the fact that under the **projected unit method** the **current service cost** will increase as the members of the scheme approach retirement.

(k) The **fair value** of the scheme **assets**, the present value of the scheme **liabilities** based on the accounting assumptions and the resulting surplus or deficit should be disclosed in a note to the financial statements. Where the **asset** or **liability** in the balance sheet differs from the surplus or deficit in the scheme, an explanation of the difference should be given. An analysis of the movements during the period in the surplus or deficit in the scheme should be given.

Appendix III
Illustrative Examples and Practical Considerations

This Appendix contains illustrative examples and practical considerations for general guidance and does not form part of the Financial Reporting Standard. The best form of reporting will depend on individual circumstances.

EXAMPLE: STATEMENT OF TOTAL RECOGNISED GAINS AND LOSSES

	2002	2001 as restated
	£	£
Profit for the financial year	29,000	7,000
Unrealised surplus on revaluation of property	4,000	6,000
Unrealised (loss) /gain on trade investment	(3,000)	7,000
Total recognised gains and losses relating to the year	30,000	20,000
Prior year adjustment (as explained in note x)	(10,000)	
Total gains and losses recognised since last annual report	20,000	

EXAMPLE: DISCLOSURE – DEFINED CONTRIBUTION PENSION SCHEME

The company operates a defined contribution pension scheme. The assets of the scheme are held separately from those of the company in an independently administered fund. The pension cost charge represents contributions payable by the company to the fund and amounted to £50,000 (2001 £45,000). Contributions totalling £2,500 (2001 £1,500) were payable to the fund at the year-end and are included in creditors.

EXAMPLE: DISCLOSURE – DEFINED BENEFIT PENSION SCHEME[56]

The company operates a pension scheme providing benefits based on final pensionable pay. The assets of the scheme are held separately from those of the company, being invested with insurance companies.

The contributions are determined by a qualified actuary on the basis of triennial valuations using the projected unit method. The most recent valuation was as at 31 December 2005 which has been updated to reflect conditions at the balance sheet date. The assumptions that have the most significant effect on the results of the valuation are those relating to the rate of return on investments and the rate of increase in salaries and pensions. It was assumed that the investment returns would be 6 per cent per year, that salary increases would average 4 per cent per year and that present and future pensions would increase at the rate of 3 per cent per year.

The pension charge for the year was £46,000 (2005 £25,000). This included £12,000 (2005 £nil) in respect of past service costs. The contributions of the company and employees will remain at 10 per cent and 5 per cent of earnings respectively.

---

[56] *This example reflects the disclosure requirements of paragraph 1 of Appendix II.*

The defined benefit scheme is closed to new members and so under the projected unit method the current service cost would be expected to increase over time as members of the scheme approach retirement.

Value of scheme assets and liabilities	2006	2005
	£	£
Market value of assets	1,488,000	962,000
Present value of scheme liabilities	(1,009,000)	(758,000)
Pension scheme surplus/(deficit)	479,000	204,000
Related deferred tax asset/(liability)	(144,000)	(61,000)
Net pension scheme asset/(liability)	335,000	143,000

Movements in year	2006	2005
	£	£
Pension scheme surplus/(deficit) at beginning of year	204,000	92,000
Current service cost	(34,000)	(25,000)
Cash contribution	25,000	35,000
Past service costs	(12,000)	0
Other finance income	20,000	11,000
Actuarial gain	276,000	91,000
Pension scheme surplus/(deficit) at end of year	479,000	204,000

PRACTICAL CONSIDERATIONS: STOCKS AND LONG-TERM CONTRACTS

Many of the problems involved in arriving at the amount at which stocks and long-term contracts are stated in financial statements are of a practical nature rather than resulting from matters of principle. The following paragraphs discuss some particular areas in which difficulty may be encountered.

The allocation of overheads

1   Production overheads are included in the cost of conversion together with direct labour, direct expenses and subcontracted work. This inclusion is a necessary corollary of the principle that expenditure should be included to the extent to which it has been incurred in bringing the product 'to its present location and condition'. However, all abnormal conversion costs (such as exceptional spoilage, idle capacity and other losses) that are avoidable under normal operating conditions need, for the same reason, to be excluded.

2   Where firm sales contracts have been entered into for the provision of goods or services to customer's specification, overheads relating to design, and marketing and selling costs incurred before manufacture, may be included in arriving at cost.

3   The costing methods adopted by a business are usually designed to ensure that all direct material, direct labour, direct expenses and subcontracted work are identified and charged on a reasonable and consistent basis, but problems arise on the allocation of overheads,

which must usually involve the exercise of personal judgement in the selection of an appropriate convention.

The classification of overheads necessary to achieve this allocation takes the function of the overhead as its distinguishing characteristic (e.g. whether it is a function of production, marketing, selling or administration), rather than whether the overhead tends to vary with time or with volume. **4**

The costs of general management, as distinct from functional management, are not directly related to current production and are, therefore, excluded from the cost of conversion and, hence, from the cost of stocks and long-term contracts. **5**

In the case of smaller organisations whose management may be involved in the daily administration of each of the various functions, particular problems may arise in practice in distinguishing these general management overheads. In such organisations the costs of management may fairly be allocated on suitable bases to the functions of production, marketing, selling and administration. **6**

Problems may also arise in allocating the costs of central service departments, the allocation of which should depend on the function or functions that the department is serving. For example, the accounts department will normally support the following functions: **7**

(a)   production – by paying direct and indirect production wages and salaries, by controlling purchases and by preparing periodic financial statements for the production units;

(b)   marketing and distribution – by analysing sales and by controlling the sales ledger; and

(c)   general administration – by preparing management accounts and annual financial statements and budgets, by controlling cash resources and by planning investments.

Only those costs of the accounts department that can reasonably be allocated to the production function fall to be included in the cost of conversion.

The allocation of overheads included in the valuation of stocks and long-term contracts needs to be based on the company's normal level of activity, taking one year with another. The governing factor is that the cost of unused capacity should be written off in the current year. In determining what constitutes 'normal' the following factors need to be considered: **8**

(a)   the volume of production that the production facilities are intended by their designers and by management to produce under the working conditions (e.g. single or double shift) prevailing during the year;

(b)   the budgeted level of activity for the year under review and for the ensuing year; and

(c)   the level of activity achieved both in the year under review and in previous years.

Although temporary changes in the load of activity may be ignored, persistent variation should lead to revision of the previous norm.

Where management accounts are prepared on a marginal cost basis, it will be necessary to add to the figure of stocks so arrived at the appropriate proportion of those production overheads not already included in the marginal cost. **9**

The adoption of a conservative approach to the valuation of stocks and long-term contracts has sometimes been used as one of the reasons for omitting selected production overheads. In so far as the circumstances of the business require an element of prudence in determining the amount at which stocks and long-term contracts are stated, this needs to be taken into account in the determination of net realisable value and not by the exclusion from cost of selected overheads. **10**

Methods of costing

11   It is frequently not practicable to relate expenditure to specific units of stocks and longterm contracts. The ascertainment of the nearest approximation to cost gives rise to two problems:

(a)   the selection of an appropriate method for relating costs to stocks and long-term contracts (e.g. job costing, batch costing, process costing, standard costing);

(b)   the selection of an appropriate method for calculating the related costs where a number of identical items have been purchased or made at different times (e.g. unit cost, average cost or 'first in, first out' (FIFO)).

12   In selecting the methods referred to in paragraph 11(a) and (b), management must exercise judgement to ensure that the methods chosen provide the fairest practicable approximation to cost. Furthermore, where standard costs are used they need to be reviewed frequently to ensure that they bear a reasonable relationship to actual costs obtaining during the period. Methods such as base stock and 'last in, first out' (LIFO) are not usually appropriate methods of stock valuation because they often result in stocks being stated in the balance sheet at amounts that bear little relationship to recent cost levels. When this happens, not only is the presentation of current assets misleading, but there is potential distortion of subsequent results if stock levels reduce and out-of-date costs are drawn into the profit and loss account.

13   The method of arriving at cost by applying the latest purchase price to the total number of units in stock is unacceptable in principle because it is not necessarily the same as actual cost and, in times of rising prices, will result in the taking of a profit that has not been realised.

14   One method of arriving at cost, in the absence of a satisfactory costing system, is the use of selling price less an estimated profit margin. This is acceptable only if it can be demonstrated that the method gives a reasonable approximation of the actual cost.

15   In industries where the cost of minor by-products is not separable from the cost of the principal products, stocks of such by-products may be stated in accounts at their net realisable value. In this case the costs of the main products are calculated after deducting the net realisable value of the by-products.

The determination of net realisable value

16   The initial calculation of provisions to reduce stocks from cost to net realisable value may often be made by the use of formulae based on predetermined criteria. The formulae normally take account of the age, movements in the past, expected future movements and estimated scrap values of the stock, as appropriate. Whilst the use of such formulae establishes a basis for making a provision that can be consistently applied, it is still necessary for the results to be reviewed in the light of any special circumstances that cannot be anticipated in the formulae, such as changes in the state of the order book.

17   Where a provision is required to reduce the value of finished goods below cost, the stocks of the parts and subassemblies held for the purpose of the manufacture of such products, together with stocks on order, need to be reviewed to determine if provision is also required against such items.

Where stocks of spares are held for sale, special consideration of the factors in paragraph 16   **18**
will be required in the context of:

(a)   the number of units sold to which they are applicable;
(b)   the estimated frequency with which a replacement spare is required; and
(c)   the expected useful life of the unit to which they are applicable.

Events occurring between the balance sheet date and the date of completion of the financial   **19**
statements need to be considered in arriving at the net realisable value at the balance sheet
date (e.g. a subsequent reduction in selling prices). However, no reduction falls to be made
when the realisable value of material stocks is less than the purchase price, provided that
the goods into which the materials are to be incorporated can still be sold at a profit after
incorporating the materials at cost price.

The application of net realisable value

The principal situations in which net realisable value is likely to be less than cost are where   **20**
there has been:

(a)   an increase in costs or a fall in selling price;
(b)   physical deterioration of stocks;
(c)   obsolescence of products;
(d)   a decision as part of a company's marketing strategy to manufacture and sell products
      at a loss; and
(e)   errors in production or purchasing.

Furthermore, when stocks are held that are unlikely to be sold within the turnover period
normal in that company (i.e. excess stocks), the impending delay in realisation increases
the risk that the situations outlined in (a)-(c) above may occur before the stocks are sold
and needs to be taken into account in assessing net realisable value.

Long-term contracts

In ascertaining costs of long-term contracts it is not normally appropriate to include interest   **21**
payable on borrowed money. However, in circumstances where sums borrowed can be
identified as financing specific long-term contracts, it may be appropriate to include such
related interest in cost, in which circumstances the inclusion of interest and the amount of
interest so included should be disclosed in a note to the financial statements.

In some businesses, long-term contracts for the supply of services or manufacture and   **22**
supply of goods exist where the prices are determined and invoiced according to separate
parts of the contract. In these businesses the most appropriate method of reflecting profits
on each contract is usually to match costs against performance of the separable parts of
the contract, treating each such separable part as a separate contract. In such instances,
however, future revenues from the contract need to be compared with future estimated
costs and provision made for any foreseen loss.

Turnover (ascertained in a manner appropriate to the industry, the nature of the contracts   **23**
concerned and the contractual relationship with the customer) and related costs should
be recorded in the profit and loss account as contract activity progresses. Turnover may
sometimes be ascertained by reference to valuation of the work carried out to date. In
other cases, there may be specific points during a contract at which individual elements
of work done with separately ascertainable sales and values and costs can be identified
and appropriately recorded as turnover (e.g. because delivery or customer acceptance has
taken place.

24   In determining whether the stage has been reached at which it is appropriate to recognise profit, account should be taken of the nature of the business concerned. It is necessary to define the earliest point for each particular contract before which no profit is taken up, the overriding principle being that there can be no attributable profit until the outcome of a contract can reasonably be foreseen. Of the profit that in the light of all the circumstances can be foreseen with a reasonable degree of certainty to arise on completion of the contract, there should be regarded as earned to date only that part which prudently reflects the amount of work performed to date. The method used for taking up such profit needs to be consistently applied.

25   In calculating the total estimated profit on the contract, it is necessary to take into account not only the total costs to date and the total estimated further costs to completion (calculated by reference to the same principles as were applied to cost to date) but also the estimated future costs of rectification and guarantee work, and any other future work to be undertaken under the terms of the contract. These are then compared with the total sales value of the contract. In considering future costs, it is necessary to have regard to likely increases in wages and salaries, to likely increases in the price of raw materials and to rises in general overheads, so far as these items are not recoverable from the customer under the terms of the contract.

26   Where approved variations have been made to a contract in the course of it and the amount to be received in respect of these variations has not yet been settled and is likely to be a material factor in the outcome, it is necessary to make a conservative estimate of the amount likely to be received and this is then treated as part of the total sales value. On the other hand, allowance needs to be made for foreseen claims or penalties payable arising out of delays in completion or from other causes.

27   The settlement of claims arising from circumstances not envisaged in the contract or arising as an indirect consequence of approved variations is subject to a high level of uncertainty relating to the outcome of future negotiations. In view of this, it is generally prudent to recognise receipts in respect of such claims only when negotiations have reached an advanced stage and there is sufficient evidence of the acceptability of the claim in principle to the purchaser, with an indication of the amount involved also being available.

28   The amounts to be included in the year's profit and loss account will be both the appropriate amount of turnover and the associated costs of achieving that turnover, to the extent that these amounts exceed corresponding amounts recognised in previous years. The estimated outcome of a contract that extends over several accounting years will nearly always vary in the light of changes in circumstances and for this reason the result of the year will not necessarily represent the proportion of the total profit on the contract that is appropriate to the amount of work carried out in the period; it may also reflect the effect of changes in circumstances during the year that affect the total profit estimated to accrue on completion.

PRACTICAL CONSIDERATIONS – CONSIGNMENT STOCK

29   In determining whether consignment stock is in substance an asset of the dealer, it is necessary to identify whether the dealer has access to the benefits of the stock and exposure to the risks inherent in those benefits. Therefore, to assist in using paragraph 8.9 of the FRSSE, the following table is provided.

Indications that the stock is not an asset of the dealer at delivery	Indications that the stock is an asset of the dealer at delivery
The manufacturer can require the dealer to return stock (or to transfer stock to another dealer) without compensation or Penalty paid by the dealer to prevent returns/transfers of stock at the manufacturer's request.	The manufacturer cannot require the dealer to return or transfer stock or Financial incentives given to persuade the dealer to transfer stock at the manufacturer's request.
The dealer has unfettered right to return stock to the manufacturer without penalty and actually exercises the right in practice. The manufacturer bears obsolescence risk, e.g.: – obsolete stock is returned to the manufacturer without penalty or – financial incentives given by the manufacturer to prevent stock being returned to it (e.g. on model change or if it becomes obsolete).	The dealer has no right to return stock or is commercially compelled not to exercise its right of return. The dealer bears obsolescence risk, e.g.: – penalty charged if the dealer returns stock to the manufacturer or – obsolete stock cannot be returned to the manufacturer and no compensation is paid by the manufacturer for losses due to obsolescence.
Stock transfer price charged by the manufacturer is based on the manufacturer's list price at date of transfer of legal title. The manufacturer bears slow movement risk, e.g.: – transfer price set independently of time for which the dealer holds stock, and there is no deposit.	Stock transfer price charged by the manufacturer is based on the manufacturer's list price at date of delivery. The dealer bears slow movement risk, e.g.: – the dealer is effectively charged interest as transfer price or other payments to the manufacturer vary with time for which the dealer holds stock or – the dealer makes a substantial interestfree deposit that varies with the levels of stock held.

PRACTICAL CONSIDERATIONS – DEBT FACTORING

30   To assist in using paragraphs 8.10 to 8.12 of the FRSSE, the following table is provided.

Indications that derecognition is appropriate (debts are not an asset of the seller)	Indications that a linked presentation is appropriate	Indications that a separate presentation is appropriate (debts are an asset of the seller)
Transfer is for a single, non-returnable fixed sum.	Some non-returnable proceeds received, but the seller has rights to further sums from the factor (or vice versa) whose amount depends on whether or when debtors pay.	Finance cost varies with speed of collection of debts, e.g.: – by adjustment to consideration for original transfer *or* – subsequent transfers priced to recover costs of earlier transfers.
There is no recourse to the seller for losses.	There is either no recourse for losses, or such recourse has a fixed monetary ceiling.	There is full recourse to the seller for losses.
The factor is paid all amounts received from the factored debts (and no more). The seller has no rights to further sums from the factor.	The factor is paid only out of amounts collected from the factored debts, and the seller has no right or obligation to repurchase debts.	The seller is required to repay amounts received from the factor on or before a set date, regardless of timing or amounts of collections from debtors.

PRACTICAL CONSIDERATIONS – BILL AND HOLD ARRANGEMENTS

31   Under a bill and hold arrangement, a seller enters into a contractual arrangement with a customer for the supply of goods where there is transfer of title but physical delivery is deferred to a later date.

Analysis

32   The purpose of the analysis below is to determine whether, in the circumstances described in paragraph 37, the seller should:

(a)   recognise turnover and a right to consideration; or
(b)   continue to recognise the goods as stock.

33   In accordance with the general principles set out in Section 4 of the FRSSE the goods cease to be assets of the seller and become assets of the customer (and in exchange the seller obtains the **right to consideration**) when the seller transfers to the customer access to the significant benefits relating to the goods and exposure to the risks inherent in those benefits. From the customer's perspective, the principal benefits and risks include:

Benefits

(a)   the right to obtain the goods as and when required;
(b)   the sole right to the goods for their sale to a third party and the future cash flows from such a sale; and
(c)   insulation from changes in prices charged by the seller (e.g. because the seller has revised its standard price list).

Risks

(a)   slow movement, resulting in increased costs of financing and holding of the goods, and an increased risk of obsolescence; and
(b)   being compelled to take delivery of goods that have become obsolete or not readily saleable, resulting in no onward sale or a sale at a reduced price.

In order for the seller to have the right to recognise changes in its assets or liabilities, and turnover, arising from its **right to consideration** in respect of the bill and hold arrangement, the terms of the contractual arrangement between the seller and the customer should include all of the following characteristics: **34**

(a)   the goods should be complete and ready for delivery;
(b)   the seller should not have retained any significant **performance obligations** other than the safekeeping of the goods and their shipment when the customer requests this;
(c)   subject to any rights of return, the seller should have obtained the **right to consideration** regardless of whether the goods are shipped, at the customer's request, to its delivery address. Where rights of return are granted, particular consideration is required of the commercial substance of the related sales, especially the transfer of risk. Rights of return are addressed at paragraphs 43-53 below;
(d)   the goods should be identified separately from the seller's other stock and should not be capable of being used to fill other orders that are received between the date of the bill and hold sale and shipment of the goods to the customer; and
(e)   the bill and hold terms should be in accordance with the commercial objectives of the customer and not the seller. For example, where the delay in the delivery of the goods is to meet the customer's need for flexibility in the timing and location of delivery, and the conditions set out in paragraphs (a) to (d) above are met, it will be appropriate for the seller to recognise changes in assets or liabilities, and turnover.

Accounting

Substance of the transaction is that the goods represent an asset of the customer

Where it is concluded that the stock is an asset of the customer, resulting in the seller having a **right to consideration**, the seller should recognise the related changes in its assets or liabilities, and turnover.   **35**

Substance of the transaction is that the goods represent an asset of the seller

Where it is concluded that the stock remains an asset of the seller, it should be retained on the seller's balance sheet. Any amounts received from the customer should be included within creditors in accordance with paragraph 4.2 of the FRSSE.   **36**

PRACTICAL CONSIDERATIONS – SALES WITH RIGHTS OF RETURN

Features

37   The terms of contractual arrangements may allow customers to return goods that they have purchased and obtain a refund or release from the **obligation** to pay.

38   Rights of return may be included explicitly or implicitly within contractual arrangements. Alternatively, they may arise through statutory requirements.

Analysis

39   The purpose of the analysis below is to determine the effect of rights of return on a seller's recognition of changes in its assets or liabilities, and turnover.

40   The inclusion of rights of return in a contractual arrangement may affect both the quantification of the seller's **right to consideration**, compared to an otherwise identical arrangement which does not have these rights, and the point at which the seller should recognise that right. This is because rights of return give rise to a contractual **obligation** on the part of the seller to transfer economic benefits to its customer and in some cases oblige the seller to defer recognition of the sales transaction so long as substantially all of the risks associated with the goods are retained.

41   The seller's recognition of its **right to consideration** and contractual **obligation** to transfer economic benefits to its customer in respect of rights of return are linked transactions. In consequence, changes in the seller's assets or liabilities should reflect the loss expected to arise from the rights of return. Turnover should exclude the sales value of estimated returns.

42   A seller will generally be able to estimate reliably the sales value of returns, having regard to risk, which may be less than its maximum potential **obligation**. It will generally be possible to derive a **reliable** estimate from historical experience of the amount of comparable goods returned as a proportion of comparable sales.

43   If a seller is unable to estimate reliably the expected value of returns, the maximum potential amount should be calculated in accordance with the terms of its contractual arrangement with the customer and excluded from turnover.

44   In some cases, the risk of return may be so significant that substantially all of the risks associated with the goods are retained by the seller and accordingly the seller does not have the **right to consideration**. In such circumstances the seller should not recognise any changes in its assets or liabilities, and turnover, from the transaction. Any amounts received from the customer should be accounted for as a payment in advance, in accordance with paragraph 4.2 of the FRSSE.

Accounting

45   A seller should record changes in its assets or liabilities, and turnover, to the extent that its **performance** has earned it the **right to consideration**, taking account of any expected loss. The amount recorded as turnover should exclude the sales value of estimated returns from the total sales value of the goods supplied to customers.

At each reporting date, the seller should review its estimate of returns, having regard **46**
to changes in expectations and the expiry of contractual rights of return. Subsequent
adjustments to the estimate should be recorded within revenue.

Where a seller has been precluded from recognising changes in its assets or liabilities, **47**
and turnover, because substantially all of the risks associated with the goods are retained
and so it has not earned the **right to consideration**, it should recognise these changes and
turnover on the earlier of the dates on which:

(a) it is capable of estimating the level of returns with **reliability**; and
(b) the right of return expires or is surrendered.

PRACTICAL CONSIDERATIONS – PRESENTATION OF TURNOVER AS PRINCIPAL OR AS AGENT

Features

A seller may act on its own account when contracting with its customers for the supply of **48**
goods in return for the right to consideration. In such transactions the seller is frequently
referred to as a principal.

Alternatively, a seller may act as an intermediary, earning a fee or commission in return for **49**
arranging the provision of goods or services on behalf of a principal. In such transactions,
the seller is frequently referred to as an agent.

Analysis

The purpose of the analysis below is to determine whether a seller obtains the right to **50**
consideration by performing its contractual obligations:

(a) as principal in an exchange transaction with its customer; or
(b) as agent in relation to a transaction between its principal and the principal's customer.

The general principles of the standard require that, in order for a seller to account for **51**
exchange transactions as principal, it should normally have exposure to all significant
benefits and risks associated with at least one of the following:

(a) Selling price: the ability, within economic constraints, to establish the selling price
     with the customer, either directly or, where the selling price of an item is fixed,
     indirectly by providing additional goods or services or adjusting the terms of a linked
     transaction; or
(b) Stock: exposure to the risks of damage, slow movement and obsolescence, and
     changes in suppliers' prices.

Where the seller has not disclosed that it is acting as agent, there is a rebuttable presumption **52**
that it is acting as principal.

Additional factors which indicate that a seller may be acting as principal include: **53**

(a) performance of part of the services, or modification to the goods supplied;
(b) assumption of credit risk; and
(c) discretion in supplier selection.

54   In contrast, where a seller acts as agent it will not normally be exposed to the majority of the benefits and risks associated with the exchange transaction. Agency arrangements will typically include the following characteristics:

(a)   the seller has disclosed the fact that it is acting as agent;

(b)   once the seller has confirmed its customer's order with a third party, the seller will normally have no further involvement in the performance of the ultimate supplier's contractual obligations;

(c)   the amount that the seller earns is predetermined, being either a fixed fee per transaction or a stated percentage of the amount billed to the customer; and

(d)   the seller bears no stock or credit risk, other than in circumstances where it receives additional consideration from the ultimate supplier in return for its assumption of this risk.

Accounting

Seller acts as principal

55   Where the substance of a transaction is that the seller acts as principal, it should report turnover based on the gross amount received or receivable in return for its performance under the contractual arrangement.

Seller acts as agent

56   Where the substance of a transaction is that the seller acts as agent, it should report as turnover the commission or other amounts received or receivable in return for its performance under the contractual arrangement. Any amounts received or receivable from the customer that are payable to the principal should not be included in the agent's turnover.

Illustrations

57   A seller acts as a building contractor for the construction of a new office block. An analysis of the arrangement shows that the terms of the seller's contract with its customer include a negotiated selling price, credit risk for amounts due from the customer, primary responsibility for the construction and quality of the new building and discretion as to whether it carries out the work itself or employs subcontractors. The seller is acting as principal and should account for the gross amount of turnover, regardless of whether it carries out the work itself or employs subcontractors to carry out part or all of the construction activities.

58   A seller acts as an online retailer from a website, where it advertises holidays. An analysis of the arrangement shows that it acts as an intermediary between its customers and the ultimate sellers of the holidays and that it does not set the selling price. Its contractual terms of business include an exclusion of any liability to its customers once they have been put in touch with the ultimate sellers. The seller is paid a fee for each customer that purchases a holiday from an ultimate seller and has no involvement in the transaction after it has put the customer in touch with the ultimate seller. The seller is acting as agent and its turnover should include only the fees it receives from the ultimate seller.

59   A department store provides space for concessionaires to sell products and receives a fixed amount of rental income from the concessionaire. An analysis of the factors discussed in paragraphs 57-60 shows that the concessionaire is acting as principal in an exchange transaction with its customers and is entitled to the amounts received from the sale of the goods and services. In these circumstances, the concessionaire should include within its turnover the amounts received or receivable in respect of the sale of the goods and services. The department store should not include within its turnover the value of the concessionaire's sales.

Disclosure – Seller acts as agent

Where a seller acts as agent, it is encouraged, where practicable, to disclose the gross value of sales throughput as additional, non-statutory information. Where such disclosure is given, a brief explanation of the relationship of recognised turnover to the gross value of sales throughput should be given.   **60**

PRACTICAL CONSIDERATIONS – CLASSIFICATION OF PREFERENCE SHARES

Paragraph 12.1 of the FRSSE provides an example of a preference share that is classified as a financial liability. The following analysis provides further guidance on the classification of preference shares as financial liabilities or equity instruments.   **61**

Illustrative features of preference shares

A company issues preference shares that: **62**

(a) carry a fixed right to cumulative dividends;
(b) have the same voting rights as the ordinary shares;
(c) the issuer is under no obligation to redeem these shares (but may be able to choose to redeem them); and
(d) in a formal winding up the preference shares rank above the ordinary shares and receive par value.

Analysis

In determining whether the preference shares are a financial liability or an equity instrument the issuer will need to assess the particular rights attaching to the shares.   **63**

In the straightforward case where the preference shares provide for redemption on a set date they would be classified as financial liabilities. The classification is clear from looking at the rights attached to the shares i.e. at the set redemption date the issuer has an obligation to transfer financial assets to the holder of the preference shares.   **64**

For preference shares that the issuer is not obliged to redeem the appropriate classification is determined by the other rights that attach to them (i.e. based on an assessment of the substance of the contractual arrangements and by reference to the definitions of financial liabilities and equity instruments). Therefore only when the distributions to the holders of the preference shares are at the discretion of the issuer will such shares be classified as equity instruments. It should be noted there is a difference between an expectation of dividend payments and an obligation.   **65**

One feature of the above preference shares is that the holders are entitled to fixed rights to cumulative dividends which are not at the discretion of the issuer. This would indicate that the issuer has an obligation to transfer financial assets to the holders of the preference shares. The shares would therefore be classified as financial liabilities[57].   **66**

---

[57] *In arriving at this conclusion, it is assumed that the dividend represents a market rate of return and that the instrument was issued at fair value.*

EXAMPLE: CASH FLOW STATEMENT

Entities are encouraged, but not required, to report some cash flow information using the indirect method. An example of a presentation of an indirect method of cash flow statement is given below, as an indication of the type of statements that smaller entities may wish to include in their financial statements. Comparative figures are not shown in the example.

	£	£
Cash generated from operations		
Operating profit/(loss)	(5,050)	
Reconciliation to cash generated from operations:		
Depreciation	245	
Increase in stocks	(194)	
Decrease in trade debtors	67,440	
Decrease in trade creditors	(4,678)	
Increase in other creditors	3,127	
		60,890
Cash from other sources		
Interest received	150	
Issues of shares for cash	5,500	
New long-term bank borrowings	4,500	
Proceeds from sale of tangible fixed assets	50	
		10,200
Application of cash		
Interest paid	(3,000)	
Tax paid	(29,220)	
Dividends paid	(10,000)	
Purchase of fixed assets	(10,500)	
Repayment of amounts borrowed	(3,000)	
		(55,720)
Net increase in cash		15,370
Cash at bank and in hand less overdrafts at beginning of year		(4,321)
Cash at bank and in hand less overdrafts at end of year		11,049
Consisting of:		
Cash at bank and in hand		11,549
Overdrafts included in bank loans and overdrafts falling due within one year		(500)
		11,049

Major non-cash transactions: finance leases

During the year the company entered into finance lease arrangements in respect of assets with a total capital value at the inception of the leases of £2,850.

EXAMPLE: DISCOUNTING WHEN MAKING A PROVISION

A company faces a fine for operating without due regard to safety legislation. The company has been notified of the case and expects to lose it but does not expect the fine (of £100,000) to be payable for five years. How much should be provided for if the amount and timing of the fine is assumed to be certain and the market rate on relevant government bonds is five per cent?

The discounted amount for the payment of £100,000 to be made in five years' time is:

$$\frac{£100,000}{(1 + (5/100))^5} = £78,353$$

Therefore, in the current year £78,353 is recorded as an expense and a provision in the company's books, rather than £100,000.

In the subsequent years the discount will unwind, increasing the amount of the provision and resulting in a debit to the profit and loss account (shown as a financial expense separate from interest) as follows:

	£
year 1 (78,353 × 6 5%)	3,918
year 2 ((78,353 + 3,918) × 6 5%)	4,113
year 3 etc	4,319
year 4 etc	4,535
year 5 etc	4,762
	21,647
Add amount originally recorded	78,353
Total provision at end of year 5	100,000

Appendix IV
The Development of the FRSSE

1   For many years there has been different reporting by different types of company: the requirements for listed public companies have been more onerous than for private companies and those for larger companies more onerous than for smaller companies. In particular, the provisions of the EC Fourth and Seventh Company Law Directives have been adopted in the UK and the Republic of Ireland, through which the disclosure requirements for large, medium-sized and small companies have been varied, allowing small companies more extensive exemptions both in the abbreviated accounts to be filed with the registrar of companies and in the statutory accounts for shareholders.

2   The application of accounting standards for smaller companies has also been an issue for standard-setters. The Board, prompted by the concern to reduce burdens on business, asked the Consultative Committee of Accountancy Bodies (CCAB) to establish a Working Party to examine the issue and to undertake wide consultation with a view to recommending criteria for exempting certain types of entity from accounting standards on the grounds of size or relative lack of public interest.

3   The CCAB Working Party published a Consultative Document in November 1994. This proposed that the Board should exempt all entities that met the Companies Act definition of a small company from compliance with all but the five accounting standards and the UITF Abstract noted below, which would continue to apply.

SSAP 4	*Accounting for government grants*
SSAP 9	*Stocks and long-term contracts*
SSAP 13	*Accounting for research and development*
SSAP 17	*Accounting for post balance sheet events*
SSAP 18	*Accounting for contingencies*
UITF Abstract 7	*True and fair view override disclosures*

4   Comments in response to that Consultative Document supported the use of the small companies threshold and a change in the present system whereby small entities were required to comply with almost all accounting standards. However, there was no clear support for the proposal of piecemeal application of a limited number of standards. Analysis of the comments identified a number of recurrent themes, including the need for guidance on measurement issues and the suggestion that a codification of all standards should be undertaken as well as a comprehensive review of those standards that were perceived as needing revision or updating, particularly in the context of their application to smaller entities. On the latter point, the amount of time needed for this codification and review was recognised, as was the observation that it might not provide a complete solution for the issues faced by smaller entities.

5   Prompted by the comments received, the proposals in the DTI's Consultative Document 'Accounting Simplifications' published in May 1995 and the wish to focus on the needs of smaller entities, the CCAB Working Party proposed in its Paper 'Designed to fit', published in December 1995, that there should be a specific Financial Reporting Standard for Smaller Entities. To demonstrate that this approach was feasible, practical and capable of delivering benefits to those involved with financial statements for smaller entities, a draft FRSSE was included in 'Designed to fit'.

Letters of comment received in response to 'Designed to fit' indicated general support **6** for a FRSSE that would apply to small companies and groups, as defined in companies legislation. Accordingly, the CCAB Working Party recommended to the Board that it should publish, as part of its due process, an Exposure Draft containing the proposed FRSSE, amended as appropriate to incorporate comments made on the draft contained in 'Designed to fit'.

The Board, largely accepting the CCAB Working Party's recommendations, duly published **7** an Exposure Draft of the proposed FRSSE in December 1996, based on the proposals in 'Designed to fit', but with three main differences. First, the proposed FRSSE in the Exposure Draft was capable of application to small groups, unlike the proposals in 'Designed to fit'. Secondly, guidance on debt factoring arrangements was included in the Exposure Draft. Lastly, the requirement in 'Designed to fit' for a summarised cash flow statement was omitted. This led to the issue of the FRSSE in November 1997.

LINK WITH COMPANIES LEGISLATION

The FRSSE is linked with accounts drawn up in Great Britain under Schedule 8 to the **8** Companies Act 1985[58] for the following reasons:

(a) it allows the establishment of a clearly distinguishable regime, i.e. the relevant statutory Schedule and the FRSSE. The importance of this was enhanced by the implementation of the Companies Act 1985 (Accounts of Small and Medium-Sized Companies and Minor Accounting Amendments) Regulations 1997 (SI 1997/220), which established a revised Schedule 8, containing all of the provisions applying to small companies; and

(b) it creates the link with the Schedule 8 provisions on a true and fair view, which may be of assistance to standard-setters and others in justifying different disclosure and any simplified measurement regime.

MATTERS CONSIDERED IN THE DEVELOPMENT OF THE FRSSE ISSUED IN NOVEMBER 1997

Application to small groups

Small groups are not required by law to prepare consolidated accounts, and therefore in **9** practice not many do so, at least on a statutory basis. The Board, however, agreed that it would be unfair to those small groups that voluntarily prepare group accounts, if they were not able to take advantage of the provisions in the FRSSE. To import all the necessary requirements from accounting standards and UITF Abstracts into the FRSSE to deal with consolidated accounts would have added substantially to its length and complexity, even though it would have been of interest to only a small percentage of entities. Accordingly, the Board preferred to extend the FRSSE in certain areas and then require small groups adopting the FRSSE to follow those accounting standards and UITF Abstracts that deal with consolidated financial statements. This approach was supported by the majority of respondents to the Exposure Draft commenting on the matter.

Cash flow statements

Consistently with the views of the majority of respondents to 'Designed to fit', the Exposure **10** Draft did not propose any cash flow disclosures based on *FRS 1 (Revised 1996) Cash Flow*

[58] *The equivalent legislation in Northern Ireland is Schedule 8 to the Companies (Northern Ireland) Order 1986. There is no equivalent to Schedule 8 in companies legislation in the Republic of Ireland. See the derivation table on the FRC website for Republic of Ireland legal requirements.*

Statements. The majority of respondents to the Exposure Draft supported the deletion of the cash flow requirements. However, given that management of cash is fundamental to the success of small businesses, the Board agreed with the minority of respondents, mainly representing users of the financial statements, that a cash flow statement is important. It provides a useful focus for discussions with management, as well as a reference point for subsequent more detailed analysis that users might require. Despite this, the Board recognised the difficulty of mandating a cash flow requirement when, previously, small entities had been exempt from such a requirement. Furthermore, the Board acknowledged that a cash flow format based on *FRS 1 (Revised 1996)* was not necessarily suitable or appropriate for smaller businesses.

11   The Board, therefore, while not mandating cash flow statements, strongly encourages smaller entities to provide such a statement voluntarily. Consultations suggested that it would be preferable to advocate only one method of cash flow presentation, for consistency and comparability. The direct method of cash flow statement, in a format similar to an entity's own cash forecasts and management accounts, may provide a link between management's cash projections and the financial statements. However, the indirect method is helpful in understanding the connection between the cash generated during a period and the resulting profit. Following consultation, the Board encourages the presentation of a cash flow statement using the indirect method as it is generally held to be more useful and better understood by many users of financial statements, as well as less costly to prepare.

Related party disclosures

12   About half of the respondents to the Board's Exposure Draft of the FRSSE believed that the FRSSE should not include any of the provisions from FRS 8 Related Party Disclosures. They argued that they were unnecessary, given that Parts II and III of Schedule 6 to the Companies Act 1985 require the disclosure of dealings in favour of directors and connected persons. Furthermore, if there was a material transaction with a related party, possibly executed at other than fair value, then, where there was any doubt whether applying any provision of the FRSSE would be sufficient to give a true and fair view, adequate explanation in the notes to the accounts of the transaction or arrangement concerned and the treatment adopted would be required (paragraph 2.5).

13   The Board, however, shared the view of the other respondents that related party disclosures are needed for a proper understanding of an entity's operations and for a true and fair view, given that material related party transactions are generally more prevalent in smaller businesses. It also noted that, in respect of dealings in favour of directors and connected persons, the statutory provisions apply equally to companies of all sizes and although the provisions overlapped the disclosure requirements in FRS 8 in many respects, the FRS was broader in scope and, in particular, expressed more clearly than the Act the spirit of Schedule 6. It also clarified, to the benefit of both preparers and auditors, the disclosures necessary to meet the fundamental requirement that accounts should give a true and fair view.

14   The Board, however, accepted that the full requirements of FRS 8 were unduly onerous and could be reduced for smaller entities, without compromising the benefit of the disclosures. Accordingly, the FRSSE requires that only those related party transactions that are material to the reporting entity need be disclosed in the notes to the financial statements, even though the FRS requires the disclosure of some transactions that are material only in relation to the other related party.

FRS 5

The FRSSE requires regard to be had to the substance of any arrangement or transaction,   **15**
or series of such, into which an entity has entered. But it does not contain the extensive
discussion in FRS 5 *Reporting the Substance of Transactions* on reflecting the substance
of transactions. This is because small entities generally do not enter into complex
transactions. However, the Board was advised that debt factoring and consignment stock
may be a common feature of such entities and accordingly the provisions, principally in
FRS 5's Application Notes, are likely to be of value to small entities. The relevant guidance
in FRS 5 has therefore been included in the FRSSE.

SUBSEQUENT AMENDMENTS TO THE FRSSE

The FRSSE (effective March 1999)

On issuing the FRSSE, the Board acknowledged that it would need to be revised and   **16**
updated periodically to reflect developments in financial reporting. The first such revision
was issued in December 1998, and incorporated the relevant aspects of FRSs 9-11 and
UITF Abstracts 18-22. The main changes were to align the requirements for entities
applying the FRSSE with the basic measurement requirements of *FRS 10 Goodwill and
Intangible Assets*, which was issued in December 1997, and FRS 11 *Impairment of Fixed
Assets and Goodwill*, which was issued in July 1998.

The measurement requirements in the FRSSE were simplified, compared with those of   **17**
FRS 10 and FRS 11, by:

(a)   setting 20 years as a maximum, rather than a presumed maximum that may be
     rebutted, for the useful economic lives assigned to intangible assets and goodwill
     arising on the acquisition of unincorporated businesses, thereby removing the need
     for annual exercises to forecast and discount future cash flows;

(b)   removing the exception that allows recognition of internally developed intangible
     assets with market values and revaluation of any intangible asset with a market value;

(c)   omitting the detailed requirements for calculating value in use (as part of recoverable
     amount) and the subsequent monitoring of cash flows for five years following an
     impairment review where recoverable amount has been based on value in use.

The Board acknowledged that in principle the options for smaller entities applying the   **18**
FRSSE would be more restricted than those for entities applying FRS 10. However,
the Board is of the opinion that it would not, in practice, be restricting the options, as
smaller entities would rarely be in a position to take advantage of them. The Board has
not incorporated the detailed requirements from FRS 11 in the FRSSE, in order to allow
smaller entities greater flexibility by enabling simpler calculations to be used where
appropriate, given that detailed cash flow projections of smaller businesses are often not
readily available.

The FRSSE (effective March 2000)

The second revision of the FRSSE was issued in December 1999. It incorporated the   **19**
relevant aspects, modified and simplified where appropriate for smaller entities, of the
four Financial Reporting Standards (FRSs 12-15) that were issued between July 1998 and
June 1999.

The main changes were to update and add to the material relating to provisions and fixed   **20**
assets, to reflect the issue of *FRSs 12 Provisions, contingent liabilities and contingent*

assets and 15 *Tangible fixed assets*. FRSs 13 and 14, which deal with financial instruments and earnings per share, respectively, were not addressed.

21   The detailed rules of FRS 12 relating to discounting were omitted from the FRSSE, as were the majority of the disclosure requirements. The requirements of FRS 15 were also simplified for inclusion in the FRSSE, particularly those relating to revaluations and the disclosure requirements.

The FRSSE (effective June 2002)

22   The third revision of the FRSSE was issued in December 2001. It incorporated the relevant aspects, modified and simplified where appropriate for smaller entities of the four Financial Reporting Standards (FRSs 16-19) that were issued between July 1999 and June 2001.

23   The main changes were to update the requirements relating to current and deferred tax to reflect the issue of FRS 16 *Current tax* and FRS 19 *Deferred tax*. The requirement for discounting of deferred tax balances in FRS 19 was not included and a number of presentational and disclosure requirements were omitted.

24   A new Appendix II was added to the FRSSE setting out the requirements for accounting for defined benefit schemes included in FRS 17 *Retirement benefits*. Some of the requirements of FRS 18 *Accounting policies* were incorporated into the FRSSE to ensure the framework underpinning the definition, selection and disclosure of accounting policies by FRSSE entities is consistent with that applied by other companies.

The FRSSE (effective January 2005)

25   The fourth edition of the FRSSE was issued in April 2005. In developing this revision, the Board considered the relevant aspects, modified and simplified as appropriate for smaller entities, of the two Financial Reporting Standards (FRS 20 and 21), amendments to FRS 5 and FRS 17 and eight UITF Abstracts (UITF Abstracts 31 to 38) that were issued between June 2001 and November 2004. The Board also considered the requirements of relevant companies legislation.

26   The main changes were to update the requirements for post balance sheet events to be consistent with FRS 21 and to incorporate the principles on revenue recognition from Application Note G to FRS 5. Specific guidance on 'bill and hold arrangements', 'sales with rights of return' and 'presentation of turnover as principal or as agent' were also included in Appendix III as these are transactions commonly undertaken by smaller entities. An additional disclosure example for a defined contribution pension scheme was also included in Appendix III.

27   The Board decided not to introduce any of the requirements from FRS 20 (IFRS 2) *Sharebased Payment* into the FRSSE but proposed to consider further in a future update. It also decided not to reflect the requirements of UITF Abstracts 31 to 38 other than UITF Abstract 34 *Pre-contract costs* which deals with the costs incurred in bidding for and securing contracts to supply goods or services of the FRSSE. The Board also incorporated the requirements of UITF Abstract 40 as guidance in Appendix III.

The FRSSE (effective January 2007)

The amendments made to the January 2005 version of the FRSSE are largely based   28
upon those proposed in the Exposure Draft on amending the FRSSE that was published
in April 2006. In developing this revision, the Board was again advised by its specialist
Committee on Accounting for Smaller Entities (CASE).

This fifth edition of the FRSSE was published in January 2007 and incorporates the   29
relevant aspects, modified and simplified where appropriate for smaller entities, of the
eight new Financial Reporting Standards (FRS 22 to FRS 29), two amendments to FRSs
(FRS 2 and FRS 26) and two UITF Abstracts (UITF 39 and UITF 40) that have been
issued since October 2004, when the last Exposure Draft of amendments to the FRSSE
was published. It also considers FRS 20 *Share-based payment*, which was not addressed
in the last amendment of the FRSSE, and changes in the company law financial reporting
requirements affecting smaller entities.

The main question asked by the Board in publishing the Exposure Draft was whether the   30
FRSSE should require smaller entities to apply the key principles of FRS20 for share-
based payment arrangements. The majority of respondents argued against this proposal on
the grounds that share-based payments were relatively uncommon for smaller entities and
that the costs of complying with FRS20 are likely to outweigh the benefits obtained by
users of small company accounts. The Board acknowledged these arguments and accepted
CASE's proposals that cash settled transactions should be reported at the entity's best
estimate of the expenditure required to settle the liability at the balance sheet date and that
equity settled arrangements should be reported on a disclosure only basis.

The other main issue arising from consultation relates to the FRS 25 requirements for   31
classifying capital instruments as either debt or equity. Respondents commented this was
a difficult issue for smaller entities, particularly in terms of preference shares, and one
where illustrative guidance in the FRSSE would be welcomed. The FRSSE (effective
January 2007) therefore includes working examples that are intended to assist smaller
entities in applying the presentation requirements of FRS 25.

A number of other minor changes have been made to the FRSSE (effective January 2007)   32
to reflect recent changes in company law and to make some presentational changes. The
most significant presentational change has been to remove Appendices V to VII, thereby
helping to make the FRSSE a more manageable document. The Board acknowledges that
smaller entities find the derivation information included in these Appendices helpful and
is therefore committed to making it freely available on the FRC website.

The FRSSE (effective April 2008)

The amendments made to the FRSSE (effective January 2007) reflect the impact of the   33
Companies Act 2006. The Board decided to issue an updated version of the FRSSE to
ensure it continued to accurately reflect company law requirements, as set out in the
Companies Act 2006. Updating the FRSSE would also ensure that it retains is usefulness
as a 'one-stop shop'. In issuing this version of the FRSSE (effective April 2008), the Board
was advised by its Committee on Accounting for Smaller Entities (CASE).

In carrying out a review of the FRSSE (effective January 2007) there were two amendments   34
to accounting standards to consider and five new UITF Abstracts. The Board decided that
it was not necessary, at this stage, to update the accounting requirements of the FRSSE for
these developments.

35   The impact of the Companies Act 2006 is not significant in terms of smaller company accounting, although there are some substantive changes. These include increases to the thresholds for companies qualifying as small and increases in the thresholds for reporting political and charitable donations.

36   The derivation table available on the FRC website provides a full cross-reference between the Companies Act 2006 and the legislative requirements set out in the FRSSE (effective April 2008). It also retains separate columns showing the equivalent references for the FRSSE (effective January 2007) to the 1985 Companies Act and relevant legislation in Northern Ireland and the Republic of Ireland. The Companies Act 2006 represents United Kingdom legislation, unlike the Companies Act 1985 which only covered Great Britain. For this reason, the FRSSE (effective April 2008) does not require separate derivations for Northern Ireland.

37   There have been no changes to the legal requirements in the Republic of Ireland.

37D   In April 2014 the FRC issued *Amendments to the Financial Reporting Standard for Smaller Entities (effective April 2008) and the Financial Reporting Standard for Smaller Entities (effective January 2015) – Micro-entities*. The amendments made to the FRSSE reflect the impact of the Small Companies (Micro-Entities' Accounts) Regulations 2013. As a result micro-entities will be able to prepare micro-entity accounts in compliance with the FRSSE.

Editor's note: Amendments to the FRSSE – Micro-entities (April 2014) has added this paragraph 37D.

The FRSSE (effective January 2015)

38   In November 2012 the FRC[59] amended the FRSSE as a consequence of the significant changes that were made to UK and Republic of Ireland financial reporting standards at this date. In November 2012 the FRC revised extant Financial Reporting Standards, withdrawing its existing financial reporting standards and supplementary literature from 1 January 2015 and replacing them with revised financial reporting requirements, based on International Financial Reporting Standards (for example, the IFRS for SMEs was used as a basis for FRS 102 *The Financial Reporting Standard applicable in the UK and Republic of Ireland*). The FRSSE (effective April 2008) was amended as a consequence of these changes.

39   The consequential amendments to the FRSSE were to update references in the FRSSE (effective April 2008) to accounting standards that were withdrawn or for greater consistency with legislation. In addition, the FRC explained that where an entity applying the FRSSE undertakes a new transaction for which it has no existing accounting policy it should have regard to FRS 102, not as a mandatory document but as a means of establishing current practice. The FRC removed the reference to the accounting standards applicable to consolidated financial statements because the general requirements in the FRSSE for developing accounting policies for transactions or events that are not dealt with in the FRSSE are equally applicable to consolidated financial statements.

40   The FRC made two further amendments to the FRSSE:

(a)   it introduced a requirement which is consistent with the EU Directives, that if an entity is unable to make a reliable estimate of the useful life of goodwill or intangible assets, the life shall be presumed not to exceed five years.

---

[59] *The Financial Reporting Council (FRC) became the prescribed body for issuing accounting standards on 2 July 2012; the prescribed body was previously the Accounting Standards Board (ASB).*

(b)   it clarified that an entity shall assess annually whether there is any indication that an asset should be written down. This will assist entities applying the existing requirement for fixed assets and goodwill to be carried at no more than their recoverable amount.

These amendments relate to applying existing company law requirements.

RELATIONSHIP WITH OTHER FRC DOCUMENTS

The FRSSE is designed to provide smaller entities with a single accounting standard that **41** is focused on their particular circumstances. Smaller entities that choose to adopt the FRSSE are exempt from other accounting standards. The FRC accepts that the FRSSE is not comprehensive and that there may be issues of general application on which guidance will be sought. Preparers may come across transactions on which accounting guidance is not provided in the FRSSE. This raises the question of whether, in the absence of guidance within the FRSSE, preparers would be required to follow FRS 102 *The Financial Reporting Standard applicable in the UK and Republic of Ireland* to the extent that it provides guidance on transactions of relevance to the smaller entity. The FRC's view, formulated after consultation with legal advisers and others, is that users expect financial statements to be prepared using accepted practice. If a practice was clearly established and accepted, it should be followed unless there were good reasons to depart from it. Accordingly, preparers should have regard to FRSs (including FRS 102 *The Financial Reporting Standard applicable in the UK and Republic of Ireland*), not as mandatory documents, but as a means of establishing current practice.

In relation to earlier versions of the FRSSE, some respondents asked that there should be **42** specific cross-references within the FRSSE to SSAPs, other FRSs and UITF Abstracts (the equivalent cross references would now be to FRS 102 *The Financial Reporting Standard applicable in the UK and Republic of Ireland*). The FRC rejected this suggestion because the inclusion of cross-references would lead to preparers having to consider those other pronouncements in all cases, as well as the FRSSE, thereby lengthening checklists and adding to the burden. Furthermore, it is recognised that as new FRSs are issued (including FRS 102 *The Financial Reporting Standard applicable in the UK and Republic of Ireland*) that amend generally accepted accounting practice as it applies to larger entities, it may not be appropriate for such rules to apply to smaller entities.

FRED 63
Draft amendments to FRS 101
Reduced Disclosure Framework – 2015/16 cycle

(December 2015)

Contents

SUMMARY

(i)   With effect from 1 January 2015, the Financial Reporting Council (FRC) revised financial reporting standards in the United Kingdom and Republic of Ireland. The revisions fundamentally reformed financial reporting, replacing the extant standards with five Financial Reporting Standards:

  (a)   FRS 100 *Application of Financial Reporting Requirements*;
  (b)   FRS 101 *Reduced Disclosure Framework*;
  (c)   FRS 102 *The Financial Reporting Standard applicable in the UK and Republic of Ireland*;
  (d)   FRS 103 *Insurance Contracts*; and
  (e)   FRS 104 *Interim Financial Reporting*.

  The FRC has also issued FRS 105 *The Financial Reporting Standard applicable to the Micro-entities Regime* to support the implementation of the new micro-entities regime.

  This FRED proposes limited amendments to FRS 101.

(ii)   The FRC's overriding objective in setting accounting standards is to enable users of accounts to receive high-quality understandable financial reporting proportionate to the size and complexity of the entity and users' information needs.

(iii)   In meeting this objective, the FRC aims to provide succinct financial reporting standards that:

  (a)   have consistency with international accounting standards through the application of an IFRS-based solution unless an alternative clearly better meets the overriding objective;
  (b)   reflect up-to-date thinking and developments in the way entities operate and the transactions they undertake;
  (c)   balance consistent principles for accounting by all UK and Republic of Ireland entities with practical solutions, based on size, complexity, public interest and users' information needs;
  (d)   promote efficiency within groups; and
  (e)   are cost-effective to apply.

Draft amendments to FRS 101

(iv)   After considering the 2015/16 annual review of FRS 101 this FRED proposes amendments to FRS 101 to provide certain disclosure exemptions in relation to IFRS 15 *Revenue from Contracts with Customers* and clarify a legal requirement relating to the order in which the notes to the financial statements are presented.

INVITATION TO COMMENT

1   The FRC is requesting comments on FRED 63 by 31 March 2016. The FRC is committed to developing standards based on evidence from consultation with users, preparers and others. Comments are invited in writing on all aspects of the draft standard. In particular, comments are sought in relation to the questions below.

> **Question 1**
>
> The principles for determining whether disclosure exemptions from EU-adopted IFRS should be available in FRS 101 are set out in paragraph 9 of the Accounting Council's Advice. These are relevance, cost considerations and avoiding gold plating.
>
> Qualifying entities have limited external users of the financial statements. These external users are likely to be providers of credit with a greater focus on information that supports the statement of financial position of the qualifying entity, when compared with detailed analysis of performance as required by some of the disclosures in IFRS 15 *Revenue from Contracts with Customers*. Do you agree?
>
> **Question 2**
>
> Do you consider that additional refinements could be made to the principles set out in paragraph 9 of the Accounting Council's Advice that, when applied, would help to increase further the cost-effectiveness of FRS 101?
>
> **Question 3**
>
> Do you agree with the proposed amendments to FRS 101? If not, why not?
>
> **Question 4**
>
> In relation to the Consultation stage impact assessment do you have any comments on the costs and benefits identified? Please provide evidence to support your views of the quantifiable costs or benefits of these proposals.

Information on how to submit comments and the FRC's policy in relation to responses is set out on page 13.   2

[DRAFT] AMENDMENTS TO FRS 101 *REDUCED DISCLOSURE FRAMEWORK*

[Draft] Amendments to FRS 101

The following paragraphs set out the [draft] amendments to FRS 101 *Reduced Disclosure Framework* (inserted text is underlined).   1

Paragraph 8(eA) is inserted as follows: 2

8(eA) The requirements of the second sentence of paragraph 110 and paragraphs 113 to 115, 118 to 127 and 129 of IFRS 15 *Revenue from Contracts with Customers.*

[Draft] Amendments to Appendix II: Note on Legal Requirements

The following paragraphs set out the [draft] amendments to Appendix II: *Note on Legal Requirements* (inserted text is underlined).   3

Paragraph A2.11A and the sub-heading preceding it are inserted as follows: 4

Notes to the financial statements

A2.11A Paragraph 42(2) of the Regulations requires the notes to the financial statements to be presented in the order in which, where relevant, the items to which they relate are presented in the statement of financial position and the income statement. A qualifying entity preparing financial statements in accordance with FRS 101 shall have regard to this requirement when determining a systematic manner for the presentation of its notes to the financial statements in accordance with paragraphs 113 and 114 of IAS 1.

THE ACCOUNTING COUNCIL'S ADVICE TO THE FRC TO ISSUE FRED 63 *DRAFT AMENDMENTS TO FRS 101 – 2015/16 CYCLE*

Introduction

1   This report provides an overview of the main issues that have been considered by the Accounting Council in advising the Financial Reporting Council (FRC) to issue FRED 63 *Draft amendments to FRS 101 Reduced Disclosure Framework – 2015/16 cycle.*

2   The FRC, in accordance with the *Statutory Auditors (Amendment of Companies Act 2006 and Delegation of Functions etc) Order 2012* (SI 2012/1741), is a prescribed body for issuing accounting standards in the UK. The *Foreword to Accounting Standards* sets out the application of accounting standards in the Republic of Ireland.

3   In accordance with the FRC Codes and Standards: procedures, any proposal to issue, amend or withdraw a code or standard is put to the FRC Board with the full advice of the relevant Councils and/or the Codes & Standards Committee. Ordinarily, the FRC Board will only reject the advice put to it where:

   (a)   it is apparent that a significant group of stakeholders has not been adequately consulted;

   (b)   the necessary assessment of the impact of the proposal has not been completed, including an analysis of costs and benefits;

   (c)   insufficient consideration has been given to the timing or cost of implementation; or

   (d)   the cumulative impact of a number of proposals would make the adoption of an otherwise satisfactory proposal inappropriate.

4   The FRC has established the Accounting Council as the relevant Council to assist it in the setting of accounting standards.

Advice

5   The Accounting Council is advising the FRC to issue FRED 63 *Draft amendments to FRS 101 Reduced Disclosure Framework – 2015/16 cycle.*

6   The Accounting Council advises that these proposals will ensure that FRS 101 *Reduced Disclosure Framework* continues to be effective in providing disclosure reductions when compared with EU-adopted IFRS and maintains consistency with company law.

7   When these draft amendments are finalised the Accounting Council's Advice to the FRC in respect of these amendments will be added into FRS 101.

Background

The Accounting Council advised the FRC to update FRS 101 at regular intervals to ensure   **8** that the reduced disclosure framework continues to be effective in providing disclosure reductions when compared with EU-adopted IFRS. An annual review is carried out to consider changes in IFRS and their potential impact on FRS 101.

Draft amendments to FRS 101

The Accounting Council advised the FRC that the following principles should be applied   **9** when determining which of the disclosure requirements in EU-adopted IFRS should be applied by qualifying entities:

1   Relevance:
     Does the disclosure requirement provide information that is capable of making a difference to the decisions made by the users of the financial statements of a qualifying entity?
2   Cost constraint on useful financial reporting:
     Does the disclosure requirement impose costs on the preparers of the financial statements of a qualifying entity that are not justified by the benefits to the users of those financial statements?
3   Avoid gold plating:
     Does the disclosure requirement override an existing exemption provided by company law in the UK?

IASB projects completed since the 2014/15 cycle

The IASB has completed four projects since those considered in the review for the 2014/15   **10** cycle, which was performed in August 2014. In addition, one project was brought forward for consideration as part of this review.

	IASB project	Date issued	Date effective	Date endorsed in the EU
1	Equity Method in Separate Financial Statements (Amendments to IAS 27)	Aug 2014	1 Jan 2016	Expected Q4 2015
2	Sale or Contribution of Assets between an Investor and its Associate or Joint Venture (Amendments to IFRS 10 and IAS 28)	Sept 2014	1 Jan 2016	Postponed
3	Annual Improvements to IFRSs (2012 – 2014 Cycle)	Sept 2014	1 Jan 2016	Expected Q4 2015
4	Investment Entities: Applying the Consolidation Exception (Amendments to IFRS 10, IFRS 12 and IAS 28)	Dec 2014	1 Jan 2016	Expected Q1 2016
5	Disclosure Initiative (Amendments to IAS 1)	Dec 2014	1 Jan 2016	Expected Q4 2015

The amendments[1] resulting from these five projects were reviewed in the context of the   **11** reduced disclosure framework for any amendments that:

[1] *The full IASB documents setting out the amendments for each project are available on the IASB website (www. ifrs.org).*

(a)   alter disclosure requirements, as consideration will need to be given to whether changes should be made to the disclosure exemptions permitted in FRS 101; and/or

(b)   are inconsistent with current UK legal requirements, as consideration will need to be given to whether changes should be made to the Application Guidance: *Amendments to International Financial Reporting Standards as Adopted in the European Union for Compliance with the Act and the Regulations* to FRS 101.

12   The Accounting Council advises that only limited amendment to FRS 101 are necessary in relation to these amendments to IFRS. These are discussed below.

Equity method in separate financial statements

13   Following changes that implemented the EU Accounting Directive, company law now permits the use of the equity method in an entity's individual financial. As a result, the Accounting Council advises that no amendments to FRS 101 are necessary in relation to the recent amendment to IAS 27 *Separate Financial Statements*.

Disclosure initiative

14   The Accounting Council notes that this project was intended to clarify existing requirements and give greater guidance, particularly on the application of materiality to disclosures, the levels of aggregation (or disaggregation) permitted and the order in which notes might be presented. As a result it did not change disclosure requirements.

15   However, one area where additional guidance was included relates to the systematic manner in which the notes to the financial statements are presented. Company law contains a requirement about the order in which the notes to the financial statements shall be presented. The amendments to IAS 1 *Presentation of Financial Statements* paragraphs 113 and 114 do not require entities to present notes to the financial statements in an order that would conflict with this legal requirement. However, some of the examples of how to present notes in a systematic manner are unlikely to comply with company law. Therefore the Accounting Council advises including an additional paragraph (paragraph A2.11A) in Appendix II: *Note on legal requirements* to discuss this issue.

IFRS 15 Revenue from Contracts with Customers

16   The disclosure requirements of IFRS 15 have been compared to the principles set out in paragraph 9. In doing so, the Accounting Council considered further how the principle of 'relevance' should be applied in the context of disclosure by qualifying entities. It noted that qualifying entities usually have few users of their financial statements, and particularly few users that would be external to the group the qualifying entity is part of. Any external users are likely to be providers of credit to the qualifying entity.

17   The Accounting Council considered that the interest a provider of credit has in the financial statements of a qualifying entity is generally likely to be focused on information about the liquidity and solvency of the qualifying entity, that might be relevant to the ability of the qualifying entity to pay (or repay) any credit advanced. This would mean that in relation to detailed disclosures, there would be greater interest in information supporting the statement of financial position, rather than information supporting the income statement. The Accounting Council therefore advises refining the application of the principle of 'relevance' in relation to disclosure by a qualifying entity to note that information supporting items in the income statement is less likely to make a difference to users' decisions than information supporting items in the statement of financial position.

As a result, the Accounting Council advises that significant disclosure exemptions from **18** IFRS 15 should be available to qualifying entities. The Accounting Council also noted that, in addition, there are company law requirements relating to disaggregation of turnover and that IAS 1 contains requirements relating to judgements having a significant effect on the amounts recognised in an entity's financial statements.

The Accounting Council advises that disclosure exemptions from paragraphs 113 to **19** 115, 118 to 127 and 129 should be available. In addition, an exemption from the second sentence of paragraph 110 should be provided to remove the cross-references to these later paragraphs.

Effective date

Paragraph 8 of FRS 101 notes that the exemptions are available from when the relevant **20** standard is applied. Therefore there is no need to amend the effective date for these proposed amendments. However, it should be noted that the change in company law to permit the equity method in individual financial statements is effective from 1 January 2016 (or 1 January 2015 if it is applied early), which is the same date as the amendment to IAS 27 *Separate Financial Statements*.

CONSULTATION STAGE IMPACT ASSESSMENT

Introduction

The Financial Reporting Council (FRC) is committed to a proportionate approach to the **1** use of its powers, making effective use of impact assessments and having regard to the impact of regulation on small enterprises.

Draft amendments to FRS 101

FRS 101 *Reduced Disclosure Framework* is an optional standard that is intended to enable **2** cost-efficient financial reporting within groups, particularly those applying EU-adopted IFRS in their consolidated financial statements. Therefore it is only applied by those qualifying entities that consider it a cost-effective option for the preparation of their individual financial statements.

FRS 101 requires an entity to apply EU-adopted IFRS subject to specified disclosure **3** exemptions. Therefore without intervention to amend FRS 101, an entity applying FRS 101 would need to provide all the disclosures required by IFRS 15 *Revenue from Contracts with Customers* from the date that it applies that standard.

The draft amendments to FRS 101 provide disclosure exemptions from certain of the **4** disclosures that would otherwise be required by IFRS 15, and are therefore expected to reduce the cost of compliance with FRS 101.

Conclusion

The FRC believes that the draft amendments to FRS 101 will have a positive impact on **5** financial reporting and reduce the costs of compliance.

> This draft is issued by the Financial Reporting Council for comment. It should be noted that the draft may be modified in the light of comments received before being issued in final form.

For ease of handling, we prefer comments to be sent by e-mail to:

ukfrs@frc.org.uk

Comments may also be sent in hard copy to:

Jenny Carter
Financial Reporting Council
8th Floor
125 London Wall
London
EC2Y 5AS

Comments should be despatched so as to be received no later than 31 March 2016.

The FRC's policy is to publish on its website all responses to formal consultations issued by the FRC unless the respondent explicitly requests otherwise. A standard confidentiality statement in an e-mail message will not be regarded as a request for non-disclosure. The FRC does not edit personal information (such as telephone numbers or postal or e-mail addresses) from submissions; therefore, only information that you wish to be published should be submitted.

The FRC aims to publish responses within 10 working days of receipt.

The FRC will publish a summary of the consultation responses, either as part of, or alongside, its final decision.

FRED 64
Draft amendments to FRS 103
Insurance Contracts – Solvency II

(December 2015)

Contents

SUMMARY

(i)   With effect from 1 January 2015, the Financial Reporting Council (FRC) revised financial reporting standards in the United Kingdom and Republic of Ireland. The revisions fundamentally reformed financial reporting, replacing the extant standards with five Financial Reporting Standards:

(a)   FRS 100 *Application of Financial Reporting Requirements*;
(b)   FRS 101 *Reduced Disclosure Framework*;
(c)   FRS 102 *The Financial Reporting Standard applicable in the UK and Republic of Ireland*;
(d)   FRS 103 *Insurance Contracts*; and
(e)   FRS 104 *Interim Financial Reporting*.

The FRC has also issued FRS 105 *The Financial Reporting Standard applicable to the Micro-entities Regime* to support the implementation of the new micro-entities regime.

This FRED proposes limited amendments to FRS 103 as a result of the implementation of Solvency II.

(ii)   The FRC's overriding objective in setting accounting standards is to enable users of accounts to receive high-quality understandable financial reporting proportionate to the size and complexity of the entity and users' information needs.

(iii)   In meeting this objective, the FRC aims to provide succinct financial reporting standards that:

(a)   have consistency with international accounting standards through the application of an IFRS-based solution unless an alternative clearly better meets the overriding objective;
(b)   reflect up-to-date thinking and developments in the way entities operate and the transactions they undertake;
(c)   balance consistent principles for accounting by all UK and Republic of Ireland entities with practical solutions, based on size, complexity, public interest and users' information needs;
(d)   promote efficiency within groups; and
(e)   are cost-effective to apply.

Draft amendments to FRS 103

(iv)   This FRED proposes amendments to FRS 103 to update the terminology and definitions used for changes in the regulatory framework. Established accounting policies can continue to be applied if an entity so chooses.

INVITATION TO COMMENT

The FRC is requesting comments on FRED 64 by 28 February 2016. The FRC is committed to developing standards based on evidence from consultation with users, preparers and others. Comments are invited in writing on all aspects of the draft standard. In particular, comments are sought in relation to the questions below.

1

> **Question 1**
>
> Do you agree with the amendments proposed to FRS 103 and the related Implementation Guidance? If not, why not?
>
> **Question 2**
>
> Have you identified any other amendments that you consider should be made to FRS 103 or the related Implementation Guidance as a result of the changes in the regulatory framework? If so, please provide details of your proposed amendments and the rationale for them.

Information on how to submit comments and the FRC's policy in relation to responses is set out on page 22.

2

[DRAFT] AMENDMENTS TO FRS 103 *INSURANCE CONTRACTS*

[Draft] Amendments to Section 1 Scope

1   The following paragraph sets out the [draft] amendments to Section 1 Scope (inserted text is underlined).

2   Paragraph 1.11A in inserted as follows:

> 1.11A In [month 2016] amendments were made to this FRS, to update it for changes in the regulatory framework. An entity shall apply these amendments for accounting periods ending on or after 1 January 2016.

[Draft] Amendments to Section 3 Recognition and Measurement: Requirements for entities with long-term insurance business

3   The following paragraphs set out the [draft] amendments to Section 3 *Recognition and Measurement: Requirements for entities with long-term insurance business* (deleted text is struck through, inserted text is underlined).

4   Paragraph 3.1 is amended as follows:

> 3.1 This section sets out requirements for entities applying this FRS that are carrying out **long-term insurance business**:
>
> (a)   Paragraphs 3.3 to 3.10 and 3.16 to 3.18 apply to all long-term insurance business.
>
> (b)   Paragraphs 3.11 to 3.15 apply to **with-profits business** and with-profits funds, to which the **Prudential Regulatory Authority (PRA) realistic capital regime** is being applied, either voluntarily or compulsorily of an entity that has, or had at any time since 31 December 2004, with-profits liabilities greater than £500 million.

5   Paragraph 3.7 is amended as follows:

> 3.7 **Acquisition costs** shall not be deferred for with-profits funds to which the PRA realistic capital regime is being applied, either voluntarily or compulsorily within the scope of paragraph 3.1(b).

6   Paragraph 3.11 is amended as follows:

> 3.11 The established accounting treatment for long-term insurance business is to measure liabilities for policyholder benefits under the **modified statutory solvency established long-term insurance business liability basis (MSSB)**. This FRS requires those with-profits funds within the scope of the PRA realistic capital regime to use the **realistic value of liabilities** as the basis for the estimated value of the liabilities to be included in the **financial statements**.

7   Paragraph 3.12 is amended as follows:

> 3.12 For with-profits funds to which the PRA realistic capital regime is being applied, either voluntarily or compulsorily:
>
> (a)   liabilities to policyholders arising from with-profits business shall be stated at the amount of the realistic value of liabilities adjusted to exclude the shareholders' share of projected future **bonuses**;

(b) **reinsurance recoveries** that are recognised shall be measured on a basis that is consistent with the value of the policyholder liabilities to which the reinsurance applies;

(c) an amount may be recognised for the **present value** of future profits on **non-participating business** written in a with-profits fund if:

(i) ~~the non-participating business is measured on a realistic basis for the purposes of the regulatory returns made under the PRA realistic capital regime;~~

(ii) ~~the value is determined in accordance with the PRA regulations; and~~

(iii) the determination of the realistic value of liabilities in that with-profits fund takes account, directly or indirectly, of this value;

(d) where a with-profits life fund has an interest in a subsidiary or associate and the determination of the realistic value of liabilities to with-profits policyholders takes account of a value of that interest at an amount in excess of the net amounts included in the entity's consolidated accounts, an amount may be recognised representing this excess; and

(e) adjustments to reflect the consequential tax effects of (a) to (d) above shall be made.

Adjustments from the ~~MSSB~~ established long-term insurance business liability basis necessary to meet the above requirements, including the recognition of an amount in accordance with paragraph 3.12(c) or 3.12(d), shall be included in **profit or loss**. An amount equal and opposite to the net amount of these adjustments shall be transferred to or from the **fund for future appropriations (FFA)** and also included in profit or loss.

[Draft] Amendments to Appendix I: Glossary

The following glossary terms and definitions, and footnote 8 (subsequent footnotes will be renumbered sequentially), are deleted:

8

~~INSPRU~~	~~See **Prudential sourcebook for insurers (INSPRU).**~~
~~**Prudential sourcebook for insurers (INSPRU)**~~	~~The section of the PRA Handbook detailing the prudential rules for **insurers, including capital** requirements, credit, market and **liquidity risk.**~~
~~**realistic capital regime**~~	~~As set out in section 1.3 of INSPRU8.~~
~~**statutory solvency basis**~~	~~The basis of determination of **insurance liabilities** in accordance with rule 1 of **INSPRU.**~~

~~8 References to the PRA's Prudential sourcebook for insurers, and to individual rules therein, are to the rules made on 1 April 2013 by the FCA and PRA Handbook Designation (General Modifications) Instrument 2013.~~

The following glossary terms and definitions are amended as follows (deleted text is struck through, inserted text is underlined):

9

equalisation provisions	As defined in the relevant regulatory framework (eg ~~INSPRU~~).

gross premium method	A form of actuarial valuation of **liabilities** arising under long-term insurance contracts where the premiums brought into account are the full amounts receivable under the contract. The method includes explicit estimates of cash flows for: (a) premiums, adjusted for renewals and lapses; (b) expected claims and for **with-profits business** future regular but not occasional or terminal **bonuses**; (c) costs of maintaining contracts; and (d) future renewal expenses. Cash flows are discounted at the valuation interest rate. The methodology may be set out in the relevant regulatory framework. For UK companies this is included in the **PRA** Handbook. The discount rate is based on the expected return on the assets deemed to back the **liabilities** as prescribed by the PRA Handbook. This may be further constrained by a maximum rate set by the PRA. This will be adjusted to reflect any further risks although, under this method, most of the key risks will be reflected in the modelling of the cash flows. For **linked business**, allowance may be made for the purchase of future units required by the contract terms and credit is taken for future charges permitted under those terms.
long-term fund	The fund or funds maintained by an undertaking in respect of its **long-term insurance business** in accordance with the **PRA** rules.

~~modified statutory solvency~~ established long-term insurance business liability basis ~~(MSSB)~~	~~The~~ A basis for determining insurance liabilities which ~~is~~: (a) is appropriate to the entity; (b) is consistent from year to year without arbitrary changes; (c) is consistent with the method of valuing assets; (d) includes appropriate margins for adverse deviation of relevant factors; (e) recognises the distribution of profits in an appropriate way over the duration of each **insurance contract**; and (f) is in accordance with generally accepted actuarial practice. ~~the statutory solvency basis~~ The established long-term insurance liability basis shall include adjustment~~s~~ed ~~for the following~~ items: (a) to defer new business **acquisition costs** incurred where the benefit of such costs will be obtained in subsequent **reporting periods**; and (b) to treat investment, resilience and similar reserves, or reserves held in respect of general contingencies or the specific contingency that the fund will be closed to new business, where such items are held in respect of **long-term insurance business** ~~within the~~ **long-term fund**, as reserves rather than provisions. These are included, as appropriate, within shareholders' capital and reserves or the **fund for future appropriations (FFA)**. The basis applied by an entity shall be consistent with accounting policies applied in periods ending before 1 January 2016.
mutual	As defined in the **PRA** ~~Handbook~~ Rulebook.
net premium method	An actuarial valuation of **liabilities** arising under long-term **insurance contracts** where the premium brought into account at any valuation date is that which, on the valuation assumptions regarding interest, mortality and disability, will exactly provide for the benefits guaranteed. A variation of the net premium method involves **zillmerisation**. The detailed methodology for UK companies is included in regulations contained in the **PRA** ~~Handbook~~ Rulebook.
non-participating business	**Long-term insurance business** where **policyholders** are not entitled to share in the surplus of the relevant ~~long-term fund~~ long-term business.

principles and practices of financial management (PPFM)	The statement that the ~~PRA~~ Financial Conduct Authority requires each **with-profits** life fund to make available to its **policyholders** containing, inter alia, a description of the fund's investment management and bonus distribution policies.
realistic value of liabilities	~~That element~~ The sum of~~:~~ (a) the with-profits benefits reserve; (b) the future policy-related **liabilities**; and (c) the realistic current **liabilities** of the fund, ~~amount defined by rule 1.3.40 in INSPRU,~~ excluding current **liabilities** ~~falling within the definition in rule 1.3.190~~ that are recognised separately in the **statement of financial position**. The method for determining the realistic value of liabilitiesshall be consistent with that applied in periods ending before1 January 2016.
regulatory capital resources	An entity's capital resources as calculated in accordance with the ~~capital resources table in INSPRU~~ regulatory framework.

[Draft] Amendments to Appendix IV: Note on legal requirements

10   The following paragraphs set out the [draft] amendments to Appendix IV: *Note on legal requirements* (deleted text is struck through, inserted text is underlined).

11   The table in paragraph A4.3 is amended as follows (only the line that is amended is shown here):

Legislation	Overview of requirements
~~Industrial and Provident Societies Act 1965~~ Co-operative and Community Benefit Societies Act 2014	The Insurance Accounts Directive (Miscellaneous Insurance Undertakings) Regulations 2008 require every society that is an insurance undertaking to prepare its financial statements substantially as though it were a company registered under the Companies Act 2006.

[DRAFT] AMENDMENTS TO IMPLEMENTATION GUIDANCE TO ACCOMPANY FRS 103 *INSURANCE CONTRACTS*

[Draft] Amendments to Implementation Guidance – Section 1 Guidance for entities
with long-term insurance business

The following paragraphs set out the [draft] amendments to Implementation Guidance –   **12**
Section 1 *Guidance for entities with long-term insurance business* (deleted text is struck
through, inserted text is underlined).

Paragraph IG1.1 is amended as follows (footnote 1 is not amended and is not repeated   **13**
here):

> IG1.1 An entity may, but is not required to, adopt the requirements of paragraph 3.12
> of **FRS 103** *Insurance Contracts* for UK[1] **with-profits business** that does not fall
> within the scope of the **PRA realistic capital regime** or for which the PRA has
> granted a full waiver from compliance with this regime paragraph 3.1(b) of FRS 103.
> If an entity changes its **accounting policy** for such with-profits business it shall only
> do so in accordance with paragraph 2.3 of FRS 103.

Paragraph IG1.2 is amended as follows: **14**

> IG1.2 The shareholders' share of projected future **bonuses** deducted in accordance
> with paragraph 3.12(a) of FRS 103 should be calculated as the value of future
> transfers to shareholders calculated using market consistent financial assumptions,
> and assuming that transfers take place at a level consistent with those assumptions
> within the PRA realistic balance sheet. Where an explicit assumption is not required
> in order to calculate the **liabilities** under the PRA's approach then continuation of the
> current profit sharing arrangements should be assumed unless the firm has plans to
> change this approach. Non-economic projection assumptions should be consistent
> with those used elsewhere in the realistic balance sheet. The amount deducted in
> accordance with this paragraph should be taken to the **fund for future appropriations
> (FFA)**. If shareholders transfers have been included as part of the PRA **realistic** value
> **of liabilities**y (or otherwise included in liabilities) then the amount of such transfers
> should be taken out of liabilities and included in the FFA, together with any related
> tax liability. If shareholders transfers have not been set up as part of the PRA realistic
> value of liabilitiesy or elsewhere, no adjustment is required.

Paragraph IG1.3 is amended as follows and 'realistic value of liabilities' is no longer   **15**
shown in bold type:

> IG1.3 Under the PRA realistic capital regime, a In determining the realistic value
> of liabilities, a with-profits life fund may take account of includes within assets the
> value of future profits expected to arise from any **non-participating business** that
> forms part of the with-profits fund—sometimes referred to as the **value of in-force
> life assurance business (VIF)**. Excluding the VIF from the **statement of financial
> position** whilst recognising the realistic value of liabilities in full, and valuing the non-
> participating liabilities in the with-profits fund on a statutory basis, would give rise to
> an inconsistency in the fund's net assets. An entity is therefore permitted to recognise
> the VIF if that business has been taken into account in measuring the liability, in the
> circumstances of paragraph 3.12(c) of FRS 103, even though there is not a direct link
> between the value of the asset and the amount of the liabilities. Where there is not a
> direct link between the value of the business and the amount of realistic liabilities,
> but the value is taken into account in determining those liabilities, it is appropriate
> to recognise the total value of the business. Although not separately identifiable, any
> excess value over that included in realistic liabilities will be taken to the FFA.

16   Paragraph IG1.4 is amended as follows:

IG1.4 Paragraph 3.12(c) of FRS 103 permits an amount to be recognised for VIF on non-participating business written in a with-profits fund when~~: (i) the non-participating business is measured on this basis for the purposes of the regulatory returns made under the PRA realistic capital regime; (ii) the VIF is calculated on the basis used in the PRA realistic capital regime; and (iii)~~ the determination of the realistic value of liabilities takes account of this value either directly or indirectly. Where with-profits **policyholders** are entitled to a share of the profits on non-participating business it would generally be expected that the determination of the realistic liabilities would take account, directly or indirectly, of the value of future profits on this business.

17   Paragraph IG1.6 is amended as follows:

IG1.6 The VIF recognised within assets ~~for regulatory purposes~~ as described in paragraph IG1.3~~2~~ is determined as the discounted value of future profits expected to arise from the policies, taking into account liabilities relating to the policies measured on the ~~a **statutory solvency**~~ **established long-term insurance business liability** basis. ~~When~~ This includes adjustments ~~are made onto a **modified statutory solvency basis (MSSB)**~~ for the purposes of the **financial statements** (for example, to adjust liabilities to exclude certain additional reserves included in the liabilities for regulatory purposes, or where future income included in the VIF covers **deferred acquisition costs** included in the ~~MSSB~~ statement of financial position)~~.;~~ ~~A~~a corresponding adjustment to the value of in-force policies will need to be made in order to ensure a consistent valuation.

18   Paragraph IG1.7 is amended as follows:

IG1.7 Paragraph 3.12 of FRS 103 requires that the VIF asset ~~recognised~~ should be taken account of in ~~determin~~ing ~~in accordance with~~ the realistic value of liabilities ~~capital regime requirements~~. Paragraph IG1.4 explains that the value calculated ~~under the realistic capital regime requirements~~ must be adjusted to ensure consistency where adjustments have been made onto the ~~MSSB~~ established long-term insurance business liability ~~measurement~~ basis in relation to non-participating contracts. The measurement of the VIF asset ~~recognised in accordance with the realistic capital regime~~ may take into account the release of capital requirements for non-participating business. It would not be appropriate to recognise this release of capital requirements within the VIF asset presented in the accounts because the ~~MSSB~~ established long-term insurance business liability basis liabilities do not include an allowance for capital. Therefore the amount of the VIF asset ~~determined for the purposes of the PRA realistic capital regime~~ should be adjusted accordingly.

19   Paragraph IG1.8 is amended as follows:

IG1.8 The profit recognition profile for non-participating contracts which do not satisfy FRS 103's definition of an insurance contract or contain a **discretionary participation feature** will be determined by the requirements of Sections 11, 12 and 23 of **FRS 102**. Where these contracts are written in a with-profits fund, paragraph IG1.4 will apply but the VIF recognised for such contracts ~~for the purposes of the PRA's realistic capital regime~~ should be adjusted to reflect the difference in the profit recognition bases between the basis used to determine the VIF ~~used in~~ taken into account in determining the realistic value of liabilities ~~capital regime~~ and the profit recognition profile determined by FRS 102.

Paragraph IG1.9 is amended as follows: 20

IG1.9 Paragraph 3.12(d) of FRS 103 permits that where a with-profits fund has an interest in a subsidiary or associate and the determination of that is valued for PRA regulatory purposes the realistic value of liabilities takes account of a value for that interest at an amount in excess of the net amounts that would be included in the entity's consolidated accounts, an amount may be recognised representing this excess if the determination of the realistic value of liabilities to with-profits policyholders takes account of this value. As explained in paragraph 3.15 of FRS 103 this situation could arise where the subsidiary or associate writes non-participating business and the value of the subsidiary or associate recognised for PRA reporting purposes incorporates the VIF of non-participating business written in the subsidiary or associate. The value of the subsidiary or associate recognised for PRA reporting purposes is reduced by the subsidiary's or associate's capital requirement as noted in rule 1.3.33(3) of INSPRU. When preparing both consolidated and non-consolidated accounts, the excess value that may be recognised should therefore be taken as the excess before deduction of the subsidiary's or associate's capital requirement.

Paragraph IG1.10 is amended as follows: 21

IG1.10 Where the amounts on a 'realistic' basis determined in accordance with paragraph 3.12 of FRS 103 are different from the amounts on the established long-term insurance business liability basis a MSSB, a corresponding amount is transferred to or from the FFA, so that there is no effect on **equity**. The potential shareholders' share corresponding to additional bonuses to policyholders that have been included in the policyholders' liability should be accounted for in the FFA. As a result, there will generally be no change in the profit for the **reporting period** except where the adjustments result in a negative balance on the FFA and the entity determines that this negative balance should result in a deduction from equity through **profit or loss**.

Paragraph IG1.11 is amended as follows: 22

IG1.11 Entities with with-profits business within the scope of paragraph 3.1(b) of FRS 103 the PRA realistic capital regime are required to measure the liability of that business in respect of **options and guarantees** relating to policyholders either at **fair value** or at an amount estimated using a **market-consistent stochastic model** in accordance with PRA regulations.

Paragraph IG1.12 is amended as follows (footnote 2 is not amended and is not repeated   23
here):

IG1.12 For all entities with **long-term insurance business**, the best basis for measuring policyholders' options and guarantees is one that includes their time value[2]. Any **deterministic approach** to valuation of a policy with a guarantee or optionality feature will generally fail to deal appropriately with the time value of the option. Therefore stochastic modelling techniques to evaluate the range of potential outcomes should be used unless a market value for the option is available. The PRA realistic capital regime regulatory framework includes a requirement to value options and guarantees on this basis. For the liabilities of businesses not falling within the scope of the PRA realistic capital regime paragraph 3.1(b) of FRS 103, entities are encouraged, but not required, to adopt these valuation techniques. Where options are not valued on this basis, additional disclosures are required; these are set out in paragraph IG3.14(c).

Paragraph IG1.13 is amended as follows: 24

IG1.13 In determining the value of guarantees and options under the PRA realistic capital regime regulatory framework, the entity will take into account under each scenario in the market-consistent stochastic modelling management actions it anticipates would be taken in response to variations in market variables (such as changing the balance of the investment portfolio between debt instruments and equity, varying the amount charged to policyholders, or varying its bonus policy) that will affect the amount payable under the guarantee or option. Such actions must be realistically capable of being implemented within the timescale assumed in the scenario analysis, and be consistent with the entity's published **principles and practices of financial managements (PPFM)**.

[Draft] Amendments to Implementation Guidance – Section 2 Guidance for entities with general insurance business or long-term insurance business

25   The following paragraph sets out the [draft] amendments to Implementation Guidance – Section 2 *Guidance for entities with general insurance business or long-term insurance business* (deleted text is struck through, inserted text is underlined).

26   Paragraph IG2.28 is amended as follows:

IG2.28 Disclosure should be made where an equalisation reserve has been established in accordance with the **PRA** ~~Handbook~~ Rulebook. Where equalisation reserves are established, an entity should disclose the following in the notes to the financial statements:

   (a)   that the amounts provided are not liabilities because they are in addition to the provisions required to meet the anticipated ultimate cost of settlement of outstanding claims at the reporting date;

   (b)   notwithstanding this, they are required by Schedule 3 to the Regulations to be included within technical provisions; and

   (c)   the impact of the equalisation reserves on **equity** and the effect of movements in the reserves on the profit or loss for the reporting period.

27   Paragraph IG2.42 is amended as follows:

IG2.42 The long-term business provision may be calculated on the **established long-term insurance liability** basis ~~used for reporting under PRA rules~~ subject to:

~~(a) reassessment of the provisions and reserves included in the statutory liabilities for solvency purposes to consider the extent to which they should be included in the long-term business provision. This will require the exclusion of the appropriate proportion of reserves (such as investment reserves, reserves to cover general contingencies and reserves to cover the specific contingency of the fund being closed to new business). Any amount in excess of the necessary provision should be disclosed in the financial statements as a reserve or in the~~ **fund for future appropriations (FFA)** ~~as appropriate; and~~

~~(b)~~ the reversal of any reduction in policyholder liabilities ~~in the regulatory returns~~ where these liabilities already implicitly take account of a pension fund surplus through future expense assumptions which reflect lower expected contributions.

28   Paragraph IG2.48 is amended as follows:

IG2.48 The net assets held to cover linked liabilities at the reporting date may differ from the technical provisions for linked liabilities. The reasons for any significant mismatching should be disclosed. ~~In practice this should apply only to overseas companies included in consolidated financial statements because of the requirements of rule 3.1.57 of~~ **INSPRU**.

In paragraph IG2.50 the first occurrence of 'FFA' is replaced by 'fund for future **29** appropriations (FFA)' in bold type.

Paragraph IG2.53 is amended as follows: **30**

> IG2.53 The investment return (which includes movements in realised and **unrealised investment gains and losses)** and related tax charges on assets representing reserves which are held within the **long-term fund** for solvency purposes under the PRA rules should be credited to the technical account for long-term business. Allocations may then be made as appropriate to the **non-technical account** in accordance with paragraphs IG2.65 and IG2.66 or to the FFA. <u>When the regulatory framework does not require the entity to set up a long-term fund for its long-term insurance business, the entity shall make the allocations as appropriate between the technical and non-technical account and disclose the basis of its allocation in the notes to the financial statements.</u>

The rubric before paragraph IG2.56 is amended as follows: **31**

> *Paragraphs IG2.56 to IG2.58 ~~provide guidance for applying the requirements of paragraphs 2 and 3 of the instructions for completing Form 47 in the PRA rules. They~~ are only relevant to long-term insurance business.*

Paragraph IG2.60 is amended as follows: **32**

> IG2.60 On consolidation, the profit or loss of any non-insurance entity belonging to the long-term ~~fund~~ <u>business</u> may be included directly in the technical account for long-term business. Where material, more detailed disclosure should be provided in the notes to the financial statements. Where an entity carrying on general insurance business is ~~owned by~~ <u>an asset of</u> the long-term ~~fund~~ <u>business</u>, the profit or loss of this business should be transferred from the non-technical account to the technical account for long-term business using new lines for this purpose.

THE ACCOUNTING COUNCIL'S ADVICE TO THE FRC TO ISSUE FRED 64 *DRAFT AMENDMENTS TO FRS 103 – SOLVENCY II*

Introduction

1   This report provides an overview of the main issues that have been considered by the Accounting Council in advising the Financial Reporting Council (FRC) to issue FRED 64 *Draft amendments to FRS 103 Insurance Contracts – Solvency II*.

2   The FRC, in accordance with the *Statutory Auditors (Amendment of Companies Act 2006 and Delegation of Functions etc) Order 2012* (SI 2012/1741), is a prescribed body for issuing accounting standards in the UK. The *Foreword to Accounting Standards* sets out the application of accounting standards in the Republic of Ireland.

3   In accordance with the *FRC Codes and Standards: procedures*, any proposal to issue, amend or withdraw a code or standard is put to the FRC Board with the full advice of the relevant Councils and/or the Codes & Standards Committee. Ordinarily, the FRC Board will only reject the advice put to it where:

(a)   it is apparent that a significant group of stakeholders has not been adequately consulted;

(b)   the necessary assessment of the impact of the proposal has not been completed, including an analysis of costs and benefits;

(c)   insufficient consideration has been given to the timing or cost of implementation; or

(d)   the cumulative impact of a number of proposals would make the adoption of an otherwise satisfactory proposal inappropriate.

4   The FRC has established the Accounting Council as the relevant Council to assist it in the setting of accounting standards.

Advice

5   The Accounting Council is advising the FRC to issue FRED 64 *Draft amendments to FRS 103 Insurance Contracts – Solvency II*.

6   The Accounting Council advises that these proposals will update FRS 103 *Insurance Contracts* for changes in the regulatory framework and ensure that established accounting policies can continue to be applied if an entity so chooses.

7   When these draft amendments are finalised the Accounting Council's Advice to the FRC in respect of these amendments will be added into FRS 103.

Background

8   When FRS 103 *Insurance Contracts* was issued in March 2014 the Accounting Council advised the FRC to review, in due course, whether or not consequential changes to FRS 103 would be required for the commencement of Solvency II.

9   As Solvency II is effective from 1 January 2016 this review is now being carried out and the Accounting Council advises that limited amendments are proposed to FRS 103 to reflect the changes in the regulatory regime. The Accounting Council does not advise making changes to FRS 103, other than those that are necessary as a result of the changes in the regulatory framework.

Draft amendments to FRS 103

FRS 103 makes a number of references to the PRA realistic capital regime, which will   **10**
be replaced by Solvency II from 1 January 2016. In addition, it refers to the Prudential
sourcebook for Insurers (INSPRU), which will be replaced from the same date. As these
references will be out of date, amendments will be required to FRS 103.

In considering the amendments that are required, the Accounting Council advises that   **11**
entities should be permitted to continue to apply established accounting practice in their
financial statements, if they choose to do so. It notes that FRS 103 already includes the
ability for an insurer to change its accounting policies for insurance contracts if it judges
certain criteria are met, and therefore there is no need to introduce specific new accounting
policies relating to Solvency II.

The Accounting Council notes that paragraph 3.1(b) of FRS 103 describes the circumstances   **12**
in which the requirements for with-profits liabilities and related assets apply, which was
based on those to which the PRA realistic capital regime applied. The Accounting Council
considered the following two options for revising the description of the scope of these
requirements:

(a)   describe more fully the current scope; or
(b)   describe the scope by reference to Solvency II.

The Accounting Council noted that describing the scope by reference to Solvency II may   **13**
extend the application of the relevant requirements of FRS 103 to entities not previously
within their scope. As the Accounting Council's aim was to limit the amount of change in
accounting policies that would be required, the Accounting Council advises describing the
current scope in paragraph 3.1(b) more fully, in order to avoid unintended consequences.

In developing a revised description for the established method of accounting for long-   **14**
term insurance business (to replace the modified statutory solvency basis), the Accounting
Council advises taking a principles-based approach to the definition. However, in order
to make it clear that entities are not expected to change accounting policies unless they
take advantage of the provisions of paragraph 2.3, the definitions of both the 'established
long-term insurance liability basis'and the 'realistic value of liabilities' make it clear
that these should be consistent with accounting policies applied in periods ending before
1 January 2016.

Effective date

The Accounting Council advises that the amendments to FRS 102 set out in this FRED   **15**
should be effective for accounting periods ending after 1 January 2016. Early adoption
should not be permitted because this is consistent with the effective date of the new
regulatory framework.

CONSULTATION STAGE IMPACT ASSESSMENT

Introduction

1   The Financial Reporting Council (FRC) is committed to a proportionate approach to the use of its powers, making effective use of impact assessments and having regard to the impact of regulation on small enterprises.

Draft amendments to FRS 103

2   The draft amendments are intended to update FRS 103 *Insurance Contracts* for changes in the regulatory framework and ensure that established accounting policies can continue to be applied if an entity so chooses. As such, an entity can apply its judgement and choice over the extent to which the changes in the regulatory framework impact on its financial reporting. These draft amendments should not result in additional costs for entities.

3   The FRC notes that some changes in the regulatory framework may, nevertheless, have a direct impact on financial reporting, for example in relation to equalisation provisions. HM Treasury has carried out an impact assessment on the transposition of the Solvency II Directive into UK law and regulation and the FRC has not carried out any further impact assessment in relation to this.

Conclusion

4   The FRC believes that the draft amendments to FRS 103 are necessary given the changes in the regulatory framework.

This draft is issued by the Financial Reporting Council for comment. It should be noted that the draft may be modified in the light of comments received before being issued in final form.

For ease of handling, we prefer comments to be sent by e-mail to:

ukfrs@frc.org.uk

Comments may also be sent in hard copy to:

Jenny Carter
Financial Reporting Council
8th Floor
125 London Wall
London
EC2Y 5AS

Comments should be despatched so as to be received no later than 28 February 2016.

The FRC's policy is to publish on its website all responses to formal consultations issued by the FRC unless the respondent explicitly requests otherwise. A standard confidentiality statement in an e-mail message will not be regarded as a request for non-disclosure. The FRC does not edit personal information (such as telephone numbers or postal or e-mail addresses) from submissions; therefore, only information that you wish to be published should be submitted.

The FRC aims to publish responses within 10 working days of receipt.

The FRC will publish a summary of the consultation responses, either as part of, or alongside, its final decision.

Part Four

Staff Education Notes and other FRC documents

FRC Policy on Developing Statements of Recommended Practice (SORPs)

(March 2016)

Contents

FRC POLICY ON DEVELOPING STATEMENTS OF RECOMMENDED PRACTICE (SORPS)

Introduction

This document sets out the Financial Reporting Council's (FRC) policy on developing Statements of Recommended Practice (SORPs), with effect from 3 March 2016. This Policy replaces the FRC's Policy and Code of Practice on SORPs dated April 2014.

The FRC is a prescribed body for issuing accounting standards in the UK and its accounting standards are also applied in the Republic of Ireland. The FRC issues technical auditing standards and ethical standards for auditors for use in the UK and Ireland[1]. The FRC also issues technical actuarial standards in the UK.

SORPs are sector-driven recommendations on financial reporting, auditing practices and actuarial practices for specialised industries, sectors or areas of work, or which supplement FRC standards and other legal and regulatory requirements in the light of special factors prevailing or transactions undertaken in that particular industry, sector or area of work that are not addressed in FRC standards. SORPs also address matters that are addressed in FRC standards, but about which additional guidance is considered necessary. Where there are policy options in FRC standards, a SORP may recommend the most appropriate option to the particular industry or sector.

SORPs may only be issued by 'SORP-making bodies'. A SORP-making body is a body that has been recognised by the FRC for the purpose of producing the SORP for a particular industry or sector. SORP-making bodies have a responsibility to act in the public interest when developing and issuing a SORP.

To be recognised as a SORP-making body, a particular industry or sectoral body must meet criteria set by the FRC and must agree to develop SORPs in accordance with this Policy.

A SORP must carry a Statement by the FRC confirming, as appropriate, that the SORP does not appear to contain any fundamental points of principle that are unacceptable in the context of current financial reporting practice, auditing practice or actuarial practice, nor does it conflict with an FRC standard or undermine the FRC's broader objectives.

Overarching Criteria for Developing a SORP

The FRC will consider authorising the development of a SORP in support of FRC standards if the circumstances warrant it, for example if one or more of the following factors are present:

(i)   there are indications that issuing a SORP will lead to higher quality financial reporting, auditing or actuarial work or conversely a risk of unacceptable quality if a SORP is not issued;

(ii)   there is evidence or a risk of inconsistent practice across different entities overall or within a particular industry leading to an unacceptable lack of comparability;

(iii)   there is an industry or sector specific need;

(iv)   changes within a particular industry or sectors means mean an FRC standard requires additional application guidance; or

(v)   there is a recognised need in the public interest to establish a benchmark for accountability of professionals.

---

[1] *The professional bodies require their members to use FRC issued auditing and ethical standards. BIS is currently considering legislative changes to provide a legal basis to underpin the use of standards.*

In certain circumstances, the FRC may, at its sole discretion, decide that it would be most appropriate if the additional guidance is issued by the FRC.

The sorts of circumstances envisaged include:

- the additional guidance is necessary to secure compliance with international obligations;
- the intention is to supplement standards through additional guidance;
- allowing the additional guidance to be issued by a trade representative or professional body could create a real or perceived conflict of interest;
- the public interest lies in maintaining independence from the profession; or
- a speedy response from the FRC is needed, at least in the first instance.

Becoming a SORP-making Body

The FRC may recognise bodies for the purpose of developing and issuing SORPs. Bodies will only be recognised where the following criteria are met:

(i) the industry or sector represented by the body in question has special financial reporting, auditing or actuarial issues and the application or interpretation of FRC standards requires clarification in order to deal with those issues;

(ii) the body in question represents the whole or a major part of the industry or sector;

(iii) the body shares the FRC's aim of:

(a) high-quality financial reporting proportionate to the size and complexity of the entity and users' information needs; or

(b) high-quality auditing work proportionate to the needs, size and complexity of the entity; or

(c) high-quality actuarial work.

(iv) the body agrees to abide by this Policy in developing its SORP;

(v) the body commits to reviewing its SORP in line with this Policy;

(vi) where an industry or sector is regulated or financed by another body, the regulator or financing body has confirmed in writing that it is content for the body seeking recognition by the FRC as a SORP-making body to promulgate SORPs for that industry or sector.

The FRC may, at its sole discretion, withdraw recognition of a SORP-making body if it considers that the above criteria are no longer met, or if the SORP-making body fails to act in accordance with this Policy.

In the event that the FRC withdraws recognition of a SORP-making body, it may publish that fact if it considers that publicity is necessary or desirable in the public interest.

DEVELOPMENT OF SORPS

1   Industry and sector bodies that wish to develop SORPs must first secure recognition by the FRC as a SORP-making body. Once recognition as a SORP-making body has been granted, a body may proceed to develop a new SORP.

Developing or revising a SORP

2   Before starting work on the development of a SORP, a SORP-making body should seek approval from the FRC, by contacting the relevant FRC Executive Director. This will ensure that the proposed SORP does not overlap with an FRC project or address a matter that the FRC would prefer to deal with itself. It should also agree with the FRC the nature and scope of the SORP.

3   A SORP should specify the types of entity or work to which the SORP is intended to apply. Where entities or work may fall within the scope of more than one SORP, the SORP to be applied will usually be the SORP with the more specific application. In such circumstances, the SORP-making body should agree with the FRC and the other relevant SORP-making bodies which SORP should apply and identify this clearly within the relevant SORPs.

4   A SORP should aim to promote consistency across the industry, sector or type of work by recommending a preferred treatment, approach or methodology. It should also seek, where practicable and appropriate, to adopt an approach or methodology that is consistent with the approach taken in similar industries, sectors or areas of work.

5   A SORP should clearly indicate those areas that relate to the subject matter of FRC standards and those that relate to other information to be provided in a document containing that subject matter. A SORP should clearly indicate which recommendations provide guidance on applying FRC standards and which go beyond the application of FRC standards (for example by recommending additional disclosure).

6   SORPs should be developed in line with current FRC standards and best practice. The provisions of a SORP cannot override the provisions of the law, regulatory requirements or FRC standards.

7   Where a more recently issued FRC standard or a change in legislation creates a conflict with the provisions of an existing SORP, the relevant provisions of the SORP will cease to have effect. The SORP-making body is responsible for updating the relevant provisions within the SORP on a timely basis to bring them into line with new legislation or FRC standards or to withdraw them as appropriate.

8   A SORP should include a clear and prominent statement along the following lines:

> "*In developing this SORP, all [accounting / auditing / actuarial] standards [and other FRC pronouncements] issued by [insert date] were considered in the development of the SORP.*"

9   After considering FRC standards in their entirety, SORP-making bodies should ensure that a SORP makes clear which sections of the relevant FRC standard(s) and other pronouncements in effect at the date of publication of the SORP have been addressed in the development of the SORP, including an indication as to their relevance to the industry, sector or work in question and an explanation of how each has been dealt with in the SORP.

10   Failure to update a SORP does not exempt reporting entities or practitioners from applying the FRC standards effective at the relevant date. Entities that operate in the public sector or

under specific legislative regimes should be guided by those regimes in assessing whether they are prevented or exempt from complying with this requirement.

SORP-making bodies should include in their SORP a statement setting out the status of the SORP with reference to FRC standards, along the following lines: **11**

> *"Entities or work complying with this SORP shall apply the [accounting / auditing / actuarial] standards applicable at the relevant reporting date (which does not preclude early application where permitted). Where the current edition of this SORP predates a change in legislation or [accounting / auditing / actuarial] standards and a conflict is thereby created, the affected provisions of this SORP cease to have effect."*

Accountability

SORPs must be drafted by the SORP-making body itself or by a properly constituted working party of the SORP-making body. The SORP-making body should inform the FRC of the arrangements it is putting in place to develop the SORP, including the membership of its working party, and provide an appropriate point of contact to the FRC. FRC staff must be accorded observer status at meetings of the SORP-making body or SORP working party, whichever is appropriate. **12**

The SORP development process must ensure: **13**

(a) the participation of a sufficiently broad range of representatives of the industry or sector concerned (including where appropriate practitioners and other regulators);

(b) independent members who represent the wider public interest, who should be in the majority where audit SORPs are concerned;

(c) where possible, users of financial statements, audit reports or actuarial information; and

(d) sufficient technical support.

The SORP-making body must provide evidence of the process followed and effective participation by stakeholders. The FRC will not normally agree to make a Statement on the SORP unless it is satisfied that: **14**

(a) in developing the SORP:

    (i) due process was followed;

    (ii) an appropriate cross-section of stakeholders was involved; and

(b) the SORP does not contain any fundamental points of principle that are unacceptable in the context of current financial reporting practice, auditing practice or actuarial practice, nor does it conflict with an FRC standard(s) or undermine the FRC's broader objectives.

Due process

Proceedings of the SORP-making body or its working party should be conducted in a spirit of openness and follow due process including open consultation. **15**

During the development or revision of a SORP, the SORP-making body is responsible for identifying potential divergence from FRC standards and must inform the FRC of any such potential divergence as soon as possible. **16**

Where a proposed SORP includes recommendations that go beyond the application of FRC standards (for example by recommending additional disclosure) the FRC will need to be satisfied that the SORP-making body has given appropriate consideration to the expected impact in terms of costs and benefits. **17**

18   Before finalising and publishing the SORP, the SORP-making body should proactively seek the views of stakeholders and should consult publicly. The preferred mechanism for public consultation is a published draft, with a minimum three month comment period. In certain circumstances a shorter period of consultation may be acceptable. The FRC will, however, need to be satisfied that the nature of the consultation and length of the comment period was appropriate.

19   In some cases, a SORP-making body may wish to seek input via a published statement of intent in advance of publishing a consultation draft. However, a published statement of intent is not an acceptable substitute for a published consultation draft and will consequently delay development of the SORP.

20   All statements of intent, consultation drafts and final SORPs should be presented to the FRC for comment before publication. The SORP-making body must allow sufficient time for any changes sought by the FRC to be incorporated prior to publication.

21   A statement should be included in a SORP consultation draft or statement of intent setting out the scope of the FRC's review, along the following lines:

> *"In accordance with the FRC's Policy on Developing Statements of Recommended Practice the FRC carried out a review of the proposed SORP focusing on those aspects relevant to the [financial statements / audit report / actuarial information] but also including aspects relevant to the FRC's broader responsibilities where appropriate."*

22   In addition, the FRC reserves the right to require a statement to be included within a statement of intent or consultation draft indicating areas of overlap with its own work and any reservations it has regarding the content of the statement of intent or consultation draft.

23   Before publishing a final SORP, the SORP-making body must provide the FRC with copies of consultation responses and comment letters, an analysis or summary of the main comments and an indication of how the comments have been dealt with. In this way the FRC can satisfy itself that stakeholder comments have been appropriately considered.

24   SORP-making bodies are expected to adopt a transparent process and accordingly, comment letters should be made publicly available unless confidentiality is requested by the respondent. SORP-making bodies should publish on their websites all responses to formal consultations. SORP-making bodies should aim to publish responses as soon as possible and within 10 days of receipt.

Consistency between SORPs

25   As SORPs should be developed in the context of current FRC standards and best practice the FRC will expect a degree of consistency between SORPs if they are addressing similar matters for different industries, sectors or work, unless there are good reasons for different approaches (for example different user needs and different legal or regulatory environments).

26   The FRC will consider consistency between SORPs as part of its review.

The FRC's 'Statement on the SORP'

27   The SORP-making body must obtain the written consent of the FRC to include a Statement on the SORP. The FRC's Statement on the SORP should be included in a prominent place in each SORP. No other reference to the FRC should be made without prior written approval of the FRC.

Maintenance of SORPs

The SORP-making body should provide the FRC with an appropriate point of contact for the purposes of reviewing and maintaining the SORP. **28**

Responsibility for maintaining a SORP falls to the body which promulgated that SORP. **29** In promulgating a SORP, the SORP-making body undertakes to review on an annual basis each SORP for which it is responsible. In particular the body should consider:

(a) any implications for the SORP of new and proposed accounting, auditing or actuarial standards – any divergence should be notified to the FRC as soon as possible;

(b) any evidence of widespread or significant failure in the relevant industry or sector to follow any part of the guidance contained in the SORP, of which the SORP-making body is aware;

(c) developments in the industry or sector which suggest that further guidance in respect of their accounting, auditing or actuarial treatment is desirable; and

(d) the continued need for the SORP.

The SORP-making body should provide the FRC with an account, in writing, of the **30** findings of its annual review, and include the current membership of the SORP-making body and any working parties. The account should also reaffirm the SORP-making body's commitment to complying with this Policy, and state whether it proposes to revise any of the SORPs for which it is responsible in the light of the findings of its annual review.

Consequential amendments to SORPs

Where it is necessary to amend a SORP in order to reflect changes in FRC standards **31** or in legislative or regulatory requirements, and the amendments will not involve new interpretation of those requirements or introduce other changes, the SORP-making body may agree with the FRC that:

(a) the requirement to publish a consultation draft would be disproportionate in the circumstances; and

(b) these changes can therefore be made by way of a shortened administrative procedure, after which the FRC will issue its Statement on the SORP.

In the event amendments are to be made via this shortened administrative procedure, the **32** SORP-making body agrees to give notice of its intention to amend the SORP on its website.

Withdrawal of the FRC's 'Statement on the SORP'

The FRC reserves the right to withdraw its Statement at any time if it considers that it is no **33** longer appropriate to maintain its Statement, for example because:

(a) the SORP is out of date;

(b) the SORP has been superseded by developments in FRC standards or by legislative or regulatory requirements;

(c) the SORP-making body does not review and/or maintain the SORP in line with this Policy; or

(d) the SORP-making body refuses to implement changes to the SORP that are requested by the FRC.

Additional Guidance

It will not normally be necessary for a SORP-making body to supplement a SORP with **34** further guidance. Material that a SORP-making body proposes to issue which offers an interpretation of FRC standards should normally be included in the SORP itself. In the event that a SORP-making body intends to issue supplementary material, the development of that material should be submitted to the same due process and scrutiny as a SORP, including review by the FRC.

35   There are, nevertheless, three sets of circumstances in which it may be desirable to publish further guidance outside the SORP itself, as follows:

(a)   an urgent need for guidance on a new accounting standard or other relevant publication issued after publication of the SORP – any such guidance should normally be incorporated into the SORP at the earliest subsequent opportunity;

(b)   further guidance is necessary in order to interpret the requirements of the SORP for a particular sub-sector; or

(c)   further guidance on the application of the SORP is necessary in order to aid practitioners.

36   In the situations cited in paragraph 35, the SORP-making body should notify the FRC and explain what guidance is proposed. The FRC may require that a reference to the FRC is included in the guidance. The guidance should not be published without the agreement of the FRC.

37   The FRC does not usually endorse guidance issued outside the SORP. However, where it is clear in relation to matters that fall within paragraph 35(a), that:

(a)   guidance is urgently needed on a significant issue and cannot be delayed until revision of the SORP; and

(b)   the SORP-making body follows the same due process that it would normally follow when revising a SORP, including review by the FRC,

then the FRC's Statement on the SORP may be attached to the guidance, thereby according it the same authority as the SORP.

38   For situations that fall within paragraphs 35(b) and (c), the SORP-making body should include in any published guidance a statement that clearly indicates the authority of that material and states that it is not part of the SORP and has not been reviewed by the FRC. An example of such a statement is set out below:

> "the overall aim of the guidance is to assist practitioners in the preparation of [financial statements / audit reports / carrying out actuarial work]. It does not form part of the [date and name of SORP], nor has it been reviewed by the FRC. It attempts to explain and illustrate what is required under [date and name of SORP] but does not carry the authority of the SORP."

Recognition of SORPs by the FRC

SORPs issued by SORP-making bodies must include the FRC's 'Statement on the SORP'.

The FRC will only issue a Statement on the SORP if it has been developed in accordance with this Policy.

FRC review of SORPs

Before issuing a Statement on the SORP, the FRC will conduct a review of the proposed SORP to determine whether the SORP:

(a)   has been developed in accordance with this Policy; and

(b)   contains fundamental points of principle that are unacceptable in the context of current practice; and

(c)   contains requirements that conflict with the requirements or principles of an FRC standard; and

(d)   supports matters that fall within the FRC's broader responsibilities, to the extent this is relevant to the industry, sector or area of work in question.

Where a SORP provides recommendations relating to other information to be provided in a document containing the financial statements / audit report / actuarial information, and the FRC believes the SORP's requirements or recommendations in relation to those areas could undermine the credibility of the document containing the financial statements / audit report / actuarial information, it will discuss the issue with the SORP-making body. If this does not resolve the issue, the FRC will consider the implications for its Statement on the SORP, and may vary its Statement to fit the circumstances.

FRC Statement on the SORP

The Statement on the SORP will:

- outline the nature of the review the FRC has undertaken;
- confirm that the SORP does not appear to contain any fundamental points of principle that are unacceptable in the context of current financial reporting practice, auditing practice or actuarial practice or to conflict with an FRC standard; and
- where relevant, confirm that the SORP does not appear to undermine the FRC's broader objectives.

The FRC will vary its Statement on the SORP to fit the circumstances of an individual SORP.

An example of the kind of Statement that will be issued is set out below:

"The aim of the Financial Reporting Council (FRC) is to promote high-quality corporate governance and reporting to foster investment. In relation to [choose one]

accounting standards applicable in the UK and Republic of Ireland, the FRC's overriding objective is to enable users of accounts to receive high-quality understandable financial reporting proportionate to the size and complexity of the entity and users' information needs. In particular industries or sectors, clarification of aspects of those standards may be needed in order for the standards to be applied in a manner that is relevant and provides useful information to users of financial statements in that industry or sector.

or

auditing standards applicable in the UK and Republic of Ireland, the FRC's overriding objective is to enable users of audit reports or other information issued by the auditor to receive high-quality understandable information and audit reports proportionate to the size and complexity of the entity and users' information needs. In particular industries or sectors, clarification of aspects of those standards may be needed in order for the standards to be applied in a manner that is relevant and provides useful information to users of audit reports or other information issued by the auditor in that industry or sector.

or

actuarial standards applicable in the UK the FRC's overriding objective is that the users for whom a piece of actuarial information was created should be able to place a high degree of reliance on the information's relevance, transparency of assumptions, completeness and comprehensibility, including the communication of any uncertainty inherent in the information. For particular actuarial work, clarification may be needed in order for the standards to be applied in a manner that is relevant and provides reliable information to the user

Such clarification in connection with accounting / auditing / actuarial standards is issued in the form of Statements of Recommended Practice (SORPs) by bodies recognised for this purpose by the FRC. The [insert name of body] has confirmed that it shares the FRC's aim of high-quality financial reporting / audit practice / actuarial work and has been recognised by the FRC for the purpose of issuing SORPs for the [industry, sector or area of work].

In accordance with the FRC's Policy on Developing Statements of Recommended Practices the FRC carried out a review of the SORP focusing on those aspects relevant to the financial statements / audit work / actuarial work but also including aspects relevant to the FRC's broader responsibilities where appropriate.

On the basis of its review, the FRC has concluded that the SORP has been developed in accordance with the FRC's Policy on SORPs and does not appear to contain any fundamental points of principlethat are unacceptable in the context of present [financial reporting practices / auditing practices / actuarial practices] or to conflict with an [accounting / auditing / actuarial] standard [or to undermine the FRC's broader objectives]."

[date]

When issuing a Statement on the SORP, the FRC is making an assessment of that SORP at a particular moment. The FRC gives no guarantee that it will not, at some point in the future, issue a pronouncement that supersedes that SORP.

FRC Governance

Responsibility for discharging the functions set out in this Policy will fall to:

- A Committee of the FRC Board, advised by the relevant Council(s), when deciding whether or not the FRC should recognise individual bodies as SORP-making bodies.
- A Committee of the FRC Board, advised by the relevant Council(s) (and its advisory groups), when deciding whether or not to issue a Statement on the SORP unless the FRC Board has specific responsibility in legislation for issuing a Statement on the SORP (where it will be advised by a Committee of the FRC Board and the relevant Council (and its advisory groups)).

The table below sets out how this will operate within the current FRC structure:

Action	Carried out by
Recognition as SORP-making body	FRC Board Committee on advice of relevant Council
Statement on a SORP	FRC Board or Board Committee on advice of relevant Council
Approval to publish draft of a SORP	Council (on advice of Council advisory groups, as appropriate)
Review of a SORP	Council advisory groups, as appropriate

True and Fair

(June 2014)

Contents

TRUE AND FAIR

Introduction

The purpose of this document is to confirm that the true and fair requirement remains of fundamental importance in IFRS and UK GAAP, whether embodied in the new standards FRS 100 – 103 or the standards they replace.

Section 393 of the Companies Act 2006 requires that the directors of a company must not approve accounts unless they are satisfied they give a true and fair view. The true and fair requirement has been fundamental to accounting in the UK for many years. It is a requirement of both UK and EU law.[1]

The introduction of IFRS in the UK did not change the fundamental requirement for accounts to give a true and fair view and the concept remains paramount in the presentation of UK company financial statements, even though the routes by which that requirement is embedded may differ slightly. Fair presentation under IFRS is equivalent to a true and fair view.

Concerns have been raised on the operation of the true and fair override in IFRS and the absence of the term 'prudence' following changes made by the IASB in 2010 during the first phase of its Conceptual Framework project. However, these changes do not affect the fundamental importance of the true and fair requirement. Whilst terminology has changed, the true and fair override requirement still exists in the same substantive form and the absence of the term 'prudence' in the 2010 Conceptual Framework does not prevent accounts prepared in accordance with IFRS from presenting a true and fair view.[2]

In this paper we discuss the continuing primacy of the true and fair requirement and its relevance to preparers, those charged with governance and auditors.

Preparation of accounts

Whilst there has been a gradual shift over time to more detailed accounting standards, the preparation of financial statements cannot be reduced to a mechanistic following of the relevant accounting standards. Objective professional judgement must be applied to ensure that financial statements give a true and fair view.

This professional judgement is all important. It applies at all stages of preparation of the accounts, for example:

- Where there is a choice of accounting policies allowed under accounting standards, ensuring that those selected are appropriate taking into account the circumstances of the company (see for example FRS 102 Section 10 and IAS 8).
- Establishing accounting policies for items not specifically covered by accounting standards or where they are ambiguous. In such circumstances the approach in IAS 8 to consider standards dealing with similar items may be appropriate; however reliance

---

[1] *The requirement that company and consolidated accounts give a true and fair view is recognised in Article 2 (3) of the 4th Company Law Directive and Article 16 (3) of the 7th Company Law Directive issued by the European Commission. Although these two Articles do not apply for accounts required to give a fair presentation in accordance with endorsed IFRS under the IAS Regulation, the true and fair principle underlying them is expressly recognised in Article 3(2) of the IAS Regulation – no IFRS standard can be endorsed if it would conflict with the principle set out in those Articles.*

[2] *The FRC has obtained two opinions from Martin Moore QC, one in 2008 and one in 2013 which are consistent with the analysis presented in this paper. Both Opinions are available on the FRC website.*

on an approved accounting treatment of a different kind of item will not necessarily give a true and fair view.

- Making judgements, for example about valuation, aimed at giving a true and fair view.
- Not using detailed accounting rules as an excuse for poor accounting
- Considering what is and what is not material.
- Giving appropriate disclosures even where not specifically required by accounting standards.
- Ensuring that significant information is not obscured by immaterial or irrelevant disclosures
- Standing back at the end of the accounts preparation process and making sure the accounts overall do give a true and fair view.

Prudence

For companies reporting under new UK GAAP, both FRS 102 Section 2 and company law require that directors make prudent judgements in their consideration of accounts, particularly where there is uncertainty.

IAS 8 requires that financial statements are prudent and 'neutral, i.e. free from bias'[3]. These characteristics are not contradictory if, consistent with the 2010 Conceptual Framework, neutrality is seen as the absence of deliberate manipulation of financial information intended to make its reception by users more or less favourable. The inclusion of both characteristics reflects the fact that the use of excessive prudence, resulting in the deliberate understatement of assets or overstatement of liabilities, does not lead to useful information. As an example, hidden reserves or excessive provisions, which may be released later at will to boost profit, are not allowed.

The relative emphasis given to those characteristics that contribute to a true and fair view concept has, like the concept itself, evolved over time. Greater emphasis on neutrality reflects concerns about the smoothing of profits. In the first phase of its revisions to the IFRS Conceptual Framework in 2010, the IASB removed explicit references to prudence as the IASB considered that its inclusion may have led to greater bias. However, as part the second phase of its review of the Conceptual Framework, the IASB is now proposing to reintroduce an explicit reference to prudence though this is not expected to be finalised until 2015.[4]

Irrespective of whether it is specifically included in the Conceptual Framework, the concept of prudence continues to underlie the preparation of accounts under both UK GAAP and IFRS through, for example, asymmetry in the recognition of profits when compared to losses and the measurement of assets and liabilities where uncertainty exists.

The importance of prudence in the development of IFRS was also confirmed by Mr Hoogervorst, Chairman of the IASB, who has said 'the basic tenets of the concept of prudence are still vital for our work. Indeed, the exercise of caution is visible in many of our standards and is also an important issue in the development of new standards.'[5]

---

[3] *IAS 8 para 10 (b) identifies prudent and neutral as characteristics of financial statements that present reliable financial information.*

[4] *See IASB Update May 2014 for a summary of the IASB's tentative decisions on the Conceptual Framework revisions.*

[5] *In a speech entitled 'The concept of Prudence: dead or alive', given in September 2012*

Reflecting the substance of transactions

IFRS and new UK GAAP, unlike the standards it replaces, do not contain separate standards that require accounts to reflect the substance of a transaction rather than its legal form where this is different. However, this does not mean that substance over form has no place in IFRS or new UK GAAP. It would be difficult for accounts to present a true and fair view if form had overridden substance.

IAS 8 states that for information to be reliable, it must be reported in accordance with economic substance, rather than strictly in adherence to its legal form.[6] Indeed if material transactions are not accounted for in accordance with their substance it is doubtful whether the accounts present a true and fair view.

True and fair and accounting standards

True and fair is not something that is merely a separate add-on to accounting standards. Rather the whole essence of standards is to provide for recognition, measurement, presentation and disclosure for specific aspects of financial reporting in a way that reflects economic reality and hence that provides a true and fair view.

Accounting standards are arrived at after extensive consultation and after full due process. Further reviews are performed to ensure that IFRS meet the criteria for endorsement by the European Commission to ensure they would give a true and fair view.

These processes should result in accounting standards that, in the vast majority of cases, are complied with when presenting a true and fair view. The statement in IAS 1 that departures from the standards should only be necessary in 'extremely rare circumstances' should be understood in the context of the consultation and other due processes that preceded the issue of the standards. It does not release directors from their legal obligation to only approve particular accounts if they are satisfied that they give a true and fair view and directors should not rely on it to avoid making appropriate judgements.

Disagreement with a particular standard does not, on its own, provide grounds for departing from it. Where the accounting standards clearly address an issue, but the requirements are insufficient to fully explain the issue, the solution is normally additional disclosure. For example, some companies have disclosed alternative measures, such as adjusted Earnings per Share measures, where such disclosures were considered necessary to provide a more complete picture of their performance.

However, where directors and auditors do not believe that following a particular accounting policy will give a true and fair view they are legally required to adopt a more appropriate policy, even if this requires a departure from a particular standard. As IAS 1 states, an entity cannot rectify inappropriate accounting policies by disclosure. These circumstances are more likely to arise where the precise circumstances were not contemplated during the development of the relevant standard.

IAS 1 paragraph 19 specifically requires departure from the requirements of a standard when compliance would conflict with the objective of financial statements.[7] Concerns have been raised as to whether this continues to ensure standards are overridden in order to present a true and fair view. These concerns arose, in part, because the IFRS Conceptual Framework states that the objective of financial statements is that they should be useful

---

and does not refer to the legal requirement that accounts present a true and fair view or are presented fairly. However such concerns are misplaced because:

- The concepts of usefulness and true and fair are, in the context of financial statements, inseparable - for financial statements to be useful they must present a true and fair view;
- IAS 1 para 24 explains that an accounting policy would conflict with the objective of financial statements 'when it does not represent faithfully the transactions, other events and conditions that it purports to present or could reasonably be expected to represent'; and
- Where the true and fair override is applied, IAS 1 requires disclosure that the departure from a particular requirement is 'to achieve a fair presentation'.

Where a company departs from a standard in order to give a true and fair view and a proper explanation is given of the reason for the departure and its effects, the Financial Reporting Review Panel will be reluctant to substitute its own judgement for that of the company's board unless it is not satisfied that the board has acted reasonably. There have been examples where the override has been used under IFRS, both inside and outside the UK.[8]

The approach to be taken by auditors

The obligations of an auditor when giving an opinion on a company's financial statements are clearly set out in sections 393 (2) and 495 to 497, Companies Act 2006. Those obligations include stating whether, in their opinion, the accounts give a true and fair view (section 495 (3)(a)).

The importance of this approach is clearly recognised in ISA (UK & I) 700, in particular, in paragraphs 8, 9 and 11 (and supported in the application material in paragraphs A10 and A11).

Against that background, it is clear that if auditors are to discharge properly their legal and professional responsibilities, they should stand back as they approach finalisation of those accounts and consider whether, viewed as a whole and in view of the issues that they have addressed in the course of the audit, the accounts do indeed give a true and fair view.

Conclusion

It will be evident from the above that the FRC expects preparers, those charged with governance and auditors:

- Always to stand back and ensure that the accounts as a whole do give a true and fair view;
- To provide additional disclosures when compliance with an accounting standard is insufficient to present a true and fair view;
- To use the true and fair override where compliance with the standards does not result in the presentation of a true and fair view; and
- To ensure that the consideration they give to these matters is evident in their deliberations and documentation.

This will help ensure that accounts in the UK continue to demonstrate the high quality that users have come to expect.

---

[8] *In the UK for example HSBC and National Express*

SEN 1
Cash flow statements

Contents

Disclaimer

This Education Note has been prepared by FRC staff for the convenience of users of FRS 102 The Financial Reporting Standard applicable in the UK and Republic of Ireland. It aims to illustrate certain requirements of FRS 102, but should not be relied upon as a definitive statement on the application of the standard. The illustrative material is not a substitute for reading the detailed requirements of FRS 102.

INTRODUCTION

In this Staff Education Note, an illustrative cash flow statement is shown first under FRS 1 *Cash flow statements (revised 1996)* and then restated to comply with Section 7 *Statement of Cash Flows* of FRS 102 *The Financial Reporting Standard applicable in the UK and Republic of Ireland.*

In contrast to FRS 1, a cash flow statement prepared under FRS 102:

- reconciles the movement in cash and cash equivalents, not just cash;
- groups cash flows into fewer headings (ie cash flows from operating, investing and financing activities);
- reconciles profit to cash flows from operating activities starting from profit for the year rather than operating profit; and
- has fewer supporting notes.

This Staff Education Note has been prepared to illustrate the format of the cash flow statement prepared in accordance with FRS 102 and assumes that there are no other changes arising from the application of FRS 102. In a full set of financial statements, comparatives would be provided.

There are no requirements in the Regulations[1] in respect of cash flow statements.

This Staff Education Note is written to highlight key areas of consideration when transitioning to FRS 102 and is not designed to be exhaustive.

This Staff Education Note is written to highlight key areas of consideration when transitioning to FRS 102 and is not designed to be exhaustive.

---

[1] *Large and Medium-sized Companies and Groups (Accounts and Reports) Regulations 2008 (SI 2008/410).*

ILLUSTRATIVE CASH FLOW STATEMENT

FRS 1 Cash flow statements (revised 1996)

Cash flow statement[2]

for the year ended 31 December 20X1

	Note	20X1 CU'000
Net cash inflow from operating activities	A	**6,889**
Returns on investments and servicing of finance		
Interest received		3,011
Interest paid		(12)
Net cash inflow from returns on investments and servicing of finance		**2,999**
Taxation		**(2,922)**
Capital expenditure		
Payments to acquire intangible fixed assets		(71)
Payments to acquire tangible fixed assets		(1,496)
Receipts from sales of tangible fixed assets		42
Capital expenditure		**(1,525)**
		5,441
Equity dividends paid		**(2,417)**
Net cash inflow before use of liquid resources and financing		
		3,024
Management of liquid resources		
Purchase of treasury bills		(650)
Sale of treasury bills		200
Net cash outflow from management of liquid resources		**(450)**
Financing		
Issue of ordinary share capital		211
Repurchase of debenture loan		(149)
Expenses paid in connection with share issue		(5)
Financing		**57**
Increase in cash	B, C	**2,631**

---

[2] *The individual categories of inflows and outflows under the standard headings should be disclosed separately in the cash flow statement, as shown here, or in the notes to the financial statements.*

ILLUSTRATIVE CASH FLOW STATEMENT

FRS 102 The Financial Reporting Standard applicable in the UK and Republic of Ireland

Cash flow statement[3]

for the year ended 31 December 20X1

	Note	20X1 CU'000
Cash flows from operating activities[4]		
Profit for the financial year[5]		6,099
Adjustments for:		
Depreciation of property, plant and equipment		869
Amortisation of intangible assets		50
Profit on disposal of property, plant and equipment		(20)
Interest paid[6]		12
Interest received[6]		(3,011)
Taxation[7]		2,922
Decrease/(increase) in trade and other receivables		(72)
Decrease/(increase) in inventories		(194)
Increase/(decrease) in trade payables		234
Cash from operations[8]		6,889
Interest paid[6]		(12)
Income taxes paid		(2,922)
Net cash generated from operating activities		3,955
Cash flows from investing activities		
Proceeds from sale of equipment		42
Purchases of property, plant and equipment		(1,496)
Purchases of intangible assets		(71)
Interest received[6]		3,011
Net cash from investing activities		1,486

[3] *FRS 102 uses the term 'Statement of Cash Flows'. No title for this statement is specified in the Regulations, therefore any title that adequately describes the statement is permitted (FRS 102 paragraph 3.22 permits any titles as long as they are not misleading).*

[4] *FRS 102 paragraph 7.7 permits entities to present cash flows from operating activities using either the indirect method or the direct method. This Education Note illustrates the indirect method, which is the method commonly applied in the UK. The reconciliation of profit or loss to cash from operations can be shown either on the face of the cash flow statement or in the notes. FRS 1 also permits operating cash flows to be presented using either the direct method or the indirect method (FRS 1 paragraph 7).*

[5] *If the indirect method is chosen, FRS 102 paragraph 7.7(a) requires the profit or loss to be adjusted for the effects of non-cash transactions. FRS 102 Section 7 does not specify which measure of profit or loss should be used, but the glossary defines profit or loss as The total of income less expenses, excluding the components of other comprehensive income. As a result, the measure of profit or loss to be used should be profit or loss for the financial year.*

[6] *For simplicity, the interest charge and income in this example are assumed to be the same as the cash flows. FRS 102 paragraph 7.15 gives a choice for interest paid and received to be included in operating cash flows or in financing and investing respectively. Here the choice has been taken to include interest paid in operating cash flows and interest received in investing cash flows.*

[7] *For simplicity, the taxation charge in this example is assumed to be the same as the cash flows.*

[8] *The cash from operations subtotal is discretionary and is used here in part to illustrate the similarity between the two cash flow statements.*

	Note	20X1 CU'000
Cash flows from financing activities		
Issue of ordinary share capital		206
Repayment of borrowings		(149)
Dividends paid[9]		(2,417)
Net cash used in financing activities		(2,360)
Net increase/(decrease) in cash and cash equivalents		3,081
Cash and cash equivalents at beginning of year[10]	A	(1,492)
Cash and cash equivalents at end of year[11]	A	1,589

ILLUSTRATIVE EXTRACTS FROM THE NOTES TO THE FINANCIAL STATEMENTS

FRS 1 Cash flow statements (revised 1996)

Notes to the financial statements

for the year ended 31 December 20X1

A. Reconciliation of operating profit to net cash inflow from operating activities

	20X1 CU'000
Operating profit	6,022
Depreciation	869
Amortisation	50
Profit on disposal of tangible assets	(20)
Increase in stock	(194)
Increase in debtors	(72)
Increase in creditors	234
Net cash inflow from operating activities	6,889

---

[9] *FRS 102 paragraph 7.16 gives a choice for dividends paid to be included either in cash flows arising from operating activities or financing activities.*

[10] *Overdrafts have been included within this opening figure as the overdraft is repayable on demand and forms an integral part of the entity's cash management (see paragraph 7.2 of FRS 102).*

[11] *It is assumed that the current asset investments shown as liquid resources in the first example have a short maturity of three months or less from the date of acquisition, are readily convertible to known amounts of cash and are subject to an insignificant risk of changes in value, and hence in the FRS 102 cash flow statement are included as part of cash and cash equivalents.*

B. Analysis of changes in net debt

	At 1 Jan 20X1 CU'000	Cash flows CU'000	Other changes CU'000	At 31 Dec 20X1 CU'000
Cash in hand, at bank	42	847		889
Overdrafts	(1,784)	1,784		
		2,631		
Debt due within one year	(149)	149	(230)	(230)
Debt due after one year	(1,262)		230	(1,032)
Current asset investments	250	450		700
Total	(2,903)	3,230	-	327

C. Reconciliation of net cash flow to movement in net debt[12]

	20X1 CU'000
Increase in cash in the period	2,631
Cash to repurchase debenture	149
Cash used to increase liquid resources	450
Change in net debt	3,230
Net debt at 1 January	(2,903)
Net funds at 31 December	327

ILLUSTRATIVE EXTRACTS FROM THE NOTES TO THE FINANCIAL STATEMENTS

FRS 102 The Financial Reporting Standard applicable in the UK and Republic of Ireland

Notes to the financial statements

for the year ended 31 December 20X1

A. Components of cash and cash equivalents[13]

	20X1 CU'000	20X2 CU'000
Cash	42	889
Overdraft	(1,784)	
Cash equivalents	250	700
	(1,492)	1,589

The Financial Reporting Lab of the FRC carried out a project on net debt reconciliations. This noted that a majority of investors use a net debt reconciliation or reconciliation of net cash flows to net debt when one is presented. It encouraged companies to consider how this might be relevant to their own circumstances and if so enhance their reporting to meet investor needs.

[12] *This reconciliation shall be given either adjoining the cash flow statement or in a note as it is here (FRS 1 paragraph 33).*

[13] *FRS 102 paragraph 7.20 requires an entity to present the components of cash and cash equivalents. It also requires a reconciliation of cash and cash equivalents as presented in the cash flow statement to the equivalent items presented in the statement of financial position (balance sheet). In addition, paragraph 7.21 of FRS 102 requires the disclosure of cash held by the entity but which is not available for use. It has been assumed that this is not the case in this example.*

OTHER SIMILARITIES AND DIFFERENCES

Exemptions

FRS 1	FRS 102

Subsidiary undertakings where 90 per cent or more of the voting rights are controlled within the group are exempt from having to prepare a cash flow statement, provided that consolidated financial statements in which the subsidiary undertakings are included are publicly available.
 	
(FRS 1 paragraph 5)
	A qualifying entity may take advantage of certain disclosure exemptions (including the preparation of a cash flow statement) provided that:
	(a) Its shareholders have been notified in writing about, and do not object to, the use of the disclosure exemptions...
	(b) It otherwise applies the recognition, measurement and disclosure requirements of this FRS.
	(c) It discloses in the notes to its financial statements:
	  (i) a brief narrative summary of the disclosure exemptions adopted; and
	  (ii) the name of the parent of the group in whose consolidated financial statements its financial statements are consolidated, and from where those financial statements may be obtained.
	
	(FRS 102 paragraph 1.11 and 1.12)
	
	A qualifying entity is a member of a group where the parent of that group prepares publicly available consolidated financial statements which are intended to give a true and fair view (of the assets, liabilities, financial position and profit or loss) and that member is included in the consolidation.
	
	(FRS 102 Glossary)

Under FRS 102, if certain conditions are met and an entity elects to take advantage of the reduced disclosures for subsidiaries (and ultimate parents), it is possible for any subsidiary and any parent company to opt out of preparing a cash flow statement. This is in contrast to FRS 1, where only 90% subsidiaries are exempt from preparing a cash flow statement. This represents a change when applying FRS 102.

Acquisitions and disposals

FRS 1	FRS 102
Individual categories of inflows and outflows should be disclosed separately, where material. (FRS 1 paragraph 7) Cash outflows from acquisitions and disposals include payments to acquire investments in subsidiary undertakings, showing separately any balances of cash and overdrafts acquired. (FRS 1 paragraph 24(a))	An entity shall present separately major classes of gross cash receipts and gross cash payments arising from investing and financing activities. The aggregate cash flows arising from acquisitions and from disposals of subsidiaries or other business units shall be presented separately and classified as investing activities. (FRS 102 paragraph 7.10)

Therefore, FRS 102 does not explicitly require the disclosure of the cash or overdrafts acquired as part of an acquisition. However, if the cash or overdraft acquired was material it may be regarded as a major class of gross cash receipts or payments and separate presentation would be required.

Foreign currency cash flows

FRS 1 / SSAP 20	FRS 102
Where a portion of a reporting entity's business is undertaken by a foreign entity, the cash flows of that entity are to be included in the cash flow statement on the basis used for translating the results of those activities in the profit and loss account of the reporting entity. (FRS 1 paragraph 41) The profit and loss account of a foreign enterprise accounted for under the closing rate/net investment method should be translated at the closing rate or at an average rate for the period. (SSAP 20 paragraph 54)	… to reconcile cash and cash equivalents at the beginning and the end of the period, the effect of exchange rate changes on cash and cash equivalents held or due in a foreign currency must be presented in the statement of cash flows. … The entity shall present the resulting unrealised gain or loss separately from cash flows from operating, investing and financing activities. (FRS 102 paragraph 7.13) An entity shall translate cash flows of a foreign subsidiary at the exchange rate between the entity's functional currency and the foreign currency at the date of the cash flow or at an exchange rate that approximates the actual rate (for example, a weighted average exchange rate for the period). (FRS 102 paragraph 7.12)

In accordance with FRS 1, the value changes recognised by translating cash held or due in a foreign currency at the balance sheet date are not required to be presented separately in the cash flow statement. However, such value changes are not cash flows as defined by FRS 102 and FRS 102 requires the separate presentation of foreign exchange differences relating to cash and cash equivalents. This will be a change when applying FRS 102.

In relation to profit and loss items, FRS 1 allows a choice between translating at the closing rate or an average rate for the period, in contrast to FRS 102 which allows a choice between the rate at the transaction rate or an average rate for the period. This represents a change when applying FRS 102.

SEN 2
Debt instruments – Amortised cost
(updated October 2015)

(October 2015)

Contents

Disclaimer

*This Education Note has been prepared by FRC staff for the convenience of users of FRS 102 **The Financial Reporting Standard applicable in the UK and Republic of Ireland**. It aims to illustrate certain requirements of FRS 102, but should not be relied upon as a definitive statement on the application of the standard. The illustrative material is not a substitute for reading the detailed requirements of FRS 102*

This Staff Education Note was updated on 27 October 2015 as a result of the issuance of Staff Education Note 16 *Financing transactions*. The guidance on financing transactions has been incorporated into Staff Education Note 16 and deleted from this Staff Education Note.

INTRODUCTION

FRS 102 *The Financial Reporting Standard applicable in the UK and Republic of Ireland*, Section 11 *Basic Financial Instruments* requires that basic debt instruments, which include basic types of loans and other receivables and payables, shall be measured at amortised cost using the effective interest method. This Education Note discusses aspects of the application of the amortised cost measurement requirements in FRS 102 and indicates whether entities should expect accounting differences on transition when applying the amortised cost measurement requirements of FRS 102 for the first time. This Education Note is written from the perspective of reporting entities that do not apply FRS 26 (IAS 39) *Financial instruments: recognition and measurement* and assumes that pre-transition accounting policies are based on the requirements of FRS 4 *Capital instruments*.

This Education Note highlights some common key areas for consideration when transitioning to FRS 102, but is not in any way meant to be exhaustive and should therefore not be used as a substitute for a thorough analysis.

AMORTISED COST MEASUREMENT REQUIREMENTS IN FRS 102

Paragraphs 11.15 to 11.20 of FRS 102 provide guidance on how to calculate amortised cost using the effective interest method. Paragraphs 11.15 and 11.16 are reproduced below:

> *11.15 The amortised cost of a financial asset or financial liability at each **reporting date** is the net of the following amounts:*
>
> (a) *the amount at which the financial asset or financial liability is measured at initial recognition;*
> (b) *minus any repayments of the principal;*
> (c) *plus or minus the cumulative amortisation using the effective interest method of any difference between the amount at initial recognition and the maturity amount;*
> (d) *minus, in the case of a financial asset, any reduction (directly or through the use of an allowance account) for impairment or uncollectability.*
>
> *Financial assets and financial liabilities that have no stated interest rate (and do not constitute a financing transaction) and are classified as payable or receivable within one year are initially measured at an undiscounted amount in accordance with paragraph 11.14(a). Therefore, (c) above does not apply to them.*
>
> *11.16 The effective interest method is a method of calculating the amortised cost of a financial asset or a financial liability (or a group of financial assets or financial liabilities) and of allocating the interest income or interest expense over the relevant period. The **effective interest rate** is the rate that exactly discounts estimated future cash payments or receipts through the expected life of the financial instrument or, when appropriate, a shorter period, to the **carrying amount** of the financial asset or financial liability. The effective interest rate is determined on the basis of the carrying amount of the financial asset or liability at initial recognition. Under the effective interest method:*
>
> (a) *the amortised cost of a financial asset (liability) is the present value of future cash receipts (payments) discounted at the effective interest rate; and*
> (b) *the interest expense (income) in a period equals the carrying amount of the financial liability (asset) at the beginning of a period multiplied by the effective interest rate for the period.*

Effective interest method

In accordance with paragraph 11.14(a) of FRS 102 debt instruments that meet the conditions of paragraphs 11.8(b) and 11.9 shall, following initial recognition, be measured at amortised cost using the effective interest method. Debt instruments include basic types of financial assets and liabilities, eg trade receivables and payables and variable or fixed rate loans. Please note that paragraph 11.14(b) also provides an alternative accounting treatment and entities may elect to measure their debt instruments at fair value which is not discussed further in this document.

Paragraphs 11.15 and 11.16 of FRS 102 (reproduced above) set out the basic principles of an amortised cost calculation and describe how the effective interest method should be applied. The effective interest rate of a debt instrument may equal its coupon rate, but, often an entity will also incur other costs or receive other income associated with the instrument, eg finance charges or premiums and discounts which affect the effective interest rate. The effective interest rate includes, besides interest, other related finance fees and charges (refer also to paragraph 11.18 of FRS 102). Please also refer to the example of an amortisation cost calculation in Section 11 of FRS 102.

It is not expected that accounting differences will arise in respect of the determination of the effective interest rate when transitioning to FRS 102, since similar principles apply under FRS 4 *Capital Instruments*, provided the interest rate of the loan is a market rate of interest (see Staff Education Note 16 *Financing transactions* for the measurement requirements applying to loans with a below market rate of interest)).

Amortisation period

In order to calculate the effective interest rate, an entity has to determine the expected life of the debt instrument. A shorter period than the expected life should be used under certain circumstances. This is typically the case when certain fees, finance charges or other transaction costs relate to a period shorter than the expected life of the debt instrument (paragraphs 11.16 and 11.18 of FRS 102).

On transition, entities should assess whether amortisation periods used to calculate the effective interest rate are in accordance with the requirements of FRS 102. Generally no accounting difference is expected, however, in some specific situations, eg debts with early redemption options differences may arise.

MEASUREMENT OF COMMON DEBT INSTRUMENTS

Overdraft repayable on demand

If a creditor has the right to demand repayment at any time, the borrower measures the liability at the undiscounted amount of cash repayable.

A standard bank overdraft repayable on demand would be measured at the principal amount of the overdraft.

Current trade debtors (receivables) and trade creditors (payables)

Under FRS 102, trade receivables (debtors) and trade payables (creditors) are recognised at the transaction price (unless the arrangement is a financing transaction as described in paragraph 11.13 of FRS 102, see Staff Education Note 16 for more detail), which in most cases is the invoiced amount (refer to the examples in paragraph 11.13 of FRS 102). In accordance with paragraph 11.14(a) of FRS 102 receivables and payables due within one year continue to be measured after their initial recognition at the undiscounted amount of cash or other consideration expected to be paid or received. Therefore in most situations short term receivables and payables are measured at their invoiced amount until they are settled or otherwise extinguished.

Trade receivables are subject to impairment and must not be stated at a value higher than their recoverable amount. More information on the accounting for impairment of trade receivables can be found in Staff Education Note 3 *Impairment of trade debtors*.

It is not expected that accounting differences will arise in respect of current trade receivables and trade payables when transitioning to FRS 102.

Loans bearing a market rate of interest

Paragraph 11.13 of FRS 102 requires that all financial assets and financial liabilities are initially recorded at the transaction price (unless it is a financing transaction as described in paragraph 11.13 of FRS 102, see Staff Education Note 16 for more detail). Loans bearing a market rate of interest will therefore be recognised at the initial value exchanged (ie the amount of the cash lent or received) including transaction costs.

Loans that meet the conditions of a basic debt instrument set out in paragraphs 11.8(b) and 11.9 of FRS 102 are measured at amortised cost after initial recognition. Provided no transaction costs have been incurred or premiums/discounts have been paid/received, for loans bearing a market rate of interest, the effective interest rate is equal to the market rate of interest at the date of initial recognition.

It is not expected that accounting differences will arise in respect of loans bearing a market rate of interest when transitioning to FRS 102.

FINANCING TRANSACTIONS

The term financing transaction is used in FRS 102 to specifically refer to transactions with deferred payments or repayments, for which there is no explicit interest rate or the interest charged is not at a market rate. Examples of such transactions include:

- the sale of goods or services, if payment is deferred beyond normal business terms or is financed at a rate of interest that is not a market rate (paragraph 11.13 of FRS 102);
- below market rate and interest-free loans between group entities; and
- below market rate and interest-free loans to or from directors.

More detailed guidance on financing transactions can be found in Staff Education Note 16.

SEN 3
Impairment of trade debtors

Contents

Disclaimer

This Education Note has been prepared by FRC staff for the convenience of users of FRS 102 The Financial Reporting Standard applicable in the UK and Republic of Ireland. It aims to illustrate certain requirements of FRS 102, but should not be relied upon as a definitive statement on the application of the standard. The illustrative material is not a substitute for reading the detailed requirements of FRS 102.

INTRODUCTION

This Staff Education Note provides information on the requirements for the impairment of financial assets measured at cost or amortised cost, specifically on the impairment of trade debtors, and is written for entities that do not currently apply FRS 26 (IAS 39) *Financial instruments: recognition and measurement.*

Both current UK accounting standards and FRS 102 *The Financial Reporting Standard applicable in the UK and Republic of Ireland* require financial assets to be carried at the lower of their carrying amount or recoverable amount. A financial asset is therefore impaired when there is a reduction in its recoverable amount below its carrying amount. However there are differences in the level of guidance provided for identifying and measuring impairments.

Please note that the FRC intends to issue a supplementary exposure draft as the IASB finalises the requirements of IFRS 9 *Financial Instruments*. The supplementary exposure draft will propose changes to Setion 11 *Basic Financial Instruments* and Section 12 *Other Financial Instruments Issues*. Therefore, paragraphs 11.21 to 11.24 of FRS 102 referred to below may be subject to change.

This Staff Education Note is written to highlight key areas of consideration when transitioning to FRS 102 and is not designed to be exhaustive.

IMPAIRMENT REQUIREMENTS OF FINANCIAL ASSETS MEASURED AT COST OR AMORTISED COST

Current UK accounting standards

There is a general requirement in company law that current assets must not be stated at more than their net realisable value. For those entities not applying FRS 26 there is little detail in current UK accounting standards on impairment of current financial assets (as opposed to fixed assets and goodwill, which are covered by FRS 11 *Impairment of fixed assets and goodwill*).

FRS 102

FRS 102 is more prescriptive, including an explicit requirement for there to be objective evidence of an impairment, which may lead to some changes in practice.

For most entities that are not financial institutions, the main financial assets that will be subject to possible impairment are trade debtors (receivables). Most entities are already likely to be making a 'bad debt provision', but they will need to ensure that their processes are consistent with the requirements of FRS 102. Application of FRS 102 will not necessarily result in a significant change in the carrying amount of trade debtors.

Extract from FRS 102

> 11.21   At the end of each reporting period, an entity shall assess whether there is objective evidence of impairment of any financial assets that are measured at cost or amortised cost. If there is objective evidence of impairment, the entity shall recognise an **impairment loss** in profit or loss immediately.

11.22 Objective evidence that a financial asset or group of assets is impaired includes observable data that come to the attention of the holder of the asset about the following loss events:

(a)   *significant financial difficulty of the issuer or obligor;*

(b)   *a breach of contract, such as a default or delinquency in interest or principal payments;*

(c)   *the creditor, for economic or legal reasons relating to the debtor's financial difficulty, granting to the debtor a concession that the creditor would not otherwise consider;*

(d)   *it has become **probable** that the debtor will enter bankruptcy or other financial reorganisation; and*

(e)   *observable data indicating that there has been a measurable decrease in the estimated future cash flows from a group of financial assets since the initial recognition of those assets, even though the decrease cannot yet be identified with the individual financial assets in the group, such as adverse national or local economic conditions or adverse changes in industry conditions.*

11.23 Other factors may also be evidence of impairment, including significant changes with an adverse effect that have taken place in the technological, market, economic or legal environment in which the issuer operates.

11.24 An entity shall assess the following financial assets individually for impairment:

(a)   *all equity instruments regardless of significance; and*

(b)   *other financial assets that are individually significant.*

*An entity shall assess other financial assets for impairment either individually or grouped on the basis of similar **credit risk** characteristics.*

IMPAIRMENT OF TRADE DEBTORS

Objective evidence

Under FRS 102, to recognise an impairment loss there must be objective evidence that the loss has occurred (ie there will be an impact on the expected future cash flows associated with the debtor), and that this is a result of one or more past events. Losses expected to arise as a result of future events may not be recognised. Paragraph 11.22 sets out examples of observable data that might be considered as objective evidence that a loss has occurred (eg the death of a debtor).

In the absence of any objective evidence or observable data indicating that a loss has occurred, there is no basis for recognising an impairment, or bad debt provision.

Individual financial assets

An entity needs to assess financial assets for impairment individually in the following circumstances:

(a)   Where the entity does not routinely provide credit, either at all, or to certain types of debtor, the entity should consider whether those assets should be part of a group of assets with similar credit characteristics, and if not they must be assessed for impairment individually;

(b)   Where the financial asset is individually significant; or

(c)   Where there is specific information about the credit risk of that financial asset (regardless of whether or not it is part of a group of financial assets with similar credit characteristics).

A group of financial assets

Paragraph 11.22(e) states that where observable data indicates that there has been a measureable decrease in the estimated future cash flows from a group of financial assets, even though the decrease cannot yet be identified on an individual asset basis, this is objective evidence that an impairment has occurred.

To apply this in practice, it may be necessary to identify groups of debtors within the overall portfolio that have similar credit risk characteristics (eg trade debtors with the same geographical location or industry sector or demographic) and then estimate the loss that is expected from that group. It is reasonable to make use of historical loss experience as a basis for this estimate, but it should be adjusted to:

(a)   reflect the effect of current conditions that did not affect the period on which the historical loss experience is based; and

(b)   remove the effects of conditions in the historical period that do not exist currently.

It may not be sufficient to only use days past due to calculate bad debt provisions (ie impairment losses on trade debtors). It is likely that the debtors will need to be stratified by more than just days past due, in order to reflect other credit risk characteristics, and the formula needs to reflect actual experience of delinquency, which is expected to continue. Such formulae would need to be kept under active review, and reflect changes in credit risk characteristics, such as a change in the customer base, not just historical loss experience.

Example

A furniture retailer which has a small chain of stores, offers extended credit terms for purchases over £2,000. In the vicinity of one store, a significant local employer announces redundancies amounting to approximately 20% of its staff. The manager of this store estimates that 40% of its debtors are currently employed by this employer, and therefore it might be expected that 8% (20% of 40%) of the debtors may lose their jobs.

Using observable data about the likely extent of default to measure the amount of the impairment (for example, historical evidence from a previous period of higher unemployment), the furniture retailer should estimate and recognise an impairment loss for the group of financial assets relating to the people employed by this particular local employer.

If there is observable data that job losses at this employer have a knock-on effect on the local economy as a whole, the impact should be considered separately. The furniture retailer should not apply this impairment to all debtors as they do not share the same credit risk characteristics of this sub-group.

SEN 4
Investment properties

Contents

Disclaimer

This Education Note has been prepared by FRC staff for the convenience of users of FRS 102 The Financial Reporting Standard applicable in the UK and Republic of Ireland. It aims to illustrate certain requirements of FRS 102, but should not be relied upon as a definitive statement on the application of the standard. The illustrative material is not a substitute for reading the detailed requirements of FRS 102.

INTRODUCTION

This Staff Education Note compares the accounting treatment for investment properties under current UK accounting standards (SSAP 19 *Accounting for Investment Properties*) and Section 16 *Investment Properties* of FRS 102 *The Financial Reporting Standard applicable in the UK and Republic of Ireland*.

This Staff Education Note is written to highlight key areas of consideration when transitioning to FRS 102 and is not designed to be exhaustive.

DEFINITION OF INVESTMENT PROPERTY

SSAP 19	FRS 102
An interest in land and/or buildings: (a) in respect of which construction work and development have been completed; and (b) which is held for its investment potential, any rental being negotiated at arm's length. (SSAP 19 paragraph 7) Exceptions to the definition: (a) a property which is owned and occupied by a company for its own purposes; and (b) a property let to and occupied by another group company is not an investment property for the purposes of its own accounts or the group accounts. (SSAP 19 paragraph 8)	Property (land or a building, or part of a building, or both) held by the owner or by the lessee under a finance lease to earn rentals or for capital appreciation or both, rather than for: (a) use in the production or supply of goods or services or for administrative purposes; or (b) sale in the ordinary course of business. (FRS 102 paragraph 16.2) A property interest that is held by a lessee under an operating lease may be classified and accounted for as investment property. (FRS 102 paragraph 16.3) Property that has a mixed use will be separated into investment property and property, plant and equipment. (FRS 102 paragraph 16.4)

FRS 102 does not exclude from investment properties those properties that are let to and occupied by group companies, which would be recognised as investment properties in individual financial statements of the lessor. In the group accounts such properties would be part of property, plant and equipment.

In certain circumstances FRS 102 permits a property held under an operating lease to be treated as an investment property. SSAP 19 is not explicit on this point, therefore this may constitute a change when applying FRS 102.

There is no requirement to separate mixed-use properties under SSAP 19, although this may occur in practice, in which case no change would be required on application of FRS 102.

INITIAL RECOGNITION

SSAP 19	FRS 102
Included at open market value. (SSAP 19 paragraph 11)	Included at cost of purchased investment property and directly attributable expenditure. (FRS 102 paragraph 16.5)

Not considered to be significantly different.

SUBSEQUENT MEASUREMENT

Recognition of gains and losses[1]

SSAP 19	FRS 102
Included at open market value. Changes in market value are taken to the statement of total recognised gains and losses (being movements on an investment property revaluation reserve), unless a deficit (or its reversal) on an individual investment property is expected to be permanent, in which case it should be charged (or credited) in the profit and loss account. (SSAP 19 paragraph 13)	Where fair value can be measured reliably without undue cost or effort the property shall be measured at fair value. Changes in fair value are recognised in profit or loss. (FRS 102 paragraph 16.7) All other investment property is accounted for as property, plant and equipment using the cost model in accordance with Section 17 *Property, plant and equipment*. (FRS 102 paragraph 16.1)

Application is unlikely to change as fair values can normally be obtained without undue cost or effort[2]. However, there is a significant presentational change required (see example below).

Example

Facts

On 1 January 20X1, the carrying amount of an entity's investment property was £1.5m. It obtains an updated valuation of £1.6m on 31 December 20X1.

SSAP 19

Under SSAP 19, the gain of £0.1m would be recognised as follows:

Dr Investment property   £0.1m

Cr Investment property revaluation reserve (STRGL)   £0.1m

---

[1] *Reference should be made to Section 29 Income Tax which sets out the accounting treatment in relation to deferred tax on investment properties.*

[2] *See paragraph 118 of the Accounting Council's Advice to the FRC in FRS 102 (and paragraphs 2.13 and 2.14 of FRS 102) for further information on 'undue cost and effort'.*

The revaluation is in accordance with the alternative accounting rules of company law, which require amounts to be transferred to a revaluation reserve.

FRS 102

Under FRS 102, the gain of £0.1m would be recognised as follows:

Dr: Investment property	£0.1m
Cr: Profit and loss	£0.1m

The revaluation is in accordance with the fair value accounting rules[3].

The profit on revaluation of investment property will not be a realised profit available for distribution. An entity may choose to transfer such gains and losses to a non-distributable reserve, but there is nothing in the law to require this.

The presentation of capital and reserves will be different on application of FRS 102 (unless entities choose to transfer gains and losses on remeasurement of investment property to a separate reserve, in which case the balance sheet may appear unchanged). Amounts that would previously have been shown in a revaluation reserve will be part of the accumulated profit and loss account.

An entity choosing not to show a separate revaluation reserve may wish to make disclosure regarding distributable and non-distributable profits. As set out in the ICAEW Technical Release 02/10 *Guidance On The Determination Of Realised Profits And Losses In The Context Of Distributions Under The Companies Act 2006*, the revaluation of an investment property is not considered realised as the fair value of the investment property is not readily convertible to cash.

Transfers to and from investment properties

SSAP 19	FRS 102
Not specifically addressed.	Provides that transfers to, or from, investment property shall only occur when the property first meets, or ceases to meet, the definition of investment property.
	(FRS 102 paragraph 16.9)
	A transfer is also made where a reliable measure of fair value is no longer available without undue cost or effort for an item of investment property measured using the fair value model.
	(FRS 102 paragraph 16.8)

Application is unlikely to change as fair values can normally be obtained without undue cost or effort.

---

[3] *See paragraph 39 of the Large and Medium-Sized Companies and Groups (Accounts and Reports) Regulations 2008.*

SEN 5
Property, plant and equipment

Contents

Disclaimer

This Education Note has been prepared by FRC staff for the convenience of users of FRS 102 The Financial Reporting Standard applicable in the UK and Republic of Ireland. It aims to illustrate certain requirements of FRS 102, but should not be relied upon as a definitive statement on the application of the standard. The illustrative material is not a substitute for reading the detailed requirements of FRS 102.

INTRODUCTION

This Staff Education Note provides a comparison of the accounting treatment for tangible fixed assets under current UK accounting standards (including FRS 15 *Tangible Fixed Assets* and FRS 5 *Reporting the substance of transactions*) and Section 17 *Property, Plant and Equipment* of FRS 102 *The Financial Reporting Standard applicable in the UK and Republic of Ireland*.

This Staff Education Note is written to highlight key areas of general application for consideration when transitioning to FRS 102 and is not designed to be exhaustive. In practice, for the majority of entities there are no significant differences in the accounting treatment of tangible fixed assets.

RECOGNITION CRITERIA FOR TANGIBLE FIXED ASSETS

FRS 15 / FRS 5	FRS 102
Does not specifically address recognition criteria for tangible assets. However, FRS 5 *Reporting the substance of transactions* sets out the general criteria that apply to the recognition of assets which states that an item that meets the definition of an asset should be recognised in the balance sheet if: (a) there is sufficient evidence of the existence of the item (including, where appropriate, evidence that a future inflow or outflow of benefit will occur); and (b) the item can be measured at a monetary amount with sufficient reliability. (FRS 5 paragraph 20)	States an entity shall apply the recognition criteria in determining whether to recognise an item of property, plant and equipment. Consequently, an entity recognises an item of property, plant and equipment when it is probable that future economic benefits associated with the item will flow to the entity, and the costs of the item can be measured reliably. (FRS 102 paragraphs 17.4 and 2.27)

Therefore, FRS 102 explicitly makes the link between at item of property, plant and equipment and the need for future economic benefits to flow to the entity, but this is unlikely to have much impact in practice.

INITIAL MEASUREMENT

Cost

FRS 15	FRS 102
Requires a tangible fixed asset to be measured initially at cost. Cost includes those costs that are directly attributable to bringing the asset into working condition for its intended use. (FRS 15 paragraphs 6) Examples of directly attributable costs include: ● acquisition costs; ● the cost of site preparation and clearance; ● initial delivery and handling costs; ● installation costs; ● professional fees; ● the estimated cost of dismantling and removing the asset and restoring the site, to the extent that it is recognised as a provision. (FRS 15 paragraph 10) If the entity chooses an accounting policy of capitalising finance costs, the cost of the construction of a tangible fixed asset may include finance costs. (FRS 15 paragraph 19)	The cost of an item of property, plant and equipment comprises the following: (a) its purchase price; (b) any costs directly attributable to bringing the asset to the location and condition necessary for it to be capable of operating in the manner intended by management including site preparation, initial delivery and handling, installation and assembly, and testing of functionality; (c) the initial estimate of the cost of dismantling and removing the item and restoring the site on which it is located, the obligation for which an entity incurs either when the item is acquired or as a consequence of having used the item during a particular period for purposes other than to produce inventories during that period; and (d) any borrowing costs capitalised. (FRS 102 paragraph 17.10)

In practice there is no difference in the cost that would be capitalised under FRS 15 and FRS 102.

SUBSEQUENT MEASUREMENT

Depreciation and separate components

FRS 15	FRS 102
Requires the depreciable amount of the tangible asset to be allocated on a systematic basis over its useful economic life. (FRS 15 paragraph 77)	Requires an entity to allocate the depreciable amount of an asset on a systematic basis over its useful life. (FRS 102 paragraph 17.18)

FRS 15	FRS 102
Notes that the fundamental objective of depreciation is to reflect in operating profit the cost of use of the tangible fixed assets in the period. (FRS 15 paragraph 78) Provides that where the tangible fixed asset comprises two or more major components with substantially different useful economic lives, each component should be accounted for separately for depreciation purposes and depreciated over its individual useful economic life. (FRS 15 paragraph 83)	Requires that if the major components of an item of property, plant and equipment have significantly different patterns of consumption of economic benefits, an entity shall allocate the initial cost of the asset to its major components and depreciate each such component separately over its useful life. Other assets shall be depreciated over their useful lives as a single asset. (FRS 102 paragraph 17.16)

Both standards require similar application of a components approach in calculating depreciation; both are based on the consumption of the asset.

Example

Depreciation of major components

On 1 January 20X1, Co A acquired an item of machinery for CU500,000. The machine is made up of two components of equal value; the computer processing unit and the mechanical parts. Management estimate that the computer processing unit has a useful life of 5 years and the mechanical parts have a useful life of 10 years. Management also estimates that the straight-line method best reflects the pattern in which the entity expects to consume the future economic benefits of all components of the machine.

Initially the cost of the machine should be allocated between the two component parts, ie CU250,000 each. Subsequently each component should be depreciated over its respective useful life.

Residual value

FRS 15	FRS 102
Where the residual value is material it should be reviewed at the end of each reporting period to take account of reasonably expected technological changes based on prices prevailing at the date of acquisition (or revaluation). (FRS 15 paragraph 95)	Factors such as a change in how an asset is used, significant unexpected wear and tear, technological advancement, and changes in market prices may indicate that the residual value or useful life of an asset has changed since the most recent annual reporting date. If such indicators are present, an entity shall review its previous estimates and, if current expectations differ, amend the residual value, depreciation method or useful life. (FRS 102 paragraph 17.19) Residual value is defined as the estimated amount that an entity would currently obtain from disposal of an asset, after deducting the estimated costs of disposal, if the asset were already of the age and in the condition expected at the end of its useful life. (FRS 102 Glossary)

There is a difference in accounting treatment between current UK accounting standards and FRS 102 in the way that residual value is determined. FRS 102 defines residual value as the estimated amount that would currently be obtained ie it takes into account future price changes, whereas FRS 15 does not.

Revaluations

FRS 15	FRS 102
Permits tangible fixed assets to be revalued only where an entity adopts a policy of revaluation. That policy must be applied to all assets within individual classes of tangible fixed assets, but not necessarily to all classes of tangible fixed assets. (FRS 15 paragraph 42)	After initial recognition, an entity shall measure all items of property, plant and equipment after initial recognition using the cost model or the revaluation model. Where the revaluation model is selected, this shall be applied to all items of property, plant and equipment in the same class.

FRS 15	FRS 102
Where a tangible fixed asset is subject to a policy of revaluation its carrying amount should be its current value as at the balance sheet date. This will be met by a full valuation at least every five years and an interim valuation in year 3. Interim valuations in years 1, 2 and 4 should be carried out where it is likely that there is material change in value. (FRS 15 paragraphs 43 and 45)	(FRS 102 paragraph 17.15) Provides that under the revaluation model an item of property plant and equipment whose fair value can be measured reliably shall be carried at revalued amount, being its fair value at the date of revaluation less any subsequent accumulated depreciation and subsequent accumulated impairment losses. Revaluations shall be made with sufficiently regularity to ensure that the carrying amount does not differ materially from that which would be determined using fair value at the end of the reporting period. (FRS 102 paragraph 17.15B)

In both cases an option to revalue items of property, plant and equipment is available, however, FRS 15 is more prescriptive with regards to the regularity of valuations (ie full valuations every 5 years and interim valuations every 3 years) however FRS 102 still expects revaluations to be performed with sufficient regularity such that the carrying amount does not differ materially from the fair value at the balance sheet date.

There is also a difference in valuation basis; FRS 15 requires entities to revalue non-specialised properties on the basis of existing use value whereas FRS 102 requires entities to revalue to fair value (which is equivalent to open market value).

Subsequent expenditure

FRS 15	FRS 102
Subsequent expenditure should be capitalised in three circumstances: (a) where the subsequent expenditure provides an enhancement of the economic benefits of the tangible fixed asset in excess of the previously assessed standard of performance. (b) where a component of the tangible fixed asset that has been treated separately for depreciation purposes and depreciated over its individual useful economic life, is replaced or restored.	The entity shall recognise the cost of an item of property, plant and equipment as an asset if, and only if: (a) it is probable that future economic benefits associated with the item will flow to the entity; and (b) the cost of the item can be measured reliably. (FRS 102 paragraph 17.4) Parts of some items of property, plant and equipment may require replacement at regular intervals (eg the roof of a building). An entity shall add to the carrying amount of an item of property, plant and equipment the cost of replacing part of such an item when that cost is incurred if the replacement part is expected to provide incremental future benefits to the entity. (FRS 102 paragraph 17.6)

FRS 15	FRS 102
(c) where the subsequent expenditure relates to a major inspection or overhaul of a tangible fixed asset that restores the economic benefits of the asset that have been consumed by the entity and have already been reflected in depreciation. (FRS 15 paragraph 36)	When each major inspection is performed, its cost is recognised in the carrying amount of the item of property, plant and equipment as a replacement if the recognition criteria are satisfied. Any remaining carrying amount of the cost of the previous major inspection (as distinct from physical parts) is derecognised. This is done regardless of whether the cost of the previous major inspection was identified in the transaction in which the item was acquired or constructed. If necessary, the estimated cost of a future similar inspection may be used as an indication of what the cost of the existing inspection component was when the item was acquired or constructed. (FRS 102 paragraph 17.7)

FRS 102 does not have an equivalent to paragraph 36(a) in FRS 15. However, in circumstances where subsequent expenditure has been incurred, the basic recognition criteria set out in paragraph 17.4 are still applicable. Therefore, in practice there is unlikely to be any change in accounting treatment as an assessment of the likelihood of future economic benefits occurring will still have to be made before an asset can be recognised.

SEN 6
Leases

Contents

Disclaimer

This Education Note has been prepared by FRC staff for the convenience of users of FRS 102 The Financial Reporting Standard applicable in the UK and Republic of Ireland. *It aims to illustrate certain requirements of FRS 102, but should not be relied upon as a definitive statement on the application of the standard. The illustrative material is not a substitute for reading the detailed requirements of FRS 102.*

INTRODUCTION

This Staff Education Note compares the accounting treatment for leases under current UK accounting standards (including SSAP 21 *Accounting for leases and hire purchase contracts*, *FRS 5 Reporting the substance of transactions* and UITF abstract 28 *Operating lease incentives*) and Section 20 *Leases* of FRS 102 *The Financial Reporting Standard applicable in the UK and Republic of Ireland*.

While the two frameworks are conceptually similar, there are some application differences that are highlighted in this Staff Education Note:

(a) Classification of leases between operating and finance
(b) Determination of whether an arrangement contains a lease
(c) Accounting for finance leases
(d) Accounting for operating leases

This Staff Education Note is written to highlight key areas of consideration when transitioning to FRS 102 and is not designed to be exhaustive.

CLASSIFICATION OF LEASES

Both SSAP 21 and FRS 102 require an entity to classify each of its leases as either a finance lease or an operating lease.

SSAP 21	FRS 102
A finance lease is defined as one that transfers substantially all the risks and rewards of ownership of an asset to the lessee.	Takes a risks and rewards approach to lease classification and has an almost identical definition for a finance lease.
There is a rebuttable presumption that if, at inception, the present value of the minimum lease payments amounts to 90% or more of the fair value of the leased asset, the lease is a finance lease. To rebut the presumption, preparers might look to other indications about risks and rewards, though this rebuttal is expected only to happen in exceptional circumstances. (SSAP 21 paragraphs 15 and 16)	Gives a list of situations which individually or in combination would normally lead to a lease being classified as a finance lease: (a) the lease transfers ownership of the asset to the lessee by the end of the lease term. (b) the lessee has the option to purchase the asset at a price that is expected to be sufficiently lower than the fair value at the date the option becomes exercisable for it to be reasonably certain, at the inception of the lease, that the option will be exercised. (c) the lease term is for the major part of the economic life of the asset even if title is not transferred. (d) at the inception of the lease the present value of the minimum lease payments amounts to at least substantially all of the fair value of the leased asset. (e) the leased assets are of such a specialised nature that only the lessee can use them without major modifications. (FRS 102 paragraph 20.5)

SSAP 21	FRS 102
	Gives a list of secondary considerations that might also lead to finance lease classification.
	(FRS 102 paragraph 20.6)
	However there is no direct equivalent to the 'bright line' 90% test under SSAP 21.

Both standards aim to identify those situations where substantially all the risks and rewards of ownership of an asset are held by a lessee, but use different specific tests or indicators. Therefore, there are unlikely to be many cases where the lease classification will change as a result of applying of FRS 102.

Example 1 Lease classification – Specialised assets

This example is designed to illustrate the different elements of the lease classification decision-making process and may not be representative of a typical lease seen in practice.

Facts

Company A leases a bespoke piece of machinery from Company B. The machinery was constructed for use in Company A's specialist business, to its specification and is used in producing an item for which Company A holds the patent, so a third party would not legally be able to use the machinery without significant alteration. The lease is for a period of seven years and the expected useful life of the machinery is at least 10 years. The present value of the minimum future lease payments is 70% of the asset's fair value at inception.

SSAP 21

The present value of the minimum lease payments is only 70% of the fair value of the asset at the inception of the lease, therefore, it may be classified as an operating lease[1].

FRS 102

Under FRS 102, the lease would pass the condition set out in paragraph 20.5(e) and so would be classified as a finance lease.

---

[1] *SSAP 21 does not rely exclusively on the '90% test'. Paragraph 16 of SSAP 21 notes 'the presumption that a lease which fails to meet the conditions in paragraph 15 (ie including the '90% test') is not a finance lease may in exceptional circumstances be rebutted'. In practice (outside this stylised example) the economics of this example are questionable and it is likely that Company A would need to consider other factors, which may result in classification as a finance lease. In which case there would be no difference in lease classification arising from application of FRS 102.*

DETERMINING WHETHER AN ARRANGEMENT CONTAINS A LEASE

SSAP 21 / FRS 5	FRS 102
SSAP 21 applies only to leases ie to arrangements that meet the definition of 'a contract between a lessor and lessee for the hire of a specific asset'. Other contracts may have some features in common with leases, but are outside the scope of SSAP 21. FRS 5 *Reporting the substance of transactions* Application Note F *Private Finance Initiative and Similar Contracts* may apply to these contracts – it is relevant to contracts for services, where an asset is necessary to perform the contracted services.	Some arrangements do not take the legal form of a lease but convey rights to use assets in return for payments. Examples of arrangements in which one entity (the supplier) may convey a right to use an asset to another entity (the purchaser), often together with related services, may include outsourcing arrangements, telecommunication contracts that provide rights to capacity and take-or-pay contracts. (FRS 102 paragraph 20.3) Determining whether an arrangement is, or contains, a lease shall be based on the substance of the arrangement and requires an assessment of whether: (a) fulfilment of the arrangement is dependent on the use of a specific asset or assets. Although a specific asset may be explicitly identified in an arrangement, it is not the subject of a lease if fulfilment of the arrangement is not dependent on the use of the specified asset. An asset is implicitly specified if, for example, the supplier owns or leases only one asset with which to fulfil the obligation and it is not economically feasible or practicable for the supplier to perform its obligation through the use of alternative assets; and (b) the arrangement conveys a right to use the asset. This will be the case where the arrangement conveys to the purchaser the right to control the use of the underlying asset. (FRS 102 paragraph 20.3A)

Example 2 Arrangement that contains a lease

Facts

Company C enters into a contract to provide electricity to Company D, and for this purpose Company C has to construct a new substation, as Company D is based on a remote island. Realistically, the only way to get the required electricity to Company D is by use of this substation, and no one else does or can benefit from its use.

FRS 5

This arrangement would not be in the scope of SSAP 21 as there is no lease over a specified asset in place; it is a contract to provide a service. The arrangement would be considered by applying FRS 5, and in particular Application Note F, and weighing up a number of risks and their economic effects.

FRS 102

Under FRS 102, the arrangement should be analysed to determine whether it conveys the right for Company D to use the substation in return for payments. In this case, Company D has obtained the right to use the substation because it has been built only to meet its needs. It should therefore be accounted for as a lease. Depending on the details of the arrangement, both parties would account for the arrangement either as an operating lease (with Company C showing income and Company D showing expense relating to the use of the substation, distinct from that for the supply of electricity) or as a finance lease, so the substation would be shown as an asset on Company D's books rather than Company C's. If it is a finance lease, Company C would recognise a receivable equal to the net investment in the lease.

Current UK accounting standards focus on the likelihood of their being variations in the profits or losses (or cash flows) arising from the use of the property subject to the arrangement and FRS 102 focuses on whether there is a right to use the specific asset. However, in considering whether an entity has a right to use an asset, it is likely entities will consider factors such as the variability of the price to be paid. In both cases the intended result is the recognition of the substance of the arrangement and UITF Information Sheet 86 *Status of Adoption into UK GAAP of IFRIC Interpretations* (recently updated as http://www.frc.org.uk/Our-Work/Publications/Accounting-and-Reporting-Policy/Status-of-Adoption-into-UK-GAAP-of-IFRIC-Interpret.aspx) noted that IFRIC 4 (from which these requirements of FRS 102 were developed) is already addressed in UK GAAP.

However, entities with service contracts (such as outsourcing arrangements, telecommunication contracts that provide rights to capacity, and take-or-pay contracts) should review whether they have a right to use certain assets when applying FRS 102 for the first time.

Example 3 Outsourcing arrangement

Facts

Company E has outsourced elements of its finance function, which are now provided by Company F. Company F uses a standard finance system for all its clients (Company F is not reliant on business from Company E), and provides data in a way which interfaces with the systems retained by Company E.

FRS 5

Although further details of the arrangement would need to be considered, it is likely that Company E would account for this as an operating cost. Company F would not show a lease, but would account for any fixed assets.

FRS 102

This outsourcing arrangement appears to be a contact for services that does not transfer the right to use the assets (Company F's finance system) from Company F to Company E, for example because Company F uses it to provide services to a large number of clients. A contract for services would be accounted for as an operating cost.

For outsourcing arrangements that are contracts for services (ie they do not confer a right to use assets) there is unlikely to be any change in accounting when applying FRS 102 for the first time.

ACCOUNTING FOR FINANCE LEASES

Initial recognition

SSAP 21	FRS 102
At the inception of the lease the sum to be recorded as both an asset and a liability should be the present value of the minimum lease payments, derived by discounting them at the interest rate implicit in the lease.	At the commencement of the lease term, a lessee shall recognise its rights of use and obligations under finance leases as assets and liabilities ... at amounts equal to the fair value of the leased asset or, if lower, the present value of the minimum lease payments, determined at the inception of the lease.
(SSAP 21 paragraph 32)	(FRS 102 paragraph 20.9)
In practice the fair value of the asset will often be a sufficiently close approximation to the present value of the minimum lease payments and may in these circumstances be substituted for it.	The present value of the minimum lease payments should be calculated using the interest rate implicit in the lease. If this cannot be determined, the lessee's incremental borrowing rate shall be used.
(SSAP 21 paragraph 33)	(FRS 102 paragraph 20.10)
Inception of a lease	***Commencement of the lease term***
The earlier of the time the asset is brought into use and the date from which rentals first accrue. (SSAP 21 paragraph 29)	The commencement of the lease term is the date from which the lessee is entitled to exercise its right to use the leased asset. It is the date of initial recognition of the lease (ie the recognition of the assets, liabilities, income or expenses resulting from the lease, as appropriate).
	The inception of the lease is the earlier of the date of the lease agreement and the date of commitment by the parties to the principal provisions of the lease.
	(FRS 102 Glossary)
	Lease classification is made at the inception of the lease.
	(FRS 102 paragraph 20.8)

FRS 102 requires finance leases to be recognised at amounts equal to the fair value of the leased asset, or if lower, the present value of the minimum lease payments. In contrast, SSAP 21 requires measurement at the present value of the minimum lease payments, but as a practical expedient permits the use of the fair value of the asset (where it is a sufficiently close approximation). On application of FRS 102, entities may need to consider the measurement of finance lease obligations on initial recognition more carefully. However, in cases where the fair value of the leased asset was deemed a sufficiently close approximation to the present value of the minimum lease payments, there is unlikely to be a material difference between the two.

For most leases, the date of inception of the lease in accordance with SSAP 21 and the date of the commencement of the lease term in accordance with FRS 102 will be the same. However, it is possible, that the timing of the initial recognition of the asset and lease obligation will differ on application of FRS 102. For example, if a lessee signs a lease agreement on 1 January 20X1 but cannot start using the lease until 1 June 20X1, under FRS 102, the inception date would be 1 January 20X1 but the commencement date would be 1 June 20X1. The asset and lease obligation would not be recognised until the commencement date of 1 June 20X1. Under SSAP 21, the asset and lease liability would be recognised on 1 January 20X1.

ACCOUNTING FOR OPERATING LEASES

Operating lease incentives

UITF 28	FRS 102
Operating lease incentives for lessors (a reduction against rental income) and lessees (a reduction against rental expense) should be allocated over the lease term or a shorter period ending on the date from which it is expected the prevailing market rental will be payable. The allocation should be on a straight line basis unless another systematic basis is more representative of the time pattern of the benefit receivable/received from the use of the asset. (UITF Abstract 28 paragraphs 14 and 15)	Operating lease incentives for lessors (a reduction against rental income) and lessees (a reduction against rental expense) shall be recognised over the lease term on a straight line basis unless another systematic basis is more representative of the time pattern of the benefit receivable/received from the use of the asset. (FRS 102 paragraphs 20.15A and 20.25A) Lease term is defined as the non-cancellable period for which the lessee has contracted to lease the asset together with any further terms for which the lessee has the option to continue to lease the asset, with or without further payment, when at the inception of the lease it is reasonably certain that the lessee will exercise the option. (FRS 102 Glossary)

In both cases, lease incentives are recognised on a straight line basis unless another systematic basis is more representative. The key difference is that the period over which operating lease incentives are recognised may be longer under FRS 102, for example where the lease term is 5 years, yet a rent review may take place after 2 years.

Disclosures

SSAP 21	FRS 102

The lessee should disclose the payments which he is committed to make in the next year, analysed between those in which the commitment expires within that year, in the second to fifth years inclusive, and over five years from the balance sheet date, showing separately the commitments in respect of leases of land and buildings and other operating leases.
 	
(SSAP 21 paragraph 56)
	A lessee shall make the following disclosures for operating leases:
	
	(a) the total of future minimum lease payments under non-cancellable operating leases for each of the following periods:
	
	   (i) not later than one year;
	
	   (ii) later than one year and not later than five years; and
	
	   (iii) later than five years.
	
	(b) lease payments recognised as an expense.
	
	(FRS 102 paragraph 20.16)

In both cases, companies (other than those subject to the small companies' regime) would be required to comply with Companies Act 2006 s410A. This requires disclosure, for material arrangements that are not reflected in the balance sheet, of:

- the nature and business purpose of the arrangements; and
- the financial impact of the arrangements on the company (not applicable to medium-sized companies).

Disclosure of operating leases will be different under FRS 102. The total future minimum lease payments due within each of the required periods will be disclosed, rather than the annual amount due to expire in the relevant year.

SEN 7
Revenue recognition

Contents

Disclaimer

This Education Note has been prepared by FRC staff for the convenience of users of FRS 102 The Financial Reporting Standard applicable in the UK and Republic of Ireland. It aims to illustrate certain requirements of FRS 102, but should not be relied upon as a definitive statement on the application of the standard. The illustrative material is not a substitute for reading the detailed requirements of FRS 102.

INTRODUCTION

This Staff Education Note provides a comparison of revenue recognition requirements set out in Section 23 *Revenue* of FRS 102 *The Financial Reporting Standard applicable in the UK and Republic of Ireland* and current UK accounting standards including:

(a)   FRS 5 *Reporting the substance of transactions*;

(b)   SSAP 9 *Stocks and long-term contracts*; and

(c)   UITF abstract 40 *Revenue recognition and service contracts*.

This Staff Education Note is written to highlight key areas of consideration when transitioning to FRS 102 and is not designed to be exhaustive. In practice, for the majority of entities, there will be no significant changes to the recognition of revenue.

BASIC PRINCIPLES

Scope and recognition

FRS 5 – Application Note G	FRS 102
Applies to any activity giving rise to revenue. Provides that a seller recognises revenue when it obtains the right to consideration in exchange for its performance. (FRS 5 paragraph G4) Provides areas of specific guidance for a number of specified types of transactions (FRS 5 paragraph G1).	Provides recognition criteria for: (a) the sale of goods; (b) rendering of services; (c) construction contracts in which the entity is the contractor; and (d) interest, royalties and dividends. (FRS 102 paragraph 23.1).

There appears to be no difference in the basic scope and recognition principles.

Measurement

FRS 5 – Application Note G	FRS 102
Requires revenue to be measured at the fair value of the right to consideration. (FRS 5 paragraph G7)	Requires revenue to be measured at the fair value of the consideration received or receivable. (FRS 102 paragraph 23.3)

If consideration is received or receivable, then it follows that the entity has a right to that consideration (under a contractual arrangement). Likewise, if an entity has a right to consideration, that consideration would be receivable by the entity.

Therefore, there appears to be no difference in the basic measurement principle.

Discounting

FRS 5 – Application Note G	FRS 102
States that where the effect of the time value of money is material, the amount of revenue recognised should be the present value of the cash inflows expected to be received. (FRS 5 paragraph G8)	Requires that where payment is deferred under a financing transaction, the fair value of the consideration is measured as the present value of all future receipts determined using an imputed rate of interest. This imputed rate of interest is either the prevailing rate for a similar instrument of an issuer with a similar credit rating or a rate that discounts the nominal value of the instrument to the current cash sales prices of the goods or services. (FRS 102 paragraph 23.5)

Both standards permit discounting, therefore there does not appear to be any significant difference in the treatment of deferred payment arrangements, although FRS 102 is more prescriptive regarding the discount rate.

Risk of default

FRS 5 – Application Note G	FRS 102
Requires that where, at the time revenue is recognised, there is a significant risk that there will be default, then an adjustment is made to the amount of revenue recognised. (FRS 5 paragraph G9)	Requires that revenue is measured at the fair value of the consideration received or receivable. Although it does not explicitly address the risk of default at the time of recognition, a fair value measurement would be expected to reflect any significant credit risk.
	Further, the revenue recognition criteria for the sale of goods or the rendering of services, requires that revenue is recognised only when it is probable (more likely than not) that the economic benefits will flow to the entity. (FRS 102 paragraph 23.10(d) and 23.14(b))

Where there is a risk of default at the time of revenue recognition, FRS 5 takes this into account when measuring revenue, which at the extreme could result in no revenue being recognised at that time. FRS 102 requires that, if the risk of default is so high that it is not probable that any payment would be received, no revenue should be recognised until receipt is probable. Therefore in practice the amount recognised may not differ.

DETAILED RECOGNITION REQUIREMENTS

Point of recognition for sale of goods

FRS 5	FRS 102
Treats the sale of goods as derecognition of the stock and recognition of a new asset, usually a debtor.	Requires that an entity shall recognise revenue from the sale of goods when all the following conditions are satisfied:

FRS 5	FRS 102
Evidence that an entity has rights or other access to benefits (and hence has an asset) is given if the entity is exposed to the risks inherent in the benefits, taking into account the likelihood of those risks having a commercial effect in practice.	(a) the entity has transferred to the buyer the significant risks and rewards of ownership of the goods;
(FRS 5 paragraph 17)	(b) the entity retains neither continuing managerial involvement to the degree usually associated with ownership nor effective control over the goods sold;
An asset should be recognised if:	(c) the amount of revenue can be measured reliably;
(a) there is sufficient evidence of the existence of the item (including, where appropriate, evidence that a future inflow or outflow of benefit will occur); and	(d) it is probable that the economic benefits associated with the transaction will flow to the entity; and
	(e) the costs incurred or to be incurred in respect of the transaction can be measured reliably.
(b) when the item can be measured at a monetary amount with sufficient reliability.	(FRS 102 paragraph 23.10)
(FRS 5 paragraph 20)	

There is unlikely to be any significant difference in the recognition of revenue recognised on the sale of goods.

Revenue recognition for rendering of services

SSAP 9, UITF Abstract 40	FRS 102
Under SSAP 9, once the outcome of a long-term contract can be assessed with reasonable certainty, attributable profit is calculated on a prudent basis and revenue recognised accordingly.	Requires that when the outcome of a transaction can be estimated reliably, an entity shall recognise revenue associated with the transaction by reference to the stage of completion of the transaction at the end of the reporting period.
(SSAP 9 paragraph 9)	The outcome of a transaction can be estimated reliably when all the following conditions are met:
	(a) the amount of revenue can be measured reliably;
	(b) it is probable that the economic benefits associated with the transaction will flow to the entity;
	(c) the stage of completion of the transaction at the end of the reporting period can be measured reliably; and
	(d) the costs incurred for the transaction and the costs to complete the transaction can be measured reliably.
	(FRS 102 paragraph 23.14)

There does not appear to be any significant difference between FRS 102 and SSAP 9 regarding the point at which profit may first be recognised on a long-term contract for the rendering of services. The SSAP 9 requirement for the outcome to be reasonably certain is normally equal to a reliable estimate.

Amount of revenue recognised on service contracts

SSAP 9, UITF Abstract 40	FRS 102
Where the outcome of a contract can be assessed with reasonable certainty, the prudently calculated attributable profit should be recognised as the difference between turnover (ascertained in a manner appropriate to the stage of completion of the contract, the business and the industry in which it operates) and the related costs. (SSAP 9 paragraphs 8 and 9)	When the outcome of a transaction involving the rendering of services can be estimated reliably, revenue is calculated by reference to the stage (or percentage) of completion of the transaction at the end of the reporting period. Further guidance is provided on applying the method. (FRS 102 paragraph 23.14)
Where the substance of a contract is that a right to consideration does not arise until the occurrence of a critical event, revenue is not recognised until that event occurs. This only applies where the right to consideration is conditional or contingent on a specified future event or outcome, the occurrence of which is outside the control of the seller. (UITF Abstract 40 paragraph 19) The amount of revenue recognised on any contract for services should reflect any uncertainties as to the amount that the customer will accept and pay. (UITF Abstract 40 paragraph 28)	When services are performed by an indeterminate number of acts over a specified period of time, an entity recognises revenue on a straight-line basis over the specified period unless there is evidence that some other method better represents the stage of completion. When a specific act is much more significant than any other act, the entity postpones recognition of revenue until the significant act is executed. (FRS 102 paragraph 23.15)
Where the outcome of long-term contracts cannot be assessed with reasonable certainty before the conclusion of the contract, no profit should be reflected in the profit and loss account in respect of those contracts, although in such circumstances, if no loss is expected it may be appropriate to show as turnover a proportion of the total contract value using a zero estimate of profit. (SSAP 9 paragraph 10)	When the outcome of the transaction involving the rendering of services cannot be estimated reliably, an entity shall recognise revenue only to the extent of the expenses recognised that are recoverable. (FRS 102 paragraph 23.16)

SSAP 9, UITF Abstract 40	FRS 102
If it is expected that there will be a loss on a contract as a whole, all of the loss should be recognised as soon as it is foreseen. (SSAP 9 paragraph 11)	When it is probable that total contract costs will exceed total contract revenue, the expected loss shall be recognised as an expense immediately. (FRS 102 paragraph 23.26)

The facts of each contract will need to be reviewed in detail to determine if there is any change the timing or amount of the revenue recognised, although the requirements of the two standards are similar. Contingent fee arrangements will normally be accounted for under paragraphs 23.14 to 23.16 of FRS 102.

Unbundling of contracts

FRS 5 Guidance Note G	FRS 102
A contractual arrangement should be accounted for as two or more separate transactions only where the commercial substance is that the individual components operate independently of each other. 'Operate independently' means that each component represents a separable good or service that the seller can provide to customers, either on a stand-alone basis or as an optional extra. Alternatively, one or more components(s) may be capable of being provided by another supplier. (FRS 5 Guidance Note G paragraph G25) Conversely, the commercial substance of two or more separate contracts may require them to be accounted for as a single transaction. (FRS 5 Guidance Note G paragraph G26)	An entity shall apply the recognition criteria to the separately identifiable components of a single transaction when necessary to reflect the substance of the transaction. For example, when the selling price of a product includes an identifiable amount for subsequent servicing. Conversely, an entity applies the recognition criteria to two or more transactions together when they are linked in such a way that the commercial effect cannot be understood without reference to the series of transactions as a whole. For example, when an entity sells goods and, at the same time, enters into a separate agreement to repurchase the goods at a later date, thus negating the substantive effect of the transaction. (FRS 102 paragraph 23.8)

Both FRS 102 and current UK accounting standards require a single contract to be accounted for as two or more separate transactions where this is necessary to reflect the commercial substance.

They also both require that more than one contract is considered together where this is necessary to understand and reflect the commercial substance.

Contracts for multiple services

UITF Abstract 40	FRS 102
Only contracts for services that constitute a single service, or a number of services that constitute a single project, are accounted for as long-term contracts. (UITF Abstract 40 paragraph 11 and 24) A contract to provide services on an on-going basis, for example a contract to provide repetitive services, is not accounted for as a long-term contract. (UITF Abstract 40 paragraph 12 and 26) Therefore, the entity would recognise revenue when and to the extent that it obtained the right to consideration in exchange for performance under FRS 5, which would be on the basis of each service performed.	For a contract for services, where those services are performed by an indeterminate number of acts over a specified period of time, an entity recognises revenue on a straight-line basis over the specified period unless there is evidence that some other method better represents the stage of completion. (FRS 102 paragraph 23.15)

In practice, since under current UK accounting standards revenue would be recognised as each service (or number of services that constitute a single project) is performed and under FRS 102 revenue would be recognised using a method representing the stage of completion, the recognition of revenue would generally be the same under both standards.

SEN 8
Government grants

Contents

Disclaimer

This Education Note has been prepared by FRC staff for the convenience of users of FRS 102 The Financial Reporting Standard applicable in the UK and Republic of Ireland. It aims to illustrate certain requirements of FRS 102, but should not be relied upon as a definitive statement on the application of the standard. The illustrative material is not a substitute for reading the detailed requirements of FRS 102.

INTRODUCTION

This Staff Education Note compares the current accounting treatment for government grants under SSAP 4 *Accounting for government grants* and Section 24 *Government Grants* of FRS 102 *Financial Reporting Standard applicable in the UK and Republic of Ireland*.

This Staff Education Note is written to highlight key areas of consideration when transitioning to FRS 102 and is not designed to be exhaustive.

RECOGNITION CRITERIA

SSAP 4	FRS 102
Government grants (a) should be recognised in the profit and loss account so as to match them with the expenditure towards which they are intended to contribute. (b) made as a contribution towards fixed assets should be recognised over the expected useful economic lives of the related assets. (c) made to finance the general activities of an enterprise over a specific period or to compensate for the loss of current or future income should be recognised in the profit and loss account of the period in respect of which they are paid. (SSAP 4 paragraph 23) In practice this might be seen as giving entities some flexibility over their accounting policies for the recognition of government grants.	Requires grants to be accounted for either based on the performance model or the accrual model. (FRS 102 paragraph 24.4) ***The performance model* requires that:** (a) A grant that does not impose specified future performance-related conditions on the recipient is recognised in income when the grant proceeds are received or receivable. (b) A grant that imposes specified future performance-related conditions on the recipient is recognised in income only when the performance-related conditions are met. (FRS 102 paragraph 24.5B) ***The accrual model* requires that:** (a) An entity classifies a grant either as a grant relating to revenue or a grant relating to assets. (b) Grants relating to revenue are recognised in income on a systematic basis over the periods in which the entity recognises the related costs for which the grant is intended to compensate. (Note: A grant that becomes receivable as compensation for expenses or losses already incurred or for the purpose of giving immediate financial support to the entity with no future related costs shall be recognised in income in the period in which it becomes receivable.) (c) Grants relating to assets are recognised in income on a systematic basis over the expected useful life of the asset. (FRS 102 paragraphs 24.5C to 24.5F)

EXAMPLE – GRANT TOWARDS A FIXED ASSET

Facts

A manufacturing company receives a government grant of £200,000 as an incentive to open a factory in a region of high unemployment. There are no further conditions associated with the grant, other than that it is used to pay for the construction of this factory. In the same year as receiving the grant, the company constructs the factory for a total cost of £600,000 and begins to use it. The company has a policy of depreciating buildings over a useful life of 50 years.

SSAP 4

Under SSAP 4 (and taking into account company law), the grant is deferred and shown as a liability. It is then released to the profit and loss account over the expected useful life of the related asset. Given that the asset's life is 50 years (and the company has no plans to relocate during this time), the entries are as follows:

Recognition of the factory (fixed asset)

Dr Fixed assets	£600,000
Cr Cash	£600,000

Initial recognition of the grant

Dr Cash	£200,000
Cr Deferred grants	£200,000

Recognition of depreciation charge on the factory (£600,000 / 50 years)

Dr Depreciation (P&L)	£12,000
Cr Fixed assets	£12,000

Release the grant to the P&L (£200,000 / 50 years)

Dr Deferred grants	£4,000
Cr P&L (grant income)	£4,000

FRS 102

Performance model

Under FRS 102, where the entity elects to apply the performance model, the whole grant is recognised in profit or loss immediately. This is because there are no provisions requiring deferral of the grant received, as the only condition was that the factory must be constructed and this condition has been fulfilled.

Recognition of the factory (fixed asset)

Dr Fixed assets	£600,000
Cr Cash	£600,000

Initial recognition of the grant

Dr Cash	£200,000
Cr Grant income (P&L)	£200,000

Recognition of depreciation charge on the factory (£600,000 / 50 years)

Dr Depreciation (P&L)	£12,000
Cr Fixed assets	£12,000

Note: If the fact pattern changed, this example may show a less stark difference between SSAP 4 and the performance model in accordance with FRS 102. For instance, if the company had an obligation to use the factory (and hence provide local employment) for a certain period following its construction, the grant would be recognised later. The mechanism for recognising the grant during the specified period would depend on the detailed terms and conditions, and would not necessarily be based on the expected useful life of the building.

Accrual model

Under FRS 102, where the entity elects to apply the accrual model, the accounting would be the same as SSAP 4.

It should be noted that paragraph 2.52 of FRS 102 does not permit an entity to offset assets and liabilities, or income and expenses, unless required or permitted by the FRS, and that paragraph 24.5G of FRS 102 explicitly prohibits the deduction of a government grant relating to an asset from the carrying amount of the fixed asset.

SEN 9
Short-term employee benefits and termination benefits

Contents

Disclaimer

This Education Note has been prepared by FRC staff for the convenience of users of FRS 102 **The Financial Reporting Standard applicable in the UK and Republic of Ireland.** *It aims to illustrate certain requirements of FRS 102, but should not be relied upon as a definitive statement on the application of the standard. The illustrative material is not a substitute for reading the detailed requirements of FRS 102.*

INTRODUCTION

This Staff Education Note provides a comparison of the accounting requirements for short-term employee benefits and termination benefits set out in Section 28 *Employee Benefits* of FRS 102 *The Financial Reporting Standard applicable in the UK and Republic of Ireland* and current UK accounting standards.

Current UK accounting standards do not include explicit requirements for accounting for short-term employee benefits or termination benefits. However, the principles set out in a number of current accounting standards may be relevant, including:

(a)   FRS 12 *Provision, contingent liabilities and contingent assets*; and

(b)   FRS 5 *Reporting the substance of transactions*.

This Staff Education Note is written to highlight key areas of consideration when transitioning to FRS 102 and is not designed to be exhaustive.

SHORT-TERM EMPLOYEE BENEFITS

Definition

Current UK accounting standards	FRS 102
Not defined, although the Companies Act 2006 requires disclosure of employee costs paid or payable in respect of the year, which includes wages, salaries and social security costs.	Short-term employee benefits are employee benefits (other than termination benefits) that are expected to be settled wholly before twelve months after the end of the reporting period in which the employees render the related service.
No further detail of components of employee costs, but the following is relevant:	(FRS 102 paragraph 28.1(a))
Accruals are liabilities to pay for goods or services that have been received or supplied but have not been paid… including amounts due to employees (for example amounts relating to accrued holiday pay).	Short-term employee benefits include items such as the following, if expected to be settled wholly before 12 months after the end of the annual reporting period in which the employees render the related service:
(FRS 12 paragraph 11(b))	(a) wages, salaries and social security contributions;
	(b) paid annual leave and paid sick leave;
	(c) profit-sharing and bonuses; and
	(d) non-monetary benefits (such as medical care, housing, cars and free or subsidised goods or services) for current employees.
	(FRS 102 paragraph 28.4)

Measurement

Current UK accounting standards	FRS 102
No explicit requirements, but employee costs would be measured at transaction amount.	When an employee has rendered service to an entity during the reporting periods, the entity shall measure the amounts at the undiscounted amount of short-term employee benefits expected to be paid in exchange for that service.
	(FRS 102 paragraph 28.5)
	An entity shall recognise the expected cost of accumulating compensated absences when the employees render service that increases their entitlement to future compensated absences, at the undiscounted additional amount that the entity expects to pay as a result of the unused entitlement that has accumulated at the end of the reporting period. The entity shall present this amount as falling due within one year at the reporting date.
	(FRS 102 paragraph 28.6)
	An entity shall recognise the cost of other (non-accumulating) compensated absences when the absences occur, at the undiscounted amount of salaries and wages paid or payable for the period of absence.
	(FRS 102 paragraph 28.7)

Current UK GAAP is much less explicit about the accounting for short-term benefits than FRS 102, but there is no conceptual difference between the two. However, in practice many UK reporting entities do not provide for holiday pay (short-term compensated absences) and will need to consider this when applying FRS 102 for the first time.

Example 1

Employees of Company A are permitted 24 days annual leave which must be taken in the holiday year which commences on 1 April. Company A's financial year end is 31 December.

At 31 December an employee, pro-rata is entitled to have taken 18 days holiday. Company A calculates from holiday records that outstanding holiday (ie holiday not taken from an allowance of 18 days) is 56 days for all employees at the same grade.

Company A considers that it is appropriate to make an accrual for the 56 days outstanding holiday measured at the average salary per day.

Overall impact

On the date of transition to FRS 102, a new provision would be recognised for short-term employee benefits with a corresponding adjustment to opening retained earnings. In future years, assuming the annual holiday allowance, the pattern of holidays taken and holiday year remain constant, the movement in the provision from one year to the next will probably be limited.

TERMINATION BENEFITS

Definition

FRS 12	FRS 102
Not defined, but referred to in FRS 12. A provision for restructuring costs would include termination benefits meeting the definition of a provision. (FRS 12 paragraph 77)	Termination benefits are employee benefits payable as a result of either: (a) an entity's decision to terminate an employee's employment before the normal retirement date; or (b) an employee's decision to accept voluntary redundancy in exchange for those benefits. (FRS 102 paragraph 28.1(d)) An entity may be committed, by legislation, by contractual or other agreements with employees or their representatives or by a constructive obligation based on business practice, custom or a desire to act equitably, to make payments (or provide other benefits) to employees when it terminates their employment. Such payments are termination benefits. (FRS 102 paragraph 28.31)

Recognition

FRS 12	FRS 102
As noted above, termination benefits would be included in a restructuring provision, which should include only the direct expenditures arising from the restructuring, which are those that are both: (a) necessarily entailed by the restructuring; and (b) not associated with the on-going activities of the entity. (FRS 12 paragraph 85)	Termination payments do not provide an entity with future economic benefits therefore an entity shall recognise them as an expense in profit or loss immediately. (FRS 102 paragraph 28.32)

FRS 12	FRS 102
A constructive obligation to restructure arises only when an entity: (a) has a detailed formal plan for the restructuring identifying at least… …the location, function, and approximate number of employees who will be compensated for terminating their services; and (b) has raised a valid expectation in those affected that it will carry out the restructuring by starting to implement that plan or announcing its main features to those affected by it. (FRS 12 paragraph 77) Negotiations with employees' representatives for termination payments may have been concluded subject only to Board approval. Once that approval has been obtained and communicated to the other parties, the entity has a constructive obligation to restructure (assuming the other conditions are met). (FRS 12 paragraph 81)	An entity shall recognise such payments as a liability and an expense only when the entity is demonstrably committed either: (a) to terminate the employment of an employee or group of employees before the normal retirement date; or (b) to provide termination benefits as a result of an offer made in order to encourage voluntary redundancy. (FRS 102 paragraph 28.34) An entity is demonstrably committed to a termination only when the entity has a detailed formal plan for the termination and is without realistic possibility of withdrawal from the plan. (FRS 102 paragraph 28.35)

There appears to be no difference in the recognition of termination benefits.

Measurement

Current UK accounting standards	FRS 102
The amount recognised as a provision should be the best estimate of the expenditure required to settle the present obligation at the balance sheet date. (FRS 12.36) Where the effect of the time value of money is material, the amount of the provision should be the present value of the expenditures expected to be required to settle the obligation. (FRS 12.45)	An entity shall measure termination benefits at the best estimate of the expenditure that would be required to settle the obligation at the reporting date. In the case of an offer made to encourage voluntary redundancy, the measurement of termination benefit shall be based on the number of employees expected to accept the offer. (FRS 102 28.36) When termination benefits are due more than twelve months after the end of the reporting period, they shall be measured at their discounted present value. (FRS 102 28.37)

FRS 102 appears to be more prescriptive in requiring discounting whenever the termination benefits are payable after more than one year. However, in practice, if the effect of the discounting was not material it may not be necessary to adjust for it.

Example 2

Company B has a 31 December year end. On 5 December 20X1 it makes a public announcement that it will close its manufacturing facilities in Wales during the next financial year. It currently employs 250 personnel in its manufacturing facilities but considers that it will be able to relocate 50 personnel within the company. It anticipates the cost of statutory redundancy for the 200 staff will be CU3m. Company B however, decides to pay a further CU5,000 as an enhancement to each employee (which is not related to future service[1]). The public announcement sets out the Company B's intentions including the enhancement of CU5,000 to each employee.

Company B recognises a liability of CU4m (being CU3m for its statutory liability and CU1m for the enhancement) in its 31 December 20X1 financial statements, being its best estimate of the amount required to settle the obligation.

---

[1] *If the payments were a 'staying bonus' to encourage employees not to leave before a certain date, they would be recognised over the period of the service (ie they would be short-term employee benefits).*

SEN 10
Employee benefits – Defined benefit plans

Contents

Disclaimer

This Education Note has been prepared by FRC staff for the convenience of users of FRS 102 The Financial Reporting Standard applicable in the UK and Republic of Ireland. *It aims to illustrate certain requirements of FRS 102, but should not be relied upon as a definitive statement on the application of the standard. The illustrative material is not a substitute for reading the detailed requirements of FRS 102.*

INTRODUCTION

This Staff Education Note compares the accounting treatment for defined benefit plans as set out in current UK accounting standards (FRS 17 *Retirement Benefits*) and Section 28 *Employee Benefits* of FRS 102 *The Financial Reporting Standard applicable in the UK and Republic of Ireland*.

In particular, it focuses on:

- multi-employer and group schemes; and
- general requirements.

This Staff Education Note is written to highlight key areas of consideration when transitioning to FRS 102 and is not designed to be exhaustive.

MULTI-EMPLOYER SCHEMES

FRS 17	FRS 102
Does not formally define multi-employer schemes but provides that where more than one employer participates in a defined benefit scheme the employer should account for the scheme as a defined benefit scheme unless: (a) the employer's contributions are set in relation to the current service period only (ie are not affected by any surplus or deficit in the scheme relating to past service of its own employees or any other members of the scheme). If this is the case, the employer should account for the contributions to the scheme as if it were a defined contribution scheme. (b) the employer's contributions are affected by a surplus or deficit in the scheme but the employer is unable to identify its share of the underlying assets and liabilities in the scheme on a consistent and reasonable basis. If this is the case, the employer should account for the contributions to the scheme as if it were a defined contribution scheme but, in addition, make specified disclosures. (FRS 17 paragraph 9)	Defines multi-employer plans to include only those where the participating employers are not under common control. (FRS 102 Glossary) Provides that multi-employer plans are classified as defined contribution or defined benefit plans on the basis of the terms of the plan, including any constructive obligation. However, where sufficient information is not available to use defined benefit accounting then the employer should account for the plan as a defined contribution plan and provide additional disclosures. (FRS 102 paragraph 28.11) Where an entity participates in a defined benefit plan, which is a multi-employer plan that is accounted for as if the plan were a defined contribution plan, and the entity has entered into an agreement with the multi-employer plan that determines how the entity will fund a deficit, the entity shall recognise a liability for the contributions payable that arise from the agreement (to the extent that they relate to the deficit) and the resulting expense in profit or loss. (FRS 102 paragraph 28.11A)

There is no change unless paragraph 28.11A of FRS 102 applies. Paragraph 28.11A applies to multi-employer schemes and requires that liabilities for contributions payable that arise from commitments to fund deficits are recognised in the statement of financial position.

GROUP SCHEMES

Recognition and measurement

FRS 17	FRS 102
Does not differentiate between group and multi-employer schemes.	States that a group plan is where an entity participates in a defined benefit plan that shares risks between entities under common control.
Provides that subsidiaries are not exempt and, where possible, will account for defined benefit schemes. However, many group schemes are run on a basis that does not enable individual companies within the group to identify their share of the underlying assets and liabilities. In these circumstances, the individual companies (including the parent company) within the group will account for the scheme as a defined contribution scheme and will give the additional disclosures required for multi-employer schemes.	Provides that an entity shall obtain information about the plan as a whole measured on the basis of assumptions that apply to the plan as a whole. If there is a contractual agreement or stated policy for charging the cost of a defined benefit plan as a whole to individual group entities, the entity shall, in its individual accounts, recognise the cost of a defined benefit plan so charged.
(FRS 17 paragraph 12)	If there is no such agreement or policy, the cost of a defined benefit plan shall be recognised in the individual accounts of the group entity which is legally responsible for the plan. The other group entities shall, in their individual accounts, recognise a cost equal to their contribution payable for the period.
	(FRS 102 paragraph 28.38)

FRS 102 does not permit the pension liability or asset to only be recognised in the consolidated financial statements, as permitted by FRS 17. Under FRS 102 at least one entity will apply defined benefit accounting depending on the policy for charging pension costs around the group. This may have an impact on distributable reserves[1].

---

[1] See ICAEW Technical Release Tech 02/10 Guidance on the Determination of Realised Profits and Losses in the Context of Distributions under the Companies Act 2006 available on the ICAEW website (www.icaew.com).

Disclosures

FRS 17	FRS 102
Requires specific disclosures to be provided for multi-employer schemes where an employer is affected by a surplus or deficit in the scheme, but is unable to identify its share of the underlying assets and liabilities in the scheme on a consistent and reasonable basis. This may apply to individual entities participating in a group pension scheme. In these circumstances the general disclosure requirements of FRS 17 do not apply. (FRS 17 paragraph 9(b))	Where an entity accounts for an allocation of the plan's cost then it makes all the disclosures required by paragraph 28.41. (FRS 102 paragraph 28.41) If the entity accounts for the plan on a contribution basis then the disclosures are restricted to: ● a general description of the plan; ● date of the most recent actuarial valuation; ● details of the plan assets; and ● details of the own equity instruments or properties occupied by the entity included in the plan assets. This information can, however, be disclosed by cross referring to another group entity's financial statements if certain criteria are met. (FRS 102 paragraph 28.41A)

There are differences in the disclosure requirements for entities participating in group defined benefit plans; however, paragraph 28.41A of FRS 102 permits cross referral if certain criteria are met..

GENERAL REQUIREMENTS

Actuarial method and assumptions

FRS 17	FRS 102
Defined benefit scheme liabilities should be measured on an actuarial basis using the projected unit method. (FRS 17 paragraph 20) Full actuarial valuations by a professionally qualified actuary should be obtained for a defined benefit scheme at intervals not exceeding three years. The actuary should review the most recent actuarial valuation at the balance sheet date and update it to reflect current conditions. (FRS 17 paragraph 35)	An entity shall use the projected unit credit method to measure its defined benefit obligation and the related expense. (FRS 102 paragraph 28.18) Does not require an entity to engage an independent actuary to perform the comprehensive actuarial valuation needed to calculate its defined benefit obligation. Nor does it require that a comprehensive actuarial valuation must be done annually. In periods between comprehensive actuarial valuations, if the principal actuarial assumptions have not changed significantly the defined benefit obligation can be measured by adjusting the prior period measurement for changes in employee demographics. (FRS 102 paragraph 28.20)

Both standards require the use of the projected unit method. However, FRS 102 does not require an independent actuary to perform the valuation nor does it stipulate how often a comprehensive valuation need be performed. Nevertheless, in practice, entities may continue to have independent actuarial valuations performed at the same regularity as they currently do.

Cost of a defined benefit plan

FRS 17	FRS 102
The change in the defined benefit asset or liability (other than arising from contributions to the scheme) should be analysed into the following components:	An entity shall recognise the cost of a defined benefit plan, except to the extent that another section of the FRS requires part or all of the cost to be recognised as part of the cost of an asset, as follows:
Periodic Costs	
(a) the current service cost; (b) the interest cost; (c) the expected return on assets; (d) actuarial gains and losses;	(a) the change in the net defined benefit liability arising from employee service rendered during the reporting period in profit or loss (ie the current service cost);
Non-Periodic Costs	(b) net interest on the net defined benefit liability during the reporting period in profit or loss;
(e) past service costs; and (f) gains and losses on settlements and curtailments. (FRS 17.50)	(c) plan introductions, benefit changes, curtailments and settlements in profit or loss; and
The current service cost should be included within operating profit.	(d) remeasurement of the net defined benefit liability in other comprehensive income.
(FRS 17 paragraph 51)	(FRS 102 paragraph 28.23)
The net of the interest cost and the expected return on assets should be included as other finance costs (or income) adjacent to interest.	The net interest on the defined benefit liability is the interest cost on the defined benefit obligation and interest income on plan assets excluding the effect of any surplus that is not recoverable.
(FRS 17 paragraph 56)	
Actuarial gains and losses should be recognised in the statement of total recognised gains and losses.	(FRS 102 paragraph 28.24A)
	Interest income on plan assets, excluding the effect of any surplus that is not recoverable, is a component of the return on plan assets, and is determined by multiplying the fair value of the plan assets by the discount rate both as determined at the start of the annual reporting period, taking account of any changes in plan assets held during the period as a result of contribution and benefit payments. The difference between the interest income on plan assets and the return on plan assets is included in the remeasurement of the net defined benefit liability.
(FRS 17 paragraph 57)	
Past service costs should be recognised in the profit and loss account on a straight-line basis over the period in which the increases in benefit vest.	
(FRS 17 paragraph 60)	
Gains and losses on settlement and curtailments not allowed for in the actuarial assumptions are recognised in the profit and loss account.	(FRS 102 paragraph 28.24B)
(FRS 17 paragraph 64)	Remeasurement of the net defined benefit liability comprises:
	(a) actuarial gains and losses; and (b) the return on plan assets, excluding amounts included in net interest on the net defined benefit liability.
	(FRS 102 paragraph 28.25)

The presentational differences between FRS 17 and FRS 102 can be illustrated as follows:

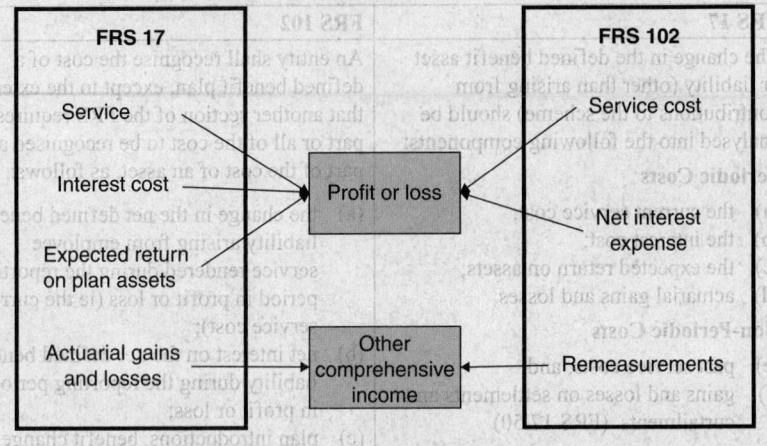

The key change from FRS 17 is the method of calculation of the interest income on the plan assets.

Disclosures

FRS 17	FRS 102
Aligned with IAS 19 prior to it being updated in June 2011. (See FRS 17 paragraphs 76 and 77)	The disclosure requirements do not vary significantly from those of FRS 17. (FRS 102 28.41)

Although the disclosure requirements in FRS 102 do not vary significantly from FRS 17, some entities may find there is a reduction in disclosures about defined benefit pension plans on application of FRS 102.

SEN 11
Foreign exchange contracts

Contents

Disclaimer

This Education Note has been prepared by FRC staff for the convenience of users of FRS 102 The Financial Reporting Standard applicable in the UK and Republic of Ireland. *It aims to illustrate certain requirements of FRS 102, but should not be relied upon as a definitive statement on the application of the standard. The illustrative material is not a substitute for reading the detailed requirements of FRS 102.*

INTRODUCTION

Entities may enter into foreign exchange contracts to manage the uncertainty of cash flows associated with debtors or creditors in foreign currencies.

For entities that do not apply FRS 26 (IAS 39) *Financial instruments: Recognition and Measurement* and thereby FRS 23 (IAS 21) *The effects of changes in foreign exchange rates* and apply SSAP 20 *Foreign currency translation* to their foreign currency transactions, there will be a change of accounting treatment under FRS 102 *The Financial Reporting Standard applicable in the UK and Republic of Ireland*.

This Staff Education Note is written to highlight key areas of consideration when transitioning to FRS 102 and is not designed to be exhaustive.

FOREIGN CURRENCY MONETARY ITEMS (EG A FOREIGN CURRENCY DEBTOR)

Initial recognition

SSAP 20	FRS 102
A transaction in a foreign currency should initially be recognised at either: (a) the exchange rate on the transaction date; or (b) where a trading transaction is covered by a related or matching forward contract, the exchange rate specified in that contract may be used. (SSAP 20 paragraph 4)	Requires a foreign currency transaction to be recorded at the spot rate at the transaction date. (FRS 102 paragraph 30.7)

Subsequent measurement

SSAP 20	FRS 102
At the year end, foreign currency monetary items should be translated using the exchange rate ruling at that date, or where appropriate, the rates of exchange fixed under the terms of the relevant transactions. Where there are related or matching forward contracts in respect of trading transactions, the rates of exchange specified in those contracts may be used. (SSAP 20 paragraph 6)	At the year end, foreign currency monetary items are required to be translated at the closing rate (i.e. the exchange rate at the reporting date) with the difference taken through profit or loss. (FRS 102 paragraphs 30.9 and 30.10)

DERIVATIVES (EG A FOREIGN EXCHANGE CONTRACT)

Current UK accounting standards	FRS 102
Derivatives are not recognised.	Requires all derivatives to be recognised at fair value with changes in fair value recognised in profit or loss. (FRS 102 paragraph 12.8)

There is no option in FRS 102 to use the contracted forward rate at the transaction or balance sheet date. For an entity that does not currently apply the SSAP 20 option of using the forward contract rate, the only difference in the accounting for the foreign exchange transaction between current UK accounting standards and FRS 102 is the recognition of a derivative (the forward foreign exchange contract) under FRS 102.

EXAMPLE

A UK entity sells goods to a US customer on 1 November 20X1. The invoice is for $100,000 for settlement in 3 months ie 31 January 20X2.

On 1 November 20X1, the entity enters into a forward contract to sell $100,000 on 31 January 20X2 at a contracted rate of £1.62:$1.

The entity has a 31 December year end.

Details of GBP to USD exchange rates are below:

Date	Spot rate (£1:$X)	Forward rate to 31 January 20X2 (£1:$X)
1 November 20X1	1.6	1.62
31 December 20X1	1.57	1.59
31 January 20X2	1.55	–

SSAP 20

Option 1: Use exchange rate specified in forward contract

This shows the accounting entries if the entity chooses to use the exchange rate specified in the forward contract as permitted by SSAP 20 paragraph 4.

At 1 November 20X1 – Transaction Date

Debtor – Recognise $100,000 at the forward rate (£1:$1.62)

Dr	Debtors	£61,728
Cr	Sales	£61,728

At 31 December 20X1 – Year End

No accounting entries required as SSAP 20 permits foreign currency monetary assets to be measured at the contracted rate.

At 31 January 20X2 – Settlement Date

Debtor – Debt is settled at the forward rate (£1:$1.62)

Dr	Cash	£61,728
Cr	Debtors	£61,728

Option 2: Use spot rate at transaction date

This shows the accounting entries if the entity uses the spot rate on the transaction date.

At 1 November 20X1 – Transaction Date

Debtor – Recognise $100,000 at the transaction date spot rate (£1: $1.6)

Dr	Debtors	£62,500
Cr	Sales	£62,500

At 31 December 20X1 – Year End

Debtor – Retranslate at y/e spot rate (£1:$1.57)

Dr	Debtors	£1,194[1]
Cr	FX gain	£1,194

At 31 January 20X2 – Settlement Date

Debtor – Retranslate at settlement date spot rate (£1: $1.55)

Dr	Debtors	£822[2]
Cr	FX gain	£822

Debtor – Settled at forward rate (£1:$1.62)

Dr	Cash	£61,728[3]
Dr	Loss on derivative	£2,788
Cr	Debtors	£64,516

FRS 102

The accounting entries for the debtor will be the same as for Option 2 under SSAP 20 however there will be additional entries for recognition and measurement of the forward contract (derivative):

At 1 November 20X1 – Transaction Date

At the transaction date the forward contract will have a fair value of zero.

At 31 December 20X1 – Year End

Derivative – Recognise at fair value

Dr	Loss on derivative	£1,165[4]
Cr	Derivative – Liability	£1,165

---

[1] *$100,000 at £1:$1.57 (£63,694) less original debtor of £62,500 equals FX gain of £1,194.*

[2] *$100,000 at £1:$1.55 (£64,516) less y/e debtor of £63,694 equals gain of £822.*

[3] *$100,000 at the forward rate of £1:$1.62*

[4] *For simplicity, the loss is calculated as the difference between $100,000 at the contracted forward rate of £1:$1.62 (£61,728) and the year end forward rate £1:$1.59 (£62,893) giving a loss of £1,165*

At 31 January 20X2 – Settlement Date

Derivative – Fair value change at settlement date

Dr	Loss on derivative		£1,623[5]
Cr	Derivative liability		£1,623

Debtor and derivative settlement

Dr	Cash		£61,728[6]
Dr	Derivative liability		£2,788
Cr	Debtors		£64,516

Summary of impact on financial statements

For y/e 31 December 20X1

	SSAP 20		FRS 102
	Option 1	Option 2	
	£	£	£
Profit and loss			
Sales	61,728	62,500	62,500
FX gain	–	1,194	1,194
Loss on derivative			(1,165)
Total	**61,728**	**63,694**	**62,529**
Balance sheet			
Debtors	61,728	63,694	63,694
Derivative liability	–	–	(1,165)
Total	**61,728**	**63,694**	**62,529**

For y/e 31 December 20X2

	SSAP 20		FRS 102
	Option 1	Option 2	
	£	£	£
Profit and loss			
Sales			
FX gain	–	822	822
Loss on derivative		(2,788)	(1,623)
Total	**–**	**(1,966)**	**(801)**
Balance sheet			
Brought forward retained profit	61,728	63,694	62,529
Carried forward retained profit	**61,728**	**61,728**	**61,728**

---

[5] *For simplicity, the loss is calculated as the difference between $100,000 at the settlement date spot rate of £1:$1.55 (£64,516) and $100,000 at the y/e forward rate of £1:$1.59 (£62,893) giving a loss of £1,623.*

[6] *$100,000 at the contracted forward rate of £1:$1.62.*

Under SSAP 20 Option 2 and FRS 102, the total impact on profit or loss over the two years is the same as Option 1. The differences arise due to the timing of recognition of the loss on the derivative:

- SSAP 20 Option 2 – the loss is recognised on settlement; and
- FRS 102 – the loss is recognised in the period in which it occurs.

The total loss on the derivative of £2,788 represents the exchange difference arising on $100,000 translated at the contracted rate (£1: $1.62) and the spot rate on the date of settlement (£1:$1.55), ie if the entity had not taken out the forward contract, it would have received £2,788 more cash on settlement of the debtor.

The net loss from currency movements is £772 (1,194 – 1,165 + 822 – 1,623), which is equal to the exchange difference arising on $100,000 translated at the spot rate (£1:$1.6) and the forward rate at 1 November 201X (£1:$1.62). This loss is recognised at initial recognition under Option 1 and recognised as part of the sales revenue.

SEN 12
Incoming resources from non-exchange transactions

Contents

Disclaimer

This Education Note has been prepared by FRC staff for the convenience of users of FRS 102 The Financial Reporting Standard applicable in the UK and Republic of Ireland. It aims to illustrate certain requirements of FRS 102, but should not be relied upon as a definitive statement on the application of the standard. The illustrative material is not a substitute for reading the detailed requirements of FRS 102.

INTRODUCTION

This Staff Education Note compares the accounting treatment for incoming resources from non-exchange transactions under current UK accounting standards and FRS 102 *The Financial Reporting Standard applicable in the UK and Republic of Ireland.*

Incoming resources from non-exchange transactions is a topic specific to public benefit entities. Non-exchange transactions include, but are not limited to, donations of cash, goods and services, and legacies.

Current UK accounting standards do not include specific requirements relating to donations, other than in relation to the receipt of tangible fixed assets as gifts or donations by charities which fall within the scope of FRS 15 *Tangible Fixed Assets*. The *Statement of Principles: Interpretation for public benefit entities* includes a discussion of donated goods and services. The Charity Commission considered this in drafting the current version of its SORP *Accounting and Reporting by Charities: A Statement of Recommended Practice.*

FRS 102 addresses this area in Section 34 *Specialised Activities*.

This Staff Education Note is written to highlight key areas of consideration when transitioning to FRS 102 and is not designed to be exhaustive.

ACCOUNTING TREATMENT

Recognition

Statement of Principles: Interpretation for public benefit entities	FRS 102
Donations of cash, goods and services should be recognised when they can be measured with sufficient reliability. (Paragraph 4.48)	There is a consistent approach between accounting for non-exchange transactions and the performance model of accounting for grants (set out in Section 24 *Government Grants*). An entity shall recognise receipts of resources from non-exchange transactions as follows: (a) Transactions that do not impose specified future performance-related conditions on the recipient are recognised as income when the resources are received or receivable; and (b) Transactions that do impose specified future performance-related conditions on the recipient are recognised in income only when the performance-related conditions are met. (c) where resources are received before the revenue recognition criteria are satisfied, a liability is recognised. (FRS 102 paragraph PBE34.67)

Statement of Principles: Interpretation for public benefit entities	FRS 102
	When applying the above requirements, an entity must take into consideration whether the resource can be measured reliably and whether the benefits of recognising the resource outweigh the costs.
	(FRS 102 paragraph PBE34.69)
	Therefore, where it is not practicable to estimate the value of the resource with sufficient reliability, the income shall be included in the financial period when the resource is sold.
	(FRS 102 paragraph PBE34.70)

The overall principle that the resources received or receivable should be capable of being measured with sufficient reliability is consistent. As an accounting standard, FRS 102 provides more detail on when resources might be considered receivable and provides further guidance on applying the principles to specific circumstances.

Measurement

Statement of Principles: Interpretation for public benefit entities	FRS 102
Measurement should be based on the current value to the recipient. (Paragraph 4.48)	An entity shall measure incoming resources from non-exchange transactions as follows:
	(a) Donated services and facilities that would otherwise have been purchased shall be measured at the value to the entity.
	(b) All other incoming resources from non-exchange transactions shall be measured at the fair value of the resources received or receivable.
	(FRS 102 paragraph PBE34.73)
	Paragraph PBE34.73(a) requires donated services and facilities to be measured at the value to the entity. This requirement only applies to those services and facilities that would otherwise have been purchased by the entity. The value placed on these services and facilities should be the estimated value to the entity of the service or facility received, this will be the price the entity estimates it would pay in the open market for a service or facility of equivalent utility to the entity.
	(FRS 102 paragraph PBE34B.15)

In many cases there will be no change in the measurement of resources received in non-exchange transactions.

Disclosures

Statement of Principles: Interpretation for public benefit entities	FRS 102
This does not generally address detailed disclosure requirements, but does recommend disclosure of the nature and scale of donated services received that have not been recognised. (Paragraph 4.51)	Disclosure is required of: (a) The nature and amounts of resources receivable from non-exchange transactions that have been recognised in the financial statements. (b) Any unfulfilled conditions or other contingencies attached to resources that have been received in non-exchange transactions, but have not yet been recognised as income. (c) An indication of any other forms of resources from non-exchange transactions from which the entity has benefited. (FRS 102 paragraph PBE34.74)

There are no differences of principle between the requirements.

EXAMPLES

Example 1 Donated goods provided to charity shops

A charity receives many donations of unwanted clothes, books etc. The charity will need to sort through the donations to identify those suitable for sale in its shops, which may need cleaning, repairing etc before being ready for sale.

Some of the donated goods will not be suitable for sale, and the charity will then need to dispose of these goods, although textiles can be sold as rags, there may be costs involved in the disposal.

Typically the donated goods have low individual second-hand values. Overall, over the course of a year, the cash proceeds from the sale of donated goods are a material source of income to the charity.

There are no performance-related conditions attached to the donated goods, and therefore, in principle, the resources should be recognised as income when the goods are received. However, in order to recognise the income, the charity must be able to measure their value reliably, and have assessed the benefits of doing so as outweighing any costs involved.

The charity believes that, because it does not receive donations of high value items and it is difficult to reliably estimate the fair value less costs to sell of individual donations, the costs of determining the value of resources received at the time of receipt, outweighs the benefits of providing users with more timely information on receipt of donated goods. Instead, the charity recognises the donated resources as income when cash has been raised from the subsequent sale of the donated goods.

The charity discloses its accounting policy for donated goods. The charity should disclose any additional information that is relevant to understanding the extent of support received by the charity through donations.

Example 2 Donated services – Volunteers

A university receives help from a number of volunteers in running its library.

The volunteers are not trained librarians, and do not work in libraries as part of their paid employment.

In accordance with FRS 102 paragraph PBE34B.11, it is not possible to reasonably quantify the value of the services provided by the volunteers, and donated services are not recognised in the financial statements.

The university provides narrative disclosure of the assistance received from its volunteer librarians.

Example 3 Donated services – Services that would otherwise have been purchased

A public benefit entity receives pro bono legal services. The public benefit entity would otherwise have had to pay for legal services.

The public benefit entity is able to make a reliable estimate of the costs it would have incurred if it had paid for the legal services, based on price it estimates it would pay in an open market. Therefore the public benefit entity recognises the value of the donated legal services as income, and a corresponding expense is also recognised.

The public benefit entity provides disclosure of the nature and amount of the donated services received.

Example 4 Donation with performance-related conditions

A local sports club that is charity receives a donation from a former member, on condition that it is spent on purchasing a specific piece of sports equipment; a rowing boat costing approximately £20,000 which must be made available for use to club members. The donor makes the donation in advance of the order being placed for the boat.

The sports club's year end falls between the order being placed for the boat, and its delivery to the club. At the year end the sports club does not recognise the donation as income; it has not yet fulfilled the performance-related conditions attached to the donation which requires the purchase of the rowing boat and for it to be made available for use to members. Instead it will recognise a liability for the full amount of the donation.

The sports club will disclose the unfulfilled performance-related conditions attached to the donation.

The following year end, after the boat has been received and made available for use , the sports club will derecognise the liability, and recognise the donation as income in full. The boat will be recognised as an item of property, plant and equipment and be depreciated over its estimated useful life.

SEN 13
Transition to FRS 102 Disclaimer

Contents

Disclaimer

This Education Note has been prepared by FRC staff for the convenience of users of FRS 102 The Financial Reporting Standard applicable in the UK and Republic of Ireland. *It aims to illustrate certain requirements of FRS 102, but should not be relied upon as a definitive statement on the application of the standard. The illustrative material is not a substitute for reading the detailed requirements of FRS 102.*

This Staff Education Note was updated on 8 January 2014 for minor typographical errors in the suggested reconciliations on pages 11 to 13.

INTRODUCTION

Section 35 Transition to this FRS of FRS 102 *The Financial Reporting Standard applicable in the UK and Republic of Ireland* applies to the first-time adoption of FRS 102 and sets out how an entity prepares its first financial statements that conform with that standard.

FRS 102 will be effective for accounting periods beginning on or after 1 January 2015, although early application is permitted. It requires the comparative and opening balance sheet at the date of transition to be restated in accordance with FRS 102; the date of transition being the beginning of the earliest period for which an entity presents full comparative information. However, the opening balance sheet itself does not need to be presented.

FRS 102 requires the presentation of reconciliations of equity determined in accordance with its previous financial reporting framework and its equity determined in accordance with FRS 102 at two dates:

(a)   the date of transition to FRS 102; and
(b)   the end of the latest period presented in the entity's most recent annual financial statements determined in accordance with its previous financial reporting framework.

FRS 102 requires the presentation of a reconciliation of profit or loss determined in accordance with its previous financial reporting framework for the latest period in the entity's most recent annual financial statements to its profit or loss determined in accordance with FRS 102 for the same period.

For example, for an entity with a 31 December year end, the first year of mandatory application will be the year ending 31 December 2015. The entity will need to restate its opening balance sheet at the date of transition (ie at 1 January 2014) and comparative balance sheet (ie at 31 December 2014) in accordance with FRS 102, although the opening balance sheet need not be presented. The entity will need to prepare reconciliations of equity at 1 January 2014 and 31 December 2014 and of its profit or loss for the year ending 31 December 2014.

This Staff Education Note is written to highlight key areas of consideration when transitioning to FRS 102 and is not designed to be exhaustive.

TRANSITIONAL PROCEDURES

FRS 102 requires the balance sheet at the date of transition to be prepared in accordance with the recognition and measurement requirements of FRS 102.

Required amendments – Retrospective restatement

For an entity with a date of transition of 1 January 2014, it is required to restate its balance sheet at 31 December 2013 by making the adjustments that are necessary to recognise and measure all assets and liabilities in accordance with FRS 102.

Paragraph 35.7 of FRS 102 requires an entity to:

(a)   recognise all assets and liabilities whose recognition is required by FRS 102 (eg forward exchange contracts);
(b)   not recognise items as assets or liabilities if FRS 102 does not permit their recognition;
(c)   reclassify items (eg into different groupings in the cash flow statement); and
(d)   restate certain assets and liabilities at a different value (eg financial instruments measured at amortised cost using the effective interest rate, which in some cases may vary from a previously used historical cost).

Paragraph 35.8 states that adjustments on transition shall be recognised in retained earnings, or where appropriate, another category within equity.

Exceptions to retrospective restatement

Paragraph 35.9 states that on first-time adoption of FRS 102, an entity shall not retrospectively change the accounting that it followed under its previous financial reporting framework for any of the following transactions:

(a) **Derecognition of financial assets and financial liabilities:**
Financial assets and liabilities derecognised under an entity's previous accounting framework before the date of transition shall not be recognised upon adoption of this FRS. Conversely, for financial assets and liabilities that would have been derecognised under this FRS in a transaction that took place before the date of transition, but that were not derecognised under an entity's previous accounting framework, an entity may choose:

   (i)   to derecognise them on adoption of this FRS; or
   (ii) to continue to recognise them until disposed of or settled.

(b) **Hedge accounting:**
An entity shall not change its hedge accounting before the date of transition to this FRS for hedging relationships that no longer exist at the date of transition. For hedging relationships that exist at the date of transition, the entity shall follow the hedge accounting requirements of Section 12 *Other Financial Instruments Issues*, including the requirements for discontinuing hedge accounting for hedging relationships that do not meet the conditions of Section 12.

(c) **Accounting estimates** (see Example 5).
(d) **Discontinued operations.**
(e) *Measuring **non-controlling interests***:

   The requirements:

   (i)   to allocate profit or loss and total comprehensive income between non-controlling interest and owners of the parent;
   (ii) for accounting for changes in the parent's ownership interest in a subsidiary that do not result in a loss of control; and
   (iii) for accounting for a loss of control over a subsidiary

   shall be applied prospectively from the date of transition to this FRS (or from such earlier date as this FRS is applied to restate business combinations).

Optional exemptions

Paragraph 35.10 provides a number of exemptions that entities may elect to use on transition to FRS 102. These aim to ease the requirements for preparation of the balance sheet at the date of transition. Some areas included in these exemptions are:

(a) **Business combinations including group reconstructions:** An entity may elect not to restate business combinations that occurred before the transition date. However, if a first-time adopter restates any business combination to comply with FRS 102, it shall restate all later combinations (see Example 2). If a first-time adopter chooses not to apply Section 19 *Business Combinations* retrospectively, the first-time adopter shall recognise and measure all of its assets and liabilities acquired or assumed in a past business combination at the date of transition to FRS 102 in accordance with the requirements of FRS 102, except for goodwill and intangible assets subsumed in goodwill.
If a first-time adopter elects not to apply Section 19 retrospectively, it will still need to apply Section 19 prospectively to any goodwill recognised in its balance sheet at

the date of transition. As noted above, the carrying amount of the goodwill would not be adjusted on transition, however it would be amortised over a finite useful life going forward. For an entity that has previously determined a finite useful life for goodwill, the entity can continue to amortise that goodwill over this period so long as it can reliably estimate that useful life. For an entity that has previously determined an indefinite useful life for goodwill, the entity will need to reassess the remaining useful life going forward. If an entity is unable to reliably estimate the useful life of goodwill, then the useful life shall not exceed five years.

(b) *Share-based payment transactions:* An entity that has not previously applied FRS 20 *Share-based payments* may elect not to apply FRS 102 to equity instruments that were granted before the date of transition, or to liabilities arising from share-based payment transactions that were settled before the transition date. An entity that has previously applied FRS 20 (IFRS 2) shall apply FRS 20 / IFRS 2 or Section 26 of FRS 102.

(c) *Fair value as deemed cost:* An entity may elect for an item of property, plant or equipment, an investment property, or an intangible asset that meets the recognition criteria and the criteria for revaluation, to be measured at its fair value at the date of transition and for that fair value to be used as the deemed cost of the item going forward.

(d) *Revaluation as deemed cost:* For a revalued item of property, plant or equipment, investment property, or intangible asset that meets the recognition criteria and the criteria for revaluation, an entity may elect to use as its deemed cost, its revalued amount either at, or before the date of transition (see Example 3).

(e) *Individual and separate financial statements:* For investments in subsidiaries, associates and jointly controlled entities, an entity may elect to use the carrying amount at the date of transition determined under its previous GAAP as its deemed cost going forward.

(f) *Compound financial instruments:* For compound financial instruments where the liability component is not outstanding at the date of transition, an entity may elect not to separate out the liability and equity components.

(g) *Service concession arrangements – Accounting by operators:* An entity may elect not to apply FRS 102 to service concessions arrangements that were entered into before the date of transition. Instead, its previous accounting policies would continue to be applied. A similar exemption is not available to grantors.

(h) *Arrangements containing a lease:* An entity may elect to determine whether an arrangement contains a lease based on the facts and circumstances existing at the date of transition, rather than when the arrangement was entered into.

(i) *Decommissioning liabilities included in the cost of property, plant and equipment:* An entity may elect to measure the component of the cost of an item of property, plant and equipment resulting from decommissioning liabilities at the date of transition rather than on the date when the obligation initially arose.

(j) *Dormant companies:* There is no requirement for dormant companies to restate the opening balance sheet at the date of transition (nor any subsequent balance sheets) until there is a change in its existing balances or the company undertakes any new transactions.

(k) *Deferred development costs as deemed cost:* An entity may elect to carry forward the carrying amount of development costs deferred in accordance with SSAP 13 *Research and development* as the deemed cost at that date (see Example 4).

(l) *Borrowing costs:* An entity electing to adopt an accounting policy of capitalising borrowing costs may elect to treat the date of transition as the date on which capitalisation of borrowing costs commences (see Example 5).

(m) *Lease incentives:* An entity may elect not to apply FRS 102 to lease incentives provided the term of the lease commenced before the date of transition. Instead, the previous accounting treatment would continue to apply.

(n) *Public benefit entity combinations:* An entity may elect not to apply FRS 102 to public benefit entity combinations that were effected before the date of transition.

However, if a public benefit entity restates any entity combination to comply with this section, it shall restate all later entity combinations.

(o) *Designation of previously recognised financial instruments:* An entity may elect to designate previously recognised financial instruments at fair value through profit or loss on the date of transition provided they meet the criteria set out in paragraph 11.14(b) of FRS 102.

Other more specialised exemptions relate to extractive activities and assets and liabilities of subsidiaries (associates and joint ventures) where transition dates may differ from the parent (entity with significant influence and venturer).

EXAMPLES

Examples 1 to 5 in this Education Note relate to Entity T which has a 31 December 2015 year end and is preparing its first set of financial statements compliant with FRS 102. Its date of transition to FRS 102 is 1 January 2014.

Example 1 Accounting estimates

At 31 December 2013, Entity T had a significant debtor balance of CU500. Entity T was concerned about the credit risk of the debtor and was in discussion with the customer as to how the debt might be settled. As a consequence Entity T had made a provision of CU250, ie for 50 per cent of the balance.

During 2014, the debtor collapsed and is currently being liquidated. As a consequence Entity T does not think it will collect any of the outstanding debt.

Although Entity T is preparing an opening balance sheet at the date of transition as at 1 January 2014, hindsight shows that its accounting estimate made on 31 December 2013 was inaccurate[1], however it does not make a transitional adjustment as paragraph 35.9(c) of FRS 102 prohibits retrospective adjustments to correct accounting estimates.

Example 2 Business combination before the date of transition

On 1 January 2010, Entity T acquired a wholly owned subsidiary and applied the requirements of FRS 6 *Acquisitions and Mergers* and FRS 7 *Fair Values in Acquisition Accounting*. In accordance with these FRSs, Entity T recognised the following opening fair values in its consolidated financial statements:

	CU	CU
Property, plant and equipment	30,000	
Goodwill	10,000	
		40,000
Stock	1,000	
Debtors	1,500	
Net current assets	2,500	
Creditors	(3,000)	
Net current liabilities		(500)
Net assets acquired at fair value		39,500

[1] *It is also possible that the amount of provision that would have been recognised in accordance with FRS 102 would have differed, not only because of the effect of hindsight, but because the requirements of FRS 102 paragraphs 11.21 to 11.25 could have led to a different value for the impairment loss to be recognised (based on the information available at 31 December 2013).*

On transition (1 January 2014):

Goodwill

Paragraph 19.23(a) of FRS 102 states that goodwill shall be considered to have a finite useful life and if an entity is unable to make a reliable estimate of the useful life, the life shall not exceed five years.

On acquisition in 2010, Entity T decided that in accordance with FRS 10 *Goodwill* and intangible assets the goodwill had an economic life of 10 years. At 31 December 2013 the carrying amount for the goodwill is therefore CU6,000[2] and has a remaining useful life of 6 years.

Entity T considers there is evidence to support the remaining economic life of 6 years and provides adequate evidence to support this. It is therefore not required to adjust the expected amortisation profile.

Fair values at acquisition

As the acquisition occurred prior to the date of transition, Entity T elects not to apply FRS 102 to this acquisition (in accordance with paragraph 35.10(a)). Entity T therefore does not review the acquired identifiable assets and liabilities, either to determine whether additional items would have been recognised if FRS 102 had been applicable at the date of acquisition, or to restate their fair values at that date if application of FRS 102 would have required recognition at a different value. However, Entity T does need to consider whether assets and liabilities acquired in the business combination which are still held on the date of transition, are recognised and measured in accordance with FRS 102 going forward.

Example 3 Revaluation as deemed cost

Entity T has two properties, A and B. Neither Property A nor Property B is an investment property. Entity T has an accounting policy to revalue its properties and to depreciate them over a useful life of 50 years.

Property A was acquired on 31 December 1980 at a cost of CU1,000 and has been revalued on a regular basis; the last time was on 31 December 2010 where its value was recorded in the financial statements at CU100,000 and its remaining useful life was 20 years. There has been no significant change in the value of Property A since that revaluation.

Property B was acquired on 31 December 2010, at a cost of CU50,000. Property B has never been revalued as it was purchased in the year of the most recent valuation and its cost was the best available evidence of its valuation. There has been no impairment in its value.

On transition (1 January 2014):

Property A

If Entity T decides not to continue its policy of revaluation, it has a choice in relation to Property A:

(a)   it could elect to use the most recent revaluation in 2010 (being CU100,000) as its deemed cost at that date and no further adjustment is required; or

(b)   it could restate the property to its original cost of CU1,000.

[2] *Being CU10,000 x 6/10 years*

If the revalued amount of CU100,000 were used as its deemed cost, in order to comply with company law the revaluation reserve would be retained and the excess depreciation would continue to be offset against it.

If the property is restated to the original cost of CU1,000 the following adjustment would be required:

Dr	Revaluation Reserve	CU84,660
Dr	Accumulated depreciation	CU14,340[3]
Cr	Property, plant and equipment	CU99,000

Property B

No adjustment is required on transition for Property B[4].

Example 4 Carrying value of development costs

Entity T had previously made an accounting policy choice to capitalise development costs meeting the criteria set out in SSAP 13 *Accounting for research and development*[5].

In 2010 Entity T undertook a programme to develop the products it acquired as part of the acquisition in Example 1 to be compatible with its own products. In accordance with SSAP 13, it capitalised CU2,500 of expenditure which it is amortising over five years. Four years later at 31 December 2013, the carrying amount of asset was therefore CU500.

Paragraph 18.8H of FRS 102 permits an entity to recognise an intangible asset arising from the development phase of an internal project providing it meets certain criteria. Entity T makes the accounting policy choice to capitalise development costs meeting the criteria set out in FRS 102.

Entity T may elect to take the carrying amount of those development costs deferred in accordance with SSAP 13 at the date of transition, to be the deemed cost going forward. Therefore, although in this example it is unlikely that there is a material difference between the carrying value of the development costs measured using SSAP 13 or FRS 102, for ease Entity T elects to retain the value determined in accordance with SSAP 13 as the deemed cost of deferred development costs and makes no adjustment to its balance sheet at the date of transition.

Example 5 Borrowing costs

Entity T decided to construct a new building for its own use. Work on the construction commenced during 2013. Entity T capitalises tangible fixed assets on the basis of cost,

---

[3] *This represents three years depreciation (from 31 December 2010 to 1 January 2014) on the revalued amount being £15,000 in total (CU100,000 x 3 / 20 years remaining) less 33 years depreciation (from 31 Dec 1980 to 1 January 2014) on the historical cost being CU660 in total (CU1,000 x 33 / 50 years) which is not adjusted for.*

[4] *The exemption to permit revaluation as deemed cost is available at the level of individual items of property, plant and equipment. Entity T could choose to revalue Property B at the date of transition and use that new valuation as deemed cost. Similarly, as an alternative to using the 2010 valuation for Property A, Entity T could revalue it at the transition date (irrespective of whether Property B is revalued at transition date).*

[5] *Research expenditure must be expensed as incurred (SSAP 13 paragraph 24), but SSAP 13 permits a choice of accounting policy for development expenditure meeting certain criteria. Development expenditure may be written off as incurred, or deferred to future periods and amortised (SSAP 13 paragraphs 25 to 28).*

in accordance with FRS 15 *Tangible Fixed Assets*, but had not previously constructed any significant assets and therefore its accounting policy did not include the capitalisation of finance costs.

As at 31 December 2013, Entity T had capitalised construction costs of CU25,000 and estimated that it still had approximately nine months of construction work ahead. Had Entity T had a policy of capitalisation, finance costs that could have been capitalised amounted to CU300.

During 2014 Entity T completes construction of the building. The total cost to be capitalised in accordance with FRS 102 (excluding borrowing costs) is CU90,000. Qualifying borrowing costs calculated in accordance with FRS 102 relating to the project as a whole are CU2,500.

On transition to FRS 102, Entity T reviews its accounting policies and decides that it will now elect to capitalise borrowing costs in accordance with Section 25 *Borrowing Costs* of FRS 102, and in accordance with paragraph 35.10(o) it elects to capitalise costs prospectively from 1 January 2014. As a result, no adjustment is made to the balance sheet at the date of transition (ie 1 January 2014); the CU300 previously written off is not capitalised, but CU2,200[6] of borrowing costs are capitalised during the year ended 31 December 2014.

REQUIRED TRANSITIONAL DISCLOSURES

Explanation of transition to FRS 102

Paragraph 35.12 states that an entity shall explain how the transition from its previous financial reporting framework to this FRS affected its reported financial position, financial performance.

Example 6 Disclosure of transition to FRS 102

These financial statements for the year ended 31 December 2015 are the first financial statements of [name] that comply with FRS 102. The date of transition to FRS 102 is 1 January 2014.

The transition to FRS 102 has resulted in a small number of changes in accounting policies compared to those used previously.

The following notes to the financial statements describe the differences between equity and profit or loss presented previously, and the amounts as restated to comply with the accounting policies selected in accordance with FRS 102 for the reporting period ended at 31 December 2014 (ie comparative information), as well as equity presented in the opening statement of financial position (ie at 1 January 2014). It also describes all the required changes in accounting policies made on first-time adoption of FRS 102.

Reconciliations of equity and profit or loss

Paragraph 35.13 states that to comply with the above an entity's first financial statements prepared using this FRS shall include:

---

[6] *The amount capitalised is £2,200 = £2,500 (total qualifying borrowing costs) - £300 (borrowing costs incurred prior to 1 January 2014 and elected not to be capitalised).*

(a)   a description of the nature of each change in accounting policy.

(b)   reconciliations of its equity determined in accordance with its previous financial reporting framework to its equity determined in accordance with this FRS for both of the following dates:

    (i)   the date of transition to this FRS; and

    (ii)   the end of the latest period presented in the entity's most recent annual financial statements determined in accordance with its previous financial reporting framework.

(c)   a reconciliation of the profit or loss determined in accordance with its previous financial reporting framework for the latest period in the entity's most recent annual financial statements to its profit or loss determined in accordance with this FRS for the same period.

Paragraph 35.14 states that if an entity becomes aware of errors made under its previous financial reporting framework, the reconciliations required shall, to the extent practicable, distinguish the correction of those errors from changes in accounting policies.

FRS 102 does not specify the format of the reconciliations of equity and profit or loss. Set out below are suggested formats for the reconciliations, and entities will need to determine the most suitable format for their reconciliations taking into account the nature and amount of their own adjustments.

Reconciliations Suggested Option 1

Reconciliation of equity

	Note	At 1 Jan 2014			At 31 Dec 2014		
		As previously stated	Effect of transition	FRS 102 (as restated)	As previously stated	Effect of transition	FRS 102 (as restated)
		CU '000	CU '000	CU '000	CU '000	CU '000	CU '000
Fixed assets		5,868	–	5,868	5,416	–	5,416
Current assets	(i) (ii)	2,475	15	2,490	2,520	17[a]	2,537
Creditors: amounts falling due within one year	(i) (iii)	(2,355)	(16)[b]	(2,371)	(1,824)	(20)[c]	(1,844)
Net current assets		120	(1)	119	696	(3)	693
Total assets less current liabilities		5,988	(1)	5,987	6,112	(3)	6,109

[a] *Made up of financial assets of CU18,000 (Note i) and the decrease in stock of CU1,000 (Note ii).*

[b] *Made up of financial liabilities of CU17,000 (Note i) less creditors amounts falling due after more than one year of CU6,000 plus the holiday pay accrual of CU5,000 (Note iii).*

[c] *Made up of financial liabilities of CU17,000 (Note i) less creditors amounts falling due after more than one year of CU3,000 plus the holiday pay accrual of CU6,000 (Note iii).*

	Note	At 1 Jan 2014			At 31 Dec 2014		
		As previously stated	Effect of transition	FRS 102 (as restated)	As previously stated	Effect of transition	FRS 102 (as restated)
		CU '000	CU '000	CU '000	CU '000	CU '000	CU '000
Creditors: amounts falling due after more than one year	(i)	(2,900)	(6)	(2,906)	(2,840)	(3)	(2,843)
Provisions for liabilities		(410)	–	(410)	(465)	–	(465)
Net assets		2,678	(7)	2,671	2,807	(6)	2,801
Capital and reserves		2,678	(7)	2,671	2,807	(6)	2,801

Reconciliation of profit or loss for the year

	Note	Year ended 31 Dec 2014		
		As previously stated	Effect of transition	FRS 102 (as restated)
		CU '000	CU '000	CU '000
Turnover		832	–	832
Cost of sales	(i) (ii)	(520)	1[d]	(519)
Gross profit		312	1	313
Administrative expenses	(i) (ii) (iii)	(65)	0[e]	(65)
Other operating income		42	–	42
Operating profit		289	1	290
Interest receivable and similar income		5	–	5
Interest payable and similar charges		(130)	–	(130)
Taxation		(35)	–	(35)
Profit on ordinary activities after taxation and for the financial year		129	1	130

Reconciliations Suggested Option 2

Reconciliation of equity

	Note	At 1 Jan 2014	At 31 Dec 2014
		CU '000	CU '000
Capital and reserves (as previously stated)		2,678	2,807
Recognition of derivative financial instruments	(i)	(2)	1
Re-measurement of stock using spot exchange rate	(ii)	–	(1)
Short-term compensated absences	(iii)	(5)	(6)
Capital and reserves (as restated)		2,671	2,801

[d] *Made up of an increase of CU1,000 (Note ii) less the reclassification of CU2,000 to administrative expenses (Note ii) giving an overall reduction in cost of sales of CU1,000.*

[e] *Made up of a profit (ie a reduction in administrative expenses) from the recognition of the derivatives of CU3,000 (Note i), an increase from the reclassification of CU2,000 (Note ii) and an increase in the holiday pay accrual of CU1,000 (Note iii) giving an overall nil effect.*

Reconciliation of profit or loss for the year

	Note	Year ended 31 Dec 2014 CU '000
Profit for the year (as previously stated)		129
Recognition of derivative financial instruments	(i)	3
Re-measurement of stock using spot exchange rate	(ii)	(1)
Short-term compensated absences	(iii)	(1)
Profit for the year (as restated)		130

Notes to the reconciliations

The following notes are applicable to both formats set out above.

Financial instruments

(i)   [Name] was not previously required to recognise derivative financial instruments on the balance sheet. Instead the effects of the derivative financial instruments were recognised in profit or loss when the instruments were settled. Derivative financial instruments are classified as 'other financial instruments' in FRS 102 and are recognised as a financial asset or a financial liability, at fair value, when an entity becomes party to the contractual provisions of the instrument. Consequently financial assets of CU15,000 and financial liabilities of CU17,000 have been recognised in the opening balance sheet at 1 January 2014. Financial assets of CU18,000 and financial liabilities of CU17,000 have been recognised in the balance sheet as at 31 December 2014. Derivatives are measured to fair value with gains (losses) from changes in fair value recognised in profit or loss. The effect on profit for the year ended 31 December 2014 is an increase of CU3,000.

(ii)   The derivative financial instruments are foreign exchange forward contracts. In applying SSAP 20 *Foreign currency translation*, [Name] previously chose to translate purchases in foreign currencies at the rate of exchange specified in a matching forward contract. This is not permitted by FRS 102, which requires purchases to be translated using the spot exchange rate on the date of the transaction. FRS 102 does not provide an exemption from measuring stock bought in a foreign currency and paid for before the transition date in accordance with its required accounting policies, but the difference is not material and accordingly no adjustment has been made. Items purchased since the transition date have been re-measured based on spot exchange rate. Consequently stock at 31 December 2014 has been reduced and cost of sales for the year end has been increased by CU1,000 and costs of CU2,000 have been reclassified as administrative expenses rather than cost of sales.

Short-term compensated absences

(iii)   Prior to applying FRS 102, [Name] did not make provision for holiday pay (ie holiday earned but not taken prior to the year-end). FRS 102 requires the cost of short-term compensated absences to be recognised when employees render the service that increases their entitlement. Consequently an additional accrual of CU5,000 at 1 January 2014 has been made to reflect this. The additional provision at 31 December 2014 is CU6,000 and the effect on profit for the year ended 31 December 2014 is an additional expense of CU1,000.

SEN 13
Transition to FRS 102
(updated October 2015)

October 2015

Contents

Disclaimer

This Education Note has been prepared by FRC staff for the convenience of users of FRS 102 The Financial Reporting Standard applicable in the UK and Republic of Ireland. It aims to illustrate certain requirements of FRS 102, but should not be relied upon as a definitive statement on the application of the standard. The illustrative material is not a substitute for reading the detailed requirements of FRS 102.

This Staff Education Note was updated as follows:

(a) on 8 January 2014 for minor typographical errors in the suggested reconciliations on pages 11 to 13; and

(b) on 28 April 2015 to clarify the examples and revise the descriptions of the transitional exemptions to align with the requirements in the August 2014 edition of FRS 102.

(c) On 27 October 2015 to align with the September 2015 edition of FRS 102.

INTRODUCTION

Section 35 *Transition to this FRS* of FRS 102 *The Financial Reporting Standard applicable in the UK and Republic of Ireland* applies to the first-time adoption of FRS 102 and sets out how an entity prepares its first financial statements that conform with that standard.

FRS 102 is effective for accounting periods beginning on or after 1 January 2015. It requires the comparative and opening balance sheet at the date of transition to be restated in accordance with FRS 102; the date of transition being the beginning of the earliest period for which an entity presents full comparative information. However, the opening balance sheet itself does not need to be presented.

FRS 102 requires the presentation of reconciliations of equity determined in accordance with its previous financial reporting framework and its equity determined in accordance with FRS 102 at two dates:

(a)   the date of transition to FRS 102; and
(b)   the end of the latest period presented in the entity's most recent annual financial statements determined in accordance with its previous financial reporting framework.

FRS 102 requires the presentation of a reconciliation of profit or loss determined in accordance with its previous financial reporting framework for the latest period in the entity's most recent annual financial statements to its profit or loss determined in accordance with FRS 102 for the same period.

For example, for an entity with a 31 December year end, the first year of mandatory application will be the year ending 31 December 2015. The entity will need to restate its opening balance sheet at the date of transition (ie at 1 January 2014) and comparative balance sheet (ie at 31 December 2014) in accordance with FRS 102, although the opening balance sheet does not need to be presented. The entity will need to prepare reconciliations of equity at 1 January 2014 and 31 December 2014 and of its profit or loss for the year ending 31 December 2014.

This Staff Education Note is written to highlight key areas of consideration when transitioning to FRS 102 and is not designed to be exhaustive.

This Staff Education Note is based on the requirements of FRS 102 issued in September 2015.

TRANSITIONAL PROCEDURES

FRS 102 requires the balance sheet at the date of transition to be prepared in accordance with the recognition and measurement requirements of FRS 102.

Required amendments – Retrospective restatement

Paragraph 35.7 of FRS 102 requires an entity to:

(a)   recognise all assets and liabilities whose recognition is required by FRS 102 (eg forward exchange contracts);
(b)   not recognise items as assets or liabilities if FRS 102 does not permit their recognition;
(c)   reclassify items (eg into different groupings in the cash flow statement); and
(d)   restate certain assets and liabilities at a different value (eg financial instruments measured at amortised cost using the effective interest rate, which in some cases may vary from a previously used historical cost).

Paragraph 35.8 of FRS 102 states that adjustments on transition shall be recognised in retained earnings, or where appropriate, another category within equity.

For example, an entity with a date of transition of 1 January 2014 is required to reassess all its assets and liabilities as at 31 December 2013 and make any adjustments that are necessary to recognise and measure them in accordance with FRS 102.

Exceptions to retrospective restatement

Paragraph 35.9 of FRS 102 states that on first-time adoption of FRS 102, an entity shall not retrospectively change the accounting that it followed under its previous financial reporting framework for any of the following transactions:

(a) ***Derecognition of financial assets and financial liabilities:***
Financial assets and liabilities derecognised under an entity's previous accounting framework before the date of transition shall not be recognised upon adoption of this FRS. Conversely, for financial assets and liabilities that would have been derecognised under this FRS in a transaction that took place before the date of transition, but that were not derecognised under an entity's previous accounting framework, an entity may choose:

    (i) to derecognise them on adoption of this FRS; or

    (ii) to continue to recognise them until disposed of or settled.

(b) [Not used]

(c) ***Accounting estimates*** (see Example 1 below).

(d) ***Discontinued operations.***

(e) *Measuring **non-controlling interests***:

    The requirements:

    (i) to allocate profit or loss and total comprehensive income between non-controlling interest and owners of the parent;

    (ii) for accounting for changes in the parent's ownership interest in a subsidiary that do not result in a loss of control; and

    (iii) for accounting for a loss of control over a subsidiary

    shall be applied prospectively from the date of transition to this FRS (or from such earlier date as this FRS is applied to restate business combinations).

Optional exemptions

Paragraph 35.10 of FRS 102 provides a number of exemptions that entities may elect to use on transition to FRS 102. These aim to ease or remove the requirements of paragraph 35.7 of FRS 102 for the restatement of assets and liabilities at the date of transition. The optional exemptions in paragraph 35.10 of FRS 102 are (some of these have been summarised):

(a) ***Business combinations including group reconstructions:*** An entity may elect not to restate business combinations that occurred before the transition date (see Example 2). However, if a first-time adopter restates any business combination to comply with FRS 102, it shall restate all later combinations. If a first-time adopter chooses not to apply Section 19 *Business Combinations* retrospectively, the first-time adopter shall recognise and measure all of its assets and liabilities acquired or assumed in a past business combination at the date of transition to FRS 102 in accordance with the requirements of FRS 102, except for goodwill and intangible assets subsumed in goodwill.
If a first-time adopter elects not to apply Section 19 retrospectively, it will still need to apply Section 19 prospectively to any goodwill recognised in its balance sheet at

the date of transition. As noted above, the carrying amount of the goodwill would not be adjusted on transition, however it would be amortised over a finite useful life going forward. For an entity that has previously determined a finite useful life for goodwill, the entity can continue to amortise that goodwill over this period so long as it is a reliable estimate of the useful life. For an entity that has previously determined an indefinite useful life for goodwill, the entity will need to reassess the remaining useful life going forward. If an entity is unable to reliably estimate the useful life of goodwill, then the useful life shall not exceed ten years.

(b) ***Share-based payment transactions (revised in July 2015):*** An entity may elect not to apply FRS 102 to equity instruments (including the equity component of an instrument that was under previous GAAP treated as a compound instrument) that were granted before the date of transition. Entities selecting this option that have previously applied FRS 20 *(IFRS 2) Share-based payments* or IFRS 2 *Share-based payments* shall continue to apply either FRS 20 or IFRS 2 to these instruments. Entities are not required to apply FRS 102 to liabilities arising from share-based payment transactions that were settled before the transition date. For small entities[1] that have not previously applied either FRS 20 or IFRS 2, the exemption is extended to all equity instruments granted before the start of the first reporting period in which the entity adopts FRS 102, provided that they apply FRS 102 for the first time before 1 January 2017.

(c) ***Fair value as deemed cost:*** An entity may elect for an item of property, plant or equipment, an investment property, or an intangible asset that meets the recognition criteria and the criteria for revaluation, to be measured at its fair value at the date of transition and for that fair value to be used as the deemed cost of the item going forward.

(d) ***Revaluation as deemed cost:*** For a revalued item of property, plant or equipment, investment property, or intangible asset that meets the recognition criteria and the criteria for revaluation, an entity may elect to use as its deemed cost, its revalued amount either at, or before the date of transition (see Example 3).

(e) [Not used]

(f) ***Individual and separate financial statements:*** For investments in subsidiaries, associates and jointly controlled entities, an entity may elect to use the carrying amount at the date of transition determined under its previous GAAP as its deemed cost going forward.

(g) ***Compound financial instruments:*** For compound financial instruments where the liability component is not outstanding at the date of transition, an entity may elect not to separate out the liability and equity components.

(h) [Not used]

(i) ***Service concession arrangements – Accounting by operators:*** An entity may elect not to apply FRS 102 to service concessions arrangements that were entered into before the date of transition. Instead, its previous accounting policies would continue to be applied. A similar exemption is not available to grantors.

(j) ***Extractive activities:*** Oil and gas exploration and evaluation assets and other oil and gas assets in development or production phases may be measured at an amount determined under previous GAAP, subject to impairment tests at the date of transition.

(k) ***Arrangements containing a lease:*** An entity may elect to determine whether an arrangement contains a lease based on the facts and circumstances existing at the date of transition, rather than when the arrangement was entered into.

(l) ***Decommissioning liabilities included in the cost of property, plant and equipment:*** An entity may elect to measure the component of the cost of an item of property, plant and equipment resulting from decommissioning liabilities at the date of transition rather than on the date when the obligation initially arose.

---

[1] *Small entities are defined in FRS 102 (refer to the Glossary).*

(m) **Dormant companies:** There is no requirement for dormant companies to restate the opening balance sheet at the date of transition (nor any subsequent balance sheets) until there is a change in its existing balances or the company undertakes any new transactions.

(n) **Deferred development costs as deemed cost:** An entity may elect to carry forward the carrying amount of development costs deferred in accordance with SSAP 13 *Research and development* as the deemed cost at that date (see Example 4).

(o) **Borrowing costs:** An entity electing to adopt an accounting policy of capitalising borrowing costs may elect to treat the date of transition as the date on which capitalisation of borrowing costs commences (see Example 5).

(p) **Lease incentives:** An entity may elect not to apply FRS 102 to lease incentives provided the term of the lease commenced before the date of transition. Instead, the previous accounting treatment would continue to apply.

(q) **Public benefit entity combinations:** An entity may elect not to apply FRS 102 to public benefit entity combinations that were effected before the date of transition. However, if a public benefit entity restates any entity combination to comply with this section, it shall restate all later entity combinations.

(r) **Assets and liabilities of subsidiaries, associates and joint ventures:** Where the transition date of a subsidiary differs from that of its parent, the subsidiary, may elect to measure its assets and liabilities either at the date of transition of the parent or at the date the subsidiary transitions to FRS 102. A similar election is available to associates and joint ventures.

(s) **Designation of previously recognised financial instruments:** An entity may elect to designate previously recognised financial instruments at fair value through profit or loss on the date of transition provided they meet the criteria set out in paragraph 11.14(b) of FRS 102.

(t) **Hedge accounting (revised in July 2014):** An entity may apply hedge accounting prior to the documentation requirements set out in paragraphs 12.18(d) and (e) of FRS 102 being met, provided the required documentation is in place no later than the date the first FRS 102 compliant financial statements are authorised for issue. Further, when a hedging relationship has ceased to exist prior to the date of transition, an entity is not required to adjust the carrying amount of a hedged item. An entity that chooses to apply IAS 39 *Financial Instruments: Recognition and Measurement* or IFRS 9 *Financial Instruments*, as permitted by FRS 102, applies IFRS 1 *First-time adoption of International Financial Reporting Standards* instead of the transitional requirements and exemptions in FRS 102, subject to certain reliefs that apply in respect of the documentation requirements.

(u) *Small entities*[2] — *fair value measurement of financial instruments:* A small entity that did not measure financial instruments at fair value under its previous GAAP is not required to restate the comparative period information to comply with the fair value measurement requirements for financial instruments (eg for derivatives) of FRS 102. This exemption is only available to small entities applying FRS 102 for the first time before 1 January 2017.

(v) **Small entities**[3] — *financing transactions involving related parties:* A small entity is not required to restate comparative information in accordance with the accounting requirements for financing transactions[4] involving related parties in Section 11 *Basic Financial Instruments*. This exemption is only available to small entities applying FRS 102 for the first time before 1 January 2017.

---

[2] *Small entities are defined in FRS 102 (refer to the Glossary).*

[3] *Small entities are defined in FRS 102 (refer to the Glossary).*

[4] *Please refer to Staff Education Note 16* Financing transactions *for more detail on this topic.*

Examples

Examples 1 to 5 in this Education Note relate to entities which have a 31 December 2015 year end and prepare their first set of financial statements that are compliant with FRS 102 as at that date. Their date of transition to FRS 102 is 1 January 2014.

Example 1 Accounting estimates

At 31 December 2013, Entity A had a debtor balance of CU500. At 31 December 2013 Entity A was concerned about the credit risk of the debtor and was in discussion with the debtor as to how the debt might be settled. As a consequence Entity A had made a provision of CU250, ie for 50 per cent of the balance as at that date. During 2014 the debtor collapsed and was liquidated.

When Entity A prepares its opening balance sheet as at 1 January 2014 in accordance with FRS 102 it no longer believes it will collect any of the outstanding debt. However, Entity A does not revise its previous estimate taking into account hindsight for preparing its opening balance sheet as at 1 January 2014, because paragraph 35.9(c) of FRS 102 prohibits retrospective adjustments to accounting estimates on the date of transition.

Example 2 Business combination before the date of transition

On 1 January 2010, Entity B acquired a wholly owned subsidiary and applied the requirements of FRS 6 *Acquisitions and Mergers* and FRS 7 *Fair Values in Acquisition Accounting*. In accordance with these FRSs, Entity B recognised the following opening fair values in its consolidated financial statements: Entity B did not recognise deferred tax in respect of any of the fair value adjustments made on acquisition.

	CU	CU
Property, plant and equipment	30,000	
Goodwill	10,000	
		40,000
Stock	1,000	
Debtors	1,500	
Net current assets	2,500	
Creditors	(3,000)	
Net current liabilities		(500)
		39,500

On transition (1 January 2014):

(1) Measurement of goodwill

Paragraph 19.23(a) of FRS 102 states that goodwill shall be considered to have a finite useful life and in the exceptional cases when an entity is unable to make a reliable estimate of the useful life, the life shall not exceed 10 years.

On acquisition in 2010, Entity B decided that in accordance with FRS 10 *Goodwill and intangible assets* the goodwill had an economic life of 15 years. At 31 December 2013 the carrying amount for the goodwill is therefore CU7,333[5] and has a remaining useful life of 11 years.

---

[5] *Being CU10,000 × 11/15 years*

Entity B considers there is evidence to support the remaining useful economic life of 11 years and provides adequate evidence to support this. It is therefore not required to adjust the expected amortisation profile.

(2) Measurement of other acquired assets and liabilities

As permitted by paragraph 35.10(a) of FRS 102 Entity B decides not to apply the requirements of Section 19 *Business Combinations and Goodwill* retrospectively to the acquired assets and liabilities. In this case Entity B is still required to recognise and measure those acquired assets and liabilities that remain within the group at the date of transition in accordance with the other first-time adoption accounting requirements set out in paragraphs 35.7 to 35.9 and paragraphs 35.10 (b) to (t) of FRS 102.

Entity B determines that no adjustments to the acquired assets and liabilities are required in accordance with the first-time adoption accounting requirements of FRS 102, except for deferred tax. Paragraph 29.6 of FRS 102 requires the recognition of deferred tax on all timing differences. Entity B still owns the acquired property, plant and equipment which were fair valued on the date of acquisition. Entity B measures the deferred tax liability on the fair value adjustments (to the extent that they have not been reduced by depreciation prior to the date of transition) based on tax rates enacted or substantively enacted at the date of transition and records the corresponding adjustment in equity.

Example 3 Revaluation as deemed cost

Entity C has two properties, A and B. Neither Property A nor Property B is an investment property. Entity C has an accounting policy to revalue its properties and to depreciate them over a useful life of 50 years.

Property A was acquired on 31 December 1980 at a cost of CU1,000 and has been revalued on a regular basis; the last time was on 31 December 2010 when its value was recorded in the financial statements at CU100,000 and its remaining useful life was 20 years. There has been no significant change in the value of Property A since that revaluation.

Property B was acquired on 31 December 2010, at a cost of CU50,000. Property B has never been revalued as it was purchased in the same year that the most recent valuation was carried out and at that time its cost was the best available evidence of its valuation. There has been no impairment in its value.

On transition (1 January 2014):

Entity C decides not to continue its policy of revaluation as permitted by FRS 102.

Property A

Paragraph 35.10(d) provides an optional exemption from restating the value of the property based on its original cost. Therefore Entity C has the following two choices in relation to Property A:

(a)   it could elect to use the most recent revaluation from 2010 (being CU100,000) as its deemed cost at that date and no further adjustment is required; or

(b)   it could restate the property to its original cost of CU1,000.

If the revalued amount of CU100,000 were used as its deemed cost, in order to comply with company law the revaluation reserve would be retained and the excess depreciation would continue to be offset against it.

If the property is restated to the original cost of CU1,000 the following adjustment would be required:

Dr	Revaluation Reserve	CU84,660
Dr	Accumulated depreciation	CU14,340[6]
Cr	Property, plant and equipment	CU99,000

Property B

No adjustment is required on transition for Property B[7].

Example 4 Carrying value of development costs

Entity D had previously made an accounting policy choice to capitalise development costs meeting the criteria set out in SSAP 13 *Accounting for research and development*.[8] In 2010 Entity D undertook a programme to develop the products it acquired as part of an earlier acquisition to make them compatible with products it had developed in-house. In accordance with SSAP 13, it capitalised CU2,500 of expenditure which it is amortising over five years. Four years later at 31 December 2013, the carrying amount of asset was therefore CU500.

Paragraph 18.8H of FRS 102 permits an entity to recognise an intangible asset arising from the development phase of an internal project providing it meets certain criteria. Entity D makes the accounting policy choice to capitalise development costs meeting the criteria set out in Section 18 *Intangible Assets other than Goodwill* of FRS 102.

As permitted by paragraph 35.10(n), Entity D may elect to take the carrying amount of those development costs deferred in accordance with SSAP 13 at the date of transition to be the deemed cost going forward. Therefore, although in this example it is unlikely that there is a material difference between the carrying value of the development costs measured using SSAP 13 or FRS 102, for ease Entity D elects to retain the value determined in accordance with SSAP 13 as the deemed cost of deferred development costs and makes no adjustment to the carrying value of the deferred development costs at the date of transition.

Example 5 Borrowing costs

Entity E decided to construct a new building for its own use. Work on the construction commenced during 2013. Entity E capitalised tangible fixed assets on the basis of cost, in accordance with FRS 15 *Tangible Fixed Assets*, but had not previously constructed any significant assets and therefore its accounting policy did not include the capitalisation of finance costs.

---

[6] *This represents three years depreciation (from 31 December 2010 to 1 January 2014) on the revalued amount being £15,000 in total (CU100,000 × 3 / 20 years remaining) less 33 years depreciation (from 31 Dec 1980 to 1 January 2014) on the historical cost being CU660 in total (CU1,000 × 33 / 50 years) which is not adjusted for.*

[7] *The exemption to permit revaluation as deemed cost is available at the level of individual items of property, plant and equipment. Entity C could choose to revalue Property B at the date of transition and use that new valuation as deemed cost. Similarly, as an alternative to using the 2010 valuation for Property A, Entity C could revalue it at the transition date (irrespective of whether Property B is revalued at transition date).*

[8] *Research expenditure must be expensed as incurred (SSAP 13 paragraph 24), but SSAP 13 permits a choice of accounting policy for development expenditure meeting certain criteria. Development expenditure may be written off as incurred, or deferred to future periods and amortised (SSAP 13 paragraphs 25 to 28).*

As at 31 December 2013, Entity E had capitalised construction costs of CU25,000 and estimated that it still had approximately nine months of construction work ahead. Had Entity E had a policy of capitalisation, finance costs that could have been capitalised amounted to CU300.

During 2014 Entity E completed construction of the building. The total cost to be capitalised in accordance with FRS 102 (excluding borrowing costs) is CU90,000. Qualifying borrowing costs calculated in accordance with FRS 102 relating to the project as a whole are CU2,500.

On transition to FRS 102, Entity E reviews its accounting policies and decides that it will now elect to capitalise borrowing costs in accordance with Section 25 *Borrowing Costs* of FRS 102, and in accordance with paragraph 35.10(o) it elects to capitalise costs prospectively from 1 January 2014. As a result, no adjustment is made to the carrying value of the asset at the date of transition (ie 1 January 2014); the CU300 previously written off are not capitalised, but CU2,200[9] of borrowing costs are capitalised during the year ended 31 December 2014.

REQUIRED TRANSITIONAL DISCLOSURES

Explanation of transition to FRS 102

Paragraph 35.12 states that an entity[10] shall explain how the transition from its previous financial reporting framework to FRS 102 affected its reported financial position and performance.

Paragraph 35.13 states that to comply with the above an entity's first financial statements prepared using FRS 102 shall include:

(a) a description of the nature of each change in accounting policy.
(b) reconciliations of its equity determined in accordance with its previous financial reporting framework to its equity determined in accordance with this FRS [FRS 102] for both of the following dates:
   (i)   the date of transition to this FRS [FRS 102]; and
   (ii) the end of the latest period presented in the entity's most recent annual financial statements determined in accordance with its previous financial reporting framework.
(c) a reconciliation of the profit or loss determined in accordance with its previous financial reporting framework for the latest period in the entity's most recent annual financial statements to its profit or loss determined in accordance with this FRS [FRS 102] for the same period.

Paragraph 35.14 states that if an entity becomes aware of errors made under its previous financial reporting framework, the reconciliations required shall, to the extent practicable, distinguish the correction of those errors from changes in accounting policies.

FRS 102 does not specify the format of the reconciliations of equity and profit or loss. Set out below are suggested formats for the reconciliations, but entities will need to determine

---

[9] *The amount capitalised is £2,200 = £2,500 (total qualifying borrowing costs) − £300 (borrowing costs incurred prior to 1 January 2014 and elected not to be capitalised).*

[10] *Small entities (as defined in the Glossary of FRS 102) are not required to make the disclosures set out in Section 35, but should consider whether they are necessary for their financial statements to give a true and fair view (paragraph 1A.17 of FRS 102). Small entities are required to make the disclosures required by paragraphs 1AC.7 to 1AC.9 of FRS 102 in respect of changes in presentation and accounting policies and correction of errors.*

the most suitable format for their reconciliations taking into account the nature and amount of their own adjustments.

Example 6 Disclosure of transition to FRS 102

Entity F prepares its first financial statements that comply with FRS 102 for the year ended 31 December 2015. Entity F's date of transition to FRS 102 is 1 January 2014. For Entity F the transition to FRS 102 has resulted in only a small number of changes in accounting policies compared to those used previously.

The following examples of notes to the financial statements of Entity F describe the differences between equity and profit or loss presented previously, and the amounts as restated to comply with the accounting policies selected in accordance with FRS 102 for the reporting period ended at 31 December 2014 (ie comparative information), as well as equity presented in the opening statement of financial position (ie at 1 January 2014). It also describes all the required changes in accounting policies made on first-time adoption of FRS 102.

Reconciliations Suggested Option 1 Reconciliation of equity

	Note	At 1 Jan 2014			At 31 Dec 2014		
		As previously stated	Effect of transition	FRS 102 (as restated)	As previously stated	Effect of transition	FRS 102 (as restated)
		CU '000	CU '000	CU '000	CU '000	CU '000	CU '000
Fixed assets		5,868	–	5,868	5,416	–	5,416
Current assets	(i) (ii)	2,475	15	2,490	2,520	17ᵃ	2,537
Creditors: amounts falling due within one year	(i) (iii)	(2,355)	(16)ᵇ	(2,371)	(1,824)	(20)ᶜ	(1,844)
Net current assets		120	(1)	119	696	(3)	693
Total assets less current liabilities		5,988	(1)	5,987	6,112	(3)	6,109
Creditors: amounts falling due after more than one year	(i)	(2,900)	(6)	(2,906)	(2,840)	(3)	(2,843)
Provisions for liabilities		(410)	–	(410)	(465)	–	(465)
Net assets		2,678	(7)	2,671	2,807	(6)	2,801
Capital and reserves		2,678	(7)	2,671	2,807	(6)	2,801

ᵃ *Made up of financial assets of CU18,000 (Note (i)) and the decrease in stock of CU1,000 (Note (ii)).*

ᵇ *Made up of financial liabilities of CU17,000 (Note (i)) less creditors amounts falling due after more than one year of CU6,000 plus the holiday pay accrual of CU5,000 (Note (iii)).*

ᶜ *Made up of financial liabilities of CU17,000 (Note (i)) less creditors amounts falling due after more than one year of CU3,000 plus the holiday pay accrual of CU6,000 (Note (iii)).*

Reconciliation of profit or loss for the year

	Note	Year ended 31 Dec 2014		
		As previously stated	Effect of transition	FRS 102 (as restated)
		CU '000	CU '000	CU '000
Turnover		832	–	832
Cost of sales	(i) (ii)	(520)	1ᵈ	(519)
Gross profit		312	1	313
Administrative expenses	(i) (ii) (iii)	(65)	0ᵉ	(65)
Other operating income		42	–	42
Operating profit		289	1	290
Interest receivable and similar income		5	–	5
Interest payable and similar charges		(130)	–	(130)
Taxation		(35)	–	(35)
Profit on ordinary activities after taxation and for the financial year		129	1	130

Reconciliations Suggested Option 2 Reconciliation of equity

		At 1 Jan 2014	At 31 Dec 2014
	Note	CU '000	CU '000
Capital and reserves (as previously stated)		2,678	2,807
Recognition of derivative financial instruments	(i)	(2)	1
Re-measurement of stock using spot exchange rate	(ii)	–	(1)
Short-term compensated absences	(iii)	(5)	(6)
Capital and reserves (as restated)		2,671	2,801

Reconciliation of profit or loss for the year

	Note	Year ended 31 Dec 2014
		CU '000
Profit for the year (as previously stated)		129
Recognition of derivative financial instruments	(i)	3
Re-measurement of stock using spot exchange rate	(ii)	(1)
Short-term compensated absences	(iii)	(1)
Profit for the year (as restated)		130

ᵈ *Made up of an increase of CU1,000 (Note (ii)) less the reclassification of CU2,000 to administrative expenses (Note (ii)) giving an overall reduction in cost of sales of CU1,000.*

ᵉ *Made up of a profit (ie a reduction in administrative expenses) from the recognition of the derivatives of CU3,000 (Note (i)), an increase from the reclassification of CU2,000 (Note (ii)) and an increase in the holiday pay accrual of CU1,000 (Note (iii)) giving an overall nil effect.*

Notes to the reconciliations

The following notes are applicable to both formats set out above.

Financial instruments

(i)   Entity F was not previously required to recognise derivative financial instruments on the balance sheet. Instead the effects of the derivative financial instruments were recognised in profit or loss when the instruments were settled. Derivative financial instruments are classified as 'other financial instruments' in FRS 102 and are recognised as a financial asset or a financial liability, at fair value, when an entity becomes party to the contractual provisions of the instrument. Consequently financial assets of CU15,000 and financial liabilities of CU17,000 have been recognised in the opening balance sheet at 1 January 2014. Financial assets of CU18,000 and financial liabilities of CU17,000 have been recognised in the balance sheet as at 31 December 2014. Derivatives are measured to fair value with gains (losses) from changes in fair value recognised in profit or loss. The effect on profit for the year ended 31 December 2014 is an increase of CU3,000.

(ii)   The derivative financial instruments are foreign exchange forward contracts. In applying SSAP 20 *Foreign currency translation*, Entity F previously chose to translate purchases in foreign currencies at the rate of exchange specified in a matching forward contract. This is not permitted by FRS 102, which requires purchases to be translated using the spot exchange rate on the date of the transaction. FRS 102 does not provide an exemption from measuring stock bought in a foreign currency and paid for before the transition date in accordance with its required accounting policies, but the difference is not material and accordingly no adjustment has been made. Items purchased since the transition date have been re-measured based on spot exchange rate. Consequently stock at 31 December 2014 has been reduced and cost of sales for the year end has been increased by CU1,000 and costs of CU2,000 have been reclassified as administrative expenses rather than cost of sales.

Short-term compensated absences

(iii) Prior to applying FRS 102, Entity F did not make provision for holiday pay (ie holiday earned but not taken prior to the year-end). FRS 102 requires the cost of short-term compensated absences to be recognised when employees render the service that increases their entitlement. Consequently an additional accrual of CU5,000 at 1 January 2014 has been made to reflect this. The additional provision at 31 December 2014 is CU6,000 and the effect on profit for the year ended 31 December 2014 is an additional expense of CU1,000.

SEN 14
Credit unions – Illustrative financial statements

Contents

	Page

Disclaimer

This Education Note has been prepared by FRC staff for the convenience of users of FRS 102 The Financial Reporting Standard applicable in the UK and Republic of Ireland. It aims to illustrate certain requirements of FRS 102, but should not be relied upon as a definitive statement on the application of the standard. The illustrative material is not a substitute for reading the detailed requirements of FRS 102.

INTRODUCTION

This Staff Education Note has been prepared from an anonymous set of credit union financial statements prepared in accordance with current accounting standards for the year ended 30 September 2009 and have not been updated for any changes in legislation or for the introduction of any potentially new financial instruments.

As a result, in some areas the disclosures in this Staff Education Note are limited (identified by a 'X') where additional information is required to be disclosed by FRS 102, but which was not required to be disclosed in the existing financial statements.

This Staff Education Note is written to illustrate some of the key differences between current accounting standards and FRS 102 *The Financial Reporting Standard applicable in the UK and Republic of Ireland* and is not designed to be exhaustive. There may be transactions that a credit union may enter into, that are not reflected in these illustrative financial statements. Credit unions should refer to relevant legislation to ensure requirements are met.

Credit Union A
30 September 2016

FSA registration number xx

Directors'
Report and
Financial
Statements

Administrative information

Directors

[Include names of directors in office at the date of authorisation of the financial statements]

Secretary
Industrial and Provident Society
Registration Number
Financial Services Authority Registration
Number
Registered Office
Auditors
Bankers
Solicitors

Contents

Directors' Report

for the year ended 30 September 2016

The Directors present their report and the financial statements for the year ended 30 September 2016.

[...]

The Directors' Report was approved by the Board of Directors on [date] and signed on its behalf by:

[Name]

Independent Auditors' Report

[...]

Revenue Account[1]

for the year ended 30 September 2016

	Note	2016 £	2015 £
Loan interest receivable and similar income	4	1,019,175	945,434
Interest payable	5	(318,670)	(435,007)
Net interest income[2]		700,505	510,427
Fees and commissions receivable	6	3,532	3,184
Fees and commissions payable[3]		(3,179)	(3,110)
Net fees and commissions receivable[4]		353	74
Other income		893	5,008
Administrative expenses	7a	(304,401)	(333,317)
Depreciation and amortisation	10	(22,214)	(24,230)
Other operating expenses	7b	(104,419)	(115,420)
Impairment losses on loans to members[5]	11e	(58,585)	(52,433)
Surplus before taxation		212,132	(9,891)
Taxation	9a	(11,024)	(26,950)
Surplus for the financial year		201,108	(36,841)
Other comprehensive income[6]		–	–
Total comprehensive income		201,108	(36,841)

---

[1] *Revenue Account is the title required by the Friendly and Industrial and Provident Societies Act 1968. FRS 102 does not require use of the title Statement of Comprehensive Income. Paragraph 4.2 permits a choice of formats. Credit Union A chooses to present its revenue account in accordance with the requirements for a profit and loss account in Schedule 2 to The Large and Medium-sized Companies and Groups (Accounts and Reports) Regulations 2008 (the Regulations).*

[2] *This subtotal is not required by Schedule 2 to the Regulations, but is often provided by financial institutions.*

[3] *In this case, bank charges have been classified as fees and commissions payable. If there are more components to fees and commissions payable it might be useful to provide a note to the financial statements showing the different components.*

[4] *This subtotal is not required by Schedule 2 to the Regulations, but is often provided by financial institutions.*

[5] *This includes provision for doubtful debts, bad debts written off and reversal of impairment losses on bad debts recovered. Writing off bad debts is not the same as derecognising the financial asset (as evidenced by the reversal of impairment losses).*

[6] *As there is no other comprehensive income, this need not necessarily be shown, although in those circumstances it would be good practice to add a footnote to confirm that there are no items of other comprehensive income. Credit Union A has chosen the single-statement approach to the Statement of Comprehensive Income.*

Balance Sheet[7]

as at 30 September 2016

	Note	2016 £	2015 £
ASSETS			
Cash, cash equivalents and liquid deposits[8]			
Cash and balances with the Bank of England[9]	15		
Loans and advances to banks	15	**1,542,720**	2,148,704
Loans and advances to members	11	**13,713,454**	12,243,266
Tangible fixed assets	10	**100,818**	114,615
Other receivables		**23,374**	22,725
Prepayments and accrued income		**22,315**	28,878
Total assets		**15,402,681**	14,558,188
LIABILITIES			
Subscribed capital – repayable on demand	12	**(13,655,585)**	(13,004,895)
Other payables	13	**(39,538)**	(46,843)
		(13,695,123)	(13,051,738)
Retained earnings		**1,707,558**	1,506,450
Total liabilities		**15,402,681**	14,558,188

The financial statements were approved, and authorised for issue, by the Board on [date] and signed on its behalf by:

[Name][10]

Statement of changes in retained earnings

for the year ended 30 September 2016

	2016 £	2015 £
As at 1 October 2015	**1,506,450**	1,543,291
Total comprehensive income for the year	**201,108**	(36,841)
As at 30 September 2016	**1,707,558**	1,506,450

---

[7] *Balance sheet is the term used in the Friendly and Industrial and Provident Societies Act 1968. FRS 102 does not require use of the title Statement of Financial Position. Credit Union A has chosen to present its balance sheet in accordance with Schedule 2 to the Large and Medium-sized Companies and Groups (Accounts and Reports) Regulations 2008 (the Regulations).*

[8] *This heading is not required by Schedule 2 to the Regulations. It has been included in order to group together the line items users might regard as cash.*

[9] *It has been assumed that Credit Union A does not hold cash with the Bank of England. If there is no cash held with the Bank of England in either year presented, there is no need to include this line item.*

[10] *The balance sheet should be signed by the secretary and two directors.*

Cash flow statement[11]

for the year ended 30 September 2016

	Note	2016 £	2015 £
Cash flows from operating activities			
Surplus/(deficit) before taxation		**212,132**	(9,891)
Adjustments for non-cash items:			
Depreciation	10	**22,214**	24,230
Impairment losses	11e	**59,746**	56,536
		81,960	80,766
Movements in:			
Accrued interest		**6,563**	44,024
Other receivables		**(649)**	(3,453)
Other payables		**8,618**	3,230
		14,532	43,801
Cash flows from changes in operating assets and liabilities			
Cash inflow from subscribed capital	12	**5,272,934**	5,019,614
Cash outflow from repaid capital	12	**(4,622,244)**	(5,035,601)
New loans to members	11a	**(7,713,518)**	(6,887,274)
Repayment of loans by members	11a	**6,183,584**	6,269,395
		(879,244)	(633,866)
Taxation paid		**(26,947)**	(37,893)
Net cash flows from operating activities		**(597,567)**	(557,083)
Cash flows from investing activities			
Purchase of property, plant and equipment	10	**(8,417)**	(10,327)
Net cash flow from managing liquid deposits		**250,000**	(1,000,000)
		241,583	(1,010,327)
Net decrease in cash and cash equivalents		**(355,984)**	(1,567,410)
Cash and cash equivalents at beginning of year		**1,148,704**	2,715,844
Cash and cash equivalents at end of year	15	**792,720**	1,148,704

Notes to the financial statements

for the year ended 30 September 2016

1. Legal and regulatory framework

Credit Union A is a society established under the Industrial and Provident Societies Act 1965, whose principal activity is to operate as a credit union, within the meaning of the Credit Unions Act 1979. Credit Union A has registered with the Financial Conduct Authority and is regulated by the Prudential Regulation Authority under the provisions of the Financial Services and Markets Act 2000.

In accordance with the regulatory environment for credit unions, deposits from members can be made by subscription for redeemable shares, deferred shares and interest-bearing shares. At present Credit Union A has only issued redeemable shares.

---

[11] *In accordance with FRS 102 paragraph 7.2, the cash flow statement reconciles cash and cash equivalents, which are highly liquid investments with a short-term maturity (three-months or less). Cash and cash equivalents will include both cash and balances at the central bank (ie Bank of England) and short-term deposits with other financial institutions. In accordance with FRS 102 paragraph 7.20, the components of cash and cash equivalents are disclosed in the notes to the financial statements.*

2. Accounting policies

Basis of preparation

These financial statements have been prepared in accordance with FRS 102 *The Financial Reporting Standard applicable in the UK and Republic of Ireland.*

The financial statements are prepared on the historical cost basis.

[If other bases were applicable, include. Areas where other bases have been applied are identified in the accounting policies below.]

First-time adoption of FRS 102

These are Credit Union A's first financial statements to comply with FRS 102. The date of transition to FRS 102 is 1 October 2014.

The transition to FRS 102 has resulted in a small number of accounting policy changes compared to those applied previously. Note 19 to the financial statements describes the differences between the retained earnings and surplus or deficit presented previously, and the amounts as restated to comply with the accounting policies selected in accordance with FRS 102 for the reporting period ended at 30 September 2015 (ie comparative information), as well as the retained earnings presented in the opening balance sheet (ie at 1 October 2014). It also describes all the required changes in accounting policies made on first-time adoption of FRS 102.

Going concern

The financial statements are prepared on the going concern basis. The directors of Credit Union A believe this is appropriate despite a mismatch in the maturity analysis of subscribed capital and loans to members, because *[...include relevant explanation, which, for example, might refer to some of the subscribed capital not being redeemable at short notice unless loans with the same member have been repaid[12]].*

Income

Loan interest receivable and similar income: Interest on both loans to members and loans to banks (ie cash and cash equivalents held on deposit with other financial institutions) is recognised using the effective interest method[13], and is calculated and accrued on a daily basis.

Fees and commissions receivable: Fees and charges either arise in connection with a specific transaction, or accrue evenly over the year. Income relating to individual transactions is recognised when the transaction is completed.

Other income: Other income is recognised when *[...]*

---

[12] *Credit Unions should consider consistency between the description of liquidity risk associated with subscribed capital (especially any that is not repayable until loans to the same member have been repaid) and the liquidity risk disclosures in note 14.*

[13] *Credit unions will need to consider whether there are other charges or fees that should be included in the calculation of the effective interest rate, rather than being classified separately.*

Taxation

The tax charge for the year reflects current tax payable. Current tax is the expected corporation tax payable for the year, using tax rates in force for the year. Credit Union A is not liable to corporation tax payable on its activities of making loans to members, and investing surplus funds, as these are not classified as a trade. However, corporation tax is payable on investment income.

As a result of the limited activities of Credit Union A from which profits are chargeable to corporation tax, it is unlikely that deferred tax will arise.

Tangible fixed assets

Tangible fixed assets comprises items of property, plant and equipment, which are stated at cost, less accumulated depreciation and any accumulated impairment losses. Cost includes expenditure that is directly attributable to the acquisition of the asset.

Deprecation is provided to write off the cost of each item of property, plant and equipment, less its estimated residual value, on a straight line basis over its estimated useful life. The categories of property, plant and equipment are depreciated as follows:

Land and buildings   10 to 25 years
Office equipment   3 to 5 years
Fixtures and fittings   5 years

Cash and cash equivalents

Cash and cash equivalents comprise cash on hand and with the Bank of England and loans and advances to banks (ie cash deposited with banks) with maturity of less than or equal to three months.

Financial assets – loans and advances to members

Loans to members are financial assets with fixed or determinable payments, and are not quoted in an active market. Loans are recognised when cash is advanced to members and measured at amortised cost using the effective interest method.

Loans are derecognised when the right to receive cash flows from the asset have expired, usually when all amounts outstanding have been repaid by the member. *[In accordance with relevant regulations]* Credit Union A does not transfer loans to third parties.

Impairment of financial assets

Credit Union A assesses, at each balance sheet date, if there is objective evidence that any of its loans to members are impaired. The loans are assessed collectively in groups that share similar credit risk characteristics, because no loans are individually significant. In addition, if, during the course of the year, there is objective evidence that any individual loan is impaired, a specific loss will be recognised.

Any impairment losses are recognised in the revenue account, as the difference between the carrying value of the loan and the net present value of the expected cash flows.

Financial liabilities – subscribed capital

Members' shareholdings in Credit Union A are redeemable and therefore are classified as financial liabilities, and described as subscribed capital. They are initially recognised at the amount of cash deposited and subsequently measured at amortised cost.

[Where a credit union has issued deferred shares, as permitted by the The Legislative Reform (Industrial and Provident Societies and Credit Unions) Order 2011, it will need to determine its accounting policy for these shares. Credit unions should consider the rights and obligations existing in relation to those deferred shares in the context of Section 22 of FRS 102, which sets out the conditions for classifying an instrument as equity, including that it can only be settled in cash in the event of liquidation. Where any deferred shares are classified as equity the dividends paid to the holders of the deferred shares will be classified as a distribution to owners and be recognised in the Statement of Changes in Retained Earnings. Credit unions will need to consider making it clear to users what the distinction is between 'dividends' recognised as interest payable and dividends recognised as distributions.]

Employee benefits

Defined contribution plans: The amounts charged as expenditure for the defined contribution plan are the contributions payableby Credit Union A for the relevant period.

Other employee benefits: Other short and long term employee benefits, including holiday pay, are recognised as an expense over the period they are earned.

Reserves

Retained earnings are the accumulated surpluses to date that have not been declared as dividends returnable to members.

3. Use of estimates and judgements

The preparation of financial statements requires the use of certain accounting estimates. It also requires the Directors to exercise judgement in applying Credit Union A's accounting policies. The areas requiring a higher degree of judgement, or complexity, and areas where assumptions or estimates are most significant to the financial statements, are disclosed below:

Impairment losses on loans to members

[Say something about how Credit Union A conducts impairment reviews and what sort of observable evidence is used.]

[Include any other areas of significant estimates or judgements, if any][14]

---

[14] *Without further information it has been assumed that Credit Union A does not have any assets, liabilities or transactions that would need to be recognised in accordance with FRS 102, and which are not already referenced in its financial statements prepared in accordance with UK accounting standards. For example, this could include arrangements with the substance, but not the form, of a lease.*

4. Loan interest receivable and similar income

	Note	2016 £	2015 £
Loan interest receivable from members		**971,911**	817,001
Bank interest receivable on cash and liquid deposits		**47,264**	128,433
Total loan interest receivable and similar income		**1,019,175**	945,434

5. Interest expense

Interest expense is the dividend paid to members for the prior year. The dividend is formally proposed by the Directors after the year end and is confirmed at the following AGM. As a result it does not represent a liability at the balance sheet date.

	Note	2016 £	2015 £
Interest paid during the year		**318,670**	435,007
Dividend rate:			
Share 1 accounts		**2.5%**	x%
Saverplus accounts		**1.0%**	x%
Interest proposed, but not recognised		**389,383**	318,670
Dividend rate:			
Share 1 accounts		**3.0%**	2.5%
Saverplus accounts		**1.5%**	1.0%

[Where a credit union has issued interest-bearing shares, as permitted by the The Legislative Reform (Industrial and Provident Societies and Credit Unions) Order 2011, it will need to consider disaggregating interest expense between that which is paid as a 'dividend' on members' deposits and that which is paid on interest-bearing shares. Additional accounting policy disclosure should also be considered.]

6. Fees and commissions receivable

	Note	2016 £	2015 £
Entrance fees		**2,265**	1,945
Insurance commission received		**872**	869
Annual service charge		**395**	370
Total fees and commissions receivable		**3,532**	3,184

7. Expenses

	Note	2016 £	2015 £
Administrative expenses	7a	**304,401**	333,317
Depreciation and amortisation	10	**22,214**	24,230
Other operating expenses	7b	**104,419**	115,420
		431,034	472,967

[This note is not required by FRS 102, but has been included as an aggregation of the costs that credit unions might currently consider to be their expenses, in case it is a metric credit unions use to manage their business.]

7a. Administrative expenses

	Note	2016	2015
		£	£
Employment costs	8b	234,175	259,535
Staff training		516	404
Directors' expenses		3,244	3,161
Other staff expenses		7,453	7,269
Auditors' remuneration	7c	4,403	5,084
Telephone		6,852	3,986
Computer maintenance		9,999	12,968
Legal and professional		9,145	18,244
General expenses		4,175	689
Printing, postage and stationery		21,622	19,123
Other insurance		2,817	2,854
Total administrative expenses		**304,401**	**333,317**

7b. Other operating expenses

Other operating expenses comprise the costs of occupying offices and regulatory and financial management costs:

	2016	2015
	£	£
Cost of occupying offices (excluding depreciation)		
Cleaning	6,680	6,762
Repairs and maintenance	4,507	4,105
Heating and lighting	4,245	4,138
	15,432	15,005
Regulatory and financial management costs		
Financial Conduct Authority and Prudential Regulation Authority fees	1,629	1,450
Association of British Credit Unions Limited dues	8,477	8,436
Financial Services Compensation Scheme levy	12,730	–
Fidelity insurance	4,838	4,838
Loan protection and life savings insurance	61,313	85,691
	88,987	100,415
	104,419	115,420

7c. Auditors' remuneration

Credit Union A voluntarily presents an analysis of its auditors' remuneration in accordance with the Companies (Disclosure of Auditor Remuneration and Liability Limitation Agreements) Regulations 2008.

	2016	2015
	£	£
Fees payable for the audit of Credit Union A's annual accounts[15]	x	x
Fees payable to Credit Union A's auditor for other services:		
Services relating to taxation	x	x
Total auditors' remuneration	**4,403**	**5,084**

---

[15] *If the auditor has changed in the last year, it should be made clear what fees have been paid to each audit firm.*

8. Employees and employment costs

8a. Number of employees[16]

The average monthly number of employees during the year were:

	2016 Number	2015 Number
Office staff	9	9

8b. Employment costs[17]

	2016 £	2015 £
Wages and salaries	186,256	209,919
Social security costs	17,834	17,872
Payments to defined contribution pension schemes	30,085	31,744
Total employment costs	**234,175**	259,535

8c. Directors' Remuneration

The Directors of Credit Union A are its key management personnel *[or, if there is a Non-Executive Board, supported by Management, then it is probably the Members of the Board, plus the Chief Executive, or Senior Management Team, depending on the circumstances]*.

	2016 £	2015 £
Short term employee benefits	x	x
Payments to defined contribution pension schemes	x	x
Total key management personnel compensation[18]	**x**	x

Short-term employee benefits include wages, salaries, social security contributions and paid annual leave.

9. Taxation

9a. Recognised in the Revenue Account

The taxation charge for the year, based on the small profits rate of Corporation Tax of 21% (2015: 20.5%, taking into account marginal relief) comprised:

	Note	2016 £	2015 £
Current tax			
UK Corporation tax	9b	11,024	26,950
Total current tax and total taxation expense recognised in the Revenue Account		**11,024**	26,950

[16] *FRS 102 does not require disclosure of the number of employees. For companies there is a legal requirement to disclose the number of employees; it is considered good practice for entities reporting in accordance with other legal/regulatory frameworks.*

[17] *This is not an explicit requirement of FRS 102. For companies there is a legal requirement to disclose employment costs disaggregated as set out in this note; it is considered good practice for entities reporting in accordance with other legal/regulatory frameworks.*

[18] *If any termination benefits have been paid to departing key management personnel, they must also be disclosed here as a separate category within total key management personnel compensation.*

9b. Reconciliation of taxation expense

Credit Union A is not liable to corporation tax payable on its activities of making loans to members, and investing surplus funds, as these are not classified as a trade. However, corporation tax is payable on investment income. As a result, the tax charge for the year differs from the standard rate of Corporation Tax. The differences are explained below:

	2016	2015
	£	£
Surplus before taxation	212,132	(9,891)
Surplus before taxation multiplied by small profits rate of corporation tax in the UK of 21% (2015: 20.5%)	44,547	(2,027)
Effects of:		
Non-taxable adjustment re holiday pay[19]	(35)	328
Non-taxable surplus/(deficit) on transactions with members	(33,488)	28,649
Total tax charge for the year	11,024	26,950

10. Tangible fixed assets

Tangible fixed assets comprise the following property, plant and equipment:

	Freehold land and buildings	Office equipment	Fixtures and fittings	Total
	£	£	£	£
Cost				
At 30 September 2015	206,064	94,089	19,806	319,959
Additions	–	7,612	805	8,417
At 30 September 2016	206,064	101,701	20,611	328,376
Depreciation				
At 30 September 2015	105,847	83,084	16,413	205,344
Charge for the year	10,045	10,497	1,672	22,214
At 30 September 2016	115,892	93,581	18,085	227,558
Net book value				
At 30 September 2016	90,172	8,120	2,526	100,818
At 30 September 2015	100,217	11,005	3,393	114,615

11. Loans and advances to members – financial assets[20]

11a. Loans and advances to members[21]

	Note	2016	2015
		£	£
As at 1 October 2015		12,389,020	11,805,223
Advanced during the year		7,713,518	6,887,274

---

[19] *In practice this tax effect would be aggregated with the one below, but has been shown separately here to illustrate the impact of the accounting change on adoption of FRS 102.*

[20] *Credit Union A does not have mortgages. Those credit unions with mortgages should consider disaggregating loans and advances to members between loans and mortgages (see FRS 102 paragraph 34.20).*

[21]*FRS 102 does not require this note, but it might be useful in providing a link between movements in lending (as shown in the cash flow statement) and the net book value of loans shown in the balance sheet.*

	Note	2016 £	2015 £
Repaid during the year		**(6,183,584)**	(6,269,395)
Gross loans and advances to members	11b	**13,918,954**	12,423,102
Impairment losses			
Individual financial assets	11b, 11d	**(29,550)**	(34,082)
Groups of financial assets	11c	**(175,950)**	(145,754)
		(205,500)	(179,836)
As at 30 September 2016		**13,713,454**	12,243,266

11b. Memorandum – Total loan assets for regulatory purposes[22]

	Note	2016 £	2015 £
Gross loans and advances to members		**13,918,954**	12,423,102
Impairment of individual financial assets		**(29,550)**	(34,082)
Total loan assets for regulatory purposes	14b	**13,889,404**	12,389,020

11c. Credit risk disclosures

Credit Union A does not offer mortgages and as a result all loans to members are unsecured, except that there are restrictions on the extent to which borrowers may withdraw their savings whilst loans are outstanding[23]. *[If there is a limit on how much may be borrowed by each member, disclose this because it provides evidence relating to credit risk concentration. This could be supplemented by any information on the average amount loaned.]*

The carrying amount of the loans to members represents Credit Union A's maximum exposure to credit risk. The following table provides information on the credit quality of loan repayments. Where loans are not impaired it is expected that the amounts repayable will be received in full.

	2016 Amount £	Proportion[24] %	2015 Amount £	Proportion %
Not impaired:				
Neither past due nor impaired	x	x	x	x
Up to 3 months past due	x	x	x	x
Between 3 and 6 months past due	x	x	x	x
Between 6 months and 1 year past due	x	x	x	x
Over 1 year past due	x	x	x	x
Sub-total: loans not impaired	x	x%	x	x%
Individually impaired:				
Not yet past due, but impaired	x	x	x	x
Up to 3 months past due	x	x	x	x
Between 3 and 6 months past due	x	x	x	x

[22] *Consideration should be given to presenting a reconciliation between the amount recognised in the balance sheet (ie after impairment losses) and the gross loans used for regulatory purposes, if there is a difference.*

[23] *Where loans are secured, disclosure about the security should be provided.*

[24] *FRS 102 does not require disclosure of the proportion of loans in each category, but this might be useful to users.*

	2016		2015	
	Amount	**Proportion**[24]	**Amount**	**Proportion**
	£	**%**	**£**	**%**
Between 6 months and 1 year past due	x	x	x	x
Over 1 year past due	x	x	x	x
Total loans	**13,918,954**	**100%**	12,423,102	100%
Impairment allowance	**(205,500)**		(179,836)	
Total carrying value	**13,713,454**		12,243,266	

Factors that are considered in determining whether loans are impaired are discussed in Note 3.

11d. Allowance account for impairment losses

	Note	2016 £	2015 £
As at 1 October 2015		**145,754**	123,300
Allowance for losses made during the year		x	x
Allowances reversed during the year		x	x
Increase in allowances during the year	11e	**30,196**	22,454
As at 30 September 2016		**175,950**	145,754

11e. Impairment losses recognised for the year

	2016 £	2015 £
Impairment of individual financial assets	**29,550**	34,082
Increase in impairment allowances during the year	**30,196**	22,454
	59,746	56,536
Reversal of impairment where debts recovered	**(1,161)**	(4,103)
Total impairment losses recognised for the year	**58,585**	52,433

12. Subscribed capital – financial liabilities[25]

	Note	2016 £	2015 £
As at 1 October 2015		**13,004,895**	13,020,882
Received during the year		**5,272,934**	5,019,614
Repaid during the year		**(4,622,244)**	(5,035,601)
As at 30 September 2016	14b	**13,655,585**	13,004,895

Deposits from members may only be made by way of subscription for shares.

[If Credit Union A had issued interest-bearing shares or had juvenile depositors, it might be useful to disaggregate this note between subscribed capital which is interest-bearing and that which is not, and separately identify deposits from juveniles.]

---

[25] *This note is not required by FRS 102 but provides a useful link between movements in subscribed capital as shown in the cash flow statement and the total deposited as shown in the balance sheet.*

13. Other payables

	2016 £	2015 £
UK Corporation Tax	11,024	26,947
Other payables	15,304	13,474
Accruals and deferred income	13,210	6,422
	39,538	46,843

14. Additional financial instruments disclosures

14a. Financial risk management

Credit Union A manages its subscribed capital and loans to members so that it earns income from the margin between interest receivable and interest payable.

The main financial risks arising from Credit Union A's activities are credit risk, liquidity risk and interest rate risk. The Board reviews and agrees policies for managing each of these risks, which are summarised below.

Credit risk: Credit risk is the risk that a borrower will default on their contractual obligations relating to repayments to Credit Union A, resulting in financial loss to Credit Union A. In order to manage this risk the Board approves Credit Union A's lending policy, and all changes to it. All loan applications are assessed with reference to the lending policy in force at the time. Subsequently loans are regularly reviewed for any factors that may indicate that the likelihood of repayment has changed. [Credit Union A also monitors its banking arrangements closely in light of the current banking situation].

Liquidity risk: Credit Union A's policy is to maintain sufficient funds in liquid form at all times to ensure that it can meet its liabilities as they fall due. The objective of Credit Union A's liquidity policy is to smooth the mismatches between maturing assets and liabilities and to provide a degree of protection against any unexpected developments that may arise. Note 2 provides further details about the impact of the maturity mismatch on the going concern status of Credit Union A.

Market risk: Market risk is generally comprised of interest rate risk, currency risk and other price risk. Credit Union A conducts all its transactions in sterling and does not deal in derivatives or commodity markets. Therefore Credit Union A is not exposed to any form of *currency risk* or *other price risk*.

Interest rate risk: Credit Union A's main interest rate risk arises from differences between the interest rate exposures on the receivables and payables that form an integral part of a credit union's operations. Credit Union A considers rates of interest receivable when deciding on the dividend rate payable on subscribed capital. Credit Union A does not use interest rate options to hedge its own positions. *[Need to describe how the interest rate risk is measured and/or monitored by the Board.]*

14b. Interest rate risk disclosures

The following table shows the average interest rates applicable to relevant financial assets and financial liabilities.

	2016		2015	
	Amount £	Average interest rate	Amount £	Average interest rate
Financial assets				
Loans to members[26]	**13,899,404**	**6.99%**	12,389,020	6.59%
Financial liabilities				
Subscribed capital[27]				
Saver 1 accounts	**12,303,282**	**3.00%**	12,574,737	2.50%
Supersaver accounts	**1,352,303**	**1.50%**	430,158	1.00%
	13,655,585	**2.85%**	13,004,895	2.45%

The interest rates applicable to loans to members are fixed and range from x% to y%. The interest payable on subscribed capital is determined on the basis of income less administrative expenses and, as can be seen above, a consistent margin is maintained between interest receivable and interest payable. As a result, the surplus for the year is not particularly sensitive to interest rate risk and no sensitivity analysis is presented[28].

[Credit unions that have issued interest-bearing shares will need to include these as a separate line item in the table above. In addition, they will need to consider the impact of the interest-bearing shares on the assumptions and discussion about sensitivity to interest rate risk.]

14c. Liquidity risk disclosures

Excluding short-term other payables, as noted in the balance sheet, Credit Union A's financial liabilities, the subscribed capital, are repayable on demand.

14d. Fair value of financial instruments

Credit Union A does not hold any financial instruments at fair value.

15. Cash and cash equivalents

	2016 £	2015 £
Cash and balances with the Bank of England	–	–
Loans and advances to banks	**1,542,720**	2,148,704
	1,542,720	2,148,704
Less: amounts maturing after three months	**(750,000)**	(1,000,000)
Total cash and cash equivalents	**792,720**	1,148,704

16. Post balance sheet events

There are no material events after the balance sheet date to disclose.

[26] *Average interest rates on loans have been calculated based on interest receivable for the year and the regulatory balance of loans outstanding at the year end.*

[27] *The interest rate for subscribed capital is based on the proposed dividend not the cash dividend paid, which effectively derives from the surplus in the prior year.*

[28] *FRS 102 requires financial institutions to provide a sensitivity analysis for each type of market risk it is exposed to. This note explains that because interest payable is determined after the end of the relevant financial year, there is a lack of sensitivity. This table showing the average interest rates receivable on loans and payable on subscribed capital is not required by FRS 102, but is useful in highlighting the margin between interest payable and receivable, which is a way in which Credit Union A manages interest rates.*

17. Contingent liabilities

Credit Union A participates in the Financial Services Compensation Scheme (FSCS) and therefore has a contingent liability, which cannot be quantified, in respect of contributions to the FSCS, as required by the Financial Services and Markets Act 2000. The Financial Conduct Authority (FCA) had provided details of how the calculation of next year's contribution towards the FSCS will be calculated and full provision has been included for this liability. However this is subject to future changes in interest rates and levels of deposits held by UK deposit takers. Therefore there is inherent uncertainty regarding the totality of the levy that Credit Union A will have to pay.

18. Related party transactions

During the year, 31 members of the Board, staff and their close family members (2015: 28 members) had loans with Credit Union A. These loans were approved on the same basis as loans to other members of Credit Union A. None of the directors, staff or their close family members, have any preferential terms on their loans.

19. Transition to FRS 102

Credit Union A has adopted FRS 102 for the first time in these financial statements for the year ended 30 September 2016. The reconciliations below highlight the key impacts on both the surplus for the financial year and the retained earnings.

Reconciliation of surplus from previous UK accounting standards to FRS 102

	2016	2015
	£	£
Surplus/(deficit) as previously reported	200,940	(35,239)
Short term employee benefits	168	(1,602)
Surplus (in accordance with FRS 102)	**201,108**	**(36,841)**

Reconciliation of retained earnings from previous UK accounting standards to FRS 102

	2016	2015
	£	£
Retained earnings	1,708,992	1,508,052
Short term employee benefits	(1,434)	(1,602)
Retained earnings (in accordance with FRS 102)	**1,707,558**	**1,506,450**

The adjustments are:

19a. Employee benefits

Under UK accounting standards, Credit Union A did not make a provision for holiday pay, ie holiday earned but not taken prior to the year end. In contrast, FRS 102 requires the cost of short-term compensated absences to be recognised when employees render the service that increases their entitlement. As a result an additional accrual has been made to reflect this.[29]

---

[29] *It has been assumed that on average staff have two days holiday earned but not yet taken at 30 September. In this case it might be argued that the impact of this adjustment is not material, and therefore need not have been processed. However, in order to illustrate this difference between current UK accounting standards and FRS 102, the adjustment has been reflected in these financial statements.*

SEN 15
Acquisitions and disposals of subsidiaries

Contents

Disclaimer

This Education Note has been prepared by FRC staff for the convenience of users of FRS 102 The Financial Reporting Standard applicable in the UK and Republic of Ireland. *It aims to illustrate certain requirements of FRS 102, but should not be relied upon as a definitive statement on the application of the standard. The illustrative material is not a substitute for reading the detailed requirements of FRS 102.*

INTRODUCTION

This Staff Education Note compares the accounting treatment for acquisitions and disposals of subsidiaries under current UK accounting standards:

- FRS 2 *Accounting for subsidiary undertakings;*
- FRS 6 *Acquisitions and mergers;* and
- FRS 10 *Goodwill and intangible assets;*

with the requirements of the following sections in FRS 102 *The Financial Reporting Standard applicable in the UK and Republic of Ireland*:

- Section 9 *Consolidated and Separate Financial Statements;*
- Section 19 *Business Combinations and Goodwill; and*
- Section 22 *Liabilities and Equity.*

It covers the following acquisition and disposal scenarios:

- Acquisition – control achieved in stages;
- Acquisition – increasing a controlling interest in a subsidiary;
- Disposal – where control is lost; and
- Disposal – where control is retained.

The term 'non-controlling interest' is used throughout this Staff Education Note and is interchangeable with the term 'minority interest'.

This Staff Education Note is written to highlight key areas of consideration when transitioning to FRS 102 and is not designed to be exhaustive.

ACQUISITION OF SUBSIDIARIES

Determination of control and acquisition date

Although articulated slightly differently, the determination of when control is achieved, and therefore the acquisition date, in most circumstances, is unlikely to be different between current UK standards and FRS 102 in practice.

Step acquisitions / Control achieved in stages

This scenario arises when an entity obtains control over another entity over a number of transactions. For example, Company A acquires 30% of Company B on 1 January 20X1, and then a further 40% on 1 January 20X2, resulting in a controlling shareholding of 70%.

In this scenario, there is no difference in the accounting treatment between current UK accounting standards and FRS 102. The identifiable net assets of Company B are included in the consolidation at the fair values on the date control is achieved (ie 1 January 20X2), rather than at the date of the earlier purchases. Prior to 1 January 20X2 Company B would be accounted for as an associate, assuming that the 30% holding gave Company A significant influence over Company B. Goodwill is also recognised at the date control is achieved and generally is calculated as the difference between:

(a) the aggregate fair value of consideration given at each acquisition stage (as determined in accordance with paragraph 19.11 of FRS 102); and

(b) the fair value of Company A's interest in the identifiable net assets of Company B at the date control is achieved.

This method agrees with paragraph 9 of Schedule 6 to the Regulations[1]. However, in rare circumstances, where this method of calculation would fail to give a true and fair view, both current UK accounting standards and paragraph A4.21 of FRS 102 allow goodwill to be calculated as the sum of goodwill arising from each purchase of an interest in the subsidiary, adjusted as necessary for any subsequent impairment. The difference between the goodwill calculated using this method and the method above is recognised in reserves.

Increasing a controlling interest in a subsidiary

This scenario arises where a parent increases its controlling holding in a subsidiary, for example from 70% to 80%.

FRS 2 *Accounting for subsidiary undertakings*	FRS 102
The identifiable assets and liabilities of that subsidiary undertaking **should be revalued to fair value and goodwill arising on the increase in interest should be calculated by reference to those fair values.** This revaluation is not required if the difference between net fair values and carrying amounts of the assets and liabilities attributable to the increase in stake is not material. (FRS 2 paragraph 51)	The identifiable assets and liabilities and a provision for contingent liabilities of the subsidiary **shall not be revalued to fair value and no additional goodwill shall be recognised at the date the controlling interest is increased.** (FRS 102 paragraph 9.19C) The transaction shall be accounted for as a transaction between equity holders and the resulting change in non-controlling interest shall be accounted for in accordance with paragraph 22.19 (FRS 102 paragraph 9.19D) An entity shall treat changes in a parent's controlling interest in a subsidiary that do not result in a loss of control as transactions with equity holders in their capacity as equity holders. Accordingly, the carrying amount of the non-controlling interest shall be adjusted to reflect the change in the parent's interest in the subsidiary's net assets. Any difference between the amount by which the non-controlling interest is so adjusted and the fair value of the consideration paid or received, if any, shall be recognised directly in equity and attributed to equity holders of the parent. An entity shall not recognise a gain or loss on these changes. Also, an entity shall not recognise any change in the carrying amounts of assets (including goodwill) or liabilities as a result of such transactions. (FRS 102 paragraph 22.19)

[1] *The Large and Medium-sized Companies and Groups (Accounts and Reports) Regulations 2008 (SI 2008/410)*

There is a significant change in accounting treatment in this situation. Currently under FRS 2, the net assets of the subsidiary are revalued to fair value at the date control is increased and goodwill is recognised at that date, whereas under FRS 102, the net assets are not revalued and no goodwill is recognised; instead the transaction is treated as a transaction with equity holders.

Example 1

Company A acquires 70% of Company B for CU120m on 1 January 20X1, when the fair value and book value of its net assets was CU90m. A year later, Company A acquires a further 10% of Company B for CU20m when the carrying amount of Company B's net assets were CU100m. The fair value of Company B's net assets at that time was CU170m.

FRS 2

1 Jan 20X1 – Acquisition

Control has been achieved. The identifiable net assets of the subsidiary are consolidated at fair value of CU90m. Goodwill is recognised as an asset at the date of acquisition amounting to CU57m:

	CUm
Cost to acquire 70% holding	120
Company A's share of identifiable net assets acquired (70% x CU90m)	(63)
Positive goodwill	57

Non-controlling interest of CU27m (30% x CU90m) is also recognised.

31 Dec 20X1 – Year end

The increase in Company B's net assets is due to profits of CU10m (CU100m - CU90m) being made during the year 20X1. This profit is split CU7m (70% x CU10m) to the equity holders of Company A (the parent) and CU3m (30% x CU10m) to the non-controlling interest.

interest. The non-controlling interest's share in Company B's net assets now totals CU30m (CU27m + CU3m)[2].

1 Jan 20X2 – Decrease in controlling interest

As a result of the acquisition of an additional 10% holding, Company A's controlling share increases from 70% to 80%, and the non-controlling interest's share falls from 30% to 20%.

The non-controlling interest's share in the net assets of Company B will decrease by CU10m ((30% – 20%) x CU100m) and will now total CU20m (CU30m - CU10m)[3].

---

[2] *This is the same as taking the non-controlling interest's share of Company B's net assets at 31 December 20X1 ie 30% x CU100m.*

[3] *This is the same as taking the new non-controlling interest's share of Company B's net assets at 1 January 20X2 ie 20% x CU100m.*

Company B's net assets are revalued to fair value of CU170m and an uplift of CU70m is recognised in the consolidation. This uplift is split CU56m (80% x CU70m) to the equity holders of Company A and CU14m (20% x CU70m) to the non-controlling interest.

Further, additional goodwill is recognised on this acquisition amounting to CU3m:

	CUm
Cost to acquire additional 10% holding	20
Company A's share of identifiable net assets acquired (10% x CU170m)	(17)
Positive goodwill	3

FRS 102

1 Jan 20X1 – Acquisition

Same as FRS 2.

31 Dec 20X1 – Year end

Same as FRS 2.

1 Jan 20X2 – Decrease in controlling interest

This acquisition is treated as a transaction between equity holders. As with FRS 2, the non-controlling interest's share in the net assets of Company B will decrease by CU10m ((30% – 20%) x CU100m) and will now total CU20m (CU30m - CU10m).

Company B's net assets are not revalued and will remain at CU100m.

No additional goodwill is recognised.

DISPOSAL OF SUBSIDIARIES

Where control is lost

This scenario arises where either a parent disposes of all of its shares in its subsidiary, or a parent disposes of some of its shares such that it no longer has a controlling holding (for example from 80% down to 40%).

There is no difference in the accounting treatment between current UK accounting standards and FRS 102. The results of the subsidiary (ie its profit or loss) will be included in the consolidation up to the date of disposal, and a gain or loss on disposal should also be recognised. This gain or loss is calculated as the difference between the fair value of the consideration received and the proportion of the identifiable net assets (including goodwill) of the subsidiary disposed of.

Where control is retained

This scenario arises where a parent disposes of some of its shares such that it still has a controlling holding (for example from 80% down to 60%).

FRS 2 *Accounting for subsidiary undertakings*	FRS 102
Where a group reduces its interest in a subsidiary undertaking, it should record any profit or loss arising calculated as the difference between the carrying amount of the net assets of that subsidiary undertaking attributable to the group's interest before the reduction and the carrying amount attributable to the group's interest after the reduction together with any proceeds received. The net assets compared should include any related goodwill not previously written off through the profit and loss account. Where the undertaking remains a subsidiary undertaking after the disposal, the non-controlling interest in that subsidiary undertaking should be increased by the carrying amount of the net identifiable assets that are now attributable to the non-controlling interest because of the decrease in the group's interest. No amount for goodwill that arose on acquisition of the group's interest in that subsidiary undertaking should be attributed to the non-controlling interest. [[amphlnl]](FRS 2 paragraph 52)	Where a parent reduces its holding in a subsidiary and control is retained, it shall be accounted for as a transaction between equity holders and the resulting change in non-controlling interest shall be accounted for in accordance with paragraph 22.19. No gain or loss shall be recognised at the date of disposal. (FRS 102 paragraph 9.19A) An entity shall treat changes in a parent's controlling interest in a subsidiary that do not result in a loss of control as transactions with equity holders in their capacity as equity holders. Accordingly, the carrying amount of the non-controlling interest shall be adjusted to reflect the change in the parent's interest in the subsidiary's net assets. Any difference between the amount by which the non-controlling interest is so adjusted and the fair value of the consideration paid or received, if any, shall be recognised directly in equity and attributed to equity holders of the parent. An entity shall not recognise a gain or loss on these changes. Also, an entity shall not recognise any change in the carrying amounts of assets (including goodwill) or liabilities as a result of such transactions. (FRS 102 paragraph 22.19)

There is a significant change in accounting treatment in this situation. Currently under FRS 2, a gain or loss is recognised on the disposal and a proportion of goodwill written off, whereas under FRS 102, no gain or loss is recognised and goodwill is not adjusted; instead the transaction is treated as a transaction with equity holders.

Example 2

Company A disposed of a proportion of its shares in Company B on 31 December 20X1 for CU100m in cash, reducing its holding from 80% to 60%. The carrying amount of the identifiable net assets of Company B in the consolidated financial statements was CU200m at that date. The carrying amount of goodwill attributable to the acquisition of Company B was CU40m at the date of disposal.

FRS 2

A gain of CU50m is recognised on disposal in the consolidated financial statements:

	CUm
Proceeds received	100
Carrying amount of identifiable net assets (inc. goodwill) attributable to group after disposal (60% x CU200m) + (60/80 x CU40m)	150
	250
Carrying amount of identifiable net assets (inc. goodwill) attributable to group before disposal (80% x CU200m) + CU40m	(200)
Gain	50

The carrying amount of goodwill is reduced by CU10m (20/80 x CU40m).

The non-controlling interest's share in the net assets of Company B will increase from 20% to 40%, ie it will increase from CU40m (20% x CU200m) to CU80m (40% x CU200m). No goodwill is attributable to the non-controlling interest.

FRS 102

No gain or loss is recognised on this disposal; instead it is treated as a transaction between equity holders.

As with FRS 2, the non-controlling interest will increase from 20% to 40%, ie it will increase from CU40m to CU80m.

The carrying amount of goodwill is not adjusted as a result of the disposal.

SEN 16
Financing transactions

(October 2015)

Contents

Disclaimer

This Education Note has been prepared by FRC staff for the convenience of users of FRS 102 The Financial Reporting Standard applicable in the UK and Republic of Ireland. *It aims to illustrate certain requirements of FRS 102, but should not be relied upon as a definitive statement on the application of the standard. The illustrative material is not a substitute for reading the detailed requirements of FRS 102.*

INTRODUCTION

Lending is a very common transaction between entities. For example, it may take the form of a formal bank loan or informal overdraft or take the form of a purchase or sale on credit. The receivable and payable recognised by the lender and borrower respectively, are accounted for in accordance with the requirements set out in Section 11 *Basic Financial Instruments* or Section 12 *Other Financial Instruments Issues* of FRS 102 *The Financial Reporting Standard applicable in the UK and Republic of Ireland.*

In some situations the seller and buyer of goods or services may agree that payment can be deferred for a period that is longer than what is normal business practice. Loans, most commonly loans between related parties, may be financed at an interest rate that is lower than the rate that would typically be charged for a similar loan or the loan may even be interest-free. FRS 102 refers to these types of lending arrangements as financing transactions. FRS 102 sets out separate accounting requirements for financing transactions which in essence require that the loan is measured as if it was a loan with a market rate of interest.

This Education Note provides guidance on the application of the measurement requirements in FRS 102 applicable to financing transactions. It also sets out a comparative analysis of the key accounting requirements for financing transactions under FRS 102 and those applicable under previous UK and Irish GAAP.

Entities are reminded that this Education Note does not cover all aspects of the accounting for financing transactions. The examples included are simplified to illustrate the application of certain aspects of the accounting requirements and do not cover all possible accounting issues. In practice entities need to take into consideration all relevant facts and circumstances of a transaction to determine the appropriate accounting.

Staff Education Note 2 *Debt instruments – Amortised cost* provides further guidance on the accounting for financial assets and financial liabilities measured at amortised cost using the effective interest method when a lending arrangement does not constitute a financing transaction in the context of FRS 102.

This Education Note does not address the accounting for public benefit entity concessionary loans made or received at or below the prevailing market rate of interest. Please refer to paragraphs PBE34.87 to PBE34.97 of FRS 102 for the applicable accounting requirements.

This Education Note is based on the requirements of FRS 102 issued in September 2015.

MEASUREMENT OF FINANCING TRANSACTIONS

The term financing transaction is used in FRS 102 to specifically refer to transactions with deferred payments or repayments, for which there is no explicit interest rate or the interest charged is not at a market rate. Examples of such transactions include:

- the sale of goods or services, if payment is deferred beyond normal business terms or is financed at a rate of interest that is not a market rate (paragraph 11.13 of FRS 102);
- below market rate and interest-free loans between group entities; and
- below market rate and interest-free loans to or from directors.

Section 11 *Basic Financial Instruments* and Section 12 *Other Financial Instruments Issues* of FRS 102 *The Financial Reporting Standard applicable in the UK and Republic of Ireland* set out specific measurement requirements for financial assets and financial liabilities where the arrangement constitutes a financing transaction. The following discussions are limited to the requirements in Section 11 and therefore only apply to financial assets and financial liabilities that are classified as basic. Please refer to paragraphs 11.8 to 11.11 of FRS 102 which specify the conditions for a financial asset or financial liability to be classified as a basic financial instrument.

Initial measurement

Paragraph 11.13 of FRS 102 sets out the initial measurement requirements for financial assets and financial liabilities. Generally financial assets and financial liabilities are measured at their transaction price, which typically is the amount of cash borrowed or the invoiced amount when goods or services are sold. However, when a financial asset or financial liability, ie a receivable or payable, originates from an arrangement that is a financing transaction, that receivable or payable is measured at the present value of the future cash payments discounted at a market rate of interest for a similar debt instrument[1] (paragraph 11.13 of FRS 102).

Below are five common examples of financing transactions where the loan has a fixed repayment date to demonstrate the application of the present value measurement requirement of paragraph 11.13 of FRS 102.

It should be noted that the present value of a financial asset or financial liability that is repayable on demand is equal to the undiscounted cash amount payable reflecting the lender's right to demand immediate repayment.

The sale of goods or services on deferred payment terms

When goods or services are sold on credit, the arrangement has in substance two components, firstly the sale of the goods or services and secondly a financing element. The two components are accounted for separately.

To that effect a seller recognises the revenue from the sale in accordance with Section 23 *Revenue* of FRS 102 and a purchaser recognises the acquired goods and services in accordance with the applicable accounting requirements in FRS 102.

When the arrangement is a financing transaction, ie when the payment for goods or services is deferred beyond normal business terms or the sale is financed at a below market rate of interest, the trade debtor and trade creditor are measured at the present value of the cash flows receivable or payable discounted at the market rate of interest for a similar receivable or payable (paragraph 11.13 of FRS 102). In practice, an entity may use the current cash selling price for the goods or services sold on an arm's length basis as an estimate for the present value of the future payments. However, if there is no cash sale alternative or the cash selling price is the same as the price when buying on credit, the entity must calculate the present value of the future cash flows.

The following numerical example demonstrates the accounting by a seller (the manufacturer) and a buyer (the customer) when payment is deferred.

Example 1: The sale of goods on deferred payment terms

A manufacturer sells a piece of machinery to a customer on credit for CU1,000 on 1 January 20X0, agreeing with the customer that full payment is due in two years' time on 31 December 20X1. Under normal business terms the piece of machinery is sold for cash and the current cash selling price is CU900. Sales taxes are ignored in this example.

---

[1] *Debt instruments include loans receivable, loans payable, trade debtors and trade creditors.*

(1) Accounting by the manufacturer

In accordance with paragraph 23.5 of FRS 102, on 1 January 20X0 the manufacturer recognises the revenue from the sale at the cash selling price of the piece of machinery of CU900. The trade receivable is also measured at the cash selling price of CU900 in accordance with paragraph 11.13 of FRS 102. The manufacturer records the following accounting entries when the piece of machinery is sold:

Dr Trade receivable	CU900
Cr Revenue	CU900

After initial recognition the manufacturer will account for the trade receivable at amortised cost using the effective interest method as demonstrated in Example 6 below. In accordance with paragraph 23.5 of FRS 102, the difference between the present value of the trade receivable of CU900 and the nominal amount of the consideration of CU1,000 is recognised as interest income using the effective interest method over the two years until payment is due from the customer.

(2) Accounting by the customer

The customer applies the requirements of Section 17 *Property, Plant and Equipment* of FRS 102. In accordance with paragraph 17.13 of FRS 102, on 1 January 20X0 the purchase of the piece of machinery is recorded at the cash selling price of CU900. The customer also records a trade payable measured at the cash selling price of CU900 in accordance with paragraph 11.13 of FRS 102. The customer records the following accounting entries when the piece of machinery is purchased:

Dr Property, plant and equipment	CU900
Cr Trade payable	CU900

After initial recognition the customer accounts for the trade payable at amortised cost using the effective interest method as demonstrated in Example 6 below.

Fixed term loans with no interest or a below market rate of interest

A loan provided or received at no or a below market rate of interest constitutes a financing transaction. Paragraph 11.13 of FRS 102 requires that such a loan is measured at the present value of the future cash receipts or payments discounted at a market rate of interest of a similar financial asset or financial liability.

The present value calculated in accordance with paragraph 11.13 of FRS 102 reflects the value of a similar loan with a market rate of interest. For loans other than those repayable on demand, a difference arises between the amount of cash received or advanced and the present value of the loan. This difference reflects that the lender has made a loan at a lower than market rate of interest and thereby has provided an additional benefit to the borrower.

FRS 102 does not set out specific accounting requirements for that difference. Where FRS 102 does not specifically address the accounting for a transaction, an entity applies judgement to determine the accounting treatment that meets the requirements of paragraph 10.4 of FRS 102, ie an entity selects an accounting policy that results in relevant and reliable information. Paragraph 10.5 sets out the sources an entity should consider for that analysis.

To determine the accounting treatment for the difference, an entity should assess the particular facts and circumstances of each arrangement. In that regard it is particularly important to establish the reasons a lender decided to make a loan at a non-market rate of interest. For example a lender may make the loan because of an ownership interest in the borrower. If so, the lender is, in its capacity as the owner, effectively making an additional investment in the entity when making a loan at a below market rate of interest. In other instances there may be related transactions to consider, for example the lender may be compensated by obtaining goods or services from the borrower at below market prices.

Where a loan is made at a non-market rate of interest and the lender and the borrower are related parties because one owns the other or the lender and borrower are owned by the same entity or person, the difference arising on initial recognition of the loan would generally be accounted for as a distribution or capital contribution.

FRS 102 sets out accounting requirements for distributions. For the entity making a distribution it represents a decrease of economic benefits that results in a decrease in equity. A distribution is not an expense and is therefore recorded as a reduction of equity (paragraphs 2.23(b) and 22.17 of FRS 102). It should be noted that in some cases a distribution may be recorded in the financial statements in accordance with FRS 102, although it may not be a distribution as a matter of law and vice versa. An entity that is subject to company law should consider whether the distribution recorded in the financial statements for reporting purposes is also a distribution as a matter of the law and if so, should assess whether it has sufficient distributable profits to make the distribution.

The entity receiving a distribution records it as an income, since it represents an increase in economic benefits that results in an increase of equity that is not related to a capital contribution from an equity investor (paragraph 2.23(a) of FRS 102). Income is recorded in total comprehensive income, either in profit or loss or in other comprehensive income. Company law prohibits the inclusion of unrealised profits within profit or loss, except where an unrealised revaluation gain arises from the application of fair value accounting. If the distribution is considered a realised profit it is recorded in profit or loss, otherwise it is recorded in other comprehensive income. An entity that is a company should assess whether the distribution received is a realised profit within the meaning of company law.

The determination of realised and distributable profits in accordance with company law is a complex area where accounting and legal requirements interface. This Education Note does not address company law issues that may be relevant in this regard. An entity may refer to Technical Release 02/10 *Guidance on realised and distributable profits under the Companies Act 2006* (Technical Release 02/10) issued by the Institute of Chartered Accountants in England and Wales and the Institute of Chartered Accounts of Scotland, or any successor document. An entity may also wish to take specialist legal advice on these matters.

Capital contributions from equity investors do not meet the definition of income (see paragraph 2.23(a) of FRS 102). A capital contribution is therefore recorded by the receiving entity as an increase in equity. The entity making a capital contribution records it as an increase in its investment in the entity receiving the capital contribution.

The Examples 2 to 5 below illustrate different scenarios of interest-free loan arrangements between related parties and demonstrate the accounting for the difference.

Example 2: Fixed term interest-free loans between a parent and its subsidiary

Loans between parents and their subsidiaries are often made on interest-free terms. It can be presumed that a loan is made on these terms because the parent owns and controls its subsidiary.

A fixed term interest free-loan consists, in substance, of two components:

(a) a loan at a market rate of interest; and
(b) a benefit or contribution to the borrower.

In the case of an interest-free loan between a parent and its subsidiary, the first component, ie the loan made at a market-rate of interest, is determined by calculating the present value of the future payments discounted at a market rate of interest of a similar loan. The second component, ie the gift or contribution to the borrower, is the measurement difference which is accounted for as a capital contribution or distribution. The accounting is demonstrated in the numerical examples below.

(1) A parent provides a fixed term interest-free loan of CU1,000 to its subsidiary. The present value of the loan using a market rate of interest for a similar loan is CU900[2]. The difference of CU100 represents an additional investment by the parent in the subsidiary. The parent would record the following accounting entries in its individual financial statements:

Dr	Loan receivable from subsidiary[3]	CU900
Dr	Investment in subsidiary[3]	CU100
Cr	Cash	CU1,000

The subsidiary would record the following accounting entries:

Dr	Cash	CU1,000
Cr	Loan repayable to parent	CU900
Cr	Capital contribution (equity)	CU100

(2) A subsidiary provides a fixed term interest-free loan of CU1,000 to its parent. The present value of the loan using a market rate of interest for a similar loan is CU900[4]. The difference of CU100 is a distribution to the parent. The parent would record the following accounting entries in its individual financial statements:

Dr	Cash	CU1,000
Cr	Loan repayable to subsidiary	CU900
Cr	Distribution received from subsidiary (profit or loss)[5]	CU100

The subsidiary would record the following accounting entries:

Dr	Loan receivable from parent	CU900
Dr	Distribution to parent (equity)[6]	CU100
Cr	Cash	CU1,000

---

[2] *See Example 6 below for the calculation of the present value and a demonstration of the subsequent accounting for an interest-free loan.*

[3] *Loans and investments are subject to impairment. An entity shall apply the relevant accounting requirements in FRS 102 to determine whether a loan or investment is impaired.*

[4] *See Example 6 below for the calculation of the present value and a demonstration of the subsequent accounting for an interest-free loan.*

[5] *Company law requires that only profits realised at the reporting date are included in profit or loss. For the purpose of this example it is assumed that the distribution is a realised profit and it is therefore recorded in profit or loss. The legal requirements on realised profits are not addressed in this Education Note. Technical Release 02/10 considers issues concerning the determination of realised profits and entities may refer to this or any successor document for more guidance.*

[6] *In accordance with paragraph 22.17 of FRS 102 a distribution is recorded as a reduction of equity. A distribution recorded in the financial statements in accordance with FRS 102 may not be a distribution as a matter of law. The legal requirements on distributable profits are not addressed in this Education Note. Technical Release 02/10 considers issues concerning the determination of distributable profits and entities may refer to this or any successor document for more guidance.*

Example 3: Fixed term interest-free loans between fellow subsidiaries

In a situation where fellow subsidiaries enter into a loan which constitutes a financing transaction, it can generally be presumed that the loan was made on the direction of their parent. However, sometimes the facts and circumstances may indicate otherwise, for example when an interest-free loan is made in return for receiving goods or services at a discounted price.

If an interest-free loan is made on the direction of the parent, the subsidiaries account for the transaction as if it had been conducted through the parent. The lending subsidiary accounts for the loan as if it had made a loan to its parent and the borrowing subsidiary accounts for the loan as if it had received a loan from its parent. The transaction is not required to be reflected in the parent's own financial statements because the parent is not directly involved.

As noted in Example 2 above, a fixed term interest-free loan consists, in substance, of two separate components. In the case of an interest-free loan between fellow subsidiaries, the first component represents a loan made at a market-rate of interest and the second component is a distribution or capital contribution. The accounting is demonstrated in the following numerical example.

A subsidiary makes a fixed term interest-free loan of CU1,000 to a fellow subsidiary. The present value of the loan using a market rate of interest for a similar loan is CU900[7]. The excess of the cash advanced over the present value of the loan of CU100 is accounted for as a distribution from the lending subsidiary. The accounting entries of the lending subsidiary are as follows:

Dr	Loan receivable from fellow subsidiary	CU900
Dr	Distribution (equity)[8]	CU100
Cr	Cash	CU1,000

The borrowing subsidiary would account for the excess of CU100 as a capital contribution and record the following accounting entries:

Dr	Cash	CU1,000
Cr	Loan repayable to fellow subsidiary	CU900
Cr	Capital contribution (equity)	CU100

Example 4: Fixed term interest-free loans between entities owned by the same person

In some instances an interest-free loan is made between entities that are not members of the same group, but the entities are related parties because they are owned and controlled by the same person. Unless the facts and circumstances indicate that the loan is made on

---

[7] *See Example 6 below for the calculation of the present value and a demonstration of the subsequent accounting for an interest-free loan.*

[8] *In accordance with paragraph 22.17 of FRS 102 a distribution is recorded as a reduction of equity. A distribution recorded in the financial statements in accordance with FRS 102 may not be a distribution as a matter of law. The legal requirements on distributable profits are not addressed in this Education Note. Technical Release 02/10 considers issues concerning the determination of distributable profits and entities may refer to this or any successor document for more guidance.*

these terms for a reason other than that the entities are controlled by the same owner, the accounting for the loan will be the same as shown in Example 3 above for a fixed term interest-free loan between fellow subsidiaries.

As noted in Example 2 above, a fixed term interest-free loan consists, in substance, of two separate components. In the case of a fixed term interest-free loan between entities that are owned by the same person, the first component represents a loan made at a market-rate of interest and the second component is a distribution or capital contribution. The accounting is demonstrated in the numerical example below.

An entity makes a fixed term interest-free loan of CU1,000 to another entity. Both entities have the same owner. The present value of the loan using a market rate of interest for a similar loan is CU900[9].

The lending entity records the following accounting entries:

Dr	Loan receivable from related party	CU900
Dr	Distribution (equity)[10]	CU100
Cr	Cash	CU1,000

The borrowing entity records the following accounting entries:

Dr	Cash	CU1,000
Cr	Loan repayable to related party	CU900
Cr	Capital contribution (equity)	CU100

Example 5: Fixed term interest-free loans between entities and their directors

A fixed term interest-free loan may be made between an entity and its director(s). The accounting for the measurement difference arising on the initial recognition of the loan will depend on whether the loan was made in the director's capacity as a shareholder or for another reason. For example, in a situation where a director is the majority shareholder it can be presumed that the loan was made in the director's capacity as a shareholder. This presumption can be rebutted, if, for example, loans between the entity and other third parties without an ownership interest in the entity (eg employees) are made on the same or similar terms.

If a fixed term interest-free loan is made between the entity and a director in its capacity as a shareholder the accounting for the loan is similar to the accounting for a fixed term interest-free loan between a parent and its subsidiary shown in Example 2 above.

As noted in Example 2, a fixed term interest-free loan consists, in substance, of two components. In the case of a fixed term loan between an entity and a director who is also a shareholder, the first component represents a loan at a market rate of interest and the second component is a capital contribution or distribution between the director and the entity. The numerical examples below demonstrate the accounting.[10]

---

[9] *In accordance with paragraph 22.17 of FRS 102 a distribution is recorded as a reduction of equity. A distribution recorded in the financial statements in accordance with FRS 102 may not be a distribution as a matter of law. The legal requirements on distributable profits are not addressed in this Education Note. Technical Release 02/10 considers issues concerning the determination of distributable profits and entities may refer to this or any successor document for more guidance.*

[10] *Only the accounting entries for the entity are shown here as it is presumed that the director is not preparing financial statements in accordance with FRS 102.*

(1)   A director provides a fixed term interest-free loan of CU1,000 to an entity owned by the director. The loan is considered to be provided by the director in his/her capacity as a shareholder. The present value of the loan using a market rate of interest of a similar loan is CU900[11]. The difference of CU100 represents an additional investment by the owner which is recorded by the entity as a capital contribution. The entity would record the following accounting entries:

Dr	Cash	CU1,000
Cr	Loan repayable to owner/director	CU900
Cr	Capital contribution (equity)	CU100

(2)   An entity provides a fixed term interest-free loan of CU1,000 to a director who also owns the entity. The loan is considered to be provided to the director in his/her capacity as a shareholder. The present value of the loan using a market rate of interest of a similar loan is CU900[11]. The difference of CU100 represents a distribution from the entity to its owner. The entity would record the following accounting entries:

Dr	Loan receivable from owner/director	CU900
Dr	Distribution to owner (equity)[12]	CU100
Cr	Cash	CU1,000

If an interest-free loan is made between an entity and a director who has no direct ownership interest in the entity, the terms of the loan and the reasons for making it should be assessed carefully as this is relevant for determining the appropriate accounting under FRS 102.

For example, an entity may offer interest-free loans to all employees, including its directors, as an additional employee benefit. Often these loans are made for a specific purpose, for example to purchase a season travel ticket. In this situation the entity accounts for the measurement difference as an employee benefit cost in accordance with Section 28 *Employee Benefits* of FRS 102.

When a director without ownership interest makes a loan to the entity, the director's motives have to be identified, as the director would not normally directly benefit from making a loan on these terms. The appropriate accounting for the measurement difference will be dependent on the individual circumstances of each transaction.

Subsequent measurement

Basic financial assets and financial liabilities are generally measured at amortised cost using the effective interest method (paragraph 11.14(a) of FRS 102). This requirement applies regardless of whether the financial asset or financial liability results from an arrangement that constitutes a financing transaction or not.

The effective interest rate is determined in accordance with the requirements of paragraphs 11.16 to 11.20 of FRS 102. Assuming that the original effective interest rate as determined at the time of the initial recognition of the loan is a fixed rate of interest, the rate is not updated for subsequent changes to the market rate of interest. The following numerical example demonstrates the subsequent accounting for an interest-free loan.

---

[11] *See Example 6 below for the calculation of the present value and a demonstration of the subsequent accounting for an interest-free loan.*

[12] *In accordance with paragraph 22.17 of FRS 102 a distribution is recorded as a reduction of equity. A distribution recorded in the financial statements in accordance with FRS 102 may not be a distribution as a matter of law. The legal requirements on distributable profits are not addressed in this Education Note. Technical Release 02/10 considers issues concerning the determination of distributable profits and entities may refer to this or any successor document for more guidance.*

Example 6: Subsequent measurement of interest-free loans

On 1 January 20X1 a subsidiary obtains an interest-free loan of CU1,000 from its parent. The loan is repayable in full on 31 December 20X2. The market rate of interest for similar loans is 5.4 per cent per annum. The net present value of the loan is CU900[13] ($1,000/1.054^2=900$). The amortised cost of the loan as at 31 December 20X1 and 20X2 is as follows:

Year	Carrying amount at 1 January	Interest accrued (5.4%)	Cash flow	Carrying amount at 31 December
	CU	CU	CU	CU
20X1	900	49	–	949
20X2	949	51	(1,000)	–

On 1 January 20X1 the parent and the subsidiary would record the accounting entries set out in Example 2 above when a parent makes an interest-free loan to its subsidiary. As described in Example 2, at initial recognition the interest-free loan is accounted for as a loan at a market-rate of interest and a capital contribution or distribution. After initial recognition the interest-free loan is treated for accounting purpose as if it was a loan at a market rate of interest with capital and interest payable at the end of the term of the loan. Interest is accounted for applying the effective interest method.

The entity receiving interest (in this example the parent) records it as an income. Income is recorded in total comprehensive income, either in profit or loss or in other comprehensive income. Company law prohibits the inclusion of unrealised profits within profit or loss, except for an unrealised revaluation gain arising from the application of fair value accounting.

If the interest income is considered a realised profit it is recorded in profit or loss, otherwise it is recorded in other comprehensive income. An entity that is a company should assess whether the interest income is a realised profit within the meaning of company law. The determination of realised profits in accordance with company law is a complex area where accounting and legal requirements interface. This Education Note does not address company law issues that may be relevant in this regard. An entity may refer to Technical Release 02/10, or any successor document. An entity may also wish to take specialist legal advice.

The entity paying interest (in this example the subsidiary) records it as an expense in profit or loss.

The parent would record the following accounting entries:

Year ended 31 December 20X1

To record the accrued interest

Dr	Loan receivable from subsidiary	CU49
Cr	Interest income[14]	CU49

---

[13] *900 is a rounded figure.*

[14] *Company law requires that only profits realised at the reporting date are included in profit or loss. For the purpose of this example it is assumed that the interest income is a realised profit. The legal requirements on realised profits are not addressed in this Education Note. Technical Release 02/10 considers issues concerning the determination of realised profits and entities may refer to this or any successor document for more guidance.*

Year ended 31 December 20X2

To record the accrued interest

Dr   Loan receivable from subsidiary   CU51
Cr   Interest income[15]   CU51

To record the loan repayment

Dr   Cash   CU1,000
Cr   Loan receivable from subsidiary   CU1,000

The subsidiary would record the following accounting entries:

Year ended 31 December 20X1

To record the accrued interest

Dr   Interest expense   CU49
Cr   Loan repayable to parent   CU49

Year ended 31 December 20X2

To record the accrued interest

Dr   Interest Expense   CU51
Cr   Loan repayable to parent   CU51

To record the loan repayment

Dr   Loan repayable to parent   CU1,000
Cr   Cash   CU1,000

Differences between FRS 102 and previous UK and Irish GAAP

The tables below present the key accounting requirements in FRS 102 and previous UK and Irish GAAP for the most common types of financing transactions[16], ie goods or services sold on deferred payment terms and loans made at a below market rate of interest.

As highlighted below accounting differences may arise on transition to FRS 102 in some cases.

---

[15] *Company law requires that only profits realised at the reporting date are included in profit or loss. For the purpose of this example it is assumed that the interest income is a realised profit. The legal requirements on realised profits are not addressed in this Education Note. Technical Release 02/10 considers issues concerning the determination of realised profits and entities may refer to this or any successor document for more guidance.*

[16] *It should be noted that previous UK and Irish GAAP did not include the term financing transaction.*

The sale of goods or services on deferred payment terms

FRS 4/ FRS 5	FRS 102
Borrower (purchaser of the goods/services on extended credit terms)	
FRS 4 *Capital instruments* characterises a capital instrument as a means of raising finance. Where a transaction relates to a purchase on credit terms that is extended to the extent that there is a financing element to the transaction, the debt is recognised at the net proceeds, assumed to be the fair value of the goods or services received. The difference between the fair value and the amount to be paid is the finance cost, to be allocated to periods over the term of the debt at a constant rate on the carrying amount. (FRS 4 paragraphs 27 and 28)	If the transaction is a financing transaction the financial liability shall be measured at the present value of the future payments discounted at a market rate of interest for a similar debt instrument. The cash price for the transaction could provide evidence of the present value of the transaction from which the effective interest rate can be calculated. (FRS 102 paragraph 11.13) The difference between the invoiced amount and the present value of the future payments is recognised as interest expense over the credit term using the effective interest method. (FRS 102 paragraph 11.14(a))
Lender (seller of the goods/services on extended credit terms)	
Revenue and the corresponding receivable are initially recognised at the present value of the cash inflows expected to be received from the customer on settlement, where the effect of the time value of money is material to the reported revenue. The unwinding of the discount should be credited to finance income as this represents a gain from a financing transaction. (FRS 5 Application Note G, paragraph G8)	Revenue is initially measured at the fair value of the consideration receivable. Where the inflow of cash is deferred, and the arrangement constitutes in effect a financing transaction, the fair value of the consideration is the present value of all future receipts determined using an imputed rate of interest. (FRS 102 paragraphs 23.3 and 23.5) The corresponding receivable shall be measured at the present value of the future payments discounted at a market rate of interest for a similar debt instrument. The cash price for the transaction could provide evidence of the present value. (FRS 102 paragraph 11.13) The difference between the invoiced amount and the present value of the future receipts is recognised as interest income over the credit term using the effective interest method. (FRS 102 paragraph 11.14(a))

Not considered to be different.

Loans at a below market rate of interest[17]

FRS 4	FRS 102
Borrower	
The loan is recognised initially at the amount of the net proceeds[18], which in most cases would be the amount borrowed. (FRS 4 paragraph 27) Finance costs are defined as the difference between the net proceeds and the total payments. (FRS 4 paragraph 8) The finance costs should be allocated over the term of the debt at a constant rate on the amount borrowed. (FRS 4 paragraph 28)	When a lending arrangement constitutes, in effect, a financing transaction, the financial liability shall be measured at the present value of the future payments discounted at a market rate of interest for a similar debt instrument. (FRS 102 paragraph 11.13) The difference between the cash received and the present value of the loan is recognised as interest expense over the period of the loan using the effective interest method. (FRS 102 paragraph 11.14(a))
Lender	
No specific accounting requirements apply (FRS 4.19 excludes investments in capital instruments from its scope) and current practice would be to recognise the loan at the amount advanced (usually the nominal value of the loan).	When a transaction constitutes, in effect, a financing transaction, the financial asset shall be measured at the present value of the future payments discounted at a market rate of interest for a similar debt instrument. (FRS 102 paragraph 11.13) The difference between the cash loaned and the present value of the loan is recognised as interest income using the effective interest method. (FRS 102 paragraph 11.14(a))

Whilst under FRS 4 a loan with a below market rate of interest was measured at the amount of the net proceeds, FRS 102 requires that such a loan is measured initially at the present value of the future cash flows discounted at a market rate. Any difference arising on initial measurement is subsequently allocated over the term of the loan using the effective interest method.

---

[17] *This analysis does not apply to entities that adopted FRS 26 (IAS 39) Financial Instruments: recognition and measurement under previous UK and Irish GAAP. The measurement requirements for a loan at non-market rate under FRS 26 are similar to those in FRS 102.*

[18] *Defined in paragraph 11 of FRS 4 as 'the fair value of the consideration received on the issue of a capital instrument after deduction of issue costs'.*

Small entities[19] that first adopt FRS 102 for an accounting period that commences before 1 January 2017 need not restate comparative information to comply with the accounting requirements of paragraph 11.13 of FRS 102 for financing transactions involving related parties[19]. Small entities that apply this transitional exemption are also permitted to determine the present value of the financial asset or financial liability at the start of the first reporting period that complies with the requirements of paragraph 11.13 of FRS 102 on the basis of the facts and circumstances existing at that date, rather than when the arrangement was entered into. See paragraph 35.10(v) of FRS 102.

---

[19]*Small entities and related parties are terms defined in FRS 102. Refer to the Glossary in FRS 102 for more detail.*

Part Five

ICAEW Technical Releases

TECH 03/08
Guidance on Materiality in Financial Reporting by UK Entities

Contents

Guidance on materiality in financial reporting by UK entities, published in June 2008 by the Institute of Chartered Accountants in England and Wales.

This Technical Release provides general guidance and does not purport to deal with all possible questions and issues that may arise in any given situation. The Institute and the authors do not accept responsibility for loss caused to any person who acts or refrains from acting in reliance on the material in this publication, whether such loss is caused by negligence or otherwise.

INTRODUCTION

The principles of Tech 32/96 *The interpretation of materiality in financial reporting* were still sound and relevant more than 10 years after it was first published. However, many of its references to UK literature were no longer current and it did not deal at all with IFRS. The Financial Reporting Committee of the Institute's Financial Reporting Faculty has therefore updated the guidance to take account of the latest UK literature and IFRS, and to make sure that its principles remain in line with the latest thinking on materiality. This will help to minimise divergent practices in the application of materiality judgements in the preparation of financial statements.

A draft of the revised guidance was published for comment as Tech 01/07 in June 2007. Tech 03/08 has been finalised in the light of comments received. References to Company Law, Accounting and Auditing Standards and other accounting, auditing and regulatory literature and material are correct as at 9 June 2008.

GUIDANCE ON MATERIALITY IN FINANCIAL REPORTING BY UK ENTITIES

SCOPE

This guidance is for preparers of financial statements ('preparers'). It considers the issue   **1**
of materiality in financial reporting, including the relevant discussion in the Statement of
Principles for Financial Reporting ('Statement of Principles') issued by the Accounting
Standards Board ('ASB') in December 1999. It is intended to help with the practical
application of the definitions and explanations of materiality. As the principles underlying
the Statement of Principles and the Framework for the Preparation and Presentation of
Financial Statements ('Framework') adopted by the International Accounting Standards
Board ('IASB') in April 2001 are consistent, it may also be useful in relation to financial
statements prepared under IFRS.

This guidance refers primarily to the financial statements of commercial entities reporting   **2**
in compliance with companies legislation and therefore intended to give a true and fair
view[1]. However, its principles can be applied more generally to financial statements
prepared by other organisations (eg, charities, pension schemes, government departments,
local authorities and public sector businesses)[2], although the assessment of users' needs
may vary (see paragraphs 20, 22, 38 and 39 below).

The principles set out in this guidance may also be relevant to other information, such   **3**
as that provided in an operating and financial review, a business review, a half-yearly
report, interim management statements, information about post balance sheet events or in
corporate governance disclosures.

Auditors apply similar concepts in arriving at judgements about materiality, but are subject   **4**
to separate guidance issued by the Auditing Practices Board ('APB'). Audit aspects of
materiality are therefore not addressed in this guidance.

---

[1] *The Companies Act 2006 s393 requires that the directors of a company must be satisfied that their accounts prepared in compliance with the Act give a true and fair view, irrespective of the accounting framework used. The Companies Act 1985 s262(2A) provides in relation to financial statements prepared under IAS that references in the relevant part of the Act to financial statements giving a true and fair view are references to their achieving a fair presentation. See also paragraph 8.2 of the Department of Trade and Industry's (now the Department for Business, Enterprise and Regulatory Reform's) Guidance for British Companies on Changes to the Accounting and Reporting Provisions of the Companies Act 1985 (revised August 2005). See also the Opinion of 21 April 2008 by Martin Moore QC, referenced in FRC Press Notice 222 Relevance of 'True and Fair' concept confirmed (http://www.frc.org.uk/press/pub1615.html).*

[2] *The ASB published its Statement of Principles for Financial Reporting: Proposed Interpretation for Public Benefit Entities in June 2007, which includes a discussion of materiality (see paragraphs 15-19 of Chapter 3).*

DEFINITION OF MATERIALITY

5   The concept of materiality is fundamental to the reporting of information. The ASB's Statement of Principles[3] defines and explains it as follows:

> 3.28 Materiality is the final test of what information should be given in a particular set of financial statements. While the paragraphs above describe the characteristics that, if present, will mean that the usefulness of the financial information has been maximised, the materiality test asks whether the resulting information content is of such significance as to require its inclusion in the financial statements.
>
> 3.29 Materiality is therefore a threshold quality that is demanded of all information given in the financial statements. Furthermore, when immaterial information is given in the financial statements, the resulting clutter can impair the understandability of the other information provided. In such circumstances, the immaterial information will need to be excluded.
>
> 3.30 An item of information is material to the financial statements if its misstatement or omission might reasonably be expected to influence the economic decisions of users of those financial statements, including their assessments of management's stewardship.
>
> 3.31 Whether information is material will depend on the size and nature of the item in question judged in the particular circumstances of the case. The principal factors to be taken into account are set out below. It will usually be a combination of these factors, rather than any one in particular, that will determine materiality.
>
> (a)   The item's size is judged in the context both of the financial statements as a whole and of the other information available to users that would affect their evaluation of the financial statements. This includes, for example, considering how the item affects the evaluation of trends and similar considerations.
>
> (b)   Consideration is given to the item's nature in relation to:
>
> > (i)   the transactions or other events giving rise to it; (ii) the legality, sensitivity, normality and potential consequences of the event or transaction;
> >
> > (ii)   the identity of the parties involved; and (iv) the particular headings and disclosures that are affected.
>
> If there are two or more similar items, the materiality of the items in aggregate as well as of the items individually needs to be considered.

GENERAL CONSIDERATIONS

6   Materiality depends on an item's size, nature and circumstances.

---

[3] *Materiality is independent of any particular accounting framework. The Statement of Principles was developed from the IASB's Framework, which in turn drew on work carried out by the US Financial Accounting Standards Board (FASB) in relation to its conceptual framework project. The principles underlying the Statement and Framework are therefore consistent. The IASB and FASB are currently working on a joint project to develop a common conceptual framework. The guidance in this Technical Release may ultimately need to be revisited in the light of the IASB/FASB project. See also paragraph 3.2 of this Overview of text on Auditors may rely on Framework for the Preparation and Presentation.*

Paragraphs 29 and 30 of the Framework deal with materiality in the context of relevance (see footnote 13 below). Paragraph 11 of IAS 1 Presentation of Financial Statements */ paragraph 7 of IAS 1 (Revised) states in relation to materiality that:*

Omissions or misstatements of items are material if they could, individually or collectively, influence the economic decisions of users taken / that users make on the basis of the financial statements. Materiality depends on the size and nature of the omission or misstatement judged in the surrounding circumstances. The size or nature of the item, or a combination of both, could be the determining factor.

Dependence on size means that materiality is quantifiable in financial terms. However, the nature and circumstances of an item are qualitative matters and so materiality is not capable of general mathematical definition. Because judgement is required to determine materiality, different people may have different views about whether an item is material. Materiality will often be indicated by a range of potential values with the eventual treatment of a particular item depending upon a full consideration of the information involved and how it will be used.

Judgements about materiality ultimately depend on how information could influence   7
the economic decisions of users of financial statements or other information ('users')[4].
According to Chapter One of the Statement of Principles:

> The objective of financial statements is to provide information about the reporting entity's financial performance and financial position that is useful to a wide range of users for assessing the stewardship[5] of the entity's management and for making economic decisions.[6]

There is a role for guidelines in reaching consistent and properly considered conclusions.   8
Nevertheless, if preparers are to be responsive to users, they should not substitute the mechanical application of rules and formulae for careful consideration of how information could influence or enhance users' economic decisions, such as whether to hold or sell investments or whether to reappoint or replace management. Preparers should also appreciate that information often has economic effects without changing economic decisions. For example, in preparing financial statements to be used to value a business for an acquisition, a relatively minor adjustment may alter the purchase price without changing the decision to proceed with the acquisition.

APPLICATIONS OF MATERIALITY

In financial reporting, the concept of materiality is applied to, inter alia, tolerances,   9
uncertainties, differences and errors, in relation to:

(a)   classes of transaction;
(b)   account balances;
(c)   disclosures; and
(d)   the financial statements as a whole.

In maintaining accounting records relating to individual transactions with other parties,   10
accuracy and precision are essential and therefore the concept of materiality does not apply.[7] Other items are recorded in accounting records based on best estimates of the outcomes of future events, fair values and the appropriate allocation of costs and revenues to different activities and periods. Such estimates are subjective and the concept of materiality is applied in determining appropriate precision tolerances that reflect the nature of the items involved.

---

[4] *The US Supreme Court has stated that an omitted fact is generally considered to be material if there is a substantial likelihood that a reasonable investor would have viewed its disclosure as significantly altering the 'total mix' of available information (TSC Industries, Inc. v. Northway, Inc.,426 US 438 [1976]).*

[5] *Stewardship is discussed in paragraph 22 below.*

[6] *This is expressed in paragraph 12 of the Framework as: 'The objective of financial statements is to provide information about the financial position, performance and changes in financial position of an entity that is useful to a wide range of users in making economic decisions.'*

[7] *The legal requirement to maintain accounting records is in Companies Act 2006 s386 and Companies Act 1985 s221.*

11   The application of materiality thresholds and tolerances is fundamental to the internal and external reporting that underpins corporate governance, the management of commercial risk and business decision-making. Managements require internal reports which highlight relevant matters and omit irrelevant detail and they supplement basic accounting records with management systems and controls which, amongst other things:

   (a)   summarise information from the accounting records which might be material in aggregate; and

   (b)   prevent and detect material misstatement of that information.

12   For internal and external financial reporting purposes it is conventional to apply low thresholds for accumulating information so that similar items can be considered in aggregate against a chosen level of materiality as the time for reporting approaches. The use of lower thresholds helps ensure that cumulative omissions (including those accumulating over more than one year) and other errors do not lead to an overall material misstatement. It is also conventional to select a monetary unit, such as a pound or a thousand pounds, and to round to the nearest unit. The chosen unit is set sufficiently low to ensure that the resulting loss of precision and detail is clearly immaterial, trivial or inconsequential.

13   In assessing the materiality of errors, account should be taken of the effect on both the balance sheet and the profit and loss account, including the effect of uncorrected errors in past years and the effect on trends.[8]

14   In the context of external reporting, legislation and regulations for different types of organisation contain requirements to report particular accounting and other information. Legislation and regulations usually specifically describe such requirements as applying only when a materiality condition is satisfied: for example, the need to include a line item shown in the accounts formats in companies legislation.

15   Application of the concept of materiality is also explicitly permitted under financial reporting standards of the ASB and the IASB and their respective interpretations ('financial reporting standards') and companies legislation in a variety of circumstances.

16   Many materiality decisions are called for in the application of financial reporting standards. Even where preparers decide to apply an individual provision of a standard – eg, in relation to measurement – they are not necessarily committed to apply all the other provisions of the standard: eg, to make specified disclosures which are immaterial[9]. The importance of such decisions is clear from paragraph 20 of the ASB's Foreword to Accounting Standards which states that the Financial Reporting Review Panel (FRRP) is concerned with material departures from financial reporting standards or the accounting provisions of companies legislation where such a departure results in the financial statements in question not giving a true and fair view.

   (The FRRP considers financial statements prepared both under UK GAAP and IFRS.)

17   In respect of other disclosures required by legislation rather than by standards (for example, directors' emoluments, auditor remuneration, staff costs), application of the concept of materiality is neither specifically permitted nor forbidden by the relevant legislation. These

---

[8] *Correction of errors is dealt with in FRS 3* Reporting Financial Performance *and IAS 8* Accounting Policies, Changes in Accounting Estimates and Errors.

[9] *Paragraph 31 of IAS 1 states that, 'Applying the concept of materiality means that a specific disclosure requirement in a Standard or an Interpretation need not be satisfied if the information is not material.' This is rephrased in paragraph 31 of IAS 1 (Revised) as 'An entity need not provide a specific disclosure required by an IFRS if the information is not material'.*

disclosures are required principally for accountability purposes and materiality should be assessed in that light (see also paragraph 27 below).

USERS

The primary focus of the Statement of Principles is on those financial statements that are intended to give a true and fair view of the reporting entity's financial performance and financial position. For most entities, those statements will be their full annual financial statements to be laid before the members as a body.

18

The Statement of Principles regards financial statements as providing information that is useful to a wide range of external users.[10] It notes a rebuttable presumption that '... financial statements that focus on the interest that investors have in the reporting entity's financial performance and financial position will, in effect, also be focusing on the common interest that all users have in that entity's financial performance and financial position.' Such users include actual and potential investors, employees, lenders, suppliers and other trade creditors, governments and their agencies, and members of the public with access to financial statements. In making judgements on materiality, preparers should therefore be concerned with identifying relevant users. Identifying groups of users for the purpose of making reporting decisions does not itself involve acknowledging a legal duty of care to such groups.

19

The expectation that preparers will address the needs of a wide range of users is mitigated by the Boards' assertions in the Statement of Principles and the Framework that:

20

(a) not all the information needs of all users can be met by financial statements (Statement of Principles paragraph 1.8 and Framework paragraph 10);

(b) financial statements that focus on the interest that investors have in the reporting entity's financial performance and financial position will, in effect, be focusing on the interest that all users have (Statement of Principles paragraph 1.11 and, in different terms, Framework paragraph 10);

(c) users can be assumed to have a reasonable knowledge of business and economic activities and accounting and a willingness to study information with reasonable diligence (Statement of Principles paragraph 3.27(c) and Framework paragraph 25).

It is therefore envisaged that judgements about materiality can generally be made on the basis of the needs of classes of knowledgeable and diligent users who are reasonable in their use of and reliance on financial statements and other information. Such users recognise the inherent limitations of financial statements and other information requiring the use of estimates and the consideration of future events. It is also important when there are large numbers of users in a group to consider representative users. Preparers should not seek to address a single hypothetical user, especially one on the brink of making a decision to buy or sell, whose decision might be changed by even a small change in a reported number or disclosure.

21

The ASB (and IASB) identify providers of risk capital as the primary users of financial statements. Consequently, in considering materiality, preparers are expected to focus on the relevance of information to the assessment of financial performance, position and adaptability and management's discharge of its stewardship responsibilities (referred to generally in this guidance as 'accountability'). In entities where the provision of risk capital is of reduced importance (eg, charities, pension schemes and government bodies),

22

---

[10] *The Framework states that 'The objective of financial statements is to provide information about the financial position, performance and changes in financial position of an entity that is useful to a wide range of users in making economic decisions.' (paragraph 12)*

the same broad financial and accountability issues are still likely to be of most interest to the relevant primary user groups.

DETERMINANTS OF MATERIALITY

23   The determinants of the materiality of an item are its size and nature as judged in the 'particular circumstances of the case' (see the Statement of Principles) or 'surrounding circumstances' (see paragraph 11 of IAS 1).[11] The tests are both quantitative and qualitative, and where the nature and circumstances are of sufficient importance it is these qualitative aspects, rather than considerations of the relative size of an item alone, that determines whether an item falls to be separately disclosed. Judgements are applied consistently within the period and from one period to the next.

24   It may be that an item should be brought to the attention of users due to its nature or the circumstances of its arising, notwithstanding that the amount might not otherwise be regarded as material. Criteria that might apply when deciding whether separate disclosure of an item is needed include the assessment of an item's nature in relation to the matters set out in paragraph 28 below.

25   Examples of such items include unlawful transactions, fines[12], penalties and illegal dividends. Further examples of qualitative items would include the inadequate or improper description of an accounting policy when it is likely that a user of the financial statements would be misled by the description, and failure to disclose a breach of regulatory requirements when it is likely that the consequent imposition of regulatory restrictions will significantly impair operating capability.

Size

26   The size of an item recognised in primary financial statements can only be expressed in terms of monetary value. In considering the materiality of uncertainties and contingencies, preparers therefore have to make best estimates of the potential monetary amounts involved, taking into account the likelihood of crystallisation. In considering the materiality of related party transactions for which no price is charged, preparers should have regard to the potential monetary amounts involved.

27   Whilst the quantification of materiality is fundamental and unavoidable, materiality can never be judged purely on the basis of absolute size.

- £1 million is a large amount but in relation to a potential misstatement of sales by a large multinational, it is likely to be immaterial.
- Conversely, in some cases the nature and circumstances of an item can be of such importance to users that a size threshold is of little practical significance in determining materiality. For example, £10,000 is a comparatively small amount but it might be seen as material, even for a large multinational, if it relates to a benefit-in-kind which has been wrongly omitted from the disclosure of directors' remuneration.

---

[11] *The Framework judges the 'relevance' of an item by reference to its materiality and, separately, its nature: 'Information is material if its omission or misstatement could influence the economic decisions of users taken on the basis of the financial statements. Materiality depends on the size of the item or error judged in the particular circumstances of its omission or misstatement.' (paragraph 30) The Statement of Principles does not subsume 'nature' within relevance; it states that 'information is relevant if it has the ability to influence the economic decisions of users and is provided in time to influence those decisions.' (paragraph 3.2)*

[12] *See FRRP Press Notice 51 dated 12 May 1998 (http://www.frc.org.uk/frrp/press/pub0110.html).*

The latter point may be particularly relevant where management accountability or corporate governance are at issue or in the context of disclosures in financial statements required by legislation (see paragraph 17 above).

Nature

The nature of an item is characterised by: 28

(a) the transactions or other events giving rise to it;
(b) the legality, sensitivity, normality and potential consequences of the event or transaction;
(c) the identity of the parties involved; and
(d) the account captions and disclosure notes affected.

Particular care should be taken not to offset items which are different in nature when they 29
might be material if considered separately; eg, an unrecorded sale and the related cost of sale, or an item and its tax effect. Conversely, the materiality of items of a similar nature should be considered in aggregate; eg, if a number of sales have not been recorded, their materiality should be considered in aggregate.

The Statement of Principles states that, 'In requiring information provided by financial 30
statements to represent faithfully what it purports to represent and to be neutral, there is an implication that the information is complete and free from error – at least within the bounds of materiality. Information that contains a material error or has been omitted for reasons other than materiality can cause the financial statements to be false or misleading and thus unreliable and deficient in terms of their relevance' (paragraph 3.16, emphasis in italics added). Creating immaterial errors deliberately or selectively correcting immaterial errors in order to influence a trend is not in accordance with UK GAAP.[13]

This is also an issue that has been highlighted in other relevant literature. For example, the 31
APB's Aggressive Earnings Management[14] states that 'as a matter of principle the APB believes that directors and management should correct all misstatements identified by the auditors' (paragraph 35); and 'auditors consider whether judgements and decisions made by the directors and management ... could be part of a pattern of bias, even though individually they may appear reasonable, to avoid the financial statements reflecting the underlying reality' (paragraph 47).

Circumstances

The materiality of information can only be judged in relation to its ultimate impact, or 32
potential impact, on users. Consequently, the materiality of a given item of a given size will depend on the context of the accounting and other information available to users.

The immediate context of an item is the entity's financial statements. Some financial 33
reporting standards and related guidance contain explicit references to the appropriate context in which to judge materiality and look beyond the immediate disclosures and captions affected by an item. It might be appropriate to focus on one or more of the following:

---

[13] *See also paragraph 41 of IAS 8, which makes it clear that 'financial statements do not comply with IFRSs if they contain ... immaterial errors made intentionally to achieve a particular presentation of an entity's financial position, financial performance or cash flows.'*

[14] *http://www.frc.org.uk/images/uploaded/documents/aggrressive.pdf [sic]*

(a)   individual disclosures;
(b)   primary statement captions and subtotals;
(c)   the relevant primary financial statement as a whole;
(d)   the financial statements as a whole; and
(e)   the entity's financial position or the scale of its operations as indicated by the financial statements.

34   Paragraph 20 of the Explanation of FRS 8 *Related Party Disclosures* provides additional guidance. It indicates that the materiality of related party transactions is to be judged not only in the broader context of the reporting entity but also in relation to an individual related party; eg, where that party is a director, key manager or some other accountable person. (This does not apply in the FRSSE, which is silent on the issue.)[15] If the disclosure of a related party transaction is considered to be sensitive (eg, for tax reasons or the nature of the transaction) this is likely to affect consideration of the transaction's materiality if disclosure might be expected to influence the users of the financial statements.

35   The financial statements of a single period for a single entity are of limited value and users generally consider such information in a wider context. It will therefore often be appropriate for preparers to modify their views on the materiality of an item in the light of:

(a)   comparative figures and trend information;
(b)   expectations including, where relevant, projections and forecasts;
(c)   the financial statements of comparable entities; and
(d)   economic and industry background information.

HALF-YEARLY STATEMENTS

36   The ASB Statement Half-Yearly Financial Reports (July 2007) states that

'materiality should be assessed by reference to the results and financial position for the half-yearly period rather than in relation to expected results and financial position for the full year' (paragraph 28).[16] Interim measurements of financial data may rely on estimates to a greater extent than annual measurements and this may be relevant when making assessments of materiality at half-yearly or other interim dates.

MAKING DECISIONS ABOUT MATERIALITY

37   Prescriptive rules which seek to reflect how users make decisions cannot address all situations and relieve preparers of the need to apply judgement. Preparers may wish to develop and maintain guidelines for their own organisation which reflect their consideration of users and the size, nature and circumstances of individual items within the financial statements. Such guidelines provide relatively objective rebuttable presumptions against which subsequent judgements about particular situations can be gauged. Preparers may have regard to the increasing precision with which materiality can be expressed during the course of preparation of financial statements. An important overall test of the appropriateness of decisions about materiality is to consider whether the resulting financial statements give a true and fair view as required by companies legislation and the regulations for many different types of entity.[17]

---

[15] *IAS 24* Related Party Disclosures *is silent on this issue. The ASB has published FRED 41 proposing to replace FRS 8 with an accounting standard based on IAS 24, and is therefore also silent on this issue.*

[16] *IAS 34* Interim Financial Reporting *similarly states that 'materiality shall be assessed in relation to the interim period financial data' (paragraph 23).*

[17] *The Companies Act 2006 requires a true and fair view for financial statements prepared both under UK GAAP and IAS.*

Materiality guidelines can be derived from answering the following questions: **38**

(a)   who are the relevant users?
(b)   what are their decision-making needs?
(c)   what types of financial information are likely to influence the decisions of the users? (For example, users of financial statements of a nonprofit organisation and users of financial statements of a commercial trading entity may focus on different information.)
(d)   for a given item, what is the appropriate context for assessing its materiality?
(e)   in what range of values do items become critical in terms of materiality?
(f)   how should particular items in these critical ranges be decided and reported?

Preparers' perceptions of users' needs can be based on: **39**

(a)   general discussions with users and other information relating to users' expectations gathered as a result of a company's corporate governance procedures;
(b)   observing users' responses to information, eg, press or analyst comment on particular disclosures, numbers, ratios or trends and the effects on decisions to hold or sell investments or to reappoint or replace management;
(c)   the impact on market prices of specific items of news; and
(d)   their own reactions and attitudes as users of financial information in similar situations.

In some cases the approach will be relatively straightforward. Where a company's bank   **40**
facility is dependent on compliance with covenants based upon financial statements, the users of those statements include investors, bankers and creditors with an interest in knowing whether the covenants are violated.[18] Their decision-making needs will at least cover the figures that are used in the covenant calculations. An item will be judged material if it will make a difference in triggering non-compliance with a covenant or in ensuring that a covenant is satisfied.

At certain critical thresholds, an assessment of users' needs will indicate a requirement for   **41**
very low levels of materiality and potentially unrealistic demands for accuracy; eg, where trends reverse, profits become losses, technical insolvency occurs, or compliance with debt covenants is in doubt. In these circumstances, preparers should:

(a)   adopt an even-handed approach in areas where the required degree of accuracy is difficult to achieve so that there is perceived to be an equal chance of mistakenly falling on either side of a critical divide;
(b)   be particularly sensitive to the potentially misleading cumulative effect of individually immaterial items or errors (see paragraph 13 above); and
(c)   consider whether the reliability of the information in relation to its potential use is such that the information should be accompanied by a clear statement of the circumstances of its preparation and its inherent limitations (see paragraph 26 above).[19]

---

[18] *Paragraph 18 of FRS 29 (IFRS 7)* Financial Instruments: Disclosures *and IFRS 7* Financial Instruments: Disclosures *require specified disclosures about defaults that occur during the period. Paragraph 67 of IAS 1 / paragraph 76 of IAS 1 (Revised) and FRS 21 (IAS 10)* Events after the balance sheet date *are relevant for disclosures of defaults that occur between the balance sheet date and the date the financial statements are authorised. (Paragraph 67 of IAS 1 / paragraph 76 of IAS 1 (Revised) sets out specified disclosures regarding the latter.)*

[19] *See also paragraph 113 of IAS 1 / paragraph 122 of IAS 1 (Revised), which requires disclosure of significant judgements made in applying the entity's accounting policies; and paragraph 116 of IAS 1 / paragraph 125 of IAS 1, which requires disclosure of assumptions about the future and other major sources of estimation uncertainty that have a significant risk of causing material adjustments in the next financial year.*

42   On the basis of experience, a preparer might reasonably decide to attach particular importance to the materiality of items in a company's financial statements in the context of the trend of earnings and the margins of other companies in the same sector. Such considerations might be particularly appropriate in situations of marginal or break-even profitability.

EVIDENCING DECISIONS

43   It may be appropriate for those preparing financial statements, whether as individuals or, collectively, as a body charged with governance, formally to document, for their own purposes, and commensurate with the size and complexity of the entity in the prevailing circumstances, their principles, policies and guidelines with regard to materiality and the main decisions they have taken. Such steps may be useful in appropriate circumstances in dealings with Regulators such as the FRRP.

desmond.wright@icaew.com

TECH 02/10
Guidance on the Determination of Realised Profits and Losses in the Context of Distributions under the Companies Act 2006

Issued by the Institute of Chartered Accountants in England and Wales and the Institute of Chartered Accountants of Scotland (the Institutes)

(October 2010)

Contents

*This Technical Release provides general guidance and does not purport to deal with
all possible questions and issues that may arise in any given situation. The Institutes
and the authors do not accept responsibility for loss caused to any person who acts or
refrains from acting in reliance on the material in this publication, whether such loss is
caused by negligence or otherwise.*

1. INTRODUCTION

1.1   This Technical Release provides guidance on realised and distributable profits under the Companies Act 2006 (the Act). Its purpose is to identify, interpret and apply the principles relating to the determination of realised profits and losses for the purposes of making distributions under the Act. It is based on the guidance originally issued as TECH 01/09 in June 2009 but includes some significant additional material, the draft version of which was issued for comment as TECH 03/09 in December 2009. For the convenience of users, paragraph numbering has been kept consistent with TECH 01/09 so far as possible and consequently some paragraph numbers are not used where material has been deleted or moved.

1.2   Comments received on TECH 03/09 were generally supportive of the proposals and did not raise any major issues of principle. Some drafting improvements have been made in the light of comments received.

1.3   The more significant changes made from the proposals in TECH 03/09 are as follows:

(a)   for profits arising from remeasurement of acquired liabilities prior to settlement, TECH 03/09 set out three options for consideration. None of the responses supported the approach in its paragraph 9.9 that such profits would be realised without any restrictions. Responses were divided between those supporting the 'readily convertible to cash' approach in its paragraph 9.7, which is consistent with the underlying principles of realisation established in previous guidance, and those supporting a departure from that approach in paragraph 9.8 which looked to whether qualifying consideration was received when the liability was assumed. The 9.7 approach is in effect an application of existing guidance and, as the Institutes have concluded that the level of support for the approach set out in paragraph 9.8 did not amount to sufficient to change 'generally accepted practice', this guidance therefore reflects the conclusion that a realised profit will arise on remeasurement of an acquired liability only when that profit is readily convertible to cash (as defined in paragraph 3.12);

(b)   for goodwill written off to reserves, TECH 03/09 proposed a single approach to realisation which would have been independent of the accounting framework adopted. However, several of the responses suggested that it would be more appropriate to apply the principles of the accounting framework actually used to prepare the financial statements. This approach has been adopted in this technical release. A consequence of this decision is that in some cases goodwill written off to reserves that had been treated as a realised loss on the basis of notional amortisation in accordance with SSAP 22 or FRS 10 will no longer be treated as a realised loss on transition to IFRSs, because the impairment model is applied and there has been no impairment;

(c)   for distributions settled by set-off, TECH 03/09 proposed two possible approaches. The approach proposed in paragraph 8.12, which was to add a new paragraph 3.11(e) to the definition of qualifying consideration, received most support and has been adopted in this technical release; and

(d)   additional guidance has been added to address the treatment of reimbursement assets arising in connection with IFRIC 5 'Rights to Interests arising from Decommissioning, Restoration and Environmental Rehabilitation Funds' (see 10.69 to 10.72).

1.4   This Technical Release reflects accounting standards in issue at 1 June 2010. It does not provide guidance on how transactions and arrangements should be accounted for. However, it has been necessary to make assumptions about accounting treatments while providing guidance on the impact on realised and distributable profits.

This Technical Release represents generally accepted practice at 1 June 2010. Whilst many of the revisions to TECH 01/09 made by this TECH 02/10 represent principles that were generally accepted prior to that date, the revisions introduced now should not be used to question the lawfulness of distributions made at an earlier date. However, balances on reserves will need to be re-examined in the light of the guidance and the position should be re-assessed before a distribution is made. **1.5**

English and Scottish Counsel have confirmed that the guidance is consistent with the law at 1 June 2010. Counsel accept no responsibility (other than to the Institutes) in relation to advice ascribed to them in this guidance. **1.6**

The Act permits companies to prepare their individual accounts using UK GAAP or EU-adopted IFRSs. This guidance applies to companies reporting under both UK GAAP and EU-adopted IFRSs except where otherwise stated. The guidance has been written on the basis of 'full' IFRSs as issued by the IASB except where otherwise stated but should be equally applicable to EU-adopted IFRSs. No reference is made to IFRS 9 'Financial instruments', which has not yet been adopted by the EU. Similarly, no consideration has been given to issues that may arise from use of the IFRS for SMEs, **1.7**

In the case of converged standards, reference to an IFRS or IAS should be read as applying to the equivalent UK standard unless the context requires otherwise. The guidance uses the IFRS terminology 'in profit or loss'. In the context of UK GAAP, this should be read as meaning 'in the profit and loss account'. References to the 'Accounting Regulations' are to the Large and Medium-sized Companies and Groups (Accounts and Reports) Regulations 2008 (SI 2008/410) and to the Small Companies and Groups (Accounts and Directors' Report) Regulations 2008 (SI 2008/409) as appropriate. **1.8**

The revised version of IAS 1 issued in 2007 makes some changes of terminology, for example referring to a statement of financial position instead of a balance sheet. It also introduced a requirement for a statement of comprehensive income which may be presented either as a single statement or as an income statement together with a separate statement showing other comprehensive income. For simplicity and consistency with UK GAAP, the previous terminology has been retained in this guidance. **1.9**

Companies should consider taking their own legal advice, particularly in relation to any matters not covered by this guidance. **1.10**

2. THE LEGAL FRAMEWORK

Introduction

The legal framework relating to the determination of realised profits and losses and of profits available for distribution consists of two elements: common law and statutory provisions. **2.1**

Those aspects of the Act that deal with matters other than those relating to the form and content of accounts continue to apply when accounts are prepared under IFRSs. All of the rules on capital maintenance in the Act therefore continue to apply. That is to say, the legal rules regarding shares (and the share premium account) continue to control, for example, payments in respect of those shares even though the shares (and related share premium) may be presented as liabilities in the accounts. For example, the ability to pay dividends on preference shares is still determined by reference to the availability of distributable profits even if those dividends are reported as an expense in accordance with IFRSs. **2.1AA**

The common law

2.1A   The 2006 Act codifies the general duties of directors under common law. However, this does not render obsolete the rules in relation to capital maintenance or duties in relation to creditors of the company which remain relevant.

2.1B   Under sections 851 and 852, any restrictions in common law or imposed by the company's articles on the sums available for distribution or the cases in which a distribution may be made, take precedence over the statutory provisions. Section 851(2) makes an exception to this rule. It provides that the amount of any distribution in kind is established by the statutory rules in sections 845 and 846 (see 2.9 – 2.9F below) and not by the applicable common law rules.

2.2   Under common law, a company cannot lawfully make a distribution out of capital. Thus, the directors must consider, both at the time of proposing the distribution and at the time it is made (see paragraph 2.10 below), whether the company, subsequent to the balance sheet date to which the 'relevant accounts' were prepared, has incurred losses that have eroded its profits available for distribution (the 'capital maintenance rule'). Guidance on the application of the capital maintenance rule to the introduction of a new accounting standard is given at 3.30 and 3.31 below. It is not practicable to give further guidance on the application of the capital maintenance rule in this Technical Release: appropriate advice will have to be taken to deal with specific circumstances.

Fiduciary and other duties and volatility

2.3   In addition, directors are subject to fiduciary and other duties in the exercise of the powers conferred on them. Examples of fiduciary and other duties include the obligation on directors to safeguard the company's assets and take reasonable steps to ensure that the company is in a position to settle its debts as they fall due. Directors must therefore specifically consider whether the company will still be solvent following a proposed distribution. Thus, directors should consider both the immediate cash flow implications of a distribution and the continuing ability of the company to pay its debts as they fall due. In reaching their decision they must take into account any change in the financial position of the company after the balance sheet date of the relevant accounts and the future cash needs of the company.

2.4   In the context of fair value accounting, volatility is an aspect where directors will need to consider their duties. The fair value of financial instruments may be volatile even though such fair value is properly determined in accordance with IAS 39 *Financial Instruments: Recognition and Measurement* (subsequently referred to as IAS 39 for brevity). Directors should consider, as a result of their duties, whether it is prudent to distribute profits arising from changes in the fair values of financial instruments considered to be volatile, even though they may otherwise be realised profits in accordance with this guidance.

2.5   Similarly, IAS 39 is based on a 'mixed measurement model' whereby some financial instruments may be included at fair value while others may be included on an amortised cost basis. This may, in some cases, lead to volatility in the profit or loss for the period. For example, an asset and a liability may provide an economic hedge but if the asset is measured at fair value and the liability is not, a profit may be reported on one but a loss not reported on the other. Although such profits may be realised profits in accordance with this guidance, directors should consider, as a result of their duties, whether it would be prudent to distribute them.

Definition of a distribution for Part 23 of the 2006 Act

A 'distribution' is defined by section 829 as every description of distribution of a company's assets to its members, whether in cash or otherwise, subject to the following exceptions:

    2.6

(a)   an issue of shares as fully or partly paid bonus shares;

(b)   the reduction of share capital;

    (i)   by extinguishing or reducing the liability of any of the members on any of the company's shares in respect of share capital not paid up; or

    (ii)   by repaying paid up share capital;

(c)   the redemption or purchase of any of the company's own shares out of capital (including the proceeds of any fresh issue of shares) or out of unrealised profits in accordance with Chapter 3, 4 or 5 of Part 18; and

(d)   a distribution of assets to members of the company on its winding-up.

Profits available for distribution

A company may make a distribution only out of profits available for that purpose (section 830(1)) (the common law position is set out in paragraph 2.2). A company's profits available for distribution are its accumulated, realised profits (so far as not previously distributed or capitalised) less its accumulated, realised losses (so far as not previously written off in a reduction or reorganisation of its share capital) (section 830(2)). Thus realised losses may not be offset against unrealised profits. Section 831 imposes a further restriction on public companies (see paragraph 2.30 below).

    2.7

Section 853(4) of the Act provides that references to realised profits and realised losses are to such profits or losses as fall to be treated as realised in accordance with principles generally accepted at the time when the accounts are prepared, with respect to the determination for accounting purposes of realised profits or losses. Section 3 below provides guidance on the application of this requirement.

    2.8

In addition, The Companies (Reduction of Share Capital) Order 2008 SI 2008/1915 ('the Order) specifies the cases in which a reserve arising from a reduction in a company's capital (ie share capital, share premium account, capital redemption reserve or redenomination reserve)[1] is to be treated as a realised profit as a matter of law. The Order also disapplies the general prohibition in section 654 on the distribution of a reserve arising from a reduction of capital. The Order provides that:

    2.8A

(a)   if an unlimited company reduces its capital, a reserve arising from the reduction is treated as a realised profit;

(b)   if a private company limited by shares reduces its capital and the reduction is supported by a solvency statement but has not been subject to an application to the court for an order confirming it, the reserve arising from the reduction is treated as a realised profit; and

(c)   if a limited company having a share capital reduces its capital and the reduction is confirmed by order of court, the reserve arising from the reduction is treated as a realised profit unless the court orders otherwise.

---

[1] *The Order refers only to share capital but section 11 of the Interpretation Act 1978 makes it plain that where an Act contains power to promote subordinate legislation, words used in that subordinate legislation have the same meaning as in the main Act. Subject to certain exceptions, the provisions of the Companies Act 2006 relating to the reduction of a company's share capital apply to any share premium account, capital redemption reserve or redenomination reserve as if they were part of paid up share capital (sections 610(4), 628(3) and 733(6)).*

These provisions are without prejudice to any contrary provisions of an order or undertaking given to the court, the resolution for, or any other resolution relevant to, the reduction of capital, or the company's memorandum or articles of association. These provisions came into effect on 1 October 2008. In accordance with The Companies Act 2006 (Commencement No.7, Transitional Provisions and Savings) Order 2008, they apply irrespective of when the reduction in capital occurred or when the reserve arose. They therefore apply to capital reductions made under the 1985 Act and those made by unlimited companies.

2.8B   Section 654 and the Order are concerned with the status of any reserve arising from the reduction of a company's capital. They do not apply to the extent that a reduction of capital takes the form of a payment to shareholders so that no reserve arises.

2.8C   Section 654 and the Order do not differentiate between a reduction of foreign currency share capital and other reductions. Thus the Order applies to such cases and the reserve arising in such cases will, subject to the requirements of the Order, be a realised profit. The amount of the realised profit arising may not be the same as the amount of the reduction due to exchange movements because the reduction is calculated by reference to rates of exchange at the date of the reduction. For example, where there is a reduction of capital with no payment to shareholders, although the reduction is calculated by reference to the exchange rates at the date of the reduction, the amount of the realised profit arising will be equal to the nominal value of the shares translated at the exchange rate ruling when the shares were issued. Section 11 explains the issues in detail.

2.8D   Section 662 is concerned with the duty of a public company to cancel any shares in itself that it holds when shares are forfeited, or surrendered to the company in lieu of forfeiture, in pursuance of the Articles, for failure to pay any sums payable in respect of the shares (and certain other situations). Unless the shares are disposed of within three years of the forfeiture or surrender, the company must cancel the shares and diminish the amount of the company's share capital by the nominal value of the shares cancelled. Section 662(4) provides that the directors of a company may take any steps necessary to enable the company to comply with this requirement without complying with the requirements of chapter 10 of Part 17 of the Act in relation to reductions of capital.

2.8E   A reserve arising from a capital reduction under section 662 will not be a distributable reserve because of the restriction imposed by section 654 (see 2.8A above). Section 654 is not disapplied by section 662(4) because Section 654 is not in chapter 10 of Part 17 of the Act, neither is it disapplied in these circumstances by the Order[2].

Distributions in kind: Meaning

2.8F   Sections 845 and 846 make provision for a distribution consisting of or including, or treated as arising in consequence of, the sale, transfer or other disposition by a company of a non-cash asset (referred to in this guidance as a 'distribution in kind'). A waiver of an amount receivable from a parent is considered as a distribution in kind, being an 'other disposition', of that receivable.

Distributions in kind: Treatment of unrealised profits

2.9   Section 846 provides that where a company makes a distribution in kind and any part of the amount at which the asset is stated in the accounts relevant to the distribution represents an

---

[2] *The Institutes believe that this may be as a result of an oversight in drafting the Order and have drawn the matter to the attention of the Department for Business, Innovation & Skills.*

unrealised profit, that profit is to be treated as realised for the purposes of the distribution. Thus if a company wishes to distribute in kind an asset with a historical cost of £100 and which is in the books at £130 (with the surplus in the revaluation reserve), the surplus of £30 is treated as realised for this purpose and only £100 of other realised profits are needed.

However, if the surplus has been capitalised, it is no longer available for this purpose and other realised profits of £130 would be needed to cover the proposed distribution.

The application of section 846 to replacement assets is considered at 10.73 below. The application of section 846 to fungible assets is considered at 10.77 below.   **2.9A**

Distributions in kind: Determination of amount

Section 845 was a new provision in the 2006 Act (not in the 1985 Act) which removed **2.9B** doubts arising from the decision in *Aveling Barford Ltd v Perion Ltd* [1989] BCLC 626 in relation to the amount of the distribution of a non-cash asset. Section 845 applies where:

(a)   at the time of the disposition of the asset, the company has profits available for distribution; and

(b)   if the amount of the distribution were to be determined in accordance with the section, the company could make the distribution without contravening Part 23.

Where section 845 applies, the amount of any distribution consisting of or arising from the **2.9C** sale, transfer or other disposition by the company of a non-cash asset should be calculated by reference to the value at which that asset is included in the company's accounts (ie its book value) as follows. If an asset is transferred for a consideration not less than its book value, the amount of the distribution is zero, but if the asset is transferred for a consideration less than its book value, the amount of the distribution is equal to that shortfall, which will therefore need to be covered by distributable profits.

In determining whether a company has profits available for distribution for the purposes **2.9D** of section 845, section 845(3) provides that the company's profits available for distribution are treated as increased by the amount (if any) by which the amount or value of any consideration for the disposition exceeds the book value of the asset. In this context, distributable profits may be 'treated as increased' from a negative starting point[3]. However, to apply section 845, a company must have profits available for distribution after any adjustment in accordance with section 845(3). This requirement is not met by a nil balance. There must be a positive balance even if it is only 1p.

The references to consideration in section 845 are not restricted to consideration that would **2.9E** meet the definition of 'qualifying consideration' in this guidance.

Appendix 1 sets out illustrative worked examples of a transfer of an asset applying **2.9F** section 845.

---

[3] *Legal interpretation of an amount being 'increased' in other contexts may be restricted to being increased from a lower amount but not from zero or below. However, in the context of section 845, such an interpretation would render sub-section (3) redundant and therefore this does not appear to be the intention of the legislation. Therefore, in this case, profits may be treated as increased from a negative starting point.*

Distributions in kind: Effect of IFRIC 17

2.9G   The amount of a distribution in kind for legal purposes will be the book value of the asset to be distributed, provided that this amount is available for distribution, because of the application of section 845 (see 2.9A to 2.9F above).

2.9H   There are no requirements in UK GAAP about accounting for distributions in kind. UK companies have almost invariably accounted for such distributions based on the book value of the asset in question. It has also been acceptable to account for such a distribution based on the fair value of the asset and recognise a profit on disposal. This treatment has been used occasionally.

2.9I   In December 2008, the IASB published IFRIC 17 *Distributions of Non-cash Assets to Owners*. It is to be applied prospectively (ie no restatement of prior periods is required) for annual periods beginning on or after 1 July 2009. The scope of IFRIC 17 excludes certain distributions, including those where the non-cash asset is controlled by the same party or parties before and after the distribution (e.g. intra-group transactions). It applies to a distribution that gives owners a choice of receiving either non-cash assets or a cash alternative. The ASB has stated (in UITF Information Sheet 88) that it has no plans to issue an Abstract based on IFRIC 17 because it has decided that the current accounting under UK GAAP is adequate.

2.9J   IFRIC 17 requires that, when accounting for a distribution of a non-cash asset, the distribution is measured at the fair value of the asset in question. The difference between the fair value of the asset and its book value is subsequently recognised in profit or loss when the distribution is settled. This will be a significant change of practice and may, in certain circumstances, have an adverse impact on the ability of a public company to make a distribution for the reasons explained below.

2.9K   IFRIC 17 requires the recognition of a liability to make the distribution when it is appropriately authorised and no longer at the discretion of the entity. In most cases this means that the liability, which will usually exceed in amount the carrying value of the asset to be distributed, will be recognised before the distribution is settled. It will not be possible to revalue the asset to fair value prior to settlement in most cases. For example, investments in subsidiaries are usually carried on the historical cost basis and it would not be regarded as acceptable to revalue, in isolation, a particular investment. Nor is it possible to anticipate the 'profit' on disposal as this arises only on 'settlement' which must necessarily be later (if only momentarily).

2.9L   If relevant accounts are drawn up after the liability has arisen but before settlement, they will include the liability for the distribution and consequentially reduced net assets. That reduction will be larger than that which will ultimately arise once the distribution is settled. The profit reverses some of the reduction to leave net assets reduced overall only by the book value of the distributed asset.

2.9M   The debit entry arising from recognition of a liability in accordance with IFRIC 17 is an advance recognition of an unsettled distribution obligation and is not a realised loss. The fact that it is recognised at an amount greater than the distribution measured under section 845, therefore, does not affect the ability of a private company to make a distribution.

2.9N   For a public company, the temporary adverse impact on the company's net assets will have an adverse impact on its ability to make a distribution which is based on those relevant accounts (e.g. a proposed final dividend) because of the net asset test in section 831. However, it will not affect the company's ability to make the non-cash distribution in question because that distribution will have been made when it was approved (see 2.10 below) and is based on earlier relevant accounts.

The test in section 831 is a statutory one which applies to the amounts shown in the 'relevant accounts' for the purposes of the distribution. There is no need to update these amounts on an ongoing basis throughout the year other than for earlier distributions as required by section 840. Therefore, the issue arises only when the 'relevant accounts' are drawn up to a date between the date of approval of the distribution and when it is settled. Provided that the period between approval and settlement does not straddle the company's year end, this issue is thus unlikely to cause a problem in practice.   **2.9O**

Date of distribution

A distribution is made when it becomes a legally binding liability of the company, regardless of the date on which it is to be settled. In the case of a final dividend, this will be when it is declared by the company in general meeting or, for private companies, by the members passing a written resolution. In the case of an interim dividend authorised under common articles of association (e.g. 1985 Act Table A), normally no legally binding liability is established prior to payment being made of the dividend. In such a case, a distribution is made only when the dividend is paid. However, in the case of an interim dividend, steps may be taken to establish a legally binding liability at an earlier date. See 9.6 to 9.18 below concerning how such a liability may be established. That guidance is written in the context of intra-group transactions. However, the guidance may also be relevant in other cases.   **2.10**

Distributable profits are consumed when a distribution is made in accordance with the previous paragraph. After that time, a shareholder's right to any unpaid dividend is as a creditor of the company rather than as a shareholder[4].   **2.10A**

Merger relief and group reconstruction relief

Where the company has entered into a transaction which gives rise to group reconstruction relief or merger relief under sections 611 or 612, it may choose under section 615 to disregard any amount that would otherwise have been included in the share premium account in determining the amount at which the acquired asset is stated in the company's balance sheet. Subject to the rules in accounting standards, the asset may therefore be stated at the nominal value of the shares issued together with any minimum premium value recognised when applying group reconstruction relief. However, it is also possible to record the asset acquired at fair value and to credit the amount of that relief to another reserve (often called a merger reserve)[5]. In such a case, that reserve is in law a profit and is initially treated as unrealised but becomes realised in a manner similar to a revaluation reserve. Thus, provided the merger reserve is not capitalised (by way of a bonus issue of shares), the decision as to whether or not to record the merger reserve should not overall have any effect on the level of the company's realised profits. The accounting choice referred to in this paragraph may be restricted by the application of accounting standards. This is considered further at 9.43 to 9.44D below.   **2.11**

---

[4] *Section 74(2)(f) of the Insolvency Act 1986 provides that a sum due to a member in his character of a member by way of dividends etc is subordinated in a liquidation to the claims of other creditors.*

[5] *As explained at 9.44B below, a third basis of measurement may be required when applying IAS 27 as revised in May 2008.*

Relevant accounts

General

2.12   Under both the Act and common law, distributions are made by individual companies and not by groups. The group accounts are therefore not relevant for the purpose of determining a company's profits available for distribution (see 10.1 to 10.3 below). The status of accounts prepared in accordance with IAS 28 or IAS 31 (ie using equity accounting) where a company has an associate or jointly controlled entity but has no subsidiaries is considered at 10.4 below.

2.13   Whether or not a distribution may be made within the terms of the Act is determined by reference to a company's 'relevant accounts'. Where it is proposed to make a distribution during the company's first accounting reference period or before any accounts have been circulated, initial accounts must be prepared. In all other cases the relevant accounts are its last annual accounts that were circulated to members[6] or interim accounts, if the proposed distribution cannot be justified by reference to the last annual accounts.

2.14   The items in these accounts to which reference is made in determining the amount of a distribution which may be made are listed in section 836(1) as profits, losses, assets, liabilities, provisions[7], share capital and reserves (including undistributable reserves). Thus, valuations or contingencies referred to in notes to the financial statements, but not incorporated in the balance sheet, do not affect the amount of realised profit calculated by reference to the relevant accounts. For example, if the relevant accounts record an unrealised profit but state in a note that, as a consequence of an event subsequent to the balance sheet date, the profit has become realised, interim accounts must nevertheless be prepared before a distribution can be made out of these profits.

2.15   Similarly, disclosures about the impact of future changes of accounting policy, such as those required by IAS 8(30), do not affect the amount of realised profit calculated by reference to the relevant accounts. However, they may be relevant to the application of the common law on capital maintenance where a distribution is to be made in the period in relation to which the change of policy will be implemented (see 3.30 and 3.31 below).

2.16   In practice it may not be sufficient to determine the amount of realised profits simply by examining the relevant accounts as further enquiries may be necessary as to the composition of the various reserves included in the balance sheet. For example, certain reserves may include both realised and unrealised profits. As there is no legal requirement for a company to distinguish in its accounts between distributable and non distributable profits as such (see 2.25 to 2.27 below), companies should keep sufficient records to enable them to distinguish between those profits which are available for distribution and those which are not.

2.17   Under section 395, a company's individual accounts must be prepared either as 'Companies Act individual accounts' or as 'IAS individual accounts'. Thus, the relevant accounts will be either its 'Companies Act individual accounts' or 'IAS individual accounts', depending on the choice made by the company. It follows that when a company elects to prepare its statutory individual accounts in accordance with EU-adopted IFRSs, it is the amounts stated in those accounts that are relevant for the purposes of justifying a distribution.

---

[6] *Where a company circulates to members a summary financial statement, the relevant accounts are the full accounts from which the summary financial statement was derived.*

[7] *Provisions are defined for this purpose in section 836(1) as, in the case of Companies Act accounts, provisions of any kind specified for this purpose by regulations under section 396 and, in the case of IAS accounts, provisions of any kind.*

The detailed requirements for relevant accounts (annual, interim or initial) are summarised in the following paragraphs. **2.18**

Annual accounts – all companies

If the company's last annual accounts constitute the relevant accounts they must be prepared under Part 15 of the Act (Accounts and Reports) and comply with the requirements of section 837. Such accounts may be either 'Companies Act individual accounts' or 'IAS individual accounts' (see 2.17 above). The requirements of section 837 are that: **2.19**

(a) the accounts must have been properly prepared in accordance with the Act (including the requirement in section 393 that they must not be approved unless the directors are satisfied that they give a true and fair view of the assets, liabilities, financial position and profit or loss of the company), subject only to matters not material for determining the lawfulness of a distribution;

(b) the accounts must have been circulated to members in accordance with section 423[8];

(c) the accounts must be accompanied, where applicable, by the report of the auditors under section 495; and

(d) if the report of the auditors is qualified, the auditors must state in writing whether in their opinion the matters in respect of which their report is qualified is material for determining the lawfulness of the distribution. The statement by the auditors, which can be subsequent to the report, must be laid before the company in general meeting in the case of a public company, or be circulated to members in accordance with section 423 in the case of a private company.

The last two sub-paragraphs do not apply where the directors of the company have taken advantage of the audit exemption conferred by sections 477(1) or 480(1).

Initial and interim accounts – public companies

Sections 838 and 839 respectively provide that interim and initial accounts of a public company must have been 'properly prepared', or have been properly prepared subject only to matters that are not material for determining, by reference to those accounts, whether the proposed distribution would contravene sections 830 or 831. A copy of the interim and initial accounts must have been delivered to the Registrar of Companies before the distribution is made (ie before the date of the distribution – see 2.10 above). **2.20**

'Properly prepared' means that the accounts must comply with sections 395 to 397 which includes the true and fair requirement in relation to Companies Act accounts[9] and the requirement to apply EU-adopted IFRSs in relation to IAS accounts. These requirements are to be applied with such modifications as are necessary because the accounts are prepared otherwise than in respect of an accounting reference period. In the case of interim accounts, the balance sheet must be signed in accordance with section 414. There is no equivalent statutory requirement for initial accounts to be signed in accordance with section 414 but, in practice, the auditors will require the accounts to be approved and signed by the directors before the report of the auditors can be signed. **2.21**

---

[8] *Where a company circulates to members a summary financial statement, the relevant accounts are the full accounts from which the summary financial statement was derived.*

[9] *There is no statutory requirement for interim and initial accounts to give a true and fair view when they are prepared under IFRSs because section 393, which imposes an overarching requirement for annual accounts to give a true and fair view, does not apply for this purpose. However, the requirements of IAS 1 impose a similar requirement to 'present fairly'.*

2.22   In requiring the interim and initial accounts to be 'properly prepared', or to be properly prepared except for matters which are not relevant in determining whether a proposed dividend would be lawful under the Act, the legislation permits a public company to omit information which is not relevant in determining whether a distribution would be lawful under the Act. In practice, therefore, interim or initial accounts will consist of a balance sheet and profit and loss account but the notes may be restricted to those matters that are relevant to a distribution. Corresponding amounts for the previous financial year would not be relevant.

2.23   Interim accounts are not required to be audited. However, initial accounts of a public company must be accompanied by a report by the auditors stating whether, in their opinion, the accounts have been 'properly prepared'. If their report is qualified (which would be the case if the company chooses to prepare initial accounts which do not give a true and fair view, as described in paragraph 2.22 above), the auditors must make an additional statement which states whether, in their opinion, the matters in respect of which their report is qualified is material for determining, by reference to the initial accounts, whether the distribution would contravene sections 830 or 831. A copy of the auditors' statement must also have been laid before the company in general meeting and delivered to the Registrar of Companies.

Initial and interim accounts – private companies

2.24   The requirements of sections 838 and 839 regarding the form and content of interim and initial accounts of public companies do not apply to private companies. Instead, the only requirement for private companies flows from the general definition at the start of those sections of interim or initial accounts as those necessary to enable a reasonable judgement to be made as to profits, losses, assets and liabilities, provisions, and share capital and reserves. Reliable management accounts which deal with these matters will often satisfy this requirement. However, management accounts sometimes do not deal with all relevant matters. For example, they may exclude tax. In these cases, appropriate adjustments need to be made to the management accounts.

Disclosure of distributable profits

2.25   There is no requirement under law or accounting standards for financial statements to distinguish between realised profits and unrealised profits or between distributable profits and non-distributable profits. Paragraph 2.16 above draws attention to the need for companies to maintain sufficient records to enable them to distinguish between those profits that are available for distribution and those which are not.

2.26   The guidance at 2.16 above is likely to be of greater significance when reporting under IFRSs or using the fair value accounting rules under UK GAAP than has previously been the case. One reason for this is that the restriction in the Accounting Regulations that only profits realised at the balance sheet date may be included in the profit and loss account does not apply in these cases.

2.27   It may be thought helpful to users of financial statements if there is an indication of which reserves are distributable but, as noted above, there is no legal requirement to do so. In some cases, there may be practical difficulties with providing such an analysis. For example, there may be uncertainties about whether certain profits are realised or unrealised. There is generally no need for directors to form a view on whether profits are realised unless they intend to utilise them to make a distribution.

Subsequent events

Under common law, a company cannot lawfully make a distribution out of capital. **2.28**
Therefore it may be necessary to take into account losses incurred after the balance sheet
date (see 2.2 above).

One or more distributions may already have been made by reference to a particular set of **2.29**
accounts; for example, an interim dividend or a purchase of own shares. In determining
the lawfulness of any proposed further distribution by reference to the same accounts, the
directors must take account of any such distributions (section 840(1)).

Public companies

A further restriction is placed on distributions by public companies (section 831). A public **2.30**
company may make a distribution only if, after giving effect to such distribution, the
amount of its net assets (as defined in section 831(2)) is not less than the aggregate of
its called up share capital and undistributable reserves as shown in the relevant accounts.

Under section 831(4) the following are undistributable reserves: **2.31**

(a)   share premium account (see also section 610);
(b)   capital redemption reserve (see also section 733);
(c)   the excess of accumulated unrealised profits, so far as not previously utilised by
      capitalisation, over the accumulated unrealised losses, so far as not previously
      written off in a reduction or reorganisation of its share capital; and
(d)   any other reserve which the company is prohibited from distributing by any
      enactment (e.g. a redenomination reserve arising under section 628), or by its articles
      of association (or equivalent).

This means that, in calculating the amount available for distribution, a public company
must reduce the amount of its net realised profits available for distribution by the amount
of its net unrealised losses. The effects of this rule in relation to holdings of own shares
through an ESOP trust and in relation to the presentation of shares as liabilities in the
balance sheet are addressed at 7.12 *et seq* and 6.24 *et seq* respectively.

Provisions

The general rule and the exception

Section 841(2) states that for the purposes of Part 23, the following are treated as realised **2.31A**
losses:

● in the case of Companies Act accounts, provisions of a kind specified for the purpose
  in regulations under section 396 (other than revaluation provisions); and
● in the case of IAS accounts, provisions of any kind (except revaluation provisions).

The Accounting Regulations[10] state that references to provisions for depreciation or
diminution in value of assets are to any amounts written off by way of providing for
depreciation or diminution in value of assets. It also states that references to provisions for
liabilities (or, in the case of insurance companies to provisions for other risks), are to any
amounts retained as reasonably necessary for the purpose of providing for any liability, the
nature of which is clearly defined and which is either likely to be incurred, or certain to be
incurred but uncertain as to the amount or as to the date on which it will arise.

---

[10] *Schedule 7 to SI 2008/409 and Schedule 9 to SI 2008/410.*

2.32   The general rule is therefore that any provision (including one for depreciation or diminution in value as well as provisions for liabilities, charges or losses) is treated as a realised loss.

2.33   As an exception to the general rule, a 'revaluation provision' which is a provision for diminution in value of a fixed asset appearing on a revaluation of all the fixed assets (other than goodwill) (section 841(3)) is not treated as a realised loss. However, this exception would not apply where the fixed asset has been sold or scrapped, because in these circumstances any loss would need to be reclassified as realised. Furthermore, unrealised losses which exceed unrealised profits are relevant to a public company in determining the amount available for distribution as the requirements of section 831 (Restrictions on the distribution of assets) referred to at 2.30 above must be satisfied.

2.34   For the exception in 2.33 above to apply, it is not necessary for a revaluation of all the fixed assets to be recorded in the accounts. Section 841(4) provides that a revaluation of all the fixed assets is treated as having taken place if (1) the directors consider the value of any assets that have not actually been revalued, (2) they are satisfied that the aggregate value of those assets is not less than that stated in the company's accounts and (3) the notes to the accounts include a statement to that effect. The notes to the accounts should also state that amounts are stated in the accounts on the basis that a revaluation of fixed assets is treated as having taken place.

2.34AA   Application of the exception in section 841 for revaluation provisions is not restricted to those circumstances where there is an offsetting unrealised profit (recognised or not). Where all of the assets are actually revalued, section 841 treats the provision as a revaluation provision without any additional restrictions.

2.34AB   Where the assets, other than the impaired one, are not actually revalued but their value is 'considered' in accordance with section 841, the directors must be satisfied that the aggregate value of those assets (ie the ones not actually revalued) at the time of their consideration was not less than the aggregate amount at which they were stated in the accounts. This does not impose any substantive additional restriction because financial reporting requirements ensure that an asset is not stated at a carrying amount which is higher than its value.

2.34AC   An unlawful return of capital might arise if a company makes a distribution out of accumulated realised profits without deducting an impairment loss which is treated as a revaluation provision in circumstances where there is an absence of any upside on other assets. The company may have made a distribution which results in its assets being less than its capital under common law (see 2.2 above). In the case of a public company, a distribution would never be possible under the statutory provisions in these circumstances because of section 831 (see 2.30 above).

Application of the exception under IFRSs

2.34A   Due to changes in accounting methods and choices as between cost and valuation, effected by the implementation of IFRSs, the question might arise as to whether the exception provided for by section 841(2) continues to be capable of use under IFRSs. The following paragraphs explain questions that might arise and the conclusion that the exception does continue to be capable of use under IFRSs.

2.34C   For example, using section 841, an impairment write down of one subsidiary may be offset by an increase in value of another subsidiary for the purposes of determining profits available for distribution (although the impairment would still have to be recorded in the profit and loss account for financial reporting purposes). Another example is where financial assets are regarded as fixed assets, such as in the case of investment companies, and any decrease in the fair value of investments may be offset by any increase in the fair value of other investments for the purposes of determining profits available for distribution (even though certain increases in fair value might be treated as unrealised for the purposes of this guidance). However, as noted at 2.34AA above, the application of the exception in section 841 is not restricted to circumstances where there is an offsetting unrealised profit.

Definition of 'fixed assets'

2.34D The definition of a 'revaluation provision' (see 2.33 above) uses the term 'fixed assets' which are defined in section 853(6) as meaning assets of a company which are intended for use on a continuing basis in the company's activities. This term is not used in IFRSs. 'Non-current assets' as defined in IAS 1 will not correspond with 'fixed assets' as defined in section 853(6), for example because the former may include long term debtors.

2.34E For the purposes of applying section 841, fixed assets are those assets that meet the section 853(6) definition of 'fixed assets'. As noted above, in 'IAS individual accounts', these will not necessarily correspond with those presented as non-current assets in the relevant accounts. However, there is nothing in section 841 that requires the fixed assets to be shown in the balance sheet as such for the section to be applied.

Ability to revalue assets

2.34F Investments in subsidiaries present a particular issue in the context of section 841 and IFRSs. Under IFRSs, only two accounting policies are available for investments in subsidiaries that are not classified as held for sale:

(a) cost (see 9.22 below); or
(b) in accordance with IAS 39, which requires such investments to be maintained at fair value.

In practice, fair value under (b) above may be precluded because the range of reasonable fair value estimates is significant and the probabilities of the various estimates cannot reasonably be assessed (see IAS 39, AG 80-81). IAS 39 requires such investments to be carried at cost. Even where a fair value policy is possible, it will require valuations to be obtained each time a balance sheet is drawn up. This is unattractive to most companies. Most companies, therefore, hold subsidiaries at cost. The issue that arises is whether it is possible to apply the exception for 'revaluation provisions' in section 841 in circumstances where the accounting policy is cost (either through choice or because IAS 39 does not permit the assets to be revalued).

2.34G Any assessment of the value of an asset can be described, for the purpose of the exception in section 841, as a revaluation, even if it is not in accordance with relevant accounting standards. In particular, the consideration of the value of an asset for the purposes of an impairment review could be described as a revaluation in this broad sense. Accordingly, section 841 does not use the term 'revaluation' as meaning a revaluation in accordance with relevant accounting standards. However, depreciation of an asset is not consideration of the value of an asset for the purposes of section 841.

2.34H It is also relevant that, for the purposes of a revaluation of all the fixed assets (or all other than goodwill) under section 841, the assets do not have to be included in the balance sheet at their revalued amounts nor do they have to be permitted to be included in the balance sheet at a valuation. In accordance with section 841(4), 'for the purposes of subsections (2) and (3) any consideration by the directors of the value at a particular time of a fixed asset is treated as a revaluation' (subject to the requirements of sub-section (4)). Section 841(4) refers to 'any consideration by the directors of the value .....' without any explicit requirement for that value to be determined on a basis that would be permitted for inclusion in the balance sheet.

2.34I   In conclusion, it is possible to apply the exception for 'revaluation provisions' in section 841 in circumstances where the accounting policy is cost (either through choice or because IAS 39 does not permit the assets to be revalued).

Asset revaluations

2.35   Special considerations apply where a fixed asset has been revalued and an unrealised profit is recorded. Where a sum written off or retained for depreciation on or after the revaluation exceeds that which would have been charged if the unrealised profit had not been made, the excess does not give rise overall to a realised loss as there is a corresponding realisation of the related revaluation surplus, to the extent that that surplus has not previously been capitalised (section 841(5)). This means that the loss arising on the depreciation of revalued fixed assets is, in effect, calculated for distribution purposes by using historical cost principles, except to the extent that the surplus has previously been capitalised.

2.36   If an asset is revalued downwards below its recoverable amount, as defined in FRS 11 or IAS 36, then the difference between that revalued amount and recoverable amount is treated as an unrealised loss as it reflects a revaluation adjustment rather than a provision as defined in section 841[11]. Such a loss would become realised in the event of a subsequent scrapping, disposal or impairment of the asset.

2.37   Under IAS 16, any revaluation loss that exceeds an existing revaluation surplus will be recognised as an expense in the income statement. Under FRS 15, such a loss would be recognised in the Statement of Total Recognised Gains and Losses to the extent that the asset's recoverable amount was greater than its revalued amount. Also, under FRS 15, where an impairment loss on a revalued asset is caused by a clear consumption of economic benefits, the loss will be taken to the profit and loss account. Under IAS 16, it will be taken to equity to the extent that there is a revaluation surplus relating to the asset. Consequently, losses may be reported differently under IFRSs and UK GAAP but the effect on accumulated realised profits will be the same.

Development costs

2.38   Section 844 requires that development costs shown as an asset should be treated as a realised loss, except where the directors justify the costs carried forward being treated as an asset. This would be the case if the costs are carried forward in accordance with applicable accounting standards. The justification must be included in a note to the accounts (section 844(3)).

2.39   [Moved to 2.1AA]

Treasury shares

2.40   Sections 724 to 732 of the Act relax, in some circumstances, the requirement that when a company purchases its own shares they are automatically cancelled. They allow certain public companies that purchase their own 'qualifying shares' out of distributable profits the option of holding them 'in treasury' (ie un-cancelled) for sale at a later date (which

---

[11] *FRS 15(70) states that where it can be demonstrated that recoverable amount is greater than the revalued amount, the difference between recoverable amount and the revalued amount is clearly not an impairment and should therefore be recognised in the statement of total recognised gains and losses as a valuation adjustment, rather than the profit and loss account.*

must be for cash) or transferring them for the purposes of, or pursuant to, an employee share scheme. The treasury shares may also be cancelled at a later date. Only 'qualifying shares' may be held in treasury. Qualifying shares are shares which are included in the Official List, traded on AIM, officially listed in another EEA[12] state or traded on a regulated market established in an EEA state. In all other cases, shares purchased are cancelled by the automatic operation of the law in accordance with section 706.

Any purchase of shares to be held in treasury has to be made out of distributable profits which will be reduced by the amount of the purchase price.   **2.41**

The Act specifies how the proceeds of sale of any treasury shares for cash affects distributable profits. Where the proceeds of sale are equal to or less than the purchase price paid by the company for the shares, the proceeds should be treated as realised profits (ie to reverse the original reduction in realised profits up to the purchase price paid). Where the proceeds of sale exceed the purchase price paid by the company for the shares, that part of the proceeds that is equal to the purchase price paid should be treated as a realised profit of the company. A sum equal to the excess should be transferred to the share premium account (ie so that the purchase and sale of shares cannot create an overall increase in realised profits). For these purposes, section 731(4) provides that the purchase price paid by the company for the shares should be determined by the application of a weighted average price method.   **2.42**

Investments in own shares through an ESOP trust are not treasury shares as a matter of law. The distributable profit implications of shares held by an ESOP trust are considered in section 7 of this guidance. The purchase by an ESOP trust of shares held as treasury shares is considered at 7.33 to 7.35.   **2.43**

Section 832 – Investment companies

Investment companies are defined in section 833. Under section 832 they are permitted, subject to meeting certain requirements in section 832(5), to make distributions in circumstances, described in the following paragraph, which would not be permitted for other public companies under section 831. However, section 832 is an alternative rather than additional test for investment companies. Accordingly, an investment company may make a distribution in accordance with section 832 regardless of whether it would meet the tests in section 831 and, although possibly more rarely, *vice versa*. However, an investment company's articles must prohibit the distribution of capital profits (see section 833(2)(c)) and the application of section 831 cannot override this.   **2.44**

An investment company may make distributions at any time out of its accumulated realised revenue profits, so far as not previously utilised by a distribution or capitalisation, less its accumulated revenue losses (whether realised or unrealised), so far as not previously written off in a reduction or reorganisation of capital duly made: **2.44A**

- if at that time the amount of its assets is at least equal to one and a half times the aggregate of its liabilities to creditors;
- if, and to the extent that, the distribution does not reduce that amount to less than one and a half times that aggregate; and
- the conditions set out in section 832(5) are met.

In most circumstances, these rules allow an investment company to ignore capital losses, whether realised or unrealised, when making a distribution.   **2.45**

---

[12] *The European Economic Area (EEA) comprises the European Union together with Norway, Iceland and Liechtenstein.*

2.46   As noted at 6.24 *et seq* in relation to section 831, the presentation of financial instruments in accordance with the substance of their contractual terms under IFRSs may affect the amount of a company's liabilities as stated in its relevant accounts. In particular, where all or part of the amount attributable to preference shares is presented as a liability, total liabilities will be increased by that amount. The amount of a company's assets is unaffected by the reclassification of shares as liabilities.

2.47   However, section 832 refers to 'liabilities to creditors'. Although 'creditors' is not defined for this purpose in the Act, this amount excludes amounts in respect of share capital and share premium that have been presented as liabilities. It also excludes other amounts due to shareholders in their capacity as such including accruals for dividends and redemption premiums that have been presented as expenses in the income statement and liabilities in the balance sheet. It would not, however, exclude general accruals, deferred income or deferred tax.

2.47A   Ordinary dividends are accrued in the balance sheet only in those rare cases where they are legally binding liabilities at the balance sheet date (see 2.10 above). However, a shareholder's right to any unpaid dividend is as a creditor of the company rather than as a shareholder (see 2.10A above). Therefore, any such liability is a liability to creditors for the purposes of section 832.

Section 843 – Long term insurance business

2.47B   The normal rules of the Act (ie the section 830 requirement for realised profits and the section 831 net assets rule) apply to insurance companies. However, for the purposes of determining whether there is a realised profit, the section 853(4) definition of realised profits, as being determined by reference to generally accepted accounting principles, is displaced in favour of special rules in the case of long-term insurance business.

2.48   Section 843 sets out special rules that apply to an authorised insurance company (as defined in section 1165), other than an insurance special purpose vehicle (as defined in section 843(8)), carrying on long-term insurance business. An amount included in the relevant part of the company's balance sheet is treated as a realised profit if it:

- represents a surplus in the fund or funds maintained by it in respect of its long-term business (as defined in sub-section (7) and which includes both with-profits life business and other life business); and
- has not been allocated to policyholders or, as the case may be, carried forward unappropriated in accordance with asset identification rules made under section 142(2) of the Financial Services and Markets Act 2000.

2.49   For this purpose the relevant part of the balance sheet is that part of the balance sheet that represents accumulated profit or loss. A surplus in the fund or funds maintained by the company in respect of its long-term business means an excess of the assets representing that fund or those funds over the liabilities of the company attributable to its long-term business, as shown by an actuarial investigation.

2.50   A deficit in the fund or funds maintained by the company in respect of its long-term business is treated as a realised loss. For this purpose, a deficit in any such fund or funds means an excess of the liabilities of the company attributable to its long-term business over the assets representing that fund or those funds, as shown by an actuarial investigation.

2.51   Subject to this, any profit or loss arising in the company's long-term business is left out of account when determining realised profits and losses.

For the purpose of these requirements, an actuarial investigation means an investigation   **2.52**
made into the financial condition of an authorised insurance company in respect of its
long-term business, by an actuary appointed as actuary to the company:

- carried out once every period of twelve months in accordance with Rules made under
  Part 10 of the Financial Services and Markets Act 2000; or
- carried out in accordance with a requirement imposed by section 166 of that Act.

Much of the guidance in this Technical Release relates to the identification of generally   **2.53**
accepted principles as to the determination of realised profits and losses in relation to
section 853(4). To that extent, it is inapplicable to long-term insurance business of
authorised insurance companies (other than special purpose vehicles) to which the above
mentioned special rule applies instead. It should not be overlooked, however, that where
such a company is a public company, it must also have regard to the section 831 net assets
test.

3. REALISED PROFITS

General

Section 830(2) of the Act defines a company's profits available for distribution as   **3.1**
'its accumulated, realised profits, so far as not previously utilised by distribution or
capitalisation, less its accumulated, realised losses, so far as not previously written off in
a reduction or reorganisation of capital duly made'. Realised profits and realised losses
are defined as 'such profits or losses of the company as fall to be treated as realised in
accordance with principles generally accepted at the time when the accounts are prepared,
with respect to the determination for accounting purposes of realised profits or losses'
(section 853(4)). It is apparent from the use of the words 'at the time when the accounts are
prepared' that the concept of a realised profit is intended to be dynamic, changing with the
development of generally accepted accounting principles, as well as bringing within the
definition profits which might not in ordinary language be called realised.

The determination of a company's profits available for distribution is derived from what   **3.2**
is recorded in its accounts which are relevant for this purpose (see 2.12 above). It is
fundamental for this purpose that the company's accounts have been properly prepared in
accordance with the law and generally accepted accounting principles. Profits available
for distribution may include amounts reported outside the profit and loss account (ie in
the Statement of Total Recognised Gains and Losses or Reconciliation of Movements in
Shareholders' Funds and their equivalents under IFRSs).

Principles of realisation

It is generally accepted that profits shall be treated as realised for the purpose of applying   **3.3**
the definition of realised profits in companies legislation only when realised in the form
of cash or of other assets the ultimate cash realisation of which can be assessed with
reasonable certainty. In this context, 'realised' may encompass profits relating to assets that
are readily realisable. This would embrace profits and losses resulting from the recognition
of changes in fair values, in accordance with relevant accounting standards, to the extent
that they are readily convertible to cash.

The principles of realisation set out in this guidance are consistent with the notion of   **3.4**
realisation as expressed in FRS 18. They are, however, relevant irrespective of whether
the relevant accounts are prepared under UK GAAP or under IFRSs. The guidance also
recognises that certain amounts may, as a matter of law, be profits (see 3.8(b) below).

3.5   In assessing whether a company has a realised profit, transactions and arrangements should not be looked at in isolation. A realised profit will arise only where the overall commercial effect on the company is such that the definition of realised profit set out in this guidance is met.

3.5A   Thus, for example, a group or series of transactions or arrangements should be viewed as a whole, particularly if they are artificial, linked (whether legally or otherwise) or circular or any combination of these. The principle in paragraph 3.5 is likely to be of particular relevance for, but not limited to, intra-group transactions which are considered in section 9 of this guidance. Further guidance on the application of the principle in paragraph 3.5 is set out at 3.43 to 3.75 below. The specific circumstances of 'cash box structures' are addressed in section 12.

3.6   A profit previously regarded as unrealised becomes realised when the relevant criteria set out in this guidance are met (for example, a revaluation surplus becomes realised when the related asset is sold for 'qualifying consideration'). Similarly, a profit previously regarded as realised becomes unrealised when the criteria set out in this guidance cease to be met. This is considered more fully at 3.28 to 3.29C below.

Definitions

3.7   The definitions which follow should be read in conjunction with the principles of realisation as well as the guidance on their interpretation set out in this Technical Release.

Profit

3.8   'Profit' for the purpose of section 853(4) comprises:

    (a)   'gains', as defined in the Accounting Standards Board's 'Statement of Principles for Financial Reporting' and 'income' as defined in the International Accounting Standards Board's 'Framework' which both convey (with different wording) increases in ownership interest not resulting from contributions from owners; and

    (b)   other amounts which are profits as a matter of law, or which are treated as profits, including:

        (i)   gratuitous contributions of assets from owners in their capacity as such; and

        (ii)   an amount taken to a so-called 'merger reserve' reflecting the extent that relief is obtained under sections 611 or 612 of the Act from the requirement to recognise a share premium account.

Realised profit

3.9   A profit is realised, as a matter of generally accepted accounting practice, where it arises from:

    (a)   a transaction where the consideration received by the company is 'qualifying consideration'; or

    (b)   an event which results in 'qualifying consideration' being received by the company in circumstances where no consideration is given by the company; or

    (c)   the recognition in the financial statements of a change in fair value, in those cases where fair value has been determined in accordance with measurement guidance in the relevant accounting standards or company law, and to the extent that the change recognised is readily convertible to cash; or

    (d)   the translation of:

        (i)   a monetary asset which comprises qualifying consideration; or

        (ii)   a liability,

denominated in a foreign currency; or

(e)   the reversal of a loss previously regarded as realised; or

(f)   a profit[13] previously regarded as unrealised (such as amounts taken to a revaluation reserve, merger reserve or other similar reserve) becoming realised as a result of:

(i)   consideration previously received by the company becoming 'qualifying consideration'; or

(ii)   the related asset being disposed of in a transaction where the consideration received by the company is 'qualifying consideration'; or

(iii)   a realised loss being recognised on the scrapping or disposal of the related asset; or

(iv)   a realised loss being recognised on the write-down for depreciation, amortisation, diminution in value or impairment of the related asset[14];

(v)   the distribution in kind of the asset to which the unrealised profit relates; or

(vi)   the receipt of a dividend in the form of qualifying consideration when no profit is recognised because the dividend is deducted from the book value of the investment to which the unrealised profit relates (e.g. as required by IAS 27 before its amendment in May 2008[15] in the case of dividends out of pre-acquisition profits of subsidiaries) (see 9.22 *et seq* below),

in which case the appropriate proportion[16] of the related unrealised profit becomes a realised profit; or

(g)   the remeasurement of a liability, to the extent that the change recognised is readily convertible to cash (see 3.9B below).

3.9A   In addition, as explained at 2.8A, The Companies (Reduction of Share Capital) Order 2008 SI 2008/1915 specifies the cases in which a reserve arising from a reduction in a company's share capital is to be treated as a realised profit as a matter of law.

3.9B   A profit arising on the remeasurement of a liability will often be the reversal of a realised loss, a foreign currency translation gain or a fair value gain, and may therefore be a realised profit in accordance with 3.9(c), (d) or (e), Paragraph 3.9(g) will be relevant in other cases such as that of a defined benefit pension liability assumed for consideration either in a separate transaction or as part of a business combination. In such a case the profit is only a realised profit in those rare cases where the change in value is readily convertible to cash as defined at 3.12 below.

Realised loss

3.10   Losses should be regarded as realised losses except to the extent that the law, accounting standards or this guidance provide otherwise. The statutory position is set out in section 2 of this guidance.

---

[13] *Where the related profit has been capitalised, it will not be available for transfer from unrealised profit to realised profit.*

[14] *If the write down is subsequently reversed, an equal amount of profit should be regarded as becoming unrealised. In other words, the amount of profit regarded as becoming realised is equal to the cumulative amount of any write down treated as a realised loss.*

[15] *Amendments to IFRS 1 First-time Adoption of IFRSs and IAS 27 Consolidated and Separate Financial Statements: Cost of an Investment in a Subsidiary, Jointly Controlled Entity or Associate.*

[16] *In the case of (iii) and (iv), the loss is treated as a realised loss under paragraph 3.15 of this guidance. However, part of this realised loss is compensated by a reclassification from unrealised to realised profit.*

Qualifying consideration

3.11   Qualifying consideration comprises:

(a)   cash; or

(b)   an asset that is readily convertible to cash; or

(c)   the release, or the settlement or assumption by another party, of all or part of a liability of the company; or

(d)   an amount receivable in any of the above forms of consideration where:

    (i)   the debtor is capable of settling the receivable within a reasonable period of time; and

    (ii)   there is a reasonable certainty that the debtor will be capable of settling when called upon to do so; and

    (iii)   there is an expectation that the receivable will be settled; or

(e)   an amount receivable from a shareholder where and to the extent that[17]:

    (i)   the company intends to make a distribution to the shareholder of an amount equal to or less than its receivable from that shareholder; and

    (ii)   the company intends to settle such distribution by off-setting against the amount receivable (in whole or in part); and

    (iii)   within the meaning of paragraph 3.5 and 3.5A of this guidance, (i) and (ii) are linked.

3.11A   For the purposes of applying paragraph 3.11 above, references to settlement include settlement by way of set-off with a liability to the same party.

Readily convertible to cash

3.12   An asset, or change in the fair value of an asset or liability, is considered to be 'readily convertible to cash' if:

(a)   a value can be determined at which a transaction in the asset or liability could occur, at the date of determination[18], in its state at that date, without negotiation and/or marketing, to either convert the asset, liability or change in fair value into cash, or to close out the asset, liability or change in fair value; and

(b)   in determining the value, information such as prices, rates or other factors that market participants would consider in setting a price is observable; and

(c)   the company's circumstances must not prevent immediate conversion to cash or close out of the asset, liability or change in fair value; for example, the company must be able to dispose of, or close out the asset, liability or the change in fair value, without any intention or need to liquidate or curtail materially the scale of its operations, or to undertake a transaction on adverse terms.

3.13   Further guidance on the application of 'readily convertible to cash' is provided in section 4 of this guidance. The position regarding fair value losses is dealt with at 4.29 *et seq* below.

---

[17] *In the case addressed by paragraph 3.11(e), it would be possible, in the absence of other accumulated realised losses, to distribute the receivable in kind under section 846. Paragraph 3.11(e) sets down generally accepted accounting practice that the receivable can be regarded as qualifying consideration in certain circumstances. The effect of this is that making a distribution settled by offset against the receivable is an alternative procedure to a distribution in kind of that receivable. This is illustrated in the example in Appendix 9.*

[18] *The reference to the date of determination is subject to the limited exception in paragraph 4.17 below for the determination of the effect that any block discount on securities traded in an active market has on realised profits.*

Application

Instances of realised profit

In addition to those instances which are readily apparent from the definition of realised profit, in applying the principles of realisation and the definitions set out above the following would constitute a realised profit: **3.14**

(a)   the receipt or accrual of investment or other income receivable in the form of qualifying consideration; or

(b)   a gain arising on a return of capital on an investment where the return is in the form of qualifying consideration; or

(c)   a gift (such as a 'capital contribution') received in the form of qualifying consideration; or

(d)   the release of a provision for a liability or loss which was treated as a realised loss; or

(e)   the reversal of a write-down or provision for diminution in value or impairment of an asset which was treated as a realised loss.

Instances of realised loss

Realised losses will include: **3.15**

(a)   a cost or expense (other than one charged to the share premium account) which results in a reduction in recorded net assets;

(b)   a loss arising on the sale or other disposal or scrapping of an asset;

(c)   the writing down, or providing for the depreciation, amortisation, diminution in value or impairment, of an asset[19], except as noted at 2.33 and 2.36 above;

(d)   the creation of, or increase in, a provision for a liability or loss (other than deferred tax in the circumstances described at 3.17 below) which results in an overall reduction in recorded net assets;

(e)   a gift made by the company (or the release of all or part of a debt due to the company or the assumption of a liability by the company) to the extent that it results in an overall reduction in recorded net assets; and

(f)   a loss arising from fair value accounting where profits on remeasurement of the same asset or liability would be treated as realised profits.

[Deleted]   **3.16**

Deferred tax

A provision for deferred tax should generally be regarded as a realised loss. However, when assets are revalued to their fair value and the gain is regarded as unrealised, the deferred tax on that gain should be treated as a reduction in that unrealised gain rather than as a realised loss.   **3.17**

Exchange of assets ('top-slicing')

Where an asset is sold partly for qualifying consideration and partly for other consideration (for example, a mixed consideration of cash and a freehold property), any profit arising is a realised profit to the extent that the fair value of the consideration received is in the form of qualifying consideration. This approach is sometimes referred to as 'top-slicing'.   **3.18**

---

[19] *Where the asset has been revalued or is otherwise represented to any extent by an unrealised profit, the appropriate proportion of the related unrealised profit becomes a realised profit, thus mitigating the effect of the realised loss – see paragraph 3.9(f) of this guidance.*

(Example: fair value of consideration received is 10, of which 4 is cash and 6 is freehold property. If the depreciated historical cost of the asset sold is 5, the total gain is 5 but the realised profit is limited to 4.)

Hedging

3.19   Where hedge accounting is obtained in accordance with the relevant accounting standards, it is necessary to consider the combined effect of both sides of the hedging relationship to determine whether there is a realised profit or loss in accordance with the criteria in this guidance.

3.20   Application of this principle in the context of hedge relationships within the individual financial statements of a company is considered at 5.1 to 5.18 of this guidance. Consideration of the effects of hedge relationships where the hedging instrument and the hedged item are held by different group companies is considered at 5.19 to 5.22.

Foreign exchange profits and losses

3.21   Paragraph 65 of SSAP 20 Foreign currency translation, which was issued in 1983, states that 'the application of paragraph 50 of this statement may result in unrealised exchange gains on unsettled long-term monetary items being taken to the profit and loss account'. Since then, however, the currency markets have become more sophisticated and companies have significantly more flexibility to crystallise exchange profits on long-term monetary items. Consequently, unless there are doubts as to the convertibility or marketability of the currency in question, foreign exchange profits arising on the retranslation of monetary items are realised, irrespective of the maturity date of the monetary item.

3.21A   This has become generally accepted practice even though the exchange difference may not be 'readily convertible to cash' at the balance sheet date. However, a profit on retranslation of a monetary asset will not be a realised profit where the underlying balance on which the exchange difference arises does not itself meet the definition of 'qualifying consideration'. For example, this may be the case for some long-term inter-company balances within groups.

3.21B   The position regarding exchange differences reported in a separate component of equity (ie not in the income statement) is considered at 5.7 below in relation to cash flow hedge accounting; and in relation to the translation of branches into the company's functional currency, the translation of the whole of a company's accounts from the company's functional currency to a presentation currency and questions of mismatch with the currency of denomination of shares are considered in section 11.

Goodwill in an individual company

3.22   Where goodwill arises in a company's individual accounts (which would be the case, for example, where the company has purchased an unincorporated business) the goodwill will become a realised loss as the goodwill is amortised or written down for impairment in accordance with relevant accounting standards.

3.23   For periods ending before 23 December 1998, purchased goodwill may have been accounted for under SSAP 22 'Accounting for goodwill' by immediate elimination against reserves. Such goodwill may have remained eliminated against reserves under UK GAAP under the transitional provisions of FRS 10. Such goodwill should be regarded as a realised loss to the extent that, had it always been recognised as an asset, it would have been amortised or impaired in accordance with FRS 10.

If the business to which the acquired goodwill relates is disposed of or closed, FRS 10 requires the profit or loss on disposal to include the goodwill previously taken to reserves to the extent that it has not previously been charged to the profit and loss account. Notional amortisation or impairment for the purposes of calculating realised profits does not affect this financial reporting requirement. However, the effect of the disposal on realised profits is therefore net of any amount already treated as a realised loss in accordance with this guidance.   **3.23A**

Goodwill may also have remained eliminated against reserves on transition to IFRSs in accordance with IFRS 1. Such goodwill should be regarded as a realised loss to the extent that, had it always been recognised as an asset under IFRSs, it would have been impaired in accordance with IFRS 3 and IAS 36. This is unaffected by any amounts of notional amortisation in accordance with FRS 10 that might have been treated as realised losses prior to transition to IFRSs.   **3.23B**

When applying IFRSs, goodwill previously written off to reserves is not taken into account in any profit or loss on subsequent disposal. However, any goodwill written off to reserves that has not previously been treated as a realised loss will become realised as a result of the disposal.   **3.23C**

Companies not wishing to make these assessments may prudently opt to regard the entire amount of goodwill written off to reserves as a realised loss.   **3.23D**

Negative goodwill in an individual company

The following guidance on negative goodwill applies under UK GAAP and IFRSs unless otherwise stated. Neither IFRS 3 nor IFRS 3 Revised (subsequently together referred to as IFRS 3) uses the term 'negative goodwill' but instead they describe that concept using different words. For simplicity, such an amount is described in this guidance as negative goodwill.   **3.24**

Negative goodwill up to the fair values of the non-monetary assets acquired should be treated as being realised in the periods in which the non-monetary assets are recovered, whether through depreciation or sale. Where the negative goodwill exceeds the value of the non-monetary assets, this excess should be treated as being realised in the periods expected to benefit. However, negative goodwill should not be treated as a realised profit in the case of a sale of the non-monetary assets where the consideration received is not qualifying consideration.   **3.25**

Under UK GAAP, negative goodwill recognised in the profit and loss account in accordance with FRS 10 therefore represents a realised profit except in the case of a sale of the non-monetary assets where the consideration received is not qualifying consideration. Where negative goodwill was accounted for under SSAP 22 in the accounts of an individual company, it would have been regarded initially as an unrealised profit. It will become a realised profit on the same basis as if it had been negative goodwill accounted for under FRS 10.   **3.26**

IFRS 3 requires the immediate recognition of negative goodwill as a profit for financial reporting purposes but this does not accelerate the realisation of negative goodwill which is as set out at 3.25 above irrespective of the accounting framework adopted.   **3.27**

Changes in circumstances including changes in accounting policies and on the adoption of IFRSs

Introduction

3.28   The treatment of a retained profit or loss as realised (or unrealised), or the recognition of an item as a profit or loss or an asset or liability, may change subsequent to its original recognition as a result of:

(a)   a change in the principles of realisation; or

(b)   a change in the law or in accounting standards or interpretations, either through an express reference to the realisation or otherwise of the profit or loss or, more commonly, through a change in the recognition or measurement of assets, liabilities, income or expenses. A company adopting IFRSs for the first time will, in effect, be making a number of changes in accounting policies; or

(c)   some other change in circumstance such that what was originally qualifying consideration under paragraph 3.11(d) is no longer so, for example, where a receivable was initially regarded as qualifying consideration but circumstances change such that there is now no expectation that the receivable will be settled in the form of qualifying consideration.

3.29   Although the effect of these changes may be to reduce or even eliminate a company's net realised profits, that would not render unlawful a distribution already made out of realised profits determined by reference to 'relevant accounts' which had been prepared in accordance with generally accepted accounting principles applicable to those accounts (this is subject to paragraphs 3.30 and 3.31 below). This is because the Act defines realised profits and losses for determining the lawfulness of a distribution as 'such profits and losses of the company as fall to be treated as realised in accordance with principles generally accepted at the time when the accounts are prepared, with respect to the determination for accounting purposes of realised profits or losses' (section 853(4), emphasis added).

3.29A   The circumstances described in paragraph 3.28(c) do not extend to the case of 'an asset that is readily convertible to cash' (which is 'qualifying consideration' under paragraph 3.11(b)). Such assets are, when received, regarded as being so highly liquid as to be treated as equivalent to cash. That is to say, the initial determination that a profit is a realised one is, if based on the qualifying consideration's being cash or 'an asset that is readily convertible to cash', definitive and unchangeable. Thus, for example, if changes in the market for a financial asset mean that from a certain point in time the asset no longer meets the 'readily convertible to cash' test, then prior fair value movements – whether profits or losses – remain as realised.

3.29B   This would be relevant if, for example, the financial asset were reclassified out of a fair value category under the amendment to IAS 39 of November 2008. To the extent that the last fair value includes amounts originally determined to be realised profits, they remain so. It is as if the profits were realised in cash and re-invested (outside of the principle in paragraph 3.5) into the financial asset in question. In such a reclassification case, it may of course be the case that the market changed, so as no longer to meet the 'readily convertible to cash' test, at an earlier date than the reclassification. In such a case the financial asset's carrying value may include realised profits and unrealised profits. Whilst the realised profits will retain that status going forward, the unrealised profits are capable at some future date of changing to realised profits under paragraph 3.9(f).

3.29C   It would be open to a company, instead of splitting the fair value movement since inception into movements that were and were not readily convertible to cash, to make a shortcut, prudent assumption that if there are cumulative net gains since inception, they are regarded as unrealised.

Timing of the effect of changes in accounting policies on distributable profits

The effects of the introduction of a new accounting standard or on the adoption of IFRSs **3.30** become relevant to the application of the common law capital maintenance rule only in relation to distributions accounted for in periods in which the change will first be recognised in the accounts. Where items will fall to be treated as liabilities under a new standard in a period after the period in which the dividend is accounted for, directors do not have to pay regard to such future liabilities merely because they are disclosed in the notes to the accounts.

Where the directors are considering the payment of an interim dividend in respect of **3.31** a financial year, and a new accounting standard may, for example, lead to items being recognised as liabilities in the accounts for that year, the directors must, under common law, have regard to the effect of these liabilities on the expected level of profits available for distribution at the end of the financial year when determining the lawfulness of the interim dividend.

For example, for a company adopting IFRSs for its individual accounts in 2010 the position **3.32** is as follows:

- any final dividend for 2009 will not be provided in the 2009 UK GAAP accounts and will first be accounted for in the 2010 accounts. Such a dividend would therefore have to have regard to the effect of adoption of IFRSs even though the 'relevant accounts' may still be those for 2009 prepared under UK GAAP;
- any interim dividend paid during 2010 would have to have regard to the effect of adoption of IFRSs even though the 'relevant accounts' may still be those for 2009 prepared under UK GAAP; and
- the 2010 accounts prepared under IFRSs would be the relevant accounts for the purposes of the final dividend approved by shareholders in 2011. The effect of a change in accounting policy known to be adopted in 2011 needs to be taken into account in determining the dividend to be approved by shareholders in 2011. The dividend will be recognised in the 2011 accounts.

The considerations set out above apply to all dividends whether in respect of shares **3.33** classified as equity or shares classified as debt (or partly shares and partly debt as a compound instrument) under either IFRSs or UK GAAP.

If the effect of a new accounting standard or guidance on profits which fall to be treated **3.34** as realised is to increase the company's accumulated profits and the company wishes to distribute an amount in excess of that which could be determined by reference to what would otherwise constitute the company's 'relevant accounts', the company is required to prepare interim accounts complying with the new accounting standard or guidance. Where a public company is in this position, those interim accounts are required to be delivered to the Registrar under section 838.

For the purposes of a dividend made by reference, under statute, to UK GAAP relevant **3.35** accounts, but at a time when the foregoing guidance requires the effect of a current year changeover to IFRSs to be considered, the directors will need to understand the consequences of adopting IFRSs for the company's profits available for distribution. There is no statutory requirement to prepare interim accounts under section 836 (and section 838 in the case of a public company) if a proposed distribution can be justified by reference to the relevant accounts. However, under common law, a company cannot lawfully make a distribution out of capital. The directors may, for example, by reason of their duties to exercise appropriate skill and care, consider preparing interim accounts under IFRSs, as of the date shortly before the time of paying the proposed dividend, to satisfy themselves that the accumulated realised profits shown in the last statutory individual accounts have not been eliminated, or reduced to such an extent that the proposed distribution would be unlawful. (It should be noted that these 'interim accounts' would not be interim accounts within the meaning of section 836(2) of the Act and section 838 would not therefore apply to them.) For a public company, the directors will also have to consider the impact of the restriction on distributions arising from section 831 (see 6.24 *et seq*). It may not always be necessary to prepare interim accounts, for example, in very straightforward cases where the directors are satisfied that no material adjustments arise from the transition to IFRSs.

3.36   The directors of a company may not yet have decided whether to adopt IFRSs for the current financial year. Similarly, they may not have decided whether to adopt early a new accounting standard that has been issued but is not mandatory for the financial year. In these cases, the company's accounting policies are those that it has previously applied until a decision is made to change them. Therefore, in applying the foregoing guidance, it is not necessary to have regard to possible changes of policy that are being considered but have not yet been agreed.

3.37   Where a company believes that the implementation of IFRSs will increase its balance of distributable profits, and it wishes to distribute those profits as increased, the guidance at 3.34 above will be relevant.

Realised profits that have been distributed and are subsequently eliminated by a change of circumstances (including a change of accounting policy)

3.38   Where the effect of a change in circumstance is that a profit previously recognised as realised can no longer be regarded as being realised, the amount of that profit should either be eliminated through a prior year adjustment or be reclassified as unrealised (as appropriate) in the relevant accounts in which the change in circumstance is first recognised.

3.38A   Where a previously recognised realised profit is eliminated through a prior year adjustment, the adjustment should be treated as a realised loss. The effect is therefore to reduce accumulated realised profits by the amount of the adjustment. If the adjustment results in accumulated realised losses, further distributions will not be possible until the shortfall is made good. To make a distribution before the shortfall is made good would amount to an unlawful return of capital, contrary to common law.

3.38B   The same approach is possible where the previously recognised realised profit is reclassified as an unrealised profit. However, as explained below, in certain circumstances, it may be possible to adopt an alternative approach and to treat the distribution as having been made, in whole or in part, out of the profit which has been reclassified as unrealised so that it reduces accumulated unrealised profits rather than accumulated realised profits. This alternative approach may reduce any adverse impact on accumulated realised profits but is more difficult to apply. Either approach is acceptable when realised profits are reclassified as unrealised profits.

3.38C   Under the alternative approach referred to in 3.38B, as profits are fungible, unless there is evidence that the profit affected by the change in circumstances has been distributed, it should be assumed that the first distribution made after the recognition of the profit was made pro rata out of all available profits shown in the relevant accounts. Accordingly, the balance remaining after that distribution would include a proportionate amount of the affected profit. Similarly each subsequent distribution would reduce proportionately the amount of the affected profit.

3.39   For example, a company has accumulated realised profits of 40 brought forward at the beginning of Year 1. During that year it makes realised profits of 60 of which 40 arose from a specific transaction in that period, and distributes 70, leaving a balance of 30. In Year 2 it generates a further 170 of realised profits and distributes 150. A change in circumstances in year 3 leads to the 40 recognised in Year 1 becoming treated as unrealised. The amount of the original profit of 40 that would be regarded as having been distributed in Year 1 would be 28 (70% [ie, 70/100] of 40), leaving 12 of the original profit to be carried forward in the closing balance of 30 at the end of Year 1. In Year 2 the amount of this 12 that would be regarded as having been distributed in Year 2 would be 9 (75% [ie, 150/200] of 12), leaving 3 of the original profit to be carried forward in the closing balance of 50 at the end of Year 2. Thus the amount of profit to be reclassified as unrealised in Year 3 as a result of the change in circumstance would be 3.

		Total	Affected profit
YEAR 1:	Brought forward	40	–
	Profit for year	60	40
	Available for distribution	100	40
	Distributed	(70)	(28)
YEAR 2:	Brought forward	30	12
	Profit for year	170	–
	Available for distribution	200	12
	Distributed	(150)	(9)
YEAR 3:	Brought forward	50	3

Where after making all reasonable enquiries it proves impracticable to obtain the information to make the allocation described at 3.38C, it would be appropriate to assume that the profit has been distributed (to the extent that there have been distributions).   **3.40**

Effect of errors

Under UK GAAP, only changes in accounting policies and correction of *fundamental* errors are accounted for by restatement of comparatives. This means that errors that are material but not 'fundamental' are accounted for in the year in which they are detected without any restatement. In contrast, IAS 8 requires all *material* errors to be corrected retrospectively through a restatement of comparatives. Consequently, correction of errors by restatement is more common when reporting under IFRSs. A distribution may have been made by reference to the original accounts which would not have been justified if the error had not occurred. The question arises of whether such a distribution would be rendered unlawful.   **3.41**

It is the error, rather than its correction, that may have the effect of making a previous distribution unlawful. The effect of reporting under IFRSs is to make such errors more visible because of the requirement for retrospective restatement for all material errors. But whether or not an error is corrected in this way does not, of itself, govern the lawfulness of a previous distribution. The effect of an error on the lawfulness of a distribution raises complex legal issues that are beyond the scope of this guidance.   **3.42**

Application of the linkage etc principle in paragraph 3.5

The principle in paragraph 3.5 above must be viewed from the perspective of an individual company to determine that company's realised profits. Therefore, if a company enters into a single transaction, that transaction cannot be linked because the concept of linkage requires the effect of two or more legally separate transactions of the same entity to be   **3.43** viewed as a single transaction in substance. The fact that a series of transactions is circular from the perspective of a group does not mean that an individual company in the group, for example that participates in a single transaction in that series, cannot realise a profit on that transaction. The normal test of realisation may be met when applied to that single transaction.

3.44   The fact that an individual company's transactions are linked for the purposes of paragraph 3.5 does not necessarily mean that a realised profit cannot arise. The normal tests of realisation may be met when applied to the overall effect of the series of transactions taken together.

3.45   For two transactions to be linked, the second transaction must have been contemplated when the first transaction was entered into. If the second transaction is entered into for genuine commercial reasons unconnected with the first transaction and was not part of a plan with the first transaction, the two transactions would not be determined as linked.

3.46   The following principles address the application of paragraph 3.5 and require the exercise of judgement.

3.47   **The application of paragraph 3.5 is not restricted to intra-group cash flows even though it is illustrated in the examples in section 9 solely in relation to intra-group situations.**

3.48   Paragraph 3.5 is also relevant to transactions with third parties. The examples in section 9 focus on intra-group transactions as these are the more common situations where the question of linkage arises. An example of a situation involving a third party where linkage must be considered is the sale of a subsidiary for cash to a third party on the condition that the cash is applied in subscribing for shares of the purchaser. The substance or overall commercial effect of the transactions is a sale with consideration in shares of the purchaser.

3.49   **The transactions do not have to be more than one of 'linked' or 'artificial' or 'circular' to fall within the principle in paragraph 3.5.**

3.50   Paragraph 3.5 states that 'a realised profit will arise only where the *overall commercial effect* on the company is such that the definition of realised profit set out in this guidance is met' (emphasis added).

3.51   Transactions need satisfy only one of the examples mentioned in paragraph 3.5A of being linked, artificial or circular, and furthermore these three cases are only particular instances of its application; that is to say, it is not limited to those cases. In practice individual transactions may fall within paragraph 3.5 because they are artificial or because collectively their effect is circular; but it is not necessary that a transaction be linked or artificial or circular for it to fall within paragraph 3.5.

3.52   **Splitting a transaction into separate steps would require consideration under the principle in paragraph 3.5.**

3.53   Taking the example discussed above of the sale of a subsidiary for shares; if this had been dealt with in one transaction it is obvious that the shares have to be evaluated to determine if they are qualifying consideration before concluding whether the profit on the transaction is realised. However, by splitting the transaction into two – a sale for cash and a subscription agreement – the commercial effect is obscured. Without proper analysis, the subscription agreement might have been overlooked and the profit determined as realised as the consideration was apparently cash. The transactions are linked. The transaction could be achieved by a single transaction of a sale for shares.

However, transactions may be linked without being artificial, or circular without being linked. Judgement is required in any determination of whether transactions fall within paragraph 3.5.   **3.54**

Other indicators of transactions that may fall within paragraph 3.5 include: **3.55**
- the transactions being entered into at the same time (although see the discussion of time delays below) and in contemplation of each other;
- the transactions being with the same counterparty (which would include entities under common control and back-to-back arrangements); and
- transactions that are not in the ordinary course of business.

Transactions may be linked 'whether legally or otherwise'.   **3.56**

Transactions will often be 'linked' when they form part of a single plan. For example, a so called 'steps plan' may exist in which a number of separate transactions are envisaged. It may be clear that the first step of the plan would never have been carried out unless there was every expectation that step two would also be carried out. In this case, it is appropriate to consider the combined effect of all of the transactions together.   **3.57**

However, this does not mean that transactions must be regarded as linked or circular just because they were planned together. For example, a company may sell some quoted investments for cash with the intention of using that cash to purchase stock. The fact that the company plans to use the cash to purchase stock does not prevent the profit on disposal[20] of the investments being a realised profit. Similarly, trading profits will be realised profits in accordance with the normal rules, even though the cash inflows are reinvested in stock or fixed assets.   **3.58**

One feature usually present for there to be linkage is that the cash flow has been generated with the intention of, or for the purpose of, undertaking the linked transaction. Trading cash flows are generated as an end in themselves and thus do not possess this feature.   **3.59**

In relation to a sale and operating leaseback, the cash inflow arising from the sale transaction will be, at least in part, offset by the future cash outflows arising from the leaseback transaction. Therefore it might be queried whether they are linked. However, it is generally accepted that such arrangements do not fall within the scope of paragraph 3.5. A sale and leaseback transaction is not entered into for the purpose of financing the future operating lease rentals. To the extent that the apparent sale's profit exceeds arm's length terms (ie the 'profit' is directly compensated for by high rentals) it is deferred anyway (under IAS 17 and SSAP 21).   **3.60**

Transactions may be linked legally by, say, being dealt with in the same contract or being in separate contracts but expressed to be inter-conditional. However, as made clear by the words 'or otherwise', it is necessary to consider more than just the legal form of linkage of transactions to understand their substance collectively, as to do otherwise may not adequately express the overall commercial effect of the arrangements.   **3.61**

For example, in the case of the so called steps plan mentioned above, there may be no legal obligation to complete step 2 following step 1. However, this may, for example, be a commercial necessity because step 1 does not make sense without step 2.   **3.62**

---

[20] *It is assumed for simplicity here that a profit is recognised on disposal of the investments, but companies applying IFRSs or FRS 26 may have recorded a profit at an earlier stage because of the need to account for the investments at fair value.*

3.63   **For a cash inflow and a cash outflow of a company to fall within paragraph 3.5, it is not necessary that the cash flows 'close the loop' by joining up at some other place in the group.**

3.64   A transaction is circular for a company if, for that company, there is a cash inflow and in another step in a series there is a cash outflow back to the same party. As discussed above, circularity is a sufficient but not a necessary feature for the application of paragraph 3.5. Another situation where paragraph 3.5 may apply is where the cash outflow at another step is to another party rather than the provider of the cash inflow. It is not necessary, for something to be linked, that the recipient of the onward cash flow passes the cash back to the original provider.

3.65   **Transactions are not linked merely because they are pre-planned but this may be evidence of linkage.**

3.66   Pre-planning (eg by way of a steps plan) is evidence that the transactions are to be entered into in contemplation of each other and the overall outcome was pre-meditated. Evidence of pre-planning may indicate that those cash flows and the transactions from which they arise should be assessed as linked in order to understand their overall commercial effect. However, as explained in the example above at 3.58 concerning a disposal of quoted investments to finance a purchase of stock, this principle does not result in normal commercial transactions in the ordinary course of business being regarded as linked.

3.67   Taking this example further, the transactions are not linked because the vendor of the stock would normally require payment in cash and would not accept quoted investments in settlement. Therefore, the substance of the transactions taken together is **not** an exchange of quoted investments for stock.

3.68   **Where paragraph 3.5 requires a series of transactions to be viewed as a whole, the consequence is that a profit, to be realised, has to be represented by an increase in qualifying consideration between the start and end points of the series.**

3.69   If a series of transactions is viewed as a whole, then it is necessary to compare the assets and liabilities, and their amounts, at the start and end of the series to determine what transaction, in substance, has occurred (changes in assets and liabilities). The transaction thus identified is tested under the other principles set out in this guidance. Thus, where paragraph 3.5 applies, it is necessary to determine the amount of qualifying consideration involved at the start and end of the linked transactions to see if there has been an increase, decrease or a net nil position. Unless there has been an increase in the amount of qualifying consideration (in any of the forms defined in paragraph 3.11), it cannot have a realised profit from that series of transactions.

3.70   **If there is a new external cash flow somewhere in a chain of intra-group transactions to which the company is party, this cannot be associated with a portion of the gross cash flows of the company in question if, after considering a series of transactions that fall within the scope of paragraph 3.5 to which the company is party, the company does not have a net increase in cash or other qualifying consideration.**

3.71   A net nil cash position (as described at 3.69 above) cannot be broken into two gross components to assert that there has been an increase in qualifying consideration that will justify recognition of a realised profit. To do so would amount to dealing with such transactions as if they were independent and so would fail to treat them, as required by paragraph 3.5, as a series that is to be assessed as a whole. Thus, where a company's transactions, taken as a whole, do not increase its qualifying consideration, they do not generate a realised profit. This is the case irrespective of whether the cash inflow has been financed from new external cash receipts elsewhere in the group.

For example, consider a company that receives a dividend of 100 from one subsidiary and reinvests the same amount in another subsidiary as equity capital, both as part of a planned corporate restructuring. There is no net increase in qualifying consideration and therefore the receipt of the dividend is not a realised profit. It does not matter that the dividend of 100 was funded from external cash receipts elsewhere in the group.   **3.72**

However, paragraphs 3.71 and 3.72 above are concerned only with circumstances where the cash inflow and cash outflow comprising the net nil position fall within paragraph 3.5. For example, paragraph 3.72 is concerned with a planned corporate restructuring. The fact that dividends are received from some subsidiaries at or about the same time as investments are made in other subsidiaries as equity capital does not automatically prevent those dividends being recognised as realised profits. To be linked, there needs to be something more than juxtapositioning of transactions, such as the dividends being necessary at this time to facilitate the investment.   **3.73**

Time does not necessarily matter when judging whether steps in a series of transactions need to be viewed as a whole. Inserting a pre-planned period of delay, for example, between intended steps will not generally break 'linkage'.   **3.74**

Time gaps in a series of transactions is a factor to judge as to whether this was an attempt to frustrate a series-of-transactions argument. Deliberate insertion of time delays is usually persuasive evidence of pre-planning and pre-meditation of the outcome. The length of the time period or periods between transactions is not, of itself, relevant. Thus, a time gap should not affect the conclusion. However, time may be a factor to consider if it gives genuine opportunity for a relevant change to occur in the series of steps. The more time that is to elapse between steps then the more time there is for commercial circumstances to change and thus for the subsequent steps, if not yet irrevocable, not to go ahead due to changed circumstances.   **3.75**

4. FAIR VALUE ACCOUNTING

Introduction

The directors of any particular company need to consider their own company's facts and circumstances in determining whether an accounting profit arising through changes in fair value is readily convertible to cash in accordance with the definition and can therefore be considered as realised for distribution purposes. Consideration should also be given to 2.3 to 2.5 above regarding volatility and directors' duties. This section provides guidance on: **4.1**

(a)   the application of the definition of 'readily convertible to cash' to particular situations (see 4.2 *et seq*);
(b)   available-for-sale investments and the fair value reserve (see 4.23 *et seq*);
(c)   the fair value option (see 4.26 *et seq*); and
(d)   losses arising from fair value accounting (see 4.29 *et seq*).

Guidance on the application of 'readily convertible to cash'

Financial instruments

The definition of 'readily convertible to cash' in paragraph 3.12 is closely but not completely aligned with the measurement guidance in IAS 39. Necessary differences remain.   **4.2**

4.3   In situations where:

(a)   the financial instrument is traded in an active market; or

(b)   the financial instrument is valued using a valuation technique whose variables include only data from observable markets,

it will generally be possible to enter into a transaction to convert the change in value to cash at short notice without any period of marketing and/or negotiation. Even when the instrument is not traded in an active market, there may be many institutions which will be prepared to quote a price based on observable market data at which a transaction could take place immediately. Such a change in value that is a profit would therefore, subject also to the test at 3.12(c) above, be regarded as realised.

4.4   However, a change in the fair value of a financial instrument that is a profit which is determined using a valuation technique where not all of the variables include data from observable markets would be regarded as unrealised. This would not be so where part of the profit can be closed out independently of the rest and that part may be realised pursuant to the guidance on close out at 4.5 and 4.6 below.

Close out

4.5   A financial asset, financial liability or change in the fair value of a financial asset or financial liability may be capable of being readily convertible to cash for the purposes of applying condition (a) of the readily convertible to cash test at 3.12 above if it could be immediately closed out, meaning the relevant contract or underlying market risk position is capable of being immediately offset in the market and the normal market practice would be to close out the position in this way. For example, risks inherent in a derivative may be eliminated by taking out other financial instruments, including derivative contracts, with an offsetting risk profile. When it is possible under normal market practice to enter into such arrangements to 'lock in' any profit on the original contract, the profit that could be 'locked in' could be regarded as readily convertible to cash. It is not necessary for an actual transaction to have occurred.

4.6   4.5 above addresses the ability to close out in the context of condition (a) of 3.12. In relation to condition (a), consideration should also be given to whether the cash flows from the close-out instrument meet the definition of qualifying consideration, in particular the criteria set out at 3.11.

4.6A   In addition, conditions (b) and (c) in 3.12 must also be considered. In the context of condition (b), consideration should be given to whether the valuation of the close-out instrument is based on observable market data.

4.7   The position regarding fair value losses is dealt with at 4.29 to 4.33 below.

Embedded derivatives

4.8   Unless the whole contract has been designated at fair value through profit or loss, an embedded derivative that is determined not to be closely related to the economic characteristics and risks of the host contract is required to be separated from its host for accounting purposes (bifurcation) and fair valued, as if it were a standalone derivative with the same terms. Changes in fair value of the embedded derivative are recognised in profit or loss. However, where a change in fair value is a profit it does not constitute a realised profit unless the embedded derivative can be closed out in the manner described above in 'Close out' or the host contract and embedded derivative together meet the 'readily convertible to cash' test (including by reference to close-out if appropriate).

Top-slicing

Fair value accounting under the relevant accounting standards involves the valuation of **4.9** the whole item or, in the case of fair value hedge accounting, a particular risk and the recognition of the change in fair value in the financial statements. Where the change is a profit, it is not necessary to have completed a transaction to determine whether the whole of the increase in fair value is to be treated as realised. The criteria for determining whether an increase in fair value that is a profit could be readily converted to cash and thus be treated as realised are set out at 3.12 above. The concept of top-slicing a gain into realised and unrealised parts as envisaged by paragraph 3.18 arises when there has been a transaction involving qualifying and other consideration. On remeasurement there is no transaction involved in the recognition of a fair value profit, hence the question of top-slicing (ie determining, by reference to mixed consideration receivable, whether part of the profit should be treated as realised as opposed to the whole of such profit) does not occur.

Unquoted equity investments

Although increases in the fair value of many financial assets will meet the test of being **4.10** 'readily convertible to cash' at 3.12 above, this will not generally be true of unquoted equity investments. The measurement of such investments at fair value may be precluded because the range of reasonable fair value estimates is significant and the probabilities of the various estimates cannot reasonably be assessed. Even where the value can be estimated sufficiently reliably to meet the requirements of IAS 39 and an increase in fair value is recognised, it is unlikely that the amount would be readily convertible to cash at the date of determination. This is because, for example, a period of marketing and/or negotiation would generally be required to dispose of such an investment.

Strategic investments

Under a company's business strategy it may hold investments for strategic purposes. **4.11** Such investments are not readily disposable in the sense required to meet condition (c) of the readily convertible to cash test at 3.12 above, as a company's strategy cannot be readily changed so as to allow the investment to be realised immediately at the date of determination. For example, the company might have a strategic investment in a listed company that qualifies to be accounted for as an associate under IAS 28. It is possible for the company to elect under IAS 28 to account for its associates (in its separate financial statements) at fair value under IAS 39 (e.g. as an available-for-sale asset, with fair value changes reported in equity). Increases in fair value of such a strategic investment might be regarded as realised but for condition (c) of the test for readily convertible to cash. Thus the fair value increases are, consequently, unrealised.

A similar analysis may be made for a company's holding of other financial assets, such **4.12** as government bonds, that are classified as available-for-sale and are thus remeasured at fair value but nevertheless are held to meet the company's business strategy or regulatory requirements. Any fair value increases of such assets are unrealised as the company cannot readily change its business strategy or regulatory compliance to allow the financial assets to be realised immediately at the date of determination.

Hedge relationships in group situations

4.12A   Under a group's hedging strategy, different companies in the group may hold the hedging instrument and the hedged item. For example, in a net investment hedge as illustrated in IFRIC 16 Hedges of a Net Investment in a Foreign Operation. The circumstances of each of the companies involved in the hedge relationship needs to be assessed at the date of determination, as the relevant company may not be in a position to realise an increase in fair value in the sense required to meet condition (c) of the readily convertible to cash test at 3.12 above. For example, the purpose of the company holding the hedging instrument is to hold it for the benefit of, or to assist, another group company, and accordingly it may not be able to dispose of or close out the hedging instrument, needing instead to seek that other company's concurrence. This is discussed further at 5.19 to 5.22 of section 5 Hedge accounting."

Investment properties

4.13   None of an increase in fair value of investment property is readily convertible to cash and is not therefore treated as a realised profit. This is because a period of marketing and/or negotiation would be required to dispose of such an investment and therefore it could not be converted to cash at the date of determination. This is not intended to preclude a profit being regarded as realised at the date of determination in those cases when the process of marketing and/or negotiation is complete at that date and legal completion occurs shortly after the date of determination.

Own credit

4.14   When liabilities (e.g. bank debt or bond issues) and over-the-counter derivative contracts are measured at fair value, their value may be affected by the reporting company's own creditworthiness. Consequently, a profit may arise in circumstances where the company's creditworthiness is deteriorating, that is, the fair value of the liability is decreasing. In such cases, it is necessary to consider whether the company would be able to realise the profit by settling the liability at its fair value. This may not be possible, particularly if the company is experiencing financial difficulties, and the relevant profit will therefore not be a realised profit. However, in most circumstances where a company is not in financial difficulties and it would be able to settle the debt at fair value, there will be no need to analyse the fair value changes between the amount attributable to marginal changes in the creditworthiness of the liability and changes due to movements in interest rates and other market factors.

4.15   It should be noted, however, that the tests set out at 3.12 above are wider than solely the ability to settle at fair value and must all be met. For example, the company must be able to settle on the date of determination without negotiation or marketing. Thus where a large volume of debt is under consideration, this is akin to a question of whether the company could refinance that large volume of debt on that date without negotiation, which would often not be the case.

Block discounts for securities traded in an active market

4.16   IAS 39 requires certain financial instruments to be valued on a basis that does not take account of the size of the holding. That is to say that the valuation included in the accounts uses the published price quotation in an active market as the best estimate of fair value and does not reflect any 'block discount' that might apply if the entire holding was disposed of at the date of determination. In the case of assets (e.g. investments) that are traded on an active market, it may be possible to dispose of the entire holding at the date of determination but it is necessary to recognise that the proceeds may be less than the value recognised in the balance sheet in accordance with IAS 39.

Holdings in financial assets traded in an active market that might be regarded as relatively small (e.g. less than 1% of a company's share capital) may nevertheless be large in relation to the volume of business done in that company's shares on a typical day in the market. For example, some such investments held by investment companies and other financial institutions fall into this category. Such investments are rarely, if ever, disposed of in a single block but are instead disposed of in a number of smaller blocks either all on the same day or over a short period of time, in accordance with normal market practice, to reduce or eliminate the effect of any block discount. In these limited circumstances, the effect of any block discount on realised profits may be calculated on the basis set out at 4.18 and 4.19 below rather than on the basis that the entire holding is disposed of in a single block on the date of determination. This is a limited departure from the principle established at 3.12(a) above.   **4.17**

Part 4 of the Statement of Recommended Practice 'Accounting for Securities by Banks' ('the SORP') issued by the British Bankers' Association contained the following guidance: **4.18**

> "61. Where a holding of a quoted security (other than one to which paragraph [62] or [63] applies)[21] is so large that it could be disposed of only at an unfavourable price or over an extended period, it should be valued at an appropriate discount to the market price. The discount should be sufficient to reflect the reduction in price resulting from the size of the holding or all future costs likely to be incurred in disposing of the interest over time in the ordinary course of business."

The SORP has been withdrawn because it is not applicable to banks reporting under IFRSs or applying FRS 26 under UK GAAP. It nevertheless provides an indication of generally accepted practice for the valuation of large holdings. Although this approach no longer applies for financial reporting purposes for companies applying IFRSs or FRS 26, it continues to be relevant to the determination of realised profits.

Where it is determined that a block discount exists in relation to a holding of securities traded in an active market, only the part of the profit that may not be realisable over a short period of time in the ordinary course of business should be treated as unrealised[22]. This would not necessarily be the same as the block discount that may apply if the entity disposed of the entire holding in a single block at the date of determination (e.g. in a forced sale), and which applies to situations other than those covered by the previous sentence for the purposes of determining the part of the profit that is unrealised.   **4.19**

Estimation of the unrealised profit referred to at 4.16 and 4.19 above will require the exercise of judgement. Directors of companies frequently have to exercise judgement in making accounting estimates. The position concerning block discounts is no different. Directors do not have to be able to quantify the unrealised profit referred to at 4.16 and 4.19 above precisely; an estimate is all that is required. It will often be clear that there is a sufficient margin of profit available for distribution (over and above the proposed   **4.20**

---

[21] *Paragraph 62 dealt with instruments held for hedging and paragraph 63 dealt with investment securities stated at cost.*

[22] *A similar adjustment is not required when an overall (ie cumulative) loss is recognised on the remeasurement of a financial instrument in accordance with IAS 39. The potential additional loss, equivalent to the block discount, that would arise on disposal of the entire holding at the date of determination is not recorded as a loss in the financial statements. Consequently, the realised loss will equal the loss reported in the financial statements, which will exclude the effect of any block discount.*

distribution) to absorb a prudent assessment of the effect of any unrealised profit attributable to block discounts.

4.21 Directors should consider their common law duty to avoid an unlawful distribution of capital. If an investment is sold after the date of determination to finance a distribution, the impact of any resulting loss (whether due to the unrealised component of a block discount or otherwise) on profits available for distribution should be considered.

4.22 The case of a block discount can be distinguished from that of investment property and most unquoted equity investments when none of the profit is treated as realised due to the period of marketing and/or negotiation required to dispose of such investments, such that the profit could not be readily converted to cash at the date of determination.

Available-for-sale financial assets and the fair value reserve

4.23 Under IAS 39, profits and losses on 'available-for-sale' financial assets are recognised directly in equity through the statement of other comprehensive income (except for dividends, interest, impairment losses and foreign exchange profits and losses on monetary items). This applies until the assets are derecognised (e.g. sold) at which time the cumulative profit or loss previously recognised in equity is recognised in profit or loss (ie 'recycled')[23].

4.24 Profits and losses arising on the remeasurement of available-for-sale financial assets will be realised or unrealised according to the same principles that would apply if the same assets had been accounted for at fair value through profit or loss (see above). For example, it would be illogical if the question of whether a profit was realised or unrealised depended on whether the directors designated the particular assets 'at fair value through profit or loss' on initial recognition, when using the fair value option in the circumstances permitted by the relevant accounting standards (see 4.26 below). However, profits on remeasurement of available-for-sale financial assets will be realised or unrealised in accordance with the principles described above, irrespective of whether they meet the requirements to be accounted for at fair value through profit or loss.

4.25 For companies reporting under IFRSs (ie directly under the IAS Regulation), there is no requirement to credit profits included in other comprehensive income on available-for-sale investments to any particular reserve. For companies reporting under UK GAAP (FRS 26), such profits will be taken to the fair value reserve in accordance with the requirements of the Accounting Regulations. There is no specific legal restriction on the distribution of profits included in the fair value reserve in either the Act or the EU Fair Value Directive (2001/65/EC) from which the provisions on fair value accounting in UK legislation are drawn. Therefore, there is no constraint on treating profits on remeasurement of available-for-sale financial assets as available for distribution if they are in all other respects realised profits in accordance with this guidance.

Fair value option

4.26 IAS 39, the EU adopted version of IAS 39 and FRS 26 contain the same conditions regarding when it is permitted to use the fair value option to designate financial instruments 'at fair value through profit or loss' on initial recognition. The conditions for using the fair value option are set out in paragraph 9 *et seq* of IAS 39.

---

[23] *Similar rules for 'available-for-sale' financial assets apply for companies using FRS 26, where the profits and losses are recognised directly in equity through the statement of total recognised gains and losses. The amendment to FRS 3 for companies using FRS 26 clarifies the position for recycling the cumulative profit or loss on a sale of an available-for-sale financial asset.*

Where the fair value option is used it is necessary to consider whether the changes in **4.27** fair value of the relevant financial instruments that are recognised in the profit and loss account meet the conditions to be treated as realised. In this respect, the guidance above on 'Financial instruments', 'Embedded derivatives', 'Own credit' and 'Block discounts' will be most relevant in interpreting the 'readily convertible to cash' criterion as defined at 3.12 above.

In addition, it is recognised that the use of the fair value option to eliminate or significantly **4.28** reduce an accounting mismatch may validly be used in place of hedge accounting for hedges of fair value exposures. Consequently, where this is the case, although the designated financial instrument that is fair valued under the fair value option and the derivative that would otherwise give rise to the accounting mismatch are not in a formal IAS 39 hedge relationship, consideration of the guidance in 5.2 to 5.6 'Fair value hedge accounting' (which contain further guidance on the principle set out at 3.19 above) would be relevant in determining the effect on realised profits of the combined effect of the designated financial instruments and the derivatives concerned.

Losses

Losses arising from fair value accounting should be treated as realised losses where profits **4.29** on remeasurement of the same asset or liability would be treated as realised profits in accordance with this guidance (see 3.15(f) above).

A loss that represents the reversal of an unrealised profit will not reduce cumulative realised **4.30** profits. Even if the loss is treated as a realised loss, for example because it represents an impairment, the unrealised profit will become realised in accordance with 3.9(f) above.

Cumulative net losses arising on fair value accounting will be unrealised only if both: **4.31**

(a) profits on remeasurement of the same asset or liability would be unrealised; and
(b) the losses would not have been recorded otherwise than pursuant to fair value accounting.

With reference to paragraph (b) above, absent fair value accounting a loss may need to be **4.32** recorded for example, in relation to an asset, on the basis of historical/ amortised costs less impairment provisions; and in relation to a liability, under either an amortised cost basis of financial instrument accounting or as an onerous contract liability.

It is well established that the recoverable amount of tangible fixed assets (e.g. properties **4.33** used in a business) may exceed their fair value (see paragraph 65 of FRS 15). In the case of other assets (including investment property), it may be more difficult to justify a recoverable amount that is greater than fair value. Each case should be considered on its merits and, where there is doubt, losses should be treated as realised.

5. HEDGE ACCOUNTING

Hedge relationships in individual companies

As stated at 3.19 above, the principle to be applied to the determination of realised profits **5.1** and losses when hedge accounting is used is as follows:

"Where hedge accounting is obtained in accordance with the relevant accounting standards, it is necessary to consider the combined effect of both sides of the hedging relationship to determine whether there is a realised profit or loss in accordance with the criteria in this guidance."

The application of this principle to different types of hedge accounting permitted by IAS 39 by companies holding both the hedging instrument and the hedged item is described at 5.2 to 5.18 below.

5.1A   Where the hedging instrument and hedged item are held in different companies within the same group a hedging relationship is established only in the group's consolidated financial statements. The general realisation principles as set out at 3.3 to 3.12 apply to the individual companies. As the hedge relationship does not exist within a single company the principle at 3.19 is inapplicable in such a case. Instead guidance on the application of these principles is provided at 5.19 to 5.22 below to assist in determining in what circumstances any profits or losses on the hedging instruments and hedged items can be treated as realised for the individual companies concerned.

Fair value hedge accounting

5.2   In the case of fair value hedges under IAS 39, the gross profits and losses on remeasuring the hedging instrument and the hedged item for the hedged risk are both recognised in profit or loss. In many instances both the profit on one and the loss on the other will be realised by reference to the readily convertible to cash and other criteria. In such cases, no special consideration of hedging aspects is required (including hedge effectiveness or ineffectiveness).

5.3   In some cases, however, the profit on either the hedged item or the hedging instrument may, absent consideration of the hedging aspect, be unrealised (e.g. if a fair value movement is not readily convertible to cash). The following paragraphs explain how the principle set out at 5.1 above should be applied in circumstances where the profit is not realised.

5.4   Where the hedge accounting relationship results in a net loss, this amount will generally be treated as a realised loss. For example, consider the situation where there is an unrealised profit on the hedged item of £90 and a realised loss on the hedging instrument of £100. The net loss of £10, which arises from hedge ineffectiveness, is recognised in the profit and loss account and is treated as a realised loss. Due to the hedge accounting relationship, the remaining £90 of the gross loss on the hedging instrument is not treated as a realised loss and is set off against the unrealised profit on the hedged item.

5.5   Where there is a net profit, it will be necessary to consider whether that profit is a realised profit. This will depend on the relationship between the gross components. For example, if there is an unrealised profit of £100 and a realised loss of £90, only the net profit of £10 will be treated as unrealised.

5.6   This approach applies irrespective of whether the profits or losses in question arise from changes in fair value of open contracts or from settled transactions. For example, the hedge accounting policy may designate a series of rolling derivatives as the hedging instrument, some of which have already been settled in cash, whereas there have been no past settlements in respect of the hedged item.

Cash flow hedge accounting

5.7   In the case of cash flow hedges under IAS 39, the portion of the profit or loss on the hedging instrument that is determined to be an effective hedge is recognised in other comprehensive income. Such profits and losses are unrealised and become realised only when the hedged transaction affects profit or loss (or IAS 39 otherwise requires the gain or loss to be recycled through profit or loss). This is based on the principle (set out in 5.1 above) that it is necessary to have regard to the combined effect of both sides of the hedge accounting relationship to determine whether there is a realised profit or loss. To the extent that the profit or loss is included in other comprehensive income (or, later on, added to the cost of a non-financial asset) in accordance with IAS 39, it must arise in connection with a valid hedge accounting relationship. It would therefore be inappropriate to consider this profit or loss in isolation from the hedged item. To the extent that any ineffective element of the profit or loss on the hedging instrument is recognised in profit or loss, that element should be assessed as to whether it is realised in accordance with normal principles (e.g. the 'readily convertible to cash' test).

The hedging principle at 5.1 above applies irrespective of whether the profits or losses in question arise from changes in fair value of open contracts or from settled transactions. The amounts taken direct to equity may, for example, include profits or losses on short-term derivative contracts that form part of a rolling-hedge strategy but which have matured. Such profits and losses should be treated as unrealised provided that IAS 39 requires them still to be deferred in equity as part of a cash flow hedge accounting relationship. **5.8**

Accounting for a cash flow hedge in accordance with IAS 39 will affect net assets although the profit or loss is regarded as unrealised. Where the cumulative net amount on the cash flow hedge component of equity (cash flow hedge reserve) is an overall unrealised loss, this may additionally restrict the ability of a public company to make distributions because of the application of section 831 (see 6.24 *et seq*). **5.9**

Net investment hedge accounting

Under IAS 39, net investment hedge accounting policies will generally arise only in the context of consolidated financial statements. Those financial statements are not relevant for the purposes of justifying distributions. However, it is possible that in some instances, in accordance with IAS 21, a branch may be treated as a foreign operation in the individual accounts of a company. In this case, net investment hedge accounting may be relevant to the individual accounts of a company. A net investment hedge under IAS 39 is accounted for similarly to a cash flow hedge. So far as the hedge accounting is concerned, the question of whether the hedged item gives rise to realised profits is dealt with in section 11. **5.10**

The circumstances where a company previously adopted hedge accounting for a foreign equity investment (ie shares) in accordance with paragraph 51 of SSAP 20 is considered below. **5.11**

Transition from SSAP 20 – Hedge accounting for foreign equity investments

Under UK GAAP, SSAP 20 permits a form of hedge accounting for foreign equity investments, subject to certain conditions. Where a company has used foreign currency borrowings to finance, or provide a hedge against, its foreign equity investments, it may denominate those investments in the appropriate foreign currencies and translate the amounts at the balance sheet date at closing rate. Where this policy is adopted, the resulting exchange differences are taken to reserves. The exchange differences on the related foreign currency borrowings are, subject to certain conditions, also taken to reserves. In some cases hedge accounting may be possible for such arrangements under IAS 39 but as a fair value hedge through profit or loss. This is subject to more stringent conditions which do not apply under UK GAAP. Therefore companies may not be able to obtain hedge accounting for such financing arrangements under IFRSs. **5.12**

The hedge accounting for foreign equity investments under SSAP 20 described above is not restricted to investments in subsidiaries but this is its most common application. This guidance assumes, for simplicity, that the equity investment is in a subsidiary. **5.13**

5.14   Where hedge accounting is not available under IAS 39, the exchange differences on the borrowings will be included in profit or loss. Unless the equity investment is held at fair value under IAS 39, there will be no offsetting difference on the investment and it is usually, in effect, frozen at its historical cost in the functional currency of the investor. It is then necessary to determine whether the exchange difference on the borrowings is realised or unrealised.

5.15   The exchange difference on the borrowings should be treated as realised in accordance with the general principles in section 3 where hedge accounting is not applied. This is irrespective of whether the purpose of the loan is for hedging an investment and of whether hedge accounting would have been permitted in the circumstances. This is the same as the position under SSAP 20 when the use of hedge accounting was optional.

5.16   It should be noted that even though hedge accounting is not available, the purpose of the loan may still be to provide an 'economic hedge' against the related equity investment. As stated at 2.3 *et seq*, although profits on the borrowings will be realised profits, directors should consider, as a result of their fiduciary and other duties, whether it would be prudent to distribute them.

5.17   Where hedge accounting was used under SSAP 20 and is not possible (or is otherwise not used) under IFRSs, it will be necessary, subject to IFRS 1, to restate the investment to either cost or fair value in accordance with IAS 27. On first-time adoption of IFRSs, paragraphs B5 and B6 of IFRS 1 will be relevant in these circumstances. They state that 'if, before the date of transition to IFRSs, an entity had designated a transaction as a hedge but the hedge does not meet the conditions for hedge accounting in IAS 39 the entity shall apply paragraphs 91 and 101 of IAS 39 to discontinue hedge accounting'. Those paragraphs require hedge accounting to be discontinued prospectively. The practical effect of this is that, if a policy of stating the investment at cost is adopted, the cumulative translation differences from applying SSAP 20 remain adjusted against the carrying value of the investment (ie the investment in the subsidiary is frozen at the amount determined by translating the historic foreign currency cost of the investment at the spot rate prevailing at the date of transition).

5.18   When this treatment is applicable, the profits and losses taken to reserves under SSAP 20 will remain within equity under IAS 39. In this case the assessment of whether those profits and losses are realised should continue to be made by reference to the net amount included within equity.

Hedge relationships in group situations

5.19   Under a group's hedging strategy, different companies in the group may hold the hedging instrument and the hedged item. For example, in a net investment hedge as illustrated in IFRIC 16 Hedges of a Net Investment in a Foreign Operation. In these cases, there is no hedge relationship within an individual company and thus the hedging principle articulated at 3.19 and as expanded upon at 5.1 to 5.18 does not apply. Accordingly, the general realisation principles as set out at 3.3 to 3.12 apply as follows.

Fair value accounting

5.20   As referred to at 4.12A, a company holding a hedging instrument in a designated group hedge relationship cannot generally readily dispose of or close out the instrument in the sense required to meet condition (c) of the readily convertible to cash test at 3.12 above. This is because the company may not be able to act unilaterally to de-designate the hedging relationship that has been created by the group so as to allow it to realise the hedging instrument immediately at the date of determination. Consequently, any fair value increases of the hedging instrument are unrealised. Decreases in fair value will need to be considered carefully to determine the extent to which they are realised by applying the guidance at 4.29 et seq.

The company holding the hedged item may not be as constrained, if at all, as to its actions as the company holding the hedging instrument. Nevertheless, it should be considered whether the company has the ability to meet condition (c) of the readily convertible to cash test at 3.12 above. Disposing of or closing out the hedged item would involve breaking the group hedge relationship and this may have adverse consequences for the group. If the company has the ability to dispose of or close out the hedged item at the date of determination and thus meet condition (c), any fair value increases of the hedged item are realised. On the other hand, if it is determined that condition (c) cannot be met, then any fair value increases of the hedged item are unrealised. Decreases in fair value will need to be considered carefully to determine the extent to which they are realised by applying the guidance at 4.29 et seq. **5.21**

Historical cost accounting

Companies not applying IAS 39 or FRS 26 but which have stand-alone derivatives or non-derivative financial instruments measure those instruments at historical cost and apply historical cost accounting. This is equally true for those that are held as part of a group hedging relationship. They could include, for example, accounting for foreign exchange differences under SSAP 20 or debtors and creditors for interest rate differentials in interest rate swaps. The general realisation principles as set out at 3.3 to 3.12 apply and normally these profits and losses are realised. Where profits on derivative and non-derivative financial instruments are realised, directors should consider whether from a group perspective it is appropriate to distribute them.' **5.22**

6. ISSUES ARISING FROM IAS 32 (AND ITS EQUIVALENT, FRS 25)

Introduction

Under IFRSs, financial instruments are presented according to the substance of the contractual arrangement, determined by the rules in IAS 32. This may differ from their legal form. For example, redeemable preference shares bearing mandatory dividends are presented as liabilities in the balance sheet and their corresponding distributions as interest charges in the income statement because the issuer has no ability to avoid payment in cash of either the principal or distributions. The substance of the contractual arrangement is therefore debt. Also, compound financial instruments are accounted for under the relevant standards using 'split accounting', whereby the proceeds of issue are split between a liability component and an equity component. Examples of compound financial instruments are convertible redeemable preference shares and convertible debt (assuming that the conversion feature itself meets the definition of equity in IAS 32). **6.1**

Under UK GAAP, FRS 25's requirements on debt and equity presentation are the same as those in IAS 32. **6.2**

The following guidance considers the implications for distributable profits of companies, for example, entering into contracts involving their own shares that may require classification in whole, or in part, as liabilities. **6.3**

The guidance summarises the ten key principles in relation to determining distributable profits when dealing with such contracts. The guidance then applies the principles to scenarios based on examples 1, 2, 4, 6 and 9 set out in the Illustrative Examples appendices to IAS 32 and FRS 25 involving contracts on own equity instruments. In addition, **6.4** other scenarios are considered involving preference shares presented as liabilities, mandatorily redeemable preference shares and convertible preference shares.

6.5 Appendix 2 to the guidance provides illustrations of the accounting and capital maintenance book-keeping entries for the eight scenarios referred to above.

6.6 The ten principles underpinning the guidance in this section are set out below. The principles are split between those applying to all companies and those specific to public companies resulting from the application of the net assets test of section 831 of the Act. The principles are those underlying statute and common law in respect of distributions and capital maintenance.

Assumptions

6.6A The contracts described in this section and in Appendix 2 do not contain a cash settlement option.

6.6B Any redemption of the relevant shares will be made out of profits available for distribution and not out of the proceeds of a fresh issue of shares for the purpose of the redemption unless the text in this section or in Appendix 2 otherwise indicates. Payment of any dividends and redemption amounts are contingent upon such payments/redemption being lawful under the Act at the time of payment/redemption, with, where appropriate, the relevant amount being deferred until such time as the Act's restrictions fall away.

6.6C The shares, contracts and convertible instruments described in this section and in Appendix 2 are denominated in the issuer's functional currency, pay dividends and are redeemed in that currency, and, where convertible are convertible into shares denominated in that currency. It is also assumed that there are no contingent settlement provisions (see paragraph 25 of IAS 32 and FRS 25) or alternate settlement options (see paragraph 26 of IAS 32 and FRS 25). The effect of foreign currency, contingent settlement provisions and/or alternate settlement options can have an impact on the accounting to deny equity treatment in certain cases.

Principles – General

6.7 **Principle 1 – A distribution or a capital repayment is not as a matter of law a loss, notwithstanding that it may be presented for accounting purposes as an interest charge in the income statement**

6.8 Section 830(2) of the Act provides that, 'a company's profits available for distribution are its accumulated, realised profits, so far as not previously utilised by distribution or capitalisation, less its accumulated, realised losses, so far as not previously written off in a reduction or reorganisation of capital duly made.' This is based on the premise that distributions are not losses. If distributions were losses they would be dealt with by the words 'less its accumulated, realised losses,' and thus the words 'so far as not previously utilised by distribution' would be superfluous.

6.9 A distribution or capital repayment may on occasion be presented as an accounting loss. For example, in some cases dividends on a preference share are presented as interest charges in the profit and loss account. Notwithstanding the accounting presentation, such distributions or capital repayments remain, as a matter of law, distributions or capital repayments for the purposes of Part 23 of the Act. Accordingly, they are not counted as losses – and thus not as realised or unrealised losses – for the purposes of Part 23 of the Act.

Principle 2 – An advance recognition of a future distribution or capital repayment is not a loss notwithstanding that it may be presented for accounting purposes as an interest charge in the income statement   **6.10**

A distribution or capital repayment is not, as a matter of law, a loss. Thus the advance recognition of a future distribution or capital repayment is not a loss either. Hence, the accrual, as an interest charge, of a dividend, or a foreign exchange translation difference, in respect of a preference share presented as debt is an advance recognition of a future distribution or capital repayment but it is not a loss for distribution purposes even though the accrual is charged as interest the profit and loss account.   **6.11**

Principle 3 – A distribution or a capital repayment consumes distributable profits when paid or when a dividend is declared by a company in general meeting   **6.12**

An accounting liability recognised for accrued unpaid dividends or a capital repayment is an advance recognition of a future distribution or capital repayment and is not, as a matter of law, a loss.   **6.13**

A distribution does not consume distributable profits until such time as, as a matter of law, the distribution occurs, e.g. when paid under the authority of the directors, under common form articles of association, or when declared by members in general meeting, or at an earlier date on which a legally binding liability to pay the dividend is established (see 2.10 above).   **6.14**

The repurchase price for shares does not consume distributable profits until such time as, as a matter of law, the distribution and/or capital repayment comprised in the price occurs. In particular, notwithstanding that there are arrangements in place that will lead to repurchase, the company is not liable to pay the purchase price, and thus distributable profits are not consumed, until the shares are actually repurchased or redeemed. It should be noted that the holder of the shares cannot sue for damages in the event of failure by the company to repurchase those shares (see section 735 of the Act).   **6.15**

Section 691(2) provides that where a limited company purchases its own shares, the shares must be paid for in cash on purchase. However, in the case of redeemable shares, section 686(2) provides that the terms of redemption may provide that the amount payable on redemption may, by agreement between the company and the holder of the shares, be paid in cash on a date later than the redemption date. This is a change from the 1985 Act which required payment on redemption. When payment on redemption is deferred, it is the current value of the redemption promise, at the redemption date, which determines the amount of distributable profits consumed. It is therefore the present value of the amount payable on redemption rather than its absolute amount which must be covered by distributable profits, at the redemption date, for the redemption to be permitted.   **6.15A**

Principle 4 – Premiums received by the issuer on written options to issue or repurchase own equity shares are profits when received   **6.16**

A premium received by the writer of an option over its own equity shares is regarded as a profit at law. This is because it is value received by the company otherwise than in payment up of a share and otherwise than for taking on a liability. In particular, a written put option is not, as a matter of law, a liability of the company; for example, the holder of the option cannot sue for damages in the event of failure by the company to repurchase the shares (see section 735 of the Act).   **6.17**

Thus to the extent that the premium is received in the form of qualifying consideration, it is a realised profit at the outset.   **6.18**

6.19 **Principle 5 – When a company issues a compound financial instrument that is legally a debt, the original credit to equity determined using split accounting is not, as a matter of law, a profit; the original credit to equity is eliminated as accounting charges, which are not as a matter of law losses, accrue upwards the amount recorded as a liability**

6.20 The initial credit to equity is not an accounting profit because in accounting terms it is the equivalent of the issue of an equity instrument. As a matter of law there is not a profit either, because the proceeds received are in consideration for taking on a liability (in which respect it is distinctly different from a legally separate option contract addressed in Principle 4) albeit a liability that is not fully reflected as such in the accounts. The liability becomes fully reflected in the accounts through an additional interest charge that is not, as a matter of law, a loss because the full instrument that is legally a debt is reflected in the balance sheet at issue albeit in different places. Thus the cumulative debit in equity arising from these additional charges is available to eliminate the initial credit.

6.21 **Principle 6 – When a company issues a compound financial instrument that is legally a share, the original credit to equity determined using split accounting is share capital, and if applicable share premium; accounting charges made to accrue upwards the amount recorded for accounting purposes as a liability component, are not, as a matter of law, losses**

6.22 The initial credit to equity as a result of split accounting is share capital, and if applicable share premium, and is reflected as such. Subsequent accounting charges, to accrue upwards the amount recorded for accounting purposes as a liability component, are not, as a matter of law, losses because they are advance recognition of a future distribution or capital repayment.

6.23 In some circumstances, there may be a debit to be recognised in equity on an issue of shares to a parent company or fellow subsidiary, where the shares do not qualify to be classified in the accounts as equity of the issuer. The shares are recognised initially by the issuer as a liability at their fair value. However, the fair value may be greater than the proceeds received for their issue because the terms are off-market and, for example, involve redemption for significant amounts above the original proceeds and/or bear coupons that are substantial. In such circumstances, this difference between fair value and proceeds, a debit, is in effect advance recognition of future distributions and/or a future capital repayment and is recognised in equity. Consequently, this debit is not a loss at initial recognition. [Principle 2]. The debit will consume distributable profits either as dividends on the shares are made, which are distributions as a matter of law, or at the date of redemption (ie when the payments are set against the liability over time or at the end). [Principle 3]

Principles – Impact of Section 831 for public companies

6.24 **Principle 7 – The treatment of certain shares wholly as liabilities under IFRSs does not in itself affect the application of the section 831 of the Act net assets test for public companies and thus does not restrict distributable profits**

6.25 Section 831 states that a public company may only make a distribution at any time:

- if at that time the amount of its net assets is not less than the aggregate of its called-up share capital and undistributable reserves (as defined); and
- if, and to the extent that, the distribution does not reduce the amount of those assets to less than that aggregate.

Section 831 defines 'net assets' for this purpose to mean the aggregate of the company's assets less the aggregate of its liabilities. By virtue of section 836, net assets for the purposes of section 831 are those shown in the 'relevant accounts' prepared in accordance with applicable accounting standards; that is, its 'IAS individual accounts', or its 'Companies Act individual accounts'. Therefore in the case of the issue of a financial instrument that is presented as debt in accordance with the substance of its contractual arrangements rather than their strict legal form, the company's net assets are unaffected for the purposes of section 831. This is because a liability is recorded (being in respect of the nominal value plus related share premium attributable to the shares) equal to the cash received as issue proceeds. **6.26**

It is less clear from the drafting of section 831 whether there is any effect on the amount of a company's 'share capital and undistributable reserves' arising from the issue of shares for which the presentation of share capital and related share premium is as a liability. In legal form there will have been an increase in share capital and related share premium. However, in accordance with section 836, the amount of share capital and undistributable reserves is determined by reference to the amount as stated in the company's relevant accounts. Accordingly, it appears that any amount of share capital and related share premium that has been presented as a liability should be excluded from the amount of share capital and undistributable reserves for the purposes of applying section 831. This is because the amount of share capital and undistributable reserves as stated in the relevant accounts excludes this amount. **6.27**

This interpretation of section 831 is consistent with the 'Guidance for British companies on changes to reporting and accounting provisions of the Companies Act 1985' (originally issued by the DTI[24] in November 2004 and updated in August 2005[25]). The DTI's guidance states that 'the interaction of section 264 and section 270(2) [of the 1985 Act, now sections 831 and 836(1) of the 2006 Act] is such that, where preference shares are classified as liabilities, they should be treated as such for the purposes of the net asset test, and should not be treated as part of called-up share capital and undistributable reserves for that purpose'. **6.28**

Consequently the issue of shares with their nominal value and related share premium presented as debt does not result in an immediate restriction in the amount of profits available for distribution by a public company under section 831, because the issue leaves both net assets and share capital and undistributable reserves (as defined) unaffected. **6.29**

When the section 831 test comes to be applied to the repurchase or redemption of the shares, it should be borne in mind that whilst the repayment of the nominal value and issue premium on the shares will leave net assets unaffected, 'share capital and undistributable reserves' will increase due to the recording of the capital redemption reserve and the inclusion in the share premium account within equity of the issue premium which has always existed and which is no longer required to be presented as a liability. Under section 831(1) the net assets must be at least equal to the 'share capital and undistributable reserves' both before (sub-section (1)(a)) and after (sub-section (1)(b)) the repayment for it to be lawful. **6.30**

Principle 8 – A debit to equity arising from an advance recognition of a future distribution or capital repayment does not form part of share capital and **6.31**

---

[24] *Now the Department for Business, Innovation & Skills.*

[25] *Guidance available from National Archives at: http://webarchive.nationalarchives.gov.uk/+/http://www.berr.gov.uk/files/file21617.doc*

undistributable reserves (as defined) for the purposes of section 831 and thus restricts distributable profits for public companies under that section

6.32   Despite not representing a realised loss or a consumption of distributable profits, nevertheless an advance recognition of a future distribution or capital repayment restricts distributable profits for public companies. This is due to the advance recognition of the distribution as a liability, reducing net assets, but the corresponding debit to equity (via the income statement/profit and loss account) not reducing 'share capital and undistributable reserves' as defined by section 831.

6.33   The above contrasts with Principle 1 because in the context of section 831, the Act gives precedence to the accounting presentation and this restricts the amount of the profits available for distribution.

6.33A   The existence of any unrealised profits does not alter this situation (e.g., such unrealised profits cannot be applied to offset the deduction, because the deduction is not an unrealised loss).

6.34   The question may arise as to whether this restriction might operate to prevent the distribution or capital repayment in question when it comes to be made, e.g. because the effect might be that the surplus of net assets over 'share capital and undistributable reserves' might be reduced to an amount less than the distribution or capital repayment to be made. However, there will be no restricting effect on the making of such amount of a distribution or capital repayment as has been recognised in advance, provided that immediately beforehand the net assets are not less than 'share capital and undistributable reserves'. This is because, accordingly, the company will meet the test in section 831(1)(a); and on the actual making of the distribution or capital repayment, which has previously been recognised as a liability, net assets are unaffected and thus remain no less than 'share capital and undistributable reserves', thereby meeting section 831(1)(b). If the shares in question were originally classified as debt, then the operation of section 831 in relation to the original issue price is as described at 6.30 above.

6.35   **Principle 9 – On initial recognition, split accounting for compound financial instruments does not restrict distributable profits for public companies under section 831**

6.36   If the compound financial instrument is legally a share (for example, a redeemable preference share with discretionary dividends) and is split into its debt and equity components, at the outset there is no effect on distributable profits. The initial liability is matched by an equal amount of cash proceeds and there is no effect on net assets. In respect of the equity component, the initial credit to equity is, at law, share capital (and share premium) and is included in 'share capital and undistributable reserves' for the purposes of the section 831 net assets test. This increase on one side of the net assets equation is balanced by the corresponding amount of cash proceeds which increases the company's net assets. Thus, 'share capital and undistributable reserves' do not exceed net assets and therefore there is no restriction on distributable profits at the outset.

6.37   If the compound financial instrument is legally a debt (for example, a convertible debt) and it is split into its debt and equity components, the initial liability is exceeded by the amount of cash proceeds, equal in amount to that of the initial credit to equity, and accordingly there is an increase in net assets. However, in respect of the initial credit to equity itself, this does not form part of 'share capital and undistributable reserves'. As a result, an increase in net assets is recorded (being the difference between the consideration received and the liability recognised) with no corresponding increase in 'share capital and undistributable reserves'. Thus the issue of this instrument contributes an excess of net assets over 'share capital and undistributable reserves'. This has the effect of reducing any pre-existing restriction on distributable profits under section 831. However, where there is no pre-existing restriction, or such a restriction is more than eliminated by the issue of this instrument, distributable profits are not created; this is because section 831 has effect only to reduce the ability to distribute realised profits.

Principle 10 – The accretion of the liability component of compound financial instruments reduces distributable profits for public companies under section 831 unless the instrument is legally a debt   **6.38**

Where the compound financial instrument is legally a share, the 'interest charge' for the accretion of the liability component is not a loss as a matter of law [Principle 6] and has no effect on the amount shown as 'share capital and undistributable reserves' in the relevant accounts. That is, the initial credit to equity (being share capital (and share premium)) cannot be used to absorb the accumulating 'interest charge' debited to retained earnings (via the profit and loss account) due to the accretion of the liability. Hence, under the section 831 net assets test, the amount that a public company can distribute is restricted by the accumulated amount of the 'interest charge' debit, which ultimately will be equal to the initial credit to equity. In other words, net assets are reduced but there is no corresponding reduction of 'share capital and undistributable reserves' and thus over time the cumulative restriction of distributable profits will equal the initial credit to equity.   **6.39**

Where a compound financial instrument is legally a debt, the accretion of the liability is an accounting loss (although not a loss as a matter of law [Principle 5]) that reduces net assets for the purposes of the section 831 net assets test (see paragraph 6.33). However this eliminates the initial increase to net assets recorded as a result of the split accounting and thus of itself does not restrict distributable profits.   **6.40**

Examples

The following examples illustrate the application of the ten principles described in 6.7 to 6.40 above. The first five examples addressed below are based on examples 1, 2, 4, 6 and 9 involving contracts on own equity instruments set out in the Illustrative Examples appendices to IAS 32 and FRS 25. Three further examples address preference shares presented as liabilities, mandatorily redeemable preference shares and convertible preference shares. The assumptions made at 6.6A to 6.6C above apply for the purposes of these examples.   **6.41**

Appendix 2 provides illustrations of the accounting and statutory capital maintenance book keeping entries for the eight examples.   **6.42**

[Assumptions]

[Moved to 6.6A]   **6.43**

[Moved to 6.6B]   **6.44**

[Moved to 6.6C]   **6.45**

Example 1 – Forward contract to repurchase own equity shares

Where a company enters into a forward contract to repurchase its own shares that are equity shares under the relevant standard, the standards require the company to set up a liability, at the outset, for the present value of the payment to be made (ie a discounted   **6.46** amount), with a corresponding debit taken directly to equity. The accounting effect is as if the equity shares had been repurchased immediately.

6.47   The initial debit to equity, for the present value of the consideration payable, is not a realised loss. This is because the eventual payment is not a loss, but is in fact a distribution (or a capital repayment to the extent not out of distributable profits) [Principle 2].

6.48   Over time the (discounted) liability is accreted up to the eventual repayment amount, with a corresponding charge to finance expense (interest) in the profit and loss account (income statement). The accretion of the liability over time up to full value of the eventual redemption amount is presented as an accounting loss – it is shown as part of the interest charge. Again, however, the ultimate payment of the full amount is either a distribution or a capital repayment and is not therefore, as a matter of law, a loss nor, therefore, a realised loss. [Principle 2]

The effect on a public company

6.49   For a public company the effect is to restrict distributable profits. [Principle 8]

Combining the accounting and statutory capital maintenance entries to complete the repurchase of non-equity shares

6.50   When payment is made to repurchase the shares, it is, for accounting purposes, set against the liability. To the extent that the payment must, in law, come out of distributable profits, the debit in reserves (ie the initial debit to equity, together with the interest charge for the accretion) is set against and consumes distributable profits. To the extent that the payment must in law be charged to capital (e.g., funded by a fresh issue), then this debit is set against called-up share capital (and share premium as the case may be). Any necessary transfer from called-up share capital to capital redemption reserve is made in the usual way.

Example 2 – Written option to repurchase own equity shares

6.51   The accounting standards require the same accounting for a written option to repurchase equity shares as for a forward to repurchase equity shares (Example 1), save that in the case of the written option, any premium received at the outset is required to be taken directly to equity. So far as accounting for the repurchase price itself is concerned, the distributable profits considerations are the same as for the forward (see *Forward contract to repurchase own equity shares* at 6.46 *et seq* above).

6.52   The option premium is regarded as a profit at law and, to the extent that the premium is received in the form of qualifying consideration, is a realised profit. [Principle 4]. As a matter of law, the repurchase price for the shares is a future distribution or capital repayment. [Principle 3]

The effect on a public company

6.53   For a public company the effect of the recognition of the liability for the present value of the payment to be made and the subsequent accretion of the liability to the payment amount, is to restrict distributable profits. [Principle 8]

Example 3 – Forward contract to issue own equity shares

6.54   A forward contract to deliver, through a fresh issue of shares, a fixed number of the company's own equity shares in exchange for a fixed amount of cash meets the definition of an equity instrument in the relevant standard because it cannot be settled otherwise than through the delivery of shares in exchange for cash (see assumptions in *6.6A to 6.6C* above). Consequently, the right to receive the cash in a future accounting period is not recognised by the company, and the standards do not require accounting entries to be made until the forward contract matures, when the company receives cash and issues shares to the contract's counterparty.

Assuming the fair value of the forward contract at inception is zero, no cash is paid or received at that date, and thus no accounting entries are required on inception. Therefore, where a company enters into a forward contract to issue equity shares, the required accounting for such an arrangement raises no issues of distributable profits.   **6.55**

The effect on a public company

There are no additional considerations for a public company.   **6.56**

Example 4 – Written option to issue own equity shares

The relevant standards require the premium received on the writing of an option to issue own shares, that are presented as equity, to be credited directly to equity. The premium stays in equity regardless of whether the option ultimately is exercised or lapses, although it may be transferred between components of equity (ie between reserves). The premium, to the extent that it is received in the form of qualifying consideration, is, in law, a realised profit at the outset. [Principle 4]   **6.57**

The effect on a public company

There are no additional considerations for a public company.   **6.58**

Example 5 – Convertible debt

Under the relevant standards, an issuer of debt convertible into the issuer's own equity shares will use split accounting (see assumptions in 6.6A to 6.6C above). That is, part of the issue proceeds are recognised as a liability, with the balance recognised directly in equity at the date the convertible debt is issued, being the component deemed to relate to the written option to issue own equity shares (the equity conversion option). There is a correspondingly higher interest charge over the life of the debt because of the need also to charge the increase in the recorded amount of the liability as interest. That additional interest is an accounting loss but is not, as a matter of law, a loss. [Principle 5]   **6.59**

The initial credit to equity is not a profit but as the liability component is fully reflected in the accounts, it offsets the additional interest charge. [Principle 5]   **6.60**

The effect on a public company

There are no additional considerations for a public company. [Principle 10]   **6.61**

Example 6 – Preference shares presented as liabilities

Where a company issues a class of preference shares that are redeemable at a specified date, or at the holders' option, and the dividends on the shares are non-discretionary and cumulative, IAS 32/FRS 25 requires that the company classifies this class of shares as a liability (ie debt). Under IAS 39/FRS 26, the liability has to be carried at inception at its fair value, which will be the sum of the nominal value of the shares and any associated   **6.62** share premium where the shares have been issued at fair value. Over the life of the shares the non-discretionary dividend is accrued between each payment date and is presented in profit or loss as an 'interest charge'. A dividend when paid is set against the accrued liability.

6.63   To the extent that the preference shares are to be redeemed contractually at a premium, the liability will need to be accreted over time such that by redemption the carrying amount of the liability is equal to the redemption price. The accretion of the redemption premium attributable to an accounting period will be presented together with the accrued dividend as the 'interest charge' for that period in profit or loss.

6.64   The presentation of the nominal value of, and any share premium associated with, the preference shares as debt has no effect on the determination of the company's realised profits and losses.

6.65   The accrued preference dividend (and any accrued redemption premium) that is presented as an 'interest charge', and thus an accounting loss, is, as a matter of law, a distribution at the time of its making and not a loss. Thus such accruals do not affect the company's realised profits. [Principles 1, 2 and 3]

The effect on a public company

6.66   For a public company, the presentation of preference shares (ie the nominal value and any associated share premium) as debt does not result in an immediate restriction in the amount of profits available for distribution by a public company under section 831. [Principle 7]

6.67   Nevertheless, the effect of the accounting for the dividends (and any redemption premium) on the preference shares should be considered. The accounting liability recognised for the accrued unpaid preference dividend (and any redemption premium) is an advance recognition for accounting purposes of the eventual distribution (and/or capital repayment) and thus does not consume distributable profits until it is actually made as a distribution (or capital repayment). [Principle 3] However, profits available for distribution by a public company under section 831 will be restricted due to the reduction in net assets. [Principle 8]

Combining the accounting and statutory capital maintenance entries to complete the redemption

6.68   When payment is made to redeem the preference shares, it is for accounting purposes, set against the debt.

6.69   However, at redemption the law requires the following, where the redemption is made out of distributable profits:

- the nominal value of the redeemed shares is added to the capital redemption reserve; and
- the redemption price consumes distributable profits equal to its amount.

6.70   Therefore to reconcile these positions, the nominal value of the redeemed shares should be credited to the capital redemption reserve. Any share premium on the original issue of the shares now being redeemed should be credited to share premium account in equity at the date of redemption. The sum of the amounts added to the capital redemption reserve and added to share premium account is applied against retained earnings; this sum combined with the accumulated 'interest charge' in respect of any redemption premium (which has built up in retained earnings over time) is equal to the amount of the redemption price that the law recognises as consuming distributable profits. As established earlier, the debit that builds up over time in retained earnings in respect of the redemption premium is the advance recognition of part of the redemption price and is disregarded as to its effect on distributable profits until the actual redemption takes place. [Principle 3]

Example 7 – Mandatorily redeemable preference shares

Under IAS 32/FRS 25, an issuer of mandatorily redeemable preference shares, which bear non-cumulative discretionary dividends, has a compound instrument and has to use split accounting (see assumptions in 6.6A to 6.6C above). That is, the standards require the company to set up a liability, at the outset, for the present value of the payment to be made on redemption of the shares. This will take into account any contractual premium to be paid on redemption. The difference between the proceeds received on issue of the shares and the net present value of the redemption amount is credited (or debited) directly to equity at the outset. Over time the (discounted) liability is accreted up to the contracted redemption price, with a corresponding 'interest charge' being expensed in profit or loss. **6.71**

As a matter of law, all of the nominal value and any associated share premium of the preference shares are share capital and share premium irrespective of where they may now be presented in the balance sheet. Consequently, the initial credit to equity is share capital/ share premium, albeit that it is the only part that is allowed by the relevant accounting standard to be shown as such, and is not a profit. The presentation of shares partly within liabilities and partly within equity has no effect on the determination of the company's realised profits and losses. **6.72**

The interest expense from the accretion up to the full amount of the redemption price is, however, presented as an accounting loss – it is shown as an 'interest charge'. Since the ultimate payment is either a distribution or a capital repayment, the interest charge is, as a matter of law, not a loss even though it is accounted for as if it were a loss. [Principle 2] **6.73**

The effect on a public company

For a public company, the effect of this IAS 32/FRS 25 accounting is to restrict the maximum amount of profits available for distribution over time by the amount of the cumulative accruals for the redemption price. [Principle 10] **6.74**

Combining the accounting and statutory capital maintenance entries to complete the redemption

For IAS 32/FRS 25 purposes, the payment to redeem the shares is set against the fully accreted liability. **6.75**

However, at redemption the law requires the following, where the redemption is made out of distributable profits: **6.76**

- no amount remains recorded in called-up share capital for the redeemed shares;
- the nominal value of the redeemed shares is added to the capital redemption reserve; and
- the redemption price consumes distributable profits equal to its amount.

Therefore to reconcile these positions, the nominal value of the redeemed shares should be credited to the capital redemption reserve in equity and the corresponding amount for this entry is used to eliminate the original credit to equity to the extent recorded as share **6.77** capital (which is now cancelled share capital). Any share premium on the original issue of the shares now being redeemed, if hitherto presented as part of the liability, should be credited to share premium account in equity at the date of redemption. The sum of the amount added to the capital redemption reserve, but not used to make a corresponding elimination of the original credit to share capital, and that added to share premium account is applied against retained earnings; this sum, combined with the accumulated 'interest charge' in respect of any redemption premium (which has built up in retained earnings over time) is equal to the amount of the redemption price that the law recognises as consuming distributable profits. As established earlier, the 'interest charge' debit in retained earnings is the advance recognition of part of the redemption price and has no effect on cumulative realised profits until the actual redemption takes place.

Example 8 – Convertible redeemable preference shares

6.78   Under IAS 32/FRS 25, convertible redeemable preference shares are a compound instrument and an issuer of such instruments will use split accounting (see assumptions in 6.6A to 6.6C above). This is similar to debt convertible into an issuer's own equity instruments as described in 6.59 *et seq* above. That is, a liability is recognised for the debt component and a credit is recognised in equity for the equity component (the equity conversion option). However, the analysis for distributable profits purposes is more akin to that for the mandatorily redeemable shares with discretionary dividends described in 6.71 *et seq* above. This is because the initial credit to equity is share capital (and share premium).

6.79   It is assumed that the preference shares are convertible at any time by the holder into ordinary shares of the issuer and are mandatorily redeemed at the end of their term if not converted. The conversion feature cannot be settled other than by an exchange of the preference shares for a fixed number of the issuer's ordinary shares.

6.80   The presentation of the shares (inclusive of their share premium) as partly debt and partly as a credit in equity has no effect on the determination of realised profits and losses.

6.81   Any accrued unpaid preference dividends and the accretion up to the full amount of the redemption price, although presented as accounting losses through the profit and loss account, are disregarded in determining whether distributable profits have been consumed until their actual payment. [Principle 6]

The effect on a public company

6.82   At the outset there is no effect on distributable profits [Principle 9]. There will be a restriction for a public company on the maximum amount of profits available for distribution over time by the amount of the cumulative accruals for the redemption price. [Principle 10]

Combining the accounting and statutory capital maintenance entries where the shares are redeemed

6.83   The same analysis applies as given in 6.71 *et seq* in respect of the mandatorily redeemable preference shares with discretionary dividends.

Combining the accounting and statutory capital maintenance entries where the shares are converted

6.84   Under IAS 32/FRS 25, when the holders exercise their option to convert the preference shares into the issuer's ordinary shares, the amount of the liability at conversion is transferred to equity.

However, to establish the impact on profits available for distribution it is necessary to re-analyse the aggregate entries in equity to establish the amounts that represent: **6.85**

- the nominal value of the ordinary shares issued on conversion;
- the relevant amount of share premium to be included in the share premium account; and
- the elimination of the 'interest charge' debit in retained earnings.

This is achieved at conversion by crediting to retained earnings an amount equal to the accumulated 'interest charge' in respect of accrued unpaid dividends and accretion to the issue price of the shares from the amount transferred from liabilities to equity. The aggregate of the balance of the transfer to equity and the initial credit to equity is equal to the total of the nominal value and share premium attributable to the ordinary shares issued on conversion. **6.86**

The allocation of part of the transfer from liabilities equal to the accrued 'interest charge' effectively reverses the 'interest charge' accounting entries. At law the debit accounting entries had not consumed distributable profits and therefore the effective reversal of these entries has no effect on the quantum of distributable profits. However, for public companies, the effective reversal of the 'interest charge' debit at conversion removes the restriction under the section 831 net assets test. **6.87**

7. EMPLOYEE SHARE SCHEMES

ESOP trusts

Introduction

Paragraphs 7.4 to 7.45 are concerned with the effect of a company's sponsorship of a trust (ESOP trust) that holds shares in the company, which may be delivered to the company's employees under an employee share scheme. This differs from the case of the direct holding of a company's own shares (treasury shares) which are addressed at paragraphs 2.40 to 2.43 above. **7.1**

The practice of employing ESOP trusts evolved partly because of restrictions on a company acquiring its own shares (s658) or acquiring shares in its parent company (section 136). These restrictions were eased from 1 December 2003 when certain companies were permitted, subject to some restrictions, to hold their own shares as treasury shares (see above). The use of ESOP trusts has, however, remained widespread. **7.2**

The provision of funds by a company to an ESOP trust to enable it to buy shares in the company or its parent company will generally fall within the definition of financial assistance for the acquisition of own shares (section 677). Such assistance is generally prohibited, subject to certain exceptions, for a public company or a subsidiary of a public company (section 678). Under the 1985 Act, similar restrictions applied to all companies until 1 October 2008. However, one of the exceptions to the general rules in section 682(2)(b) is 'the provision by the company, in good faith in the interests of the company or its holding company, of financial assistance for the purposes of an employee's share scheme'. **7.2A**

That exception is subject to a restriction in section 682(1) that the financial assistance may only be given if the company has net assets which are not thereby reduced, or to the extent that those assets are thereby reduced, the financial assistance is provided out of distributable profits. Although paragraphs 7.25 to 7.31 address the interaction of this restriction with the accounting for ESOP trusts, the general question of the lawfulness of financial assistance is not within the scope of this guidance and accordingly directors may wish to consider seeking legal advice. **7.3**

ESOP trusts under UK GAAP

7.4   Under UK GAAP, UITF Abstract 38 'Accounting for ESOP trusts' requires the sponsoring company of an ESOP trust to recognise the assets and liabilities of the trust in its own accounts whenever it had de facto control of those assets and liabilities. Where the trust purchases the company's own shares, the consideration paid for those shares should be deducted in equity until such time as the shares vest unconditionally in the company's employees. The effect of this deduction, which occurs in the individual accounts of the sponsoring company and not merely on consolidation, is considered below.

7.5   The sponsoring company of an ESOP trust may be a company other than the one whose shares are held by the trust. For example, a subsidiary may be the sponsoring company of an ESOP trust that holds shares in its parent. In this case the shares will not be 'own shares' from the perspective of the subsidiary's financial statements. The shares would be recognised as an asset in the subsidiary's balance sheet and the issues addressed in this guidance would not arise.

ESOP trusts under IFRSs

7.6   The guidance set out below in relation to investments in own shares held through an ESOP trust will be relevant to companies reporting under IFRSs if they account for investments in own shares in their individual balance sheets in a manner similar to that required by UITF Abstract 38. However, published literature suggests that a different accounting treatment may be permitted in individual accounts under IFRSs. Whereas UITF Abstract 38 requires the assets and liabilities of the trust to be included in the individual balance sheet of the sponsoring company, under IFRSs it may be acceptable to account for the ESOP trust as an investment in a subsidiary. The IFRS Interpretations Committee was asked to address the question of which of these treatments is appropriate but declined to do so on the basis that it would be unable to reach a consensus on a timely basis given the different types of trusts and arrangements that exist in practice (see IFRIC Update, November 2006, for further details).

7.7   Where the ESOP trust is accounted for as a subsidiary, any loans to the trust by the sponsoring company, to the extent that they are regarded as recoverable, may therefore be recognised as assets in the individual balance sheet of the sponsoring company even though they have been used to finance an investment in own shares by the trust. If it is necessary to write the loan down for impairment at any time then that write down will represent a realised loss. The guidance set out below concerning the effects of a deduction within equity is not relevant when the loan is recognised as an asset because the deduction within equity will arise only in the consolidated financial statements

Note of legal considerations attached to Abstract 38

7.8   A note of legal considerations attached to Abstract 38 sets out legal advice that the UITF received on the implications for distributable profits when the accounting treatment required by the Abstract is followed. The note of legal considerations is reproduced in Appendix 3 to this guidance for reference. This guidance is consistent with that note of legal considerations but additionally addresses some issues that were not covered in that note as well as considering some issues in greater depth.

7.8A   The note of legal considerations attached to UITF Abstract 38 states that although the acquisition of shares by an ESOP trust will not, of itself, result in a realised profit or loss for the company concerned, 'a company will still need to consider other transactions with the ESOP, for example a loan to the ESOP to fund acquisitions of shares, and these may affect the company's realised profits and losses'. The reference to a loan to the

ESOP might be read as implying that realised profits and losses should be determined by reference to 'narrow entity accounting' (see 7.14 below). However, this is not the case; the UITF Abstract 38 note refers to the existence of a loan as only one of a number of factors that might be relevant. The assessment of realised profits and losses for the justification of a distribution is by reference to a company's 'relevant accounts' and, as explained in paragraph 7.14 this means by reference to 'extended entity accounting'. However, see 7.25 to 7.31 regarding financial assistance by a public company.

Effect of deduction within equity on realised profits

A purchase of a company's own shares though an ESOP trust is not a distribution at law. This is because, at law, the shares have been purchased by the trust, notwithstanding that assistance may have been given by the company (by way of gift or loan, some or all of which may be ultimately irrecoverable, or by guarantee of the trust's borrowings that may ultimately be called upon to some extent). See 7.25 to 7.31 below for regulation of the transaction for a public company as financial assistance.   **7.9**

Neither does such a purchase, of itself, give rise to an immediate realised loss. Therefore, such an acquisition does not reduce the amount of profits available for distribution under section 830.   **7.10**

In addition, whilst the acquisition of shares will not, of itself, give rise to an immediate realised loss, the impact of other factors such as the granting of rights over those shares should be considered (see 7.37 to 7.41 below).   **7.11**

Effect on section 831 restriction on purchase of own shares for a public company

The consideration paid on the purchase of shares by an ESOP trust sponsored by a public company will immediately restrict the profits available for distribution by virtue of section 831 by the amount of the consideration paid. As more fully explained below, there will be an immediate reduction in net assets but no change in share capital or undistributable reserves.   **7.12**

A public company may only make a distribution at any time: **7.13**

(a)   if at that time the amount of its net assets is not less than the aggregate of its called-up share capital and undistributable reserves; and

(b)   if, and to the extent that, the distribution does not reduce the amount of those assets to less than that aggregate.

Change in net assets

Section 831 states that 'net assets' means the aggregate of the company's assets less the aggregate of its liabilities. Under section 836, net assets are those as shown in the company's 'relevant accounts' which are normally the last annual accounts under Part 15 of the Act, properly prepared under the Act; in certain circumstances, the relevant accounts are initial accounts or interim accounts, which are prepared to a similar standard. Net assets for the purposes of section 831 should therefore be determined in accordance with accounting standards and UITF Abstracts. Accordingly, the relevant accounts and the net assets should include the assets and liabilities of the ESOP trust as reported under Abstract 38 ('extended entity accounting') rather than, for example, any loan between the company and the ESOP trust ('narrow entity accounting').   **7.14**

The effect of the accounting treatment required by Abstract 38 is that, in drawing up the relevant accounts, any own shares held by an ESOP would be recorded as a deduction in   **7.15** arriving at shareholders' funds rather than as an asset. Therefore, it follows that the relevant aggregate net asset amount for the purposes of the definition in section 831(2) would be reduced by the own shares held (being the consideration paid for the shares).

7.16   Disclosure by way of note that the company also has an 'asset' of own shares held through an ESOP trust would not restore the net assets for the purposes of section 831 (see 2.14 above). If the shares are not an asset for accounting purposes they cannot be an asset for the purposes of calculating net assets when applying section 831.

Change in share capital or undistributable reserves

7.17   A company's undistributable reserves are defined in section 831. In short, they include the company's unrealised profits less its unrealised losses, except that this amount is never less than zero (ie net unrealised losses are not within the definition).

7.18   The correct characterisation, as a matter of law, of the deduction in equity is not straightforward. On the one hand the deduction should not be characterised as a loss at all (thereby rendering redundant questions of realisation) because from the point of view of the company's individual accounts (which are on an extended entity basis) the company has not lost control of the shares nor have these shares suffered any objectively measurable diminution in value. On the other hand, given that the applicable accounting treatment does not permit the company to treat the shares as an asset, some might argue that the deduction should be categorised as a loss, although the nearest equivalent could be said to be a return of capital. The characterisation which gives primacy to the substance rather than presentation is the view to be preferred and accordingly the deduction should not be characterised as a loss.

7.19   Accordingly, the deduction for own shares in equity is neither a realised loss nor an unrealised loss and does not affect the balance of undistributable reserves.

The effect on profits available for distribution under section 831

7.20   Thus with net assets reduced but share capital and undistributable reserves unaffected, the purchase of ESOP shares affects the maximum distribution permissible by virtue of the application of section 831 (the 'maximum distribution permissible'). In other words, the effect of the section is such that the profits available for distribution are restricted by a reduction in net assets that is neither a realised nor an unrealised loss.

7.21   Furthermore, the existence of any unrealised profits does not alter this situation (e.g., such unrealised profits cannot be applied to offset the deduction, because the deduction is not an unrealised loss).

Effect on section 831 restriction on subscription for own shares for a public company

7.22   A subscription for new shares in a public company by its own sponsored ESOP trust will immediately restrict the maximum distribution permissible.

7.23   The application of section 831 is considered above. In the case of a subscription for new shares, there is no change in net assets. This is because the cash subscribed for the shares by the ESOP trust is recorded in the balance sheet of the sponsoring company both before and after the subscription in accordance with Abstract 38.

7.24   However, the amount of the company's called-up share capital is increased by the nominal value of the shares issued to the trust. The amount of the company's undistributable reserves is also increased to the extent of any share premium arising on the issue, for example where the ESOP trusts subscribes for the shares at market value which is at a premium to nominal value. There is no other effect of the subscription on undistributable reserves as defined in section 831. Consequently, any excess of the company's net assets over the aggregate amount of the company's called-up share capital and undistributable reserves is reduced and hence the amount of the company's maximum distribution permissible is restricted by the amount attributable to the share issue (ie the proceeds of subscription for the shares by the trust).

The effect of the financial assistance rules in relation to a public company

Assuming that the relevant assistance is permitted by virtue of section 682(2), in the case of a public company the assistance can only be given if the company has net assets which are not thereby reduced or, to the extent that those assets are thereby reduced, if the assistance is provided out of distributable profits. **7.25**

Net assets

For the purposes of section 682, 'net assets' are defined as the amount by which the aggregate of the company's assets exceeds the aggregate of its liabilities, taking the amount of both its assets and liabilities to be as stated in the company's accounting records immediately before the financial assistance is given. This is in contrast to section 831 where, by reason of section 836, net assets are the aggregate of the company's assets less the aggregate of its liabilities as shown in the company's relevant accounts. **7.26**

Section 386 imposes a duty to keep accounting records which are sufficient to show and explain the company's transactions and to enable the directors to ensure that any balance sheet and profit and loss account prepared under Part 15 of the Act complies with the requirements of the Act. Thus the records must at least be consistent with accounting standards and interpretations by the UITF or the IFRS Interpretations Committee as the case may be. However, this does not impose an obligation to maintain the entries in the accounting records fully in accordance with accounting standards and interpretations provided that it is evident from those records how to make suitable adjustments to prepare accounts in accordance with the requirements of the Act. Accordingly, section 386 does not require net assets for the purposes of section 682 to be determined by reference to 'extended entity accounting' (as described at 7.14 above). **7.27**

Thus, in the absence of any such requirement, the company's assets and liabilities should be given their natural meaning, namely the assets and liabilities of the company as a legal person. In other words, the 'narrow entity accounting' basis is used for determining the net asset position of the company concerned and whether the financial assistance has reduced the company's net assets[26]. There is thus in this respect no change to the assessment of a company's net asset position as a result of applying Abstract 38. **7.28**

The effect of section 831 where financial assistance is provided out of distributable profits.

Where a company has provided financial assistance out of distributable profits which has reduced its net assets and shares have been acquired by an ESOP trust, section 831 does not require a further restriction in the maximum distribution permissible equal to the amount of the reduction in net assets calculated under section 682. **7.29**

---

[26] *More generally, the presentation of shares as liabilities reduces net assets as defined in section 682 for the purposes of financial assistance. The legislation refers to amounts stated in the accounting records rather than in the 'relevant accounts' because the test is a 'real time' one. However, subject to the use of 'narrow entity accounting' as described above, net assets as defined in section 682 for the purposes of financial assistance should generally be the same as net assets as defined in section 831 for the purposes of distributions by a public company. That is, the relevant shares should be treated as liabilities to creditors.*

7.30   Section 682 and section 831 are directed to different objectives. Section 682 determines the legality of the provision of financial assistance tested on a narrow entity basis. Section 831 determines the maximum distribution permissible tested on an extended entity basis. On the extended entity basis the assistance provided to the ESOP trust will not be treated as having been paid away until the shares are purchased at which point the net assets are reduced by the consideration paid for the shares (as described at 7.12 to 7.21 above).

7.31   Section 840 contains accumulation rules where distributions are proposed by reference to particular accounts and prior distributions have taken place. Section 840(2) makes it clear that financial assistance which is given out of distributable profits is taken into account in the accumulation rules. These rules continue to apply.

7.32   [Deleted]

Purchase by an ESOP trust of shares held as treasury shares by a listed public company

7.33   A purchase of treasury shares by an ESOP trust for cash will be a sale of treasury shares for cash for the purposes of section 731 (see paragraph 7.34 below). The proceeds will therefore increase distributable profits up to an amount equal to the original purchase price of the shares (ie reversing the decrease that would have occurred at the time of purchase of the treasury shares). Any excess will be credited to share premium. At the same time, the former treasury shares, now shares held by the ESOP trust, will be accounted for and treated for distributable profit purposes just as if they had been purchased at the same price from a third party, ie the entire consideration paid by the ESOP trust restricts the amount of profits available for distribution (see 7.12 to 7.31 above).

7.34   Section 727(1) states that where shares are held as treasury shares, a company may at any time '(a) sell the shares… for a cash consideration or (b) transfer the shares … for the purposes of or pursuant to an employees' shares scheme'. Section 729(1) states that where shares are held as treasury shares the company may at any time 'cancel the shares'. Section 731 deals with the treatment of the proceeds when shares 'are sold' and requires any excess over the purchase price to be credited to share premium, with the remainder to replenish distributable profits. No treatment is otherwise specified for the proceeds when shares are 'transferred' to an employee share scheme in accordance with section 727(1)(b). Section 731 does not apply exclusively to sales falling solely within section 727(1)(a) but applies to any sale of treasury shares to an ESOP trust notwithstanding that the sale might also be a transfer under section 727(1)(b).

7.35   The requirement in section 731 to transfer an amount to share premium when shares are sold for more than their purchase price applies only to treasury shares. Such a transfer is not required, or permitted, when shares held by an ESOP trust are sold in comparable circumstances. Whether or not the resulting surplus in the trust is a distributable profit from the perspective of the company is addressed at 7.42 to 7.45 below.

Effect on distributable profits for a public company when proceeds are received for sale of shares by an ESOP trust

7.36   In the case of a public company, the initial acquisition of the ESOP shares would have an immediate effect on distributable profits under section 831 because net assets were reduced without a corresponding reduction in share capital and undistributable reserves (see 7.12 to 7.21 above). However, if option holders then subscribe for the shares or the shares are sold in the market, the receipt of proceeds gives rise to an accounting entry (debit cash, credit shareholders' funds) that reverses the situation and restores distributable profits to the extent of those proceeds. That is, net assets are increased for the purposes of section 831 but there is no corresponding increase in share capital and undistributable reserves.

Realised loss when shares held by an ESOP trust are transferred to employees – where shares originally acquired externally

The purchase of shares by an ESOP trust does not, of itself, give rise to a realised loss (see 7.10 above) and, other than in the case of a public company, does not otherwise immediately affect the distribution of available profits. However, it is clear that if the shares are to be transferred to employees for less than their purchase price, the shortfall will at some time fall to be treated as a realised loss. In some cases options may be granted with an exercise price that is lower than the price at which the shares were purchased. In other cases shares may be transferred to employees for no consideration on the achievement of specified performance or service conditions. In all such cases, the difference between the purchase price of the shares and the proceeds received or receivable from the employee should be regarded as becoming a realised loss over the relevant amortisation or charging period as would be the case with a cash bonus that was contingent on future service.   **7.37**

[Deleted]   **7.38**

Where options have been granted over the shares in question but those options are 'out-of-the-money' or where there are 'surplus' shares that have not been allocated to any particular share scheme, a realised loss may also arise if the market value of the shares falls below their purchase price. A realised loss will have arisen to the extent that the fall in market price below cost is not expected to be reversed and thus that part of the cost incurred is not expected to be recovered.   **7.39**

[Moved to 7.8A]   **7.40**

Realised loss when shares held by an ESOP trust are transferred to employees – where shares originally subscribed

The subscription for shares by an ESOP trust does not, of itself, give rise to a realised loss (see 7.10 above) and, other than in the case of a public company, does not otherwise immediately affect the distribution of available profits. However, as in the case of a purchase of shares described at 7.37 to 7.39 above, a realised loss may arise if the shares are subsequently transferred to employees for less than their subscription price. In all such cases, the difference between the subscription price of the shares and the proceeds received from the employee should be regarded as becoming a realised loss over the relevant amortisation or charging period.   **7.41**

Whether a surplus on disposal of shares by an ESOP trust is a realised and distributable profit from the perspective of the sponsoring company

As explained at 7.44, a surplus on disposal of shares held by an ESOP trust is a realised profit. However, in respect of it being distributable, the directors should have regard to their wider common law duties as required by sections 851 and 852. As explained at 7.45, the profit therefore may not become distributable until some time in the future.   **7.42**

Under Abstract 38, a sponsoring company includes the assets, liabilities and transactions of its ESOP trust in its accounts as if the trust were a division or branch of the company. This is therefore not just a matter of including the trust in consolidated accounts. The assets, liabilities and transactions of the trust are included in the company's individual accounts. These are the 'relevant accounts' for the purposes of determining profits available for   **7.43** distribution. Where the trust has a surplus in the equivalent of its profit and loss account, the question arises of whether this should be reflected in the calculation of the company's realised profits.

7.44   Where the trust has a surplus (e.g. from the sale of shares at more than their purchase price), it is arguable that, just as a parent would not treat a surplus in a subsidiary as a realised profit in its own individual accounts, the parent should not regard the surplus in the trust as increasing its realised profits. But there is a clear difference in that Abstract 38 requires the assets and liabilities of the trust to be included in the company's own individual accounts. Also, Abstract 13, which was superseded by Abstract 38 and required own shares to be recognised as assets, made no mention of any legal difficulties about including any 'profits' of the trust in the company's profit and loss account. Under Abstract 38, no such profits arise to be included in the company's profit and loss account but the issue is still relevant to the determination of the company's realised profits. Where the consideration received by the trust for the sale of the shares is in the form of cash (or other 'qualifying consideration') that will be included in the company's balance sheet in accordance with the requirements of Abstract 38, the profit will be a realised profit from the company's perspective.

7.45   However, the directors should have regard to their wider common law duties as required by sections 851 and 852 (see 2.1 above). It would not be regarded as prudent to distribute an amount that represents assets that are retained in the ESOP trust and therefore not available for the general purposes of the company. If the assets of the trust are used in future to meet an expense, an equivalent amount of the gain should at that time be treated as distributable. Therefore to the extent that the realised loss arising from the expense does not exceed the previously recognised gain that was treated as undistributable, there will be no reduction in distributable profits.

Expenses for share based payments required by IFRS 2 and FRS 20

7.46   IFRS 2 (and FRS 20) require expenses to be recognised in profit or loss for cash-settled share-based payment arrangements. The credit entry will be either a cash payment or a provision. The expense recognised will therefore be a realised loss. The paragraphs which follow are concerned with equity-settled arrangements.

7.47   IFRS 2 (and FRS 20) require expenses to be recognised in profit or loss for equity-settled share-based payment arrangements. The standard requires the credit entry arising from recognition of this expense to be credited within equity but does not specify any particular component of equity.

7.48   Any expense recognised in accordance with IFRS 2 will be a realised loss. This follows from the principle that all losses should be regarded as realised losses except to the extent that the law, accounting standards or this guidance provide otherwise (see 3.10 above). However, the overall impact of the IFRS 2 expense on distributable profits will depend on the status of the credit entry in equity.

7.49   If the consideration for an issue of shares is, as a matter of law, the provision of goods or services to the company, it will be necessary to credit share capital and share premium with the fair value of those goods or services. Similarly, if shares are, as a matter of law, issued in settlement of a monetary liability, it will be necessary to credit share capital and share premium with the amount of the liability discharged. Where this is so, the credit entry to equity required by IFRS 2 cannot be a realised profit.

In the case of share options, the note of legal considerations appended to UITF Abstract 17 (now superseded by FRS 20) provided the following guidance[27]. **7.50**

> "The UITF has received legal advice on the implications for share premium account when the accounting treatment required by this Abstract is followed. It has been advised that where new shares are issued in connection with an employee share scheme the share premium account will normally have to reflect only the cash subscribed for the shares (e.g. by the employee or by an ESOP). In such cases, any difference between the cash subscribed for the shares (which must be at least as much as the nominal value, as shares cannot be issued at a discount) and the fair value at the date of grant of rights should be credited to reserves other than the share premium account. This is on the basis that the services of the employee do not, as a matter of law, form part of the consideration received for the shares issued, and the UITF has been advised that this would be the usual legal interpretation of such transactions. Exceptionally, however, the terms of a transaction might be such as to lead to the opposite interpretation, and companies may need to take legal advice on this point. In such a case, the operation of section 99(2) of the Companies Act 1985 [now section 585(1) of the Companies Act 2006] [prohibition of public company accepting undertaking to perform services in payment up of its shares] and section 103 [now section 593 of the Companies Act 2006] [non-cash consideration to be valued before allotment of shares] would also have to be considered."

However, the arrangements referred to in the last two sentences of the quoted paragraph are not typical. Instead, for example, in the case of share options, the credit to equity required by IFRS 2 will usually be a credit to reserves other than share premium account.

The note of legal considerations does not, however, address whether the credit to equity in the case of options to subscribe for shares is a realised profit. However, an unrealised reserve will be treated as having become realised by the amortisation or writing down of the related asset (see 3.9(f) above). Therefore, assuming that the IFRS 2 expense has been included in profit or loss (which would be the case except where the charge had been capitalised as part of the cost of production of an asset) the credit entry in equity will be a realised profit. The IFRS 2 expense will therefore have no net effect on distributable profits. **7.51**

The manner of settlement (e.g. subscription for new shares or purchase of shares in the market by an ESOP trust) does not affect the expense recognised under IFRS 2 or whether this is a realised loss. However, it will be necessary to consider the effect on realised profits arising from any shares held by an ESOP trust (see 7.37 to 7.41 above). **7.52**

Intra-group recharges for share-based payments

In November 2006, the IFRS Interpretations Committee issued IFRIC 11 'IFRS 2 – Group and Treasury Share Transactions' which has subsequently been incorporated into IFRS 2. The Exposure Draft upon which this was based (IFRIC D17) included some material on the treatment of inter-company recharges made within groups in connection with share-based payment arrangements. The IFRS Interpretations Committee decided not to address these issues in IFRIC 11 because it did not wish to widen the scope of the Interpretation to an issue that relates to accounting for intra-group payments generally. The appropriate accounting for such recharges is thus a matter of developing practice, including that in some cases the treatment that was set out in the draft guidance in IFRIC D17, described below, may be appropriate. **7.53**

---

[27] *The equivalent 2006 Act references have been added to the original note for ease of reference.*

7.54   The situation in question is one in which the company, being a subsidiary, makes a cash payment to its parent in relation to a share-based payment in favour of the company's own employees and where IFRS 2 requires an equity-settled share-based payment charge in the company's accounts. The proposals in IFRIC D17 envisaged that where a charge is made by the parent to the subsidiary which exceeds the expense that the subsidiary is required to recognise under IFRS 2, the excess is accounted for by the subsidiary as a distribution. For example, this may arise if a charge is made on the basis of intrinsic value at exercise date which will generally be higher than the grant date fair value recognised as an expense in accordance with IFRS 2. The accounting treatment of any such charge does not affect whether or not it is a distribution as a matter of law. In particular, if there is a commercial basis for such a charge, it will not be a distribution as a matter of law. An example of a commercial basis would be the expense that the subsidiary would have incurred if it had purchased shares in the market to satisfy the options. Consequently, it will not be unlawful for the subsidiary to make the reimbursement payment, even in the absence of distributable profits, provided that the payment is not a distribution as a matter of law.

7.55   However, the entire reimbursement payment will have the effect of reducing accumulated realised profits or increasing accumulated realised losses of the subsidiary. The debit to equity arising from the payment will first reduce the credit in equity arising from IFRS 2 which will no longer be available to offset the realised loss recognised as a result of the IFRS 2 expense. Any debit to equity in excess of this amount will be a realised loss even though it will not have been accounted for as a loss in the financial statements.

7.56   A liability may be recognised by the subsidiary where the parent has a contractual right to reimbursement at a future date. The amount of the realised loss at any date will generally be based on the amount of the liability recognised at that date but the particular facts of each case should be considered.

8. RETIREMENT BENEFIT SCHEMES

Introduction

8.1   The guidance in this section is written in terms of compliance with FRS 17 but is equally applicable when the equivalent international standard IAS 19 'Employee benefits' is being applied. When IAS 19 is being applied, the guidance should be applied to the amounts reported under that standard. For simplicity, this guidance refers throughout to the relevant requirements of FRS 17.

8.2   The guidance set out below applies both to pension schemes acquired in a business combination and those that are started by the reporting company.

Defined contribution schemes

8.3   For defined contribution retirement benefit schemes, the cost charged to the profit and loss account under FRS 17 is equal to the contributions payable to the scheme for the accounting period. The charge to the profit and loss account for the contributions payable is a realised loss.

Multi-employer schemes

8.4   Under FRS 17, some companies account for their participation in certain multi-employer defined benefit retirement benefit schemes as if they were defined contribution schemes. Where a scheme meets the criteria for this treatment in FRS 17, the position as regards realised profits and losses will be the same as for any other defined contribution scheme.

Defined benefit schemes

Summary

In summary, what is required in relation to a defined benefit scheme is to identify whether **8.5** any adjustment is required to reserves, to exclude unrealised profits, in arriving at the amount of distributable profits. To do so, it is first necessary to ascertain the cumulative amounts charged or credited in relation to the pension scheme, whether through the profit and loss account or through the statement of total recognised gains and losses (ie the total amounts taken to reserves). Paragraphs 8.11 to 8.13 determine whether that cumulative amount is realised or unrealised, with the test being different for cumulative net debits as against cumulative net credits. The cumulative net debit or credit will not be readily apparent from the accounts and so paragraphs 8.14 to 8.15 provide that it is determined from the movement in the pension scheme asset or liability on the balance sheet since inception of the scheme (ie when it is started by the company or when it was acquired in a business combination) and the cumulative net cash paid to the scheme. The cumulative cash flows may themselves be difficult to obtain and so paragraphs 8.16 to 8.17 provide a method of estimating the amounts. Paragraph 8.18 then describes some circumstances when it is possible to deduce easily, without working through these procedures, that all amounts accumulated in reserves are realised.

This calculation is unaffected by the date of adoption of FRS 17 and the accounting **8.5A** adopted previously (ie SSAP 24). A company may have established the cumulative amount in reserves for the pension scheme on adoption of FRS 17 in which case the amount can be rolled forward from year to year. However, the approach set out below will enable the position to be established at a particular date if no such calculation was performed.

General principles

It is the cumulative gain or loss credited or debited to reserves in respect of a pension **8.6** scheme, rather than the existence of a surplus or deficit, that affects the realised profits and losses of a company. This principle is illustrated in Appendix 4.

The effect of FRS 17 on reserves must be calculated to identify whether any adjustment **8.7** in respect of pensions is needed to reported reserves to arrive at realised reserves. No adjustment is required if a net cumulative loss has been taken to reserves. If a net cumulative gain has been taken to reserves, and under the guidance set out at 8.12 below that gain is in part or in full unrealised, a deduction equivalent to the unrealised element must be made to reserves in assessing the level of realised reserves.

In establishing the impact that a surplus or deficit under FRS 17 has on a company's **8.8** realised profits, it is therefore necessary to:

(a)   identify the cumulative net gain or loss taken to reserves in respect of the pension surplus or deficit; and
(b)   establish the extent to which that gain or loss is realised.

Although the various elements making up the changes in the defined benefit asset or liability **8.9** are disclosed separately in the performance statements (see paragraph 50 of FRS 17), it is the net amount that represents the cost to the company of the pension promise. Thus it is the cumulative net gain or loss taken to reserves that falls to be categorised as realised or unrealised. There is no need to distinguish that cumulative balance between amounts charged or credited in the profit and loss account and those recognised in the statement of total recognised gains and losses (STRGL). The entries in the STRGL are considered for this purpose as revisions of past estimates of the net pension cost and are not precluded from being treated as realised simply because they have passed through the STRGL rather than the profit and loss account.

8.10   The impact on reserves is not usually the same as the pension asset or liability recognised in the balance sheet. It will be different due to the net contributions paid to the scheme (see 8.15 *et seq*) and any asset or liability introduced as the result of a business combination (see 8.19 *et seq*).

8.11   A cumulative net debit in reserves in respect of the pension scheme constitutes a realised loss as it results from the creation of, or an increase in, a provision for a liability or loss resulting in an overall reduction in net assets. This follows from 2.32, 3.10 and 3.15(d) above.

8.12   A cumulative net credit in reserves in respect of the pension scheme constitutes a realised profit only to the extent that it is represented by an asset to be recovered by refunds that have been agreed by the pension scheme trustees at the balance sheet date of the relevant accounts and the refunds will take the form of qualifying consideration. This follows from 3.9(a) above which refers to 'a transaction where the consideration received by the company is 'qualifying consideration''. An asset that is recognised based on a reduction in future contributions or on expected refunds that are not agreed at the balance sheet date will not meet the definition of 'qualifying consideration'.

8.13   To the extent that a cumulative net credit in reserves exceeds any such agreed refunds it is unrealised, but it becomes realised in subsequent periods to the extent that it offsets subsequent net debits to reserves being recognised as realised losses in respect of the pension scheme (ie as the cumulative net credit reduces). This follows from 3.9(f)(iii) and (iv) above.

8.14   To establish the effect on realised profits at a particular date, a company must therefore establish the cumulative net credit or debit in reserves for the pension scheme at that date. This equals the amount of the surplus or deficit recognised before taking account of deferred tax, adjusted for:

(a)   cumulative net contributions less refunds made in respect of the pension scheme; and

(b)   in the rare cases in which the company has recognised a pension asset or liability in its individual accounts on the acquisition of an unincorporated business (in respect of the pension scheme of that business), the amount initially recognised (see 8.19 and 8.20 below).

An illustration of such a calculation is set out in Appendix 4. As explained at 8.18 below, it will often be obvious, without any calculations, that all of the amounts included in reserves arising from pension scheme accounting are realised.

8.15   Companies that are able to establish the precise amount of the cumulative net credit or debit in reserves in respect of the pension scheme will treat it as realised or unrealised in accordance with 8.11 to 8.13 above.

8.16   It may not be practicable for companies with long-established schemes to ascertain the total cumulative net contributions less refunds made since the scheme commenced, to perform with precision the analysis in 8.13 above (although, in view of their rarity, it is likely that the company would be able to identify all refunds made and these should be included in the calculation). For such schemes the estimated approach set out in this paragraph may be taken:

(a)   the calculation set out in 8.14 above may be performed initially using the amount of those cumulative net contributions the company has been able to identify; and

(b)   that calculation may be revisited subsequently, as set out in 8.17 below, if further contributions are identified that were made prior to the date of the assessment.

A company adopting the estimated approach set out at 8.16 above might be able to revise that estimate subsequently by identifying additional contributions that have been made since the scheme was established or acquired. If so, it may be able to revise upwards the amount of a net cumulative realised loss in reserves and therefore treat as realised net credits arising in subsequent periods that would otherwise be treated as unrealised.   **8.17**

It will often be obvious, without any calculations, that all of the amounts included in reserves arising from pension scheme accounting are realised. Therefore, no adjustments will be required to the amounts stated in the accounts when determining the cumulative amount of realised profits available for distribution. Other than sometimes in those rare cases where a pension asset or liability has been recognised in the company's individual accounts on a past acquisition, no adjustment is necessary if a liability is recognised in the balance sheet (ie because the net cumulative contributions cannot be negative). Where a pension asset is recognised in the balance sheet, it is only necessary to determine that the cumulative net contributions exceed this amount to be able to confirm that no adjustment is necessary. The calculations are more complex when a past acquisition is involved.   **8.18**

Acquisition of an unincorporated business

Where part of a company's pension asset or liability arose on the acquisition of an unincorporated business, it will have been recorded initially at fair value as required by FRS 7. That initial asset or liability will not have affected the company's reserves directly and must therefore be taken into account as part of the adjustment in arriving at the impact of FRS 17 on reserves.   **8.19**

FRS 17 did not change the requirement of FRS 7 to record the pension asset or liability at fair value, although it may have required fair value to be measured using a different method from that used when the acquisition was first recorded. FRS 17 paragraph 97 notes that any difference between the FRS 17 measure of fair value and that originally used 'should be treated as a change in assumptions (ie an actuarial gain or loss) arising since acquisition'. Such a difference will therefore have given rise to a gain or loss that falls to be categorised as realised or unrealised in accordance with the general approach noted above. As a result, it is the asset or liability recognised initially as part of the acquisition accounting that is taken into account (together with the net contributions paid since acquisition) in assessing the reserves position under FRS 17.   **8.20**

An actuarial gain arising from a reduction of a pension liability that was assumed in a business combination will result is an unrealised profit to the extent that it is not a reversal of post-acquisition pension expense. That is because such a reduction in a pension liability is not readily convertible to cash (see 3.9(g) and 3.9B).   **8.20A**

Deferred tax

The deferred tax asset or liability arising from different treatments of pension costs for accounting and tax purposes generally relates to the pension asset or liability in the balance sheet and is not necessarily associated with the cumulative net debit or credit in reserves.   **8.21**

The cumulative debit in reserves in respect of a deferred tax liability relating to a pension asset should be treated as a realised loss. However, to the extent that there is an unrealised cumulative net credit in reserves in respect of the pension asset, then the amount of the debit in respect of deferred tax should be treated as a reduction in that unrealised profit   **8.22** rather than as a realised loss. It is not necessary to restrict the offset by applying the tax rate to the amount of the unrealised profit.

8.23   The cumulative credit in reserves in respect of a deferred tax asset relating to a pension liability should be treated as an unrealised profit. However, to the extent that there is a realised cumulative net debit in reserves in respect of the pension liability, then the amount of the credit in respect of deferred tax should be treated as a reduction in that realised loss rather than as an unrealised profit. It is not necessary to restrict the offset by applying the tax rate to the amount of the realised loss.

8.24   The approach set out above is consistent with 3.17 above.

Companies with more than one scheme

8.25   This guidance assumes the company has only one scheme. A company that operates more than one defined benefit scheme should assess separately for each scheme the impact of an FRS 17 asset or liability on its realised profits and losses. However, there may be situations where two schemes are to merge. In such situations a company may treat any net credit to reserves that has been recorded in respect of one scheme as a reduction in the realised loss caused by a net debit in respect of the other scheme from the point at which the trustees of the schemes have irrevocably agreed that they will merge and to extent that the surplus and deficit are permitted to be offset for funding purposes. A similar argument applies in cases where a transfer has been irrevocably agreed between different schemes.

8.26   A company that operates more than one defined benefit scheme may find that it can follow 8.11 to 8.13 above for schemes formed or acquired in an acquisition of an unincorporated business relatively recently but may need to follow 8.16 above for schemes operated by the company for a longer time. This guidance does not preclude such a mixed approach.

9. INTRA-GROUP TRANSACTIONS

Introduction

9.1   Under both common law and statute, distributions are made by companies and not by groups. The group accounts are therefore not relevant for the purpose of determining realisation or distributability; for example, realised profits which are reflected in a parent's[28] own accounts may be eliminated in the group accounts, and profits retained by subsidiaries are not distributable by the parent.

9.2   The ability of a parent to control the actions of its subsidiary must also be borne in mind when considering the substance of an intra-group transaction carried out by or with that subsidiary.

9.3   It is not practicable to attempt to illustrate every circumstance in which difficulties may arise in determining whether a profit is realised. The principles set out in this guidance should be applied in relation to the group company seeking to establish a realised profit. In particular, the principle in paragraph 3.5 (linkage etc) and the related guidance at 3.43 to 3.75 should be applied. The examples which follow are intended to illustrate the factors to be considered in determining whether intra-group transactions give rise to realised profits.

---

[28] *The terms 'parent' and 'subsidiary' refer respectively to a 'parent undertaking' and a 'subsidiary undertaking' as defined in section 1162 of the Act.*

Cash pooling arrangements and group treasury functions

Groups of companies often operate cash pooling arrangements and group treasury **9.4**
functions. An example of such an arrangement is where a group company acts akin to a
banker to other group companies by accepting funds and settling debts on behalf of those
group companies. Group companies sometimes do not have their own bank accounts or
have accounts which are cleared to a central account, in the name of one group company,
at the close of business each day.

A group company may recognise a profit on a transaction which results in an increase in **9.4A**
the balance due from the group treasury company. The normal considerations apply when
assessing whether such a profit is realised. That is to say that the balance must represent
qualifying consideration and the profit must arise from a transaction or arrangement that
does not fall within paragraph 3.5 of this guidance (e.g. artificial or linked or circular). The
nature of such arrangements vary widely in practice. It is always necessary to have regard
to the particular facts and circumstances of each case.

A group company may have a 'current account' balance with another group company **9.4B**
through which many transactions, both debits and credits, are processed. There may
be a considerable 'churn' on the account even though a substantial balance remains
outstanding. The fact that there is no expectation that the core balance will be settled does
not preclude transactions processed through the account being realised profits when they
arise from normal trading transactions in the ordinary course of business. This is because
the debit entries to the account arising from these transactions are expected to be (ie they
are foreseen to be) settled by offset with credit entries on the account and therefore the
criterion in 3.11(d)(iii) can be regarded as met. However, large or unusual transactions
that result in a 'permanent' increase in the core balance will require careful consideration.

Dividends

Dividend received or receivable on an investment in a subsidiary

For a dividend received or receivable from a subsidiary to be treated as a realised profit, **9.5**
the consideration must be in the form of qualifying consideration. Accounting for
dividends receivable and payable, including payment of intra-group dividends through
inter-company accounts, is considered at 9.6 *et seq*. It will also be necessary to consider
the effect any dividend has on the value of the investment in the subsidiary and, where
its recoverable amount has fallen below its book value, to take account of the effect of
any such impairment (and, where appropriate, any consequential release from revaluation,
merger or other similar reserve).

Accrual of intra-group dividends payable and receivable

The following paragraphs deal with income that is dividend income or appropriation for **9.6**
legal purposes and which for accounting purposes is dealt with as a dividend by the paying
and receiving companies (rather than as interest under IAS 32 or FRS 25).

A dividend payable is accrued in accordance with IFRIC 17 or FRS 21 only when it is **9.7**
'appropriately authorised and no longer at the discretion of the entity'. This test will be
met when a legally binding liability is established as described at 2.10 above. A dividend
will be accrued as receivable by a parent company only when the subsidiary has a legally
binding obligation to make the distribution. IAS 10 refers to dividends 'declared' after the
balance sheet date with the implication that those 'declared' before the balance sheet date
would be accrued (by both the subsidiary and the parent). However, IFRIC 17 refers to
dividends that are declared as those that are 'appropriately authorised and no longer at the

discretion of the entity'. A dividend may therefore have been 'declared' by the directors in the everyday sense of the term but not meet the requirements for recognition in financial statements.

9.7A   [Deleted]

9.7B   Paragraph 10(b) of IFRIC 17 states that a dividend is recognised on the date when it is declared by management or the board, if the law of the jurisdiction does not require further approval. This might have been seen as requiring a change of practice in relation to interim dividends on adoption of IFRIC 17. However, it is generally agreed that this is not so because the requirement to recognise a dividend only when it is no longer at the discretion of the entity takes precedence[29]. Also, it may be said that a UK interim dividend does require further approval by the directors immediately before it is paid because of the effect of their common law duties.

9.8   Companies may have to consider paying up (or establishing a legally binding liability to pay) interim dividends before the balance sheet date to ensure that the parent company has adequate distributable reserves to support the expected level of the proposed final dividend.

9.9   [Deleted]

9.10   [Deleted]

9.11   This therefore raises the question as to what constitutes payment of an interim dividend and what steps may be taken to establish a legally binding liability. This will affect the timing of its recognition as a distribution by the paying company and as a profit by the recipient company. The question of whether a profit recorded by the recipient company is a realised profit falls to be determined under the general principles in this guidance, for example, whether it is qualifying consideration.

9.12   Where there is a transfer of cash the answer will be clear as payment has been received. This conclusion would not be affected by the cash being immediately or closely afterwards reinvested in the paying company either by way of loan or by way of capital investment, although the fact of such reinvestment will require consideration of the guidance at 9.19 below as to whether the profit is realised or unrealised in the parent company's hands.

9.13   Where the dividend is recorded on inter-company account and the effect of such an entry reduces the amount recorded as receivable from the parent to the dividend paying subsidiary, this would constitute settlement by way of set-off and would be equivalent to a payment in cash taking place at the date that the book entries were made by both companies (or the later of them if these should be different) to the extent that this does not reduce the amount recorded as receivable from the parent to the dividend-paying subsidiary below nil.

9.14   Where the dividend is recorded on inter-company account and the book entry creates or increases a liability of the paying subsidiary, the question arises as to whether the dividend falls to be treated as paid and received, or a legally binding liability is otherwise established.

9.15   Effecting the dividend via a group treasury function (see 9.4 above) where the subsidiary company instructs the group treasury function to debit the subsidiary's account and credit the parent's account, would constitute payment.

---

[29] *Paragraphs BC18-20 of IFRIC 17 explain that the Interpretation does not change the principle on when to recognise a dividend payable. The principle was moved from IAS 10 into the Interpretation and clarified but without changing the principle.*

In other circumstances, more than just entries into the accounting records of the paying and receiving company are likely to be required. If there were no doubt as to the paying subsidiary's ability to pay the dividend, a legally binding liability in respect of an individual dividend could be established by the execution, as a Deed, of an acknowledgment of liability to pay the amount entered in the accounting records as a payable by the subsidiary and a receivable by the parent company or the constitution of such liability pursuant to an enforceable contract under Scots Law. **9.16**

Any doubts about whether an interim dividend recorded by book entry is a legally binding liability can be removed by the conversion of the interim dividend into a final dividend before the year end. Under common form articles of association, this will require a recommendation by the directors and the declaration of the dividend either by approval by the members in a general meeting or, for private companies, by the members passing a written resolution. **9.17**

In scenarios other than those discussed above, the position is more complex and dependent on the specific facts and circumstances and companies in doubt as to the position may wish to seek legal advice. **9.18**

Dividend by a subsidiary to a parent which provides or reinvests the funds in the subsidiary

Investment by a parent in a subsidiary which has paid a dividend in the form of qualifying consideration does not in itself preclude that dividend from continuing to be treated as a realised profit by the parent. However, if a subsidiary pays a dividend to a parent which directly or indirectly provides the funds for the dividend or reinvests the proceeds in the subsidiary in circumstances where the transactions or arrangements fall within paragraph 3.5 of this guidance, the dividend will not represent a realised profit for the parent if it does not receive in return for the provision of funds or their reinvestment an asset which is in the form of qualifying consideration. Thus, in such a case, the profit will be unrealised if, for example: **9.19**

(a)   the provision or reinvestment of funds is in the form of:

    (i)   a subscription for shares, as the subsidiary is in effect capitalising its realised profits; or

    (ii)   a capital contribution (ie, a gift); or

    (iii) a loan which does not meet the definition of qualifying consideration; or

    (iv) a guarantee of borrowings used to fund the dividend (unless the likelihood that the guarantee will be called upon is remote); or

(b)   the subsidiary is unlikely to be able to meet its obligations under any borrowings used to fund the dividend without recourse directly or indirectly to the parent.

Dividends received out of pre-acquisition profits

The Act does not deal specifically with the onward distribution by a parent of dividends out of the pre-acquisition profits of its subsidiaries. Under UK GAAP such dividends should be treated by a parent in the same way as any other dividend which it receives from a subsidiary, including taking account of any impairment in accordance with paragraph 9.5 (see 9.21 below). The position under IFRSs is considered at 9.22 *et seq* below. **9.20**

Under UK GAAP, it has for many years been accepted that dividends received out of pre-acquisition profits of subsidiaries are treated as giving rise to a profit unless the dividend causes a diminution in the value of the investment below its book amount. This is separate **9.21** from the question of whether or not such dividends are realised profits which will depend on whether they have been received in the form of qualifying consideration.

9.22   Under IAS 27, before its amendment in May 2008[30], when investments in subsidiaries were stated using the cost model, any dividends received out of their pre-acquisition profits were credited against the cost of investment.

9.22A   In May 2008, the IASB issued an amendment to IAS 27 which removed this requirement. At the same time, it also issued an amendment to IFRS 1 which permits the use of the previous GAAP carrying amount of subsidiaries as their deemed cost on transition to IFRSs. When applying the amended Standards there will generally be no adjustment to the carrying amount of the investment in subsidiaries on transition to IFRSs so there is no effect on accumulated realised profits. This is applicable only to a parent that adopted IFRS after that amended version of IFRS 1 was applicable.

9.23   On transition to IFRSs, when applying the unamended IAS 27, companies had to determine the extent to which any dividends have been received out of the pre-acquisition profits of their subsidiaries. The May 2008 amendment has, on a prospective basis, removed this requirement and potential source of difficulty.

9.24   [Deleted]

9.25   [Deleted]

9.26   [Deleted]

9.27   [Deleted]

Sale of an asset by a parent to its subsidiary

9.28   If a parent sells an asset to a subsidiary in circumstances where the transactions or arrangements fall within paragraph 3.5 of this guidance, any profit on the sale of the asset will not represent a realised profit for the parent if it does not receive an asset which is in the form of qualifying consideration. Thus, in such a case, the profit will be unrealised if, for example:

(a)   there is an agreement or understanding regarding the repurchase of the asset by the parent; or

(b)   the parent directly or indirectly provides the funds for the purchase or reinvests the proceeds in the subsidiary where the provision or reinvestment of funds is in the form of:

   (i)   a subscription for shares; or

   (ii)   a capital contribution (ie a gift); or

   (iii) a loan which does not meet the definition of qualifying consideration; or

   (iv)   a guarantee of borrowings used to fund the purchase (unless the likelihood that the guarantee will be called upon is remote); or

(c)   the subsidiary is unlikely to be able to meet its obligations under any borrowings used to fund the purchase without recourse directly or indirectly to the parent.

---

[30] *Amendments to IFRS 1 First-time Adoption of IFRSs and IAS 27 Consolidated and Separate Financial Statements: Cost of an Investment in a Subsidiary, Jointly Controlled Entity or Associate.*

Sale of an asset by a subsidiary to a parent followed by a dividend to the parent of the resulting profit

The subsidiary should apply factors similar to those in paragraph 9.28 in determining whether it has made a realised profit on the sale of an asset to its parent.

9.29

If a subsidiary sells an asset to its parent and pays a dividend out of the resulting profit in circumstances where the transactions or arrangements, from the parent's perspective, fall within paragraph 3.5 of this guidance, the dividend will not give rise to a realised profit for the parent unless the asset which the parent purchased meets the definition of qualifying consideration. This is because the overall commercial effect of such an arrangement for the parent is similar to a dividend in kind (see paragraph 9.33).

9.30

Sale of an asset by a subsidiary to a fellow subsidiary followed by a dividend to the parent of the resulting profit

The subsidiary should apply factors similar to those in paragraph 9.28 in determining whether it has made a realised profit on the sale of an asset to its fellow subsidiary.

9.31

If a subsidiary sells an asset to a fellow subsidiary and pays a dividend to the parent out of the resulting profit in circumstances where the transactions or arrangements, from the parent's perspective, fall within paragraph 3.5 of this guidance, the dividend will not give rise to a realised profit for the parent if, for example:

9.32

(a) the parent directly or indirectly provides the funds for the purchase where the provision of funds is in the form of:

    (i) a subscription for shares; or

    (ii) a capital contribution (ie, a gift); or

    (iii) a loan which does not meet the definition of qualifying consideration; or

(b) the parent directly or indirectly reinvests the dividend (or equivalent consideration) in the subsidiary which paid the dividend or the fellow subsidiary to which the asset was sold and the asset which the parent receives from this reinvestment is not in the form of qualifying consideration; or

(c) the parent directly or indirectly guarantees any borrowings used to provide either the fellow subsidiary with the consideration for its purchase of the asset or the vendor subsidiary with funds for its dividend (in either case unless the likelihood that the guarantee will be called upon is remote) or the subsidiary in question is unlikely to be able to meet its obligations under the borrowings without recourse directly or indirectly to the parent.

Dividend in kind

A dividend in kind from a subsidiary is an unrealised profit in the hands of the parent (even where there is a cash alternative) unless the asset distributed meets the definition of qualifying consideration. However, if the non-cash asset is distributed by the parent then, following section 846, that unrealised profit would be treated by the parent as a realised profit for the purpose of that onward distribution, provided that the profit was recorded in the relevant accounts.

9.33

Return of capital contribution

Where a capital contribution is returned directly or indirectly to the donor company in circumstances where the transactions or arrangements fall within paragraph 3.5 of this guidance, it will not give rise to a realised profit in the hands of the donor.

9.34

Transfer of an asset for consideration followed by waiver of the resulting inter-company debt

9.34A   A group company may transfer an asset to another group company for consideration but subsequently waive the resulting inter-company debt. In such a case, if the purchase and release are part of a group or series of transactions or arrangements falling within paragraph 3.5 of this guidance, any profit will not represent a realised profit unless the asset originally acquired met the definition of qualifying consideration or has been disposed of for qualifying consideration. For example, where the substance of the arrangements taken together (e.g. where the waiver is a step in the plan even if undocumented) is to transfer a fixed asset for no consideration, any profit recorded by the transferee company on the debt waiver will not be a realised profit. Instead, the profit is in the nature of a revaluation of an asset acquired at no cost.

Debits within equity arising on group reconstructions

9.35   Business combinations involving entities or businesses under common control are excluded from the scope of IFRS 3, 'Business combinations'. Typical examples include a group reorganisation involving either a transfer of a company within a group or the transfer of a business from one group member to another.

9.36   When a company carries out a transaction under common control[31] such as acquiring the business of another company within the same group, the directors may determine that it is not appropriate to recognise the net assets acquired at their fair values and that it is not appropriate to recognise goodwill. For example, a company may purchase the trade and assets of a division from its parent company, the consideration being a combination of cash and shares. The directors may determine that the appropriate accounting is to recognise the net assets acquired at the transferor's book amounts. The consideration paid, say, measured at the nominal value of the shares issued plus the value of the cash element, may exceed the book amount of the net assets acquired and this will leave a debit difference to be recognised. It is not goodwill. The debit is sometimes referred to as a 'merger difference' and is recorded in equity.

9.37   A business combination involving members of the same group is completed under the direction of the controlling party, the common parent. Consequently, any excess paid by the acquirer over the book amount of the vendor's net assets is accounted for in a similar manner to a distribution or return of capital to the common parent. Distributions and returns of capital are dealt with through equity, and therefore it is logical also to recognise the debit in equity.

9.38   Such a debit directly to equity is not necessarily, however, a distribution as a matter of law. This is because the debit described above is determined on a book basis, whereas the question as to whether there would be an actual distribution is determined by whether the company gives consideration other than an issue of its shares, to its parent or a fellow subsidiary, with a fair value in excess of the fair value of the net assets and business acquired. Accordingly the debit may form part of an actual distribution or may not.

9.39   In a case where the debit in equity does not form part of an actual distribution, then at the date of acquisition the debit does not represent a loss; the acquiring company has purchased net assets worth at least the book value of the consideration given but, under the appropriate accounting, has recognised these at a lower amount. The difference between the two is the amount of the debit. As the debit is not a loss at all, it is neither realised nor unrealised.

---

[31] *As defined in IFRS 3.*

To the extent that the assets, if they had been recognised at the higher amount, would have been written down, say, by depreciation or impairment, an equivalent amount of the debit becomes a realised loss. It is a realised, rather than unrealised, loss because, had the debit been carried as an asset, any write down for depreciation or impairment would be required, by section 841 and the principles of realisation (see section 3), to be regarded as realised.

9.40

The above guidance is written in the context of IFRS 3 but is equally applicable to a group reconstruction accounted for under FRS 6.

9.41

Additional consideration for a public company

For a public company, the initial recognition of the debit will restrict the maximum amount of profits available for distribution to the extent the cash paid out (or the book value of other non-equity consideration given) is greater than the book value of the net assets acquired. This is because the acquirer's net assets as shown in the company's relevant accounts for section 836 purposes would be reduced as a result of paying out cash consideration but increased by a smaller amount by recognising the acquired net assets at a lower amount. Since the debit is neither a realised loss nor an unrealised loss it has no effect on the 'share capital and undistributable reserves' part of the section 831 net assets test. Consequently, the maximum permissible distribution would be restricted.

9.42

Merger relief and group reconstruction relief

As explained at 2.11 above, when shares are issued as consideration for the acquisition of a subsidiary, the issuing company may benefit from merger relief (section 612 of the Act) or group reconstruction relief (section 611 of the Act). In accordance with section 615 of the Act, under UK GAAP, such companies may state the cost of investment at the nominal value of the shares issued (for merger relief) or based on the minimum premium value (for group reconstruction relief). Under IFRSs, the interaction of these reliefs with the accounting for the acquired asset is complicated.

9.43

The IASB published amendments to IFRS 1 and IAS 27 in May 2008[32] that had implications for the treatment of merger relief and group reconstruction relief for accounting purposes. The amendments were effective for annual periods beginning on or after 1 January 2009. The effect of these amendments is described at 9.44A to 9.44D below.

9.43A

Before the amendment in May 2008, IAS 27 was generally considered to require the acquired asset to be booked at fair value in some or all cases. Therefore, on transition to IFRSs, it was necessary to gross up the cost of investment to the fair value at the date of acquisition and to recognise a corresponding 'merger reserve'. Although different views were expressed on this financial reporting issue, the following paragraph deals with the treatment for distributable profit purposes when the merger reserve is recorded.

9.43B

The adjustment to establish the merger reserve will have no direct impact on accumulated realised profits because the reserve will represent an unrealised profit. However, the reserve may become realised at a later date. This may, for example, occur on disposal of the investment for qualifying consideration or if the investment is written down for impairment.

9.44

---

[32] *Amendments to IFRS 1 First-time Adoption of IFRSs and IAS 27 Consolidated and Separate Financial Statements: Cost of an Investment in a Subsidiary, Jointly Controlled Entity or Associate. These amendments are separate from the revision of IAS 27, which was published in January 2008, that has no effect on the accounting in the separate financial statements of a parent.*

9.44A   In May 2008, the IASB issued an amendment to IFRS 1 which permits the use of the previous GAAP carrying amount of subsidiaries as their deemed cost on transition to IFRSs. If the exemption in the amended IFRS 1 is used, there is no adjustment to the carrying amount of the investment on transition to IFRSs and consequently no effect on accumulated realised profits. The amendment had no effect on a company that had already adopted IFRSs in a period before the amended standard was first applied.

9.44B   In May 2008, the IASB also amended IAS 27 to insert a new requirement for the accounting treatment to be adopted by a new parent company (including an intermediate parent company) established as a result of a group reorganisation when certain criteria are met. When these criteria are met[33], the new parent accounts for the cost of its investment in the original parent 'at the carrying amount of its share of the equity items shown in the separate financial statements of the original parent at the date of the reorganisation'. In practice, this means that the new parent company will record the cost of its investment in the original parent at an amount equal to the IFRS net asset value of the original parent as shown in its separate financial statements at the date of the reorganisation. This will usually differ from both the fair value of the investment and the amount that might have been recorded under UK GAAP taking into account merger relief or group reconstruction relief (see 9.43 above).

9.44C   The amendment required only prospective application to reorganisations occurring in annual periods beginning on or after 1 January 2009. No restatement was required for past reorganisations although this was permitted provided that all subsequent past reorganisations meeting the relevant criteria are restated in accordance with the amended standard.

9.44D   For future reorganisations, the application of the new requirement may have the effect of restricting the ability of a public company to make distributions because the net assets of the new parent company may (depending on the circumstances) be stated at an amount that is less than its share capital and undistributable reserves. However, for reorganisations not meeting the criteria in the amended IAS 27 and for other acquisitions, the guidance at 9.43B and 9.44 above continues to apply.

10. MISCELLANEOUS ISSUES

IAS 27, IAS 28 and IAS 31 – Separate financial statements

10.1   The balance of profits available for distribution is that available to the company, not to its group. The availability of such profits is to be judged by reference to accounts, which must therefore be the company's individual accounts. Except when initial or interim accounts are required, the 'relevant accounts' for this purpose are the individual accounts forming part of the annual accounts, whether they are 'Companies Act individual accounts' or 'IAS individual accounts' (see section 2 above).

10.2   IFRSs do not use the term 'individual accounts' but uses the term 'separate financial statements' which are defined in IAS 27 as follows:

> "Separate financial statements are those presented by a parent, an investor in an associate or a venturer in a jointly controlled entity, in which the investments are accounted for on the basis of the direct equity interests rather than on the basis of the reported results and net assets of the investee."

---

[33] *The new requirement will not apply to all group reorganisations involving the establishment of a new parent company because it applies only if all of three specified criteria are met. Reorganisations may, in practice, fail one or more of the tests.*

Where a company prepares consolidated financial statements, these 'separate financial statements' will be the company's 'IAS individual accounts' for the purposes of section 395 and therefore the relevant accounts under section 836 for the purposes of justifying any distribution.

10.3

However, where a company has an associate or jointly controlled entity but has no subsidiaries, in some circumstances IAS 28 and/or IAS 31, when considered outside the EU legal framework, require the preparation of financial statements that are neither separate financial statements nor consolidated financial statements. In such financial statements, the investments in associates and jointly controlled entities are accounted for using the equity method or proportional consolidation as appropriate (see IAS 28(4) and IAS 31(5)). In these circumstances, the company is not required by IFRSs (when considered outside of the EU legal framework) to prepare separate financial statements. One point of view is that the financial statements including investments on the basis of equity accounting and/or proportional consolidation are not relevant for the purposes of justifying distributions and that the 'separate financial statements' are the 'IAS individual accounts'.

10.4

Within the EU legal framework, an alternative point of view is that the financial statements required by IAS 28 and IAS 31 (ie those including investments on the basis of equity accounting and/or proportional consolidation) are a company's 'IAS individual accounts'. The Institutes have to date not been able to establish which view is the correct interpretation of the law and of EU-adopted IFRSs. The European Commission's Accounting Regulatory Committee has considered some related issues but has so far not provided clear guidance on this specific point.

10.5

Were the accounts including the equity accounting to be the 'IAS individual accounts', the share of results of associates/jointly-controlled-entities is not realised save to the extent that it is received as distributions in the form of qualifying consideration. Therefore the amount of a company's accumulated realised profits will be the same irrespective of which interpretation of the law is correct.

10.6

[10.7 to 10.16 moved to 2.32 *et seq* and amended.]

IFRS 1 – Fair value or revaluation as deemed cost

Under IFRS 1, a first-time adopter may elect to measure an item of property, plant and equipment at the date of transition to IFRSs at its fair value and to use that fair value as deemed cost. A first-time adopter may also elect to use a previous GAAP valuation of an item of property, plant and equipment subject to various conditions. For example, it would be possible for a company that was carrying a property at a 'frozen valuation' under the transitional provisions of FRS 15 to deem that valuation as cost on transition to IFRSs. These elections are also available for investment property when a company elects to use the cost model under IAS 40 and also, in certain limited circumstances, for intangible assets.

10.17

IFRS 1 does not specify the treatment of any revaluation reserve existing under previous GAAP or of any excess of fair value over cost when the election is used to measure the asset at fair value at the date of transition. However, it is clear that this should not be presented as a revaluation surplus because the asset is regarded as held at cost (and, for example, any subsequent fall in value would have to be charged in the income statement rather than treated as a reversal of a revaluation surplus). In the absence of any other requirement in IFRS 1, the adjustment on transition may be reflected in retained earnings.

10.18

Nevertheless, the treatment of a revaluation as deemed cost for the purposes of IFRSs does not alter the nature of the revaluation surplus which will usually be unrealised. Therefore,

10.19

companies that elect for this treatment will have to keep an analysis of the balance of retained earnings to ensure that they can identify the amount of unrealised profit included. The unrealised profit will become realised as the asset is depreciated or written down for impairment, or is sold for qualifying consideration. This is consistent with the application of section 841(5) which is summarised at 2.35 above.

10.20   The assets that are included on the basis of fair value or revaluation as deemed cost may have been depreciated under UK GAAP. Consider a tangible fixed asset that cost £100 and, at the date of transition to IFRSs, had a net book value of £50. Suppose that the fair value at the date of transition is £120 and the company elects to use this as deemed cost. The excess above original cost of £20 is clearly unrealised. It might be argued that the other £50 of the adjustment is a realised profit because it reverses the depreciation that had previously been charged as a realised loss. However, this analysis is not appropriate because the restatement to fair value is in the nature of a revaluation and it is generally accepted that depreciation is not written back to the profit and loss account on a revaluation. This is implicit in paragraph 63 of FRS 15. Similarly, when a previous valuation is treated as deemed cost, nothing of substance has occurred to cause the previously unrealised profit to become realised. This situation may be contrasted with an adjustment to depreciation that arises from a change in accounting policy for depreciation to comply with IAS 16 (see *Changes to depreciation policies* at 10.21 below). It may be possible to argue that some component of the restatement to deemed cost relates to a reconsideration of residual values and is therefore a realised profit (see 10.22 below). But, in practice, it would not usually be practicable to distinguish this component.

IFRS 1 and IAS 16 – Changes to depreciation policies

10.21   Under IFRS 1, any change in estimated useful life or depreciation pattern is accounted for prospectively from the date that the change of estimate is made provided that the depreciation methods and rates under previous GAAP are acceptable under IFRSs. However, in some cases, a company's depreciation methods and rates under previous GAAP may not be acceptable under IFRSs. If those differences have a material effect on the financial statements, the company adjusts the accumulated depreciation in its opening IFRS balance sheet retrospectively so that it complies with IFRSs (see IFRS 1 IG7).

10.22   The requirements of IAS 16 are, in general, similar to those of FRS 15 and so the depreciation methods and rates used for UK GAAP will usually be acceptable under IFRSs. However, a difference may arise because of the different way in which residual value is measured in the standards. Under FRS 15, residual values are based on the prices prevailing at the date of acquisition or revaluation of the asset. Under IAS 16, they are based on prices prevailing at the balance sheet date. Therefore, in general, cumulative depreciation will be lower under IFRSs assuming that prices are rising with inflation. Where such an effect is material, and an adjustment is made to reduce accumulated depreciation, the adjustment will be regarded as a realised profit because it represents the reversal of a previous realised loss.

IFRS 1 – Deferred tax on business combinations

10.23   The requirements of IFRS 1 and IFRS 3 for business combinations will generally be relevant only to the consolidated financial statements and therefore have no effect on distributable profits. However, in some cases it is necessary to account for a business combination in the individual accounts of a company, for example where it acquires an unincorporated business.

10.24   In some circumstances, IFRS 1 may require deferred tax to be provided in respect of assets or liabilities acquired through a previous business combination. For example, in many instances no deferred tax would have been provided on the revaluation of tangible fixed assets to fair value under UK GAAP but such a provision would be required under IFRSs. When the company is not required to restate the business combination in accordance with IFRS 3 and uses this exemption, the deferred tax provision still has to be recognised but is adjusted against retained earnings rather than against goodwill.

The tax provision will reduce accumulated realised profits available for distribution where **10.25** the transaction involved the acquisition of an unincorporated business by an individual company. It does not matter that the tax provision would not have been treated in this way had IFRS 3 been applied. It is the accounting that has actually been applied in the relevant accounts, in accordance with applicable accounting standards, which affects the amount of profits available for distribution.

IFRS 1 – Past capitalisation of revaluation reserve

Under UK GAAP, some companies have revalued assets, in particular properties and **10.26** investments in subsidiaries, and subsequently capitalised all or part of the resulting revaluation reserve through a bonus issue of shares. The issue that arises on transition to IFRSs is the status of the debit entry in reserves if revalued assets are restated to a cost basis.

Investment properties and property, plant and equipment

Under SSAP 19, investment properties are required to be included in the balance sheet **10.27** at their open market value. Under FRS 15, companies that chose to adopt a policy of revaluation for classes of tangible fixed assets (property, plant and equipment) have to ensure that those assets are carried at their current value at the balance sheet date. On transition to IFRSs, companies are not required to continue to apply a revaluation policy for their investment properties or property, plant and equipment. In effect, IFRS 1 allows companies on transition to IFRSs to state their investment properties or property, plant and equipment at depreciated historical cost, or, in the case of property, plant and equipment, at a 'deemed cost' that could be a previous valuation or fair value at the date of transition. This guidance addresses the position where a company chooses to restate to depreciated historical cost. In the case of a transition using a 'deemed cost' the revaluation survives transition and there is no restatement to consider.

Where the revaluation surplus has not been used at all for a bonus issue of shares and is **10.28** still recorded in the balance sheet at the date of transition to IFRSs, the adjustment required will be simply to eliminate the revaluation reserve and reduce the revalued assets by the same amount to restate them to their depreciated historical cost. However, if the revaluation surplus has been capitalised, in full or in part, through a past bonus issue of shares, it will not be possible to reduce the reserve in this way. Neither is it possible to apply the debit to reduce share capital by the amount of the bonus shares. The question therefore arises as to the status of the debit entry in reserves arising from reversal of the past revaluation.

Paragraph 3.15(c) above states that, with two exceptions explained at 2.33 and 3.36, **10.29** realised losses will include the writing down, or providing for depreciation, amortisation, diminution in value or impairment of an asset. However, the entry to reverse the previous revaluation surplus is not depreciation or amortisation. It also does not relate to the diminution in the value of the assets or impairment but instead relates to a reduction in the amount at which those assets are recorded in the balance sheet. The actual value of the assets remains unchanged.

The exception described at 2.36 is as follows: **10.30**

If an asset is revalued downwards below its recoverable amount, as defined in FRS 11 or IAS 36, then the difference between that revalued amount and recoverable amount is treated as an unrealised loss as it reflects a revaluation adjustment rather than a provision as defined in section 841 .Such a loss would become realised in the event of a subsequent scrapping, disposal or impairment of the asset.

10.31 This principle may be applied to the restatement of a revalued asset to its depreciated historical cost. Therefore the debit entry to reserves arising from such a restatement (which equates to the revaluation element of the carrying value that is not yet depreciated) will be an unrealised loss provided that the recoverable amount of the asset is equal to or greater than the book amount prior to the restatement. To the extent that the revaluation surplus still exists as an unrealised reserve, the unrealised loss will simply eliminate that unrealised reserve. To the extent that the revaluation surplus has been utilised, in part or in full, for a bonus issue of shares, the resulting net debit entry will represent an unrealised loss.

10.32 The entry to reverse the previous revaluation surplus is not a provision for the purposes of applying section 841(2). In the case of Companies Act individual accounts, 'provisions of a kind specified for the purposes of this paragraph by regulations under section 396 (except revaluation provisions)' are treated as realised losses. In the case of 'IAS individual accounts', 'provisions of any kind (except revaluation provisions)' are treated as realised losses. The entry to reverse the previous revaluation surplus is not a provision of the kind specified by the regulations under section 396 and is not a provision at all in the sense that the term is used for accounting purposes. On the restatement to historical cost there will be no provision deducted from the asset.

Investments in subsidiaries

10.33 Under the alternative accounting rules in the Accounting Regulations, investments in subsidiaries may be stated 'at a market value determined as at the date of their last valuation' or 'at a value determined on any basis which appears to the directors to be appropriate in the circumstances of the company'. There is no obligation under the law or UK accounting standards to keep such valuations up to date although it is necessary to consider whether the assets have become impaired. Under IFRSs, two accounting policies are available for investments in subsidiaries. The first policy is that of cost, using the IAS 27-cost method. The second is to account for such investments in accordance with IAS 39. This would require such investments to be maintained at fair value. In practice, the measurement of such equity investments at fair value may be precluded because the range of reasonable fair value estimates is significant and the probabilities of the various estimates cannot reasonably be assessed (see IAS 39, AG 80-81). Even where such a policy is possible, it will require valuations to be obtained each time a balance sheet is drawn up. This is likely to be unattractive to most companies. Therefore, most companies hold subsidiaries at cost, as determined under IAS 27.

10.34 Hence the guidance on the effect of a restatement to depreciated historical cost of a previously revalued investment property or tangible fixed asset is equally applicable to a restatement of previously revalued investments in subsidiaries on to an IAS 27-cost basis.

Effect of restatements for a public company

10.35 For a public company, the restatement of a revalued asset (whether investment property, other property, plant and equipment or investment in subsidiaries) to a cost basis will restrict its profits available for distribution under section 831 to the extent that the revaluation surplus was capitalised. The effect of the unrealised loss on the restriction imposed by section 831 may be mitigated by the existence of recognised unrealised profits.

IAS 11 – *Accounting for construction contracts*

Under UK GAAP (SSAP 9), accounting for profit on long-term contracts results in debtor balances described as 'Amounts recoverable on contracts'. This treatment was adopted when the standard was revised in 1988 because legal advice suggested that it was not possible to include the profit element in work-in-progress because of the requirement to state work-in-progress at cost. **10.36**

The accounting required for construction contracts under IAS 11 is broadly similar to that required by SSAP 9 (although the scope of the standards is different). However, IAS 11 is not specific as to the nature of the asset to be recognised. In practice the item may simply be disclosed as 'construction contracts' although it may also be included within debtors or within work-in-progress. **10.37**

Under UK GAAP it is usually clear that the debtor balance for 'Amounts recoverable on contracts' meets the definition of 'qualifying consideration' (see 3.11 above). Therefore profit recognised on such contracts is regarded as a realised profit. On the basis that this treatment has been generally accepted under UK GAAP, any profits recognised in accordance with IAS 11 should be regarded as realised profits, irrespective of how the asset is described in the balance sheet. **10.38**

IFRIC 12 Service Concession Arrangements may require a profit to be recognised by the operator in accordance with IAS 11 in relation to the construction or upgrading of the infrastructure to be used to provide a public service. Whether any such profit is a realised profit will depend on whether a financial asset or an intangible asset is recognised in accordance with IFRIC 12. This is more fully explained at 10.65 to 10.68 below. **10.38A**

IAS 12 – *Income taxes – Deferred tax*

As stated at 3.17 above, a provision for deferred tax should generally be regarded as a realised loss. However, when assets are revalued to their fair value, with any gain being recorded in the profit and loss account even though regarded as unrealised, the deferred tax on that gain should be treated as a reduction in that unrealised gain rather than as a realised loss (paragraph 14 of Appendix III to FRS 19 *Deferred tax*). **10.39**

This principle is also applicable to deferred tax provisions recognised under IAS 12, irrespective of whether profits are recognised in profit or loss, or direct in equity. For many financial instruments, profits arising from fair value accounting are realised profits (see Section 4 above). Any attributable deferred tax provision will be a realised loss. **10.40**

Deferred tax is more often recognised on unrealised profits under IFRSs than under UK GAAP. For example, the remeasurement of investment property at fair value will result in unrealised profits (see Section 4 above) on which deferred tax will have to be provided. Such a deferred tax provision is treated as a reduction in the unrealised profit rather than as a realised loss. **10.41**

When a convertible debt instrument is accounted for using 'split accounting' (see *Convertible debt* at 6.59 *et seq* above), a deferred tax provision is established and debited against the initial carrying amount of the equity component in accordance with paragraph 23 of IAS 12. This occurs if the tax base of the debt is its full amount but the book amount is lower by the amount of the equity component. The deferred tax provision reverses through profit or loss over the life of the instrument as illustrated in Example 4 in Appendix B to IAS 12. It does not represent a future cash outflow for payment of tax. The deferred tax provision should be treated as a reduction in the credit to equity rather than as a realised loss. The equity component of the financial instrument is not a profit at all and therefore **10.42** does not fall to be classified as realised or unrealised (see *Convertible debt* at 6.59 *et seq* above). An adjustment to such an item does not affect realised profits.

10.43   In some cases it may be necessary to provide for current tax on an unrealised profit. A current tax provision should be treated as a realised loss even if it arises from the taxation of an unrealised profit. This is because a provision for current tax represents a specific cash outflow that will arise irrespective of whether the related profit is realised or not.

Property, plant and equipment – asset swaps

10.44   One or more items of property, plant and equipment may be acquired in exchange for a non-monetary asset or assets, or a combination of monetary and non-monetary assets. IAS 16 requires the cost of such an item of property, plant and equipment to be measured at fair value unless the transaction lacks commercial substance or the fair value of neither the asset received nor the asset given up is reliably measurable. IAS 16 provides guidance on the circumstances in which the fair value of an asset is reliably measurable for this purpose.

10.45   A profit may therefore be recognised on such an exchange transaction in accordance with IFRSs. This profit is likely to be unrealised because an item of property, plant and equipment is unlikely to meet the definition of 'qualifying consideration' (see 3.11 above).

10.46   When a combination of property, plant and equipment and qualifying consideration (e.g. cash) is received, the guidance at 3.18 above on 'top-slicing' will be relevant.

10.47   Any profit treated as unrealised, becomes realised as the related asset is depreciated, written down for impairment or sold for qualifying consideration.

10.48   A loss arising on such a transaction is usually a realised loss. However, in some cases the loss may be similar in substance to an unrealised revaluation deficit (see 2.28 above).

10.49   For example, if a factory used in a business was exchanged for a similar factory and a loss recognised under IAS 16 by reference to the market value of the factories, the loss will be unrealised if there would have been no need to write down the original factory for impairment because its value in use was higher than its market value. It will also be necessary to consider the value in use of the new factory which might be different from the value in use of the old factory, even though their market value is the same (e.g. because one is larger than the other).

10.50   IAS 38 provides for the same accounting treatment for swaps of intangibles as that under IAS 16 in respect of property, plant and equipment, and therefore the foregoing analysis also applies to intangibles under IAS 38.

10.51   There are no specific requirements in UK accounting standards dealing with such asset swaps. The above guidance is relevant to any profit recognised under UK GAAP although it should be noted that only profits realised at the balance sheet date may be included in the profit and loss account in accordance with the Accounting Regulations[34] (although the fair value accounting rules make an exception to this general rule).

---

[34] *Paragraph 13 of Schedule 1 to SI 2008/409 and Paragraph 13 to Schedule 1 to SI 2008/410.*

Revenue – Barter transactions

When goods are sold or services rendered in exchange for dissimilar goods or services, the exchange is regarded as a transaction that generates revenue in accordance with IAS 18. The revenue is measured at the fair value of the goods or services received, adjusted by the amount of any cash or cash equivalents transferred. When the fair value cannot be measured reliably, the revenue is measured at the fair value of the goods or services given up, adjusted by the amount of any cash or cash equivalents transferred. **10.52**

When an asset is received, in determining whether any profit on such an exchange is realised or unrealised, it is necessary to determine whether such asset meets the definition of qualifying consideration. For example, when a property is received, it will be straightforward to assess whether or not it meets the definition of qualifying consideration. Any profit will not become realised until that property is depreciated, written down for impairment or sold for qualifying consideration. **10.53**

Where services are exchanged, the effect of the accounting entries is to gross up the revenue and the costs by the same amount. Accordingly, there will be no effect on profit. When services are receivable but have not yet been received at the balance sheet date, a prepayment will be recognised. A prepayment does not meet the definition of qualifying consideration. **10.54**

Where an exchange of services straddles the end of an accounting reference period, such that services are provided but not received before the balance sheet date, any profit at the year end would not be realised. Any such profit initially recognised will not become realised until the service has been received in exchange. That is, the profit will be realised by the prepayment being expensed to profit or loss when the service has been received. **10.55**

There are no specific requirements in UK accounting standards dealing with barter transactions other than UITF Abstract 26 which is concerned with barter transactions for advertising. The above guidance will be relevant to any profit recognised under UK GAAP although it should be noted that only profits realised at the balance sheet date may be included in the profit and loss account in accordance with the Accounting Regulations[35]. **10.56**

[10.57 to 10.64 withdrawn and replaced by section 11.]

IFRIC 12 Service concession arrangements

IFRIC 12 Service Concession Arrangements was issued in November 2006 and has subsequently been adopted by the EU. Service concession arrangements are arrangements whereby a government or other public sector body ('the grantor') enters into a contract with a private sector entity ('the operator') for the construction / upgrade and operation of assets with which public services are supplied, such as roads, prisons or hospitals. Private Finance Initiative (PFI) arrangements are a common example of service concession arrangements in the UK. **10.65**

The operator will often construct or upgrade the infrastructure to be used to provide the public service and the cost of this will be recovered over the life of the arrangement. This is accounted for as a construction contract under IAS 11 Construction contracts. The asset arising from the recognition of revenue in accordance with IAS 11 will be either a financial asset or an intangible asset, in accordance with IFRIC 12, depending on the terms of the arrangement. **10.66**

---

[35] *Paragraph 13 of Schedule 1 to SI 2008/409 and Paragraph 13 to Schedule 1 to SI 2008/410.*

10.67 When a financial asset is recognised in accordance with IFRIC 12, this will be an amount receivable from the grantor and therefore should normally meet the definition of qualifying consideration. Any profit arising from the recognition of revenue in the construction phase will therefore normally be a realised profit.

10.68 When an intangible asset is recognised in accordance with IFRIC 12, this will not meet the definition of qualifying consideration. Any profit arising from the recognition of revenue in the construction phase will not therefore be a realised profit. Any unrealised profit arising in the construction phase will become realised as the intangible asset is amortised or impaired over the life of the arrangement.

IFRIC 5 Decommissioning funds

10.69 IFRIC 5 'Rights to Interests arising from Decommissioning, Restoration and Environmental Rehabilitation Funds' was issued in December 2004 and subsequently adopted by the EU. Such funds are more fully described in IFRIC 5 but are typically established to provide a ring-fenced fund of assets to be used to pay for the decommissioning of an asset (e.g. a nuclear power plant) at the end of its life. IFRIC 5 applies to the financial statements of a contributor to such a fund where the assets are administered separately (either by being held in a separate legal entity or as segregated assets within another entity) and the contributor's right to access the assets is restricted. The contributor retains the obligation to pay the decommissioning costs but is able to draw on the assets in the fund to finance such costs when they are incurred.

10.70 In accordance with IFRIC 5, the contributor recognises the right to receive reimbursement from the fund as a reimbursement asset in accordance with IAS 37. The reimbursement is measured at the lower of the amount of the decommissioning obligation recognised and the contributor's share of the fair value of the net assets of the fund attributable to the contributor. Changes in the carrying value of the reimbursement asset, other than contributions to and payments from the fund, are recognised in profit or loss in the period in which the changes occur.

10.71 Paragraph 53 of IAS 37 states that a reimbursement asset is recognised when, and only when, it is virtually certain that the reimbursement will be received if the entity settled the obligation. An amount receivable which is regarded, for financial reporting purposes, as meeting this test will also generally meet the definition of qualifying consideration in paragraph 3.11(d).

10.72 That definition refers to the debtor being capable of settling the receivable within a reasonable period of time. What is a reasonable period of time is a matter of judgement and will depend on the particular facts and circumstances. Decommissioning funds may be established to pay liabilities that will not arise for many years. However, the nature of such funds is that they will generally be capable of settling the amount within a relatively short period of time if they were required to do so at the date of determination. The definition of qualifying consideration does not require actual settlement within any particular period of time.

Section 846 and replacement assets

10.73 The following paragraphs illustrate how to apply s846 (see 2.9 above) where the asset to which an unrealised reserve relates has been replaced by a different asset.

10.74 Company A has brought forward realised profits of £75,000. It previously acquired an investment (in Company B) via a share for share transfer. This transaction qualified for merger relief in accordance with section 612 and the company elected to record a merger reserve in relation to this share issue. The aggregate nominal value of the shares issued was £50,000, compared with a fair value of £500,000 such that a merger reserve of £450,000 was recorded.

Subsequently Company A transfers that investment in Company B to another subsidiary company (Company C) in exchange for shares. As a matter of accounting practice, the merger reserve which initially related to Company A's investment in Company B is now attached to the investment in Company C, ie part of the amount at which the investment in Company C is stated represents the reserve. These transactions are illustrated in the diagram below (in which 'CV' means carrying value). **10.75**

Therefore, if Company A wishes to distribute its investment in Company C to its shareholders, it can do so by applying section 846. This reserve (together with £75,000 of the brought forward realised profits) can be used to distribute Company A's investment in Company C to its shareholders. This is illustrated in the following memorandum balance sheet of Company A. **10.76**

Memorandum balance sheet of Company A

	Opening balance sheet	Share for share acquisition of Company B	After acquisition of Company B	Share for share transfer of Company B to Company C	After transfer to Company C	Distribution of Company C	After distribution of Company C
	£'000	£'000	£'000	£'000	£'000	£'000	£'000
Investment in Company B		500	500	(500)	-		-
Investment in Company C	10		10	500	510	(510)	-
Other net assets	90		90		90		90
Net assets	100	500	600	-	600	(510)	90
Share capital / premium	25	50	75		75		75
Merger reserve (Company B)		450	450	(450)	-		-
Merger reserve (Company C)				450	450	(450)	-
P&L reserves (realised)	75		75		75	(60)	15
Capital and reserves	100	500	600	-	600	(510)	90

Section 846 and fungible assets

The following paragraphs provide guidance on the distribution in kind of fungible assets such as shares or loan notes that have been received as consideration for the sale of another asset. For example, Company A has 1,000 £1 loan notes which are transferable in multiples of £1 and represent an unrealised profit of £900. If the company makes a distribution in kind of £500 of loan notes, the question is whether the unrealised profit might be regarded as becoming realised through the application of section 846 either:

10.77

* to the extent of £450 on the basis that the realisation of 50% of the asset results in the realisation of 50% of the profit; or
* to the extent of £500 through the application of a 'top slicing' rule similar to the one in 3.18 below for exchanges of assets.

The first (ie pro rata) approach is correct. This is a matter of the statutory construction of section 846 rather than a matter of generally accepted accounting practice.

10.78

Section 846 is reproduced below for ease of reference.

10.79

846 Distributions in kind: treatment of unrealised profits

(1) *This section applies where—*

   (a) *a company makes a distribution consisting of or including, or treated as arising in consequence of, the sale, transfer or other disposition by the company of a non-cash asset, and*

   (b) *any part of the amount at which that asset is stated in the relevant accounts represents an unrealised profit.*

(2) *That profit is treated as a realised profit—*

   (a) *for the purpose of determining the lawfulness of the distribution in accordance with this Part (whether before or after the distribution takes place), and*

   (b) *for the purpose of the application, in relation to anything done with a view to or in connection with the making of the distribution, of any provision of regulations under section 396 under which only realised profits are to be included in or transferred to the profit and loss account.*

The profit that is to be treated as realised in accordance with sub-section (2) is the unrealised profit referred to in sub-section (1)(b). The reference in sub-section (1)(b) to 'that asset' means the asset to be distributed. Therefore, it is necessary to identify 'that asset' which in the above example is not a single asset of £500 of loan notes but an aggregation of assets comprising 500 £1 loan notes. Naturally, if the loan notes were transferable only in units of £100 the distribution would consist of 5 assets. Therefore, in the above example, the distribution of £500 of loan notes results in the realisation of £450 of profit because that is the amount of unrealised profit attributable to those loan notes. In other words, the unrealised profit must be treated as spread evenly across each unit of the fungible asset and section 846 applied to each unit separately.

10.80

Paragraph 3.18 refers to the use of a top-slicing approach where an asset is sold partly for qualifying consideration and partly for other consideration and a realised profit falls to be assessed under generally accepted accounting principles. That guidance is not relevant to the application of section 846 which is not concerned with the disposal of an asset for mixed consideration but with the recharacterisation of an existing unrealised profit under that the specific provision of that section. In addition, that guidance is not relevant to the attribution of an unrealised profit, at the point of its arising, among one or more assets.

10.81

10.82   As illustrated in Appendix 8, this conclusion, may lead to unexpected results in some cases. In particular, the maximum distribution possible as a distribution in kind may be less than would be the case if all of the loan notes were redeemed or sold for qualifying consideration.

11. FOREIGN CURRENCY SHARE CAPITAL AND USE OF PRESENTATION CURRENCIES

Introduction

11.1   The guidance in this section deals with matters arising from mismatches between any of the currency of share capital, the company's functional currency and the company's presentation currency. The accounting context in which this section is written is IFRS, ie IAS 21. So far as UK GAAP is concerned, if FRS 23 is applicable then this is converged with IAS 21; if SSAP 20 is applicable, the issues and principles are, however, the same because SSAP 20 differs only in minor details from IAS 21 for these purposes, although SSAP 20 does not include a free choice of presentation currency.

11.2.   The main points at issue might be briefly put as follows: what is the effect of a translation of the whole of the accounts of a company into a presentation currency of free choice; and what is the effect of the share capital's being denominated in a currency other than the functional currency?

11.3   The first matter is similar to the issue of translation of an autonomous branch which was previously addressed at paragraphs 10.57-10.64 (which have now been withdrawn and replaced by the guidance in this section). However, that case is not one of free choice of presentation currency. Rather, it is a necessity to translate the results of the branch into the functional currency of the company of which it is legally a part. In the case of use of a presentation currency, there is an arbitrary choice as to the units in which to show the accounts for mere presentation purposes.

11.4   [Not used]

11.5   [Not used]

Principles

11.6   Paragraphs 11.7 to 11.34 set out seven principles to be applied in relation to foreign currency share capital and the use of presentation currencies. Examples of the application of the principles are set out in Appendix 5.

11.7   **Principle 1: Realised profits and losses are measured by reference to the functional currency of the company.**

11.8   **Principle 2: An accounting gain or loss arising upon the retranslation of the whole of the accounts from the company's functional currency to a presentation currency, is not a profit or a loss as a matter of law. Such an amount therefore cannot be a realised profit or loss.**

11.9   IAS 21 requires foreign currency assets, liabilities and transactions to be measured using a company's functional currency. This is defined as the currency of the primary economic environment in which the entity operates. Functional currency is a matter of fact and is not an accounting policy choice. However, IAS 21 also permits a company to present its financial statements in a currency other than its functional currency. Such a currency is referred to as a presentation currency and may be freely chosen.

The 'relevant accounts' for the purposes of justifying a distribution are determined in accordance with section 836 but will generally be the company's most recent statutory individual accounts. Although the face of those accounts shows amounts in presentation currency, the functional currency amounts underlie and form part of those relevant accounts. Realised profits and losses are determined by reference to these functional currency amounts. The functional-to-presentation translation gain or loss, which also appears in the relevant accounts, is not a profit or loss at law, for the reasons explained below. **11.10**

The presentation currency is an arbitrary choice as to the units in which to show the accounts for mere presentation purposes. The functional-to-presentation translation is a book-keeping or accounting exercise. The accounting gain or loss arising from that process is an arithmetical difference which does not spring from any functional substance. There has been no profit or loss but merely a change in calibration. Thus such changes are not characterised as a profit or loss as a matter of law. **11.11**

Principle 3: The profit or loss arising upon the necessary retranslation of an autonomous branch, from its functional currency into the functional currency of the company, is a realised profit or a loss to the extent that the branch net assets were qualifying consideration when the profit or loss arose. **11.12**

A company has only a single pool of realised profits available for distribution, irrespective of its having one or more autonomous branches, with a functional currency different from that of the rest of the company. That single pool is measured by reference to the functional currency of the rest of the company. Thus in the case of a foreign operation (branch) with a functional currency that is different from the functional currency of the company, the translation is not an arbitrary one but one made of necessity to state the branch asset and results in the company's functional currency. It therefore has substance and is a profit or loss at law. **11.13**

Whether that profit or loss is a realised one depends upon the nature of the assets and liabilities on which they arise. A profit that arises on retranslation of an asset which comprises qualifying consideration, or a liability, is a realised profit in accordance with paragraph 3.9(d) above. A profit arising on the retranslation of assets which do not comprise qualifying consideration (e.g. property, plant and equipment) is an unrealised profit. A loss arising on retranslation of an asset or liability is a realised loss unless it is the reversal of an unrealised profit on that same asset or liability. The gross profits and losses on retranslation (rather than the net amount) should be assessed separately. It is therefore possible, for example, that there is a realised loss to be taken into account when determining profits available for distribution, even though the net amount taken direct to equity is a profit. **11.14**

The analysis in the previous paragraph will apply only in straightforward situations where the composition of the company's assets has not changed significantly during the period. For example, it would not be appropriate to regard the exchange difference related to the amount of the opening cash balance (ie, the beginning to the end of year exchange difference computed in relation to that part of the opening net assets equal to the opening cash balance) as realised if that cash balance did not exist throughout the period (eg because it was invested in assets such as property, plant and equipment which would not comprise qualifying consideration). **11.15**

The exchange difference taken to equity will also include the difference between the profit or loss for the period translated at actual (or average) rate and that profit or loss translated at closing rate. The profit or loss for the period arises on changes in the amounts and/or composition of the company's assets and liabilities (e.g. on an exchange of stocks for cash). **11.16**

11.17   Thus taking together the exchange differences on retranslation of the profit or loss for the period and on the opening net assets, the total amount arises in relation to an asset base that changes throughout the year. To establish whether this exchange difference is realised, partly realised or unrealised will require careful analysis of the facts. Appendix 6 gives two examples of this, illustrating why this calculation needs to be done. Ideally, it would be necessary to compute and assess exchange differences continually. In practice when conducting the analysis, reasonable approximations may be made. The approximations will depend on the facts of any case, for example the rate of change in the composition of the balance sheet between various asset/ liability categories.

11.18   **Principle 4: Where a company's shares, irrespective of whether those shares are classified as equity or debt for accounting purposes, are denominated in a currency other than the company's functional currency, the adjustment arising upon any translation for accounting purposes of the share capital is not a profit or loss at law. Such an amount therefore cannot be a realised profit or loss.**

11.19   Where shares are classified as equity under accounting standards and their currency differs from the company's functional currency, then the company will either retranslate those shares into functional currency at each balance sheet date or will leave them at their original historical amounts, although typically the latter is adopted in the case of ordinary shares. Accounting standards do not have anything to say about the translation of shares classified as equity, or at least not directly. In IAS 21 the requirement to accumulate the translation differences in the currency translation reserve rules out any question of allocating any of them against capital. In the case of retranslation the resulting difference does not pass through profit or loss and is not a gain or loss for accounting purposes. Where the shares are classified as debt (eg certain preference shares), retranslation is mandatory and the resulting difference is an accounting gain or loss flowing through profit or loss.

11.20   In both cases, the shares remain share capital as a matter of law. Any retranslation of share capital for accounting purposes (whether equity or debt classified) is a bookkeeping or accounting exercise. The gain or loss arising from that process is an arithmetical difference which does not spring from any substance in law. There has been no profit or loss but merely a change in calibration. Thus such changes are not characterised as profits or losses as a matter of law.

11.21   **Principle 5: Where a company's shares, whether those shares are classified as equity or debt for accounting purposes, are denominated in a currency other than the company's functional currency, the common law has the effect of restricting distributions where to do otherwise would result in the net assets' falling below the functional currency worth of the share capital.**

11.22   Under statute, shares (whether of a private or a public company) must be of a fixed nominal amount (s542). There is a rule of law that where the share capital is denominated in another currency (other than the functional currency) the share capital is in fact fixed as that other currency amount.

11.23   Further, the common law provides that a company may not distribute its capital (see 2.2 above). In relation to the currency of shares, this rule is not concerned with whether or not share capital has been retranslated in the accounts or with the nature of any translation adjustments. It is concerned with a question of fact as to value of the assets compared with the amount of the share capital. Since the amount of the capital is the currency amount, then for such a comparison to be effected the share capital must be stated in the same terms as value of the net assets. Thus the current worth of the share capital in functional currency terms must be compared with the net assets in functional currency. To the extent that a distribution would result in the net assets falling below the current functional currency worth of the share capital, the ability to make such a distribution is restricted.

Thus an increase in the functional currency worth of the share capital may restrict distributions to less than the amount available under Part 23's statutory rules. On the other hand, a decrease will neither restrict nor augment the ability to make a distribution. The effect of a share capital decrease will be to increase the difference between net assets and share capital (assuming no other amounts within equity – see below for other cases) so as to exceed the Part 23 realised profits (and any unrealised profits). However, the maximum amount that may be distributed can never exceed the amount permitted by Part 23. **11.24**

Principle 6: Share premium account, and similar capital accounts, do not have a currency of denomination but are amounts of record in the books of account in functional currency. **11.25**

Share premium account is different from share capital in this context. Share capital is required by statute to be of fixed amount and therefore has a currency of denomination. Share premium account is not so required. Furthermore, share premium was, prior to the statutory requirement to treat it as if it were part of a company's capital, in law a profit. It is thus an amount of record arising on the occasion of a share issue. The amount is determined at that time and in the functional currency since that is the currency of substance for the keeping of accounts. **11.26**

A capital redemption reserve is of the same nature as a share premium account. It is not required by statute to have a fixed amount. It is an amount of record arising on the occasion of a share redemption or repurchase. The amount is determined at that time and in the functional currency. It should be noted that the amount determined at that time will be by reference to the then functional currency worth of the shares redeemed or repurchased. This is because those shares, up to the moment of their redemption or repurchase, represent capital of that currency. Thus the nominal value of those shares, by reference to which the statutory rules for determining capital redemption reserve operate, is as a matter of fact a non-functional currency amount; its functional currency worth must be determined at the date of redemption or repurchase. **11.27**

Principle 5 identifies a possible restricting effect upon distributions in relation to share capital where there is a mismatch between that capital's denomination and the functional currency. Since share premium and similar capital accounts do not have currencies of denomination, but are amounts of record in functional currency, no equivalent issue arises in relation to share premium and similar capital accounts; that is to say, there is no concept of variation in the worth of, eg, share premium to be concerned about. **11.28**

It should be noted, however, that share premium is brought into the calculation of the restricting effect arising from a variation in the worth of the share capital under Principle 5. The common law prohibition on distribution of capital covers both share capital and share premium account. Thus, where a company has a share premium account, the restricting effect under Principle 5 is computed by comparison of the net assets with the aggregate of the functional currency worth of the share capital and the functional currency amount of record of the share premium account. **11.29**

The common law principles of maintenance of capital apply to any reserve which the Act says must be treated as if it were part of the paid up share capital of the company. It therefore includes, in addition to a share premium account, a capital redemption reserve under section 733 and a redenomination reserve under section 626. The treatment of a **11.30** share premium account described in 2.29 above therefore applies to any capital redemption reserve or redenomination reserve.

11.31   Principle 7: The application of the s831 statutory net assets test operates by reference to amounts as shown upon the face of the accounts in presentation currency.

11.32   The s831 net assets test (see 2.30 above) applies only to public companies. It is a statutory test formulated in terms of amounts set out in the relevant accounts required by the Act: net assets, share capital and undistributable reserves (as defined). It therefore operates by reference to whatever is shown in presentation currency in those accounts.

11.33   It may be noted here that s831 operates upon figures in presentation currency whereas, as described at Principles 1 and 2, s830's realised profits test draws upon functional currency amounts. This is because s830 deals with profits and losses and in law the functional-to-presentation translation does not yield a profit or loss. It is therefore necessary for s830 to begin with the amounts in the relevant accounts but to take from them only the amounts that are profits and losses in law. On the other hand s831 asks only that certain accounts figures be compared (eg, in a similar way to that described at 6.24ff above whereby shares classified as debt count as a reduction of net assets rather than an increase to share capital for the s831 test).

11.34   It should be noted that where share capital is retranslated, the amount within reserves arising as a result of the retranslation is not a profit or loss at law (see Principle 2). Nor is that translation difference presented as share capital. Thus the difference cannot be included, for the operation of the s831 test, as share capital or as undistributable reserves. Thus, in particular, any debit difference cannot be an unrealised loss to be deducted from the unrealised profits component of 'undistributable reserves'.

11.35   Principle 8: A reduction of foreign currency share capital is calculated by reference to the rate of exchange at the date of the reduction.

11.36   The amount of the reserve so arising is a matter of accounting practice. That reserve will be the functional currency amount (see paragraph 11.7) of:

(a)   the amount previously recorded in relation to the now-reduced nominal value;

(b)   plus or minus any amounts previously recorded for retranslation of the share capital (if it was retranslated – see paragraphs 11.18-11.20);

(c)   less any amounts repaid translated at the rate at the date of repayment.

Put simply, the reserve is the aggregate net amount left over, in functional currency, after all of the share capital being reduced, any associated retranslation amounts and any repayment have been removed from the accounts. Appendix 7 contains illustrative examples of a company's position in several scenarios for capital reductions where there have been movements in the exchange rate between the functional currency and foreign share capital currency.

11.37   It should be noted that the amount of the reserve so arising is not the same as the amount of the reduction. In law the amount of the reduction would be the currency nominal value reduced at the functional currency exchange rate at the date that the reduction becomes effective. This is because the amount of the capital, and thus of the reduction, is the currency amount (see paragraph 11.22). It can be meaningfully stated at the effective date only at the rate applicable that day. For example, if the amount was repaid on reduction it would be that amount that would actually be repaid and accounted for as a cash payment. The realised profits arising on the reduction, on the other hand, are not determined by reference to the reduction amount but to the reserve arising, which is an accounting matter and may be a different figure.

The reserve may be thought of as comprising a number of components, one of which is the **11.38** reduction amount, as follows, in the functional currency:

(a) a credit for the reduced nominal value, to the extent not paid out, at the reduction date exchange rate;

(b) a credit for any previously recorded balance, representing the reduced nominal value, that has not been eliminated by (a) above and/ or by any repayment;

(c) a debit for any previously recorded balance, representing the reduced nominal value, that has been over-eliminated by (a) above and/ or by any repayment; and

(d) a credit or debit, as the case may be, to replace any reserves entry for prior accounting retranslation of the reduced element of the shares since this is associated with the shares' nominal value that no longer exists.

In relation to the last component, such a prior reserves entry arises only where the shares were retranslated for accounting purposes; in effect it anticipated the reduction of the shares (it is the difference between the nominal value at historical rate and an amount equal to what is now the reduction amount) and so should be brought into account in reduction accounting.

12. CASH BOX STRUCTURES

Introduction to the cash box share issue method

The so-called 'cash box' method of effecting an issue of shares for cash has been employed **12.1** from time to time over at least two decades. They have recently become commonplace. Whilst they have previously been seen in relation to acquisition funding, more recently they also have been seen in connection with debt repayment or regulatory capital increases. Some companies undertaking such issues have been advised by their lawyers that the arrangement does not give rise to any share premium. As a consequence the question arises as to the status of the reserve recorded instead of share premium: is it a realised profit?

Brief details

Although there are slight variations in the schemes put forward, a common case would be **12.2** as follows (in this case a placing):

- There are four parties involved: the Company; NewCo, a newly incorporated non-UK subsidiary of which the company holds 89 of 100 ordinary shares (worth a trivial amount); a bank, that owns the other 11 shares (worth a trivial amount); and the placees who will put up a substantial amount of cash.
- The placees pay over the cash subscription amount to the bank, which, as principal, subscribes that cash amount for preference shares in NewCo.
- The Company allots ordinary shares (being equity shares under s548) to the placees, in consideration for which the bank transfers to it the 11 NewCo ordinary shares and the NewCo preference shares.
- NewCo redeems its preference shares (now held by the Company) in cash for the amount of the placing proceeds.

No share premium account?

In relation to the penultimate bullet, it is assumed here, for the purposes of what follows, that **12.3** there is merger relief under s612 and thus no share premium account falls to be recorded. That is a question of law, which will depend on the particular facts and circumstances of the case. Companies may wish to take legal advice. This Technical Release offers none.

Accounting entries

12.4   In terms of accounting entries, where there is no share premium account there will instead be an other reserve. This would arise because either:

- the Company chooses to record a reserve at the point of acquiring the shares in NewCo in the same way that a company may choose to record a merger reserve in lieu of share premium in any case of the application of s612. This amount is a profit at law, in the same way as merger relief reserves generally (see paragraph 3.8(b)(ii)); or

- the Company could (under UK GAAP) choose to record its investment in NewCo at the nominal value of the shares and thus no reserve arises at this point. However, once the investment in NewCo is redeemed for cash, the Company will record a profit on the redemption in the same amount.

12.5   Either way, the Company finds itself with a merger reserve or a profit reserve and the same question applies to them both: is the reserve realised? The method by which the reserve was recorded makes no difference to the question.

The framework for considering whether the reserve is a realised profit?

12.6   The reserve is akin to one arising where a company receives a capital contribution from shareholders. Paragraphs 12.7 to 12.15 below consider, in effect, whether the assessment of realisation of that reserve proceeds in any different fashion from that of a conventional capital contribution reserve.

Prior to considering the use of the funds

12.7   Following redemption of the Newco preference shares, the cash proceeds thereof will, subject to the question of linkage set out below, fall to be treated as 'qualifying consideration' in the hands of the Company (see paragraph 3.9(a) or (f), depending on whether as an accounting entry the reserve arises on redemption by NewCo or on issue by the Company). *Prima facie,* and subject to what follows, the reserve would therefore be considered a realised profit.

Questions of the use of the funds

12.8   Sometimes the reason for the placing or rights issue – and a reason will always be given to the market – is to obtain funds for an acquisition. The precise circumstances of the acquisition will vary. It is possible that the acquisition and placing/ rights issue are conditional upon each other; or they might occur on the same day; or the acquisition may be announced at the placing date but still itself be conditional; or there may in some industries be regulatory restrictions on the use of the cash proceeds.

12.9   In other cases the company may have raised the funds in connection with a need to recapitalise a subsidiary. For example, it is possible that the company may be compelled by regulatory requirements immediately to subscribe for equity share capital in a subsidiary; or it may be a commercial necessity to recapitalise a subsidiary. Other cases might include a capitalisation of the company itself for regulatory reasons; or to fund the repayment of the company's own debt.

12.10   In this context the question arises as to whether the reserve should therefore be deemed to relate to the intended application of the funds (ie with the placing/ rights issue and the application of the funds being a series of related transactions) rather than to the immediate cash proceeds of the placing/ rights issue.

This can be split into two questions: **12.11**

- Does the use of the funds need to be considered in terms of the 'linkage' principle in paragraph 3.5?
- If so, will the use of the funds be found to be linked under that provision?

Should linkage be considered?

Paragraph 3.5 is of general application and contains no exceptions. There is nothing   **12.12**
in a cash box structure that marks it out as fundamentally different and warranting the
insertion of an exception to paragraph 3.5. The effect of the application of paragraph 3.5
has therefore to be considered.

Two other observations may be noted at this juncture. First, it would be unjustifiable to halt   **12.13**
the analysis at the conversion of the NewCo preference shares into cash, and not to go on to
consider whether there should be brought into the analysis the conversion of the cash into
some other asset; it is a commercial reality that cash boxes are not carried out in a vacuum.

Second, if the question of linkage were not addressed, all manner of intra-group transactions   **12.14**
might claim to result in realised profits.

Conclusion as to framework to be employed in the assessment of realisation

Thus, all of the normal rules of realisation, including the effect of the application of   **12.15**
paragraph 3.5 (linkage etc), apply. The assessment therefore proceeds in no different a way
from that of the case of a conventional capital contribution.

The effect of the application of paragraph 3.5

Paragraphs 12.7 to 12.15 above establish that a cash-box share issue and its wider context   **12.16**
should be considered under the paragraph 3.5 principle of linkage etc. Paragraphs 12.17
to 12.35 look at the application of that principle to some scenarios detailing the use
of the cash raised. The questions are: is the use of the funds linked; and if so, does the
linked transaction, taken together with the equity issue, result in an increase in qualifying
consideration for the company issuing the shares?

Recapitalisation of the company for regulatory reasons

Suppose that the company is subject to a regulatory regime that requires it to maintain a   **12.17**
specified level of net assets. The company's position and performance has deteriorated and
it needs to raise funds, by an equity issue, to maintain its regulatory compliance and hence
the continuation of its business. The cash received is employed as working capital.

Unless the company needs to hold the funds raised in some particular asset within its   **12.18**
business, eg if the regulatory requirement is to hold the funds in a particular type of asset,
then there is no linked transaction. Accordingly, the profit is a realised one. Even so, it
seems unlikely that in practice the company would make a distribution from it as to do so
would reduce the company's regulatory capital again.

If there were a need to hold the funds in some particular asset category, then consideration   **12.19**
would need to be given as to whether the specific asset meets the definition of qualifying
consideration (see 3.11). To the extent that the asset is qualifying consideration the reserve
that is created would be realised (albeit its distribution may not be a practical proposition
from a regulatory perspective as noted above).

Recapitalisation of a subsidiary company, with equity, for regulatory reasons

12.20 The company is a holding company that holds a subsidiary that is subject to a regulatory regime that requires it to maintain a specified level of net assets. The subsidiary's position and performance has deteriorated and the subsidiary needs to raise funds, by an equity issue, to maintain its regulatory compliance and hence the continuation of its business. The company (that is, the holding company of the regulated subsidiary) raises the cash by an equity issue of its own and uses the cash to subscribe for equity in the subsidiary.

12.21 The regulatory necessity to recapitalise the subsidiary is enough for the company's onward investment of the funds to be linked. In this case the cash has been invested in equity shares in a subsidiary which will not be qualifying consideration (see 4.10), and thus the reserve is unrealised.

Recapitalisation of a subsidiary company, with equity, out of commercial necessity

12.22 The case here is similar to that above save that the subsidiary is not regulated. It is, however, in financial difficulties and needs funds to continue in business. The company (that is, the holding company of the troubled subsidiary) raises the cash by an equity issue of its own and uses the cash to subscribe for equity in the subsidiary.

12.23 The commercial necessity to recapitalise the subsidiary is enough for the company's onward investment of the funds to be linked. As with the previous example the cash has been invested in equity shares in a subsidiary, which will not be qualifying consideration (see 4.10), and thus the reserve is unrealised.

Recapitalisation of a subsidiary company, with inter-company debt, out of commercial necessity

12.24 Assume that the facts are the same as the previous example except that the cash raised by the company is lent to the subsidiary rather than the company's subscribing for subsidiary shares.

12.25 Again the commercial necessity to recapitalise the subsidiary is enough for the company's onward lending of the funds to be linked. In this case, the cash has been turned into an inter-company debt receivable. Whilst an inter-company debt receivable can be qualifying consideration (see 3.11(d)), where the funds have been lent to the subsidiary in view of, say, its troubled financial condition, then it is very unlikely that the debt would meet the tests necessary to be qualifying consideration and as such the reserve would be unrealised. A loan to a financially troubled subsidiary may also be on subordinated terms (such as a contingent loan) and so would make it even less likely that the definition of qualifying consideration would be met.

Repayment of the company's own debt

12.26 In this scenario the cash raised as new equity is used to repay some of the company's debt. There might be a variety of reasons for this. For example, the company may be rebalancing its gearing ratio for the long term, say because credit markets will not enable it to sustain the previous high level. Or it might be that the company needs to repay that debt in order to survive and has no other sources of liquidity but an equity raising.

12.27 The commercial necessity to repay debt, or even the management intention to do so, is enough for the company's debt repayment to be linked. However, this does not prevent a realised profit arising. The reserve will in fact be realised as release or settlement of debt is itself a form of qualifying consideration (see 3.11(c)).

However, if the debt arose from the acquisition of an asset that does not meet the definition of qualifying consideration and the repayment through the equity issue was planned at the time of the acquisition of the asset, the reserve will be unrealised.   **12.28**

Raising cash to be used to fund possible, unspecified acquisitions

In this scenario the company believes that there will be opportunities, in the medium term, to acquire some companies on favourable terms. It therefore raises cash now in order to move quickly if a target is identified.   **12.29**

There is not a strong enough nexus between the fund raising and an actual, specific acquisition. Acquisitions are the motivation, but there is not a specific target. In addition, a change in commercial circumstances is a realistic possibility (in a similar way to the sufficient time elapsing during in a planned transaction sequence such that commercial circumstances could change and the rest of the sequence not go ahead – see paragraph 3.74 above). The nexus is too weak for there to be linkage under paragraph 3.5.   **12.30**

Thus subject to any arrangement or intention to hold the funds in non-qualifying consideration form, here a realised profit will result.   **12.31**

Using the cash received to fund a specific acquisition – where the placing and acquisition are inter-conditional

The company raises equity funds from placees and the placing and the acquisition are conditional upon each other.   **12.32**

The acquisition is linked (legally in this case). As the linked use of the cash is to acquire an equity investment that thereby becomes a subsidiary, the reserve will not be realised as the investment is not qualifying consideration as it is not readily convertible to cash (see 4.10).   **12.33**

Other acquisition funding cases

Other acquisition funding cases will require careful examination to determine the level of linkage. The above two examples are at the opposite ends of the spectrum, one where the cash will be used to fund an acquisition, the other where it may or may not be used but in any event not immediately. Obviously there will be situations between these two extremes where judgement will need to be exercised. It should be recalled, however, that legal linkage is not a necessary test for linkage to exist. Simultaneously effecting a fund raising and an acquisition would also be very strong linkage; and few other types of circumstances are likely to be as non-specific and subject to change as the scenario involving possible but unspecified acquisitions.   **12.34**

Disclosure

The July 2008 edition of the ASB newsletter *Inside Track* noted that the UITF had received a request for guidance about cash box structures. The UITF decided not to address this issue because it was a matter of the application of company law and was already being addressed by the Institutes. However, the issue reached the UITF agenda because some companies had failed to explain adequately, in their financial statements, why no share premium account arose on an issue of share at an apparent premium. When cash box   **12.35** structures are used, it is important that directors consider the adequacy of disclosures about their use and the consequential effect on items in financial statements.

LC, 29.10.10

Liz.Cole@icaew.com

Appendix 1
Examples of the application of sections 845 and 846

EXAMPLE 1 – TRANSFER OF AN ASSET AT BOOK VALUE APPLYING SECTION 845

A company has profits available for distribution of £10,000 on its profit and loss account. It sells a non-cash asset to its parent for a consideration of £20,000 which is equal to its book value. The market value of the asset is £60,000.

The company can apply section 845 in these circumstances and, as explained below, applying this section the distribution would be lawful. Section 845(2) provides that the amount of the distribution is taken to be zero because the amount of the consideration for the transfer is not less than the book value of the asset. Section 845(3) provides that, for the purposes of section 845(1)(a), the company's profits available for distribution are treated as increased by the amount (if any) by which the amount or value of any consideration for the transfer exceeds the book value of the asset. The adjustment in this case is therefore zero and the profits available for distribution in accordance with section 845(1)(a) are treated as £10,000. The company may therefore lawfully make the transfer of the asset because the distributable profits are treated as £10,000 and the amount of the distribution is treated as zero. Thus immediately after the transfer the company's distributable reserves remain £10,000.

Realised profits brought forward	10,000
Adjustment for section 845(3)	—
Profits available for distribution	10,000
Distribution measured in accordance with section 845	—
Balance carried forward on reserves	£10,000

Had the asset been revalued immediately before transfer to its market value of £60,000 the position (using section 846) would have been as follows:

Realised profits brought forward	10,000
Unrealised profit arising from revaluation from book value (£20,000) to market value (£60,000) of the non-cash asset to be transferred to the parent	40,000
Profits treated as available for distribution in accordance with section 846	50,000
Distribution measured as the difference between the fair value of the asset (£60,000) and the consideration received (£20,000)	(40,000)
Balance carried forward on reserves	£10,000

Thus, it can be seen that, section 845 gives the same position before and after the transfer in this example as is given by revaluing the asset and using section 846. The balance carried forward on reserves is a realised profit.

EXAMPLE 2 – TRANSFER OF AN ASSET AT ABOVE BOOK VALUE APPLYING SECTION 845 WHERE THERE IS INITIALLY A POSITIVE BALANCE OF DISTRIBUTABLE RESERVES

A company has profits available for distribution of £10,000 on its profit and loss account. It sells a non-cash asset to its parent for a consideration of £50,000 which exceeds its book value of £20,000. The market value of the asset is £60,000.

The company can apply section 845 in these circumstances and, as explained below, applying this section the distribution would be lawful. Section 845(2) provides that the amount of the distribution is taken to be zero because the amount of the consideration for the transfer is not less than the book value of the asset. Section 845(3) provides that, for the purposes of section 845(1)(a), the company's profits available for distribution are treated as increased by the amount (if any) by which the amount or value of any consideration for the transfer exceeds the book value of the asset. The adjustment in this case is therefore £30,000 and the profits available for distribution in accordance with section 845(1)(a) are treated as £40,000. The company may therefore lawfully make the transfer of the asset because the distributable profits are treated as £40,000 and the amount of the distribution is treated as zero.

Realised profits brought forward	10,000
Adjustment for section 845(3):	–
Increase in profits treated as available for distribution due to the consideration being in excess of the book value (£50,000 less £20,000)	30,000
Profits treated as available for distribution	40,000
Distribution measured in accordance with section 845	–
Balance carried forward on reserves	£40,000

Whether or not the increase in reserves of £30,000 after the transfer is a realised profit depends on whether the consideration for the transfer is qualifying consideration.

If it is now assumed that the company revalued the asset to its market value of £60,000 it can again be seen that sections 845 and 846 give the same position after the transfer.

Realised profits brought forward	10,000
Unrealised profit arising from revaluation from book value (£20,000) to market value (£60,000) of the non-cash asset to be transferred to the parent	40,000
Profits treated as available for distribution in accordance with section 846	50,000
Distribution measured as the difference between the fair value of the asset (£60,000) and the consideration received (£50,000)	(10,000)
Balance carried forward on reserves	£40,000

EXAMPLE 3 – TRANSFER OF AN ASSET AT BELOW BOOK VALUE APPLYING SECTION 845

A company has profits available for distribution of £10,000 on its profit and loss account. It sells a non-cash asset to its parent for a consideration of £15,000 which is £5,000 below its book value of £20,000. The market value of the asset is £60,000.

The company can apply section 845 in these circumstances and, as explained below, applying this section the distribution would be lawful. Section 845(2) provides that the amount of the distribution is taken to be £5,000 because the amount of the consideration for the transfer is £15,000 and the book value of the asset is £20,000. Section 845(3) provides that, for the purposes of section 845(1)(a), the company's profits available for distribution are treated as increased by the amount (if any) by which the amount or value of any consideration for the transfer exceeds the book value of the asset. The adjustment in this case is therefore zero and the profits available for distribution in accordance with section 845(1)(a) are treated as £10,000. The company may therefore lawfully make the transfer of the asset because the distributable reserves are treated as £10,000 and the amount of the distribution is treated as £5,000. Thus immediately after the transfer the company's distributable reserves are £5,000.

Realised profits brought forward	10,000
Adjustment for section 845(3)	
Profits available for distribution	10,000
Distribution measured in accordance with section 845 (£20,000 – £15,000)	5,000
Balance carried forward on reserves	£5,000

The balance carried forward on reserves is a realised profit.

Again, if it is now assumed that the company revalued the asset to its market value of £60,000 it can be seen that sections 845 and 846 give the same position after the transfer.

Realised profits brought forward	10,000
Unrealised profit arising from revaluation from book value (£20,000) to market value (£60,000) of the non-cash asset to be transferred to the parent	40,000
Profits treated as available for distribution in accordance with section 846	50,000
Distribution measured as the difference between the fair value of the asset (£60,000) and the consideration received (£15,000)	(45,000)
Balance carried forward on reserves	£5,000

EXAMPLE 4 – TRANSFER OF AN ASSET AT ABOVE BOOK VALUE APPLYING SECTION 845 WHERE THERE IS INITIALLY A NEGATIVE BALANCE OF DISTRIBUTABLE RESERVES

A company has an accumulated deficit of £10,000 on its profit and loss account (ie it has a deficit on its profits available for distribution). It sells a non-cash asset to its parent for a consideration of £50,000 compared with a book value of £20,000 and a market value of £60,000.

The company can apply section 845 in these circumstances although it starts with a negative balance of distributable profits. Section 845(3) provides that, for the purposes of section 845(1)(a), the company's profits available for distribution are treated as increased by the amount (if any) by which the amount or value of any consideration for the transfer exceeds the book value of the asset. The adjustment in this case is therefore £30,000 and the profits available for distribution in accordance with section 845(1)(a) are treated as £20,000. Section 845(2) provides that the amount of the distribution is taken to be zero because the amount of the consideration for the transfer is not less than the book value of the asset. The company may therefore lawfully make the transfer of the asset because the distributable reserves are treated as £20,000 and the amount of the distribution is treated as zero.

Realised losses brought forward	(10,000)
Adjustment for section 845(3):	
Increase in profits treated as available for distribution due to the consideration being in excess of the book value (£50,000 less £20,000)	30,000
Profits treated as available for distribution	20,000
Distribution measured in accordance with section 845	
Balance carried forward on reserves	£20,000

Although the entire profit of £30,000 has been treated as realised for the purposes of the distribution, the balance carried forward on reserves falls to be treated in accordance with the normal rules. The analysis of reserves carried forward on reserves will depend on whether the transfer of the asset was for qualifying consideration. If the transfer was for qualifying consideration, the whole of the balance of £20,000 carried forward will be a realised profit. If the transfer was not for qualifying consideration, the profit arising on the transfer of the asset will be an unrealised profit and the analysis of reserves will be as follows:

Realised losses	(10,000)
Unrealised profit	30,000
Balance on reserves	£20,000

The same position is achieved by revaluing the asset and applying section 846. The asset could be revalued from £20,000 to £60,000 (its market value) which results in an unrealised profit of £40,000. The distribution is measured at £10,000 being the difference between the fair value of the asset and the consideration received on disposal. In accordance with section 846(2), the unrealised profit of £40,000 is treated as a realised profit for the purposes of determining the lawfulness of the distribution which consists of the sale of the non-cash asset. The profits treated as available for distribution under section 846 are therefore £30,000 which is adequate to cover the distribution of £10,000. This may be summarised as follows:

Realised losses brought forward	(10,000)
Unrealised profit arising from revaluation from book value (£20,000) to market value (£60,000) of the non-cash asset to be transferred to the parent	40,000
Profits treated as available for distribution in accordance with section 846	30,000
Distribution measured as the difference between the fair value of the asset (£60,000) and the consideration received (£50,000)	(10,000)
Balance carried forward on reserves	£20,000

The analysis of reserves carried forward will depend on whether the transfer of the non-cash asset was for qualifying consideration in the same way as described above under section 845.

The distribution in kind of the non-cash asset may therefore, in effect, be made out of unrealised profits without making good the shortfall on realised profits first. Whether or not the consideration for the transfer meets the definition of qualifying consideration has no effect of the lawfulness of the transfer but affects the disposition of the reserves following the transfer.

Appendix 2
Numerical illustrations for section 6

The following are numerical illustrations of the eight examples discussed in Section 6 of the guidance. The illustrations reflect the application of the 10 Principles in 6.7 to 6.40 of Section 6. The assumptions set out in 6.43 to 6.45 of Section 6 apply to these numerical illustrations.

These illustrations are based on simple terms and conditions of the types of financial instruments concerned. Therefore, they cannot, and do not, purport to be representative of the accounting that may flow from more complex terms and conditions. Determining whether a financial instrument is debt, equity or is a compound instrument and/or contains embedded derivatives depends on a rigorous analysis of the relevant instruments' full terms and conditions.

IFRSs and converged UK GAAP (e.g. using FRS 26 'Financial instruments: Recognition and Measurement' and the fair value accounting rules in the Act) do not distinguish between profits that are realised and those that are not. Furthermore, as certain classes of share capital and their associated share premium have to be classified as liabilities and others split into debt and equity components, it is no longer possible to point to one place in the balance sheet that represents all of a company's share capital and share premium. Hence companies will need to maintain sufficient records to enable the tracking of their actual share capital and share premium and realised profits and thus their distributable profits. Companies may choose to do this in the form of memorandum accounts dealing with shares and options in relation to shares according to their legal form. Although, a company's annual statutory accounts prepared in accordance with IFRSs or converged UK GAAP will form their relevant accounts for the purposes of section 836 of the Act, it will be necessary to reconcile these back to records such as these memorandum accounts to understand the legal position in respect of their share capital, share premium, realised and distributable profits. Such memorandum accounts are illustrated below in addition to the balance sheet position under IFRSs/converged UK GAAP.

In the memorandum accounts, the realised profits available are shown for illustrative purposes as a separate component of equity.

In the IFRS/converged UK GAAP accounts, 'Other reserves' represent amounts taken to equity for accounting purposes but which do not form part of 'share capital and undistributable reserves'. For public companies in these illustrations, the expression 'share capital and undistributable reserves' for the purposes of section 831 comprises 'Share capital', 'Share premium' and 'Capital redemption reserve'. The P&L reserve is taken initially to be comprised wholly of realised profits.

For the avoidance of doubt, these illustrations do not purport to define the headings or reserve names within which amounts, thrown up only by IFRS/ converged UK GAAP accounting, must as a matter of accounting convention be maintained within equity.

EXAMPLE 1 – FORWARD CONTRACT TO REPURCHASE OWN EQUITY SHARES (SECTION 6, 6.46 – 6.50)

A company has entered into a forward contract to repurchase 100 of its own equity shares from a third party in 5 years' time and the shares are to be cancelled on repurchase. These shares have a nominal value of £100 and are to be bought back for £100 (present value assumed to be £70). The company will buy the shares back, assuming it has sufficient distributable profits, and cancel them.

Under IAS 32/FRS 25, as the company will be required to deliver cash, the forward contract meets the definition of a financial liability.

Journal entries for the IFRS / converged UK GAAP balance sheet

On Day 1:

Dr	Equity – Other reserves	£70
Cr	Liability	£70

Being the recognition of the liability under the forward contract.

Note that the liability amount is the discounted present value of the redemption amount and is assumed to be £70 in this example. This recognises that the company has purchased an interest in itself on day 1 with the consideration being deferred.

The debit of £70 that has been recorded in other reserves is not an accounting loss and does not affect distributable profits on day 1.

Public company
The recognition of the liability reduces net assets and hence restricts distributable profits for public companies as a result of the section 831 net assets test.

During the 5 years:

Dr	Profit & Loss – Interest expense	£30
Cr	Liability	£30

Being the accretion of the discounted liability to the redemption amount of £100.

Private company
Although the interest is charged to the profit and loss account, it is not a loss for the purposes of Part VIII of the Act. Thus it is not a realised loss.

Public company
However, for a public company, although realised profits have not decreased, net assets have decreased (as the liability has increased). Hence there is a restriction through the operation of section 831 on the profits available for distribution of £100 in total immediately prior to repurchase as a result of this transaction.

On settlement of the contract:

Dr	Liability	£100
Cr	Cash	£100

Being the payment (or distribution) to settle the forward contract.

Dr Equity – Profit & Loss reserve	£70
Cr Equity – Other reserves	£70

Being the entry to reflect the consumption of distributable profits in the Profit & Loss reserve as a result of the payment to settle the forward contract.

Dr Equity – Share capital	£100
Cr Equity – Capital redemption reserve	£100

Being the transfer to maintain the capital of the company.

Memorandum balance sheet

	Before entering into forward	Enter into forward to repurchase shares	After entering into forward	Entries during the 5 years	Before repurchase	Repurchase entries	After repurchase
	£	£	£	£	£	£	£
Cash	100	0	0	0	100	(100)	0
Assets	200	0	0	0	200	0	200
Net assets	**300**	**0**	**0**	**0**	**300**	**(100)**	**200**
Share capital	200	0	0	0	200	(100)	100
Share premium	0	0	0	0	0	0	0
Capital redemption reserve	0	0	0	0	0	100	100
Realised profits	100	0	0	0	100⁺	(100)	0
Shareholders' funds	**300**	**0**	**0**	**0**	**300**	**(100)**	**200**

⁺£100 represents the maximum profits available for distribution but for a public company this will be restricted by £100, immediately prior to repurchase, through the operation of section 831, which is applied to the section 836 relevant accounts (ie the IFRS / converged UK GAAP balance sheet below) which show that net assets are equal to share capital and undistributable reserves.

For the purposes of section 831, in this illustration 'share capital and undistributable reserves' comprise 'Share capital', 'Share premium' and 'Capital redemption reserve'.

IFRS / converged UK GAAP balance sheet

	Before entering into forward	Enter into forward to repurchase shares	After entering into forward	Entries during the 5 years	Before repurchase	Repurchase entries	After repurchase
	£	£	£	£	£	£	£
Cash	100	0	100	0	100	(100)	0
Assets	200	0	200	0	200	0	200
Liabilities	0	(70)	(70)	(30)	(100)	100	0
Net assets	**300**	**(70)**	**230**	**(30)**	**200**	**0**	**200**
Share capital	200	0	200	0	200	(100)	100
Share premium	0	0	0	0	0	0	0
Capital redemption reserve	0	0	0	0	0	100	100
Other reserves	0	(70)	(70)	0	(70)	70	0
P&L reserve	100	0	100	(30)	70	(70)	0
Shareholders' equity	**300**	**(70)**	**230**	**(30)**	**200**	**0**	**200**

EXAMPLE 2 – WRITTEN OPTION TO REPURCHASE OWN EQUITY SHARES (SECTION 6, 6.51 TO 6.53)

A company writes an option to repurchase 100 of its own equity shares from a third party in 5 years' time. These shares have a nominal value of £100 and will be bought back for £100 (present value assumed to be £70). If the option is exercised by the third party, the company intends to buy the shares back out of profits, assuming it has sufficient distributable profits, and to cancel them. The company receives a premium of £5 on issue of the option.

Under IAS 32/FRS 25, as the company will be required to deliver cash on exercise of the option, the contract meets the definition of a financial liability. The premium received on the issue of the option is required to be taken directly to equity.

Journal entries for the IFRS / converged UK GAAP balance sheet

On Day 1:

Dr   Cash   £5
Cr   Equity – Other reserves   £5

Being the recognition of the premium received.

The option premium is a realised profit because the premium is regarded as a profit at law and has been received in the form of cash. For the purposes of this illustration, the premium has been credited to other reserves on initial receipt and has remained there on exercise (but it could be taken to P&L reserve as illustrated in example 4).

Dr   Equity – Other reserves   £70
Cr   Liability   £70

Being the recognition of the liability under the written option.

Note that the liability amount is the discounted present value of the redemption amount and is assumed to be £70 in this example. This recognises that the company has purchased an interest in itself on day 1 with the consideration being deferred.

The debit of £70 that has been recorded in other reserves is not an accounting loss and does not affect distributable profits on day 1.

Public company
The recognition of the liability reduces net assets but not share capital and undistributable reserves and hence restricts distributable profits by £70 for public companies as a result of the section 831 net assets test.

During the 5 years:

Dr   Profit & Loss – Interest expense   £30
Cr   Liability   £30

Being the accretion over 5 years of the discounted liability to the redemption value of £100.

Private company
Although the interest is charged to the profit and loss account, it is not a loss for the purposes of Part VIII of the Act. Thus it is not a realised loss.

Public company

However, for a public company, although realised profits have not decreased, net assets have decreased (as the liability has increased). Hence there is a restriction through the operation of section 831 on profits available for distribution of the amount recognised a liability as a result of this transaction (in this case £100).

On settlement of the contract:

Dr	Liability	£100
Cr	Cash	£100

Being the payment (or distribution) to settle the forward contract.

Dr	Equity – Share capital	£100
Cr	Equity – Capital redemption reserve	£100

Being the transfer to maintain the capital of the company.

Dr	Equity – Profit & Loss reserve	£70
Cr	Equity – Other reserves	£70

Being the entry to reflect the consumption of distributable profits in the Profit & Loss reserve as a result of the payment on exercise.

Memorandum balance sheet

	Before issuing option	Issue of option to repurchase shares	After issuing option	Entries during the 5 years	Before exercise	Exercise entries	After exercise
	£	£	£	£	£	£	£
Cash	100	5	105	0	105	(100)	5
Assets	200	0	200	0	200	0	200
Net assets	**300**	**5**	**305**	**0**	**305**	**(100)**	**205**
Share capital	200	0	200	0	200	(100)	100
Share premium	0	0	0	0	0	0	0
Capital redemption reserve	0	0	0	0	0	100	100
Realised profits	100	5	105	0	105⁺	(100)	5
Shareholders' funds	**300**	**0**	**305**	**0**	**305**	**(100)**	**205**

⁺*£105 represents the maximum profits available for distribution but for a public company this will be restricted by £100, immediately prior to exercise, through the operation of section 831, which is applied to the section 836 relevant accounts (ie the IFRS / converged UK GAAP balance sheet below) which show that net assets only exceed share capital and undistributable reserves by £5.*

For the purposes of section 831, in this illustration 'share capital and undistributable reserves' comprise 'Share capital', 'Share premium' and 'Capital redemption reserve'.

IFRS / converged UK GAAP balance sheet

	Before issuing option	Issue of option to repurchase shares	After issuing option	Entries during the 5 years	Before exercise	Exercise entries	After exercise
	£	£	£	£	£	£	£
Cash	100	5	105	0	105	(100)	5
Assets	200	0	200	0	200	0	200
Liabilities	0	(70)	(70)	(30)	(100)	100	0
Net assets	**300**	**(65)**	**235**	**(30)**	**205**	**0**	**205**
Share capital	200	0	200	0	200	(100)	100
Share premium	0	0	0	0	0	0	0
Capital redemption reserve	0	0	0	0	0	100	100
Other reserves	0	(65)	(65)	0	(65)	70	5
P&L reserve	100	0	100	(30)	70	(70)	0
Shareholders' equity	**300**	**(65)**	**235**	**(30)**	**205**	**0**	**205**

EXAMPLE 3 – FORWARD CONTRACT TO ISSUE OWN EQUITY SHARES (SECTION 6, 6.54 TO 6.56)

A company contracts with a third party that the latter will subscribe in one year's time for 100 of the company's £1 ordinary shares for a fixed price of £2 each. The contract cannot be settled other than by an exchange of the fixed amount of cash (£200) for the fixed number (100) of shares. It is assumed that the fair value of the forward contract at inception is zero and thus no cash is paid or received at that date. The functional currency of the company is pounds sterling.

No accounting entries are made on inception of the contract because no cash is paid or received since the contract's initial fair value is zero. This forward contract to deliver a fixed number of the company's own shares in exchange for a fixed amount of cash in the company's functional currency meets the definition of an equity instrument in IAS 32. There are no other settlement alternatives otherwise than through the delivery of shares in exchange for cash. Consequently, the right to receive the cash in one year's time is not recognised by the company. Therefore, where a company enters into a forward contract to issue ordinary shares, the IAS 32/FRS 25 accounting for such an arrangement raises no issues of distributable profits.

No accounting entries are made until the forward contract matures in one year's time, when the company receives £200 in cash and issues 100 ordinary shares to the contract's counterparty.

Journal entries for the IFRS / converged UK GAAP balance sheet

On settlement of the contract:

Dr	Cash	£200
Cr	Equity – Share capital	£100
Cr	Equity – Share premium	£100

Being the issue of the shares at a premium of £1 per share for £200 in cash.

Memorandum balance sheet

	Before entering into forward	Enter into forward to issue shares	After entering into forward	On settlement of the contract	After settlement
	£	£	£	£	£
Cash	100	0	100	200	300
Assets	200	0	200	0	200
Liabilities	0	0	0	0	0
Net assets	**300**	**0**	**300**	**200**	**500**
Share capital	200	0	200	100	300
Share premium	0	0	0	100	100
Capital redemption reserve	0	0	0	0	0
Other reserves	0	0	0	0	0
Realised profits	100	0	100[+]	0	100
Shareholders' equity	**300**	**0**	**300**	**200**	**500**

⁺*£100 represents the maximum profits available for distribution. For a public company there is no restriction through the operation of section 831, which is applied to the section 836 relevant accounts (ie the IFRS / converged UK GAAP balance sheet below) which show that net assets exceeds share capital and undistributable reserves by £100.*

For the purposes of section 831, in this illustration 'share capital and undistributable reserves' comprise 'Share capital', 'Share premium' and 'Capital redemption reserve'.

IFRS / converged UK GAAP balance sheet

	Before entering into forward	Enter into forward to issue shares	After entering into forward	On settlement of the contract	After settlement
	£	£	£	£	£
Cash	100	0	100	200	300
Assets	200	0	200	0	200
Liabilities	0	0	0	0	0
Net assets	**300**	**0**	**300**	**200**	**500**
Share capital	200	0	200	100	300
Share premium	0	0	0	100	100
Capital redemption reserve	0	0	0	0	0
Other reserves	0	0	0	0	0
P&L reserve	100	0	100	0	100
Shareholders' equity	**300**	**0**	**300**	**200**	**500**

EXAMPLE 4 – WRITTEN OPTION TO ISSUE OWN EQUITY SHARES (SECTION 6, 6.57 TO 6.58)

A company issues an option allowing the holder to subscribe for 100 £1 ordinary shares for £1 each in one years' time. The functional currency of the company is pounds sterling. The option cannot be settled other than by an exchange of the cash in the functional currency of the company for the fixed number of shares. The holder makes an immediate payment of £5 to the company for the granting of this option.

The option is an equity instrument. Accordingly, the £5 received is credited directly to equity funds. The £5 is not an accounting profit. The £5 credit remains in equity funds irrespective of whether the option is exercised or lapses. If the option is exercised, the £100 is also credited directly to equity funds in the normal way.

Journal entries for the IFRS / converged UK GAAP balance sheet

On Day 1:

Dr	Cash	£5
Cr	Equity – Other reserves	£5

Being the receipt of the option premium.

In law the premium received is a profit at the outset, and a realised profit because it is received in cash. For the purposes of this illustration the premium has been credited to Other reserves on initial receipt and is transferred to the Profit & Loss reserve when the option is exercised.

On Exercise:

Dr	Cash	£100
Cr	Equity – Share capital	£100
Dr	Equity – Other reserves	£5
Cr	Equity – Profit & Loss reserve	£5

Being the entries for the issue of the new ordinary shares and receipt of the subscription monies and the transfer of the option premium to Profit & Loss reserve.

Memorandum balance sheet

	Before issuing option	Issue of option to issue shares	After issuing option	On exercise	After exercise
	£	£	£	£	£
Cash	100	5	105	100	205
Assets	200	0	200	0	200
Liabilities	0	0	0	0	0
Net assets	**300**	**5**	**305**	**100**	**405**
Share capital	200	0	200	100	300
Share premium	0	0	0	0	0
Capital redemption reserve	0	0	0	0	0
Other reserves	0	0	0	0	0

	Before issuing option	Issue of option to issue shares	After issuing option	On exercise	After exercise
	£	£	£	£	£
Realised profits	100	5	105†	0	105
Shareholders' equity	**300**	**0**	**305**	**100**	**405**

†£105 *represents the maximum profits available for distribution. For a public company there will be no restriction through the operation of section 831, which is applied to the section 836 relevant accounts (ie the IFRS / converged UK GAAP balance sheet below) which show that net assets exceed share capital and undistributable reserves by £105.*

For the purposes of section 831, in this illustration 'share capital and undistributable reserves' comprise 'Share capital', 'Share premium' and 'Capital redemption reserve'.

IFRS / converged UK GAAP balance sheet

	Before issuing option	Issue of option to issue shares	After issuing option	On exercise	After exercise
	£	£	£	£	£
Cash	100	5	105	100	205
Assets	200	0	200	0	200
Liabilities	0	0	0	0	0
Net assets	**300**	**5**	**305**	**100**	**405**
Share capital	200	0	200	100	300
Share premium	0	0	0	0	0
Capital redemption reserve	0	0	0	0	0
Other reserves	0	5	5	(5)	0
P&L reserve	100	0	100	5	105
Shareholders' equity	**300**	**5**	**305**	**100**	**405**

EXAMPLE 5 – CONVERTIBLE DEBT (SECTION 6, 6.59 TO 6.61)

A company issues a 5% £100 10-year convertible bond for £100. The bond is convertible, at the holder's option, into 100 £1 ordinary shares at the end of year 10. If not converted the bond is redeemable at the end of year 10 at par. The conversion feature cannot be settled other than by an exchange of the bond for the fixed number of shares. The company's functional currency is pounds sterling. There are no other features of the bond's terms and conditions that would deny equity treatment for the equity conversion option.

IAS 32/FRS 25 require, where their conditions are met, that convertible debt is split into its constituent components of an unconvertible debt (assumed fair value, £60) and a written option to subscribe for ordinary shares (the equity conversion option). The latter component is accounted for in the same way as the stand-alone written option described in Example 4 above.

Journal entries for the IFRS / converged UK GAAP balance sheet

On Day 1:

Dr	Cash	£100
Cr	Liability	£60
Cr	Equity – Other reserves	£40

Being the recognition of the constituent components.

The split accounting is determined by computing the fair value of the debt component and assigning to the equity component the difference between the value of the debt and the proceeds of the bond issue. The fair value of the debt component is calculated as the present value of the repayment at maturity plus the present value of the future coupon payments (which are lower than those for an unconvertible debt due to the presence of the conversion opportunity). The discount rate used in calculating the present values is the prevailing market interest rate at the date the bonds were issued for a similar debt without the conversion option. For the purposes of this illustration, it is assumed that the split accounting is determined as £60 attributable to the liability component and £40 to the equity component.

The initial credit to equity is not a profit. It is not an accounting profit because in accounting terms it is the equivalent of an equity instrument. As a matter of law, it is not a profit either, because the proceeds received are in consideration for taking on a liability, albeit a liability that is not fully reflected in the accounts.

Over the 10 year life of debt:

Dr	Profit & Loss – Interest expense	£90
Cr	Cash	£50
Cr	Liability	£40

Being the recognition of 10 annual coupons of £5 each and the total additional interest of £40 to accrete the liability up to the redemption value. The allocation of the £90 among the 10 years' profit and loss accounts is determined using the appropriate method stipulated under the relevant accounting standard.

Dr	Equity – Other reserves	£40
Cr	Equity – Profit & Loss reserve	£40

As the change to the liability becomes fully reflected in the accounts as a loss by virtue of the initial treatment through the additional interest charge, then the portion of the proceeds (£40) initially credited directly to equity offsets the impact of the initial treatment. For the purposes of this illustration, the amounts have been transferred from the Other reserves to the Profit & Loss reserve to reflect this.

At maturity (if conversion occurs):

Dr   Liability   £100
Cr   Equity – Share capital)   £100

If the debt converts, the £100 is credited direct to shareholders' funds.

At maturity on redemption (if conversion does not occur):

Dr   Liability   £100
Cr   Cash   £100

Recording the cash settlement of the liability.

Conversion

Memorandum balance sheet

	Before issuing convertible debt	Issue of convertible debt	After issuing convertible debt	Entries during the 10 years	Before conversion	Conversion entries	After conversion
	£	£	£	£	£	£	£
Cash	100	100	200	(50)	150	0	150
Assets	250	0	250	0	250	0	250
Liabilities	0	(100)	(100)	0	(100)	100	0
Net assets	**350**	**0**	**350**	**(50)**	**300**	**100**	**400**
Share capital	200	0	200	0	200	100	300
Share premium	0	0	0	0	0	0	0
Capital redemption reserve	0	0	0	0	0	0	0
Other reserves	0	0	0	0	0	0	0
Realised profits	150	0	150	(50)	100[+]	0	100
Shareholders' equity	**350**	**0**	**350**	**(50)**	**300**	**100**	**400**

[+]£100 represents the maximum profits available for distribution. For a public company there is no restriction through the operation of section 831, which is applied to the section 836 relevant accounts (ie the IFRS / converged UK GAAP balance sheet below) which show that net assets exceed share capital and undistributable reserves by £100.

For the purposes of section 831, in this illustration 'share capital and undistributable reserves' comprise 'Share capital', 'Share premium' and 'Capital redemption reserve'.

IFRS / converged UK GAAP balance sheet

	Before issuing convertible debt	Issue of convertible debt	After issuing convertible debt	Entries during the 10 years	Before conversion	Conversion entries	After conversion
	£	£	£	£	£	£	£
Cash	100	100	200	(50)	150	0	150
Assets	250	0	250	0	250	0	250
Liabilities	0	(60)	(60)	(40)	(100)	100	0
Net assets	**350**	**40**	**390**	**(90)**	**300**	**100**	**400**
Share capital	200	0	200	0	200	100	300
Share premium	0	0	0	0	0	0	0
Capital redemption reserve	0	0	0	0	0	0	0
Other reserves	0	40	40	(40)	0	0	0
P&L reserve	150	0	150	(50)	100	0	100
Shareholders' equity	**350**	**40**	**390**	**(90)**	**300**	**100**	**400**

Redemption

Memorandum balance sheet

	Before issuing convertible debt	Issue of convertible debt	After issuing convertible debt	Entries during the 10 years	Before Redemption	Redemption entries	After redemption
	£	£	£	£	£	£	£
Cash	100	100	200	(50)	150	(100)	50
Assets	250	0	250	0	250	0	250
Liabilities	0	(100)	(100)	0	(100)	100	0
Net assets	**350**	**0**	**350**	**(50)**	**300**	**0**	**300**
Share capital	200	0	200	0	200	0	200
Share premium	0	0	0	0	0	0	0
Capital redemption reserve	0	0	0	0	0	0	0
Other reserves	0	0	0	0	0	0	0
Realised profits	150	0	150	(50)	100[*]	0	100
Shareholders' equity	**350**	**0**	**350**	**(50)**	**300**	**0**	**300**

[*]*£100 represents the maximum profits available for distribution. For a public company there is no restriction through the operation of section 831, which is applied to the section 836 relevant accounts (ie the IFRS / converged UK GAAP balance sheet below) which show that net assets exceed share capital and undistributable reserves by £100.*

For the purposes of section 831, in this illustration "share capital and undistributable reserves comprise 'Share capital', 'Share premium' and 'Capital redemption reserve'.

IFRS / converged UK GAAP balance sheet

	Before issuing convertible debt	Issue of convertible debt	After issuing convertible debt	Entries during the 10 years	Before Redemption	Redemption entries	After redemption
	£	£	£	£	£	£	£
Cash	100	100	200	(50)	150	(100)	50
Assets	250	0	250	0	250	0	250
Liabilities	0	(60)	(60)	(40)	(100)	100	0
Net assets	**350**	**40**	**390**	**(90)**	**300**	**0**	**300**
Share capital	200	0	200	0	200	0	200
Share premium	0	0	0	0	0	0	0
Capital redemption reserve	0	0	0	0	0	0	0
Other reserves	0	40	40	(40)	0	0	0
P&L reserve	150	0	150	(50)	100	0	100
Shareholders' equity	**350**	**40**	**390**	**(90)**	**300**	**0**	**300**

EXAMPLE 6 – PREFERENCE SHARES PRESENTED AS LIABILITIES (SECTION 6, 6.62 TO 6.70)

A company issues for £110 (being fair value) in cash 100 of its 5% £1 preference shares which are mandatorily redeemable in 5 years' time for £125. The 5% coupons are non-discretionary, cumulative and payable annually. At redemption the company redeems them wholly out of distributable profits.

On issue of the redeemable preference shares the company is required to present these shares as a financial liability of £110, because the issuer has an obligation to transfer cash to the holder of the shares for both the principal and coupons and £110 is the fair value of the shares.

Journal entries for the IFRS / converged UK GAAP balance sheet

On day 1:

Dr	Cash	£110
Cr	Liability	£110

Being the recognition of the financial liability under IAS 32/FRS 25.

Entries during the 5 years:

Dr	Profit & Loss – Interest expense	£40
Cr	Cash	£25
Cr	Liability	£15

Being the recognition of the £5 annual non-discretionary dividends and the accretion of the liability over time, such that by redemption, the carrying amount of the liability is equal to the redemption price of £125. The allocation of the £40 among the 5 years' profit and loss accounts is determined using the appropriate method stipulated by the relevant accounting standard.

The presentation of the nominal value of £100 of, and the £10 of share premium associated with, the preference shares as a debt has no effect on the determination of the company's realised profits. The accrued dividend and the accrued redemption premium that is presented as an 'interest charge' in the profit and loss account, and thus an accounting loss, is not, as a matter of law, a loss, as it is a distribution at the time it is actually made as such in law. Hence it is not until dividends (and the redemption premium) take legal effect that distributable profits are consumed by the distribution.

Public company

Notwithstanding that there is no consumption of distributable profits until such time that the dividends (and redemption premium) have legal effect, the accounting liability recognised for accrued but unpaid preference dividends and the accreted redemption premium reduces net assets. Therefore under section 831 there is a restriction on profits available for distribution equal to the amount of the reduction in net assets. Just before redemption, and assuming that the preference dividends have been paid, the section 831 restriction will be equal to the reduction in net assets of £15. This can be observed by comparing the realised profits in the Memorandum balance sheet (£175) with the Profit & Loss reserve (£160) in the IFRS / converged UK GAAP balance sheet.

Entries on redemption:

Dr	Liability	£125
Cr	Cash	£125

At the end of year 5, the company delivers £125 in cash to the shareholder, who delivers 100 of the company's (£1) redeemable preference shares. The company sets its cash payment of £125 against the financial liability.

Capital maintenance considerations

In addition, the company has to comply with the Act. Consequently, under section 733 of the Act there has to be a credit to capital redemption reserve equal to the nominal value of the preference shares redeemed that had been presented within liabilities. A corresponding debit is also made to distributable profits (the rationale for which is set out below).

At the same time the £10 of share premium, previously represented by the accounting liability, now falls to be included in the share premium account. A corresponding debit is made to distributable profits (the rationale for which is set out below).

Additional entries required on redemption due to capital maintenance rules:

Dr	Equity – Profit & Loss reserve	£110
Cr	Equity – Capital redemption reserve	£100
Cr	Equity – Share premium	£10

Being the entry to the Profit & Loss reserve which together with the debit for the accrued redemption premium (£15) ensures that £125 of distributable profits is consumed by the redemption price, as required by law. The entry to the Capital redemption reserve is the entry to reflect the legal preservation of the company's capital on redemption out of distributable profits. The £10 entry to the share premium account reflects the legal preservation of the initial share premium.

Memorandum balance sheet

	Before issuing preference shares	Issue of preference shares	After issuing preference shares	Entries during the 5 years	Before redemption	Redemption entries	After redemption
	£	£	£	£	£	£	£
Cash	100	110	210	(25)	185	(125)	60
Assets	300	0	300	0	300	0	300
Liabilities	0	0	0	0	0	0	0
Net assets	**400**	**110**	**510**	**(25)**	**485**	**(125)**	**360**
Share capital	200	100	300	0	300	(100)	200
Share premium	0	10	10	0	10	0	10
Capital redemption reserve	0	0	0	0	0	100	100
Realised profits	200	0	200	(25)	175⁺	(125)	50
Shareholders' equity	**400**	**110**	**510**	**(25)**	**485**	**(125)**	**360**

£175 represents the maximum profits available for distribution but for a public company this will be restricted by £15 through the operation of section 831, which is applied to the section 836 relevant accounts (ie the IFRS / converged UK GAAP balance sheet below) which show that net assets only exceed share capital and undistributable reserves by £160.

For the purposes of section 831, in this illustration 'share capital and undistributable reserves' comprise 'Share capital', 'Share premium' and 'Capital redemption reserve'.

IFRS / converged UK GAAP balance sheet

	Before issuing preference shares	Issue of preference shares	After issuing preference shares	Entries during the 5 years	Before redemption	Redemption entries	After redemption
	£	£	£	£	£	£	£
Cash	100	110	210	(25)	185	(125)	60
Assets	300	0	300	0	300	0	300
Liabilities	0	(110)	(110)	(15)	(125)	125	0
Net assets	**400**	**0**	**400**	**(40)**	**360**	**0**	**360**
Share capital	200	0	200	0	200	0	200
Share premium	0	0	0	0	0	10	10
Capital redemption reserve	0	0	0	0	0	100	100
P&L reserve	200	0	200	(40)	160	(110)*	50
Shareholders' equity	**400**	**0**	**400**	**(40)**	**360**	**0**	**360**

Redemption price consumption of distributable profits of £125 = £110 debit at redemption + £15 debit over period to redemption as the additional interest charge (£40-£25).

EXAMPLE 7 – MANDATORILY REDEEMABLE PREFERENCE SHARES (SECTION 6, 6.71 TO 6.77)

A company issues £100 nominal value of its £1 preference shares for £110 in cash. These shares are redeemable in 5 years' time for £125. Dividends are discretionary and non-cumulative. Under IAS 32/FRS 25 paragraphs 28 and AG37, these shares contain both a liability (assumed fair value, £90) and an equity component. Hence the instrument is classified as debt with an equity component for the dividend feature. It is assumed that over the five years, a total of £50 of discretionary dividends are paid. The accounting is set out below:

Journal entries for the IFRS / converged UK GAAP balance sheet

On Day 1:

Dr	Cash	£110
Cr	Liability	£90
Cr	Equity – Share capital	£20

Being the cash receipt on issuing the shares and recording of the appropriate liability and equity components.

Note that the fair value of the liability amount is the discounted present value of the redemption amount and is assumed to be £90 in this example. The balance (£20) of the proceeds is allocated to the equity component. For ease of this illustration, it is assumed that the entire share premium (£10) is included in the liability and that the credit to equity (£20) is all share capital.

The £20 credit to equity is not an accounting profit and as a matter of law forms part of share capital. This applies irrespective of the allocation of the £20 between share capital and share premium.

Public company

For the purposes of section 831, there is no restriction on profits available for distribution on issue of the preference shares as share capital and undistributable profits have increased by £20 and this is equal to the increase in net assets. The presentation of the balance (£90) of the shares and share premium has no impact on the section 831 calculation.

During the 5 years:

Dr	Profit & Loss – Interest expense	£35
Cr	Liability	£35

Being the accretion of the discounted liability to the redemption amount of £125.

Private company

The presentation of the discounted present value of the redemption amount of the preference shares as a liability has no effect on the determination of the company's realised profits. The interest expense from the accretion up to the full amount of the redemption price is presented as an accounting loss – as it is shown as an 'interest charge'. Since the ultimate payment is either a distribution or a capital repayment, the 'interest charge' is, as a matter of law, not a loss even though it is accounted for as if it were a loss.

Public company

However, for a public company, although realised profits have not decreased, net assets have decreased (as the liability has increased) over the 5 years. Hence, through the operation of section 831, there is a restriction on distributions of the amount recognised as a liability, £35 in this case, by the redemption date. This can be observed by comparing the realised profits in the Memorandum balance sheet (£200) with the Profit & Loss reserve (£165) in the IFRS / converged UK GAAP balance sheet.

During the 5 years:

Dr	Equity – Profit & Loss reserve	£50
Cr	Cash	£50

Being the payment of the discretionary dividends during the term of the instrument.

On redemption:

Dr	Liability	£125
Cr	Cash	£125

Being the payment to redeem the shares.

Capital maintenance considerations

The company has to comply with the Act. Consequently, under section 733 of the Act there has to be a credit to capital redemption reserve equal to the nominal value of the preference shares redeemed that had been presented within liabilities. A corresponding debit is also made to distributable profits adjusted for the £20 originally taken to share capital (the rationale for which is set out below).

At the same time the £10 of share premium, previously represented by the accounting liability, now falls to be included in the share premium account. A corresponding debit is made to distributable profits (the rationale for which is set out below).

Additional entries required on redemption due to capital maintenance rules:

Dr	Equity – Profit & Loss reserve	£90
Cr	Equity – Capital redemption reserve	£100
Dr	Equity – Share capital	£20
Cr	Equity – Share premium	£10

Being the entry to the Profit & Loss reserve which together with the debit for the accrued redemption premium (£35) ensures that £125 of distributable profits is consumed by the redemption price, as required by law. The entry to the Capital redemption reserve is the entry to reflect the legal preservation of the company's capital on redemption out of distributable profits. The £20 debit to share capital is to eliminate the £20 originally recorded in respect to the shares which are now cancelled as a result of the redemption. The £10 entry to the share premium account reflects the legal preservation of the initial share premium. This share premium credit (£10), taken together with the capital redemption reserve credit, to the extent not matched by the elimination of share capital (£100 – 20 = £80), gives rise to a corresponding £90 debit to the profit and loss reserve, as referred to above.

Memorandum balance sheet

	Before issuing preference shares	Issue of preference shares	After issuing preference shares	Entries during the 5 years	Before redemption	Redemption entries	After redemption
	£	£	£	£	£	£	£
Cash	100	110	210	(50)	160	(125)	35
Assets	250	0	250	0	250	0	250
Net assets	**350**	**110**	**460**	**(50)**	**410**	**(125)**	**285**
Share capital	100	100	200	0	200	(100)	100
Share premium	0	10	10	0	10	0	10
Capital redemption reserve	0	0	0	0	0	100	100
Realised profits	250	0	250	(50)	200[+]	(125)	75
Shareholders' funds	**350**	**110**	**460**	**(50)**	**410**	**(125)**	**285**

[+]*£200 represents the maximum profits available for distribution but for a public company this will be restricted by £35 through the operation of section 831, which is applied to the section 836 relevant accounts (ie the IFRS / converged UK GAAP balance sheet below) which show that net assets only exceed share capital and undistributable reserves by £165.*

For the purposes of section 831, in this illustration 'share capital and undistributable reserves' comprise 'Share capital', 'Share premium' and 'Capital redemption reserve'.

IFRS / converged UK GAAP balance sheet

	Before issuing preference shares	Issue of preference shares	After issuing preference shares	Entries during the 5 years	Before redemption	Redemption entries	After redemption
	£	£	£	£	£	£	£
Cash	100	110	210	(50)	160	(125)	35
Assets	250	0	250	0	250	0	250
Liabilities	0	(90)	(90)	(35)	(125)	125	0
Net assets	**350**	**20**	**370**	**(85)**	**285**	**0**	**285**
Share capital	100	20	120	0	120	(20)	100
Share premium	0	0	0	0	0	0	0
Capital redemption reserve	0	0	0	0	0	100	100
P&L reserve	250	0	250	(85)	165	(90)*	75
Shareholders' equity	**350**	**20**	**370**	**(85)**	**285**	**0**	**285**

*Redemption price consumption of distributable profits of £125 = £90 debit at redemption + £35 debit over period to redemption as the additional interest charge.

EXAMPLE 8 – CONVERTIBLE REDEEMABLE PREFERENCE SHARES (SECTION 6, 6.78 TO 6.87)

A company issues for £100 in cash a non-cumulative 10% £100 10-year preference share. The 10% coupons are non-discretionary. The preference share is convertible at the holder's option at any time into 100 £1 ordinary shares. If the holder does not exercise its option to convert, the preference share is mandatorily redeemable for £100 at the end of year 10. The company's functional currency is pounds sterling. There are no other features of the preference share's terms and conditions that would deny equity treatment for the equity conversion option.

Under IAS 32 and FRS 25 paragraph 28, the convertible redeemable preference share is a compound instrument. The preference share has to be split accounted to separate the debt and equity components. The liability component comprises the host redeemable preference share and the non-discretionary coupons (assumed fair value, £60) and the equity component comprises the equity conversion option. The accounting is set out below:

Journal entries for the IFRS / converged UK GAAP balance sheet

On Day 1:

Dr	Cash	£100
Cr	Liability	£60
Cr	Equity – Share capital	£40

Being the recognition of the constituent liability and equity components.

The split accounting is determined by computing the fair value of the debt component and assigning to the equity component the difference between value of the debt component and the proceeds of the preference share issue. The fair value of the debt component is calculated as the present value of the repayment at final maturity (the only date at which cash could be paid) plus the present value of the future coupon payments (which are lower than those for an unconvertible preference share due to the presence of the conversion opportunity). The discount rate used in calculating the present values is the prevailing market coupon rate at the date the preference shares were issued for a similar preference shares without the conversion option. For the purposes of this illustration, it is assumed that the split accounting determined that £60 is the fair value attributable to the liability component and £40 to the equity component.

The £40 credit to equity is not an accounting profit and as a matter of law forms part of share capital.

During the 10 years:

Dr	Profit & Loss – Interest expense	£140
Cr	Cash	£100
Cr	Liability	£40

Being the recognition of the 10% coupon on the preference shares and the accretion of the liability component up to the redemption value.

Private company

The presentation of the discounted present value of the redemption amount of the preference shares as a liability has no effect on the determination of the company's realised profits. The interest expense from the accretion up to the full amount of the redemption price is presented as an accounting loss – as it is shown as an 'interest charge'. Since the ultimate payment is either a distribution or a capital repayment, the 'interest charge' is, as a matter of law, not a loss even though it is accounted for as if it were a loss.

Public company

However, for a public company, although realised profits have not decreased, net assets have decreased (as the liability has increased) over the 5 years. Hence, through the operation of section 831, there is a restriction on distributions of the amount recognised as a liability, £40 in this case, by the redemption date. This can be observed by comparing the realised profits in the Memorandum balance sheet (£150) with the Profit & Loss reserve (£110) in the IFRS / converged UK GAAP balance sheet.

On conversion (if conversion occurs):

Dr	Liability	£100
Cr	Equity – Share capital	£100

Being the recognition of the equity issued to settle the liability.

In addition, the company has to respect the fact that as a matter of law there is only £100 of share capital in issue (not £140 taking this journal together with the original issue journal).

Additional entries on conversion

Dr	Equity – Share capital	£40
Cr	Equity – Profit & Loss reserve	£40

Being the entries to reflect the elimination of the prior accumulated debits to the profit and loss reserve in respect of the redemption price, with the corresponding adjustment taken to share capital leaving the balance there correctly representing just £100 of share capital, wholly classified as equity, post-conversion.

On redemption (if conversion does not occur):

Dr	Liability	£100
Cr	Cash	£100

Being the recognition of the settlement of the liability in cash.

Capital maintenance considerations

In addition, the company has to comply with the Act. Consequently, under section 733 of the Act there has to be a credit to capital redemption reserve equal to the nominal value of the preference shares redeemed that had been presented within liabilities. However, only £40 of this is matched by a corresponding debit to eliminate the share capital now cancelled on redemption. The balance of £60 is debited to the profit and loss reserve (see below).

Additional entries required on redemption due to capital maintenance rules:

Dr	Equity – Profit & Loss reserve	£60
Dr	Equity – Share capital	£40
Cr	Equity – Capital redemption reserve	£100

Being the entries required to reflect the cancellation and preservation of the company's capital on redemption and the charging of the balance of £60 against realised profits; together with the £40- already charged to the profit and loss reserves, which now consumes realised profits, this brings the total consumption of realised profits, on redemption, to the £100 redemption price in accordance with law.

Conversion

Memorandum balance sheet

	Before issuing preference shares	Issue of preference shares	After issuing preference shares	Entries during the 10 years	Before conversion	Conversion entries	After conversion
	£	£	£	£	£	£	£
Cash	200	100	300	(100)	200	0	200
Assets	250	0	250	0	250	0	250
Liabilities	0	0	0	0	0	0	0
Net assets	450	100	550	(100)	450	0	450
Share capital	200	100	300	0	300	0	300
Share premium	0	0	0	0	0	0	0
Other reserves	0	0	0	0	0	0	0
Realised profits	250	0	250	(100)	150[+]	0	150
Shareholders' equity	450	100	550	(100)	450	0	450

[+]*£150 represents the maximum profits available for distribution but for a public company this will be restricted by £40, immediately prior to conversion, through the operation of section 831, which is applied to the section 836 relevant accounts (ie the IFRS / converged UK GAAP balance sheet below) which show that net assets only exceed share capital and undistributable reserves by £110.*

For the purposes of section 831, in this illustration 'share capital and undistributable reserves' comprise 'Share capital', 'Share premium' and 'Capital redemption reserve'.

IFRS / converged UK GAAP balance sheet

	Before issuing preference shares	Issue of preference shares	After issuing preference shares	Entries during the 10 years	Before conversion	Conversion entries	After conversion
	£	£	£	£	£	£	£
Cash	200	100	300	(100)	200	0	200
Assets	250	0	250	0	250	0	250
Liabilities	0	(60)	(60)	(40)	(100)	100	0
Net assets	450	40	490	(140)	350	100	450
Share capital	200	40	240	0	240	60	300
Share premium	0	0	0	0	0	0	0
Capital redemption reserve							
Other reserves	0	0	0	0	0	0	0
P&L reserve	250	0	250	(140)	110	40	150
Shareholders' equity	450	40	490	(140)	350	100	450

Redemption

Memorandum balance sheet

	Before issuing preference shares	Issue of preference shares	After issuing preference shares	Entries during the 10 years	Before the redemption	Redemption entries redemption	After redemption
	£	£	£	£	£	£	£
Cash	200	100	300	(100)	200	(100)	100
Assets	250	0	250	0	250	0	250
Liabilities	0	0	0	0	0	0	0
Net assets	**450**	**100**	**550**	**(100)**	**450**	**100**	**350**
Share capital	200	100	300	0	300	(100)	200
Share premium	0	0	0	0	0	0	0
Capital redemption reserve	0	0	0	0	0	100	100
Other reserves	0	0	0	0	0	0	0
Realised profits	250	0	250	(100)	150[+]	(100)	50
Shareholders' equity	**450**	**100**	**550**	**(100)**	**450**	**(100)**	**350**

[+]*£150 represents the maximum profits available for distribution but for a public company this will be restricted by £40 through the operation of section 831, which is applied to the section 836 relevant accounts (ie the IFRS / converged UK GAAP balance sheet below) which show that net assets only exceed share capital and undistributable reserves by £110.*

For the purposes of section 831, in this illustration 'share capital and undistributable reserves' comprise 'Share capital', 'Share premium' and 'Capital redemption reserve'.

IFRS / converged UK GAAP balance sheet

	Before issuing preference shares	Issue of preference shares	After issuing preference shares	Entries during the 10 years	Before the redemption	Redemption entries redemption	After redemption
	£	£	£	£	£	£	£
Cash	200	100	300	(100)	200	(100)	100
Assets	250	0	250	0	250	0	250
Liabilities	0	(60)	(60)	(40)	(100)	100	0
Net assets	**450**	**40**	**490**	**(140)**	**350**	**0**	**350**
Share capital	200	40	240	0	240	(40)	200
Share premium	0	0	0	0	0	0	0
Capital redemption reserve	0	0	0	0	0	100	100
Other reserves	0	0	0	0	0	0	0
P&L reserve	250	0	250	(140)	110	(60)*	50
Shareholders' equity	**450**	**40**	**490**	**(140)**	**350**	**0**	**350**

Redemption price consumption of distributable profits of £100 = £60 debit at redemption + £40 debit over period to redemption as the additional interest charge.

Appendix 4
Numerical illustrations for section 8

DISTINGUISHING THE CUMULATIVE GAIN OR LOSS IN RESERVES FROM THE PENSION SURPLUS OR DEFICIT

It is the cumulative gain or loss credited or debited to reserves in respect of a pension scheme, rather than the existence of a surplus or deficit, that affects the realised profits and losses of a company. Consider the example below of a scheme set up at the start of the year. For simplicity, current and deferred tax is ignored. The scheme has a surplus of 4 at the end of the year that would be reported on the company's balance sheet as an asset. Contributions have been paid which are equal to the expense recognised in the profit and loss account of 20. An actuarial gain of 4 has also been recognised in the STRGL.

	Increase/ (decrease) in pension asset	(Reduction) in cash balance	Amount debited/ (credited) in reserves
Brought forward	0		
Debited to profit and loss	(20)		20
Credited in STRGL	4		(4)
Contributions paid	20	(20)	
Carried forward	4	(20)	16

The net effect on the balance sheet in the above example is:

Dr	Pension asset	4	
Dr	Reserves	16	
Cr	Cash		20

It is the cumulative loss of 16 in the above example that has been debited to reserves in respect of the pension scheme that falls to be treated as realised, rather than any notional 'credit' relating to the asset of 4.

ESTABLISHING THE EFFECT ON REALISED PROFITS AT A PARTICULAR DATE

This example illustrates the application of paragraph 8.14 of the guidance in the case where the company has recognised a pension asset on acquisition of an unincorporated business.

In 2005, a company acquired an unincorporated business and the fair values of the net assets recognised included a pension asset of 20. At 31 December 2007, cumulative post-acquisition contributions of 4 have been made and the asset has reduced to 18. The cumulative amount included in reserves is calculated as follows:

Surplus recognised in balance sheet	18
Cumulative net contributions	(4)
Surplus recognised on acquisition	(20)
Amount included in reserves (debit)	(6)

Another way of expressing the same calculation is as follows:

Cumulative net contributions	(4)
Surplus recognised in balance sheet	18
Less: Surplus recognised on acquisition	(20)
Decrease in surplus recognised	(2)
Amount included in reserves (debit)	(6)

It can be seen from this example that there must be a cumulative debit in reserves if the asset recognised in the balance sheet is less than the amount recognised on acquisition provided that the cumulative net post-acquisition contributions are not negative and the scheme has not been combined with any other scheme.

Appendix 5
Illustrative examples of the effect of the principles relating to foreign currency set out in section 11

EXAMPLE 1 – ILLUSTRATION OF PRINCIPLES 1 AND 2 (FUNCTIONAL CURRENCY STRENGTHENS)

Principle 1: Realised profits and losses are measured by reference to the functional currency of the company.

Principle 2: An accounting gain or loss arising upon the retranslation of the whole of the accounts from the company's functional currency to a presentation currency, is not a profit or a loss as a matter of law. Such an amount therefore cannot be a realised profit or loss.

Facts:

Type of company	Private
Functional currency	Sterling
Share capital currency	Sterling
Presentation currency	Dollars
Opening exchange rate	£1 = $1.6
Average exchange rate	£1 = $1.7
Closing exchange rate (sterling has strengthened against the dollar)	£1 = $1.8

The company began the year with no cumulative translation difference (eg, there has been no exchange rate variation to date).

The company's assets and profits are as shown in the table below.

The company's functional and presentation balance sheets and income statements are as follows:

	Opening balance sheet	Profit	Retranslation difference	Closing balance sheet
In functional currency	£	£		£
Share capital	100			100
Profit and loss account reserve (all realised)	20	30		50
Net assets	120	30		150
In presentation currency	$ (at $1.6)	$ (at $1.7)	$	$
Share capital	160			160
Profit and loss account reserve	32	51		83
Cumulative translation difference	–		27	27
Net assets	192	51	27	270*

Net assets of £150 translated at £1 = $1.8.

What are this company's realised profits for the purposes of Part 23?

In accordance with principle 1, the realised profits are measured in the functional currency. In accordance with principle 2, the cumulative translation difference of $27 is not a realised profit. The realised profits are therefore £50. The company could, therefore, so far as the Act is concerned, distribute £50, being $90 in presentation terms (£50 at $1.8) (note that the $83 shown in the profit and loss account reserve is the accumulation of functional currency profits translated at historical presentation rates). The retranslation process has no effect on the determination of realised profits, which occurs at the level of the underlying functional numbers.

Public companies should give consideration to principle 7 when applying the s831 net assets test, as the test operates by reference to the amounts shown in presentation currency, in contrast with the fact that realised profits are measured in the functional currency. In this example there is no restricting effect as the difference between the net assets of $270 and share capital of $160 is $110, which equates to £61 when translated at the closing rate, which is greater than the realised profits in functional currency terms.

EXAMPLE 2 – ILLUSTRATION OF PRINCIPLES 1 AND 2 (FUNCTIONAL CURRENCY WEAKENS)

Principle 1: Realised profits and losses are measured by reference to the functional currency of the company.

Principle 2: An accounting gain or loss arising upon the retranslation of the whole of the accounts from the company's functional currency to a presentation currency, is not a profit or a loss as a matter of law. Such an amount therefore cannot be a realised profit or loss.

Facts:

Type of company	Private
Functional currency	Sterling
Share capital currency	Sterling
Presentation currency	Dollars
Opening exchange rate	£1 = $1.6
Average exchange rate	£1 = $1.5
Closing exchange rate (sterling has weakened against the dollar)	£1 = $1.3

The company began the year with no cumulative translation difference (eg, there has been no exchange rate variation to date).

The company's assets and profits are as shown in the table below.

The company's functional and presentation balance sheets and income statements are as follows:

	Opening balance sheet	Profit	Retranslation difference	Closing balance sheet
In functional currency	£	£		£
Share capital	100			100
Profit and loss account reserve (all realised)	20	30		50
Net assets	120	30		150
In presentation currency	$ (at $1.6)	$ (at $1.5)	$	$
Share capital	160			160
Profit and loss account reserve	32	45		77
Cumulative translation difference	–		(42)	(42)
Net assets	192	45	(42)	195*

*Net assets of £150 translated at £1 = $1.3.

What are this company's realised profits for the purposes of Part 23?

In accordance with principle 1, the realised profits are measured in the functional currency. In accordance with principle 2, the cumulative translation difference of $(42) not a realised loss. The realised profits are therefore £50. The company could, therefore, so far as the Act is concerned, distribute £50, being $65 in presentation terms (£50 at $1.3) (note that the $77 shown in the profit and loss account reserve is the accumulation of functional currency profits translated at historical presentation rates). The retranslation process has no effect on the determination of realised profits, which occurs at the level of the underlying functional numbers.

Public companies should give consideration to principle 7 when applying the s831 net assets test, as the test operates by reference to the amounts shown in presentation currency, in contrast with the fact that realised profits are measured in the functional currency. Example 7 follows the same fact pattern as above but is for a public company and illustrates the resulting restriction.

EXAMPLE 3 – ILLUSTRATION OF PRINCIPLE 3

Principle 3: The profit or loss arising upon the necessary retranslation of an autonomous branch, from its functional currency into the functional currency of the company, is a realised profit or a loss to the extent that the branch net assets during the period, in relation to which the components of that profit or loss arise, were qualifying consideration.

Facts:

Functional currency of company	Sterling
Functional currency of branch	Dollars
Presentation currency of company*	Sterling
Opening exchange rate	£1 = $2.0
Closing exchange rate	£1 = $1.5

This example is not concerned with presentation currency issues. A presentation currency is included as a simplifying assumption.

The company began the year with no cumulative translation difference (ie, there has been no exchange rate variation to date).

For simplicity and illustrative purposes it has been assumed that there has been no trading during the period, no interest has accrued on the loan and there are no intercompany balances.

The branch's functional currency balance sheets are as follows:

	Opening balance sheet $	Closing balance sheet $
Property, plant and equipment (land)	30	30
Cash	30	30
Loans	(6)	(6)
Net assets	54	54
Represented by:		
Retained profits (all realised)	54	54

When included in the functional currency balance sheet of the company (which currency is also its presentation currency), the assets and liabilities of the branch will be stated as follows:

	£ (at $2.0)	£ (at $1.5)
Property, plant and equipment (land)	15	20
Cash	15	20
Loans	(3)	(4)
Net assets	27	36
Represented by:		
Cumulative translation difference		9
Profit and loss account reserve	27	27
Total	27	36

What are this company's realised profits, in relation to its branch, for the purposes of Part 23?

In accordance with principle 3, the cumulative translation difference needs to be analysed with reference to the assets and liabilities that give rise to the difference. In the example above, there is a net profit of 9 which comprises:

Retranslation gain on property, plant and equipment	5
Retranslation gain on cash	5
Retranslation loss on loans	(1)
Total	9

The gain on the property, plant and equipment is not a realised gain, as these assets do not constitute qualifying consideration. The gain on the cash balance held will be a realised gain as cash is qualifying consideration. The loss on the translation of the loan is a realised loss. Therefore, despite a net gain recorded in equity of 9, only 4 of this constitutes realised profit. In total the company's realised profits in relation to its branch are £31. Note that this amount is the realised profits of the branch measured in the company's functional currency in accordance with Principle 1; although the branch has profits of $54 in its branch functional currency of dollars, there is no concept of realised profits at branch level but only at company level where the functional currency is sterling and thus the $54 figure is of itself of no relevance.

If in the example above the company did not have any assets that comprise qualifying consideration, for example, if the cash was instead say an investment property then despite there being a net gain of 9 recognised in equity, the impact on distributable profits would be a reduction of 1, as the loss of the loan would be realised but the gains unrealised.

EXAMPLE 4 – ILLUSTRATION OF PRINCIPLE 4

Principle 4: Where a company's shares, whether those shares are classified as equity or debt for accounting purposes, are denominated in a currency other than the company's functional currency, the adjustment arising upon any translation for accounting purposes of the share capital is not a profit or loss at law. Such an amount therefore cannot be a realised profit or loss.

Facts:

Functional currency	Sterling
Presentation currency	Sterling
Share capital currency	Euro
Nominal value of shares	€90
Opening exchange rate	£1 = €1.8
Closing exchange rate	£1 = €2.0
Share classified as	Accounting equity
Share capital retranslated at balance sheet date	Yes

There have been no translation differences on the share capital prior to the opening balance sheet.

The company has no other foreign (ie, non-sterling) assets or liabilities.

The company's functional and presentation currency balance sheets and income statements are as follows:

	Opening balance sheet	Profit	Retranslation difference	Closing balance sheet
	£ (at €1.8)	£	£	£ (at €2.0)
Share capital	50			45
Reserve for translation difference on share capital			5	5
Profit and loss account reserve (all realised)	490	270		760
Net assets	540	270	540	810

What are this company's realised profits for the purposes of Part 23?

It is only the profits represented in the retained profit account that are realised (£760). The translation difference of £5 that arises in the above scenario is not a profit at law, and as such the amount cannot be a realised profit. The same would apply if the closing balance sheet exchange rate was £1 = €1.5 meaning that the share capital was stated at £60, the resulting debit balance of £10 would not be a realised loss.

Public companies should give consideration to principle 7 when applying the s831 net assets test, as the test operates by reference to the amounts shown in the accounts. Therefore, the s831 test is applied by reference to share capital recorded at £45, even though the difference of £5 shown above for the retranslation of share capital is not realised (in this particular case there is no restricting effect, since £810 of net assets less £45 of share capital exceeds the realised profits of £760). The s831 test only determines the maximum amount of realised profits that are distributable; it does not have an impact on the calculation of realised profits for the purposes of Part 23.

If the shares were measured at their historical amount (ie not retranslated) there would be no foreign currency movement in respect of the share capital as they remain at their historical amounts (although please see example principle 5 as the current currency worth of the shares would need to be considered).

Shares classified as an accounting liability

Suppose that the facts are the same as before but instead the shares are classified as an accounting liability. In this scenario IAS 21 requires the liability to be retranslated at each balance sheet date, and the foreign exchange difference that arises will be recognised in the income statement. Even though the shares are presented as an accounting liability, they remain share capital as a matter of law; any exchange difference arising on the retranslation is the result of an accounting exercise rather than a profit or loss in law; and the company's realised profits would be as above. However, consideration will need to be given to the other principles (such as the current currency worth of share capital) to determine whether there is any restriction as to the amounts that can be distributed.

EXAMPLE 5 – ILLUSTRATION OF PRINCIPLE 5

Principle 5: Where a company's shares, whether those shares are classified as equity or debt for accounting purposes, are denominated in a currency other than the company's functional currency, the common law has the effect of restricting distributions where to do otherwise would result in the net assets' falling below the functional currency worth of the share capital.

Facts:

Functional currency	Sterling
Presentation currency	Sterling
Share capital currency	Euro
Nominal value of shares	€90
Opening exchange rate	£1 = €2.0
Closing exchange rate	£1 = €1.8
Share classified as	Accounting equity
Share capital retranslated at balance sheet date	No

Assume shares were issued when the exchange rate was £1 = €2.0.

The company has no other foreign (ie, non-sterling) assets or liabilities. The company's functional and presentation balance sheets and income statements are as follows:

	Opening balance sheet	Profit	Closing balance sheet
	£	£	£
Share capital	45		45
Profit and loss account reserve (all realised)	495	270	765
Net assets	540	270	810

What are this company's realised profits for the purposes of Part 23, and what is the maximum amount that the company could distribute?

For the purposes of Part 23, the company's realised profits are £765.

Even though the company has not translated its share capital it still needs to take account of what is the current currency worth of its shares. At the balance sheet date, the €90 of share capital would be worth £50. Therefore when comparing the current worth of the share capital and the net assets in functional currency terms, any distribution would be limited to £760 (£810 – £50).

EXAMPLE 6 – ILLUSTRATION OF PRINCIPLE 6

Principle 6: Share premium account, and similar capital accounts, do not have a currency of denomination but are amounts of record in the books of account in functional currency.

Facts:

Functional currency	Sterling
Presentation currency	Sterling
Currency shares denominated in	Euro
Nominal value of shares (in denomination currency)	€90
Consideration originally received for share issue	€100
Opening exchange rate	£1 = €2.0
Closing exchange rate	£1 = €1.8
Share classified as	Accounting equity
Share capital retranslated at balance sheet date	No
Assume shares were issued when the exchange rate was £1 = €2.0.	
Share premium fixed in sterling at historical rate (€100-€90, at £1 = €2.0)	£5

The company has no other foreign (ie, non-sterling) assets or liabilities.

The company's balance sheets and income statements are as follows:

	Opening balance sheet	Profit	Closing balance sheet
	£	£	£
Share capital	45		45
Share premium	5		5
Profit and loss account reserve (all realised)	490	270	760
Net assets	540	270	810

What are this company's realised profits for the purposes of Part 23, and what is the maximum amount that the company could distribute?

For the purposes of Part 23, the company's realised profits are £760.

As illustrated in example 5, the company needs to take account of what the current currency worth of the share capital is. As before at the balance sheet date the €90 of share capital (the amount initially issued) would be worth £50. Therefore, there may be a restricting effect due to the increase in the currency worth of the shares as a result of the exchange rate movement. There is, however, no equivalent variation in worth in relation to the share premium; but the share premium account is capital that may not be distributed. Thus under Principle 5 this company compares its net assets of £810 with the aggregate of the current functional currency worth of its share capital (£50) and the functional currency amount of record of its share premium (£5), amounting to £55, and finds that the result does have a restricting effect: ie, £755 is less than the realised profits of £760.

Thus only £755 of the realised profits would be distributable.

It should be noted that in this computation the existence of a share premium account has not, however, increased the restriction. (Eg, if the company had not issued the shares at a premium and had correspondingly lower net assets, then Principle 5 would still yield a £5 restriction: £805 – 50 = £755 vs £760 realised.) What should be appreciated is that had the share premium account in this Example 6 been omitted from the capital side of the Principle 5 calculation, then the company would incorrectly have concluded that there was no restriction (£810 net assets less £50 share capital = £760 vs £760 realised, ie no apparent restriction) and could have inadvertently distributed part of its capital.

EXAMPLE 7 – ILLUSTRATION OF PRINCIPLE 7

Principle 7: The application of the s831 statutory net assets test operates by reference to amounts as shown upon the face of the accounts in presentation currency.

Facts:

Type of company	Public
Functional currency	Sterling
Share capital currency	Sterling
Presentation currency	Dollars
Opening exchange rate	£1 = $1.6
Average exchange rate	£1 = $1.5
Closing exchange rate	£1 = $1.3

The facts are the same as Example 2 except the company is a public company.

The company began the year with no cumulative translation difference (eg, there has been no exchange rate variation to date).

Its assets and profits are as shown in the table below.

The company's functional and presentation balance sheets and income statements are as follows:

	Opening balance sheet	Profit	Retranslation difference	Closing balance sheet
In functional currency	£	£		£
Share capital	100			100
Profit and loss account reserve (all realised)	20	30		50
Net assets	120	30		150
In presentation currency	$ (at $1.6)	$ (at $1.5)	$	$
Share capital	160			160
Profit and loss account reserve	32	45		77
Cumulative translation difference	–		(42)	(42)
Net assets	192	45	(42)	195*

*Net assets of £150 translated at £1 = $1.3.

What are this company's realised profits for the purposes of Part 23, and how much can be distributed under Part 23?

In accordance with principle 1, the realised profits are measured in the functional currency. The realised profits are therefore £50 (see example 2). In accordance with principle 2, the cumulative translation difference of $(42) is not a realised loss. If it were a private company, the company could, therefore, so far as the Act is concerned, distribute £50, being $65 in presentation terms (£50 at $1.3).

However, a public company is subject to s831 (see 2.30 – 2.31 above). In summary, a public company may make a distribution only if, after giving effect to such distribution, the amount of its net assets (as defined in s831(2)) is not less than the aggregate of its called-up share capital and undistributable reserves (as defined in s831(4)) as shown in the relevant accounts. This calculation is performed using figures taken directly from the presentational currency accounts.

The cumulative translation reserve does not meet the s831(4) definition of an undistributable reserve (nor is it share capital), therefore the purposes of s831 the amount that could be distributed is calculated below:

	$
Net assets	195
Share capital	(160)
Undistributable reserves	–
Amount that can be distributed under s831	35

The company could under Part 23 distribute only $35, rather than the full £50 ($65) of realised profits (see above).

Note that this restriction is correctly expressed in dollars since it is derived according to the statutory formula from amounts expressed on the face of the accounts in presentation dollars. This is so even though the realised profits, the distribution of which it restricts, are themselves in sterling (in accordance with Principle 1). In order to ascertain the effect of this restriction on any particular distribution, it is necessary to compare the dollar worth of that distribution with this $35 figure. The dollar worth of the distribution would be computed at the exchange rate applying at the date of making the distribution (see [TECH 01/09] paragraph 2.10 as to this date).

Appendix 6
Foreign currency branch examples

EXAMPLE 1 – ILLUSTRATION OF A NON-TRADING BRANCH THAT PURCHASES AND HOLDS PPE

Principle 3: The profit or loss arising upon the necessary retranslation of an autonomous branch, from its functional currency into the functional currency of the company, is a realised profit or a loss to the extent that the branch net assets were qualifying consideration when the profit or loss arose.

The simplified illustration below demonstrates the effect on realised profits from changes in the composition of a branch's net assets (in this case purchasing and holding PPE). In analysing a net retranslation gain or loss, regard must be had to the nature of the changing asset base on which they arise. In practice, when conducting the analysis, reasonable approximations may be made.

See illustration on next page.

Assumptions

Company with a sterling functional currency establishes a branch which has a dollar functional currency

All cash flows happen at the end of the month

All of the branch's transactions are transacted in Dollars

Background

The branch starts the period with cash, which it uses to purchase land. No further transactions are undertaken

Start of period

Actions	$	£
Exchange rate – £1 =		2
PPE (land)	0	0
Cash	300	150
	300	150
Foreign exchange	0	0

Day 1 — Buys land for $300

Actions	$	£		Period	Cumulative
Exchange rate – £1 =		2			
PPE (land)	300	150			
Cash	0	0			
	300	150			
Foreign exchange		0			
FX differences				Period	Cumulative
PPE (land)				0	0
Cash				0	0
				0	0

Day 365 — Unrealised gain

Actions	$	£		Period	Cumulative
Exchange rate – £1 =		1.8			
PPE (land)	300	167			
Cash	0	0			
	300	167			
Foreign exchange		17			
		0			
FX differences				Period	Cumulative
PPE (land)				17	17
Cash				0	0
				17	17

Even though the branch has been dormant since it purchased the land, we can not assume that the foreign exchange difference of 17 arising in the year on the opening balance sheet is realised just because the balance sheet was represented by cash on day 1.

EXAMPLE 2 – ILLUSTRATION OF A TRADING BRANCH AND THE IMPORTANCE OF THE COMPOSITION OF FOREIGN EXCHANGE MOVEMENTS

Principle 3: The profit or loss arising upon the necessary retranslation of an autonomous branch, from its functional currency into the functional currency of the company, is a realised profit or a loss to the extent that the branch net assets were qualifying consideration when the profit or loss arose.

The simplified illustration below demonstrates the effect on realised profits from changes in the composition of a branch's net assets (in this case building up inventory to a peak and then running it down again). In analysing a net retranslation gain or loss, regard must be had to the nature of the changing asset base on which they arise. In practice, when conducting the analysis, reasonable approximations may be made.

See illustration on next page.

Assumptions

Company with a sterling functional currency establishes a branch which has a dollar functional currency.

All cash flows happen at the end of the month.

The loan that the branch has taken out is non-interest bearing

All of the branch's transactions are transacted in Dollars

Background

The branch obtains a loan at the start of the period, which it uses to purchase inventory in the first half. It then starts to run down the inventory.

Start of period

Obtain loan of $300

Actions	$	£
Exchange rate – £1 =		2
Inventory	100	50
Cash	200	100
Loan	(300)	(150)
	0	0
Trading profit (realised)	0	0
Foreign exchange	0	0

Month 1

Buys inventory for $100

Actions	$	£
Exchange rate – £1 =		2.2
Inventory	200	91
Cash	100	45
Loan	(300)	(136)
	0	0
Trading profit (realised)	0	0

FX differences	Period	Cumulative	
Inventory	(4.5)	(4.5)	
Realisation of inventory			
FX *			
Cash	(9.1)	(9.1)	
Loan	13.6	13.6	
	0.0	0.0	

Month 2

Sells $50 of inventory for $100

Actions	$	£
Exchange rate – £1 =		1.9
Inventory	150	79
Cash	200	105
Loan	(300)	(158)
	50	26
Trading profit (realised)	50	26
Foreign exchange	50	26

FX differences	Period	Cumulative	
Inventory	13.0	8.5	Unrealised gain
Realisation of inventory	1.3	1.3	Realised gain *
FX *			
Cash	7.2	(1.9)	Realised loss
Loan	(21.5)	(7.9)	Realised loss
	0.0	0.0	

*See separate sheet on pages 160-161

If the opening and closing cash balance is looked at in isolation, one might assume that when calculating the realised profits of the branch, foreign currency movements on the cash balance would not have an adverse effect on the amounts that can be distributed – the balance at the start and end of the period is the same and there has been a favourable change in the exchange rate – the $200 that at the start of period was worth £100 is now worth £105.

On that assumption, one might conclude that all that needs to be considered is the foreign exchange movements on the loan balance, as the foreign exchange movements on the inventory will be unrealised gains.

However as can be seen from the foreign exchange movements that arise in the period, there is actually a cumulative foreign exchange loss on cash balance during the period. This will be a realised loss. The realised profits at the end of the period are £17 (£26 trading profit less £10 realised foreign exchange loss (on the cash and the loan) and a £1 realised gain in relation to foreign exchange movements that have arisen on the sale of inventory (see separate sheet).

The example above is a simplified example which demonstrates that when analysing a net retranslation gain or loss, regard must be had to the nature of the changing asset base on which they arise. When conducting the analysis in a more complicated scenario reasonable approximations may be made.

Analysis of movements from the company's perspective of changes in the composition of the branch's net assets

	Inventory		Cash		Loan	
	$	£	$	£	$	£
Balance at start of period (£1:$2)	100	50.0	200.0	100.0	(300.0)	(150.0)
FX during period						
$100 @ £1:$2.2 – $100 @ £1:$2		(4.5)				
$200 @ £1:$2.2 – $200 @ £1:$2				(9.1)		
$300 @ £1:$2.2 – $300 @ £1:$2						13.6
Cashflow movements						
$100 @ £1=$2.2			(100.0)	(45.5)		
Inventory movements						
$100 @ £1=$2.2	100.0	45.5				
End of month 1 (£1:$2.2)	200.0	90.9	100.0	45.5	300.0	(136.4)
FX during period						
$200 @ £1:$2 – $100 @ £1:$1.9		14.4				
$100 @ £1:$2 – $200 @ £1:$1.9				7.2		
$300 @ £1:$2 – $300 @ £1:$1.9						(21.5)
Sub-total before trading profits		105.3		52.6		(157.9)
Cumulative FX		9.8		(1.9)		(7.9)

Inventory movements						
Sale of $50	(50.0)	(25.0)*1	(1.3)*2	(26.3)*3		(300.0)
Realisation of inventory FX movement						
Cashflow movements						
Realisation of historic cost of inventory		100.0	25.0*1			
Realisation of inventory FX			1.3*2			
Trading profit			26.3*4			
			52.6*5			
End of month 2 (£1:$1.9)	150.0	200.0	105.3		(300.0)	(157.9)
	78.9					
Cumulative FX at end of month 2	8.5	(1.9)				(7.9)

*1 On a FIFO basis $50 of inventory sold was originally £25 (at £1:$2). Whilst this example assumes a FIFO approach, other methods may be adopted according to normal considerations.

*2 This difference, between (*1) and (*2) is the FX gain in inventory realised as a result of its sale for cash.

*3 Inventory of $50 removed from the inventory balance when the rate is £1:$1.9.

*4 Calculated as the difference between the proceeds received ($100 @ £1:$1.9) and the carrying amount of inventory sold ($50 @ £1:$1.9)

*5 This equals $100 at £1:$1.9 (the exchange rate on the date of the transaction) and is comprised of the 3 components above

Appendix 7
Illustrative examples of a company's position in several scenarios for capital reductions where there have been movements in the exchange rate between the functional currency and foreign share capital currency

Facts:

Functional currency	Sterling
Presentation currency	Sterling
Share capital currency	Dollars
Nominal value of shares	$200
Opening exchange rate	£1 = $2.0
Closing exchange rate	See the illustrations below for alternates
Share classified as	Accounting equity
Share capital retranslated at balance sheet date	See the illustrations below for alternates

Assume that the shares were issued when the exchange rate was £1 = $2.0, and the proceeds received on issue were converted into sterling.

Assume that the company has no other foreign (ie, non-sterling) assets or liabilities.

Please see the illustrations below for a company's position in several scenarios.

	Reduction of currency shares capital £1 = $x 1.00				Exclusive of repayment £1 = $x 4.00			
	Share capital	Retrans entry	Redux reserve	Total	Share capital	Retrans entry	Redux reserve	Total
	£	£	£	£	£	£	£	£
Without retranslation b/f	100			100	100			100
Reduction	(200)		200	0	(50)		50	0
Un(over) eliminated	100		(100)	0	(50)		50	0
c/f	0	0	100	100	0	0	100	100
With retranslation b/f	200	(100)		100	50	50		100
Reduction	(200)		200	0	(50)		50	0
Un(over) eliminated	0	0	100	0	0	(50)	50	0
	0	0	100	100	0	0	100	100

Where an overall debit is left behind as a consumption of amounts available for distribution it is assumed that either the company had such amounts available prior to the reduction or that, if such a reduction may be validly effected, the consequence is that the company has a deficit (an excess utilisation of realised profits) which must be made good before any further distribution can be made.

	Reduction of currency shares capital				With repayment			
	£1 = $x 1.00						£1 = $x 4.00	
	Share capital	Retrans entry	Redux reserve	Total	Share capital	Retrans entry	Redux reserve	Total
	£	£	£	£	£	£	£	£
Without retranslation b/f	100			100	100			100
Repayment	(200)			(200)	(50)			(50)
Un(over) eliminated	100		(100)	0	(50)		50	0
	0	0	100	100	0	0	50	50
With retranslation b/f	200	(100)		100	50	50		100
Repayment	(200)			(200)	(50)			(50)
Un(over) eliminated	0	100	(100)	0	0	(50)	50	0
	0	0	100	100	0	0	50	50

Where an overall debit is left behind as a consumption of amounts available for distribution it is assumed that either the company had such amounts available prior to the reduction or that, if such a reduction may be validly effected, the consequence is that the company has a deficit (an excess utilisation of realised profits) which must be made good before any further distribution can be made.

Appendix 8
Example of application of section 846 to fungible assets

Company A has a freehold property with a book value of £100 and a fair value of £1,000. The company would be unable to distribute the property as a distribution in kind because it does not have sufficient distributable reserves.

Freehold property	100
	100
Share capital	50
Realised profits	50
	100

If Company A sells the freehold property in exchange for 1,000 £1 loan notes which represents qualifying consideration, the position is as follows:

Loan notes receivable	1,000
	1,000
Share capital	50
Realised profits	950
	1,000

As the loan notes represent qualifying consideration, the profit of £900 is a realised profit and Company A can make a distribution equal to its accumulated realised profits of £950.

Alternatively, if Company A sells the freehold property in exchange for £1,000 of loan notes which do not represent qualifying consideration, the position is as follows:

Loan notes receivable	1,000
	1,000
Share capital	50
Realised profits	50
Unrealised profits	900
	1,000

As the loan notes are fungible assets, the distribution of a proportion of the loan notes results in the realisation of the same proportion of the unrealised reserve. Every £1 loan note represents 90p of unrealised profit. Therefore, the element of each loan note which is not a profit is 10p. As realised profits are £50, only 500 loan notes may be distributed (because distribution of each £1 loan note will consume 10p of realised profits) The balance sheet after such a distribution would be as follows:

Loan notes receivable	500
	500
Share capital	50
Realised profits	–
Unrealised profits	450
	500

No further distribution of the remaining loan notes is possible because the distribution of £1 of loan notes would cause only 90p of unrealised profit to become realised and there are no other realised profits available. The maximum distribution possible as a distribution in kind is therefore less than would be the case if all of the loan notes were redeemed or sold for qualifying consideration.

Appendix 9
Example of application of 3.11(E) for distribution by set off

This example is concerned with the scenario where a subsidiary wishes to make a distribution to its parent of an unrealised profit and the distribution would result in the elimination, or reduction, of the asset which represents the unrealised profit.

The subsidiary has an unrealised profit which is represented by a balance due from its parent company. Without considering paragraph 3.11(e), the balance would not meet the definition of qualifying consideration because it would fail to meet one or more of the three criteria specified in paragraph 3.11(d).

The subsidiary's balance sheet is as follows.

Amount receivable from parent	130
Other assets	20
	150
Share capital	10
Unrealised profit related to amount receivable from parent	130
Realised profit	10
	150

The company could lawfully make a distribution in kind of the £130 receivable by applying section 846 of the 2006 Act and treating the unrealised profit as realised for the purposes of the distribution (see paragraph 2.9). Following the distribution, its balance sheet would be as follows.

Amount receivable from parent	–
Other assets	20
	20
Share capital	10
Unrealised profit related to amount receivable from parent	–
Realised profit	10
	20

The same effect is achieved through a waiver of the balance. A waiver by a subsidiary of a balance due to it by its parent would be classified legally as a distribution in kind (see paragraph 2.8E).

However, the legal position is different if the company instead declares a dividend of £130 with the intention of settling it through inter-company account. Section 846 is not applicable because there is no transfer of a non-cash asset. To declare the dividend, the company needs to have realised profits of £130 or more.

The definition of qualifying consideration in paragraph 3.11 addresses these circumstances, specifically at 3.11(e). It confirms that for the purposes of assessing the lawfulness of such a proposed distribution, the amount receivable from the shareholder is qualifying consideration where and to the extent that:

(i)   the company intends to make a distribution to the shareholder of an amount equal to or less than its receivable from that shareholder; and

(ii)   the company intends to settle such distribution by off-setting against the amount receivable (in whole or in part); and

(iii) within the meaning of paragraph 3.5 of this guidance, (i) and (ii) are linked.

These conditions are met in the circumstances described above and therefore it is lawful for the subsidiary to make a distribution of £130 by set off.

The above example is concerned only with whether the distribution may lawfully be made by the subsidiary. It does not address whether the receipt of the distribution by the parent is a realised profit. For example, where the profit in the subsidiary arises from a hive up of assets, the guidance at 3.5 concerning arrangements that are artificial, linked or circular is relevant.

TECH 14/13FRF
Disclosure of auditor remuneration

(December 2013)

Contents

Paragraphs

INTRODUCTION

TABLE OF QUESTIONS

Appendix

Guidance on the disclosure of auditor remuneration for the audit of accounts and other (non-audit) services, in accordance with the requirements of the Companies (Disclosure of Auditor Remuneration and Liability Limitation Agreements) Regulations 2008 (Statutory Instrument 2008/489) as amended.

ABOUT ICAEW

ICAEW is a professional membership organisation, supporting over 140,000 chartered accountants around the world. Through our technical knowledge, skills and expertise, we provide insight and leadership to the global accountancy and finance profession.

Our members provide financial knowledge and guidance based on the highest professional, technical and ethical standards. We develop and support individuals, organisations and communities to help them achieve long-term, sustainable economic value.

The ICAEW Financial Reporting Faculty is recognised internationally as a leading authority on financial reporting. The faculty is responsible for formulating ICAEW policy on financial reporting issues and makes submissions to standard setters and other external bodies. The faculty also provides an extensive range of services to its members, providing practical assistance in dealing with common financial reporting problems.

INTRODUCTION

This Technical Release provides guidance on the application of the legal requirement for companies to disclose in their individual and group accounts the remuneration receivable by the company's auditor and the auditor's associates for the audit of accounts and other (non-audit) services. It aims to ensure that directors (or their equivalents for entities other than companies) and auditors understand the nature and purpose of the requirement and, in particular, the basis for deciding into which category a service provided by the auditor falls.

The detailed legal requirements are set out in the Companies (Disclosure of Auditor Remuneration and Liability Limitation Agreements) Regulations 2008 (Statutory Instrument 2008/489)[1] ('the 2008 Regulations'). These requirements were amended by the Companies (Disclosure of Auditor Remuneration and Liability Limitation Agreements) (Amendment) Regulations 2011 (Statutory Instrument 2011/2198)[2] ('the 2011 Regulations'). The list of categories into which 'other' services must be analysed was amended to align it more closely with the requirements of the EU Audit Directive and with the Auditing Practices Board's Ethical Standards. At the same time, the opportunity was taken to ensure that the amount disclosed for audit of the company's accounts includes such fees for services provided by the 'associates' of the auditor.

References in this Technical Release to 'the Regulations' are to the 2008 Regulations as amended by the 2011 Regulations unless the context requires otherwise.

This guidance supersedes the draft guidance published in December 2011 as TECH 04/11 FRF, This final guidance is substantively unchanged from the draft guidance. However, additional guidance has been added to the answer to question 46 to clarify the relationship between the requirements of the 2011 Regulations and the contents of the illustrative template for communicating information on audit and non-audit services to those charged with governance that is appended to the Auditing Practices Board's Ethical Standard 1 *Integrity, objectivity and independence*.

All companies are required to disclose the fees payable to the auditor for the audit of their financial statements. However, small and medium-sized companies (SMEs) are exempt from the requirements relating to disclosures for other services.

In addition to legislative measures for disclosure, auditors are bound by the Auditing Practices Board's Ethical Standards. In particular, Ethical Standard 5 *Non-audit services provided to audit clients* imposes certain constraints and safeguards in relation to the provision of non-audit services. Ethical Standard 5 includes a definition of audit-related services which is reproduced in paragraph 38.1 of this Technical Release. Also, as noted above, Ethical Standard 1 *Integrity, objectivity and independence* includes an illustrative template for communicating information on audit and non-audit services to those charged with governance.

References to 'the Act', or 'sections' or 'schedules' within this guidance are to the Companies Act 2006, or sections of, or to schedules to, that Act, unless otherwise stated.

References in this guidance to 'auditor' and 'auditors' are identical in meaning unless otherwise required by the context.

The Regulations use the term 'subsidiary' to mean a subsidiary undertaking as defined in section 1162; the same usage is adopted in this guidance.

This guidance should be read in conjunction with the Regulations. It does not purport to deal with all aspects of the Regulations, but only with certain areas where it is considered that additional guidance would be helpful.

[1] *www.legislation.gov.uk/uksi/2008/489/contents/made*

[2] *www.legislation.gov.uk/uksi/2011/2198/contents/made*

TABLE OF QUESTIONS

The Regulations and other general issues

Q1. When did the 2011 Regulations take effect

Q2. To which companies do the Regulations apply?

Q3. To which other types of entity do the Regulations apply?

Q4. Where does the information required by the Act have to be disclosed?

Q5. Do comparative figures have to be given?

Q6. How is the necessary information obtained?

Q7. What is an associate of a company's auditor?

Q8. What is a 'distant associate' of a company's auditor?

Q9. What is the definition of a small or medium-sized company?

Q10. What do SMEs have to disclose?

Q11. What do companies that are not SMEs have to disclose in their individual accounts if they are not a member of a group?

Q12. What do companies that are not SMEs have to disclose in their individual accounts if they are a member of a group

Q13. What is an associate of a company?

Q14. Is disclosure required of fees receivable by the company's auditor in respect of the company's 'associates', 'joint ventures' and 'joint arrangements' as defined by accounting standards?

Q15. What about audit-assist fees?

Q16. What is an associated pension scheme of a company?

Q17. What disclosure is required in respect of associated pension schemes?

Q18. How will the information for associated pension schemes be obtained?

Q19. What is included in the audit fee?

Q20. Is it permissible to provide a sub-total of audit fees together with the fees for the statutory audits of subsidiaries?

Q21. What is disclosed where there has been a change of auditor?

Q22. What is disclosed in relation to joint auditors?

Q23. What should be disclosed as the audit fee in group accounts?

Q24. If an auditor that is not an associate of the parent company's auditor performs the audit of a subsidiary, does that mean that the group has joint auditors?

Q26. Are there exemptions for the accounts of companies in a group?

Q27. Can a parent company that takes advantage of the permission not to publish its individual profit and loss account/income statement under section 408 also not publish the information about its own audit fee and fees for other services?

Q28. Which entities and which auditors' fees have to be considered for inclusion?

Q29. What is included in 'Other services'?

Q30. What disclosure should be made if a single fee is agreed (and a single engagement letter is in place) for the audit and for the provision of services in addition to the audit of the accounts?

Q31. Will complying with the Regulations ensure compliance with the Audit Directive?

Q32. Are the categories consistent with those required by the US Securities and Exchange Commission (SEC)?

Q33. Is it necessary to disclose the eight services specified in Schedule 2A in the order in which they are listed in the Schedule?

Q34. Are sub-analyses required?

Q35. Is it necessary to disclose nil or immaterial amounts?

Q36. Is it necessary to disclose the aggregated total of fees for other services?

Q37. What is included in Category 1 'The auditing of accounts of any associate of the company'?

Q38. What is included in Category 2 'Audit-related assurance services'?

Q39. Should fees for the review of the half-yearly report be included in Category 2?

Q40. What is included in Category 3 'Taxation compliance services' and Category 4 'All taxation advisory services not falling within paragraph 3'?

Q41. What is included in Category 5 'Internal audit services'?

Q42. What is included in Category 6 'All assurance services not falling within paragraphs 1 to 5'?

Q43. What is included in Category 7 'All services relating to corporate finance transactions entered into, or proposed to be entered into, by or on behalf of the company or any of its associates not falling within paragraphs 1 to 6'?

Q44. What is included in Category 8 'All non-audit services not falling within paragraphs 2 to 7'?

Q45. Are amounts receivable by the company's auditor from third parties ever disclosable?

Q46. Does information about other services performed after the period end need to be disclosed in the accounts?

Q47. Is any narrative disclosure required?

Q48. Where should transition fees be disclosed?

Q49. Should the amounts disclosed include irrecoverable VAT?

Q50. What is the exemption for 'distant associates'?

The Regulations and other general issues

Q1   When did the 2011 Regulations take effect

1.1   The 2011 Regulations apply to financial years beginning on or after 1 October 2011. Early adoption was permitted, enabling concurrent adoption of the 2011 Regulations and the APB's revised Ethical Standards.

Q2   To which companies do the Regulations apply?

2.1   The Regulations apply to all companies, irrespective of whether their annual accounts are prepared in accordance with UK GAAP or EU-adopted IFRS. This includes SMEs. However, SMEs do not have to make such extensive disclosures as other companies, since they are outside the scope of the non-audit service disclosure requirements (see paragraphs 9.1 - 10.3 below).

2.2   Certain exemptions also apply to the accounts of companies in a group (see paragraphs 26.1 – 26.6 below).

2.3   The Regulations apply to companies incorporated in the United Kingdom, which includes Northern Ireland.

Q3   To which other types of entity do the Regulations apply?

3.1   Entities that are incorporated under the Act (or previous legislation) and those entities that have to comply with the requirements of the Act because of other legislation have to comply with the Regulations. Examples include charitable companies incorporated under the Act, limited liability partnerships and qualifying partnerships under the Partnership (Accounts) Regulations 2008 (statutory instrument 2008/569[3]).

3.2   References to 'company/ies' within this guidance should be read as encompassing such other entities.

3.3   The Regulations do not apply to registered overseas companies (ie, companies that have registered a UK establishment with the UK Registrar of Companies). The financial statements of such companies for filing with the Registrar of Companies will, depending on the circumstances, be either prepared in accordance with requirements applicable in their country of incorporation or prepared in accordance with the requirements of the Overseas Companies Regulations 2009 (Statutory Instrument 2009/1801). The disclosures specified in these Overseas Companies Regulations do not include auditor's remuneration. Furthermore, financial statements prepared under those Regulations need not be audited.

---

[3] *The definition of qualifying partnership in statutory instrument 2008/569 has been amended in respect of financial years beginning on or after 1 October 2013 by SI 2013/2005*

Where does the information required by the Act have to be disclosed? Q4

The Regulations require the information to be disclosed in the notes to the annual accounts. 4.1
They are subject to audit. When the disclosures are given elsewhere in the annual report (eg,
in the audit committee report), the notes should cross reference to where the disclosures
are given. Moreover, the information should be clearly identified as audited information
wherever it is shown.

Do comparative figures have to be given? Q5

Yes. The Regulations are silent on the matter of comparative figures but, as the information 5.1
is required to be given in the notes to the annual accounts (see paragraph 4.1 above),
FRS 28 *Corresponding amounts*, paragraph 3.14 of FRS 102 *The Financial Reporting
Standard Applicable in the UK and Ireland* or IAS 1 *Presentation of financial statements*
applies.

How is the necessary information obtained? Q6

The directors of the company are responsible for ensuring the company's compliance with 6.1
the Regulations. They will generally be able to do this from information available within
the accounting records of the company and its associates that are subsidiaries.

The Regulations require the auditor to 'supply the directors of the company with such 6.2
information as is necessary to enable the disclosure required by [the Regulations] to be
made' (*Regulation 7*). For listed companies, Ethical Standard 1 requires the auditor to
provide the audit committee with a detailed analysis of audit and non-audit fees. For
other companies, it generally should be sufficient to supply the directors with a list of
the auditor's associates (see paragraphs 7.1 to 7.4 below). Some auditors may wish, as a
matter of client service, to go further than required by law and supply their clients with the
relevant amounts of fees for disclosure purposes.

The directors will generally need to contact the trustees of associated pension schemes 6.3
(see paragraph 16.1 below) to obtain the necessary information in respect of those
schemes. Under normal circumstances, the list of the auditor's associates should be
sufficient to enable the directors to obtain the information from the trustees. However, if
the trustees refuse to provide the information to the directors, the auditor is required by
Regulation 7 to supply the directors with the necessary information regarding services by
it and its associates to the company's associated pension schemes, even though the pension
schemes are not legally part of the group. ICAEW was advised by the DTI (now BIS)
that this specific statutory obligation overrides any general legal or contractual duty of
confidentiality owed by the auditor to its pension scheme client.

Associates of a company's auditor

What is an associate of a company's auditor? Q7

Associates of a company's auditor are defined in Schedule 1 to the Regulations. Associates 7.1
of a company's auditor include bodies corporate and partnerships outside the UK. The
definition is comprehensive and designed to capture a wide range of individuals and
organisations with connections to the auditor. Associates include (but are not limited to)
any entity controlled by the auditor or under common control or otherwise affiliated or
associated with the auditor through the use of a common name or through the sharing of
significant common professional resources.

7.2   Paragraph 1(d) of schedule 1 to the Regulations includes as an associate 'any person who is party to an arrangement with the company's auditors, with or without any other person, under which costs, profits, quality control, business strategy or significant professional resources are shared.' This appears to cover a wide variety of arrangements and to have been intended to capture the concept of an auditor's 'network' which is now defined in the EU Audit Directive. It means the larger structure which is aimed at cooperation and to which a statutory auditor or an audit firm belongs and which is clearly aimed at profit or cost-sharing or shares common ownership, control or management, common quality-control policies and procedures, a common business strategy, the use of a common brand name or a significant part of professional resources. As the intention of paragraph 1(d) is to capture something that should be considered as part of the auditor's network despite the lack of a common name, then an agreement with another party not part of the network to share costs or profits on a particular engagement would not appear to make the other party necessarily an associate of the auditor.

7.3   Reference should be made to the definition of 'associates of a company's auditor' in the Regulations[4] which is not reproduced in this Technical Release. Some relationships are caught even where the degree of influence may be insignificant, for example any partnership which has a partner in common with the company's auditor is considered an associate of the company's auditor.

7.4   Similarly, if a partner in an audit firm is also a director (such as a non-executive) of a company that supplies cleaning services to a client of that audit firm, payments for the supply of those services are required to be disclosed in that client's accounts, within 'All non-audit services not falling within paragraphs 2 to 7' (see paragraph 44.1 below). Each auditor will have to assess the specific circumstances in deciding whether an associate relationship exists. However, such services may be covered by the de minimis exemption for services provided by distant associates (see paragraphs 8.1-3 and 50.1-3 below). Also, as stated at paragraph 29.4 below, the Regulations require disclosure only of fees for services and therefore no disclosure is required of fees for any supply of goods.

Q8   What is a 'distant associate' of a company's auditor?

8.1   The 2008 Regulations introduced a new exemption from disclosure of certain fees for services supplied by a 'distant associate' of a company's auditors. However, the exemption is available only if:

(a)   the associate meets the definition of a 'distant associate' (see paragraph 8.3 below);

(b)   the services fall within 'All non-audit services not falling within paragraphs 2 to 7)' (ie, they are not any of the seven specified categories described at paragraph 29.2 below, for example taxation compliance services etc.); and

(c)   the fees in question do not exceed £10,000 or a lower limit in some cases (see paragraphs 50.1 to 50.3 below).

All three conditions must be met.

8.2   The exemption was included in the 2008 Regulations in response to concern that the definition of associates of the auditor was too broad and included entities which would not ordinarily be thought of as connected with the auditor. However, rather than narrowing the definition of associates, the Government agreed to this limited disclosure exemption. The limited exemption from disclosure is described at paragraphs 50.1 to 50.3 below.

---

[4] *See paragraphs 1-3 of Schedule 1 to the Regulations*

Distant associates are a sub-set of associates and are defined in the Regulations[5] by **8.3** reference to a list of numbered sub-paragraphs within the definition of associates. The definition is not reproduced here and is of limited relevance due to the narrowness of the exemption. However, the definition of a 'distant associate' includes, where the auditor is a partnership or an LLP, any body corporate of which a partner in the company's auditor is a director.

Small and medium-sized companies

What is the definition of a small or medium-sized company? **Q9**

A company is small in relation to a financial year if the small companies regime, as defined **9.1** in section 381, applies to that financial year. A company is medium-sized in relation to a financial year if it qualifies as medium-sized in relation to that year under section 465 and is not excluded from being medium-sized under section 467(1) (*Regulations Reg 3(2)*). In addition to meeting the size criteria, it is important to consider whether the company might be ineligible for the exemption because it falls within one of the ineligible categories eg, members of a group containing public companies and certain financial services companies cannot qualify as small or medium-sized companies. In practice, the test is the same as the one that determines whether the company is entitled to file abbreviated accounts.

What do SMEs have to disclose? **Q10**

In the accounts required to be sent to members under section 423, SMEs are required **10.1** to disclose only the fee receivable by their auditor (including any benefits in kind) for the audit of those accounts (*Regulation 4*). This is the case whether those accounts are individual or group accounts. For SMEs, the amount disclosed excludes any services provided by associates of the auditor (see paragraph 11.2 below).

If small companies prepare abbreviated accounts for filing with the Registrar of Companies, **10.2** the abbreviated accounts need not include this disclosure. However, if a medium-sized company prepares abbreviated accounts, there is no exemption from disclosure of auditor's remuneration for audit services in those abbreviated accounts.

For companies that are subject to the small companies regime, section 444(1) makes **10.3** optional the filing with the Registrar of Companies of the directors' report and the profit and loss account and related notes. Such accounts should include the disclosure of auditor's remuneration for auditing the accounts because this disclosure is required by the Regulations and cannot be construed as a note to the profit and loss account.

Other companies' individual accounts

What do companies that are not SMEs have to disclose in their individual accounts **Q11**
if they are not a member of a group?

Companies that are not SMEs must disclose in their individual accounts: **11.1**

(a) the fee receivable by their auditor or associates of their auditor for the auditing of those accounts (see paragraphs 19.1 - 19.11 below) (*Regulation 5(1)(a)*);
(b) any fees receivable by their auditor or associates of their auditor for the supply of other services to the company or its associates (see paragraph 13.1 below – a company which is not a member of a group may still have an associated pension scheme for this purpose) (*Regulation 5(1)(b)*).

---

[5] *See paragraph 1-3 of Schedule 1 to the Regulations*

11.2   Prior to the amendments made to the Regulations in 2011, the disclosure of fees receivable for auditing of the accounts did not include fees receivable by the associates of the auditor. This anomaly was addressed by the 2011 Regulations. An equivalent amendment was not made in the case of SMEs (see paragraph 10.1 above), presumably because the issue is unlikely to be relevant to most SMEs.

Q12   What do companies that are not SMEs have to disclose in their individual accounts if they are a member of a group

12.1   Regulation 5 requires the disclosures to be made in a note to the 'annual accounts' which are defined in section 471 to include a company's individual accounts and any group accounts. This could be seen as indicating that separate disclosures are not required for the company and for the group. However, the fact that Regulation 6(2) provides an exemption for the individual accounts of a parent (subject to certain conditions – see paragraphs 26.1 to 26.6 below) confirms that separate disclosures are expected unless the exemption applies.

12.2   Separate disclosure is therefore required in the individual accounts and any group accounts of fees for auditing the accounts of the company. However, the amount to be disclosed will be the same because it relates to fees for auditing the 'annual accounts'. There is no requirement to disclose separately the fee for auditing the individual accounts of the parent company.

12.3   The disclosures about fees for other services relate to services supplied to the company or its associates, irrespective of whether group accounts are prepared. The amount disclosed will include (in Category 1) fees for auditing the accounts of subsidiaries. Where the exemption (see paragraphs 26.1 to 26.6 below) does not apply, the amounts to be disclosed will nevertheless generally be the same for the individual accounts and for the group accounts.

Q13   What is an associate of a company?

13.1   A company's associates for the purposes of the Regulations are its subsidiaries (except where its control over a subsidiary is subject to severe long-term restrictions) and associated pension schemes (*Regulation 3(2)(c)*) (in both cases including those outside the UK). The terminology in the Regulations is potentially confusing because it uses the term 'associates' to include subsidiaries.

Q14   Is disclosure required of fees receivable by the company's auditor in respect of the company's 'associates', 'joint ventures' and 'joint arrangements' as defined by accounting standards?

14.1   Disclosure is not required of remuneration for work performed for 'associates' and 'joint ventures' as defined in accounting standards, whether equity accounted or proportionately consolidated. However, where any work performed by the company's auditor on such entities goes towards supporting an opinion on the group accounts (eg, auditing accounting policy alignments), this will be part of the group audit and will fall to be included in the group audit fee disclosure. Additional voluntary disclosure of the audit fee of an 'associate', 'joint venture' or 'joint arrangement' may be desirable as good practice if such interests are substantial.

Q15   What about audit-assist fees?

15.1   Work may be undertaken within the audit firm as part of the audit by non-audit professionals. For example, they may be involved in reviewing work such as tax computations, actuarial valuations or property valuations. Such work is regarded as 'audit-assist' and the fee for such work is included in the audit fee for disclosure purposes. Where tax work, for example, is carried out for a single fee covering both compliance and audit-assist work, then the fee should be apportioned between the two types of service.

Pension schemes

What is an associated pension scheme of a company? Q16

An 'associated pension scheme' is a scheme for the provision of benefits for or in respect **16.1** of directors or employees (or former directors or employees) of the company or any subsidiary of the company where:

(a) the benefits consist of or include any pension, lump sum, gratuity or other like benefit given or to be given on retirement or on death or in anticipation of retirement or, in connection with past service, after retirement or death; and

(b) either:

(i) a majority of the trustees are appointed by (or by a person acting on behalf of) the company or a subsidiary of the company; or

(ii) the company, or a subsidiary of the company, exercises a dominant influence over the appointment of the auditor (if any) of the scheme.

(Regulation 3(1))

The requirements apply equally to overseas pension schemes - for example, the pension schemes of overseas subsidiaries - and UK pension schemes. This definition includes both defined benefit and defined contribution schemes. Industry-wide schemes are not thought likely to fall within this definition.

It is important to note that part (b)(i) of the definition is a test about potential influence **16.2** over the appointment of auditors and does not refer to the way in which the company and the pension scheme trustees interact after the trustees' appointment.

Under the Pensions Act 1995, the scheme auditor must be appointed by the trustees. In **16.3** considering whether a scheme is an associated pension scheme under part (b)(ii) of the definition above, the company will need to understand the process adopted by the trustees in making the appointment of the scheme auditor and to assess the level of influence over that process exercised by the company (or by any of its subsidiaries). Since the company's other associates are its subsidiaries (other than those over which the company's rights are severely restricted), it might be helpful to the directors to consider the definition of 'actual exercise of dominant influence' given in FRS 2 *Accounting for subsidiary undertakings*:

The actual exercise of dominant influence is the exercise of an influence that achieves the result that the operating and financial policies of the undertaking influenced are set in accordance with the wishes of the holder of the influence and for the holder's benefit whether or not those wishes are explicit. The actual exercise of dominant influence is identified by its effect in practice rather than by the way in which it is exercised.

or the equivalent requirements of FRS 102 *The Financial Reporting Standard Application in the UK and Ireland* where that standard is used.

What disclosure is required in respect of associated pension schemes? Q17

The Regulations require disclosure of fees receivable by a company's auditor and associates **17.1** of the company's auditor from the company's 'associated pension schemes' for services supplied to those schemes. This applies irrespective of whether or not the company's auditor or any of its associates is the auditor of the pension scheme.

The same information must be disclosed in respect of associated pension schemes as is **17.2** required for the company (or group) – ie, using the same non-audit service categories. It must be disclosed separately from the information for the company and/or group.

17.3 This might be achieved, for example, by the use of a columnar layout with separate columns for the group and associated pension schemes. However, where the range of services supplied to the pension schemes is limited, it may be more appropriate to provide the amounts and descriptions of services supplied in the form of a separate narrative paragraph.

Q18 **How will the information for associated pension schemes be obtained?**

18.1 The directors of the company will generally need to contact the trustees of associated pension schemes to obtain the necessary information in respect of those schemes. Paragraph 6.3 above addresses this issue further.

The audit fee for companies' individual accounts

Q19 **What is included in the audit fee?**

19.1 The audit fee includes all remuneration receivable for work carried out as part of the audit of the accounts of the company. It includes, for example, the fee for reporting on directors' remuneration for quoted companies, in accordance with regulations. It also includes fees for all work carried out to satisfy the auditor's responsibilities under the law and auditing standards in relation to material accompanying the accounts such as the directors' report, the strategic report and any corporate governance statements.

19.2 When the company is a parent company, the audit fee to be disclosed is that for the annual accounts (ie, its individual accounts and, if prepared, any group accounts). There is no requirement to disclose separately the fee for auditing the individual accounts of the parent company. This will be included in the amount disclosed for the audit of the annual accounts. This is because Regulation 5 requires disclosure of the fees for auditing the 'annual accounts' which is a term defined in section 471 to include the individual accounts and, where required, the group accounts. See paragraphs 12.1 to 12.3 above.

19.3 In the context of a group audit, work will often be performed on a subsidiary's accounts by both a head office audit team and a subsidiary audit team from the parent company's auditor or an associate thereof. For the purposes of disclosure, it will generally be reasonable to allocate the fee for all such work performed by the head office team to the group audit fee, and the fee for all such work performed by the subsidiary audit team to the subsidiary's audit fee, which will fall to be included in Category 1 under 'Other services' in the group's disclosure (see paragraph 37.2 below) and as the subsidiary's audit fee in its own individual statutory accounts (where it is a UK company).

19.4 Where a subsidiary has been invoiced separately (ie, where the parent has not been invoiced with a single fee for the entire group (see paragraph 25.1 below)), the fee will generally relate to all the work performed at that subsidiary (including work common to both the consolidation pack and the local statutory accounts, work relating solely to the local statutory accounts and work relating solely to the audit of the consolidation pack). It will generally be reasonable to show the combined amount as being the subsidiary's audit fee for the purposes of disclosure in the subsidiary's own annual accounts and to be included in Category 1 of 'Other services' in the disclosures in the group accounts (see paragraph 37.2 below).

19.5 However, in those cases where the fee for the work relating solely to the audit of the consolidation pack is clearly identifiable, its classification should be considered separately from that of the remaining subsidiary audit fee.

19.6 In the group accounts, if the subsidiary is audited by the parent company auditor or an associate thereof, any clearly identifiable element of the subsidiary fee relating solely to the audit of the subsidiary's consolidation pack would be disclosed within the group audit fee because it relates to the audit of the parent company's annual accounts. Prior to the amendments made by the 2011 Regulations, the position was more complicated because fees for services supplied by associates of the auditor could not be included in audit services. The position is now the same irrespective of whether the services are supplied by the auditor or by an associate of the auditor.

In the accounts of the subsidiary, any such clearly identifiable element of the subsidiary fee **19.7** relating solely to the consolidation pack will be disclosed within Category 2 'Audit related assurance services' – although in practice, there may not be such a clearly identifiable element. This is because the services supplied are directly related to auditing the parent's accounts and not those of the subsidiary. Using the language of Ethical Standard 5 (see paragraph 38.1 below) these services are 'extended audit work'. They cannot be included in Category 1 because the parent company is not an associate of its subsidiary (see paragraph 29.6 below). The subsidiary will often be exempt from making disclosures about 'other services' (see paragraphs 26.1 to 26.6 below).

The fee disclosed for the audit of the annual accounts is conventionally the fee for the year **19.8** on which the auditor is reporting. This is confirmed in Regulation 5(1)(a) which requires the fee to be disclosed for 'the auditing of those accounts'. This is not a time-sensitive phrase, but rather calls for disclosure of the fee for a particular audit regardless of the year in which the work is performed or the fee is expensed. However, this is not intended to suggest that any necessary adjustment for over and under-accruals of previous year audit fees may not be included within the disclosure of audit fees for the current year (see paragraph 19.9 below). It may be helpful to disclose the effect of such adjustments when the amount is material to the fees disclosed or to the trend in disclosed audit fees.

If the audit fee charged in the year includes an amount for work carried out in the previous **19.9** year by the previous auditor (if, for example, the fee has been under-accrued), it is recommended that this amount is disclosed separately. There is no explicit requirement for separate disclosure where there has been no change of auditors.

In all cases, the disclosure of the audit fees will include payments to reimburse the auditor **19.10** for expenses incurred in conducting the audit and any benefits in kind received by the auditor (*Regulation 3(1) – definition of remuneration*). Where remuneration includes benefits in kind, their nature and estimated money value must be disclosed in the notes (*Regulations 4(2) and 5(2)*).

Fees paid to an associate of the auditor for the audit of a branch of the company **19.11** are included in fees for audit services. Prior to the amendments made by the 2011 Regulations, the position was more complicated because fees for services supplied by associates of the auditor could not be included in audit services. The position is now the same irrespective of whether the services are supplied by the auditor or by an associate of the auditor.

Is it permissible to provide a sub-total of audit fees together with the fees for the **Q20**
statutory audits of subsidiaries?

Sub-totals are permitted (but not required) by the Regulations. Sub-totals are, however, **20.1** included in Ethical Standard 1's illustrative template for communicating information on audit and non-audit services provided to those charged with governance and companies may wish to include these subtotals in their accounts. In any event, companies may wish to sub-total the fees for the audit of the accounts of the company itself together with fees for the audits of the accounts of its subsidiaries, which are required to be disclosed within the relevant category within 'Other services' in accordance with the Regulations.

More than one auditor

Q21   What is disclosed where there has been a change of auditor?

21.1   Where more than one person or firm has been appointed as a company's auditor in respect of the period to which the accounts relate, separate disclosure is required in respect of remuneration of each such auditor (and of its associates in the case of a company that is not an SME) (*Regulations 4(3) and 5(5)*). This would, for example, apply where there had been a change of auditor.

Q22   What is disclosed in relation to joint auditors?

22.1   Remuneration receivable by each joint auditor should be disclosed separately.

The audit fee for groups

Q23   What should be disclosed as the audit fee in group accounts?

23.1   In group accounts, the audit fee disclosed is the fee receivable by the auditor of the parent company or its associates in respect of the auditing of the accounts of that company including their work on the consolidated accounts. This includes the fee for work performed by the parent company auditor and its associates on consolidation returns from members of the group, although it will generally exclude the amount for work on those returns performed by a subsidiary's audit team from the parent company auditor (see paragraphs 19.3 to 19.6 above). Fees receivable by the parent company auditor or its associates in respect of the audits of subsidiaries, separate from the audit for group accounts purposes, should not be included here but instead should be disclosed within Category 1 of 'Other services' unless fees relating solely to the consolidation returns are clearly identifiable (see paragraphs 19.3 - 19.6 above and 38.1 below) (*Regulation 5(1)(a)*).

23.2   There is likely to be a significant variation in the way that different groups analyse the total cost of auditing the group between audit fees and Category 1 of 'Other services'. This will, in part, depend on the legal structure but will also be a matter of judgement about how fees are allocated. A group which has most of its operating subsidiaries in jurisdictions where there is no statutory audit requirement will disclose most of the cost of auditing the group as a whole as audit fees. Conversely, a UK based group where all of the subsidiaries are subject to statutory audit requirements will disclose most of the cost of auditing the group as a whole as Category 1 of 'Other services' if the approach suggested by paragraph 19.4 is applied. Consequently, the total of the two amounts is likely to be of interest to users of the financial statements. Companies may consider presenting a sub-total of the two separate amounts that are required by law (see paragraph 20.1 above).

Q24   If an auditor that is not an associate of the parent company's auditor performs the audit of a subsidiary, does that mean that the group has joint auditors?

24.1   No. Fees paid by subsidiaries to unassociated auditors (sometimes referred to as 'secondary auditors') are not disclosable, although voluntary disclosure is not prohibited.

Q25   What is disclosable if the parent company's auditor invoices a single fee to the parent for all the group company audits?

25.1   Where the parent company's auditor invoices a single fee to the parent for the audit of the entire group, the disclosure is as follows:

- Subsidiary – Regulation 5(1)(a) requires disclosure of the audit fee regardless of who has borne it. Therefore the appropriate fee needs to be allocated to each UK subsidiary for disclosure purposes in its annual accounts.
- Group – The fee for the audit of the group accounts needs to exclude amounts not in respect of the audit of the group/consolidated accounts (ie, in respect of the annual accounts of the subsidiaries).
- Where the group itself allocates fees around the group companies, this will often be an appropriate basis for disclosure.

It is necessary to apportion the group audit fee between the companies in the group for the purposes of disclosure even if the cost has not been recharged. A reasonable approximation is acceptable and this should not involve a great deal of work. **25.2**

Are there exemptions for the accounts of companies in a group? **Q26**

The fee for auditing the individual accounts of each company must be disclosed in that company's accounts (other than the parent itself (see paragraph 19.2 above)). However, it is not necessary to disclose in the **individual** accounts of a parent or of a consolidated subsidiary amounts receivable by the company's auditor or its associates in respect of other (non-audit) services, where the information is required to be given in the group accounts required to be prepared in accordance with the Act, and the individual accounts state that the group accounts are required to give that information. This applies whether those group accounts are Companies Act group accounts or IAS group accounts). (*Regulation 6(2)*) A consolidated UK subsidiary is eligible for the exemption even if its auditor is different from that of its parent. **26.1**

As explained in paragraph 26.1 above, the exemption under the Regulations applies only where the group accounts upon which the exemption depends are prepared as a requirement of the Act. Therefore a company that is a subsidiary of a foreign immediate or ultimate parent and either has no subsidiaries or takes exemption from preparing group accounts under section 400 or section 401, is not eligible for the exemption in Regulation 6(2)(b). It must therefore disclose in its individual accounts fees for other services under Regulation 5(1)(b) and thus has to give the full disclosure discussed at paragraph 11.1(b) above, including in respect of services to its (unconsolidated) associates, if relevant. This is because the foreign parent's group accounts will not be prepared in accordance with the Act. ('Foreign' includes both parents that are incorporated elsewhere in the European Economic Area and those that are not.) **26.2**

The exemption under the Regulations is available only where the parent company is 'required to prepare' group accounts in accordance with the Act. This could be read as implying that the exemption is not available where the parent company is entitled to one of the exemptions under section 400 or section 401 but chooses voluntarily to prepare group accounts. This is not so provided that the group accounts are deemed to be required as described in paragraph 26.4 below. The exemption from disclosing 'other services' in the individual accounts will be available provided that group accounts are actually prepared and make the disclosures required by the Regulations, and that the individual accounts include the exemption statement that is a requirement for the exemption. **26.3**

An intermediate parent company is exempt under section 400 or section 401 from the requirement to prepare group accounts if, inter alia, it discloses in its individual accounts that it is taking advantage of that exemption. If it elects to prepare group accounts as part of its annual accounts and it does not make that disclosure it will therefore be preparing group accounts because it is required to do so, and not 'voluntarily' so far as the Act is concerned. The company and its consolidated subsidiaries will thus be eligible to take advantage in their **individual** accounts of the exemption from disclosing non-audit **26.4** services in Regulation 6(2) discussed in paragraph 26.1 above (see paragraph 26.6 below for **group** accounts).

26.5   If a subsidiary's accounts are approved before those of the parent, there can be no absolute certainty that the parent will prepare consolidated accounts and make the disclosures required by the Regulations. It may be reasonable, in some cases, for the subsidiary to assume that the parent will meet its legal obligations in due course and so the exemption from the Regulations should be available. This might be so, for example, where the parent is a UK listed company. However, the subsidiary's directors should in all cases make such enquiries as they consider necessary to establish that the exemption will be available. If they are in any doubt, the exemption should not be used. The UK parent company may be entitled to an exemption from preparing consolidated accounts under section 400 or section 401. Where this is the case, the subsidiary should establish whether or not the parent intends to use the exemption and consider the risk that any such decision might subsequently be reversed.

26.6   The exemptions considered in this section are for the individual accounts of a parent and its subsidiaries. There is no exemption in relation to any **group** accounts. Therefore an intermediate holding company which is a subsidiary of another UK company but prepares group accounts (eg, because it has listed debt or because it falls into the circumstances discussed at paragraph 26.4 above) has no exemption from the disclosure in its **group** accounts of 'Other services'. This is so even though its parent prepares group accounts and makes disclosures in accordance with the Regulations.

Q27   Can a parent company that takes advantage of the permission not to publish its individual profit and loss account/income statement under section 408 also not publish the information about its own audit fee and fees for other services?

27.1   Section 408 does not permit details of a company's audit fee and fees for other services to be excluded when advantage is taken of the exemption from publishing in its annual accounts the company's individual profit and loss account. The disclosures on audit fees and fees for other services are required specifically by the Regulations, rather than generally as a note to the profit and loss account/income statement. However, if a company is required to[6] prepare group accounts as part of its annual accounts, then it will be exempt from providing information about the fees for its individual accounts anyway (provided that it makes the necessary exemption statement), as discussed at paragraph 26.1 above. As also explained at paragraph 19.2 above, there is no requirement to disclose separately the fee for auditing the individual accounts of the parent company.

Other services

Q28   Which entities and which auditors' fees have to be considered for inclusion?

28.1   The stipulation in Regulation 6(1) to apply Regulation 5(1)(b) as if the undertakings included in the consolidation were a single company has the following effect. If, under EU-adopted IFRS, the consolidation includes an undertaking that is not a subsidiary undertaking as a matter of law, then the parent company's disclosure of the group's fees for other services will include services provided to that undertaking.

28.2   The fact that the undertakings included in the consolidation are treated as a single company does not mean that fees other than those paid to the parent company's auditors and its associates are included in the disclosure (so fees paid to any 'secondary auditors' are excluded).

[6] *As explained at paragraph 26.1 et seq, a company may be 'required to' prepare group accounts when it makes use of certain exemptions.*

What is included in 'Other services'?

Q29

The aggregate amount receivable by the auditor (and its associates) for each of the eight categories of service set out in Schedule 2A to the Regulations must be disclosed by companies that are not SMEs (*Regulation 5(3)*).

29.1

For ease of reference, the complete list of categories of 'Other services' set out in Schedule 2A to the Regulations is as follows:

29.2

(1)   The auditing of accounts of any associate of the company.
(2)   Audit-related assurance services.
(3)   Taxation compliance services.
(4)   All taxation advisory services not falling within paragraph 3.
(5)   Internal audit services.
(6)   All assurance services not falling within paragraphs 1 to 5.
(7)   All services relating to corporate finance transactions entered into, or proposed to be entered into, by or on behalf of the company or any of its associates not falling within paragraphs 1 to 6.
(8)   All non-audit services not falling within paragraphs 2 to 7.

Where one fee covers more than one category of service, some reasonable form of apportionment should be used to allocate the fee between the relevant categories.

29.3

The Regulations require disclosure only of fees for services and therefore no disclosure is required of fees for any supply of goods that the auditor or its associates might make. However, the definition of remuneration in Regulation 3 includes payments in respect of expenses and benefits in kind.

29.4

As explained at paragraph 19.8 above, the fee disclosed for the audit of the annual accounts is conventionally the fee for the year on which the auditor is reporting. The same approach should be used for any fees for auditing the accounts of the company's associates (which will be included in Category 1 of 'Other services') and for regulatory filings that relate to the signing of an audit opinion (which generally will be included in Category 2 of 'Other services'). Other fees which are unrelated to the audit for a particular year should be calculated on an accruals basis (ie, for work carried out in the period). The amount disclosed should be the amount charged to income or capitalised within assets (for example, fees relating to due diligence work) or included within issue costs of debt or equity during the company's reporting period.

29.5

The Regulations require disclosure of 'any remuneration receivable by the company's auditors or [their associates] for the supply of other services to the company or its associates'. The associates of a company are defined in the Regulations as being most subsidiaries (see paragraph 13.1 above) and all associated pension schemes but do not include parent companies. Therefore, fees for services that are supplied by a company's auditor (or its associates) to its parent company do not have to be disclosed in the subsidiary's accounts.

29.6

For example, consider a company that is a subsidiary of a foreign parent. Its auditor may provide services which do not relate to the audit of the company but are necessary for the consolidated accounts of the foreign parent. For example, they might relate to the audit of a consolidation return under US GAAP. In this case, whether the services have been supplied to the parent or the subsidiary will depend on the facts. In some cases it will be clear that the services were supplied to the foreign parent although the work may physically have been carried out at the premises of the UK subsidiary company. Where this is the case, the fees for these services will not be included in the amounts disclosed by the subsidiary for 'Other services'. Factors to consider when determining which company

29.7

the services have been supplied to include the addressee of the engagement letter and any reports. The identity of the company which paid the fees may be a relevant factor where the other evidence is unclear or conflicting about the identity of the company to which the services were supplied. But payment of fees is not itself the basis for disclosure where the services have clearly been supplied to another company. However, where such services have been supplied to the subsidiary and are clearly identifiable they generally will fall within the appropriate 'Other services' category. In relation to this specific example, they would be within Category 2 (see paragraph 19.7 above).

Q30   What disclosure should be made if a single fee is agreed (and a single engagement letter is in place) for the audit and for the provision of services in addition to the audit of the accounts?

30.1   Where a single fee has been agreed for the audit and other services (for example, a review of the interim financial information) the auditor should provide a reasonable breakdown of the total fee into the different services.

Q31   Will complying with the Regulations ensure compliance with the Audit Directive?

31.1   Yes. The EU Audit Directive (2006/43/EC) amended the Fourth and Seventh Company Law Directives to introduce requirements into EU law on disclosure of auditor's remuneration for audit and non-audit services. These requirements were implemented in the UK as part of the implementation of the Companies Act 2006 through the 2008 Regulations. One of the stated purposes of the revised classification of non-audit services under the 2011 Regulations is to link more clearly with the requirements of the amended Fourth and Seventh Directives.

Q32   Are the categories consistent with those required by the US Securities and Exchange Commission (SEC)?

32.1   No. SEC registrants are required to conform to two similar but separate requirements, and are required to present additional information in order to comply with SEC requirements. Similarly, disclosures presented in accordance with SEC requirements do not fulfil the UK disclosure requirements.

Q33   Is it necessary to disclose the eight services specified in Schedule 2A in the order in which they are listed in the Schedule?

33.1   Disclosing other services in the order in which they are listed is not a requirement. Companies may, however, wish to follow this order. Alternatively they may wish to use the order included in Ethical Standard 1's illustrative template for communicating information on audit and non-audit services to those charged with governance or some other order.

33.2   However, care is required to ensure that the description of the categories is accurate. For example, the Ethical Standard's illustrative template lists 'other assurance services' immediately below 'audit related assurance services' but clarifies by way of footnote that the former excludes any tax or internal audit assurance services which would be included in those categories lower down the page.

Q34   Are sub-analyses required?

34.1   Sub-analysis of the individual categories is not required, but may be desirable in some instances. For example, category 6 'All assurance services not falling within paragraphs 1 to 5' will include assurance engagements such as those which involve reporting on historical financial information which is included in an investment circular. It may be helpful to disclose such amounts separately because they might otherwise be expected to be included in Category 7 'All services relating to corporate finance transactions ...'. Similarly, it may be helpful to provide a sub-analysis of Category 8 'All non-audit services not falling within paragraphs 2 to 7' as this may include fees relating to a variety of services (see paragraphs 44.1 to 44.2 below).

Is it necessary to disclose nil or immaterial amounts?   **Q35**

Nil amounts do not have to be disclosed. Therefore, categories for which there are no   **35.1**
amounts in the current year or the prior year may be omitted. However, there is no explicit
exemption from disclosing immaterial amounts.

Information in the notes to the financial statements is often reported in thousands or even   **35.2**
millions of units of the presentation currency. IAS 1 paragraph 53 confirms that this
may be acceptable so long as the level of rounding in presentation is disclosed (ie, it is
clear that the amounts are, for example, thousands of pounds) and material information
is not omitted. This is also acceptable under UK GAAP although there is no specific
pronouncement on it. The same approach would appear to be acceptable for the disclosure
of auditor's remuneration based on past practice unless, of course, the level of rounding
renders the disclosure meaningless.

Is it necessary to disclose the aggregated total of fees for other services?   **Q36**

No.   **36.1**

What is included in Category 1 'The auditing of accounts of any associate of the   **Q37**
company'?

Category 1 includes fees receivable by the auditor or its associates for the auditing of   **37.1**
the accounts of subsidiaries and associated pension schemes (both inside and outside the
UK). The reference to 'accounts' is not limited to statutory accounts and may include
consolidation returns or non-statutory accounts. However, fees receivable by the parent
company's auditor or its associates for work on the consolidated accounts will be included
in the amount disclosed as the group audit fee (see paragraph 23.1 above). The group audit
fee will generally include fees receivable for the parent company's auditor's head office
team's review of consolidation returns of subsidiaries (and any clearly identifiable element
of the subsidiary fee relating solely to the audit of the subsidiary's consolidation pack
(see paragraphs 19.3 to 19.7)).

Fees receivable by the parent company auditor or its associates in respect of the audit of   **37.2**
subsidiaries, separate from their audit of the group accounts, should be disclosed in the
group accounts within Category 1.

A subsidiary will usually be exempt in its individual accounts from disclosing fees paid   **37.3**
for 'Other services' as described in paragraph 26.1. However, where that is not the case,
in a UK subsidiary's accounts, any clearly identifiable fee paid to the subsidiary's auditor
for the audit of that subsidiary's consolidation return, to the extent that the auditor's work
was not necessary for the audit of the subsidiary's own accounts, is disclosed under the
appropriate category (see paragraph 19.7 above) unless the services have been supplied
to the parent in which case no disclosure will be required in the subsidiary's accounts
(see paragraph 29.7 above). The fee for this work may be material and clearly identifiable
if, for example, the consolidation return and the subsidiary's own accounts are prepared
using different accounting frameworks. Another example would be the audit of information
at the subsidiary in support of hedge documentation prepared at group level in accordance
with IAS 39 / FRS 26 *Financial instruments: Recognition and measurement* / Section 12
of FRS 102 *The Financial Reporting Standard applicable in the UK and Ireland* for the
purposes of achieving hedge accounting in the group accounts but that was not relevant for

the subsidiary as it may not have hedged the exposure or may have hedged in a different manner for the purposes of its own accounts.

Q38   What is included in Category 2 'Audit-related assurance services'?

38.1   The Explanatory Note to the 2011 Regulations explains that the categories have been updated to correlate with the requirements of APB Ethical Standard 5. Therefore, although the Regulations themselves do not include a definition of 'audit-related assurance services', it is appropriate to refer to Ethical Standard 5 which defines 'audit-related services' as 'those non-audit services ... that are largely carried out by members of the engagement team where the work involved is closely related to the work performed in the audit and the threats to auditor independence are clearly insignificant and, as a consequence, safeguards need not be applied'[7].

Paragraph 55 of Ethical Standard 5 states that audit-related services are:

- reporting required by law or regulation to be provided by the auditor;
- reviews of interim financial information;
- reporting on regulatory returns;
- reporting to a regulator on client assets;
- reporting on government grants;
- reporting on internal financial controls when required by law or regulation; and
- extended audit work that is authorised by those charged with governance performed on financial information and/or financial controls where the work is integrated with the audit work and is performed on the same principal terms and conditions.

The Ethical Standard does not include specific examples of extended audit work but work on auditing consolidation returns could fall into this category (see paragraph 19.7 above).

38.2   Paragraph 57 of Ethical Standard 5 notes that some services other than those listed in paragraph 55 may be considered by the auditor to be closely related to an audit. However, paragraph 56 states that only those non-audit services listed in paragraph 55 are described as audit-related in communications with those charged with governance. This approach should be applied also to disclosures in financial statements.

38.3   Some of the services listed in paragraph 55 of Ethical Standard 5 may not strictly involve giving assurance, for example an agreed upon procedures report in connection with a regulatory return or grant application. However, a footnote to Ethical Standard 1's illustrative template states that audit-related assurance services 'will, and will only, include those services which are identified as audit related services in paragraph 55 of ES 5'. Also, guidance issued by BIS[8] indicates that audit-related assurance services should include all those services listed in paragraph 55 of Ethical Standard 5. It therefore appears to be intended that category 2 is completely aligned with paragraph 55 of Ethical Standard 5.

38.4   The services included in Category 2 are not restricted to those which are required by to be performed by the company's auditors except in relation to the first bullet in paragraph 38.1 above. It is sufficient that the services are those defined as audit-related services by the Ethical Standard. However, such services are conventionally performed by the auditor.

38.5   When performing an audit, an approach may be taken whereby work performed on internal controls forms an integral part of the audit procedures for the UK audit and is also sufficient for the signing of the report under section 404 of the US Sarbanes Oxley

---

[7] *Ethical Standard 5 paragraph 54*

[8] *Explanatory text, paragraph 16.*

Act ('the section 404 report'). Consequently, in this case, the fees for work on internal controls will be included in the audit fee disclosure. If there is additional work performed on internal controls to give the section 404 report or on preparing the report itself that would not be required for the UK audit (eg, controls are tested that are not relied upon for the UK audit), any fee relating to this work also falls within Category 2.

In the group financial statements, only the fees relating to work performed on internal controls within the parent company and over the consolidation process should be included in the group audit fee. To the extent that work is performed as part of the audit on the internal controls of a subsidiary, these fees form part of the fee for auditing the subsidiary. As such, from a group perspective, they will fall to be included in Category 1. However, if the work on the internal controls of the subsidiary is only carried out for the purposes of the section 404 report, the fees will fall to be disclosed within Category 2.

Should fees for the review of the half-yearly report be included in Category 2?   Q39

There is no statutory requirement in the UK for a review by the auditor of the half-yearly report. Where a review is performed the fees will be included within Category 2 because it is specifically listed by the Ethical Standards as part of the definition of audit-related services.   39.1

Auditors may carry out work at the time of the review of the half-yearly report which is a necessary and integral part of the audit of the full year financial statements. Fees for such work are for audit services and should not be included within Category 2. It is only the incremental cost of reviewing the half-yearly report which will be included in Category 2.   39.2

What is included in Category 3 'Taxation compliance services' and Category 4 'All taxation advisory services not falling within paragraph 3'?   Q40

Fees for tax compliance services (for example, preparing and submitting tax computations, subsequent discussions and correspondence with HMRC etc.) should be disclosed under Category 3.   40.1

Fees for tax work carried out as part of the audit of the accounts (for example, auditing tax provisions) should be included as part of the amount receivable in respect of the audit of the accounts of the company (or of its associates, as appropriate, in which case the fees would fall to be included within Category 1) (see paragraphs 15.1, 23.1 or 37.1 above, as appropriate).   40.2

Fees for all other tax advisory services should be disclosed under Category 4. This will include, for example, fees for tax advisory services in relation to corporate finance transactions.   40.3

What is included in Category 5 'Internal audit services'?   Q41

Ethical Standard 5 paragraph 58 discusses what internal audit services might constitute.   41.1

Internal audit services should be distinguished from extended audit work. Paragraph 68 of Ethical Standard 5 notes that if extended audit work on financial information and/or financial controls is authorised by those charged with governance, it will be considered an 'audit-related service' provided that it is integrated with the work performed in the audit and performed largely by the existing audit team, and is performed on the same principal terms and conditions as the audit.   41.2

Q42   What is included in Category 6 'All assurance services not falling within paragraphs 1 to 5'?

42.1   The following are examples of assurance services that generally would not fall into categories higher on the list, and which therefore fall into Category 6:

- assurance reporting on historical financial information which is included in an investment circular[9];
- non-regulatory reporting on internal controls or corporate governance matters;
- environmental audits, providing assurance on corporate responsibility reports and similar services;
- reports under sections 93 and 1150 concerning recent allotments of shares for non-cash consideration;
- reports under sections 593 and 1150 concerning valuation of non-cash consideration for shares; and
- reports under sections 599 and 1150 concerning transfer of non-cash asset in initial period.

42.2   Paragraph 7 of the IFAC Framework defines an 'assurance engagement' as 'an engagement in which a practitioner expresses a conclusion designed to enhance the degree of confidence of the intended users other than the responsible party about the outcome of the evaluation or measurement of a subject matter against criteria'.

Q43   What is included in Category 7 'All services relating to corporate finance transactions entered into, or proposed to be entered into, by or on behalf of the company or any of its associates not falling within paragraphs 1 to 6'?

43.1   As explained at paragraph 42.1 above, certain corporate finance services, for example relating to historical financial information may fall within the definition of assurance services and therefore be included in Category 6. Some other corporate finance services (ie, in addition to reporting on historical financial information) may involve assurance and therefore will be included in Category 6.

43.2   Other corporate finance services will fall within Category 7. For example this will include work on long-form reports, irrespective of whether the company is the vendor or purchaser.

43.3   Other examples of corporate finance services given in paragraph 126 of Ethical Standard 5 include the following but the provision of some of these services by auditors is prohibited or restricted:

- to identify possible purchasers for parts of the audited entity's business and provide advisory services in the course of such sales; or
- to identify possible 'targets' for the audited entity to acquire; or
- to advise the audited entity on how to fund its financing requirements; or
- to act as sponsor on admission to listing on the London Stock Exchange, or as Nominated Advisor on the admission of the audited entity on the Alternative Investments Market (AIM); or
- to act as financial adviser to audited entity offerors or offerees in connection with public takeovers.

Such services, where permitted, would generally fall within category 7.

Q44   What is included in Category 8 'All non-audit services not falling within paragraphs 2 to 7'?

---

[9] *For example, the APB's illustrative template refers to reports prepared under SIR 2000 (Revised) Investment reporting standards applicable to public reporting engagements on historical financial information*

The following are examples of services that generally would not fall into categories higher on the list, and which therefore fall into Category 8:   **44.1**

- advice on accounting matters (where this is unrelated to the auditing of the accounts);
- provision of accounting services;
- secondments of the auditor's staff to the audit client;
- financial and non-financial services provided by a company of which a partner in the audit firm is a director (see paragraph 7.4 above, in particular the cleaning services example);
- actuarial valuation services
- other valuation services;
- information technology services;
- litigation support services;
- legal services;
- recruitment and remuneration services; and
- restructuring services.

This is not intended to be an exhaustive list and the precise nature of the engagement may put individual fees into a different category. The provision by auditors of some of the services listed above is restricted by Ethical Standard 5, depending upon the exact nature of the services and whether the company is a listed company.

While it is not necessary to show individual amounts for the different services, narrative   **44.2**
explanation of the nature of the services included in the category may be helpful to the user. This may be particularly useful when there are no amounts, or only immaterial amounts, disclosed in the earlier categories (eg, such that the largest single amount is described as 'Other').

Other issues

Are amounts receivable by the company's auditor from third parties ever disclosable?   **Q45**

Fees may be payable by third parties to a company's auditor for work carried out by them   **45.1**
under separate engagements unrelated to the audit and under instructions from a third party but nevertheless in relation to their mutual client. Examples include litigation support work, where the auditor may report directly to the solicitors; and credit investigation reports, where the report may be made to the bank. In each case, the fees may be payable by the third party, but the service is provided in relation to the audit client. Since the substance of the service is that it has been rendered to the audit client, the fee should be subject to disclosure. Such fees should be disclosed in the appropriate category or categories; in these examples, they would fall into Category 8 'All non-audit services not falling within paragraphs 2 to 7'.

The key point is that disclosure does not depend on which company pays the fees but on   **45.2**
which company the services are supplied to. These will often be the same but this will not always be the case.

For example, banks sometimes require their customers to appoint accountants to prepare   **45.3**
reports as a condition of continued lending. The bank's customer will normally pay the fees. The accountants appointed may coincidentally be the auditor of the bank. It would be unusual for the bank to require the work to be performed by their auditor although they may appear on a shortlist of approved firms. In many cases it will be clear that the services are being supplied to the bank's customer rather than to the bank itself. In fact, if the accountants were also the auditor of the bank's customer, it would be expected that the fees would be disclosed as 'Other services' in that company's accounts. Consequently, it would not be expected that the amounts would also be disclosed as 'Other services' in the bank's

accounts. In each case, directors will need to consider the particular arrangements and form a view on whether the services are being supplied to the bank or to the bank's customer.

45.4   The illustrative template appended to Ethical Standard 1 *Integrity, objectivity and independence* includes a line item for 'Non-audit services in respect of the audited entity provided to a third party'. A footnote explains that such services are included as non-audit services for the purposes of ethical standards and gives the example of transaction-related services, in respect of an audited entity's financial information, provided to a prospective acquirer of the audited entity. These services would not be in substance supplied to the audited entity and so would not be included in the statutory disclosures. It appears that the intention of the additional line item on the template is to ensure that fees for such services are disclosed **in addition** to those required to be disclosed by law.

45.5   This was made clear in the template by:

- stating in a note to the template that 'Disclosures required under UK company legislation are indicated by those categories in bold type above. Fuller information can be provided by companies if desired';
- ensuring that the heading 'Non-audit services in respect of the audited entity provided to a third party' is not in bold type;
- placing this line item below the 'total fees' line so as to make it clear that any amount disclosed against this heading is not included in the amount for 'total fees' in the template, which is clearly the total of the nine bold (statutory disclosure) headings; and
- explaining (by cross reference from the heading for this line item to footnote 26 to Ethical Standard 1) that such services are 'non-audit services' for the purposes of the ethical standards and cross referring from this footnote to paragraph 12 of Ethical Standard 5, which establishes this.

45.6   There should therefore not be any duplication in the amounts disclosed under the statutory headings and under the line item 'Non-audit services in respect of the audited entity provided to a third party'.

45.7   The template appended to Ethical Standard 1 is for communication with the audit committee and there is no statutory requirement to disclose 'Non-audit services in respect of the audited entity provided to a third party' in the financial statements. However, if the amount is significant, the company should consider whether disclosure would be appropriate as good corporate governance practice.

Q46   Does information about other services performed after the period end need to be disclosed in the accounts?

46.1   The Regulations do not require disclosure of information about any services performed after the period end or about any contracts for services not yet performed. However, such information will need to be reported internally where relevant corporate governance procedures are in place. As indicated in paragraph 19.8 above, audit work performed after the year end will generally relate to the audit of the annual accounts for the year just ended.

Q47   Is any narrative disclosure required?

47.1   The Regulations do not require any narrative disclosures. In the case of listed companies, if the auditor provides non-audit services narrative disclosure should be provided to explain how the auditor's objectivity and independence is safeguarded (*UK Corporate Governance Code provision C.3.8*).

The Guidance on Audit Committees published by the Financial Reporting Council includes recommendations for the content of this explanation. Where the auditor provides non-audit services other than audit-related services, these include: **47.2**

- an explanation for each significant engagement, or category of engagements;
- what the services are;
- why the audit committee concluded that it was in the interests of the company to purchase them from the external auditor (rather than another supplier); and
- how auditor independence and objectivity has been safeguarded.

These disclosures are typically provided in a corporate governance statement or audit committee report rather than in the financial statements.

Companies should consider whether additional footnote disclosure would help explain the nature of the non-audit services including Category 6 'All assurance services not falling within paragraphs 1 to 5' and Category 8 'All non-audit services not falling within paragraphs 2 to 7'.   **47.3**

Where fees for non-audit services have changed significantly between years, companies should consider whether an explanation of the reasons for the changes may be helpful. This may be the case, particularly, where there are significant one-off services relating to a specific transaction. For example, in the year of an initial public offering (IPO), there will be significant reporting accountant fees that will not recur.   **47.4**

Where a parent company has made a substantial acquisition and its auditor or an associate of the auditor has taken on the audits of the acquired companies for the first time, it may be useful to provide a comparison with the fees charged in the previous year by the previous auditor of these companies.   **47.5**

Paragraph 22 of Ethical Standard 4 requires that, in the case of listed companies, the audit engagement partner should disclose to the audit committee, in writing, any contingent fee arrangements for non-audit services provided by the auditor or its associates. This is included on the illustrative template included in Ethical Standard 1. Consideration should be given to including similar disclosures in the financial statements or in the disclosures under the UK Corporate Governance Code described at paragraph 47.1 above.   **47.6**

Where should transition fees be disclosed?   **Q48**

In most cases, the work performed by the auditor on IFRS transition would be necessary to enable them to give their opinion on the first IFRS financial statements, including the reconciliations required by IFRS 1. Where this is so, the fees are for the audit of the accounts and should be disclosed as audit fees. This is so even if they are billed separately. It is also the case where a separate report is provided on the transition work unless this significantly increased the scope of the auditor's work.   **48.1**

Where the work performed by the auditor goes significantly beyond what would be required of them as auditors to give their opinion on the financial statements, the fees will most likely be included in Category 2 'Audit-related assurance services' because it will normally be extended audit work. This will depend on the exact nature of the services provided.   **48.2**

The IFRS transition work may be done at the same time as the auditor's review of the company's first IFRS interim report. However, it will generally be disclosed as relating to the audit rather than the interim review because it would have been required irrespective of whether an interim review was performed.   **48.3**

48.4   The same principles will apply for fees incurred when companies transition from current UK GAAP to the new UK GAAP regime that is effective for periods beginning on or after 1 January 2015.

Q49   Should the amounts disclosed include irrecoverable VAT?

49.1   The amounts disclosed should exclude VAT, whether it is recoverable or not. This is because the focus of the Regulations is on what is receivable by the auditor.

Q50   What is the exemption for 'distant associates'?

50.1   Disclosure is not required of remuneration receivable for the supply of services falling within paragraph 8 of Schedule 2A (ie, 'All non-audit services not falling within paragraphs 2 to 7') supplied by a 'distant associate' (see paragraphs 8.1 to 8.3 above) of the company's auditor where the total remuneration receivable for all of those services supplied by that associate does not exceed either:

- £10,000; or
- 1% of the total audit remuneration received by the company's auditor in the most recent financial year of the auditor which ended no later than the end of the financial year of the company to which the accounts relate.

50.2   For this purpose 'financial year of the auditor' means:

- the period of not more than 18 months in respect of which the auditor's profit and loss account is required to be made up (whether by law or by or in accordance with the auditor's constitution (if any)); or
- failing any such requirement, the period of 12 months beginning with 1 April.

58.3   Also, 'total audit remuneration received' means the total remuneration received for the auditing pursuant to legislation (including that of countries and territories outside the United Kingdom) of any accounts of any person.

APPENDIX
Example of disclosure of services provided by the company's auditor and its associates

BACKGROUND

X plc is a large trading company which has two smaller trading subsidiaries: Y Ltd, a company incorporated under the Companies Act and Z SA, a company incorporated in France. X plc also has a material joint venture, A Ltd and a pension scheme, the X plc pension scheme, which is operated for the benefit of staff employed by X plc and Y Ltd.

Each entity referred to above pays fees to X plc's auditor (D'Green & Co) and its associates as follows:

X plc pays D'Green & Co:

- £1 million to the audit practice for the year end audit, of which £200,000 is in respect of the audit of the consolidated accounts and £800,000 is in respect of the audit of the company's accounts.
- £400,000 to the audit practice for their review of the consolidated interim report.
- £500,000 to the tax practice, of which £200,000 is in respect of work performed by the tax department to assist the auditor in their audit of the tax numbers in the consolidated accounts and £300,000 is for tax compliance work for the company.
- £500,000 for corporate finance services which includes £200,000 for assurance services on historical financial information and £50,000 for taxation advisory services in connection with the transaction.

Y Ltd pays D'Green & Co:

- £67,000 to the audit practice, of which £60,000 is in respect of the year end audit, including both work on the statutory accounts of Y Ltd and work on the group consolidation pack and £7,000 is in respect of work performed contributing to D'Green & Co's review of the interim financial statements.
- £10,000 to the tax practice for tax compliance work.

Z SA pays the French firm of D'Green & Co (an associate of the UK firm):

- £25,000 to the audit practice for the year end audit, including both work on the statutory accounts of Z SA and work on the group consolidation pack.
- £7,000 to the tax practice for tax compliance work.

A Ltd pays D'Green & Co:

- £7,500 to the audit practice for the audit of the statutory accounts of A Ltd. No additional fees are paid by A Ltd for the audit of information to be included in the X Plc consolidated accounts: instead, this is included in the audit fee paid by X Plc.
- £5,000 to the tax practice for tax compliance work.

The X plc pension scheme pays D'Green & Co:

- £4,000 to the assurance practice for the audit of the pension scheme.
- £2,000 to the assurance practice for the audit of a return submitted to the pension regulator.

DISCLOSURE IN NOTES TO ACCOUNTS

The disclosure of auditor remuneration in X plc's group and individual accounts and Y Ltd's individual accounts will be as shown below. Comparative information has not been included in this example but is required for disclosure in accounts. The information has been given in tabular format but this is not required by the legislation and a narrative format for some or all of the information (for example, that relating to associated pension schemes) would be acceptable.

X plc	£'000s	
Fees payable to the company's auditor for the audit of the company's annual accounts	1,200	
Fees payable to the company's auditor and its associates for other services:		
Audit of the accounts of subsidiaries*	85	*(Category 1)†*
Audit-related assurance services	407	*(Category 2)*
Tax compliance services	317	*(Category 3)*
Tax advisory services	50	*(Category 4)*
Other assurance services	200	*(Category 6)*
Corporate finance services‡	250	*(Category 7)*
Fees in respect of the X plc pension scheme:		
Audit	4	*(Category 1)*
Other services pursuant to legislation	2	*(Category 2)*
Fees paid to D'Green & Co and its associates for non-audit services to the company itself are not disclosed in the individual accounts of X plc because the company's consolidated accounts are required to disclose such fees on a consolidated basis.		

Additional voluntary disclosure of fees paid by X plc's joint venture may be desirable, as good practice, if the associate is particularly material (see paragraph 14.1 of TECH 14/13).

†References to categories of fees for other services are provided as a link to the Analysis of fees - working schedules given below. Reference to the categories is not required by legislation nor is publication of the Analysis of fees.*

‡Excluding amounts included within tax advisory services and other assurance services.*

Y Ltd	£'000s
Fees for the audit of the company	60
Fees paid to the company's auditor, D'Green & Co, and its associates for services other than the statutory audit of the company are not disclosed in Y Ltd's accounts since the consolidated accounts of Y Ltd's parent, X plc, are required to disclose non-audit fees on a consolidated basis.	

ANALYSIS OF FEES - WORKING SCHEDULES

The following table has been prepared to aid understanding of the disclosures shown above. There is no requirement to publish such an analysis.

The table analyses the fees paid by companies in the group to D'Green & Co and its associates and shows how the fees feed into the categories in the disclosure above. The audit fee disclosable in X plc's group and individual accounts is one and the same number (see paragraph 17.2 above). Although Y Ltd has taken the exemption from presenting information about fees (other than the statutory audit fee) paid to D'Green & Co and its associates, this table analyses them to show how they would fall to be disclosed if the exemption was not available or Y Ltd elected not to apply it.

	X plc group	Y Ltd
Fees paid by X plc		
Audit of group accounts - £200,000	Audit fee	
Audit of individual accounts - £800,000	Audit fee	
Interim review fee - £400,000	Category 2	
Tax audit fee - £200,000	Audit fee	
Tax compliance fee - £300,000	Category 3	
Tax advice on CF transaction - £50,000	Category 4	
Assurance services on CF transaction - £200,000	Category 6	
Other corporate finance services - £250,000	Category 7	
Fees paid by Y Ltd		
Year end audit of Y Ltd - £60,000	Category 1	Audit fee
Work contributing to the interim review by D'Green & Co of the consolidated accounts - £7,000	Category 2	Category 2
Tax compliance fee - £10,000	Category 3	Category 3
Fees paid by Z SA		
Year end audit of Z SA - £25,000	Category 1	
Tax compliance fee - £7,000	Category 3	

TECH 05/16BL
Exposure Draft of updated guidance on the determination of realised profits and losses in the context of distributions under the Companies Act 2006

Issued by the Institute of Chartered Accountants in England and Wales and the Institute of Chartered Accountants of Scotland
(the Institutes)

(March 2016)

Contents

ISBN 978-1-78363-648-8

INVITATION TO COMMENT

Since TECH 02/10 was issued in 2010, there have been changes to International Financial Reporting Standards (IFRSs). There have also been changes to UK accounting standards, principally in the form of FRS 102 *The Financial Reporting Standard applicable in the UK and Republic of Ireland* which is based on, but not necessarily the same as, IFRSs. The principles set out in TECH 02/10 apply to the revised financial reporting requirements which do not raise any fundamentally new issues for realised and distributable profits. However, it is now appropriate to refresh the guidance and update references as necessary. The opportunity has also been taken to address certain new issues which have been identified.

This draft guidance is based on TECH 02/10 marked up to show the proposed amendments. In addition to updating references to standards and removing obsolete material the following main changes are proposed:

- Additional guidance has been added at 2.6A to 2.6D concerning the definition of a distribution. This has been applied to certain intragroup off-market loans at 9.55.
- Additional guidance has been added at 9.45 to 9.56 to address the consequences of accounting for intragroup off-market loans. In accordance with FRS 102 (and IFRSs) these are recognised initially at fair value rather than face value, The guidance addresses the nature of the difference in value and subsequent interest income and expense under the law and for distributable profits.
- The guidance on retirement benefit schemes in section 8 has been completely rewritten on a simplified basis because the previous material was mainly concerned with transition from SSAP 24 to FRS 17.
- New paragraphs 2.47C–2.47E have been added to draw attention to the very considerable doubt concerning the operation of s843's special rule for long term insurance business, in relation to accounts for years ending on or after 1 January 2016, as a result of Solvency II. ICAEW understands that Government is actively considering changing the law to address this issue.
- The guidance on deferred tax has been reorganised. It has been clarified that, unless it is the reversal of a realised loss, a deferred tax credit which results in the recognition of a deferred tax asset will generally be an unrealised profit because a deferred tax asset does not usually meet the definition of qualifying consideration (see 3.17D).

The draft guidance deals with some issues about the interpretation of the law. To this extent, the draft guidance should be regarded as having immediate effect. In particular, this applies to the guidance concerning the definition of a distribution and its application to intragroup off-market loans.

The draft guidance also deals with questions of what profits and losses fall to be treated as realised in accordance with principles generally accepted, at the time when the accounts are prepared, with respect to the determination for accounting purposes of realised profits and losses. It is not possible to conclude on what is generally accepted until comments on the draft guidance have been received and considered.

Comments are sought on all aspects of the draft guidance but particularly those highlighted above. Comments on single issues or briefly confirming agreement with the draft guidance are welcome. Please also comment if you believe that FRS 101, FRS 102 or changes to IFRSs raise any other issues that you believe need to be addressed in the guidance. If you do not agree with the draft guidance, please give your reasons and suggest alternative approaches that might be considered.

Comments should preferably be emailed to distributableprofits2016@icaew.com. Alternatively, they may be sent to the following address (in which case a copy in electronic format is also requested if possible).
Business Law
The Institute of Chartered Accountants in England and Wales
Chartered Accountants' Hall
PO Box 433
Moorgate Place
London
EC2P 2BJ

Comments should be despatched so as to be received no later than Thursday 9 June 2016. All comments will be regarded as on the public record unless confidentiality is requested.

1. INTRODUCTION

This is an outline of the Introduction which is expected to appear in the finalised guidance. It will be updated for the outcome of the consultation. It is similar to the Introduction to TECH 02/10. However, is not shown as a mark-up because the changes are extensive due to the equivalent material in TECH 02/10 dealing with amendments being made to the guidance at that time.

1.1   This Technical Release provides guidance on realised and distributable profits under the Companies Act 2006 (the Act). Its purpose is to identify, interpret and apply the principles relating to the determination of realised profits and losses for the purposes of making distributions under the Act. It is based on the guidance previously issued as TECH 02/10 in October 2010 but has been updated as proposed in [this consultation] which was issued for comment in March 2016. For the convenience of users, paragraph numbering has been kept consistent with TECH 02/10 so far as possible and consequently some paragraph numbers are not used where material has been deleted or moved.

1.2   [*Insert summary of comments received in response to the consultation.*]

1.3   [*Insert summary of any significant changes made to the proposals in the light of comments received.*]

1.4   This Technical Release reflects accounting standards in issue at 31 December 2015. It does not provide guidance on how transactions and arrangements should be accounted for. However, it has been necessary to make assumptions about accounting treatments while providing guidance on the impact on realised and distributable profits.

1.5   This Technical Release represents generally accepted practice at 31 December 2015. Whilst many of the revisions to TECH 02/10 made by [the finalised guidance] represent principles that were generally accepted prior to that date, the revisions introduced now should not be used to question the lawfulness of distributions made at an earlier date. However, balances on reserves will need to be re-examined in the light of the guidance [when finalised] and the position should be re-assessed before a distribution is made.

1.6   English and Scottish Counsel have confirmed that the [draft] guidance is consistent with the law at 31 December 2015. Counsel accept no responsibility (other than to the Institutes) in relation to advice ascribed to them in this guidance.

1.7   The Act permits companies to prepare their individual accounts using UK GAAP or EU-adopted IFRSs. This guidance applies to companies reporting under both UK GAAP and EU-adopted IFRSs except where otherwise stated. The guidance has been written on the basis of 'full' IFRSs as issued by the IASB except where otherwise stated but should be equally applicable to EU-adopted IFRSs. No reference is made to IFRS 9 'Financial instruments', [which has not yet been adopted by the EU]. However, IFRS 9 does not appear to raise any substantive new issues about realised and distributable profits. References to accounting for financial instruments in accordance with IAS 39 should be read as applying to the equivalent requirements of FRS 102 for companies applying that standard.

1.8   Reference to an IFRS or IAS should be read as applying to the equivalent requirements of UK standards unless the context requires otherwise. For example, references to accounting for financial instruments in accordance with IAS 39 should be read as applying to the equivalent requirements of FRS 102 for companies applying that standard. The guidance uses the terminology 'in profit or loss' but this has the same meaning as 'in the profit and loss account'. References to the 'Accounting Regulations' are to the Large and Medium-sized Companies and Groups (Accounts and Reports) Regulations 2008 (SI 2008/410) and to the Small Companies and Groups (Accounts and Directors' Report) Regulations 2008 (SI 2008/409) as appropriate. Where relevant, these take into account the amendments made up to 31 December 2015.

IFRSs and FRS 102 use terminology that is different from that in the Companies Act 2006, **1.9** for example referring to a statement of financial position instead of a balance sheet. IFRSs and FRS 102 also include a requirement for a statement of comprehensive income which may be presented either as a single statement or as an income statement together with a separate statement showing other comprehensive income. For simplicity, company law terminology has generally been used in this guidance.

FRS 101 *Reduced Disclosure Framework* generally requires recognition and measurement **1.10** on a basis that is consistent with IFRSs as adopted by the EU. It does not, therefore, raise any new issues about realised and distributable profits.

Certain companies are permitted to prepare their accounts in accordance with the micro- **1.11** entities regime in company law and in accordance with FRS 105 *The Financial Reporting Standard applicable to the Micro-entities Regime*. Accounts prepared in accordance with the micro-entities regime are 'presumed' to give a true and fair view if prepared in accordance with the applicable legal requirements (s393(2A)). Such accounts will generally be a company's 'relevant accounts' for the purposes of determining distributable profits. The micro-entities regime does not raise any new issues in relation to distributable profits and is not generally referred to separately in this Technical Release.

Companies should consider taking their own legal advice, particularly in relation to any **1.12** matters not covered by this guidance.

2. THE LEGAL FRAMEWORK

Introduction

The legal framework relating to the determination of realised profits and losses and of **2.1** profits available for distribution consists of two elements: common law and statutory provisions.

Those aspects of the Act that deal with matters other than those relating to the form and **2.1AA** content of accounts continue to apply <u>irrespective of the accounting framework under which the accounts are prepared</u>when accounts are prepared under IFRSs. All of the rules on capital maintenance in the Act therefore continue to apply <u>regardless of whether the accounts are prepared under IFRSs or FRS 102</u>. T<s>That is to say,</s> the legal rules regarding shares (and the share premium account) continue to control, for example, payments in respect of those shares even though the shares (and related share premium) may be presented as liabilities in the accounts. For example, the ability to pay dividends on preference shares is still determined by reference to the availability of distributable profits even if those dividends are reported as an expense<s>in accordance with IFRSs</s>.

The common law

The 2006 Act codifies the general duties of directors under common law. However, this **2.1A** does not render obsolete the rules in relation to capital maintenance or duties in relation to creditors of the company which remain relevant.

Under sections 851 and 852, any restrictions in common law or imposed by the company's **2.1B** articles on the sums available for distribution or the cases in which a distribution may be made, take precedence over the statutory provisions. Section 851(2) makes an exception to this rule. It provides that the amount of any distribution in kind is established by the statutory rules in sections 845 and 846 (see 2.9–2.9F below) and not by the applicable common law rules.

2.2   Under common law, a company cannot lawfully make a distribution out of capital. Thus, the directors must consider, both at the time of proposing the distribution and at the time it is made (see paragraph 2.10 below), whether the company, subsequent to the balance sheet date to which the 'relevant accounts' were prepared, has incurred losses that have eroded its profits available for distribution (the 'capital maintenance rule'). Guidance on the application of the capital maintenance rule to the introduction of a new accounting standard is given at 3.30 and 3.31 below. It is not practicable to give further guidance on the application of the capital maintenance rule in this Technical Release: appropriate advice will have to be taken to deal with specific circumstances.

Fiduciary and other duties and volatility

2.3   In addition, directors are subject to fiduciary and other duties in the exercise of the powers conferred on them. Examples of fiduciary and other duties include the obligation on directors to safeguard the company's assets and take reasonable steps to ensure that the company is in a position to settle its debts as they fall due. Directors must therefore specifically consider whether the company will still be solvent following a proposed distribution. Thus, directors should consider both the immediate cash flow implications of a distribution and the continuing ability of the company to pay its debts as they fall due. In reaching their decision they must take into account any change in the financial position of the company after the balance sheet date of the relevant accounts and the future cash needs of the company. An expectation of future trading losses is a factor to take into account when making this assessment.

2.4   In the context of fair value accounting, volatility is an aspect where directors will need to consider their duties. The fair value of financial instruments may be volatile even though such fair value is properly determined in accordance with ~~IAS 39 *Financial Instruments: Recognition and Measurement* (subsequently referred to as IAS 39 for brevity)~~accounting standards. Directors should consider, as a result of their duties, whether it is prudent to distribute profits arising from changes in the fair values of financial instruments considered to be volatile, even though they may otherwise be realised profits in accordance with this guidance.

2.5   Accounting standards are~~Similarly, IAS 39 is~~ based on a ""mixed measurement model"" whereby some financial instruments may be included at fair value while others may be included on an amortised cost basis. This may, in some cases, lead to volatility in the profit or loss for the period. For example, an asset and a liability may provide an economic hedge but if the asset is measured at fair value and the liability is not, a profit may be reported on one but a loss not reported on the other. Although such profits may be realised profits in accordance with this guidance, directors should consider, as a result of their duties, whether it would be prudent to distribute them.

Definition of a distribution for Part 23 of the 2006 Act

2.6   A ""distribution"" is defined by section 829 as every description of distribution of a company's assets to its members, whether in cash or otherwise, subject to the following exceptions:

(a)   an issue of shares as fully or partly paid bonus shares;
(b)   the reduction of share capital;

(i)   by extinguishing or reducing the liability of any of the members on any of the company's shares in respect of share capital not paid up; or

(ii)   by repaying paid up share capital;

(c)   the redemption or purchase of any of the company's own shares out of capital (including the proceeds of any fresh issue of shares) or out of unrealised profits in accordance with Chapter 3, 4 or 5 of Part 18; and

(d)   a distribution of assets to members of the company on its winding-up.

The above statutory definition is wide. The case law, which is as applicable to the question of whether a distribution under section 829 has been made as it is to the question of whether there has been a return of capital, is clear that it does not matter what label is put on a transaction. It is its purpose and substance that matters. In particular an undervalue transaction with a shareholder or sister company is capable of being a distribution, because it involves in substance an element of gift to the transferee. However, the state of mind of those orchestrating an undervalue transaction may be relevant. It would be necessary to consider what advice they took, how they tested the market and how the actual terms were negotiated – whether the transaction and terms were arrived at because the other party was a shareholder or sister company.   **2.6A**

It should be noted that when considering the state of mind of those orchestrating the transaction, it is not a matter of whether they explicitly intended to effect a distribution, but whether the intended substance of the transaction is something that, regardless of its label, is a distribution, eg, knowingly transferring an asset at undervalue to a shareholder. For the application of this principle to intragroup loans on off-market terms see paragraph 9.55 below.   **2.6B**

The definition of a distribution refers to distributions of assets, but it is clear that a distribution can arise from the assumption of a liability if the company does not receive consideration of the same amount. That is because the liability commits the company to transfer assets at a future date and its assets are therefore reduced when entering into the commitment.   **2.6C**

In October 2014, ICAEW issued TECH16/14 Guidance on donations by a company to its parent charity. This provides guidance on the status under company law of charitable donations made by a company to its parent that is a registered charity. It concludes, based on the illustrative circumstances which it describes, that such payments are distributions as a matter of law and therefore can be lawfully made only out of distributable profits.   **2.6D**

Profits available for distribution

A company may make a distribution only out of profits available for that purpose (section 830(1)) (the common law position is set out in paragraph 2.2). A company's profits available for distribution are its accumulated, realised profits (so far as not previously distributed or capitalised) less its accumulated, realised losses (so far as not previously written off in a reduction or reorganisation of its share capital) (section 830(2)). Thus realised losses may not be offset against unrealised profits. Section 831 imposes a further restriction on public companies (see paragraph 2.30 below).   **2.7**

Section 853(4) of the Act provides that references to realised profits and realised losses are to such profits or losses as fall to be treated as realised in accordance with principles generally accepted at the time when the accounts are prepared, with respect to the determination for accounting purposes of realised profits or losses. Section 3 below provides guidance on the application of this requirement.   **2.8**

2.8A   In addition, The Companies (Reduction of Share Capital) Order 2008 SI 2008/1915 ("the Order") specifies the cases in which a reserve arising from a reduction in a company's capital (ie, share capital, share premium account, capital redemption reserve or redenomination reserve)[1] is to be treated as a realised profit as a matter of law. The Order also disapplies the general prohibition in section 654 on the distribution of a reserve arising from a reduction of capital. The Order provides that:

(a)   if an unlimited company reduces its capital, a reserve arising from the reduction is treated as a realised profit;

(b)   if a private company limited by shares reduces its capital and the reduction is supported by a solvency statement but has not been subject to an application to the court for an order confirming it, the reserve arising from the reduction is treated as a realised profit; and

(c)   if a limited company having a share capital reduces its capital and the reduction is confirmed by order of court, the reserve arising from the reduction is treated as a realised profit unless the court orders otherwise.

These provisions are without prejudice to any contrary provisions of an order or undertaking given to the court, the resolution for, or any other resolution relevant to, the reduction of capital, or the company's memorandum or articles of association. These provisions came into effect on 1 October 2008. In accordance with The Companies Act 2006 (Commencement No.7, Transitional Provisions and Savings) Order 2008, they apply irrespective of when the reduction in capital occurred or when the reserve arose. They therefore apply to capital reductions made under the 1985 Act and those made by unlimited companies.

2.8B   Section 654 and the Order are concerned with the status of any reserve arising from the reduction of a company's capital. They do not apply to the extent that a reduction of capital takes the form of a payment to shareholders so that no reserve arises.

2.8C   Section 654 and the Order do not differentiate between a reduction of foreign currency share capital and other reductions. Thus the Order applies to such cases and the reserve arising in such cases will, subject to the requirements of the Order, be a realised profit. The amount of the realised profit arising may not be the same as the amount of the reduction due to exchange movements because the reduction is calculated by reference to rates of exchange at the date of the reduction. For example, where there is a reduction of capital with no payment to shareholders, although the reduction is calculated by reference to the exchange rates at the date of the reduction, the amount of the realised profit arising will be equal to the nominal value of the shares translated at the exchange rate ruling when the shares were issued. Section 11 explains the issues in detail.

2.8D   Section 662 is concerned with the duty of a public company to cancel any shares in itself that it holds when shares are forfeited, or surrendered to the company in lieu of forfeiture, in pursuance of the Articles, for failure to pay any sums payable in respect of the shares (and certain other situations). Unless the shares are disposed of within three years of the forfeiture or surrender, the company must cancel the shares and diminish the amount of the company's share capital by the nominal value of the shares cancelled. Section 662(4) provides that the directors of a company may take any steps necessary to enable the company to comply with this requirement without complying with the requirements of chapter 10 of Part 17 of the Act in relation to reductions of capital.

---

[1] *The Order refers only to share capital but section 11 of the Interpretation Act 1978 makes it plain that where an Act contains power to promote subordinate legislation, words used in that subordinate legislation have the same meaning as in the main Act. Subject to certain exceptions, the provisions of the Companies Act 2006 relating to the reduction of a company's share capital apply to any share premium account, capital redemption reserve or redenomination reserve as if they were part of paid up share capital (sections 610(4), 628(3) and 733(6)).*

A reserve arising from a capital reduction under section 662 will not be a distributable reserve because of the restriction imposed by section 654 (see 2.8A above). Section 654 is not disapplied by section 662(4) because sSection 654 is not in chapter 10 of Part 17 of the Act, neither is it disapplied in these circumstances by the Order[2].   **2.8E**

Distributions in kind: Meaning

Sections 845 and 846 make provision for a distribution consisting of or including, or treated as arising in consequence of, the sale, transfer or other disposition by a company of a non-cash asset (referred to in this guidance as a 'distribution in kind').   **2.8F**

Section 1163 defines a non-cash asset to mean any property or interest in property, other than cash. It also states that a reference to the transfer or acquisition of a non-cash asset includes: **2.8G**

(a)   the creation or extinction of an estate or interest in, or a right over, any property; and
(b)   the discharge of a liability of any person, other than a liability for a liquidated sum.

Therefore, a distribution which arises from the discharge of a liability for a liquidated sum is not within the scope of sections 845 and 846. The amount of such a distribution is the amount of the liquidated sum as stated in the relevant accounts, whether or not a provision has been made against it. This is because the amount of any provision has consumed distributable profits at the time it was made. To do otherwise would result in double counting the amount of the provision as a loss and as a distribution.

A waiver of an amount receivable from a parent is ~~considered as~~ a distribution ~~in kind~~but is not within the scope of sections 845 and 846, ~~being an "'other disposition", of that receivable~~.   **2.8H**

Distributions in kind: Treatment of unrealised profits

Section 846 provides that where a company makes a distribution in kind and any part of the amount at which the asset is stated in the accounts relevant to the distribution represents an unrealised profit, that profit is to be treated as realised for the purposes of the distribution. Thus if a company wishes to distribute in kind an asset with a historical cost of £100 and which is in the books at £130 (with the surplus in the revaluation reserve), the surplus of £30 is treated as realised for this purpose and only £100 of other realised profits are needed. However, if the surplus has been capitalised, it is no longer available for this purpose and other realised profits of £130 would be needed to cover the proposed distribution.   **2.9**

The application of section 846 to replacement assets is considered at 10.73 below. The application of section 846 to fungible assets is considered at 10.77 below.   **2.9A**

Distributions in kind: Determination of amount

Section 845 was a new provision in the 2006 Act (not in the 1985 Act) which removed doubts arising from the decision in Aveling Barford Ltd v Perion Ltd [1989] BCLC 626 in relation to the amount of the distribution of a non-cash asset. Section 845 applies where: **2.9B**

(a)   at the time of the disposition of the asset, the company has profits available for distribution; and
(b)   if the amount of the distribution were to be determined in accordance with the section, the company could make the distribution without contravening Part 23.

[2] *The Institutes believe that this may be as a result of an oversight in drafting the Order and have drawn the matter to the attention of the Department for Business, Innovation & Skills.*

2.9C   Where section 845 applies, the amount of any distribution consisting of or arising from the sale, transfer or other disposition by the company of a non-cash asset should be calculated by reference to the value at which that asset is included in the company's accounts (ie, its book value) as follows. If an asset is transferred for a consideration not less than its book value, the amount of the distribution is zero, but if the asset is transferred for a consideration less than its book value, the amount of the distribution is equal to that shortfall, which will therefore need to be covered by distributable profits.

2.9D   In determining whether a company has profits available for distribution for the purposes of section 845, section 845(3) provides that the company's profits available for distribution are treated as increased by the amount (if any) by which the amount or value of any consideration for the disposition exceeds the book value of the asset. In this context, distributable profits may be 'treated as increased' from a negative starting point[3]. However, to apply section 845, a company must have profits available for distribution after any adjustment in accordance with section 845(3). This requirement is not met by a nil balance. There must be a positive balance, even if it is only 1p, immediately before the transfer of the asset. However, the balance may be nil after the transfer when the asset is transferred at below book value such as to eliminate the whole of the positive balance.

2.9E   The references to consideration in section 845 are not restricted to consideration that would meet the definition of 'qualifying consideration' in this guidance.

2.9F   Appendix 1 sets out illustrative worked examples of a transfer of an asset applying section 845.

Distributions in kind: Effect of IFRIC 17

2.9G   The amount of a distribution in kind for legal purposes will be the book value of the asset to be distributed, provided that this amount is available for distribution, because of the application of section 845 (see 2.9A to 2.9F above).

2.9H   There are no requirements in FRS 102~~UK GAAP~~ about accounting for distributions in kind except for a disclosure requirement to disclose the fair value of any such non-cash assets distributed (FRS 102.22.18), except when the assets are ultimately controlled by the same parties both before and after the distribution. UK companies have almost invariably accounted for such distributions based on the book value of the asset in question. It has also been acceptable to account for such a distribution based on the fair value of the asset and recognise a profit on disposal. ~~This treatment has been used occasionally.~~

2.9I   ~~In December 2008, the IASB published IFRIC 17 *Distributions of Non-cash Assets to Owners*. It is to be applied prospectively (ie no restatement of prior periods is required) for annual periods beginning on or after 1 July 2009. The scope of IFRIC 17 excludes certain distributions, including those where the non-cash asset is controlled by the same party or parties before and after the distribution (e.g. intra-group transactions). It applies to a distribution that gives owners a choice of receiving either non-cash assets or a cash alternative. The ASB has stated (in UITF Information Sheet 88) that it has no plans to issue an Abstract based on IFRIC 17 because it has decided that the current accounting under UK GAAP is adequate.~~[Deleted]

---

[3] *Legal interpretation of an amount being 'increased' in other contexts may be restricted to being increased from a lower amount but not from zero or below. However, in the context of section 845, such an interpretation would render sub-section (3) redundant and therefore this does not appear to be the intention of the legislation. Therefore, in this case, profits may be treated as increased from a negative starting point.*

Under IFRSs, IFRIC 17 Distributions of Non-cash Assets to Owners requires that, when accounting for a distribution of a non-cash asset, the distribution is measured at the fair value of the asset in question. The difference between the fair value of the asset and its book value is subsequently recognised in profit or loss when the distribution is settled. This ~~will be a significant change of practice and~~ may, in certain circumstances, have an adverse impact on the ability of a public company to make a distribution for the reasons explained below. **2.9J**

IFRIC 17 requires the recognition of a liability to make the distribution when it is appropriately authorised and no longer at the discretion of the entity. In most cases this means that the liability, which will usually exceed in amount the carrying value of the asset to be distributed, will be recognised before the distribution is settled. It will not be possible to revalue the asset to fair value prior to settlement in most cases. For example, investments in subsidiaries are usually carried on the historical cost basis and it would not be regarded as acceptable to revalue, in isolation, a particular investment. Nor is it possible to anticipate the 'profit' on disposal as this arises only on 'settlement' which must necessarily be later (if only momentarily). **2.9K**

If relevant accounts are drawn up after the liability has arisen but before settlement, they will include the liability for the distribution and consequentially reduced net assets. That reduction will be larger than that which will ultimately arise once the distribution is settled. The profit reverses some of the reduction to leave net assets reduced overall only by the book value of the distributed asset. **2.9L**

The debit entry arising from recognition of a liability in accordance with IFRIC 17 is ~~the~~an ~~advance~~ recognition of an unsettled distribution obligation and is not a ~~realised~~ loss. The fact that it is recognised at an amount greater than the distribution measured under section 845, therefore, does not affect the ability of a private company to make a distribution. **2.9M**

For a public company, the temporary adverse impact on the company's net assets will have an adverse impact on its ability to make a distribution which is based on those relevant accounts (~~e.g.~~eg, a proposed final dividend) because of the net asset test in section 831. However, it will not affect the company's ability to make the non-cash distribution in question because that distribution will have been made when it was approved (see 2.10 below) and is based on earlier relevant accounts. **2.9N**

The test in section 831 is a statutory one which applies to the amounts shown in the ~~""""~~"relevant accounts~~""""~~" for the purposes of the distribution. There is no need to update these amounts on an ongoing basis throughout the year other than for earlier distributions as required by section 840. Therefore, the issue arises only when the 'relevant accounts' are drawn up to a date between the date of approval of the distribution and when it is settled. Provided that the period between approval and settlement does not straddle the company's year end, this issue is thus unlikely to cause a problem in practice. **2.9O**

Date of distribution

A distribution is made when it becomes a legally binding liability of the company, regardless of the date on which it is to be settled. In the case of a final dividend, this will be when it is declared by the company in general meeting or, for private companies, by the members passing a written resolution. In the case of an interim dividend authorised under common articles of association (eg, Model articles for private companies limited by shares[4]~~1985 Act Table A~~), normally no legally binding liability is established prior to **2.10**

---

[4] *As contained in Schedule 1 to the Companies (Model Articles) Regulations 2008, SI 2008/3229.*

payment being made of the dividend. In such a case, a distribution is made only when the dividend is paid. However, in the case of an interim dividend, steps may be taken to establish a legally binding liability at an earlier date. See 9.6 to 9.18 below concerning how such a liability may be established. That guidance is written in the context of intra-group transactions. However, the guidance may also be relevant in other cases.

2.10A   Distributable profits are consumed when a distribution is made in accordance with the previous paragraph. After that time, a shareholder's right to any unpaid dividend is as a creditor of the company rather than as a shareholder[5].

2.11   Where the company has entered into a transaction which gives rise to group reconstruction relief or merger relief under sections 611 or 612, it may choose under section 615 to disregard any amount that would otherwise have been included in the share premium account in determining the amount at which the acquired asset is stated in the company's balance sheet. Subject to the rules in accounting standards, the asset may therefore be stated at the nominal value of the shares issued together with any minimum premium value recognised when applying group reconstruction relief. However, it is also possible to record the asset acquired at fair value and to credit the amount of that relief to another reserve (often called a merger reserve)[6]. In such a case, that reserve is in law a profit and is initially treated as unrealised but becomes realised in a manner similar to a revaluation reserve. Thus, provided the merger reserve is not capitalised (by way of a bonus issue of shares), the decision as to whether or not to record the merger reserve should not overall have any effect on the level of the company's realised profits. The accounting choice referred to in this paragraph may be restricted by the application of accounting standards. This is considered further at 9.43 to 9.44D below.

Relevant accounts

General

2.12   Under both the Act and common law, distributions are made by individual companies and not by groups. The group accounts are therefore not relevant for the purpose of determining a company's profits available for distribution ~~(see 10.1 to 10.3 below)~~. The effect of the inclusion of profits and losses arising from equity accounting in individual accounts is considered at 10.1 to 10.3 below. ~~The status of accounts prepared in accordance with IAS 28 or IAS 31 (ie using equity accounting) where a company has an associate or jointly controlled entity but has no subsidiaries is considered at 10.4 below.~~

2.13   Whether or not a distribution may be made within the terms of the Act is determined by reference to a company's 'relevant accounts'. Where it is proposed to make a distribution during the company's first accounting reference period or before any accounts have been circulated, initial accounts must be prepared. In all other cases the relevant accounts are its last annual accounts that were circulated to members[7] or interim accounts made up to a more recent date, if the proposed distribution cannot be justified by reference to the last annual accounts.

---

[5] *Section 74(2)(f) of the Insolvency Act 1986 provides that a sum due to a member in his character of a member by way of dividends etc is subordinated in a liquidation to the claims of other creditors.*

[6] *As explained at 9.44B below, a third basis of measurement may be required when applying IAS 27 as revised in May 2008.*

[7] ~~*Where a company circulates to members a summary financial statement, the relevant accounts are the full accounts from which the summary financial statement was derived.*~~

The items in these accounts to which reference is made in determining the amount of a distribution which may be made are listed in section 836(1) as profits, losses, assets, liabilities, provisions[8], share capital and reserves (including undistributable reserves). Thus, valuations or contingencies referred to in notes to the financial statements, but not incorporated in the balance sheet, do not affect the amount of realised profit calculated by reference to the relevant accounts. For example, if the relevant accounts record an unrealised profit but state in a note that, as a consequence of an event subsequent to the balance sheet date, the profit has become realised, interim accounts must nevertheless be prepared before a distribution can be made out of these profits.   **2.14**

Similarly, disclosures about the impact of future changes of accounting policy, such as those required by IAS 8(30), do not affect the amount of realised profit calculated by reference to the relevant accounts. However, they may be relevant to the application of the common law on capital maintenance where a distribution is to be made in the period in relation to which the change of policy will be implemented (see 3.30 and 3.31 below).   **2.15**

In practice it may not be sufficient to determine the amount of realised profits simply by examining the relevant accounts as further enquiries may be necessary as to the composition of the various reserves included in the balance sheet. For example, certain reserves may include both realised and unrealised profits. As there is no legal requirement for a company to distinguish in its accounts between distributable and non-_-distributable profits as such (see 2.25 to 2.27 below), companies should keep sufficient records to enable them to distinguish between those profits which are available for distribution and those which are not.   **2.16**

Under section 395, a company's individual accounts must be prepared either as """"Companies Act individual accounts"""' or as """"IAS individual accounts"""'. Thus, the relevant accounts will be either its """"Companies Act individual accounts"""' or """"IAS individual accounts"""', depending on the choice made by the company. It follows that when a company elects to prepare its statutory individual accounts in accordance with EU-adopted IFRSs, it is the amounts stated in those accounts that are relevant for the purposes of justifying a distribution.   **2.17**

The detailed requirements for relevant accounts (annual, interim or initial) are summarised in the following paragraphs.   **2.18**

Annual accounts – all companies

If the company's last annual accounts constitute the relevant accounts they must be prepared under Part 15 of the Act (Accounts and Reports) and comply with the requirements of section 837. Such accounts may be either """"Companies Act individual accounts"""' or """"IAS individual accounts"""' (see 2.17 above). The requirements of section 837 are that: **2.19**

(a)   the accounts must have been properly prepared in accordance with the Act (including the requirement in section 393 that they must not be approved unless the directors are satisfied that they give a true and fair view of the assets, liabilities, financial position and profit or loss of the company), subject only to matters not material for determining the lawfulness of a distribution;

(b)   the accounts must have been circulated to members in accordance with section 423[9];

---

[8] *Provisions are defined for this purpose in section 836(1) as, in the case of Companies Act accounts, provisions of any kind specified for this purpose by regulations under section 396 and, in the case of IAS accounts, provisions of any kind.*

[9] ~~*Where a company circulates to members a summary financial statement, the relevant accounts are the full accounts from which the summary financial statement was derived.*~~

(c)   the accounts must be accompanied, where applicable, by the report of the auditors under section 495; and

(d)   if the report of the auditors is qualified, the auditors must state in writing whether in their opinion the matters in respect of which their report is qualified is material for determining the lawfulness of the distribution. The statement by the auditors, which can be subsequent to the report, must be laid before the company in general meeting in the case of a public company, or be circulated to members in accordance with section 423 in the case of a private company.

The last two sub-paragraphs do not apply where the directors of the company have taken advantage of anthe audit exemption from auditconferred by sections 477(1) or 480(1).

Initial and interim accounts – public companies

2.20   Sections 838 and 839 respectively provide that interim and initial accounts of a public company must have been 'properly prepared', or have been properly prepared subject only to matters that are not material for determining, by reference to those accounts, whether the proposed distribution would contravene sections 830 or 831. A copy of the interim and initial accounts must have been delivered to the Registrar of Companies before the distribution is made (ie, before the date of the distribution – see 2.10 above).

2.21   'Properly prepared' means that the accounts must comply with sections 395 to 397 which includes the true and fair requirement in relation to Companies Act accounts[10] and the requirement to apply EU-adopted IFRSs in relation to IAS accounts. These requirements are to be applied with such modifications as are necessary because the accounts are prepared otherwise than in respect of an accounting reference period. In the case of interim accounts, the balance sheet must be signed in accordance with section 414. There is no equivalent statutory requirement for initial accounts to be signed in accordance with section 414 but, in practice, the auditors will require the accounts to be approved and signed by the directors before the report of the auditors can be signed.

2.22   In requiring the interim and initial accounts to be 'properly prepared', or to be properly prepared except for matters which are not relevant in determining whether a proposed dividend would be lawful under the Act, the legislation permits a public company to omit information which is not relevant in determining whether a distribution would be lawful under the Act. In practice, therefore, interim or initial accounts will consist of a balance sheet and profit and loss account but the notes may be restricted to those matters that are relevant to a distribution. Corresponding amounts for the previous financial year would not be relevant.

2.23   Interim accounts are not required to be audited. However, initial accounts of a public company must be accompanied by a report by the auditors stating whether, in their opinion, the accounts have been 'properly prepared'. If their report is qualified (which would be the case if the company chooses to prepare initial accounts which do not give a true and fair view, as described in paragraph 2.22 above), the auditors must make an additional statement which states whether, in their opinion, the matters in respect of which their report is qualified is material for determining, by reference to the initial accounts, whether the distribution would contravene sections 830 or 831. A copy of the auditors' statement must also have been laid before the company in general meeting and delivered to the Registrar of Companies.

---

[10] *There is no statutory requirement for interim and initial accounts to give a true and fair view when they are prepared under IFRSs because section 393, which imposes an overarching requirement for annual accounts to give a true and fair view, does not apply for this purpose. However, the requirements of IAS 1 impose a similar requirement to 'present fairly'.*

The requirements of sections 838 and 839 regarding the form and content of interim and initial accounts of public companies do not apply to private companies. Instead, the only requirement for private companies flows from the general definition at the start of those sections of interim or initial accounts as those necessary to enable a reasonable judgement to be made as to profits, losses, assets and liabilities, provisions, and share capital and reserves. Reliable management accounts which deal with these matters will often satisfy this requirement. However, management accounts sometimes do not deal with all relevant matters. For example, they may exclude tax. In these cases, appropriate adjustments need to be made to the management accounts.   **2.24**

Disclosure of distributable profits

There is no requirement under law or accounting standards for financial statements to distinguish between realised profits and unrealised profits or between distributable profits and non-distributable profits. Paragraph 2.16 above draws attention to the need for companies to maintain sufficient records to enable them to distinguish between those profits that are available for distribution and those which are not.   **2.25**

The guidance at 2.16 above is likely to be of greater significance when reporting under IFRSs or using the fair value accounting rules under UK GAAP than has previously been the case. One reason for this is that the restriction in the Accounting Regulations that only profits realised at the balance sheet date may be included in the profit and loss account does not apply in these cases.   **2.26**

It may be thought helpful to users of financial statements if there is an indication of which reserves are distributable but, as noted above, there is no legal requirement to do so[11]. In some cases, there may be practical difficulties with providing such an analysis. For example, there may be uncertainties about whether certain profits are realised or unrealised. There is generally no need for directors to form a view on whether profits are realised unless they intend to utilise them to make a distribution.   **2.27**

Subsequent events

Under common law, a company cannot lawfully make a distribution out of capital. Therefore it may be necessary to take into account losses incurred after the balance sheet date (see 2.2 above).   **2.28**

One or more distributions may already have been made by reference to a particular set of accounts; for example, an interim dividend or a purchase of own shares. In determining the lawfulness of any proposed further distribution by reference to the same accounts, the directors must take account of any such distributions (section 840(1)).   **2.29**

Public companies

A further restriction is placed on distributions by public companies (section 831). A public company may make a distribution only if, after giving effect to such distribution, the   **2.30**

---

[11] *On 24 November 2015, the FRC's Financial Reporting Lab issued a report '"'Disclosure of dividends policy and practice: exploring how companies can make dividend disclosures more relevant for investors"'". The report can be downloaded from the FRC website at https://www.frc.org.uk/News-and-Events/FRC-Press/Press/2015/November/ Making-dividends-disclosures-more-relevant-for-inv.aspx.*

amount of its net assets (as defined in section 831(2)) is not less than the aggregate of its called up share capital and undistributable reserves as shown in the relevant accounts.

2.31   Under section 831(4) the following are undistributable reserves:

(a)   share premium account (see also section 610);

(b)   capital redemption reserve (see also section 733);

(c)   the excess of accumulated unrealised profits, so far as not previously utilised by capitalisation, over the accumulated unrealised losses, so far as not previously written off in a reduction or reorganisation of its share capital; and

(d)   any other reserve which the company is prohibited from distributing by any enactment (e.g.eg. a redenomination reserve arising under section 628), or by its articles of association (or equivalent).

In relation to (c), the reference to 'excess' means that this amount can never be negative. Net unrealised losses cannot therefore be deducted although net unrealised profits must be added.

This means that, in calculating the amount available for distribution, a public company must reduce the amount of its net realised profits available for distribution by the amount of its net unrealised losses. The effects of this rule in relation to holdings of own shares through an ESOP trust and in relation to the presentation of shares as liabilities in the balance sheet are addressed at 7.12 *et seq* and 6.24 *et seq* respectively.

Provisions

The general rule and the exception

2.31A   Section 841(2) states that for the purposes of Part 23, the following are treated as realised losses:

- in the case of Companies Act accounts, provisions of a kind specified for the purpose in regulations under section 396 (other than revaluation provisions); and
- in the case of IAS accounts, provisions of any kind (except revaluation provisions).

The Accounting Regulations[12] state that references to provisions for depreciation or diminution in value of assets are to any amounts written off by way of providing for depreciation or diminution in value of assets. It also states that references to provisions for liabilities (or, in the case of insurance companies to provisions for other risks), are to any amounts retained as reasonably necessary for the purpose of providing for any liability, the nature of which is clearly defined and which is either likely to be incurred, or certain to be incurred but uncertain as to the amount or as to the date on which it will arise.

2.32   The general rule is therefore that any provision (including one for depreciation or diminution in value as well as provisions for liabilities, charges or losses) is treated as a realised loss.

2.33   As an exception to the general rule, a 'revaluation provision' which is a provision for diminution in value of a fixed asset appearing on a revaluation of all the fixed assets (other than goodwill) (section 841(3)) is not treated as a realised loss. However, this exception would not apply where the fixed asset has been sold or scrapped, because in these circumstances any loss would need to be reclassified as realised. Furthermore, unrealised losses which exceed unrealised profits are relevant to a public company in determining the

[12] *Schedule 7 to SI 2008/409 and Schedule 9 to SI 2008/410.*

amount available for distribution as the requirements of section 831 (Restrictions on the distribution of assets) referred to at 2.30 above must be satisfied.

An example of applying section 841 is that an impairment write down of one subsidiary may be offset by an increase in value of another subsidiary for the purposes of determining profits available for distribution (although the impairment would still have to be recorded in the profit and loss account for financial reporting purposes). Another example is where financial assets are regarded as fixed assets, such as in the case of investment companies, and any decrease in the fair value of investments may be offset by any increase in the fair value of other investments for the purposes of determining profits available for distribution (even though certain increases in fair value might be treated as unrealised for the purposes of this guidance). However, as noted at 2.34AA below, the application of the exception in section 841 is not restricted to circumstances where there is an offsetting unrealised profit.   **2.33A**

For the exception in 2.33 above to apply, it is not necessary for a revaluation of all the fixed assets to be recorded in the accounts. Section 841(4) provides that a revaluation of all the fixed assets is treated as having taken place if (1) the directors consider the value of any assets that have not actually been revalued, (2) they are satisfied that the aggregate value of those assets is not less than that stated in the company's accounts and (3) the notes to the accounts include a statement to that effect. The notes to the accounts should also state that amounts are stated in the accounts on the basis that a revaluation of fixed assets is treated as having taken place.   **2.34**

Application of the exception in section 841 for revaluation provisions is not restricted to those circumstances where there is an offsetting unrealised profit (recognised or not). Where all of the assets are actually revalued, section 841 treats the provision as a revaluation provision without any additional restrictions.   **2.34AA**

Where the assets, other than the impaired one, are not actually revalued but their value is 'considered' in accordance with section 841, the directors must be satisfied that the aggregate value of those assets (ie, the ones not actually revalued) at the time of their consideration was not less than the aggregate amount at which they were stated in the accounts. This does not impose any substantive additional restriction because financial reporting requirements ensure that an asset is not stated at a carrying amount which is higher than its value.   **2.34AB**

An unlawful return of capital might arise if a company makes a distribution out of accumulated realised profits without deducting an impairment loss which is treated as a revaluation provision in circumstances where there is an absence of any upside on other assets. The company may have made a distribution which results in its assets being less than its capital under common law (see 2.2 above). In the case of a public company, a distribution would never be possible under the statutory provisions in these circumstances because of section 831 (see 2.30 above).   **2.34AC**

Application of the exception under IFRSs and FRS 102

Due to changes in accounting methods and choices as between cost and valuation, effected by the implementation of IFRSs and FRS 102, the question might arise as to whether the exception provided for by section 841(2) continues to be capable of use under IFRSs and FRS 102. The following paragraphs explain questions that might arise and the conclusion that the exception does continue to be capable of use under IFRSs and FRS 102.   **2.34A**

[Deleted]   **2.34B**

2.34C   ~~For example, using section 841, an impairment write down of one subsidiary may be offset by an increase in value of another subsidiary for the purposes of determining profits available for distribution (although the impairment would still have to be recorded in the profit and loss account for financial reporting purposes). Another example is where financial assets are regarded as fixed assets, such as in the case of investment companies, and any decrease in the fair value of investments may be offset by any increase in the fair value of other investments for the purposes of determining profits available for distribution (even though certain increases in fair value might be treated as unrealised for the purposes of this guidance). However, as noted at 2.34AA above, the application of the exception in section 841 is not restricted to circumstances where there is an offsetting unrealised profit.~~ [Deleted]

Definition of ""fixed assets""

2.34D   The definition of a ""revaluation provision"" (see 2.33 above) uses the term ""fixed assets"" which are defined in section 853(6) as meaning assets of a company which are intended for use on a continuing basis in the company's activities. This term is not used in IFRSs. "'Non-current assets" as defined in IAS 1 will not correspond with "'fixed assets" as defined in section 853(6), for example because the former may include long term debtors.

2.34E   For the purposes of applying section 841, fixed assets are those assets that meet the section 853(6) definition of "'fixed assets". As noted above, in "'IAS individual accounts", these will not necessarily correspond with those presented as non-current assets in the relevant accounts. However, there is nothing in section 841 that requires the fixed assets to be shown in the balance sheet as such for the section to be applied.

Ability to revalue assets

2.34F   Investments in subsidiaries present a particular issue in the context of section 841 and IFRSs. Under IFRSs, three~~only two~~ accounting policies are available for investments in subsidiaries that are not classified as held for sale:

   (a)   cost (see 9.22 below); or

   (b)   in accordance with IAS 39, which requires such investments to be maintained at fair value; or

   (c)   using the equity method as described in IAS 28.

   In practice, fair value under (b) above may be precluded because the range of reasonable fair value estimates is significant and the probabilities of the various estimates cannot reasonably be assessed (see IAS 39, AG 80–81). IAS 39 requires such investments to be carried at cost. Even where a fair value policy is possible, it will require valuations to be obtained each time a balance sheet is drawn up. This is unattractive to most companies. Most companies, therefore, hold subsidiaries at cost. The issue that arises is whether it is possible to apply the exception for "'revaluation provisions" in section 841 in circumstances where the accounting policy is cost (either through choice or because IAS 39 does not permit the assets to be revalued).

2.34FA   The same issue arises in connection with FRS 102 which permits a choice of accounting policy for investments in subsidiaries. These are cost, fair value through profit or loss and fair value through other comprehensive income.

2.34G   Any assessment of the value of an asset can be described, for the purpose of the exception in section 841, as a revaluation, even if it is not in accordance with relevant accounting standards. In particular, the consideration of the value of an asset for the purposes of an impairment review could be described as a revaluation in this broad sense. Accordingly, section 841 does not use the term "revaluation" as meaning a revaluation in accordance with relevant accounting standards. However, depreciation of an asset is not consideration of the value of an asset for the purposes of section 841.

It is also relevant that, for the purposes of a revaluation of all the fixed assets (or all other than goodwill) under section 841, the assets do not have to be included in the balance sheet at their revalued amounts nor do they have to be permitted to be included in the balance sheet at a valuation. In accordance with section 841(4), "for the purposes of sub-sections (2) and (3) any consideration by the directors of the value at a particular time of a fixed asset is treated as a revaluation" (subject to the requirements of sub-section (4)). Section 841(4) refers to "any consideration by the directors of the value ...." without any explicit requirement for that value to be determined on a basis that would be permitted for inclusion in the balance sheet. **2.34H**

In conclusion, it is possible to apply the exception for "revaluation provisions" in section 841 in circumstances where the accounting policy is cost (either through choice or because IAS 39 does not permit the assets to be revalued). **2.34I**

Asset revaluations

Special considerations apply where a fixed asset has been revalued and an unrealised profit is recorded. Where a sum written off or retained for depreciation on or after the revaluation exceeds that which would have been charged if the unrealised profit had not been made, the excess does not give rise overall to a realised loss as there is a corresponding realisation of the related revaluation surplus, to the extent that that surplus has not previously been capitalised (section 841(5)). This means that the loss arising on the depreciation of revalued fixed assets is, in effect, calculated for distribution purposes by using historical cost principles, except to the extent that the surplus has previously been capitalised. **2.35**

If an asset is revalued downwards below its recoverable amount, as defined in FRS 102~~11~~ or IAS 36, then the difference between that revalued amount and recoverable amount is treated as an unrealised loss as it reflects a revaluation adjustment rather than a provision as defined in section 841[13]. Such a loss would become realised in the event of a subsequent scrapping, disposal or impairment of the asset. **2.36**

[Deleted]~~Under IAS 16, any revaluation loss that exceeds an existing revaluation surplus will be recognised as an expense in the income statement. Under FRS 15, such a loss would be recognised in the Statement of Total Recognised Gains and Losses to the extent that the asset's recoverable amount was greater than its revalued amount. Also, under FRS 15, where an impairment loss on a revalued asset is caused by a clear consumption of economic benefits, the loss will be taken to the profit and loss account. Under IAS 16, it will be taken to equity to the extent that there is a revaluation surplus relating to the asset. Consequently, losses may be reported differently under IFRSs and UK GAAP but the effect on accumulated realised profits will be the same.~~ **2.37**

Development costs

Section 844 requires that development costs shown as an asset should be treated as a realised loss, except where the directors justify the costs carried forward being treated **2.38**

---

[13] ~~FRS 15(70) states that where it can be demonstrated that recoverable amount is greater than the revalued amount, the difference between recoverable amount and the revalued amount is clearly not an impairment and should therefore be recognised in the statement of total recognised gains and losses as a valuation adjustment, rather than the profit and loss account.~~

as an asset. This would be the case if the costs are carried forward in accordance with applicable accounting standards. The justification must be included in a note to the accounts (section 844(3)).

2.39   [Moved to 2.1AA]

Treasury shares

2.40   Sections 724 to 732 of the Act relax, in some circumstances, the requirement that when a company purchases its own shares they are automatically cancelled. They allow ~~certain public~~ companies that purchase their own ~~"~~'qualifying shares~~"~~' out of distributable profits the option of holding them ~~"~~'in treasury~~"~~' (ie, un-cancelled) for sale at a later date (which must be for cash) or transferring them for the purposes of, or pursuant to, an employee share scheme. The treasury shares may also be cancelled at a later date. ~~Only~~ 'qualifying shares' ~~may be held in treasury. Qualifying shares are shares which are included in the Official List, traded on AIM, officially listed in another EEA[14] state or traded on a regulated market established in an EEA state.~~ In all other cases, shares purchased are cancelled by the automatic operation of the law in accordance with section 706.

2.41   Any purchase of shares to be held in treasury has to be made out of distributable profits which will be reduced by the amount of the purchase price.

2.42   The Act specifies how the proceeds of sale of any treasury shares for cash affects distributable profits. Where the proceeds of sale are equal to or less than the purchase price paid by the company for the shares, the proceeds should be treated as realised profits (ie, to reverse the original reduction in realised profits up to the purchase price paid). Where the proceeds of sale exceed the purchase price paid by the company for the shares, that part of the proceeds that is equal to the purchase price paid should be treated as a realised profit of the company. A sum equal to the excess should be transferred to the share premium account (ie, so that the purchase and sale of shares cannot create an overall increase in realised profits). For these purposes, section 731(4) provides that the purchase price paid by the company for the shares should be determined by the application of a weighted average price method.

2.43   Investments in own shares through an ESOP trust are not treasury shares as a matter of law. The distributable profit implications of shares held by an ESOP trust are considered in section 7 of this guidance. The purchase by an ESOP trust of shares held as treasury shares is considered at 7.33 to 7.35.

Section 832 – Investment companies

2.44   Investment companies are defined in section 833[15]. Under section 832[16] they are permitted, subject to meeting ~~a certain~~ requirements in section 832(5), to make distributions in circumstances, described in the following paragraph, which would not be permitted for other public companies under section 831. However, section 832 is an alternative rather than additional test for investment companies. Accordingly, an investment company may make a distribution in accordance with section 832 regardless of whether it would meet the

---

[14] *The European Economic Area (EEA) comprises the European Union together with Norway, Iceland and Liechtenstein.*

[15] *As amended by The Companies Act 2006 (Amendment of Part 23) (Investment Companies) Regulations 2012 (SI 2012/952).*

[16] *As amended by The Companies Act 2006 (Amendment of Part 23) (Investment Companies) Regulations 2012 (SI 2012/952).*

tests in section 831 and, although possibly more rarely, vice versa. ~~However, an investment company's articles must prohibit the distribution of capital profits (see section 833(2)(c)) and the application of section 831 cannot override this.~~

An investment company may make distributions at any time out of its accumulated realised revenue profits, so far as not previously utilised by a distribution or capitalisation, less its accumulated revenue losses (whether realised or unrealised), so far as not previously written off in a reduction or reorganisation of capital duly made: **2.44A**

- if at that time the amount of its assets is at least equal to one and a half times the aggregate of its liabilities to creditors;
- if, and to the extent that, the distribution does not reduce that amount to less than one and a half times that aggregate; and
- the conditions set out in section 832(5) are met.

In most circumstances, these rules allow an investment company to ignore capital losses, whether realised or unrealised, when making a distribution. **2.45**

As noted at 6.24 *et seq* in relation to section 831, the presentation of financial instruments in accordance with the substance of their contractual terms under IFRSs may affect the amount of a company's liabilities as stated in its relevant accounts. In particular, where all or part of the amount attributable to preference shares is presented as a liability, total liabilities will be increased by that amount. The amount of a company's assets is unaffected by the reclassification of shares as liabilities. **2.46**

However, section 832 refers to "'liabilities to creditors'". Although "'creditors'" is not defined for this purpose in the Act, this amount excludes amounts in respect of share capital and share premium that have been presented as liabilities. It also excludes other amounts due to shareholders in their capacity as such including accruals for dividends and redemption premiums that have been presented as expenses in the income statement and liabilities in the balance sheet. It would not, however, exclude general accruals, deferred income or deferred tax. **2.47**

Ordinary dividends are accrued in the balance sheet only in those rare cases where they are legally binding liabilities at the balance sheet date (see 2.10 above). However, a shareholder's right to any unpaid dividend is as a creditor of the company rather than as a shareholder (see 2.10A above). Therefore, any such liability is a liability to creditors for the purposes of section 832. **2.47A**

Section 843 – Long term insurance business

The normal rules of the Act (ie, the section 830 requirement for realised profits and the section 831 net assets rule) apply to insurance companies. However, for the purposes of determining whether there is a realised profit, the section 853(4) definition of realised profits, as being determined by reference to generally accepted accounting principles, is displaced in favour of special rules in the case of long-term insurance business, as set out in section 843. Paragraphs 2.48–2.53 below describe the operation of those special rules when the relevant accounts are for a year ending 31 December 2015 or earlier. Those rules are based on the regulatory regime applicable to such insurance companies through to that date. **2.47B**

From 1 January 2016, however, the new and very different Solvency II regulatory regime will apply to most insurance companies. There is ~~very~~ considerable doubt whether section 843 is capable of applying to accounts drawn up to that or subsequent dates by companies falling under Solvency II, since Solvency II, unlike the previous regulatory **2.47C** regime on which section 843 was derived, is not based on a general approach of funds or asset identification rules. On that basis, when these insurers determine whether there is a realised profit with reference to accounts for periods ending on or after 1 January 2016, the section 853(4) definition of realised profits (as being determined by reference to generally accepted accounting principles, ie, as set out in the rest of this Technical Release) would apply as it applies to all other companies.

2.47D   Given the large and varied investment portfolios held by such insurance companies, it is likely that the application of section 853(4) will involve significant effort and will lead to some part of the accumulated profits, perhaps a significant part, being unrealised. Note that after 1 January 2016 a set of 31 December 2015 accounts remain relevant accounts for distributions until subsequent statutory annual or interim accounts are drawn up (see paragraphs 2.12–2.24 above), and to that extent distributions can be determined based on such 31 December 2015 accounts and section 843. However, that is a short-term expedient, it will be spent once accounts are drawn up to a later date, and will not assist, eg, March 2016 year -ends.

2.47E   As noted in the Invitation to Comment, ICAEW understands that Government is actively considering changing the law to address this issue. This guidance will be updated in the light of any amendment made to the law before the revised guidance is finalised.

2.48   Section 843 sets out special rules that apply to an authorised insurance company (as defined in section 1165), other than an insurance special purpose vehicle (as defined in section 843(8)), carrying on long-term insurance business. An amount included in the relevant part of the company's balance sheet is treated as a realised profit if it:

- represents a surplus in the fund or funds maintained by it in respect of its long-term business (as defined in sub-section (7) and which includes both with-profits life business and other life business); and
- has not been allocated to policyholders or, as the case may be, carried forward unappropriated in accordance with asset identification rules made under section 142(2) of the Financial Services and Markets Act 2000.

2.49   For this purpose the relevant part of the balance sheet is that part of the balance sheet that represents accumulated profit or loss. A surplus in the fund or funds maintained by the company in respect of its long-term business means an excess of the assets representing that fund or those funds over the liabilities of the company attributable to its long-term business, as shown by an actuarial investigation.

2.50   A deficit in the fund or funds maintained by the company in respect of its long-term business is treated as a realised loss. For this purpose, a deficit in any such fund or funds means an excess of the liabilities of the company attributable to its long-term business over the assets representing that fund or those funds, as shown by an actuarial investigation.

2.51   Subject to this, any profit or loss arising in the company's long-term business is left out of account when determining realised profits and losses.

2.52   For the purpose of these requirements, an actuarial investigation means an investigation made into the financial condition of an authorised insurance company in respect of its long-term business, by an actuary appointed as actuary to the company:

- carried out once every period of twelve months in accordance with Rules made under Part 10 of the Financial Services and Markets Act 2000; or
- carried out in accordance with a requirement imposed by section 166 of that Act.

2.53   Much of the guidance in this Technical Release relates to the identification of generally accepted principles as to the determination of realised profits and losses in relation to section 853(4). To that extent, it is inapplicable to long-term insurance business of authorised insurance companies (other than special purpose vehicles) to which the above mentioned special rule applies instead. It should not be overlooked, however, that where such a company is a public company, it must also have regard to the section 831 net assets test.

3. REALISED PROFITS

General

Section 830(2) of the Act defines a company's profits available for distribution as 'its accumulated, realised profits, so far as not previously utilised by distribution or capitalisation, less its accumulated, realised losses, so far as not previously written off in a reduction or reorganisation of capital duly made'. Realised profits and realised losses are defined as 'such profits or losses of the company as fall to be treated as realised in accordance with principles generally accepted at the time when the accounts are prepared, with respect to the determination for accounting purposes of realised profits or losses' (section 853(4)). It is apparent from the use of the words 'at the time when the accounts are prepared' that the concept of a realised profit is intended to be dynamic, changing with the development of generally accepted accounting principles, as well as bringing within the definition profits which might not in ordinary language be called realised.   **3.1**

The determination of a company's profits available for distribution is derived from what is recorded in its accounts which are relevant for this purpose (see 2.12 above). It is fundamental for this purpose that the company's accounts have been properly prepared in accordance with the law and generally accepted accounting principles. Profits available for distribution may include amounts reported outside the profit and loss account (ie, as other comprehensive income or in the statement of changes in equity~~in the Statement of Total Recognised Gains and Losses or Reconciliation of Movements in Shareholders' Funds and their equivalents under IFRSs~~).   **3.2**

Principles of realisation

It is generally accepted that profits shall be treated as realised for the purpose of applying the definition of realised profits in companies legislation only when realised in the form of cash or of other assets the ultimate cash realisation of which can be assessed with reasonable certainty. In this context, "~~'~~realised~~'~~" may encompass profits relating to assets that are readily realisable. This would embrace profits and losses resulting from the recognition of changes in fair values, in accordance with relevant accounting standards, to the extent that they are readily convertible to cash.   **3.3**

[Deleted]~~The principles of realisation set out in this guidance are consistent with the notion of realisation as expressed in FRS 18. They are, however, relevant irrespective of whether the relevant accounts are prepared under UK GAAP or under IFRSs. The guidance also recognises that certain amounts may, as a matter of law, be profits (see 3.8(b) below).~~   **3.4**

In assessing whether a company has a realised profit, transactions and arrangements should not be looked at in isolation. A realised profit will arise only where the overall commercial effect on the company is such that the definition of realised profit set out in this guidance is met.   **3.5**

Thus, for example, a group or series of transactions or arrangements should be viewed as a whole, particularly if they are artificial, linked (whether legally or otherwise) or circular or any combination of these. The principle in paragraph 3.5 is likely to be of particular relevance for, but not limited to, intra-group transactions which are considered in section 9   **3.5A** of this guidance. Further guidance on the application of the principle in paragraph 3.5 is set out at 3.43 to 3.75 below. The specific circumstances of 'cash box structures' are addressed in section 12.

3.6   A profit previously regarded as unrealised becomes realised when the relevant criteria set out in this guidance are met (for example, a revaluation surplus becomes realised when the related asset is sold for 'qualifying consideration'). Similarly, a profit previously regarded as realised becomes unrealised when the criteria set out in this guidance cease to be met. This is considered more fully at 3.28 to 3.29C below.

Definitions

3.7   The definitions which follow should be read in conjunction with the principles of realisation as well as the guidance on their interpretation set out in this Technical Release.

Profit

3.8   'Profit' for the purpose of section 853(4) comprises:

(a)   ~~'gains', as defined in the Accounting Standards Board's 'Statement of Principles for Financial Reporting' and~~ 'income' as defined in the IASB's Conceptual Framework and Section 2 of FRS 102~~International Accounting Standards Board's 'Framework'~~ which both convey ~~(with different wording)~~ increases in ownership interest not resulting from contributions from owners; and

(b)   other amounts which are profits as a matter of law, or which are treated as profits, including:

(i)   gratuitous contributions of assets from owners in their capacity as such; and

(ii)   an amount taken to a so-called 'merger reserve' reflecting the extent that relief is obtained under sections 611 or 612 of the Act from the requirement to recognise a share premium account.

Realised profit

3.9   A profit is realised, as a matter of generally accepted accounting practice, where it arises from:

(a)   a transaction where the consideration received by the company is 'qualifying consideration'; or

(b)   an event which results in 'qualifying consideration' being received by the company in circumstances where no consideration is given by the company; or

(c)   the recognition in the financial statements of a change in fair value, in those cases where fair value has been determined in accordance with measurement guidance in the relevant accounting standards or company law, and to the extent that the change recognised is readily convertible to cash; or

(d)   the translation of:

(i)   a monetary asset which comprises qualifying consideration; or

(ii)   a liability,

denominated in a foreign currency; or

(e)   the reversal of a loss previously regarded as realised; or

(f)   a profit[17] previously regarded as unrealised (such as amounts taken to a revaluation reserve, merger reserve or other similar reserve) becoming realised as a result of:

---

[17] *Where the related profit has been capitalised, it will not be available for transfer from unrealised profit to realised profit.*

(i)   consideration previously received by the company becoming 'qualifying consideration'; or

(ii)   the related asset being disposed of in a transaction where the consideration received by the company is 'qualifying consideration'; or

(iii)   a realised loss being recognised on the scrapping or disposal of the related asset; or

(iv)   a realised loss being recognised on the write-down for depreciation, amortisation, diminution in value or impairment of the related asset[18];

(v)   the distribution in kind of the asset to which the unrealised profit relates; or

(vi)   the receipt of a dividend in the form of qualifying consideration when no profit is recognised because the dividend is deducted from the book value of the investment to which the unrealised profit relates (eg, a dividend which is credited to the cost of investment because it is in substance a return of capital~~as required by IAS 27 before its amendment in May 2008[19] in the case of dividends out of pre-acquisition profits of subsidiaries~~) (see 9.22 *et seq* below),

in which case the appropriate proportion[20] of the related unrealised profit becomes a realised profit; or

(g)   the remeasurement of a liability, to the extent that the change recognised is readily convertible to cash (see 3.9B below).

In addition, as explained at 2.8A, The Companies (Reduction of Share Capital) Order 2008 SI 2008/1915 specifies the cases in which a reserve arising from a reduction in a company's share capital is to be treated as a realised profit as a matter of law.   **3.9A**

A profit arising on the remeasurement of a liability will often be the reversal of a realised loss, a foreign currency translation gain or a fair value gain, and may therefore be a realised profit in accordance with 3.9(c), (d) or (e), Paragraph 3.9(g) will be relevant in other cases such as that of a defined benefit pension liability assumed for consideration either in a separate transaction or as part of a business combination. In such a case the profit is only a realised profit in those rare cases where the change in value is readily convertible to cash as defined at 3.12 below.   **3.9B**

In relation to paragraph 3.9(f)(ii) above, when the asset disposed of is a fungible asset, the disposal of a proportion of that asset for qualifying consideration will result in the realisation of the same proportion of the previously unrealised profit. The rationale for this is similar to that set out in paragraphs 10.77 to 10.82 below regarding section 846 and fungible assets.   **3.9C**

Realised loss

Losses should be regarded as realised losses except to the extent that the law, accounting standards or this guidance provide otherwise. The statutory position is set out in section 2 of this guidance.   **3.10**

---

[18] *If the write down is subsequently reversed, an equal amount of profit should be regarded as becoming unrealised. In other words, the amount of profit regarded as becoming realised is equal to the cumulative amount of any write down treated as a realised loss.*

[19] ~~*Amendments to IFRS 1 First-time Adoption of IFRSs and IAS 27 Consolidated and Separate Financial Statements: Cost of an Investment in a Subsidiary, Jointly Controlled Entity or Associate.*~~

[20] *In the case of (iii) and (iv), the loss is treated as a realised loss under paragraph 3.15 of this guidance. However, part of this realised loss is compensated by a reclassification from unrealised to realised profit.*

3.10A   The instances of unrealised losses referred to in this guidance are:

    (a)   'revaluation provisions' as defined in section 841(3) which are an exception to the general rule that all other provisions are realised losses (see paragraphs 2.31A to 2.34I above);

    (b)   a downwards revaluation of fixed assets to below their recoverable amount (see paragraphs 2.36 above);

    (c)   some losses arising from fair value accounting, but only when two criteria are met (see paragraph 4.31 below); and

    (d)   deferred tax provided on revalued assets when the deferred tax is treated as a reduction of the unrealised profit rather than as a separate realised loss (see paragraph 3.17 below).

Qualifying consideration

3.11   Qualifying consideration comprises:

    (a)   cash; or

    (b)   an asset that is readily convertible to cash; or

    (c)   the release, or the settlement or assumption by another party, of all or part of a liability of the company; or

    (d)   an amount receivable in any of the above forms of consideration where:

        (i)   the debtor is capable of settling the receivable within a reasonable period of time; and

        (ii)   there is a reasonable certainty that the debtor will be capable of settling when called upon to do so; and

        (iii)   there is an expectation that the receivable will be settled; or

    (e)   an amount receivable from a shareholder where and to the extent that[21]:

        (i)   the company intends to make a distribution to the shareholder of an amount equal to or less than its receivable from that shareholder; and

        (ii)   the company intends to settle such distribution by off-setting against the amount receivable (in whole or in part); and

        (iii)   within the meaning of paragraph 3.5 and 3.5A of this guidance, (i) and (ii) are linked.

3.11A   For the purposes of applying paragraph 3.11 above, references to settlement include settlement by way of set-off with a liability to the same party.

Readily convertible to cash

3.12   An asset, or change in the fair value of an asset or liability, is considered to be "'readily convertible to cash'" if:

    (a)   a value can be determined at which a transaction in the asset or liability could occur, at the date of determination[22], in its state at that date, without negotiation and/or

---

[21] *In the case addressed by paragraph 3.11(e), it would be possible, in the absence of other accumulated realised losses, to distribute the receivable in kind under section 846. Paragraph 3.11(e) sets down generally accepted accounting practice that the receivable can be regarded as qualifying consideration in certain circumstances. The effect of this is that making a distribution settled by offset against the receivable is an alternative procedure to a distribution in kind of that receivable. This is illustrated in the example in Appendix 9.*

[22] *The reference to the date of determination is subject to the limited exception in paragraph 4.17 below for the determination of the effect that any block discount on securities traded in an active market has on realised profits.*

marketing, to either convert the asset, liability or change in fair value into cash, or to close out the asset, liability or change in fair value; and

(b) in determining the value, information such as prices, rates or other factors that market participants would consider in setting a price is observable; and

(c) the company's circumstances must not prevent immediate conversion to cash or close out of the asset, liability or change in fair value; for example, the company must be able to dispose of, or close out the asset, liability or the change in fair value, without any intention or need to liquidate or curtail materially the scale of its operations, or to undertake a transaction on adverse terms.

Further guidance on the application of "'readily convertible to cash'" is provided in section 4 of this guidance. The position regarding fair value losses is dealt with at 4.29 *et seq* below. **3.13**

Application

Instances of realised profit

In addition to those instances which are readily apparent from the definition of realised profit, in applying the principles of realisation and the definitions set out above the following would constitute a realised profit: **3.14**

(a) the receipt or accrual of investment or other income receivable in the form of qualifying consideration; or

(b) a gain arising on a return of capital on an investment where the return is in the form of qualifying consideration; or

(c) a gift (such as a 'capital contribution') received in the form of qualifying consideration; or

(d) the release of a provision for a liability or loss which was treated as a realised loss; or

(e) the reversal of a write-down or provision for diminution in value or impairment of an asset which was treated as a realised loss.

Instances of realised loss

Realised losses will include: **3.15**

(a) a cost or expense (other than one charged to the share premium account) which results in a reduction in recorded net assets;

(b) a loss arising on the sale or other disposal or scrapping of an asset;

(c) the writing down, or providing for the depreciation, amortisation, diminution in value or impairment, of an asset[23], except as noted at 2.33 and 2.36 above;

(d) the creation of, or increase in, a provision for a liability or loss (other than deferred tax in the circumstances described at 3.17 below) which results in an overall reduction in recorded net assets;

(e) a gift made by the company (or the release of all or part of a debt due to the company or the assumption of a liability by the company) to the extent that it results in an overall reduction in recorded net assets; and

(f) a loss arising from fair value accounting where profits on remeasurement of the same asset or liability would be treated as realised profits.

[Deleted] **3.16**

---

[23] *Where the asset has been revalued or is otherwise represented to any extent by an unrealised profit, the appropriate proportion of the related unrealised profit becomes a realised profit, thus mitigating the effect of the realised loss – see paragraph 3.9(f) of this guidance.*

Deferred tax

3.17   A provision for deferred tax should generally be regarded as a realised loss. However, when assets are revalued to their fair value and the gain is regarded as unrealised, the deferred tax on that gain should be treated as a reduction in that unrealised gain rather than as a realised loss.

3.17A   This principle is applicable to deferred tax provisions recognised in accordance with accounting standards, irrespective of whether profits are recognised in profit or loss, or in other comprehensive income. For many financial instruments, profits arising from fair value accounting are realised profits (see Section 4 below). Any attributable deferred tax provision will be a realised loss. [Moved from 10.40]

3.17B   For companies applying IFRSs, when a convertible debt instrument is accounted for using 'split accounting' (see Convertible debt at 6.59 et seq below), a deferred tax provision is established and debited against the initial carrying amount of the equity component in accordance with paragraph 23 of IAS 12. This occurs if the tax base of the debt is its full amount but the book amount is lower by the amount of the equity component. The deferred tax provision reverses through profit or loss over the life of the instrument as illustrated in Example 4 in Appendix B to IAS 12. It does not represent a future cash outflow for payment of tax. The deferred tax provision should be treated as a reduction in the credit to equity rather than as a realised loss. The equity component of the financial instrument is not a profit at all and therefore does not fall to be classified as realised or unrealised (see Convertible debt at 6.59 et seq below). An adjustment to such an item does not affect realised profits. This issue does not arise under FRS 102 because initial recognition of a compound instrument does not result in any tax accounting. [Moved from 10.42]

3.17C   In some cases it may be necessary to provide for current tax on an unrealised profit. A current tax provision should be treated as a realised loss even if it arises from the taxation of an unrealised profit. This is because a provision for current tax represents a specific cash outflow that will arise irrespective of whether the related profit is realised or not. [Moved from 10.43]

3.17D   A credit in profit or loss for deferred tax will often be attributable to a realised loss and can be regarded as a reduction in that realised loss. If this is not the case, and the credit results in the recognition of a deferred tax asset in accordance with accounting standards, the resulting profit will generally be an unrealised profit because a deferred tax asset does not usually meet the definition of qualifying consideration.

Exchange of assets ('top-slicing')

3.18   Where an asset is sold partly for qualifying consideration and partly for other consideration (for example, a mixed consideration of cash and a freehold property), any profit arising is a realised profit to the extent that the fair value of the consideration received is in the form of qualifying consideration. This approach is sometimes referred to as 'top-slicing'. (Example: fair value of consideration received is £10m, of which £4m is cash and £6m is freehold property. If the depreciated historical cost of the asset sold is £5m, the total gain is £5m but the realised profit is limited to £4m.)

3.18A   The consideration received may comprise a combination of assets and liabilities. For example, this will often be the case on a transfer of trade and assets for no consideration (eg, a 'hive down' or 'hive across'). To apply the 'top slicing' rule in this case, any liabilities should first be deducted from the amount of qualifying consideration received. The profit will be realised only to the extent of any net balance of qualifying consideration received. For example, if a capital contribution received comprises investment property of £100,000 and cash of £50,000 together with a bank loan of £70,000, none of the resulting profit of £80,000 is realised because the net amount of qualifying consideration received is negative.

Hedging

Where hedge accounting is obtained in accordance with the relevant accounting standards, it is necessary to consider the combined effect of both sides of the hedging relationship to determine whether there is a realised profit or loss in accordance with the criteria in this guidance.   **3.19**

Application of this principle in the context of hedge relationships within the individual financial statements of a company is considered at 5.1 to 5.18 of this guidance. Consideration of the effects of hedge relationships where the hedging instrument and the hedged item are held by different group companies is considered at 5.19 to 5.22.   **3.20**

Foreign exchange profits and losses

~~U~~Paragraph 65 of SSAP 20 Foreign currency translation, which was issued in 1983, states that 'the application of paragraph 50 of this statement may result in unrealised exchange gains on unsettled long-term monetary items being taken to the profit and loss account'. ~~Since then, however, the currency markets have become more sophisticated and companies have significantly more flexibility to crystallise exchange profits on long-term monetary items. Consequently,~~ unless there are doubts as to the convertibility or marketability of the currency in question, foreign exchange profits arising on the retranslation of monetary items are realised, irrespective of the maturity date of the monetary item.   **3.21**

This has become generally accepted practice even though the exchange difference may not be 'readily convertible to cash' at the balance sheet date. However, a profit on retranslation of a monetary asset will not be a realised profit where the underlying balance on which the exchange difference arises does not itself meet the definition of 'qualifying consideration'. For example, this may be the case for some long-term inter-company balances within groups.   **3.21A**

The position regarding exchange differences reported in a separate component of equity (ie, not in the income statement) is considered at 5.7 below in relation to cash flow hedge accounting; and in relation to the translation of branches into the company's functional currency, the translation of the whole of a company's accounts from the company's functional currency to a presentation currency and questions of mismatch with the currency of denomination of shares are considered in section 11.   **3.21B**

Goodwill in an individual company

Where goodwill arises in a company's individual accounts (which would be the case, for example, where the company has purchased an unincorporated business) the goodwill will become a realised loss as the goodwill is amortised or written down for impairment in accordance with relevant accounting standards.   **3.22**

For periods ending before 23 December 1998, purchased goodwill may have been accounted for under SSAP 22 ~~"~~'Accounting for goodwill~~"~~' by immediate elimination against reserves. Such goodwill may have remained eliminated against reserves under UK GAAP under the transitional provisions of FRS 10 and will remain there on transition to FRS 102. Such goodwill should be regarded as a realised loss to the extent that, had it always been recognised as an asset, it would have been amortised or impaired in accordance with FRS 10.   **3.23**

3.23A   If the business to which the acquired goodwill relates is disposed of or closed, FRS 10 requireds the profit or loss on disposal to include the goodwill previously taken to reserves to the extent that it hads not previously been charged to the profit and loss account. Notional amortisation or impairment for the purposes of calculating realised profits diddoes not affect this financial reporting requirement. However, the effect of the disposal on realised profits wasis therefore net of any amount already treated as a realised loss in accordance with this guidance. FRS 102 does not include any similar requirement about goodwill previously written off to reserves.

3.23B   Goodwill may also have remained eliminated against reserves on transition to IFRSs in accordance with IFRS 1 or on transition to FRS 102 in accordance with sSection 35 of FRS 102. Such goodwill should be regarded as a realised loss to the extent that, had it always been recognised as an asset under IFRSs, it would have been impaired in accordance with IFRS 3 and IAS 36. This is unaffected by any amounts of notional amortisation in accordance with FRS 10 or FRS 102 that might have been treated as realised losses prior to transition to IFRSs.

3.23C   When applying IFRSs, goodwill previously written off to reserves is not taken into account in any profit or loss on subsequent disposal. However, any goodwill written off to reserves that has not previously been treated as a realised loss will become realised as a result of the disposal. The same will apply under FRS 102.

3.23D   Companies not wishing to make these assessments may prudently opt to regard the entire amount of goodwill written off to reserves as a realised loss.

Negative goodwill in an individual company

3.24   The following guidance on negative goodwill applies under UK GAAP and IFRSs unless otherwise stated. Neither IFRS 3 does not usenor IFRS 3 Revised (subsequently together referred to as IFRS 3) uses the term "'negative goodwill'" but instead they describes that concept using different words. For simplicity, such an amount is described in this guidance as negative goodwill.

3.25   Negative goodwill up to the fair values of the non-monetary assets acquired should be treated as being realised in the periods in which the non-monetary assets are recovered, whether through depreciation or sale. Where the negative goodwill exceeds the value of the non-monetary assets, this excess should be treated as being realised in the periods expected to benefit. However, negative goodwill should not be treated as a realised profit in the case of a sale of the non-monetary assets where the consideration received is not qualifying consideration.

3.26   Under UK GAAP, negative goodwill recognised in the profit and loss account in accordance with FRS 10 or FRS 102 therefore represents a realised profit except in the case of a sale of the non-monetary assets where the consideration received is not qualifying consideration. Where negative goodwill was accounted for under SSAP 22 in the accounts of an individual company, it would have been regarded initially as an unrealised profit. It will become a realised profit on the same basis as if it had been negative goodwill accounted for under FRS 10 or FRS 102.

3.27   IFRS 3 requires the immediate recognition of negative goodwill as a profit for financial reporting purposes but this does not accelerate the realisation of negative goodwill which is as set out at 3.25 above irrespective of the accounting framework adopted.

Changes in circumstances including changes in accounting policies and on the adoption of IFRSs and FRS 102

Introduction

The treatment of a retained profit or loss as realised (or unrealised), or the recognition of an item as a profit or loss or an asset or liability, may change subsequent to its original recognition as a result of: **3.28**

(a)   a change in the principles of realisation; or

(b)   a change in the law or in accounting standards or interpretations, either through an express reference to the realisation or otherwise of the profit or loss or, more commonly, through a change in the recognition or measurement of assets, liabilities, income or expenses. A company adopting IFRSs or FRS 102 for the first time will, in effect, be making a number of changes in accounting policies; or

(c)   some other change in circumstance such that what was originally qualifying consideration under paragraph 3.11(d) is no longer so, for example, where a receivable was initially regarded as qualifying consideration but circumstances change such that there is now no expectation that the receivable will be settled in the form of qualifying consideration.

Although the effect of these changes may be to reduce or even eliminate a company's net realised profits, that would not render unlawful a distribution already made out of realised profits determined by reference to 'relevant accounts' which had been prepared in accordance with generally accepted accounting principles applicable to those accounts (this is subject to paragraphs 3.30 and 3.31 below). This is because the Act defines realised profits and losses for determining the lawfulness of a distribution as 'such profits and losses of the company as fall to be treated as realised in accordance with principles generally accepted **at the time when the accounts are prepared**, with respect to the determination for accounting purposes of realised profits or losses' (section 853(4), emphasis added). **3.29**

The circumstances described in paragraph 3.28(c) do not extend to the case of "an asset that is readily convertible to cash" (which is "qualifying consideration" under paragraph 3.11(b)). Such assets are, when received, regarded as being so highly liquid as to be treated as equivalent to cash. That is to say, the initial determination that a profit is a realised one is, if based on the qualifying consideration's being cash or "an asset that is readily convertible to cash", definitive and unchangeable. Thus, for example, if changes in the market for a financial asset mean that from a certain point in time the asset no longer meets the "readily convertible to cash" test, then prior fair value movements – whether profits or losses – remain as realised. **3.29A**

This would be relevant if, for example, the financial asset were reclassified out of a fair value category under ~~the amendment to~~ IAS 39 ~~of November 2008~~. To the extent that the last fair value includes amounts originally determined to be realised profits, they remain so. It is as if the profits were realised in cash and re-invested (outside of the principle in paragraph 3.5) into the financial asset in question. In such a reclassification case, it may of course be the case that the market changed, so as no longer to meet the "readily convertible to cash" test, at an earlier date than the reclassification. In such a case the financial asset's carrying value may include realised profits and unrealised profits. Whilst the realised profits will retain that status going forward, the unrealised profits are capable at some future date of changing to realised profits under paragraph 3.9(f). **3.29B**

It would be open to a company, instead of splitting the fair value movement since inception into movements that were and were not readily convertible to cash, to make a shortcut, prudent assumption that if there are cumulative net gains since inception, they are regarded as unrealised. **3.29C**

Timing of the effect of changes in accounting policies on distributable profits

3.30 The effects of the introduction of a new accounting standard or on the adoption of IFRSs or FRS 102 become relevant to the application of the common law capital maintenance rule only in relation to distributions accounted for in periods in which the change will first be recognised in the accounts. Where items will fall to be treated as liabilities under a new standard in a period after the period in which the dividend is accounted for, directors do not have to pay regard to such future liabilities merely because they are disclosed in the notes to the accounts.

3.31 Where the directors are considering the payment of an interim dividend in respect of a financial year, and a new accounting standard may, for example, lead to items being recognised as liabilities in the accounts for that year, the directors must, under common law, have regard to the effect of these liabilities on the expected level of profits available for distribution at the end of the financial year when determining the lawfulness of the interim dividend.

3.32 For example, for a company adopting IFRSs for the first time in its individual accounts in 201610 the position is as follows:

- any dividends accounted for in the 2015 accounts (eg. interim dividends paid during the year) do not have to have regard to the effect of adoption of IFRSs;
- any final dividend for 201509 will not be provided in the 201509 UK GAAP accounts and will first be accounted for in the 201610 accounts. Such a dividend would therefore have to have regard to the effect of adoption of IFRSs even though the "relevant accounts" may still be those for 201509 prepared under UK GAAP;
- any interim dividend paid during 201610 would have to have regard to the effect of adoption of IFRSs even though the "relevant accounts" may still be those for 201509 prepared under UK GAAP; and
- the 201610 accounts prepared under IFRSs would be the relevant accounts for the purposes of the final dividend approved by shareholders in 201711. The effect of a change in accounting policy known to be adopted in 201711 needs to be taken into account in determining the dividend to be approved by shareholders in 201711. The dividend will be recognised in the 201711 accounts.

3.33 The considerations set out above apply to all dividends whether in respect of shares classified as equity or shares classified as debt (or partly shares and partly debt as a compound instrument) under either IFRSs or UK GAAP.

3.34 If the effect of a new accounting standard or guidance on profits which fall to be treated as realised is to increase the company's accumulated profits and the company wishes to distribute an amount in excess of that which could be determined by reference to what would otherwise constitute the company's 'relevant accounts', the company is required to prepare interim accounts complying with the new accounting standard or guidance. Where a public company is in this position, those interim accounts are required to be delivered to the Registrar under section 838.

3.35 For the purposes of a dividend made by reference, under statute, to previousUK GAAP relevant accounts, but at a time when the foregoing guidance requires the effect of a current year changeover to a new GAAPIFRSs to be considered, the directors will need to understand the consequences of adopting the new GAAPIFRSs for the company's profits available for distribution. There is no statutory requirement to prepare interim accounts under section 836 (and section 838 in the case of a public company) if a proposed distribution can be justified by reference to the relevant accounts. However, under common law, a company cannot lawfully make a distribution out of capital. The directors may, for example, by reason of their duties to exercise appropriate skill and care, consider preparing interim accounts under the new GAAPIFRSs, as of the date shortly before the time of paying the proposed dividend, to satisfy themselves that the accumulated realised profits shown in the last statutory individual accounts have not been eliminated, or reduced to such an extent that the proposed distribution would be unlawful. (It should be noted that these "'interim accounts"' would not be interim accounts within the meaning of section 836(2) of the Act and section 838 would not therefore apply to them.) For a public company, the directors will also have to consider the impact of the restriction on distributions arising from section 831 (see 6.24 *et seq*). It may not always be necessary to prepare interim accounts, for example, in very straightforward cases where the directors are satisfied that no material adjustments arise from the transition to the new GAAPIFRSs.

3.36 The directors of a company may not yet have decided whether to adopt a new GAAPIFRSs for the current financial year. Similarly, they may not have decided whether to adopt early a new accounting standard that has been issued but is not mandatory for the financial year. In these cases, the company's accounting policies are those that it has previously applied until a decision is made to change them. Therefore, in applying the foregoing guidance, it is not necessary to have regard to possible changes of policy that are being considered but have not yet been agreed.

3.37 Where a company believes that the implementation of a new GAAPIFRSs will increase its balance of distributable profits, and it wishes to distribute those profits as increased, the guidance at 3.34 above will be relevant.

Realised profits that have been distributed and are subsequently eliminated by a change of circumstances (including a change of accounting policy)

3.38 Where the effect of a change in circumstance is that a profit previously recognised as realised can no longer be regarded as being realised, the amount of that profit should either be eliminated through a prior year adjustment or be reclassified as unrealised (as appropriate) in the relevant accounts in which the change in circumstance is first recognised.

3.38A Where a previously recognised realised profit is eliminated through a prior year adjustment, the adjustment should be treated as a realised loss. The effect is therefore to reduce accumulated realised profits by the amount of the adjustment. If the adjustment results in accumulated realised losses, further distributions will not be possible until the shortfall is made good. To make a distribution before the shortfall is made good would amount to an unlawful return of capital, contrary to common law.

3.38B The same approach is possible where the previously recognised realised profit is reclassified as an unrealised profit. However, as explained below, in certain circumstances, it may be possible to adopt an alternative approach and to treat the distribution as having been made, in whole or in part, out of the profit which has been reclassified as unrealised so that it reduces accumulated unrealised profits rather than accumulated realised profits. This alternative approach may reduce any adverse impact on accumulated realised profits but is more difficult to apply. Either approach is acceptable when realised profits are reclassified as unrealised profits.

3.38C Under the alternative approach referred to in 3.38B, as profits are fungible, unless there is evidence that the profit affected by the change in circumstances has been distributed, it should be assumed that the first distribution made after the recognition of the profit was made pro rata out of all available profits shown in the relevant accounts. Accordingly, the balance remaining after that distribution would include a proportionate amount of the affected profit. Similarly each subsequent distribution would reduce proportionately the amount of the affected profit.

3.39   For example, a company has accumulated realised profits of 40 brought forward at the beginning of Year 1. During that year it makes realised profits of 60 of which 40 arose from a specific transaction in that period, and distributes 70, leaving a balance of 30. In Year 2 it generates a further 170 of realised profits and distributes 150. A change in circumstances in year 3 leads to the 40 recognised in Year 1 becoming treated as unrealised. The amount of the original profit of 40 that would be regarded as having been distributed in Year 1 would be 28 (70% [ie, 70/100] of 40), leaving 12 of the original profit to be carried forward in the closing balance of 30 at the end of Year 1. In Year 2 the amount of this 12 that would be regarded as having been distributed in Year 2 would be 9 (75% [ie, 150/200] of 12), leaving 3 of the original profit to be carried forward in the closing balance of 50 at the end of Year 2. Thus the amount of profit to be reclassified as unrealised in Year 3 as a result of the change in circumstance would be 3.

		Total	Affected profit
YEAR 1:	Brought forward	40	–
	Profit for year	60	40
	Available for distribution	100	40
	Distributed	(70)	(28)
YEAR 2:	Brought forward	30	12
	Profit for year	170	–
	Available for distribution	200	12
	Distributed	(150)	(9)
YEAR 3:	Brought forward	50	3

3.40   Where after making all reasonable enquiries it proves impracticable to obtain the information to make the allocation described at 3.38C, it would be appropriate to assume that the profit has been distributed (to the extent that there have been distributions).

Effect of errors

3.41   ~~Under UK GAAP, only changes in accounting policies and correction of~~ *fundamental* ~~errors are accounted for by restatement of comparatives. This means that errors that are material but not 'fundamental' are accounted for in the year in which they are detected without any restatement. In contrast,~~ IAS 8 and FRS 102 requires all *material* errors to be corrected retrospectively through a restatement of comparatives. ~~Consequently, correction of errors by restatement is more common when reporting under IFRSs.~~ A distribution may have been made by reference to the original accounts which would not have been justified if the error had not occurred. The question arises of whether such a distribution would be rendered unlawful.

3.42   It is the error, rather than its correction, that may have the effect of making a previous distribution unlawful. W~~The effect of reporting under IFRSs is to make such errors more visible because of the requirement for retrospective restatement for all material errors. But~~ whether or not an error is corrected in this way does not, of itself, govern the lawfulness of a previous distribution. The effect of an error on the lawfulness of a distribution raises complex legal issues that are beyond the scope of this guidance.

Application of the linkage etc principle in paragraph 3.5

3.43   The principle in paragraph 3.5 above must be viewed from the perspective of an individual company to determine that company's realised profits. Therefore, if a company enters into a single transaction, that transaction cannot be linked because the concept of linkage requires the effect of two or more legally separate transactions of the same entity to be viewed as a single transaction in substance. The fact that a series of transactions is circular from the perspective of a group does not mean that an individual company in the group, for example that participates in a single transaction in that series, cannot realise a profit on that transaction. The normal test of realisation may be met when applied to that single transaction.

The fact that an individual company's transactions are linked for the purposes of paragraph 3.5 does not necessarily mean that a realised profit cannot arise. The normal tests of realisation may be met when applied to the overall effect of the series of transactions taken together.   **3.44**

For two transactions to be linked, the second transaction must have been contemplated when the first transaction was entered into. If the second transaction is entered into for genuine commercial reasons unconnected with the first transaction and was not part of a plan with the first transaction, the two transactions would not be determined as linked.   **3.45**

The following principles address the application of paragraph 3.5 and require the exercise of judgement.   **3.46**

The application of paragraph 3.5 is not restricted to intra-group cash flows even though it is illustrated in the examples in section 9 solely in relation to intra-group situations.   **3.47**

Paragraph 3.5 is also relevant to transactions with third parties. The examples in section 9 focus on intra-group transactions as these are the more common situations where the question of linkage arises. An example of a situation involving a third party where linkage must be considered is the sale of a subsidiary for cash to a third party on the condition that the cash is applied in subscribing for shares of the purchaser. The substance or overall commercial effect of the transactions is a sale with consideration in shares of the purchaser.   **3.48**

The transactions do not have to be more than one of 'linked' **or** 'artificial' **or** 'circular' **to fall within the principle in paragraph 3.5.**   **3.49**

Paragraph 3.5 states that "'a realised profit will arise only where the *overall commercial effect* on the company is such that the definition of realised profit set out in this guidance is met"' (emphasis added).   **3.50**

Transactions need satisfy only one of the examples mentioned in paragraph 3.5A of being linked, artificial or circular, and furthermore these three cases are only particular instances of its application; that is to say, it is not limited to those cases. In practice individual transactions may fall within paragraph 3.5 because they are artificial or because collectively their effect is circular; but it is not necessary that a transaction be linked or artificial or circular for it to fall within paragraph 3.5.   **3.51**

Splitting a transaction into separate steps would require consideration under the principle in paragraph 3.5.   **3.52**

Taking the example discussed above of the sale of a subsidiary for shares; if this had been dealt with in one transaction it is obvious that the shares have to be evaluated to determine if they are qualifying consideration before concluding whether the profit on the transaction is realised. However, by splitting the transaction into two – a sale for cash and a subscription agreement – the commercial effect is obscured. Without proper analysis, the   **3.53** subscription agreement might have been overlooked and the profit determined as realised as the consideration was apparently cash. The transactions are linked. The transaction could be achieved by a single transaction of a sale for shares.

3.54   However, transactions may be linked without being artificial, or circular without being linked. Judgement is required in any determination of whether transactions fall within paragraph 3.5.

3.55   Other indicators of transactions that may fall within paragraph 3.5 include:

- the transactions being entered into at the same time (although see the discussion of time delays below) and in contemplation of each other;
- the transactions being with the same counterparty (which would include entities under common control and back-to-back arrangements); and
- transactions that are not in the ordinary course of business.

3.56   **Transactions may be linked "'whether legally or otherwise'".**

3.57   Transactions will often be 'linked' when they form part of a single plan. For example, a so called 'steps plan' may exist in which a number of separate transactions are envisaged. It may be clear that the first step of the plan would never have been carried out unless there was every expectation that step two would also be carried out. In this case, it is appropriate to consider the combined effect of all of the transactions together.

3.58   However, this does not mean that transactions must be regarded as linked or circular just because they were planned together. For example, a company may sell some quoted investments for cash with the intention of using that cash to purchase stock. The fact that the company plans to use the cash to purchase stock does not prevent the profit on disposal[24] of the investments being a realised profit. Similarly, trading profits will be realised profits in accordance with the normal rules, even though the cash inflows are reinvested in stock or fixed assets.

3.59   One feature usually present for there to be linkage is that ~~the cash flow has been~~:

- ~~the cash inflow has been~~ generated with the intention <u>or purpose of undertaking the linked cash outflow, or vice versa,</u>; or ~~for the purpose of, undertaking the linked transaction~~
- <u>the cash outflow would not have occurred without the linked cash inflow, or vice versa.</u>

Trading cash flows are generated as an end in themselves and thus do not possess this feature.

3.60   In relation to a sale and operating leaseback, the cash inflow arising from the sale transaction will ~~be~~, at ~~be~~ least in part, <u>be</u> offset by the future cash outflows arising from the leaseback transaction. Therefore it might be queried whether they are linked. However, it is generally accepted that such arrangements do not fall within the scope of paragraph 3.5. A sale and leaseback transaction is not entered into for the purpose of financing the future operating lease rentals. To the extent that the apparent sale's profit exceeds arm's length terms (ie, the 'profit' is directly compensated for by high rentals) it is deferred anyway (under IAS 17 and <u>FRS 102</u>~~SSAP 21~~).

3.61   Transactions may be linked legally by, say, being dealt with in the same contract or being in separate contracts but expressed to be inter-conditional. However, as made clear by

---

[24] *It is assumed for simplicity here that a profit is recognised on disposal of the investments, but companies applying IFRSs or FRS 26 may have recorded a profit at an earlier stage because of the need to account for the investments at fair value.*

the words "'or otherwise'", it is necessary to consider more than just the legal form of linkage of transactions to understand their substance collectively, as to do otherwise may not adequately express the overall commercial effect of the arrangements.

For example, in the case of the so called steps plan mentioned above, there may be no **3.62** legal obligation to complete step 2 following step 1. However, this may, for example, be a commercial necessity because step 1 does not make sense without step 2 or because step 2 is necessitated by step 1.

For a cash inflow and a cash outflow of a company to fall within paragraph 3.5, it is **3.63** **not necessary that the cash flows** 'close the loop' **by joining up at some other place in** **the group.**

A transaction is circular for a company if, for that company, there is a cash inflow and in **3.64** another step in a series there is a cash outflow back to the same party. As discussed above, circularity is a sufficient but not a necessary feature for the application of paragraph 3.5. Another situation where paragraph 3.5 may apply is where the cash outflow at another step is to another party rather than the provider of the cash inflow. It is not necessary, for something to be linked, that the recipient of the onward cash flow passes the cash back to the original provider.

Transactions are not linked merely because they are pre-planned but this may be **3.65** **evidence of linkage.**

Pre-planning (eg, by way of a steps plan) is evidence that the transactions are to be entered **3.66** into in contemplation of each other and the overall outcome was pre-meditated. Evidence of pre-planning may indicate that those cash flows and the transactions from which they arise should be assessed as linked in order to understand their overall commercial effect. However, as explained in the example above at 3.58 concerning a disposal of quoted investments to finance a purchase of stock, this principle does not result in normal commercial transactions in the ordinary course of business being regarded as linked.

Taking this example further, the transactions are not linked because the vendor of the **3.67** stock would normally require payment in cash and would not accept quoted investments in settlement. Therefore, the substance of the transactions taken together is **not** an exchange of quoted investments for stock.

Where paragraph 3.5 requires a series of transactions to be viewed as a whole, the **3.68** **consequence is that a profit, to be realised, has to be represented by an increase in** **qualifying consideration between the start and end points of the series.**

If a series of transactions is viewed as a whole, then it is necessary to compare the assets **3.69** and liabilities, and their amounts, at the start and end of the series to determine what transaction, in substance, has occurred (changes in assets and liabilities). The transaction thus identified is tested under the other principles set out in this guidance. Thus, where paragraph 3.5 applies, it is necessary to determine the amount of qualifying consideration involved at the start and end of the linked transactions to see if there has been an increase, decrease or a net nil position. Unless there has been an increase in the amount of qualifying consideration (in any of the forms defined in paragraph 3.11), there cannot be~~it cannot have~~ a realised profit from that series of transactions.

If there is a new external cash flow somewhere in a chain of intra-group transactions **3.70** **to which the company is party, this cannot be associated with a portion of the gross** **cash flows of the company in question if, after considering a series of transactions that**

fall within the scope of paragraph 3.5 to which the company is party, the company does not have a net increase in cash or other qualifying consideration.

3.71   A net nil cash position (as described at 3.69 above) cannot be broken into two gross components to assert that there has been an increase in qualifying consideration that will justify recognition of a realised profit. To do so would amount to dealing with such transactions as if they were independent and so would fail to treat them, as required by paragraph 3.5, as a series that is to be assessed as a whole. Thus, where a company's transactions, taken as a whole, do not increase its qualifying consideration, they do not generate a realised profit. This is the case irrespective of whether the cash inflow has been financed from new external cash receipts elsewhere in the group.

3.72   For example, consider a company that receives a dividend of 100 from one subsidiary and reinvests the same amount in another subsidiary as equity capital, both as part of a planned corporate restructuring. There is no net increase in qualifying consideration and therefore the receipt of the dividend is not a realised profit. It does not matter that the dividend of 100 was funded from external cash receipts elsewhere in the group.

3.73   However, paragraphs 3.71 and 3.72 above are concerned only with circumstances where the cash inflow and cash outflow comprising the net nil position fall within paragraph 3.5. For example, paragraph 3.72 is concerned with a planned corporate restructuring. The fact that dividends are received from some subsidiaries at or about the same time as investments are made in other subsidiaries as equity capital does not automatically prevent those dividends being recognised as realised profits. To be linked, there needs to be something more than juxtapositioning of transactions, such as the dividends being necessary at this time to facilitate the investment.

3.74   **Time does not necessarily matter when judging whether steps in a series of transactions need to be viewed as a whole. Inserting a pre-planned period of delay, for example, between intended steps will not generally break "linkage".**

3.75   Time gaps in a series of transactions is a factor to judge as to whether this was an attempt to frustrate a series-of-transactions argument. Deliberate insertion of time delays is usually persuasive evidence of pre-planning and pre-meditation of the outcome. The length of the time period or periods between transactions is not, of itself, relevant. Thus, a time gap should not affect the conclusion. However, time may be a factor to consider if it gives genuine opportunity for a relevant change to occur in the series of steps. The more time that is to elapse between steps then the more time there is for commercial circumstances to change and thus for the subsequent steps, if not yet irrevocable, not to go ahead due to changed circumstances.

4. FAIR VALUE ACCOUNTING

Introduction

4.1   The directors of any particular company need to consider their own company's facts and circumstances in determining whether an accounting profit arising through changes in fair value is readily convertible to cash in accordance with the definition and can therefore be considered as realised for distribution purposes. Consideration should also be given to 2.3 to 2.5 above regarding volatility and directors' duties. This section provides guidance on:

    (a)   the application of the definition of 'readily convertible to cash' to particular situations (see 4.2 *et seq*);

    (b)   available-for-sale investments and the fair value reserve (see 4.23 *et seq*);

    (c)   the fair value option (see 4.26 *et seq*); and

    (d)   losses arising from fair value accounting (see 4.29 *et seq*).

Guidance on the application of "~~"~~readily convertible to cash~~"~~"

Financial instruments

The definition of ~~"~~readily convertible to cash~~"~~ in paragraph 3.12 is closely but not completely aligned with the definition of Level 1 and Level 2 within the fair value hierarchy in IFRS 13 Fair Value Measurement. In particular, paragraph 3.12(c) imposes some additional restrictions so that not all Level 1 and Level 2 valuations will result in realised profits.~~measurement guidance in IAS 39. Necessary differences remain.~~ **4.2**

In situations where: **4.3**

(a) the financial instrument is traded in an active market; or

(b) the financial instrument is valued using a valuation technique whose variables include only data from observable markets,

it will generally be possible to enter into a transaction to convert the change in value to cash at short notice without any period of marketing and/or negotiation. Even when the instrument is not traded in an active market, there may be many institutions which will be prepared to quote a price based on observable market data at which a transaction could take place immediately. Such a change in value that is a profit would therefore, subject also to the test at 3.12(c) above, be regarded as realised.

However, a change in the fair value of a financial instrument that is a profit which is determined using a valuation technique where not all of the variables include data from observable markets would be regarded as unrealised. This would not be so where part of the profit can be closed out independently of the rest and that part may be realised pursuant to the guidance on close out at 4.5 and 4.6 below. **4.4**

Close out

A financial asset, financial liability or change in the fair value of a financial asset or financial liability may be capable of being readily convertible to cash for the purposes of applying condition (a) of the readily convertible to cash test at 3.12 above if it could be immediately closed out, meaning the relevant contract or underlying market risk position is capable of being immediately offset in the market and the normal market practice would be to close out the position in this way. For example, risks inherent in a derivative may be eliminated by taking out other financial instruments, including derivative contracts, with an offsetting risk profile. When it is possible under normal market practice to enter into such arrangements to ~~"~~lock in~~"~~ any profit on the original contract, the profit that could be ~~"~~locked in~~"~~ could be regarded as readily convertible to cash. It is not necessary for an actual transaction to have occurred. **4.5**

4.5 above addresses the ability to close out in the context of condition (a) of 3.12. In relation to condition (a), consideration should also be given to whether the cash flows from the close-out instrument meet the definition of qualifying consideration, in particular the criteria set out at 3.11. **4.6**

In addition, conditions (b) and (c) in 3.12 must also be considered. In the context of condition (b), consideration should be given to whether the valuation of the close-out instrument is based on observable market data. **4.6A**

The position regarding fair value losses is dealt with at 4.29 to 4.33 below. **4.7**

Embedded derivatives

4.8   Unless the whole contract has been designated at fair value through profit or loss, an embedded derivative that is determined not to be closely related to the economic characteristics and risks of the host contract is required to be separated from its host for accounting purposes (bifurcation) and fair valued, as if it were a standalone derivative with the same terms. Changes in fair value of the embedded derivative are recognised in profit or loss. However, where a change in fair value is a profit it does not constitute a realised profit unless the embedded derivative can be closed out in the manner described above in "'Close out'" or the host contract and embedded derivative together meet the "'readily convertible to cash'" test (including by reference to close-out if appropriate).

Top-slicing

4.9.   Fair value accounting under the relevant accounting standards involves the valuation of the whole item or, in the case of fair value hedge accounting, a particular risk and the recognition of the change in fair value in the financial statements. Where the change is a profit, it is not necessary to have completed a transaction to determine whether the whole of the increase in fair value is to be treated as realised. The criteria for determining whether an increase in fair value that is a profit could be readily converted to cash and thus be treated as realised are set out at 3.12 above. The concept of top-slicing a gain into realised and unrealised parts as envisaged by paragraph 3.18 arises when there has been a transaction involving qualifying and other consideration. On remeasurement there is no transaction involved in the recognition of a fair value profit, hence the question of top-slicing (ie, determining, by reference to mixed consideration receivable, whether part of the profit should be treated as realised as opposed to the whole of such profit) does not occur.

Unquoted equity investments

4.10   Although increases in the fair value of many financial assets will meet the test of being "'readily convertible to cash'" at 3.12 above, this will not generally be true of unquoted equity investments. The measurement of such investments at fair value may be precluded because the range of reasonable fair value estimates is significant and the probabilities of the various estimates cannot reasonably be assessed. Even where the value can be estimated sufficiently reliably to meet the requirements of IAS 39 and an increase in fair value is recognised, it is unlikely that the amount would be readily convertible to cash at the date of determination. This is because, for example, a period of marketing and/or negotiation would generally be required to dispose of such an investment.

Strategic investments

4.11   Under a company's business strategy it may hold investments for strategic purposes. Such investments are not readily disposable in the sense required to meet condition (c) of the readily convertible to cash test at 3.12 above, as a company's strategy cannot be readily changed so as to allow the investment to be realised immediately at the date of determination. For example, the company might have a strategic investment in a listed company that qualifies to be accounted for as an associate under IAS 28. It is possible for the company to elect under IAS 28 to account for its associates (in its separate financial statements) at fair value under IAS 39 (e.g. eg, as an available-for-sale asset, with fair value changes reported in equity). Increases in fair value of such a strategic investment might be regarded as realised but for condition (c) of the test for readily convertible to cash. Thus the fair value increases are, consequently, unrealised.

A similar analysis may be made for a company's holding of other financial assets, such as government bonds, that are classified as available-for-sale and are thus remeasured at fair value but nevertheless are held to meet the company's business strategy or regulatory requirements. Any fair value increases of such assets are unrealised as the company cannot readily change its business strategy or regulatory compliance to allow the financial assets to be realised immediately at the date of determination. **4.12**

Hedge relationships in group situations

Under a group's hedging strategy, different companies in the group may hold the hedging instrument and the hedged item. For example, in a net investment hedge as illustrated in IFRIC 16 Hedges of a Net Investment in a Foreign Operation. The circumstances of each of the companies involved in the hedge relationship needs to be assessed at the date of determination, as the relevant company may not be in a position to realise an increase in fair value in the sense required to meet condition (c) of the readily convertible to cash test at 3.12 above. For example, the purpose of the company holding the hedging instrument is to hold it for the benefit of, or to assist, another group company, and accordingly it may not be able to dispose of or close out the hedging instrument, needing instead to seek that other company's concurrence. This is discussed further at 5.19 to 5.22 of section 5 Hedge accounting." **4.12A**

Investment properties

None of an increase in fair value of investment property is readily convertible to cash and is not therefore treated as a realised profit. This is because a period of marketing and/or negotiation would be required to dispose of such an investment and therefore it could not be converted to cash at the date of determination. This is not intended to preclude a profit being regarded as realised at the date of determination in those cases when the process of marketing and/or negotiation is complete at that date and legal completion occurs shortly after the date of determination. **4.13**

Own credit

When liabilities (e.g.eg, bank debt or bond issues) and over-the-counter derivative contracts are measured at fair value, their value may be affected by the reporting company's own creditworthiness. Consequently, a profit may arise in circumstances where the company's creditworthiness is deteriorating, that is, the fair value of the liability is decreasing. In such cases, it is necessary to consider whether the company would be able to realise the profit by settling the liability at its fair value. This may not be possible, particularly if the company is experiencing financial difficulties, and the relevant profit will therefore not be a realised profit. However, in most circumstances where a company is not in financial difficulties and it would be able to settle the debt at fair value, there will be no need to analyse the fair value changes between the amount attributable to marginal changes in the creditworthiness of the liability and changes due to movements in interest rates and other market factors. **4.14**

It should be noted, however, that the tests set out at 3.12 above are wider than solely the ability to settle at fair value and must all be met. For example, the company must be able to settle on the date of determination without negotiation or marketing. Thus where a large volume of debt is under consideration, this is akin to a question of whether the company could refinance that large volume of debt on that date without negotiation, which would often not be the case. **4.15**

Block discounts for securities traded in an active market

4.16   IFRS 13~~IAS 39~~ requires certain financial instruments to be valued on a basis that does not take account of the size of the holding. That is to say that the valuation included in the accounts uses the published price quotation in an active market as the best estimate of fair value and does not reflect any "'block discount"' that might apply if the entire holding was disposed of at the date of determination. In the case of assets (~~e.g.~~eg, investments) that are traded on an active market, it may be possible to dispose of the entire holding at the date of determination but it is necessary to recognise that the proceeds may be less than the value recognised in the balance sheet in accordance with IAS 39.

4.17   Holdings in financial assets traded in an active market that might be regarded as relatively small (~~e.g.~~eg, less than 1% of a company's share capital) may nevertheless be large in relation to the volume of business done in that company's shares on a typical day in the market. For example, some such investments held by investment companies and other financial institutions fall into this category. Such investments are rarely, if ever, disposed of in a single block but are instead disposed of in a number of smaller blocks either all on the same day or over a short period of time, in accordance with normal market practice, to reduce or eliminate the effect of any block discount. In these limited circumstances, the effect of any block discount on realised profits may be calculated on the basis set out at 4.18 and 4.19 below rather than on the basis that the entire holding is disposed of in a single block on the date of determination. This is a limited departure from the principle established at 3.12(a) above.

4.18   Part 4 of the Statement of Recommended Practice "'Accounting for Securities by Banks"' ("'the SORP"') issued by the British Bankers' Association contained the following guidance:

> "'61. Where a holding of a quoted security (other than one to which paragraph [62] or [63] applies)[25] is so large that it could be disposed of only at an unfavourable price or over an extended period, it should be valued at an appropriate discount to the market price. The discount should be sufficient to reflect the reduction in price resulting from the size of the holding or all future costs likely to be incurred in disposing of the interest over time in the ordinary course of business."'

The SORP was~~has been~~ withdrawn because it was~~is~~ not applicable to banks reporting under IFRSs or applying FRS 26 under UK GAAP. It nevertheless provides an indication of generally accepted practice for the valuation of large holdings. Although this approach no longer applies for financial reporting purposes ~~for companies applying IFRSs or FRS 26~~, it continues to be relevant to the determination of realised profits.

4.19   Where it is determined that a block discount exists in relation to a holding of securities traded in an active market, only the part of the profit that may not be realisable over a short period of time in the ordinary course of business should be treated as unrealised[26]. This would not necessarily be the same as the block discount that may apply if the entity disposed of the entire holding in a single block at the date of determination (~~e.g.~~eg, in a forced sale), and which applies to situations other than those covered by the previous sentence for the purposes of determining the part of the profit that is unrealised.

---

[25] *Paragraph 62 dealt with instruments held for hedging and paragraph 63 dealt with investment securities stated at cost.*

[26] *A similar adjustment is not required when an overall (ie cumulative) loss is recognised on the remeasurement of a financial instrument in accordance with IAS 39. The potential additional loss, equivalent to the block discount, that would arise on disposal of the entire holding at the date of determination is not recorded as a loss in the financial statements. Consequently, the realised loss will equal the loss reported in the financial statements, which will exclude the effect of any block discount.*

Estimation of the unrealised profit referred to at 4.16 and 4.19 above will require the exercise of judgement. Directors of companies frequently have to exercise judgement in making accounting estimates. The position concerning block discounts is no different. Directors do not have to be able to quantify the unrealised profit referred to at 4.16 and 4.19 above precisely; an estimate is all that is required. It will often be clear that there is a sufficient margin of profit available for distribution (over and above the proposed distribution) to absorb a prudent assessment of the effect of any unrealised profit attributable to block discounts. **4.20**

Directors should consider their common law duty to avoid an unlawful distribution of capital. If an investment is sold after the date of determination to finance a distribution, the impact of any resulting loss (whether due to the unrealised component of a block discount or otherwise) on profits available for distribution should be considered. **4.21**

The case of a block discount can be distinguished from that of investment property and most unquoted equity investments when none of the profit is treated as realised due to the period of marketing and/or negotiation required to dispose of such investments, such that the profit could not be readily converted to cash at the date of determination. **4.22**

Available-for-sale financial assets and the fair value reserve

Under IAS 39, profits and losses on "available-for-sale" financial assets are recognised indirectly in equity through the statement of other comprehensive income (except for dividends, interest, impairment losses and foreign exchange profits and losses on monetary items). This applies until the assets are derecognised (e.g.eg. sold) at which time the cumulative profit or loss previously recognised in equity is recognised in profit or loss (ie, "recycled")[27]. **4.23**

Profits and losses arising on the remeasurement of available-for-sale financial assets will be realised or unrealised according to the same principles that would apply if the same assets had been accounted for at fair value through profit or loss (see above). For example, it would be illogical if the question of whether a profit was realised or unrealised depended on whether the directors designated the particular assets "at fair value through profit or loss" on initial recognition, when using the fair value option in the circumstances permitted by the relevant accounting standards (see 4.26 below). However, profits on remeasurement of available-for-sale financial assets will be realised or unrealised in accordance with the principles described above, irrespective of whether they meet the requirements to be accounted for at fair value through profit or loss. **4.24**

For companies reporting under IFRSs (ie, directly under the IAS Regulation), there is no requirement to credit profits included in other comprehensive income on available-for-sale investments to any particular reserve. FRS 102 does not have a category of 'available-for-sale' financial assets, However, fFor companies reporting under FRS 101 or applying the option in FRS 102 to apply IAS 39 recognition and measurement requirementsUK GAAP (FRS 26), such profits maywill be taken to the fair value reserve in accordance with the requirements of the Accounting Regulations. There is no specific legal restriction on the distribution of profits included in the fair value reserve in either the Act or the EU Fair Value Directive (2001/65/EC) from which the provisions on fair value accounting in UK legislation are drawn. Therefore, there is no constraint on treating profits on **4.25**

[27] *Similar rules for 'available-for-sale' financial assets apply for companies using FRS 26, where the profits and losses are recognised directly in equity through the statement of total recognised gains and losses. The amendment to FRS 3 for companies using FRS 26 clarifies the position for recycling the cumulative profit or loss on a sale of an available-for-sale financial asset.*

remeasurement of available-for-sale financial assets as available for distribution if they are in all other respects realised profits in accordance with this guidance.

Fair value option

4.26   IAS 39~~, the EU adopted version of IAS 39 and FRS 26~~ contains ~~the same~~ conditions regarding when it is permitted to use the fair value option to designate financial instruments "'at fair value through profit or loss''" on initial recognition. The conditions for using the fair value option are set out in paragraph 9 *et seq* of IAS 39.

4.27   Where the fair value option is used it is necessary to consider whether the changes in fair value of the relevant financial instruments that are recognised in the profit and loss account meet the conditions to be treated as realised. In this respect, the guidance above on "'Financial instruments'", "'Embedded derivatives'", "'Own credit'" and "'Block discounts'" will be most relevant in interpreting the "'readily convertible to cash'" criterion as defined at 3.12 above.

4.28   In addition, it is recognised that the use of the fair value option to eliminate or significantly reduce an accounting mismatch may validly be used in place of hedge accounting for hedges of fair value exposures. Consequently, where this is the case, although the designated financial instrument that is fair valued under the fair value option and the derivative that would otherwise give rise to the accounting mismatch are not in a formal IAS 39 hedge relationship, consideration of the guidance in 5.2 to 5.6 "'Fair value hedge accounting'" (which contain further guidance on the principle set out at 3.19 above) would be relevant in determining the effect on realised profits of the combined effect of the designated financial instruments and the derivatives concerned.

Losses

4.29   Losses arising from fair value accounting should be treated as realised losses where profits on remeasurement of the same asset or liability would be treated as realised profits in accordance with this guidance (see 3.15(f) above).

4.30   A loss that represents the reversal of an unrealised profit will not reduce cumulative realised profits. Even if the loss is treated as a realised loss, for example because it represents an impairment, the unrealised profit will become realised in accordance with 3.9(f) above.

4.31   Cumulative net losses arising on fair value accounting will be unrealised only if both:

(a)   profits on remeasurement of the same asset or liability would be unrealised; and

(b)   the losses would not have been recorded otherwise than pursuant to fair value accounting.

4.32   With reference to paragraph (b) above, absent fair value accounting a loss may need to be recorded for example, in relation to an asset, on the basis of historical/ amortised costs less impairment provisions; and in relation to a liability, under either an amortised cost basis of financial instrument accounting or as an onerous contract liability.

4.33   It is well established that the recoverable amount of tangible fixed assets (~~e.g.~~eg, properties used in a business) may exceed their fair value ~~(see paragraph 65 of FRS 15)~~. In the case of other assets (including investment property), it may be more difficult to justify a recoverable amount that is greater than fair value. Each case should be considered on its merits and, where there is doubt, losses should be treated as realised.

5. HEDGE ACCOUNTING

Hedge relationships in individual companies

As stated at 3.19 above, the principle to be applied to the determination of realised profits   **5.1**
and losses when hedge accounting is used is as follows:

> "'Where hedge accounting is obtained in accordance with the relevant accounting
> standards, it is necessary to consider the combined effect of both sides of the hedging
> relationship to determine whether there is a realised profit or loss in accordance with
> the criteria in this guidance.'"

The application of this principle to different types of hedge accounting permitted by IAS 39
by companies holding both the hedging instrument and the hedged item is described at 5.2
to 5.18 below. The criteria for hedge accounting in FRS 102 are different from those in
IAS 39, but the same three types of hedge accounting are permitted. This guidance is
equally applicable to hedge accounting under FRS 102.

Where the hedging instrument and hedged item are held in different companies within   **5.1A**
the same group a hedging relationship is established only in the group's consolidated
financial statements. The general realisation principles as set out at 3.3 to 3.12 apply to the
individual companies. As the hedge relationship does not exist within a single company the
principle at 3.19 is inapplicable in such a case. Instead guidance on the application of these
principles is provided at 5.19 to 5.22 below to assist in determining in what circumstances
any profits or losses on the hedging instruments and hedged items can be treated as realised
for the individual companies concerned.

Fair value hedge accounting

In the case of fair value hedges under IAS 39, the gross profits and losses on remeasuring   **5.2**
the hedging instrument and the hedged item for the hedged risk are both recognised in
profit or loss. In many instances both the profit on one and the loss on the other will be
realised by reference to the readily convertible to cash and other criteria. In such cases,
no special consideration of hedging aspects is required (including hedge effectiveness or
ineffectiveness).

In some cases, however, the profit on either the hedged item or the hedging instrument may,   **5.3**
absent consideration of the hedging aspect, be unrealised (e.g.eg, if a fair value movement
is not readily convertible to cash). The following paragraphs explain how the principle set
out at 5.1 above should be applied in circumstances where the profit is not realised.

Where the hedge accounting relationship results in a net loss, this amount will generally be   **5.4**
treated as a realised loss. For example, consider the situation where there is an unrealised
profit on the hedged item of £90 and a realised loss on the hedging instrument of £100. The
net loss of £10, which arises from hedge ineffectiveness, is recognised in the profit or and
loss account and is treated as a realised loss. Due to the hedge accounting relationship, the
remaining £90 of the gross loss on the hedging instrument is not treated as a realised loss
and is set off against the unrealised profit on the hedged item.

Where there is a net profit, it will be necessary to consider whether that profit is a realised   **5.5**
profit. This will depend on the relationship between the gross components. For example,
if there is an unrealised profit of £100 and a realised loss of £90, only the net profit of £10
will be treated as unrealised.

5.6   This approach applies irrespective of whether the profits or losses in question arise from changes in fair value of open contracts or from settled transactions. For example, the hedge accounting policy may designate a series of rolling derivatives as the hedging instrument, some of which have already been settled in cash, whereas there have been no past settlements in respect of the hedged item.

Cash flow hedge accounting

5.7   In the case of cash flow hedges under IAS 39, the portion of the profit or loss on the hedging instrument that is determined to be an effective hedge is recognised in other comprehensive income. Such profits and losses are unrealised and become realised only when the hedged transaction affects profit or loss (or IAS 39 otherwise requires the gain or loss to be recycled through profit or loss). This is based on the principle (set out in 5.1 above) that it is necessary to have regard to the combined effect of both sides of the hedge accounting relationship to determine whether there is a realised profit or loss. To the extent that the profit or loss is included in other comprehensive income (or, later on, added to the cost of a non-financial asset) in accordance with IAS 39, it must arise in connection with a valid hedge accounting relationship. It would therefore be inappropriate to consider this profit or loss in isolation from the hedged item. To the extent that any ineffective element of the profit or loss on the hedging instrument is recognised in profit or loss, that element should be assessed as to whether it is realised in accordance with normal principles (~~e.g.~~eg, the ~~""~~'readily convertible to cash~~"~~'' test).

5.8   The hedging principle at 5.1 above applies irrespective of whether the profits or losses in question arise from changes in fair value of open contracts or from settled transactions. The amounts taken direct to equity may, for example, include profits or losses on short-term derivative contracts that form part of a rolling-hedge strategy but which have matured. Such profits and losses should be treated as unrealised provided that IAS 39 requires them still to be deferred in equity as part of a cash flow hedge accounting relationship.

5.9   Accounting for a cash flow hedge in accordance with IAS 39 will affect net assets although the profit or loss is regarded as unrealised. Where the cumulative net amount on the cash flow hedge component of equity (cash flow hedge reserve) is an overall unrealised loss, this may additionally restrict the ability of a public company to make distributions because of the application of section 831 (see 6.24 *et seq*).

Net investment hedge accounting

5.10   Under IAS 39, net investment hedge accounting policies will generally arise only in the context of consolidated financial statements. Those financial statements are not relevant for the purposes of justifying distributions. However, it is possible that in some instances, in accordance with IAS 21, a branch may be treated as a foreign operation in the individual accounts of a company. In this case, net investment hedge accounting may be relevant to the individual accounts of a company. A net investment hedge under IAS 39 is accounted for similarly to a cash flow hedge. So far as the hedge accounting is concerned, the question of whether the hedged item gives rise to realised profits is dealt with in section 11.

5.11   The circumstances where a company previously adopted hedge accounting for a foreign equity investment (ie, shares) in accordance with paragraph 51 of SSAP 20 are~~is~~ considered below.

Transition from SSAP 20 – Hedge accounting for foreign equity investments

5.12   Under <u>old</u> UK GAAP, SSAP 20 permitted~~s~~ a form of hedge accounting for foreign equity investments, subject to certain conditions. Where a company ha<u>d</u>s used foreign currency borrowings to finance, or provide a hedge against, its foreign equity investments, it ~~could~~may denominate those investments in the appropriate foreign currencies and translate the amounts at the balance sheet date at closing rate. Where this policy was~~is~~ adopted, the resulting exchange differences were~~are~~ taken to reserves. The exchange differences on the related foreign currency borrowings were~~are~~, subject to certain conditions, also taken to reserves. In some cases hedge accounting may be possible for such arrangements under IAS 39 or FRS 102 but as a fair value hedge through profit or loss. This is subject to more stringent conditions which did~~do~~ not apply under SSAP 20~~UK GAAP~~. Therefore companies may not be able to obtain hedge accounting for such financing arrangements under IFRSs or FRS 102.

The hedge accounting for foreign equity investments under SSAP 20 described above is not restricted to investments in subsidiaries but this is its most common application. This guidance assumes, for simplicity, that the equity investment is in a subsidiary.   **5.13**

Where hedge accounting is not available under IAS 39 or FRS 102, the exchange differences on the borrowings will be included in profit or loss. Unless the equity investment is held at fair value under IAS 39 or FRS 102, there will be no offsetting difference on the investment and it is usually, in effect, frozen at its historical cost in the functional currency of the investor. It is then necessary to determine whether the exchange difference on the borrowings arising subsequent to the date of transition is realised or unrealised.   **5.14**

The exchange difference on the borrowings should be treated as realised in accordance with the general principles in section 3 where hedge accounting is not applied. This is irrespective of whether the purpose of the loan is for hedging an investment and of whether hedge accounting would have been permitted in the circumstances. This is the same as the position under SSAP 20 when the use of hedge accounting was optional.   **5.15**

It should be noted that even though hedge accounting is not available, the purpose of the loan may still be to provide an "~~'~~economic hedge~~'~~" against the related equity investment. As stated at 2.3 *et seq*, although profits on the borrowings will be realised profits, directors should consider, as a result of their fiduciary and other duties, whether it would be prudent to distribute them.   **5.16**

Where hedge accounting was used under SSAP 20 and is not possible (or is otherwise not used) under IFRSs or FRS 102, it will not usually be necessary~~, subject to IFRS 1,~~ to restate the investment to ~~either cost or fair value in accordance with IAS 27~~. Paragraph D15 of IFRS 1 and paragraph 35.10(f)(ii) of FRS 102 permit the use of a deemed cost based on the previous GAAP carrying amount at the date of transition. ~~On first-time adoption of IFRSs, paragraphs B5 and B6 of IFRS 1 will be relevant in these circumstances. They state that 'if, before the date of transition to IFRSs, an entity had designated a transaction as a hedge but the hedge does not meet the conditions for hedge accounting in IAS 39 the entity shall apply paragraphs 91 and 101 of IAS 39 to discontinue hedge accounting'. Those paragraphs require hedge accounting to be discontinued prospectively.~~ The practical effect of this is that, if a policy of stating the investment at cost is adopted and the transitional exemption is used, the cumulative translation differences from applying SSAP 20 remain adjusted against the carrying value of the investment (ie, the investment in the subsidiary is frozen at the amount determined by translating the historic foreign currency cost of the investment at the spot rate prevailing at the date of transition).   **5.17**

When this treatment is applicable, the profits and losses taken to reserves under SSAP 20 will remain within equity under IAS 39 or FRS 102. In this case the assessment of whether those profits and losses are realised should continue to be made by reference to the net amount included within equity in accordance with the principle set out in paragraph 3.19 above.   **5.18**

Hedge relationships in group situations

5.19   Under a group's hedging strategy, different companies in the group may hold the hedging instrument and the hedged item. For example, in a net investment hedge as illustrated in IFRIC 16 Hedges of a Net Investment in a Foreign Operation. In these cases, there is no hedge relationship within an individual company and thus the hedging principle articulated at 3.19 and as expanded upon at 5.1 to 5.18 does not apply. Accordingly, the general realisation principles as set out at 3.3 to 3.12 apply as follows.

Fair value accounting

5.20   As referred to at 4.12A, a company holding a hedging instrument in a designated group hedge relationship cannot generally readily dispose of or close out the instrument in the sense required to meet condition (c) of the readily convertible to cash test at 3.12 above. This is because the company may not be able to act unilaterally to de-designate the hedging relationship that has been created by the group so as to allow it to realise the hedging instrument immediately at the date of determination. Consequently, any fair value increases of the hedging instrument are unrealised. Decreases in fair value will need to be considered carefully to determine the extent to which they are realised by applying the guidance at 4.29 et seq.

5.21   The company holding the hedged item may not be as constrained, if at all, as to its actions as the company holding the hedging instrument. Nevertheless, it should be considered whether the company has the ability to meet condition (c) of the readily convertible to cash test at 3.12 above. Disposing of or closing out the hedged item would involve breaking the group hedge relationship and this may have adverse consequences for the group. If the company has the ability to dispose of or close out the hedged item at the date of determination and thus meet condition (c), any fair value increases of the hedged item are realised. On the other hand, if it is determined that condition (c) cannot be met, then any fair value increases of the hedged item are unrealised. Decreases in fair value will need to be considered carefully to determine the extent to which they are realised by applying the guidance at 4.29 et seq.

Historical cost accounting

5.22   [Deleted]~~Companies not applying IAS 39 or FRS 26 but which have stand-alone derivatives or non-derivative financial instruments measure those instruments at historical cost and apply historical cost accounting. This is equally true for those that are held as part of a group hedging relationship. They could include, for example, accounting for foreign exchange differences under SSAP 20 or debtors and creditors for interest rate differentials in interest rate swaps. The general realisation principles as set out at 3.3 to 3.12 apply and normally these profits and losses are realised. Where profits on derivative and non-derivative financial instruments are realised, directors should consider whether from a group perspective it is appropriate to distribute them."~~

6. ISSUES ARISING FROM IAS 32 AND SECTION 22 OF FRS 102 ~~(AND ITS EQUIVALENT, FRS 25)~~

Introduction

6.1   Under IFRSs, financial instruments are presented according to the substance of the contractual arrangement, determined by the rules in IAS 32. This may differ from their legal form. For example, redeemable preference shares bearing mandatory dividends are presented as liabilities in the balance sheet and their corresponding distributions as interest charges in the income statement because the issuer has no ability to avoid payment in cash of either the principal or distributions. The substance of the contractual arrangement is therefore debt. Also, compound financial instruments are accounted for under the relevant standards using "split accounting", whereby the proceeds of issue are split between a liability component and an equity component. Examples of compound financial instruments are convertible redeemable preference shares and convertible debt (assuming that the conversion feature itself meets the definition of equity in IAS 32).

Under UK GAAP, FRS 10225's requirements on debt and equity presentation are very **6.2** similar tothe same as those in IAS 32 in terms of underlying principles and terminology. However, IAS 32 contains more specific requirements in some areas (eg. puttable instruments) and as a result some classification differences may arise in rare cases. For simplicity, the guidance refers to the requirements of IAS 32 rather than those of FRS 102. However, it is equally applicable to the same accounting when applied under FRS 102. In that case, references to amounts presented as liabilities should be read as meaning those amounts presented as liabilities in accordance with FRS 102. One specific difference is that FRS 102 does not require recognition of a liability for the present value of the future cash outflow in the case of a forward contract or written option to purchase own equity shares.

The following guidance considers the implications for distributable profits of companies, **6.3** for example, entering into contracts involving their own shares that may require classification in whole, or in part, as liabilities.

The guidance summarises the ten key principles in relation to determining distributable **6.4** profits when dealing with such contracts. The guidance then applies the principles to some common scenarios based on examples 1, 2, 4, 6 and 9 set out in the Illustrative Examples appendices to IAS 32 and FRS 25 involving contracts on own equity instruments. In addition, other scenarios are considered involving preference shares presented as liabilities, mandatorily redeemable preference shares and convertible preference shares.

Appendix 2 to the guidance provides illustrations of the accounting and capital maintenance **6.5** book-keeping entries for the eight scenarios referred to above.

The ten principles underpinning the guidance in this section are set out below. The **6.6** principles are split between those applying to all companies and those specific to public companies resulting from the application of the net assets test of section 831 of the Act. The principles are those underlying statute and common law in respect of distributions and capital maintenance.

Assumptions

The contracts described in this section and in Appendix 2 do not contain a cash settlement **6.6A** option.

Any redemption of the relevant shares will be made out of profits available for distribution **6.6B** and not out of the proceeds of a fresh issue of shares for the purpose of the redemption unless the text in this section or in Appendix 2 otherwise indicates. Payment of any dividends and redemption amounts are contingent upon such payments/redemption being lawful under the Act at the time of payment/redemption, with, where appropriate, the relevant amount being deferred until such time as the Act's restrictions fall away.

The shares, contracts and convertible instruments described in this section and in **6.6C** Appendix 2 are denominated in the issuer's functional currency, pay dividends and are redeemed in that currency, and, where convertible are convertible into shares denominated in that currency. It is also assumed that there are no contingent settlement provisions (see paragraph 25 of IAS 32 and FRS 25) or alternate settlement options (see paragraph 26 of IAS 32 and FRS 25). The effect of foreign currency, contingent settlement provisions and/or alternate settlement options can have an impact on the accounting to deny equity treatment in certain cases.

Principles – General

6.7   **Principle 1 – A distribution or a capital repayment is not as a matter of law a loss, notwithstanding that it may be presented for accounting purposes as an interest charge in the income statement**

6.8   Section 830(2) of the Act provides that, "'a company's profits available for distribution are its accumulated, realised profits, so far as not previously utilised by distribution or capitalisation, less its accumulated, realised losses, so far as not previously written off in a reduction or reorganisation of capital duly made.'" This is based on the premise that distributions are not losses. If distributions were losses they would be dealt with by the words "'less its accumulated, realised losses,'" and thus the words "'so far as not previously utilised by distribution'" would be superfluous.

6.9   A distribution or capital repayment may on occasion be presented as an accounting loss. For example, in some cases dividends on a preference share are presented as interest charges in the profit and loss account. Notwithstanding the accounting presentation, such distributions or capital repayments remain, as a matter of law, distributions or capital repayments for the purposes of Part 23 of the Act. Accordingly, they are not counted as losses – and thus not as realised or unrealised losses – for the purposes of Part 23 of the Act.

6.10   **Principle 2 – An advance recognition of a future distribution or capital repayment is not a loss notwithstanding that it may be presented for accounting purposes as an interest charge in the income statement**

6.11   A distribution or capital repayment is not, as a matter of law, a loss. Thus the advance recognition of a future distribution or capital repayment is not a loss either. Hence, the accrual, as an interest charge, of a dividend, or a foreign exchange translation difference, in respect of a preference share presented as debt is an advance recognition of a future distribution or capital repayment but it is not a loss for distribution purposes even though the accrual is charged as interest the profit and loss account.

6.12   **Principle 3 – A distribution or a capital repayment consumes distributable profits when paid or when a dividend is declared by a company in general meeting**

6.13   An accounting liability recognised for accrued unpaid dividends or a capital repayment is an advance recognition of a future distribution or capital repayment and is not, as a matter of law, a loss.

6.14   A distribution does not consume distributable profits until such time as, as a matter of law, the distribution occurs, e.g. eg, when paid under the authority of the directors, under common form articles of association, or when declared by members in general meeting, or at an earlier date on which a legally binding liability to pay the dividend is established (see 2.10 above).

6.15   The repurchase price for shares does not consume distributable profits until such time as, as a matter of law, the distribution and/or capital repayment comprised in the price occurs. In particular, notwithstanding that there are arrangements in place that will lead to repurchase, the company is not liable to pay the purchase price, and thus distributable profits are not consumed, until the shares are actually repurchased or redeemed. It should be noted that the holder of the shares cannot sue for damages in the event of failure by the company to repurchase those shares (see section 735 of the Act).

Section 691(2) provides that where a limited company purchases its own shares, the shares must be paid for in cash on purchase. This restriction does not, however, apply when a private limited company is purchasing shares for the purposes of or pursuant to an employees' share scheme (section 691(3)). IHowever, in the case of redeemable shares, section 686(2) provides that the terms of redemption may provide that the amount payable on redemption may, by agreement between the company and the holder of the shares, be paid in cash on a date later than the redemption date. This is a change from the 1985 Act which required payment on redemption. When payment on redemption is deferred, it is the current value of the redemption promise, at the redemption date, which determines the amount of distributable profits consumed. It is therefore the present value of the amount payable on redemption rather than its absolute amount which must be covered by distributable profits, at the redemption date, for the redemption to be permitted. The imputed interest expense arising from the use of the present value will, however, reduce distributable profits subsequent to the redemption date. **6.15A**

Principle 4 – Premiums received by the issuer on written options to issue or repurchase own equity shares are profits when received **6.16**

A premium received by the writer of an option over its own equity shares is regarded as a profit at law. This is because it is value received by the company otherwise than in payment up of a share and otherwise than for taking on a liability. In particular, a written put option is not, as a matter of law, a liability of the company; for example, the holder of the option cannot sue for damages in the event of failure by the company to repurchase the shares (see section 735 of the Act). **6.17**

Thus to the extent that the premium is received in the form of qualifying consideration, it is a realised profit at the outset. **6.18**

Principle 5 – When a company issues a compound financial instrument that is legally a debt, the original credit to equity determined using split accounting is not, as a matter of law, a profit; the original credit to equity is eliminated as accounting charges, which are not as a matter of law losses, accrue upwards the amount recorded as a liability **6.19**

The initial credit to equity is not an accounting profit because in accounting terms it is the equivalent of the issue of an equity instrument. As a matter of law there is not a profit either, because the proceeds received are in consideration for taking on a liability (in which respect it is distinctly different from a legally separate option contract addressed in Principle 4) albeit a liability that is not fully reflected as such in the accounts. The liability becomes fully reflected in the accounts through an additional interest charge that is not, as a matter of law, a loss because the full instrument that is legally a debt is reflected in the balance sheet at issue albeit in different places. Thus the cumulative debit in equity arising from these additional charges is available to eliminate the initial credit. **6.20**

Principle 6 – When a company issues a compound financial instrument that is legally a share, the original credit to equity determined using split accounting is share capital, and if applicable share premium; accounting charges made to accrue upwards the amount recorded for accounting purposes as a liability component, are not, as a matter of law, losses **6.21**

6.22   The initial credit to equity as a result of split accounting is share capital, and if applicable share premium, and is reflected as such. Subsequent accounting charges, to accrue upwards the amount recorded for accounting purposes as a liability component, are not, as a matter of law, losses because they are advance recognition of a future distribution or capital repayment.

6.23   In some circumstances, there may be a debit to be recognised in equity on an issue of shares to a parent company or fellow subsidiary, where the shares do not qualify to be classified in the accounts as equity of the issuer. The shares are recognised initially by the issuer as a liability at their fair value. However, the fair value may be greater than the proceeds received for their issue because the terms are off-market and, for example, involve redemption for significant amounts above the original proceeds and/or bear coupons that are substantial. In such circumstances, this difference between fair value and proceeds, a debit, is in effect advance recognition of future distributions and/or a future capital repayment and is recognised in equity. Consequently, this debit is not a loss at initial recognition. [Principle 2]. The debit will consume distributable profits either as dividends on the shares are made, which are distributions as a matter of law, or at the date of redemption (ie, when the payments are set against the liability over time or at the end). [Principle 3]

Principles – Impact of Section 831 for public companies

6.24   **Principle 7 – The treatment of certain shares wholly as liabilities under IFRSs does not in itself affect the application of the section 831 of the Act net assets test for public companies and thus does not restrict distributable profits**

6.25   Section 831 states that a public company may only make a distribution at any time:

- if at that time the amount of its net assets is not less than the aggregate of its called-up share capital and undistributable reserves (as defined); and
- if, and to the extent that, the distribution does not reduce the amount of those assets to less than that aggregate.

6.26   Section 831 defines "'net assets"' for this purpose to mean the aggregate of the company's assets less the aggregate of its liabilities. By virtue of section 836, net assets for the purposes of section 831 are those shown in the "'relevant accounts"' prepared in accordance with applicable accounting standards; that is, its "'IAS individual accounts"', or its "'Companies Act individual accounts"'. Therefore in the case of the issue of a financial instrument that is presented as debt in accordance with the substance of its contractual arrangements rather than their strict legal form, the company's net assets are unaffected for the purposes of section 831. This is because a liability is recorded (being in respect of the nominal value plus related share premium attributable to the shares) equal to the cash received as issue proceeds.

6.27   It is less clear from the drafting of section 831 whether there is any effect on the amount of a company's "'share capital and undistributable reserves"' arising from the issue of shares for which the presentation of share capital and related share premium is as a liability. In legal form there will have been an increase in share capital and related share premium. However, in accordance with section 836, the amount of share capital and undistributable reserves is determined by reference to the amount as stated in the company's relevant accounts. Accordingly, it appears that any amount of share capital and related share premium that has been presented as a liability should be excluded from the amount of share capital and undistributable reserves for the purposes of applying section 831. This is because the amount of share capital and undistributable reserves as stated in the relevant accounts excludes this amount.

This interpretation of section 831 is consistent with the "*Guidance for British companies on changes to reporting and accounting provisions of the Companies Act 1985*" (originally issued by the DTI[28] in November 2004 and updated in August 2005[29]). The DTI's guidance states that "the interaction of section 264 and section 270(2) [of the 1985 Act, now sections 831 and 836(1) of the 2006 Act] is such that, where preference shares are classified as liabilities, they should be treated as such for the purposes of the net asset test, and should not be treated as part of called-up share capital and undistributable reserves for that purpose".   **6.28**

Consequently the issue of shares with their nominal value and related share premium presented as debt does not result in an immediate restriction in the amount of profits available for distribution by a public company under section 831, because the issue leaves both net assets and share capital and undistributable reserves (as defined) unaffected.   **6.29**

When the section 831 test comes to be applied to the repurchase or redemption of the shares, it should be borne in mind that whilst the repayment of the nominal value and issue premium on the shares will leave net assets unaffected, "share capital and undistributable reserves" will increase due to the recording of the capital redemption reserve and the inclusion in the share premium account within equity of the issue premium which has always existed and which is no longer required to be presented as a liability. Under section 831(1) the net assets must be at least equal to the "share capital and undistributable reserves" both before (sub-section (1)(a)) and after (sub-section (1)(b)) the repayment for it to be lawful.   **6.30**

Principle 8 – A debit to equity arising from an advance recognition of a future distribution or capital repayment does not form part of share capital and undistributable reserves (as defined) for the purposes of section 831 and thus restricts distributable profits for public companies under that section   **6.31**

Despite not representing a realised loss or a consumption of distributable profits, nevertheless an advance recognition of a future distribution or capital repayment restricts distributable profits for public companies. This is due to the advance recognition of the distribution as a liability, reducing net assets, but the corresponding debit to equity (via the income statement/profit and loss account) not reducing "share capital and undistributable reserves" as defined by section 831.   **6.32**

The above contrasts with Principle 1 because in the context of section 831, the Act gives precedence to the accounting presentation and this restricts the amount of the profits available for distribution.   **6.33**

The existence of any unrealised profits does not alter this situation (~~e.g.~~eg. such unrealised profits cannot be applied to offset the deduction, because the deduction is not an unrealised loss).   **6.33A**

The question may arise as to whether this restriction might operate to prevent the distribution or capital repayment in question when it comes to be made, ~~e.g.~~eg. because the effect might be that the surplus of net assets over "share capital and undistributable reserves" might be reduced to an amount less than the distribution or capital repayment to be made. However, there will be no restricting effect on the making of such amount of a distribution or capital repayment as has been recognised in advance, provided that immediately beforehand the net assets are not less than "share capital and undistributable   **6.34**

---

[28] *Now the Department for Business, Innovation & Skills.*

[29] *Guidance available from National Archives at: http://webarchive.nationalarchives.gov.uk/+/http://www.berr.gov. uk/files/file21617.doc*

reserves["]. This is because, accordingly, the company will meet the test in section 831(1)(a); and on the actual making of the distribution or capital repayment, which has previously been recognised as a liability, net assets are unaffected and thus remain no less than ["'share capital and undistributable reserves"], thereby meeting section 831(1)(b). If the shares in question were originally classified as debt, then the operation of section 831 in relation to the original issue price is as described at 6.30 above.

6.35   Principle 9 – On initial recognition, split accounting for compound financial instruments does not restrict distributable profits for public companies under section 831

6.36   If the compound financial instrument is legally a share (for example, a redeemable preference share with discretionary dividends) and is split into its debt and equity components, at the outset there is no effect on distributable profits. The initial liability is matched by ~~a part~~ an ~~equal amount~~ of the cash proceeds equal to the liability and there is no effect on net assets in relation to the liability component. In respect of the equity component equating to the balance of the proceeds, the initial credit to equity is, at law, share capital (and share premium) and is included in ["'share capital and undistributable reserves"] for the purposes of the section 831 net assets test. This increase on one side of the net assets equation is balanced by the corresponding amount of cash proceeds which increases the company's net assets (ie, net assets increase by the amount of the equity component). Thus, ["'share capital and undistributable reserves"] do not exceed net assets and therefore there is no restriction on distributable profits at the outset.

6.37   If the compound financial instrument is legally a debt (for example, a convertible debt) and it is split into its debt and equity components, the initial liability is exceeded by the amount of cash proceeds, equal in amount to that of the initial credit to equity, and accordingly there is an increase in net assets. However, in respect of the initial credit to equity itself, this does not form part of ["'share capital and undistributable reserves"]. As a result, an increase in net assets is recorded (being the difference between the consideration received and the liability recognised) with no corresponding increase in ["'share capital and undistributable reserves"]. Thus the issue of this instrument contributes an excess of net assets over ["'share capital and undistributable reserves"]. This has the effect of reducing any pre-existing restriction on distributable profits under section 831. However, where there is no pre-existing restriction, or such a restriction is more than eliminated by the issue of this instrument, distributable profits are not created; this is because section 831 has effect only to reduce the ability to distribute realised profits.

6.38   Principle 10 – The accretion of the liability component of compound financial instruments reduces distributable profits for public companies under section 831 unless the instrument is legally a debt

6.39   Where the compound financial instrument is legally a share, the ["'interest charge"'] for the accretion of the liability component is not a loss as a matter of law [Principle 6] and has no effect on the amount shown as ["'share capital and undistributable reserves"'] in the relevant accounts. That is, the initial credit to equity (being share capital (and share premium)) cannot be used to absorb the accumulating ["'interest charge"'] debited to retained earnings (via the profit and loss account) due to the accretion of the liability. Hence, under the section 831 net assets test, the amount that a public company can distribute is restricted by the accumulated amount of the ["'interest charge"'] debit, which ultimately will be equal to the initial credit to equity. In other words, net assets are reduced but there is no corresponding reduction of 'share capital and undistributable reserves' and thus over time the cumulative restriction of distributable profits will equal the initial credit to equity.

Where a compound financial instrument is legally a debt, the accretion of the liability is an accounting loss (although not a loss as a matter of law [Principle 5]) that reduces net assets for the purposes of the section 831 net assets test (see paragraph 6.33). However this eliminates the initial increase to net assets recorded as a result of the split accounting and thus of itself does not restrict distributable profits.   **6.40**

Examples

The following examples illustrate the application of the ten principles described in 6.7 to 6.40 above. The first five examples addressed below are based on examples 1, 2, 4, 6 and 9 involving contracts on own equity instruments set out in the Illustrative Examples appendices to IAS 32 ~~and FRS 25~~. Three further examples address preference shares presented as liabilities, mandatorily redeemable preference shares and convertible preference shares. The assumptions made at 6.6A to 6.6C above apply for the purposes of these examples.   **6.41**

Appendix 2 provides illustrations of the accounting and statutory capital maintenance book-keeping entries for the eight examples.   **6.42**

[Assumptions]

[Moved to 6.6A]   **6.43**

[Moved to 6.6B]   **6.44**

[Moved to 6.6C]   **6.45**

Example 1 – Forward contract to repurchase own equity shares

Where a company enters into a forward contract to repurchase its own shares that are equity shares under the relevant standard, the standards require the company to set up a liability, at the outset, for the present value of the payment to be made (ie, a discounted amount), with a corresponding debit taken directly to equity. The accounting effect is as if the equity shares had been repurchased immediately. <u>This accounting entry is not required by FRS 102.</u>   **6.46**

The initial debit to equity, for the present value of the consideration payable, is not a realised loss. This is because the eventual payment is not a loss, but is in fact a distribution (or a capital repayment to the extent not out of distributable profits) [Principle 2].   **6.47**

Over time the (discounted) liability is accreted up to the eventual repayment amount, with a corresponding charge to finance expense (interest) in the profit and loss account (income statement). The accretion of the liability over time up to full value of the eventual redemption amount is presented as an accounting loss – it is shown as part of the interest charge. Again, however, the ultimate payment of the full amount is either a distribution or a capital repayment and is not therefore, as a matter of law, a loss nor, therefore, a realised loss. [Principle 2]   **6.48**

The effect on a public company

For a public company the effect is to restrict distributable profits. [Principle 8]   **6.49**

Combining the accounting and statutory capital maintenance entries to complete the repurchase of non-equity shares

6.50   When payment is made to repurchase the shares, it is, for accounting purposes, set against the liability. To the extent that the payment must, in law, come out of distributable profits, the debit in reserves (ie, the initial debit to equity, together with the interest charge for the accretion) is set against and consumes distributable profits. To the extent that the payment must in law be charged to capital (e.g., funded by a fresh issue), then this debit is set against called-up share capital (and share premium as the case may be). Any necessary transfer from called-up share capital to capital redemption reserve is made in the usual way.

Example 2 – Written option to repurchase own equity shares

6.51   The accounting standards require the same accounting for a written option to repurchase equity shares as for a forward to repurchase equity shares (Example 1), save that in the case of the written option, any premium received at the outset is required to be taken directly to equity. So far as accounting for the repurchase price itself is concerned, the distributable profits considerations are the same as for the forward (see *Forward contract to repurchase own equity shares* at paragraph 6.46 *et seq* above). As noted at paragraph 6.46 above, the initial accounting entry to recognise the present value of the future payments to be made is not required by FRS 102.

6.52   The option premium is regarded as a profit at law and, to the extent that the premium is received in the form of qualifying consideration, is a realised profit. [Principle 4]. As a matter of law, the repurchase price for the shares is a future distribution or capital repayment. [Principle 3]

The effect on a public company

6.53   For a public company the effect of the recognition of the liability for the present value of the payment to be made and the subsequent accretion of the liability to the payment amount, is to restrict distributable profits. [Principle 8]

Example 3 – Forward contract to issue own equity shares

6.54   A forward contract to deliver, through a fresh issue of shares, a fixed number of the company's own equity shares in exchange for a fixed amount of cash meets the definition of an equity instrument in the relevant standard because it cannot be settled otherwise than through the delivery of shares in exchange for cash (see assumptions in *6.6A to 6.6C* above). Consequently, the right to receive the cash in a future accounting period is not recognised by the company, and the standards do not require accounting entries to be made until the forward contract matures, when the company receives cash and issues shares to the contract's counterparty.

6.55   Assuming the fair value of the forward contract at inception is zero, no cash is paid or received at that date, and thus no accounting entries are required on inception. Therefore, where a company enters into a forward contract to issue equity shares, the required accounting for such an arrangement raises no issues of distributable profits.

The effect on a public company

6.56   There are no additional considerations for a public company.

Example 4 – Written option to issue own equity shares

The relevant standards require the premium received on the writing of an option to issue   **6.57**
own shares, that are presented as equity, to be credited directly to equity. The premium
stays in equity regardless of whether the option ultimately is exercised or lapses, although
it may be transferred between components of equity (ie, between reserves). The premium,
to the extent that it is received in the form of qualifying consideration, is, in law, a realised
profit at the outset. [Principle 4]

The effect on a public company

There are no additional considerations for a public company.   **6.58**

Example 5 – Convertible debt

Under the relevant standards, an issuer of debt convertible into the issuer's own equity   **6.59**
shares will use split accounting (see assumptions in 6.6A to 6.6C above). That is, part of
the issue proceeds are recognised as a liability, with the balance recognised directly in
equity at the date the convertible debt is issued, being the component deemed to relate to
the written option to issue own equity shares (the equity conversion option). There is a
correspondingly higher interest charge over the life of the debt because of the need also
to charge the increase in the recorded amount of the liability as interest. That additional
interest is an accounting loss but is not, as a matter of law, a loss. [Principle 5]

The initial credit to equity is not a profit but as the liability component is fully reflected in   **6.60**
the accounts, it offsets the additional interest charge. [Principle 5]

The effect on a public company

There are no additional considerations for a public company. [Principle 10]   **6.61**

Example 6 – Preference shares presented as liabilities

Where a company issues a class of preference shares that are redeemable at a specified   **6.62**
date, or at the holders' option, and the dividends on the shares are non-discretionary and
cumulative, IAS 32/FRS 25 requires that the company classifies this class of shares as a
liability (ie, debt). Under IAS 39/FRS 26, the liability has to be carried at inception at its
fair value, which will be the sum of the nominal value of the shares and any associated
share premium where the shares have been issued at fair value. Over the life of the shares
the non-discretionary dividend is accrued between each payment date and is presented in
profit or loss as an "'interest charge'". A dividend when paid is set against the accrued
liability.

To the extent that the preference shares are to be redeemed contractually at a premium, the   **6.63**
liability will need to be accreted over time such that by redemption the carrying amount
of the liability is equal to the redemption price. The accretion of the redemption premium
attributable to an accounting period will be presented together with the accrued dividend
as the "'interest charge'" for that period in profit or loss.

The presentation of the nominal value of, and any share premium associated with, the   **6.64**
preference shares as debt has no effect on the determination of the company's realised
profits and losses.

6.65   The accrued preference dividend (and any accrued redemption premium) that is presented as an "'interest charge'", and thus an accounting loss, is, as a matter of law, a distribution at the time of its making and not a loss. Thus such accruals do not affect the company's realised profits. [Principles 1, 2 and 3]

The effect on a public company

6.66   For a public company, the presentation of preference shares (ie, the nominal value and any associated share premium) as debt does not result in an immediate restriction in the amount of profits available for distribution by a public company under section 831. [Principle 7]

6.67   Nevertheless, the effect of the accounting for the dividends (and any redemption premium) on the preference shares should be considered. The accounting liability recognised for the accrued unpaid preference dividend (and any redemption premium) is an advance recognition for accounting purposes of the eventual distribution (and/or capital repayment) and thus does not consume distributable profits until it is actually made as a distribution (or capital repayment). [Principle 3] However, profits available for distribution by a public company under section 831 will be restricted due to the reduction in net assets. [Principle 8]

Combining the accounting and statutory capital maintenance entries to complete the redemption

6.68   When payment is made to redeem the preference shares, it is for accounting purposes, set against the debt.

6.69   However, at redemption the law requires the following, where the redemption is made out of distributable profits:

- the nominal value of the redeemed shares is added to the capital redemption reserve; and
- the redemption price consumes distributable profits equal to its amount.

6.70   Therefore to reconcile these positions, the nominal value of the redeemed shares should be credited to the capital redemption reserve. Any share premium on the original issue of the shares now being redeemed should be credited to share premium account in equity at the date of redemption. The sum of the amounts added to the capital redemption reserve and added to share premium account is applied against retained earnings; this sum combined with the accumulated "'interest charge'" in respect of any redemption premium (which has built up in retained earnings over time) is equal to the amount of the redemption price that the law recognises as consuming distributable profits. As established earlier, the debit that builds up over time in retained earnings in respect of the redemption premium is the advance recognition of part of the redemption price and is disregarded as to its effect on distributable profits until the actual redemption takes place. [Principle 3]

Example 7 – Mandatorily redeemable preference shares

6.71   Under IAS 32/~~FRS 25~~, an issuer of mandatorily redeemable preference shares, which bear non-cumulative discretionary dividends, has a compound instrument and has to use split accounting (see assumptions in 6.6A to 6.6C above). That is, the standards require the company to set up a liability, at the outset, for the present value of the payment to be made on redemption of the shares. This will take into account any contractual premium to be paid on redemption. The difference between the proceeds received on issue of the shares and the net present value of the redemption amount is credited (or debited) directly to equity at the outset. Over time the (discounted) liability is accreted up to the contracted redemption price, with a corresponding "'interest charge'" being expensed in profit or loss.

As a matter of law, all of the nominal value and any associated share premium of the preference shares are share capital and share premium irrespective of where they may now be presented in the balance sheet. Consequently, the initial credit to equity is share capital/ share premium, albeit that it is the only part that is allowed by the relevant accounting standard to be shown as such, and is not a profit. The presentation of shares partly within liabilities and partly within equity has no effect on the determination of the company's realised profits and losses.   **6.72**

The interest expense from the accretion up to the full amount of the redemption price is, however, presented as an accounting loss – it is shown as an "'interest charge'". Since the ultimate payment is either a distribution or a capital repayment, the interest charge is, as a matter of law, not a loss even though it is accounted for as if it were a loss. [Principle 2]   **6.73**

The effect on a public company

For a public company, the effect of this IAS 32/FRS 25 accounting is to restrict the maximum amount of profits available for distribution over time by the amount of the cumulative accruals for the redemption price. [Principle 10]   **6.74**

Combining the accounting and statutory capital maintenance entries to complete the redemption

For IAS 32/FRS 25 purposes, the payment to redeem the shares is set against the fully accreted liability.   **6.75**

However, at redemption the law requires the following, where the redemption is made out of distributable profits: **6.76**

- no amount remains recorded in called-up share capital for the redeemed shares;
- the nominal value of the redeemed shares is added to the capital redemption reserve; and
- the redemption price consumes distributable profits equal to its amount.

Therefore to reconcile these positions, the nominal value of the redeemed shares should be credited to the capital redemption reserve in equity and the corresponding amount for this entry is used to eliminate the original credit to equity to the extent recorded as share capital (which is now cancelled share capital). Any share premium on the original issue of the shares now being redeemed, if hitherto presented as part of the liability, should be credited to share premium account in equity at the date of redemption. The sum of the amount added to the capital redemption reserve, but not used to make a corresponding elimination of the original credit to share capital, and that added to share premium account is applied against retained earnings; this sum, combined with the accumulated "'interest charge'" in respect of any redemption premium (which has built up in retained earnings over time) is equal to the amount of the redemption price that the law recognises as consuming distributable profits. As established earlier, the "'interest charge'" debit in retained earnings is the advance recognition of part of the redemption price and has no effect on cumulative realised profits until the actual redemption takes place.   **6.77**

Example 8 – Convertible redeemable preference shares

Under IAS 32/FRS 25, convertible redeemable preference shares are a compound instrument and an issuer of such instruments will use split accounting (see assumptions   **6.78** in 6.6A to 6.6C above). This is similar to debt convertible into an issuer's own equity instruments as described in 6.59 *et seq* above. That is, a liability is recognised for the debt component and a credit is recognised in equity for the equity component (the equity conversion option). However, the analysis for distributable profits purposes is more akin to that for the mandatorily redeemable shares with discretionary dividends described in 6.71 *et seq* above. This is because the initial credit to equity is share capital (and share premium).

6.79   It is assumed that the preference shares are convertible at any time by the holder into ordinary shares of the issuer and are mandatorily redeemed at the end of their term if not converted. The conversion feature cannot be settled other than by an exchange of the preference shares for a fixed number of the issuer's ordinary shares.

6.80   The presentation of the shares (inclusive of their share premium) as partly debt and partly as a credit in equity has no effect on the determination of realised profits and losses.

6.81   Any accrued unpaid preference dividends and the accretion up to the full amount of the redemption price, although presented as accounting losses through the profit and loss account, are disregarded in determining whether distributable profits have been consumed until their actual payment. [Principle 6]

The effect on a public company

6.82   At the outset there is no effect on distributable profits [Principle 9]. There will be a restriction for a public company on the maximum amount of profits available for distribution over time by the amount of the cumulative accruals for the redemption price. [Principle 10]

Combining the accounting and statutory capital maintenance entries where the shares are redeemed

6.83   The same analysis applies as given in 6.71 *et seq* in respect of the mandatorily redeemable preference shares with discretionary dividends.

Combining the accounting and statutory capital maintenance entries where the shares are converted

6.84   Under IAS 32/FRS 25, when the holders exercise their option to convert the preference shares into the issuer's ordinary shares, the amount of the liability at conversion is transferred to equity.

6.85   However, to establish the impact on profits available for distribution it is necessary to re-analyse the aggregate entries in equity to establish the amounts that represent:

- the nominal value of the ordinary shares issued on conversion;
- the relevant amount of share premium to be included in the share premium account; and
- the elimination of the "interest charge" debit in retained earnings.

6.86   This is achieved at conversion by crediting to retained earnings an amount equal to the accumulated "interest charge" in respect of accrued unpaid dividends and accretion to the issue price of the shares from the amount transferred from liabilities to equity. The aggregate of the balance of the transfer to equity and the initial credit to equity is equal to the total of the nominal value and share premium attributable to the ordinary shares issued on conversion.

The allocation of part of the transfer from liabilities equal to the accrued "~~'~~interest charge~~''~~" effectively reverses the "~~'~~interest charge~~''~~" accounting entries. At law the debit accounting entries had not consumed distributable profits and therefore the effective reversal of these entries has no effect on the quantum of distributable profits. However, for public companies, the effective reversal of the "~~'~~interest charge~~''~~" debit at conversion removes the restriction under the section 831 net assets test.   **6.87**

7. EMPLOYEE SHARE SCHEMES

ESOP trusts

Introduction

Paragraphs 7.4 to 7.45 are concerned with the effect of a company's sponsorship of a trust (ESOP trust) that holds shares in the company, which may be delivered to the company's employees under an employee share scheme. This differs from the case of the direct holding of a company's own shares (treasury shares) which are addressed at paragraphs 2.40 to 2.43 above.   **7.1**

The practice of employing ESOP trusts evolved partly because of restrictions on a company acquiring its own shares (s658) or acquiring shares in its parent company (section 136). These restrictions have been~~were~~ eased now that~~from 1 December 2003 when certain~~ companies are~~were~~ permitted~~, subject to some restrictions,~~ to hold their own shares as treasury shares (see paragraph 7.1 above). The use of ESOP trusts has, however, remained widespread.   **7.2**

The provision of funds by a company to an ESOP trust to enable it to buy shares in the company or its parent company will generally fall within the definition of financial assistance for the acquisition of own shares (section 677). Such assistance is generally prohibited, subject to certain exceptions, for a public company or a subsidiary of a public company (section 678). ~~Under the 1985 Act, similar restrictions applied to all companies until 1 October 2008.~~ However, one of the exceptions to the general rules in section 682(2) (b) is 'the provision by the company, in good faith in the interests of the company or its holding company, of financial assistance for the purposes of an employee's share scheme'.   **7.2A**

That exception is subject to a restriction in section 682(1) that the financial assistance may only be given if the company has net assets which are not thereby reduced, or to the extent that those assets are thereby reduced, the financial assistance is provided out of distributable profits. Although paragraphs 7.25 to 7.31 address the interaction of this restriction with the accounting for ESOP trusts, the general question of the lawfulness of financial assistance is not within the scope of this guidance and accordingly directors may wish to consider seeking legal advice.   **7.3**

ESOP trusts under UK GAAP

FRS 102~~Under UK GAAP, UITF Abstract 38~~ 'Accounting for ESOP trusts' requires the sponsoring company of an ESOP trust to recognise the assets and liabilities of the trust in its own accounts whenever it had de facto control of those assets and liabilities. Where the trust purchases the company's own shares, the consideration paid for those shares should be deducted in equity until such time as the shares vest unconditionally in the company's employees. The effect of this deduction, which occurs in the individual accounts of the sponsoring company and not merely on consolidation, is considered below.   **7.4**

7.5   The sponsoring company of an ESOP trust may be a company other than the one whose shares are held by the trust. For example, a subsidiary may be the sponsoring company of an ESOP trust that holds shares in its parent. In this case the shares will not be ~~"~~'own shares~~"~~' from the perspective of the subsidiary's financial statements. The shares would be recognised as an asset in the subsidiary's balance sheet and the issues addressed in this guidance would not arise.

ESOP trusts under IFRSs

7.6   The guidance set out below in relation to investments in own shares held through an ESOP trust will be relevant to companies reporting under IFRSs if they account for investments in own shares in their individual balance sheets in a manner similar to that required by FRS 102~~UITF Abstract 38~~. However, published literature suggests that a different accounting treatment may be permitted in individual accounts under IFRSs. Whereas FRS 102~~UITF Abstract 38~~ requires the assets and liabilities of the trust to be included in the individual balance sheet of the sponsoring company, under IFRSs it may be acceptable to account for the ESOP trust as an investment in a subsidiary. The IFRS Interpretations Committee was asked to address the question of which of these treatments is appropriate but declined to do so on the basis that it would be unable to reach a consensus on a timely basis given the different types of trusts and arrangements that exist in practice (see IFRIC Update, November 2006, for further details).

7.7   Where the ESOP trust is accounted for as a subsidiary, any loans to the trust by the sponsoring company, to the extent that they are regarded as recoverable, may therefore be recognised as assets in the individual balance sheet of the sponsoring company even though they have been used to finance an investment in own shares by the trust. If it is necessary to write the loan down for impairment at any time then that write down will represent a realised loss. The guidance set out below concerning the effects of a deduction within equity is not relevant when the loan is recognised as an asset because the deduction within equity will arise only in the consolidated financial statements.

Note of legal considerations attached to Abstract 38

7.8   [Deleted]~~A note of legal considerations attached to Abstract 38 sets out legal advice that the UITF received on the implications for distributable profits when the accounting treatment required by the Abstract is followed. The note of legal considerations is reproduced in Appendix 3 to this guidance for reference. This guidance is consistent with that note of legal considerations but additionally addresses some issues that were not covered in that note as well as considering some issues in greater depth.~~

7.8A   [Deleted]~~The note of legal considerations attached to UITF Abstract 38 states that although the acquisition of shares by an ESOP trust will not, of itself, result in a realised profit or loss for the company concerned, 'a company will still need to consider other transactions with the ESOP, for example a loan to the ESOP to fund acquisitions of shares, and these may affect the company's realised profits and losses'. The reference to a loan to the ESOP might be read as implying that realised profits and losses should be determined by reference to 'narrow entity accounting' (see 7.14 below). However, this is not the case; the UITF Abstract 38 note refers to the existence of a loan as only one of a number of factors that might be relevant. The assessment of realised profits and losses for the justification of a distribution is by reference to a company's 'relevant accounts' and, as explained in paragraph 7.14 this means by reference to 'extended entity accounting'. However, see 7.25 to 7.31 regarding financial assistance by a public company.~~

Effect of deduction within equity on realised profits

A purchase of a company's own shares though an ESOP trust is not a distribution at law. This is because, at law, the shares have been purchased by the trust, notwithstanding that assistance may have been given by the company (by way of gift or loan, some or all of which may be ultimately irrecoverable, or by guarantee of the trust's borrowings that may ultimately be called upon to some extent). See 7.25 to 7.31 below for regulation of the transaction for a public company as financial assistance.   **7.9**

Neither does such a purchase, of itself, give rise to an immediate realised loss. Therefore, such an acquisition does not reduce the amount of profits available for distribution under section 830.   **7.10**

In addition, whilst the acquisition of shares will not, of itself, give rise to an immediate realised loss, the impact of other factors such as the granting of rights over those shares should be considered (see 7.37 to 7.41 below).   **7.11**

Effect on section 831 restriction on purchase of own shares for a public company

The consideration paid on the purchase of shares by an ESOP trust sponsored by a public company will immediately restrict the profits available for distribution by virtue of section 831 by the amount of the consideration paid. As more fully explained below, there will be an immediate reduction in net assets but no change in share capital or undistributable reserves.   **7.12**

A public company may only make a distribution at any time: **7.13**

(a)   if at that time the amount of its net assets is not less than the aggregate of its called-up share capital and undistributable reserves; and

(b)   if, and to the extent that, the distribution does not reduce the amount of those assets to less than that aggregate.

Change in net assets

Section 831 states that "'net assets'" means the aggregate of the company's assets less the aggregate of its liabilities. Under section 836, net assets are those as shown in the company's "'relevant accounts'" which are normally the last annual accounts under Part 15 of the Act, properly prepared under the Act; in certain circumstances, the relevant accounts are initial accounts or interim accounts, which are prepared to a similar standard. Net assets for the purposes of section 831 should therefore be determined in accordance with accounting standards ~~and UITF Abstracts~~. Accordingly, the relevant accounts and the net assets should include the assets and liabilities of the ESOP trust as reported under FRS 102~~Abstract 38~~ ("'extended entity accounting'") rather than, for example, any loan between the company and the ESOP trust ("'narrow entity accounting'").   **7.14**

The effect of the accounting treatment required by FRS 102~~Abstract 38~~ is that, in drawing up the relevant accounts, any own shares held by an ESOP trust would be recorded as a deduction in arriving at shareholders' funds rather than as an asset. Therefore, it follows that the relevant aggregate net asset amount for the purposes of the definition in section 831(2) would be reduced by the own shares held (being the consideration paid for the shares).   **7.15**

Disclosure by way of note that the company also has an "'asset'" of own shares held through an ESOP trust would not restore the net assets for the purposes of section 831 (see 2.14 above). If the shares are not an asset for accounting purposes they cannot be an asset for the purposes of calculating net assets when applying section 831.   **7.16**

Change in share capital or undistributable reserves

7.17   A company's undistributable reserves are defined in section 831. In short, they include the company's unrealised profits less its unrealised losses, except that this amount is never less than zero (ie, net unrealised losses are not within the definition).

7.18   The correct characterisation, as a matter of law, of the deduction in equity is not straightforward. On the one hand the deduction should not be characterised as a loss at all (thereby rendering redundant questions of realisation) because from the point of view of the company's individual accounts (which are on an extended entity basis) the company has not lost control of the shares nor have these shares suffered any objectively measurable diminution in value. On the other hand, given that the applicable accounting treatment does not permit the company to treat the shares as an asset, some might argue that the deduction should be categorised as a loss, although the nearest equivalent could be said to be a return of capital. The characterisation which gives primacy to the substance rather than presentation is the view to be preferred and accordingly the deduction should not be characterised as a loss.

7.19   Accordingly, the deduction for own shares in equity is neither a realised loss nor an unrealised loss and does not affect the balance of undistributable reserves.

The effect on profits available for distribution under section 831

7.20   Thus with net assets reduced but share capital and undistributable reserves unaffected, the purchase of ESOP trust shares affects the maximum distribution permissible by virtue of the application of section 831 (the "'maximum distribution permissible"'). In other words, the effect of the section is such that the profits available for distribution are restricted by a reduction in net assets that is neither a realised nor an unrealised loss.

7.21   Furthermore, the existence of any unrealised profits does not alter this situation (e.g.eg. such unrealised profits cannot be applied to offset the deduction, because the deduction is not an unrealised loss).

Effect on section 831 restriction on subscription for own shares for a public company

7.22   A subscription for new shares in a public company by its own sponsored ESOP trust will immediately restrict the maximum distribution permissible.

7.23   The application of section 831 is considered above. In the case of a subscription for new shares, there is no change in net assets. This is because the cash subscribed for the shares by the ESOP trust is recorded in the balance sheet of the sponsoring company both before and after the subscription in accordance with FRS 102Abstract 38.

7.24   However, the amount of the company's called-up share capital is increased by the nominal value of the shares issued to the trust. The amount of the company's undistributable reserves is also increased to the extent of any share premium arising on the issue, for example where the ESOP trusts subscribes for the shares at market value which is at a premium to nominal value. There is no other effect of the subscription on undistributable reserves as defined in section 831. Consequently, any excess of the company's net assets over the aggregate amount of the company's called-up share capital and undistributable reserves is reduced and hence the amount of the company's maximum distribution permissible is restricted by the amount attributable to the share issue (ie, the proceeds of subscription for the shares by the trust).

The effect of the financial assistance rules in relation to a public company

Assuming that the relevant assistance is permitted by virtue of section 682(2), in the case of **7.25** a public company the assistance can only be given if the company has net assets which are not thereby reduced or, to the extent that those assets are thereby reduced, if the assistance is provided out of distributable profits.

Net assets

For the purposes of section 682, "'net assets''' are defined as the amount by which the **7.26** aggregate of the company's assets exceeds the aggregate of its liabilities, taking the amount of both its assets and liabilities to be as stated in the company's accounting records immediately before the financial assistance is given. This is in contrast to section 831 where, by reason of section 836, net assets are the aggregate of the company's assets less the aggregate of its liabilities as shown in the company's relevant accounts.

Section 386 imposes a duty to keep accounting records which are sufficient to show and **7.27** explain the company's transactions and to enable the directors to ensure that any balance sheet and profit and loss account prepared under Part 15 of the Act complies with the requirements of the Act. Thus the records must at least be consistent with accounting standards and interpretations issued by the IASB or FRCUITF or the IFRS Interpretations Committee as the case may be. However, this does not impose an obligation to maintain the entries in the accounting records fully in accordance with accounting standards and interpretations provided that it is evident from those records how to make suitable adjustments to prepare accounts in accordance with the requirements of the Act. Accordingly, section 386 does not require net assets for the purposes of section 682 to be determined by reference to "'extended entity accounting''' (as described at 7.14 above).

Thus, in the absence of any such requirement, the company's assets and liabilities should **7.28** be given their natural meaning, namely the assets and liabilities of the company as a legal person. In other words, the "'narrow entity accounting''' basis is used for determining the net asset position of the company concerned and whether the financial assistance has reduced the company's net assets[30]. There is thus in this respect no change to the assessment of a company's net asset position as a result of applying FRS 102Abstract 38.

The effect of section 831 where financial assistance is provided out of distributable profits.

Where a company has provided financial assistance out of distributable profits which has **7.29** reduced its net assets and shares have been acquired by an ESOP trust, section 831 does not require a further restriction in the maximum distribution permissible equal to the amount of the reduction in net assets calculated under section 682.

Section 682 and section 831 are directed to different objectives. Section 682 determines the **7.30** legality of the provision of financial assistance tested on a narrow entity basis. Section 831 determines the maximum distribution permissible tested on an extended entity basis. On the extended entity basis the assistance provided to the ESOP trust will not be treated as

---

[30] *More generally, the presentation of shares as liabilities reduces net assets as defined in section 682 for the purposes of financial assistance. The legislation refers to amounts stated in the accounting records rather than in the 'relevant accounts' because the test is a 'real time' one. However, subject to the use of 'narrow entity accounting' as described above, net assets as defined in section 682 for the purposes of financial assistance should generally be the same as net assets as defined in section 831 for the purposes of distributions by a public company. That is, the relevant shares should be treated as liabilities to creditors.*

having been paid away until the shares are purchased at which point the net assets are reduced by the consideration paid for the shares (as described at 7.12 to 7.21 above).

7.31   Section 840 contains accumulation rules where distributions are proposed by reference to particular accounts and prior distributions have taken place. Section 840(2) makes it clear that financial assistance which is given out of distributable profits is taken into account in the accumulation rules. These rules continue to apply.

7.32   [Deleted]

Purchase by an ESOP trust of shares held as treasury shares by a ~~listed~~ public company

7.33   A purchase of treasury shares by an ESOP trust for cash will be a sale of treasury shares for cash for the purposes of section 731 (see paragraph 7.34 below). The proceeds will therefore increase distributable profits up to an amount equal to the original purchase price of the shares (ie, reversing the decrease that would have occurred at the time of purchase of the treasury shares). Any excess will be credited to share premium. At the same time, the former treasury shares, now shares held by the ESOP trust, will be accounted for and treated for distributable profit purposes just as if they had been purchased at the same price from a third party, ie, the entire consideration paid by the ESOP trust restricts the amount of profits available for distribution (see 7.12 to 7.31 above).

7.34   Section 727(1) states that where shares are held as treasury shares, a company may at any time "'(a) sell the shares … for a cash consideration or (b) transfer the shares … for the purposes of or pursuant to an employees' shares scheme'". Section 729(1) states that where shares are held as treasury shares the company may at any time "'cancel the shares'". Section 731 deals with the treatment of the proceeds when shares "'are sold'" and requires any excess over the purchase price to be credited to share premium, with the remainder to replenish distributable profits. No treatment is otherwise specified for the proceeds when shares are "'transferred'" to an employee share scheme in accordance with section 727(1) (b). Section 731 does not apply exclusively to sales falling solely within section 727(1)(a) but applies to any sale of treasury shares to an ESOP trust notwithstanding that the sale might also be a transfer under section 727(1)(b).

7.35   The requirement in section 731 to transfer an amount to share premium when shares are sold for more than their purchase price applies only to treasury shares. Such a transfer is not required, or permitted, when shares held by an ESOP trust are sold in comparable circumstances. Whether or not the resulting surplus in the trust is a distributable profit from the perspective of the company is addressed at 7.42 to 7.45 below.

Effect on distributable profits for a public company when proceeds are received for sale of shares by an ESOP trust

7.36   In the case of a public company, the initial acquisition of the ESOP shares would have an immediate effect on distributable profits under section 831 because net assets were reduced without a corresponding reduction in share capital and undistributable reserves (see 7.12 to 7.21 above). However, if option holders then subscribe for the shares or the shares are sold in the market, the receipt of proceeds gives rise to an accounting entry (debit cash, credit shareholders' funds) that reverses the situation and restores distributable profits to the extent of those proceeds. That is, net assets are increased for the purposes of section 831 but there is no corresponding increase in share capital and undistributable reserves.

Realised loss when shares held by an ESOP trust are transferred to employees – where
shares originally acquired externally

The purchase of shares by an ESOP trust does not, of itself, give rise to a realised loss   **7.37**
(see 7.10 above) and, other than in the case of a public company, does not otherwise
immediately affect the distribution of available profits. However, it is clear that if the
shares are to be transferred to employees for less than their purchase price, the shortfall
will at some time fall to be treated as a realised loss. In some cases options may be granted
with an exercise price that is lower than the price at which the shares were purchased. In
other cases shares may be transferred to employees for no consideration on the achievement
of specified performance or service conditions. In all such cases, the difference between
the purchase price of the shares and the proceeds received or receivable from the employee
should be regarded as becoming a realised loss over the relevant amortisation or charging
period as would be the case with a cash bonus that was contingent on future service.

[Deleted]   **7.38**

Where options have been granted over the shares in question but those options are ""out-   **7.39**
of-the-money"" or where there are ""surplus"" shares that have not been allocated to any
particular share scheme, a realised loss may also arise if the market value of the shares
falls below their purchase price. A realised loss will have arisen to the extent that the fall
in market price below cost is not expected to be reversed and thus that part of the cost
incurred is not expected to be recovered.

[Moved to 7.8A]   **7.40**

Realised loss when shares held by an ESOP trust are transferred to employees – where
shares originally subscribed

The subscription for shares by an ESOP trust does not, of itself, give rise to a realised   **7.41**
loss (see 7.10 above) and, other than in the case of a public company, does not otherwise
immediately affect the distribution of available profits. However, as in the case of a
purchase of shares described at 7.37 to 7.39 above, a realised loss may arise if the shares
are subsequently transferred to employees for less than their subscription price. In all such
cases, the difference between the subscription price of the shares and the proceeds received
from the employee should be regarded as becoming a realised loss over the relevant
amortisation or charging period.

Whether a surplus on disposal of shares by an ESOP trust is a realised and distributable
profit from the perspective of the sponsoring company

As explained at 7.44, a surplus on disposal of shares held by an ESOP trust is a realised   **7.42**
profit. However, in respect of it being distributable, the directors should have regard to
their wider common law duties as required by sections 851 and 852. As explained at 7.45,
the profit therefore may not become distributable until some time in the future.

Under FRS 102Abstract 38, a sponsoring company includes the assets, liabilities and   **7.43**
transactions of its ESOP trust in its accounts as if the trust were a division or branch
of the company. This is therefore not just a matter of including the trust in consolidated
accounts. The assets, liabilities and transactions of the trust are included in the company's
individual accounts. These are the ""relevant accounts"" for the purposes of determining
profits available for distribution. Where the trust has a surplus in the equivalent of its profit
and loss account, the question arises of whether this should be reflected in the calculation
of the company's realised profits.

7.44   Where the trust has a surplus (~~e.g.~~eg, from the sale of shares at more than their purchase price), it is arguable that, just as a parent would not treat a surplus in a subsidiary as a realised profit in its own individual accounts, the parent should not regard the surplus in the trust as increasing its realised profits. But there is a clear difference in that FRS 102~~Abstract 38~~ requires the assets and liabilities of the trust to be included in the company's own individual accounts. ~~Also, Abstract 13, which was superseded by Abstract 38 and required own shares to be recognised as assets, made no mention of any legal difficulties about including any 'profits' of the trust in the company's profit and loss account. Under Abstract 38, no such profits arise to be included in the company's profit and loss account but the issue is still relevant to the determination of the company's realised profits.~~ Where the consideration received by the trust for the sale of the shares is in the form of cash (or other "~~'~~qualifying consideration~~''~~") that will be included in the company's balance sheet in accordance with the requirements of FRS 102~~Abstract 38~~, the profit will be a realised profit from the company's perspective.

7.45   However, the directors should have regard to their wider common law duties as required by sections 851 and 852 (see 2.1 above). It would not be regarded as prudent to distribute an amount that represents assets that are retained in the ESOP trust and therefore not available for the general purposes of the company. If the assets of the trust are used in future to meet an expense, an equivalent amount of the gain should at that time be treated as distributable. Therefore to the extent that the realised loss arising from the expense does not exceed the previously recognised gain that was treated as undistributable, there will be no reduction in distributable profits.

Expenses for share based payments ~~required by IFRS 2 and FRS 20~~

7.46   IFRS 2 ~~(~~and FRS 102~~20)~~ require expenses to be recognised in profit or loss for cash-settled share-based payment arrangements. The credit entry will be either a cash payment or a provision. The expense recognised will therefore be a realised loss. The paragraphs which follow are concerned with equity-settled arrangements.

7.47   IFRS 2 ~~(~~and FRS 102~~20)~~ require expenses to be recognised in profit or loss for equity-settled share-based payment arrangements. The standard requires the credit entry arising from recognition of this expense to be credited within equity but does not specify any particular component of equity.

7.48   Any expense recognised in accordance with IFRS 2 or FRS 102 will be a realised loss. This follows from the principle that all losses should be regarded as realised losses except to the extent that the law, accounting standards or this guidance provide otherwise (see 3.10 above). However, the overall impact of the IFRS 2 or FRS 102 expense on distributable profits will depend on the status of the credit entry in equity.

7.49   If the consideration for an issue of shares is, as a matter of law, the provision of goods or services to the company, it will be necessary to credit share capital and share premium with the fair value of those goods or services. Similarly, if shares are, as a matter of law, issued in settlement of a monetary liability, it will be necessary to credit share capital and share premium with the amount of the liability discharged. Where this is so, the credit entry to equity required by IFRS 2 or FRS 102 cannot be a realised profit.

7.50   In the case of share options, the note of legal considerations appended to UITF Abstract 17 is still relevant, despite that Abstract being superseded by FRS 20 and FRS 102, and it~~(now superseded by FRS 20)~~ provided the following guidance[31].

---

[31] *The equivalent 2006 Act references have been added to the original note for ease of reference.*

"'The UITF has received legal advice on the implications for share premium account when the accounting treatment required by this Abstract is followed. It has been advised that where new shares are issued in connection with an employee share scheme the share premium account will normally have to reflect only the cash subscribed for the shares (e.g.eg, by the employee or by an ESOP trust). In such cases, any difference between the cash subscribed for the shares (which must be at least as much as the nominal value, as shares cannot be issued at a discount) and the fair value at the date of grant of rights should be credited to reserves other than the share premium account. This is on the basis that the services of the employee do not, as a matter of law, form part of the consideration received for the shares issued, and the UITF has been advised that this would be the usual legal interpretation of such transactions. Exceptionally, however, the terms of a transaction might be such as to lead to the opposite interpretation, and companies may need to take legal advice on this point. In such a case, the operation of section 99(2) of the Companies Act 1985 [now section 585(1) of the Companies Act 2006] [prohibition of public company accepting undertaking to perform services in payment up of its shares] and section 103 [now section 593 of the Companies Act 2006] [non-cash consideration to be valued before allotment of shares] would also have to be considered."'

However, the arrangements referred to in the last two sentences of the quoted paragraph are not typical. Instead, for example, in the case of share options, the credit to equity required by IFRS 2 or FRS 102 will usually be a credit to reserves other than share premium account.

7.51 The note of legal considerations does not, however, address whether the credit to equity in the case of options to subscribe for shares is a realised profit. However, an unrealised reserve will be treated as having become realised by the amortisation or writing down of the related asset (see 3.9(f) above). Therefore, assuming that the IFRS 2 or FRS 102 expense has been included in profit or loss (which would be the case except where the charge had been capitalised as part of the cost of production of an asset) the credit entry in equity will be a realised profit. The IFRS 2 or FRS 102 expense will therefore have no net effect on distributable profits.

7.52 The manner of settlement (e.g.eg, subscription for new shares or purchase of shares in the market by an ESOP trust) does not affect the expense recognised under IFRS 2 or FRS 102 or whether this is a realised loss. However, it will be necessary to consider the effect on realised profits arising from any shares held by an ESOP trust (see 7.37 to 7.41 above).

Intra-group recharges for share-based payments

7.53 In November 2006, the IFRS Interpretations Committee issued IFRIC 11 "'IFRS 2 – Group and Treasury Share Transactions"' which has subsequently been incorporated into IFRS 2. The Exposure Draft upon which this was based (IFRIC D17) included some material on the treatment of inter-company recharges made within groups in connection with share-based payment arrangements. The IFRS Interpretations Committee decided not to address these issues in IFRIC 11 because it did not wish to widen the scope of the Interpretation to an issue that relates to accounting for intra-group payments generally. The appropriate accounting for such recharges is thus a matter of developing practice, including that in some cases the treatment that was set out in the draft guidance in IFRIC D17, described below, may be appropriate.

7.54 The situation in question is one in which the company, being a subsidiary, makes a cash payment to its parent in relation to a share-based payment in favour of the company's own employees and where IFRS 2 requires an equity-settled share-based payment charge in the company's accounts. The proposals in IFRIC D17 envisaged that where a charge is made by the parent to the subsidiary which exceeds the expense that the subsidiary is required to recognise under IFRS 2, the excess is accounted for by the subsidiary as a distribution. For example, this may arise if a charge is made on the basis of intrinsic value at exercise date which will generally be higher than the grant date fair value recognised as an expense in accordance with IFRS 2. The accounting treatment of any such charge does not affect whether or not it is a distribution as a matter of law. In particular, if there is a commercial basis for such a charge, it will not be a distribution as a matter of law. An example of a commercial basis would be the expense that the subsidiary would have incurred if it had purchased shares in the market to satisfy the options. Consequently, it will not be unlawful for the subsidiary to make the reimbursement payment, even in the absence of distributable profits, provided that the payment is not a distribution as a matter of law.

7.55   However, the entire reimbursement payment will have the effect of reducing accumulated realised profits or increasing accumulated realised losses of the subsidiary. The debit to equity arising from the payment will first reduce the credit in equity arising from IFRS 2 which will no longer be available to offset the realised loss recognised as a result of the IFRS 2 expense. Any debit to equity in excess of this amount will be a realised loss even though it will not have been accounted for as a loss in the financial statements.

7.56   A liability may be recognised by the subsidiary where the parent has a contractual right to reimbursement at a future date. The amount of the realised loss at any date will generally be based on the amount of the liability recognised at that date but the particular facts of each case should be considered.

8. RETIREMENT BENEFIT SCHEMES

Introduction

8.1   The guidance in this section is written in terms of compliance with IAS 19 but is equally applicable to the very similar requirements of sSection 28 of FRS 102. Companies transitioning from FRS 102 to IFRSs or vice versa should often see no change of accounting treatment and therefore no impact on distributable reserves. However, companies transitioning from FRS 17 to either IAS 19 or FRS 102 may see a change of accounting treatment, particularly when they were accounting for their participation in group multi-employer defined benefit schemes as if they were defined contribution schemes.

Defined contribution schemes

8.2   For defined contribution schemes, or those accounted for as defined contribution schemes, the cost charged to profit or loss under IAS 19 is a realised loss.

Defined benefit schemes

8.3   For a defined benefit scheme, it is the cumulative amounts charged or credited to reserves which must be assessed as realised or unrealised. This is true irrespective of whether those amounts have been reported in profit or loss or in other comprehensive income. The assessment is as follows:

8.4   A cumulative charge is a realised loss.

8.5   A cumulative credit is a realised profit only to the extent that it is represented by an asset that is to be recovered by refunds that have been agreed by the pension scheme trustees at the balance sheet date of the relevant accounts and the refunds will take the form of cash or other qualifying consideration.

In most cases, there will be a cumulative realised loss and therefore no need to make any adjustment to what has already flowed through total comprehensive income (ie, that is already in reserves) in arriving at the amount of distributable profits. The few cases when adjustment may be required are when: **8.6**

- the scheme is in surplus (see paragraphs 8.11 and 8.12 below); or
- the scheme was acquired as part of a trade and assets acquisition (see paragraphs 8.13 and 8.14 below)

It will usually be obvious that there is a cumulative charge within reserves and it will not be necessary to quantify that cumulative charge. In the absence of a trade and assets acquisition, it is only necessary to determine that the cumulative net contributions to the scheme since its inception exceed any pension scheme asset recognised in the balance sheet to be able to confirm that there is a cumulative charge within reserves. When this is the case, no adjustment will be required in arriving at distributable profits. **8.7**

In other cases, the cumulative net debit or credit within reserves is calculated by adjusting the cumulative net contributions less refunds made in respect of the scheme for: **8.8**

- the amount of any surplus or deficit recognised in the balance sheet before taking account of deferred tax; and
- the amount initially recognised in respect of a trade and assets purchase.

It may not be practical for companies with long-established schemes to ascertain the net contributions less refunds to perform this calculation. In those rare cases where such a calculation is necessary, it is possible to use an estimated approach using only the amount of net contributions that the company is able to identify. **8.9**

A company adopting the estimated approach in 8.9 above might be able to revise that estimate subsequently by identifying additional contributions that have been made since the scheme was established or acquired. If so, it may be able to revise upwards the amount of a net cumulative realised loss in reserves and therefore treat as realised net credits arising in subsequent periods that would otherwise be treated as unrealised. **8.10**

When a scheme is in surplus, this may be because there has been a cumulative amount credited to reserves. In such a case, adjustment will be required to arrive at distributable profit, unless the cumulative credit meets the test at paragraph 8.5 above. **8.11**

A surplus might also arise if there has been a cumulative charge (ie, if contributions have been greater than that charge). No adjustment is required in this case. **8.12**

The need for adjustment is more difficult to identify when the pension scheme has been acquired as part of a business combination. This is because the original business combination accounting will have involved the initial recognition of an asset or liability for the pension scheme at the date of business combination. Whilst that initial recognition has no effect on accumulated reserves of the acquiring company, and hence no effect on distributable profits, it makes identification of potential cases of cumulative post-acquisition credits less readily apparent (eg, a year-end surplus might not be a result of a cumulative post-acquisition credit but of the acquired position). **8.13**

Further, where there is a cumulative post-acquisition credit, it may be partly represented by (a) a pension scheme asset on that balance sheet and partly by (b) the reversal of an acquisition date deficit. A credit represented by (b) is never a realised profit because such a reduction in a pension liability is not readily convertible to cash (see paragraphs 3.9(g) and 3.9B above). The credit represented by (a) is tested under the principles set out at paragraph 8.5 above. **8.14**

8.15   Companies transitioning to IAS 19 from FRS 17 may have to adopt defined benefit accounting for the first time if they previously were accounting for their participation in group multi-employer defined benefit schemes as if they were defined contribution schemes. Any such adjustment for financial reporting purposes will usually have an equal effect on the cumulative realised profits and therefore on distributable reserves. The exception is those rare cases referred to above when this would result in a restatement to a cumulative net credit within reserves, which will require more detailed assessment.

The guidance in this section is written in terms of compliance with FRS 17 but is equally applicable when the equivalent international standard IAS 19 'Employee benefits' is being applied. When IAS 19 is being applied, the guidance should be applied to the amounts reported under that standard. For simplicity, this guidance refers throughout to the relevant requirements of FRS 17.

8.2   The guidance set out below applies both to pension schemes acquired in a business combination and those that are started by the reporting company.

Defined contribution schemes

8.3   For defined contribution retirement benefit schemes, the cost charged to the profit and loss account under FRS 17 is equal to the contributions payable to the scheme for the accounting period. The charge to the profit and loss account for the contributions payable is a realised loss.

Multi-employer schemes

8.4   Under FRS 17, some companies account for their participation in certain multi-employer defined benefit retirement benefit schemes as if they were defined contribution schemes. Where a scheme meets the criteria for this treatment in FRS 17, the position as regards realised profits and losses will be the same as for any other defined contribution scheme.

Defined benefit schemes

Summary

8.5   In summary, what is required in relation to a defined benefit scheme is to identify whether any adjustment is required to reserves, to exclude unrealised profits, in arriving at the amount of distributable profits. To do so, it is first necessary to ascertain the cumulative amounts charged or credited in relation to the pension scheme, whether through the profit and loss account or through the statement of total recognised gains and losses (ie the total amounts taken to reserves). Paragraphs 8.11 to 8.13 determine whether that cumulative amount is realised or unrealised, with the test being different for cumulative net debits as against cumulative net credits. The cumulative net debit or credit will not be readily apparent from the accounts and so paragraphs 8.14 to 8.15 provide that it is determined from the movement in the pension scheme asset or liability on the balance sheet since inception of the scheme (ie when it is started by the company or when it was acquired in a business combination) and the cumulative net cash paid to the scheme. The cumulative cash flows may themselves be difficult to obtain and so paragraphs 8.16 to 8.17 provide a method of estimating the amounts. Paragraph 8.18 then describes some circumstances when it is possible to deduce easily, without working through these procedures, that all amounts accumulated in reserves are realised.

8.5A   This calculation is unaffected by the date of adoption of FRS 17 and the accounting adopted previously (ie SSAP 24). A company may have established the cumulative amount in reserves for the pension scheme on adoption of FRS 17 in which case the amount can be rolled forward from year to year. However, the approach set out below will enable the position to be established at a particular date if no such calculation was performed.

General principles

It is the cumulative gain or loss credited or debited to reserves in respect of a pension scheme, rather than the existence of a surplus or deficit, that affects the realised profits and losses of a company. This principle is illustrated in Appendix 4.   **8.6**

The effect of FRS 17 on reserves must be calculated to identify whether any adjustment in respect of pensions is needed to reported reserves to arrive at realised reserves. No adjustment is required if a net cumulative loss has been taken to reserves. If a net cumulative gain has been taken to reserves, and under the guidance set out at 8.12 below that gain is in part or in full unrealised, a deduction equivalent to the unrealised element must be made to reserves in assessing the level of realised reserves.   **8.7**

In establishing the impact that a surplus or deficit under FRS 17 has on a company's realised profits, it is therefore necessary to: **8.8**

(a)   identify the cumulative net gain or loss taken to reserves in respect of the pension surplus or deficit; and
(b)   establish the extent to which that gain or loss is realised.

Although the various elements making up the changes in the defined benefit asset or liability are disclosed separately in the performance statements (see paragraph 50 of FRS 17), it is the net amount that represents the cost to the company of the pension promise. Thus it is the cumulative net gain or loss taken to reserves that falls to be categorised as realised or unrealised. There is no need to distinguish that cumulative balance between amounts charged or credited in the profit and loss account and those recognised in the statement of total recognised gains and losses (STRGL). The entries in the STRGL are considered for this purpose as revisions of past estimates of the net pension cost and are not precluded from being treated as realised simply because they have passed through the STRGL rather than the profit and loss account.   **8.9**

The impact on reserves is not usually the same as the pension asset or liability recognised in the balance sheet. It will be different due to the net contributions paid to the scheme (see 8.15 et seq) and any asset or liability introduced as the result of a business combination (see 8.19 et seq).   **8.10**

A cumulative net debit in reserves in respect of the pension scheme constitutes a realised loss as it results from the creation of, or an increase in, a provision for a liability or loss resulting in an overall reduction in net assets. This follows from 2.32, 3.10 and 3.15(d) above.   **8.11**

A cumulative net credit in reserves in respect of the pension scheme constitutes a realised profit only to the extent that it is represented by an asset to be recovered by refunds that have been agreed by the pension scheme trustees at the balance sheet date of the relevant accounts and the refunds will take the form of qualifying consideration. This follows from 3.9(a) above which refers to 'a transaction where the consideration received by the company is 'qualifying consideration''. An asset that is recognised based on a reduction in future contributions or on expected refunds that are not agreed at the balance sheet date will not meet the definition of 'qualifying consideration'.   **8.12**

8.13 To the extent that a cumulative net credit in reserves exceeds any such agreed refunds it is unrealised, but it becomes realised in subsequent periods to the extent that it offsets subsequent net debits to reserves being recognised as realised losses in respect of the pension scheme (ie as the cumulative net credit reduces). This follows from 3.9(f)(iii) and (iv) above.

8.14 To establish the effect on realised profits at a particular date, a company must therefore establish the cumulative net credit or debit in reserves for the pension scheme at that date. This equals the amount of the surplus or deficit recognised before taking account of deferred tax, adjusted for:

(a) cumulative net contributions less refunds made in respect of the pension scheme; and

(b) in the rare cases in which the company has recognised a pension asset or liability in its individual accounts on the acquisition of an unincorporated business (in respect of the pension scheme of that business), the amount initially recognised (see 8.19 and 8.20 below).

An illustration of such a calculation is set out in Appendix 4. As explained at 8.18 below, it will often be obvious, without any calculations, that all of the amounts included in reserves arising from pension scheme accounting are realised.

8.15 Companies that are able to establish the precise amount of the cumulative net credit or debit in reserves in respect of the pension scheme will treat it as realised or unrealised in accordance with 8.11 to 8.13 above.

8.16 It may not be practicable for companies with long-established schemes to ascertain the total cumulative net contributions less refunds made since the scheme commenced, to perform with precision the analysis in 8.13 above (although, in view of their rarity, it is likely that the company would be able to identify all refunds made and these should be included in the calculation). For such schemes the estimated approach set out in this paragraph may be taken:

(a) the calculation set out in 8.14 above may be performed initially using the amount of those cumulative net contributions the company has been able to identify; and

(b) that calculation may be revisited subsequently, as set out in 8.17 below, if further contributions are identified that were made prior to the date of the assessment.

8.17 A company adopting the estimated approach set out at 8.16 above might be able to revise that estimate subsequently by identifying additional contributions that have been made since the scheme was established or acquired. If so, it may be able to revise upwards the amount of a net cumulative realised loss in reserves and therefore treat as realised net credits arising in subsequent periods that would otherwise be treated as unrealised.

8.18 It will often be obvious, without any calculations, that all of the amounts included in reserves arising from pension scheme accounting are realised. Therefore, no adjustments will be required to the amounts stated in the accounts when determining the cumulative amount of realised profits available for distribution. Other than sometimes in those rare cases where a pension asset or liability has been recognised in the company's individual accounts on a past acquisition, no adjustment is necessary if a liability is recognised in the balance sheet (ie because the net cumulative contributions cannot be negative). Where a pension asset is recognised in the balance sheet, it is only necessary to determine that the cumulative net contributions exceed this amount to be able to confirm that no adjustment is necessary. The calculations are more complex when a past acquisition is involved.

Acquisition of an unincorporated business

Where part of a company's pension asset or liability arose on the acquisition of an unincorporated business, it will have been recorded initially at fair value as required by FRS 7. That initial asset or liability will not have affected the company's reserves directly and must therefore be taken into account as part of the adjustment in arriving at the impact of FRS 17 on reserves. **8.19**

FRS 17 did not change the requirement of FRS 7 to record the pension asset or liability at fair value, although it may have required fair value to be measured using a different method from that used when the acquisition was first recorded. FRS 17 paragraph 97 notes that any difference between the FRS 17 measure of fair value and that originally used 'should be treated as a change in assumptions (ie an actuarial gain or loss) arising since acquisition'. Such a difference will therefore have given rise to a gain or loss that falls to be categorised as realised or unrealised in accordance with the general approach noted above. As a result, it is the asset or liability recognised initially as part of the acquisition accounting that is taken into account (together with the net contributions paid since acquisition) in assessing the reserves position under FRS 17. **8.20**

An actuarial gain arising from a reduction of a pension liability that was assumed in a business combination will result is an unrealised profit to the extent that it is not a reversal of post-acquisition pension expense. That is because such a reduction in a pension liability is not readily convertible to cash (see 3.9(g) and 3.9B). **8.20A**

Deferred tax

The deferred tax asset or liability arising from different treatments of pension costs for accounting and tax purposes generally relates to the pension asset or liability in the balance sheet and is not necessarily associated with the cumulative net debit or credit in reserves. **8.21**

The cumulative debit in reserves in respect of a deferred tax liability relating to a pension asset should be treated as a realised loss. However, to the extent that there is an unrealised cumulative net credit in reserves in respect of the pension asset, then the amount of the debit in respect of deferred tax should be treated as a reduction in that unrealised profit rather than as a realised loss. It is not necessary to restrict the offset by applying the tax rate to the amount of the unrealised profit. **8.22**

The cumulative credit in reserves in respect of a deferred tax asset relating to a pension liability should be treated as an unrealised profit. However, to the extent that there is a realised cumulative net debit in reserves in respect of the pension liability, then the amount of the credit in respect of deferred tax should be treated as a reduction in that realised loss rather than as an unrealised profit. It is not necessary to restrict the offset by applying the tax rate to the amount of the realised loss. **8.23**

The approach set out above is consistent with 3.17 above. **8.24**

Companies with more than one scheme

This guidance assumes the company has only one scheme. A company that operates more than one defined benefit scheme should assess separately for each scheme the impact of an FRS 17 asset or liability on its realised profits and losses. However, there may be situations where two schemes are to merge. In such situations a company may treat any net credit to reserves that has been recorded in respect of one scheme as a reduction in the realised loss caused by a net debit in respect of the other scheme from the point at which the trustees of the schemes have irrevocably agreed that they will merge and to extent that the surplus and **8.25** deficit are permitted to be offset for funding purposes. A similar argument applies in cases where a transfer has been irrevocably agreed between different schemes.

8.26   A company that operates more than one defined benefit scheme may find that it can follow 8.11 to 8.13 above for schemes formed or acquired in an acquisition of an unincorporated business relatively recently but may need to follow 8.16 above for schemes operated by the company for a longer time. This guidance does not preclude such a mixed approach.

9. INTRA-GROUP TRANSACTIONS

Introduction

9.1   Under both common law and statute, distributions are made by companies and not by groups. The group accounts are therefore not relevant for the purpose of determining realisation or distributability; for example, realised profits which are reflected in a parent's[32] own accounts may be eliminated in the group accounts, and profits retained by subsidiaries are not distributable by the parent.

9.2   The ability of a parent to control the actions of its subsidiary must also be borne in mind when considering the substance of an intra-group transaction carried out by or with that subsidiary.

9.3   It is not practicable to attempt to illustrate every circumstance in which difficulties may arise in determining whether a profit is realised. The principles set out in this guidance should be applied in relation to the group company seeking to establish a realised profit. In particular, the principle in paragraph 3.5 (linkage etc) and the related guidance at 3.43 to 3.75 should be applied. The examples which follow are intended to illustrate the factors to be considered in determining whether intra-group transactions give rise to realised profits.

Cash pooling arrangements and group treasury functions

9.4   Groups of companies often operate cash pooling arrangements and group treasury functions. An example of such an arrangement is where a group company acts akin to a banker to other group companies by accepting funds and settling debts on behalf of those group companies. Group companies sometimes do not have their own bank accounts or have accounts which are cleared to a central account, in the name of one group company, at the close of business each day.

9.4A   A group company may recognise a profit on a transaction which results in an increase in the balance due from the group treasury company. The normal considerations apply when assessing whether such a profit is realised. That is to say that the balance must represent qualifying consideration and the profit must arise from a transaction or arrangement that does not fall within paragraph 3.5 of this guidance (e.g.eg, artificial or linked or circular). The nature of such arrangements vary widely in practice. It is always necessary to have regard to the particular facts and circumstances of each case.

9.4B   A group company may have a ""current account"" balance with another group company through which many transactions, both debits and credits, are processed. There may be a considerable ""churn"" on the account even though a substantial balance remains outstanding. The fact that there is no expectation that the core balance will be settled does not preclude transactions processed through the account being realised profits when they

---

[32] *The terms ""parent"" and ""subsidiary"" refer respectively to a ""parent undertaking"" and a ""subsidiary undertaking"" as defined in section 1162 of the Act.*

arise from normal trading transactions in the ordinary course of business. This is because the debit entries to the account arising from these transactions are expected to be (ie, they are foreseen to be) settled by offset with credit entries on the account and therefore the criterion in 3.11(d)(iii) can be regarded as met. However, large or unusual transactions that result in a "'permanent"' increase in the core balance will require careful consideration.

Dividends

Dividend received or receivable on an investment in a subsidiary

For a dividend received or receivable from a subsidiary to be treated as a realised profit, **9.5**
the consideration must be in the form of qualifying consideration. Accounting for dividends receivable and payable, including payment of intra-group dividends through inter-company accounts, is considered at 9.6 *et seq*. It will also be necessary to consider the effect any dividend has on the value of the investment in the subsidiary and, where its recoverable amount has fallen below its book value, to take account of the effect of any such impairment (and, where appropriate, any consequential release from revaluation, merger or other similar reserve).

Accrual of intra-group dividends payable and receivable

The following paragraphs deal with income that is dividend income or appropriation for **9.6**
legal purposes and which for accounting purposes is dealt with as a dividend by the paying and receiving companies (rather than as interest under IAS 32 or FRS 102~~25~~).

A dividend payable is accrued in accordance with IFRIC 17 or FRS 102~~21~~ only when it is **9.7**
"'appropriately authorised and no longer at the discretion of the entity"'. This test will be met when a legally binding liability is established as described at 2.10 above. A dividend will be accrued as receivable by a parent company only when the subsidiary has a legally binding obligation to make the distribution. Paragraph 32.8 of FRS 102~~IAS 10~~ refers to dividends "'declared"' after the end of the reporting period~~balance sheet date~~ with the implication that those "'declared"' before then~~the balance sheet date~~ would be accrued (by both the subsidiary and the parent). However, IFRIC 17 refers to dividends that are declared as those that are "'appropriately authorised and no longer at the discretion of the entity"'. A dividend may therefore have been 'declared' by the directors in the everyday sense of the term but not meet the requirements for recognition in financial statements.

[Deleted] **9.7A**

Paragraph 10(b) of IFRIC 17 states that a dividend is recognised on the date when it is **9.7B**
declared by management or the board, if the law of the jurisdiction does not require further approval. This might have been seen as requiring a change of practice in relation to interim dividends on adoption of IFRIC 17. However, it is generally agreed that this is not so because the requirement to recognise a dividend only when it is no longer at the discretion of the entity takes precedence[33]. Also, it may be said that a UK interim dividend does require further approval by the directors immediately before it is paid because of the effect of their common law duties.

Companies may have to consider paying up (or establishing a legally binding liability to **9.8**
pay) interim dividends before the balance sheet date to ensure that the parent company

---

[33] *Paragraphs BC18–20 of IFRIC 17 explain that the Interpretation does not change the principle on when to recognise a dividend payable. The principle was moved from IAS 10 into the Interpretation and clarified but without changing the principle.*

has adequate distributable reserves to support the expected level of the proposed final dividend.

9.9   [Deleted]

9.10   [Deleted]

9.11   This therefore raises the question as to what constitutes payment of an interim dividend and what steps may be taken to establish a legally binding liability. This will affect the timing of its recognition as a distribution by the paying company and as a profit by the recipient company. The question of whether a profit recorded by the recipient company is a realised profit falls to be determined under the general principles in this guidance, for example, whether it is qualifying consideration.

9.12   Where there is a transfer of cash the answer will be clear as payment has been received. This conclusion would not be affected by the cash being immediately or closely afterwards reinvested in the paying company either by way of loan or by way of capital investment, although the fact of such reinvestment will require consideration of the guidance at 9.19 below as to whether the profit is realised or unrealised in the parent company's hands.

9.13   Where the dividend is recorded on inter-company account and the effect of such an entry reduces the amount recorded as receivable from the parent to the dividend paying subsidiary, this would constitute settlement by way of set-off and would be equivalent to a payment in cash taking place at the date that the book entries were made by both companies (or the later of them if these should be different) to the extent that this does not reduce the amount recorded as receivable from the parent to the dividend-paying subsidiary below nil.

9.14   Where the dividend is recorded on inter-company account and the book entry creates or increases a liability of the paying subsidiary, the question arises as to whether the dividend falls to be treated as paid and received, or a legally binding liability is otherwise established.

9.15   Effecting the dividend via a group treasury function (see 9.4 above) where the subsidiary company instructs the group treasury function to debit the subsidiary's account and credit the parent's account, would constitute payment.

9.16   In other circumstances, more than just entries into the accounting records of the paying and receiving company are likely to be required. If there were no doubt as to the paying subsidiary's ability to pay the dividend, a legally binding liability in respect of an individual dividend could be established by the execution, as a Deed, of an acknowledgment of liability to pay the amount entered in the accounting records as a payable by the subsidiary and a receivable by the parent company or the constitution of such liability pursuant to an enforceable contract under Scots Law.

9.17   Any doubts about whether an interim dividend recorded by book entry is a legally binding liability can be removed by the conversion of the interim dividend into a final dividend before the year end. Under common form articles of association, this will require a recommendation by the directors and the declaration of the dividend either by approval by the members in a general meeting or, for private companies, by the members passing a written resolution.

9.18   In scenarios other than those discussed above, the position is more complex and dependent on the specific facts and circumstances and companies in doubt as to the position may wish to seek legal advice.

Dividend by a subsidiary to a parent which provides or reinvests the funds in the subsidiary

Investment by a parent in a subsidiary which has paid a dividend in the form of qualifying consideration does not in itself preclude that dividend from continuing to be treated as a realised profit by the parent. However, if a subsidiary pays a dividend to a parent which directly or indirectly provides the funds for the dividend or reinvests the proceeds in the subsidiary in circumstances where the transactions or arrangements fall within paragraph 3.5 of this guidance, the dividend will not represent a realised profit for the parent if it does not receive in return for the provision of funds or their reinvestment an asset which is in the form of qualifying consideration. Thus, in such a case, the profit will be unrealised if, for example: **9.19**

(a) the provision or reinvestment of funds is in the form of:

    (i) a subscription for shares, as the subsidiary is in effect capitalising its realised profits; or

    (ii) a capital contribution (ie, a gift); or

    (iii) a loan which does not meet the definition of qualifying consideration in the parent's accounts; or

    (iv) a guarantee of borrowings used to fund the dividend (unless the likelihood that the guarantee will be called upon is remote); or

(b) the subsidiary is unlikely to be able to meet its obligations under any borrowings used to fund the dividend without recourse directly or indirectly to the parent.

~~Dividends received out of pre-acquisition profits~~

[Deleted]~~The Act does not deal specifically with the onward distribution by a parent of dividends out of the pre-acquisition profits of its subsidiaries. Under UK GAAP such dividends should be treated by a parent in the same way as any other dividend which it receives from a subsidiary, including taking account of any impairment in accordance with paragraph 9.5 (see 9.21 below). The position under IFRSs is considered at 9.22 *et seq* below.~~ **9.20**

[Deleted]~~Under UK GAAP, it has for many years been accepted that dividends received out of pre-acquisition profits of subsidiaries are treated as giving rise to a profit unless the dividend causes a diminution in the value of the investment below its book amount. This is separate from the question of whether or not such dividends are realised profits which will depend on whether they have been received in the form of qualifying consideration.~~ **9.21**

[Deleted]~~Under IAS 27, before its amendment in May 2008³⁴, when investments in subsidiaries were stated using the cost model, any dividends received out of their pre-acquisition profits were credited against the cost of investment.~~ **9.22**

[Deleted]~~In May 2008, the IASB issued an amendment to IAS 27 which removed this requirement. At the same time, it also issued an amendment to IFRS 1 which permits the use of the previous GAAP carrying amount of subsidiaries as their deemed cost on transition to IFRSs. When applying the amended Standards there will generally be no adjustment to the carrying amount of the investment in subsidiaries on transition to IFRSs so there is no effect on accumulated realised profits. This is applicable only to a parent that adopted IFRS after that amended version of IFRS 1 was applicable.~~ **9.22A**

---

³⁴ ~~*Amendments to IFRS 1 First-time Adoption of IFRSs and IAS 27 Consolidated and Separate Financial Statements: Cost of an Investment in a Subsidiary, Jointly Controlled Entity or Associate.*~~

9.23   [Deleted]~~On transition to IFRSs, when applying the unamended IAS 27, companies had to determine the extent to which any dividends have been received out of the pre-acquisition profits of their subsidiaries. The May 2008 amendment has, on a prospective basis, removed this requirement and potential source of difficulty.~~

9.24   [Deleted]

9.25   Deleted]

9.26   [Deleted]

9.27   [Deleted]

Sale of an asset by a parent to its subsidiary

9.28   If a parent sells an asset to a subsidiary in circumstances where the transactions or arrangements fall within paragraph 3.5 of this guidance, any profit on the sale of the asset will not represent a realised profit for the parent if it does not receive an asset which is in the form of qualifying consideration. Thus, in such a case, the profit will be unrealised if, for example:

(a)   there is an agreement or understanding regarding the repurchase of the asset by the parent; or

(b)   the parent directly or indirectly provides the funds for the purchase or reinvests the proceeds in the subsidiary where the provision or reinvestment of funds is in the form of:

   (i)   a subscription for shares, as the subsidiary is in effect capitalising realised profits; or

   (ii)   a capital contribution (ie, a gift); or

   (iii) a loan which does not meet the definition of qualifying consideration in the parent's accounts; or

   (iv)   a guarantee of borrowings used to fund the purchase (unless the likelihood that the guarantee will be called upon is remote); or

(c)   the subsidiary is unlikely to be able to meet its obligations under any borrowings used to fund the purchase without recourse directly or indirectly to the parent.

Sale of an asset by a subsidiary to a parent followed by a dividend to the parent of the resulting profit

9.29   The subsidiary should apply factors similar to those in paragraph 9.28 in determining whether it has made a realised profit on the sale of an asset to its parent.

9.30   If a subsidiary sells an asset to its parent and pays a dividend out of the resulting profit in circumstances where the transactions or arrangements, from the parent's perspective, fall within paragraph 3.5 of this guidance, the dividend will not give rise to a realised profit for the parent unless the asset which the parent purchased meets the definition of qualifying consideration. This is because the overall commercial effect of such an arrangement for the parent is similar to a dividend in kind (see paragraph 9.33).

Sale of an asset by a subsidiary to a fellow subsidiary followed by a dividend to the parent of the resulting profit

9.31   The subsidiary should apply factors similar to those in paragraph 9.28 in determining whether it has made a realised profit on the sale of an asset to its fellow subsidiary.

If a subsidiary sells an asset to a fellow subsidiary and pays a dividend to the parent out **9.32** of the resulting profit in circumstances where the transactions or arrangements, from the parent's perspective, fall within paragraph 3.5 of this guidance, the dividend will not give rise to a realised profit for the parent if, for example:

(a)   the parent directly or indirectly provides the funds for the purchase where the provision of funds is in the form of:

  (i)   a subscription for shares, as the subsidiary is in effect capitalising its retained profits; or

  (ii)   a capital contribution (ie, a gift); or

  (iii)   a loan which does not meet the definition of qualifying consideration in the parent's accounts; or

(b)   the parent directly or indirectly reinvests the dividend (or equivalent consideration) in the subsidiary which paid the dividend or the fellow subsidiary to which the asset was sold and the asset which the parent receives from this reinvestment is not in the form of qualifying consideration; or

(c)   the parent directly or indirectly guarantees any borrowings used to provide either the fellow subsidiary with the consideration for its purchase of the asset or the vendor subsidiary with funds for its dividend (in either case unless the likelihood that the guarantee will be called upon is remote) or the subsidiary in question is unlikely to be able to meet its obligations under the borrowings without recourse directly or indirectly to the parent.

Dividend in kind

A dividend in kind from a subsidiary is an unrealised profit in the hands of the parent **9.33** (even where there is a cash alternative) unless the asset distributed meets the definition of qualifying consideration. However, if the non-cash asset is distributed by the parent then, following section 846, that unrealised profit would be treated by the parent as a realised profit for the purpose of that onward distribution, provided that the profit was recorded in the relevant accounts.

Return of capital contribution

Where a capital contribution is returned directly or indirectly to the donor company in **9.34** circumstances where the transactions or arrangements fall within paragraph 3.5 of this guidance, it will not give rise to a realised profit in the hands of the donor.

Transfer of an asset for consideration followed by waiver of the resulting inter-company debt

A group company may transfer an asset to another group company for consideration **9.34A** but subsequently waive the resulting inter-company debt. In such a case, if the purchase and release are part of a group or series of transactions or arrangements falling within paragraph 3.5 of this guidance, any profit will not represent a realised profit unless the asset originally acquired met the definition of qualifying consideration or has been disposed of for qualifying consideration. For example, where the substance of the arrangements taken together (e.g. eg. where the waiver is a step in the plan even if undocumented) is to transfer a fixed asset for no consideration, any profit recorded by the transferee company on the debt waiver will not be a realised profit. Instead, the profit is in the nature of a revaluation of an asset acquired at no cost.

Debits within equity arising on group reconstructions

9.35   Business combinations involving entities or businesses under common control are excluded from the scope of IFRS 3, "'Business combinations''". Typical examples include a group reorganisation involving either a transfer of a company within a group or the transfer of a business from one group member to another.

9.36   When a company carries out a <u>business combination</u>transaction under common control[35] such as acquiring the business of another company within the same group, the directors may determine that it is not appropriate to recognise the net assets acquired at their fair values and that it is not appropriate to recognise goodwill. For example, a company may purchase the trade and assets of a division from its parent company, the consideration being a combination of cash and shares. The directors may determine that the appropriate accounting is to recognise the net assets acquired at the transferor's book amounts. The consideration paid, say, measured at the nominal value of the shares issued plus the value of the cash element, may exceed the book amount of the net assets acquired and this will leave a debit difference to be recognised. It is not goodwill. The debit is sometimes referred to as a "'merger difference''" and is recorded in equity.

9.37   A business combination involving members of the same group is completed under the direction of the controlling party, the common parent. Consequently, any excess paid by the acquirer over the book amount of the vendor's net assets is accounted for in a similar manner to a distribution or return of capital to the common parent. Distributions and returns of capital are dealt with through equity, and therefore it is logical also to recognise the debit in equity.

9.38   Such a debit directly to equity is not necessarily, however, a distribution as a matter of law. This is because the debit described above is determined on a book basis, whereas the question as to whether there would be an actual distribution is determined by whether the company gives consideration other than an issue of its shares, to its parent or a fellow subsidiary, with a fair value in excess of the fair value of the net assets and business acquired. Accordingly the debit may form part of an actual distribution or may not.

9.39   In a case where the debit in equity does not form part of an actual distribution, then at the date of acquisition the debit does not represent a loss; the acquiring company has purchased net assets worth at least the book value of the consideration given but, under the appropriate accounting, has recognised these at a lower amount. The difference between the two is the amount of the debit. As the debit is not a loss at all, it is neither realised nor unrealised.

9.40   To the extent that the assets, if they had been recognised at the higher amount, would have been written down, say, by depreciation or impairment, an equivalent amount of the debit becomes a realised loss. It is a realised, rather than unrealised, loss because, had the debit been carried as an asset, any write down for depreciation or impairment would be required, by section 841 and the principles of realisation (see section 3), to be regarded as realised.

9.41   The above guidance is written in the context of IFRS 3 but is equally applicable to a group reconstruction accounted for under FRS 102.

Additional consideration for a public company

9.42   For a public company, the initial recognition of the debit will restrict the maximum amount of profits available for distribution to the extent the cash paid out (or the book

---

[35] *As defined in IFRS 3.*

value of other non-equity consideration given) is greater than the book value of the net assets acquired. This is because the acquirer's net assets as shown in the company's relevant accounts for section 836 purposes would be reduced as a result of paying out cash consideration but increased by a smaller amount by recognising the acquired net assets at a lower amount. Since the debit is neither a realised loss nor an unrealised loss it has no effect on the "'share capital and undistributable reserves²' part of the section 831 net assets test. Consequently, the maximum permissible distribution would be restricted.

Merger relief and group reconstruction relief

As explained at 2.11 above, when shares are issued as consideration for the acquisition of a subsidiary, the issuing company may benefit from merger relief (section 612 of the Act) or group reconstruction relief (section 611 of the Act). In accordance with section 615 of the Act, under FRS 102~~UK GAAP~~, such companies may state the cost of investment at the nominal value of the shares issued (for merger relief) or based on the minimum premium value (for group reconstruction relief). Under IFRSs, the interaction of these reliefs with the accounting for the acquired asset is complicated. **9.43**

The IASB published amendments to IFRS 1 and IAS 27 in May 2008³⁶ that had implications for the treatment of merger relief and group reconstruction relief for accounting purposes. The amendments were effective for annual periods beginning on or after 1 January 2009. The effect of these amendments is described at 9.44A to 9.44D below. **9.43A**

Before the amendment in May 2008, IAS 27 was generally considered to require the acquired asset to be booked at fair value in some or all cases. Therefore, on transition to IFRSs, it was necessary to gross up the cost of investment to the fair value at the date of acquisition and to recognise a corresponding "'merger reserve²'. Although different views were expressed on this financial reporting issue, the following paragraph deals with the treatment for distributable profit purposes when the merger reserve is recorded. **9.43B**

The adjustment to establish the merger reserve will have no direct impact on accumulated realised profits because the reserve will represent an unrealised profit. However, the reserve may become realised at a later date. This may, for example, occur on disposal of the investment for qualifying consideration or if the investment is written down for impairment. **9.44**

In May 2008, the IASB issued an amendment to IFRS 1 which permits the use of the previous GAAP carrying amount of subsidiaries as their deemed cost on transition to IFRSs. If the exemption in the amended IFRS 1 is used, there is no adjustment to the carrying amount of the investment on transition to IFRSs and consequently no effect on accumulated realised profits. The amendment had no effect on a company that had already adopted IFRSs in a period before the amended standard was first applied. **9.44A**

In May 2008, the IASB also amended IAS 27 to insert a new requirement for the accounting treatment to be adopted by a new parent company (including an intermediate parent company) established as a result of a group reorganisation when certain criteria are met. When these criteria are met³⁷, the new parent accounts for the cost of its investment **9.44B**

---

³⁶ *Amendments to IFRS 1 First-time Adoption of IFRSs and IAS 27 Consolidated and Separate Financial Statements: Cost of an Investment in a Subsidiary, Jointly Controlled Entity or Associate. These amendments are separate from the revision of IAS 27, which was published in January 2008, that has no effect on the accounting in the separate financial statements of a parent.*

³⁷ *The new requirement will not apply to all group reorganisations involving the establishment of a new parent company because it applies only if all of three specified criteria are met. Reorganisations may, in practice, fail one or more of the tests.*

in the original parent [11] *at the carrying amount of its share of the equity items shown in the separate financial statements of the original parent at the date of the reorganisation[11]*. In practice, this means that the new parent company will record the cost of its investment in the original parent at an amount equal to the IFRS net asset value of the original parent as shown in its separate financial statements at the date of the reorganisation. This will usually differ from both the fair value of the investment and the amount that might have been recorded under UK GAAP taking into account merger relief or group reconstruction relief (see 9.43 above).

9.44C   The amendment required only prospective application to reorganisations occurring in annual periods beginning on or after 1 January 2009. No restatement was required for past reorganisations although this was permitted provided that all subsequent past reorganisations meeting the relevant criteria are restated in accordance with the amended standard.

9.44D   For future reorganisations, the application of the new requirement may have the effect of restricting the ability of a public company to make distributions because the net assets of the new parent company may (depending on the circumstances) be stated at an amount that is less than its share capital and undistributable reserves. However, for reorganisations not meeting the criteria in the amended IAS 27 and for other acquisitions, the guidance at 9.43B and 9.44 above continues to apply.

Intragroup loans on off-market terms

9.45   The accounting treatment of some intragroup loans will change on adoption of FRS 102 compared with old (non-FRS 26) UK GAAP. The accounting treatment required by FRS 102 is the same as that required under IFRSs. This will apply to interest free loans and other loans not at a market rate of interest unless they are repayable on demand. In summary, this treatment results in initial recognition of capital contributions and distributions for accounting purposes together with the recognition of imputed interest income and expense over the life of the loan. Where the loans are at a market rate, no initial accounting issues arise as the initial carrying amount, being the present value of the future cash flows discounted at the market rate, will equate to the sum advanced.

9.46   Transactions affected by these requirements may take a variety of forms. They may involve payment of interest at above or below market rates. They may take the form of loans from a parent to its subsidiary or from a subsidiary to its parent or from one subsidiary to a fellow subsidiary. For simplicity, the following description assumes that the loans are interest free, but the same principles apply in other cases.

Interest-free loan from parent to subsidiary

9.47   If a parent advances a cash sum as an interest-free loan to its subsidiary, the accounting treatment may be summarised as follows:

- the parent recognises a loan receivable equal to the present value of the future cash flows discounted at the market rate of interest;
- the parent debits the cost of investment in its subsidiary with the amount of the capital contribution, being the difference between the above and the sum advanced;
- the subsidiary recognises a loan payable at the same amount as that recorded by the parent and credits equity with the amount of the capital contribution, being the difference between that and the sum advanced;
- the parent recognises interest income equal to the amount of the capital contribution over the term of the loan; and

- the subsidiary recognises interest expense equal to the amount of the capital contribution over the term of the loan.

The parent's debit to the cost of investment in the subsidiary has no distributable profit implications, assuming that it does not result in a need to write down the investment for impairment.

9.48

The credit to equity in the subsidiary's accounts is not an accounting profit. As a matter of law, there is not a profit either because the proceeds received are in consideration for taking on a liability (ie, in accordance with the legal form of the transaction rather than its substance, which determines the accounting treatment). The credit to equity, being neither an accounting profit nor a profit in law, is, therefore, not a realised profit. This conclusion is consistent with the guidance on a compound financial instrument at paragraphs 6.19 and 6.20 above.

9.49

The interest expense recognised by the subsidiary is an accounting charge, which is not, as a matter of law, a loss. The cumulative debit within equity arising from this additional charge is available to eliminate the initial credit to equity for the capital contribution (see paragraph 9.49 above). This conclusion is consistent with the guidance on a compound financial instrument at paragraphs 6.19 and 6.20 above.

9.50

The interest income recognised by the parent (ie, accruing the recognised asset up to the sum repayable at maturity) is, as a matter of principle, not considered a linked transaction. This is because:

9.51

- the loan has not been made with the intention, or purpose, to facilitate the payment of the interest (see paragraph 3.59 above); and
- the time between advance and repayment is such that circumstances of the subsidiary may change and repayment will not be made, ie, default (see paragraph 3.75 above).

This conclusion assumes that the loan has been entered into for genuine business purposes rather than with the specific intention of creating distributable reserves.

If making the loan and making the capital contribution are not regarded as linked transactions, the interest income recognised by the parent, being a profit recognised under paragraph 3.8(a) above, will be a realised profit. This is different from the treatment of the capital contribution (see paragraph 9.49 above) because that is not a profit as defined in paragraph 3.8 above.

9.52

Interest-free loan from subsidiary to parent

If a subsidiary advances a cash sum as an interest-free loan to its parent, the accounting treatment may be summarised as follows:

9.53

- the subsidiary recognises a loan receivable equal to the present value of the future cash flows discounted at a market rate of interest;
- the subsidiary recognises a distribution made to its parent, being the difference between the above and the sum advanced;
- the parent recognises a loan payable at the same amount as recorded by the subsidiary and a distribution received from the subsidiary, being the difference between that and the sum advanced;
- the parent recognises interest expense equal to the amount of the distribution over the term of the loan; and
- the subsidiary recognises interest income equal to the amount of the distribution over the term of the loan.

9.54   Consistent with the analysis set out at paragraph 9.50 above, making the loan and making the distribution should not be regarded as linked transactions. Therefore:

- the receipt of the distribution by the parent will be a realised profit;
- the interest expense recognised by the parent will be a realised loss; and
- the interest income recognised by the subsidiary will be a realised profit.

9.55   This transaction is accounted for as a distribution by the subsidiary. It is also a distribution as a matter of law because it is at undervalue. This is necessarily, and therefore intentionally, the effect of an interest-free loan. It is unrealistic to suppose that those terms arose other than as a result of the parent–subsidiary relationship (see paragraphs 2.6A and 2.6B above). An interest-free loan which is legally repayable on demand may also be a distribution as a matter of law if it is at undervalue (eg, if there is no ability to repay it immediately) even though there is no distribution for accounting purposes.

Interest-free loan from subsidiary to fellow subsidiary

9.56   When one subsidiary makes an interest-free loan to another subsidiary, the first subsidiary accounts for making a distribution and the second subsidiary accounts for the receipt of a capital contribution. This raises no new issues not already considered at paragraphs 9.45 to 9.55 above. The parent does not generally record any accounting entries.

10. MISCELLANEOUS ISSUES

Profits and losses arising from equity accounting IAS 27, IAS 28 and IAS 31 – Separate financial statements

10.1   The balance of profits available for distribution is that available to the company, not to the group. The availability of such profits is to be judged by reference to accounts which must therefore be the company's individual accounts.

10.2   IFRS permits the use of equity accounting for subsidiaries, associates and joint ventures in separate financial statements and thus a company's individual accounts. However, the share of profits of subsidiaries, associates and joint ventures is not a realised profit except to the extent that it is received as distributions in the form of qualifying consideration. Therefore, the amount of a company's accumulated realised profits will be the same irrespective of whether equity accounting is used in the IAS individual accounts.

10.3   Cumulative losses arising from equity accounting (ie, those that are not the reversal of profits from equity accounting) should be regarded as realised losses to the extent that a loss would be recorded for impairment of the investment had equity accounting not been used. The balance of profits available for distribution is that available to the company, not to its group. The availability of such profits is to be judged by reference to accounts, which must therefore be the company's individual accounts. Except when initial or interim accounts are required, the 'relevant accounts' for this purpose are the individual accounts forming part of the annual accounts, whether they are 'Companies Act individual accounts' or 'IAS individual accounts' (see section 2 above).

10.2   IFRSs do not use the term 'individual accounts' but uses the term 'separate financial statements' which are defined in IAS 27 as follows:

'Separate financial statements are those presented by a parent, an investor in an associate or a venturer in a jointly controlled entity, in which the investments are accounted for on the basis of the direct equity interests rather than on the basis of the reported results and net assets of the investee.'

~~Where a company prepares consolidated financial statements, these 'separate financial statements' will be the company's 'IAS individual accounts' for the purposes of section 395 and therefore the relevant accounts under section 836 for the purposes of justifying any distribution.~~ **10.3**

~~However, where a company has an associate or jointly controlled entity but has no subsidiaries, in some circumstances IAS 28 and/or IAS 31, when considered outside the EU legal framework, require the preparation of financial statements that are neither separate financial statements nor consolidated financial statements. In such financial statements, the investments in associates and jointly controlled entities are accounted for using the equity method or proportional consolidation as appropriate (see IAS 28(4) and IAS 31(5)). In these circumstances, the company is not required by IFRSs (when considered outside of the EU legal framework) to prepare separate financial statements. One point of view is that the financial statements including investments on the basis of equity accounting and/ or proportional consolidation are not relevant for the purposes of justifying distributions and that the "separate financial statements" are the 'IAS individual accounts'.~~ **10.4**

~~Within the EU legal framework, an alternative point of view is that the financial statements required by IAS 28 and IAS 31 (ie those including investments on the basis of equity accounting and/or proportional consolidation) are a company's 'IAS individual accounts'. The Institutes have to date not been able to establish which view is the correct interpretation of the law and of EU-adopted IFRSs. The European Commission's Accounting Regulatory Committee has considered some related issues but has so far not provided clear guidance on this specific point.~~ **10.5**

~~Were the accounts including the equity accounting to be the 'IAS individual accounts', the share of results of associates/jointly-controlled-entities is not realised save to the extent that it is received as distributions in the form of qualifying consideration. Therefore the amount of a company's accumulated realised profits will be the same irrespective of which interpretation of the law is correct.~~ **10.6**

[10.4 to 10.6 deleted]

[10.7 to 10.16 moved to 2.32 *et seq* and amended.]

IFRS 1 – Fair value or revaluation as deemed cost on transition

Under IFRS 1 (and FRS 102), a first-time adopter may elect to measure an item of property, plant and equipment at the date of transition to IFRSs at its fair value and to use that fair value as deemed cost. A first-time adopter may also elect to use a previous GAAP valuation of an item of property, plant and equipment subject to various conditions. ~~For example, it would be possible for a company that was carrying a property at a 'frozen valuation' under the transitional provisions of FRS 15 to deem that valuation as cost on transition to IFRSs.~~ These elections are also available for investment property when a company elects to use the cost model under IAS 40 and also, in certain limited circumstances, for intangible assets. **10.17**

IFRS 1 does not specify the treatment of any revaluation reserve existing under previous GAAP or of any excess of fair value over cost when the election is used to measure the asset at fair value at the date of transition. However, it is clear that this should not be presented as a revaluation surplus because the asset is regarded as held at cost (and, for example, any subsequent fall in value would have to be charged in the income statement rather than treated as a reversal of a revaluation surplus). In the absence of any other requirement in IFRS 1, the adjustment on transition may be reflected in retained earnings. **10.18**

10.18A   Similar considerations apply to the exemptions available on first-time adoption of FRS 101 and FRS 102. However, in those cases, the company will be applying the statutory alternative accounting rules and therefore the excess of the valuation over depreciated cost is presented as a revaluation reserve even though the assets are said to be at 'cost'.

10.19   Nevertheless, the treatment of a revaluation as deemed cost for the purposes of IFRSs does not alter the nature of the revaluation surplus which will usually be unrealised. Therefore, companies that elect for this treatment will have to keep an analysis of the balance of retained earnings to ensure that they can identify the amount of unrealised profit included. The unrealised profit will become realised as the asset is depreciated or written down for impairment, or is sold for qualifying consideration. This is consistent with the application of section 841(5) which is summarised at 2.35 above.

10.20   The assets that are included on the basis of fair value or revaluation as deemed cost may have been depreciated under UK GAAP. Consider a tangible fixed asset that cost £100 and, at the date of transition to IFRSs, had a net book value of £50. Suppose that the fair value at the date of transition is £120 and the company elects to use this as deemed cost. The excess above original cost of £20 is clearly unrealised. It might be argued that the other £50 of the adjustment is a realised profit because it reverses the depreciation that had previously been charged as a realised loss. However, this analysis is not appropriate because the restatement to fair value is in the nature of a revaluation and it is generally accepted that depreciation is not written back to the profit and loss account on a revaluation. ~~This is implicit in paragraph 63 of FRS 15.~~ Similarly, when a previous valuation is treated as deemed cost, nothing of substance has occurred to cause the previously unrealised profit to become realised. This situation may be contrasted with an adjustment to depreciation that arises from a change in accounting policy for depreciation to comply with IAS 16 (see *Changes to depreciation policies* at 10.21 below). It may be possible to argue that some component of the restatement to deemed cost relates to a reconsideration of residual values and is therefore a realised profit (see 10.22 below). But, in practice, it would not usually be practicable to distinguish this component.

~~IFRS 1 and IAS 16—~~*Changes to depreciation policies on transition*

10.21   Depreciation policies under FRS 15, FRS 102 and IAS 16 are likely to be similar and only rarely will adjustments be necessary to those policies on transition between these GAAPs. A potential exception to this rule relates to the basis of determination of residual value.~~Under IFRS 1, any change in estimated useful life or depreciation pattern is accounted for prospectively from the date that the change of estimate is made provided that the depreciation methods and rates under previous GAAP are acceptable under IFRSs. However, in some cases, a company's depreciation methods and rates under previous GAAP may not be acceptable under IFRSs. If those differences have a material effect on the financial statements, the company adjusts the accumulated depreciation in its opening IFRS balance sheet retrospectively so that it complies with IFRSs (see IFRS 1 IG7).~~

10.22   The requirements of IAS 16 and FRS 102 are, in general, similar to those of FRS 15 ~~and so the depreciation methods and rates used for UK GAAP will usually be acceptable under IFRSs~~. However, a difference may arise because of the different way in which residual value is measured in the standards. Under FRS 15, residual values were~~are~~ based on the prices prevailing at the date of acquisition or revaluation of the asset. Under IAS 16 and FRS 102, they are based on prices prevailing at the balance sheet date. Therefore, in general, cumulative depreciation will be lower under IAS 16 and FRS 102~~IFRSs~~ assuming that prices are rising with inflation. Where such an effect is material, and an adjustment is made to reduce accumulated depreciation, the adjustment will be regarded as a realised profit because it represents the reversal of a previous realised loss.

IFRS 1—Deferred tax on business combinations

The requirements of IFRS 1 and IFRS 3 for business combinations will generally be relevant only to the consolidated financial statements and therefore have no effect on distributable profits. However, in some cases it is necessary to account for a business combination in the individual accounts of a company, for example where it acquires an unincorporated business. **10.23**

In some circumstances, IFRS 1 may require deferred tax to be provided in respect of assets or liabilities acquired through a previous business combination. For example, in many instances no deferred tax would have been provided on the revaluation of tangible fixed assets to fair value under old UK GAAP but such a provision would be required under IFRSs. When the company is not required to restate the business combination in accordance with IFRS 3 and uses this exemption, the deferred tax provision still has to be recognised but is adjusted against retained earnings rather than against goodwill. **10.24**

The tax provision will reduce accumulated realised profits available for distribution where the transaction involved the acquisition of an unincorporated business by an individual company. It does not matter that the tax provision would not have been treated in this way had IFRS 3 been applied. It is the accounting that has actually been applied in the relevant accounts, in accordance with applicable accounting standards, which affects the amount of profits available for distribution. **10.25**

A similar issue can arise on transition to FRS 102 and similar considerations apply. **10.25A**

IFRS 1—Past capitalisation of revaluation reserve

~~SUnder UK GAAP,~~ some companies have revalued assets, in particular properties and investments in subsidiaries, and subsequently capitalised all or part of the resulting revaluation reserve through a bonus issue of shares. The issue that arises on transition to IFRSs or FRS 102 is the status of the debit entry in reserves if revalued assets are restated to a cost basis. **10.26**

Investment properties and property, plant and equipment

~~Under SSAP 19, investment properties are required to be included in the balance sheet at their open market value. Under FRS 15, companies that chose to adopt a policy of revaluation for classes of tangible fixed assets (property, plant and equipment) have to ensure that those assets are carried at their current value at the balance sheet date. On transition to IFRSs, companies are not required to continue to apply a revaluation policy for their investment properties or property, plant and equipment. In effect, IFRS 1 allows companies on transition to IFRSs to state their investment properties or property, plant and equipment at depreciated historical cost, or, in the case of property, plant and equipment, at a 'deemed cost' that could be a previous valuation or fair value at the date of transition. This guidance addresses the position where a company chooses to restate to depreciated historical cost. In the case of a transition using a 'deemed cost' the revaluation survives transition and there is no restatement to consider.~~On transition to IFRSs or FRS 102, a company is permitted to make different accounting policy choices about the revaluation of certain assets. For example, a company that has previously had a policy of revaluing property, plant and equipment may decide to revert to historical cost accounting for those assets. Similarly, a company ~~which~~that has previously revalued its investment in subsidiaries may decide to restate them on the basis of cost less impairment. **10.27**

Where the revaluation surplus has not been used at all for a bonus issue of shares and is still recorded in the balance sheet at the date of transition to IFRSs, the adjustment required **10.28** will be simply to eliminate the revaluation reserve and reduce the revalued assets by the same amount to restate them to their depreciated historical cost. However, if the revaluation surplus has been capitalised, in full or in part, through a past bonus issue of shares, it will not be possible to reduce the reserve in this way. Neither is it possible to apply the debit to reduce share capital by the amount of the bonus shares. The question therefore arises as to the status of the debit entry in reserves arising from reversal of the past revaluation.

10.29   Paragraph 3.15(c) above states that, with two exceptions explained at 2.33 and 23.36, realised losses will include the writing down, or providing for depreciation, amortisation, diminution in value or impairment of an asset. However, the entry to reverse the previous revaluation surplus is not depreciation or amortisation. It also does not relate to the diminution in the value of the assets or impairment but instead relates to a reduction in the amount at which those assets are recorded in the balance sheet. The actual value of the assets remains unchanged.

10.30   The exception described at 2.36 is as follows:

> If an asset is revalued downwards below its recoverable amount, as defined in FRS 102++ or IAS 36, then the difference between that revalued amount and recoverable amount is treated as an unrealised loss as it reflects a revaluation adjustment rather than a provision as defined in section 841-. Such a loss would become realised in the event of a subsequent scrapping, disposal or impairment of the asset.

10.31   This principle may be applied to the restatement of a revalued asset to its depreciated historical cost. Therefore the debit entry to reserves arising from such a restatement (which equates to the revaluation element of the carrying value that is not yet depreciated) will be an unrealised loss provided that the recoverable amount of the asset is equal to or greater than the book amount prior to the restatement. To the extent that the revaluation surplus still exists as an unrealised reserve, the unrealised loss will simply eliminate that unrealised reserve. To the extent that the revaluation surplus has been utilised, in part or in full, for a bonus issue of shares, the resulting net debit entry will represent an unrealised loss.

10.32   The entry to reverse the previous revaluation surplus is not a provision for the purposes of applying section 841(2). In the case of Companies Act individual accounts, "'provisions of a kind specified for the purposes of this paragraph by regulations under section 396 (except revaluation provisions)'" are treated as realised losses. In the case of "'IAS individual accounts'", "'provisions of any kind (except revaluation provisions)'" are treated as realised losses. The entry to reverse the previous revaluation surplus is not a provision of the kind specified by the regulations under section 396 and is not a provision at all in the sense that the term is used for accounting purposes. On the restatement to historical cost there will be no provision deducted from the asset.

Investments in subsidiaries

10.33   Under the alternative accounting rules in the Accounting Regulations, investments in subsidiaries may be stated 'at a market value determined as at the date of their last valuation' or 'at a value determined on any basis which appears to the directors to be appropriate in the circumstances of the company'. There is no obligation under the law or UK accounting standards to keep such valuations up to date although it is necessary to consider whether the assets have become impaired. Under IFRSs, two accounting policies are available for investments in subsidiaries. The first policy is that of cost, using the IAS 27 cost method. The second is to account for such investments in accordance with IAS 39. This would require such investments to be maintained at fair value. In practice, the measurement of such equity investments at fair value may be precluded because the range of reasonable fair value estimates is significant and the probabilities of the various estimates cannot reasonably be assessed (see IAS 39, AG 80-81). Even where such a policy is possible, it will require valuations to be obtained each time a balance sheet is drawn up. This is likely to be unattractive to most companies. Therefore, most companies hold subsidiaries at cost, as determined under IAS 27.[Deleted]

[Deleted]Hence the guidance on the effect of a restatement to depreciated historical cost of a previously revalued investment property or tangible fixed asset is equally applicable to a restatement of previously revalued investments in subsidiaries on to an IAS 27 cost basis. **10.34**

Effect of restatements for a public company

For a public company, the restatement of a revalued asset (whether investment property, other property, plant and equipment or investment in subsidiaries) to a cost basis will restrict its profits available for distribution under section 831 to the extent that the revaluation surplus was capitalised. The effect of the unrealised loss on the restriction imposed by section 831 may be mitigated by the existence of recognised unrealised profits. **10.35**

IAS 11 – Accounting for construction contracts

Under old UK GAAP (SSAP 9), accounting for profit on long-term contracts results in debtor balances described as "'Amounts recoverable on contracts'". This treatment was adopted when the standard was revised in 1988 because legal advice suggested that it was not possible to include the profit element in work-in-progress because of the requirement to state work-in-progress at cost. **10.36**

The accounting required for construction contracts under IAS 11 and FRS 102 is broadly similar to that required by SSAP 9 (although the scope of the requirementsstandards is different). However, IAS 11 and FRS 102 areis not specific as to the nature of the asset to be recognised. In practice the item may simply be disclosed as "'construction contracts'" although it may also be included within debtors or within work-in-progress. **10.37**

Under old UK GAAP it wasis usually clear that the debtor balance for "'Amounts recoverable on contracts'" metmeets the definition of "'qualifying consideration'" (see 3.11 above). Therefore profit recognised on such contracts wasis regarded as a realised profit. On the basis that this treatment has been generally accepted under old UK GAAP, any profits recognised in accordance with IAS 11 or FRS 102 should be regarded as realised profits, irrespective of how the asset is described in the balance sheet. **10.38**

IFRIC 12 Service Concession Arrangements (and the equivalent requirements of FRS 102) may require a profit to be recognised by the operator in accordance with IAS 11 in relation to the construction or upgrading of the infrastructure to be used to provide a public service. Whether any such profit is a realised profit will depend on whether a financial asset or an intangible asset is recognised in accordance with IFRIC 12 or FRS 102. This is more fully explained at 10.65 to 10.68 below. **10.38A**

IAS 12 – Income taxes – Deferred tax

[Deleted – see 3.17 to 3.17D]]As stated at 3.17 above, a provision for deferred tax should generally be regarded as a realised loss. However, when assets are revalued to their fair value, with any gain being recorded in the profit and loss account even though regarded as unrealised, the deferred tax on that gain should be treated as a reduction in that unrealised gain rather than as a realised loss (paragraph 14 of Appendix III to FRS 19 *Deferred tax*). **10.39**

10.40   [Deleted]~~This principle is also applicable to deferred tax provisions recognised under IAS 12, irrespective of whether profits are recognised in profit or loss, or direct in equity. For many financial instruments, profits arising from fair value accounting are realised profits (see Section 4 above). Any attributable deferred tax provision will be a realised loss.~~

10.41   [Deleted]~~Deferred tax is more often recognised on unrealised profits under IFRSs than under UK GAAP. For example, the remeasurement of investment property at fair value will result in unrealised profits (see Section 4 above) on which deferred tax will have to be provided. Such a deferred tax provision is treated as a reduction in the unrealised profit rather than as a realised loss.~~

10.42   ~~When a convertible debt instrument is accounted for using 'split accounting' (see *Convertible debt* at 6.59 et seq above), a deferred tax provision is established and debited against the initial carrying amount of the equity component in accordance with paragraph 23 of IAS 12. This occurs if the tax base of the debt is its full amount but the book amount is lower by the amount of the equity component. The deferred tax provision reverses through profit or loss over the life of the instrument as illustrated in Example 4 in Appendix B to IAS 12. It does not represent a future cash outflow for payment of tax. The deferred tax provision should be treated as a reduction in the credit to equity rather than as a realised loss. The equity component of the financial instrument is not a profit at all and therefore does not fall to be classified as realised or unrealised (see *Convertible debt* at 6.59 et seq above). An adjustment to such an item does not affect realised profits.~~[Deleted]

10.43   ~~In some cases it may be necessary to provide for current tax on an unrealised profit. A current tax provision should be treated as a realised loss even if it arises from the taxation of an unrealised profit. This is because a provision for current tax represents a specific cash outflow that will arise irrespective of whether the related profit is realised or not.~~[Deleted]

Property, plant and equipment – asset swaps

10.44   One or more items of property, plant and equipment may be acquired in exchange for a non-monetary asset or assets, or a combination of monetary and non-monetary assets. IAS 16 requires the cost of such an item of property, plant and equipment to be measured at fair value unless the transaction lacks commercial substance or the fair value of neither the asset received nor the asset given up is reliably measurable. IAS 16 provides guidance on the circumstances in which the fair value of an asset is reliably measurable for this purpose.

10.45   A profit may therefore be recognised on such an exchange transaction in accordance with IFRSs. This profit is likely to be unrealised because an item of property, plant and equipment is unlikely to meet the definition of "'qualifying consideration'" (see 3.11 above).

10.46   When a combination of property, plant and equipment and qualifying consideration (~~e.g.~~eg. cash) is received, the guidance at 3.18 above on "'top-slicing'" will be relevant.

10.47   Any profit treated as unrealised, becomes realised as the related asset is depreciated, written down for impairment or sold for qualifying consideration.

10.48   A loss arising on such a transaction is usually a realised loss. However, in some cases the loss may be similar in substance to an unrealised revaluation deficit (see 2.28 above).

10.49   For example, if a factory used in a business was exchanged for a similar factory and a loss recognised under IAS 16 by reference to the market value of the factories, the loss will be unrealised if there would have been no need to write down the original factory for impairment because its value in use was higher than its market value. It will also be necessary to consider the value in use of the new factory which might be different from the value in use of the old factory, even though their market value is the same (~~e.g.~~eg. because one is larger than the other).

IAS 38 provides for the same accounting treatment for swaps of intangibles as that under IAS 16 in respect of property, plant and equipment, and therefore the foregoing analysis also applies to intangibles under IAS 38.   **10.50**

FRS 102 includes similar requirements to those of IFRSs~~There are no specific requirements in UK accounting standards dealing with such asset swaps~~. The above guidance is relevant to any profit recognised under UK GAAP although it should be noted that only profits realised at the balance sheet date may be included in the profit and loss account in accordance with the Accounting Regulations[38] (although the fair value accounting rules make an exception to this general rule).   **10.51**

Revenue – Barter transactions

Some barter transaction result in the recognition of revenue and profit in accordance with applicable accounting standards. The following guidance is applicable in such cases under IFRSs and UK GAAP. However, under UK GAAP it should be noted that only profits realised at the balance sheet date may be included in the profit and loss account in accordance with the Accounting Regulations[39].~~When goods are sold or services rendered in exchange for dissimilar goods or services, the exchange is regarded as a transaction that generates revenue in accordance with IAS 18. The revenue is measured at the fair value of the goods or services received, adjusted by the amount of any cash or cash equivalents transferred. When the fair value cannot be measured reliably, the revenue is measured at the fair value of the goods or services given up, adjusted by the amount of any cash or cash equivalents transferred.~~   **10.52**

When an asset is received, in determining whether any profit on such an exchange is realised or unrealised, it is necessary to determine whether such asset meets the definition of qualifying consideration. For example, when a property is received, it will be straightforward to assess whether or not it meets the definition of qualifying consideration. Any profit will not become realised until that property is depreciated, written down for impairment or sold for qualifying consideration.   **10.53**

Where services are exchanged, the effect of the accounting entries is to gross up the revenue and the costs by the same amount. Accordingly, there will be no effect on profit. When services are receivable but have not yet been received at the balance sheet date, a prepayment will be recognised. A prepayment does not meet the definition of qualifying consideration.   **10.54**

Where an exchange of services straddles the end of an accounting reference period, such that services are provided but not received before the balance sheet date, any profit at the year end would not be realised. Any such profit initially recognised will not become realised until the service has been received in exchange. That is, the profit will be realised by the prepayment being expensed to profit or loss when the service has been received.   **10.55**

---

[38] *Paragraph 13 of Schedule 1 to SI 2008/409 and Paragraph 13 ~~of~~to Schedule 1 to SI 2008/410.*

[39] *Paragraph 13 of Schedule 1 to SI 2008/409 and Paragraph 13 of Schedule 1 to SI 2008/410.*

10.56   ~~There are no specific requirements in UK accounting standards dealing with barter transactions other than UITF Abstract 26 which is concerned with barter transactions for advertising. The above guidance will be relevant to any profit recognised under UK GAAP although it should be noted that only profits realised at the balance sheet date may be included in the profit and loss account in accordance with the Accounting Regulations⁴⁰.~~ [Deleted]

[10.57 to 10.64 withdrawn and replaced by section 11.]

~~IFRIC 12~~ *Service concession arrangements*

10.65   ~~IFRIC 12 Service Concession Arrangements was issued in November 2006 and has subsequently been adopted by the EU.~~ Service concession arrangements <u>are addressed in IFRIC 12 Service Concession Arrangements and</u> are arrangements whereby a government or other public sector body ('the grantor') enters into a contract with a private sector entity ('the operator') for the construction / upgrade and operation of assets with which public services are supplied, such as roads, prisons or hospitals. Private Finance Initiative (PFI) arrangements are a common example of service concession arrangements in the UK.

10.66   The operator will often construct or upgrade the infrastructure to be used to provide the public service and the cost of this will be recovered over the life of the arrangement. This is accounted for as a construction contract under IAS 11 Construction contracts. The asset arising from the recognition of revenue in accordance with IAS 11 will be either a financial asset or an intangible asset, in accordance with IFRIC 12, depending on the terms of the arrangement.

10.67   When a financial asset is recognised in accordance with IFRIC 12, this will be an amount receivable from the grantor and therefore should normally meet the definition of qualifying consideration. Any profit arising from the recognition of revenue in the construction phase will therefore normally be a realised profit.

10.68   When an intangible asset is recognised in accordance with IFRIC 12, this will not meet the definition of qualifying consideration. Any profit arising from the recognition of revenue <u>in excess of cost</u> in the construction phase will not therefore be a realised profit. Any unrealised profit arising in the construction phase will become realised as the intangible asset is amortised or impaired over the life of the arrangement.

10.68A   <u>FRS 102 includes similar requirements to those of IFRIC 12.</u>

IFRIC 5 Decommissioning funds

10.69   <u>Decommissioning</u>~~IFRIC 5 'Rights to Interests arising from Decommissioning, Restoration and Environmental Rehabilitation Funds' was issued in December 2004 and subsequently adopted by the EU. Such~~ funds are more fully described in IFRIC 5 <u>Decommissioning, Restoration and Environmental Rehabilitation Funds</u> but are typically established to provide a ring-fenced fund of assets to be used to pay for the decommissioning of an asset (~~e.g.~~<u>eg</u>, a nuclear power plant) at the end of its life. IFRIC 5 applies to the financial statements of a contributor to such a fund where the assets are administered separately (either by being held in a separate legal entity or as segregated assets within another entity) and the contributor's right to access the assets is restricted. The contributor retains the obligation to pay the decommissioning costs but is able to draw on the assets in the fund to finance such costs when they are incurred.

---

⁴⁰ ~~Paragraph 13 of Schedule 1 to SI 2008/409 and Paragraph 13 to Schedule 1 to SI 2008/410.~~

In accordance with IFRIC 5, the contributor recognises the right to receive reimbursement from the fund as a reimbursement asset in accordance with IAS 37-. The reimbursement is measured at the lower of the amount of the decommissioning obligation recognised and the contributor's share of the fair value of the net assets of the fund attributable to the contributor. Changes in the carrying value of the reimbursement asset, other than contributions to and payments from the fund, are recognised in profit or loss in the period in which the changes occur. **10.70**

Paragraph 53 of IAS 37 states that a reimbursement asset is recognised when, and only when, it is virtually certain that the reimbursement will be received if the entity settled the obligation. An amount receivable which is regarded, for financial reporting purposes, as meeting this test will also generally meet the definition of qualifying consideration in paragraph 3.11(d). **10.71**

That definition refers to the debtor being capable of settling the receivable within a reasonable period of time. What is a reasonable period of time is a matter of judgement and will depend on the particular facts and circumstances. Decommissioning funds may be established to pay liabilities that will not arise for many years. However, the nature of such funds is that they will generally be capable of settling the amount within a relatively short period of time if they were required to do so at the date of determination. The definition of qualifying consideration does not require actual settlement within any particular period of time. **10.72**

Section 846 and replacement assets

The following paragraphs illustrate how to apply s846 (see 2.9 above) where the asset to which an unrealised reserve relates has been replaced by a different asset. **10.73**

Company A has brought forward realised profits of £75,000. It previously acquired an investment (in Company B) via a share for share transfer. This transaction qualified for merger relief in accordance with section 612 and the company elected to record a merger reserve in relation to this share issue. The aggregate nominal value of the shares issued was £50,000, compared with a fair value of £500,000 such that a merger reserve of £450,000 was recorded. **10.74**

Subsequently Company A transfers that investment in Company B to another subsidiary company (Company C) in exchange for shares. As a matter of accounting practice, the merger reserve which initially related to Company A's investment in Company B is now attached to the investment in Company C, ie, part of the amount at which the investment in Company C is stated represents the reserve. These transactions are illustrated in the diagram below (in which 'CV' means carrying value). **10.75**

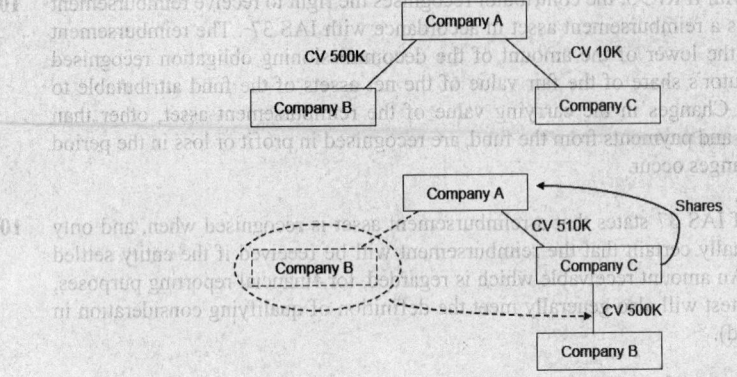

10.76   Therefore, if Company A wishes to distribute its investment in Company C to its shareholders, it can do so by applying section 846. This reserve (together with £75,000 of the brought forward realised profits) can be used to distribute Company A's investment in Company C to its shareholders. This is illustrated in the following memorandum balance sheet of Company A.

Memorandum balance sheet of Company A

	Opening balance sheet £'000	Share for share acquisition of Company B £'000	After acquisition of Company B £'000	Share for share transfer of Company B to Company C £'000	After transfer to Company C £'000	Distribution of Company C £'000	After distribution of Company C £'000
Investment in Company B		500	500	(500)	–	–	–
Investment in Company C	10		10	500	510	(510)	–
Other net assets	90		90	–	90		90
Net assets	**100**	**500**	**600**	**–**	**600**	**(510)**	**90**
Share capital / premium	25	50	75		75		75
Merger reserve (Company B)		450	450	(450)			
Merger reserve (Company C)				450	450	(450)	
P&L reserves (realised)	75		75		75	(60)	15
Capital and reserves	**100**	**500**	**600**	**–**	**600**	**(510)**	**90**

Section 846 and fungible assets

10.77   The following paragraphs provide guidance on the distribution in kind of fungible assets such as shares or loan notes that have been received as consideration for the sale of another asset. For example, Company A has 1,000 £1 loan notes which are transferable in multiples of £1 and represent an unrealised profit of £900. If the company makes a distribution in kind of £500 of loan notes, the question is whether the unrealised profit might be regarded as becoming realised through the application of section 846 either:

- to the extent of £450 on the basis that the realisation of 50% of the asset results in the realisation of 50% of the profit; or
- to the extent of £500 through the application of a "'top slicing''' rule similar to the one in 3.18 below for exchanges of assets.

10.78   The first (ie, pro rata) approach is correct. This is a matter of the statutory construction of section 846 rather than a matter of generally accepted accounting practice.

10.79   Section 846 is reproduced below for ease of reference.

846 Distributions in kind: treatment of unrealised profits

1   *This section applies where—*
   (a)   *a company makes a distribution consisting of or including, or treated as arising in consequence of, the sale, transfer or other disposition by the company of a non-cash asset, and*
   (b)   *any part of the amount at which that asset is stated in the relevantaccounts represents an unrealised profit.*

2   *That profit is treated as a realised profit—*
   (a)   *for the purpose of determining the lawfulness of the distribution in accordance with this Part (whether before or after the distribution takes place), and*
   (b)   *for the purpose of the application, in relation to anything done with a view to or in connection with the making of the distribution, of any provision of regulations under section 396 under which only realised profits are to be included in or transferred to the profit and loss account.*

10.80   The profit that is to be treated as realised in accordance with sub-section (2) is the unrealised profit referred to in sub-section (1)(b). The reference in sub-section (1)(b) to 'that asset' means the asset to be distributed. Therefore, it is necessary to identify "'that asset''' which in the above example is not a single asset of £500 of loan notes but an aggregation of assets comprising 500 £1 loan notes. Naturally, if the loan notes were transferable only in units of £100 the distribution would consist of 5 assets. Therefore, in the above example, the distribution of £500 of loan notes results in the realisation of £450 of profit because that is the amount of unrealised profit attributable to those loan notes. In other words, the unrealised profit must be treated as spread evenly across each unit of the fungible asset and section 846 applied to each unit separately.

10.81   Paragraph 3.18 refers to the use of a top-slicing approach where an asset is sold partly for qualifying consideration and partly for other consideration and a realised profit falls to be assessed under generally accepted accounting principles. That guidance is not relevant to the application of section 846 which is not concerned with the disposal of an asset for mixed consideration but with the recharacterisation of an existing unrealised profit under that the specific provision of that section. In addition, that guidance is not relevant to the attribution of an unrealised profit, at the point of its arising, among one or more assets.

As illustrated in Appendix 8, this conclusion, may lead to unexpected results in some cases. In particular, the maximum distribution possible as a distribution in kind may be less than would be the case if all of the loan notes were redeemed or sold for qualifying consideration.   **10.82**

11. FOREIGN CURRENCY SHARE CAPITAL AND USE OF PRESENTATION CURRENCIES

Introduction

The guidance in this section deals with matters arising from mismatches between any of the currency of share capital, the company's functional currency and the company's presentation currency. The accounting context in which this section is written is IFRS but will also be applicable to companies applying FRS 102., ie IAS 21. So far as UK GAAP is concerned, if FRS 23 is applicable then this is converged with IAS 21; if SSAP 20 is applicable, the issues and principles are, however, the same because SSAP 20 differs only in minor details from IAS 21 for these purposes, although SSAP 20 does not include a free choice of presentation currency.   **11.1**

The main points at issue might be briefly put as follows: **11.2**

(a) What is the effect of a translation of the whole of the accounts of a company into a presentation currency of free choice?;

(b) What is the effect of the retranslation of an autonomous branch from its functional currency into the functional currency of the company?; and

(c) What is the effect of the share capital's being denominated in a currency other than the functional currency?

The first matter is similar to the second in accounting termsissue of translation of an autonomous branch which was previously addressed at paragraphs 10.57 -10.64 (which have now been withdrawn and replaced by the guidance in this section). However, the secondthat case is not one of free choice of presentation currency. Rather, it is a necessity to translate the results of the branch into the functional currency of the company of which it is legally a part. In the case of use of a presentation currency, there is an arbitrary choice as to the units in which to show the accounts for mere presentation purposes. The legal analysis for the purpose of determining distributable profits is therefore different.   **11.3**

[DeletedNot used]   **11.4**

[DeletedNot used]   **11.5**

Principles

Paragraphs 11.7 to 11.384 set out eightseven principles to be applied in relation to foreign currency share capital and the use of presentation currencies. Examples of the application of the principles are set out in Appendix 5.   **11.6**

Principle 1: Realised profits and losses are measured by reference to the functional currency of the company.   **11.7**

Principle 2: An accounting gain or loss arising upon the retranslation of the whole of the accounts from the company's functional currency to a presentation currency, is not a profit or a loss as a matter of law. Such an amount therefore cannot be a realised profit or loss.   **11.8**

11.9   IAS 21 requires foreign currency assets, liabilities and transactions to be measured using a company's functional currency. This is defined as the currency of the primary economic environment in which the entity operates. Functional currency is a matter of fact and is not an accounting policy choice. However, IAS 21 also permits a company to present its financial statements in a currency other than its functional currency. Such a currency is referred to as a presentation currency and may be freely chosen.

11.10   The "'relevant accounts'" for the purposes of justifying a distribution are determined in accordance with section 836 but will generally be the company's most recent statutory individual accounts. Although the face of those accounts shows amounts in presentation currency, the functional currency amounts underlie and form part of those relevant accounts. Realised profits and losses are determined by reference to these functional currency amounts. The functional-to-presentation translation gain or loss, which also appears in the relevant accounts, is not a profit or loss at law, for the reasons explained below.

11.11   The presentation currency is an arbitrary choice as to the units in which to show the accounts for mere presentation purposes. The functional-to-presentation translation is a book-keeping or accounting exercise. The accounting gain or loss arising from that process is an arithmetical difference which does not spring from any functional substance. There has been no profit or loss but merely a change in calibration. Thus such changes are not characterised as a profit or loss as a matter of law.

11.12   **Principle 3: The profit or loss arising upon the necessary retranslation of an autonomous branch, from its functional currency into the functional currency of the company, is a realised profit or a loss to the extent that the branch net assets were qualifying consideration when the profit or loss arose.**

11.13   A company has only a single pool of realised profits available for distribution, irrespective of its having one or more autonomous branches, with a functional currency different from that of the rest of the company. That single pool is measured by reference to the functional currency of the rest of the company. Thus in the case of a foreign operation (branch) with a functional currency that is different from the functional currency of the company, the translation is not an arbitrary one but one made of necessity to state the branch asset and results in the company's functional currency. It therefore has substance and is a profit or loss at law.

11.14   Whether that profit or loss is a realised one depends upon the nature of the assets and liabilities on which ~~it~~they arises. A profit that arises on retranslation of an asset which comprises qualifying consideration, or a liability, is a realised profit in accordance with paragraph 3.9(d) above. A profit arising on the retranslation of assets which do not comprise qualifying consideration (~~e.g.~~eg, property, plant and equipment) is an unrealised profit. A loss arising on retranslation of an asset or liability is a realised loss unless it is the reversal of an unrealised profit on that same asset or liability. The gross profits and losses on retranslation (rather than the net amount) should be assessed separately. It is therefore possible, for example, that there is a realised loss to be taken into account when determining profits available for distribution, even though the net amount taken direct to equity is a profit.

11.15   The analysis in the previous paragraph will apply only in straightforward situations where the composition of the company's assets has not changed significantly during the period. For example, it would not be appropriate to regard the exchange difference related to the amount of the opening cash balance (ie, the beginning to the end of year exchange difference computed in relation to that part of the opening net assets equal to the opening cash balance) as realised if that cash balance did not exist throughout the period (eg, because it was invested in assets such as property, plant and equipment which would not comprise qualifying consideration).

The exchange difference taken to equity will also include the difference between the profit or loss for the period translated at actual (or average) rate and that profit or loss translated at closing rate. The profit or loss for the period arises on changes in the amounts and/or composition of the company's assets and liabilities (e.g.eg, on an exchange of stocks for cash). **11.16**

Thus taking together the exchange differences on retranslation of the profit or loss for the period and on the opening net assets, the total amount arises in relation to an asset base that changes throughout the year. To establish whether this exchange difference is realised, partly realised or unrealised will require careful analysis of the facts. Appendix 6 gives two examples of this, illustrating why this calculation needs to be done. Ideally, it would be necessary to compute and assess exchange differences continually. In practice when conducting the analysis, reasonable approximations may be made. The approximations will depend on the facts of any case, for example the rate of change in the composition of the balance sheet between various asset/ liability categories. **11.17**

Principle 4: Where a company's shares, irrespective of whether those shares are classified as equity or debt for accounting purposes, are denominated in a currency other than the company's functional currency, the adjustment arising upon any translation for accounting purposes of the share capital is not a profit or loss at law. Such an amount therefore cannot be a realised profit or loss. **11.18**

Where shares are classified as equity under accounting standards and their currency differs from the company's functional currency, then the company will either retranslate those shares into functional currency at each balance sheet date or will leave them at their original historical amounts, although typically the latter is adopted in the case of ordinary shares. Accounting standards do not have anything to say about the translation of shares classified as equity, or at least not directly. In IAS 21 the requirement to accumulate the translation differences in the currency translation reserve rules out any question of allocating any of them against capital. In the case of retranslation the resulting difference does not pass through profit or loss and is not a gain or loss for accounting purposes. Where the shares are classified as debt (eg, certain preference shares), retranslation is mandatory and the resulting difference is an accounting gain or loss flowing through profit or loss. **11.19**

In both cases, the shares remain share capital as a matter of law. Any retranslation of share capital for accounting purposes (whether equity or debt classified) is a book-keeping or accounting exercise. The gain or loss arising from that process is an arithmetical difference which does not spring from any substance in law. There has been no profit or loss but merely a change in calibration. Thus such changes are not characterised as profits or losses as a matter of law. **11.20**

Principle 5: Where a company's shares, whether those shares are classified as equity or debt for accounting purposes, are denominated in a currency other than the company's functional currency, the common law has the effect of restricting distributions where to do otherwise would result in the net assets' falling below the functional currency worth of the share capital. **11.21**

Under statute, shares (whether of a private or a public company) must be of a fixed nominal amount (s542). There is a rule of law that where the share capital is denominated in another currency (other than the functional currency) the share capital is in fact fixed as that other currency amount. **11.22**

11.23   Further, the common law provides that a company may not distribute its capital (see 2.2 above). In relation to the currency of shares, this rule is not concerned with whether or not share capital has been retranslated in the accounts or with the nature of any translation adjustments. It is concerned with a question of fact as to value of the assets compared with the amount of the share capital. Since the amount of the capital is the currency amount, then for such a comparison to be effected the share capital must be stated in the same terms as value of the net assets. Thus the current worth of the share capital in functional currency terms must be compared with the net assets in functional currency. To the extent that a distribution would result in the net assets falling below the current functional currency worth of the share capital, the ability to make such a distribution is restricted.

11.24   Thus an increase in the functional currency worth of the share capital may restrict distributions to less than the amount available under Part 23's statutory rules. On the other hand, a decrease will neither restrict nor augment the ability to make a distribution. The effect of a share capital decrease will be to increase the difference between net assets and share capital (assuming no other amounts within equity – see below for other cases) so as to exceed the Part 23 realised profits (and any unrealised profits). However, the maximum amount that may be distributed can never exceed the amount permitted by Part 23.

11.25   **Principle 6: Share premium account, and similar capital accounts, do not have a currency of denomination but are amounts of record in the books of account in functional currency.**

11.26   Share premium account is different from share capital in this context. Share capital is required by statute to be of fixed amount and therefore has a currency of denomination. Share premium account is not so required. Furthermore, share premium was, prior to the statutory requirement to treat it as if it were part of a company's capital, in law a profit. It is thus an amount of record arising on the occasion of a share issue. The amount is determined at that time and in the functional currency since that is the currency of substance for the keeping of accounts.

11.27   A capital redemption reserve is of the same nature as a share premium account. It is not required by statute to have a fixed amount. It is an amount of record arising on the occasion of a share redemption or repurchase. The amount is determined at that time and in the functional currency. It should be noted that the amount determined at that time will be by reference to the then functional currency worth of the shares redeemed or repurchased. This is because those shares, up to the moment of their redemption or repurchase, represent capital of that currency. Thus the nominal value of those shares, by reference to which the statutory rules for determining capital redemption reserve operate, is as a matter of fact a non-functional currency amount; its functional currency worth must be determined at the date of redemption or repurchase.

11.28   Principle 5 identifies a possible restricting effect upon distributions in relation to share capital where there is a mismatch between that capital's denomination and the functional currency. Since share premium and similar capital accounts do not have currencies of denomination, but are amounts of record in functional currency, no equivalent issue arises in relation to share premium and similar capital accounts; that is to say, there is no concept of variation in the worth of, eg, share premium to be concerned about.

11.29   It should be noted, however, that share premium is brought into the calculation of the restricting effect arising from a variation in the worth of the share capital under Principle 5. The common law prohibition on distribution of capital covers both share capital and share premium account. Thus, where a company has a share premium account, the restricting effect under Principle 5 is computed by comparison of the net assets with the aggregate of the functional currency worth of the share capital and the functional currency amount of record of the share premium account.

The common law principles of maintenance of capital apply to any reserve which the Act says must be treated as if it were part of the paid up share capital of the company. It therefore includes, in addition to a share premium account, a capital redemption reserve under section 733 and a redenomination reserve under section 626. The treatment of a share premium account described in 2.29 above therefore applies to any capital redemption reserve or redenomination reserve.   **11.30**

Principle 7: The application of the s831 statutory net assets test operates by reference   **11.31**
to amounts as shown upon the face of the accounts in presentation currency.

The section 831 net assets test (see 2.30 above) applies only to public companies. It is a statutory test formulated in terms of amounts set out in the relevant accounts required by the Act: net assets, share capital and undistributable reserves (as defined). It therefore operates by reference to whatever is shown in presentation currency in those accounts.   **11.32**

It may be noted here that s831 operates upon figures in presentation currency whereas, as described at Principles 1 and 2, s830's realised profits test draws upon functional currency amounts. This is because s830 deals with profits and losses and in law the functional-to-presentation translation does not yield a profit or loss. It is therefore necessary for s830 to begin with the amounts in the relevant accounts but to take from them only the amounts that are profits and losses in law. On the other hand s831 asks only that certain accounts figures be compared (eg, in a similar way to that described at 6.24 to 6.30ff above whereby shares classified as debt count as a reduction of net assets rather than an increase to share capital for the s831 test).   **11.33**

It should be noted that where share capital is retranslated, the amount within reserves arising as a result of the retranslation is not a profit or loss at law (see Principle 2). Nor is that translation difference presented as share capital. Thus the difference cannot be included, for the operation of the s831 test, as share capital or as undistributable reserves. Thus, in particular, any debit difference cannot be an unrealised loss to be deducted from the unrealised profits component of "'undistributable reserves'".   **11.34**

Principle 8: A reduction of foreign currency share capital is calculated by reference to   **11.35**
the rate of exchange at the date of the reduction.

The amount of the reserve so arising is a matter of accounting practice. That reserve will be the functional currency amount (see paragraph 11.7) of: **11.36**

(a)   the amount previously recorded in relation to the now-reduced nominal value;
(b)   plus or minus any amounts previously recorded for retranslation of the share capital (if it was retranslated – see paragraphs 11.18–11.20);
(c)   less any amounts repaid translated at the rate at the date of repayment.

Put simply, the reserve is the aggregate net amount left over, in functional currency, after all of the share capital being reduced, any associated retranslation amounts and any repayment have been removed from the accounts. Appendix 7 contains illustrative examples of a company's position in several scenarios for capital reductions where there have been movements in the exchange rate between the functional currency and foreign share capital currency.

It should be noted that the amount of the reserve so arising is not the same as the amount of the reduction. In law the amount of the reduction would be the currency nominal value reduced at the functional currency exchange rate at the date that the reduction becomes   **11.37** effective. This is because the amount of the capital, and thus of the reduction, is the currency amount (see paragraph 11.22). It can be meaningfully stated at the effective date only at the rate applicable that day. For example, if the amount was repaid on reduction it would be that amount that would actually be repaid and accounted for as a cash payment. The realised profits arising on the reduction, on the other hand, are not determined by reference to the reduction amount but to the reserve arising, which is an accounting matter and may be a different figure.

11.38   The reserve may be thought of as comprising a number of components, one of which is the reduction amount, as follows, in the functional currency:

(a)   a credit for the reduced nominal value, to the extent not paid out, at the reduction date exchange rate;

(b)   a credit for any previously recorded balance, representing the reduced nominal value, that has not been eliminated by (a) above and/ or by any repayment;

(c)   a debit for any previously recorded balance, representing the reduced nominal value, that has been over-eliminated by (a) above and/ or by any repayment; and

(d)   a credit or debit, as the case may be, to replace any reserves entry for prior accounting retranslation of the reduced element of the shares since this is associated with the shares' nominal value that no longer exists.

In relation to the last component, such a prior reserves entry arises only where the shares were retranslated for accounting purposes; in effect it anticipated the reduction of the shares (it is the difference between the nominal value at historical rate and an amount equal to what is now the reduction amount) and so should be brought into account in reduction accounting.

12. CASH BOX STRUCTURES

Introduction to the cash box share issue method

12.1   The so-called "cash box" method of effecting an issue of shares for cash has been employed from time to time over at least two decades. They have recently become commonplace. Whilst they have previously been seen in relation to acquisition funding, more recently they also have been seen in connection with debt repayment or regulatory capital increases. Some companies undertaking such issues have been advised by their lawyers that the arrangement does not give rise to any share premium. As a consequence the question arises as to the status of the reserve recorded instead of share premium: is it a realised profit?

Brief details

12.2   Although there are slight variations in the schemes put forward, a common case would be as follows (in this case a placing):

- There are four parties involved: the Company; NewCo, a newly incorporated non-UK subsidiary of which the company holds 89 of 100 ordinary shares (worth a trivial amount); a bank, that owns the other 11 shares (worth a trivial amount); and the placees who will put up a substantial amount of cash.
- The placees pay over the cash subscription amount to the bank, which, as principal, subscribes that cash amount for preference shares in NewCo.
- The Company allots ordinary shares (being equity shares under s548) to the placees, in consideration for which the bank transfers to it the 11 NewCo ordinary shares and the NewCo preference shares.
- NewCo redeems its preference shares (now held by the Company) in cash for the amount of the placing proceeds.

No share premium account?

In relation to the penultimate bullet, it is assumed here, for the purposes of what follows, that there is merger relief under s612 and thus no share premium account falls to be recorded. That is a question of law, which will depend on the particular facts and circumstances of the case. Companies may wish to take legal advice. This Technical Release offers none. **12.3**

Accounting entries

In terms of accounting entries, where there is no share premium account there will instead be an other reserve. This would arise because either: **12.4**

- the Company chooses to record a reserve at the point of acquiring the shares in NewCo in the same way that a company may choose to record a merger reserve in lieu of share premium in any case of the application of s612. This amount is a profit at law, in the same way as merger relief reserves generally (see paragraph 3.8(b)(ii)); or
- the Company could (under UK GAAP) choose to record its investment in NewCo at the nominal value of the shares and thus no reserve arises at this point. However, once the investment in NewCo is redeemed for cash, the Company will record a profit on the redemption in the same amount.

Either way, the Company finds itself with a merger reserve or a profit reserve and the same question applies to them both: is the reserve realised? The method by which the reserve was recorded makes no difference to the question. **12.5**

The framework for considering whether the reserve is a realised profit?

The reserve is akin to one arising where a company receives a capital contribution from shareholders. Paragraphs 12.7 to 12.15 below consider, in effect, whether the assessment of realisation of that reserve proceeds in any different fashion from that of a conventional capital contribution reserve. **12.6**

Prior to considering the use of the funds

Following redemption of the Newco preference shares, the cash proceeds thereof will, subject to the question of linkage set out below, fall to be treated as ""qualifying consideration"" in the hands of the Company (see paragraph 3.9(a) or (f), depending on whether as an accounting entry the reserve arises on redemption by NewCo or on issue by the Company). *Prima facie*, and subject to what follows, the reserve would therefore be considered a realised profit. **12.7**

Questions of the use of the funds

Sometimes the reason for the placing or rights issue – and a reason will always be given to the market – is to obtain funds for an acquisition. The precise circumstances of the acquisition will vary. It is possible that the acquisition and placing/ rights issue are conditional upon each other; or they might occur on the same day; or the acquisition may be announced at the placing date but still itself be conditional; or there may in some industries be regulatory restrictions on the use of the cash proceeds. **12.8**

In other cases the company may have raised the funds in connection with a need to recapitalise a subsidiary. For example, it is possible that the company may be compelled by regulatory requirements immediately to subscribe for equity share capital in a subsidiary; or it may be a commercial necessity to recapitalise a subsidiary. Other cases might include **12.9** a capitalisation of the company itself for regulatory reasons; or to fund the repayment of the company's own debt.

12.10   In this context the question arises as to whether the reserve should therefore be deemed to relate to the intended application of the funds (ie, with the placing/ rights issue and the application of the funds being a series of related transactions) rather than to the immediate cash proceeds of the placing/ rights issue.

12.11   This can be split into two questions:

- Does the use of the funds need to be considered in terms of the "'linkage'" principle in paragraph 3.5?
- If so, will the use of the funds be found to be linked under that provision?

Should linkage be considered?

12.12   Paragraph 3.5 is of general application and contains no exceptions. There is nothing in a cash box structure that marks it out as fundamentally different and warranting the insertion of an exception to paragraph 3.5. The effect of the application of paragraph 3.5 has therefore to be considered.

12.13   Two other observations may be noted at this juncture. First, it would be unjustifiable to halt the analysis at the conversion of the NewCo preference shares into cash, and not to go on to consider whether there should be brought into the analysis the conversion of the cash into some other asset; it is a commercial reality that cash boxes are not carried out in a vacuum.

12.14   Second, if the question of linkage were not addressed, all manner of intra-group transactions might claim to result in realised profits.

Conclusion as to framework to be employed in the assessment of realisation

12.15   Thus, all of the normal rules of realisation, including the effect of the application of paragraph 3.5 (linkage etc), apply. The assessment therefore proceeds in no different a way from that of the case of a conventional capital contribution.

The effect of the application of paragraph 3.5

12.16   Paragraphs 12.7 to 12.15 above establish that a cash-box share issue and its wider context should be considered under the paragraph 3.5 principle of linkage etc. Paragraphs 12.17 to 12.35 look at the application of that principle to some scenarios detailing the use of the cash raised. The questions are: is the use of the funds linked; and if so, does the linked transaction, taken together with the equity issue, result in an increase in qualifying consideration for the company issuing the shares?

Recapitalisation of the company for regulatory reasons

12.17   Suppose that the company is subject to a regulatory regime that requires it to maintain a specified level of net assets. The company's position and performance has deteriorated and it needs to raise funds, by an equity issue, to maintain its regulatory compliance and hence the continuation of its business. The cash received is employed as working capital.

12.18   Unless the company needs to hold the funds raised in some particular asset within its business, eg, if the regulatory requirement is to hold the funds in a particular type of asset, then there is no linked transaction. Accordingly, the profit is a realised one. Even so, it seems unlikely that in practice the company would make a distribution from it as to do so would reduce the company's regulatory capital again.

If there were a need to hold the funds in some particular asset category, then consideration would need to be given as to whether the specific asset meets the definition of qualifying consideration (see 3.11). To the extent that the asset is qualifying consideration the reserve that is created would be realised (albeit its distribution may not be a practical proposition from a regulatory perspective as noted above).   **12.19**

Recapitalisation of a subsidiary company, with equity, for regulatory reasons

The company is a holding company that holds a subsidiary that is subject to a regulatory regime that requires it to maintain a specified level of net assets. The subsidiary's position and performance has deteriorated and the subsidiary needs to raise funds, by an equity issue, to maintain its regulatory compliance and hence the continuation of its business. The company (that is, the holding company of the regulated subsidiary) raises the cash by an equity issue of its own and uses the cash to subscribe for equity in the subsidiary.   **12.20**

The regulatory necessity to recapitalise the subsidiary is enough for the company's onward investment of the funds to be linked. In this case the cash has been invested in equity shares in a subsidiary which will not be qualifying consideration (see 4.10), and thus the reserve is unrealised.   **12.21**

Recapitalisation of a subsidiary company, with equity, out of commercial necessity

The case here is similar to that above save that the subsidiary is not regulated. It is, however, in financial difficulties and needs funds to continue in business. The company (that is, the holding company of the troubled subsidiary) raises the cash by an equity issue of its own and uses the cash to subscribe for equity in the subsidiary.   **12.22**

The commercial necessity to recapitalise the subsidiary is enough for the company's onward investment of the funds to be linked. As with the previous example the cash has been invested in equity shares in a subsidiary, which will not be qualifying consideration (see 4.10), and thus the reserve is unrealised.   **12.23**

Recapitalisation of a subsidiary company, with inter-company debt, out of commercial necessity

Assume that the facts are the same as the previous example except that the cash raised by the company is lent to the subsidiary rather than the company's subscribing for subsidiary shares.   **12.24**

Again the commercial necessity to recapitalise the subsidiary is enough for the company's onward lending of the funds to be linked. In this case, the cash has been turned into an inter-company debt receivable. Whilst an inter-company debt receivable can be qualifying consideration (see 3.11(d)), where the funds have been lent to the subsidiary in view of, say, its troubled financial condition, then it is very unlikely that the debt would meet the tests necessary to be qualifying consideration and as such the reserve would be unrealised. A loan to a financially troubled subsidiary may also be on subordinated terms (such as a contingent loan) and so would make it even less likely that the definition of qualifying consideration would be met.   **12.25**

Repayment of the company's own debt

12.26   In this scenario the cash raised as new equity is used to repay some of the company's debt. There might be a variety of reasons for this. For example, the company may be rebalancing its gearing ratio for the long term, say because credit markets will not enable it to sustain the previous high level. Or it might be that the company needs to repay that debt in order to survive and has no other sources of liquidity but an equity raising.

12.27   The commercial necessity to repay debt, or even the management intention to do so, is enough for the company's debt repayment to be linked. However, this does not prevent a realised profit arising. The reserve will in fact be realised as release or settlement of debt is itself a form of qualifying consideration (see 3.11(c)).

12.28   However, if the debt arose from the acquisition of an asset that does not meet the definition of qualifying consideration and the repayment through the equity issue was planned at the time of the acquisition of the asset, the reserve will be unrealised.

Raising cash to be used to fund possible, unspecified acquisitions

12.29   In this scenario the company believes that there will be opportunities, in the medium term, to acquire some companies on favourable terms. It therefore raises cash now in order to move quickly if a target is identified.

12.30   There is not a strong enough nexus between the fund raising and an actual, specific acquisition. Acquisitions are the motivation, but there is not a specific target. In addition, a change in commercial circumstances is a realistic possibility (in a similar way to the sufficient time elapsing during in a planned transaction sequence such that commercial circumstances could change and the rest of the sequence not go ahead – see paragraph 3.74 above). The nexus is too weak for there to be linkage under paragraph 3.5.

12.31   Thus subject to any arrangement or intention to hold the funds in non-qualifying consideration form, here a realised profit will result.

Using the cash received to fund a specific acquisition – where the placing and acquisition are inter-conditional

12.32   The company raises equity funds from placees and the placing and the acquisition are conditional upon each other.

12.33   The acquisition is linked (legally in this case). As the linked use of the cash is to acquire an equity investment that thereby becomes a subsidiary, the reserve will not be realised as the investment is not qualifying consideration as it is not readily convertible to cash (see 4.10).

Other acquisition funding cases

12.34   Other acquisition funding cases will require careful examination to determine the level of linkage. The above two examples are at the opposite ends of the spectrum, one where the cash will be used to fund an acquisition, the other where it may or may not be used but in any event not immediately. Obviously there will be situations between these two extremes where judgement will need to be exercised. It should be recalled, however, that legal linkage is not a necessary test for linkage to exist. Simultaneously effecting a fund raising and an acquisition would also be very strong linkage; and few other types of circumstances are likely to be as non-specific and subject to change as the scenario involving possible but unspecified acquisitions.

Disclosure

The July 2008 edition of the ASB newsletter *Inside Track* noted that the UITF had received **12.35** a request for guidance about cash box structures. The UITF decided not to address this issue because it was a matter of the application of company law and was already being addressed by the Institutes. However, the issue reached the UITF agenda because some companies had failed to explain adequately, in their financial statements, why no share premium account arose on an issue of share at an apparent premium. When cash box structures are used, it is important that directors consider the adequacy of disclosures about their use and the consequential effect on items in financial statements.

LC, 29.10.10

Liz.Cole@icaew.com

www.icaew.com

www.icas.org.uk

Appendix 1
Examples of the application of sections 845 and 846

EXAMPLE 1 – TRANSFER OF AN ASSET AT BOOK VALUE APPLYING SECTION 845

A company has profits available for distribution of £10,000 on its profit and loss account. It sells a non-cash asset to its parent for a consideration of £20,000 which is equal to its book value. The market value of the asset is £60,000.

The company can apply section 845 in these circumstances and, as explained below, applying this section the distribution would be lawful. Section 845(2) provides that the amount of the distribution is taken to be zero because the amount of the consideration for the transfer is not less than the book value of the asset. Section 845(3) provides that, for the purposes of section 845(1)(a), the company's profits available for distribution are treated as increased by the amount (if any) by which the amount or value of any consideration for the transfer exceeds the book value of the asset. The adjustment in this case is therefore zero and the profits available for distribution in accordance with section 845(1)(a) are treated as £10,000. The company may therefore lawfully make the transfer of the asset because the distributable profits are treated as £10,000 and the amount of the distribution is treated as zero. Thus immediately after the transfer the company's distributable reserves remain £10,000.

Realised profits brought forward	10,000
Adjustment for section 845(3)	–
Profits available for distribution	10,000
Distribution measured in accordance with section 845	–
Balance carried forward on reserves	£10,000

Had the asset been revalued immediately before transfer to its market value of £60,000 the position (using section 846) would have been as follows:

Realised profits brought forward	10,000
Unrealised profit arising from revaluation from book value (£20,000) to market value (£60,000) of the non-cash asset to be transferred to the parent	40,000
Profits treated as available for distribution in accordance with section 846	50,000
Distribution measured as the difference between the fair value of the asset (£60,000) and the consideration received (£20,000)	(40,000)
Balance carried forward on reserves	£10,000

Thus, it can be seen that, section 845 gives the same position before and after the transfer in this example as is given by revaluing the asset and using section 846. The balance carried forward on reserves is a realised profit.

EXAMPLE 2 – TRANSFER OF AN ASSET AT ABOVE BOOK VALUE APPLYING SECTION 845 WHERE THERE IS INITIALLY A POSITIVE BALANCE OF DISTRIBUTABLE RESERVES

A company has profits available for distribution of £10,000 on its profit and loss account. It sells a non-cash asset to its parent for a consideration of £50,000 which exceeds its book value of £20,000. The market value of the asset is £60,000.

The company can apply section 845 in these circumstances and, as explained below, applying this section the distribution would be lawful. Section 845(2) provides that the amount of the distribution is taken to be zero because the amount of the consideration for the transfer is not less than the book value of the asset. Section 845(3) provides that, for the purposes of section 845(1)(a), the company's profits available for distribution are treated as increased by the amount (if any) by which the amount or value of any consideration for the transfer exceeds the book value of the asset. The adjustment in this case is therefore £30,000 and the profits available for distribution in accordance with section 845(1)(a) are treated as £40,000. The company may therefore lawfully make the transfer of the asset because the distributable profits are treated as £40,000 and the amount of the distribution is treated as zero.

Realised profits brought forward	10,000
Adjustment for section 845(3):	
Increase in profits treated as available for distribution due to the consideration being in excess of the book value (£50,000 less £20,000)	30,000
Profits treated as available for distribution	40,000
Distribution measured in accordance with section 845	–
Balance carried forward on reserves	£40,000

Whether or not the increase in reserves of £30,000 after the transfer is a realised profit depends on whether the consideration for the transfer is qualifying consideration.

If it is now assumed that the company revalued the asset to its market value of £60,000 it can again be seen that sections 845 and 846 give the same position after the transfer.

Realised profits brought forward	10,000
Unrealised profit arising from revaluation from book value (£20,000) to market value (£60,000) of the non-cash asset to be transferred to the parent	40,000
Profits treated as available for distribution in accordance with section 846	50,000
Distribution measured as the difference between the fair value of the asset (£60,000) and the consideration received (£50,000)	(10,000)
Balance carried forward on reserves	£40,000

EXAMPLE 3 – TRANSFER OF AN ASSET AT BELOW BOOK VALUE APPLYING SECTION 845

A company has profits available for distribution of £10,000 on its profit and loss account. It sells a non-cash asset to its parent for a consideration of £15,000 which is £5,000 below its book value of £20,000. The market value of the asset is £60,000.

The company can apply section 845 in these circumstances and, as explained below, applying this section the distribution would be lawful. Section 845(2) provides that the amount of the distribution is taken to be £5,000 because the amount of the consideration for the transfer is £15,000 and the book value of the asset is £20,000. Section 845(3) provides that, for the purposes of section 845(1)(a), the company's profits available for distribution are treated as increased by the amount (if any) by which the amount or value of any consideration for the transfer exceeds the book value of the asset. The adjustment in this case is therefore zero and the profits available for distribution in accordance with section 845(1)(a) are treated as £10,000. The company may therefore lawfully make the transfer of the asset because the distributable reserves are treated as £10,000 and the amount of the distribution is treated as £5,000. Thus immediately after the transfer the company's distributable reserves are £5,000.

Realised profits brought forward	10,000
Adjustment for section 845(3)	–
Profits available for distribution	10,000
Distribution measured in accordance with section 845 (£20,000 – £15,000)	5,000
Balance carried forward on reserves	£5,000

The balance carried forward on reserves is a realised profit.

Again, if it is now assumed that the company revalued the asset to its market value of £60,000 it can be seen that sections 845 and 846 give the same position after the transfer.

Realised profits brought forward	10,000
Unrealised profit arising from revaluation from book value (£20,000) to market value (£60,000) of the non-cash asset to be transferred to the parent	40,000
Profits treated as available for distribution in accordance with section 846	50,000
Distribution measured as the difference between the fair value of the asset (£60,000) and the consideration received (£15,000)	(45,000)
Balance carried forward on reserves	£5,000

EXAMPLE 4 – TRANSFER OF AN ASSET AT ABOVE BOOK VALUE APPLYING SECTION 845 WHERE THERE IS INITIALLY A NEGATIVE BALANCE OF DISTRIBUTABLE RESERVES

A company has an accumulated deficit of £10,000 on its profit and loss account (ie, it has a deficit on its profits available for distribution). It sells a non-cash asset to its parent for a consideration of £50,000 compared with a book value of £20,000 and a market value of £60,000.

The company can apply section 845 in these circumstances although it starts with a negative balance of distributable profits. Section 845(3) provides that, for the purposes of section 845(1)(a), the company's profits available for distribution are treated as increased by the amount (if any) by which the amount or value of any consideration for the transfer exceeds the book value of the asset. The adjustment in this case is therefore £30,000 and the profits available for distribution in accordance with section 845(1)(a) are treated as £20,000. Section 845(2) provides that the amount of the distribution is taken to be zero because the amount of the consideration for the transfer is not less than the book value of the asset. The company may therefore lawfully make the transfer of the asset because the distributable reserves are treated as £20,000 and the amount of the distribution is treated as zero.

Realised losses brought forward	(10,000)
Adjustment for section 845(3):	
Increase in profits treated as available for distribution due to the consideration being in excess of the book value (£50,000 less £20,000)	30,000
Profits treated as available for distribution	20,000
Distribution measured in accordance with section 845	–
Balance carried forward on reserves	£20,000

Although the entire profit of £30,000 has been treated as realised for the purposes of the distribution, the balance carried forward on reserves falls to be treated in accordance with the normal rules. The analysis of reserves carried forward on reserves will depend on whether the transfer of the asset was for qualifying consideration. If the transfer was for qualifying consideration, the whole of the balance of £20,000 carried forward will be a realised profit. If the transfer was not for qualifying consideration, the profit arising on the transfer of the asset will be an unrealised profit and the analysis of reserves will be as follows:

Realised losses	(10,000)
Unrealised profit	30,000
Balance on reserves	£20,000

The same position is achieved by revaluing the asset and applying section 846. The asset could be revalued from £20,000 to £60,000 (its market value) which results in an unrealised profit of £40,000. The distribution is measured at £10,000 being the difference between the fair value of the asset and the consideration received on disposal. In accordance with section 846(2), the unrealised profit of £40,000 is treated as a realised profit for the purposes of determining the lawfulness of the distribution which consists of the sale of the non-cash asset. The profits treated as available for distribution under section 846 are therefore £30,000 which is adequate to cover the distribution of £10,000. This may be summarised as follows:

Realised losses brought forward	(10,000)
Unrealised profit arising from revaluation from book value (£20,000) to market value (£60,000) of the non-cash asset to be transferred to the parent	40,000
Profits treated as available for distribution in accordance with section 846	30,000
Distribution measured as the difference between the fair value of the asset (£60,000) and the consideration received (£50,000)	(10,000)
Balance carried forward on reserves	£20,000

The analysis of reserves carried forward will depend on whether the transfer of the non-cash asset was for qualifying consideration in the same way as described above under section 845.

The distribution in kind of the non-cash asset may therefore, in effect, be made out of unrealised profits without making good the shortfall on realised profits first. Whether or not the consideration for the transfer meets the definition of qualifying consideration has no effect of the lawfulness of the transfer but affects the disposition of the reserves following the transfer.

Appendix 2
Numerical illustrations for section 6

The following are numerical illustrations of the eight examples discussed in Section 6 of the guidance. The illustrations reflect the application of the 10 Principles in 6.7 to 6.40 of Section 6. The assumptions set out in 6.~~6A~~43 to 6.~~6C~~45 of Section 6 apply to these numerical illustrations.

These illustrations are based on simple terms and conditions of the types of financial instruments concerned. Therefore, they cannot, and do not, purport to be representative of the accounting that may flow from more complex terms and conditions. Determining whether a financial instrument is debt, equity or is a compound instrument and/or contains embedded derivatives depends on a rigorous analysis of the relevant instruments' full terms and conditions.

IFRSs ~~and converged UK GAAP (e.g. using FRS 26 'Financial instruments: Recognition and Measurement' and the fair value accounting rules in the Act)~~ do not distinguish between profits that are realised and those that are not. <u>Under FRS 102 unrealised profits may be included in the profit and loss account when applying fair value accounting.</u> Furthermore, as certain classes of share capital and their associated share premium have to be classified as liabilities and others split into debt and equity components, it is no longer possible to point to one place in the balance sheet that represents all of a company's share capital and share premium. Hence companies will need to maintain sufficient records to enable the tracking of their actual share capital and share premium and realised profits and thus their distributable profits. Companies may choose to do this in the form of memorandum accounts dealing with shares and options in relation to shares according to their legal form. Although, a company's annual statutory accounts prepared in accordance with IFRSs or <u>FRS 102</u>~~converged UK GAAP~~ will form their relevant accounts for the purposes of section 836 of the Act, it will be necessary to reconcile these back to records such as these memorandum accounts to understand the legal position in respect of their share capital, share premium, realised and distributable profits. Such memorandum accounts are illustrated below in addition to the balance sheet position under IFRSs<u> and FRS 102</u>/~~converged UK GAAP~~.

In the memorandum accounts, the realised profits available are shown for illustrative purposes as a separate component of equity.

In the IFRS/<u>FRS 102</u>~~converged UK GAAP~~ accounts, "<u>'</u>Other reserves<u>'</u>" represent amounts taken to equity for accounting purposes but which do not form part of "<u>'</u>share capital and undistributable reserves<u>'</u>". For public companies in these illustrations, the expression "<u>'</u>share capital and undistributable reserves<u>'</u>" for the purposes of section 831 comprises "<u>'</u>Share capital<u>'</u>", "<u>'</u>Share premium<u>'</u>" and "<u>'</u>Capital redemption reserve<u>'</u>" . The P&L reserve is taken initially to be comprised wholly of realised profits.

For the avoidance of doubt, these illustrations do not purport to define the headings or reserve names within which amounts, thrown up only by IFRS/<u>FRS 102</u>~~converged UK GAAP~~ accounting, must as a matter of accounting convention be maintained within equity.

EXAMPLE 1 – FORWARD CONTRACT TO REPURCHASE OWN EQUITY SHARES (SECTION 6, 6.46 – 6.50)

A company has entered into a forward contract to repurchase 100 of its own equity shares from a third party in 5 years' time and the shares are to be cancelled on repurchase. These shares have a nominal value of £100 and are to be bought back for £100 (present value assumed to be £70). The company will buy the shares back, assuming it has sufficient distributable profits, and cancel them.

Under IAS 32/~~FRS 25~~, as the company will be required to deliver cash, the forward contract meets the definition of a financial liability.

Journal entries for the IFRS[41] / converged UK GAAP balance sheet

On Day 1:

Dr	Equity – Other reserves	£70
Cr	Liability	£70

Being the recognition of the liability under the forward contract.

Note that the liability amount is the discounted present value of the redemption amount and is assumed to be £70 in this example. This recognises that the company has purchased an interest in itself on day 1 with the consideration being deferred.

The debit of £70 that has been recorded in other reserves is not an accounting loss and does not affect distributable profits on day 1.

Public company

The recognition of the liability reduces net assets and hence restricts distributable profits for public companies as a result of the section 831 net assets test.

During the 5 years:

Dr	Profit & Loss – Interest expense	£30
Cr	Liability	£30

Being the accretion of the discounted liability to the redemption amount of £100.

Private company

Although the interest is charged to the profit and loss account, it is not a loss for the purposes of Part VIII of the Act. Thus it is not a realised loss.

Public company

However, for a public company, although realised profits have not decreased, net assets have decreased (as the liability has increased). Hence there is a restriction through the operation of section 831 on the profits available for distribution of £100 in total immediately prior to repurchase as a result of this transaction.

---

[41] *FRS 102 does not require the recognition of the liability of £70.*

On settlement of the contract:

Dr   Liability   £100

Cr   Cash   £100

Being the payment (or distribution) to settle the forward contract.

Dr   Equity – Profit & Loss reserve   £70

Cr   Equity – Other reserves   £70

Being the entry to reflect the consumption of distributable profits in the Profit & Loss reserve as a result of the payment to settle the forward contract.

Dr   Equity – Share capital   £100

Cr   Equity – Capital redemption reserve   £100

Being the transfer to maintain the capital of the company.

Memorandum balance sheet

	Before entering into forward	Enter into forward to repurchase shares	Enter into forward to repurchase shares	Entries during the 5 years	Before repurchase	Repurchase entries	After repurchase
	£	£	£	£	£	£	£
Cash	100	0	0	0	100	(100)	0
Assets	200	0	0	0	200	0	200
Net assets	**300**	**0**	**0**	**0**	**300**	**(100)**	**200**
Share capital	200	0	0	0	200	(100)	100
Share premium	0	0	0	0	0	0	0
Capital redemption reserve	0	0	0	0	0	100	100
Realised profits	100	0	0	0	100[+]	(100)	0
Shareholders' funds	**300**	**0**	**0**	**0**	**300**	**(100)**	**200**

[+]*£100 represents the maximum profits available for distribution but for a public company this will be restricted by £100, immediately prior to repurchase, through the operation of section 831, which is applied to the section 836 relevant accounts (ie, the IFRS/ converged UK GAAP balance sheet below) which show that net assets are equal to share capital and undistributable reserves.*

For the purposes of section 831, in this illustration "'share capital and undistributable reserves"' comprise "'Share capital"', "'Share premium"' and "'Capital redemption reserve"'.

IFRS/converged UK GAAP balance sheet

	Before entering into forward	Enter into forward to repurchase shares	After entering into forward	Entries during the 5 years	Before repurchase	Repurchase entries	After repurchase
	£	£	£	£	£	£	£
Cash	100	0	100	0	100	(100)	0
Assets	200	0	200	0	200	0	200
Liabilities	0	(70)	(70)	(30)	(100)	100	0
Net assets	**300**	**(70)**	**230**	**(30)**	**200**	**0**	**200**
Share capital	200	0	200	0	200	(100)	100
Share premium	0	0	0	0	0	0	0
Capital redemption reserve	0	0	0	0	0	100	100
Other reserves	0	(70)	(70)	0	(70)	70	0
P&L reserve	100	0	100	(30)	70	(70)	0
Shareholders' equity	**300**	**(70)**	**230**	**(30)**	**200**	**0**	**200**

EXAMPLE 2 – WRITTEN OPTION TO REPURCHASE OWN EQUITY SHARES (SECTION 6, 6.51 TO 6.53)

A company writes an option to repurchase 100 of its own equity shares from a third party in 5 years' time. These shares have a nominal value of £100 and will be bought back for £100 (present value assumed to be £70). If the option is exercised by the third party, the company intends to buy the shares back out of profits, assuming it has sufficient distributable profits, and to cancel them. The company receives a premium of £5 on issue of the option.

Under IAS 32/~~FRS 25~~, as the company will be required to deliver cash on exercise of the option, the contract meets the definition of a financial liability. The premium received on the issue of the option is required to be taken directly to equity.

Journal entries for the IFRS[42] / ~~converged UK GAAP~~ balance sheet

On Day 1:

Dr	Cash	£5
Cr	Equity – Other reserves	£5

Being the recognition of the premium received.

The option premium is a realised profit because the premium is regarded as a profit at law and has been received in the form of cash. For the purposes of this illustration, the premium has been credited to other reserves on initial receipt and has remained there on exercise (but it could be taken to P&L reserve as illustrated in example 4).

Dr	Equity – Other reserves	£70
Cr	Liability	£70

Being the recognition of the liability under the written option.

Note that the liability amount is the discounted present value of the redemption amount and is assumed to be £70 in this example. This recognises that the company has purchased an interest in itself on day 1 with the consideration being deferred.

The debit of £70 that has been recorded in other reserves is not an accounting loss and does not affect distributable profits on day 1.

Public company

The recognition of the liability reduces net assets but not share capital and undistributable reserves and hence restricts distributable profits by £70 for public companies as a result of the section 831 net assets test.

During the 5 years:

Dr	Profit & Loss – Interest expense	£30
Cr	Liability	£30

Being the accretion over 5 years of the discounted liability to the redemption value of £100.

Private company

Although the interest is charged to the profit and loss account, it is not a loss for the purposes of Part VIII of the Act. Thus it is not a realised loss.

Public company

However, for a public company, although realised profits have not decreased, net assets have decreased (as the liability has increased). Hence there is a restriction through the operation of section 831 on profits available for distribution of the amount recognised a liability as a result of this transaction (in this case £100).

On settlement of the contract:

Dr	Liability	£100
Cr	Cash	£100

Being the payment (or distribution) to settle the forward contract.

Dr	Equity – Share capital	£100
Cr	Equity – Capital redemption reserve	£100

Being the transfer to maintain the capital of the company.

Dr	Equity – Profit & Loss reserve	£70
Cr	Equity – Other reserves	£70

Being the entry to reflect the consumption of distributable profits in the Profit & Loss reserve as a result of the payment on exercise.

Memorandum balance sheet

	Before issuing option	Issue of option to repurchase shares	After issuing option	Entries during the 5 years	Before exercise	Exercise entries	After exercise
	£	£	£	£	£	£	£
Cash	100	5	105	0	105	(100)	5
Assets	200	0	200	0	200	0	200
Net assets	**300**	**5**	**305**	**0**	**305**	**(100)**	**205**
Share capital	200	0	200	0	200	(100)	100
Share premium	0	0	0	0	0	0	0
Capital redemption reserve	0	0	0	0	0	100	100
Realised profits	100	5	105	0	105+	(100)	5
Shareholders' funds	**300**	**0**	**305**	**0**	**305**	**(100)**	**205**

+£105 represents the maximum profits available for distribution but for a public company this will be restricted by £100, immediately prior to exercise, through the operation of section 831, which is applied to the section 836 relevant accounts (ie, the IFRS / converged UK GAAP balance sheet below) which show that net assets only exceed share capital and undistributable reserves by £5.

For the purposes of section 831, in this illustration "'share capital and undistributable reserves"' comprise "'Share capital"', "'Share premium"' and "'Capital redemption reserve"'.

IFRS / converged UK GAAP balance sheet

	Before issuing option	Issue of option to repurchase shares	After issuing option	Entries during the 5 years	Before exercise	Exercise entries	After exercise
	£	£	£	£	£	£	£
Cash	100	5	105	0	105	(100)	5
Assets	200	0	200	0	200	0	200
Liabilities	0	(70)	(70)	(30)	(100)	100	0
Net assets	300	(65)	235	(30)	205	0	205
Share capital	200	0	200	0	200	(100)	100
Share premium	0	0	0	0	0	0	0
Capital redemption reserve	0	0	0	0	0	100	100
Other reserves	0	(65)	(65)	0	(65)	70	5
P&L reserve	100	0	100	(30)	70	(70)	0
Shareholders' equity	300	(65)	(65)	(30)	205	0	205

EXAMPLE 3 – FORWARD CONTRACT TO ISSUE OWN EQUITY SHARES (SECTION 6, 6.54 TO 6.56)

A company contracts with a third party that the latter will subscribe in one year's time for 100 of the company's £1 ordinary shares for a fixed price of £2 each. The contract cannot be settled other than by an exchange of the fixed amount of cash (£200) for the fixed number (100) of shares. It is assumed that the fair value of the forward contract at inception is zero and thus no cash is paid or received at that date. The functional currency of the company is pounds sterling.

No accounting entries are made on inception of the contract because no cash is paid or received since the contract's initial fair value is zero. This forward contract to deliver a fixed number of the company's own shares in exchange for a fixed amount of cash in the company's functional currency meets the definition of an equity instrument in IAS 32. There are no other settlement alternatives otherwise than through the delivery of shares in exchange for cash. Consequently, the right to receive the cash in one year's time is not recognised by the company. Therefore, where a company enters into a forward contract to issue ordinary shares, the IAS 32/FRS 25 accounting for such an arrangement raises no issues of distributable profits.

No accounting entries are made until the forward contract matures in one year's time, when the company receives £200 in cash and issues 100 ordinary shares to the contract's counterparty.

Journal entries for the IFRS-/-FRS 102converged UK GAAP balance sheet

On settlement of the contract:

Dr Cash	£200	
Cr Equity – Share capital		£100
Cr Equity – Share premium		£100

Being the issue of the shares at a premium of £1 per share for £200 in cash.

Memorandum balance sheet

	Before entering into forward	Enter into forward to issue shares	After entering into forward	On settlement of the contract	After settlement
	£	£	£	£	£
Cash	100	0	100	200	300
Assets	200	0	200	0	200
Liabilities	0	0	0	0	0
Net assets	**300**	**0**	**300**	**200**	**500**
Share capital	200	0	200	100	300
Share premium	0	0	0	100	100
Capital redemption reserve	0	0	0	0	0
Other reserves	0	0	0	0	0
Realised profits	100	0	100+	0	100
Shareholders' equity	**300**	**0**	**300**	**200**	**500**

'*£100 represents the maximum profits available for distribution. For a public company there is no restriction through the operation of section 831, which is applied to the section 836 relevant accounts (ie. the IFRS-/FRS 102converged UK GAAP balance sheet below) which show that net assets exceeds share capital and undistributable reserves by £100.*

For the purposes of section 831, in this illustration "'share capital and undistributable reserves'" comprise "'Share capital'", "'Share premium'" and "'Capital redemption reserve'".

IFRS-/FRS 102converged UK GAAP balance sheet

	Before entering into forward	Enter into forward to issue shares	After entering into forward	On settlement of the contract	After settlement
	£	£	£	£	£
Cash	100	0	100	200	300
Assets	200	0	200	0	200
Liabilities	0	0	0	0	0
Net assets	**300**	**0**	**300**	**200**	**500**
Share capital	200	0	200	100	300
Share premium	0	0	0	100	100
Capital redemption reserve	0	0	0	0	0
Other reserves	0	0	0	0	0
P&L reserve	100	0	100	0	100
Shareholders' equity	**300**	**0**	**300**	**200**	**500**

EXAMPLE 4 – WRITTEN OPTION TO ISSUE OWN EQUITY SHARES (SECTION 6, 6.57 TO 6.58)

A company issues an option allowing the holder to subscribe for 100 £1 ordinary shares for £1 each in one years' time. The functional currency of the company is pounds sterling. The option cannot be settled other than by an exchange of the cash in the functional currency of the company for the fixed number of shares. The holder makes an immediate payment of £5 to the company for the granting of this option.

The option is an equity instrument. Accordingly, the £5 received is credited directly to equity funds. The £5 is not an accounting profit. The £5 credit remains in equity funds irrespective of whether the option is exercised or lapses. If the option is exercised, the £100 is also credited directly to equity funds in the normal way.

Journal entries for the IFRS-/-FRS 102converged UK GAAP balance sheet

On Day 1:

Dr Cash	£5	
Cr Equity – Other reserves		£5

Being the receipt of the option premium.

In law the premium received is a profit at the outset, and a realised profit because it is received in cash. For the purposes of this illustration the premium has been credited to Other reserves on initial receipt and is transferred to the Profit & Loss reserve when the option is exercised.

On Exercise:

Dr Cash	£100	
Cr Equity – Share capital		£100
Dr Equity – Other reserves	£5	
Cr Equity – Profit & Loss reserve		£5

Being the entries for the issue of the new ordinary shares and receipt of the subscription monies and the transfer of the option premium to Profit & Loss reserve.

Memorandum balance sheet

	Before issuing option	Issue of option to issue shares	After issuing option	On exercise	After exercise
	£	£	£	£	£
Cash	100	5	105	100	205
Assets	200	0	200	0	200
Liabilities	0	0	0	0	0
Net assets	**300**	**5**	**305**	**100**	**405**
Share capital	200	0	200	100	300
Share premium	0	0	0	0	0
Capital redemption reserve	0	0	0	0	0
Other reserves	0	0	0	0	0
Realised profits	100	5	105[+]	0	105
Shareholders' equity	**300**	**0**	**305**	**100**	**405**

[+]*£105 represents the maximum profits available for distribution. For a public company there will be no restriction through the operation of section 831, which is applied to the section 836 relevant accounts (ie. the IFRS-/~~FRS 102~~converged UK GAAP balance sheet below) ~which show that net assets exceed share capital and undistributable reserves by £105.*

For the purposes of section 831, in this illustration "'share capital and undistributable reserves'" comprise "'Share capital'", "'Share premium'" and "'Capital redemption reserve'".

IFRS-/~~FRS 102~~converged UK GAAP *balance sheet*

	Before issuing option	Issue of option to issue shares	After issuing option	On exercise	After exercise
	£	£	£	£	£
Cash	100	5	105	100	205
Assets	200	0	200	0	200
Liabilities	0	0	0	0	0
Net assets	**300**	**5**	**305**	**100**	**405**
Share capital	200	0	200	100	300
Share premium	0	0	0	0	0
Capital redemption reserve	0	0	0	0	0
Other reserves	0	5	5	(5)	0
P&L reserve	100	0	100	5	105
Shareholders' equity	**300**	**5**	**305**	**100**	**405**

EXAMPLE 5 – CONVERTIBLE DEBT (SECTION 6, 6.59 TO 6.61)

A company issues a 5% £100 10-year convertible bond for £100. The bond is convertible, at the holder's option, into 100 £1 ordinary shares at the end of year 10. If not converted the bond is redeemable at the end of year 10 at par. The conversion feature cannot be settled other than by an exchange of the bond for the fixed number of shares. The company's functional currency is pounds sterling. There are no other features of the bond's terms and conditions that would deny equity treatment for the equity conversion option.

IAS 32/~~FRS 25~~ requires, where its~~their~~ conditions are met, that convertible debt is split into its constituent components of an unconvertible debt (assumed fair value, £60) and a written option to subscribe for ordinary shares (the equity conversion option). The latter component is accounted for in the same way as the stand-alone written option described in Example 4 above.

Journal entries for the IFRS-/~~FRS 102~~converged ~~UK GAAP~~ balance sheet

On Day 1:

Dr	Cash	£100
Cr	Liability	£60
Cr	Equity – Other reserves	£40

Being the recognition of the constituent components.

The split accounting is determined by computing the fair value of the debt component and assigning to the equity component the difference between the value of the debt and the proceeds of the bond issue. The fair value of the debt component is calculated as the present value of the repayment at maturity plus the present value of the future coupon payments (which are lower than those for an unconvertible debt due to the presence of the conversion opportunity). The discount rate used in calculating the present values is the prevailing market interest rate at the date the bonds were issued for a similar debt without the conversion option. For the purposes of this illustration, it is assumed that the split accounting is determined as £60 attributable to the liability component and £40 to the equity component.

The initial credit to equity is not a profit. It is not an accounting profit because in accounting terms it is the equivalent of an equity instrument. As a matter of law, it is not a profit either, because the proceeds received are in consideration for taking on a liability, albeit a liability that is not fully reflected in the accounts.

Over the 10 year life of debt:

Dr	Profit & Loss – Interest expense	£90
Cr	Cash	£50
Cr	Liability	£40

Being the recognition of 10 annual coupons of £5 each and the total additional interest of £40 to accrete the liability up to the redemption value. The allocation of the £90 among the 10 years' profit and loss accounts is determined using the appropriate method stipulated under the relevant accounting standard.

Dr	Equity – Other reserves	£40	
Cr	Equity – Profit & Loss reserve		£40

As the change to the liability becomes fully reflected in the accounts as a loss by virtue of the initial treatment through the additional interest charge, then the portion of the proceeds (£40) initially credited directly to equity offsets the impact of the initial treatment. For the purposes of this illustration, the amounts have been transferred from the Other reserves to the Profit & Loss reserve to reflect this.

At maturity (if conversion occurs):

Dr	Liability	£100	
Cr	Equity – Share capital)		£100

If the debt converts, the £100 is credited direct to shareholders' funds.

At maturity on redemption (if conversion does not occur):

Dr	Liability	£100	
Cr	Cash		£100

Recording the cash settlement of the liability.

Conversion

Memorandum balance sheet

	Before issuing convertible debt	Issue of convertible debt	After issuing convertible debt	Entries during the 10 years	Before conversion	Conversion entries	After conversion
	£	£	£	£	£	£	£
Cash	100	100	200	(50)	150	0	150
Assets	250	0	250	0	250	0	250
Liabilities	0	(100)	(100)	0	(100)	100	0
Net assets	**350**	**0**	**350**	**(50)**	**300**	**100**	**400**
Share capital	200	0	200	0	200	100	300
Share premium	0	0	0	0	0	0	0
Capital redemption reserve	0	0	0	0	0	0	0
Other reserves	0	0	0	0	0	0	0
Realised profits	150	0	150	(50)	100[+]	0	100
Shareholders' equity	**350**	**0**	**350**	**(50)**	**300**	**100**	**400**

[+] *£100 represents the maximum profits available for distribution. For a public company there is no restriction through the operation of section 831, which is applied to the section 836 relevant accounts (ie, the IFRS-/FRS 102converged UK GAAP balance sheet below) which show that net assets exceed share capital and undistributable reserves by £100.*

For the purposes of section 831, in this illustration "'share capital and undistributable reserves'" comprise "'Share capital'", "'Share premium'" and "'Capital redemption reserve'".

IFRS-/ FRS 102converged UK GAAP balance sheet

	Before issuing convertible debt	Issue of convertible debt	After issuing convertible debt	Entries during the 10 years	Before conversion	Conversion entries	After conversion
	£	£	£	£	£	£	£
Cash	100	100	200	(50)	150	0	150
Assets	250	0	250	0	250	0	250
Liabilities	0	(60)	(60)	(40)	(100)	100	0
Net assets	**350**	**40**	**390**	**(90)**	**300**	**100**	**400**
Share capital	200	0	200	0	200	100	300
Share premium	0	0	0	0	0	0	0
Capital redemption reserve	0	0	0	0	0	0	0
Other reserves	0	40	40	(40)	0	0	0
P&L reserve	150	0	150	(50)	100	0	100
Shareholders' equity	**350**	**40**	**390**	**(90)**	**300**	**100**	**400**

Redemption

Memorandum balance sheet

	Before issuing convertible debt	Issue of convertible debt	After issuing convertible debt	Entries during the 10 years	Before redemption	Redemption entries	After redemption
	£	£	£	£	£	£	£
Cash	100	100	200	(50)	150	(100)	50
Assets	250	0	250	0	250	0	250
Liabilities	0	(100)	(100)	0	100	100	0
Net assets	**350**	**0**	**350**	**(50)**	**300**	**0**	**300**
Share capital	200	0	200	0	200	0	200
Share premium	0	0	0	0	0	0	0
Capital redemption reserve	0	0	0	0	0	0	0
Other reserves	0	0	0	0	0	0	0
Realised profits	150	0	150	(50)	100[+]	0	100
Shareholders' equity	**350**	**0**	**350**	**(50)**	**300**	**0**	**300**

[+]*£100 represents the maximum profits available for distribution. For a public company there is no restriction through the operation of section 831, which is applied to the section 836 relevant accounts (ie, the IFRS-/ FRS 102converged UK GAAP balance sheet below) which show that net assets exceed ⁻share capital and undistributable reserves by £100.*

For the purposes of section 831, in this illustration "'share capital and undistributable reserves comprise "'Share capital"', "'Share premium"' and "'Capital redemption reserve"'.

IFRS-/ FRS 102converged UK GAAP balance sheet

	Before issuing convertible debt	Issue of convertible debt	After issuing convertible debt	Entries during the 10 years	Before redemption	Redemption entries	After redemption
	£	£	£	£	£	£	£
Cash	100	100	200	(50)	150	(100)	50
Assets	250	0	250	0	250	0	250
Liabilities	0	(60)	(60)	(40)	(100)	100	0
Net assets	**350**	**40**	**390**	**(90)**	**300**	**0**	**300**
Share capital	200	0	200	0	200	0	200
Share premium	0	0	0	0	0	0	0
Capital redemption reserve	0	0	0	0	0	0	0
Other reserves	0	40	40	(40)	0	0	0
P&L reserve	150	0	150	(50)	100	0	100
Shareholders' equity	**350**	**40**	**390**	**(90)**	**300**	**0**	**300**

EXAMPLE 6 – PREFERENCE SHARES PRESENTED AS LIABILITIES (SECTION 6, 6.62 TO 6.70)

A company issues for £110 (being fair value) in cash 100 of its 5% £1 preference shares which are mandatorily redeemable in 5 years' time for £125. The 5% coupons are non-discretionary, cumulative and payable annually. At redemption the company redeems them wholly out of distributable profits.

On issue of the redeemable preference shares the company is required to present these shares as a financial liability of £110, because the issuer has an obligation to transfer cash to the holder of the shares for both the principal and coupons and £110 is the fair value of the shares.

Journal entries for the IFRS-/~~FRS 102~~converged ~~UK GAAP~~ balance sheet

On day 1:

Dr	Cash	£110	
Cr	Liability		£110

Being the recognition of the financial liability under IAS 32/~~FRS 25~~.

Entries during the 5 years:

Dr	Profit & Loss – Interest expense	£40	
Cr	Cash		£25
Cr	Liability		£15

Being the recognition of the £5 annual non-discretionary dividends and the accretion of the liability over time, such that by redemption, the carrying amount of the liability is equal to the redemption price of £125. The allocation of the £40 among the 5 years' profit and loss accounts is determined using the appropriate method stipulated by the relevant accounting standard.

The presentation of the nominal value of £100 of, and the £10 of share premium associated with, the preference shares as a debt has no effect on the determination of the company's realised profits. The accrued dividend and the accrued redemption premium that is presented as an "interest charge" in the profit and loss account, and thus an accounting loss, is not, as a matter of law, a loss, as it is a distribution at the time it is actually made as such in law. Hence it is not until dividends (and the redemption premium) take legal effect that distributable profits are consumed by the distribution.

Public company

Notwithstanding that there is no consumption of distributable profits until such time that the dividends (and redemption premium) have legal effect, the accounting liability recognised for accrued but unpaid preference dividends and the accreted redemption premium reduces net assets. Therefore under section 831 there is a restriction on profits available for distribution equal to the amount of the reduction in net assets. Just before redemption, and assuming that the preference dividends have been paid, the section 831 restriction will be equal to the reduction in net assets of £15. This can be observed by comparing the realised profits in the Memorandum balance sheet (£175) with the Profit & Loss reserve (£160) in the IFRS-/~~FRS 102~~converged ~~UK GAAP~~ balance sheet.

Entries on redemption:

Dr	Liability	£125
Cr	Cash	£125

At the end of year 5, the company delivers £125 in cash to the shareholder, who delivers 100 of the company's (£1) redeemable preference shares. The company sets its cash payment of £125 against the financial liability.

Capital maintenance considerations

In addition, the company has to comply with the Act. Consequently, under section 733 of the Act there has to be a credit to capital redemption reserve equal to the nominal value of the preference shares redeemed that had been presented within liabilities. A corresponding debit is also made to distributable profits (the rationale for which is set out below).

At the same time the £10 of share premium, previously represented by the accounting liability, now falls to be included in the share premium account. A corresponding debit is made to distributable profits (the rationale for which is set out below).

Additional entries required on redemption due to capital maintenance rules:

Dr	Equity – Profit & Loss reserve	£110
Cr	Equity – Capital redemption reserve	£100
Cr	Equity – Share premium	£10

Being the entry to the Profit & Loss reserve which together with the debit for the accrued redemption premium (£15) ensures that £125 of distributable profits is consumed by the redemption price, as required by law. The entry to the Capital redemption reserve is the entry to reflect the legal preservation of the company's capital on redemption out of distributable profits. The £10 entry to the share premium account reflects the legal preservation of the initial share premium.

Memorandum balance sheet

	Before issuing preference shares	Issue of preference shares	After issuing preference shares	Entries during the 5 years	Before redemption	Redemption entries	After redemption
	£	£	£	£	£	£	£
Cash	100	110	210	(25)	185	(125)	60
Assets	300	0	300	0	300	0	300
Liabilities	0	0	0	0	0	0	0
Net assets	**400**	**110**	**510**	**(25)**	**485**	**(125)**	**360**
Share capital	200	100	300	0	300	(100)	200
Share premium	0	10	10	0	10	0	10
Capital redemption reserve	0	0	0	0	0	100	100
Realised profits	200	0	200	(25)	175+	(125)	50
Shareholders' equity	**400**	**110**	**510**	**(25)**	**485**	**(125)**	**360**

⁺*£175 represents the maximum profits available for distribution but for a public company this will be restricted by £15 through the operation of section 831, which is applied to the section 836 relevant accounts (ie, the IFRS+/FRS 102converged UK GAAP balance sheet below) which show that net assets only exceed share capital and undistributable reserves by £160.*

For the purposes of section 831, in this illustration "'share capital and undistributable reserves"' comprise "'Share capital"', "'Share premium"' and "'Capital redemption reserve"'.

IFRS+/FRS 102converged UK GAAP balance sheet

	Before issuing preference shares	Issue of preference shares	After issuing preference shares	Entries during the 5 years	Before redemption	Redemption entries	After redemption
	£	£	£	£	£	£	£
Cash	100	110	210	(25)	185	(125)	60
Assets	300	0	300	0	300	0	300
Liabilities	0	(110)	(110)	(15)	(125)	125	0
Net assets	**400**	**0**	**400**	**(40)**	**360**	**0**	**360**
Share capital	200	0	200	0	200	0	200
Share premium	0	0	0	0	0	10	10
Capital redemption reserve	0	0	0	0	0	100	100
P&L reserve	200	0	200	(40)	160	(110)*	50
Shareholders' equity	**400**	**0**	**400**	**(40)**	**360**	**0**	**360**

Redemption price consumption of distributable profits of £125 = £110 debit at redemption + £15 debit over period to redemption as the additional interest charge (£40-£25).

EXAMPLE 7 – MANDATORILY REDEEMABLE PREFERENCE SHARES (SECTION 6, 6.71 TO 6.77)

A company issues £100 nominal value of its £1 preference shares for £110 in cash. These shares are redeemable in 5 years' time for £125. Dividends are discretionary and non-cumulative. Under IAS 32/~~FRS 25~~ paragraphs 28 and AG37, these shares contain both a liability (assumed fair value, £90) and an equity component. Hence the instrument is classified as debt with an equity component for the dividend feature. It is assumed that over the five years, a total of £50 of discretionary dividends are paid. The accounting is set out below:

Journal entries for the IFRS~~/~~/~~FRS 102~~converged ~~UK GAAP~~ balance sheet

On Day 1:

Dr	Cash	£110	
Cr	Liability		£90
Cr	Equity – Share capital		£20

Being the cash receipt on issuing the shares and recording of the appropriate liability and equity components.

Note that the fair value of the liability amount is the discounted present value of the redemption amount and is assumed to be £90 in this example. The balance (£20) of the proceeds is allocated to the equity component. For ease of this illustration, it is assumed that the entire share premium (£10) is included in the liability and that the credit to equity (£20) is all share capital.

The £20 credit to equity is not an accounting profit and as a matter of law forms part of share capital. This applies irrespective of the allocation of the £20 between share capital and share premium.

Public company

For the purposes of section 831, there is no restriction on profits available for distribution on issue of the preference shares as share capital and undistributable profits have increased by £20 and this is equal to the increase in net assets. The presentation of the balance (£90) of the shares and share premium has no impact on the section 831 calculation.

During the 5 years:

Dr	Profit & Loss – Interest expense	£35	
Cr	Liability		£35

Being the accretion of the discounted liability to the redemption amount of £125.

Private company

The presentation of the discounted present value of the redemption amount of the preference shares as a liability has no effect on the determination of the company's realised profits. The interest expense from the accretion up to the full amount of the redemption price is presented as an accounting loss – as it is shown as an ""interest charge"". Since the ultimate payment is either a distribution or a capital repayment, the ""interest charge"" is, as a matter of law, not a loss even though it is accounted for as if it were a loss.

Public company

However, for a public company, although realised profits have not decreased, net assets have decreased (as the liability has increased) over the 5 years. Hence, through the operation of section 831, there is a restriction on distributions of the amount recognised as a liability, £35 in this case, by the redemption date. This can be observed by comparing the realised profits in the Memorandum balance sheet (£200) with the Profit & Loss reserve (£165) in the IFRS~/~FRS 102converged UK GAAP balance sheet.

During the 5 years:

Dr	Equity – Profit & Loss reserve	£50
Cr	Cash	£50

Being the payment of the discretionary dividends during the term of the instrument.

On redemption:

Dr	Liability	£125
Cr	Cash	£125

Being the payment to redeem the shares.

Capital maintenance considerations

The company has to comply with the Act. Consequently, under section 733 of the Act there has to be a credit to capital redemption reserve equal to the nominal value of the preference shares redeemed that had been presented within liabilities. A corresponding debit is also made to distributable profits adjusted for the £20 originally taken to share capital (the rationale for which is set out below).

At the same time the £10 of share premium, previously represented by the accounting liability, now falls to be included in the share premium account. A corresponding debit is made to distributable profits (the rationale for which is set out below).

Additional entries required on redemption due to capital maintenance rules:

Dr	Equity – Profit & Loss reserve	£90	
Cr	Equity – Capital redemption reserve		£100
Dr	Equity – Share capital	£20	
Cr	Equity – Share premium		£10

Being the entry to the Profit & Loss reserve which together with the debit for the accrued redemption premium (£35) ensures that £125 of distributable profits is consumed by the redemption price, as required by law. The entry to the Capital redemption reserve is the entry to reflect the legal preservation of the company's capital on redemption out of distributable profits. The £20 debit to share capital is to eliminate the £20 originally recorded in respect to the shares which are now cancelled as a result of the redemption. The £10 entry to the share premium account reflects the legal preservation of the initial share premium. This share premium credit (£10), taken together with the capital redemption reserve credit, to the extent not matched by the elimination of share capital (£100 – 20 =£80), gives rise to a corresponding £90 debit to the profit and loss reserve, as referred to above.

Memorandum balance sheet

	Before issuing preference shares	Issue of preference shares	After issuing preference shares	Entries during the 5 years	Before redemption	Redemption entries	After redemption
	£	£	£	£	£	£	£
Cash	100	110	210	(50)	160	(125)	35
Assets	250	0	250	0	250	0	250
Net assets	**350**	**110**	**460**	**(50)**	**410**	**(125)**	**285**
Share capital	100	100	200	0	200	(100)	100
Share premium	0	10	10	0	10	0	10
Capital redemption reserve	0	0	0	0	0	100	100
Realised profits	250	0	250	(50)	200+	(125)	75
Shareholders' funds	**350**	**110**	**460**	**(50)**	**410**	**(125)**	**285**

+£200 represents the maximum profits available for distribution but for a public company this will be restricted by £35 through the operation of section 831, which is applied to the section 836 relevant accounts (ie. the ~~IFRS+/~~FRS 102 ~~converged UK GAAP~~ balance sheet below) which show that net assets only exceed share capital and undistributable reserves by £165.

For the purposes of section 831, in this illustration "~~"~~share capital and undistributable reserves~~"~~" comprise "~~"~~Share capital~~"~~", "~~"~~Share premium~~"~~" and "~~"~~Capital redemption reserve~~"~~".

IFRS+/FRS 102 converged UK GAAP balance sheet

	Before issuing preference shares	Issue of preference shares	After issuing preference shares	Entries during the 5 years	Before redemption	Redemption entries	After redemption
	£	£	£	£	£	£	£
Cash	100	110	210	(50)	160	(125)	35
Assets	250	0	250	0	250	0	250
Liabilities	0	(90)	(90)	(35)	(125)	125	0
Net assets	**350**	**20**	**370**	**(85)**	**285**	**0**	**285**
Share capital	100	20	120	0	120	(20)	100
Share premium	0	0	0	0	0	10	10
Capital redemption reserve	0	0	0	0	0	100	100
P&L reserve	250	0	250	(85)	165	(90)*	75
Shareholders' equity	**350**	**20**	**370**	**(85)**	**285**	**0**	**285**

*Redemption price consumption of distributable profits of £125 = £90 debit at redemption + £35 debit over period to redemption as the additional interest charge.

EXAMPLE 8 – CONVERTIBLE REDEEMABLE PREFERENCE SHARES (SECTION 6, 6.78 TO 6.87)

A company issues for £100 in cash a non-cumulative 10% £100 10-year preference share. The 10% coupons are non-discretionary. The preference share is convertible at the holder's option at any time into 100 £1 ordinary shares. If the holder does not exercise its option to convert, the preference share is mandatorily redeemable for £100 at the end of year 10. The company's functional currency is pounds sterling. There are no other features of the preference share's terms and conditions that would deny equity treatment for the equity conversion option.

Under IAS 32 ~~and FRS 25~~ paragraph 28, the convertible redeemable preference share is a compound instrument. The preference share has to be split accounted to separate the debt and equity components. The liability component comprises the host redeemable preference share and the non-discretionary coupons (assumed fair value, £60) and the equity component comprises the equity conversion option. The accounting is set out below:

Journal entries for the IFRS~~+/FRS 102~~ ~~converged UK GAAP~~ balance sheet

On Day 1:

Dr Cash	£100	
Cr Liability		£60
Cr Equity – Share capital		£40

Being the recognition of the constituent liability and equity components.

The split accounting is determined by computing the fair value of the debt component and assigning to the equity component the difference between value of the debt component and the proceeds of the preference share issue. The fair value of the debt component is calculated as the present value of the repayment at final maturity (the only date at which cash could be paid) plus the present value of the future coupon payments (which are lower than those for an unconvertible preference share due to the presence of the conversion opportunity). The discount rate used in calculating the present values is the prevailing market coupon rate at the date the preference shares were issued for a similar preference shares without the conversion option. For the purposes of this illustration, it is assumed that the split accounting determined that £60 is the fair value attributable to the liability component and £40 to the equity component.

The £40 credit to equity is not an accounting profit and as a matter of law forms part of share capital.

During the 10 years:

Dr Profit & Loss – Interest expense	£140	
Cr Cash		£100
Cr Liability		£40

Being the recognition of the 10% coupon on the preference shares and the accretion of the liability component up to the redemption value.

Private company

The presentation of the discounted present value of the redemption amount of the preference shares as a liability has no effect on the determination of the company's realised profits. The interest expense from the accretion up to the full amount of the redemption price is presented as an accounting loss – as it is shown as an "'interest charge"'. Since the ultimate payment is either a distribution or a capital repayment, the "'interest charge"' is, as a matter of law, not a loss even though it is accounted for as if it were a loss.

Public company

However, for a public company, although realised profits have not decreased, net assets have decreased (as the liability has increased) over the 5 years. Hence, through the operation of section 831, there is a restriction on distributions of the amount recognised as a liability, £40 in this case, by the redemption date. This can be observed by comparing the realised profits in the Memorandum balance sheet (£150) with the Profit & Loss reserve (£110) in the IFRS+/FRS 102~~converged UK GAAP~~ balance sheet.

On conversion (if conversion occurs):

Dr Liability	£100	
Cr Equity – Share capital		£100

Being the recognition of the equity issued to settle the liability.

In addition, the company has to respect the fact that as a matter of law there is only £100 of share capital in issue (not £140 taking this journal together with the original issue journal).

Additional entries on conversion

Dr Equity – Share capital	£40	
Cr Equity – Profit & Loss reserve		£40

Being the entries to reflect the elimination of the prior accumulated debits to the profit and loss reserve in respect of the redemption price, with the corresponding adjustment taken to share capital leaving the balance there correctly representing just £100 of share capital, wholly classified as equity, post-conversion.

On redemption (if conversion does not occur):

Dr Liability	£100	
Cr Cash		£100

Being the recognition of the settlement of the liability in cash.

Capital maintenance considerations

In addition, the company has to comply with the Act. Consequently, under section 733 of the Act there has to be a credit to capital redemption reserve equal to the nominal value of the preference shares redeemed that had been presented within liabilities. However, only £40 of this is matched by a corresponding debit to eliminate the share capital now cancelled on redemption. The balance of £60 is debited to the profit and loss reserve (see below).

Additional entries required on redemption due to capital maintenance rules:

Dr   Equity – Profit & Loss reserve   £60
Dr   Equity – Share capital   £40
Cr   Equity – Capital redemption reserve   £100

Being the entries required to reflect the cancellation and preservation of the company's capital on redemption and the charging of the balance of £60 against realised profits; together with the £40- already charged to the profit and loss reserves, which now consumes realised profits, this brings the total consumption of realised profits, on redemption, to the £100 redemption price in accordance with law.

Conversion

Memorandum balance sheet

	Before issuing preference shares	Issue of preference shares	After issuing preference shares	Entries during the 10 years	Before conversion	Conversion entries	After conversion
	£	£	£	£	£	£	£
Cash	200	100	300	(100)	200	0	200
Assets	250	0	250	0	250	0	250
Liabilities	0	0	0	0	0	0	0
Net assets	**450**	**100**	**550**	**(100)**	**450**	**0**	**450**
Share capital	200	100	300	0	300	0	300
Share premium	0	0	0	0	0	0	0
Other reserves	0	0	0	0	0	0	0
Realised profits	250	0	250	(100)	150[+]	0	150
Shareholders' equity	**450**	**100**	**550**	**(100)**	**450**	**0**	**450**

[+]*£150 represents the maximum profits available for distribution but for a public company this will be restricted by £40, immediately prior to conversion, through the operation of section 831, which is applied to the section 836 relevant accounts (ie, the IFRS+/FRS 102converged UK GAAP balance sheet below) which show that net assets only exceed share capital and undistributable reserves by £110.*

For the purposes of section 831, in this illustration "'share capital and undistributable reserves'" comprise "'Share capital'", "'Share premium'" and "'Capital redemption reserve'".

IFRS+/FRS 102converged UK GAAP balance sheet

	Before issuing preference shares	Issue of preference shares	After issuing preference shares	Entries during the 10 years	Before conversion	Conversion entries	After conversion
	£	£	£	£	£	£	£
Cash	200	100	300	(100)	200	0	200
Assets	250	0	250	0	250	0	250
Liabilities	0	(60)	(60)	(40)	(100)	100	0
Net assets	**450**	**40**	**490**	**(140)**	**350**	**100**	**450**
Share capital	200	40	240	0	240	60	300
Share premium	0	0	0	0	0	0	0
Capital redemption reserve	0	0	0	0	0	0	0
Other reserves	0	0	0	0	0	0	0
P&L reserve	250	0	250	(140)	110	40	150
Shareholders' equity	**450**	**40**	**490**	**(140)**	**350**	**100**	**450**

Redemption

Memorandum balance sheet

	Before issuing preference shares	Issue of preference shares	After issuing preference shares	Entries during the 10 years	Before redemption	Redemption entries	After redemption
	£	£	£	£	£	£	£
Cash	200	100	300	(100)	200	(100)	100
Assets	250	0	250	0	250	0	250
Liabilities	0	0	0	0	0	0	0
Net assets	**450**	**100**	**550**	**(100)**	**450**	**(100)**	**350**
Share capital	200	100	300	0	300	(100)	200
Share premium	0	0	0	0	0	0	0
Capital redemption reserve	0	0	0	0	0	100	100
Other reserves	0	0	0	0	0	0	0
Realised profits	250	0	250	(100)	150[+]	(100)	50
Shareholders' equity	**450**	**100**	**550**	**(100)**	**450**	**(100)**	**350**

[+]*£150 represents the maximum profits available for distribution but for a public company this will be restricted by £40 through the operation of section 831, which is applied to the section 836 relevant accounts (ie. the IFRS+/FRS 102converged UK GAAP balance sheet below) which show that net assets only exceed share capital and undistributable reserves by £110.*

For the purposes of section 831, in this illustration "'share capital and undistributable reserves"' comprise "'Share capital"', "'Share premium"' and "'Capital redemption reserve"'.

IFRS+/FRS 102 converged UK GAAP balance sheet

	Before issuing preference shares	Issue of preference shares	After issuing debt	Entries during the 10 years	Before redemption	Redemption entries	After redemption
	£	£	£	£	£	£	£
Cash	200	100	300	(100)	200	(100)	100
Assets	250	0	250	0	250	0	250
Liabilities	0	(60)	(60)	(40)	(100)	100	0
Net assets	**450**	**40**	**490**	**(140)**	**350**	**0**	**350**
Share capital	200	40	240	0	240	(40)	200
Share premium	0	0	0	0	0	0	0
Capital redemption reserve	0	0	0	0	0	100	100
Other reserves	0	0	0	0	0	0	0
P&L reserve	250	0	250	(140)	110	(60)*	50
Shareholders' equity	**450**	**40**	**490**	**(140)**	**350**	**0**	**350**

*Redemption price consumption of distributable profits of £100 = £60 debit at redemption + £40 debit over period to redemption as the additional interest charge.

Appendix 3
~~Note of legal considerations reproduced from uitf abstract 38~~

~~[Deleted]The equivalent 2006 Act references have been added to the original note for ease of reference.~~

~~FRS 5 is not intended to affect the legal characterisation of a transaction, or to change the situation at law achieved by the parties to it (paragraph 46). Shares acquired by ESOP trusts and included in the balance sheet under this Abstract are not treasury shares as defined in the Companies Act 1985 (as amended by the Companies (Acquisition of Own Shares) (Treasury Shares) Regulations 2003) [s724 of the 2006 Act] or as defined by the Companies Act 1990 in the Republic of Ireland. Nor does the inclusion of the shares in the company's balance sheet as a deduction in arriving at shareholders' funds imply that they have been purchased by the company as a matter of law or that they are required to be cancelled, which would be the consequence of such a purchase except for shares held as treasury shares (in Great Britain sections 162(2) and 160(4) of the Companies Act 1985) [s706 of the 2006 Act].43~~

~~The UITF has received legal advice on the implications for companies' distributable profits when the accounting treatment required by this Abstract is followed. It has been advised that in Great Britain:~~

~~(a) Section 264 of the Companies Act 1985 [s831 of the 2006 Act] provides that a public company may only make a distribution if, and to the extent that, this will not reduce the company's net assets to less than an amount equal to the aggregate of its called up share capital and undistributable reserves. Section 270 [s836 of the 2006 Act] applies for the purposes of determining whether a distribution can be made without contravening sections 263, 264 or 265 [s830, s831 and s832 of the 2006 Act]. It provides that the amount of a distribution which can be made is determined by reference, inter alia, to the company's assets and liabilities as stated in the company's accounts. These are normally the company's last annual accounts (but may be initial or interim accounts). As the effect of the accounting treatment required by this Abstract would be that, in drawing up the accounts in question, any shares held by an ESOP would be recorded as a deduction in arriving at shareholders' funds rather than as an asset, it follows that the relevant aggregate asset value for the purposes of the definition of net assets in section 264(2) [s831(2) of the 2006 Act] would be reduced by a corresponding amount.~~

~~(b) In calculating a company's distributable profits, it is necessary to determine its "accumulated, realised profits so far as not previously utilised by distribution or capitalisation, less its accumulated, realised losses, so far as not previously written off in a reduction or reorganisation of capital duly made" (section 263(3) of the Companies Act 1985) [s830(2) of the 2006 Act].~~

~~The acquisition of shares by an ESOP does not, of itself, affect the company's realised profits or realised losses. The accounting treatment required by this Abstract, which requires a deduction in arriving at shareholders' funds and that no gain or loss should be recognised in the profit and loss account, is consistent with this analysis. This analysis holds good notwithstanding that an acquisition of treasury shares, with~~

~~43 The corresponding references in Northern Ireland are to articles 172(2) and 170(4) of the Companies (Northern Ireland) Order 1986 and in the Republic of Ireland to sections 211(2) and 208(a) of the Companies Act 1990. The corresponding references for the Republic of Ireland indicate the provisions dealing with the same topic as the sections in the Companies Act 1985 and are not identical in all cases. The Republic of Ireland references should be consulted for further information.~~

which an acquisition of shares by an ESOP has similarities, involves a deduction from distributable profits.

Although the acquisition of shares by an ESOP will not, of itself, result in a realised profit or loss for the company concerned, a company will still need to consider other transactions with the ESOP, for example a loan to the ESOP to fund acquisitions of shares, and these may affect the company's realised profits and losses.

(c)   In determining whether a company has sufficient distributable profits and net assets in order lawfully to pay a dividend to its shareholders, under section 270(2) of the Companies Act 1985 [s836(1) of the 2006 Act] the relevant accounts are the company's own individual accounts and not its consolidated accounts.

Appendix 4

[Deleted]

NUMERICAL ILLUSTRATIONS FOR SECTION 8

Distinguishing the cumulative gain or loss in reserves from the pension surplus or deficit

It is the cumulative gain or loss credited or debited to reserves in respect of a pension scheme, rather than the existence of a surplus or deficit, that affects the realised profits and losses of a company. Consider the example below of a scheme set up at the start of the year. For simplicity, current and deferred tax is ignored. The scheme has a surplus of 4 at the end of the year that would be reported on the company's balance sheet as an asset. Contributions have been paid which are equal to the expense recognised in the profit and loss account of 20. An actuarial gain of 4 has also been recognised in the STRGL.

	Increase/ (decrease) in pension asset	(Reduction) in cash balance	Amount debited/ (credited) in reserves
Brought forward	0		
Debited to profit and loss	(20)		20
Credited in STRGL	4		(4)
Contributions paid	20	20	
Carried forward	4	(20)	16

The net effect on the balance sheet in the above example is:

Dr Pension asset	4	
Dr Reserves	16	
Cr Cash		20

It is the cumulative loss of 16 in the above example that has been debited to reserves in respect of the pension scheme that falls to be treated as realised, rather than any notional 'credit' relating to the asset of 4.

Establishing the effect on realised profits at a particular date

This example illustrates the application of paragraph 8.14 of the guidance in the case where the company has recognised a pension asset on acquisition of an unincorporated business.

In 2005, a company acquired an unincorporated business and the fair values of the net assets recognised included a pension asset of 20. At 31 December 2007, cumulative post-acquisition contributions of 4 have been made and the asset has reduced to 18. The cumulative amount included in reserves is calculated as follows:

Surplus recognised in balance sheet	18
Cumulative net contributions	(4)
Surplus recognised on acquisition	(20)
Amount included in reserves (debit)	(6)

Another way of expressing the same calculation is as follows:

Cumulative net contributions		(4)
Surplus recognised in balance sheet	18	
Less: Surplus recognised on acquisition	(20)	
Decrease in surplus recognised		(2)
Amount included in reserves (debit)		(6)

It can be seen from this example that there must be a cumulative debit in reserves if the asset recognised in the balance sheet is less than the amount recognised on acquisition provided that the cumulative net post-acquisition contributions are not negative and the scheme has not been combined with any other scheme.

Appendix 5
Illustrative examples of the effect of the principles relating to foreign currency set out in section 11

EXAMPLE 1 – ILLUSTRATION OF PRINCIPLES 1 AND 2 (FUNCTIONAL CURRENCY STRENGTHENS)

Principle 1: Realised profits and losses are measured by reference to the functional currency of the company.

Principle 2: An accounting gain or loss arising upon the retranslation of the whole of the accounts from the company's functional currency to a presentation currency, is not a profit or a loss as a matter of law. Such an amount therefore cannot be a realised profit or a loss.

Facts:

Type of company	Private
Functional currency	Sterling
Share capital currency	Sterling
Presentation currency	Dollars
Opening exchange rate	£1 = $1.6
Average exchange rate	£1 = $1.7
Closing exchange rate (sterling has strengthened against the dollar)	£1 = $1.8

The company began the year with no cumulative translation difference (eg, there has been no exchange rate variation to date).

The company's assets and profits are as shown in the table below.

The company's functional and presentation balance sheets and income statements are as follows:

	Opening balance sheet	Profit	Retranslation difference	Closing balance sheet
In functional currency	£	£		£
Share capital	100			100
Profit and loss account reserve (all realised)	20	30		50
Net assets	120	30		150
In presentation currency	$	$	$	$
	(at $1.6)	(at $1.7)		
Share capital	160			160
Profit and loss account reserve	32	51		83
Cumulative translation difference	–		27	27
Net assets	192	51	27	270*

*Net assets of £150 translated at £1 = $1.8.

What are this company's realised profits for the purposes of Part 23?

In accordance with principle 1, the realised profits are measured in the functional currency. In accordance with principle 2, the cumulative translation difference of $27 is not a realised profit. The realised profits are therefore £50. The company could, therefore, so far as the Act is concerned, distribute £50, being $90 in presentation terms (£50 at $1.8) (note that the $83 shown in the profit and loss account reserve is the accumulation of functional currency profits translated at historical presentation rates). The retranslation process has no effect on the determination of realised profits, which occurs at the level of the underlying functional numbers.

Public companies should give consideration to principle 7 when applying the s831 net assets test, as the test operates by reference to the amounts shown in presentation currency, in contrast with the fact that realised profits are measured in the functional currency. In this example there is no restricting effect as the difference between the net assets of $270 and share capital of $160 is $110, which equates to £61 when translated at the closing rate, which is greater than the realised profits in functional currency terms.

EXAMPLE 2 – ILLUSTRATION OF PRINCIPLES 1 AND 2 (FUNCTIONAL CURRENCY WEAKENS)

Principle 1: Realised profits and losses are measured by reference to the functional currency of the company.

Principle 2: An accounting gain or loss arising upon the retranslation of the whole of the accounts from the company's functional currency to a presentation currency, is not a profit or a loss as a matter of law. Such an amount therefore cannot be a realised profit or loss.

Facts:

Type of company	Private
Functional currency	Sterling
Share capital currency	Sterling
Presentation currency	Dollars
Opening exchange rate	£1 = $1.6
Average exchange rate	£1 = $1.5
Closing exchange rate (sterling has weakened against the dollar)	£1 = $1.3

The company began the year with no cumulative translation difference (eg, there has been no exchange rate variation to date).

The company's assets and profits are as shown in the table below.

The company's functional and presentation balance sheets and income statements are as follows:

	Opening balance sheet	Profit	Retranslation difference	Closing balance sheet
In functional currency	£	£		£
Share capital	100			100
Profit and loss account reserve (all realised)	20	30		50
Net assets	120	30		150
In presentation currency	$	$	$	$
	(at $1.6)	(at $1.5)		
Share capital	160			160
Profit and loss account reserve	32	45		77
Cumulative translation difference	–		(42)	(42)
Net assets	192	45	(42)	195*

*Net assets of £150 translated at £1 = $1.3.

What are this company's realised profits for the purposes of Part 23?

In accordance with principle 1, the realised profits are measured in the functional currency. In accordance with principle 2, the cumulative translation difference of $(42) not a realised loss. The realised profits are therefore £50. The company could, therefore, so far as the Act is concerned, distribute £50, being $65 in presentation terms (£50 at $1.3) (note that the $77 shown in the profit and loss account reserve is the accumulation of functional currency profits translated at historical presentation rates). The retranslation process has no effect on the determination of realised profits, which occurs at the level of the underlying functional numbers.

Public companies should give consideration to principle 7 when applying the s831 net assets test, as the test operates by reference to the amounts shown in presentation currency, in contrast with the fact that realised profits are measured in the functional currency. Example 7 follows the same fact pattern as above but is for a public company and illustrates the resulting restriction.

EXAMPLE 3 – ILLUSTRATION OF PRINCIPLE 3

Principle 3: The profit or loss arising upon the necessary retranslation of an autonomous branch, from its functional currency into the functional currency of the company, is a realised profit or a loss to the extent that the branch net assets during the period, in relation to which the components of that profit or loss arise, were qualifying consideration.

Facts:

Functional currency of company	Sterling
Functional currency of branch	Dollars
Presentation currency of company*	Sterling
Opening exchange rate	£1 = $2.0
Closing exchange rate	£1 = $1.5

This example is not concerned with presentation currency issues. A presentation currency is included as a simplifying assumption.

The company began the year with no cumulative translation difference (ie, there has been no exchange rate variation to date).

For simplicity and illustrative purposes it has been assumed that there has been no trading during the period, no interest has accrued on the loan and there are no intercompany balances.

The branch's functional currency balance sheets are as follows:

	Opening balance sheet $	Closing balance sheet $
Property, plant and equipment (land)	30	30
Cash	30	30
Loans	(6)	(6)
Net assets	54	54
Represented by:		
Retained profits (all realised)	54	54

When included in the functional currency balance sheet of the company (which currency is also its presentation currency), the assets and liabilities of the branch will be stated as follows:

	£ (at $2.0)	£ (at $1.5)
Property, plant and equipment (land)	15	20
Cash	15	20
Loans	(3)	(4)
Net assets	27	36
Represented by:		
Cumulative translation difference		9
Profit and loss account reserve	27	27
Total	27	36

What are this company's realised profits, in relation to its branch, for the purposes of Part 23?

In accordance with principle 3, the cumulative translation difference needs to be analysed with reference to the assets and liabilities that give rise to the difference. In the example above, there is a net profit of 9 which comprises:

Retranslation gain on property, plant and equipment	5
Retranslation gain on cash	5
Retranslation loss on loans	(1)
Total	9

The gain on the property, plant and equipment is not a realised gain, as these assets do not constitute qualifying consideration. The gain on the cash balance held will be a realised gain as cash is qualifying consideration. The loss on the translation of the loan is a realised loss. Therefore, despite a net gain recorded in equity of 9, only 4 of this constitutes realised profit. In total the company's realised profits in relation to its branch are £31. Note that this amount is the realised profits of the branch measured in the company's functional currency in accordance with Principle 1; although the branch has profits of $54 in its branch functional currency of dollars, there is no concept of realised profits at branch level but only at company level where the functional currency is sterling and thus the $54 figure is of itself of no relevance.

If in the example above the company did not have any assets that comprise qualifying consideration, for example, if the cash was instead say an investment property then despite there being a net gain of 9 recognised in equity, the impact on distributable profits would be a reduction of 1, as the loss of the loan would be realised but the gains unrealised.

EXAMPLE 4 – ILLUSTRATION OF PRINCIPLE 4

Principle 4: Where a company's shares, whether those shares are classified as equity or debt for accounting purposes, are denominated in a currency other than the company's functional currency, the adjustment arising upon any translation for accounting purposes of the share capital is not a profit or loss at law. Such an amount therefore cannot be a realised profit or loss.

Facts:

Functional currency	Sterling
Presentation currency	Sterling
Share capital currency	Euro
Nominal value of shares	€90
Opening exchange rate	£1 = €1.8
Closing exchange rate	£1 = €2.0
Share classified as	Accounting equity
Share capital retranslated at balance sheet date	Yes

There have been no translation differences on the share capital prior to the opening balance sheet.

The company has no other foreign (ie, non-sterling) assets or liabilities.

The company's functional and presentation currency balance sheets and income statements are as follows:

	Opening balance sheet	Profit	Retranslation difference	Closing balance sheet
	£	£	£	£
	(at €1.8)			(at €2.0)
Share capital	50			45
Reserve for translation difference on share capital			5	5
Profit and loss account reserve (all realised)	490	270		760
Net assets	540	270	540	810

What are this company's realised profits for the purposes of Part 23?

It is only the profits represented in the retained profit account that are realised (£760). The translation difference of £5 that arises in the above scenario is not a profit at law, and as such the amount cannot be a realised profit. The same would apply if the closing balance sheet exchange rate was £1 = €1.5 meaning that the share capital was stated at £60, the resulting debit balance of £10 would not be a realised loss.

Public companies should give consideration to principle 7 when applying the s831 net assets test, as the test operates by reference to the amounts shown in the accounts. Therefore, the s831 test is applied by reference to share capital recorded at £45, even though the difference of £5 shown above for the retranslation of share capital is not realised (in this particular case there is no restricting effect, since £810 of net assets less £45 of share capital exceeds the realised profits of £760). The s831 test only determines the maximum amount of realised profits that are distributable; it does not have an impact on the calculation of realised profits for the purposes of Part 23.

If the shares were measured at their historical amount (ie, not retranslated) there would be no foreign currency movement in respect of the share capital as they remain at their historical amounts (although please see example principle 5 as the current currency worth of the shares would need to be considered).

Shares classified as an accounting liability

Suppose that the facts are the same as before but instead the shares are classified as an accounting liability. In this scenario IAS 21 requires the liability to be retranslated at each balance sheet date, and the foreign exchange difference that arises will be recognised in the income statement. Even though the shares are presented as an accounting liability, they remain share capital as a matter of law; any exchange difference arising on the retranslation is the result of an accounting exercise rather than a profit or loss in law; and the company's realised profits would be as above. However, consideration will need to be given to the other principles (such as the current currency worth of share capital) to determine whether there is any restriction as to the amounts that can be distributed.

EXAMPLE 5 – ILLUSTRATION OF PRINCIPLE 5

Principle 5: Where a company's shares, whether those shares are classified as equity or debt for accounting purposes, are denominated in a currency other than the company's functional currency, the common law has the effect of restricting distributions where to do otherwise would result in the net assets' falling below the functional currency worth of the share capital.

Facts:

Functional currency	Sterling
Presentation currency	Sterling
Share capital currency	Euro
Nominal value of shares	€90
Opening exchange rate	£1 = €2.0
Closing exchange rate	£1 = €1.8
Share classified as	Accounting equity
Share capital retranslated at balance sheet date	No

Assume shares were issued when the exchange rate was £1 = €2.0.

The company has no other foreign (ie, non-sterling) assets or liabilities.

The company's functional and presentation balance sheets and income statements are as follows:

	Opening balance sheet	Profit	Closing balance sheet
	£	£	£
Share capital	45		45
Profit and loss account reserve (all realised)	495	270	765
Net assets	540	270	810

What are this company's realised profits for the purposes of Part 23, and what is the maximum amount that the company could distribute?

For the purposes of Part 23, the company's realised profits are £765.

Even though the company has not translated its share capital it still needs to take account of what is the current currency worth of its shares. At the balance sheet date, the €90 of share capital would be worth £50. Therefore when comparing the current worth of the share capital and the net assets in functional currency terms, any distribution would be limited to £760 (£810 − £50).

EXAMPLE 6 – ILLUSTRATION OF PRINCIPLE 6

Principle 6: Share premium account, and similar capital accounts, do not have a currency of denomination but are amounts of record in the books of account in functional currency.

Facts:

Functional currency	Sterling
Presentation currency	Sterling
Currency shares denominated in	Euro
Nominal value of shares (in denomination currency)	€90
Consideration originally received for share issue	€100
Opening exchange rate	£1 = €2.0
Closing exchange rate	£1 = €1.8
Share classified as	Accounting equity
Share capital retranslated at balance sheet date	No

Assume shares were issued when the exchange rate was £1 = €2.0.

Share premium fixed in sterling at historical rate (€100-€90, at £1 = €2.0)   £5

The company has no other foreign (ie, non-sterling) assets or liabilities.

The company's balance sheets and income statements are as follows:

	Opening balance sheet	Profit	Closing balance sheet
	£	£	£
Share capital	45		45
Share premium	5		5
Profit and loss account reserve (all realised)	490	270	760
Net assets	540	270	810

What are this company's realised profits for the purposes of Part 23, and what is the maximum amount that the company could distribute?

For the purposes of Part 23, the company's realised profits are £760.

As illustrated in example 5, the company needs to take account of what the current currency worth of the share capital is. As before at the balance sheet date the €90 of share capital (the amount initially issued) would be worth £50. Therefore, there may be a restricting effect due to the increase in the currency worth of the shares as a result of the exchange rate movement. There is, however, no equivalent variation in worth in relation to the share premium; but the share premium account is capital that may not be distributed. Thus under Principle 5 this company compares its net assets of £810 with the aggregate of the current functional currency worth of its share capital (£50) and the functional currency amount of record of its share premium (£5), amounting to £55, and finds that the result does have a restricting effect: ie, £755 is less than the realised profits of £760.

Thus only £755 of the realised profits would be distributable.

It should be noted that in this computation the existence of a share premium account has not, however, increased the restriction. (Eg, if the company had not issued the shares at a premium and had correspondingly lower net assets, then Principle 5 would still yield a £5 restriction: £805 – 50 = £755 vs £760 realised.) What should be appreciated is that had the share premium account in this Example 6 been omitted from the capital side of the Principle 5 calculation, then the company would incorrectly have concluded that there was no restriction (£810 net assets less £50 share capital = £760 vs £760 realised, ie, no apparent restriction) and could have inadvertently distributed part of its capital.

EXAMPLE 7 – ILLUSTRATION OF PRINCIPLE 7

Principle 7: The application of the s831 statutory net assets test operates by reference to amounts as shown upon the face of the accounts in presentation currency.

Facts:

Type of company	Public
Functional currency	Sterling
Share capital currency	Sterling
Presentation currency	Dollars
Opening exchange rate	£1 = $1.6
Average exchange rate	£1 = $1.5
Closing exchange rate	£1 = $1.3

The facts are the same as Example 2 except the company is a public company.

The company began the year with no cumulative translation difference (eg, there has been no exchange rate variation to date).

Its assets and profits are as shown in the table below.

The company's functional and presentation balance sheets and income statements are as follows:

	Opening balance sheet	Profit	Retranslation difference	Closing balance sheet
In functional currency	£	£		£
Share capital	100			100
Profit and loss account reserve (all realised)	20	30		50
Net assets	120	30		150
In presentation currency	$	$	$	$
	(at $1.6)	(at $1.5)		
Share capital	160			160
Profit and loss account reserve	32	45		77
Cumulative translation difference	–		(42)	(42)
Net assets	192	45	(42)	195*

Net assets of £150 translated at £1 = $1.3.

What are this company's realised profits for the purposes of Part 23, and how much can be distributed under Part 23?

In accordance with principle 1, the realised profits are measured in the functional currency. The realised profits are therefore £50 (see example 2). In accordance with principle 2, the cumulative translation difference of $(42) is not a realised loss. If it were a private company, the company could, therefore, so far as the Act is concerned, distribute £50, being $65 in presentation terms (£50 at $1.3).

However, a public company is subject to s831 (see 2.30 – 2.31 above). In summary, a public company may make a distribution only if, after giving effect to such distribution, the amount of its net assets (as defined in s831(2)) is not less than the aggregate of its called-up share capital and undistributable reserves (as defined in s831(4)) as shown in the relevant accounts. This calculation is performed using figures taken directly from the presentational currency accounts.

The cumulative translation reserve does not meet the s831(4) definition of an undistributable reserve (nor is it share capital), therefore the purposes of s831 the amount that could be distributed is calculated below:

	$
Net assets	195
Share capital	(160)
Undistributable reserves	–
Amount that can be distributed under s831	35

The company could under Part 23 distribute only $35, rather than the full £50 ($65) of realised profits (see above).

Note that this restriction is correctly expressed in dollars since it is derived according to the statutory formula from amounts expressed on the face of the accounts in presentation dollars. This is so even though the realised profits, the distribution of which it restricts, are themselves in sterling (in accordance with Principle 1). In order to ascertain the effect of this restriction on any particular distribution, it is necessary to compare the dollar worth of that distribution with this $35 figure. The dollar worth of the distribution would be computed at the exchange rate applying at the date of making the distribution (see [TECH 01/09] paragraph 2.10 as to this date).

Appendix 6
Foreign currency branch examples

EXAMPLE 1 – ILLUSTRATION OF A NON-TRADING BRANCH THAT PURCHASES AND HOLDS PPE

Principle 3: The profit or loss arising upon the necessary retranslation of an autonomous branch, from its functional currency into the functional currency of the company, is a realised profit or a loss to the extent that the branch net assets were qualifying consideration when the profit or loss arose.

The simplified illustration below demonstrates the effect on realised profits from changes in the composition of a branch's net assets (in this case purchasing and holding PPE). In analysing a net retranslation gain or loss, regard must be had to the nature of the changing asset base on which they arise. In practice, when conducting the analysis, reasonable approximations may be made.

See illustration on next page.

Assumptions

Company with a sterling functional currency establishes a branch which has a dollar functional currency

All cash flows happen at the end of the month

All of the branch's transactions are transacted in Dollars

Background

The branch starts the period with cash, which it uses to purchase land. No further transactions are undertaken

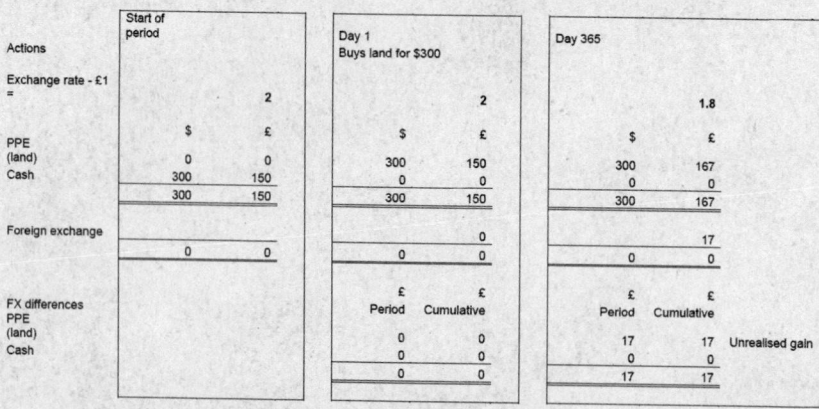

Even though the branch has been dormant since it purchased the land, we can not assume that the foreign exchange difference of 17 arising in the year on the opening balance sheet is realised just because the balance sheet was represented by cash on day 1.

EXAMPLE 2 – ILLUSTRATION OF A TRADING BRANCH AND THE IMPORTANCE OF THE COMPOSITION OF FOREIGN EXCHANGE MOVEMENTS

Principle 3: The profit or loss arising upon the necessary retranslation of an autonomous branch, from its functional currency into the functional currency of the company, is a realised profit or a loss to the extent that the branch net assets were qualifying consideration when the profit or loss arose.

The simplified illustration below demonstrates the effect on realised profits from changes in the composition of a branch's net assets (in this case building up inventory to a peak and then running it down again). In analysing a net retranslation gain or loss, regard must be had to the nature of the changing asset base on which they arise. In practice, when conducting the analysis, reasonable approximations may be made.

See illustration on next page.

Assumptions

Company with a sterling functional currency establishes a branch which has a dollar functional currency.

All cash flows happen at the end of the month.

The loan that the branch has taken out is non-interest bearing

All of the branch's transactions are transacted in Dollars

Background

The branch obtains a loan at the start of the period, which it uses to purchase inventory in the first half. It then starts to run down the inventory.

Actions	Start of period		Month 1		Month 2	
	Obtain loan of $300 Purchase inventory for $100		Buys inventory for $100		Sells $50 of inventory for $100	
Exchange rate - £1 =		2		2.2		1.9
	$	£	$	£	$	£
Inventory	100	50	200	91	150	79
Cash	200	100	100	45	200	105
Loan	(300)	(150)	(300)	(136)	(300)	(158)
	0	0	0	0	50	26
Trading profit (realised)			0	0	50	26
Foreign exchange				0		0
	0	0	0	0	50	26

FX differences			Period	Cumulative	Period	Cumulative
			£	£	£	£
Inventory			(4.5)	(4.5)	13.0	8.5	Unrealised gain
Realisation of inventory FX (*1)					1.3	1.3	Realised gain *1
Cash			(9.1)	(9.1)	7.2	(1.9)	Realised loss
Loan			13.6	13.6	(21.5)	(7.9)	Realised loss
			0.0	0.0	0.0	0.0	

*1 - See separate sheet on pages 160-161

If the opening and closing cash balance is looked at in isolation, one might assume that when calculating the realised profits of the branch, foreign currency movements on the cash balance would not have an adverse effect on the amounts that can be distributed – the balance at the start and end of the period is the same and there has been a favourable change in the exchange rate – the $200 that at the start of period was worth £100 is now worth £105.

On that assumption, one might conclude that all that needs to be considered is the foreign exchange movements on the loan balance, as the foreign exchange movements on the inventory will be unrealised gains.

However as can be seen from the foreign exchange movements that arise in the period, there is actually a cumulative foreign exchange loss on cash balance during the period. This will be a realised loss. The realised profits at the end of the period are £17 (£26 trading profit less £10 realised foreign exchange loss (on the cash and the loan) and a £1 realised gain in relation to foreign exchange movements that have arisen on the sale of inventory (see separate sheet).

The example above is a simplified example which demonstrates that when analysing a net retranslation gain or loss, regard must be had to the nature of the changing asset base on which they arise. When conducting the analysis in a more complicated scenario reasonable approximations may be made.

Analysis of movements from the company's perspective of changes in the composition of the branch's net assets

	Inventory $	Inventory £	Cash $	Cash £	Loan $	Loan £
Balance at start of period (£1:$2)	100	50.0	200.0	100.0	(300.0)	(150.0)
FX during period						
$100 @ £1:$2.2 - $100 @ £1:$2		(4.5)				
$200 @ £1:$2.2 - $200 @ £1:$2				(9.1)		
$300 @ £1:$2.2 - $300 @ £1:$2						13.6
Cashflow movements						
$100 @ £1=$2.2			(100.0)	(45.5)		
Inventory movements						
$100 @ £1=$2.2	100.0	45.5				
End of month 1 (£1:$2.2)	200.0	90.9	100.0	45.5	(300.0)	(136.4)
FX during period						
$200 @ £1:$2 - $100 @ £1:$1.9		14.4				
$100 @ £1:$2 - $200 @ £1:$1.9				7.2		
$300 @ £1:$2 - $300 @ £1:$1.9						(21.5)
Sub-total before trading profits		105.3		52.6		(157.9)
Cumulative FX		9.8		(1.9)		(7.9)
Inventory movements						
Sale of $50	(50.0)	(25.0) *1				
Realisation of inventory FX movement		(1.3) *2				
		(26.3) *3				
Cashflow movements						
Realisation of historic cost of inventory			100.0	25.0 *1		
Realisation of inventory FX				1.3 *2		
Trading profit				26.3 *4		
				52.6 *5		
End of month 2 (£1:$1.9)	150.0	78.9	200.0	105.3	(300.0)	(157.9)
Cumulative FX at end of month 2		8.5		(1.9)		(7.9)

*1   On a FIFO basis $50 of inventory sold was originally £25 (at £1:$2).
    Whilst this example assumes a FIFO approach, other methods may be adopted according to normal considerations.
*2   This difference, between (*1) and (*2) is the FX gain in inventory realised as a result of its sale for cash.
*3   Inventory of $50 removed from the inventory balance when the rate is £1:$1.9.
*4   Calculated as the difference between the proceeds received ($100 @ £1:$1.9) and the carrying amount of inventory sold ($50 @ £1:$1.9)
*5   This equals $100 at £1:$1.9 (the exchange rate on the date of the transaction) and is comprised of the 3 components above

Appendix 7
Illustrative examples of a company's position in several scenarios for capital reductions where there have been movements in the exchange rate between the functional currency and foreign share capital currency.

Facts:

Functional currency	Sterling
Presentation currency	Sterling
Share capital currency	Dollars
Nominal value of shares	$200
Opening exchange rate	£1 = $2.0
Closing exchange rate	See the illustrations below for alternates
Share classified as	Accounting equity
Share capital retranslated at balance sheet date	See the illustrations below for alternates

Assume that the shares were issued when the exchange rate was £1 = $2.0, and the proceeds received on issue were converted into sterling.

Assume that the company has no other foreign (ie, non-sterling) assets or liabilities.

Please see the illustrations below for a company's position in several scenarios.

	Reduction of currency shares capital £1 = $x 1.00				Exclusive of repayment £1 = $x 4.00			
	Share capital	Retrans entry	Redux reserve	Total	Share capital	Retrans entry	Redux reserve	Total
	£	£	£	£	£	£	£	£
Without retranslation b/f	100			100	100			100
Reduction	(200)		200	0	(50)		50	0
Un(over) eliminated	100		(100)	0	(50)		50	0
c/f	0	0	100	100	0	0	100	100
With retranslation b/f	200	(100)		100	50	50		100
Reduction	(200)		200	0	(50)		50	0
Un(over) eliminated	0	0	100	0	0	(50)	50	0
	0	0	100	100	0	0	100	100

	Reduction of currency shares capital				With repayment		
	£1 = $x 1.00				£1 = $x 4.00		
	Share capital	Retrans entry	Redux reserve/(distr'n)	Total	Share capital	Retrans entry	Redux reserve/(distr'n)	Total
	£	£	£	£	£	£	£	£
Without retranslation b/f	100			100	100			100
Repayment	(200)			(200)	(50)			(50)
Un(over) eliminated	100		(100)	0	(50)		50	0
	0	0	(100)	(100)	0	0	50	50
With retranslation b/f	200	(100)		100	50	50		100
Repayment	(200)			(200)	(50)			(50)
Un(over) eliminated	0	100	(100)	0	0	(50)	50	0
	0	0	(100)	(100)	0	0	50	50

Where an overall debit is left behind as a consumption of amounts available for distribution it is assumed that either the company had such amounts available prior to the reduction or that, if such a reduction may be validly effected, the consequence is that the company has a deficit (an excess utilisation of realised profits) which must be made good before any further distribution can be made.

Appendix 8
Example of application of section 846 to fungible assets

Company A has a freehold property with a book value of £100 and a fair value of £1,000. The company would be unable to distribute the property as a distribution in kind because it does not have sufficient distributable reserves.

Freehold property	100
	100
Share capital	50
Realised profits	50
	100

If Company A sells the freehold property in exchange for 1,000 £1 loan notes which represents qualifying consideration, the position is as follows:

Loan notes receivable	1,000
	1,000
Share capital	50
Realised profits	950
	1,000

As the loan notes represent qualifying consideration, the profit of £900 is a realised profit and Company A can make a distribution equal to its accumulated realised profits of £950.

Alternatively, if Company A sells the freehold property in exchange for £1,000 of loan notes which do not represent qualifying consideration, the position is as follows:

Loan notes receivable	1,000
	1,000
Share capital	50
Realised profits	50
Unrealised profits	900
	1,000

As the loan notes are fungible assets, the distribution of a proportion of the loan notes results in the realisation of the same proportion of the unrealised reserve. Every £1 loan note represents 90p of unrealised profit. Therefore, the element of each loan note which is not a profit is 10p. As realised profits are £50, only 500 loan notes may be distributed (because distribution of each £1 loan note will consume 10p of realised profits) The balance sheet after such a distribution would be as follows:

Loan notes receivable	500
	500
Share capital	50
Realised profits	–
Unrealised profits	450
	500

No further distribution of the remaining loan notes is possible because the distribution of £1 of loan notes would cause only 90p of unrealised profit to become realised and there are no other realised profits available. The maximum distribution possible as a distribution in kind is therefore less than would be the case if all of the loan notes were redeemed or sold for qualifying consideration.

Appendix 9
Example of application of 3.11(E) for distribution by set off

This example is concerned with the scenario where a subsidiary wishes to make a distribution to its parent of an unrealised profit and the distribution would result in the elimination, or reduction, of the asset which represents the unrealised profit.

The subsidiary has an unrealised profit which is represented by a balance due from its parent company. Without considering paragraph 3.11(e), the balance would not meet the definition of qualifying consideration because it would fail to meet one or more of the three criteria specified in paragraph 3.11(d).

The subsidiary's balance sheet is as follows.

Amount receivable from parent	130
Other assets	20
	150
Share capital	10
Unrealised profit related to amount receivable from parent	130
Realised profit	10
	150

The company could lawfully make a distribution in kind of the £130 receivable by applying section 846 of the 2006 Act and treating the unrealised profit as realised for the purposes of the distribution (see paragraph 2.9). Following the distribution, its balance sheet would be as follows.

Amount receivable from parent	–
Other assets	20
	20
Share capital	10
Unrealised profit related to amount receivable from parent	–
Realised profit	10
	20

The same effect is achieved through a waiver of the balance. A waiver by a subsidiary of a balance due to it by its parent would be classified legally as a distribution in kind (see paragraph 2.8E).

However, the legal position is different if the company instead declares a dividend of £130 with the intention of settling it through inter-company account. Section 846 is not applicable because there is no transfer of a non-cash asset. To declare the dividend, the company needs to have realised profits of £130 or more.

The definition of qualifying consideration in paragraph 3.11 addresses these circumstances, specifically at 3.11(e). It confirms that for the purposes of assessing the lawfulness of such a proposed distribution, the amount receivable from the shareholder is qualifying consideration where and to the extent that:

(i)   the company intends to make a distribution to the shareholder of an amount equal to or less than its receivable from that shareholder; and

(ii)   the company intends to settle such distribution by off-setting against the amount receivable (in whole or in part); and

(iii)   within the meaning of paragraph 3.5 of this guidance, (i) and (ii) are linked.

These conditions are met in the circumstances described above and therefore it is lawful for the subsidiary to make a distribution of £130 by set off.

The above example is concerned only with whether the distribution may lawfully be made by the subsidiary. It does not address whether the receipt of the distribution by the parent is a realised profit. For example, where the profit in the subsidiary arises from a hive up of assets, the guidance at 3.5 concerning arrangements that are artificial, linked or circular is relevant.